READER'S DIGEST 1984 ALMANAC AND YEARBOOK

PUBLISHED ANNUALLY BY
THE READER'S DIGEST ASSOCIATION, INC.
PLEASANTVILLE, NEW YORK 10570

Reader's Digest

1984 ALMANAC AND YEARBOOK

A specially commissioned work
prepared by
David C. Whitney Associates, Inc.,
with the editors of
The Reader's Digest Association, Inc.

Editor: David C. Whitney
Associate Editors: Lynn Augenblick, Melvin Wolfson

Library of Congress Catalog Card Number 66-14383

ISBN 0-89577-177-2
ISSN 0079-9831

Printed in the United States of America

CONTENTS

The main sections of the *Reader's Digest 1984 Almanac and Yearbook* are listed below along with the contents of each. To find specific information on persons, places, or subjects, turn to the alphabetical *Index* with its more than 9,000 references on pages 978–1024.

MAJOR NEWS DEVELOPMENTS: 1983

For the convenience of the reader who seeks the entire year's news at a glance, following is a listing of some of 1983's major events and developments with references to the page numbers on which they are reviewed in words and pictures.

The many events and developments that affected the United States and the world in 1983 are examined in detail throughout the *Reader's Digest 1984 Almanac and Yearbook.*

For the reader who wishes to review the events of the year in the order in which they happened, pages 8–30 provide a month-by-month, day-by-day chronology.

Facing each monthly summary of events is a FOCUS page providing details of a major event or development.

The main body of the *Almanac* contains 38 sections arranged alphabetically from *Accidents and Disasters* to *Women's Rights.* Within these sections other articles examine additional important happenings of 1983. Each section also contains the latest facts and statistics on thousands of persons, places, and events.

To find a specific fact the reader should consult the alphabetical *Index* on pages 987–1024.

QUICK QUIZ questions at the bottom of right-hand pages in the sections *History* and *Nations of the World* guide the curious reader to interesting information throughout the *Reader's Digest 1984 Almanac and Yearbook.*

JANUARY

3 **98th Congress convenes:** House swears in 269 Democrats and 165 Republicans; Senate swears in 54 Republicans and 46 Democrats.
3 **Building collapse in Turkey kills 50:** Occurs in city of Diyarbakir.
3 **New prime minister named in Peru:** Fernando Schwalb takes office as President Fernando Belaúnde Terry swears in 9 cabinet members in sweeping reorganization.
5 **New Secretary of Transportation named:** President Reagan nominates Elizabeth Dole to succeed Drew Lewis, who resigned in December.
5 **Texas congressman resigns:** Rep. Phil Gramm (D-Tex.) resigns to seek reelection as a Republican two days after Democratic Party's steering and policy committee voted, 26–4, to strip him of seat on House Budget Committee because of his support of Reagan policies.
5 **Automobile industry reports low sales:** Says 1982 car sales of 7,978,487 represents 6.3% decline from 1981; weakest performance since 1963.
7 **December unemployment at 10.8%,** up from November's revised figure of 10.7%, Labor Department announces. Average unemployment for 1982 was 9.7%; highest since 1941.
7 **Embargo on arms sales to Guatemala lifted:** Five-year-old embargo cancelled because of "significant steps" by government to end human rights abuses, Reagan administration says.
10 **Stock market hits record high:** Dow Jones average closes at 1,092.35; day's volume is 101.9 million shares.
11 **Secretary of Health and Human Services resigns:** Richard H. Schweiker to take job in private industry; President Reagan names Margaret M. Heckler to succeed him.
12 **Reagan fires U.S. arms control director:** Eugene Rostow dismissed as director of U.S. Arms Control and Disarmament Agency because of internal policy divisions; Kenneth L. Adelman named to replace Rostow.
12 **Retail sales up 3% in 1982:** Commerce Department reports 1982 retail sales totaled $1,070 billion.
14 **Producer prices rose only 3.5% in 1982:** Labor Department reports increase in wholesale prices was lowest since 1971.
14 **Anticrime bill vetoed:** President Reagan vetoes bill approved by 97th Congress because it would have created cabinet-level position for official to oversee federal efforts to combat narcotics trafficking.
14 **Records set for three 1982 harvests:** Agriculture Department says production of 8.4 billion bushels of corn, 2.81 billion bushels of wheat, and 2.28 billion bushels of soybeans were records.
16 **Air crash in Turkey kills 47:** Turkish Airlines Boeing 727 crashes on landing in Ankara after flight from Istanbul.
16–31 **Storms batter southern California:** Violent rainstorms blamed for 11 deaths, 21 injuries, and $70 million in property damage.
17 **Alabama governer inaugurated:** George C. Wallace is first to win fourth term as governor of Alabama.
18 **South Africa to control Namibia:** Dissolves National Assembly and resumes direct control of territory following resignation of multiracial Namibia Council of Ministers.
18 **UN Lebanon peacekeeping force extended:** UN Security Council votes, 13–0, to keep forces in Lebanon for another 6 months.
18 **Thatcher cleared in Falklands inquiry:** British government panel clears government of Prime Minister Margaret Thatcher of blame for Britain's failure to anticipate or prevent Argentina's capture of Falkland Islands in April 1982 which led to 2-month war.
18 **Housing starts decline:** Commerce Department reports work started on 1,061 million units in 1982; lowest number since 1946.
19 **Real GNP for 1982 fell 1.8%:** Commerce Department says decrease in "real" gross national product was worst since 1946.
19 **Suriname to form new government:** Hank Herrenberg, ambassador to the Netherlands, named by military leaders to head government.
21 **Human rights progress seen in El Salvador:** Reagan administration certifies to Congress that government of El Salvador made progress in curbing human-rights abuses, making it eligible to receive $25 million in military aid in fiscal 1983.
21 **Consumer price rise lowest since 1972:** Labor Department says inflation rate for 1982 was 3.9%.
23 **Soviet satellite falls from space:** *Cosmos 1402* plunges through atmosphere; debris falls harmlessly into Indian Ocean.
25 **President speaks on State of the Union:** In annual message to Congress, President Reagan says "America is on the mend."
25 **New code of canon law signed by Pope:** John Paul II signs first revision in Catholic Church's canon law since 1917 codification; to take effect Nov. 27.
25 **New family law in Greece:** Greek parliament passes legislation saying man is no longer legally head of family with final say on all matters; law intended to give married women equal voice in family affairs.
26 **Trade deficit sets record:** Commerce Department says 1982 trade deficit of $42.7 billion reached all-time high.
28 **Lebanon explosion kills 30:** Car packed with explosives blows up in Shtaura, Lebanon, outside building belonging to Yasir Arafat's Al Fatah Palestinian guerrilla organization.
29 **Nigeria expels illegal immigrants:** Orders all unskilled illegal immigrants to leave; hundreds of thousands flee.
30 **Pro football Super Bowl XVII:** Washington Redskins win, 27–17, over Miami Dolphins at Pasadena, Calif.
31 **Single-family home sales decline:** Commerce Department reports sale of 413,000 single-family homes in 1982 was lowest in the 20 years government has been keeping track.
31 **Price of gold rises:** Price in New York closes at $510.10, highest since April 8, 1981.
31 **Independent truckers begin strike:** Nation's independent truckers begin parking vehicles in nationwide strike to protest higher taxes on gasoline and diesel fuel, excise taxes on trucking equipment, and bigger fees for registration of large trucks.

VIOLENT STORMS BATTER CALIFORNIA

FOCUS

United Press Int'l.

Gale force winds and rain hit northern California on Jan. 26 with winds gusting to 70 miles per hour. That, combined with unusually high tides, effectively closed a Marin County bridge and flooded access roads. *Right,* the tide smashes into a sea wall at Fort Point road at the south end of the Golden Gate Bridge, causing the road to collapse and forcing its closure.

An estimated $70 million in damage was caused by a series of storms that battered the California coast in January. The four storms, Jan. 16–31, caused 11 deaths and damaged more than 3,000 homes. Mudslides and floods collapsed highways, closed bridges, and ruined farm crops.

After a short respite, the violent weather resumed, Feb. 27–March 5, when another tropical storm hit the Pacific coast. Thirteen persons died as a result, and damage was estimated at more than $200 million. Once again, coastal erosion, heavy crop damage, and extensive landslides were reported. A tornado hit Los Angeles and Pasadena on March 1, damaging 100 homes and ripping off part of the roof of the Los Angeles Convention Center.

The latter storm severely curtailed many of the activities planned for the visit of Britain's Queen Elizabeth II. She was prevented from sailing up the coast on the royal yacht *Britannia* from Los Angeles to President Reagan's ranch at Santa Barbara. Several outdoor ceremonies had to be scrapped.

The series of storms played havoc with farmers' planting seasons and were expected to cause consumers to pay higher prices for lettuce, strawberries, celery, broccoli, orchard fruits and nursery plants.

Economic damage was also felt in a drop in tourism.

FEBRUARY

1–March 13 Thousands die in Indian violence: Death toll estimated at 3,000 in violence between immigrants and natives of state of Assam sparked by government insistence on holding state elections despite Assamese demands that Muslim immigrants be stricken from election rolls and deported.

4 Nation's unemployment rate falls to 10.4%: First decrease in unemployment in 17 months, Labor Department reports.

5 PLO offices in Lebanon bombed: 22 die as car packed with explosives blows up outside Palestine Liberation Organization (PLO) research center in Beirut.

5 Former CIA agent convicted: Edwin P. Wilson found guilty in federal court in Houston, Tex., on four counts involving illegal exports of explosives to Libya in 1977.

6 Philippine coal-mine explosion kills 15: Blast occurs in mine shaft at Danao, on Cebu Island.

8 Israeli inquiry results released: Special state commission investigating 1982 massacre of Palestinian civilians in West Beirut refugee camps, says Israeli military leaders bore indirect responsibility; finds Defense Minister Ariel Sharon and three Israeli generals guilty of neglectful behavior and recommends Sharon's dismissal.

9 General Motors to recall X-cars: GM announces it will recall 240,000 1980 X-model autos to modify reportedly defective braking system.

10 Retail sales rose 0.1% in January, Commerce Department reports.

10 Independent truckers strike ends: Leaders of Independent Truckers Assn. end 11-day strike after receiving assurances from congressmen that scheduled increases in federal fuel taxes and user fees would be reviewed.

11 Snowstorm cripples mid-Atlantic states: Blizzard heaps accumulations of 18–22 inches across area, paralyzing New York and Washington, D.C., metropolitan areas; 15 die.

11 Ship sinks in storm off Virginia coast: Coal carrier *Marine Electric* overturns off Chincoteague, Va.; 31 crew members killed.

11 Record drop in January producer prices: Labor Department reports index of prices producers paid for finished goods fell 1% in January; largest drop ever.

13 President of Cyprus wins new term: President Spyros Kyprianou elected to five-year term; wins 57% of vote.

13 Fire in Italian movie theater kills 64: Flames sweep through theater in Turin.

14 Stock market reaches new high: Dow Jones average closes at 1,097.10.

14 Judge blocks birth-control rule: New York City federal district judge blocks implementation of Reagan administration regulation requiring parental notification by federally funded clinics when minors received birth-control prescriptions.

14 Tennessee bank declared insolvent: United American Bank of Knoxville closed by Tennessee banking commission; fourth-largest commercial-bank failure since 1933; bank is acquired and reopened Feb. 15 by First Tennessee National Corp.

15 Lebanese army takes control of East Beirut: 4,000 Lebanese army troops move across line after Christian militia cedes area it had controlled since 1975–76 civil war.

15 American Stock Exchange hits record high: Amex Index closes at 384.72.

16 Reagan orders EPA probe: President says he has ordered complete investigation by Justice Department into charges made that Environmental Protection Agency (EPA) personnel had shredded documents subpoenaed by Congress. See page 11.

16 January housing starts soar: Commerce Department reports housing starts increased 35.9% in January, highest increase on record.

16–17 Brush fires in Australia kill 71: Gale-force winds spread brush fires across Victoria and southeast coast of Australia; damage estimated at more than $97 million; two men later were charged with starting fires.

17 GM and Toyota sign pact: General Motors Corp. and Toyota Motor Co. of Japan sign agreement to jointly produce subcompact automobile at a Fremont, Calif., GM plant.

19 Rail collision in Mexico kills 100: Freight train collides with disabled passenger train near Guaymas.

20 Blizzard in Lebanon kills 38: Strands hundreds of motorists on Beirut-Damascus highway; many victims freeze to death in cars.

22 U.S. offers buyout of dioxin-tainted town: Federal government offers to buy all businesses and homes in Times Beach, Mo., after tests continue to show dangerously high levels of dioxin in town's soil; Environmental Protection Agency (EPA) Anne M. Burford authorizes Federal Emergency Management Agency to spend estimated $33 million to demolish town's buildings and relocate 2,400 residents.

23 Greek ferry boat sinks, killing 28: *Chrissie Avgi* sinks off Euboea, Greece.

24 Chrysler posts first profit since 1977: Chrysler Corp. announces $170.1 million profit for 1982.

24 Stock market tops 1,100 mark: Dow Jones average closes at 1,121.81, up 24.87 points for day; highest close to date.

25 Consumer prices rose 0.2% in January: Bureau of Labor Statistics reports slight rise after 0.3% decline in December 1982.

25 Prime rate dips to 10.5%: Several major banks drop prime rate to lowest level since November 1978.

25 New prime minister named in Suriname: Errol Alibux picked for post by strong man Col. Desi Bouterse; new 12-member cabinet installed Feb. 28.

26–March 7 Queen Elizabeth II visits U.S.: Travels through Western states; is entertained by President Reagan at his California ranch; bad weather hampers sightseeing.

27 Senegalese president wins reelection: President Abdou Diouf and ruling Socialist Party receive 85% of vote in national elections.

28 February farm prices jump 3.1%: Agriculture Department announces increase of 3.1% in prices received by farmers for their raw agricultural products.

CONTROVERSY SWIRLS AROUND EPA

FOCUS

Controversy between Congress and the Reagan administration over the way the Environmental Protection Agency (EPA), was being run dominated headlines in the early months of 1983.

EPA head Anne M. Gorsuch had been cited for contempt of Congress in December 1982 for refusing to release documents subpoenaed by the House in its investigation of the agency's work with a $1.6 billion toxic waste cleanup fund.

On Feb. 7, President Reagan dismissed Rita M. Lavelle, head of the agency's toxic waste cleanup fund, after she refused to resign at the request of Mrs. Gorsuch. Ms. Lavelle's office handled the material involved in the House's contempt citation, and she had been alleged to use political favoritism in dealing with polluting companies.

At a news conference of Feb. 16, President Reagan stressed that he "would never invoke executive privilege to cover up wrongdoing," and said he had ordered a Justice Department investigation into charges against the EPA. Mrs. Gorsuch had maintained that she withheld the documents on orders of President Reagan by his exercise of executive privilege.

As controversy increased, Mrs. Gorsuch, who remarried and became Anne McGill Burford on Feb. 20, resigned. More than 20 other high-ranking EPA officials resigned or were fired in the wake of the controversy.

Mrs. Burford was absolved of the contempt charges by the House Public Works Committee on June 24.

President Reagan named William D. Ruckelshaus as his nominee to head the EPA, on March 21. Ruckelshaus had been the first administrator of the EPA in 1970-73. A popular choice, he was confirmed by the Senate in a 97-0 vote on May 17, and sworn in May 18.

Also on May 18, the House voted 413-0 to find Rita Lavelle in contempt of Congress for refusing to honor a subpoena to appear before the House Energy and Commerce Committee's investigations subcommittee on March 21.

A Federal district court jury found Ms. Lavelle not guilty of contempt of Congress on July 22. However, she then was indicted on Aug. 4 on charges of perjury and obstructing a congressional investigation. Trial was set for November.

In the meantime, the Justice Department announced on Aug. 11 that it had not found sufficient evidence to warrant criminal prosecution of Anne McGill Burford or five other former EPA officials it had investigated. Thus, Ms. Lavelle became the only former EPA official actually indicted as a result of the investigation into mismanagement of the EPA.

Wide World

Rita M. Lavelle meets reporters on Feb. 13 in her first public appearance after being fired by President Reagan from her job as assistant administrator of the EPA.

On Dec. 1, a federal jury found Ms. Lavelle guilty of four counts of perjury and impeding a Congressional investigation of the hazardous waste program. The perjury charges stemmed from her testimony to Congress that she did not know that the Aerojet-General Corporation, her employer before she entered government, had dumped hazardous materials at the Stringfellow Acid Pits site in California. According to Lavelle, she disqualified herself from the investigation just as soon as she learned of Aerojet-General's involvement in June 1982. Prosecution witnesses convinced the jury that she knew of the inquiry before June 1982 and tipped off the company in hopes of private gain.

The jury found her not guilty of lying to a Congressional committee when she said under oath that she had not used the toxic waste cleanup program to help elect Republican candidates win elections.

With sentencing scheduled for Jan. 9, 1984, Ms. Lavelle faced a possible prison term of up to 20 years and $19,000 in fines. She was expected to appeal.

MARCH

1 Steelworkers approve concessions: Presidents of United Steelworkers locals ratify 41-month contract containing concessions in wages and benefits; first time in history of steel unions that concessions are granted on national level.

1 Chinese ferry capsizes, killing 150: Occurs in thunderstorms on Sanshui River in Guangdong province.

1 Pacific storm hits California: 8 die and 21 are injured in devastating storm that hurls tornadoes into Los Angeles and Pasadena.

2 January economic indicators rise 3.5%: Increase in index of leading economic indicators is highest since July 1950 and second highest in history, Commerce Department reports.

2 Single-family home sales rose in January: Commerce Department reports rise of 9.9% in sales of new single-family homes is highest in 28 months.

2–10 Pope visits Central America: John Paul II travels to Costa Rica, Nicaragua, Panama, El Salvador, Guatemala, Honduras, Belize, Haiti.

5 Labor Party wins Australian elections: Leader Robert Hawke's Labor Party ousts 8-year-old conservative government of Prime Minister Malcolm Fraser; Labor wins 75 seats in 125-member House of Representatives and 30 seats in 64-member Senate.

6 National elections held in West Germany: Chancellor Helmut Kohl's conservative coalition capture 244 seats in 498-member lower house of parliament with 48.8% of popular vote.

7 Turkish coal mine blast kills 98: Gas explosion tears through Armatcuk mine near Eregli.

7 Landslide in China kills 270: Engulfs village in northwest China.

7–12 Third World summit held in India: Representatives of 101 nonaligned nations meet in New Delhi; focus on world economy and disarmament.

9 EPA administrator resigns: President Reagan accepts resignation of Environmental Protection Agency administrator Anne Burford; William D. Ruckelshaus named to succeed her on March 21. See page 11.

10 February retail sales dropped 0.4%, Commerce Department reports.

10 Reagan proclaims coastal economic zone: President proclaims 200-mile wide coastal economic zone in which U.S. will exercise sole rights over all resources; result of U.S. refusal to sign Law of the Sea Treaty in 1982.

11 Inventories dropped 0.6% in February: Commerce Department announces inventories of unsold goods at lowest level since May 1981.

12 Air crash in Venezuela kills 18: DC-9 aircraft goes down in flames at airport at Barquisimeto, Venezuela.

12 Landslide in Pakistan kills 84: Hits village of Phupan, in Himalayan foothills.

16 February housing starts rose 2.9%: Commerce Department reports February level is highest since September 1979.

17 1982 balance of payments gap is posted: Commerce Department reports balance of payments on current accounts showed 1982 deficit of $8.09 billion, largest since 1978.

18 Producer Price Index rose 0.1% in February, Labor Department reports.

20 Floods in northern Peru and Bolivia kill 260: Caused by heavy rains and mudslides.

20–21 Elections held in Finland: Social Democrats win 26.8% of vote, good for 57 seats, and conservatives capture 22.2%, good for 44 seats; Communist Party loses 8 of its 25 seats.

21 European currencies realigned: Members of European Monetary System agree to realign their currencies in relation to the others; German mark increases 5.5%, while French franc is devalued 2.5%; Dutch guilder raised 3.5%, Danish krone raised 2.5%, Belgian and Luxembourg franc by 1.5% each; Italian lira devalued 2.5% and Irish pound devalued 3.5%.

22 Nicaragua reports Honduran invasion: Charges, in meeting of UN Security Council, that U.S.-backed rebels invaded Nicaragua three weeks earlier from bases in Honduras.

22 Labor Party candidate wins Israeli post: Opposition candidate Chaim Herzog elected president of Israel.

22 Rules on infant care implemented: Reagan administration implements rules, issued March 7, designed to prevent federally funded hospitals from denying food or medical care to handicapped infants; Federal district judge in Washington strikes down rule on April 14.

23 President calls for antimissile technology: In major speech, President Reagan calls for development of antiballistic missile system that could destroy Soviet missiles before they reached their targets.

23 Consumer prices fell 0.2% in February, Labor Department reports.

23 Artificial heart recipient dies: Dr. Barney B. Clark, first human to have artificial heart implanted on Dec. 2, 1982, dies of massive circulatory collapse, shock, and failure of all organs in his body except the artificial heart.

23 British pound at lowest rate against dollar: Closes in London at $1.46; lowest rate ever.

24 Stock prices set record: Dow Jones average closes at 1,145.90; highest ever.

25 Congress passes Social Security reform bill: Provisions include acceleration of scheduled payroll-tax increases, increases in taxes on self-employed, delay cost-of-living increases, raising retirement age, and extending coverage to federal workers and employees of nonprofit institutions.

25 France announces austerity measures: Includes tax increases, forced loans to government, and restrictions on amount of money French citizens can take abroad.

27 Pakistan ends press censorship: General Zia Pakistan's military ruler, announces end of three years of formal restraint on press.

30 Reagan offers compromise on missiles: President Reagan offers to reduce number of intermediate-range missiles scheduled to be deployed in Europe in exchange for Soviet reduction of missiles in Europe and Asia; both sides to have same number of warheads. See page 13.

31 Earthquake in Colombia kills 240: Devastates southwestern city of Popayan.

REAGAN CALLS FOR "STAR WARS" WEAPONS

FOCUS

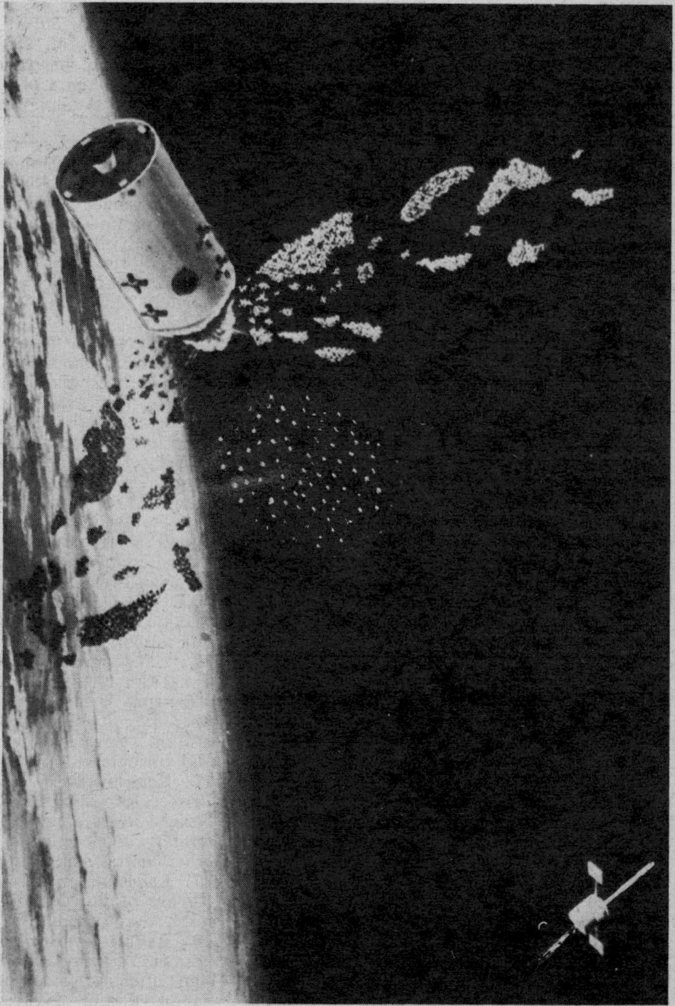

Soviet ASAT (anti-satellite) weapon can destroy a space satellite by shooting it down with a burst of shrapnel as shown in this illustration from booklet on Soviet military power released by the Department of Defense. The Soviets are believed to have successfully tested the ASAT several times. The U.S. also is said to have tested an ASAT system.

United Press Int'l.

In a TV address to the nation on March 23, President Reagan announced his support for a new strategic military policy that would rely on defensive weapons rather than retaliation to deter the Soviets from an atomic attack.

"I call upon the scientific community who gave us nuclear weapons," the President said, "to turn their great talents to the cause of mankind and world peace: to give us the means of rendering these nuclear weapons impotent and obsolete."

In what became known as his "Star Wars" address, the President declared:

"I am directing a comprehensive and intensive effort to define a long-term research and development program to begin to achieve our ultimate goal of eliminating the threat posed by strategic nuclear missiles."

Weapons scientists later said such a defensive system would depend upon the development of powerful lasers. Some estimated that deployment of such a weapons system in the early years of the next century could cost over $1 trillion.

APRIL

1 New gas tax goes into effect: 5-cent-a-gallon increase in federal gasoline tax becomes effective; expected to be passed along to consumers.
1 March unemployment is unchanged: Labor Department reports same 10.1% rate reported for January and February.
1 Thousands protest nuclear weapons: Form human chain stretching 14 miles across British countryside; sponsored by Campaign for Nuclear Disarmament.
2 Gromyko rejects missile proposal: Soviet Foreign Minister Andrei A. Gromyko calls President Reagan's proposal of interim agreement limiting medium-range missiles in Europe "unacceptable."
4–9 New space shuttle completes mission: In inaugural flight, space shuttle *Challenger* carries four astronauts; two take first space walk by Americans in nine years, spending nearly four hours outside spacecraft.
5 France expels 47 Soviets: Accuses diplomats, journalists, others of espionage.
6–12 Floods hit deep South: Deluge of rain causes extensive flooding in Mississippi, Alabama, Tennesse, Louisiana; kills 15, displaces more than 52,000; causes estimated $625 million in damage.
7 U.S. and Chinese cultural programs cancelled: China cancels sports and cultural exchanges with U.S. for remainder of 1983 in response to U.S. granting political asylum to Chinese tennis star Hu Na on April 4.
11–14 Holocaust survivors gather: Estimated 15,000 survivors of Holocaust gather in Washington, D.C., to commemorate loss of millions of Jews in World War II.
12 Chicago elects first black mayor: U.S. Rep. Harold Washington (D–Ill.) wins 52% of vote in bitter election.
14 Arms control director approved: Senate, in 57–42 vote, confirms appointment of Kenneth L. Adelman as director of Arms Control and Disarmament Agency.
18 American embassy in Beirut attacked: Carbomb explodes just outside embassy, demolishing building; 63 killed, including 17 Americans; Pro-Iranian group, Islamic Jihad, takes responsibility. See page 15.
18 South Korean disco fire kills 25: Blaze sweeps through disco in Taegu; 70 injured.
20 First quarter GNP rises 3.1%: Commerce Department announces growth of real Gross National Product for first quarter of 1983 is highest rise since first quarter of 1981.
20 States can ban nuclear power plants: Supreme Court rules unanimously that states can prohibit development of nuclear power plants if ban is caused by doubts about economics of nuclear power, rather than safety.
21 U.S. expels three Soviet diplomats: FBI announces two members of Soviet mission to UN and a military intelligence officer are asked to leave because of unrelated espionage activities.
22 Social Security increase announced: Nation's 36 million Social Security recipients will receive 3.5% cost-of-living increase in benefit checks in January 1984.
22 Soviet space mission aborted: Three cosmonauts return safely to earth after failure of docking of their *Soyuz T-8* spacecraft, launched April 20, with orbiting *Salyut 7* space station.
22 Discovery of Hitler diaries announced: West German magazine *Stern* says it has obtained 60 volumes of hitherto unknown diaries written by Adolph Hitler in 1932–45; later found to have been forgeries. See page 685.
22 Convicted murderer executed: John Louis Evans 3d dies in Holman (Ala.) prison; first to be put to death in Alabama since 1965.
22 Consumer prices rose 0.1% in March: Labor Department says Consumer Price Index rose at annual rate of 0.4% in first quarter; lowest quarterly rise since third quarter of 1965.
22 British inflation at 15-year low: Britain announces March rate of 4.6% is lowest level in 15 years.
24 U.S. prison inmates at record high: Justice Department announces number of prison inmates in 1982 was 412,303.
24 Austrian socialists lose majority: Chancellor Bruno Kreisky's Socialist Party loses clear majority in Parliament in national elections; Kreisky, chancellor since 1970, announces resignation; on April 25, socialists choose education minister Fred Sinowatz to succeed Kreisky.
24 Turkey lifts ban on political activity: National Security Council sets May 16 as date for formal establishment of new political parties.
26 San Francisco mayor survives recall: Mayor Dianne Feinstein wins 81% of vote in recall election sought by splinter group opposing mayor's support for gun control.
26 U.S. education criticized: 18-member National Commission on Excellence releases report criticizing U.S. education; calls for significant upgrading of school systems; says erosion of education "threatens our very future as a nation and a people."
27 Reagan asks more aid for Central America: In speech to joint session of Congress, President Reagan urges approval of package of increased military and economic aid to El Salvador and other central American nations.
27 Landslide in Ecuador kills 100: Engulfs convoy of buses and trucks on highway 180 miles south of Quito.
29 Italian government resigns: Coalition government of Prime Minister Amintore Fanfani resigns after losing support of socialists; President Sandro Pertini dissolves parliament on May 4; calls general elections for June 26–27.
29 Stock market at record high: Dow Jones industrial average closes at all-time high of 1,226.20.
29 Economic indicators up in March: Commerce Department announces March increase of 1.5% in index of leading economic indicators is seventh consecutive monthly gain.
29 April farm prices rise 2.2%: Agriculture Department says gain is fourth consecutive monthly increase.
30 U.S. Navy plane crashes; 15 killed: Turboprop C-131 crashes on takeoff from Jacksonville, Fla., Naval Air Station.

BOMB DAMAGES U.S. EMBASSY IN BEIRUT

FOCUS

Wide World

U.S. Ambassador to Lebanon Robert Dillon talks to reporters after bomb damaged U.S. embassy in Beirut.

The United States embassy in Beirut, Lebanon, was shattered by a powerful bomb on April 18. The explosion occurred at midday, when most embassy employees were at work and the streets were clogged with people. Witnesses reported seeing a van force its way into the embassy compound seconds before the blast occurred.

The explosion shook all of West Beirut and broke windows up to a mile away. It severely damaged the eight-story, horseshoe-shaped building. The bomb completely demolished the central section, which housed the cafeteria where many employees were just sitting down to lunch.

Ambassador Robert Dillon, who was in his top-floor office at the time, escaped with minor cuts and bruises, but 63 others were killed, including 17 Americans. Among the American victims were CIA Middle East analyst Robert C. Ames, 49, and William R. McIntyre, 52, deputy director of the Agency for International Development in Beirut.

Special U.S. envoys Philip Habib and Morris Draper were not in the building.

President Reagan called the bombing a "cowardly act," and said the United States would not be deterred from its efforts to bring peace to the region and negotiate the withdrawal of foreign troops from Lebanon.

A pro-Iranian group, Islamic Jihad (Holy War), took responsibility for the bombing in telephone calls to some news agencies, but other news organizations got calls from different groups claiming responsibility.

By the end of August, civil strife escalated in Lebanon, endangering the UN peacekeeping force. After several U.S. Marines were killed in Lebanon, the Reagan administration announced on Sept. 13 that the marines could call on U.S. naval and air power to defend themselves. See page 27.

MAY

1 U.S. per capita income gain slowed in 1982: Commerce Department reports 5.3% gain is lowest since 1966; 1982 per capita income was $11,056.

2 Earthquake hits central California: Epicenter near Coalinga; measures 6.5 on Richter scale; 50 hurt; damage estimated at $50 million.

2 Flash flood in Peru kills 50: Sweeps over bridge on Pan American Highway, near Chepen.

2 Court strikes down California vagrancy law: Supreme Court rules, 7–2, that state cannot give police power to arrest person who fails to produce proper identification on demand.

2 Court upholds Texas school residency law: Supreme Court rules, 8–1, that a local public school district may deny free education to student who is not valid district resident.

3 Pastoral letter approved by bishops: Roman Catholic bishops of U.S., meeting at Chicago, approve, 238–9, amended third draft of 150-page pastoral letter denouncing nuclear arms race.

3 San Diego elects new mayor: Republican Roger Hedgecock chosen to serve 19 months of unexpired term of Pete Wilson, who won election to U.S. Senate in November 1982.

4 Iran dissolves Communist Party: Accuses it of spying for Soviet Union; expels 18 Soviet diplomats.

5 Air crash in Thailand kills 31: Royal Thai Air Force C-123 crashes on landing at Ta Khli Air Base near Bangkok.

5 Israeli president sworn in: Chaim Herzog takes office, succeeding Yitzhak Navon.

6 Israel and Lebanon agree on troop withdrawal: Accept U.S.-mediated proposal calling for simultaneous withdrawal of Israeli and Syrian troops and Palestine Liberation Organization (PLO); Syria rejects plan on May 13; Israeli and Lebanese negotiators sign final text of agreement on May 17.

6 Stocks close at record high: Dow Jones average closes at 1,232.59; highest close to date.

6 April unemployment unchanged: Remains at March level of 10.1%.

6 Trade deficit shrinks in first quarter: Commerce Department reports first-quarter deficit narrowed to $8.4 billion, down from $12.1 billion in fourth quarter of 1982.

6 Finland installs new government: Premier Kalevi Sorsa sworn in along with four-party coalition government.

7 Fire in Istanbul, Turkey, kills 42: Sweeps through downtown *Hotel Washington;* 60 hurt.

8 Gunpowder explodes in Mexican church: 34 killed in crowded Roman Catholic church in Tlapacoya, Mexico.

9–10 OECD summit held in Paris: Officials of 24 member nations of Organization for Economic Cooperation (OECD) issue communiqué urging priority to be given to "increased output and employment."

11 April retail sales rose 1.6%, Commerce Department reports.

13 New president takes office in Yugoslavia: Mika Spiljak succeeds Peta Stambolic.

13 April industrial output jumped 2.1%: Largest monthly rise since August 1975, Federal Reserve Board reports.

15 Transportation deaths at 20-year low: National Transportation Safety Board releases preliminary figures showing 43,990 deaths in 1982 on highways and in other areas of transportation; down 11% from 49,301 in 1981.

17 Ruckelshaus confirmed as EPA head: Senate unanimously confirms William D. Ruckelshaus to be new administrator of Environmental Protection Agency (EPA). See page 11.

17 Premier ousted in Upper Volta: President Jean-Baptiste Ouedraogo announces purge; Premier Thomas Sankara and other members of ruling People's Salvation Council arrested.

18 House cites ex-EPA official for contempt: Votes, 413–0, to cite Rita Lavelle, former head of toxic waste program, for contempt of Congress for failing to comply with subpoena to testify before a House subcommittee. See page 11.

18–23 Gulf Coast and Southeastern states hit by storms: Ravaged by 59 tornadoes; 32 die in Texas, Mississippi, Missouri, Georgia, Tennessee, and Louisiana.

20 Car bomb rocks Pretoria, South Africa: 17 killed, 188 injured in terrorist attack outside headquarters of South African air force; African Nationalist Congress (ANC) takes responsibility; South Africa stages reprisal raid on suburb of Maputo, Mozambique, on May 23, reports killing 64 persons, disputed by ANC.

25 U.S. Navy commander killed in El Salvador: Lt. Cmdr. Albert A. Schaufelberger, deputy commander of U.S. military group in El Salvador, shot and killed by left-wing guerrilla group.

25 President replaces civil-rights panelists: Dismisses three of six members of U.S. Civil Rights Commission; new appointees are Morris Abram, John Bunzel, Robert Destro; dismissed are Mary Frances Berry, Blandina Cardenas Ramirez, Rabbi Murray Saltzman.

25 Nile River steamer sinks: 317 die as *10th of Ramadan* catches fire after engine-room explosion in lake behind Aswan Dam in Egypt.

26 Earthquake in Japan kills 102: Quake measures 7.7 on Richter scale, induces tidal waves on western coast of Honshu.

26 New government formed in Iceland: Steingrimur Hermannsson named premier and head of center-right government.

27 Trade deficit widens in April: Commerce Department reports increase to $4.6 billion.

28–30 Leaders of industrial nations meet: President Reagan and heads of state of Britain, France, Japan, West Germany, Canada, Italy meet at Williamsburg, Va., to discuss world economic issues. See page 17.

30 State of emergency declared in Peru: President Fernando Belaunde Terry takes action to combat terrorism by leftist guerrillas.

31 Leading economic indicators up 1.1% in May: Commerce Department reports 10th consecutive monthly gain.

31 Court rules on spouses' tax obligations: Supreme Court rules, 5–4, that a federal judge may order the sale of married couple's home to satisfy one spouse's federal unpaid tax obligation even if other spouse owes no taxes.

ECONOMIC SUMMIT HELD AT WILLIAMSBURG

FOCUS

President Reagan and British Prime Minister Margaret Thatcher hold talks at Williamsburg, Va., summit.

The leaders of France, Britain, Japan, Canada, West Germany, Italy, the U.S., and the European Common Market met in Williamsburg, Va., on May 28–30, for an economic summit conference.

As host to the ninth in a series of summits involving the industrialized Western nations, the U.S. chose Colonial Williamsburg, the Rockefeller-financed restoration of the colonial capital of Virginia, as the setting for the Memorial Day weekend events.

Each conference participant arrived by helicopter on May 28, then transferred to an open horse-drawn carriage carrying footmen dressed in green britches, gold vests, and tricornered hats. Each visitor was welcomed by President Reagan at the Governor's Palace where they listened to the various national anthems and watched a fife-and-bugle corps march across the green.

At the end of the first day of discussions, May 29, the leaders called on the Soviet Union to negotiate reduction of nuclear weapons and warned that Soviet attempts to divide the Western nations would not be successful.

The summit concluded on May 30, with the issuance of a 1,200-word Williamsburg Declaration on Economic Recovery and a 500-word Annex.

The Declaration pledged cooperative efforts to help economic recovery, not only in the West, but throughout the world. It included a strong commitment to elimination of trade barriers, with the highest priority given to developing nations. Also highlighted was the intention to increase aid to developing nations in the areas of industry, food, energy, and trade.

The leaders pledged "enhanced" efforts to promote greater "convergence" of economic policies, with an emphasis on stabilizing exchange rates.

The world leaders also agreed to expand cooperation to protect the environment, to use natural resources in more efficient ways, and to increase health research.

The Annex reaffirmed the objectives of noninflationary growth of income and employment, promotion of exchange market stability, and reinforced cooperation with the International Monetary Fund.

Though the documents offered few concrete suggestions on achieving the stated goals, the leaders apparently felt encouraged about the spirit of cooperation evidenced.

The 1984 economic summit meeting will take place in Britain.

JUNE

1 Special envoy sworn in: Former U.S. Sen. Richard B. Stone of Florida sworn in as special envoy to Latin America with rank of ambassador; takes fact-finding trip on June 2–14.

2 Air crash in Cincinnati kills 23: Air Canada DC-9 catches fire in flight; makes emergency landing at Greater Cincinnati Airport while in flames; 23 aboard survive.

3 U.S. unemployment dipped slightly in May: Labor Department reports decrease to 10% from 10.1%.

5 Boat accident in Soviet Union kills at least 100: Passenger vessel *Aleksandr Suvorov* strikes rail bridge in Volga River at Ulyanovsk; some estimates say 240 die.

6 Court upholds "windfall profits" tax: Supreme Court unanimously upholds Crude Oil Windfall Profit Tax Act of 1980.

8 Search warrants on anonymous tips backed: Supreme Court rules, 6–3, to expand police powers to obtain search warrants on the basis of anonymous tips; Court avoids ruling on whether illegally seized evidence could be admissible in court if police acted in good faith.

8–12 OAU meeting held in Ethiopia: 19th summit of Organization of African Unity convenes in Addis Ababa; delegates call for direct negotiations between Morocco and Polisario guerrillas of Western Sahara.

9 British prime minister scores victory: Prime Minister Margaret Thatcher and her Conservative government win parliamentary majority of 144 seats in general elections.

9 American business expansion down: Report prepared by Commerce Department says American business plans to spend $305.5 billion on expansion and modernization projects in 1983; down 3.1% from 1982 adjusted level.

10 New Presbyterian church formed: Merger of United Presbyterian Church in the U.S.A. and Presbyterian Church in the United States results in new 3.2 million-member denomination called The Presbyterian Church (U.S.A.). See page 703.

10 Producer Price Index up first time in 1983: Labor Department reports rise of 0.3% in May.

10 Retail sales up 2.1% in May, Commerce Department reports.

10 Rail crash in Egypt kills 24: Speeding train slams into rear of stationary train 30 miles south of Cairo; 47 injured.

11 Coal-mine explosion in Yugoslavia kills 21.

13 Court sets penalty for "frivolous" appeal: Supreme Court votes, 5–3, to penalize appellant $500 for filing "frivolous" appeal; first time in history such action taken.

13 U.S. spacecraft departs solar system: *Pioneer 10,* launched in 1972, crosses orbit of Neptune, becomes first man-made object to leave solar system.

15 Supreme Court reaffirms right to abortion: Votes, 6–3, to curb power of state and local governments to limit access to legal abortions.

16 Senators raise salaries: Senate votes, 49–47, to raise salary of senators to $69,800, same as that of congressmen, effective July 1; defers previously-approved 30% limit on earnings from speeches to Jan. 1, 1984.

16 May housing starts rose 19.1%, Commerce Department reports: highest level since September 1979.

16 Andropov named president of Soviet Union: Soviet Communist Party leader Yuri Andropov is formally elected president of Soviet Union.

16 Indonesia ship accident kills 80: Inter-island ferry sinks in Banda Sea.

16–23 Pope visits native Poland: John Paul II receives tumultuous welcome wherever he goes; meets with Polish leader, Gen. Wojciech Jaruzelski and Solidarity leader Lech Walesa; urges restoration of human rights. See page 19.

17 Stock prices at record high: Dow Jones average rises 11.02 points to close at 1,248.30, highest level in history to date.

18 President reappoints Federal Reserve head: President Reagan announces appointment of Paul A. Volcker to second term as chairman of Federal Reserve Board.

18 President appointed in China: National People's Congress names Li Xiannian to mainly ceremonial post, vacant since 1968.

18–24 First American woman launched in space: Dr. Sally K. Ride and four male astronauts complete near-perfect mission aboard space shuttle *Challenger.*

20 Health insurance plans may not discriminate: Supreme Court rules, 7–2, that company medical plans must cover pregnancies of employees' wives to same extent they cover all other dependents' medical expenses.

22 Coal-mine explosion in Hungary kills 36: Occurs in town of Oroszlany.

22 May Consumer Price index rose 0.5%, Labor Department reports.

23 Supreme Court voids "legislative veto": Historic 7–2 vote rules unconstitutional the "legislative veto" used by Congress to delegate authority to President and then block his actions under law when it disagrees.

23 Congress approves 1984 budget: Compromise budget resolutions approved by both houses; new budget mandates higher taxes, lower defense spending, and higher domestic spending than proposed by Reagan administration.

23 EPA eases clean-air sanctions: Environmental Protection Agency administrator William Ruckelshaus announces EPA would not impose strict economic sanctions on communities that fail to meet clean-air standards set by Congress if they have made reasonable efforts to improve air quality.

24 Court backs auto passive-restraints rule: Supreme Court unanimously affirms ruling that National Highway Traffic Safety Administration (NHTSA) acted improperly in 1981 when it attempted to repeal regulation requiring passive restraints in 1984-model cars.

24 Austerity plan approved in Portugal: Parliament approves plan for tighter credit, new taxes, lower government spending, and higher prices for some consumer goods.

30 Leak of Carter campaign papers to be probed: FBI announces formal investigation into how Ronald Reagan's 1980 campaign staff acquired secret papers on President Carter's reelection campaign.

POPE JOHN PAUL II VISITS POLAND

FOCUS

Pope John Paul II returned to Poland on June 16 for a one-week visit to his homeland. According to sources at the Vatican, the pope felt he needed to return because of the events that took place after his first visit to Poland as pope in 1979 . . . the Dec. 13, 1981, imposition of martial law, outlawing of the Solidarity labor union, and the jailing of its leaders.

On his arrival, John Paul II kissed the ground and was greeted with chants of "Solidarity, Solidarity." His remarks upon landing in Warsaw included references to Poland as "a mother who has suffered much and who ever suffers anew." He regretted he could not personally visit all of those imprisoned, referring to the jailed Solidarity activists.

The pontiff met privately with Gen. Wojciech Jaruzelski, head of the government, on June 17, following a televised exchange of speeches. In his remarks, John Paul II expressed hope that social reforms agreed upon in 1980, permitting independent labor unions and more personal freedoms, might gradually be put into effect. Gen. Jaruzelski responded by defending martial law.

During the evening of June 17, the pope celebrated mass at a Warsaw soccer stadium before more than a million people. There, as he did throughout his visit, he stressed Polish nationalism and urged restoration of basic human rights.

On June 18 the pope visited World War II memorials in Warsaw, and made an unscheduled visit to put flowers at a memorial commemorating the 1943 Jewish ghetto uprising against the Nazis. He then flew to the Niepokalanow monastery where he celebrated mass in honor of Rev. Maksymilian Kolbe, a monk who gave his life for a fellow inmate at the Auschwitz concentration camp.

The pope then flew to Czestochowa to visit the nation's holiest shrine, the Black Madonna at Jasna Gora. There the pontiff told a crowd of over a million that the workers' struggle of 1980 "touched hearts and consciences."

In another mass at the monastery on June 19 the pope told another crowd of one million that, as a son of Poland, he feels its wish to live "in truth, in freedom, in justice, and social solidarity."

Huge crowds greeted the pope during the rest of his tour, which included Poznan, Katowice, Wroclaw, and Krakow. In Krakow, more than 2 million persons attended an outdoor mass.

On June 23, the pope was allowed to meet with Solidarity founder Lech Walesa, in the resort town of Zakopane. The night before the pope's meeting with Walesa, Gen. Jaruzelski unexpectedly flew to Krakow to meet with John Paul II. The details of both meetings were kept secret.

A month later, on July 22, martial law was lifted, but the government adopted new laws to restrict human freedoms.

Pope John Paul II also travelled to Central America, France, and Austria in 1983. See page 704.

Pope John Paul II salutes cheering crowd at Warsaw's soccer stadium just before holding high mass on June 17, the second day of his visit to Poland.

Wide World

JULY

1 Air crash in Guinea kills 23: North Korean-owned Ilyushin-62 goes down near town of Labe.
1 U.S. and Belau sign nuclear transport accord: Agreement bars U.S. from testing or storing nuclear weapons in area but permits transportation of materials through Belau; must be ratified by both congresses.
4 Death row prisoners reach record level: Justice Department announces that 1,050 prisoners on death row at end of 1982 was largest number ever—22.7% more than in 1981.
4–8 CARICOM meeting held: Nations composing Caribbean Community and Common Market (CARICOM) meet at Port of Spain, Trinidad; admit Bahamas as 13th member; call for end to foreign intervention in Central America and endorse efforts of Contadora group (Mexico, Colombia, Venezuela, Panama) to evolve peaceful solution to problems in area.
6 Supreme Court bars pension inequality: Rules, 5–4, that employee retirement plans can not pay women lower monthly pension benefits than are paid to men.
6 Court okays "protective" auto searches: Supreme Court rules, 6–3, that police can conduct a "protective" search of passenger area of a car without a warrant if they believe that concealed weapons are in the auto.
8 June unemployment dropped to 9.8%: Labor Department reports decline from 10% in May.
11 Air crash in Ecuador kills 119: Ecuadorian Boeing 737 hits mountain on landing at Cuenca.
11 U.S. sues Alabama on racial bias: Reagan administration files first school desegregation suit; charges Alabama maintained system of racial discrimination, denying qualified black applicants admission to traditionally white public colleges and universities.
15 Industrial production up 1.1% in June: Federal Reserve Board reports production of nation's factories showed seventh consecutive monthly gain.
15 U.S. and Greece agree on military bases: Announce pact allowing operation of U.S. military bases in Greece until 1988; U.S. agrees to seek $500 million in military credits for Greece in new fiscal year, a $280 million increase.
15 Typhoon in Philippines kills 45: Typhoon Vera hits main island of Luzon.
15 Car bomb at Paris airport kills 7: Bomb explodes in suitcase at Turkish Airlines check-in counter; responsibility claimed by Armenian Secret Army for the Liberation of Armenia.
15 June producer prices up 0.5%: Labor Department reports gain in Producer Price Index is highest in seven months.
15 Cruise missile tests allowed by Canada: Canadian government announces U.S. is to be allowed to test cruise missiles over northern Canada, beginning in January 1984.
16 British helicopter accident kills 20: British Airways helicopter shuttling passengers to Scilly Islands crashes in English Channel.
18 Central American policy commission created: President Reagan announces establishment of 12-member bipartisan commission to make long-term recommendations on U.S. policy in Central America; to be headed by former Secretary of State Henry Kissinger.
18 U.S. industrial capacity at 16-month high: Federal Reserve Board reports American industry operated at 74.5% capacity in June; highest since February 1982.
20 Stock market soars 30.74 points: Dow Jones Average closes at 1,227.86; highest one-day rise since Nov. 30, 1982.
20 House censures two Congressmen: Reps. Daniel B. Crane (R-Ill.) and Gerry E. Studds (D-Mass.) censured after Crane admits having sexual relations with female House page and Studds admits relationship with male page.
21 Poland formally lifts martial law: Polish authorities announce end of 19 months of martial law and decree partial amnesty for nation's political prisoners; new curbs are enacted, extending tight government control until 1985.
21 Record low temperature recorded: Thermometer at Vostok Soviet research station in Antarctica records −126.9° F.
22 Consumer prices rose 0.2% in June: Labor Department reports 12-month inflation rate of 2.6% is lowest since 1967.
22 Mideast negotiator steps down: President Reagan announces resignation of Philip C. Habib as chief Middle East negotiator; to be replaced by deputy national security adviser Robert C. McFarlane.
22 Former EPA official cleared of contempt: Federal jury in Washington, D.C., acquits Rita Lavelle of contempt of Congress charges levied after she failed to appear before House energy subcommittee in March. See page 11.
23 Mudslide in Japan kills 120: Heavy rain causes flooding, mudslides in Honshu, Japan.
24–Aug. 1 Violence flares in Sri Lanka: More than 200 dead in week of violent clashes between Buddhist Sinhalese majority and Hindu Tamil minority; daily curfew imposed July 26.
26 Congress approves MX missile funding: Senate approves $2.6 billion in funds for production of MX missile; House approved same figure July 20 but reduced it to $2.2 billion on July 21; bills go to conference committee.
27 Turkish Embassy in Lisbon attacked: Band of Armenian terrorists blow up building; 7 die.
28 Congress repeals withholding on interest: House and Senate approve compromise bill repealing withholding of income tax from interest and dividend payments, originally scheduled to go into effect Aug. 5.
28 House cancels aid to Nicaraguan rebels: Votes, 228–195, to ban by Sept. 30 all secret aid to rebels fighting Nicaraguan government.
28 Commission on organized crime named: President Reagan names 20-member commission, headed by Judge Irving R. Kaufman, to analyze organized crime and recommend remedies.
29 Trade deficit narrowed in June: Commerce Department reports U.S. merchandise trade deficit at $4.9 billion; down from record $6.9 billion in May.
29 Farm prices dipped 2.2% in July, reports Agriculture Department.

COURT DUMPS CONGRESSIONAL VETO

FOCUS

United Press Int'l.

Jagdish Rai Chadha, 38, a British citizen who lives in Berkeley, Calif., initiated the suit that caused the Supreme Court to rule that the legislative veto is unconstitutional. He began his litigation in 1975 in an effort to remain in the U.S. after the House of Representatives vetoed a ruling by the Immigration and Naturalization Service that would have let him stay in this country even though his student visa had expired.

In its most far-reaching decision of the year, the Supreme Court ruled by a vote of 7 to 2 on June 23 that Congress cannot restrict the powers of the President by use of the legislative veto.

Congress had written the legislative veto into 196 laws since first beginning to do so in 1932 during the administration of President Hoover. It enabled Congress to grant the President authority to carry out a measure while retaining the right for either or both houses to veto the way he planned to exercise the authority.

The majority opinion of the Court, written by Chief Justice Warren E. Burger, declared that the legislative veto was unconstitutional because it upset the checks and balances on the three branches of government that had been designed by the Founding Fathers.

"To preserve those checks, and maintain the separation of powers," Chief Justice Burger wrote, "the carefully defined limits on the power of each branch must not be eroded. To accomplish what has been attempted by one house of Congress in this case requires action in conformity with the express procedures of the Constitution's presciption for legislative action: passage by a majority of both Houses and presentment to the President. . . .

"There is no support in the Constitution or decisions of this Court for the proposition that the cumbersomeness and delays often encountered in complying with explicit constitutional standards may be avoided, either by the Congress or by the President. With all the obvious flaws of delay, untidiness, and potential for abuse, we have not yet found a better way to preserve freedom than by making the exercise of power subject to the carefully crafted restraints spelled out in the Constitution."

AUGUST

2 U.S. poverty rate rose in 1982: Census Bureau reports rate of 15% was highest since 1956; number of Americans classified as poor increased by 2.6 million to 34.4 million.

2 Women over 40 need more breast X rays: American Cancer Society says women over 40 years of age should have breast X rays or mammograms every one or two years to aid early detection of breast cancer.

3 GM sued on X-car problem: U.S. Justice Department files suit against General Motors Corporation, charging GM sold 1980 X-model automobiles knowing they had serious brake defects.

4 Italy gets socialist premier: Bettino Craxi sworn in as Italy's first socialist prime minister; heads 5-party coalition, 44th government since World War II.

4 Former EPA official indicted: Rita Lavelle indicted by federal grand jury on five felony counts of lying to Congress and the agency about her actions when she headed the Environmental Protection Agency's toxic-waste clean-up program. See page 11.

5 Unemployment dropped in July: Labor Department announces decline to 9.3%, down from 9.8% in June.

5 Coup in Upper Volta leaves 13 dead: Former Prime Minister Thomas Sankara, 35, seizes government from President Jean-Baptiste Ouedraogo; 15 wounded; national revolutionary council to govern nation.

5 Boat sinks off Indonesia: 104 drown as *Sumber Wangi* sinks in Java Sea north of Masalembo Island.

5 Second-quarter trade deficit widens: Commerce Department reports second-quarter deficit at record $14.9 billion, up from $8.9 billion in first quarter.

6 Nigerian president reelected: Voters give President Shehu Shagari second 4-year term; he receives 47% of vote in six-candidate election.

8 Guatemalan government overthrown: Defense Minister Brig. Gen. Oscar Humberto Mejia Victores installed as chief of state after military overthrows President Efrain Rios Montt; second coup in nation in 17 months.

8 U.S. banks raise prime rate to 11%: Half-point increase is first since February 1982.

11 Ex-EPA officials cleared: Justice Department reports insufficient evidence of criminal wrongdoing to prosecute former Environmental Protection Agency head Anne McGill Burford and five former aides. See page 11.

11–12 Protest held in Chile: 27 die during nationwide protest against government as police attack demonstrators; 1,200 arrested.

14 President Reagan meets with Mexican leader in La Paz, Mexico: President Miguel de la Madrid Hurtado warns U.S. "show of force" in Central America might aggravate internal conflicts in area.

14–15 Pope visits shrine at Lourdes, France: John Paul II concludes pilgrimage by celebrating Feast of the Assumption with open-air mass.

15 Paraguayan president sworn in for 7th term: Gen. Alfredo Stroessner has ruled since 1954.

16 U.S. admits it aided Nazi: Justice Department says U.S. Army employed former Gestapo officer Klaus Barbie, now facing trial in France for war crimes, as spy in Germany following World War II and then helped him escape to South America.

18 Hurricane Alicia slams into Texas coast: 18 die; damage estimated at $1.6 billion; Houston and Galveston extensively damaged.

18 Andropov offers weapons moratorium: Soviet President Yuri P. Andropov announces "unilateral moratorium" on deployment of antisatellite weapons at Moscow meeting with nine U.S. senators.

19 U.S. and China sign textile accord: Five-year agreement permits 3.5% rate of growth of textile exports to U.S. over five years.

21 Philippine opposition leader assassinated: Benigno S. Aquino Jr. shot to death as he disembarks from plane in which he returned to Manila after self-imposed 3-year exile; President Ferdinand Marcos denies involvement; appoints 5-judge panel to probe killing.

21 Elections held in Mauritius: Three-party alliance of Prime Minister Aneerood Jugnauth sweeps to victory in general elections.

21 Telephone strike ends: Executive board of Communications Workers of America approves new contract ending 15-day nationwide strike.

23 July consumer prices rose 0.4%: Labor Department reports gain translates to annual rate of 4.8%.

25 U.S. and Soviet Union sign grain agreement: Five-year accord gives Soviets guarantees that supplies will not be interrupted.

26 State of emergency lifted in Chile: President Augusto Pinochet Ugarte says he will lift state of emergency, in effect since 1978.

26 Mexico reschedules debt payment: Mexico and international bankers sign agreement rescheduling over eight years payment of $11.4 billion government debt.

27 Floods on French-Spanish border kill 37: Heavy rains inundate Basque country in Spain.

27 Anniversary of civil-rights march marked: More than 250,000 people gather in Washington, D.C., to commemorate 1963 march on Washington led by late Dr. Martin Luther King Jr.; most speakers criticize Reagan policies.

28 Israeli premier announces resignation: Prime Minister Menachem Begin tells cabinet he intends to resign; actually submits resignation Sept. 15.

29 American marines killed in Lebanon: Civil strife between Christians and Muslims results in death of two U.S. Marines; four French military personnel are killed on Aug. 30.

29 July trade deficit third worst on record: Commerce Department announces expansion of deficit to $6.36 billion.

30–Sept. 5 Space shuttle completes flight: Space shuttle *Challenger* accomplishes both launch and landing at night; carries first U.S. black astronaut, Guion S. Bluford.

31 August farm prices climbed 4.6%: Department of Agriculture announces sharpest one-month increase in more than three years.

RECORD DROUGHT SCORCHES MIDWEST

FOCUS

A record-breaking drought withered many of the crops in the nation's midwestern Farm Belt in 1983. The month of August was the hottest on record, according to the National Weather Service, with temperatures averaging 4 degrees above normal in over half of the nation. The summer for the U.S. as a whole, was the 17th hottest on record. The heat, combined with a much lower-than-normal amount of rainfall, claimed at least 220 lives across the nation and an estimated $10 billion in crops.

As of Nov. 1, the nation's corn crop stood at 4.12 billion bushels, a drop of 51% from 1982. Average corn yields dropped to 80 bushels an acre from 134 an acre in Illinois. Iowa farmers harvested an average of 85 bushels an acre, compared with 121 in 1982.

Soybeans also were affected by the drought. U.S. soybean production averaged 25 bushels an acre, compared with 32 a year earlier. Total soybean production was 1.54 billion bushels, a drop of 42.9% from 1983.

Most areas of the Midwest sought aid for the problem-plagued farmers. On Sept. 2, Secretary of Agriculture John R. Block designated 57 counties in Indiana as drought disaster areas, the first of several hundred such designations that would allow farmers to become eligible for low-interest government loans and other financial help.

On Dec. 3, Secretary Block loosened eligibility rules for selling government-owned corn to livestock producers affected by the drought. Farmers would be able to buy feed at discount prices during December.

City dwellers also were affected by the record heat, and some cities, such as St. Louis, Mo., set up "cooling centers" where residents who lacked air conditioning could go for relief from the heat. During five days of over-100° temperatures in July, 42 deaths were reported in the St. Louis, metropolitan area.

The government estimated that $5.7 billion was spent on air conditioning in July and August, compared with a normal $4.8 billion.

Europe also suffered from the heat wave. On July 28, Prague, Czechoslovakia, recorded its hottest day ever with a temperature of 101°. Armbug, West Germany measured 104° on the same day, and 101° was recorded in Nuremberg.

Farmer Walter Yoder, of Harrisonville, Mo., husks an ear of corn on his son's farm on Sept. 17, revealing damage caused by record drought during summer of 1983. The Yoders and other farmers were forced to find alternative sources of feed for their herds of dairy cattle. The 1983 corn crop was down 51% from 1982.

Wide World

SEPTEMBER

1 Soviets shoot down passenger plane: Korean Air Lines Boeing 747 shot down near Sakhalin Island in Sea of Japan after overflying Soviet airspace during New York-to-Seoul flight; all 269 aboard killed. See page 25.
1 U.S. increases offshore Lebanon forces: President Reagan orders 2,000-member Marine force to join warships off Beirut to "assure safety" of Marines in Lebanon.
1 Washington's Sen. Henry Jackson dies: Democrat served nearly 43 years in Congress; elected senator in 1952; Daniel J. Evans, Republican governor of Washington in 1965–77, appointed to vacant Senate seat Sept. 8 and sworn in on Sept. 12.
1–18 Flooding in India kills 400: Monsoon rains deluge scores of villages in five Indian states.
2 Unemployment rose slightly in August: Labor Department says jobless rate, including U.S. military personnel based domestically, rose 0.1% to 9.4%.
5 U.S. average per capita income rose in 1982: Commerce Department says 5% increase brought average income to $11,107 in 1982.
7 Ireland approves anti-abortion amendment: Referendum results show 841,233 voting for amendment with 416,136 against.
7 Marshall Islanders vote for self-government: Approve plebiscite on adopting form of limited independence from U.S.; compact of free association requires ratification by U.S. congress; Marshall Islands to receive about $1.5 billion in economic aid over 15 years.
8–11 Violence in Chile kills 10: Antigovernment protests call for resignation of President Augusto Pinochet Ugarte; hundreds reported wounded and arrested.
9 Wholesale prices rose 0.4% in August: Bureau of Labor Statistics announces increase in Producer Price Index.
10–13 Pope John Paul II visits Vienna: During trip to Austria, pope warns against abortion and urges U.S. and Soviets to negotiate for peace in good faith.
11 FBI reports decrease in crime: 1982 rate is 4% less than 1981 rate, with 5,553 crimes reported for every 100,000 persons.
12 Coal mine blast in South Africa kills 64: Methane gas explosion rips through coal mine in Hlobane, South Africa.
13 Air support authorized in Lebanon: Reagan administration announces U.S. Marines in peacekeeping force are authorized to call for U.S. naval artillery and air strikes for their own protection.
13 Retail sales fell 1.4% in August: Commerce Department reports biggest drop since June 1982.
19 St. Christopher and Nevis becomes independent: Oldest British colony in Caribbean remains member of British Commonwealth; first prime minister is Kennedy Simonds.
19 August housing starts rose 8.4% in August: Commerce Department reports adjusted annual rate of 1,935,000 units; highest since August 1978.
20 UN General Assembly opens: 38th annual General Assembly elects Jorge Illueca, vice president of Panama, as president.
20 Hottest August on record reported: National Weather Service reports month of August was hottest on record; claimed at least 220 lives and caused $10 billion in damage to crops. See page 23.
21 Vietnam veterans form lobby group: Twelve groups of Vietnam War veterans announce formation of national coalition to lobby on behalf of veterans of Vietnam War.
21 Cancer treatment ordered for Tennessee girl: Tennessee Supreme Court orders chemotherapy treatments for 12-year-old girl with rare form of bone cancer despite protests by her parents, members of fundamentalist denomination that forbids medicine, vaccines, and shots.
23 Air crash in Abu Dhabi kills 111: Gulf Air Boeing 737 jetliner crashes and burns in mountains of sheikdom of United Arab Emirates.
23 Consumer prices rose 0.4% in August, Labor Department reports.
23 St. Christopher and Nevis joins UN: Becomes 158th member of United Nations.
25 Lebanon cease-fire announced: Governments of Syria and Lebanon say warring factions of Lebanon agree to abide by cease-fire as result of Saudi Arabian negotiation; took effect on Sept. 26.
25 National day of protest held in Uruguay: More than 25,000 march through Montevideo to protest military government.
26 Stock market hits record high: Dow Jones average closes at 1,260.77, highest close ever.
26 Reagan addresses UN: President speaks to General Assembly; calls on Soviet Union to reduce tension; offers concessions to break deadlock at Geneva talks on reduction of missiles.
26 Kenya elects new parliament: Voters unseat 40% of parliament, including five cabinet ministers.
26 *Australia II* wins America's Cup race: For first time in 132 years, foreign challenger wins coveted cup; defeats *Liberty* 4 races to 3.
26 IMF to lend Brazil $11 billion: International Monetary Fund agrees to provide Brazil with package of loans and credits through 1984.
28 Rail, bus crash in Yugoslavia kills 25: Commuter train collides with bus near Gospic.
28 Passenger vessel sinks in Nicaragua: 127 die as *Santa Elena* catches fire in Lake Nicaragua.
28 August trade deficit is highest ever: Commerce Department announces record trade gap of $7.19 billion; blamed on strong U.S. dollar and increased demand for imported goods.
29 Congress approves war powers compromise: Senate votes, 54–46, to approve resolution declaring 1973 War Powers Resolution to apply to situation in Lebanon and authorizes deployment of U.S. Marines there for additional 18 months; House had approved measure, 270–161, on Sept. 28.
30 Leading economic indicators fell in August: Commerce Department reports decrease of 0.1%; first decline since August 1982.
30 September farm prices declined 1.4%, Agriculture Department reports.
30 EPA bans pesticide: Environmental Protection Agency bans use of pesticide ethylene dibromide (EDB) as soil fumigant and orders farmers to phase out use on crops and food products; had been determined to be cause of cancer and birth defects.
30–Oct. 3 Arizona flooding widespread: 15 die, thousands made homeless in flooding southeastern Arizona; more than $300 million in property damage.

SOVIETS SHOOT DOWN CIVILIAN AIRLINER

FOCUS

United Press Int'l.

South Korean 747 jetliner was shot down by Soviet SU-15 fighters after it strayed into Soviet air space on Sept. 1.

The world was shocked and horrified on Sept. 1, 1983, when it learned that an unarmed Korean Air Lines 747 passenger plane had been shot down over the Sea of Japan, with 269 people aboard. All aboard the New York-to-Seoul flight perished, including 61 Americans.

Apparently straying into Soviet air space, the plane was destroyed by a Soviet SU-15 fighter plane firing an air-to-air missile, after the airline pilot, according to the Soviet Union, ignored efforts by Soviet pilots to establish radio contact. However, tapes supplied by Japanese ground stations, and played at the United Nations on Sept. 6, followed the voice of the Soviet pilot during the attack, and did not indicate any effort by him to contact the KAL pilot or to establish that the plane was, indeed, a civilian aircraft.

In the hours and days just after the attack, the Soviet Union denied it had even shot the plane down. It admitted firing warning shots, but not until Sept. 6, did the Soviet government admit the plane had been shot down. The government claimed, however, that the fighter pilots "could not have known" that the South Korean plane was a civilian airliner.

The Soviets maintained that the aircraft was carrying out espionage activities for the United States. Reagan administration officials announced on Sept. 4, that a U.S. RC-135 reconnaissance plane had been in the area a few hours earlier, but that it had never entered Soviet air space and had already landed in Alaska by the time of the KAL downing.

President Reagan termed the incident a "horrifying act of violence" and on Sept. 14, the House of Representatives voted 416-0 to condemn the action as "one of the most infamous and reprehensible acts in history."

At the United Nations on Sept. 12, the Soviet Union vetoed a Security Council resolution deploring the Soviet action.

Following the lead of the U.S., European airline pilots on Sept. 12 began a boycott of flights to the Soviet Union. Many other nations followed suit. On Sept. 16, the U.S. told the Soviet Union that Soviet Foreign Minister Andrei A. Gromyko would not be allowed to land at a civilian airport if he flew to New York to attend a UN General Assembly meeting. Although Gromyko was promised landing rights at a military airport, he did not attend the UN meeting.

The boycotts against flights to the Soviet Union ended in October, when the 17 nations involved agreed to resumption of flights.

The full story of KAL Flight 007 may never be known, because the wreckage and the "black box" containing the flight recorder could not be recovered. On Nov. 5, the U.S. called off its two-month search.

Hampered by rough weather, the searchers were unable to find any large sections of the plane. Several bodies and bits and pieces of wreckage turned up on some Japanese beaches.

The Soviet Union refused to allow search ships to enter waters in Soviet territory.

OCTOBER

4 Reagan proposes reduction in arms: President Reagan, in nationally televised speech, offers new proposal to reduce U.S. and Soviet long-range nuclear arsenals; proposal would allow modernization of strategic arsenals but require destruction of old nuclear warheads when new ones are deployed.

4 Railroads announce merger: Santa Fe Industries, Inc. and Southern Pacific Co. announce agreement for merger that would form third-largest rail system in U.S.

4 U.S. automakers end 1983 model year: General Motors, Ford, and Chrysler end with 16.7% increase in sales; first increase since 1978.

5 Lech Walesa awarded Nobel Peace Prize: Founder of outlawed Polish trade union Solidarity wins coveted award. See page 69.

7 September unemployment down 0.3% to 9.1%: Labor Department reports lowest level in 18 months.

9 Burma bomb blast kills South Koreans: Bomb explodes at wreath-laying ceremony in Rangoon, killing four South Korean cabinet members and 15 others; motorcade of South Korean President Chun Doo Hwan had been delayed by traffic; North Korea blamed for terrorist act.

9 Interior Secretary James G. Watt resigns: Steps down after racial joke spurs calls for ouster; President Reagan names national security adviser William P. Clark to replace Watt on Oct. 13.

10 Stock market hits record high: Dow Jones average closes at 1,284.65.

10 New premier elected in Israel: Yitzhak Shamir becomes prime minister after 60–53 vote in parliament; devaluation of shekel by 18.7% announced on Oct. 11.

12 Japan's ex-premier convicted for bribery: Former Prime Minister Kakuei Tanaka is found guilty of taking an estimated $2 million in bribes from Lockheed Corp. in 1972–74; sentenced to four years in prison and amount of bribes; Tanaka refuses to give up seat in parliament; plans appeal.

14 Producer prices up slightly in September: Labor Department reports 0.2% increase in prices paid for finished goods.

14 Industrial production up 1.5% in September: Federal Reserve Board reports tenth consecutive monthly gain in output of nation's factories, utilities, and mines.

14–15 Floods in India kill 42: Storms occur in Uttar Pradesh.

16 U.S., Canada sign environmental pact: Accord aims at reducing phosphorus pollution in Great Lakes.

17 Reagan names new national security adviser: Appoints Robert C. McFarlane to replace William P. Clark.

17 Industrial production at 78.1% of capacity: Federal Reserve Board reports highest level since October 1981, when American industry operated at 78.6% of capacity.

17 Reagan okays campaign committee: President Reagan formally notifies Federal Election Commission of formation of campaign committee to seek reelection, but refrains from announcing definite plans to be a candidate.

18 GM settles bias suit: General Motors Corp. and Equal Employment Opportunity Commission announce accord, in 10-year-old employment discrimination complaint, in which GM would commit some $42.5 million to the hiring, training, and promotion of women and minorities in its plants.

19 Prime minister of Grenada killed: Maurice Bishop killed by soldiers after being held under house arrest since Oct. 13; 16-member military council assumes leadership of nation Oct. 20 with Gen. Hudson Austin in command.

19 Congress approves King holiday: Senate votes 78–22 to designate third Monday in January, beginning in 1986, as a federal holiday in honor of Rev. Martin Luther King Jr.; House had approved the legislation in August.

19 September housing starts dip 13.5%: Commerce Department announces plunge, attributed to high mortgage rates.

20 GNP up 7.9% in third quarter: Commerce Department reports brisk growth of gross national product in third quarter of 1983.

21 Irish president reelected: Patrick J. Hillery wins second 7-year term.

22 Intruder crashes country club to see Reagan: Charles R. Harris, 45, of August, Ga., crashes truck through gates of Augusta National Golf Course, takes seven hostages, including White House aides, and demands to speak to President Reagan, who was playing golf there; hostages released and intruder surrenders with no injuries.

22–23 European demonstrators oppose missiles: An estimated 2 million persons took part in demonstrations in West Germany, Britain, Italy and other European cities to protest deployment of U.S. cruise and Pershing II missiles in Europe.

23 Beirut terrorist attack kills 240 Marines: See page 27.

25 U.S., troops land in Grenada: President Reagan announces predawn action to rescue U.S. citizens. See page 29.

25 Consumer Price Index jumps 0.5% in September, Labor Department reports.

26 Oil-drilling ship sinks in China Sea: 5,930-ton *Glomar Java Sea* sinks during typhoon; 81 die.

28 Earthquake in Idaho kills two children: Quake rocks eight northwestern states; registers 6.9 on Richter scale; deaths occur in Challis, Idaho.

28 September trade deficit narrows: Commerce Department reports trade gap at $5.81 billion, smaller than August's record of $7.19 billion.

30 Earthquake in Turkey kills 1,233: Levels 50 villages in eastern Turkey; measures 7.1 on Richter scale.

30 Argentina election: Raul Alfonsin of moderate Radical Civic Union is elected president with 52% of vote, ending nearly 8 years of military rule and reducing influence of Peronist Party; Radicals also win majority in lower house of legislature.

30 Zambia's president sworn in for fifth term: Kenneth Kaunda takes oath for fifth time, after receiving 93% of vote on Oct. 27.

31 Lebanese reconciliation talks begin: Representatives of Lebanese government, Maronite Christian community, antigovernment Druse and Shiite Muslim groups, and observers from Saudi Arabia and Syria meet in Geneva, Switzerland, in attempt to settle fate of strife-torn Lebanon.

241 U.S. MARINES KILLED IN BEIRUT BLAST

FOCUS

Wide World

The U.S. Flag hangs limply from a piece of wreckage as rescue workers search for victims in the bombed ruins of the U.S. Marine command center near Beirut International airport.

At dawn on Oct. 23 a terrorist driving a large yellow truck rammed through a barbed wire fence at the U.S. Marine compound near Beirut International Airport in Lebanon. He sped past two sentry posts where the Marines on duty were armed, on orders, with unloaded weapons. Then he smashed the truck into the main headquarters building, detonating several tons of high explosives that destroyed the building. Some 241 Marines were killed.

Almost at the same time, another terrorist crashed his bomb-laden truck into headquarters of French forces in Beirut, killing 56.

Both the American and French troops were part of an international peacekeeping force sent to Lebanon in August 1982, first to ensure the safe evacuation of PLO guerrillas from the city, and later to aid the Lebanese army in its attempt to stop fighting among rival factions in the war-torn country. In September 1983 Congress ordered the Marines to be withdrawn in 18 months unless Congress agrees to an extension of time (see page 157).

Six months before the bombing of the U.S. and French headquarters, the U.S. embassy in Beirut was wrecked by a similar terrorist truck-bomb. See page 15.

U.S. officials blamed Syria for the acts of the terrorists but took no retaliatory action until the Syrians fired on American reconnaissance planes on Dec. 3. The following day 28 U.S. planes bombed Syrian positions. Two of the planes were shot down, and one American pilot was imprisoned by the Syrians.

More Marines were killed in artillery duels with guerrillas in the days that followed. U.S. warships retaliated with bombardment of guerrilla positions.

NOVEMBER

1 Fire on Navy carrier kills 6: Flames race through engine room of aircraft carrier *Ranger* in Arabian Sea; 35 injured.

1 Postal Service to seek rate increase: Will ask for 15% increase, raising cost of mailing first-class letter from 20¢ to 23¢; to go into effect in October 1984.

2 Ruling party wins Vanuatu elections: Ruling National Party of Prime Minister Walter Lini wins 33 seats in 39-seat parliament; first general election since independence in 1980.

2 UN General Assembly scores Grenada action: Resolution "deeply deploring" U.S. "armed intervention in Grenada" approved 108–9; 27 abstain.

2 South Africans approve new charter: About 66% of white voters approve new constitution providing new rights for people of Indian or mixed-race descent, but not blacks.

3 Rumsfeld named to Mideast post: President Reagan names former Defense Secretary Donald H. Rumsfeld as new special Mideast envoy, succeeding Robert C. McFarlane.

4 October unemployment drops to 8.7%: Labor Department reports 0.4% decrease.

4 Bomb destroys Israeli headquarters in Lebanon: 60 die as truck loaded with explosives crashes into Israeli compound in Tyre, Lebanon; hours later Israeli jets strike at Palestinian targets along Beirut-Damascus highway.

6 Turkey holds general elections: Independent conservative Motherland Party wins 212 of 400 seats in parliament; its leader, Turgut Ozal, to be prime minister.

6 Earthquake in China kills 30: Hits Shandong province; measures 5.9 on Richter scale.

7 Bomb explodes in U.S. Capitol: Dynamite explosion causes damage but no injuries at 11 P.M. outside office of Senate Minority Leader Robert C. Byrd.

8 U.S. holds elections: See page 245.

8–14 President Reagan visits Asia: Meets leaders of Japan and South Korea.

8 Air crash in Angola kills 126: Angolan Boeing 737 crashes after takeoff from Lubango.

9 Ruling panel named in Grenada: Governor General Sir Paul Scoon names 9-member advisory council as interim government; Meredith Alister McIntyre to head panel; main task is to prepare for free elections.

10 Iran severs economic ties with France: Action is protest against sale of French warplanes and missiles to Iraq.

12 Train derailment in Texas kills 4: Amtrak train bound from Chicago to San Antonio derails near Marshall, Tex.

14 U.S. cruise missiles arrive in Britain: First of NATO's new generation of medium-range missiles to be deployed in Western Europe.

15 Turkish Cypriots declare independence: Rauf Denktash, leader of Turkish Cypriots, declares establishment of Turkish Republic of Northern Cyprus; move condemned by Cyprus' President Spyros Kyprianou; Turkey recognizes new nation.

15 U.S. Naval officer assassinated in Athens: Two unidentified gunmen kill Capt. George Tsantes, 53, head of naval section of joint U.S. military assistance group in Greece.

16 U.S. troops to leave Grenada by Dec. 23: Reagan administration says U.S. combat troops in Grenada will be home for Christmas.

16 PLO Leader's stronghold falls: Syrian-backed Palestinian rebels fight way into Beddawi refugee camp near Tripoli, Lebanon, last stronghold of PLO leader Yasir Arafat.

18 Congress adjourns after raising debt ceiling: Lawmakers give final approval to legislation raising national debt ceiling to $1,490 billion and authorizing $250 billion Defense Department budget; adjourns 98th Congress to January.

18 Argentina claims nuclear capacity: Government announces it has developed technology to make enriched uranium that can be used in bombs; says technology will be used only for peaceful purposes.

18 New secretary of interior confirmed: Senate votes, 71–18, in favor of appointment of William P. Clark; sworn in Nov. 21.

19 Trains collide in Texas: 4 die as tanker-truck train rams into back of parked freight train in Baytown, Tex.

21 October personal income rose 1.2%: Biggest rise in 25 months, Commerce Department reports.

21 Ferry sinks off Philippines: 200 dead and missing as ferry *Dona Cassandra* sinks in typhoon off Mindanao Island.

22 John F. Kennedy remembered: Memorial services in Washington, D.C., and across U.S. commemorate 20th anniversary of assassination of 35th president.

23 Consumer prices rose 0.4% in October, Bureau of Labor Statistics reports.

23 Soviets break off arms talks: Soviet Union walks out of talks with U.S. in Geneva, Switzerland, on medium-range nuclear missiles. See page 31.

24 Palestinians, Israelis exchange prisoners: Palestine Liberation Organization (PLO) releases six Israelis held more than 14 months; Israel releases 4,500 Arab prisoners from southern Lebanon detention center.

27 Air crash in Spain kills 183: Colombian Avianca Boeing 747 crashes five miles east of Madrid airport; 11 survive.

27–28 Blizzard paralyzes upper Midwest: Denver, Colo., airport closed after 15 to 20 inches of snow; travelers stranded; weather blamed for 56 deaths since Nov. 21.

28 Space shuttle *Columbia* blasts off: Carries 6-man crew and European-built Spacelab research laboratory. See page 748.

28 Nigerian plane crash kills 53: Nigeria Airways Fokker F-28 crashes near Enugu.

28 President approves cooperation with Israel: Administration officials announce resumption of delivery of American-made cluster bomb artillery shells and delay in repayment of American military aid during next fiscal year.

29 Stock prices at record high: Dow Jones average soars 17.38 points to close at 1,287.20, highest ever.

U.S. TROOPS LAND IN GRENADA

FOCUS

United Press Int'l.

U.S. Marines, with automatic rifles at the ready, patrol a road in Grenada after overcoming resistance by communist forces that opposed the landing of U.S. troops in October.

Many Americans first became aware of the small Caribbean island nation Grenada in March when President Reagan displayed aerial photos on TV that indicated the island was being turned into a Cuban military base.

Grenada again burst into the news when its Marxist Prime Minister was overthrown by other members of his government in a coup on Oct. 12. A week later he was killed by the new leaders, who clamped a martial law curfew on the nation.

The Organization of Eastern Caribbean States and the governor general of Grenada appealed to President Reagan to intervene. The U.S. government also feared for the safety of several hundred American students who were attending medical school on the island.

Shortly before dawn on Oct. 25, some 1,900 U.S. Marines and U.S. Army paratroops made a surprise landing on Grenada, accompanied by police units from six Caribbean island nations.

Cuban troops and those of Grenada's Marxist leaders put up stiff resistance, but were quickly overwhelmed. The American students were flown to safety in the U.S.

Total casualties were 18 American troops killed and 116 wounded; 45 Grenadians killed and 337 wounded; and 24 Cubans killed and 59 wounded.

The last U.S. combat troops were withdrawn on Dec. 15, leaving behind about 300 noncombat servicemen to help Caribbean peacekeeping forces.

DECEMBER

1 **EPA official guilty:** See page 13.
2 **November unemployment falls to 8.2%:** Lowest level since January 1982.
3 **Concrete barriers installed at White House:** To impede any terrorist attempting to ram gate.
4 **Syrians down American jets:** American fighter-bombers strike Syrian targets in Lebanon in response to Syrian antiaircraft attacks on unarmed reconnaissance aircraft Dec. 3; two U.S. carrier jets shot down; one American airman captured, one killed.
4 **Eight U.S. Marines killed in Beirut:** Syrian-backed militiamen bombard Beirut airport.
4 **Reagan warns Syria:** U.S. president vows retaliation for any military actions against U.S.
4 **Opposition candidate wins in Venezuela:** Jaime Lusinchi of Democratic Action party wins presidential election.
6 **Bomb on Jerusalem bus kills 6.**
6 **Common Market summit ends in deadlock:** Meeting of European Economic Community leaders in Athens, Greece, ends in deadlock over proposed cuts in farm spending and British demand for a $1 billion budget refund.
7 **Jetliners collide on runway in Spain:** 93 killed as Iberia Airlines Boeing 727 crashes broadside into Aviaco DC-9 in fog at Madrid airport.
8 **Space shuttle *Columbia* returns:** Arrives at Edwards Air Force Base, Calif., eight hours behind schedule because of computer malfunctions; 10-day flight is longest shuttle mission and first test of Spacelab research facility.
8 **U.S. lifts ban on arms sales to Argentina:** State Department announces President Reagan will lift ban effective Dec. 10; ban began in 1978 because of nation's human rights violations.
9 **U.S. sues Shell Oil Co. for $1.9 billion:** Justice Department files suit for damage to environment allegedly caused by Shell's pesticide factory on grounds of Army's Rocky Mountain Arsenal, near Denver.
10 **Argentine president sworn in:** Raúl Ricardo Alfonsin inaugurated, ending nearly eight years of military rule; pledges restoration of human rights, improvement of economy.
10 **NOW endorses Mondale:** National Organization for Women gives first endorsement in its history to former Vice President Mondale.
11 **Pope joins in Lutheran rite:** John Paul II joins service at Evangelical Lutheran Church in Rome; first time a Pope has ever done so.
11 **Bangladesh military leader becomes president:** Lieut. Gen. Hussain Mohammed Ershad, head of military government, proclaims himself president and dissolves cabinet.
12 **U.S. embassy in Kuwait attacked:** 5 killed as truck loaded with explosives smashes into embassy compound; 62 injured.
13 **U.S. and Portugal sign Azores agreement:** Extends U.S. rights to use air base in Azores for seven more years.
13 **Turkish premier takes office:** Prime Minister Turkut Ozal takes office after President Gen. Kenan Everen approves cabinet appointments.
15 **Last U.S. combat troops leave Grenada:** 190 men and commanding general fly home; 300 U.S. noncombat soldiers remain on island.
15 **Reagan administration announces Israel aid:** Will give Israel $1.4 billion in military aid in 1985 fiscal year, beginning Oct. 1, 1984; none must be repaid.
15 **Ruling party wins Jamaica elections:** Jamaica Labor Party of Prime Minister Seaga wins all six contested seats in parliament; first one-party parliament in Jamaica history.
16 **New cease-fire in Lebanon:** Announced in Damascus, Syria, by representatives of Lebanese army and Muslim militia forces; Beirut airport opens for first time in 16 days.
16 **November producer prices decline:** Producer Price Index decreased 0.2%.
17 **Bomb explodes outside London store:** Car bomb blast outside Harrod's department store kills 6; 95 injured; Irish Republican Army takes responsibility.
17 **Fire in Spanish disco kills 81:** Sweeps through discotheque in Madrid.
17–31 **Record cold wave grips U.S.:** More than 100 persons freeze to death.
18 **Japanese elections held:** Ruling Liberal Democratic Party suffers setback, failing to win majority in lower house.
19 **Greyhound strike ends:** Bus drivers and other workers approve 7.8% pay cut to end 7-week strike; return to work on Dec. 21.
20 **PLO guerrillas leave Lebanon:** Yasir Arafat and 4,000 followers evacuated from Tripoli, Lebanon, in Greek ships escorted by French warships.
22 **PLO-Egypt reconciliation:** PLO leader Yasir Arafat embraces Egypt's President Hosni Mubarak in Cairo, ending 6-year split since Egypt signed peace treaty with Israel.
29 **U.S. resigns from UNESCO:** Will leave on Dec. 31, 1984, because UNESCO has "politicized" issues.
30 **Coup in Nigeria:** Maj. Gen. Mohammed Buhari overthrows Nigeria's elected civilian government.

LATE FOOTBALL BOWL RESULTS

Dec. 10 **Independence:** Air Force 9, Miss. 3.
Dec. 17 **Florida Citrus:** Tenn. 30, Md. 23.
Dec. 22 **Hall of Fame:** W. Virginia 20, Ky. 16.
Dec. 23 **Holiday:** Brig. Young 21, Mo. 17.
Dec. 24 **Sun Bowl:** Alabama 28, SMU 7.
Dec. 24 **Pro Football AFC First Round Playoffs:** Seattle 31, Denver 7.
Dec. 26 **Pro Football NFC First Round Playoffs:** Los Angeles 24, Dallas 17.
Dec. 26 **Aloha:** Penn State 13, Wash. 10.
Dec. 29 **Liberty:** Notre D. 19, Boston C. 18.
Dec. 30 **Peach:** Florida State 28, N.C. 3.
Dec. 30 **Gator Bowl:** Florida, 14, Iowa 6.
Dec. 31 **Bluebonnet:** Okla. St. 24, Baylor 14.
Dec. 31 **AFC and NFC Playoffs:** Seattle 27, Miami 20; San F. 24, Detroit 23.

1984

Jan. 1 **AFC and NFC Playoffs:** Washington 51, L.A. Rams 7; L.A. Raiders 38, Pittsburgh 10.
Jan. 2 **Cotton Bowl:** Georgia 10, Texas 9.
Jan. 2 **Fiesta Bowl:** Ohio St. 28, Pittsburgh 23.
Jan. 2 **Orange Bowl:** Miami 31, Nebraska 30.
Jan. 2 **Rose Bowl:** UCLA 45, Illinois 9.
Jan. 2 **Sugar Bowl:** Auburn 9, Michigan 7.

SOVIETS BREAK OFF DISARMAMENT TALKS

FOCUS

Nuns took part in this prayer for an end to the arms race and a parade sponsored by the Catholics for Peace in Chicago in May. It was only one of hundreds of peace demonstrations that took part in many countries throughout the year.

Soviet leaders broke off all formal talks on disarmament or nuclear arms limitations in 1983 to show their anger over the deployment in Europe of new U.S. Pershing II and cruise missiles.

President Reagan and other Western leaders contended deployment of the missiles in West Germany, Britain, Italy, and the Netherlands was essential as a counterforce to Soviet nuclear missiles aimed at Western Europe.

Throughout the year the Soviet Union had made repeated threats, especially against West Germany, in an effort to influence European opinion against installation of the U.S. missiles.

As the first of the new U.S. weapons began arriving in Europe, the Soviets on Nov. 23 halted talks with U.S. diplomats in Geneva that had sought to reach agreement on limiting the number of medium range missiles in Europe.

On Dec. 8 the Soviet Union ended a conference with Americans in Geneva on limiting long-range nuclear missiles, refusing to set a date for resumption of the discussion.

Less than a week later, on Dec. 15, an East-West conference on reduction of armed forces in Europe in Vienna was broken off with no date set for another session.

The next possibility for U.S.-Soviet arms reduction talks lies with the Conference on European Disarmament in Stockholm, Sweden, that has been scheduled for Jan. 17, 1984.

QUOTABLE QUOTES: 1983

ONLY ONE WIFE

"I feel like Nathan Hale—I regret that I have but one wife to give to my country's infrastructure. TV dinners are a small price to pay."

—**Sen. Robert Dole** (R-Kan.), commenting on the nomination of his wife, Elizabeth Dole, to be Secretary of Transportation, on Jan. 26, 1983.

A SHORT NAME PAYS OFF

"I owe a lot to luck, loyalty, and a short name. If I'd been Friedrick Dürrenmatt, I'd never have made it."

—Playwright **Neil Simon,** at ceremonies naming a Broadway theater after him, on June 29, 1983.

IT'S BEEN A PLEASURE

"All in all it has been a pleasure to be able to help people."

—**Barney Clark,** world's first heart transplant recipient in interview March 2, 1983, three weeks before he died.

TRYING HARDER PAYS OFF

"I was chosen because I was qualfied for the position. The fact that I was black was not a factor. I've always had to try harder in my life to achieve things, so this is regular."

—**Vanessa Williams,** commenting on being named Miss America, on Sept. 18, 1983.

IT MUST NOT BE REPEATED

"It has to be told, it has to be relived so it won't be repeated. Coming here is like ripping open an old wound, but it has to be done."

—**Regina Rapaport,** Holocaust survivor, at the Holocaust commemoration in Washington, D.C., on April 11, 1983.

WHO COULD OBJECT?

"Unless you're planning a life of crime for your child, I can't see why any parent would object."

—**Bettie Anne Brophy,** mother of young child being finger-printed for identification purposes in Linden, N.J., on Jan. 25, 1983.

WHAT NEXT?

"Today, Neptune, yesterday, Pluto, and tomorrow, on to the stars."

—**Jack Dyer,** chief of spacecraft operations for *Pioneer 10* space probe, as it crossed out of our solar system and continued into space, on June 13, 1983.

THAT'S NO EXCUSE

"We can no longer tolerate the vacuous notion that we can get along with the present structure 'because we have always done it that way.' "

—**Chief Justice Warren E. Burger,** calling for a new federal court system, on Feb. 6, 1983.

COMPUTERS ARE NECESSARY

"In an age that demands computer literacy, a school without a computer is like a school without a library."

—**Sen. Frank R. Lautenberg** (D-N.J.), on June 7, 1983.

WE'LL WAVE GOODBYE

"If in the judicious determination of the members of the United Nations they feel they were not welcome and treated with the hostly consideration that is their due, the United States strongly encourages member states to seriously consider removing themselves and this organization from the soil of the United States. We will put no impediment in your way and we will be at the dockside bidding you a farewell as you set off into the sunset."

—U.S. delegate to the UN Charles M. Lichenstein, in response to Soviet charge that American actions in denying Foreign Minister Andrei Gromyko permission to land a Soviet plane at New York area public airports raised questions about the suitability of the U.S. as host nation, on Sept. 19, 1983.

NO WORSE JOB

"I don't know of anything that is worse than the job I have, and having to make the calls that I have made."

—**President Ronald Reagan,** discussing the phone calls he made to families of U.S. military persons killed in Beirut, Lebanon, and Grenada.

GET MAD!

"I want you to get damn mad about the current state of affairs. I want you to get so mad that you use your new degree and your common sense to kick America off dead center."

—**Lee A. Iacocca,** chairman of the board of Chrysler Corporation, at commencement exercises at the University of Michigan at Ann Arbor, on May 29, 1983.

ALL TICKETY-BOO

"Everything's going tickety-boo so far."

—Astronaut **Paul J. Weitz,** aboard space shuttle *Challenger,* on April 4, 1983.

NO WAY OUT

"There is no clear way out. We cannot retreat under fire and if we were to declare war we wouldn't know who to declare war against."

—**Sen. Alan Cranston** (D-Calif.), discussing the terrorist bombing of U.S. Marine barracks in Lebanon, on Oct. 23, 1983.

LET US RECALL

"Traces of bigotry still mar America. So each year on Martin Luther King Day, let us not only recall Dr. King, but rededicate ourselves to the commandments he believed in and sought to live every day. "Thou shalt love thy God with all thy heart and thou shall love thy neighbor as thyself.' "

—**President Ronald Reagan,** signing bill creating federal holiday to honor Martin Luther King Jr., on Nov. 2, 1983.

Accidents and Disasters

Wide World

Beach homes along West Beach of Galveston Island, Tex., were destroyed Aug. 18 by Hurricane Alicia as it pounded the island with 100-mile-an-hour winds that caused high tides. Damage from the hurricane was estimated at $1.6 billion in the areas around Houston and Galveston. Eighteen persons died as a result of the storm.

HIGHLIGHTS: 1983

Four of the worst air disasters of 1983 occurred within a span of 30 days. On Nov. 8, an Angolan Airlines Boeing 737 crashed on takeoff from Lubango, Angola, killing all 126 aboard. Officials blamed the crash on technical problems, but a South African-backed guerrilla group, UNITA, claimed to have shot down the aircraft.

Next, on Nov. 27, a Colombian Boeing 747 crashed and exploded in Spain 5 miles east of Madrid's Barajas Airport, killing 183. Eleven passengers survived the accident, which occurred in clear skies. The flight was Avianca Airlines' regular flight from Paris to Bogotá, Colombia.

On the following day, Nov. 28, a Nigeria Airways Fokker F-28 fell on approach to the airport in Enugu, Nigeria. The crash, during a flight from Lagos, Nigeria, killed 53 persons; 19 passengers survived.

Then, on Dec. 7, two jetliners collided in heavy fog on the ground at Madrid's Barajas Airport, killing 93. The collision came as an Iberia Airlines Boeing 727 was moving down a runway at 150 miles per hour in preparation for takeoff. It crashed into an Aviaco airlines DC-9 that had taxied onto the same runway. Officials blamed lack of ground radar and multicolored warning lights for the crash. Forty-two passengers from the Iberia jet survived. Officials said the airport was not closed because the visibility was 300 yards.

The worst aircraft disaster of 1983 occurred on Sept. 29, when an unarmed Korean Air Lines Boeing 747 was shot down by Soviet fighter planes over the Sea of Japan, killing all 269 aboard. See page 25.

DISASTROUS HURRICANES AND TYPHOONS

DATE AND NAME	PLACE	DEATHS	REMARKS
1703, Nov. 26–27	England	8,000	Hurricane
1864, Oct. 5	Calcutta, India	50,000	Much of city stripped by cyclone
1876, Oct. 31	Bakarganj, India (now Bangladesh)	200,000	Storm surge inundates city
1881, Oct. 8	Indochina	300,000	Typhoon and storm surge
1882, June 5	Bombay, India	100,000	Cyclone and storm surge
1899, Aug. 8	Puerto Rico	3,369	San Ciriaco hurricane
1900, Aug. 27–Sept. 15	Texas	6,000	$25 million damage caused by storm tide that inundates Galveston island
1906, Sept. 18	Hong Kong	10,000	Typhoon
1909, Sept. 14–21	Louisiana and Mississippi	350	Wide extent of Louisiana coast inundated; $5 million damage
1915, Aug. 5–25	Texas and Louisiana	275	12-foot storm tide inundates Galveston to depth of 5–6 feet; $50 million damage
1915, Sept. 22–Oct. 1	Middle Gulf Coast	275	90% of buildings destroyed over large area of Louisiana south of New Orleans; $13 million damage
1919, Sept. 2–15	Florida, Louisiana, and Texas	287	Hurricane severe both in Florida and Texas; over 500 casualties in ships lost at sea; $22 million damage
1926, Sept. 11–22	Florida and Alabama	243	Very severe in Miami area and from Pensacola into southern Alabama; $73 million damage
1926, Oct. 20	Havana, Cuba	600	Hurricane strikes city and suburbs
1928, Sept. 6–20	Southern Florida	1,836	Wind-driven waters of Lake Okeechobee overflow into populated areas; $25 million damage
1930, Sept. 3	Santo Domingo, Dominican Rep.	2,000	Hurricane
1931, Sept. 10	British Honduras (Belize)	1,000	Hurricane and tidal wave destroys city of Belize
1934, Sept. 21	Honshu, Japan	4,000	Typhoon causes $50 million property damage
1935, Aug. 29–Sept. 10	Southern Florida	408	"Labor Day Storm"; barometer reading of 26.35 inches on Long Key lowest on record in Western Hemisphere; $6 million damage
1935, Oct. 21	Haiti	2,150	Hurricane
1938, Sept. 10–22	Long Island, New York; southern New England	600	Very heavy wind causes $306 million damage in New England
1940, Aug. 5–15	Georgia and Carolinas	50	Heavy flooding; $2 million damage
1942, Oct. 16	Bengal India	40,000	Cyclone
1944, Sept. 9–16	North Carolina to New England	46	$102 million damage
1944, Oct. 12–23	Florida	18	Warnings prevent heavier casualties; $10 million damage
1944, Dec. 18	South China Sea	800	Three U.S. ships lost in typhoon
1947, Sept. 4–21	Florida and Middle Gulf Coast	51	$55 million damage on east coast of Florida and in Louisiana and Mississippi
1947, Sept. 15–19	Honshu, Japan	1,000	Typhoon and floods
1949, Oct. 27	Southeastern India	1,000	Cyclone
1949, Oct. 31– Nov. 2	Philippines	1,000	Typhoon
1951, Dec. 9–10	Philippines	569	Typhoon leaves 60,000 homeless
1952, Oct. 22	Philippines	431	Southern Luzon hit by typhoon
1953, Sept. 26	Vietnam	1,000	Typhoon and floods
1954, Aug. 25–31 Carol	North Carolina to New England	60	$439 million property losses greatest of any single storm to this date
1954, Sept. 2–14	New Jersey to New England	21	Edna causes $41 million damage in New England
1954, Sept. 26	Northern Japan	1,218	Typhoon causes train ferry to capsize
1954, Oct. 5–18 Hazel	South Carolina to New York	95	$200 million damage in exposed North Carolina shore areas; storm retains destructive intensity through Middle Atlantic states
1954, Oct. 12	Southwestern Haiti	410	Hurricane Hazel leaves 250,000 homeless
1955, Aug. 3–14 Connie	North Carolina	25	Heavy rainfall from North Carolina to New England; $46 million damage
1955, Aug. 16–20 Diane	North Carolina to New England	187	Heavy rainfall with near-maximum runoff causes severe floods through Northeast; $714 million damage exceeds any prior storm
1955, Sept. 19	Tampico, Mexico	300	Hurricane Hilda
1955, Sept. 22–28	West Indies and Mexico	712	Hurricane Janet
1956, Aug. 1	China	2,161	Typhoon devastates Hopen and Honan provinces
1956, Sept. 21–30 Flossy	Louisiana to Florida	15	$10 million damage over area from New Orleans and mouth of Mississippi to western Florida
1957, June 26–29 Audrey	Texas to Alabama	390	Storm surge over 12 feet by Gulf waters floods flat Louisiana coast; $138 million damage
1958, Sept. 27–28	Japan	679	Typhoon Ida strikes central Honshu

DISASTROUS HURRICANES AND TYPHOONS *(continued)*

DATE AND NAME	PLACE	DEATHS	REMARKS
1958, Oct. 30–Nov. 5	East Pakistan (Bangladesh)	500	Cyclone
1959, Aug. 20	China	720	Typhoon Iris strikes coast of Fukien Province
1959, Sept. 17–19	South Korea	669	Typhoon Sarah
1959, Sept. 26–27	Japan	4,580	Typhoon Vera strikes central Honshu
1959, Oct. 27–28	Mexico	960	Hurricane, flood, and mud slides on Pacific coast
1960, Sept. 9–13 Donna	Florida to New England	50	$426 million damage; first storm with hurricane winds to travel up Atlantic coast in 75 years
1960, Oct. 10, 31	East Pakistan (Bangladesh)	14,000	Two cyclones strike Bay of Bengal area
1961, May 9	East Pakistan (Bangladesh)	2,000	Cyclone and storm surge
1961, Sept. 11–14 Carla	Texas	46	Hurricane Carla causes $408 million damage along Texas coast
1961, Sept. 16–17	Japan	172	Typhoon strikes Honshu and other islands
1961, Oct. 31	British Honduras (Belize)	262	Hurricane Hattie devastates Belize
1961, Nov. 12	Southern Mexico	436	Hurricane Tara
1962, Sept. 1	Hong Kong	400	Typhoon Wanda
1962, Oct. 27	Thailand	769	Cyclone
1963, May 28–29	East Pakistan (Bangladesh)	22,000	Cyclone and storm surge leave 1 million homeless
1963, Oct. 1–9	Caribbean Sea	7,200	Hurricane Flora
1964, June 13–14	West Pakistan	250	High winds and floods
1964, Aug. 22	Caribbean Sea	214	Hurricane Cleo sweeps through Guadeloupe and Haiti
1964, Aug. 28–Sept. 16 Dora	Florida and Georgia	5	First hurricane to hit northeastern Florida during this century; $250 million damage
1964, Sept. 28–Oct. 5 Hilda	Louisiana, Mississippi, Carolinas, and Georgia	38	Hurricane and six tornadoes cause $125 million damage
1964, Dec. 22	Ceylon (Sri Lanka)	800	Cyclone hits east coast, principally Trincomalee
1965, May 12	East Pakistan (Bangladesh)	13,000	Cyclone and storm leaves 5–7 million homeless
1965, Sept. 7–12 Betsy	Florida and Louisiana	87	Strikes Miami and devastates New Orleans; damage estimated at $1.42 billion
1965, Oct. 1–9	Northern Mariana Islands	208	Typhoon Carmen
1965, Dec. 15	East Pakistan (Bangladesh)	25,000	Cyclone and storm surge
1966, Sept. 25	Japan	318	Typhoon Ida strikes Japan with winds to 200 mph
1966, Sept. 25–Oct. 11	West Indies, Fla., Mexico	1,000	Hurricane Inez carries 135–145 mph winds
1967, July 9	Southwestern Japan	263	Typhoon Billie causes landslides and floods
1967, Sept. 5–22 Beulah	Texas	15	Severe flooding and 115 tornadoes cause $208 million damage
1968, April 11	East Pakistan (Bangladesh)	200	Cyclone
1968, May 9–10	Burma	1,000	Cyclone leaves 17,200 homeless
1969, May 19–20	Andhra Pradesh, India	608	Cyclone leaves 20,000 homeless
1969, Aug. 17–20 Camille	Mississippi and Louisiana coasts	324	Most destructive hurricane in U.S. history; winds up to 200 mph and tides up to 24 feet; thousands homeless; $1.42 billion damage
1970, Aug. 3–5 Celia	Texas	11	Port Aransas and Aransas Pass suffer worst destruction; causes $454 million damage
1970, Sept. 15	Philippines	300	Typhoon strikes Luzon
1970, Oct. 14	Philippines	575	Typhoon strikes Luzon Island; 193 missing
1970, Oct. 18	Philippines	631	Typhoon strikes Mindanao Island; 284 missing
1970, Nov. 12–13	East Pakistan (Bangladesh)	500,000	Cyclone and storm surge devastates coastal areas
1970, Nov. 20	Philippines	120	Typhoon strikes Manila
1971, Aug. 16–17	Hong Kong	100	Typhoon Rose
1971, Oct. 29–30	India	10,000	Cyclone and tidal wave strike Orissa State
1972, June 17–23 Agnes	Florida to New York	105	Costliest storm in U.S. history with over $4 billion in damage; Pennsylvania is hardest hit with $1.2 billion damage and 48 deaths
1973, April–June	Bangladesh	427	Storms and floods leave 10,000 homeless
1973, April 29–May 2	Indonesia	1,650	Storm and tidal wave hit Flores and Palue islands
1973, Nov. 8	Bangladesh	127	Cyclone in Bay of Bengal sinks fishing fleet
1974, March 25	Bangladesh	300	Storm hits coast Bay of Bengal
1974, June 11	Luzon, Philippines	71	Typhoon Dinah strikes Luzon
1974, July 6	Japan and South Korea	108	Typhoon Gilda causes over $300 million damages
1974, Sept. 7–8	Louisiana	1	Hurricane Carmen causes $150 million damage
1974, Sept. 19–20	Honduras	2,000	Hurricane Fifi leaves 115,000 homeless
1974, Nov. 28	Bangladesh	500	Cyclone hits Bay of Bengal coast
1974, Dec. 25	Darwin, Australia	48	Cyclone destroys port city; 35,000 homeless
1975, May 9	Northern Burma	130	Tropical storm damages 20 towns
1975, Sept. 15–27 Eloise	Puerto Rico, Florida, Northeastern states	61	Puerto Rico hardest hit by 130 mph winds, thousands homeless; severe floods in East Coast states; $420 million damage
1976, May 20–22	Philippines	215	Typhoon Olga leaves 630,000 homeless
1976, Aug. 9–10 Belle	Atlantic Coast, North Carolina to New England	1	Long Island, N.Y., hardest hit by 90 mph winds, 200,000 persons evacuated before storm; $250 million damage

DISASTROUS HURRICANES AND TYPHOONS *(continued)*

DATE AND NAME	PLACE	DEATHS	REMARKS
1976, Sept. 8–13	Japan	104	Typhoon Fran causes flood; 325,000 homeless
1976, Oct. 1	Baja California, Mexico	630	Hurricane Liza breaks dam outside La Paz
1977, July 25	Southern Taiwan	28	Typhoon Thelma destroys 20,000 homes
1977, July 30	Taipei, Taiwan	45	Typhoon Vera hits northern Taiwan, steel bridge collapses in Taipei
1977, Nov. 12	Tamil Nadu, India	400	Cyclone strikes southern India
1977, Nov. 14	Philippines	80	Typhoon whips fire in Manila hotel, killing 47
1977, Nov. 19	Andhra Pradesh, India	over 20,000	Cyclone causes flooding and tidal waves
1978, April 4	Bay of Bengal	1,000	Storm sinks about 100 boats
1978, April 16	Eastern India	173	Tornado hits 10 villages; over 600 injured
1978, Oct. 27	Luzon, Philippines	314	Typhoon Rita leaves 50,000 homeless and estimated $85.4 million damages
1978, Nov. 24	Sri Lanka	500	Cyclone strikes coastal area
1979, April 18	Philippines	29	Typhoon causes $3 million damage
1979, May 12	Andhra Pradesh, India	607	Cyclone leaves 2.5 million homeless and causes $850 million in damage
1979, Aug. 29–Sept. 7, David	Caribbean and eastern United States	1,380	Dominica and Dominican Republic hardest hit; total damage more than $1 billion
1979, Sept. 12 Frederic	Florida, Alabama, Mississippi	8	Evacuation of 500,000 people prevents high loss of life; $1.5 billion damage
1979, Oct. 19	Japan	52	Typhoon Tip ravages Japan; sets off gas-tank fire at U.S. Marine base, killing 12
1980, Aug. 4–11	Caribbean and U.S. Gulf Coast	272	Hurricane Allen, worst Caribbean storm in history, caused more than $1 billion damage
1980, Sept. 15	Central Vietnam	164	Typhoon Ruth wipes out rice crop
1981, July 1	Central Philippines	120	Tropical storm causes flash floods, mudslides
1981, Sept. 20	Northern Philippines	21	Typhoon wrecks Philippine Navy destroyer and sinks freighter
1981, Oct. 9	North Pacific coast of Mexico	65	Tropical storm breaks two dams
1981, Nov. 2	West Coast of India	1,300	Tropical storm sinks fishing fleet off Rajpara
1981, Nov. 24	Luzon, Philippines	204	Typhoon causes tidal waves, floods
1981, Nov. 29–Dec. 5	Thailand	37	Typhoon causes flash floods
1981, Dec. 11	India, Bangladesh	27	Typhoon batters coast
1981, Dec. 26–27	Philippines	185	Typhoon Lee destroys more than 24,000 houses
1982, March 27–28	Philippines	50	Typhoon Nelson causes high waves and flooding
1982, June 3	Orissa, India	200	Hurricane lashes coastal region, 200,000 left homeless
1982, Aug. 2	Central Japan	62	Typhoon Bess causes torrential rain
1982, Aug. 13–14	South Korea	38	Typhoon Cecil causes flooding and mudslides
1982, Sept. 12	Central Japan	26	Typhoon Judy causes flooding, landslides
1982, Sept. 17–20	Guatemala, El Salvador	1,315	Hurricane Olivia sweeps across Central America
1982, Nov. 9	Gujurat, India	275	Hurricane displaces 5,000,000 people
1982, Nov. 24	Hawaii	1	Hurricane Iwa causes $200 million damage.
1983, July 15	Philippines	45	Typhoon Vera sweeps through southern part of Luzon Island.
1983, Aug. 18	Texas	18	Hurricane Alicia devastates Galveston and Houston; $1.6 billion in damage.

MAJOR U.S. TORNADOES SINCE 1900

Source: National Oceanic and Atmospheric Administration

DATE	PLACE	DEATHS	INJURED	DAMAGE
1900, Nov. 20	Arkansas, Mississippi, Tennessee	73	many	$ 500,000
1903, June 1	Gainesville, Georgia	98	190	$ 1,000,000
1905, May 10	Snyder, Oklahoma	87	49	$ 20,000
1908, April 24	Lamar and Wayne counties, Mississippi	100	649	$ 880,000
1909, March 8	Dallas and Monroe counties, Arkansas	64	671	$ 640,000
1913, March 23	Omaha, Nebraska	95	—	$ 3,500,000
1916, June 5	Arkansas (series of tornadoes)	83	400	millions
1917, March 23	New Albany, Indiana	45	—	$ 2,000,000
1917, May 26	Mattoon and Charleston, Illinois	101	638	$ 2,500,000
1917, May 27	Tennessee and Kentucky	70	—	$ 2,000,000
1919, June 22	Fergus Falls, Minnesota	59	—	$ 3,500,000
1920, March 28	Alabama and Georgia	50	—	$ 1,400,000
1920, March 28	Chicago, Illinois, and vicinity	28	—	$ 3,000,000
1920, April 20	Oktibbeha County, Mississippi, and Franklin County, Ala.	87	—	$ 1,500,000
1920, May 2	Rogers, Mayes, and Cherokee counties in Oklahoma	64	—	$ 180,000
1921, April 15	Cass County, Texas; Hempstead, Miller, Pike counties, Ark.	61	—	$ 1,300,000
1924, April 30	Central South Carolina	67	—	$ 1,000,000
1924, June 28	Lorain and Sandusky, Ohio	85	—	$ 12,000,000
1925, March 18	Missouri, Illinois, Indiana	689	1,980	$ 17,000,000
1926, Nov. 25	Belleville to Portland, Arkansas	53	—	$ 630,000

MAJOR U.S. TORNADOES SINCE 1900 *(continued)*

DATE	PLACE	DEATHS	INJURED	DAMAGE
1927, April 12	Rock Springs, Texas	74	—	$ 1,200,000
1927, May 9	Randolph County, Arkansas; Poplar Bluff, Missouri	92	—	$ 2,300,000
1927, Sept. 29	St. Louis, Missouri	72	—	$ 22,000,000
1929, April 25	Southeastern and central Georgia	40	—	$ 850,000
1930, May 6	Hill and Ellis counties, Texas	41	—	$ 2,100,000
1932, March 21	Alabama (series of tornadoes)	268	1,874	$ 5,000,000
1933, May 1	Webster and Bienville Parishes, Louisiana	23	400	$ 1,300,000
1936, April 2	Cordele, Georgia	23	500	$ 3,000,000
1936, April 5	Tupelo, Mississippi	216	700	$ 3,500,000
1936, April 6	Gainesville, Georgia	203	934	$ 13,000,000
1938, Sept. 29	Charleston, South Carolina	32	150	$ 2,000,000
1939, April 16	Drew County, Arkansas	27	62	$ 20,000
1942, March 16	Central to northeastern Mississippi	75	525	$ 1,400,000
1942, April 27	Rogers and Mayes counties, Oklahoma	52	181	$ 2,000,000
1944, June 25	Ravenna, Ohio; Pennsylvania; West Virginia; Maryland	150	867	$ 4,200,000
1945, April 12	Oklahoma and Arkansas	102	689	$ 4,000,000
1946, Jan. 4	Northeastern Texas	30	335	$ 2,700,000
1947, April 9	Texas, Oklahoma, Kansas	169	983	$ 9,800,000
1948, March 19	Bunker Hill and Gillespie, Illinois	33	449	$ 3,800,000
1949, Jan. 3	Louisiana and Arkansas	58	439	$ 1,500,000
1949, May 21	Cape Girardeau, Missouri	23	130	$ 3,500,000
1952, March 21–22	Arkansas, Missouri, and Tennessee (series of tornadoes)	208	1,154	$ 14,000,000
1953, May 11	Waco, Texas	114	597	$ 41,000,000
1953, June 8	Flint to Lakeport, Michigan	116	867	$ 19,000,000
1953, June 9	Central and eastern Massachusetts	90	1,288	$ 52,000,000
1953, Dec. 5	Vicksburg, Mississippi	38	270	$ 25,000,000
1955, May 25	Blackwell, Oklahoma	20	280	$ 8,000,000
1955, May 25	Udall, Kansas	80	270	$ 2,200,000
1956, April 3	Southern Michigan	18	340	$ 11,000,000
1956, April 15	Birmingham, Alabama	25	200	$ 1,500,000
1957, May 20	Williamsburg, Kansas, to Ruskin Heights, Missouri	44	531	millions
1959, Feb. 10	St. Louis, Missouri	21	345	millions
1964, Oct. 3	Lafourche Parish, Louisiana	22	165	$ 500,000
1965, April 11	Illinois, Michigan, Indiana, and Ohio (series of tornadoes)	226	3,000	$620,500,000
1966, March 3	Mississippi and western Alabama	58	531	$ 18,500,000
1966, June 8	Topeka, Kansas, and Vicinity	16	406	$100,000,000
1967, April 21	Boone, McHenry, and Cook counties, Ill.; Kent County, Mich.	57	982	$ 18,000,000
1968, May 15–16	Arkansas, Illinois, Indiana, Iowa, Minnesota, Mississippi, Missouri, Nebraska, Ohio, Tennessee, and Wisconsin	72	1,000	$ 51,000,000
1969, Jan. 23	Jefferson to Newton counties, Mississippi	32	241	$ 500,000
1969, July 4	Northern Ohio (storm and tornadoes)	41	—	substantial
1970, April 17	Texas Panhandle	25	200	$ 5,000,000
1970, May 11	Lubbock, Texas	26	500	$135,000,000
1971, Feb. 21	Mississippi, Louisiana, Tennessee (series of tornadoes)	121	1,600	$ 19,000,000
1973, May 26–28	10 states in South and Midwest (series of 195 tornadoes)	47	—	$ 55,000,000
1974, April 3–4	13 states in South and Midwest (148 tornadoes)	329	6,142	$540,000,000
1974, June	Tulsa and Drumright, Okla., hit by about 20 tornadoes	26	294	$ 23,500,000
1975, Jan. 10	Series of tornadoes in Mississippi, Alabama, and Louisana	15	298	$ 5,000,000
1975, Feb. 22	Tornadoes, thunderstorms, and hail in Oklahoma	4	91	$ 5,000,000
1975, March 24	Atlanta, Ga., about 500 homes, including Governor's mansion, badly damaged	3	152	$ 56,500,000
1975, March 28	Warren, Ark., tornado hits center of city	7	50	$ 5,000,000
1975, May 6	Omaha, Neb., 10 or more tornadoes destroy over 1,000 homes	3	133	$400,000,000
1976, March 26–29	Arkansas and Mississippi, series of tornadoes	8	249	$ 27,000,000
1977, April 4	Northwest of Birmingham, Alabama	22	130	$ 15,000,000
1977, Aug. 21	Lake Mattooon, Illinois, resort area	6	56	$ 5,000,000
1978, April 18	Series of tornadoes hits southeastern Mississippi	4	31	$ 500,000
1978, May 4	Hits elementary school in Pinellas County, Florida	3	94	$ 3,000,000
1978, July 4–5	Cuts 75-mile path in North Dakota and Minnesota	9	73	$ 5,000,000
1978, Sept. 16	Destroys businesses and farms near Grinnell, Iowa	6	45	$ 5,000,000
1978, Dec. 3	Three series of tornadoes in Arkansas and Louisiana	4	250	$100,000,000
1979, April 9–11	Series of tornadoes in Texas and Oklahoma	60	800	$300,000,000
1980, May 12–13	Series of tornadoes in Missouri, Pennsylvania, Michigan	7	—	$100,000,000
1980, June 3	Grand Island, Nebraska	4	134	$140,000,000
1981, April 4	Series of tornadoes in Wisconsin, neighboring states	8	125	$ 9,000,000
1981, June 13–15	Series of tornadoes in Midwest and East	20	99	$ 10,000,000
1982, April 2	Tornadoes hit Arkansas, Texas, Missouri	27	383	$ 50,000,000
1982, May 11–13	Tornadoes hit southwest U.S.	3	16	$220,000,000
1982, May 29	Tornado strikes southern Illinois	10	181	$100,000,000
1983, May 18–23	Series of tornadoes in Texas, Tennessee, Mississippi, and neighboring states cause floods	32	100	$ 41,000,000

MAJOR VOLCANIC DISASTERS

DATE	PLACE	DEATHS	REMARKS
A.D. 79, Aug. 24–26	Pompeii, Herculaneum, Italy	16,000	Mt. Vesuvius erupts; destroys these towns
1169	Sicily	15,000	Mt. Etna erupts
1631, Dec. 16	Italy	4,000	Mt. Vesuvius erupts; destroys five towns
1669	Sicily	20,000	Mt. Etna erupts for 40 days
1772	Java, Indonesia	3,000	Mt. Papandayan erupts
1783	Iceland	9,000	Mt. Hekla erupts; 20 villages obliterated
1815	Sumbawo, Indonesia	12,000	Tambora explodes, followed by tidal waves
1883, Aug. 26–28	Indonesia	35,000	Krakatau erupts, followed by tidal wave
1902, April 8	Guatemala	1,000	Santa Maria erupts
1902, May	Saint Vincent, West Indies	2,000	Soufrière volcano erupts
1902, May 8	Martinique, West Indies	40,000	Mt. Pelée erupts, wiping out city of St. Pierre
1911	Philippines	1,400	Mt. Taal, on Luzon, erupts
1919	Java, Indonesia	5,000	Mt. Kelud erupts, 100 villages destroyed
1951, Jan. 18–21	New Guinea	3,000	Mt. Lamington erupts
1963, March	Bali, Indonesia	1,500	Mt. Agung erupts, leaving 85,000 homeless
1965, Sept. 28	Philippines	500	Mt. Taal, on Luzon, erupts
1966, April 28	Java, Indonesia	1,000	Mt. Kelud erupts; nine villages destroyed
1968, July 29	Costa Rica	100	Mt. Arenal erupts for first time in 500 years
1973, Jan. 23	Heimaey, Iceland	—	Kirkjufell Volcano erupts; 5,000 homeless
1979, Feb. 20	Java, Indonesia	175	Mt. Sinila erupts; 6 villages destroyed
1979, Sept. 12	Catania, Sicily	9	Mt. Etna erupts, 24 injured
1980, May 18	Cascade Mtns., Washington	57	Mount St. Helens erupts; $1.6 billion in damages
1982, March 28	Pichucalco, Mexico	100	Chichón volcano erupts; 20,000 evacuated
1982, April 9	Java, Indonesia	30	Galunggung volcano erupts; 30,000 homeless

PRINCIPAL WORLD FLOODS

DATE	PLACE	DEATHS	REMARKS
1228	Holland	100,000	Sea flood in Friesland
1642	China	300,000	Yellow River dikes collapse at K'ai-feng
1787	Eastern India	10,000	Storm drives seawater inland 20 miles
1861	Sacramento, California	700	Sacramento River overflows banks
1874	Western Pennsylvania	220	River floods
1874	Mill River Valley, Mass.	144	Dam bursts
1881	Mississippi and Ohio rivers	138	Rivers flood; $15,000,000 damage
1887	Honan, China	900,000	Yellow River overflows
1889, May 31	Johnstown, Pennsylvania	2,209	Dam bursts on South Fork Reservoir
1896	Sanriku, Japan	22,000	Tidal wave caused by earthquake
1900, Sept. 8	Galveston, Texas	6,000	Tidal wave caused by hurricane
1903, May–June	Kansas, Missouri, Miss. rivers	100	Rivers flood; $40,000,000 damage
1903, June 15	Heppner, Oregon	325	Flash flood following cloudburst
1911	China	100,000	Yangtze River overflows
1912, March	Bolivar County, Mississippi	200	Mississippi River floods; $70,000,000 damage
1913, March 25–27	Ohio and Indiana	732	$180,873,000 damage
1913, Dec. 1–5	Texas	177	Brazos River floods; $9,000,000 damage
1915, Aug. 17	Galveston, Texas	300	Tidal wave caused by hurricane
1921, June	Pueblo, Colorado	120	Arkansas River floods
1921, September	Texas	215	Rivers flood; $19,000,000 damage
1927, Spring	Mississippi River Valley	313	Mississippi River floods; $284,118,000 damage
1927, November	New England	88	Winooski River floods; $45,578,000 damage
1928, March 13	Santa Paula, California	450	St. Francis Dam collapses
1928, Sept. 13	Lake Okeechobee, Florida	1,836	Flood caused by hurricane
1935, May–June	Kansas	110	Republican and Kansas rivers flood
1935, July	Pennsylvania	52	Susquehanna River tributaries flood
1936, March–April	New England, Pennsylvania	107	Rivers flood; $270,000,000 damage
1937, Jan.–Feb.	Ohio and Miss. river valleys	137	1 million homeless; $417,685,000 damage
1938, March	Southern California	79	Streams flood; $24,500,000 damage
1939, July	Kentucky	78	Licking and Kentucky rivers flood
1939	China	1 million	Floods in north, followed by starvation
1940, August	Va., Tenn., N. and S. Carolina	40	Floods cause $12,000,000 damage
1942, May	Pennsylvania	33	Delaware and Susquehanna rivers flood
1943, April–June	Midwest	60	Mississippi River and tributaries flood
1946, April 1	Hawaii	173	Tidal wave caused by earthquake in Alaska
1947	Honshu Island, Japan	2,000	Flooding after typhoon
1947, May–July	Middle West	29	Missouri and Upper Mississippi valleys flood; $235,000,000 damage
1948, May–June	Columbia River, Washington	35	$101,725,000 damage
1950, June	West Virginia	31	Rivers flood in central part of state
1951, June–July	Kansas and Missouri valleys	41	50,000 homeless in floods; $923,224,000 damage
1951, August	Manchuria	1,800	Flood; some estimates of dead as high as 5,000
1953, Feb. 1	Northwest Europe	1,850	Storm floods Netherlands and North Sea coast
1954, August	Iran	2,000	Flash flood
1955, Aug. 18–21	Northeastern U.S.	187	Hurricane-caused floods; $714,079,000 damage

PRINCIPAL WORLD FLOODS *(continued)*

DATE	PLACE	DEATHS	REMARKS
1955, Oct. 7–12	Pakistan and India	1,700	Flood
1955, December	California, Oregon, Washington	61	Streams and rivers flood; $154,532,000 damage
1956, August	China	2,000	Three provinces flood after typhoon
1957	Kyushu Island, Japan	513	Flood
1957, April–June	Tex., Ark., Kan., La., Mo., Okla.	18	Floods cause $105,000,000 damage
1958, July	Iowa	19	Flash floods on E. Nishnabotna River cause $5,850,000 damage
1959, November	Western Mexico	2,000	Flood
1959, Dec. 2	Frejus, France	412	Collapse of dam and flood
1960, Feb. 29	Agadir, Morocco	12,000	Tidal wave caused by earthquake
1960, October	East Pakistan (Bangladesh)	10,000	Tidal wave
1961, July	Charleston, West Virginia	22	Flash floods on streams cause $3,238,000 damage
1962, Feb. 17	West Germany	342	Storm breaks North Sea dikes
1963, March	Ohio River Valley	26	Floods cause $97,600,000 damage
1963, Sept. 27	Barcelona, Spain	445	Flash flood west and north of city
1963, Oct. 9	Northern Italy	2,000	Vaiont Dam collapses
1963, Nov. 14–15	Haiti	500	Flood and landslides
1964, June 8–9	Northern Montana	31	Floods cause $54,279,000 damage
1964, December	California and Oregon	40	Floods cause $415,832,000 damage
1965, March–May	Midwest	16	Missouri, Upper Mississippi, and Red River of the North flood
1965, June	Nebraska	16	South Platte River floods; $415,076,000 damage
1965, June 18–19	Sanderson, Texas	26	Flash flood causes $2,715,000 damage
1965, June	Kansas and Missouri	16	Flood causes $58,340,000 damage
1966, Jan. 11–13	Rio de Janeiro, Brazil	405	Floods and landslides leave 50,000 homeless
1966, April–May	Texas	14	Sabine and Trinity rivers flood
1966, Nov. 3–4	Arno Valley, Italy	113	Art treasures in Florence damaged and destroyed
1967, Jan.–March	Brazil	1,200	Heavy rains in Rio de Janeiro and São Paulo states
1967, Nov. 26	Lisbon, Portugal	464	Record rainfall causes heavy flooding
1967, Nov. 30	Java, Indonesia	160	Irrigation dam collapses
1968, May	Northern New Jersey	—	Floods cause $166,690,000 damage
1968, Aug. 7–14	Western India	1,000	Widespread flooding kills 80,000 cattle
1968, Oct. 3–7	Northeastern India	900	Torrential rains cause flooding
1969, Jan. 18–26	Southern California	91	Floods, mudslides cause $399,233,000 damage
1969, March–April	Upper Midwestern states	—	Snowmelt floods cause $151,000,000 damage
1969, March 16	Northeastern Brazil	218	Flash floods
1969, July 4	Ohio and Michigan	33	Flash floods cause $87,915,000 damage
1969, Aug. 20–22	Virginia and West Virginia	153	Floods caused by Hurricane Camille
1969, October	Tunisia	500	Heavy rains cause flash floods
1970, January	California	18	Sacramento River floods
1970, May–June	Romania	215	Danube River flood causes $500 million damages
1970, July	Uttar Pradesh, India	600	Buses swept away by flooding of Alaknanda River
1970, September	India	600	Floods from Bombay to Calcutta; 20,000 homeless
1970, September	Arizona	23	Floods cause $5,000,000 damage
1970, October	Puerto Rico	50	Floods cause $62,000,000 damage
1970, October	South Vietnam	193	Worst floods in six years leave 200,000 homeless
1970, November	Colombia	250–750	Heavy flooding on the Magdalena River
1971, Feb. 26	Rio de Janeiro, Brazil	130	Flash flood
1971, April 26–28	Salvador, Brazil	140	Flood from heavy rains
1971, July 29	Afghanistan	1,000	Flood caused by landslide into a reservoir
1972, Feb. 26	Buffalo Creek, West Virginia	125	Coal-waste dam collapses
1972, June 9–10	Rapid City, South Dakota	237	Canyon Lake Dam collapses in flash flood
1972, June 21–27	East Coast United States	105	Hurricane Agnes causes $4,019,721,000 damage
1972, July 1–Aug. 7	Philippines	454	Floods from heavy rains
1972, mid-July	Japan	370	Landslides and floods from heavy rains
1972, Aug. 18–19	Seoul, South Korea	296	Flash floods from worst rains in nation's history
1973, April–May	Mississippi, Ohio, Missouri rivers	33	Valley floods; $1,154,770,000 damage
1973, Aug. 19–31	Pakistan	1,500	Floods in Punjab destroys 3,000 villages
1973, Oct. 19–20	Spain	190	Floods and mudslides in southern Spain
1974, March–May	Brazil	2,000	Ten states devasted by floods; 300,000 homeless
1974, July–August	Bangladesh and India	2,750	Flood damage estimated at $2 billion
1974, Sept. 14	Nelson Landing, Nevada	14	Flash flood causes $1,000,000 damage
1974, Nov. 23	Texas	13	Flash floods in Travis, Hays, and Comal counties
1976, June	Bangladesh	143	Floods result from monsoon rains
1976, July 31–Aug. 1	Big Thompson Canyon, Colorado	139	Flash flood causes $50,000,000 damage
1976, July	Mexico	120	Floods caused by two weeks of rain in central Mexico
1976, August	Pakistan	316	Flood waters flow from Himalayas
1976, November	Indonesia	136	Floods caused by torrential rains in East Java
1977, April 4–6	Southeastern U.S. states	40	Tornadoes cause flooding; $275,000,000 damage
1977, June 30	Karachi, Pakistan	400	Rains flood low-lying slum dwellings
1977, July 9	Anyang, South Korea	188	Heavy rains trigger floods and mudslides
1977, July 19–20	Johnstown, Pennsylvania	74	Rains cause dam to burst; $200,000,000 damage
1977, Sept. 12–13	Kansas City, Missouri	25	Flash floods cause $140,000,000 damage

PRINCIPAL WORLD FLOODS *(continued)*

DATE	PLACE	DEATHS	REMARKS
1977, Nov. 2–3	Athens and Piraeus, Greece	25	Rivers flooded after torrential rains
1977, Nov. 6	Toccoa, Georgia	39	Dam bursts after 4 days of rain
1978, July 9	Afghanistan-Pakistan border	122	Torrential rains cause flooding
1978, Aug. 4–8	Southern and Central Texas	26	Flash flood cause $50,000,000 damage
1978, Aug. 13	Northern India	450	Monsoon rains cause flooding of Ganges River
1978, Aug. 18	Acajutla, El Salvador	100	Tidal wave strike summer resort town
1978, September	Northern India	1,500	Heavy rains trigger floods and mudslides
1979, Aug. 11	Morvi, India	1,335	Rain-soaked dam collapses
1979, October	Egypt	42	Worst floods in 25 years leaves 25,000 homeless
1980, Feb. 13–22	Southern California, Arizona	36	Heavy rains bring $320,000,000 damage
1980, August	India	987	Floods from monsoon rains in Uttar Pradesh
1980, Aug. 31	Ibadan, Nigeria	240	Flood from 12-hour rainstorm
1980, Sept. 17	Orissa, India	203	Flash floods from overflow of Mahanadi River
1981, Jan. 26	Laingsburg, South Africa	130	Torrential rains flood Buffels River
1981, May 25	Austin, Texas	13	Rains cause flash floods; $20,000,000 damage
1981, July 12–15	Sichuan Province, China	753	Yangtze River overflows; $1,140,000,000 damage
1981, July 19–25	Northwest India	550	Swollen rivers overflow banks
1982, Jan. 3–6	San Francisco Bay Area	36	Floods cause $280 million damage
1982, Jan. 23–27	Peru	800	Chontayacu and Huallaga rivers flood
1982, March 26	Peru	220	Heavy rains cause floods, landslides
1982, May 12	Guangdong, China	430	Worst floods in 30 years leave 450,000 homeless
1982, May 24–28	Nicaragua, Honduras	226	Floods cause $200 million damage; 65,000 homeless
1982, June 3	Sumatra Island, Indonesia	176	Flooding destroys farmland; 2,500 homeless
1982, July 23	Nagasaki, Japan	307	Heaviest rains in 25 years cause floods
1982, Aug.–Sept.	Northeastern India	600	Torrential rains leave 2.2 million homeless
1982, Dec. 2–10	Mississippi Valley, U.S.	22	Floods cause $600,000,000 damage; 34,000 homeless
1983, March 20	Northern Peru and Bolivia	260	Floods and mudslides bury towns
1983, April 6–12	Southern states, United States	15	Floods cause $625 million damage
1983, May 2	Pacasmayo, Peru	50	Flash floods sweep across Pan American Highway
1983, June 22–26	Gujarat, India	500	Heavy rains result in flooding
1983, July 23	Honshu, Japan	120	Floods cause landslides
1983, Oct. 14–15	Uttar Pradesh, India	42	Heavy rains bring flooding

WORLD EARTHQUAKES AND AVALANCHES

The strength of an earthquake is measured by the 9-point Richter scale developed in the 1930s by Dr. Charles Francis Richter of the California Institute of Technology. Each point on the Richter scale stands for a magnitude 10 times greater than the previous number. Thus an earthquake with a Richter number of 9 would be 100,000,000 times as strong as a tremor with a Richter number of 1. No earthquake has yet been recorded with a Richter number of 9.

The great San Francisco earthquake of 1906 is calculated to have had a Richter number of 8.3.

526, May 20	Antioch, Syria	250,000	Earthquake
551, July 9	Beirut, Lebanon	—	Destroyed by earthquake
856, December	Corinth, Greece	45,000	Earthquake
936	Constantinople	—	Destroyed by earthquake
1057	Hopeh Province near Peking, China	25,000	Earthquake
1268	Cilicia, Asia Minor	60,000	Earthquake
1290, Sept. 27	Hopeh Province near Peking, China	100,000	Earthquake
1293, May 20	Kamakura, Japan	30,000	Earthquake
1531, Jan. 26	Lisbon, Portugal	30,000	Earthquake
1556, Jan. 24	Shensi, China	830,000	Earthquake
1667, November	Shemakha, East Azerbaijan	80,000	Earthquake
1693, Jan. 11	Catania, Italy	60,000	Earthquake
1703, Dec. 30	Tokyo, Japan	200,000	Earthquake
1737, Oct. 11	Calcutta, India	300,000	Earthquake
1755, June 7	Northern Persia	40,000	Earthquake
1755, Nov. 1	Lisbon, Portugal	60,000	Earthquake destroys most of city
1783, Feb. 4	Southern Italy and Sicily	50,000	Wide-ranging earthquake; Messina ravaged
1797, Feb. 4	Cuzco, Peru, and Quito, Ecuador	40,000	Earthquakes destroy cities
1811, Dec. 15	New Madrid, Missouri	—	Heaviest recorded earthquake in North America
1822, Sept. 5	Aleppo, Syria	22,000	Earthquake
1828, Dec. 28	Honshu, Japan	30,000	Earthquake
1868, Aug. 13–15	Peru and Ecuador	25,000	Earthquakes razes towns; $300 million loss
1875, May 16	Venezuela and Colombia	16,000	Earthquake
1886, Aug. 31	Charleston, South Carolina	60	Earthquake severely damages city
1896, June 15	Sanriku coast, Japan	22,000	Earthquakes and seismic sea wave
1906, April 18	San Francisco, California	700	Earthquake followed by fire; $500 million loss
1906, Aug. 16	Chile	1,500	Earthquake; $100 million loss
1908, Dec. 28	Southern Italy and Sicily	75,000	Earthquake
1915, Jan. 13	Central Italy	30,000	Earthquake
1918, Oct. 11	Puerto Rico	116	Earthquake and tidal wave; $4 million damage

WORLD EARTHQUAKES AND AVALANCHES *(continued)*

DATE	PLACE	DEATHS	REMARKS
1920, Dec. 16	Kansu, China	180,000	Earthquake destroys 10 cities
1923, Sept. 1	Yokohama and Tokyo, Japan	143,000	Earthquake destroys all of Yokohama, half of Tokyo
1932, Dec. 26	Kansu, China	70,000	Earthquake
1933, March 10	Long Beach, California	115	Earthquake; about $40 million loss
1935, May 31	Quetta, Baluchistan, India	60,000	Earthquake
1939, Jan. 24	Chile	30,000	Earthquake
1939, Dec. 27	Anatolia, Turkey	23,000	Series of earthquakes followed by floods
1946, May 31	Eastern Turkey	1,300	Earthquake
1946, Dec. 21	Southern Japan	2,000	Earthquake and six seismic sea waves
1948, June 28	Fukui, Japan	5,131	Earthquake and fire destroys most of Fukui
1949, Aug. 5	Ecuador	6,000	Earthquake heavily damages 50 towns
1950, Aug. 15	Assam, India	1,500	Earthquake and widespread flooding
1953, Feb. 12	Eastern Iran	1,000	Earthquake destroys town of Trud
1953, March 18	Northwestern Turkey	1,200	Earthquake; 50,000 homeless
1954, Sept. 9–12	Algeria	1,600	Earthquake destroys most of Orléansville
1956, June 10–17	Northern Afghanistan	2,000	Series of earthquakes
1957, July 2	Iran	2,500	Earthquakes along shores of Caspian Sea
1957, Dec. 2	Outer Mongolia	1,200	Earthquake
1957, Dec. 13	Western Iran	2,000	Earthquake
1960, Feb. 29	Agadir, Morocco	12,000	Earthquake, seismic sea wave, and fire
1960, May 21–30	Chile	5,700	Earthquake and seismic sea waves
1962, Jan. 10	Peru	2,000	Avalanche on Huascarán, extinct volcano
1962, Sept. 1	Northwestern Iran	10,000	Earthquake
1963, July 26	Skoplje, Yugoslavia	1,100	Earthquake destroys most of city
1964, March 27	Alaska	131	Earthquake and seismic sea wave
1965, March 28	Near Santiago, Chile	400	Earthquake
1966, Jan. 11–13	Rio de Janeiro, Brazil	300	Landslide caused by record rain
1966, Aug. 19	Turkey	2,529	Earthquake; 100,000 homeless
1967, July 29	Venezuela	236	Earthquake extending from Andes to Caribbean Sea
1968, Jan. 15	Western Sicily	224	Series of earthquakes destroys several towns
1968, Aug. 2	Manila, Philippines	207	Earthquake
1968, Aug. 15	Donggala, Indonesia	200	Earthquake
1968, Aug. 31	Northeastern Iran	13,000	Earthquake, world's worst in 30 years
1969, Feb. 23	Celebes Island, Indonesia	600	Earthquake and seismic sea waves
1970, March 28	Western Turkey	1,089	Earthquakes
1970, May 31	Northern Peru	60,000	Earthquake and avalanche
1970, Dec. 12	Cauca Valley, Colombia	200	Avalanche
1971, Feb. 9	Southern California	64	Earthquake in San Fernando Valley
1971, July 9	North central Chile	90	Earthquake
1972, Jan. 26	Bogotá, Colombia	70	Torrential rains cause landslide
1972, April 10	Southwestern Iran	5,374	Earthquake
1972, Dec. 23	Managua, Nicaragua	10,000	Capital city destroyed by earthquake
1973, Jan. 30	Mexico	52	Earthquake makes 22,000 homeless
1973, Aug. 28	Mexico	527	Earthquake damages 67 villages
1974, April 25	Peru	750	Landslides destroy three villages
1974, June 28	Colombia	200	Landslide on eastern slope of Andes
1974, Sept. 30	Colombia	90	Landslide buries small town
1974, Oct. 3	Lima, Peru	78	Earthquake and tidal wave hit coast
1974, Dec. 28	Pakistan	5,300	Earthquake near Chinese border; 16,000 injured
1975, Feb. 4	Manchuria, China	Unknown	Widespread destruction by earthquake
1975, July 8	Pagan, Burma	—	Hundreds of ancient temples destroyed
1975, Sept. 6	Eastern Turkey	2,200	Village of Lice destroyed; 3,500 injured
1976, Feb. 4	Guatemala, Honduras	22,934	Earthquake leaves 1,277,000 homeless
1976, May 6	Northern Italy	968	Earthquake devastates Friuli area of northern Italy
1976, June 26	Western New Guinea	443	Earthquake results in mud and rock slides
1976, July 14	Bali, Indonesia	500	Earthquake
1976, July 28	Tientsin-Tangshan, China	242,000	Strongest quake since 1964; 164,000 injured
1976, Aug. 17	Philippines	8,000	Earthquake off southern island of Mindanao
1976, Oct. 29	West Iran, Indonesia	133	Earthquake hits remote jungle area
1976, Nov. 24	Turkey	3,790	Earthquake in eastern Turkey; 50,000 homeless
1977, March 4	Bucharest, Romania	1,541	Earthquake almost destroys central city
1977, March 22	Southern Iran	167	Earthquake causes heavy damage
1977, April 6	Western Iran	352	Destroys mountain villages
1977, Aug. 19	Indonesia	150	Quake causes tidal waves
1977, Nov. 23	Western Argentina	100	Earthquake destroys town of Caucete
1977, Dec. 20	Southeastern Iran	519	Earthquake near Zarand leaves thousands homeless
1978, Sept. 16	Northeastern Iran	25,000	Earthquake destroys whole villages
1979, Jan. 16	Qaen, Iran	199	Earthquake strikes three villages in northeast Iran
1979, April 15	Yugoslavia	235	Earthquake jolts Adriatic coast; 80,000 homeless
1979, April 30	West Sumatra, Indonesia	82	Landslide caused by burst of crater on Merapi volcano
1979, July 18	Lomblem Island, Indonesia	539	Landslide on Mt. Werung causes tidal wave
1979, Aug. 6	San Francisco, Calif.	—	Strong quake jolts northern California
1979, Sept. 12	Yapen Island, Indonesia	100	Earthquake causes tidal wave; 10,000 homeless
1979, Oct. 15	California–Mexico border	—	Earthquake causes property damage; injures 70

WORLD EARTHQUAKES AND AVALANCHES *(continued)*

DATE	PLACE	DEATHS	REMARKS
1979, Nov. 14	Northeastern Iran	248	Earthquake rocks 14 villages
1979, Nov. 23	Western Colombia	300	Earthquake causes $20 million damage
1979, Dec. 12	Colombia–Ecuador border	133	Six coastal towns flattened by earthquake
1980, Oct. 10	Algeria	2,950	Quake destroys Al Asnam; 300,000 homeless
1980, Nov. 23	Southern Italy	2,735	Quakes flatten 133 villages; 300,000 homeless
1981, Jan. 18	Irian Jaya, Indonesia	250	Earthquake destroys 14 villages
1981, Jan. 24	Sichuan, China	150	Earthquake disrupts communication
1981, May 20	Java, Indonesia	184	Landslide hits villages on Mt. Semeru
1981, June 11	Kerman, Iran	1,600	Quake flattens town of Golbaf
1981, July 28	Kerman, Iran	1,500	Second quake in 6 weeks devastates area
1981, Sept. 12–13	Gilgit, Northern Pakistan	212	Quake causes much damage
1982, Dec. 13	North Yemen	2,000	Many towns and villages destroyed
1982, Dec. 16	Afghanistan	500	Occurs in Hindu-Kush mountain range
1983, March 7	Northwest China	270	Landslide destroys villages
1983, March 12	Phupan, Pakistan	84	Landslide engulfs village
1983, March 31	Popayán, Colombia	240	Earthquake devastates town
1983, April 27	Ecuador	100	Landslide buries highway in Chimborazo province
1983, May 26	Honshu, Japan	102	Quake sets off tidal wave
1983, July 28	Gachalá, Colombia	160	Mudslide buries workers at hydroelectric project
1983, Oct. 30	Turkey	1,333	50 villages in eastern Turkey leveled
1983, Nov. 6	Shandong province, China	30	Measures 5.9 on Richter scale
1983, Dec. 21, Dec. 24	Guinea	443	Two quakes destroy score of villages

WORLD'S WORST FIRES AND EXPLOSIONS

DATE	PLACE	DEATHS	REMARKS
1666, Sept. 2–6	London, England	—	Fire destroys many public buildings, 89 churches and over 13,200 houses; 200,000 homeless
1835, Dec. 16	New York, New York	—	Nearly 700 buildings burned; $20 million loss
1836, Feb. 14	St. Petersburg, Russia	700	Theater fire
1842, May 5–7	Hamburg, Germany	100	More than 4,000 buildings destroyed
1845, April 10	Pittsburgh, Pennsylvania	—	1,000 buildings destroyed in fire; $6 million loss
1846, June 12	Quebec, Canada	200	Theater fire
1851, May 4	St. Louis, Missouri	—	Much of city burned; $15 million loss
1863, Dec. 8	Santiago, Chile	2,000	Church burned while filled with worshipers
1866, July 4	Portland, Maine	—	City almost totally destroyed by fire; $10 million loss
1866, Oct. 13	Quebec, Canada	—	2,500 buildings burned
1871, Oct. 8–9	Chicago, Illinois	300	3½ square miles devastated by fire; 18,000 buildings lost; 100,000 homeless; $200 million loss
1871, Oct. 8–14	Michigan and Wisconsin	1,000	Great forest fire devastates large area
1872, Nov. 9–11	Boston, Massachusetts	—	Fire; 600 buildings ruined; $75 million loss
1876, Dec. 5	Brooklyn, New York	295	Conway's Theater fire
1877, June 20	St. John, New Brunswick, Canada	100	Fire; $12,500,000 property loss
1881, Dec. 8	Vienna, Austria	640	Ring Theater fire
1883, Jan. 13	Berdichev, Russia	270	Theater fire
1887, May 25	Paris, France	200	Opéra Comique fire
1887, Sept. 4	Exeter, England	200	Theater fire
1888, May 25	Oporto, Portugal	200	Baquet Theater fire
1889, June 6	Seattle, Washington	—	Fire loss about $10 million
1889, Aug. 4	Spokane, Washington	—	Fire destroys business district
1894, Sept. 1	Hinckley, Minnesota	418	160,000 forest acres burned; $25 million loss
1897, May 4	Paris, France	150	Fire at charity bazaar
1889, March 17	New York, New York	45	Windsor Hotel fire
1900, June 30	Hoboken, New Jersey	300	Pier burned; property damage, $4,627,000
1902, Sept. 20	Birmingham, Alabama	115	Church fire
1903, Dec. 30	Chicago, Illinois	639	Iroquois Theater fire
1904, Feb. 7–8	Baltimore, Maryland	—	Fire; 75 city blocks destroyed; $85 million loss
1906, March 10	Courrières, France	1,060	Mine explosion
1906, April 18	San Francisco, California	700	Following earthquake, fire devastates 4 square miles; property damage about $500 million
1907, Dec. 6	Monongah, West Virginia	362	Coal-mine explosion
1908, Jan. 13	Boyertown, Pennsylvania	173	Fire from motion-picture machine explosion
1908, March 4	Collinwood, Ohio	161	School fire
1908, April 12	Chelsea, Massachusetts	—	Destroyed by fire; $17 million loss
1909, Feb. 15	Acapulco, Mexico	250	Flores Theater fire
1909, Nov. 13	Cherry, Illinois	259	Coal-mine fire
1911, March 25	New York, New York	145	Triangle Shirtwaist Factory fire
1913, Oct. 22	Dawson, New Mexico	263	Mine fire
1914, June 25–26	Salem, Massachusetts	—	1,700 buildings burned; $14 million loss
1914, Dec. 15	Fukuoka, Japan	687	Coal-mine disaster at Hojo Colliery
1916, July 30	Black Tom Island, Jersey City, N.J.	—	German war sabotage; $220 million loss
1917, April 10	Eddystone, Pennsylvania	133	Munitions plant explosion
1917, Dec. 6	Halifax, Nova Scotia	1,500	Explosion of war material; $35 million damage
1918, Oct. 4–5	Morgan Station, New Jersey	64	Gillespie Loading Co. explosion

WORLD'S WORST FIRES AND EXPLOSIONS *(continued)*

DATE	PLACE	DEATHS	REMARKS
1918, Oct. 13–15	Minnesota and Wisconsin	1,000	Forest fires; $100 million loss
1919, June 20	San Juan, Puerto Rico	150	Mayaguez Theater fire
1921 Sept. 21	Oppau, Germany	600	Ammonium-nitrate plant explosion
1922, Sept. 13	Smyrna, Turkey	—	Fire almost totally destroys city; 100,000 homeless
1923, May 17	Kershaw County, N.C.	77	Fire in school during presentation of play
1928, May 19	Mather, Pennsylvania	194	Coal-mine explosion
1929, May 15	Crile Hospital, Cleveland, Ohio	125	Poisonous fumes cause mass suffocation
1930, April 21	Columbus, Ohio	317	Fire at Ohio State Penitentiary
1934, March 22	Hakodate, Japan	1,500	Fire destroys largest city north of Tokyo
1934, May 19	Chicago, Illinois	—	Union Stockyards burn; $10 million loss
1934, Sept. 22	Wrexham, Wales	265	Coal-mine explosion
1937, Feb. 13	Antung, Manchuria	658	Theater fire
1937, March 18	New London, Texas	413	Schoolhouse destroyed by natural-gas explosion
1938, Nov. 12–16	Changsha, China	2,000	Fire levels city
1939, March 1	Osaka, Japan	500	Munitions explosion destroys part of Osaka
1939, July 10	Peñaranda de Bracamonte, Spain	100	Town demolished by munitions factory explosion
1939, Nov. 14	Lagunillas, Venezuela	500	Oil town built on Lake Maracaibo destroyed by fire
1940, April 23	Natchez, Mississippi	198	Dance-hall fire
1941, May 31	Jersey City, New Jersey	—	Waterfront fire; $25 million loss
1941, June 8	Smederevo, Yugoslavia	1,000	Explosion of ammunition plant; town destroyed
1942, April 26	Honkeiko Colliery, Manchuria	1,549	Worst mine disaster in history
1942, May 1	Tessenderlo, Belgium	250	Chemical works explosion
1942, Nov. 28	Boston, Massachusetts	493	Cocoanut Grove nightclub fire
1942, Dec. 13	St. John's, Newfoundland	100	Knights of Columbus Hostel fire panic
1943, May 7	Sandoná, Colombia	103	Municipal Palace demolished by fire
1944, April 14	Bombay, India	1,500	Ship's fire causes explosion of ammunition
1944, July 6	Hartford, Connecticut	168	Audience panics in circus "Big Top" fire
1944, July 17	Port Chicago, California	300	Two ammunition-dump explosions
1944, Oct. 20	Cleveland, Ohio	121	Liquid-gas tanks explode; fire burns 50 blocks
1946, June 5	Chicago, Illinois	60	La Salle Hotel fire
1946, Dec. 7	Atlanta, Georgia	119	Winecoff Hotel fire
1947, March 25	Centralia, Illinois	111	Coal-mine explosion
1947, April 16	Texas City, Texas	468	Explosion of French ship *Grandcamp* ruins city
1947, Aug. 20	Cádiz, Spain	400	Shipyard explosion
1947, Oct. 25	Bar Harbor, Maine	—	Forest fire; estimated loss at $30 million
1948, March 9	Tsingtao, China	200	Ammunition storehouse explosion
1948, July 28	Ludwigshafen, Germany	200	I. G. Farben Company explosions and fire
1948, Sept. 22	Hong Kong	135	Fire and chemical explosion in warehouse
1949, Sept. 4	Chungking, China	1,700	Central part of city burns; 100,000 homeless
1950, May 19	South Amboy, New Jersey	30	Munitions barges explode
1951, May 13	Kano, Nigeria	100	Movie house burns
1951, Dec. 21	West Frankfort, Illinois	119	Coal-mine explosion
1955, Feb. 17	Near Yokohama, Japan	97	Home for aged women burns
1956, Aug. 7	Cali, Colombia	1,100	Seven trucks carrying dynamite explode
1956, Aug. 8	Marcinelle, Belgium	263	Coal-mine fires
1957, Feb. 17	Warrenton, Missouri	72	Home for aged burns
1958, Feb. 19	Near Asansol, India	180	Coal-mine explosion
1958, June 23	Santo Amaro, Brazil	100	Fireworks explosion
1958, Dec. 1	Chicago, Illinois	93	Parochial-school fire
1958, Dec. 16	Bogotá, Colombia	84	Department-store fire
1960, Jan. 21	Coalbrook, South Africa	437	Coal-mine cave-ins and explosion
1960, Feb. 22	Zwickau, East Germany	123	Explosion in Karl Marx Mine
1960, March 4	Havana, Cuba	75	French munitions ship explodes
1960, July 14	Guatemala City, Guatemala	200	Hospital for insane swept by fire
1960, Nov. 13	Amude, Syria	152	Movie-house fire
1961, July 8	Dolna Suce, Czechoslovakia	108	Coal-mine gas explosion
1961, Dec. 17	Niteroi, Brazil	323	Circus-tent fire
1962, Feb. 7	Saar, Germany	298	Coal-mine explosion
1963, May 4	Diourbel, Senegal	64	Theater fire
1963, Oct. 31	Indianapolis, Indiana	73	Explosion at State Fair coliseum
1963, Nov. 9	Fukuoka, Japan	458	Coal-mine disaster
1963, Nov. 23	Fitchville, Ohio	63	Fire burns rest home
1964, July 23	Bone, Algeria	100	Explosion aboard Egyptian munitions ship
1965, May 28	Bihar, India	400	Mine disaster
1965, June 1	Fukuoka, Japan	237	Coal-mine disaster at Yamano Colliery
1965, June 8	Kakanj, Yugoslavia	108	Mine disaster
1965, Aug. 9	Searcy, Arkansas	53	Explosion in a Titan 11 missile silo
1967, May 22	Brussels, Belgium	322	Fire in L'Innovation department store
1968, April 6	Richmond, Indiana	43	Explosion and fire; nearly two city blocks wrecked
1968, Nov. 20	Mannington, West Virginia	78	Fire and explosions in coal mine
1969, March 31	Barroteran, Mexico	183	Coal-mine explosion
1969, Nov. 7	Buffelstein, South Africa	64	Explosion in gold mine
1970, Jan. 9	Marietta, Ohio	31	Private nursing-home fire

WORLD'S WORST FIRES AND EXPLOSIONS *(continued)*

DATE	PLACE	DEATHS	REMARKS
1970, April 9	Osaka, Japan	73	Gas-leak explosions at subway construction site
1970, Nov. 1	Saint-Laurent-du-Pont, France	144	Fire in dance hall
1970, Dec. 30	Wooton, Kentucky	38	Coal-mine explosion
1971, Dec. 25	Seoul, South Korea	163	Hotel fire
1972, March 11	Minsk, Soviet Union	100	Factory fire and/or explosion
1972, May 2	Kellogg, Idaho	91	Sunshine silver-mine fire
1972, May 13	Osaka, Japan	115	Nightclub fire
1972, June 6	Wankie, Rhodesia	427	Coal-mine explosion
1973, Feb. 10	Staten Island, New York City	40	Oil storage-tank explosion
1973, June 24	New Orleans, Louisiana	32	Nightclub fire
1973, Aug. 2	Douglas, Isle of Man, Britain	51	Amusement-park fire
1973, Sept. 1	Copenhagen, Denmark	35	Hotel fire; 20 Americans killed
1973, Nov. 29	Kumamoto, Japan	101	Department-store fire; 2,500 shoppers saved
1974, Feb. 1	São Paulo, Brazil	189	Fire in 25-story skyscraper; 293 injured
1974, June 17	Lahore, Pakistan	40	Store building destroyed by fire
1974, Dec. 27	Lievin, France	42	Explosion and fire in coal mine
1975, Jan. 22	Manila, Philippines	51	Factory fire; 79 injured
1975, Dec. 12	Mecca, Saudi Arabia	138	Muslim pilgrims' tent-city fire; 151 injured
1975, Dec. 27	Dhanbad, India	431	Explosion floods coal mine
1976, April 13	Lapua, Finland	40	Ammunition-factory explosion
1976, Dec. 31	Chlebovice, Czechoslovakia	43	Gas explosion in coal mine
1977, Feb. 25	Moscow, Soviet Union	45	Fire in Rossiya Hotel, world's largest hotel
1977, May 28	Southgate, Kentucky	164	Nightclub fire, more than 100 injuries
1977, June 9	Abidjan, Ivory Coast	41	Nightclub fire
1977, June 26	Columbia, Tennessee	42	Maurcy County Jail fire traps inmates and visitors
1977, Aug. 2	Moatize, Mozambique	150	Explosion in coal mine; 9 killed in later rioting
1977, Nov. 14	Manila, Philippines	47	Hotel fire fanned by winds of typhoon
1977, Dec. 22	Westwego, Louisiana	35	Explosion in grain elevator
1978, July 11	Tarragona, Spain	181	Tank truck explodes and falls into campsite
1978, Aug. 19	Abadan, Iran	430	Enemies of Shah set fire in movie theater
1978, Nov. 2	Huimanguillo, Mexico	52	Gas pipeline explodes
1978, Dec. 1	Klerksdorp, South Africa	41	Gold-mine fire
1979, Feb. 15	Warsaw, Poland	49	Explosion in savings bank; 110 injured
1979, July 12	Saragossa, Spain	71	Oil tank explodes in luxury hotel
1979, July 29	Tuticorin, India	104	Fire in movie theater
1979, Oct. 10	Bytom, Poland	34	Coal-mine fire
1979, Oct. 31	Czechowice-Dziedzice, Poland	63	Coal-mine fire
1980, Jan. 1	Chapais, Quebec	45	Fire in social club
1980, Jan. 31	Guatemala City, Guatemala	39	Fire in Spanish Embassy
1980, May 20	Kingston, Jamaica	157	Fire in home for poor and elderly
1980, Aug. 2	Bologna, Italy	81	Terrorist bomb explodes in railroad station
1980, Aug. 15	Baghdad, Iraq	59	Fire in movie theater
1980, Aug. 16	London, England	37	Fire in adjoining social clubs
1980, Oct. 24	Ortuella, Spain	51	Explosion in elementary school
1980, Nov. 2	Gorna Grupa, Poland	50	Fire in mental hospital
1980, Nov. 16	Bangkok, Thailand	60	Explosion in munitions plant
1980, Nov. 19	Kawaji, Japan	44	Fire in resort hotel
1980, Nov. 22	Las Vegas, Nevada	84	Fire in MGM Grand resort hotel and casino
1980, Nov. 24	Danaciobasi, Turkey	97	Explosion at village engagement party
1980, Dec. 3	Northern Romania	49	Explosion in Livezeni coal mine
1980, Dec. 4	Harrison, New York	26	Fire in motel conference center
1981, Jan. 9	Keansburg, New Jersey	31	Fire in nursing home
1981, Feb. 7	Bangalore, India	71	Circus tent catches fire
1981, Feb. 14	Dublin, Ireland	46	Fire in discotheque
1981, Sept. 3	Northern Czechoslovakia	65	Explosion in Zaluzi coal mine
1981, Oct. 16	Hokkaido, Japan	93	Explosion in coal mine caused by methane gas
1982, Feb. 8	Tokyo, Japan	32	Fire in luxury hotel
1982, April 25	Todi, Italy	34	Fire in antiques exhibit
1982, May 12	Zenica, Yugoslavia	39	Explosion in coal mine caused by methane gas
1982, Nov. 3	Salang Pass Tunnel, Afghanistan	c.1,100	Explosion caused by oil tank truck
1982, Nov. 11	Tyre, Lebanon	89	Explosion in Israeli army headquarters
1982, Dec. 19	Caracas, Venezuela	132	Fuel-tank fire and explosions at power plant
1983, Feb. 13	Turin, Italy	64	Fire in movie theater
1983, Feb. 16–17	Australia	71	Brush fires in two Australian southern states
1983, March 7	Eregli, Turkey	98	Coal-mine explosion
1983, April 18	Taegu, South Korea	25	Fire in disco
1983, May 7	Istanbul, Turkey	42	Hotel fire
1983, May 8	Tlapacoya, Mexico	34	Gunpowder explodes in church
1983, June 7	Serbia, Yugoslavia	21	Coal-mine explosion
1983, June 22	Oroszlay, Hungary	36	Coal-mine explosion
1983, Sept. 12	Natal, South Africa	64	Coal-mine explosion
1983, Dec. 17	Madrid, Spain	79	Fire in discotheque
1983, Dec. 17	Amsterdam, Netherlands	13	Gambling club burns

WORLD'S WORST AIRCRAFT DISASTERS

DATE	AIRCRAFT	DEATHS	REMARKS
1921, Aug. 24	English dirigible R-38 (U.S. ZR-2)	62	Breaks in two over Hull, England
1928, Dec. 21	French dirigible *Dixmude*	52	Vanishes over Mediterranean Sea or Sahara Desert
1930, Oct. 5	English dirigible R-101	47	Crashes near Beauvais, France
1933, April 4	U.S. dirigible *Akron II*	73	Crashes off new Jersey coast
1935, May 18	Soviet aircraft *Maxim Gorky*	49	Collides with a small plane over Moscow
1937, May 6	German zeppelin *Hindenburg*	36	Burns at mooring in Lakehurst, N.J.
1938, July 24	Military stunt plane	53	Crashes into grandstand in Bogotá, Colombia
1944, Aug. 23	U.S. bomber	76	Crashes into school in Freckleton, England
1945, July 28	U.S. bomber	13	Crashes into Empire State Building
1949, Nov. 1	P-38 fighter and DC-4 airliner	55	Collide above airport in Washington, D.C.
1950, March 12	English airliner	80	Crashes near Cardiff, Wales
1952, March 27	Two Soviet planes	70	Collide over Tula Airport, Moscow
1952, Dec. 20	U.S. Air Force plane	87	Crashes at Larson Air Force Base, Wash.
1953, June 18	U.S. Air Force Globemaster	129	Crashes near Tokyo, Japan
1955, Oct. 6	Airliner, DC-4	66	Crashes in mountains near Laramie, Wyo.
1956, June 20	Venezuelan airliner	74	Crashes in Atlantic 40 miles south of New York City
1956, June 30	Two airliners	128	Collide over Grand Canyon, Ariz.
1957, Aug. 11	Chartered Canadian airliner	79	Crashes near Quebec, Canada
1958, May 18	Belgian airliner	65	Crashes in Casablanca, Morocco
1958, Aug. 14	Dutch airliner	99	Crashes in ocean west of Ireland
1958, Oct. 17	Soviet jet airliner	75	Crashes in Kanash, Soviet Union
1959, Feb. 3	U.S. turboprop airliner	65	Crashes into East River, New York City
1959, June 26	U.S. luxury airliner	68	Explodes near Milan, Italy
1960, Feb. 25	U.S. Navy and Brazilian planes	61	Collide over Rio de Janeiro
1960, March 17	Turboprop airliner	63	Mid-air explosion over Tell City, Ind.
1960, Aug. 29	French airliner	63	Crashes into sea near Dakar, Senegal
1960, Sept. 18	U.S. DC-6AB	80	Crashes on takeoff from Guam
1960, Oct. 4	U.S. Electra	62	Crashes into harbor at takeoff in Boston, Mass.
1960, Dec. 16	U.S. DC-8 and U.S. Constellation	134	Collide over New York City
1961, Feb. 15	Belgian jet airliner	73	Crashes near Berg, Belgium
1961, May 10	French airliner	79	Crashes in Ghadames, Libya
1961, Sept. 1	U.S. Constellation	78	Crashes after takeoff in Chicago, Ill.
1961, Sept. 10	U.S. charter plane	83	Crashes in Shannon, Ireland
1961, Nov. 8	U.S. charter plane	77	Crashes in Richmond, Va.
1962, March 1	U.S. B-707	95	Explodes as it crashes into Jamaica Bay, N.Y. City
1962, March 4	English DC-7	111	Crashes in jungle near Douala, Cameroon
1962, March 16	U.S. Super Constellation	107	Crashes into western Pacific Ocean
1962, June 3	French B-707	130	Crashes at takeoff in Paris, France
1962, June 22	French B-707	113	Crashes near Guadeloupe, West Indies
1962, July 7	Italian DC-8	94	Crashes near Bombay, India
1962, Nov. 27	Brazilian jet airliner	97	Crashes and burns in Lima, Peru
1963, Feb. 1	British and Turkish planes	95	Collide over Ankara, Turkey
1963, June 3	U.S. military chartered airliner	101	Crashes in Pacific Ocean off British Columbia
1963, Nov. 29	Canadian airliner	118	Crashes after takeoff in Montreal, Canada
1963, Dec. 8	U.S. B-707/121	81	Crashes near Elkton, Md.
1964, Feb. 25	U.S. DC-8	58	Crashes in Lake Pontchartrain, La.
1964, Feb. 29	English Britannia	83	Crashes near Innsbruck, Austria
1964, March 1	U.S. Constellation	85	Crashes near Lake Tahoe, Calif.
1964, May 11	U.S. military C-135 transport	75	Crashes at Clark Air Force Base, the Philippines
1965, Feb. 6	Chilean DC-6B	87	Crashes in the Andes
1965, Feb. 8	U.S. DC-7B	84	Plunges into Atlantic near Kennedy Airport, N.Y. City
1965, May 20	Pakistani jet airliner	119	Crashes near Cairo, Egypt
1965, June 25	U.S. Air Force transport	84	Crashes into mountains near Los Angeles, Calif.
1965, Nov. 8	U.S. B-727	58	Crashes during landing near Cincinnati, Ohio
1965, Dec. 11	U.S. Air Force transport C-123	85	Crashes into mountain near Nhatrang, South Vietnam
1966, Jan. 24	Indian B-707	117	Crashes into Mont Blanc, France
1966, Feb. 4	Japanese B-727	133	Plunges into Tokyo Bay during landing
1966, March 5	British B-707	124	Catches fire above Mt. Fuji and crashes on slopes
1966, April 22	U.S. Lockheed Electra	82	Crashes near Ardmore, Okla.
1966, Sept. 1	British turboprop	95	Crashes during landing in Belgrade, Yugoslavia
1966, Nov. 24	TABSO Airways, Ilyushin-18	82	Crashes at Bratislava, Czechoslovakia
1966, Dec. 24	Flying Tiger CL-44	111	Cargo flight crashes at Danang, South Vietnam
1967, April 20	Swiss jetliner	126	Crashes while landing at Nicosia, Cyprus
1967, June 3	British DC-6	88	Crashes into Mt. Canigou in French Pyrenees
1967, Nov. 20	U.S. Convair jetliner	69	Crashes on landing near Cincinnati, Ohio
1968, April 20	South African Boeing 707	122	Crashes near Windhoek, South West Africa
1968, May 3	U.S. jetliner	85	Crashes in central Texas during thunderstorm
1968, Sept. 11	French Caravelle jetliner	95	Catches fire and crashes off French Riveria
1969, March 16	Venezuelan DC-9	155	Crashes into suburb of Maracaibo, Venezuela
1969, March 20	Egyptian IL-18	91	Crashes on landing at Aswan airport, Egypt
1969, June 4	Mexican jet	79	Flies into mountain near Monterrey, Mexico
1969, Sept. 9	U.S. DC-9 and Piper Cherokee	83	Collide over Shelbyville, Ind.
1969, Sept. 20	U.S. Phantom and Vietnamese DC-4	77	Collide near Danang, South Vietnam

WORLD'S WORST AIRCRAFT DISASTERS *(continued)*

DATE	AIRCRAFT	DEATHS	REMARKS
1969, Nov. 20	Nigerian VC-10	87	Crashes near Iju, Nigeria
1969, Dec. 8	Greek DC-6B	90	Crashes on mountain near Athens during storm
1970, Feb. 15	Dominican Airways DC-9	102	Crashes into sea after takeoff from Santo Domingo
1970, July 4	British four-engine Comet	112	Crashes into mountain in Spain
1970, July 5	Canadian DC-8	109	Crashes near Toronto airport
1970, Aug. 9	Peruvian Electra	101	Crashes near Cuzco
1970, Nov. 14	U.S. DC-9	75	Crashes near Kenova, W.Va.
1970, Dec. 31	Aeroflot Ilyushin-18	90	Crashes at takeoff from Leningrad
1971, May 23	Yugoslav TU-134A	78	Crashes and burns on island off Rijeka, Yugoslavia
1971, July 30	Japanese Boeing 727 and F-86	162	Collide over Morioka, Japan
1971, Sept. 4	Alaska Airlines Boeing 727	111	Crashes in Tongass National Forest, Alaska
1972, Jan. 7	Iberian Airlines Caravelle	104	Crashes near island of Ibiza, Spain
1972, March 14	Danish Sterling Airways charter	112	Crashes near Gulf of Oman
1972, May 6	Alitalia DC-8	115	Crashes into mountain on Sicily
1972, June 18	BEA Trident-1	118	Crashes after takeoff at London
1972, June	Antonov-10	108	Crashes near Kharkov in the Ukraine
1972, Aug. 14	E. German Ilyushin-62	156	Crashes after takeoff from Schönefeld Airport
1972, Oct. 3	Soviet Ilyushin-18	106	Crashes near Black Sea resort of Sochi
1972, Oct. 13	Soviet Ilyushin-62	176	Crashes near Sheremetyevo Airport
1972, Dec. 3	Spanish charter jet	155	Crashes in Canary Islands
1972, Dec. 29	Eastern Airlines L-1011 jet	101	Crashes in Everglades near Miami, Fla.
1973, Jan. 22	Royal Jordanian Airways 707	176	Crashes in fog at Kano, Nigeria
1973, Feb. 19	Soviet jetline	77	Crashes in landing at Prague, Czechoslovakia
1973, Feb. 21	Libyan airliner	108	Shot down by Israeli jets near Suez Canal
1973, April 10	British charter flight	105	Hits mountain near Basel, Switzerland
1973, July 11	Brazilian 707 jet	122	Burns on crashing near Paris, France
1973, July 23	Pan American 707 jet	78	After takeoff, crashes near Tahiti
1973, July 31	Delta Air Lines DC-9	89	Hits seawall while landing in fog, Boston, Mass.
1973, Aug. 13	Aviaco Airline Caravelle	85	Hits trees while landing in fog, La Coriena, Spain
1973, Dec. 22	Charter Caravelle airliner	106	Crashes into mountain near Tangier, Morocco
1974, Jan. 31	Pan American 707 jet	92	Landing crash at Pago Pago, American Samoa
1974, March 3	Turkish Airlines DC-10	346	Falls near Paris after cargo door blows off
1974, April 4	Chartered DC-4	77	Takeoff crash at Francistown, Botswana
1974, April 22	Pan American 707	107	Crashes into mountainside on Bali, Indonesia
1974, April 27	Soviet turboprop airliner	118	Takeoff crash at Leningrad
1974, Sept. 8	TWA 707 airliner	88	Falls in Ionian Sea off Greece in storm
1974, Sept. 11	Eastern Airlines DC-9	72	Landing crash at Charlotte, N.C.
1974, Dec. 1	TWA 727 jet airliner	92	Crashes during landing at Washington, D.C.
1974, Dec. 4	Dutch DC-8 jet airliner	191	Falls during landing approach on Sri Lanka
1974, Dec. 22	Venezuelan airliner	77	Takeoff crash at Maturín, Venezuela
1975, April 4	Air Force C-5A Galaxy	155	Planeload of war orphans crashes in South Vietnam
1975, June 24	Eastern Airlines Boeing 727	113	Crashes at Kennedy Airport, New York City
1975, Aug. 3	Moroccan Boeing 707 airliner	188	Strikes mountain near Agadir, Morocco
1975, Aug. 20	Czechoslovak Ilyushin 62	126	Landing crash near Damascus, Syria, airport
1975, Oct. 25	Bolivian Air Force Convair 440	70	Hits mountain near La Paz, Bolivia
1975, Oct. 30	Yugoslav DC-9 airliner	68	Crashes landing in fog at Prague, Czechoslovakia
1976, Jan. 1	Lebanese Boeing 707 airliner	82	Explodes in storm over Arabian Desert
1976, July 28	Czechoslovak Ilyushin 18	70	Falls into lake near Bratislava, Czechoslovakia
1976, Sept. 4	Venezuelan Air Force transport	68	Crashes on landing at U.S. air base in Azores
1976, Sept. 10	British Trident and Yugoslav DC-9	176	Collide near Zagreb, Yugoslavia
1976, Sept. 19	Turkish Boeing 727	155	Strikes Karakaya Mountain in Turkey
1976, Oct. 6	Cuban DC-8 airliner	73	Explodes after takeoff from Barbados
1976, Oct. 12	Indian Airlines Caravelle	95	Crashes after takeoff from Bombay
1976, Oct. 13	Chartered Boeing 707	100	Falls into downtown street in Santa Cruz, Bolivia
1976, Nov. 28	Soviet Tupolev TU-104	72	Crashes after takeoff from Moscow
1976, Dec. 25	Egyptian Boeing 707	72	Crashes into factory at Bangkok, Thailand
1977, March 27	Pan Am 747 and KLM 747	581	Jets collide on airport runway at Santa Cruz de Tenerife, Canary Islands; aviation's worst disaster
1977, April 4	Southern Airways DC-9	71	Crashes in hailstorm at New Hope, Ga.
1977, May 27	Soviet IL-62	66	Crashes on landing at Havana, Cuba
1977, Nov. 19	Portuguese Boeing 727	130	Crashes on landing at Funchal, Madeira, airport
1977, Dec. 4	Malaysian jetliner	100	Explodes in southern Malaysia after being hijacked
1978, Jan. 1	Air India Boeing 747	213	Explodes and crashes in sea near Bombay, India
1978, March 16	Bulgarian Tupolev-134	73	Crashes after takeoff from Sofia, Bulgaria
1978, Sept. 25	Boeing 727 and Cessna 172	144	Collide over San Diego, Calif.
1978, Nov. 15	Icelandic Airlines DC-8	183	Crashes short of runway at Colombo, Sri Lanka
1978, Dec. 23	Alitalia Airlines DC-9	108	Crashes into sea short of Palermo, Italy, airport
1979, March 18	Soviet TU-104	90	Crashes on takeoff from Moscow's Vnukovo Airport
1979, May 25	American Airline DC-10	273	Crashes on takeoff from Chicago airport
1979, Aug. 11	Two Soviet TU-134 jets	173	Collide over Ukraine in bad weather
1979, Oct. 31	Western Airlines DC-10	73	Crashes on landing at Mexico City airport
1979, Nov. 26	Pakistan Int'l Airlines Boeing 707	156	Crashes after takeoff from Jidda, Saudi Arabia
1979, Nov. 28	Air New Zealand DC-10	257	Crashes in Antarctica during sightseeing flight

WORLD'S WORST AIRCRAFT DISASTERS *(continued)*

DATE	AIRCRAFT	DEATHS	REMARKS
1980, Jan. 21	Iran Air Boeing 727	128	Crashes in mountains near Teheran, Iran
1980, March 14	Polish IL-62 jetliner	87	Crashes on landing in Warsaw, Poland
1980, April 25	British Boeing 727	146	Hits mountain in Tenerife, Canary Islands
1980, June 28	Itavia Airlines DC-9	81	Falls into Tyrrhenian Sea on flight to Sicily
1980, July 7	Soviet TU-154	163	Crashes on takeoff from Alma Ata, Soviet Union
1980, Aug. 19	Saudi Arabian Lockheed Tri-star	301	Flames trap passengers after landing at Riyadh
1980, Sept. 13	Florida Commuter Airlines DC-3	34	Crashes into Atlantic Ocean on flight to Bahamas
1980, Sept. 14	Saudi Arabian C-130 transport	89	Catches fire and plunges into desert near Medina
1980, Dec. 21	Colombian Caravelle Jet	68	Crashes in northern desert of Colombia
1981, Feb. 7	Soviet ILA26 jet	70	Crashes near Leningrad, Soviet Union
1981, Aug. 22	Taiwanese Boeing 737	110	Explodes and crashes near Sanyi, Taiwan
1981, Dec. 1	Yugoslav DC-9 jetliner	174	Hits mountain near Ajaccio, Corsica
1982, Jan. 13	Air Florida Boeing 737	78	Crashes on takeoff from Washington, D.C.
1982, Feb. 3	French army aircraft	36	Crashes into mountain during training flight
1982, April 26	Chinese Trident jetliner	112	Strikes mountain near Guilin, China
1982, June 8	Brazilian Boeing 727	137	Crashes into mountain near Fortaleza, Brazil
1982, July 6	Soviet IL-62 jetliner	90	Burns after takeoff from Moscow
1982, July 9	Pan Am 727 jetliner	154	Crashes on takeoff from New Orleans, La.
1982, Sept. 13	Spantax Airlines DC-10	52	Crashes as pilot aborts takeoff from Málaga, Spain
1982, Dec. 9	Nicaraguan MI-8 helicopter	84	Crashes in mountains of Nicaragua
1983, Jan. 16	Turkish Airlines Boeing 727	47	Crashes on landing in Ankara, Turkey
1983, July 11	Ecuadorian Boeing 737	119	Explodes trying to land at Cuenca, Ecuador
1983, Sept. 1	Korean Air Lines Boeing 747	269	Shot down over Sea of Japan by Soviet Union
1983, Sept. 23	Gulf Air Boeing 737	111	Crashes on landing in Abu Dhabi
1983, Nov. 8	Angolan Boeing 737	126	Crashes on takeoff from Lubango, Angola
1983, Nov. 27	Colombian Boeing 747	183	Crashes on landing approach to Madrid, Spain, airport
1983, Nov. 28	Nigerian Fokker F-28	53	Crashes on landing at Lagos, Nigeria
1983, Dec. 7	Iberian Boeing 727 and Aviaco DC-9	93	Collide on runway at Madrid, Spain, airport

SHIPWRECKS AND MARINE DISASTERS

DATE	CRAFT	DEATHS	REMARKS
1831, July 19	*Lady Sherbrooke*	263	Sinks off Cape May, N.J.
1833, May 11	*Lady of the Lake*	215	Strikes iceberg while bound for Quebec
1840, Jan. 13	*Lexington,* steam ferry	146	Burned in Long Island Sound
1850, March 29	*Royal Adelaide*	400	Wrecked off Margate, England
1852, March 26	*Birkenhead,* troopship	454	Wrecked; bound for Cape of Good Hope
1853, Sept. 29	*Annie Jane,* immigrant vessel	348	Wrecked off Scotland
1854, March	*City of Glasgow*	450	Vanishes; bound for Philadelphia from Liverpool
1854, Sept. 27	*Arctic*	322	Sinks near Grand Banks, off Newfoundland
1857, Sept. 12	*Central America*	400	Sinks in storm; bound for New York from Havana
1858, Sept. 13	*Austria*	471	Burns on Hamburg–New York run
1859, April 27	*Pomona*	386	Wrecked off Ireland
1859, Oct. 25	*Royal Charter*	450	Wrecked in Irish Sea
1860, Sept. 8	*Lady Elgin,* excursion steamer	300	Collides with lumber ship on Lake Michigan
1865, April 27	*Sultana,* river steamer	1,450	Explodes and sinks in Memphis, Tenn.
1867, Oct. 29	*Rhone* and *Wye,* mail boats	1,000	Wrecked in storm; St. Thomas, West Indies
1870, Sept. 17	*Captain,* English warship	472	Founders off Finistère, France
1871, July 30	*Westfield,* Staten Island (N.Y.) ferry	104	Boiler explosion at slip in New York City
1873, April 1	*Atlantic,* English steamer	547	Wrecked off Nova Scotia
1878, Sept. 3	*Princess Alice,* English steamer	700	Collides and sinks in River Thames
1890, Sept. 19	*Ertogrul,* Turkish frigate	540	Burns off Japanese coast
1891, March 17	*Utopia,* British steamer	574	Collides and sinks off Gibraltar
1895, March 14	*Reina Regenta,* Spanish cruiser	400	Founders in Atlantic near Gibraltar
1898, Feb. 15	*Maine,* U.S. battleship	264	Blown up in Havana Harbor
1898, July 4	*Bourgogne* and *Cromartyshire*	560	Collide near Sable Island off Nova Scotia
1904, June 15	*General Slocum*	1,000	Burns in East River, New York City
1904, June 28	*Norge*	600	Wrecked on Rockall Reef off Scotland
1912, April 15	*Titanic*	1,502	Strikes iceberg and sinks in North Atlantic
1912, Sept. 28	*Kichemaru*	1,000	Sinks off coast of Japan
1914, May 29	*Empress of Ireland*	1,024	Strikes Norwegian collier in St. Lawrence River
1915, May 7	*Lusitania*	1,195	Sunk by German submarine off coast of Ireland
1915, July 24	*Eastland,* excursion steamer	812	Capsizes in Chicago River, Ill.
1916, Aug. 29	*Hsin Yu*	1,000	Sinks off coast of China
1917, July 9	*Vanguard,* English warship	800	Blown up at Scapa Flow dock off northern Scotland
1918, July 12	*Kawachi,* Japanese battleship	500	Explodes in Tokayama Bay, Japan
1919, Jan. 17	*Chaonia*	460	Wrecked in Strait of Messina, Italy
1921, March 18	*Hong Kong*	1,000	Wrecked on rocks off Swatow in South China Sea
1926, Oct. 16	Chinese troopship	1,200	Explodes in Yangtze River, China
1927, Oct. 25	*Principessa Mafalda,* Italian liner	326	Sinks off coast of Brazil
1928, Nov. 12	*Vestris*	113	Founders off Virginia Capes
1931, June 14	French excursion steamer	450	Overturns in Bay of Biscay storm off St. Nazaire
1934, Sept. 8	*Morro Castle*	137	Burns off coast of New Jersey near Asbury Park
1939, May 23	*Squalus,* U.S. submarine	26	Sinks off New Hampshire coast

SHIPWRECKS AND MARINE DISASTERS *(continued)*

DATE	CRAFT	DEATHS	REMARKS
1939, June 1	*Thetis,* British submarine	99	Sinks in Irish Sea
1939, June 15	*Phenix,* French submarine	63	Sinks off Indochina
1941, June 16	O-9, U.S. submarine	33	Sinks in test dive off Maine coast
1942, Feb. 9	*Normandie,* French liner	1	Burns at Hudson River pier, New York City
1942, Oct. 2	*Queen Mary* and *Curacao*	338	Liner rams and sinks British cruiser
1942, Oct. 26	Jewish refugee ship	200	Wrecked in Sea of Marmara, Turkey
1944, Dec. 17–18	Three U.S. Third Fleet destroyers	790	Capsize during typhoon in Philippine Sea
1945, Jan. 30	*Wilhelm Gustloff,* German ship	6,100	Sunk by Russian submarine in Baltic Sea
1945, April 9	U.S. Liberty ship	360	Explodes in harbor at Bari, Italy
1945, July 29	*Indianapolis,* U.S. cruiser	883	Sunk by Japanese torpedo in Pacific Ocean
1946, Aug. 2	*Vitya*	295	Sinks in Lake Nyasa, Tanganyika
1947, Jan. 19	*Himara*	392	Hits mine and sinks off Athens, Greece
1947, July 17	*Ramdas,* coastal steamer	550	Sinks off Bombay, India
1948, Jan. 28	*Joo Maru,* freighter	250	Hits mine and sinks in Inland Sea, Japan
1948, Feb. 28	Steamer	160	Sinks during pirate attack near Amoy, China
1948, June 11	*Kjoebenhavn,* Danish liner	140	Hits mine and sinks off coast of Jutland
1948, Dec. 3	Steamer	1,140	Explodes and sinks south of Shanghai
1949, Jan. 27	Chinese liner and collier	600	Collide and sink off south coast of China
1949, Sept. 17	*Noronic,* Great Lakes liner	130	Burns at pier in Toronto, Canada
1950, Jan. 12	*Truculent,* English submarine	65	Rammed by tanker in Thames Estuary
1951, April 16	*Affray,* English submarine	75	Sinks off Isle of Wight, near southern England
1952, April 26	*Hobson,* U.S. destroyer, and *Wasp,* aircraft carrier	176	Collide; *Hobson* sinks in Atlantic Ocean
1953, Jan. 9	South Korean passenger liner	249	Sinks in heavy seas off Pusan, South Korea
1953, Jan. 31	Ferry	132	Sinks in storm off Northern Ireland
1953, Aug. 1	*Monique*	120	Vanishes near New Caledonia in South Pacific
1954, May 26	*Bennington,* U.S. aircraft carrier	103	Explodes and burns off Quonset Point, R.I.
1954, Sept. 26	*Toya Maru,* Japanese ferry	1,172	Sinks in Tsugaru Strait, Japan
1956, June 3	Pakistani liner	199	Wrecked in storm in Bay of Bengal
1956, July 26	*Andrea Doria* and *Stockholm*	50	Collide; *Andrea Doria* sinks off Massachusetts
1957, April 10	Two pilgrimage boats	150	Sink in Godavari River, India
1957, July 14	Soviet ship	270	Runs aground in storm in Caspian Sea
1958, Jan. 26	Japanese ferry	170	Vanishes in Inland Sea
1958, March 1	Turkish ferry	238	Sinks near Istanbul, in Sea of Marmara
1959, May 8	Nile River excursion boat	150	Sinks north of Cairo, Egypt
1960, Dec. 19	*Constellation,* U.S. aircraft carrier	50	Burns in Brooklyn Navy Yard, New York
1961, April 8	*Dara,* English liner	212	Burns in Persian Gulf
1961, July 8	*Save*	259	Runs aground and explodes in Mozambique
1961, Sept. 3	*Vencedor,* excursion ship	150	Sinks near Buenaventura, Colombia
1963, April 10	*Thresher,* U.S. nuclear submarine	129	Sinks in North Atlantic
1963, May 4	Motor launch	206	Sinks in Upper Nile
1963, Aug. 17	*Midori Maru,* Japanese ferry	128	Sinks in East China Sea
1963, Dec. 23	*Lakonia,* Greek liner	155	Sinks after fire in Atlantic north of Madeira
1964, Feb. 11	*Voyager,* destroyer, and *Melbourne,* aircraft carrier	85	Collide; *Voyager* sinks near Ulladulla, Australia
1965, Feb. 11	Four fishing trawlers	100	Sink in Bering Sea
1965, May 24	African ferry	150	Capsizes in Shire River, Malawi
1965, Nov. 13	*Yarmouth Castle,* cruise ship	90	Catches fire and sinks in Caribbean
1966, Dec. 8	*Heraklion,* Greek ferry	217	Sinks in storm in Sea of Crete
1967, July 29	*Forrestal,* U.S. aircraft carrier	134	Crippled by fire off Vietnam
1968, Jan. 26	*Dakar,* Israeli submarine	69	Sinks in eastern Mediterranean Sea
1968, May 27	*Scorpion,* U.S. nuclear submarine	99	Sinks in Atlantic Ocean southwest of Azores
1969, June 2	*Frank E. Evans,* U.S. destroyer, and *Melbourne,* aircraft carrier	74	Collide; *Evans* breaks in half, bow section sinks
1970, March 4	*Eurydice,* French submarine	57	Sinks in Mediterranean near Toulon, France
1970, April 12	Soviet submarine	88	Sinks in Atlantic off Spain
1970, Aug. 1	*Christena,* motor launch	125	Capsizes and sinks in Caribbean off St. Kitts
1970, Dec. 15	South Korean ferry	308	Capsizes in Korea Strait
1971, Nov. 21	*Beethoven II*	106	Sinks off Philippines
1974, Feb. 22	South Korean tugboat	157	Capsizes in Chungmu harbor, South Korea
1974, May 1	Bangladesh motor launch	250	Capsizes in coastal waters off Bangladesh
1974, Sept. 12	Soviet guided-missile destroyer	350	Explodes and sinks in Black Sea
1975, Aug. 9	Two Chinese riverboats	500	Collide and sink in West River, near Canton
1975, Nov. 10	U.S. ore carrier *Edmund Fitzgerald*	29	Sank during storm on Lake Superior
1975, Dec. 18	Burmese coastal schooner	70	Capsizes in storm in Andaman Sea
1976, Oct. 20	Tanker and ferry *George Prince*	78	Collide in Mississippi River
1976, Dec. 23	Egyptian passenger ship *Patria*	170	311 rescued in Red Sea sinking
1976, Dec. 30	*Grand Zenith,* Panamanian tanker	38	Sinks off Cape Cod, Mass.
1977, Jan. 17	U.S. Navy launch and freighter	46	Collide in Barcelona, Spain, harbor
1977, Sept. 25	Egyptian ferry	50	Capsizes in Nile River near Cairo
1978, April 8	Burmese coastal transport	100	Capsizes in Bay of Bengal
1978, June 17	Steam showboat *Whippoorwill*	15	Overturned by tornado on Lake Pomona, Kans.
1978, Oct. 12	Liberian tanker *Spyros*	59	Explodes in Singapore harbor; 90 injured

SHIPWRECKS AND MARINE DISASTERS *(continued)*

DATE	CRAFT	DEATHS	REMARKS
1978, Dec. 2	Vietnamese refugee boat	143	Sinks in rough seas off Pasir Puteh, Malaysia
1979, Jan. 8	French oil tanker *Betelgeuse*	50	Explodes while unloading at Bantry, Ireland
1979, March 31	Vietnamese refugee boat	100	Capsizes while being towed to sea off Malaysia
1979, Nov. 15	Romanian tanker and Greek freighter	47	Collide in Bosporus off Istanbul, Turkey
1979, Nov. 25	Chinese drilling rig *Bo Hai # 2*	72	Collapses while being towed in Bohai Gulf
1980, Feb. 27	Chinese ferry	276	Capsizes during storm in southern China river
1980, March 27	Oil rig platform *Alexander L Kielland*	128	Collapses, overturns in stormy North Sea
1980, April 22	Philippine ferry and oil tanker	300	Collide off Mindoro Island, Philippines
1980, May 9	Freighter *Summit Venture*	35	Rams into bridge at Tampa Bay, Fla.
1980, Aug. 22	Mexican ferry	50	Sinks off Ciudad del Carmen, Mexico
1980, Oct. 25	Freighter *S.S. Poet*	34	Disappears after leaving Philadelphia, Pa.
1981, Jan. 6	Brazilian ferry *Novo Amapo*	230	Sinks in Jari River
1981, Jan. 27	Indonesian ferry	374	Sinks in storm in Java Sea
1981, Feb. 26	Soviet freighter *Komsomolets Nakhodki*	38	Sinks in storm near Hakodate, Japan
1981, Sept. 19	Amazon riverboat *Sobral Santos*	252	Sinks at port of Obidos, Brazil
1981, Oct. 26	Haitian refugee boat	33	Breaks apart just off Hillsborough Beach, Fla.
1981, Dec. 29	Italian freighter *Marina d'Equa*	30	Sinks in storm in Bay of Biscay
1982, Feb. 15	Oil-drilling rig *Ocean Ranger*	84	Sinks in storm off Newfoundland, Canada
1982, Feb. 16	Soviet freighter *Mekhanik Tarasov*	33	Sinks near Halifax, Nova Scotia
1982, March 28	Burmese ferry	129	Capsizes in canal in Burma
1982, April 11	Burmese ferry	160	Capsizes near Henzada, Burma
1982, June 17	Philippine passenger ferry *Queen Helen*	36	Explodes in Sulu Sea, Philippines
1982, Aug. 8	Indonesian ferry	300	Capsizes off coast of Celebes, Indonesia
1982, Sept. 4	Indian ferry	35	Capsizes in swollen river in Orissa, India
1982, Oct. 17	Indonesian steamer *Karya Tambangan*	58	Sinks in Java Sea
1983, Feb. 11	Coal transport *Marine Electric*	31	Overturns off coast of Virginia
1983, March 1	Chinese ferry boat	150	Capsizes near Canton, China
1983, May 25	Egyptian ferry *10th of Ramadan*	317	Catches fire and sinks in Nile River
1983, June 5	Soviet river boat *Aleksandr Suvorov*	240	Rams railway bridge on Volga River
1983, June 16	Indonesian inter-island ferry	80	Lost in Banda Sea
1983, Aug. 5	Indonesian passenger boat *Sumber Wangi*	104	Sinks in Java Sea
1983, Sept. 28	Nicaraguan passenger ferry *Santa Elena*	127	Sinks in Lake Nicaragua
1983, Oct. 26	Drilling ship *Glomar Java Sea*	81	Disappears in South China Sea
1983, Nov. 21	Philippine ferry *Dona Cassandra*	200	Sinks in typhoon off Mindanao Island

WORLD RAILROAD DISASTERS

DATE	PLACE	DEATHS	REMARKS
1856, July 17	Near Philadelphia, Pennsylvania	66	Train wrecked
1857, March 17	Near Hamilton, Ontario, Canada	60	Train derailed on bridge over Desjardins Canal
1864, July 15	Near Lackawaxen, Pennsylvania	65	Two trains collide
1876, Dec. 29	Ashtabula, Ohio	92	Bridge collapses in snowstorm
1879, Dec. 28	Dundee, Scotland	78	Train falls from Tay Bridge
1881, June 24	Cuautla, Mexico	200	Train falls into river
1882, July 13	Near Tchnery, Russia	150	Train derailed
1887, Aug. 10	Chatsworth, Illinois	81	Train wrecked as burning bridge collapsed
1888, Oct. 10	Mud Run, Pennsylvania	62	Locomotive hits standing excursion train
1889, June 12	Near Armagh, Ireland	80	Train collision
1891, June 14	Near Basel, Switzerland	100	Train collision
1896, July 30	Atlantic City, New Jersey	60	Train wrecked
1903, Dec. 23	Laurel Run, Pennsylvania	78	Train wrecked
1904, Aug. 7	Eden, Colorado	96	Train wrecked
1904, Sept. 24	New Market, Tennessee	56	Train wrecked
1906, Dec. 30	Washington, D.C.	53	Train wrecked
1910, March 1	Wellington, Washington	96	Avalanche throws two trains into canyon
1910, March 21	Green Mountain, Iowa	55	Passenger train wrecked
1915, May 22	Quintinshill, near Gretna, Scotland	227	Troop train collides with local train
1917, Dec. 12	Modane, France	550	Troop train derailed near Mont Cénis tunnel
1918, June 22	Ivanhoe, Indiana	68	Train rams circus train
1918, July 9	Near Nashville, Tennessee	101	Two trains collide head-on
1918, Nov. 1	Brooklyn, New York	92	Five-car rapid transit train derailed
1937, July 16	Near Patna, India	107	Delhi–Calcutta Express derailed
1938, Dec. 19	Babacena, Minas Gerais, Brazil	90	Freight and passenger trains collide head-on
1938, Dec. 25	Near Kishinev, Romania	100	Passenger trains collide
1939, Dec. 22	Near Magdeburg, Germany	132	Two express trains collide
1939, Dec. 22	Near Friedrichshafen, Germany	99	Train wrecked
1940, Jan. 29	Osaka, Japan	200	Passenger trains collide and burn
1943, Sept. 6	Philadelphia, Pennsylvania	79	Nine cars of Congressional Limited derailed
1943, Dec. 16	Rennert, North Carolina	72	Two streamliners collide
1944, Jan. 16	León Province, Spain	500	Train wrecked inside tunnel
1944, March 2	Salerno, Italy	521	Train stalls in tunnel; mass suffocation
1944, Dec. 31	Near Ogden, Utah	50	Two sections of Pacific Limited wrecked
1945, Feb. 1	Cazadero, Mexico	100	Train with religious pilgrims hit by freight train
1946, March 20	Near Aracaju, Brazil	185	Train wrecked

WORLD RAILROAD DISASTERS *(continued)*

DATE	PLACE	DEATHS	REMARKS
1947, Aug. 3	Sumatra, East Indies	400	Train wrecked
1948, March 31	Osaka, Japan	70	Express hits electric train
1949, April 28	Near Johannesburg, South Africa	73	Three trains collide
1949, Oct. 22	Nowy Dwor, Poland	200	Danzig–Warsaw Express derailed
1950, April 6	Near Tanguá, Brazil	108	Train falls into flooded Indios River
1950, May 7	Bihar State, India	81	Punjab mail train crashes near Jasidih
1950, Nov. 22	Jamaica, New York	78	Train collides with standing commuter train
1951, Feb. 6	Woodbridge, New Jersey	84	Commuter train falls through temporary overpass
1952, March 4	Near Rio de Janeiro, Brazil	119	Two passenger trains collide
1952, July 9	Near Rzepin, Poland	160	Train wrecked
1952, Oct. 8	Harrow, England	112	Commuter train hit by two express trains
1953, Dec. 24	Near Wairoa, New Zealand	155	Wellington–Auckland Express falls into stream
1954, Jan. 21	North of Karachi, Pakistan	60	Mail express wrecked
1954, Jan. 31	Near Seoul, South Korea	56	Train crashes
1954, Sept. 28	East of Hyderabad, India	137	Express falls from flood-damaged bridge
1955, April 3	Near Guadalajara, Mexico	300	Train falls into canyon
1956, Sept. 2	Near Secunderabad, India	121	Two coaches fall into river as bridge collapses
1956, Nov. 23	Marudaiyar River, India	143	Express train plunges down river embankment
1957, Sept. 1	Jamaica, British West Indies	178	Train pitches into ravine
1957, Sept. 29	Near Montgomery, West Pakistan	250	Express crashes into standing oil train
1957, Oct. 20	Near Instanbul, Turkey	89	Two trains collide at high speed
1957, Dec. 4	Near London, England	90	Commuter trains collide; bridge collapses
1958, March 7	Santa Cruz, Brazil	67	Three commuter trains collide
1958, May 8	Near Rio de Janeiro, Brazil	128	Two trains collide head-on
1958, Sept. 15	Newark Bay, Elizabethport, N.J.	48	Train plunges through lift bridge
1959, May 28	Java, Indonesia	92	Train plunges into ravine
1959, June 5	São Paulo, Brazil	60	Two trains collide head-on
1960, May 15	Leipzig, East Germany	59	Local train and express collide
1960, Nov. 14	Pardubice, Czechoslovakia	110	Two passenger trains collide
1961, Dec. 23	Cantanzaro, Italy	69	Train car plummets into gorge
1962, Jan. 8	Woerden, Netherlands	91	Passenger trains collide
1962, May 3	Tokyo, Japan	163	Two commuter trains collide with freight train
1962, May 31	Voghera, Italy	63	Passenger train collide with freight train
1962, July 21	Dumraon, India	69	Passenger train and freight train collide
1964, Jan. 4	Jajinci, Yugoslavia	66	Commuter train hits stalled passenger train
1964, Feb. 1	Altamirano, Argentina	70	Express rams stalled freight train
1964, July 26	Oporto, Portugal	94	Train wrecked
1965, Oct. 5	Near Durban, South Africa	100	Passenger train derails
1965, Dec. 9	Burma	76	Two trains collide head-on near Toungoo
1966, June 13	Bombay, India	60	Two suburban trains collide
1967, July 6	Langenweddingen, East Germany	82	Train collides with gasoline truck
1969, July 14	Jaipur, India	85	Freight train collides with passenger train
1970, Feb. 1	Buenos Aires, Argentina	139	Two passenger trains collide
1970, Feb. 16	Northern Nigeria	81	Train wreck
1972, June 4	Jessore, Bangladesh	76	Two passenger trains collide in station
1972, June 16	Vierzy, France	107	Two trains collide in tunnel cave-in
1972, July 21	Lebrija, Spain	76	Two passenger trains collide head-on
1972, Oct. 6	Saltillo, Mexico	208	Speeding passenger train derails on curve
1972, Oct. 30	Chicago, Illinois	44	Commuter train crushed from behind by another
1974, March 27	Laurenço Marques, Mozambique	60	Head-on collision of two trains
1974, Aug. 30	Zagreb, Yugoslavia	153	Passenger train derails in station
1974, Nov. 7	Cotonou, Dahomey	80	Two passenger trains collide
1975, Feb. 28	London, England	41	Subway train crashes in blind tunnel; 70 injured
1977, Jan. 18	Granville, Australia	82	Commuter train derails on bridge, which collapses
1977, Oct. 10	Naini, India	61	Passenger train hits freight train stopped at station
1977, Nov. 11	Iri, South Korea	57	Freight train explodes at railroad station
1978, April 15	Bologna, Italy	45	Mudslide causes collision; 120 injured
1979, Jan. 5	Turkey	56	Two express trains crash in blizzard near Ankara
1979, Jan. 26	Chuadanga, Bangladesh	70	Express train derails
1979, Aug. 21	Tailing Chan, Thailand	65	Freight train rams commuter train
1979, Sept. 13	Stalac, Yugoslavia	60	Freight train crashes into express train
1979, Oct. 30	Djibouti	50	Train derails and crashes near Ethiopian border
1980, June 7	Empageni, South Africa	45	Freight train hits bus filled with shoppers
1980, Aug. 19	Northern Poland	62	Passenger train collides with freight train
1981, March 8	Coronel Brandsen, Argentina	45	Passenger train collides with two derailed freight cars
1981, May 14	Kyongsan, South Korea	54	Commuter train rams express train
1981, June 6	Bihar, India	268	Train goes off bridge into Bagmati River
1981, June 21	Gagry, Soviet Union	70	Express train and local train collide
1982, Jan. 27	Agra, India	66	Freight train collides with express train in fog
1982, Jan. 27	El Asnam, Algeria	130	Derails during trip from Algiers to Oran
1982, July 11	Tepic, Mexico	120	Train derails, plunges down 800-foot gorge
1983, Feb. 19	Empalme, Mexico	100	Two trains collide
1983, Aug. 31	Pojuca, Brazil	42	Tank cars explode

Animals in the News

Wide World

Staten Island (N.Y.) Zoo's Galápagos tortoise, Jalopy, is given a warm welcome home Sept. 8 after undergoing experimental therapy in Arizona for a recurring tumor. His movement is aided by a dolly since undergoing surgery in 1981 to remove a tumor in his left front leg. The borough of Staten Island proclaimed Sept. 8 as Jalopy Day.

HIGHLIGHTS: 1983

RARE CONDORS HATCH IN CALIFORNIA

A California condor was hatched for the first time in captivity, at the San Diego (Calif.) Zoo, on March 30.

The chick, weighing half a pound, emerged from its shell with the aid of two bird keepers using surgical instruments. The egg had been laid on Feb. 2, in the wilds of Ventura County, Calif., and taken from the nest on Feb. 23 as part of the California Condor Recovery program. The program is designed to replenish the species, which is in danger of extinction.

The new chick, named Sisquoc, after a condor preserve in Santa Barbara County, was fed a diet of finely chopped mice by a zoo keeper wearing a condor puppet on his hand.

Shortly after birth Sisquoc was taken to the San Diego Wild Animal Park, about 30 miles from the zoo. It was to become part of a captive population of five breeding pairs, whose offspring would be set free in the mountains of central California.

A second condor chick, named Tecuya, was hatched on April 5, and two more were born in May and June. Blood tests determined that Sisquoc is a male and the other three chicks are female. They are kept at the San Diego Wild Animal Park with other large vultures in a complex of pens topped with coils of barbed wire. Officials do not want them to get too used to people, for fear it would damage their relationships with other condors. Thus, even the staff who feed them and clean their cages make only two quick visits each day. Condors reach full growth at about a year, and sexual maturity at about five. Adult condors weigh 16 to 22 pounds and have a wingspan of 9 feet.

EPIDEMIC KILLS FAMED AUSTRIAN HORSES

A herpes epidemic struck the stud farm for Austria's famed Lippizaner killing 39 mares and foals. The disease, equine rhinopneumonitis, is induced by a herpes virus, and appeared not to affect any of the male horses.

The disease did not spread to the famed Royal Spanish Riding School in Vienna, where the Lippizaner horses perform ballet maneuvers and aerial feats. The Lippizaner horses made their first United States tour in nearly 20 years in 1982, and a Lippizaner stallion was presented to President Reagan.

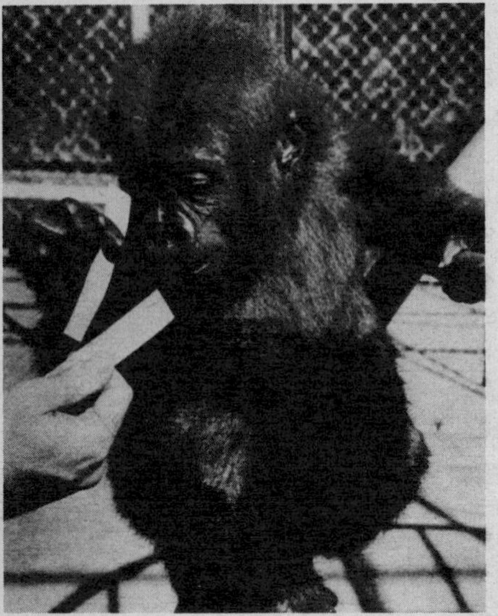

United Press Int'l.

Kanda the Great, a gorilla at the Dallas, Tex., zoo, shows how he makes his football picks. For two weeks in November, Kanda's won-loss record was 19–7–1, better than a panel of local sportswriters.

HIGHLIGHTS: 1983 *(continued)*

Austria's Agriculture Ministry runs the stud farm, in Piber, Austria, as well as the Riding School.

The Lippizaner originated in the 16th century, in an area that is now Yugoslavia, as a result of crossbreeding of Arab and Spanish breeds of horses.

PANDA GIVES BIRTH BUT CUB DIES

The first panda cub ever born in the United States died within three hours, on July 21. Born to Ling-Ling, at the Washington (D.C.) Zoo, the cub appeared normal at birth. Later tests determined the cause of death to be a lung infection that developed before birth.

The giant panda and her mate, Hsing-Hsing arrived in the United States in 1972, gifts from China. The two pandas resisted mating with one another until March 1983, but Ling-Ling was also artificially inseminated. Because of giant panda's large size and the small size of their offspring, it is difficult to tell when a panda is pregnant. Normal gestation varies from 97 to 165 days for giant pandas, and zoo officials, alerted by rising levels of female hormones in Ling-Ling's urine, began a "panda watch" on July 11. Staffed by volunteers, observers were on round-the-clock duty to be alert for an imminent delivery. On July 20, Ling-Ling was observed to be carrying bamboo to the corner of her cage and building a nest. She also rubbed carrots up and down on her body, which was unusual behavior for her. Late that night, she could be seen licking the genital area, and then becoming restless, with occasional groans.

Films of the birth, taken with monitoring equipment from the National Geographic Society, showed Ling-Ling lying on her back when the 6-inch, 4.8-ounce male cub emerged from the birth canal. The cub fell to the floor, motionless, until Ling-Ling brushed against it, and it started wriggling and squealing. Then Ling-Ling picked it up in her mouth and cradled it. Three hours later it appeared to stop moving, but the mother panda kept cradling it to her body. It was not until about eleven hours later that Ling-Ling moved to the other side of the cage, and zoo officials could remove the small body. Zoo spokesman Bob Hoage said that she didn't search for the cub after its removal but she did spend a lot of time holding an apple, perhaps believing it was her cub.

The death of the firstborn is not uncommon in the animal world, and often helps reinforce maternal instincts necessary to rearing of subsequent offspring.

BIRDS DISAPPEAR FROM PACIFIC ISLAND

Nearly all 17 million adult birds on Christmas Island, in the central Pacific, seemed to have disappeared, according to a National Science Foundation report in March.

Dr. Ralph W. Schreiber, curator of ornithology at the Natural History Museum of Los Angeles County said that when he visited the island in November 1982, it was devoid of birds. The adult birds apparently left their nestlings behind to die.

PREGNANCY PERIOD OF ANIMALS

ANIMAL	PREGNANCY	AVERAGE IN LITTER	ANIMAL	PREGNANCY	AVERAGE IN LITTER	ANIMAL	PREGNANCY	AVERAGE IN LITTER
Baboon	6 months	1	Fox	51 days	4–10	Mouse	19–21 days	1–9
Cat	9 weeks	1–6	Goat	151 days	1–3	Pig	113 days	4–6
Cow	280 days	1–2	Gorilla	8½ months	1–2	Rabbit	1 month	4
Chimpanzee	226 days	1	Horse	330 days	1	Sheep	148 days	2
Dog	61 days	1–4	Kangaroo	38–40 days	1	Squirrel	44 days	4
Dolphin	8–9 months	1	Lion	108 days	4	Tiger	100 days	2–4
Elephant	21 months	1	Mink	6 weeks	4–8	Zebra	12 months	1

According to Dr. Schreiber, when he left the island in July 1982, it was teeming with bird life. Christmas Island was home to 14 million sooty terns, about 1.5 million wedge-tailed shearwaters, and over a million birds of 16 other species.

He termed the "population crash" the largest of its kind ever reported and believed it may have been caused by an abrupt change in Pacific water temperatures that seriously disrupted fishing along the northwestern coast of South America. The phenomenon, which involved changes in wind patterns, salinity, ocean currents, and sea levels, is known as "El Niño."

The missing birds normally fed on fish and squid, and it was possible the changes in ocean conditions might have disrupted the birds' feeding patterns, forcing them to abandon their young and go elsewhere for food.

On a follow-up visit to Christmas Island in June, Dr. Schreiber and his wife found that about 1% of the birds had returned. Though they were encouraged by seeing some of the birds return, the Schreibers were still mystified as to what happened to the others. They believe that most of the birds died and that only the survivors would return to the island. All birds that disappeared were sea birds, able to live aloft for months at a time.

Christmas Island is the world's largest coral atoll, located just north of the equator in the central Pacific. It is part of the republic of Kiribati.

COUPLE AWARDED JOINT CUSTODY OF DOG

A childless couple was awarded joint custody of their dog, in accordance with California's child-custody laws.

In September, Judge John Wooley of Orange County (Calif.) Superior Court handed down his ruling to Rex and Judi Wheatland, of Santa Ana, after a year of bitter divorce proceedings.

The dog, Runaway, is a cockapoo, a cross between a cocker spaniel and a poodle. They acquired the dog in 1981 from Mrs. Wheatland's sister, and, according to Rex Wheatland, it became the "nucleus of our family." He added that when he and Judi split up, she took off and hid with Runaway, and he had to tail her in order to find the dog.

Judge Wooley ruled that as a child substitute the dog should be jointly owned and shared and that neither owner could take her out of state without permission from the other. He ordered the Wheatlands to share the dog on a monthly basis.

PYTHON CRUSHES OWNER TO DEATH

Robert J. Vierling, 42, of Winchester, Mo., was crushed to death by his pet python, in April. His wife, Christine, found his body

Herman, a 14-day-old water buffalo, stands beside its surrogate mother on March 31, at the University of Florida's Veterinary Medical Teaching Hospital. Herman is the result of the first known embryo transfer in his species.

Wide World

HIGHLIGHTS: 1983 *(continued)*

and thought he had suffered a heart attack. An autopsy found that he had been crushed to death.

Vierling had complete trust in the 16-foot, 100-pound Burmese python and often played with it on the bed. The snake was taken to the St. Louis (Mo.) Zoo for safekeeping.

FIRST SPACE CHIMP DIES

Ham, the chimpanzee who rode a Redstone rocket in a suborbital space flight Jan. 31, 1961, died at the North Carolina Zoological Park on Jan. 17, 1983, at age 26.

The flight preceded by three months the first suborbital flight of Alan B. Shepard Jr., the first American in space. The chimpanzee showed no ill effects after his ride in space.

JULIEANN, COME HOME?

A pregnant heifer, in the spirit of the well-known novel *Lassie, Come Home*, traveled 35 miles over barbed-wire fences and pastureland to her home in Geneva, Fla.

Sidney Kraftsow sold Julieann, a pregnant, 700-pound 2-year-old purebred Brahman heifer, to rancher Read Hayes, of Orange County, on March 6. Hayes reported that she jumped out of her pen that night, leaped over two four-foot barbed-wire fences, and made her way north. Twenty hours later, on Monday, March 7, she strolled back onto Kraftsow's farm, sporting only a few scratches.

The two men decided to let her bear her calf at the Kraftsow farm, then Hayes would claim her again, this time building higher fences around her pen. He bought her for breeding purposes.

FIRST TEST-TUBE BABOON BORN

A female black baboon, believed the first nonhuman primate conceived in a laboratory dish, was born in San Antonio, Tex., on July 25.

The tiny female, named E.T. for embryo transfer, was born six months after its test-tube fertilization. Dr. Thomas J. Kuehl, head of the Southwest Foundation for Research and Education's prenatal biology program, said E.T. was the 10th attempt, and first success, in a program that began in November 1982. He said the success rate for humans and baboons appears to be about the same, "a dismal ten percent," for unknown reasons.

An 8-year-old female baboon that had never been pregnant was chosen to be the foster mother, and would continue to care for E.T. until she was 12 or 16 weeks old.

TWIN GORILLAS BORN IN OHIO

On Oct. 26, 1983, Bridgette, a gorilla, gave birth to twins, the first such birth in captivity in the Northern Hemisphere, at the Columbus, Ohio, zoo. The twins, both male, weighed 4.8 pounds each. Officials at the Henry Doorly Zoo in Omaha, Neb., had sent Bridgette to the Columbus to mate with its gorilla, Oscar, on the condition that her firstborn be returned to Nebraska. What to do with the second-born twin was yet to be decided.

A miniature condominium floats in a large pond at the Society for the Prevention of Cruelty to Animals (S.P.C.A.) enclosure at Salinas, Calif., in January. Officials hoped the condo, which houses 12 ducks, would protect them from bobcats coming down from the nearby hills. They pounce on the ducks, which are sound sleepers and easy targets.

United Press Int'l.

HIGHLIGHTS: 1983

EARLIEST MOZART SYMPHONY DISCOVERED

Gunnar Thygesen, librarian of the Odense Symphony in Denmark, announced in February 1983 the discovery and authentication of the first symphony written by Wolfgang Amadeus Mozart at about age nine. Believed to have been composed in London in 1765, it is the only one of Mozart's 41 symphonies that is written in A-minor.

The three-movement work was found in a group of manuscripts that had been handed over to the Odense Symphony by the town council after it had cleared out some rooms in the county hall in 1943. The uncatalogued material remained in the library until 1982, when Thygesen had a chance to go through it. The existence of the symphony had been known for many years, but not its whereabouts.

NATIONAL GALLERY OF ART EXPANDS

The West Building of Washington, D.C.'s National Gallery of Art opened to the public on Feb. 3 after a $16.7 million renovation, which provides a new 4,000-square-foot exhibition area. The new area has allowed the gallery to increase its exhibition of sculpture and graphic arts and expand its temporary exhibition program.

Paul Mellon, son of Andrew W. Mellon, who founded the National Gallery, presented the institution on Jan. 27 with 93 works from his private collection. The bequest of 50 paintings included six Monets, two Gauguins, two Cassatts, a Renoir, a Van Gogh, and *The Lighthouse at Honfleur,* one of the last privately owned paintings by Jacques Seurat. Also included in Mellon's donation were 24 sculptures and 19 prints and drawings. Mellon is the gallery's board chairman. The gift was thought to be the largest single donation ever made by one individual to the National Gallery at one time.

Art historian and scholar S. J. Freedberg was named chief curator of the National Gallery of Art on Feb. 28.

AMERICAN DANCERS WIN AWARDS

Three Americans won prizes in the 11th International Ballet Competition held in Varna, Bulgaria, in July. Katherine Healy, 14, of Bryn Mawr, Pa., was awarded the gold medal in the junior division. She performed with Greg Larson, 18, of Austin, Tex., who was not competing.

Trained in New York at the School of American Ballet, Katherine has been in several New York City Ballet productions, is a professional ice skater, and appeared in the 1982 film *Six Weeks.*

Bonnie Moore, 18, of Phoenix, Ariz., won a third prize in the junior division. She performed with John Goding of the Washington Ballet, who won an award for choreography. Bonnie shared third prize with French dancer Christine Landault.

Maria Teresa Del Real, 20, of Miami, Fla., won a third prize in the senior division. She performed with Miguel Campaneria who, though a noncompetitor, won a special award as best partner.

A design by 8-year-old Danny LaBoccetta, of New York City, will be the basis of the contemporary issue Christmas stamp to be issued in October 1984. The cheerful Santa Claus with a sack of toys was one of two chosen from more than a half-million entries in a nationwide project sponsored by the U. S. Postal Service. The other finalist was Molly LaRue, 18, of Shaker Heights, Ohio, whose design featured stick figure art.

U. S. Postal Service

HIGHLIGHTS: 1983 *(continued)*

The "Special Distinction of the Youth Organization of Varna," the contest's highest award, went to Sylvie Guillem of France. A junior division competitor, she is a member of the Paris Opera Ballet.

METROPOLITAN OPERA HAS 100TH BIRTHDAY

New York's Metropolitan Opera celebrated its 100th anniversary on Oct. 22, with a two-part, daylong concert featuring some of the world's greatest opera stars. Among the highlights of the day were performances by such luminaries as Joan Sutherland, Placido Domingo, Luciano Pavarotti, Birgit Nilsson, Kiri Te Kanawa, as well as the introduction of a group of guests who did not perform, such as Risë Stevens, Dorothy Kirsten, Zinka Milanov, and Patrice Munsel. Together, the two concerts grossed $1.45 million.

The Met inaugurated its 100th season on Sept. 26 with Jessye Norman, Placido Domingo, and Tatiana Troyanos in Hector Berlioz's *Les Troyens.* The opening night performance grossed $601,000.

BERNSTEIN UNVEILS NEW OPERA

Composer Leonard Bernstein's newest opera, *A Quiet Place*, had its premier performance in Houston, Tex., on June 17. The somber work is a sequel to an earlier Bernstein opera, *Trouble in Tahiti*, about a strained marriage in suburbia. The new work looks at the same couple 30 years later.

VIOLINISTS SHARE FIRST PRIZE

The 1983 International American Music Competition held at Carnegie Hall in September, awarded the first prize to two musicians. It was the first time the competition had split the prize.

The two winners were Maryvonne Le Dizes-Richard, 43, of France, and Robert Davidovici 37, who was born in Romania, grew up in Australia, and is now artist-in-residence at North Texas State University. For the competition, he played solo pieces by Hugh Aitken, Bach, Cage, Copland, Bartók, and George Crumb. Miss Le Dizes-Richard played American music by Carter, Copland, Glass, Ives, and Melby, as well as other pieces by Bach, Beethoven, and Berio. Each contestant was required to play at least 50 minutes of American music in the final recital.

Joel Smirnoff, 33, of Cambridge, Mass., won second prize. Soviet-born Mischa Lefkowitz, 29, now of California, won third prize.

ART WORKS FETCH RECORD PRICES

In 12 days of auctions in May at Sotheby Parke Bernet and Christie's auction houses, more than $67 million was spent for Impressionist and 20th century artworks.

On May 18, $37.4 million was realized at Sotheby's, the highest figure ever achieved at one auction. A highlight of that sale was $3.74 million paid for *Waiting*, an 1882 pastel by Degas. It was the highest ever paid at auction for an Impressionist painting. The purchasers were two California institutions—the Norton Simon Museum of Pasadena and the J. Paul Getty Museum of Malibu. A second Degas, *The Cafe Concert*, went for $3.4 million to an unidentified buyer.

At Christie's, on May 17, an unidentified purchaser paid $1.1 million for Mary Cassatt's *Reading le Figaro*, an 1883 portrait of her mother. It was the highest price paid at auction for a painting by Cassatt.

A price record was set on June 3 at Sotheby's for a 20th century American work of art when $1.87 million was paid for the Charles Sheeler painting of the Ford motor plant in River Rouge, Mich. Titled *Classic Landscape*, the work is an idealized depiction of the auto plant, showing none of the unpleasant aspects of manufacturing.

A private Japanese collector on June 27 paid $2,156,000 at Christie's for *Composition With Red, Blue, and Yellow* by Dutch modernist Piet Mondrian, the highest price ever paid at auction for a work of abstract art.

An 18th century French cabinet that was used in the study of King Louis XVI at Versailles fetched a record $1.39 million on July 8 at Sotheby's. The cabinet, bought by an anonymous New Jersey collector, is ebony and lacquer with gilt-bronze mounts. It was attributed to 18th century French cabinetmaker Adam Weisweiller and was delivered to Versailles on Jan. 11, 1784, according to the original bill of lading. The previous record for an auctioned piece of furniture was set in 1979 for a King Louis XV corner, which sold for $1.27 million in Monaco.

A mural by the late abstract expressionist painter Mark Rothko fetched $1,815,000 on Nov. 9 at an auction at Sotheby's. It was a record price paid for a contemporary painting.

At the same auction, an 82-by-118-inch silkscreen mural of singer Elvis Presley by Andy Warhol sold for $148,500.

An 18th century Chippendale desk, carved in Newport, R.I., about 1765, was sold by Sotheby's in January for $687,500, the highest price ever paid at auction for a piece of American furniture. The previous record was set in 1980, when $390,000 was paid for a Newport blockfront chest of drawers.

AMERICAN SYMPHONY ORCHESTRAS

Source: American Symphony Orchestra League

MAJOR ORCHESTRAS	DIRECTOR	OTHER INFORMATION
Atlanta Symphony Orchestra	Robert Shaw	Founded 1945; Shaw became director in 1966
Baltimore Symphony Orchestra	Sergiu Comissiona	Founded 1916; Comissiona became director in 1968
Boston Symphony Orchestra	Seiji Ozawa	Founded 1881; also performs as Boston Pops, under John Williams
Buffalo Philharmonic Orchestra	Julius Rudel	Founded 1935; Rudel became director in 1979
Chicago Symphony Orchestra	Sir Georg Solti	Founded 1891; Solti joined orchestra in 1969
Cincinnati Symphony Orchestra	Michael Gielen	Founded 1895; Gielen became director in 1980
Cleveland Orchestra	Christoph von Dohnanyi	Founded 1918; von Dohnanyi named director in 1983
Dallas Symphony Orchestra	Eduarto Mata	Founded 1900; Mata became director in 1977
Denver Symphony Orchestra	Gaetano Delogu	Founded 1933; Delogu became director in 1979
Detroit Symphony Orchestra	Antal Dorati	Founded 1914; Dorati became director in 1977
Houston Symphony Orchestra	Sergiu Comissiona	Founded 1913; Comissiona became music advisor, 1979
Indianapolis Symphony Orchestra	John Nelson	Founded 1930; Nelson joined orchestra in 1976
Los Angeles Philharmonic	Carlo Maria Giulini	Founded 1919; Giulini joined orchestra in 1977
Milwaukee Symphony Orchestra	Lukas Foss	Founded 1930; Foss joined orchestra in 1980
Minnesota Symphony Orchestra	Neville Marriner	Founded 1903 as Minneapolis Symphony Orchestra; Marriner joined orchestra in 1979
National Symphony Orchestra	Mstislav Rostropovich	Founded 1931 as orchestra of Washington, D.C.; Rostropovich became director in 1977
New Orleans Philharmonic	Philippe Entremont	Founded 1935; Entremont joined orchestra in 1980
New York Philharmonic	Zubin Mehta	America's oldest orchestra, founded in 1842; Leonard Bernstein is director emeritus; Mehta named director beginning 1978–79 season
Oregon Symphony Orchestra	James DePriest	Founded 1896; DePriest became director in 1980
Philadelphia Orchestra	Riccardo Muti	Founded 1900; Muti became director in 1980
Pittsburgh Symphony	André Previn	Founded 1927; Previn joined orchestra in 1975
Rochester Philharmonic	David Zinman	Founded 1929; Zinman named music advisor in 1973
St. Louis Symphony Orchestra	Leonard Slatkin	Founded 1880; Slatkin named music director in 1979
St. Paul Chamber Orchestra	Pinchas Zukerman	Founded 1959; Zukerman became music director, 1980
San Antonio Symphony Orchestra	Lawrence Leighton Smith	Founded 1937; Smith joined orchestra in 1980
San Diego Symphony	David Atherton	Founded 1927; became major orchestra in 1980
San Francisco Symphony Orchestra	Edo de Waart	Founded 1911; de Waart became director in 1977
Seattle Symphony Orchestra	Gerard Schwarz	Founded 1903; Schwarz became interim adviser in 1983
Syracuse Symphony Orchestra	Christopher Keene	Founded 1924; Keene joined orchestra in 1975
Utah Symphony Orchestra	Varujan Kojian	Founded 1926; Kojian joined orchestra in 1980

LEADING U. S. OPERA COMPANIES

Source: Central Opera Service

MAJOR OPERAS	DIRECTOR	OTHER INFORMATION
Baltimore Opera Company	Jay Holbrook	Founded 1941; Holbrook appointed in 1980
Cincinnati Opera Association	James de Blasis	Founded 1921; de Blasis appointed in 1973
Cleveland Opera Company	David Bamberger	Founded 1976, with Bamberger as director
Connecticut Opera Association	George Osborne	Founded 1942; Osborne appointed in 1979
Dallas Opera Company	Plato Karayanis	Founded 1957; Karayanis appointed in 1977
Fort Worth Opera Association	Dwight Bowes	Founded 1946; Bowes appointed in 1982
Greater Miami Opera Association	Robert Herman	Founded 1941; Herman appointed in 1973
Houston Grand Opera	David Gockley	Founded 1956; Gockley appointed in 1972
Kentucky Opera Assn. (Louisville)	Thomson Smillie	Founded 1952; Smillie appointed in 1981
Lyric Opera of Chicago	Ardis Krainik	Founded 1954; Krainik appointed in 1981
Lyric Opera of Kansas City	Russell Patterson	Founded 1958, with Patterson as director
Metropolitan Opera Association (N.Y.)	Anthony A. Bliss	Founded 1883; Bliss appointed in 1975
Michigan Opera Theatre (Detroit)	David Di Chiera	Founded 1966, with Di Chiera as director
Minnesota Opera Company (St. Paul)	Wesley Balk	Founded 1964; Balk appointed in 1974
New Orleans Opera Association	Arthur Cosenza	Founded 1943; Cosenza appointed in 1966
New York City Opera	Beverly Sills	Founded 1944; Sills appointed in 1979
Opera Colorado (Denver)	Nathaniel Merrill	Founded 1982, with Merrill as director
Opera Company of Boston	Sarah Caldwell	Founded 1958, with Caldwell as director
Opera Company of Philadelphia	Margaret Everitt	Founded 1975; Everitt appointed in 1980
Opera Theatre of St. Louis	Richard Gaddes	Founded 1976, with Gaddes as director
Pittsburgh Opera	Tito Capobianco	Founded 1940; Capobianco appointed in 1983
Portland Opera Association	Robert Bailey	Founded 1951; Bailey appointed in 1982
San Diego Opera Association	Ian Campbell	Founded 1965; Campbell appointed in 1983
San Francisco Opera Association	Terence McEwen	Founded 1923; McEwen appointed in 1982
Santa Fe Opera	John Crosby	Founded 1957, with Crosby as director
Seattle Opera Association	Speight Jenkins	Founded 1962, Jenkins appointed in 1983
Tulsa Opera Inc.	Edward Purrington	Founded 1948; Purrington appointed in 1975
Virginia Opera Association (Norfolk)	Peter Mark	Founded 1974, with Mark as artistic director
Washington Opera Company	Martin Feinstein	Founded 1957; Feinstein appointed in 1979

MUSICIANS, COMPOSERS, SINGERS, DANCERS*

Licia Albanese (1913–), Italian soprano who was one of the principal singers at the Metropolitan Opera after her debut in 1940.

Marian Anderson (1902–), American contralto who achieved worldwide fame as a concert artist.

Johann Christian Bach (1735–82), German composer; J.S. Bach's 18th child. He spent much of his life in the court of England's George III, where he wrote operas and many symphonies.

Johann Sebastian Bach (1685–1750), German composer. A master of counterpoint, he was among the most influential composers of all time. His works include the six Brandenburg Concertos (1721), the B Minor Mass (1733–38), and many keyboard works.

Karl Philipp Emanuel Bach (1714–88), J.S. Bach's fifth child. With Haydn and Mozart, he helped develop the sonata form, which dominated instrumental music for two centuries.

George Balanchine (1904–83), Russian-American ballet dancer and choreographer; director of ballet at the Metropolitan Opera (1934–37) and the New York City Ballet (since 1948).

Samuel Barber (1910–81), American composer whose outstanding works include an overture to *The School for Scandal* (1931), *Adagio for Strings* (1936), and *Essays for Orchestra* (1937).

Sir John Barbirolli (1899–1970), English conductor who led the British National Opera (1926–27), the New York Philharmonic (1937–42), and the Houston Symphony.

Béla Bartók (1881–1945), Hungarian composer whose music combines folk elements with an extremely modern style. His works include three piano concertos (1926, 1931, 1945) and the *Concerto for Orchestra* (1944).

Mikhail Baryshnikov (1948–), Russian ballet dancer with Kirov Ballet who defected to the West in 1974; became guest artist for world's leading ballet companies; choreographed *The Nutcracker Suite* for American Ballet Theatre in 1976; made film debut in *The Turning Point* (1976); named director of American Ballet Theatre in 1980.

Sir Thomas Beecham (1879–1961), English conductor who organized the London Philharmonic Orchestra in 1932 and the Royal Philharmonic in 1946.

Ludwig van Beethoven (1770–1827), German composer who ranks among the greatest musical geniuses of all time. His masterpieces include 9 symphonies, 32 piano sonatas, 17 string quartets, and 5 piano concertos.

Alban Berg (1885–1935), Austrian atonal composer and pupil of Arnold Schoenberg. His opera *Wozzeck* (1914–1920) is considered his masterpiece.

Irving Berlin (1888–), American composer of popular songs, including *God Bless America.*

Hector Berlioz (1803–69), French composer and exponent of the Romantic movement. The *Symphonie Fantastique* (1830–31) and *Harold in Italy* (1834) are among his greatest works.

Leonard Bernstein (1918–), American conductor and composer (*Jeremiah Symphony*, 1941–44; *West Side Story,* 1957) who was musical director of the New York Philharmonic Orchestra (1958–69).

Georges Bizet (1838–75), French composer whose *Carmen* (1873–74) is one of the world's most popular operas.

Jussi Bjorling (1911–60), Swedish tenor who appeared in major European and American opera houses in over 50 leading roles.

Ernest Bloch (1880–1959), Swiss-American composer of the opera *Macbeth* (1903–09) and the *Israel Symphony* (1912–16).

Aleksandr Borodin (1833–87), Russian composer of nationalistic music, including the unfinished opera *Prince Igor.*

Johannes Brahms (1833–97), German composer of four symphonies (1855–76, 1877, 1883, 1884–85), *The Academic Festival Overture* (1880), *The Tragic Overture* (1880–81), one violin and two piano concertos, and much chamber music.

Alexander Brailowsky (1896–1976), Russian-born pianist noted for his playing of Chopin.

Benjamin Britten (1913–76), English composer whose opera *Peter Grimes* (1945) was one of few modern operas to achieve worldwide acclaim.

Anton Bruckner (1824–96), Austrian composer whose works utilize romantic themes in an expanded sonata structure. He wrote nine symphonies, the last unfinished, and four masses.

Ferruccio Busoni (1866–1924), Italian composer whose most popular compositions are the *Comedy Overture* (1897), the *Pianoforte Concerto* (1903–04), and *Doctor Faust* (1916–24).

William Byrd (1543–1623), English organist and composer called the father of English music for his masses, madrigals, chamber and keyboard music.

John Cage (1912–), American composer who employs random, nonmusical sounds to create highly experimental works.

Maria Callas (1923–77), Greek-American soprano who appeared in the major opera houses of Europe and the United States. Her greatest roles included Tosca and Norma.

Elliott Carter (1908–), American composer of the ballet *Pocahontas* (1939) and the Second String Quartet (1959), for which he received the 1960 Pulitzer Prize in music.

Enrico Caruso (1873–1921), Italian tenor and one of the world's most celebrated opera stars. He sang with the New York Metropolitan Opera from 1903 to 1920.

Robert Casadesus (1899–1972), French pianist who earned a reputation as a major artist.

Pablo Casals (1876–1973), Spanish cellist and conductor generally regarded as the world's greatest cellist. A distinguished conductor, he formed the Orquesta Pau Casals in Barcelona in 1919.

Feodor Chaliapin (1873–1938), Russian basso who sang in the major European opera houses and at the Metropolitan Opera (1907–08, 1921–29).

Lucia Chase (1907–), ballerina and co-director of the American Ballet Theatre (1945–80).

Frédéric Chopin (1810–49), Polish-French composer of highly romantic compositions for the piano. His works include 27 études, 25 preludes, 13 polonaises, and 2 concertos.

Van Cliburn (1934–), American pianist, gained worldwide fame by winning 1958 International Tchaikovsky Piano Competition in Moscow.

Aaron Copland (1900–), American composer whose highly successful works include *Music for the Theater* (1925), *Saga of the Prairie* (1937), *Billy the Kid* (1938), *Rodeo* (1942), *Appalachian Spring* (1944), and *Nonet* (1960).

Franco Corelli (1923–), Italian tenor who made his operatic debut at the Spoleto (Italy) Festival in 1952 and debuted with the New York Metropolitan Opera in 1961.

Henry Cowell (1897–1965), American composer whose unconventional music includes the five *Hymn-and-Fuguing Tunes* (1941–55).

Merce Cunningham (1919–), American dancer and choreographer who performed with the Martha

* See pages 981–986 for 1983 deaths, and see pages 271–282 for popular musicians and composers.

Graham Company (1940–45) before forming his own dance company in 1952.

Walter Damrosch (1862–1950), American conductor. Organized Damrosch Opera Company (1895) and led Metropolitan Opera Orchestra (1885–91, 1900–02) and New York Symphony (1903–27).

Alexandra Danilova (1906–), Russian ballerina and choreographer. She was the prima ballerina with the Ballet Russe de Monte Carlo (1938–58).

Claude Debussy (1862–1918), French composer and founder of the impressionistic school. His best works include *L'Après-midi d'un faune* (1892–94), *La Mer* (1905), the opera *Pelléas et Mélisande* (1902), and many pieces for piano solo.

Léo Delibes (1836–91), French composer best known for *Sylvia* (1876) and other ballets.

Frederick Delius (1862–1934), English composer whose best-known compositions include *A Village Romeo and Juliet* (1900–01), *Sea Drift* (1903), and *Mass of Life* (1904–05).

Victoria de Los Angeles (1923–), Spanish soprano who sang in Madrid, Milan, and Paris before joining the Metropolitan Opera in 1950.

Agnes De Mille (1909–), ballerina and choreographer who created the first noteworthy American ballet, *Rodeo* (1938). She was the first to use ballet in musical comedies such as *Oklahoma!* (1943) and *Carousel* (1945).

Sergei Diaghilev (1872–1929), Russian ballet director who founded the famous Diaghilev's Ballet Russe in Paris in 1909.

David Diamond (1915–), American composer of dissonant, rhythmic music, including *Psalm* (1936), *Rounds* (1944).

Anton Dolin (1904–), English ballet dancer and choreographer who performed with Diaghilev's Ballet Russe (1921–25) and the Ballet Theater in New York. He formed several ballet companies.

Gaetano Donizetti (1797–1848), Italian composer of operas. *Lucia di Lammermoor* (1835) is his most popular creation.

Anton Dvorák (1841–1904), Czech composer whose works were strongly influenced by Bohemian folk music. He completed nine symphonies, including the New World Symphony.

Emma Eames (1865–1952), American soprano who starred at the Metropolitan Opera from 1891 to 1909. Her greatest performances were in *Tosca, Don Giovanni,* and *Aïda.*

André Eglevsky (1917–77), American ballet dancer who performed at the Ballet Russe de Monte Carlo (1939–42) and the Ballet Theater (1942–46). He was *premier danseur* at the New York City Ballet (1951–58).

Sir Edward Elgar (1857–1934), English composer whose distinctly British pieces include the five *Pomp and Circumstance* marches (1901–30) and *Enigma Variations* (1899).

Duke Ellington (1899–1974), American jazz musician and composer; best-known pieces are *Mood Indigo, Sophisticated Lady,* and *Harlem.*

Mischa Elman (1891–1967), Russian-American violinist who began his long and successful career at the age of twelve.

Manuel de Falla (1876–1946), Spanish composer whose nationalistic music includes *La Vida Breve,* (1903), *El Amor Brujo* (1915), and *Nights in the Gardens of Spain* (1916).

Geraldine Farrar (1882–1967), American soprano who enjoyed tremendous popularity during her career with the Metropolitan Opera (1906–22). Her most famous performances were in *Madame Butterfly* and *Carmen.*

Eileen Farrell (1920–), American soprano who sang on radio and in concerts before her successful opera debuts in San Francisco (1956) and at the Metropolitan Opera (1960).

Suzanne Farrell (1943–), American ballerina with the New York City Ballet in 1961–69 and since 1975.

Gabriel Fauré (1845–1924), French organist and composer whose works include the lyric drama *Pénélope* (1913).

Arthur Fiedler (1894–1979), American conductor, who led the Boston Pops Orchestra (1930–79).

Kirsten Flagstad (1895–1962), Norwegian soprano hailed as one of the greatest Wagnerian sopranos of this century. She sang at the Metropolitan Opera (1935–37; 1950–52).

Carlisle Floyd (1926–), American composer whose operas include *Susannah* (1953–54) and *The Passion of Jonathan Wade* (1962).

Mikhail Fokine (1880–1942), Russian choreographer and ballet dancer who is considered the founder of modern ballet.

Dame Margot Fonteyn (1919–), English ballerina who won international acclaim. She was *prima ballerina assoluta* of the Royal Ballet.

Lukas Foss (1922–), German-American composer of avant-garde music and a noted conductor.

Stephen Foster (1826–64), American composer of popular folk ballads, including *Oh! Susannah* (1848) and *Old Folks at Home* (1851).

Zino Francescatti (1905–), French violinist who has given concerts all over the world and is considered one of the greatest living musicians.

César Franck (1822–90), French composer and organist whose important works include the Symphony in D minor (1886–88).

Wilhelm Furtwängler (1886–1954), German conductor who led virtually all the great European orchestras as well as the New York Philharmonic.

Amelita Galli-Curci (1882–1963), Italian soprano who won wide U.S. acclaim at the Chicago (until 1942) and Metropolitan (1926–30) operas.

Mary Garden (1877–1967), Scottish soprano who became a sensational star as a result of her performances throughout Europe and with the Manhattan (1907–10) and Chicago (1910–31) operas.

George Gershwin (1898–1937), American composer of the popular song *Swanee* (1919), *Rhapsody in Blue* (1924), *Concerto in F* for piano and orchestra (1925), *An American in Paris* (1928), and the folk opera *Porgy and Bess* (1935).

Walter Gieseking (1895–1956), German pianist noted for his performances of Debussy.

Beniamino Gigli (1890–1957), Italian tenor who was regarded as Caruso's successor at the Metropolitan Opera (1920–32; 1938–39).

Mikhail I. Glinka (1804–57), Russian composer regarded as father of the Russian national school. His works include *Kamarinskaya* (1848).

Christoph Willibald von Gluck (1714–87), German composer and influential reformer of the opera. His greatest works are *Alceste* (1767) and *Iphigénie en Tauride* (1778).

Aleksandr Godunov (1949–) Russian-ballet dancer who starred with the Bolshoi Ballet of Moscow in 1971–79. He defected to the U.S. in 1979, joining the American Ballet Theatre.

Glenn Gould (1932–82), Canadian pianist best known as interpreter of keyboard music of Bach.

Morton Gould (1913–), American composer and pianist. His works, in the traditional vein, include *Latin American Symphonette* (1940).

Charles Gounod (1818–93), French composer of the well-known operas *Faust* (1859) and *Romeo and Juliette* (1867).

Martha Graham (1894–), American dancer, choreographer, director, and teacher of modern dance. She formed her own company in 1929.

MUSICIANS *(continued)*

Edvard Hagerup Grieg (1843–1907), Norwegian composer whose music was inspired by Norwegian folk tunes: the *Piano Concerto in A Minor* (1868) and the *Peer Gynt Suite* (1876).

Oscar Hammerstein II (1895–1960), American librettist for musicals. Wrote *The Desert Song* (1926) with Sigmund Romberg, *Show Boat* (1927) with Jerome Kern, and many with Richard Rogers, such as *Oklahoma!* (1943), *South Pacific* (1949), *The King and I* (1951), and *The Sound of Music* (1959).

George Frideric Handel (1685–1759), German composer of baroque music. In addition to the *Messiah* (1741) and other oratorios, he wrote operas, cantatas, and chamber music.

Howard Hanson (1896–1981), American composer of highly romantic works, the best known of which is the *Romantic Symphony* (1930).

Roy Harris (1898–1979), American composer whose best-known works are his *Third Symphony* (1939) and the *Cumberland Concerto* (1951).

Melissa Hayden (1923–), Canadian-born ballerina who starred with New York City Ballet in 1950–73.

Franz Joseph Haydn (1732–1809), Austrian composer who wrote the first important symphonies in the classical sonata-allegro form. He composed more than 100 symphonies and 80 string quartets.

Jascha Heifetz (1901–), Russian-American violinist and one of the foremost artists in his field. Before coming to New York (1917), he played in St. Petersburg, Kiev, Berlin, and Vienna.

Victor Herbert (1859–1924), Irish-American cellist, conductor, and composer best known for his operettas *Babes in Toyland* (1903), *Naughty Marietta* (1910), and *Sweethearts* (1913).

Paul Hindemith (1895–1963), German composer who employed highly advanced and varied methods of composition. His most important work is the symphony *Mathis der Maler* (1934).

Arthur Honegger (1892–1955), French composer whose best-known works include the tone poem *Pacific 231* (1923) and the oratorios *King David* (1921) and *Joan of Arc at the Stake* (1935).

Vladimir Horowitz (1904–), Russian-American pianist who has enjoyed great popularity during his career on the U.S. concert stage (since 1928).

Engelbert Humperdinck (1854–1921), German composer of the opera *Hansel and Gretel* (1893).

Doris Humphrey (1895–1958), dancer and choreographer who developed new dance approaches.

Vincent d'Indy (1851–1931), French composer; his masterpiece is the *Symphony Cévenole* (1886).

Charles Ives (1874–1954), American composer whose music captures the spirit of America. His works include the *Third Symphony* (1901–04) and the *Concord Sonata* (1909–15).

Robert Joffrey (1930–), American dancer, choreographer, and director of the Robert Joffrey Ballet Company, which he founded in 1956.

Um Kalthoum (1899–1975), Arab concert singer who was Egypt's most popular star from 1922 to 1972.

Herbert von Karajan (1908–), Austrian conductor who has directed the leading orchestras in Austria and Germany and has made highly successful guest appearances in the U.S.

Jerome David Kern (1885–1945), American composer of musicals, including *Show Boat* (1927).

Aram Khatchaturian (1903–78), Soviet-Armenian composer known for the lively "Sabre Dance" in his ballet *Gayane* (1924) and for his ballet *Spartacus* (1954).

Ralph Kirkpatrick (1911–), American harpsichordist and musicologist. He is an authority on the music of Domenico Scarlatti.

Zoltán Kodály (1882–1967), Hungarian composer whose music combines folk themes with a romantic style. His most famous works are the *Psalmus Hungaricus* (1923) for chorus, and the opera *Hâry Jânos* (1925–26).

André Kostelanetz (1901–80), Russian-American conductor. He directed orchestras on radio and TV for CBS and made many recordings.

Serge Koussevitzky (1874–1951), Russian conductor who directed the Russian State Symphony (1917–20), the Grand Opera of Moscow (1918–20), and the Boston Symphony Orchestra (1924–49).

Fritz Kreisler (1875–1962), Austrian-American violinist and composer who won international fame for his performances in Europe and the U.S.

Wanda Landowska (1877–1959), Polish-American harpsichordist, considered the greatest modern master of that instrument. She is best remembered for her recording of Bach's *Well-Tempered Clavier.*

Leonid Lavrosky (1905–), Russian choreographer who directed the Leningrad Opera and Ballet (1938–44) and the Bolshoi Theater (1944–64).

Lilli Lehmann (1848–1929), German soprano and one of the foremost Wagnerian opera stars. She sang throughout Europe and with the Metropolitan Opera (1885–89; 1891–92).

Lotte Lehmann (1888–1976), German soprano who sang with the Hamburg (1909), the Vienna State (1914–38), and the New York Metropolitan (1934–45) operas. She later was stage director of the Metropolitan.

Erich Leinsdorf (1912–), Austrian-American conductor who led the New York Metropolitan Opera (1938–43; 1956–62), the Cleveland Orchestra (1943–44), the Rochester (N.Y.) Orchestra (1945–54), and the Boston Symphony (1962–69).

Ruggiero Leoncavallo (1858–1919), Italian composer whose best known work is *I Pagliacci* (1892).

Josef Lhévinne (1874–1944), Russian-American pianist and teacher who taught at the Moscow Conservatory (1902–06) and for many years at the Juilliard Graduate School in New York.

José Limón (1908–72), dancer, choreographer, and teacher who was with the Humphrey-Weidman Company and later formed his own dance group.

Jenny Lind (1820–87), Swedish soprano whose magnificent voice and dramatic ability made her the idol of opera lovers throughout Europe. She toured the U.S. from 1850 to 1852.

Franz Liszt (1811–86), Hungarian composer whose virtuosity as a pianist has never been equaled. His compositions include the *Faust Symphony* (1854–57), *Les Préludes* (1856), and 20 Hungarian rhapsodies (1851–86).

Jean Baptiste Lully (1632–87), French operatic composer who wrote the first French operas and founded the Paris Opera in 1672. His works include *Alceste* (1674), *Thésée* (1675), *Psyché* (1678), *Armide* (1686), and *Acis et Galatée* (1687).

Edward MacDowell (1861–1908), American composer whose best-known works are *Indian Suite* (1897) and the *Piano Concerto No. 2* (1890).

Gustav Mahler (1860–1911), Austrian composer and perhaps the last important member of the late Romantic school of symphonists. He wrote 10 great symphonies, the last unfinished, and the song cycle *Das Lied von der Erde* (1908).

Natalia Makarova (1940–), Russian ballerina who defected from Kirov Ballet in 1970; has since appeared with world's leading ballet companies.

Gian Francesco Malipiero (1882–), Italian composer of operas (*L'Orfeide,* 1918–21; *Guilio Cesare,* 1935), symphonies (*Impressions from Nature I, II, and III,* 1910–22), choral and chamber music.

Alicia Markova (1910–), English ballerina who achieved recognition for her performances with the Diaghilev Ballet Russe (1925–32); the Vic-Wells

Ballet (1932–35), where she was prima ballerina; and the Ballet Russe de Monte Carlo (1938–41).

Giovanni Martinelli (1885–1969), Italian tenor who made his debut in Milan (1910) and sang at the Metropolitan Opera (1913–46) in over 50 leading roles.

Pietro Mascagni (1863–1945), Italian composer whose best-known work is *Cavalleria rusticana* (1890).

Jules Massenet (1842–1912), French composer of over 20 operas, including *Manon* (1884), *Werther* (1892), *Thaïs* (1894), and *Don Quichotte* (1910).

Léonide Massine (1896–1979), Russian-American ballet dancer and choreographer who worked with Diaghilev's Ballet Russe (1914–20), the Ballet Russe de Monte Carlo (1932–42), and the Ballet Theater in New York (1942–44).

Patricia McBride (1942–), American-born ballerina; principal dancer with New York City ballet since 1959.

John McCormack (1884–1945), Irish-American tenor. A major operatic star in London and New York, he confined his last years to concerts.

Zubin Mehta (1936–), Indian-American conductor of the New York Philharmonic Orchestra, appointed in 1978.

Dame Nellie Melba (1859–1931), Australian soprano who sang with tremendous success in Brussels (1887), London (1889), Paris (1889–91), and New York (1893–96; 1907–20).

Lauritz Melchior (1890–1973), Danish tenor who appeared in Copenhagen (1913–21), Bayreuth (1925–26), and at the Metropolitan Opera (1926–50), where he was the leading Wagnerian tenor.

Felix Mendelssohn (1809–47), German composer whose beautiful music includes the Overture to *A Midsummer Night's Dream* (1826), the *Scotch Symphony* (1830–42), a violin concerto (1844), the opera *Elijah* (1846), and chamber music.

Peter Mennin (1923–83), American composer who was president of the Juilliard School of Music since 1962. Among his works are seven symphonies and eight choral works.

Gian-Carlo Menotti (1911–), Italian-American composer best known for his operas *Amahl and the Night Visitors* (1951) and *The Saint of Bleecker Street* (1954), which won a Pulitzer Prize in 1955.

Yehudi Menuhin (1916–), American violinist who gave his first concert at the age of seven.

Robert Merrill (1917–), American baritone at the Metropolitan Opera since the early 1950s.

Giacomo Meyerbeer (1791–1864), German composer and master of the French grand opera. Among his works are *Les Huguenots* (1836) and *L'Africaine* (1838–63).

Darius Milhaud (1892–1974), French composer best known for his operas *Le Pauvre Matelot* (1926) and *Christophe Colombe* (1928).

Dimitri Mitropoulos (1896–1960), Greek conductor who led the Paris Symphony (1932), the Minneapolis Symphony (1937–49), and the New York Philharmonic (1950–58).

Igor Moiseyev (1906–), Russian dancer and choreographer who was with the Bolshoi Theatre (1924–39). In 1936 he organized the Moiseyev Dance Company.

Pierre Monteux (1875–1964), French conductor who directed the Metropolitan Opera (1917–19), the Boston Symphony (1919–24), the Paris Symphony (1928–35), the San Francisco Symphony (1935–52), and the London Symphony (1962–64).

Claudio Monteverdi (1567–1643), Italian composer credited with writing the first significant operas, including *Orfeo* (1607), *The Return of Ulysses* (1641), and *The Coronation of Poppea* (1642).

Grace Moore (1901–47), American soprano who sang at the Metropolitan Opera (1928–32, 1934–35, 1937–39) and made several films. She was killed in a plane crash at the height of her career.

Wolfgang Amadeus Mozart (1756–91), Austrian composer who epitomized the classical tradition with 41 symphonies, over 30 piano concertos, concertos for other instruments, chamber music, masses, and such operas as *Don Giovanni* (1787) and *The Magic Flute* (1791).

Charles Münch (1891–1968), French conductor who directed the Paris Philharmonic Orchestra (1938–46), the Boston Symphony (1949–62), and the Berkshire Music Center (1951–62).

Patrice Munsel (1925–), American soprano who made her debut at the Metropolitan Opera in 1943 and has also appeared in films.

Modest Mussorgsky (1839–81), Russian composer whose best-known work is the opera *Boris Godunov* (1874).

Bronislava Nijinska (1891–1971), Russian dancer and choreographer associated with the Diaghilev Ballet Russe until 1924.

Vaslav Nijinsky (1890–1950), Russian ballet dancer considered by many to be the greatest of all time. He began dancing at the age of 10. He performed with the Diaghilev Ballet Russe (1909–17) until he was committed to an insane asylum.

Birgit Nilsson (1918–), Swedish singer considered the greatest living Wagnerian soprano. Her triumphant debut at the Metropolitan Opera (1959) made front-page news.

Lillian Nordica (1857–1914), American soprano most famous for her Wagnerian roles. In addition to many appearances in Europe, she starred at the Metropolitan Opera from 1893 to 1909.

Rudolf Nureyev (1938–), Russian ballet dancer who has been called a second Nijinsky. He starred with the Kirov Ballet before defecting to the West in 1961 while on a trip to London. Since then Nureyev has been the principal dancer and choreographer for the Royal Ballet.

Jacques Offenbach (1819–80), French composer of over 100 operettas. His masterpiece is the opera *Tales of Hoffmann* (1877–80), which was not produced until after his death.

David Oistrakh (1908–74), Russian violinist hailed as one of the greatest 20th century musicians.

Carl Orff (1895–1982), German composer: best known for cantata *Carmina Burana* (1936).

Eugene Ormandy (1899–), Hungarian-American conductor who came to the U.S. in 1920. He led the Minneapolis Symphony (1931–35) and the Philadelphia Orchestra (1938–79).

Ignace Jan Paderewski (1860–1941), Polish pianist and composer who enjoyed tremendous international popularity as a performer. His best-known composition is the *Minuet in G* for piano (1899).

Niccolò Paganini (1782–1840), Italian violinist considered the world's greatest violin virtuoso. He charmed audiences throughout Europe.

Giovanni Palestrina (1524–94), Italian composer of polyphonic sacred motets and masses and of secular madrigals. His works rank among the most important of the Italian Renaissance.

Luciano Pavarotti, (1935–), Italian tenor: Made operatic debut in Reggio Emilia, Italy, in 1961; debuted with the New York Metropolitan Opera on Nov. 23, 1968.

Anna Pavlova (1881–1931), Russian ballerina who won international recognition for her magnificent performances in Europe and America.

Jan Peerce (1904–), American tenor who sang on radio and at the Radio City Music Hall (1932–37) before joining the Metropolitan Opera in 1941.

Roberta Peters (1930–), American operatic soprano: debuted with Metropolitan Opera in 1950; recorded operas; appeared in several motion pictures.

Gregor Piatigorsky (1903–76), Russian-born concert cellist, made his American debut in 1929. He became a U.S. citizen in 1942.

Ezio Pinza (1892–1957), Italian basso who sang at

MUSICIANS *(continued)*

the Metropolitan Opera (1926–48). In 1949 he was featured in the Broadway musical *South Pacific.*

Walter Piston (1894–1976), American composer who was awarded two Pulitzer Prizes in music for his Third (1948) and Seventh (1961) symphonies.

Ildebrando Pizzetti (1880–1968), Italian composer whose operas *Fedra* (1909–12) and *Debora e Jaele* (1915–21) are his most popular works.

Lily Pons (1904–76), French soprano who sang at the Metropolitan Opera from 1931 to 1959.

Rosa Ponselle (1897–1981), American soprano who gave outstanding performances at the Metropolitan Opera (1918–37) and in London (1929–31).

Cole Porter (1893–1964), American composer of musical comedies, including *Kiss Me, Kate* (1948) and *Silk Stockings* (1955), and the songs *Night and Day* and *Begin the Beguine.*

Francis Poulenc (1899–1963), French composer whose works include *Concert Champêtre* (1927–28) and the Mass in G (1937).

Leontyne Price (1927–), American soprano who has sung on Broadway and in major opera houses. She made her debut with the Metropolitan Opera in 1961.

William Primrose (1903–82), Scottish violist regarded as one of the world's finest.

Sergei Prokofiev (1891–1953), Russian composer and piano virtuoso. His distinctive works include the First (1916–17) and Fifth (1944) symphonies, *Peter and the Wolf* (1936), and the ballet *Romeo and Juliette* (1935–36).

Giacomo Puccini (1858–1924), Italian composer of the universally popular operas *La Bohème* (1896), *Tosca* (1900), and *Madame Butterfly* (1904).

Henry Purcell (1659–95), English composer believed by some authorities to be England's greatest. His works include the opera *Dido and Aeneas* (1689) and religious music.

Sergei Rachmaninov (1873–1943), Russian composer and pianist. Among his best works are the Second Piano Concerto (1901), the Second Symphony (1907), and Rhapsody on a Theme of Paganini (1934).

Maurice Ravel (1875–1937), French composer whose works include the ballet *Daphnis et Chloé* (1909–11) and *Rhapsodie Espagnole* (1907) and *Bolero* (1928) for orchestra.

Fritz Reiner (1888–1963), Hungarian conductor who directed the Cincinnati Orchestra (1922–31), the Pittsburgh Orchestra (1938–48), and the Chicago Orchestra (1953–62).

Ottorino Respighi (1879–1936), Italian composer known for his symphonic poems *The Fountains of Rome* (1917) and *The Pines of Rome* (1924).

Sviatoslav Richter (1914–), Russian pianist acclaimed as a distinguished virtuoso.

Wallingford Riegger (1885–1961), American composer of highly original works, including four symphonies and Music for Brass Choir (1948–49).

Nicholas Rimsky-Korsakov (1844–1908), Russian nationalist composer of the *Spanish Capriccio* (1887), *Scheherazade* (1888), and *Easter Overture* (1888).

Jerome Robbins (1918–), American dancer and choreographer who joined the Ballet Theater in New York (1940–44) and in 1959 became associate musical director of the New York City Ballet.

Paul Robeson (1898–1976), American black concert singer and actor, noted for his singing in *Showboat* (1936) and as the Moor in *Othello.*

Richard Rodgers (1902–79), American composer of musicals. Teamed with librettist Oscar Hammerstein II on many, including *Oklahoma!* (1943), *South Pacific* (1949), *The King and I* (1951), and *The Sound of Music* (1959).

Sigmund Romberg (1887–1951), American composer of operettas and musicals, including *The Student Prince* (1924) and *The Desert Song* (1926).

Gioacchino Rossini (1792–1868), Italian composer best known for his operas *The Barber of Seville* (1816) and *William Tell* (1829).

Anton Rubenstein (1829–94), Russian pianist and composer whose renowned mastery of the keyboard ranked second only to that of Liszt.

Arthur Rubinstein (1887–1982), Polish-American musician considered one of the greatest pianists.

Ruth St. Denis (1877–1968), American dancer, choreographer, and pioneer in the development of modern dance in the U.S.

Charles Camille Saint-Saëns (1835–1921), French composer of the opera *Samson et Dalila* (1868–75), three symphonies, and five piano concertos.

Alessandro Scarlatti (1660–1725), Italian composer of 115 operas.

Domenico Scarlatti (1685–1757), Italian composer and harpsichordist; son of A. Scarlatti. His roughly 500 sonatas are among the first important keyboard works written in this form.

Alexander Schneider (1908–), Russian-American violinist and conductor. A member of the Budapest String Quartet (1938–68), he is also a major participant in the Casals summer music festivals.

Arnold Schoenberg (1874–1951), Austrian composer and creator of the 12-tone (atonal) method. His works include *Verklärte Nacht* (1899), the Variations for Orchestra (1928), and an unfinished opera, *Moses und Aron* (1932–51).

Franz Schubert (1797–1828), Austrian composer of over 600 songs; nine symphonies, of which the "Unfinished" (1822) is best known; and the "Trout" Quintet in A Major (1819).

William Schuman (1910–), American composer; president of Lincoln Center in New York (1962–68). His works include the *American Festival Overture* (1939).

Robert Schumann (1810–56), German romantic composer of the Piano Concerto in A Minor (1841–45) and the Spring (1841) and Rhenish (1850) symphonies.

Ernestine Schumann-Heink (1861–1936), Austrian-American contralto. She appeared at the Chicago Opera (1898), the Metropolitan Opera (1899–1904), and in many concerts.

Antonio Scotti (1866–1936), Italian baritone who enjoyed great popularity as a member of the Metropolitan Opera (1899–1933).

Aleksandr Scriabin (1872–1915), Russian pianist whose notable works include *Divine Poem* (1903) and *Prometheus: A Poem of Fire* (1909–10).

Andrés Segovia (1893–), Spanish guitarist noted for his interpretation of classical works.

Marcella Sembrich (1858–1935), Polish soprano who sang in the great European opera houses and with the Metropolitan Opera (1898–1909).

Peter Serkin (1947–), American pianist and son of Rudolf Serkin. He is among the most accomplished of the younger keyboard artists.

Rudolf Serkin (1903–), Austrian-American pianist who ranks among the best contemporary artists. He has toured widely and since 1951 has directed the Marlboro (Vt.) School of Music.

Roger Sessions (1896–), American composer: Orchestral Suite from *The Black Maskers* (1928) and four symphonies (1927, 1946, 1957, 1958).

Ted Shawn (1891–1972), American dancer, choreographer, and teacher. With Ruth St. Denis he founded the influential Denishawn School for Modern Dance.

Dimitri Shostakovich (1906–75), Russian composer who won international acclaim with such symphonies as the Fifth (1937) and Ninth (1945).

Jean Sibelius (1865–1957), Finnish composer of stirring nationalist music and seven symphonies.

Cesare Siepi (1923–), Italian bass and a member of the New York Metropolitan Opera since 1950.

Beverly Sills (1929–), American soprano, made her debut with the New York City Opera in 1955 and with the Metropolitan Opera in 1975; appointed director of New York City Opera in 1978.
Bedřich Smetana (1824–84), Czech nationalist composer whose well-known works include the opera *The Bartered Bride* (1866) and the symphonic poem *My Country* (1874–79).
Michael Somes (1917–), English ballet dancer who began his career with the Sadler's Wells Ballet Company in 1935 and was a leading dancer with the Royal Ballet in London.
John Philip Sousa (1854–1932), American band-master and composer of over 100 marches including *The Stars and Stripes Forever* (1897).
Eleanor Steber (1916–), American soprano who sang with the Metropolitan Opera from 1940.
William Steinberg (1899–1978), German–American conductor of the Pittsburgh Symphony (1952–75) and Boston Symphony (1969–71) orchestras.
Issac Stern (1920–), American violinist who has given outstanding performances throughout the world.
Risë Stevens (1913–), American mezzo-soprano who sang throughout the world and with the Metropolitan Opera from the 1930s through the 1950s.
Karlheinz Stockhausen (1928–), German composer whose avant-garde works include *Kontrapunkte* (1952) and *Koutackte* (1960) for electronic sounds, percussion, and piano.
Leopold Stokowski (1882–1977), American conductor who led the Cincinnati Symphony (1909–12), the Philadelphia Orchestra (1912–36), and the New York Philharmonic (1945–50). In 1962 he founded the American Symphony in New York.
Johann Strauss Jr. (1825–99), Austrian conductor and composer of more than 400 waltzes, including *The Blue Danube* (1866) and *Tales from the Vienna Woods* (1868).
Richard Strauss (1864–1949), German composer whose major works are the symphonic poems *Don Juan* (1888) and *Till Eulenspiegel* (1894–95) and the opera *Der Rosenkavalier* (1911).
Igor Stravinsky (1882–1971), Russian–French composer considered the father of modern music. Among his most important works are the ballets *The Firebird* (1910) and *The Rite of Spring* (1913).
Sir Arthur Sullivan (1842–1900), English composer (with W. S. Gilbert) of operettas, including *H.M.S. Pinafore* (1878) and *The Mikado* (1885).
Joan Sutherland (1926–), Australian soprano. In 1961 she made a spectacular debut at the Metropolitan Opera.
George Szell (1897–1970), Hungarian conductor who led the Berlin State Opera (1924–30), the Metropolitan Opera (1942–45), and the Cleveland Orchestra (1946–70).
Maria Tallchief (1925–), American ballerina who danced with the Ballet Russe de Monte Carlo (1942–47) and was the prima ballerina at the New York City Ballet (1954–55) and at the American Ballet Theatre (1960).
Deems Taylor (1885–1966), American composer: *Through the Looking Glass* (1922) for orchestra, and the opera *The King's Henchmen* (1927).
Paul Taylor (1930–), American dancer and choreographer who performed with the Martha Graham Company (1955–61) and the New York City Ballet (1959–61).
Peter Ilich Tchaikovsky (1840–93), Russian composer. His works include six symphonies, the *Romeo and Juliet Overture* (1870), the Piano Concerto in B Flat Minor (1875), the ballet *Swan Lake* (1876), and a concerto for violin and orchestra.
Renata Tebaldi (1922–), Italian soprano who has performed in Milan (1949–54, 1959), London (1950), San Francisco (1950), and at the Metropolitan Opera (since 1955).
Twyla Tharp (1941–), American choreographer who uses popular and jazz music to blend ballet with modern dance.
Virgil Thomson (1896–), American composer of the opera *Four Saints in Three Acts* (1928).
Lawrence Tibbett (1896–1960), American baritone who starred at the Metropolitan Opera (1923–50) and in several films.
Arturo Toscanini (1867–1957), Italian conductor renowned for his artistry. He led the orchestras at the La Scala Opera (1898–1903) and Metropolitan Opera (1908–15), and the New York Philharmonic (1927–36) and NBC Symphony (1937-54).
Helen Traubel (1899–1972), American soprano who excelled in Wagnerian roles at the Metropolitan Opera (1939–53), and sang with leading orchestras.
Richard Tucker (1914–75), American tenor who starred with the Metropolitan Opera (1945–75).
Antony Tudor (1909–), English dancer and choreographer who worked with the Rambert Ballet (1930–38), Sadler's Wells Ballet (1931–36), and American Ballet Theater (1939–56). He became ballet director of the Metropolitan Opera in 1957.
Galina Ulanova (1910–), Russian ballerina considered one of the greatest dancers since Anna Pavlova. She appeared with the Bolshoi Theatre from 1935, becoming prima ballerina in 1944.
Ralph Vaughan Williams (1872–1958), English composer. *Three Norfolk Rhapsodies* (1905–07) and the opera *Hugh the Drover* (1911–14).
Giuseppe Verdi (1813–1901), Italian composer of such well-known operas as *Rigoletto* (1851), *La Traviata* (1853), *Don Carlos* (1867), *Aïda* (1871), *Otello* (1886), and *Falstaff* (1893).
Heitor Villa-Lobos (1887–1959), Brazilian composer: *Amazonas* (1917), the *Bachiana brasileira* (1930), and the Chorós No. 11 (1941).
Antonio Vivaldi (1675-1741), Italian composer of over 40 operas who is best-known for his violin concertos *The Seasons* and the *Tempesta di Màre.*
Richard Wagner (1813–83), German romantic opera composer. *Tannhäuser* (1843–45), *Lohengrin* (1846–48), and *Die Meistersinger* (1862–67).
Bruno Walter (1876–1962), German conductor who directed the New York Philharmonic (1923–33, 1947–49).
Sir William Walton (1902–83), British composer whose works include the oratoria *Belshazzar's Feast* (1931) and the opera *Troilus and Cressida* (1954).
Leonard Warren (1911–60), American baritone who won acclaim at the Metropolitan Opera (1939–60), where he died onstage.
André Watts (1943–), American pianist who made his debut at the age of nine and has played with numerous major orchestras.
Carl Maria von Weber (1786–1826), German composer who began the Romantic movement in German opera. Among his operas are *Der Freischütz* (1821) and *Oberon* (1826).
Anton von Webern (1883–1945), Austrian composer and pupil of Arnold Schoenberg. A leading atonal composer, he is best known for *Five Pieces for Orchestra* (1911–13) and *Variations* (1940).
Charles Weidman (1901–75), American dancer, choreographer, and director who helped develop modern dance; founded own company in 1941.
Kurt Weill (1900–50), German composer for the stage. *The Threepenny Opera* (1928), *One Touch of Venus* (1943), and *Street Scene* (1947).
Hugo Wolf (1860–1903), Austrian composer known for more than 250 songs composed by setting the poems of others to music.
Igor Youskevitch (1912–), Russian ballet dancer with the Ballet Russe de Monte Carlo (1938) and the Ballet Theater in New York (1946–56).

FAMOUS PAINTERS, SCULPTORS, AND ARCHITECTS

Famous artists, sculptors, architects, and painters are included in the following list. Where it was thought helpful to the reader, the artist is described according to the movement or school to which he belonged. In most cases one or more works typical of each artist's output are mentioned. See pages 981–986 for 1983 deaths.

A glossary describing the artistic movements and schools mentioned in connection with many of the artists can be found on page 68.

Leone Battista Alberti (1404–72), Florentine architect and a pioneer in Renaissance church design: the Church of Sant'Andrea (1470) in Mantua.
Andrea del Sarto (1486–1531), Florentine painter of religious frescoes: *The Birth of the Virgin* (1514).
Fra Angelico (c.1400–55), Florentine painter of religious subjects: *Annunciation* (c.1440–50).
Alexander Archipenko (1887–1964), Ukrainian-American abstract sculptor: *Boxers* (1935).
Jean Arp (1887–1966), French surrealist and Dadaist painter and sculptor: *Constellation According to the Laws of Chance* (1932), wood relief.
John James Audubon (1785?–1851), American ornithologist and artist noted for his finely detailed illustrations of American wildlife: *The Birds of America* (1827–38).
Francis Bacon (1910–), English surrealist painter: *Study After Velázquez's Portrait of Pope Innocent X* (1953).
James Barry (1741–1806), Anglo-Irish painter: *The Progress of Human Culture* (1777–83).
Fra Bartolommeo (1475–1517), Italian painter of the High Renaissance: *Marriage of St. Catherine.*
Aubrey Vincent Beardsley (1872–98), English illustrator in black and white: *Isolde* (c.1890).
Max Beckmann (1884–1950), German expressionist painter: *Self-portrait with a Saxophone* (1930).
Giovanni Bellini (c.1430–1516), Venetian religious painter: *St. Francis in Ecstasy* (c.1485).
George Wesley Bellows (1882–1925), American realistic painter: *Stag at Sharkey's* (1907), *Up the Hudson* (1908).
Thomas Hart Benton (1889–1975), American regional painter: *Lonesome Road, Cotton Pickers.*
Giovanni Lorenzo Bernini (1598–1680), Italian baroque sculptor: *David* (1623), *Ecstasy of St. Teresa* (1645–52).
George Caleb Bingham (1811–79), American regional painter: *The County Election* (c.1851).
Umberto Boccioni (1882–1916), Italian futurist painter and sculptor: *The City Rises* (1910).
Giovanni da Bologna (1524–1608), French-born mannerist sculptor who worked in Florence: *The Rape of the Sabines* (1583).
Pierre Bonnard (1867–1947) French postimpressionist painter: *Man and Woman* (1900), *Nude Washing* (c.1922).
Francesco Borromini (1599–1677), Italian baroque architect: San Carlo alle Quattro Fontane, in Rome (begun in 1638).
Hieronymus Bosch or **Jerome Bos** (c.1450–1516), Flemish painter of bizarre fantasies: *The Garden of Delights* (1500).
Sandro Botticelli (Alessandro di Mariano dei Filipepi, c.1444–1510), Florentine religious and allegorical painter: *Primavera* (1477–78), *The Birth of Venus* (c.1480).
Edmé Bouchardon (1698–1762), French sculptor of religious subjects and portrait busts: *Christ Leaning on His Cross* (1745).
François Boucher (1703–70), French rococo painter: *The Triumph of Venus* (1740).
Constantin Brancusi (1876–1957), Romanian abstract sculptor: *The Kiss* (1908), *Bird in Space* (1919).
Georges Braque (1882–1963), French cubist painter: *Still Life, "Melody"* (1914), *The Bike* (1952).
Il Bronzino (Agnolo di Cosimo di Mariano, 1503–72), Florentine mannerist painter: *Eleanor de Toledo and Her Son* (c.1550).
Pieter Bruegel the Elder (c.1525–69), Flemish landscape painter: *The Return of the Hunters* (1565), *Peasant Wedding* (1565).
Filippo Brunelleschi (1377–1446), Florentine architect who produced the first important early Renaissance architecture: dome for the cathedral in Florence (1420–36).
Bernard Buffet (1928–), French painter whose work derives from several modern schools: *Landscape in Provence* (1957).
Charles Burchfield (1893–1967), American painter of landscapes and urban scenes, especially in watercolor: *Ice Glare* (1933).
Edward Coley Burne-Jones (1833–98), English Pre-Raphaelite painter: *Love Among the Ruins* (1894).
Alexander Calder (1898–1976), American abstract sculptor who introduced the mobile and the stabile forms: *Lobster Trap and Fish Tail* (1939).
Antonio Canova (1757–1822), Venetian neoclassic sculptor: *Pauline Bonaparte Borghese* (1808).
Michelangelo Merisi da Caravaggio (1573–1610), Italian baroque painter: *Calling of St. Matthew* (1598–99).
Jean Baptiste Carpeaux (1827–75), French romantic sculptor: *The Dance* (in Paris Opéra, 1865–69).
Mary Cassatt (1845–1926), American impressionist painter: *Mother and Child at a Boating Party.*
Andrea del Castagno (c.1423–57), Florentine religious painter: *Last Supper* (1445–50).
Benvenuto Cellini (1500–71), Italian mannerist sculptor: *Perseus with the Head of Medusa* (c.1545).
Paul Cézanne (1839–1906), French painter who began the postimpressionist movement: *Fruit Bowl, Glass and Apples* (1879–82), *Mont Sainte-Victoire Seen from Bibemus Quarry* (1898–1900).
Marc Chagall (1889–), Russian expressionist painter: *I and the Village* (1911), *The Grey House* (1917).
Jean Baptiste Chardin (1699–1779), French genre painter: *Return from Market* (1739).
Giorgio de Chirico (1888–1978), Italian surrealist painter: *The Anguish of Departure* (1913–14).
Frederick Edwin Church (1826–1900), American landscape painter: *Niagara Falls* (1857), *The Heart of the Andes* (1859); his *Icebergs* (1861) was sold in 1979 for record price of $2.5 million.
Giovanni Cimabue (Cenni di Pepo, c.1240–1302), Florentine painter of religious frescoes: *Madonna of St. Francis,* in the church at Assisi.
Claude Lorrain (1600–82), French landscape painter: *View of the Campagna* (c.1650).
Clodion (Claude Michel, 1738–1814), French rococo sculptor: *Bacchante and a Satyr, Montesquieu* (1779–83).
Thomas Cole (1801–48), American landscape painter and member of the Hudson River School: *The Oxbow of the Connecticut* (1836).
John Constable (1776–1837), English landscape painter: *Hampstead Heath* (1821).
John Singleton Copley (1738–1815), American painter of portraits (*Mrs. Thomas Boylston, 1766*) and romanticized historic works (*Watson and the Shark, 1778*).
Jean Baptiste Camille Corot (1796–1875), French romantic landscape painter: *The Bridge at Narni (1826), Homer and the Shepherds* (1845).

Correggio (Antonio Allegri, 1494–1534), Italian mannerist painter: *Assumption of the Virgin* (c.1525), *Jupiter and Io* (c.1532).

Gustave Courbet (1819–77), French realist painter: *The Stone Breakers* (1849), *Painter's Studio* (1855).

Lucas I. Cranach (1472–1553), German painter, etcher, and woodcut designer: Made portraits of notable contemporaries, including Martin Luther.

John Steuart Curry (1897–1946), American artist who painted scenes of Midwestern life: *Baptism in Kansas* (1928), *Tornado over Kansas* (1929).

Salvador Dali (1904–), Spanish surrealist painter: *Persistence of Memory* (1931).

Honoré Daumier (1808–79), French painter, sculptor, and caricaturist of the realist school: *The Third-Class Carriage* (1862), *Don Quixote Attacking the Windmills* (1866).

Jacques Louis David (1748–1825), French neoclassic painter: *The Death of Marat* (1793), *The Rape of the Sabines* (1799).

Leonardo da Vinci (1452–1519), Italian painter, architect, and sculptor: Was influential leader of Renaissance art. Paintings include *Last Supper* (c.1495–97) and *Mona Lisa* (c.1503–05). He was also an innovator and inventor in the physical sciences and engineering.

Stuart Davis (1894–1964), U.S. semiabstract painter: *The Barber Shop* (1930), *Visa* (1951).

Edgar Degas (1834–1917), French impressionist painter: *Prima Ballerina* (1876), *Absinthe Drinkers* (1876), *Ballet Class* (c.1878).

Willem de Kooning (1904–), Dutch-American abstract expressionist painter: *Woman I* (1950–52).

Ferdinand Victor Eugène Delacroix (1798–1863), French romantic painter: *Massacre of Scio* (1822–24), *Frédéric Chopin* (1838).

André Derain (1880–1954), French fauvist painter: *Seascape* and *Collioure* (both c.1905).

Donatello (Donato di Niccolò di Betto Bardi, c.1386–1466), Florentine sculptor of the Renaissance: statues include *St. Mark* (1411–13); panels include *St. George and the Dragon* (1415–17).

Jean Dubuffet (1901–), French surrealist painter: *Landscape with Two Personages* (1952).

Marcel Duchamp (1887–1968), French cubist and Dadaist painter: *Nude Descending a Staircase* (1913).

Raoul Dufy (1877–1953), French painter influenced by the impressionists and fauvists: *Casino at Nice* (1927), *Deauville, Drying the Sails* (1933).

Albrecht Dürer (1471–1528), German Renaissance painter and engraver: *The Four Horsemen of the Apocalypse* (1497–98).

Thomas Eakins (1844–1916), American realist painter: *The Gross Clinic* (1875).

Charles Eames (1907-78), U.S. architect and designer: Responsible for first mass-produced molded plastic chair used in many public waiting rooms; his luxury lounge chairs regarded as ultimate in comfort.

Sir Jacob Epstein (1880–1959), American sculptor: the Oscar Wilde Memorial (1911), *Adam, Jacob and the Angel* (1939).

Max Ernst (1891–1976), German-American surrealist painter: *Two Children Are Threatened by a Nightingale* (1924), *Euclid* (1945).

Lyonel Feininger (1871–1956), American cubist painter: *Church in the Market Place* (1929).

Jean Honoré Fragonard (1732–1806), French rococo painter: *The Swing* (c.1765); *The Progress of Love* (c.1771), a series of painted panels.

Thomas Gainsborough (1727–88), English landscape and portrait painter: *Robert Andrews and His Wife* (c.1748–50), *The Mall* (1783).

Paul Gauguin (1848–1903), French postimpressionist painter: *The Yellow Christ* (1890).

Jean Louis André Théodore Géricault (1791–1824), French romantic painter: *Mounted Officer of the Imperial Guard* (1812), *Raft of the Medusa* (1818–19).

Lorenzo Ghiberti (c.1378–1455), Florentine sculptor of religious subjects: *The Sacrifice of Isaac*, (1401–02), a set of bronze doors for the Baptistery in Florence.

Domenico Ghirlandaio (1449–94), Florentine painter of religious subjects: *Saint Jerome* (1480).

Alberto Giacometti (1901–66), Swiss sculptor, mainly of the surrealist school: *The Palace at 4 A.M.* (1932–33), *Man Pointing* (1947).

Giorgione (c.1478–1510), Venetian painter who influenced art in Venice: *The Tempest*.

Giotto (di Bondone, c.1266–1337), Florentine artist generally considered one of the founders of modern, naturalist painting: religious frescoes in the Arena Chapel in Padua (1305–06).

William James Glackens (1870–1938), American realist painter: *Chez Mouquin* (1905).

Arshile Gorky (1904–48), American abstract expressionist painter: *Agony* (1947).

Francisco José de Goya y Lucientes (1746–1828), Spanish painter, etcher, and lithographer whose work covers a wide range, from official portraits to satire: *The Family of Charles IV* (1800), *The Third of May, 1808* (1814–15).

El Greco (Domenikos Theotokopoulos, c.1541–1614), Greek mannerist painter who spent most of his career in Spain: *Burial of the Count of Orgaz* (1586), *View of Toledo*.

Juan Gris (1887–1927), Spanish cubist painter: *Still Life Before an Open Window* (1915).

George Grosz (1893–1959), German-American expressionist painter: *Germany, A Winter's Tale* (1918).

Mathias Grünewald (c.1480–1528), German Gothic painter: *Isenheim Altarpiece* (c.1510–15).

Francesco Guardi (1712–93), Venetian landscape painter, especially scenes of the city: *Venice, Piazza San Marco* (1765).

Frans Hals (c.1580–1666), Dutch portrait and genre painter: *The Jolly Toper* (1627), *Malle Bobbe* (c.1650).

William M. Hartnett (1848–92), American still-life painter: *The Social Club* (1879).

Meindert Hobbema (1638–1709), Dutch landscape painter: *Avenue at Middelharnis* (1689).

Hans Hofmann (1880–1966), German-American abstract expressionist painter: *Elegy* (1950).

William Hogarth (1697–1764), English painter and engraver who did satiric studies of English society: *The Rake's Progress* (c.1735).

Katsushika Hokusai (1760–1849), Japanese painter whose work influenced Western landscape art: *Views of Famous Bridges* (1823–35), *Hundred Views of Mount Fuji* (1835).

Hans Holbein the Younger (c.1497–1543), German portrait painter: *Erasmus of Rotterdam* (c.1523), *Sir Thomas More* (1527), *Henry VIII* (1540).

Winslow Homer (1836–1910), American romantic painter, especially of seascapes: *The Gulfstream* (1889), *Breaking Storm* and *Maine Coast* (1894).

Pieter de Hooch (c.1629–84), Dutch genre painter: *Delft After the Explosion* (1654).

Edward Hopper (1882–1967), American regional painter and engraver: *Early Sunday Morning* (1930), *Night Hawks* (1942).

Jean Antoine Houdon (1741–1828), French neoclassic sculptor: *Morpheus* (1777), *Girl Shivering* (1783).

Jean Auguste Dominique Ingres (1780–1867), French neoclassic painter: *Vow of Louis XIII* (1824).

George Inness (1825–94), American landscape painter: *Delaware Valley* (1865), *Niagara* (1889).

Augustus John (1878–1961), English landscape and portrait painter: *The Marchesa Casati* (1919), *An Irish Bay* (1911–14).

PAINTERS, SCULPTORS, AND ARCHITECTS *(continued)*

Jasper Johns (1930–), American pop artist: *Map* (1962).

Philip Cortelyou Johnson (1906–), American architect who helped plan the Seagram Building and Lincoln Center, both in New York City.

Inigo Jones (1573–1652), English architect deeply influenced by Italian Renaissance styles: the banquet hall at Whitehall Palace (1619–22).

Vasili Kandinsky (1866–1944), Russian painter who originated modern abstract painting, or tachisme: *Black Patch* (1921), *Movement I* (1935).

Rockwell Kent (1882–1971), American illustrator and painter: illustrated *Moby Dick*, *Beowulf*, and *The Canterbury Tales.*

Paul Klee (1879–1940), Swiss painter of fantastic, often humorous subjects: *The Twittering Machine* (1922), *Park Near Lucerne* (1938).

Franz Kline (1910–62), American abstract expressionist painter, best known for an extensive series of paintings which he numbered rather than giving them titles.

Oskar Kokoschka (1886–1980), Austrian expressionist painter: *Hans Tietze and His Wife* (1909).

Le Corbusier (Charles Edouard Jeanneret, 1887–1965), Franco-Swiss architect who was a major influence on modern architecture: Savoye House, Poissy, France (1929–31), Secretariat Building, Chandigarh, India (1952–56).

Doris Emrick Lee (1905–), American painter: *Thanksgiving* (1935).

Fernand Léger (1881–1955), French cubist painter: *The City* (1919), *Women in an Interior* (1922).

Emanuel Gottlieb Leutze (1816–68), German-American historical painter: *Washington Crossing the Delaware* (1851).

Roy Lichtenstein (1923–), American pop artist: *Step-on Can with Leg*, a diptych (1961).

Jacques Lipchitz (1891–1973), French-Lithuanian sculptor whose works bear cubist influences: *Man with a Guitar* (1915).

Fra Filippo Lippi (c.1406–69), Italian painter of religious subjects: *Madonna with Saints* (c.1432).

Richard Lippold (1915–), American abstract sculptor, best known for his elaborate wire constructions: *The Sun* (1953–56).

Aristide Maillol (1861–1944), French sculptor of the female nude: *Seated Woman* (c.1901).

Édouard Manet (1832–83), French painter usually associated with the impressionist movement: *Luncheon on the Grass* (1863), *The Fife Player* (1866).

John Marin (1870–1953), American expressionist painter best known for watercolors: *Maine Islands* (1922), *Gray Sea* (1924).

Masaccio (Tommaso Guidi, c.1401–28), Florentine painter of frescoes in Italian churches: *Madonna and Child* (1426).

Henri Matisse (1869–1954), French painter and leader of the fauvist movement: *The Joy of Life* (1905–06), *Harmony in Red* (1908–09).

Michelangelo Buonarroti (1475–1564), Italian painter, sculptor, and architect who was a leading figure in Renaissance art. His most famous paintings include the frescoes in the Sistine Chapel. Among his many statues are those of *David* (1501–04) and *Moses* (c.1513–15). He is generally considered the greatest sculptor and draftsman.

Ludwig Miës van der Rohe (1886–1969), German-American architect: Lake Shore apartments, Chicago (1950–52), Seagram Building, New York (with Philip Johnson, 1955–57).

John Millais (1829–96), English portrait and genre painter and, for a while, a key member of the Pre-Raphaelites: *The Carpenter's Shop* (1850).

Jean François Millet (1814–75), French romantic painter: *The Sower* (c.1850), *Angelus* (1859).

Joan Miró (1893–), Spanish surrealist painter: *Carnival of Harlequin* (1924–25).

Amedeo Modigliani (1884–1920), Italian painter who lived in France, and whose work combines influences from various schools: *Boy in a Blue Jacket* (1918), *Reclining Nude* (c.1919).

Piet Mondrian (1872–1944), Dutch abstract expressionist painter whose canvases are painted in simple horizontal and vertical stripes: *Composition with Red, Blue, and Yellow* (1930).

Claude Monet (1840–1926), French painter who was among the leaders of the impressionists: *Sailboat at Argenteuil* (1875).

Henry Moore (1898–), English abstract sculptor: *Recumbent Figure* (1938), *Locking Piece* (1963–65).

Grandma Moses (Anna Mary Robertson Moses, 1860–1961), American primitive painter of rural and domestic scenes: *Hurrah for Christmas* (1939).

Robert Motherwell (1915–), American abstract expressionist painter: *Elegy for the Spanish Republic* (1953–54).

Edvard Munch (1863–1944), Norwegian expressionist painter: *The Scream* (1893), *Dance of Life* (1900).

Bartolomé Esteban Murillo (1617?–82), Spanish portrait and religious painter: *Birth of the Virgin* (c.1655), *Marriage of St. Catherine* (1682).

Louise Nevelson (1900–), American sculptor in wood whose work shows cubist and surrealist influences: *Sky Cathedral* (1958).

Georgia O'Keeffe (1887–), American regional painter of the Southwest: *Black Cross, New Mexico* (1929).

Claes Oldenburg (1929–), American pop artist whose sculpture consists of rearranged junk and huge realistic objects, such as a giant lipstick, *Feasible Monument* (1969).

José Clemente Orozco (1883–1949), Mexican social-realist mural painter: *An Epic of American Civilization* (1934), at Dartmouth College.

Charles Willson Peale (1741–1827), American portrait painter: *George Washington* (1780).

I.M. (Ieoh Ming) Pei (1917–), Chinese-born architect: John Hancock Tower, Boston; National Gallery of Art East Building, Washington, D.C.; John F. Kennedy Library, Boston.

Claude Perrault (1613–88), French architect who designed much of the Louvre.

Perugino (Pietro Vannucci, c.1445–1523), Italian painter of religious subjects, and the teacher of Raphael: *Crucifixion with Saints* (1496).

Phidias of Athens (c.500–432 B.C.), Greek sculptor: *Athena* (c.447–439 B.C.) in the Parthenon, a building whose construction he may have supervised.

Pablo Picasso (1881–1973), Spanish painter and sculptor who helped found cubism and who produced major works in styles ranging from neoclassicism to surrealism. Paintings include *Woman in White* (1923), *The Three Dancers* (1925), *Guernica* (1937). Sculptures include *Woman's Head* (1909).

Piero della Francesca (c.1420–92), Italian painter of religious subjects: *The Flagellation of Christ* (c.1441–51), *The Story of the True Cross* (c.1452).

Camille Pissarro (1830–1903), French impressionist painter: *Le Fond de l'Hermitage* (1879), *The Boulevard Montmartre* (1897).

Jackson Pollock (1912–56), American abstract expressionist painter noted for his "action paintings": *Convergence* (1952).

Polycletus of Argos (400s B.C.), Greek sculptor whose *Doryphorus* or *Spear-Bearer* (c.450–440 B.C.) was held to represent ideal human proportions.

Nicolas Poussin (1594–1665), French painter noted for his heroic classic style: *The Rape of the Sabine Women* (c.1636–37).

Praxiteles (300s B.C.), Greek sculptor: *Hermes* (c.330–320 B.C.), *Aphrodite of Cnidus* (c.330 B.C.).
Maurice Prendergast (1859–1924), American impressionist painter: *Ponte della Paglia* (1899).
Pierre Proudhon (1758–1823), French romantic painter: *Empress Josephine* (1805).
Sir Henry Raeburn (1756–1823), Scottish portrait painter: *The Macnab* (c.1803), *Lord Newton* (c.1806).
Raphael Santi or **Sanzio** (1483–1520), Italian painter: numerous *Madonnas; The School of Athens* (1509–12), a fresco in the Vatican Palace.
Robert Rauschenberg (1925–), American pop artist: *Reservoir* (1961).
Odilon Redon (1840–1916), French symbolist painter and lithographer: *Cyclops* (1895–1900).
Rembrandt Harmenszoom van Rijn (1606–69), Dutch painter and greatest of the northern European Renaissance artists: *The Supper in Emmaus* (1648), *Aristotle Contemplating the Bust of Homer* (1653), *The Polish Rider* (1655), numerous *Self-Portraits.*
Frederic Remington (1861–1909), American painter and sculptor of cowboys and Indians: *The Bronco Buster* (1895), *The Cheyenne* (1901).
Pierre Auguste Renoir (1841–1919), French impressionist painter: *Moulin de la Galette* (1876), *Luncheon of the Boating Party* (1880–81).
Sir Joshua Reynolds (1723–92), English portrait painter: *Garrick Between Comedy and Tragedy* (1760–61), *Dr. Beattie (The Triumph of Truth).* He was also a writer of considerable repute.
Diego Rivera (1886–1957), Mexican muralist and fresco painter.
Luca della Robbia (1400–82), Italian sculptor: *The Madonna of the Rose Garden* (c.1430).
Norman Rockwell (1894–1978), U.S. painter and illustrator: won popularity for realistic paintings of everyday life, many appearing as covers for *The Saturday Evening Post.*
Auguste Rodin (1840–1917), French impressionist sculptor: *The Thinker* (1879–89), *The Kiss* (1896–98), *Balzac* (1892–97).
Dante Gabriel Rossetti (1828–82), English romantic painter and poet, and leading member of the Pre-Raphaelites: *Girlhood of Mary Virgin* (1849), *Mary Magdalene* (1878).
Mark Rothko (1903–70), American abstract expressionist painter: *Orange, Red, Yellow* (1961), *Slate Blue and Brown on Plum* (1958) typify his studies in simple color contrasts.
Georges Rouault (1871–1958), French expressionist painter whose works often use dark lines to suggest stained glass: *Head of Christ* (1905), *Three Judges* (1913), *The Old King* (1916–37).
Henri Rousseau (1844–1910), French primitivist painter: *The Snake Charmer* (1907), *The Dream* (1910).
Peter Paul Rubens (1577–1640), Flemish baroque painter: *Raising of the Cross* (1609–10), *The Judgment of Paris* (1639).
Jacob van Ruisdael (c.1628–82), Dutch landscape painter: *The Jewish Graveyard* (c.1655).
Charles Marion Russell (1864–1926), American painter and sculptor of scenes of the West: *Bronc to Breakfast.*
Albert Pinkham Ryder (1847–1917), American painter of romantic and fantastic subjects: *Toilers of the Sea, Flying Dutchman, The Forest of Arden, The Race Track, or Death on a Pale Horse.*
Eero Saarinen (1910–61), Finnish-American architect: TWA Terminal, Kennedy Airport, New York; American Embassy, London.
Augustus Saint-Gaudens (1848–1907), American realist sculptor: Shaw Memorial, Boston; statue of General Sherman, New York City.
John Singer Sargent (1856–1925), American portrait and landscape painter: *Portrait of Madame X* (1884), *Robert Louis Stevenson* (1887).
Georges Seurat (1859–91), French postimpressionist painter who used tiny dots of color to create mosaiclike effects in his works: *Sunday Afternoon on the Island of La Grande Jatte* (1884–86).
Ben Shahn (1898–1969), American expressionist painter: *The Passion of Sacco and Vanzetti* (1931–32).
Paul Signac (1863–1935), French neoimpressionist painter: *The Harbor at Saint-Tropez* (1893).
Alfred Sisley (1839–99), Anglo-French impressionist painter: *Square at Argenteuil* (1872).
John Sloan (1871–1951), American realist painter of everyday life: *McSorley's Bar* (1912).
David Smith (1906–65), American abstract sculptor best known for his works in welded metal: *Lectern Sentinel* (1961).
Chaim Soutine (1894–1943), Russian-French expressionist painter: *The Madwoman* (1920).
Jan Steen (1626–79), Dutch genre painter: *Grace Before Meat* (c.1665).
Philip Wilson Steer (1860–1940), English impressionist painter: *The Bridge, Etaples* (1887), *Chepstow Castle* (1905).
Frank Stella (1937–), American modernist painter best known for his "shaped canvases": *Sinjerli II* (1969).
Joseph Stella (1877–1946), U.S. semiabstract painter of subjects of the Industrial Age: *The Bridge* (1922).
Clyfford Still (1904–80), American abstract expressionist painter: *Jamais* (1944).
Edward Durell Stone (1902-78), U.S. architect: John F. Kennedy center in Washington, D.C.; General Motors building in New York City; U.S. embassy in New Delhi, India.
Gilbert Stuart (1755–1828), American portrait painter: *George Washington, John Adams.*
Louis Henry Sullivan (1856–1924), American architect and a pioneer in the design of skyscrapers: Roosevelt College building, Chicago (1887–89), Chicago Stock Exchange.
Lorado Taft (1860–1936), American sculptor: *Fountain of Time* (1922), *Solitude of the Soul* (1901), *Black Hawk* (1911).
Yves Tanguy (1900–55), French-American surrealist painter: *Mama, Papa Is Wounded* (1927).
Albert Bertel Thorvaldsen (1770–1844), Danish neoclassical sculptor: *Jason* (1802), *Cupid and Psyche* (1807).
Giovanni Battista Tiepolo (1696–1770), Venetian rococo painter of frescoes: several in Doge's Palace, Venice; Episcopal Palace, Würzburg.
Tintoretto (c.1518–94), Venetian mannerist painter: *Christ Before Pilate* (1566–67), *Bacchus and Ariadne* (1577), *The Last Supper* (1592–94).
Titian (Tiziano Vecellio, 1490?–1576), Venetian painter and one of the masters of Renaissance art: *Bacchanal* (1518), *Rape of Europa* (1559), *Christ Crowned with Thorns* (1570).
Henri de Toulouse-Lautrec (1864–1901), French postimpressionist painter and lithographer best known for his character studies: *Jane Avril* (1890), *At the Moulin Rouge* (1892).
John Trumbull (1756–1843), American painter of Revolutionary War scenes; his murals hang in U.S. Capitol.
Joseph Mallord William Turner (1775–1851), English romantic landscape painter: *The Grand Canal* (1835), *Rain, Steam, and Speed* (1844).
Maurice Utrillo (1883–1955), French painter of street scenes: *Rooftops at Sarcelle* (1909).
Sir Anthony Van Dyck (1599–1641), Flemish portrait and religious painter: *Portrait of Charles I Hunting* (c.1635), *The Vision of St. Augustine* and *Lamentation* (both 1634–35).
Jan Van Eyck (c.1390–1441), Flemish religious

PAINTERS, SCULPTORS, AND ARCHITECTS *(continued)*
painter: *Ghent Altarpiece* (1425–32).

Vincent Van Gogh (1853–90), Dutch postimpressionist painter who worked mainly in France: *The Sunflowers* (1888), *Starry Night* (1889), several self-portraits.

Jan Van Goyen (1596–1656), Dutch artist who was among the founders of the Dutch and Flemish school of landscape painting: *Windmill by the River* (1642).

Diego Velázquez (1599–1660), Spanish portrait painter: *Borrachos* (1629), *The Maids of Honor* (1656), *The Water-Carrier of Seville* (1619–21), *The Surrender of Breda* (1634–35).

Jan Vermeer (1632–75), Dutch genre painter: *Officer and Laughing Girl* (c.1655–60), *The Letter* (1666).

Paolo Veronese (1528–88), Venetian painter of religious and allegorical subjects: *Christ in the House of Levi* (1573), *The Rape of Europa* (1576), *Marriage at Cana* (1563).

Andrea del Verrocchio (1435–88), Florentine painter and sculptor: *Baptism of Christ* (c.1470), *Putto with a Dolphin* (c.1470).

Maurice de Vlaminck (1876–1958), French fauvist painter: *On the Banks of the Seine* (1906).

Andy Warhol (1927–), American pop artist: *Campbell's Soup Can.*

Antoine Watteau (1684–1721), French baroque painter: *Gilles* (c.1716), *Pilgrimage to Cythera* (1717), *The Fatigues of War* or *Troop March* (1712–15), *Gersaint's Shop Sign* (1720).

Max Weber (1881–1961), American abstract and cubist painter: *Chinese Restaurant* (1915).

Benjamin West (1738–1820), American painter of romantic and heroic scenes: *Death of General Wolfe* (1770).

Rogier van der Weyden (1399–1464), Flemish painter of religious subjects: *The Last Judgment* (c.1446).

James Abbott McNeill Whistler (1834–1903), American painter and etcher whose work shows influences both of French impressionists and English academic painters: *Arrangement in Gray and Black*; *The Artist's Mother* (1871), *The Falling Rocket* (1874).

Grant Wood (1891–1942), American painter of rural Midwest scenes: *American Gothic* (1930), *Daughters of the Revolution* (1932).

Sir Christopher Wren (1632–1723), English architect who worked in the neoclassic style: St. Paul's Cathedral, London.

Frank Lloyd Wright (1869–1959), American architect who pioneered in radical designs: Johnson Wax Building, Racine, Wis. (1936–39); the Guggenheim Museum, New York City (1946–59).

Andrew Wyeth (1917–), American romantic realist painter: *Winter* (1946), *Christina's World* (1948).

MAJOR ART MOVEMENTS

Abstract expressionism, American painting style that reached peak in 1940s and 1950s. Form and color are emphasized for their own sake, and works seldom contain identifiable objects. Earlier European movement producing similar results (for example, Kandinsky's paintings) was called *tachisme.*

Art nouveau, ornate style that originated in the late 1800s. Among best-known artists in style were Louis C. Tiffany and René Lalique.

Barbizon School, group of French artists in mid-1800s; including Millet, who painted romantic landscapes and pastoral scenes.

Baroque, predominantly Italian style of art and architecture that reached peak in the mid-1600s. Baroque works are ornate and dramatic.

Cubism, early movement in painting and, to lesser extent, in sculpture. It reduced all shapes to simple geometric forms, or distorted objects by simultaneously presenting them from several different angles. Founders of cubism were Braque and Picasso.

Dadaism, movement originating in 1916 in France, expressing nihilistic protest against all previous art and culture. One of its leaders, Marcel Duchamp, attached labels to ordinary commercial products (for example, bicycle wheels, drinking fountains) and called them art.

Expressionism, 20th century northern European movement in painting. Usually ordinary subjects were given distorted shapes, and colors were exaggerated to produce strong emotional effects.

Fauvism, French movement of painters who exhibited together in Paris from about 1903 to 1905. Their use of distorted design and wild colors caused them to be called *Les fauves* (beasts) by some critics. Their leaders included Matisse and Rouault.

Futurism, Italian art movement of early 1900s, glorifying mechanical age, speed, and motion.

Genre painting, type of picture, usually of small size, that represents everyday life in unidealized manner. Examples, which are found through ages, include many peasant and tavern and household scenes depicted by Dutch painters of 1600s.

Impressionism, most important art movement of 1800s, mainly centered around Paris. Impressionistic painters were primarily concerned with effects of natural light in their spontaneous and undetailed portrayals of subjects in their artwork.

Mannerism, movement between 1520 and 1600 mainly in Italy, although probably the greatest mannerist painter was Greek-Spanish El Greco. Human figure was central subject, but it was posed in dramatically strained positions, or its shape was elongated.

Minimal art, kind of abstract painting developed in 1960s, eliminating emotions or symbolism.

Neoclassicism, movement of 1700s that arose in reaction to excesses of baroque and rococo art. Painters, and especially sculptors, consciously imitated styles and subject matter of ancient Greek and Roman art.

New realism, movement of 1970s, in which paintings are executed with photographic realistic detail.

Op art, movement of 1960s, emphasizing optical illusion through creation of complex geometric constructions or designs.

Pop art, New York-centered movement of 1960s, in which everyday examples of graphic design are illustrated or reproduced, often greatly enlarged. Comic strips and advertising art are favorite subjects.

Postimpressionism, loosely knit movement of late 1800s, mainly in rejection of impressionism. Cézanne usually considered founder of movement, although work has little in common with other postimpressionists.

Pre-Raphaelite, English movement of mid-1800s emphasizing purity and use of moral and religious themes. Leaders included Millais and Rossetti.

Realism, movement begun by Courbet in mid-1800s, depicting real people in everyday situations.

Rococo, movement in art and architecture that began in France in 1700s and spread to Germany and Austria. Prettiness, gaiety, and ornate delicacy characterize rococo art.

Romanticism, movement of early 1800s reacting against neoclassicism by combining realistic details and expression of emotions. Constable and Turner were leaders of romanticism.

Surrealism, essentially an outgrowth from cubism; its subject matter consists of fantastic, dreamlike objects and scenes. Surrealism reached its peak in works by Picasso, Dali, and Ernst.

Awards and Prizes

Wide World

Lech Walesa, leader of the outlawed Polish Solidarity labor union movement, won the Nobel Peace Prize in 1983. He said he would donate the $190,000 prize to the Roman Catholic Church for a fund to aid private farmers in Poland.

HIGHLIGHTS: 1983

Nobel Prizes were awarded in 1983 to five Americans, one Briton, and one Pole.

The five Americans were:

India-born Subrahmanyan Chandrasekhar, 73, an astrophysicist at the University of Chicago, co-winner of the Nobel Prize for Physics.

William Fowler, 72, professor of physics at the California Institute of Technology, co-winner of the Nobel Prize for Physics.

Canadian-born Henry Taube, 67, professor of chemistry at Sanford University, winner of the Nobel Prize for Chemistry.

French-born Gerard Debreu, 62, professor of mathematics and economics at the University of California at Berkeley, awarded the Nobel Prize for Economics.

Barbara McClintock, 81, director of the Cold Spring Harbor Laboratory in New York, winner of the Nobel Prize for Medicine.

British novelist William Golding, 72, won the Nobel Prize in Literature, and Polish labor leader Lech Walesa, 40, was awarded the Nobel Prize for Peace.

NOBEL PRIZES

Nobel Prizes are awarded each year to persons who have made important contributions for the good of humanity.

The awards were established in the will of Alfred Bernhard Nobel (1833–96), a Swedish chemist who became wealthy from his invention of dynamite in 1867. He regretted that dynamite had been used as an instrument of war, and left a fund of about $9 million to establish the Nobel Prizes to encourage peace and progress.

Six prizes are awarded each year in chemistry, economics, literature, peace, physics, and physiology or medicine. The first prizes were awarded in 1901. The economics prize was added in 1969. Each prize in 1983 carried a monetary award of about $190,000, divided when there was more than one recipient.

The Royal Academy of Science in Sweden picks the prizewinners in physics, chemistry, and economics. The medical faculty of Stockholm's Caroline Institute chooses the winner in the field of physiology or medicine. The Swedish Academy of Literature names the literature winner. The Norwegian parliament elects a committee of five persons to select the winner of the prize for peace.

A total of 179 Americans have received awards. The British are second with 83. Some 57 Germans have won Nobel Prizes, French 44, Swedes 29, Russians 14, Swiss 14, Dutch 11, Danes, 11, Italians 10, Austrians 9, Belgians 8, Norwegians 7, Japanese 6, Spanish 5, Canadians 4, Irish 4, Argentinians 4, Australians 3, Poles 3, and Indians 3. Two Nobel Prizes have been won by Israelis, Chileans, Hungarians, Finns, and Greeks. One each have been won by an Egyptian, an Icelander, a Czech, a Yugoslav, a Guatemalan, a South African, a Vietnamese, a Portuguese, a Pakistani, a Bulgarian, a Mexican, and a Colombian.

NOBEL CHEMISTRY PRIZES

YEAR	NAME AND NATIONALITY	AWARDED FOR:
1901	**Jacobus H. van't Hoff**, Dutch	Discovery of laws of chemical dynamics and osmotic pressure in solutions.
1902	**Emil Fischer**, German	Work on sugar and purine syntheses.
1903	**Svante A. Arrhenius**, Swedish	Electrolytic theory of dissociation.
1904	**Sir William Ramsay**, British	Discovery of inert gaseous elements in air and determination of their place in periodic system.
1905	**Johann von Baeyer**, German	Work on organic dyes and hydroaromatic compounds.
1906	**Henri Moissan**, French	Study and isolation of element fluorine and development of electric furnace named after him.
1907	**Eduard Buchner**, German	Biochemical researches and discovery of cell-free fermentation.
1908	**Ernest Rutherford**, British	Studies of disintegration of elements, and chemistry of radioactive substances.
1909	**Wilhelm Ostwald**, German	Work on catalysis and studies of fundamental principles governing chemical equilibria and rates of reaction.
1910	**Otto Wallach**, German	Pioneer work in field of alicyclic compounds.
1911	**Marie Curie**, French (Polish-born)	Discovery of elements radium and polonium, isolation of radium and study of its nature and compounds.
1912	**Victor Grignard**, French	Discovery of Grignard reagent.
	Paul Sabatier, French	Method of hydrogenating organic compounds in presence of finely disintegrated metals.
1913	**Alfred Werner**, Swiss (German-born)	Work on linkage of atoms in molecules.
1914	**Theodore W. Richards**, U.S.	Determinations of atomic weight of many chemical elements.
1915	**Richard M. Willstätter**, German	Researches on plant pigments, especially chlorophyll.
1916	No award	
1917	No award	
1918	**Fritz Haber**, German	Synthesis of ammonia from its elements.
1919	No award	
1920	**Walther H. Nernst**, German	Work in thermochemistry.
1921	**Frederick Soddy**, British	Studies of chemistry of radioactive substances, and investigations into origin and nature of isotopes.
1922	**Francis W. Aston**, British	Discovery, by means of his mass spectrograph, of isotopes in a large number of nonradioactive elements.
1923	**Fritz Pregl**, Austrian	Invention of method of microanalysis of organic substances.
1924	No award	
1925	**Richard A. Zsigmondy**, German (Austrian-born)	Demonstration of heterogeneous nature of colloid solutions.
1926	**Theodor Svedberg**, Swedish	Work on dispersion systems and colloid chemistry.
1927	**Heinrich O. Wieland**, German	Studies of constitution of bile acids and related substances.
1928	**Adolf O. R. Windaus**, German	Research into constitution of sterols and their connection with vitamins.
1929	**Arthur Harden**, British **Hans von Euler–Chelpin**, Swedish (German-born)	Investigations on fermentation of sugar and fermentative enzymes.
1930	**Hans Fischer**, German	Researches into constitution of hemin and chlorophyll.
1931	**Friedrich Bergius**, German **Carl Bosch**, German	Contributions to invention and development of chemical high-pressure methods.
1932	**Irving Langmuir**, U.S.	Discoveries and investigations in surface chemistry.
1933	No award	
1934	**Harold C. Urey**, U.S.	Discovery of heavy hydrogen.
1935	**Frédéric Joliot-Curie**, French **Irène Joliot-Curie**, French	Synthesis of new radioactive elements.
1936	**Peter J. W. Debye**, Dutch	Knowledge of molecular structure by studies of dipole moments, diffraction of X rays, and electrons in gases.

1937	**Walter N. Haworth**, British	Research on carbohydrates and vitamin C.
	Paul Karrer, Swiss (Russian-born)	Investigations on carotenoids, flavins, and vitamins A and B_2.
1938	**Richard Kuhn**, German (Austrian-born)	Work on carotenoids and vitamins. (Prize declined.)
1939	**Adolf F. J. Butenandt**, German	Work on sex hormones. (Prize declined under political pressure.)
	Leopold Ružička, Swiss	Work on polymethylenes and higher terpenes.
1940–42	No award	
1943	**Georg de Hevesy**, Hungarian	Work on use of isotopes as tracers in chemistry.
1944	**Otto Hahn**, German	Discovery of fission of heavy nuclei.
1945	**Artturi I. Virtanen**, Finnish	Research and inventions in agricultural and nutrition chemistry.
1946	**James B. Sumner**, U.S.	Discovery that enzymes can be crystallized.
	John H. Northrop, U.S. **Wendell M. Stanley**, U.S.	Preparation of enzymes and virus proteins in pure form.
1947	**Sir Robert Robinson**, British	Investigation of plant products of biological importance.
1948	**Arne W. K. Tiselius**, Swedish	Research on electrophoresis and adsorption analysis.
1949	**William F. Giauque**, U.S.	Contributions in field of chemical thermodynamics, particularly behavior of substances at extremely low temperatures.
1950	**Kurt Alder**, German **Otto P. H. Diels**, German	Discovery and development of diene synthesis.
1951	**Edwin M. McMillan**, U.S. **Glenn T. Seaborg**, U.S.	Discoveries in chemistry of transuranium elements.
1952	**Archer J. P. Martin**, British **Richard L. M. Synge**, British	Invention of partition chromatography, method for analysis of mixtures.
1953	**Hermann Staudinger**, German	Discoveries in field of macromolecular chemistry.
1954	**Linus C. Pauling**, U.S.	Research into nature of chemical bond and its application.
1955	**Vincent du Vigneaud**, U.S.	Work on biochemically important sulfur compounds, especially for first synthesis of polypeptide hormone.
1956	**Sir Cyril N. Hinshelwood**, British **Nikolai N. Semenov**, Russian	Researches into mechanism of chemical reactions.
1957	**Lord Todd (Alexander R. Todd)**, British	Work on nucleotides and nucleotide coenzymes.
1958	**Frederick Sanger**, British	Work on structure of proteins, especially of insulin.
1959	**Jaroslav Heyrovsky**, Czech	Discovery and development of polarographic methods of analysis.
1960	**Willard F. Libby**, U.S.	Method to use carbon-14 for age determination in archaeology, geology, geophysics, and other branches of science.
1961	**Melvin Calvin**, U.S.	Research on carbon dioxide assimilation in plants.
1962	**Sir John C. Kendrew**, British **Max F. Perutz**, British (Austrian-born)	Studies of structures of globular proteins.
1963	**Giulio Natta**, Italian **Karl Ziegler**, German	Discoveries in chemistry and technology of high polymers.
1964	**Dorothy Crowfoot Hodgkin**, British	Discovery by X-ray techniques of structure of important biochemical substances.
1965	**Robert B. Woodward**, U.S.	Techniques for syntheses of complicated organic compounds.
1966	**Robert S. Mulliken**, U.S.	Fundamental work on chemical bonds and electronic structure of molecules by molecular orbital method.
1967	**Manfred Eigen**, German **Ronald G. W. Norrish**, British **Sir George Porter**, British	Studies of extremely fast chemical reactions effected by disturbing equilibrium by means of very short pulses of energy.
1968	**Lars Onsager**, U.S. (Norwegian-born)	Discovery of reciprocal relations that bear his name, which are fundamental to thermodynamics of irreversible processes.
1969	**Derek H. R. Barton**, British **Odd Hassel**, Norwegian	Work to develop and apply concept of conformation in chemistry.
1970	**Luis F. Leloir**, Argentine (French-born)	Discovery of sugar nucleotides and their role in biosynthesis of carbohydrates.
1971	**Gerhard Herzberg**, Canadian (German-born)	Studies in electronic structure and geometry of molecules, particularly free radicals.
1972	**Christian B. Anfinsen**, U.S. **Stanford Moore**, U.S. **William H. Stein**, U.S.	Research relating to chemical structure and biologic reactions of protein ribonuclease.
1973	**Ernest Otto Fischer**, German **Geoffrey Wilkinson**, British	Research on merging of organic and metallic compounds, seeking solution to automobile exhaust pollution.
1974	**Paul J. Flory**, U.S.	Pioneering analytical methods for studying long-chain molecules, leading to development of many plastics and synthetic materials.
1975	**John Warcus Cornforth**, British (Australian-born) **Vladimir Prelog**, Swiss (Yugoslav-born)	Research in field of stereochemistry, study of how properties of chemical compounds are affected by arrangement of their atoms.
1976	**William N. Lipscomb**, U.S.	Studies on structure and bonding of compounds called boranes, providing new insight into nature of chemical bonding.
1977	**Ilya Prigogine**, Belgian (Russian-born)	Lifetime contributions to nonequilibrium thermodynamics, particularly theory of dissipative structures that helps explain how living organisms use energy and how life originated.
1978	**Peter Mitchell**, British	Research on energy transformations in living cells and formulation of the chemiosmotic theory of how cells convert food into metabolic energy.
1979	**Herbert C. Brown**, U.S. (British-born) **Georg Wittig**, West German	Development of boron and phosphorus compounds linking large molecules, enabling mass production of many pharmaceuticals and industrial chemicals.
1980	**Paul Berg**, U.S.	Pioneering work in gene-splicing or genetic engineering.
	Walter Gilbert, U.S. **Frederick Sanger**, British	Determining the chemical structure of nucleic acids in regard to DNA used in gene-splicing.
1981	**Roald Hoffman**, Swedish **Kenichi Fukui**, Japanese	Applying theories of quantum mathematics to predict course of chemical reactions.
1982	**Aaron Klug**, British (South African-born)	Developing three-dimensional electron microscope images revealing the structure of viruses and other tiny biological organisms.
1983	**Henry Taube**, U.S. (Canadian-born)	Discovery of the way electrons transfer between molecules in chemical reactions

NOBEL ECONOMICS PRIZES

1969	**Ragnar Frisch**, Norwegian **Jan Tinbergen**, Dutch	Development of mathematical models for analyzing economic activity.
1970	**Paul A. Samuelson**, U.S.	Raising level of scientific analysis in economic theory.
1971	**Simon Kuznets**, U.S.	Working out methods to determine country's gross national product.
1972	**Kenneth J. Arrow**, U.S. **Sir John R. Hicks**, British	Pioneering studies in theory of general economic equilibrium.
1973	**Wassily Leontief**, U.S. (Russian-born)	Development of "input-output" method of economic analysis used by most industrial nations.
1974	**Gunnar Myrdal**, Swedish **Friedrich A. von Hayek**, Austrian	Pioneering work in theory of money and economic fluctuations.
1975	**Leonid V. Kantorovich**, Russian **Tjalling C. Koopmans**, U.S. (Dutch-born)	Contributions to theory of optimum allocation of resources.
1976	**Milton Friedman**, U.S.	Achievements in consumption analysis, monetary history and theory, and demonstration of complexity of stabilization policy.
1977	**Bertil Ohlin**, Swedish **James Edward Meade**, British	For pathbreaking contributions to theory of international trade and international capital movement.
1978	**Herbert Simon**, U.S.	Pioneering research into how businesses and other organizations make economic decisions.
1979	**Sir Arthur Lewis**, British (St. Lucian-born) **Theodore W. Schultz**, U.S.	For efforts to solve economic problems of need and poverty in world and to find solutions for developing nations.
1980	**Lawrence Klein**, U.S.	For development of econometric models to analyze economic fluctuations.
1981	**James Tobin**, U.S.	Development of "portfolio selection theory."
1982	**George J. Stigler**, U.S.	Studies of industry and government regulation.
1983	**Gerard Debreu**, U.S. (French-born)	Refining and confirming Adam Smith's theory of supply and demand by use of mathematical models.

NOBEL LITERATURE PRIZES

1901	**Sully-Prudhomme (Renáe Prudhomme)**, French
1902	**C. M. T. Mommsen**, German
1903	**Björnstjerne Björnson**, Norwegian
1904	**Frédéric Mistral**, French **José Echegaray**, Spanish
1905	**Henryk Sienkiewicz**, Polish
1906	**Giosuè Carducci**, Italian
1907	**Rudyard Kipling**, British
1908	**Rudolf C. Eucken**, German
1909	**Selma Lagerlöf**, Swedish
1910	**Paul J. L. Heyse**, German
1911	**Count Maurice Maeterlinck**, Belgian
1912	**Gerhart Hauptmann**, German
1913	**Rabindranath Tagore**, Indian
1914	No award
1915	**Romain Rolland**, French
1916	**Carl G. von Heidenstam**, Swedish
1917	**Karl A. Gjellerup**, Danish **Henrik Pontoppidan**, Danish
1918	No award
1919	**Carl F. G. Spitteler**, Swiss
1920	**Knut Hamsun**, Norwegian
1921	**Anatole France**, French
1922	**Jacinto Benavente**, Spanish
1923	**William Butler Yeats**, Irish
1924	**Wladyslaw S. Reymont**, Polish
1925	**George Bernard Shaw**, British (Irish-born)
1926	**Grazia Deledda**, Italian
1927	**Henri Bergson**, French
1928	**Sigrid Undset**, Norwegian (Danish-born)
1929	**Thomas Mann**, German
1930	**Sinclair Lewis**, U.S.
1931	**Erik A. Karlfeldt**, Swedish
1932	**John Galsworthy**, British
1933	**Ivan A. Bunin**, French (Russian-born)
1934	**Luigi Pirandello**, Italian
1935	No award
1936	**Eugene O'Neill**, U.S.
1937	**Roger Martin du Gard**, French
1938	**Pearl S. Buck**, U.S.
1939	**Frans E. Sillanpää**, Finnish
1940–43	No award
1944	**Johannes V. Jensen**, Danish
1945	**Gabriela Mistral**, Chilean
1946	**Hermann Hesse**, Swiss (German-born)
1947	**André Gide**, French
1948	**T. S. Eliot**, British (U.S.-born)
1949	**William Faulkner**, U.S.
1950	**Bertrand Russell**, British
1951	**Pär F. Lagerkvist**, Swedish
1952	**François Mauriac**, French
1953	**Sir Winston Churchill**, British
1954	**Ernest Hemingway**, U.S.
1955	**Halldór K. Laxness**, Icelandic
1956	**Juan Ramón Jiménez**, Spanish
1957	**Albert Camus**, French
1958	**Boris L. Pasternak**, Russian (Prize declined)
1959	**Salvatore Quasimodo**, Italian
1960	**Saint-John Perse**, French
1961	**Ivo Andrić**, Yugoslavian
1962	**John Steinbeck**, U.S.
1963	**George Seferis**, Greek
1964	**Jean-Paul Sartre**, French (Prize declined)
1965	**Mikhail Sholokhov**, Russian
1966	**Shmuel Yosef Agnon**, Israeli (Austrian-born) **Nelly Sachs**, Swedish (German-born)
1967	**Miguel Angel Asturias**, Guatemalan
1968	**Yasunari Kawabata**, Japanese
1969	**Samuel Beckett**, Irish
1970	**Aleksandr I. Solzhenitsyn**, Russian
1971	**Pablo Neruda**, Chilean
1972	**Heinrich Böll**, German
1973	**Patrick White**, Australian
1974	**Eyvind Johnson**, Swedish **Harry Edmund Martinson**, Swedish
1975	**Eugenio Montale**, Italian
1976	**Saul Bellow**, U.S.
1977	**Vicente Aleixandre**, Spanish
1978	**Isaac Bashevis Singer**, U.S. (Polish-born)
1979	**Odysseus Elytis**, Greek
1980	**Czeslaw Milosz**, U.S. (Polish-born)
1981	**Elias Canetti**, Bulgarian
1982	**Gabriel García Márquez**, Colombian
1983	**William Golding**, British

NOBEL PEACE PRIZES

1901	**Jean H. Dunant**, Swiss **Frédéric Passy**, French
1902	**Elie Ducommun**, Swiss **Charles A. Gobat**, Swiss
1903	**Sir William R. Cremer**, British
1904	**Institute of International Law**
1905	**Baroness Bertha von Suttner**, Austrian
1906	**Theodore Roosevelt**, U.S.
1907	**Ernesto T. Moneta**, Italian **Louis Renault**, French
1908	**Klas P. Arnoldson**, Swedish **Fredrik Bajer**, Danish
1909	**Auguste M. F. Beernaert**, Belgian **Paul H. B. B. d'Estournelles de Constant**, French
1910	**Permanent International Peace Bureau**
1911	**Tobias M. C. Asser**, Dutch **Alfred H. Fried**, Austrian
1912	**Elihu Root**, U.S.
1913	**Henri Lafontaine**, Belgian
1914–16	No award
1917	**International Committee of the Red Cross**
1918	No award
1919	**Woodrow Wilson**, U.S.
1920	**Léon V. A. Bourgeois**, French
1921	**Karl H. Branting**, Swedish **Christian L. Lange**, Norwegian
1922	**Fridtjof Nansen**, Norwegian
1923	No award
1924	No award
1925	**Sir J. Austen Chamberlain**, British **Charles G. Dawes**, U.S.
1926	**Aristide Briand**, French **Gustav Stresemann**, German
1927	**Ferdinand Buisson**, French **Ludwig Quidde**, German
1928	No award
1929	**Frank B. Kellogg**, U.S.
1930	**Lars O. N. Söderblom**, Swedish
1931	**Jane Addams**, U.S. **Nicholas Murray Butler**, U.S.
1932	No award
1933	**Sir Norman Angell**, British
1934	**Arthur Henderson**, British
1935	**Carl von Ossietzky**, German
1936	**Carlos Saavedra Lamas**, Argentinian
1937	**Viscount Cecil of Chelwood**, British
1938	**International Office for Refugees**
1939	No award
1940	No award
1941	No award
1942	No award
1943	No award
1944	**International Committee of the Red Cross**
1945	**Cordell Hull**, U.S.
1946	**Emily G. Balch**, U.S. **John R. Mott**, U.S.
1947	**Friends Service Council**, British **American Friends Service Committee**
1948	No award
1949	**Lord John Boyd Orr of Brechin**, British
1950	**Ralph J. Bunche**, U.S.
1951	**Léon Jouhaux**, French
1952	**Albert Schweitzer**, French (German-born)
1953	**George C. Marshall**, U.S.
1954	**Office of UN High Commissioner for Refugees**
1955	No award
1956	No award
1957	**Lester B. Pearson**, Canadian
1958	**Georges Pire**, Belgian
1959	**Philip J. Noel-Baker**, British
1960	**Albert J. Luthuli**, South African
1961	**Dag Hammarskjöld**, Swedish (posthumous)
1962	**Linus C. Pauling**, U.S.
1963	**International Committee of the Red Cross** **Red Cross Societies League**
1964	**Martin Luther King Jr.**, U.S.
1965	**United Nations Children's Fund (UNICEF)**
1966	No award
1967	No award
1968	**René Cassin**, French
1969	**International Labor Organization (ILO)**
1970	**Norman E. Borlaug**, U.S.
1971	**Willy Brandt**, German
1972	No award
1973	**Henry A. Kissinger**, U.S. (German-born) **Le Duc Tho**, North Vietnamese
1974	**Eisaku Sato**, Japanese **Sean MacBride**, Irish
1975	**Andrei D. Sakharov**, Russian
1976	**Betty Williams** and **Mairead Corrigan**, organizers of peace movement to resist terrorist violence in Northern Ireland
1977	**Amnesty International**, organization that exposes governmental violations of human rights
1978	**Anwar al-Sadat**, president of Egypt, and **Menachem Begin**, prime minister of Israel, for Mideast peace initiative to end three decades of conflict
1979	**Mother Teresa**, Indian (Albanian-born), for charitable work in helping poor of Calcutta.
1980	**Adolfo Pérez Esquivel**, Argentinian, a leading human-rights advocate.
1981	**Office of UN High Commissioner for Refugees**
1982	**Alfonso García Robles**, Mexican, and **Alva Reimer Myrdal**, Swedish, for their work promoting disarmament
1983	**Lech Walesa**, Polish, for his avoidance of violence in labor struggle with Poland's communist government

NOBEL PHYSICS PRIZES

1901	**Wilhelm C. Roentgen**, German	Discovery of Roentgen rays (X rays).
1902	**Hendrik A. Lorentz**, Dutch **Pieter Zeeman**, Dutch	Researches into influence of magnetism upon radiation phenomena.
1903	**Antoine Henri Becquerel**, French	Discovery of spontaneous radioactivity.
	Marie Curie, French (Polish-born) **Pierre Curie**, French	Joint researches on radiation phenomena discovered by A. Henri Becquerel.
1904	**Lord Rayleigh (John W. Strutt)** British	Investigations of densities of most important gases and discovery of argon.
1905	**Philipp E. A. von Lenard**, German (Hungarian-born)	Work on cathode rays.
1906	**Sir Joseph John Thomson**, British	Theoretical and experimental investigations on conduction of electricity by gases.
1907	**Albert A. Michelson**, U.S. (German-born)	Optical precision instruments for spectroscopic and meteorological investigations.
1908	**Gabriel Lippmann**, French (Luxembourgian-born)	Method of reproducing colors photographically based on phenomenon of interference.
1909	**Guglielmo Marconi**, Italian **Carl F. Braun**, German	Development of radio (wireless telegraphy).
1910	**Johannes D. van der Waals**, Dutch	Work on equation of state for gases and liquids.
1911	**Wilhelm Wien**, German	Discoveries regarding laws of heat radiation.
1912	**Nils G. Dalén**, Swedish	Invention of automatic regulators to be used with gas accumulators for illuminating lighthouses and buoys.
1913	**Heike Kamerlingh-Onnes**, Dutch	Investigations on properties of matter at lower temperatures, which led to production of liquid helium.
1914	**Max von Laue**, German	Discovery of diffraction of X rays by crystals.

NOBEL PHYSICS PRIZES *(continued)*

1915	**Sir William H. Bragg,** British **Sir William L. Bragg,** British	The analysis of crystal structure by means of X rays.
1916	No award	
1917	**Charles G. Barkla,** British	Discovery of characteristic Roentgen radiation of elements.
1918	**Max K. E. L. Planck,** German	Discovery of energy quanta.
1919	**Johannes Stark,** German	Discovery of Doppler effect in canal rays and splitting of spectral lines in electric fields.
1920	**Charles E. Guillaume,** French (Swiss-born)	Discovery of anomalies in nickel-steel alloys.
1921	**Albert Einstein,** U.S. (German-born)	Studies in theoretical physics, and especially for discovery of law of photoelectric effect.
1922	**Niels Bohr,** Danish	Investigation of atomic structure and radiation.
1923	**Robert A. Millikan,** U.S.	Work on elementary charge of electricity and on photoelectric effect.
1924	**Karl M. G. Siegbahn,** Swedish	Discoveries and research in field of X-ray spectroscopy.
1925	**James Franck,** German **Gustav Hertz,** German	Discovery of laws governing impact of electron upon atom.
1926	**Jean B. Perrin,** French	Work on discontinuous structure of matter, and especially for discovery of sedimentation equillibrium.
1927	**Arthur H. Compton,** U.S.	Discovery of Compton effect concerning increase in wave length of X rays and gamma rays scattered by electrons.
	Charles T. R. Wilson, British (Scottish-born)	Method of making paths of electrically charged particles visible by condensation of vapor.
1928	**Owen W. Richardson,** British	Work on thermionics, phenomena associated with emission of electrically charged particles by heated body, and for discovery of Richardson's law.
1929	**Prince Louis-Victor de Broglie,** French	Discovery of wave nature of electrons.
1930	**Sir Chandrasekhara V. Raman,** Indian	Work on scattering of light and discovery of Raman effect.
1931	No award	
1932	**Werner Heisenberg,** German	Creation of quantum mechanics, which led to discovery of allotropic forms of hydrogen.
1933	**Paul A. M. Dirac,** British **Erwin Schrödinger,** Austrian	Extensions of atomic theory.
1934	No award	
1935	**Sir James Chadwick,** British	Discovery of neutron.
1936	**Carl D. Anderson,** U.S.	Discovery of positron.
	Victor F. Hess, Austrian	Discovery of cosmic radiation.
1937	**Clinton J. Davisson,** U.S. **George P. Thomson,** British	Experimental discovery of diffraction of electrons by crystals.
1938	**Enrico Fermi,** U.S. (Italian-born)	Demonstrations of existence of new radioactive elements produced by neutron irradiation, and discovery of nuclear reactions caused by slow neutrons.
1939	**Ernest O. Lawrence,** U.S.	Invention and development of cyclotron and results obtained from its use in investigation of artificial radioactive elements.
1940	No award	
1941	No award	
1942	No award	
1943	**Otto Stern,** U.S. (German-born)	Contribution to development of molecular-ray method and discovery of magnetic moment of proton.
1944	**Isidor Isaac Rabi,** U.S.	Resonance method for recording magnetism of atomic nuclei.
1945	**Wolfgang Pauli,** U.S.	Discovery of exclusion, or Pauli, principle in quantum physics.
1946	**Percy Williams Bridgman,** U.S.	Invention of apparatus to produce extremely high pressures, and resulting discoveries in field of high-pressure physics.
1947	**Sir Edward V. Appleton,** British	Investigations of physics of upper atmosphere and discovery of Appleton layer of ionosphere.
1948	**Patrick M. S. Blackett,** British	Development of Wilson cloud-chamber method and resulting discoveries in fields of nuclear physics and cosmic radiation.
1949	**Hideki Yukawa,** Japanese	Theoretical prediction of existence of mesons.
1950	**Cecil F. Powell,** British	Development of photographic method of studying nuclear processes and resulting discoveries regarding mesons.
1951	**Sir John D. Cockroft,** British **Ernest T. S. Walton,** Irish	Research on transmutation of atomic nuclei by artificially accelerated atomic particles.
1952	**Felix Bloch,** U.S. (Swiss-born) **Edward M. Purcell,** U.S.	Development of new methods for nuclear-magnetic precision measurements and related discoveries.
1953	**Frits Zernike,** Dutch	Demonstration of phase-contrast method, and invention of phase-contrast microscope.
1954	**Max Born,** British (German-born)	Fundamental research in quantum mechanics.
	Walther Bothe, German	Coincidence method of counting, used in nuclear and cosmic-ray research.
1955	**Polykarp Kusch,** U.S. (German-born)	Precise determination of magnetic moment of electron.
	Willis E. Lamb, U.S.	Discoveries concerning fine structure of hydrogen spectrum.
1956	**John Bardeen,** U.S. **Walter H. Brattain,** U.S. **William Shockley,** U.S.	Research on semiconductors and discovery of transistor.
1957	**Tsung-Dao Lee,** U.S. (Chinese-born) **Chen Ning Yang,** U.S. (Chinese-born)	Investigation of parity laws, which led to important discoveries regarding elementary particles.
1958	**Paval A. Cherenkov,** Russian **Ilya M. Frank,** Russian **Igor J. Tamm,** Russian	Discovery and interpretation of Cherenkov effect.

1959	**Owen Chamberlain,** U.S. .... **Emilio G. Segrè,** U.S. (Italian-born)	Discovery of antiproton.
1960	**Donald A. Glaser,** U.S.	Invention of bubble chamber.
1961	**Robert Hofstadter,** U.S. .... **Rudolf L. Mössbauer,** German	Studies of electron scattering with resulting discoveries concerning structure of nucleons. Studies of resonance absorption of gamma radiation and resulting discovery of Mössbauer effect.
1962	**Lev D. Landau,** Russian	Theories of condensed matter, especially liquid helium.
1963	**Maria Goeppert-Mayer,** U.S. .... **J. Hans D. Jensen,** German **Eugene P. Wigner,** U.S.	Discoveries concerning nuclear shell structures. Contribution to theory of atomic nucleus and elementary particles.
1964	**Nikolai G. Basov,** Russian .... **Aleksandr M. Prokhorov,** Russian **Charles H. Townes,** U.S.	Fundamental work in field of quantum electronics, leading to construction of maser-laser oscillators and amplifiers.
1965	**Richard P. Feynman,** U.S. .... **Julian S. Schwinger,** U.S. **Sin-itiro Tomonaga,** Japanese	Research in quantum electrodynamics, which contributed to understanding of elementary particles in high-energy physics.
1966	**Alfred Kastler,** French	Discovery and development of optical methods for studying Herzian resonances in atoms.
1967	**Hans A. Bethe,** U.S. (German-born)	Contributions to theory of nuclear reaction, especially discoveries concerning energy production of stars.
1968	**Luis W. Alvarez,** U.S.	Contributions to physics of subatomic particles, in particular discovery of large number of resonance states.
1969	**Murray Gell-Mann,** U.S.	Contributions and discoveries concerning classification of elementary particles and their interactions.
1970	**Hannes O. G. Alfvén,** Swedish .... **Louis E. F. Néel,** French	Contributions and discoveries in magnetohydrodynamics with applications in plasma physics. Discoveries and work in ferromagnetism and antiferromagnetism with applications in solid-state physics.
1971	**Dennis Gabor,** British (Hungarian-born)	Invention of system of three-dimensional photography known as holography.
1972	**John Bardeen,** U.S. .... **Leon N. Cooper,** U.S. **John R. Schrieffer,** U.S.	Development of superconductivity theory of certain metals at very low temperatures.
1973	**Ivar Giaever,** U.S. (Norwegian-born) ... **Leo Esaki,** Japanese **Brian D. Josephson,** British	Developments relating to miniature electronic semiconductors and superconductors. Discovery of "Josephson effects" of electric supercurrent.
1974	**Antony Hewish,** British **Sir Martin Ryle,** British	Studies of universe using radiotelescopes; Dr. Hewish discovered pulsars in 1967.
1975	**L. James Rainwater,** U.S. .... **Aage Bohr,** Danish **Ben Roy Mottelson,** Danish (U.S.-born)	Discovery and explanation of fact that nuclei of some atoms are not spherical because of connection between collective motion and particle motion in atomic nucleus.
1976	**Burton Richter,** U.S. .... **Samuel C. C. Ting,** U.S.	Independent discoveries of Psi or J particle, heavy elementary particle believed smallest building block of matter.
1977	**John H. Van Vleck,** U.S. .... **Philip W. Anderson,** U.S. .... **Sir Nevill F. Mott,** British	Founding modern magnetism by explaining magnetic properties of solids and how foreign ion or atom behaves in crystal. Discoveries made separately in sold-state physics that led to use of amorphous material, such as glass, in electronic switching and memory devices.
1978	**Robert W. Wilson,** U.S. .... **Arno A. Penzias,** U.S. (German-born) **Pyotr Leontevitch Kapitsa,** Russian	Discovery of cosmic microwave background radiation, confirming "big bang" theory of creation of universe. Basic research in low-temperature physics.
1979	**Steven Weinberg,** U.S. .... **Abdus Salam,** Pakistani **Sheldon L. Glashow,** U.S.	Development of theory of weak interactions, regarded as a major step toward unifying knowledge of four major forces of nature: gravity, electromagnetism, force that holds together atomic nuclei, and weak force that causes radioactive decay in some atomic nuclei.
1980	**James W. Cronin,** U.S. .... **Val L. Fitch,** U.S.	Discovery in 1964 of asymmetry in behavior of subatomic particles, later used to explain "big bang" theory of birth of universe.
1981	**Nicolaas Bloemberger,** U.S. .... **Arthur Schawlow,** U.S. **Kai M. Siegbahn,** Swedish	Development of laser spectroscopy and high-resolution electron spectroscopy.
1982	**Kenneth Geddes Wilson,** U.S.	Solving the complex interactions that occur when matter changes from one form to another, as when water boils.
1983	**Subrahmanyan Chandrasekhar,** U.S. .... (India-born) **William A. Fowler,** U.S.	Research and theories concerning evolution of stars, especially white dwarf stars. Study of nuclear reactions in stars and development of theory of formation of chemical elements in universe.

NOBEL PHYSIOLOGY OR MEDICINE PRIZES

1901	**Emil A. von Behring**, German	Work on serum therapy, especially for use against diphtheria.
1902	**Sir Ronald Ross**, British	Investigation of how malaria parasites enter the body.
1903	**Niels R. Finsen**, Danish	Contribution to treatment of tuberculous skin diseases, especially lupus vulgaris, with concentrated light radiation.
1904	**Ivan P. Pavlov**, Russian	Work on physiology of digestion.
1905	**Robert Koch**, German	Investigations and discoveries in relation to tuberculosis.
1906	**Camillo Golgi**, Italian **Santiago Ramón y Cajal**, Spanish	Work on structure of nervous system.
1907	**Charles L. A. Laveran**, French	Work on role played by protozoa in causing diseases.
1908	**Paul Ehrlich**, German **Élie Metchnikoff**, French (Russian-born)	Work on immunity.
1909	**Emil T. Kocher**, Swiss	Work on physiology, pathology, and surgery of thyroid gland.
1910	**Albrecht Kossel**, German	Contributions to knowledge of cell chemistry made through his work on proteins, including nucleic substances.
1911	**Allvar Gullstrand**, Swedish	Work on dioptrics of eye.
1912	**Alexis Carrel**, U.S.	Work on vascular suture and transplantation of blood vessels and organs.
1913	**Charles R. Richet**, French	Work on anaphylaxis and allergies.
1914	**Robert Bárány**, Hungarian	Work on physiology and pathology of inner ear.
1915–18	No award	
1919	**Jules Bordet**, Belgian	Discoveries relating to immunity.
1920	**Schack A. S. Krogh**, Danish	Discovery of capillary motor-regulating mechanism.
1921	No award	
1922	**Archibald V. Hill**, British **Otto F. Meyerhof**, German	Discovery relating to production of heat in muscle. Discovery of fixed relationship between consumption of oxygen and metabolism of lactic acid in muscle.
1923	**Frederick G. Banting**, Canadian **John J. R. Macleod**, Canadian	Discovery of insulin.
1924	**Willem Einthoven**, Dutch	Discovery of mechanism of electrocardiogram.
1925	No award	
1926	**Johannes A. G. Fibiger**, Danish	Experimental production of cancerlike growth in rats.
1927	**Julius Wagner-Jauregg**, Austrian	Use of malaria inoculation to treat paralysis and mental deterioration associated with syphilis.
1928	**Charles J. H. Nicolle**, French	Work on typhus.
1929	**Christiaan Eijkman**, Dutch **Sir Frederick G. Hopkins**, British	Discovery of health defects due to vitamin B_1 deficiency. Discovery of growth-stimulating vitamins.
1930	**Karl Landsteiner**, U.S. (Austrian-born)	Discovery of human blood groups.
1931	**Otto H. Warburg**, German	Discovery of nature and mode of action of respiratory enzyme.
1932	**Edgar D. Adrian**, British **Sir Charles S. Sherrington**, British	Discoveries regarding functions of nerve cells.
1933	**Thomas H. Morgan**, U.S.	Discoveries concerning role of chromosome in heredity.
1934	**George R. Minot**, U.S. **William P. Murphy**, U.S. **George H. Whipple**, U.S.	Discoveries concerning liver therapy in cases of anemia.
1935	**Hans Spemann**, German	Discovery of organizer effect in embryonic development.
1936	**Sir Henry H. Dale**, **British** **Otto Loewi**, U.S. (Austrian-born)	Discoveries relating to chemical transmission of nerve impulses.
1937	**Albert Szent-Györgyi von Nagyrapolt** U.S. (Hungarian-born)	Studies in body metabolism with special reference to role of vitamin C and fumaric acid.
1938	**Corneille J. F. Heymans**, Belgian	Discovery of role played by sinus and aortic mechanisms in regulation of respiration.
1939	**Gerhard Domagk**, German	Discovery of antibacterial effects of drug prontosil. (Prize declined under political pressure; awarded later.)
1940	No award	
1941	No award	
1942	No award	
1943	**Henrik C. P. Dam**, Danish **Edward A. Doisy**, U.S.	Discovery of vitamin K. Discovery of chemical nature of vitamin K.
1944	**Joseph Erlanger**, U.S. **Herbert S. Gasser**, U.S.	Discoveries relating to highly differentiated functions of single nerve fibers.
1945	**Sir Alexander Fleming**, British **Ernst B. Chain**, British (German-born) **Sir Howard W. Florey**, British (Australian-born)	Discovery of penicillin and its curative effect in various infectious diseases.
1946	**Hermann J. Muller**, U.S.	Discovery of production of mutations by means of X rays.
1947	**Carl F. Cori**, U.S. (Czech-born) **Gerty T. Cori**, U.S. (Czech-born) **Bernardo A. Houssay**, Argentine	Discovery of course of catalytic conversion of glycogen. Discovery of part played by hormone of anterior pituitary lobe in metabolism of sugar.
1948	**Paul H. Müller**, Swiss	Discovery of high efficiency of DDT as insecticide.
1949	**Walter R. Hess**, Swiss **Antonio Moniz**, Portuguese	Discovery of functional organization of interbrain as coordinator of activities of internal organs. Discovery of value of prefrontal lobotomy in certain psychoses.
1950	**Philip S. Hench**, U.S. **Edward C. Kendall**, U.S. **Tadeus Reichstein**, Swiss (Polish-born)	Discoveries relating to hormones of adrenal cortex, their structure and biological effects.
1951	**Max Theiler**, U.S. (S. African-born)	Discoveries concerning yellow fever and how to combat it.
1952	**Selman A. Waksman**, U.S.	Discovery of streptomycin, first antibiotic effective against TB.
1953	**Hans A. Krebs**, British (German-born) **Fritz A. Lipmann**, U.S. (German-born)	Discovery of citric acid cycle. Discovery of coenzyme A and its importance for intermediary metabolism.

1954	**John F. Enders**, U.S. **Federick C. Robbins**, U.S. **Thomas H. Weller**, U.S.	Discovery of ability of poliomyelitis viruses to grow in cultures of various types of tissue.
1955	**Alex H. T. Theorell**, Swedish	Discoveries concerning oxidation enzymes.
1956	**Andráe F. Cournand**, U.S. (French-born) **Werner Forssmann**, German **Dickinson W. Richards Jr.**, U.S.	Discoveries concerning heart catheterization and pathological changes in circulatory system.
1957	**Daniel Bovet**, Italian (Swiss-born)	Discoveries relating to synthetic compounds that inhibit action of certain body substances.
1958	**George W. Beadle**, U.S. **Edward L. Tatum**, U.S. **Joshua Lederberg**, U.S.	Discovery that genes act by regulating definite chemical events. Discoveries concerning genetic recombination and organization of genetic material of bacteria.
1959	**Arthur Kornberg**, U.S. **Severo Ochoa**, U.S. (Spanish-born)	Discovery of mechanisms in biological synthesis of RNA and DNA.
1960	**Sir F. Macfarlane Burnet**, Australian **Peter B. Medawar**, British (Brazilian-born)	Discovery of acquired immunological tolerance.
1961	**Georg von Békésy**, U.S. (Hungarian-born)	Discoveries of physical mechanism of stimulation within cochlea of inner ear.
1962	**Francis H. C. Crick**, British **James D. Watson**, U.S. **Maurice H. F. Wilkins**, British	Discoveries concerning molecular structure of nuclear acids and its significance for information transfer in living material.
1963	**Sir John C. Eccles**, Australian **Alan L. Hodgkin**, British **Andrew F. Huxley**, British	Discoveries concerning nerve-cell membrane.
1964	**Konrad E. Bloch**, U.S. **Feodor Lynen**, German	Discoveries concerning mechanism and regulation of cholesterol and fatty-acid metabolism.
1965	**François Jacob**, French **André Lwoff**, French **Jacques Monod**, French	Discovery of regulatory processes in body cells that contribute to genetic control of enzymes and virus synthesis.
1966	**Charles B. Huggins**, U.S. **Francis Peyton Rous**, U.S.	Discoveries concerning hormonal treatment of cancer of prostate gland. Discovery of tumor-inducing viruses in chickens.
1967	**Ragnar Granit**, Swedish (Finnish-born) **Haldan Keffer Hartline**, U.S. **George Wald**, U.S.	Discoveries concerning primary chemical and physiological visual processes in eye.
1968	**Robert W. Holley**, U.S. **Har Gobind Khorana**, U.S. (Indian-born) **Marshall W. Nirenberg**, U.S.	Explanation of genetic code that determines function of cells.
1969	**Max Delbrück**, U.S. (German-born) **Alfred D. Hershey**, U.S. **Salvador D. Luria**, U.S. (Italian-born)	Discoveries concerning reproductive mechanism and genetic structure of viruses.
1970	**Julius Axelrod**, U.S. **Ulf von Euler**, Swedish **Bernard Katz**, British	Basic research in chemistry of nerve transmission.
1971	**Earl W. Sutherland Jr.**, U.S.	Discoveries concerning mechanisms of action of hormones.
1972	**Gerald M. Edelman**, U.S. **Rodney Porter**, British	Determination of antibody's exact chemical structure.
1973	**Karl von Frisch**, Austrian **Konrad Lorenz**, Austrian **Nikolaas Tinbergen**, British (Dutch-born)	Discoveries in individual and social behavior patterns of birds and bees in relation to natural selection and survival of species.
1974	**Albert Claude**, U.S. (Luxembourgian-born) **Christian Rene de Duve**, Belgian **George Emil Palade**, U.S. (Romanian-born)	Founding science of cell biology, pioneering in use of electron microscope to study living cells, and discovering such cell parts as ribosomes and lysosomes.
1975	**David Baltimore**, U.S. **Howard Martin Temin**, U.S. **Renato Dulbecco**, U.S. (Italian-born)	Research discoveries concerning interaction between tumor viruses and genetic material of living cell.
1976	**Baruch S. Blumberg**, U.S. **D. Carleton Gajdusek**, U.S.	Research that led to test for hepatitis virus in donated blood and to experimental vaccine against hepatitis. Discovery of virus causing kuru disease among cannibals in New Guinea, transmitted through eating of human brains.
1977	**Rosalyn S. Yalow**, U.S. **Roger C. L. Guillemin**, U.S. (French-born) **Andrew V. Schally**, U.S. (Polish-born)	Development of radioimmunoassay, use of radioactive materials to measure hormones and other substances in blood and tissues. Discovery and synthesis of peptide hormones produced by hypothalmus in brain, providing greater understanding of brain's control of body's chemistry.
1978	**Daniel Nathans**, U.S. **Hamilton O. Smith**, U.S. **Werner Arber**, Swiss	Research that made possible gene splicing or recombinant DNA to create mutant life forms by discovering and using enzymes called *restriction endonucleases.*
1979	**Allan McLeod Cormack**, U.S. **Godfrey Newbold Hounsfield**, British	Development of computerized axial tomography (CAT), an X-ray scanning technique used in medical diagnosis of patients.
1980	**George D. Snell**, U.S. **Baruj Benacerraf**, U.S. (Venezuelan-born) **Jean Dausset**, French	Identification of the HLA antigens, or histocompatability system, in human cells, leading to more successful surgical transplants of human organs.
1981	**David H. Hubel**, U.S. **Roger W. Sperry**, U.S. **Torsten N. Wiesel**, U.S. (Swedish-born)	Research on human brain organization and function.
1982	**Sune Bergstrom**, Swedish **Bengt Samuelsson**, Swedish **John R. Vane**, British	Research on prostaglandins, explaining how the hormone-like substances are formed in human body and how they defend cells from disease.
1983	**Barbara McClintock**, U.S.	Discovery that genes of corn can move from one place in the chromosomes of a plant to another, changing the characteristics of future plants.

PULITZER PRIZES

The Pulitzer Prizes are the most prestigious awards made each year in the United States for journalism, literature, and music. The prizes were established under terms of the will of Joseph Pulitzer (1847–1911), a Hungarian immigrant who in 1878 founded one of America's great newspapers, the *St. Louis* (Mo.) *Post-Dispatch,* and then in 1883 purchased New York City's *The World,* making it into a crusading newspaper with the largest circulation in the United States.

Upon his death in 1911, Pulitzer left $2 million to found a graduate school of journalism at Columbia University in New York City with the provision that after the school had operated for at least three years prizes should be awarded annually for the advancement of journalism, literature, music, and public service. The Columbia University School of Journalism was founded in 1912. The first Pulitzer Prizes began to be awarded in 1917.

Each prize carries an award of $1,000 except for the gold medal award to a newspaper for meritorious public service.

Prizes in journalism are awarded in 12 categories. Prizes in literature, drama, and music are awarded in seven areas. In addition, special awards are made from time to time.

LOCAL INVESTIGATIVE REPORTING

1953 Edward J. Mowery, *New York World-Telegram & Sun*
1954 Alvin S. McCoy, *Kansas City* (Mo.) *Star*
1955 Roland K. Towery, *Cuero* (Tex.) *Record*
1956 Arthur Daley, *New York Times*
1957 Wallace Turner and William Lambert, *Portland Oregonian*
1958 George Beveridge, *Washington Evening Star*
1959 John Harold Brislin, *Scranton* (Pa.) *Tribune and Scrantonian*
1960 Mariam Ottenberg, *Washington Evening Star*
1961 Edgar May, *Buffalo Evening News*
1962 George Bliss, *Chicago Tribune*
1963 Oscar O'Neal Griffin Jr., *Pecos* (Tex.) *Independent and Enterprise*
1964 James V. Magee, Albert V. Gaudiosi, and Frederick A. Meyer, *Philadelphia Bulletin*
1965 Gene Goltz, *Houston Post*
1966 John A. Frasca, *Tampa* (Fla.) *Tribune*
1967 Gene Miller, *Miami Herald*
1968 J. Anthony Lukas, *New York Times*
1969 Albert Delugach and Denny Walsh, *St. Louis Globe-Democrat*
1970 Harold E. Martin, *Montgomery* (Ala.) *Advertiser*
1971 William Hugh Jones, *Chicago Tribune*
1972 Ann DeSantis, S. A. Kurkjian, T. Leland, and G. M. O'Neill, *Boston Globe*
1973 *Sun* Newspapers, Omaha, Nebr.
1974 William Sherman, *New York Daily News*
1975 *Indianapolis Star*
1976 Staff of *Chicago Tribune*
1977 Acel Moore and Wendell Rawls Jr., *Philadelphia Inquirer*
1978 Anthony R. Dolan, *Stamford* (Conn.) *Advocate*
1979 Gilbert M. Paul and Elliot G. Jaspin, *Pottsville* (Pa.) *Republican*
1980 Stephen A. Kurkjian, Alexander B. Hawes Jr., Nils J. Bruzelius, Joan Vennochi, and Robert Porterfield, *Boston Globe*
1981 Clark Hallas and Robert B. Lowe, *Arizona Daily Star*
1982 Paul Henderson, *Seattle Times*
1983 Loretta Tofani, *Washington Post,* for articles on conditions in Maryland detention center

LOCAL GENERAL REPORTING

1953 *Providence* (R.I.) *Journal and Evening Bulletin*
1954 *Vicksburg* (Miss.) *Sunday Post-Herald*
1955 Caro Brown, *Alice* (Tex.) *Daily Echo*
1956 Lee Hills, *Detroit Free Press*
1957 *Salt Lake Tribune*
1958 *Fargo* (N.D.) *Forum*
1959 Mary Lou Werner, *Washington Evening Star*
1960 Jack Nelson, *Atlanta Constitution*
1961 Sanche de Gramont, *New York Herald Tribune*
1962 Robert D. Mullins, *Deseret News,* Salt Lake City, Utah
1963 Sylvan Fox, Anthony Shannon, and William Longgood, *New York World-Telegram & Sun*
1964 Norman C. Miller, *Wall Street Journal*
1965 Melvin H. Ruder, *Hungry Horse* (Mont.) *News*
1966 Staff, *Los Angeles Times*
1967 Robert V. Cox, *Chambersburg* (Pa.) *Public Opinion*
1968 *Detroit Free Press*
1969 John Fretterman, *Louisville Courier-Journal*
1970 Thomas Fitzpatrick, *Chicago Sun-Times*
1971 *Akron* (Ohio) *Beacon Journal*
1972 R. I. Cooper and J. W. Machacek, *Rochester* (N.Y.) *Times-Union*
1973 *Chicago Tribune*
1974 Arthur M. Petacque and Hugh F. Hough, *Chicago Sun-Times*
1975 *Xenia* (Ohio) *Daily Gazette*
1976 Gene Miller, *Miami Herald*
1977 Margo Huston, *Milwaukee Journal*
1978 Richard Whitt, *Louisville* (Ky.) *Courier-Journal*
1979 Staff of *San Diego* (Calif.) *Evening Tribune*
1980 Staff of *Philadelphia Inquirer*
1981 Staff of *Longview* (Wash.) *Daily News* for reporting of Mount St. Helens volcanic eruption
1982 *Kansas City Star* and *Kansas City Times* for coverage of Hyatt Regency Hotel disaster
1983 Staff of *Ft. Wayne (Ind.) News-Sentinel* for coverage of 1982 flood

NATIONAL REPORTING

1942 Louis Stark, *New York Times*
1943 No award
1944 Dewey L. Fleming, *Sun,* Baltimore
1945 James B. Reston, *New York Times*
1946 Edward A. Harris, *St. Louis Post-Dispatch*
1947 Edward T. Folliard, *Washington Post*
1948 Bert Andrews, *New York Herald Tribune,* and Nat S. Finney, *Minneapolis Tribune*
1949 Charles P. Trussell, *New York Times*
1950 Edwin O. Guthman, *Seattle Times*
1951 No award
1952 Anthony Leviero, *New York Times*
1953 Don Whitehead, Associated Press
1954 Richard Wilson, Cowles Newspapers
1955 Anthony Lewis, *Washington Daily News*
1956 Charles Bartlett, *Chattanooga* (Tenn.) *Times*
1957 James Reston, *New York Times*
1958 Relman Morin, Associated Press
1959 Howard Van Smith, *Miami News*
1960 Vance Trimble, Scripps-Howard
1961 Edward R. Cony, *Wall Street Journal*

1962 Nathan G. Caldwell and Gene S. Graham, *Nashville Tennessean*
1963 Anthony Lewis, *New York Times*
1964 Merriman Smith, United Press International
1965 Louis Kohlmeier, *Wall Street Journal*
1966 Haynes Johnson, *Washington Evening Star*
1967 Monroe W. Karmin and Stanley W. Penn, *Wall Street Journal*
1968 Howard James, *Christian Science Monitor,* and Nathan Kotz, *Register,* Des Moines, Iowa
1969 Robert Cahn, *Christian Science Monitor*
1970 William J. Seton, *Chicago Daily News*
1971 Lucinda Franks and Thomas Powers, United Press International
1972 Jack Anderson, syndicated columnist
1973 Robert Boyd and Clark Hoyt, the Knight. Newspapers
1974 James R. Polk, *Washington Star-News,* and Jack White, *Providence* (R.I.) *Journal-Bulletin*
1975 Donald L. Barlett and James B. Steel *Philadelphia Inquirer*
1976 James Risser, *Register,* Des Moines, Iowa
1977 Walter Mears, Associated Press
1978 Gaylord Shaw, *Los Angeles Times*
1979 James Risser, *Register,* Des Moines, Iowa
1980 Bette Swenson Orsini and Charles Stafford, *St. Petersburg* (Fla.) *Times*
1981 John H. Crewdson, *New York Times*
1982 Rick Atkinson, *Kansas City Times*
1983 Staff of *Boston Globe,* for "War and Peace in the Nuclear Age" supplement

INTERNATIONAL CORRESPONDENCE

1942 Laurence E. Allen, Associated Press
1943 Ira Wolfert, North American Newspaper Alliance
1944 Daniel DeLuce, Associated Press
1945 Mark S. Watson, *Sun,* Baltimore
1946 Homer W. Bigart, *New York Herald Tribune*
1947 Eddy Gilmore, Associated Press
1948 Paul W. Ward, *Sun,* Baltimore
1949 Price Day, *Sun,* Baltimore
1950 Edmund Stevens, *Christian Science Monitor*
1951 Keyes Beech and Fred Sparks, *Chicago Daily News,* Homer Bigart and Marguerite Higgins, *New York Herald Tribune,* Relman Morin and Don Whitehead, Associated Press
1952 John M. Hightower, Associated Press
1953 Austin Wehrwein, *Milwaukee Journal*
1954 Jim G. Lucas, Scripps-Howard Newspapers
1955 Harrison Salisbury, *New York Times*
1956 William Randolph Hearst Jr., Kingsbury Smith, and Frank Conniff, International News Service
1957 Russell Jones, United Press
1958 *New York Times*
1959 Joseph Martin and Philip Santora, *New York Daily News*
1960 A.M. Rosenthal, *New York Times*
1961 Lynn Heinzerling, Associated Press
1962 Walter Lippmann, New York Herald Tribune Syndicate
1963 Hal Hendrix, *Miami News*
1964 Malcolm W. Browne, Associated Press
David Halberstam, *New York Times*
1965 J.A. Livingston, *Philadelphia Bulletin*
1966 Peter Arnett, Associated Press
1967 R.J. Hughes, *Christian Science Monitor*
1968 Alfred Friendly, *Washington Post*
1969 William Tuohy, *Los Angeles Times*
1970 Seymour M. Hersh, Dispatch News Service
1971 Jimmie Lee Hoagland, *Washington Post*
1972 Peter R. Kann, *Wall Street Journal*
1973 Max Frankel, *New York Times*
1974 Hedrick Smith, *New York Times*
1975 William Mullen and Ovie Carter, *Chicago Tribune*
1976 Sydney H. Schanberg, *New York Times*
1977 No award
1978 Henry Kamm, *New York Times*
1979 Richard Ben Cramer, *Philadelphia Inquirer*
1980 Joel Brinkley and Jay Mather, *Louisville* (Ky.) *Courier-Journal* for Cambodia coverage
1981 Shirley Christian, *Miami Herald*
1982 John Darnton, *New York Times,* for reporting on Poland's crisis

FEATURE WRITING

1979 Jon D. Franklin, *Baltimore Evening Sun*
1980 Madeline Blais, *Miami Herald*
1981 Theresa Carpenter, *The Village Voice*
1982 Saul Pett, *Associated Press*
1983 Nan Robertson, *New York Times,* for account of her experience with toxic shock sysdrome

EDITORIAL WRITING

1917 *New York Tribune*
1918 *Courier-Journal,* Louisville, Ky.
1919 No award
1920 Harvey E. Newbranch, *Evening World-Herald,* Omaha
1921 No award
1922 Frank M. O'Brien, *New York Herald*
1923 William Allen White, *Emporia* (Kans.) *Gazette*
1924 *Boston Herald; Frank I. Cobb, New York World*
1925 *Charleston* (S.C.) *News and Courier*
1926 Edward M. Kingsbury, *New York Times*
1927 F.L. Bullard, *Boston Herald*
1928 Grover Cleveland Hall, *Montgomery* (Ala.) *Advertiser*
1929 Louis I. Jaffee, *Norfolk Virginian-Pilot*
1930 No award
1931 Charles S. Ryckman, *Fremont* (Nebr.) *Tribune*
1932 No award
1933 *Kansas City Star*
1934 E.P. Chase, *Atlantic* (Iowa) *News-Telegraph*
1935 No award
1936 Felix Morley, *Washington Post*
George B. Parker, Scripps-Howard
1937 John W. Owens, *Baltimore Sun*
1938 W.W. Waymack, *Register and Tribune,* Des Moines, Iowa
1939 Ronald G. Callvert, Portland *Oregonian*
1940 Bart Howard, *St. Louis Post-Dispatch*
1941 Reuben Maury, *New York Daily News*
1942 Geoffrey Parsons, *New York Herald Tribune*
1943 Forrest W. Seymour, *Register and Tribune,* Des Moines, Iowa
1944 Henry J. Haskell, *Kansas City Star*
1945 George W. Potter, *Providence* (R.I.) *Journal-Bulletin*
1946 Hodding Carter, *Delta Democrat-Times,* Greenville, Miss.
1947 William Grimes, *Wall Street Journal*
1948 Virginius Dabney, *Richmond* (Va.) *Times-Dispatch*
1949 John H. Crider, *Boston Herald*
Herbert Elliston, *Washington Post*
1950 Carl M. Saunders, *Jackson* (Mich.) *Citizen Patriot*
1951 William Fitzpatrick, *New Orleans States*
1952 Louis LaCoss, *St. Louis Globe-Democrat*
1953 Vermont Royster, *Wall Street Journal*
1954 Don Murray, *Boston Herald*
1955 Royce Howes, *Detroit Free Press*
1956 Lauren K. Soth, *Register and Tribune,* Des Moines, Iowa
1957 Buford Boone, *Tuscaloosa* (Ala.) *News*
1958 Harry S. Ashmore, *Arkansas Gazette,* Little Rock
1959 Ralph McGill, *Atlanta Constitution*

PULITZER PRIZES *(continued)*

1960 Lenoir Chambers, *Norfolk Virginian-Pilot*
1961 William J. Dorvillier, *San Juan* (P.R.) *Star*
1962 Thomas M. Storke, *Santa Barbara* (Calif.) *News-Press*
1963 Ira B. Harkey Jr., *Pascagoula* (Miss.) *Chronicle*
1964 Hazel Smith, *Lexington* (Miss.) *Advertiser*
1965 John R. Harrison, *Gainesville* (Fla.) *Sun*
1966 Robert Lasch, *St. Louis Post-Dispatch*
1967 Eugene C. Patterson, *Atlanta Constitution*
1968 John S. Knight, Knight Newspapers
1969 Paul Greenberg, *Pine Bluff* (Ark.) *Commercial*
1970 Philip Geyelin, *Washington Post*
1971 Horance G. Davis Jr., *Gainesville* (Fla.) *Sun*
1972 J. Strohmeyer, *Bethlehem* (Pa.) *Globe-Times*
1973 Roger B. Linscott, *Berkshire Eagle*, Mass.
1974 F. Gilman Spencer, *Trenton Trentonian*
1975 John Daniell Maurice, *Charleston* (W.Va.) *Daily Mail*
1976 Philip P. Kerby, *Los Angeles Times*
1977 Warren L. Lerude, Foster Church, Norman F. Cardoza, *Reno Evening Gazette* and *Nevada State Journal*
1978 Meg Greenfield, *Washington Post*
1979 Edwin M. Yoder Jr., *Washington Star*
1980 Robert L. Bartley, *Wall Street Journal*
1981 No award
1982 Jack Rosenthal, *New York Times*
1983 Editorial board, *Miami Herald*

CARTOON PULITZER PRIZES

1922 Rollin Kirby, *New York World*
1923 No award
1924 Jay Norwood Darling, *New York Tribune*
1925 Rollin Kirby, *New York World*
1926 Daniel R. Fitzpatrick, *St. Louis Post-Dispatch*
1927 Nelson Harding, *Brooklyn Daily Eagle*
1928 Nelson Harding, *Brooklyn Daily Eagle*
1929 Rollin Kirby, *New York World*
1930 Charles R. Macauley, *Brooklyn Daily Eagle*
1931 Edmund Duffy, *Baltimore Sun*
1932 John McCutcheon, *Chicago Tribune*
1933 H.M. Talburt, *Washington Daily News*
1934 Edmund Duffy, *Baltimore Sun*
1935 Ross A. Lewis, *Milwaukee Journal*
1936 No award
1937 Clarence Daniel Batchelor, *N.Y. Daily News*
1938 Vaughn Shoemaker, *Chicago Daily News*
1939 Charles G. Werner, *Daily Oklahoman*, Oklahoma City
1940 Edmund Duffy, *Baltimore Sun*
1941 Jacob Burck, *Chicago Times*
1942 Herbert L. Block (Herblock), Newspaper Enterprise Association Service
1943 Jay Norwood Darling, *N.Y. Herald Tribune*
1944 Clifford K. Berryman, *Washington Evening Star*
1945 William (Bill) Mauldin, United Features Syndicate, Inc.
1946 Bruce Russell, *Los Angeles Times*
1947 V. Shoemaker, *Chicago Daily News*
1948 Reuben L. (Rube) Goldberg, *New York Sun*
1949 Lute Pease, *Newark*, (N.J.) *Evening News*
1950 James T. Berryman, *Washington Evening Star*
1951 Reginald W. Manning, *Arizona Republic*, Phoenix, Ariz.
1952 Fred L. Packer, *New York Mirror*
1953 Edward D. Kuekes, *Cleveland Plain Dealer*
1954 Herbert L. Block (Herblock), *Washington Post & Times-Herald*
1955 Daniel R. Fitzpatrick, *St. Louis Post-Dispatch*
1956 Robert York, *Louisville Times*
1957 Tom Little, *Nashville Tennessean*
1958 Bruce M. Shanks, *Buffalo Evening News*
1959 William (Bill) Mauldin, *St. Louis Post-Dispatch*
1960 No award
1961 Carey Orr, *Chicago Tribune*
1962 E.S. Valtman, *Hartford* (Conn.) *Times*
1963 Frank Miller, *Des Moines Register*
1964 Paul Conrad, *Denver Post*
1965 No award
1966 Don Wright, *Miami News*
1967 Patrick B. Oliphant, *Denver Post*
1968 E. G. Payne, *Charlotte* (N.C.) *Observer*
1969 John Fischetti, *Chicago Daily News*
1970 Thomas Darcy, *Newsday*, Garden City, N.Y.
1971 Paul Conrad, *Los Angeles Times*
1972 J. K. MacNelly, *Richmond* (Va.) *News Leader*
1973 No award
1974 Paul Szep, *Boston Globe*
1975 Garry Trudeau, creator of "Doonesbury"
1976 Tony Auth, political cartoonist, *Philadelphia Inquirer*
1977 Paul Szep, *Boston Globe*
1978 J. K. MacNelly, *Richmond* (Va.) *News Leader*
1979 Herbert L. Block (Herblock), *Washington Post*
1980 Don Wright, *Miami News*
1981 Mike Peters, *Dayton* (Ohio) *Daily News*
1982 Ben Sargent, *Austin* (Tex.) *American-Statesman*
1983 Richard Locher, *Chicago Tribune*

NEWS PHOTOGRAPHY PULITZER PRIZES

1942 Milton Brooks, *Detroit News*
1943 Frank Noel, Associated Press
1944 Frank Filan, Associated Press
1945 Joe Rosenthal, Associated Press
1946 No award
1947 Arnold Hardy, amateur photographer
1948 Frank Cushing, *Boston Traveler*
1949 Nathaniel Fein, *New York Herald Tribune*
1950 Bill Crouch, *Oakland* (Calif.) *Tribune*
1951 Max Desfor, Associated Press
1952 John Robinson and Don Ultang, *Des Moines Register and Tribune*
1953 William M. Gallagher, *Flint* (Mich.) *Journal*
1954 Mrs. Walter M. Schau, photographer
1955 John L. Gaunt Jr., *Los Angeles Times*
1956 *New York Daily News*
1957 Harry A. Trask, *Boston Traveler*
1958 William C. Beall, *Washington Daily News*
1959 William Seaman, *Minneapolis Star*
1960 Andrew Lopez, United Press International
1961 Yasushi Nagao, Mainichi Newspapers, Tokyo, Japan
1962 Paul Vathis, Associated Press
1963 Hector Rondon, Caracas, Venezuela
1964 Robert H. Jackson, *Dallas Times Herald*
1965 Horst Faas, Associated Press
1966 Kyoichi Sawada, United Press International
1967 Jack R. Thornell, Associated Press
1968 Rocco Morabito, *Jacksonville* (Fla.) *Journal*
1969 Edward T. Adams, Associated Press
1970 Steve Starr, Associated Press
1971 John Paul Filo, amateur photographer
1972 H. Faas, M. Laurent, Associated Press
1973 Huynh Cong Ut, Associated Press
1974 Anthony K. Roberts, freelance
1975 Gerald H. Gay, *Seattle Times*
1976 Stanley Forman, *Boston Herald-American*
1977 Stanley Forman, *Boston Herald-American*, and Neal Ulevich, Associated Press
1978 John W. Blair, freelance

1979 Thomas J. Kelley III, *Pottstown* (Pa.) *Mercury*
1980 Unidentified photographer of Iranian firing squad
1981 Larry C. Price, *Fort Worth Star-Telegram*
1982 Ron Edmonds, Associated Press
1983 Bill Foley, Associated Press

FEATURE PHOTOGRAPHY PULITZER PRIZES

1968 Toshio Sakai, United Press International
1969 Moneta Sleet Jr., *Ebony* magazine
1970 Dallas Kinney, *Palm Beach* (Fla.) *Post*
1971 Jack Dykinga, *Chicago Sun-Times*
1972 Dave Kennerly, United Press International
1973 B. Lanker, *Topeka* (Kans.) *Capital-Journal*
1974 Slava Veder, Associated Press
1975 Matthew Lewis, *Washington Post*
1976 Photographic staff of *Louisville Courier-Journal and Times*
1977 Robin Hood, *News-Free Press*, Chattanooga, Tenn.
1978 J. Ross Baughman, freelance
1979 Staff of *The Boston Herald-American*
1980 Erwin H. Hagler, *Dallas Times Herald*
1981 Taro M. Yamasaki, *Detroit Free Press*
1982 John H. White, *Chicago Sun-Times*
1983 James B. Dickman, *Dallas Times Herald*

MERITORIOUS PUBLIC SERVICE

1918 *New York Times*
1919 *Milwaukee Journal*
1920 No award
1921 *Boston Post*
1922 *World*, New York
1923 *Memphis Commercial Appeal*
1924 *World*, New York
1925 No award
1926 *Enquirer Sun*, Columbus, Ga.
1927 *Canton* (Ohio) *Daily News*
1928 *Indianapolis Times*
1929 *Evening World*, New York
1930 No award
1931 *Atlanta Constitution*
1932 *Indianapolis News*
1933 *New York World-Telegram*
1934 *Medford* (Oreg.) *Mail Tribune*
1935 *Sacramento* (Calif.) *Bee*
1936 *Cedar Rapids* (Iowa) *Gazette*
1937 *St. Louis Post-Dispatch*
1938 *Bismarck* (N.D.) *Tribune*
1939 *Miami Daily News*
1940 *Waterbury* (Conn.) *Republican and American*
1941 *St. Louis Post-Dispatch*
1942 *Los Angeles Times*
1943 *World-Herald*, Omaha, Nebr.
1944 *New York Times*
1945 *Detroit Free Press*
1946 *Scranton* (Pa.) *Times*
1947 *Baltimore Sun*
1948 *St. Louis Post-Dispatch*
1949 *Nebraska State Journal*
1950 *Chicago Daily News; St. Louis Post-Dispatch*
1951 *Miami Herald; Brooklyn Eagle*
1952 *St. Louis Post-Dispatch*
1953 *News Reporter*, Whiteville, N.C.
Tabor City (N.C.) *Tribune*
1954 Newsday, Garden City, N.Y.
1955 *Columbus* (Ga.) *Ledger and Sunday Ledger-Enquirer*
1956 *Watsonville* (Calif.) *Register-Pajaronian*
1957 *Chicago Daily News*
1958 *Arkansas Gazette*, Little Rock
1959 *Utica* (N.Y.) *Observer-Dispatch*
Utica (N.Y.) *Daily Press*
1960 *Los Angeles Times*
1961 *Amarillo* (Tex.) *Globe-Times*
1962 *Panama City* (Fla.) *News-Herald*
1963 *Chicago Daily News*
1964 *St. Petersburg* (Fla.) *Times*
1965 *Hutchinson* (Kans.) *News*
1966 *Boston Globe*
1967 *Louisville Courier-Journal; Milwaukee Journal*
1968 *Riverside* (Calif.) *Press*
1969 *Los Angeles Times*
1970 *Newsday*, Garden City, N.Y.
1971 *Winston-Salem* (N.C.) *Journal and Sentinel*
1972 *New York Times*
1973 *Washington Post*
1974 *Newsday*, Garden City, N.Y.
1975 *Boston Globe*
1976 *Anchorage* (Alaska) *Daily News*
1977 *Lufkin* (Tex.) *News*
1978 *Philadelphia Inquirer*
1979 *Point Reyes* (Calif.) *Light*, for Synanon exposé
1980 Gannett News Service, for exposing mismanagement of funds of Pauline Fathers
1981 *Charlotte* (N.C.) *Observer*, for exposure of "brown lung" disease among textile workers
1982 *Detroit News*, for exposure of Navy cover-ups of circumstances of shipboard deaths
1983 Jackson, Miss., *Clarion Ledger*, for investigation of Mississippi public school system.

CRITICISM PULITZER PRIZES

1970 Ada Louise Huxtable, *New York Times*
1971 Harold C. Schonberg, *New York Times*
1972 Frank L. Peters Jr., *St. Louis Post-Dispatch*
1973 Ronald Powers, *Chicago Sun-Times*
1974 Emily Genauer, *Newsday* syndicate
1975 Roger Ebert, *Chicago Sun-Times*
1976 Alan M. Kriegsman, *Washington Post*
1977 William McPherson, *Washington Post*
1978 Walter Kerr, *New York Times*
1979 Paul Gapp, *Chicago Tribune*
1980 William A. Henry III, TV critic, *Boston Globe*
1981 Jonathan Yardley, book critic, *Washington Star*
1982 Martin Bernheimer, music critic, *Los Angeles Times*
1983 Manuela Hoelterhoff, *Wall Street Journal*

COMMENTARY PULITZER PRIZES

1970 Marquis Childs, *St. Louis Post-Dispatch*
1971 William A. Caldwell, *Record*, Hackensack, N.J.
1972 Mike Royko, *Chicago Daily News*
1973 David S. Broder, *Washington Post*
1974 Edwin A. Roberts Jr., *National Observer*
1975 Mary McGrory, *Washington Star*
1976 Walter W. (Red) Smith, sports columnist, *New York Times*
1977 George F. Will, syndicated columnist, Washington Post Writers Group
1978 William Safire, columnist, *New York Times*
1979 Russell Baker, columnist, *New York Times*
1980 Ellen H. Goodman, columnist, *Boston Globe*
1981 Dave Anderson, sports columnist, *N.Y. Times*
1982 Art Buchwald, *Los Angeles Times* syndicate
1983 Claude Sitton, Raleigh, N.C., *News & Observer*

REPORTING PULITZER PRIZES: 1948–1952

1948 George E. Goodwin, *Atlanta Journal*
1949 Malcolm Johnson, *Sun*, New York
1950 Meyer Berger, *New York Times*
1951 Edward Montgomery, *San Francisco Examiner*
1952 George de Carvalho, *San Francisco Chronicle*

PULITZER PRIZES *(continued)*

SPECIAL PULITZER PRIZE CITATIONS

1938 *Edmonton Journal*, for defending freedom of the press in Alberta, Canada.
1941 *New York Times*, for the public educational value of its foreign news reporting
1944 To Mrs. William Allen White, for interest and services during previous seven years as member of Advisory Board of the Graduate School of Journalism, Columbia University. Byron Price, Director of the Office of Censorship, for the creation and administration of the newspaper and radio codes.
1945 The cartographers of the American press, whose maps of the war fronts helped notably to clarify and increase public information on the progress of the armies and navies engaged in World War II.
1947 (Pulitzer Centennial year) Columbia University and the Graduate School of Journalism, for their efforts to maintain and advance the high standards governing the Pulitzer Prize awards.
1948 To Dr. Frank Diehl Fackenthal, a scroll indicating appreciation of his interest and service during the preceding years.
1951 Cyrus L. Sulzberger, of *New York Times*, for his exclusive interview with Archbishop Aloysius Stepinac of Yugoslavia.
1952 *Kansas City Star*, for the news coverage of the great regional flood of 1951 in Kansas and northwestern Missouri.
Max Case, of *New York Journal-American*, for his exposures of corruption in basketball.
1953 *New York Times*, for the section of its Sunday edition headed *Review of the Week*, which for 17 years brought enlightened commentary to its readers.
1958 Walter Lippmann, nationally syndicated columnist of *New York Herald Tribune*, for his wisdom, perception, and responsibility.
1964 Gannett Newspapers, Rochester, N.Y., for their program *The Road to Integration*, a distinguished example of the use of a newspaper group's resources to complement the work of its individual newspapers.
1973 James T. Flexner, for *George Washington*, a four-volume biography.
1976 Scott Joplin (1868–1917), special Bicentennial year award for his contributions to American music with such compositions as *Maple Leaf Rag*.
1976 John Hohenberg, for 22 years of service as administrator of the Pulitzer Prizes.
1977 Alex Haley, for *Roots*, an "important contribution to the literature of slavery."
1978 E. B. White, for contributions to literature; Richard L. Strout, for contributions to journalism.
1982 Milton Babbitt, for life work as distinguished composer.

FICTION PULITZER PRIZES

1918 *His Family*, by Ernest Poole
1919 *The Magnificent Ambersons*, by Booth Tarkington
1920 No award
1921 *The Age of Innocence*, by Edith Wharton
1922 *Alice Adams*, by Booth Tarkington
1923 *One of Ours*, by Willa Cather
1924 *The Able McLaughlins*, by Margaret Wilson
1925 *So Big*, by Edna Ferber
1926 *Arrowsmith*, by Sinclair Lewis
1927 *Early Autumn*, by Louis Bromfield
1928 *The Bridge of San Luis Rey*, by Thornton Wilder
1929 *Scarlet Sister Mary*, by Julia Peterkin
1930 *Laughing Boy*, by Oliver LaFarge
1931 *Years of Grace*, by Margaret Ayer Barnes
1932 *The Good Earth*, by Pearl S. Buck
1933 *The Store*, by T.S. Stribling
1934 *Lamb in His Bosom*, by Caroline Miller
1935 *Now in November*, by Josephine W. Johnson
1936 *Honey in the Horn*, by Harold L. Davis
1937 *Gone with the Wind*, by Margaret Mitchell
1938 *The Late George Apley*, by John Phillips Marquand
1939 *The Yearling*, by Marjorie Kinnan Rawlings
1940 *The Grapes of Wrath*, by John Steinbeck
1941 No award
1942 *In This Our Life*, by Ellen Glasgow
1943 *Dragon's Teeth*, by Upton Sinclair
1944 *Journey in the Dark*, By Martin Flavin
1945 *A Bell for Adano*, by John Hersey
1946 No award
1947 *All the King's Men*, by Robert Penn Warren
1948 *Tales of the South Pacific*, by James Michener
1949 *Guard of Honor*, by James Gould Cozzens
1950 *The Way West*, by A. B. Guthrie Jr.
1951 *The Town*, by Conrad Richter
1952 *The Caine Mutiny*, by Herman Wouk
1953 *The Old Man and the Sea*, by Ernest Hemingway
1954 No Award
1955 *A Fable*, by William Faulkner
1956 *Andersonville*, by MacKinlay Kantor
1957 No award
1958 *A Death in the Family*, by James Agee
1959 *The Travels of Jaimie McPheeters*, by Robert Lewis Taylor
1960 *Advise and Consent*, by Allen Drury
1961 *To Kill a Mockingbird*, by Harper Lee
1962 *The Edge of Sadness*, by Edwin O'Connor
1963 *The Reivers*, by William Faulkner
1964 No award
1965 *The Keepers of the House*, by Shirley Ann Grau
1966 *The Collected Stories of Katherine Anne Porter*, by Katherine Anne Porter
1967 *The Fixer*, by Bernard Malamud
1968 *The Confessions of Nat Turner*, by William Styron
1969 *House Made of Dawn*, by N. Scott Momaday
1970 *Collected Stories*, by Jean Stafford
1971 No award
1972 *Angle of Repose*, by Wallace Stegner
1973 *The Optimist's Daughter*, by Eudora Welty
1974 No award
1975 *The Killer Angels*, by Michael Shaara
1976 *Humboldt's Gift*, by Saul Bellow
1977 No award
1978 *Elbow Room*, by James Alan McPherson
1979 *The Stories of John Cheever*, by John Cheever
1980 *The Executioner's Song*, by Norman Mailer
1981 *A Confederacy of Dunces*, John Kennedy Toole
1982 *Rabbit Is Rich*, John Updike
1983 *The Color Purple*, Alice Walker

DRAMA PULITZER PRIZES

1917 No award
1918 *Why Marry?*, by Jesse L. Williams
1919 No award
1920 *Beyond the Horizon*, By Eugene O'Neill
1921 *Miss Lulu Bett*, by Zona Gale
1922 *Anna Christie*, by Eugene O'Neill
1923 *Icebound*, by Owen Davis
1924 *Hell-Bent for Heaven*, by Hatcher Hughes
1925 *They Knew What They Wanted*, by Sidney Howard
1926 *Craig's Wife*, by George Kelly
1927 *In Abraham's Bosom*, by Paul Green

1928 *Strange Interlude,* by Eugene O'Neill
1929 *Street Scene,* by Elmer L. Rice
1930 *The Green Pastures,* by Marc Connelly
1931 *Alison's House,* by Susan Glaspell
1932 *Of Thee I Sing,* by George S. Kaufman, Ira Gershwin, and Morris Ryskind
1933 *Both Your Houses,* by Maxwell Anderson
1934 *Men in White,* by Sidney Kingsley
1935 *The Old Maid,* by Zoe Akins
1936 *Idiot's Delight,* by Robert E. Sherwood
1937 *You Can't Take It with You,* by Moss Hart and George S. Kaufman
1938 *Our Town,* by Thornton Wilder
1939 *Abe Lincoln in Illinois,* by Robert E. Sherwood
1940 *The Time of Your Life,* by William Saroyan
1941 *There Shall Be No Night,* by Robert E. Sherwood
1942 No award
1943 *The Skin of Our Teeth,* by Thornton Wilder
1944 No award
1945 *Harvey,* by Mary Chase
1946 *State of the Union,* by Russel Crouse and Howard Lindsay
1947 No award
1948 *A Streetcar Named Desire,* by Tennessee Williams
1949 *Death of a Salesman,* by Arthur Miller
1950 *South Pacific,* by Richard Rogers, Oscar Hammerstein II, and Joshua Logan
1951 No award
1952 *The Shrike,* by Joseph Kramm
1953 *Picnic,* by William Inge
1954 *The Teahouse of the August Moon,* by John Patrick
1955 *Cat on a Hot Tin Roof,* by Tennessee Williams
1956 *Diary of Anne Frank,* by Albert Hackett and Frances Goodrich
1957 *Long Day's Journey Into Night,* by Eugene O'Neill
1958 *Look Homeward, Angel,* by Ketti Frings
1959 *J. B.,* by Archibald MacLeish
1960 *Fiorello!* by Jerome Weidman and George Abbott
1961 *All the Way Home,* by Tad Mosel
1962 *How to Succeed in Business Without Really Trying,* by Frank Loesser and Abe Burrows
1963–64 No award
1965 *The Subject Was Roses,* by Frank Gilroy
1966 No award
1967 *A Delicate Balance,* by Edward Albee
1968 No award
1969 *The Great White Hope,* by Howard Sackler
1970 *No Place to Be Somebody,* by Charles Gordone
1971 *The Effect of Gamma Rays on Man-in-the-Moon Marigolds,* by Paul Zindel
1972 No award
1973 *That Championship Season,* by Jason Miller
1974 No award
1975 *Seascape,* by Edward Albee
1976 *A Chorus Line,* produced by Joseph Papp
1977 *The Shadow Box,* by Michael Cristofer
1978 *The Gin Game,* by Donald L. Coburn
1979 *Buried Child,* by Sam Shepard
1980 *Talley's Folly,* by Lanford Wilson
1981 *Crimes of the Heart,* by Beth Henley
1982 *A Soldier's Play,* by Charles Fuller
1983 *'Night, Mother,* by Marsha Norman

HISTORY PULITZER PRIZES

1917 *With Americans of Past and Present Days,* by J. J. Jusserand
1918 *A History of the Civil War, 1861–65,* by James Ford Rhodes
1919 No award
1920 *The War with Mexico,* by Justin H. Smith
1921 *The Victory at Sea,* William Sowden Sims and Burton J. Hendrick
1922 *The Founding of New England,* by James Truslow Adams
1923 *The Supreme Court in United States History,* by Charles Warren
1924 *The American Revolution—A Constitutional Interpretation,* by Charles McIlwain
1925 *A History of the American Frontier,* by Frederic L. Paxson
1926 *The History of the United States,* by Edward Channing
1927 *Pinckney's Treaty,* by Samuel Flagg Bemis
1928 *Main Currents in American Thought* (2 vols.), by Vernon Louis Parrington
1929 *The Organization and Administration of the Union Army, 1861–1865,* by Fred Albert Shannon
1930 *The War of Independence,* by Claude H. Van Tyne
1931 *The Coming of the War: 1914,* by Bernadotte E. Schmitt
1932 *My Experiences in the World War,* by John J. Pershing
1933 *The Significance of Sections in American History,* by Frederick J. Turner
1934 *The People's Choice,* by Herbert Agar
1935 *The Colonial Period of American History,* by Charles McLean Andrews
1936 *The Constitutional History of the United States,* by Andrew C. McLaughlin
1937 *The Flowering of New England,* by Van Wyck Brooks
1938 *The Road to Reunion, 1865–1900,* by Paul Herman Buck
1939 *A History of American Magazines,* by Frank Luther Mott
1940 *Abraham Lincoln: The War Years,* by Carl Sandburg
1941 *The Atlantic Migration, 1607–1860,* by Marcus Lee Hansen
1942 *Reveille in Washington,* by Margaret Leech
1943 *Paul Revere and the World He Lived In,* by Esther Forbes
1944 *The Growth of American Thought,* by Merle Curti
1945 *Unfinished Business,* by Stephen Bonsal
1946 *The Age of Jackson,* by Arthur M. Schlesinger Jr.
1947 *Scientists Against Time,* by James Phinney Baxter III
1948 *Across the Wide Missouri,* by Bernard DeVoto
1949 *The Disruption of American Democracy,* by Roy Franklin Nichols
1950 *Art and Life in America,* by Oliver W. Larkin
1951 *The Old Northwest: Pioneer Period, 1815–1840,* by R. Carlyle Buley
1952 *The Uprooted,* by Oscar Handlin
1953 *The Era of Good Feelings, by George Dangerfield*
1954 *A Stillness at Appomattox,* by Bruce Catton
1955 *Great River: The Rio Grande in North American History,* by Paul Horgan
1956 *Age of Reform,* by Richard Hofstadter
1957 *Russia Leaves the War: Soviet-American Relations,* 1917–1920, by George F. Kennan
1958 *Banks and Politics in America—From the Revolution to the Civil War,* by Bray Hammond
1959 *The Republican Era: 1869–1901,* by Leonard D. White, assisted by Jean Schneider
1960 *In the Days of McKinley,* by Margaret Leech
1961 *Between War and Peace: The Potsdam Conference,* by Herbert Feis
1962 *The Triumphant Empire: Thunder-Clouds Gather in the West,* by Lawrence H. Gipson
1963 *Washington: Village and Capital, 1800–1878,* by Constance McLaughlin Green
1964 *Puritan Village: The Formation of a New England Town,* by Sumner Chilton Powell

PULITZER PRIZES *(continued)*

1965 *The Greenback Era,* by Irwin Unger
1966 *Life of the Mind in America: From the Revolution to the Civil War,* by Perry Miller
1967 *Exploration and Empire: The Explorer and Scientist in the Winning of the American West,* by William H. Goetzmann
1968 *The Ideological Origins of the American Revolution,* by Bernard Bailyn
1969 *Origins of the Fifth Amendment,* by Leonard Levy
1970 *Present at the Creation: My Years in the State Department,* by Dean G. Acheson
1971 *Roosevelt: The Soldier of Freedom, 1940–1945,* by James MacGregor Burns
1972 *Neither Black Nor White,* by C. N. Degler
1973 *People of Paradox: An Inquiry Concerning the Origin of American Civilization,* by Michael Kammen
1974 *The Americans: The Democratic Experience,* by Daniel J. Boorstin
1975 *Jefferson and His Time,* by Dumas Malone
1976 *Lamy of Santa Fe,* by Paul Horgan
1977 *The Impending Crisis,* by David M. Potter
1978 *The Visible Hand: The Managerial Revolution in American Business,* by Alfred D. Chandler Jr.
1979 *The Dred Scott Case,* by Don E. Fehrenberger
1980 *Been in the Storm So Long,* by Leon F. Litwack
1981 *American Education: The National Experience, 1783–1876,* by Lawrence A. Cremin
1982 *Mary Chestnut's Civil War,* by C. Vann Woodward, editor
1983 *The Transformation of Virginia, 1740–1790,* by Rhys L. Isaac

BIOGRAPHY/AUTOBIOGRAPHY

1917 *Julia Ward Howe,* by Laura E. Richards, Maude H. Elliot, and Florence H. Hall
1918 *Benjamin Franklin, Self-Revealed,* by William Cabell Bruce
1919 *The Education of Henry Adams,* by Henry Adams
1920 *The Life of John Marshall* (4 vols.), by Albert J. Beveridge
1921 *The Americanization of Edward Bok,* by Edward Bok
1922 *A Daughter of the Middle Border,* by Hamlin Garland
1923 *The Life and Letters of Walter H. Page,* by Burton J. Hendrick
1924 *From Immigrant to Inventor,* by Michael Pupin
1925 *Barrett Wendell and His Letters,* by M. A. DeWolfe Howe
1926 *The Life of Sir William Osler* (2 vols.), by Harvey Cushing
1927 *Whitman,* by Emory Holloway
1928 *The American Orchestra and Theodore Thomas,* by Charles Edward Russell
1929 *The Training of an American: The Earlier Life and Letters of Walter H. Page,* by Burton J. Hendrick
1930 *The Raven,* by Marquis James
1931 *Charles W. Eliot,* by Henry James
1932 *Theodore Roosevelt,* by Henry F. Pringle
1933 *Grover Cleveland,* by Allan Nevins
1934 *John Hay,* by Tyler Dennett
1935 *R.E. Lee,* by Douglas Southall Freeman
1936 *The Thought and Character of William James,* by Ralph Barton Perry
1937 *Hamilton Fish,* by Allan Nevins
1938 *Pedlar's Progress,* by Odell Shepard
Andrew Jackson, by Marquis James
1939 *Benjamin Franklin,* by Carl Van Doren
1940 *Woodrow Wilson, Life and Letters, Volumes VII and VIII,* by Ray Stannard Baker
1941 *Jonathan Edwards,* by Ola E. Winslow
1942 *Crusader in Crinoline,* by Forrest Wilson
1943 *Admiral of the Ocean Sea,* by Samuel Eliot Morison
1944 *The American Leonardo: The Life of Samuel F. B. Morse,* by Carleton Mabee
1945 *George Bancroft: Brahmin Rebel,* by Russell Blaine Nye
1946 *Son of the Wilderness,* by Linnie M. Wolfe
1947 *The Autobiography of William Allen White,* by William Allen White
1948 *Forgotten First Citizen: John Bigelow,* by Margaret Clapp
1949 *Roosevelt and Hopkins,* by Robert E. Sherwood
1950 *John Quincy Adams and the Foundations of American Foreign Policy,* by Samuel Bemis
1951 *John C. Calhoun: American Portrait,* by Margaret Louise Coit
1952 *Charles Evans Hughes,* by Merlo J. Pusey
1953 *Edmund Pendleton 1721–1803,* by David J. Mays
1954 *The Spirit of St. Louis,* by Charles A. Lindbergh
1955 *The Taft Story,* by William S. White
1956 *Benjamin Henry Latrobe,* by T. F. Hamlin
1957 *Profiles in Courage,* by John F. Kennedy
1958 *George Washington, Volumes I-VI,* by Douglas Southall Freeman; *Volume VII,* by Mary Ashworth and John Carroll
1959 *Woodrow Wilson, American Prophet,* by Arthur Walworth
1960 *John Paul Jones,* by Samuel Eliot Morison
1961 *Charles Sumner and the Coming of the Civil War,* by David Donald
1962 No award
1963 *Henry James,* by Leon Edel
1964 *John Keats,* by Walter Jackson Bate
1965 *Henry Adams,* by Ernest Samuels
1966 *A Thousand Days,* by Arthur Schlesinger Jr.
1967 *Mr. Clemens and Mark Twain,* by Justin Kaplan
1968 *Memoirs (1925–1950),* by George F. Kennan
1969 *The Man from New York: George Quinn and His Friends,* by Benjamin Reid
1970 *Huey Long,* by T. Harry Williams
1971 *Robert Frost: The Years of Triumph, 1915–1938,* by Lawrance R. Thompson
1972 *Eleanor and Franklin,* by J. P. Lash
1973 *Luce and His Empire,* by W. A. Swanberg
1974 *O'Neill, Son and Artist,* by Louis Sheaffer
1975 *The Power Broker: Robert Moses and the Fall of New York,* by Robert A. Caro
1976 *Edith Wharton: A Biography,* by Richard Warrington Baldwin Lewis
1977 *A Prince of Our Disorder* (T. E. Lawrence), by John E. Mack
1978 *Samuel Johnson,* by Walter Jackson Bate
1979 *Days of Sorrow and Pain: Leo Baeck and the Berlin Jews,* by Leonard Baker
1980 *The Rise of Theodore Roosevelt,* by Edmund Morris
1981 *Peter the Great: His Life and World,* by Robert K. Massie
1982 *Grant: A Biography,* by William S. McFeely
1983 *Growing Up,* by Russell Baker

GENERAL NONFICTION

1962 *The Making of the President 1960,* by Theodore H. White
1963 *The Guns of August,* by Barbara Tuchman
1964 *Anti-intellectualism in American Life,* by Richard Hofstadter
1965 *O Strange New World,* by Howard Mumford Jones
1966 *Wandering Through Winter,* by Edwin Way Teale
1967 *The Problem of Slavery in Western Culture,* by David Brion Davis
1968 *Rousseau and Revolution,* by Will and Ariel Durant

1969 *So Human an Animal: How We Are Shaped by Surroundings and Events,* by René Dubos
The Armies of the Night, by Norman Mailer
1970 *Gandhi's Truth,* by Erik H. Erikson
1971 *The Rising Sun,* by John Toland
1972 *Stilwell and the American Experience in China, 1911–1945,* by Barbara W. Tuchman
1973 *Fire in the Lake,* by Frances FitzGerald *Children of Crisis,* by Robert Coles
1974 *The Denial of Death,* by Ernest Becker
1975 *Pilgrim at Tinker Creek,* by Annie Dillard
1976 *Why Survive? Being Old in America,* by Robert N. Butler
1977 *Beautiful Swimmers: Watermen, Crabs and the Chesapeake Bay,* by William W. Warner
1978 *The Dragons of Eden,* by Carl Sagan
1979 *On Human Nature,* by Edward O. Wilson
1980 *An Eternal Golden Braid,* by Douglas R. Hofstadter
1981 *Fin-de-Siecle Vienna: Politics and Culture,* by Carl E. Schorske
1982 *The Soul of a New Machine,* by Tracy Kidder
1983 *Is There No Place on Earth for Me?* by Susan Sheehan

POETRY PULITZER PRIZES

1918 *Love Songs,* by Sara Teasdale
1919 *Corn Huskers,* by Carl Sandburg
Old Road to Paradise, by Margaret Widdemer
1920–21 No awards
1922 *Collected Poems,* by Edwin Arlington Robinson
1923 *The Ballad of the Harp-Weaver; A Few Figs from Thistles;* eight sonnets in *American Poetry,* 1922, *A Miscellany,* by Edna St. Vincent Millay
1924 *New Hampshire: A Poem with Notes and Grace Notes,* by Robert Frost
1925 *The Man Who Died Twice,* by Edwin Arlington Robinson
1926 *What's O'Clock,* by Amy Lowell
1927 *Fiddler's Farewell,* by Leonora Speyer
1928 *Tristram,* by Edwin Arlington Robinson
1929 *John Brown's Body,* by Stephen Vincent Benét
1930 *Selected Poems,* by Conrad Aiken
1931 *Collected Poems,* by Robert Frost
1932 *The Flowering Stone,* by George Dillon
1933 *Conquistador,* by Archibald MacLeish
1934 *Collected Verse,* by Robert Hillyer
1935 *Bright Ambush,* by Audrey Wurdemann
1936 *Strange Holiness,* by R. P. Tristram Coffin
1937 *A Further Range,* by Robert Frost
1938 *Cold Morning Sky,* by Marya Zaturenska
1939 *Selected Poems,* by John Gould Fletcher
1940 *Collected Poems,* by Mark Van Doren
1941 *Sunderland Capture,* by Leonard Bacon
1942 *The Dust Which Is God,* by William Benét
1943 *A Witness Tree,* by Robert Frost
1944 *Western Star,* by Stephen Vincent Benét
1945 *V-Letter and Other Poems,* by Karl Shapiro
1946 No award
1947 *Lord Weary's Castle,* by Robert Lowell
1948 *The Age of Anxiety,* by W. H. Auden
1949 *Terror and Decorum,* by Peter Viereck
1950 *Annie Allen,* by Gwendolyn Brooks
1951 *Complete Poems,* by Carl Sandburg
1952 *Collected Poems,* by Marianne Moore
1953 *Collected Poems 1917–1952,* by Archibald MacLeish
1954 *The Waking,* by Theodore Roethke
1955 *Collected Poems,* by Wallace Stevens
1956 *Poems—North & South,* by Elizabeth Bishop
1957 *Things of This World,* by Richard Wilbur
1958 *Promises: Poems 1954–56,* by Robert Penn Warren
1959 *Selected Poems 1928–1958,* by Stanley Kunitz
1960 *Heart's Needle,* by W. D. Snodgrass
1961 *Times Three: Selected Verse from Three Decades,* by Phyllis McGinley
1962 *Poems,* by Alan Dugan
1963 *Pictures from Breughel,* by William Carlos Williams
1964 *At the End of the Open Road,* by Louis Simpson
1965 *77 Dream Songs,* by John Berryman
1966 *Selected Poems,* by Richard Eberhart
1967 *Live or Die,* by Anne Sexton
1968 *The Hard Hours,* by Anthony Hecht
1969 *Of Being Numerous,* by George Oppen
1970 *Untitled Subjects,* by Richard Howard
1971 *The Carrier of Ladders,* by W. S. Merwin
1972 *Collected Poems,* by James Wright
1973 *Up Country,* by Maxine Winokur Kumin
1974 *The Dolphin,* by Robert Lowell
1975 *Turtle Island,* by Gary Snyder
1976 *Self-Portrait in a Convex Mirror,* by John Ashbery
1977 *Divine Comedies,* by James Merrill
1978 *Collected Poems,* by Howard Nemerov
1979 *Now and Then,* by Robert Penn Warren
1980 *Selected Poems,* by Donald Rodney Justice
1981 *The Morning of the Poem,* by James Schuyler
1982 *The Collected Poems,* by Sylvia Plath
1983 *Selected Poems,* by Galway Kinnell

MUSIC PULITZER PRIZES

1943 *Secular Cantata No. 2,* by William Schuman
1944 *Symphony No. 4, opus 34,* by Howard Hanson
1945 *Appalachian Spring,* by Aaron Copland
1946 *The Canticle of the Sun,* by Leo Sowerby
1947 *Symphony No. 3,* by Charles Ives
1948 *Symphony No. 3,* by Walter Piston
1949 *Louisiana Story,* by Virgil Thomson
1950 *The Consul,* by Gian-Carlo Menotti
1951 *Giants in the Earth,* by Douglas S. Moore
1952 *Symphony Concertante,* by Gail Kubik
1953 No award
1954 *Concerto for Two Pianos and Orchestra,* by Quincy Porter
1955 *The Saint of Bleecker Street,* by Gian-Carlo Menotti
1956 *Symphony No. 3,* by Ernst Toch
1957 *Meditations on Ecclesiastes,* by Norman Dello Joio
1958 The score of *Vanessa,* by Samuel Barber
1959 *Concerto for Piano and Orchestra,* by John La Montaine
1960 *Second String Quartet,* by Elliott C. Carter Jr.
1961 *Symphony No. 7,* by Walter Piston
1962 *The Crucible,* by Robert Ward
1963 *Piano Concerto No. 1,* by Samuel Barber
1964–65 No awards
1966 *Variations for Orchestra,* by Leslie Bassett
1967 *Quartet No. 3,* by Leon Kirchner
1968 *Echoes of Time and the River,* by George Crumb
1969 *String Quartet No. 3,* by Karel Husa
1970 *Time's Encomium,* by Charles W. Wuorinen
1971 *Synchronisms No. 6,* by Mario Davidovsky
1972 *Windows,* by Jacob Druckman
1973 *String Quartet No. 3,* by Elliott Carter
1974 *Notturno,* by Donald Martino; special citation to Roger Sessions
1975 *From the Diary of Virginia Woolf,* by D. Argento
1976 *Air Music,* 10 études for orchestra, by Ned Rorem
1977 *Visions of Terror and Wonder,* by Richard Wernick
1978 *Déjà Vu for Percussion Quartet and Orchestra,* by Michael Colgrass
1979 *Aftertones of Infinity,* by Joseph Schwantner
1980 *In Memory of a Summer Day,* by David Del Tredici
1981 No award
1982 *Concerts for Orchestra,* by Roger Sessions
1983 *Three Movements for Orchestra,* by Ellen T. Zwilich

HALL OF FAME FOR GREAT AMERICANS

The Hall of Fame for Great Americans was established in 1900 by Dr. Henry Mitchell MacCracken, chancellor of New York University, to honor United States citizens.

MEMBERS OF THE HALL OF FAME	ELECTED
Adams, John (1735–1826), 2d U.S. President	1900
Adams, John Quincy (1767–1848), 6th U.S. President	1905
Addams, Jane (1860–1935), reformer	1965
Agassiz, Louis (1807–73), naturalist	1915
Anthony, Susan B. (1820–1906), social reformer	1950
Audubon, John James (1785?–1851), ornithologist, artist	1900
Bancroft, George (1800–91), historian and diplomat	1910
Barton, Clara (1821–1912), founder of American Red Cross	1976
Beecher, Henry Ward (1813–87), theologian	1900
Bell, Alexander Graham (1847–1922), inventor	1950
Boone, Daniel (1734–1820), frontiersman	1915
Booth, Edwin (1833–93), actor	1925
Brandeis, Louis D. (1856–1941), jurist	1973
Brooks, Phillip (1835–93), theologian	1910
Bryant, William Cullen (1794–1878), writer	1910
Burbank, Luther (1849–1926), horticulturist	1976
Carnegie, Andrew (1835–1919), steelmaker and philanthropist	1976
Carver, George Washington (1859?–1943), chemist	1973
Channing, William Ellery (1780–1842), theologian	1900
Choate, Rufus (1799–1859), lawyer and legislator	1915
Clay, Henry (1777–1852), statesman	1900
Clemens, Samuel Langhorne (Mark Twain; 1835–1910), novelist	1920
Cleveland, Grover (1837–1908), 22d and 24th U.S. President	1935
Cooper, James Fenimore (1789–1851), novelist	1910
Cooper, Peter (1791–1883), philanthropist	1900
Cushman, Charlotte (1816–76), actress	1915
Eads, James (1820–87), engineer	1920
Edison, Thomas Alva (1847–1931), inventor	1960
Edwards, Jonathan (1703–58), theologian	1900
Emerson, Ralph Waldo (1803–82), poet and essayist	1900
Farragut, David Glasgow (1801–70), naval officer	1900
Foster, Stephen (1826–64), composer	1940
Franklin, Benjamin (1706–90), statesman and inventor	1900
Fulton, Robert (1765–1815), inventor	1900
Gibbs, Josiah (1839–1903), physicist	1950
Gorgas, William Crawford (1854–1920), physician	1950
Grant, Ulysses S. (1822–85), Union general and 18th U.S. President	1900
Gray, Asa (1810–88), botanist	1900
Hamilton, Alexander (1755?–1804), statesman	1915
Hawthorne, Nathaniel (1804–64), author	1900
Henry, Joseph (1797–1878), physicist	1915
Henry, Patrick (1736–99), statesman	1920
Holmes, Oliver Wendell (1809–94), writer	1910
Holmes, Oliver Wendell, Jr. (1841–1935), Supreme Court associate justice	1965
Hopkins, Mark (1802–87), educator	1915
Howe, Elias (1819–67), inventor	1915
Irving, Washington (1783–1859), author and diplomat	1900
Jackson, Andrew (1767–1845), 7th U.S. President	1910
Jackson, Stonewall (1824–63), Confederate general	1955
Jefferson, Thomas (1743–1826), 3d U.S. President	1900
Jones, John Paul (1747–92), naval commander	1925
Kent, James (1763–1847), jurist	1900
Lanier, Sidney (1842–81), poet and musician	1945
Lee, Robert E. (1807–70), Confederate general	1900
Lincoln, Abraham (1809–65), 16th U.S. President	1900
Longfellow, Henry Wadsworth (1807–82), poet	1900
Lowell, James Russell (1819–91), poet	1905
Lyon, Mary (1797–1849), educator	1905
MacDowell, Edward Alexander (1861–1908), composer	1960
Madison, James (1751–1836), 4th U.S. President	1905
Mann, Horace (1796–1859), educator	1900
Marshall, John (1755–1835), Chief Justice of U.S.	1900
Maury, Matthew Fontaine (1806–73), naval officer and oceanographer	1930
Michelson, Albert (1852–1931), physicist	1970
Mitchell, Maria (1818–89), astronomer	1905
Monroe, James (1758–1831), 5th U.S. President	1930
Morse, Samuel F. B. (1791–1872), inventor	1900
Morton, William (1819–68), dentist	1920
Motley, John Lothrop (1814–77), historian	1910
Newcomb, Simon (1835–1909), astronomer	1935
Paine, Thomas (1737–1809), political writer	1945
Palmer, Alice (1855–1902), educator	1920
Parkman, Francis (1823–93), historian	1915
Peabody, George (1795–1869), philanthropist	1900
Penn, William (1644–1718), colonial leader	1935
Poe, Edgar Allan (1809–49), poet and author	1910
Reed, Walter (1851–1902), physician	1945
Roosevelt, Franklin Delano (1882–1945), 32d U.S. President	1973
Roosevelt, Theodore (1858–1919), 26th U.S. President	1950
Saint-Gaudens, Augustus (1848–1907), sculptor	1920
Sherman, William Tecumseh (1820–91), Union general	1905
Sousa, John Philip (1854–1932), bandleader	1973
Story, Joseph (1779–1845), Supreme Court associate justice	1900
Stowe, Harriet Beecher (1811–96), novelist	1910
Stuart, Gilbert (1755–1828), painter	1900
Thayer, Sylvanus (1785–1872), military educator	1965
Thoreau, Henry David (1817–62), essayist and poet	1960
Wald, Lillian (1867–1940), social worker	1970
Washington, Booker T. (1856–1915), educator	1945
Washington, George (1732–99), Revolutionary War general and 1st U.S. President	1900
Webster, Daniel (1782–1852), statesman	1900
Westinghouse, George (1846–1914), inventor	1955
Whistler, James A. McNeill (1834–1903), painter	1930
Whitman, Walt (1819–92), poet	1930
Whitney, Eli (1765–1825), inventor	1900
Whittier, John Greenleaf (1807–92), poet	1905
Willard, Emma (1787–1870), educator	1905
Willard, Frances Elizabeth (1839–98), reformer	1910
Williams, Roger (1603?–83), colonial leader	1920
Wilson, Woodrow (1856–1924), 28th U.S. President	1950
Wright, Orville (1871–1948), inventor	1965
Wright, Wilbur (1867–1912), inventor	1955

SPINGARN MEDAL

The highest award each year to blacks for achievement, the gold Spingarn Medal was established in 1914 by Elias Spingarn, chairman of the board of the National Association for the Advancement of Colored People (NAACP). Medals awarded since 1961 include:

YEAR	NAME	FIELD
1961	Kenneth B. Clark	Education
1962	Robert C. Weaver	Government
1963	Medgar W. Evers	Civil rights
1964	Roy Wilkins	Civil rights
1965	Leontyne Price	Music
1966	John H. Johnson	Publishing
1967	Edward W. Brooke	Government
1968	Sammy Davis Jr.	Entertainment
1969	Clarence M. Mitchell Jr.	Government
1970	Jacob Lawrence	Painting
1971	Leon H. Sullivan	Economic opportunity
1972	Gordon Parks	The Arts
1973	Wilson C. Riles	Education
1974	Damon J. Keith	Law
1975	Henry Aaron	Sports
1976	Alvin Ailey	Dance
1977	Alex Haley	Literature
1978	Andrew Young	Government
1979	W. Rayford Logan	Education
1980	Coleman A. Young	Government
1981	Benjamin Elijah Mays	Education
1982	Lena Horne	Entertainment

Books

Wide World

Thousands of people journey to the tiny northeast Iowa village of Burr Oak each year to visit the old Masters Hotel, one of the childhood homes of author Laura Ingalls Wilder, known for her "Little House" books. The hotel and its grounds were completely restored by residents. The Ingalls family lived there in 1876–1878.

HIGHLIGHTS: 1983

SUMMER BOOK SALES UP

The summer of 1983 found about three-fourths of the bookstores polled by *Publishers Weekly* reporting gains in sales compared with 1982. The most important reason for the upswing in sales was the economic recovery.

Among the more successful sellers in nonfiction during the summer were business books, including *In Search of Excellence, Megatrends,* and *One Minute Manager.* Other popular nonfiction titles were *The Price of Power, Creating Wealth, Blue Highways,* and *Jane Fonda's Workout Book.*

The summer's most popular fiction books included *The Little Drummer Girl, August, Christine, Voice of the Heart,* and *Hollywood Wives.* Many booksellers lamented the fact that there was no runaway bestseller.

In the paperback category, booksellers reported strong sales of *Master of the Game, Dinner at the Homesick Restaurant, The Man from St. Petersburg, Lace,* and *Cinnamon Skin.*

Most of those polled were optimistic about fall sales and expected to find bestsellers in James Michener's *Poland,* Stephen King's *Pet Sematary,* James Herriot's *The Best of James Herriot,* and Erma Bombeck's *Motherhood: The Second Oldest Profession.*

High expectations for fall were also pinned on sales for paperbacks that are reprints of hardcover bestsellers. They included *Space, In Search of Excellence, One Minute Manager,* and *Valley of the Horses.*

NEW GRIMM TALE DISCOVERED

The New York firm of Farrar, Straus & Giroux is planning to publish a newly discovered tale by Wilhelm Grimm, who with his brother Jakob published the world renowned *Grimm's Fairy Tales* in 1812–15.

The manuscript was written in German in 1816 to a girl named Milli, whom the author had never met. It remained in the possession of the girl's family until 1974, when it was consigned to a West German auction house, which sold it to Martin Bresslauer, a New York dealer in rare books. He, in turn, forgot about it until early 1983, when he gave it to a dealer in early children's manuscripts,

HIGHLIGHTS: 1983 *(continued)*

Justin Schiller Ltd., on consignment for $26,000. Farrar, Straus & Giroux paid "a substantial five-figure price," and plans to bring it out in 1984 or early 1985 with illustrations by Maurice Sendak.

The tale is about a little girl who is sent away into the woods because her mother fears an impending war. The child spends what she believes are three days, but are really thirty years, serving an old man who reveals himself to be St. Joseph. He gives her a rosebud as she leaves to return to her mother, telling her she will return when the rose is in full bloom. The girl and her mother are reunited for one night, and are found dead the next day, with the fully-bloomed rose between them.

USE OF PUBLIC LIBRARIES FOUND TO INCREASE

Herbert Goldhor, director of the Library Research Center at the University of Illinois, in Urbana, Ill., reported in July on a study he made of circulation in the nation's public libraries from 1941–1982. During those years, he found that circulation rose 160%, while the population increased only 70%.

Goldhor said that estimated circulation of all library materials, including audiovisual materials, as well as books and magazines, reached 1.07 billion in 1982.

U.S. BOOK TITLES PUBLISHED

Source: *Publishers Weekly*

CLASSIFICATION	1950	1955	1960	1965	1970	1975	1980	1981	1982
Agriculture	152	168	156	270	265	456	461	474	435
Art	357	347	470	971	1,169	1,561	1,691	1,693	1,713
Biography	603	833	879	685	1,536	1,968	1,891	1,860	1,687
Business	250	312	305	•537	797	820	1,185	1,342	1,314
Education	256	274	348	954	1,178	1,038	1,011	1,172	1,035
Fiction	1,907	2,073	2,440	3,241	3,137	3,805	2,835	5,655	2,448
General Works	345	387	282	634	846	1,113	1,643	1,743	2,338
History	516	665	865	1,682	1,995	1,823	2,220	2,321	2,139
Home Economics	193	255	197	300	321	728	879	1,108	1,019
Juveniles	1,059	1,485	1,725	2,895	2,640	2,292	2,859	3,102	2,827
Language	148	168	228	527	472	438	529	761	569
Law	298	305	394	436	604	915	1,102	1,448	1,450
Literature	591	660	736	1,686	3,085	1,904	1,686	1,777	1,704
Medicine	443	534	520	1,218	1,476	2,282	3,292	3,788	3,201
Music	113	103	98	300	404	305	357	398	342
Philosophy, Psychology	340	314	480	979	1,280	1,374	1,429	1,465	1,393
Poetry, Drama	531	493	492	994	1,474	1,501	1,179	1,183	1,021
Religion	727	849	1,104	1,855	1,788	1,778	2,055	2,278	2,053
Science	705	801	1,089	2,562	2,358	2,942	3,109	3,375	3,110
Sociology, Economics	515	520	754	3,242	5,912	6,590	7,152	7,801	7,400
Sports, Recreation	188	200	286	591	799	1,225	971	1,264	982
Technology	497	477	698	1,153	1,141	1,720	2,337	2,313	2,311
Travel	288	366	466	883	1,394	794	504	472	459
TOTAL	11,022	12,589	15,012	28,595	36,071	39,372	42,377	48,793	42,950

U.S. BOOK PUBLISHING SALES

Source: Association of American Publishers

TYPE OF SALES	1975	1980	1981	1982	Percent change from '81
Trade (retail stores)	$ 549,200,000	$1,271,300,000	$1,353,700,000	$1,355,500,000	0.1%
Adult hardbound	313,400,000	695,900,000	735,600,000	671,600,000	−8.7%
Adult paperback	111,200,000	364,600,000	384,700,000	452,000,000	17.5%
Juvenile	124,600,000	210,800,000	233,400,000	231,800,000	−6.8%
Religious	154,600,000	351,400,000	360,100,000	390,000,000	8.3%
Professional	501,200,000	999,100,000	1,140,700,000	1,230,500,000	7.9%
Technical and scientific	175,500,000	334,800,000	391,100,000	431,400,000	10.3%
Business and other	242,300,000	424,400,000	492,700,000	530,600,000	7.7%
Medical	83,400,000	239,900,000	256,900,000	268,500,000	4.5%
Book clubs	303,400,000	538,300,000	571,100,000	590,000,000	3.3%
Mail-order books	279,800,000	566,900,000	653,600,000	604,600,000	−7.5%
Mass-market paperbacks	356,200,000	653,300,000	735,600,000	823,100,000	11.9%
University presses	48,800,000	80,700,000	86,000,000	92,400,000	7.5%
Textbooks	1,173,700,000	1,893,000,000	2,073,300,000	2,193,900,000	5.8%
Elementary and secondary	643,100,000	940,300,000	998,600,000	1,051,500,000	5.3%
College	530,600,000	952,700,000	1,074,700,000	1,142,400,000	6.3%
Standardized tests	36,700,000	67,200,000	62,600,000	69,700,000	11.4%
Subscription reference	258,100,000	384,700,000	386,200,000	396,600,000	2.7%
Other	189,000,000	233,500,000	242,200,000	225,100,000	−7.6%
TOTAL	$3,810,000,000	$7,039,400,000	$7,665,100,000	$7,971,500,000	4.0%

BESTSELLERS AND NOTEWORTHY BOOKS: 1983

Nonfiction and fiction books in the following table include most of those mentioned during 1983 on bestseller lists of the *New York Times* and *Publishers Weekly* as well as other noteworthy books published in 1983.

NONFICTION

The Anatomy of Power, John Kenneth Galbraith (Houghton Mifflin; $14.95). In-depth look at public and private power in the U.S.
American Couples, Philip Blumenstein and Pepper Schwartz (Morrow; $19.95). Study of relationships in U.S. today.
Ben-Gurion: Prophet of Fire, Dan Kurzman (Simon & Schuster; $19.95). Biography of first prime minister of Israel.
Benjamin Franklin: A Biography, Ronald W. Clark (Random House; $20). Biography of Franklin, focusing on his involvement with science.
The Best of James Herriot: Favorite Memories of a Country Vet, James S. Herriot (St. Martin's; $19.95). Essays and stories by British veterinarian, author of *All Creatures Great and Small.*
Betrayers of the Truth: Fraud and Deceit in the Halls of Science, William Broad and Nicholas Wade (Simon & Schuster; $15.50). Discussion of fraud, plagiarism, and deceit that plague scientific community.
Blue Highways, William Least Heat Moon (Atlantic/Little, Brown; $17.50). Saga of trip along back roads of America.
Charlie Company: What Vietnam Did to Us, Peter Goldman and Tony Fuller (Morrow; $15.95). Lives of 64 men from U.S. Army infantry company after Vietnam War.
Creating Wealth, Robert G. Allen (Simon & Schuster; $14.95). Advice on real estate investment.
Cults in America: Programmed for Paradise, Willa Appel (Holt, Rinehart and Winston; $15.95). Anthropologist looks at methods and characteristics of cults.
Dashiell Hammett: A Life, Diane Johnson (Random House; $17.95). Biography of American author of mystery stories.
Dear Bess: The Letters from Harry to Bess Truman, 1910–59, Robert H. Ferrell (Norton; $19.95). Collection of letters from late U.S. President Harry S. Truman to his wife over 40-year span.
Delta Force: The U.S. Counterterrorist Unit and the Iran Hostage Rescue Mission, Col. Charlie E. Beckwith and Donald Knox (Harcourt Brace Jovanovich; $14.95). Story behind the attempt to rescue U.S. hostages in Iran.
The Discoverers, Daniel J. Boorstin (Random House; $25). Historical survey of all types of discovery.
Fatal Vision, Joe McGinniss (Putnam; $17.95). Inside look at trial of former Green Beret Dr. Jeffrey MacDonald, convicted of killing his wife and children.
A General's Life: An Autobiography, Omar N. Bradley and Clay Blair (Simon & Schuster; $19.95). Life story of World War II general and former chairman of Joint Chiefs of Staff.
Growing Up, Russell Baker (Congdon & Weed; $15). Memoir by *New York Times* columnist.
Home Before Morning: The Story of an Army Nurse in Vietnam, Lynda Van Devaner (Beaufort Books; $16.95). Life as surgical nurse in Vietnam combat zone.
How to Avoid Love and Marriage, Dan Greenburg and Suzanne O'Malley (Freundlich Books; $9.95). Humorous look at marriage and love.
How to Live to Be 100 or More, George Burns (Putnam; $11.95). Advice on diet, exercise, and sex by octogenarian comedian.
In Search of Excellence: Lessons from America's Best-Run Companies, Thomas J. Peters and Robert H. Waterman Jr. (Harper & Row; $19.95). Experiences of some of the nation's best-run firms.
In the Spirit of Crazy Horse, Peter Mathiessen (Viking; $20.95). Reconstruction of 1975 murder of four American Indians by FBI agents at Wounded Knee, and discussion of status of Indians in today's United States.
The Last Lion: Winston Spencer Churchill; Visions of Glory: 1874–1932, William Manchester (Little, Brown; $25). Biography of fabled British politician.
The Love You Make, Peter Brown and Stephen Gaines (McGraw-Hill; $14.95). Story of The Beatles, by friend and business associate.
Louis Armstrong: An American Genius, James Lincoln Collier (Oxford University Press; $17.95). Biography of renowned musician.
Margaret Mead and Samoa: The Making and Unmaking of an Anthropological Myth, Derek Freeman (Harvard University Press; $20). Australian anthropology professor refutes Margaret Mead's 1928 study *Coming of Age in Samoa.*
Megatrends: Ten New Directions Transforming Our Lives, John Naisbitt (Warner; $15.95). Predictions about America in the 1980s.
Minor Characters, Joyce Johnson (Houghton Mifflin; $13.95). Young woman recalls years spent as companion of Jack Kerouac.
Motherhood: The Second Oldest Profession, Erma Bombeck (McGraw-Hill; $12.95). Humorous look at being a parent.
On Wings of Eagles, Ken Follett (Morrow; $17.95). Account of 1978 rescue of two American executives from Iranian jails, by Dallas businessman Ross Perot.
The One Minute Manager, Kenneth Blanchard and Spencer Johnson (Morrow; $15). Advice on increasing productivity on the job.
Out on a Limb, Shirley MacLaine (Bantam; $15.95). Actress's mid-life identity crisis.
Outrageous Acts and Everyday Rebellions, Gloria Steinem (Holt, Rinehart and Winston; $14.95). Collection of essays of feminist activist.
The Partners: Inside America's Most Powerful Law Firms, James B. Stewart (Simon & Schuster; $16.95). Life in some of the nation's elite law firms.
Pontiff, Gordon Thomas and Max Morgan-Witts (Doubleday; $17.95). Study of Popes John Paul II, Paul VI, and John Paul I.
The Price of Power: Kissinger in the Nixon White House, Seymour M. Hersh (Summit; $19.95). Kissinger's influence on former President Richard M. Nixon.

BESTSELLERS: 1983 *(continued)*

Royal Service: My Twelve Years as Valet to Prince Charles, Stephen P. Barry (Macmillan; $14.95). Inside look at life of Britain's Prince Charles.
Salvador, Joan Didion (Simon & Schuster; $12.95). Description of life in El Salvador.
What's Ahead for the Economy: The Challenge and the Chance, Louis Rukeyser (Simon & Schuster; $15.95). Theories on improving the economy of the U.S.
While Reagan Slept, Art Buchwald (Putnam; $14.95). Collection of humorist's columns from 1981–83.
Why the Jews?: The Reason for the World's Greatest Hatred, Dennis Prager and Joseph Telushkin (Simon & Schuster; $14.95). Discussion of reasons for anti-Semitism.
The Youngest Science: Notes of a Science Watcher, Lewis Thomas, M.D. (Viking; $14.95). Collection of essays by medical researcher who wrote *Lives of a Cell* and *The Medusa and the Snail.*

FICTION

Act of Darkness, Francis King (Little, Brown; $14.95). British family in India in 1930s is torn apart after brutal death of small son.
The Anatomy Lesson, Philip Roth (Farrar, Straus & Giroux; $13.95). Jewish author turns 40 and has writer's block.
Ancient Evenings, Norman Mailer (Little, Brown; $19.95). Story of three reincarnations of ancient Egyptian.
Ascent into Hell, Andrew M. Greeley (Warner Books; $16.50). Man leaves priesthood after impregnating nun and becomes commodities trader in secular world.
The Auerbach Will, Stephen Birmingham (Little, Brown; $15.95). Heirs of prominent Jewish family battle over matriarch's will.
August, Judith Rossner (Houghton Mifflin; $15.95). Relationship of female psychiatrist and young patient.
Balefire, Kenneth Goddard (Bantam; $14.95). International terrorist puts into motion first stage of planned attacks against 1984 Olympics in California.
Banker, Dick Francis (Putnam; $14.95). British investment banker become involved in purchase of race horse.
Cal, Bernard Mac Laverty (George Braziller; $10.95). Young man, growing up in Northern Ireland, wrestles with political issues.
Changes, Danielle Steel (Delacorte; $15.95). TV anchorwoman from New York and California doctor try to merge households.
Christine, Stephen King (Viking; $16.95). Teenager buys old car that turns out to be haunted.
Decision, Allen Drury (Doubleday; $17.95). Young man blows up atomic energy plant, injuring daughters of two Supreme Court justices.
The Delta Star, Joseph Wambaugh (Morrow; $15.95). Los Angeles policeman investigates death of woman.
Ellis Island, Fred Mustard Stewart (Morrow; $15.95). Lives of five people who arrive in America in 1907 aboard the same boat.
Emerald, Phyllis A. Whitney (Doubleday; $14.95). Young woman uncovers secret in life of aging film star.
Exocet, Jack Higgins (Stein and Day; $14.95). Russians become involved in Falkland Islands war of 1982.
Firefox Down! Craig Thomas (Bantam; $14.95). Sequel to *Firefox* about fate of U.S. pilot who steals plane from under noses of Soviets.
Floating Dragon, Peter Straub (Putnam; $15.95). Ghost appears in small Connecticut town and wreaks havoc on inhabitants.
Godplayer, Robin Cook (Putnam; $14.95). Unexplained deaths occur in Boston hospital.
Heartburn, Nora Ephron (Knopf; $11.95). Autobiographical tale of crumbling marriage.
Hollywood Wives, Jackie Collins (Simon & Schuster; $16.95). Wife of aging screen star attempts to help his career.
Icebreaker, John Gardner (Putnam; $10.95). Secret Agent 007 tries to prevent formation of a Fourth Reich.
Karpov's Brain, Gerald Green (Morrow/A Perigord Press Book; $15.95). Soviet neurosurgeon disconnects hemispheres of brain of noted KGB man during surgery, by author of *The Last Angry Man.*
Legion, William Peter Blatty (Simon & Schuster; $14.95). Sequel to *The Exorcist* in which police officer tries to find vicious killer in Washington, D.C.
Light a Penny Candle, Maeve Binchey (Viking; $17.75). Friendship between English girl and Irish girl in 1940s to 1960s.
The Little Drummer Girl, John le Carré (Knopf; $15.95). Israeli agents hunt for man who planted bomb in home of Israeli diplomat in West Germany.
The London Embassy, Paul Theroux (Houghton Mifflin; $13.95). Tales of life as employee in American Embassy in London.
The Madness of a Seduced Woman, Susan Fromberg Schaeffer (Dutton; $16.95). Woman in Vermont in early 1900s has abortion after being betrayed by her lover; then must stand trial.
Mandarin, Robert S. Elegant (Simon & Schuster; $17.95). Saga of two merchant families in China in 1860s.
Marie Blythe, Howard Frank Mosher (Viking; $17.95). French Canadian child comes to live in northern Vermont in 1899.
The Mists of Avalon, Marion Zimmer Bradley (Knopf; $16.95). Four women who played leading roles in Arthurian legend tell their stories.
Monimbo, Robert Moss and Arnaud De Borchgrave (Simon & Schuster; $15.95). Cuban leader Fidel Castro tries to stir up racial tension in the U.S.
Partisans, Alistair MacLean (Doubleday, $14.95). Adventure involving a plot to annihilate Tito's partisans in Yugoslavia in World War II.
Pet Sematary, Stephen King (Doubleday; $15.95). Horrifying things happen to urban family after moving to Maine, near old cemeteries.
Poland, James A. Michener (Random House; $17.95). Historical epic of three Polish families, from Middle Ages to present.

The Seduction of Peter S., Lawrence Sanders (Putnam; $14.95). Out-of-work actor finds success in running male house of prostitution.

So Many Partings, Cathy Cash Spellman (Delacorte; $16.95). Family saga involving Irish immigrant who arrives in U.S. in 1900.

A Spark of Goodness, Charles Brady (Houghton Mifflin; $14.95). Teenage delinquents experience wilderness camping as part of rehabilitation.

Stand We at Last, Zoe Fairbairns (Houghton Mifflin; $15.95). Four generations of women in one family, from Victorian England to American college campuses in 1960s.

A Stolen Past, John Knowles (Holt, Rinehart and Winston/A William Abrahams Book; $14.95). Writer returns to alma mater to lecture about book he wrote and must confront his past.

Sudden Death, Rita Mae Brown (Bantam; $13.95). Romance between woman tennis pro and female intellectual.

The Summer of Katya, Trevanian (Crown; $12.95). Doctor falls in love with young girl in French village in 1938.

This Family of Women, Richard Peck (Delacorte; $14.95). Saga of lives of group of related women over three generations.

Tiger the LURP Dog, Kenn Miller (Atlantic-Little, Brown; $14.95). Experiences of group of regular army men in Vietnam, and their mascot.

The Transfer, Thomas Palmer (Ticknor & Fields; $14.95). Owner of marine salvage company in Miami gets drawn into drug trade.

Trinity's Child, William Prochnau (A Boston Book/Putnam; $16.95). As World War III gets under way, Secretary of Interior becomes President of U.S. in midst of chaos.

Voice of the Heart, Barbara Taylor Bradford (Doubleday; $17.95). Lives of actress and British noble family are intertwined.

War Toys, Hampton Howard (Stein and Day; $14.95). Ex-CIA computer whiz is framed by CIA agent and French policeman.

The Warlord, Malcolm Bosse (Simon & Schuster; $17.95). Chinese warlord tries to bring some order to his chaotic country in 1927.

White Gold Wielder, Stephen R. Donaldson (Ballantine/A Del Ray Book; $14.95). Third book in science-fiction series *Second Chronicles of Thomas Covenant.*

Who Killed the Robins Family? Bill Adler and Thomas Chastain (Morrow; $9.95). Readers are invited to solve mystery, and publisher offers $10,000 prize to winner.

A Woman of Consequence, Sondra Gotlieb (St. Martin's; $12.95). Life of wife of Canadian prime minister, by wife of Canadian ambassador to U.S.

The World Is Made of Glass, Morris West (Morrow; $15.95). Fictional account of Swiss analyst Carl Jung's involvement with woman patient, based on Jung's autobiography.

BOOK AND LITERATURE AWARDS: 1983

AMERICAN BOOK AWARDS: 1983

The American Book Awards, sponsored by the American Booksellers Association, for books published in 1982, included:

HARDCOVER BOOKS:

Fiction: *The Color Purple,* Alice Walker.

First novel: *The Women of Brewster Place,* Gloria Naylor.

General nonfiction: *China: Alive in the Bitter Sea,* Fox Butterfield.

History: *Voices of Protest: Huey Long, Father Coughlin and the Great Depression,* Alan Brinkley.

Autobiography/Biography: *Isak Dinesen: The Life of a Storyteller,* Judith Thurman.

Poetry: (Tie) *Selected Poems,* Galway Kinnell, and *Country Music,* Charles Wright.

Science: *'Subtle is the Lord . . .' The Science and Life of Albert Einstein,* Abraham Pais.

Translation: Baudelaire's *Fleurs du Mal,* Richard Howard.

Children's books, fiction: *Homesick: My Own Story,* Jean Fritz.

Children's picture books: (Tie) *Miss Rumphius,* Barbara Cooney, and *Doctor De Soto,* William Steig.

Children's books, nonfiction: *Chimney Sweeps,* James Cross Giblin.

PAPERBACK BOOKS:

Fiction: *The Collected Stories of Eudora Welty* (Harvest/HBJ).

General nonfiction: *National Defense,* James Fallows.

History: *Utopian Thought in the Western World,* Frank E. Manuel and Fritzie P. Manuel.

Science: *The Mathematical Experience,* Philip J. Davis and Reuben Hersh.

Children's books, fiction: (Tie) *A Place Apart,* Paula Fox, and *Marked by Fire,* Joyce Carol Thomas.

Children's picture books: *A House Is a House for Me,* Mary Ann Hoberman.

BANCROFT PRIZES

The annual Bancroft Prizes of Columbia University, recognizing books of exceptional merit and distinction in American history, included:

John P. Demos, for *Entertaining Satan: Witchcraft and the Culture of Early New England.*

Nick Salvatore, for *Eugene V. Debs: Citizen and Socialist.*

EDGAR ALLAN POE AWARDS

The annual Edgar Allan Poe Awards, presented by the Mystery Writers of America, Inc., included:

Best Mystery Novel: *Billingsgate Shoal,* Rick Boyer.

Best First Novel: *The Butcher's Boy,* Thomas Perry.

Best Fact Crime: *The Vatican Connection,* Richard Hammer.

Best Juvenile Mystery: *The Murder of Hound Dog Bates,* Robbie Branscum.

AMERICAN LIBRARY ASSOCIATION AWARDS

The American Library Association awards, presented annually by the Children's Services Division of the American Library Association to the most distinguished books for children published in the U.S., included:

John Newberry Medal: Cynthia Voigt, for *Dicey's Song.*

Randolph J. Caldecott Medal: Marcia Brown, for *Shadow.*

NATIONAL BOOK CRITICS CIRCLE AWARDS

The 1983 National Book Critics Circle Awards, included:

Best fiction novel: *George Mills,* Stanley Elkin.

General nonfiction: *The Path to Power: The Years of Lyndon Johnson,* Robert A. Caro.

Poetry: *Antarctic Traveller,* Katha Pollitt.

Criticism: *The Second American Revolution and Other Essays,* 1976–1982, Gore Vidal.

BESTSELLERS OF THE PAST

The following were the bestselling books in the U.S. from 1921 to 1982. Sources for these lists are *70 Years of Best Sellers,* by Alice Payne Hackett (Bowker), and *Publishers Weekly.*

FICTION BESTSELLERS

1921	**Main Street,** Sinclair Lewis
1922	**If Winter Comes,** A.S.M. Hutchinson
1923	**Black Oxen,** Gertrude Atherton
1924	**So Big,** Edna Ferber
1925	**Soundings,** A. Hamilton Gibbs
1926	**The Private Life of Helen of Troy,** John Erskine
1927	**Elmer Gantry,** Sinclair Lewis
1928	**The Bridge of San Luis Rey,** Thornton Wilder
1929	**All Quiet on the Western Front,** Erich Remarque
1930	**Cimarron,** Edna Ferber
1931	**The Good Earth,** Pearl S. Buck
1932	**The Good Earth,** Pearl S. Buck
1933	**Anthony Adverse,** Hervey Allen
1934	**Anthony Adverse,** Hervey Allen
1935	**Green Light,** Lloyd C. Douglas
1936	**Gone with the Wind,** Margaret Mitchell
1937	**Gone with the Wind,** Margaret Mitchell
1938	**The Yearling,** Marjorie K. Rawlings
1939	**The Grapes of Wrath,** John Steinbeck
1940	**How Green Was My Valley,** Richard Llewellyn
1941	**The Keys of the Kingdom,** A.J. Cronin
1942	**The Song of Bernadette,** Franz Werfel
1943	**The Robe,** Lloyd C. Douglas
1944	**Strange Fruit,** Lillian Smith
1945	**Forever Amber,** Kathleen Winsor
1946	**The King's General,** Daphne du Maurier
1947	**The Miracle of the Bells,** Russell Janney
1948	**The Big Fisherman,** Lloyd C. Douglas
1949	**The Egyptian,** Mika Waltari
1950	**The Cardinal,** Henry Morton Robinson
1951	**From Here to Eternity,** James Jones
1952	**The Silver Chalice,** Thomas B. Costain
1953	**The Robe,** Lloyd C. Douglas
1954	**Not as a Stranger,** Morton Thompson
1955	**Marjorie Morningstar,** Herman Wouk
1956	**Don't Go Near the Water,** William Brinkley
1957	**By Love Possessed,** James Gould Cozzens
1958	**Doctor Zhivago,** Boris Pasternak
1959	**Exodus,** Leon Uris
1960	**Advise and Consent,** Allen Drury
1961	**The Agony and the Ecstasy,** Irving Stone
1962	**Ship of Fools,** Katherine Anne Porter
1963	**The Shoes of the Fisherman,** Morris L. West
1964	**The Spy Who Came in from the Cold,** John Le Carré
1965	**The Source,** James A. Michener
1966	**Valley of the Dolls,** Jacqueline Susann
1967	**The Arrangement,** Elia Kazan
1968	**Airport,** Arthur Hailey
1969	**Portnoy's Complaint,** Philip Roth
1970	**Love Story,** Erich Segal
1971	**Wheels,** Arthur Hailey
1972	**Jonathan Livingston Seagull,** Richard Bach
1973	**Jonathan Livingston Seagull,** Richard Bach
1974	**Centennial,** James A. Michener
1975	**Ragtime,** E.L. Doctorow
1976	**Trinity,** Leon Uris
1977	**The Silmarillion,** J.R.R. Tolkien
1978	**Chesapeake,** James A. Michener
1979	**The Matarese Circle,** Robert Ludlum
1980	**The Covenant,** James Michener
1981	**Noble House,** James Clavell
1982	**E.T. The Extra-Terrestrial Storybook,** William Kotzwinkle

NONFICTION BESTSELLERS

1921	**The Outline of History,** H.G. Wells
1922	**The Outline of History,** H.G. Wells
1923	**Etiquette,** Emily Post
1924	**Diet and Health,** Lulu Hunt Peters
1925	**Diet and Health,** Lulu Hunt Peters
1926	**The Man Nobody Knows,** B. Barton
1927	**The Story of Philosophy,** Will Durant
1928	**Disraeli,** André Maurois
1929	**The Art of Thinking,** Ernest Dimnet
1930	**The Story of San Michele,** Axel Munthe
1931	**Education of a Princess,** Grand Duchess Marie
1932	**The Epic of America,** James Truslow Adams
1933	**Life Begins at Forty,** Walter B. Pitkin
1934	**While Rome Burns,** Alexander Woollcott
1935	**North to the Orient,** Anne Morrow Lindbergh
1936	**Man the Unknown,** Alexis Carrel
1937	**How to Win Friends and Influence People,** Dale Carnegie
1938	**The Importance of Living,** Lin Yutang
1939	**Days of Our Years,** Pierre van Paassen
1940	**I Married Adventure,** Osa Johnson
1941	**Berlin Diary,** William L. Shirer
1942	**See Here, Private Hargrove,** Marion Hargrove
1943	**Under Cover,** John Roy Carlson
1944	**I Never Left Home,** Bob Hope
1945	**Brave Men,** Ernie Pyle
1946	**The Egg and I,** Betty MacDonald
1947	**Peace of Mind,** Joshua Loth Liebman
1948	**Crusade in Europe,** Dwight D. Eisenhower
1949	**White Collar Zoo,** Clare Barnes Jr.
1950	**Betty Crocker's Picture Cook Book**
1951	**Look Younger, Live Longer,** Gaylord Hauser
1952	**The Holy Bible: Revised Standard Version**
1953	**The Holy Bible: Revised Standard Version**
1954	**The Holy Bible: Revised Standard Version**
1955	**Gift from the Sea,** Anne Morrow Lindbergh
1956	**Arthritis and Common Sense,** Dan Dale Alexander
1957	**Kids Say the Darndest Things,** Art Linkletter
1958	**Kids Say the Darndest Things,** Art Linkletter
1959	**Twixt 12 and 20,** Pat Boone
1960	**Folk Medicine,** D.C. Jarvis
1961	**The New English Bible: The New Testament**
1962	**Calories Don't Count,** Dr. Herman Taller
1963	**Happiness Is a Warm Puppy,** Charles M. Schultz
1964	**Four Days,** American Heritage and UPI
1965	**How to Be a Jewish Mother,** Dan Greenburg
1966	**How to Avoid Probate,** Norman F. Dacey
1967	**Death of a President,** William Manchester
1968	**Better Homes and Gardens New Cook Book**
1969	**American Heritage Dictionary of the English Language,** ed. William Morris
1970	**Everything You Always Wanted to Know About Sex,** David Reuben, M.D.
1971	**The Sensuous Man,** "M"
1972	**The Living Bible,** Kenneth Taylor
1973	**The Living Bible,** Kenneth Taylor
1974	**The Total Woman,** Marabel Morgan
1975	**Angels: God's Secret Agents,** Billy Graham
1976	**The Final Days,** Bob Woodward and Carl Bernstein
1977	**Roots,** Alex Haley
1978	**If Life Is a Bowl of Cherries—What Am I Doing in the Pits?,** Erma Bombeck
1979	**Aunt Erma's Cope Book,** Erma Bombeck
1980	**Crisis Investing,** Douglas R. Casey
1981	**The Beverly Hills Diet,** Judy Mazel
1982	**Jane Fonda's Workout Book,** Jane Fonda

CHARACTERS IN FAMOUS BOOKS

How many of the characters listed below can you identify with the name of the book in which they appear?

You can check whether you are right by noting the number of the character and then looking to see if that number follows the title of the book you have named from the table of well-known books listed at the bottom of this page.

1. Roberta Alden	33. Edward Cummings	65. Tom Joad	97. Nataly Rostóva
2. Fern Arable	34. Cunegonde	66. Robert Jordan	98. Emma Roualt
3. Aunt Chloe	35. Edmond Dantès	67. Stanislaus Katczinsky	99. Lady Rowena
4. Aunt Em	36. Wendy Darling	68. Will Kennicott	100. Evangeline St. Clare
5. Aunt Polly	37. Stephen Dedalus	69. Kincaid	101. Gerald Scales
6. Sophia Baines	38. Arthur Dimmesdale	70. Elizabeth Lavenza	102. Penrod Schofield
7. David Balfour	39. Nicole Diver	71. Simon Legree	103. Ebeneezer Scrooge
8. Horace Benbow	40. Temple Drake	72. John Little	104. Bill Sikes
9. Jane Bennet	41. Dulcinea del Toboso	73. Prince Manfred	105. Mattie Silver
10. Bernabò of Genoa	42. C. Auguste Dupin	74. Jo March	106. Julien Sorel
11. Pierre Bezúkhov	43. Léon Dupuis	75. Mr. Micawber	107. Willie Stark
12. Leopold Bloom	44. Tess Durbeyfield	76. Carol Milford	108. Alan Breck Stewart
13. Raff Brinker	45. Catherine Earnshaw	77. Mole	109. Becky Thatcher
14. John Brooke	46. Sondra Finchley	78. William Morel	110. John Thornton
15. Buck	47. Robert Fitzooth	79. Scarlett O'Hara	111. Tiny Tim
16. Natty Bumppo	48. Henry Fleming	80. O-Lan	112. Tinker Bell
17. Rhett Butler	49. Phileas Fogg	81. Sugar-Boy O'Sheean	113. Toad
18. Mr. By-Ends	50. Zenobia Frome	82. Doctor Pangloss	114. Topsy
19. Philip Carey	51. Mastro Geppetto	83. Sancho Panza	115. Trampas
20. Eppie Cass	52. Dr. Gibbs	84. Passepartout	116. Betsey Trotwood
21. Holden Caulfield	53. Joe Green	85. Pilar	117. Jean Valjean
22. Harvey Cheyne	54. Griffin	86. Popeye	118. Hilda van Gleck
23. Chingachgook	55. Clyde Griffiths	87. Porfiry	119. Rip Van Winkle
24. Nick Chopper	56. Griselda	88. Hester Prynne	120. Robert Walton
25. Christian	57. Heathcliff	89. Queequeg	121. Wang Lung
26. Angel Clare	58. Uriah Heep	90. Peter Quint	122. Mrs. Waters
27. Jim Conklin	59. Captain Hook	91. Raskolnikov	123. Emily Webb
28. Nana Coupeau	60. Injun Joe	92. Rebecca	124. Sophia Western
29. Ichabod Crane	61. Isabella	93. Christopher Robin	125. Wife of Bath
30. Bob Cratchit	62. Ishmael	94. Mr. Rochester	126. Wilbur
31. Art Croft	63. Javert	95. Mildred Rogers	127. Ashley Wilkes
32. Sam Croft	64. Miss Jessel	96. Rose of Sharon	128. George Willard

WELL-KNOWN BOOKS AND THEIR AUTHORS

The Adventures of Pinocchio, Carlo Collodi (51)
The Adventures of Tom Sawyer, Mark Twain (5, 60, 109)
All Quiet on the Western Front, Erich Remarque (67)
All the King's Men, Robert Penn Warren (81, 107)
An American Tragedy, Theodore Dreiser (1, 46, 55)
Around the World in Eighty Days, Jules Verne (49, 84)
Black Beauty, Anna Sewell (53)
The Call of the Wild, Jack London (15, 110)
Candide, François de Voltaire (34, 82)
Canterbury Tales, Geoffrey Chaucer (125)
Captains Courageous, Rudyard Kipling (22)
The Castle of Otranto, Horace Walpole (61, 73)
The Catcher in the Rye, J.D. Salinger (21)
Charlotte's Web, E.B. White (2, 126)
A Christmas Carol, Charles Dickens (30, 103, 111)
The Count of Monte Cristo, Alexandre Dumas (35)
Crime and Punishment, Feodor Dostoyevsky (87, 91)
David Copperfield, Charles Dickens (58, 75, 116)
Decameron, Giovanni Boccaccio (10)
Don Quixote, Miguel de Cervantes Saavedra (41, 83)
Ethan Frome, Edith Wharton (50, 105)
For Whom the Bell Tolls, Ernest Hemingway (66, 85)
Frankenstein, Mary Wollstonecraft Shelley (70, 120)
Gone With the Wind, Margaret Mitchell (17, 79, 127)
The Good Earth, Pearl S. Buck (80, 121)
The Grapes of Wrath, John Steinbeck (65, 96)
Hans Brinker, Mary Mapes Dodge (13, 118)
The Invisible Man, H.G. Wells (54)
Ivanhoe, Sir Walter Scott (92, 99)
Jane Eyre, Charlotte Brontë (94)
Kidnapped, Robert Louis Stevenson (7, 108)
The Last of the Mohicans, James Fenimore Cooper (16, 23)
Les Misérables, Victor Hugo (63, 117)
Little Women, Louisa May Alcott (14, 74)
Madame Bovary, Gustave Flaubert (43, 98)
Main Street, Sinclair Lewis (68, 76)
The Merry Adventures of Robin Hood, Howard Pyle (47, 72)
The Murders in the Rue Morgue, Edgar Allan Poe (42)
Moby-Dick, Herman Melville (62, 89)
The Naked and the Dead, Norman Mailer (32, 33)
Nana, Emile Zola (28)
Of Human Bondage, W. Somerset Maugham (19, 95)
The Old Wives' Tale, Arnold Bennett (6, 101)
Oliver Twist, Charles Dickens (104)
Our Town, Thornton Wilder (52, 123)
The Ox-Bow Incident, Walter Van Tilburg Clark (31, 69)
Penrod and Sam, Booth Tarkington (102)
Peter and Wendy, Sir James Barrie (36, 59, 112)
The Pilgrim's Progress, John Bunyan (18, 25)
Pride and Prejudice, Jane Austen (9)
The Red and the Black, Stendhal (106)
The Red Badge of Courage, Stephen Crane (27, 48)
Sanctuary, William Faulkner (8, 40, 86)
The Scarlet Letter, Nathaniel Hawthorne (38, 88)
Silas Marner, George Eliot (20)
Sketchbook, Washington Irving (29, 119)
Sons and Lovers, D.H. Lawrence (78)
Tender Is the Night, F. Scott Fitzgerald (39)
Tess of the D'Urbervilles, Thomas Hardy (26, 44)
Tom Jones, Henry Fielding (122, 124)
The Turn of the Screw, Henry James (64, 90)
Ulysses, James Joyce (12, 37)
Uncle Tom's Cabin, Harriet Beecher Stowe (3, 71, 100, 114)
The Virginian, Owen Wister (115)
War and Peace, Leo Tolstoy (11, 97)
When We Were Very Young, A.A. Milne (93)
The Wind in the Willows, Kenneth Grahame (77, 113)
Winesburg, Ohio, Sherwood Anderson (128)
The Wizard of Oz, Lyman Frank Baum (4, 24)
Wuthering Heights, Emily Brontë (45, 57)

AUTHORS AND WRITERS

Authors, writers, poets, and dramatists whose works are of enduring interest are listed below in alphabetical order. Birth dates and nationalities are given, along with the titles of the authors' most famous works, and their major literary prizes.

See pages 981–986 for deaths of authors and writers in 1983.

George Abbott (1887–), American playwright and producer: won a Pulitzer Prize as coauthor of musical comedy *Fiorello!* (1959).

Henry Adams (1838–1918), American historian who idealized Middle Ages and deplored materialistic modern civilization: *Mont-Saint-Michel and Chartres* (1904); *The Education of Henry Adams* (1906) won Pulitzer Prize in 1919.

James Truslow Adams (1878–1949), American historian: won a Pulitzer Prize for *The Founding of New England* (1921).

Samuel Hopkins Adams (1871–1958), American writer. His articles about fraudulent patent medicines stirred enactment in 1906 of first Pure Food and Drug Act. Wrote several biographies and novels.

Joseph Addison (1672–1719), English essayist. His essays in the *Tatler, Spectator,* and *Guardian* periodicals were noted for excellence of style.

George Ade (1866–1944), American humorist and playwright: *Fables in Slang* (1899), *The Sultan of Sulu* (1902), *The College Widow* (1904).

Aeschylus (525–456 B.C.), Greek tragic poet. Of his estimated 90 dramas, only 7 survive, including *Prometheus Bound* and *Oresteia,* a trilogy.

James Agee (1909–55), American essayist and novelist: *Let Us Now Praise Famous Men* (1941) is a powerful documentary on Alabama sharecroppers; *A Death in the Family* (1955), a novel, won a 1958 Pulitzer Prize.

Conrad Aiken (1889–1973), American poet: *Selected Poems* (1929) won a Pulitzer Prize.

Edward Albee (1928–), American playwright: *Who's Afraid of Virginia Woolf?* (1962), *Tiny Alice* (1964); *A Delicate Balance* (1966) and *Seascape* (1974) both won Pulitzer Prizes.

Louisa May Alcott (1832–88), American children's writer: *Little Women* (1868–69), *Little Men* (1871).

Horatio Alger (1832–99), American author: *Ragged Dick* (1867), *Tattered Tom* (1871).

Nelson Algren (1909–81), American novelist: *The Man with the Golden Arm* (1949), *A Walk on the Wild Side* (1956).

Hervey Allen (1889–1949), American author: *Anthony Adverse* (1933).

Hans Christian Andersen (1805–75), Danish writer of fairy tales: *The Emperor's New Clothes.*

Maxwell Anderson (1888–1959), American playwright: *Elizabeth the Queen* (1930), *Winterset* (1935), *Joan of Lorraine* (1946); *Both Your Houses* (1932) won a Pulitzer Prize.

Sherwood Anderson (1876–1941), American novelist: *Winesburg, Ohio* (1919), short stories.

Jean Anouilh (1910–), French playwright: *Waltz of the Toreadors* (1952), *Becket* (1959).

Aristophanes (c. 450–388 B.C.), Greek comic dramatist. Of his 40 or more plays, 11 are extant, including *Clouds, Lysistrata,* and *Frogs.*

Matthew Arnold (1822–88), English poet and critic. His romantic pessimism is expressed in such poems as "Dover Beach."

Sholem Asch (1880–1957), Polish-American novelist: *The Nazarene* (1939), *Moses* (1951), *The Prophet* (1955).

Isaac Asimov (1920–), Russian–American author: science-fiction trilogy *Foundation* (1951–53).

Louis Auchincloss (1917–), American novelist: *The Rector of Justin* (1964), *A World of Profit* (1968), *The Winthrop Covenant* (1976), *The Dark Lady* (1977).

W. H. (Wystan Hugh) Auden (1907–73), Anglo-American poet: *The Age of Anxiety* (1947) won a Pulitzer Prize.

Jane Austen (1775–1817), English novelist whose books often satirize manners: *Pride and Prejudice* (1813), *Emma* (1815).

Sir Francis Bacon (1561–1626), English essayist and philosopher: *The Advancement of Learning* (1605), an effort to summarize all science; *Novum Organum* (1620), an inductive analysis of knowledge; *History of Henry VII* (1622); and *Maxims of the Law* (1637).

James Baldwin (1924–), American novelist and essayist who portrays aspects of black problems: *Go Tell It on the Mountain* (1953), a novel.

Honoré de Balzac (1799–1850), French novelist and dramatist: *The Chouans* (1829), *Droll Stories* (1832–37), *Old Goriot* (1834).

George Bancroft (1800–91): American historian: 10-volume *History of the United States* (1834–74).

Imamu Amiri Baraka, formerly known as **LeRoi Jones** (1934–), American dramatist and essayist: *Dutchman* (1964) and *The Slave* (1966).

Sir James Matthew Barrie (1860–1937), Scottish playwright and novelist: best-known play was *Peter Pan* (1904). Novels include *The Little Minister* (1891).

Philip Barry (1896–1949), American playwright: *The Philadelphia Story* (1939).

John Barth (1930–), U.S. novelist: *The Sot-Weed Factor* (1960), *Giles Goat-Boy* (1966), *Letters* (1979).

John Bartlett (1820–1905), American bookseller and writer: *Familiar Quotations* (1855).

Charles Baudelaire (1821–67), French poet and leader of the French symbolist movement: *Les Fleurs du Mal* (1857).

Samuel Beckett (1906–), Irish-born French novelist and playwright: *Malone Dies* (1951), a novel; *Waiting for Godot* (1952), his best-known play. He won a Nobel Prize in 1969.

Sir Max Beerbohm (1872–1956), English parodist and critic: *Poet's Corner* (1904), satiric essay; *Zuleika Dobson* (1912), a novel.

S. N. Behrman (1893–1973), American playwright: *Brief Moment* (1931), *No Time for Comedy* (1939).

Saul Bellow (1915–), Canadian-born American novelist; awarded 1976 Nobel Prize: *The Adventures of Augie March* (1953), *Herzog* (1964), *Mr. Sammler's Planet* (1970), all of which won National Book Awards; *Humboldt's Gift* (1975) won 1976 Pulitzer Prize.

Robert C. Benchley (1889-1945), American humorist: *Inside Benchley* (1942).

Stephen Vincent Benét (1898–1943), American poet: *John Brown's Body* (1928) and *Western Star* (1943) won Pulitzer Prizes.

Arnold Bennett (1867–1931), English novelist: *The Old Wives' Tale* (1908), *Clayhanger* (1910).

John Berryman (1914–72), American poet: *77 Dream Songs* (1963) won a Pulitzer Prize, and *His Toy* (1968) won a National Book Award.

Ambrose Bierce (1842–1914?), American critic and short-story writer: *In the Midst of Life* (1898).

Josh Billings (real name **Henry Wheeler Shaw,** 1818–85), American humorist: *Josh Billings' Farmers' Allminax* (1869–80).

William Blake (1757–1827), English poet and mystic: *Songs of Innocence* (1789), *Songs of Experience* (1794).

Robert Bly (1926–), American poet: *The Light*

Around the Body (1967) won a National Book Award.

Giovanni Boccaccio (1313–75), Italian poet: the *Decameron* (1348–53), the *Filostrato* (c. 1338).

James Boswell (1740–95), Scottish biographer and diarist: *Life of Samuel Johnson* (1791).

Elizabeth Bowen (1899–1973), Anglo-Irish novelist: *The Death of the Heart* (1938).

Ray Bradbury (1920–), American sci-fi author: *Martian Chronicles* (1950), *Fahrenheit 451* (1953).

Anne Bradstreet (c. 1612–1672), American poet: *The Tenth Muse Lately Sprung Up in America* (1650).

Bertolt Brecht (1898–1956), German dramatist and poet. Borrowing freely from past writers, he combined polemics and lyricism in such plays as *The Threepenny Opera* (1928), *Mother Courage* (1940).

Louis Bromfield (1896–1956): American novelist: *Early Autumn* (1926) won a Pulitzer Prize.

Charlotte Brontë (1816–55), English novelist: *Jane Eyre* (1847).

Emily Brontë (1818–48), English novelist: *Wuthering Heights* (1847).

Rupert Brooke (1887–1915), English poet: his work treats the horrors of World War I.

Gwendolyn Brooks (1917–), American poet: *Annie Allen* (1949) won a Pulitzer Prize.

Van Wyck Brooks (1886–1963), American critic and historian: *The Flowering of New England* (1936) won a Pulitzer Prize.

Elizabeth Barrett Browning (1806–61), English poet and translator who was the wife of Robert Browning.

Robert Browning (1812–89), English dramatic poet: *The Ring and the Book (1869).*

William Cullen Bryant (1794–1878), American poet: *Thanatopsis* (1817).

Pearl S. Buck (1892–1973), American novelist: *The Good Earth* (1931) won Nobel Prize and Pulitzer Prize in 1932.

John Bunyan (1628–88), English allegorist: *Pilgrim's Progress* (1678).

Edmund Burke (1729–97), English essayist and orator: *American Taxation* (1774) and *Letter to the Sheriff of Bristol* (1777) pleaded cause of American colonists.

Robert Burns (1759–96), Scottish lyric poet and ballad writer: "The Cotter's Saturday Night."

Edgar Rice Burroughs (1875–1950), American adventure and science-fiction writer, best known for his many Tarzan jungle stories.

John Burroughs (1837–1921), American outdoors writer: *Camping and Tramping with Roosevelt* (1907), *Under the Apple-Trees* (1916).

George Gordon, Lord Byron (1788–1824), English lyric poet: *Don Juan* (1819–24).

James Branch Cabell (1879–1958), American novelist: *Jurgen* (1919).

Caius Julius Caesar (100?–44 B.C.), Roman statesman and historian: *The Gallic Wars.*

James Mallahan Cain (1892–1977), American crime novelist: *The Postman Always Rings Twice* (1934), *Double Indemnity* (1936), *Mildred Pierce* (1941).

Erskine Caldwell (1903–), American novelist: *Tobacco Road* (1932), *God's Little Acre* (1933).

(Janet) Taylor Caldwell (1900–), American novelist: *Dear and Glorious Physician* (1959), *Testimony of Two Men* (1968), *Captains and Kings* (1972).

Albert Camus (1913–60), French essayist and novelist. His *Myth of Sisyphus* (1955) was an existentialist essay. His novels include *The Stranger* (1946) and *The Plague* (1948). He won a Nobel Prize in 1957.

Karel Capek (1890–1938), Czech dramatist: *R.U.R.* (*Rossum's Universal Robots,* 1921).

Truman Capote (1924–), American short-story writer and essayist: *Other Voices, Other Rooms* (1948); *In Cold Blood* (1965), a documentary; *Music for Chameleons* (1980).

Thomas Carlyle (1795–1881), Scottish critic and historical essayist: *The French Revolution* (1837).

Lewis Carroll (real name **Charles Lutwidge Dodgson**; 1832–98), British mathematician and author: *Alice's Adventures in Wonderland* (1865).

Joyce Cary (1888–1957), Anglo-Irish novelist: *The Horse's Mouth* (1944).

Giovanni Casanova (1752–98), Italian memoirist. His amorous and adventurous *Memoirs* were not published in their complete form until 1960–61.

Willa Cather (1873–1947), American novelist: *O Pioneers!* (1913), *My Antonia* (1918); *One of Ours* (1922) won a Pulitzer Prize.

Bruce Catton (1899–1978), American historian: *A Stillness at Appomattox* (1953) won a Pulitzer Prize.

Caius Valerius Catullus (84?–54 B.C.), Roman poet. Of his numerous lyric poems, 116 are extant.

Miguel de Cervantes Saavedra (1547?–1616), Spanish novelist: *Don Quixote* (1614).

Raymond Chandler (1888–1959), American mystery and detective novelist: *The Big Sleep* (1939).

François René de Chateaubriand (1768–1848), French essayist and novelist. Best known for his autobiography, *Mémoires d'outre-tombe* (1850).

Geoffrey Chaucer (1343?–1400), English poet: *Canterbury Tales* (c. 1387), *Troilus and Criseyde* (c. 1385).

John Cheever (1912–82), American novelist: *The Wapshot Chronicle* (1951), *Bullet Park* (1969), *Falconer* (1977); *The Stories of John Cheever* (1978) won a Pulitzer Prize.

Anton Chekhov (1860–1904), Russian dramatist and short-story writer. After achieving success in short fiction he produced several great plays, including *The Sea Gull* (1896) and *The Cherry Orchard* (1904).

G. K. (Gilbert Keith) Chesterton (1874–1936), English novelist, poet, and critic who created the "Father Brown" detective story series.

Agatha Christie (1891–1976), English mystery novelist: *The Murder of Roger Ackroyd* (1926) and more than 50 other crime novels.

Sir Winston Churchill (1874–1965), English statesman and historian: *History of the English-Speaking Peoples* (4 vols., 1956–58).

John Ciardi (1916–), American poet: *As If: Poems New and Selected* (1955).

Marcus Tullius Cicero (106–43 B.C.), Roman statesman and orator: wrote many essays.

Arthur C. Clarke (1917–), British science-fiction author: *Against the Fall of Night* (1953); coauthor of movie *2001: A Space Odyssey* (1968).

Jean Cocteau (1891–1963), French dramatist, novelist, and poet: *Les Enfants Terribles* (1929), a drama.

Robert Peter Tristram Coffin (1892–1955), American writer: *Strange Holiness* (1935) won a Pulitzer Prize.

Samuel Taylor Coleridge (1772–1834), English poet and critic: collaborated with Wordsworth in the book of verse *Lyrical Ballads* (1798); *Biographia Literaria* (1817), essays on criticism.

Colette (full name **Sidonie Gabrielle Colette**; 1873–1954), French novelist and a leading feminist: *Chéri* (1920), *Gigi* (1945).

Padraic Colum (1881–1972), Irish-American novelist, dramatist, and poet. He was a leader of the Irish literary revival during the early 20th century.

Ivy Compton-Burnett (1892–1969), English novelist: *Brother and Sister* (1929).

William Congreve (1670–1729), English comic dramatist: *The Way of the World* (1700).

Marc Connelly (1890–1980), American playwright: *Green Pastures* (1930) won a Pulitzer Prize.

Joseph Conrad (1857–1924), Polish-born British novelist and short-story writer: *Lord Jim* (1900), *Typhoon* (1903); *Tales of Hearsay* (1925), stories.

James Fenimore Cooper (1789–1851), American novelist: *The Last of the Mohicans* (1826).

Noel Coward (1899–1973), English playwright and

AUTHORS AND WRITERS *(continued)*
composer: *Private Lives* (1930); *Blithe Spirit* (1941).
Malcolm Cowley (1898–), American literary critic: *Exile's Return* (1934), *The Literary Situation* (1954), *The Faulkner-Cowley File* (1966).
James Gould Cozzens (1903–78), American novelist: *Guard of Honor* (1948) won a Pulitzer Prize; *By Love Possessed* (1957).
Hart Crane (1899–1932), U.S. poet: *The Bridge* (1930).
Stephen Crane (1871–1900), American novelist: *The Red Badge of Courage* (1895).
A. J. Cronin (1896–1981), British author: *The Keys of the Kingdom* (1941).
Russel Crouse, see Howard Lindsay.
E. E. (Edward Estin) Cummings (1894–1962), American poet. His books of lyric verse, including *Tulips and Chimneys* (1923), experimented with unusual typographical styles.
Richard Henry Dana Jr. (1815–1882), American author: *Two Years Before the Mast* (1840).
Gabriele D'Annunzio (1863–1938), Italian poet, novelist, playwright: *La città morta* (1898), a play.
Dante Alighieri (1265–1321), Italian epic poet. His *Divine Comedy* ranks as the most important literary work of the Middle Ages.
Owen Davis (1874–1956), American playwright: *Icebound* (1923) won a Pulitzer Prize.
Clarence S. Day Jr. (1874–1935), American author: *Life with Father* (1935).
Thomas De Quincey (1785–1859), English author: *Confessions of an English Opium Eater* (1821).
Daniel Defoe (1660–1731), English novelist and journalist: *Robinson Crusoe* (1720), *Moll Flanders* (1722), *Journal of the Plague Year* (1722).
Charles Dickens (1812–70), English novelist: *Pickwick Papers* (1836), *Oliver Twist* (1837–39), *David Copperfield* (1849–50), *Great Expectations* (1860–61).
James Dickey (1925–), American poet and novelist: *Into the Stone* (1960), poetry; *Deliverance* (1970).
Emily Dickinson (1830–86), American poet. Her lyric poems reflect solitude and preoccupation with death.
Denis Diderot (1713–84), French encyclopedist and novelist.
George Dillon (1906–68), American poet: *The Flowering Stone* (1931) won a Pulitzer Prize.
Isak Dinesen (real name **Karen Blixen**; 1885–1962), Danish novelist: *Seven Gothic Tales* (1934).
E. L. (Edgar Lawrence) Doctorow (1931–), American novelist: *The Book of Daniel* (1971), *Ragtime* (1975), *Loon Lake* (1980).
J. P. (James Patrick) Donleavy (1926–), American novelist: *The Ginger Man* (1955), *Schultz* (1979).
John Donne (1572–1631), English poet and preacher noted for his metaphysical and devotional poems.
Hilda Doolittle ("H. D."; 1886–1961), American poet of the American Imagist movement.
John Dos Passos (1896–1970), American novelist: *U.S.A.*, a trilogy consisting of *The 42d Parallel* (1930), *1919* (1932), and *The Big Money* (1936).
Feodor Dostoyevsky (1821–81), Russian novelist: *Memoirs from the House of the Dead* (1861–62), *Crime and Punishment* (1866), *The Idiot* (1868), *The Possessed* (1871–72), *The Brothers Karamazov* (1879–80).
Lloyd C. Douglas (1877–1951), American author: *Magnificent Obsession* (1929), *Green Light* (1935), *The Robe* (1942), *The Big Fisherman* (1948).
Sir Arthur Conan Doyle (1859–1930), Scottish mystery novelist and creator of Sherlock Holmes.
Theodore Dreiser (1871–1945), American novelist: *Sister Carrie* (1900), *An American Tragedy* (1925).
Allen Drury (1918–), U.S. novelist: *Advise and Consent* (1960) won a Pulitzer Prize; *Anna Hastings* (1977); *The Hill of Summer* (1981).
John Dryden (1631–1700), English poet, dramatist, and critic: *Fables, Ancient and Modern* (1699).
Alexandre Dumas, père (1802–70), French novelist and dramatist: *The Count of Monte Cristo* (1844) and *The Three Musketeers* (1844).
Alexandre Dumas, fils (1824–95), French dramatist: *Monsieur Alphonse* (1873), *Denise* (1885).
Will Durant (1885–), U.S. historian and philosopher: *The Story of Philosophy* (1926), *The Story of Civilization* (12 vols., begun in 1935); *Rousseau and Revolution* (1967) won a Pulitzer Prize for nonfiction.
Lawrence Durrell (1912—), English novelist: *The Alexandria Quartet* (1958–60), *Tunc* (1968).
Richard Eberhart (1904–), American poet: *Selected Poems* (1965) won a Pulitzer Prize.
Leon Edel (1907–), American literary historian and biographer: *Henry James* (1953–72), a 5-volume biography. The third volume, *Henry James: The Middle Years* (1962), won a Pulitzer Prize and a National Book Award.
Ilya Ehrenberg (1891–1967), Russian novelist: *A Street in Moscow* (1930), *Out of Chaos* (1934).
George Eliot (real name **Marian Evans**; 1819–80), English novelist: *Silas Marner* (1861).
T. S. (Thomas Stearns) Eliot (1888–1965), American-born English poet and critic: *The Lovesong of J. Alfred Prufrock* (1917), *The Wasteland* (1922). He won a Nobel Prize in 1948.
Ralph Ellison (1914–), American novelist: *Invisible Man* (1952).
Ralph Waldo Emerson (1803–82), American essayist and poet; developed transcendentalist philosophy.
Euripides (485?–406 B.C.), Greek tragic dramatist. Of about 92 plays 19 are extant, including *Medea* (431 B.C.) and *Electra* (413 B.C.).
James T. Farrell (1904–79), American novelist: *Studs Lonigan* (1932–35), a trilogy.
William Faulkner (1897–1962), American novelist: *The Sound and the Fury* (1929) and *Light in August* (1932). He won a Nobel Prize in 1949 and Pulitzer Prizes for *A Fable* (1954) and *The Reivers* (1962).
Edna Ferber (1885–1968), American novelist: *So Big* (1924) won a Pulitzer Prize; *Show Boat* (1926); *Cimarron* (1930); *Giant* (1952).
Lawrence Ferlinghetti (1919–), American beat-generation poet; *A Coney Island of the Mind* (1958).
Eugene Field (1850–95), American poet and journalist: best known for children's poems "Little Boy Blue" and "Wynken, Blynken, and Nod."
Henry Fielding (1707–54), English novelist and dramatist: *Joseph Andrews* (1742), *Tom Jones* (1749).
Edward Fitzgerald (1809–83), English poet, translated Omar Khayyam's *Rubaiyat* in 1859.
F. (Francis) Scott Fitzgerald (1896–1940), American novelist and short-story writer: *This Side of Paradise* (1920), *The Great Gatsby* (1925).
Gustave Flaubert (1821–80), French novelist: *Madame Bovary* (1857).
Ford Madox Ford (real name **Ford Madox Hueffer**; 1873–1939), English novelist and poet: *The Good Soldier* (1915), *Parade's End* (1924–28), a tetralogy published in one volume in 1950.
E. M. (Edward Morgan) Forster (1879–1970), English novelist and critic: *A Passage to India* (1924), a novel; *Aspects of the Novel* (1927), criticism.
John Fowles (1926–), English novelist: *The Collector* (1963), *The Magus* (1966), *The French Lieutenant's Woman* (1970), *Mantissa* (1982).
Anatole France (real name **Anatole Jacques Thibault**; 1844–1924), French novelist and satirist: *Balthasar* (1889), short stories; won a Nobel Prize in 1921.
Douglas Southall Freeman (1886–1953), American historian: *R. E. Lee*, 4 vols. (1934), and *George Washington*, 7 vols. (1948–57) won Pulitzer Prizes.
Robert Frost (1874–1963), American lyric poet captured much of the American rural spirit. He won four Pulitzer Prizes for *New Hampshire* (1923), *Collected*

Poems (1930), *A Further Range* (1936), and *A Witness Tree* (1942).

Christopher Fry (1907–), English dramatist and translator: *The Lady's Not for Burning* (1949).

John Galsworthy (1867–1933), English novelist and playwright: *The Forsyte Saga* (1922), a trilogy.

Erle Stanley Gardner (1889–1970), American detective-story writer: *The Case of the Velvet Claws* (1933) was his first novel featuring the lawyer Perry Mason.

William H. Gass (1924–), American novelist and critic: *Omensetter's Luck* (1966), a novel; *In the Heart of the Heart of the Country* (1968).

John Gay (1685–1732), English dramatist and poet: *The Beggar's Opera* (1728).

Jean Genet (1910–), French novelist and dramatist: *The Balcony* (1957) and *The Blacks* (1959), dramas; *Miracle of the Rose* (1951), a novel.

Edward Gibbon (1737–94), English historian: *The Decline and Fall of the Roman Empire* (1776–88).

André Gide (1869–1951), French novelist: *The Immoralist* (1902), *Straight Is the Gate* (1909); awarded 1947 Nobel Prize.

Allen Ginsberg (1926–), American poet of beat and hippie movements: *Howl and Other Poems* (1955). His *The Fall of America: Poems of These States* (1973) won a National Book Award.

Jean Giraudoux (1882–1944), French dramatist: *Tiger at the Gates* (1935).

Ellen Glasgow (1874–1945), American novelist: *In This Our Life* (1941) won a Pulitzer Prize.

Johann Wolfgang von Goethe (1749–1832), German poet and dramatist. His greatest work was the dramatic poem *Faust* (1808 and 1833).

Nikolai Vasilyevich Gogol (1809–52), Russian novelist, short-story writer, and playwright: *The Inspector General* (1836), a play; *Dead Souls* (1842), a novel.

William Golding (1911–), English novelist: *Lord of the Flies* (1954) and *Darkness Visible* (1979); won 1983 Nobel Prize in Literature.

Oliver Goldsmith (1730?–74), Irish novelist, poet, and dramatist: *The Vicar of Wakefield* (1766), a novel; *She Stoops to Conquer* (1773), a drama.

Maxim Gorki (real name **Aleksey Maximovich Pyeshkov**; 1868–1936), Russian dramatist and novelist: *The Lower Depths* (1902), play; *Mother* (1907), novel.

Gunter Grass (1927–), German novelist: *The Tin Drum* (1959), *Local Anaesthetic* (1970), *The Meeting at Telgate* (1981).

Shirley Ann Grau (1929–), American novelist: *The Keepers of the House* (1964), which won a Pulitzer Prize; *The Condor Passes* (1971).

Robert Graves (1895–), English poet, novelist, and critic. Besides much lyric verse, he wrote such novels as *I, Claudius* (1934).

Thomas Gray (1716–71), English poet: "Elegy Written in a Country Churchyard" (1750).

Graham Greene (1904–), English novelist: *The Power and the Glory* (1940); *The Comedians* (1966); *A Sort of Life* (1971), autobiography; *The Honorary Consul* (1973); *The Human Factor* (1978); *Monsignor Quixote* (1982).

Lady Augusta Gregory (1852–1932), Irish dramatist and founder of Dublin's Abbey Theatre: her plays include *The Rising of the Moon* (1907).

Zane Grey (1872–1939), U.S. novelist of Old West: *The Last of The Plainsmen* (1908), *Riders of The Purple Sage* (1912).

John Gunther (1901–70), American author: *Inside Europe* (1936), *Inside Asia* (1939).

A. B. Guthrie Jr. (1901–), American novelist: *The Big Sky* (1947); *The Way West* (1949) won a Pulitzer Prize.

Alex Haley (1921–), American author: *Roots* (1976) won a special Pulitzer Prize.

James Norman Hall, see Charles Nordhoff.

Dashiell Hammett (1894–1961), U.S. detective-story writer: created Sam Spade in *The Maltese Falcon* (1930) and Nick and Nora Charles in *The Thin Man* (1934).

Knut Hamsun (1859–1952), Norwegian novelist: *Growth of the Soil* (1920), *Mysteries* (1927). He won a Nobel Prize in 1920.

Lorraine Hansberry (1930–65), American black playwright: *A Raisin in the Sun* (1959).

Thomas Hardy (1840–1928), English novelist, poet, and dramatist: *Tess of the D'Urbervilles* (1891) and *Jude the Obscure* (1895), novels.

Joel Chandler Harris (1848–1908), American novelist and short-story writer who recorded Southern dialect: *Uncle Remus: His Songs and His Sayings* (1881).

Moss Hart (1904–61), American playwright and stage director: co-winner of Pulitzer Prize for *You Can't Take It With You* (1936). Wrote many plays and musicals including *Lady in the Dark* (1941), *Winged Victory* (1943).

Bret Harte (1836–1902), American western author: *The Luck of Roaring Camp* (1870).

Gerhart Hauptmann (1862–1946), German dramatist, poet, and novelist: *Before Dawn* (1889), a play.

Nathaniel Hawthorne (1804–64), American novelist and short-story writer: *The Scarlet Letter* (1850), *The House of Seven Gables* (1851).

Heinrich Heine (1797–1856), German poet: His lyrics used in songs of Schubert, Liszt, and Schumann.

Robert A. Heinlein (1907–), American science-fiction author: *Stranger in a Strange Land* (1961), *The Past Through Tomorrow* (1967).

Joseph Heller (1923–), U.S. novelist: *Catch-22* (1961), *Something Happened* (1974), *Good as Gold* (1979).

Lillian Hellman (1905–), American playwright: *The Children's Hour* (1934), *The Little Foxes* (1939), *Watch on the Rhine* (1941); *An Unfinished Woman* (1969), autobiography.

Ernest Hemingway (1899–1961), American novelist and short-story writer: *A Farewell to Arms* (1929); *For Whom the Bell Tolls* (1940); *The Old Man and the Sea* (1952) won a Pulitzer Prize. He was awarded a Nobel Prize in 1954.

O. Henry (William Sydney Porter; 1862–1910), U.S. short-story writer of about 300 stories memorable for concise plotting and surprise endings.

Herodotus (484?–425 B.C.), Greek historian: *History of the Persian Wars.*

Robert Herrick (1591–1674), English poet. His highly polished verse reflects classical influences.

John Hersey (1914–), American novelist and journalist: *A Bell for Adano* (1944) won a Pulitzer Prize; *Hiroshima* (1946), *The Walnut Door* (1977).

Hermann Hesse (1877–1962), German poet and novelist: *Steppenwolf* (1927), *Magister Ludi* (1949). He won a Nobel Prize in 1946.

Robert Silliman Hillyer (1895–1961), American poet: *Collected Verse* (1933) won a Pulitzer Prize.

Laura Z. Hobson (1900–), U.S. novelist: *Gentleman's Agreement* (1947); *Over and Above* (1979); *Untold Millions* (1982).

Oliver Wendell Holmes (1809–94), American poet, essayist: "Old Ironsides" (1830), a poem; *Autocrat of the Breakfast Table* (1858), sketches.

Homer (c. 800–700 B.C.), Greek epic poet: the *Odyssey*, the *Iliad.*

Gerard Manley Hopkins (1844–89), English mystical poet: "The Windhover" (1918).

Horace (65–8 B.C.), Latin poet. He published three books of *Odes* and two books of *Satires.*

Paul Horgan (1903–), American author: won Pulitzer Prizes for *Great River* (1954) and *Lamy of Santa Fe* (1975).

A. E. (Alfred Edward) Housman (1859–1936), English poet: *A Shropshire Lad* (1896).

AUTHORS AND WRITERS *(continued)*

William Dean Howells (1837–1920), American novelist and critic: *The Rise of Silas Lapham* (1885), *A Hazard of New Fortunes* (1890).

Victor Hugo (1802–85), French novelist, poet, and dramatist: novels include *Notre Dame de Paris* (1831) and *Les Misérables* (1862).

Aldous Huxley (1894–1963), English novelist and essayist: *Brave New World* (1932).

Henrik Ibsen (1828–1906), Norwegian dramatist. He pioneered social realism in such plays as *A Doll's House* (1879) and *Rosmersholm* (1886).

William Inge (1913–73), American dramatist: *Come Back, Little Sheba* (1950); *Picnic* (1952) won a Pulitzer Prize; *The Dark at the Top of the Stairs* (1958).

Eugene Ionesco (1912–), French dramatist. A pioneer in the theater of the absurd, his plays include *The Chairs* (1952) and *Rhinoceros* (1960).

Washington Irving (1783–1859), American editor and short-story writer: "Rip Van Winkle" and "The Legend of Sleepy Hollow" (both 1820).

Christopher Isherwood (1904–), English dramatist and novelist. His collection of sketches, *Goodbye to Berlin* (1939), was adapted for the stage in 1951 by John Van Druten as *I Am a Camera,* as was the musical *Cabaret* in 1971.

Henry James (1843–1916), American novelist and short-story writer: *Wings of the Dove* (1902), *The Ambassadors* (1903), *The Golden Bowl* (1904).

Marquis James (1891–1955), American author: won Pulitzer Prizes for biographies *The Raven* (1929) and *Andrew Jackson* (1937).

Randall Jarrell (1914–65), American poet: *Little Friend, Little Friend* (1945), poems of World War II.

Robinson Jeffers (1887–1962), American poet: *Give Your Heart to the Hawks* (1933).

Samuel Johnson (1709–84), English essayist, critic, poet, and lexicographer: his essays in *The Rambler* helped establish literary standards; famous for his witty *Dictionary of the English Language* (1755).

James Jones (1921–77), American novelist: *From Here to Eternity* (1951) won a National Book Award.

Ben Jonson (1573?–1637), English dramatist and poet: *Volpone* (1606), *The Alchemist* (1610).

James Joyce (1882–1941), Irish novelist, poet, and short-story writer. He applied poetic techniques to his novels, *A Portrait of the Artist as a Young Man* (1916), *Ulysses* (1922), and *Finnegans Wake* (1939). *Dubliners* (1914) is a short-story collection.

Juvenal (55?–135), Roman satirical poet.

Franz Kafka (1883–1924), Austrian novelist: *Amerika* (1927), *The Castle* (1930), *The Trial* (1937).

MacKinlay Kantor (1904–77), American novelist, won a Pulitzer Prize for *Andersonville* (1955).

George S. Kaufman (1889–1961), American playwright and director: co-recipient of Pulitzer Prizes for *Of Thee I Sing* (1931) and *You Can't Take It With You* (1936).

Nikos Kazantzakis (1883?–1957), Greek novelist: *Zorba the Greek* (1946).

Alfred Kazin (1915–), American critic: *On Native Grounds* (1942), *The Inmost Leaf* (1955).

John Keats (1795–1821), English poet: "Ode on a Grecian Urn" and "To a Nightingale" (both 1820).

George Edward Kelly (1887–1974), American playwright: *Craig's Wife* (1925) won a Pulitzer Prize.

Rudyard Kipling (1865–1936), English poet, novelist, and short-story writer: *The Light That Failed* (1890), *Barrack Room Ballads* (1892), *The Jungle Book* (1894), *Captains Courageous* (1897), *Kim* (1901), *Just So Stories* (1902); won a Nobel Prize in 1907.

George Lyman Kittredge (1860–1941), American literary scholar: *Shakespeare* (1916).

Arthur Koestler (1905–83), British-Hungarian political novelist: *Darkness at Noon* (1941).

Oliver La Farge (1901–63), American author: *Laughing Boy* (1929) won a Pulitzer Prize.

Jean de La Fontaine (1621–95), French fabulist and poet: *Fables choisies mises en vers* (1668–94) consists of about 230 fables.

Pär Lägerkvist (1891–1974), Swedish Nobel Prize-winning author: *Barabas* (1951).

Charles Lamb (1775–1834), English essayist and critic. With his sister Mary he wrote the children's book *Tales from Shakespeare* (1807).

Sidney Lanier (1842–81), American poet and critic: *Poems* (1887).

Ring Lardner (1885–1933), American satirist and short-story writer: *You Know Me, Al* (1916).

D. H. (David Herbert) Lawrence (1885–1930), English novelist, poet, and critic: *Sons and Lovers* (1913), *Lady Chatterley's Lover* (1928).

Harper Lee (1926–), American novelist: *To Kill a Mockingbird* (1960) won a Pulitzer Prize.

Cecil Day Lewis (1904–72), English essayist and novelist: *Overtures to Death* (1938), poems. He became poet laureate of England in 1968.

C. S. (Clive Staples) Lewis (1898–1963), English religious essayist and poet: *The Allegory of Love* (1936), *The Screwtape Letters* (1942).

Sinclair Lewis (1885–1951), American novelist: *Main Street* (1920), *Babbitt* (1922), *Elmer Gantry* (1927); *Arrowsmith* (1925) won a Pulitzer Prize. He won a Nobel Prize in 1930.

Howard Lindsay (1889–1968) American playwright: coauthor with Russel Crouse (1893–1966) of Pulitzer Prize-winning *State of the Union* (1945) and long-running *Life with Father* (1939), in which Lindsay starred as actor.

Vachel Lindsay (1879–1931), American poet: *General William Booth Enters into Heaven* (1913).

Livy (59 B.C.–A.D. 17), Roman historian; 35 books of his 142-book *History of Rome* are extant.

Jack London (1876–1916), American novelist: *The Call of the Wild* (1903), *Martin Eden* (1909).

Henry Wadsworth Longfellow (1807–82), American poet: *Evangeline* (1847).

Federico García Lorca (1899–1936), Spanish poet and dramatist: *Blood Wedding* (1938).

Amy Lowell (1874–1925), American poet, pioneered free verse: *Sword Blades and Poppy Seeds* (1914); *What's O'Clock* (1925) won a Pulitzer Prize.

James Russell Lowell (1819–91), American poet and essayist: *A Fable for Critics* (1848).

Robert Lowell (1917–77), American poet and critic: *Lord Weary's Castle* (1946) and *The Dolphin* (1973) won Pulitzer Prizes.

Ross Macdonald (pseudonym of **Kenneth Millar**; 1915–), American mystery writer: *The Chill* (1964), *The Underground Man* (1971), *The Blue Hammer* (1976).

Niccolò Machiavelli (1469–1527), Italian essayist and dramatist: *The Prince* (1532).

Archibald MacLeish (1892–1982), American poet and dramatist. He won Pulitzer Prizes for poetry with *Conquistador* (1932) and *Collected Poems* (1952). His drama *J. B.* (1958) also won a Pulitzer Prize.

Norman Mailer (1923–), American novelist and essayist: *The Naked and the Dead* (1948), *Why Are We in Vietnam?* (1967). *The Armies of the Night* (1968) and *The Executioner's Song* (1979) won Pulitzer Prizes.

Bernard Malamud (1914–), American novelist: *The Natural* (1952), *The Assistant* (1957), *Dubin's Lives* (1979); *The Fixer* (1966) won a National Book Award and a Pulitzer Prize; *God's Grace* (1982).

Stéphane Mallarmé (1842–98), French poet: *L'Après-Midi d'un faune* (1887).

Sir Thomas Malory (died 1471), English writer of romances: *Morte D'Arthur* (1485).

André Malraux (1901–76), French novelist: *Man's*

Fate (1933); *The Voices of Silence* (1953), essays.

Thomas Mann (1875–1955), German novelist: *The Magic Mountain* (1927) and *Joseph and His Brothers* (1934–44); won Nobel Prize in 1929.

Katherine Mansfield (1888–1923), British short-story writer: *The Garden Party* (1922).

Edwin Markham (1852–1940), American poet: "The Man with the Hoe" (1899).

Christopher Marlowe (1564–93), English dramatist and poet: *Tamburlaine the Great* (1587?), *Dr. Faustus* (1588?).

John P. Marquand (1893–1960), American novelist: *The Late George Apley* (1937) won a Pulitzer Prize.

John Masefield (1878–1967), English poet laureate (1930–67): *Salt Water Ballads* (1902).

Edgar Lee Masters (1869–1950), American poet: *Spoon River Anthology* (1915).

W. Somerset Maugham (1874–1965), English novelist and playwright: *Of Human Bondage* (1915), *The Moon and Sixpence* (1919), *The Razor's Edge* (1944).

Guy de Maupassant (1850–93), French novelist and short-story writer. *Une Vie* (1883) is his best novel. His 300 masterful short stories include "The Necklace" and "The Piece of String."

François Mauriac (1885–1970), French novelist: *The Desert of Love* (1925). He won a Nobel Prize in 1952.

André Maurois (1885–1967), French novelist and biographer: *Ariel* (1923), a life of Shelley; *Proust*, (1949); *Memoirs* (1970).

Mary McCarthy (1912–), American novelist and essayist: *The Groves of Academe* (1952), *The Group* (1963), *Cannibals and Missionaries* (1979), novels.

Carson McCullers (1917–67), American novelist and playwright: *Member of the Wedding* (1946).

Phyllis McGinley (1905–78), American poet: *Times Three: Selected Verse from Three Decades* (1961) won a Pulitzer Prize.

Herman Melville (1819–91), American novelist. His allegorical *Moby-Dick*, (1851) is his masterpiece. His last great book, *Billy Budd*, was published in 1924.

H. L. (Henry Louis) Mencken (1880–1956), American satirist, editor, and essayist: *Prejudices* (1919–27), *Treatise on Right and Wrong* (1934), *The American Language* (1919, 1946, 1948).

George Meredith (1828–1909), English novelist: *The Ordeal of Richard Feverel* (1859), *The Egoist* (1879).

W. S. Merwin (1927–), American poet: *The Carrier of Ladders* (1970) won a Pulitzer Prize.

James A. Michener (1907–), American novelist: *Tales of the South Pacific* (1947) won a Pulitzer Prize; *The Source* (1965), *Centennial* (1974), *Chesapeake* (1978), *The Covenant* (1980), *Space* (1982), *Poland* (1983).

John Stuart Mill (1806–73), English philosopher: *Essay on Liberty* (1859), *Utilitarianism* (1863).

Edna St. Vincent Millay (1892–1950), American poet best remembered for her sonnets. *The Ballad of the Harp-Weaver* (1922) won a Pulitzer Prize.

Arthur Miller (1915–), American playwright: *Death of a Salesman* (1949) won a Pulitzer Prize; *The Crucible* (1953), *A View From the Bridge* (1955), *After the Fall* (1964), *The Price* (1968).

Henry Miller (1891–1980), American novelist: *Tropic of Cancer* (1934), *Tropic of Capricorn* (1939).

Joaquin Miller (1839?–1913), American poet; *Song of the Sierras* (1871), *Life Among the Modocs* (1873).

A. A. (Alan Alexander) Milne (1882–1956), English poet and children's writer: *Winnie-the-Pooh* (1926).

Czeslaw Milosz (1911–), Polish-born American poet: *Postwar Polish Poetry* (1965), *Bells in Winter* (1978); won Nobel Prize in 1980.

John Milton (1608–74), English poet. His epic *Paradise Lost* (1667) is a literary landmark.

Margaret Mitchell (1900–49), American novelist: *Gone with the Wind* (1936) won a Pulitzer Prize.

Jean Baptiste Molière (1622–73), French dramatist and one of the great comic playwrights of all time. His works include *The Miser* (1668) and *The Doctor in Spite of Himself* (1666).

Michel Eyquem de Montaigne (1533–92), French essayist and one of the world's great literary stylists.

Marianne Moore (1887–1972), American poet: *Collected Poems* (1951) won a Pulitzer Prize; *O to Be a Dragon* (1959).

Alberto Moravia (1907–), Italian novelist: *Two Women* (1957), *The Empty Canvas* (1961).

Sir Thomas More (1478–1535), English essayist: *Utopia* (1516).

Samuel Eliot Morison (1887–1976), American historian: *Admiral of the Ocean Sea* (1942) and *John Paul Jones* (1959) won Pulitzer Prizes.

Christopher Morley (1890–1957), American novelist and editor: *Kitty Foyle* (1939), a novel.

Iris Murdoch (1919–), Anglo-Irish novelist: *The Bell* (1958), *A Severed Head* (1961), *The Sacred and Profane Love Machine* (1974).

Vladimir Nabokov (1899–1977), Russian-American novelist: *Lolita* (1955), *Pnin* (1957), *Pale Fire* (1962), *Ada* (1969).

Ogden Nash (1902–71), American humorous poet: *Hard Lines* (1931), *I'm a Stranger Here Myself* (1938), *You Can't Get There From Here* (1957).

Robert Nathan (1894–), American author: novel *Portrait of Jennie* (1940), poetry *The Green Leaf: Collected Poems* (1950).

Allan Nevins (1890–1971) American historian: won Pulitzer Prizes for *Grover Cleveland* (1933) and *Hamilton Fish* (1936).

Charles Bernard Nordhoff (1887–1947) and **James Norman Hall** (1887–1951), American writing team: *Lafayette Flying Corps* (1920), *Mutiny on the Bounty* (1932), *The Hurricane* (1935).

Frank Norris (1870–1902), American novelist: *McTeague* (1899), *The Octopus* (1901), *The Pit* (1902).

Joyce Carol Oates (1938–), American novelist and critic: *Them* (1969), a novel, won a National Book Award; *Childworld* (1976); *Unholy Loves* (1979); *Bellefleur* (1980), *Angel of Light* (1981).

Sean O'Casey (1884–1964), Irish playwright: *The Shadow of a Gunman* (1923), *Juno and the Paycock* (1924), *The Plough and the Stars* (1926).

Edwin O'Connor (1918–1968), American novelist: *The Last Hurrah* (1956); *The Edge of Sadness* (1961) won a Pulitzer Prize.

Flannery O'Connor (1925–64), American novelist and short-story writer: *Wise Blood* (1952); *The Violent Bear It Away* (1960); *Complete Stories* (1971).

Clifford Odets (1906–63), American playwright: *Waiting for Lefty* (1935), *Golden Boy* (1937).

Sean O'Faoláin (1900–), Irish author: *King of the Beggars* (1938), biographies of Irish statesmen; *I Remember! I Remember!* (1961), short stories.

Liam O'Flaherty (1897–), Irish novelist: *The Informer* (1925).

John O'Hara (1905–70), American novelist and short-story writer: *Appointment in Samarra* (1934), *Butterfield 8* (1935), *Pal Joey* (1940), novels.

Omar Khayyam (11th century), Persian poet: *The Rubaiyat*.

Eugene O'Neill (1888–1953), American dramatist: *Mourning Becomes Electra* (1931) and *The Iceman Cometh* (1946). Four of his plays won Pulitzer Prizes: *Beyond the Horizon* (1919), *Anna Christie* (1921), *Strange Interlude* (1927), and *Long Day's Journey Into Night* (1941); won Nobel Prize in 1936.

José Ortega y Gasset (1883–1955), Spanish essayist and critic: *Meditations on Quixote* (1914), *The Revolt of the Masses* (1930).

George Orwell (1903–50), English satirist: *Animal Farm* (1946), *Nineteen Eighty-Four* (1949).

AUTHORS AND WRITERS *(continued)*

Ovid (43 B.C.A.D. 18), Latin poet: *Metamorphoses.*

Thomas Paine (1737–1809), American political essayist. His pamphlet *Common Sense* (1776) promoted America's independence from Britain.

Dorothy Parker (1893–1967), American poet and short-story writer: *Enough Rope* (1926), verse; *After Such Pleasures* (1933), *Here Lies* (1939), stories.

Boris Pasternak (1890–1960), Soviet poet, novelist, and translator of Shakespeare into Russian: *Doctor Zhivago* (1957), a novel; forced by his government to decline 1958 Nobel Prize.

Samuel Pepys (1633–1703), English diarist; presents vivid picture of Restoration London.

St.-John Perse (real name **Marie R.A.A.S. Léger;** 1887–1975), French poet who won a Nobel Prize in 1960. One of his best-known works is the long poem *Anabase* (1924).

Francesco Petrarch (1304–74), Italian poet of the Latin and Italian languages. He was among the first and greatest of the Renaissance poets and a popularizer of the sonnet form.

Harold Pinter (1930–), English dramatist: *The Birthday Party* (1957), *The Caretaker* (1959).

Luigi Pirandello (1867–1936), Italian playwright: *Six Characters in Search of an Author* (1920).

Sylvia Plath (1932–63), American poet and novelist: *Ariel* (1965), poems; *The Bell Jar* (1971), a novel.

Plutarch (45?–125), Greek biographer and essayist. His *Parallel Lives* is a collection of 46 biographies of notable Greek and Roman figures.

Edgar Allan Poe (1809–49), American poet and short-story writer: "The Raven" (1845) and "The Bells" (1847), poems; "The Fall of the House of Usher" (1839), and "The Gold Bug" (1843), stories.

Alexander Pope (1688–1744), English poet. His *Essay on Criticism* (1711) and *Essay on Man* (1734) used rhymed couplets in popularizing dominant ideas of the time; *The Rape of the Lock* (1714) is a landmark among mock-heroic poems.

Katherine Anne Porter (1890–1980), American short-story writer and novelist: *Pale Horse, Pale Rider* (1939), short stories; *Ship of Fools* (1962), a novel. Her *Collected Stories* (1965) won a National Book Award and a Pulitzer Prize.

Ezra Pound (1885–1972), American expatriate poet. He dominated the imagism and vorticism movements of early 1900s; best known for his serial poems, *Cantos* (1925–60).

John Boynton Priestley (1894–), English novelist: *The Good Companions* (1929).

Marcel Proust (1871–1922), French novelist. From 1913 to 1922 he produced 16-volume masterpiece, *Remembrance of Things Past.*

Aleksandr Sergeyevich Pushkin (1799–1837), Russian poet: *Eugene Onegin* (1828).

Salvatore Quasimodo (1901–68), Italian poet. His poems, philosophical interpretations of man's history, won a Nobel Prize in 1959.

Ellery Queen, pen name of Frederic Dannay (1905–82) and Manfred Lee (1905–1971), American detective-story writing team: Books featured detective Ellery Queen.

Francois Rabelais (1494?–1553), French satirist: *Gargantua* and *Pantagruel* (both 1532).

Jean Baptiste Racine (1639–99), French dramatist: *Britannicus* (1669) and *Bérénice* (1670).

Ayn Rand (1905–82), American novelist: *The Fountainhead* (1943), *Atlas Shrugged* (1957).

Marjorie Kinnan Rawlings (1896–1953), American novelist: *The Yearling* (1938) won a Pulitzer Prize.

Erich Maria Remarque (1897–1970), German-American novelist: *All Quiet on the Western Front* (1929), *Three Comrades* (1938).

Kenneth Rexroth (1905–82), American poet and critic: *Natural Numbers* (1963), poems; *Assays* (1961), essays; *The Morning Star* (1979).

Elmer Rice (1892–1967), American playwright: *Street Scene* (1929) won a Pulitzer Price; *Dream Girl* (1945).

I. A. (Ivor Armstrong) Richards (1893–1979), Anglo-American critic, pioneer in New Criticism movement: *Principles of Literary Criticism* (1925).

Samuel Richardson (1689–1761), English novelist: *Pamela* (1740), *Clarissa* (1747–48).

Conrad Richter (1890–1968), American novelist: *The Town* (1950) won a Pulitzer Prize.

James Whitcomb Riley (1849–1916), American poet best-known for Indiana dialect verse: *Rhymes of Childhood* (1890).

Rainer Maria Rilke (1875–1926), German poet; wrote on themes of spiritual isolation.

Arthur Rimbaud (1854–91), French poet: *A Season in Hell* (1873), *Les Illuminations* (1886).

Mary Roberts Rinehart (1876–1958), American mystery novelist: *The Circular Staircase* (1908).

Kenneth Roberts (1885–1957), American historical novelist: *Arundel* (1930), *Northwest Passage* (1937).

Edwin Arlington Robinson (1869–1935), American poet: *Collected Poems* (1921), *The Man Who Died Twice* (1924), and *Tristam* (1927) won Pulitzer Prizes.

Theodore Roethke (1908–63), American poet: *The Waking* (1953) won a Pulitzer Prize.

Romain Rolland (1866–1944), French novelist and biographer: biographies of Beethoven (1903) and Tolstoy (1911); 10-volume novel *Jean-Christophe* (1904–12) won a Nobel Prize in 1915.

Ole Edvart Rolvaag (1876–1931), Norwegian-American novelist: *Giants in the Earth* (1927).

Edmond Rostand (1868–1918), French dramatist and poet: *Cyrano de Bergerac* (1897).

Philip Roth (1933–), American novelist and short-story writer: *Goodbye Columbus* (1959), *Portnoy's Complaint* (1969), *The Ghost Writer* (1979).

Jean Jacques Rousseau (1712–78), French philosopher, novelist, and essayist: *The Social Contract* (1762), *Confessions* (1782).

John Ruskin (1819–1900), English critic and essayist: *The Seven Lamps of Architecture* (1849).

George Russell (**"A.E."**; 1867–1935), Irish poet: *Homeward: Songs by the Way* (1894).

Saki (real name **Hector Hugh Munro;** 1870–1916), English short-story writer. His stories are minor classics of satiric humor.

J. D. (Jerome David) Salinger (1919–), American novelist and short-story writer: *The Catcher in the Rye* (1951), *Franny and Zooey* (1961).

George Sand (real name **Amandine A. L. Dupin, Baronne Dudevant;** 1804–76), French novelist and playwright. She wrote about 80 novels that enjoyed wide popularity in their time.

Carl Sandburg (1878–1967), American poet and biographer. He wrote numerous poems celebrating America and an epic 6-volume biography of Abraham Lincoln (1926–39). *Cornhuskers* (1918), *Abraham Lincoln: The War Years* (1939), and *Complete Poems* (1950) won Pulitzer Prizes.

George Santayana (1863–1952), American poet and essayist. His *The Life of Reason* (1905–06) studied the development of human reason.

William Saroyan (1908–81), American novelist, dramatist, and short-story writer: *My Name Is Aram* (1940), short stories; *The Human Comedy* (1943), a novel. *The Time of Your Life* (1939), a play, won a Pulitzer Prize.

Jean Paul Sartre (1905–80), French philosopher, novelist, and playwright: *Being and Nothingness* (1943), a treatise on existentialism; *No Exit* (1944) and *Dirty Hands* (1948), plays; declined a Nobel Prize in 1964.

Siegfried Sassoon (1886–1967), English poet. Much of

his work derives from bitterness about World War I: *Counterattack* (1918).

Friedrich von Schiller (1759–1805), German dramatist, historian, and poet: *Wallenstein* (1798–99), a dramatic trilogy. His lyric "Ode to Joy" (1785) was used by Beethoven in his Ninth Symphony.

Delmore Schwartz (1913–66), American poet, critic, and editor: *Shenandoah* (1941).

Sir Walter Scott (1771–1832), British novelist and poet: *The Lady of the Lake* (1810), a poem; *Ivanhoe* (1820), a novel.

Lucius Annaeus Seneca (3 B.C.?–A.D. 65), Roman dramatist: *Phaedra* and *Thyestes.*

Robert Service (1874–1958), Canadian poet best known for popular Yukon ballads: *Songs of a Sourdough* (1907).

William Shakespeare (1564–1616), English dramatist and poet. In addition to his purely poetic works such as *Venus and Adonis* (1593) and the *Sonnets* (1609), he wrote comic, tragic, and historical dramas, including *The Merchant of Venice* (1597), *Henry IV* (two parts, 1597), *Hamlet* (1600–01), and *Macbeth* (1606?).

Karl Jay Shapiro (1913–), American writer: *V-Letter and Other Poems* (1944) won a Pulitzer Prize.

George Bernard Shaw (1856–1950), Irish-born dramatist, critic: *Man and Superman* (1903), *Major Barbara* (1905), *Pygmalion* (1912); won Nobel Prize in 1925.

Irwin Shaw (1913–), American novelist: *The Young Lions* (1948), *Rich Man, Poor Man* (1970); *Beggarman, Thief* (1977); *Top of the Hill* (1979); *Acceptable Losses* (1982).

Wilfrid Sheed (1930–), Anglo-American critic and novelist: editor of *G. K. Chesterton's Essays and Poems* (1957); *Max Jamison* (1970), a novel; *Transatlantic Blues* (1978); *Clare Booth Luce* (1982).

Mary Wollstonecraft Shelley (1797–1851), English author: *Frankenstein* (1818).

Percy Bysshe Shelley (1792–1822), English romantic poet: *Prometheus Unbound* (1820).

Richard Brinsley Sheridan (1751–1816), English dramatist: *The Rivals* (1775), *The School for Scandal* (1777).

Robert E. Sherwood (1896–1955), American author: plays, *Waterloo Bridge* (1930), *Idiot's Delight* (1936), *Abe Lincoln in Illinois* (1938), and *There Shall Be No Night* (1940) all won Pulitzer Prizes. Biography *Roosevelt and Hopkins* (1947) also won a Pulitzer Prize.

William L. Shirer (1904–), American journalist: *The Rise and Fall of the Third Reich* (1960).

Mikhail Sholokhov (1905–), Russian novelist: *The Silent Don* (1941); won Nobel Prize in 1965.

Neil Simon (1927–), American playwright: *Come Blow Your Horn* (1961); *Barefoot in the Park* (1963); *The Odd Couple* (1965); *Plaza Suite* (1968); *The Prisoner of Second Avenue* (1971); *California Suite* (1976); *They're Playing Our Song* (1979).

Upton Sinclair (1878–1968), American novelist: *The Jungle* (1906), *King Coal* (1917); *Dragon's Teeth* (1943) won a Pulitzer Prize.

Isaac Bashevis Singer (1904–), Polish-American author: won National Book Awards for *A Day of Pleasure: Stories of a Boy Growing Up in Warsaw* (1969) and *A Crown of Feathers* (1973); *Shosha* (1978); won 1978 Nobel Prize for Literature.

Dame Edith Sitwell (1887–1964), English poet and critic: *Rustic Elegies* (1927).

Aleksandr I. Solzhenitsyn (1918–), Russian novelist: *The Cancer Ward* (1968), *August 1914* (1972), *The Gulag Archipelago, 1918–1956* (1973). He won a Nobel Prize for literature in 1970.

Susan Sontag (1933–), American critic and novelist: *Against Interpretation* (1966), essays; *Death Kit* (1967), a novel.

Sophocles (496–406 B.C.), Greek dramatist: *Oedipus Rex* and *Electra.*

Muriel Spark (1918–), English novelist and short-story writer: *The Comforters* (1957), *The Prime of Miss Jean Brodie* (1961), *Territorial Rights* (1979).

Stephen Spender (1909–), English poet, critic, and editor. Much of his poetry is social protest.

Edmund Spenser (1552–99), English poet: *The Faerie Queene.*

Jean Stafford (1915–79), American novelist and short-story writer: *Boston Adventure* (1944). Her *Collected Stories* won a Pulitzer Prize in 1970.

Sir Richard Steele (1672–1729), English essayist and dramatist. With Joseph Addison he founded and contributed essays to the *Tatler* and the *Spectator.*

Wallace Stegner (1909–), American author: *Angle of Repose* (1971) won a Pulitzer Prize for fiction.

Gertrude Stein (1874–1946), American expatriate poet and critic: *Three Lives* (1908) and *The Autobiography of Alice B. Toklas* (1933).

John Steinbeck (1902–1968), American novelist: *The Grapes of Wrath* (1939) won a Pulitzer Prize; *East of Eden* (1952). He was awarded a Nobel Prize in 1962.

Stendhal (real name **Marie Henri Beyle;** 1783–1842), French novelist: *The Red and the Black* (1831), *The Charterhouse of Parma* (1839).

Laurence Sterne (1713–68), English novelist: *Tristram Shandy* (1760–67).

Wallace Stevens (1879–1955), American poet: *Harmonium* (1923); *Notes Toward a Supreme Fiction* (1942); *Collected Poems* (1954) won a Pulitzer Prize.

Robert Louis Stevenson (1850–94), Scottish novelist and poet: *Treasure Island* (1883), *A Child's Garden of Verses* (1885).

Irving Stone (1903–), American author: *Lust for Life* (1934), *The Agony and the Ecstasy* (1961), *The Origin* (1980).

Rex Todhunter Stout (1886–1975), American detective-story writer; wrote many books around fictional fat detective Nero Wolfe.

Harriet Beecher Stowe (1811–96), American novelist: *Uncle Tom's Cabin* (1852).

August Strindberg (1849–1912), Swedish dramatist and novelist: best known for such naturalistic dramas as *The Father* (1887) and *Miss Julie* (1888).

Jessee Hilton Stuart (1907–), American author: *Taps for Private Tussie* (1965).

William Styron (1925–), American novelist: *Lie Down in Darkness* (1951); *The Confessions of Nat Turner* (1967), which won a Pulitzer Prize; *Sophie's Choice* (1979).

Jacqueline Susann (1921–74), American novelist: *Valley of the Dolls* (1966), which sold a record 17 million copies; *The Love Machine* (1969), *Once Is Not Enough* (1973), *Dolores* (1976).

Jonathan Swift (1667–1745), English satirist, poet, and essayist: *Tale of a Tub* (1704), *Gulliver's Travels* (1726), *A Modest Proposal* (1729).

Algernon Charles Swinburne (1837–1909), English poet and critic: *Songs Before Sunrise* (1871).

John Millington Synge (1871–1909), Irish dramatist and poet: *Riders to the Sea* (1904), *Playboy of the Western World* (1907).

Cornelius Tacitus (55?–117?), Roman historian who recorded contemporary history of Rome.

Booth Tarkington (1869–1946), American novelist: *The Magnificent Ambersons* (1918) and *Alice Adams* (1922) won Pulitzer Prizes.

Allen Tate (1899–1979), American poet and critic: *Mr. Pope and Other Poems* (1928).

Sara Teasdale (1884–1933), American poet: *Love Songs* (1917) won first Pulitzer Prize for poetry in 1918; *Flame and Shadow* (1920), *Strange Victory* (1933).

Alfred Lord Tennyson (1809–92), English poet: *In Memoriam* (1850), *Idylls of the King* (1859–85).

William Makepeace Thackeray (1811–63), English novelist: *Vanity Fair* (1847–48).

Dylan Thomas (1914–53), Welsh poet. A major 20th

AUTHORS AND WRITERS *(continued)*
century lyric poet, he also wrote a drama for voices, *Under Milk Wood* (1954).

Henry David Thoreau (1817–62), American essayist and poet, champion of the individual against social organization: *Walden; or, Life in the Woods* (1854).

James Thurber (1894–1961), American humorist: *The Owl in the Attic and Other Perplexities* (1931), *My Life and Hard Times* (1934).

Alexis de Tocqueville (1805–59), French essayist and politician who studied and wrote extensively about the early days of the United States: *De la démocratie en Amérique* (4 vols., 1835–40).

J. R. R. Tolkien (1892–1973), British novelist: *The Hobbit* (1937), *Lord of the Rings* trilogy (1954–56), *The Silmarillion* (1977).

Leo Tolstoy (1828–1910), Russian novelist: *War and Peace* (1862–69), *Anna Karenina* (1875–77).

Arnold Toynbee (1889–1975), English historian: *A Study of History* (10 vols., 1934–54).

Lionel Trilling (1905–1975), American critic: *The Liberal Imagination* (1950).

Anthony Trollope (1815–82), English novelist: *The Warden* (1855), *Barchester Towers* (1857).

Thomas Tryon (1926–), American novelist: *The Other* (1971), *Lady* (1974).

Barbara Tuchman (1912–), American author: *The Guns of August* (1962) and *Stilwell and the American Experience in China, 1911–1945* (1971) both won Pulitzer Prizes; *A Distant Mirror: The Calamitous Fourteenth Century* (1978).

Ivan Turgenev (1818–83), Russian novelist and dramatist: *Fathers and Sons* (1861), a novel.

Mark Twain (real name **Samuel Clemens;** 1835–1910), American author: *Tom Sawyer* (1876), *Huckleberry Finn* (1884).

Louis Untermeyer (1885–1977), American poet and anthologist. He edited *Modern American Poetry* (1919, frequently revised).

John Updike (1932–), American novelist: *Rabbit, Run* (1960), *The Centaur* (1963), *Couples* (1968), *Bech: A Book* (1970), *Rabbit Redux* (1971), *Rabbit Is Rich* (1981), *Bech is Bach* (1982).

Leon Uris (1924–), American novelist: *Exodus* (1958), *Trinity* (1976).

Paul Valéry (1871–1945), French poet and critic. *Charmes* (1922) is his best verse collection.

S. S. Van Dine (real name **Willard Huntington Wright;** 1888–1939), American detective-story author. His books featured the amateur detective Philo Vance.

Mark Van Doren (1894–1972), American poet and critic: *Collected Poems* (1939) won Pulitzer Prize.

Thorstein Veblen (1857–1929), American essayist and social scientist: *The Theory of the Leisure Class* (1899).

Jules Verne (1828–1905), French novelist and a pioneer in science fiction: *Twenty Thousand Leagues Under the Sea* (1870).

Gore Vidal (1925–), American author: *Visit to a Small Planet* (1956), a play for TV; *Washington, D.C.* (1967), *Burr* (1973), *1876* (1976).

Virgil (70–19 B.C.), Roman poet. His masterpiece is the unfinished epic the *Aeneid.*

François Marie Arouet de Voltaire (1694–1778), French novelist, dramatist, critic, and poet. He was at his best in such short novels as *Candide* (1759).

Kurt Vonnegut Jr. (1922–), American novelist: *Mother Night* (1961), *Slaughterhouse-Five* (1969), *Jailbird* (1979), *Palm Sunday* (1981), *Deadeye Dick* (1982).

Horace Walpole (1717–97), English novelist: *The Castle of Otranto* (1764).

Robert Penn Warren (1905–), American novelist, poet, editor, and biographer. His novel *All the King's Men* (1946) won a Pulitzer Prize, as did *Promises: Poems 1954–1956* (1957), and *Now and Then* (1978).

Evelyn Waugh (1903–66), English novelist: *Decline and Fall* (1928), *Brideshead Revisited* (1945), *The Loved One* (1948).

Noah Webster (1758–1843), American lexicographer: *An American Dictionary of the English Language* (1800–28) set standard for American lexicography.

H. G. (Herbert George) Wells (1866–1946), English novelist and social historian: *The Time Machine* (1895), *The War of the Worlds* (1898).

Eudora Welty (1909–), American novelist and short-story writer: *Delta Wedding* (1946). *The Optimist's Daughter* (1972) won a Pulitzer Prize.

Franz Werfel (1890–1945), Austrian-born author: *The Song of Bernadette* (1941).

Jessamyn West (1907–), American author: *The Friendly Persuasion* (1945).

Nathanael West (1902–40), American novelist: *The Day of the Locust* (1939).

Rebecca West (1892–1983), English novelist and journalist: *The Return of the Soldier* (1918).

Edith Wharton (1862–1937), American novelist and short-story writer: *Ethan Frome* (1911); *The Age of Innocence* (1920) won a Pulitzer Prize.

E. B. White (1899–), American author: *One Man's Meat* (1942), *The Points of My Compass* (1962); *Stuart Little* (1945) and *Charlotte's Web* (1952), children's classics.

Walt Whitman (1819–92), American poet: *Leaves of Grass* (1855).

John Greenleaf Whittier (1807–92), American poet: *Snowbound* (1866).

Oscar Wilde (1854–1900), Anglo-Irish dramatist, novelist, and poet: *The Picture of Dorian Gray* (1891), a novel; *The Importance of Being Earnest* (1899), a play; *Ballad of Reading Gaol* (1898), a poem.

Thornton Wilder (1897–1975), American novelist and dramatist. He won Pulitzer Prizes for the novel *The Bridge of San Luis Rey* (1927) and the plays *Our Town* (1938) and *Skin of Our Teeth* (1942).

Tennessee Williams (1911–83), American playwright: *The Glass Menagerie* (1944), *The Rose Tattoo* (1950); *A Streetcar Named Desire* (1947) and *Cat on a Hot Tin Roof* (1955) both won Pulitzer Prizes.

William Carlos Williams (1883–1963), American poet and novelist. *Paterson* (1946) is a long poem evoking the atmosphere of his native New Jersey; *Pictures from Breughel* (1962) won a Pulitzer Prize.

Edmund Wilson (1895–1972), American critic: *Axel's Castle* (1931), *The Scrolls from the Dead Sea* (1955; revised edition 1969).

Thomas Wolfe (1900–38), American novelist: *Look Homeward, Angel* (1929), *Of Time and the River* (1935), *You Can't Go Home Again* (1940).

Virginia Woolf (1882–1941), English novelist: *Mrs. Dalloway* (1925), *To the Lighthouse* (1927).

William Wordsworth (1770–1850), English poet: "Tintern Abbey" (1800); "Ode: Intimations of Immortality" (1807).

Herman Wouk (1915–), American novelist: *The Caine Mutiny* (1951) won a Pulitzer Prize; *Marjorie Morningstar* (1955); *The Winds of War* (1971); *War and Remembrance* (1978).

Richard Wright (1908–60), American novelist: *Native Son* (1940); *Black Boy* (1945), autobiography.

Philip Gordon Wylie (1902–71), American author: *Generation of Vipers* (1942).

William Butler Yeats (1865–1939), Irish poet: *The Wild Swans at Coole* (1919); *The Tower* (1928); won a Nobel Prize in 1923.

Yevgeny Yevtushenko (1933–), Russian poet. His verse deals mainly with social protest.

Émile Zola (1840–1902), French novelist and critic, one of the most important novelists of the naturalist school. His works include the 20-volume series *Les Rougon-Macquart* (1871–93).

Calendars, Time and Holidays

FEDERAL, STATE, AND RELIGIOUS HOLIDAYS AND SPECIAL DAYS: 1984

JANUARY

1	**New Year's Day** (U.S. federal holiday)	Sunday
6	**Epiphany** (Armenian Christmas)	Friday
8	**Battle of New Orleans Day** (Louisiana)	Sunday
15	**Martin Luther King's Birthday** (b. 1929)	Sunday
19	**Robert E. Lee's Birthday** (born 1807)	Thursday
26	**Gen. Douglas MacArthur Day** (Arkansas)	Thursday
30	**F.D. Roosevelt's Birthday** (Ky.) (b. 1882)	Monday

FEBRUARY

1	**National Freedom Day** (118th anniversary of signing of resolution to end slavery)	Wednesday
1	**Chinese New Year** (Year of the Rat)	Wednesday
2	**Groundhog Day**	Thursday
12	**Lincoln's 175th Birthday** (born 1809)	Sunday
12	**Georgia Day** (Georgia)	Sunday
14	**Valentine's Day**	Tuesday
14	**Admission Day** (Arizona)	Tuesday
15	**Susan B. Anthony's Birthday** (born 1820)	Wednesday
20	**Washington's Birthday** (U.S. fed. holiday)	Monday
22	**Washington's 252d Birthday** (born 1732)	Wednesday

MARCH

2	**Texas Independence Day** (Texas)	Friday
2	**World Day of Prayer** (Christian)	Friday
6	**Shrove Tuesday, Mardi Gras** (Alabama, Florida, Louisiana)	Tuesday
6	**Town Meeting Day** (Vermont)	Tuesday
7	**Ash Wednesday** (Christian)	Wednesday
15	**Andrew Jackson's Birthday** (TN) (b. 1767)	Thursday
17	**St. Patrick's Day**	Saturday
17	**Evacuation Day** (Massachusetts)	Saturday
18	**Purim** (Jewish)	Sunday
20	**Spring begins** at 5:25 A.M. EST	Tuesday
23	**Kuhio Day** (Hawaii)	Friday
25	**Maryland Day** (Maryland)	Sunday
26	**Seward's Day** (Alaska)	Monday

APRIL

1	**April Fool's Day**	Sunday
13	**Thomas Jefferson's Birthday** (born 1743)	Friday
14	**Pan American Day**	Saturday
15	**Palm Sunday** (Christian)	Sunday
16	**Patriots' Day** (Massachusetts, Maine)	Monday
17	**First Day of Passover,** Pesach (Jewish)	Tuesday
19	**Maundy Thursday** (Christian)	Thursday
20	**Good Friday** (Christian)	Friday
21	**San Jacinto Day** (Texas)	Saturday
22	**Easter** (Christian)	Sunday
22	**Arbor Day** (Nebraska)	Sunday
23	**Easter Monday** (North Carolina)	Monday
23	**Fast Day** (New Hampshire)	Monday
23	**Confederate Memorial Day** (Ala., Miss.)	Monday
27	**Arbor Day** (Utah)	Friday
29	**Daylight Saving Time begins** (clocks set ahead one hour at 2 A.M.)	Sunday

MAY

1	**May Day,** Loyalty Day, Law Day	Sunday
8	**Harry Truman's Birthday** (Mo.) (born 1884)	Sunday
10	**Confederate Memorial Day** (South Carolina)	Thursday
11	**Minnesota Day** (Minnesota)	Friday
13	**Mother's Day**	Sunday
19	**Armed Forces Day**	Saturday
21	**Queen's Birthday** (Canada)	Monday
28	**Memorial Day** (U.S. federal holiday)	Monday
31	**Ascension Day,** Holy Thursday (Christian)	Thursday
31	**First Day of Ramadan** (Islamic)	Thursday

JUNE

3	**Jefferson Davis' Birthday** (actual—born 1808)	Sunday
4	**Jefferson Davis' Birthday** (So. States)	Monday
6	**Shavuot, Feast of Weeks** (Jewish)	Wednesday
9	**Queen's Official Birthday** (Britain)	Saturday
10	**Pentecost,** Whitsunday (Christian)	Sunday
14	**Flag Day,** 207th anniversary of U.S. Flag	Thursday
17	**Father's Day**	Sunday
21	**Summer begins** at 1:02 A.M. EDT	Thursday
24	**Corpus Christi** (Christian)	Sunday
29	**Festival of the End of Ramadan** (Islamic)	Friday

JULY

1	**Canada Day** (117th anniv. of Canada)	Sunday
4	**Independence Day** (208th anniversary of U.S. Declaration of Independence)	Wednesday
24	**Pioneer Day** (Utah)	Tuesday

AUGUST

8	**Victory Day** (Rhode Island) (39th anniversary of end of World War II)	Wednesday
16	**Bennington Battle Day** (Vermont)	Thursday
17	**Admission Day** (Hawaii)	Friday
27	**L. B. Johnson's Birthday** (TX) (born 1908)	Monday
30	**Huey Long's Birthday** (LA) (born 1893)	Thursday

SEPTEMBER

3	**Labor Day** (U.S. federal holiday)	Monday
9	**Admission Day** (California)	Sunday
9	**National Grandparents Day**	Sunday
12	**Defenders' Day** (Maryland)	Wednesday
16	**Mexico's Independence Day**	Sunday
17	**Citizenship Day** (197th anniversary of signing of U.S. Constitution)	Monday
22	**Autumn begins** at 4:33 P.M. EDT	Wednesday
27	**Rosh Hashana,** Jewish New Year, first day of year 5745 of Jewish era	Thursday
27	**Islamic New Year** (Year 1405 of Islamic Era)	Thursday
28	**American Indian Day**	Friday
30	**Gold Star Mother's Day**	Sunday

OCTOBER

6	**Yom Kippur,** Day of Atonement (Jewish)	Saturday
8	**Columbus Day** (U.S. federal holiday)	Monday
8	**Pioneers' Day** (South Dakota)	Monday
8	**Canadian Thanksgiving Day** (Canada)	Monday
9	**Leif Erikson Day (Minnesota)**	Tuesday
11	**Sukkot,** First day of Tabernacles (Jewish)	Thursday
18	**Alaska Day** (Alaska)	Thursday
28	**Standard Time begins** (clocks set back one hour at 2 A.M.)	Sunday
31	**Halloween**	Wednesday
31	**Nevada Day** (Nevada)	Wednesday

NOVEMBER

1	**All Saints' Day** (Christian)	Thursday
2	**World Community Day**	Friday
4	**Will Rogers' Birthday** (Okla.) (b. 1879)	Sunday
6	**Election Day**	Tuesday
11	**Veterans Day** (U.S. federal holiday)	Friday
22	**Thanksgiving Day** (U.S. federal holiday)	Thursday
23	**Day after Thanksgiving** (Okla., Wash.)	Friday

DECEMBER

2	**First Sunday in Advent** (Christian)	Sunday
6	**St. Nicholas Day** (Orthodox)	Thursday
10	**Wyoming Day** (Wyoming)	Monday
15	**Bill of Rights Day,** 193d anniversary	Saturday
19	**First day of Hanukkah** (Jewish)	Wednesday
21	**Winter begins** at 11:23 A.M. EST	Friday
25	**Christmas Day** (Christian)	Tuesday
31	**New Year's Eve** (Watch Night)	Monday

SPECIAL MONTHS, WEEKS, AND DAYS: 1984

The President of the United States regularly issues proclamations throughout the year designating certain months, weeks, and days for special observance.

JANUARY

1 **New Year's Day,** U.S. federal holiday.
13 **Stephen Foster Memorial Day,** since 1952.

FEBRUARY

1–29 **American Heart Month,** since 1964.
1 **National Freedom Day,** 118th anniversary of resolution to end slavery, annually since 1949.
20 **Washington's Birthday,** U.S. federal holiday, third Monday in February; actual birthday Feb. 22, 1732.

MARCH

1–31 **Red Cross Month,** since 1943.
4–10 **Save Your Vision Week,** first week, since 1963.
18–24 **National Poison Prevention Week,** third week of March, since 1962.

APRIL

1–30 **Cancer Control Month,** since 1939.
13 **Thomas Jefferson's Birthday** (born 1743), issued annually since 1938.
8–14 **Pan American Week,** week that includes Pan American Day, since 1946.
14 **Pan American Day,** observes Pan American Union's 54th anniversary; annually since 1940.

MAY

1–31 **Older Americans Month,** since 1963, previously called Senior Citizens Month until 1974.
1–31 **Steelmark Month,** annually since 1967.
1 **Law Day,** issued each year since 1958.
1 **Loyalty Day,** proclaimed annually since 1959.
3 **National Day of Prayer,** first Thursday of May, since 1952.
13 **Mother's Day,** issued annually for second Sunday in May since congressional resolution in 1914.
15 **Peace Officers Memorial Day,** since 1963.
13–19 **Police Week,** proclaimed since 1962 for week that includes Peace Officers Memorial Day.
13–19 **National Transportation Week,** since 1960.
18 **National Defense Transportation Day,** issued each year for third Friday in May, since 1957.
19 **Armed Forces Day,** always third Saturday in May since 1950.
20–26 **World Trade Week,** week that includes National Maritime Day, since 1948.
22 **National Maritime Day,** since 1933.
28 **Prayer for Peace, Memorial Day,** U.S. federal holiday, last Monday in May since 1971.

JUNE

3–9 **National Safe Boating Week,** issued annually for week commencing with first Sunday in June.
10–16 **National Flag Week,** issued annually since 1966 for week that includes Flag Day.
11–17 **National Little League Baseball Week,** week beginning second Monday in June, since 1959.
14 **Flag Day,** observes 207th anniversary of adoption of first national flag by Congress, since 1941.
17 **Father's Day,** third Sunday in June, since 1971.

JULY

4 **Independence Day,** U.S. federal holiday, 208th anniversary of U.S. Declaration of Independence.
15–21 **Captive Nations Week,** third week of July, issued annually since 1959.
25–31 **National Farm Safety Week,** week beginning on July 25, issued annually since 1944.

AUGUST

19 **National Aviation Day,** since 1939.
26 **Women's Equality Day,** since 1973.

SEPTEMBER

3 **Labor Day,** U.S. federal holiday, always on first Monday in September.
9 **National Grandparents Day,** first Sunday after Labor Day, since 1978.
10–16 **National Hispanic Heritage Week,** week that includes Sept. 15–16; annually since 1968.
17 **Citizenship Day,** 197th anniversary of signing of U.S. Constitution, issued since 1952.
17–23 **Constitution Week,** week beginning Sept. 17, annual since 1955.
29 **National Hunting and Fishing Day,** fourth Saturday in September, since 1979.
30 **Gold Star Mother's Day,** last Sunday in September, since 1936.

OCTOBER

3 **Child Health Day,** first Monday in October, since 1959.
7–13 **Minority Enterprise Development Week,** issued for first week in October.
7–13 **National Employ the Handicapped Week,** first week of October, since 1945.
7–13 **Fire Prevention Week,** week that includes Oct. 9, since 1925.
8 **Columbus Day,** U.S. federal holiday, second Monday in October, issued since 1934.
9 **Leif Erikson Day,** issued annually since 1964.
11 **General Pulaski Memorial Day,** since 1929.
14–20 **National School Lunch Week,** week beginning second Sunday in October, since 1962.
15 **White Cane Safety Day,** since 1964.
21–27 **National Forest Products Week,** week beginning with third Sunday in October; since 1960.
24 **United Nations Day,** always issued for Oct. 24 since 1948, by request of UN General Assembly.
31 **National UNICEF Day,** issued annually to fall on Halloween since 1967.

NOVEMBER

11 **Veterans Day,** U.S. federal holiday, 66th anniversary of end of World War I in 1918.
11–17 **American Education Week,** second week in November, annually since 1921.
16–22 **National Farm-City Week,** week ending on Thanksgiving Day, annually since 1955.
22 **Thanksgiving Day,** U.S. federal holiday, always proclaimed for fourth Thursday in November.

DECEMBER

2 **Pan American Health Day,** since 1940.
10 **Human Rights Day,** since 1949.
10–16 **Human Rights Week,** week of Dec. 10–16, annually since 1958.
15 **Bill of Rights Day,** issued annually for Dec. 15 since 1962, observing 193d anniversary date of ratification of Bill of Rights in 1791.
17 **Pan American Aviation Day,** proclaimed for Dec. 17 each year since 1940.
17 **Wright Brothers Day,** issued annually for Dec. 17 since 1963, observing 80th anniversary of the first successful airplane flight in 1903.
25 **Christmas Day,** U.S. federal holiday.

DATES OF EASTER: 1984–2007

1984	April 22	1988	April 3	1992	April 19	1996	April 7	2000	April 23	2004	April 11
1985	April 7	1989	March 26	1993	April 11	1997	March 30	2001	April 15	2005	March 27
1986	March 30	1990	April 15	1994	April 3	1998	April 12	2002	March 31	2006	April 16
1987	April 19	1991	March 31	1995	April 16	1999	April 4	2003	April 20	2007	April 8

UNITED STATES TIME ZONES

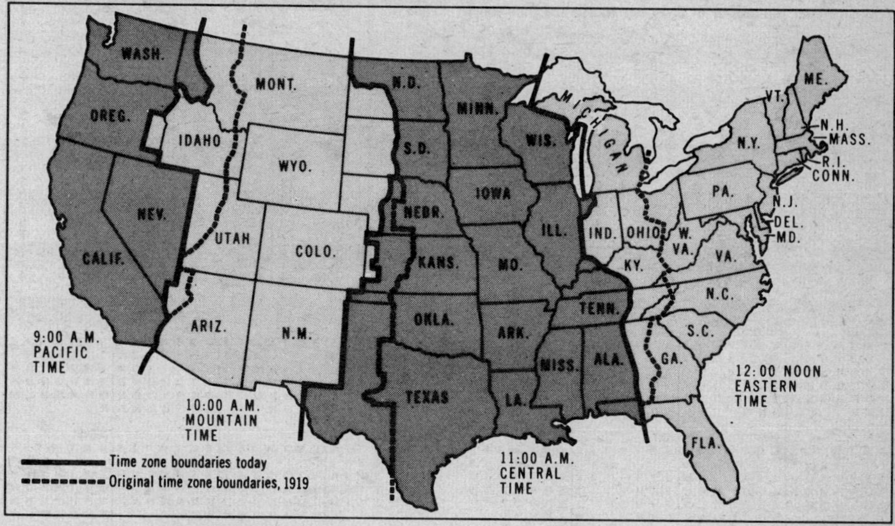

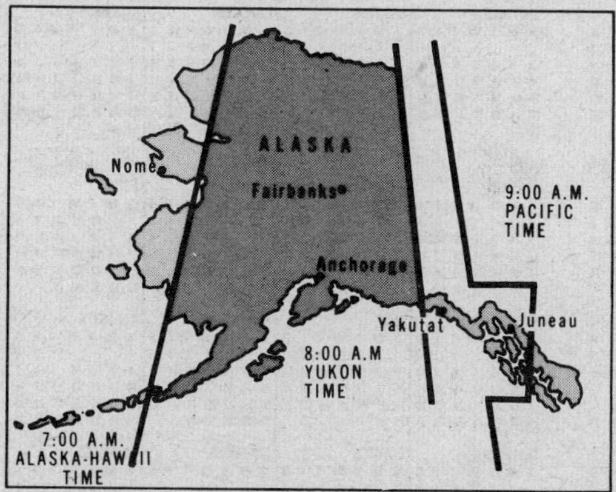

The map above shows time-zone boundaries (solid line), which in most places have moved westward somewhat from those that first went into effect on Jan. 1, 1919 (broken line).

Daylight-saving time begins at 2 A.M. on the last Sunday in April (April 29, 1984) and ends on the last Sunday in October (Oct. 28, 1984). Clocks are set ahead one hour in the spring and set back one hour in the fall.

If it had been possible to ask for the time at exactly the same moment in a number of U.S. towns in 1873, the variety of answers would have been puzzling: 12:12 P.M. in New York, 11:08 A.M. in Memphis, and so on across the nation. Yet each answer would have been right, for "Sun time" prevailed throughout much of the world until the late 1800s.

In November 1883, U.S. and Canadian rail companies agreed to set up zones for each 15 degrees of longitude with uniform time in each zone.

Most of the country went along quickly with this orderly system, but Congress did not pass a Standard Time Act until 1917. In 1966 Congress passed a Uniform Time Act urging all states to adopt daylight-saving time during half of the year from spring to fall.

As an energy conservation measure Congress passed a law in 1974 establishing year-round daylight-saving time. It was modified to eight months of daylight time in 1975, and reverted to six months in 1976.

Areas of the nation that do not observe daylight-saving time include Arizona, Hawaii, most of Indiana, Puerto Rico, the Virgin Islands, and American Samoa.

The longitudes of the standard meridians for U.S. standard time zones are Atlantic 60° W., Eastern 75° W., Central 90° W., Mountain 105° W., Pacific 120° W., Yukon 135° W., Alaska-Hawaii 150° W., and Bering 165° W.

PAST AND FUTURE CALENDARS: 1776–2014

Directions: Choose year you want in key below. Number opposite year is number of calendar to use for that year.

1776	9	1795	5	1814	7	1833	3	1852	12	1871	1
1777	4	1796	13	1815	1	1834	4	1853	7	1872	9
1777	5	1797	1	1816	9	1835	5	1854	1	1873	4
1779	6	1798	2	1817	4	1836	13	1855	2	1874	5
1780	14	1799	3	1818	5	1837	1	1856	10	1875	6
1781	2	1800	4	1819	6	1838	2	1857	5	1876	14
1782	3	1801	5	1820	14	1839	3	1858	6	1877	2
1783	4	1802	6	1821	2	1840	11	1859	7	1878	3
1784	12	1803	7	1822	3	1841	6	1860	8	1879	4
1785	7	1804	8	1823	4	1842	7	1861	3	1880	12
1786	1	1805	3	1824	12	1843	1	1862	4	1881	7
1787	2	1806	4	1825	7	1844	9	1863	5	1882	1
1788	10	1807	5	1826	1	1845	4	1864	13	1883	2
1789	5	1808	13	1827	2	1846	5	1865	1	1884	10
1790	6	1809	1	1828	10	1847	6	1866	2	1885	5
1791	7	1810	2	1829	5	1848	14	1867	3	1886	6
1792	8	1811	3	1830	6	1849	2	1868	11	1887	7
1793	3	1812	11	1831	7	1850	3	1869	6	1888	8
1794	4	1813	6	1832	8	1851	4	1870	7	1889	3

1890	4	1915	6	1940	9	1965	6	1990	2
1891	5	1916	14	1941	4	1966	7	1991	3
1892	13	1917	2	1942	5	1967	1	1992	11
1893	1	1918	3	1943	6	1968	9	1993	6
1894	2	1919	4	1944	14	1969	4	1994	7
1895	3	1920	12	1945	2	1970	5	1995	1
1896	11	1921	7	1946	3	1971	6	1996	9
1897	6	1922	1	1947	4	1972	14	1997	4
1898	7	1923	2	1948	12	1973	2	1998	5
1899	1	1924	10	1949	7	1974	3	1999	6
1900	2	1925	5	1950	1	1975	4	2000	14
1901	3	1926	6	1951	2	1976	12	2001	2
1902	4	1927	7	1952	10	1977	7	2002	3
1903	5	1928	8	1953	5	1978	1	2003	4
1904	13	1929	3	1954	6	1979	2	2004	12
1905	1	1930	4	1955	7	1980	10	2005	7
1906	2	1931	5	1956	8	1981	5	2006	1
1907	3	1932	13	1957	3	1982	6	2007	2
1908	11	1933	1	1958	4	1983	7	2008	10
1909	6	1934	2	1959	5	1984	8	2009	5
1910	7	1935	3	1960	13	1985	3	2010	6
1911	1	1936	11	1961	1	1986	4	2011	7
1912	9	1937	6	1962	2	1987	5	2012	8
1913	4	1938	7	1963	3	1988	13	2013	3
1914	5	1939	1	1964	11	1989	1	2014	4

1 — 1989

JANUARY

S	M	T	W	T	F	S
1	2	3	4	5	6	7
8	9	10	11	12	13	14
15	16	17	18	19	20	21
22	23	24	25	26	27	28
29	30	31				

FEBRUARY

S	M	T	W	T	F	S
			1	2	3	4
5	6	7	8	9	10	11
12	13	14	15	16	17	18
19	20	21	22	23	24	25
26	27	28				

MARCH

S	M	T	W	T	F	S
			1	2	3	4
5	6	7	8	9	10	11
12	13	14	15	16	17	18
19	20	21	22	23	24	25
26	27	28	29	30	31	

APRIL

S	M	T	W	T	F	S
						1
2	3	4	5	6	7	8
9	10	11	12	13	14	15
16	17	18	19	20	21	22
23	24	25	26	27	28	29
30						

MAY

S	M	T	W	T	F	S
	1	2	3	4	5	6
7	8	9	10	11	12	13
14	15	16	17	18	19	20
21	22	23	24	25	26	27
28	29	30	31			

JUNE

S	M	T	W	T	F	S
				1	2	3
4	5	6	7	8	9	10
11	12	13	14	15	16	17
18	19	20	21	22	23	24
25	26	27	28	29	30	

JULY

S	M	T	W	T	F	S
						1
2	3	4	5	6	7	8
9	10	11	12	13	14	15
16	17	18	19	20	21	22
23	24	25	26	27	28	29
30	31					

AUGUST

S	M	T	W	T	F	S
		1	2	3	4	5
6	7	8	9	10	11	12
13	14	15	16	17	18	19
20	21	22	23	24	25	26
27	28	29	30	31		

SEPTEMBER

S	M	T	W	T	F	S
					1	2
3	4	5	6	7	8	9
10	11	12	13	14	15	16
17	18	19	20	21	22	23
24	25	26	27	28	29	30

OCTOBER

S	M	T	W	T	F	S
1	2	3	4	5	6	7
8	9	10	11	12	13	14
15	16	17	18	19	20	21
22	23	24	25	26	27	28
29	30	31				

NOVEMBER

S	M	T	W	T	F	S
			1	2	3	4
5	6	7	8	9	10	11
12	13	14	15	16	17	18
19	20	21	22	23	24	25
26	27	28	29	30		

DECEMBER

S	M	T	W	T	F	S
					1	2
3	4	5	6	7	8	9
10	11	12	13	14	15	16
17	18	19	20	21	22	23
24	25	26	27	28	29	30
31						

2 — 1990

JANUARY

S	M	T	W	T	F	S
	1	2	3	4	5	6
7	8	9	10	11	12	13
14	15	16	17	18	19	20
21	22	23	24	25	26	27
28	29	30	31			

FEBRUARY

S	M	T	W	T	F	S
				1	2	3
4	5	6	7	8	9	10
11	12	13	14	15	16	17
18	19	20	21	22	23	24
25	26	27	28			

MARCH

S	M	T	W	T	F	S
				1	2	3
4	5	6	7	8	9	10
11	12	13	14	15	16	17
18	19	20	21	22	23	24
25	26	27	28	29	30	31

APRIL

S	M	T	W	T	F	S
1	2	3	4	5	6	7
8	9	10	11	12	13	14
15	16	17	18	19	20	21
22	23	24	25	26	27	28
29	30					

MAY

S	M	T	W	T	F	S
		1	2	3	4	5
6	7	8	9	10	11	12
13	14	15	16	17	18	19
20	21	22	23	24	25	26
27	28	29	30	31		

JUNE

S	M	T	W	T	F	S
					1	2
3	4	5	6	7	8	9
10	11	12	13	14	15	16
17	18	19	20	21	22	23
24	25	26	27	28	29	30

JULY

S	M	T	W	T	F	S
1	2	3	4	5	6	7
8	9	10	11	12	13	14
15	16	17	18	19	20	21
22	23	24	25	26	27	28
29	30	31				

AUGUST

S	M	T	W	T	F	S
			1	2	3	4
5	6	7	8	9	10	11
12	13	14	15	16	17	18
19	20	21	22	23	24	25
26	27	28	29	30	31	

SEPTEMBER

S	M	T	W	T	F	S
						1
2	3	4	5	6	7	8
9	10	11	12	13	14	15
16	17	18	19	20	21	22
23	24	25	26	27	28	29
30						

OCTOBER

S	M	T	W	T	F	S
	1	2	3	4	5	6
7	8	9	10	11	12	13
14	15	16	17	18	19	20
21	22	23	24	25	26	27
28	29	30	31			

NOVEMBER

S	M	T	W	T	F	S
				1	2	3
4	5	6	7	8	9	10
11	12	13	14	15	16	17
18	19	20	21	22	23	24
25	26	27	28	29	30	

DECEMBER

S	M	T	W	T	F	S
						1
2	3	4	5	6	7	8
9	10	11	12	13	14	15
16	17	18	19	20	21	22
23	24	25	26	27	28	29
30	31					

3 — 1985

JANUARY

S	M	T	W	T	F	S
		1	2	3	4	5
6	7	8	9	10	11	12
13	14	15	16	17	18	19
20	21	22	23	24	25	26
27	28	29	30	31		

FEBRUARY

S	M	T	W	T	F	S
					1	2
3	4	5	6	7	8	9
10	11	12	13	14	15	16
17	18	19	20	21	22	23
24	25	26	27	28		

MARCH

S	M	T	W	T	F	S
					1	2
3	4	5	6	7	8	9
10	11	12	13	14	15	16
17	18	19	20	21	22	23
24	25	26	27	28	29	30
31						

APRIL

S	M	T	W	T	F	S
	1	2	3	4	5	6
7	8	9	10	11	12	13
14	15	16	17	18	19	20
21	22	23	24	25	26	27
28	29	30				

MAY

S	M	T	W	T	F	S
			1	2	3	4
5	6	7	8	9	10	11
12	13	14	15	16	17	18
19	20	21	22	23	24	25
26	27	28	29	30	31	

JUNE

S	M	T	W	T	F	S
						1
2	3	4	5	6	7	8
9	10	11	12	13	14	15
16	17	18	19	20	21	22
23	24	25	26	27	28	29
30						

JULY

S	M	T	W	T	F	S
	1	2	3	4	5	6
7	8	9	10	11	12	13
14	15	16	17	18	19	20
21	22	23	24	25	26	27
28	29	30	31			

AUGUST

S	M	T	W	T	F	S
				1	2	3
4	5	6	7	8	9	10
11	12	13	14	15	16	17
18	19	20	21	22	23	24
25	26	27	28	29	30	31

SEPTEMBER

S	M	T	W	T	F	S
1	2	3	4	5	6	7
8	9	10	11	12	13	14
15	16	17	18	19	20	21
22	23	24	25	26	27	28
29	30					

OCTOBER

S	M	T	W	T	F	S
		1	2	3	4	5
6	7	8	9	10	11	12
13	14	15	16	17	18	19
20	21	22	23	24	25	26
27	28	29	30	31		

NOVEMBER

S	M	T	W	T	F	S
					1	2
3	4	5	6	7	8	9
10	11	12	13	14	15	16
17	18	19	20	21	22	23
24	25	26	27	28	29	30

DECEMBER

S	M	T	W	T	F	S
1	2	3	4	5	6	7
8	9	10	11	12	13	14
15	16	17	18	19	20	21
22	23	24	25	26	27	28
29	30	31				

4 — 1986

JANUARY

S	M	T	W	T	F	S
			1	2	3	4
5	6	7	8	9	10	11
12	13	14	15	16	17	18
19	20	21	22	23	24	25
26	27	28	29	30	31	

FEBRUARY

S	M	T	W	T	F	S
						1
2	3	4	5	6	7	8
9	10	11	12	13	14	15
16	17	18	19	20	21	22
23	24	25	26	27	28	

MARCH

S	M	T	W	T	F	S
						1
2	3	4	5	6	7	8
9	10	11	12	13	14	15
16	17	18	19	20	21	22
23	24	25	26	27	28	29
30	31					

APRIL

S	M	T	W	T	F	S
		1	2	3	4	5
6	7	8	9	10	11	12
13	14	15	16	17	18	19
20	21	22	23	24	25	26
27	28	29	30			

MAY

S	M	T	W	T	F	S
				1	2	3
4	5	6	7	8	9	10
11	12	13	14	15	16	17
18	19	20	21	22	23	24
25	26	27	28	29	30	31

JUNE

S	M	T	W	T	F	S
1	2	3	4	5	6	7
8	9	10	11	12	13	14
15	16	17	18	19	20	21
22	23	24	25	26	27	28
29	30					

JULY

S	M	T	W	T	F	S
		1	2	3	4	5
6	7	8	9	10	11	12
13	14	15	16	17	18	19
20	21	22	23	24	25	26
27	28	29	30	31		

AUGUST

S	M	T	W	T	F	S
					1	2
3	4	5	6	7	8	9
10	11	12	13	14	15	16
17	18	19	20	21	22	23
24	25	26	27	28	29	30
31						

SEPTEMBER

S	M	T	W	T	F	S
	1	2	3	4	5	6
7	8	9	10	11	12	13
14	15	16	17	18	19	20
21	22	23	24	25	26	27
28	29	30				

OCTOBER

S	M	T	W	T	F	S
			1	2	3	4
5	6	7	8	9	10	11
12	13	14	15	16	17	18
19	20	21	22	23	24	25
26	27	28	29	30	31	

NOVEMBER

S	M	T	W	T	F	S
						1
2	3	4	5	6	7	8
9	10	11	12	13	14	15
16	17	18	19	20	21	22
23	24	25	26	27	28	29
30						

DECEMBER

S	M	T	W	T	F	S
	1	2	3	4	5	6
7	8	9	10	11	12	13
14	15	16	17	18	19	20
21	22	23	24	25	26	27
28	29	30	31			

5 — 1987

JANUARY

S	M	T	W	T	F	S
				1	2	3
4	5	6	7	8	9	10
11	12	13	14	15	16	17
18	19	20	21	22	23	24
25	26	27	28	29	30	31

FEBRUARY

S	M	T	W	T	F	S
1	2	3	4	5	6	7
8	9	10	11	12	13	14
15	16	17	18	19	20	21
22	23	24	25	26	27	28

MARCH

S	M	T	W	T	F	S
1	2	3	4	5	6	7
8	9	10	11	12	13	14
15	16	17	18	19	20	21
22	23	24	25	26	27	28
29	30	31				

APRIL

S	M	T	W	T	F	S
			1	2	3	4
5	6	7	8	9	10	11
12	13	14	15	16	17	18
19	20	21	22	23	24	25
26	27	28	29	30		

MAY

S	M	T	W	T	F	S
					1	2
3	4	5	6	7	8	9
10	11	12	13	14	15	16
17	18	19	20	21	22	23
24	25	26	27	28	29	30
31						

JUNE

S	M	T	W	T	F	S
	1	2	3	4	5	6
7	8	9	10	11	12	13
14	15	16	17	18	19	20
21	22	23	24	25	26	27
28	29	30				

JULY

S	M	T	W	T	F	S
			1	2	3	4
5	6	7	8	9	10	11
12	13	14	15	16	17	18
19	20	21	22	23	24	25
26	27	28	29	30	31	

AUGUST

S	M	T	W	T	F	S
						1
2	3	4	5	6	7	8
9	10	11	12	13	14	15
16	17	18	19	20	21	22
23	24	25	26	27	28	29
30	31					

SEPTEMBER

S	M	T	W	T	F	S
		1	2	3	4	5
6	7	8	9	10	11	12
13	14	15	16	17	18	19
20	21	22	23	24	25	26
27	28	29	30			

OCTOBER

S	M	T	W	T	F	S
				1	2	3
4	5	6	7	8	9	10
11	12	13	14	15	16	17
18	19	20	21	22	23	24
25	26	27	28	29	30	31

NOVEMBER

S	M	T	W	T	F	S
1	2	3	4	5	6	7
8	9	10	11	12	13	14
15	16	17	18	19	20	21
22	23	24	25	26	27	28
29	30					

DECEMBER

S	M	T	W	T	F	S
		1	2	3	4	5
6	7	8	9	10	11	12
13	14	15	16	17	18	19
20	21	22	23	24	25	26
27	28	29	30	31		

6 — 1982

JANUARY

S	M	T	W	T	F	S
					1	2
3	4	5	6	7	8	9
10	11	12	13	14	15	16
17	18	19	20	21	22	23
24	25	26	27	28	29	30
31						

FEBRUARY

S	M	T	W	T	F	S
	1	2	3	4	5	6
7	8	9	10	11	12	13
14	15	16	17	18	19	20
21	22	23	24	25	26	27
28						

MARCH

S	M	T	W	T	F	S
	1	2	3	4	5	6
7	8	9	10	11	12	13
14	15	16	17	18	19	20
21	22	23	24	25	26	27
28	29	30	31			

APRIL

S	M	T	W	T	F	S
				1	2	3
4	5	6	7	8	9	10
11	12	13	14	15	16	17
18	19	20	21	22	23	24
25	26	27	28	29	30	

MAY

S	M	T	W	T	F	S
						1
2	3	4	5	6	7	8
9	10	11	12	13	14	15
16	17	18	19	20	21	22
23	24	25	26	27	28	29
30	31					

JUNE

S	M	T	W	T	F	S
		1	2	3	4	5
6	7	8	9	10	11	12
13	14	15	16	17	18	19
20	21	22	23	24	25	26
27	28	29	30			

JULY

S	M	T	W	T	F	S
				1	2	3
4	5	6	7	8	9	10
11	12	13	14	15	16	17
18	19	20	21	22	23	24
25	26	27	28	29	30	31

AUGUST

S	M	T	W	T	F	S
1	2	3	4	5	6	7
8	9	10	11	12	13	14
15	16	17	18	19	20	21
22	23	24	25	26	27	28
29	30	31				

SEPTEMBER

S	M	T	W	T	F	S
			1	2	3	4
5	6	7	8	9	10	11
12	13	14	15	16	17	18
19	20	21	22	23	24	25
26	27	28	29	30		

OCTOBER

S	M	T	W	T	F	S
					1	2
3	4	5	6	7	8	9
10	11	12	13	14	15	16
17	18	19	20	21	22	23
24	25	26	27	28	29	30
31						

NOVEMBER

S	M	T	W	T	F	S
	1	2	3	4	5	6
7	8	9	10	11	12	13
14	15	16	17	18	19	20
21	22	23	24	25	26	27
28	29	30				

DECEMBER

S	M	T	W	T	F	S
			1	2	3	4
5	6	7	8	9	10	11
12	13	14	15	16	17	18
19	20	21	22	23	24	25
26	27	28	29	30	31	

7 1983

JANUARY

S	M	T	W	T	F	S
						1
2	3	4	5	6	7	8
9	10	11	12	13	14	15
16	17	18	19	20	21	22
23	24	25	26	27	28	29
30	31					

FEBRUARY

S	M	T	W	T	F	S
		1	2	3	4	5
6	7	8	9	10	11	12
13	14	15	16	17	18	19
20	21	22	23	24	25	26
27	28					

MARCH

S	M	T	W	T	F	S
		1	2	3	4	5
6	7	8	9	10	11	12
13	14	15	16	17	18	19
20	21	22	23	24	25	26
27	28	29	30	31		

APRIL

S	M	T	W	T	F	S
					1	2
3	4	5	6	7	8	9
10	11	12	13	14	15	16
17	18	19	20	21	22	23
24	25	26	27	28	29	30

MAY

S	M	T	W	T	F	S
1	2	3	4	5	6	7
8	9	10	11	12	13	14
15	16	17	18	19	20	21
22	23	24	25	26	27	28
29	30	31				

JUNE

S	M	T	W	T	F	S
			1	2	3	4
5	6	7	8	9	10	11
12	13	14	15	16	17	18
19	20	21	22	23	24	25
26	27	28	29	30		

JULY

S	M	T	W	T	F	S
					1	2
3	4	5	6	7	8	9
10	11	12	13	14	15	16
17	18	19	20	21	22	23
24	25	26	27	28	29	30
31						

AUGUST

S	M	T	W	T	F	S
	1	2	3	4	5	6
7	8	9	10	11	12	13
14	15	16	17	18	19	20
21	22	23	24	25	26	27
28	29	30	31			

SEPTEMBER

S	M	T	W	T	F	S
				1	2	3
4	5	6	7	8	9	10
11	12	13	14	15	16	17
18	19	20	21	22	23	24
25	26	27	28	29	30	

OCTOBER

S	M	T	W	T	F	S
						1
2	3	4	5	6	7	8
9	10	11	12	13	14	15
16	17	18	19	20	21	22
23	24	25	26	27	28	29
30	31					

NOVEMBER

S	M	T	W	T	F	S
		1	2	3	4	5
6	7	8	9	10	11	12
13	14	15	16	17	18	19
20	21	22	23	24	25	26
27	28	29	30			

DECEMBER

S	M	T	W	T	F	S
				1	2	3
4	5	6	7	8	9	10
11	12	13	14	15	16	17
18	19	20	21	22	23	24
25	26	27	28	29	30	31

8 (LEAP YEAR) 1984

JANUARY

S	M	T	W	T	F	S
1	2	3	4	5	6	7
8	9	10	11	12	13	14
15	16	17	18	19	20	21
22	23	24	25	26	27	28
29	30	31				

FEBRUARY

S	M	T	W	T	F	S
			1	2	3	4
5	6	7	8	9	10	11
12	13	14	15	16	17	18
19	20	21	22	23	24	25
26	27	28	29			

MARCH

S	M	T	W	T	F	S
				1	2	3
4	5	6	7	8	9	10
11	12	13	14	15	16	17
18	19	20	21	22	23	24
25	26	27	28	29	30	31

APRIL

S	M	T	W	T	F	S
1	2	3	4	5	6	7
8	9	10	11	12	13	14
15	16	17	18	19	20	21
22	23	24	25	26	27	28
29	30					

MAY

S	M	T	W	T	F	S
		1	2	3	4	5
6	7	8	9	10	11	12
13	14	15	16	17	18	19
20	21	22	23	24	25	26
27	28	29	30	31		

JUNE

S	M	T	W	T	F	S
					1	2
3	4	5	6	7	8	9
10	11	12	13	14	15	16
17	18	19	20	21	22	23
24	25	26	27	28	29	30

JULY

S	M	T	W	T	F	S
1	2	3	4	5	6	7
8	9	10	11	12	13	14
15	16	17	18	19	20	21
22	23	24	25	26	27	28
29	30	31				

AUGUST

S	M	T	W	T	F	S
			1	2	3	4
5	6	7	8	9	10	11
12	13	14	15	16	17	18
19	20	21	22	23	24	25
26	27	28	29	30	31	

SEPTEMBER

S	M	T	W	T	F	S
						1
2	3	4	5	6	7	8
9	10	11	12	13	14	15
16	17	18	19	20	21	22
23	24	25	26	27	28	29
30						

OCTOBER

S	M	T	W	T	F	S
	1	2	3	4	5	6
7	8	9	10	11	12	13
14	15	16	17	18	19	20
21	22	23	24	25	26	27
28	29	30	31			

NOVEMBER

S	M	T	W	T	F	S
				1	2	3
4	5	6	7	8	9	10
11	12	13	14	15	16	17
18	19	20	21	22	23	24
25	26	27	28	29	30	

DECEMBER

S	M	T	W	T	F	S
						1
2	3	4	5	6	7	8
9	10	11	12	13	14	15
16	17	18	19	20	21	22
23	24	25	26	27	28	29
30	31					

9 (LEAP YEAR)

JANUARY

S	M	T	W	T	F	S
	1	2	3	4	5	6
7	8	9	10	11	12	13
14	15	16	17	18	19	20
21	22	23	24	25	26	27
28	29	30	31			

FEBRUARY

S	M	T	W	T	F	S
				1	2	3
4	5	6	7	8	9	10
11	12	13	14	15	16	17
18	19	20	21	22	23	24
25	26	27	28	29		

MARCH

S	M	T	W	T	F	S
					1	2
3	4	5	6	7	8	9
10	11	12	13	14	15	16
17	18	19	20	21	22	23
24	25	26	27	28	29	30
31						

APRIL

S	M	T	W	T	F	S
	1	2	3	4	5	6
7	8	9	10	11	12	13
14	15	16	17	18	19	20
21	22	23	24	25	26	27
28	29	30				

MAY

S	M	T	W	T	F	S
			1	2	3	4
5	6	7	8	9	10	11
12	13	14	15	16	17	18
19	20	21	22	23	24	25
26	27	28	29	30	31	

JUNE

S	M	T	W	T	F	S
						1
2	3	4	5	6	7	8
9	10	11	12	13	14	15
16	17	18	19	20	21	22
23	24	25	26	27	28	29
30						

JULY

S	M	T	W	T	F	S
	1	2	3	4	5	6
7	8	9	10	11	12	13
14	15	16	17	18	19	20
21	22	23	24	25	26	27
28	29	30	31			

AUGUST

S	M	T	W	T	F	S
				1	2	3
4	5	6	7	8	9	10
11	12	13	14	15	16	17
18	19	20	21	22	23	24
25	26	27	28	29	30	31

SEPTEMBER

S	M	T	W	T	F	S
1	2	3	4	5	6	7
8	9	10	11	12	13	14
15	16	17	18	19	20	21
22	23	24	25	26	27	28
29	30					

OCTOBER

S	M	T	W	T	F	S
		1	2	3	4	5
6	7	8	9	10	11	12
13	14	15	16	17	18	19
20	21	22	23	24	25	26
27	28	29	30	31		

NOVEMBER

S	M	T	W	T	F	S
					1	2
3	4	5	6	7	8	9
10	11	12	13	14	15	16
17	18	19	20	21	22	23
24	25	26	27	28	29	30

DECEMBER

S	M	T	W	T	F	S
1	2	3	4	5	6	7
8	9	10	11	12	13	14
15	16	17	18	19	20	21
22	23	24	25	26	27	28
29	30	31				

10 (LEAP YEAR)

JANUARY

S	M	T	W	T	F	S
		1	2	3	4	5
6	7	8	9	10	11	12
13	14	15	16	17	18	19
20	21	22	23	24	25	26
27	28	29	30	31		

FEBRUARY

S	M	T	W	T	F	S
					1	2
3	4	5	6	7	8	9
10	11	12	13	14	15	16
17	18	19	20	21	22	23
24	25	26	27	28	29	

MARCH

S	M	T	W	T	F	S
						1
2	3	4	5	6	7	8
9	10	11	12	13	14	15
16	17	18	19	20	21	22
23	24	25	26	27	28	29
30	31					

APRIL

S	M	T	W	T	F	S
		1	2	3	4	5
6	7	8	9	10	11	12
13	14	15	16	17	18	19
20	21	22	23	24	25	26
27	28	29	30			

MAY

S	M	T	W	T	F	S
				1	2	3
4	5	6	7	8	9	10
11	12	13	14	15	16	17
18	19	20	21	22	23	24
25	26	27	28	29	30	31

JUNE

S	M	T	W	T	F	S
1	2	3	4	5	6	7
8	9	10	11	12	13	14
15	16	17	18	19	20	21
22	23	24	25	26	27	28
29	30					

JULY

S	M	T	W	T	F	S
		1	2	3	4	5
6	7	8	9	10	11	12
13	14	15	16	17	18	19
20	21	22	23	24	25	26
27	28	29	30	31		

AUGUST

S	M	T	W	T	F	S
					1	2
3	4	5	6	7	8	9
10	11	12	13	14	15	16
17	18	19	20	21	22	23
24	25	26	27	28	29	30
31						

SEPTEMBER

S	M	T	W	T	F	S
	1	2	3	4	5	6
7	8	9	10	11	12	13
14	15	16	17	18	19	20
21	22	23	24	25	26	27
28	29	30				

OCTOBER

S	M	T	W	T	F	S
			1	2	3	4
5	6	7	8	9	10	11
12	13	14	15	16	17	18
19	20	21	22	23	24	25
26	27	28	29	30	31	

NOVEMBER

S	M	T	W	T	F	S
						1
2	3	4	5	6	7	8
9	10	11	12	13	14	15
16	17	18	19	20	21	22
23	24	25	26	27	28	29
30						

DECEMBER

S	M	T	W	T	F	S
	1	2	3	4	5	6
7	8	9	10	11	12	13
14	15	16	17	18	19	20
21	22	23	24	25	26	27
28	29	30	31			

11 (LEAP YEAR)

JANUARY

S	M	T	W	T	F	S
			1	2	3	4
5	6	7	8	9	10	11
12	13	14	15	16	17	18
19	20	21	22	23	24	25
26	27	28	29	30	31	

FEBRUARY

S	M	T	W	T	F	S
						1
2	3	4	5	6	7	8
9	10	11	12	13	14	15
16	17	18	19	20	21	22
23	24	25	26	27	28	29

MARCH

S	M	T	W	T	F	S
1	2	3	4	5	6	7
8	9	10	11	12	13	14
15	16	17	18	19	20	21
22	23	24	25	26	27	28
29	30	31				

APRIL

S	M	T	W	T	F	S
			1	2	3	4
5	6	7	8	9	10	11
12	13	14	15	16	17	18
19	20	21	22	23	24	25
26	27	28	29	30		

MAY

S	M	T	W	T	F	S
					1	2
3	4	5	6	7	8	9
10	11	12	13	14	15	16
17	18	19	20	21	22	23
24	25	26	27	28	29	30
31						

JUNE

S	M	T	W	T	F	S
	1	2	3	4	5	6
7	8	9	10	11	12	13
14	15	16	17	18	19	20
21	22	23	24	25	26	27
28	29	30				

JULY

S	M	T	W	T	F	S
			1	2	3	4
5	6	7	8	9	10	11
12	13	14	15	16	17	18
19	20	21	22	23	24	25
26	27	28	29	30	31	

AUGUST

S	M	T	W	T	F	S
						1
2	3	4	5	6	7	8
9	10	11	12	13	14	15
16	17	18	19	20	21	22
23	24	25	26	27	28	29
30	31					

SEPTEMBER

S	M	T	W	T	F	S
		1	2	3	4	5
6	7	8	9	10	11	12
13	14	15	16	17	18	19
20	21	22	23	24	25	26
27	28	29	30			

OCTOBER

S	M	T	W	T	F	S
				1	2	3
4	5	6	7	8	9	10
11	12	13	14	15	16	17
18	19	20	21	22	23	24
25	26	27	28	29	30	31

NOVEMBER

S	M	T	W	T	F	S
1	2	3	4	5	6	7
8	9	10	11	12	13	14
15	16	17	18	19	20	21
22	23	24	25	26	27	28
29	30					

DECEMBER

S	M	T	W	T	F	S
		1	2	3	4	5
6	7	8	9	10	11	12
13	14	15	16	17	18	19
20	21	22	23	24	25	26
27	28	29	30	31		

12 (LEAP YEAR)

JANUARY

S	M	T	W	T	F	S
				1	2	3
4	5	6	7	8	9	10
11	12	13	14	15	16	17
18	19	20	21	22	23	24
25	26	27	28	29	30	31

FEBRUARY

S	M	T	W	T	F	S
1	2	3	4	5	6	7
8	9	10	11	12	13	14
15	16	17	18	19	20	21
22	23	24	25	26	27	28
29						

MARCH

S	M	T	W	T	F	S
	1	2	3	4	5	6
7	8	9	10	11	12	13
14	15	16	17	18	19	20
21	22	23	24	25	26	27
28	29	30	31			

APRIL

S	M	T	W	T	F	S
				1	2	3
4	5	6	7	8	9	10
11	12	13	14	15	16	17
18	19	20	21	22	23	24
25	26	27	28	29	30	

MAY

S	M	T	W	T	F	S
						1
2	3	4	5	6	7	8
9	10	11	12	13	14	15
16	17	18	19	20	21	22
23	24	25	26	27	28	29
30	31					

JUNE

S	M	T	W	T	F	S
		1	2	3	4	5
6	7	8	9	10	11	12
13	14	15	16	17	18	19
20	21	22	23	24	25	26
27	28	29	30			

JULY

S	M	T	W	T	F	S
				1	2	3
4	5	6	7	8	9	10
11	12	13	14	15	16	17
18	19	20	21	22	23	24
25	26	27	28	29	30	31

AUGUST

S	M	T	W	T	F	S
1	2	3	4	5	6	7
8	9	10	11	12	13	14
15	16	17	18	19	20	21
22	23	24	25	26	27	28
29	30	31				

SEPTEMBER

S	M	T	W	T	F	S
			1	2	3	4
5	6	7	8	9	10	11
12	13	14	15	16	17	18
19	20	21	22	23	24	25
26	27	28	29	30		

OCTOBER

S	M	T	W	T	F	S
					1	2
3	4	5	6	7	8	9
10	11	12	13	14	15	16
17	18	19	20	21	22	23
24	25	26	27	28	29	30
31						

NOVEMBER

S	M	T	W	T	F	S
	1	2	3	4	5	6
7	8	9	10	11	12	13
14	15	16	17	18	19	20
21	22	23	24	25	26	27
28	29	30				

DECEMBER

S	M	T	W	T	F	S
			1	2	3	4
5	6	7	8	9	10	11
12	13	14	15	16	17	18
19	20	21	22	23	24	25
26	27	28	29	30	31	

13 (LEAP YEAR) 1988

JANUARY

S	M	T	W	T	F	S
					1	2
3	4	5	6	7	8	9
10	11	12	13	14	15	16
17	18	19	20	21	22	23
24	25	26	27	28	29	30
31						

FEBRUARY

S	M	T	W	T	F	S
	1	2	3	4	5	6
7	8	9	10	11	12	13
14	15	16	17	18	19	20
21	22	23	24	25	26	27
28	29					

MARCH

S	M	T	W	T	F	S
		1	2	3	4	5
6	7	8	9	10	11	12
13	14	15	16	17	18	19
20	21	22	23	24	25	26
27	28	29	30	31		

APRIL

S	M	T	W	T	F	S
					1	2
3	4	5	6	7	8	9
10	11	12	13	14	15	16
17	18	19	20	21	22	23
24	25	26	27	28	29	30

MAY

S	M	T	W	T	F	S
1	2	3	4	5	6	7
8	9	10	11	12	13	14
15	16	17	18	19	20	21
22	23	24	25	26	27	28
29	30	31				

JUNE

S	M	T	W	T	F	S
			1	2	3	4
5	6	7	8	9	10	11
12	13	14	15	16	17	18
19	20	21	22	23	24	25
26	27	28	29	30		

JULY

S	M	T	W	T	F	S
					1	2
3	4	5	6	7	8	9
10	11	12	13	14	15	16
17	18	19	20	21	22	23
24	25	26	27	28	29	30
31						

AUGUST

S	M	T	W	T	F	S
	1	2	3	4	5	6
7	8	9	10	11	12	13
14	15	16	17	18	19	20
21	22	23	24	25	26	27
28	29	30	31			

SEPTEMBER

S	M	T	W	T	F	S
				1	2	3
4	5	6	7	8	9	10
11	12	13	14	15	16	17
18	19	20	21	22	23	24
25	26	27	28	29	30	

OCTOBER

S	M	T	W	T	F	S
						1
2	3	4	5	6	7	8
9	10	11	12	13	14	15
16	17	18	19	20	21	22
23	24	25	26	27	28	29
30	31					

NOVEMBER

S	M	T	W	T	F	S
		1	2	3	4	5
6	7	8	9	10	11	12
13	14	15	16	17	18	19
20	21	22	23	24	25	26
27	28	29	30			

DECEMBER

S	M	T	W	T	F	S
				1	2	3
4	5	6	7	8	9	10
11	12	13	14	15	16	17
18	19	20	21	22	23	24
25	26	27	28	29	30	31

14 (LEAP YEAR)

JANUARY

S	M	T	W	T	F	S
						1
2	3	4	5	6	7	8
9	10	11	12	13	14	15
16	17	18	19	20	21	22
23	24	25	26	27	28	29
30	31					

FEBRUARY

S	M	T	W	T	F	S
		1	2	3	4	5
6	7	8	9	10	11	12
13	14	15	16	17	18	19
20	21	22	23	24	25	26
27	28	29				

MARCH

S	M	T	W	T	F	S
			1	2	3	4
5	6	7	8	9	10	11
12	13	14	15	16	17	18
19	20	21	22	23	24	25
26	27	28	29	30	31	

APRIL

S	M	T	W	T	F	S
						1
2	3	4	5	6	7	8
9	10	11	12	13	14	15
16	17	18	19	20	21	22
23	24	25	26	27	28	29
30						

MAY

S	M	T	W	T	F	S
	1	2	3	4	5	6
7	8	9	10	11	12	13
14	15	16	17	18	19	20
21	22	23	24	25	26	27
28	29	30	31			

JUNE

S	M	T	W	T	F	S
				1	2	3
4	5	6	7	8	9	10
11	12	13	14	15	16	17
18	19	20	21	22	23	24
25	26	27	28	29	30	

JULY

S	M	T	W	T	F	S
						1
2	3	4	5	6	7	8
9	10	11	12	13	14	15
16	17	18	19	20	21	22
23	24	25	26	27	28	29
30	31					

AUGUST

S	M	T	W	T	F	S
		1	2	3	4	5
6	7	8	9	10	11	12
13	14	15	16	17	18	19
20	21	22	23	24	25	26
27	28	29	30	31		

SEPTEMBER

S	M	T	W	T	F	S
					1	2
3	4	5	6	7	8	9
10	11	12	13	14	15	16
17	18	19	20	21	22	23
24	25	26	27	28	29	30

OCTOBER

S	M	T	W	T	F	S
1	2	3	4	5	6	7
8	9	10	11	12	13	14
15	16	17	18	19	20	21
22	23	24	25	26	27	28
29	30	31				

NOVEMBER

S	M	T	W	T	F	S
			1	2	3	4
5	6	7	8	9	10	11
12	13	14	15	16	17	18
19	20	21	22	23	24	25
26	27	28	29	30		

DECEMBER

S	M	T	W	T	F	S
					1	2
3	4	5	6	7	8	9
10	11	12	13	14	15	16
17	18	19	20	21	22	23
24	25	26	27	28	29	30
31						

WORLD TIME ZONES

The world is divided into 24 time zones, each 15° longitude wide. The longitudinal meridian passing through Greenwich, England, is the starting point, and is called the *prime meridian.*

Travelers heading west should set their watches back one hour for each time zone passed. Those going east must set their watches ahead one hour. The twelfth zone is divided by the 180th meridian (International Date Line). When the line is crossed going west, the date is advanced one day. When crossed going east, the date becomes a day earlier.

The table below gives the time in countries around the world when it is noon (Eastern Standard Time) in New York City. An asterisk (*) indicates that it is the next day.

COUNTRY	DIFFERENCE	TIME
Afghanistan	+ 9½	9:30 p.m.
Albania	+ 6	6:00 p.m.
Algeria	+ 5	5:00 p.m.
Angola	+ 6	6:00 p.m.
Argentina	+ 2	2:00 p.m.
Australia		
Perth	+14	2:00 a.m.*
Adelaide	+15½	3:30 a.m.*
Sydney	+16	4:00 a.m.*
Austria	+ 6	6:00 p.m.
Azores	+ 4	4:00 p.m.
Bahamas	0	12:00 noon
Bahrain	+ 8	8:00 p.m.
Bangladesh	+10½	10:30 p.m.
Barbados	+ 1	1:00 p.m.
Belgium	+ 6	6:00 p.m.
Benin	+ 6	6:00 p.m.
Bermuda	+ 1	1:00 p.m.
Bolivia	+ 1	1:00 p.m.
Botswana	+ 7	7:00 p.m.
Brazil (Rio)	+ 2	2:00 p.m.
Britain	+ 5	5:00 p.m.
Bulgaria	+ 7	7:00 p.m.
Burma	+11½	11:30 p.m.
Burundi	+ 7	7:00 p.m.
Cambodia	+12	12:00 mid.
Cameroon	+ 6	6:00 p.m.
Canada		
Victoria, B.C.	− 3	9:00 a.m.
Edmonton, Alta.	− 2	10:00 a.m.
Winnipeg, Man.	− 1	11:00 a.m.
Montreal, Que.	0	12:00 noon
Halifax, N.S.	+ 1	1:00 p.m.
St. John's, Nfld.	+ 1½	1:30 p.m.
Canary Is.	+ 5	5:00 p.m.
Cape Verde	+ 3	3:00 p.m.
Central Africa	+ 6	6:00 p.m.
Chad	+ 6	6:00 p.m.
Chile	+ 2	2:00 p.m.
China	+13	1:00 a.m.*
Colombia	0	12:00 noon
Comoros	+ 8	8:00 p.m.
Congo	+ 6	6:00 p.m.
Costa Rica	− 1	11:00 a.m.
Cuba	0	12:00 noon
Cyprus	+ 7	7:00 p.m.
Czechoslovakia	+ 6	6:00 p.m.
Denmark	+ 6	6:00 p.m.
Djibouti	+ 8	8:00 p.m.
Dominican Rep.	0	12:00 noon
Ecuador	0	12:00 noon
Egypt	+ 7	7:00 p.m.
El Salvador	− 1	11:00 a.m.
Equatorial Guinea	+ 6	6:00 p.m.
Ethiopia	+ 8	8:00 p.m.
Fiji	+17	5:00 a.m.*
Finland	+ 7	7:00 p.m.
France	+ 6	6:00 p.m.
Gabon	+ 6	6:00 p.m.
Gambia	+ 5	5:00 p.m.
Germany, East	+ 6	6:00 p.m.
Germany, West	+ 6	6:00 p.m.

COUNTRY	DIFFERENCE	TIME
Ghana	+ 5	5:00 p.m.
Greece	+ 7	7:00 p.m.
Grenada	+ 1	1:00 p.m.
Guam	+15	3:00 a.m.*
Guatemala	− 1	11:00 a.m.
Guinea	+ 5	5:00 p.m.
Guinea-Bissau	+ 4	4:00 p.m.
Guyana	+ 1¼	1:15 p.m.
Haiti	0	12:00 noon
Honduras	− 1	11:00 a.m.
Hungary	+ 6	6:00 p.m.
Iceland	+ 5	5:00 p.m.
India	+10½	10:30 p.m.
Indonesia	+12	12:00 mid.
Iran	+ 8½	8:30 p.m.
Iraq	+ 8	8:00 p.m.
Ireland	+ 5	5:00 p.m.
Israel	+ 7	7:00 p.m.
Italy	+ 6	6:00 p.m.
Ivory Coast	+ 5	5:00 p.m.
Jamaica	0	12:00 noon
Japan	+14	2:00 a.m.*
Jordan	+ 7	7:00 p.m.
Kenya	+ 8	8:00 p.m.
Korea, North	+14	2:00 a.m.*
Korea, South	+14	2:00 a.m.*
Kuwait	+ 8	8:00 p.m.
Laos	+12	12:00 mid.
Lebanon	+ 7	7:00 p.m.
Lesotho	+ 7	7:00 p.m.
Liberia	+ 5	5:00 p.m.
Libya	+ 7	7:00 p.m.
Liechtenstein	+ 6	6:00 p.m.
Luxembourg	+ 6	6:00 p.m.
Madagascar	+ 8	8:00 p.m.
Malawi	+ 7	7:00 p.m.
Malaysia	+12½	12:30 a.m.*
Maldives	+10	10:00 p.m.
Mali	+ 5	5:00 p.m.
Malta	+ 6	6:00 p.m.
Mauritania	+ 5	5:00 p.m.
Mauritius	+ 9	9:00 p.m.
Mexico (Mexico City)	− 1	11:00 a.m.
Midway Is.	− 6	6:00 a.m.
Mongolia	+13	1:00 a.m.*
Morocco	+ 5	5:00 p.m.
Mozambique	+ 7	7:00 p.m.
Nauru	+16½	4:30 a.m.*
Nepal	+10½	10:30 p.m.
Netherlands	+ 6	6:00 p.m.
New Zealand	+18	6:00 a.m.*
Nicaragua	− 1	11:00 a.m.
Niger	+ 6	6:00 p.m.
Nigeria	+ 6	6:00 p.m.
Norway	+ 6	6:00 p.m.
Oman	+ 9	9:00 p.m.
Pakistan	+10	10:00 p.m.
Panama	0	12:00 noon
Papua New Guinea	+15	3:00 a.m.*
Paraguay	+ 2	2:00 p.m.
Peru	− 0	12:00 noon

COUNTRY	DIFFERENCE	TIME
Philippines	+13	1:00 a.m.*
Poland	+ 6	6:00 p.m.
Portugal	+ 5	5:00 p.m.
Puerto Rico	+ 1	1:00 p.m.
Qatar	+ 8	8:00 p.m.
Romania	+ 7	7:00 p.m.
Rwanda	+ 7	7:00 p.m.
Samoa	− 6	6:00 a.m.
San Marino	+ 6	6:00 p.m.
Saudi Arabia	Sun time	c.8:00 p.m.
Senegal	+ 5	5:00 p.m.
Seychelles	+ 9	9:00 p.m.
Sierra Leone	+ 5	5:00 p.m.
Singapore	+ 7½	12:30 a.m.*
Solomons	+16	4:00 a.m.*
Somalia	+ 8	8:00 p.m.
South Africa	+ 7	7:00 p.m.
Soviet Union		
Moscow	+ 8	8:00 p.m.
Gorki	+ 9	9:00 p.m.
Sverdlovsk	+10	10:00 p.m.
Tashkent	+11	11:00 p.m.
Novosibirsk	+12	12:00 mid.
Irkutsk	+13	1:00 a.m.*
Yakutsk	+14	2:00 a.m.*
Vladivostok	+15	3:00 a.m.*
Spain	+ 6	6:00 p.m.
Sri Lanka	+10½	10:30 p.m.
Sudan	+ 7	7:00 p.m.
Suriname	+ 1½	1:30 p.m.
Swaziland	+ 7	7:00 p.m.
Sweden	+ 6	6:00 p.m.
Switzerland	+ 6	6:00 p.m.
Syria	+ 7	7:00 p.m.
Taiwan	+13	1:00 a.m.*
Tanzania	+ 8	8:00 p.m.
Thailand	+12	12:00 mid.
Togo	+ 5	5:00 p.m.
Tonga	− 6	6:00 a.m.
Trinidad-Tobago	+ 1	1:00 p.m.
Tunisia	+ 6	6:00 p.m.
Turkey	+ 7	7:00 p.m.
Uganda	+ 8	8:00 p.m.
United Arab Em.	+ 9	9:00 p.m.
United States		
Honolulu	− 5	7:00 a.m.
Anchorage	− 4	8:00 a.m.
Los Angeles	− 3	9:00 a.m.
Denver	− 2	10:00 a.m.
Chicago	− 1	11:00 a.m.
New York	0	12:00 noon
Upper Volta	+ 5	5:00 p.m.
Uruguay	+ 2	2:00 p.m.
Venezuela	+ 1	1:00 p.m.
Vietnam	+12	12:00 mid.
Virgin Islands	+ 1	1:00 p.m.
Yemen, North	+ 8	8:00 p.m.
Yemen, South	+ 8	8:00 p.m.
Yugoslavia	+ 6	6:00 p.m.
Zaire (Kinshasa)	+ 6	6:00 p.m.
Zambia	+ 7	7:00 p.m.
Zimbabwe	+ 7	7:00 p.m.

Cities

The 100th anniversary of the Brooklyn Bridge was celebrated in New York City on May 24 with a gigantic fireworks show that featured nearly 10,000 rockets and other pyrotechnics. Designed by John Roebling, the bridge was completed in 1883 across the East River, connecting Manhattan Island and Brooklyn. Now dwarfed by Manhattan's skyscrapers, the bridge's towers were the highest structures in the city at the time they were built.

HIGHLIGHTS: 1983

NEW ORLEANS WORLD'S FAIR

The New Orleans World's Fair, opening on May 12, 1984, and running six months to Nov. 11, will cover 82 acres on the bank of the Mississippi River near the city's famous French Quarter. Its theme will be "The World of Rivers—Fresh Water as a Source of Life."

Hoping to attract more visitors than the 11 million who attended the Knoxville, Tenn., world exposition in 1982, its promoters are emphasizing entertainment. Some 20 stages will feature the jazz New Orleans is noted for as well as dancers, singers, and other entertainers. The fair will remain open until 3 a.m. each night to accommodate late

20 LARGEST CITIES IN U.S.

RANK	CITY AND STATE	POPULATION
1	New York City, N.Y.[1]	7,071,639
2	Chicago, Ill.[1]	3,005,072
3	Los Angeles, Calif.[1]	2,968,579
4	Philadelphia, Pa.[1]	1,688,210
5	Houston, Tex.[1]	1,595,138
6	Detroit, Mich.[1]	1,203,339
7	Dallas, Tex.[1]	904,078
8	San Diego, Calif.[1]	875,538
9	Phoenix, Ariz.[1]	789,704
10	Baltimore, Md.[1]	786,741
11	San Antonio, Tex.[1]	785,880
12	Indianapolis, Ind.[1]	700,807
13	San Francisco, Calif.[1]	678,974
14	Memphis, Tenn.[1]	646,356
15	Washington, D.C.[1]	638,432
16	Milwaukee, Wis.[1]	636,297
17	San Jose, Calif.[1]	629,531
18	Cleveland, Ohio[1]	573,822
19	Columbus, Ohio[1]	565,032
20	Boston, Mass.[1]	562,994

[1] U.S. 1980 Census

HIGHLIGHTS: 1983 *(continued)*

revelers.

Cultural exhibits will be housed in a large building that will become the city's new convention center.

The next world's fair scheduled for the U.S. will be in Chicago, in 1992, celebrating the 500th anniversary of Columbus' discovery of America.

MOST LIVABLE CITY—FORT WAYNE, IND.

The U.S. Conference of Mayors on June 13 named Fort Wayne, Ind., as the nation's "Most Livable City." Fort Wayne won out over 44 other contenders in a competition in which *livable cities* were defined as those that "creatively use urban arts to improve their economic viability."

In February, Fort Wayne had been one of eight cities chosen for the All-American City award by the National Municipal League.

Fort Wayne was helped in winning the awards by a $100 million redevelopment project that included building an art gallery, a convention center, and a botanical garden.

Second and third places in the livable city competition went to Albuquerque, N.M., and Charleston, S.C.

Other winners of the 1983 All-American City award were Santa Ana, Calif.; Durham, N.C.; Ames, Iowa; Ann Arbor, Mich.; Santa Rosa, Calif.; Salem, Ore., and San Antonio, Texas.

TALE OF TWO TEXAS CITIES

In Houston, the nation's fifth-largest city, only 12% of the voters turned out on June 11 to vote down a $2.35 billion bond issue to build the first 18.5-mile section of a modern urban rail transit system. The vote was 62% no and 38% yes.

In Dallas, the nation's seventh-largest city, 27% of the voters went to the polls on Aug. 13 to approve a 1-cent sales tax to finance a $8.75 billion rail transit system. The vote was 58% yes and 42% no.

The plan calls for DART (the Dallas Area Rapid Transit) to construct 160 miles of rail lines, including a 3.4 mile subway, to serve Dallas and 13 other nearby cities.

WASHINGTON IS HIGH SPENDER

The U.S. Census Bureau reported in 1983 that city governments spend an average of $563.54 per capita.

The city with the highest per capita expenditure was Washington, D.C., at $3,142.

LARGEST U.S. METROPOLITAN AREAS

RANK	METROPOLITAN AREA	POPULATION
1	New York City, N.Y.-N.J.[1]	9,120,346
2	Los Angeles-Long Beach, Calif.[1]	7,477,503
3	Chicago, Ill.	7,103,624
4	Philadelphia, Pa.-N.J.[1]	4,716,818
5	Detroit, Mich.[1]	4,353,413
6	San Francisco-Oakland, Calif.[1]	3,250,630
7	Washington, D.C.-Md.-Va.[1]	3,060,922
8	Dallas-Fort Worth, Texas[1]	2,974,805
9	Houston, Texas[1]	2,905,353
10	Boston, Mass.-N.H.[1]	2,763,357
11	Nassau-Suffolk, N.Y.[1]	2,605,813
12	St. Louis, Mo.-Ill.[1]	2,356,460
13	Pittsburgh, Pa.[1]	2,263,894
14	Baltimore, Md.[1]	2,174,023
15	Minneapolis-St. Paul, Minn.[1]	2,113,533
16	Atlanta, Ga.[1]	2,029,710
17	Newark, N.J.[1]	1,965,969
18	Anaheim-Santa Ana, Calif.[1]	1,932,709
19	Cleveland, Ohio[1]	1,898,825
20	San Diego, Calif.[1]	1,861,846

WORLD'S LARGEST METROPOLITAN AREAS

RANK	METROPOLITAN AREA	POPULATION
1	Mexico City, Mexico[2]	13,993,866
2	Tokyo, Japan[2]	11,696,373
3	Shanghai, China[2]	10,820,000
4	Buenos Aires, Argentina[2]	9,910,000
5	New York City, N.Y.-N.J.[1]	9,120,346
6	Peking, China[4]	8,626,050
7	Paris, France[2]	8,612,531
8	São Paulo, Brazil[2]	8,407,500
9	Calcutta, India[2]	8,297,000
10	Moscow, Soviet Union[2]	8,011,000
11	Manila, Philippines[4]	7,800,000
12	Bombay, India	7,605,000
13	Seoul, South Korea[4]	7,500,000
14	Los Angeles-Long Beach, Calif.[1]	7,477,503
15	Chicago, Ill.[1]	7,103,624
16	London, Britain[2]	7,028,200
17	Cairo, Egypt[2,3]	5,074,016
18	Delhi, India[2]	4,891,000
19	Philadelphia, Pa.-N.J.[1]	4,716,818
20	Jakarta, Indonesia[2,3]	4,576,009

[1] U.S. 1980 Census. [2] 1979 UN Demographic Yearbook. [3] City only. [4] Official estimate.

LARGEST METROPOLITAN AREAS OF THE WORLD

Source: Censuses and official estimates by national governments

Altogether 41 American metropolitan areas with populations of more than 930,000 make up about one-fifth of the world's 206 largest metropolitan areas as shown below.

CITY	POPULATION
Adana, Turkey	1,234,735
Addis Ababa, Ethiopia	1,277,159
Ahmedabad, India	1,741,522
Alexandria, Egypt	2,317,705
Algiers, Algeria	2,000,000
Alma-Ata, Soviet Union	910,000
Amsterdam, Neth.	957,941
Anaheim, California	1,932,709
Ankara, Turkey	2,572,562
Athens, Greece	2,101,103
Atlanta, Georgia	2,029,710
Baghdad, Iraq	1,657,424
Baku, Soviet Union	1,550,000
Baltimore, Maryland	2,174,023
Bandung, Indonesia	1,201,730
Bangalore, India	1,653,779
Bangkok, Thailand	4,178,000
Barcelona, Spain	1,742,345
Beirut, Lebanon	938,940
Belo Horizonte, Brazil	1,937,200
Berlin (East), E. Ger.	1,145,743
Berlin (West), W. Ger.	1,902,750
Birmingham, Britain	2,358,980
Bogotá, Colombia	4,324,000
Bombay, India	7,605,000
Boston, Massachusetts	2,763,357
Brasília, Brazil	1,306,400
Brisbane, Australia	942,636
Brussels, Belgium	1,008,715
Bucharest, Romania	1,929,360
Budapest, Hungary	2,058,000
Buenos Aires, Argentina	9,910,000
Buffalo, New York	1,242,826
Bursa, Turkey	960,035
Cairo, Egypt	5,074,016
Calcutta, India	8,297,000
Cali, Colombia	1,382,000
Canton, China	1,840,000
Cape Town, South Africa	1,490,935
Caracas, Venezuela	2,849,191
Casablanca, Morocco	1,753,400
Changchun, China	975,000
Chelyabinsk, Soviet Un.	1,042,000
Chengtu, China	1,107,000
Chicago, Illinois	7,103,624
Chungking, China	2,121,000
Cincinnati, Ohio–Ky.	1,401,491
Cleveland, Ohio	1,898,825
Cologne, W. Germany	976,136
Columbus, Ohio	1,093,316
Copenhagen, Denmark	1,391,634
Curitiba, Brazil	943,400
Dallas, Texas	2,974,805
Damascus, Syria	1,156,000
Delhi, India	3,647,023
Denver, Colorado	1,620,902
Detroit, Michigan	4,353,413
Dhaka, Bangladesh	1,730,253
Dnepropetrovsk, Sov. Un.	1,083,000
Donetsk, Soviet Union	1,032,000
Durban, South Africa	960,792
Erevan, Soviet Union	1,036,000
Fort Lauderdale, Florida	1,018,200
Fortaleza, Brazil	1,306,800
Fukuoka, Japan	1,070,951
Fushun, China	985,000
Giza, Egypt	1,230,446
Glasgow, Scotland	1,727,625
Gorky, Soviet Union	1,358,000
Guadalajara, Mexico	2,467,657
Guayaquil, Ecuador	1,116,280
Hamburg, W. Germany	1,653,043
Hanoi, Vietnam	1,000,000
Harbin, China	1,552,000
Havana, Cuba	1,861,442
Houston, Texas	2,905,353
Hyderabad, India	1,796,339
Inchon, S. Korea	1,084,730
Indianapolis, Indiana	1,166,575
Istanbul, Turkey	3,864,493
Izmir, Turkey	1,660,529
Jakarta, Indonesia	4,576,009
Johannesburg, So. Af.	1,726,073
Kanpur, India	1,275,242
Kansas City, Mo.–Kans.	1,327,106
Karachi, Pakistan	3,498,634
Kawasaki, Japan	1,043,674
Kazan, Soviet Union	1,002,000
Kharkov, Soviet Union	1,464,000
Kiev, Soviet Union	2,192,000
Kinshasa, Zaire	2,242,297
Kitakyushu, Japan	1,068,415
Kobe, Japan	1,372,086
Konya, Turkey	1,425,910
Kuibyshev, Soviet Union	1,226,000
Kyoto, Japan	1,467,700
Lagos, Nigeria	1,476,837
Lahore, Pakistan	2,165,372
Leeds, Britain	1,735,700
Leningrad, Soviet Union	4,638,000
Lille, France	943,915
Lima, Peru	4,278,800
Lisbon, Portugal	1,611,887
Liverpool, Britain	1,226,310
Lodz, Poland	1,086,700
London, Britain	7,028,200
Los Angeles, California	7,477,503
Lyon, France	1,185,919
Madras, India	3,169,930
Madrid, Spain	3,200,067
Manchester, Britain	2,389,260
Manila, Philippines	7,800,000
Marseille, France	1,076,897
Medellín, Colombia	1,589,000
Melbourne, Australia	2,578,527
Mexico City, Mexico	14,750,182
Miami, Florida	1,625,781
Milan, Italy	1,706,268
Milwaukee, Wisconsin	1,397,143
Minneapolis, Minn.–Wis.	2,113,533
Minsk, Soviet Union	1,276,000
Monterrey, Mexico	2,018,625
Montevideo, Uruguay	1,173,254
Montreal, Canada	2,828,349
Moscow, Soviet Union	8,099,000
Munich, W. Germany	1,299,693
Nagoya, Japan	2,089,332
Nanking, China	1,419,000
Naples, Italy	1,225,227
Nassau–Suffolk, N.Y.	2,605,813
Netzahualcoyotl, Mexico	2,331,151
New Orleans, La.	1,187,073
New York, New York	9,120,346
Newark, New Jersey	1,965,969
Nova Ignacu, Brazil	1,183,600
Novosibirsk, Soviet Union	1,328,000
Odessa, Soviet Union	1,057,000
Omsk, Soviet Union	1,028,000
Osaka, Japan	2,682,221
Paris, France	8,612,531
Peking, China	8,626,050
Perm, Soviet Union	1,008,000
Philadelphia, Pa.	4,716,818
Phoenix, Arizona	1,509,052
Pittsburgh, Pa.	2,263,894
Poona, India	1,135,034
Port Arthur, China	1,508,000
Portland, Oreg.–Wash.	1,242,594
Porto, Portugal	1,314,794
Pôrto Alegre, Brazil	1,221,000
Prague, Czechoslovakia	1,193,135
Pusan, South Korea	3,160,276
Rangoon, Burma	1,586,422
Recife, Brazil	1,432,800
Rio de Janeiro, Brazil	5,539,100
Riverside–San Bernardino, California	1,558,182
Rochester, New York	971,230
Rome, Italy	2,897,505
Rostov-on-Don, Sov. Un.	946,000
Rotterdam, Netherlands	1,016,170
Sacramento, California	1,014,002
Saigon, Vietnam	1,825,297
St. Louis, Mo.–Ill.	2,356,460
Salt Lake City, Utah	936,255
Salvador, Brazil	1,501,700
San Antonio, Texas	1,071,954
San Diego, California	1,861,846
San Francisco, Calif.	3,250,630
San Jose, California	1,295,071
San Juan, Puerto Rico	1,083,664
Santiago, Chile	3,853,275
São Paulo, Brazil	8,732,000
Sapporo, Japan	1,371,108
Seattle–Everett, Wash.	1,607,469
Seoul, South Korea	8,366,756
Shanghai, China	10,820,000
Shenyang, China	2,411,000
Sian, China	1,310,000
Singapore, Singapore	2,390,800
Sofia, Bulgaria	1,014,059
Stockholm, Sweden	1,384,310
Surabaja, Indonesia	1,556,255
Sverdlovsk, Soviet Un.	1,225,000
Sydney, Australia	3,280,900
Taegu, South Korea	1,607,458
Taipei, Taiwan	1,769,568
Taiyuan, China	1,020,000
Tampa–St. Petersburg, Fla.	1,569,134
Tashkent, Soviet Union	1,816,000
Tbilisi, Soviet Union	1,080,000
Teheran, Iran	4,496,159
Tel Aviv–Yato, Israel	1,219,900
Tientsin, China	4,280,000
Tokyo, Japan	11,687,222
Torino, Italy	1,181,567
Toronto, Canada	2,998,947
Tsingtao, China	1,121,000
Turin, Italy	1,190,621
Ufa, Soviet Union	986,000
Vancouver, Canada	1,268,183
Vienna, Austria	1,592,800
Volgograd, Soviet Union	939,000
Warsaw, Poland	1,542,500
Washington, D.C.	3,060,922
Wuhan, China	2,146,000
Yokohama, Japan	2,763,270

LARGEST U.S. CITIES

Source: U.S. Census Bureau 1980 Census.

Among the largest cities in the U.S., those that grew at the fastest rates since 1970 were Aurora, Colo. (111.5%), Mesa, Ariz. (141.8%), Lexington-Fayette, Ky. (88.8%), and Arlington, Tex. (77.5%).

Cities whose populations declined at the highest rates were St. Louis, Mo. (−27.2%), Buffalo, N.Y. (−22.7%), Cleveland, Ohio (−23.6.%), and Detroit, Mich. (−20.5%).

CITY AND STATE	POPULATION
Abilene, Texas	98,315
Akron, Ohio	237,177
Albany, N.Y.	101,727
Albuquerque, N. Mex.	332,239
Alexandria, Va.	103,217
Allentown, Pa.	103,758
Amarillo, Texas	149,230
Anaheim, Calif.	219,494
Anchorage, Alaska	174,431
Ann Arbor, Mich.	107,969
Arlington, Texas	160,113
Atlanta, Ga.	425,022
Aurora, Colo.	158,588
Austin, Texas	345,890
Bakersfield, Calif.	105,611
Baltimore, Md.	786,741
Baton Rouge, La.	219,844
Bayamón, Puerto Rico	195,965
Beaumont, Texas	118,102
Berkeley, Calif.	103,328
Birmingham, Ala.	284,413
Boise, Idaho	102,160
Boston, Mass.	562,994
Bridgeport, Conn.	142,546
Brockton, Mass.	95,172
Buffalo, N.Y.	357,870
Caguas, Puerto Rico	118,020
Cambridge, Mass.	95,322
Canton, Ohio	93,077
Carolina, Puerto Rico	165,207
Cedar Rapids, Iowa	110,243
Charlotte, N.C.	315,417
Chattanooga, Tenn.	169,728
Chesapeake, Va.	114,186
Chicago, Ill.	3,005,072
Cincinnati, Ohio	385,457
Cleveland, Ohio	573,822
Colorado Springs, Colo.	214,821
Columbia, S.C.	101,229
Columbus, Ga.	169,441
Columbus, Ohio	565,032
Concord, Calif.	103,763
Corpus Christi, Texas	231,134
Dallas, Texas	904,078
Davenport, Iowa	103,264
Dayton, Ohio	193,536
Dearborn, Mich.	90,660
Decatur, Ill.	93,896
Denver, Colo.	492,365
Des Moines, Iowa	191,003
Detroit, Mich.	1,203,339
Duluth, Minn.	92,811
Durham, N.C.	100,538
East Los Angeles, Calif.	110,017
El Paso, Texas	425,259
Elizabeth, N.J.	106,201
Erie, Pa.	119,123
Eugene, Oreg.	105,624
Evansville, Ind.	130,496
Fall River, Mass.	92,574
Flint, Mich.	159,611
Fort Lauderdale, Fla.	153,279
Fort Wayne, Ind.	172,349
Fort Worth, Texas	385,164
Fremont, Calif.	131,945
Fresno, Calif.	217,129
Fullerton, Calif.	102,034
Garden Grove, Calif.	123,307
Garland, Texas	138,857
Gary, Ind.	151,953
Glendale, Ariz.	97,172
Glendale, Calif.	139,060
Grand Rapids, Mich.	181,843
Greensboro, N.C.	155,642
Hammond, Ind.	93,714
Hampton, Va.	122,617
Hartford, Conn.	136,392
Hayward, Calif.	94,342
Hialeah, Fla.	145,254
Hollywood, Fla.	121,323
Honolulu, Hawaii	365,048
Houston, Texas	1,595,138
Huntington Beach, Calif.	170,505
Huntsville, Ala.	142,513
Independence, Mo.	111,806
Indianapolis, Ind.	700,807
Inglewood, Calif.	94,245
Irving, Texas	109,943
Jackson, Miss.	202,895
Jacksonville, Fla.	540,920
Jersey City, N.J.	223,532
Kansas City, Kans.	161,148
Kansas City, Mo.	448,033
Knoxville, Tenn.	175,045
Koolaupoko, Hawaii	109,373
Lakewood, Colo.	113,808
Lansing, Mich.	130,414
Laredo, Texas	91,449
Las Vegas, Nev.	164,674
Lexington, Ky.	204,165
Lincoln, Nebr.	171,932
Little Rock, Ark.	158,915
Livonia, Mich.	104,814
Long Beach, Calif.	361,355
Los Angeles, Calif.	2,968,579
Louisville, Ky.	298,694
Lowell, Mass.	92,418
Lubbock, Texas	173,979
Macon, Ga.	116,896
Madison, Wis.	170,616
Manchester, N.H.	90,936
Mayaguez, Puerto Rico	95,886
Memphis, Tenn.	646,174
Mesa, Ariz.	152,453
Miami, Fla.	346,865
Miami Beach, Fla.	96,298
Milwaukee, Wis.	636,297
Minneapolis, Minn.	370,951
Mobile, Ala.	200,452
Modesto, Calif.	106,602
Montgomery, Ala.	177,857
Nashville, Tenn.	455,651
New Bedford, Mass.	98,478
New Haven, Conn.	126,101
New Orleans, La.	557,927
New York City, N.Y.	7,071,639
Newark, N.J.	329,248
Newport News, Va.	144,903
Norfolk, Va.	266,979
Oakland, Calif.	339,337
Odessa, Tex.	90,027
Oklahoma City, Okla.	403,484
Omaha, Nebr.	313,939
Orange, Calif.	91,450
Orlando, Fla.	128,291
Oxnard, Calif.	108,195
Parma, Ohio	92,548
Pasadena, Calif.	118,072
Pasadena, Texas	112,560
Paterson, N.J.	137,970
Peoria, Ill.	124,160
Philadelphia, Pa.	1,688,210
Phoenix, Ariz.	789,704
Pittsburgh, Pa.	423,959
Ponce, Puerto Rico	188,219
Portland, Oreg.	366,383
Portsmouth, Va.	104,577
Providence, R.I.	156,804
Pueblo, Colo.	101,686
Raleigh, N.C.	150,255
Reno, Nev.	100,756
Richmond, Va.	219,214
Riverside, Calif.	170,591
Roanoke, Va.	100,220
Rochester, N.Y.	241,741
Rockford, Ill.	139,712
Sacramento, Calif.	275,741
St. Louis, Mo.	453,085
St. Paul, Minn.	270,230
St. Petersburg, Fla.	238,647
Salt Lake City, Utah	163,034
San Antonio, Texas	786,023
San Bernardino, Calif.	118,794
San Diego, Calif.	875,538
San Francisco, Calif.	678,974
San Jose, Calif.	629,531
San Juan, Puerto Rico	432,973
Santa Ana, Calif.	204,023
Savannah, Ga.	141,651
Seattle, Wash.	493,846
Shreveport, La.	205,820
South Bend, Ind.	109,727
Spokane, Wash.	171,300
Springfield, Ill.	100,054
Springfield, Mass.	152,319
Springfield, Mo.	133,116
Stamford, Conn.	102,466
Sterling Heights, Mich.	108,999
Stockton, Calif.	149,779
Sunnyvale, Calif.	106,618
Syracuse, N.Y.	170,105
Tacoma, Wash.	158,501
Tampa, Fla.	271,523
Tempe, Ariz.	106,920
Toledo, Ohio	354,635
Topeka, Kans.	115,266
Torrance, Calif.	129,881
Trenton, N.J.	92,124
Tucson, Ariz.	330,537
Tulsa, Okla.	360,919
Virginia Beach, Va.	262,199
Waco, Texas	101,261
Warren, Mich.	161,134
Washington, D.C.	638,432
Waterbury, Conn.	103,266
Wichita, Kans.	279,835
Wichita Falls, Texas	94,201
Winston-Salem, N.C.	131,885
Worcester, Mass.	161,799
Yonkers, N.Y.	195,351
Youngstown, Ohio	115,436

LARGEST U.S. METROPOLITAN AREAS

Source: U.S. Census Bureau 1980 census.

Among the largest metropolitan areas, those that grew at the fastest rate from 1970 to 1980 were Fort Myers, Fla. (95.1%), Ocala, Fla. (77.4%), Las Vegas, Nev. (69.5%), Sarasota, Fla. (68.0%), West Palm Beach–Boca Raton, Fla. (65.3%), and Fort Lauderdale, Fla. (64.2%).

METROPOLITAN AREA	POPULATION
Akron, Ohio	660,328
Albany–Schenectady, N.Y.	795,019
Albuquerque, N. Mex.	454,499
Allentown–Bethlehem–Easton, Pa.–N.J.	635,481
Anaheim–Santa Ana–Garden Grove, Calif.	1,932,709
Ann Arbor, Mich.	264,748
Appleton–Oshkosh, Wis.	291,369
Atlanta, Ga.	2,029,710
Atlantic City, N.J.	194,119
Augusta, Ga.–S.C.	327,372
Austin, Texas	536,688
Bakersfield, Calif.	403,089
Baltimore, Md.	2,174,023
Baton Rouge, La.	494,151
Battle Creek, Mich.	187,338
Beaumont–Port Arthur–Orange, Texas	375,497
Biloxi, Miss.	191,918
Binghamton, N.Y.–Pa.	301,336
Birmingham, Ala.	847,487
Boston, Mass.–N.H.	2,763,357
Bridgeport, Conn.	395,455
Brownsville, Texas	209,727
Buffalo, N.Y.	1,242,826
Canton, Ohio	404,421
Charleston, S.C.	430,462
Charleston, W.Va.	269,595
Charlotte–Gastonia, N.C.	637,218
Chattanooga, Tenn.–Ga.	426,540
Chicago, Ill.	7,103,624
Cincinnati, Ohio–Ky.	1,401,491
Cleveland, Ohio	1,898,825
Colorado Springs, Colo.	317,458
Columbia, S.C.	410,088
Columbus, Ga.–Ala.	239,196
Columbus, Ohio	1,093,316
Corpus Christi, Texas	326,228
Dallas–Fort Worth, Texas	2,974,805
Davenport–Rock Island–Moline, Iowa–Ill.	383,958
Dayton, Ohio	830,070
Daytona Beach, Fla.	258,762
Denver–Boulder, Colo.	1,620,902
Des Moines, Iowa	338,048
Detroit, Mich.	4,353,413
Duluth–Superior, Minn.	266,650
El Paso, Texas	479,899
Erie, Pa.	279,780
Eugene–Springfield, Ore.	275,226
Evansville, Ind.–Ky.	309,408
Fayetteville, N.C.	247,160
Flint, Mich.	521,589
Fort Lauderdale–Hollywood, Fla.	1,018,200
Fort Myers, Fla.	205,266
Fort Smith, Ark.–Okla.	203,511
Fort Wayne, Ind.	382,961
Fresno, Calif.	514,621
Galveston, Texas	195,940
Gary, Ind.	642,781
Grand Rapids, Mich.	601,680
Greensboro–Winston Salem–High Point, N.C.	827,252
Greenville, S.C.	569,066
Hamilton–Middletown, O.	258,787
Harrisburg, Pa.	466,576
Hartford, Conn.	726,114
Honolulu, Hawaii	762,565
Houston, Texas	2,905,353
Huntington–Ashland, W.Va.–Ky.–Ohio	311,350
Huntsville, Ala.	308,593
Indianapolis, Ind.	1,166,575
Jackson, Miss.	320,425
Jacksonville, Fla.	737,541
Jersey City, N.J.	556,972
Johnson City–Kingsport–Bristol, Tenn.–Va.	433,638
Johnstown, Pa.	264,506
Kalamazoo, Mich.	279,192
Kansas City, Mo.–Kans.	1,327,106
Killeen–Temple, Texas	214,656
Knoxville, Tenn.	476,517
Lakeland–Winter Haven, Fla.	321,652
Lancaster, Pa.	362,346
Lansing, Mich.	471,565
Las Vegas, Nev.	463,087
Lawrence-Haverhill, Mass.	281,981
Lexington–Fayette, Ky.	317,629
Lima, Ohio	218,244
Lincoln, Nebr.	192,884
Little Rock–North Little Rock, Ark.	393,774
Long Branch–Asbury Park, N.J.	503,173
Lorain–Elyria, Ohio	274,909
Los Angeles–Long Beach	7,477,503
Louisville, Ky.–Ind.	906,152
Lowell, Mass.	233,410
Lubbock, Texas	211,651
Macon, Ga.	253,794
Madison, Wis.	323,545
McAllen–Pharr–Edinburg, Texas	283,229
Melbourne–Titusville–Cocoa, Fla.	272,959
Memphis, Tenn.-Ark.-Miss.	913,472
Miami, Fla.	1,625,781
Milwaukee, Wis.	1,397,143
Minneapolis–St. Paul, Minn.–Wis.	2,113,533
Mobile, Ala.	443,536
Modesto, Calif.	265,900
Montgomery, Ala.	272,687
Nashville–Davidson, Tenn.	850,505
Nassau–Suffolk, N.Y.	2,605,813
New Brunswick–Perth Amboy, N.J.	595,893
New Haven, Conn.	417,592
New London–Norwich, Ct.	248,554
New Orleans, La.	1,187,073
New York City, N.Y.–N.J.	9,120,346
Newark, N.J.	1,965,969
Newburgh–Mid't'n, N.Y.	259,603
Newport News, Va.	364,449
Norfolk–Portsmouth–Virginia Beach, Va.	806,951
Northeast Pennsylvania	640,396
Oklahoma City, Okla.	834,088
Omaha, Nebr.–Iowa	569,614
Orlando, Fla.	700,055
Oxnard–Ventura–Simi Valley, Calif.	529,174
Paterson–Passaic, N.J.	447,585
Pensacola, Fla.	289,782
Peoria, Ill.	365,864
Philadelphia, Pa.–N.J.	4,716,818
Phoenix, Ariz.	1,509,052
Pittsburgh, Pa.	2,263,894
Ponce, Puerto Rico	252,420
Portland, Oreg.–Wash.	1,242,594
Poughkeepsie, N.Y.	245,055
Providence–Pawtucket–Warwick, R.I.	919,216
Provo-Orem, Utah	218,106
Raleigh–Durham, N.C.	531,167
Reading, Pa.	312,509
Reno, Nevada	193,623
Richmond, Va.	632,015
Riverside–San Bernardino, Calif.	1,558,182
Roanoke, Va.	224,341
Rochester, N.Y.	971,230
Rockford, Ill.	279,514
Sacramento, Calif.	1,014,002
Saginaw, Mich.	228,059
St. Louis, Mo.–Ill.	2,356,460
Salem, Oreg.	249,895
Salinas–Monterey, Calif.	290,444
Salt Lake City–Ogden, Ut.	936,255
San Antonio, Texas	1,071,954
San Diego, Calif.	1,861,846
San Francisco–Oakland	3,250,630
San Jose, Calif.	1,295,071
San Juan, Puerto Rico	1,083,664
Santa Barbara, Calif.	298,694
Santa Cruz, Calif.	188,141
Santa Rosa, Calif.	299,681
Sarasota, Fla.	202,251
Savannah, Ga.	230,728
Seattle–Everett, Wash.	1,607,469
Shreveport, La.	376,710
South Bend, Ind.	280,772
Spokane, Wash.	341,835
Springfield, Ill.	187,789
Springfield, Mo.	207,704
Springfield–Chicopee–Holyoke, Mass.–Conn.	530,668
Stamford, Conn.	198,854
Stockton, Calif.	347,342
Syracuse, N.Y.	642,971
Tacoma, Wash.	485,643
Tampa–St. Petersburg, Fl.	1,569,134
Toledo, Ohio–Mich.	791,599
Trenton, N.J.	307,863
Tucson, Ariz.	531,443
Tulsa, Okla.	689,434
Utica–Rome, N.Y.	320,180
Vallejo–Napa, Calif.	334,402
Visalia–Tulare, Calif.	245,738
Washington, D.C.–Md.–Va.	3,060,922
Waterbury, Conn.	228,178
West Palm Beach, Fla.	576,863
Wichita, Kans.	411,313
Wilmington, Del.–N.J.–Md.	523,221
Worcester, Mass.	372,940
York, Pa.	381,255
Youngstown–Warren, O.	531,350

U.S. CITIES, ZIP CODES, AND POPULATIONS

Cities and communities with 6,000 or more people and the ZIP CODES for these places are listed on the following pages.

Population figures for cities and communities are for the U.S. Census of April 1, 1980, except for those places noted.

An asterisk (*) after a ZIP CODE number indicates the place has more than one code. So you should check a ZIP CODE directory for the code for a specific street address.

ALABAMA (Ala or AL)

PLACE AND ZIP CODE		POP.[1]	PLACE AND ZIP CODE		POP.[1]	PLACE AND ZIP CODE		POP.[1]
Alabaster	35007	7,079	Forestdale	35214	10,814	Oxford	36203	8,939
Albertville	35950	12,039	Fort Payne	35967	11,485	Ozark	36360	13,188
Alexander City	35010	13,807	Fultondale	35068	6,217	Pelham	35124	6,759
Andalusia	36420	10,415	Gadsden	35901*	47,565	Pell City	35125	6,616
Anniston	36201*	29,185	Gardendale	35071	7,928	Phenix City	36867	26,928
Arab	35016	5,967	Greenville	36037	7,807	Pleasant Grove	35127	7,102
Athens	35611	14,558	Guntersville	35976	7,041	Prattville	36067	18,647
Atmore	36502	8,789	Hartselle	35640	8,858	Prichard	36610	39,541
Attalla	35954	7,737	Homewoood	35209	21,412	Rainbow City	35901	6,299
Auburn	36830	28,471	Hoover	35216	19,792	Roanoke	36274	5,896
Bay Minette	36507	7,455	Hueytown	35023	13,469	Russellville	35653	8,195
Bessemer	35020	31,729	Huntsville	35813*	142,513	Saks	—	11,118
Birmingham	35203*	284,413	Irondale	35210	6,510	Saraland	36571	9,833
Boaz	35957	7,151	Jackson	36545	6,073	Scottsboro	35768	14,758
Brewton	36426	6,680	Jacksonville	36265	9,735	Selma	36701	26,684
Center Point	35215	23,317	Jasper	35501	11,894	Sheffield	35660	11,903
Chickasaw	36611	7,402	Lanett	36863	6,897	Sylacauga	35150	12,708
Cullman	35055	13,084	Leeds	35094	8,638	Talladega	35160	19,128
Decatur	35602*	42,002	Midfield	35228	6,203	Tarrant City	35217	8,148
Demopolis	36732	7,678	Mobile	36601*	200,452	Theodore	36582	6,392
Dothan	36303*	48,750	Montgomery	36119*	177,857	Tillman's Corner	—	15,941
Enterprise	36330	18,033	Mountain Brook	35223	19,718	Troy	36081	12,945
Eufaula	36027	12,097	Muscle Shoals	35660	8,911	Tuscaloosa	35403*	75,211
Fairfield	35064	13,242	Northport	35476	14,291	Tuscumbia	35674	9,137
Fairhope	36532	7,286	Opelika	36801	21,896	Tuskegee	36083	13,327
Florence	35631*	37,029	Opp	36467	7,204	Vestavia Hills	35216	15,722

ALASKA (Alas. or AK)

PLACE AND ZIP CODE		POP.[1]	PLACE AND ZIP CODE		POP.[1]	PLACE AND ZIP CODE		POP.[1]
Anchorage	99502*	174,431	Juneau	99801	19,528	Kodiak	99615	4,756
Fairbanks	99701	22,645	Ketchikan	99901	7,198	Sitka	99835	7,803

ARIZONA (Ariz. or AZ)

PLACE AND ZIP CODE		POP.[1]	PLACE AND ZIP CODE		POP.[1]	PLACE AND ZIP CODE		POP.[1]
Apache Junction	85220	9,935	Glendale	85301*	97,172	Prescott	86301	20,055
Avondale	85323	8,168	Globe	85501	6,886	Safford	85546	7,010
Bisbee	85603	7,154	Green Valley	85614	7,999	Scottsdale	85251*	88,622
Bulkhead City–Riviera	86430	10,364	Kingman	86401	9,257	Sierra Vista	85635	24,937
Casa Grande	85222	14,971	Lake Havasu City	86403	15,737	South Tucson	85725	6,554
Chandler	85224	29,673	Mesa	85201*	152,453	Sun City	85351*	40,505
Coolidge	85228	6,851	Nogales	85621	15,683	Tempe	85282	106,920
Douglas	85607	13,058	Paradise Valley	85253	10,832	Tucson	85726*	330,537
Eloy	85231	6,240	Peoria	85345	12,307	Winslow	86047	7,921
Flagstaff	86001	34,743	Phoenix	85026*	789,704	Yuma	85364	42,481

ARKANSAS (Ark. or AR)

PLACE AND ZIP CODE		POP.[1]	PLACE AND ZIP CODE		POP.[1]	PLACE AND ZIP CODE		POP.[1]
Arkadelphia	71923	10,005	Hope	71801	10,290	Pine Bluff	71601*	56,636
Batesville	72501	8,263	Hot Springs	71901	35,781	Rogers	72756	17,429
Benton	72015	17,717	Jacksonville	72076	27,589	Russellville	72801	14,031
Bentonville	72712	8,756	Jonesboro	72401	31,530	Searcy	72143	13,612
Blytheville	72315	23,844	Little Rock	72231*	158,915	Sherwood	72116	10,306
Camden	71701	15,356	Magnolia	71753	11,909	Siloam Springs	72761	7,940
Conway	72032	20,375	Malvern	72104	10,163	Springdale	72764	23,458
Crossett	71635	6,706	Marianna	72360	6,220	Stuttgart	72160	10,941
Dumas	71639	6,091	Monticello	71655	8,259	Texarkana	75502	21,459
El Dorado	71730	25,270	Morrilton	72110	7,355	Trumann	72472	6,405
Fayetteville	72701	36,608	Mountain Home	72653	8,066	Van Buren	72956	12,020
Forrest City	72335	13,803	Newport	72112	8,339	Warren	71671	7,646
Fort Smith	72901*	71,626	North Little Rock	72114*	64,388	West Helena	72390	11,367
Harrison	72601	9,567	Osceola	72370	8,881	West Memphis	72301	28,138
Helena	72342	9,598	Paragould	72450	15,248	Wynne	72396	7,805

[1] 1980 Census.

CALIFORNIA (Calif., Cal., or CA)

PLACE AND ZIP CODE		POP.[1]
Alameda	94501	63,852
Alamo	94507	8,505
Albany	94706	15,130
Alhambra	91802*	64,615
Alondra Park	90249	12,096
Altadena	91001	40,983
Alum Rock	95116	16,890
Anaheim	92803*	219,494
Anderson	96007	7,381
Antioch	94509	42,683
Apple Valley	92307	14,305
Aptos	95003	7,039
Arcadia	91006	45,993
Arcata	95521	12,850
Arden–Arcade	95825	87,570
Arroyo Grande	93420	11,290
Artesia	90701	14,301
Arvin	93203	6,863
Ashland	94577	13,893
Atascadero	93422	16,232
Atherton	94025	7,797
Atwater	95301	17,530
Auburn	95603	7,540
Avocado Heights	91745	11,721
Azusa	91702	29,380
Bakersfield	93302*	105,611
Baldwin Park	91706	50,554
Banning	92220	14,020
Barstow	92311	17,690
Baywood–Las Osas	—	10,933
Beaumont	92223	6,818
Bell	90201	25,450
Bell Gardens	90201	34,117
Bellflower	90706	53,441
Belmont	94002	24,505
Ben Lomond	95005	7,238
Benicia	94510	15,376
Berkeley	94704*	103,328
Beverly Hills	90213*	32,367
Big Bear	92314	11,151
Bloomington	92316	12,781
Blythe	92225	6,805
Bonita	92002	6,257
Brawley	92227	14,946
Brea	92621	27,913
Broderick–Bryte	95605	10,194
Buena Park	90622	64,165
Burbank	91505*	84,625
Burlingame	94010	26,173
Calexico	92231	14,412
Calwa	93725	6,640
Camarillo	93010	37,797
Camarillo Heights	93010	6,341
Campbell	95008	26,910
Canyon Country	91351	15,728
Capistrano Beach	92624	6,168
Capitola	95010	9,095
Cardiff-by-the-Sea	92007	10,054
Carlsbad	92008	35,490
Carmichael	95608	43,108
Carpinteria	93013	10,835
Carson	90745	81,221
Casa de Oro–Mt. Helix	—	19,651
Castle Pk.–Otay	—	44,011
Castro Valley	94546	44,011
Ceres	95307	13,281
Cerritos	90701	53,020
Cherryland	94541	9,425
Chico	95926	26,716
Chico North	—	11,733
Chico West	—	6,337
Chino	91710	40,165
Chula Vista	92010	83,927
Citrus	—	12,450
Citrus Heights	95610	85,911
Claremont	91711	31,028
Clovis	93612	33,021
Coachella	92236	9,129
Coalinga	93210	6,593
Colton	92324	21,310
Commerce	90040	10,509
Compton	90220*	81,347
Concord	94520*	103,763
Corcoran	93212	6,454
Corona	91720	37,791
Coronado	92118	18,790
Corte Madera	94925	8,074
Costa Mesa	92626*	82,562
Country Club	—	9,585
Covina	91722*	32,746
Crestline	92325	6,715
Cudahy	90201	18,275
Culver City	90230	38,139
Cupertino	95014	34,297
Cypress	90630	40,391
Daly City	94015*	78,427
Dana Point	92629	10,602
Danville	94526	26,446
Davis	95616	36,640
Del Aire	90250	8,487
Delano	93215	16,491
Diamond Bar	91765	28,045
Dinuba	93618	9,907
Dixon	95620	7,541
Downey	90241*	82,602
Duarte	91010	16,766
Dublin	94568	13,496
East Compton	—	6,435
East Hemet	—	14,712
East La Mirada	90638	9,688
East Los Angeles	90022	110,017
East Palo Alto	94303	18,191
Edwards	93523	8,554
El Cajon	92020*	73,892
El Centro	92243	23,996
El Cerrito	94530	22,731
El Monte	91734*	79,494
El Paso de Robles	93446	9,163
El Segundo	90245	13,752
El Sobrante	94803	10,535
El Toro	92630	38,153
El Toro Station	92709	7,632
Elk Grove	95624	10,959
Encinitas	92024	10,796
Escondido	92025	64,355
Eureka	95501	24,153
Fair Oaks	95628	22,602
Fairfax	94930	7,391
Fairfield	94533	58,099
Fallbrook	92028	14,041
Farmersville	93223	5,544
Fillmore	93015	9,602
Florence–Graham	90001	48,662
Florin	95823	16,523
Folsom	95630	11,003
Fontana	92335	36,991
Foothill Farms	95841	13,700
Fortuna	95540	7,591
Foster City	94404	23,287
Fountain Valley	92708	55,080
Freedom	95019	6,416
Fremont	94538*	131,945
Fresno	93706*	217,129
Fullerton	92631*	102,034
Galt	95632	5,514
Garden Acres	—	7,361
Garden Grove	92640*	123,307
Gardena	90247*	45,165
Gilroy	95020	21,641
Glen Avon	—	8,444
Glendale	91209*	139,069
Glendora	91740	38,500
Grand Terrace	92324	8,498
Grass Valley	95945	6,697
Grover City	93433	8,827
Hacienda Heights	91745	49,422
Half Moon Bay	94019	7,282
Hanford	93230	20,958
Hawaiian Gdns.	90716	10,548
Hawthorne	90250	56,447
Hayward	94544*	94,342
Healdsburg	95448	7,217
Hemet	92343	22,454
Hermosa Beach	90254	18,070
Hesperia	92345	13,540
Highland	92346	10,908
Hillsborough	94010	10,372
Hollister	95023	11,488
Huntington Beach	92647*	170,505
Huntington Park	90255	45,932
Imperial Beach	92032	22,689
Indio	92201	21,611
Inglewood	90311*	94,245
Irvine	92714	62,134
La Canada–Flintridge	91011	20,153
La Crescenta–Montrose	91214	16,531
La Habra	90631	45,232
La Mesa	92041	50,308
La Mirada	90638	40,986
La Palma	90623	15,399
La Puente	91747*	30,882
La Riviera	—	10,906
La Verne	91750	23,508
Ladera Heights	90045	6,647
Lafayette	94549	20,837
Laguna Beach	92651*	17,901
Laguna Hills	92653	33,600
Laguna Niguel	92677	12,237
Lake Arrowhead	92352	6,272
Lakeside	92040	23,921
Lakewood	90714	74,654
Lamont	93241	9,616
Lancaster	93534	48,027
Larkspur	94939	11,064
Lawndale	90260	23,460
Lemon Grove	92045	20,780
Lemoore	93245	8,832
Lennox	90304	18,445
Leucadia	92024	9,478
Lincoln Village	—	6,476
Linda	95901	10,225
Lindsay	93247	6,936
Live Oak	95953	11,482
Livermore	94550	48,349
Lodi	95240	35,221
Loma Linda	92354	10,694
Lomita	90717	18,807

[1] 1980 Census.

CALIFORNIA *(continued)*

PLACE AND ZIP CODE		POP.[1]
Lompoc	93436	26,267
Long Beach	90809*	361,355
Los Alamitos	90720	11,529
Los Altos	94022	25,769
Los Altos Hills	94022	7,421
Los Angeles	90052*	2,968,579
Los Banos	93635	10,341
Los Gatos	95030	26,906
Lucas Valley–Marinwood	—	6,409
Lynwood	90262	48,409
Madera	93637	21,732
Manhattan Beach	90266	31,542
Manteca	95336	24,925
Marina	93933	20,647
Marina del Ray	90291	6,336
Martinez	94553	22,582
Marysville	95901	9,898
Maywood	90270	21,810
McKinleyville	95521	7,772
Meiners Oaks-Miramonte	93023	9,512
Menlo Park	94025	26,369
Merced	95340	36,499
Mill Valley	94941	12,967
Millbrae	94030	20,058
Milpitas	95035	37,820
Mira Loma	91752	8,707
Mission Viejo	92675	50,666
Modesto	95350*	106,602
Monrovia	91016	30,531
Montclair	91763	22,628
Montebello	90640	52,929
Monterey	93940*	27,558
Monterey Park	91754	54,338
Moraga Town	94556	15,014
Morgan Hill	95037	17,060
Morro Bay	93442	9,064
Mountain View	94042	58,665
Muscoy	92405	6,188
Napa	94558	50,879
National City	92050	48,772
Newark	94560	32,126
Newhall	91321	12,029
Newport Beach	92660*	62,556
Norco	91760	21,126
North Auburn	—	7,619
North Fair Oaks	94025	10,308
North Highlands	95660	37,825
Norwalk	90650	85,286
Novato	94947	43,916
Oakdale	95361	8,474
Oakland	94615*	339,337
Oceanside	92054*	76,698
Oildale	93308	23,382
Ojai	93023	6,816
Olivehurst	95961	8,929
Ontario	91761*	88,820
Orange	92667	91,450
Orangevale	95662	20,585
Orinda	94563	16,843
Oroville	95965*	8,683
Oxnard	93030	108,195
Pacific Grove	93950	15,775
Pacifica	94044	36,866
Palm Desert	92260	11,801
Palm Springs	92263	32,359
Palmdale	93550	12,277
Palo Alto	94303*	55,225
Palos Verdes Est.	90274	14,376
Paradise	95969	22,571
Paramount	90723	36,407
Parkway–Sacramento South	95823	26,815
Pasadena	91109*	118,072
Perris	92370	6,827
Petaluma	94952	33,834
Pico Rivera	90660	53,387
Piedmont	94611	10,498
Pinole	94564	14,253
Pittsburg	94565	33,034
Placentia	92670	35,041
Placerville	95667	6,739
Pleasant Hill	94523	25,124
Pleasanton	94566	35,160
Pomona	91766	92,742
Port Hueneme	93041	17,803
Porterville	93257	19,707
Poway	92064	32,263
Quartz Hill	93534	7,421
Ramona	92065	8,173
Rancho Cordova	95670	42,881
Rancho Cucamonga	91730	55,250
Rancho Mirage	92270	6,281
Rancho Palos Verdes	90274	36,577
Red Bluff	96080	9,490
Redding	96001	41,995
Redlands	92373	43,619
Redondo Beach	90277*	57,102
Redwood City	94064*	54,951
Reedley	93654	11,071
Rialto	92376	37,474
Richmond	94802*	74,676
Ridgecrest	93555	15,929
Rio del Mar	—	7,067
Rio Linda	95673	7,359
Riverbank	95367	5,695
Riverside	92507*	170,591
Rocklin	95677	7,344
Rodeo	94572	8,286
Rohnert Park	94928	22,965
Rolling Hills Est.	90274	7,701
Roseland	95401	7,915
Rosemead	91770	42,604
Rosemont	—	18,882
Roseville	95678	24,347
Rossmoor	90720	10,457
Rowland Heights	91748	28,252
Rubidoux	92506	17,048
Sacramento	95813*	275,741
Salinas	93907*	80,479
San Anselmo	94960	12,067
San Bernardino	92403*	118,794
San Bruno	94066	35,417
San Carlos	94070	24,710
San Clemente	92672	27,325
San Diego	92199*	875,538
San Dimas	91773	24,014
San Fernando	91341*	17,731
San Francisco	94101*	678,974
San Gabriel	91776	30,072
San Jacinto	92383	7,098
San Jose	95101*	629,531
San Juan Capistrano	92690*	18,959
San Leandro	94577*	63,952
San Lorenzo	94580	20,545
San Luis Obispo	93401	34,252
San Marcos	92069	17,479
San Marino	91108	13,307
San Mateo	94402*	77,640
San Pablo	94806	19,750
San Rafael	94901*	44,700
San Ramon	94583	22,356
Sanger	93657	12,542
Santa Ana	92711*	204,023
Santa Barbara	93102*	74,414
Santa Clara	95050*	87,700
Santa Cruz	95060*	41,483
Santa Fe Springs	90670	14,520
Santa Maria	93456	39,685
Santa Monica	90406*	88,314
Santa Paula	93060	20,552
Santa Rosa	95402*	83,320
Santee	92071	47,080
Saratoga	95070	29,261
Saugus-Bouquet Canyon	91350	16,283
Sausalito	94965	7,338
Scotts Valley	95066	6,891
Seal Beach	90740	25,975
Seaside	93955	36,567
Selma	93662	10,942
Shafter	93263	7,010
Sierra Madre	91024	10,837
Simi Valley	93065*	77,500
Solana Beach	92075	13,047
Sonoma	95476	6,054
Soquel	95073	6,212
South El Monte	91733	16,623
South Gate	90280	66,784
South Laguna	92677	6,013
S. Lake Tahoe	95705	20,681
South Modesto	95350	12,492
South Oroville	—	7,246
South Pasadena	91030	22,681
S. San Francisco	94080	49,393
South San Jose Hl	91744	16,049
South Whittier	90605	43,815
South Yuba	95991	7,530
Spring Valley	92077	40,191
Stanford	94305	11,045
Stanton	90680	23,723
Stockton	95208*	149,779
Suisun City	94585	11,087
Sun City	92381	8,460
Sunnymead	92388	11,554
Sunnyvale	94086*	106,618
Susanville	96130	6,520
Tamalpais–Homestead Valley	—	8,511
Tara Hills–Mt. Manor	—	9,471
Temple City	91780	28,972
Thousand Oaks	91360*	77,072
Tiburon	94920	6,685
Torrance	90510*	129,881
Tracy	95376	18,428
Tulare	93274	22,530
Turlock	95380	26,287
Tustin	92680	32,317
Tustin–Foothills	92705	26,174
Twentynine Palms	92277	7,465
Ukiah	95482	12,035
Union City	94587	39,406
Upland	91786	47,647
Vacaville	95688	43,367
Valencia	91355	12,163
Valinda	91744	18,700

[1] 1980 Census.

CALIFORNIA *(continued)*

PLACE AND ZIP CODE		POP.[1]	PLACE AND ZIP CODE		POP.[1]	PLACE AND ZIP CODE		POP.[1]
Vallejo	94590	80,303	Walnut Creek W.	94596	5,893	West Whittier–Los Nietos	90605	21,001
Ventura	93002*	74,393	Walnut Park	90255	11,811	Westminster	92683	71,133
Victorville	92392	14,220	Wasco	93280	9,613	Westmont	90047	27,916
View Park–Windsor Hills	90043	12,101	Watsonville	95076	23,662	Whittier	90605*	68,558
Villa Park	92667	7,137	West Athens	90044	8,531	Willowbrook	90222	30,845
Vine Hill–Pacheco	—	6,129	West Carson	90502	17,997	Woodland	95695	30,235
Visalia	93277	49,729	West Covina	91793	81,292	Yorba Linda	92686	28,254
Vista	92083	35,834	West Hollywood	90069	35,703	Yuba City	95991	18,736
Walnut	91789	12,478	West Pittsburg	—	10,244	Yucaipa	92399	23,345
Walnut Creek	94596*	53,490	W. Puente Valley	91746	20,445	Yucca Valley	92284	8,294
			W. Sacramento	95691	10,875			

COLORADO (Colo. or CO)

PLACE AND ZIP CODE		POP.[1]	PLACE AND ZIP CODE		POP.[1]	PLACE AND ZIP CODE		POP.[1]
Alamosa	81101	6,830	Durango	81301	11,649	Littleton	80120*	28,631
Applewood	—	12,040	Englewood	80110*	30,021	Longmont	80501	42,942
Arvada	80001	84,576	Evergreen	80439	6,376	Loveland	80537	30,215
Aurora	80010*	158,588	Federal Heights	80221	7,846	Montrose	81401	8,722
Boulder	80302	76,685	Fort Carson	80913	13,219	Northglenn	80233	29,847
Brighton	80601	12,773	Fort Collins	80521*	65,092	Pueblo	81003*	101,686
Broomfield	80020	20,730	Fort Morgan	80701	8,768	Salida	81201	4,870
Canon City	81212	13,037	Fountain	80817	8,324	Security–Widefield	80911	18,768
Castlewood	—	16,413	Golden	80401*	12,237	Sherrelwood	—	17,629
Cimarron Hills	81220	6,597	Grand Junction	81501	27,956	Southglenn	80161	37,787
Colorado Springs	80901*	214,821	Greeley	80631	53,006	Sterling	80751	11,385
Columbine	—	23,523	Gunnison	81230	5,785	Thornton	80229	40,343
Commerce City	80022	16,234	Ken Caryl	—	10,661	Trinidad	81082	9,663
Cortez	81321	7,095	La Junta	81050	8,338	Welby	—	9,668
Craig	81625	8,133	Lafayette	80026	8,985	Westminster	80030	50,211
Denver	80202*	492,365	Lakewood	80215	113,808	Westminister East	80030	6,002
Derby	—	8,578	Lamar	81052	7,713	Wheat Ridge	80033	30,293

CONNECTICUT (Conn. or CT)

PLACE AND ZIP CODE		POP.[1]	PLACE AND ZIP CODE		POP.[1]	PLACE AND ZIP CODE		POP.[1]
Ansonia	06401	19,039	Ledyard †	06339	13,735	Sherwood Manor	—	6,303
Avon †	06001	11,201	Litchfield †	06759	7,605	Somers †	06071	8,473
Berlin	06037	15,121	Madison †	06443	14,031	South Windsor †	06074	17,198
Bethel	06801	18,755	Manchester	06040	31,058	Southbury †	06488	14,156
Bloomfield	06002	18,608	Mansfield †	06250	20,634	Southington †	06489	36,879
Bridgeport	06602*	142,546	Meriden	06450	57,118	Southwood Acres	—	9,779
Bristol	06010	57,370	Middlebury †	06762	5,995	Stafford †	06075	9,268
Brookfield †	06804	12,872	Middletown	06457	39,040	Stamford	06904*	102,466
Canton †	06019	7,635	Milford	06460	49,101	Stonington †	06378	16,220
Clinton †	06413	11,195	Monroe †	06468	14,010	Storrs	06268	11,394
Colchester †	06415	7,761	Montville †	06353	16,455	Stratfield–Brooklawn	—	8,890
Conning Towers–Nautilus Park	—	9,665	Naugatuck	06770	26,456	Stratford †	06497	50,541
Coventry †	06238	8,895	New Britain	06050	73,840	Suffield †	06078	9,294
Cromwell †	06416	10,265	New Canaan †	06840	17,931	Thomaston †	06787	6,276
Danbury	06810	60,470	New Fairfield †	06810	11,260	Thompson †	06277	8,141
Darien †	06820	18,892	New Haven	06511*	126,101	Tolland †	06084	9,694
Derby	06418	12,346	New London	06320	28,842	Torrington †	06790	30,987
East Hampton †	06424	8,572	Newington †	06111	28,841	Trumbull †	06611	32,989
East Hartford †	06108	52,563	Newtown †	06470	19,107	Vernon †	06066	27,974
East Haven †	06512	25,028	North Branford †	06471	11,554	Wallingford	06492	17,821
East Lyme †	06333	13,870	North Haven †	06473	22,080	Waterbury	06701*	103,266
East Windsor †	06088	8,925	Norwalk	06856*	77,767	Waterford †	06385	17,843
Ellington †	06029	9,711	Norwich	06360	38,074	Watertown †	06795	19,489
Enfield	06082	48,151	Oakville	06779	8,737	West Hartford †	06107	61,301
Fairfield †	06430	54,849	Old Lyme †	06371	6,159	West Haven	06516	53,184
Farmington †	06032	16,407	Old Saybrook †	06475	9,287	Weston †	06883	8,284
Glastonbury	06033	27,049	Orange †	06477	13,237	Westport †	06880	25,290
Granby †	06035	7,956	Oxford †	06483	6,634	Wethersfield †	06109	26,013
Greenwich †	06830	59,578	Plainfield †	06374	12,774	Willimantic	06226	14,652
Griswold †	06351	8,967	Plainville †	06062	16,401	Wilton †	06897	15,351
Groton	06340	10,086	Plymouth †	06782	10,732	Winchester †	06094	10,841
Guilford †	06437	17,375	Prospect †	06712	6,807	Windham †	06280	21,062
Haddam †	06438	6,383	Putnam	06260	6,855	Windsor	06095	17,517
Hamden †	06514	51,071	Redding †	06875	7,272	Windsor Locks †	06096	12,190
Hartford	06101*	136,392	Ridgefield	06877	26,066	Winsted	06098	8,092
Kensington	06037	7,502	Rocky Hill †	06067	14,559	Wolcott †	06716	13,008
Killingly †	06239	14,519	Seymour †	06483	13,434	Woodbridge †	06525	7,761
			Shelton	06484	31,314	Woodbury †	06798	6,942

[1] 1980 Census. † Town or township (includes rural population).

DELAWARE (Del. or DE)

PLACE AND ZIP CODE		POP.[1]
Brookside	—	15,255
Claymont	19703	10,022
Dover	19901	23,507
Edgemoor	19809	7,397
Elsmere	19805	6,493
Newark	19711	25,247
Talleyville	19803	6,880
Wilmington	19850*	70,195
Wilmington Manor	—	9,233

FLORIDA (Fla. or FL)

PLACE AND ZIP CODE		POP.[1]
Altamonte Springs	32701	22,028
Apopka	32703	6,019
Arcadia	33821	6,002
Atlantic Beach	32233	7,847
Auburndale	33823	6,501
Aventura	—	9,698
Avon Park	33825	8,026
Azalea Park	32803	8,301
Bartow	33830	14,780
Bayonet Point	—	14,945
Bayshore Gdns.	33507	14,945
Beacon Square	—	6,513
Bellair–Mdwbrk. Terr.	—	12,144
Belle Glade	33430	16,535
Bellview	32620	15,439
Boca Raton	33432	49,505
Boynton Beach	33435	35,624
Bradenton	33506*	30,228
Brandon	33511	41,826
Brent	32503	21,872
Broadview Park	—	6,022
Browardale	—	7,409
Brownsville	—	18,058
Callaway	32401	7,154
Cape Canaveral	32920	5,733
Cape Coral	33904	32,103
Carol City	33055	47,349
Casselberry	32707	15,247
Century Village	—	10,619
Clearwater	33575*	85,528
Cocoa	32922	16,096
Cocoa Beach	32931	10,926
Cocoa West	32922	6,432
Coconut Creek	—	6,288
Collier City	—	7,135
Collier Manor–Cresthaven	—	7,045
Conway	32809	24,027
Cooper City	33328	10,140
Coral Gables	33134	43,241
Coral Springs	33065	37,349
Coral Terrace	—	22,702
Crestview	32536	7,617
Crystal Lake	—	6,827
Cutler	—	15,593
Cutler Ridge	33157	20,886
Cypress Gardens	33880	8,043
Cypress Lake	—	8,721
Dania	33004	11,811
Davie	33314	20,877
Daytona Beach	32015*	54,176
De Land	32720	15,354
Deerfield Beach	33441	39,193
Del Rio	—	7,409
Delray Beach	33444	34,325
Deltona	32725	15,710
Dunedin	33528	30,203
East Naples	—	12,127
Edgewater	32032	6,726
Egypt Lake	33614	11,932
Elfers	33531	11,396
Englewood	33533	9,633
Ensley	32504	14,422
Eustis	32726	9,453
Fairview Shores	—	10,174
Fern Park	32730	8,890
Fernandina Beach	32034	7,224
Ferry Pass	32504	16,910
Florida City	33034	6,174
Forest City	32751	6,819
Fort Lauderdale	33310*	153,279
Fort Myers	33906*	36,638
Fort Pierce	33454*	33,802
Ft. Walton Beach	32548	20,829
Gainesville	32602	81,371
Gifford	32960	6,240
Gladview	—	18,919
Glenvar Hts.	—	13,216
Golden Glades	—	23,154
Goldenrod	—	13,682
Gonzales	32560	6,084
Goulds	33170	7,078
Greenacres City	—	8,780
Gulf Gate Est.	—	9,284
Gulfport	33737	11,180
Haines City	33844	10,799
Hallandale	33009	36,517
Hialeah	33010*	145,254
Hobe Sound	33455	6,822
Holden Heights	32805	13,864
Holiday	33590	18,392
Holly Hill	32017	9,953
Hollywood	33022*	121,323
Homestead	33030*	20,668
Homestead Base	33039	7,594
Immokalee	33934	11,038
Inwood	33880	6,668
Ives Estates	—	12,623
Jacksonville	32203*	540,920
Jacksonville Bch.	32250	15,462
Jasmine Estates	—	11,995
Jensen Beach	33457	6,639
Jupiter	33458	9,868
Kendale Lakes	—	32,769
Kendall	33156	73,758
Kendall Green	—	6,768
Key Biscayne	33149	6,313
Key Largo	33037	7,447
Key West	33040	24,382
Killearn	—	8,700
Kings Point	—	8,724
Kissimmee	32741	15,487
Lake Carroll	—	13,012
Lake City	32055	9,257
Lake Lucerne	—	9,762
Lake Magdalene	33612	13,331
Lake Park	33403	6,909
Lake Wales	33853*	8,466
Lake Worth	33461*	27,048
Lakeland	33802*	47,406
Lakeland Highlands	—	10,426
Lakeside	—	10,534
Lantana	33462	8,048
Largo	33540*	58,977
Lauderdale Lakes	33313	25,426
Lauderhill	33313	37,271
Laurel	33545	6,368
Lealman	—	19,873
Leesburg	32748	13,191
Lehigh Acres	33936	9,604
Leisure City	—	17,905
Leto	33614	9,003
Lighthouse Point	33064	11,488
Lindgren Acres	—	11,986
Live Oak	32060	6,732
Lockhart	32860	10,569
Longwood	32750	10,029
Lynn Haven	32444	6,239
Maitland	32751	8,763
Mango-Seffner	33584	6,439
Marathon	33050	7,568
Margate	33063	35,900
Marianna	32446	7,006
Melbourne	32901*	46,536
Merritt Island	32952	30,708
Miami	33152*	346,865
Miami Beach	33139	96,298
Miami Gardens–Utopia–Carver	—	9,025
Miami Lakes	—	9,809
Miami Shores	33153	9,244
Miami Springs	33166	12,350
Milton	32570	7,206
Mims	32754	7,583
Miramar	33023	32,813
Myrtle Grove	32506	14,238
Naples	33941*	17,581
Naranja-Princeton	33032	10,381
New Port Richey	33552*	11,196
New Port Richey East	—	6,147
New Smyrna Beach	32069	13,557
Niceville	32578	8,543
Norland	33169	19,471
N. Andrews Gardens	—	8,967
North Fort Myers	33903	22,808
North Lauderdale	33068	18,653
North Miami	33161	42,566
N. Miami Beach	33160	36,553
North Naples	33940	7,950
N. Palm Beach	33408	11,344
North Port	33596	6,205
Oak Ridge	—	15,477
Oakland Park	33334	23,035
Ocala	32678*	37,170
Ocoee	32761	7,803
Ojus	33163	17,344
Olympia Hts.	33165	33,112
Oneco	33558	6,417
Opa–Locka	33054	14,460
Orange Park	32073	8,766
Orlando	32802*	128,291
Orlovista	32861	6,474
Ormond Beach	32074	21,378
Ormond-by-the-Sea	32074	7,665
Pahokee	33476	6,346
Palatka	32077	10,175
Palm Bay	32905	18,560
Palm Beach	33480	9,729
Palm Beach Gardens	—	14,407
Palm River–Clair Mel	—	14,447
Palm Springs	—	8,166
Palmetto	33561	8,637
Palmetto Estates	—	11,116
Panama City	32401*	33,346
Pembroke Pines	33024	35,776

[1] 1980 Census.

FLORIDA *(continued)*

PLACE AND ZIP CODE		POP.[1]	PLACE AND ZIP CODE		POP.[1]	PLACE AND ZIP CODE		POP.[1]
Pensacola	32501*	57,619	Satellite Beach	32937	9,163	Titusville	32780	31,910
Perrine	33157	16,129	Scott Lake	—	14,154	Town 'n' Country	33685	37,834
Perry	32347	8,254	Sebring	33870	8,736	Treasure Island	33740	6,316
Pine Castle	32859	9,992	Siesta Key	33578	7,010	Union Park	32817	19,175
Pine Hills	32808	35,771	Sky Lake	—	6,692	University	33124	24,514
Pinellas Park	33565	32,811	South Apopka	32703	5,687	Valparaiso	32580	6,142
Pinewood	—	16,252	South Bradenton	—	14,297	Venice	33595*	12,153
Plant City	33566	17,064	South Daytona	32021	11,252	Venice Gardens	—	6,568
Plantation	33317	48,653	South Miami	33143	10,944	Vero Beach	32960	16,176
Pompano Beach	33060*	52,618	South Miami Hts.	—	23,559	Villas	—	8,724
Pompano Beach			South Patrick Shores	—	9,816	Warrington	32507	15,792
Highlands	—	16,154	South Venice	33595	8,075	Washington Park	—	7,240
Port Charlotte	33952	25,770	Southgate	33579	7,322	Wekiva Springs	—	13,386
Port Orange	32019	18,756	Spring Hill	33526	6,468	West Bradenton	—	8,767
Port St. Lucie	33452	14,690	Springfield	32401	7,220	West Little River	—	32,492
Punta Gorda	33950*	6,797	Stuart	33494	9,467	West Miami	33144	6,076
Quincy	32351	8,591	Sunny Isles	—	12,564	West Palm Beach	33401*	63,305
Richmond Hts.	—	8,577	Sunrise	33304	39,681	West Pensacola	—	24,371
Riviera Beach	33404	26,489	Sunset	—	13,531	Westchester	—	29,272
Rockledge	32955	11,877	Sweetwater	—	8,251	Westview	—	9,102
Safety Harbor	33572	6,461	Tallahassee	32301*	81,548	Westwood Lakes	—	11,478
St. Augustine	32084	11,985	Tamarac	33321	29,376	Wilton Manors	33334	12,742
St. Cloud	32769	7,840	Tamiami	33144	17,607	Winston	—	9,315
St. Petersburg	33730*	238,647	Tampa	33630*	271,523	Winter Garden	32787	6,789
St. Petersbg. Bch.	33706	9,354	Tanglewood	—	8,229	Winter Haven	33880	21,119
Sanford	32771	23,176	Tarpon Springs	33589*	13,251	Winter Park	32789*	22,339
Sarasota	33578	48,868	Temple Terrace	33617	11,097	Winter Springs	32708	10,475
Sarasota Springs	—	13,860	Tice	33905	6,645	Wright	32548	13,011

GEORGIA (Ga. or GA)

PLACE AND ZIP CODE		POP.[1]	PLACE AND ZIP CODE		POP.[1]	PLACE AND ZIP CODE		POP.[1]
Albany	31706*	74,425	East Point	30344	37,486	North Druid Hills	—	12,438
Americus	31709	16,120	Fair Oaks	30060	8,486	Panthersville	—	11,366
Athens	30603*	42,549	Fairview	—	6,558	Peachtree City	30269	6,429
Atlanta	30304*	425,022	Fitzgerald	31750	10,187	Perry	31069	9,453
Augusta	30901*	47,532	Forest Park	30050	18,782	Riverdale	30274	7,121
Bainbridge	31717	10,553	Fort Benning S.	—	15,074	Rome	30161	29,654
Belvedere Park	—	17,776	Fort Gordon	30905	14,069	Roswell	30077	23,337
Blakely	31723	5,880	Fort Stewart	31314	15,031	St. Simons	31522	6,566
Brunswick	31520*	17,605	Fort Valley	31030	9,000	Sandersville	31082	6,137
Buford	30518	6,578	Gainesville	30501	15,280	Sandy Springs	30358	46,877
Cairo	31728	8,777	Garden City	31408	6,895	Savannah	31401*	141,651
Camilla	31730	5,414	Gresham Park	—	6,232	Scottdale	30079	8,770
Candler-McAfee	—	27,306	Griffin	30223	20,728	Smyrna	30080	20,312
Carrollton	30117	14,078	Hapeville	30354	6,166	Snellville	30278	8,514
Cartersville	30120	9,247	Hinesville	31313	11,309	South Augusta	—	51,072
Cedartown	30125	8,619	Jesup	31545	9,418	Statesboro	30458	14,866
Chamblee	30341	7,137	La Fayette	30728	6,517	Swainsboro	30401	7,602
College Park	30354	24,632	La Grange	30240	24,204	Sylvester	31791	5,860
Columbus	31908*	169,441	Lawrenceville	30245	8,928	Thomaston	30286	9,682
Conley	30027	6,033	Lithia Springs	30057	9,145	Thomasville	31792	18,463
Conyers	30207*	6,567	Mableton	30059	25,111	Thomson	30824	7,001
Cordele	31015	11,184	Macon	31213*	116,896	Tifton	31794	13,749
Covington	30209	10,586	Marietta	30060	30,805	Toccoa	30577	9,104
Dalton	30720	20,548	Martinez	30907	16,472	Tucker	30084	25,399
Decatur	30030*	18,404	Midway-Hardwick	31320	8,977	Valdosta	31601*	37,596
Dock Junction	—	6,189	Milledgeville	31061	12,176	Vidalia	30474	10,393
Doraville	30340	7,414	Monroe	30655	8,854	Warner Robbins	31093	39,893
Douglas	31533	10,980	Moultrie	31768	15,105	Waycross	31501	19,371
Douglasville	30134	7,641	Mountain Park	—	9,425	Waynesboro	30830	5,760
Druid Hills	30333	12,700	Newnan	30263	11,449	West Augusta	—	24,242
Dublin	31021	16,083	North Atlanta	30319	30,521	Wilmington Is	31410	7,546
Dunwoody	30338	17,768	North Decatur	30033	11,830	Winder	30680	6,705

HAWAII (HI)

PLACE AND ZIP CODE		POP.[1]	PLACE AND ZIP CODE		POP.[1]	PLACE AND ZIP CODE		POP.[1]
Ahuimanu	—	6,238	Kaneohe	96744	29,919	Nanakuli	96792	8,185
Aiea	96701	32,879	Kihei	96753	5,644	Pearl City	96782	42,575
Ewa Beach	96706	14,369	Lahaina	96761	16,095	Schofield Barracks	96857	18,851
Hilo	96720	35,269	Makaha	—	6,582	Wahiawa	96786	16,911
Honolulu	96820*	365,048	Makakilo City	—	7,691	Waianae	96792	7,941
Kahului	96732	12,978	Mililani	96789	21,365	Wailuku	96793	10,260
Kailua	96734	35,812	Mokapu	—	11,615	Waipahu	96797	29,139

[1] 1980 Census.

IDAHO (Ida. or ID)

PLACE AND ZIP CODE		POP.[1]
Ammon	83401	4,669
Blackfoot	83221	10,065
Boise City	83708*	102,160
Burley	83318	8,761
Caldwell	83605	17,699
Chubbuck	83202	7,052
Coeur D'Alene	83814	19,913
Idaho Falls	83401	39,734
Jerome	83338	6,891
Lewiston	83501	27,986
Meridian	83642	6,658
Moscow	83843	16,513
Mountain Home	83647	7,540
Nampa	83651	25,112
Payette	83661	5,448
Pocatello	83201	46,340
Post Falls	83854	5,736
Rexburg	83440	11,559
Rupert	83350	5,476
Twin Falls	83301	26,209
Weiser	83672	4,771

ILLINOIS (Ill. or IL)

PLACE AND ZIP CODE		POP.[1]
Addison	60101	29,826
Alsip	60658	17,134
Alton	62002	34,171
Arlington Heights	60004*	66,116
Aurora	60507*	81,293
Barrington	60010	9,029
Bartlett	60103	13,254
Bartonville	61607	6,137
Batavia	60510	12,574
Beardstown	62618	6,338
Belleville	62220*	41,580
Bellwood	60104	19,811
Belvidere	61008	15,176
Bensenville	60106	16,106
Benton	62812	7,778
Berwyn	60402	46,849
Bethalto	62010	8,630
Bloomingdale	60108	12,659
Bloomington	61701	44,189
Blue Island	60406	21,855
Bolingbrook	60439	37,261
Bourbonnais	60914	13,280
Boulder Hill	—	9,333
Bradley	60915	11,008
Bridgeview	60455	14,155
Broadview	60153	8,618
Brookfield	60513	19,395
Buffalo Grove	60090	22,230
Burbank	60459	28,462
Cahokia	62206	18,904
Calumet City	60409	39,697
Calumet Park	60643	8,788
Canton	61520	14,626
Carbondale	62901	26,414
Carmi	62821	6,264
Carol Stream	—	15,472
Carpentersville	60110	23,272
Cary	60013	6,640
Centralia	62801	15,126
Centreville	—	9,747
Champaign	61820	58,267
Charleston	61920	19,355
Chester	62233	8,401
Chicago	60607*	3,005,072
Chicago Heights	60411	37,026
Chicago Ridge	60415	13,473
Chillicothe	61523	6,176
Cicero	60650	61,232
Clarendon Hills	60514	6,870
Clinton	61727	8,014
Collinsville	62234	19,613
Country Club Hills	60477	14,676
Countryside	—	6,290
Crest Hill	60435	9,252
Crestwood	—	10,852
Creve Coeur	61611	6,851
Crystal Lake	60014	18,590
Danville	61832	38,985
Darien	60559	14,536
De Kalb	60115	33,157
Decatur	62521*	93,896
Deerfield	60015	17,430
Des Plaines	60018*	53,568
Dixon	61021	15,701
Dolton	60419	24,766
Downers Grove	60515	42,691
Du Quoin	62832	6,594
East Alton	62024	7,096
East Moline	61244	20,907
East Peoria	61611	22,385
East St. Louis	62201*	55,200
Edwardsville	62025	12,480
Effingham	62401	11,270
Elgin	60120	63,668
Elk Grove Village	60007	28,679
Elmhurst	60126	44,276
Elmwood Park	60635	24,016
Evanston	60204*	73,706
Evergreen Park	60642	22,260
Fairview Heights	62208	12,414
Flossmoor	60422	8,423
Forest Park	60130	15,177
Fox Lake	60020	6,831
Franklin Park	60131	17,507
Freeport	61032	26,266
Galesburg	61401	35,305
Geneseo	61254	6,373
Geneva	60134	9,881
Glen Ellyn	60137	23,852
Glencoe	60022	9,200
Glendale Heights	60137	23,163
Glenview	60025*	32,060
Glenwood	60425	10,538
Granite City	62040	36,815
Gurnee	60031	7,179
Hanover Park	60103	28,719
Harrisburg	62946	10,410
Harvey	60426	35,810
Harwood Heights	60656	8,228
Hazel Crest	60429	13,973
Herrin	62948	10,708
Hickory Hills	60457	13,778
Highland	62249	7,122
Highland Park	60035*	30,611
Hillside	60162	8,279
Hinsdale	60521	16,726
Hoffman Estates	60195	37,272
Homewood	60430	19,724
Hoopeston	60942	6,411
Itasca	60143	7,129
Jacksonville	62650	20,284
Jerseyville	62052	7,506
Joliet	60436*	77,956
Justice	60458	10,552
Kankakee	60901	30,141
Kewanee	61443	14,508
La Grange	60525	15,693
La Grange Park	60525	13,359
La Salle	61301	10,347
Lake Forest	60045	15,245
Lake Zurich	60047	8,225
Lansing	60438	29,039
Libertyville	60048	16,520
Lincoln	62656	16,327
Lincolnwood	60645	11,921
Lindenhurst	—	6,220
Lisle	60532	13,638
Litchfield	62056	7,204
Lockport	60441	9,170
Lombard	60148	36,879
Loves Park	61111	13,192
Lyons	60534	9,925
Macomb	61455	19,863
Marion	62959	14,031
Markham	60426	15,172
Matteson	60443	10,223
Mattoon	61938	19,293
Maywood	60153	27,998
McHenry	60050	10,908
Melrose Park	60160*	20,735
Mendota	61342	7,134
Metropolis	62960	7,171
Midlothian	60445	14,274
Milan	61264	6,264
Moline	61265	46,278
Monmouth	61462	10,706
Morris	60450	8,833
Morton	61550	14,178
Morton Grove	60053	23,747
Mount Carmel	62863	8,908
Mount Prospect	60056	52,634
Mount Vernon	62864	17,193
Mundelein	60060	17,053
Murphysboro	62966	9,866
Naperville	60566	42,601
Niles	60648	30,363
Normal	61761	35,672
Norridge	60656	16,483
North Chicago	60064	38,774
North Park	—	15,806
North Riverside	60546	6,764
Northbrook	60062	30,778
Northlake	60164	12,166
Oak Brook	60521	6,676
Oak Forest	60452	26,096
Oak Lawn	60454*	60,590
Oak Park	60301*	54,887
O'Fallon	62269	12,241
Olney	62450	9,026
Orland Park	60462	23,045
Ottawa	61350	18,166
Palatine	60067	32,166
Palos Heights	60463	11,096
Palos Hills	60465	16,654
Pana	62557	6,040
Paris	61944	9,885
Park Forest	60466	26,222
Park Forest South	60466	6,245
Park Ridge	60068	38,704
Pekin	61554	33,967
Peoria	61601*	124,160
Peoria Heights	61614	7,453
Peru	61354	10,886
Pontiac	61764	11,227
Princeton	61356	7,342
Prospect Heights	60070	11,823

[1] 1980 Census.

ILLINOIS *(continued)*

PLACE AND ZIP CODE		POP.[1]
Quincy	62301*	42,554
Rantoul	61866	20,161
Richton Park	60471	9,403
River Forest	60305	12,392
River Grove	60171	10,368
Riverdale	60627	13,233
Riverside	60546	9,236
Robbins	60472	8,853
Robinson	62454	7,285
Rochelle	61068	8,982
Rock Falls	61071	10,633
Rock Island	61201	46,928
Rockford	61125*	139,712
Rolling Meadows	60008	20,167
Romeoville	60441	15,519
Roselle	60194*	17,034
Round Lake Bch.	60073	12,921
St. Charles	60174	17,492
Salem	62881	7,813
Sauk Village	60411	10,906
Schaumberg	60194	53,305
Schiller Park	60176	11,458
Silvis	61282	7,130
Skokie	60076*	60,278
South Holland	60473	24,977
Springfield	62703*	100,054
Steger	60475	9,269
Sterling	61081*	16,281
Streamwood	60103	23,456
Streator	61364*	14,795
Summit	60501	10,110
Sycamore	60178	9,219
Taylorville	62568	11,386
Tinley Park	60477	26,178
Urbana	61801	35,978
Vandalia	62471	5,338
Vernon Hills	60061	9,827
Villa Park	60181	23,155
Warrenville	60555	7,519
Washington	61571	10,364
Washington Park	62204	8,223
Waukegan	60085*	67,653
West Chicago	60185	12,550
West Frankfort	62896	9,437
Westchester	60153	17,730
Western Springs	60558	12,876
Westmont	60559	17,353
Wheaton	60187	43,043
Wheeling	60090	23,266
Wilmette	60091	28,221
Winnetka	60093	12,772
Wood Dale	60191	11,251
Wood River	62095	12,446
Woodridge	60517	21,767
Woodstock	60098	11,725
Worth	60482	11,592
Zion	60099	17,865

INDIANA (Ind. or IN)

PLACE AND ZIP CODE		POP.[1]
Alexandria	46001	6,028
Anderson	46018*	64,695
Auburn	46706	8,122
Bedford	47421	14,410
Beech Grove	46107	13,196
Bloomington	47401	52,044
Bluffton	46714	8,705
Boonville	47601	6,300
Brazil	47834	7,852
Brownsburg	46112	6,242
Carmel	46032	18,272
Cedar Lake	46303	8,754
Chesterton	46304	8,531
Clarksville	47130	15,164
Columbus	47201	30,614
Connersville	47331	17,023
Crawfordsville	47933	13,325
Crown Point	46307	16,455
Decatur	46733	8,649
Dyer	46311	9,555
East Chicago	46312	39,786
Elkhart	46515	41,305
Elwood	46036	10,867
Evansville	47708*	130,496
Fort Wayne	46802*	172,349
Frankfort	46041	15,168
Franklin	46131	11,563
Gary	46401*	151,953
Gas City	46933	6,370
Goshen	46526*	19,665
Greencastle	46135	8,403
Greenfield	46140	11,299
Greensburg	47240	9,254
Greenwood	46142	19,327
Griffith	46319	17,026
Hammond	46320*	93,714
Hartford City	47348	7,622
Highland	46322	25,935
Hobart	46342	22,987
Huntington	46750	16,202
Indianapolis	46206*	700,807
Jasper	47546	9,097
Jeffersonville	47130	21,220
Kendallville	46755	7,299
Kokomo	46902	47,808
La Porte	46350*	21,796
Lafayette	47901*	43,011
Lake Station	46405	14,294
Lawrence	46226	25,591
Lebanon	46052	11,456
Linton	47441	6,315
Logansport	46947	17,731
Madison	47250	12,472
Marion	46952	35,874
Martinsville	46151	11,311
Merrillville	46410	27,677
Michigan City	46360	36,850
Mishawaka	46544	40,201
Mount Vernon	47620	7,656
Muncie	47302*	77,216
Munster	46321	20,671
New Albany	47150	37,103
New Castle	47362	20,056
New Haven	46774	6,714
Noblesville	46060	12,056
Peru	46970	13,764
Plainfield	46168	9,191
Plymouth	46563	7,693
Portage	46368	27,409
Portland	47371	7,074
Princeton	47670	8,976
Richmond	47374	41,349
Rushville	46173	6,113
Schererville	46375	13,209
Seymour	47274	15,050
Shelbyville	46176	14,989
South Bend	46624*	109,727
South Haven	—	6,679
Speedway	46224	12,641
Tell City	47586	8,704
Terre Haute	47808*	61,125
Valparaiso	46383	22,247
Vincennes	47591	20,857
Wabash	46992	12,985
Warsaw	46580	10,647
Washington	47501	11,325
West Lafayette	47906	21,247

IOWA (Ia. or IA)

PLACE AND ZIP CODE		POP.[1]
Algona	50511	6,289
Ames	50010	45,775
Ankeny	50021	15,429
Atlantic	50022	7,789
Bettendorf	52722	27,381
Boone	50036	12,602
Burlington	52601	29,529
Carroll	51401	9,705
Cedar Falls	50613	36,322
Cedar Rapids	52401*	110,243
Centerville	52544	6,558
Charles City	50616	8,778
Cherokee	51012	7,004
Clear Lake City	50428	7,458
Clinton	52732*	32,828
Clive	50053*	6,064
Coralville	52241	7,687
Council Bluffs	51501	56,449
Creston	50801	8,429
Davenport	52802*	103,264
Decorah	52101	7,991
Denison	51442	6,675
Des Moines	50318*	191,003
Dubuque	52001	62,321
Estherville	51334	7,518
Fairfield	52556	9,428
Fort Dodge	50501	29,423
Fort Madison	52627	13,520
Grinnell	50112	8,868
Independence	50644	6,392
Indianola	50125	10,843
Iowa City	52240	50,508
Iowa Falls	50126	6,174
Keokuk	52632	13,536
Knoxville	50138	8,143
Le Mars	51031	8,276
Maquoketa	52060	6,313
Marion	52302	19,474
Marshalltown	50158	26,938
Mason City	50401	30,144
Mount Pleasant	52641	7,322
Muscatine	52761	23,467
Newton	50208	15,292
Oelwein	50662	7,564
Oskaloosa	52577	10,989
Ottumwa	52501	27,381
Pella	50219	8,349
Perry	50220	7,053
Red Oak	51566	6,810
Shenandoah	51601	6,274
Sioux City	51101*	82,003
Spencer	51301	11,726
Storm Lake	50588	8,814
Urbandale	50322	17,869
Washington	52353	6,584
Waterloo	50701*	75,985
Waverly	50677	8,444
Webster City	50595	8,572
West Des Moines	50265	21,894
Windsor Heights	—	5,474

[1] 1980 Census.

KANSAS (Kan., Kans., or KS)

Place and Zip Code		Pop.[1]	Place and Zip Code		Pop.[1]	Place and Zip Code		Pop.[1]
Abilene	67410	6,752	Great Bend	67530	16,608	Mission	66205	8,643
Arkansas City	67005	13,201	Hays	67601	16,301	Newton	67114	16,332
Atchison	66002	11,407	Haysville	67060	8,006	Olathe	66061	37,258
Augusta	67010	6,968	Hutchinson	67501	40,284	Ottawa	66067	11,016
Bonner Springs	66012	6,266	Independence	67301	10,598	Overland Park	66204	81,784
Chanute	66720	10,506	Iola	66749	6,938	Parsons	67357	12,898
Coffeyville	67337	15,185	Junction City	66441	19,305	Pittsburg	66762	18,770
Colby	67701	5,544	Kansas City	66110*	161,148	Prairie Village	66208	24,657
Concordia	66901	6,847	Lansing	66043	5,307	Pratt	67124	6,885
Derby	67037	9,786	Lawrence	66044	52,738	Roeland Park	66203	7,962
Dodge City	67801	18,001	Leavenworth	66048	33,656	Russell	67665	5,427
El Dorado	67042	10,510	Leawood	66206	13,360	Salina	67401	41,843
Emporia	66801	25,287	Lenexa	66215	18,639	Shawnee	66212	29,653
Fort Riley North	—	16,086	Liberal	67901	14,911	Topeka	66603*	115,266
Fort Scott	66701	8,893	Manhattan	66502	32,664	Wellington	67152	8,212
Garden City	67846	18,256	McPherson	67460	11,753	Wichita	67276*	279,835
Goodland	67735	5,708	Merriam	66203	10,794	Winfield	67156	10,736

KENTUCKY (Ky., Ken., or KY)

Place and Zip Code		Pop.[1]	Place and Zip Code		Pop.[1]	Place and Zip Code		Pop.[1]
Ashland	41101	27,064	Fort Knox	40121	31,055	Morehead	40351	7,789
Bardstown	40004	6,155	Fort Mitchell	41017	7,310	Murray	42071	14,248
Bellevue	41073	7,678	Fort Thomas	41075	16,012	Newberg	—	24,612
Berea	40403	8,226	Frankfort	40601	25,973	Newport	41071*	21,587
Beuchel	—	6,855	Franklin	42134	7,738	Nicholasville	40356	10,319
Bowling Green	42101	40,450	Georgetown	40324	10,972	Okolona	40219	20,039
Campbellsville	42718	8,715	Glasgow	42141	12,958	Owensboro	42301	54,450
Corbin	40701	8,075	Harrodsburg	40330	7,265	Paducah	42001	29,315
Covington	41011*	49,574	Hazard	41701	5,371	Paris	40361	7,935
Cynthiana	41031	5,881	Henderson	42420	24,834	Pleasure Rdg. Pk.	40258	27,332
Danville	40422	12,942	Highview	—	13,286	Princeton	42445	7,073
Dayton	41074	6,979	Hopkinsville	42240	27,318	Radcliff	40160	14,519
Edgewood	41017	7,239	Independence	41051	7,998	Richmond	40475	21,705
Elizabethtown	42701	15,380	Jeffersontown	40299	15,795	Russellville	42276	7,520
Elsmere	—	7,203	Lebanon	40033	6,590	St. Matthews	40207	13,519
Erlanger	41018	14,470	Lexington–Fayette	40511*	204,165	Shively	40216	16,645
Fairdale	40118	7,315	Louisville	40231*	298,694	Somerset	42501	10,649
Fern Creek	40291	16,866	Madisonville	42431	16,979	Valley Station	40272	24,474
Flatwoods	41139	8,354	Mayfield	42066	10,705	Versailles	40383	6,427
Florence	41042	15,586	Maysville	41056	7,983	Westwood	41101	5,973
Fort Campbell N.	—	17,211	Middlesboro	40965	12,251	Winchester	40391	15,216

LOUISIANA (La. or LA)

Place and Zip Code		Pop.[1]	Place and Zip Code		Pop.[1]	Place and Zip Code		Pop.[1]
Abbeville	70510	12,391	Harahan	70183	11,384	Port Allen	70767	6,114
Alexandria	71301	51,565	Harvey	70058	22,709	Poydras	—	5,722
Arabi	70032	10,248	Houma	70360	32,602	Prien	—	6,224
Avondale	—	6,699	Jeanerette	70544	6,511	Raceland	70394	6,302
Baker	70714	12,865	Jefferson	—	15,550	Rayne	70578	9,066
Bastrop	71220	15,527	Jennings	70546	12,401	Reserve	70084	7,288
Baton Rouge	70821*	219,844	Kenner	70062	66,382	River Edge	—	17,146
Bayou Cane	—	15,723	Lafayette	70501*	81,961	Ruston	71270*	20,585
Bogalusa	70427	16,976	Lake Charles	70601*	75,226	St. Martinville	70582	7,965
Bossier City	71111*	50,817	Lake Providence	71254	6,361	Scotlandville	70807	15,113
Broadmoor	70185	7,051	Laplace	70068	16,112	Shreveport	71102*	205,820
Brownsville–Bawcomville	—	7,252	Leesville	71446*	9,054	Slidell	70458	26,718
			Mandeville	70448	6,076	Springhill	71075	6,516
Bunkie	71322	5,364	Mansfield	71052	6,485	Sulphur	70663	19,709
Chalmette	70043	33,847	Marrero	70072	36,548	Tallulah	71282	11,341
Claiborne	—	6,278	Metairie	70009	164,160	Terrytown	—	23,548
Covington	70433	7,892	Minden	71055	15,084	Thibodaux	70301	15,810
Crowley	70526	16,036	Monroe	71203*	51,597	Timberlane	—	11,579
De Ridder	70634	11,057	Morgan City	70380	16,114	Vidalia	71373	5,936
Denham Springs	70726	8,412	Moss Bluff	70601	7,004	Ville Plate	70586	9,201
Donaldsonville	70346	7,901	Natchitoches	71457	16,664	Violet	70092	11,678
Estelle	—	12,724	New Iberia	70560	32,766	Waggman	—	9,004
Eunice	70535	12,479	New Orleans	70113*	557,927	West Monroe	71291	14,993
Franklin	70538	9,584	Oakdale	71463	7,155	Westwego	70094	12,663
Gonzales	70737	7,287	Opelousas	70570	18,903	Winnfield	71483	7,311
Gretna	70053	20,615	Pineville	71360	12,034	Winnsboro	71295	5,921
Hammond	70401	15,043	Plaquemine	70764	7,521	Zachary	70791	7,297

[1] 1980 Census.

MAINE (Me. or ME)

PLACE AND ZIP CODE		POP.[1]
Auburn	04210	23,128
Augusta	04330	21,819
Bangor	04401	31,643
Bath	04530	10,246
Belfast	04915	6,243
Biddeford	04005	19,638
Brewer	04412	9,017
Brunswick	04011	10,990
Cape Elizabeth †	04107	7,838
Caribou	04736	9,916
Fairfield †	04937	6,113
Falmouth †	04105	6,853
Farmington †	04938	6,730
Gardiner	04345	6,485
Gorham †	04038	10,101
Houlton †	04730	6,766
Kennebunk †	04043	6,621
Lewiston	04240	40,481
Limestone †	04750	8,719
Lisbon †	04250	8,769
Millinocket	04462	7,567
Old Orchard Beach	04064	6,023
Old Town	04468	8,422
Orono	04473	9,981
Portland	04101*	61,572
Presque Isle	04769	11,172
Rockland	04841	7,919
Rumford	04276	6,256
Saco	04072	12,921
Sanford	04073	10,268
Scarborough †	04074	11,347
Skowhegan	04976	6,517
South Portland	04106	22,712
Waterville	04901	17,779
Wells †	04090	8,211
Westbrook	04092	14,976
Windham †	—	11,282
Yarmouth †	04096	6,585
York †	03909	8,465

MARYLAND (Md. or MD)

PLACE AND ZIP CODE		POP.[1]
Aberdeen	21001	11,533
Adelphi	20783	12,530
Andrews	20331	10,064
Annapolis	21401*	31,740
Arbutus	21227	20,163
Arnold	21012	12,285
Aspen Hill	20906	47,455
Baltimore	21233*	786,741
Bel Air	21014	7,814
Bel Air South	—	9,140
Beltsville	20705	12,760
Bethesda	20814	63,022
Bladensburg	20710	7,691
Bowie	20715	33,695
Brooklyn Park	21225	11,508
Calverton	—	7,649
Cambridge	21613	11,703
Camp Springs	20748	16,118
Cape St. Clair	21401	6,022
Carney	—	21,488
Catonsville	21228	33,208
Chevy Chase	20815	12,232
Chillum	20783	32,775
Clinton	20735	16,438
Cockeysville	21030	17,013
Colesville	20904	14,359
College Park	20740	23,614
Columbia	21045*	52,518
Coral Hills	20027	11,602
Crofton	21114	12,009
Cumberland	21502	25,933
District Heights	20747	6,799
Dundalk	21222	71,293
East Riverdale	—	14,117
Easton	21601	7,536
Edgemere	21219	9,078
Edgewood	21040	19,455
Elkton	21921	6,468
Ellicott City	21043	21,784
Essex	21221	39,614
Ferndale	21061	14,314
Forestville	20747	16,401
Fort Meade	20755	14,083
Frederick	21701	28,086
Friendly	—	8,848
Frostburg	21532	7,715
Gaithersburg	20877	26,424
Germantown	20874	9,721
Glassmanor	—	7,751
Glen Burnie	21061	37,263
Goddard	20771	6,147
Green Haven	21122	6,577
Greenbelt	20770	17,332
Hagerstown	21740	34,132
Halfway	—	8,659
Havre De Grace	21078	8,763
Hillandale	—	9,686
Hillcrest Heights	20031	17,021
Hyattsville	20780*	12,709
Joppatowne	21085	11,348
Kentland	20785	8,596
Kettering	—	6,972
Lake Shore	21122	10,181
Langley Park	20787	14,038
Lanham–Seabr'k.	20706	15,814
Lansdowne–Baltimore Hlds.	21227	16,759
Laurel	20707	12,103
Lexington Park	20653	10,361
Linthicum	21090	7,457
Londontowne	—	6,052
Lochearn	—	26,908
Lutherville–Timonium	21093	16,871
Maryland City	—	6,949
Middle River	21220	26,756
Milford Mill	—	20,354
Montgomery Vill.	20879	18,725
Mount Rainier	20712	7,361
New Carrollton	20784	12,632
North Bethesda	—	22,671
North Kensington	—	9,039
North Laurel	—	6,093
Odenton	21113	13,270
Olney	20832	13,026
Overlea	21206	12,965
Owings Mills	21117	9,526
Oxon Hill	20745	36,267
Palmer Park	20785	7,986
Parkville	21234	35,159
Pasadena	21122	7,439
Perry Hall	21128	13,455
Pikesville	21208	22,555
Potomac	20854	40,402
Randallstown	21133	25,927
Redland	—	10,759
Reisterstown	21136	19,385
Riviera Beach	21122	8,812
Rockville	20850*	43,811
Rosedale	21237	19,956
Rossville	—	8,646
St. Charles	—	13,921
Salisbury	21801	16,429
Security	—	29,453
Severn	21144	20,147
Severna Park	21146	21,253
Silver Spring	20907*	72,893
South Gate	21061	24,185
S. Kensington	20795	9,344
South Laurel	20810	18,034
Suitl'd.–Silver Hill	20746	32,164
Takoma Park	20912	16,231
Tantallon	—	9,945
Temple Hills	20748	6,630
Towson	21204	51,083
Waldorf	20601	9,782
Walker Mill	20028	10,651
Westminster	21157	8,808
Wheaton	20902	48,598
White Oak	20903	13,700

MASSACHUSETTS (Mass. or MA)

PLACE AND ZIP CODE		POP.[1]
Abington †	02351	13,517
Acton †	01720	17,544
Acushnet †	02743	8,704
Adams	01220	6,857
Agawam †	01001	26,271
Amesbury	01913	12,236
Amherst	01002	17,773
Andover	01810	8,445
Arlington	02174	48,219
Ashland †	01721	9,165
Athol	01331	8,708
Attleboro	02703	34,196
Auburn †	01501	14,845
Ayer †	01432*	6,993
Barnstable †	02630	30,898
Bedford †	01730	13,067
Belchertown †	01007	8,339
Bellingham †	02019	14,300
Belmont †	02178	26,100
Beverly	01915	37,655
Billerica †	01821	36,727
Blackstone †	01504	6,570
Boston	02205*	562,994
Bourne †	02532	13,874
Braintree †	02134	36,337
Bridgewater	02324	6,781
Brockton	02403	95,172
Brookline †	02146	55,062
Burlington †	01803	23,486
Cambridge	02138*	95,322
Canton †	02021	18,182
Carver †	02330	6,988
Charlton †	01507	6,719
Chatham †	02633	6,071
Chelmsford †	01824	31,174
Chelsea	02150	25,431
Chicopee	01021*	55,112
Clinton †	01510	12,771
Cochituate	01778	6,126
Cohasset †	02025	7,174
Concord †	01742	16,293
Dalton †	01226	6,797

1 1980 Census. † Town or township.

MASSACHUSETTS *(continued)*

PLACE AND ZIP CODE		POP.[1]
Danvers †	01923	24,100
Dartmouth †	02714	23,966
Dedham †	02026	25,298
Deerfield †	01342	4,517
Dennis †	02638	12,360
Dracut †	01826	21,249
Dudley †	01570	8,717
Duxbury †	02332	11,807
E. Bridgewater †	02333	9,945
E. Longmeadow †	01028	12,905
Easthampton †	01027	15,580
Easton †	02334	16,623
Everett	02149	37,195
Fairhaven †	02719	15,759
Fall River	02722*	92,574
Falmouth	02540*	5,720
Fitchburg	01420	39,580
Fort Devens	01433	9,546
Foxborough	02035	5,697
Framingham †	01701	65,113
Franklin	02038	9,296
Freetown †	—	7,058
Gardner	01440	17,900
Gloucester	01930	27,768
Grafton †	01519	11,238
Grt. Barrington †	01230	7,405
Greenfield	01301	14,198
Groton †	01450	6,154
Groveland †	01834	5,040
Halifax †	02338	5,513
Hamilton †	01936	6,960
Hampden †	01036	4,745
Hanover †	02339	11,358
Hanson †	02341	8,617
Harvard †	01451	12,170
Harwich †	02645	8,971
Haverhill	01830	46,865
Hingham	02043	5,742
Holbrook †	02343	11,140
Holden †	01520	13,336
Holliston †	01746	12,622
Holyoke	01040	44,678
Hopkinton †	01748	7,114
Hudson	01749	14,156
Hull †	02045	9,714
Hyannis	02601	9,118
Ipswich †	01938	11,158
Kingston †	02364	7,362
Lakeville †	—	5,931
Lancaster †	01523	6,334
Lawrence	01842*	63,175
Lee †	01238	6,247
Leicester †	01524	9,446
Lenox †	01240	6,523
Leominster	01453	34,508
Lexington †	02173	29,479
Lincoln †	01773	7,098
Littleton †	01460	6,970
Longmeadow †	01106	16,301
Lowell	01853*	92,418
Lunenburg †	01462	8,405
Lynn	01901*	78,471
Ludlow †	01056	18,150
Lynnfield †	01940	11,267
Malden	02148	53,386
Manchester †	01944	5,424
Mansfield	02048	6,786
Marblehead †	01945	20,126
Marlborough	01752	30,617
Marshfield †	02050	20,916
Mattapoisett †	02739	5,597
Maynard †	01754	9,590
Medfield	02052	6,108
Medford	02155	58,076
Medway †	02053	8,447
Melrose	02176	30,055
Methuen †	01844	36,701
Middleboro	02346	7,012
Milford	01757	21,730
Millbury †	01527	11,808
Millis †	02054	6,908
Milton †	02186	25,860
Monson †	01057	7,315
Montague †	01351	8,011
Nantucket †	02554	5,087
Natick †	01760	29,461
Needham †	02161	27,901
New Bedford	02741*	98,478
Newburyport	01950	15,900
Newton	02154	83,622
Norfolk †	02056	6,363
North Adams	01247	18,063
North Andover †	01845	20,129
N. Attleboro †	02760*	21,095
North Reading †	01864	11,455
Northampton	01060	29,286
Northborough	01532	5,670
Northbridge †	01534	12,246
Norton †	02766	12,690
Norwell †	02061	9,182
Norwood †	02062	29,711
Orange †	01364	6,844
Orleans †	02653	5,306
Oxford	01540	6,369
Palmer †	01069	11,389
Peabody	01960	45,976
Pembroke †	02359	13,487
Pepperell †	01463	8,061
Pinehurst	01866	6,588
Pittsfield	01201	51,974
Plainville †	02762	5,857
Plymouth	02360	7,232
Quincy	02169	84,743
Randolph †	02368	28,218
Raynham	02767	9,085
Reading †	01867	22,678
Rehoboth †	02769	7,570
Revere	02151	42,423
Rockland †	02370	15,695
Rockport †	01966	6,345
Salem	01970	38,220
Salisbury †	01950	5,973
Sandwich †	02563	8,727
Saugus †	01906	24,746
Scituate	02066	5,351
Seekonk †	02771	12,269
Sharon	02067	5,976
Shirley †	01464	5,124
Shrewsbury †	01545	22,674
Somerset †	02721	18,813
Somerville	02143	77,372
South Hadley †	01075	16,399
South Yarmouth	02664	7,525
Southborough †	01772	6,193
Southbridge	01550	12,882
Southwick †	01077	7,382
Spencer	01562	6,350
Springfield	01101*	152,319
Sterling †	01564	5,440
Stoneham †	02180	21,424
Stoughton †	02072	26,710
Stow †	01775	5,144
Sturbridge †	01566	5,976
Sudbury †	01776	14,027
Sutton †	—	5,855
Swampscott †	01907	13,837
Swansea †	02777	15,461
Taunton	02780	45,001
Templeton †	01468	6,070
Tewksbury †	01876	24,635
Topsfield †	01983	5,709
Townsend †	01469	7,201
Tyngsborough †	01879	5,683
Uxbridge †	01569	8,374
Wakefield †	01880	24,895
Walpole	02081	5,274
Waltham	02154	58,200
Ware	01082	6,806
Wareham †	02571	18,457
Watertown †	02172	34,384
Wayland †	01778	12,170
Webster	01570	11,175
Wellesley †	02181	27,209
West Boylston †	01583	6,204
W. Bridgewater †	02379	6,359
W. Springfield †	01089	27,042
Westborough †	01581	13,619
Westfield	01085	36,465
Westford †	01886	13,434
Westminster †	01473	5,139
Weston †	02193	11,169
Westport †	02790	13,763
Westwood †	02090	13,212
Weymouth †	02169	55,601
Whitinsville	01588	5,379
Whitman †	02382	13,534
Wilbraham †	01095	12,053
Williamstown	01267	4,798
Wilmington †	01887	17,471
Winchendon †	01475	7,019
Winchester †	01890	20,701
Winthrop †	02152	19,294
Woburn	01801	36,626
Worcester	01613	161,799
Wrentham †	02093	7,580
Yarmouth †	02675	18,449

MICHIGAN (Mich. or MI)

PLACE AND ZIP CODE		POP.[1]
Adrian	49221	21,276
Albion	49224	11,059
Allen Park	48101	34,196
Alma	48801	9,652
Alpena	49707	12,214
Ann Arbor	48106*	107,969
Avon	—	40,779
Battle Creek	49016*	35,724
Bay City	48706*	41,593
Beecher	—	17,178
Benton Harbor	49022	14,707
Benton Heights	—	6,787
Berkley	48072	18,637
Beverly Hills	48009	11,598
Big Rapids	49307	14,361
Birmingham	48012*	21,698
Bloomfield	—	42,876
Burton	—	29,276

1 1980 Census. † Town or township.

MICHIGAN *(continued)*

PLACE AND ZIP CODE		POP.[1]	PLACE AND ZIP CODE		POP.[1]	PLACE AND ZIP CODE		POP.[1]
Cadillac	49601	10,199	Hazel Park	48030	20,914	Okemos	48864	8,882
Carrollton	48724	7,482	Highland Park	48203	27,909	Owosso	48867	16,455
Center Line	48015	9,293	Hillsdale	49242	7,432	Petoskey	49770	6,097
Charlotte	48813	8,251	Holland	49423*	26,281	Plymouth	48170	9,986
Clawson	48017	15,103	Holt	48842	10,097	Pontiac	48056*	76,715
Clinton	49236	72,400	Houghton	49931	7,512	Port Huron	48060	33,981
Coldwater	49036	9,461	Howell	48843	6,976	Portage	49081	38,157
Cutlerville	49508	8,256	Huntington Wds.	48070	6,937	River Rouge	48218	12,912
Davison	48423	6,087	Inkster	48141	35,190	Riverview	48192	14,569
Dearborn	48120*	90,660	Ionia	48846	5,920	Rochester	48063	7,203
Dearborn Heights	48127	67,706	Iron Mountain	49801	8,341	Romulus	48174	24,857
Detroit	48233*	1,203,339	Ironwood	49938	7,741	Roseville	48066	54,311
Dowagiac	49047	6,307	Ishpeming	49849	7,538	Royal Oak	48068*	70,893
East Detroit	48021	38,280	Jackson	49201*	39,739	Saginaw	48605*	77,508
E. Grand Rapids	49506	10,914	Jenison	49428	16,330	St. Clair Shores	48080	76,210
East Lansing	48823	51,392	Kalamazoo	49001*	79,722	St. Johns	48879	7,376
Eastwood	—	7,186	Kentwood	49508	30,438	St. Joseph	49085	9,622
Ecorse	48229	14,447	Kingsford	49801	5,290	Saline	48176	6,483
Escanaba	49829	14,355	Lakeview	48850	13,345	Sault Ste. Marie	49783	14,448
Fair Plain	—	8,289	Lambertville	48144	6,341	South Haven	49090	5,943
Farmington	48024	11,022	Lansing	48924*	130,414	Southfield	48037	75,568
Farmington Hills	48024	58,056	Lapeer	48446	6,198	Southgate	48195	32,058
Fenton	48430	8,098	Lincoln Park	48146	45,105	Springfield	—	5,917
Ferndale	48220	26,227	Livonia	48150*	104,814	Sterling Heights	48077	108,999
Flat Rock	48134	6,853	Ludington	49431	8,937	Sturgis	49091	9,468
Flint	48502*	159,611	Madison Heights	48071	35,375	Taylor	48180	77,568
Flushing	48433	8,624	Manistee	49660	7,665	Tecumseh	49286	7,320
Fraser	48026	14,560	Marquette	49855	23,288	Three Rivers	49093	7,015
Garden City	48135	35,640	Marshall	49068	7,201	Traverse City	49684	15,516
Grand Blanc	48439	6,848	Marysville	48040	7,345	Trenton	48183	22,762
Grand Haven	49417	11,763	Mason	48854	6,019	Troy	48099	67,102
Grand Ledge	48837	6,920	Melvindale	48122	12,322	Walker	49504	15,088
Grand Rapids	49501*	181,843	Menominee	49858	10,099	Warren	48089	161,134
Grandville	49418	12,412	Midland	48640	37,269	Waterford	48095	64,250
Greenville	48838	8,019	Monroe	48161	23,531	Wayne	48184	21,159
Grosse Ile	48138	9,320	Mount Clemens	48043*	18,806	West Bloomfield	48033	41,962
Grosse Pointe	48236	5,901	Mt. Pleasant	48858	23,746	Westland	48185	84,603
Grosse Pt. Farms	48236	10,551	Muskegon	49440*	40,823	Westwood	—	8,519
Grosse Pointe Park	48236	13,639	Muskegon Heights	49444	14,611	Whitelake—		
Grosse Pointe Wds.	48236	18,886	Niles	49120	13,115	Seven Harbors	—	7,557
Hamtramck	48212	21,300	Northview	—	11,662	Wixom	48096	6,705
Harper Woods	48225	16,361	Northville	48167	5,698	Woodhaven	48183	10,902
Harrison	48625	23,649	Norton Shores	49441	22,025	Wyandotte	48192	34,006
Haslett	48840	7,025	Novi	48050	22,525	Wyoming	49509	59,616
Hastings	49058	6,418	Oak Park	48237	31,537	Ypsilanti	48197	24,031

MINNESOTA (Minn. or MN)

PLACE AND ZIP CODE		POP.[1]	PLACE AND ZIP CODE		POP.[1]	PLACE AND ZIP CODE		POP.[1]
Albert Lea	56007	19,200	Eagan	55121	20,700	Marshall	56258	11,161
Alexandria	56308	7,608	East Bethel	55005	6,626	Mendota Heights	55050	7,288
Andover	—	9,387	East Grand Forks	56721	8,537	Minneapolis	55401*	370,951
Anoka	55303	15,634	Eden Prairie	55344	16,263	Minnetonka	55343	38,683
Apple Valley	55124	21,818	Edina	55424	46,073	Moorhead	56560	29,998
Arden Hills	—	8,012	Elk River	55330	6,785	Mound	55364	9,280
Austin	55912	23,020	Fairmont	56031	11,506	Mounds View	55112	12,593
Bemidji	56601	10,949	Faribault	55021	16,241	New Brighton	55112	23,269
Blaine	55433	28,558	Fergus Falls	56537	12,519	New Hope	55428	23,087
Bloomington	55420	81,831	Fridley	55432	30,228	New Ulm	56073	13,755
Brainerd	56401	11,489	Golden Valley	55427	22,775	North Mankato	56001	9,145
Brooklyn Center	55429	31,230	Grand Rapids	55744	7,934	North St. Paul	55109	11,921
Brooklyn Park	55444	43,332	Ham Lake	—	7,832	Northfield	55057	12,562
Burnsville	55337	35,674	Hastings	55033	12,827	Oakdale	—	12,123
Champlin	55316	9,006	Hermantown	—	6,759	Orono	—	6,845
Chanhassen	55317	6,359	Hibbing	55746	21,193	Owatonna	55060	18,632
Chaska	55318	8,346	Hopkins	55343	15,336	Plymouth	55427	31,615
Cloquet	55720	11,142	Hutchinson	55350	9,244	Prior Lake	55372	7,284
Columbia Heights	55421	20,029	Inver Grove Hts.	55075	17,171	Ramsey	55303	10,093
Coon Rapids	55433	35,826	Lakeville	55044	14,790	Red Wing	55066	13,736
Cottage Grove	55016	18,994	Little Canada	—	7,102	Richfield	55423	37,851
Crookston	56716*	8,628	Little Falls	56345	7,250	Robbinsdale	55422	14,422
Crystal	55422	25,543	Mankato	56001*	28,646	Rochester	55901*	57,890
Detroit Lakes	56501	7,106	Maple Grove	—	20,525	Roseville	55113	35,820
Duluth	55806*	92,811	Maplewood	55109	26,990	St. Anthony	55418	7,981

[1] 1980 Census.

MINNESOTA *(continued)*

PLACE AND ZIP CODE		POP.[1]	PLACE AND ZIP CODE		POP.[1]	PLACE AND ZIP CODE		POP.[1]
St. Cloud	56301	42,566	South St. Paul	55075	21,235	West St. Paul	55118	18,527
St. Louis Park	55416	42,931	Spring L. Park	56680	6,477	White Bear Lake	55110	22,538
St. Paul	55101*	270,230	Stillwater	55082	12,290	Willmar	56201	15,895
St. Peter	56082	9,056	Thief River Falls	56701	9,105	Winona	55987*	25,075
Shakopee	55379	9,941	Virginia	55792	11,056	Woodbury	55125	10,297
Shoreview	55112	17,300	Waseca	56093	8,219	Worthington	56187	10,243

MISSISSIPPI (Miss. or MS)

PLACE AND ZIP CODE		POP.[1]	PLACE AND ZIP CODE		POP.[1]	PLACE AND ZIP CODE		POP.[1]
Aberdeen	39730	7,184	Greenwood	38930	20,115	N. Gulfport	—	6,660
Amory	38821	7,307	Grenada	38901	12,641	N. Long Beach	—	7,063
Bay St. Louis	39520	7,850	Gulfport	39503*	39,676	Ocean Springs	39564	14,504
Biloxi	39530*	49,311	Hattiesburg	39401	40,829	Orange Grove	—	13,476
Booneville	38829	6,199	Holly Springs	38635	7,285	Oxford	38655	9,882
Brandon	39042	9,626	Indianola	38751	8,221	Pascagoula	39567	29,318
Brookhaven	39601	10,800	Jackson	39205*	202,895	Pearl	39208	18,602
Canton	39046	11,116	Kosciusko	39090	7,415	Petal	39465	8,476
Clarksdale	38614	21,137	Laurel	39440	21,897	Philadelphia	39350	6,434
Cleveland	38732	14,524	Leland	38756	6,667	Picayune	39466	10,361
Clinton	39056	14,660	Long Beach	39560	7,967	Southaven	38671	16,071
Columbia	39429	7,733	Louisville	39339	7,323	Starkville	39759	15,169
Columbus	39701	27,503	McComb	39648	12,331	Tupelo	38801	23,905
Corinth	38834	13,839	Meridian	39301	46,577	Vicksburg	39180	25,434
D'Iberville	—	13,369	Moss Point	39563	18,998	West Point	39773	9,123
Gautier	39553	8,917	Natchez	39120	22,209	Winona	38967	6,177
Greenville	38701	40,613	New Albany	38652	7,072	Yazoo City	39194	12,092

MISSOURI (Mo. or MO)

PLACE AND ZIP CODE		POP.[1]	PLACE AND ZIP CODE		POP.[1]	PLACE AND ZIP CODE		POP.[1]
Affton	63123	23,181	Florissant	63033*	55,372	Monett	65708	6,148
Arnold	63010	19,141	Fulton	65251	11,046	Neosho	64850	9,493
Aurora	65605	6,437	Gladstone	64118	24,990	Nevada	64772	9,044
Ballwin	63011	12,656	Glendale	63122	6,035	O'Fallon	63366	8,677
Bellefontaine Neighbors	63137	12,082	Grandview	64030	24,561	Olivette	63132	7,952
			Hannibal	63401	18,811	Overland	63114	19,620
Belton	64012	12,708	Harrisonville	64701	6,372	Perryville	63775	7,343
Berkeley	63134	15,922	Hazelwood	63042*	12,935	Pine Lawn	63120	6,600
Blue Springs	64015	25,927	Higginsville	64037	4,595	Poplar Bluff	63901	17,139
Boonville	65233	6,959	Independence	64051*	111,806	Raytown	64133	31,826
Brentwood	63144	8,209	Jackson	63755	7,827	Richmond Hts.	63117	11,516
Bridgeton	63044	18,445	Jefferson City	65101	33,619	Rolla	65401	13,303
Cape Girardeau	63701	34,361	Jennings	63136	17,217	St. Ann	63074	15,523
Carthage	64836	11,104	Joplin	64801	39,023	St. Charles	63301	37,739
Caruthersville	63830	7,958	Kansas City	64108*	448,033	St. Johns	63114	7,854
Chillicothe	64601	9,089	Kennett	63857	10,145	St. Joseph	64501*	76,691
Clayton	63105	14,306	Kirksville	63501	17,167	St. Louis	63155*	453,085
Clinton	64735	8,366	Kirkwood	63122	27,987	St. Peters	63376	15,700
Columbia	65201	62,061	Ladue	63124	9,376	Sappington	63126	11,388
Concord	—	20,896	Lebanon	65536	9,507	Sedalia	65301	20,927
Crestwood	63126	12,815	Lees Summit	64063	28,741	Sikeston	63801	17,431
Creve Coeur	63141	11,736	Lemay	63125	35,424	Spanish Lake	—	20,632
Dellwood	63136	6,200	Liberty	64068	16,251	Springfield	65801*	133,116
Des Peres	63131	7,953	Malden	63863	6,096	Trenton	64683	6,811
Dexter	63841	7,043	Manchester	63011	6,191	University City	63130	42,738
Ellisville	—	6,233	Maplewood	63143	10,960	Warrensburg	64093	13,807
Excelsior Springs	64024	10,424	Marshall	65340	12,781	Washington	63090	9,251
Farmington	63640	8,270	Maryville	64468	9,558	Webb City	64870	7,309
Ferguson	63135	24,549	Mexico	65265	12,276	Webster Groves	63119	23,097
Festus	63028	7,574	Moberly	65270	13,418	West Plains	65775	7,741

MONTANA (Mont. or MT)

PLACE AND ZIP CODE		POP.[1]	PLACE AND ZIP CODE		POP.[1]	PLACE AND ZIP CODE		POP.[1]
			Great Falls	59403*	56,725	Miles City	59301	9,602
Anaconda–Deer Lodge	59711*	12,518	Havre	59501	10,891	Missoula	59806	33,388
Billings	59101*	66,842	Helena	59601*	23,938	Missoula South	—	5,557
Billings Heights	59101	8,480	Kalispell	59901*	10,648	Orchard Homes	—	10,837
Bozeman	59715	21,645	Laurel	59044	5,481	Sidney	59270	5,726
Butte-Silver Bow	59701	37,205	Lewiston	59457	7,104			
Glendive	59330	5,978	Livingston	59047	6,994			

NEBRASKA (Neb., Nebr., or NE)

PLACE AND ZIP CODE		POP.[1]	PLACE AND ZIP CODE		POP.[1]	PLACE AND ZIP CODE		POP.[1]
Alliance	69301	9,920	Blair	68008	6,418	Gering	69341	7,760
Beatrice	68310	12,891	Columbus	68601	17,328	Grand Island	68801	33,180
Bellevue	68005	21,813	Fremont	68025	23,979	Hastings	68901	23,045

[1] 1980 Census.

PLACE AND ZIP CODE		POP.[1]	PLACE AND ZIP CODE		POP.[1]	PLACE AND ZIP CODE		POP.[1]
NEBRASKA *(continued)*								
Holdrege	68949	5,624	Nebraska City	68410	7,127	Scottsbluff	69361	14,156
Kearney	68847	21,158	Norfolk	68701	19,449	Sidney	69162	6,010
La Vista	68128	9,588	North Platte	69101	24,509	South Sioux City	68776	9,339
Lexington	68850	7,040	Omaha	68108*	313,939	York	68467	7,723
Lincoln	68501*	171,932	Papillion	68133	6,399			
McCook	69001	8,404	Plattsmouth	68048	6,295			
NEVADA (Nev. or NV)								
Boulder City	89005	9,590	Incline Village	89450	6,225	Reno	89510*	100,756
Carson City	89701	32,022	Las Vegas	89114*	164,674	Sparks	89431	40,780
East Las Vegas	89112	6,449	Nellis A.F.B.	—	7,476	Sunrise Manor	—	44,155
Elko	89801	8,758	North Las Vegas	89030	42,739	Sun Valley	89431	8,222
Henderson	89015	24,363	Paradise	89132	84,818	Winchester	—	19,728
NEW HAMPSHIRE (N.H. or NH)								
Amherst †	03031	8,243	Hampton	03842	6,779	Nashua	03061	67,865
Bedford †	03102	9,481	Hanover	03755	6,861	Newport †	03773	6,229
Berlin	03570	13,084	Hooksett †	03106	7,303	Pelham †	03076	8,090
Claremont	03743	14,557	Hudson	03051	6,248	Plaistow †	03865	5,609
Concord	03301	30,400	Keene	03431	21,449	Portsmouth	03801	26,254
Conway †	03818	7,158	Laconia	03246	15,575	Raymond †	03077	5,453
Derry	03038	12,248	Lebanon	03766	11,134	Rochester	03867	21,560
Dover	03820	22,377	Littleton †	03561	5,558	Salem †	03079	24,124
Durham	03824	8,448	Londonderry †	03053	13,598	Seabrook †	03874	5,917
Exeter	03833	8,947	Manchester	03103*	90,936	Somersworth	03878	10,350
Franklin	03235	7,901	Merrimack †	03054	15,406	Swanzey †	—	5,183
Goffstown †	03045	11,315	Milford	03055	6,269	Windham †	03087	5,664
NEW JERSEY (N.J. or NJ)								
Aberdeen †	—	17,235	Crestwood Village	—	7,965	Hawthorne	07506	18,200
Absecon	08201	6,859	Dover	07801	14,681	Hazlet	07730	23,013
Asbury Park	07712	17,015	Dumont	07628	18,334	Highland Park	08904	13,396
Atlantic City	08401*	40,199	Dunellen	08812	6,593	Hillsdale	07642	10,495
Audubon	08106	9,533	East Brunswick †	08816	37,711	Hillside	07205	21,440
Barrington	08007	7,418	East Hanover	07936	9,319	Hoboken	07030	42,460
Bayonne	07002	65,047	East Orange	07019	77,878	Holiday City—		
Beachwood	08722	7,687	East Rutherford	07073	7,849	Berkeley	—	9,019
Belleville	07109	35,367	East Windsor †	—	21,041	Hopatcong	07843	15,531
Bellmawr	08031	13,721	Eatontown	07724	12,703	Irvington	07111	61,493
Belmar	07719	6,771	Edgewater Park	—	9,273	Jersey City	07303*	223,532
Bergenfield	07621	25,568	Edison †	08818*	70,193	Keansburg	07734	10,613
Berkeley Heights	07922	12,549	Elizabeth	07207*	106,201	Kearny	07032	35,735
Bernardsville	07924	6,715	Elmwood Park	07407	18,377	Kendall Park	08824	7,419
Bloomfield	07003	47,792	Emerson	07630	7,793	Kenilworth	07033	8,221
Bloomingdale	07403	7,867	Englewood	07631	23,701	Keyport	07735	7,413
Bogota	07603	8,344	Ewing Township	—	34,842	Kinnelon	07405	7,770
Boonton	07005	8,620	Fair Lawn	07410	32,229	Lake Mohawk	—	8,498
Bound Brook	08805	9,710	Fairfield †	07006	7,987	Lakewood	08701	22,863
Bridgeton	08302	18,795	Fairview	07022	10,519	Laurence Harbor	08879	6,737
Brigantine	08203	8,318	Fanwood	07023	7,767	Leonia	07605	8,027
Browns Mills	08015	10,568	Florence	08518	7,677	Lincoln Park	07035	8,806
Budd Lake	07828	6,523	Florham Park	07932	9,359	Linden	07036	37,836
Burlington	08016	10,246	Fort Lee	07024	32,449	Lindenwold	08021	18,196
Butler	07405	7,616	Franklin Lakes	07417	8,769	Linwood	08221	6,144
Caldwell	07006	7,624	Freehold	07728	10,020	Little Falls	07424	11,496
Camden	08101*	84,910	Garfield	07026	26,803	Little Ferry	07643	9,399
Candlewood	—	6,166	Gilford Park	—	6,528	Livingston	07039	28,040
Carlstadt	07072	6,166	Glassboro	08028	14,574	Lodi	07644	23,956
Carney's Point	08069	7,574	Glen Ridge	07028	7,855	Long Branch	07740	29,819
Carteret	07008	20,598	Glen Rock	07452	11,497	Lyndhurst	07071	20,326
Cedar Grove	07009	12,600	Gloucester City	08030	13,121	Madison	07940	15,357
Chatham	07928	8,537	Gordon's Corner	—	6,320	Madison Park	—	7,447
Cherry Hill †	08034*	68,785	Guttenberg	07093	7,340	Manville	08835	11,278
Cinnaminson	08077	16,072	Hackensack	07602*	36,039	Maple Shade	08052	20,525
Clark	07066	16,699	Hackettstown	07840	8,850	Maplewood	07040	22,950
Clayton	08312	6,013	Haddon Heights	08035	8,361	Margate City	08402	9,179
Cliffside Park	07010	21,464	Haddonfield	08033	12,337	Marlton	08053	9,411
Clifton	07015*	74,388	Haledon	07508	6,607	Matawan	07747	8,837
Closter	07624	8,164	Hammonton	08037	12,298	Maywood	07607	9,895
Collingswood	08108	15,838	Hanover Township	—	11,846	Mercerville	08619	25,446
Cranford	07016	24,573	Harrison	07029	12,242	Metuchen	08840	13,762
Cresskill	07626	7,609	Hasbrouck Hts.	07604	12,166	Middlesex	08846	13,480

1 1980 Census. † Town or township (includes rural population).

NEW JERSEY *(continued)*

PLACE AND ZIP CODE		POP.[1]	PLACE AND ZIP CODE		POP.[1]	PLACE AND ZIP CODE		POP.[1]
Middletown	07748	62,298	Phillipsburg	08865	16,647	Stratford	08084	8,005
Midland Park	07432	7,381	Pine Hill	08021	8,684	Succasunna	07876	10,931
Millburn	07041	19,543	Piscataway	08854	42,223	Summit	07901	21,071
Milltown	08850	7,136	Pitman	08071	9,744	Teaneck	07666	39,007
Millville	08332	24,815	Plainfield	07061*	45,555	Tenafly	07670	13,552
Montclair	07042*	38,321	Pleasantville	08232	13,435	Tinton Falls	07724	7,740
Montvale	07645	7,318	Point Pleasant	08742	17,747	Toms River	08753	7,465
Moorestown	08057	13,695	Pompton Lakes	07442	10,660	Totowa	07512	11,448
Morristown	07960*	16,614	Princeton	08540	12,035	Trenton	08650*	92,124
Mt. Holly	08060	10,818	Rahway	07065*	26,723	Twin Rivers	—	7,742
Mountainside	07092	7,118	Ramblewood	08054	6,475	Union	07083	50,184
Neptune †	—	28,336	Ramsey	07446	12,899	Union Beach	07735	6,354
New Brunswick	08901*	41,442	Raritan	08869	6,128	Union City	07087	55,593
New Milford	07646	16,876	Red Bank	07701	12,031	Upper Saddle R.	07458	7,958
New Providence	07974	12,426	Ridgefield	07657	10,294	Ventnor City	08406	11,704
Newark	07102*	329,248	Ridgefield Park	07660	12,738	Verona	07044	14,166
Newton	07860	7,748	Ridgewood	07451*	25,208	Vineland	08360	53,753
North Arlington	07032	16,587	Ringwood	07456	12,625	Waldwick	07463	10,802
North Bergen †	07047	47,019	River Edge	07661	11,111	Wallington	07057	10,741
North Haledon	07508	8,177	River Vale	07675	9,489	Wanaque	07465	10,025
North Plainfield	07060	19,108	Riverside	08075	7,941	Washington	07882	6,429
Northfield	08225	7,795	Rockaway	07866	6,852	Washington †	07882	9,550
Nutley	07110	28,998	Roselle	07203	20,641	Watchung	07060	15,290
Oakland	07436	13,443	Roselle Park	07204	13,377	Wayne	07470	46,474
Ocean City	08226	13,949	Rumson	07760	7,623	Weehawken	07087	13,168
Ocean Twnshp. †	07712	23,570	Runnemede	08078	9,461	West Caldwell	07006	11,407
Old Bridge †	08857	51,515	Rutherford	07070*	19,068	West Freehold	—	9,929
Oradell	07649	8,658	Saddle Brook	07662	14,084	W. Long Branch	07764	7,380
Orange	07051*	31,136	Salem	08079	6,959	West New York	07093	39,194
Palisades Park	07650	13,732	Sayreville	08872	20,969	West Orange	07052	39,510
Palmyra	08065	7,085	Scotch Plains	07076	20,774	West Paterson	07424	11,293
Paramus	07652	26,474	Secaucus	07094	13,719	Westfield	07091*	30,447
Park Ridge	07656	8,515	Silverton	—	7,236	Westwood	07675	10,714
Parsippany—	07054	49,868	Somers Point	08244	10,330	White Horse	—	10,098
Troy Hills			Somerset	08873	21,731	White Meadow Lk.	—	8,429
Passaic	07055	52,463	Somerville	08876*	11,973	Williamstown	08094	5,768
Paterson	07510*	137,970	South Amboy	08879	8,322	Willingboro	08046	39,912
Paulsboro	08066	6,944	South Orange †	07079	15,864	Wood-Ridge	07075	7,929
Pennsauken	—	33,775	South Plainfield	07080	20,521	Woodbridge †	07095	90,074
Pennsville †	08070	13,848	South River	08882	14,361	Woodbury	08096	10,353
Pequannock †	—	13,776	Spotswood	08884	7,840	Wyckoff	07481	15,500
Perth Amboy	08861*	38,951	Springfield	07081	13,955	Yardville	08620	9,414

NEW MEXICO (N.M., N. Mex., or NM)

Alamogordo	88310	24,024	Grants	87020	11,439	Rio Rancho Est.	—	9,985
Albuquerque	87101*	332,239	Hobbs	88240	29,153	Roswell	88201	39,676
Artesia	88210	10,385	Las Cruces	88001*	45,086	Santa Fe	87501*	48,953
Carlsbad	88220	25,496	Las Vegas	87701	14,322	Shiprock	87420	7,237
Clovis	88101	31,194	Los Alamos	87544	11,039	Silver City	88061*	9,887
Deming	88030	9,964	Lovington	88260	9,727	Socorro	87801	7,173
Espanola	87532*	6,803	North Valley	—	12,868	South Valley	—	38,898
Farmington	87401	31,222	Portales	88130	9,940	Tucumcari	88401*	6,765
Gallup	87301*	18,167	Raton	87740	8,225	White Rock	87544	6,560

NEW YORK (N.Y. or NY)

Albany	12212	101,727	Bayville	11709	7,034	Cedarhurst	11516	6,162
Albion	14411	4,897	Beacon	12508	12,937	Center Moriches	11934	5,703
Alfred	14802	4,967	Bellmore	11710	18,431	Centereach	11720	30,136
Amityville	11701	9,076	Bethpage	11714	18,555	Centerport	11721	6,576
Amsterdam	12010	21,872	Binghamton	13902*	55,860	Central Islip	11722	19,734
Arlington	12603	11,305	Bohemia	11716	9,308	Cheektowaga	14225	92,145
Auburn	13021	32,548	Brentwood	11717	44,321	Clifton Knolls	—	5,636
Babylon	11702*	12,388	Briarcliff Manor	10510	7,115	Cobleskill	12043	5,272
Baldwin	11510	34,525	Brighton	11235	35,776	Cohoes	12047	18,144
Baldwinsville	13027	6,446	Brockport	14420	9,776	Cold Spring Hbr.	11724	5,336
Ballston Spa	12020	4,711	Bronxville	10708	6,267	Colonie	12212	8,869
Batavia	14020	16,703	Buffalo	14240*	357,870	Commack	11725	34,719
Bath	14810	6,042	Canandaigua	14424	10,419	Congers	10920	7,123
Bay Shore	11706*	10,784	Canastota	13032	4,773	Copiague	11726	20,132
Bayberry-Lynelle Mdws.	—	14,813	Canton	13617	7,055	Coram	11727	24,752
Bayport	11705	9,282	Catskill	12414	4,718	Corning	14830	12,953

[1] 1980 Census. † Town or township (includes rural population).

NEW YORK *(continued)*

PLACE AND ZIP CODE		POP.[1]
Cortland	13045	20,138
Croton-on-Hudson	10520	6,889
Dansville	14437	4,979
De Witt	13214	9,024
Deer Park	11729	30,394
Delmar	12054	8,423
Depew	14043	19,819
Dix Hills	11746	26,693
Dobbs Ferry	10522	10,053
Dunkirk	14048	15,310
East Aurora	14052	6,803
East Glenville	—	6,537
East Hills	11577	7,160
East Islip	11730	13,852
E. Massapequa	11758	13,987
East Meadow	11554	39,317
East Northport	11731	20,187
East Patchogue	11772	18,139
East Rochester	14445	7,596
East Rockaway	11518	10,917
Eastchester	10709	20,305
Elmira	14901*	35,327
Elmont	11003	27,592
Elwood	11731	11,847
Endicott	13760	14,457
Endwell	13760	13,745
Fairmount	13219	13,415
Farmingdale	11735	7,946
Farmingville	11738	13,398
Floral Park	11001*	16,805
Fort Salonga	—	19,550
Franklin Square	11010	29,051
Fredonia	14063	11,126
Freeport	11520	38,272
Fulton	13069	13,312
Garden City	11530	22,927
Garden City Park	11530	7,712
Gates-N. Gates	—	115,244
Geneseo	14454	6,746
Geneva	14456	15,133
Glen Cove	11542	24,618
Glens Falls	12801	15,897
Gloversville	12078	17,836
Great Neck	11022*	9,168
Greece	14616	16,177
Greenlawn	11740	13,869
Greenville	12083	8,706
Hamburg	14075	10,582
Hampton Bays	11946	7,256
Harrison	10528	23,046
Hartsdale	10530	10,216
Hastings-on-Hudson	10706	8,573
Hauppauge	11787	20,960
Haverstraw	10927	8,800
Hempstead	11551*	40,404
Herkimer	13350	8,383
Herricks	11040	8,123
Hewlett	11557	6,986
Hicksville	11802*	43,245
Holbrook	11741	24,382
Holtsville	11742	13,515
Hornell	14843	10,234
Horseheads	14845	7,348
Hudson	12534	7,986
Hudson Falls	12839	7,419
Huntington	11743	21,727
Huntington Sta.	11746	28,769
Ilion	13357	9,450
Inwood	11696	8,228
Irondequoit	14617	57,648
Islip	11751	13,438
Ithaca	14850	28,732
Jamestown	14701	35,775
Jefferson Valley–Yorktown	10535	13,380
Jericho	11753	12,739
Johnson City	13790	17,126
Johnstown	12095	9,360
Kenmore	14217	18,474
Kings Park	11754	16,131
Kingston	12401	24,481
Lackawanna	14218	22,701
Lake Carmel	—	7,295
Lake Grove	11755	9,692
Lake Ronkonkoma	11779	38,336
Lancaster	14086	13,056
Larchmont	10538	6,308
Latham	12110	11,182
Lawrence	11559	6,175
Levittown	11756	57,045
Lindenhurst	11757	26,919
Little Falls	13365	6,156
Lockport	14094	24,844
Locust Grove	11791	9,670
Long Beach	11561	34,073
Loudonville	12211	11,480
Lynbrook	11563	20,424
Mahopac	10541	7,681
Malone	12953	7,668
Malverne	11565	9,262
Mamaroneck	10543	17,616
Manhasset	11030	8,485
Massapequa	11758	24,454
Massapequa Park	11762	19,779
Massena	13662	12,851
Mastic	11950	10,413
Mastic Beach	11951	8,318
Mattydale	13211	7,511
Medford	11763	20,418
Medina	14103	6,392
Melville	11747	8,139
Merrick	11566	24,478
Middletown	10940	21,454
Miller Place	11764	7,877
Mineola	11501	20,757
Monsey	10952	12,380
Monticello	12701	6,306
Mount Kisco	10549	8,025
Mount Sinai	11766	6,591
Mount Vernon	10551*	66,713
Nanuet	10954	12,578
Nesconset	11767	10,706
New Cassel	11590	9,635
New Castle †	10514	15,425
New City	10956	35,859
New Hyde Park	11040	9,801
New Rochelle	10802*	70,794
New Windsor †	12550	19,534
New York	10001*	7,071,639
Newark	14513	10,017
Newburgh	12550	23,438
Niagara Falls	14302*	71,384
Niagara Town	—	9,648
North Amityville	11701	13,140
North Babylon	11703	19,019
North Bay Shore	—	35,020
North Bellmore	11710	20,630
North Bellport	—	7,432
N. Great River	11739	11,416
N. Lindenhurst	11757	11,511
N. Massapequa	11758	21,385
North Merrick	11566	12,848
North New Hyde Park	11040	15,114
N. Patchogue	—	7,126
N. Syracuse	13212	7,970
N. Tarrytown	10591	7,994
N. Tonawanda	14120	35,760
North Valley Stream	11580	14,530
North Wantagh	11793	12,677
Northport	11768	7,651
Norwich	13815	8,082
Nyack	10960	6,428
Oakdale	11769	8,090
Oceanside	11572	33,639
Ogdensburg	13669	12,375
Old Bethpage	11804	6,215
Olean	14760	18,207
Oneida	13421	10,810
Oneonta	13820	14,933
Ossining	10562	20,196
Oswego	13126	19,793
Oyster Bay	11771	6,497
Patchogue	11772*	11,291
Pearl River	10965	15,893
Peekskill	10566	18,236
Pelham	10803	6,848
Pelham Manor	10803	6,130
Pitcher Hill	—	6,063
Plainedge	11714	9,629
Plainview	11803	28,037
Plattsburgh	12901	21,057
Pleasantville	10570	6,749
Port Chester	10573	23,565
Port Jefferson	11777	6,731
Port Jefferson Station	11776	17,009
Port Jervis	12771	8,699
Port Washington	11050	14,521
Potsdam	13676	10,635
Poughkeepsie	12601*	29,757
Rensselaer	12144	9,047
Ridge	11961	8,977
Riverhead	11901	6,339
Rochester	14692*	241,741
Rockville Centre	11570	25,412
Rocky Point	11778	7,012
Roessleville	12205	11,685
Rome	13440	43,826
Roosevelt	11575	14,109
Roslyn Heights	11577	6,546
Rotterdam	12303	22,933
Rye	10580	15,083
St. James	11780	12,122
Salamanca	14779	6,890
Saratoga Springs	12866	23,906
Sayville	11782	12,013
Scarsdale	10583	17,650
Schenectady	12301*	67,972
Scotchtown	10940	7,352
Scotia	12302	7,280
Seaford	11783	16,117
Selden	11784	17,259
Seneca Falls	13148	7,466
Setauket–East Setauket	11733	10,176
Shirley	11967	18,072
Smithtown	11787	30,906

[1] 1980 Census. † Township.

NEW YORK *(continued)*

PLACE AND ZIP CODE		POP.[1]	PLACE AND ZIP CODE		POP.[1]	PLACE AND ZIP CODE		POP.[1]
Solvay	13209	7,140	Troy	12180*	56,638	West Islip	11795	29,533
Sound Beach	11789	8,071	Tuckahoe	10707	6,076	West Nyack	10994	8,553
S. Farmingdale	11735	16,439	Uniondale	11553	20,016	West Point	10996	8,105
S. Huntington	11746	14,854	Utica	13504*	75,632	West Sayville	11796	8,185
S. Westbury	11590	9,732	Valley Cottage	10989	8,214	West Seneca	14224	51,210
Southport	14904	8,329	Valley Stream	11580*	35,769	Westbury	11590*	13,871
Spring Valley	10977	20,537	Walden	12586	5,659	Westmere	—	6,881
Stony Brook	11790	16,155	Wantagh	11793	19,817	Westvale	—	6,169
Stony Point	10980	8,686	Watertown	13601	27,861	White Plains	10602*	46,999
Suffern	10901	10,794	Watervliet	12189	11,354	Williamsville	14221	6,017
Syosset	11791	9,818	Wellsville	14895	5,769	Williston Park	11596	8,216
Syracuse	13220*	170,105	West Amityville	—	6,623	Woodbury	11797	7,043
Tappan	10983	8,267	West Babylon	11704	41,699	Woodmere	11598	17,205
Tarrytown	10591	10,648	West Haverstraw	10993	9,181	Wyandanch	11798	13,215
Thornwood	10594	7,197	West Hempstead	11552	18,536	Yonkers	10701*	195,351
Tonawanda	14150	18,693	West Hills	—	6,071	Yorktown Heights	10598	7,696

NORTH CAROLINA (N.C. or NC)

Albemarle	28001	15,110	Henderson	27536	13,522	Reidsville	27320	12,492
Asheboro	27203	15,252	Hendersonville	28739	6,862	Roanoke Rapids	27870	14,702
Asheville	28810	53,583	Hickory	28601	20,757	Rockingham	28379	8,300
Boone	28607*	10,191	High Point	27260*	63,808	Rocky Mount	27801	41,283
Burlington	27215	37,266	Jacksonville	28540*	18,259	Roxboro	27573	7,532
Carrboro	27510	7,336	Kannapolis	28081	34,564	St. Stephens	—	10,797
Cary	27511	21,763	Kernersville	27284	6,802	Salisbury	28144	22,677
Chapel Hill	27514	32,421	King	27021	8,757	Sanford	27330*	14,773
Charlotte	28228*	315,473	Kings Grant	—	6,562	Shelby	28150	15,310
Clemmons	27012	7,401	Kings Mountain	28086	9,080	Smithfield	27577	7,288
Clinton	28328	7,552	Kinston	28501	25,234	Southern Pines	28387	8,620
Concord	28025	16,942	Laurinburg	28352	11,480	Spring Lake	28390	6,273
Dunn	28334	8,962	Lenoir	28645	13,748	Statesville	28677	18,622
Durham	27701*	100,831	Lexington	27292	15,711	Tarboro	27886	8,634
Eden	27288	15,672	Lumberton	28358	18,241	Thomasville	27360	14,144
Elizabeth City	27909	14,004	Mint Hill	28212	7,915	Trinity	27370	6,878
Fayetteville	28302*	59,507	Monroe	28110	12,639	Washington	27889	8,418
Forest City	28043	7,688	Mooresville	28115	8,575	Waynesville	28786	6,765
Garner	27529	10,073	Morganton	28655	13,763	West Concord	—	5,859
Gastonia	28052	47,333	Mount Airy	27030	6,862	White Oak	28399	6,058
Goldsboro	27530	31,871	New Bern	28560*	14,557	Whiteville	28472	5,565
Graham	27253	8,674	Newton	28658	7,624	Williamston	27892	6,159
Greensboro	27420*	155,642	North Belmont	28012	10,762	Wilmington	28402*	44,000
Greenville	27834	35,740	Oxford	27565	7,603	Wilson	27893	34,424
Havelock	28532	17,718	Raleigh	27611*	150,255	Winston-Salem	27102*	131,885

NORTH DAKOTA (N.D., or N. Dak., or ND)

Bismarck	58501*	44,485	Grand Forks	58201*	43,765	Tatman †	—	5,439
Devils Lake	58301	7,442	Jamestown	58401	16,280	Valley City	58072	7,774
Dickinson	58601	15,924	Mandan	58554	15,513	Wahpeton	58075	9,064
Fargo	58102	61,383	Mekinock †	58258	9,011	West Fargo	58078	10,099
Grafton	58237	5,293	Minot	58701	32,843	Williston	58801	13,336

OHIO (O. or OH)

Akron	44309*	237,177	Bedford Heights	44146	13,214	Brooklyn	44144	12,342
Alliance	44601	24,315	Bellaire	43906	8,241	Brunswick	44212	28,104
Amherst	44001	10,638	Bellefontaine	43311	11,888	Bryan	43506	7,879
Ashland	44805	20,326	Bellevue	44811	8,187	Bucyrus	44820	13,433
Ashtabula	44004	23,449	Belpre	45714	7,193	Cambridge	43725	13,573
Athens	45701	19,743	Berea	44017	19,567	Campbell	44405	11,619
Aurora	44202	8,177	Bexley	43209	13,405	Canton	44711*	93,077
Austintown	44515	33,636	Blacklick Estates	43004	11,223	Celina	45822	9,137
Avon	44011	7,241	Blue Ash	45242	9,506	Centerville	45459	18,886
Avon Lake	44012	13,222	Boardman	44512	39,161	Cheviot	45211	9,888
Barberton	44203	29,751	Bowling Green	43402	25,728	Chillicothe	45601	23,420
Bay Village	44140	17,846	Brecksville	44141	10,132	Cincinnati	45234*	385,457
Beachwood	44122	9,983	Bridgetown	—	11,460	Circleville	43113	11,700
Beavercreek	—	31,589	Broadview Heights	44147	10,920	Cleveland	44101*	573,822
Bedford	44146	15,056	Brook Park	44142	26,195	Cleveland Heights	44118	56,438

[1] 1980 Census. † Town or township (includes rural population).

OHIO *(continued)*

PLACE AND ZIP CODE		POP.[1]
Columbus	43216*	565,032
Conneaut	44030	13,835
Coshocton	43812	13,405
Cuyahoga Falls	44222*	43,890
Dayton	45401*	193,536
Deer Park	45236	6,745
Defiance	43512	16,810
Delaware	43015	18,780
Delhi Hills	—	27,647
Delphos	45833	7,314
Dover	44622	11,782
East Cleveland	44112	36,957
East Liverpool	43920	16,687
Eastlake	44094	22,104
Eaton	45320	6,839
Elyria	44035*	57,538
Englewood	45322	11,329
Euclid	44117	59,999
Fairborn	45324	29,702
Fairfield	45014	30,777
Fairlawn	44313	6,100
Fairview Park	44126	19,311
Findlay	45840	35,594
Forest Park	45405	18,675
Fort McKinley	—	10,161
Fostoria	44830	15,743
Franklin	45005	10,711
Fremont	43420	17,834
Gahanna	43230	18,001
Gallipolis	45631	5,576
Garfield Heights	44125	34,938
Geneva	44041	6,655
Girard	44420	12,517
Grandview Hts.	43212	7,420
Greenville	45331	12,999
Groesbeck	45224	9,594
Grove City	43123	16,816
Hamilton	45012*	63,189
Heath	43055	6,969
Hilliard	43026	8,008
Hillsboro	45133	6,356
Howland	—	7,441
Hubbard	44425	9,245
Huber Heights	45424	35,480
Huron	44839	7,123
Independence	44131	6,607
Ironton	45638	14,290
Jackson	45640	6,675
Kent	44240*	26,164
Kenton	43326	8,605
Kenwood	43606	9,928
Kettering	45429	61,186
Lakewood	44107	61,963
Lancaster	43130	34,953
Lebanon	45036	9,636
Lima	45802*	47,827
Lincoln Village	43228	10,548
Logan	43138	6,557
London	43140	6,958
Lorain	44052*	75,416
Louisville	44641	7,996
Loveland	45140	9,106
Lyndhurst	44124	18,092

PLACE AND ZIP CODE		POP.[1]
Macedonia	44056	6,571
Madeira	45243	9,341
Mansfield	44901*	53,927
Maple Heights	44137	29,735
Marietta	45750	16,467
Marion	43302	37,040
Martins Ferry	43935	9,331
Marysville	43040	7,414
Mason	45040	8,692
Massillon	44646	30,557
Maumee	43537	15,747
Mayfield Heights	44124	21,550
Medina	44256	15,268
Mentor	44060	42,065
Mentor-on-Lake	44060	7,919
Miamisburg	45342	15,304
Middleburg Hts.	44017	16,218
Middletown	45042	43,719
Monfort Heights	—	9,745
Montgomery	45242	10,088
Mount Healthy	45231	7,562
Mount Vernon	43050	14,323
Napoleon	43545	8,614
New Carlisle	45344	6,498
New Philadelphia	44663	16,883
Newark	43055	41,200
Niles	44446	23,088
North Canton	44720	14,228
North College Hill	45239	11,114
North Madison	—	8,741
North Olmsted	44070	36,486
North Ridgeville	44039	21,522
North Royalton	44133	17,671
Northbrook	—	8,357
Northview	—	9,973
Norton	44203	12,242
Norwalk	44857	14,358
Norwood	45212	26,342
Oakwood	45873	9,372
Oberlin	44074	8,660
Oregon	43619	18,675
Orrville	44667	7,511
Overlook-Page Manor	45431	14,825
Oxford	45056	17,655
Painesville	44077	16,391
Parma	44129	92,548
Parma Heights	44130	23,112
Pepper Pike	44124	6,177
Perry Heights	—	9,206
Perrysburg	43551	10,215
Piqua	45356	20,480
Pisgah	—	15,660
Port Clinton	43452	7,223
Portage Lakes	—	11,310
Portsmouth	45662	25,943
Ravenna	44266	11,987
Reading	45215	12,843
Reynoldsburg	43068	20,661
Richmond Heights	44143	10,095
Rittman	44270	6,063
Rocky River	44116	21,084
St. Marys	45885	8,414

PLACE AND ZIP CODE		POP.[1]
Salem	44460	12,869
Sandusky	44870	31,360
Sandusky South	—	6,548
Seven Hills	44131	13,650
Shaker Heights	44120	32,487
Sharonville	45241	10,108
Sheffield Lake	44054	10,484
Shelby	44875	9,646
Shiloh	44878	11,735
Sidney	45365	17,657
Silverton	—	6,172
Solon	44139	14,341
South Euclid	44121	25,713
Springdale	45246	10,111
Springfield	45501	72,563
Steubenville	43952	26,400
Stow	44224	25,303
Streetsboro	44240	9,055
Strongsville	44136	28,577
Struthers	44471	13,624
Sylvania	43560	15,527
Tallmadge	44278	15,269
Tiffin	44883	19,549
Toledo	43601*	354,635
Toronto	43964	6,934
Trenton	45067	6,401
Trotwood	45426	7,802
Troy	45373	19,086
Twinsburg	44087	7,632
Uhrichsville	44683	6,130
University Heights	44118	15,401
Upper Arlington	43221	35,648
Upper Sandusky	43351	5,967
Urbana	43078	10,762
Van Wert	45891	11,035
Vandalia	45377	13,161
Vermilion	44089	11,012
Wadsworth	44281	15,166
Wapakoneta	45895	8,402
Warren	44481*	56,629
Warrensville Hts.	44122	16,565
Washington	43160	12,682
Wauseon	43567	6,173
Wellston	45692	6,016
West Carrollton	45418	13,148
Westerville	43081	23,414
Westlake	44145	19,483
White Oak	—	9,563
Whitehall	43213	21,299
Wickliffe	44092	16,790
Willard	44890	5,720
Willoughby	44094	19,329
Willoughby Hills	44094	8,612
Willowick	44094	17,834
Wilmington	45177	10,431
Woodbourne-Hyde Park	—	8,826
Wooster	44691	19,289
Worthington	43085	15,016
Wyoming	45215	8,282
Xenia	45385	24,653
Youngstown	44501*	115,436
Zanesville	43701	28,655

OKLAHOMA (Okla. or OK)

PLACE AND ZIP CODE		POP.[1]
Ada	74820	15,902
Altus	73521	23,101
Alva	73717	6,416
Anadarko	73005	6,378
Ardmore	73401	23,689
Bartlesville	740[illegible]3	34,568
Bethany	730[illegible]	22,038
Bixby	74008	6,969
Blackwell	74631	8,400
Broken Arrow	74012	35,761
Chickasha	73018	15,828
Choctaw	73020	7,520
Claremore	74017	12,085
Clinton	73601	8,796
Cushing	74023	7,720

[1] 1980 Census.

OKLAHOMA *(continued)*

PLACE	ZIP CODE	POP.[1]
Del City	73155	28,523
Duncan	73533	22,517
Durant	74701	11,972
Edmond	73034	34,637
El Reno	73036	15,486
Elk City	73644	9,579
Enid	73701	50,363
Frederick	73542	6,153
Guthrie	73044	10,312
Guymon	73942	8,492
Henryetta	74437	6,432
Hugo	74743	7,172
Idabel	74745	7,622
Jenks	74037	5,876
Lawton	73501*	80,054
Marlow	73055	5,017
McAlester	74501	17,255
Miami	74354	14,237
Midwest City	73141	49,559
Moore	73160	35,063
Muskogee	74401	40,011
Mustang	73064	7,496
Norman	73070*	68,020
Oklahoma City	73125*	403,484
Okmulgee	74447	16,263
Owasso	74055	6,149
Pauls Valley	73075	5,664
Perry	73077	5,796
Ponca City	74601	26,238
Poteau	74953	7,089
Pryor Creek	74361	8,483
Sallisaw	74955	6,403
Sand Springs	74063	13,121
Sapulpa	74066	15,853
Seminole	74868	8,590
Shawnee	74801*	26,506
Stillwater	74074	38,268
Sulphur	73086	5,516
Tahlequah	74464	9,708
The Village	73120	11,114
Tulsa	74101*	360,919
Turley	74156	6,336
Vinita	74301	6,740
Wagoner	74467	6,191
Warr Acres	73123	9,940
Weatherford	73096	9,640
Woodward	73801	13,610
Yukon	73099	17,112

OREGON (Ore., Oreg., or OR)

PLACE	ZIP CODE	POP.[1]
Albany	97321	26,678
Aloha	97005	28,353
Altamonte	—	19,805
Ashland	97520	14,943
Astoria	97103	9,998
Baker	97814	9,471
Beaverton	97005	31,926
Bend	97701	17,263
Canby	97013	7,659
Cedar Hills	97225	9,619
Centennial	—	22,118
Central Point	97502	6,357
City of the Dalles	97058	10,820
Coos Bay	97420	14,424
Corvallis	97333	40,960
Cottage Grove	97424	7,148
Cully	—	10,569
Dallas	97338	8,530
Errol Heights	—	10,847
Eugene	97401*	105,624
Forest Grove	97116	11,449
Four Corners	97301	11,331
Garden Home–Whitford	97223	6,926
Gladstone	97027	9,500
Grants Pass	97526	15,032
Gresham	97030	33,005
Hazelwood	—	25,541
Hayesville	—	9,213
Hermiston	97838	9,408
Hillsboro	97123	27,664
Keizer	97303	18,592
Klamath Falls	97601*	16,661
La Grande	97850	11,354
Lake Oswego	97034	22,527
Lebanon	97355	10,413
McMinnville	97128	14,080
Medford	97501	39,603
Milwaukie	97222	17,931
Monmouth	97361	5,594
Newberg	97132	10,394
Newport	97365	7,519
North Bend	97459	9,779
North Springfield	—	6,140
Oak Grove	97268	11,640
Ontario	97914	8,814
Oregon City	97045	14,673
Parkrose	97220	21,108
Pendleton	97801	14,521
Portland	97208*	366,383
Powellhurst	—	20,132
Raleigh Hills	97225	6,517
Redmond	97756	6,452
River Road	—	10,370
Roseburg	97470	16,644
St. Helens	97051	7,064
Salem	97301*	89,233
Santa Clara	—	14,288
Springfield	97477	41,621
Sweet Home	97386	6,921
Tigard	97223	14,286
Troutdale	97060	5,908
Tualatin	97062	7,483
West Linn	97068	12,956
Wilkes–Rockwood	—	23,216
Woodburn	97071	11,196

PENNSYLVANIA (Pa., Penn., or PA)

PLACE	ZIP CODE	POP.[1]
Aliquippa	15001	17,094
Allentown	18101*	103,758
Altoona	16603*	57,078
Ambler	19002	6,628
Ambridge	15003	9,575
Archbald	18403	6,295
Arnold	15068	6,853
Avalon	—	6,240
Baldwin	15234	24,712
Beaver Falls	15010	12,525
Bellefonte	16823	6,300
Bellevue	15202	10,128
Berwick	18603	11,850
Bethel Park	15102	34,755
Bethlehem	18016*	70,419
Blakely	18447	7,438
Bloomsburg	17815	11,717
Bradford	16701	11,211
Brentwood	15227	11,861
Bridgeville	15017	6,154
Bristol	19007	10,867
Brookhaven	19015	7,912
Butler	16001	17,026
Camp Hill	17011	8,422
Canonsburg	15317	10,459
Carbondale	18407	11,255
Carlisle	17013	18,314
Carnot–Moon	—	11,102
Carnegie	15106	10,099
Castle Shannon	15234	10,164
Catasauqua	18032	6,711
Chambersburg	17201	16,174
Chester	19013*	45,794
Clairton	15025	12,188
Clarion	16214	6,198
Clearfield	16830	7,580
Clifton Heights	19018	7,320
Coatesville	19320	10,698
Collingdale	19023	9,539
Columbia	17512	10,466
Connellsville	15425	10,319
Conshohocken	19428	8,475
Coraopolis	15108	7,308
Corry	16407	7,149
Crafton	15205	7,623
Darby	19023	11,513
Dickson City	18519	6,699
Donora	15033	7,524
Dormont	15216	11,275
Downingtown	19335	7,650
Doylestown	18901	8,717
DuBois	15801	9,290
Dunmore	18512	16,781
Duquesne	15110	10,094
East Norriton	—	12,711
E. Stroudsburg	18301	8,039
Easton	18042	26,027
Economy	—	9,538
Edinboro	16412	6,324
Elizabethtown	17022	8,233
Ellwood City	16117	9,998
Emmaus	18049	11,001
Ephrata	17522	11,095
Erie	16515*	119,123
Farrell	16121	8,645
Folcroft	19032	8,231
Forest Hills	15540	8,198
Franklin	16323	8,146
Franklin Park	—	6,135
Fullerton	18052	8,055
Gettysburg	17325	7,194
Glassport	15045	6,242
Glenolden	19036	7,633
Greensburg	15601	17,558
Greenville	16125	7,730
Grove City	16127	8,162
Hanover	17331	14,890
Harrisburg	17105*	53,264
Hatboro	19040	7,579
Hazleton	18201	27,318
Hellertown	18055	6,025

[1] 1980 Census.

PENNSYLVANIA *(cont.)*

PLACE AND ZIP CODE		POP.[1]
Hershey	17033	13,249
Homeacre–Lyndora	16045	8,333
Horsham	19044	9,900
Huntingdon	16652	7,042
Indiana	15701	16,051
Jeannette	15644	13,106
Jefferson	15344	8,643
Johnstown	15901*	35,496
Kingston	18704	15,681
Lancaster	17604*	54,725
Lansdale	19446	16,526
Lansdowne	19050	11,891
Latrobe	15650	10,799
Lebanon	17042	25,711
Lewistown	17044	9,830
Lititz	17543	7,590
Lock Haven	17745	9,617
Lower Burrell	15068	13,200
Mahanoy City	17948	6,167
McKees Rocks	15136	8,742
McKeesport	15134*	31,012
Meadville	16335	15,544
Mechanicsburg	17055	9,487
Media	19063*	6,119
Middletown	17057	10,122
Millersville	17551	7,668
Milton	17847	6,730
Monaca	15061	7,661
Monessen	15062	11,928
Monroeville	15146	30,977
Moosic	18507	6,068
Morrisville	19067	9,845
Mount Carmel	17851	8,190
Mount Lebanon	15228	34,414
Munhall	15120	14,535
Murrysville	15668	16,036
Nanticoke	18634	13,044
New Brighton	15066	7,364
New Castle	16101*	33,621
New Cumberland	17070	8,051
New Kensington	15068*	17,660
Norristown	19401*	34,684
North Braddock	15104	8,711
North Versailles	15137	13,294
Northampton	18067	8,240
Norwood	19074	6,647
Oakmont	15139	7,039
Oil City	16301	13,881
Old Forge	18518	9,304
Palmyra	17078	7,228
Penn Hills	15235	57,632
Philadelphia	19104*	1,688,210
Phoenixville	19460	14,165
Pittsburgh	15219*	423,959
Pittston	18640*	9,930
Pleasant Hills	15236	9,374
Plum	15239	25,390
Plymouth	18651	7,605
Pottstown	19464	22,729
Pottsville	17901	18,195
Prospect Park	19076	6,593
Punxsutawney	15767	7,479
Quakertown	18951	8,867
Reading	19603*	78,686
Ridley Park	19078	7,889
St. Marys	15857	6,417
Sayre	18840	6,951
Scranton	18505*	88,117
Shamokin	17872	10,357
Sharon	16146	19,057
Sharon Hill	19079	6,221
Shenandoah	17976	7,589
Somerset	15501	6,474
Souderton	18964	6,657
S. Williamsport	17701	6,581
Springfield	19064	25,326
State College	16801*	36,130
Steelton	17113	6,484
Sunbury	17801	12,292
Swissvale	15218	11,345
Tamaqua	18252	8,843
Tarentum	15084	6,419
Taylor	18517	7,246
Titusville	16354	6,884
Turtle Creek	15145	6,959
Tyrone	16686	6,346
Uniontown	15401	14,510
Upper Darby	19082	84,054
Upper Merion	—	26,138
Upper St. Clair	15241	19,083
Vandergrift	15690	6,823
Warminster	18974	35,463
Warren	16365	12,146
Washington	15301	18,363
Waynesboro	17268	9,726
West Chester	19380	17,435
West Goshen	—	7,998
West Mifflin	15122	26,552
West View	15229	7,648
Westmont	—	6,113
White Oak	15131	9,480
Whitehall	18052	15,143
Wilkes-Barre	18701*	51,551
Wilkinsburg	15221	23,669
Williamsport	17701	33,401
Wilson	15025	7,564
Wyomissing	19610	6,551
Yeadon	19050	11,727
York	17405*	44,619

RHODE ISLAND (R.I. or RI)

PLACE AND ZIP CODE		POP.[1]
Barrington	02806	16,174
Bristol	02809	20,128
Burrillville †	02830	13,164
Central Falls	02863	16,995
Coventry †	02816	27,065
Cranston	02910	71,992
Cumberland †	02864	27,069
Cumberland Hill	02864	5,421
East Greenwich †	02818	10,211
East Providence	02914	50,980
Glocester †	—	7,550
Greenville	02828	7,576
Hopkinton †	02833	6,406
Johnston †	02919	24,907
Lincoln †	02865	16,949
Middletown †	02840	17,216
Narragansett †	02882	12,088
Newport	02840	29,259
N. Kingstown †	02852*	21,938
N. Providence	02908	29,188
N. Smithfield †	02876	9,972
Pawtucket	02860*	71,204
Portsmouth †	02871	14,257
Providence	02940*	156,804
Scituate †	02857	8,405
Smithfield †	02917	16,886
S. Kingstown †	02879	20,414
Tiverton	02878	7,653
Warren †	02885	10,640
Warwick	02887*	87,123
West Warwick	02893	27,026
Westerly †	02891	18,580
Woonsocket	02895	45,914

SOUTH CAROLINA (S.C. or SC)

PLACE AND ZIP CODE		POP.[1]
Aiken	29801	14,978
Anderson	29621*	27,638
Beaufort	29902	8,634
Belvedere	29841	6,859
Bennettsville	29512	8,774
Berea	29611	13,164
Brookdale	—	6,123
Camden	29020	7,462
Capitol View	—	10,456
Cayce	29033	11,701
Charleston	29401*	69,510
Chester	29706	6,820
Clemson	29631	8,118
Clinton	29325	8,596
Columbia	29201*	101,229
Conway	29526	10,240
Darlington	29532	7,989
Dentsville	29204	13,579
Dillon	29536	7,060
Dorchester Terrace–Brentwood	29405	7,862
Easley	29640	14,264
Florence	29501*	29,842
Forest Acres	29260	6,062
Gaffney	29340	13,453
Gantt	—	13,719
Georgetown	29440	10,144
Goose Creek	29445	17,811
Greenville	29602*	58,242
Greenwood	29646	21,613
Greer	29651	10,525
Hanahan	29410	13,224
Hartsville	29550	7,631
Hilton Head Is.	29928*	11,344
Homeland Park	—	6,720
James Island	29412*	24,124
Ladson	29456	13,246
Lake City	29560	6,731
Lancaster	29720	9,703
Laurens	29360	10,587
Marion	29571	7,700
Mauldin	29662	8,143
Mt. Pleasant	29464	14,209
Mullins	29574	6,068
Myrtle Beach	29577	18,446
Newberry	29108	9,866
North Augusta	29841	13,593
North Charleston	29406	62,562
North Trenholm	—	10,962
Oak Grove	—	7,092
Orangeburg	29115	14,933
Parris Island	29905	7,752
Pinehurst–Sheppard Park	—	6,936
Rock Hill	29730	35,327
St. Andrews (Charleston)	—	9,908

[1] 1980 Census. † Town or township.

SOUTH CAROLINA *(continued)*

PLACE AND ZIP CODE		POP.[1]
St. Andrews (Richland)	—	20,245
Sans Souci	29609	8,393
Seneca	29678	7,436
Seven Oaks	—	16,604
Simpsonville	29681	9,037
South Sumter	—	7,096
Spartanburg	29301*	43,826
Summerville	29483	6,706
Sumter	29150	24,890
Taylors	29687	15,801
Union	29379	10,523
Wade Hampton	—	20,180
Walterboro	29488	6,706
Welcome	—	6,922
West Columbia	29169	10,409
Woodfield	—	9,588
York	29745	6,412

SOUTH DAKOTA (S.D., S.Dak., or SD)

PLACE AND ZIP CODE		POP.[1]
Aberdeen	57401	25,851
Brookings	57006	14,951
Huron	57350	13,000
Madison	57042	6,210
Mitchell	57301	13,916
Pierre	57501	11,973
Rapid City	57701	46,492
Sioux Falls	57101*	81,343
Spearfish	57783	5,251
Vermillion	57069	10,136
Watertown	57201	15,649
Yankton	57078	12,011

TENNESSEE (Tenn. or TN)

PLACE AND ZIP CODE		POP.[1]
Alcoa	37701	6,870
Athens	37303	12,080
Bartlett	38134	17,170
Bloomingdale	37660	12,088
Bolivar	38008	6,597
Brentwood	37027	9,431
Bristol	37620	23,986
Brownsville	38012	9,307
Cedar Bluff	—	10,654
Chattanooga	37401*	169,728
Clarksville	37040	54,777
Cleveland	37311	26,415
Collierville	38017	7,839
Colonial Heights	37663	6,744
Columbia	38401	26,571
Concord	37922	8,569
Cookeville	38501	20,535
Covington	38019	6,065
Crossville	38555	6,394
Dayton	37321	5,913
Dickson	37055	7,040
Dyersburg	38024	15,856
Eagleton Village	—	5,331
East Ridge	37412	21,236
Elizabethton	37643	12,431
Fayetteville	37334	7,559
Franklin	37064	12,407
Gallatin	37066	17,191
Germantown	38138	21,482
Goodlettsville	37072	8,327
Greeneville	37743	14,097
Halls	38040	10,363
Harriman	37748	8,303
Harrison	37341	6,206
Hendersonville	37075	26,561
Humboldt	38343	10,209
Jackson	38301	49,131
Johnson City	37601	39,753
Kingsport	37662*	32,027
Knoxville	37901*	175,045
La Follette	37766	8,198
Lawrenceburg	38464	10,184
Lebanon	37087	11,872
Lewisburg	37091	8,760
Lexington	38351	5,934
Lynn Garden	37665	7,213
Manchester	37355	7,250
Martin	38237	8,898
Maryville	37801	17,480
McMinnville	37110	10,683
Memphis	38101*	646174
Milan	38358	8,083
Middle Valley	—	11,420
Millington	38053*	20,236
Morristown	37814	19,683
Murfreesboro	37130	32,845
Nashville–Davidson	37202*	455,651
Newport	37821	7,580
Oak Ridge	37830	27,662
Paris	38242	10,728
Powell	37849	7,220
Pulaski	38478	7,184
Red Bank	37415	13,129
Ripley	38063	6,366
Savannah	38372	6,992
Shelbyville	37160	13,530
Signal Mountain	37377	5,818
Smyrna	37167	8,839
Soddy–Daisy	37379	8,388
Springfield	37172	10,814
Summit	—	8,307
Tullahoma	37388	15,800
Union City	38261	10,436
Winchester	37398	5,821

TEXAS (Tex. or TX)

PLACE AND ZIP CODE		POP.[1]
Abilene	79604*	98,315
Alamo Heights	78209	6,252
Aldine	—	12,623
Alice	78332	20,961
Allen	75002	8,314
Alvin	77511	16,515
Amarillo	79120*	149,230
Andrews	79714	11,061
Angleton	77515	13,929
Aransas Pass	78336	7,173
Arlington	76010*	160,113
Athens	75751	10,197
Atlanta	75551	6,272
Austin	78710*	345,890
Balch Springs	75180	13,746
Bay City	77414	17,837
Baytown	77520	56,923
Beaumont	77704*	118,102
Bedford	76021	20,821
Beeville	78102	14,574
Bellaire	77401	14,950
Bellmead	76705	7,569
Belton	76513	10,660
Benbrook	76126	13,579
Big Spring	79720	24,804
Bonham	75418	7,338
Borger	79007	15,837
Breckenridge	76024	6,921
Brenham	77833	10,966
Bridge City	77611	7,667
Brownfield	79316	10,387
Brownsville	78520	84,997
Brownwood	76801	19,396
Bryan	77801	44,337
Burkburnett	76354	10,668
Burleson	76028	11,734
Canyon	79015	10,724
Carrizo Springs	78834	6,886
Carrollton	75006	40,595
Carthage	75633	6,447
Cedar Hill	75104	6,849
Champions	—	14,692
Channelview	77530	17,471
Cleburne	76031	19,218
Cloverleaf	—	17,317
Clute	77531	9,577
College Station	77840*	37,272
Colleyville	76034	6,700
Commerce	75428	8,136
Conroe	77301*	18,034
Copperas Cove	76522	19,469
Corpus Christi	78408*	232,134
Corsicana	75110	21,712
Crockett	75835	7,405
Crystal City	78839	8,334
Cuero	77954	7,124
Dalhart	79022	6,854
Dallas	75260*	904,078
De Soto	75115	15,538
Deer Park	77536	22,648
Del Rio	78840	30,034
Denison	75020	23,884
Denton	76201*	48,063
Dickinson	77539	7,505
Donna	78537	9,952
Dumas	79029	12,194
Duncanville	75116	27,781
Eagle Pass	78852	21,407
Edinburg	78539	24,075
El Campo	77437	10,462
El Paso	79910*	425,259
Ennis	75119	12,110
Euless	76039	24,002
Falfurrias	78355	6,103
Farmers Branch	75234	24,863
Forest Hills	75702	11,684
Fort Stockton	79735	8,688
Fort Worth	76101*	385,164
Fredericksburg	78624	6,412
Freeport	77541	13,444
Friendswood	77546	10,719
Gainesville	76240	14,081
Galena Park	77547	9,879
Galveston	77553*	61,902
Garland	75040*	138,857
Gatesville	76528	6,260
Georgetown	78626	9,468
Gladewater	75647	6,548
Gonzales	78629	7,152
Graham	76046	9,170

[1] 1980 Census.

TEXAS *(continued)*

PLACE AND ZIP CODE		POP.[1]	PLACE AND ZIP CODE		POP.[1]	PLACE AND ZIP CODE		POP.[1]
Grand Prairie	75051	71,462	Lufkin	75901	28,562	Round Rock	78664	12,740
Grapevine	76051	11,801	Mansfield	76063	8,102	Rowlett	75088	7,522
Greenville	75401	22,161	Marlin	76661	7,099	Saginaw	76179	5,736
Groves	77619	17,090	Marshall	75670	24,921	San Angelo	76902*	73,240
Haltom City	76117	29,014	Mathis	78368	5,667	San Antonio	78284*	786,023
Harker Heights	76541	7,345	McAllen	78501	66,281	San Benito	78586	17,988
Harlingen	78550	43,543	McKinney	75069	16,256	San Juan	78589	7,608
Henderson	75652	11,473	Mercedes	78570	11,851	San Marcos	78666	23,420
Hereford	79045	15,853	Mesquite	75149	67,053	Santa Fe	—	6,172
Highland Park	75205	8,909	Mexia	76667	7,094	Schertz	78154	7,262
Highlands	77562	6,467	Midland	79702*	70,525	Seagoville	75159	7,304
Hillsboro	76645	7,397	Mineral Wells	76067	14,468	Seguin	78155	17,854
Hitchcock	77563	6,142	Mission	78572	22,653	Seminole	79360	6,080
Hondo	78861	6,057	Missouri City	77459	24,423	Sherman	75090	30,413
Houston	77201*	1,595,138	Monahans	79756	8,397	Silsbee	77656	7,684
Humble	77338*	6,729	Mt. Pleasant	75455	11,003	Sinton	78387	6,044
Huntsville	77340	23,936	Nacogdoches	75961	27,149	Slaton	79364	6,804
Hurst	76053	31,420	Nederland	77627	16,855	Snyder	79549	12,705
Iowa Park	76367	6,184	New Braunfels	78130	22,402	South Houston	77587	13,293
Irving	75061*	109,943	N. Richland Hills	76118	30,592	Stephenville	76401	11,881
Jacinto City	77029	8,953	Odessa	79760*	90,027	Sugar Land	77478	8,826
Jacksonville	75766	12,264	Orange	77630	23,628	Sulphur Springs	75482	12,804
Jasper	75951	6,959	Palestine	75801	15,948	Sweetwater	79556	12,242
Katy	77450	5,660	Pampa	79065	21,396	Taylor	76574	10,619
Kermit	79745	8,015	Paris	75460	25,498	Temple	76501	42,354
Kerrville	78028	15,276	Pasadena	77501*	112,560	Terrell	75160	13,269
Kilgore	75662	11,332	Pearland	77581*	13,248	Texarkana	75501	31,271
Killeen	76541*	46,296	Pearsall	78061	7,383	Texas City	77590	41,201
Kingsville	78363	28,808	Pecos	79772	12,855	The Colony	75028	11,586
Kingwood	77339	16,261	Perryton	79070	7,991	The Woodlands	77380	8,443
Kirby	—	6,435	Pharr	78577	21,381	Tyler	15712*	70,508
La Marque	77568	15,372	Plainview	79072	22,187	Universal City	78148	10,720
La Porte	77571	14,062	Plano	75074	72,331	University Park	78201	22,254
Lake Jackson	77566	19,102	Pleasanton	78064	6,346	Uvalde	78801	14,178
Lamesa	79331	11,790	Port Arthur	77640	61,251	Vernon	76384	12,695
Lampasas	76550	6,165	Port Lavaca	77979	10,911	Victoria	77901	50,695
Lancaster	75146	14,807	Port Neches	77651	13,944	Vidor	77662	11,834
Laredo	78041*	91,449	Portland	78374	12,023	Waco	76701*	101,261
League City	77573	16,578	Raymondville	78580	9,493	Watauga	76148	10,284
Leon Valley	—	9,088	Richardson	75080	72,496	Waxahachie	75165	14,624
Levelland	79336	13,809	Richland Hills	76681	7,977	Weatherford	76086	12,049
Lewisville	75067	24,273	Richmond	77469	9,692	Weslaco	78596	19,331
Liberty	77575	7,945	Rio Grande City	78582	8,930	West Univ. Place	77005	12,010
Littlefield	79339	7,409	River Oaks	77019	6,890	Wharton	77488	9,033
Live Oak	—	8,183	Robinson	76706	6,074	White Settlement	76108	13,508
Lockhart	78644	7,953	Robstown	78380	12,100	Wichita Falls	76307*	94,201
Longview	75602*	62,762	Rockwall	75087	5,939	Woodway	76710	7,091
Lubbock	79408*	173,979	Rosenberg	77471	17,833	Yoakum	77995	6,148

UTAH (Ut. or UT)

PLACE AND ZIP CODE		POP.[1]	PLACE AND ZIP CODE		POP.[1]	PLACE AND ZIP CODE		POP.[1]
American Fork	84003	12,693	Midvale	84047	10,146	South Cottonwood	—	11,117
Bennion	—	9,575	Mount Olympus	—	16,068	South Jordan	—	7,492
Bountiful	84010	32,877	Murray	84107	25,750	South Ogden	84403	11,366
Brigham City	84302	15,596	North Ogden	84404	9,309	South Salt Lake	84115	10,413
Cedar City	84720	10,972	Ogden	84401*	64,407	Spanish Fork	84660	9,825
Centerville	84014	8,069	Orem	84057	52,399	Springville	84663	12,101
Clearfield	84015*	17,982	Payson	84651	8,246	Sunset	—	5,733
Cottonwood	84121	11,554	Pleasant Grove	84062	10,833	Taylorsville	—	17,448
Cottonwood Hts.	—	22,665	Price	84501	9,086	Tooele	84074	14,335
Holladay	84117	22,189	Provo	84601	74,108	Union–East Midvale	—	9,665
Kaysville	84037	9,811	Riverdale	—	6,031	Val Verda	—	6,422
Kearns	84118	21,353	Riverton	84065	7,293	Vernal	84078	6,600
Layton	84041	22,862	Roy	84067	19,694	Washington Terrace	84403	8,212
Lehi	84043	6,848	St. George	84770	11,350	West Jordan	84084	27,315
Logan	84321	26,844	Salt Lake City	84119*	163,034	West Valley	—	72,433
Magna	84044	13,138	Sandy City	84070	52,210	White City	—	7,267

VERMONT (Vt. or VT)

PLACE AND ZIP CODE		POP.[1]	PLACE AND ZIP CODE		POP.[1]	PLACE AND ZIP CODE		POP.[1]
Barre	05641	9,824	Burlington	05401*	37,712	Essex Junction	05452	7,033
Bennington	05201	9,349	Colchester †	05446	12,629	Hartford †	05047	7,963
Brattleboro	05301	8,596	Essex †	05451	14,392	Middlebury	05753	5,591

[1] 1980 Census. † Town or township.

VERMONT *(continued)*

PLACE AND ZIP CODE		POP.[1]
Milton †	05468	6,829
Montpelier	05602	8,241
Northfield †	05663	5,435
Rutland	05701	18,436
St. Albans	05478	7,308
St. Johnsbury	05819	7,150
S. Burlington	05401	10,679
Springfield	05156	5,603
Winooski	05404	6,318

VIRGINIA (Va. or VA)

PLACE AND ZIP CODE		POP.[1]
Alexandria	22313*	103,217
Annadale	—	49,524
Arlington	22210*	152,599
Bailey's Crossroads	22041	12,564
Belle Haven	23306	6,520
Bellwood	—	6,439
Blacksburg	24060	30,638
Bon Air	23235	16,224
Bristol	24201	19,042
Buena Vista	24416	6,717
Burke	22015	33,835
Cave Spring	—	21,862
Centreville	22020	7,473
Chantilly	22021	12,259
Charlottesville	22906*	39,916
Chesapeake	23320*	114,486
Chester	23831	11,728
Christiansburg	24073	10,345
Collinsville	24078	7,517
Colonial Heights	23834	16,509
Covington	24426	9,063
Culpeper	22701	6,621
Dale City	22193	33,127
Danville	24541	45,642
Dumbarton	—	8,149
Dunn Loring	22027	6,077
East Highland Park	—	11,797
Fairfax	22030	19,390
Falls Church	22046*	9,515
Farmville	23901	6,067
Fort Belvoir	22060	7,726
Fort Hunt	—	14,294
Fort Lee	23801	9,784
Franconia	22310	8,476
Franklin	23851	7,308
Fredericksburg	22404*	15,322
Front Royal	22630	11,126
Galax	24333	6,524
Glen Allen	23060	6,202
Groveton	—	18,860
Hampton	23670*	122,617
Harrisonburg	22801	19,671
Herndon	22070*	11,449
Highland Springs	23075	12,146
Hollins	24019	12,295
Hopewell	23860	23,397
Hybla Valley	—	15,333
Idylwood	—	11,982
Jefferson	—	24,342
Lake Barcroft	—	8,725
Lake Ridge	—	11,072
Lakeside	23228	12,289
Laurel	23060	10,569
Leesburg	22075	8,357
Lexington	24450	7,292
Lincolnia	22312	10,350
Lynchburg	24506*	66,743
Madison Heights	24572	14,146
Manassas	22110	15,438
Manassas Park	22111	6,524
Mantua	—	6,524
Marion	24354	7,029
Martinsville	24112	18,149
McLean	22101*	35,664
Mechanicsville	23111	9,269
Merrifield	22116	7,525
Mount Vernon	22121*	24,058
Newington	22122*	8,313
Newport News	23607*	144,903
Norfolk	23501*	266,979
N. Springfield	22151	9,538
Oakton	22124	19,150
Petersburg	23804*	41,055
Pimmit Hills	22043	6,658
Poquoson	23662	8,726
Portsmouth	23705*	104,577
Pulaski	24301	10,106
Quantico Station	—	7,121
Radford	24141	13,225
Reston	22090	36,407
Richmond	23232*	219,214
Roanoke	24022*	100,220
Rose Hill	24281	11,926
Salem	24153	23,958
Seven Corners	22044	6,058
South Boston	24592	7,093
Springfield	22150*	21,435
Staunton	24401	21,857
Sterling Park	—	16,080
Suffolk	23434	47,621
Sugarland Run	—	6,258
Timberlake	24502	9,697
Tuckahoe	23229	39,868
Tyson's Corner	—	10,065
University Hts.	—	6,736
Vienna	22180	15,469
Vinton	24179	8,027
Virginia Beach	23450*	262,199
Waynesboro	22980	15,329
West Springfield	22152	25,012
Williamsburg	23185	9,870
Winchester	22601	20,217
Wolf Trap	—	9,875
Woodbridge	22191	24,004
Wytheville	24382	7,135

WASHINGTON (Wash. or WA)

PLACE AND ZIP CODE		POP.[1]
Aberdeen	98520	18,739
Alderwood Manor	98036	16,524
Anacortes	98221	9,013
Auburn	98002	26,417
Bellevue	98009*	73,903
Bellingham	98225	45,794
Bothell	98011	7,943
Boulevard Park	—	8,382
Bremerton	98310*	36,208
Burien	98148	23,189
Cascade	98055	16,939
Centralia	98531	11,555
Chehalis	98532	6,100
Cheney	99004	7,630
Clarkston	99403	6,903
Des Moines	98108	7,378
Dishman	99213	10,169
E. Renton Highlands	—	12,033
E. Wenatchee Beach	—	11,410
Eastgate	98007	8,341
Edmonds	98020	27,679
Ellensburg	98926	11,752
Esperance	—	11,120
Everett	98201*	54,413
Fort Lewis	98433	23,761
Hazel Dell	98665	15,386
Hoquiam	98550	9,719
Inglewood	98011	12,467
Juanita	98033	17,232
Kelso	98626	11,129
Kenmore	98028	7,281
Kennewick	99336	34,397
Kent	98031	22,961
Kingsgate	—	12,652
Kirkland	98033	18,779
Lacey	98503	13,940
Lake Forest North	—	7,995
Lakeland North	—	11,648
Lakes District	—	54,533
Longview	98632	31,052
Lynnwood	98036	22,641
Martha Lake	—	7,022
Mercer Island	98040	21,522
Moses Lake	98837	10,629
Mount Vernon	98273	13,009
Mountlake Terrace	98043	16,534
Newport Hills	98006	12,245
North City	98155	13,551
North Hill	—	10,170
North Marysville	—	15,159
Oak Harbor	98277	12,271
Olympia	98501*	27,447
Opportunity	99214	21,241
Orchards	98662	8,828
Parkland	98444	23,355
Pasco	99301	18,425
Port Angeles	98362	17,311
Port Townsend	98368	6,067
Poverty Bay	—	8,353
Pullman	99163	23,579
Puyallup	98371	18,251
Redmond	98052	23,318
Renton	98057*	30,612
Richland	99352	33,578
Richmond Highlands	—	24,463
Riverton	—	14,182
Rose Hill	—	7,616
Seattle	98109*	493,846
Sedro-Woolley	98284	6,110
Shelton	98584	7,629
Sheridan Beach	—	6,873
Silver Lake–Fircrest	—	10,299
Spanaway	98387	8,868
Spokane	99210*	171,300
Sunnyside	98944	9,225
Tacoma	98413*	158,501
Toppenish	98948	6,517
Tumwater	98501	6,705
University Place	98466	20,381
Valley Ridge	—	17,961
Vancouver	98661*	42,834
Veradale	99037	7,256
Walla Walla	99362	25,618
Wenatchee	98801	17,257
West Federal Way	—	16,872
West Pasco	—	5,729
White Center–Shorewood	—	19,362
Yakima	98903*	49,826
Zenith–Saltwater	—	8,982

[1] 1980 Census. † Town or township.

WEST VIRGINIA (W. Va. or WV)

PLACE	ZIP CODE	POP.[1]
Beckley	25801	20,492
Bluefield	24701	16,060
Bridgeport	26330	6,604
Buckhannon	26201	6,820
Charleston	25301*	63,968
Clarksburg	26301	22,371
Dunbar	25064	9,285
Elkins	26241	8,536
Fairmont	26554	23,863
Grafton	26354	6,845
Huntington	25704*	63,684
Keyser	26726	6,569
Martinsburg	25401	13,063
Morgantown	26505	27,605
Moundsville	26041	12,419
New Martinsville	26155	7,109
Nitro	25143	8,074
Oak Hill	25901	7,120
Parkersburg	26101	39,946
Point Pleasant	25550	5,682
Princeton	24740	7,493
St. Albans	25177	12,402
S. Charleston	25303	15,968
Vienna	26105	11,618
Weirton	26062	25,371
Weston	26452	6,250
Westover	26505	4,884
Wheeling	26003	43,070
Williamson	25661	5,219

WISCONSIN (Wis., Wisc., or WI)

PLACE	ZIP CODE	POP.[1]
Allouez	—	14,882
Antigo	54409	8,653
Appleton	54911	58,913
Ashland	54806	9,115
Ashwaubenon	54304	14,486
Baraboo	53913	8,081
Beaver Dam	53916	14,149
Beloit	53511	35,207
Berlin	54923	5,478
Brookfield	53005	34,035
Brown Deer	53209	12,921
Burlington	53105	8,385
Cedarburg	53012	9,005
Chippewa Falls	54729	12,270
Cudahy	53110	19,547
De Pere	54115	14,892
Delavan	53115	5,684
Eau Claire	54701	51,509
Elm Grove	53122	6,735
Fond du Lac	54935	35,863
Fort Atkinson	53538	9,785
Fox Point	53217	7,649
Franklin	53132	16,871
Germantown	53022	10,729
Glendale	53209	13,882
Grafton	53024	8,381
Green Bay	54305*	87,889
Greendale	53129	16,928
Greenfield	53220	31,467
Hales Corners	53130	7,110
Hartford	53027	7,046
Hartland	53029	5,559
Howard	54303	8,240
Hudson	54016	5,434
Janesville	53545	51,071
Jefferson	53549	5,647
Kaukauna	54130	11,310
Kenosha	53141*	77,685
Kimberly	54136	5,881
La Crosse	54601	48,347
Lake Geneva	53147	5,612
Little Chute	54140	7,907
Madison	53707*	170,616
Manitowoc	54220	32,547
Marinette	54143	11,965
Marshfield	54449	18,290
Menasha	54952	14,728
Menomonee Falls	53051	27,845
Menomonie	54751	12,769
Mequon	53092	16,193
Merrill	54452	9,578
Middleton	53562	11,848
Milwaukee	53201*	636,297
Monona	53716	8,809
Monroe	53566	10,027
Muskego	53150	15,277
Neenah	54956	22,432
New Berlin	53151	30,529
New London	54961	6,210
Oak Creek	53154	16,932
Oconomowoc	53066	9,909
Onalaska	54650	9,249
Oshkosh	54901	49,620
Platteville	53818	9,580
Plymouth	53073	6,027
Port Washington	53074	8,612
Portage	53901	7,896
Prairie du Chien	53821	5,859
Racine	53401*	85,725
Rhinelander	54501	7,873
Rice Lake	54868	7,691
Ripon	54971	7,111
River Falls	54022	9,019
St. Francis	53207	10,042
Shawano	54166	7,013
Sheboygan	53081	48,085
Shorewood	53211	14,327
S. Milwaukee	53172	21,069
Sparta	54656	6,934
Stevens Point	54481	22,970
Stoughton	53589	7,589
Sturgeon Bay	54235	8,847
Sun Prairie	53590	12,931
Superior	54880	29,571
Tomah	54660	7,204
Two Rivers	54241	13,354
Watertown	53094	18,113
Waukesha	53186	50,365
Waupun	53963	8,132
Wausau	54401	32,426
Wausau West–Rib Mountain	—	6,005
Wauwatosa	53213	51,308
West Allis	53214	63,982
West Bend	53095	21,484
Weston	—	8,775
Whitefish Bay	53217	14,930
Whitewater	53190	11,520
Wisconsin Rapids	54494	17,995

WYOMING (Wyo., or WY)

PLACE	ZIP CODE	POP.[1]
Casper	82601*	51,016
Cheyenne	82001	47,283
Cody	82414	6,790
Douglas	82633	6,030
Evanston	82930	6,421
Gillette	82716	12,134
Green River	82935	12,807
Jackson	83001	4,511
Lander	82520	7,867
Laramie	82070*	24,410
Powell	82435	5,310
Rawlins	82301	11,547
Riverton	82501	9,247
Rock Springs	82901	19,458
Sheridan	82801	15,146
Torrington	82240	5,441
Wheatland	82201	5,816
Worland	82401	6,391

DIST. OF COLUMBIA (D.C. or DC)

PLACE	ZIP CODE	POP.[1]
Washington	20013*	638,432

GUAM (GU)

PLACE	ZIP CODE	POP.[1]
Tamuning	96911	13,527

VIRGIN ISLANDS (V.I. or VI)

PLACE	ZIP CODE	POP.[1]
Charlotte Amalie	00801	11,756

PUERTO RICO (P.R. or PR)

PLACE	ZIP CODE	POP.[1]
Aguada †	00602	31,521
Aguadilla †	00603	52,627
Aibonito †	00609	22,230
Arecibo †	00612	86,660
Bayamon †	00619	195,965
Cabo Rojo †	00623	33,909
Caguas †	00625	118,020
Canovanas †	00629	31,934
Carolina †	00630	165,207
Catano †	00632	26,318
Cayey †	00633	40,927
Cidra †	00639	28,135
Coamo †	00640	30,752
Corozal †	00643	28,218
Fajardo †	00648	32,011
Guayama †	00654	40,137
Guaynabo †	00657	80,857
Hatillo †	00659	28,973
Humacao †	00661	45,916
Isabela †	00662	37,451
Juana Diaz †	00665	43,464
Juncos †	00666	25,433
Lares †	00669	26,742
Las Piedras †	00671	22,425
Manati †	00701	36,480
Mayaguez †	00708	95,886
Moca †	00716	29,309
Ponce †	00731	188,219
Rio Grande †	00745	34,326
Salinas †	00751	26,494
San German †	00753	32,941
San Juan †	00936*	432,973
San Lorenzo †	00754	32,333
San Sebastian †	00755	35,877
Toa Alta †	00758	31,946
Toa Baja †	00759	78,119
Trujillo Alto †	00760	51,389
Utuado †	00761	34,384
Vega Alta †	00762	28,255
Vega Baja †	00763	46,841
Yabucoa †	00767	30,589
Yauco †	00768	37,682

[1] 1980 Census. † Town or township.

AREAS, LATITUDES, LONGITUDES, AND ELEVATIONS OF U.S. CITIES

Sources: National Oceanic and Atmospheric Administration (elevations of weather stations); Bureau of the Census

STATE AND CITY	AREA (sq. mi.)	LATITUDE °	LATITUDE ′	LONGITUDE °	LONGITUDE ′	ELEVATION (ft.)
ALABAMA						
Anniston	14.9	33	35	85	51	599
Bessemer	15.1	33	22	87	01	540
Birmingham	98.5	33	34	86	45	620
Dothan	70.5	31	12	85	21	300
Florence	21.4	34	48	87	41	578
Gadsden	35.4	34	02	86	00	565
Huntsville	113.5	34	42	86	35	600
Mobile	123.0	30	41	88	15	211
Montgomery	128.3	32	18	86	24	221
Tuscaloosa	43.2	33	14	87	37	170
ALASKA						
Anchorage	1,732.0	61	10	150	01	114
Fairbanks	31.4	64	49	147	52	436
Juneau	2,626.0	58	22	134	35	12
Sitka	2,938.0	57	04	135	21	15
ARIZONA						
Flagstaff	64.1	35	08	111	40	7,006
Mesa	67.6	33	25	111	52	1,230
Phoenix	324.0	33	27	112	04	1,083
Scottsdale	88.4	33	30	111	55	1,227
Tempe	37.9	33	26	111	56	1,150
Tucson	98.8	32	15	110	57	2,444
Yuma	18.4	32	44	114	37	240
ARKANSAS						
Fort Smith	46.4	35	39	94	09	793
Hot Springs	22.7	34	31	93	03	680
Little Rock	79.4	34	46	92	19	512
Pine Bluff	21.6	34	13	92	01	215
Texarkana	13.6	33	27	94	00	361
CALIFORNIA						
Altadena	8.5	34	11	118	08	1,127
Bakersfield	73.6	35	25	119	03	495
Berkeley	10.9	37	52	122	15	345
Burlingame	4.3	37	35	122	21	10
Chula Vista	17.7	32	36	117	06	9
Concord	29.3	37	58	121	59	195
El Centro	5.3	32	46	115	34	–30
Fairfield	27.0	38	16	122	02	38
Fresno	65.6	36	46	119	43	328
Fullerton	22.1	33	53	117	55	330
Hayward	39.0	37	39	121	59	715
Long Beach	49.8	33	49	118	09	34
Los Angeles	464.7	34	03	118	14	270
Modesto	24.9	37	39	121	00	91
Oakland	53.9	37	48	122	16	30
Oxnard	24.0	34	12	119	11	49
Palm Springs	76.0	33	50	116	30	425
Palo Alto	24.6	37	27	122	08	25
Pasadena	23.1	34	09	118	09	864
Pomona	22.8	34	04	117	49	740
Redwood City	33.7	37	29	122	14	31
Richmond	32.8	37	56	122	21	55
Riverside	71.8	33	57	117	23	840
Sacramento	96.1	38	35	121	30	19
Salinas	15.1	36	40	121	36	85
San Bernardino	53.2	34	08	117	16	1,125
San Diego	320.0	32	44	117	10	13
San Francisco	46.4	37	47	122	25	52
San Jose	158.0	37	21	121	54	67
San Mateo	11.7	37	32	122	18	21
Santa Ana	27.4	33	45	117	52	115
Santa Barbara	18.7	34	25	119	41	5
Santa Clara	19.1	37	21	121	56	88
Santa Monica	8.2	34	00	118	30	15
Santa Rosa	26.6	38	27	122	42	167
Stockton	40.0	38	00	121	19	12
Torrance	20.5	33	48	118	20	110
Ventura	15.2	34	17	119	17	105
Whittier	12.8	33	58	118	02	340
COLORADO						
Boulder	19.5	40	00	105	16	5,420
Colorado Springs	103.4	38	49	104	43	6,090
Denver	110.6	39	45	104	59	5,320
Lakewood	35.6	39	45	105	08	5,637
Pueblo	33.2	38	17	104	31	4,639
CONNECTICUT						
Bridgeport	14.7	41	10	73	08	7
Danbury	46.5	41	23	73	28	510
Hartford	17.8	41	48	72	39	19
Manchester	26.9	41	46	72	29	420
Milford	23.4	41	12	73	05	30
New Haven	18.9	41	18	72	56	24
Norwalk	22.3	41	07	73	25	37
Norwich	28.6	41	32	72	04	20
Stamford	38.1	41	08	73	33	190
DELAWARE						
Wilmington	10.5	39	40	75	36	74
DIST. OF COLUMBIA						
Washington	62.7	38	56	77	02	10
FLORIDA						
Clearwater	22.4	27	58	82	46	65
Fort Lauderdale	29.2	26	06	80	12	16
Gainesville	32.2	29	38	82	22	92
Jacksonville	759.7	30	30	81	42	26
Key West	9.0	24	34	81	48	6
Miami	34.3	25	48	80	16	7
Orlando	39.5	28	26	81	20	85
Pensacola	24.1	30	28	87	12	112
St. Petersburg	55.5	27	46	82	38	8
Tampa	84.4	27	58	82	32	19
GEORGIA						
Albany	42.6	31	32	84	08	180
Atlanta	131.0	33	39	84	26	1,010
Augusta	16.8	33	22	81	58	148
Columbus	217.5	32	31	84	56	385
Macon	49.6	32	42	83	39	354
Savannah	56.8	32	08	81	12	46
HAWAII						
Hilo	54.3	19	43	155	04	27
Honolulu	87.0	21	20	157	55	7
IDAHO						
Boise	39.3	43	34	116	13	2,838
Idaho Falls	12.8	43	31	112	04	4,730
Lewiston	16.1	46	23	117	01	1,413
Pocatello	22.4	42	55	112	36	4,454
ILLINOIS						
Aurora	25.5	41	45	88	21	690
Belleville	12.2	38	30	89	51	450
Bloomington	14.2	40	31	89	00	785
Chicago	228.1	41	47	87	45	607

STATE AND CITY	AREA (sq. mi.)	LATITUDE °	LATITUDE ′	LONGITUDE °	LONGITUDE ′	ELEVATION (ft.)
Decatur	37.1	39	51	88	58	670
Elgin	19.3	42	02	88	16	758
Joliet	23.5	41	33	88	05	550
Peoria	41.0	40	40	89	41	652
Rockford	38.8	42	12	89	06	724
Springfield	39.8	39	50	89	40	588
Waukegan	20.3	42	21	87	53	700
INDIANA						
Evansville	37.3	37	58	87	33	384
Fort Wayne	52.6	41	00	85	12	791
Gary	39.4	41	37	87	23	597
Indianapolis	352.0	39	44	86	17	792
Muncie	21.9	40	11	85	21	957
South Bend	36.3	41	42	86	19	773
Terre Haute	26.3	39	21	87	25	555
IOWA						
Cedar Rapids	53.9	41	53	91	42	840
Davenport	59.5	41	31	90	34	568
Des Moines	66.1	41	32	93	39	938
Dubuque	22.7	42	24	90	42	1,056
Iowa City	21.7	41	39	91	32	640
Sioux City	51.5	42	24	96	23	1,103
Waterloo	62.0	42	33	92	24	868
KANSAS						
Dodge City	10.5	37	46	99	58	2,582
Emporia	8.4	38	20	96	12	1,209
Lawrence	19.1	38	58	95	16	1,000
Salina	18.9	38	48	97	38	1,257
Topeka	49.4	39	04	95	38	877
Wichita	101.4	37	39	97	26	1,321
KENTUCKY						
Bowling Green	26.1	37	00	86	26	536
Covington	14.7	39	04	84	40	869
Lexington-Fayette	284.7	38	02	84	36	966
Louisville	60.0	38	14	85	46	462
Owensboro	11.2	37	46	87	09	420
LOUISIANA						
Baton Rouge	61.6	30	32	91	09	64
Lafayette	27.1	30	13	92	01	37
Lake Charles	27.2	30	07	93	13	9
Monroe	24.5	32	33	92	07	80
New Orleans	199.4	29	56	90	08	6
Shreveport	80.9	32	28	93	49	254
MAINE						
Bangor	35.4	44	48	68	49	163
Lewiston	34.9	44	06	70	13	180
Portland	23.2	43	39	70	19	43
MARYLAND						
Baltimore	80.3	39	17	76	37	14
Rockville	11.8	39	07	77	06	400
Towson	14.0	39	23	76	34	390
MASSACHUSETTS						
Boston	47.2	42	22	71	02	15
Brockton	21.5	42	03	71	00	80
Fall River	33.7	41	43	71	08	190
Framingham	24.9	42	17	71	25	170
Haverhill	31.8	42	46	71	04	60
Holyoke	21.0	42	12	72	36	98
Lawrence	6.6	42	42	71	10	57
New Bedford	18.7	41	38	70	56	120
Provincetown	7.3	42	04	70	12	30
Springfield	31.7	42	07	72	35	190
Worcester	37.4	42	16	71	52	986

STATE AND CITY	AREA (sq. mi.)	LATITUDE °	LATITUDE ′	LONGITUDE °	LONGITUDE ′	ELEVATION (ft.)
MICHIGAN						
Ann Arbor	24.6	42	18	83	43	900
Bay City	10.8	43	37	83	52	590
Dearborn	23.8	42	19	83	14	607
Detroit	135.6	42	25	83	01	623
Flint	32.4	42	58	83	44	770
Grand Rapids	43.4	42	53	85	31	784
Kalamazoo	24.6	42	18	85	34	760
Lansing	35.3	42	47	84	36	841
Pontiac	18.7	42	39	83	18	974
Saginaw	17.4	43	32	84	05	662
MINNESOTA						
Duluth	67.3	46	50	92	11	1,438
Minneapolis	55.1	44	53	93	13	834
Rochester	18.7	43	55	92	30	1,297
MISSISSIPPI						
Biloxi	19.7	30	24	88	54	15
Gulfport	20.0	30	23	89	08	35
Jackson	106.2	32	19	90	05	330
Meridian	35.4	32	20	88	45	290
MISSOURI						
Columbia	41.9	38	49	92	13	887
Independence	80.6	39	06	94	25	1,000
Jefferson City	24.0	38	34	92	11	640
Kansas City	316.3	39	00	94	32	870
St. Louis	61.4	38	37	90	11	446
Springfield	64.9	37	14	93	23	1,268
MONTANA						
Billings	20.3	45	46	108	29	3,097
Great Falls	16.1	47	29	111	22	3,662
Helena	13.3	46	36	112	00	3,828
NEBRASKA						
Lincoln	60.0	40	49	96	42	1,150
Omaha	90.9	41	22	96	01	1,309
NEVADA						
Carson City	145.6	39	09	119	46	4,651
Las Vegas	55.0	36	05	115	10	2,162
Reno	31.0	39	30	119	47	4,404
NEW HAMPSHIRE						
Concord	64.1	43	12	71	30	346
Manchester	32.1	43	00	71	28	170
Nashua	31.3	42	47	71	30	188
NEW JERSEY						
Atlantic City	10.7	39	23	74	26	11
Jersey City	13.2	40	44	74	03	135
Newark	24.1	40	42	74	10	11
Paterson	8.3	40	54	74	09	100
Trenton	7.0	40	13	74	46	56
NEW MEXICO						
Albuquerque	95.3	35	03	106	37	5,311
Santa Fe	31.5	35	39	105	58	6,800
NEW YORK						
Albany	21.6	42	45	73	48	275
Binghamton	10.4	42	13	75	59	1,590
Buffalo	41.8	42	56	78	44	705
New York	301.5	40	47	73	58	132
Rochester	34.2	43	07	77	40	547
Schenectady	10.2	42	50	73	55	225
Syracuse	23.8	43	07	76	07	410
Utica	16.8	43	09	75	23	718
White Plains	9.6	41	04	73	43	397

AREAS, LATITUDES, LONGITUDES, AND ELEVATIONS OF U.S. CITIES *(continued)*

STATE AND CITY	AREA (sq. mi.)	LATITUDE °	LATITUDE ′	LONGITUDE °	LONGITUDE ′	ELEVATION (ft.)
NORTH CAROLINA						
Asheville	28.7	35	36	82	32	2,242
Charlotte	139.7	35	13	80	56	735
Durham	40.6	36	02	78	58	406
Fayetteville	33.0	35	13	80	56	735
Greensboro	60.3	36	05	79	57	897
High Point	31.5	35	58	79	59	912
Raleigh	53.8	35	47	78	42	400
Winston-Salem	60.7	36	05	80	13	770
NORTH DAKOTA						
Bismarck	18.8	46	51	100	33	1,720
Fargo	25.7	46	54	96	48	896
Grand Forks	13.1	47	56	97	05	830
Minot	12.9	48	16	101	17	1,713
OHIO						
Akron	57.5	41	05	81	31	1,007
Canton	19.5	40	46	81	23	1,020
Cincinnati	78.1	39	09	84	31	761
Cleveland	79.0	41	29	81	43	690
Columbus	180.9	39	57	83	07	875
Dayton	48.4	39	46	84	11	745
Hamilton	19.4	39	24	84	34	590
Lima	12.3	40	45	84	05	870
Mansfield	25.5	40	49	82	31	1,295
Toledo	84.2	41	39	83	32	595
Warren	14.8	41	09	80	49	900
Youngstown	34.5	41	16	80	40	1,178
OKLAHOMA						
Lawton	44.6	34	37	98	27	1,150
Oklahoma City	603.6	35	28	97	33	1,200
Tulsa	185.6	36	11	95	54	668
OREGON						
Eugene	32.5	44	07	123	13	364
Portland	103.3	45	36	122	36	21
Salem	36.8	44	55	123	01	195
PENNSYLVANIA						
Allentown	17.5	40	39	75	26	387
Altoona	9.1	40	30	78	28	1,320
Erie	21.7	42	05	80	11	732
Harrisburg	7.7	40	13	76	51	338
Lancaster	6.4	40	01	76	17	255
Philadelphia	136.0	39	57	75	09	35
Pittsburgh	55.4	40	27	80	00	747
Reading	9.6	40	19	75	56	270
Scranton	24.8	41	25	75	40	746
Wilkes-Barre	7.3	41	20	75	44	930
York	5.2	39	54	76	44	640
RHODE ISLAND						
Newport	7.7	41	31	71	19	20
Providence	18.9	41	44	71	26	51
Woonsocket	7.8	41	59	71	30	115
SOUTH CAROLINA						
Charleston	25.5	32	47	79	56	9
Columbia	107.1	33	59	81	01	242
Greenville	27.9	34	52	82	24	1,010
SOUTH DAKOTA						
Aberdeen	6.5	45	27	98	26	1,296
Huron	5.3	44	22	98	13	1,277
Pierre	12.7	44	23	100	17	1,734
Rapid City	22.0	44	04	103	16	3,370
Sioux Falls	40.7	43	34	96	44	1,418

STATE AND CITY	AREA (sq. mi.)	LATITUDE °	LATITUDE ′	LONGITUDE °	LONGITUDE ′	ELEVATION (ft.)
TENNESSEE						
Chattanooga	123.8	35	02	85	12	665
Knoxville	77.1	35	57	83	55	895
Memphis	264.1	35	09	90	03	205
Nashville-Davidson	479.5	36	07	86	41	590
TEXAS						
Abilene	75.9	32	25	99	41	1,784
Amarillo	80.1	35	14	101	42	3,607
Arlington	79.1	32	44	97	07	630
Austin	116.0	30	18	97	42	597
Beaumont	72.9	30	06	94	06	20
Brownsville	27.8	25	54	97	26	19
Corpus Christi	104.0	27	46	97	30	44
Dallas	333.0	32	51	96	51	481
El Paso	239.2	31	48	106	24	3,918
Fort Worth	240.2	32	45	97	20	616
Galveston	48.2	29	18	94	48	7
Houston	556.4	29	45	95	22	96
Laredo	19.7	27	30	99	28	396
Odessa	29.4	31	53	102	24	2,910
San Antonio	262.7	29	32	98	28	788
Waco	74.1	31	37	97	13	500
Wichita Falls	49.2	33	58	98	29	994
UTAH						
Ogden	26.1	41	15	111	57	4,350
Provo	35.0	40	13	111	40	4,470
Salt Lake City	75.2	40	46	111	53	4,320
VERMONT						
Burlington	10.8	44	28	73	12	400
Montpelier	10.6	44	12	72	34	1,126
VIRGINIA						
Alexandria	15.0	38	48	77	05	70
Lynchburg	49.5	37	20	79	12	916
Newport News	65.3	37	01	76	27	50
Norfolk	53.0	36	54	76	12	22
Richmond	60.1	37	30	77	20	164
Roanoke	43.1	37	19	79	58	1,149
WASHINGTON						
Bellingham	22.5	48	45	122	29	140
Everett	23.3	47	59	122	11	60
Olympia	16.8	46	58	122	54	195
Seattle	144.6	47	39	122	18	19
Spokane	51.7	47	40	117	25	1,875
Tacoma	47.7	47	15	122	26	267
WEST VIRGINIA						
Charleston	28.0	38	21	81	39	600
Huntington	15.9	38	25	82	27	565
Wheeling	13.4	40	06	80	42	659
WISCONSIN						
Appleton	15.8	44	15	88	23	730
Green Bay	43.2	44	29	88	08	682
Kenosha	15.4	42	33	87	48	600
La Crosse	16.5	43	52	91	15	651
Madison	53.9	43	08	89	20	858
Milwaukee	95.8	42	57	87	54	672
Oshkosh	13.5	44	03	88	33	753
Racine	13.8	42	43	87	52	695
WYOMING						
Casper	13.9	42	51	106	18	5,195
Cheyenne	14.9	41	09	104	49	6,126
Laramie	9.7	41	19	105	35	7,173

Climate and Weather

Wide World

Skier glides down New York's Fifth Avenue past Rockefeller Center after storm dumped foot of snow on city on Feb. 11–12, 1983. Hundreds of motorists were stranded on snow-clogged highways throughout the northeast as result of the weekend storm.

HIGHLIGHTS: 1983

In a long-range forecast, the National Weather Service predicted that the winter of 1983–84 would bring warmer than normal weather to both the East and West coasts of the United States. However, the forecast said that the central portion of the country might expect colder than usual winter weather with heavy rains and snowstorms.

Throughout the winter of 1982–83 storms brought heavy snowfalls to the Rocky Mountains and the central Plains states. Denver recorded a total of 100 inches of snow, including three storms with 18 or more inches.

The Northeastern states were blanketed by

STORMS FORECAST FOR 1984

Based on a research study of the relationship of bad storms to phases of the Moon, the worst storms each month in 1984 may take place in the following periods.

January 3–5	**July** 15–17
January 21–23	**July** 29–31
February 2–4	**August** 14–16
February 19–21	**August** 27–29
March 3–5	**September** 13–15
March 20–22	**September** 25–27
April 2–4	**October** 12–14
April 18–20	**October** 25–27
May 1–2	**November** 11–13
May 17–19	**November** 23–25
June 1–2	**December** 11–13
June 16–18	**December** 23–25
June 29–30	

HIGHLIGHTS: 1983 *(continued)*

one of the century's greatest snowstorms on Feb. 11–12, with Philadelphia receiving a record 22 inches.

Southern California was battered in January and again in March by storms that sent coastal waves crashing over seawalls and caused massive property damage. Mudslides damaged homes and highways. See page 9.

A spring blizzard on March 26 dumped up to 18 inches of snow across the Midwest, snarling traffic.

Heavy rains and melting mountain snow in May to July brought major floods in the Colorado River basin. The central business district of Salt Lake City flooded in May from the heavy runoff from local mountains. In June thousands of persons fled from their homes as floodgates had to be opened at Colorado River dams, sweeping away many riverside homes and businesses. Flooding of popular recreation areas hurt the tourist industry in the region.

Summer brought the worst drought to the Midwest since the "dust bowl" of the 1930s while a heat wave killed hundreds of persons. August was the hottest month recorded this century with temperatures in half the nation averaging 4 degrees above normal. See page 23.

The worst storm of the year, Hurricane Alicia, struck Galveston and Houston on Aug. 17–18 with sustained winds of 103 mph and gusts to 135 mph. The storm caused business and property losses estimated at $2.4 billion to $3.8 billion. Sixteen persons were killed, but most residents of the heavily populated area had sufficient warning to find safe shelters.

A polar cold front in the third week of September brought below-normal temperatures from the Great Lakes to the Texas Panhandle. Temperatures fell as much as 60 degrees overnight. Heavy rains caused flooding from Wisconsin to Texas. Arizona was hard hit by flooding caused by heavy rainfall from September 29 to October 2.

The winter of 1983–84 got off to an early start as three storms in rapid succession in late November struck the Rocky Mountain states and swept across the Middle West to the Great Lakes, hitting cities and towns from Denver to Minneapolis. More than 50 persons were killed by the early winter weather. The second storm, a blizzard with winds to 50 mph, dropped up to 2 feet of snow across the central part of the country. Schools in many localities had to suspend classes. Airports and highways were closed as snow drifted to 9 feet deep, stranding thousands of Thanksgiving weekend travelers. Motorists trapped on interstate highways had to be rescued by snowplows. The wind-chill factor dropped as low as 45 degrees below zero. Such cities as Norfolk, Neb., Sioux City, Iowa, and Minneapolis, Minn., reported heavier snowfalls during November than ever before recorded.

EL NIÑO BLAMED FOR BAD WEATHER

An oceanic phenomenon called El Niño was blamed by meteorologists for bad weather that caused death, destruction, and property losses in many parts of the world.

Ordinarily, winds blow steadily westward across the Pacific Ocean at the equator. As the winds drag surface water with them, the sea level in the western Pacific is higher than in the eastern Pacific.

From time to time the wind shifts around to blow toward the east. This causes the sea level to rise along South America's west coast and keeps surface water warmer. This condition has been called El Niño, meaning "The Child," because it usually happens around the Christmas season.

However, in 1982 El Niño appeared much earlier than usual, in May, and lingered for more than 17 months, to October 1983.

El Niño changed the normal pattern of the jet stream, the high winds that blow from west to east across North America. El Niño was blamed for droughts in the United States, South America, Africa, Indonesia, Australia, Hawaii, and Mexico. It also was believed to have caused damaging rainstorms and floods in Ecuador, Peru, China, and California.

EARLY COLD TRAPS SHIPS

When temperatures unexpectedly fell to 20 degrees below zero in early October in the Arctic region, some 90 Soviet ships were trapped as ice sealed off navigational channels. One freighter sank and at least 30 were damaged. The Soviet Union mounted a huge effort to free the vessels with nuclear-powered icebreakers. The Soviet propaganda organ *Pravda* blamed government meteorologists for bad weather forecasting.

NEW RECORD LOW TEMPERATURE

Soviet scientists on July 21 recorded the world's lowest air temperature at 128.6 degrees below zero. The temperature was set at the Soviet Vostok station atop a 11,200-foot mountain in Antarctica. The world's previous record low of 126.9 degrees below zero had been set at the same station on Aug. 24, 1960.

WEATHER STRESS INDEX

The National Oceanic and Atmospheric Administration announced the development of a new index called the weather-stress index to measure discomfort. The new index adds humidity to temperature and wind-speed figures to calculate wind chill.

RECORD HIGH AND LOW TEMPERATURES

Source: Environmental Data Service, NOAA, U.S. Department of Commerce

	RECORD HIGH TEMPERATURES			RECORD LOW TEMPERATURES		
	Temp. (F.)	Date	Location	Temp. (F.)	Date	Location
World	136°	Sept. 13, 1922	Al Aziziyah, Libya,	–128.6°	July 21, 1983	Vostock Research Station, Antarctica
United States	134°	July 10, 1913	Greenland Ranch, California	–79.8°	Jan. 23, 1971	Prospect Creek Camp, Alaska
Alabama	112°	Sept. 5, 1925	Centerville	–27°	Jan. 30, 1966	New Market
Alaska	100°	June 27, 1915	Fort Yukon	–79.8°	Jan. 23, 1971	Prospect Creek Camp
Arizona	127°	July 7, 1905*	Parker	–40°	Jan. 7, 1971	Hawley Lake
Arkansas	120°	Aug. 10, 1936	Ozark	–29°	Feb. 13, 1905	Pond
California	134°	July 10, 1913	Greenland Ranch	–45°	Jan. 20, 1937	Boca
Colorado	118°	July 11, 1888	Bennett	–60°	Feb. 1, 1951	Taylor Park
Connecticut	105°	July 22, 1926	Waterbury	–32°	Feb. 16, 1943	Falls Village
Delaware	110°	July 21, 1930	Millsboro	–17°	Jan. 17, 1893	Millsboro
Dist. of Columbia	106°	July 20, 1930*	Washington	–15°	Feb. 11, 1899	Washington
Florida	109°	June 29, 1931	Monticello	– 2°	Feb. 13, 1899	Tallahassee
Georgia	113°	May 27, 1978	Greenville	–17°	Jan. 27, 1940	CCC Camp F-16
Hawaii	100°	Apr. 27, 1931	Pahala	12°	May 17, 1979	Mauna Kea
Idaho	118°	July 28, 1934	Orofino	–60°	Jan. 16, 1943	Island Park Dam
Illinois	117°	July 14, 1954	E. St. Louis	–35°	Jan. 22, 1930	Mt. Carroll
Indiana	116°	July 14, 1936	Collegeville	–35°	Feb. 2, 1951	Greensburg
Iowa	118°	July 20, 1934	Keokuk	–47°	Jan. 12, 1912	Washta
Kansas	121°	July 24, 1936*	Alton (near)	–40°	Feb. 13, 1905	Lebanon
Kentucky	114°	July 28, 1930	Greensburg	–34°	Jan. 28, 1963	Cynthiana
Louisiana	114°	Aug. 10, 1936	Plain Dealing	–16°	Feb. 13, 1899	Minden
Maine	105°	July 10, 1911*	North Bridgton	–48°	Jan. 19, 1925	Van Buren
Maryland	109°	July 10, 1936*	Cumberland & Frederick	–40°	Jan. 13, 1912	Oakland
Massachusetts	107°	Aug. 2, 1975	New Bedford and Chester	–34°	Jan. 18, 1957	Birch Hill Dam
Michigan	112°	July 13, 1936	Mio	–51°	Feb. 9, 1934	Vanderbilt
Minnesota	114°	July 6, 1936*	Moorhead	–59°	Feb. 16, 1903*	Pokegama Dam
Mississippi	115°	July 29, 1930	Holly Springs	–19°	Jan. 30, 1966	Corinth 4 SW
Missouri	118°	July 14, 1954*	Warsaw & Union	–40°	Feb. 13, 1905	Warsaw
Montana	117°	July 5, 1937	Medicine Lake	–70°	Jan. 20, 1954	Rogers Pass
Nebraska	118°	July 24, 1936*	Minden	–47°	Feb. 12, 1899	Camp Clarke
Nevada	122°	June 23, 1954*	Overton	–50°	Jan. 8, 1937	San Jacinto
New Hampshire	106°	July 4, 1911	Nashua	–46°	Jan. 28, 1925	Pittsburg
New Jersey	110°	July 10, 1936	Runyon	–34°	Jan. 5, 1904	River Vale
New Mexico	116°	July 10, 1934*	Orogrande	–50°	Feb. 1, 1951	Gavilan
New York	108°	July 22, 1926	Troy	–52°	Feb. 9, 1934	Stillwater Reservoir
North Carolina	109°	Sept. 7, 1954*	Weldon	–29°	Jan. 30, 1966	Mt. Mitchell
North Dakota	121°	July 6, 1936	Steele	–60°	Feb. 15, 1936	Parshall
Ohio	113°	July 21, 1934*	Gallipolis (near)	–39°	Feb. 10, 1899	Milligan
Oklahoma	120°	July 26, 1943*	Tishomingo	–27°	Jan. 18, 1930*	Watts
Oregon	119°	Aug. 10, 1938*	Pendleton	–54°	Feb. 10, 1933*	Seneca
Pennsylvania	111°	July 10, 1936*	Phoenixville	–42°	Jan. 5, 1904	Smethport
Rhode Island	104°	Aug. 2, 1975	Providence	–23°	Jan. 11, 1942	Kingston
South Carolina	111°	June 28, 1954*	Camden	–20°	Jan. 18, 1977	Caesars Head
South Dakota	120°	July 5, 1936	Gannvalley	–58°	Feb. 17, 1936	McIntosh
Tennessee	113°	Aug. 9, 1930*	Perryville	–32°	Dec. 30, 1917	Mountain City
Texas	120°	Aug. 12, 1936	Seymour	–23°	Feb. 8, 1933*	Seminole
Utah	116°	June 28, 1892	Saint George	–50°	Jan. 5, 1913*	Strawberry Tunnel
Vermont	105°	July 4, 1911	Vernon	–50°	Dec. 30, 1933	Bloomfield
Virginia	110°	July 15, 1954	Balcony Falls	–29°	Feb. 10, 1899	Monterey
Washington	118°	Aug. 5, 1961*	Ice Harbor Dam	–48°	Dec. 30, 1968	Mazama & Winthrop
West Virginia	112°	July 10, 1936*	Martinsburg	–37°	Dec. 30, 1917	Lewisburg
Wisconsin	114°	July 13, 1936	Wisconsin Dells	–54°	Jan. 24, 1922	Danbury
Wyoming	114°	July 12, 1900	Basin	–63°	Feb. 9, 1933	Moran

* Also on earlier dates at same or other places in the state.

WEATHER IN U.S. STATES, CITIES, AND TERRITORIES

Source: *Local Climatological Data,* Environmental Data Service, NOAA

PLACE	TEMPERATURE RECORDS				NUMBER OF HOT AND COLD DAYS[1]			NUMBER OF SUNNY AND CLOUDY DAYS[1]			NUMBER OF STORMY DAYS[1]		
	High	Date	Low	Date	Hot[2]	Freezing[3]	Below zero[4]	Clear	Partly cloudy	Overcast	Rain[5]	Snow[6]	Fog[7]
ALABAMA													
Birmingham	107°	July 1930	−10°	Feb. 1899	56	56	0	—	—	—	104	0	—
Huntsville	104°	July 1966	−11°	Jan. 1966	44	72	0	84	113	168	109	0	13
Mobile	104°	July 1952	− 1°	Feb. 1899	92	25	0	116	109	140	107	0	42
Montgomery	107°	July 1881	− 5°	Feb. 1899	84	40	0	116	92	157	95	0	12
ALASKA													
Anchorage	86°	June 1953	−38°	Feb. 1947	6[8]	196	13	50	61	254	134	16	25
Barrow	78°	July 1927	−56°	Feb. 1924	0	333	161	—	—	—	107	2	44
Fairbanks	99°	July 1919	−66°	Jan. 1934	36[8]	215	61	65	68	232	124	21	14
Juneau	90°	July 1975	−22°	Jan. 1972	20[8]	112	0	—	—	—	229	8	23
Kodiak	86°	June 1953	−12°	Feb. 1971	7[8]	85	0	72	67	226	209	7	12
Nome	86°	July 1977	−47°	Jan. 1919	7[8]	239	52	91	75	199	150	32	17
ARIZONA													
Flagstaff	97°	July 1973	−30°	Jan. 1937	8	181	0	154	99	113	96	31	—
Phoenix	118°	July 1958	16°	Jan. 1913	172	0	0	206	86	73	28	0	0
Tucson	112°	June 1902	6°	Jan. 1913	136	4	0	184	104	77	54	0	0
Winslow	109°	July 1971	−19°	Dec. 1898	68	124	0	—	—	—	51	0	—
Yuma	123°	Sept. 1950	22°	Jan. 1937	195	0	0	202	104	59	15	0	—
ARKANSAS													
Fort Smith	113°	Aug. 1936	−15°	Feb. 1899	61	72	0	108	97	160	103	1	19
Little Rock	110°	Aug. 1936	−13°	Feb. 1899	70	52	0	—	—	—	86	0	12
CALIFORNIA													
Bakersfield	118°	July 1908	13°	Dec. 1905	121	2	0	188	75	102	38	0	27
Fresno	115°	July 1905	17°	Jan. 1913	124	4	0	172	73	120	46	0	48
Long Beach	111°	Oct. 1961	25°	Jan. 1963	36	0	0	178	98	89	27	0	30
Los Angeles	110°	Sept. 1963	23°	Jan. 1937	34	0	0	—	—	—	29	0	—
Sacramento	115°	June 1961	17°	Dec. 1932	71	4	0	184	71	110	60	0	31
San Diego	111°	Sept. 1963	25°	Jan. 1913	5	0	0	148	108	109	36	0	30
San Francisco	106°	June 1961	20°	Dec. 1932	3	0	0	155	86	124	74	0	7
Stockton	114°	July 1972	19°	Jan. 1963	117	2	0	178	66	121	57	0	—
COLORADO													
Alamosa	93°	July 1971	−50°	Jan. 1948	4	211	35	155	124	87	66	7	—
Colorado Springs	100°	June 1954	−32°	Jan. 1883	23	147	4	114	131	120	105	4	17
Denver	105°	Aug. 1878	−30°	Feb. 1936	43	115	3	106	131	128	82	19	12
Grand Junction	105°	July 1976	−23°	Jan. 1963	65	125	0	130	102	133	82	3	8
Pueblo	105°	July 1973	−31°	Feb. 1951	66	129	5	147	97	122	65	8	—
CONNECTICUT													
Bridgeport	103°	July 1957	−20°	Feb. 1934	4	101	3	85	112	168	111	3	—
Hartford	102°	July 1966	−26°	Jan. 1961	13	123	10	78	104	183	119	7	13
DELAWARE													
Wilmington	107°	Aug. 1918	−15°	Feb. 1934	18	101	2	89	106	170	103	3	21
DIST. OF COLUMBIA													
Washington	106°	July 1930	−15°	Feb. 1899	33	61	0	87	108	170	108	2	5
FLORIDA													
Jacksonville	105°	July 1942	10°	Feb. 1899	98	37	0	108	134	123	95	0	36
Key West	97°	Aug. 1956	41°	Jan. 1886	53	0	0	125	145	95	99	0	3
Miami	100°	July 1942	26°	Dec. 1934	94	1	0	85	183	97	114	0	3
Orlando	103°	Sept. 1921	20°	Jan. 1977	139	10	0	99	159	107	99	0	21
Pensacola	103°	Aug. 1947	7°	Feb. 1899	53	24	0	129	120	116	78	0	33
Tallahassee	104°	June 1933	− 2°	Feb. 1899	88	53	0	107	113	145	101	0	36
Tampa	98°	June 1977	18°	Dec. 1962	68	10	0	117	163	85	89	0	16
West Palm Beach	101°	July 1942	27°	Jan. 1977	107	1	0	92	166	107	111	0	3
GEORGIA													
Athens	108°	July 1930	− 3°	Feb. 1899	75	59	0	123	106	136	97	0	27
Atlanta	103°	July 1952	− 9°	Feb. 1899	60	52	0	110	108	147	97	0	22
Augusta	106°	July 1952	− 2°	Jan. 1982	77	76	0	130	121	114	104	0	17
Columbus	106°	Sept. 1925	− 3°	Feb. 1899	87	47	0	121	97	147	95	0	7
Macon	106°	June 1954	3°	Jan. 1966	85	43	0	130	107	128	96	0	11
Savannah	105°	July 1879	8°	Feb. 1899	78	38	0	110	109	146	91	0	24
HAWAII													
Hilo	94°	May 1966	51°	May 1910	1	0	0	73	163	129	242	0	0
Honolulu	93°	Oct. 1979	53°	Feb. 1976	9	0	0	86	222	57	97	0	0

[1] Average per year. [2] Highest temperature 90° F. or above. [3] Lowest temperature 32° F. or below. [4] Lowest temperature 0° F. or below. [5] Rain of 0.01 inch or more. [6] Snow of 1 inch or more. [7] Visibility of 1/4 mile or less. [8] Days 70° F. and above.

WEATHER IN U.S. STATES, CITIES, AND TERRITORIES *(continued)*

PLACE	TEMPERATURE RECORDS				NUMBER OF HOT AND COLD DAYS[1]			NUMBER OF SUNNY AND CLOUDY DAYS[1]			NUMBER OF STORMY DAYS[1]		
	High	Date	Low	Date	Hot[2]	Freezing[3]	Below zero[4]	Clear	Partly cloudy	Overcast	Rain[5]	Snow[6]	Fog[7]
IDAHO													
Boise	111°	July 1960	−23°	Dec. 1972	55	119	0	130	68	167	94	6	16
Lewiston	117°	July 1939	−23°	Dec. 1919	44	68	0	89	67	209	101	3	—
Pocatello	105°	July 1931	−31°	Jan. 1949	46	169	3	114	85	166	103	14	19
ILLINOIS													
Chicago	105°	July 1934	−26°	Jan. 1982	6	138	14	73	112	180	121	9	11
Moline	106°	Aug. 1936	−27°	Jan. 1979	1	137	15	97	116	152	113	6	11
Peoria	113°	July 1936	−27°	Jan. 1884	7	118	15	89	105	171	117	7	31
Rockford	112°	July 1936	−25°	Jan. 1924	3	146	15	97	92	176	104	6	3
Springfield	112°	July 1954	−24°	Feb. 1905	21	110	6	107	100	158	116	6	15
INDIANA													
Evansville	108°	July 1936	−23°	Feb. 1951	26	95	0	97	109	159	109	1	16
Fort Wayne	106°	July 1936	−24°	Jan. 1918	2	125	11	70	109	186	124	7	19
Indianapolis	107°	July 1934	−25°	Jan. 1884	10	124	10	79	84	202	132	7	24
South Bend	109°	July 1934	−22°	Jan. 1943	3	118	7	59	87	219	147	28	30
IOWA													
Des Moines	110°	July 1936	−30°	Jan. 1884	12	118	12	115	96	154	94	8	14
Sioux City	111°	July 1939	−35°	Jan. 1912	22	138	15	97	117	151	82	9	14
Waterloo	112°	Aug. 1936	−34°	Mar. 1962	3	155	27	100	87	178	103	7	11
KANSAS													
Concordia	116°	Aug. 1936	−25°	Feb. 1899	35	107	5	113	113	139	83	3	13
Dodge City	109°	July 1978	−26°	Feb. 1899	71	104	2	126	102	137	86	4	21
Topeka	114°	July 1936	−25°	Feb. 1899	25	105	5	103	100	162	94	3	9
Wichita	114°	Aug. 1936	−22°	Feb. 1899	55	99	2	117	99	149	82	2	10
KENTUCKY													
Lexington	108°	July 1936	−21°	Jan. 1963	6	101	4	72	100	193	123	2	19
Louisville	107°	July 1901	−20°	Jan. 1963	26	92	1	83	105	177	111	3	5
LOUISIANA													
Baton Rouge	110°	Aug. 1909	2°	Feb. 1899	91	22	0	103	122	140	101	0	30
Lake Charles	104°	Aug. 1951	12°	Jan. 1948	68	12	0	104	116	145	99	0	68
New Orleans	102°	June 1954	7°	Feb. 1899	99	12	0	84	124	157	103	0	15
Shreveport	110°	Aug. 1909	− 5°	Feb. 1899	79	38	0	87	117	161	90	0	22
MAINE													
Caribou	96°	May 1977	−41°	Feb. 1955	0	179	29	54	94	217	163	30	—
Portland	103°	Aug. 1975	−39°	Feb. 1943	1	146	14	92	80	193	131	15	40
MARYLAND													
Baltimore	107°	July 1936	− 7°	Jan. 1963	22	99	1	108	94	163	103	2	13
MASSACHUSETTS													
Boston	104°	July 1911	−18°	Feb. 1934	11	95	3	102	91	172	120	10	21
Worcester	102°	July 1911	−24°	Feb. 1943	3	138	7	82	107	176	143	15	—
MICHIGAN													
Detroit	105°	July 1934	−24°	Dec. 1872	9	104	2	79	104	183	143	10	9
Flint	108°	July 1936	−28°	Feb. 1916	2	141	10	66	98	201	131	11	16
Grand Rapids	108°	July 1936	−24°	Feb. 1899	7	139	6	66	83	216	115	12	22
Lansing	102°	Aug. 1918	−33°	Feb. 1875	7	144	12	68	93	204	126	11	23
Marquette	108°	July 1901	−27°	Feb. 1888	3	199	30	—	—	—	163	48	44
Sault Ste. Marie	98°	Aug. 1947	−37°	Feb. 1934	0	207	27	70	97	198	145	31	36
MINNESOTA													
Duluth	106°	July 1936	−41°	Jan. 1885	0	185	37	81	103	181	136	15	67
International Falls	103°	July 1923	−49°	Jan. 1896	4	180	45	69	110	186	121	17	18
Minn.-St. Paul	108°	July 1936	−34°	Jan. 1970	1	146	27	102	104	159	120	18	7
Rochester	108°	July 1936	−42°	Jan. 1887	1	156	28	88	88	189	119	15	34
MISSISSIPPI													
Jackson	107°	July 1930	− 5°	Jan. 1940	90	46	0	122	103	140	90	0	22
Meridian	105°	Aug. 1943	− 7°	Jan. 1940	106	50	0	106	107	152	90	0	24
MISSOURI													
Columbia	113°	July 1954	−26°	Feb. 1899	25	98	5	102	91	172	111	5	18
Kansas City	113°	Aug. 1936	−22°	Feb. 1899	17	99	7	106	103	156	98	4	14
St. Louis	115°	July 1954	−23°	Jan. 1864	20	91	4	107	97	161	120	6	6
Springfield	113°	July 1954	−29°	Feb. 1899	48	93	1	103	87	175	104	4	23

[1] Average per year. [2] Highest temperature 90°F. or above. [3] Lowest temperature 32°F. or below. [4] Lowest temperature 0°F. or below. [5] Rain of 0.01 inch or more. [6] Snow of 1 inch or more. [7] Visibility of 1/4 mile or less.

WEATHER IN U.S. STATES, CITIES, AND TERRITORIES *(continued)*

PLACE	TEMPERATURE RECORDS				NUMBER OF HOT AND COLD DAYS[1]			NUMBER OF SUNNY AND CLOUDY DAYS[1]			NUMBER OF STORMY DAYS[1]		
	High	Date	Low	Date	Hot[2]	Freezing[3]	Below zero[4]	Clear	Partly cloudy	Overcast	Rain[5]	Snow[6]	Fog[7]
MONTANA													
Billings	112°	July 1901	−49°	Feb. 1899	42	142	6	114	95	156	96	12	18
Great Falls	107°	July 1933	−49°	Feb. 1936	24	150	7	88	103	174	98	15	12
Helena	105°	Aug. 1969	−42°	Jan. 1957	17	171	6	110	75	180	88	9	10
Missoula	105°	July 1973	−33°	Jan. 1957	19	175	3	85	69	211	132	14	33
NEBRASKA													
Grand Island	117°	July 1936	−34°	Feb. 1899	28	134	7	113	124	128	79	6	13
Lincoln	115°	July 1936	−33°	Jan. 1974	34	129	7	119	109	137	83	6	11
Omaha	114°	July 1936	−32°	Jan. 1884	26	135	15	—	—	—	78	8	11
NEVADA													
Elko	107°	July 1890	−43°	Jan. 1937	75	183	0	142	90	133	77	8	4
Las Vegas	117°	July 1942	8°	Jan. 1963	134	12	0	197	80	88	23	0	1
Reno	106°	July 1931	−19°	Jan. 1890	70	162	0	152	82	131	52	5	2
NEW HAMPSHIRE													
Concord	102°	July 1966	−37°	Feb. 1943	4	166	21	78	90	197	133	19	30
NEW JERSEY													
Atlantic City	106°	June 1969	−10°	Jan. 1977	23	121	3	80	120	165	98	2	29
Newark	105°	July 1966	−14°	Feb. 1934	21	92	2	86	134	146	104	5	6
NEW MEXICO													
Albuquerque	105°	June 1974	−17°	Jan. 1971	69	124	0	162	105	98	57	1	5
Roswell	110°	July 1958	−29°	Feb. 1905	69	82	0	148	107	110	54	3	18
NEW YORK													
Albany	104°	July 1911	−28°	Jan. 1971	5	157	16	64	97	204	132	15	20
Binghamton	103°	July 1936	−28°	Jan. 1893	0	140	9	56	83	226	154	20	40
Buffalo	99°	Aug. 1948	−21°	Feb. 1934	0	129	4	43	93	229	170	20	13
New York City	107°	July 1966	−15°	Feb. 1934	16	70	1	—	—	—	109	5	—
Rochester	102°	July 1936	−22°	Feb. 1934	5	134	11	56	91	218	166	33	11
Syracuse	102°	July 1936	−26°	Jan. 1966	9	132	9	50	84	231	164	31	8
NORTH CAROLINA													
Asheville	99°	July 1936	− 7°	Jan. 1966	17	102	0	104	118	143	109	3	67
Cape Hatteras	97°	June 1952	8°	Dec. 1880	6	59	0	122	95	148	117	1	8
Charlotte	104°	Sept. 1954	− 5°	Feb. 1899	31	75	0	118	105	142	97	1	20
Greensboro	102°	July 1977	− 7°	Jan. 1940	30	91	0	126	96	143	96	3	20
Raleigh	105°	July 1952	− 2°	Feb. 1899	39	92	0	115	97	153	94	1	24
NORTH DAKOTA													
Bismarck	114°	July 1936	−45°	Feb. 1936	16	174	27	95	112	158	93	7	14
Fargo	114°	July 1936	−48°	Jan. 1887	8	175	34	100	100	165	99	7	17
OHIO													
Akron	104°	Aug. 1918	−22°	Jan. 1982	3	126	8	60	95	210	156	20	22
Cincinnati	109°	July 1934	−25°	Jan. 1977	13	119	9	84	93	188	130	5	16
Cleveland	103°	July 1941	−19°	Jan. 1963	3	125	8	55	93	217	163	23	11
Columbus	106°	July 1936	−20°	Feb. 1899	5	121	8	73	90	202	142	8	11
Dayton	108°	July 1901	−28°	Feb. 1899	10	117	10	70	93	202	135	5	23
Toledo	105°	July 1936	−17°	Jan. 1963	5	141	12	75	103	187	137	11	16
Youngstown	100°	July 1954	−18°	Jan. 1963	7	129	11	51	81	233	158	18	26
OKLAHOMA													
Oklahoma City	113°	Aug. 1936	−17°	Feb. 1899	63	74	1	122	86	157	94	0	15
Tulsa	115°	Aug. 1936	−16°	Jan. 1930	65	64	1	123	95	147	89	0	12
OREGON													
Astoria	101°	July 1942	6°	Dec. 1972	1	16	0	39	95	231	189	0	39
Eugene	106°	Aug. 1972	−12°	Dec. 1972	16	52	0	62	75	228	147	0	78
Medford	115°	July 1946	−10°	Dec. 1919	58	63	0	118	67	180	105	1	61
Portland	107°	July 1965	− 3°	Feb. 1950	17	30	0	54	93	218	161	1	46
Salem	108°	July 1941	−12°	Dec. 1972	19	69	0	65	97	203	142	0	43
PENNSYLVANIA													
Allentown	105°	July 1966	−12°	Jan. 1961	12	113	5	82	109	174	119	8	11
Erie	99°	Sept. 1953	−16°	Feb. 1875	1	129	8	56	90	219	170	26	13
Harrisburg	107°	July 1966	−14°	Jan. 1912	14	107	3	85	112	168	114	10	5
Philadelphia	106°	Aug. 1918	−11°	Feb. 1934	15	98	1	94	114	157	104	3	8
Pittsburgh	103°	July 1936	−20°	Feb. 1899	2	140	9	55	106	204	156	18	13

[1] Average per year. [2] Highest temperature 90°F. or above. [3] Lowest temperature 32°F. or below. [4] Lowest temperature 0°F. or below. [5] Rain of 0.01 inch or more. [6] Snow of 1 inch or more. [7] Visibility of 1/4 mile or less.

WEATHER IN U.S. STATES, CITIES, AND TERRITORIES *(continued)*

PLACE	TEMPERATURE RECORDS				NUMBER OF HOT AND COLD DAYS[1]			NUMBER OF SUNNY AND CLOUDY DAYS[1]			NUMBER OF STORMY DAYS[1]		
	High	Date	Low	Date	Hot[2]	Freezing[3]	Below zero[4]	Clear	Partly cloudy	Overcast	Rain[5]	Snow[6]	Fog[7]
RHODE ISLAND													
Providence	104°	Aug. 1975	−17°	Feb. 1934	18	114	5	86	104	175	117	9	20
SOUTH CAROLINA													
Charleston	104°	June 1944	7°	Feb. 1899	73	50	0	120	109	136	92	0	20
Columbia	107°	June 1954	− 2°	Feb. 1899	62	77	0	111	113	141	105	0	12
Greenville	101°	July 1977	− 6°	Jan. 1966	39	76	0	132	105	128	100	1	19
SOUTH DAKOTA													
Aberdeen	115°	July 1936	−46°	Jan. 1912	23	175	38	105	95	166	61	6	—
Rapid City	110°	July 1973	−33°	Feb. 1936	23	150	9	108	140	117	88	4	19
Sioux Falls	110°	July 1936	−42°	Feb. 1899	20	147	23	119	100	146	97	6	10
TENNESSEE													
Bristol	102°	July 1952	−15°	Jan. 1966	6	115	2	81	110	174	126	5	44
Chattanooga	106°	July 1952	−10°	Jan. 1966	48	80	0	91	115	159	109	0	20
Knoxville	104°	July 1930	−16°	Jan. 1884	32	79	0	88	114	163	116	3	29
Memphis	106°	July 1952	−13°	Dec. 1963	68	47	0	115	106	144	93	0	10
Nashville	107°	July 1952	−15°	Jan. 1963	33	80	1	97	96	172	107	2	16
TEXAS													
Abilene	111°	Aug. 1943	− 9°	Jan. 1947	107	30	0	131	99	135	65	1	7
Amarillo	108°	June 1953	−16°	Feb. 1899	66	97	2	135	91	139	89	1	28
Austin	109°	Aug. 1954	− 2°	Jan. 1949	119	10	0	106	110	149	87	0	34
Brownsville	104°	Sept. 1947	12°	Feb. 1899	148	0	0	101	126	138	84	0	27
Dallas–Fort Worth	112°	Aug. 1936	− 8°	Feb. 1899	104	33	0	126	103	136	82	0	15
El Paso	112°	July 1979	− 8°	Jan. 1962	100	54	0	171	100	94	61	2	4
Galveston	101°	July 1932	8°	Feb. 1899	35	2	0	—	—	—	94	0	—
Houston	108°	Aug. 1909	5°	Jan. 1940	118	11	0	95	113	157	97	0	28
San Antonio	107°	Aug. 1909	0°	Jan. 1949	114	21	0	75	129	161	92	0	21
UTAH													
Salt Lake City	107°	July 1960	−30°	Feb. 1933	59	97	0	89	104	172	99	15	12
VERMONT													
Burlington	101°	Aug. 1944	−30°	Jan. 1957	3	146	22	57	86	222	165	26	12
VIRGINIA													
Norfolk	105°	Aug. 1918	2°	Feb. 1895	31	76	0	115	95	155	112	1	13
Richmond	107°	Aug. 1918	−12°	Jan. 1940	43	102	0	94	110	161	105	1	18
Roanoke	105°	July 1936	−12°	Dec. 1917	25	113	0	106	102	157	98	5	14
WASHINGTON													
Olympia	103°	July 1941	− 7°	Jan. 1972	14	75	0	40	84	241	178	2	109
Seattle–Tacoma	100°	June 1955	0°	Jan. 1950	6	22	0	52	97	216	155	1	43
Spokane	108°	Aug. 1961	−30°	Jan. 1888	20	133	0	85	93	187	100	8	40
Walla Walla	113°	Aug. 1961	−29°	Jan. 1875	39	48	0	109	95	161	114	3	—
Yakima	111°	July 1928	−25°	Feb. 1950	40	115	0	111	94	160	72	7	15
WEST VIRGINIA													
Charleston	108°	July 1931	−17°	Dec. 1917	18	114	2	82	106	177	158	12	77
Huntington	108°	July 1930	−15°	Jan. 1963	16	106	2	61	108	196	136	5	48
Parkersburg	106°	Aug. 1918	−27°	Feb. 1899	7	111	0	—	—	—	122	7	—
WISCONSIN													
Green Bay	104°	July 1936	−36°	Jan. 1888	5	158	20	87	94	184	107	10	12
Madison	107°	July 1936	−37°	Jan. 1951	5	162	16	94	95	176	115	10	23
Milwaukee	105°	July 1934	−26°	Jan. 1982	2	136	14	81	99	185	111	10	20
WYOMING													
Casper	104°	July 1954	−40°	Jan. 1972	38	161	8	86	104	175	95	14	5
Cheyenne	100°	June 1954	−38°	Jan. 1875	8	154	4	96	130	139	99	13	25
Sheridan	106°	July 1954	−41°	Dec. 1919	30	176	10	115	119	131	89	10	3
AMERICAN SAMOA													
Pago Pago	92°	Feb. 1977	62°	July 1964	9	0	0	6	119	240	275	0	0
GUAM													
Taguac	95°	Sept. 1957	54°	Mar. 1965	2	0	0	4	119	242	296	0	—
PACIFIC ISLANDS													
Johnston Island	89°	Nov. 1969	62°	Dec. 1964	0	0	0	118	157	90	174	0	0
Kwajalein Island	97°	Oct. 1958	69°	Dec. 1963	7	0	0	21	89	255	212	0	0
Wake Island	93°	Aug. 1978	64°	Dec. 1954	53	0	0	135	135	95	184	0	0
PUERTO RICO													
San Juan	96°	June 1975	60°	Mar. 1957	152	0	0	48	208	109	199	0	0

[1] Average per year. [2] Highest temperature 90°F. or above. [3] Lowest temperature 32°F. or below. [4] Lowest temperature 0°F. or below. [5] Rain of 0.01 inch or more. [6] Snow of 1 inch or more. [7] Visibility of 1/4 mile or less.

WEATHER IN FOREIGN COUNTRIES AND CITIES

Source: Environmental Data Service, *Climates of the World*

COUNTRY AND CITY	TEMPERATURES (in degrees Fahrenheit)						RAINFALL (in inches)				
	Extremes		Daily Average Range								
	Low	High	Jan.	April	July	Oct.	Annual	Jan.	Apr.	July	Oct.
Afghanistan: Kabul	– 6	104	18–36	43–66	61–92	42–73	12.6	3.1	0.3	0.1	T
Algeria: Algiers	32	107	49–59	55–68	70–83	63–74	30.0	4.4	1.6	T	3.1
Angola: Luanda	58	98	.74–83	75–85	65–74	71–79	12.7	1.0	4.6	T	0.2
Argentina: Buenos Aires	22	104	63–85	53–72	42–57	50–69	37.4	3.1	3.5	2.2	3.4
Australia: Canberra	14	109	55–82	44–67	33–52	43–68	23.0	1.9	1.6	1.8	2.2
Austria: Vienna	–14	98	26–34	41–57	59–75	44–55	25.6	1.5	2.0	3.0	2.0
Bahamas: Nassau	41	94	65–77	69–81	75–88	73–85	46.4	1.4	2.5	5.8	6.5
Bangladesh: Dhaka	43	108	56–77	74–92	79–88	75–88	73.9	0.3	5.4	13.0	5.3
Barbados: Bridgetown	61	95	70–83	72–86	74–86	73–86	50.3	2.6	1.4	5.8	7.0
Bermuda: Hamilton	40	99	58–68	59–71	73–85	69–79	57.6	4.4	4.1	4.5	5.8
Bolivia: La Paz	26	80	43–63	40–65	33–62	40–66	22.6	4.5	1.3	0.4	1.6
Brazil: Brasília	46	93	65–80	62–82	51–78	64–82	54.0	9.0	3.4	0.0	4.9
Rio de Janeiro	46	102	73–84	69–80	63–75	66–77	42.6	4.9	4.2	1.6	3.1
Britain: London	9	99	35–44	40–56	55–73	44–58	22.9	2.0	1.8	2.0	2.3
Bulgaria: Sofia	–17	99	22–34	41–62	57–82	42–63	25.0	1.3	2.3	2.4	2.1
Burma: Mandalay	44	111	55–82	77–101	78–93	73–89	32.6	0.1	1.2	2.7	4.3
Canada: Edmonton, Alta.	–57	99	–3–16	28–52	50–74	30–51	18.0	0.9	1.0	3.3	0.8
Montreal, Que.	–35	97	6–21	33–50	61–78	40–54	40.8	3.8	2.6	3.7	3.4
Ottawa, Ont.	–38	102	3–21	31–51	58–81	37–54	34.3	2.9	2.7	3.4	2.9
St. John, N.B.	–24	93	11–28	32–43	54–69	41–54	42.6	4.1	3.2	3.1	4.1
Vancouver, B.C.	2	92	32–41	40–58	54–74	44–57	57.4	8.6	3.3	1.2	5.8
Winnipeg, Man.	–54	108	–13–7	27–48	55–79	31–51	21.2	0.9	1.4	3.1	1.5
Canary Islands: Las Palmas	46	99	58–70	61–71	67–77	67–79	8.6	1.4	0.5	T	1.1
Central Africa: Bangui	57	101	68–90	71–91	69–85	69–87	60.8	1.0	5.3	8.9	7.9
Chad: N'Djamena	47	114	57–93	74–107	72–92	70–97	29.3	0.0	0.1	6.7	1.4
Chile: Santiago	24	99	53–85	45–74	37–59	45–72	14.2	0.1	0.5	3.0	0.6
China: Canton	31	101	49–65	65–77	77–91	67–85	63.6	0.9	6.8	8.1	3.4
Shanghai	–3	109	16–33	45–68	73–90	48–68	21.0	0.2	0.5	7.6	0.6
Tientsin	–30	112	–7–13	36–60	58–82	31–50	11.5	0.6	1.5	0.7	1.7
Colombia: Bogotá	30	75	48–67	51–67	50–64	50–66	41.8	2.3	5.8	2.0	6.3
Congo: Brazzaville	54	98	69–88	71–91	63–82	70–89	58.0	6.3	7.0	T	5.4
Costa Rica: San José	49	92	58–75	62–79	62–77	60–77	70.8	0.6	1.8	8.3	11.8
Cuba: Havana	43	104	65–79	69–84	75–89	73–85	48.2	2.8	2.3	4.9	6.8
Cyprus: Nicosia	23	116	42–58	50–74	69–97	58–81	14.6	2.9	0.8	T	0.9
Czechoslovakia: Prague	–16	101	25–34	40–55	58–74	44–54	19.3	0.9	1.5	2.6	1.2
Denmark: Copenhagen	– 3	91	29–36	37–50	55–72	42–53	23.3	1.6	1.7	2.2	3.2
Dominican R.: Santo Domingo	59	98	66–84	69–85	72–88	72–87	55.8	2.4	3.9	6.4	6.0
Ecuador: Quito	25	86	46–67	47–69	44–71	46–71	43.9	3.9	6.9	0.8	4.4
Egypt: Cairo	34	117	47–65	57–83	70–96	65–86	1.1	0.2	0.1	0.0	T
El Salvador: San Salvador	45	105	60–90	65–93	65–89	65–87	70.0	0.3	1.7	11.5	9.5
Ethiopia: Addis Ababa	32	94	43–75	50–77	50–69	45–75	48.7	0.5	3.4	11.8	0.6
Finland: Helsinki	–23	89	17–27	31–43	57–71	37–45	27.6	2.2	1.7	2.3	2.9
France: Marseille	9	101	38–53	41–59	58–78	57–76	23.2	1.9	2.0	0.6	3.7
Paris	1	105	32–42	41–60	55–76	44–59	22.3	1.5	1.7	2.1	2.2
Germany, East: Berlin	–15	96	26–35	38–55	55–74	41–55	23.1	1.9	1.7	3.1	1.7
Germany, West: Hamburg	– 4	92	28–35	39–51	56–69	44–53	28.9	2.1	1.8	3.4	2.6
Munich	–14	99	23–33	37–54	54–72	40–53	34.1	1.7	2.7	4.7	2.2
Ghana: Accra	59	100	73–87	76–88	73–81	74–85	28.5	1.3	3.2	1.8	2.5
Greece: Athens	20	109	42–54	52–67	72–90	60–74	15.8	2.2	0.8	0.2	1.7
Guadeloupe: Basse-Terre	54	92	64–77	65–79	68–81	68–81	140.4	9.2	7.3	17.6	12.4
Guam: Agana	54	95	72–84	73–86	72–87	73–86	88.5	4.6	3.0	9.0	13.1
Guatemala: Guatemala City	41	90	53–73	58–82	60–78	60–76	51.8	0.3	1.2	8.0	6.8
Guinea: Conakry	63	96	72–88	73–90	72–83	73–87	169.0	0.1	0.9	51.1	14.6
Haiti: Port-au-Prince	58	101	68–87	71–89	74–94	72–90	53.3	1.3	6.3	2.9	6.7
Honduras: Tegucigalpa	58	96	67–82	72–87	73–88	71–86	96.1	8.9	3.3	6.4	13.5
Hong Kong: Victoria	32	97	56–64	67–75	78–87	73–81	85.1	1.3	5.4	15.0	4.5
Hungary: Budapest	–10	103	26–35	44–62	61–82	45–61	24.2	1.5	2.0	2.0	2.1
Iceland: Reykjavik	4	74	28–36	33–43	48–58	36–44	33.9	4.0	2.1	2.0	3.4
India: Calcutta	44	111	55–80	76–97	79–90	74–89	63.0	0.4	1.7	12.8	4.5
New Delhi	31	115	43–71	68–97	80–95	64–93	25.2	0.9	0.3	7.1	0.4
Indonesia: Jakarta	66	98	74–84	75–87	73–87	74–87	70.8	11.8	5.8	2.5	4.4
Iran: Tehran	– 5	109	27–45	49–71	72–99	53–76	9.7	1.8	1.4	0.1	0.3
Iraq: Baghdad	18	121	39–60	57–85	76–110	61–92	5.5	0.9	0.5	T	0.1
Ireland: Dublin	8	86	35–47	38–54	51–67	43–57	29.7	2.7	1.9	2.8	2.7
Ireland, Northern: Belfast	14	82	34–42	38–53	52–65	44–55	38.2	4.2	2.4	3.5	3.8
Israel: Jerusalem	26	107	41–55	50–73	63–87	59–81	19.7	5.1	0.9	0.0	0.3
Italy: Rome	20	104	39–54	46–68	64–88	53–73	29.5	3.3	2.0	0.4	4.3

T = trace, less than 0.05 inch. [1] Average daily minimum and maximum temperatures.

COUNTRY AND CITY	TEMPERATURES (in degrees Fahrenheit)						RAINFALL (in inches)				
	Extremes		Daily Average Range								
	Low	High	Jan.	April	July	Oct.	Annual	Jan.	Apr.	July	Oct.
Jamaica: Kingston	56	97	67–86	70–87	73–90	73–88	31.5	0.9	1.2	1.5	7.1
Japan: Tokyo	17	101	29–47	46–63	70–83	55–69	61.6	1.9	5.3	5.6	8.2
Jordan: Amman	21	109	39–54	49–73	65–89	57–81	10.9	2.7	0.6	0.0	0.2
Kenya: Nairobi	41	87	54–77	58–75	51–69	55–76	41.8	1.5	8.3	0.6	2.1
Korea, South: Seoul	–12	99	15–32	41–62	70–84	45–67	49.2	1.2	3.0	14.8	1.6
Lebanon: Beirut	30	107	51–62	58–72	73–87	69–81	35.1	7.5	2.2	T	2.0
Liberia: Monrovia	62	97	71–89	72–90	72–80	72–86	174.9	0.2	11.7	24.2	25.2
Libya: Tripoli	33	114	47–61	57–72	71–85	65–80	15.1	3.2	0.4	T	1.6
Madagascar: Antananarivo	34	95	61–79	58–76	48–68	54–80	53.4	11.8	2.1	0.3	2.4
Malaysia: Kuala Lumpur	64	99	72–90	74–91	72–90	73–89	96.1	6.2	11.5	3.9	9.8
Mali: Bamako	47	117	61–91	76–103	71–89	71–93	44.1	T	0.6	11.0	1.7
Malta: Valletta	34	105	51–59	56–66	72–84	66–76	20.3	3.3	0.8	T	2.7
Martinique: Fort-de-France	56	96	69–83	71–86	74–86	73–87	80.4	4.7	3.9	9.4	9.7
Mauritania: Nouakchott	44	115	57–85	64–90	74–89	71–91	6.2	T	T	0.5	0.4
Mauritius: Port-Louis	50	95	73–86	70–82	62–75	64–80	50.6	8.5	5.0	2.3	1.6
Mexico: Acapulco	60	97	70–85	71–87	75–89	74–88	55.1	0.3	T	9.1	6.7
Chihuahua	12	102	36–65	51–81	66–89	51–79	15.4	0.2	0.2	3.6	0.9
Mexico City	24	92	42–66	52–78	54–74	50–70	23.0	0.2	0.7	4.5	1.6
Monterrey	25	107	48–68	62–84	71–90	64–80	22.9	0.6	1.3	2.4	3.0
Veracruz	53	98	66–77	72–83	74–87	73–85	65.7	0.9	0.8	4.1	6.9
Morocco: Rabat	32	118	46–63	52–71	63–82	58–77	19.8	2.6	1.7	T	1.9
Mozambique: Maputo	45	114	71–86	66–83	55–76	64–82	29.9	5.1	2.1	0.5	1.9
Netherlands: Amsterdam	3	95	34–40	43–52	59–69	48–56	25.6	2.0	1.6	2.6	2.8
New Zealand: Wellington	29	88	56–69	51–63	42–53	48–60	47.4	3.2	3.8	5.4	4.0
Nigeria: Lagos	60	104	74–88	77–89	74–83	74–85	72.3	1.1	5.9	11.0	8.1
Norway: Oslo	–21	93	20–30	34–50	56–73	37–49	26.9	1.7	1.6	2.9	2.9
Pakistan: Islamabad	25	118	38–62	59–86	77–98	57–89	36.5	2.5	1.9	8.1	0.6
Panama: Panama City	63	97	71–88	74–90	74–87	73–85	69.7	1.0	2.9	7.1	10.1
Papua N.G.: Port Moresby	64	98	76–89	75–87	73–83	75–86	39.8	7.0	4.2	1.1	1.4
Paraguay: Asunción	29	110	71–95	65–84	53–74	62–86	51.8	5.5	5.2	2.2	5.5
Peru: Lima	49	93	66–82	63–80	57–67	58–71	1.6	0.1	T	0.3	0.1
Philippines: Manila	58	101	69–86	73–93	75–88	74–88	82.0	0.9	1.3	17.0	7.6
Poland: Warsaw	–22	98	21–30	38–54	56–75	41–54	22.0	1.2	1.5	3.0	1.7
Portugal: Lisbon	29	103	46–56	52–64	63–79	57–69	27.0	3.3	2.4	0.2	3.1
Puerto Rico: San Juan	60	94	67–81	69–84	74–87	73–87	64.2	4.7	3.7	6.3	5.8
Romania: Bucharest	–18	105	20–33	41–63	61–86	44–65	22.8	1.5	1.6	2.3	1.6
Samoa, American: Pago Pago	67	98	75–87	76–87	74–83	75–85	193.6	24.5	16.5	10.0	14.9
Saudi Arabia: Riyadh	19	113	46–70	64–89	78–107	61–94	3.2	0.1	1.0	0.0	0.0
Senegal: Dakar	53	109	64–79	65–81	76–88	76–89	21.3	T	T	3.5	1.5
Seychelles: Victoria	67	92	76–83	77–86	75–81	75–83	92.5	15.2	7.2	3.3	6.1
Singapore: Singapore	66	97	73–86	75–88	75–88	74–87	95.0	9.9	7.4	6.7	8.2
Solomons: Tulagi	68	96	76–88	76–88	76–86	76–87	123.4	14.3	10.0	7.6	8.7
Somalia: Mogadiscio	59	97	73–86	78–90	73–83	76–86	16.9	T	2.3	2.5	0.9
South Africa: Cape Town	28	103	60–78	53–72	45–63	52–70	20.0	0.6	1.9	3.5	1.2
Soviet Union: Leningrad	–36	91	12–23	31–45	57–71	37–45	19.2	1.0	1.0	2.5	1.8
Moscow	–49	96	9–21	31–47	55–76	34–46	24.8	1.5	1.9	3.0	2.7
Spain: Madrid	14	102	33–47	44–64	62–87	48–66	16.5	1.1	1.7	0.4	1.9
Sri Lanka: Colombo	59	99	72–86	76–88	77–85	75–85	92.3	3.5	9.1	5.3	13.7
Sudan: Khartoum	41	118	59–90	72–105	77–101	75–104	6.2	T	T	2.1	0.2
Suriname: Paramaribo	62	99	72–85	73–86	73–87	73–91	91.0	8.4	9.0	9.1	3.0
Sweden: Stockholm	–26	97	23–31	32–45	55–70	39–48	22.4	1.5	1.5	2.8	2.1
Switzerland: Bern	–9	96	26–35	39–56	56–74	42–55	38.5	1.9	3.0	4.4	3.5
Syria: Damascus	21	113	36–53	49–75	64–96	54–81	8.6	1.7	0.5	T	0.4
Tahiti: Papeete	61	93	72–89	72–89	68–86	70–87	74.7	13.2	6.8	2.6	3.4
Taiwan: Taipei	32	101	53–66	64–77	76–92	68–80	72.7	3.8	5.3	8.8	5.5
Tanzania: Dar es Salaam	59	96	77–83	73–86	66–83	69–85	41.9	2.6	11.4	1.2	1.6
Thailand: Bangkok	50	104	67–89	78–95	76–90	76–88	57.8	0.2	2.3	6.9	9.9
Togo: Lomé	58	94	72–85	74–86	71–80	72–83	31.0	0.6	4.6	2.8	2.4
Trinidad-Tob.: Port of Spain	52	101	69–87	69–90	71–88	71–89	64.2	2.7	2.1	8.6	6.7
Tunisia: Tunis	30	118	43–58	51–70	68–90	59–77	16.5	2.5	1.4	0.1	2.0
Turkey: Istanbul	17	100	36–45	45–61	65–81	54–67	31.5	3.7	1.9	1.7	3.8
Uganda: Kampala	53	97	65–83	64–79	62–77	63–81	46.2	1.8	6.9	1.8	3.8
Upper Volta: Ouagadougou	48	118	60–92	79–103	74–91	74–95	35.2	T	0.6	8.0	1.3
Uruguay: Montevideo	25	109	62–83	53–71	43–58	49–68	37.4	2.9	3.9	2.9	2.6
Venezuela: Caracas	45	91	56–75	60–81	61–78	61–79	32.9	0.9	1.3	4.3	4.3
Vietnam: Hanoi	41	108	58–68	70–80	79–92	72–84	69.4	0.8	3.6	11.9	3.5
Virgin Is., U.S.: Charlotte Amalie	63	92	71–82	74–85	77–88	76–87	43.7	2.5	2.2	3.2	5.6
Yugoslavia: Belgrade	–14	107	27–37	45–64	61–84	47–65	24.6	1.6	2.2	1.9	2.7
Zaire: Kinshasa	58	97	70–87	71–89	64–81	70–88	53.3	5.3	7.7	0.1	4.7
Zambia: Lusaka	39	100	63–78	59–79	49–73	64–88	32.9	9.1	0.7	T	0.4
Zimbabwe: Harare	32	95	60–78	55–78	44–70	58–83	32.6	7.7	1.1	T	1.1

CAUSES OF CLIMATE AND WEATHER

Source: Environmental Data Service, U.S. Department of Commerce

The climate of a place is the long-term normal weather for a given day, month, season, or year. It is the weather we expect for spring in our hometown or for vacation time at our favorite camping grounds. These expectations are based on weather data collected over a relatively long period, usually several decades.

In contrast, weather is the current or recent state of the atmosphere. Both can be described in terms of temperature, pressure, humidity, sunshine, winds, clouds, and precipitation. For example, temperature in weather is the present temperature at a place, while temperature in climate is the average temperature for the location, determined from previous records.

The underlying causes of weather and climate are heat from the Sun and the rotation of the Earth. The radiant energy of the Sun and the constant rotation of the Earth about its axis serve to set up circulation patterns within the atmosphere. These circulation patterns carry heat and moisture from the equator to the poles, across land and sea, and over flat land and mountains. Patterns of winds, rainfall, cloudiness, and temperature tend to remain relatively steady at any given location on Earth. Weather tends to follow the same pattern year after year. These patterns determine the climate of a place.

Briefly, climate is controlled by latitude, land surfaces and sources of moisture, prevailing winds, ocean currents, elevation, and mountain barriers.

LATITUDE

Heat from the Sun reaches the Earth after passing through approximately 93 million miles of space. The rays reaching the equator appear to come from nearly directly overhead. At points nearer the poles, the Sun appears lower in the sky. The position of the Sun causes warm climates in the equatorial regions and successively cooler climates toward the poles—thus the higher the latitude, the cooler the climate.

Seasons modify the latitude effect because of the tilt of the axis of the Earth. The Earth's axis is tilted 23.5 degrees from a line perpendicular to the plane that contains the Sun and the Earth's orbit around the Sun. Beginning about September 21 and ending about March 21, the north end of the axis points away from the Sun, so the rays from the Sun are more slanting in the Northern Hemisphere and more directly overhead in the Southern Hemisphere.

The length of daylight, hence the length of time a location receives solar heat, increases as we move from the pole to the equator during winter. During summer, the length of daylight increases north of the equator, but the more slanted rays of the Sun keep the higher latitudes cooler than the low latitudes.

LAND SURFACES AND SOURCES OF MOISTURE

Land and water surfaces react differently to the incoming rays of the Sun. In general, land surfaces are heated rapidly by the Sun, but the heat does not penetrate deeply, so land surfaces also cool rapidly. On the other hand, water warms up slowly, holds a much larger quantity of heat than the land surface, and cools slowly.

As a result the surface layer of air over the continents is warmer in summer and colder in winter than that over the oceans. Because warm air rises, permitting air from cooler areas to flow in to replace it, there is a net inflow of cool ocean air onto continents in summer and an outflow from the continents in winter. Land and sea breezes result from a similar situation in coastal areas, where the land is colder than the water at night and early morning but warmer later in the day.

Sources of moisture—oceans, gulfs, lakes, and other large bodies of water—have a major influence on the climate of an area. Places in the interior of continents usually tend to be hotter and drier in summer and colder in winter than coastal areas, and usually have greater differences between daily high and low temperatures.

PREVAILING WINDS

The uneven heating of the Earth by the Sun is the main cause of wind systems. The equatorial regions receive considerably more solar heat per square mile than do the polar regions. Warm equatorial surface air rises and is replaced by cooler surface air flowing in from the poles. The unequal heating of the Earth's surface together with its rotation produces a general global movement of air.

The global air movement causes a worldwide pattern of prevailing winds. Surface winds in the Northern Hemisphere are arranged in three broad belts: the northeast trades (from the northeast) in the tropics and subtropics; the prevailing westerlies (from the west to southwest) in the middle latitudes; and the polar easterlies (from the northeast) in the polar region.

HIGH- AND LOW-PRESSURE AREAS

The rotation of the Earth about its axis causes winds to turn to the right (clockwise) in the Northern Hemisphere. For example, a wind blowing from south to north turns toward the east. Similarly, a north wind turns toward the west. The resulting huge whirling masses of air are called high-pressure areas (also called highs or anticyclones). Between these highs are low-pressure areas (also called lows or cyclones) that rotate to the left (counterclockwise). Air tends to flow inward toward low-pressure centers and outward from high-pressure areas.

AIR MASSES

When temperature and humidity are very much the same throughout any level in a high-pressure area, the high is called an *air mass.* Four general types of air masses are recognized in the United States: (1) cold dry air masses that move in from Canada, generally traveling south-eastward; (2) cool moist air masses that generally travel eastward across the states from the Pacific Ocean; (3) warm moist air masses that move in from the Pacific, the Gulf of Mexico, or the Atlantic; and (4) warm dry air masses that may move from the southwest.

STORMS

Most storms and active weather occur in and around the low-pressure areas between highs.

The Canadian highs bring cool dry conditions. As they move into an area, they usually are preceded by showers along or adjacent to a cold front. The Pacific highs, also preceded by fronts, are moister and somewhat warmer than the Canadian highs.

Lows bring in warm humid air from the Pacific, the Gulf of Mexico, or the Atlantic. Lows are usually accompanied by widespread rain or snow.

The migrating highs and lows occur more frequently, are more intense, and travel faster in winter than in summer. Average motion is 750 miles per day in winter and 500 in summer.

The air masses that prevail over an area determine its climate. For example, the southeastern states are dominated in summer by a moist tropical air mass associated with a high-pressure area located offshore. The southerly winds on the west side of this high bring moist air from the Gulf of Mexico into these states. In winter the southern states are invaded by Canadian air masses that bring cold fronts across the area about once every five days.

Severe local storms, such as thunderstorms and tornadoes, and tropical cyclones up to hurricane intensity are superimposed on the general climatic pattern.

Winds in the upper atmosphere tend to "steer" moving air masses at lower levels. The jet stream, a meandering current of air at 30,000 to 50,000 feet, moves air masses in a generally eastward direction.

SEMIPERMANENT HIGHS AND LOWS

Wind and storm patterns are strongly influenced by the locations and intensities of semipermanent high- and low-pressure areas.

The Aleutian low is the semipermanent pressure system that dominates the northern end of the North Pacific. This low intensifies and expands in winter and weakens and moves to the northwest in summer. Its average central pressure in February is 29.50 inches.

The Pacific high, another semipermanent pressure system, intensifies and expands in summer. The average summer pressure at the center of this high is 30.27 inches at its center, about 1,600 miles west of San Francisco. In its summer position, this semipermanent Pacific high effectively blocks the passage of storms into the California-Oregon-Washington coastal area, steering them instead to the coast of British Columbia. In autumn and winter this high becomes weak, and its center moves to the southwest. In this new position, it cannot block the movement of storms to the coast, so there is an increase in the frequency of storms reaching the Washington coast by September. By late November and December, storms reach the coast as far south as southern California.

The semipermanent pressure systems in the Atlantic are the Icelandic low and the Bermuda (or Azores) high. Many of the storms associated with migratory low-pressure areas in the central and eastern United States tend to drift toward the Icelandic low. The favored path of these storms is across the Great Lakes and along the valley of the St. Lawrence River.

During summer, the Bermuda high has a marked effect on the eastern states. This high is strongest in summer when it lies off the East Coast and brings a southerly flow of warm moist maritime air from the Caribbean Sea. On occasion, this warm moist air is carried into the Arizona-New Mexico area, bringing welcome rainfall.

OCEAN CURRENTS

Well-established ocean currents have a great effect on the climates of coastal areas. Perhaps the best-known ocean current is the Gulf Stream that carries warm waters from the Florida Straits northward along the Atlantic coast and then northeastward and eastward to the British Isles. Winds blowing across this warm stream of water pick up heat and moisture and bring them over the East Coast.

The climate of the East Coast is also affected by the cold Labrador Current, which flows southward as far as Norfolk, Va. This current is responsible for frequent fogs over the coast.

The Japanese Current is the major ocean current affecting the West Coast. This current reaches the west coast of the continent at about the latitude of the United States-Canada border. Here it branches. One branch, the Alaska Current, turns northward bringing a milder warmer climate to coastal British Columbia and Alaska. The other branch, the California Current, turns southward bringing cooler water along the shore of Washington, Oregon, and California. During winter, the Davidson Current moves in from southeast of the California Current, bringing warmer weather to the coast.

ELEVATION

Temperature in the atmosphere decreases with increasing elevation, or altitude. The usual rate of decrease is 3.3 °F. per 1,000 feet. The climatic mean temperature on a mountain generally is 3.3 °F. lower per 1,000 feet of elevation than that of nearby lower altitude stations.

MOUNTAIN BARRIERS

Mountain ranges not only have colder temperatures at higher elevations but they also act as barriers to block the flow of prevailing winds and the movement of storms.

Air flowing upward on the slopes of a mountain barrier tends to drop much of its moisture on the windward side of the range. This is the reason deserts lie to the east of the Coast Ranges and the Cascade–Sierra Nevada ranges of California.

Because mountain ranges in the United States run north and south, they block the flow of the prevailing westerlies. Moisture-laden air from the Pacific is forced up the slopes of the Coast and Cascade–Sierra Nevada ranges where it dumps most of its moisture. In the east the Appalachian Mountains tend to block the flow of Atlantic air into the interior but permit the free passage of the cold arctic and polar air masses of Canada over the central and eastern two-thirds of the United States.

The lack of an east-west mountain barrier allows a northward flow of warm maritime tropical air far northward into the interior.

BE YOUR OWN WEATHER FORECASTER

Source: NOAA, U.S. Department of Commerce

You can forecast weather merely by observing the direction from which the wind blows and reading the level of air pressure on a barometer.

The following table summarizes wind and barometer indications of approaching weather that are generally applicable to most U.S. regions.

WIND DIRECTION	BAROMETER (reduced to sea level)	WEATHER FORECAST
SW to NW	30.10 to 30.20 and steady	Fair, with slight temperature changes for 1 to 2 days
SW to NW	30.10 to 30.20, rising rapidly	Fair, followed within 2 days by rain
SW to NW	30.20 and above, stationary	Continued fair with no decided temperature change
SW to NW	30.20 and above, falling slowly	Slowly rising temperature and fair for 2 days
S to SW	30.00 or below, rising slowly	Clearing within a few hours and fair for several days
S to E	29.80 or below, falling rapidly	Severe storm imminent, followed within 24 hours by clearing and in winter by colder temperatures
S to SE	30.10 to 30.20, falling slowly	Rain within 24 hours
S to SE	30.10 to 30.20, falling rapidly	Wind increasing in force; rain within 12 to 24 hours
SE to NE	30.10 to 30.20, falling slowly	Rain in 12 to 18 hours
SE to NE	30.10 to 30.20, falling rapidly	Increasing wind; rain within 12 hours
SE to NE	30.00 or below, falling slowly	Rain will continue 1 to 2 days
SE to NE	30.00 or below, falling rapidly	Rain with high wind, followed within 36 hours by clearing, and in winter by colder temperatures
E to NE	30.10 and above, falling slowly	In summer, with light winds, rain may not fall for several days; in winter, rain within 24 hours
E to NE	30.10 and above, falling rapidly	In summer, rain probable within 12 to 24 hours; in winter, rain or snow with increasing winds
E to N	29.80 or below, falling rapidly	Severe northeast gale; in summer, heavy rain; in winter, heavy snow followed by cold wave
Easterly	29.80 or below, rising rapidly	Clearing and colder

CLOUD FORMATIONS—AND WHAT THEY MEAN

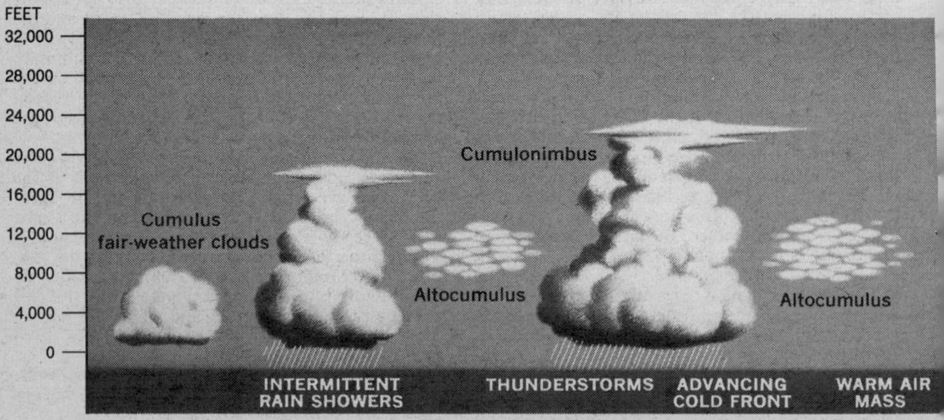

WIND CHILL—WHY YOU FEEL COLDER THAN THE THERMOMETER

Source: Environmental Data Service, NOAA, U.S. Department of Commerce

In winter the stronger the wind the colder the weather seems. The wind causes the chill that you *feel* to be even colder than the temperature *shown* on your thermometer. The following wind-chill table prepared by the National Weather Service can help you find what the equivalent wind-chill temperature is when you know the thermometer temperature and the wind speed. For example, if the thermometer shows a temperature of 15° and you know that the wind speed is 10 mph, then look in the table and you will see that the wind-chill temperature you will feel is 3° below zero.

	THERMOMETER TEMPERATURES IN DEGREES FAHRENHEIT													
	35°	30°	25°	20°	15°	10°	5°	0°	-5°	-10°	-15°	-20°	-25°	-30°
WIND SPEED	EQUIVALENT WIND–CHILL TEMPERATURES (HOW COLD YOU SEEM TO FEEL)													
5 mph	32°	27°	22°	16°	11°	6°	0°	- 5°	-10°	-15°	-21°	-26°	-31°	- 36°
10 mph	22°	16°	10°	3°	- 3°	- 9°	-15°	-22°	-27°	-34°	-40°	-46°	-52°	- 58°
15 mph	16°	9°	2°	- 5°	-11°	-18°	-25°	-31°	-38°	-45°	-51°	-58°	-65°	- 72°
20 mph	12°	4°	- 3°	-10°	-17°	-24°	-31°	-39°	-46°	-53°	-60°	-67°	-74°	- 81°
25 mph	8°	1°	- 7°	-15°	-22°	-29°	-36°	-44°	-51°	-59°	-66°	-74°	-81°	- 88°
30 mph	6°	-2°	-10°	-18°	-25°	-33°	-41°	-49°	-56°	-64°	-71°	-79°	-86°	- 93°
35 mph	4°	-4°	-12°	-20°	-27°	-35°	-43°	-52°	-58°	-67°	-74°	-82°	-89°	- 97°
40 mph	3°	-5°	-13°	-21°	-29°	-37°	-45°	-53°	-60°	-69°	-76°	-84°	-92°	-100°
45 mph	2°	-6°	-14°	-22°	-30°	-38°	-46°	-54°	-62°	-70°	-78°	-85°	-93°	-102°
50 mph	0°	-7°	-17°	-24°	-31°	-38°	-47°	-56°	-63°	-70°	-79°	-88°	-96°	-103°

BEAUFORT WIND SCALE

The Beaufort wind scale indicates wind strength by a series of numbers. it was developed in 1805 by a British admiral, Sir Francis Beaufort, to help gauge wind speed without an instrument.

BEAUFORT NUMBER	WIND NAME	SPEED (mph)	OBSERVED EFFECT OF WIND
0	Calm	0–1	Calm. Smoke rises straight up into the air.
1	Light Air	1–3	Weather vanes remain motionless. Smoke drifts slightly with wind.
2	Light Breeze	4–7	Weather vanes active. You can feel wind on your face. Leaves rustle.
3	Gentle Breeze	8–12	Light flags fill out with wind. Twigs on trees move.
4	Moderate Breeze	13–18	The wind picks up dust and loose paper. Small tree branches sway.
5	Fresh Breeze	19–24	Waves break on inland waters. Small trees sway in the wind.
6	Strong Breeze	25–31	Using an umbrella becomes difficult. Large tree branches sway.
7	Near Gale	32–38	Walking against the wind is difficult. Entire large trees sway.
8	Gale	39–46	Walking against the wind is almost impossible. Twigs break off trees.
9	Strong Gale	47–54	Shingles blown off house roofs. Some damage to buildings.
10	Storm	55–63	Entire trees blown over and uprooted. Much damage to buildings.
11	Violent Storm	64–72	Severe damage to crops, trees, and property.
12	Hurricane	73–82	Widespread violent destruction.

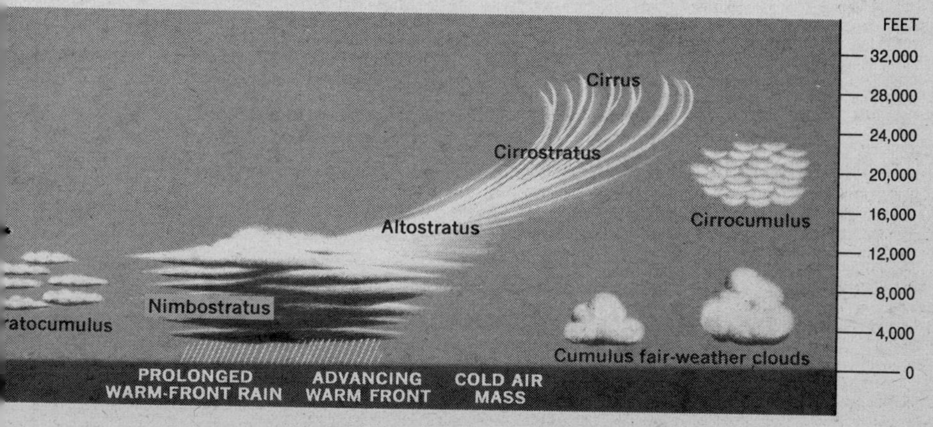

RECORD U.S. BLIZZARDS AND SNOWSTORMS

Source: Environmental Data Service, NOAA, U.S. Department of Commerce

DATE	PLACE	DEPTH	DESCRIPTION
1717, Feb. 19–24	New England	60–72 in.	The "great snow"; drifts cover many one-story houses
1888, March 11–14	Northeast States	40–50 in.	Snow and winds to 70 mph; over 400 deaths
1899, Feb. 11–14	Washington, D.C.	35.2 in.	Record snowfall in one month for capital
1901, April 19–21	Watertown, Ohio	45 in.	Greatest 24-hour snowfall in state
1911, Jan.	Tamarack, Calif.	390 in.	Greatest U.S. snowfall in one month
1921, April 14–15	Silver Lake, Colo.	95 in.	Record snowfall of 75.8 inches in 24 hours
1921, Nov. 17–20	The Dalles, Oreg.	54 in.	Record snowfall for state
1922, Jan. 27–29	Washington, D.C.	28 in.	Snow collapses Knickerbocker theater, killing 98
1928, April 27–28	Bayard, W. Va.	34 in.	Record 24-hour snowfall (34 inches) for state
1933, Jan. 18–19	Giant Forest, Calif.	60 in.	Record 24-hour snowfall for state
1935, Jan. 20–24	Winthrop, Wash.	52 in.	Record 24-hour snowfall for state
1940, Jan. 18–22	Watertown, N.Y.	69 in.	Record snowfall for state
1940, Jan. 23–24	Louisville, Miss.	15.5 in.	Record 24-hour snowfall for state
1940, Nov. 11–12	Iowa to Minnesota	—	144 deaths; subzero temperatures; high winds
1946, January	Stampede Pass, Wash.	192.9 in.	Record snowfall in one month
1946, Nov. 2–6	New Mexico	36 in.	Unprecedented heavy snowfall
1947, March 2–5	Readsboro, Vt.	50 in.	Record snowfall for state
1947, March 2–5	Peru, Mass.	47 in.	Record snowfall for state
1949, Jan. 1–6	Colorado to Dakotas	7–30 in.	39 deaths; severe blizzard; 70 mph winds
1950, March 25–27	Dumont, S.D.	60 in.	Record snowfall for state
1950, Nov. 23–28	Ohio, Pa., West Virginia	33–57 in.	Record snowfall for three states
1951, March 10–14	Iowa City, Iowa	27.2 in.	Record snowfall for state
1955, April 2–5	Colorado to Dakotas	30–52 in.	One of heaviest and latest spring snowstorms
1956, March 16–17	New England, New York, Pa.	20 in.	Crippling winds and snowstorm
1958, Feb. 13–19	North Carolina to New Jersey	36 in.	43 deaths; damage $500 million
1958, March 19–22	Virginia to New England	17–30 in.	Severe snowstorm; 49 deaths
1959, Feb. 13–19	Mt. Shasta Ski Bowl, Calif.	189 in.	Greatest U.S. snowfall in one storm
1959, March 11–13	New England, New York	20 in.	Blizzard conditions; transportation paralyzed
1960, Feb. 18–20	Maryland to New England	20–36 in.	Damage in millions of dollars
1961, Jan. 19–20	North Carolina to New York	10–30 in.	37 deaths; many cities paralyzed
1961, Feb. 3–5	North Carolina to New England	10–36 in.	73 deaths; drifts of 15 feet
1964, Feb. 2–5	N.M., Okla., Texas	18–36 in.	Second heaviest storm in Panhandle's history
1966, Jan. 29–31	Virginia to New England	12–36 in.	50 deaths; drifts to 20 feet
1966, March 2–5	Nebraska to Dakotas	12–36 in.	15 deaths; 100,000 cattle killed; drifts to 30 feet
1967, Jan. 26–27	Chicago and Midwest	23 in.	Record snow and ice storms; high winds
1969, Feb. 9–10	New York and New England	15 in.	Worst storm to hit New York City in 8 years
1969, February	Mt. Washington, N.H.	172.8 in.	State record for one-month snowfall
1973, Feb. 10–11	Georgia and Carolinas	15–21 in.	Worst storm in South in this century
1974, Dec. 1–2	Michigan, Ohio	17–20 in.	Record 19.2 in. of snow paralyzes Detroit
1975, Jan. 10–12	N.D., S.D., Neb., Kan., Mo., Iowa, Minn., Wis.	8–15 in.	Winds of 80 mph drift snow to 20 feet; over 60 killed, hundreds injured; over $15 million damage
1977, Jan. 1–31	West Virginia	104 in.	West Virginia record for one-month snowfall
1977, Jan. 28–Feb. 1	Ill., Ind., Ohio, N.Y., Pa.	12–71 in.	Blizzard with winds to 69 mph kills 75 persons
1978, Jan. 26–27	Midwestern and Eastern states	12–34 in.	Called "worst blizzard of century"; 100 killed; winds gust to 100 mph; snow drifts to 25 feet
1978, Feb. 6–7	Northeast states	18–38 in.	Winds to 100 mph cause 40-foot coastal waves
1979, Jan. 13–14	Chicago and Midwest	20.7 in.	Heavy snowfall paralyzes Chicago
1980, March 2	Middle Atlantic and Southern states	10–28 in.	Surprise blizzard paralyzes mid-Atlantic area; Florida citrus crop damaged; 36 killed
1982, Jan. 20–23	Northern Minnesota	38 in.	Blizzard paralyzes area
1982, Jan. 31	St. Louis, Mo., and Midwest	18–22 in.	Blizzard immobilizes area
1982, January	Muskegon, Mich.	89 in.	Record snow total for one month
1982, Dec. 24–25	Denver, Colo.	24 in.	Blizzard strands holiday travelers
1983, Feb. 11–12	Northeast states	17–35 in.	Record 22 in. of snow in Philadelphia
1983, Nov. 27–28	Rocky Mts. and Central Plains	15–22 in.	Blizzards blamed for over 50 deaths

U.S. AND WORLD RECORD RAINFALLS

DURATION	DEPTH	LOCATION	DATE
1 minute (world record)	1.50 in.	Barst, Guadeloupe	Nov. 26, 1970
1 minute (U.S. record)	1.23 in.	Unionville, Maryland	July, 4, 1956
15 minutes (world record)	7.80 in.	Plumb Point, Jamaica	May 12, 1916
1 hour (U.S. record)	12.00 in.	Holt, Missouri	June 22, 1947
1 hour (U.S. record)	12.00 in.	Kilauea plantation, Kauai, Hawaii	Jan. 24–25, 1956
12 hours (world record)	52.76 in.	Belouve, Réunion	Feb. 28–29, 1964
24 hours (world record)	73.62 in.	Cilaos, Réunion	March 15–16, 1952
24 hours (U.S. record)	43.00 in.	Alvin, Texas	July 25–26, 1979
1 month (world record)	366.14 in.	Cherrapunji, India	July 1861
1 month (U.S. record)	107.00 in.	Puu Kukui, Maui, Hawaii	March 1942
1 year (world record)	1,041.78 in.	Cherrapunji, India	Aug. 1860–July 1861
1 year (U.S. record)	578.00 in.	Puu Kukui, Maui, Hawaii	1950

Congress of the United States

United Press Int'l.

In a mass swearing-in ceremony on Jan. 3, 1983, Speaker of the House Thomas O'Neill gave the oath of office to 81 freshmen U.S. Representatives as members of the 98th Congress. Some held their children while being sworn in.

HIGHLIGHTS: 1983

Republicans picked up one seat in each house of Congress in 1983. This gave the GOP a 55–45 majority in the Senate and reduced the Democratic majority in the house to 267–167 with one vacancy.

The Republican gain in the Senate came when Daniel J. Evans, former governor of Washington in 1965–77, defeated Democratic Rep. Mike Lowry in November in a race to fill the seat of Sen. Henry M. Jackson, who died on Sept. 1.

The vacancy in the House occurred with the death on Dec. 3 of Rep. Clement J. Zablocki (D-Wis.), chairman of the House Foreign Relations Committee.

The additional Republican seat in the House came about when Rep. Phil Gramm of Texas resigned his seat on Jan. 5 and quit the Democratic Party after the party leadership removed him from the House Budget Committee because of his support for President Reagan's economic policies. Gramm returned home and in a special election on Feb. 12 defeated Democratic opponents to regain his House seat as a Republican.

Several new faces were added to the House of Representatives without changing the parties' balance of power.

HIGHLIGHTS: 1983 *(continued)*

Republican state senator Daniel L. Schaefer won a special Colorado election on March 29 to win the seat left vacant by the death on Dec. 27, 1982, of former astronaut Jack Swigert.

Democrat Sala Burton won a California special election on June 21 to fill the seat left vacant by the death of her husband, Rep. Phillip Burton (D-Calif) on April 10.

Democratic labor leader Charles A. Hayes won a special election in Illinois on Aug. 23 to fill the seat vacated when Rep. Harold Washington (D-Ill.) became mayor of Chicago.

Gary Ackerman, a Democratic state senator, won a special New York election on March 1 to fill the seat vacated by the death on Jan. 4 of Rep. Benjamin S. Rosenthal (D-N.Y.).

Democrat George W. "Buddy" Darden won a special Georgia runoff election on Nov. 8 for the seat vacated by the death of Rep. Larry P. McDonald (D-Ga.) in the crash of a South Korean airliner shot down by Soviet fighter planes on Sept. 1. See page 25.

FIRST SESSION OF 98th CONGRESS

The first session of the 98th Congress lasted 319 days, from Jan. 3 to Nov. 18, 1983, when members adjourned for a six-week vacation until reconvening in January 1984.

The session was the shortest for a non-election year since the first session of the 89th Congress in 1965. More than 8,400 bills and resolutions were introduced. However, only about 2% of the measures were passed by Congress and signed by the President.

LEGISLATIVE VETO UNCONSTITUTIONAL

The Supreme Court on June 23 took away one of the major powers Congress had voted itself when the legislative veto on the executive branch was found to be unconstitutional. See page 21.

NEW FEDERAL HOLIDAY

President Reagan on Nov. 2 signed into law legislation establishing a new federal holiday to honor slain civil-rights leader Dr. Martin Luther King Jr. Beginning in 1986, the holiday will be proclaimed for the third Monday each January.

Establishment of the 10th federal holiday was hailed by civil-rights groups, which had lobbied for the legislation for 15 years.

The Senate approved the bill 78–22 on Oct. 19, overcoming opposition by Sen. Jesse Helms (R-N.C.), who had objected to King's anti-Vietnam War policy and had accused King of having links with the Communist Party.

Senate Majority Leader Howard H. Baker Jr. (R-Tenn.) hailed the holiday as a symbol of national unity.

Earlier, on Aug. 2, the House passed the measure, 338–90, where opponents objected to the cost in lost time by federal workers.

SOCIAL SECURITY OVERHAUL

An important measure approved in 1983 was the overhaul of Social Security in an effort to prevent the system from going broke.

The Senate passed the measure, 58–14, on March 25. The House had approved it 243-102 on March 24.

The revisions in Social Security were expected to raise $165 billion over the next 7 years to keep the retirement and disability benefit system in the black into the next century.

The measure provided that the retirement age will be raised from 65 to 67 by the year 2027. And benefits for early retirement at age 62 would be reduced to 70% by 2027.

Beginning on Jan. 1, 1984, Social Security is extended to include all employees of nonprofit organizations, all new federal employees, all members of Congress, federal judges, the President, the Vice President, and major federal political appointees and civil servants.

The new law also prohibits state and local governments from withdrawing their employees from Social Security.

For the first time beneficiaries with higher-than-average-incomes will have to pay income tax on their Social Security benefits. The benefits will be taxed as regular income if an individual's adjusted gross income combined with half the Social Security benefits exceeds $25,000. The limit for couples was set at $32,000.

Payroll taxes for self-employed persons were increased 33% to equal the combined taxes paid by employers and employees. However, the impact of the increase was to be offset by tax credits to the self-employed in the period 1984–89.

Employer and employee payroll taxes were increased from 6.7% in 1983 to 7% in 1984, to 7.15% in 1988, to 7.51% in 1989, and to 7.65% in 1990.

Cost-of-living increases in Social Security benefits were delayed from July 1983 to January 1984.

Future cost-of-living increases would be based on the lower of increases in the Consumer Price Index or average wages, if Social Security trust funds were running short.

The bonus for persons delaying retirement beyond age 65 would be increased from 3% added benefits per year to 8% a year by 2008.

The measure also extended unemployment benefits for individuals who had exhausted 39 weeks of regular jobless benefits, and it provided a multitude of new regulations for the Medicare system that were designed to reduce soaring medical costs.

PAY FOR REDUCED MILK SUPPLIES

Giving in to pressure from farm state congressional leaders, President Reagan on Nov. 29 signed into law a measure that for the first time will pay dairy farmers not to produce additional milk.

Earlier the President had fought the measure. His budget advisers said it would result in consumers paying $1.8 billion more for milk in 1984 while doing little to reduce swelling dairy surpluses. About 10% more milk is produced each year than consumers are willing to buy. The government for many years has helped dairy farmers keep dairy prices artificially high by purchasing the extra milk. The cost to taxpayers for such government purchases of surplus milk was about $2.7 billion in 1983. The President had tried to get Congress to reduce the $13.10 per 100 pounds price that the government pays for surplus milk, believing that this would force dairy farmers to reduce production.

Under the new law, dairy farmers who reduce their milk production from 5% to 30% will be paid $10 per 100 pounds for the milk that is not produced.

Congress helped force the President to sign the measure by tying to it other farm measures favored by the administration—continuation of price supports for tobacco farmers and aid to drought-stricken livestock ranchers. Farmers in drought areas will be able to purchase from the government surplus livestock feed at $2 a bushel.

The House approved a conference committee version of the measure on Nov. 18 after the Senate had passed it a day earlier.

Congress did not take final action on a separate measure that would have enabled debt-ridden farmers to delay repayment of Farmers Home Administration loans. Congress also failed to act on administration requests for a measure to block legislated increases in government price supports.

NATIONAL DEFENSE

Congress approved a $250 billion national defense appropriation for 1984—the largest such measure ever approved in peacetime. See pages 459–461.

WAR POWERS INVOKED

After the first U.S. Marines were killed in combat in Lebanon on Aug. 29, Congress invoked for the first time the 1973 War Powers Resolution designed to give Congress control over the President's use of armed forces in foreign conflicts.

In a resolution passed by the Senate, 54–46, on Sept. 29 and approved by the House 253–156 a few hours later, Congress formally authorized the President to keep U.S. armed forces in Lebanon for 18 more months. The Marines were sent into Lebanon in August 1982 as part of a multinational peacekeeping force to support Lebanon's government.

HOW A BILL BECOMES A LAW

The process by which a bill becomes a law is long and complicated. Following is a summary of steps in the passage of legislation by Congress.

Introduction of Bill. The bill is introduced in the House by a representative or in the Senate by a senator. Sometimes to speed up action the same bill is introduced in both houses at the same time. All tax bills must be introduced in the House, but the Senate is free to amend them.

First Reading. The title of the bill is read to the House or Senate. It is given a number, and it is printed.

Assignment to Committee. The Speaker of the House, or the Vice President in the Senate, assigns each bill to a committee for consideration.

Committee Consideration. The committee may hold hearings on the bill, and then rewrite or amend it. The committee also can decide to table the bill, or kill it.

Committee Approval. If the committee approves the bill, it is sent to the floor to await its turn on the calendar. The bill can be pushed ahead of others in the House by the House Rules Committee or in the Senate by the majority leaders.

Second Reading. When the bill reaches the floor of the House or Senate, it is read in full and then debated. It may be amended or it may be returned to committee. The time for debate is limited in the House but is unlimited in the Senate unless a two-thirds majority votes to impose limits. At the end of the debate the House or Senate votes on the bill.

Third Reading. Only the title of the bill is read, and another vote is taken, usually by roll call.

Consideration by Other House of Congress. After a bill is passed by one house, it must go through the same process already described in the other house. If it is amended during the process by the other house and then is passed on third reading by a majority vote, it is returned to the house that originated the bill.

Approval of Amendments by Originating House. When a bill is returned to the house of Congress in which it originated, it is debated and a vote is taken to decide whether the majority approves the amended version of the bill.

Conference Committee. If the majority of the house in which the bill originated rejects the other house's amendments, the bill is sent to a conference committee composed of both representatives and senators. The conference committee revises the bill to reconcile the differences between its two versions.

Final Approval by House and Senate. After the conference committee reports out its revised version of the bill, the House and the Senate each must vote again. If a majority in each house votes to approve the bill, it then is sent to the President.

Presidential Signature. If the President signs the bill, it immediately becomes law.

Becoming a Law Without Presidential Signature. If Congress is in session the bill automatically becomes law 10 days after the President receives it, excluding Sundays, even though he does not sign it.

Regular Veto. The President may within 10 days veto the bill by returning it to Congress with an explanation of why he refuses to approve it.

Pocket Veto. If Congress adjourns within the 10-day period of presidential consideration, the bill automatically is killed if the President does not sign it.

Overriding a Veto. If the President vetoes a bill, Congress can make it become law if both the House and the Senate again pass the bill, each by a two-thirds majority.

HIGHLIGHTS: 1983 *(continued)*

The President agreed to give Congress formal reports every 60 days on the status of affairs in Lebanon.

After 239 U.S. Marines were killed by a terrorist bomb in Lebanon on Oct. 23 (see page 27), Democrats sought passage of a new resolution that would limit to three months the remaining time for U.S. armed forces in Lebanon. However, in the rush for adjournment the new measure failed to come before either house for a vote.

After President Reagan ordered U.S. troops to land on Grenada on Oct. 25 (see page 29), the House voted, 403–23, on Nov. 1 to invoke the War Powers Resolution and set a 60-day time limit on the time American armed forces could remain on the island. The Senate on Oct. 28 had approved a similar measure by 64–20; however, it was attached as an amendment to a bill raising the national debt limit—a bill that was defeated in the Senate by a vote of 39–56 on Oct. 31. The Senate took no further action to revive consideration of applying the War Powers Resolution to Grenada.

EL SALVADOR CERTIFICATION VETOED

President Reagan on Nov. 30 vetoed a bill that would have required him to certify to Congress every six months that human rights were improving in El Salvador if that Central American country were to continue receiving U.S. military aid.

The House had approved the measure on Sept. 30 and the Senate on Nov. 17. The President exercised a pocket veto by not signing the bill within 10 days after it came to him.

Opponents of the Reagan administration's policies in Central America said the veto was likely to increase violence in El Salvador if that country's government felt it no longer had to improve human rights.

Military aid to El Salvador earlier had been set by Congress at $81.3 million in fiscal 1983 and $64.8 million in fiscal 1984. The appropriation requires that aid be cut by 30% if the government of El Salvador does not bring to trial those accused of slaying four American churchwomen in 1980.

CONGRESSIONAL PAY RAISE

Senators voted themselves a 15% pay raise, increasing their salaries to $69,800 to match those of House members who gave themselves a matching raise in December 1982.

The legislation provided that starting on Jan. 1, 1984, senators cannot receive more than $20,940 in honoraria for lectures, articles, or special appearances. The House already had set the same ceiling on honoraria for its members.

Congress also appropriated $38 million for its mailing costs—an average of more than $70,000 per legislator.

However, Congress was not so liberal with other federal employees, authorizing only a 3.5% pay increase for white-collar government workers effective Jan. 1, 1984.

TAXES AND SPENDING

The fiscal 1984 budget resolution adopted by Congress in June called for a $73 billion increase in taxes over the period 1984–86. The resolution also provided for spending cuts of $12.3 billion in the same period.

However, Congress failed to act on any measure to increase taxes or cut spending.

Just before adjourning for the rest of the year, Congress raised the public debt limit to $1.49 trillion, an increase of $101 billion.

REVENUE SHARING

A three-year extension of federal revenue-sharing grants to local governments was approved by voice vote in both houses of Congress on Nov. 17. The measure provided the same annual $4.6 billion level of spending as previously authorized in 1980–83.

The House had sought a $450 million-a-year increase in this program, but gave in to administrative warnings that the measure would be vetoed if the spending level was raised.

TUITION TAX CREDIT KILLED

The Senate by 59–38 on Nov. 16 defeated the tuition tax-credit plan that had been strongly supported by President Reagan.

The plan would have provided parents whose children attend private school with tax credits for part of their tuition expenses.

President Reagan had asked for the measure as a means of providing more competition between private and public schools, saying, "Without a race there can be no champion; without competition to excel in our educational system we will not have excellence."

Opponents had claimed that encouraging parents to move their children from public schools to private schools would cause a decline in the quality of public schools.

NEW FEDERALLY FUNDED HOUSING

By linking together unrelated legislation in a single package, Congress approved on Nov. 18 the first new federally funded housing program during the Reagan administration.

An example of the art of logrolling, the measure combined a Democratic-sponsored $15.6 billion housing bill, a Republican-sponsored $8.4 billion contribution to the International Monetary Fund, and $302 million in supplementary appropriations for a variety of projects.

The legislation was described by one senator as "mating a turkey and a camel.

UNITED STATES SENATE IN 1984

Republicans control the U.S. Senate in the 98th Congress, with 55 members to the Democrats' 45.

The U.S. Senate with 100 members is the smaller but the more influential of the two houses of Congress.

The Senate's presiding officer is Vice President Bush.

Senate officers chosen for the 98th Congress include:

President Pro Tempore Strom Thurmond (R-S.C.), Republican Floor Leader Howard H. Baker (R-Tenn.), Democratic Floor Leader Robert C. Byrd (D-W. Va.), Republican Whip Ted Stevens (R-Alaska), and Democratic Whip Alan Cranston (D-Calif.)

Thurmond is the senior Republican senator, having served since Nov. 7, 1956.

The senior Democratic senator is John D. Stennis of Mississippi, who has served since Nov. 5, 1947.

U.S. senators are elected for terms of 6 years. A senator must be at least 30 years of age, a citizen for 9 years, and a resident of the state he represents.

Senators' salaries were raised to $69,800 on July 1, 1983. Salaries of the president pro tem and majority and minority leaders were raised to $78,900.

In addition each senator receives free office space, staff salaries, travel expenses, and other allowances averaging $400,000 or more annually.

Dates in the table show when each senator took office. An asterisk (*) indicates a freshman (first-term) senator.

Alabama	*Howell Heflin (D), Jan. 3, 1979 *Jeremiah Denton (R), Jan. 2, 1981	**Montana**	John Melcher (D), Jan. 3, 1977 *Max Baucus (D), Dec. 15, 1978
Alaska	Theodore F. Stevens (R), Dec. 24, 1968 *Frank H. Murkowski (R), Jan. 3, 1981	**Nebraska**	Edward Zorinsky (D), Dec. 28, 1976 *J. James Exon (D), Jan. 3, 1979
Arizona	Barry Goldwater (R), Jan. 3, 1969 *Dennis DeConcini (D), Jan. 3, 1977	**Nevada**	Paul Laxalt (R), Dec. 18, 1974 *Chic Hecht (R), Jan. 3, 1983
Arkansas	Dale Bumpers (D), Jan. 3, 1975 *David Pryor (D), Jan. 3, 1979	**New Hampshire**	*Gordon Humphrey (R), Jan. 3, 1979 *Warren Rudman (R), Jan. 3, 1981
California	Alan Cranston (D), Jan. 3, 1969 *Pete Wilson (R), Jan. 3, 1983	**New Jersey**	*Bill Bradley (D), Jan. 3, 1979 *Frank R. Lautenberg (D), Jan. 3, 1983
Colorado	Gary Hart (D), Jan. 3, 1975 *William L. Armstrong (R), Jan. 3, 1979	**New Mexico**	Pete V. Domenici (R), Jan. 3, 1973 *Jeff Bingaman (D), Jan. 3, 1983
Connecticut	Lowell P. Weicker Jr. (R), Jan. 3, 1971 *Christopher J. Dodd (D), Jan. 3, 1981	**New York**	Daniel P. Moynihan (D), Jan. 3, 1977 *Alfonse M. D'Amato (R), Jan. 3, 1981
Delaware	William V. Roth Jr. (R), Jan. 1, 1971 Joseph R. Biden Jr. (D), Jan. 3, 1973	**North Carolina**	Jesse A. Helms (R), Jan. 3, 1973 *John P. East (R), Jan. 3, 1981
Florida	Lawton Chiles (D), Jan. 3, 1971 *Paula Hawkins (R), Jan. 3, 1981	**North Dakota**	Quentin N. Burdick (D), Aug. 8, 1960 *Mark Andrews (R), Jan. 3, 1981
Georgia	Sam Nunn (D), Nov. 8, 1972 *Mack Mattingly (R), Jan. 3, 1981	**Ohio**	John H. Glenn (D), Dec. 24, 1974 Howard M. Metzenbaum (D), Dec. 29, 1976
Hawaii	Daniel K. Inouye (D), Jan. 3, 1963 Spark M. Matsunaga (D), Jan. 3, 1977	**Oklahoma**	*David L. Boren (D), Jan. 3, 1979 *Don Nickles (R), Jan. 3, 1981
Idaho	James A. McClure (R), Jan. 3, 1973 *Steven D. Symms (R), Jan. 3, 1981	**Oregon**	Mark O. Hatfield (R), Jan. 10, 1967 Robert W. Packwood (R), Jan. 3, 1969
Illinois	Charles H. Percy (R), Jan. 3, 1967 *Alan J. Dixon (D), Jan. 3, 1981	**Pennsylvania**	H. John Heinz III (R), Jan. 3, 1977 *Arlen Specter (R), Jan. 3, 1981
Indiana	Richard G. Lugar (R), Jan. 3, 1977 *Dan Quayle (R), Jan. 3, 1981	**Rhode Island**	Claiborne Pell (D), Jan. 3, 1961 John H. Chafee (R), Dec. 29, 1976
Iowa	*Roger Jepson (R), Jan. 3, 1979 *Charles E. Grassley (R), Jan. 3, 1981	**South Carolina**	Strom Thurmond (R), Nov. 7, 1956 Ernest F. Hollings (D), Nov. 9, 1966
Kansas	Robert Dole (R), Jan. 3, 1969 *Nancy L. Kassebaum (R), Dec. 23, 1978	**South Dakota**	*Larry Pressler (R), Jan. 3, 1979 *James Abdnor (R), Jan. 3, 1981
Kentucky	Walter (Dee) Huddleston (D), Jan. 3, 1973 Wendell H. Ford (D), Dec. 28, 1974	**Tennessee**	Howard H. Baker Jr. (R), Jan. 3, 1967 James R. Sasser (D), Jan. 3, 1977
Louisiana	Russell B. Long (D), Dec. 31, 1948 J. Bennett Johnston Jr. (D), Nov. 14, 1972	**Texas**	John G. Tower (R), June 15, 1961 Lloyd M. Bentsen Jr. (D), Jan. 3, 1971
Maine	*William S. Cohen (R), Jan. 3, 1979 George J. Mitchell (D), May 8, 1980	**Utah**	Jake Garn (R), Dec. 21, 1974 Orrin G. Hatch (R), Jan. 3, 1977
Maryland	Charles McC. Mathias Jr. (R), Jan. 3, 1969 Paul S. Sarbanes (D), Jan. 3, 1977	**Vermont**	Robert T. Stafford (R), Sept. 16, 1971 Patrick J. Leahy (D), Jan. 3, 1975
Massachusetts	Edward M. Kennedy (D), Nov. 7, 1962 *Paul E. Tsongas (D), Jan. 3, 1979	**Virginia**	*John W. Warner (R), Jan. 2, 1979 *Paul S. Trible Jr. (R), Jan. 3, 1983
Michigan	Donald W. Riegle Jr. (D), Dec. 30, 1976 *Carl Levin (D), Jan. 3, 1979	**Washington**	*Daniel J. Evans (R), Sept. 12, 1983 *Slade Gorton (R), Jan. 3, 1981
Minnesota	David Durenberger (R), Nov. 8, 1978 *Rudy Boschwitz (R), Dec. 30, 1978	**West Virginia**	Jennings Randolph (D), Nov. 5, 1958 Robert C. Byrd (D), Jan. 3, 1959
Mississippi	John Stennis (D), Nov. 5, 1947 *Thad Cochran (R), Dec. 27, 1978	**Wisconsin**	William Proxmire (D), Aug. 28, 1957 *Robert W. Kasten Jr. (R), Jan. 3, 1981
Missouri	Thomas F. Eagleton (D), Dec. 28, 1968 John C. Danforth (R), Dec. 27, 1976	**Wyoming**	Malcolm Wallop (R), Jan. 3, 1977 *Alan K. Simpson (R), Jan. 1, 1979

U.S. HOUSE OF REPRESENTATIVES IN 1984

Democrats control the U.S. House of Representatives in the 98th Congress, with 267 votes to the Republicans' 167, and 1 vacancy.

The chief officers of the House in the 98th Congress include: Speaker of the House Thomas P. O'Neill Jr. (D-Mass.), Democratic Floor Leader Jim Wright (D-Texas), Republican Floor Leader Robert H. Michel (R-Ill.), Democratic Whip Thomas S. Foley (D-Wash.), and Republican Whip Trent Lott (R-Miss.).

The senior Democrat is Jamie L. Whitten of Mississippi, who has served since Nov. 4, 1941. The senior Republican is John J. Rhodes of Arizona, who has served since Jan. 3, 1953.

The larger house of Congress (435 members) represents the people more directly than the Senate. Three powers are delegated exclusively to the House: (1) it originates all bills for raising revenue, (2) it elects the President if there is no electoral majority, and (3) it impeaches federal officials.

A representative must be at least 25 years of age, a citizen of the U.S. for 7 years, and a resident of the state he represents.

The salaries of representatives were raised 15% to $69,800 on Dec. 18, 1982. At the same time the majority and minority leaders were raised to $78,900.

In addition each representative receives other allowances.

An asterisk (*) in the table below indicates a freshman member (one serving his first term in the House).

Congressional districts within a state are indicated by numerals. A representative-at-large is shown as AL.

ALABAMA
1. Jack Edwards (R)
2. William L. Dickinson (R)
3. William Nichols (D)
4. Tom Bevill (D)
5. Ronnie G. Flippo (D)
6. Ben Erdreich (D)*
7. Richard C. Shelby (D)

ALASKA
AL Donald E. Young (R)

ARIZONA
1. John McCain (R)*
2. Morris K. Udall (D)
3. Bob Stump (R)
4. Eldon D. Rudd (R)
5. Jim McNulty (D)*

ARKANSAS
1. Bill Alexander Jr. (D)
2. Ed Bethune (R)
3. John Hammerschmidt (R)
4. Beryl F. Anthony Jr. (D)

CALIFORNIA
1. Douglas H. Bosco (D)*
2. Eugene A. Chappie (R)
3. Robert T. Matsui (D)
4. Vic Fazio (D)
5. Sala Burton (D)*
6. Barbara Boxer (D)*
7. George Miller III (D)
8. Ronald V. Dellums (D)
9. Fortney H. Stark (D)
10. Don Edwards (D)
11. Tom Lantos (D)
12. Ed Zschau (R)*
13. Norman Y. Mineta (D)
14. Norman D. Shumway (R)
15. Tony Coelho (D)
16. Leon E. Panetta (D)
17. Charles Pashayan Jr. (R)
18. Richard Lehman (D)*
19. R. J. Lagomarsino (R)
20. William Thomas (R)*
21. Bobbi Fiedler (R)
22. Carlos J. Moorhead (R)
23. Anthony Beilenson (D)
24. Henry A. Waxman (D)
25. Edward R. Roybal (D)
26. Howard L. Berman (D)*
27. Mel Levine (D)*
28. Julian C. Dixon (D)
29. Augustus F. Hawkins (D)
30. Matthew G. Martinez (D)
31. Mervyn M. Dymally (D)
32. Glenn M. Anderson (D)
33. David Dreier (R)
34. Esteban Torres (D)*
35. Jerry Lewis (R)
36. George E. Brown Jr. (D)
37. Al McCandless (R)*
38. Jerry M. Patterson (D)
39. William Dannemeyer (R)
40. Robert E. Badham (R)
41. Bill Lowery (R)
42. Dan Lungren (R)
43. Ron Packard (R)*
44. Jim Bates (D)*
45. Duncan L. Hunter (R)

COLORADO
1. Patricia Schroeder (D)
2. Timothy E. Wirth (D)
3. Ray Kogovsek (D)
4. Hank Brown (R)
5. Ken Kramer (R)
6. Daniel L. Schaefer (R)*

CONNECTICUT
1. Barbara B. Kennelly (D)
2. Samuel Gejdenson (D)
3. Bruce A. Morrison (D)*
4. Stewart B. McKinney (R)
5. William Ratchford (D)
6. Nancy L. Johnson (R)*

DELAWARE
AL Thomas R. Carper (D)*

FLORIDA
1. Earl Hutto (D)
2. Don Fuqua (D)
3. Charles E. Bennett (D)
4. Bill Chappell Jr. (D)
5. Bill McCollum (R)
6. Kenneth MacKay (D)*
7. Sam Gibbons (D)
8. C.W. Young (R)
9. Michael Bilirakis (R)*
10. Andrew P. Ireland (D)
11. Bill Nelson (D)
12. Tom Lewis (R)*
13. Connie Mack (R)*
14. Daniel Mica (D)
15. E. Clay Shaw Jr. (R)
16. Larry Smith (D)*
17. William Lehman (D)
18. Claude Pepper (D)
19. Dante B. Fascell (D)

GEORGIA
1. Lindsay Thomas (D)*
2. Charles F. Hatcher (D)
3. Richard Ray (D)*
4. Elliott H. Levitas (D)
5. Wyche Fowler Jr. (D)
6. Newt Gingrich (R)
7. George Darden (D)*
8. J. Roy Rowland (D)*
9. Ed Jenkins (D)
10. Doug Barnard Jr. (D)

HAWAII
1. Cecil Heftel (D)
2. Daniel Akaka (D)

IDAHO
1. Larry Craig (R)
2. George Hansen (R)

ILLINOIS
1. Charles A. Hayes (D)*
2. Gus Savage (D)*
3. Martin A. Russo (D)
4. George M. O'Brien (R)
5. William Lipinski (D)*
6. Henry J. Hyde (R)
7. Cardiss Collins (D)
8. Dan Rostenkowski (D)
9. Sidney R. Yates (D)
10. John E. Porter (R)
11. Frank Annunzio (D)
12. Philip M. Crane (R)
13. John N. Erlenborn (R)
14. Tom Corcoran (R)
15. Edward R. Madigan (R)
16. Lynn M. Martin (R)
17. Lane Evans (D)*
18. Robert H. Michel (R)
19. Daniel B. Crane (R)
20. Richard J. Durbin (D)*
21. Melvin Price (D)
22. Paul Simon (D)

INDIANA
1. Katie Hall (D)*
2. Philip R. Sharp (D)
3. John Hiler (R)
4. Daniel R. Coats (R)
5. Elwood H. Hillis (R)
6. Daniel L. Burton (R)*
7. John T. Myers (R)
8. Francis X. McCloskey (D)*
9. Lee H. Hamilton (D)
10. Andrew Jacobs Jr. (D)

IOWA
1. James Leach (R)
2. Tom Tauke (R)
3. Cooper Evans (R)
4. Neal Smith (D)
5. Tom Harkin (D)
6. Berkley Bedell (D)

KANSAS
1. Pat Roberts (R)
2. Jim Slattery (D)*
3. Larry Winn Jr. (R)
4. Dan Glickman (D)
5. Robert Whittaker (R)

KENTUCKY
1. Carroll Hubbard Jr. (D)
2. William H. Natcher (D)
3. Romano L. Mazzoli (D)
4. M. G. (Gene) Snyder (R)
5. Harold Rogers (R)
6. Larry J. Hopkins (R)
7. Carl D. Perkins (D)

LOUISIANA
1. Robert L. Livingston Jr. (R)
2. Lindy Boggs (D)
3. W.J. (Billy) Tauzin (D)
4. Buddy Roemer (D)
5. Jerry Huckaby (D)
6. Henson Moore (R)
7. John B. Breaux (D)
8. Gillis W. Long (D)

MAINE
1. John R. McKernan Jr. (R)*
2. Olympia Snowe (R)

MARYLAND
1. Roy Dyson (D)
2. Clarence D. Long (D)
3. Barbara A. Mikulski (D)
4. Marjorie S. Holt (R)
5. Steny H. Hoyer (D)
6. Beverly Byron (D)
7. Parren J. Mitchell (D)
8. Michael Barnes (D)

MASSACHUSETTS
1. Silvio O. Conte (R)
2. Edward P. Boland (D)
3. Joseph D. Early (D)
4. Barney Frank (D)
5. James Shannon (D)
6. Nicholas Mavroules (D)
7. Edward J. Markey (D)
8. Thomas P. O'Neill Jr. (D)
9. John (Joe) Moakley (D)
10. Gerry E. Studds (D)
11. Brian J. Donnelly (D)

MICHIGAN
1. John Conyers Jr. (D)
2. Carl D. Pursell (R)
3. Howard Wolpe (D)
4. Mark Siljander (R)
5. Harold S. Sawyer (R)
6. M. Robert Carr (D)*
7. Dale E. Kildee (D)
8. Bob Traxler (D)
9. Guy A. Vander Jagt (R)
10. Don Albosta (D)
11. Robert W. Davis (R)
12. David E. Bonior (D)
13. G. W. Crockett Jr. (D)
14. Dennis M. Hertel (D)
15. William D. Ford (D)
16. John D. Dingell (D)
17. Sander Levin (D)*
18. William S. Broomfield (R)

MINNESOTA
1. Timothy J. Penny (D)*
2. Vin Weber (R)
3. Bill Frenzel (R)
4. Bruce F. Vento (D)
5. Martin O. Sabo (D)
6. Gerry Sikorski (D)*
7. Arlan Stangeland (R)
8. James L. Oberstar (D)

MISSISSIPPI
1. Jamie L. Whitten (D)
2. Webb Franklin (R)*
3. G. V. Montgomery (D)
4. Wayne Dowdy (D)
5. Trent Lott (R)

MISSOURI
1. William L. Clay (D)
2. Robert A. Young (D)
3. Richard A. Gephardt (D)
4. Ike Skelton (D)
5. Alan Wheat (D)*
6. E. Thomas Coleman (R)
7. Gene Taylor (R)
8. Bill Emerson (R)
9. Harold L. Volkmer (D)

MONTANA
1. Pat Williams (D)
2. Ron Marlenee (R)

NEBRASKA
1. Douglas K. Bereuter (R)
2. Hal Daub (R)
3. Virginia Smith (R)

NEVADA
1. Harry Reid (D)*
2. Barbara Vucanovich (R)*

NEW HAMPSHIRE
1. Norman D'Amours (D)
2. Judd Gregg (R)

NEW JERSEY
1. James J. Florio (D)
2. William J. Hughes (D)
3. James J. Howard (D)
4. Christopher H. Smith (R)
5. Marge Roukema (R)
6. Bernard J. Dwyer (D)
7. Matthew J. Rinaldo (R)
8. Robert A. Roė (D)
9. Robert Torricelli (D)*
10. Peter W. Rodino Jr. (D)
11. Joseph G. Minish (D)
12. Jim Courter (R)
13. Edwin B. Forsythe (R)
14. Frank J. Guarini (D)

NEW MEXICO
1. Manuel Lujan Jr. (R)
2. Joe Skeen (R)
3. Bill Richardson (D)*

NEW YORK
1. William Carney (R)
2. Thomas J. Downey (D)
3. Robert J. Mrazek (D)*
4. Norman F. Lent (R)
5. Raymond J. McGrath (R)
6. Joseph P. Addabbo (D)
7. Gary Ackerman (D)*
8. James H. Scheuer (D)
9. Geraldine Ferraro (D)
10. Charles E. Schumer (D)
11. Edolphus Towns (D)*
12. Major R. Owens (D)*
13. Stephen J. Solarz (D)
14. Guy V. Molinari (R)
15. S. William Green (R)
16. Charles B. Rangel (D)
17. Theodore S. Weiss (D)
18. Robert Garcia (D)
19. Mario Biaggi (D)
20. Richard L. Ottinger (D)
21. Hamilton Fish Jr. (R)
22. Benjamin A. Gilman (R)
23. Samuel S. Stratton (D)
24. Gerald Solomon (R)
25. Sherwood Boehlert (R)*
26. David O'B. Martin (R)
27. George Wortley (R)
28. Matthew F. McHugh (D)
29. Frank Horton (R)
30. Barber B. Conable Jr. (R)
31. Jack F. Kemp (R)
32. John J. LaFalce (D)
33. Henry J. Nowak (D)
34. Stanley N. Lundine (D)

NORTH CAROLINA
1. Walter B. Jones (D)
2. I.T. Valentine Jr. (D)*
3. Charles Whitley (D)
4. Ike F. Andrews (D)
5. Stephen L. Neal (D)
6. Charles R. Britt (D)*
7. Charles G. Rose III (D)
8. W. G. (Bill) Hefner (D)
9. James G. Martin (R)
10. James T. Broyhill (R)
11. James M. Clarke (D)*

NORTH DAKOTA
AL Byron L. Dorgan (D)

OHIO
1. Thomas A. Luken (D)
2. Bill Gradison (R)
3. Tony P. Hall (D)
4. Michael Oxley (R)
5. Delbert L. Latta (R)
6. Bob McEwen (R)
7. Michael DeWine (R)*
8. Thomas N. Kindness (R)
9. Marcy Kaptur (D)*
10. Clarence E. Miller (R)
11. Dennis E. Eckart (D)
12. John R. Kasich (R)*
13. Donald J. Pease (D)
14. John F. Seiberling Jr. (D)
15. Chalmers P. Wylie (R)
16. Ralph S. Regula (R)
17. Lyle Williams (R)
18. Douglas Applegate (D)
19. Edward F. Feighan (D)*
20. Mary Rose Oakar (D)
21. Louis Stokes (D)

OKLAHOMA
1. James R. Jones (D)
2. Mike Synar (D)
3. Wes Watkins (D)
4. Dave McCurdy (D)
5. Mickey Edwards (R)
6. Glenn English (D)

OREGON
1. Les AuCoin (D)
2. Bob Smith (R)*
3. Ron Wyden (D)
4. James Weaver (D)
5. Denny Smith (R)

PENNSYLVANIA
1. Thomas F. Foglietta (D)
2. William H. Gray III (D)
3. Robert A. Borski (D)*
4. Joseph P. Kolter (D)*
5. Richard T. Schulze (R)
6. Gus Yatron (D)
7. Robert W. Edgar (D)
8. Peter H. Kostmayer (D)*
9. E. G. (Bud) Shuster (R)
10. Joseph M. McDade (R)
11. Frank Harrison (D)*
12. John P. Murtha (D)
13. Lawrence Coughlin (R)
14. William J. Coyne (D)
15. Donald L. Ritter (R)
16. Robert S. Walker (R)
17. George W. Gekas (R)*
18. Doug Walgren (D)
19. William F. Goodling (R)
20. Joseph M. Gaydos (D)
21. Thomas J. Ridge (R)*
22. Austin J. Murphy (D)
23. William Clinger Jr. (R)

RHODE ISLAND
1. F. J. St. Germain (D)
2. Claudine Schneider (R)

SOUTH CAROLINA
1. Thomas F. Hartnett (R)
2. Floyd D. Spence (R)
3. Butler D. Derrick Jr. (D)
4. Carroll Campbell Jr. (R)
5. John Spratt (D)*
6. Robert M. Tallon Jr. (D)*

SOUTH DAKOTA
AL Tom Daschle (D)

TENNESSEE
1. James H. Quillen (R)
2. John J. Duncan (R)
3. Marilyn Bouquard (D)
4. Jim Cooper (D)*
5. Bill Boner (D)
6. Albert Gore Jr. (D)
7. Don Sundquist (R)*
8. Ed Jones (D)
9. Harold E. Ford (D)

TEXAS
1. Sam B. Hall Jr. (D)
2. Charles Wilson (D)
3. Steve Bartlett (R)*
4. Ralph M. Hall (D)
5. John Bryant (D)*
6. Phil Gramm (R)
7. Bill Archer (R)
8. Jack Fields (R)
9. Jack Brooks (D)
10. J. J. Pickle (D)
11. Marvin Leath (D)
12. James C. Wright Jr. (D)
13. Jack Hightower (D)
14. William N. Patman (D)
15. Eligio de la Garza (D)
16. Ronald Coleman (D)*
17. Charles Stenholm (D)
18. Mickey Leland (D)
19. Kent Hance (D)
20. Henry B. Gonzalez (D)
21. Tom Loeffler (R)
22. Ron Paul (R)
23. Abraham Kazen Jr. (D)
24. Martin Frost (D)
25. Mike Andrews (D)*
26. Tom Vandergriff (D)*
27. Solomon P. Ortiz (D)*

UTAH
1. James V. Hansen (R)
2. Dan Marriott (R)
3. Howard C. Nielson (R)*

VERMONT
AL James M. Jeffords (R)

VIRGINIA
1. Herbert Bateman (R)*
2. G. William Whitehurst (R)
3. Thomas J. Bliley Jr. (R)
4. Norman Sisisky (D)*
5. W. C. (Dan) Daniel (D)
6. James Olin (D)*
7. J. Kenneth Robinson (R)
8. Stanford E. Parris (R)
9. Frederick Boucher (D)*
10. Frank R. Wolf (R)

WASHINGTON
1. Joel Pritchard (R)
2. Al Swift (D)
3. Don Bonker (D)
4. Sid Morrison (R)*
5. Thomas S. Foley (D)
6. Norman D. Dicks (D)
7. Mike Lowry (D)
8. Rodney Chandler (R)*

WEST VIRGINIA
1. Alan B. Mollohan (D)*
2. Harley O. Staggers Jr. (D)*
3. Robert E. Wise (D)*
4. Nick J. Rahall II (D)

WISCONSIN
1. Les Aspin (D)
2. Robert W. Kastenmeier (D)
3. Steve Gunderson (R)
4. Vacant
5. James Moody (D)*
6. Thomas E. Petri (R)
7. David R. Obey (D)
8. Tobias A. Roth (R)
9. F. J. Sensenbrenner Jr. (R)

WYOMING
AL Richard Cheney (R)

COMMITTEES OF CONGRESS

The fate of legislation introduced in Congress depends to a large extent on what happens to it in House or Senate committees. Before a bill goes back to either house for a vote, the committee can revise it, change it beyond recognition, or simply bottle it up.

Committee chairmen, who achieve their positions largely through seniority, have considerable influence in determining which measures will or will not become law. They also can use pressure to get their favorite bills passed.

A committee's importance is determined by the kind of legislation it handles. The House Ways and Means Committee and the Senate Finance Committee are responsible for all tax, tariff, and Social Security legislation.

The House Rules Committee decides which bills will go to the floor of the House. The House and Senate Appropriations Committees consider appropriation measures, and the House and Senate Budget Committees establish the federal budget for each fiscal year.

Listed below are the permanent committees, their chairmen, and members by party (D-Democrat; R-Republican) during the second session of the 98th Congress in 1984.

COMMITTEE, CHAIRMAN, AND MEMBERSHIP	JURISDICTION	COMMITTEE, CHAIRMAN, AND MEMBERSHIP
SENATE		HOUSE
Agriculture, Nutrition, and Forestry Jesse A. Helms (R-N.C.) R-10, D-8	All matters dealing with agriculture, including farm credit and security, crop insurance, soil conservation, and rural electrification; **and (Senate only) forestry; human nutrition, including school nutrition programs**	**Agriculture** E. de la Garza (D-Tex.) D-26, R-15
Appropriations Mark O. Hatfield (R-Oreg.) R-15, D-14	All matters pertaining to the appropriations of government revenues	**Appropriations** Jamie L. Whitten (D-Miss.) D-36, R-21
Armed Services John G. Tower (R-Texas) R-10, D-8	Military affairs, including aeronautical and space activities concerned with weapons systems; **and (Senate only) Panama Canal and Canal Zone**	**Armed Services** Melvin Price (D-Ill.) D-28, R-16
Banking, Housing, and Urban Affairs Jake Garn (R-Utah) R-10, D-8	All financial matters other than taxes and appropriations, particulary those concerned with banking and currency, including public and private housing matters; urban affairs	**Banking, Finance, and Urban Affairs** Ferdinand J. St. Germain (D-R.I.) D-29, R-17
Budget Pete V. Domenici (R-N.M.) R-12, D-10	Reviews presidential budget proposals; considers advice of congressional budget office and other committees regarding federal expenditures	**Budget** James R. Jones (D-Okla.) D-20, R-11
Commerce, Science, and Commerce Robert W. Packwood (R-Oreg.) R-9, D-8	Interstate transportation and communications, inland waterways, civil aeronautics; **(Senate only) science; weather; (House only) foreign commerce, railroad labor, securities and exchanges, interstate oil compacts, natural gas and public health, regulation of interstate transmission of power (except between government projects)**	**Energy and Commerce** John D. Dingell (D-Mich.) D-27, R-15
	Merchant Marine, Coast Guard, Coast and Geodetic Survey, fisheries and wildlife Maintenance and operation of Panama Canal and administration of Canal Zone	**Merchant Marine and Fisheries** Walter B. Jones (D-N.C.) D-25, R-14
Energy and Natural Resources James A. McClure (R-Idaho) R-11, D-9	Energy regulation, conservation; research and development; solar energy; oil and gas; hydroelectric power; coal; naval petroleum; mining; public parks; recreation areas; public lands	**Interior and Insular Affairs** Morris K. Udall (D-Ariz.) D-25, R-14
Environment and Public Works Robert T. Stafford (R-Vt.) R-9, D-7	Environment in general; environmental research; fisheries and wildlife; ocean dumping; solid waste disposal; pollution; public works; dams and bridges; federal buildings	(In House split among several committees)

SENATE COMMITTEE, CHAIRMAN, AND MEMBERSHIP	JURISDICTION	HOUSE COMMITTEE, CHAIRMAN, AND MEMBERSHIP
Select Ethics Ted Stevens (R-Alaska) R-3, D-3	Standards and conduct of members and employees; recommends remedies for unethical conduct	**Standards of Official Conduct** Louis Stokes (D-Ohio) D-6, R-6
Finance Robert Dole (R-Kan.) R-11, D-9	All matters pertaining to taxes, tariffs, import quotas, social security, and social welfare	**Ways and Means** Dan Rostenkowski (D-Ill.) D-23, R-12
Foreign Relations Charles H. Percy (R-Ill.) R-9, D-8	Relations of the United States with foreign nations and international organizations, including the Red Cross, diplomatic service, United Nations, foreign loans, **and (Senate only) treaties**	**Foreign Affairs** Vacant D-24, R-13
Governmental Affairs William V. Roth Jr. (R-Del.) R-10, D-8	Reorganization of the Executive Branch, and governmental relationships between federal, state, and local governments; civil service; **and (Senate only) between U.S. and international organizations; District of Columbia**	**Government Operations** Jack Brooks (D-Texas) D-25, R-14
Judiciary Strom Thurmond (R-S.C.) R-10, D-8	Federal courts and judges, civil rights, civil liberties, constitutional amendments, interstate compacts, immigration and naturalization, apportionment of representatives, meetings of Congress, and members' attendance; **(Senate only)** claims against the United States; **(House only)** presidential succession and impeachment	**Judiciary** Peter W. Rodino Jr. (D-N.J.) D-20, R-11
Labor and Human Resources Orrin G. Hatch (R-Utah) R-10, D-8	Health, education, public welfare, labor, arts, child development, migratory labor, handicapped, health research, aging	**Education and Labor** Carl D. Perkins (D-Ky.) D-20, R-11
Rules and Administration Charles McC. Mathias Jr. (R-Md.) R-7, D-5	General administration of the Senate and management of the Library of Congress and the Smithsonian Institution; **(House only)** rules and orders of business of the House	**Rules** Claude D. Pepper (D-Fla.) D-9, R-4
Select Indian Affairs Mark Andrews (R-N.D.) R-4, D-3	All legislation on Indian affairs; Indian problems in education, health, and other areas; Indian claims against the United States	(Indian affairs under House Interior and Insular Affairs Committee)
Select Small Business Lowell P. Weicker Jr. (R-Conn.) R-10, D-9	Study and investigation of the problems of small business and of legislation affecting small business	**Small Business** Parren J. Mitchell (D-Md.) D-26, R-15
Veterans Affairs Alan K. Simpson (R-Wyo.) R-7, D-5	Veterans pensions, armed forces life insurance, rehabilitation, education, medical care and treatment of veterans, veterans hospitals	**Veterans Affairs** G.V. Montgomery (D-Miss.) D-21, R-12
(see **Senate Governmental Affairs Committee**)	Operation of all municipal affairs of the District of Columbia except for the appropriation of money for its operation	**District of Columbia** Ronald V. Dellums (D-Calif.) D-7, R-4
—	House administration; printing and correction of the Congressional Record; federal elections; and management of the Library of Congress; supervision of the Smithsonian Institution	**House Administration** Augustus F. Hawkins (D-Calif.) D-12, R-7
—	All matters pertaining to the postal and civil services; the census; the National Archives	**Post Office and Civil Service** William D. Ford (D-Mich.) D-15, R-9
—	Public buildings and roads; flood control, improvement of rivers and harbors; stream pollution; waterpower; and transportation	**Public Works and Transportation** James J. Howard (D-N.J.) D-30, R-18
—	Nonmilitary scientific research, development, and administration of all matters in energy and space and aeronautical activities; National Science Foundation; National Weather Service	**Science and Technology** Don Fuqua (D-Fla.) D-26, R-15
Select Committee on Aging John Heinz (R-Pa.) R-8, D-7	Investigation of problems of aged.; (Senate only) cannot send legislation to floor	**Select Aging** Claude Pepper (D-Fla.) D-38, R-22
Select Intelligence Barry Goldwater (R-Ariz.) R-8, D-7	Legislation, and budgets of CIA, FBI, and other intelligence agencies of the federal government	**Select Intelligence** Edward P. Boland (D-Mass.) D-9, R-5

POLITICAL MAKEUP OF CONGRESS: 1789–1984

CONGRESS	YEARS	PRESIDENT AND PARTY		HOUSE OF REPRESENTATIVES			SENATE		
				Majority Party	Minority Party	Other	Majority Party	Minority Party	Other
1st	1789–1791	G. Washington	Fed	Fed-38	AF-26	—	Fed-17	AF-9	—
2d	1791–1793	G. Washington	Fed	Fed-37	DR-33	—	Fed-16	DR-13	—
3d	1793–1795	G. Washington	Fed	DR-57	Fed-48	—	Fed-17	DR-13	—
4th	1795–1797	G. Washington	Fed	Fed-54	DR-52	—	Fed-19	DR-13	—
5th	1797–1799	J. Adams	Fed	Fed-58	DR-48	—	Fed-20	DR-12	—
6th	1799–1801	J. Adams	Fed	Fed-64	DR-42	—	Fed-19	DR-13	—
7th	1801–1803	T. Jefferson	DR	DR-69	Fed-36	—	DR-18	Fed-13	—
8th	1803–1805	T. Jefferson	DR	DR-102	Fed-39	—	DR-25	Fed-9	—
9th	1805–1807	T. Jefferson	DR	DR-116	Fed-25	—	DR-27	Fed-7	—
10th	1807–1809	T. Jefferson	DR	DR-118	Fed-24	—	DR-28	Fed-6	—
11th	1809–1811	J. Madison	DR	DR-94	Fed-48	—	DR-28	Fed-6	—
12th	1811–1813	J. Madison	DR	DR-108	Fed-36	—	DR-30	Fed-6	—
13th	1813–1815	J. Madison	DR	DR-112	Fed-68	—	DR-27	Fed-9	—
14th	1815–1817	J. Madison	DR	DR-117	Fed-65	—	DR-25	Fed-11	—
15th	1817–1819	J. Monroe	DR	DR-141	Fed-42	—	DR-34	Fed-10	—
16th	1819–1821	J. Monroe	DR	DR-156	Fed-27	—	DR-35	Fed-7	—
17th	1821–1823	J. Monroe	DR	DR-158	Fed-25	—	DR-44	Fed-4	—
18th	1823–1825	J. Monroe	DR	DR-187	Fed-26	—	DR-44	Fed-4	—
19th	1825–1827	J. Q. Adams	Co	Co-105	Ja-97	—	Co-26	Ja-20	—
20th	1827–1829	J. Q. Adams	Co	Ja-119	Co-94	—	Ja-28	Co-20	—
21st	1829–1831	A. Jackson	D	D-139	NR-74	—	D-26	NR-22	—
22d	1831–1833	A. Jackson	D	D-141	NR-58	14	D-25	NR-21	2
23d	1833–1835	A. Jackson	D	D-147	AM-53	60	D-20	NR-20	8
24th	1835–1837	A. Jackson	D	D-145	W-98	—	D-27	W-25	—
25th	1837–1839	M. Van Buren	D	D-108	W-107	24	D-30	W-18	4
26th	1839–1841	M. Van Buren	D	D-124	W-118	—	D-28	W-22	—
27th	1841–1843	W. H. Harrison J. Tyler	W W	W-133	D-102	6	W-28	D-22	2
28th	1843–1845	J. Tyler	W	D-142	W-79	1	W-28	D-25	1
29th	1845–1847	J. K. Polk	D	D-143	W-77	6	D-31	W-25	—
30th	1847–1849	J. K. Polk	D	W-115	D-108	4	D-36	W-21	1
31st	1849–1851	Z. Taylor M. Filmore	W W	D-112	W-109	9	D-35	W-25	2
32d	1851–1853	M. Fillmore	W	D-140	W-88	5	D-35	W-24	3
33d	1853–1855	F. Pierce	D	D-159	W-71	4	D-38	W-22	2
34th	1855–1857	F. Pierce	D	R-108	D-83	43	D-42	R-15	5
35th	1857–1859	J. Buchanan	D	D-131	R-92	14	D-39	R-20	5
36th	1859–1861	J. Buchanan	D	R-113	D-101	23	D-38	R-26	2
37th	1861–1863	A. Lincoln	R	R-106	D-42	28	R-31	D-11	7
38th	1863–1865	A. Lincoln	R	R-103	D-80	—	R-39	D-12	—
39th	1865–1867	A. Lincoln A. Johnson	U U	U-145	D-46	—	U-42	D-10	—
40th	1867–1869	A. Johnson	U	R-143	D-49	1	R-42	D-11	—
41st	1869–1871	U. S. Grant	R	R-170	D-73	—	R-61	D-11	2
42d	1871–1873	U. S. Grant	R	R-139	D-104	—	R-57	D-17	—
43d	1873–1875	U. S. Grant	R	R-203	D-88	2	R-54	D-19	1
44th	1875–1877	U. S. Grant	R	D-181	R-107	5	R-46	D-29	1
45th	1877–1879	R. B. Hayes	R	D-156	R-137	—	R-39	D-36	1
46th	1879–1881	R. B. Hayes	R	D-150	R-128	15	D-43	R-33	—
47th	1881–1883	J. A. Garfield C. A. Arthur	R R	R-152	D-130	11	R-37	D-37	2
48th	1883–1885	C. A. Arthur	R	D-200	R-119	6	R-40	D-36	—
49th	1885–1887	G. Cleveland	D	D-182	R-140	3	R-41	D-34	1
50th	1887–1889	G. Cleveland	D	D-170	R-151	4	R-39	D-37	—
51st	1889–1891	B. Harrison	R	R-173	D-156	1	R-47	D-37	—
52d	1891–1893	B. Harrison	R	D-231	R-88	14	R-47	D-39	2

CONGRESS	YEARS	PRESIDENT AND PARTY	HOUSE OF REPRESENTATIVES			SENATE		
			Majority Party	Minority Party	Other	Majority Party	Minority Party	Other
53d	1893–1895	G. Cleveland . . . . . . D	D-220	R-126	10	D-44	R-38	6
54th	1895–1897	G. Cleveland . . . . . . D	R-246	D-104	7	R-44	D-39	5
55th	1897–1899	W. McKinley . . . . R	R-206	D-134	17	R-46	D-34	10
56th	1899–1901	W. McKinley . . . . R	R-185	D-163	9	R-53	D-26	11
57th	1901–1903	W. McKinley . . . . R T. Roosevelt . . . . R	R-198	D-153	6	R-56	D-29	5
58th	1903–1905	T. Roosevelt . . . . R	R-207	D-178	1	R-58	D-32	—
59th	1905–1907	T. Roosevelt . . . . R	R-250	D-136	—	R-58	D-32	—
60th	1907–1909	T. Roosevelt . . . . R	R-222	D-164	—	R-61	D-29	2
61st	1909–1911	W. H. Taft . . . . R	R-219	D-172	—	R-59	D-32	1
62d	1911–1913	W. H. Taft . . . . R	D-228	R-162	1	R-49	D-42	—
63d	1913–1915	W. Wilson . . . . D	D-290	R-127	18	D-51	R-44	1
64th	1915–1917	W. Wilson . . . . D	D-231	R-193	11	D-56	R-39	1
65th	1917–1919	W. Wilson . . . . D	D-210 [1]	R-216	9	D-53	R-42	1
66th	1919–1921	W. Wilson . . . . D	R-237	D-191	7	R-48	D-47	1
67th	1921–1923	W. G. Harding . . . . . R	R-300	D-132	3	R-59	D-37	—
68th	1923–1925	W. G. Harding . . . . . R C. Coolidge . . . . R	R-225	D-207	3	R-51	D-43	2
69th	1925–1927	C. Coolidge . . . . R	R-247	D-183	5	R-54	D-40	2
70th	1927–1929	C. Coolidge . . . . R	R-237	D-195	3	R-48	D-47	1
71st	1929–1931	H. Hoover . . . . R	R-267	D-163	5	R-56	D-39	1
72d	1931–1933	H. Hoover . . . . R	D-216 [2]	R-218	1	R-48	D-47	1
73d	1933–1935	F. D. Roosevelt . . . . D	D-313	R-117	5	D-59	R-36	1
74th	1935–1937	F. D. Roosevelt . . . . D	D-322	R-103	10	D-69	R-25	2
75th	1937–1939	F. D. Roosevelt . . . . D	D-333	R-89	13	D-75	R-17	4
76th	1939–1941	F. D. Roosevelt . . . . D	D-262	R-169	4	D-69	R-23	4
77th	1941–1943	F. D. Roosevelt . . . . D	D-267	R-162	6	D-66	R-28	2
78th	1943–1945	F. D. Roosevelt . . . . D	D-222	R-209	4	D-57	R-38	1
79th	1945–1947	F. D. Roosevelt . . . . D Harry S. Truman . . . D	D-243	R-190	2	D-57	R-38	1
80th	1947–1949	Harry S. Truman . . . D	R-246	D-188	1	R-51	D-45	—
81st	1949–1951	Harry S. Truman . . . D	D-263	R-171	1	D-54	R-42	—
82d	1951–1953	Harry S. Truman . . . D	D-234	R-199	2	D-48	R-47	1
83d	1953–1955	D. D. Eisenhower . . R	R-221	D-213	1	R-48	D-46	2
84th	1955–1957	D. D. Eisenhower . . R	D-232	R-203	—	D-48	R-47	1
85th	1957–1959	D. D. Eisenhower . . R	D-234	R-201	—	D-49	R-47	—
86th	1959–1961	D. D. Eisenhower . . R	D-283	R-153	—	D-64	R-34	—
87th	1961–1963	John F. Kennedy . . . D	D-262	R-175	—	D-64	R-36	—
88th	1963–1965	John F. Kennedy . . . D Lyndon B. Johnson . D	D-258	R-176	1	D-67	R-33	—
89th	1965–1967	Lyndon B. Johnson . D	D-295	R-140	—	D-68	R-32	—
90th	1967–1969	Lyndon B. Johnson . D	D-248	R-187	—	D-64	R-36	—
91st	1969–1971	Richard Nixon . . . . . R	D-243	R-192	—	D-58	R-42	—
92d	1971–1973	Richard Nixon . . . . . R	D-255	R-180	—	D-54	R-44	2
93d	1973–1975	Richard Nixon . . . . . R Gerald Ford . . . . R	D-242	R-192	1	D-56	R-42	2
94th	1975–1977	Gerald Ford . . . . R	D-291	R-144	—	D-60	R-37	2
95th	1977–1979	Jimmy Carter . . . . . D	D-292	R-143	—	D-61	R-38	1
96th	1979–1981	Jimmy Carter . . . . . D	D-277	R-158	—	D-58	R-41	1
97th	1981–1983	Ronald Reagan . . . . R	D-242	R-192	1	R-53	D-46	1
98th	1983–1985	Ronald Reagan . . . . R	D-267	R-167	1	R-55	D-45	—

Political party abbreviations: AF—Antifederalist; AM—Anti-Masonic; Co—Coalition; D—Democrat; DR—Democratic-Republican; Fed—Federalist; Ja—Jacksonian; NR—National Republican; R—Republican; U—Unionist; W—Whig.

[1] Democrats organized House with help of other parties. [2] Democrats organized House because of Republican deaths.

SPEAKERS OF THE HOUSE OF REPRESENTATIVES: 1789–1984

The speaker of the U.S. House of Representatives is the third most important position in the federal government after President and Vice President. He presides over the House and is the recognized leader of the majority party in the House of Representatives.

There are several ways in which the speaker can become President without being elected to that office, including:

If both the office of President and Vice President should become vacant as a result of the deaths or resignations of the incumbents.

If the office of Vice President is vacant and the incumbent President should die or resign before a new Vice President is sworn in.

If the President-elect and the Vice President-elect are found not to be qualified to take office on Inauguration Day.

Rep. Thomas P. O'Neill Jr. (D-Mass.) was chosen speaker without opposition in December 1976 after the retirement of Rep. Carl Albert (D-Okla.), who had held the position since 1971. O'Neill has served in Congress since 1953 from the same district once represented by President John Kennedy.

Only one speaker ever has become President: James K. Polk of Tennessee, who served in the position in 1835–39.

CONGRESS	SPEAKER	PARTY	CONGRESS	SPEAKER	PARTY
1st (1789–91)	Frederick A. C. Muhlenberg	Federalist	47th (1881–83)	J. Warren Keifer	Republican
2d (1791–93)	Jonathan Trumbull	Federalist	48th (1883–85)	John G. Carlisle	Democrat
3d (1793–95)	Frederick A. C. Muhlenberg	Federalist	49th (1885–87)	John G. Carlisle	Democrat
4th (1795–97)	Jonathan Dayton	Federalist	50th (1887–89)	John G. Carlisle	Democrat
5th (1797–99)	Jonathan Dayton	Federalist	51st (1889–91)	Thomas B. Reed	Republican
	George Dent	Dem.-Rep.	52d (1891–93)	Charles F. Crisp	Democrat
6th (1799–1801)	Theodore Sedgwick	Federalist	53d (1893–95)	Charles F. Crisp	Democrat
7th (1801–03)	Nathaniel Macon	Dem.-Rep.	54th (1895–97)	Thomas B. Reed	Republican
8th (1803–05)	Nathaniel Macon	Dem.-Rep.	55th (1897–99)	Thomas B. Reed	Republican
9th (1805–07)	Nathaniel Macon	Dem.-Rep.	56th (1899–1901)	David B. Henderson	Republican
10th (1807–09)	Joseph B. Varnum	Dem.-Rep.	57th (1901–03)	David B. Henderson	Republican
11th (1809–11)	Joseph B. Varnum	Dem.-Rep.	58th (1903–05)	Joseph G. Cannon	Republican
12th (1811–13)	Henry Clay	Dem.-Rep.	59th (1905–07)	Joseph G. Cannon	Republican
13th (1813–15)	Henry Clay	Dem.-Rep.	60th (1907–09)	Joseph G. Cannon	Republican
	Langdon Cheves	Dem.-Rep.	61st (1909–11)	Joseph G. Cannon	Republican
14th (1815–17)	Henry Clay	Dem.-Rep.	62d (1911–13)	Champ Clark	Democrat
15th (1817–19)	Henry Clay	Dem.-Rep.	63d (1913–15)	Champ Clark	Democrat
16th (1819–21)	Henry Clay	Dem.-Rep.	64th (1915–17)	Champ Clark	Democrat
	John W. Taylor	Dem.-Rep.	65th (1917–19)	Champ Clark	Democrat
17th (1821–23)	Philip P. Barbour	Dem.-Rep.	66th (1919–21)	Frederick H. Gillett	Republican
18th (1823–25)	Henry Clay	Dem.-Rep.	67th (1921–23)	Frederick H. Gillett	Republican
19th (1825–27)	John W. Taylor	Dem.-Rep.	68th (1923–25)	Frederick H. Gillett	Republican
20th (1827–29)	Andrew Stevenson	Democrat	69th (1925–27)	Nicholas Longworth	Republican
21st (1829–31)	Andrew Stevenson	Democrat	70th (1927–29)	Nicholas Longworth	Republican
22d (1831–33)	Andrew Stevenson	Democrat	71st (1929–31)	Nicholas Longworth	Republican
23d (1833–35)	Andrew Stevenson	Democrat	72d (1931–33)	John N. Garner	Democrat
	John Bell	Whig	73d (1933–35)	Henry T. Rainey	Democrat
24th (1835–37)	James K. Polk	Democrat	74th (1935–37)	Joseph W. Byrns	Democrat
25th (1837–39)	James K. Polk	Democrat		William B. Bankhead	Democrat
26th (1839–41)	Robert M. T. Hunter	Democrat	75th (1937–39)	William B. Bankhead	Democrat
27th (1841–43)	John White	Whig	76th (1939–41)	William B. Bankhead	Democrat
28th (1843–45)	John W. Jones	Democrat		Sam Rayburn	Democrat
29th (1845–47)	John W. Davis	Democrat	77th (1941–43)	Sam Rayburn	Democrat
30th (1847–49)	Robert C. Winthrop	Whig	78th (1943–45)	Sam Rayburn	Democrat
31st (1849–51)	Howell Cobb	Democrat	79th (1945–47)	Sam Rayburn	Democrat
32d (1851–53)	Linn Boyd	Democrat	80th (1947–49)	Joseph W. Martin Jr.	Republican
33d (1853–55)	Linn Boyd	Democrat	81st (1949–51)	Sam Rayburn	Democrat
34th (1855–57)	Nathaniel P. Banks	American	82d (1951–53)	Sam Rayburn	Democrat
35th (1857–59)	James L. Orr	Democrat	83d (1953–55)	Joseph W. Martin Jr.	Republican
36th (1859–61)	William Pennington	Whig	84th (1955–57)	Sam Rayburn	Democrat
37th (1861–63)	Galusha A. Grow	Republican	85th (1957–59)	Sam Rayburn	Democrat
38th (1863–65)	Schuyler Colfax	Republican	86th (1959–61)	Sam Rayburn	Democrat
39th (1865–67)	Schuyler Colfax	Republican	87th (1961–63)	Sam Rayburn	Democrat
40th (1867–69)	Schuyler Colfax	Republican	88th (1963–65)	John W. McCormack	Democrat
	Theodore M. Pomeroy	Republican	89th (1965–67)	John W. McCormack	Democrat
41st (1869–71)	James G. Blaine	Republican	90th (1967–69)	John W. McCormack	Democrat
42d (1871–73)	James G. Blaine	Republican	91st (1969–71)	John W. McCormack	Democrat
43d (1873–75)	James G. Blaine	Republican	92d (1971–73)	Carl Albert	Democrat
44th (1875–77)	Michael C. Kerr	Democrat	93d (1973–75)	Carl Albert	Democrat
	Samuel S. Cox	Democrat	94th (1975–77)	Carl Albert	Democrat
	Milton Sayler	Democrat	95th (1977–79)	Thomas P. O'Neill Jr.	Democrat
	Samuel J. Randall	Democrat	96th (1979–81)	Thomas P. O'Neill Jr.	Democrat
45th (1877–79)	Samuel J. Randall	Democrat	97th (1981–83)	Thomas P. O'Neill Jr.	Democrat
46th (1879–81)	Samuel J. Randall	Democrat	98th (1983–85)	Thomas P. O'Neill Jr.	Democrat

Crime

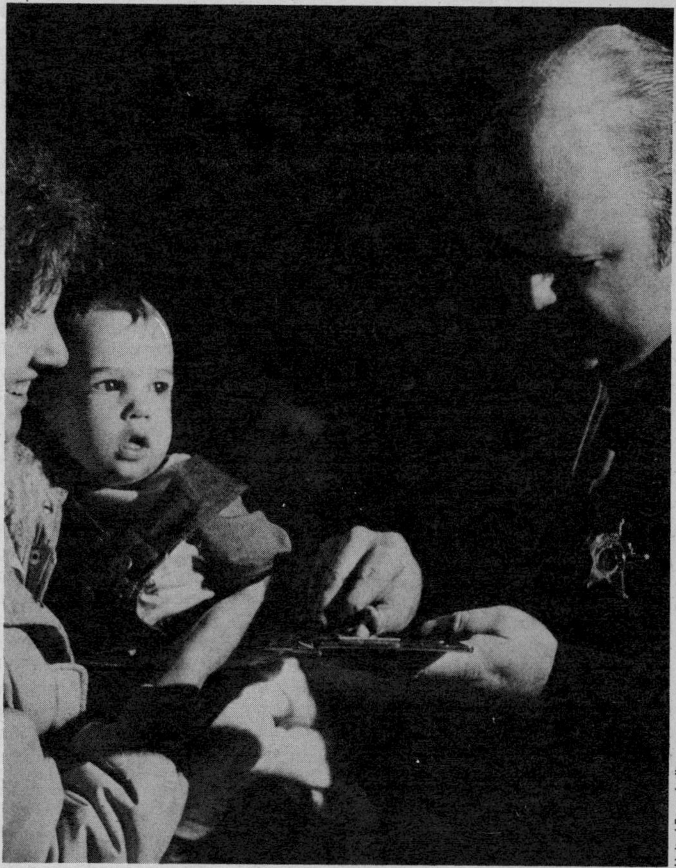

United Press Int'l.

Cuyahoga County Deputy Sheriff Bob Szudarek fingerprints eight month-old Michael Marunowski in Cleveland, Ohio, as part of a program to provide identification of kidnapped and missing children. Similar programs were conducted in many parts of the nation as authorities sought to improve efforts at finding the estimated 150,000 children who are abducted each year. Officials say that 20,000 to 40,000 missing children cases remain unsolved each year.

HIGHLIGHTS: 1983

NO. 1 CRIME PROBLEM—DRUGS

Vice President George Bush, former head of the CIA, was placed in charge of a new federal effort to stop the smuggling of drugs into the U.S. In the Reagan administration's war against the $80 billion criminal narcotics industry, Bush said he would coordinate activities of the CIA, military intelligence agencies, and domestic crime fighters to intercept drug smugglers.

Called the National Narcotics Border Interdiction System, the program set up regional offices in New York City; El Paso, Texas; New Orleans, La.; Long Beach, Calif., and Chicago.

Francis M. "Bud" Mullen Jr., who coordinated the FBI's Abscam investigation of corruption in Congress, became administrator of the Drug Enforcement Administration in October. The U.S. Senate finally confirmed his appointment after a delay of 19 months. He had headed the agency as acting administrator since July 1981.

Mullen accused Cuba's President Fidel Castro of aiding drug smuggling to finance subversive activities in Latin America.

OVERCROWDED PRISONS

As more and more criminals have been imprisoned each year, the prisons and jails of the United States have become overcrowded. Throughout the nation in 1983 lawsuits

HIGHLIGHTS: 1983 *(continued)*

brought on behalf of inmates have caused courts to order the release of prisoners in New York City, Chicago, Pittsburgh, Grand Rapids, Mich., and elsewhere. In all, some 14,000 prisoners in the U.S. have been released in the past three years with shortened sentences because of the prison conditions.

Alabama called a special session of its legislature in November that approved a $9 million prison construction and expansion program to meet a federal court order that would trigger a mass release of prisoners on March 15, 1984, if overcrowding is not alleviated.

Obeying a federal court order, New York City in the first two weeks of November released 613 prisoners on low bail or no bail. By the end of November, 55 of those released had been rearrested, 35 on felonies that included burglary and narcotics charges. Arrest warrants were issued for 75 others who failed to show up for scheduled court appearances.

In South Carolina, 330 prisoners were freed on Sept. 16 before their sentences had been completed because state prisons were crowded with 15% more prisoners than their capacity.

The U.S. Department of Justice reported that during the first half of 1983 the number of prisoners in federal and state facilities grew by 4.2%, increasing to 431,829. This brought the number of prisoners per 100,000 population to 177. See table on opposite page for 1981–82 statistics on prisoners.

In mid-1983 the states with the most prisoners were California, 37,238; Texas, 36,963; New York, 29,802; and Florida, 27,830.

States with the largest percentages of increases in prisoners in 1983 were North Dakota, 24.8%; Tennessee, 14.2%; Hawaii, 13.9%; and Oklahoma, 13.6%.

Ten states reported fewer prisoners in the first six months of 1983. The largest declines were in West Virginia, 9.2; Connecticut, 5.2; and Michigan, 3.9%.

BIGGEST BRITISH ROBBERY

Overshadowing the Great Train Robbery and other thrillers, six masked gunmen stole $40 million in gold and $175,000 in diamonds from a security vault at Heathrow Airport near London on Nov. 26. The robbers overpowered six guards, poured gasoline over one, and threatened to set him on fire if the others refused to cooperate.

The nearly three tons of stolen gold consisted of 6,800 bars in 76 boxes that had been brought to the Brinks-Mat Ltd. vault only a few hours before the robbery. Officials said the gold occupied a space of about 42 cubic feet.

The thieves also took an unknown amount of scrap gold and travelers checks.

Scotland Yard detectives at first said they had no solid clue as to who the robbers were or how they managed to break through the elaborate alarms, heavy automatic doors, and other security precautions at the heavily guarded warehouse building. But eight days later one of the company's guards, John Black, 31, was arrested on charges of taking part in the robbery and soon after seven other persons were jailed.

U.S. CRIME RATE: 1960–1982

Source: Federal Bureau of Investigation

YEAR	REPORTED CRIMES		VIOLENT CRIMES [2]		PROPERTY CRIMES [3]		MURDERS		ROBBERIES	
	Total	Rate [1]	Total	Rate [1]	Total	Rate [1]	Total	Rate [1]	Total	Rate [1]
1960	3,384,200	1,887.2	288,460	160.9	3,095,700	1,726.3	9,110	5.1	107,840	60.1
1962	3,752,200	2,019.8	301,510	162.3	3,450,700	1,857.5	8,530	4.6	110,860	59.7
1963	4,109,500	2,180.3	316,970	168.2	3,792,500	2,012.1	8,640	4.6	116,470	61.8
1964	4,564,600	2,388.1	364,220	190.6	4,200,400	2,197.5	9,360	4.9	130,390	68.2
1965	4,739,400	2,449.0	387,390	200.2	4,352,000	2,248.8	9,960	5.1	138,690	71.7
1966	5,223,500	2,670.8	430,180	220.0	4,793,300	2,450.9	11,040	5.6	157,990	80.8
1967	5,903,400	2,989.7	499,930	253.2	5,403,500	2,736.5	12,240	6.2	202,910	102.8
1968	6,720,200	3,370.2	595,010	298.4	6,125,200	3,071.8	13,800	6.9	262,840	131.8
1969	7,410,900	3,680.0	661,870	328.7	6,749,000	3,351.3	14,760	7.3	298,850	148.4
1970	8,098,000	3,984.5	738,820	363.5	7,359,200	3,621.0	16,000	7.9	349,860	172.1
1971	8,588,200	4,164.7	816,500	396.0	7,771,700	3,768.8	17,780	8.6	387,700	188.0
1972	8,248,800	3,961.4	834,900	401.0	7,413,900	3,560.4	18,670	9.0	376,290	180.7
1973	8,718,100	4,154.4	875,910	417.4	7,842,200	3,737.0	19,640	9.4	384,220	183.1
1974	10,253,448	4,850.4	974,716	461.1	9,278,732	4,389.3	20,711	9.8	442,397	209.3
1975	11,256,566	5,281.7	1,026,284	481.5	10,230,282	4,800.2	20,505	9.6	464,973	218.2
1976	11,304,788	5,266.4	986,578	459.6	10,318,210	4,806.8	18,784	8.8	420,214	195.8
1977	10,935,777	5,055.1	1,009,499	466.6	9,926,278	4,588.4	19,121	8.8	404,847	187.1
1978	11,141,334	5,109.3	1,061,826	486.9	10,079,508	4,622.4	19,555	9.0	417,038	191.3
1979	12,152,730	5,521.5	1,178,539	535.5	10,974,191	4,986.0	21,456	9.7	466,881	212.1
1980	13,295,400	5,899.9	1,308,898	580.8	11,986,501	5,319.1	23,044	10.2	548,809	243.5
1981	13,290,256	5,799.9	1,321,906	576.9	11,968,350	5,223.0	22,516	9.8	574,134	250.6
1982	12,857,218	5,553.1	1,285,705	555.3	11,571,513	4,997.8	21,012	9.1	536,888	231.9

[1] Crimes per 100,000 population. [2] Violent crimes include murder, forcible rape, robbery, and aggravated assault. [3] Property crimes include burglary, larceny, and auto theft.

STATE AND FEDERAL PRISONERS

Source: U.S. Department of Justice, Bureau of Justice Statistics

From 1981 to 1982 the number of prisoners held by federal and state authorities increased by 42,915—the largest rise since records began to be kept in 1925.

The prison rate, the number of prisoners per 100,000 population, rose from 153 to 170 during the year with the number of female prisoners increasing more rapidly than that of men prisoners.

REGION AND STATE	TOTAL			SHORT TERM PRISONERS [1]			PRISON RATE [2]
	1982	1981	Percent change	1982	1981	Percent change	
United States	412,303	369,388	11.6	17,929	15,868	13.0	170
Male	394,654	353,932	11.5	16,609	14,642	13.4	336
Female	17,649	15,456	14.2	1,320	1,226	7.7	14
Federal institutions	29,673	28,133	5.5	6,021	5,964	1.0	10
State institutions	382,630	341,255	12.1	11,908	9,904	20.2	160
Northeast	59,751	54,013	10.6	2,974	2,835	4.9	115
Maine	1,007	992	1.5	226	186	21.5	69
New Hampshire	445	398	11.8	0	0	—	47
Vermont	599	534	12.2	164	139	18.0	84
Massachusetts	4,431	3,889	13.9	NA	98	—	77
Rhode Island	1,037	962	7.8	255	273	−6.6	82
Connecticut	5,674	5,263	7.8	2,068	1,915	8.0	114
New York	27,910	25,599	9.0	0	0	—	158
New Jersey	8,126	7,011	15.9	201	150	34.0	107
Pennsylvania	10,522	9,365	12.4	60	74	−18.9	88
North Central	77,553	72,348	7.2	1,214	895	35.6	130
Ohio	17,317	14,968	15.7	0	0	—	160
Indiana	8,827	8,022	10.0	532	463	14.9	152
Illinois	13,875	13,206	5.1	281	210	33.8	119
Michigan	14,737	15,157	−2.8	0	0	—	162
Wisconsin	4,662	4,416	5.6	94	0	—	96
Minnesota	2,081	2,024	2.8	0	0	—	50
Iowa	2,829	2,670	6.0	120	116	3.4	93
Missouri	7,283	6,489	12.2	0	0	—	147
North Dakota	359	280	28.2	46	62	−25.8	47
South Dakota	791	693	14.1	36	31	16.1	109
Nebraska	1,680	1,653	1.6	105	13	707.7	99
Kansas	3,112	2,770	12.3	0	0	—	129
South	180,388	159,712	12.9	5,511	3,926	40.4	224
Delaware	2,064	1,712	20.6	557	464	20.0	250
Maryland	11,012	9,335	18.0	585	0	—	244
District of Columbia	4,152	3,479	19.3	801	547	46.4	531
Virginia	10,079	9,388	7.4	364	375	−2.9	177
West Virginia	1,498	1,565	−4.3	2	0	—	77
North Carolina	16,578	15,791	5.0	1,220	937	30.2	255
South Carolina	9,161	8,538	7.3	508	528	−3.8	270
Georgia	14,320	12,444	15.1	406	67	506.0	247
Florida	27,830	23,589	18.0	691	389	77.6	261
Kentucky	4,051	4,167	−2.8	0	0	—	110
Tennessee	8,046	7,897	1.9	0	0	—	173
Alabama	8,687	7,657	13.5	225	458	−50.9	215
Mississippi	5,484	4,624	18.6	125	130	−3.8	210
Arkansas	3,819	3,328	14.8	27	31	−12.9	166
Louisiana	10,935	9,415	16.1	0	0	—	251
Oklahoma	6,390	5,281	21.0	0	0	—	201
Texas	36,282	31,502	15.2	0	0	—	237
West	64,938	55,182	17.7	2,209	2,248	−1.7	139
Montana	917	831	10.3	0	3	—	114
Idaho	1,036	957	8.3	0	0	—	107
Wyoming	677	587	15.3	0	0	—	135
Colorado	3,286	2,772	18.5	0	2	—	108
New Mexico	1,842	1,497	23.0	135	152	−11.2	126
Arizona	5,994	5,223	14.8	8	24	−66.7	209
Utah	1,216	1,140	6.7	17	14	21.4	77
Nevada	2,653	2,116	25.4	0	0	—	301
Washington	6,264	5,336	17.4	0	0	—	148
Oregon	3,867	3,295	17.4	0	3	—	146
California	34,459	29,202	18.0	1,049	1,289	−18.6	135
Alaska	1,301	1,019	27.7	450	311	44.7	194
Hawaii	1,426	1,207	18.1	550	450	22.2	88

[1] Prisoners sentenced to 1 year or less, or unsentenced. [2] Number of prisoners per 100,000 population. NA = not available.

CRIME IN THE STATES: 1982

Source: Federal Bureau of Investigation

An estimated 12,857,218 criminal offenses were reported to law-enforcement agencies in 1982, down 3.3% from 1981. Property crimes decreased 3.3%, while the number of violent crimes fell by 2.7%.

Nevada had the highest crime rate in the nation, with 7,901.0 per 100,000 population. Florida was second with 7,465.2 and California third with 7,285.5. California continues to lead the nation with the largest number of crimes—1,801,256.

West Virginia had the lowest crime rate—2,511.2. North Dakota reported the fewest number of crimes—17,742.

STATE	REPORTED CRIMES		VIOLENT CRIMES [2]		PROPERTY CRIMES [3]		MURDERS		ROBBERIES	
	Total	Rate[1]	Total	Rate[1]	Total	Rate[1]	Total	Rate[1]	Total	Rate[1]
U.S. TOTAL	**12,857,218**	**5,553.1**	**1,285,705**	**555.3**	**11,571,513**	**4,997.8**	**21,012**	**9.1**	**536,888**	**231.9**
Alabama	182,701	4,633.6	17,653	447.7	165,048	4,185.8	417	10.6	4,417	112.0
Alaska	27,211	6,212.6	2,732	623.7	24,479	5,588.8	81	18.5	586	133.8
Arizona	203,946	7,131.0	14,785	517.0	189,161	6,614.0	236	8.3	4,537	158.6
Arkansas	88,697	3,871.5	7,438	324.7	81,259	3,546.9	187	8.2	1,805	78.8
California	1,801,256	7,285.5	201,429	814.7	1,599,827	6,470.7	2,779	11.2	91,988	372.1
Colorado	215,584	7,079.9	15,354	504.2	200,230	6,575.7	182	6.0	4,587	150.6
Connecticut	171,129	5,427.5	12,597	399.5	158,532	5,028.0	164	5.2	6,574	208.5
Delaware	38,437	6,384.9	3,370	559.8	35,067	5,825.1	32	5.3	737	122.4
Florida	777,577	7,465.2	93,411	896.8	684,166	6,568.4	1,409	13.5	31,002	297.6
Georgia	294,060	5,214.8	26,963	478.2	267,097	4,736.6	713	12.6	8,716	154.6
Hawaii	65,448	6,584.3	2,542	255.7	62,906	6,328.6	31	3.1	1,560	156.9
Idaho	39,403	4,083.2	2,501	259.2	36,902	3,824.0	24	2.5	292	30.3
Illinois	551,465	4,817.1	51,955	453.8	499,510	4,363.3	1,005	8.8	23,456	204.9
Indiana	242,338	4,429.5	16,444	300.6	225,894	4,128.9	355	6.5	5,966	109.0
Iowa	120,166	4,136.5	5,018	172.7	115,148	3,963.8	67	2.3	1,051	36.2
Kansas	119,244	4,952.0	8,088	335.9	111,156	4,616.1	138	5.7	2,095	87.0
Kentucky	130,854	3,568.4	11,550	315.0	119,304	3,253.4	355	9.7	3,568	97.3
Louisiana	231,674	5,311.2	29,185	669.1	202,489	4,642.1	698	16.0	9,275	212.6
Maine	43,731	3,859.8	1,847	163.0	41,884	3,696.7	24	2.1	345	30.5
Maryland	256,428	6,012.4	36,254	850.0	220,174	5,162.3	432	10.1	15,377	360.5
Massachusetts	318,171	5,503.7	33,031	571.4	285,140	4,932.4	219	3.8	12,359	213.8
Michigan	618,001	6,784.5	59,806	656.6	558,195	6,128.0	827	9.1	24,699	271.1
Minnesota	184,110	4,454.6	9,062	219.3	175,048	4,235.4	95	2.3	4,188	101.3
Mississippi	91,137	3,572.6	7,515	294.6	83,622	3,278.0	358	14.0	1,863	73.0
Missouri	244,966	4,947.8	25,078	506.5	219,888	4,441.3	479	9.7	9,554	193.0
Montana	34,709	4,333.2	1,801	224.8	32,908	4,108.4	31	3.9	265	33.1
Nebraska	62,660	3,950.8	3,641	229.6	59,019	3,721.2	31	2.0	982	61.9
Nevada	69,608	7,901.0	7,096	805.4	62,512	7,095.6	120	13.6	3,697	419.6
New Hampshire	36,416	3,829.2	1,187	124.8	35,229	3,704.4	21	2.2	322	33.9
New Jersey	422,191	5,676.1	45,175	607.4	377,016	5,068.8	482	6.5	22,880	307.6
New Mexico	89,798	6,607.7	9,982	734.5	79,816	5,873.1	158	11.6	1,715	126.2
New York	1,142,202	6,468.1	174,833	990.1	967,369	5,478.1	2,013	11.4	107,843	610.7
North Carolina	273,458	4,543.2	26,865	446.3	246,593	4,096.9	545	9.1	5,168	85.9
North Dakota	17,742	2,648.1	414	61.8	17,328	2,586.3	5	0.7	85	12.7
Ohio	532,594	4,935.5	47,126	436.7	485,468	4,498.8	676	6.3	19,809	183.6
Oklahoma	165,917	5,222.4	14,103	443.9	151,814	4,778.5	344	10.8	4,218	132.8
Oregon	173,973	6,567.5	12,529	473.0	161,444	6,094.5	136	5.1	4,433	167.3
Pennsylvania	409,670	3,452.8	42,767	360.4	366,903	3,092.3	678	5.7	20,806	175.4
Rhode Island	51,388	5,364.1	3,849	401.8	47,539	4,962.3	35	3.7	1,099	114.7
South Carolina	171,718	5,361.2	23,061	720.0	148,657	4,641.2	348	10.9	3,921	122.4
South Dakota	18,276	2,644.9	684	99.0	17,592	2,545.9	19	2.7	118	17.1
Tennessee	205,278	4,413.6	19,586	421.1	185,692	3,992.5	452	9.7	8,173	175.7
Texas	962,977	6,302.2	88,178	577.1	874,799	5,725.1	2,466	16.1	33,618	220.0
Utah	82,891	5,334.0	4,440	285.7	78,451	5,048.3	53	3.4	1,344	86.5
Vermont	24,210	4,691.9	655	126.9	23,555	4,564.9	12	2.3	119	23.1
Virginia	233,683	4,255.7	16,970	309.1	216,713	3,946.7	405	7.4	6,708	122.2
Washington	266,680	6,282.2	17,251	406.4	249,429	5,875.8	185	4.4	5,003	117.9
West Virginia	48,919	2,511.2	3,405	174.8	45,514	2,336.4	102	5.2	970	49.8
Wisconsin	211,524	4,439.1	9,077	190.5	202,447	4,248.6	148	3.1	3,393	71.2
Wyoming	24,116	4,804.0	1,527	304.2	22,589	4,499.8	46	9.2	172	34.3

1 Crimes per 100,000 population. 2 Violent crimes include murder, forcible rape, robbery, and aggravated assault.
3 Property crimes include burglary, larceny of $50 or more, and auto theft.

CRIME IN U.S. METROPOLITAN AREAS: 1982

Source: Federal Bureau of Investigation

Atlantic City, N.J., once again was the metropolitan area with the highest crime rate in the United States in 1982, counting 12,889.7 crimes per 100,000 population. Miami, Fla., was in second place with a rate of 10,289.4. Las Vegas, Nev., was third with a rate of 9,614.4; West Palm Beach, Fla., was fourth with a rate of 8,877.2; and Gainesville, Fla., was fifth with a rate of 8,842.5.

Other metropolitan areas with a crime rate of more than 8,500 per 100,000 population were Lubbock, Tex., and Bakersfield, Calif.

Among the nation's 10 largest metropolitan areas, New York, N.Y.-N.J. had the highest rate with 8,496.6; Detroit, Mich., was second with 8,175.4; Los Angeles-Long Beach, Calif., was third with 8,172.2; Dallas, Tex., was fourth with 8,047.6; and San Francisco-Oakland, Calif., was fifth with 7,775.3.

	TOTAL CRIMES		VIOLENT CRIMES[2]		PROPERTY CRIMES[3]		MURDERS		ROBBERIES	
	Number	Rate[1]	Total	Rate[1]	Total	Rate[1]	Total	Rate[1]	Total	Rate[1]
Akron, Ohio	33,372	5,043.3	2,316	350.0	31,056	4,693.3	24	3.6	785	118.6
Albany-Schenectady, N.Y.	29,299	3,656.8	2,175	271.5	27,124	3,385.4	20	2.5	554	69.1
Albuquerque, N. Mex.	35,368	7,512.1	3,597	764.0	31,771	6,748.1	42	8.9	1,029	218.6
Allentown-Easton, Pa.-N.J.	21,676	3,386.2	1,248	195.0	20,428	3,191.2	26	4.1	465	72.6
Amarillo, Tex.	11,801	6,305.7	920	491.6	10,881	5,814.1	25	13.4	234	125.0
Anaheim-Santa Ana, Calif.	123,268	6,092.3	8,407	415.5	114,861	5,676.8	83	4.1	3,665	181.1
Ann Arbor, Mich.	18,523	7,168.3	1,285	497.3	17,238	6,671.1	16	6.2	257	99.5
Appleton-Oshkosh, Wis.	12,573	4,290.6	311	106.1	12,262	4,184.4	4	1.4	49	16.7
Asheville, N.C.	6,518	3,574.1	401	219.9	6,117	3,354.2	13	7.1	93	51.0
Atlanta, Ga.	145,842	6,946.2	15,104	719.4	130,738	6,226.8	265	12.6	5,794	276.0
Atlantic City, N.J.	24,722	12,889.7	1,894	987.5	22,828	11,902.2	27	14.1	832	433.8
Austin, Tex.	40,564	7,060.1	2,188	380.8	38,376	6,679.3	79	13.7	754	131.2
Bakersfield, Calif.	35,902	8,510.2	3,328	788.9	32,574	7,721.4	62	14.7	1,138	269.8
Baltimore, Md.	151,261	6,867.9	25,841	1,173.3	125,420	5,694.6	294	13.3	11,245	510.6
Baton Rouge, La.	39,786	7,705.7	4,560	883.2	35,226	6,822.6	73	14.1	969	187.7
Battle Creek, Mich.	10,453	5,697.9	774	421.9	9,679	5,276.0	9	4.9	191	104.1
Beaumont-Port Arthur, Tex.	24,275	6,006.1	3,198	791.2	21,077	5,214.8	43	10.6	858	212.3
Biloxi-Gulfport, Miss.	12,333	6,610.0	1,012	542.4	11,321	6,067.6	29	15.5	279	149.5
Binghamton, N.Y.-Pa.	9,413	3,094.5	265	87.1	9,148	3,007.4	4	1.3	70	23.0
Birmingham, Ala.	52,457	6,222.7	5,108	605.9	47,349	5,616.8	134	15.9	1,729	205.1
Boise, Idaho	9,134	5,167.5	713	403.4	8,421	4,764.1	5	2.8	93	52.6
Boston, Mass.	197,983	6,031.3	22,328	680.2	175,655	5,351.1	173	5.3	10,056	306.3
Bradenton, Fla.	10,023	6,201.5	850	525.9	9,173	5,675.6	12	7.4	194	120.0
Bridgeport, Conn.	47,679	5,842.1	3,263	399.8	44,416	5,442.3	50	6.1	1,764	216.1
Brockton, Mass.	23,068	5,654.9	1,984	486.4	21,084	5,168.6	14	3.4	369	90.5
Brownsville, Tex.	13,306	5,926.0	951	423.5	12,355	5,502.5	23	10.2	162	72.1
Canton, Ohio	15,951	3,940.9	1,149	283.9	14,802	3,657.0	17	4.2	436	107.7
Cedar Rapids, Iowa	9,291	5,479.6	313	184.6	8,978	5,295.0	4	2.4	95	56.0
Charleston, S.C.	28,711	6,674.3	3,955	919.4	24,756	5,754.9	55	12.8	1,125	261.5
Charleston, W. Va.	11,341	4,327.5	840	320.5	10,501	4,006.9	13	5.0	359	137.0
Charlotte-Gastonia, N.C.	49,952	7,672.5	5,155	791.8	44,797	6,880.7	66	10.1	1,198	184.0
Chattanooga, Tenn.-Ga.	24,167	5,557.6	1,887	433.9	22,280	5,123.6	49	11.3	459	105.6
Chicago, Ill.	375,943	5,283.3	38,193	536.7	337,750	4,746.6	834	11.7	20,311	285.4
Cincinnati, Ohio-Ky.-Ind.	75,994	5,450.4	6,707	481.0	69,287	4,969.4	83	6.0	2,324	166.7
Cleveland, Ohio	101,554	5,345.9	12,730	670.1	88,824	4,675.8	250	13.2	6,328	333.1
Colorado Springs, Colo.	21,993	6,546.2	1,575	468.8	20,418	6,077.4	15	4.5	495	147.3
Columbia, S.C.	28,289	6,831.4	3,868	934.1	24,421	5,897.3	49	11.8	907	219.0
Columbus, Ga.-Ala.	11,483	4,629.8	985	397.1	10,498	4,232.7	25	10.1	388	156.4
Columbus, Ohio	72,404	6,634.1	6,065	555.7	66,339	6,078.4	100	9.2	2,957	270.9
Corpus Christi, Tex.	26,499	7,559.1	2,257	643.8	24,242	6,915.3	53	15.1	556	158.6
Dallas-Fort Worth, Tex.	257,239	8,047.6	22,950	718.0	234,289	7,329.6	509	15.9	9,293	290.7
Davenport, Iowa-Ill.	19,277	5,011.0	1,421	369.4	17,856	4,641.6	7	1.8	387	100.6
Dayton, Ohio	53,821	6,488.0	5,087	613.2	48,734	5,874.7	74	8.9	2,743	330.7
Daytona Beach, Fla.	20,203	7,439.4	1,821	670.6	18,382	6,768.8	24	8.8	471	173.4
Denver-Boulder, Colo.	135,923	7,961.0	10,176	596.0	125,747	7,365.0	121	7.1	3,625	212.3
Des Moines, Iowa	26,283	7,795.3	1,222	362.4	25,061	7,432.9	18	5.3	388	115.1
Detroit, Mich.	350,214	8,175.4	38,148	890.5	312,066	7,284.9	614	14.3	20,372	475.6
El Paso, Tex.	31,048	6,005.3	4,151	802.9	26,897	5,202.4	46	8.9	956	184.9
Erie, Pa.	10,055	3,587.5	860	306.8	9,195	3,280.6	9	3.2	340	121.3
Eugene-Springfield, Oreg.	17,894	6,503.8	685	249.0	17,209	6,254.8	14	5.1	256	93.0
Evansville, Ind.-Ky.	14,494	4,707.8	1,116	362.5	13,378	4,345.3	14	4.5	287	93.2
Fall River, Mass.	23,524	4,914.0	1,832	382.7	21,692	4,531.3	6	1.3	491	102.6
Fayetteville, N.C.	15,921	6,285.1	1,468	579.5	14,453	5,705.6	22	8.7	456	180.0
Flint, Mich.	40,452	7,857.7	4,308	836.8	36,144	7,020.9	42	8.2	1,077	209.2
Ft. Collins, Col.	9,015	5,758.4	466	297.7	8,549	5,460.8	3	1.9	45	28.7
Ft. Lauderdale-Hollywood, Fla.	88,329	8,122.4	8,748	804.4	79,581	7,317.9	149	13.7	4,004	368.2

1 Crimes per 100,000 population. 2 Violent crimes includes murder, forcible rape, robbery, and aggravated assault. 3 Property crimes include burglary, larceny of $50 or more, and auto theft.

CRIME IN U.S. METROPOLITAN AREAS *(continued)*

	TOTAL CRIMES		VIOLENT CRIMES [2]		PROPERTY CRIMES [3]		MURDERS		ROBBERIES	
	Number	Rate[1]	Total	Rate[1]	Total	Rate[1]	Total	Rate[1]	Total	Rate[1]
Fort Wayne, Ind.	17,288	4,536.0	986	258.7	16,302	4,277.3	25	6.6	420	110.2
Fresno, Calif.	42,686	8,013.6	4,036	757.7	38,650	7,255.9	71	13.3	1,610	302.2
Gainesville, Fla.	14,107	8,842.5	1,580	990.4	12,527	7,852.1	18	11.3	276	173.0
Galveston-Texas City, Tex.	13,193	6,283.6	1,364	649.7	11,829	5,634.0	22	10.5	492	234.3
Gary-Hammond-E. Chicago, Ind.	34,550	5,397.6	3,241	506.3	31,309	4,891.2	117	18.3	1,359	212.3
Grand Rapids, Mich.	33,099	5,536.8	2,646	442.6	30,453	5,094.2	34	5.7	752	125.8
Green Bay, Wis.	8,512	4,765.4	212	118.7	8,300	4,646.7	1	0.6	53	29.7
Greensboro-Winston-Salem-High Point, N.C.	42,068	4,955.6	4,649	547.6	37,419	4,407.9	62	7.3	931	109.7
Greenville-Spartanburg, S.C.	34,082	5,784.1	3,973	674.3	30,109	5,109.8	45	7.6	597	101.3
Hagerstown, Md.	3,369	2,936.7	298	259.8	3,071	2,676.9	6	5.2	54	47.1
Hamilton-Middletown, Ohio	14,638	5,653.7	939	362.7	13,699	5,291.1	8	3.1	276	106.6
Harrisburg, Pa.	18,153	4,045.7	1,391	310.0	16,762	3,735.7	14	3.1	619	138.0
Hartford, Conn.	57,938	6,176.0	5,078	541.3	52,860	5,634.7	57	6.1	2,728	290.8
Honolulu, Hawaii	50,600	6,444.4	2,151	273.9	48,449	6,170.4	25	3.2	1,457	185.6
Houston, Texas	237,341	7,612.8	23,791	763.1	213,550	6,849.7	879	28.2	14,413	462.3
Huntington, W.Va.-Ky.-Ohio	12,343	3,957.5	1,060	339.9	11,283	3,617.7	14	4.5	219	70.2
Huntsville, Ala.	15,546	4,932.2	815	258.6	14,731	4,673.7	22	7.0	242	76.8
Indianapolis, Ind.	64,951	5,579.5	5,721	491.4	59,230	5,088.0	93	8.0	2,516	216.1
Jackson, Miss.	22,111	6,907.5	1,450	453.0	20,661	6,454.5	65	20.3	719	224.6
Jacksonville, Fla.	56,129	7,001.4	6,742	841.0	49,387	6,160.4	104	13.0	2,363	294.8
Jersey City, N.J.	37,608	6,683.1	4,786	850.5	32,822	5,832.6	74	13.2	2,805	498.5
Johnstown, Pa.	5,071	1,912.6	476	179.5	4,595	1,733.1	6	2.3	43	16.2
Kankakee, Ill.	5,964	5,770.2	458	443.1	5,506	5,327.1	7	6.8	176	170.3
Kansas City, Mo.-Kans.	92,491	6,897.0	10,411	776.3	82,080	6,120.6	134	10.0	3,723	277.6
Killeen-Temple, Tex.	9,621	4,167.4	811	351.3	8,810	3,816.1	18	7.8	259	112.2
Knoxville, Tenn.	20,424	4,203.3	1,503	309.3	18,921	3,894.0	35	7.2	618	127.2
Lake Charles, La.	10,690	6,150.5	923	531.0	9,767	5,619.5	20	11.5	193	111.0
Lakeland-Winter Haven, Fla.	22,816	6,509.9	2,811	802.0	20,005	5,707.8	36	10.3	540	154.1
Lancaster, Pa.	10,544	2,903.0	496	136.6	10,048	2,766.4	4	1.1	155	42.7
Las Vegas, Nev.	48,920	9,614.4	5,378	1,057.0	43,542	8,557.4	101	19.8	3,069	603.2
Lexington-Fayette, Ky.	20,535	6,464.6	1,442	454.0	19,093	6,010.6	40	12.6	467	147.0
Lima, Ohio	9,270	4,243.0	595	272.3	8,675	3,970.7	3	1.4	169	77.4
Lincoln, Nebr.	11,440	5,851.6	443	226.6	10,997	5,625.0	2	1.0	99	50.6
Little Rock, Ark.	32,189	8,149.5	3,200	810.2	28,989	7,339.3	47	11.9	1,011	256.0
Long Branch, N.J.	24,233	4,819.7	2,130	423.6	22,103	4,396.1	15	3.0	600	119.3
Los Angeles-Long Beach	639,177	8,172.2	99,330	1,270.0	539,847	6,902.2	1,416	18.1	50,983	651.8
Louisville, Ky.-Ind.	51,451	5,671.3	4,055	447.0	47,396	5,224.4	58	6.4	2,127	234.5
Lubbock, Tex.	19,379	8,510.8	1,914	840.6	17,465	7,670.2	26	11.4	326	143.2
Lynchburg, Va.	6,279	3,969.6	378	239.0	5,901	3,730.6	8	5.1	52	32.9
Macon, Ga.	12,554	4,776.4	879	334.4	11,675	4,441.9	25	9.5	243	92.5
Madison, Wis.	19,155	5,992.6	638	199.6	18,517	5,793.0	7	2.2	202	63.2
Manchester, N.H.	12,186	4,261.9	379	132.6	11,807	4,129.3	2	0.7	141	49.3
McAllen-Pharr, Tex.	14,471	4,795.2	1,195	396.0	13,276	4,399.2	15	5.0	125	41.4
Melbourne-Titusville, Fla.	17,691	6,007.5	1,435	487.3	16,256	5,520.2	17	5.8	248	84.2
Memphis, Tenn.-Ark.-Miss.	63,416	6,822.7	8,318	894.9	55,098	5,927.8	143	15.4	4,573	492.0
Miami, Fla.	176,195	10,289.4	27,206	1,588.8	148,989	8,700.6	508	29.7	12,546	732.7
Milwaukee, Wis.	76,987	5,429.7	4,465	314.9	72,522	5,114.8	77	5.4	2,341	165.1
Minneapolis-St. Paul, Minn.	126,543	5,897.3	7,720	359.8	118,823	5,537.6	70	3.3	3,934	183.3
Mobile, Ala.	34,117	7,594.6	3,749	834.5	30,368	6,760.0	73	16.3	1,176	261.8
Montgomery, Ala.	13,462	4,804.9	1,041	371.6	12,421	4,433.4	29	10.4	310	110.6
Muskegon, Mich.	13,200	7,456.6	1,423	803.8	11,777	6,652.8	6	3.4	225	127.1
Nashville, Tenn.	46,726	5,511.7	4,081	481.4	42,645	5,030.4	101	11.9	1,829	215.7
New Brunswick, N.J.	27,564	4,573.0	1,889	313.4	25,675	4,259.6	19	3.2	659	109.3
New Haven, Conn.	43,852	5,689.8	3,004	389.8	40,848	5,300.0	42	5.4	1,777	230.6
New London-Norwich, Conn.	9,859	4,059.4	614	252.8	9,245	3,806.6	7	2.9	177	72.9
New Orleans, La.	92,916	7,557.9	13,085	1,064.3	79,831	6,493.5	311	25.3	6,413	521.6
New York, N.Y.-N.J.	778,586	8,496.6	149,646	1,633.1	628,940	6,863.6	1,749	19.1	98,750	1,077.6
Newark, N.J.	118,913	5,977.8	19,592	984.9	99,321	4,992.9	178	8.9	10,802	543.0
Newport News-Hampton, Va.	18,381	4,898.0	1,439	383.5	16,942	4,514.6	33	8.8	541	144.2
Norfolk, Va.-N.C.	49,148	5,957.2	4,293	520.4	44,855	5,436.9	87	10.5	1,880	227.9
Northeast, Pa.	15,923	2,526.5	930	147.6	14,993	2,379.0	25	4.0	292	46.3
Ocala, Fla.	9,182	7,099.1	887	685.8	8,295	6,413.3	14	10.8	171	132.2
Oklahoma City, Okla.	63,098	7,185.9	5,838	664.9	57,260	6,521.0	112	12.8	2,165	246.6
Omaha, Nebr.-Iowa	33,070	5,773.1	2,890	504.5	30,180	5,268.6	28	4.9	814	142.1
Orlando, Fla.	61,340	8,110.7	7,230	956.0	54,110	7,154.7	79	10.4	2,038	269.5
Oxnard, Calif.	25,066	4,506.4	2,105	378.4	22,961	4,128.0	32	5.8	759	136.5
Parkersburg-Marietta, W.Va.-O.	5,441	3,360.6	255	157.5	5,186	3,203.1	3	1.9	74	45.7

[1] Crimes per 100,000 population. [2] Violent crimes includes murder, forcible rape, robbery, and aggravated assault.
[3] Property crimes include burglary, larceny of $50 or more, and auto theft.

	TOTAL CRIMES		VIOLENT CRIMES[2]		PROPERTY CRIMES[3]		MURDERS		ROBBERIES	
	Number	Rate[1]	Total	Rate[1]	Total	Rate[1]	Total	Rate[1]	Total	Rate[1]
Paterson-Passaic, N.J.	29,767	6,562.0	3,865	852.0	25,902	5,709.9	36	7.9	2,400	529.1
Pensacola, Fla.	21,085	6,809.4	2,721	878.8	18,364	5,930.7	25	8.1	551	177.9
Peoria, Ill.	18,154	4,948.6	1,739	474.0	16,415	4,474.6	18	4.9	445	121.3
Philadelphia, Pa.-N.J.	233,406	4,937.2	29,681	627.8	203,725	4,309.3	477	10.1	15,144	320.3
Phoenix, Ariz.	124,490	7,819.4	8,590	539.5	115,900	7,279.8	135	8.5	3,084	193.7
Pittsburgh, Pa.	73,156	3,226.5	8,733	385.2	64,423	2,841.4	103	4.5	5,022	221.5
Portland, Maine	12,191	5,608.8	616	283.4	11,575	5,325.4	8	3.7	137	63.0
Portland, Oreg.-Wash.	99,621	7,935.1	8,766	698.2	90,855	7,236.9	74	5.9	3,665	291.9
Poughkeepsie, N.Y.	8,552	3,472.7	781	317.1	7,771	3,155.5	5	2.0	283	114.9
Providence-Warwick, R.I.	45,984	5,251.8	3,496	399.3	42,488	4,852.5	35	4.0	1,043	119.1
Provo-Orem, Utah	8,611	3,720.1	290	125.3	8,321	3,594.8	3	1.3	59	25.5
Pueblo, Colo.	8,758	6,583.4	773	581.1	7,985	6,002.4	9	6.8	168	126.3
Racine, Wis.	10,887	6,203.1	847	482.6	10,040	5,720.5	6	3.4	229	130.5
Raleigh-Durham, N.C.	34,316	6,349.9	2,266	419.3	32,050	5,930.6	59	10.9	733	135.6
Reading, Pa.	9,374	2,989.2	778	248.1	8,596	2,741.1	8	2.6	328	104.6
Reno, Nev.	14,122	6,617.1	1,076	504.2	13,046	6,112.9	16	7.5	472	221.2
Richmond, Va.	40,937	6,376.4	3,513	547.2	37,424	5,829.2	89	13.9	1,668	259.8
Riverside, Calif.	127,953	7,918.2	12,262	758.8	115,691	7,159.4	160	9.9	3,959	245.0
Roanoke, Va.	12,653	5,486.6	580	251.5	12,073	5,235.1	19	8.2	243	105.4
Rochester, N.Y.	53,608	5,479.3	3,757	384.0	49,851	5,095.3	42	4.3	1,397	142.8
Rockford, Ill.	18,774	6,678.3	1,526	542.8	17,248	6,135.5	13	4.6	509	181.1
Sacramento, Calif.	88,759	8,356.4	6,807	640.9	81,952	7,715.5	84	7.9	3,070	289.0
Saginaw, Mich.	18,404	8,203.1	1,887	841.1	16,517	7,362.0	29	12.9	490	218.4
St. Cloud, Minn.	4,981	3,006.0	78	47.1	4,903	2,958.9	3	1.8	19	11.5
St. Louis, Mo.-Ill.	141,414	5,988.0	16,323	691.2	125,091	5,296.9	349	14.8	6,528	276.4
Salem, Oreg.	16,526	6,538.0	1,011	400.0	15,515	6,138.0	8	3.2	204	80.7
Salinas-Monterey, Calif.	18,727	6,296.5	1,578	530.6	17,149	5,766.0	29	9.8	496	166.8
Salt Lake City-Ogden, Utah	63,834	6,406.7	3,478	349.1	60,356	6,057.6	41	4.1	1,223	122.7
San Antonio, Tex.	77,781	6,739.6	6,708	581.2	71,073	6,158.3	213	18.5	2,394	207.4
San Diego, Calif.	118,669	6,080.8	10,642	545.3	108,027	5,535.5	124	6.4	4,894	250.8
San Francisco, Calif.	263,528	7,775.3	29,670	875.4	233,858	6,899.9	338	10.0	15,030	443.5
San Jose, Calif.	91,765	6,768.2	5,843	431.0	85,922	6,337.3	61	4.5	2,590	191.0
Santa Barbara, Calif.	19,728	6,307.0	1,373	438.9	18,355	5,868.1	15	4.8	320	102.3
Santa Cruz, Calif.	12,035	6,129.9	765	389.6	11,270	5,740.2	6	3.1	195	99.3
Santa Rosa, Calif.	18,492	6,022.1	1,057	344.2	17,435	6,677.8	11	3.6	268	87.3
Sarasota, Fla.	12,604	5,807.8	863	397.7	11,741	5,410.2	13	6.0	224	103.2
Savannah, Ga.	19,840	8,501.8	1,917	821.5	17,923	7,680.3	40	17.1	689	295.2
Seattle-Everett, Wash.	119,634	7,241.9	8,180	495.2	111,454	6,746.7	72	4.4	3,053	184.8
Shreveport, La.	22,680	5,796.4	2,429	620.8	20,251	5,175.6	63	16.1	521	133.2
Sioux City, Iowa-Nebr.	6,842	5,834.9	229	195.3	6,613	5,639.7	5	4.3	41	35.0
South Bend, Ind.	17,057	6,122.1	978	351.0	16,079	5,771.1	10	3.6	432	155.1
Spokane, Wash.	19,820	5,631.1	1,196	339.8	18,624	5,291.3	18	5.1	338	96.0
Springfield, Ill.	12,205	6,504.9	1,197	638.0	11,008	5,867.0	5	2.7	320	170.6
Springfield, Mo.	13,663	6,564.2	545	261.8	13,118	6,302.4	8	3.8	170	81.7
Springfield, Ohio	8,012	4,363.0	664	361.6	7,348	4,001.4	5	2.7	249	135.6
Stockton, Calif.	30,056	8,236.9	2,275	623.5	27,781	7,613.4	71	19.5	913	250.2
Syracuse, N.Y.	29,202	4,503.0	1,717	264.8	27,485	4,238.2	13	2.0	857	132.2
Tacoma, Wash.	33,940	6,810.2	2,657	533.1	31,283	6,277.1	26	5.2	780	156.5
Tallahassee, Fla.	11,229	6,566.2	1,031	602.9	10,198	5,963.3	16	9.4	205	119.9
Tampa-St. Petersburg, Fla.	120,719	7,153.4	14,836	879.1	105,883	6,274.3	147	8.7	3,987	236.3
Terre Haute, Ind.	7,096	4,027.9	346	196.4	6,750	3,831.5	3	1.7	95	53.9
Texarkana, Tex.-Ark.	6,087	4,592.0	444	334.9	5,643	4,257.0	6	4.5	64	48.3
Toledo, Ohio-Mich.	46,315	5,865.3	3,269	414.0	43,046	5,451.4	34	4.3	1,645	208.3
Topeka, Kans.	10,243	5,438.4	710	377.0	9,533	5,061.4	7	3.7	227	120.5
Trenton, N.J.	19,943	6,440.1	1,849	597.1	18,094	5,843.0	16	5.2	1,062	342.9
Tucscon, Ariz.	46,072	8,223.8	3,597	642.1	42,475	7,581.7	53	9.5	1,062	189.6
Tulsa, Okla.	44,288	6,165.1	3,704	515.6	40,584	5,649.5	59	8.2	1,205	167.7
Utica-Rome, N.Y.	9,647	2,993.3	361	112.0	9,286	2,881.3	6	1.9	133	41.3
Vallejo-Fairfield-Napa, Calif.	18,591	5,434.0	1,600	467.7	16,991	4,966.3	21	6.1	390	114.0
Waco, Tex.	12,551	6,822.7	989	537.6	11,562	6,285.1	33	17.9	268	145.7
Washington, D.C.-Md.-Va.	195,746	6,324.5	24,900	804.5	170,846	5,520.0	334	10.8	14,826	479.0
West Palm Beach, Fla.	53,346	8,877.2	5,978	994.8	47,368	7,882.4	75	12.5	1,570	261.3
Wichita, Kans.	30,195	7,178.0	2,084	495.4	28,111	6,682.6	42	10.0	718	170.7
Wichita Falls, Tex.	8,844	6,312.0	775	553.1	8,069	5,758.9	19	13.6	270	192.7
Williamsport, Pa.	4,001	3,363.7	169	142.1	3,832	3,221.6	4	3.4	37	31.1
Wilmington, Del.-N.J.-Md.	33,325	6,286.4	2,863	540.1	30,462	5,746.3	19	3.6	737	139.0
Wilmington, N.C.	8,981	6,286.6	832	582.4	8,149	5,704.2	12	8.4	172	120.4
Yakima, Wash.	12,366	7,016.8	792	449.4	11,574	6,567.4	8	4.5	205	116.3
York, Pa.	11,803	3,090.7	556	145.6	11,247	2,945.1	6	1.6	235	61.5
Youngstown-Warren, Ohio	23,742	4,470.5	2,894	544.9	20,848	3,925.6	29	5.5	889	167.4

[1] Crimes per 100,000 population. [2] Violent crimes includes murder, forcible rape, robbery, and aggravated assault. [3] Property crimes include burglary, larceny of $50 or more, and auto theft.

HISTORIC ASSASSINATIONS

44 B.C. (March 15) Julius Caesar, Roman general and dictator, stabbed to death in Roman Senate by Brutus, Cimber, Cassius, Casca and others.
1792 (March 16) Gustavus III, king of Sweden, shot at masked ball by assassin hired by nobles.
1793 (July 13) Jean Marat, French Revolutionary leader, stabbed by Charlotte Corday.
1801 (March 24) Paul I, czar of Russia, slain by Russian nobles after he refused to abdicate.
1865 (April 14) Abraham Lincoln, 16th U.S. President, shot by John Wilkes Booth in Ford's Theater in Washington, D.C. Died next day.
1881 (March 13) Alexander II, czar of Russia, assassinated by Russian terrorist.
1881 (July 2) James A. Garfield, 20th U.S. President, shot by disappointed job seeker Charles J. Guiteau. Died Sept. 19, 1881.
1898 (Sept. 10) Elizabeth, empress of Austria, assassinated in Geneva by Italian anarchist.
1900 (July 29) Humbert I, king of Italy, killed by Gaetano Bresci in Monza, Italy.
1901 (Sept. 6) William McKinley, 25th U.S. President, shot by anarchist Leon Czolgosz in Buffalo, N.Y. Died eight days later.
1903 (June 11) Alexander I, king of Serbia, and his wife, assassinated in Belgrade.
1908 (Feb. 1) Carlos I, king of Portugal, and his son, the crown prince, shot in Lisbon.
1913 (Feb. 22) Francisco I. Madero, president of Mexico, shot by guard after being imprisoned by Gen. Victoriano Huerta.
1913 (March 18) George I, king of Greece, assassinated during second Balkan War.
1914 (June 28) Francis Ferdinand, archduke of Austria-Hungary, and his wife, shot by Serbian nationalist in Sarajevo, starting World War I.
1916 (Dec. 30) Grigori Rasputin, Russian monk, poisoned, stabbed, and shot by nobles who hated his influence on Czar Nicholas II.
1918 (July 16) Nicholas II, czar of Russia, his wife, and children, shot in Ekaterinburg.
1919 (April 10) Emiliano Zapata, Mexican revolutionary and reformer, killed in ambush by agents of President Venustiano Carranza.
1923 (July 20) Pancho Villa, Mexican revolutionary, assassinated at his estate in Durango.
1928 (July 17) Alvaro Obregón, president of Mexico, killed by Roman Catholic fanatic.
1934 (July 25) Engelbert Dollfuss, Austrian chancellor, assassinated by Nazis.
1934 (Oct. 9) Alexander I, king of Yugoslavia, killed by terrorist in Marseille, France.
1935 (Sept. 8) Huey P. Long, U.S. senator from Louisiana and candidate for Democratic presidential nomination, shot by Dr. Carl A. Weiss. Died two days later.
1940 (Aug. 20) Leon Trotsky, Russian revolutionary exile, stabbed by Stalinist agent Ramón Mercader in Mexico City. Died next day.
1948 (Jan. 30) Mohandas Gandhi, leader of India, shot by Nathuram Godse, Hindu who blamed Gandhi for partition of India.
1951 (July 20) Abdullah ibn Hussein, king of Jordan, assassinated in Jerusalem.
1955 (Jan. 2) José Antonio Remón, president of Panama, killed by machine-gunner.
1956 (Sept. 21) Anastasio Somoza, president of Nicaragua, shot during election campaign dance. Died eight days later.
1957 (July 26) Carlos Castillo Armas, president of Guatemala, shot by a palace guard.
1958 (July 14) Faisal II, king of Iraq, killed in revolt by Abdul Karim Kassem.
1959 (Sept. 25) Solomon Bandaranaike, prime minister of Ceylon, shot by Buddhist monk.
1960 (Aug. 29) Hazza Majali, premier of Jordan, killed by time bomb in his office.
1961 (May 30) Rafael L. Trujillo, dictator and president of the Dominican Republic, slain.
1963 (Jan. 13) Sylvanus Olympio, president of Togo, killed by former soldiers in Lomé.
1963 (Nov. 1-2) Ngo Dinh Diem, president of South Vietnam, and his brother slain.
1963 (Nov. 22) John F. Kennedy, U.S. President, shot by Lee Harvey Oswald in Dallas.
1966 (Sept. 6) Hendrik F. Verwoerd, prime minister of South Africa, stabbed in parliament in Cape Town by Dimitrio Stifanos.
1968 (April 4) Martin Luther King Jr., U.S. civil-rights leader, shot by ex-convict James Earl Ray in Memphis.
1968 (June 5) Robert F. Kennedy, U.S. senator from New York, shot by Sirhan Sirhan in Los Angeles while celebrating California presidential primary victory. Died next day.
1969 (Oct. 15) A. A. Shermarke, president of Somalia, assassinated in Las Anos, Somalia.
1973 (March 2) Cleo A. Noel Jr., U.S. ambassador, slain in Khartoum, Sudan, by Arab terrorists.
1974 (Aug. 19) Rodger P. Davies, U.S. ambassador, slain by Greek Cypriots in embassy at Nicosia, Cyprus.
1975 (Feb. 11) Madagascar head of state Col. Richard Ratsimandrava slain in ambush.
1975 (March 25) King Faisal of Saudi Arabia shot by nephew during palace reception.
1975 (April 13) President N'Garta Tombalbaye of Chad slain in military coup.
1975 (Aug. 15) Bangladesh President Mujibur Rahman killed by army officers in coup.
1976 (Feb. 13) Nigeria's head of state, Gen. Murtala Ramat Muhammed, killed in unsuccessful coup.
1976 (June 16) U.S. Ambassador to Lebanon Francis Meloy Jr. assassinated by terrorists.
1976 (July 21) British Ambassador to Ireland Christopher Biggs slain in Ireland.
1977 (Feb. 3) Ethiopia's chief of state Gen. Teferi Bante assassinated in coup, reportedly by Mengistu Haile Mariam, who became dictator.
1977 (March 18) Congo's President Marien Ngouabi assassinated in Brazzaville.
1977 (Oct. 11) North Yemen's President Ibrahim al-Hamdi and his brother assassinated in Sana.
1978 (April 27) Afghanistan's President Mohammad Daoud slain in communist coup in Kabul.
1978 (June 24) North Yemen's President Ahmed Hussein al-Ghashmi assassinated by South Yemen envoy.
1978 (Nov. 18) U.S. Rep. Leo J. Ryan and 4 other Americans assassinated in Guyana by California religious sect; then its 914 members kill selves.
1978 (Nov. 27) San Francisco's Mayor George Moscone assassinated by former official Dan White.
1979 (Feb. 14) Adolph Dubs, U.S. Ambassador to Afghanistan, killed in police shootout with terrorists.
1979 (Aug. 27) Britain's Earl Mountbatten of Burma assassinated by Irish terrorists.
1979 (Sept 14) Afghanistan's President Noor Taraki slain by his prime minister, Hafizullah Amin.
1979 (Oct. 26) South Korean President Park Chung Hee assassinated at dinner by intelligence chief.
1981 (May 30) Bangladesh President Ziaur (Zia) Rahman slain in unsuccessful coup by army officers.
1981 (Aug. 30) Iran's President Mohammed Ali Rajai, Prime Minister Mohammed Jad Bahonar, and 3 others assassinated by bomb planted in office by opponents.
1981 (Oct. 6) Egyptian President Anwar al-Sadat assassinated at military parade by Muslim fanatics.
1982 (Sept. 14) Lebanon's President-elect Bashir Gemayel killed with 25 others in Beirut bomb blast.

Earth

Wide World

The Pacific Coast shoreline is being nibbled away by storms such as this one in February that washed away the soil underneath a trailer court at Pacifica, Calif., leaving only paving overhanging the seaside cliff.

HIGHLIGHTS: 1983

CALIFORNIA MADE OF ALIEN LAND

About 85% of California is made up of land that originally was not part of North America, according to Dr. M. Clark Blake Jr. of the U.S. Geological Survey.

His report, made to a meeting of the American Geophysical Union, said that 160 million to 200 million years ago California was formed from islands, parts of the ocean floor, and pieces of other continents that became attached to North America.

Magnetism in some of California's rock formations indicate that they were formed south of the equator.

Some rocks contain fossils unlike those discovered elsewhere in North America but like some found in China.

As the sea reclaimed part of the California coastline with violent storms in 1983, waves uncovered the remains of a prehistoric mammoth in a cliff south of Half Moon Bay in February.

PREHISTORY OF PACIFIC ISLANDS

The Pacific island nations Fiji, Vanuatu, and Tonga separated from each other about 5 to 8 million years ago, according to a report by Earth scientists of the University of California. Before that time the islands made up a single group called the Vitiaz arc, the scientists told a meeting of the American Geophysical Union.

HIGHLIGHTS: 1983 *(continued)*

The research team, headed by Professor of Earth Sciences James Gill, said a split in the ocean bed caused the islands to move apart into their present locations.

The scientists made their conclusions after a lengthy study of volcanic rock formations on the islands.

PREHISTORIC MAN EXHIBIT

For the first time, scientists in 1984 will be able to make direct comparisons of most of the existing fossils of man's prehistoric ancestors that have been found.

The fossils will be assembled from 23 institutions around the world at the American Museum of Natural History in New York City.

After scientists have had an opportunity to study them, the fossils will be shown to the public from April 16 to Sept. 9, 1984, in an exhibition called "Ancestors: Four Million Years of Humanity."

Dr. Ian Tattersall, curator of the department of anthropology at the Museum of Natural History, called the fossils to be assembled "the crown jewels of anthropology."

The fossils being provided include those of Neanderthal man, Heidelberg Man, Java Man, and more ancient specimens found in Ethiopia and Tanzania.

SURVIVORS IN THE ICE AGE

Australian scientists reported that a cave found in Tasmania contains huge deposits of stone tools and other artifacts showing that it was occupied by humans 20,500 years ago during the Ice Age.

The 2,000-foot-long limestone cave was discovered by scientists of the Australian National University.

WHEN WHALES LIVED ON LAND

Dr. Philip D. Gingerich of the University of Michigan at Ann Arbor reported the finding in Pakistan of a 50-million-year-old prehistoric animal believed to be the oldest known ancestor of the whale. He said the animal was believed to have lived on land, but slipped into the sea to catch fish for food.

He said the creature was about 6 feet long and might have weighed about 600 pounds.

His report said that finding the fossil provides confirmation of a theory that the earliest whales lived on land before becoming adapted to living in the sea.

VOLCANIC ERUPTIONS

Throughout the year Mount Kilauea on Hawaii Island spewed out lava that rolled down its sides. The lava flow destroyed some houses in its path but caused no deaths.

Mount Etna on the Italian island of Sicily also continued to erupt, destroying many houses with its lava flow. Efforts to divert the rivers of molten rock by blasting with dynamite proved ineffective.

Mount St. Helens in Washington continued to build a dome in its crater that scientists said might explode at some unforeseeable time, bringing new disaster to the region. The U.S. Geologic Survey estimated that a break in the Spirit Lake dam near the volcano could unloose over 2 billion cubic yards of sediment in a gigantic mud slide that could engulf the Columbia River port towns of Longview and Kelso.

The U.S. Geologic Survey reported that a study of 35 volcanos in the Western states had identified eight that are "capable of extremely destructive eruptions." These were Mount St. Helens, the Mono-Inyo Craters and Long Valley Caldera near California's Mammoth Lakes, Mount Lassen and Mount Shasta in California, Mount Rainier and Mount Baker in Washington, and Mount Hood in Oregon.

The study said that frequent earthquakes on the California-Nevada border indicated that molten rock was flowing into an underground reservoir and might presage a volcanic explosion greater than any recorded in history.

A huge volcanic eruption in the region about 700,000 years ago sent streams of lava 1,000-feet deep rushing through the valleys, accompanied by clouds of ash that spread across Kansas and Missouri.

The scientists said they did not have enough evidence either to predict or to discount that such an eruption could happen again.

TRANSFER OF LANDSAT CONTROL

Operation of the Landsat earth remote-sensing satellite system was transferred on Feb. 1, 1984, from the National Aeronautics and Space Administration (NASA) to the National Environmental Satellite, Data, and Information Service (NESDIS). NESDIS is a service within the Commerce Department's National Oceanic and Atmospheric Administration (NOAA).

The Landsat program began with the launching of the first Landsat satellite in 1972. Three more Landsat satellites were put into orbit in 1975, 1978, and 1982. Only Landsat 4 remained operational in 1984.

The satellites, which provide large-scale views of the Earth's surface, have provided valuable information for agricultural and urban planning, geologic exploration, land management studies, and snow melt and flood runoff analysis.

NASA retained control of an experimental instrument aboard Landsat 4 called the Thematic Mapper while developing computer analysis programs for its data.

FACTS ABOUT THE EARTH

Age of Earth: 4.6 to 5 billion years.
Area of Earth: *Total area,* 196,940,000 square miles; *Land area,* 30%, 57,506,000 square miles; *Water area,* 70%, 139,434,000 square miles.
Atmosphere of Earth: Extends about 1,000 miles above surface; *Chemical composition,* nitrogen 78%, oxygen 21%, argon and other gases 1%.
Circumference of Earth: *Polar circumference* (distance around Earth at poles), 24,859.82 miles; *Equatorial circumference* (distance at equator), 24,901.55 mi.
Density of Earth: 5.52 (water has density of 1).
Diameter of Earth: *Polar diameter* (through Earth from pole to pole), 7,899.83 miles; *Equatorial diameter* (through Earth at equator), 7,926.41 miles.
Distance of Moon from Earth: *Closest distance,* 221,456 miles; *Farthest distance,* 252,711 miles; *Average distance,* 238,875 miles.
Distance of Sun from Earth: *Closest distance,* 91.4 million miles; *Farthest distance,* 94.5 million miles; *Average distance,* 92.9 million miles.
Escape Velocity from Earth: 7 miles per second.
Inclination of Earth on Axis: 23° 27′.
Interior of Earth: *Crust,* made up of igneous, sedimentary, and metamorphic rock, extends 20 miles deep under continents and about 5 miles deep under oceans; *Mantle,* layer of solid rock about 1,800 miles thick beneath Earth's crust, has temperatures of 1600° to 4400°F.; *Outer Core,* 1,400-mile thick layer of molten iron and nickel between mantle and inner core, has temperatures of 4000° to 9000°F.; *Inner Core,* ball of solid iron and nickel at Earth's center with diameter of about 1,600 miles, with temperature of about 9,000°F.
Period of Revolution of Earth around Sun: 1 year (or 365 days, 6 hours, 9 minutes, 9.54 seconds).
Period of Rotation of Earth on Axis: 1 day (or 23 hours, 56 minutes, 4.09 seconds).
Speed of Earth in Orbit around Sun: 18.5 miles per second.
Volume of Earth: 260 billion cubic miles.
Weight or Mass of Earth: 6,586,000,000,000,000,000,000 tons (or 6.586 sextillion tons).

The seven cameras aboard Landsat 4 provide photographs that have 10 times the clarity of the earlier satellites. They can identify individual buildings in any city, providing details of objects up to 90 feet wide.

Scientists said that they can determine sources of pollution by studying Landsat photographs of smoke from industrial plants and the type of silt and sediment emptying into the oceans from rivers.

The Landsat photos also were expected to improve forecasts of food supplies by identifying exactly what crops are being raised throughout the world.

"Our new Landsat can distinguish very nicely between rice fields and soybean fields that lie right next to each other," Landsat project scientist Vincent Salomonson said. "The older satellites could never do that."

PREPARING FOR THE WORST

Scientists warned in 1983 that stress along the Midwest's New Madrid Fault Zone has built to the point that a severe earthquake could occur at any time. The fault line runs from southern Illinois through Kentucky, Missouri, Tennessee, and Arkansas.

The most violent earthquakes in U.S. history centered on New Madrid, Mo., in the winter of 1811–12, causing widespread damage but few casualties because of the sparse population of the region at that time.

The Federal Emergency Management Agency stepped up efforts to prepare for the havoc that such an earthquake could cause today. At a meeting held in St. Louis in July, disaster managers from the states that would be affected were asked to press for stiffer codes to force the construction of earthquake-proof buildings.

William R. Beaty, director of Missouri's emergency management agency, estimated that 26 gas and oil pipelines crossing the fault would be broken by a medium-sized earthquake.

ROMAN DISCOVERY OF AMERICA

Did Roman explorers discover America more than 1,000 years before Columbus made his voyage? Archaeologist Robert Marx hopes to answer that question in 1984 by an underwater search of Guanabara Bay on the coast of Brazil.

Pottery found on the bottom of the bay has been identified by scientists at the University of Massachusetts as having been made by Romans about 200 B.C.

Marx hopes his 1984 expedition will find wreckage of the ship that carried the pottery to help determine how it got there.

MUMMY MYSTERY

X rays taken of an Egyptian mummy at the Minneapolis Institute of Arts revealed a mystery that easily could provide the plot for a novel. The mummy was identified by an inscription on the coffin as the body of Tashat, the teenage daughter of the treasurer of the Temple of Amon in Thebes.

X rays revealed that the girl had slashes across the bottoms of her feet, a broken arm, and broken ribs. Between her legs was the embalmed skull of an adult man whose skull had been fractured by a blow. Scientists said it was the only known example of two skulls having been embalmed as a single mummy.

CONTINENTAL MOVEMENT

Scientists at the Naval Surface Weapons Center in Dahlgren, Va., reported that a study of 10 years of data from navigational satellites has revealed new information on the movement of the continents.

They said Europe is moving east at about 4 inches a year, while Australia is drifting north at about 6 inches per year.

EXTREMES OF THE EARTH

Source: National Geographic Society

Highest mountain	Mt. Everest, Nepal–China; 29,028 feet
Lowest point on surface	Dead Sea, Israel–Jordan; –1,312 feet below sea level
Greatest ocean depth	Mariana Trench, Pacific Ocean; 35,810 feet
Highest volcano	Chimborazo, Ecuador; 20,561 feet
Largest desert	Sahara, North Africa; over 3 million square miles
Largest island	Greenland; 840,000 square miles
Longest river	Nile, Africa; 4,145 miles
Highest waterfall	Angel Falls, Venezuela; 3,212 feet
Largest lake	Caspian Sea, Asia; 143,244 square miles
Rainiest spot	Mt. Waialeale, Hawaii; average 460 inches a year
Deepest lake	Baykal, U.S.S.R.; 5,315 ft.
Driest spot	Atacama Desert, Chile; rainfall barely measurable
Northernmost town	Ny Alesund, Spitsbergen, Norway
Southernmost town	Puerto Williams, Chile
Lowest town	Villages along Dead Sea; 1,299 feet below sea level
Largest gorge	Grand Canyon, Colorado River, Arizona; 277 miles long, 600 feet to 18 miles wide, 1 mile deep
Deepest gorge	Hells Canyon, Snake River, Idaho; 7,900 feet deep
Strongest wind	231 mph; record in 1924 at Mt. Washington, New Hampshire
Greatest tides	Bay of Fundy, Nova Scotia; 53 feet

SEVEN CONTINENTS

Source: National Geographic Society

NAME	AREA (in square miles)	% OF WORLD'S LAND	HIGHEST POINT (in feet)	LOWEST POINT (feet below sea level)	TEMPERATURE RECORDS HIGHEST (with date)	LOWEST (with date)
Asia	16,999,000	29.7	Mt. Everest Nepal–China (29,028)	Dead Sea, Israel–Jordan (1,312)	Tirat Zevi, Israel 129.0 ° F. (June 21, 1942)	Oymyakon, Soviet Union –89.9 ° F. (Feb. 6, 1933)
Africa	11,688,000	20.4	Mt. Kilimanjaro, Tanzania (19,340)	Lake Assal, Djibouti (512)	Al Aziziyah, Libya 136.0 ° F. (Sept. 13, 1922)	Ifrane, Morocco –11.2 ° F. (Feb. 11, 1935)
North America	9,366,000	16.3	Mt. McKinley, Alaska (20,320)	Death Valley, California (282)	Death Valley, California 134.0 ° F. (July 10, 1913)	Snag, Yukon, Canada –81.0 ° F. (Feb. 3, 1947)
South America	6,881,000	12.0	Mt. Aconcagua, Argentina (22,834)	Valdes Peninsula, Argentina (131)	Rivadavia, Argentina 120.0 ° F. (Dec. 11, 1905)	Sarmiento, Argentina –27.4 ° F. (June 1, 1907)
Antarctica	5,100,000	8.9	Vinson Massif (16,864)	Not known	Esperanza Station 58.3 ° F. (Oct. 20, 1956)	Vostok –127.0 ° F. (Aug. 24, 1960)
Europe	4,017,000	7.0	Mt. Elbrus, Soviet Union (18,510)	Caspian Sea, Soviet Union (92)	Seville, Spain 122.0 ° F. (Aug. 4, 1881)	Ust' Schchugor, Soviet Union –67.0 ° F.
Australia	2,966,000	5.2	Mt. Kosciusko, New South Wales (7,310)	Lake Eyre, South Australia (52)	Cloncurry, Queensland 127.6 ° F. (Jan. 16, 1889)	Charlotte Pass, New S. Wales –8.0 ° F. (July 22, 1947)

OCEANS OF THE EARTH AND THEIR GREATEST DEPTHS

Source: National Geographic Society

OCEANS	AREA (in sq. mi.)	PERCENT OF WORLD'S WATER	GREATEST DEPTH IN OCEANS Location	Feet
Pacific Ocean	64,186,000	46.0%	Mariana Trench, off the Mariana Islands	35,810
Atlantic Ocean	33,420,000	23.9%	Puerto Rico Trench, off Puerto Rico	28,374
Indian Ocean	28,350,000	20.3%	Java Trench, off Java	23,376
Arctic Ocean	3,662,000	2.6%	Eurasia Basin	16,804

SEAS OF THE EARTH AND THEIR AVERAGE DEPTHS

SEAS	AREA (sq. mi.)	AVERAGE DEPTH (feet)
South China Sea	1,148,500	4,802
Caribbean Sea	971,400	8,448
Mediterranean Sea	969,100	4,926
Bering Sea	873,000	4,893
Gulf of Mexico	582,100	5,297
Sea of Okhotsk	537,500	3,192
Sea of Japan	391,100	5,468
Hudson Bay	281,900	305
East China Sea	256,600	620
Andaman Sea	218,100	3,667
Black Sea	196,100	3,906
Red Sea	174,900	1,764
North Sea	164,900	308
Baltic Sea	147,500	180
Yellow Sea	113,500	121

EARTH HISTORY

The rocks of the Earth's crust tell scientists the history of our planet. Because the rocks form layers, or *strata*, the dating of various eras and periods of Earth history relates to the age of these rocks.

AZOIC ERA

The Earth began during this era, about 4.6 to 5 billion years ago when the solar system formed around the Sun. The oldest rocks found on the Moon, dated as 4.66 billion years old, are believed to be from this era. Meteorites, thought to have formed at the same time as the Earth, have been dated by the radioactive technique as being 4.7 billion years old. The air and the oceans formed.

ARCHEOZOIC ERA

Beginning about 3.5 billion years ago, life originated in the warm seas in the form of bacteria and algae. Some kinds of chert, slate, and marble formed in this period contain fossils of these early types of life.

PROTEROZOIC ERA

About 1.2 billion years ago, the first animals began to live in the oceans. These were invertebrates, or animals without backbones. They included sponges, jellyfish, and worms. Rocks that formed in this era included many metal ores, such as iron and copper. Land thrust up as continents.

PALEOZOIC ERA

Much more is known of this era than of earlier eras because of the plentiful supply of fossils that have been found. The era is divided into six major periods.

Cambrian Period began about 600 million years ago and lasted about 120 million years. Most of North America was covered with seas. Mountains formed in Vermont. Fossils of small sea animals called trilobites date from this period. The first fish appeared.

Ordovician Period began about 500 million years ago and lasted about 45 million years. Corals and animals with shells developed in the seas.

Silurian Period began about 435 million years ago and lasted 30 million years. Gas, oil, and salt deposits formed. The first animals that breathed air appeared.

Devonian Period began about 405 million years ago and lasted 60 million years. Sharks and other large fish lived in the seas. The first amphibian animals crawled onto the land. Forests covered the swampy land.

Carboniferous Period began 345 million years ago and lasted about 70 million years. It is often divided into two equal-length periods called the *Mississippian* and *Pennsylvanian*. The first land animals with backbones, the reptiles, appeared. Huge coal deposits formed.

Permian Period began about 275 million years ago and lasted about 50 million years. The Appalachian Mountains formed in North America. The first plants with seeds developed—trees with cones.

MESOZOIC ERA

This was the era of the dinosaurs.

Triassic Period began about 225 million years ago and lasted 45 million years. The first dinosaurs and turtles appeared.

Jurassic Period began 180 million years ago and lasted about 50 million years. The mountains of the Sierra Nevada and California Coast ranges were formed. Dinosaurs reached their biggest size. Small mammals began living on the land. Birds began to fly.

Cretaceous Period began about 130 million years ago and lasted about 65 million years. The Rocky Mountains formed in North America. The huge dinosaurs died out. Plants with flowers appeared.

CENOZOIC ERA

Tertiary Period began about 65 million years ago and lasted about 62 million years.

Paleocene Epoch began 65 million years ago and lasted about 10 million years. Erosion formed soil in which flowering plants flourished. The earliest primates appeared.

Eocene Epoch began about 55 million years ago and lasted about 15 million years. Modern mammals appeared, including whales, camels, and monkeys.

Oligocene Epoch began 40 million years ago and lasted 14 million years. Large grazing animals appeared, as did primitive apes.

Miocene Epoch began 26 million years ago and lasted about 12 million years. Dogs, elephants, and apes became common throughout Asia and Africa.

Pliocene Epoch began 14 million years ago and lasted about 11 million years. The Cascade Mountains formed in North America. Most modern kinds of animals appeared, as well as the first men.

Quaternary Period began about 3,100,000 years ago and lasts to the present day.

Pleistocene Epoch lasted over 3,000,000 years. During this Ice Age, glaciers formed over most of North America and Eurasia four times. Prehistoric man hunted, made tools, tamed animals, and began farming.

Holocene Epoch covers the most recent 10,000 years, since the retreat of the last glaciers. Civilization developed.

U.S. GEOGRAPHIC CENTERS AND HIGHEST AND LOWEST POINTS

Source: Geological Survey, U.S. Department of the Interior

STATE	GEOGRAPHIC CENTER [1] County and Locality	HIGHEST POINT [2] Name and Elevation (in feet)	LOWEST POINT Name and Elevation (in feet)
UNITED STATES	Butte Co., S.D. (West of Castle Rock)	Mt. McKinley (20,320)	Death Valley (−282)
Alabama	Chilton (12 mi. SW of Clanton)	Cheaha Mountain (2,407)	Gulf of Mexico [3]
Alaska	63° 50′ N, 152° 00′ W, 60 miles NW of Mt. McKinley	Mt. McKinley (20,320)	Pacific Ocean [3]
Arizona	Yavapai (55 mi. ESE of Prescott)	Humphreys Peak (12,633)	Colorado River(70)
Arkansas	Pulaski (12 mi. NW of Little Rock)	Magazine Mountain (2,753)	Ouachita River (55)
California	Madera (38 mi. E of Madera)	Mt. Whitney (14,494)	Death Valley (−282)
Colorado	Park (30 mi. NW of Pikes Peak)	Mt. Elbert (14,433)	Arkansas River (3,350)
Connecticut	Hartford (at East Berlin)	Mt. Frissell, on south slope (2,380)	Long Island Sound [3]
Delaware	Kent (11 mi. S of Dover)	Ebright Road (442)	Atlantic Ocean [3]
District of Columbia	Near 4th and L Streets NW	Tenleytown (410)	Potomac River (1)
Florida	Hernando (12 mi. NNW of Brooksville)	Sec. 30, T6N, R20'W, Walton Co. (345)	Atlantic Ocean [3]
Georgia	Twiggs (18 mi. SE of Macon)	Brasstown Bald (4,784)	Atlantic Ocean [3]
Hawaii	Hawaii (20° 15′ N, 156° 20′ W, off Maui Island)	Mauna Kea (13,796)	Pacific Ocean [3]
Idaho	Custer (at Custer, SW of Challis)	Borah Peak (12,662)	Snake River (710)
Illinois	Logan (28 mi. NE of Springfield)	Charles Mound (1,235)	Mississippi River (279)
Indiana	Boone (14 mi. NNW of Indianapolis)	Franklin T, Wayne Co. (1,257)	Ohio River (320)
Iowa	Story (5 mi. NE of Ames)	Sec. 29, T100N, R41W, Osceola Co. (1,670)	Mississippi River (480)
Kansas	Barton (15 mi. NE of Great Bend)	Mt. Sunflower (4,039)	Verdigris River (680)
Kentucky	Marion (3 mi. NNW of Lebanon)	Black Mountain (4,145)	Mississippi River (257)
Louisiana	Avoyelles Parish (3 mi. SE of Marksville)	Driskill Mountain (535)	New Orleans (−5)
Maine	Piscataquis (18 mi. N of Dover)	Mt. Katahdin (5,268)	Atlantic Ocean [3]
Maryland	Prince Georges (4½ miles NW of Davidsonville)	Backbone Mountain (3,360)	Atlantic Ocean [3]
Massachusetts	Worcester (north part of city of Worcester)	Mt. Greylock (3,491)	Atlantic Ocean [3]
Michigan	Wexford (5 mi. NNW of Cadillac)	Mt. Arvon (1,979)	Lake Erie (572)
Minnesota	Crow Wing (10 mi. SW of Brainerd)	Eagle Mountain, Cook Co. (2,301)	Lake Superior (602)
Mississippi	Leake (9 mi. WNW of Carthage)	Woodall Mountain (806)	Gulf of Mexico [3]
Missouri	Miller (20 mi. SW of Jefferson City)	Taum Sauk Mountain (1,772)	St. Francis River (230)
Montana	Fergus (12 mi. W of Lewistown)	Granite Peak (12,799)	Kootenai River (1,800)
Nebraska	Custer (10 mi. NW of Broken Bow)	Johnson T. Kimball Co. (5,426)	SE corner of state (840)
Nevada	Lander (26 mi. SE of Austin)	Boundary Peak (13,143)	Colorado River (470)
New Hampshire	Belknap (3 mi. E. of Ashland)	Mt. Washington (6,288)	Atlantic Ocean [3]
New Jersey	Mercer (5 mi. SE of Trenton)	High Point (1,803)	Atlantic Ocean [3]
New Mexico	Torrance (12 mi. SSW of Willard)	Wheeler Peak (13,161)	Red Bluff Reservoir (2,817)
New York	Madison (12+ mi. S of Oneida and 26+ mi. SW of Utica)	Mt. Marcy (5,344)	Atlantic Ocean [3]
North Carolina	Chatham (10 mi. NW of Sanford)	Mt. Mitchell (6,684)	Atlantic Ocean [3]
North Dakota	Sheridan (5 mi. SW of McClusky)	White Butte, Slope Co. (3,506)	Red River (750)
Ohio	Delaware (25 mi. NNE of Columbus)	Campbell Hill (1,550)	Ohio River (433)
Oklahoma	Oklahoma (8 mi. N of Oklahoma City)	Black Mesa (4,973)	Little River (287)
Oregon	Crook (25 mi. SSE of Prineville)	Mt. Hood (11,239)	Pacific Ocean [3]
Pennsylvania	Centre (2½ mi. SW of Bellefonte)	Mt. Davis (3,213)	Delaware River [3]
Rhode Island	Kent (1 mi. SSW of Crompton)	Jerimoth Hill (812)	Atlantic Ocean [3]
South Carolina	Richland (13 mi. SE of Columbia)	Sassafras Mountain (3,560)	Atlantic Ocean [3]
South Dakota	Hughes (8 mi. NE of Pierre)	Harney Peak (7,242)	Big Stone Lake (962)
Tennessee	Rutherford (5 mi. NE of Murfreesboro)	Clingmans Dome (6,643)	Mississippi River (182)
Texas	McCulloch (15 mi. NE of Brady)	Guadalupe Peak (8,749)	Gulf of Mexico [3]
Utah	Sanpete (3 mi. N of Manti)	Kings Peak (13,528)	Beaverdam Creek (2,000)
Vermont	Washington (3 mi. E of Roxbury)	Mt. Mansfield (4,393)	Lake Champlain (95)
Virginia	Buckingham (5 mi. SW of Buckingham)	Mt. Rogers (5,729)	Atlantic Ocean [3]
Washington	Chelan (10 mi. WSW of Wenatchee)	Mt. Rainier (14,410)	Pacific Ocean [3]
West Virginia	Braxton (4 mi. E of Sutton)	Spruce Knob (4,863)	Potomac River (240)
Wisconsin	Wood (9 mi. SE of Marshfield)	Timms Hill, Price Co. (1,951)	Lake Michigan (581)
Wyoming	Fremont (58 mi. ENE of Lander)	Gannett Peak (13,804)	Belle Fourche River (3,100)

[1] Approximate [2] Sec. = section; T = township; R = range; N = north; W = west; S = south; [3] Sea level.

PREHISTORIC MAN

In the 1600s people believed that man had lived on Earth for less than 6,000 years. But with Charles Darwin's publication of the theory of evolution in 1859, anthropologists began searching for a "missing link" that might prove man had evolved from a lower primate.

The most ancient complete human skull was found by anthropologist Richard Leakey in Kenya in 1972. It has been dated as 2.9 million years old. His parents, anthropologists Louis and Mary Leakey, first proved in 1959–63 that man had lived over 1 million years ago.

Anthropologists classify prehistoric humans into several genera based largely on brain shape and size.

HOMO SAPIENS—500,000 B.C. TO PRESENT

Two general types of prehistoric men have skulls about the size of modern men, and are classified as *Homo sapiens.*

Cro-Magnon Man was like modern man, standing about 6 feet tall. He was named after fossils found at Cro-Magnon, France, by Edouard Larter in 1868. The oldest remains of Cro-Magnon Man have been dated as about 35,000 years old.

Neanderthal Man had a brain the size of modern man's, but was somewhat shorter and had heavier bones. Fossils of Neanderthal Man were the first remains of prehistoric man to be found, creating a scientific sensation at the time of their discovery in 1856 in the Neander Valley near Düsseldorf, Germany, by Johann C. Fuhlrott.

Neanderthals are believed to have lived from about 500,000 to 25,000 B.C. in many parts of the world. Fossil remains of this type were found in Zambia (then Northern Rhodesia) in 1921 and called Rhodesian Man. Similar fossil remains found in Java, Indonesia, from 1931 to 1936 were called Solo Man. Other Neanderthaloid fossils were found by anthropologists at Steinheim, Germany, in 1933; at Swanscombe, England, in 1935–36; in caves at Mount Carmel (now in Israel) from 1929 to 1934; and at Shanidar, Iraq, in 1957.

HOMO ERECTUS—1,700,000 TO 500,000 B.C

Homo erectus was a smaller type of man about 5 feet tall with a brain about three-fourths the size of the brain of modern man.

Heidelberg Man. A fossil jaw discovered near Heidelberg, Germany, in 1907 by Otto Schoetensack dates to about 500,000 B.C. Identification has been difficult because no other parts of the skull were found.

Java Man, who made tools, hunted, and used fire, lived from about 1,000,000 to 500,000 B.C. Fossil remains of this primitive man were discovered in Java, Indonesia, by Eugène Dubois in 1891.

Peking Man. Several 500,000-year-old skulls were found near Peking, China, in 1927 by Davidson Black. They are believed to be of the type *Homo erectus,* although at least one skull was as large as that of a modern man.

Kenya Man. Richard Leakey discovered a skull identified as *Homo erectus* near Lake Turkana (Rudolf) in Kenya in 1975. It was dated as 1.5 million years old.

Yuanmou Man. Fossil teeth discovered in China in 1965 have been dated as 1.7 million years old.

HOMO HABILIS—3,750,000 TO 1,500,000 B.C.

Scientists disagree as to whether certain fossils found in Africa should be classified as early man or as primates. They were called *Homo habilis* (skilled man) by their discoverers, the Leakeys, because they used stone tools.

Olduvai Man. The first skulls of an early type of man that used stone tools were found at Olduvai Gorge in Tanganyika in 1959–63 by the Leakeys. These remains have been dated as 1.8 million years old. The discovery provided the first evidence that man had lived more than a million years ago.

Laetolil Man. Jaws and teeth of 11 adults and children were discovered by Mary Leakey in the Laetolil area of Tanzania in 1975. The fossils were dated as between 3.35 and 3.75 million years old.

HOMINOIDS—14,000,000 TO 1,300,000 B.C.

Hominoids are extinct primates that had features similar both to apes and to man.

The earliest of hominoid fossils, called *Ramapithecus,* have been found in Africa, Europe, Pakistan, and India These bones have been dated up to 14 million years old.

The next known hominoid was *Australopithecus,* a small apelike creature that lived in Africa 5.5 million to 1.3 million years ago.

The *Australopithecus* stood about 4 feet tall. His brain was about one-third the size of that of modern man. The first fossils of this type were found at Taung, South Africa, in 1924 by Raymond A. Dart.

Parts of jawbones, teeth, and leg bones were found in 1973–77 by American anthropologist Donald Johanson in Ethiopia. They were dated as 2.9 to 3.6 million years old and identified as a new species named *Australopithecus afarensis,* or Afar ape-man.

HIGHEST MOUNTAINS

Source: National Geographic Society

Mountain ranges were formed when landmasses were pushed up. As time passed, the mountains wore away by weathering and erosion.

The Himalaya range in Asia includes Mt. Everest, the highest peak in the world.

The highest mountains in Europe lie in the Caucasus, a range in the Soviet Union that divides Europe and Asia.

In western Europe the tallest peaks are the Alps, which are located in Switzerland, Italy, France, West Germany, and Austria.

NAME	LOCATION	FEET	NAME	LOCATION	FEET
Highest Peaks in North America			**Highest Peaks in South America**		
McKinley	Alaska	20,320	Aconcagua	Argentina	22,834
Logan	Canada	19,850	Ojos del Salado	Argentina–Chile	22,572
Pico de Orizaba	Mexico	18,700	Bonete	Argentina	22,546
St. Elias	Alaska–Canada	18,008	Tupungato	Argentina–Chile	22,310
Popocatépetl	Mexico	17,887	Pissis	Argentina	22,241
Foraker	Alaska	17,400	Mercedario	Argentina	22,211
Iztaccihuatl	Mexico	17,343	Huascarán	Peru	22,205
Lucania	Canada	17,147	Llullaillaco	Argentina–Chile	22,057
King	Canada	16,971	El Libertador	Argentina	22,047
Steele	Canada	16,644	Cachi	Argentina	22,047
Bona	Alaska	16,421	Yerupaja	Peru	21,709
Blackburn	Alaska	16,390	Galán	Argentina	21,654
Sanford	Alaska	16,237	El Muerto	Argentina–Chile	21,457
South Buttress	Alaska	15,885	Sajama	Bolivia	21,391
Wood	Canada	15,885	Nacimiento	Argentina	21,302
Vancouver	Alaska–Canada	15,700	Illimani	Bolivia	21,201
Churchill	Alaska	15,638	Coropuna	Peru	21,083
Fairweather	Alaska	15,300	Laudo	Argentina	20,997
Zinantecatl (Toluca)	Mexico	15,016	Ancohuma	Bolivia	20,958
Hubbard	Alaska–Canada	15,015	Ausangate	Peru	20,945
Bear	Alaska	14,831	Toro	Argentina–Chile	20,932
Walsh	Canada	14,780	Illampu	Bolivia	20,873
East Buttress	Alaska	14,730	Tres Cruces	Argentina–Chile	20,853
Matlalcueyetl	Mexico	14,636	Huandoy	Peru	20,852
Hunter	Alaska	14,573	Parinacota	Bolivia–Chile	20,768
Alverstone	Alaska–Canada	14,565	Tórtolas	Argentina–Chile	20,745
Browne Tower	Alaska	14,530	Ampato	Peru	20,702
Whitney	California	14,494	Cóndor	Argentina	20,669
Elbert	Colorado	14,433	Salcantay	Peru	20,574
Massive	Colorado	14,421	Chimborazo	Ecuador	20,561
Harvard	Colorado	14,420	Huancarhuas	Peru	20,531
Rainier	Washington	14,410	Famatina	Argentina	20,505
Williamson	California	14,375	Pumasillo	Peru	20,492
Blanca Peak	Colorado	14,345	Solo	Argentina	20,492
La Plata Peak	Colorado	14,336	Polleras	Argentina	20,456
Uncompahgre Peak	Colorado	14,309	Pular	Chile	20,423
Crestone Peak	Colorado	14,294	Chañi	Argentina	20,341
Lincoln	Colorado	14,286	Aucanquilcha	Chile	20,295
Grays Peak	Colorado	14,270	Juncal	Argentina–Chile	20,276
Antero	Colorado	14,269	Negro	Argentina	20,184
Torreys Peak	Colorado	14,267	Quela	Argentina	20,128
Castle Peak	Colorado	14,265	Condoriri	Bolivia	20,095
Quandary Peak	Colorado	14,265	Palermo	Argentina	20,079
Evans	Colorado	14,264	Solimana	Peru	20,068
Longs Peak	Colorado	14,255	San Juan	Argentina–Chile	20,049
McArthur	Canada	14,253	Sierra Nevada	Argentina–Chile	20,023
Wilson	Colorado	14,246	Antofalla	Argentina	20,013
White	California	14,246	Marmolejo	Argentina–Chile	20,013
North Palisade	California	14,242	Chachani	Peru	19,931
Shavano Peak	Colorado	14,229	Chaupi Orko	Peru–Bolivia	19,682

NAME	LOCATION	FEET
Highest Peaks in Asia		
Everest	Nepal–China (Tibet)	29,028
K2 (Godwin-Austen)	Pakistan (Kashmir)	28,250
Kanchenjunga	Nepal–India (Sikkim)	28,208
Lhotse I	Nepal–China (Tibet)	27,923
Makalu I	Nepal–China (Tibet)	27,824
Lhotse II	Nepal–China (Tibet)	27,560
Dhaulagiri	Nepal	26,810
Manaslu I	Nepal	26,760
Cho Oyu	Nepal–China (Tibet)	26,750
Nanga Parbat	Pakistan (Kashmir)	26,660
Annapurna	Nepal	26,504
Gasherbrum	Pakistan (Kashmir)	26,470
Broad	Kashmir	26,400
Gosainthan	China (Tibet)	26,287
Annapurna II	Nepal	26,041
Gyachung Kang	Nepal–China (Tibet)	25,910
Disteghil Sar	Pakistan (Kashmir)	25,858
Himalchuli	Nepal	25,801
Nuptse	Nepal–China (Tibet)	25,726
Masherbrum	Pakistan (Kashmir)	25,660
Nanda Devi	India	25,645
Rakaposhi	Pakistan (Kashmir)	25,550
Kamet	India–China (Tibet)	25,447
Namcha Barwa	China (Tibet)	25,445
Gurla Mandhata	China (Tibet)	25,355
Ulugh Muz Tagh	China (Tibet-Sinkiang)	25,340
Kungur	China (Sinkiang)	25,325
Tirich Mir	Pakistan	25,230
Makalu II	Nepal–China (Tibet)	25,120
Minya Konka	China	24,900
Kula Gangri	Bhutan–China (Tibet)	24,784
Changtzu	Nepal–China (Tibet)	24,780
Muz Tagh Ata	China (Sinkiang)	24,757
Skyang Kangri	Pakistan (Kashmir)	24,750
Communism Peak	Soviet Union	24,590
Jongsang Peak	Nepal–India (Sikkim)	24,472
Pobedy Peak	Soviet Union–China	24,406
Sia Kangri	Pakistan (Kashmir)	24,350
Haramosh Peak	Pakistan	24,270
Istoro Nal	Pakistan	24,240
Tent Peak	Nepal–India (Sikkim)	24,165
Chomo Lhari	Bhutan–China (Tibet)	24,040
Chamlang	Nepal	24,012
Kabru	Nepal–India (Sikkim)	24,002
Alung Gangri	China (Tibet)	24,000
Baltoro Kangri	Pakistan (Kashmir)	23,990
Mussu Shan	China (Sinkiang)	23,890
Mana	India	23,860
Baruntse	Nepal	23,688
Nepal Peak	Nepal–India (Sikkim)	23,500
Amne Machin	China	23,490
Gauri Sankar	Nepal–China (Tibet)	23,440
Badrinath	India	23,420
Nunkun	Pakistan (Kashmir)	23,410
Lenina Peak	Soviet Union	23,405
Pyramid	Nepal–India (Sikkim)	23,400
Api	Nepal	23,399
Pauhunri	India–China (Tibet)	23,385
Trisul	India	23,360
Kangto	India–China (Tibet)	23,260
Nyenchhen Thanglha	China (Tibet)	23,255
Trisuli	India	23,210
Dunagiri	India	23,184
Lombo Kangra	China (Tibet)	23,165

NAME	LOCATION	FEET
Highest Peaks in Europe		
Elbrus	Soviet Union	18,510
Shkara	Soviet Union	17,064
Dykh Tau	Soviet Union	17,054
Kashtan Tau	Soviet Union	16,877
Dzhangi Tau	Soviet Union	16,565
Kazbek	Soviet Union	16,558
Mont Blanc	France–Italy (Alps)	15,771
Monte Rosa	Italy–Switzerland (Alps)	15,203
Dom	Switzerland (Alps)	14,911
Liskamm	Switzerland (Alps)	14,852
Weisshorn	Switzerland (Alps)	14,780
Täschhorn	Switzerland (Alps)	14,733
Matterhorn	Switzerland (Alps)	14,690
Dent Blanche	Switzerland (Alps)	14,293
Nadelhorn	Switzerland (Alps)	14,196
Grand Combin	Switzerland (Alps)	14,154
Lenzspitze	Switzerland (Alps)	14,088
Finsteraarhorn	Switzerland (Alps)	14,022
Castor	Switzerland (Alps)	13,865
Zinalrothorn	Switzerland (Alps)	13,849
Hohberghorn	Switzerland (Alps)	13,842
Alphubel	Switzerland (Alps)	13,799
Rimpfischhorn	Switzerland (Alps)	13,776
Aletschhorn	Switzerland (Alps)	13,763
Strahlhorn	Switzerland (Alps)	13,747
Dent d'Hérens	Switzerland (Alps)	13,686
Breithorn	Switzerland (Alps)	13,665
Bishorn	Switzerland (Alps)	13,645
Jungfrau	Switzerland (Alps)	13,642
Highest Peaks in Africa		
Kilimanjaro (2 peaks):		
Kibo	Tanzania	19,340
Mawenzi	Tanzania	16,896
Kenya	Kenya	17,058
Margherita	Uganda–Zaire	16,763
Ras Dashan	Ethiopia	15,158
Meru	Tanzania	14,979
Karisimbi	Rwanda–Zaire	14,787
Elgon	Kenya–Uganda	14,178
Batu	Ethiopia	14,131
Gugē	Ethiopia	13,780
Toubkal	Morocco	13,655
Birhan	Ethiopia	13,628
Highest Peaks in the Pacific and Southeast Asia		
Jaya	Indonesia (Irian Jaya)	16,500
Pilimsit	Indonesia (Irian Jaya)	15,748
Trikora	Indonesia (Irian Jaya)	15,585
Mandala	Indonesia (Irian Jaya)	15,420
Wilhelm	Papua New Guinea	14,793
Highest Peaks in Antarctica		
Vinson Massif		16,864
Tyree		16,290
Shinn		15,750
Gardner		15,375
Epperly		15,100

MAJOR VOLCANOES

About 600 active and 10,000 inactive or dormant volcanoes are found along three belts, closely matching the earthquake regions of the world.

The "ring of fire" includes the Pacific coasts of North and South America and Asia.

A second belt extends from the Mediterranean to the East Indies, and a third lies along the midocean ridges of the major oceans.

Volcanic activity is deceptively sporadic—brief periods of outgassing or eruption, followed by unpredictably longer dormant periods.

Many volcanoes began their eruptions on the bed of the sea. Italy's Etna and Vesuvius were submarine volcanoes originally.

Cones are inevitably modified by eruptions. Thus some heights are approximate.

See also *Major Volcanic Disasters,* page 38.

NAME	LOCATION	HEIGHT
AFRICA AND INDIAN OCEAN		
Kilimanjaro	Tanzania	19,340
Cameroon Mt.	Cameroon	13,350
Teide	Tenerife Island	12,198
Nyiragongo	Zaire	11,400
Nyamlagira	Zaire	10,028
Fogo	Cape Verde	9,281
Piton de la Fournaise	Réunion	8,630
Tristan da Cunha	Atlantic Ocean	6,760
ANTARCTICA		
Erebus	Rosa Island	12,450
ASIA AND PACIFIC OCEAN		
Klyuchevskaya	Soviet Union	15,584
Mauna Kea	Hawaii	13,796
Mauna Loa	Hawaii	13,680
Kerinci	Indonesia	12,467
Fuji	Japan	12,388
Rinjani	Indonesia	12,224
Tolbachik	Soviet Union	12,080
Semeru	Indonesia	12,060
Ichinskaya	Soviet Union	11,880
Kronotskaya	Soviet Union	11,575
Koryakskaya	Soviet Union	11,339
Slamet	Indonesia	11,247
Raung	Indonesia	10,932
Shiveluch	Soviet Union	10,771
Dempo	Indonesia	10,364
Welirang	Indonesia	10,354
Agung	Indonesia	10,308
Sundoro	Indonesia	10,285
Plosky Tolbachik	Soviet Union	10,121
Ciremay	Indonesia	10,098
Ontake	Japan	10,049
Gede	Indonesia	9,705
Merapi	Indonesia	9,548
Bezymyannaya	Soviet Union	9,514
Apo	Philippines	9,369
Tambora	Indonesia	9,353
Ruapehu	New Zealand	9,175
Peuetsagoe	Indonesia	9,121
Bromo	Indonesia	9,088
Avachinskaya	Soviet Union	9,026
Api Siau	Indonesia	8,856
Mayon	Philippines	7,943
Ngauruhoe	New Zealand	7,516
Sarychev	Kurile Islands	4,910
Karimsky	Soviet Union	4,875
Kilauea	Hawaii	4,077
Sakurazima	Kyushu, Japan	3,657
Suwanosezima	Ryukyus	2,620
Usu	Hokkaido, Japan	2,385
Shin-dake	Ryukyus	2,100
EUROPE		
Etna	Italy	10,791
Beeren Berg	Norway	7,470
Askja	Iceland	4,954
Europe *(continued)*		
Hekla	Iceland	4,892
Vesuvius	Italy	4,190
Katla	Iceland	3,182
Stromboli	Italy	3,038
Leirhnukur	Iceland	2,132
NORTH AMERICA		
Citlaltepec	Mexico	18,700
Popocatépetl	Mexico	17,887
Wrangell	Alaska	14,163
Colima	Mexico	12,988
Torbert	Alaska	11,413
Spurr	Alaska	11,069
Baker	Washington	10,778
Lassen	California	10,457
Redoubt	Alaska	10,197
Iliamna	Alaska	10,016
Mount St. Helens	Washington	9,671*
Shishaldin	Alaska (Aleutians)	9,387
Pavlof	Alaska	8,261
Veniaminof	Alaska	8,225
Griggs	Alaska	7,600
Paricutín	Mexico	7,451
St. Augustine	Alaska	3,969
CENTRAL AMERICA AND CARIBBEAN SEA		
Tajumulco	Guatemala	13,845
Tacaná	Guatemala	13,428
Acatenango	Guatemala	12,992
Fuego	Guatemala	12,582
Santa Maria	Guatemala	12,372
Atitlán	Guatemala	11,565
Irazú	Costa Rica	11,260
San Pedro	Guatemala	9,921
Póas	Costa Rica	8,859
Pacaya	Guatemala	8,346
San Miguel	El Salvador	6,988
San Cristóbal (El Viejo)	Nicaragua	5,842
Arenal	Costa Rica	5,092
La Soufrière	Guadeloupe	4,812
SOUTH AMERICA		
Chimborazo	Ecuador	20,561
Guallatiri	Chile	19,882
Lascar	Chile	19,652
Cotopaxi	Ecuador	19,347
Misti	Peru	19,098
Cayambe	Ecuador	18,996
Tupungatito	Chile	18,504
Sangay	Ecuador	17,159
Tungurahua	Ecuador	16,512
Cotacachi	Ecuador	16,204
Pichincha	Ecuador	15,696
Puracé	Colombia	15,604
Reventador	Ecuador	11,431
Lautaro	Chile	11,090
Llaima	Chile	10,239
Villarrica	Chile	9,318

* Estimated 1,500 feet sheared off during 1980 eruption.

PRINCIPAL DESERTS

Once simply used for an uninhabited, or "deserted" place, the term *desert* is now commonly applied to regions that have little rainfall, scanty vegetation, and limited human use.

Of the three types of deserts commonly recognized, only a few *tropical* deserts, such as the Libyan part of the Sahara, resemble the popular image of a hot, dry, sandy expanse.

Middle latitude deserts lie in the "rainshadow" of a mountain barrier (as deserts in the southwestern U.S.), or deep within the moisture-starved interiors of continents (the Gobi).

Polar deserts occur because moisture is "locked up" as ice and snow.

Desert landscapes range from flat, sandy plains to mountainous plateaus. The rocks of deserts are typically eroded into fantastic shapes by the action of wind-driven sand.

DESERT	LOCATION	SIZE	REMARKS
NORTH AMERICA			
Black Rock	Humboldt and Pershing counties, Nevada	An area of 1,000 square miles	A barren plain practically devoid of vegetation; from its surface, alkaline dust is blown into vast clouds by the summer winds.
Colorado	Arid region of southeastern California	200 miles long; maximum width of 50 miles	The soil of its Imperial Valley is highly productive when irrigated.
Death Valley	Eastern California and Southwestern Nevada	2,936 square miles	Yielded much borax in the 19th century.
Mohave	Southern California; northeast of Los Angeles extends into Mohave County, Arizona	15,000 square miles	Needles, on the Arizona-California boundary, is one of the hottest towns in the United States.
Painted Desert	Coconino and Navajo counties in northern Arizona	200 miles long; 15–30 miles wide	Within the desert are seven Hopi villages; the Painted Desert is so called because of its coloring, caused by centuries of erosion exposing brilliantly colored rock formations.
SOUTH AMERICA			
Atacama	Northern Chile	600 miles long	An area of rich nitrate and copper deposits.
AFRICA			
Kalahari	South Africa; the Orange River marks its southern limit	120,000 square miles	Hottentots and Bushmen inhabit the area.
Namib	Namibia	800 miles long; 30–100 miles wide	Long, narrow desert plain along Atlantic coast.
Sahara	North Africa; on the west the desert extends to the Atlantic coast	Over 3,000,000 square miles	Nomadic herding is still an important activity in the desert, but in recent years there has been petroleum extraction; the Libyan and Nubian deserts are part of the Sahara.
ASIA			
Dasht i Kavir	Iran, from the Caspian Sea to the Persian Gulf	300 miles long; 100 miles wide	Saline swamps and dry salt areas.
Gobi	Extends 1,500 miles from Manchuria to Sinkiang Province, China	500,000 square miles	Many paleontological finds, including dinosaur eggs, have been made there.
Kara Kum	Asiatic Soviet Union	110,000 square miles	The Kara Kum has a number of "old river beds" that may have been either channels or tributaries of the Amu.
Kizil-Kum	Asiatic Soviet Union	370 by 220 miles	The surface is characterized by stationary sands with sparse vegetation.
Negev	Southern Israel	4,700 square miles	Barren expanses of sand, now dotted with prosperous farms, orchards, and towns; has King Solomon's mines and the Dead Sea.
An Nafud	Northern Saudi Arabia	An average width of 200 miles	Huge area of sand dunes, populated only by a few nomads.
Rub al-Khali (Empty Quarter)	Southern Saudi Arabia	300,000 square miles	Practically unexplored; it may contain large tracts of hard gravel or limestone deposits.
Syrian	Northernmost Saudi Arabia, extending into Jordan, Syria, and Iraq	——	The oasis of Al Jawf has extensive palm groves and a population of more than 10,000.
Taklamakan	Central Asia, in the Chinese province of Sinkiang	125,000 square miles	Ancient trade routes cross this desert, and there are reports of buried cities; the Chinese exploded their first atomic bomb there in 1964.
Thar (Indian)	Northwestern India, between the Gulf of Cutch and the Arabian Sea on the south	100,000 square miles	Camel caravans still traverse the desert; parts of the Thar are disputed between India and Pakistan.
AUSTRALIA			
Great Australian	Much of central and western Australia	——	Primitive Bushmen live in this area, which Australians prefer to call "Sparselands."

MAJOR ISLANDS

Source: National Geographic Society

Islands are bodies of land surrounded by water. Continents are islands in the strict sense of the word, differing from other islands only in size.

The largest islands in the world are, in square miles: Greenland (840,000); New Guinea (306,000); Borneo (280,100); Madagascar (226,658); Baffin (195,928); Sumatra (165,000); Honshu (87,805); Great Britain (84,200); Victoria (83,896); and Ellesmere (75,767).

The largest islands of the United States, in square miles, are: Hawaii (4,037); Kodiak (3,670); and Puerto Rico (3,515).

Islands in minor waters (in square miles): Manitoulin (Canada), Lake Huron (1,068); Singapore, Singapore Strait (239); Isle Royale, Mich., Lake Superior (209); Pinang (Malaysia), Strait of Malacca (110); Staten Island, N.Y. (59); Manhattan, N.Y. (22).

NAME	AREA (in sq. miles)
ARCTIC OCEAN	
Canadian	
Axel Heiberg	16,671
Baffin	195,928
Banks	27,033
Devon	21,331
Ellesmere	75,767
Melville	16,274
Prince of Wales	12,872
Southampton	15,913
Victoria	83,896
Soviet Union	
Franz Josef Land	8,000
Novaya Zemlya	35,000
Wrangel	2,800
Norwegian	
Svalbard	23,940
Nordaustlandet	5,410
Spitsbergen	15,060
ATLANTIC OCEAN	
British Isles	
Great Britain, mainland	84,200
Hebrides	2,744
Ireland	32,599
Man	227
Orkney Is.	390
Shetland Is.	567
Skye	670
Other Atlantic Islands	
Anticosti (Canada)	3,066
Azores (Portugal)	902
Bahamas	5,353
Bermuda Is. (Britain)	20
Canary Is. (Spain)	2,808
Cape Breton (Canada)	3,981
Cape Verde Is.	1,750
Faeroe Is. (Denmark)	540
Falkland Is. (Britain)	4,700
Fernando Po (Equatorial Guinea)	785
Greenland (Denmark)	840,000
Iceland	39,769
Long Island (New York)	1,396
Madeira Is. (Portugal)	307
Marajó (Brazil)	15,528
Martha's Vineyard (Massachusetts)	91
Nantucket (Massachusetts)	46
Newfoundland (Canada)	42,030
Prince Edward (Canada)	2,184
South Georgia (Britain)	1,450
Tierra del Fuego (Chile and Argentina)	17,800
BALTIC SEA	
Aland (Finland)	581
Bornholm (Denmark)	227
Gotland (Sweden)	1,164
CARIBBEAN SEA	
Antigua	108
Barbados	166
Cuba	44,218
Isle of Youth	1,182
Dominica	290
Guadeloupe (France)	687
Hispaniola (Haiti and Dominican Republic)	29,530
Jamaica	4,244
Martinique (France)	425
Puerto Rico (U.S.)	3,515
Trinidad	1,864
Virgin Is. (U.S.)	132
INDIAN OCEAN	
Andaman Is. (India)	2,500
Madagascar	226,658
Mauritius	720
Pemba (Tanzania)	380
Réunion (France)	969
Seychelles	107
Sri Lanka	25,332
Zanzibar (Tanzania)	640
Persian Gulf	
Bahrain	258
MEDITERRANEAN SEA	
Balearic Is. (Spain)	1,936
Corfu (Greece)	229
Corsica (France)	3,365
Crete (Greece)	3,186
Cyprus	3,572
Elba (Italy)	86
Euboea (Greece)	1,409
Malta	122
Rhodes (Greece)	542
Sardinia (Italy)	9,262
Sicily (Italy)	9,822
PACIFIC OCEAN	
Aleutian Is. (Alaska)	6,821
Caroline (U.S. Trust Territory)	473
Galápagos Is. (Ecuador)	3,043
Guadalcanal (Britain)	2,500
Guam (U.S.)	209
Hainan (China)	13,000
Hawaiian Is. (U.S.)	6,450
Hawaii	4,037
Oahu	593
Hong Kong (Britain)	29
Japan	145,809
Hokkaido	30,144
Honshu	87,805
Iwo Jima	8
Kyushu	14,114
Okinawa	459
Shikoku	7,049
Kodiak (Alaska)	3,670
Marquesas Is. (France)	492
Marshall Is. (U.S. Trust)	70
Nauru	8
New Caledonia (France)	6,530
New Guinea (Indonesia–Papua New Guinea)	306,000
New Zealand	103,883
North	44,035
South	58,305
Northern Mariana Is. (U.S.)	184
Philippines	115,831
Leyte	2,787
Luzon	40,880
Mindanao	36,775
Mindoro	3,790
Negros	4,907
Palawan	4,554
Panay	4,446
Samar	5,050
Quemoy	56
Sakhalin (Soviet Union)	29,500
Samoa Islands	1,177
American Samoa	77
Tutuila	52
Western Samoa	1,101
Savaii	670
Upolu	429
Tahiti (France)	402
Taiwan	13,823
Tasmania (Australia)	26,178
Vancouver (Canada)	12,079
Vanuatu	5,700
Viti Levu (Fiji)	4,109
Indonesia	
Bali	2,147
Borneo (with Malaysia–Britain)	280,100
Celebes	69,000
Java	48,900
Moluccas	28,766
Sumatra	165,000
Timor	11,570
Papua New Guinea	
New Britain	14,093
New Ireland	3,707

LONGEST RIVERS

Source: National Geographic Society

RIVER	EMPTIES INTO	MILES
NORTH AMERICA		
Albany (Canada)	James Bay	610
Arkansas (Colo.–Ark.)	Mississippi River	1,459
Athabasca (Canada)	Lake Athabasca	765
Back (Canada)	Chantrey Inlet	605
Brazos (Texas)	Gulf of Mexico	1,210
Canadian (N.M.–Okla.)	Arkansas River	906
Churchill (Canada)	Hudson Bay	1,000
Cimarron (Colo.–Okla.)	Arkansas River	600
Colorado (Colo.–Mexico)	Gulf of California	1,450
Colorado (Texas)	Matagorda Bay	840
Columbia (U.S.–Canada)	Pacific Ocean	1,243
Cumberland (Ky.–Tenn.)	Ohio River	720
Fraser (Brit. Col.)	Strait of Georgia	850
Green (Utah–Wyo.)	Colorado River	730
James (N.D.–S.D.)	Missouri River	710
Kuskokwim (Alaska)	Kuskokwim Bay	800
Mackenzie (Canada)	Beaufort Sea	2,635
Mississippi (Minn.–La.)	Gulf of Mexico	2,348
Mississippi–Missouri–Red Rock (Mont.–La.)	Gulf of Mexico	3,710
Missouri (Mont.–Mo.)	Mississippi River	2,315
Missouri–Red Rock (Mont.–Mo.)	Mississippi River	2,533
Nelson (Canada)	Hudson Bay	1,600
North Canadian (Okla.)	Canadian River	760
North Platte (Wyo.–Nebr.)	Platte River	680
Ohio (Pa.–Ill.)	Mississippi River	981
Ohio–Allegheny (Pa.–Ill.)	Mississippi River	1,306
Ottawa (Canada)	St. Lawrence River	790
Peace (Canada)	Slave River	1,195
Pecos (N.M.–Tex.)	Rio Grande	735
Red (Okla.–Tex.–La.)	Mississippi River	1,270
Rio Grande (Colo.–Mexico)	Gulf of Mexico	1,885
Saguenay (Canada)	St. Lawrence River	434
St. Lawrence (N.Y.–Canada)	Gulf of St. Lawrence	800
Saskatchewan (Canada)	Lake Winnipeg	1,205
Snake (Wyo.–Wash.)	Columbia River	1,038
Tennessee–French Broad (N.C.–Ky.)	Ohio River	900
Trinity (Canada)	Trinity Bay	715
Usumacinta (Mexico)	Gulf of Mexico	270
White (Ark.–Mo.)	Mississippi River	720
Yukon (Alaska–Canada)	Bering Sea	1,979
SOUTH AMERICA		
Amazon (Brazil)	Atlantic Ocean	4,000
Japura (Colombia–Brazil)	Amazon River	1,750
Madeira (Brazil)	Amazon River	2,013
Magdalena (Colombia)	Caribbean Sea	956
Negro (Brazil)	Amazon River	1,400
Orinoco (Venezuela)	Atlantic Ocean	1,600
Paraguay (Paraguay)	Paraná River	1,584
Paraná (Argentina)	Rio de la Plata	2,485
Pilcomayo (Arg.-Paraguay)	Paraguay River	1,000
Purus (Peru–Brazil)	Amazon River	2,100
Rio Theodore Roosevelt (Brazil)	Aripciana River	400
São Francisco (Brazil)	Atlantic Ocean	1,988
Tocantins (Brazil)	Pará River	1,677
Uruguay (Arg.–Uruguay)	Rio de la Plata	1,000
EUROPE		
Bug S. (Poland–Soviet Union)	Dnieper River	532
Bug W. (Soviet Union–Poland)	Wisla River	481
Danube (W. Germany—Romania)	Black Sea	1,776
Daugava–Dvina (Soviet Union)	Gulf of Riga	634
Dnieper (Soviet Union)	Black Sea	1,420
Dniester (Soviet Union)	Black Sea	877
Don (Soviet Union)	Sea of Azov	1,224
Drava (Yugoslavia)	Danube River	447
Ebro (Spain)	Mediterranean Sea	565
Elbe (E. Germany)	North Sea	724
Loire (France)	Bay of Biscay	634
Meuse (Belgium–France)	North Sea	580
Oder (E. Germany–Poland)	Baltic Sea	567
Rhine (Switz.–Netherlands)	North Sea	820
Rhone (France–Switz.)	Mediterranean Sea	505
Seine (France)	English Channel	496
Tajo or Tagus (Spain–Port.)	Atlantic Ocean	626
Tisza (Hungary)	Danube River	600
Ural (Soviet Union)	Caspian Sea	1,575
Volga (Soviet Union)	Caspian Sea	2,194
Weser (W. Germany)	North Sea	454
Wisla (Poland)	Baltic Sea	675
AFRICA		
Gambia (Gambia)	Atlantic Ocean	700
Niger (Nigeria)	Gulf of Guinea	2,590
Nile (Sudan–Egypt)	Mediterranean Sea	4,145
Orange (South Africa)	Atlantic Ocean	1,300
Zaire or Congo (Zaire–Congo)	Atlantic Ocean	2,900
Zambezi (Zambia–Mozambique)	Indian Ocean	1,700
ASIA		
Amu (Soviet Union)	Aral Sea	1,578
Amur (Soviet Union)	Tatar Strait	2,744
Angara (Soviet Union)	Yenisey River	1,151
Brahmaputra	Bay of Bengal	1,800
Euphrates (Syria–Iraq)	Persian Gulf	2,235
Ganges (India–Bangladesh)	Bay of Bengal	1,560
Hsi (China)	South China Sea	1,200
Indus (Pakistan)	Arabian Sea	1,800
Irrawaddy (Burma)	Bay of Bengal	1,337
Lena (Soviet Union)	Laptev Sea	2,734
Mekong (SE Asia)	South China Sea	2,600
Ob–Irtysh (Soviet Union)	Gulf of Ob	3,362
Salween (Burma)	Gulf of Martaban	1,500
Sungari (China)	Amur River	1,150
Syr Darya (Soviet Union)	Aral Sea	1,370
Tigris (Iraq)	Euphrates River	1,180
Chang Jiang or Yangtze (China)	East China Sea	3,964
Huang or Yellow (China)	Yellow Sea	2,903
Yenisey (Soviet Union)	Kara Sea	2,543
AUSTRALIA		
Murray–Darling	Indian Ocean	2,310

FAMOUS WATERFALLS

Source: National Geographic Society

There are tens of thousands of waterfalls scattered over the Earth, hundreds of them of considerable magnitude. The highest waterfalls in the world are: Angel (Venezuela), 3,212 feet; Yosemite (California), 2,425 feet; Southern Mardalsfossen (Norway), 2,149 feet; Tugela (South Africa), 2,014 feet; Cuquenán (Venezuela), 2,000 feet; Sutherland (New Zealand), 1,904 feet.

On the basis of annual flow combined with considerable height, Guaira, between Brazil and Paraguay, is the world's greatest waterfall; its estimated annual flow is 470,000 cusecs (cubic feet per second). A greater volume of water passes over Boyoma Falls, in Zaire, the former Democratic Republic of the Congo, but not one of its seven falls, spread over a distance of 60 miles, is higher than 10 feet.

The estimated annual flows of other great waterfalls are: Niagara (Canada and United States), 212,200 cusecs; Paulo Afonso (Brazil), 100,000; Urubupunga (Brazil), 97,000; Iguazú (Argentina and Brazil), 61,600; Patos-Maribondo (Brazil), 53,000; Victoria (Zambia and Zimbabwe), 35,400; and Kaieteur (Guyana), 23,400.

LOCATION AND NAME	FEET HIGH[1]
AFRICA	
Angola	
Duque de Braganca	344
Ruacana, Cuene R.	406
Ethiopia	
Del Verme, Dawa R.	98
Fincha	508
T'is Isat, Blue Nile	140
Lesotho	
Maletsunyane [2]	630
South Africa	
Aughrabies [2], Orange R.	480
Howick, Umgeni R.	311
Tugela [3]	2,014
Highest single fall	597
Tanzania–Zambia	
Kalambo [2]	726
Uganda	
Kabalega (Murchison) Victoria Nile R.	130
Zambia	
Chirombo	880
Zimbabwe and Zambia	
Victoria [2], Zambezi R.	343
ASIA	
India	
Cauvery [2]	330
Gokak [2], Ghataprabha R.	170
Jog [2] (Gersoppa), Sharavathi R.	830
Japan	
Kegon [2], Daiya R.	330
Laos	
Khon Cataracts [4], Mekong R.	70
AUSTRALASIA	
Australia	
New South Wales	
Wentworth [3]	614
Wollomombi	1,100
Queensland	
Coomera	210
Tully	885
Wallaman [3]	1,137
New Zealand	
Bowen	540
Helena	890
Stirling	505
Sutherland [3], Arthur R.	1,904
EUROPE	
Austria	
Gastein [3]	492
Golling [2, 3], Schwarzbach R.	250
Krimml [3]	1,312
France	
Gavarnie [3]	1,385
Great Britain	
Scotland: Glomach	370
Wales: Rhaiadr	240
Iceland	
Detti	144
Italy	
Frua [4], Toce R.	470
Norway	
Mardalsfossen (Northern)	1,535
Mardalsfossen [3] (Southern)	2,149
Skjeggedal [3, 5], Nybuai R.	1,378
Skykkje [5]	984
Vetti	900
Vöring, Bjoreio R.	597
Sweden	
Handöl [3]	427
Tannforsen, Are R.	120
Switzerland	
Diesbach [3]	394
Giessbach [4]	984
Handegg, Aare R.	150
Iffigen	120
Pissevache, Salanfe R.	213
Reichenbach [3]	656
Simmen [3]	459
Staubbach	984
Trümmelbach [3]	1,312
NORTH AMERICA	
Canada	
Alberta	
Panther, Nigel Cr.	600
British Columbia	
Della	1,443
Takakkaw, Daly Glacier	1,200
Northwest Territories	
Virginia, S. Nahanni R.	294
Quebec	
Montmorency	274
Canada–United States	
Niagara [6]	
American	182
Horseshoe	173
Mexico	
El Salto	218
United States	
California	
Feather [2], Fall R.	640
Yosemite Natl. Park:	
Bridal Veil [2]	620
Nevada [2], Merced R.	594
Ribbon [5]	1,612
Silver Strand [5], Meadow Br.	1,170
Yosemite [3, 5]	2,425
Colorado	
Seven [3], S. Cheyenne Cr.	300
Hawaii	
Akaka	442
Idaho	
Shoshone [5], Snake R.	212
Twin, Snake R.	120
New York	
Taughannock [2]	215
Oregon	
Multnomah [3]	620
Tennessee	
Fall Creek	256
Washington	
Mt. Rainier Natl. Park:	
Narada, Paradise R.	168
Sluiskin, Paradise R.	300
Palouse	197
Snoqualmie [5]	268
Wisconsin	
Big Manitou [2, 4], Black R.	165
Wyoming	
Yellowstone Natl. Park:	
Tower	132
Yellowstone (upper) [2]	109
Yellowstone (lower) [2]	308
SOUTH AMERICA	
Argentina–Brazil	
Iguazú	230
Brazil	
Glass	1,325
Herval	400
Patos-Maribondo, Grande R.	115
Paulo Afonso, São Francisco R.	275
Urubupunga, Paraná R.	40
Colombia	
Catarata de Candelas, Cusiana R.	984
Tequendama, Bogotá R.	427
Guyana	
Kaieteur, Potaro R.	741
Great Kamarang R.	1,600
Marina [3], Ipobe R.	500
Venezuela	
Angel [2, 3]	3,212
Cuquenán	2,000

1 Height means total drop whether in one or more leaps. 2 Falls greatly diminish seasonally. 3 Falls consist of more than one leap. 4 Cascade-type falls. 5 Falls dry part of year. 6 Niagara's cataract is divided by Goat Island into two waterfalls.

LARGEST LAKES IN EACH U.S. STATE

Source: National Geographic Society

STATE	LAKE	AREA (sq. miles)	MAX. DEPTH (feet)	SHORE-LINE (miles)
Alabama	Guntersville[1,3,5]	106	68	949
	Eufaula[2,3,5]	71	90	640
Alaska	Iliamna[1,4]	1,115	987	—
Arizona	Theodore Roosevelt[1,3]	27	280	88
	Powell[2,3]	252	580	1,800
Arkansas	Ouachita[1,3]	75	207	975
	Bull Shoals[2,3]	71	250	740
California	Salton Sea[1,4]	375	50	—
	Tahoe[2,4]	191	1,645	71
Colorado	Blue Mesa[1,3,5]	14	342	96
	Navajo[2,3,5]	24	388	150
Connecticut	Candlewood[1,3]	8	85	65
	Colebrook River[2,3]	2	140	13
Delaware	Lum's Pond[1,3]	0.3	10	7
Florida	Okeechobee[1,4]	700	15	96
	Seminole[2,3]	59	27	—
Georgia	Sidney Lanier[1,3]	59	156	540
	Clark Hill[2,3]	109	145	1,200
Hawaii	Waita[1,3,5]	0.7	29	4
Idaho	Pend Oreille[1,4]	148	1,237	226
Illinois	Carlyle[3,5]	41	40	83
	Michigan[2,4]	22,300	923	1,660
Indiana	Monroe[1,3,5]	17	70	150
	Michigan[2,4]	22,300	923	1,660
Iowa	Rathbun[1,3,5]	17	102	180
Kansas	Tuttle Creek[1,3,5]	25	90	112
Kentucky	Cumberland[1,3]	79	183	1,255
	Kentucky[2,3]	250	71	2,380
Louisiana	Pontchartrain[1,4]	621	18	112
	Toledo Bend[2,3,5]	284	92	1,200
Maine	Moosehead[1,4]	117	246	190
Maryland	Deep Creek[1,3]	7	72	65
	Youghiogheny[2,3,5]	4	115	38
Massachusetts	Quabbin[1,3,5]	39	150	118
Michigan	Houghton[1,4]	31	20	30
	Superior[2,4]	31,700	1,333	2,980
Minnesota	Red[1,4]	451	31	123
	Superior[2,4]	31,700	1,333	2,980
Mississippi	Ross Barnett[1,3,5]	52	55	105
	Pickwick[2,3]	67	—	496
Missouri	Harry S. Truman[1,3,5]	87	125	958
	Bull Shoals[2,3,5]	71	250	740
Montana	Fort Peck[1,3,5]	389	210	1,650
	Koocanusa[2,3]	73	350	224
Nebraska	McConaughy[1,3]	55	142	105
	Lewis and Clark[2,3]	27	50	90
Nevada	Pyramid[1,4]	169	330	66
	Mead[2,3]	247	432	550
New Hamp.	Winnipesaukee[1,4]	70	180	240
	Umbagog[2,4]	12	—	—
New Jersey	Hopatcong[1,4]	4	58	32
	Greenwood[2,4]	3	52	14
New Mexico	Elephant Butte[1,3,5]	58	157	250
	Navajo[2,3,5]	24	388	150
New York	Oneida[1,4]	79	55	58
	Erie[2,4]	9,910	210	856
North Carolina	Mattamusket[1,4]	67	5	—
	John H. Kerr[2,3,5]	76	105	800
North Dakota	Sakakawea[1,3]	575	180	1,600
	Oahe[2,3,5]	556	200	2,250
Ohio	Grand[1,2]	22	10	60
	Erie[2,4]	9,910	210	856
Oklahoma	Eufaula[1,3]	160	87	600
	Texoma[2,3]	139	142	580
Oregon	Upper Klamath[1,4]	143	50	165
	Goose[2,4]	194	24	90
Pennsylvania	Raystown[1,3,5]	13	186	115
	Erie[2,4]	9,910	210	856
Rhode Island	Scituate[1,3,5]	5	94	38
South Carolina	Marion[1,3]	173	40	330
	Clark Hill[2,3]	123	150	1,200
South Dakota	Francis Case[1,3,5]	159	140	540
	Oahe[2,3,5]	556	200	2,250
Tennessee	Watts Bar[1,3]	61	61	771
	Kentucky[2,3]	250	71	2,380
Texas	Sam Rayburn[1,3,5]	179	73	560
	Toledo Bend[2,3,5]	284	92	1,200
Utah	Great Salt[1,4]	1,680	34	335
	Powell[2,3]	252	560	1,960
Vermont	Bomoseen[1,4]	4	65	22
	Champlain[2,4]	437	400	379
Virginia	Smith Mountain[1,3]	31	200	500
	John H. Kerr[2,3,5]	76	105	800
Washington	F.D. Roosevelt[1,3]	123	375	151
West Virginia	Summersville[1,3]	4	267	65
Wisconsin	Winnebago[1,4]	215	21	85
	Superior[2,4]	31,700	1,333	2,980
Wyoming	Yellowstone[1,4]	137	309	110
	Flaming Gorge[2,3,5]	66	437	—

[1] Entirely within state. [2] Shared with another state or states. [3] Man-made. [4] Natural. [5] Reservoir.

WORLD'S LARGEST LAKES

Source: National Geographic Society

LAKE AND LOCATION	AREA (sq. miles)	LENGTH (miles)	MAX. DEPTH (feet)
Caspian Sea (U.S.S.R.-Iran)	143,244	760	3,363
Superior (U.S.-Canada)	31,700	350	1,333
Victoria (Uganda-Tanzania-Kenya)	26,828	250	270
Aral Sea (U.S.S.R.)	24,904	280	220
Huron (U.S.-Canada)	23,000	206	750
Michigan (U.S.)	22,300	307	923
Tanganyika (Zaire-Burundi-Tanzania-Zambia)	12,700	420	4,823
Baykal (U.S.S.R.)	12,162	395	5,315
Great Bear (Canada)	12,096	192	1,463
Nyasa or Malawi (Tanzania-Mozambique-Malawi)	11,150	360	2,280
Great Slave (Canada)	11,031	298	2,015
Erie (U.S.-Canada)	9,910	241	210
Winnipeg (Canada)	9,417	266	60
Ontario (U.S.-Canada)	7,550	193	802
Balkhash (U.S.S.R.)	7,115	376	85
Ladoga (U.S.S.R.)	6,835	124	738
Chad (Chad-Niger-Nigeria)	6,300	175	24
Maracaibo (Venezuela)	5,217	133	115
Onega (U.S.S.R.)	3,710	145	328
Eyre (Australia)	3,600	90	4
Volta (Ghana)	3,276	250	—
Titicaca (Peru-Bolivia)	3,200	122	922
Nicaragua (Nicaragua)	3,100	102	230
Athabasca (Canada)	3,064	208	407
Reindeer (Canada)	2,568	143	—
Turkana (Kenya-Ethiopia)	2,473	154	240
Issyk Kul (U.S.S.R.)	2,355	115	2,303

COAST AND SHORELINE OF THE UNITED STATES

Source: National Ocean Service, National Oceanic and Atmospheric Administration

STATE	GENERAL COASTLINE [1]	TIDAL SHORELINE [2]
United States	**12,383**	**88,633**
Atlantic Coast	**2,069**	**28,673**
Connecticut	—	618
Delaware	28	381
Florida (Atlantic only)	580	3,331
Georgia	100	2,344
Maine	228	3,478
Maryland	31	3,190
Massachusetts	192	1,519
New Hampshire	13	131
New Jersey	130	1,792
New York	127	1,850
North Carolina	301	3,375
Pennsylvania	—	89
Rhode Island	40	384
South Carolina	187	2,876
Virginia	112	3,315
Gulf Coast	**1,631**	**17,141**
Alabama	53	607
Florida (Gulf only)	770	5,095
Louisiana	397	7,721
Mississippi	44	359
Texas	367	3,359
Pacific Coast	**7,623**	**40,298**
Alaska	5,580	31,383
California	840	3,427
Hawaii	750	1,052
Oregon	296	1,410
Washington	157	3,026
Arctic Coast, Alaska	**1,060**	**2,521**

[1] Statute mile length of general outline of seacoast. Measurements made with unit measure of 30 minutes of latitude on charts as near scale of 1:1,200,000 as possible. [2] Statute mile length of shoreline of outer coast, offshore islands, sounds, bays, rivers, and creeks to the head of tidewater or to point where tidal waters narrow to 100 feet wide.

TIDE RANGES IN THE UNITED STATES

Source: National Ocean Service, National Oceanic and Atmospheric Administration

Listed below are the average tidal ranges for 1984. "Average range" is the difference in height between average high and low tides. "Spring range" is the average range occurring semimonthly due to a new or full moon. "Diurnal range" is the difference in height between average higher high tide and average lower low tide.

EAST COAST LOCATION	AVERAGE RANGE	SPRING RANGE
Portland, Maine	9.1 ft.	10.4 ft.
Boston, Massachusetts	9.5 ft.	11.0 ft.
New London, Connecticut	2.6 ft.	3.1 ft.
The Battery, New York City	4.5 ft.	5.4 ft.
Atlantic City, New Jersey	4.1 ft.	5.0 ft.
Hampton Roads, Virginia	2.5 ft.	3.0 ft.
Charleston, South Carolina	5.2 ft.	6.1 ft.
Savannah, Georgia	7.4 ft.	8.6 ft.
Miami, Fla. (E. end of causeway)	2.5 ft.	2.4 ft.

WEST COAST LOCATION	AVERAGE RANGE	DIURNAL RANGE
Seattle, Washington	7.6 ft.	11.3 ft.
Coos Bay, Oregon	5.6 ft.	7.3 ft.
Crescent City, California	5.1 ft.	6.9 ft.
San Francisco, California	4.1 ft.	5.8 ft.
Santa Barbara, California	3.6 ft.	5.3 ft.
Los Angeles, California	3.8 ft.	5.4 ft.
San Diego, California	4.1 ft.	5.7 ft.
Honolulu, Hawaii	1.2 ft.	1.9 ft.
Cordova, Alaska	11.1 ft.	12.4 ft.

GREAT LAKES SYSTEM OF NORTH AMERICA

Source: National Ocean Service, National Oceanic and Atmospheric Administration

GENERAL LAKE DIMENSIONS	LAKE SUPERIOR	LAKE MICHIGAN	LAKE HURON	LAKE ST. CLAIR	LAKE ERIE	LAKE ONTARIO
Length in miles	350	307	206	26	241	193
Breadth in miles	160	118 [1]	183 [2]	24	57	53
Length of coastline in miles (including islands)	2,726	1,638	3,827 [3]	257	871	712
Areas in square miles:						
Total water surface	31,700 [4]	22,300 [5]	23,000 [6]	490 [7]	9,910	7,550 [8]
Water surface, United States	20,600 [4]	22,300 [5]	9,100 [6]	198 [7]	4,980	3,560 [8]
Water surface, Canada	11,100 [4]	—	13,900 [6]	292 [7]	4,930	3,990 [8]
Drainage basin (land) total	49,300 [4]	45,600 [5]	51,700 [6]	6,930 [7]	22,720	27,300 [8]
Drainage basin land, United States	16,900 [4]	45,600 [5]	16,200 [6]	2,852 [7]	18,000	15,200 [8]
Drainage basin land, Canada	32,400 [4]	—	35,500 [6]	4,080 [7]	4,720	12,100 [8]
Drainage basin (land and water) total	81,000 [4]	67,900 [5]	74,700 [7]	7,420 [7]	32,630 [8]	34,850 [8]
Maximum depth, feet	1,333	923	750	21 [9]	210	802
Average depth, feet	489	279	195	10	62	283
Volume of water in cubic miles	2,900	1,180	850	1	116	393
Length of outflow river (shown under lake from which it flows), approximate miles:						
St. Marys	70					
St. Clair			27			
Detroit				32		
Niagara					37	
St. Lawrence						502

[1] Measured at wide point through Green Bay. [2] Measured at wide point through Georgian Bay. [3] Includes Georgian Bay and North Channel. [4] Including St. Marys River above Brush Point. [5] Lake Michigan including Green Bay. [6] Including St. Marys River below Brush Point, North Channel, and Georgian Bay. [7] Lake St. Clair and St. Clair and Detroit Rivers. [8] Lake Ontario including Niagara River and St. Lawrence River above Iroquois Dam. [9] Maximum natural depth; dredged navigation channel has 27.5–foot depth.

Ecology and Environment

Protest march in Arlington, Va., in February against environmental policies of the Reagan administration was one of hundreds throughout the nation in 1983. Love Canal survivor Lois Gibbs, *center*, led marchers from Maryland and Virginia in demonstrating for faster action by the federal government to clean up toxic waste sites.

Wide World

HIGHLIGHTS: 1983

ENVIRONMENTAL SHAKE-UP

Although President Reagan repeatedly defended the environmental policies of his administration against attacks from Democrats and environmental groups, he made an effort to appease his critics with two major administrative changes.

After weeks of congressional investigation into charges that the Environmental Protection Agency (EPA) favored industry and made decisions to aid Republican candidates, President Reagan on March 21 replaced Anne McGill Burford as head of the EPA with William Ruckelshaus, who had been the first administrator of the agency under President Nixon.

Ruckelshaus quickly restored the integrity of EPA. He won plaudits from environmental group spokesmen.

Some 23 of the agency's leading officials resigned. Rita M. Lavelle, administrator of the EPA's toxic-waste program, was convicted

HIGHLIGHTS: 1983 *(continued)*

more than eight months later of lying to congressional investigators. See page 11.

James Watt, who had been under intensive fire from environmentalists throughout his tenure as secretary of the interior, resigned on Oct. 9 and was replaced a few days later by William P. Clark, who had been President Reagan's national-security adviser.

Watt's downfall came because of a flippant remark he had made on Sept. 21. While addressing a group of lobbyists, Watt described a special commission appointed to study coal-leasing as "every kind of mix you can have. I have a black, a woman, two Jews, and a cripple." Although Watt apologized to the President the next day, admitting his remarks were "morally offensive," Republican senators, who saw his continuation in office as a political liability, demanded his ouster.

Environmental groups denounced Clark's appointment because of his lack of experience in the field. A spokesman for the Sierra Club, Polly Freeman, declared, "William Clark has no environmental record—obviously that's of great concern to us, especially given the fact that Watt's lieutenants in interior are prepared to go on with his policies."

ACID RAIN SOLUTION SOUGHT

The National Clean Air coalition denounced EPA Administrator Ruckelshaus in November for failing to act to solve the problem of acid rain. Acid rain, caused by pollutants in the air, has been blamed for the death of freshwater wildlife in lakes and damage to crops, forests, and buildings.

Environmental groups have called on the EPA to establish stricter rules on coal-burning utilities and industrial plants that contaminate the air with sulfur dioxide, the main pollutant in acid rain. They have estimated that 28 million tons of sulfur dioxide go up in smoke each year.

It has been estimated that from $2.5 billion to $5 billion must be spent each year to reduce the amount of sulfur dioxide emitted into the air.

The Edison Electric Institute, a trade association of electrical utilities, estimated that electricity bills to consumers would be increased as much as one-third if utilities must foot the bill for cleaner air.

Environmentalists declared that the Edison Electric Institute figures were a "scare tactic," countering with statistics to show that the clean-up would cost less than $25 annually per capita.

THE GREAT CHICKEN MASSACRE

In an effort to save the nation's $9.5 billion poultry industry from disaster, the U.S. Department of Agriculture quarantined much of Pennsylvania and New Jersey to prevent the spread of avian influenza which had infected chicken flocks in those states. The disease does not affect humans.

To limit spread of the disease, some 500 federal and state workers killed some 4 million chickens in Pennsylvania and New Jersey during November. The dead chickens were buried in landfills.

Federal authorities estimated that only about 1% of the poultry farms in the region had become infected.

A federal disaster fund of $12.6 million was allocated to reimburse farmers for the chickens that were killed.

No live chickens were allowed to be shipped out of the quarantined area, even from farms whose flocks showed no infection.

WORLD'S POPULATION GROWTH: 1975–2000

Source: U.S. Census Bureau

Estimates of how large the world's population will be by the year 2000 depend on how widely and how quickly the world's people accept family planning methods to reduce population growth.

	World	Africa	Asia and Oceania	Latin America	Soviet Union and Eastern Europe	Northern America, Western Europe Japan, Australia, and New Zealand
Total population (millions):						
1975	4,090	399	2,274	324	384	708
2000	6,350	814	3,630	636	460	809
Net growth, 1975 to 2000:						
Persons (millions)	2,260	415	1,356	312	76	101
Percent	55%	104%	60%	96%	20%	14%
Birthrate (per 1,000 persons):						
1975	30.4	46.7	33.7	37.2	17.7	14.8
2000	25.6	38.5	25.9	28.7	15.9	14.5
Death rate (per 1,000 persons):						
1975	12.3	19.0	13.0	8.9	9.7	9.6
2000	9.1	11.3	8.7	5.7	10.5	10.5
Rate of natural increase:						
1975	1.8%	2.8%	2.1%	2.8%	0.8%	0.5%
2000	1.7%	2.7%	1.7%	2.3%	0.5%	0.4%

BUYING OUT TIMES BEACH

The EPA announced in February a $33 million plan to purchase the entire town of Times Beach, Mo., because it had become contaminated with the highly toxic chemical dioxin. Most of the 800 families who lived in Times Beach moved elsewhere, but a few families remained.

Guards were posted to prevent anyone but residents or those with special permission from entering the town.

However, eight months after the buy-out plan was announced by the government only 43 of the properties in Times Beach actually had been sold to the government. Arguments between property owners and government appraisers over the value of the remaining properties delayed their sale.

Meanwhile, a health study by federal and state authorities that was released in mid-October compared 68 persons who had been exposed to dioxin with a control group of 36 persons who had no exposure to the substance.

The study found no health differences between the two groups. However, former residents of Times Beach continued to worry over their exposure to dioxin.

U.S. Postal Service

A 20-cent stamp to be issued in 1984 commemorates the 50th anniversary of cooperative federal, state, and local efforts to abate soil erosion and preserve water resources. In 1934 the newly formed Soil Erosion Service began working directly with farmers in demonstration projects. In the following year the soil Conservation Service was created in the Department of Agriculture.

WORDS IN ECOLOGY AND ENVIRONMENT

abiotic environment—nonliving parts of environment, including air, soil, water, climate, weather, and nonliving nutrients
acclimatization—way plant or animal adjusts to changes of climate
adaptation—way plant or animal adjusts to live in certain environment
aerosol—fine particles of liquids, dust, smoke, or solids that remain suspended in air for long periods of time
air pollution—poisoning of air by ash, bacteria, dust gases, pollen, smoke, and other substances, both man-made and natural
balance of nature—stability of population of each of many kinds of animals and plants living in certain environment
biodegradable—easily decomposed by normal biological processes without environmental damage
biome—large community of animals and plants living together in specific climate and region, as in tropical rain forest
biosphere—life-sustaining part of world, including soil, rock, bodies of water, and lower atmosphere
biotic environment—living plants, animals, and microorganisms and their interaction in certain area
community—animals and plants that live together and depend upon each other
conservation—protection and management of environment to preserve resources and basic ingredients needed for life
defoliant—chemical agent that causes leaves to fall from trees and plants
ecology—study of relationship of plants, animals, and people to each other and to their environments
ecosystem—system of relationships within given community that supports life of each kind of plant and animal in area
effluent—liquid or gaseous waste discharged into environment
emission standard—legal limit for discharge of waste material
endangered species—animal in danger of extinction
environment—living and nonliving things in certain area and forces and conditions that affect them
Environmental Protection Agency (EPA)—federal agency responsible for protecting environment by controlling pollution
erosion—gradual wearing away of natural resource, such as soil by wind and floods
eutrophication—unwholesome condition of fresh-water, marked by decrease in oxygen, caused by sewage or chemical-fertilizer runoff
fallout—dropping to earth of dust or particles carried in air, such as radioactive fallout resulting from explosion of atomic bomb
flood control—building of dams, dikes, and reservoirs in effort to prevent destruction by floods and water erosion
fluorocarbon—aerosol gas propellant, considered harmful to atmosphere
food chain—series or chain of plants and animals that depend upon each other for food supply to live; for example, man eats fish, which eat shrimp, which eat algae
greenhouse effect—warming of atmosphere by buildup of carbon dioxide, water vapor, and ozone, preventing normal dissipation of heat from earth surface
habitat—area in which plant or animal lives
herbicide—chemical agent for controlling or destroying weeds and unwanted plant growth
inversion—condition in atmosphere that occurs when warm layer of air is trapped between two cooler layers of air, sometimes causing smog to linger over area
meltdown—disintegration of reactor core in nuclear power plant resulting from cooling-system failure, with possible release of toxic radioactivity
natural selection—process that results in specific kinds of animals and plants surviving in particular environment
noise pollution—unwanted, disagreeable sounds
ozone layer—region of ozone gas in stratosphere serving as shield against solar radiation
particulates—tiny particles of dust or soot in air
pesticide—chemical agent for controlling or destroying unwanted animals, insects, or plants
pH—symbol with scale of numbers from 0 to 14 to indicate whether water or soil is acid or alkaline; pH 7 is neutral, while pH numbers below 7 are acid and pH numbers above 7 are alkaline
pollutant—any substance that adversely affects natural environment
pollution—discharge of waste materials that cause adverse and unpleasant effects to environment
population density—relationship of total number of plants, animals, or people to area of region where they live, such as number of people per square mile
primary consumer—animal that eats plants and then is eaten by another kind of animal
primary producer—plant that produces engery from Sun and then provides energy to animal that eats it
recycling—process to convert waste materials into useful materials, such as recycling of waste paper, glass, and aluminum
runoff—water from rain, snow, or industrial waste that flows over ground surface and discharges into streams
secondary consumer—animal that depends upon eating primary consumer for its energy; for example, fish that lives on shrimp for food is secondary consumer because shrimp is primary consumer, deriving its energy from eating algae
soil pollution—damage to soil, such as destruction of microscopic organisms in the soil by pesticides
waste disposal—process of getting rid of waste materials such as garbage or sewage
water pollution—discharge of waste materials into body of water
web of life—dependence of living things upon each other for survival

The Economy

Home Banking Service unveiled by Bank of America in San Francisco on Nov. 30 enables personal computer user never to have to stand in line while paying bills, transferring funds from one account to another, inquiring about account balances, and reviewing current statements.

Wide World

HIGHLIGHTS: 1983

NATION'S ECONOMY REVISES

Triggered by consumer spending, the nation's economy reversed course in 1983. The Commerce Department reported in November that for the 14th month in a row the Index of Leading Economic Indicators continued to show an increase.

Fatter paychecks and optimism about the future brought consumers flocking to stores where the jingle of cash registers recorded increasing profits for businessmen.

Commerce Secretary Malcolm Baldridge said, "We can expect the current economic expansion to continue," as he pointed out that the 14-month upswing in the economic indicators was the second longest since World War II. It was exceeded only by a 17-month rise after the recession of 1973–75.

The Commerce Department also reported in November that corporate profits rose more

HIGHLIGHTS: 1983 *(continued)*

sharply than in any previous recovery since World War II. Profits, which had fallen 18.1% during the recession, rose 52.1% in the first three quarters compared with the same period in the previous year. Altogether corporate profits in the third quarter rose at a seasonally adjusted annual rate of $246.2 billion compared with $218.2 billion in the second quarter.

During the third quarter the gross national product (GNP) rose to an annual rate of $3.36 trillion, an increase of 11.2% over the previous year. Adjusted for inflation, the rate showed an increase of 7.7%.

Personal income rose steadily throughout the year, reaching an annual rate of $2.82 trillion in October. This translated into an average $10,259 of personal income for each man, woman, and child in the U.S.

While consumers were spending more, they also were saving more. Personal savings rose to $131.8 billion in October compared with $116.3 billion the previous month. The

U.S. EMPLOYMENT AND UNEMPLOYMENT: 1900–1983

Source: U.S. Bureau of Labor Statistics

Year	Potential Labor Force[1]	Not in Labor Force[2]	Armed Services	Total Civil Labor Force	Employed in Agriculture	Employed in Nonfarm jobs	Unemployed	Percent Unemployed
1900	57,950,000	28,877,000	124,000	28,376,000	11,050,000	15,906,000	1,420,000	5.0%
1910	71,580,000	33,413,000	141,000	36,709,000	11,260,000	23,299,000	2,150,000	5.9%
1920	82,739,000	41,125,000	380,000	41,340,000	10,440,000	28,768,000	2,132,000	5.2%
1930	98,723,000	49,893,000	260,000	48,523,000	10,340,000	33,843,000	4,340,000	8.9%
1933	99,150,000	48,019,000	250,000	50,882,000	10,090,000	27,962,000	12,830,000	25.2%
1940	100,147,000	47,136,000	540,000	55,640,000	9,540,000	37,980,000	8,120,000	14.6%
1950	106,164,000	42,787,000	1,169,000	58,918,000	7,160,000	51,758,000	3,288,000	5.2%
1955	111,747,000	44,660,000	2,064,000	62,170,000	6,450,000	55,722,000	2,852,000	4.3%
1960	119,106,000	46,617,000	1,861,000	65,778,000	5,458,000	60,318,000	3,852,000	5.4%
1965	128,459,000	52,058,000	1,946,000	71,088,000	4,361,000	66,726,000	3,366,000	4.4%
1969	136,573,000	53,602,000	2,238,000	77,902,000	3,606,000	74,296,000	2,832,000	3.4%
1970	139,203,000	54,315,000	2,118,000	78,678,000	3,463,000	75,215,000	4,093,000	4.8%
1971	142,189,000	55,834,000	1,973,000	79,367,000	3,394,000	75,972,000	5,016,000	5.8%
1972	145,939,000	57,091,000	1,813,000	82,153,000	3,484,000	78,669,000	4,882,000	5.5%
1973	148,870,000	57,667,000	1,774,000	85,064,000	3,470,000	81,594,000	4,355,000	4.8%
1974	151,841,000	58,171,000	1,721,000	86,794,000	3,515,000	83,279,000	5,166,000	5.5%
1975	154,831,000	59,377,000	1,678,000	85,845,000	3,408,000	82,438,000	7,929,000	8.3%
1976	157,818,000	59,991,000	1,668,000	88,752,000	3,331,000	85,421,000	7,406,000	7.6%
1977	160,689,000	60,025,000	1,656,000	92,017,000	3,283,000	88,734,000	6,991,000	6.9%
1978	153,541,000	59,659,000	1,631,000	96,048,000	3,387,000	92,661,000	6,202,000	6.0%
1979	166,460,000	59,900,000	1,597,000	98,824,000	3,347,000	95,477,000	6,137,000	5.8%
1980	169,349,000	60,806,000	1,604,000	99,303,000	3,364,000	95,938,000	7,637,000	7.0%
1981	171,775,000	61,460,000	1,645,000	100,397,000	3,368,000	97,030,000	8,723,000	7.5%
1982	173,939,000	62,067,000	1,668,000	99,526,000	3,401,000	96,125,000	10,578,000	9.5%
1983[3]	176,474,000	62,737,000	1,695,000	112,042,000	3,407,000	99,252,000	9,383,000	8.2%

1 Americans 16 years and older not in institutions, such as prisons and mental hospitals. 2 Includes dependent wives and husbands, and full-time students. 3 October 1983 data.

EMPLOYEES[1] IN U.S. INDUSTRIES: 1900–1983

Source: U.S. Bureau of Labor Statistics

Year	Total	Mining	Construction	Manufacturing	Transportation & Public Utilities	Wholesale & Retail Trade	Finance, Insurance, and Real Estate	Services	Government: Federal	Government: State & Local
1900	15,178	637	1,147	5,468	2,282	2,502	308	1,740	1,094	
1910	21,697	1,068	1,342	7,828	3,366	3,570	483	2,410	1,630	
1920	27,434	1,180	850	10,702	4,317	4,012	902	3,100	2,371	
1930	29,424	1,009	1,372	9,562	3,685	5,797	1,475	3,376	526	2,622
1934	25,953	883	862	8,501	2,750	5,281	1,319	3,058	652	2,647
1940	32,376	925	1,294	10,985	3,038	6,750	1,502	3,681	996	3,206
1950	45,197	901	2,364	15,241	4,034	9,386	1,888	5,357	1,928	4,098
1960	54,189	712	2,926	16,796	4,004	11,391	2,629	7,378	2,270	6,083
1970	70,880	623	3,588	19,367	4,515	15,040	3,645	11,548	2,731	9,823
1975	76,945	752	3,525	18,323	4,542	17,060	4,165	13,892	2,748	11,937
1976	79,382	779	3,576	18,997	4,582	17,755	4,271	14,551	2,733	12,138
1977	82,471	813	3,851	19,682	4,713	18,516	4,467	15,303	2,727	12,399
1978	86,697	851	4,229	20,505	4,923	19,542	4,724	16,252	2,753	12,919
1979	89,823	958	4,463	21,040	5,136	20,192	4,975	17,112	2,773	13,147
1980	90,406	1,027	4,346	20,285	5,146	20,310	5,160	17,890	2,866	13,375
1981	91,156	1,139	4,188	20,170	5,165	20,547	5,298	18,619	2,772	13,259
1982	89,596	1,143	3,911	18,853	5,081	20,401	5,340	19,064	2,739	13,064
1983[2]	91,716	1,033	4,326	19,195	5,079	20,752	5,484	20,084	2,713	13,050

1 All figures in thousands (add 000). Excludes farm workers, proprietors, self-employed, domestics. 2 October 1983 data.

national savings rate rose to 5.5% of disposable income in October compared with 4.9% in September.

UNEMPLOYMENT

The rate of unemployment in the United States fell to 8.2% in October, the lowest level in 22 months according to Department of Labor statistics. The unemployment rate had fallen 2.6 percentage points from the high of 10.8% that had been reached in December 1982.

Not counting members of the armed forces, the civilian unemployment level fell to 8.4%.

Altogether 104,356,000 Americans were employed in October, with 102,671,000 civilian workers and 1,685,000 in the armed forces. This represented an increase of 740,000 workers during the month. Some 2.8 million more persons were working at jobs in October than 10 months earlier.

The Labor Department said there were about 9.4 million unemployed workers in October. The rate of unemployment for black teenagers remained exceptionally high, at 46.2%.

INFLATION

Although consumers saw sharp increases of food prices at supermarkets, the overall inflation in prices for the 12 months ending in October had fallen to a rate of 2.9%. Because prices were increasing at a faster rate during the third quarter of 1983, the annual rate of inflation for the calendar year was expected to be about 4%.

U.S. GROSS NATIONAL PRODUCT

Source: U.S. Bureau of Economic Analysis

The gross national product (GNP) is the total national output of goods and services valued at market prices. It includes all consumer purchases of goods and services, private investment expenditures, the net value of exports less imports, and government purchases of goods and services. The United States has the highest GNP of any country in the world. The following amounts are in $ billions (add 000,000,000).

YEAR	GNP	GROWTH RATE	YEAR	GNP	GROWTH RATE
1910	$ 35.3	2.8%	1965	$ 688.1	8.2%
1915	$ 40.0	0.8%	1970	$ 982.4	5.0%
1920	$ 91.5	4.3%	1974	$1,412.9	8.1%
1925	$ 93.1	8.4%	1975	$1,528.8	8.2%
1930	$ 90.4	9.8%	1976	$1,708.2	11.7%
1932	$ 58.0	14.7%	1977	$1,918.0	12.3%
1933	$ 55.6	1.8%	1978	$2,156.1	12.4%
1935	$ 72.2	9.9%	1979	$2,413.9	11.9%
1940	$ 99.7	16.1%	1980	$2,633.1	8.9%
1945	$211.9	1.7%	1981	$2,954.1	12.2%
1950	$286.2	10.9%	1982	$3,073.0	4.0%
1955	$399.3	9.0%	1983*	$3,360.3	11.2%
1960	$506.0	4.0%			

* Data annualized for first 9 months of 1983.

CONSUMER AND PRODUCER PRICE INDEXES: 1955–1983

Source: U.S. Department of Labor, Bureau of Labor Statistics

YEAR	CONSUMER PRICES (1967 = 100) All items		Commodities		Services		PRODUCER PRICES (1967 = 100) All commodities		Farm products, food, and feeds		Industrial commodities	
	Index	Percent change	Index	Percent change	Index	Percent change	Index	Percent change	Index	Percent change	Index	Percent change
1955	80.2	–0.4%	85.1	–0.9%	70.9	2.0%	87.8	0.2%	91.2	–4.7%	86.9	2.2%
1959	87.3	0.8%	90.7	0.1%	80.8	2.9%	94.8	0.2%	93.5	–4.7%	95.3	1.8%
1960	88.7	1.6%	91.5	0.9%	83.5	3.3%	94.9	0.1%	93.7	0.2%	95.3	0%
1961	89.6	1.0%	92.0	0.5%	85.2	2.0%	94.5	–0.4%	93.7	0.0%	94.8	–0.5%
1962	90.6	1.1%	92.8	0.9%	86.8	1.9%	94.8	0.3%	94.7	1.1%	94.8	0%
1963	91.7	1.2%	93.6	0.9%	88.5	2.0%	94.5	–0.3%	93.8	–1.0%	94.7	–0.1%
1964	92.9	1.3%	94.6	1.1%	90.2	1.9%	94.7	0.2%	93.2	–0.6%	95.2	0.5%
1965	94.5	1.7%	95.7	1.2%	92.2	2.2%	96.6	2.0%	97.1	4.2%	96.4	1.3%
1966	97.2	2.9%	98.2	2.6%	95.8	3.9%	99.8	3.3%	103.5	6.6%	98.5	2.2%
1967	100.0	2.9%	100.0	1.8%	100.0	4.4%	100.0	0.2%	100.0	–3.4%	100.0	1.5%
1968	104.2	4.2%	103.7	3.7%	105.2	5.2%	102.5	2.5%	102.4	2.4%	102.5	2.5%
1969	109.8	5.4%	108.4	4.5%	112.5	6.9%	106.5	3.9%	108.0	5.5%	106.0	3.4%
1970	116.3	5.9%	113.5	4.7%	121.6	8.1%	110.4	3.7%	111.7	3.4%	110.0	3.8%
1971	121.3	4.3%	117.4	3.4%	128.4	5.6%	114.0	3.3%	113.9	2.0%	114.1	3.7%
1972	125.3	3.3%	120.9	3.0%	133.3	3.8%	119.1	4.5%	122.4	7.5%	117.9	3.3%
1973	133.1	6.2%	129.9	7.4%	139.1	4.4%	134.7	13.1%	159.1	30.0%	125.9	6.8%
1974	147.7	11.0%	145.5	12.0%	152.1	9.3%	160.1	18.9%	177.4	11.5%	153.8	22.2%
1975	161.2	9.1%	158.4	8.9%	166.6	9.5%	174.9	9.2%	184.2	3.8%	171.5	11.5%
1976	170.5	5.8%	165.2	4.3%	180.4	8.3%	182.9	4.6%	183.1	–0.6%	182.3	6.3%
1977	181.5	6.5%	174.7	5.8%	194.3	7.7%	194.2	6.1%	188.8	3.1%	195.1	7.0%
1978	195.3	7.6%	187.1	7.1%	210.9	8.5%	209.3	7.8%	206.6	9.4%	209.4	7.3%
1979	217.7	11.5%	219.4	17.3%	249.3	18.2%	249.7	19.3%	234.6	13.6%	253.1	20.9%
1980	246.8	13.4%	233.9	6.6%	270.3	8.4%	268.8	7.6%	244.7	4.3%	274.8	8.6%
1981	272.3	10.2%	253.6	8.4%	305.7	13.1%	293.4	9.2%	251.5	2.8%	304.1	10.6%
1982	288.6	6.0%	263.8	4.0%	333.3	9.0%	299.3	2.0%	248.9	–1.0%	312.3	2.7%
1983*	301.8	2.9%	274.5	3.0%	349.0	2.7%	305.3	2.0%	259.2	4.1%	317.2	1.6%

* Data for October 1983.

WORLD TRADE BY NATIONS: 1970–1982

Source: United Nations

The value of exports and imports fell more than $262 billion in 1982 as the world suffered an economic recession. U.S. exports decreased to $212.3 billion and imports to $254.9 billion.

In 1982 the U.S. continued as the leading exporting nation in foreign trade, followed by West Germany, Japan, Britain, France, Soviet Union, Saudi Arabia, Italy, Canada, and Netherlands.

	IMPORTS[1]				EXPORTS[1]			
	1970	1975	1981	1982	1970	1975	1981	1982
WORLD	**$328,597**	**$903,980**	**$2,035,229**	**$1,919,683**	**$314,309**	**$874,948**	**$1,978,973**	**$1,832,022**
Afghanistan	112	349	—	—	86	223	—	—
Algeria	1,257	5,999	10,891	—	1,009	4,699	14,486	9,164
Argentina	1,694	3,947	9,485	5,324	1,773	2,961	9,151	7,511
Australia	4,543	9,995	23,768	24,187	4,770	11,945	21,767	22,002
Austria	3,549	9,390	21,048	19,557	2,856	7,518	15,845	15,685
Bahamas	337	2,697	—	—	90	2,216	—	—
Bahrain	247	1,158	4,124	3,730	274	1,147	4,347	3,789
Bangladesh	—	874	2,699	2,300	—	303	791	769
Barbados	118	217	560	550	40	107	220	257
Belgium-Luxembourg	11,413	30,789	62,464	58,007	11,600	28,804	55,705	52,392
Bolivia	159	558	909	496	190	445	893	832
Brazil	2,849	13,703	24,007	22,637	2,739	8,670	22,743	20,190
Britain	21,689	53,489	102,722	99,656	19,346	44,114	102,820	96,994
Bulgaria	1,831	5,408	—	—	2,004	4,691	—	—
Burma	169	250	373	408	108	172	455	380
Burundi	22	62	167	214	24	32	71	88
Cameroon	242	599	1,428	1,205	232	448	1,122	998
Canada	13,360	34,105	66,193	55,064	16,119	32,682	69,978	68,498
Central Africa	34	69	—	—	31	48	—	—
Chad	61	133	—	—	30	48	—	—
Chile	930	1,338	6,364	3,529	1,234	1,552	3,906	3,822
China	—	7,490	21,566	19,529	—	7,260	21,560	21,474
Colombia	843	1,495	5,199	4,937	727	1,465	2,956	3,235
Congo	57	170	—	—	31	179	—	—
Costa Rica	317	694	1,008	887	231	493	1,209	872
Cuba	1,311	3,883	—	—	1,049	3,684	—	—
Cyprus	235	308	1,165	1,221	108	152	556	564
Czechoslovakia	3,695	9,077	14,658	15,499	3,792	8,356	14,876	15,734
Denmark	4,407	10,370	17,803	17,162	3,356	8,713	16,250	15,527
Dominican Rep.	278	773	1,450	1,248	214	894	1,188	768
Ecuador	274	943	—	56	190	897	—	—
Egypt	787	3,934	8,839	7,755	762	1,402	3,233	3,120
El Salvador	214	598	986	883	228	513	792	696
Ethiopia	172	296	738	—	122	240	374	—
Fiji	104	269	632	515	68	170	311	285
Finland	2,636	7,626	14,202	13,382	2,306	5,503	14,015	13,127
France	19,114	53,992	120,924	115,405	17,935	52,227	100,497	92,268
Gabon	80	471	—	—	121	942	—	—
Gambia	18	60	122	97	17	48	27	44
Germany, East	4,847	11,290	20,181	21,743	4,581	10,088	19,858	20,196
Germany, West	29,814	74,936	163,934	155,856	34,189	90,176	176,043	176,428
Ghana	411	791	1,106	—	458	807	1,063	—
Greece	1,958	5,321	8,677	10,023	642	2,286	4,292	4,297
Guatemala	284	733	1,673	1,362	299	624	1,226	1,173
Guyana	134	344	436	283	133	365	367	256
Haiti	52	143	—	—	41	81	—	—
Honduras	221	404	949	—	179	303	760	—
Hungary	2,506	7,176	9,128	8,825	2,317	6,091	8,712	8,795
Iceland	157	488	980	942	147	307	859	685
India	2,124	6,385	15,654	14,088	2,026	4,355	8,373	8,111
Indonesia	1,002	4,770	13,271	16,858	1,108	7,103	22,260	22,293
Iran	1,662	10,343	—	—	2,623	20,212	10,548	17,610
Iraq	509	4,215	—	—	1,100	8,297	10,530	10,230
Ireland	1,573	3,779	10,603	9,701	1,039	3,192	7,706	8,064
Israel	1,422	4,109	7,801	7,848	734	1,835	5,343	4,901
Italy	14,970	38,536	91,022	86,211	13,206	34,995	75,187	73,481

[1] All figures in millions of U.S. dollars (add 000,000).

	IMPORTS[1] 1970	1975	1981	1982	EXPORTS[1] 1970	1975	1981	1982
Ivory Coast	$388	$1,127	—	$2,384	$469	$1,182	$2,537	—
Jamaica	525	1,124	1,473	1,470	347	759	974	820
Japan	18,881	57,880	143,287	131,932	19,318	55,840	152,016	138,911
Jordan	184	728	3,149	3,241	34	153	732	737
Kenya	442	980	2,069	—	305	644	1,188	—
Korea, South	1,984	7,274	26,131	24,251	835	5,081	21,254	21,853
Kuwait	625	2,388	6,948	—	1,901	9,184	16,339	13,294
Lebanon	567	—	—	—	198	—	—	—
Liberia	150	332	477	—	213	394	531	—
Libya	554	3,542	8,382	—	2,366	6,840	15,576	13,951
Madagascar	170	367	—	—	145	294	—	—
Malawi	86	251	360	314	60	139	242	259
Malaysia	1,490	3,908	13,132	—	1,763	4,188	12,884	—
Mali	47	177	365	—	33	54	155	—
Malta	161	377	855	790	39	167	448	421
Mauritania	56	177	265	273	89	174	259	179
Mauritius	76	332	554	463	69	298	354	362
Mexico	2,320	6,570	24,161	15,042	1,282	2,992	20,041	2,101
Morocco	684	2,568	4,356	4,315	488	1,617	2,320	2,062
Mozambique	324	417	—	—	156	202	—	—
Netherlands	13,426	34,836	65,921	62,583	11,774	35,099	68,732	66,322
New Zealand	1,245	3,140	5,684	5,752	1,225	2,151	5,563	5,524
Nicaragua	198	517	—	—	179	375	—	—
Niger	58	101	—	—	32	91	—	—
Nigeria	1,059	6,041	—	—	1,239	7,994	20,210	16,677
Norway	3,702	9,706	15,652	15,487	2,457	7,234	18,220	17,587
Oman	18	765	2,288	—	495	1,416	4,422	4,123
Pakistan	1,171	2,158	5,342	5,298	723	1,035	2,880	2,381
Panama	357	901	1,540	—	106	280	315	309
Papua New Guinea	268	476	1,104	—	103	440	859	753
Paraguay	64	178	506	586	64	177	296	378
Peru	619	2,390	3,803	—	1,048	1,291	3,255	—
Philippines	1,286	3,776	7,946	—	1,142	2,294	5,722	4,852
Poland	3,608	12,536	15,224	10,248	3,548	10,282	13,182	11,208
Portugal	1,582	3,844	9,799	9,521	949	1,938	4,147	4,167
Qatar	—	410	1,949	—	236	1,809	5,691	4,329
Romania	1,960	5,342	12,458	—	1,851	5,341	12,610	—
Rwanda	29	96	—	—	25	42	—	—
Saudi Arabia	692	4,214	35,244	40,654	2,424	29,676	120,240	79,123
Senegal	193	583	861	—	152	460	442	—
Sierra Leone	116	185	311	—	101	121	153	—
Singapore	2,461	8,134	27,608	28,047	1,554	5,376	20,967	20,788
Solomons	11	29	76	—	8	16	66	—
Somalia	45	155	199	—	31	89	200	317
South Africa	3,566	7,557	21,006	—	2,151	4,636	—	—
Soviet Union	11,732	36,971	78,210	77,793	12,800	33,316	87,399	86,949
Spain	4,716	16,234	32,159	31,535	2,388	7,669	20,337	20,522
Sri Lanka	389	751	1,803	1,771	342	559	1,021	1,015
Sudan	284	1,033	1,529	1,285	298	438	658	499
Suriname	115	252	568	—	135	277	474	—
Sweden	7,004	17,861	28,845	27,573	6,792	17,382	28,683	26,822
Switzerland	6,486	13,303	30,696	28,670	5,152	12,957	27,042	26,024
Syria	357	1,685	5,040	4,028	203	930	2,103	2,026
Tanzania	318	773	1,140	—	259	372	566	—
Thailand	1,299	3,280	10,014	8,544	710	2,377	6,918	6,953
Togo	65	174	435	—	55	126	208	—
Trinidad-Tobago	542	1,471	3,115	3,697	480	1,754	3,725	3,072
Tunisia	306	1,424	3,779	3,287	182	856	2,497	1,959
Turkey	894	4,739	8,928	8,753	588	1,401	4,703	5,701
Uganda	172	200	—	—	282	267	—	—
United Arab Emir.	267	2,669	9,648	—	550	6,970	20,240	16,420
UNITED STATES	39,756	103,843	273,352	254,884	42,590	108,050	233,739	212,275
Upper Volta	49	151	338	—	18	44	75	—
Uruguay	231	556	1,599	1,041	233	384	1,215	1,027
Vanuatu	13	34	58	—	12	10	33	—
Venezuela	1,641	5,329	11,807	—	3,197	8,799	20,125	18,694
Western Samoa	14	37	—	—	5	7	—	—
Yemen, North	32	294	—	—	3	11	—	—
Yemen, South	200	323	—	—	135	172	—	—
Yugoslavia	2,874	7,697	15,817	—	1,679	4,072	10,929	—
Zaire	533	905	672	—	781	865	662	—
Zambia	477	929	1,047	—	1,001	810	1,056	1,059
Zimbabwe	329	802	1,472	1,430	367	923	1,406	1,250

WORLD PRODUCTION: 1970–1982

Source: United Nations

	1970	1975	1979	1980	1981	1982
POPULATION						
World total	3,610,000,000	4,033,000,000	4,357,000,000	4,432,000,000	4,508,000,000	4,586,000,000
AGRICULTURE						
Barley [1]	139,426,000	153,000,000	158,000,000	159,000,000	155,000,000	160,000,000
Cocoa beans [1] (chocolate)	1,507,000	1,544,000	1,657,000	1,621,000	1,640,000	1,587,000
Corn (maize) [1]	261,548,000	326,000,000	419,000,000	396,000,000	451,000,000	455,000,000
Cotton [1]	11,738,000	12,294,000	13,900,000	13,900,000	15,300,000	14,700,000
Eggs (hen) [1]	21,132,000	23,600,000	27,500,000	28,300,000	29,200,000	29,800,000
Livestock						
Cattle [2]	1,086,955,000	1,194,749,000	1,194,240,000	1,201,810,000	1,209,833,000	—
Hogs [2]	545,565,000	682,899,000	762,410,000	797,957,000	779,324,000	—
Horses [2]	64,227,000	66,102,000	64,569,000	65,784,000	66,192,000	—
Sheep [2]	1,075,322,000	1,063,316,000	1,087,962,000	1,117,964,000	1,130,751,000	—
Milk [1]	396,054,000	430,000,000	466,000,000	471,000,000	473,000,000	483,000,000
Peanuts [1]	18,300,000	19,300,000	18,800,000	18,600,000	19,300,000	19,200,000
Potatoes [1]	312,134,000	285,000,000	288,000,000	230,000,000	258,000,000	255,000,000
Rice [1]	308,578,000	360,000,000	377,000,000	399,000,000	412,000,000	411,000,000
Tobacco [1]	4,678,000	5,416,000	5,420,000	5,284,000	5,965,000	6,058,000
Wheat [1]	318,319,000	356,000,000	429,000,000	446,000,000	454,000,000	481,000,000
Wool [1]	2,768,000	2,638,000	2,734,000	2,810,000	2,845,000	2,856,000
FISHING						
Total catch [1]	70,000,000	68,600,000	71,300,000	72,400,000	74,800,000	—
ENERGY						
Coal [1,3]	1,774,000,000	1,889,000,000	2,686,000,000	2,732,000,000	2,742,000,000	2,861,000,000
Electricity [4]	4,846,000,000	6,331,000,000	7,999,000,000	8,244,000,000	8,357,000,000	8,226,000,000
Natural gas [5]	2,241,198	11,106,503	12,996,200	13,126,400	13,326,700	13,531,100
Petroleum [1]	2,253,000,000	2,575,000,000	3,127,000,000	2,975,000,000	2,789,000,000	2,625,000,000
FOOD AND BEVERAGES						
Coffee [1]	3,869,000	4,652,000	5,053,000	4,799,000	6,032,000	4,934,000
Flour (wheat) [1]	121,450,000	125,700,000	133,600,000	137,200,000	138,700,000	—
Meat [1]	84,567,000	122,800,000	138,000,000	141,000,000	143,000,000	145,000,000
Sugar [1]	72,896,000	81,600,000	88,900,000	83,900,000	92,300,000	100,400,000
Tea [1]	1,078,000	1,547,000	1,819,000	1,866,000	1,864,000	1,925,000
FOREST PRODUCTS						
Natural Rubber [1]	3,100,000	3,315,000	3,860,000	3,845,000	3,685,000	3,750,000
Paper (newsprint) [1]	21,535,000	20,948,000	25,300,000	26,400,000	26,600,000	21,030,000
Sawnwood [7]	404,425	404,000	451,000	439,000	419,000	—
Wood pulp [1]	104,445,000	81,100,000	92,900,000	95,200,000	94,300,000	—
MINERALS AND METALS						
Aluminum [1]	9,445,000	11,856,000	17,907,000	18,699,000	18,741,000	18,687,000
Copper [1]	6,221,000	7,250,000	8,598,000	8,389,000	8,712,000	8,690,000
Iron (pig iron) [1]	439,300,000	456,000,000	540,000,000	527,000,000	516,000,000	512,000,000
Iron ore [1]	424,100,000	483,000,000	736,000,000	743,000,000	708,000,000	695,000,000
Lead [1]	3,146,000	3,150,000	5,049,000	4,729,000	4,764,000	4,781,000
Steel (crude) [1]	576,000,000	615,000,000	739,000,000	703,000,000	692,000,000	761,000,000
Tin [1]	183,600	176,000	213,000	209,000	207,000	202,000
Zinc [1]	4,664,000	4,700,000	6,056,000	5,820,000	5,858,000	5,903,000
MANUFACTURED PRODUCTS						
Automobiles [2]	22,550,000	25,220,000	31,360,000	28,880,000	27,720,000	6,740,000
Buses and trucks [2]	6,780,000	7,960,000	10,260,000	9,580,000	9,380,000	2,310,000
Cement [1]	569,000,000	703,000,000	856,000,000	868,000,000	736,000,000	746,000,000
Fertilizer (nitrogenous) [1]	30,200,000	42,500,000	119,000,000	124,500,000	119,600,000	—
Ships (merchant) [10]	21,690,000	34,200,000	11,460,000	13,570,000	17,030,000	17,170,000

1 Metric tons 2 Units 3 Including some brown coal and lignite. 4 Megawatts, 5 Teracalories. 6 Hectoliters. 7 Cubic meters. 8 Metric carats. 9 Kilograms. 10 Gross tons launched.

Education

While other schools struggle to meet their budgets, the well-to-do Beverly Hills, Calif., school district receives about $100,000 a month as revenue from this oil well that pumps about 3,000 barrels a day. Standing next to the high school soccer field, the well is camouflaged as an observation tower to avoid an offensive appearance to the movie stars and other wealthy residents of the district.

United Press Int'l.

HIGHLIGHTS: 1983

A national debate on the quality of American education and what can be done to improve it was touched off in April by a report of the 18-member bipartisan National Commission on Excellence in Education that had been appointed by Secretary of Education T.H. Bell in 1981.

"Our nation is at risk," the report stated. "Our once unchallenged preeminence in commerce, industry, science, and technological innovation is being overtaken by competitors throughout the world. . . .

"We report to the American people that while we can take great pride in what our

RISING COLLEGE AND UNIVERSITY EXPENDITURES: 1961–1984

Source: U.S. Department of Education

1961–1962	$ 8,500,000,000
1965–1966	$ 15,200,000,000
1970–1971	$ 27,100,000,000
1972–1973	$ 31,400,000,000
1973–1974	$ 34,300,000,000
1974–1975	$ 38,900,000,000
1975–1976	$ 42,700,000,000
1976–1977	$ 46,300,000,000
1977–1978	$ 49,500,000,000
1978–1979	$ 54,200,000,000
1979–1980	$ 62,500,000,000
1980–1981	$ 70,500,000,000
1981–1982*	$ 76,600,000,000
1982–1983*	$ 82,500,000,000
1983–1994*	$ 89,000,000,000

* Estimates.

U.S. ELEMENTARY AND SECONDARY SCHOOL ENROLLMENT: 1955–1990

Source: National Center for Educational Statistics, U.S. Department of Education

YEAR [1]	TOTAL PUBLIC AND NONPUBLIC			PUBLIC			PRIVATE [2]		
	K-12	K-8	9-12	K-12	K-8	9-12	K-12	K-8	9-12
1955	35,280,000	27,717,000	7,563,000	30,680,000	23,917,000	6,763,000	4,600,000	3,800,000	800,000
1960	42,181,000	32,492,000	9,689,000	36,281,000	27,692,000	8,589,000	5,900,000	4,800,000	1,100,000
1965	48,473,000	35,463,000	13,010,000	42,173,000	30,563,000	11,610,000	6,300,000	4,900,000	1,400,000
1970	51,272,000	36,629,000	14,643,000	45,909,000	32,577,000	13,332,000	5,363,000	4,052,000	1,311,000
1971	51,215,000	36,120,000	15,095,000	46,081,000	32,265,000	13,816,000	5,134,000	3,855,000	1,279,000
1972	50,737,000	35,569,000	15,168,000	45,744,000	31,831,000	,913,000	4,993,000	3,738,000	1,255,000
1973	50,380,000	35,031,000	15,349,000	45,429,000	31,353,000	14,077,000	4,950,000	3,678,000	1,272,000
1974	50,028,000	34,596,000	15,432,000	45,053,000	30,921,000	14,132,000	4,975,000	3,675,000	1,300,000
1975	49,834,000	34,211,000	15,623,000	44,791,000	30,487,000	14,304,000	5,043,000	3,724,000	1,319,000
1976	49,484,000	33,831,000	15,653,000	44,317,000	30,006,000	14,311,000	5,167,000	3,825,000	1,342,000
1977	48,716,000	33,133,000	15,583,000	43,577,000	29,336,000	14,240,000	5,140,000	3,797,000	1,343,000
1978	47,636,000	32,060,000	15,576,000	42,550,000	28,328,000	14,223,000	5,085,000	3,732,000	1,353,000
1979	46,679,000	31,585,000	15,094,000	40,984,000	27,665,000	13,319,000	5,100,000	3,700,000	1,360,000
1980	45,948,000	31,316,000	14,633,000	40,987,000	27,647,000	13,313,000	4,962,000	3,642,000	1,320,000
1981	45,148,000	30,869,000	14,279,000	40,148,000	27,269,000	12,879,000	5,000,000	3,600,000	1,400,000
1982 [2]	44,400,000	30,700,000	13,700,000	39,500,000	27,100,000	12,400,000	4,900,000	3,600,000	1,300,000
1983 [2]	44,000,000	30,600,000	13,400,000	39,100,000	27,000,000	12,100,000	4,900,000	3,600,000	1,300,000
1984 [2]	44,039,000	30,505,000	13,534,000	39,039,000	26,905,000	12,134,000	5,000,000	3,600,000	1,400,000
1985 [2]	44,166,000	30,551,000	13,615,000	39,166,000	26,951,000	12,215,000	5,000,000	3,600,000	1,400,000
1986 [2]	44,556,000	31,059,000	13,497,000	39,456,000	27,359,000	12,097,000	5,100,000	3,700,000	1,400,000
1987 [2]	45,004,000	31,787,000	13,217,000	39,804,000	27,987,000	11,817,000	5,200,000	3,800,000	1,400,000
1988 [2]	45,358,000	32,522,000	12,836,000	40,158,000	28,722,000	11,436,000	5,200,000	3,800,000	1,400,000
1989 [2]	45,905,000	33,347,000	12,558,000	40,605,000	29,447,000	11,158,000	5,300,000	3,900,000	1,400,000
1990 [2]	46,667,000	34,244,000	12,423,000	41,267,000	30,244,000	11,023,000	5,400,000	4,000,000	1,400,000

[1] Fall enrollment. [2] Estimated.

HIGHLIGHTS: 1983 *(continued)*

schools and colleges have historically accomplished and contributed to the United States and the well-being of the people, the educational foundations of our society are presently being eroded by a rising tide of mediocrity that threatens our very future as a nation and a people. What was unimaginable a generation ago has begun to occur—others are matching and surpassing our educational attainments. . . .

"If an unfriendly foreign power had attempted to impose on America the mediocre educational performance that exists today, we might well have viewed it as an act of war. As it stands, we have allowed this to happen to ourselves."

The commission recommended:

—That salaries of teachers be increased and that their contracts be extended from 9 months to 11 months.

—That merit rather than seniority become the basis for raises, promotions, and tenure for teachers.

—That students spend more time in school, with the school day lengthened to 7 hours and the school year increased from 200 to 220 days.

—That students be required to do "far more homework."

—That high schools require rigorous study in basic subjects, including English, mathematics, science, social studies, and computer science. Greater emphasis on foreign languages also was called for.

—That colleges and universities toughen admission standards in testing students for their skills in basic subjects.

President Reagan applauded the report. In the months that followed he made many speeches before educational groups, calling for implementation of the commission's proposals by state and local governments.

Democrats called for an increase in the amount the federal government spends on education, a proposal opposed by the President.

U.S. HIGH SCHOOL GRADUATES: 1869–1991

Source: National Center for Educational Statistics, U.S. Department of Education

YEAR	GRADUATES	YEAR	GRADUATES	YEAR	GRADUATES	YEAR	GRADUATES
1869–70	16,000	1951–52	1,196,500	1967–68	2,702,000	1979–80	3,058,000
1879–80	23,634	1953–54	1,276,100	1968–69	2,829,000	1980–81	3,026,000
1889–90	43,731	1955–56	1,421,000	1969–70	2,896,000	1981–82 [1]	2,937,000
1899–1900	94,883	1957–58	1,513,000	1970–71	2,944,000	1982–83 [1]	2,795,000
1909–10	156,429	1959–60	1,864,000	1971–72	3,008,000	1983–84 [1]	2,680,000
1919–20	311,266	1960–61	1,971,000	1972–73	3,043,000	1984–85 [1]	2,614,000
1929–30	666,904	1961–62	1,925,000	1973–74	3,080,000	1985–86 [1]	2,599,000
1939–40	1,221,475	1962–63	1,950,000	1974–75	3,140,000	1986–87 [1]	2,648,000
1943–44	1,019,233	1963–64	2,290,000	1975–76	3,155,000	1987–88 [1]	2,710,000
1945–46	1,080,033	1964–65	2,665,000	1976–77	3,161,000	1988–89 [1]	2,626,000
1947–48	1,189,909	1965–66	2,632,000	1977–78	3,134,000	1989–90 [1]	2,444,000
1949–50	1,199,700	1966–67	2,679,000	1978–79	3,134,000	1990–91 [1]	2,350,000

[1] Estimated.

U.S. COLLEGES AND UNIVERSITIES: 1983–1984

Source: Adapted from *College Facts Chart 83–84* by National Beta Club, Box 730, Spartanburg, SC 29304

Information in the following table provides a general guide to attending more than 3,400 specific colleges and universities.

The chart includes information collected by The National Beta Club, founded in 1934, a nonprofit leadership-service organization for secondary school students throughout the U.S. Membership is selected by each school administration from students who demonstrate worthy character, good mentality, creditable achievement, and commendable attitude.

No reference to accreditation is made or implied. Inclusion of an institution does not constitute approval or endorsement of that institution.

Following are explanations of the main column headings in the table:

Name and Address. The schools are grouped by states to make it easier for you to locate them.

Level. Two-year programs—Junior **(J)**; four-year programs—Senior **(S)**; graduate program **(G)**; professional degree program **(P)**.

Type. Most colleges are now coordinate or coeducational **(C)**, but some are for women only **(W)** and some are for men only **(M)**.

Affiliation. Schools supported by taxes are **Public**, Community **(Comm)**, or **State.**

Private schools largely without church support are independent **(Ind)**. The listing of a church may indicate indirect support or direct control.

Enrollment and Teachers figures are for the 1982–1983 school year.

Tuition and Fees are the average cost for the 1982–1983 school year. For variations, including nonresident costs, consult the institution directly.

Board and Room. These are average costs for housing and food available *on the campus.* A dash (—) means room and board are *not available on the campus* or that the school did not provide this information.

Total Cost. These are average costs for state residents. In most cases the cost does not include laundry or other personal expenses.

NAME	ADDRESS	FOUNDED	AFFILIATION	LEVEL/TYPE	ENROLLMENT	TEACHERS	TUITION & FEES	BOARD & ROOM	TOTAL COST
ALABAMA									
Alabama A.&M. University	Normal, AL 35762	1875	State	S-G/C	4,135	327	$ 784	$1,768	$ 2,552
Alabama Christian College	Montgomery, AL 36193	1942	C of Chr	S/C	1,956	78	$ 2,880	$3,000	$ 5,880
Alabama State University	Montgomery, AL 36195	1874	State	S-G/C	4,044	212	$ 660	$1,320	$ 1,980
Alexander City St. Jr. College	Alexander City, AL 35010	1965	State	J/C	1,284	76	$ 375	—	$ 375
Athens State College	Athens, AL 35611	1822	State	S/C	1,027	40	$ 675	$1,380	$ 2,055
Auburn University	Auburn, AL 36849	1856	State	S-G/C	18,401	1,470	$ 990	$1,800	$ 2,790
At Montgomery	Montgomery, AL 36193	1969	State	S-G/C	5,153	173	$ 1,000	$2,500	$ 3,500
Birmingham School of Law	Birmingham, AL 35203	1915	Independ	P/C	300	27	$ 1,000	—	$ 1,000
Birmingham-Southern College	Birmingham, AL 35254	1856	Methodist	S-G/C	1,553	103	$ 3,990	$2,040	$ 6,050
Brewer State Jr. College	Fayette, AL 35555	1969	State	J/C	737	25	$ 375	—	$ 375
Chattahoochee Val. Comm. Col.	Phenix City, AL 36867	1973	State	J/C	1,447	58	$ 375	—	$ 375
Comm. College of the Air Force	Maxwell AFB, AL 36112	1972	Federal	J/C	156,776	11,234	—	—	—
Concordia College	Selma, AL 36701	1922	Lutheran	J/C	200	14	$ 1,700	$1,850	$ 3,550
Enterprise State Jr. College	Enterprise, AL 36331	1965	State	J/C	1,938	44	$ 375	—	$ 375
Faulkner State Jr. College	Bay Minette, AL 36502	1965	State	J/C	1,359	60	$ 375	$1,585	$ 1,960
Gadsden State Jr. College	Gadsden, AL 35999	1965	State	J/C	3,572	111	$ 380	$1,395	$ 1,775
Geo. C. Wallace St. Comm. Col.	Dothan, AL 36303	1965	State	J/C	3,026	97	$ 375	—	$ 375
Geo. C. Wallace St. Comm. Col.	Selma, AL 36701	1965	State	J-T/C	1,300	58	$ 375	—	$ 525
Huntingdon College	Montgomery, AL 36106	1854	Un. Meth	S/C	743	76	$ 2,850	$2,250	$ 5,100
Jacksonville State University	Jacksonville, AL 36265	1883	State	S-G/C	6,509	340	$ 750	$1,390	$ 2,140
Jefferson Davis St. Jr. College	Brewton, AL 36426	1965	State	J/C	935	24	$ 375	—	$ 375
Jefferson State Jr. College	Birmingham, AL 35215	1963	State	J/C	6,749	318	$ 387	—	$ 387
John C. Calhoun St. Comm. C.	Decatur, AL 35602	1965	State	J/C	6,011	257	$ 600	—	$ 600
Judson College	Marion, AL 36756	1838	Baptist	S/W	538	41	$ 2,530	$2,050	$ 4,580
Lawson State Comm. College	Birmingham, AL 35221	1965	State	J/C	1,786	84	$ 400	—	$ 400
Livingston University	Livingston, AL 35470	1835	State	S-G/C	1,458	82	$ 948	$1,560	$ 2,508
Lomax-Hannon Jr. College	Greenville, AL 36037	1893	AME	J/C	129	12	$ 1,985	$1,479	$ 3,464
Lurleen B. Wallace St. Jr. Col.	Andalusia, AL 36420	1969	State	J/C	801	29	$ 375	—	$ 375
Marion Military Institute	Marion, AL 36756	1842	Independ	J/M	462	32	$ 4,200	$2,200	$ 6,400
Miles College	Birmingham, AL 35208	1905	CME	S/C	586	43	$ 3,000	$1,850	$ 4,850
Mobile College	Mobile, AL 36613	1961	Baptist	S/C	1,002	943	$ 2,176	$1,860	$ 4,036
Northeast Ala. St. Jr. College	Rainsville, AL 35986	1965	State	J/C	957	50	$ 375	—	$ 375
Northwest Ala. St. Jr. College	Phil Campbell, AL 35581	1981	State	J/C	1,041	61	$ 375	—	$ 375
Oakwood College	Huntsville, AL 35896	1896	7-D Adv	S/C	1,418	74	$ 3,846	$2,016	$ 5,862
Patrick Henry St. Jr. College	Monroeville, AL 36460	1963	State	J/C	691	49	$ 375	—	$ 1,875
Samford University	Birmingham, AL 35229	1841	Baptist	S-G/C	4,048	285	$ 3,400	$2,300	$ 5,700
S.D. Bishop St. Jr. College	Mobile, AL 36690	1936	State	J/C	1,619	46	$ 327	—	$ 327
Selma University	Selma, AL 36701	1878	Baptist	J-S/C	342	32	$ 1,477	$1,620	$ 3,097
Snead State Jr. College	Boaz, AL 35957	1935	State	J/C	1,170	35	$ 375	$1,350	$ 1,725
Southeastern Bible College	Birmingham, AL 35256	1935	Independ	S-G/C	200	21	$ 2,600	$1,800	$ 4,400
Southern Union St. Jr. College	Wadley, AL 36276	1922	State	J/C	1,691	87	$ 500	$1,267	$ 1,767
Spring Hill College	Mobile, AL 36608	1830	Catholic	S-G/C	900	78	$ 4,700	$2,600	$ 7,300
Stillman College	Tuscaloosa, AL 35403	1876	Presby	S/C	523	43	$ 2,180	$2,003	$ 4,183
Talladega College	Talladega, AL 35160	1867	Independ	S/C	538	62	$ 2,950	$2,050	$ 5,000
Troy State University	Troy, AL 36082	1887	State	S-G/C	7,317	419	$ 900	$1,530	$ 2,430
Fort Rucker/Dothan	Dothan, AL 36302	1961	State	S-G/C	1,582	71	$ 825	—	$ 825
Montgomery Branch	Montgomery, AL 36195	1965	State	S-G/C	2,020	132	$ 1,000	—	$ 1,250
Tuskegee Institute	Tuskegee Inst., AL 36088	1881	Independ	S-G/C	3,577	337	$ 3,000	$2,000	$ 5,000
University of Alabama	University, AL 35486	1831	State	S-G/C	16,022	1,407	$ 1,074	$2,020	$ 3,094
Birmingham	Birmingham, AL 35294	1966	State	S-G/C	14,530	1,522	$ 1,245	—	$ 1,245
Huntsville	Huntsville, AL 35899	1950	State	S-G/C	6,025	389	$ 1,048	$ 975	$ 2,023
University of Montevallo	Montevallo, AL 35115	1896	State	S-G/C	2,600	155	$ 1,030	$1,723	$ 2,723
University of North Alabama	Florence, AL 35632	1872	State	S-G/C	5,270	223	$ 940	$1,866	$ 2,806
University of South Alabama	Mobile, AL 36608	1963	State	S-G/C	9,411	591	$ 1,245	$1,845	$ 3,090
Walker College	Jasper, AL 35501	1938	Independ	J/C	712	45	$ 1,050	$1,550	$ 2,600

ALASKA

NAME	ADDRESS	FOUNDED	AFFILIATION	LEVEL/TYPE	ENROLLMENT	TEACHERS	TUITION & FEES	BOARD & ROOM	TOTAL COST
Alaska Bible College	Glennallen, AK 99588	1966	Independ	S/C	81	16	$ 1,480	$2,640	$ 4,120
Alaska Pacific University	Anchorage, AK 99508	1959	Un. Meth	S-G/C	1,450	95	$ 3,190	$2,924	$ 6,114
Sheldon Jackson College	Sitka, AK 99835	1878	Independ	S/C	230	31	$ 3,160	$3,000	$ 6,160
University of Alaska									
Anchorage	Anchorage, AK 99508	1976	State	S-G/C	3,869	269	$ 648	—	$ 648
Anchorage Comm. College	Anchorage, AK 99508	1954	State	J/C	11,311	505	$ 650	—	$ 650
Fairbanks	Fairbanks, AK 99701	1917	State	S-G/C	5,754	382	$ 778	$2,100	$ 2,878
Juneau	Juneau, AK 99801	1956	State	S-G/C	2,206	71	$ 700	$3,000	$ 3,700
Kenai Peninsula Comm. Col.	Soldotna, AK 99669	1964	State	J/C	1,328	88	$ 630	—	$ 630
Ketchikan Community Col.	Ketchikan, AK 99901	1954	State	J/C	1,200	83	$ 600	—	$ 600
Kodiak Community College	Kodiak, AK 99615	1968	State	J/C	952	60	$ 500	—	$ 500
Kuskokwim Community Col.	Bethel, AK 99559	1972	State	J/C	652	16	$ 600	$4,500	$ 5,100
Matanuska-Susitna Comm. Col.	Palmer, AK 99645	1957	State	J/C	1,056	65	$ 622	—	—
Northwest Community Col.	Nome, AK 99762	1975	State	J/C	399	31	$ 630	—	$ 630
Prince William Sound Comm. Col.	Valdez, AK 99686	1978	State	J/C	562	4	$ 620	$4,600	$ 5,220
Sitka Community College	Sitka, AK 99835	1962	State	J/C	735	37	$ 700	—	$ 700
Tanana Valley Comm. College	Fairbanks, AK 99701	1974	State	J/C	2,200	122	$ 788	$2,100	$ 2,888

ARIZONA

NAME	ADDRESS	FOUNDED	AFFILIATION	LEVEL/TYPE	ENROLLMENT	TEACHERS	TUITION & FEES	BOARD & ROOM	TOTAL COST
American Grad. Sch. Int. Man.	Glendale, AZ 85306	1946	Independ	G/C	1,037	95	$ 5,000	$2,350	$ 7,350
American Independian Bible College	Phoenix, AZ 85021	1957	A of God	S/C	67	8	$ 1,584	$1,726	$ 3,310
Arizona State University	Tempe, AZ 85287	1885	State	S-G/C	39,319	2,059	$ 755	$6,400	$ 7,155
Arizona Western College	Yuma, AZ 85364	1961	State	J/C	3,999	257	$ 360	$1,930	$ 2,290
Central Arizona College	Coolidge, AZ 85228	1969	State	J/C	5,175	347	$ 316	$1,710	$ 2,026
Cochise College	Douglas, AZ 85607	1962	Independ	J/C	3,944	250	$ 380	$1,602	$ 1,982
College of Ganado	Ganado, AZ 86505	1970	Independ	J/C	213	11	$ 1,452	$3,458	$ 4,910
Devry Inst. of Technology	Phoenix, AZ 85016	1967	Independ	S/C	4,763	205	$ 3,300	—	$ 3,300
Eastern Arizona College	Thatcher, AZ 85552	1888	State	J/C	3,889	200	$ 322	$1,900	$ 2,222
Embry-Riddle Aeronautical Univ.	Prescott, AZ 86301	1926	Independ	S-G/C	855	75	$ 3,000	$2,300	$ 5,300
Grand Canyon College	Phoenix, AZ 85061	1949	Baptist	S/C	1,220	64	$ 2,933	$2,190	$ 5,123
Jan Hus University	Scottsdale, AZ 85251	1972	Independ	P/C	—	—	$ 3,000	$2,000	$ 5,000
Maricopa County Comm. Col.	Phoenix, AZ 85034	1963	County	J/C	59,315	2,241	$ 220	—	$ 220
Glendale Comm. College	Glendale, AZ 85301	1966	County	J/C	13,415	424	$ 264	—	$ 264
Maricopa Tech. Comm. Col.	Phoenix, AZ 85034	1968	County	J/C	3,466	149	$ 264	—	$ 264
Mesa Comm. College	Mesa, AZ 85202	1965	County	J/C	14,674	445	$ 264	—	$ 264
Phoenix College	Phoenix, AZ 85013	1920	County	J/C	12,729	495	$ 264	—	$ 264
Rio Salado Comm. College	Phoenix, AZ 85003	1978	County	J/C	10,050	302	$ 264	—	$ 264
Scottsdale Comm. College	Scottsdale, AZ 85253	1970	County	J/C	7,356	229	$ 264	—	$ 264
South Mountain Comm. Col.	Phoenix, AZ 85040	1978	County	J/C	1,394	85	$ 264	—	$ 264
Mohave Comm. College	Kingman, AZ 86401	1970	State	J/C	3,297	215	$ 206	—	$ 206
Navajo Community College	Tsaile, AZ 86556	1968	Private	J/C	1,419	65	$ 730	$2,320	$ 3,050
Northern Arizona University	Flagstaff, AZ 86011	1899	State	S-G/C	11,665	630	$ 755	$1,800	$ 2,555
Northland Pioneer College	Holbrook, AZ 86025	1973	State	J/C	6,377	400	$ 120	—	$ 120
Ottawa University	Phoenix, AZ 85015	1977	Baptist	S/C	500	30	$ 1,728	—	$ 1,728
Pima Community College	Tucson, AZ 85709	1967	State	J/C	21,780	1,026	$ 360	—	$ 360
Prescott Center College	Prescott, AZ 86301	1975	Private	S/C	133	18	$ 3,675	—	$ 3,675
University of Arizona	Tucson, AZ 85721	1885	State	S-G/C	30,292	1,446	$ 755	$2,278	$ 3,033
University of Phoenix	Phoenix, AZ 85004	1978	Independ	S-G/C	2,400	380	$ 3,450	—	$ 3,450
Western International Univ.	Phoenix, AZ 85021	1978	Independ	S-G/C	850	15	$ 1,350	—	$ 1,350
Yavapai College	Prescott, AZ 86301	1970	State	J/C	5,536	327	$ 400	$1,880	$ 2,280

ARKANSAS

NAME	ADDRESS	FOUNDED	AFFILIATION	LEVEL/TYPE	ENROLLMENT	TEACHERS	TUITION & FEES	BOARD & ROOM	TOTAL COST
Arkansas Baptist College	Little Rock, AR 72202	1884	Baptist	S/C	210	13	$ 1,340	$1,304	$ 2,654
Arkansas College	Batesville, AR 72501	1872	Presby	S/C	514	57	$ 3,300	$1,596	$ 4,896
Arkansas State University	State Univ., AR 72467	1909	State	S-G/C	7,448	302	$ 720	$1,622	$ 2,342
Beebe Campus	Beebe, AR 72012	1927	State	J/C	714	30	$ 540	$1,140	$ 1,680
Arkansas Tech University	Russellville, AR 72801	1909	State	S-G/C	3,255	155	$ 750	$1,440	$ 2,190
Central Baptist College	Conway, AR 72032	1952	Baptist	S-G/C	292	22	$ 720	$1,120	$ 1,840
College of the Ozarks	Clarksville, AR 72830	1834	Presby	S/C	694	46	$ 1,480	$1,350	$ 2,830
Crowley's Ridge College	Paragould, AR 72450	1964	C of Chr	J/C	107	12	$ 1,910	$1,598	$ 3,508
East Arkansas Comm. College	Forrest City, AR 72335	1974	State	J/C	1,155	25	$ 600	—	$ 600
Garland County Comm. College	Hot Springs, AR 71913	1973	State	J/C	1,807	83	$ 432	—	$ 432
Harding University	Searcy, AR 72143	1924	C of Chr	S-G/C	2,847	166	$ 2,943	$1,924	$ 4,867
Henderson State University	Arkadelphia, AR 71923	1890	State	S-G/C	2,636	145	$ 720	$1,336	$ 2,056
Hendrix College	Conway, AR 72032	1884	Un. Meth	S/C	962	66	$ 3,680	$1,640	$ 5,320
John Brown University	Siloam Springs, AR 72761	1919	Independ	S/C	768	50	$ 2,700	$2,100	$ 4,800
Mississippi County Comm. Col.	Blytheville, AR 72315	1975	State	J/C	1,180	65	$ 432	—	$ 432
North Arkansas Comm. College	Harrison, AR 72601	1974	State	J/C	901	50	$ 600	$1,800	$ 2,400
Ouachita Baptist University	Arkadelphia, AR 71923	1886	Baptist	S/C	1,691	110	$ 2,650	$1,720	$ 4,370
Philander Smith College	Little Rock, AR 72202	1877	Un. Meth	S/C	637	61	$ 1,300	$2,000	$ 3,300
Phillips County Comm. College	Helena, AR 72342	1965	State	J/C	1,775	45	$ 464	—	$ 464
Shorter College	N. Little Rock, AR 72114	1886	AME	J/C	161	14	$ 1,400	$1,890	$ 3,290
Southern Arkansas University	Magnolia, AR 71753	1909	State	S-G/C	2,070	136	$ 750	$1,430	$ 2,180
El Dorado Branch	El Dorado, AR 71730	1975	State	J/C	518	40	$ 552	—	$ 552
Tech Branch	East Camden, AR 71701	1967	State	J/C	691	51	$ 552	$1,360	$ 1,912
Southern Baptist College	Walnut Ridge, AR 72476	1941	Baptist	J/C	402	27	$ 2,062	$1,490	$ 3,552
University of Arkansas	Fayetteville, AR 72701	1871	State	S-G/C	15,108	1,097	$ 390	$ 875	$ 1,265
Medical Sciences Campus	Little Rock, AR 72205	1879	State	S-G/C	1,652	404	$ 2,000	$2,000	$ 4,000
at Little Rock	Little Rock, AR 72204	1927	State	S-G/C	10,065	400	$ 800	—	$ 800
at Monticello	Monticello, AR 71655	1909	State	S/C	1,817	97	$ 720	$1,510	$ 2,230
at Pine Bluff	Pine Bluff, AR 71601	1873	State	S/C	2,731	149	$ 710	$1,493	$ 2,203
University of Central Arkansas	Conway, AR 72032	1907	State	S-G/C	5,875	274	$ 720	$1,688	$ 2,408
Westark Community College	Fort Smith, AR 72912	1928	State	J/C	3,684	98	$ 492	—	$ 492

NAME	ADDRESS	FOUNDED	AFFILIATION	LEVEL/TYPE	ENROLLMENT	TEACHERS	TUITION & FEES	BOARD & ROOM	TOTAL COST
CALIFORNIA									
Allan Hancock Joint Comm. College	Santa Maria, CA 93454	1920	Public	J/C	8,898	339	$ 20	—	$ 20
Ambassador College	Pasadena, CA 91129	1947	C of God	S/C	642	49	$ 1,550	$2,100	$ 3,650
American Christian Theol. Sem.	Anaheim, CA 92806	1973	Int-Den	P/C	65	9	$ 3,075	—	$ 3,075
American College of Law	Anaheim, CA 92805	1971	Independ	P/C	137	22	$ 2,500	—	$ 2,500
American River College	Sacramento, CA 95841	1955	State	J/C	23,819	594		—	—
Antelope Valley Comm. Col.	Lancaster, CA 93534	1929	District	J/C	7,446	286	$ 100	—	$ 100
Antioch University West	San Francisco, CA 94118	1852	Independ	S-G/C	994	49	$ 4,650	—	$ 4,650
Armstrong College	Berkeley, CA 94704	1918	Independ	S-G/C	542	42	$ 2,226	—	$ 2,226
Art Center Col. of Design	Pasadena, CA 91103	1930	Independ	S/C	1,126	168	$ 4,310	$2,750	$ 7,060
Azusa Pacific College	Azusa, CA 91702	1899	Independ	S-G/C	2,302	139	$ 4,700	$2,300	$ 7,000
Bakersfield College	Bakersfield, CA 93305	1913	Public	J/C	11,715	500	$ 2,219	$2,200	$ 4,419
Barstow College	Barstow, CA 92311	1959	State	J/C	1,738	54	—	—	$ 2,150
Berean Bible College	San Diego, CA 92105	1970	Independ	T/C	200	20	$ 915	—	$ 915
Bethany Bible College	Santa Cruz, CA 95066	1919	A of God	S/C	515	41	$ 2,410	$1,990	$ 4,400
Biola University	La Mirada, CA 90639	1908	Independ	S-G/C	3,096	253	$ 4,470	$2,522	$ 6,992
Brooks College	Long Beach, CA 90804	1970	Independ	J/C	850	74	$ 3,780	$2,780	$ 6,560
Brooks Institute	Santa Barbara, CA 93108	1946	Independ	S-G/C	800	36	$ 4,650	—	$ 4,650
Butte College	Oroville, CA 95965	1967	State	J/C	11,000	110	$ 40	—	—
Cabrillo College	Aptos, CA 95003	1959	Comm	J/C	11,460	225	$ 154	$4,946	$ 5,100
California Baptist College	Riverside, CA 92504	1950	Baptist	S-G/C	660	70	$ 3,320	$2,200	$ 5,520
California Christian College	Fresno, CA 93703	1955	Baptist	S/C	30	6	$ 1,200	$1,600	$ 2,800
California Christian Univ.	Adelanto, CA 92301	1971	Christian	S-G/C	47	2	$ 1,580	—	$ 1,580
California Coast University	Santa Ana, CA 92701	1973	Independ	S-G/C	5,000	—	$ 2,500	—	$ 2,500
Calif. Col. of Arts & Crafts	Oakland, CA 94618	1907	Private	P/C	822	155	$ 5,190	$1,040	$ 6,230
California Col. of Commerce	Long Beach, CA 90813	1921	Independ	S-G/C	150	10	$ 1,650	—	$ 1,650
Calif. Col. of Podiatric Med.	San Francisco, CA 94115	1914	Independ	P/C	428	38	$ 9,665	—	$ 9,665
Calif. Graduate Institute	Los Angeles, CA 90024	1968	Independ	G/C	400	50	$ 2,500	—	$ 2,500
Calif. Inst. of the Arts	Valencia, CA 91355	1961	Independ	S-G/C	854	159	$ 6,200	$3,625	$ 9,825
California Institute of Technology	Pasadena, CA 91125	1891	Independ	S-G/C	1,810	337	$ 8,600	$3,500	$12,100
Calif. International University	Los Angeles, CA 90057	1974	Independ	S-G/C	20	4	$ 2,600	—	$ 2,600
Calif. Lutheran College	Thousand Oaks, CA 91360	1959	Lutheran	S-G/C	2,511	235	$ 5,010	$2,400	$ 7,410
Calif. Maritime Academy	Vallejo, CA 94590	1929	State	S/C	500	32	$ 1,309	$3,159	$ 4,468
Calif. Missionary Baptist Inst.	Bellflower, CA 90706	1957	Baptist	G/C	48	16	$ 500	—	—
Calif. Polytechnic State Univ.	San Luis Obispo, CA 93407	1901	State	S-G/C	15,648	950	$ 603	$2,500	$ 3,103
California School of Professional Psychology	Berkeley, CA 94704	1970	Independ	G/C	248	90	$ 6,915	$4,560	$11,475
Calif. Sch. of Prof. Psychology	Fresno, CA 93721	1973	Independ	G/C	146	27	$ 6,900	$4,510	$11,410
Calif. Sch. of Prof. Psychology	Los Angeles, CA 90057	1970	Independ	G/C	266	64	$ 6,910	$4,740	$11,650
Calif. Sch. of Prof. Psychology	San Diego, CA 92121	1972	Independ	G/C	237	81	$ 6,900	$4,770	$11,670
Calif. State College									
Bakersfield	Bakersfield, CA 93309	1965	State	S-G/C	3,335	145	$ 650	$2,552	$ 3,502
San Bernardino	San Bernardino, CA 92407	1962	State	S-G/C	5,060	—	$ 600	$2,400	$ 3,000
Stanislaus	Turlock, CA 95380	1957	State	S-G/C	4,600	279	$ 600	$2,300	$ 2,900
California State Polytechnic University	Pomona, CA 91768	1938	State	S-G/C	16,558	1,063	$ 788	$2,880	$ 3,668
California State University									
Chico	Chico, CA 95929	1887	State	S-G/C	14,024	666	$ 600	$2,300	$ 2,900
Dominguez Hills	Carson, CA 90747	1962	State	S-G/C	8,307	500	$ 650	$1,422	$ 2,072
Fresno	Fresno, CA 93740	1911	State	S-G/C	16,171	1,029	$ 530	$2,228	$ 2,758
Fullerton	Fullerton, CA 92634	1959	State	S-G/C	23,399	1,388	$ 694	—	$ 694
Hayward	Hayward, CA 94542	1967	State	S-G/C	11,624	477	$ 468	—	$ 468
Long Beach	Long Beach, CA 90840	1949	State	S-G/C	32,034	1,686	$ 600	$2,800	$ 3,400
Los Angeles	Los Angeles, CA 90032	1947	State	S-G/C	21,863	617	$ 666	—	$ 666
Northridge	Northridge, CA 91330	1958	State	S-G/C	28,111	1,571	$ 519	—	$ 519
Sacramento	Sacramento, CA 95819	1947	State	S-G/C	21,671	1,225	$ 671	$2,601	$ 3,272
Canada College	Redwood City, CA 94061	1968	Public	J/C	8,315	264	$ 40	—	$ 40
Casa Loma Institute of Technology	Lake View Terrace, CA 91342	1966	Independ	J/C	120	10	$ 4,450	$5,914	$10,364
Center for Early Education	Los Angeles, CA 90048	1939	Independ	S-G/C	54	8	$ 2,640	—	$ 2,640
Cerritos College	Norwalk, CA 90650	1956	Public	J/C	22,950	260	—	—	—
Cerro Coso Comm. College	Ridgecrest, CA 93555	1973	State	J/C	3,934	201	$ 20	—	$ 20
Chabot College	Hayward, CA 94545	1961	Public	J/C	19,770	800	$ 36	—	$ 36
Chaffey Comm. College	Alta Loma, CA 91701	1883	State	J/C	12,700	280	$ 45	—	$ 45
Chapman College	Orange, CA 92666	1861	D of Chr	S-G/C	1,465	135	$ 6,220	$2,700	$ 8,920
Christian Heritage College	El Cajon, CA 92021	1970	Church	S/C	383	18	$ 2,800	$1,600	$ 4,400
Christian Life College	Stockton, CA 95205	1953	Un Pent	P/C	150	18	$ 1,050	$1,635	$ 2,685
Church Div. Sch. of Pacific	Berkeley, CA 94709	1893	Episcopal	G/C	104	14	$ 3,150	$2,500	$ 5,650
Citrus Belt Law School	Riverside, CA 92506	1971	Independ	P/C	135	15	$ 1,740	—	$ 1,740
Citrus College	Azusa, CA 91702	1915	Independ	J/C	10,052	345	$ 70	—	—
City College of San Francisco	San Francisco, CA 94112	1935	State	J/C	26,000	1,099		—	—
City Univ. School of Law	Los Angeles, CA 90017	1976	Independ	S-G/C	80	—	$ 1,700	—	$ 1,850
Claremont McKenna College	Claremont, CA 91711	1946	Independ	S/C	831	—	$ 7,250	$2,800	$12,000
Claremont Graduate School	Claremont, CA 91711	1925	Independ	G/C	1,182	126	$ 6,300	—	$ 6,300
Cleveland Chiropractic College	Los Angeles, CA 90004	1908	Independ	P/C	630	43	$ 6,500	—	$ 6,500
Coast. School of Deep Sea Diving, Inc.	Oakland, CA 94601	1950	Private	P/C	250	6	$ 1,395	$1,100	$ 2,495
Cogswell College	San Francisco, CA 94108	1887	Independ	S/C	452	56	$ 1,350	$4,080	$ 5,430
Coleman College	La Mesa, CA 92041	1963	Independ	S-G/C	851	50	$ 5,625	—	—
College of Alameda	Alameda, CA 94501	1970	State	J/C	6,760	183	—	—	—
College of the Canyons	Valencia, CA 91355	1969	State	J/C	3,498	109	$ 22	—	$ 22
College of the Desert	Palm Desert, CA 92260	1958	State	J/C	10,042	236	$ 150	—	$ 150
College of Marin	Kentfield, CA 94904	1926	Public	J/C	7,400	162	—	—	—

NAME	ADDRESS	FOUNDED	AFFILIATION	LEVEL/TYPE	ENROLLMENT	TEACHERS	TUITION & FEES	BOARD & ROOM	TOTAL COST
CALIFORNIA *(continued)*									
College of Notre Dame	Belmont, CA 94002	1851	Independ	S-G/C	1,371	113	$ 5,100	$3,100	$ 8,200
College of the Redwoods	Eureka, CA 95501	1964	Independ	J/C	8,605	550	—	$2,900	$ 4,400
College of San Mateo	San Mateo, CA 94402	1923	State	J/C	15,000	250	—	—	—
College of the Sequoias	Visalia, CA 93277	1925	State	J/C	7,372	160	$ 20	—	$ 20
College of the Siskiyous	Weed, CA 96094	1957	State	J/C	2,862	144	$ 35	$2,420	$ 2,455
Columbia College	Columbia, CA 95310	1968	State	J/C	2,915	44	$ 12	—	$ 12
Columbia College-Hollywood	Hollywood, CA 90038	1952	Independ	J-S/C	354	40	$ 3,000	—	$ 3,000
Columbia Pacific University	Mill Valley, CA 94941	1978	Independ	S-G/C	1,350	200	$ 2,800	—	$ 2,800
Common College	Woodside, CA 94062	1971	Independ	S/C	8	20	$ 4,000	—	$ 4,000
Compton Community College	Compton, CA 90221	1927	Public	J/C	5,000	350	$ 20	—	$ 20
Contra Costa College	San Pablo, CA 94806	1950	Public	J/C	9,300	267	—	—	—
Cosumnes River College	Sacramento, CA 95823	1970	Public	J/C	6,625	192	—	—	—
Crafton Hills College	Yucaipa, CA 92399	1972	Public	J/C	4,018	49	—	—	—
Cuesta College	San Luis Obispo, CA 93403	1965	State	J/C	5,893	185	$ 40	—	$ 40
Cuyamaca College	El Cajon, CA 92020	1978	State	J/C	2,820	108	—	—	—
Cypress College	Cypress, CA 90630	1966	State	J/C	14,468	196	$ 50	—	$ 50
De Anza College	Cupertino, CA 95014	1967	Public	J/C	24,569	810	$ 27	—	$ 89
Deep Springs College	Deep Springs, CA 89010	1917	Independ	J/M	24	8	—	—	—
Diablo Valley College	Pleasant Hill, CA 94523	1949	District	J/C	19,892	494	$ 52	—	$ 52
Dominican Col. of San Rafael	San Rafael, CA 94901	1890	Catholic	S-G/C	618	104	$ 4,900	$3,500	$ 8,400
Dominican School of Philosophy and Theology	Berkeley, CA 94709	1932	Catholic	S-G/C	120	15	$ 2,410	—	—
Don Bosco Technical Institute	Rosemead, CA 91770	1969	Catholic	J/M	324	38	$ 1,850	—	$ 1,850
D-Q University	Davis, CA 95617	1970	Private	J/C	197	31	$ 3,205	$2,849	$ 6,054
East Los Angeles College	Monterey Park, CA 91754	1945	State	J/C	20,534	624	—	—	—
El Camino College	Torrance, CA 90506	1947	Public	J/C	30,820	722	$ 10	—	$ 10
Empire College	Santa Rosa, CA 95401	1959	Independ	P/C	210	9	$ 4,000	—	$ 4,000
Empire College Sch. of Law	Santa Rosa, CA 95401	1959	Independ	P/C	106	16	$ 2,000	—	$ 2,000
Ernest Holmes College School of Ministry	Los Angeles, CA 90020	1972	Church	P/C	62	8	$ 2,250	—	$ 2,250
Eubanks Cons. of Music & Arts	Los Angeles, CA 90043	1951	Independ	S-G/C	400	32	$ 1,800	—	$ 1,800
Evangelical Christian College	Fresno, CA 93726	1946	Pent	S/C	80	8	$ 1,000	$1,500	$ 2,750
Evergreen Valley College	San Jose, CA 95135	1975	State	J/C	10,147	400	$ 10	—	$ 10
Feather River College	Quincy, CA 95971	1968	State	J/C	1,400	60	$ 15	$3,500	$ 4,000
Fielding Institute	Santa Barbara, CA 93105	1974	Independ	G/C	458	38	$ 5,220	—	$ 5,940
Foot Hills College	Los Altos Hills, CA 94022	1958	State	J/C	13,892	480	—	—	—
Fresno City College	Fresno, CA 93741	1910	State	J/C	14,947	421	$ 80	—	$ 80
Fresno Pacific College	Fresno, CA 93702	1944	Independ	S-G/C	812	55	$ 4,000	$2,500	$ 6,500
Fuller Theological Seminary	Pasadena, CA 91101	1947	Independ	G/C	2,728	126	$ 3,744	—	$ 3,744
Fullerton College	Fullerton, CA 92634	1913	State	J/C	19,733	503	$ 13	—	$ 13
Gavilan College	Gilroy, CA 95020	1919	State	J/C	3,250	64	$ 135	—	$ 135
Glendale Community College	Glendale, CA 91208	1927	State	J/C	12,185	375	$ 25	—	$ 25
Glendale Univ. Col. of Law	Glendale, CA 91206	1967	Independ	P/C	185	15	$ 3,772	—	$ 3,772
Gold. Gate Bapt. Theol. Sem.	Mill Valley, CA 94941	1944	Baptist	G/C	628	30	$ 700	—	—
Golden Gate University	San Francisco, CA 94105	1901	Independ	S-G/C	11,500	850	$ 5,000	—	$ 5,000
Golden State University	San Marcos, CA 92069	1977	Independ	S-G/C	2,311	206	$ 2,940	—	$ 2,940
Grace Bible Institute	Long Beach, CA 90807	1974	Brethren	S/C	197	18	$ 594	—	$ 594
Grace Graduate School	Long Beach, CA 90807	1974	Brethren	G/C	84	17	$ 1,500	—	$ 1,500
Graduate Theol. Union	Berkeley, CA 94709	1962	Independ	G/C	294	125	$ 4,990	—	$ 9,500
Grantham Col. of Engineering	Los Angeles, CA 90034	1951	Independ	S/C	715	—	—	—	—
Grossmont College	El Cajon, CA 92020	1961	Public	J/C	14,403	499	—	—	—
Hartnell College	Salinas, CA 93901	1920	Public	J/C	7,182	258	—	—	—
Harvey Mudd College	Kingston Hall, CA 91711	1955	Independ	S-G/C	500	68	$ 7,900	$3,450	$11,350
Hebrew Union College	Los Angeles, CA 90007	1875	Jewish	G/C	60	22	$ 4,300	—	$12,000
Holy Names College	Oakland, CA 94619	1868	Catholic	S-G/C	678	95	$ 4,950	$2,800	$ 7,750
Humboldt State University	Arcata, CA 95221	1913	State	S-G/C	7,228	500	$ 725	$2,700	$ 3,425
Humphreys College	Stockton, CA 95207	1896	Independ	J/C	370	40	$ 2,090	$1,900	$ 3,990
Humphreys College School of Law	Fresno, CA 93721	1896	Independ	P/C	30	9	$ 1,750	—	$ 1,750
Imperial Valley College	Imperial, CA 92251	1922	State	J/C	4,666	99	$ 72	—	—
Indian Valley College	Novato, CA 94947	1971	Public	J/C	3,500	67	—	—	—
Inst. of Buddhist Studies	Berkeley, CA 94704	1966	Buddhist	G/C	10	8	$ 1,140	—	$ 1,140
International College	Los Angeles, CA 90024	1970	Independ	S-G/C	337	150	$ 3,600	—	$ 7,975
Jesuit School of Theology	Berkeley, CA 94709	1934	Catholic	P/C	196	35	$ 3,015	—	—
John F. Kennedy University	Orinda, CA 94563	1964	Independ	S-G/C	1,800	400	$ 2,475	—	$ 2,475
Kensington University	Glendale, CA 91206	1976	Independ	S-G/C	1,200	—	$ 1,900	—	$ 1,950
Kings River Comm. College	Reedley, CA 93654	1926	State	J/C	3,289	125	$ 32	$2,228	$ 2,260
Lake Tahoe Comm. College	Lake Tahoe, CA 95702	1974	Public	J/C	1,800	78	$ 60	—	$ 60
Laney Comm. College	Oakland, CA 94607	1953	Public	J/C	12,191	346	$ 10	—	$ 10
Lassen College	Susanville, CA 96130	1925	State	J/C	3,000	350	$ 22	$2,100	$ 2,122
Laurence University	Santa Barbara, CA 93101	1973	Independ	G/C	120	16	$ 2,250	—	$ 2,250
L.I.F.E. Bible College	Los Angeles, CA 90026	1923	4 Square	S/C	460	22	$ 2,055	$2,025	$ 4,080
Lincoln University	San Francisco, CA 94118	1919	Independ	S-G/C	549	63	$ 2,500	—	$ 2,500
Linda Vista Bapt. Bible College	El Cajon, CA 92021	1946	Ind. Bapt.	S-G/C	85	9	$ 1,620	$1,400	$ 3,020
Living Word Bible College	Pasadena, CA 91107	1971	Gospel	J/C	45	11	$ 1,245	—	$ 1,245
Loma Linda University	Loma Linda, CA 92350	1905	7-D Adv	S-G/C	5,157	—	$ 5,490	$2,451	$ 7,941
Long Beach Comm. College	Long Beach, CA 90808	1927	Public	J/C	25,357	1,102	—	—	—
Los Angeles Baptist College	Newhall, CA 91321	1927	Baptist	S/C	310	28	$ 3,450	$2,170	$ 6,000
Los Angeles City College	Los Angeles, CA 90029	1929	Public	J/C	20,174	—	$ 100	—	$ 100
Los Ang. Col. of Chiropractic	Whittier, CA 90609	1911	Independ	P/C	708	48	$ 6,150	—	$ 6,150
Los Angeles Cultural Center	Los Angeles, CA 90006	1966	Independ	T-P/C	400	30	$ 1,500	—	$ 1,500
Los Angeles Harbor College	Wilmington, CA 90744	1949	Public	J/C	11,786	342	—	—	—
Los Angeles Pierce College	Woodland Hills, CA 91371	1947	State	J/C	24,770	572	$ 14	—	$ 14

CALIFORNIA *(continued)*

NAME	ADDRESS	FOUNDED	AFFILIATION	LEVEL/TYPE	ENROLLMENT	TEACHERS	TUITION & FEES	BOARD & ROOM	TOTAL COST
Los Angeles Southwest College	Los Angeles, CA 90047	1967	State	J/C	5,400	125	—	—	—
Los Angeles Trade-Tech. Col.	Los Angeles, CA 90015	1929	Public	J/C	17,000	485	—	—	—
Los Angeles Valley College	Van Nuys, CA 91401	1949	State	J/C	22,358	650	—	—	—
Los Medanos College	Pittsburg, CA 94565	1973	Public	J/C	5,000	190	—	—	—
Loyola Marymount University	Los Angeles, CA 90045	1911	Catholic	S-G/C	6,433	351	$ 5,500	$2,675	$ 8,175
Magna Carta University College of Law	San Francisco, CA 94080	1974	Independ	P/C	80	8	$ 1,000	—	$ 1,200
Marymount Palos Verdes Col.	Rancho Palos Verdes, CA 90274	1933	Catholic	J/C	520	44	$ 4,185	$3,600	$ 7,785
Mendocino College	Ukiah, CA 95482	1972	State	J/C	3,604	165	$ 4	—	—
Menlo College	Atherton, CA 94025	1927	Independ	J-S/C	644	71	$ 6,490	$3,450	$ 9,940
Mennonite Brethren Bible Seminary	Fresno, CA 93727	1955	Mennon	G/C	162	21	$ 2,640	—	$ 2,640
Merced College	Merced, CA 95340	1962	Public	J/C	7,800	120	$ 20	—	—
Merritt College	Oakland, CA 94602	1954	State	J/C	8,951	130	—	—	—
Mills College	Oakland, CA 94613	1852	Independ	S-G/W	907	135	$ 7,220	$3,500	$10,720
Miracosta College	Oceanside, CA 92056	1934	State	J/C	11,682	241	—	—	—
Modesto Junior College	Modesto, CA 95350	1921	State	J/C	10,996	374	$ 108	—	$ 108
Monterey Institute of International Studies	Monterey, CA 93940	1955	Private	S-G/C	444	60	$ 5,450	$3,600	$ 9,050
Monterey Peninsula College	Monterey, CA 93940	1947	State	J/C	7,517	321	$ 20	—	$ 20
Moorpark College	Moorpark, CA 93021	1967	State	J/C	9,865	132	$ 15	—	$ 15
Mount St. Mary's College	Los Angeles, CA 90049	1925	Catholic	S-G/W	1,099	132	$ 5,000	$3,025	$ 8,025
Mt. San Antonio Comm. Col.	Walnut, CA 91789	1946	State	J/C	22,934	722	$ 44	—	$ 44
Mt. San Jacinto Comm. College	San Jacinto, CA 92383	1963	State	J/C	3,678	43	$ 15	—	$ 15
Music and Arts Institute of San Francisco	San Francisco, CA 94115	1934	Independ	S-G/C	92	22	$ 2,365	$3,000	$ 5,365
Napa College	Napa, CA 94558	1942	Public	J/C	9,044	409	—	—	—
National Technical Schools	Los Angeles, CA 90037	1905	Independ	J/C	950	55	$ 2,850	—	$ 2,850
National University	San Diego, CA 92108	1971	Independ	S-G/C	7,539	504	$ 3,420	—	$ 3,420
Naval Postgraduate School	Monterey, CA 93940	1909	Federal	G/C	1,450	200	—	—	—
New College of California	San Francisco, CA 94110	1971	Independ	S-G/C	550	45	$ 3,000	—	$ 3,000
Northern Calif. Bible College	San Jose, CA 95122	1971	Church	S/C	120	10	$ 700	—	$ 750
Northrop University	Inglewood, CA 90306	1947	Independ	S-G/C	1,852	143	$ 4,950	$3,414	$ 8,364
Nyingma Institute	Berkeley, CA 94709	1973	Buddhist	G/C	200	25	$ 1,500	$1,200	$ 1,700
Occidental College	Los Angeles, CA 90041	1887	Independ	S-G/C	1,593	126	$ 7,995	$3,300	$11,295
Ohlone College	Fremont, CA 94538	1966	Public	J/C	8,294	354	—	—	—
Orange Coast College	Costa Mesa, CA 92626	1948	Public	J/C	32,000	841	$ 26	—	$ 26
Otis Art Institute	Los Angeles, CA 90057	1897	Independ	S-G/C	1,674	110	$ 5,350	$3,000	$ 8,350
Oxnard College	Oxnard, CA 93033	1975	Public	J/C	5,749	245	$ 45	—	$ 45
Pacific Christian College	Fullerton, CA 92631	1928	Christian	S-G/C	432	38	$ 2,486	$2,538	$ 5,024
Pacific Coast Baptist Bible College	San Dimas, CA 91773	1967	Baptist	S/C	383	24	$ 1,000	$2,200	$ 3,200
Pacific Oaks College	Pasadena, CA 91103	1945	Independ	S-G/C	300	30	$ 3,840	—	$ 3,840
Pacific School of Religion	Berkeley, CA 94709	1866	Int-Den	G/C	217	12	$ 3,021	$2,743	$ 5,764
Pacific States University	Los Angeles, CA 90006	1928	Independ	S-G/C	850	46	$ 2,160	—	$ 2,160
Pacific Union College	Angwin, CA 94508	1882	7-D Adv	S-G/C	1,592	144	$ 5,490	$2,145	$ 7,635
Pacific Western University	Encino, CA 91436	1976	Independ	S-G/C	3,000	—	$ 1,900	—	$ 1,900
Palo Verde Comm. College	Blythe, CA 92225	1947	Public	J/C	710	32	$ 20	—	$ 40
Palomar Community College	San Marcos, CA 92069	1946	Public	J/C	19,344	640	$ 12	—	$ 12
Pasadena City College	Pasadena, CA 91001	1924	Public	J/C	32,000	320	$ 120	—	$ 120
Pasadena Col. of Chiropractic	Pasadena, CA 91103	1971	Independ	P/C	250	27	$ 5,600	—	$ 5,600
Patten College	Oakland, CA 94601	1945	Int-Den	S/C	144	15	$ 2,472	$2,421	$ 4,893
Peninsula Univ. Col. of Law	Mountain View, CA 94043	1975	Independ	P/C	150	15	$ 1,400	—	$ 1,400
Pepperdine University	Malibu, CA 90265	1937	C of Chr	S-G/C	6,531	390	$ 7,520	$3,400	$10,920
Pitzer College	Claremont, CA 91711	1963	Independ	S/C	740	63	$ 8,610	$2,675	$11,285
Point Loma College	San Diego, CA 92106	1902	Nazarene	S-G/C	1,870	97	$ 4,029	$2,100	$ 6,129
Pomona College	Claremont, CA 91711	1887	Independ	S/C	1,390	153	$ 8,048	$3,270	$11,318
Porterville College	Porterville, CA 93257	1927	State	J/C	2,254	152	$ 30	—	$ 30
Rancho Arroyo Voc. Tech. Institute	Sacramento, CA 95826	1965	Independ	T/C	48	9	$ 4,000	—	$ 4,000
Rand Graduate Institute	Santa Monica, CA 90406	1970	Independ	G/C	54	17	$ 6,500	—	$ 6,500
Rio Hondo Comm. College	Whittier, CA 90608	1960	State	J/C	12,436	419	—	—	—
Riverside City College	Riverside, CA 92506	1916	State	J/C	14,721	523	$ 30	—	$ 30
Sacramento City College	Sacramento, CA 95822	1916	State	J/C	16,009	360	—	—	—
Saddleback College	Mission Viejo, CA 92692	1967	State	J/C	24,625	1,017	—	—	—
St. Joseph's College	Mountain View, CA 94039	1925	Catholic	S/M	101	12	$ 3,500	$ 750	$ 4,250
St. Mary's College of Calif.	Moraga, CA 94575	1863	Catholic	S-G/C	2,779	223	$ 5,400	$2,940	$ 8,340
St. Stephens Colleges & Seminary	Los Angeles, CA 90003	1952	Baptist	S-G/C	3,300	200	$ 3,778	—	$ 3,778
San Bernardino Bible College	Colton, CA 92324	1969	Independ	S/C	44	9	$ 630	—	$ 630
San Bernardino Valley College	San Bernardino, CA 92410	1926	Public	J/C	15,256	500	$ 33	—	—
San Diego City College	San Diego, CA 92101	1914	Public	J/C	16,838	853	—	—	—
San Diego Mesa College	San Diego, CA 92111	1962	State	J/C	20,900	—	—	—	—
San Diego State University	San Diego, CA 92182	1897	State	S-G/C	31,265	2,065	$ 581	$2,500	$ 3,081
Imperial Valley Campus	Calexico, CA 92231	1960	State	S-G/C	379	15	$ 581	—	—
San Fernando Valley College of Law	Sepulveda, CA 91343	1962	Independ	P/C	220	16	$ 2,148	—	$ 2,148
San Francisco Art Institute	San Francisco, CA 94133	1874	Independ	S-G/C	640	60	$ 5,110	—	—
San Fran. Bapt. Theol. Sem.	San Francisco, CA 94109	1958	Baptist	G/M	20	7	$ 1,400	—	—
San Francisco College of Mortuary Science	San Francisco, CA 94109	1932	Independ	J/C	50	8	$ 2,700	—	$ 2,700
San Francisco Cons. of Music	San Francisco, CA 94122	1917	Independ	S-G/C	225	65	$ 5,030	$3,375	$ 8,405
San Francisco State University	San Francisco, CA 94132	1899	State	S-G/C	24,467	1,752	$ 432	$4,110	$ 4,542

NAME	ADDRESS	FOUNDED	AFFILIATION	LEVEL/TYPE	ENROLLMENT	TEACHERS	TUITION & FEES	BOARD & ROOM	TOTAL COST
CALIFORNIA *(continued)*									
San Joaquin College of Law	Fresno, CA 93726	1969	Independ	P/C	165	23	$ 2,800	—	$ 2,800
San Joaquin Delta College	Stockton, CA 95207	1963	State	J/C	22,700	741	—	—	—
San Jose Bible College	San Jose, CA 95108	1939	Christian	S/C	190	16	$ 2,400	$1,800	$ 4,200
San Jose City College	San Jose, CA 95128	1921	State	J/C	13,253	179	$ 10	—	$ 10
San Jose State University	San Jose, CA 95192	1857	State	S-G/C	25,427	1,734	$ 590	$2,484	$ 3,074
Santa Ana College	Santa Ana, CA 92715	1915	State	J/C	25,772	700	$ 10	—	$ 10
Santa Barbara City College	Santa Barbara, CA 93109	1908	Public	J/C	10,823	165	$ 10	—	$ 10
Santa Monica College	Santa Monica, CA 90405	1929	State	J/C	23,199	898	$ 10	—	$ 10
Santa Rosa Junior College	Santa Rosa, CA 95401	1918	Public	J/C	23,000	734	$ 20	$1,500	$ 1,520
School of Theol. at Claremont	Claremont, CA 91711	1885	Methodist	G/C	402	28	$ 4,100	$2,715	$ 6,815
Scripps College	Claremont, CA 91711	1926	Independ	S/W	620	80	$ 7,938	$3,588	$11,526
Shasta College	Redding, CA 96099	1949	State	J/C	12,574	460	$ 16	$2,533	$ 2,549
Shiloh Bible College	Oakland, CA 94602	1967	Church	S-G/C	410	34	$ 300	—	$ 300
Sierra College	Rocklin, CA 95677	1914	State	J/C	9,838	129	$ 50	$2,220	$ 2,270
Simpson College	San Francisco, CA 94134	1921	Mission	S-G/C	265	23	$ 3,200	$2,200	$ 5,400
Skadron College of Business	San Bernardino, CA 92410	1907	Independ	T/C	380	25	$ 3,150	$1,800	$ 5,000
Skyline College	San Bruno, CA 94066	1969	State	J/C	8,450	120	$ 160	—	$ 160
Solano Community College	Suisun City, CA 94585	1945	State	J/C	10,000	359	$ 13	—	$ 413
Sonoma State University	Rohnert Park, CA 94928	1960	State	S-G/C	5,554	333	$ 710	$2,700	$ 3,410
South Bay Col. of Business	Hawthorne, CA 90250	1965	Independ	J/C	954	30	$ 4,095	—	$ 4,095
Southern Calif. Bible College	San Diego, CA 92115	1970	Independ	S/C	105	14	$ 1,500	—	$ 1,500
Southern Calif. College	Costa Mesa, CA 92626	1927	A of God	S/C	782	56	$ 1,698	$1,178	$ 2,876
Southern California College of Optometry	Fullerton, CA 92631	1904	Independ	P/C	401	70	$ 7,100	—	$ 7,100
So. Calif. Comm. Bible College	Norwalk, CA 90650	1971	Non-Den	S-G/C	170	16	$ 795	—	$ 795
So. Calif. Conserv. of Music	Sun Valley, CA 91352	1972	Independ	P/C	85	30	$ 700	—	$ 700
So. Calif. Inst. of Architecture	Santa Monica, CA 90404	1972	Independ	S-G/C	387	46	$ 3,350	—	$ 3,350
Southwestern College	Chula Vista, CA 92010	1960	State	J/C	12,333	415	$ 20	—	$ 20
Sw. Univ. School of Law	Los Angeles, CA 90005	1911	Independ	G/C	1,660	95	$ 5,700	—	$ 5,700
Stanford University	Stanford, CA 94305	1885	Private	S-G/C	13,075	1,267	$ 9,027	$3,937	$12,964
Starr King Sch. for the Ministry	Berkeley, CA 94709	1904	Unitarian	G/C	52	10	$ 2,750	—	$ 2,750
Taft College	Taft, CA 93268	1921	State	J/C	1,280	67	$ 2,159	$1,730	$ 3,700
Thomas Aquinas College	Santa Paula, CA 93060	1969	Catholic	S/C	113	15	$ 5,245	$2,735	$ 7,980
Union University	Los Angeles, CA 90033	1973	Private	S-G/C	200	15	$ 3,600	—	$ 4,100
United College of Business	Hollywood, CA 90028	1969	Independ	T/C	600	16	$ 4,000	—	$ 4,000
U.S. International University	San Diego, CA 92131	1952	Independ	S-G/C	3,500	225	$ 5,025	$2,772	$ 7,797
University of California									
Berkeley Campus	Berkeley, CA 94720	1868	State	S-G/C	29,308	1,600	$ 1,430	$7,562	$ 8,992
Davis Campus	Davis, CA 95616	1905	State	S-G/C	19,321	1,346	$ 1,290	$2,600	$ 3,890
Hastings College of Law	San Francisco, CA 94102	1868	State	G/C	1,500	53	$ 1,239	—	$ 1,239
Irvine Campus	Irvine, CA 92717	1965	State	S-G/C	11,270	491	$ 1,215	$3,070	$ 4,285
Los Angeles Campus	Los Angeles, CA 90024	1919	State	S-G/C	34,568	3,000	$ 1,344	$2,390	$ 3,734
Riverside Campus	Riverside, CA 92521	1954	State	S-G/C	4,787	374	$ 1,350	$2,645	$ 3,995
San Diego Campus	La Jolla, CA 92093	1912	State	S-G/C	12,319	850	$ 1,196	$3,300	$ 4,496
Santa Barbara Campus	Santa Barbara, CA 93106	1944	State	S-G/C	16,163	847	$ 1,362	$2,570	$ 3,932
Santa Cruz Campus	Santa Cruz, CA 95064	1965	State	S-G/C	6,819	455	$ 1,267	$3,057	$ 4,324
University of Judaism	Los Angeles, CA 90077	1947	Independ	S-G/C	208	40	$ 3,040	$5,490	$ 8,530
University of La Verne	La Verne, CA 91750	1891	Independ	S-G/C	1,349	94	$ 5,550	$2,750	$ 8,300
Univ. of Oriental Studies	Los Angeles, CA 90006	1973	Independ	S-G/C	25	10	$ 4,000	—	$ 5,500
University of Redlands	Redlands, CA 92373	1907	Independ	S-G/C	1,217	115	$ 6,865	$2,860	$ 9,725
University of San Diego	San Diego, CA 92110	1949	Catholic	S-G/C	5,003	317	$ 5,760	$3,088	$ 8,848
University of San Francisco	San Francisco, CA 94117	1855	Catholic	S-G/C	6,500	277	$ 5,380	$3,124	$ 9,504
University of Santa Clara	Santa Clara, CA 95053	1851	Catholic	S-G/C	7,266	438	$ 5,607	$3,030	$ 8,637
University of Southern California	Los Angeles, CA 90089	1880	Independ	S-G/C	29,411	1,668	$ 7,928	$3,442	$11,370
University of the Pacific	Stockton, CA 95211	1851	Independ	S-G/C	5,884	367	$ 7,780	$3,262	$11,042
Univ. of West Los Angeles	Culver City, CA 90230	1966	Independ	S-P/C	715	54	$ 2,200	—	—
Ventura College	Ventura, CA 93003	1925	State	J/C	13,664	173	$ 95	—	$ 95
Ventura College of Law	Ventura, CA 93001	1969	Independ	P/C	150	15	$ 2,200	—	$ 2,200
Victor Valley College	Victorville, CA 92392	1960	Public	J/C	4,312	69	$ 16	—	$ 16
West Coast University	Los Angeles, CA 90020	1909	Independ	S-G/C	1,822	162	$ 3,063	—	$ 3,063
West Hills Community College	Coalinga, CA 93210	1932	State	J/C	2,313	136	$ 1,550	—	$ 1,550
West Los Angeles College	Culver City, CA 90230	1968	District	J/C	12,620	171	—	—	$ 2,200
West Valley College	Saratoga, CA 95070	1963	Public	J/C	16,458	180	$ 28	—	$ 28
Western State University College of Law	Fullerton, CA 92631	1966	Independ	S-G/C	1,326	68	$ 4,170	—	$ 4,170
Western State University College of Law	San Diego, CA 92101	1969	Independ	P/C	779	32	$ 4,170	—	$ 4,170
Western State College of Engineering	Inglewood, CA 90301	1946	Independ	S/C	112	14	$ 2,300	—	$ 2,300
Westmont College	Santa Barbara, CA 93108	1940	Independ	S-C	1,010	80	$ 5,870	$2,960	$ 8,830
Whittier College	Whittier, CA 90608	1887	Independ	S-G/C	1,541	137	$ 6,861	$2,706	$ 9,567
Woodbury University	Los Angeles, CA 90017	1884	Independ	S-G/C	1,203	88	$ 4,100	—	$ 4,100
World College West	San Rafael, CA 94912	1973	Independ	S/C	65	10	$ 4,500	$2,700	$ 7,200
Wright Institute	Berkeley, CA 94704	1968	Private	G/C	156	25	$ 5,900	—	—
Yeshiva Univ. of Los Angeles	Los Angeles, CA 90035	1977	Jewish	S/M	65	11	$ 2,300	$2,500	$ 4,800
Yuba College	Marysville, CA 95901	1927	State	J/C	8,463	440	$ 28	$2,500	$ 2,528
COLORADO									
Adams State College	Alamosa, CO 81102	1921	State	S-G/C	2,009	85	$ 986	$2,000	$ 2,986
Aims Community College	Greeley, CO 80634	1967	Public	J/C	6,300	329	$ 396	—	$ 396
Arapahoe Community College	Littleton, CO 80120	1965	State	J/C	6,488	208	$ 716	—	$ 716

COLORADO *(continued)*

NAME	ADDRESS	FOUNDED	AFFILIATION	LEVEL/TYPE	ENROLLMENT	TEACHERS	TUITION & FEES	BOARD & ROOM	TOTAL COST
Baptist Bible Col. of Denver	Broomfield, CO 80020	1952	Baptist	S-G/C	159	15	$ 2,710	$2,440	$ 5,150
Belleview College	Westminster, CO 80030	1921	P/Fire	S/C	25	5	$ 1,800	$1,250	$ 3,050
Colorado College	Colorado Spgs., CO 80903	1874	Independ	S/C	1,968	137	$ 6,950	$2,400	$ 9,350
Colorado Mountain College	Glenwood Spgs., CO 81602	1967	Public	J/C	8,150	630	$ 382	$2,100	$ 2,482
Colorado Northwest. Comm. College	Rangely, CO 81648	1962	Public	J/C	2,540	242	$ 580	$1,950	$ 2,530
Colorado School of Mines	Golden, CO 80401	1874	State	S-G/C	2,948	240	$ 2,550	$2,450	$ 5,000
Colorado State University	Fort Collins, CO 80523	1870	State	S/C	18,909	965	$ 1,190	$2,750	$ 3,940
Colorado Technical College	Colorado Spgs., CO 80907	1965	Independ	J-S/C	602	40	$ 3,500	—	—
Community College of Denver	Denver, CO 80218	1967	State	J/C	16,800	302	$ 650	—	$ 650
Auraria Campus	Denver, CO 80204	1970	State	J/C	4,843	80	—	—	—
Fort Range Comm. College	Westminster, CO 80030	1968	State	J/C	5,679	264	$ 689	—	$ 689
Red Rocks Campus	Golden, CO 80401	1969	State	J/C	4,950	91	—	—	—
Denver Conservative Baptist Theological Seminary	Denver, CO 80210	1950	Baptist	G/C	491	44	$ 2,880	$1,300	$ 4,180
Fort Lewis College	Durango, CO 81301	1933	State	S/C	3,503	184	$ 827	$2,025	$ 2,852
Iliff School of Theology	Denver, CO 80210	1892	Methodist	G/C	339	21	$ 2,670	$ 860	$ 3,530
Lamar Community College	Lamar, CO 81052	1937	State	J/C	523	39	$ 819	$1,998	$ 2,817
Loretto Heights College	Denver, CO 80236	1918	Independ	S/C	811	106	$ 4,900	$2,700	$ 7,600
Mesa College	Grand Junction, CO 81502	1925	State	S/C	4,457	146	$ 1,000	$2,138	$ 3,138
Metropolitan State College	Denver, CO 80204	1963	State	S/C	17,384	713	$ 900	—	$ 900
Nat. Col.–Colo. Springs Ext.	Colorado Spgs., CO 80932	1974	Private	S/C	193	31	$ 2,406	—	$ 2,406
Nat. College of Business–Ext.	Denver, CO 80221	1974	Private	S/C	118	11	$ 2,190	—	$ 2,190
Nat. College of Business–Ext.	Pueblo, CO 81004	1975	Private	S/C	130	17	$ 2,349	—	$ 2,349
Northeastern Junior College	Sterling, CO 80751	1941	District	J/C	1,537	62	$ 705	$2,130	$ 2,835
Otero Junior College	La Junta, CO 81050	1941	State	J/C	850	41	$ 771	$2,145	$ 2,916
Pikes Peak Comm. College	Colorado Spgs., CO 80906	1967	State	J/C	6,034	499	$ 670	—	$ 670
Pueblo Vocational Comm. Col.	Pueblo, CO 81004	1933	State	T/C	1,070	85	$ 678	—	$ 678
Regis College	Denver, CO 80221	1877	Catholic	S/C	1,057	69	$ 5,700	$3,150	$ 8,850
Rockmont College	Denver, CO 80226	1914	Independ	S/C	306	26	$ 3,640	$2,330	$ 5,970
St. Thomas Theol. Seminary	Denver, CO 80210	1907	Catholic	S-G/M	114	25	$ 2,310	$2,250	$ 4,560
Trinidad State Junior College	Trinidad, CO 81082	1925	State	J/C	1,199	50	$ 621	$2,124	$ 2,745
U.S. Air Force Academy	USAF, CO 80840	1955	Federal	S/C	4,400	575	—	—	—
University of Colorado	Boulder, CO 80309	1876	State	S-G/C	22,177	1,500	$ 1,335	$2,423	$ 3,758
Colorado Springs Campus	Colorado Spgs., CO 80933	1965	State	S-G/C	5,288	307	$ 825	—	$ 825
Denver	Denver, CO 80202	1938	State	S-G/C	10,720	464	$ 798	—	$ 798
Health Sciences Center	Denver, CO 80262	1883	State	S-G/C	1,385	705	—	—	—
University of Denver	Denver, CO 80208	1864	Independ	S-G/C	8,296	650	$ 6,696	$2,950	$ 9,646
University of Northern Colo.	Greeley, CO 80639	1889	State	S-G/C	9,671	573	$ 1,105	$2,400	$ 3,505
University of Southern Colo.	Pueblo, CO 81001	1933	State	S-G/C	4,856	262	$ 974	$2,280	$ 3,254
Western Bible College	Denver, CO 80465	1948	Int-Den	S/C	218	20	$ 2,700	$1,950	$ 4,650
Western Colorado College of Business	Grand Junction, CO 81502	1976	Independ	T/C	50	5	$ 1,950	—	$ 1,950
Western Colorado University	Grand Junction, CO 81502	1971	Independ	S-G/C	300	8	$ 2,550	—	$ 2,550
Western State College of Colo.	Gunnison, CO 81230	1901	State	S-G/C	2,950	160	$ 700	$1,950	$ 2,650

CONNECTICUT

NAME	ADDRESS	FOUNDED	AFFILIATION	LEVEL/TYPE	ENROLLMENT	TEACHERS	TUITION & FEES	BOARD & ROOM	TOTAL COST
Albertus Magnus College	New Haven, CT 06511	1925	Catholic	S/W	499	56	$ 4,700	$2,900	$ 7,600
Bridgeport Engineering Inst.	Bridgeport, CT 06606	1924	Independ	S/C	901	91	$ 1,800	—	$ 1,800
Central Conn. State University	New Britain, CT 06050	1849	State	S-G/C	12,487	624	$ 931	$2,446	$ 3,377
Connecticut College	New London, CT 06320	1911	Independ	S-G/C	1,933	232	$ 8,750	$2,700	$11,450
Eastern Conn. State University	Willimantic, CT 06226	1889	Public	S-G/C	3,416	208	$ 914	$2,186	$ 3,100
Fairfield University	Fairfield, CT 06430	1924	Catholic	S-G/C	4,960	286	$ 5,650	$3,095	$ 8,745
Greater Hartford Comm. Col.	Hartford, CT 06105	1967	State	J/C	3,776	80	$ 520	—	$ 520
Hartford College For Women	Hartford, CT 06105	1939	Independ	J/W	221	35	$ 4,600	$2,850	$ 7,450
Hartford Graduate Center	Hartford, CT 06120	1955	Independ	G/C	1,931	42	—	—	—
Hartford State Tech. College	Hartford, CT 06106	1946	State	T/C	1,983	78	$ 492	—	$ 492
Holy Apostles Sem./College	Cromwell, CT 06416	1957	Catholic	S-G/C	152	24	$ 2,000	$2,200	$ 4,200
Housatonic Community Col.	Bridgeport, CT 06608	1967	State	J/C	2,649	91	$ 434	—	$ 434
Manchester Community Col.	Manchester, CT 06040	1963	State	J/C	6,500	210	$ 434	—	$ 434
Mattatuck Community College	Waterbury, CT 06708	1967	State	J/C	4,136	90	$ 434	—	$ 434
Middlesex Community College	Middletown, CT 06067	1966	State	J/C	2,986	84	$ 434	—	$ 654
Mitchell College	New London, CT 06320	1938	Independ	J/C	544	28	$ 5,400	$2,700	$ 8,100
Morse School of Business	Hartford, CT 06103	1860	Independ	J/C	850	70	$ 2,600	—	$ 2,600
Mount Sacred Heart College	Hamden, CT 06514	1954	Catholic	J/W	14	9	—	—	—
Northwest Conn. Comm. Col.	Winsted, CT 06098	1965	State	J/C	2,371	105	$ 334	—	$ 334
Norwalk Comm. College	Norwalk, CT 06854	1961	State	J/C	3,511	92	$ 434	—	$ 434
Norwalk State Tech. College	Norwalk, CT 06854	1961	State	T/C	2,021	104	$ 492	—	$ 492
Post College	Waterbury, CT 06708	1890	Independ	J-S/C	1,484	69	$ 4,000	$2,500	$ 6,500
Quinnipiac College	Hamden, CT 06518	1929	Independ	S-G/C	3,631	342	$ 4,700	$2,500	$ 7,200
Sacred Heart University	Bridgeport, CT 06606	1963	Independ	S-G/C	5,072	257	$ 3,450	—	—
St. Alphonsus College	Suffield, CT 06078	1963	Catholic	S/M	68	17	$ 2,700	$1,800	$ 4,500
St. Basil's College	Stamford, CT 06902	1939	Catholic	S/M	7	9	$ 3,000	$2,600	$ 5,600
St. Joseph College	West Hartford, CT 06117	1932	Catholic	S-G/W	1,212	122	$ 4,820	$2,900	$ 7,720
Southern Conn. State College	New Haven, CT 06515	1893	State	S-G/C	10,846	621	$ 792	$2,242	$ 3,034
Thames Valley St. Tech. College	Norwich, CT 06360	1963	State	T/C	1,147	45	$ 492	—	$ 492
Trinity College	Hartford, CT 06106	1823	Independ	S-G/C	1,800	142	$ 8,320	$3,050	$11,370
Tunxis Community College	Farmington, CT 06032	1970	State	J/C	4,435	166	$ 434	—	$ 434
U.S. Coast Guard Academy	New London, CT 06320	1876	Federal	S/C	939	115	—	—	—
University of Bridgeport	Bridgeport, CT 06601	1927	Independ	S-G/C	6,344	272	$ 5,963	$3,104	$ 9,069
University of Connecticut	Storrs, CT 06268	1881	State	S-G/C	22,800	1,141	$ 1,470	$2,330	$ 3,800
Health Center	Farmington, CT 06032	1961	State	G/C	1,107	298	—	—	—

NAME	ADDRESS	FOUNDED	AFFILIATION	LEVEL/TYPE	ENROLLMENT	TEACHERS	TUITION & FEES	BOARD & ROOM	TOTAL COST
CONNECTICUT *(continued)*									
University of Hartford	West Hartford, CT 06117	1877	Independ	S-G/C	8,563	639	$ 6,970	$3,847	$10,183
University of New Haven	West Haven, CT 06516	1920	Independ	S-G/C	7,298	350	$ 4,120	$2,278	$ 6,398
Waterbury State Tech. College	Waterbury, CT 06708	1964	State	J/C	1,968	113	$ 453	—	$ 453
Wesleyan University	Middletown, CT 06457	1831	Independ	S-G/C	3,006	275	$ 9,100	$3,300	$12,400
Western Conn. State College	Danbury, CT 06810	1903	State	S-G/C	5,996	222	$ 931	$2,123	$ 3,054
Yale University	New Haven, CT 06520	1701	Independ	S-G/C	10,369	1,708	$ 9,050	$3,930	$12,980
DELAWARE									
Delaware State College	Dover, DE 19901	1891	State	S-G/C	2,151	144	$ 700	$2,000	$ 2,700
Delaware Tech. & Comm. Col.	Dover, DE 19901	1967	State	T/C	9,281	620	$ 576	—	$ 576
Goldey Beacom College	Wilmington, DE 19808	1886	Independ	S/C	1,863	78	$ 3,050	$1,759	$ 4,800
University of Delaware	Newark, DE 19711	1833	State	S-G/C	18,600	1,050	$ 1,367	$2,254	$ 3,621
Wesley College	Dover, DE 19901	1873	Methodist	S/C	1,218	49	$ 5,450	$2,750	$ 8,110
Widener University									
Brandywine College	Wilmington, DE 19803	1965	Independ	J/C	756	48	$ 3,950	$2,750	$ 6,700
Delaware Law School	Wilmington, DE 19803	1971	Independ	P/C	864	53	$ 5,100	—	$ 5,100
School of Hotel & Restaurant Management	Wilmington, DE 19803	1981	Independ	S/C	292	10	$ 4,300	$2,750	$ 7,050
University College	Wilmington, DE 19803	1980	Independ	S/C	695	51	$ 996	—	$ 996
Wilmington College	New Castle, DE 19720	1967	Independ	S-G/C	1,003	70	$ 3,000	$1,100	$ 4,100
DISTRICT OF COLUMBIA									
American University	Washington, DC 20016	1893	Methodist	S-G/C	11,548	936	$ 7,070	$3,453	$10,523
Antioch School of Law	Washington, DC 20009	1852	Independ	G/C	469	45	$ 5,780	—	$ 5,780
Beacon College	Washington, DC 20009	1971	Independ	S-G/C	175	—	$ 3,000	—	$ 3,000
Benjamin Franklin University	Washington, DC 20036	1925	Independ	S-G/C	415	26	$ 2,700	—	$ 2,700
Catholic University of America	Washington, DC 20064	1887	Catholic	S-G/C	7,057	427	$ 6,000	$3,350	$ 9,350
Gallaudet College	Washington, DC 20002	1864	Private	S-G/C	1,510	219	$ 1,654	$2,560	$ 4,214
George Washington University	Washington, DC 20052	1821	Independ	S-G/C	19,150	1,712	$ 6,248	$3,690	$ 9,938
Georgetown University	Washington, DC 20057	1789	Catholic	S-G/C	12,020	1,578	$ 6,830	$2,750	$ 9,580
Howard University	Washington, DC 20059	1867	Independ	S-G/C	11,624	1,992	$ 2,550	$2,367	$ 4,917
Mount Vernon College	Washington, DC 20007	1875	Independ	S/W	489	40	$ 5,600	$3,800	$ 9,400
Sch. of Ad. Inter. Stud.-J.H.U.	Washington, DC 20036	1943	Independ	G/C	383	117	$ 8,140	$4,600	$12,740
Southeastern University	Washington, DC 20024	1879	Independ	S-G/C	1,593	308	$ 3,525	—	$ 3,525
Strayer College	Washington, DC 20005	1904	Independ	S/C	1,773	67	$ 2,976	—	$ 2,976
Trinity College	Washington, DC 20017	1897	Catholic	S-G/W	1,158	87	$ 5,900	$3,800	$ 9,700
USDA Graduate School	Washington, DC 20250	1921	Independ	G-C	25,000	700	$ 345	—	$ 345
Univ. of the Dist. of Columbia	Washington, DC 20008	1976	Public	J-S/C	14,107	568	$ 364	—	$ 364
Washington Musical Institute	Washington, DC 20016	1928	Independ	S-G/C	180	6	—	—	—
Wesley Theological Seminary	Washington, DC 20016	1882	Un. Meth	G/C	358	40	$ 3,150	$1,620	$ 4,770
FLORIDA									
Apostolic Bible School	Lakeland, FL 33801	1934	Church	J/C	17	7	$ 140	—	$ 140
Art Inst. of Fort Lauderdale	Fort Lauderdale, FL 33316	1968	Independ	T/C	1,225	55	$ 4,000	—	$ 8,000
Baptist Bible Institute	Graceville, FL 32440	1943	Baptist	S/C	399	20	$ 956	$ 544	$ 1,500
Barry University	Miami Shores, FL 33161	1940	Catholic	S-G/C	3,218	220	$ 4,700	$2,500	$ 7,200
Bauder College	Fort Lauderdale, FL 33334	1964	Independ	J/C	463	23	$ 4,390	$1,850	$ 6,240
Bethune-Cookman College	Daytona Beach, FL 32015	1904	Un. Meth	S/C	1,636	120	$ 3,212	$2,212	$ 5,424
Biscayne College	Miami, FL 33054	1961	Catholic	S-G/C	3,200	350	$ 2,300	$2,700	$ 5,000
Brevard Community College	Cocoa, FL 32922	1960	State	J/C	11,000	628	$ 608	—	$ 608
Broward Community College	Fort Lauderdale, FL 33301	1960	State	J/C	22,515	726	$ 570	—	$ 570
Central Florida Bible College	Orlando, FL 32856	1957	Church	S/C	130	10	$ 1,962	$1,077	$ 3,039
Central Florida Comm. College	Ocala, FL 32678	1957	State	J/C	3,195	99	$ 576	—	$ 576
Chipola Junior College	Marianna, FL 32446	1947	State	J/C	1,173	52	$ 510	$1,550	$ 2,000
Clearwater Christian College	Clearwater, FL 33519	1965	Independ	S/C	227	22	$ 2,137	$2,300	$ 4,437
College of Boca Raton	Boca Raton, FL 33431	1963	Independ	S/C	500	60	$ 5,000	$2,200	$ 7,200
College of the Palm Beaches	W. Palm Beach, FL 33401	1926	Independ	S-G/C	350	15	$ 1,800	—	$ 1,800
Daytona Beach Comm. College	Daytona Beach, FL 32015	1958	State	J/C	21,000	638	$ 584	—	$ 584
Eckerd College	St. Petersburg, FL 33712	1958	Presby	S/C	1,102	69	$ 5,495	$2,360	$ 7,855
Edison Community College	Fort Myers, FL 33907	1962	State	J/C	5,647	244	$ 540	—	$ 540
Edward Waters College	Jacksonville, FL 32209	1866	AME	S/C	867	53	$ 2,280	$3,100	$ 5,380
Embry-Riddle Aero. University	Daytona Beach, FL 32010	1926	Independ	S-G/C	5,765	293	$ 2,930	$2,350	$ 5,280
Faith Bible College	Milton, FL 32570	1974	Baptist	S/C	18	9	$ 800	—	—
Flagler College	St. Augustine, FL 32084	1968	Independ	S/C	985	77	$ 2,830	$1,800	$ 4,630
Florida A&M University	Tallahassee, FL 32307	1887	State	S-G/C	4,689	428	$ 795	$1,782	$ 2,577
Florida Atlantic University	Boca Raton, FL 33431	1961	State	S-G/C	9,292	322	$ 900	$2,445	$ 3,345
Florida Baptist College	Lakeland, FL 33802	1968	Baptist	S-G/C	45	9	$ 680	$ 900	$ 1,580
Florida Beacon College	Largo, FL 33541	1956	Independ	G/C	45	12	$ 1,365	$1,617	$ 2,982
Florida Bible College	Kissimmee, FL 32741	1962	Independ	S/C	168	17	$ 1,850	$2,600	$ 4,450
Florida College	Temple Terrace, FL 33617	1946	Independ	J/C	447	36	$ 2,200	$1,500	$ 3,700
Florida Inst. of Bible Studies	West Palm Beach, FL 33411	1975	Baptist	S-G/C	33	10	$ 445	$3,600	$ 3,900
Florida Inst. of Technology	Melbourne, FL 32901	1958	Independ	S-G/C	5,222	289	$ 4,182	$2,370	$ 6,552
Florida International University	Miami, FL 33199	1965	State	S-G/C	13,640	670	$ 867	—	$ 867
Fla. Jr. Col. at Jacksonville	Jacksonville, FL 32202	1966	State	J/C	15,647	348	$ 480	—	$ 480
Florida Keys Comm. College	Key West, FL 33040	1965	State	J/C	1,700	35	$ 480	$2,570	$ 3,050
Florida Memorial College	Miami, FL 33054	1879	Baptist	S/C	1,001	72	$ 2,540	$1,900	$ 4,440
Florida Southern College	Lakeland, FL 33802	1885	Methodist	S/C	1,938	176	$ 3,645	$2,350	$ 5,995
Florida State University	Tallahassee, FL 32306	1857	State	S-G/C	22,020	1,500	$ 841	$2,100	$ 2,941
Florida Theological Center	Miami, FL 33135	1979	Presby.	G/M	15	2	$ 1,700	—	$ 1,700
Fort Lauderdale College	Fort Lauderdale, FL 33301	1940	Private	S/C	936	36	$ 2,020	—	$ 2,020
Freedom Seminary	Orlando, FL 32805	1973	Independ	S-G/C	1,050	85	$ 1,100	—	$ 1,100

FLORIDA *(continued)*

NAME	ADDRESS	FOUNDED	AFFILIATION	LEVEL/TYPE	ENROLLMENT	TEACHERS	TUITION & FEES	BOARD & ROOM	TOTAL COST
Gulf Coast Comm. College	Panama City, FL 32401	1957	State	J/C	4,000	74	$ 550	—	$ 550
Heritage College	Orlando, FL 32808	1976	Baptist	J-S/C	66	8	$ 1,000	$1,800	$ 2,800
Hillsborough Comm. College	Tampa, FL 33622	1968	State	J/C	12,142	173	$ 540	—	$ 540
Hobe Sound Bible College	Hobe Sound, FL 33455	1960	Independ	S/C	240	25	$ 1,650	$1,500	$ 3,150
Independian River Comm. College	Fort Pierce, FL 33450	1959	State	J/C	9,500	140	$ 500	—	$ 500
International Fine Arts College	Miami, FL 33132	1965	Independ	J/C	255	23	$ 5,985	$1,800	$ 7,785
Jacksonville University	Jacksonville, FL 32211	1934	Independ	S-G/C	2,419	191	$ 4,380	$2,490	$ 6,870
Jones College	Jacksonville, FL 32211	1918	Independ	S/C	1,605	70	$ 1,873	—	$ 1,873
Lake City Comm. College	Lake City, FL 32055	1947	State	J/C	2,872	114	$ 544	$1,420	$ 1,964
Lakeland College	Lakeland, FL 33803	1929	Independ	J/C	238	8	$ 3,420	—	$ 3,420
Lake-Sumter Comm. College	Leesburg, FL 32748	1962	State	J/C	2,076	99	$ 648	—	$ 648
Landmark Baptist College	Haines City, FL 33844	1979	Baptist	S-G/C	90	15	$ 1,800	$1,900	$ 3,700
Liberty Bible College	Pensacola, FL 32506	1966	Int-Den	S-G/C	300	18	$ 1,200	$1,600	$ 2,800
Luther Rice Seminary	Jacksonville, FL 32207	1962	Independ	P/C	2,100	25	$ 1,200	—	$ 1,200
Manatee Junior College	Bradenton, FL 33506	1957	State	J/C	6,604	248	$ 578	—	$ 578
Miami Christian College	Miami, FL 33167	1949	Int-Den	S/C	321	12	$ 2,750	$2,080	$ 4,830
Miami-Dade Comm. College	Miami, FL 33176	1960	State	J/C	42,226	804	$ 570	—	$ 570
Nassau Baptist College	Yulee, FL 32097	1974	Baptist	G/C	25	4	$ 250	—	$ 250
North Florida Junior College	Madison, FL 32340	1958	State	J/C	865	42	$ 420	$1,570	$ 1,990
Nova University	Ft. Lauderdale, FL 33314	1964	Independ	S-G/C	5,655	176	$ 3,500	$2,500	$ 6,000
Okaloosa-Walton Jr. College	Niceville, FL 32578	1963	State	J/C	6,518	135	$ 510	—	$ 510
Orlando College	Orlando, FL 32810	1953	Baptist	S/C	1,121	58	$ 1,922	—	$ 1,922
Palm Beach Atlantic College	W. Palm Beach, FL 33401	1968	Baptist	S/C	651	30	$ 2,100	$1,500	$ 3,600
Palm Beach Baptist Bible Inst.	Loxahatchee, FL 33470	1975	Baptist	S-G/C	20	5	$ 320	$5,000	$ 5,320
Palm Beach Junior College	Lake Worth, FL 33461	1933	State	J/C	13,115	489	$ 608	—	$ 608
Pasco-Hernando Comm. Col.	Dade City, FL 33525	1967	State	J/C	3,018	178	$ 550	—	$ 550
Pensacola Christian College	Pensacola, FL 32523	1974	Independ	S-G/C	800	50	$ 1,600	$1,600	$ 3,200
Pensacola Junior College	Pensacola, FL 32504	1948	State	J/C	16,659	678	$ 495	—	$ 495
Polk Community College	Winter Haven, FL 33881	1964	State	J/C	5,566	180	$ 462	—	$ 462
Prospect Hall College	Hollywood, FL 33020	1929	Independ	J/C	400	30	$ 3,600	—	$ 3,600
Ringling School of Art	Sarasota, FL 33580	1931	Independ	S/C	459	30	$ 3,500	$2,000	$ 5,500
Roger Williams College	Tampa, FL 33617	1936	Baptist	P/C	—	15	$ 2,500	—	$ 2,500
Rollins College	Winter Park, FL 32789	1885	Independ	S-G/C	1,362	104	$ 5,936	$2,640	$ 8,576
St. John Vianney Col. Sem.	Miami, FL 33165	1959	Catholic	S/M	65	22	$ 1,900	$1,850	$ 3,750
St. John's River Comm. College	Palatka, FL 32077	1958	State	J/C	1,656	97	$ 480	—	$ 480
St. Leo College	Saint Leo, FL 33574	1889	Catholic	S/C	1,160	67	$ 3,888	$1,335	$ 5,218
St. Petersburg Junior College	St. Petersburg, FL 33733	1927	State	J/C	16,357	311	$ 570	—	$ 570
St. Vincent De Paul Reg. Sem.	Boynton Beach, FL 33435	1963	Church	G/C	106	38	$ 1,350	$3,650	$ 5,000
Santa Fe Comm. College	Gainesville, FL 32601	1966	State	J/C	7,354	220	$ 570	—	$ 570
Sarasota Theological Sem.	Sarasota, FL 33579	1979	Independ	G/C	—	—	$ 500	—	$ 500
Seminole Community College	Sanford, FL 32771	1965	State	J/C	5,172	203	$ 550	—	$ 550
S. E. Col. of the Assem. of God	Lakeland, FL 33801	1935	A of God	S/C	1,092	44	$ 848	$1,550	$ 2,398
South Florida Junior College	Avon Park, FL 33825	1965	State	J/C	1,080	32	$ 660	—	$ 660
Southern College	Orlando, FL 32807	1968	Independ	J/C	650	34	$ 1,930	—	$ 1,930
Spurgeon Baptist Bible College	Mulberry, FL 33860	1970	Baptist	S/C	64	9	$ 1,680	$1,750	$ 3,430
Stetson University	DeLand, FL 32720	1883	Baptist	S-G/C	2,903	201	$ 4,740	$1,995	$ 6,735
Tallahassee Comm. College	Tallahassee, FL 32304	1965	State	J/C	4,971	185	$ 420	—	$ 420
Talmudic College of Florida	Miami Beach, FL 33140	1974	Jewish	S-G/M	112	8	$ 2,100	$2,000	$ 4,100
Tampa College	Tampa, FL 33607	1890	Independ	S/C	1,412	65	$ 1,700	—	$ 1,700
Tampa Tech. Institute	Tampa, FL 33610	1948	Independ	T/C	1,813	57	$ 3,920	—	$ 3,920
Transylvania Bible College	Lakeworth, FL 33463	1975	Int-Den	S/C	16	4	$ 450	—	$ 450
Trinity Baptist College	Jacksonville, FL 32205	1974	Baptist	S/C	307	19	$ 1,700	$2,100	$ 3,800
Trinity College	Dunedin, FL 33528	1932	Independ	S-G/C	100	20	$ 1,000	$1,200	$ 2,200
United Bible Col. & Seminary	Orlando, FL 32858	1979	Independ	G/C	130	7	$ 450	—	$ 450
United Electronics Institute	Tampa, FL 33606	1967	Independ	J/C	956	24	$ 4,200	—	—
University of Central Florida	Orlando, FL 32816	1963	State	S-G/C	14,180	546	$ 936	$2,322	$ 3,258
University of Florida	Gainesville, FL 32611	1853	State	S-G/C	33,400	1,813	$ 841	$2,674	$ 3,515
University of Miami	Coral Gables, FL 33124	1925	Private	S-G/C	20,067	1,257	$ 5,700	$2,550	$ 9,075
University of North Florida	Jacksonville, FL 32216	1965	State	S-G/C	5,622	163	$ 849	—	$ 849
University of Sarasota	Sarasota, FL 33577	1973	Independ	G/C	160	9	$ 4,275	—	$ 4,275
University of South Florida	Tampa, FL 33620	1956	State	S-G/C	25,743	1,145	$ 886	$2,198	$ 2,721
New College	Sarasota, FL 33580	1960	Public	S/C	350	47	$ 946	$2,140	$ 3,086
University of Tampa	Tampa, FL 33606	1931	Independ	S-G/C	2,206	251	$ 5,678	$2,782	$ 8,460
University of West Florida	Pensacola, FL 32514	1963	State	S-G/C	5,217	344	$ 840	$1,780	$ 2,620
Valencia Community College	Orlando, FL 32802	1967	State	J/C	11,123	670	$ 570	—	$ 570
Walden University	Naples, FL 33940	1970	Independ	G/C	200	10	$ 6,900	$1,000	$ 7,900
Warner Southern College	Lake Wales, FL 33853	1968	C of God	S/C	304	43	$ 3,400	$1,750	$ 5,150
Webber College	Babson Park, FL 33827	1927	Independ	S/C	308	15	$ 3,090	$2,080	$ 5,170
Yeshiva Gedolah Rabbin. Col.	Miami Beach, FL 33139	1973	Jewish	S-G/M	60	3	$ 2,000	$2,000	$ 4,000

GEORGIA

NAME	ADDRESS	FOUNDED	AFFILIATION	LEVEL/TYPE	ENROLLMENT	TEACHERS	TUITION & FEES	BOARD & ROOM	TOTAL COST
Abraham Baldwin Agri. College	Tifton, GA 31793	1908	State	J/C	2,215	105	$ 633	$1,905	$ 2,538
Agnes Scott College	Decatur, GA 30030	1889	Independ	S/W	533	80	$ 5,575	$2,250	$ 7,825
Albany Junior College	Albany, GA 31707	1963	State	J/C	1,911	90	$ 450	—	$ 450
Albany State College	Albany, GA 31705	1903	State	S-G/C	1,832	136	$ 855	$1,650	$ 2,505
Amer. Col. for Applied Arts	Atlanta, GA 30342	1975	Independ	S/C	171	20	$ 4,035	$1,875	$ 5,910
Andrew College	Cuthbert, GA 31740	1854	Un. Meth	J/C	330	22	$ 1,938	$2,049	$ 3,993
Armstrong State College	Savannah, GA 31406	1935	State	S-G/C	2,992	189	$ 800	—	$ 1,000
Atlanta Area Tech. School	Atlanta, GA 30310	1967	Public	T/C	1,900	125	$ 200	—	$ 200
Atlanta Christian College	East Point, GA 30344	1937	Christian	S/C	178	18	$ 1,800	$1,750	$ 3,550
Atlanta College of Art	Atlanta, GA 30309	1928	Independ	S/C	271	32	$ 4,325	$3,305	$ 7,630
Atlanta Junior College	Atlanta, GA 30310	1974	State	J/C	1,585	64	$ 489	—	$ 489
Atlanta University	Atlanta, GA 30314	1867	Independ	S-G/C	1,082	144	$ 3,600	$1,250	$ 4,850
Augusta Area Tech. School	Augusta, GA 30906	1961	State	T/C	2,600	125	$ 150	—	$ 150

GEORGIA *(continued)*

NAME	ADDRESS	FOUNDED	AFFILIATION	LEVEL/TYPE	ENROLLMENT	TEACHERS	TUITION & FEES	BOARD & ROOM	TOTAL COST
Augusta College	Augusta, GA 30910	1925	State	S-G/C	4,159	174	$ 750	—	$ 750
Bainbridge Junior College	Bainbridge, GA 31717	1973	State	J/C	662	31	$ 519	—	$ 519
Berry College	Mt. Berry, GA 30149	1902	Independ	S-G/C	1,521	104	$ 3,780	$2,310	$ 6,090
Brenau College	Gainesville, GA 30501	1878	Private	S-G/W	652	91	$ 3,360	$3,140	$ 6,500
Brewton-Parker College	Mt. Vernon, GA 30445	1904	Baptist	J/C	1,060	60	$ 1,500	$1,500	$ 3,300
Brunswick Junior College	Brunswick, GA 31523	1961	State	J/C	1,254	52	$ 651	—	$ 651
Carver Bible Inst. & College	Atlanta, GA 30313	1943	Church	S/C	125	11	$ 850	$1,666	$ 2,747
Clark College	Atlanta, GA 30314	1869	Un. Meth	S/C	1,966	125	$ 3,315	$1,750	$ 5,065
Clayton Junior College	Morrow, GA 30260	1969	State	J/C	3,692	148	$ 585	—	$ 585
Columbia Theological Sem.	Decatur, GA 30031	1828	Presby	P/C	444	37	$ 2,800	$2,211	$ 5,011
Columbus College	Columbus, GA 31993	1958	State	S-G/C	4,245	192	$ 734	—	$ 734
Dalton Junior College	Dalton, GA 30720	1963	State	J/C	1,755	78	$ 519	—	$ 519
DeKalb Community College	Clarkston, GA 30021	1964	Public	J/C	16,501	945	$ 810	—	$ 810
DeVry Inst. of Technology	Atlanta, GA 30341	1969	Independ	S/C	2,567	127	$ 3,300	—	$ 3,300
Draughon's Junior College	Savannah, GA 31406	1899	Independ	J/C	654	41	$ 2,125	—	$ 2,100
Emanuel County Jr. College	Swainsboro, GA 30401	1973	State	J/C	444	23	$ 534	—	$ 534
Emmanuel College	Franklin Spgs., GA 30639	1919	Pent H	J/C	342	32	$ 1,980	$1,674	$ 3,654
Emory University	Atlanta Spgs., GA 30322	1836	Methodist	S-G/C	8,228	1,250	$ 6,850	$3,050	$ 9,900
Floyd Junior College	Rome, GA 30163	1970	State	J/C	1,627	55	$ 519	—	$ 519
Fort Valley State College	Fort Valley, GA 31030	1895	State	S-G/C	1,722	146	$ 855	$1,650	$ 2,505
Gainesville Junior College	Gainesville, GA 30503	1964	State	J/C	1,679	56	$ 534	—	$ 534
Gammon Theological Seminary	Atlanta, GA 30314	1883	Un. Meth	G/C	133	33	$ 2,900	$1,200	$ 3,000
Georgia College	Milledgeville, GA 31061	1889	State	S-G/C	3,468	131	$ 780	$1,440	$ 2,220
Georgia Inst. of Technology	Atlanta, GA 30332	1885	State	S-G/C	11,396	673	$ 1,200	$2,650	$ 3,850
Georgia Military College	Milledgeville, GA 31061	1879	Independ	J/C	348	21	$ 1,662	$3,209	$ 4,871
Fort Gordon	Fort Gordon, GA 30905	1971	Independ	J/C	611	62	$ 1,620	—	$ 1,620
Moody AFB	Moody AFB, GA 31699	1973	Independ	J/C	116	8	$ 1,620	—	$ 1,620
Georgia Southern College	Statesboro, GA 30460	1906	State	S-G/C	6,830	311	$ 822	$1,455	$ 2,277
Georgia Southwestern College	Americus, GA 31709	1906	State	S-G/C	2,329	116	$ 834	$1,620	$ 2,454
Georgia State University	Atlanta, GA 30303	1913	State	S-G/C	21,335	749	$ 915	—	$ 915
Gordon Junior College	Barnesville, GA 30204	1852	State	J/C	1,451	60	$ 549	$1,380	$ 1,929
Immanuel Baptist Schools	Atlanta, GA 30316	1952	Baptist	S-G/C	70	5	$ 625	—	$ 625
Interden. Theological Center	Atlanta, GA 30314	1958	Independ	G/C	301	30	$ 2,560	$3,800	$ 6,360
John Marshall Law School	Atlanta, GA 30308	1933	Independ	G/C	200	14	$ 1,200	—	$ 1,200
Kennesaw College	Marietta, GA 30061	1963	State	S/C	4,789	142	$ 699	—	$ 699
LaGrange College	LaGrange, GA 30240	1831	Methodist	S-G/C	960	67	$ 2,425	$1,525	$ 3,950
Life Chiropractic College	Marietta, GA 30060	1974	Independ	P/C	1,607	101	$ 3,638	$4,281	$ 7,919
Macon Junior College	Macon, GA 31297	1968	State	J/C	2,968	85	$ 519	—	$ 519
Medical College of Georgia	Augusta, GA 30912	1828	State	P/C	2,362	795	$ 1,690	$ 930	$ 2,620
Mercer University	Macon, GA 31207	1833	Baptist	S-G/C	2,953	217	$ 4,530	$2,196	$ 6,726
Mercer Univ. in Atlanta	Atlanta, GA 30341	1964	Baptist	S-G/C	1,808	76	$ 2,631	—	$ 2,631
Mercer Univ. Sch. of Pharmacy	Atlanta, GA 30312	1903	Baptist	P/C	323	35	$ 4,650	—	$ 4,650
Middle Georgia College	Cochran, GA 31014	1884	State	J/C	1,395	79	$ 600	$1,500	$ 2,100
Morehouse College	Atlanta, GA 30314	1867	Independ	S-G/M	1,931	125	$ 3,100	$2,200	$ 5,475
Morris Brown College	Atlanta, GA 30314	1881	AME	S/C	1,326	100	$ 3,100	$1,900	$ 5,000
North Georgia College	Dahlonega, GA 30597	1873	State	S-G/C	1,984	93	$ 801	$1,410	$ 2,211
North Ga. Tech. & Voc. School	Clarkesville, GA 30523	1943	State	T/C	700	48	$ 60	$1,140	$ 1,200
Oglethorpe University	Atlanta, GA 30319	1835	Independ	S-G/C	1,160	68	$ 4,490	$2,460	$ 6,800
Oxford College of Emory Univ.	Oxford, GA 30267	1836	Methodist	J/C	522	33	$ 4,900	$2,300	$ 7,200
Paine College	Augusta, GA 30901	1882	Methodist	S/C	842	60	$ 2,800	$1,600	$ 4,400
Phillips College	Augusta, GA 30902	1948	Independ	J/C	600	25	$ 2,000	—	$ 2,050
Phillips College	Columbus, GA 31901	1951	Independ	J/C	575	30	$ 4,000	—	$ 4,000
Piedmont College	Demorest, GA 30535	1897	Congreg	S/C	450	38	$ 1,848	$2,250	$ 4,098
Reinhardt College	Waleska, GA 30183	1883	Methodist	J/C	497	37	$ 1,775	$1,800	$ 3,575
Savannah State College	Savannah, GA 31404	1890	State	S-G/C	2,115	144	$ 855	$1,560	$ 2,415
Shorter College	Rome, GA 30161	1873	Baptist	S/C	780	63	$ 2,950	$1,850	$ 4,800
South Georgia College	Douglas, GA 31533	1906	State	J/C	1,244	62	$ 606	$1,485	$ 2,091
Southern Technical Institute	Marietta, GA 30064	1948	State	S/C	3,300	134	$ 774	$2,100	$ 2,874
Spelman College	Atlanta, GA 30314	1881	Independ	S/W	1,457	110	$ 3,500	$2,525	$ 6,025
Thomas County Comm. College	Thomasville, GA 31792	1950	Private	J/C	440	29	$ 1,700	—	$ 1,700
Tift College	Forsyth, GA 31029	1847	Baptist	S/W	656	33	$ 2,520	$2,340	$ 4,860
Toccoa Falls College	Toccoa Falls, GA 30598	1907	Private	S/C	665	49	$ 2,500	$1,850	$ 4,350
Truett-McConnell College	Cleveland, GA 30528	1946	Baptist	J/C	852	111	$ 2,262	$1,650	$ 3,912
University of Georgia	Athens, GA 30602	1785	State	S-G/C	25,886	1,424	$ 1,242	$2,040	$ 3,282
Valdosta State College	Valdosta, GA 31698	1906	State	S-G/C	5,600	211	$ 400	$1,500	$ 1,900
Waycross Junior College	Waycross, GA 31501	1976	State	J/C	542	17	$ 528	—	$ 528
Wesleyan College	Macon, GA 31297	1836	Methodist	S/W	400	58	$ 3,800	$2,325	$ 6,125
West Georgia College	Carrollton, GA 30118	1933	State	S-G/C	6,050	241	$ 834	$1,506	$ 2,340
Woodrow Wilson Col. of Law	Atlanta, GA 30308	1932	Independ	G/C	300	18	$ 1,980	—	$ 1,980
Young Harris College	Young Harris, GA 30582	1886	Un. Meth	J/C	517	35	$ 2,190	$1,890	$ 4,080

GUAM

NAME	ADDRESS	FOUNDED	AFFILIATION	LEVEL/TYPE	ENROLLMENT	TEACHERS	TUITION & FEES	BOARD & ROOM	TOTAL COST
University of Guam	Mangilao, GU 96913	1952	State	S-G/C	2,660	187	$ 700	$3,050	$ 3,750

HAWAII

NAME	ADDRESS	FOUNDED	AFFILIATION	LEVEL/TYPE	ENROLLMENT	TEACHERS	TUITION & FEES	BOARD & ROOM	TOTAL COST
Brig. Young U./Hawaii Camp.	Laie, HI 96762	1955	Mormon	S-G/C	1,945	116	$ 1,150	$1,960	$ 3,010
Chaminade Univ. of Honolulu	Honolulu, HI 96816	1955	Catholic	S-G/C	2,164	162	$ 3,288	$2,580	$ 5,868
Hawaii Loa College	Kaneohe, HI 96744	1963	Ecumen.	S/C	389	39	$ 4,000	$2,900	$ 6,900
Hawaii Pacific College	Honolulu, HI 96813	1965	Independ	S/C	2,526	138	$ 2,900	—	$ 2,900
University of Hawaii									
At Manoa	Honolulu, HI 96822	1907	State	S-G/C	21,065	1,615	$ 481	$1,541	$ 2,022
At Hilo	Hilo, HI 96720	1947	State	S/C	3,478	253	$ 330	$1,437	$ 1,767
West Oahu College	Aiea, HI 96701	1976	State	S/C	410	21	$ 400	—	$ 400

HAWAII *(continued)*

NAME	ADDRESS	FOUNDED	AFFILIATION	LEVEL/TYPE	ENROLLMENT	TEACHERS	TUITION & FEES	BOARD & ROOM	TOTAL COST
Honolulu Community College	Honolulu, HI 96817	1920	State	J/C	5,331	217	$ 90	—	$ 90
Kapiolani Community College	Honolulu, HI 96814	1946	State	J/C	5,560	198	$ 90	—	$ 90
Kauai Community College	Lihue, HI 96766	1928	State	J/C	1,272	61	$ 90	—	$ 90
Leeward Community College	Pearl City, HI 96782	1968	State	J/C	6,261	212	$ 90	—	$ 90
Maui Community College	Kahului, HI 96732	1931	State	J/C	2,308	95	$ 90	$1,040	$ 1,130
Windward Community College	Kaneohe, HI 96744	1972	State	J/C	1,568	57	$ 90	—	$ 90

IDAHO

NAME	ADDRESS	FOUNDED	AFFILIATION	LEVEL/TYPE	ENROLLMENT	TEACHERS	TUITION & FEES	BOARD & ROOM	TOTAL COST
Boise State University	Boise, ID 83725	1932	State	S-G/C	11,241	511	$ 801	$3,000	$ 3,801
College of Idaho	Caldwell, ID 83605	1891	Presby	S-G/C	773	82	$ 4,830	$2,358	$ 7,188
College of Southern Idaho	Twin Falls, ID 83301	1965	State	J/C	5,000	110	$ 600	$1,800	$ 2,400
Idaho State University	Pocatello, ID 83209	1901	State	S-G/C	12,119	405	$ 805	$1,840	$ 2,645
Lewis-Clark State College	Lewiston, ID 83501	1893	State	S/C	2,046	110	$ 740	$1,970	$ 2,710
North Idaho College	Coeur d'Alene, ID 83814	1933	Public	J-T/C	2,457	156	$ 530	$2,100	$ 2,630
Northwest Nazarene College	Nampa, ID 83651	1913	Nazarene	S-G/C	1,258	92	$ 3,735	$1,965	$ 5,700
Ricks College	Rexburg, ID 83440	1888	Mormon	J/C	6,539	249	$ 1,250	$2,120	$ 3,370
University of Idaho	Moscow, ID 83843	1889	State	S-G/C	9,185	731	$ 816	$1,954	$ 4,300

ILLINOIS

NAME	ADDRESS	FOUNDED	AFFILIATION	LEVEL/TYPE	ENROLLMENT	TEACHERS	TUITION & FEES	BOARD & ROOM	TOTAL COST
American Academy of Art	Chicago, IL 60604	1923	Independ	J/C	944	48	$ 3,880	—	$ 3,880
American Conserv. of Music	Chicago, IL 60603	1886	Independ	S-G/C	339	120	$ 3,600	—	$ 3,600
Augustana College	Rock Island, IL 61201	1860	Lutheran	S-G/C	2,352	147	$ 5,196	$2,337	$ 7,533
Aurora College	Aurora, IL 60507	1893	Adv/Chr	S-G/C	1,414	62	$ 4,300	$2,500	$ 6,800
Barat College	Lake Forest, IL 60045	1907	Independ	S/C	650	40	$ 4,800	$2,300	$ 7,100
Belleville Area College	Belleville, IL 62221	1948	State	J/C	12,500	650	$ 608	—	$ 608
Bethany Theological Seminary	Oak Brook, IL 60521	1905	Brethren	P/C	121	19	$ 2,304	$1,060	$ 3,346
Blackburn College	Carlinville, IL 62606	1837	Presby	S/C	510	52	$ 3,810	$1,290	$ 5,100
Black Hawk College	Moline, IL 61265	1946	Public	J/C	20,000	283	$ 825	—	$ 825
East Campus	Kewanee, IL 61443	1967	Public	J/C	866	64	$ 885	—	$ 885
Bradley University	Peoria, IL 61625	1897	Private	S-G/C	5,637	432	$ 5,000	$2,200	$ 6,700
Carl Sandburg College	Galesburg, IL 61401	1966	State	J/C	4,000	110	$ 612	—	$ 612
Catholic Theological Union	Chicago, IL 60615	1968	Catholic	G/C	330	37	$ 3,000	$3,000	$ 6,000
Chicago Col. of Osteo. Med.	Chicago, IL 60615	1900	Independ	P/C	396	272	$ 8,500	—	—
Chicago State University	Chicago, IL 60628	1867	State	S-G/C	7,389	286	$ 798	—	$ 798
Chicago Theol. Seminary	Chicago, IL 60637	1855	C of Chr	G/C	146	13	$ 2,800	$2,100	$ 8,000
City Colleges of Chicago	Chicago, IL 60601	1911	State	J/C	128,975	1,332	$ 600	—	$ 600
Chicago City-Wide College	Chicago, IL 60601	1975	State	J/C	16,063	63	$ 600	—	$ 600
Chicago Urban Skills Inst.	Chicago, IL 60609	1970	State	J/C	44,842	91	$ 15	—	$ 15
Daley College	Chicago, IL 60652	1960	State	J/C	9,997	138	$ 600	—	$ 600
Kennedy-King College	Chicago, IL 60621	1934	State	J/C	9,886	264	$ 600	—	$ 600
Loop College	Chicago, IL 60601	1962	State	J/C	9,863	182	$ 600	—	$ 600
Malcolm X College	Chicago, IL 60612	1911	State	J/C	7,716	174	$ 600	—	$ 600
Olive-Harvey College	Chicago, IL 60628	1957	State	J/C	8,167	152	$ 600	—	$ 600
Truman College	Chicago, IL 60645	1956	State	J/C	12,043	167	$ 600	—	$ 600
Wright College	Chicago, IL 60634	1934	State	J/C	10,425	192	$ 600	—	$ 600
College of Dupage	Glen Ellyn, IL 60137	1966	State	J/C	24,034	1,229	$ 720	—	$ 720
College of Lake County	Grayslake, IL 60030	1967	State	J/C	13,089	576	$ 990	—	$ 990
College of St. Francis	Joliet, IL 60435	1930	Catholic	S-G/C	1,522	198	$ 3,834	$2,224	$ 6,058
Columbia College Chicago	Chicago, IL 60605	1890	Independ	S-G/C	4,257	375	$ 3,500	—	$ 3,500
Concordia Teachers College	River Forest, IL 60305	1864	Lutheran	S-G/C	1,318	87	$ 3,300	$2,140	$ 5,440
Danville Area Comm. College	Danville, IL 61832	1946	Public	J/C	4,100	140	$ 650	—	$ 650
De Lourdes College	Des Plaines, IL 60016	1927	Catholic	S/W	278	27	$ 1,350	—	$ 1,350
DePaul University	Chicago, IL 60604	1898	Independ	S-G/C	12,867	763	$ 4,290	$2,847	$ 7,137
DeVry Institute of Technology	Chicago, IL 60618	1931	Independ	S/C	5,450	178	$ 3,300	—	$ 3,300
DeVry Institute of Technology	Lombard, IL 60148	1982	Independ	S/C	1,038	50	$ 3,300	—	$ 3,300
Dr. William M. Scholl College of Podiatric Medicine	Chicago, IL 60610	1912	Independ	P/C	600	89	$ 9,515	—	$ 9,515
Eastern Illinois University	Charleston, IL 61920	1895	State	S-G/C	9,926	530	$ 1,283	$1,990	$ 3,273
Elgin Community College	Elgin, IL 60120	1949	State	J/C	6,500	394	$ 630	—	$ 630
Elmhurst College	Elmhurst, IL 60126	1871	C of Chr	S/C	3,534	155	$ 4,550	$2,400	$ 6,950
Emmaus Bible School	Oak Park, IL 60301	1941	Non-Den	J/C	167	12	$ 1,275	$1,995	$ 3,270
Eureka College	Eureka, IL 61530	1855	Independ	S/C	537	51	$ 3,500	$2,000	$ 5,500
Felician College	Chicago, IL 60659	1926	Catholic	J/C	414	37	$ 1,860	—	$ 1,860
Garrett-Evang. Theol. Sem.	Evanston, IL 60201	1853	Un. Meth	G/C	363	39	$ 3,195	$2,228	$ 5,423
George Williams College	Downers Grove, IL 60515	1890	Independ	S-G/C	1,705	110	$ 4,941	$2,277	$ 7,218
Governors State University	Park Forest S., IL 60466	1969	State	S-G/C	4,886	320	$ 934	—	$ 934
Greenville College	Greenville, IL 62246	1892	Fr. Meth	S/C	755	49	$ 4,587	$2,170	$ 6,757
Hebrew Theological College	Skokie, IL 60077	1922	Jewish	S-G/C	122	22	$ 2,120	$2,490	$ 4,610
Highland Community College	Freeport, IL 61032	1962	State	J/C	2,480	47	$ 512	—	$ 512
Illinois Benedictine College	Lisle, IL 60532	1887	Catholic	S-G/C	1,623	122	$ 4,600	$2,500	$ 7,100
Illinois Central College	East Peoria, IL 61635	1966	District	J/C	14,911	602	$ 512	—	$ 512
Illinois College	Jacksonville, IL 62650	1829	Presby	S/C	767	75	$ 3,300	$2,000	$ 5,300
Illinois College of Optometry	Chicago, IL 60616	1955	Independ	P/C	548	46	$ 6,560	$1,245	$ 7,805
Ill. Eastern Comm. Colleges									
Frontier Comm. College	Fairfield, IL 62837	1977	Public	J/C	3,906	228	$ 288	—	$ 288
Lincoln Trail College	Robinson, IL 62454	1969	Public	J/C	1,906	106	$ 288	—	$ 288
Olney Central College	Olney, IL 62450	1962	Public	J/C	2,798	118	$ 288	—	$ 288
Wabash Valley College	Mt. Carmel, IL 62863	1960	Public	J/C	2,709	185	$ 288	—	$ 288
Illinois Inst. of Technology	Chicago, IL 60616	1892	Independ	S-G/C	5,818	455	$ 6,390	$3,000	$ 9,390
Chicago-Kent Col. of Law	Chicago, IL 60606	1888	Independ	P/C	1,032	91	$ 6,105	—	$ 6,105
Illinois State University	Normal, IL 61761	1857	State	S-G/C	19,817	1,100	$ 1,157	$2,088	$ 3,245
Illinois Valley Comm. College	Oglesby, IL 61348	1924	State	J/C	4,540	173	$ 320	—	$ 320
Illinois Wesleyan University	Bloomington, IL 61701	1850	Methodist	S/C	1,623	126	$ 5,730	$2,445	$ 8,175

NAME	ADDRESS	FOUNDED	AFFILIATION	LEVEL/TYPE	ENROLLMENT	TEACHERS	TUITION & FEES	BOARD & ROOM	TOTAL COST
ILLINOIS *(continued)*									
John A. Logan College	Carterville, IL 62918	1967	State	J/C	2,530	101	$ 365	—	$ 365
John Marshall Law School	Chicago, IL 60604	1899	Independ	P/C	1,651	90	$ 5,090	$5,200	$10,290
Joliet Junior College	Joliet, IL 60436	1901	State	J/C	10,280	391	$ 450	—	$ 450
Judson College	Elgin, IL 60120	1963	Baptist	S/C	426	47	$ 4,910	$2,290	$ 7,200
Kankakee Community College	Kankakee, IL 60901	1966	State	J/C	3,727	57	$ 585	—	$ 585
Kaskaskia College	Centralia, IL 62801	1940	State	J/C	2,949	54	$ 450	—	$ 450
Kendall College	Evanston, IL 60201	1934	Methodist	S/C	396	31	$ 3,710	$2,200	$ 5,910
Kishwaukee College	Malta, IL 60150	1968	Public	J/C	3,925	182	$ 328	—	$ 328
Knox College	Galesburg, IL 61401	1837	Independ	S/C	963	86	$ 6,909	$2,391	$ 9,300
Lake Forest College	Lake Forest, IL 60045	1857	Presby	S-G/C	1,050	83	$ 7,710	$2,310	$10,020
Lake Land College	Mattoon, IL 61938	1966	Public	J/C	3,940	92	$ 780	—	$ 780
Lewis & Clark Comm. College	Godfrey, IL 62035	1970	State	J/C	6,000	267	$ 436	—	$ 436
Lewis University	Romeoville, IL 60441	1932	Independ	S-G/C	2,747	179	$ 4,768	$2,200	$ 6,968
Lincoln Christian College	Lincoln, IL 62656	1944	Christian	S-G/C	489	31	$ 2,720	$1,640	$ 4,360
Lincoln College	Lincoln, IL 62656	1865	Independ	J/C	1,662	97	$ 4,300	$2,300	$ 6,600
Lincoln Land Comm. College	Springfield, IL 62708	1967	State	J/C	7,067	348	$ 493	—	$ 493
Loyola Univ. of Chicago	Chicago, IL 60611	1870	Catholic	S-G/C	15,857	1,245	$ 4,250	$2,500	$ 6,850
Niles College	Chicago, IL 60631	1961	Catholic	S/M	143	25	$ 4,227	$1,350	$ 5,577
Lutheran School of Theology	Chicago, IL 60615	1860	Lutheran	P/C	308	28	$ 1,800	—	—
MacCormac College	Chicago, IL 60604	1904	Independ	J/C	716	49	$ 3,150	—	$ 3,150
MacMurray College	Jacksonville, IL 62650	1846	Un. Meth.	S/C	632	75	$ 4,870	$1,330	$ 7,200
Mallinckrodt College	Wilmette, IL 60091	1918	Catholic	J-S/W	285	38	$ 2,430	—	$ 2,430
McCormick Theological Sem.	Chicago, IL 60637	1829	Presby	G/C	568	25	$ 2,810	$2,605	$ 5,415
McHenry County College	Crystal Lake, IL 60014	1967	State	J/C	3,979	186	$ 660	—	$ 660
McKendree College	Lebanon, IL 62254	1828	Un. Meth.	S/C	764	65	$ 3,706	$2,100	$ 6,756
Meadville/Lombard Theol. School	Chicago, IL 60637	1844	Unit. Univ.	G/C	36	4	$ 6,450	$4,000	$10,450
Midwest Col. of Engineering	Lombard, IL 60148	1967	Independ	S-G/C	255	50	$ 4,320	—	$ 4,320
Midwest Montessori Teach. Tr. Ctr.	Chicago, IL 60622	1964	Independ	S-G/C	102	11	$ 1,850	—	$ 1,850
Millikin University	Decatur, IL 62522	1901	Presby	S/C	1,546	142	$ 5,057	$2,255	$ 7,312
Monmouth College	Monmouth, IL 61462	1853	Presby	S/C	649	71	$ 5,960	$2,240	$ 8,200
Moody Bible Institute	Chicago, IL 60610	1886	Independ	S/C	1,301	69	—	$2,620	$ 2,620
Moraine Valley Comm. College	Palos Hills, IL 60465	1969	Public	J/C	13,267	325	$ 647	—	$ 647
Morton College	Cicero, IL 60650	1924	State	J/C	4,345	196	$ 570	—	$ 570
Mundelein College	Chicago, IL 60660	1929	Catholic	S-G/W	1,282	130	$ 4,500	$2,352	$ 6,852
Nat. College of Chiropractic	Lombard, IL 60148	1906	Independ	P/C	1,000	80	$ 4,270	$2,500	$ 6,770
North Central College	Naperville, IL 60566	1861	Un. Meth.	S/C	1,401	105	$ 4,800	$2,500	$ 7,300
North Park College	Chicago, IL 60625	1891	Evang	S/C	1,171	77	$ 4,900	$2,100	$ 7,000
Northeastern Illinois Univ.	Chicago, IL 60625	1961	State	S-G/C	10,349	527	$ 774	—	$ 774
No. Baptist Theological Sem.	Lombard, IL 60148	1913	Baptist	G/C	204	22	$ 2,050	$3,300	$ 5,350
Northern Illinois University	DeKalb, IL 60115	1895	State	S-G/C	25,676	1,251	$ 1,264	$2,200	$ 3,464
Northwestern University	Evanston, IL 60201	1851	Independ	P/C	15,703	1,783	$ 8,895	$3,380	$12,275
Oakton Community College	Des Plaines, IL 60016	1969	State	J/C	9,655	484	$ 402	—	$ 402
Olivet Nazarene College	Kankakee, IL 60901	1907	Nazarene	S-G/C	1,946	112	$ 3,505	$2,045	$ 5,550
Parkland College	Champaign, IL 61821	1966	Public	J/C	9,199	505	$ 510	—	$ 510
Parks Col. of St. Louis Univ.	Cahokia, IL 62206	1927	Catholic	S/C	1,051	70	$ 1,735	$1,130	$ 2,865
Prairie State College	Chicago Hgts, IL 60411	1958	State	J/C	5,920	378	$ 576	—	$ 576
Principia College	Elsah, IL 62028	1898	Independ	S/C	771	75	$ 6,135	$3,465	$ 9,600
Quincy College	Quincy, IL 62301	1859	Catholic	S/C	1,800	100	$ 4,300	$2,130	$ 6,430
Reid Col. of Detect. of Deception	Chicago, IL 60606	1947	Independ	G/C	12	4	$ 2,800	—	$ 2,800
Rend Lake College	Ina, IL 62846	1967	State	J/C	3,025	112	$ 480	—	$ 480
Richland Community College	Decatur, IL 62526	1971	State	J/C	3,312	222	$ 630	—	$ 630
Robert Morris College	Carthage, IL 62321	1965	Independ	J/W	487	30	$ 3,900	$3,400	$ 7,300
Chicago Branch	Chicago, IL 60601	1965	Independ	J/C	864	46	$ 3,900	—	$ 3,900
Rock Valley College	Rockford, IL 61101	1964	State	J/C	11,660	779	$ 670	—	$ 670
Rockford College	Rockford, IL 61101	1847	Independ	S-G/C	1,500	115	$ 4,990	$2,350	$ 7,340
Roosevelt University	Chicago, IL 60605	1945	Independ	S-G/C	6,601	475	$ 4,200	$2,600	$ 6,800
Rosary College	River Forest, IL 60305	1901	Catholic	S-G/C	1,686	150	$ 4,350	$2,500	$ 6,850
Saint Xavier College	Chicago, IL 60655	1847	Catholic	S-G/C	2,346	137	$ 3,240	$2,280	$ 5,520
Sangamon State University	Springfield, IL 62708	1969	State	S-G/C	3,327	208	$ 850	—	—
Sauk Valley College	Dixon, IL 61021	1965	Public	J/C	4,200	61	$ 640	—	$ 640
Sch. of the Art Inst. of Chicago	Chicago, IL 60603	1866	Independ	S-G/C	1,535	159	$ 5,550	—	$ 5,550
Seabury-Western Theol. Sem.	Evanston, IL 60201	1933	Episcopal	G/C	97	10	$ 4,030	$2,300	$ 9,500
Sherwood Music School	Chicago, IL 60605	1895	Independ	S/C	56	37	$ 2,200	—	$ 2,200
Southeastern Illinois College	Harrisburg, IL 62946	1960	Independ	J/C	2,753	65	$ 540	—	$ 2,710
Southern Illinois University	Carbondale, IL 62901	1869	State	S-G/C	23,733	1,698	$ 1,307	$2,224	$ 3,551
So. Ill. Univ. at Edwardsville	Edwardsville, IL 62026	1957	State	S-G/C	11,098	635	$ 1,182	$2,343	$ 3,525
Spertus College of Judaica	Chicago, IL 60613	1925	Independ	S-G/C	233	15	$ 2,450	—	$ 2,450
Spoon River College	Canton, IL 61520	1959	Public	J/C	2,071	147	$ 688	—	$ 688
Springfield College in Illinois	Springfield, IL 62702	1929	Catholic	J/C	485	47	$ 2,850	—	$ 2,850
State Community College	St. Louis, IL 62201	1969	State	J/C	1,815	42	$ 360	—	$ 360
Thornton Community College	South Holland, IL 60473	1927	State	J/C	11,133	288	$ 656	—	$ 656
Trinity Christian College	Palos Heights, IL 60463	1959	Independ	S/C	440	50	$ 4,290	$2,000	$ 6,290
Trinity College	Deerfield, IL 60015	1897	Independ	S/C	563	58	$ 4,545	$2,400	$ 6,945
Triton College	River Grove, IL 60171	1964	State	J/C	23,934	1,139	$ 610	—	$ 610
University of Chicago	Chicago, IL 60637	1891	Private	S-G/C	9,096	1,055	$ 8,034	$4,500	$12,534
University of Illinois	Urbana, IL 61801	1867	State	S-G/C					
Chicago Circle Campus	Chicago, IL 60680	1965	State	S-G/C	25,262	2,304	$ 1,350	—	$ 1,350
Medical Center Campus	Chicago, IL 60680	1896	State	G/C	4,259	1,236	$ 1,644	$3,750	$ 5,394
Urbana-Champaign Campus	Urbana, IL 61801	1867	State	S-G/C	34,914	2,289	$ 1,410	$2,670	$ 4,080
Vandercook College of Music	Chicago, IL 60616	1909	Independ	S-G/C	177	36	$ 3,200	$2,500	$ 5,700
Waubonsee Community Col.	Sugar Grove, IL 60554	1966	State	J/C	6,510	300	$ 635	—	$ 635
Western Illinois University	Macomb, IL 61455	1899	State	S-G/C	12,411	731	$ 1,245	$1,990	$ 3,235
Wheaton College	Wheaton, IL 60187	1860	Independ	S-G/C	2,490	200	$ 5,280	$2,660	$ 7,940
William Rainey Harper College	Palatine, IL 60067	1965	State	J/C	•24,835	1,074	$ 804	—	$ 804

INDIANA

NAME	ADDRESS	FOUNDED	AFFILIATION	LEVEL/TYPE	ENROLLMENT	TEACHERS	TUITION & FEES	BOARD & ROOM	TOTAL COST
Ancilla College	Donaldson, IN 46513	1937	Catholic	J/C	440	23	$ 1,200	—	$ 1,200
Anderson College	Anderson, IN 46012	1917	C of God	S-G/C	2,008	163	$ 4,160	$1,660	$ 5,820
Ball State University	Muncie, IN 47306	1918	State	S-G/C	19,488	870	$ 1,275	$1,890	$ 3,165
Bethel College	Mishawaka, IN 46545	1947	Mission	S-G/C	410	30	$ 3,300	$2,000	$ 5,300
Butler University	Indianapolis, IN 46208	1855	Independ	S-G/C	4,030	300	$ 5,004	$2,300	$ 7,304
Calumet College	Whiting, IN 46394	1951	Catholic	S/C	1,269	55	$ 1,655	—	$ 1,655
Christian Theol. Seminary	Indianapolis, IN 46208	1924	D of Chr	G/C	342	35	$ 2,280	—	$ 2,280
Concordia Theol. Seminary	Fort Wayne, IN 46825	1846	Lutheran	G/M	553	35	$ 2,880	$1,875	$ 4,755
DePauw University	Greencastle, IN 46135	1837	Methodist	S-G/C	2,334	192	$ 6,700	$2,800	$ 9,500
Earlham College	Richmond, IN 47374	1847	Friends	S/C	1,069	105	$ 6,900	$2,325	$ 9,225
Elkhart Inst. of Technology	Elkhart, IN 46516	1882	Independ	T/C	130	6	$ 1,710	$1,480	$ 3,190
Fort Wayne Bible College	Fort Wayne, IN 46807	1904	Mission	S/C	450	50	$ 3,188	$2,050	$ 5,238
Franklin College of Indiana	Franklin, IN 46131	1834	Baptist	S/C	536	59	$ 4,990	$2,160	$ 7,150
Goshen Biblical Seminary	Elkhart, IN 46517	1946	Mennon	G/C	139	9	$ 1,960	$4,240	$ 6,200
Goshen College	Goshen, IN 46526	1894	Mennon	S/C	1,122	114	$ 4,375	$2,015	$ 6,390
Grace College	Winona Lake, IN 46590	1948	Brethren	S/C	916	60	$ 3,850	$2,200	$ 6,050
Hanover College	Hanover, IN 47243	1827	Presby	S/C	994	72	$ 3,800	$1,940	$ 5,740
Herron School of Art of Ind. Univ.	Indianapolis, IN 46202	1902	State	S-G/C	370	56	$ 1,288	$2,340	$ 4,428
Holy Cross Junior College	Notre Dame, IN 46556	1966	Catholic	J/C	314	21	$ 1,500	—	$ 1,500
Huntington College	Huntington, IN 46750	1897	Brethren	S-G/C	438	60	$ 4,375	$1,935	$ 6,310
Indiana Central University	Indianapolis, IN 46227	1902	Independ	S-G/C	3,388	237	$ 4,450	$2,220	$ 6,670
Indiana Inst. of Technology	Fort Wayne, IN 46803	1930	Independ	S/C	566	46	$ 3,750	$2,220	$ 5,970
Indiana North. Grad. Sch. of Professional Management	Gas City, IN 46933	1963	Independ	G/C	50	10	$ 2,400	—	$ 2,400
Indiana State University	Terre Haute, IN 47809	1865	State	S-G/C	12,091	636	$ 1,147	$1,581	$ 2,728
Ind. State Univ. Evansville	Evansville, IN 47712	1965	State	S/C	3,586	173	$ 992	—	$ 992
Indiana University	Bloomington, IN 47405	1820	State	S-G/C	80,774	3,289	—	—	—
Bloomington	Bloomington, IN 47405	1820	State	S-G/C	32,711	1,414	$ 1,328	$1,977	$ 3,305
East	Richmond, IN 47374	1971	State	J/C	1,448	29	$ 1,118	—	$ 1,118
Kokomo	Kokomo, IN 46902	1945	State	S/C	2,808	54	$ 1,118	—	$ 1,118
Northwest	Gary, IN 46408	1948	State	S-G/C	4,897	140	$ 1,118	—	$ 1,118
Purdue Univ. at Fort Wayne	Fort Wayne, IN 46805	1964	State	S-G/C	5,101	143	$ 1,119	—	$ 1,119
Purdue Univ. at Indianapolis	Indianapolis, IN 46202	1969	State	S-G/C	23,258	1,260	$ 1,208	—	$ 1,208
South Bend	South Bend, IN 46634	1941	State	S-G/C	5,912	151	$ 1,118	—	$ 1,118
Southeast	New Albany, IN 47150	1941	State	S-G/C	4,640	98	$ 1,118	—	$ 1,118
Indiana Vocational Technical College	Indianapolis, IN 46206	1963	State	T/C	26,298	1,305	$ 960	—	$ 960
Central Indiana	Indianapolis, IN 46202	1966	State	T/C	4,142	62	$ 960	—	$ 960
Columbus	Columbus, IN 47201	1967	State	T/C	1,860	110	$ 960	—	$ 960
Kokomo	Kokomo, IN 46901	1968	State	T/C	1,447	79	$ 960	—	$ 960
Lafayette	Lafayette, IN 47903	1968	State	T/C	1,482	51	$ 960	—	$ 960
Muncie	Muncie, IN 47302	1968	State	T/C	2,194	43	$ 960	—	$ 960
Northeast	Fort Wayne, IN 46805	1968	State	T/C	3,375	221	$ 960	—	$ 960
Northwest	Gary, IN 46408	1948	State	S-G/C	4,897	140	$ 1,118	—	$ 1,118
South Bend	South Bend, IN 46619	1967	State	T/C	2,374	145	$ 960	—	$ 960
Southcentral	Sellersburg, IN 47172	1968	State	T/C	1,395	102	$ 960	—	$ 960
Southeast	Madison, IN 47250	1968	State	T/C	565	44	$ 960	—	$ 960
Southwest	Evansville, IN 47710	1968	State	T/C	1,706	107	$ 960	—	$ 960
Wabash Valley	Terre Haute, IN 47802	1966	State	T/C	1,559	76	$ 960	—	$ 960
Whitewater	Richmond, IN 47374	1968	State	T/C	905	63	$ 960	—	$ 960
Manchester College	Manchester, IN 46962	1889	Brethren	S-G/C	1,011	100	$ 4,380	$1,920	$ 6,500
Marian College	Indianapolis, IN 46222	1851	Catholic	S/C	855	75	$ 3,500	$1,930	$ 5,430
Marion College	Marion, IN 46952	1920	Wesleyan	S-G/C	1,096	95	$ 4,210	$2,000	$ 6,210
Mennonite Biblical Seminary	Elkhart, IN 46517	1946	Mennon	G/C	92	22	$ 1,960	$4,240	$ 6,200
Oakland City College	Oakland City, IN 47660	1885	Baptist	S-G/C	562	36	$ 3,600	$1,767	$ 5,367
Purdue University	West Lafayette, IN 47907	1869	State	S-G/C	32,455	3,100	$ 1,350	$2,100	$ 3,450
Calumet	Hammond, IN 46323	1876	State	S-G/C	7,716	233	$ 1,400	—	$ 1,400
North Central Campus	Westville, IN 46391	1947	State	J-S-G/C	2,544	145	$ 1,318	—	$ 1,318
Rose-Hulman Institute of Technology	Terre Haute, IN 47803	1874	Independ	S-G/M	1,322	95	$ 5,400	$2,425	$ 7,825
St. Francis College	Fort Wayne, IN 46808	1890	Catholic	S-G/C	1,276	80	$ 3,360	$2,100	$ 5,460
St. Joseph's College	Rensselaer, IN 47978	1889	Catholic	S/C	962	70	$ 4,300	$2,200	$ 6,500
St. Mary-of-The-Woods College	St. Mary/Woods, IN 47876	1840	Catholic	S/W	704	76	$ 4,400	$2,080	$ 6,480
St. Mary's College	Notre Dame, IN 46556	1844	Catholic	S/W	1,839	173	$ 5,834	$2,829	$ 8,663
St. Meinrad College	St. Meinrad, IN 47577	1861	Catholic	S/M	180	40	$ 2,618	$2,987	$ 5,605
Taylor University	Upland, IN 46989	1846	Independ	S/C	1,470	100	$ 4,424	$2,216	$ 6,640
Tri-State University	Angola, IN 46703	1884	Independ	S/C	1,100	75	$ 4,341	$2,100	$ 6,441
Union Bible Seminary	Westfield, IN 46074	1911	Int-Den	S/C	95	10	$ 1,000	$1,900	$ 2,900
University of Evansville	Evansville, IN 47702	1854	Methodist	S-G/C	4,761	257	$ 4,965	$2,337	$ 7,302
University of Notre Dame	Notre Dame, IN 46556	1842	Catholic	S-G/C	9,042	737	$ 5,950	$2,065	$ 8,015
Valparaiso Technical Institute	Valparaiso, IN 46383	1824	Private	T/C	235	12	$ 2,810	$2,900	$ 5,710
Valparaiso University	Valparaiso, IN 46383	1859	Lutheran	S-G/C	3,772	270	$ 4,782	$2,350	$ 7,132
Vincennes University	Vincennes, IN 47591	1801	State	J/C	6,174	284	$ 980	$1,880	$ 2,860
Wabash College	Crawfordsville, IN 47933	1832	Independ	S/M	789	74	$ 5,780	$2,485	$ 8,265

IOWA

NAME	ADDRESS	FOUNDED	AFFILIATION	LEVEL/TYPE	ENROLLMENT	TEACHERS	TUITION & FEES	BOARD & ROOM	TOTAL COST
American Institute of Business	Des Moines, IA 50321	1921	Independ	J/C	1,131	55	$ 2,580	$1,170	$ 3,750
Briar Cliff College	Sioux City, IA 51104	1930	Catholic	S/C	1,342	70	$ 3,150	$1,600	$ 4,750
Buena Vista College	Storm Lake, IA 50588	1891	Presby	S/C	1,403	54	$ 5,400	$2,140	$ 7,540
Central University of Iowa	Pella, IA 50219	1853	Reformed	S/C	1,473	93	$ 5,100	$2,000	$ 7,100
Clarke College	Dubuque, IA 52001	1843	Catholic	S-G/C	892	93	$ 4,500	$1,950	$ 6,450
Clinton Community College	Clinton, IA 52732	1946	State	J/C	897	44	$ 349	—	$ 349
Coe College	Cedar Rapids, IA 52402	1851	Presby	S/C	1,448	100	$ 5,810	$2,020	$ 7,830
Cornell College	Mt. Vernon, IA 52314	1853	Methodist	S/C	830	70	$ 6,010	$2,186	$ 8,196

NAME	ADDRESS	FOUNDED	AFFILIATION	LEVEL/TYPE	ENROLLMENT	TEACHERS	TUITION & FEES	BOARD & ROOM	TOTAL COST
IOWA *(continued)*									
Des Moines Area Comm. Col.	Ankeny, IA 50021	1966	State	J/C	5,698	192	$ 900	—	$ 900
Boone Campus	Boone, IA 50036	1927	State	J/C	731	26	$ 900	—	$ 900
Urban Campus	Des Moines, IA 50314	1972	State	J/C	785	22	$ 900	—	$ 900
Divine Word College	Epworth, IA 52045	1912	Catholic	S/M	88	23	$ 3,200	$1,200	$ 4,400
Dordt College	Sioux Center, IA 51250	1955	Reformed	S/C	1,077	75	$ 4,200	$1,610	$ 5,810
Drake University	Des Moines, IA 50311	1881	Independ	S-G/C	6,492	350	$ 5,750	$2,650	$ 8,400
Eastern Iowa Comm. Col. Dist.									
Clinton Community College	Clinton, IA 52732	1946	State	J/C	1,136	55	$ 783	—	$ 783
Muscatine Community College	Muscatine, IA 52761	1929	State	J/C	913	46	$ 797	—	$ 797
Scott Community College	Bettendorf, IA 52722	1966	State	J/C	2,244	120	$ 795	—	$ 795
Ellsworth Community College	Iowa Falls, IA 50126	1890	State	J/C	976	58	$ 720	$1,740	$ 2,460
Faith Baptist Bible College	Ankeny, IA 50021	1924	Baptist	S-G/C	415	23	$ 1,375	$ 990	$ 2,365
Graceland College	Lamoni, IA 50140	1895	Lat Day	S/C	1,086	80	$ 4,445	$1,845	$ 6,290
Grand View College	Des Moines, IA 50316	1896	Lutheran	S/C	1,247	104	$ 3,750	$1,750	$ 5,500
Grinnell College	Grinnell, IA 50112	1846	Independ	S/C	1,181	105	$ 7,070	$2,170	$ 9,240
Hawkeye Inst. of Technology	Waterloo, IA 50704	1966	State	T/C	2,049	129	$ 711	—	$ 711
Independian Hills Comm. College	Ottumwa, IA 52501	1966	State	J/C	2,105	121	$ 630	$1,500	$ 2,130
Iowa Central Comm. College	Fort Dodge, IA 50501	1966	State	J/C	2,780	112	$ 800	$1,860	$ 2,660
Iowa Lakes Comm. College	Estherville, IA 51334	1967	State	J/C	1,761	83	$ 685	—	$ 685
Iowa State University	Ames, IA 50011	1858	State	S-G/C	24,906	1,725	$ 1,104	$1,868	$ 2,972
Iowa Wesleyan College	Mt. Pleasant, IA 52641	1842	Methodist	S/C	750	60	$ 4,900	$1,990	$ 6,890
Iowa Western Comm. College	Clarinda, IA 51632	1966	State	J/C	351	24	$ 900	$2,500	$ 3,400
Iowa Western Comm. College	Council Bluffs, IA 51502	1966	State	J/C	3,312	136	$ 804	$2,395	$ 3,199
Kirkwood Comm. College	Cedar Rapids, IA 52406	1966	State	J/C	5,917	198	$ 700	—	$ 700
Loras College	Dubuque, IA 52001	1839	Catholic	S-G/C	1,784	125	$ 4,500	$2,160	$ 6,660
Luther College	Decorah, IA 52101	1861	Lutheran	S/C	2,082	155	$ 5,600	$1,900	$ 7,500
Marshalltown Comm. College	Marshalltown, IA 50158	1927	State	J/C	1,478	90	$ 620	—	$ 620
Marycrest College	Davenport, IA 52804	1939	Catholic	S-G/C	1,400	65	$ 4,140	$1,990	$ 6,130
Morningside College	Sioux City, IA 51106	1894	Methodist	S-G/C	1,295	100	$ 4,970	$1,780	$ 6,750
Mount Mercy College	Cedar Rapids, IA 52402	1928	Catholic	S/C	1,167	90	$ 4,285	$2,015	$ 6,300
Mount St. Clare College	Clinton, IA 52732	1928	Catholic	J-S/C	362	41	$ 3,040	$2,000	$ 5,040
North Iowa Area Comm. Col.	Mason City, IA 50401	1918	State	J/C	2,158	122	$ 600	$1,750	$ 2,350
Northeast Iowa Tech. Institute	Calmar, IA 52132	1967	Public	T/C	1,173	107	$ 757	$ —	$ 3,820
Northwest Iowa Tech. Col.	Sheron, IA 51201	1966	State	J/C	499	40	$ 895	—	$ 895
Northwestern College	Orange City, IA 51041	1882	Reformed	S/C	892	54	$ 4,200	$1,700	$ 5,900
Palmer Col. of Chiropractic	Davenport, IA 52803	1895	Independ	P/C	1,913	121	$ 3,900	$4,650	$ 8,550
Saint Ambrose College	Davenport, IA 52803	1882	Catholic	S-G/C	2,138	157	$ 4,940	$2,100	$ 7,040
Simpson College	Independianola, IA 50125	1860	Un. Meth	S/C	1,065	73	$ 5,375	$1,935	$ 7,310
Sioux Empire College	Hawarden, IA 51023	1965	Independ	J/C	401	31	$ 2,800	$1,300	$ 4,100
Southeastern Comm. College	W. Burlington, IA 52655	1966	State	J/C	2,420	99	$ 660	—	$ 660
Southwestern Comm. College	Creston, IA 50801	1966	State	J/C	659	41	$ 696	$1,700	$ 2,360
University of Dubuque	Dubuque, IA 52001	1852	Presby	S/C	1,117	75	$ 4,575	$1,800	$ 6,375
University of Iowa	Iowa City, IA 52242	1847	State	S-G/C	28,140	1,579	$ 1,104	$1,976	$ 3,080
University of Northern Iowa	Cedar Falls, IA 50613	1876	State	S-G/C	11,963	683	$ 1,050	$1,700	$ 2,750
Univ. of Ost. Med. & Hlth. Sci.	Des Moines, IA 50312	1898	Independ	P/C	777	92	$11,750	—	$11,750
Upper Iowa University	Fayette, IA 52142	1857	Independ	S/C	380	35	$ 4,450	$2,330	$ 6,780
Vennard College	University Park, IA 52595	1910	Independ	S/C	201	14	$ 2,080	$1,840	$ 3,920
Waldorf College	Forest City, IA 50436	1903	Lutheran	J/C	444	38	$ 4,750	$2,020	$ 6,770
Wartburg College	Waverly, IA 50677	1852	Lutheran	S/C	1,131	81	$ 5,210	$1,990	$ 7,200
Wartburg Theological Sem.	Dubuque, IA 52001	1854	Lutheran	P/C	262	20	$ 1,500	$1,530	$ 3,030
Western Iowa Tech. Comm. Col	Sioux City, IA 51102	1967	State	J/C	1,435	104	$ 828	—	$ 828
Westmar College	LeMars, IA 51031	1890	Un. Meth	S/C	505	40	$ 4,526	$2,158	$ 6,684
William Penn College	Oskaloosa, IA 52577	1873	Friends	S/C	500	38	$ 5,460	$1,790	$ 7,250
KANSAS									
Allen County Comm. College	Iola, KS 66749	1923	State	J/C	1,000	90	$ 410	$1,500	$ 1,910
Baker University	Baldwin City, KS 66006	1858	Un. Meth	S-G/C	775	61	$ 3,500	$2,225	$ 5,727
Barton Co. Comm. College	Great Bend, KS 67530	1965	State	J/C	3,461	115	$ 455	$1,650	$ 2,105
Benedictine College	Atchison, KS 66002	1858	Catholic	S/C	965	94	$ 4,020	$2,030	$ 6,050
Bethany College	Lindsborg, KS 67456	1881	Lutheran	S/C	926	75	$ 3,490	$2,180	$ 5,670
Bethel College	North Newton, KS 67117	1887	Mennon	S/C	662	88	$ 3,830	$2,150	$ 5,980
Butler County Comm. College	El Dorado, KS 67042	1927	State	J/C	3,195	77	$ 570	$1,936	$ 2,710
Central Baptist Theol. Sem.	Kansas City, KS 66102	1901	Baptist	P/C	161	19	$ 1,350	$ 675	$ 2,025
Central College	McPherson, KS 67460	1884	Methodist	J/C	307	23	$ 3,600	$2,100	$ 5,700
Cloud County Comm. College	Concordia, KS 66901	1965	State	J/C	1,929	95	$ 544	—	—
Coffeyville Comm. Jr. College	Coffeyville, KS 67337	1923	State	J/C	1,692	52	$ 320	$1,299	$ 1,619
Colby Community College	Colby, KS 67701	1964	State	J/C	1,622	55	$ 570	$1,650	$ 2,220
Cowley County Comm. College	Arkansas City, KS 67005	1922	County	J/C	2,193	79	$ 450	$1,850	$ 2,300
Dodge City Comm. College	Dodge City, KS 67801	1935	State	J/C	1,602	95	$ 491	$1,720	$ 2,211
Donnelly College	Kansas City, KS 66102	1949	Catholic	J/C	710	49	$ 1,100	—	$ 1,170
Emporia State University	Emporia, KS 66801	1863	State	S-G/C	5,768	240	$ 880	$1,910	$ 2,790
Fort Hays State University	Hays, KS 67601	1902	State	S-G/C	5,513	298	$ 832	$1,860	$ 2,692
Fort Scott Comm. Jr. College	Fort Scott, KS 66701	1919	State	J/C	1,399	104	$ 510	$1,680	$ 2,190
Friends Bible College	Haviland, KS 67059	1917	Friends	S/C	150	21	$ 3,500	$1,550	$ 5,050
Friends University	Wichita, KS 67213	1898	Friends	S/C	826	70	$ 3,795	$1,750	$ 5,545
Garden City Comm. College	Garden City, KS 67846	1919	State	J/C	1,697	68	$ 500	$1,650	$ 2,150
Haskell Independian Jr. College	Lawrence, KS 66044	1884	Federal	J/C	984	49	—	—	—
Hesston College	Hesston, KS 67062	1909	Mennon	J/C	582	61	$ 3,700	$1,950	$ 5,650
Highland Comm. Jr. College	Highland, KS 66035	1858	Public	J/C	1,250	76	$ 550	$1,800	$ 2,350
Hutchinson Comm. Jr. College	Hutchinson, KS 67501	1928	State	J/C	2,652	210	$ 486	$1,800	$ 2,286
Independence Comm. College	Independence, KS 67301	1925	State	J/C	945	75	$ 480	$1,600	$ 2,080
Johnson County Comm. Col.	Overland Park, KS 66210	1967	County	J/C	7,698	364	$ 525	—	$ 525
Kansas City Kans. Comm. Col.	Kansas City, KS 66112	1923	State	J/C	3,970	224	$ 430	—	$ 430
Kansas Newman College	Wichita, KS 67213	1933	Catholic	S/C	763	67	$ 3,565	$1,890	$ 5,455

KANSAS *(continued)*

NAME	ADDRESS	FOUNDED	AFFILIATION	LEVEL/TYPE	ENROLLMENT	TEACHERS	TUITION & FEES	BOARD & ROOM	TOTAL COST
Kansas State University	Manhattan, KS 66502	1863	State	S-G/C	19,220	1,545	$ 926	$1,860	$ 2,786
Kansas Technical Institute	Salina, KS 67401	1965	State	T/C	628	33	$ 495	$1,650	$ 2,145
Kansas Wesleyan	Salina, KS 67401	1886	Methodist	S/C	578	44	$ 3,785	$2,226	$ 6,011
Labette Comm. Jr. College	Parsons, KS 67357	1923	Public	J/C	2,200	35	$ 450	$1,550	$ 2,000
Manhattan Christian College	Manhattan, KS 66502	1927	Independ	S/C	294	19	$ 1,740	$2,000	$ 3,740
Marymount College of Kansas	Salina, KS 67401	1922	Catholic	S/C	706	56	$ 3,550	$2,000	$ 5,550
McPherson College	McPherson, KS 67460	1887	Brethren	S/C	496	51	$ 3,800	$2,075	$ 5,875
Mid-America Nazarene College	Olathe, KS 66061	1966	Nazarene	S/C	1,386	85	$ 2,592	$2,118	$ 4,710
Neosho Cnty. Comm. Jr. Col.	Chanute, KS 66720	1936	State	J/C	857	49	$ 430	$1,450	$ 1,880
Ottawa University	Ottawa, KS 66067	1865	Baptist	S/C	450	40	$ 3,730	$2,193	$ 5,923
Pittsburg State University	Pittsburg, KS 66762	1903	State	S-G/C	5,438	289	$ 726	$1,950	$ 2,676
Pratt Community College	Pratt, KS 67124	1938	State	J/C	2,662	124	$ 514	$1,835	$ 2,349
St. John's College	Winfield, KS 67156	1893	Lutheran	S/C	266	29	$ 3,300	$1,925	$ 5,800
St. Mary College	Leavenworth, KS 66048	1923	Catholic	S/W	802	84	$ 3,100	$2,035	$ 5,135
St. Mary of the Plains College	Dodge City, KS 67801	1952	Catholic	S/C	640	45	$ 5,510	$2,000	$ 5,800
Seward County Comm. College	Liberal, KS 67901	1967	State	J/C	1,694	59	$ 480	$1,850	$ 2,330
Southwestern College in Kansas	Winfield, KS 67156	1885	Methodist	S/C	640	61	$ 3,495	$2,107	$ 5,602
Sterling College	Sterling, KS 67579	1887	Presby	S/C	393	41	$ 3,850	$1,850	$ 5,700
Tabor College	Hillsboro, KS 67063	1908	Mennon	S/C	421	43	$ 3,450	$2,100	$ 5,550
University of Kansas	Lawrence, KS 66045	1866	State	S-G/C	24,400	1,331	$ 820	$1,892	$ 2,712
Col. of Health Sciences	Kansas City, KS 66103	1905	State	S-G/C	2,507	720	—	—	—
Washburn Univ. of Topeka	Topeka, KS 66621	1865	City	S-G/C	6,515	287	$ 1,224	$2,160	$ 3,384
Wichita State University	Wichita, KS 67208	1895	State	S-G/C	17,187	762	$ 943	$2,050	$ 2,993

KENTUCKY

NAME	ADDRESS	FOUNDED	AFFILIATION	LEVEL/TYPE	ENROLLMENT	TEACHERS	TUITION & FEES	BOARD & ROOM	TOTAL COST
Alice Lloyd College	Pippa Passes, KY 41844	1923	Independ	J-S/C	483	23	$ 2,230	$1,550	$ 3,780
Asbury College	Wilmore, KY 40390	1890	Independ	S/C	1,183	108	$ 3,514	$2,205	$ 5,719
Ashland Comm. College	Ashland, KY 41101	1957	State	J/C	1,775	47	$ 414	—	$ 414
Bellarmine College	Louisville, KY 40205	1950	Catholic	S-G/C	2,730	138	$ 3,600	$2,190	$ 5,790
Berea College	Berea, KY 40404	1855	Independ	S/C	1,599	150	$ 118	$1,629	$ 1,747
Brescia College	Owensboro, KY 42301	1950	Catholic	S/C	912	78	$ 3,000	$1,860	$ 4,860
Campbellsville College	Campbellsville, KY 42718	1906	Baptist	S/C	700	43	$ 2,880	$2,100	$ 4,980
Centre College of Kentucky	Danville, KY 40422	1819	Independ	S/C	718	65	$ 5,960	$2,500	$ 8,460
Cumberland College	Williamsburg, KY 40769	1889	Baptist	S-G/C	1,747	92	$ 2,380	$1,576	$ 3,956
Eastern Kentucky University	Richmond, KY 40475	1906	State	S-G/C	13,041	680	$ 850	$1,950	$ 2,800
Elizabethtown Comm. College	Elizabethtown, KY 42701	1964	State	J/C	2,187	50	$ 414	—	$ 414
Georgetown College	Georgetown, KY 40324	1829	Baptist	S-G/C	1,246	94	$ 3,256	$2,146	$ 5,402
Hazard Community College	Hazard, KY 41701	1968	State	J/C	514	20	$ 414	—	$ 414
Henderson Community Col.	Henderson, KY 42420	1960	State	J/C	1,042	28	$ 414	—	$ 414
Hopkinsville Comm. College	Hopkinsville, KY 42240	1965	State	J/C	1,164	29	$ 414	—	$ 414
Jefferson Comm. College	Louisville, KY 40202	1968	State	J/C	5,261	131	$ 414	—	$ 414
Southwest Campus	Louisville, KY 40272	1972	State	J/C	1,334	131	$ 414	—	$ 414
Kentucky Christian College	Grayson, KY 41143	1919	Christian	S/C	709	28	$ 4,200	—	$ 4,200
Kentucky State University	Frankfort, KY 40601	1886	State	S-G/C	2,323	107	$ 674	$1,690	$ 2,324
Kentucky Wesleyan College	Owensboro, KY 42301	1858	Methodist	S/C	942	52	$ 3,670	$1,970	$ 5,640
Lees Junior College	Jackson, KY 41339	1883	Presby	J/C	320	25	$ 2,400	$1,800	$ 4,200
Lexington Technical Institute	Lexington, KY 40506	1965	State	T/C	2,462	60	$ 740	—	$ 740
Lexington Theol. Seminary	Lexington, KY 40508	1865	D of Chr	P/C	124	14	$ 2,710	$1,300	$ 4,010
Lindsey Wilson College	Columbia, KY 42728	1903	Methodist	J/C	428	29	$ 2,640	$2,288	$ 4,928
Louisville Presby. Theol. Sem.	Louisville, KY 40205	1853	Presby	G/C	267	26	$ 2,700	$2,180	$ 4,880
Madisonville Community Col.	Madisonville, KY 42431	1968	State	J/C	1,263	23	$ 414	—	$ 414
Maysville Comm. College	Maysville, KY 41056	1968	State	J/C	571	21	$ 414	—	$ 414
Midway College	Midway, KY 40347	1847	D of Chr	J/W	350	55	$ 2,700	$2,200	$ 4,900
Morehead State University	Morehead, KY 40351	1922	State	S-G/C	6,370	402	$ 816	$1,800	$ 2,631
Murray State University	Murray, KY 42071	1923	State	S-G/C	6,299	351	$ 367	$ 785	$ 2,304
Northern Kentucky University	Highland Hgts., KY 41076	1968	State	S-G/C	9,358	444	$ 714	$1,200	$ 1,914
Paducah Community College	Paducah, KY 42001	1932	State	J/C	1,885	46	$ 414	—	$ 414
Pikeville College	Pikeville, KY 41501	1889	Presby	S/C	620	45	$ 2,500	$1,500	$ 4,000
Prestonsburg Comm. College	Prestonsburg, KY 41653	1964	State	J/C	906	27	$ 414	—	$ 414
St. Catharine College	Springfield, KY 40061	1931	Catholic	J/C	227	23	$ 2,350	$1,800	$ 4,150
Somerset Community College	Somerset, KY 42501	1965	State	J/C	1,128	34	$ 414	—	$ 414
Southeast Community College	Cumberland, KY 40823	1960	State	J/C	624	26	$ 414	—	$ 414
Southern Baptist Theol. Sem.	Louisville, KY 40280	1859	Baptist	G/C	2,561	75	$ 600	$2,000	$ 2,600
Spaulding College	Louisville, KY 40203	1814	Catholic	S-G/C	977	89	$ 2,972	$1,850	$ 4,822
Sue Bennett College	London, KY 40741	1896	Methodist	J/C	286	29	$ 1,615	$1,320	$ 2,935
Thomas More College	Fort Mitchell, KY 41017	1921	Catholic	S/C	1,224	118	$ 4,250	$2,400	$ 6,650
Transylvania University	Lexington, KY 40508	1780	D of Chr	S/C	750	67	$ 5,320	$2,280	$ 7,600
Union College	Barbourville, KY 40906	1879	Methodist	S-G/C	836	72	$ 3,550	$1,760	$ 5,310
University of Kentucky	Lexington, KY 40506	1865	State	S-G/C	22,275	1,452	$ 740	$2,078	$ 2,818
Center at Fort Knox	Fort Knox, KY 40121	1959	State	S/C	385	34	$ 846	—	$ 846
University of Louisville	Louisville, KY 40292	1798	State	S-G/C	19,744	1,713	$ 877	$1,470	$ 2,347
Western Kentucky University	Bowling Green, KY 42101	1906	State	S-G/C	13,200	600	$ 800	$1,700	$ 2,500

LOUISIANA

NAME	ADDRESS	FOUNDED	AFFILIATION	LEVEL/TYPE	ENROLLMENT	TEACHERS	TUITION & FEES	BOARD & ROOM	TOTAL COST
Andrew Jackson University	Baton Rouge, LA 70808	1980	Independ	S-G/C	1,500	275	$ 3,000	$3,000	$ 6,000
College of Asiatic Disc.	Baton Rouge, LA 70808	1980	Independ	P/C	1,000	75	$ 2,000	$3,000	$ 5,000
Baptist Christian College	Shreveport, LA 71115	1961	Baptist	S/C	360	15	$ 2,300	$2,000	$ 4,300
Bossier Parish Comm. College	Bossier City, LA 71111	1967	State	J/C	1,463	57	$ 270	—	$ 270
Centenary Col. of Louisiana	Shreveport, LA 71134	1825	Methodist	S-G/C	1,502	109	$ 3,570	$2,330	$ 5,900
Delgado College	New Orleans, LA 70119	1921	State	J/C	9,918	242	$ 350	—	$ 350
Dillard University	New Orleans, LA 70122	1869	Private	S-G/C	1,142	99	$ 3,300	$2,310	$ 5,610
Georgia Military College	Barksdale AFB, LA 71110	1976	Independ	J/C	251	12	$ 1,620	—	$ 1,620
Grambling State University	Grambling, LA 71245	1901	State	S-G/C	3,970	232	$ 755	$1,736	$ 2,491

NAME	ADDRESS	FOUNDED	AFFILIATION	LEVEL/TYPE	ENROLLMENT	TEACHERS	TUITION & FEES	BOARD & ROOM	TOTAL COST
LOUISIANA *(continued)*									
Louisiana College	Pineville, LA 71359	1906	Baptist	S/C	1,306	85	$ 2,250	$1,837	$ 4,087
Louisiana State Univ. System	Baton Rouge, LA 70893	1860	State	—	—	—	—	—	—
Agricultural & Mech. College	Baton Rouge, LA 70803	1860	State	S-G/C	30,300	1,553	$ 801	$1,876	$ 2,677
Alexandria	Alexandria, LA 71303	1960	State	J/C	1,713	86	$ 410	—	$ 410
Cent. for Agri. Sci. & Rur. Dev.	Baton Rouge, LA 70803	1972	State	—	—	—	—	—	—
Eunice	Eunice, LA 70535	1967	State	J/C	1,543	82	$ 380	—	$ 380
Medical Center	New Orleans, LA 70112	1931	State	P/C	2,553	517	$ 570	$ 840	$ 1,410
Paul M. Herbert Law Center	Baton Rouge, LA 70803	1906	State	P/C	800	53	$ 1,188	$1,876	$ 3,064
Shreveport	Shreveport, LA 71105	1967	State	S-G/C	4,280	162	$ 680	—	$ 680
University of New Orleans	New Orleans, LA 70122	1958	State	S-G/C	15,901	598	$ 744	$1,874	$ 2,618
Louisiana Tech University	Ruston, LA 71272	1894	State	S-G/C	11,169	515	$ 760	$1,770	$ 2,530
Loyola University	New Orleans, LA 70118	1912	Catholic	S-G/C	4,682	324	$ 4,016	$2,800	$ 6,816
McNeese State University	Lake Charles, LA 70609	1939	State	S-G/C	7,351	328	$ 673	$1,560	$ 2,233
Nicholls State University	Thibodaux, LA 70301	1948	State	S-G/C	7,226	280	$ 652	$1,540	$ 2,192
Northeast Louisiana Univ.	Monroe, LA 71209	1931	State	S-G/C	11,075	406	$ 634	$1,544	$ 2,178
Northwest State Univ. of La.	Natchitoches, LA 71457	1884	State	S-G/C	6,481	255	$ 681	$1,590	$ 2,271
Notre Dame Seminary School of Theology	New Orleans, LA 70118	1923	Catholic	G/C	98	18	$ 2,450	$2,030	$ 4,480
Our Lady of Holy Cross Col.	New Orleans, LA 70114	1916	Catholic	S/C	760	110	$ 2,600	—	$ 2,600
St. Bernard Parish Comm. Col.	Chalmette, LA 70043	1968	State	J/C	1,246	23	$ 55	—	$ 55
St. Joseph Seminary College.	St. Benedict, LA 70457	1891	Catholic	S-G/M	129	33	$ 2,025	$2,300	$ 4,325
St. Mary's Dominican College	New Orleans, LA 70118	1910	Catholic	S/W	870	48	$ 4,200	$2,950	$ 7,150
Southeastern Louisiana Univ.	Hammond, LA 70402	1925	State	S-G/C	9,531	275	$ 740	$1,140	$ 2,150
Southern University System	Baton Rouge, LA 70813								
A & M College	Baton Rouge, LA 70813	1880	State	S-G/C	9,072	547	$ 683	$1,974	$ 2,657
Shreveport Campus	Shreveport, LA 71107	1964	State	J/C	696	48	$ 477	—	$ 477
Southern Univ. in New Orleans	New Orleans, LA 70126	1959	State	S/C	2,662	99	$ 649	—	$ 649
Tulane University	New Orleans, LA 70118	1834	Independ	S-G/C	10,511	879	$ 7,300	$3,000	$10,300
Newcomb College	New Orleans, LA 70118	1886	Independ	S/W	1,662	139	$ 6,500	$2,620	$ 9,120
University of Southwest La.	Lafayette, LA 70504	1898	State	S-G/C	15,729	640	$ 652	$1,614	$ 2,266
Xavier Univ. of Louisiana	New Orleans, LA 70125	1925	Catholic	S-G/C	2,194	166	$ 3,472	$2,140	$ 5,612
MAINE									
Andover College	Portland, ME 04101	1966	Independ	J/C	488	24	$ 2,050	—	$ 2,050
Bangor Theological Seminary	Bangor, ME 04401	1814	C of Chr	P/C	86	22	$ 2,935	$1,950	$ 4,885
Bates College	Lewiston, ME 04240	1855	Independ	S/C	1,452	122	$11,500	—	$11,500
Beal College	Bangor, ME 04401	1891	Independ	J/C	350	31	$ 2,650	$1,400	$ 4,050
Bowdoin College	Brunswick, ME 04011	1794	Independ	S/C	1,378	100	$ 8,635	$3,230	$11,865
Casco Bay College	Portland, ME 04101	1863	Independ	J/C	363	19	$ 2,555	—	$ 2,555
Central Maine Voc. Tech. Inst.	Auburn, ME 04210	1964	State	T/C	2,347	158	$ 635	$1,650	$ 2,285
Colby College	Waterville, ME 04901	1813	Independ	S/C	1,666	141	$ 8,330	$3,050	$11,380
College of the Atlantic	Bar Harbor, ME 04609	1969	Private	S/C	163	29	$ 5,475	$2,335	$ 7,810
Eastern Maine Voc. Tech. Inst.	Bangor, ME 04401	1966	State	T/C	607	53	$ 600	$1,605	$ 2,205
Husson College	Bangor, ME 04401	1898	Independ	S-G/C	1,499	110	$ 4,275	$2,625	$ 6,900
Kennebec Valley Vocational Tech. Inst.	Waterville, ME 04901	1970	State	T/C	260	28	$ 700	—	$ 700
Maine Maritime Academy	Castine, ME 04420	1941	State	P/C	644	60	$ 2,460	$2,745	$ 5,205
Mid-State College	Auburn, ME 04210	1916	Independ	J/C	175	14	$ 1,970	$ 800	$ 2,770
Augusta Campus	Augusta, ME 04330	1916	Independ	J/C	145	10	$ 1,970	—	$ 1,970
New England Bapt. Bible Col.	Portland, ME 04101	1980	Baptist	S/C	27	6	$ 1,565	—	$ 1,565
North. Maine Voc. Tech. Inst.	Presque Isle, ME 04769	1963	State	T/C	577	49	$ 665	$1,605	$ 2,270
Portland School of Art	Portland, ME 04046	1882	Independ	P/C	270	32	$ 4,700	—	$ 4,700
St. Joseph's College	North Windham, ME 04062	1912	Catholic	S/C	497	59	$ 3,875	$2,000	$ 5,875
South. Maine Voc. Tech. Inst.	South Portland, ME 04106	1946	State	J/C	1,415	97	$ 655	$1,605	$ 2,160
Thomas College	Waterville, ME 04901	1894	Independ	S-G/C	1,040	30	$ 5,130	$2,805	$ 7,935
Unity College	Unity, ME 04988	1965	Independ	J-S/C	336	31	$ 4,440	$2,600	$ 7,040
University of Maine									
Augusta	Augusta, ME 04330	1965	State	J/C	3,423	222	$ 670	—	$ 1,500
Bangor Comm. College	Bangor, ME 04401	1974	State	J/C	919	82	$ 1,455	$2,620	$ 4,075
Farmington	Farmington, ME 04938	1864	State	S/C	1,880	110	$ 1,365	$2,210	$ 3,575
Fort Kent	Fort Kent, ME 04743	1878	State	S/C	679	25	$ 1,350	$2,500	$ 3,850
Machias	Machias, ME 04654	1909	State	S/C	782	35	$ 1,515	$2,625	$ 4,140
Orono	Orono, ME 04469	1865	State	S-G/C	11,651	621	$ 1,425	$2,680	$ 4,105
Presque Isle	Presque Isle, ME 04769	1903	State	S/C	1,187	76	$ 1,438	$2,559	$ 3,997
School of Law	Portland, ME 04102	1961	State	G/C	225	24	$ 1,860	—	$ 1,860
University of New England	Biddeford, ME 04005	1939	Independ	S/C	429	32	$ 4,950	$2,700	$ 7,650
University of So. Maine	Gorham, ME 04103	1878	State	S-G/C	8,166	351	$ 1,434	$2,315	$ 3,749
Wash. County Voc. Tech. Inst.	Calais, ME 04619	1969	State	T/C	321	31	$ 630	$ 703	$ 1,333
Westbrook College	Portland, ME 04103	1831	Independ	J-S/C	1,036	106	$ 5,400	$2,700	$ 8,100
MARYLAND									
Allegany Community College	Cumberland, MD 21502	1961	State	J/C	4,900	150	$ 700	—	$ 700
Anne Arundel Comm. College	Arnold, MD 21012	1961	State	J/C	8,694	512	$ 800	—	$ 800
Baltimore Hebrew College	Baltimore, MD 21215	1919	Independ	S-G/C	249	21	$ 1,128	—	$ 1,128
Bowie State College	Bowie, MD 20715	1865	State	S-G/C	2,233	120	$ 1,030	$2,532	$ 2,286
Capitol Inst. of Technology	Laurel, MD 20708	1964	Independ	J-S/C	821	40	$ 3,492	—	$ 3,492
Catonsville Comm. College	Catonsville, MD 21228	1956	County	J/C	10,274	496	$ 514	—	$ 514
Cecil Comm. College	North East, MD 21901	1968	Public	J/C	1,455	60	$ 560	—	$ 560
Charles County Comm. College	La Plata, MD 20646	1958	State	J/C	4,003	189	$ 675	—	$ 675
Chesapeake College	Wye Mills, MD 21679	1965	Public	J/C	2,889	30	$ 450	—	$ 450
Col. of Notre Dame of Md.	Baltimore, MD 21210	1896	Independ	S/W	1,689	125	$ 4,000	$2,800	$ 6,800
Columbia Union College	Takoma Park, MD 20912	1904	7-D Adv	S/C	915	89	$ 4,800	$2,390	$ 7,190

NAME	ADDRESS	FOUNDED	AFFILIATION	LEVEL/TYPE	ENROLLMENT	TEACHERS	TUITION & FEES	BOARD & ROOM	TOTAL COST
MARYLAND *(continued)*									
Comm. College of Baltimore	Baltimore, MD 21215	1947	City	J/C	8,930	148	$ 560	—	$ 560
Coppin State College	Baltimore, MD 21216	1900	State	S-G/C	2,307	144	$ 1,045	—	$ 1,045
Dundalk Community College	Baltimore, MD 21222	1971	Independ	J/C	2,709	166	$ 550	—	$ 550
Eastern Christian College	Bel Air, MD 21014	1959	Christian	S/C	65	9	$ 1,120	$1,420	$ 2,860
Essex Community College	Baltimore, MD 21237	1957	State	J/C	10,000	500	$ 632	—	$ 632
Frederick Comm. College	Frederick, MD 21701	1957	State	J/C	3,043	161	$ 750	—	$ 750
Frostburg State College	Frostburg, MD 21532	1898	State	S-G/C	3,654	250	$ 1,300	$1,990	$ 3,290
Garrett Community College	McHenry, MD 21541	1971	County	J/C	620	56	$ 650	—	$ 650
Goucher College	Baltimore, MD 21204	1885	Independ	S-G/W	1,041	143	$ 7,000	$3,500	$10,500
Hagerstown Business College	Hagerstown, MD 21740	1938	Independ	J/C	294	20	$ 1,720	$2,800	$ 4,520
Hagerstown Junior College	Hagerstown, MD 21740	1946	Public	J/C	2,456	55	$ 807	—	$ 807
Harford Community College	Bel Air, MD 21014	1957	Public	J/C	4,706	221	$ 628	—	$ 628
Hood College	Frederick, MD 21701	1893	C of Chr	S-G/W	1,686	154	$ 5,510	$2,765	$ 8,275
Howard Community College	Columbia, MD 21044	1969	Independ	J/C	3,650	181	$ 759	—	$ 759
Johns Hopkins University	Baltimore, MD 21218	1876	Independ	S-G/C	3,140	333	$ 7,600	$3,200	$10,800
Loyola College	Baltimore, MD 21210	1852	Catholic	S-G/C	6,110	320	$ 4,530	$2,675	$ 7,205
Maryland Institute of Art	Baltimore, MD 21217	1826	Independ	S-G/C	911	81	$ 5,300	—	—
Montgomery College	Rockville, MD 20850	1946	State	J/C	19,966	978	$ 957	—	$ 957
Morgan State University	Baltimore, MD 21239	1867	State	S-G/C	4,721	260	$ 1,216	$3,340	$ 4,556
Mount St. Mary's College	Emmitsburg, MD 21727	1808	Catholic	S-G/C	1,410	83	$ 4,700	$2,200	$ 6,900
Ner Israel Rabbinical College	Baltimore, MD 21208	1933	Jewish	S-G/M	295	12	$ 2,000	$2,500	$ 4,500
Peabody Institute J.H.U.	Baltimore, MD 21202	1857	Independ	S-G/C	418	108	$ 6,400	$3,000	$ 9,400
Prince George's Comm. Col.	Largo, MD 20772	1958	Public	J/C	15,354	628	$ 650	—	$ 650
St. John's College	Annapolis, MD 21404	1696	Independ	S/C	386	46	$ 7,200	$2,700	$ 9,900
St. Mary's Col. of Maryland	St. Mary's City, MD 20686	1839	State	S/C	1,296	107	$ 1,505	$2,680	$ 4,185
St. Mary's Sem. & University	Baltimore, MD 21210	1791	Catholic	P/C	606	84	$ 3,500	$2,600	$ 6,100
Salisbury State College	Salisbury, MD 21801	1922	State	S-G/C	4,341	257	$ 1,324	$2,420	$ 3,744
Sojourner-Douglas College	Baltimore, MD 21205	1972	Independ	S/C	452	43	$ 3,970	—	$ 3,970
Towson State University	Baltimore, MD 21204	1866	State	S-G/C	14,858	805	$ 1,322	$3,227	$ 4,549
United States Naval Academy	Annapolis, MD 21402	1845	Federal	S/C	4,588	475	—	—	—
University of Baltimore	Baltimore, MD 21201	1925	State	S-G/C	5,379	252	$ 1,125	—	$ 1,125
University of Maryland									
Baltimore City Campus	Baltimore, MD 21201	1807	State	S-G/C	4,777	1,092	$ 815	$ 965	$ 1,780
Baltimore County Campus	Baltimore, MD 21228	1966	State	S-G/C	6,753	292	$ 1,224	$2,590	$ 3,814
College Park Campus	College Park, MD 20742	1856	State	S-G/C	37,528	2,054	$ 1,185	—	—
Eastern Shore Campus	Princess Anne, MD 21853	1886	State	S-G/C	1,214	90	$ 968	$2,400	$ 3,368
University College	College Park, MD 20740	1947	State	S-G/C	11,273	664	$ 2,040	$ 922	$ 2,040
Villa Julie College	Stevenson, MD 21153	1952	Independ	J/C	910	114	$ 2,850	—	$ 2,850
Washington Bible College	Lanham, MD 20706	1938	Independ	S-G/C	530	30	$ 2,660	$2,440	$ 5,100
Washington College	Chestertown, MD 21620	1782	Independ	S/C	684	65	$ 4,650	$2,250	$ 6,900
Western Maryland College	Westminster, MD 21157	1867	Independ	S-G/C	1,818	133	$ 5,650	$2,200	$ 7,850
Wor-Wic Tech. Comm. College	Salisbury, MD 21801	1976	State	J/C	642	79	$ 600	—	$ 600
MASSACHUSETTS									
American International College	Springfield, MA 01109	1885	Private	S-G/C	2,196	80	$ 4,500	$2,400	$ 6,900
Amherst College	Amherst, MA 01002	1821	Independ	S/C	1,534	140	$ 8,255	$2,750	$11,005
Andover Newton Theol. Sch.	Newton Centre, MA 02159	1807	Independ	G/C	453	63	$ 3,400	$2,000	$ 5,400
Anna Maria College	Paxton, MA 01612	1946	Catholic	S-G/C	1,655	140	$ 4,640	$2,760	$ 7,150
Aquinas Junior College	Newton, MA 02158	1961	Catholic	J/W	306	26	$ 3,000	—	$ 3,000
Aquinas Junior College	Milton, MA 02186	1956	Catholic	J/W	356	22	$ 3,100	—	$ 3,100
Arthur D. Little Man. Ed. Inst.	Cambridge, MA 02140	1972	Independ	G/C	57	30	$10,875	—	—
Assumption College	Worcester, MA 01609	1904	Catholic	S-G/C	2,800	180	$ 5,330	$2,785	$ 8,115
Atlantic Union College	South Lancaster, MA 01561	1882	7-D Adv	S/C	597	65	$ 5,546	$2,250	$ 7,796
Babson College	Babson Park, MA 02157	1919	Independ	S-G/C	3,210	123	$ 6,970	$3,260	$10,230
Bay Path Junior College	Longmeadow, MA 01106	1897	Independ	J/W	682	30	$ 4,000	$3,600	$ 7,600
Bay State Junior College	Boston, MA 02116	1946	Independ	J/C	650	35	$ 3,750	$3,050	$ 6,800
Becker Jr. Col.–Leicester	Leicester, MA 01524	1887	Independ	J/C	505	42	$ 3,100	$2,400	$ 5,500
Becker Jr. Col.–Worcester	Worcester, MA 01609	1887	Independ	J/C	710	50	$ 3,100	$2,400	$ 5,500
Bentley College	Waltham, MA 02154	1917	Independ	S-G/C	10,170	320	$ 5,600	$3,135	$ 8,735
Berklee College of Music	Boston, MA 02215	1945	Independ	S/C	2,463	213	$ 3,820	$2,710	$ 6,530
Berkshire Christian College	Lenox, MA 01240	1897	Adv Chr	S/C	140	20	$ 2,900	$2,900	$ 5,800
Berkshire Community College	Pittsfield, MA 01201	1960	State	J/C	1,967	106	$ 780	—	$ 780
Blue Hills Tech. Institute	Canton, MA 02021	1966	Public	T/C	545	35	$ 2,600	—	$ 2,600
Boston College	Chestnut Hill, MA 02167	1863	Catholic	S-G/C	14,069	861	$ 6,820	$3,750	$10,570
Boston Conserv. of Music	Boston, MA 02215	1867	Independ	S-G/C	411	86	$ 4,720	$2,990	$ 7,710
Boston State College	Boston, MA 02115	1852	State	S-G/C	5,231	280	$ 720	—	$ 720
Boston University	Boston, MA 02215	1869	Independ	S-G/C	28,157	2,600	$ 8,420	$3,780	$12,200
Bradford College	Bradford, MA 01830	1803	Independ	J-S/C	390	42	$ 6,235	$3,390	$ 9,625
Brandeis University	Waltham, MA 02254	1948	Independ	S-G/C	3,557	461	$ 8,745	$3,620	$12,365
Bridgewater State College	Bridgewater, MA 02324	1840	State	S-G/C	4,622	267	$ 1,106	$1,806	$ 2,912
Bristol Community College	Fall River, MA 02720	1965	State	J/C	2,618	154	$ 733	—	$ 733
Bunker Hill Comm. College	Charlestown, MA 02129	1973	State	J/C	3,193	138	$ 739	—	$ 739
Burdett School	Boston, MA 02199	1879	Independ	J/W	649	23	$ 3,500	$3,000	$ 6,500
Cambridge College	Cambridge, MA 02138	1971	Independ	G/C	300	36	$ 5,600	—	$ 5,600
Cape Cod Community College	West Barnstable, MA 02668	1960	State	J/C	5,000	145	$ 785	—	$ 785
Central New Eng. Col. of Tech.	Worcester, MA 01610	1888	Independ	J-S/C	1,813	141	$ 4,000	—	$ 4,000
Chamberlayne Junior College	Boston, MA 02116	1892	Independ	J/C	800	60	$ 3,660	$3,030	$ 6,990
Clark University	Worcester, MA 01610	1887	Independ	S-G/C	3,156	220	$ 7,790	$2,610	$10,400
College of the Holy Cross	Worcester, MA 01610	1843	Jesuit	S-G/C	2,504	201	$ 6,800	$3,100	$ 9,900
Col. of Our Lady of the Elms	Chicopee, MA 01013	1928	Catholic	S/W	756	71	$ 4,350	$2,480	$ 6,830
Curry College	Milton, MA 02186	1879	Independ	S-G/C	1,504	102	$ 5,750	$3,300	$ 9,050
Dean Junior College	Franklin, MA 02038	1865	Independ	J/C	2,232	143	$ 4,445	$2,210	$ 6,655
Eastern Nazarene College	Quincy, MA 02169	1918	Nazarene	S-G/C	841	60	$ 3,641	$2,175	$ 5,816
Emerson College	Boston, MA 02116	1880	Independ	S-G/C	2,229	150	$ 6,700	$4,100	$10,800

MASSACHUSETTS *(continued)*

NAME	ADDRESS	FOUNDED	AFFILIATION	LEVEL/TYPE	ENROLLMENT	TEACHERS	TUITION & FEES	BOARD & ROOM	TOTAL COST
Emmanuel College	Boston, MA 02115	1919	Catholic	S-G/W	1,165	90	$ 5,500	$2,900	$ 8,400
Endicott College	Beverly, MA 01915	1939	Independ	J/W	810	70	$ 5,150	$2,950	$ 8,100
Episcopal Divinity School	Cambridge, MA 02138	1867	Episcopal	G/C	125	21	$ 4,200	$1,900	$ 6,100
Fisher Junior College	Boston, MA 02116	1903	Independ	J/W	643	41	$ 4,200	$3,650	$ 7,850
Fitchburg State College	Fitchburg, MA 01420	1894	State	S-G/C	3,777	228	$ 1,041	$2,048	$ 3,089
Forsyth Sch. For Den. Hygienists	Boston, MA 02115	1916	Independ	J/C	200	20	$ 4,800	$3,600	$ 8,400
Framingham State College	Framingham, MA 01701	1839	State	S-G/C	3,166	162	$ 940	$1,800	$ 2,740
Franklin Institute of Boston	Boston, MA 02116	1908	Independ	J/C	540	39	$ 4,200	$3,500	$ 7,700
Gordon College	Wenham, MA 01984	1889	Independ	S/C	1,059	78	$ 5,460	$2,502	$ 7,962
Gordon-Conwell Theol. Sem.	So. Hamilton, MA 01982	1884	Independ	G/C	660	52	$ 3,270	$2,060	$ 5,330
Greenfield Comm. College	Greenfield, MA 01301	1962	State	J/C	1,570	85	$ 371	—	$ 371
Hampshire College	Amherst, MA 01002	1965	Independ	S/C	1,150	97	$ 9,260	$2,890	$12,150
Harvard University	Cambridge, MA 02138	1636	Independ	S-G/C	25,500	—	$ 9,035	$4,115	$13,250
Hebrew College	Brookline, MA 02146	1921	Independ	S-G/C	249	13	$ 725	—	—
Hellenic College/Holy Cross	Brookline, MA 02146	1937	Orthodox	S-G/C	249	41	$ 3,200	$2,100	$ 5,300
Holyoke Community College	Holyoke, MA 01040	1946	State	J/C	3,218	180	$ 779	—	$ 779
Laboure Junior College	Boston, MA 02124	1971	Catholic	J/C	673	59	$ 4,800	$2,000	$ 6,800
Lasell Junior College	Newton, MA 02166	1851	Independ	J/C	538	76	$ 4,895	$3,048	$ 7,943
Lesley College	Cambridge, MA 02138	1909	Independ	S-G/W	2,571	204	$ 6,000	$3,745	$ 9,745
Mass. Bay Comm. College	Wellesley Hills, MA 02181	1961	State	J/C	4,360	231	$ 740	—	$ 740
Mass. College of Art	Boston, MA 02215	1873	State	S-G/C	2,100	110	$ 1,100	—	$ 1,100
Mass. College of Pharmacy	Boston, MA 02115	1823	Independ	P/C	995	80	$ 4,734	$3,600	$ 8,334
Mass. Inst. of Technology	Cambridge, MA 02139	1861	Independ	S-G/C	9,475	1,867	$ 9,600	$3,880	$13,480
Mass. Maritime Academy	Buzzards Bay, MA 02532	1891	State	S/C	839	60	$ 1,193	$2,560	$ 3,753
Massasoit Commmunity Col.	Brockton, MA 02402	1966	State	J/C	7,174	155	$ 714	—	$ 714
Merrimack College	North Andover, MA 01845	1947	Catholic	S/C	2,165	135	$ 5,350	$3,150	$ 8,500
Middlesex Community College	Bedford, MA 01730	1970	State	J/C	6,872	416	$ 363	—	$ 363
Mount Holyoke College	South Hadley, MA 01075	1837	Independ	S/W	1,978	195	$ 8,600	$3,075	$11,675
Mount Ida Junior College	Newton Centre, MA 02159	1899	Independ	J-S/C	815	79	$ 4,500	$3,100	$ 7,600
Mount Wachusett Comm. Col.	Gardner, MA 01440	1963	State	J/C	1,684	94	$ 765	—	$ 765
New Eng. Col. of Optometry	Boston, MA 02115	1894	Private	P/C	349	93	$ 9,020	—	$ 9,020
New Eng. Conser. of Music	Boston, MA 02115	1867	Independ	S-G/C	726	160	$ 6,250	$3,425	$ 9,675
New Eng. Inst. of App. Arts & Sci.	Boston, MA 02215	1907	Independ	J/C	113	11	$ 6,000	—	$ 6,000
New England School of Law	Boston, MA 02116	1908	Independ	P/C	900	60	$ 3,175	—	$ 3,175
Newbury Junior College	Boston, MA 02115	1962	Private	J/C	3,492	286	$ 4,250	$2,600	$ 6,850
Nichols College	Dudley, MA 01570	1815	Independ	S-G/C	992	60	$ 4,500	$2,600	$ 7,100
North Adams State College	North Adams, MA 01247	1894	State	S-G/C	2,171	113	$ 1,136	$1,100	$ 2,236
North Shore Comm. College	Beverly, MA 01915	1965	State	J/C	2,791	167	$ 714	—	$ 714
Northeastern University	Boston, MA 02115	1898	Private	S-G/C	41,729	2,615	$ 5,745	$3,930	$ 9,675
Northern Essex Comm. Col.	Haverhill, MA 01830	1961	State	J/C	6,782	367	$ 800	—	$ 800
Pine Manor College	Chestnut Hill, MA 02167	1911	Independ	S/W	551	55	$ 7,200	$4,200	$11,400
Quincy Junior College	Quincy, MA 02169	1958	Public	J/C	1,797	151	$ 1,090	—	$ 1,090
Quinsigamund Comm. College	Worcester, MA 01606	1963	State	J/C	5,100	300	$ 900	—	$ 900
Radcliffe College	Cambridge, MA 02138	1879	Independ	S/W	2,479	—	$ 9,035	$4,115	$13,150
Regis College	Weston, MA 02193	1927	Catholic	S-G/W	1,191	99	$ 5,405	$3,100	$ 8,505
Roxbury Community College	Roxbury, MA 02115	1973	State	J/C	999	71	$ 634	—	$ 634
St. Hyacinth Col. Seminary	Granby, MA 01033	1927	Catholic	S/M	42	24	$ 3,000	$3,000	$ 6,000
St. John's Seminary College	Brighton, MA 02135	1968	Catholic	S/M	113	26	$ 2,100	$2,100	$ 4,200
Salem State College	Salem, MA 01970	1854	State	S-G/C	5,306	278	$ 745	$1,600	$ 2,345
Sch. of the Mus. of Fine Arts	Boston, MA 02115	1876	Private	S-G/C	595	71	$ 4,555	—	—
Simmons College	Boston, MA 02115	1899	Independ	S-G/W	2,834	267	$ 7,104	$3,488	$10,602
Simon's Rock of Bard College	Gt. Barrington, MA 01230	1966	Independ	S/C	312	50	$ 8,600	$2,600	$11,200
Smith College	Northampton, MA 01063	1871	Independ	S/W	2,574	260	$ 8,430	$3,400	$11,830
Southeastern Mass. University	No. Dartmouth, MA 02747	1895	State	S-G/C	5,364	295	$ 1,037	$3,200	$ 4,237
Springfield College	Springfield, MA 01109	1885	Independ	S-G/C	2,137	127	$ 4,500	$2,385	$ 6,885
Springfield Tech. Comm. Col.	Springfield, MA 01105	1967	State	J/C	3,647	186	$ 775	—	$ 775
Stonehill College	North Easton, MA 02356	1948	Catholic	S/C	2,745	204	$ 5,110	$2,870	$ 7,980
Suffolk University	Boston, MA 02108	1906	Private	S-G/C	6,200	377	$ 3,990	—	$ 3,990
Swain School of Design	New Bedford, MA 02740	1881	Independ	P/C	155	17	$ 3,900	—	$ 6,500
Swedenborg Sch. of Religion	Newton, MA 02158	1881	Swed	G/C	12	5	$ 1,200	$ 309	$ 1,509
Tufts University	Medford, MA 02155	1852	Independ	S-G/C	7,122	994	$ 7,886	$3,830	$11,716
Flet. Sch. of Law and Dip.	Medford, MA 02155	1933	Independ	G/C	275	35	$ 7,600	$4,000	$11,600
University of Lowell	Lowell, MA 01854	1894	State	S-G/C	9,528	584	$ 1,223	$2,328	$ 3,551
Univ. of Mass./Amherst	Amherst, MA 01003	1863	State	S-G/C	19,226	1,100	$ 1,700	$2,400	$ 4,100
Wellesley College	Wellesley, MA 02181	1875	Independ	S/W	2,262	295	$ 8,630	$3,340	$11,970
Wentworth Inst. of Tech.	Boston, MA 02115	1904	Independ	T-S/C	3,282	161	$ 4,535	$3,140	$ 7,675
Western New England College	Springfield, MA 01119	1919	Independ	S-G/C	5,364	308	$ 4,580	$2,800	$ 7,380
Westfield State College	Westfield, MA 01086	1838	State	S-G/C	2,864	158	$ 1,050	$2,100	$ 3,150
Weston School of Theology	Cambridge, MA 02138	1922	Catholic	P/C	265	32	$ 3,300	$4,200	$ 7,500
Wheaton College	Norton, MA 02766	1834	Independ	S/W	1,268	128	$ 8,200	$3,315	$11,515
Wheelock College	Boston, MA 02215	1888	Independ	J-S-G/C	1,125	125	$ 6,200	$3,250	$ 9,450
Williams College	Williamstown, MA 01267	1793	Independ	S/C	1,999	225	$ 7,016	$2,660	$ 9,676
Woods Hole Oceanog. Inst.	Woods Hole, MA 02543	1930	Private	G/C	98	20	$13,300	—	$13,300
Worcester Polytechnic Inst.	Worcester, MA 01609	1865	Independ	S-G/C	3,782	225	$ 7,392	$2,830	$10,222
Worcester State College	Worcester, MA 01602	1874	State	S-G/C	3,917	171	$ 993	$1,886	$ 2,879

MICHIGAN

NAME	ADDRESS	FOUNDED	AFFILIATION	LEVEL/TYPE	ENROLLMENT	TEACHERS	TUITION & FEES	BOARD & ROOM	TOTAL COST
Adrian College	Adrian, MI 49221	1859	Methodist	S-G/C	1,222	81	$ 5,376	$2,022	$ 7,398
Albion College	Albion, MI 49224	1835	Methodist	S/C	1,811	117	$ 5,850	$2,630	$ 8,480
Alma College	Alma, MI 48801	1886	Presby	S/C	1,255	95	$ 5,980	$2,516	$ 8,496
Alpena Community College	Alpena, MI 49707	1952	State	J/C	1,845	90	$ 682	$2,040	$ 2,970
Andrews University	Berrien Springs, MI 49104	1874	7-D Adv	S-G/C	2,851	208	$ 5,203	$2,730	$ 7,933

NAME	ADDRESS	FOUNDED	AFFILIATION	LEVEL/TYPE	ENROLLMENT	TEACHERS	TUITION & FEES	BOARD & ROOM	TOTAL COST
MICHIGAN *(continued)*									
Aquinas College	Grand Rapids, MI 49506	1922	Catholic	S-G/C	2,784	110	$ 4,790	$2,436	$ 7,226
Baker Jr. College of Business	Flint, MI 48507	1911	Independ	J/C	1,765	70	$ 2,250	$1,175	$ 3,425
Bay De Noc Comm. College	Escanaba, MI 49829	1963	State	J/C	1,624	126	$ 2,671	$ 900	$ 3,571
Calvin College	Grand Rapids, MI 49506	1876	Reformed	S-G/C	3,838	242	$ 4,280	$1,980	$ 6,260
Calvin Theological Seminary	Grand Rapids, MI 49506	1876	Reformed	P/C	212	18	$ 2,545	—	$ 2,545
Center for Creative Studies	Detroit, MI 48202	1926	Private	S/C	1,078	125	$ 4,300	$2,300	$ 6,600
Central Michigan University	Mt. Pleasant, MI 48859	1892	State	S-G/C	16,191	760	$ 1,507	$2,120	$ 3,627
Chapin Junior Col. of Business	Oxford, MI 48051	1981	Independ	J/C	15	5	$ 1,850	$2,000	$ 3,850
Cleary College	Ypsilanti, MI 48197	1883	Independ	S/C	1,006	52	$ 2,760	—	$ 2,760
Concordia College	Ann Arbor, MI 48105	1963	Lutheran	S/C	540	61	$ 2,750	$2,106	$ 4,856
Cranbrook Academy of Art	Bloomfield Hills, MI 48013	1932	Independ	P/C	140	10	$ 5,060	$2,400	$ 7,460
Davenport College of Business	Grand Rapids, MI 49503	1866	Independ	J/C	4,511	150	$ 3,938	$2,250	$ 6,188
Delta College	Univ. Center, MI 48710	1961	State	J/C	10,195	385	$ 825	$2,100	$ 2,925
Detroit College of Business	Dearborn, MI 48126	1936	Independ	S/C	2,965	195	$ 2,733	—	$ 2,733
Detroit College of Law	Detroit, MI 48201	1891	Private	P/C	877	65	$ 3,800	—	—
Eastern Michigan University	Ypsilanti, MI 48197	1849	State	S-G/C	18,745	822	$ 1,481	$2,278	$ 3,759
Faithway Baptist College	Belleville, MI 48111	1974	Baptist	S-G/C	80	18	$ 1,580	$2,300	$ 3,880
Ferris State College	Big Rapids, MI 49307	1884	State	S-G/C	11,008	488	$ 1,671	$2,316	$ 3,987
Gen. Motors Eng. & Mgmt. Inst.	Flint, MI 48502	1919	Private	S/C	2,424	135	$ 2,464	$1,900	$ 4,364
Glen Oaks Community College	Centreville, MI 49032	1965	Public	J/C	1,511	73	$ 704	—	$ 704
Gogebic Community College	Ironwood, MI 49938	1932	Public	J/C	1,517	80	$ 650	$1,500	$ 2,150
Grace Bible College	Grand Rapids, MI 49509	1939	Gospel	S/C	170	20	$ 1,830	$2,100	$ 3,930
Grand Rapids Baptist College	Grand Rapids, MI 49505	1941	Baptist	S/C	816	54	$ 3,320	$2,260	$ 5,580
Grand Rapids Baptist Sem.	Grand Rapids, MI 49505	1941	Baptist	G/C	261	13	$ 2,550	—	$ 2,550
Grand Rapids Junior College	Grand Rapids, MI 49503	1914	State	J/C	7,300	323	$ 1,100	—	$ 1,100
Grand Valley State Colleges	Allendale, MI 49401	1960	State	S-G/C	6,366	325	$ 1,380	$2,290	$ 3,670
Great Lakes Bible College	Lansing, MI 48901	1949	C of Chr	S/C	186	17	$ 2,000	$2,350	$ 4,350
Henry Ford Community College	Dearborn, MI 48128	1938	Public	J/C	16,160	217	$ 870	—	$ 870
Highland Park Comm. College	Highland Park, MI 48203	1918	State	J/C	2,650	125	$ 732	—	$ 732
Hillsdale College	Hillsdale, MI 49242	1844	Independ	S/C	1,044	75	$ 5,720	$2,680	$ 8,400
Hope College	Holland, MI 49423	1866	Reformed	S/C	2,530	152	$ 5,410	$2,410	$ 7,820
Jackson Community College	Jackson, MI 49201	1928	State	J/C	6,980	428	$ 868	—	$ 868
Jordan College	Cedar Springs, MI 49319	1967	Independ	S/C	1,050	66	$ 2,200	$1,500	$ 3,700
Kalamazoo College	Kalamazoo, MI 49007	1833	Baptist	S/C	1,235	94	$ 6,400	$2,600	$ 9,000
Kalamazoo Valley Comm. Col.	Kalamazoo, MI 49009	1967	State	J/C	8,127	243	$ 672	—	$ 672
Kellogg Community College	Battle Creek, MI 49016	1956	State	J/C	7,300	232	$ 667	—	$ 667
Kendall School of Design	Grand Rapids, MI 49503	1928	Independ	S/C	577	55	$ 3,345	$1,710	$ 5,055
Kirtland Community College	Roscommon, MI 48653	1966	State	J/C	1,400	75	$ 700	—	$ 700
Lake Michigan College	Benton Harbor, MI 49022	1946	State	J/C	3,324	200	$ 710	—	$ 710
Lake Superior State College	Sault Ste. Marie, MI 49783	1946	State	S/C	2,494	103	$ 1,452	$2,500	$ 3,952
Lansing Community College	Lansing, MI 48901	1957	State	J/C	20,407	1,213	$ 565	—	$ 565
Lawrence Inst. of Technology	Southfield, MI 48075	1932	Independ	S/C	5,868	270	$ 2,040	—	$ 2,040
Lewis College of Business	Detroit, MI 48235	1929	Private	J/C	533	28	$ 5,328	—	$ 5,328
Macomb County Comm. College	Warren, MI 48093	1954	State	J/C	30,410	822	$ 825	—	$ 825
Madonna College	Livonia, MI 48150	1947	Catholic	S-G/C	3,506	170	$ 1,950	$2,030	$ 3,980
Marygrove College	Detroit, MI 48221	1910	Catholic	S-G/C	1,189	98	$ 4,050	$2,250	$ 6,300
Mercy College of Detroit	Detroit, MI 48220	1941	Catholic	S-G/C	2,142	210	$ 3,390	$1,680	$ 5,070
Michigan Christian College	Rochester, MI 48063	1959	C of Chr	J/C	346	28	$ 2,610	$2,110	$ 4,720
Michigan State University	East Lansing, MI 48824	1855	State	S-G/C	40,627	2,511	$ 1,727	$2,259	$ 3,986
Michigan Technical Institute	Ann Arbor, MI 48107	1915	Independ	T/C	350	18	$ 3,500	—	$ 3,500
Michigan Tech. University	Houghton, MI 49931	1885	State	S-G/C	7,634	400	$ 1,512	$2,208	$ 3,720
Mid Michigan Comm. College	Harrison, MI 48625	1965	State	J/C	1,573	80	$ 661	—	$ 661
Midrasha College of Jewish Studies	Southfield, MI 48076	1948	Independ	S/C	707	20	$ 900	—	$ 900
Midwestern Baptist College	Pontiac, MI 48053	1954	Baptist	S-G/C	220	28	$ 1,620	$ 720	$ 2,340
Monroe County Comm. College	Monroe, MI 48161	1964	State	J/C	2,711	120	$ 456	—	$ 456
Montcalm Community College	Sidney, MI 48885	1965	State	J/C	756	48	$ 774	—	$ 774
Mott Community College	Flint, MI 48502	1923	State	J/C	10,787	411	$ 675	—	$ 675
Muskegon Business College	Muskegon, MI 49442	1885	Independ	J/C	1,312	60	$ 2,160	$1,700	$ 4,000
Muskegon Community College	Muskegon, MI 49442	1926	Public	J/C	5,009	195	$ 620	—	$ 620
Nazareth Col. at Kalamazoo	Nazareth, MI 49074	1924	Catholic	S/C	571	61	$ 5,170	$2,530	$ 7,700
North Central Michigan College	Petoskey, MI 49770	1958	State	J/C	1,862	80	$ 750	$2,200	$ 2,950
Northeastern School of Com.	Bay City, MI 48706	1880	Independ	T/C	175	8	$ 1,800	—	$ 1,800
Northern Michigan University	Marquette, MI 49855	1899	State	S-G/C	8,164	373	$ 1,500	$2,418	$ 3,918
Northwestern Michigan College	Traverse City, MI 49684	1951	State	J/C	3,448	105	$ 1,035	$2,210	$ 3,245
Northwood Institute	Midland, MI 48640	1959	Private	S/C	1,833	80	$ 3,765	$2,030	$ 5,795
Oakland Community College	Bloomfield Hills, MI 48013	1964	State	J/C	25,359	296	$ 730	—	$ 730
Oakland University	Rochester, MI 48063	1957	State	S-G/C	11,721	546	$ 1,550	$1,172	$ 2,722
Olivet College	Olivet, MI 49076	1844	UC Chr	S/C	570	51	$ 5,080	$2,350	$ 7,430
Reformed Bible College	Grand Rapids, MI 49506	1939	Independ	S/C	225	18	$ 2,620	$2,100	$ 4,720
Sacred Heart Seminary College	Detroit, MI 48206	1919	Catholic	S/M	195	15	$ 2,550	$1,600	$ 4,150
Saginaw Valley State College	Univ. Center, MI 48710	1963	State	S-G/C	4,426	245	$ 1,711	$2,369	$ 4,080
St. Clair County Comm. College	Port Huron, MI 48060	1923	County	J/C	3,879	200	$ 825	—	$ 825
St. John's Provincial Sem.	Plymouth, MI 48170	1949	Catholic	G/C	210	22	$ 1,800	$3,600	$ 5,400
St. Mary's College	Orchard Lake, MI 48033	1885	Catholic	S/C	256	40	$ 2,300	$2,300	$ 4,600
Schoolcraft College	Livonia, MI 48152	1961	State	J/C	8,717	318	$ 634	$1,100	$ 1,734
Shaw College	Detroit, MI 48202	1936	Independ	S/C	456	33	$ 3,900	$2,214	$ 6,114
Siena Heights College	Adrian, MI 49221	1919	Catholic	S-G/C	1,750	103	$ 3,700	$2,200	$ 5,900
Southwestern Michigan College	Dowagiac, MI 49047	1964	State	J/C	2,742	150	$ 720	—	$ 720
Spring Arbor College	Spring Arbor, MI 49283	1873	Methodist	J-S/C	975	103	$ 4,590	$2,008	$ 6,598
Saints Cyril & Methodistodius Sem.	Orchard Lake, MI 48033	1885	Catholic	G/C	102	16	$ 2,100	$2,580	$ 4,680
Suomi College	Hancock, MI 49930	1896	Lutheran	J/C	558	44	$ 5,400	$2,300	$ 7,700
Thomas M. Cooley Law School	Lansing, MI 48901	1972	Independ	P/C	1,119	51	$ 4,215	—	$ 4,215

MICHIGAN *(continued)*

NAME	ADDRESS	FOUNDED	AFFILIATION	LEVEL/TYPE	ENROLLMENT	TEACHERS	TUITION & FEES	BOARD & ROOM	TOTAL COST
University of Detroit	Detroit, MI 48221	1877	Catholic	S-G/C	6,270	275	$ 4,770	$2,400	$ 7,170
University of Michigan	Ann Arbor, MI 48109	1817	State	S-G/C	34,895	2,800	$ 2,500	$2,800	$ 5,300
Dearborn Campus	Dearborn, MI 48128	1959	State	S-G/C	6,575	336	$ 1,328	—	$ 1,328
Flint Campus	Flint, MI 48502	1956	State	S-G/C	5,025	227	$ 1,356	—	$ 1,356
Walsh College of Accounting	Troy, MI 48084	1922	Independ	S-P/C	1,819	76	$ 2,075	—	$ 2,075
Washtenaw Community College	Ann Arbor, MI 48106	1965	State	J/C	8,247	492	$ 583	—	$ 583
Wayne County Comm. College	Detroit, MI 48226	1969	State	J/C	20,000	753	$ 930	—	$ 930
Wayne State University	Detroit, MI 48202	1868	State	S-G/C	29,775	1,800	$ 1,990	$1,200	$ 3,190
West Shore Community College	Scottsville, MI 49454	1967	State	J/C	940	67	$ 650	—	$ 650
Western Michigan University	Kalamazoo, MI 49008	1903	State	S-G/C	18,965	890	$ 1,475	$2,250	$ 3,725
William Tyndale College	Farmington Hls, MI 48018	1945	Independ	S/C	320	27	$ 2,396	$2,200	$ 4,596

MINNESOTA

NAME	ADDRESS	FOUNDED	AFFILIATION	LEVEL/TYPE	ENROLLMENT	TEACHERS	TUITION & FEES	BOARD & ROOM	TOTAL COST
Anoka-Ramsey Comm. College	Coon Rapids, MN 55433	1965	State	J/C	3,880	175	$ 855	—	$ 855
Arrowhead Comm. Col.—Itasca	Grand Rapids, MN 55744	1922	State	J/C	1,000	50	$ 800	—	$ 800
Hibbing Campus	Hibbing, MN 55746	1916	State	J/C	794	45	$ 900	—	$ 900
Vermillion Campus	Ely, MN 55731	1922	State	J/C	496	28	$ 912	$1,900	$ 2,812
Augsburg College	Minneapolis, MN 55454	1869	Lutheran	S/C	1,502	184	$ 5,160	$2,335	$ 7,495
Austin Community College	Austin, MN 55912	1940	State	J/C	887	50	$ 855	—	$ 855
Bemidji State University	Bemidji, MN 56601	1919	State	S-G/C	4,311	215	$ 1,009	$1,470	$ 2,479
Bethany Lutheran College	Mankato, MN 56001	1926	Lutheran	J/C	246	25	$ 3,170	$2,010	$ 5,180
Bethel College & Seminary	St. Paul, MN 55112	1871	Baptist	S/C	2,067	170	$ 4,900	$2,220	$ 7,176
Brainerd Community College	Brainerd, MN 56401	1938	State	J/C	580	30	$ 876	—	$ 876
Carleton College	Northfield, MN 55057	1866	Independ	S/C	1,877	187	$ 7,810	$2,390	$10,200
College of Saint Benedict	St. Joseph, MN 56374	1913	Catholic	S/W	2,262	140	$ 4,940	$2,120	$ 7,060
College of St. Catherine	St. Paul, MN 55105	1905	Catholic	S-G/W	2,285	206	$ 4,920	$2,200	$ 7,120
College of St. Scholastica	Duluth, MN 55811	1912	Catholic	S-G/C	1,165	88	$ 4,667	$2,223	$ 6,890
College of St. Teresa	Winona, MN 55987	1907	Catholic	S/W	553	62	$ 4,960	$1,950	$ 6,910
College of St. Thomas	St. Paul, MN 55105	1885	Catholic	S-G/C	5,854	323	$ 4,700	$2,260	$ 6,960
Concordia College	Moorhead, MN 56560	1891	ALC	S/C	2,553	194	$ 5,305	$1,795	$ 7,100
Concordia College	St. Paul, MN 55104	1893	Lutheran	S/C	718	54	$ 3,855	$1,830	$ 5,685
Crosier Seminary Jr. College	Onamia, MN 56359	1922	Catholic	J/M	20	15	$ 1,915	$1,765	$ 3,680
Dr. Martin Luther College	New Ulm, MN 56073	1884	Lutheran	S/C	722	71	$ 1,635	$1,400	$ 3,035
E. W. Cook Inst. of Psychother.	Faribault, MN 55021	1971	Independ	G/C	16	18	$ 388	—	$ 388
Fergus Falls Community College	Fergus Falls, MN 56537	1960	State	J/C	665	36	$ 876	—	$ 876
Golden Valley Lutheran College	Minneapolis, MN 55422	1967	Independ	J/C	527	49	$ 4,860	$2,312	$ 7,172
Gustavus Adolphus College	St. Peter, MN 56082	1862	Lutheran	S/C	2,307	143	$ 6,000	$2,150	$ 8,150
Hamline University	St. Paul, MN 55104	1854	Methodist	S-G/C	1,882	140	$ 5,975	$2,400	$ 8,375
Inver Hills Comm. College	Inver Grove Hts., MN 55075	1970	State	J/C	4,148	192	$ 855	—	$ 855
Itasca Community College	Grand Rapids, MN 55721	1922	State	J/C	996	100	$ 650	—	$ 650
Lakewood Community College	White Bear La., MN 55110	1967	State	J/C	4,262	146	$ 855	—	$ 855
Luther-Northwestern Seminary	St. Paul, MN 55108	1976	Lutheran	P/C	841	49	$ 1,620	$2,365	$ 3,985
Macalester College	St. Paul, MN 55105	1874	Presby	S/C	1,695	165	$ 6,800	$2,350	$ 9,150
Mankato State University	Mankato, MN 56001	1867	State	S-G/C	12,400	550	$ 1,100	$1,500	$ 2,600
Mayo Foundation	Rochester, MN 55905	1915	Independ.	G/C	1,245	812	—	—	—
Mesabi Community College	Virginia, MN 55792	1918	State	J/C	933	29	$ 1,080	—	$ 1,080
Metropolitan State University	St. Paul, MN 55101	1971	State	S/C	3,406	350	$ 798	—	$ 798
Minneap. Col. of Art & Design	Minneapolis, MN 55404	1886	Private	S/C	509	57	$ 4,500	$2,100	$ 6,600
Minneapolis Comm. College	Minneapolis, MN 55403	1965	State	J/C	3,100	175	$ 855	—	$ 855
Minnesota Bible College	Rochester, MN 55901	1913	Christian	S/C	98	15	$ 1,800	$1,700	$ 3,500
Moorhead State University	Moorhead, MN 56560	1887	State	S-G/C	7,591	343	$ 998	$1,411	$ 2,409
National Col. of Bus.-Ext.	St. Paul, MN 55104	1974	Private	S/C	246	27	$ 2,400	—	$ 2,400
Normandale Community College	Bloomington, MN 55431	1968	State	J/C	5,853	172	$ 742	—	$ 742
North Central Bible College	Minneapolis, MN 55404	1930	A of God	J-S/C	937	38	$ 2,810	$1,752	$ 4,562
North Hennepin Comm. College	Minneapolis, MN 55445	1966	State	J/C	4,867	169	$ 657	—	$ 657
Northland Community College	Thief Riv. Falls, MN 56701	1965	State	J/C	565	28	$ 900	—	$ 900
Northwestern College	Roseville, MN 55113	1902	Independ	S/C	891	75	$ 3,900	$2,010	$ 5,910
Pillsbury Baptist Bible College	Owatonna, MN 55060	1954	Baptist	S/C	602	55	$ 2,050	$1,950	$ 4,000
Rainy River Comm. College	Intl. Falls, MN 56649	1967	State	J/C	550	32	$ 912	$2,700	$ 3,612
Rochester Community College	Rochester, MN 55901	1915	State	J/C	3,278	145	$ 825	—	$ 825
St. Cloud State University	St. Cloud, MN 56301	1869	State	S-G/C	11,608	579	$ 1,025	$1,437	$ 2,462
St. John's University	Collegeville, MN 56321	1857	Catholic	S-G/M	2,028	150	$ 4,900	$2,390	$ 7,290
St. Mary's College	Winona, MN 55987	1912	Catholic	S-G/C	1,404	109	$ 4,750	$2,610	$ 6,910
St. Mary's Junior College	Minneapolis, MN 55454	1964	Catholic	J/C	760	81	$ 2,700	—	$ 2,700
St. Olaf College	Northfield, MN 55057	1874	ALC	S/C	3,062	296	$ 6,075	$2,075	$ 8,150
St. Paul Bible College	Bible College, MN 55375	1916	C & Miss	S/C	593	49	$ 2,864	$2,320	$ 5,184
St. Paul Seminary	St. Paul, MN 55105	1894	Catholic	G/M	84	13	$ 3,510	$4,115	$ 7,625
Southwest State University	Marshall, MN 56258	1963	State	S/C	2,011	102	$ 1,250	$1,600	$ 4,050
United Theological Seminary	New Brighton, MN 55112	1960	UC Chr	G/C	225	18	$ 3,300	—	$ 6,100
University of Minnesota	Minneapolis, MN 55455	1851	State	S-G/C	47,383	4,800	$ 1,633	$2,755	$ 4,388
Duluth Campus	Duluth, MN 55812	1947	State	S-G/C	7,734	450	$ 1,576	$2,755	$ 4,331
Morris Campus	Morris, MN 56267	1960	State	S/C	1,583	115	$ 1,605	$2,755	$ 4,360
Technical College, Crookston	Crookston, MN 56716	1966	State	T/C	1,149	53	$ 1,432	$2,755	$ 4,187
Technical College, Waseca	Waseca, MN 56093	1971	State	T/C	1,113	39	$ 1,450	$2,755	$ 4,205
Walden University	Minneapolis, MN 55402	1970	Independ	G/C	180	250	$ 4,500	$ 500	$ 5,000
Wm. Mitchell College of Law	St. Paul, MN 55105	1900	Independ	P/C	1,151	199	$ 3,700	—	$ 3,700
Willmar Community College	Willmar, MN 56201	1962	State	J/C	761	47	$ 855	—	$ 855
Winona State University	Winona, MN 55987	1858	State	S-G/C	5,304	225	$ 1,020	$1,323	$ 2,343
Worthington Comm. College	Worthington, MN 56187	1936	State	J/C	575	30	$ 900	—	$ 3,900

MISSISSIPPI

NAME	ADDRESS	FOUNDED	AFFILIATION	LEVEL/TYPE	ENROLLMENT	TEACHERS	TUITION & FEES	BOARD & ROOM	TOTAL COST
Alcorn State University	Lorman, MS 39096	1871	State	S-G/C	2,442	149	$ 825	$1,475	$ 2,300
Belhaven College	Jackson, MS 39202	1883	Presby	S/C	938	61	$ 3,000	$1,640	$ 4,640
Blue Mountain College	Blue Mountain, MS 38610	1873	Baptist	S/W	352	32	$ 2,130	$1,530	$ 3,660

NAME	ADDRESS	FOUNDED	AFFILIATION	LEVEL/TYPE	ENROLLMENT	TEACHERS	TUITION & FEES	BOARD & ROOM	TOTAL COST
MISSISSIPPI *(continued)*									
Coahoma Junior College	Clarksdale, MS 38614	1949	State	J/C	1,999	56	$ 530	$1,670	$ 2,200
Copiah-Lincoln Junior College	Wesson, MS 39191	1928	State	J/C	1,229	79	$ 400	$1,110	$ 1,510
Natchez Campus	Natchez, MS 39120	1971	State	J/C	531	32	$ 450	—	$ 450
Delta State University	Cleveland, MS 38733	1925	State	S-G/C	3,480	187	$ 770	$1,206	$ 1,976
East Central Junior College	Decatur, MS 39327	1928	State	J/C	917	53	$ 456	$1,080	$ 1,536
East Mississippi Jr. College	Scooba, MS 39358	1927	State	J/C	1,130	146	$ 390	$ 945	$ 1,335
Hinds Junior College	Raymond, MS 39154	1917	State	J/C	8,023	466	$ 370	$ 980	$ 1,350
Holmes Junior College	Goodman, MS 39079	1925	State	J/C	1,349	55	$ 440	$1,000	$ 1,440
Itawamba Junior College	Fulton, MS 38843	1948	Public	J/C	4,599	144	$ 260	$1,100	$ 1,360
Jackson State University	Jackson, MS 39217	1877	State	S-G/C	6,523	379	$ 949	$ 823	$ 1,772
Jones County Junior College	Ellisville, MS 39437	1927	State	J/C	2,856	155	$ 440	$1,320	$ 1,760
Magnolia Bible College	Kosciusko, MS 39090	1976	C of Chr	S/C	66	10	$ 610	$2,200	$ 2,810
Mary Holmes College	West Point, MS 39773	1892	Presby	J/C	475	20	$ 1,250	$1,550	$ 2,800
Meridian Junior College	Meridian, MS 39301	1937	Public	J/C	2,600	170	$ 255	—	$ 255
Mid South Christian College	Senatobia, MS 38668	1959	C of Chr	S/C	40	8	$ 1,226	$1,430	$ 2,656
Millsaps College	Jackson, MS 39210	1890	Methodist	S-G/C	1,203	94	$ 4,655	$1,900	$ 6,555
Mississippi Baptist Seminary	Jackson, MS 39209	1942	Baptist	P/C	500	91	$ 350	—	$ 350
Mississippi College	Clinton, MS 39058	1826	Baptist	S-G/C	2,688	196	$ 2,904	$1,730	$ 4,634
Clarke College	Newton, MS 39345	1908	Baptist	J/C	139	29	$ 1,876	$1,600	$ 3,476
Mississippi Delta Jr. College	Moorhead, MS 38761	1926	State	J/C	1,817	101	$ 375	$ 950	$ 1,325
Miss. Gulf Coast Jr. College									
Jackson County Campus	Gautier, MS 39553	1965	State	J/C	4,117	90	$ 454	—	$ 454
Jefferson Davis Campus	Gulfport, MS 39501	1965	State	J/C	3,261	93	$ 454	—	$ 454
Perkinston Campus	Perkinston, MS 39573	1911	State	J/C	977	47	$ 454	$ 836	$ 1,290
Mississippi State University	Mississippi State, MS 39762	1878	State	S-G/C	12,049	730	$ 1,132	$1,870	$ 3,002
Mississippi Univ. for Women	Columbus, MS 39701	1884	State	S-G/W	1,894	129	$ 800	$1,580	$ 2,380
Mississippi Valley State Univ.	Itta Bena, MS 38941	1950	State	S-G/C	2,479	158	$ 800	$1,333	$ 2,133
Natchez Junior College	Natchez, MS 39120	1885	Baptist	J/C	50	8	$ 810	$ 800	$ 1,600
Northeast Mississippi Jr. Col.	Booneville, MS 38829	1948	State	J/C	2,247	135	$ 480	$1,580	$ 2,060
Northwest Mississippi Jr. Col.	Senatobia, MS 38668	1927	State	J/C	2,800	170	$ 630	$1,050	$ 1,680
Pearl River Junior College	Poplarville, MS 39470	1909	State	J/C	2,772	106	$ 350	$ 954	$ 1,435
Prentiss Normal & Indust. Inst.	Prentiss, MS 39474	1907	Private	J/C	153	15	$ 1,895	$1,543	$ 3,438
Reformed Theological Seminary	Jackson, MS 39209	1964	Church	G/C	303	20	$ 2,225	—	$ 2,225
Rust College	Holly Springs, MS 38635	1866	Methodist	S/C	848	42	$ 2,125	$1,800	$ 3,925
Southeastern Baptist College	Laurel, MS 39440	1948	Baptist	S/C	154	18	$ 1,080	$1,130	$ 2,210
Southwest Mississippi Jr. Col.	Summit, MS 39666	1918	State	J/C	1,421	73	$ 350	$1,000	$ 1,350
Tougaloo College	Tougaloo, MS 39174	1869	D of Chr	S/C	775	79	$ 2,450	$1,320	$ 3,770
University of Mississippi	University, MS 38677	1844	State	S-G/C	9,412	525	$ 1,167	$1,920	$ 3,087
Medical Center	Jackson, MS 39216	1955	State	S-G/C	1,733	464	$ 3,000	$4,500	$ 7,500
University of Southern Miss.	Hattiesburg, MS 39406	1910	State	S-G/C	10,792	612	$ 1,040	$1,604	$ 2,644
Utica Junior College	Utica, MS 39175	1903	State	J/C	1,240	62	$ 370	$1,137	$ 1,507
Wesley Biblical Seminary	Jackson, MS 39206	1974	Tr-Den	G/C	83	15	$ 1,965	—	$ 1,965
Wesley College	Florence, MS 39073	1944	Methodist	S/C	67	14	$ 1,250	$1,550	$ 3,000
William Carey College	Hattiesburg, MS 39401	1906	Baptist	S-G/C	2,943	107	$ 2,280	$1,810	$ 4,090
Wood Junior College	Mathiston, MS 39752	1886	Methodist	J/C	448	43	$ 1,440	$1,792	$ 3,232
MISSOURI									
Avila College	Kansas City, MO 64145	1916	Catholic	S/C	1,876	170	$ 3,650	$1,850	$ 5,500
Calvary Bible College	Kansas City, MO 64147	1932	Independ	S-G/C	523	30	$ 2,280	$1,880	$ 4,160
Cardinal Glennon College	St. Louis, MO 63119	1900	Catholic	S/M	98	28	$ 2,335	$1,250	$ 3,585
Central Bible College	Springfield, MO 65802	1922	A of God	S/C	906	53	$ 2,010	$1,960	$ 3,970
Central Christian College	Moberly, MO 65270	1957	Christian	S/C	119	10	$ 1,250	$1,580	$ 2,830
Central Methodist College	Fayette, MO 65248	1854	Methodist	S/C	578	42	$ 4,250	$1,950	$ 6,200
Central Missouri State Univ.	Warrensburg, MO 64093	1871	State	S-G/C	9,526	497	$ 738	$1,700	$ 2,438
Cleveland Chiropractic College	Kansas City, MO 64131	1922	Independ	P/C	400	45	$ 3,220	—	$ 3,220
Columbia College	Columbia, MO 65216	1851	D of Chr	S/C	674	53	$ 4,425	$2,200	$ 6,625
Conception Seminary College	Conception, MO 64433	1886	Catholic	S/M	100	24	$ 2,440	$2,240	$ 4,680
Concordia Seminary	St. Louis, MO 63105	1839	Lutheran	P/C	735	42	$ 2,240	$1,710	$ 3,950
Cottey Junior College	Nevada, MO 64772	1884	Independ	J/W	362	31	$ 2,200	$1,800	$ 4,000
Covenant Theological Sem.	St. Louis, MO 63141	1956	Presby	P/C	142	16	$ 2,888	$ 540	$ 3,428
Crowder College	Neosho, MO 64850	1963	State	J/C	1,290	40	$ 340	$1,390	$ 1,730
Culver-Stockton College	Canton, MO 63435	1853	D of Chr	S/C	710	49	$ 3,850	$1,850	$ 5,700
Drury College	Springfield, MO 65802	1873	D of Chr	S-G/C	1,024	70	$ 3,875	$1,810	$ 5,685
East Central Junior College	Union, MO 63084	1968	Public	J/C	2,234	90	$ 532	—	$ 532
Eden Theological Seminary	St. Louis, MO 63119	1850	UC Chr	G/C	204	12	$ 3,000	—	$ 6,000
Evangel College	Springfield, MO 65802	1955	A of God	S/C	1,809	120	$ 2,667	$2,020	$ 4,687
Fontbonne College	St. Louis, MO 63105	1917	Catholic	S-G/C	905	115	$ 4,100	$1,150	$ 5,250
Georgia AFB	Whiteman AFB 65305	1974	Independ	J/C	255	29	$ 1,620	—	$ 1,620
Hannibal-Lagrange College	Hannibal, MO 63401	1858	Baptist	S/C	578	57	$ 2,950	$ 900	$ 3,850
Harris-Stowe State College	St. Louis, MO 63103	1857	State	S/C	1,027	77	$ 650	—	$ 650
Jefferson College	Hillsboro, MO 63050	1963	State	J/C	3,048	163	$ 360	—	$ 360
Kansas City Art Institute	Kansas City, MO 64111	1885	Independ	S/C	438	49	$ 6,150	$1,255	$ 7,405
Kemper Military Sch. and Col.	Boonville, MO 65233	1844	Independ	J/C	125	16	$ 3,230	$3,420	$ 6,650
Kirksville Col. of Osteo. Med.	Kirksville, MO 63501	1892	Independ	P/C	526	71	$13,250	$3,900	$17,150
Lincoln University of Missouri	Jefferson City, MO 65101	1866	State	S-G/C	2,700	315	$ 700	$2,140	$ 2,840
Lindenwood Colleges	St. Charles, MO 63301	1827	Independ	S-G/C	1,974	155	$ 4,600	$2,950	$ 7,550
Logan College of Chiropractic	Chesterfield, MO 63017	1935	Independ	P/C	680	56	$ 3,240	—	$ 3,240
Maryville College	St. Louis, MO 63141	1872	Independ	S-G/C	1,927	133	$ 4,550	$2,310	$ 6,860
Metropolitan Comm. College	Kansas, MO 64111	1915	Local	J/C					
Longview Comm. College	Lee's Summit, MO 64063	1969	Public	J/C	7,213	131	$ 600	—	$ 600
Maple Woods Comm. College	Kansas City, MO 64156	1969	Public	J/C	3,283	96	$ 600	—	$ 600
Penn Valley Comm. College	Kansas City, MO 64111	1915	Public	J/C	7,829	179	$ 600	—	$ 600

MISSOURI *(continued)*

NAME	ADDRESS	FOUNDED	AFFILIATION	LEVEL/TYPE	ENROLLMENT	TEACHERS	TUITION & FEES	BOARD & ROOM	TOTAL COST
Pioneer Comm. College	Kansas City, MO 64111	1976	Public	J/C	1,553	15	$ 600	—	$ 600
Midwestern Bapt. Theol. Sem.	Kansas City, MO 64118	1957	Baptist	P/C	625	20	$ 450	—	$ 450
Mineral Area College	Flat River, MO 63601	1965	State	J/C	1,604	65	$ 360	—	$ 360
Missouri Baptist College	St. Louis, MO 63141	1968	Baptist	S/C	406	35	$ 2,600	$1,800	$ 4,400
Missouri Inst. of Technology	Kansas City, MO 64114	1931	Independ	S/C	2,425	119	$ 3,300	—	$ 3,300
Missouri Southern State Col.	Joplin, MO 64801	1937	State	S/C	4,478	189	$ 640	$1,330	$ 1,970
Missouri Valley College	Marshall, MO 65340	1889	Presby	S/C	412	47	$ 3,400	$1,880	$ 5,280
Missouri Western St. College	St. Joseph, MO 64507	1915	State	S/C	4,284	213	$ 830	$1,530	$ 2,360
Moberly Junior College	Moberly, MO 65270	1927	Public	J/C	1,029	60	$ 730	$1,100	$ 1,830
National College of Business	Kansas City, MO 64138	1975	Private	S/C	124	9	$ 2,298	—	$ 2,298
Nazarene Theological Sem.	Kansas City, MO 64131	1945	Nazarene	P/C	426	24	$ 1,080	—	$ 1,080
Northeast Missouri St. Univ.	Kirksville, MO 63501	1867	State	S-G/C	6,960	296	$ 620	$1,480	$ 2,100
Northwest Missouri St. Univ.	Maryville, MO 64468	1905	State	S-G/C	5,147	225	$ 875	$1,620	$ 2,495
Ozark Bible College	Joplin, MO 64801	1942	Christian	S/C	641	41	$ 1,440	$1,500	$ 2,940
Park College	Parkville, MO 64152	1875	RLDS	S-G/C	817	51	$ 3,740	$1,990	$ 5,730
Rockhurst College	Kansas City, MO 64110	1910	Catholic	S-G/C	3,205	198	$ 4,010	$2,250	$ 4,010
St. Louis College of Pharmacy	St. Louis, MO 63110	1864	Independ	S/C	634	44	$ 3,800	$2,250	$ 6,050
St. Louis Comm. College	St. Louis, MO 63110	1962	Public	J/C	32,367	1,607	$ 615	—	$ 615
Florissant Valley	Ferguson, MO 63135	1963	Public	J/C	12,069	488	$ 615	—	$ 615
Forest Park	St. Louis, MO 63110	1963	Public	J/C	7,989	521	$ 615	—	$ 615
Meramec	Kirkwood, MO 63122	1963	Public	J/C	12,309	598	$ 615	—	$ 615
St. Louis Conserv. of Music	St. Louis, MO 63130	1923	Independ	S-G/C	102	48	$ 4,500	—	$ 4,500
St. Louis University	St. Louis, MO 63103	1818	Catholic	S-G/C	10,179	2,348	$ 4,990	$2,520	$ 7,510
St. Mary's College of O'Fallon	O'Fallon, MO 63366	1921	Catholic	J/C	617	59	$ 2,626	—	$ 2,626
St. Mary's Seminary College	Perryville, MO 63775	1818	Catholic	S/M	66	14	$ 2,892	$1,750	$ 4,732
St. Paul School of Theology	Kansas City, MO 64127	1958	Methodist	P/C	216	17	$ 2,550	$2,400	$ 4,900
St. Paul's College	Concordia, MO 64020	1883	Lutheran	J/C	74	20	$ 2,370	$2,066	$ 4,436
School of the Ozarks	Point Lookout, MO 65726	1906	Independ	S/C	1,230	83	—	—	—
Southeast Missouri State Univ.	Cape Girardeau, MO 63701	1873	State	S-G/C	9,017	410	$ 600	$1,550	$ 2,150
Southwest Baptist College	Bolivar, MO 65613	1878	Baptist	S-G/C	1,530	76	$ 3,200	$1,400	$ 4,600
Southwest Missouri St. Univ.	Springfield, MO 65804	1905	State	S-G/C	15,051	673	$ 792	$1,445	$ 2,237
State Fair Community College	Sedalia, MO 65301	1966	Public	J/C	1,575	50	$ 360	—	—
Stephens College	Columbia, MO 65215	1833	Independ	S/W	1,295	126	$ 5,175	$2,325	$ 7,500
Tarkio College	Tarkio, MO 64491	1883	Presby	S/C	440	28	$ 3,700	$2,240	$ 5,940
Three Rivers Comm. College	Poplar Bluff, MO 63901	1966	State	J/C	1,895	118	$ 400	—	$ 400
Trenton Junior College	Trenton, MO 64683	1925	Public	J/C	555	39	$ 612	—	$ 1,900
University of Health Sciences	Kansas City, MO 64124	1916	Independ	G/C	622	82	$11,000	—	$11,000
University of Missouri System	Columbia, MO 65211								
Columbia Campus	Columbia, MO 65211	1839	State	S-G/C	24,763	1,950	$ 1,267	$1,850	$ 3,117
Kansas City Campus	Kansas City, MO 64110	1933	State	S-G/C	11,419	848	$ 1,294	$2,063	$ 3,357
Rolla Campus	Rolla, MO 65401	1870	State	S-G/C	7,795	776	$ 1,428	$2,388	$ 3,816
St. Louis Campus	St. Louis, MO 63121	1963	State	S-G/C	12,035	566	$ 1,296	—	—
Washington University	St. Louis, MO 63130	1853	Private	G/C	10,700	2,446	$ 7,954	$3,224	$11,178
Webster College	St. Louis, MO 63119	1915	Independ	S-G/C	5,539	984	$ 4,200	$2,450	$ 6,650
Wentworth Mil. Acad. & Jr. Col.	Lexington, MO 64067	1880	Independ	J/M	92	21		—	—
Westminster College	Fulton, MO 65251	1851	Independ	S/C	693	54	$ 4,700	$2,300	$ 7,000
William Jewell College	Liberty, MO 64068	1849	Baptist	S/C	1,570	160	$ 3,810	$1,880	$ 5,690
William Woods College	Fulton, MO 65251	1870	D of Chr	S/W	815	64	$ 5,050	$2,115	$ 7,165

MONTANA

NAME	ADDRESS	FOUNDED	AFFILIATION	LEVEL/TYPE	ENROLLMENT	TEACHERS	TUITION & FEES	BOARD & ROOM	TOTAL COST
Carroll College	Helena, MT 59625	1909	Catholic	S/C	1,358	103	$ 3,140	$2,076	$ 5,216
College of Great Falls	Great Falls, MT 59405	1932	Catholic	S-G/C	1,312	81	$ 3,100	$1,670	$ 4,770
Dawson Community College	Glendive, MT 59330	1940	State	J/C	900	41	$ 650	$2,420	$ 3,070
Eastern Montana College	Billings, MT 59101	1927	State	S-G/C	4,177	160	$ 732	$2,250	$ 2,982
Flathead Valley Comm. College	Kalispell, MT 59901	1967	State	J/C	1,808	139	$ 375	$2,800	$ 3,175
Miles Community College	Miles City, MT 59301	1939	State	J/C	1,075	40	$ 525	$1,950	$ 2,475
Mont. Col. of Min. Sci. & Tech.	Butte, MT 59701	1893	State	G/C	2,217	110	$ 675	$2,265	$ 2,940
Montana State University	Bozeman, MT 59717	1893	State	S-G/C	11,233	720	$ 730	$2,100	$ 2,830
Northern Montana College	Havre, MT 59501	1913	State	S-G/C	1,687	111	$ 651	$2,000	$ 2,651
Rocky Mountain College	Billings, MT 59102	1878	Int-Den	S/C	388	40	$ 3,498	$2,194	$ 6,692
University of Montana	Missoula, MT 59812	1893	State	S-G/C	9,101	484	$ 825	—	—
Western Montana College	Dillon, MT 59725	1893	State	S/C	984	44	$ 667	$2,056	$ 2,723

NEBRASKA

NAME	ADDRESS	FOUNDED	AFFILIATION	LEVEL/TYPE	ENROLLMENT	TEACHERS	TUITION & FEES	BOARD & ROOM	TOTAL COST
Bellevue College	Bellevue, NE 68005	1965	Independ	S/C	2,785	85	$ 1,320	—	$ 1,320
Central Tech. Comm. Col. Area	Grand Island, NE 68802	1973	Local	T/C	—	—	—	—	—
Hastings Campus	Hastings, NE 68901	1966	Local	T/C	2,217	76	$ 522	$1,323	$ 1,845
Grand Island Campus	Grand Island, NE 68802	1975	Local	T/C	1,816	92	$ 522	—	$ 522
Platte Campus	Columbus, NE 68601	1967	Local	T/C	2,535	44	$ 522	$1,323	$ 1,845
Chadron State College	Chadron, NE 69337	1911	State	S-G/C	1,977	103	$ 846	$1,666	$ 2,512
College of Saint Mary	Omaha, NE 68124	1923	Catholic	S/W	1,141	154	$ 4,052	$1,810	$ 5,862
Concordia Teachers College	Seward, NE 68434	1894	Lutheran	S-G/C	1,066	88	$ 3,800	$1,920	$ 5,720
Creighton University	Omaha, NE 68178	1878	Independ	S-G/C	5,682	986	$ 4,456	$2,204	$ 6,660
Dana College	Blair, NE 68008	1884	Lutheran	S/C	595	49	$ 4,020	$1,655	$ 5,675
Doane College	Crete, NE 68333	1872	UC Chr	S/C	646	58	$ 4,410	$1,710	$ 6,120
Grace College of the Bible	Omaha, NE 68108	1943	Independ	S/C	312	21	$ 2,550	$1,750	$ 4,300
Hastings College	Hastings, NE 68901	1882	Presby	S/C	777	56	$ 3,820	$1,760	$ 5,580
Kearney State College	Kearney, NE 68849	1903	State	S-G/C	7,276	250	$ 872	$1,506	$ 2,378
McCook Community College	McCook, NE 69001	1926	State	J/C	520	40	$ 500	$1,362	$ 1,862
Met. Tech. Comm. College	Omaha, NE 68103	1974	State	J/C	6,168	278	$ 681	—	$ 681
Midland Lutheran College	Fremont, NE 68025	1883	Lutheran	S/C	857	58	$ 4,280	$1,910	$ 6,190
Mid-Plains Community College	North Platte, NE 69101	1968	Public	J/C	1,989	51	$ 550	$1,550	$ 2,100
Nebraska Christian College	Norfolk, NE 68701	1945	C of Chr	S/C	172	16	$ 1,338	$1,650	$ 2,988

NAME	ADDRESS	FOUNDED	AFFILIATION	LEVEL/TYPE	ENROLLMENT	TEACHERS	TUITION & FEES	BOARD & ROOM	TOTAL COST
NEBRASKA *(continued)*									
Nebraska Wesleyan Univ.	Lincoln, NE 68504	1887	Methodist	S/C	1,063	99	$ 4,380	$1,850	$ 6,230
Northeast Tech. Comm. Col.	Norfolk, NE 68701	1928	State	T/C	1,686	110	$ 648	$1,600	$ 2,248
Peru State College	Peru, NE 68421	1867	State	S/C	950	47	$ 875	$1,748	$ 2,623
Platte Valley Bible College	Scottsbluff, NE 69361	1951	C of Chr	S/C	37	6	$ 1,000	$1,200	$ 2,200
Southeast Community College	Lincoln, NE 68520	1973	Public	T/C					
Fairbury/Beatrice Campus	Fairbury, NE 68352	1941	Public	T/C	328	17	$ 560	$1,500	$ 2,060
Lincoln Campus	Lincoln, NE 68520	1967	Public	T/C	4,157	103	$ 560	—	$ 560
Milford Beatrice Campus	Milford, NE 68405	1941	Public	T/C	1,228	93	$ 560	$1,454	$ 2,014
Union College	Lincoln, NE 68506	1891	7-D Adv	S/C	1,024	83	$ 5,450	$2,050	$ 7,500
University of Nebraska	Lincoln, NE 68583	1869	State	S-G/C	979	88	$ 4,835	$1,900	$ 6,735
Lincoln	Lincoln, NE 68588	1869	State	S-G/C	24,006	1,072	$ 1,128	$1,825	$ 2,953
Medical Center	Omaha, NE 68105	1902	State	S-G/C	2,031	144	$ 2,588	—	$ 2,588
Omaha	Omaha, NE 68132	1908	State	S-G/C	15,333	393	$ 1,064	—	$ 1,064
Sch. of Tech. Agriculture	Curtis, NE 69025	1965	State	T/C	310	31	$ 769	$1,485	$ 2,254
Wayne State College	Wayne, NE 68787	1910	State	S-G/C	2,321	94	$ 837	$1,632	$ 2,469
Western Tech. Comm. College	Scottsbluff, NE 69361	1973	Public	J/C	—	—	—	—	—
Nebraska Western College	Scottsbluff, NE 69361	1926	Public	J/C	1,398	78	$ 615	$1,700	$ 2,315
Nebraska Western Col.-Practical Nursing	Alliance, NE 69301	1958	State	T/C	42	4	$ 520	—	$ 520
West. Nebraska Technical College	Sidney, NE 69162	1965	State	T/C	660	45	$ 570	$1,560	$ 2,130
York College	York, NE 68467	1890	C of Chr	J/C	456	29	$ 2,270	$2,300	$ 4,570
NEVADA									
Northern Nevada Comm. Col.	Elko, NV 89801	1968	State	J/C	1,725	90	$ 510	—	$ 510
Reno Business College	Reno, NV 89502	1902	Independ	J/C	250	26	$ 2,585	—	—
Sierra Nevada College	Incline Village, NV 89450	1969	Independ	S/C	180	36	$ 2,500	—	$ 2,500
Univ. of Nevada, Las Vegas	Las Vegas, NV 89154	1957	State	S-G/C	11,452	472	$ 930	$2,469	$ 3,399
Univ. of Nevada, Reno	Reno, NV 89557	1864	State	S-G/C	9,577	479	$ 930	$2,110	$ 3,040
NEW HAMPSHIRE									
Antioch/New Eng. Grad. Cen.	Keene, NH 03431	1964	Independ	G/C	396	70	$ 4,000	—	$ 4,000
Castle Junior College	Windham, NH 03087	1963	Catholic	J/W	126	12	$ 1,900	—	$ 1,900
Colby-Sawyer College	New London, NH 03257	1837	Independ	S/W	579	53	$ 6,390	$2,600	$ 8,990
Daniel Webster College	Nashua, NH 03063	1965	Independ	S/C	475	27	$ 4,990	$2,600	$ 7,590
Dartmouth College	Hanover, NH 03755	1769	Independ	S-G/C	4,376	309	$ 9,090	$3,490	$12,580
Franklin Pierce College	Rindge, NH 03461	1962	Independ	S/C	973	65	$ 5,950	$2,640	$ 8,590
Hesser College	Manchester, NH 03101	1900	Independ	J/C	1,708	97	$ 3,050	$1,100	$ 4,150
Keene State College	Keene, NH 03431	1909	State	S/C	3,850	175	$ 1,300	$2,200	$ 3,500
Lebanon College	Lebanon, NH 03766	1957	Independ	J/C	1,800	120	—	—	—
Magdalen College	Bedford, NH 03102	1973	Catholic	S/C	70	7	$ 3,200	$2,000	$ 5,200
McIntosh College	Dover, NH 03820	1896	Independ	J/C	400	18	$ 2,100	—	$ 2,100
Merrimack Valley College	Manchester, NH 03102	1967	State	J/C	469	39	$ 1,110	—	$ 1,110
Nathaniel Hawthorne College	Antrim, NH 03440	1962	Independ	J-S/C	382	30	$ 5,100	$2,100	$ 7,200
New England College	Henniker, NH 03242	1946	Independ	S-G/C	1,618	116	$ 6,190	$2,830	$ 9,020
New Hampshire College	Manchester, NH 03104	1932	Independ	S-G/C	1,540	72	$ 6,160	$3,100	$ 9,260
New Hampshire Tech. Inst.	Concord, NH 03301	1965	State	T/C	2,147	72	$ 992	$1,760	$ 2,752
N.H. Voc. Tech. College	Berlin, NH 03570	1966	State	T/C	349	32	$ 1,230	—	$ 1,230
N.H. Voc. Tech. College	Claremont NH 03743	1967	State	T/C	338	38	$ 935	—	$ 935
N.H. Voc. Tech. College	Laconia, NH 03246	1967	State	J/C	244	21	$ 930	—	$ 930
N.H. Voc. Tech. College	Manchester, NH 03102	1945	State	J/C	450	35	$ 925	—	$ 925
N.H. Voc. Tech. College	Nashua, NH 03063	1967	State	T/C	314	25	$ 945	—	$ 945
N.H. Voc. Tech. College	Stratham, NH 03885	1945	State	T/C	268	25	$ 1,232	—	$ 1,232
Notre Dame College	Manchester, NH 03104	1950	Catholic	S-G/W	716	70	$ 3,100	$2,150	$ 5,250
Plymouth State College	Plymouth, NH 03264	1871	State	S/C	3,458	182	$ 1,447	$2,062	$ 3,509
Rivier College	Nashua, NH 03060	1933	Catholic	S-G/W	2,218	154	$ 4,000	$2,600	$ 6,600
St. Anselm's College	Manchester, NH 03102	1889	Catholic	S/C	1,795	157	$ 4,750	$2,450	$ 7,200
University of New Hampshire	Durham, NH 03824	1866	State	S-G/C	12,246	620	$ 1,837	$2,387	$ 4,225
White Pines College	Chester, NH 03036	1965	Independ	J/C	223	26	$ 3,600	$2,400	$ 6,000
NEW JERSEY									
Assumption College for Sisters	Mendham, NJ 07945	1953	Catholic	J/W	23	10	$ 1,200	$1,100	$ 2,300
Atlantic Community College	Mays Landing, NJ 08330	1964	County	J/C	3,718	140	$ 804	$2,500	$ 3,304
Bergen Community College	Paramus, NJ 07652	1965	Public	J/C	11,422	470	$ 690	—	$ 2,066
Berkeley School	Little Falls, NJ 07424	1931	Independ	J/C	600	22	$ 4,200	$3,300	$ 7,500
Bloomfield College	Bloomfield, NJ 07003	1868	Independ	S/C	1,898	145	$ 4,350	$2,380	$ 6,730
Brookdale Community College	Lincroft, NJ 07738	1967	State	J/C	11,712	147	$ 610	—	$ 610
Burlington County College	Pemberton, NJ 08068	1968	County	J/C	6,981	92	$ 672	—	$ 672
Caldwell College	Caldwell, NJ 07006	1939	Catholic	S/W	768	67	$ 3,750	$2,500	$ 6,250
Camden County College	Blackwood, NJ 08012	1967	Public	J/C	8,816	345	$ 634	—	$ 634
Centenary College	Hackettstown, NJ 07840	1867	Independ	J-S/W	1,290	126	$ 4,300	$3,600	$ 7,900
College of Saint Elizabeth	Convent Sta., NJ 07961	1899	Catholic	S/W	880	94	$ 4,670	$2,500	$ 7,170
County College of Morris	Randolph, NJ 07869	1965	Public	J/C	12,012	558	$ 765	$3,500	$ 4,265
Cumberland County College	Vineland, NJ 08360	1963	Public	J/C	2,419	93	$ 695	—	$ 695
Devry Technical Institute	Woodbridge, NJ 07095	1969	Independ	S/C	2,432	100	$ 3,300	—	$ 3,300
Don Bosco College	Newton, NJ 07860	1928	Catholic	S/M	78	21	$ 2,860	$1,925	$ 4,785
Drew University	Madison, NJ 07940	1866	Methodist	S-G/C	2,335	178	$ 6,980	$2,614	$ 9,594
Essex County College	Newark, NJ 07102	1968	State	J/C	6,500	200	$ 700	—	$ 700
Fairleigh Dickinson Univ.									
Edward Williams College	Hackensack, NJ 07601	1942	Independ	J/C	717	54	$ 3,960	$2,633	$ 6,593
Florham-Madison Campus	Madison, NJ 07940	1942	Independ	S-G/C	4,974	278	$ 4,826	$2,633	$ 7,459
Rutherford Campus	Rutherford, NJ 07070	1942	Independ	S-G/C	4,172	266	$ 4,826	$2,633	$ 7,459
Teaneck-Hackensack	Teaneck, NJ 07666	1942	Independ	S-G/C	7,970	700	$ 4,826	$2,633	$ 7,459
Felician College	Lodi, NJ 07644	1942	Catholic	S/W	631	48	$ 2,800	—	$ 2,800

NEW JERSEY *(continued)*

NAME	ADDRESS	FOUNDED	AFFILIATION	LEVEL/TYPE	ENROLLMENT	TEACHERS	TUITION & FEES	BOARD & ROOM	TOTAL COST
Georgian Court College	Lakewood, NJ 08701	1908	Catholic	S-G/W	1,499	116	$ 3,500	$2,100	$ 5,600
Glassboro State College	Glassboro, NJ 08028	1923	State	S-G/C	9,134	353	$ 1,164	$2,150	$ 3,314
Gloucester County College	Sewell, NJ 08080	1968	Public	J/C	3,743	138	$ 600	—	$ 600
Hudson County Comm. Col.	Jersey City, NJ 07306	1977	State	J/C	3,600	170	$ 700	—	$ 700
Immaculate Conception Sem.	Darlington, NJ 07430	1861	Catholic	G/C	177	36	$ 2,200	$2,200	$ 4,400
Jersey City State College	Jersey City, NJ 07305	1929	State	S-G/C	6,539	510	$ 552	—	$ 552
Kean College of New Jersey	Union, NJ 07083	1855	State	S-G/C	12,984	735	$ 1,400	$2,550	$ 3,950
Mercer County Comm. College	Trenton, NJ 08690	1966	County	J/C	10,248	380	$ 640	—	$ 640
Middlesex County College	Edison, NJ 08818	1964	County	J/C	12,400	380	$ 750	—	$ 750
Monmouth College	W. Long Branch, NJ 07764	1933	Independ	S-G/C	4,067	198	$ 5,210	$2,350	$ 7,560
Montclair State College	Upper Montclair, NJ 07043	1908	State	S-G/C	14,754	762	$ 1,276	$3,264	$ 4,540
New Brunswick Theol. Sem.	New Brunswick, NJ 08901	1784	Reformed	G/C	110	15	$ 2,160	$1,040	$ 3,200
New Jersey Inst. of Tech.	Newark, NJ 07102	1881	State	S-G/C	6,874	276	$ 1,706	$2,600	$ 4,306
Northeastern Bible College	Essex Falls, NJ 07021	1950	Independ	S/C	301	35	$ 3,600	$2,390	$ 5,990
Ocean County College	Toms River, NJ 08753	1964	County	J/C	5,542	239	$ 690	—	$ 690
Passaic County Comm. College	Paterson, NJ 07509	1968	County	J/C	2,894	166	$ 690	—	$ 690
Princeton Theol. Seminary	Princeton, NJ 08540	1812	Presby	G/C	888	76	$ 2,500	$2,465	$ 4,965
Princeton University	Princeton, NJ 08544	1746	Private	S-G/C	6,031	607	$ 9,450	$3,460	$13,910
Rabbinical Col. of America	Morristown, NJ 07960	1956	Jewish	S/M	230	14	$ 3,000	$2,500	$ 5,500
Ramapo Col. of New Jersey	Mahwah, NJ 07430	1969	State	S/C	4,515	200	$ 1,184	$3,100	$ 4,284
Rider College	Lawrenceville, NJ 08648	1865	Independ	S-G/C	5,462	280	$ 4,500	$2,420	$ 6,920
Rutgers, State Univ. of N.J.	New Brunswick, NJ 08540	1766	State	S-G/C					
Camden Campus	Camden, NJ 08102	1935	State	S/C	1,192	—	—	—	—
Camden Col. of Arts & Sci.	Camden, NJ 08102	1927	State	S/C	2,786	162	$ 1,586	—	$ 1,586
College of Engineering	New Brunswick, NJ 08903	1864	State	S/C	2,136	86	$ 1,682	$2,140	$ 3,822
College of Nursing	Newark, NJ 07102	1956	State	S/C	492	44	$ 1,573	—	$ 1,573
College of Pharmacy	New Brunswick, NJ 08903	1892	State	S/C	694	30	$ 1,682	$2,140	$ 3,822
Cook College	New Brunswick, NJ 08903	1921	State	S/C	2,926	125	$ 1,670	$2,140	$ 3,810
Douglass College	New Brunswick, NJ 08903	1918	State	S/W	3,482	224	$ 1,674	$2,140	$ 3,814
Livingston College	New Brunswick, NJ 08903	1969	State	S/C	3,246	204	$ 1,686	$2,140	$ 3,826
Mason Gross Sch. of the Arts	New Brunswick, NJ 08903	1976	State	S-G/C	451	12	$ 1,682	$2,140	$ 3,822
Newark Campus	Newark, NJ 07102	1934	State	S/C	1,961	36	—	—	—
Newark Col. of Arts & Sci.	Newark, NJ 07105	1946	State	S/C	3,722	214	$ 1,584	—	$ 1,584
Rutgers College	New Brunswick, NJ 08903	1766	State	S/C	8,110	506	$ 1,682	$2,140	$ 3,822
University College	New Brunswick, NJ 08903	1934	State	S/C	3,299	101	—	—	—
Saint Peter's College	Jersey City, NJ 07306	1872	Catholic	S-G/C	4,199	411	$ 4,340	—	$ 4,340
Salem Comm. College	Penns Grove, NJ 08069	1972	State	J/C	1,266	30	$ 725	—	$ 725
Seton Hall University	So. Orange, NJ 07079	1856	Catholic	S-G/C	9,532	609	$ 4,296	$2,300	$ 6,596
Seton Hall Univ. Sch. of Law	Newark, NJ 07102	1951	Catholic	P/C	1,193	70	$ 4,296	$2,300	$ 6,596
Shelton College	Cape May, NJ 08204	1907	Independ	S/C	60	13	$ 1,800	$1,700	$ 3,500
Somerset County College	Somerville, NJ 08876	1966	Public	J/C	4,885	211	$ 690	—	$ 690
Stevens Inst. of Technology	Hoboken, NJ 07030	1870	Independ	S-G/C	3,098	185	$ 7,500	$3,550	$11,050
Stockton State College	Pomona, NJ 08240	1969	State	S/C	5,056	227	$ 1,212	$2,620	$ 4,582
Thomas A. Edison State Col.	Trenton, NJ 08625	1972	State	S-G/C	2,887	—	$ 145	—	$ 145
Trenton State College	Trenton, NJ 08625	1855	State	S-G/C	9,955	509	$ 1,384	$2,735	$ 4,119
Union County College	Cranford, NJ 07016	1933	Public	J/C	9,536	278	$ 700	—	$ 700
Univ. of Med. & Dent. of N.J.	Newark, NJ 07103	1956	State	P/C	2,345	735	$ 5,500	—	$ 5,500
Upsala College	East Orange, NJ 07019	1893	Lutheran	S-G/C	1,210	102	$ 4,718	$2,520	$ 8,238
Wirths Campus	Sussex, NJ 07461	1979	Lutheran	J/C	153	30	$ 2,400	—	$ 2,400
Westminster Choir College	Princeton, NJ 08540	1926	Independ	S-G/C	417	60	$ 5,000	$2,400	$ 7,400
William Paterson Col. of N.J.	Wayne, NJ 07470	1855	State	S-G/C	12,129	577	$ 1,155	$2,290	$ 3,445

NEW MEXICO

NAME	ADDRESS	FOUNDED	AFFILIATION	LEVEL/TYPE	ENROLLMENT	TEACHERS	TUITION & FEES	BOARD & ROOM	TOTAL COST
College of Santa Fe	Santa Fe, NM 87501	1947	Catholic	S/C	1,000	80	$ 3,500	$2,700	$ 6,200
College of the Southwest	Hobbs, NM 88240	1956	Independ	S/C	205	24	$ 1,215	$ 720	$ 1,935
Eastern New Mexico Univ.	Portales, NM 88130	1934	State	S-G/C	3,730	207	$ 875	$1,585	$ 2,460
Clovis Campus	Clovis, NM 88101	1961	State	J/C	1,674	82	$ 162	—	$ 162
Eastern N.M. Univ.–Roswell	Roswell, NM 88201	1958	State	J/C	1,525	56	$ 417	—	$ 417
Inst. of Amer. Independian Arts	Santa Fe, NM 87501	1962	Federal	J/C	212	19	—	—	—
National College of Business	Albuquerque, NM 87198	1975	Private	S/C	263	32	$ 2,355	—	$ 2,355
New Mexico Highlands Univ.	Las Vegas, NM 87701	1893	State	S-G/C	2,312	134	$ 530	$1,550	$ 2,080
N. M. Inst. of Min. & Tech.	Socorro, NM 87801	1889	State	S-G/C	1,371	140	$ 838	$2,200	$ 3,038
New Mexico Junior College	Hobbs, NM 88240	1965	Public	J/C	2,309	95	$ 165	—	$ 165
New Mexico Military Inst.	Roswell, NM 88201	1891	State	J/C	925	62	$ 325	$1,670	$ 2,308
New Mexico State University	Las Cruces, NM 88033	1888	State	S-G/C	15,700	691	$ 940	$1,650	$ 2,341
Alamogordo Branch	Alamogordo, NM 88310	1958	State	J/C	1,298	30	$ 384	—	$ 384
Carlsbad Branch	Carlsbad, NM 88220	1950	State	J/C	875	60	$ 400	—	$ 400
Grants Branch	Grants, NM 87020	1968	State	J/C	479	39	$ 360	—	$ 360
St. John's College	Santa Fe, NM 87501	1964	Independ	S-G/C	342	44	$ 7,200	$2,800	$10,000
S.W. Independian Polytechnic Inst.	Albuquerque, NM 87184	1971	Federal	T/C	570	50	—	—	—
University of Albuquerque	Albuquerque, NM 87140	1920	Independ	S-G/C	1,807	120	$ 3,150	$2,630	$ 5,780
University of New Mexico	Albuquerque, NM 87131	1889	State	S-G/C	23,701	1,367	$ 840	$1,950	$ 2,790
Western New Mexico Univ.	Silver City, NM 88061	1893	State	S-G/C	1,570	92	$ 830	$1,658	$ 3,000

NEW YORK

NAME	ADDRESS	FOUNDED	AFFILIATION	LEVEL/TYPE	ENROLLMENT	TEACHERS	TUITION & FEES	BOARD & ROOM	TOTAL COST
Academy of Aeronautics	Flushing, NY 11371	1932	Independ	J-T/C	1,780	56	$ 3,600	—	$ 3,600
Adelphi University	Garden City, NY 11530	1896	Independ	S-G/C	11,208	367	$ 5,030	$2,688	$ 7,718
Albany Business College	Albany, NY 12210	1857	Independ	J/C	495	18	$ 3,200	—	$ 4,500
Albany College of Pharmacy	Albany, NY 12208	1881	Independ	S/C	550	42	$ 3,100	—	$ 6,500
Albany Law School of Union Univ.	Albany, NY 12208	1851	Independ	G/C	709	40	$ 5,900	—	—
Albany Med. Col. of Union U.	Albany, NY 12208	1839	Independ	P/C	575	—	$14,200	$1,100	$15,300
Alfred University	Alfred, NY 14802	1836	Independ	S-G/C	2,372	211	$ 7,240	$2,660	$ 9,900
Amer. Acad. of Dramatic Arts	New York, NY 10016	1884	Independ	J/C	589	35	$ 3,300	—	$ 3,300

NAME	ADDRESS	FOUNDED	AFFILIATION	LEVEL/TYPE	ENROLLMENT	TEACHERS	TUITION & FEES	BOARD & ROOM	TOTAL COST
NEW YORK *(continued)*									
Amer. Acad. McAllister Inst.	New York, NY 10003	1926	Independ	J/C	190	15	$ 4,120	—	$ 4,120
Bank Street College of Ed.	New York, NY 10025	1916	Independ	G/C	595	40	$ 1,710	$5,650	$ 7,360
Bard College	Ann'dal.-on-Hud., NY 12504	1860	Independ	S-G/C	815	90	$ 9,450	$3,050	$12,500
Barnard College	New York, NY 10027	1889	Independ	S/W	2,416	250	$ 8,985	$2,440	$11,425
Berkeley School	Hicksville, NY 11801	1961	Independ	T/C	385	15	$ 4,200	—	$ 4,200
Berkeley School	New York, NY 10174	1936	Independ	T/C	548	16	$ 4,200	—	$ 4,200
Berkeley School	White Plains, NY 10604	1945	Independ	T/C	830	27	$ 4,200	$3,300	$ 7,500
Beth Israel School of Nursing	New York, NY 10003	1904	Independ	J/C	156	28	$ 2,655	$1,975	$ 4,630
Boricua College	New York, NY 10032	1974	Independ	S/C	1,061	98	$ 3,500	—	$ 3,500
Bramson ORT Tech. Institute	New York, NY 10010	1977	Independ	J/C	200	19	$ 2,700	$2,000	$ 4,700
Briarcliffe Sec. School	Hicksville, NY 11801	1966	Independ	J/W	400	26	$ 3,200	—	$ 3,200
Brooklyn Law School	Brooklyn, NY 11201	1901	Independ	P/C	1,400	39	$ 5,000	—	$ 5,000
Bryant & Stratton Bus. Inst.	Buffalo, NY 14202	1854	Independ	J/C	3,436	118	$ 3,195	—	$ 3,195
Bryant & Stratton Bus. Inst.	Rochester, NY 14604	1973	Independ	P/C	837	30	$ 3,220	—	$ 3,220
Bryant & Stratton Bus. Inst.	Williamsville, NY 14221	1977	Independ	J/C	1,008	27	$ 2,985	—	$ 2,985
Bryant & Stratton Powelson Bus. Inst.	Syracuse, NY 13202	1926	Independ	J/C	983	40	$ 3,195	$1,680	$ 4,875
Canisius College	Buffalo, NY 14208	1870	Independ	S-G/C	4,354	271	$ 4,650	$2,450	$ 7,100
Cathedral Col. of Imm. Conc.	Douglaston, NY 11362	1914	Catholic	S/M	103	31	$ 3,500	$2,000	$ 5,500
Cazenovia College	Cazenovia, NY 13035	1824	Independ	J/C	600	57	$ 4,800	$2,500	$ 7,300
Central City Business Institute	Syracuse, NY 13203	1904	Independ	T/C	1,200	60	$ 2,495	$1,800	$ 4,295
Christ the King Seminary	East Aurora, NY 14052	1855	Catholic	G/M	175	23	$ 4,600	—	$ 4,600
City University of New York									
Bernard M. Baruch College	New York, NY 10010	1919	Public	S-G/C	15,238	720	$ 1,126	—	$ 1,126
Borough of Manhat. Comm. Col.	New York, NY 10007	1963	Public	J/C	9,867	579	$ 1,074	—	$ 1,074
Bronx Community College	Bronx, NY 10453	1957	Public	J/C	6,690	469	$ 1,145	—	$ 1,145
Brooklyn College	Brooklyn, NY 11210	1930	City	S-G/C	15,568	1,314	$ 998	—	$ 998
City College of New York	New York, NY 10031	1847	City	S-G/C	13,500	800	$ 1,075	—	$ 1,075
College of Staten Island	Staten Island, NY 10301	1976	City	S-G/C	11,500	370	$ 1,075	—	$ 1,075
Grad. Sch. and Univ. Center	New York, NY 10036	1961	City	G/C	3,431	326	$ 1,900	—	$ 1,900
Herbert H. Lehman College	Bronx, NY 10468	1931	City	S-G/C	9,591	664	$ 1,126	—	$ 1,126
Hostos Community College	Bronx, NY 10472	1970	City	J/C	4,008	341	$ 537	—	$ 1,075
Hunter College	New York, NY 10021	1870	City	S-G/C	17,373	1,091	$ 1,075	—	$ 1,075
John Jay Col. of Crim. Justice	New York, NY 10019	1964	City	S-G/C	5,880	404	$ 1,275	—	$ 1,275
Kingsborough Comm. College	Brooklyn, NY 11235	1964	City	J/C	9,212	683	$ 1,075	—	$ 1,075
LaGuardia Comm. College	L.I.C., NY 11101	1971	City	J/C	6,863	249	$ 1,075	—	$ 1,075
Medgar Evers College	Brooklyn, NY 11225	1969	City	J/C	2,639	181	$ 1,126	$5,309	$ 6,435
New York City Tech Col.	Brooklyn, NY 11201	1946	City	J/C	12,260	964	$ 1,122	—	$ 1,122
Queens College	Flushing, NY 11367	1937	City	S-G/C	17,335	1,524	$ 1,206	—	$ 1,206
Queensborough Comm. Col.	Bayside, NY 11364	1958	City	J/C	12,970	600	$ 1,095	—	$ 1,095
York College	Jamaica, NY 11451	1966	City	S/C	4,119	270	$ 1,075	—	$ 1,075
Clarkson College of Technology	Potsdam, NY 13676	1896	Independ	S-G/C	4,037	234	$ 6,950	$3,280	$10,230
Colgate Roch./Bexley/ Crozer	Rochester, NY 14620	1817	Ecumen	G/C	226	18	$ 3,130	$1,660	$ 5,010
Colgate University	Hamilton, NY 13346	1819	Independ	S-G/C	2,630	219	$ 8,300	$3,020	$11,320
College for Human Services	New York, NY 10014	1964	Independ	S-G/C	550	25	$ 3,960	—	$ 3,960
College of Insurance	New York, NY 10038	1962	Independ	S-G/C	1,622	200	$ 2,288	$3,300	$ 7,876
College of Mt. Saint Vincent	Riverdale, NY 10471	1847	Independ	S/C	1,147	84	$ 4,950	$3,000	$ 7,950
College of New Rochelle	New Rochelle, NY 10801	1904	Independ	S-G/C	990	66	—	—	$ 3,450
Graduate School	New Rochelle, NY 10801	1969	Independ	G/C	916	112	$ 4,800	$3,000	$ 7,800
School of Arts & Sciences	New Rochelle, NY 10801	1904	Independ	S-G/W	916	112	$ 4,800	$3,000	$ 7,800
School of New Resources	New Rochelle, NY 10801	1972	Independ	S/C	3,493	400	$ 3,120	—	$ 3,120
School of Nursing	New Rochelle, NY 10801	1976	Independ	S/C	330	17	$ 4,950	$3,000	$ 7,950
College of Saint Rose	Albany, NY 12203	1920	Independ	S-G/C	2,728	179	$ 4,400	$2,400	$ 6,800
Colum. Mem. Hosp. Sch. of Nur.	Hudson, NY 12534	1900	Independ	S/C	120	10	$ 1,948	—	$ 1,948
Columbia University	New York, NY 10027	1754	Independ	S-G/C	18,200	4,600	$ 8,942	$3,809	$12,751
Columbia College	New York, NY 10027	1754	Independ	S/C	2,918	530	$ 8,942	$3,808	$12,751
Sch. of Eng. & Ap. Sci.	New York, NY 10027	1754	Independ	S-G/C	2,080	108	$ 8,942	$3,808	$12,751
Sch. of General Studies	New York, NY 10027	1947	Independ	S/C	3,100	400	$ 8,122	—	$ 8,122
Teachers College	New York, NY 10027	1889	Independ	G/C	4,450	275	$ 5,280	—	$ 5,280
Concordia College	Bronxville, NY 10708	1881	Lutheran	J-S/C	457	50	$ 4,050	$2,260	$ 6,310
Cooper Union	New York, NY 10003	1859	Independ	S-G/C	978	159	$ 300	—	$ 300
Cornell University									
Endowed Division	Ithaca, NY 14853	1865	Independ	S-G/C	7,371	1,016	$ 8,900	$3,250	$12,150
Statutory Division	Ithaca, NY 14853	1865	State	S-G/C	4,853	803	$ 3,740	$3,250	$ 6,990
Medical College	New York, NY 10021	1865	Independ	G/C	575	446	$12,650	—	$12,650
Culinary Inst. of America	Hyde Park, NY 12538	1946	Independ	J/C	1,800	80	$ 6,000	$1,200	$ 7,200
Daemen College	Amherst, NY 14226	1947	Private	S/C	1,520	130	$ 4,660	$2,400	$ 7,060
Dominican College of Blauvelt	Orangeburg, NY 10962	1952	Independ	S/C	1,713	116	$ 3,000	—	$ 3,000
Dowling College	Oakdale, NY 11769	1959	Independ	S-G/C	2,153	163	$ 3,700	$2,100	$ 5,800
D'Youville College	Buffalo, NY 14201	1908	Independ	S-G/C	1,179	117	$ 4,000	$2,180	$ 6,180
Elizabeth Seton College	Yonkers, NY 10701	1960	Independ	J/C	1,284	180	$ 3,325	$2,650	$ 5,975
Elmira College	Elmira, NY 14901	1855	Independ	S-G/C	2,548	189	$ 5,900	$2,400	$ 8,300
Five Towns College	Seaford, NY 11783	1972	Independ	J/C	322	24	$ 3,200	—	$ 3,200
Fordham University	Bronx, NY 10458	1841	Independ	S-G/C	14,000	860	$ 5,500	$2,800	$ 8,300
Friends World College	Huntington, NY 11743	1965	Independ	S/C	162	20	$ 4,200	$3,500	$ 7,700
General Theological Seminary	New York, NY 10011	1817	Episcopal	G/C	167	38	$ 3,800	$3,355	$ 7,155
Hamilton College	Clinton, NY 13323	1812	Independ	S/C	1,642	153	$ 8,600	$2,850	$11,450
Hartwick College	Oneonta, NY 13820	1928	Independ	S/C	1,426	102	$ 7,100	$2,600	$ 9,700
Helene Fuld Sch. of Nursing	New York, NY 10035	1975	Independ	P/C	131	15	$ 4,020	—	$ 4,020
Hilbert College	Hamburg, NY 14075	1957	Independ	J/C	619	50	$ 2,950	$2,050	$ 5,000
Hobart College	Geneva, NY 14456	1822	Independ	S/M	1,050	122	$ 8,100	$2,730	$10,830
Hofstra University	Hempstead, NY 11550	1935	Independ	S-G/C	10,809	637	$ 4,950	$2,729	$ 7,670
Houghton College	Houghton, NY 14744	1883	Wesleyan	S/C	1,178	88	$ 4,450	$2,100	$ 6,550
Buffalo Suburban Campus	West Seneca, NY 14224	1969	Wesleyan	J/C	75	11	$ 4,400	$2,000	$ 6,400
Institute of Design and Con.	Brooklyn, NY 11201	1947	Independ	J/C	250	20	$ 1,820	—	$ 1,820

NAME	ADDRESS	FOUNDED	AFFILIATION	LEVEL/TYPE	ENROLLMENT	TEACHERS	TUITION & FEES	BOARD & ROOM	TOTAL COST
NEW YORK *(continued)*									
Iona College	New Rochelle, NY 10801	1940	Independ	S-G/C	6,304	378	$ 4,200	$2,700	$ 6,900
Ithaca College	Ithaca, NY 14850	1892	Independ	S-G/C	5,111	407	$ 6,026	$2,688	$ 8,714
Jamestown Business College	Jamestown, NY 14701	1886	Independ	J/C	290	12	$ 2,455	$1,800	$ 4,255
Jewish Theol. Sem. of America	New York, NY 10027	1886	Jewish	S-G/C	457	96	$ 3,070	$1,960	$ 5,030
Juilliard School	New York, NY 10023	1905	Independ	S-G/C	975	160	$ 5,000	—	—
Katherine Gibbs School	New York, NY 10166	1918	Independ	T/C	600	27	$ 5,150	—	$ 5,150
Keuka College	Keuka Park, NY 14478	1890	Independ	S/W	500	55	$ 5,560	$1,980	$ 7,540
King's College	Briarcliff Man., NY 10510	1938	Private	S/C	801	66	$ 4,660	$1,800	$ 6,460
Laboratory Inst./Merchandising	New York, NY 10022	1939	Independ	S/C	241	28	$ 4,670	—	$ 8,670
LeMoyne College	Syracuse, NY 13214	1946	Catholic	S/C	2,144	182	$ 4,380	$2,200	$ 6,580
Long Island University									
A. & M. Schwartz Col. of Phar.	Brooklyn, NY 11201	1886	Independ	P/C	950	43	$ 3,600	$2,750	$ 6,350
Brooklyn Center	Brooklyn, NY 11201	1926	Independ	S-G/C	6,817	406	$ 4,790	$2,620	$ 7,140
C. W. Post Center	Greenvale, NY 11548	1954	Independ	S-G/C	13,041	766	$ 5,400	$3,000	$ 8,400
Southampton College	Southampton, NY 11968	1963	Independ	S-G/C	1,215	68	$ 5,200	$3,100	$ 8,300
L.I. Col. Hosp. Sch. of Nursing	Brooklyn, NY 11201	1883	Independ	P/C	134	11	$ 2,000	—	$ 2,000
Manhattan College	Riverdale, NY 10471	1853	Independ	S-G/C	4,900	340	$ 4,200	$3,000	$ 7,200
Manhattan School of Music	New York, NY 10027	1917	Independ	S-G/C	712	186	$ 5,600	—	$ 5,600
Manhattanville College	Purchase, NY 10577	1841	Independ	S-G/C	1,289	153	$ 7,000	$3,250	$10,250
Mannes College of Music	New York, NY 10021	1916	Independ	S-G/C	200	50	$ 5,000	—	$ 9,000
Maria College	Albany, NY 12208	1958	Independ	J/C	841	63	$ 2,230	—	—
Maria Regina College	Syracuse, NY 13208	1961	Catholic	J/W	523	31	$ 2,600	$1,800	$ 4,400
Marist College	Poughkeepsie, NY 12601	1946	Independ	S-G/C	2,552	166	$ 4,767	$3,100	$ 7,867
Maryknoll Sch. of Theology	Maryknoll, NY 10545	1912	Catholic	P/C	176	41	$ 3,000	$4,400	$ 7,400
Marymount College	Tarrytown, NY 10591	1907	Independ	S/W	1,271	119	$ 5,365	$3,340	$ 8,705
Marymount Manhattan College	New York, NY 10021	1936	Independ	S/W	2,214	156	$ 4,070	—	$ 4,070
Mater Dei College	Ogdensburg, NY 13669	1960	Catholic	J/C	426	37	$ 2,466	$2,000	$ 4,466
Medaille College	Buffalo, NY 14214	1875	Independ	S/C	808	82	$ 3,650	—	$ 3,650
Mercy College	Dobbs Ferry, NY 10522	1950	Independ	J-S-G/C	8,331	669	$ 3,060	—	$ 3,060
Yorktown Campus	Yorktown Hghts., NY 10598	1978	Independ	S/C	1,152	—	$ 3,036	—	$ 3,036
Molloy College	Rockville Centre, NY 11570	1955	Catholic	S/C	1,287	174	$ 3,676	—	$ 3,676
Monroe Business Institute	Bronx, NY 10468	1933	Independ	J/C	1,613	69	$ 1,190	—	$ 1,190
Mount Saint Alphonsus Sem.	Esopus, NY 12429	1907	Catholic	G/M	50	14	$ 1,500	$1,500	$ 3,000
Mount Saint Mary College	Newburgh, NY 12550	1959	Independ	S/C	1,038	81	$ 3,696	$2,297	$ 5,993
Nazareth Col. of Rochester	Rochester, NY 14610	1924	Independ	S-G/C	2,422	93	$ 4,200	$2,500	$ 6,700
New School for Social Res.	New York, NY 10011	1919	Independ	S-G/C	12,835	1,100	$ 5,780	$3,000	$ 8,780
New York Chiropractic Col.	Old Brookville, NY 11545	1919	Independ	P/C	650	103	$ 6,750	—	$ 6,750
New York Col. of Pod. Med.	New York, NY 10035	1911	Independ	P/C	508	95	$10,000	—	$16,000
New York Inst. of Technology	Old Westbury, NY 11568	1955	Independ	S-G/C	13,000	650	$ 3,784	$2,550	$ 6,334
New York Law School	New York, NY 10013	1891	Independ	G/C	1,400	130	$ 6,000	$7,000	$13,000
N.Y. Medical College	Valhalla, NY 10595	1860	Independ	P/C	1,153	2,088	$16,175	$6,052	$22,227
New York Sch. of Int. Design	New York, NY 10022	1916	Independ	S/C	841	72	$ 3,890	—	$ 3,890
New York Theol. Seminary	New York, NY 10001	1900	Independ	P/C	207	26	$ 2,000	—	$ 2,000
New York University	New York, NY 10003	1831	Independ	S-G/C	45,255	6,579	$ 7,200	$3,700	$10,900
Niagara University	Niagara Univ., NY 14109	1856	Catholic	S-G/C	3,839	267	$ 4,370	$2,650	$ 7,020
Nyack College	Nyack, NY 10960	1882	Christian	S-G/C	763	63	$ 4,038	$2,260	$ 6,298
Pace University									
College of White Plains	White Plains, NY 10603	1923	Independ	S/C	1,751	150	$ 4,660	$3,000	$ 7,660
New York City Campus	New York, NY 10038	1906	Independ	S-G/C	30,356	1,417	$ 4,660	$2,700	$ 7,360
Plsntville/Briarcliff Cam.	Pleasantville, NY 10570	1963	Independ	G/C	5,092	452	$ 3,560	$3,050	$ 6,610
Parsons School of Design	New York, NY 10011	1896	Independ	S-G/C	2,710	609	$ 6,320	$3,590	$ 9,910
Paul Smith's Col. of Arts & Sci.	Paul Smith, NY 12970	1946	Independ	J/C	893	78	$ 3,790	$2,540	$ 6,330
Polytechnic Institute of N.Y.	Brooklyn, NY 11201	1854	Independ	S-G/C	3,281	230	$ 7,000	$2,450	$ 9,450
Graduate Center	White Plains, NY 10605	1845	Independ	G/C	407	—	$ 7,000	—	$ 7,000
Long Island Center	Farmingdale, NY 11735	1845	Independ	S-G/C	1,242	—	$ 7,000	$2,450	$ 9,450
Pratt Institute	Brooklyn, NY 11205	1887	Private	S-G/C	4,320	502	$ 5,410	$1,480	$ 6,890
Rensselaer Polytechnic Inst.	Troy, NY 12181	1824	Independ	S-G/C	4,501	382	$ 8,600	$2,918	$11,518
Roberts Wesleyan College	Rochester, NY 14624	1866	Methodist	S/C	613	53	$ 4,364	$2,262	$ 6,626
Rochester Business Institute	Rochester, NY 14604	1863	Independ	J/C	219	11	$ 2,650	—	$ 2,650
Rochester Institute of Tech.	Rochester, NY 14623	1829	Independ	S-G/C	16,259	1,075	$ 5,559	$3,162	$ 8,841
Rockefeller University	New York, NY 10021	1901	Independ	G/C	96	—	—	$ 528	$ 528
Russell Sage College	Troy, NY 12180	1916	Independ	S-G/W	1,450	131	$ 5,700	$2,916	$ 8,616
Junior Col. of Albany	Albany, NY 12208	1957	Independ	J/C	1,000	49	$ 3,600	—	$ 3,600
St. Bonaventure University	St. Bonaventure, NY 14778	1858	Independ	S-G/C	2,751	197	$ 4,615	$2,565	$ 7,180
St. Francis College	Brooklyn, NY 11201	1884	Private	S/C	2,839	161	$ 3,475	—	$ 3,475
St. John Fisher College	Rochester, NY 14618	1948	Independ	S/C	2,332	196	$ 4,994	$2,833	$ 7,827
St. John's University	Jamaica, NY 11439	1870	Catholic	S-G/C	18,961	881	$ 3,900	—	$ 3,900
Staten Island	Staten Island, NY 10301	1870	Catholic	S-G/C	2,168	34	$ 3,178	$3,500	$ 6,678
St. Joseph's College	Brooklyn, NY 11205	1916	Independ	S/C	1,008	140	$ 3,020	—	$ 3,020
Suffolk Campus	Patchogue, NY 11772	1916	Independ	S/C	1,318	158	$ 3,020	—	$ 3,020
St. Joseph's Seminary	Yonkers, NY 10704	1896	Catholic	P/M	73	27	—	—	—
St. Lawrence University	Canton, NY 13617	1856	Independ	S-G/C	2,300	161	$ 7,800	$2,710	$10,510
St. Thomas Aquinas College	Sparkill, NY 10976	1952	Independ	S/C	1,973	100	$ 3,300	$1,200	$ 4,500
St. Vladimir's Orth. Theo. Sem.	Tuckahoe, NY 10701	1938	E Orth	G/C	45	20	$ 1,650	$1,750	$ 3,400
Sarah Lawrence College	Bronxville, NY 10708	1928	Independ	S-G/C	935	132	$ 9,280	$3,850	$13,130
School of Visual Arts	New York, NY 10010	1947	Independ	S-G/C	4,900	594	$ 5,200	$2,100	$ 7,300
Sem. of the Im. Conception	Huntington, NY 11743	1930	Catholic	G/C	204	32	—	—	—
Siena College	Loudonville, NY 12211	1937	Independ	S/C	3,473	195	$ 4,395	$2,885	$ 7,280
Skidmore College	Saratoga Spgs., NY 12866	1911	Independ	S/C	2,152	170	$ 8,050	$3,450	$11,500
State University of N.Y.									
Adirondack Comm. College	Glen Falls, NY 12801	1960	State	J/C	3,019	162	$ 810	—	$ 810
Agricultural & Tech. College	Alfred, NY 14802	1908	State	J/C	4,173	220	$ 1,265	$2,340	$ 3,605
Agricultural & Tech. College	Canton, NY 13617	1907	State	J/C	2,638	121	$ 1,239	$2,625	$ 3,864
Agricultural & Tech. College	Cobleskill, NY 12043	1916	State	T/C	2,762	142	$ 1,196	$2,300	$ 3,496

NAME	ADDRESS	FOUNDED	AFFILIATION	LEVEL/TYPE	ENROLLMENT	TEACHERS	TUITION & FEES	BOARD & ROOM	TOTAL COST
NEW YORK *(continued)*									
Agricultural & Tech. College	Delhi, NY 13753	1913	State	J/C	2,448	136	$ 1,253	$2,450	$ 3,703
Agricultural & Tech. College	Farmingdale, NY 11735	1912	State	J/C	13,427	618	$ 1,216	$2,410	$ 3,175
Agricultural & Tech. College	Morrisville, NY 13408	1908	State	J/C	3,040	138	$ 1,350	$2,490	$ 5,010
Broome Community College	Birmingham, NY 13902	1946	State	J/C	6,671	459	$ 796	—	$ 796
Cayuga County Comm. Col.	Auburn, NY 13021	1953	State	J/C	3,218	162	$ 1,056	—	$ 1,056
Clinton Comm. College	Plattsburgh, NY 12901	1966	State	J/C	1,500	80	$ 900	—	—
Columbia-Greene Comm. C	Hudson, NY 12534	1969	State	J/C	1,420	54	$ 970	—	$ 970
Comm. Col. of Finger Lakes	Canandaigua, NY 14424	1965	State	J/C	3,070	84	$ 1,025	—	$ 1,025
Corning Community College	Corning, NY 14830	1957	State	J/C	3,799	133	$ 1,227	$2,500	$ 3,725
Downstate Medical Center	Brooklyn, NY 11203	1860	State	S-G/C	1,424	793	$ 4,300	$1,600	$ 5,900
Dutchess Community Col.	Poughkeepsie, NY 12601	1957	State	J/C	7,205	399	$ 975	—	$ 975
Empire State College	Saratoga Spgs., NY 12866	1971	State	J-S-G/C	5,201	294	$ 1,630	—	$ 1,630
Erie Community College	Williamsville, NY 14221	1946	County	J/C	13,011	800	$ 875	—	$ 1,600
Fashion Institute of Tech.	New York, NY 10001	1944	State	J-S/C	11,685	583	$ 1,160	$2,500	$ 3,660
Fulton-Montgomery Comm. Col.	Johnstown, NY 12095	1963	State	J/C	1,850	67	$ 885	—	$ 885
Genesee Comm. College	Batavia, NY 14020	1966	State	J/C	2,423	136	$ 868	—	$ 868
Herkimer Co. Comm. Col.	Herkimer, NY 13350	1966	State	J/C	2,255	93	$ 687	—	$ 687
Hudson Valley Comm. Col.	Troy, NY 12180	1953	State	J/C	8,167	280	$ 950	—	$ 950
Jamestown Comm. College	Jamestown, NY 14701	1950	State	J/C	4,300	240	$ 1,050	$2,300	$ 3,350
Jefferson Comm. College	Watertown, NY 13601	1961	State	J/C	1,805	105	$ 1,150	—	$ 3,200
Maritime College	Bronx, NY 10465	1874	State	S-G/C	924	76	$ 1,855	$2,600	$ 4,455
Mohawk Valley Comm. Col.	Utica, NY 13501	1946	State	J/C	4,057	165	$ 1,100	$2,300	$ 3,400
Monroe Community College	Rochester, NY 14623	1961	State	J/C	11,138	547	$ 1,060	—	$ 1,060
Nassau Community College	Garden City, NY 11530	1959	State	J/C	23,089	1,107	$ 1,100	—	$ 1,100
N.Y. Sch. of Indus. and L.R. at Cornell U.	Ithaca, NY 14853	1944	State	S-G/C	725	48	$ 2,500	$3,390	$ 5,890
N.Y. St. Col. of Agr. & Life Sciences	Ithaca, NY 14850	1904	State	S-G/C	4,000	400	$ 3,300	$3,050	$ 7,400
N.Y. St. Col. of Ceramics	Alfred, NY 14802	1900	State	S-G/C	762	50	$ 2,200	$2,660	$ 4,860
N.Y. St. Col. of Env. Sci. & Forestry	Syracuse, NY 13210	1925	State	S-G/C	1,709	104	$ 1,300	$1,650	$ 2,950
N.Y. State College of Human Eco. at Cornell Univ.	Ithaca, NY 14853	1925	State	G/C	1,380	115	$ 3,300	$3,050	$ 6,350
N.Y. State Col. of Optometry	New York, NY 10010	1971	State	P/C	260	100	$ 4,370	—	$ 4,370
N.Y. St. Col. of Technology	Utica, NY 13502	1966	State	S-G/C	3,338	163	$ 1,200	—	$ 1,200
N.Y. St. Col. of Vet. Med.	Ithaca, NY 14853	1894	State	P/C	319	136	$ 6,965	$4,012	$10,977
Niagara County Comm. Col.	Sanborn, NY 14132	1962	State	J/C	4,375	290	$ 870	—	$ 870
North Country Comm. Col.	Saranac Lake, NY 12983	1968	State	J/C	1,513	46	$ 1,000	—	$ 1,000
Onondaga Comm. College	Syracuse, NY 13215	1962	State	J/C	7,513	449	$ 1,100	—	$ 1,100
Orange County Comm. Col.	Middletown, NY 10940	1950	State	J-T/C	2,583	133	$ 1,115	—	$ 1,115
Rockland Comm. College	Suffern, NY 10901	1959	State	J/C	8,462	360	$ 910	—	$ 910
Schenectady Co. Comm. Col.	Schenectady, NY 12308	1967	State	J/C	3,164	168	$ 1,193	—	$ 1,193
State U. College	Brockport, NY 14420	1867	State	S-G/C	7,400	400	$ 1,160	$2,108	$ 3,268
State U. College	Buffalo, NY 14222	1867	State	S-G/C	10,085	556	$ 1,155	$2,400	$ 3,555
State U. College	Cortland, NY 13045	1868	State	S-G/C	5,994	340	$ 1,075	$2,170	$ 3,245
State U. College	Fredonia, NY 14063	1826	State	S-G/C	5,192	307	$ 1,159	$2,408	$ 3,567
State U. College	Geneseo, NY 14454	1867	State	S-G/C	5,231	290	$ 1,175	$2,110	$ 3,285
State U. College	New Paltz, NY 12561	1885	State	S-G/C	7,450	417	$ 1,264	$2,360	$ 3,624
State U. College	Old Westbury, NY 11568	1966	State	S/C	3,755	210	$ 1,400	$2,100	$ 4,750
State U. College	Oneonta, NY 13820	1889	State	S-G/C	6,124	387	$ 1,075	$2,220	$ 3,295
State U. College	Oswego, NY 13126	1861	State	S-G/C	7,815	403	$ 1,050	$2,290	$ 3,340
State U. College	Plattsburgh, NY 12901	1889	State	S-G/C	5,645	291	$ 1,155	$2,164	$ 3,319
State U. College	Potsdam, NY 13676	1867	State	S-G/C	4,600	222	$ 1,500	$2,500	$ 4,000
State U. College	Purchase, NY 10577	1967	State	S/C	3,681	192	$ 1,175	$2,327	$ 3,502
State University of N.Y.	Albany, NY 12222	1844	State	S-G/C	15,726	830	$ 1,075	$2,170	$ 3,245
State University of N.Y.	Binghamton, NY 13901	1950	State	S-G/C	11,725	615	$ 1,491	$2,790	$ 4,281
State University of N.Y.	Buffalo, NY 14260	1846	State	S-G/C	26,839	1,939	$ 1,453	$2,490	$ 3,943
State University of N.Y.	Stony Brook, NY 11794	1957	State	S-G/C	16,181	1,250	$ 1,155	$2,538	$ 3,693
Suffolk County Comm. Col.	Selden, NY 11784	1959	State	J/C	21,500	370	$ 1,000	—	$ 1,000
Sullivan County Comm. Col.	Loch Sheldrake, NY 12759	1962	State	J/C	1,650	90	$ 1,056	—	$ 1,056
Tompkins Cort. Comm. Col.	Dryden, NY 13053	1968	State	J/C	3,472	172	$ 1,075	—	$ 1,075
Ulster County Comm. Col.	Stone Ridge, NY 12484	1961	State	J/C	2,250	93	$ 1,118	—	$ 3,518
Upstate Medical Center	Syracuse, NY 13210	1834	State	P/C	927	258	$ 1,400	$3,000	$ 6,000
Westchester Comm. College	Valhalla, NY 10595	1946	State	J/C	8,639	173	$ 1,000	—	$ 1,000
Stenotype Institute	New York, NY 10019	1937	Independ	J/C	190	7	$ 3,300	—	$ 3,300
Stenotype Institute	Hicksville, NY 11802	1969	Independ	J/C	106	9	$ 3,300	—	$ 3,300
Syracuse University	Syracuse, NY 13210	1871	Independ	S-G/C	21,122	1,948	$ 6,884	$3,460	$10,344
Utica College	Utica, NY 13502	1946	Independ	S/C	2,343	178	$ 5,000	$2,300	$ 7,300
Technical Career Institute	New York, NY 10001	1974	Independ	T/C	1,919	75	$ 4,000	—	$ 4,000
Tobe-Coburn Sch. of Fashion	New York, NY 10021	1937	Independ	J/C	325	14	$ 5,880	—	$ 5,880
Touro College	New York, NY 10036	1970	Independ	S-G/C	2,107	220	$ 3,590	$2,400	$ 5,990
Trocaire College	Buffalo, NY 14220	1958	Independ	J/C	984	97	$ 2,600	—	$ 2,600
Union College	Schenectady, NY 12308	1795	Independ	S-G/C	3,389	206	$ 8,155	$2,840	$10,995
Union Theological Seminary	New York, NY 10027	1836	Independ	P/C	400	35	$ 3,800	$4,000	$ 7,800
U.S. Merchant Marine Acad.	Kings Point, NY 11024	1943	Federal	S/C	1,100	81			
U.S. Military Academy	West Point, NY 10996	1802	Federal	S/C	4,500	650	—	—	—
University of Rochester	Rochester, NY 14627	1850	Independ	S-G/C	8,668	—	$ 7,790	$3,389	$11,179
Utica School of Commerce	Utica, NY 13501	1896	Independ	J/C	335	17	$ 2,440	—	$ 2,440
Vassar College	Poughkeepsie, NY 12601	1861	Independ	S-G/C	2,250	210	$ 8,360	$3,440	$11,800
Villa Maria College of Buffalo	Buffalo, NY 14225	1960	Catholic	J/C	824	69	$ 2,280	—	$ 2,280
Wadhams Hall Sem. Col.	Ogdensburg, NY 13669	1924	Catholic	S/M	68	16	$ 2,480	$2,200	$ 4,680
Wagner College	Staten Island, NY 10301	1883	Independ	S-G/C	2,380	113	$ 5,150	$3,100	$ 8,250
Webb Inst. of Naval Arch	Glen Cove, NY 11542	1889	Independ	S/C	79	14		$2,750	$ 2,750
Wells College	Aurora, NY 13026	1868	Independ	S/W	500	55	$ 6,960	$2,500	$ 9,460
Westchester Business Inst.	White Plains, NY 10602	1915	Independ	J/C	550	25	$ 3,900	—	$ 3,900
William Smith College	Geneva, NY 14456	1908	Independ	S/W	750	122	$ 8,100	$2,730	$10,830
Wood School	New York, NY 10017	1879	Independ	J/W	488	26	$ 4,700	—	$ 4,700

NAME	ADDRESS	FOUNDED	AFFILIATION	LEVEL/ TYPE	ENROLLMENT	TEACHERS	TUITION & FEES	BOARD & ROOM	TOTAL COST
NEW YORK *(continued)*									
Yeshiva University	New York, NY 10033	1886	Independ	S-G/C	4,384	2,716	$ 5,845	$2,845	$ 8,690
Rabbi I. Elchanan Theol. Sem.	New York, NY 10033	1896	Jewish	P/M	268	18	$ 2,010	$2,645	$ 4,655
NORTH CAROLINA									
Appalachian State University	Boone, NC 28608	1899	State	S-G/C	10,051	548	$ 733	$1,460	$ 2,193
Ashevil.-Buncombe Tech. Col.	Asheville, NC 28801	1959	State	T/C	2,600	155	$ 185	—	$ 185
Atlantic Christian College	Wilson, NC 27893	1902	D of Chr	S/C	1,546	93	$ 2,994	$1,490	$ 4,484
Barber-Scotia College	Concord, NC 28025	1867	Presby	S/C	374	30	$ 2,423	$1,879	$ 4,302
Beaufort County Comm. Col.	Washington, NC 27889	1967	State	J/C	1,200	45	$ 150	—	$ 150
Belmont Abbey College	Belmont, NC 28012	1876	Catholic	S/C	805	60	$ 3,902	$1,970	$ 5,872
Bennett College	Greensboro, NC 27420	1873	Methodist	S/W	543	56	$ 3,000	$1,400	$ 4,400
Brevard College	Brevard, NC 28712	1853	Methodist	J/C	745	52	$ 2,920	$2,070	$ 4,990
Caldwell Community College	Hudson, NC 28645	1964	State	J/C	2,330	174	$ 156	—	$ 156
Campbell University	Buies Creek, NC 27506	1887	Baptist	S-G/C	3,190	168	$ 3,930	$1,765	$ 5,695
Cape Fear Technical Inst.	Wilmington, NC 28401	1959	State	T/C	1,950	87	$ 156	—	$ 156
Carteret Technical College	Morehead City, NC 28557	1963	State	T/C	1,025	70	$ 126	—	$ 126
Catawba College	Salisbury, NC 28144	1851	UC Chr	S/C	986	70	$ 3,970	$1,925	$ 5,895
Catawba Valley Tech. College	Hickory, NC 28601	1960	State	T/C	2,400	85	$ 160	—	$ 160
Cecils Junior College	Asheville, NC 28806	1905	Independ	J/C	350	20	$ 2,112	—	$ 2,112
Central Carolina Tech. College	Sanford, NC 27330	1962	State	T/C	2,079	150	$ 156	—	$ 156
Central Piedmont Comm. Col.	Charlotte, NC 28235	1963	State	J/C	25,928	979	$ 120	—	$ 120
Chowan College	Murfreesboro, NC 27855	1848	Baptist	J/C	1,078	68	$ 2,615	$1,875	$ 4,490
Coastal Carolina Comm. Col.	Jacksonville, NC 28540	1964	State	J/C	2,744	114	$ 132	—	$ 132
College of the Albemarle	Elizabeth City, NC 27909	1960	State	J/C	1,459	46	$ 145	—	$ 145
Craven Community College	New Bern, NC 28560	1965	State	J/C	1,816	95	$ 144	—	$ 144
Davidson College	Davidson, NC 28036	1837	Presby	S/C	1,395	103	$ 5,310	$2,190	$ 7,500
Davidson County Comm. Col.	Lexington, NC 27292	1958	State	J/C	2,597	135	$ 140	—	$ 140
Duke University	Durham, NC 27706	1838	Methodist	S-G/C	9,565	1,442	$ 6,964	$3,374	$10,338
Durham Technical Institute	Durham, NC 27703	1961	State	T/C	3,875	226	$ 168	—	$ 168
East Carolina University	Greenville, NC 27834	1907	State	S-G/C	13,311	665	$ 666	$1,756	$ 2,422
Cherry Point Center	Cherry Point, NC 28533	1965	State	S-G/C	550	35	$ 840	—	$ 840
Elizabeth City State University	Elizabeth City, NC 27909	1891	State	S/C	1,532	125	$ 782	$1,780	$ 2,562
Elon College	Elon College, NC 27244	1889	UC Chr	S/C	2,580	150	$ 2,700	$1,740	$ 4,440
Fayetteville State University	Fayetteville, NC 28301	1867	State	S-G/C	2,410	185	$ 694	$1,550	$ 2,394
Fort Bragg-Pope AFB Center	Fort Bragg, NC 28307	1972	State	S/C	3,174	45	$ 840	—	$ 840
Fayetteville Technical Inst.	Fayetteville, NC 28303	1961	State	J/C	5,788	171	$ 123	—	$ 123
Forsyth Technical Institute	Winston Salem, NC 27103	1960	State	T/C	3,118	98	$ 180	—	$ 180
Gardner-Webb College	Boiling Springs, NC 28017	1905	Baptist	S/C	1,760	80	$ 3,300	$2,200	$ 5,500
Gaston College	Dallas, NC 28034	1963	State	J/C	3,318	139	$ 135	—	$ 135
Greensboro College	Greensboro, NC 27401	1838	Methodist	S/C	585	51	$ 3,820	$2,170	$ 5,990
Guilford College	Greensboro, NC 27410	1837	Quaker	S/C	1,622	121	$ 4,890	$2,215	$ 7,105
Guilford Technical Institute	Jamestown, NC 27282	1965	Public	T/C	4,175	125	$ 184	—	$ 184
Haywood Technical Institute	Clyde, NC 28721	1965	State	T/C	950	75	$ 156	—	$ 156
High Point College	High Point, NC 27262	1924	Methodist	S/C	1,355	69	$ 3,640	$1,650	$ 5,290
Isothermal Community College	Spindale, NC 28160	1964	State	J/C	2,711	100	$ 145	—	$ 145
Johnson C. Smith University	Charlotte, NC 28216	1867	Independ	S/C	1,192	90	$ 2,860	$1,640	$ 4,500
John Wesley College	High Point, NC 27260	1932	Independ	S/C	96	8	$ 1,650	—	$ 1,650
King's College	Charlotte, NC 28204	1901	Private	T/C	400	15	$ 4,300	$2,900	$ 7,200
Lees-McRae College	Banner Elk, NC 28604	1900	Presby	J/C	709	44	$ 2,797	$1,722	$ 4,519
Lenoir Community College	Kinston, NC 28501	1958	State	J/C	2,119	70	$ 165	—	$ 165
Lenoir-Rhyne College	Hickory, NC 28603	1891	LCA	S-G/C	1,382	100	$ 4,130	$1,738	$ 5,868
Livingstone College	Salisbury, NC 28144	1879	AME	S/C	618	63	$ 2,610	$2,046	$ 4,656
Louisburg College	Louisburg, NC 27549	1787	Methodist	J/C	728	49	$ 3,025	$1,650	$ 4,675
Mars Hill College	Mars Hill, NC 28754	1856	Baptist	S/C	1,279	104	$ 3,650	$1,660	$ 5,310
Martin Community College	Williamston, NC 27892	1968	State	J/C	704	49	$ 132	—	$ 132
Meredith College	Raleigh, NC 27607	1891	Baptist	S/W	1,615	131	$ 3,050	$1,350	$ 4,400
Methodist College	Fayetteville, NC 28301	1956	Methodist	S/C	780	50	$ 3,280	$1,970	$ 5,250
Mitchell Community College	Statesville, NC 28677	1852	State	J/C	1,303	45	$ 144	—	$ 144
Montreat-Anderson College	Montreat, NC 28757	1916	Presby	J/C	388	29	$ 2,776	$2,164	$ 4,940
Mount Olive College	Mount Olive, NC 28365	1951	Baptist	J/C	400	35	$ 2,400	$2,000	$ 4,400
N.C. A. & T. State University	Greensboro, NC 27411	1891	State	S-G/C	5,200	277	$ 819	$1,774	$ 2,593
N.C. Central University	Durham, NC 27707	1910	State	S-G/C	4,990	344	$ 682	$1,624	$ 2,306
N.C. School of the Arts	Winston-Salem, NC 27107	1965	State	S-G/C	520	90	$ 666	$2,002	$ 2,668
N.C. State University	Raleigh, NC 27650	1889	State	S-G/C	22,468	1,213	$ 682	$2,100	$ 2,782
N.C. Wesleyan College	Rocky Mount, NC 27801	1956	Methodist	S/C	940	59	$ 3,600	$1,925	$ 5,525
Peace College	Raleigh, NC 27604	1857	Presby	J/W	456	35	$ 2,600	$2,250	$ 4,850
Pembroke State University	Pembroke, NC 28372	1887	State	S-G/C	2,301	124	$ 548	$1,210	$ 1,758
Pfeiffer College	Misenheimer, NC 28109	1885	Methodist	S/C	813	78	$ 3,700	$1,890	$ 5,590
Piedmont Bible College	Winston-Salem, NC 27101	1945	Baptist	S/C	405	24	$ 2,120	$1,530	$ 3,650
Pitt Comm. College	Greenville, NC 27834	1962	State	T/C	2,771	175	$ 162	—	$ 162
Queens College	Charlotte, NC 28274	1857	Presby	S-G/W	1,103	69	$ 4,600	$2,600	$ 6,560
Randolph Technical College	Asheboro, NC 27203	1962	State	T/C	1,189	50	$ 132	$3,000	$ 3,132
Richmond Technical Institute	Hamlet, NC 28345	1964	State	T/C	1,092	95	$ 135	—	$ 135
Rockingham Community Col.	Wentworth, NC 27375	1966	Public	J/C	2,094	135	$ 144	—	$ 144
Rowan Technical Institute	Salisbury, NC 28144	1963	State	T/C	2,064	135	$ 177	—	$ 177
Rutledge Col. of Charlotte	Charlotte, NC 28202	1977	Independ	J/C	380	14	$ 1,512	—	$ 1,512
Sacred Heart College	Belmont, NC 28012	1892	Catholic	S/C	395	43	$ 3,270	$2,080	$ 5,350
St. Andrew's Presbyterian Col.	Laurinburg, NC 28352	1896	Presby	S/C	756	55	$ 3,950	$1,950	$ 5,900
St. Augustine's College	Raleigh, NC 27610	1867	Episcopal	S/C	1,581	102	$ 3,300	$1,800	$ 5,100
St. Mary's College	Raleigh, NC 27611	1842	Episcopal	J/W	503	42	$ 3,830	$2,990	$ 6,820
Salem College	Winston-Salem, NC 27108	1772	Moravian	S/W	699	67	$ 4,600	$3,100	$ 7,700
Sandhills Community College	Carthage, NC 28327	1963	State	J/C	2,126	106	$ 184	—	—
Shaw University	Raleigh, NC 27611	1865	Baptist	S/C	1,753	58	$ 2,570	$1,330	$ 3,900
Southeast. Bapt. Theol. Sem.	Wake Forest, NC 27587	1951	Baptist	G/C	1,250	38	$ 500	$1,800	$ 2,300

NORTH CAROLINA *(continued)*

NAME	ADDRESS	FOUNDED	AFFILIATION	LEVEL/TYPE	ENROLLMENT	TEACHERS	TUITION & FEES	BOARD & ROOM	TOTAL COST
Southeastern Comm. College	Whiteville, NC 28472	1965	State	J/C	1,911	63	$ 142	—	$ 142
Southwestern Technical Col.	Sylva, NC 28779	1964	State	T/C	1,077	39	$ 170	—	$ 170
Surry Community College	Dobson, NC 27017	1964	State	J/C	2,243	93	$ 135	—	$ 135
Technical Inst. of Alamance	Haw River, NC 27258	1958	State	T/C	1,875	45	$ 168	—	$ 168
Univ. of N.C. at Asheville	Asheville, NC 28814	1927	State	S/C	2,520	166	$ 628	$1,670	$ 2,298
Univ. of N.C. at Chapel Hill	Chapel Hill, NC 27514	1789	State	S-G/C	22,016	1,884	$ 701	$2,375	$ 4,000
Univ. of N.C. at Charlotte	Charlotte, NC 28223	1946	State	S/C	10,069	671	$ 648	$1,860	$ 2,508
Univ. of N.C. at Greensboro	Greensboro, NC 27412	1891	State	S-G/C	10,126	628	$ 744	$1,744	$ 2,488
Univ. of N.C. at Wilmington	Wilmington, NC 28406	1947	State	S-G/C	5,334	302	$ 645	$1,945	$ 2,590
Wake Forest University	Winston-Salem, NC 27109	1834	Baptist	S-G/C	4,795	479	—	—	$ 8,000
Wake Technical College	Raleigh, NC 27603	1963	Public	J/C	3,254	126	$ 140	—	$ 140
Warren Wilson College	Swannanoa, NC 28778	1894	Presby	S/C	535	86	$ 3,950	$1,608	$ 5,558
Wayne Community College	Goldsboro, NC 27530	1957	State	J/C	2,330	102	$ 180	—	$ 180
Western Carolina University	Cullowhee, NC 28723	1889	State	S-G/C	6,066	382	$ 713	$1,575	$ 2,288
Western Piedmont Comm. Col.	Morganton, NC 28655	1964	State	J/C	1,934	92	$ 135	—	$ 135
Wilkes Community College	Wilkesboro, NC 28697	1965	State	J/C	2,781	61	$ 190	—	$ 190
Wilson County Tech. Institute	Wilson, NC 27893	1958	State	T/C	1,356	44	$ 171	—	$ 171
Wingate College	Wingate, NC 28174	1896	Baptist	S/C	1,481	78	$ 2,773	$1,820	$ 4,593
Winston-Salem State Univ.	Winston-Salem, NC 27110	1892	State	S/C	2,259	169	$ 611	$1,813	$ 2,424

NORTH DAKOTA

NAME	ADDRESS	FOUNDED	AFFILIATION	LEVEL/TYPE	ENROLLMENT	TEACHERS	TUITION & FEES	BOARD & ROOM	TOTAL COST
Bismarck Junior College	Bismarck, ND 58501	1939	City	J/C	2,325	89	$ 720	$1,400	$ 2,120
Dickinson State College	Dickinson, ND 58601	1918	State	J-S/C	1,202	88	$ 810	$1,600	$ 2,410
Jamestown College	Jamestown, ND 58401	1883	Presby	S/C	637	54	$ 4,300	$1,575	$ 5,875
Lake Region Junior College	Devils Lake, ND 58301	1941	State	J/C	751	40	$ 760	$1,430	$ 2,190
Mary College	Bismarck, ND 58501	1958	Catholic	S/C	1,121	73	$ 2,960	$1,622	$ 4,582
Mayville State College	Mayville, ND 58257	1889	State	S/C	694	55	$ 702	$1,344	$ 2,046
Minot State College	Minot, ND 58701	1913	State	S-G/C	2,760	132	$ 681	$1,200	$ 1,881
North Dakota State Sch. of Sci.	Wahpeton, ND 58075	1903	State	J/C	3,398	185	$ 630	$1,600	$ 2,230
North Dakota State University	Fargo, ND 58105	1890	State	S-G/C	8,932	450	$ 732	$1,695	$ 2,427
Bottineau Branch	Bottineau, ND 58318	1907	State	J/C	441	26	$ 697	$1,347	$ 2,044
Northwest Bible College	Minot, ND 58701	1934	C of God	S/C	114	7	$ 941	$ 745	$ 1,686
University of North Dakota	Grand Forks, ND 58202	1883	State	S-G/C	11,103	630	$ 904	$1,738	$ 2,642
Williston Center	Williston, ND 58801	1957	State	J/C	607	42	$ 948	$1,500	$ 2,448
Valley City State College	Valley City, ND 58072	1890	State	S/C	1,081	71	$ 783	$1,410	$ 2,193

OHIO

NAME	ADDRESS	FOUNDED	AFFILIATION	LEVEL/TYPE	ENROLLMENT	TEACHERS	TUITION & FEES	BOARD & ROOM	TOTAL COST
Air Force Inst. of Technology	Wright-Pat. AFB, OH 45433	1919	Federal	G/C	962	105	—	—	—
Antioch University	Yellow Springs, OH 45387	1852	Independ	S-G/C					
Antioch College	Yellow Springs, OH 45387	1852	Independ	S/C	626	47	$ 6,330	$2,510	$ 8,840
Antioch International	Yellow Springs, OH 45387	1852	Independ	S-G/C	124	10	$ 3,775	—	$ 3,775
Art Academy of Cincinnati	Cincinnati, OH 45202	1887	Independ	S/C	225	28	$ 3,535	—	$ 3,535
Ashland College	Ashland, OH 44805	1878	Brethren	S-G/C	2,837	97	$ 5,706	$2,394	$ 8,100
Athenaeum of Ohio	Cincinnati, OH 45230	1829	Catholic	G/M	178	42	$ 2,800	$2,200	$ 5,000
Baldwin-Wallace College	Berea, OH 44017	1845	Methodist	S-G/C	3,755	207	$ 5,181	$2,553	$ 7,734
Bliss College	Columbus, OH 43214	1899	Independ	J/C	411	23	$ 2,784	$4,320	$ 7,104
Bluffton College	Bluffton, OH 45817	1899	Mennonite	S/C	601	514	$ 4,320	$1,810	$ 6,130
Borromeo College of Ohio	Wickliffe, OH 44092	1954	Catholic	S/M	107	25	$ 3,250	$1,700	$ 4,950
Bowling Green State Univ.	Bowling Green, OH 43403	1910	State	S-G/C	16,335	731	$ 1,614	$1,756	$ 3,370
Firelands College	Huron, OH 44839	1946	State	J/C	1,325	63	$ 1,404	—	$ 1,404
Capital University	Columbus, OH 43209	1850	Lutheran	S-G/C	2,560	190	$ 5,870	$2,429	$ 8,299
Case Western Reserve Univ.	Cleveland, OH 44106	1826	Independ	S-G/C	8,584	1,532	$ 7,230	$2,980	$10,210
Cedarville College	Cedarville, OH 45314	1887	Baptist	S/C	1,750	74	$ 3,374	$2,190	$ 5,564
Central Ohio Technical Col.	Newark, OH 43055	1971	State	T/C	1,230	95	$ 1,030	—	$ 1,030
Central State University	Wilberforce, OH 45384	1887	State	S/C	2,420	110	$ 1,290	$2,607	$ 3,897
Cincinnati Bible Seminary	Cincinnati, OH 45204	1924	Christian	S-G/C	854	41	$ 2,050	$2,000	$ 4,050
Cincinnati Col. of Mort. Sci.	Cincinnati, OH 45206	1882	Independ	P/C	111	7	$ 3,480	$3,356	$ 6,836
Cincinnati Technical College	Cincinnati, OH 45223	1966	State	T/C	3,962	200	$ 1,140	—	$ 1,140
Circleville Bible College	Circleville, OH 43113	1948	Christian	P/C	215	15	$ 2,600	$1,740	$ 4,340
Clark Technical College	Springfield, OH 45501	1962	State	T/C	2,652	137	$ 1,350	—	$ 1,350
Cleveland Institute of Art	Cleveland, OH 44106	1882	Independ	S/C	540	116	$ 4,700	$3,000	$ 7,700
Cleveland Institute of Music	Cleveland, OH 44106	1920	Independ	S-G/C	269	65	$ 6,865	$2,870	$ 9,735
Cleveland State University	Cleveland, OH 44115	1964	State	S-G/C	18,944	729	$ 1,497	—	—
College of Mount St. Joseph	Mt. St. Joseph, OH 45051	1920	Catholic	S/W	1,887	144	$ 4,096	$2,438	$ 6,534
College of Wooster	Wooster, OH 44691	1866	Presby	S/C	1,760	156	$ 9,650	—	$ 9,650
Columbus Col. of Art & Design	Columbus, OH 43215	1879	Independ	S/C	876	67	$ 4,350	$1,100	$ 5,450
Columbus Tech. Institute	Columbus, OH 43216	1963	State	T/C	9,300	500	$ 1,008	—	$ 1,008
Cuyahoga Community College	Cleveland, OH 44115	1963	State	J/C					
Eastern Campus	Warrensv. Twp., OH 44122	1971	State	J/C	5,930	202	$ 810	—	$ 810
Metropolitan Campus	Cleveland, OH 44115	1963	State	J/C	8,063	467	$ 810	—	$ 810
Western Campus	Parma, OH 44130	1966	State	J/C	13,012	441	$ 810	—	$ 810
Defiance College	Defiance, OH 43512	1850	UC Chr	S/C	834	59	$ 4,274	$2,079	$ 6,353
Denison University	Granville, OH 43023	1831	Independ	S/C	2,149	165	$ 6,670	$2,360	$ 9,030
Dyke College	Cleveland, OH 44114	1848	Independ	S/C	1,441	100	$ 2,900	—	$ 2,900
Findlay College	Findlay, OH 45840	1882	C of God	S/C	1,206	91	$ 4,740	$2,180	$ 6,920
Franklin University	Columbus, OH 43215	1902	Private	S/C	4,983	214	$ 2,100	—	$ 2,100
Hebrew Union College	Cincinnati, OH 45220	1875	Hebrew	G/C	600	150	$ 5,000	$3,000	$ 8,000
Heidelberg College	Tiffin, OH 44883	1850	UC Chr	S/C	844	79	$ 5,620	$2,270	$ 7,890
Hiram College	Hiram, OH 44234	1850	D Chr	S/C	1,158	80	$ 6,659	$2,019	$ 8,678
Hocking Technical College	Nelsonville, OH 45764	1968	State	T/C	3,523	237	$ 846	$1,900	$ 2,746
Jefferson Technical College	Steubenville, OH 43952	1966	State	T/C	1,789	100	$ 600	—	$ 600
John Carroll University	Univ. Hts., OH 44118	1886	Catholic	S-G/C	3,767	253	$ 4,352	$2,500	$ 6,852
Kent State University	Kent, OH 44242	1910	State	S-G/C	19,615	972	$ 1,712	$1,950	$ 3,662
Ashtabula Campus	Ashtabula, OH 44004	1958	State	J/C	1,010	60	$ 1,440	—	$ 1,440

NAME	ADDRESS	FOUN-DED	AFFILI-ATION	LEVEL/TYPE	ENROLL-MENT	TEACH-ERS	TUITION & FEES	BOARD & ROOM	TOTAL COST
OHIO *(continued)*									
East Liverpool Campus	East Liverpool, OH 43920	1965	State	J/C	665	37	$1,440	—	$ 1,440
Geauga Campus	Burton, OH 44021	1964	State	J/C	324	31	$1,440	—	$ 1,440
Salem Campus	Salem, OH 44460	1962	State	J/C	574	16	$1,440	—	$ 1,440
Stark Campus	Canton, OH 44720	1946	State	J/C	1,923	91	$1,440	—	$ 1,440
Trumbull Campus	Warren, OH 44483	1954	State	J/C	1,537	4	$1,440	—	$ 1,440
Tuscarawas Campus	New Phila., OH 44663	1962	State	J/C	962	73	$1,440	—	$ 1,440
Kenyon College	Gambier, OH 43022	1824	Episcopal	S/C	1,400	156	$7,090	$2,455	$ 9,545
Kettering Col. of Med. Arts	Kettering, OH 45429	1967	Church	J/C	530	65	$3,084	$1,500	$ 4,584
Lake Erie College	Painesville, OH 44077	1865	Independ	S-G/W	1,005	92	$6,140	$2,400	$ 8,540
Lakeland Community College	Mentor, OH 44060	1967	State	J/C	9,234	398	$ 945	—	$ 945
Lima Technical College	Lima, OH 45804	1971	State	T/C	2,324	142	$ 945	—	$ 945
Lorain County Comm. College	Elyria, OH 44035	1963	State	J/C	6,692	343	$ 922	—	$ 922
Lourdes College	Sylvania, OH 43560	1958	Catholic	J-S/C	750	38	$1,650	—	$ 1,650
Malone College	Canton, OH 44709	1892	Friends	S/C	872	42	$4,523	$2,250	$ 6,773
Marietta College	Marietta, OH 45750	1835	Independ	S-G/C	1,336	103	$6,500	$2,250	$ 8,750
Methodist Theol. Sch. of Ohio	Delaware, OH 43015	1958	Methodist	G/C	227	22	$2,700	$1,335	$ 4,035
Miami-Jacobs Junior College	Dayton, OH 45401	1864	Independ	J/C	659	31	$2,350	—	$ 2,350
Miami University	Oxford, OH 45056	1809	State	S-G/C	14,888	901	$2,090	$1,990	$ 4,080
Hamilton Campus	Hamilton, OH 45011	1968	State	J/C	1,777	48	$1,850	—	$ 1,850
Middletown Campus	Middletown, OH 45042	1965	State	J/C	1,689	57	$1,850	—	$ 1,850
Mount Union College	Alliance, OH 44601	1846	Methodist	S/C	968	71	$6,630	$2,030	$ 8,660
Mount Vernon Bible College	Mt. Vernon, OH 43050	1959	4 Square	S/C	74	8	$1,350	$1,785	$ 3,135
Mount Vernon Nazarene Col.	Mt. Vernon, OH 43050	1966	Nazarene	S/C	1,027	73	$3,109	$1,924	$ 5,033
Muskingum Area Tech. Col.	Zanesville, OH 43701	1969	State	T/C	1,422	70	$ 780	—	$ 780
Muskingum College	New Concord, OH 43762	1837	Presby	S/C	1,017	66	$5,830	$2,260	$ 8,090
Northwest Technical College	Archbold, OH 43502	1968	State	J/C	920	54	$1,080	—	$ 1,080
Notre Dame College of Ohio	Cleveland, OH 44121	1922	Catholic	S/W	723	63	$3,500	$2,150	$ 5,650
Oberlin College	Oberlin, OH 44074	1833	Independ	S/C	2,743	226	$8,640	$3,050	$11,690
Ohio Col. of Podiatric Med.	Cleveland, OH 44106	1916	Independ	P/C	596	73	$8,500	$3,300	$11,800
Ohio Dominican College	Columbus, OH 43219	1911	Catholic	S/C	1,019	75	$4,390	$2,500	$ 6,890
Ohio Inst. of Technology	Columbus, OH 43209	1952	Independ	S/C	4,333	174	$3,300	—	$ 3,300
Ohio Northern University	Ada, OH 45810	1871	Methodist	S/C	2,759	168	$4,710	$2,010	$ 6,720
Ohio State University	Columbus, OH 43210	1870	State	S-G/C	53,438	6,020	$1,458	$2,514	$ 3,972
Agricul. Tech. Institute	Wooster, OH 44691	1972	State	T/C	705	55	$1,413	—	—
Lima Campus	Lima, OH 45804	1960	State	S/C	901	58	$1,413	—	—
Mansfield Campus	Mansfield, OH 44906	1958	State	S/C	1,095	47	$1,413	—	—
Marion Campus	Marion, OH 43302	1957	State	J/C	729	62	$1,413	—	—
Newark Campus	Newark, OH 43055	1957	State	S/C	911	66	$1,413	—	—
Ohio University	Athens, OH 45701	1804	State	S-G/C	14,600	753	$1,680	$2,409	$ 4,089
Belmont County Campus	St. Clairsville, OH 43950	1957	State	J-S/C	935	60	$1,320	—	$ 1,320
Chillicothe Campus	Chillicothe, OH 45601	1946	State	J/C	1,162	75	$1,320	—	$ 1,320
Ironton Campus	Ironton, OH 45638	1956	State	J/C	890	—	$1,200	—	$ 1,200
Zanesville Campus	Zanesville, OH 43701	1946	State	J-S/C	904	65	$1,320	—	$ 1,320
Ohio Wesleyan University	Delaware, OH 43015	1842	Methodist	S/C	1,941	148	$6,785	$2,715	$ 9,500
Otterbein College	Westerville, OH 43081	1847	Methodist	S/C	1,661	93	$6,009	$2,424	$ 8,433
Owens Technical College	Toledo, OH 43699	1965	State	T/C	4,351	240	$ 936	—	$ 936
Penn-Ohio College	Youngstown, OH 44507	1941	Independ	J/C	250	20	$1,563	—	$ 1,563
Pontifical Col. of Josephinum	Columbus, OH 43085	1888	Catholic	S-G/M	202	43	$2,372	$1,870	$ 4,150
Ray. Walters Gen. & Tech. Col.	Cincinnati, OH 45236	1967	State	J/C	3,750	140	$1,671	—	$ 1,671
Rio Grande Col. & Comm. Col.	Rio Grande, OH 45674	1876	Independ	J-S/C	1,267	70	$1,035	$1,920	$ 2,955
St. Mary Seminary	Cleveland, OH 44108	1848	Catholic	G/C	72	18	$3,024	$1,500	$ 4,524
Shawnee State Comm. College	Portsmouth, OH 45662	1975	State	J/C	2,325	202	$ 990	—	$ 990
Sinclair Community College	Dayton, OH 45402	1887	State	J/C	18,662	823	$ 900	—	$ 900
Southern Ohio College	Cincinnati, OH 45237	1927	Independ	J/C	1,454	82	$2,320	$2,600	$ 4,900
Buckeye College Division	Akron, OH 44312	1968	Independ	J/C	468	25	$2,440	—	$ 2,440
Fairfield Branch	Fairfield, OH 45014	1968	Independ	J/C	901	90	$2,244	—	$ 2,244
Tech. Studies Division	Cincinnati, OH 45225	1968	Independ	T/C	455	33	$3,795	—	$ 3,795
Southern State Comm. College	Hillsboro, OH 45133	1975	State	J/C	1,450	78	$ 972	—	$ 972
Tiffin University	Tiffin, OH 44883	1888	Private	S/C	510	26	$2,700	$1,550	$ 5,000
United Theological Seminary	Dayton, OH 45406	1871	Methodist	G/C	278	21	$3,108	$3,440	$ 6,548
University of Akron	Akron, OH 44325	1870	State	S-G/C	26,569	1,453	$1,430	$2,130	$ 3,560
Wayne General & Tech. Col.	Orrville, OH 44667	1972	State	J/C	900	87	$1,430	—	$ 1,430
University of Cincinnati	Cincinnati, OH 45221	1819	State	S-G/C	37,906	1,981	$1,920	$2,680	$ 4,600
University of Dayton	Dayton, OH 45469	1850	Catholic	S-G/C	10,692	656	$4,330	$2,434	$ 6,764
University of Steubenville	Steubenville, OH 43952	1946	Catholic	J-S-G/C	915	54	$4,170	$2,500	$ 6,670
University of Toledo	Toledo, OH 43606	1872	State	S-G/C	21,386	1,194	$1,359	$2,289	$ 3,648
Urbana College	Urbana, OH 43078	1850	Sweden	S/C	565	65	$3,450	$2,400	$ 5,850
Ursuline College	Pepper Pike, OH 44124	1871	Catholic	S-G/W	1,264	99	$3,400	$2,040	$ 5,440
Walsh College	Canton, OH 44720	1958	Catholic	S/C	1,150	91	$3,550	$2,150	$ 5,700
Wilberforce University	Wilberforce, OH 45384	1856	AME	S/C	975	50	$3,400	$1,850	$ 5,250
Wilmington College	Wilmington, OH 45177	1870	Quaker	S/C	822	72	$4,935	$2,145	$ 7,080
Wittenberg University	Springfield, OH 45501	1845	Lutheran	S/C	2,298	140	$7,131	$2,385	$ 9,516
Wright State University	Dayton, OH 45435	1967	State	S-G/C	13,888	773	$1,470	$2,010	$ 3,480
Piqua Resident Cred. Cent.	Piqua, OH 45356	1969	State	S-G/C	49	7	$1,221	—	$ 1,221
Western Ohio Branch Cam.	Celina, OH 45822	1969	State	J/C	940	62	$1,311	—	$ 1,311
Xavier University	Cincinnati, OH 45207	1831	Catholic	S-G/C	6,950	372	$4,598	$2,515	$ 7,113
Youngstown State University	Youngstown, OH 44555	1908	State	S-G/C	15,584	785	$1,245	$1,995	$ 3,240
OKLAHOMA									
Bacone College	Muskogee, OK 74401	1880	Baptist	J/C	386	38	$1,850	$1,900	$ 3,750
Bartlesville Wesleyan College	Bartlesville, OK 74003	1909	Wesleyan	S/C	823	70	$3,170	$2,110	$ 5,280
Bethany Nazarene College	Bethany, OK 73008	1899	Nazarene	S-G/C	1,416	107	$2,816	$2,048	$ 4,864
Cameron University	Lawton, OK 73505	1908	State	S/C	5,200	182	$ 600	$1,800	$ 2,400

OKLAHOMA *(continued)*

NAME	ADDRESS	FOUNDED	AFFILIATION	LEVEL/TYPE	ENROLLMENT	TEACHERS	TUITION & FEES	BOARD & ROOM	TOTAL COST
Carl Albert Junior College	Poteau, OK 74953	1934	State	J/C	2,072	55	$ 400	—	$ 400
Central State University	Edmond, OK 73034	1890	State	S-G/C	12,309	449	$ 433	$1,245	$ 1,678
Connors State College	Warner, OK 74469	1907	State	J/C	1,497	65	$ 350	$1,200	$ 1,550
East Central University	Ada, OK 74820	1909	State	S-G/C	3,948	175	$ 500	$1,485	$ 1,985
Eastern Okla. State College	Wilburton, OK 74578	1909	State	J/C	1,986	68	$ 400	$1,200	$ 1,600
El Reno Junior College	El Reno, OK 73036	1938	State	J/C	1,500	60	$ 385	—	$ 385
Hillsdale Free Will Baptist Col.	Moore, OK 73153	1959	Baptist	J-S/C	168	20	$ 600	$1,700	$ 2,300
Langston University	Langston, OK 73050	1897	State	S/C	2,152	91	$ 448	$1,677	$ 2,125
Midwest Christian College	Oklahoma City, OK 73111	1946	Christian	S/C	110	15	$ 1,250	$1,767	$ 3,017
Murray State College	Tishomingo, OK 73460	1908	State	J/C	1,501	41	$ 403	$1,780	$ 2,183
Northeastern Okla. A&M Col.	Miami, OK 74354	1919	State	J/C	3,044	98	$ 380	$1,364	$ 1,744
Northeastern State University	Tahlequah, OK 74464	1846	State	S-G/C	6,586	267	$ 512	$1,564	$ 2,076
Northern Oklahoma College	Tonkawa, OK 74653	1901	State	J/C	2,000	78	$ 300	$ 950	$ 1,500
Northwestern Okla. State Univ.	Alva, OK 73717	1897	State	S-G/C	2,100	75	$ 525	$1,360	$ 1,885
Oklahoma Baptist University	Shawnee, OK 74801	1910	Baptist	S/C	1,488	100	$ 2,506	$1,635	$ 4,141
Oklahoma Christian College	Oklahoma City, OK 73111	1950	C of Chr	S/C	1,721	78	$ 2,500	$1,810	$ 4,310
Oklahoma City University	Oklahoma City, OK 73106	1904	Methodist	S-G/C	3,158	140	$ 2,883	$1,590	$ 4,473
Okla. Col. of Osteo. Med. & Surg.	Tulsa, OK 74101	1972	State	P/C	260	32	$ 2,420	—	$ 2,420
Okla. Missionary Baptist Col.	Marlow, OK 73055	1954	Baptist	S-P/C	60	10	$ 350	—	$ 350
Okla. Panhandle State Univ.	Goodwell, OK 73939	1909	State	S/C	1,392	69	$ 710	$1,600	$ 2,310
Oklahoma State University	Stillwater, OK 74078	1890	State	S-G/C	23,053	1,090	$ 765	$2,028	$ 2,793
Okla. St. U. Sch. of Tech. Train.	Okmulgee, OK 74447	1946	State	T/C	3,292	167	$ 495	$1,600	$ 2,295
Okla. State U. Tech. Institute	Oklahoma City, OK 73107	1961	State	J/C	2,688	193	$ 550	—	$ 550
Oral Roberts University	Tulsa, OK 74171	1965	Independ	S-G/C	4,046	360	$ 3,600	$2,200	$ 5,800
Oscar Rose Junior College	Midwest City, OK 73110	1969	State	J/C	9,250	301	$ 325	—	$ 325
Phillips University	Enid, OK 73702	1906	Christian	S-G/C	1,132	74	$ 3,200	$2,000	$ 5,200
Rogers State College	Claremore, OK 74017	1907	State	J/C	2,558	130	$ 450	$1,840	$ 2,290
St. Gregory's College	Shawnee, OK 74801	1875	Catholic	J/C	342	34	$ 2,175	$1,945	$ 4,120
Sayre Junior College	Sayre, OK 73662	1938	State	J/C	368	19	$ 300	$ 800	$ 1,100
Seminole Junior College	Seminole, OK 74868	1931	State	J/C	1,575	55	$ 392	$1,700	$ 2,092
South Okla. City Jr. College	Oklahoma City, OK 73159	1972	State	J/C	7,721	249	$ 333	—	$ 333
Southeastern Okla. State Univ.	Durant, OK 74701	1909	State	S-G/C	4,248	216	$ 495	$1,420	$ 1,915
Southwestern Okla. State Univ.	Weatherford, OK 73096	1901	State	S-G/C	4,839	211	$ 506	$1,155	$ 1,660
Spartan School of Aeronautics	Tulsa, OK 74151	1928	Independ	T/C	1,950	80	$ 4,700	—	$ 4,700
Tulsa Junior College	Tulsa, OK 74135	1968	State	J/C	15,153	550	$ 350	—	$ 350
University of Oklahoma	Norman, OK 73019	1890	State	S-G/C	21,532	871	$ 795	$2,125	$ 2,920
Health Sciences Center	Oklahoma City, OK 73190	1892	State	S-G/C	3,127	750	$ 1,200	—	$ 6,450
Univ. of Sci. and Arts of Okla.	Chickasha, OK 73018	1908	State	S/C	1,440	92	$ 550	$1,500	$ 2,050
University of Tulsa	Tulsa, OK 74104	1894	Independ	S-G/C	6,127	316	$ 3,700	$1,850	$ 5,550
Western Okla. State College	Altus, OK 73521	1926	State	J/C	1,943	56	$ 325	—	$ 325

OREGON

NAME	ADDRESS	FOUNDED	AFFILIATION	LEVEL/TYPE	ENROLLMENT	TEACHERS	TUITION & FEES	BOARD & ROOM	TOTAL COST
Blake College	Eugene, OR 97405	1961	Independ	S/C	14	3	$ 3,300	$1,700	$ 5,000
Blue Mountain Comm. College	Pendleton, OR 97801	1962	State	J/C	1,400	68	$ 540	—	$ 540
Central Oregon Comm. College	Bend, OR 97701	1949	Public	J/C	2,003	64	$ 540	$2,366	$ 2,906
Chemeketa Comm. College	Salem, OR 97309	1969	County	J/C	10,044	830	$ 600	—	$ 600
Clackamas Comm. College	Oregon City, OR 97045	1966	State	J/C	9,524	154	$ 540	—	$ 540
Clatsop Community College	Astoria, OR 97103	1958	State	J/C	3,500	200	$ 576	—	$ 576
Columbia Christian College	Portland, OR 97220	1956	C of Chr	S/C	232	29	$ 3,300	$1,962	$ 5,962
Concordia College	Portland, OR 97211	1905	Lutheran	S/C	392	38	$ 3,780	$2,515	$ 6,295
Eastern Oregon State College	La Grande, OR 97850	1929	State	S-G/C	1,881	80	$ 1,400	$2,200	$ 3,600
George Fox College	Newberg, OR 97132	1891	Friends	S/C	746	60	$ 5,025	$2,310	$ 7,335
Judson Baptist College	The Dalles, OR 97058	1956	Baptist	S/C	247	34	$ 3,900	$2,200	$ 6,100
Lane Community College	Eugene, OR 97405	1965	Local	J/C	7,748	372	$ 561	—	$ 561
Lewis and Clark College	Portland, OR 97219	1867	Independ	S-G/C	3,066	308	$ 7,000	$2,800	$ 9,800
Linfield College	McMinnville, OR 97128	1849	Baptist	S-G/C	1,496	100	$ 5,560	$2,210	$ 8,770
Linn-Benton Community Col.	Albany, OR 97321	1967	Local	J/C	14,500	425	$ 600	—	$ 600
Mount Angel Seminary	St. Benedict, OR 97373	1887	Catholic	S-G/M	100	25	$ 2,075	$1,920	$ 3,995
Mt. Hood Community College	Gresham, OR 97030	1965	State	J/C	9,727	566	$ 615	$2,520	$ 3,135
Multnomah Sch. of the Bible	Portland, OR 97220	1936	Independ	S-G/C	697	35	$ 3,280	$1,830	$ 5,110
Northwest Christian College	Eugene, OR 97401	1895	D of Chr	S/C	227	19	$ 3,150	$2,045	$ 5,555
Oregon Graduate Center	Beaverton, OR 97006	1963	Independ	G/C	74	25	$ 6,200	—	$ 6,200
Oregon Inst. of Technology	Klamath Falls, OR 97601	1947	State	S-T/C	2,650	160	$ 1,387	$2,327	$ 3,714
Oregon State University	Corvallis, OR 97331	1868	State	S-G/C	16,764	1,580	$ 1,356	$2,100	$ 3,456
Pacific N.W. College of Art	Portland, OR 97205	1909	Independ	S/C	201	33	$ 3,550	—	$ 3,550
Pacific University	Forest Grove, OR 97116	1849	Private	S-G/C	1,071	76	$ 5,560	$2,370	$ 7,930
Portland Community College	Portland, OR 97219	1961	Public	J/C	30,913	1,647	$ 570	—	$ 570
Portland State University	Portland, OR 97207	1955	State	S-G/C	14,449	728	$ 1,356	—	$ 1,356
Reed Institute	Portland, OR 97202	1909	Independ	S-G/C	1,128	114	$ 7,070	$2,750	$ 9,820
Rogue Community College	Grants Pass, OR 97526	1971	State	J/C	2,448	189	$ 504	—	$ 504
Southern Oregon State Col.	Ashland, OR 97520	1926	State	S-G/C	4,300	229	$ 1,280	$2,200	$ 3,480
Southw. Oregon Comm. Col.	Coos Bay, OR 97420	1961	State	J/C	3,877	195	$ 540	—	$ 540
Treasure Valley Comm. Col.	Ontario, OR 97914	1961	State	J/C	1,400	26	$ 600	—	$ 600
Umpqua Community College	Roseburg, OR 97470	1964	State	J/C	4,813	151	$ 615	—	$ 615
University of Oregon	Eugene, OR 97403	1876	State	S-G/C	15,405	1,342	$ 1,450	$2,150	$ 3,600
School of Dentistry	Portland, OR 97201	1900	State	P/C	364	140	$ 3,296	$5,200	$ 8,496
University of Portland	Portland, OR 97203	1902	Catholic	S-G/C	2,872	181	$ 5,100	$2,400	$ 7,500
Warner Pacific College	Portland, OR 97215	1937	C of God	S-G/C	441	50	$ 4,500	$2,100	$ 6,690
Western Baptist College	Salem, OR 97301	1935	Baptist	S/C	280	30	$ 3,864	$2,160	$ 6,024
Western Cons. Baptist Sem.	Portland, OR 97215	1927	Baptist	G/C	521	43	$ 3,000	—	$ 3,000
Western Evangelical Sem.	Portland, OR 97222	1945	Int-Den	G/C	208	16	$ 3,450	—	$ 3,450
Western Oregon State College	Monmouth, OR 97361	1882	State	S-G/C	2,478	204	$ 1,351	$2,250	$ 3,601
Western States Chirop. Col.	Portland, OR 97230	1908	Independ	G/C	445	46	$ 5,271	$2,984	$11,643
Willamette University	Salem, OR 97301	1842	Methodist	S-G/C	1,859	165	$ 6,040	$2,550	$ 9,340

NAME	ADDRESS	FOUN-DED	AFFILI-ATION	LEVEL/TYPE	ENROLL-MENT	TEACH-ERS	TUITION & FEES	BOARD & ROOM	TOTAL COST
PANAMA CANAL									
Panama Canal College	APO, Miami 34002	1933	Federal	J/C	1,750	81	—	—	—
PENNSYLVANIA									
Academy of the New Church Col.	Bryn Athyn, PA 19009	1876	Church	J-S/C	162	45	$ 1,437	$1,476	$ 2,913
Albright College	Reading, PA 19604	1856	Methodist	S/C	2,110	123	$ 6,220	$2,290	$ 8,510
Allegheny College	Meadville, PA 16335	1815	Methodist	S/C	1,948	134	$ 6,480	$2,295	$ 8,775
Allentown Col. of St. F. De S.	Center Valley, PA 18034	1965	Catholic	S/C	1,101	103	$ 4,370	$2,600	$ 6,970
Alliance College	Cambrdg. Spgs., PA 16403	1912	Independ	J-S/C	288	39	$ 2,900	$2,480	$ 5,380
Alvernia College	Reading, PA 19607	1958	Catholic	S/C	771	69	$ 2,250	$1,900	$ 4,150
American College	Bryn Mawr, PA 19010	1927	Independ	G/C	1,800	—	—	—	—
Antioch Univ., Philadelphia	Philadelphia, PA 19108	1852	Independ	S-G/C	681	21	$ 3,700	—	$ 3,700
Baptist Bible College	Clarks Summit, PA 18411	1932	Baptist	S-G/C	732	37	$ 3,390	$1,964	$ 5,354
Beaver College	Glenside, PA 19038	1853	Presby	S-G/C	2,533	158	$ 5,920	$2,650	$ 8,570
Biblical Theological Seminary	Hatfield, PA 19440	1971	Independ	G/C	148	8	$ 2,890	—	$ 2,890
Bloomsburg State College	Bloomsburg, PA 17815	1839	State	S-G/C	6,240	334	$ 1,602	$1,444	$ 3,046
Bryn Mawr College	Bryn Mawr, PA 19010	1885	Independ	S-G/W	1,815	174	$ 8,345	$3,655	$12,000
Bucknell University	Lewisburg, PA 17837	1846	Independ	S-G/C	3,325	230	$ 8,330	$2,135	$10,465
Bucks County Comm. College	Newtown, PA 18940	1964	Public	J/C	9,879	201	$ 1,045	—	$ 1,045
Butler County Comm. College	Butler, PA 16001	1965	State	J/C	2,171	140	$ 1,044	—	$ 1,044
Cabrini College	Wayne, PA 19087	1957	Catholic	S/C	757	65	$ 4,145	$2,650	$ 6,795
California State College	California, PA 15419	1852	State	S-G/C	4,529	263	$ 1,654	$1,630	$ 3,284
Carlow College	Pittsburgh, PA 15213	1929	Catholic	S-G/W	963	102	$ 5,310	$2,930	$ 8,240
Carnegie-Mellon University	Pittsburgh, PA 15213	1900	Private	S-G/C	5,998	435	$ 7,550	$3,150	$10,700
Cedar Crest College	Allentown, PA 18104	1867	UCC	S/W	1,030	98	$ 5,600	$2,600	$ 8,200
Chatham College	Pittsburgh, PA 15232	1869	Independ	S/W	666	84	$ 5,425	$2,645	$ 8,070
Chestnut Hill College	Philadelphia, PA 19118	1924	Catholic	S-G/W	1,088	100	$ 3,450	$2,450	$ 5,900
Cheyney State College	Cheyney, PA 19319	1837	State	S-G/C	1,643	176	$ 820	$ 830	$ 1,650
Christ the Saviour Seminary	Johnstown, PA 15906	1940	Church	S/M	20	8	$ 1,265	$ 800	$ 2,065
Clarion University	Clarion, PA 16214	1867	State	S-G/C	5,460	265	$ 1,644	$1,720	$ 3,364
Venango Campus	Oil City, PA 16301	1961	State	J-T/C	506	34	$ 1,628	—	$ 1,628
College Misericordia	Dallas, PA 18612	1924	Catholic	S/C	1,232	106	$ 3,770	$2,250	$ 6,017
Combs College of Music	Philadelphia, PA 19119	1885	Independ	S-G/C	130	37	$ 3,760	$2,050	$ 5,810
Comm. Col. of Allegheny Co.	Pittsburgh, PA 15222	1966	Public	J/C	—	—	—	—	—
Allegheny Campus	Pittsburgh, PA 15212	1966	Public	J/C	7,485	148	$ 871	—	$ 871
Boyce Campus	Monroeville, PA 15146	1966	Public	J/C	3,944	77	$ 871	—	$ 871
College Center North	Pittsburgh, PA 15237	1972	Public	J/C	3,616	37	$ 871	—	$ 871
South Campus	Pittsburgh, PA 15122	1967	Public	J/C	4,659	80	$ 871	—	$ 871
Comm. Col. of Beaver County	Monaca, PA 15061	1966	Public	J/C	2,400	100	$ 1,000	—	$ 1,000
Comm. Col. of Philadelphia	Philadelphia, PA 19130	1964	State	J/C	13,410	359	$ 946	—	$ 946
Curtis Institute of Music	Philadelphia, PA 19103	1924	Independ	P/C	160	65	$ 125	—	$ 125
Delaware County Comm. Col.	Media, PA 19063	1967	Public	J/C	7,209	498	$ 750	—	$ 750
Del. Val. Col. of Sci. & Agri.	Doylestown, PA 18901	1896	Independ	S/C	1,620	89	$ 4,300	$2,050	$ 6,350
Dickinson College	Carlisle, PA 17013	1773	Methodist	S/C	1,813	125	$ 7,560	$2,655	$10,215
Dickinson School of Law	Carlisle, PA 17013	1834	Independ	P/C	529	46	$ 4,055	$2,130	$ 6,185
Drexel University	Philadelphia, PA 19104	1891	Independ	S-G/C	12,474	654	$ 3,870	$2,285	$ 6,155
Dropsie Col. for Hebrew & Cognate	Philadelphia, PA 19132	1907	Private	G/C	43	10	$ 4,200	—	$ 4,200
Dubois Business College	Dubois, PA 15801	1883	Independ	J/C	285	27	$ 3,200	—	$ 3,200
Duquesne University	Pittsburgh, PA 15282	1878	Catholic	S-G/C	6,298	453	$ 5,130	$2,382	$ 7,512
East Stroudsburg State Col.	E. Stroudsburg, PA 18301	1893	State	S-G/C	4,070	225	$ 1,605	$1,674	$ 3,279
Eastern Baptist Theol. Sem.	Philadelphia, PA 19151	1925	Baptist	G/C	334	33	$ 2,880	$2,000	$ 4,880
Eastern College	St. Davids, PA 19087	1953	Baptist	S/C	845	70	$ 5,230	$2,000	$ 7,230
Edinboro State College	Edinboro, PA 16444	1857	State	S-G/C	5,636	347	$ 1,632	$1,460	$ 3,092
Elizabethtown College	Elizabethtown, PA 17022	1899	Brethren	S/C	1,510	134	$ 5,395	$2,490	$ 7,885
Evangelical Sch. of Theology	Myerstown, PA 17067	1953	Evangel	P/C	67	11	$ 2,900	—	$ 3,200
Franklin and Marshall College	Lancaster, PA 17604	1787	Independ	S/C	2,071	137	$ 7,530	$2,670	$10,200
Gannon University	Erie, PA 16541	1933	Catholic	S-G/C	4,203	225	$ 3,420	$1,800	$ 5,220
Geneva College	Beaver Falls, PA 15010	1848	Presby	S/C	1,175	58	$ 4,400	$2,230	$ 6,630
Gettysburg College	Gettysburg, PA 17325	1832	Lutheran	S/C	1,925	170	$ 6,720	$2,400	$ 9,120
Gratz College	Philadelphia, PA 19141	1895	Jewish	S-G/C	250	18	$ 450	—	$ 450
Grove City College	Grove City, PA 16127	1876	Presby	S/C	2,200	122	$ 2,620	$1,650	$ 4,270
Gwynedd-Mercy College	Gwynedd Valley, PA 19437	1948	Catholic	J-S/C	2,196	146	$ 3,600	$2,500	$ 5,100
Hahnemann University	Philadelphia, PA 19102	1848	Independ	J-S-G/C	1,900	350	$ 8,000	—	$ 8,000
Harcum Junior College	Bryn Mawr, PA 19010	1915	Private	J/W	989	62	$ 3,100	$2,200	$ 5,300
Harrisburg Area Comm. Col.	Harrisburg, PA 17110	1964	State	J/C	6,459	276	$ 708	—	$ 708
Haverford College	Haverford, PA 19041	1833	Quaker	S/C	1,021	115	$ 8,080	$2,820	$10,900
Holy Family College	Philadelphia, PA 19114	1954	Catholic	S/C	1,309	131	$ 3,600	—	$ 3,600
Immaculata College	Immaculata, PA 19345	1920	Catholic	S/W	1,672	56	$ 3,375	$2,550	$ 5,925
Indiana Univ. of Pennsylvania	Indiana, PA 15705	1875	State	S-G/C	11,806	640	$ 1,632	$1,672	$ 3,304
Armstrong County Campus	Kittanning, PA 16201	1963	State	J/C	412	18	$ 1,632	$1,672	$ 3,304
Punxsutawney Campus	Punxsutawney, PA 15767	1962	State	J/C	285	13	$ 1,632	$1,672	$ 3,304
Juniata College	Huntingdon, PA 16652	1876	Independ	S/C	1,318	90	$ 5,985	$2,340	$ 9,425
Keystone Junior College	La Plume, PA 18440	1868	Independ	J/C	1,030	82	$ 3,600	$2,350	$ 5,950
King's College	Wilkes-Barre, PA 18711	1946	Catholic	S/C	2,306	124	$ 4,500	$2,460	$ 6,960
Kutztown State College	Kutztown, PA 19530	1866	State	S-G/C	5,861	270	$ 1,594	$1,664	$ 3,258
La Roche College	Pittsburgh, PA 15237	1963	Catholic	S-G/C	1,613	123	$ 3,425	$2,510	$ 5,935
La Salle College	Philadelphia, PA 19141	1863	Catholic	S-G/C	6,400	270	$ 4,150	$2,500	$ 6,800
Lackawanna Junior College	Scranton, PA 18505	1884	Independ	J/C	1,092	90	$ 2,370	—	$ 2,370
Lafayette College	Easton, PA 18042	1826	Presby	S/C	2,047	158	$ 7,725	$1,400	$ 9,125
Lancaster Bible College	Lancaster, PA 17601	1933	Independ	S/C	359	21	$ 3,526	$2,060	$ 5,586
Lancaster Theological Sem.	Lancaster, PA 17603	1825	UC Chr	P/C	242	26	$ 3,390	$2,210	$ 5,600
Lebanon Valley College	Annville, PA 17003	1866	Methodist	S/C	1,208	94	$ 5,360	$2,400	$ 7,760
Lehigh County Comm. College	Schnecksville, PA 18078	1966	Public	J/C	3,500	80	$ 840	—	$ 840

PENNSYLVANIA *(continued)*

NAME	ADDRESS	FOUNDED	AFFILIATION	LEVEL/TYPE	ENROLLMENT	TEACHERS	TUITION & FEES	BOARD & ROOM	TOTAL COST
Lehigh University	Bethlehem, PA 18015	1865	Independ	S-G/C	6,310	413	$ 8,000	$2,900	$10,900
Lincoln University	Lincoln Univ., PA 19352	1854	State	S-G/C	1,222	98	$ 1,750	$2,065	$ 3,815
Lock Haven State College	Lock Haven, PA 17745	1870	State	S/C	2,606	165	$ 1,604	$1,648	$ 3,252
Lutheran Theol. Sem./Gtysbrg.	Gettysburg, PA 17325	1826	Lutheran	G/C	275	22	$ 1,700	$1,700	$ 3,400
Lutheran Theol. Sem. at Phil.	Philadelphia, PA 19119	1864	Lutheran	G/C	234	27	$ 1,600	$2,180	$ 3,780
Luzerne County Comm. Col.	Nanticoke, PA 18634	1967	State	J/C	2,600	70	$ 990	—	$ 990
Lycoming College	Williamsport, PA 17701	1812	Methodist	S/C	1,205	75	$ 5,580	$2,380	$ 7,960
Lyon School of Business	New Castle, PA 16101	1894	Independ	J/C	120	12	$ 3,270	$2,295	$ 5,565
Manor Junior College	Jenkintown, PA 19046	1947	Catholic	J/W	392	50	$ 3,400	$2,200	$ 5,600
Mansfield State College	Mansfield, PA 16933	1857	State	S-G/C	2,713	199	$ 1,693	$1,764	$ 3,457
Mary Immaculate Seminary	Northampton, PA 18067	1939	Catholic	G/M	40	16	$ 2,100	$2,100	$ 4,200
Marywood College	Scranton, PA 18509	1915	Catholic	S-G/W	2,966	161	$ 3,100	$2,100	$ 5,200
Medical Col. of Pennsylvania	Philadelphia, PA 19129	1850	Independ	P/C	454	252	$10,850	—	$10,850
Mercyhurst College	Erie, PA 16546	1926	Catholic	S-G/C	1,606	100	$ 4,980	$1,975	$ 6,955
Messiah College	Grantham, PA 17027	1909	Brethren	S/C	1,502	101	$ 4,400	$2,250	$ 6,650
Millersville University	Millersville, PA 17551	1855	State	S-G/C	6,414	304	$ 1,598	$1,800	$ 3,398
Montgomery Co. Comm. Col.	Blue Bell, PA 19422	1964	County	J/C	7,993	350	$ 990	—	$ 990
Moore College of Art	Philadelphia, PA 19103	1844	Independ	S/W	591	76	$ 5,200	$2,500	$ 7,700
Moravian College	Bethlehem, PA 18018	1742	Moravian	S/C	1,788	134	$ 6,275	$2,340	$ 8,615
Moravian Theological Sem.	Bethlehem, PA 18018	1807	Moravian	P/C	101	19	$ 3,220	$2,475	$ 5,695
Mount Aloysius Jr. College	Cresson, PA 16630	1939	Catholic	J/C	530	40	$ 3,150	$2,050	$ 5,200
Muhlenberg College	Allentown, PA 18104	1848	Lutheran	S/C	2,353	135	$ 6,585	$2,165	$ 8,750
Neumann College	Aston, PA 19014	1965	Catholic	S/C	847	72	$ 3,433	—	$ 3,433
New School of Music	Philadelphia, PA 19103	1942	Independ	S/C	81	35	$ 4,435	—	$ 4,435
Nrthmptn Co. Area Comm. Col.	Bethlehem, PA 18017	1966	Public	J/C	4,608	329	$ 960	—	$ 960
Northeastern Chrstn. Jr. Col.	Villanova, PA 19085	1959	C of Chr	J/C	206	33	$ 2,875	$2,400	$ 5,275
Pendle Hill	Wallingford, PA 19086	1930	Quaker	S-G/C	40	8	—	—	$ 5,800
Pennco Tech.	Bristol, PA 19007	1961	Independ	T/C	625	44	$ 3,300	—	$ 3,300
Pa. College of Optometry	Philadelphia, PA 19141	1919	Independ	P/C	579	63	$ 9,966	$1,623	$11,589
Pa. College of Podiatric Med.	Philadelphia, PA 19107	1963	Independ	P/C	476	153	$ 9,500	$3,800	$13,300
Pennsylvania State Univ.	Univ. Park, PA 16802	1855	State	S-G/C	36,162	1,688	$ 2,118	$2,274	$ 4,392
Allentown Campus	Fogelsville, PA 18057	1912	State	J/C	866	22	$ 1,827	—	$ 1,827
Altoona Campus	Altoona, PA 16603	1929	State	J/C	2,428	110	$ 1,827	$2,274	$ 4,101
Beaver Campus	Monaca, PA 15061	1964	State	J/C	1,391	53	$ 1,827	$2,274	$ 4,101
Behrend College	Erie, PA 16563	1926	State	S-G/C	1,850	103	$ 2,010	$2,274	$ 4,284
Berks Campus	Reading, PA 19608	1924	State	J/C	1,491	53	$ 1,827	—	$ 1,827
Capitol Campus	Middletown, PA 17057	1966	State	S-G/C	2,711	114	$ 2,118	$2,274	$ 4,392
Delaware County Campus	Media, PA 19063	1966	State	J/C	1,673	67	$ 1,827	—	$ 1,827
DuBois Campus	DuBois, PA 15801	1935	State	J/C	827	41	$ 1,827	—	$ 1,827
Fayette Campus	Uniontown, PA 15401	1934	State	J/C	871	50	$ 1,827	—	$ 1,827
Hazleton Campus	Hazleton, PA 18201	1934	State	J/C	1,342	52	$ 1,827	$2,274	$ 4,101
Hershey Medical Center	Hershey, PA 17033	1964	State	P/C	517	290	$ 6,681	—	$ 6,681
McKeesport Campus	McKeesport, PA 15132	1947	State	J/C	1,521	58	$ 1,827	$2,274	$ 4,101
Mont Alto Campus	Mont Alto, PA 17237	1929	State	J/C	966	48	$ 1,827	$2,274	$ 4,101
New Kensington Campus	New Kensington, PA 15068	1958	State	J/C	1,329	44	$ 1,827	$2,274	$ 4,101
Ogontz Campus	Abington, PA 19001	1950	State	J/C	3,192	115	$ 1,827	—	$ 1,827
Schuylkill Campus	Schuylkill, PA 17972	1934	State	J/C	962	36	$ 1,827	—	$ 1,827
Shenango Valley Campus	Sharon, PA 16146	1965	State	J/C	922	47	$ 1,827	—	$ 1,827
Wilkes-Barre Campus	Wilkes-Barre, PA 18708	1916	State	J/C	754	38	$ 1,827	—	$ 1,827
Worthington Scrntn. Camp.	Dunmore, PA 18512	1923	State	J/C	1,537	62	$ 1,827	—	$ 1,827
York Campus	York, PA 17403	1926	State	J/C	1,341	59	$ 1,827	—	$ 1,827
Philadelphia College of Bible	Langhorne, PA 19047	1913	Independ	S/C	573	33	$ 3,360	$2,600	$ 5,960
Phila. Col. of Osteo. Medicine	Philadelphia, PA 19131	1899	Independ	P/C	833	104	$ 9,450	—	$ 9,450
Phila. Col. of Perform. Arts	Philadelphia, PA 19102	1870	Independ	S-G/C	346	150	$ 5,570	$1,950	$ 7,520
Phila. Col. of Pharm. and Sci.	Philadelphia, PA 19104	1821	Independ	S-G/C	1,107	134	$ 5,000	$2,300	$ 7,300
Phila. Col. of Textiles & Sci.	Philadelphia, PA 19144	1884	Private	S-G/C	3,091	185	$ 4,400	$2,850	$ 7,250
Pierce Junior College	Philadelphia, PA 19102	1865	Independ	J/C	2,120	106	$ 3,160	$1,250	$ 4,410
Pinebrook Junior College	Coopersburg, PA 18036	1969	Fellow	J/C	105	20	$ 3,050	$2,040	$ 5,090
Pittsburgh Theol. Seminary	Pittsburgh, PA 15206	1794	Presby	G/C	371	20	$ 2,694	$2,000	$ 4,694
Point Park College	Pittsburgh, PA 15222	1960	Private	S-G/C	2,666	172	$ 4,300	$2,210	$ 6,510
Reading Area Comm. College	Reading, PA 19603	1971	Public	J/C	1,552	94	$ 1,250	—	$ 1,250
Reconstructionist Rab. Col.	Philadelphia, PA 19095	1968	Jewish	G/C	39	18	$ 3,000	—	$ 3,000
Reformed Presby. Theol. Sem.	Pittsburgh, PA 15208	1810	Presby	G/C	49	6	$ 1,200	$1,000	$ 2,200
Robert Morris College	Coraopolis, PA 15108	1921	Independ	S-G/C	5,765	200	$ 2,880	$2,000	$ 4,880
Rosemont College	Rosemont, PA 19010	1921	Catholic	S/W	608	87	$ 5,045	$3,170	$ 8,215
St. Charles Borromeo Sem.	Philadelphia, PA 19151	1832	Catholic	G/M	235	37	$ 2,215	$1,800	$ 4,015
St. Francis College	Loretto, PA 15940	1847	Catholic	S-G/C	1,565	85	$ 4,534	$2,350	$ 6,884
St. Joseph's University	Philadelphia, PA 19131	1852	Catholic	S-G/C	6,200	340	$ 4,600	$3,000	$ 7,600
St. Vincent College	Latrobe, PA 15650	1846	Catholic	S/C	1,060	86	$ 4,210	$2,070	$ 6,280
Seton Hill College	Greensburg, PA 15601	1883	Catholic	S/W	968	82	$ 4,500	$2,400	$ 6,900
Shippensburg University	Shippensburg, PA 17257	1871	State	S-G/C	5,862	271	$ 1,646	$1,620	$ 3,266
Slippery Rock State College	Slippery Rock, PA 16057	1889	State	S-G/C	5,782	337	$ 1,480	$1,582	$ 3,062
Spring Garden College	Chestnut Hill, PA 19118	1851	Independ	S/C	1,425	110	$ 4,350	—	$ 4,350
Susquehanna University	Selinsgrove, PA 17870	1858	Lutheran	S/C	1,409	116	$ 5,815	$2,445	$ 8,260
Swarthmore College	Swarthmore, PA 19081	1864	Quaker	S-G/C	1,278	153	$ 8,430	$3,260	$11,690
Temple University	Philadelphia, PA 19122	1884	State	S-G/C	29,643	2,703	$ 2,616	$2,835	$ 5,451
Theol. Sem. of Ref. Epis. Ch.	Philadelphia, PA 19104	1886	Episcopal	G/C	70	6	$ 1,200	$ 800	$ 2,000
Thiel College	Greenville, PA 16125	1866	Lutheran	S/C	810	75	$ 4,990	$2,398	$ 7,388
Thomas Jefferson University	Philadelphia, PA 19107	1824	Private	S-G/C	1,796	96	$ 6,100	$1,250	$ 7,350
Jefferson Medical College	Philadelphia, PA 19107	1824	Private	P/C	897	1,792	$ 8,800	—	$14,428
U.S. Army War College	Carlisle Bar, PA 17013	1901	Federal	P/C	690	58	—	—	—
United Wesleyan College	Allentown, PA 18103	1921	Wesleyan	S/C	123	16	$ 3,120	$2,000	$ 5,120
University of Pennsylvania	Philadelphia, PA 19104	1740	Independ	S-G/C	22,317	3,682	$ 8,000	$3,614	$11,614

PENNSYLVANIA *(continued)*

NAME	ADDRESS	FOUNDED	AFFILIATION	LEVEL/ TYPE	ENROLLMENT	TEACHERS	TUITION & FEES	BOARD & ROOM	TOTAL COST
University of Pittsburgh	Pittsburgh, PA 15260	1787	State	S-G/C	29,358	2,682	$ 2,318	$2,450	$ 4,768
Bradford Campus	Bradford, PA 16701	1963	State	S/C	1,023	69	$ 2,310	$2,500	$ 4,810
Greensburg Campus	Greensburg, PA 15601	1963	State	J/C	1,274	54	$ 2,090	$1,190	$ 3,280
Johnstown Campus	Johnstown, PA 15904	1927	State	S/C	3,227	163	$ 2,280	$2,110	$ 4,390
Titusville Campus	Titusville, PA 16354	1963	State	J/C	435	38	$ 2,160	$2,020	$ 4,180
University of Scranton	Scranton, PA 18510	1888	Catholic	S-G/C	4,594	241	$ 4,170	$2,330	$ 6,500
Ursinus College	Collegeville, PA 19426	1869	C of Chr	S/C	1,168	105	$ 5,550	$2,550	$ 8,100
Valley Forge Christian College	Phoenixville, PA 19460	1939	A of God	S/C	411	23	$ 2,860	$2,328	$ 5,188
Valley Forge Military Jr. Col.	Wayne, PA 19087	1928	Independ	J/M	115	17	$ 3,650	$4,155	$ 7,805
Villa Maria College	Erie, PA 16505	1925	Catholic	S/W	622	84	$ 4,350	$2,400	$ 7,500
Villanova University	Villanova, PA 19085	1842	Catholic	S-G/C	11,603	698	$ 5,555	$3,440	$ 8,995
Washington and Jefferson Col.	Washington, PA 15301	1781	Independ	S/C	1,018	89	$ 6,110	$2,190	$ 8,300
Waynesburg College	Waynesburg, PA 15370	1849	Presby	S/C	758	67	$ 5,010	$2,250	$ 7,260
West Chester University of Pennsylvania	West Chester, PA 19380	1871	State	S-G/C	9,704	523	$ 1,526	$1,750	$ 3,276
Westminster College	New Wilmington, PA 16142	1852	Presby	S-G/C	1,588	115	$ 5,500	$2,134	$ 7,634
Westminster Theol. Seminary	Glenside, PA 19038	1929	Independ	G/C	422	26	$ 2,500	$2,820	$ 5,320
Westmoreland Co. Comm. Col.	Youngwood, PA 15697	1970	County	J/C	3,241	158	$ 816	—	$ 816
Widener University	Chester, PA 19013	1821	Independ	S-G/C	3,811	217	$ 5,760	$2,620	$ 8,380
University College	Chester, PA 19013	1980	Independ	J-S/C	1,321	108	$ 1,236	—	$ 1,236
Wilkes College	Wilkes-Barre, PA 18766	1933	Independ	S-G/C	1,950	170	$ 4,900	$2,480	$ 7,380
Williamsport Area Comm. Col.	Williamsport, PA 17701	1965	State	T/C	3,701	161	$ 1,236	—	$ 1,236
Wilson College	Chambersburg, PA 17201	1869	Presby	S/W	265	35	$ 6,072	$2,280	$ 8,352
Yorktown Business Institute	York, PA	1976	Independ	J/C	214	26	$ 3,600	—	—
York Col. of Pennsylvania	York, PA 17405	1776	Independ	S-G/C	4,364	216	$ 2,990	$1,924	$ 4,914

PUERTO RICO

NAME	ADDRESS	FOUNDED	AFFILIATION	LEVEL/ TYPE	ENROLLMENT	TEACHERS	TUITION & FEES	BOARD & ROOM	TOTAL COST
Catholic. Univ. of Puerto Rico	Ponce, PR 00732	1948	Catholic	S-G/C					
Ponce Campus	Ponce, PR 00732	1948	Catholic	S-G/C	9,201	398	$ 1,626	$1,200	$ 2,826
Arecibo Branch Campus	Arecibo, PR 00612	1960	Catholic	S/C	1,453	46	$ 1,626	$1,200	$ 2,826
Guayma Branch Campus	Guayama, PR 00654	1969	Catholic	T/C	1,152	53	$ 1,626	$1,200	$ 2,826
Mayaguez Branch Campus	Mayaguez, PR 00709	1975	Catholic	T/C	978	67	$ 1,626	$1,200	$ 2,826
School of Law	Ponce, PR 00732	1961	Catholic	P/C	285	26	$ 3,300	$1,200	$ 4,500
Inter Amer. Un. of Puerto Rico	San Juan, PR 00936	1912	Independ	S-G/C					
Inter American Univ. of P.R.	Hato Rey, PR 00919	1962	Independ	S-G/C	16,608	758	$ 1,600	—	$ 1,600
Inter American Univ. of P.R.	San German, PR 00753	1912	Independ	S-G/C	7,431	299	$ 1,600	$1,150	$ 2,750
Aquadilla Regional College	Aquadilla, PR 00603	1957	Independ	J/C	2,603	117	$ 1,600	—	$ 1,600
Arecibo Regional College	Arecibo, PR 00612	1957	Independ	J/C	3,604	202	$ 1,600	—	$ 1,600
Barranquitas Regional Col.	Barranquitas, PR 00615	1957	Independ	J/C	1,366	64	$ 1,600	—	$ 1,600
Fajardo Regional College	Fajardo, PR 00648	1965	Independ	J/C	1,816	82	$ 1,600	—	$ 1,600
Guayama Regional College	Guayama, PR 00654	1958	Independ	J/C	1,256	89	$ 1,600	—	$ 1,600
Ponce Regional College	Ponce, PR 00731	1962	Independ	J/C	2,100	114	$ 1,600	—	$ 1,600
School of Law	Santurce, PR 00910	1961	Independ	G/C	870	48	$ 3,400	—	$ 3,400
School of Optometry	Hato Rey, PR 00918	1980	Independ	P/C	87	15	$ 7,660	—	$ 7,660
Puerto Rico Junior College	Rio Piedras, PR 00928	1949	Independ	J/C	4,413	238	$ 1,550	—	$ 1,550
Metropolitan University College	Rio Piedras, PR 00928	1980	Independ	S/C	4,358	165	$ 1,550	—	$ 1,550
University of Puerto Rico	San Juan, PR 00936	1903	State	J-S-G/C	51,273	2,994	$ 2,600	$1,500	$ 3,100
Univ. of the Sacred Heart	Santurce, PR 00914	1935	Catholic	J-S/C	7,032	324	$ 1,400	$ 900	$ 2,300
University of Turabo	Caguas, PR 00625	1972	Independ	S-G/C	6,470	254	$ 1,550	—	$ 1,550

RHODE ISLAND

NAME	ADDRESS	FOUNDED	AFFILIATION	LEVEL/ TYPE	ENROLLMENT	TEACHERS	TUITION & FEES	BOARD & ROOM	TOTAL COST
Barrington College	Barrington, RI 02806	1900	Independ	S/C	531	61	$ 5,440	$2,650	$ 8,090
Brown University	Providence, RI 02912	1764	Independ	S-G/C	6,942	487	$ 8,427	$3,135	$11,562
Bryant College	Smithfield, RI 02917	1863	Independ	S-G/C	6,582	280	$ 3,750	$2,630	$ 6,380
Johnson & Wales College	Providence, RI 02903	1914	Independ	S/C	3,838	140	$ 4,000	$2,500	$ 6,500
New England Inst. of Tech.	Providence, RI 02907	1940	Independ	T/C	1,471	85	$ 4,125	—	$ 4,125
Newport Col.–Salve Regina	Newport, RI 02840	1934	Catholic	S-G/C	1,960	220	$ 5,350	$3,100	$ 8,450
Providence College	Providence, RI 02918	1917	Catholic	S-G/C	3,552	224	$ 5,317	$3,100	$ 8,417
Rhode Island College	Providence, RI 02908	1854	State	S-G/C	8,732	376	$ 1,061	$2,650	$ 3,711
Rhode Island Junior College	Warwick, RI 02886	1964	State	J/C	12,149	325	$ 690	—	$ 690
Rhode Island Sch. of Design	Providence, RI 02915	1877	Independ	P/C	1,670	197	$ 7,570	$3,250	$10,820
Roger Williams College	Bristol, RI 02809	1948	Independ	S/C	4,193	340	$ 4,496	$2,842	$ 7,338
University of Rhode Island	Kingston, RI 02881	1888	State	S-G/C	14,155	850	$ 1,294	$3,082	$ 4,376

SOUTH CAROLINA

NAME	ADDRESS	FOUNDED	AFFILIATION	LEVEL/ TYPE	ENROLLMENT	TEACHERS	TUITION & FEES	BOARD & ROOM	TOTAL COST
Aiken Technical College	Aiken, SC 29801	1969	State	T/C	1,023	97	$ 600	—	$ 600
Allen University	Columbia, SC 29204	1870	Methodist	S/C	240	25	$ 2,981	$1,870	$ 4,851
Anderson College	Anderson, SC 29621	1911	Baptist	J/C	1,044	60	$ 2,640	$1,790	$ 4,430
Baptist College at Charleston	Charleston, SC 29411	1960	Baptist	S/C	1,800	103	$ 4,140	$2,484	$ 6,624
Beaufort Technical College	Beaufort, SC 29902	1972	State	T/C	1,684	76	$ 480	—	$ 480
Benedict College	Columbia, SC 29204	1870	Independ	S/C	1,371	87	$ 2,936	$1,600	$ 4,536
Bob Jones University	Greenville, SC 29614	1927	Independ	S-G/C	6,207	332	—	—	$ 4,610
Central Wesleyan College	Central, SC 29630	1906	Wesleyan	S/C	414	38	$ 3,990	$1,990	$ 5,980
Chesterfield-Marlb. Tech. Col.	Cheraw, SC 29520	1968	State	J/C	672	42	$ 480	—	$ 480
Citadel	Charleston, SC 29409	1842	State	S-G/M	3,320	194	$ 1,100	$1,670	$ 2,770
Claflin College	Orangeburg, SC 29115	1869	Methodist	S/C	670	56	$ 2,552	$1,665	$ 4,217
Clemson University	Clemson, SC 29631	1889	State	S-G/C	12,093	720	$ 1,402	$1,830	$ 3,232
Clinton Junior College	Rock Hill, SC 29731	1894	Methodist	J/C	116	10	$ 900	$1,100	$ 2,000
Coker College	Hartsville, SC 29550	1908	Independ	S/C	300	48	$ 4,235	$2,300	$ 6,535
College of Charleston	Charleston, SC 29424	1770	State	S-G/C	5,394	324	$ 1,120	$1,850	$ 2,970
Columbia Bible College	Columbia, SC 29203	1923	Int-Den	S-G/C	877	49	$ 2,700	$2,025	$ 4,725
Columbia College	Columbia, SC 29203	1854	Methodist	S-G/W	1,095	77	$ 4,200	$2,300	$ 6,500
Columbia Junior College	Columbia, SC 29203	1935	Independ	J/C	650	40	$ 1,425	$ 900	$ 2,325
Converse College	Spartanburg, SC 29301	1889	Independ	S-G/W	952	80	$ 4,575	$2,875	$ 7,450

SOUTH CAROLINA *(continued)*

NAME	ADDRESS	FOUNDED	AFFILIATION	LEVEL/TYPE	ENROLLMENT	TEACHERS	TUITION & FEES	BOARD & ROOM	TOTAL COST
Denmark Tech. College	Denmark, SC 29042	1948	State	T/C	743	45	$ 600	$2,160	$ 2,760
Erskine College	Due West, SC 29639	1839	Presby	S/C	573	48	$ 4,480	$2,150	$ 6,630
Florence-Darl. Tech. College	Florence, SC 29501	1963	State	T/C	2,325	170	$ 610	—	—
Francis Marion College	Florence, SC 29501	1970	State	S-G/C	2,911	138	$ 940	$2,040	$ 2,980
Furman University	Greenville, SC 29613	1826	Baptist	S-G/C	2,573	169	$ 4,800	$2,746	$ 7,546
Greenville Technical College	Greenville, SC 29606	1962	State	T/C	6,385	300	$ 465	—	$ 465
Holmes Col. of the Bible	Greenville, SC 29601	1898	Independ	S/C	165	16	—	—	—
Horry-Georgetown Tech. Col.	Conway, SC 29526	1966	State	T/C	1,419	40	$ 450	—	$ 450
Lander College	Greenwood, SC 29646	1872	State	S-G/C	2,004	92	$ 1,150	$1,620	$ 2,770
Limestone College	Gaffney, SC 29340	1845	Independ	S/C	1,540	99	$ 3,940	$1,960	$ 5,900
Lutheran Theol. South. Sem.	Columbia, SC 29203	1830	Lutheran	P/C	177	15	$ 1,600	$2,200	$ 3,820
Medical Univ. of S. Carolina	Charleston, SC 29425	1824	State	P/C	2,507	703	$ 1,062	$2,500	$ 3,562
Midlands Technical College	Columbia, SC 29202	1974	State	T/C	5,840	406	$ 800	—	$ 800
Morris College	Sumter, SC 29150	1908	Baptist	S/C	628	53	$ 2,548	$1,667	$ 4,215
Newberry College	Newberry, SC 29108	1856	Lutheran	S/C	742	76	$ 4,500	$2,100	$ 6,600
North Greenville College	Tigerville, SC 29688	1892	Baptist	J/C	580	37	$ 2,450	$1,813	$ 4,263
Orangeburg-Calhoun Tech. Col.	Orangeburg, SC 29115	1968	State	T/C	1,408	112	$ 495	—	$ 495
Piedmont Technical College	Greenwood, SC 29646	1966	State	T/C	1,701	120	$ 525	—	$ 525
Presbyterian College	Clinton, SC 29325	1880	Presby	S/C	923	75	$ 4,520	$2,170	$ 6,690
Rutledge College	Charleston, SC 29406	1911	Private	J/C	475	21	$ 1,800	—	$ 1,800
Rutledge College	Columbia, SC 29202	1911	Independ	J/C	647	18	$ 1,840	—	$ 1,840
Rutledge College	Spartanburg, SC 29303	1910	Independ	J/C	380	18	$ 1,620	—	$ 1,620
Sherman Col. of Strgt. Chiro.	Spartanburg, SC 29304	1973	Independ	P/C	384	30	$ 4,040	—	$ 4,040
South Carolina State College	Orangeburg, SC 29117	1896	State	S-G/C	3,901	236	$ 810	$1,764	$ 2,574
Southern Methodist College	Orangeburg, SC 29115	1956	Methodist	S/C	52	12	$ 1,370	$1,700	$ 3,070
Spartanburg Methodist College	Spartanburg, SC 29301	1911	Methodist	J/C	1,072	65	$ 2,500	$1,880	$ 4,380
Spartanburg Tech. College	Spartanburg, SC 29303	1963	State	T/C	2,100	86	$ 460	—	$ 460
Sumter Area Tech. College	Sumter, SC 29150	1963	State	T/C	1,754	172	$ 504	—	$ 504
Tri-County Tech. College	Pendleton, SC 29670	1962	State	T/C	2,635	66	$ 480	—	$ 480
Trident Tech. College	Charleston, SC 29411	1974	State	T/C	6,268	300	$ 700	—	$ 700
Univ. of South Carolina	Columbia, SC 29208	1801	State	S-G/C	24,498	1,229	$ 1,190	$1,983	$ 3,173
Aiken Campus	Aiken, SC 29801	1961	State	S/C	1,835	134	$ 850	—	$ 850
Beaufort Campus	Beaufort, SC 29902	1959	State	J/C	687	38	$ 820	—	$ 820
Coastal Carolina College	Conway, SC 29526	1959	State	S/C	2,511	116	$ 850	—	$ 850
Lancaster Campus	Lancaster, SC 29720	1959	State	J/C	798	46	$ 840	—	$ 840
Salkehatchie Campus	Allendale, SC 29810	1965	State	J/C	473	30	$ 820	—	$ 820
Spartanburg Campus	Spartanburg, SC 29303	1967	State	S/C	2,583	155	$ 850	—	$ 850
Sumter Campus	Sumter, SC 29150	1966	State	J/C	1,141	49	$ 820	—	$ 820
Union Campus	Union, SC 29379	1965	State	J/C	265	30	$ 820	—	$ 820
Voorhees College	Denmark, SC 29042	1897	Episcopal	S/C	625	56	$ 2,446	$2,000	$ 4,446
Williamsburg Tech.	Kingstree, SC 29556	1969	State	T/C	385	41	$ 500	—	$ 500
Winthrop College	Rock Hill, SC 29733	1886	State	S-G/C	4,881	260	$ 1,012	$1,396	$ 2,408
Wofford College	Spartanburg, SC 29301	1854	Methodist	S/C	1,074	75	$ 4,295	$2,300	$ 6,595
York Technical College	Rock Hill, SC 29730	1962	State	T/C	2,380	154	$ 360	—	$ 360

SOUTH DAKOTA

NAME	ADDRESS	FOUNDED	AFFILIATION	LEVEL/TYPE	ENROLLMENT	TEACHERS	TUITION & FEES	BOARD & ROOM	TOTAL COST
Augustana College	Sioux Falls, SD 57197	1860	Lutheran	S-G/C	1,968	171	$ 5,200	$1,795	$ 6,995
Black Hills State College	Spearfish, SD 57783	1883	State	S/C	2,080	95	$ 1,179	$1,568	$ 2,747
Dakota State College	Madison, SD 57042	1881	State	S/C	1,151	63	$ 1,150	$1,570	$ 2,720
Dakota Wesleyan University	Mitchell, SD 57301	1885	Methodist	S/C	511	57	$ 3,222	$1,917	$ 5,139
Freeman Junior College	Freeman, SD 57029	1900	Mennon	J/C	105	15	$ 3,075	$1,500	$ 4,575
Huron College	Huron, SD 57350	1883	Presby	S/C	377	49	$ 3,700	$2,300	$ 6,000
Lake Area Voc. Tech. Inst.	Watertown, SD 57201	1965	State	T/C	815	61	$ 1,128	$2,565	$ 3,683
Mount Marty College	Yankton, SD 57078	1936	Catholic	S-G/C	585	62	$ 3,925	$1,860	$ 5,805
National College of Business	Rapid City, SD 57701	1941	Private	S/C	1,101	84	$ 4,155	$2,540	$ 6,695
Rapid City Division	Rapid City, SD 57709	1974	Private	S/C	162	25	$ 2,350	—	$ 2,350
Sioux Falls Extension	Sioux Falls, SD 57101	1974	Private	S/C	341	23	$ 2,352	—	$ 2,352
North Amer. Baptist Seminary	Sioux Falls, SD 57105	1858	Baptist	P/C	175	10	$ 2,600	—	$ 2,600
Northern State College	Aberdeen, SD 57401	1901	State	S-G/C	2,700	115	$ 1,076	$1,403	$ 2,479
Presentation College	Aberdeen, SD 57401	1951	Catholic	J/C	312	38	$ 3,300	$1,500	$ 4,800
Sioux Falls College	Sioux Falls, SD 57105	1883	Baptist	S-G/C	872	74	$ 3,600	$1,840	$ 5,440
S. D. School of Mines & Tech.	Rapid City, SD 57701	1885	State	S-G/C	2,805	116	$ 1,313	$1,650	$ 2,963
South Dakota State University	Brookings, SD 57007	1881	State	S-G/C	7,389	397	$ 1,070	$1,444	$ 2,514
University of South Dakota	Vermillion, SD 57069	1862	State	S-G/C	6,175	415	$ 1,878	$1,500	$ 3,378
Springfield Campus	Springfield, SD 57062	1881	State	S/C	784	61	$ 1,000	$1,430	$ 2,430
Yankton College	Yankton, SD 57078	1881	UC Chr	S/C	273	45	$ 3,960	$2,080	$ 6,040

TENNESSEE

NAME	ADDRESS	FOUNDED	AFFILIATION	LEVEL/TYPE	ENROLLMENT	TEACHERS	TUITION & FEES	BOARD & ROOM	TOTAL COST
American Baptist College	Nashville, TN 37207	1924	Baptist	S-P/C	180	12	$ 1,500	$1,300	$ 2,800
Aquinas Junior College	Nashville, TN 37205	1961	Catholic	J/C	340	34	$ 1,950	—	$ 1,950
Austin Peay State University	Clarksville, TN 37040	1927	State	S-G/C	5,060	262	$ 798	$ 900	$ 1,698
Belmont College	Nashville, TN 37203	1951	Baptist	S/C	1,927	94	$ 2,700	$2,100	$ 4,800
Bethel College	McKenzie, TN 38201	1842	Presby	S/C	471	53	$ 2,400	$1,725	$ 4,125
Bristol College	Bristol, TN 37621	1895	Independ	S/C	582	35	$ 1,850	—	$ 1,850
Bryan College	Dayton, TN 37321	1930	Independ	S/C	544	47	$ 3,250	$2,450	$ 5,700
Carson-Newman College	Jefferson City, TN 37760	1851	Baptist	S/C	1,731	131	$ 3,308	$1,720	$ 5,028
Chatta. St. Tech. Comm. Col.	Chattanooga, TN 37406	1965	State	J/C	5,347	100	$ 465	—	$ 465
Christian Brothers College	Memphis, TN 38104	1871	Catholic	S/C	1,525	123	$ 3,700	$2,835	$ 6,535
Cleveland State Comm. College	Cleveland, TN 37311	1967	State	J/C	3,544	165	$ 468	—	$ 468
Columbia State Comm. College	Columbia, TN 38401	1966	State	J/C	2,969	110	$ 462	—	$ 462
Covenant College	Lookout Mtn., TN 37350	1955	Presby	S/C	542	49	$ 4,310	$2,490	$ 6,800
Cumberland Col. of Tennessee	Lebanon, TN 37087	1842	Independ	J/C	617	44	$ 2,690	$1,740	$ 4,430
David Lipscomb College	Nashville, TN 37203	1891	C of Chr	S/C	2,262	147	$ 2,598	$1,860	$ 4,458
East Tennessee State Univ.	Johnson City, TN 37614	1911	State	S-G/C	9,628	485	$ 860	$1,730	$ 2,590
Emmanuel School of Religion	Johnson City, TN 37601	1961	Christian	G/C	148	12	$ 1,235	—	$ 1,235

TENNESSEE *(continued)*

NAME	ADDRESS	FOUNDED	AFFILIATION	LEVEL/TYPE	ENROLLMENT	TEACHERS	TUITION & FEES	BOARD & ROOM	TOTAL COST
Fisk University	Nashville, TN 37203	1866	Independ	S-G/C	757	90	$ 4,900	$2,085	$ 6,985
Freed-Hardeman College	Henderson, TN 38340	1869	C of Chr	S/C	1,239	85	$ 2,850	$1,900	$ 4,750
Free Will Baptist Bible College	Nashville, TN 37205	1942	Baptist	S-G/C	510	33	$ 1,800	$1,900	$ 3,700
Hiwassee College	Madisonville, TN 37354	1849	Methodist	J/C	918	36	$ 1,995	$1,935	$ 3,930
Jackson State Comm. College	Jackson, TN 38301	1967	State	J/C	2,981	128	$ 480	—	$ 480
John A. Gupton College	Nashville, TN 37203	1946	Independ	J/C	55	12	$ 2,191	—	$ 2,191
Johnson Bible College	Knoxville, TN 37920	1893	Christian	S/C	369	24	$ 1,600	$2,260	$ 3,860
King College	Bristol, TN 37620	1867	Presby	S/C	434	47	$ 3,620	$2,330	$ 5,950
Knoxville College	Knoxville, TN 37921	1875	Presby	S/C	512	33	$ 2,880	$1,938	$ 4,818
Lambuth College	Jackson, TN 38301	1843	Methodist	S/C	758	65	$ 3,500	$1,810	$ 5,310
Lane College	Jackson, TN 38301	1882	CME	S/C	731	40	$ 2,247	$1,520	$ 3,767
Lee College	Cleveland, TN 37311	1918	C of Chr	S/C	1,122	68	$ 2,200	$1,800	$ 4,000
LeMoyne-Owen College	Memphis, TN 38126	1870	UC Chr	S/C	1,073	70	$ 2,450	—	$ 2,450
Lincoln Memorial University	Harrogate, TN 37752	1897	Private	S-G/C	1,380	74	$ 2,400	$1,800	$ 4,200
Martin College	Pulaski, TN 38478	1870	Methodist	J/C	335	24	$ 2,200	$1,975	$ 4,175
Maryville College	Maryville, TN 37801	1819	Presby	S/C	583	54	$ 4,000	$1,995	$ 5,995
Meharry Medical College	Nashville, TN 37208	1876	Independ	P/C	747	270	$ 8,100	$6,000	$13,400
Memphis Academy of Arts	Memphis, TN 38112	1936	Independ	S/C	208	24	$ 3,100	—	$ 3,100
Memphis State University	Memphis, TN 38152	1912	State	S-G/C	20,744	850	$ 832	$ 900	$ 1,732
Middle Tenn. State University	Murfreesboro, TN 37132	1911	State	S-G/C	10,933	612	$ 760	$1,724	$ 2,484
Milligan College	Milligan Col., TN 37682	1866	Christian	S/C	600	62	$ 3,400	$2,500	$ 5,900
Morristown College	Morristown, TN 37814	1881	Methodist	J/C	142	14	$ 1,985	$1,864	$ 3,849
Motlow State Community Col.	Tullahoma, TN 37388	1969	State	J/C	2,244	95	$ 470	—	$ 470
Nashville State Tech. Institute	Nashville, TN 37209	1970	State	J/C	5,744	75	$ 378	—	$ 378
Scarritt College	Nashville, TN 37203	1924	Methodist	G/C	97	9	$ 3,400	$2,800	$ 6,200
Southern Col. of Optometry	Memphis, TN 38104	1932	Independ	P/C	533	36	$ 5,650	—	$ 5,650
Southern Missionary College	Collegedale, TN 37315	1892	7-D Adv	S/C	1,801	122	$ 4,160	$2,030	$ 6,190
Southwestern at Memphis	Memphis, TN 38112	1848	Presby	S/C	1,006	118	$ 5,670	$2,743	$ 8,413
State Tech. Inst. at Memphis	Memphis, TN 38134	1967	State	J/C	7,365	392	$ 504	—	$ 504
Tennessee State University	Nashville, TN 37203	1912	State	S-G/C	8,126	476	$ 2,256	$1,826	$ 4,082
Tennessee Tech. University	Cookeville, TN 38501	1915	State	S-G/C	7,869	530	$ 780	$1,790	$ 2,570
Tennessee Temple University	Chattanooga, TN 37404	1946	Baptist	S-G/C	3,598	160	$ 2,182	$2,158	$ 4,340
Tennessee Wesleyan College	Athens, TN 37303	1857	Methodist	S/C	516	56	$ 3,000	$2,415	$ 5,415
Tomlinson College	Cleveland, TN 37311	1966	CofG Proph	J/C	242	14	$ 1,900	$1,860	$ 3,760
Trevecca Nazarene College	Nashville, TN 37203	1901	Nazarene	S/C	972	78	$ 2,900	$2,000	$ 4,900
Tusculum College	Greeneville, TN 37743	1794	Presby	S/C	370	37	$ 3,500	$2,210	$ 5,710
Union University	Jackson, TN 38301	1825	Baptist	S/C	1,374	71	$ 2,450	$1,570	$ 4,020
University of Tennessee	Knoxville, TN 37916	1794	State	S-G/C					
Center for the Health Sci.	Memphis, TN 38163	1850	State	P/C	2,026	74	$ 3,492	$2,108	$ 5,600
Chattanooga Campus	Chattanooga, TN 37402	1886	State	S-G/C	7,544	255	$ 786	$2,286	$ 3,072
Knoxville Campus	Knoxville, TN 37996	1794	State	S-G/C	27,041	1,245	$ 867	$1,803	$ 2,670
Martin Campus	Martin, TN 38238	1927	State	S-G/C	5,525	258	$ 846	$1,715	$ 2,561
University of the South	Sewanee, TN 37375	1857	Episcopal	S/C	996	96	$ 7,185	$1,850	$ 9,035
Vanderbilt University	Nashville, TN 37240	1875	Independ	S-G/C	8,782	138	$ 6,950	$2,976	$ 9,926
Walters State Comm. College	Morristown, TN 37814	1970	State	J/C	3,730	77	$ 426	—	$ 426

TEXAS

NAME	ADDRESS	FOUNDED	AFFILIATION	LEVEL/TYPE	ENROLLMENT	TEACHERS	TUITION & FEES	BOARD & ROOM	TOTAL COST
Abilene Christian University	Abilene, TX 79799	1906	C of Chr	S-G/C	4,546	286	$ 2,830	$1,860	$ 4,680
Alvin Community College	Alvin, TX 77511	1949	State	J/C	3,724	196	$ 200	—	$ 200
Amarillo College	Amarillo, TX 79179	1929	State	J/C	5,950	310	$ 254	—	$ 254
Amber University	Garland, TX 75041	1971	Independ	S-G/C	1,068	31	$ 1,800	—	$ 1,800
American Technological Univ.	Killeen, TX 76540	1973	Independ	S-G/C	487	35	$ 1,500	$1,800	$ 3,300
Angelina College	Lufkin, TX 75902	1968	State	J/C	2,200	130	$ 260	$1,500	$ 1,760
Angelo State University	San Angelo, TX 76909	1928	State	S-G/C	5,834	221	$ 420	$2,506	$ 2,926
Arlington Baptist College	Arlington, TX 76012	1939	Baptist	S/C	381	24	$ 1,350	$1,450	$ 2,800
Austin College	Sherman, TX 75090	1849	Presby	S-G/C	1,186	91	$ 4,600	$2,260	$ 6,860
Austin Community College	Austin, TX 78768	1972	State	J/C	15,362	725	$ 372	—	$ 372
Austin Presbyterian Theo. Sem.	Austin, TX 78705	1902	Presby	G/C	208	17	$ 3,420	$2,250	$ 5,670
Bauder Fashion College	Arlington, TX 76010	1967	Independ	T/C	476	35	$ 3,710	$2,680	$ 6,390
Baylor College of Dentistry	Dallas, TX 75246	1905	Private	G/C	665	285	$ 2,200	—	$ 2,200
Baylor College of Medicine	Houston, TX 77030	1900	Independ	P/C	902	1,182	$ 968	—	$ 968
Baylor University	Waco, TX 76798	1845	Baptist	S-G/C	10,473	587	$ 3,104	$2,436	$ 5,540
School of Nursing	Dallas, TX 75231	1909	Baptist	S-G/C	426	23	$ 1,845	$1,509	$ 3,354
Bee County College	Beeville, TX 78102	1965	Public	J/C	2,154	100	$ 230	$ 965	$ 1,195
Bishop College	Dallas, TX 75241	1889	Baptist	S/C	1,100	54	$ 4,100	$ 935	$ 5,035
Blinn College	Brenham, TX 77833	1883	Independ	J/C	3,243	144	$ 461	$1,050	$ 1,511
Brazosport College	Lake Jackson, TX 77566	1968	State	J/C	3,643	180	$ 175	—	$ 175
Central Texas College	West Killeen, TX 76542	1967	State	J/C	8,440	185	$ 250	$1,566	$ 1,816
Cisco Junior College	Cisco, TX 76437	1909	State	J/C	1,788	63	$ 308	$1,500	$ 1,808
Clarendon Junior College	Clarendon, TX 79221	1898	Public	J/C	1,033	28	$ 96	$1,300	$ 1,396
College of the Mainland	Texas City, TX 77591	1967	State	J/C	3,008	62	$ 108	—	$ 108
Commonwealth Col. of Fun. Serv.	Houston, TX 77006	1936	Independ	T/C	100	4	$ 3,200	—	$ 3,200
Concordia Lutheran College	Austin, TX 78705	1926	Lutheran	S/C	437	41	$ 2,400	$2,170	$ 4,570
Cooke County College	Gainesville, TX 76240	1924	Public	J/C	1,750	63	$ 324	$2,016	$ 2,340
Corpus Christi State Univ.	Corpus Christi, TX 78412	1971	State	S-G/C	3,340	136	$ 328	—	—
Dallas Baptist College	Dallas, TX 75211	1898	Baptist	S-G/C	1,337	73	$ 2,790	$2,200	$ 4,990
Dallas Bible College	Dallas, TX 75228	1940	Independ	S-G/C	199	30	$ 2,500	$1,800	$ 4,300
Dallas Christian College	Dallas, TX 75234	1950	Christian	S/C	166	18	$ 1,764	$1,660	$ 3,424
Dallas Theological Seminary	Dallas, TX 75204	1924	Independ	G/C	1,663	65	$ 3,400	$2,200	$ 5,600
Del Mar College	Corpus Christi, TX 78404	1935	State	J/C	8,620	530	$ 210	—	$ 210
Devry Inst. of Technology	Dallas, TX 75062	1969	Independ	S/C	2,015	86	$ 3,300	—	$ 3,300
East Texas Baptist College	Marshall, TX 75670	1912	Baptist	S/C	895	58	$ 2,600	$2,000	$ 4,600
East Texas State University	Commerce, TX 75428	1889	State	S-G/C	7,768	341	$ 394	$2,150	$ 2,544
Texarkana	Texarkana, TX 75501	1972	State	S-G/C	1,138	33	$ 260	—	$ 260

TEXAS *(continued)*

NAME	ADDRESS	FOUNDED	AFFILIATION	LEVEL/TYPE	ENROLLMENT	TEACHERS	TUITION & FEES	BOARD & ROOM	TOTAL COST
Eastfield College	Mesquite, TX 75150	1970	Public	J/C	8,969	320	$ 200	—	$ 200
El Centro College	Dallas, TX 75211	1965	State	J/C	7,000	200	$ 800	—	$ 800
El Paso Comm. College Dist.	El Paso, TX 79998	1969	State	J/C	11,209	564	$ 244	—	$ 244
Episc. Theol. Sem. of the S.W.	Austin, TX 78768	1951	Episcopal	G/C	90	11	$ 2,340	—	$ 2,340
Frank Phillips College	Borger, TX 79007	1948	State	J/C	950	26	$ 382	$1,190	$ 1,572
Galveston College	Galveston, TX 77550	1967	State	J/C	1,649	99	$ 150	—	$ 150
Georgia Military College	Kingsville NAS, TX 78363	1972	Independ	J/C	61	5	$ 1,620	—	$ 1,620
Grayson County Junior College	Denison, TX 75020	1965	State	J/C	6,000	123	$ 210	$1,736	$ 1,946
Gulf-Coast Bible College	Houston, TX 77270	1953	C of Chr	S/C	366	21	$ 2,520	$1,200	$ 3,720
Hardin-Simmons University	Abilene, TX 79698	1891	Baptist	S-G/C	1,948	129	$ 2,950	$1,980	$ 4,930
Henderson County Jr. College	Athens, TX 75751	1946	State	J/C	3,451	165	$ 206	$1,510	$ 1,716
Hill Junior College	Hillsboro, TX 76645	1962	State	J/C	990	30	$ 500	$2,000	$ 2,500
Houston Baptist University	Houston, TX 77074	1960	Baptist	S-G/C	2,995	130	$ 3,350	$1,780	$ 5,130
Houston Comm. Col. System	Houston, TX 77270	1971	State	J/C	45,243	1,548	$ 532	—	$ 532
Howard Co. Jr. College Dist.	Big Spring, TX 79720	1946	State	J/C	1,173	82	$ 250	$1,500	$ 1,750
Howard College	Big Spring, TX 79720	1945	State	J/C	1,050	67	$ 250	$1,825	$ 2,075
Southw. Col. Inst. for the Deaf	Big Spring, TX 79720	1979	State	J/C	117	22	$ 250	$1,825	$ 2,075
Howard Payne University	Brownwood, TX 76801	1889	Baptist	S/C	1,320	81	$ 2,480	$1,870	$ 4,350
Huston-Tillotson College	Austin, TX 78702	1876	UC Chr	S/C	577	42	$ 2,686	$2,018	$ 4,704
Incarnate Word College	San Antonio, TX 78209	1881	Catholic	S-G/C	1,357	112	$ 3,732	$1,946	$ 5,678
Jacksonville College	Jacksonville, TX 75766	1899	Baptist	J/C	300	25	$ 1,560	$1,800	$ 3,360
Jarvis Christian College	Hawkins, TX 75765	1912	Christian	S/C	551	48	$ 2,771	$1,780	$ 4,551
Kilgore College	Kilgore, TX 75662	1935	State	J/C	4,389	150	$ 330	$1,500	$ 1,830
Lamar University	Beaumont, TX 77710	1923	State	S-G/C	14,600	1,000	$ 244	$1,300	$ 2,700
Orange Campus	Orange, TX 77630	1969	State	J/C	985	48	$ 400	—	$ 400
Laredo Junior College	Laredo, TX 78040	1946	Public	J/C	3,871	115	$ 299	—	$ 299
Laredo State University	Laredo, TX 78040	1969	State	S-G/C	900	49	$ 407	—	$ 407
Lee College	Baytown, TX 77520	1934	State	J/C	6,211	188	$ 250	—	$ 250
LeTourneau College	Longview, TX 75607	1946	Independ	S/C	1,037	65	$ 3,796	$2,130	$ 5,926
Lon Morris College	Jacksonville, TX 75766	1854	Methodist	J/C	360	24	$ 2,700	$2,250	$ 4,950
Lubbock Christian College	Lubbock, TX 79407	1957	C of Chr	S/C	997	75	$ 2,600	$1,600	$ 4,200
McLennan Community College	Waco, TX 76708	1965	State	J/C	4,184	196	$ 240	—	$ 240
McMurry College	Abilene, TX 79697	1923	Methodist	S/C	1,413	128	$ 2,900	$1,746	$ 4,646
Midland College	Midland, TX 79701	1969	State	J/C	3,255	187	$ 260	—	$ 260
Midwestern State University	Wichita Falls, TX 76308	1922	State	S-G/C	4,818	159	$ 465	$1,380	$ 1,845
Mountain View College	Dallas, TX 75211	1970	State	J/C	5,979	243	$ 210	—	$ 210
Navarro College	Corsicana, TX 75110	1946	State	J/C	2,358	135	$ 424	$1,950	$ 2,374
North Harris County College	Houston, TX 77073	1974	State	J/C	9,495	169	$ 160	—	$ 160
North Texas State University	Denton, TX 76203	1890	State	S-G/C	18,782	800	$ 450	$2,200	$ 2,650
Northwood Institute of Texas	Cedar Hill, TX 75104	1966	Independ	J/C	300	14	$ 3,645	$2,900	$ 6,545
Oblate Col. of the Southwest	San Antonio, TX 78216	1903	Catholic	G/C	101	22	$ 3,108	—	$ 3,108
Odessa College	Odessa, TX 79762	1946	State	J/C	4,098	138	$ 355	$1,980	$ 2,335
Our Lady of the Lake Univ.	San Antonio, TX 78285	1911	Catholic	S-G/C	1,577	98	$ 3,200	$2,200	$ 5,400
Pan American University	Edinburg, TX 78539	1927	State	S-G/C	7,972	360	$ 316	$2,120	$ 2,436
Brownsville Campus	Brownsville, TX 78520	1973	State	S-G/C	974	70	$ 498	—	$ 498
Panola Junior College	Carthage, TX 75633	1947	State	J/C	1,094	48	$ 178	$1,750	$ 1,928
Paris Junior College	Paris, TX 75460	1924	Local	J/C	2,239	120	$ 388	$1,926	$ 2,314
Paul Quinn College	Waco, TX 76704	1872	AME	S/C	467	38	$ 2,165	$1,850	$ 4,015
Prairie View A&M University	Prairie View, TX 77445	1876	State	S-G/C	4,495	288	$ 460	$2,100	$ 2,560
Ranger Junior College	Ranger, TX 76470	1926	State	J/C	825	55	$ 400	$2,000	$ 2,400
Rice University	Houston, TX 77251	1891	Independ	S-G/C	3,881	420	$ 3,885	$3,400	$ 7,285
Richland College	Dallas, TX 75243	1972	State	J/C	14,000	308	$ 240	—	$ 240
St. Edward's University	Austin, TX 78704	1885	Catholic	S-G/C	2,575	150	$ 3,000	$2,516	$ 5,516
St. Mary's Univ. of San Antonio	San Antonio, TX 78284	1852	Catholic	S-G/C	3,311	162	$ 4,112	$ 960	$ 5,072
St. Philip's College	San Antonio, TX 78203	1898	District	J/C	6,910	217	$ 180	—	$ 180
Sam Houston State University	Huntsville, TX 77341	1879	State	S-G/C	10,470	486	$ 460	$2,095	$ 2,555
San Antonio College	San Antonio, TX 78247	1925	State	J/C	19,751	935	$ 250	—	$ 250
San Jacinto College, Central	Pasadena, TX 77505	1961	State	J/C	13,350	512	$ 205	—	$ 205
San Jacinto College, North	Houston, TX 77049	1974	State	J/C	3,650	165	$ 200	—	$ 200
Schreiner College	Kerrville, TX 78028	1923	Presby	J/C	517	41	$ 1,440	$1,050	$ 2,490
South Plains College	Levelland, TX 79336	1957	State	J/C	3,399	118	$ 244	$1,522	$ 1,766
South Texas College of Law	Houston, TX 77002	1923	Private	P/C	1,164	36	$ 3,800	$4,662	$ 8,462
Southern Bible College	Houston, TX 77078	1958	C of Chr	J-S/C	121	15	$ 1,800	$1,680	$ 3,480
Southern Methodist Univ.	Dallas, TX 75275	1911	Methodist	S-G/C	9,150	520	$ 6,300	$1,645	$ 7,945
Southwest Adventist College	Keene, TX 76059	1893	7-D Adv	S/C	712	45	$ 4,698	$2,390	$ 7,088
Southw. Assembly of God Col.	Waxahachie, TX 75165	1927	A of God	S/C	591	31	$ 1,652	$1,890	$ 3,542
Southw. Baptist Theol. Sem.	Fort Worth, TX 76122	1908	Baptist	G/C	3,853	155	$ 600	$2,016	$ 2,616
Southwest Christian College	Terrell, TX 75160	1949	C of Chr	J/C	232	18	$ 2,202	$1,406	$ 3,608
Southwest Texas Junior Col.	Uvalde, TX 78801	1946	Public	J/C	2,200	114	$ 416	$1,660	$ 2,076
Southwest Texas State Univ.	San Marcos, TX 78666	1899	State	S-G/C	16,397	651	$ 448	$1,993	$ 2,441
Southwestern University	Georgetown, TX 78626	1840	Methodist	S/C	990	80	$ 4,300	$2,680	$ 6,980
Stephen F. Austin State Univ.	Nacogdoches, TX 75962	1923	State	S-G/C	11,989	585	$ 450	$2,500	$ 2,950
Sul Ross State University	Alpine, TX 79832	1917	State	S-G/C	1,840	76	$ 476	$2,000	$ 3,376
Uvalde Study Center	Uvalde, TX 78801	1973	State	S-G/C	503	40	$ 282	—	$ 282
Tarleton State University	Stephenville, TX 76402	1899	State	S-G/C	4,231	141	$ 420	$1,830	$ 2,250
Tarrant County Junior College	Fort Worth, TX 76102	1965	State	J/C					
Northeast Campus	Hurst, TX 76059	1965	State	J/C	10,910	381	$ 120	—	$ 120
Northwest Campus	Fort Worth, TX 76179	1965	State	J/C	4,550	174	$ 120	—	$ 120
South Campus	Fort Worth, TX 76102	1965	State	J/C	10,703	320	$ 120	—	$ 120
Temple Junior College	Temple, TX 76501	1926	State	J/C	2,499	107	$ 338	$2,691	$ 3,029
Texarkana Community College	Texarkana, TX 75501	1927	State	J/C	3,923	116	$ 115	—	$ 115
Texas A&I University	Kingsville, TX 78363	1925	State	S-G/C	5,245	252	$ 375	$1,888	$ 2,263
Texas A&M University	College Station, TX 77843	1876	State	S-G/C	36,127	2,093	$ 452	$2,433	$ 2,885
Galveston Campus	Galveston, TX 77553	1971	State	S/C	590	69	$ 369	$2,810	$ 3,179

NAME	ADDRESS	FOUNDED	AFFILIATION	LEVEL/ TYPE	ENROLLMENT	TEACHERS	TUITION & FEES	BOARD & ROOM	TOTAL COST
TEXAS *(continued)*									
Texas Chiropractic College	Pasadena, TX 77505	1908	Independ	P/C	516	39	$ 4,500	—	$ 5,500
Texas Christian University	Fort Worth, TX 76129	1873	Christian	S-G/C	6,881	386	$ 4,140	$1,720	$ 5,860
Texas College	Tyler, TX 75702	1894	CME	S/C	619	43	$ 2,381	$1,925	$ 4,306
Texas College of Osteo. Med.	Fort Worth, TX 76107	1970	State	P/C	365	150	$ 1,050	—	$ 2,765
Texas Lutheran College	Seguin, TX 78155	1891	Lutheran	S/C	980	75	$ 3,000	$1,825	$ 4,825
Texas Southern University	Houston, TX 77004	1947	State	S-G/C	8,331	470	$ 900	$1,035	$ 1,935
Texas Southmost College	Brownsville, TX 78520	1926	State	J/C	4,182	194	$ 308	—	$ 308
Texas State Tech. Institute	Waco, TX 76705	1965	State	T/C					
Amarillo Campus	Amarillo, TX 79111	1970	State	T/C	1,175	97	$ 372	$2,580	$ 2,952
Harlingen Campus	Harlingen, TX 78850	1969	State	T/C	1,900	110	$ 372	$2,860	$ 3,232
Sweetwater Campus	Sweetwater, TX 79556	1970	State	T/C	749	54	$ 372	$2,860	$ 3,232
Waco Campus	Waco, TX 76705	1965	State	T/C	5,186	340	$ 372	$3,024	$ 3,396
Texas Tech. University	Lubbock, TX 79409	1923	State	S-G/C	22,216	1,550	$ 689	$2,000	$ 2,689
Texas Tech. University Health Center Sci.	Lubbock, TX 79430	1969	State	P/C	554	270	$ 480	—	$ 480
Texas Wesleyan College	Fort Worth, TX 76105	1891	Methodist	S-G/C	1,603	84	$ 3,000	$2,140	$ 5,140
Texas Woman's University	Denton, TX 76204	1901	State	S-G/W	7,827	384	$ 340	$2,382	$ 2,722
Trinity University	San Antonio, TX 78284	1869	Independ	S-G/C	3,303	214	$ 4,600	$2,575	$ 7,175
Tyler Junior College	Tyler, TX 75711	1926	State	J/C	7,313	329	$ 130	$1,736	$ 1,836
University of Dallas	Irving, TX 75061	1956	Catholic	S-G/C	2,684	184	$ 4,030	$2,400	$ 6,430
Univ. of Houston Central Camp.	Houston, TX 77004	1927	State	S-G/C	30,545	2,329	$ 400	$2,275	$ 2,675
Clear Lake City Campus	Houston, TX 77058	1971	State	S-G/C	6,580	320	$ 360	—	$ 360
Downtown College Campus	Houston, TX 77002	1974	State	S/C	6,353	273	$ 380	$3,000	$ 3,380
Victoria Campus	Victoria, TX 77901	1973	State	S-G/C	836	61	$ 232	—	$ 232
Univ. of Mary Hardin-Baylor	Belton, TX 76513	1845	Baptist	S-G/C	1,160	76	$ 2,390	$2,220	$ 4,610
University of St. Thomas	Houston, TX 77006	1947	Catholic	S-G/C	2,040	181	$ 3,200	$2,800	$ 6,000
Univ. of Texas at Arlington	Arlington, TX 76019	1895	State	S-G/C	22,171	1,302	$ 466	—	$ 466
Univ. of Texas at Austin	Austin, TX 78712	1883	State	S-G/C	48,039	2,188	$ 452	$2,694	$ 3,146
Univ. of Texas at Dallas	Richardson, TX 75080	1969	State	S-G/C	7,376	384	$ 394	—	$ 394
Univ. of Texas at El Paso	El Paso, TX 79968	1913	State	S-G/C	15,129	660	$ 396	$1,920	$ 2,316
Univ. of Texas at San Antonio	San Antonio, TX 78285	1969	State	S-G/C	11,145	482	$ 420	—	$ 420
Univ. of Texas at Tyler	Tyler, TX 75701	1971	State	S-G/C	2,623	149	$ 380	—	$ 380
Univ. of Tex. Health Sci. Center	Dallas, TX 75235	1943	State	S-G/C	1,322	581	$ 300	—	$ 300
Univ. of Tex. Health Sci. Center	Houston, TX 77225	1972	State	P/C	2,733	1,000	$ 320	—	$ 320
Dental Branch	Houston, TX 77025	1905	State	P/C	694	159	$ 484	—	$ 484
Univ. of Tex. Health Sci. Center	San Antonio, TX 78284	1959	State	P/C	2,332	640	$ 480	—	$ 480
Univ. of Texas Med. Branch	Galveston, TX 77550	1891	State	P/C	1,653	700	$ 569	—	$ 9,764
Univ. of Texas of Permian Bas.	Odessa, TX 79762	1969	State	S-G/C	1,825	105	$ 348	—	$ 348
Vernon Regional Jr. College	Vernon, TX 76384	1970	State	J/C	1,594	74	$ 400	$ 450	$ 850
Victoria College	Victoria, TX 77901	1925	State	J/C	2,640	125	$ 150	—	$ 300
Wayland Baptist College	Plainview, TX 79072	1906	Baptist	S-G/C	1,570	118	$ 1,950	$2,600	$ 4,550
Weatherford College	Weatherford, TX 76086	1869	State	J/C	1,990	65	$ 400	$1,900	$ 2,300
West Texas State University	Canyon, TX 79016	1910	State	S-G/C	6,805	364	$ 450	$1,980	$ 2,430
Western Texas College	Snyder, TX 79549	1969	Public	J/C	1,266	44	$ 250	$1,500	$ 1,750
Wharton County Junior College	Wharton, TX 77488	1946	Public	J/C	2,475	145	$ 300	$1,380	$ 1,680
Wiley College	Marshall, TX 75670	1873	Methodist	S/C	540	50	$ 2,430	$1,754	$ 4,184
UTAH									
Brigham Young University	Provo, UT 84602	1875	Mormon	S-G/C	27,990	1,572	$ 1,340	$2,100	$ 3,440
College of Eastern Utah	Price, UT 84501	1938	State	J/C	1,105	48	$ 693	$2,000	$ 2,693
Dixie College	St. George, UT 84770	1911	State	J/C	2,010	80	$ 696	$1,500	$ 2,196
Snow College	Ephraim, UT 84627	1888	Independ	J/C	1,411	52	$ 666	$1,761	$ 2,427
Southern Utah State College	Cedar City, UT 84720	1897	State	S/C	2,378	140	$ 735	$1,545	$ 2,280
Stevens Henager College	Ogden, UT 84401	1891	Independ	J/C	332	19	$ 2,502	—	$ 2,502
Provo	Provo, UT 84001	1891	Independ	J/C	426	26	$ 2,502	—	$ 2,502
University of Utah	Salt Lake City, UT 84112	1850	State	S-G/C	24,364	1,373	$ 906	$2,500	$ 3,406
Utah State University	Logan, UT 84322	1888	State	S-G/C	11,112	706	$ 925	$2,100	$ 3,025
Utah Technical Col. at Provo	Provo, UT 84603	1941	State	T/C	5,593	229	$ 627	—	$ 627
Utah Tech. Col. at Salt Lake	Salt Lake City, UT 84131	1948	Independ	T/C	7,108	439	$ 576	—	$ 576
Weber State College	Ogden, UT 84408	1889	State	S-G/C	10,000	450	$ 760	$2,000	$ 2,760
Westminster College	Salt Lake City, UT 84105	1875	Independ	S-G/C	1,233	52	$ 3,770	$2,816	$ 6,586
VERMONT									
Bennington College	Bennington, VT 05201	1925	Private	S-G/C	634	75	$10,750	$2,760	$13,510
Burlington College	Burlington, VT 05401	1972	Independ	S/C	150	30	$ 3,700	—	$ 3,700
Castleton State College	Castleton, VT 05735	1787	State	S-G/C	2,043	105	$ 1,560	$2,614	$ 4,174
Champlain College	Burlington, VT 05402	1878	Independ	J/C	1,605	105	$ 3,950	$2,975	$ 6,925
Col. of St. Joseph the Provider	Rutland, VT 05701	1952	Catholic	S-G/C	338	32	$ 3,990	$2,438	$ 6,428
College of the Americas	Brookfield, VT 05036	1972	Independ	S-G/C	—	—	—	—	—
Community Col. of Vermont	Montpelier, VT 05602	1970	State	J/C	2,045	227	$ 900	—	$ 900
Ethan Allen Community Col.	Manchester Ctr., VT 05255	1973	Independ	J/C	100	18	$ 1,510	—	$ 1,510
Goddard College	Plainfield, VT 05667	1938	Independ	S-G/C	175	35	$ 6,700	$2,000	$ 8,700
Green Mountain College	Poultney, VT 05764	1834	Independ	J-S/C	333	37	$ 5,600	$3,200	$ 8,800
Johnson State College	Johnson, VT 05656	1828	State	S-G/C	1,194	80	$ 1,866	$2,614	$ 4,480
Lyndon State College	Lyndonville, VT 05851	1911	State	S-G/C	1,060	55	$ 1,718	$2,822	$ 4,540
Marlboro College	Marlboro, VT 05344	1946	Independ	S/C	197	34	$ 7,726	$2,880	$10,606
Middlebury College	Middlebury, VT 05753	1800	Independ	S-G/C	1,900	179	$10,350	$1,450	$11,800
Norwich University Military Col. of Vermont	Northfield, VT 05663	1819	Independ	S-G/C	1,490	145	—	—	$ 9,500
Norwich University	Montpelier, VT 05602	1834	Independ	J-S/C	1,023	61	$ 4,650	$3,030	$ 7,680
St. Michael's College	Winooski, VT 05404	1903	Catholic	S-G/C	2,195	115	$ 5,900	$2,500	$ 8,500
School for Int. Training	Brattleboro, VT 05301	1964	Independ	S-G/C	735	32	$ 6,200	$3,217	$ 9,417
Southern Vermont College	Bennington, VT 05201	1926	Private	J-S/C	713	42	$ 3,480	$2,790	$ 6,270
Trinity College	Burlington, VT 05401	1925	Catholic	S/C	867	64	$ 4,690	$2,640	$ 7,330

NAME	ADDRESS	FOUNDED	AFFILIATION	LEVEL/TYPE	ENROLLMENT	TEACHERS	TUITION & FEES	BOARD & ROOM	TOTAL COST
VERMONT *(continued)*									
University of Vermont...	Burlington, VT 05405 ...	1791	State	S-G/C	11,103	764	$ 2,466	$2,612	$ 5,078
Vermont Law School....	South Royalton, VT 05068	1972	Independ	P/C	375	34	$ 6,250	—	$ 6,250
Vermont Technical College	Randolph Ctr., VT 05061	1957	State	T/C	801	67	$ 1,914	$2,614	$ 4,528
VIRGINIA									
Apprentice School......	Newport News, VA 23607	1919	Independ	T/C	906	17	$ 91	—	$ 91
Averett College	Danville, VA 24541	1859	Baptist	S-G/C	916	59	$ 3,450	$2,500	$ 5,950
Bluefield College	Bluefield, VA 24605	1922	Baptist	S/C	488	37	$ 2,276	$2,200	$ 4,476
Bridgewater College	Bridgewater, VA 22812 .	1880	Church	S/C	898	70	$ 4,315	$2,485	$ 6,700
CBN University	Virginia Beach, VA 23463	1977	Independ	G/C	212	25	$ 4,000	—	$ 4,000
Christendom Col........	Front Royal, VA 22630 ..	1977	Catholic	S/C	96	17	$ 3,570	$2,300	$ 5,870
Christopher Newport College	Newport News, VA 23606	1961	State	S/C	4,289	146	$ 1,350	—	$ 1,350
College of William and Mary	Williamsburg, VA 23185 .	1693	State	S-G/C	6,521	476	$ 1,574	$2,687	$ 4,261
Richard Bland College	Petersburg, VA 23805 ..	1960	State	J/C	1,135	46	$ 810	—	$ 810
Eastern Mennonite College	Harrisonburg, VA 22801	1917	Mennon	S/C	949	75	$ 4,356	$2,004	$ 6,360
Eastern Mennonite Seminary	Harrisonburg, VA 22801	1948	Mennon	G/C	82	25	$ 1,856	$2,004	$ 3,860
Eastern Virginia Medical Sch.	Norfolk, VA 23501	1973	Independ	P/C	347	125	$ 9,450	$4,725	$16,925
Emory & Henry College .	Emory, VA 24327	1836	Methodist	S/C	769	55	$ 3,585	$2,115	$ 5,700
Ferrum College	Ferrum, VA 24088	1913	Methodist	J-S/C	1,639	80	$ 3,950	$1,790	$ 5,740
George Mason University	Fairfax, VA 22030	1957	State	S-G/C	14,930	741	$ 1,176	$1,572	$ 2,748
Hampden-Sydney College	Hampden-Sdny, VA 23943	1776	Presby	S/M	750	62	$ 6,520	$2,030	$ 8,550
Hampton Institute	Hampton, VA 23668	1868	Independ	S-G/C	3,824	260	$ 3,215	$1,500	$ 4,715
Hollins College	Hollins Col., VA 24020 ..	1842	Independ	S/W	963	90	$ 6,500	$3,150	$ 9,650
Institute of Textile Tech.	Charlottesville, VA 22902	1944	Independ	G/C	20	—	—	—	—
James Madison University	Harrisonburg, VA 22807	1908	State	S-G/C	9,048	521	$ 1,506	$2,164	$ 3,670
Liberty Baptist College ..	Lynchburg, VA 24506 ...	1971	Baptist	S/C	3,419	183	$ 2,270	$2,600	$ 4,870
Longwood College	Farmville, VA 23901	1839	Public	S-G/C	2,724	155	$ 1,650	$2,100	$ 3,750
Lynchburg College	Lynchburg, VA 24501 ...	1903	D of Chr	S/C	2,357	154	$ 5,350	$2,750	$ 8,100
Mary Baldwin College ...	Staunton, VA 24401	1842	Presby	S/W	835	58	$ 5,250	$3,600	$ 8,850
Mary Washington College	Fredericksburg, VA 22401	1908	State	S-G/C	2,935	143	$ 1,198	$2,512	$ 3,710
Marymount Col. of Virginia	Arlington, VA 22207	1950	Catholic	S-G/C	1,650	97	$ 4,620	$2,900	$ 7,520
National Business College	Roanoke, VA 24011	1886	Independ	J/C	888	75	$ 2,304	$2,091	$ 4,395
National Grad. University	Arlington, VA 22201	1967	Private	G/C	33	9	$ 3,850	—	$ 3,850
Norfolk College	Norfolk, VA 23510	1952	Independ	T/C	370	14	$ 4,000	—	$ 4,000
Norfolk State College ...	Norfolk, VA 23504	1935	State	S-G/C	7,346	402	$ 862	$1,920	$ 2,782
Old Dominion University	Norfolk, VA 23508	1930	State	S-G/C	14,705	580	$ 1,080	$2,378	$ 3,458
Presby. Sch. of Christian Ed.	Richmond, VA 23227 ...	1914	Presby	G/C	97	17	$ 2,500	$1,827	$ 4,327
Protestant Episc. Theol. Sem.	Alexandria, VA 22304 ...	1823	Episcopal	G/C	224	18	$ 3,200	$2,320	$ 5,520
Radford University	Radford, VA 24142	1910	State	S-G/C	5,903	300	$ 1,380	$2,424	$ 3,804
Randolph-Macon College	Ashland, VA 23005	1830	Methodist	S/C	925	92	$ 5,500	$2,450	$ 7,950
Randolph-Macon Woman's Col.	Lynchburg, VA 24503 ...	1891	Methodist	S/W	767	90	$ 6,500	$3,000	$ 9,500
Roanoke College	Salem, VA 24153	1842	Lutheran	S/C	1,385	72	$ 5,200	$2,250	$ 7,450
St. Paul's College.......	Lawrenceville, VA 23868	1888	Episcopal	S/C	687	52	$ 2,760	$1,850	$ 4,610
Shenandoah C. & Cons. Music	Winchester, VA 22601 ..	1875	Methodist	S-G/C	874	125	$ 3,750	$2,500	$ 7,500
Southern Seminary Jr. College	Buena Vista, VA 24416 ..	1867	Independ	J/W	286	31	$ 4,600	$2,200	$ 6,800
Sweet Briar College	Sweet Briar, VA 24595 ..	1901	Independ	S/W	739	76	$ 6,700	$2,250	$ 8,950
Union Theol. Sem. in Virginia	Richmond, VA 23227 ...	1812	Presby	G/C	260	23	$ 2,200	—	—
University of Richmond .	Richmond, VA 23173 ...	1830	Baptist	S-G/C	4,469	299	$ 6,120	$2,170	$ 8,290
University of Virginia ...	Charlottesville, VA 22903	1819	State	S-G/C	17,118	1,681	$ 1,586	$2,328	$ 3,914
Clinch Valley College ..	Wise, VA 24293	1954	State	S/C	1,200	40	$ 1,100	$1,700	$ 2,800
Falls Church Regl. Center	Falls Church, VA 22042 .	1949	State	S-G/C	2,750	225	—	—	—
Virginia Commonw. Univ.	Richmond, VA 23284 ...	1838	State	S-G/C	20,211	1,570	$ 1,495	$2,629	$ 4,124
Virginia Com. Col. Sys.									
Blue Ridge Comm. College	Weyers Cave, VA 24486 .	1967	State	J/C	2,017	46	$ 558	—	$ 558
Central Virginia Comm. Col.	Lynchburg, VA 24502 ...	1967	State	J/C	3,683	68	$ 558	—	$ 558
Dabney S. Lancaster Com. Col.	Clifton Forge, VA 24422 .	1967	State	J/C	921	26	$ 558	—	$ 558
Danville Comm. College	Danville, VA 24541	1968	State	J/C	2,377	70	$ 558	—	$ 558
Eastern Shore Comm. College	Melfa, VA 23410	1971	State	J/C	345	11	$ 558	—	$ 558
Germanna Comm. College	Locust Grove, VA 22508	1970	State	J/C	1,641	29	$ 558	—	$ 558
John Tyler Comm. College	Chester, VA 23831	1967	State	J/C	4,020	75	$ 558	—	$ 558
J. S. Reynolds Comm. College	Richmond, VA 23241 ...	1972	State	J/C	10,162	150	$ 558	—	$ 558
Lord Fairfax Comm. College	Middletown, VA 22645 ..	1970	State	J/C	1,763	34	$ 558	—	$ 558
Mountain Emp. Comm. Col.	Big Stone Gap, VA 24219	1972	State	J/C	2,014	44	$ 558	—	$ 558
New River Comm. College	Dublin, VA 24084.......	1970	State	J/C	3,044	56	$ 558	—	$ 558
Northern Va. Comm. College	Annandale, VA 22003 ...	1966	State	J/C	34,235	498	$ 558	—	$ 558
Patrick Henry Comm. College	Martinsville, VA 24112 ..	1971	State	J/C	1,344	31	$ 558	—	$ 558
Paul D. Camp Comm. College	Franklin, VA 23851	1971	State	J/C	1,115	30	$ 558	—	$ 558
Piedmont Va. Comm. College	Charlottesville, VA 22901	1972	State	J/C	3,348	55	$ 558	—	$ 558
Rappahannock Comm. Col.	Glenns, VA 23149	1970	State	J/C	1,259	28	$ 558	—	$ 558
Southside Va. Comm. College	Alberta, VA 23821	1970	State	J/C	1,256	39	$ 558	—	$ 558
Southwest Va. Comm. College	Richlands, VA 24641	1967	State	J/C	2,683	56	$ 558	—	$ 558
Thomas Nelson Comm. Col.	Hampton, VA 23670	1968	State	J/C	6,284	122	$ 558	—	$ 558
Tidewater Comm. College	Portsmouth, VA 23703 ..	1968	State	J/C	15,035	262	$ 558	—	$ 558
Va. Highlands Comm. College	Abingdon, VA 24210	1969	State	J/C	1,438	52	$ 558	—	$ 558
Va. Western Comm. College	Roanoke, VA 24015.....	1966	State	J/C	5,478	113	$ 558	—	$ 558
Wytheville Comm. College	Wytheville, VA 24382 ...	1967	State	J/C	1,552	47	$ 558	—	$ 558
Virginia Intermont College	Bristol, VA 24201	1884	Baptist	S/C	623	64	$ 3,525	$2,200	$ 5,725
Virginia Military Institute	Lexington, VA 24450....	1839	State	S/M	1,321	139	$ 1,150	$1,895	$ 3,045
Virginia Poly. Inst. & St. Univ.	Blacksburg, VA 24061 ..	1872	State	S-G/C	21,584	1,960	$ 1,281	$1,503	$ 2,784
Virginia State University.	Petersburg, VA 23803 ..	1882	State	S-G/C	4,003	222	$ 1,430	$2,200	$ 3,630
Virginia Union University	Richmond, VA 23220 ...	1865	Baptist	S-G/C	1,295	75	$ 2,910	$2,000	$ 4,910
Virginia Wesleyan College	Norfolk, VA 23502......	1961	Methodist	S/C	848	68	$ 4,390	$2,440	$ 6,830
Washington and Lee Univ.	Lexington, VA 24450....	1749	Independ	S-G/M	1,714	168	$ 5,800	$2,720	$ 8,520

NAME	ADDRESS	FOUNDED	AFFILIATION	LEVEL/TYPE	ENROLLMENT	TEACHERS	TUITION & FEES	BOARD & ROOM	TOTAL COST
VIRGIN ISLANDS									
College of the Virgin Islands	St. Thomas, VI 00802	1962	State	S-G/C	2,744	240	$ 507	$ 1,930	$ 2,437
WASHINGTON									
Bellevue Comm. College	Bellevue, WA 98007	1966	State	J/C	9,570	372	$ 519	—	$ 519
Big Bend Comm. College	Moses Lake, WA 98837	1961	State	J/C	1,787	119	$ 519	$ 2,340	$ 2,859
Central Washington University	Ellensburg, WA 98926	1890	State	S-G/C	6,989	314	$ 1,017	$ 2,365	$ 3,382
City University	Bellevue, WA 98008	1973	Independ	S-G/C	2,800	153	$ 1,600	—	$ 1,600
Clark College	Vancouver, WA 98663	1937	State	J/C	10,000	150	$ 581	—	$ 2,100
Columbia Basin College	Pasco, WA 99301	1955	State	J/C	6,000	200	$ 535	—	$ 535
Cornish Institute of Allied Arts	Seattle, WA 98102	1914	Independ	S/C	532	114	$ 4,050	—	$ 4,050
Eastern Washington University	Cheney, WA 99004	1882	State	S-G/C	8,155	358	$ 1,017	$ 2,325	$ 3,342
Edmonds Community College	Lynnwood, WA 98036	1967	State	J/C	6,364	230	$ 525	—	$ 525
Everett Community College	Everett, WA 98201	1941	State	J/C	5,847	220	$ 519	—	$ 519
Evergreen State College	Olympia, WA 98505	1967	State	S-G/C	2,611	134	$ 942	$ 2,310	$ 3,252
Fort Steilacoom Comm. College	Tacoma, WA 98498	1967	State	J/C	9,331	417	$ 528	—	$ 528
Gonzaga University	Spokane, WA 99258	1887	Catholic	S-G/C	3,532	280	$ 5,250	$ 2,570	$ 7,820
Grays Harbor College	Aberdeen, WA 98520	1930	State	J/C	2,460	136	$ 519	—	$ 519
Green River Comm. College	Auburn, WA 90002	1965	State	J/C	6,550	103	$ 481		$ 481
Heritage College	Toppenish, WA 98948	1907	Christian	S-G/C	365	29	$ 2,280	—	$ 2,280
Highline Community College	Midway, WA 98032	1961	State	J/C	9,900	378	$ 519	—	$ 519
Lower Columbia Comm. College	Longview, WA 98632	1934	State	J/C	3,850	95	$ 581	—	$ 581
Northwest College	Kirkland, WA 98033	1934	A of God	J-S/C	719	30	$ 2,799	$ 1,734	$ 4,533
Olympic College	Bremerton, WA 98310	1946	State	J/C	6,005	275	$ 519	—	$ 519
Olympic Technical Community College	Olympia, WA 98502	1970	State	J/C	3,334	42	$ 600	—	$ 600
Pacific Lutheran University	Tacoma, WA 98447	1890	Lutheran	S-G/C	3,582	231	$ 5,632	$ 2,536	$ 8,168
Peninsula College	Port Angeles, WA 98362	1961	State	J/C	2,411	122	$ 513	$ 2,160	$ 2,673
Puget Sound Col. of the Bible	Edmonds, WA 98020	1950	Christian	P/C	151	12	$ 2,250	$ 1,875	$ 4,125
St. Martin's College	Lacey, WA 98503	1895	Catholic	S-G/C	1,050	62	$ 5,110	$ 2,560	$ 7,670
Seattle Comm. Col. District	Seattle, WA 98119	1966	State	J/C	20,672	902	$ 505	—	$ 505
North Seattle Comm. College	Seattle, WA 98103	1970	State	J/C	9,625	340	$ 288	—	$ 288
Seattle Central Comm. Col.	Seattle, WA 98122	1966	State	J/C	10,668	481	$ 288	—	$ 288
South Seattle Comm. College	Seattle, WA 98106	1970	State	J/C	8,120	297	$ 288	—	$ 288
Seattle Pacific University	Seattle, WA 98119	1891	Methodist	S-G/C	2,720	180	$ 4,845	$ 2,646	$ 7,491
Seattle University	Seattle, WA 98122	1891	Catholic	S-G/C	4,547	299	$ 5,085	$ 2,198	$ 7,283
Shoreline Comm. College	Seattle, WA 98133	1964	State	J/C	7,088	305	$ 1,386	—	$ 1,386
Skagit Valley College	Mount Vernon, WA 98273	1926	State	J/C	4,204	226	$ 519	—	$ 519
Spokane Community College	Spokane, WA 99207	1963	State	J/C	6,036	209	$ 581	—	$ 581
Spokane Falls Comm. College	Spokane, WA 99204	1970	State	J/C	4,844	123	$ 596	—	$ 596
Tacoma Comm. College	Tacoma, WA 98465	1965	State	J/C	5,822	350	$ 508	—	$ 508
University of Puget Sound	Tacoma, WA 98416	1888	Methodist	S-G/C	3,159	185	$ 5,870	$ 2,810	$ 8,680
University of Washington	Seattle, WA 98195	1861	State	S-G/C	34,468	2,497	$ 1,176	$ 2,600	$ 3,776
Walla Walla College	College Pl., WA 99324	1892	7-D Adv	S-G/C	1,802	133	$ 5,470	$ 1,632	$ 7,102
Walla Walla Community College	Walla Walla, WA 99362	1967	State	J/C	4,495	196	$ 519	—	$ 519
Washington State University	Pullman, WA 99164	1890	State	S-G/C	16,746	1,014	$ 1,176	$ 2,325	$ 3,501
Wenatchee Valley College	Wenatchee, WA 98801	1939	State	J/C	2,765	125	$ 519	$ 2,400	$ 2,919
Western Washington University	Bellingham, WA 98225	1893	State	S-G/C	9,352	505	$ 1,017	$ 2,300	$ 3,317
Whatcom Community College	Bellingham, WA 98226	1969	State	J/C	2,200	107	$ 674	—	$ 674
Whitman College	Walla Walla, WA 99362	1859	Independ	S/C	1,229	111	$ 5,850	$ 2,470	$ 8,320
Whitworth College	Spokane, WA 99251	1890	Presby	S-G/C	1,802	69	$ 5,590	$ 2,325	$ 7,915
Yakima Valley Comm. College	Yakima, WA 98907	1928	State	J/C	4,230	242	$ 540	$ 2,505	$ 3,045
WEST VIRGINIA									
Alderson-Broaddus College	Philippi, WV 26416	1871	Baptist	S/C	827	81	$ 4,440	$ 1,660	$ 6,100
Appalachian Bible Institute	Bradley, WV 25818	1950	Independ	S/C	209	16	$ 2,200	$ 1,900	$ 4,100
Beckley College	Beckley, WV 25801	1933	Independ	J/C	1,581	72	$ 960	—	$ 960
Bethany College	Bethany, WV 26032	1840	D of Chr	S/C	778	79	$ 5,910	$ 2,155	$ 8,065
Bluefield State College	Bluefield, WV 24701	1895	State	S/C	2,743	192	$ 594	—	$ 594
Greenbriar Comm. Col. Ctr.	Lewisburg, WV 24901	1969	State	J/C	400	30	$ 350	$ 1,500	$ 1,850
Concord College	Athens, WV 24712	1872	State	S/C	2,262	82	$ 754	$ 2,110	$ 2,864
Davis & Elkins College	Elkins, WV 26241	1904	Presby	S/C	952	56	$ 4,808	$ 2,341	$ 7,149
Fairmont State College	Fairmont, WV 26554	1867	State	S/C	5,190	152	$ 754	$ 2,124	$ 2,878
Glenville State College	Glenville, WV 26351	1872	State	S/C	1,785	84	$ 564	$ 2,040	$ 2,706
Marshall University	Huntington, WV 25701	1837	State	S-G/C	11,741	450	$ 650	$ 2,230	$ 2,880
Ohio Valley College	Parkersburg, WV 26101	1958	C of Chr	S/C	275	28	$ 2,480	$ 2,300	$ 4,780
Parkersburg Community Col.	Parkersburg, WV 26101	1971	State	J/C	3,419	170	$ 440	—	$ 440
Salem College	Salem, WV 26426	1888	Independ	S-G/C	650	46	$ 3,900	$ 2,000	$ 5,900
Shepherd College	Shepherdstown, WV 25443	1871	State	S/C	3,138	156	$ 576	$ 1,755	$ 2,331
Southern West Va. Comm. Col.	Logan, WV 25601	1971	State	J/C	1,778	55	$ 456	—	$ 456
University of Charleston	Charleston, WV 25304	1888	Independ	S/G-C	2,215	90	$ 3,498	$ 2,470	$ 5,968
West Liberty State College	West Liberty, WV 26074	1837	State	S/C	2,512	150	$ 604	$ 1,974	$ 2,578
West Va. Col. of Grad. Studies	Institute, WV 25313	1972	State	G/C	2,988	166	$ 420	—	$ 420
West Va. Inst. of Technology	Montgomery, WV 25136	1895	State	S-G/C	3,366	190	$ 594	$ 2,231	$ 2,825
West Va. Northern Comm. Col.	Wheeling, WV 26003	1972	State	J/C	3,814	221	$ 440	—	$ 440
West Va. Sch. of Osteo. Med.	Lewisburg, WV 24901	1972	State	P/C	231	30	$12,834	$ 1,312	$14,146
West Virginia State College	Institute, WV 25112	1891	State	S-T/C	4,414	206	$ 600	$ 2,090	$ 2,690
West Virginia University	Morgantown, WV 26506	1867	State	S-G/C	21,337	2,251	$ 840	$ 2,510	$ 3,350
Potomac State College	Keyser, WV 26726	1901	State	J/C	1,105	56	$ 602	$ 1,880	$ 2,482
West Virginia Wesleyan College	Buckhannon, WV 26201	1890	Methodist	S-G/C	1,579	115	$ 4,300	$ 2,450	$ 6,750
Wheeling College	Wheeling, WV 26003	1954	Catholic	S-G/C	988	88	$ 4,350	$ 2,400	$ 6,750
WISCONSIN									
Alverno College	Milwaukee, WI 53215	1936	Independ	S-G/W	1,359	130	$ 4,116	$ 1,800	$ 5,916
Beloit College	Beloit, WI 53511	1846	Independ	S-G/C	1,081	83	$ 6,918	$ 2,240	$ 9,158

NAME	ADDRESS	FOUNDED	AFFILIATION	LEVEL/TYPE	ENROLLMENT	TEACHERS	TUITION & FEES	BOARD & ROOM	TOTAL COST
WISCONSIN *(continued)*									
Blackhawk Technical Institute	Janesville, WI 53545	1968	State	T/C	2,287	77	$ 610	—	$ 610
Cardinal Stritch College	Milwaukee, WI 53217	1937	Catholic	S-G/C	1,261	134	$ 3,990	$2,225	$ 6,215
Carroll College	Waukesha, WI 53186	1846	Presby	S/C	1,108	76	$ 6,080	$2,060	$ 8,140
Carthage College	Kenosha, WI 53141	1847	Lutheran	S-G/C	1,040	77	$ 4,870	$2,125	$ 6,995
Concordia College Wisconsin	Mequon, WI 53092	1881	Lutheran	S/C	658	45	$ 3,600	$2,200	$ 5,800
District One Tech. Institute	Eau Claire, WI 54701	1911	Public	T/C	3,922	209	$ 625	—	$ 625
Edgewood College	Madison, WI 53711	1927	Catholic	S/C	793	81	$ 3,800	$2,000	$ 5,800
Fox Valley Technical Institute	Appleton, WI 54913	1967	State	T/C	2,995	—	$ 585	—	$ 585
Gateway Technical Institute	Kenosha, WI 53142	1912	Independ	T/C	8,860	196	$ 700	—	$ 700
Holy Redeemer College	Waterford, WI 53185	1968	Catholic	S/M	48	19	$ 2,400	$1,875	$ 4,275
Immanuel Lutheran College	Eau Claire, WI 54701	1959	Lutheran	S/C	61	11	$ 680	$1,275	$ 1,955
Institute of Paper Chemistry	Appleton, WI 54912	1929	Independ	G/C	104	43	$ 3,000	$2,000	$ 5,000
Lakeland College	Sheboygan, WI 53081	1862	UC Chr	S/C	564	36	$ 4,180	$2,190	$ 6,645
Lawrence University	Appleton, WI 54912	1847	Independ	S/C	1,150	108	$ 7,176	$2,214	$ 9,390
Madison Area Tech. College	Madison, WI 53703	1912	District	J/C	9,000	328	$ 544	—	$ 544
Marian College of Fond du Lac	Fond du Lac, WI 54935	1936	Catholic	S/C	530	66	$ 3,750	$1,500	$ 5,250
Marquette University	Milwaukee, WI 53233	1881	Independ	S-G/C	14,834	873	$ 4,810	$2,800	$ 7,610
Medical College of Wisconsin	Milwaukee, WI 53226	1913	Independ	P/C	1,030	739	$ 8,000	—	$ 8,000
Mid-State Tech. Institute	Wis. Rapids, WI 54494	1967	Public	T/C	2,200	90	$ 600	$2,275	$ 2,875
Milton College	Milton, WI 53563	1844	Independ	S/C	375	37	$ 3,950	$1,970	$ 5,920
Milwaukee Area Tech. College	Milwaukee, WI 53203	1912	State	T/C	42,738	1,976	$ 630	—	$ 630
Milwaukee Sch. of Engineering	Milwaukee, WI 53201	1903	Independ	S-G/C	2,400	105	$ 4,110	$1,845	$ 5,955
Moraine Park Tech. Institute	Fond du Lac, WI 54935	1967	Independ	T/C	5,545	142	$ 600	—	$ 600
Mount Mary College	Milwaukee, WI 53222	1913	Catholic	S/W	1,111	120	$ 3,900	$1,850	$ 5,750
Mount Senario College	Ladysmith, WI 54848	1963	Independ	S/C	516	57	$ 3,710	$1,995	$ 5,705
Nashotah House	Nashotah, WI 53058	1842	Episcopal	G/C	74	12	$ 3,630	$2,760	$ 6,390
Nicolet Col. & Tech. Institute	Rhinelander, WI 54501	1968	Public	J/C	1,267	82	$ 700	—	$ 700
North Central Tech. Institute	Wausau, WI 54401	1912	Public	T/C	3,400	135	$ 630	—	$ 630
Northeast Wis. Tech. Institute	Green Bay, WI 54303	1913	State	T/C	6,024	230	$ 1,000	—	$ 1,000
Northland College	Ashland, WI 54806	1892	UC Chr	S/C	696	55	$ 4,835	$2,450	$ 7,285
Northwestern College	Watertown, WI 53094	1865	Lutheran	S/M	275	20	$ 1,500	$1,400	$ 2,900
Ripon College	Ripon, WI 54971	1851	Independ	S/C	933	70	$ 6,632	$1,960	$ 8,592
St. Norbert College	De Pere, WI 54115	1898	Catholic	S/C	1,733	115	$ 4,835	$2,336	$ 7,171
Silver Lake College	Manitowoc, WI 54220	1935	Catholic	S/C	427	65	$ 3,600	$3,785	$ 7,385
Univ. of Wisconsin System	Madison, WI 53706	1971	State	S-G/C	159,354	6,951			
UW—Eau Claire	Eau Claire, WI 54701	1916	State	S-G/C	10,833	495	$ 1,120	$1,914	$ 3,034
UW—Green Bay	Green Bay, WI 54301	1965	State	S-G/C	4,929	233	$ 1,030	$2,150	$ 3,180
UW—La Crosse	La Crosse, WI 54601	1901	State	S-G/C	8,225	423	$ 1,116	$1,656	$ 2,772
UW—Madison	Madison, WI 53706	1848	State	S-G/C	42,230	2,291	$ 1,152	$2,225	$ 4,572
UW—Milwaukee	Milwaukee, WI 53211	1885	State	S-G/C	26,400	850	$ 1,160	$2,400	$ 3,500
UW—Oshkosh	Oshkosh, WI 54901	1871	State	S-G/C	10,942	547	$ 985	$1,325	$ 2,310
UW—Parkside	Kenosha, WI 53141	1969	State	S-G/C	6,000	343	$ 982	—	$ 982
UW—Platteville	Platteville, WI 53818	1866	State	S-G/C	5,406	341	$ 800	$ 930	$ 1,730
UW—River Falls	River Falls, WI 54022	1874	State	S-G/C	5,334	265	$ 1,055	$1,896	$ 2,951
UW—Stevens Point	Stevens Point, WI 54481	1894	State	S-G/C	9,208	236	$ 1,069	$1,956	$ 3,025
UW—Stout	Menomonie, WI 54751	1893	State	S-G/C	7,600	395	$ 1,100	$ 900	$ 2,000
UW—Superior	Superior, WI 54880	1893	State	S-G/C	2,171	150	$ 969	$2,010	$ 2,979
UW—Whitewater	Whitewater, WI 53190	1868	State	S-G/C	10,321	525	$ 1,100	$1,600	$ 2,700
Univ. of Wis. Centers	Madison, WI 53703	1971	State	J/C	10,379	421			
Baraboo/Sauk County	Baraboo, WI 53913	1968	State	J/C	532	21	—	—	—
Barron County	Rice Lake, WI 54868	1966	State	J/C	367	22	—	—	—
Fond du Lac	Fond du Lac, WI 54935	1933	State	J/C	609	27	—	—	—
Fox Valley	Menasha, WI 54952	1933	State	J/C	1,175	41	—	—	—
Manitowoc County	Manitowoc, WI 54220	1933	State	J/C	463	20	—	—	—
Marathon County	Wausau, WI 54401	1933	State	J/C	1,268	49	—	—	—
Marinette County	Marinette, WI 54143	1936	State	J/C	481	15	—	—	—
Marshfield/Wood County	Marshfield, WI 54449	1964	State	J/C	661	26	—	—	—
Richland	Richland Center, WI 53581	1967	State	J/C	305	16	—	—	—
Rock County	Janesville, WI 53545	1966	State	J/C	868	31	—	—	—
Sheboygan County	Sheboygan, WI 53081	1933	State	J/C	695	31	—	—	—
Washington County	West Bend, WI 53095	1933	State	J/C	758	30	—	—	—
Waukesha County	Waukesha, WI 53186	1966	State	J/C	2,204	76	—	—	—
Viterbo College	La Crosse, WI 54601	1931	Catholic	S/C	1,165	110	$ 4,000	$1,870	$ 5,870
Waukesha County Tech. Inst.	Pewaukee, WI 53072	1923	State	T/C	8,829	181	$ 1,500	—	$ 1,500
Western Wisconsin Tech. Inst.	La Crosse, WI 54601	1912	State	T/C	4,868	183	$ 900	$2,100	$ 3,000
Wisconsin Cons. of Music	Milwaukee, WI 53208	1899	Independ	S-G/C	107	35	$ 2,300	—	$ 2,300
Wis. Independianhead Tech. Inst.	Shell Lake, WI 54871	1972	State	T/C	804	44	$ 540	—	—
Ashland	Ashland, WI 54806	1929	State	T/C	341	20	$ 835	—	$ 835
New Richmond	New Richmond, WI 54017	1967	State	T/C	786	28	$ 835	—	$ 835
Rice Lake	Rice Lake, WI 54868	1941	State	T/C	798	44	$ 835	—	$ 835
Superior Campus	Superior, WI 54880	1912	State	T/C	890	46	$ 835	—	$ 835
Wisconsin Lutheran College	Milwaukee, WI 53226	1973	Lutheran	J/C	106	24	$ 4,240	$2,275	$ 6,515
Wisconsin Luth. Seminary	Mequon, WI 53092	1863	Lutheran	G/M	227	16	$ 1,200	$1,400	$ 2,600

WYOMING

NAME	ADDRESS	FOUNDED	AFFILIATION	LEVEL/TYPE	ENROLLMENT	TEACHERS	TUITION & FEES	BOARD & ROOM	TOTAL COST
Casper College	Casper, WY 82601	1945	State	J/C	4,389	215	$ 380	$2,150	$ 2,530
Central Wyoming College	Riverton, WY 82501	1966	State	J/C	1,415	51	$ 384	$1,500	$ 1,884
Eastern Wyoming College	Torrington, WY 82240	1948	State	J/C	957	71	$ 330	$1,600	$ 1,930
Laramie County Comm. College	Cheyenne, WY 82007	1968	State	J/C	4,266	208	$ 438	—	$ 438
Northwest Comm. College	Powell, WY 82435	1946	State	J/C	1,866	75	$ 430	$1,900	$ 2,330
Sheridan College	Sheridan, WY 82801	1948	State	J/C	1,164	50	$ 440	$1,868	$ 2,308
University of Wyoming	Laramie, WY 82071	1886	State	S-G/C	10,025	724	$ 616	$2,152	$ 2,768
Western Wyoming College	Rock Springs, WY 82901	1959	State	J/C	6,183	49	$ 395	$1,875	$ 2,270

ENROLLMENTS IN SCHOOLS, COLLEGES, AND UNIVERSITIES: 1983–1984

Source: U.S. Department of Education; National Center for Education Statistics

	ELEMENTARY AND SECONDARY SCHOOLS[1]		COLLEGES AND UNIVERSITIES[2]
	K-8	9-12	Total
UNITED STATES	27,000,000	12,200,000	12,425,780
Alabama	508,000	208,000	167,753
Alaska	64,000	26,000	24,556
Arizona	362,000	150,000	210,683
Arkansas	303,000	125,000	76,972
California	2,835,000	1,253,000	1,842,963
Colorado	384,000	162,000	171,821
Connecticut	324,000	141,000	162,194
Delaware	58,000	32,000	32,454
Dist. of Col.	62,000	25,000	82,793
Florida	1,044,000	438,000	436,606
Georgia	739,000	310,000	198,367
Hawaii	110,000	50,000	51,788
Idaho	147,000	57,000	42,975
Illinois	1,265,000	571,000	683,969
Indiana	646,000	330,000	253,529
Iowa	332,000	161,000	147,962
Kansas	282,000	121,000	141,661
Kentucky	456,000	189,000	144,159
Louisiana	559,000	213,000	176,505
Maine	144,000	63,000	47,719
Maryland	448,000	229,000	234,585
Massachusetts	572,000	301,000	407,557
Michigan	1,138,000	597,000	508,240
Minnesota	465,000	233,000	214,133
Mississippi	328,000	138,000	105,932
Missouri	538,000	246,000	244,238
Montana	108,000	44,000	36,811
Nebraska	186,000	79,000	94,390
Nevada	97,000	56,000	42,212
New Hampshire	106,000	51,000	52,208
New Jersey	757,000	384,000	322,284
New Mexico	192,000	76,000	63,483
New York	1,722,000	931,000	1,012,421
North Carolina	762,000	322,000	300,910
North Dakota	83,000	34,000	36,224
Ohio	1,234,000	582,000	532,361
Oklahoma	433,000	167,000	168,186
Oregon	307,000	137,000	141,312
Pennsylvania	1,136,000	598,000	529,341
Rhode Island	87,000	49,000	68,351
South Carolina	424,000	181,000	136,727
South Dakota	86,000	36,000	35,074
Tennessee	586,000	233,000	201,806
Texas	2,210,000	831,000	758,839
Utah	290,000	96,000	99,481
Vermont	63,000	26,000	30,648
Virginia	674,000	287,000	281,026
Washington	506,000	227,000	227,812
West Virginia	268,000	105,000	82,891
Wisconsin	493,000	272,000	276,176
Wyoming	77,000	27,000	22,713

[1] Public schools, Fall 1983 estimate. [2] Public and private, Fall 1982 data.

LARGEST U.S. UNIVERSITY AND COLLEGE LIBRARIES

Source: U.S. Department of Education; National Center for Education Statistics

RANK	INSTITUTION OR BRANCH	VOLUMES	STAFF	OPERATING COSTS		
				Total	Salaries	Books
1	Harvard University (Massachusetts)	10,409,228	802	$24,525,046	$15,128,979	$5,782,416
2	Yale University (Connecticut)	8,178,741	587	16,870,675	10,489,365	3,750,284
3	University of Michigan—Ann Arbor	6,561,427	449	13,839,587	8,412,124	3,643,519
4	University of Illinois (Urbana Campus)	6,240,615	408	12,528,142	7,383,435	4,019,841
5	University of California—Berkeley	6,117,424	388	20,189,652	14,027,167	3,662,962
6	University of California—Los Angeles	5,269,667	443	23,431,994	14,483,920	4,837,147
7	Columbia University (New York)	5,192,448	416	12,280,201	8,358,524	2,672,123
8	University of Texas at Austin	4,846,764	459	15,725,380	9,433,523	4,847,047
9	Stanford University (California)	4,658,033	522	18,537,416	11,781,649	4,723,935
10	University of Chicago (Illinois)	4,565,591	250	8,007,810	4,553,911	2,019,816
11	University of Wisconsin—Madison	4,184,038	339	13,038,168	7,976,374	3,384,052
12	Univ. of Minnesota—Minneapolis-St. Paul	3,945,397	288	11,908,116	7,722,330	2,781,213
13	Ohio State University, Main Campus	3,554,217	271	9,193,283	5,596,577	2,220,789
14	Cornell University, Endowed Colleges (New York)	3,552,452	300	9,485,109	5,549,040	2,586,195
15	Princeton University (New Jersey)	3,430,242	339	10,127,485	6,310,903	2,911,000
16	Indiana University at Bloomington	3,403,309	313	9,555,349	5,960,615	2,689,608
17	Duke University (North Carolina)	3,106,259	243	7,975,293	4,606,784	2,533,700
18	University of Pennsylvania	3,054,234	231	8,998,967	5,816,932	1,915,557
19	University of Washington	3,035,229	318	10,503,735	7,103,833	2,750,266
20	University of North Carolina at Chapel Hill	3,032,509	289	10,284,105	5,713,702	3,520,919
21	Northwestern University (Illinois)	2,889,402	258	8,367,411	5,316,907	2,244,989
22	New York University	2,698,879	266	9,437,605	5,808,832	2,344,351
23	University of Virginia, Main Campus	2,466,733	262	8,461,821	4,908,498	2,575,328
24	University of Iowa	2,412,577	171	7,057,759	3,811,817	2,794,902
25	Johns Hopkins University (Maryland)	2,260,219	174	5,428,882	2,875,201	1,695,551
26	University of Florida	2,231,509	172	8,482,904	4,834,992	2,468,646
27	University of Southern California	2,180,580	219	8,539,793	4,929,933	2,546,932
28	University of Georgia	2,141,617	223	6,946,855	3,756,668	2,590,782
29	University of Utah	2,119,959	241	4,724,848	2,620,391	1,469,126
30	University of Kansas, Main Campus	2,117,187	161	6,792,461	3,604,035	2,390,836
31	University of Missouri—Columbia	2,117,156	153	5,124,404	2,677,060	1,873,419
32	Michigan State University	2,099,099	193	7,396,874	3,142,141	2,296,850
33	University of Pittsburgh, Main Campus (PA)	2,026,135	238	7,442,539	4,781,972	1,992,216
34	Syracuse University, Main Campus (New York)	2,010,009	201	5,767,464	3,395,097	1,600,356
35	Louisiana State University and A&M College	1,965,311	144	6,865,066	3,238,880	2,951,934
36	University of Hawaii at Manoa	1,947,481	166	7,151,319	4,222,289	2,271,865

Elections

United Press Int'l.

Former Vice President Walter Mondale looks forward to heavy campaigning in 1984 in his race for the Democratic Party's presidential nomination. Mondale led in public-opinion polls as he and other presidential hopefuls prepared to battle for first place in the long series of primaries.

HIGHLIGHTS: 1983

PRESIDENTIAL HOPEFULS

Although President Reagan held back on formally announcing his candidacy for reelection in 1984, other Republicans assumed he eventually would do so. No major Republican candidate spoke up to oppose him for the party's nomination.

On the other hand, eight leading candidates scrambled for the Democratic Party's presidential nomination:

Former Vice President Walter F. Mondale seemed likely to be the winner. Throughout 1983 he received endorsements by labor unions and womens' groups, and he led in public-opinion polls.

Former astronaut Sen. John Glenn (D-Ohio) sought the support of conservative Democrats.

Sen. Alan Cranston (D-Calif.) appealed to those calling for a freeze on nuclear weapons.

Rev. Jesse Jackson counted on support by blacks and civil-rights groups.

Others actively seeking the Democratic nomination included Sen. Gary Hart (D-Colo.), Sen. Ernest F. Hollings (D-S.C.), former 1972

HIGHLIGHTS: 1983 *(continued)*

Democratic presidential nominee George McGovern of South Dakota, and former Gov. Reubin Askew of Florida.

After scores of presidential primaries in 1984, the winner of the nomination finally will be chosen by the Democratic National Convention in San Francisco in July.

MORE TV DEBATES LIKELY

More TV debates between presidential candidates are likely in the 1984 presidential campaign because of a new ruling by the Federal Communications Commission (FCC).

The FCC voted unanimously, 3–0, on Nov. 8 that broadcasters could sponsor election campaign debates between major party candidates without having to give equal time to minor party candidates.

The 50-year-old "equal time" rule had required broadcasters to give all candidates the same opportunity to present their views.

Congress voted a one-time exception in 1960 that permitted the historic TV debate between John Kennedy and Richard Nixon.

The rule was modified by the FCC in 1975 to allow broadcasters to air as news events debates that were arranged by outside nonpartisan groups. Under this rule the League of Women Voters organized the 1976 debates between Gerald Ford and Jimmy Carter and the 1980 debate between Carter and Ronald Reagan. However, the broadcasters had criticized the League's arrangements for the debates as being dull and unprofessional.

DEBATE BOOK CONTROVERSY

A book by a *Time* magazine White House reporter revealed in June that Ronald Reagan's staff had a copy of the briefing book used by President Carter to prepare for the 1980 campaign debate.

President Reagan's aides admitted having used the material but said they could not remember who had given it to them. The President himself denied any previous knowledge of the matter, ordering the Justice Department to investigate whether any crimes had been committed.

Subsequent investigations by a congressional subcommittee and by the FBI failed to reveal who provided the papers to the Reagan campaign.

GAINS BY WOMEN AND BLACKS

No major trends favoring Republicans or Democrats were seen in special congressional elections. See page 155.

Women made advances in several elections. Kentucky voters chose their first woman governor, Democrat Martha Layne Collins. Two big-city women mayors won reelection: Kathy Whitmire in Houston and Dianne Feinstein in San Francisco.

First-time black mayors were elected in Chicago, Philadelphia, Charlotte, N.C., and Flint, Mich.

PERCENT VOTING BY AGE, RACE, AND REGION

Source: *U.S. Census Bureau*

Teenagers increased their participation in congressional elections in 1982 for the first time since winning the right to vote with the 26th Amendment to the Constitution in 1971.

	CONGRESSIONAL ELECTIONS					PRESIDENTIAL ELECTIONS				
	1982	1978	1974	1970	1966	1980	1976	1972	1968	1964
UNITED STATES										
Total, voting age [1]	165,483	151,646	141,299	120,701	112,800	157,085	146,548	136,203	116,535	110,604
Percent voted	48.5	45.9	44.7	54.6	55.4	59.2	59.2	63.0	67.8	69.3
White	49.9	47.3	46.3	56.0	57.0	60.9	60.9	64.5	69.1	70.7
Black	43.0	37.2	33.8	43.5	41.7	50.5	48.7	52.1	57.6	58.5
Spanish origin [2]	25.3	23.5	22.9	NA	NA	29.9	31.8	37.5	NA	NA
Male	48.7	46.6	46.2	56.8	58.2	59.1	59.6	64.1	69.8	71.9
Female	48.4	45.3	43.4	52.7	53.0	59.4	58.8	62.0	66.0	67.0
18 to 24 years old	24.8	23.5	23.8	30.4	31.1	39.9	42.2	49.6	50.4	50.9
25 to 44 years old	45.4	43.1	42.2	51.9	53.1	58.7	58.7	62.7	66.6	69.0
45 to 64 years old	62.2	58.5	56.9	64.2	64.5	69.3	68.7	70.8	74.9	75.9
65 years and over	59.9	55.9	51.4	57.0	56.1	65.1	62.2	63.5	65.8	66.3
NORTH AND WEST										
Total, voting age [1]	110,126	102,894	96,505	83,515	78,355	106,524	99,403	93,653	81,594	78,174
Percent voted	51.9	48.9	48.8	59.0	60.9	61.0	61.2	66.4	71.0	74.6
White	53.1	50.0	50.0	59.8	61.7	62.4	62.6	67.5	71.8	74.7
Black	48.5	41.3	37.9	51.4	52.1	52.8	52.2	56.7	64.8	72.0
SOUTH										
Total, voting age [1]	55,357	48,752	44,794	37,186	34,445	50,561	47,145	42,550	34,941	32,429
Percent voted	41.8	39.6	36.0	44.7	43.0	55.6	54.9	55.4	60.1	56.7
White	42.9	41.1	37.4	46.4	45.1	57.4	57.1	57.0	61.9	59.5
Black	38.3	33.5	30.0	36.8	32.9	48.2	45.7	47.8	51.6	44.0

[1] Numbers in thousands, add (000). [2] Persons of Spanish origin may be of any race. NA = not available.

PRESIDENTIAL ELECTION RESULTS: 1980

Official returns for the 1980 presidential election showed that over 86 million Americans went to the polls, the largest number in history. But only about 53% of the nation's eligible voters cast ballots.

Independent candidate John Anderson received a substantial number of votes, more than 6.6% of all that were cast.

Other minor party candidates receiving a significant number of votes were Ed Clark (Libertarian), 920,049, and Barry Commoner (Citizens), 232,533.

	POPULAR VOTE					ELECTORAL VOTE	
States	Reagan	Carter	Anderson	Others	Totals	Reagan	Carter
Totals	**43,898,770**	**35,480,948**	**5,719,222**	**1,397,911**	**86,496,851**	**489**	**49**
Alabama	654,192	636,730	16,481	34,526	1,341,929	9	
Alaska	86,112	41,842	11,155	857	158,445	3	
Arizona	529,688	246,843	76,952	20,462	873,945	6	
Arkansas	403,164	398,041	22,468	13,909	837,582	6	
California	4,522,994	3,082,943	739,618	237,383	8,582,938	45	
Colorado	652,264	368,009	130,633	33,544	1,184,450	7	
Connecticut	677,210	541,732	171,807	15,536	1,406,285	8	
Delaware	111,252	105,754	16,288	2,374	235,668	3	
Dist. of Col.	23,313	130,231	16,131	4,204	172,889		3
Florida	2,046,951	1,419,475	189,692	30,809	3,686,927	17	
Georgia	654,168	890,955	36,055	15,627	1,596,805		12
Hawaii	130,112	135,879	32,021	5,275	303,287		4
Idaho	290,699	110,192	27,058	9,482	437,431	4	
Illinois	2,358,049	1,981,413	346,754	63,505	4,749,721	26	
Indiana	1,255,656	844,197	111,639	30,541	2,242,033	13	
Iowa	676,026	508,672	115,633	17,330	1,317,661	8	
Kansas	566,812	326,150	68,231	18,602	979,795	7	
Kentucky	635,274	617,417	31,127	11,809	1,295,627	9	
Louisiana	792,853	708,453	26,345	20,940	1,548,591	10	
Maine	238,522	220,974	53,327	10,188	523,011	4	
Maryland	680,606	726,161	119,537	14,192	1,540,496		10
Massachusetts	1,057,631	1,053,802	382,539	30,118	2,524,090	14	
Michigan	1,915,225	1,661,532	275,223	57,745	3,909,725	21	
Minnesota	873,268	954,173	174,997	49,478	2,051,916		10
Mississippi	441,089	429,281	12,036	9,344	891,750	7	
Missouri	1,074,181	931,182	77,920	16,541	2,099,824	12	
Montana	206,814	118,032	29,281	9,825	363,952	4	
Nebraska	419,214	166,424	44,854	9,041	639,533	5	
Nevada	155,017	66,666	17,651	4,358	243,692	3	
New Hampshire	221,705	108,864	49,693	3,728	383,990	4	
New Jersey	1,546,557	1,147,364	234,632	47,131	2,975,684	17	
New Mexico	250,779	167,826	29,459	8,173	456,237	4	
New York	2,893,831	2,728,372	467,801	111,955	6,201,959	41	
North Carolina	915,018	875,635	52,800	12,380	1,855,833	13	
North Dakota	193,695	79,189	23,640	4,592	301,116	3	
Ohio	2,206,545	1,752,414	254,472	70,172	4,283,603	25	
Oklahoma	695,570	402,026	38,284	13,828	1,149,708	8	
Oregon	571,044	456,890	112,389	41,193	1,181,516	6	
Pennsylvania	2,261,872	1,937,540	292,921	69,168	4,561,501	27	
Rhode Island	154,793	198,342	59,819	3,013	415,967		4
South Carolina	439,277	428,220	13,868	6,893	888,258	8	
South Dakota	198,343	103,855	21,431	4,074	327,703	4	
Tennessee	787,761	783,051	35,991	10,813	1,617,616	10	
Texas	2,510,705	1,881,147	111,613	38,171	4,541,636	26	
Utah	439,687	124,266	30,284	9,915	604,152	4	
Vermont	94,628	81,952	31,761	4,958	213,299	3	
Virginia	989,609	752,174	95,418	28,831	1,866,032	12	
Washington	865,244	650,193	185,073	41,884	1,742,394	9	
West Virginia	334,206	367,462	31,691	4,356	737,715		6
Wisconsin	1,088,845	981,584	160,657	42,135	2,273,221	11	
Wyoming	110,700	49,427	12,072	4,514	176,713	3	

ELECTORAL VOTE BY STATES FOR PRESIDENT: 1936–1980

	1936	1940	1944	1948	1952	1956	1960	1964	1968	1972	1976	1980
Democratic	523	449	432	303	89	73	303	486	191	17	297	49
Republican	8	82	99	189	442	457	219	52	301	520	240	489
Other	—	—	—	39[1]	—	1[2]	15[3]	—	46[4]	1[5]	1[6]	—
Alabama	D-11	D-11	D-11	O-11[1]	D-11	D-10[2]	D-5[3]	R-10	O-10[4]	R-9	D-9	R-9
Alaska	—	—	—	—	—	—	R-3	D-3	R-3	R-3	R-3	R-3
Arizona	D-3	D-3	D-4	D-4	R-4	R-4	R-4	R-5	R-5	R-6	R-6	R-6
Arkansas	D-9	D-9	D-9	D-9	D-8	D-8	D-8	D-6	O-6[4]	R-6	D-6	R-6
California	D-22	D-22	D-25	D-25	R-32	R-32	R-32	D-40	R-40	R-45	R-45	R-45
Colorado	D-6	R-6	R-6	D-6	R-6	R-6	R-6	D-6	R-6	R-7	R-7	R-7
Connecticut	D-8	D-8	D-8	R-8	R-8	R-8	D-8	D-8	D-8	R-8	R-8	R-8
Delaware	D-3	D-3	D-3	R-3	R-3	R-3	D-3	D-3	R-3	R-3	D-3	R-3
Dist. of Col.	—	—	—	—	—	—	—	D-3	D-3	D-3	D-3	D-3
Florida	D-7	D-7	D-8	D-8	R-10	R-10	R-10	D-14	R-14	R-17	D-17	R-17
Georgia	D-12	D-12	D-12	D-12	D-12	D-12	D-12	R-12	O-12[4]	R-12	D-12	D-12
Hawaii	—	—	—	—	—	—	D-3	D-4	D-4	R-4	D-4	D-4
Idaho	D-4	D-4	D-4	D-4	R-4	R-4	R-4	D-4	R-4	R-4	R-4	R-4
Illinois	D-29	D-29	D-28	D-28	R-27	R-27	D-27	D-26	R-26	R-26	R-26	R-26
Indiana	D-14	R-14	R-13	R-13	R-13	R-13	R-13	D-13	R-13	R-13	R-13	R-13
Iowa	D-11	R-11	R-10	D-10	R-10	R-10	R-10	D-9	R-9	R-8	R-8	R-8
Kansas	D-9	R-9	R-8	R-8	R-8	R-8	R-8	D-7	R-7	R-7	R-7	R-7
Kentucky	D-11	D-11	D-11	D-11	D-10	R-10	R-10	D-9	R-9	R-9	D-9	R-9
Louisiana	D-10	D-10	D-10	O-10[1]	D-10	R-10	D-10	R-10	O-10[4]	R-10	D-10	R-10
Maine	R-5	R-5	R-5	R-5	R-5	R-5	R-5	D-4	D-4	R-4	R-4	R-4
Maryland	D-8	D-8	D-8	R-8	R-9	R-9	D-9	D-10	D-10	R-10	D-10	D-10
Massachusetts	D-17	D-17	D-16	D-16	R-16	R-16	D-16	D-14	D-14	D-14	D-14	R-14
Michigan	D-19	R-19	D-19	R-19	R-20	R-20	D-20	D-21	D-21	R-21	R-21	R-21
Minnesota	D-11	D-11	D-11	D-11	R-11	R-11	D-11	D-10	D-10	R-10	D-10	D-10
Mississippi	D-9	D-9	D-9	O-9[1]	D-8	D-8	O-8[3]	R-7	O-7[4]	R-7	D-7	R-7
Missouri	D-15	D-15	D-15	D-15	R-13	D-13	D-13	D-12	R-12	R-12	D-12	R-12
Montana	D-4	D-4	D-4	D-4	R-4	R-4	R-4	D-4	R-4	R-4	R-4	R-4
Nebraska	D-7	R-7	R-6	R-6	R-6	R-6	R-6	D-5	R-5	R-5	R-5	R-5
Nevada	D-3	D-3	D-3	D-3	R-3	R-3	D-3	D-3	R-3	R-3	R-3	R-3
New Hampshire	D-4	D-4	D-4	R-4	R-4	R-4	R-4	D-4	R-4	R-4	R-4	R-4
New Jersey	D-16	D-16	D-16	R-16	R-16	R-16	D-16	D-17	R-17	R-17	R-17	R-17
New Mexico	D-3	D-3	D-4	D-4	R-4	R-4	D-4	D-4	R-4	R-4	R-4	R-4
New York	D-47	D-47	D-47	R-47	R-45	R-45	D-45	D-43	D-43	R-41	D-41	R-41
North Carolina	D-13	D-13	D-14	D-14	D-14	D-14	D-14	D-13	R-12[4]	R-13	D-13	R-13
North Dakota	D-4	R-4	R-4	R-4	R-4	R-4	R-4	D-4	R-4	R-3	R-3	R-3
Ohio	D-26	D-26	R-25	D-25	R-25	R-25	R-25	D-26	R-26	R-25	D-25	R-25
Oklahoma	D-11	D-11	D-10	D-10	R-8	R-8	R-7[3]	D-8	R-8	R-8	R-8	R-8
Oregon	D-5	D-5	D-6	R-6	R-6	R-6	R-6	D-6	R-6	R-6	R-6	R-6
Pennsylvania	D-36	D-36	D-35	R-35	R-32	R-32	D-32	D-29	D-29	R-27	D-27	R-27
Rhode Island	D-4	D-4	D-4	D-4	R-4	R-4	D-4	D-4	D-4	R-4	D-4	D-4
South Carolina	D-8	D-8	D-8	O-8[1]	D-8	D-8	D-8	R-8	R-8	R-8	D-8	R-8
South Dakota	D-4	R-4	R-4	R-4	R-4	R-4	R-4	D-4	R-4	R-4	R-4	R-4
Tennessee	D-11	D-11	D-12	D-11[1]	R-11	R-11	R-11	D-11	R-11	R-10	D-10	R-10
Texas	D-23	D-23	D-23	D-23	R-24	R-24	D-24	D-25	D-25	R-26	D-26	R-26
Utah	D-4	D-4	D-4	D-4	R-4	R-4	R-4	D-4	R-4	R-4	R-4	R-4
Vermont	R-3	R-3	R-3	R-3	R-3	R-3	R-3	D-3	R-3	R-3	R-3	R-3
Virginia	D-11	D-11	D-11	D-11	R-12	R-12	R-12	D-12	R-12	R-11[5]	R-12	R-12
Washington	D-8	D-8	D-8	D-8	R-9	R-9	R-9	D-9	R-9	R-9	R-8[6]	R-9
West Virginia	D-8	D-8	D-8	D-8	D-8	R-8	D-8	D-7	D-7	R-6	D-6	D-6
Wisconsin	D-12	D-12	R-12	D-12	R-12	R-12	R-12	D-12	R-12	R-11	D-11	R-11
Wyoming	D-3	D-3	R-3	D-3	R-3	R-3	R-3	D-3	R-3	R-3	R-3	R-3

D=Democratic; R=Republican; O=Other.

1936: Roosevelt (D), Landon (R); **1940:** Roosevelt (D), Willkie (R); **1944:** Roosevelt (D), Dewey (R); **1948:** Truman (D), Dewey (R); **1952:** Eisenhower (R); Stevenson (D); **1956:** Eisenhower (R), Stevenson (D); **1960:** Kennedy (D), Nixon (R); **1964:** Johnson (D), Goldwater (R); **1968:** Nixon (R), Humphrey (D); **1972:** Nixon (R), McGovern (D); **1976:** Carter (D), Ford (R); **1980:** Reagan (R), Carter (D). [1] 39 electoral votes cast for States' Rights Democratic candidates: Ala. 11; La. 10; Miss. 9; S.C. 8; Tenn. 1. [2] 1 electoral vote cast for Walter B. Jones. [3] 15 electoral votes cast for Harry F. Byrd: Ala. 6; Miss. 8; Okla. 1. [4] 46 electoral votes cast for George C. Wallace: Ala. 10; Ark. 6; Ga. 12; La. 10; Miss. 7; N.C. 1. [5] 1 electoral vote cast for John Hospers. [6] 1 electoral vote cast for Ronald Reagan.

VOTE[1] BY STATES FOR MAJOR POLITICAL PARTIES: 1972–1980

REGION AND STATE	1972 ELECTION				1976 ELECTION				1980 ELECTION			
	Total	Democratic	Republican	% for winner	Total	Democratic	Republican	% for winner	Total	Democratic	Republican	% for winner
Total	**77,719**	**29,170**	**47,170**	**R-60.7**	**81,556**	**40,831**	**39,148**	**D-50.1**	**86,497**	**35,481**	**43,643**	**R-50.5**
Northeast	19,953	8,277	11,483	R-57.5	19,520	9,929	9,272	D-50.9	18,528	7,862	8,974	R-48.7
North Central	23,192	9,127	13,711	R-59.1	24,155	11,671	11,995	R-49.7	24,243	10,026	12,579	R-51.9
South	20,046	6,087	13,666	R-68.2	23,198	12,520	10,394	D-54.0	24,966	11,303	12,834	R-51.4
West	14,529	5,679	8,309	R-57.2	14,682	6,711	7,488	R-51.0	15,429	5,472	8,565	R-55.5
Alabama	1,006	257	729	R-72.4	1,183	659	504	D-55.7	1,342	637	654	R-48.7
Alaska	95	33	55	R-58.1	124	44	72	R-57.9	158	42	86	R-54.3
Arizona	623	199	403	R-64.7	743	296	419	R-56.4	874	247	530	R-60.6
Arkansas	651	200	449	R-68.9	768	499	268	D-65.0	838	398	403	R-48.1
California	8,368	3,476	4,602	R-55.0	7,867	3,742	3,882	R-49.3	8,583	3,083	4,523	R-52.7
Colorado	954	330	597	R-62.6	1,082	460	584	R-54.0	1,185	368	652	R-55.1
Connecticut	1,384	555	811	R-58.6	1,382	648	719	R-52.1	1,406	542	677	R-48.2
Delaware	236	92	140	R-59.6	236	123	110	D-52.0	236	106	111	R-47.2
Dist. of Columbia	163	128	35	D-78.1	169	138	28	D-81.6	174	130	23	D-74.7
Florida	2,583	718	1,858	R-71.9	3,151	1,636	1,470	D-51.9	3,687	1,419	2,047	R-55.5
Georgia	1,175	290	881	R-75.0	1,467	979	484	D-66.7	1,597	891	654	D-52.5
Hawaii	270	101	169	R-62.5	291	147	140	D-50.6	303	136	130	D-44.9
Idaho	310	81	199	R-64.2	344	127	204	R-59.3	437	110	291	R-66.5
Illinois	4,723	1,913	2,788	R-59.0	4,719	2,271	2,364	R-50.1	4,750	1,981	2,358	R-49.6
Indiana	2,126	709	1,405	R-66.1	2,220	1,015	1,184	R-53.3	2,242	844	1,256	R-56.0
Iowa	1,226	496	706	R-57.6	1,279	620	633	R-49.5	1,318	508	676	R-51.3
Kansas	916	270	620	R-67.7	958	430	503	R-52.5	980	326	567	R-57.8
Kentucky	1,067	371	676	R-63.4	1,167	616	532	D-52.8	1,296	617	635	R-49.0
Louisiana	1,051	298	687	R-65.3	1,278	661	587	D-51.7	1,549	708	793	R-51.2
Maine	417	161	256	R-61.5	483	232	236	R-48.9	523	221	239	R-45.6
Maryland	1,354	506	829	R-61.3	1,440	760	673	D-52.8	1,540	726	681	D-47.1
Massachusetts	2,459	1,333	1,112	D-54.2	2,548	1,429	1,030	D-56.1	2,524	1,054	1,058	R-41.9
Michigan	3,490	1,459	1,962	R-56.2	3,654	1,697	1,894	R-51.8	3,910	1,662	1,915	R-49.0
Minnesota	1,742	802	898	R-51.6	1,950	1,070	819	D-54.9	2,052	954	873	D-46.5
Mississippi	646	127	505	R-78.2	769	381	367	D-49.6	892	429	441	R-49.5
Missouri	1,856	697	1,154	R-62.2	1,954	998	927	D-51.1	2,100	931	1,074	R-51.2
Montana	318	120	184	R-57.9	329	149	174	R-52.8	364	118	207	R-56.8
Nebraska	576	170	406	R-70.5	608	234	360	R-59.2	640	166	419	R-65.6
Nevada	182	66	116	R-63.7	202	92	101	R-50.2	244	67	155	R-63.6
New Hampshire	334	116	214	R-64.0	340	148	186	R-54.7	384	109	222	R-57.7
New Jersey	2,997	1,102	1,846	R-61.6	3,014	1,445	1,510	R-50.1	2,976	1,147	1,547	R-52.0
New Mexico	386	141	236	R-61.0	418	201	211	R-50.5	456	168	251	R-55.0
New York	7,166	2,951	4,193	R-58.5	6,534	3,390	3,101	D-51.9	6,202	2,728	2,638	R-46.7
North Carolina	1,519	439	1,055	R-69.5	1,679	927	742	D-55.2	1,856	876	915	R-49.3
North Dakota	281	100	174	R-62.1	297	136	153	R-51.6	301	79	194	R-64.3
Ohio	4,095	1,559	2,442	R-59.6	4,112	2,012	2,001	D-48.9	4,284	1,752	2,207	R-51.5
Oklahoma	1,030	247	759	R-73.7	1,092	532	546	R-50.0	1,150	402	696	R-60.5
Oregon	928	393	487	R-52.4	1,030	490	492	R-47.8	1,182	457	571	R-48.3
Pennsylvania	4,592	1,797	2,715	R-59.1	4,621	2,329	2,206	D-50.4	4,562	1,938	2,262	R-49.6
Rhode Island	416	195	220	R-53.0	411	228	181	D-55.4	416	198	155	D-47.6
South Carolina	674	187	477	R-70.8	803	451	346	D-56.2	888	428	439	R-49.5
South Dakota	307	140	166	R-54.2	301	147	152	R-50.4	328	104	198	R-60.5
Tennessee	1,201	357	813	R-67.7	1,476	826	634	D-55.9	1,618	783	788	R-48.7
Texas	3,471	1,154	2,299	R-66.2	4,072	2,082	1,953	D-51.1	4,542	1,881	2,511	R-55.3
Utah	478	126	324	R-67.6	541	182	338	R-62.4	604	124	440	R-72.8
Vermont	187	68	117	R-62.7	188	81	102	R-54.4	213	82	95	R-44.4
Virginia	1,457	439	988	R-67.8	1,697	814	837	R-49.3	1,866	752	990	R-53.0
Washington	1,471	568	837	R-56.9	1,556	717	778	R-50.0	1,742	650	865	R-49.6
West Virginia	762	277	485	R-63.6	751	436	315	D-58.0	738	367	334	D-49.7
Wisconsin	1,853	810	989	R-53.4	2,104	1,040	1,005	D-49.4	2,273	982	1,089	R-47.9
Wyoming	146	44	100	R-69.0	156	62	93	R-59.3	177	49	111	R-62.6

D=Democratic; R=Republican; O=Other. **1972:** Nixon (R), McGovern (D); **1976:** Carter (D), Ford (R); **1980:** Reagan (R), Carter (D). Vote in thousands (add 000). [1]Totals include votes for all candidates.

ELECTING OR REPLACING A PRESIDENT

PRIMARY ELECTIONS

The first step in choosing a President comes in state primary elections or party caucuses in which voters choose delegates to attend a national political party convention. The candidates for delegate may or may not be bound to vote for a certain presidential candidate.

Many states hold *presidential preference primaries* in which voters can choose between several hopeful presidential candidates who are listed on the ballot.

PRESIDENTIAL NOMINATING CONVENTIONS

Since the 1830s the major political parties have held presidential nominating conventions. For many years the delegates were chosen by party leaders, and so the selection of presidential candidates was largely controlled by political bosses. Today most delegates are chosen in state primary elections. By winning a majority of state primaries, a presidential hopeful can be assured of selection as the party's presidential candidate by the national convention.

THE ELECTORAL COLLEGE

When you vote in a November presidential election, you vote for a slate of electors who in turn vote in December in the Electoral College for the candidate of your choice.

If no candidate for President wins a majority of the 538 electors' votes, the House of Representatives decides (with each state having one vote) who shall be President from among the three candidates having the largest number of votes in the Electoral College. But if the House fails to choose a President by January 20, the Vice President-elect acts as President until the House selects a President. (Two Presidents were chosen by the House of Representatives: Thomas Jefferson and John Quincy Adams.)

If no candidate for Vice President wins a majority of the electors' votes, the Senate decides between the two candidates who received the largest number of votes in the electoral College. (One Vice President was chosen by the Senate: Richard M. Johnson.)

IF A NOMINEE OR PRESIDENT-ELECT DIES

If a presidential or vice-presidential nominee dies between the adjournment of the nominating convention that chose him and Election Day: Democratic Party rules provide that their national committee can fill the vacancy, with each state or territory's delegation eligible to cast the same number of votes it had at that year's nominating convention. Republican national conventions have always authorized their national committee to do the same.

If a President-elect or a Vice President-elect dies between Election Day and the mid-December Electoral College meeting: In theory, the electors are free to vote for anyone they please. But national party rules for filing vacancies still would be in effect, and each elector probably would respect his national committee's decision. But in a close contest, just a few defecting electors could change the outcome.

If a President-elect or a Vice President-elect dies between the electors' meeting and January 6, when Congress counts the vote: Most constitutional experts believe that the 12th Amendment compels Congress to count all electoral votes cast if the person voted for was alive when the electors cast their ballots. Section 3 of the 20th Amendment would then become applicable: "If, at the time fixed for the beginning of the term of the President, the President-elect shall have died, the Vice-President-elect shall become President."

Upon becoming President, he then would be authorized under the 25th Amendment to nominate a new Vice President (who must be confirmed by Congress). Similarly, if the Vice President-elect should die, he would still be declared the winner, and the new President would be able to nominate his replacement.

If a President-elect or a Vice President-elect dies between the vote count in Congress Inauguration Day: If a President-elect dies, the same 20th Amendment provisions would elevate the Vice President-elect to the presidency. Should a Vice President-elect die, the 25th Amendment authorizes the new President to name a Vice President, subject to congressional approval.

If neither a President-elect nor a Vice President-elect is qualified on Inauguration Day: The order of succession follows the sequence that is listed in the next paragraph.

IF A PRESIDENT DIES, RESIGNS, OR IS REMOVED

When a President dies, resigns, or is removed from office, the Vice President becomes President. If the office of Vice President is vacant, the order of succession is Speaker of the House, President pro tempore of the Senate, and then the members of the cabinet in this order: State; Treasury; Defense; Justice; Interior; Agriculture; Commerce; Labor; Health and Human Services; Housing and Urban Development; Transportation; Energy and Education.

IF A PRESIDENT CANNOT PERFORM HIS DUTIES

When the President cannot exercise the powers and duties of his office for any reason, such as physical or mental illness, the Vice President can become Acting President in one of three ways:

1. The President himself may notify in writing the President pro tempore of the Senate and the Speaker of the House of his incapacity.

2. The Vice President and a majority of the principal officers of the executive departments can notify in writing the heads of both houses of Congress of the President's incapacity.

3. If the President declares in writing that no inability exists, but the Vice President and a majority of the executive department heads disagree, Congress decides the issue. The President continues or resumes the powers of office unless within 21 days (23 days if Congress was not in session at the time of notification) two-thirds of both houses of Congress vote that the President is unable to discharge his duties.

Energy and Resources

Members of neighborhood parent groups in New York's Westchester County listen with dismay to radio report on June 9, announcing that the Nuclear Regulatory Commission had voted, 3–2, to let the Indian Point nuclear power plant continue to operate. The suburban parents had sought to shut down the plant because they claimed that emergency plans were inadequate to evacuate the 300,000 people living near Indian Point.

Wide World

HIGHLIGHTS: 1983

HOME HEATING FUELS

The Census Bureau reported the results of a study on the use of various fuels for home heating in the four decades from 1940 to 1980.

Coal or coke, which was used to heat the majority of homes in 1940, fell to sixth place in home heating by 1980, continuing to be used by fewer than 1% of all homes.

Natural gas, which overtook coal as the most popular fuel in 1960, was used by the majority of homes in 1980—53.1%.

Electricity, which heated fewer than 1% of homes in 1940, has risen to second place, providing heat in 18.4% of households in 1980.

Fuel oil, which had climbed to second place in 1960 when it heated almost one-third of all American homes, fell to third place in 1980—accounting for 18.2%.

Bottled liquefied petroleum gas (LP gas) was in fourth place as a home heating fuel, having risen from use in less than 1% of homes in 1940 to 5.6% in 1980.

Wood was in second place in 1940, being used to heat one-fourth of all homes, but by 1970 it had fallen to 1.3%. High fuel oil prices caused wood to regain some of its lost popularity by 1980 when its usage rose to 3.2%, giving it fifth place among the fuels.

HIGHLIGHTS: 1983 *(continued)*

Solar panels and other fuels provided less than 1% of home heating in 1980.

The Census Bureau said that more than half of all American homes had air conditioning by 1980, with an average of 5,000 homes per day adding air conditioning in the previous two decades.

A survey by the U.S. Department of Energy found that the total amount of fuel used to heat homes in 1981–82 remained unchanged at 9.5 quadrillion BTU, ending a three-year trend of falling usage. However, rising fuel prices caused homeowners to spend 14% more for heating fuel—a total of $85 billion.

COMMERCIAL SOLAR POWER

A huge commercial solar-power electric generating plant began operation 50 miles east of San Luis Obispo, Calif., in November 1983, just eight months after contracts for its construction were signed.

The plant, built by ARCO Solar Industries, Inc., a subsidiary of Atlantic Richfield Co., began producing enough electricity to serve 500 homes. When it reaches full production in 1985, the plant will produce 16.5 megawatts, enough to power 6,400 homes.

Built on a 640-acre site, the plant will use about 4 million photovoltaic cells mounted in 756 huge 1,088-square-foot solar panel clusters on 17.5-foot-high steel posts. Each cluster is controlled by a computer to keep it pointing directly at the sun. Weather records indicate the sun shines 300 days each year at the location.

Electricity produced by the plant is purchased by the Pacific Gas & Electric Co. and fed into its power grid that serves some 3.5 million customers.

The government of California has pledged to produce 10% of the state's power needs by 1990 by such renewable sources as the sun and wind.

To accomplish the goal, the state allows tax credits to producers of alternate power and forces utilities to purchase the power at a price equivalent to producing the electricity by using fossil fuels.

50TH BIRTHDAY CELEBRATION

The 50th anniversary of the start of construction of Grand Coulee Dam on the Columbia River was celebrated on July 16, 1983. Begun in 1933 and completed in 1941, the 500-foot-high dam and its 24 generators make up the largest hydroelectric plant in the United States and the second largest in the world.

During construction of the dam, 77 of the 8,000 workers were killed.

The project produced 555 billion kilowatt hours of electricity in its first 50 years, providing consumers in Oregon and Washington inexpensive power at half the average cost of electricity in the nation as a whole.

About 400,000 tourists visit Grand Coulee Dam each year.

U.S. ENERGY PRODUCTION: 1940–2000

Source: U.S. Department of Energy, Energy Information Administration

YEAR	TOTAL [1]	COAL	OIL [2]	NATURAL GAS	OTHER [3]
1940	25,088	53.3%	31.3%	11.9%	3.5%
1950	34,540	42.3%	35.5%	18.0%	4.2%
1960	41,790	26.6%	39.2%	30.3%	3.9%
1970	62,510	24.1%	36.6%	34.7%	4.6%
1975	60,060	25.3%	33.5%	32.7%	8.5%
1979	63,850	27.6%	28.3%	31.4%	12.6%
1980	64,810	28.8%	31.6%	30.7%	8.8%
1981	64,430	28.6%	31.8%	30.6%	9.0%
1982	63,560	29.0%	32.4%	28.5%	10.1%
1985 [4]	63,200	32.1%	32.2%	24.1%	11.4%
1990 [4]	69,100	34.6%	27.9%	23.7%	13.7%
1995 [4]	85,800	39.2%	24.7%	21.8%	14.2%
2000 [4]	100,700	40.2%	19.7%	17.5%	24.9%

[1] In trillions of BTUs. [2] Includes natural-gas plant liquids. [3] Includes nuclear, hydropower, and geothermal energy sources. [4] Estimated under mid-demand/mid-supply assumptions.

REDUCED OIL IMPORTS

The Department of Energy reported that net oil imports by the United States in 1982 fell to 27.7% of total oil consumption, the lowest level since 1972.

U.S. dependence on members of the Organization of Petroleum Exporting Countries (OPEC) also continued to decline. The U.S. received only 41.9% of its gross petroleum imports from OPEC members compared with 70.3% in 1977.

The amount of oil imported from Saudi Arabia dropped 51% in 1982 as that country, which had been the main supplier of U.S. oil imports since 1976, fell to second place behind Mexico, a non-OPEC source.

Altogether net U.S. petroleum imports declined to 4.23 million barrels per day in 1982, less than half the 8.57 million barrels per day that were imported in 1977.

Meanwhile, the U.S. government continued to pump about 250,000 barrels a day of into underground storage vaults of the Strategic Petroleum Reserve. The reserve, which by mid-1983 contained about 330 million barrels of oil, is planned to hold 750 million barrels by the late 1980s at a cost of about $23 billion. Oil from the reserve would be used to ease shortages if a crisis in the Middle East were to cut off oil shipments to the U.S.

A report by the Congressional Research Service in September said that a cutoff of oil from the Middle East could cause a fall of 4% to 9% in the nation's gross national product (GNP).

Technician George Mazaris checks growth of a gallium arsenide solar cell in a new lab facility at Lewis Research Center in Cleveland, Ohio. Known as an organometallic-vapor phase epitaxy (OME-VPE) reactor, the equipment is capable of depositing hundreds of combinations of up to 13 different elements controlled to a fraction of the thickness of human hair. It is a key tool in the center's effort to advance the state-of-the art of photovoltaic systems for producing electric power in space. Although all of the solar-cell technology work at the center is focused on space uses, gains from these efforts are expected to lead to improvements in solar cells designed for general consumer use.

NASA

ENERGY RESERVES OF THE WORLD AND OF THE UNITED STATES

Source: U.S. Department of Energy, Energy Information Administration, 1983

At current rates of production, the United States' reserves of petroleum will be used up in nine years—by 1993; natural-gas reserves will be used up in 10 years—by 1994; and uranium reserves in 13 years—by 1997, according to data released in 1983 by the U.S. Department of Energy.

ENERGY SOURCES	WORLD	UNITED STATES	U.S. % OF WORLD TOTAL
PETROLEUM[1] (in barrels):			
Estimated recoverable petroleum reserves, 1982	670,300,000,000	29,400,000,000	4.1%
Annual petroleum production	21,699,980,000	3,125,000,000	14.4%
Years remaining that known petroleum reserves would last at present rate of consumption	30 years	9 years	—
NATURAL GAS (in cubic feet):			
Estimated recoverable natural-gas reserves, 1982 ...	2,915,000,000,000,000	201,700,000,000,000	8.1%
Annual natural-gas production	54,930,000,000,000	19,420,000,000,000	36.6%
Years remaining that known natural-gas reserves would last at present rate of production	50 years	10 years	—
URANIUM[2] (in short tons):			
Known recoverable uranium reserves, 1983	2,271,100	180,000	7.9%
Annual uranium production	57,197	13,400	23.4%
Years remaining known uranium reserves would last at present rate of production	40 years	13 years	—
COAL (in short tons):			
Estimated recoverable coal reserves, 1979	975,120,000,000	246,100,000,000	25.2%
Annual coal production	4,119,000,000	824,000,000	19.0%
Years remaining known coal reserves would last at present rate of production	237 years	315 years	—

[1] Including natural-gas plant liquids. [2] Containing U_3O_8.

U.S. CONSUMPTION OF ENERGY AND ENERGY RESOURCES: 1950–2000

Source: Energy Information Administration, U.S. Department of Energy

YEAR	COAL (tons)	NATURAL GAS (cu. ft.)	PETROLEUM (barrels)[2]	ELECTRICITY	
				Hydro and geothermal power (megawatt hrs.)	Nuclear power (megawatt hrs.)
1950	494,100,000	5,770,000,000,000	2,357,000,000	102,700,000	—
1955	447,000,000	8,690,000,000,000	3,086,000,000	120,300,000	—
1960	398,000,000	11,970,000,000,000	3,586,000,000	153,700,000	500,000
1961	390,300,000	12,490,000,000,000	3,641,000,000	157,600,000	1,700,000
1962	402,200,000	13,270,000,000,000	3,796,000,000	172,300,000	2,300,000
1963	423,500,000	13,970,000,000,000	3,921,000,000	169,300,000	3,200,000
1964	445,700,000	14,810,000,000,000	4,034,000,000	182,500,000	3,300,000
1965	472,000,000	15,280,000,000,000	4,202,000,000	197,000,000	3,700,000
1966	497,700,000	16,450,000,000,000	4,411,000,000	199,200,000	5,500,000
1967	491,400,000	17,390,000,000,000	4,585,000,000	224,900,000	7,700,000
1968	509,800,000	18,630,000,000,000	4,902,000,000	225,600,000	12,500,000
1969	516,400,000	20,060,000,000,000	5,106,000,000	261,100,000	13,900,000
1970	523,200,000	21,140,000,000,000	5,364,000,000	253,400,000	21,800,000
1971	501,600,000	21,790,000,000,000	5,553,000,000	273,600,000	38,100,000
1972	524,200,000	22,100,000,000,000	5,990,000,000	284,100,000	54,100,000
1973	562,600,000	22,050,000,000,000	6,317,000,000	291,700,000	83,500,000
1974	558,400,000	21,220,000,000,000	6,078,000,000	319,400,000	114,000,000
1975	562,600,000	19,540,000,000,000	5,958,000,000	312,500,000	172,500,000
1976	603,800,000	19,950,000,000,000	6,391,000,000	299,100,000	191,100,000
1977	625,300,000	19,520,000,000,000	6,727,000,000	244,600,000	250,900,000
1978	625,200,000	19,630,000,000,000	6,879,000,000	306,200,000	276,400,000
1979	680,500,000	20,240,000,000,000	6,757,000,000	307,300,000	255,200,000
1980	702,700,000	19,880,000,000,000	6,242,000,000	305,200,000	251,100,000
1981	732,600,000	19,400,000,000,000	5,861,000,000	300,800,000	272,700,000
1982*	707,400,000	17,940,000,000,000	5,568,000,000	348,800,000	282,800,000
1985	805,000,000	15,172,000,000,000	6,645,000,000	315,500,000	387,100,000
1990	936,000,000	16,256,850,000,000	6,295,000,000	343,300,000	595,100,000
1995	1,398,240,000	18,801,130,000,000	5,689,860,000	353,230,000	779,950,000
2000	1,652,140,000	17,749,790,000,000	5,754,050,000	417,340,000	1,393,270,000

* Preliminary data.

U.S. CONSUMPTION OF ENERGY IN TRILLIONS OF BTUs[1]: 1950–2000

Source: Energy Information Administration, U.S. Department of Energy

YEAR	COAL		NATURAL GAS	PETRO-LEUM[2]	ELECTRICITY			TOTAL ENERGY USAGE	
	Anthra-cite	Bituminous and Lignite			Hydro	Geothermal	Nuclear	Total BTUs[3]	Change From Prior Year
1950	991	11,900	5,970	13,320	1,440	—	—	33,621	+8.1
1955	579	10,940	9,000	17,260	1,410	—	—	39,170	+9.6
1960	426	9,690	12,390	19,920	1,660	—	10	44,082	+3.9
1962	346	9,830	13,730	21,050	1,820	—	27	46,803	+4.6
1963	336	10,360	14,400	21,700	1,770	—	38	48,610	+3.9
1964	344	10,900	15,290	22,300	1,910	—	39	50,780	+4.5
1965	309	11,580	15,770	23,250	2,060	—	44	52,990	+4.4
1966	271	12,210	17,000	24,130	2,070	—	64	55,990	+5.7
1967	251	11,990	17,940	25,280	2,340	—	90	57,890	+3.4
1968	234	12,420	19,210	26,980	2,340	—	141	61,320	+5.9
1969	203	12,520	20,680	28,340	2,660	—	153	64,530	+5.2
1970	190	12,470	21,800	29,520	2,650	10	240	66,830	+3.6
1971	170	11,840	22,470	30,560	2,860	10	413	68,300	+2.2
1972	136	12,310	22,700	32,950	2,940	30	584	71,630	+4.9
1973	129	13,170	22,510	34,840	3,010	43	910	74,610	+4.2
1974	120	12,760	21,730	33,050	3,310	53	1,270	72,760	−2.5
1975	111	12,710	19,950	32,730	3,220	70	1,900	70,710	−2.8
1976	112	13,620	20,350	34,830	3,070	78	2,110	74,510	+5.4
1977	115	14,000	19,930	37,180	2,510	77	2,700	76,330	+2.4
1978		13,850	20,000	37,970	3,140	60	3,020	78,180	+2.4
1979		15,110	20,670	37,120	3,140	80	2,710	78,910	+0.9
1980		15,460	20,390	34,200	3,120	110	2,740	75,990	−3.7
1981		15,970	19,930	31,930	3,070	120	2,970	73,980	−2.6
1982[4]		15,420	18,430	30,330	3,570	100	3,080	70,920	−4.1
1985[5]		19,197	19,465	36,200		3,133	4,118	81,101	—
1990[5]		20,100	16,500	34,300		3,212	6,331	80,443	—
1995[5]		29,551	19,403	31,647		3,532	5,879	90,012	—
2000[5]		34,917	18,318	32,004		14,173	10,502	99,914	—

[1] One British Thermal Unit (BTU) is the quantity of heat required to raise the temperature of 1 pound of water 1 degree Fahrenheit at or near 39.2°F. [2] Including liquids from natural-gas plants. [3] Does not include synthetics, solar technology, and new technologies. [4] Preliminary. [5] Estimated under Mid Supply/Mid Demand Assumptions.

ENERGY PRICES: 1951–1982

Source: Energy Information Administration; Edison Electric Institute

YEAR	CRUDE OIL[1]	GASOLINE[2]	HEATING OIL[1]	ELECTRICITY[3]	BITUMINOUS COAL[4]	ANTHRACITE COAL[4]	NATURAL GAS[5]
1951	$ 2.53	$0.272	—	$0.0281	$ 4.92	$ 9.94	$0.76
1953	2.68	0.287	—	0.0274	4.92	9.87	0.87
1954	2.78	0.290	—	0.0270	4.52	8.76	0.89
1955	2.77	0.291	—	0.0265	4.50	8.00	0.89
1956	2.79	0.299	$0.152	0.0261	4.82	8.33	0.91
1957	3.09	0.310	0.160	0.0256	5.08	9.11	0.93
1958	3.01	0.304	0.151	0.0254	4.86	9.14	0.98
1959	2.90	0.305	0.153	0.0251	4.77	8.55	1.01
1960	2.88	0.311	0.150	0.0262	4.69	8.01	1.03
1961	2.89	0.308	0.156	0.0260	4.58	8.26	1.07
1962	2.90	0.306	0.156	0.0256	4.48	7.99	1.04
1963	2.89	0.304	0.160	0.0251	4.39	8.64	1.05
1964	2.88	0.304	0.161	0.0245	4.45	8.93	1.05
1965	2.86	0.312	0.160	0.0239	4.44	8.51	1.05
1966	2.88	0.321	0.164	0.0234	4.54	8.08	1.04
1967	2.92	0.332	0.169	0.0231	4.62	8.15	1.04
1968	2.94	0.337	0.174	0.0225	4.67	8.78	1.04
1969	3.09	0.348	0.178	0.0221	4.99	9.91	1.05
1970	3.18	0.357	0.185	0.0222	6.26	11.03	1.09
1971	3.39	0.364	0.196	0.0232	7.07	12.08	1.15
1972	3.39	0.361	0.197	0.0242	7.66	12.40	1.21
1973	3.89	0.388	0.228	0.0254	8.53	13.65	1.29
1974	6.87	0.532	0.360	0.0310	15.75	22.19	1.43
1975	7.67	0.567	0.377	0.0351	19.23	32.26	1.71
1976	8.19	0.590	0.406	0.0373	19.43	33.92	1.98
1977	8.57	0.622	0.460	0.0405	19.82	34.86	2.35
1978	9.00	0.626	0.494	0.0431	21.78	35.25	2.56
1979	12.64	0.857	0.656	0.0464	23.65	41.06	2.98
1980	21.59	1.191	0.978	0.0536	24.52	42.51	3.68
1981	31.77	1.311	1.205	0.0620	26.29	44.28	4.29
1982	28.54	1.222	1.185	0.0686	27.30	47.00	

[1] Cost per barrel at wellhead. [2] Cost per gallon. [3] Cost per kwh (residential). [4] Cost per short ton. [5] Residential cost per thousand cubic feet.

HOW TO SAVE ENERGY AND MONEY ON HOME APPLIANCES

Source: U.S. Department of Energy; Edison Electric Institute

If you let a single 100-watt light bulb burn steadily all year long, it would use 876 kilowatt-hours (kwh) of electricity. At a cost of 7.25¢ per kwh, this would add $63.51 to your electric bill. If you substituted a 60-watt bulb, *you would save $25.40.*

The average annual energy use and annual energy cost of common electrical appliances in a typical American home are shown in the following table.

ELECTRIC APPLIANCE	ANNUAL ENERGY USE	ANNUAL COST	ELECTRIC APPLIANCE	ANNUAL ENERGY USE	ANNUAL COST
Air conditioner	860 kwh	$62.35	Iron	60 kwh	$ 4.35
Broiler	85 kwh	6.16	Lighting	1,100 kwh	79.75
Can opener	3 kwh	0.22	Microwave oven	190 kwh	13.78
Clock	17 kwh	1.23	Radio	86 kwh	6.24
Clothes dryer	993 kwh	71.99	Radio-phonograph	109 kwh	7.90
Coffee maker	140 kwh	10.15	Range	730 kwh	52.93
Dishwasher	903 kwh	65.47	Refrigerator (17.5 cu. ft.)	2,250 kwh	163.13
Electric blanket	147 kwh	10.66	Sewing machine	11 kwh	
Fan (attic)	290 kwh	21.03	Shaver	1 kwh	0.07
Fan (furnace)	650 kwh	47.13	Television (black and white)	100 kwh	7.25
Fluorescent light	260 kwh	18.85	Television (color)	320 kwh	23.20
Food freezer (16 cu. ft.)	1,820 kwh	131.95	Toaster	39 kwh	2.83
Food mixer	2 kwh	0.15	Vacuum cleaner	46 kwh	3.34
Food waste disposer	7 kwh	0.51	Waffle iron	20 kwh	1.45
Frying pan	100 kwh	7.25	Washer (clothes)	1,250 kwh	90.63
Hair dryer	25 kwh	1.81	Water heater (all-electric)	5,422 kwh	393.10
Hot plate	90 kwh	6.53			

* 7.25¢ per kwh is the 1983 national average for residential users.

WORLD'S LARGEST HYDROELECTRIC GENERATING PLANTS

Source: *Water Power & Dam Construction;* In part, U.S. Bureau of Reclamation, Department of the Interior

RANK	DAM	LOCATION	CAPACITY (in megawatts) Present	Ultimate	BEGAN OPERATION
1	Itaipú (Paraná River)	Brazil–Paraguay	2,800	12,600	1983
2	Guri (Caroni River)	Venezuela	2,300	10,060	1968
3	Tucuruí (Tocantins River)	Brazil	—	8,000	UC
4	Grand Coulee (Columbia River)	Washington	6,494	6,494	1942
5	Sayano-Shushensk (Yenisei River)	Soviet Union	6,400	6,400	1980
6	Corpus Posadas (Paraná River)	Argentina–Paraguay	—	6,000	UC
7	Krasnoyarsk (Yenisei River)	Soviet Union	6,000	6,000	1968
8	La Grande 2 (La Grande River)	Quebec, Canada	2,000	5,328	1982
9	Churchill Falls (Churchill River)	Newfoundland, Canada	5,225	5,225	1971
10	Bratsk (Angara River)	Soviet Union	4,500	4,500	1964
11	Ust-Ilim (Angara River)	Soviet Union	3,675	4,500	1974
12	Yacyretá-Apipe (Paraná River)	Argentina–Paraguay	2,700	4,050	UC
13	Cabora Bassa (Zambezi River)	Mozambique	2,000	4,000	1975
14	Rogun (Vakhsh River)	Soviet Union	—	3,600	UC
15	Paulo Afonso (São Francisco River)	Brazil	1,524	3,409	1979
16	Ilha Solteira (Paraná River)	Brazil	3,200	3,200	1955
17	Gezhouba (Changjiang River)	China	—	2,715	UC
18	Bennett W.A.C. (Peace River)	British Columbia, Canada	2,700	2,700	1967
19	John Day (Columbia River)	Oregon–Washington	2,160	2,700	1969
20	Nurek (Vakhsh River)	Soviet Union	900	2,700	1976
21	Revelstoke (Columbia River)	British Columbia, Canada	900	2,700	1983
22	São-Simao (Paranaiba River)	Brazil	2,680	2,680	1979
23	Mica (Columbia River)	British Columbia, Canada	1,736	2,610	1976
24	Volgograd 22d Congress (Volga R.)	Soviet Union	2,563	2,563	1958
25	Itaparica (São Francisco River)	Brazil	—	2,500	UC
26	Chicoasen (Grijalva River)	Mexico	2,400	2,400	1981
27	Chapetón (Paraná River)	Argentina	—	2,304	UC
28	Ataturk (Euphrates River)	Turkey	—	2,400	UC
29	Volga–V.I. Lenin (Volga River)	Soviet Union	2,300	2,300	1958
30	Iron Gates (Danube River)	Romania–Yugoslavia	2,300	2,300	1970
31	La Grande 3 (La Grande River)	Quebec, Canada	1,200	2,300	1982
32	Foz Do Areia (Iguacu River)	Brazil	2,250	2,250	1983
33	Bath County (Bath Creek)	Virginia	—	2,100	UC
34	High Aswan (Nile River)	Egypt	2,100	2,100	1967
35	Tarbela (Indus River)	Pakistan	1,400	2,100	1977
36	Chief Joseph (Columbia River)	Washington–Oregon	2,069	2,069	1955

WORLD'S HIGHEST DAMS

Source: *Water Power & Dam Construction;* in part, U.S. Bureau of Reclamation

RANK	NAME, LOCATION	TYPE	HEIGHT (feet)	COMPLETED
1	Rogun, Soviet Union	E	1,099	UC
2	Nurek, Soviet Union	E	984	1980
3	Grande Dixence, Switz.	G	935	1962
4	Inguri, Soviet Union	A	892	UC
5	Boruca, Costa Rica	E	876	UC
6	Vaiont, Italy	A	860	1961
7	Chicoasén, Mexico	R	856	1981
8	Tehri, India	E	856	UC
9	Kishau, India	E,R	830	UC
10	Guavio, Colombia	E	820	UC
11	Mica, Canada	E,R	804	1973
12	Sayano-Shushensk, USSR	A	804	1980
13	Mauvoisin, Switzerland	A	778	1957
14	Chivor, Colombia	R	778	1975
15	Oroville, California	E	771	1968
16	Chirkei, Soviet Union	A	764	1977
17	Bhakra, India	G	742	1963
18	El Cajón, Honduras	A	742	UC
19	Hoover, Arizona–Nevada	A,G	725	1936
20	Contra, Switzerland	A	722	1965
21	Dabaklamm, Austria	A	722	UC
22	Mratinje, Yugoslavia	A	722	1975
23	Dworshak, Idaho	G	719	1974
24	Glen Canyon, Arizona	A	709	1964
25	Toktogol, Soviet Union	G	705	1978

WORLD'S LARGEST DAMS

Source: *Water Power & Dam Construction;* in part, U.S. Bureau of Reclamation

RANK	NAME, LOCATION	VOLUME (cubic yds.)	COMPLETED
1	New Cornelia Tailings, Ariz.	274,016,000	1973
2	Tarbela, Pakistan	159,204,000	1976
3	Fort Peck, Montana	125,627,000	1940
4	Yacyretá-Apipe, Arg.–Para.	105,944,000	UC
5	Guri, Venezuela	99,012,000	UC
6	Rogun, Soviet Union	92,995,000	UC
7	Oahe, South Dakota	92,000,000	1960
8	Mangla, Pakistan	85,868,000	1967
9	Gardiner, Canada	85,592,000	1968
10	Tucuruí, Brazil	84,101,000	UC
11	Afsluitdijk, Netherlands	82,963,000	1932
12	Oroville, California	78,005,000	1968
13	San Luis, California	77,669,000	1967
14	Garrison, North Dakota	66,503,000	1956
15	Cochiti, New Mexico	65,698,000	1975
16	Tabqua, Syria	60,166,000	1976
17	Bennett W.A.C., Canada	57,157,000	1967
18	Boruca, Costa Rica	56,242,000	UC
19	Nurek, Soviet Union	55,810,000	1980
20	High Aswan, Egypt	55,745,000	1970
21	Kiev, Soviet Union	55,457,000	1964
22	Saratov, Soviet Union	52,841,000	1967
23	Mission Tailings, Arizona	52,433,000	1973
24	Fort Randall, S. Dakota	50,199,000	1956
25	Chapetón, Argentina	49,584,000	UC

E = Earth; UC = Under Construction; G = Gravity; A = Arch; R = Rockfill; MA = Multi-arch.

ELECTRICITY GENERATED BY ATOMIC POWER

Source: International Atomic Energy Agency

In 1983 a total of 25 countries had 297 operating reactors producing 173,039 megawatts of electricity. A total of 216 more were under construction or planned with an additional power output of 204,780 megawatts. Only 29 years earlier, in 1954, there were just two atomic reactors in the world that could generate electricity. They had a total output of 7.4 megawatts of electricity.

RANK	COUNTRY	NUMBER OF REACTORS	ELECTRICITY OUTPUT (in megawatts)
1	United States	80	62,376
2	France	32	23,355
3	Soviet Union	40	17,219
4	Japan	25	16,587
5	West Germany	15	9,831
6	Sweden	10	7,330
7	Canada	14	7,278
8	Britain	32	6,462
9	Belgium	6	3,473
10	Taiwan	4	3,110
11	Finland	4	2,156
12	Spain	4	1,973
13	Switzerland	4	1,940
14	East Germany	5	1,694
15	Bulgaria	4	1,632
16	Italy	3	1,232
17	South Korea	2	1,193
18	India	4	809
19	Czechoslavakia	2	762
20	Yugoslavia	1	632
21	Brazil	1	626
22	Netherlands	2	501
23	Hungary	1	408
24	Argentina	1	335
25	Pakistan	1	125
	TOTAL	297	173,039

WORLD'S LARGEST OPERATING ATOMIC ELECTRIC POWER REACTORS

Source: International Atomic Energy Agency

RANK	NAME	LOCATION	TYPE OF REACTOR*	ELECTRICITY NET OUTPUT (in megawatts)	BEGAN COMMERCIAL OPERATION
1	Grand Gulf–1	Port Gibson, Mississippi	BWR	1,255	1983
2	Biblis–B	Biblis, Hesse, West Germany	PWR	1,240	1977
3	KKU Unterweser	Stadland, West Germany	PWR	1,230	1979
4	KKG-Grafenrheinfeld	Grafenrheinfeld, Bayern, West Germany	PWR	1,225	1982
5	McGuire–1	Cornelius, North Carolina	PWR	1,180	1982
6	Sequoyah–1	Daisy, Tennessee	PWR	1,148	1981
7	Sequoyah–2	Daisy, Tennessee	PWR	1,148	1982
8	Biblis–A	Biblis, Hesse, West Germany	PWR	1,146	1975
9	Ohi–1	Ohi, Fukui, Japan	PWR	1,120	1978
10	Ohi–2	Ohi, Fukui, Japan	PWR	1,120	1979
11	Salem–2	Salem, New Jersey	PWR	1,115	1981
12	San Onofre–1	San Clemente, California	PWR	1,100	1983
13	Trojan	Prescott, Oregon	PWR	1,095	1976
14	Salem–1	Salem, New Jersey	PWR	1,090	1977
15	LaSalle–1	Seneca, Illinois	BWR	1,078	1982
16	Browns Ferry–1	Decatur, Alabama	BWR	1,067	1974
17	Browns Ferry–2	Decatur, Alabama	BWR	1,067	1975
18	Browns Ferry–3	Decatur, Alabama	BWR	1,067	1977
19	Fukushima 1–6	Futaba, Fukushima, Japan	BWR	1,067	1979
20	Fukushima II–1	Naraha, Fukushima, Japan	BWR	1,067	1982
21	Tokai–2	Tokaimura, Ibaraki, Japan	BWR	1,056	1978
22	Peach Bottom–2	York County, Pennsylvania	BWR	1,050	1974
23	Susquehanna–1	Salem, Pennsylvania	BWR	1,050	1983
24	Donald C. Cook–1	Bridgman, Michigan	PWR	1,045	1975
25	Donald C. Cook–2	Bridgman, Michigan	PWR	1,045	1978
26	Zion–1	Zion, Illinois	PWR	1,040	1973
27	Zion–2	Zion, Illinois	PWR	1,040	1974
28	Peach Bottom–3	York County, Pennsylvania	BWR	1,035	1974
29	Indian Point–3	Peekskill, New York	PWR	965	1976
30	Novo Voronezh–5	Novovoronezh, Soviet Union	PWR	953	1981
31	Kuosheng–1	Kuosheng, Taiwan	BWR	951	1982
32	Kuosheng–2	Kuosheng, Taiwan	BWR	951	1982
33	Leningrad–1	Leningrad, Soviet Union	LWGR	950	1974
34	Leningrad–2	Leningrad, Soviet Union	LWGR	950	1975
35	Leningrad–3	Leningrad, Soviet Union	LWGR	950	1979
36	Leningrad–4	Leningrad, Soviet Union	LWGR	950	1981
37	Kursk–1	Kursk, Soviet Union	LWGR	950	1976
38	Kursk–2	Kursk, Soviet Union	LWGR	950	1979
39	Kursk–3	Kursk, Soviet Union	LWGR	950	1983
40	Chernobyl–1	Chernobyl, Soviet Union	LWGR	950	1978
41	Chernobyl–2	Chernobyl, Soviet Union	LWGR	950	1978
42	Chernobyl–3	Pripyat, Kiev, Soviet Union	LWGR	950	1982
43	Smolensk–1	Desnogorsk, Soviet Union	LWGR	950	1983

*PWR = Pressurized light-water-moderated and cooled reactor. BWR = Boiling light-water-cooled and moderated reactor. LWGR = Light-water-cooled, graphite-moderated reactor.

LEADING PRODUCERS OF ENERGY AND RESOURCES

Source: United Nations, *1981 Statistical Yearbook*

The 8 leading producing nations are listed for each of 24 major types of energy or resources. The U.S. ranks among the 8 top producers in 19 of the following basic resources and leads in 6.

COUNTRY	AMOUNT
BAUXITE (Aluminum Ore)[1]	
World	**88,571,000**
Australia	27,629,000
Jamaica	12,052,000
Guinea	11,759,000
Suriname	4,893,000
Soviet Union	4,600,000
Brazil	4,152,000
Yugoslavia	3,138,000
Greece	3,095,000

COUNTRY	AMOUNT
FISH CATCHES[1]	
World	**72,187,100**
Japan	10,410,400
Soviet Union	9,412,100
China	4,235,300
United States	3,645,500
Chile	2,816,700
Peru	2,731,400
India	2,423,500
Norway	2,401,700

COUNTRY	AMOUNT
LEAD ORE[1]	
World	**3,508,900**
United States	549,600
Soviet Union	525,000
Australia	407,000
Canada	273,800
Peru	183,600
Mexico	145,500
Yugoslavia	121,500
Bulgaria	110,000

COUNTRY	AMOUNT
RUBBER, SYNTHETIC[1]	
World	**7,075,000**
United States	2,000,000
Japan	885,000
W. Germany	421,300
France	341,900
Italy	288,000
Britain	248,200
Brazil	243,800
Canada	200,000

CEMENT[1]	
World	**867,720,000**
Soviet Union	125,049,000
Japan	88,957,000
China	79,860,000
United States	67,675,000
W. Germany	34,551,000
France	29,100,000
Spain	28,752,000
Brazil	25,879,000

FORESTRY (Roundwood)[4]	
World	**3,020,300**
Soviet Union	356,000
United States	322,300
China	224,600
Brazil	217,300
India	214,700
Canada	161,400
Indonesia	157,200
Nigeria	99,500

LIGNITE (Brown Coal)[1]	
World	**1,014,116,800**
E. Germany	210,033,760
Soviet Union	207,792,200
Czechoslov.	104,587,010
W. Germany	99,379,220
United States	56,657,142
Yugoslavia	55,727,272
Bulgaria	37,633,766
Poland	27,724,675

SILVER[1]	
World	**10,122**
Mexico	1,473
Soviet Union	1,430
Peru	1,232
Canada	1,037
United States	974
Australia	792
Poland	766
Japan	268

COAL[1]	
World	**1,818,418,000**
United States	592,967,000
Soviet Union	427,671,000
China	423,571,000
Poland	132,048,000
Britain	106,258,000
South Africa	103,617,000
W. Germany	88,720,000
India	87,931,000

GAS, LPG[1]	
World	**121,211,060**
United States	50,090,090
Saudi Arabia	10,711,068
Soviet Union	8,994,851
Canada	8,319,176
Japan	7,810,811
Mexico	4,297,297
France	3,119,691
W. Germany	2,277,992

NICKEL[1]	
World	**733,540**
Canada	194,947
Soviet Union	154,000
New Caledonia	86,975
Australia	64,893
Cuba	38,230
Indonesia	36,626
South Africa	29,030
Philippines	25,381

STEEL (Crude)[1]	
World	**706,472,000**
Soviet Union	147,941,000
Japan	111,395,000
United States	101,456,000
W. Germany	43,838,000
China	37,120,000
Italy	26,501,000
France	23,176,000
Poland	18,648,000

COPPER ORE[1]	
World	**7,956,300**
United States	1,175,300
Soviet Union	1,150,000
Chile	1,063,000
Zambia	713,000
Canada	708,400
Zaire	459,000
Peru	360,800
Poland	360,400

GAS, NATURAL[6]	
World	**13,313,781**
United States	4,992,895
Soviet Union	3,859,687
Canada	655,789
Netherlands	636,062
Romania	364,850
Britain	328,125
Norway	252,597
Mexico	225,718

PAPER (Newsprint)[1]	
World	**26,210,000**
Canada	8,620,000
United States	4,101,000
Japan	2,566,000
Finland	1,570,000
Sweden	1,534,000
China	1,498,000
Soviet Union	1,353,000
W. Germany	606,000

TIN CONCENTRATES[1]	
World	**199,500**
Malaysia	61,404
Thailand	33,685
Indonesia	32,527
Bolivia	27,271
Australia	10,391
Brazil	6,930
Zaire	3,159
Britain	3,028

DIAMONDS[2]	
World	**41,189,000**
Soviet Union	10,850,000
Zaire	10,235,000
South Africa	8,522,000
Botswana	5,101,000
Namibia	1,560,000
Ghana	1,200,000
Sierra Leone	850,000
Venezuela	825,000

GOLD[5]	
World	**955,000**
South Africa	675,000
Canada	50,620
Japan	37,842
United States	29,590
Philippines	20,025
Australia	16,921
Brazil	15,958
Papua, N.G.	14,532

PETROLEUM[1]	
World	**2,789,429,100**
Soviet Union	609,000,680
Saudi Arabia	491,132,730
United States	421,804,670
Venezuela	111,578,400
China	101,220,080
Indonesia	78,662,310
United A. Emir.	72,872,077
Nigeria	71,191,884

URANIUM[1]	
World	**43,998**
United States	13,500
Canada	8,400
South Africa	6,700
Niger	4,500
Namibia	3,939
France	2,824
Australia	2,600
Gabon	1,000

ELECTRICITY[3]	
World	**8,357,049**
United States	2,365,057
Soviet Union	1,326,003
Japan	583,252
Canada	377,626
W. Germany	368,772
France	282,480
Britain	277,731
Italy	181,756

IRON ORE[1]	
World	**502,740,000**
Soviet Union	132,885,000
Australia	61,319,000
Brazil	60,528,000
United States	44,592,000
China	37,500,000
Canada	31,283,000
India	25,742,000
South Africa	16,471,000

RUBBER, NATURAL[1]	
World	**3,820,000**
Malaysia	1,486,200
Indonesia	1,020,000
Thailand	501,100
India	155,400
Sri Lanka	133,200
Liberia	69,500
Philippines	58,800
Vietnam	50,000

ZINC[1]	
World	**5,624,600**
Canada	894,600
Soviet Union	785,000
Australia	518,000
Peru	476,900
United States	334,900
Mexico	238,200
Japan	238,100
Ireland	229,000

[1] In metric tons. [2] In metric carats. [3] In millions of kilowatt hours. [4] In thousands of cubic meters. [5] In kilograms. [6] In trillions of calories.

Entertainment

United Press Int'l.

Director Richard Attenborough, *left,* and actor Ben Kingsley hold up Oscars they received on April 11 at the 55th annual Academy Award presentations. Attenborough was honored as best director. As producer, he also received the Oscar for best picture for his epic production of *Gandhi.* Kingsley received his award as best actor for his portrayal of the legendary Indian leader Mahatma Gandhi. The film won a total of eight Academy Awards.

HIGHLIGHTS: 1983

SUMMER MOVIE BOX OFFICES SIZZLE

Perhaps it was the record heat that drove patrons to air-conditioned movie theaters in the summer of 1983, or perhaps it was the unusually varied array of films. In any case, moviegoers spent more than $1.5 billion during the period between Memorial Day and Labor Day, an increase of 8% over the same period in 1982.

The season's biggest hit was *Return of the Jedi,* the third film in the *Star Wars* trilogy. Produced by George Lucas and directed by Richard Marquand, the film featured *Star Wars* actors Carrie Fisher, Harrison Ford, and Mark Hamill.

Return of the Jedi grossed $6,219,929 on May 25, its opening day—the highest single-day gross in motion-picture history. Even that was surpassed, however, on May 29, when it grossed a record $8,440,105. By the end of the summer the film had grossed $232.3 million.

Flashdance, at $87.5 million, was the season's second most profitable film, followed by *Trading Places,* with $80.6 million. Other films grossing more than $50 million were *War-Games, Octopussy, Superman III,* and *Staying Alive.*

Although *Jaws 3-D* did blockbuster business of $13.4 million on its opening weekend in July, it failed to live up to expectations and ended the summer with a gross of only $42.3 million.

JAPANESE FILM WINS CANNES PRIZE

The Ballad of Narayama, a Japanese film that tells of 19th century life in a poor Japanese village, won the Golden Palm award, the top prize at the Cannes Film Festival in May. The only American film to win an award at the festival was an eight-minute short, *Too Much Oregano,* produced and directed by Kerry Feltham. It shared the Jury Prize for best short subject film. Italian actor Gian Maria Volonte won the best actor award for his role in a Swiss film, *The Death of Mario Ricci.* The best actress award went to West Germany's Hanna Schygula for her role in the Italian film *Storia de Piera.*

Instead of the traditional director's prize, the jury, presided over by American writer William Styron, presented a joint prize for Creative Cinema to French director Robert Bresson for the film *L'Argent* (Money) and to exiled Soviet director Andrei Tarkovsky for his Italian-made film *Nostalgia.*

The Special Grand Prize went to Monty Python's comedy *The Meaning of Life,* a British entry.

THEATER HALL OF FAME INDUCTS 10

The Theater Hall of Fame, established in 1972 to recognize lifetime achievement in the theater, added 10 notables to its roster during 1983. They were chosen by drama critics and editors from around the country under the auspices of the American Theater Critics Association and must have worked in theater for at least 25 years.

The 1983 inductees included director Peter Brook, actress Mildred Dunnock, drama critic Walter Kerr, and playwrights Neil Simon and Sidney Kingsley. Honored posthumously were actress Mrs. John Drew, producer Kermit Bloomgarden, composer Vincent Youmans, and playwrights Ben Hecht and Charles MacArthur.

HELEN HAYES THEATER

In July the Little Theater on New York's West 44th Street, was renamed the Helen Hayes Theater. The 82-year-old actress was present at the dedication, as were many other Broadway luminaries, including Colleen Dewhurst, Ellen Burstyn, and Joseph Papp. All paid tribute to the legendary actress. All had been active in 1982 in trying to prevent demolition of the first Helen Hayes Theater, on West 46th Street. That building was torn down in the spring of 1982 to make way for a hotel.

ANNIE CLOSES ON BROADWAY

The popular Broadway musical *Annie* closed on Jan. 2, 1983, after 2,377 performances, making it the ninth longest-running show in Broadway history. At the end of the final performance, its original stars, Andrea McArdle as Annie, Reid Shelton as Daddy Warbucks, and Dorothy Loudon as Miss Hannigan, appeared on stage. Also present were the five girls who played the red-headed orphan during the show's long run. The cast, along with the famous alumni, joined in an emotional rendition of "Tomorrow," the show's most popular song.

DONAHUE LOSES LAWSUIT

A jury in Denver, Colo., on May 13, awarded $5.9 million damages to a woman who was denied information concerning the whereabouts of her missing son by the staff of the Donahue TV show.

Willow Lynne Cramlet, of Arvada, Colo., filed the $10 million damage suit in 1981 against Multimedia Program Productions Inc. of Cincinnati, producers of the *Donahue* show, after being denied information on the

20th Century Fox Television

Actor Alan Alda as Hawkeye stands on the set of television show *M*A*S*H* during its final episode, broadcast on Feb. 28. The award-winning series ended after 10½ years and 14 Emmy awards. Originally a feature film, the series was about a group of Army surgeons who comprise the 4077th Mobile Army Surgical Hospital during the Korean War. The final episode depicted the breaking up of the unit as the war ended. The Feb. 28 broadcast garnered an estimated audience of 125 million, making it the most-watched single program in television history, according to CBS. Throughout the country, people marked the occasion with "Farewell to M*A*S*H" parties. A new series, called *AfterMASH,* premiered in September, involving the post-Korean War experiences of the characters of Colonel Potter, Corporal Klinger, and Father Mulcahy, but not Hawkeye.

United Press Int'l.

Michael Bennett, *center*, producer and director of *A Chorus Line*, stands on stage of New York's Shubert Theater on Sept. 29, 1983, along with 330 present and past cast members of the show, which became the longest-running Broadway production that day, with its 3,389th performance. Previously, the longest-running Broadway show had been *Grease*, which played 3,388 performances. To celebrate the milestone, the 330 dancers and singers dispersed throughout the theater, even to the balconies and the orchestra, to sing and dance in a rousing finale. They then united onstage. *A Chorus Line*, which opened July 25, 1975, had grossed an estimated $260 million worldwide by June 30, 1983 and been seen by 22,300,000 people in the United States.

whereabouts of her ex-husband, Wayne R. Anderson, who had appeared on two segments of the show and described the circumstances surrounding his abduction of their three-year-old son Eland on Dec. 29, 1979.

A fugitive warrant for Anderson had been issued in 1981 in Colorado, charging felony interference with child custody, and Ms. Cramlet's suit charged that police should have been called. Instead, *Donahue* staffers baby-sat for the child while his father was being interviewed.

Defense lawyers for the *Donahue* show tried to convince the jury that promising anonymity to someone who was breaking the law was accepted journalistic practice. A first trial, in 1982, ended in a hung jury. The May award included $1.7 million in actual damages and $4.2 in punitive damages. An appeal by Multimedia was planned.

The story had a surprise ending, however, when publicity about the case brought about a reunion between mother and son. A Tulsa, Okla., resident phoned Ms. Cramlet after reading news accounts of the case and seeing pictures of the boy in newspapers and on television. The anonymous tipster thought that a boy known as "Jeff" living with his father near the University of Tulsa might be her missing son. When Ms. Cramlet, her lawyers, and police went to the indicated address, the man and his son had moved. But they were able to trace them to a new apartment through elementary school records. When they arrived at the apartment, Anderson was arrested and Ms. Cramlet was reunited with her son. According to the police, the child seemed confused and did not recognize his mother. However, by mentioning things they used to do together, she gained the boy's confidence. As she took him home to Denver, he seemed to be remembering her more and more.

SCOTT JOPLIN STAMP ISSUED

The U.S. Postal Service issued a 20-cent commemorative stamp in July honoring ragtime composer Scott Joplin. The dedication ceremony took place on the lot which formerly was the site of the Maple Leaf Club in Sedalia, Mo., where Joplin performed and composed the *Maple Leaf Rag* and other works.

MOVIES: 1983

Beyond the Limit (PG): Drama set in South America based on Graham Greene's novel *The Honorary Consul;* with Richard Gere, Michael Caine; director, John Mackenzie; Paramount.
The Big Chill (R): Comedy about reunion of former college students of 1960s; with Tom Berenger, Kevin Kline, Glenn Close, Jeff Goldblum; director, Lawrence Kasdan; Columbia.
The Black Stallion Returns (PG): Sequel to *Black Stallion,* about horse that is stolen by Arabs and transported to Sahara; with Kelly Reno, Vincent Spano, Allen Goorwitz; director, Robert Dalva; MGM/UA.
Blue Skies Again (PG): Comedy about girl who tries out for major league baseball team; with Harry Hamlin, Mimi Rogers, Kenneth McMillan; director, Richard Michaels; Warner Bros.
Blue Thunder (R): Fantasy/action movie about fascist conspiracy to deny civil right to citizens of Los Angeles; with Roy Scheider, Warren Oates, Candy Clark; director, John Badham; Columbia.
Brainstorm (PG): Supernatural thriller about research team experimenting with brain waves; with Natalie Wood, Christopher Walken, Louise Fletcher; director, Douglas Trumbull; MGM/United Artists.
Breathless (R): Hoodlum gets romantically involved with college girl in Los Angeles after accidentally killing cop while driving stolen car; with Richard Gere, Valerie Kaprisky, Art Metrano; director, Jim McBride; Orion.
Crackers (PG): Comedy about gang of safecrackers in San Francisco; with Donald Sutherland, Jack Warden, Sean Penn; director, Louis Malle.
Cross Creek (PG): Story of writer Marjorie Kinnan Rawlings' life in Florida Everglades in late 1920s; with Mary Steenburgen, Rip Torn, Malcolm McDowell; director, Martin Ritt; Thorn EMI Films.
Daniel (R): Son seeks truth about parents who were tried and executed for espionage after World War II; with Timothy Hutton, Edward Asner, Lindsay Crouse, Amanda Plummer; director, Sidney Lumet; Paramount.
Deal of the Century (R): Comic satire dealing with insanity of arms and weapons industry; with Chevy Chase, Gregory Hines; director, William Friedkin; Warner Bros.
Eddie and the Cruisers (PG): Drama about rock-and-roll star who dies mysteriously; with Tom Berenger, Michael Pare, Joe Pantoliano; director, Martin Davidson; Embassy Pictures.
Educating Rita (PG): Comedy about young female hair-dresser who seeks intellectual fulfillment; with Julie Walters, Michael Caine; Columbia.
Enigma (PG): American-born radio broadcaster is sent on espionage mission to East Germany; with Martin Sheen, Sam Neill, Brigitte Fossey; director, Jeannot Szwarc; Embassy Pictures.
Exposed (R): Beautiful college drop-out moves to New York, becomes famous model overnight, and falls in love with violinist; with Nastassia Kinski, Rudolf Nureyev, Harvey Keitel; director, James Toback; MGM/UA.
The Final Option (R): Female terrorist captures group of American diplomats; with Richard Widmark, Lewis Collins, Judy Davis; director, Ian Sharp; M-G-M/UA.
Flashdance (R): Beautiful working girl escapes realities of life through dancing; with Jennifer Beals, Michael Nouri; director, Adrian Lyne; Paramount.
Hanna K (PG): Love affair set in Israel between woman lawyer and Palestinian; with Jill Clayburgh; director, Costa-Gavras; Universal.
Heart Like A Wheel (PG): Biography of Shirley Muldowney, first professional female race car driver; with Bonnie Bedelia, Beau Bridges; director, Jonathan Kaplan; 20th Century-Fox.
Heat and Dust (R): British girl travels to India to investigate infamous scandal between long dead great-aunt and Indian prince; with Julie Christie, Christopher Cazenove; director, James Ivory; Universal.
High Road To China (PG): Wealthy young woman hires aviator to help her find father lost in China; with Tom Selleck, Bess Armstrong, Jack Weston; director, Brian G. Hutton; Warner Bros.
Independence Day (PG): Young woman photographer, living in small Southwestern town, has affair with hometown man; with Kathleen Quinlan, David Keith, Frances Sternhagen; director, Robert Mandel; Warner Bros.
Jaws 3-D (PG): Film in 3-D about aquarium threatened by great white shark; with Dennis Quaid, Bess Armstrong, Simon MacCorkindale; director, Joe Alves; Universal.
The King of Comedy (R): Television star is kidnapped by one of his fans; with Robert De Niro, Jerry Lewis, Diahnne Abbott; director, Martin Scorsese; 20th Century-fox.
Let's Spend the Night Together (PG): Story of rock group Rolling Stones as portrayed in concert; with Mick Jagger, Keith Richards, Charlie Watts; director, Hal Ashby; Embassy Pictures.
Local Hero (PG): Houston oil man travels to Scottish fishing town to buy oil refinery, becoming bewitched by its beauty and townsfolk; with Burt Lancaster, Peter Riegert, Fulton Mackay; director, Bill Forsyth; Warner Bros.
The Lonely Lady (R): Teenage novelist who matures into Academy Award-winning screenwriter; with Pia Zadora; director Peter Sasny; Universal.
Lords of Discipline (R): Suspenseful story about brutal and sometimes vicious customs new cadets encounter when they enter military school; with David Keith, Robert Prosky, G.D. Spradlin; director, Franc Roddam; Paramount.
Lovesick (PG): Psychiatrist falls in love with one of his patients; with Dudley Moore, Elizabeth McGovern, Alec Guinness; director, Marshall Brickman; Warner Bros.
The Man from Snowy River (PG): Early 1900s story about young mountain man; with Kirk Douglas, Tom Burlinson, Terence Donovan; director, George Miller; 20th Century-Fox.
Man, Woman and Child (R): Professor and wife adopt child he fathered during an affair 10 years earlier; with Martin Sheen, Blythe Danner, Craig T. Nelson; director, Dick Richards; Paramount.

Movie ratings: G = general, all ages admitted; PG = all ages admitted, but parental guidance suggested; R = restricted, persons under 17 must be accompanied by parent or guardian; X = no one under 17 admitted.

Max Dugan Returns (PG): Teacher and teenage son, living in Venice, California, are visited by her long-absent father; with Marsha Mason, Jason Robards, Donald Sutherland; director, Herbert Ross; 20th Century-Fox.

Monty Python's The Meaning of Life (R): Series of comical skits depicting life by Monty Python troupe; with Graham Chapman, John Cleese; director, Terry Jones; Universal.

Never Say Never Again (PG): James Bond searches for group that stole nuclear warheads; with Sean Connery, Barbara Carrera, Max von Sydow; director, Irvin Kershner; Warner Bros.

Octopussy (PG): James Bond accepts mission to destroy Russian general who plans to attack NATO countries in Europe; with Roger Moore, Maud Adams, Louis Jourdan; director, John Glen; MGM/UA.

The Pirates of Penzance (G): Musical about band of pirates, loosely based on Gilbert and Sullivan *H.M.S. Pinafore;* with Kevin Kline, Angela Lansbury, Linda Ronstadt; director, Wilford Leach; Universal.

Porky's II: The Next Day (R): Sequel about high school students playing pranks in and out of classroom; with Dan Monahan, Wyatt Knight; director, Bob Clark; 20th-Century-Fox.

Psycho II (R): Sequel to Hitchcock's 1960 thriller about Norman Bates, schizoid killer, just released from mental institution; with Anthony Perkins, Vera Miles, Meg Tilley; director, Richard Franklin; Universal-Oak Production.

Return of the Jedi (PG): Sequel to *Star Wars* and *The Empire Strikes Back* about intergalactic warfare between good and evil; with Mark Hamill, Harrison Ford, Carrie Fisher; director, Richard Marquand; 20th-Century-Fox.

The Right Stuff (PG): Story about early years of U.S. Space program; with Sam Shepard, Ed Harris, Mary Jo Deschanel; director, Philip Kaufman; Warner Bros.

Romantic Comedy (PG): Two playwrights, working together, fall in love; with Mary Steenburgen, Dudley Moore; director, Arthur Hiller, MGM/UA.

Rumble Fish (R): Young boy idolizes his older gangleader brother; with Matt Dillon, Mickey Rourke, Diane Lane; director, Francis Ford Coppola; Universal.

Scarface (R): Young immigrant in America becomes powerful mobster; with Al Pacino; director, Brian De Palma.

Silkwood (PG): Drama depicting life of Karen Silkwood, union activist and laboratory technician; with Meryl Streep; director, Mike Nichols; ABC Films.

Spacehunter: Adventures in the Forbidden Zone (PG): Spaceship from Earth sets out for planet Terra in mid-21st Century; with Peter Strauss, Molly Ringwald, Ernie Hudson; director, Lamont Johnson; Columbia.

Star 80 (R): Model-actress is brutally murdered by estranged husband; with Mariel Hemingway, Cliff Robertson, Carroll Baker; director, Bob Fosse; Warner Bros.

Staying Alive (PG): sequel to *Saturday Night Fever* about male dancer living in Manhattan; with John Travolta, Cynthia Rhodes, Finola Huges; director, Sylvester Stallone; Paramount.

The Sting II (PG): Sequel to *The Sting,* about two con men living in New York in 1940s; with Jackie Gleason, Mac Davis, Teri Garr; director, Jeremy Paul Kagan; Universal.

Stroker Ace (PG): Comedy about scheming race-car champion; with Burt Reynolds, Ned Beatty, Loni Anderson; director, Hal Needham; Universal/Warner Bros.

Superman III (PG): Superman again battles forces of evil; with Christopher Reeve, Richard Pryor, director, Richard Lester; Warner Bros.

Table for Five (PG): Divorced father tries to renew friendship with his three children after five-year absence; with Jon Voight, Richard Crenna, Marie-Christine Barrault; director, Robert Lieberman; Warner Bros.

Tender Mercies (PG): Former country singer drifts into Texas prairie town and marries lonely proprietress of rundown motel; with Robert Duvall, Tess Harper, Betty Buckley; director, Bruce Beresford.

Terms of Endearment (PG): Story of mother-daughter relationship spanning 30 years; with Shirley MacLaine, Debra Winger, Jack Nicholson.

Testament (PG): California town copes with aftermath of nuclear holocaust; with Jane Alexander, William Devane; director, Lynne Littman; Paramount.

Threshold (PG): Famous cardiac surgeon successfully implants world's first self-contained artificial heart in human patient; with Donald Sutherland, Jeff Goldblum, Allan Nicholls; director, Richard Pearce; 20th Century-Fox.

Trading Places (R): Comedy about relationship between black con artist and white businessman; with Dan Aykroyd, Eddie Murphy, Ralph Bellamy; director, John Landis; Paramount.

Twilight Zone—The Movie (PG): Spinoff from Rod Serling's television series about unnatural phenomena; with Dan Aykroyd, Vic Morrow, director, John Landis, Warner Bros.

Under Fire (R): Journalists in Nicaragua cover civil war and overthrow of General Anastasio Somoza in 1979; with Nick Nolte, Gene Hackman, Joanna Cassidy; director, Roger Spottiswoode.

War Games (PG): High school computer genius unknowingly taps into America's missile defense system; with Matthew Broderick, director, John Badham; MGM/UA.

Without a Trace (PG): Drama about anguished mother whose young son disappears on way to school; with Kate Nelligan, Judd Hirsch, director, Stanley R. Jaffe, 20th Century-Fox.

The Year of Living Dangerously (PG): Romantic melodrama about young Australian journalist who is covering 1960s revolution in Indonesia; with Mel Gibson, Sigourney Weaver, Linda Hunt; director, Peter Weir; MGM/UA.

Yentl (PG): Issac Bashevis Singer's short story about rabbi's orphaned daughter who enters Yeshiva disguised as male; with Barbra Streisand, Mandy Patinkin, Amy Irving; director, Barbra Streisand.

Zelig (PG): Comedy, in mock documentary form about emotional misfit living in 1920s who has love affair with his psychiatrist; with Woody Allen, Mia Farrow, John Buckwalter; director, Woody Allen; Orion Pictures/Warner Bros.

ACADEMY AWARD WINNERS

Source: American Academy of Motion Picture Arts and Sciences

YEAR	BEST PICTURE	BEST ACTOR	BEST ACTRESS	BEST DIRECTOR
1927–28	*Wings*	Emil Jannings, *The Last Command, The Way of All Flesh*	Janet Gaynor, *Seventh Heaven, Street Angel, Sunrise*	Frank Borzage, *Seventh Heaven;* Lewis Milestone, *Two Arabian Knights*
1928–29	*Broadway Melody*	Warner Baxter, *In Old Arizona*	Mary Pickford, *Coquette*	Frank Lloyd, *The Divine Lady*
1929–30	*All Quiet on the Western Front*	George Arliss, *Disraeli*	Norma Shearer, *The Divorcee*	Lewis Milestone, *All Quiet on the Western Front*
1930–31	*Cimarron*	Lionel Barrymore, *A Free Soul*	Marie Dressler, *Min and Bill*	Norman Taurog, *Skippy*
1931–32	*Grand Hotel*	Wallace Beery, *The Champ* Fredric March, *Dr. Jekyll and Mr. Hyde*	Helen Hayes, *The Sin of Madelon Claudet*	Frank Borzage, *Bad Girl*
1932–33	*Cavalcade*	Charles Laughton, *The Private Life of Henry VIII*	Katharine Hepburn, *Morning Glory*	Frank Lloyd, *Cavalcade*
1934	*It Happened One Night*	Clark Gable, *It Happened One Night*	Claudette Colbert, *It Happened One Night*	Frank Capra, *It Happened One Night*
1935	*Mutiny on the Bounty*	Victor McLaglen, *The Informer*	Bette Davis, *Dangerous*	John Ford, *The Informer*
1936	*The Great Ziegfeld*	Paul Muni, *The Story of Louis Pasteur*	Luise Rainer, *The Great Ziegfeld*	Frank Capra, *Mr. Deeds Goes to Town*
1937	*The Life of Emile Zola*	Spencer Tracy, *Captains Courageous*	Luise Rainer, *The Good Earth*	Leo McCarey, *The Awful Truth*
1938	*You Can't Take It with You*	Spencer Tracy, *Boys Town*	Bette Davis, *Jezebel*	Frank Capra, *You Can't Take It with You*
1939	*Gone with the Wind*	Robert Donat, *Goodbye, Mr. Chips*	Vivien Leigh, *Gone with the Wind*	Victor Fleming, *Gone with the Wind*
1940	*Rebecca*	James Stewart, *The Philadelphia Story*	Ginger Rogers, *Kitty Foyle*	John Ford, *The Grapes of Wrath*
1941	*How Green Was My Valley*	Gary Cooper, *Sergeant York*	Joan Fontaine, *Suspicion*	John Ford, *How Green Was My Valley*
1942	*Mrs. Miniver*	James Cagney, *Yankee Doodle Dandy*	Greer Garson, *Mrs. Miniver*	William Wyler, *Mrs. Miniver*
1943	*Casablanca*	Paul Lukas, *Watch on the Rhine*	Jennifer Jones, *The Song of Bernadette*	Michael Curtiz, *Casablanca*
1944	*Going My Way*	Bing Crosby, *Going My Way*	Ingrid Bergman, *Gaslight*	Leo McCarey, *Going My Way*
1945	*The Lost Weekend*	Ray Milland, *The Lost Weekend*	Joan Crawford, *Mildred Pierce*	Billy Wilder, *The Lost Weekend*
1946	*The Best Years of Our Lives*	Fredric March, *The Best Years of Our Lives*	Olivia de Havilland, *To Each His Own*	William Wyler, *The Best Years of Our Lives*
1947	*Gentleman's Agreement*	Ronald Colman, *A Double Life*	Loretta Young, *The Farmer's Daughter*	Elia Kazan, *Gentleman's Agreement*
1948	*Hamlet*	Laurence Olivier, *Hamlet*	Jane Wyman, *Johnny Belinda*	John Huston, *Treasure of Sierra Madre*
1949	*All the King's Men*	Broderick Crawford, *All the King's Men*	Olivia de Havilland, *The Heiress*	Joseph L. Mankiewicz, *A Letter to Three Wives*
1950	*All About Eve*	Jose Ferrer, *Cyrano de Bergerac*	Judy Holliday, *Born Yesterday*	Joseph L. Mankiewicz, *All About Eve*
1951	*An American in Paris*	Humphrey Bogart, *The African Queen*	Vivien Leigh, *A Streetcar Named Desire*	George Stevens, *A Place in the Sun*
1952	*The Greatest Show on Earth*	Gary Cooper, *High Noon*	Shirley Booth, *Come Back, Little Sheba*	John Ford, *The Quiet Man*
1953	*From Here to Eternity*	William Holden, *Stalag 17*	Audrey Hepburn, *Roman Holiday*	Fred Zinnemann, *From Here to Eternity*
1954	*On the Waterfront*	Marlon Brando, *On the Waterfront*	Grace Kelly, *The Country Girl*	Elia Kazan, *On the Waterfront*
1955	*Marty*	Ernest Borgnine, *Marty*	Anna Magnani, *The Rose Tattoo*	Delbert Mann, *Marty*
1956	*Around the World in 80 Days*	Yul Brynner, *The King and I*	Ingrid Bergman, *Anastasia*	George Stevens, *Giant*
1957	*The Bridge on the River Kwai*	Alec Guinness, *The Bridge on the River Kwai*	Joanne Woodward, *The Three Faces of Eve*	David Lean, *The Bridge on the River Kwai*
1958	*Gigi*	David Niven, *Separate Tables*	Susan Hayward, *I Want to Live*	Vincente Minnelli, *Gigi*
1959	*Ben-Hur*	Charlton Heston, *Ben-Hur*	Simone Signoret, *Room at the Top*	William Wyler, *Ben-Hur*
1960	*The Apartment*	Burt Lancaster, *Elmer Gantry*	Elizabeth Taylor, *Butterfield 8*	Billy Wilder, *The Apartment*
1961	*West Side Story*	Maximilian Schell, *Judgment at Nuremberg*	Sophia Loren, *Two Women*	Jerome Robbins, Robert Wise, *West Side Story*
1962	*Lawrence of Arabia*	Gregory Peck, *To Kill a Mockingbird*	Anne Bancroft, *The Miracle Worker*	David Lean, *Lawrence of Arabia*
1963	*Tom Jones*	Sidney Poitier, *Lilies of the Field*	Patricia Neal, *Hud*	Tony Richardson, *Tom Jones*
1964	*My Fair Lady*	Rex Harrison, *My Fair Lady*	Julie Andrews, *Mary Poppins*	George Cukor, *My Fair Lady*
1965	*Sound of Music*	Lee Marvin, *Cat Ballou*	Julie Christie, *Darling*	Robert Wise, *Sound of Music*

YEAR	BEST PICTURE	BEST ACTOR	BEST ACTRESS	BEST DIRECTOR
1966	*A Man for All Seasons*	Paul Scofield, *A Man for All Seasons*	Elizabeth Taylor, *Who's Afraid of Virginia Woolf?*	Fred Zinnemann, *A Man for All Seasons*
1967	*In the Heat of the Night*	Rod Steiger, *In the Heat of the Night*	Katharine Hepburn, *Guess Who's Coming to Dinner?*	Mike Nichols, *The Graduate*
1968	*Oliver!*	Cliff Robertson, *Charly*	Katharine Hepburn, *The Lion in Winter;* Barbra Streisand, *Funny Girl*	Sir Carol Reed, *Oliver!*
1969	*Midnight Cowboy*	John Wayne, *True Grit*	Maggie Smith, *The Prime of Miss Jean Brodie*	John Schlesinger, *Midnight Cowboy*
1970	*Patton*	George C. Scott, *Patton*	Glenda Jackson, *Women in Love*	Franklin J. Schaffner, *Patton*
1971	*The French Connection*	Gene Hackman, *The French Connection*	Jane Fonda, *Klute*	William Friedkin, *The French Connection*
1972	*The Godfather*	Marlon Brando, *The Godfather*	Liza Minnelli, *Cabaret*	Bob Fosse, *Cabaret*
1973	*The Sting*	Jack Lemmon, *Save the Tiger*	Glenda Jackson, *A Touch of Class*	George Roy Hill, *The Sting*
1974	*The Godfather, Part II*	Art Carney, *Harry and Tonto*	Ellen Burstyn, *Alice Doesn't Live Here Anymore*	Francis Ford Coppola, *The Godfather, Part II*
1975	*One Flew Over the Cuckoo's Nest*	Jack Nicholson, *One Flew Over the Cuckoo's Nest*	Louise Fletcher, *One Flew Over the Cuckoo's Nest*	Milos Forman, *One Flew Over the Cuckoo's Nest*
1976	*Rocky*	Peter Finch, *Network*	Faye Dunaway, *Network*	John Avildsen, *Rocky*
1977	*Annie Hall*	Richard Dreyfuss, *The Goodbye Girl*	Diane Keaton, *Annie Hall*	Woody Allen, *Annie Hall*
1978	*The Deer Hunter*	Jon Voight, *Coming Home*	Jane Fonda, *Coming Home*	Michael Cimino, *The Deer Hunter*
1979	*Kramer vs. Kramer*	Dustin Hoffman, *Kramer vs. Kramer*	Sally Field, *Norma Rae*	Robert Benton, *Kramer vs. Kramer*
1980	*Ordinary People*	Robert DeNiro, *Raging Bull*	Sissy Spacek, *Coal Miner's Daughter*	Robert Redford, *Ordinary People*
1981	*Chariots of Fire*	Henry Fonda, *On Golden Pond*	Katharine Hepburn, *On Golden Pond*	Warren Beatty, *Reds*
1982	*Gandhi*	Ben Kingsley, *Gandhi*	Meryl Streep, *Sophie's Choice*	Richard Attenborough, *Gandhi*

OTHER ACADEMY AWARDS IN 1983:

The 55th annual Oscars for 1982 films were presented by the American Academy of Motion Picture Arts and Sciences on April 11, 1983.
Best foreign-language film: *Volver a Empezar* (Spain).
Best supporting actor: Louis Gossett Jr., *An Officer and a Gentleman.*
Best supporting actress: Jessica Lange, *Tootsie.*
Best screenplay, adapted: *Missing,* Costa Gavras and Donald Stewart.
Best screenplay, original: *Gandhi,* John Briley.
Best cinematography: *Gandhi,* Billy Williams and Ronnie Taylor.
Best film editing: *Gandhi,* John Bloom.
Best visual effects: *E.T.,* Carlo Rambaldi, Dennis Muren, Kenneth F. Smith.
Best original music score: *E.T.,* John Williams.
Best original song: "Up Where We Belong," from *An Officer and a Gentleman.*
Best original score and adaptation: *Victor/Victoria,* Henry Mancini and Leslie Bricusse.
Best art direction: *Gandhi,* Stuart Craig and Bob Laing, art direction; set decoration, Michael Seirton.
Costume design: *Gandhi,* John Mollo, Bhanu Athaiya.
Best sound: *E.T.,* Buzz Knudson, Robert Glass, Don Digirolamo, Gene Cantamessa.
Documentary—feature: *Just Another Missing Kid.*
Documentary—short subject: *If You Love This Planet.*
Short subjects—animated: *Tango.*
Short subjects—live: *A Shocking Accident.*
Special achievement, sound effects: *E.T.,* Charles L. Campbell and Ben Burtt.
Best makeup: *Quest for Fire,* Sarah Monzani and Michele Burke.
Honorary Award: Mickey Rooney.
Jean Hersholt Award: Walter Mirisch.
Best scientific-technical achievement: August Arnold and Erich Kaestner.

1983 NEW YORK FILM CRITICS AWARDS

The annual awards for 1982 film achievements presented by the New York Film Critics Circle included:
Best film: *Gandhi.*
Best actor: Ben Kingsley, *Gandhi.*
Best actress: Meryl Streep, *Sophie's Choice.*
Best supporting actor: John Lithgow, *The World According to Garp.*
Best supporting actress: Jessica Lange, *Tootsie.*
Best director: Sydney Pollack, *Tootsie.*
Best screenplay: L. Gelbart, Murray Schisgal, *Tootsie.*
Best cinematography: Nestor Almendros, *Sophie's Choice.*
Best foreign film: *Time Stands Still* (Hungary).

1983 NATIONAL SOCIETY OF FILM CRITICS

The 17th annual motion-picture awards by the National Society of Film Critics included:
Best film: *Tootsie.*
Best actor: Dustin Hoffman, *Tootsie.*
Best actress: Meryl Streep, *Sophie's Choice.*
Best supporting actor: Mickey Rourke, *Diner.*
Best supporting actress: Jessica Lange, *Tootsie.*
Best director: Steven Spielberg, *E.T.*
Best screenplay: *Tootsie,* M. Schisgal, Larry Gelbart.

1983 GOLDEN GLOBE MOVIE AWARDS

The Hollywood Foreign Press Association's 40th annual Golden Globe movie awards included:
Best dramatic film: *E.T.*
Best musical or comedy: *Tootsie.*
Best actor, drama: Ben Kingsley, *Gandhi.*
Best actress, drama: Meryl Streep, *Sophie's Choice.*
Best actor, comedy or musical: Dustin Hoffman, *Tootsie.*
Best actress, comedy or musical: Julie Andrews, *Victor/Victoria.*
Best supporting actor: Louis Gossett Jr., *An Officer and a Gentleman.*
Best supporting actress: Jessica Lange, *Tootsie.*
Best director: Richard Attenborough, *Gandhi.*
Best screenplay: John Briley, *Gandhi.*
Best foreign film: *Gandhi.*
Best original score: *E.T.,* John Williams.

STAGE PLAYS ON AND OFF BROADWAY: 1983

***All's Well That Ends Well:** Shakespeare's comedy about young wife who romantically pursues nobleman husband who rejected her after forced marriage; with Margaret Tyzack, Philip Franks, Harriet Walter; opened April 13, 1983.
Amen Corner: Musical about woman who becomes preacher in Harlem; with Ruth Brown, Rhetta Hughes; opened Nov. 7, 1983.
American Buffalo: Revival of drama by David Mamet about smalltime Chicago hustler; with J.J. Johnston, James Hayden, Al Pacino; director, Arvin Brown; opened Oct. 27, 1983.
Baby: Musical about three couples who are expecting babies; book, Sybille Pearson; music, David Shire, lyricist and director, Richard Maltby Jr.; opened Nov. 20, 1983.
Brighton Beach Memoirs: Comedy-drama by Neil Simon about Jewish families living in Brooklyn during Depression years; with Matthew Broderick, who won Tony award for best featured actor, Joyce Van Patten, Elizabeth Franz; director, Gene Saks, who won Tony award for best director; opened March 27, 1983.
***Brothers:** Drama by George Sibbald about union leader in New England shipbuilding town; with Carroll O'Connor; director, Carroll O'Connor; opened Nov. 30, 1983.
***The Caine Mutiny Court Martial:** Revival of drama by Herman Wouk about trial of World War II navy destroyer lieutenant accused of plotting mutiny when ship's captain goes berserk; with Michael Moriarty, John Rubinstein, Jay O. Sanders; director, Arthur Sherman; opened May 5, 1983.
Cats: Musical based on poems of T.S. Eliot about cats; won seven Tony awards including best musical and best director; director, Trevor Nunn; music, Andrew Lloyd Webber; choreographer, Gillian Lynne, opened Oct. 7, 1982.
A Chorus Line: Highly acclaimed musical about Broadway director who must choose people for a chorus line; conceived, choreographed, directed by Michael Bennett; music, Marvin Hamlisch; lyrics, Edward Kleban; book, James Kirkwood; Broadway's longest running show opened July 25, 1975.
***Dance a Little Closer:** Musical by Alan Jay Lerner based on 1936 play *Idiot's Delight* by Robert Sherwood about international group of travelers in Austrian Alps; with Don Chastain, Len Cariou, Diane Pennington; director, Alan Jay Lerner; music Charles Strouse; choreographer, Billy Wilson; opened May 11, 1983.
Doonesbury: Musical based on Pulitzer Prize-winning cartoon characters; with Kate Burton, Mark Linn-Baker; music, Elizabeth Swados; book and lyrics, Garry Trudeau; director, Jacques Levy; opened Nov. 21, 1983.
Dreamgirls: Musical about group of black female singers and rise to fame in 1960s; won five Tony awards; director and choreographer, Michael Bennett; book and lyrics, Tom Eyen; opened Dec. 20, 1981.
***Edmund Kean:** One-man play by Raymond FitzSimons, based on life of great British actor of early 19th century; with Ben Kingsley; director, Alison Sutcliffe; opened Sept. 27, 1983.

***The Flying Karamazov Brothers:** Comic variety show with five juggler-comics; with Paul David Magid, Randy Nelson, Timothy Daniel Furst, Sam Williams, Howard Jay Patterson; director, Phil Friedman; opened May 10, 1983.
42d Street: Musical, based on 1932 film, about chorus girl who achieves stardom on Broadway; won Tony awards for best play, choreography; director and choreographer, Gower Champion; music and lyrics, Harry Warren and Al Dubin; book, Michael Stewart and Mark Bramble; opened Aug. 25, 1980.
The Glass Menagerie: Revival of Tennessee Williams drama about relationship between mother and spinster daughter; with Jessica Tandy, Amanda Plummer; opened Dec. 1, 1983.
***Goodnight Grandpa:** Comedy-drama by Walter Landau about relationship between two elderly Russian Jews who emigrated to United States when they were youths; with Milton Berle, David Rosenbaum, Laurie Heineman; director, Jay Broad; opened off-Broadway March 2, 1983.
***The Guys in the Truck:** Comedy by Howard Reitsnyder about television sports crew; with Howard Laskawy, Lawrence Guardino, Geoffrey Ewing; director, David Black; opened June 19, 1983.
Heartbreak House: Revival of George Bernard Shaw's comedy; with Rex Harrison, Rosemary Harris; opened November 15, 1983.
***K-2:** Drama by Patrick Meyers about two mountain climbers trapped on icy ledge of Himlayan mountainside; with Jeffrey De Munn, Jay Patterson; director, Terry Schreiber; opened March 30, 1983.
La Cage Aux Folles: Musical about homosexual love affair; with Gene Barry, George Hearn, Brian Kelly; director, Arthur Laurents; music and lyrics, Jerry Herman; opened Aug. 21, 1983.
Marilyn: An American Fable: Musical based on life of Marilyn Monroe; with Alyson Reed, Scott Bakula; director and choreographer, Kenny Ortega; music and lyrics, Jeanne Napoli, Doug Frank, Gary Portnoy, Beth Lawrence, Norman Thalheimer; opened Nov. 20, 1983.
***Merlin:** Musical in which wizard uses powers to help Britain's proper king reach throne; with Doug Henning, Rebecca Wright, Chita Rivera, Edmund Lyndeck; opened Feb. 13, 1983.
My One and Only: Musical comedy by Peter Stone and Timothy S. Mayer incorporating music of George and Ira Gershwin from their shows about romance between aviator determined to make first trans-Atlantic solo flight and female swimmer; won four Tony awards including best actor and choreographer; with Charles "Honi" Coles, who won Tony award for best featured actor, Tommy Tune, Twiggy, Denny Dillon; director and choreographer, Thommie Walsh and Tommy Tune; opened May 1, 1983.
'Night Mother: Marsha Norman's drama about relationship of young divorcee who wishes to commit suicide, and her mother; won 1983 Pulitzer Prize for drama; with Anne Pitoniak, Kathy Bates; director, Tom Moore; opened March 31, 1983.

* Closed.

Nine: Musical based on Fellini's *8½*, about Italian director's hedonistic lifestyle; won five Tony awards, including best musical and best musical director; director, Tommy Tune; opened May 9, 1982.

Noises Off: Comedy by Michael Frayn about British acting troupe; with Dorothy Loudon, Brian Murray, Paxton Whitehead; opened Dec. 11, 1983.

On Your Toes: Revival of musical comedy by Richard Rogers about ballet impressario; with Natalia Makarova, who won Tony award for best actress, George S. Irving, Dina Merrill; director, George Abbott; choreographer, George Balanchine; opened March 6, 1983.

***Porgy and Bess:** Revival of musical about black couple fighting for better life during Depression; with Edward Strauss, Priscilla Baskerville, Luvenia Garner; music, George Gershwin; lyrics, DuBose Heyward, Ira Gershwin; director, Jack O'Brien; opened April 7, 1983.

***Private Lives:** Revival of comedy by Noel Coward about married life; with Richard Burton, Elizabeth Taylor, Kathryn Walker; director, Milton Katselas; opened May 8, 1983.

Quartermaine's Terms: Comedy-drama by Simon Gray about lives of faculty members of British language school; with Roy Poole, John Cunningham, Dana Ivey; opened off-Broadway Feb. 24, 1983.

***Show Boat:** Revival of Kern-Hammerstein musical about romance and heartbreak of 19th century river show people; with Lonette Mckee, Donald O'Connor, Richard Dix; director, Michael Kahn; opened April 24, 1983.

Tallulah: Musical revue about life of entertainer; with Helen Gallagher; book, Tony Lang; music, Arthur Siegel; lyrics, Mae Richard; director and choreographer, David Holdgrive; opened off-Broadway Oct. 30, 1983.

The Tap Dance Kid: Musical about talented child dancer whose father wants him to become a lawyer; with Sam Wright, Hinton Battle, Hattie Winston; director, Vivian Matalon; book, Charles Blackwell; lyrics, Robert Lorick; music, Henry Krieger; opened December 1983.

Torch Song Trilogy: Comedy by Harvey Fierstein about complicated personal life of homosexual drag performer; won Tony award for best play; with Harvey Fierstein, who won Tony award for best actor, Court Miller; director, Peter Pope; opened June 10, 1982.

You Can't Take It With You: Revival of Kaufman-Hart musical about antics of eccentric American family in 1930s; with Elizabeth Wilson, Carol Androsky, Rosetta Le Noire; director, Ellis Rabb; musical staging; Reed Jones; opened April 4, 1983.

Zorba: Musical about Englishman who settles in Greek village; with Anthony Quinn, Lila Kedrova; director, Michael Cacoyannis; choreographer, Graciela Daniele; opened Oct. 16, 1983.

* Closed.

THEATER AWARDS: 1983

DRAMA DESK AWARDS: 1983

Awarded annually by the drama critics, editors, and reporters of New York City, the choices for the 1982–83 season included:

Outstanding play: *Torch Song Trilogy.*
Outstanding musical: *Little Shop of Horrors.*
Outstanding dramatic actress: Jessica Tandy, *Foxfire.*
Outstanding dramatic actor: Harvey Fierstein, *Torch Song Trilogy.*
Outstanding musical actress: Natalia Makarova, *On Your Toes.*
Outstanding dramatic director: Trevor Nunn, *All's Well That Ends Well.*
Outstanding musical director: George Abbott, *On Your Toes.*
Featured dramatic actress: Judith Ivey, *Steaming.*
Featured dramatic actor: Alan Feinstein, *A View From the Bridge.*
Featured musical actress: Karla Burns, *Showboat.*
Featured musical actor: Charles "Honi" Coles, *My One and Only.*

TONY AWARDS: 1983

The 37th annual Antoinette Perry (Tony) awards sponsored by the American Theatre Wing and the League of N.Y. Theatres for the Broadway season from May 11, 1982, to May 15, 1983.

Best play: *Torch Song Trilogy,* by Harvey Fierstein.
Best musical: *Cats.*
Best musical book: *Cats,* T.S. Eliot.
Best musical score: *Cats,* by Andrew Lloyd Webber.
Best dramatic actor: Harvey Fierstein, *Torch Song Trilogy.*
Best dramatic actress: Jessica Tandy, *Foxfire.*
Best musical actor: Tommy Tune, *My One and Only.*
Best musical actress: Natalia Makarova, *On Your Toes.*
Best featured actor in a play: Matthew Broderick, *Brighton Beach Memoirs.*
Featured actress in a play: Judith Ivey, *Steaming.*
Best featured actor, musical: Charles "Honi" Coles, *My One and Only.*
Best featured actress, musical: Betty Buckley, *Cats.*
Best director, drama: Gene Saks, *Brighton Beach Memoirs.*
Best director, musical: Trevor Nunn, *Cats.*
Best choreographer: Tommy Tune and Thommie Walsh, *My One and Only.*
Best scenic designer: Ming Cho Lee, *K2.*
Best designer: John Napier, *Cats.*
Best lighting designer: David Hersey, *Cats.*
Reproduction of a play or musical: *On Your Toes.*
Special Tony Awards: The Oregon Shakespeare Festival Association.
Theatre Award '83: The Theatre Collection, Museum of The City of New York.

OBIE AWARDS: 1983

Prizes for the best off-Broadway plays and performances are awarded annually by the *Village Voice:*

Distinguished playwriting: Caryl Churchill, *Top Girls;* Tina Howe, *The Art of Dining, Museum, Painted Churches;* David Mamet, *Edmond;* Harry Kondoleon, most promising young playwright.
Distinguished directing: Gregory Mosher, *Edmond;* Gary Sinise, *True West.*
Distinguished performances: Ernest Abuba, *Yellow Fever;* Christine Baranski, *A Midsummer Night's Dream;* Glenn Close, *The Singular Life of Albert Nubbs;* Jeff Daniels, *Johnny Got His Gun;* Ruth Maleczech, *Hajj;* John Malkovich, *True West;* Donald Moffat, *Painting Churches;* Ray Wise, *The Tooth of Crime.*
Sustained achievement: Lanford Wilson, Marshall Mason, Circle Repertory Company.

MOST POPULAR MADE-FOR-TV MOVIES: 1982–1983 SEASON

Source: *Variety;* average Nielsen rating in millions of viewers.

RANK	SERIES	NET-WORK	RAT-ING
1.	The Thorn Birds, Parts 1–4	ABC	42.1*
2.	The Winds of War, Parts 1–7	ABC	38.5*
3.	V, Parts 1–2	NBC	26.3*
4.	The Blue & The Gray, Pts. 1–3	CBS	25.8*
5.	The Royal Romance of Charles and Diana	CBS	24.0
6.	Drop-Out Father	CBS	23.8
7.	Intimate Agony	ABC	23.5
8.	The A Team	NBC	23.0
9.	Forbidden Love	CBS	22.8
10.	Something So Right	CBS	22.6
11.	The Executioner's Song, Pt. 1–2	NBC	22.4*
12.	Rage of Angels, Parts 1–2	NBC	22.2*
13.	Knight Rider	NBC	21.7
13.	I Was A Mail Order Bride	CBS	21.7
15.	Little Gloria...Happy At Last, Parts 1–2	NBC	21.6*
16.	Remembrance of Love	NBC	21.3
17.	Bare Essence, Pts. 1–2	CBS	21.1*
18.	Money on the Side	ABC	21.0
19.	Murder in Coweta County	CBS	20.9
20.	Summer Girl	CBS	20.5
21.	Confessions of a Married Man	ABC	20.4
22.	Tales of the Gold Monkey	ABC	20.2
23.	Seven Brides for Seven Brothers	CBS	19.9
24.	Malibu, Parts 1–2	CBS	19.8*
25.	Grace Kelly	ABC	19.7
25.	M.A.D.D.: Mothers Against Drunk Drivers	NBC	19.7
27.	Divorce Wars: A Love Story	ABC	19.4
28.	Thursday's Child	CBS	19.3
28.	Kentucky Woman	CBS	19.3
28.	Witness for the Prosecution	CBS	19.3
31.	Scruples, Parts 1–2	CBS	19.2
31.	Baby Sister	ABC	19.2

* Average rating of episodes.

MOST POPULAR TV SERIES: 1982–1983 SEASON

Source: *Variety;* average Nielsen rating in millions of viewers.

RANK	SERIES	NET-WORK	RAT-ING
1.	60 Minutes	CBS	25.5
2.	Dallas	CBS	24.6
3.	M*A*S*H	CBS	22.6
3.	Magnum, P.I.	CBS	22.6
5.	Dynasty	ABC	22.4
6.	Three's Company	ABC	21.2
7.	Simon & Simon	CBS	21.0
8.	Falcon Crest	CBS	20.7
9.	Love Boat	ABC	20.3
10.	The A Team	NBC	20.1
10.	NFL Monday Night Football	ABC	20.1
12.	The Jeffersons	CBS	20.0
12.	Newhart	CBS	20.0
14.	The Fall Guy	ABC	19.4
14.	The Mississippi	CBS	19.4
16.	9 to 5	ABC	19.3
17.	One Day at a Time	ABC	19.1
18.	Hart to Hart	ABC	18.9
19.	Gloria	CBS	18.7
19.	Trapper John, M.D.	CBS	18.7
19.	Goodnight, Beantown	CBS	18.7
22.	Knot's Landing	CBS	18.6
23.	Hill Street Blues	NBC	18.4
23.	Ryan's Four	ABC	18.4
25.	That's Incredible	ABC	18.3
25.	Archie Bunker's Place	CBS	18.3
27.	ABC Monday Movie	ABC	18.0
28.	Laverne & Shirley	ABC	17.8
29.	ABC Sunday Movie	ABC	17.6
30.	CBS Tuesday Movie	CBS	17.5
31.	Happy Days	ABC	17.4
31.	Little House: A New Beginning	NBC	17.4
33.	Real People	NBC	17.2
33.	Dukes of Hazzard	CBS	17.2
35.	NBC Sunday Movie	NBC	17.1
35.	Facts of Life	NBC	17.1
37.	Fantasy Island	ABC	16.6
38.	Too Close for Comfort	ABC	16.5
39.	NBC Monday Movie	NBC	16.4
40.	High Performance	ABC	16.0
41.	Alice	CBS	15.8
42.	Matt Houston	ABC	15.7
43.	Benson	ABC	15.6
44.	Condo	ABC	15.5
44.	Private Benjamin	CBS	15.5
44.	It Takes Two	ABC	15.5
47.	CBS Saturday Movie	CBS	15.4
48.	Knight Rider	NBC	15.3
48.	20/20	ABC	15.3
48.	Silver Spoons	NBC	15.3
48.	Diff'rent Strokes	NBC	15.3
52.	Chips	NBC	15.2
52.	T.J. Hooker	ABC	15.2
52.	Amanda's	ABC	15.2
52.	Cagney & Lacey	CBS	15.2
56.	Family Ties	NBC	15.1
57.	Walt Disney	CBS	15.0
58.	Square Pegs	CBS	14.8
59.	Mama's Family	NBC	14.6
60.	New Odd Couple	ABC	14.5
61.	CBS Wednesday Movie	CBS	14.4
62.	Gimme a Break	NBC	14.2
62.	Baby Makes Five	ABC	14.2
62.	Quincy, M.E.	NBC	14.2
65.	Seven Brides for Seven Brothers	CBS	13.9
66.	Father Murphy	NBC	13.8
67.	At Ease	ABC	13.7
68.	Remington Steele	NBC	13.5
68.	Tales of the Gold Monkey	ABC	13.5
70.	Joanie Loves Chachi	ABC	13.4
70.	Fame	NBC	13.4
70.	Filthy Rich	CBS	13.4
73.	Cheers	NBC	13.1
73.	Ace Crawford, Private Eye	CBS	13.1
75.	Small & Frye	CBS	12.8
75.	Foot in the Door	CBS	12.8
77.	Tucker's Witch	CBS	12.7
78.	Zorro & Son	CBS	12.6
79.	Love, Sidney	NBC	12.4
80.	Ripley's Believe It or Not	ABC	12.2
80.	Bring 'Em Back Alive	CBS	12.2
82.	Gun Shy	CBS	12.1
82.	Star of the Family	ABC	12.1
84.	Bare Essence	NBC	11.9
85.	Powers of Matthew Star	NBC	11.6
86.	St. Elsewhere	NBC	11.4
87.	ABC Friday Movie	ABC	11.2
88.	Wizards & Warriors	CBS	11.1
88.	Gavilan	NBC	11.1
88.	Casablanca	NBC	11.1
91.	Greatest American Hero	ABC	10.8

TELEVISION AND RADIO AWARDS: 1983

EMMY AWARDS: 1983

The prime-time and daytime Emmy awards, for the 1982–83 season included:

Best dramatic series: *Hill Street Blues* (NBC).
Best actress, drama series: Tyne Daly, *Cagney and Lacey* (CBS).
Best actor, drama series: Ed Flanders, *St. Elsewhere* (NBC).
Best supporting actress, drama series: Doris Roberts, *St. Elsewhere* (NBC).
Best supporting actor, drama series: James Coco, *St. Elsewhere* (NBC).
Best comedy series: *Cheers* (NBC).
Best actress, comedy series: Shelley Long, *Cheers* (NBC).
Best actor, comedy series: Judd Hirsch, *Taxi* (NBC).
Best supporting actress, comedy series: Carol Kane, *Taxi* (NBC).
Best limited series: *Nicholas Nickleby* (SYN).
Best drama special: *Special Bulletin* (NBC).
Best variety, music, or comedy program: *Motown 25: Yesterday, Today, Forever* (NBC).
Best actress, limited series or special: Barbara Stanwyck, *The Thorn Birds, Part 1* (ABC).
Best actor, limited series or special: Tommy Lee Jones, *The Executioner's Song* (NBC).
Best supporting actress, limited series or special: Jean Simmons, *The Thorn Birds* (ABC).
Best supporting actor, limited series or special: Richard Kiley, *The Thorn Birds, Part 1* (ABC).
Best children's program: *Big Bird In China* (NBC).
Best daytime drama series: *The Young and the Restless* (CBS).
Best actress, daytime series: Dorothy Lyman, *All My Children* (ABC).
Best actor, daytime series: Robert Woods, *One Life to Live* (ABC).
Best supporting actress, daytime series: Louise Shaffer, *Ryan's Hope* (ABC).
Best supporting actor, daytime series: Darnell Williams, *All My Children,* (ABC).
Best talk or service daytime series: *The Old House* (PBS).
Best host or hostess, daytime talk or service series: Phil Donahue, *Donahue* (SYN).
Best game or audience participation daytime show: *The $25,000 Pyramid* (NBC).
Best variety series, daytime: *The Merv Griffin Show* (SYN).

PEABODY AWARDS: 1983

The George Foster Peabody Broadcasting Awards are presented annually and administered by the School of Journalism, University of Georgia, for distinguished and meritorious public service rendered by radio and TV.

Individual Awards: Texaco, Inc., The Texaco Foundation, and Metropolitan Opera Assn. for their radio and TV presentations of great opera; Warner Amex Satellite Entertainment Company for overall programming for children and young people on *Nickelodeon: The First Channel for Kids;* CBS Entertainment and Cinetex Int. for *The Wall;* British Broadcasting Corp., Paramount Television and Operation Prime-Time for *Smiley's People;* NBC and Highgate Pictures for *The Electric Grandmother;* NBC News for *The Man Who Shot the Pope: A Study in Terrorism;* ABC News for *ABC News Closeup/"Vietnam Requiem";* CBS News for *Julliard and Beyond: A Life in Music;* Daniel Wilson Productions and Taurus Film for *Blood and Honor: Youth Under Hitler;* Television Corporation of America for *784 Days That Changed America—From Watergate to Resignation;* Alistair Cooke for his contribution to broadcasting.

Television Awards: KOCO-TV, Oklahoma City, for *Oklahoma Shame* series about abuse, neglect and questionable deaths in homes for mentally retarded; WCVB-TV, Boston, for *Ground Zero: Victory Road,* about hypothetical nuclear attack on Boston; KYW-TV, Philadelphia, for *Sweet Nothing,* on excessive consumption of sugar; WWL-TV, New Orleans for *The Search for Alexander,* about a museum exhibition; NBC-TV, Margie-Lee Enterprises, Inc., and Blue Marble Co., Inc. for *Skeezer,* about use of dog by therapists in treatment of emotionally disturbed children; WQED, Pittsburgh, for *Stravinsky's "Firebird" by the Dance Theater of Harlem;* KQED-TV, San Francisco for *Current Affairs/The Case of Dashiell Hammett,* biographical sketch of American mystery writer; KGMB-TV, Honolulu, and Lee Productions, Inc. for *Beyond the Great Wall: Journey to the End of China;* WAGA-TV, Atlanta, for *Paradise Saved,* about Georgia barrier island; WBBM-TV, Chicago, for *Killing Crime: A Police Cop-Out,* about irregularities in crime reporting; WTSP-TV, St. Petersburg, Fla., for *Prisoners of the Harvest,* about migrant farm workers.

Radio Awards: National Public Radio for *The Sunday Show;* C.B.C. Radio for *Morningside/1905,* about events of 1905; WMAL, Washington, D.C., for *They Served with Honor,* about dedication of Vietnam Veterans Memorial; NBC Radio News for *Banks on the Brink* about the banking industry; National Public Radio for *Taylor Made Piano: A Jazz History;* Mutual Broadcasting System for *The Larry King Show;* The Radio Foundation, New York, for *The Bob and Ray Public Radio Show.*

WRITERS GUILD TV AWARDS: 1983

Original anthology: Ernest Kinoy, *Skokie* (CBS).
Anthology from another source: E. Nick Alexander, *Of Mice and Men* (NBC).
Dramatic-episodic: Michael Wagner, "The World According to Freedom," *Hill Street Blues* (NBC).
Comedy-episodic: Tony Sheehan, "Hunger Strike," *Barney Miller* (ABC).
Variety: Richard Alfieri, Rita Mae Brown, Rick Mitz, Norman Lear, Arthur Seidelman, *I Love Liberty* (ABC).
Current events documentary: Judy Reemtsma, *People Like Us* (CBS).
Feature documentary: Perry Wolff, *The Museum of Modern Art Presents Pablo Picasso: A Retrospective* (CBS).

GOLDEN GLOBE TV AWARDS: 1983

The Hollywood Foreign Press Association's 40th annual Golden Globe TV awards included:

Best series, drama: *Hill Street Blues* (NBC).
Best series, musical or comedy: Fame (NBC).
Best miniseries: *Brideshead Revisited* (PBS).
Best actor, drama: John Forsythe, *Dynasty* (ABC).
Best actress, drama: Joan Collins, *Dynasty* (ABC).
Best actor, musical or comedy: Alan Alda, *M*A*S*H* (CBS).
Best actress, musical or comedy: Debbie Allen, *Fame* (NBC).
Best supporting actor, series: Lionel Stander, *Hart to Hart* (ABC).
Best supporting actress, series: Shelley Long, *Cheers* (NBC).
Best actor, drama special: Anthony Andrews, *Brideshead Revisited* (PBS).
Best actress, drama special: Ingrid Bergman, *A Woman Called Golda* (Ind).

CHRISTOPHER TV AWARDS: 1983

To ABC for... *FDR—ABC News Presentation, Night of 100 Stars.*
To NBC for... *NBC White Paper: Facing Up to the Bomb, Oh, Boy! Babies!*
To CBS for... *Lois Gibbs and the Love Canal, The Scarlet Pimpernel.*
To PBS for... *Brooklyn Bridge, Roses in December: The Story of Jean Donovan.*
To Independent Network for... *A Woman Called Golda, Blood and Honor.*
To WNET for... *The Flight of the Condor.*

MUSIC AWARDS: 1983

GRAMMY AWARDS

The 25th annual Grammy awards, presented by the National Academy of Recording Arts and Sciences, included:

Record of the year: *Rosanna,* Toto.
Album of the year: *Toto IV,* Toto.
Song of the year: *Always on My Mind,* Johnny Christopher, Mark James, Wayne Thompson, songwriters.
Best new artist: *Men at Work.*
Best instrumental arrangement: *Flying.*
Best arrangement accompanying vocalist: *Rosanna* (track from *Toto IV*), Jerry Hey, David Paich, Jeff Porcaro.
Best album package: *Get Closer,* Kosh with Ron Larson.
Best female pop vocal performance: *You Should Hear How She Talks About You,* Melissa Manchester.
Best male pop vocal: *Truly,* Lionel Richie.
Best pop vocal performance by duo, group, or chorus: *Up Where We Belong,* Joe Cocker and Jennifer Warnes.
Best pop instrumental performance: *Chariots of Fire,* Ernie Watts.
Best rhythm and blues female vocal performance: *And I Am Telling You I'm Not Going,* Jennifer Holliday.
Best rhythm and blues male vocal performance: *Sexual Healing,* Marvin Gaye.
Best rhythm and blues performance by duo, group, or chorus: *Let It Whip,* Dazz Band, and *Wanna Be with You,* Earth, Wind & Fire.
Best rhythm & blues song: *Turn Your Love Around,* Jay Graydon, Steve Lukather, Bill Champlin.
Best rhythm and blues instrumental performance: *Sexual Healing,* Marvin Gaye.
Best female rock vocal performance: *Shadows of the Night,* Pat Benatar.
Best male rock vocal performance: *Hurts So Good,* John Cougar.
Best duo or group rock performance with vocal: *Eye of the Tiger,* Survivor.
Best rock instrumental performance: *D.N.A.,* A Flock of Seagulls.
Best female jazz vocal performance: *Gershwin Live,* Sarah Vaughan.
Best male jazz vocal performance: *An Evening with George Shearing and Mel Torme,* Mel Torme.
Best jazz instrumental performance: *We Want Miles,* Miles Davis.
Best group jazz instrumental performance: *More Live,* Phil Wood Quartet.
Best jazz group vocal performance: *Route 66,* The Manhattan Transfer.
Best big-band jazz performance: *Warm Breeze,* Count Basie and His Orchestra.
Best contemporary soul gospel performance: *Higher Plane,* Al Green.
Best female country vocal performance: *Break It to Me Gently,* Juice Newton.
Best male country vocal performance: *Always on My Mind,* Willie Nelson.
Best country vocal performance by a duo or group: *Mountain Music,* Alabama.
Best country instrumental performance: *Alabama Jubilee,* Roy Clark.
Best country song: *Always on My Mind,* Johnny Christopher, Wayne Thompson, Mark James.
Best ethnic recording: *Queen Ida and the Bon Temps Zydeco Band on Tour,* Queen Ida.
Best children's recording: *In Harmony 2,* Lucy Simon and David Levine.
Comedy record: *Live on the Sunset Strip,* Richard Pryor.
Best instrumental composition: *Flying (Theme—from E.T.—The Extra-Terrestrial),* John Williams.
Original score for motion-picture or television special: *E.T.—The Extra-Terrestrial,* John Williams, composer.
Best cast show album: *Dreamgirls.*
Classical album of the year: *Bach: The Goldberg Variations,* Glenn Gould, Samuel Carter, producers.
Best opera recording: *Wagner: Der Ring des Nibelungen,* Pierre Boulez, conductor.
Best classical choral performance: *Berlioz: La Damnation de Faust,* Margaret Hillis, chorus director.
Best classical solo performance with orchestra: *Elgar: Concerto for Violin in B Minor,* Itzhak Perlman, Daniel Barenboim, conductor, Chicago Symphony.
Best solo classical performance: *Bach: The Goldberg Variations,* Glenn Gould.
Best classical vocal: *Verdi: Arias (Leontyne Price Sings Verdi),* Leontyne Price, Zubin Mehta, conductor.

NARM BESTSELLING RECORD AWARDS

The National Association of Recording Merchandisers awards for bestselling records, presented in 1983, included:

Hit single: *Eye of the Tiger,* Survivor.
Bestselling album: *Business as Usual,* Men at Work.
Male artist: *American Fool,* John Cougar.
Female artist: *Bella Donna,* Stevie Nicks.
Group album: *Business as Usual,* Men at Work.
Male soul artist: *Lionel Richie,* Lionel Richie.
Female soul artist: *Jump to It,* Aretha Franklin.
Soul album, group: *Gap Band IV,* Gap Band.
Male country artist: *Always on My Mind,* Willie Nelson.
Female country artist: *Quiet Lies,* Juice Newton.
Country album, group: *Mountain Music,* Alabama.
Film soundtrack: *Chariots of Fire.*
Broadway cast album: *Dreamgirls.*
Children's album: *Annie.*
Jazz album: *Breakin' Away,* Al Jarreau.
Classical album: *Luciano,* Luciano Pavarotti.
Gospel/spiritual album: *Precious Lord,* Al Green.

ACADEMY OF COUNTRY MUSIC AWARDS

The Academy of Country Music awards, presented in 1983, included:

Entertainer of the year: Alabama.
Female vocalist of the year: Sylvia.
Male vocalist of the year: Ronnie Milsap.
Song of the year: *Are the Good Times Really Over,* Merle Haggard.
Album of the year: *Always on My Mind,* Willie Nelson.
Single record of the year: *Always on My Mind,* Willie Nelson.
Top vocal group: Alabama.

AMERICAN MUSIC AWARDS

Chosen by a sample of 30,000 record buyers, the 1983 American Music Awards included:

Best pop/rock single: *Truly,* Lionel Richie.
Best soul single: *Sexual Healing,* Marvin Gaye.
Country single: *Love Will Turn You Around,* Kenny Rogers.
Best pop/rock group: Daryl Hall & John Oates.
Best soul group: Kool and the Gang.
Best country group: Alabama.
Best pop/rock album: *Always on My Mind,* Willie Nelson.
Best soul album: *Jump to It,* Aretha Franklin.
Best country album: *Always on My Mind,* Willie Nelson.
Best country vocalists: Barbara Mandrell, Kenny Rogers.
Best soul vocalists: Diana Ross, Lionel Richie.
Best female pop/rock vocalist: Olivia Newton-John.
Best male pop/rock vocalists: John Cougar, Rick Springfield.

SHOW BUSINESS PERSONALITIES

Personalities of the theater, film, TV, and entertainment world are included in the following list. ffieal names follow show business names.

Members of the Theater Hall of Fame, are marked with (T). Members of the Entertainment Hall of Fame, elected by the nation's entertainment editors, are marked with (E). American Academy of Motion Picture Arts and Sciences award winners are indicated with (A) and the year for which the Oscar was given.

See also *Musicians, Composers, Singers, Dancers,* pages 58–63; *Authors and Writers,* pages 94–102. See pages 981–986 for 1983 deaths of show business personalities.

Abbott and Costello: Bud Abbott (1895–1974), Lou Costello (1906–59), comedy team
George Abbott (1887–), theatrical producer, T
Betty Ackerman (1928–), actress
Roy Acuff (1903–), country music singer
Don Adams (1927–), actor
Edie Adams (Elizabeth Edith Enke; 1929–), singer
Joey Adams (1911–), comedian
Julie Adams (1927–), actress
Maude Adams (Maude Kiskadden; 1872–1953), actress, T
Dawn Addams (1930–), actress
Larry Adler (1914–), musician
Luther Adler (1903–), actor
Richard Adler (1932–), songwriter
John Agar (1921–), actor
Brian Aherne (1902–), British actor
Anouk Aimee (Françoise Sorya; 1932–), actress
Claude Akins (1918–), actor
Anna Maria Alberghetti (1936–), Italian-born singer
Eddie Albert (Eddie Heimberger; 1908–), actor
Edward Albert (1951–), actor, son of Eddie Albert
Jack Albertson (1907–81), actor, A-1968
Lola Albright (1925–), actress
Alan Alda (1936–), actor, son of Robert Alda
Robert Alda (Alphonso d'Abruzzo; 1914–), actor
Fred Allen (John F. Sullivan; 1894–1956), actor, comedian
Gracie Allen (1906–64), comedienne, wife of George Burns
Mel Allen (1913–), sportscaster
Steve Allen (1921–), entertainer
Viola Allen (1867–1948), actress, T
Woody Allen (Allen Konigsberg; 1935–), comedian, writer, director, A-1977
Fran Allison (1924–), actress
June Allyson (Ella Geisman; 1923–), actress
Herb Alpert (1937–), musician
Robert Altman (1925–), film director
Don Ameche (Dominic Amici; 1908–), actor
Ames Brothers: Joe (1924–), Gene (1925–), Vic (1926–78), Ed (1927–), singing group
Leon Ames (Leon Waycoff; 1903–), actor
Nancy Ames (1937–), singer
Morey Amsterdam (1912–), actor and comedian
Eddie "Rochester" Anderson (1905–77), actor
Dame Judith Anderson (Frances Margaret Anderson; 1898–), Australian actress, T
Lynn Anderson (1947–), country music singer
Bibi Andersson (1935–), Swedish actress
Ursula Andress (1936–), Swiss-born actress
Andrews Sisters: LaVerne (1913–67), Maxine (1916–), Patty (1918–), singing group in 1940s
Dana Andrews (Carver Daniel Andrews; 1909–), actor
Julie Andrews (Julia Wells; 1935–), actress and singer, A-1964
Pier Angeli (1933–71), Italian-born actress
Margaret Anglin (1876–1958), actress, T
Paul Anka (1941–), singer and composer
Ann-Margret (Ann-Margret Olsson; 1941–), Swedish-born actress
Michael Ansara (1922–), actor
Michelangelo Antonioni (1912–), Italian film director
Roscoe "Fatty" Arbuckle (1887–1933), comedian
Eve Arden (Eunice Quedens; 1912–), actress
Alan Arkin (1935–), actor and director
Harold Arlen (1905–), composer
Richard Arlen (1899–1976), actor, T
George Arliss (1868–1946), British actor, A-1929–30, T
Louis Armstrong (1900–71), jazz musician and singer
Desi Arnaz (1915–), Cuban-born actor and producer
Desi Arnaz Jr. (1953–), actor, son of Desi
Lucie Arnaz (1951–), actress, daughter of Desi
James Arness (James Aurness; 1923–), actor, brother of Peter Graves
Eddie Arnold (1918–), country music singer
Edward Arnold (1890–1956), actor
Beatrice Arthur (Bernice Frankel; 1926–), actress
Jean Arthur (Gladys Greene; 1905–), actress
Jane Asher (1945–), actress
Elizabeth Ashley (1940–), actress
Edward Asner (1929–), actor
Fred Astaire (Frederick Austerlitz; 1899–), dancer and actor, T, E, A-1949
John Astin (1930–), actor
Mary Astor (1906–), actress, A-1941
Chet Atkins (1924–), country music singer
Richard Attenborough (1923–), actor, director (A-1982)
Lionell Atwill (1885–1946), British actor
Mischa Auer (1905–67), Russian-born actor
Jean-Pierre Aumont (1913–), actor
Gene Autry (1907–), singer and cowboy actor
Frankie Avalon (1939–), singer
John Avildsen (1942–), director, A-1976
Lew Ayres (1908–), actor
Charles Aznavour (1924–), French singer, actor
Lauren Bacall (Betty Joan Perske; 1924–), actress
Burt Bacharach (1928–), musician and composer
Jim Backus (1913–), actor
Buddy Baer (1915–), actor, brother of Max
Max Baer (1909–59), boxer and actor
Joan Baez (1941–), folk singer
Pearl Bailey (1918–), singer
Barbara Bain (1934–), actress
Fay Bainter (1892–1968), actress, A-1938
Bill Baird (1904–), puppeteer
Carroll Baker (1932–), actress
Josephine Baker (1906–75), singer
George Balanchine (1904–), choreographer, E
Ina Balin (1937–), actress
Lucille Ball (1910–), comedienne
Kaye Ballard (Catherine Balotta; 1926–), actress and comedienne
Martin Balsam (1919–), actor, A-1965
Anne Bancroft (Anne Italiano; 1931–), actress, A-1962
Tallulah Bankhead (1903–68), actress, T
Vilma Banky (1903–), silent-film star
Theda Bara (1890–1955), actress, first "vamp"
Brigitte Bardot (1934–), French actress
Lynn Bari (1917–), actress
Phineas T. Barnum (1810–91), showman
Gene Barry (Eugene Klass; 1921–), actor
John Barry (1933–), British composer
Ethel Barrymore (1879–1959), actress, A-1944, T
John Barrymore (John Blythe; 1882–1942), actor, T
Lionel Barrymore (1878–1954), actor, A-1930–31, T
Richard Barthelmess (1895–1963), actor
Freddie Bartholomew (1924–), child actor in 1930s
Eva Bartok (1926–), actress
James Barton (1890–1962), actor
Richard Basehart (1919–), actor
Count Basie (1904–), musician
Shirley Bassey (1937–), singer
Alan Bates (1930–), British actor
Anne Baxter (1923–), actress, A-1946
Les Baxter (1922–), musical arranger and composer
Warner Baxter (1889–1951), actor, A-1928–29
Nora Bayes (1880–1928), vaudeville entertainer, T
Orson Bean (1928–), actor and comedian
The Beatles: George Harrison (1943–), John Lennon (1940–80), Paul McCartney (1942–), Ringo Starr (1940–), British rock group
Cecil Beaton (1904–80), British photographer, designer
Warren Beatty (1937–), actor, director, A-1981
Sidney Bechet (1897–1959), jazz sax musician
Bee Gees: Barry Gibb (1946–), Robin Gibb (1949–), Maurice Gibb (1949–), singers, composers
Noah Beery (1884–1946), actor
Noah Beery Jr. (1916–), actor
Wallace Beery (1889–1949), actor, A-1931–32
Ed Begley (1901–70), actor, A-1962
Leon Bix Beiderbecke (1903–31), jazz cornetist
Harry Belafonte (1927–), singer and actor
David Belasco (1854–1931), impresario, T
Barbara Bel Geddes (1922–), actress
Norman Bel Geddes (1900–58), scenic designer, T
Ralph Bellamy (1904–), actor

SHOW BUSINESS PERSONALITIES *(continued)*

Jean-Paul Belmondo (1933–), French actor
John Belushi (1950–82), actor
Robert C. Benchley (1889–1945), humorist and author
William Bendix (1906–64), actor
Richard Benjamin (1938–), actor
Constance Bennett (1905–65), actress, sister of Joan
Joan Bennett (1910–), actress, sister of Constance
Michael Bennett (1943–), director
Richard Bennett (1873–1944), actor, T, father of Constance and Joan
Tony Bennett (1926–), singer
Jack Benny (Joseph Kubelsky; 1894–1974), comedian, E
George Benson (1943–), blues guitarist and singer
Robert Benton (1932–), director, A-1979
Gertrude Berg (1899–1966), actress
Candice Bergen (1946–), actress, daughter of Edgar
Edgar Bergen (1903–78), ventriloquist
Polly Bergen (1930–), singer
Senta Berger (1941–), Austrian actress
Ingmar Bergman (1918–), Swedish film director, A-1956, E
Ingrid Bergman (1915–82), Swedish actress, A-1944, 1956, 1974
Busby Berkeley (1895–1976), dance director
Milton Berle (Milton Berlinger; 1908–), comedian
Shelley Berman (1926–), comedian
Herschel Bernardi (1923–), actor
Sarah Bernhardt (Rosine Bernard; 1844–1923), French actress, T
Ben Bernie (1893–1943), bandleader
Chuck Berry (1926–), rock singer and composer
Bernardo Bertolucci (1940–), Italian film director
Richard Beymer (1939–), actor
Charles Bickford (1889–1967), actor
Theodore Bikel (1924–), Austrian-born actor, singer
David Birney (1940–), actor
Joey Bishop (Joseph Gottlieb; 1919–), comedian
Jacqueline Bisset (1944–), actress
Bill Bixby (1934–), actor
Cilla Black (Priscilla White; 1943–), British singer
Karen Black (1942–), actress
Honor Blackman (1929–), actress
Sidney Blackmer (1895–1973), actor
Vivian Blaine (Vivienne Stapleton; 1921–), singer, actress
Janet Blair (1921–), actress
Linda Blair (1959–), actress
Amanda Blake (Beverly Louise Neill; 1931–), actress
Eubie Blake (1883–1983), jazz pianist, composer
Robert Blake (Michael Gubitosi; 1933–), actor
Ronee Blakely (1946–), actress
Mel Blanc (1908–), cartoon voiceman
Joan Blondell (1909–79), actress
Claire Bloom (1931–), British actress
Ben Blue (1900–75), comedian
Monte Blue (1890–1963), actor
Ann Blyth (1928–), actress
Dirk Bogarde (Derek Van den Bogaerde; 1921–), British actor
Humphrey Bogart (1899–1957), actor, A-1951, E
Peter Bogdanovich (1940–), film director
Mary Boland (1880–1965), actress
John Boles (1895–1969), singer and actor
Ray Bolger (1904–), dancer and actor, T
Robert Bolt (1924–), playwright
Sonny Bono (1940–), singer, teamed with Cher
Debby Boone (1956–), singer, daughter of Pat Boone
Pat Boone (1934–), singer
Richard Boone (1917–81), actor
Edwin Booth (1833–93), actor, T
Shirley Booth (1907–), actress, A-1952, T
Victor Borge (1909–), Danish-born pianist and comedian
Ernest Borgnine (1917–), actor, A-1955
Frank Borzage (1893–1962), director, A-1927–28, 1931–32
Tom Bosley (1927–), actor
Connee Boswell (1907–76), singer
Clara Bow (1905–65), actress, known as "It Girl"
David Bowie (David Jones; 1947–), rock singer
Lee Bowman (1914–79), actor
Stephen Boyd (1928–77), Irish-born actor
William Boyd (1898–1972), cowboy actor (Hopalong Cassidy)
Charles Boyer (1899–1978), French actor
Peter Boyle (1933–), actor
Eddie Bracken (1920–), comedian and actor
Alice Brady (1893–1939), actress, T, A-1937
Scott Brady (Gerald Tierney; 1924–), actor
Marlon Brando (1924–), actor, A-1954, 1972
Keefe Brasselle (1923–), actor
Rossano Brazzi (1916–), Italian actor
Jacques Brel (1929–78), singer, composer
Walter Brennan (1894–1974), actor, A-1936, 1938, 1940
George Brent (1904–79), Irish-born actor
Teresa Brewer (1931–), singer
Fanny Brice (Fannie Borach; 1891–1951), actress and singer, T
Beau Bridges (1941–), actor, son of Lloyd Bridges
Lloyd Bridges (1913–), actor
David Brinkley (1920–), newscaster
Frederick Brisson (1915–), Danish-born producer
May Britt (Maybritt Wilkins; 1936–), Swedish-born actress
Barbara Britton (1920–80), actress
James Brolin (1942–), actor
Charles Bronson (Charles Burchinsky; 1922–), actor
Geraldine Brooks (Geraldine Stroock, 1925-77), actress
Mel Brooks (Melvin Kaminsky; 1926–), comedian
James Brown (1934–), singer
Jim Brown (1936–), actor and football star
Joe E. Brown (1892–1973), comedian
Johnny Mack Brown (1904–74), actor
Les Brown (1912–), bandleader
Dave Brubeck (1920–), jazz pianist, combo leader
Lenny Bruce (1926–66), comedian
Anita Bryant (1940–), singer
Yul Brynner (1916–), Russian-born actor, A-1956
Edgar Buchanan (1902–79), actor
Horst Buchholz (1933–), German actor
Genevieve Bujold (1942–), actress
Luis Buñuel (1900–83), Spanish director
Billie Burke (1885–1970), actress, T
Carol Burnett (1934–), comedienne
George Burns (Nathan Birnbaum, 1896–), comedian, A-1975
Raymond Burr (1917–), Canadian-born actor
Abe Burrows (1910–), playwright and director
Ellen Burstyn (Edna Gilhooley; 1932–), actress, A-1974
Richard Burton (Richard Jenkins; 1925–), Welsh actor
Francis X. Bushman (1883–1966), actor
Red Buttons (Aaron Schwatt; 1919–), actor and comedian, A-1957
Ruth Buzzi (1936–), comedienne
Edd Byrnes (1933–), actor
James Caan (1939–), actor
Bruce Cabot (1904–73), actor
Sebastian Cabot (1918–77), British actor
Sid Caesar (1922–), comedian
James Cagney (1900–), actor, A-1942, E
Jeanne Cagney (1919–), actress, sister of James
Sammy Cahn (1913–), composer
Michael Caine (Maurice Micklewhite; 1933–), British actor
Zoe Caldwell (1933–), actress
Louis Calhern (Carl Vogt; 1895–1956), actor
Michael Callan (Martin Calinff; 1935–), actor
Cab Calloway (1907–), jazz musician, bandleader
Corinne Calvet (1925–), French actress
Godfrey Cambridge (1933–76), comedian and actor
Rod Cameron (1912–), actor
Joseph Campanella (1923–), actor
Glen Campbell (1937–), singer
Mrs. Patrick Campbell (1865–1940), British actress, T
Dyan Cannon (1937–), actress
Judy Canova (1916–83), actress
Cantinflas (Mario Moreno; 1913–), Mexican comedian
Eddie Cantor (Edward Iskowitz; 1892–1964), comedian and singer, T
Lana Cantrell (1944–), singer
Frank Capra (1897–), Italian-born film director, A-1934, 1936, 1938
Capucine (1935–), French actress
Claudia Cardinale (1939–), Italian actress
Harry Carey (1878–1947), actor
MacDonald Carey (1913–), actor
Kitty Carlisle (Catherine Holzman; 1915–), actress
Richard Carlson (1912–77), actor
Hoagy Carmichael (1899–1981), songwriter
Judy Carne (Joyce Botterill; 1939–), British-born comedienne, singer
Art Carney (1918–), actor, A-1974
Karen (1950–83) and **Richard** (1945–) **Carpenter,** sing-ing team
Leslie Caron (1931–), French actress and dancer
Vikki Carr (Florencia Bisenta de Casillas; 1941–), singer
David Carradine (1940–), actor, son of John
John Carradine (1906–), actor

Keith Carradine (1950–), actor, son of John
Leo Carrillo (1880–1961), actor
Diahann Carroll (1935–), singer and actress
Leo G. Carroll (1892–1972), British actor
Madeleine Carroll (1906–), British actress
Pat Carroll (1927–), comedienne
Jack Carson (1910–63), comedian and actor
Johnny Carson (1925–), television personality
Jack Carter (1923–), comedian
Mrs. Leslie Carter (1862–1937), actress, T
Maybelle Carter (1909–78), country music singer
Johnny Cash (1932–), country music singer
Peggy Cass (1926–), comedienne
John Cassavetes (1929–), actor and director
David Cassidy (1950–), singer and actor
Jack Cassidy (1927–76), actor
Shaun Cassidy (1958–), singer and actor
Irene Castle (Irene Foote; 1893–1969) and **Vernon Castle** (Vernon Blythe; 1885–1918), wife-husband dance team
Joan Caulfield (1922–), actress
Dick Cavett (1936–), television personality
Bennett Cerf (1898–1971), television panelist, publisher
George Chakiris (1933–), actor, A-1961
Richard Chamberlain (1935–), actor
Gower Champion (1921–80), T, and Marge Champion (1925–), husband-wife dance team
John Chancellor (1927–), television commentator
Jeff Chandler (1918–61), actor
Lon Chaney (1883–1930), actor
Lon Chaney Jr. (1907–73), actor
Carol Channing (1921–), actress, T
Harry Chapin (1942–81), singer
Sir Charles Chaplin (1889–1977), British comic actor
Geraldine Chaplin (1944–), actress, daughter of Charles
Sydney Chaplin (1926–), actor, son of Charles
Cyd Charisse (Tula Finklea; 1923–), actress and dancer
Ray Charles (1932–), musician
Charley Chase (1893–1940), comedian and director
Chevy Chase (1944–), comedian
Ruth Chatterton (1893–1961), actress, T
Paddy Chayefsky (1923–81), playwright, A-1976
Chubby Checker (Ernest Evans; 1941–), singer
Cher (Cherilyn LaPierre; 1946–), singer, TV personality
Maurice Chevalier (1888–1972), French actor, A-1958
Julia Child (1912–), television personality
Julie Christie (1941–), British actress, A-1965
Jordon Christopher (1941–), actor and musician
Edwin P. Christy (1815–62), showman and minstrel
June Christy (1925–), singer
Michael Cimino (1943–), director, A-1978
Ina Claire (Ina Fagan; 1892–), actress, T
Eric Clapton (1945—), rock singer
Bobby Clark (1888–1960), comedian, T
Dane Clark (Bernard Zanville; 1913–), actor
Dick Clark (1929–), television personality
Petula Clark (1932–), British singer and actress
Roy Clark (1933–), country music singer
Jill Clayburgh (1945–), actress
Jan Clayton (1925–), actress
Montgomery Clift (1920–66), actor
Rosemary Clooney (1928–), singer
Lee J. Cobb (Leo Jacob; 1911–76), actor, T
Charles Coburn (1877–1961), actor, A-1943
James Coburn (1928–), actor
Imogene Coca (1920–), comedienne
Joe Cocker (John Robert Cocker; 1944–), singer
James Coco (1920–), actor and comedian
George M. Cohan (1878–1942), musician, composer, T
Myron Cohen (1902–), comedian
Claudette Colbert (Lily Claudette Chauchoin; 1905–), actress, A-1934
Nat King Cole (1919–65), singer and musician
Natalie Cole (1950–), singer, daughter of Nat King Cole
Constance Collier (1878–1955), British actress, T
Joan Collins (1933–), British-born actress
Judy Collins (1939–), singer
Bud Collyer (1908–69), actor and TV personality
Ronald Colman (1891–1958), British actor, A-1947
Jerry Colonna (1904–), comedian
John Coltrane (1926–67), jazz sax musician
Russ Columbo (1908–34), singer
Betty Comden (1919–), lyricist. T
Anjanette Comer (1941–), actress
Perry Como (1912–), singer
Eddie Condon (1905–73), dixieland bandleader
Ray Conniff (1916–), bandleader, music arranger
Chester Conklin (1886–71), silent-film comedian
Sean Connery (1930–), Scottish-born actor
Chuck Connors (1921–), actor
Robert Conrad (1935–), actor
William Conrad (1920–), actor
Hans Conreid (1915–82), actor
Richard Conte (1915–75), Italian-born actor
Tim Conway (1933–), actor
Rita Coolidge (1944–), singer
Jackie Coogan (1914–), child star in silent movies
Alistair Cooke (Alfred Alistaire; 1908–), British author, television personality
Alice Cooper (Vincent Furnier; 1948–), rock singer
Gary Cooper (1901–61), actor, A-1941, 1952
Jackie Cooper (1922–), child movie star in 1930s
Francis Ford Coppola (1939–), director, writer, A-1974
Ellen Corby (1913–), actress
Jeff Corey (1914–), actor
Wendell Corey (1914–68), actor
Katharine Cornell (1898–1974), stage actress, T
Charles Correll (1890–1972), radio actor, "Andy"
Bill Cosby (1938–), actor and comedian
Dolores Costello (1905–79), actress, wed John Barrymore
Joseph Cotten (1905–), actor
Tom Courtenay (1937–), British actor
Noel Coward (1899–1973), British playwright, actor, and composer, T, A-1941
Jane Cowl (1890–1950), actress, T
Wally Cox (1924–73), comic actor
Buster Crabbe (1907–83), actor, Olympic swim champion
Jeanne Crain (1925–), actress
Bob Crane (1928–78), TV star of *Hogan's Heroes*
Broderick Crawford (1910–), actor, A-1949
Joan Crawford (Lucille le Sueur; 1908–77), actress, A-1945
Michael Crawford (1942–), actor
Richard Crenna (1926–), actor
Michael Crichton (1942–), film director, screenwriter
Donald Crisp (1880–1974), British actor, A-1941
Linda Cristal (1936–), actress
Michael Cristofer (1946–), actor and playwright
Jim Croce (1943–73), rock singer
Walter Cronkite (1916–), newscaster
Hume Cronyn (1911–), Canadian actor, T
Bing Crosby (Harry Lillis Crosby; 1904–77), singer and actor, E, A-1944
Bob Crosby (1913–), musician, brother of Bing
David Crosby (1941–), rock musician
Russel Crouse (1893–1966), playwright, T
Brandon Cruz (1962–), actor
Xavier Cugat (1900–), Spanish-born bandleader
George Cukor (1899–1983), director, A-1964
Bill Cullen (1920–), television personality
John Cullum (1930–), actor
Robert Culp (1930–), actor
Robert Cummings (1908–), actor
Tony Curtis (Bernard Schwarz; 1925–), actor
Michael Curtiz (1888–1962), Hungarian-born director, A-1943
Peter Cushing (1913–), British actor
Charlotte Cushman (1816–75), Shakespearean actress, T
Arlene Dahl (1924–), actress
Dan Dailey (1915–78), actor and dancer
Abby Dalton (1935–), actress
Arnold Daly (1875–1927), actor
Augustin Daly (1838–99), playwright, theater manager, T
John Daly (1914–), newscaster, TV personality
Vic Damone (Vito Farinola; 1928–), singer
Bill Dana (1924–), comedian
Dorothy Dandridge (1923–65), actress
Rodney Dangerfield (1921–), comedian
Bebe Daniels (1901–71), actress, wife of Ben Lyon
Kim Darby (1948–), actress
Denise Darcel (1925–), actress
Bobby Darin (1927–73), singer
Linda Darnell (1923–65), actress
James Darren (1936–), actor
Danielle Darrieux (1917–), French actress
Jane Darwell (1880–1967), actress, A-1940
Howard Da Silva (1909–), actor
Jules Dassin (1911–), director, actor, and writer
Claude Dauphin (1905–78), French actor
John Davidson (1941–), singer
Marion Davies (Marion Douras; 1898–1961), actress
Ann B. Davis (1908–), actress
Bette Davis (1908–), actress, A-1935, 1938
Billy Davis Jr. (1940–), singer
Joan Davis (1908–61), comedienne
Mac Davis (1942–), songwriter
Miles Davis (1927–), jazz trumpet player
Ossie Davis (1917–), playwright and actor

SHOW BUSINESS PERSONALITIES *(continued)*
Sammy Davis Jr. (1925–), actor, singer, and dancer
Anthony Dawson (1916–), British actor
Dennis Day (1917–), singer
Doris Day (Doris Kappelhoff; 1924–), actress and singer
Laraine Day (Laraine Johnson; 1920–), actress
James Dean (1931–55), actor
Jimmy Dean (1928–), singer and entertainer
Rosemary De Camp (1913–), actress
Yvonne De Carlo (Peggy Middleton; 1922–), Canadian actress
Frances Dee (1907–), actress
Kiki Dee (Pauline Matthews; 1947–), rock singer
Ruby Dee (Ruby Ann Wallace; 1924–), actress
Sandra Dee (Alexandra Zuck; 1942–), actress
Don Defore (1917–), actor
Gloria De Haven (1925–), actress
Olivia de Havilland (1916–), British-born actress, sister of Joan Fontaine, A-1946, 1949
Albert Dekker (1905–68), Dutch-born actor
Dino De Laurentiis (1919), Italian producer
Alain Delon (1935–), French actor
Dolores Del Rio (1905–83), Mexican actress
Dom DeLuise (1933–), actor and comedian
William Demarest (1892–), actor
Agnes De Mille (1909–), choreographer, T
Cecil B. De Mille (1881–1959), director
Carol Dempster (1902–), actress
Catherine Deneuve (1943–), French actress
Robert De Niro (1943–), actor, A-1974, 1980
Richard Denning (1914–), actor
Sandy Dennis (1937–), actress, A-1966
Bob Denver (1935–), comedian
John Denver (Henry John Deutchendorf Jr.; 1943–), singer
Bo Derek (Mary Cathleen Collins; 1957–), actress
John Derek (Derek Harris; 1926–), actor
Bruce Dern (1936–), actor
Vittorio De Sica (1902–74), Italian actor and director
William Devane (1937–), actor
Andy Devine (1905–77), actor and comedian
Colleen Dewhurst (1926–), Canadian-born actress, T
Brandon de Wilde (1942–72), child actor
Susan Dey (1952–), actress
Neil Diamond (1941–), singer and songwriter
Angie Dickinson (Angeline Brown; 1931–), actress
Bo Diddley (1928–), singer and musician
Marlene Dietrich (Maria von Losch; 1902–), German-born actress
Dudley Digges (1879–1947), Irish actor, T
Phyllis Diller (Phyllis Driver; 1917–), comedienne
Bradford Dillman (1930–), actor
Walt Disney (1901–66), cartoonist and producer, E
Richard Dix (Ernest Brimmer; 1894–1949), actor
Fats Domino (1928–), jazz musician and composer
Phil Donahue (1935–), television personality
Troy Donahue (Merle Johnson; 1937–), actor
James Donald (1917–), British actor
Peter Donald (1918–), actor
Robert Donat (1905–58), British actor, A-1939
Brian Donlevy (1899–1972), Irish-born actor
Diana Dors (Diana Fluk; 1931–), British actress
Jimmy Dorsey (1904–57), bandleader, brother of Tommy
Tommy Dorsey (1905–56), trombonist and bandleader
Kirk Douglas (Issur Demsky; 1916–), actor
Melvyn Douglas (Melvyn Hesselburg; 1901–81), actor, A-1963, 1979
Michael Douglas (1945–), actor, producer, son of Kirk
Mike Douglas (Michael D. Dowd Jr.; 1925–), television personality
Paul Douglas (1907–59), actor
Morton Downey (1902–), bandleader and singer
Hugh Downs (1921–), television personality
Alfred Drake (Alfredo Capurro; 1914–), Italian-born singer and actor, T
Marie Dressler (Leila Koeber; 1869–1934), actress, A-1930–31, T
John Drew (1853–1927), actor, T, uncle of Barrymores
Richard Dreyfuss (1949–), actor, A-1977
James Drury (1934–), actor
Eddy Duchin (1905–51), musician
Peter Duchin (1937–), musician
Howard Duff (1917–), actor
Patty Duke (1946–), actress, A-1962; wed to John Astin
Keir Dullea (1939–), actor
Faye Dunaway (1941–), actress, A-1976
Isadora Duncan (1877–1927), dancer
Sandy Duncan (1946–), actress
James Dunn (1905–67), actor, A-1945
Michael Dunn (Gary Neil Miller; 1934–73), dwarf actor
Irene Dunne (1904–), actress
Mildred Dunnock (1900–), actress, T
Jimmy Durante (1893–1980), comedian
Deanna Durbin (1922–), Canadian actress, singer, A-1938
Dan Duryea (1907–68), actor
Eleanora Duse (1858–1924), Italian actress, T
Bob Dylan (Robert Zimmerman; 1941–), folk singer, composer
Jeanne Eagels (1894–1929), actress, T
Clint Eastwood (1930–), actor
Shirley Eaton (1936–), British actress
Buddy Ebsen (Christian Rudolph Ebsen; 1908–), comedian, actor
Billy Eckstine (1914–), singer
Duane Eddy (1938–), rock musician
Nelson Eddy (1901–67), singer and actor
Barbara Eden (Barbara Huffman; 1934–), actress
Ralph Edwards (1913–), entertainer
Vince Edwards (1928–), actor
Richard Egan (1921–), actor
Samantha Eggar (1940–), British actress
Sergei Eisenstein (1898–1948), Russian film director
Anita Ekberg (1931–), Swedish actress
Britt Ekland (1942–), Swedish actress
Florence Eldridge (Florence McKechnie; 1901–), actress, wed to Fredric March, T
Yvonne Elliman (1953–), rock singer
Duke Ellington (Edward Kennedy Ellington; 1899–1974), bandleader and composer, E
Leif Erickson (1914–), actor
Stuart Erwin (1903–67), comedian
Ruth Etting (1898–1978), dancer and singer
Dale Evans (Frances Butts; 1912–), singer, actress, wed to Roy Rogers
Dame Edith Evans (1888–1976), British actress
Maurice Evans (1901–), Welsh actor, T
Chad Everett (Raymond Cramton; 1937–), actor
Everly Brothers: Don (1937–) and Phil (1939–), country music singers
Tom Ewell (S. Yewell Tompkins; 1909–), comic actor
Fabian (Fabian Forte; 1942–), singer
Nanette Fabray (Nanette Fabares;1922–), actress
Douglas Fairbanks (Julius Ullman; 1883–1939), actor, husband of Mary Pickford.
Douglas Fairbanks Jr. (1909–), actor and producer
Percy Faith (1908–76), orchestra conductor
Peter Falk (1927–), actor
Barry Farber (1930–), radio personality
James Farentino (1938–), actor
Donna Fargo (1945–), country music singer
Felicia Farr (1932–), actress
Geraldine Farrar (1882–1967), opera singer and actress
Charles Farrell (1901–), actor
Glenda Farrell (1904–71), actress
Mia Farrow (1945–), actress, daughter of Maureen O'Sullivan
Farrah Fawcett-Majors (1947–), actress
Alice Faye (Alice Leppert; 1915–), singer, actress, wed to Phil Harris
Marty Feldman (1933–82), British comic actor
Barbara Feldon (1941–), actress
Jose Feliciano (1945–), singer
Federico Fellini (1920–), Italian writer and director
Edith Fellows (1923–), actress
Fernandel (1903–71), French comedian
José Ferrer (1912–), actor and director, A-1950, T
Mel Ferrer (1917–), actor and director
Stepin Fetchit (Lincoln Perry; 1902–), comedian
Betty Field (1918–73), actress
Sally Field (1946–), actress, A-1979
Dorothy Fields (1905–74), lyricist
Gracie Fields (Grace Stansfield; 1898–1979), British singer and comedienne
Totie Fields (1931–78), comedienne
W. C. Fields (William Dukinfield; 1879–1946), comedian and actor, T
Peter Finch (William Mitchell; 1916–77), Australian actor, A-1976
Albert Finney (1936–), British actor
Carrie Fisher (1956–), actress, daughter of Eddie Fisher and Debbie Reynolds
Eddie Fisher (1928–), singer
Minnie Maddern Fiske (1865–1932), actress, T
Clyde Fitch (1865–1932), playwright, T
Barry Fitzgerald (William Shields; 1888–1961), Irish actor, A-1944

Ella Fitzgerald (1918–), singer
Geraldine Fitzgerald (1912–), actress
Roberta Flack (1939–), rock singer
Lester Flatt (1914–79), bluegrass musician
Peggy Fleming (1948–), Olympic ice skater
Rhonda Fleming (Marilyn Louis; 1923–), actress
Victor Fleming (1883–1949), director, A-1939
Louise Fletcher (1935–), actress, A-1975
Errol Flynn (1909–59), actor
Nina Foch (1924–), actress
Dan Fogelberg (1951–), rock singer
Red Foley (1910–68), country music singer
Henry Fonda (1905–82), actor, T, A-1981
Jane Fonda (1937–), actress, A-1971, 1978
Peter Fonda (1939–), actor
Frank Fontaine (1920–78), singer and comedian
Joan Fontaine (Joan de Havilland; 1917–), British-born actress, A-1941, sister of Olivia de Havilland
Lynn Fontanne (1887–1983), actress, T, wife of Alfred Lunt
Bryan Forbes (1926–), actor, writer, and director
Glenn Ford (Gwyllyn Ford; 1916–), Canadian-born actor
Harrison Ford (1942–), actor
John Ford (Sean O'Feeney; 1895–1973), director, A-1935, 1940, 1941, 1952
Paul Ford (1901–76), actor
Tennessee Ernie Ford (1919–), country music singer
Milos Forman (1932–), Czech-born director, A-1975
Edwin Forrest (1806–72), actor, T
John Forsythe (John Freund; 1918–), actor
Bob Fosse (1927–), director, A-1972, T
Jodie Foster (1962–), actress
Preston Foster (1904–70), actor
Redd Foxx (John Sanford; 1922–), actor
Eddie Foy Jr. (1905–), actor and dancer
Peter Frampton (1950–), singer
Anthony Franciosa (Anthony Papaleo; 1928–), actor
Anne Francis (1932–), actress
Arlene Francis (1908–), television personality
Connie Francis (Constance Franconero; 1938–), singer
Kay Francis (Katherine Gibbs; 1899–1968), actress
James Franciscus (1934–), actor
Aretha Franklin (1942–), singer
William Frawley (1887–1966), actor and comedian
Bud Freeman (1906–), musician
Mona Freeman (Monica Freeman; 1926–), actress
William Friedkin (1939–), director, A-1973
Rudolf Friml (1879–1972), composer, T
Charles Frohmann (1860–1815), producer, T
Jane Froman (1911–80), singer
David Frost (1939–), television personality
David Frye (1934–), impressionist
Allen Funt (1914–), television personality
Betty Furness (1916–), television personality
Martin Gabel (1912–), actor and producer
Jean Gabin (1904–76), French actor
Clark Gable (1901–60), actor, A-1934
Eva Gabor (1926–), actress, sister of Zsa Zsa
Zsa Zsa Gabor (Sari Gabor; 1923–), Hungarian-born actress
Crystal Gayle (Brenda Gayle Webb; 1951–), singer
Rita Gam (1928–), actress
Joe Garagiola (1926–), television personality
Greta Garbo (Greta Gustafson; 1905–), Swedish actress
Ava Gardner (Lucy Johnson; 1922–), actress
John Garfield (Julius Garfinkle; 1913–52), actor
Art Garfunkel (1941–), singer and composer
William Gargan (1905–79), actor
Judy Garland (Frances Gumm; 1922–69), singer and actress, E, A-1939, mother of Liza Minnelli
Erroll Garner (1923–77), pianist, composer
James Garner (James Baumgarner; 1928–), actor
Peggy Ann Garner (1931–), child star in 1940s, A-1945
Leif Garrett (1961–), actor, singer
Dave Garroway (1913–82), entertainer
Greer Garson (1908–), Irish-born actress, A-1942
John Gary (1932–), singer
Vittorio Gassman (1922–), Italian actor
Larry Gatlin (1949–), country music singer
John Gavin (1935–), actor
William Gaxton (1894–1963), actor
Marvin Gaye (1939–), singer and songwriter
Gloria Gaynor (1949–), singer
Janet Gaynor (Laura Gainer; 1906–), actress, A-1927-28
Mitzi Gaynor (Francesca Mitzi von Gerber; 1930–), actress and singer
Ben Gazzara (Biago Anthony Gazzara; 1931–), actor
Will Geer (1902–78), actor
Judy Geeson (1950–), British actress
Leo Genn (1905–), British actor
Bobbie Gentry (Roberta Streeter; 1944–), singer
Grace George (1879–1961), actress, T
Richard Gere (1950–), actor
Ira Gershwin (1896–1983), lyricist, T, brother of George
Stan Getz (1927–), saxophonist
Andy Gibb (1958–), singer
Georgia Gibbs (1926–), singer
Hoot Gibson (1892–1962), cowboy actor
Mel Gibson (1956–), actor
Sir John Gielgud (1904–), British actor, T, A-1981
Billy Gilbert (1894–1971), actor and musician
John Gilbert (1897–1936), actor
Jack Gilford (1907–), actor
Dizzy Gillespie (John Birks Gillespie; 1917–), jazz trumpeter, developed bop
William Gillette (1855–1937), actor, T
Hermione Gingold (1897–), British comedienne
Dorothy Gish (1898–1968), actress, sister of Lillian
Lillian Gish (Lillian de Guiche; 1896–), actress, T
George Givot (1903–), actor
Jackie Gleason (1916–), comedian, actor
James Gleason (1886–1959), actor
George Gobel (1920–), comedian
Jean Luc Godard (1930–), French film director
Paulette Goddard (Marion Levy; 1911–), actress
Arthur Godfrey (1903–83), radio and TV personality
John Golden (1874–1955), playwright and producer, T
Bobby Goldsboro (1942–), country music singer
Sam Goldwyn (Samuel Goldfish; 1882–1974), director, producer, A-1946
Benny Goodman (1909–), jazz clarinetist, bandleader
Dody Goodman (1929–), actress
Ruth Gordon (1896–), actress, playwright, A-1968, T
Lesley Gore (1946–), actress
Eydie Gormé (1935–), singer, wed to Steve Lawrence
Frank Gorshin (1932–), actor
Marjoe Gortner (1945–), actor
Freeman Gosden (1899–1982), radio actor, "Amos"
Louis Gossett Jr. (1937–), actor, A-1982
Elliott Gould (Elliott Goldstein; 1938–), actor
Morton Gould (1913–), composer
Robert Goulet (1933–), Canadian singer
Betty Grable (1916–73), actress
Martha Graham (1894–), dancer
Gloria Grahame (Gloria Hallward; 1924–81), actress, A-1952
Farley Granger (1925–), actor
Stewart Granger (James Stewart; 1913–), British actor
Cary Grant (Archibald Leach; 1904–), British-born actor
Kathryn Grant (1933–), actress
Lee Grant (Lyova Rosenthal; 1929–), actress, A-1975
Bonita Granville (1923–), actress and producer
Ben Grauer (1908–77), radio and television announcer
Peter Graves (Peter Aurness; 1925–), actor, brother of James Arness
Kathryn Grayson (1922–), actress and singer
Buddy Greco (1926–), singer
José Greco (1918–), Italian-born dancer
Adolph Green (1915–), actor and lyricist, T
Al Green (1946–), country music singer
Lorne Greene (1915–), Canadian-born actor
Sidney Greenstreet (1879–1954), British-born actor
Charlotte Greenwood (1893–78), comedienne, dancer, T
Joan Greenwood (1921–), British actress and director
Dick Gregory (1932–), comedian
Joyce Grenfell (Joyce Phipps; 1910–79), British actress
Joel Grey (Joel Katz; 1932–), actor, A-1972
Merv Griffin (1925–), television entertainer
Andy Griffith (1926–), actor
D.W. Griffith (1875–1948), 1st major U.S. film director, E
Hugh Griffith (1912–80), Welsh actor, A-1959
Tammy Grimes (1934–), actress
Harry Guardino (1925–), actor
Sir Alec Guinness (1914–), British actor, A-1957
Sacha Guitry (1885–1957), French writer-director
Arlo Guthrie (1947–), singer and actor
Sir Tyrone Guthrie (1900–71), British director, T
Woody Guthrie (1912–67), folk singer and composer
Edmund Gwenn (1875–1959), British actor, A-1947
Fred Gwynne (1924–), actor
Buddy Hackett (Leonard Hacker; 1924–), comedian
Joan Hackett (1934–83), actress
Gene Hackman (1930–), actor, A-1971
Uta Hagen (1919–), actress
Merle Haggard (1937–), country music singer
Larry Hagman (1930–), actor, son of Mary Martin
Alan Hale (Rufus Alan McKahan; 1892–1950), actor

SHOW BUSINESS PERSONALITIES *(continued)*

Alan Hale Jr. (1918–), actor, son of Alan
Bill Haley (1925–81), singer and songwriter, said to have coined phrase "rock and roll"
Jack Haley (1902–79), comedian
Monty Hall (1923–), television personality
George Hamilton (1939–), actor
Marvin Hamlisch (1945–), composer and pianist
Oscar Hammerstein II (1895–1960), composer, T
Walter Hampden (1879–1955), actor, T
Susan Hampshire (1941–), actress
Lionel Hampton (1914–), jazz pianist, combo leader
W. C. Handy (1873–1958), blues composer
Otto Harbach (1873–1963), playwright, librettist, T
Ann Harding (1902–81), actress
Sir Cedric Hardwicke (1893–1964), British actor
Oliver Hardy (1892–1957), comedian with Stan Laurel
Earl of Harewood (1923–), British impresario
Jean ("platinum blonde") Harlow (Harlean Carpenter; 1911–37), actress
Valerie Harper (1940–), actress
Barbara Harris (1937–), actress
Emmylou Harris (1949–), country music singer
Julie Harris (1925–), actress, T
Phil Harris (1906–), actor and comedian
Richard Harris (1933–), Irish actor
Rosemary Harris (1930–), British actress
Sam H. Harris (1872–1941), producer, T
George Harrison (1943–), singer, musician (Beatles)
Rex Harrison (Reginald Carey; 1908–), British actor, A-1964, T
Lorenz Hart (1895–1943), lyricist, T
William S. Hart (1870–1946), silent-screen cowboy star
David Hartman (1935–), television personality
Elizabeth Hartman (1945–), actress
Laurence Harvey (1928–73), Lithuanian-born actor
Signe Hasso (1910–), Swedish actress
Hurd Hatfield (1918–), actor
Donny Hathaway (1945–72), singer
Henry Hathaway (1898–), director
June Haver (1926–), actress, wife of Fred MacMurray
June Havoc (June Hovick; 1916–), actress, sister of Gypsy Rose Lee
Jack Hawkins (1910–73), British actor
Howard Hawks (1896–77), director, A-1975
Goldie Hawn (1945–), comedienne, A-1969
Jill Haworth (1946–), British actress
Sessue Hayakawa (1890–1973), Japanese actor
Sterling Hayden (1916–), actor
Helen Hayes (Helen Brown; 1901–), actress, A-1931–32, 1970, T
Isaac Hayes (1942–), composer
Leland Hayward (1902–71), producer
Louis Hayward (1909–), South African-born actor
Susan Hayward (Edythe Marriner; 1919–75), actress, A-1958
Rita Hayworth (Marguerite Cansino; 1918–), actress
Edith Head (1907–81), costume designer, A-1949, 1951, 1952, 1973
Joey Heatherton (1944–), actress
Eileen Heckart (1919–), actress
Van Heflin (Emmet Evan Heflin; 1910–71), actor, A-1942, 1972
Lillian Hellman (1905–), playwright, T
David Hemmings (1942–), British actor
Florence Henderson (1934–), singer and actress
Skitch Henderson (Lyle Russell Cedric; 1918–), musician
Jimi Hendrix (1943–70), singer
Sonja Henie (1913–69), Norwegian ice skater and actress
Paul Henreid (1907–), Austrian-born actor
Audrey Hepburn (1929–), Belgian-born actress, A-1953
Katharine Hepburn (1909–), actress, A-1932–33, 1967, 1968, 1981, E, T
Hugh Herbert (1897–1952), comedian
Victor Herbert (1859–1924), Irish-American composer, T
Woody Herman (1913–), jazz clarinetist, bandleader
James A. Herne (1839–1901), playwright and actor, T
Jean Hersholt (1886–1956), Danish-born actor
Charlton Heston (1924–), actor, A-1959
Eddie Heywood (1926–), jazz musician
Hildegarde (1906–), singer
George Roy Hill (1922–), director, A-1973
Wendy Hiller (1912–), British actress, A-1958
Earl (Fatha) Hines (1906–83), jazz pianist
Mimi Hines (1933–), actress and singer
Pat Hingle (1924–), actor
Al Hirt (1922–), jazz musician
Alfred Hitchcock (1899–1980), British director, E
Raymond Hitchcock (1865–1929), actor, T
Don Ho (1930–), Hawaiian singer
Eddie Hodges (1947–), actor
John Hodiak (1914–55), actor
Dustin Hoffman (1937–), actor, A-1979
Hal Holbrook (1925–), actor and impersonator
William Holden (William Beedle; 1918–81), actor, A-1953
Geoffrey Holder (1930–), choreographer
Billie Holiday (1915–59), blues singer
Judy Holliday (Judith Tuvim; 1923–65), actress, A-1950
Earl Holliman (Anthony Numkena; 1928–), actor
Stanley Holloway (1890–1982), British actor
Buddy Holly (1936–59), country and rock singer
Celeste Holm (1919–), actress, A-1947
Jack Holt (1888–1951), actor
Tim Holt (1918–73), actor, son of Jack
Oscar Homolka (1901–78), Austrian-born actor
Bob Hope (Leslie Townes Hope; 1903–), comedian, E, A-1940, 1944, 1952 (honorary awards)
Mary Hopkin (1950–), singer
Arthur Hopkins (1878–1950), producer, T
Miriam Hopkins (1902–72), actress
Dennis Hopper (1936–), actor
De Wolf Hopper (1858–1935), actor, T
Hedda Hopper (1890–1966), columnist, wife of De Wolf
William Hopper (1915–70), actor, son of Hedda
Lena Horne (1918–), singer and actress
Edward Everett Horton (1888–1970), actor
Harry Houdini (Ehrich Weiss; 1874–1926), magician
John Houseman (Jacques Haussmann; 1902–), actor, producer, T, A-1973
Eugene Howard (1881–1965), vaudevillian, T
Joe Howard (1867–1961), vaudevillian
Ken Howard (1944–), actor
Leslie Howard (Leslie Stainer; 1893–1943), British actor, T
Ron Howard (1954–), actor
Trevor Howard (1916–), British actor
Willie Howard (1886–1949), vaudevillian, T
Sally Ann Howes (1934–), actress and singer
Rock Hudson (Roy Fitzgerald; 1925–), actor
Howard Hughes (1905–76), movie producer, director
Henry Hull (1890–1977), actor, T
Josephine Hull (1886–1957), actress, A-1950
Engelbert Humperdinck (Arnold Dorsey; 1937–), singer
Marsha Hunt (1917–), actress
Kim Hunter (Janet Cole; 1922–), actress, A-1951
Tab Hunter (Art Gelian; 1931–), actor
Chet Huntley (1911–74), newscaster
Sol Hurok (1888–1974), impresario
Olivia Hussey (1952–), actress
Ruth Hussey (Ruth Carol O'Rourke; 1917–), actress
John Huston (1906–), writer, director, actor, A-1948
Walter Huston (Walter Houghston; 1884–1950), actor, T, A-1948, father of John
Betty Hutton (Betty Thornburg; 1921–), actress
Lauren Hutton (Mary Hutton; 1944–), actress
Tim Hutton (1960–), actor, A-1980
Janis Ian (1951–), singer
Marty Ingels (1936–), comedian
John Ireland (1915–), Canadian actor
José Iturbi (1895–1980), Spanish-born musician
Burl Ives (Burl Iele Ivanhoe; 1909–), actor and folk singer, A-1958
Anne Jackson (1925–), actress, wife of Eli Wallach
Glenda Jackson (1936–), British actress, A-1970, 1973
Kate Jackson (1949–), actress
Mahalia Jackson (1911–72), spiritual singer
Michael Jackson (1958–), rock singer
Sam Jaffe (1891–), actor
Dean Jagger (1903–), actor, A-1949
Mick Jagger (1944–), musician
Dennis James (1917–), television personality
Harry James (1916–83), musician and bandleader
Joni James (1930–), singer
Elsie Janis (1889–1956), musical-comedy star, T
Emil Jannings (1886–1950), German actor, A-1927–28
David Janssen (David Meyer; 1930–80), actor
Renée Jeanmaire (1924–), French dancer and actress
Joseph Jefferson (1829–1905), actor, T
Waylon Jennings (1933–), country music singer
George E. Jessel (1898–1981), entertainer
Billy Joel (1949–), rock singer
Elton John (Reginald Dwight; 1947–), rock singer
Glynis Johns (1923–), South African-born actress
Ben Johnson (1920–), actor, A-1971
Celia Johnson (1908–82), British actress
Chic Johnson (1892–1962), comedian with Ole Olsen
Rafer Johnson (1935–), actor, Olympic athlete

Van Johnson (1916–), actor
Al Jolson (Asa Yoelson; 1880–1950), singer, starred in first talking picture, T
Allan Jones (1907–), singer, actor
Buck Jones (1889–1942), cowboy actor
Carolyn Jones (1929–83), singer and actress
Dean Jones (1935–), actor
Jack Jones (1938–), singer
James Earl Jones (1931–), actor
Jennifer Jones (Phyllis Isley; 1919–), actress, A-1943
Robert E. Jones (1887–1954), designer and director, T
Shirley Jones (1934–), actress and singer, A-1960
Spike Jones (Lindley Armstrong Jones; 1911–65), musician and comedian
Tom Jones (Thomas Jones Woodward; 1940–), rock singer
Janis Joplin (1943–70), singer
Scott Joplin (1868–1917), ragtime composer
Victor Jory (1902–82), actor
Louis Jourdan (Louis Gendre; 1919–), French actor
Curt Jurgens (1915–82), German actor
Madeline Kahn (1942–), actress
Ida Kaminska (1899–1980), Polish-born actress
Garson Kanin (1912–), playwright
Gabriel Kaplan (1945–), comedian
Boris Karloff (William Pratt; 1885–1969), British-born actor
Danny Kaye (David Kaminsky; 1913–), comedian and actor, A-1954
Sammy Kaye (1910–), musician and bandleader
Elia Kazan (1909–), Turkish-born director and writer, T, A-1947, 1954
Lainie Kazan (1940–), singer
Stacy Keach (1941–), actor
Buster Keaton (Joseph Francis Keaton; 1895–1966), comedian and actor, A-1959
Diane Keaton (1949–), actress, A-1977
Lila Kedrova (1918–), Russian-French actress, A-1964
Howard Keel (1919–), actor and singer
Ruby Keeler (Ethel Keeler; 1909–), actress
Laura Keene (1820–73), actress and theater manager, T
Bob Keeshan (1927–), TV personality *(Captain Kangaroo)*
Harvey Keitel (1941–), actor
Brian Keith (1921–), actor
Cecil Kellaway (1893–1973), South African-born actor
Marthe Keller (1946–), actress
Sally Kellerman (1937–), actress
Emmett Kelly (1898–79), clown
Gene Kelly (1912–), dancer and actor, A-1951
Grace Kelly (1928–82), actress, A-1954
Patsy Kelly (1910–81), comedienne
Eddie Kendricks (1940–), singer
Arthur Kennedy (1914–), actor
George Kennedy (1925–), actor, A-1967
Stan Kenton (Stanley Newcomb; 1912–79), jazz pianist and bandleader
Jerome Kern (1885–1945), composer, T
Deborah Kerr (1921–), British actress
Larry Kert (1930–), actor, singer
Evelyn Keyes (1919–), actress
Richard Kiley (1922–), actor and singer
Alan King (Irwin Alan Kniberg; 1927–), comedian
B.B. King (1925–), blues singer
Carole King (1941–), singer and composer
Dennis King (1897–1971), British-born actor
Ben Kingsley (1943–), actor, A-1982
Sidney Kingsley (1906–), playwright, T
Lisa Kirk (1925–), actress and singer
Phyllis Kirk (Phyllis Kirkegaard; 1930–), actress
Dorothy Kirsten (1919–), singer
Eartha Kitt (1928–), singer
Werner Klemperer (1920–), German-born actor
Robert Klein (1942–), comedian
Jack Klugman (1922–), actor
Evel Knievel (Robert Craig, 1938–), daredevil motorcyclist
Gladys Knight (1944–), rock singer
Shirley Knight (1937–), actress, T
Don Knotts (1924–), actor
Sir Alexander Korda (1893–1956), Hungarian-British movie producer
Harvey Korman (1927–), actor
Ernie Kovacs (1919–62), comedian and comic actor
Stanley Kramer (1913–), director
Kris Kristofferson (1936–), actor and singer
Gene Krupa (1909–73), jazz drummer
Stanley Kubrick (1928–), producer and director
Akira Kurosawa (1910–), Japanese director
Kay Kyser (1905–), musician and bandleader
Alan Ladd (1913–64), actor
Bert Lahr (Irving Lahrheim; 1895–1967), comedian, T
Frankie Laine (Frank Paul Lo Vecchio; 1913–), singer
Veronica Lake (Constance Ockleman; 1919–73), actress
Hedy Lamarr (Hedwig Kiesler; 1915–), Austrian-born actress
Fernando Lamas (1915–82), Argentinian actor
Dorothy Lamour (Dorothy Kaumeyer; 1914–), actress
Burt Lancaster (1913–), actor, A-1960
Elsa Lanchester (Elizabeth Sullivan; 1902–), British actress
Martin Landau (1933–), actor
Michael Landon (Michael Orowitz; 1937–), actor and director
Fritz Lang (1890–1976), Austrian-born director
Walter Lang (1898–1972), director
Harry Langdon (1884–1944), comedian
Hope Lange (1931–), actress
Jessica Lange (1949–), actress, A-1982
Frank Langella (1940–), actor
Francis Langford (1914–), singer
Lily Langtry (Emily Charlotte Le Breton; 1856–1929), British actress, T
Angela Lansbury (1925–), British-born actress, T
Robert Lansing (Robert H. Broom; 1929–), actor
Mario Lanza (Alfredo Cocozza; 1921–59), singer and actor
Julius La Rosa (1930–), singer
Jesse L. Lasky (1880–1958), producer
Louise Lasser (1940–), actress
Sir Harry Lauder (Harry MacLennan; 1870–1950), Scottish comedian
Charles Laughton (1889–1962), British-American actor, A-1932–33, wed to Elsa Lanchester
Stan Laurel (Arthur Jefferson; 1890–1965), British-born comedian, teamed with Oliver Hardy
Piper Laurie (Rosetta Jacobs; 1932–), actress
Peter Lawford (1923–), British-born actor
Carol Lawrence (Carol Maria Laraia; 1935–), dancer and actress
Gertrude Lawrence (Gertrude Klasen; 1898–1952), British actress, singer, T
Steve Lawrence (Steve Liebowitz; 1935–), singer, wed to Eydie Gormé
Vicki Lawrence (1949–), actress, singer
Cloris Leachman (1926–), actress, A-1971
David Lean (1908–), British director, A-1957, 1962
Huddie "Lead Belly" Ledbetter (1888–1949), folk singer
Brenda Lee (1944–), singer
Canada Lee (1907–1952), actor
Christopher Lee (1922–), British actor
Gypsy Rose Lee (Louise Hovick; 1914–70), dancer, sister of June Havoc
Peggy Lee (Norma Egstrom; 1920–), singer
Eva Le Gallienne (1899–), British-born actress, T
Janet Leigh (Jeanette Morrison; 1927–), actress
Vivien Leigh (Vivien Hartley; 1913–67), British actress, A-1939, 1951
Margaret Leighton (1922–76), British actress
Jack Lemmon (1925–), actor, A-1955, 1973
John Lennon (1940–80), British rock-and-roll singer, musician (Beatles)
Lennon Sisters: Dianne (1939–), Janet (1946–), Kathy (1943–), Peggy (1941–), singing group
Lotte Lenya (Caroline Blamauer; 1898–1981), Austrian-born actress and singer
Jack E. Leonard (1911–73), comedian
Sheldon Leonard (Sheldon Bershad; 1907–), actor and director
Alan Jay Lerner (1918–), librettist and lyricist
Mervyn LeRoy (1900–), actor and director
Joan Leslie (1925–), actress
Jerry Lester (1911–), comedian
Oscar Levant (1906–72), musician and comedian
Sam Levene (1906–80), actor
Sam Levenson (1911–80), humorist
Joseph E. Levine (1905–), producer
Jerry Lewis (Joseph Levitch; 1926–), comedian, teamed with Dean Martin
Jerry Lee Lewis (1935–), country music artist
Joe E. Lewis (1902–71), comedian
Shari Lewis (Shari Hurwitz; 1934–), puppeteer
Ted Lewis (1891–1971), musician and vaudevillian
Wladziu Valentino Liberace (1920–), pianist
Beatrice Lillie (Constance Sylvia Munston; 1898–), British comedienne, T
Elmo Lincoln (Otto Elmo Linkenhelter; 1889–1952), actor, first film Tarzan
Jenny Lind (1820–87), Swedish singer

SHOW BUSINESS PERSONALITIES *(continued)*
Hal Linden (Harold Lipshitz; 1931–), actor
Viveca Lindfors (1920–), Swedish-born actress
Pia Lindstrom (1938–), newscaster, daughter of Ingrid Bergman
Art Linkletter (1912–), entertainer
Virna Lisi (1937–), Italian actress
Cleavon Little (1939–), actor
Rich Little (1938–), Canadian-born comedian
Jay Livingston (1915–), composer
Mary Livingstone (1909–), comedienne, wed to Jack Benny
Frank Lloyd (1888–1960), Scottish-born director, A-1928–29, 1932–33
Harold Lloyd (1893–1971), comedian, A-1952
Gene Lockhart (1891–1957), Canadian actor
June Lockhart (1925–), actress, daughter of Gene
Margaret Lockwood (Margaret Day; 1916–), British actress
Frank Loesser (1910–69), songwriter
Ella Logan (1913–69), singer and actress
Joshua Logan (1908–), director and producer, T
Kenny Loggins (1948–), rock musician
Gina Lollobrigida (1928–), Italian actress
Carole Lombard (Jane Peters; 1908–42), actress, wed to Clark Gable
Guy Lombardo (1902–77), musician and bandleader
Julie London (Julie Peck; 1926–), singer and actress
Trini Lopez (1937–), singer
Jack Lord (1930–), actor
Pauline Lord (1890–1950), actress, T
Sophia Loren (Sophia Scicoloni; 1934–), Italian actress, A-1961
Peter Lorre (Laszlo Löewenstein; 1904–64), Hungarian-born actor
Dorothy Loudon (1932–), actress
Anita Louise (1915–70), actress
Tina Louise (1935–), actress
Bessie Love (1898–), actress
Frank Lovejoy (1912–62), actor
Edmund Lowe (1892–1971), actor
Myrna Loy (Myrna Williams; 1905–), actress
Ernst Lubitsch (1892–1947), German-born producer
Bela Lugosi (Arisztid Olt, 1888–1956), Hungarian-born actor
Paul Lukas (1895–1971), Hungarian-born actor, A-1943
Sidney Lumet (1924–), director
William Lundigan (1914–75), actor
Alfred Lunt (1893–1977), actor, wed to Lynn Fontanne, T
Ida Lupino (1918–), actress and director
Paul Lynde (1927–82), comedian
Carol Lynley (1942–), actress
Diana Lynn (1924–71), actress
Jeffrey Lynn (1909–), actor
Loretta Lynn (1932–), country music singer
Ben Lyon (1901–79), actor, husband of Bebe Daniels
James MacArthur (1937–), actor, son of Helen Hayes
Jeanette MacDonald (1907–65), singer and actress
Jack MacGouran (1918–73), Irish actor
Ali MacGraw (1938–), actress
Ted Mack (1904–76), television personality
Gisele MacKenzie (Marie LaFeche; 1927–), singer
Shirley MacLaine (Shirley Beaty; 1934–), actress, sister of Warren Beatty
Barton MacLane (1900–69), actor
Fred MacMurray (1908–), actor
Patrick MacNee (1922–), British actor
Gordon MacRae (1921–), singer and actor
Sheila MacRae (1924–), comedienne
George Macready (1909–73), actor
Bill Macy (1922–), actor
Donald Madden (1933–83), actor
Guy Madison (Robert Moseley; 1922–), actor
Patrick Magee (1924–), British actor
Anna Magnani (1908–73), Italian actress, A-1955
Marjorie Main (1890–1975), actress
Lee Majors (1940–), television actor
Miriam Makeba (1932–), singer
Karl Malden (Mladen Sekulovich; 1914–), actor, A-1951
Dorothy Malone (Dorothy Maloney; 1925–), actress, A-1956
Rouben Mamoulian (1897–), Russian-born director, T
Melissa Manchester (1951–), singer
Henry Mancini (1922–), musician and composer
Barry Manilow (1946–), singer and composer
Joseph L. Mankiewicz (1909–), director, writer, and producer, A-1949, 1950
Delbert Mann (1920–), director, A-1955
Jayne Mansfield (Vera Jane Palmer; 1933–67), actress
Richard Mansfield (1857–1907), German-Amer. actor, T
Robert B. Mantell (1854–1928), actor, T
Marcel Marceau (1923–), French pantomimist
Fredric March (Frederick Bickel; 1897–1975), actor, **A-1931–32, 1946, T**
Julia Marlowe (Sarah Frances Frost; 1865–1950), Shakespearean actress, T
Jean Marsh (1934–), actress
E. G. Marshall (1910–), actor
Herbert Marshall (1890–1966), British actor
Penny Marshall (1942–), actress
Dean Martin (Dino Crocetti; 1917–), singer and actor, teamed with Jerry Lewis
Dick Martin (1922–), television comedian
Mary Martin (1913–), singer and actress, T
Ross Martin (1920–81), actor
Steve Martin (1945–), comedian
Tony Martin (Alvin Morris; 1913–), singer
Al Martino (1927–), singer
Lee Marvin (1924–), actor, A-1965
Marx Brothers: Chico (1886–1961), Harpo (1888–1964), Groucho (1890–1977), Gummo (1897–1977), Zeppo (1901–1979), comedy team
James Mason (1909–), British actor
Marsha Mason (1942–), actress
Raymond Massey (1896–1983), Canadian-born actor
Marcello Mastroianni (1924–), Italian actor
Johnny Mathis (1935–), singer
Walter Matthau (Walter Matasschanskayasky; 1920–), actor, A-1966
Victor Mature (1916–), actor
Marilyn Maxwell (Marvel Maxwell; 1922–72), actress
Elaine May (1932–), comedienne and writer
Louis B. Mayer (1885–1957), producer, A-1950
Curtis Mayfield (1942–), singer and songwriter
Virginia Mayo (Virginia Jones; 1922–), actress
Andrea McArdle (1964–), actress and singer
Mary Margaret McBride (1899–1976), radio personality
David McCallum (1933–), Scottish-born actor
Mercedes McCambridge (1918–), actress, A-1949
Leo McCarey (1898–1969), director, A-1937, 1944
Kevin McCarthy (1914–), actor
Paul McCartney (1942–), British singer (Beatles)
Doug McClure (1935–), actor
Marilyn McCoo (1943–), singer
Patty McCormack (1945–), actress
Myron McCormick (1907–62), actor
Tim McCoy (1891–1978), cowboy actor
Joel McCrea (1905–), actor
Hattie McDaniel (1895–1952), actress, A-1939
Marie McDonald (1924–65), comedienne
Roddy McDowall (1928–), British-born actor
Darren McGavin (1925–), actor
Fibber McGee (1896–), comedian
Molly McGee (1898–1961), comedienne
Patrick McGoohan (1928–), actor
Maureen McGovern (1949–), folk singer
Dorothy McGuire (1919–), actress
Frank McHugh (1899–1981), actor
Siobhan McKenna (1923–), Irish actress
Rod McKuen (1933–), singer and composer
Victor McLaglen (1883–1959), British-born actor, A-1935
Ed McMahon (1923–), actor and television personality
Kristy McNichol (1963–), actress
Steve McQueen (1932–80), actor
Audrey Meadows (1929–), actress
Jayne Meadows (1926–), actress
Anne Meara (1929–), comedienne
Donald Meek (1880–1946), Scottish-born actor
Ralph Meeker (Ralph Rathgeber; 1920–), actor
Melanie (1947–), singer
Sergio Mendes (1941–), jazz musician
Adolphe Menjou (1890–1963), actor
Helen Menken (1901–66), actress, T
Johnny Mercer (1909–76), popular-music composer
Melina Mercouri (1915–), Greek actress
Burgess Meredith (George Burgess; 1909–), actor, T
Una Merkel (1903–), actress
Ethel Merman (Ethel Zimmerman; 1908–), singer and actress, T
David Merrick (1911–), stage producer, T
Dina Merrill (Nedenia Rumbough; 1925–), actress
Gary Merrill (1914–), actor
Bette Midler (1945–), singer and comedienne
Jo Mielziner (1901–76), scenic designer, T
Toshiro Mifune (1920–), Japanese actor
Sarah Miles (1941–), British actress

Sylvia Miles (1932–), actress
Vera Miles (Vera Ralston; 1929–), actress
Lewis Milestone (1895–1980), director, A-1927–28, 1929–30
Ray Milland (Reginald Truscott-Jones; 1905–), actor, A-1945
Ann Miller (Lucy Collier; 1919–), dancer
Glenn Miller (1909–44), jazz trombonist and bandleader
Henry Miller (1860–1926), actor and theater manager, T
Marilyn Miller (Mary Reynolds; 1898–1936), actress, T
Mitch Miller (1911–), musician
Roger Miller (1936–), country music singer
Steve Miller (1943–), rock guitarist
Hayley Mills (1946–), actress, daughter of John
John Mills (1908–), British actor, A-1970
Juliet Mills (1941–), actress, daughter of John
Mills Brothers: Herbert (1912–), Harry (1913–82), Donald (1915–), singing group.
Martin Milner (1927–), actor
Yvette Mimieux (1942–), actress
Sal Mineo (1939–76), actor
Liza Minnelli (1945–), singer and actress, A-1972, daughter of Judy Garland and Vincente Minnelli
Vincente Minnelli (1913–), director, A-1958
Carmen Miranda (1914–55), Portuguese-born singer
Cameron Mitchell (Cameron Mizell; 1918–), actor
Joni Mitchell (1943–), folk singer
Thomas Mitchell (1898–1962), actor, A-1939
Robert Mitchum (1917–), actor
Tom Mix (1880–1940), cowboy actor
Helena Modjeska (1845–1909), Polish-American actress, T
Ferenc Molnar (1878–1952), Hungarian-born playwright, T
Thelonious Monk (1918–82), bop jazz pianist, composer
Marilyn Monroe (Norma Jean Baker; 1926–62), actress, sex symbol of 1960s
Vaughn Monroe (1911–73), musician and bandleader
Ricardo Montalban (1920–), Mexican actor
Yves Montand (Ivo Levi; 1921–), French singer, actor
Elizabeth Montgomery (1933–), actress
George Montgomery (George Letz; 1916–), actor
Robert Montgomery (1904–81), actor, father of Elizabeth
Colleen Moore (Kathleen Morrison; 1900–), actress
Garry Moore (Thomas Garrison Morfit; 1915–), television personality
Grace Moore (1902–47), operatic singer and film actress
Mary Tyler Moore (1936–), actress
Melba Moore (Beatrice Moore; 1945– , actress and singer
Roger Moore (1928–), British actor
Terry Moore (Helen Koford; 1932–), actress
Victor Moore (1876–1962), vaudeville comedian, actor, T
Agnes Moorehead (1906–74), actress
Jeanne Moreau (1928–), French actress
Rita Moreno (Rosita Dolores Alverio; 1931–), actress, A-1961
Dennis Morgan (Stanley Morner; 1910–), actor
Frank Morgan (Francis Wupperman; 1890–1949), actor
Helen Morgan (1900–41), actress and singer
Henry Morgan (1915–), comedian
Jane Morgan (Florence Currier; 1916–), singer
Michael Moriarty (1942–), actor
Robert Morley (1908–), British actor
Chester Morris (1901–70), actor
Robert Morse (1931–), actor
Jelly Roll Morton (1885–1941), jazz pianist, composer
Zero Mostel (1915–77), actor, singer, and comedian
Roger Mudd (1928–), newcaster
Maria Muldaur (1943–), folk singer
Edward Mulhare (1921–), British actor
Paul Muni (1896–1967), actor, A-1936, T
Patrice Munsel (1925–), singer
Audie Murphy (1924–71), actor, World War II hero
George Murphy (1904–), actor and dancer
Anne Murray (1947–), singer
Arthur Murray (1895–), dancer, husband of Kathryn
Don Murray (1929–), actor
Jan Murray (1917–), comedian
Kathryn Murray (1906–), dancer, wife of Arthur
Mae Murray (Marie Adrienne Koenig; 1885–1965), actress
Edward R. Murrow (1908–65), radio and TV newscaster
Jim Nabors (1933–), comedian and singer
Conrad Nagel (1897–1970), actor
J. Carrol Naish (1900–73), actor
Graham Nash (1942–), rock musician
George Jean Nathan (1882–1958), drama critic, author, T
Mildred Natwick (1908–), actress
Alla Nazimova (1879–1945), Russian-born actress, T
Patricia Neal (1926–), actress, A-1963
Pola Negri (1899–), Polish-born actress
Barry Nelson (Robert Neilson; 1920–), actor
David Nelson (1936–), actor, son of Ozzie
Harriet Hilliard Nelson (Peggy Lou Snyder; 1914–), actress, wife of Ozzie
Ozzie Nelson (1906–75), actor and bandleader
Rick Nelson (1940–), actor and singer, son of Ozzie
Willie Nelson (1933–), country music singer
Cathleen Nesbitt (1889–82), British actress
Bob Newhart (1929–), comedian
Anthony Newley (1931–), British actor and writer
Edwin Newman (1919–), news commentator
Paul Newman (1925–), actor and director
Randy Newman (1943–), singer
Julie Newmar (Julia Newmeyer; 1933–), actress
Wayne Newton (1942–), singer
Olivia Newton-John (1948–), singer
Mike Nichols (Michael Peschkowsky; 1931–), German-born comedian and director, A-1967
Red Nichols (1905–65), jazz cornetist and combo leader
Jack Nicholson (1937–), actor, A-1975
Stevie Nicks (1948–), rock singer
Leonard Nimoy (1931–), actor
David Niven (1909–83), Scottish-born actor, A-1958
Lloyd Nolan (1903–), actor
Nick Nolte (1940–), actor
Mabel Normand (Mabel Fortescue; 1894–1930), silent-movie comedienne
John Ringling North (1903–), circus owner
Sheree North (Dawn Bethel; 1933–), actress
Kim Novak (Marilyn Novak; 1933–), actress
Ramon Novarro (1899–1968), Mexican actor
Elliott Nugent (1900–80), director and writer
Rudolf Nureyev (1938–), Russian-born dancer
Jack Oakie (Lewis D. Offield; 1903–78), comedian
Annie Oakley (1860–1926), Wild West performer, T
Warren Oates (1932–82), actor
Merle Oberon (1911–79), British actress
Hugh O'Brian (Hugh Krampke; 1925–), actor
Edmond O'Brien (1915–), actor, A-1954
Margaret O'Brien (1937–), child actress, A-1944
Pat O'Brien (1899–1983), actor
Carroll O'Connor (1923–), actor
Donald O'Connor (1925–), actor and dancer
Odetta (1930–), folk singer and actress
Clifford Odets (1906–63), playwright, T
Maureen O'Hara (Maureen Fitzsimmons; 1920–), Irish-born actress
Dennis O'Keefe (1908–68), actor
Warner Oland (1880–1938), Swedish-born actor
Edna May Oliver (1883–1942), actress
Susan Oliver (1937–), actress
Lord Laurence Olivier (1907–), British actor and director, A-1944, 1948, T, E
Ole Olsen (1892–1963), vaudeville star with Chic Johnson
Ryan O'Neal (1941–), actor
Tatum O'Neal (1964–), child actress, A-1973
Eugene O'Neill (1888–1953), playwright, T, E
Jennifer O'Neill (1949–), Brazilian-born actress
Jerry Orbach (1935–), singer and actor
Roy Orbison (1936–), country music singer
Tony Orlando (1944–), singer
Donny Osmond (1957–), singer, brother of Marie
Marie Osmond (1959–), singer, sister of Donny
Maureen O'Sullivan (1911–), Irish-born actress
Peter O'Toole (1934–), Irish actor
Reginald Owen (1887–1972), British actor
Buck Owens (1929–), country music singer
Jack Paar (1918–), television personality
Al Pacino (1939–), actor
Geraldine Page (1924–), actress, T
Patti Page (Clara Anne Fowler; 1927–), singer
Janis Paige (1922–), actress
Jack Palance (Walter Palanuik; 1920–), actor
Betsy Palmer (1929–), actress
Lilli Palmer (1914–), German-born British actress
Franklin Pangborn (1894–1958), comedian
Irene Papas (1926–), Greek actress
Joseph Papp (Joseph Papirofsky; 1921–), producer
Charlie "Bird" Parker (1920–55), jazz sax musician
Eleanor Parker (1922–), singer and actress
Fess Parker (1926–), actor
Bert Parks (Bert Jacobson; 1914–), television personality
Larry Parks (1914–75), actor
Michael Parks (1938–), actor
Estelle Parsons (1927–), actress, A-1967
Dolly Parton (1946–), country music singer
Joseph Pasternak (1901–), Hungarian-born producer
Katina Paxinou (1900–73), Greek actress, A-1943
Freda Payne (1945–), singer

SHOW BUSINESS PERSONALITIES *(continued)*
John Payne (1912–), actor
Minnie Pearl (Sarah Ophelia Colley Cannon, 1912–), country music singer
Gregory Peck (1916–), actor, A-1962
Sam Peckinpah (1926–), director
Arthur Penn (1922–), director
George Peppard (1929–), actor
Anthony Perkins (1932–), actor
Osgood Perkins (1892–1937), actor, T
Valerie Perrine (1943–), actress
Bernadette Peters (1944–), actress
Jean Peters (1926–), actress
Edith Piaf (1915–63), French singer
Mary Pickford (Gladys Smith; 1893–79), Canadian-born actress, A-1928–29, 1976
Molly Picon (1898–), actress, T
Walter Pidgeon (1897–), Canadian-born actor
Zasu Pitts (1898–1963), comedienne and actress
Donald Pleasence (1919–), British actor
Suzanne Pleshette (1937–), actress
Joan Plowright (1929–), actress
Christopher Plummer (1927–), Canadian actor
Sidney Poitier (1924–), actor, A-1963
Roman Polanski (1933–), Polish director
Michael Pollard (1939–), actor
Carlo Ponti (1910–), Italian producer, wed to Sophia Loren
Cole Porter (1893–1964), composer, T, E
Tom Poston (1927–), actor
Dick Powell (1904–63), actor, director, and producer
Eleanor Powell (1912–82), dancer and actress
Jane Powell (Suzanne Burce; 1929–), dancer and singer
William Powell (1892–), actor
Tyrone Power (1913–58), actor
Stefanie Powers (Stefania Federkiewicz; 1942–), actress
Otto Preminger (1906–), Austrian-born producer
Paula Prentiss (Paula Ragusa; 1939–), actress
Elvis Presley (1935–77), singer, actor
Robert Preston (Robert Messervey; 1917–), actor
Andre Previn (1929–), composer and music arranger
Ray Price (1926–), country music singer
Vincent Price (1911–), actor
Charley Pride (1938–), country music singer
Louis Prima (1912–78), singer
Harold Prince (1928–), producer, T
Freddie Prinze (1954–77), actor
Dorothy Provine (1937–), actress
Juliet Prowse (1937–), South African-born actress
Richard Pryor (1940–), comedian
Anthony Quayle (1913–), British actor and director
Richard Quine (1920–), actor and director
Anthony Quinn (1915–), actor, A-1952, 1956
David Rabe (1940–), playwright
Deborah Raffin (1953–), actress
George Raft (George Ranft; 1895–1980), actor
Luise Rainer (1912–), Austrian actress, A-1936, 1937
Claude Rains (1889–1967), British actor
Bonnie Raitt (1950–), singer
John Raitt (1917–), singer
Marjorie Rambeau (1889–1970), actress
Sally Rand (1904–79), striptease fan dancer
Tony Randall (Leonard Rosenberg; 1920–), actor
J. Arthur Rank (1888–1972), British producer
Basil Rathbone (1892–1967), South African-born actor
Dan Rather (1931–), newscaster
Gregory Ratoff (1897–1961), Russian-born actor, director
Lou Rawls (1935–), singer
Martha Raye (Margaret Yvonne Reed; 1916–), actress
Gene Raymond (1908–), actor
Ronald Reagan (1911–), actor and politician
Harry Reasoner (1923–), newscaster
Otis Redding (1941–67), blues singer
Helen Reddy (1942–), singer
Robert Redford (1936–), actor, director, A-1980
Lynn Redgrave (1944–), British actress
Sir Michael Redgrave (1908–), British actor, father of Lynn and Vanessa
Vanessa Redgrave (1937–), British actress, A-1977
Sir Carol Reed (1906–76), British director, A-1968
Donna Reed (1921–), actress, A-1953
Della Reese (Deloreese Patricia Early; 1932–), singer
Jim Reeves (1923–64), country music singer
Ada Rehan (1860–1916), actress, T
Carl Reiner (1923–), actor, writer, and director
Robert Reiner (1947–), actor, son of Carl
Max Reinhardt (1873–1943), Austrian producer
Lee Remick (1935–), actress
Michael Rennie (1909–71), British actor
Alain Resnais (1922–), French director
Anne Revere (1903–), actress, A-1945
Burt Reynolds (1936–), actor
Debbie Reynolds (Mary Frances Reynolds; 1932–), actress, singer, and dancer
Buddy Rich (1917–), jazz drummer and bandleader
Charlie Rich (1932–), country music singer
Sir Ralph Richardson (1902–83), British actor, T
Tony Richardson (1929–), British director, A-1963
Nelson Riddle (1921–), bandleader
Don Rickles (1928–), comedian
Diana Rigg (1938–), British actress
Ringling Bros.: Albert (1852–1916), Otto (1858–1911), Alfred (1861–1919), Charles Edward (1863–1926), John (1866–1936), circus managers
Minnie Riperton (1948–79), singer
Cyril Ritchard (1896–1977), British actor
Tex Ritter (1907–74), country music singer
Thelma Ritter (1905–69), actress
Ritz Brothers: Al (1901–65), Jim (1903–), Harry (1906–), comedy team
Chita Rivera (1933–), singer and actress
Geraldo Rivera (1943–), newscaster
Joan Rivers (Joan Molinsky; 1937–), comedienne
Hal Roach (1892–), director and producer
Jason Robards Jr. (1920–), actor, A-1976, 1977, T
Jerome Robbins (1918–), dancer and choreographer, T, A-1961
Cliff Robertson (1925–), actor, A-1968
Dale Robertson (1923–), actor
Paul Robeson (1898–1976), singer and actor, T
Bill "Bojangles" Robinson (1878–1949), dancer
Edward G. Robinson (Emanuel Goldenberg; 1893–1973), actor, A-1972
Jimmie Rodgers (1897–1933), country music singer
Richard Rodgers (1902–79), composer, T, E
Buddy Rogers (1904–), actor, wed to Mary Pickford
Ginger Rogers (Virginia McMath; 1911–), actress and dancer, A-1940
Kenny Rogers (1941–), rock musician
Paul Rogers (1917–), British actor
Roy Rogers (Leonard Sly; 1912–), singer, cowboy actor
Will Rogers (1879–1935), humorist, T
Gilbert Roland (1905–), Mexican actor
Cesar Romero (1907–), actor
Linda Ronstadt (1946–), singer
Mickey Rooney (Joe Yule; 1922–), actor, A-1938
Pat Rooney (1880–1962), dancer and songwriter
Billy Rose (1899–1966), showman
George Rose (1920–), British actor, T
Diana Ross (1944–), singer
Katharine Ross (1943–), actress
Roberto Rossellini (1906–77), Italian director
Lillian Roth (1910–80), singer
Richard Roundtree (1943–), actor
Dan Rowan (1922–), television comedian
Gena Rowlands (1936–), actress
Charles Ruggles (1890–1970), actor
Janice Rule (1931–), actress
Barbara Rush (1930–), actress
Harold Russell (1914–), actor, A-1946
Jane Russell (1921–), actress
Lillian Russell (1861–1922), actress, T
Nipsey Russell (1924–), comedian
Rosalind Russell (1912–76), actress
Margaret Rutherford (1892–1972), British actress, A-1963
Irene Ryan (1903–73), actress
Robert Ryan (1913–73), actor
Bobby Rydell (1942–), singer
Mort Sahl (1926–), comedian
Eva Marie Saint (1930–), actress, A-1954
Susan Saint James (Susan Miller; 1946–), actress
Jill St. John (1940–), actress
Buffy Sainte-Marie (1941–), folk singer
Soupy Sales (Milton Hines; 1927–), comedian
George Sanders (1906–72), British actor, A-1950
Diana Sands (1934–73), actress
Tommy Sands (1937–), singer
Samantha Sang (1953–), singer
Michael Sarrazin (1940–), actor
Telly Savalas (1924–), actor
John Saxon (1935–), actor
Leo Sayer (1948–), rock musician
Boz Scaggs (William Royce Scaggs; 1944–), rock singer
Franklin Schaffner (1920–), director, A-1970
Dore Schary (1905–80), writer and producer
Roy Scheider (1934–), actor
Maria Schell (1926–), Austrian actress

Maximilian Schell (1930–), Austrian actor, A-1961
Joseph M. Schenck (1878–1961), Russian-born producer, founder of 20th Century-Fox, A-1950
Joseph Schildkraut (1895–1964), Austrian actor, A-1937
John Schlesinger (1926–), British director, A-1969
Romy Schneider (Rose-Marie Albach-Retty; 1938–82), Austrian actress
Avery Schreiber (1935–), comedian
Paul Scofield (1922–), British actor, A-1966
George C. Scott (1927–), actor and director, A-1970
Lizabeth Scott (Emma Matzo; 1922–), actress
Martha Scott (1914–), actress
Randolph Scott (Randolph Crane; 1903–), actor
Zachary Scott (1914–65), actor
Earl Scruggs (1924–), country music singer
John Sebastian (1944–), singer and composer
Jean Seberg (1938–79), actress
Neil Sedaka (1939–), singer and composer
Pete Seeger (1919–), folk singer
George Segal (1940–), actor
Bob Seger (1945–), rock musician
Tom Selleck (1945–), actor
Peter Sellers (1925–80), British comedian and actor
David O. Selznick (1902–65), producer
Mack Sennett (1884–1960), producer, director, A-1937
Rod Serling (1924–75), writer and producer
Eric Sevareid (1912–), television commentator
Doc Severinson (1927–), bandleader
Ravi Shankar (1920–), sitar player
Omar Sharif (Michael Shalhouz; 1933–), Egyptian actor
William Shatner (1931–), actor
Artie Shaw (Arthur Arshawsky; 1910–), jazz clarinetist and bandleader
Robert Shaw (1927–78), actor and writer
Dick Shawn (1929–), actor
Moira Shearer (1926–), Scottish-born dancer
Norma Shearer (1904–83), actress, A-1929–30
George Shearing (1920–), jazz pianist and composer
Martin Sheen (Ramon Estevez; 1940–), actor
Cybill Shepherd (1950–), actress
Ann Sheridan (1915–67), actress
Dinah Shore (Frances Rose Shore; 1917–), singer and TV personality
Bobby Short (1936–), jazz pianist
Lee Shubert (1883–1953) and **J. J. Shubert** (1880–1963), theater managers and producers, T
Sylvia Sidney (1910–), actress
Simone Signoret (Simone Kaminker; 1921–), German-born actress, A-1959
Phil Silvers (Philip Silversmith; 1912–), actor
Alastair Sim (1900–76), Scottish actor
Jean Simmons (1929–), British actress
Carly Simon (1945–), singer, wife of James Taylor
Neil Simon (1927–), playwright, T
Paul Simon (1940–), singer and composer
Simone Simon (1914–), French actress
Nina Simone (1933–), jazz vocalist
Frank Sinatra (1915–), singer and actor, A-1953, E
Frank Sinatra Jr. (1944–), singer, son of Frank
Nancy Sinatra (1940–), actress, daughter of Frank
Red Skelton (1910–), comedian
Cornelia Otis Skinner (1901–79), actress and writer
Otis Skinner (1858–1942), actor, T, father of Cornelia
Alison Skipworth (1870–1952), comedienne
Spyros Skouras (1893–1971), Greek-born film executive
Walter Slezak (1902–83), Austrian-born actor
Gracie Slick (1939–), rock singer
Alexis Smith (1921–), actress
Sir C. Aubrey Smith (1863–1948), British actor
Bessie Smith (1898?–1937), blues singer
Howard K. Smith (1914–), television commentator
Kate Smith (1909–), singer
Maggie Smith (1934–), British actress, A-1969, 1978
Smothers Brothers: Tom (1937–) and **Dick** (1939–), comedians and singers
Carrie Snodgress (1945–), actress
Hank Snow (1914–), country music singer
Suzanne Somers (1948–), actress
Elke Sommer (Elke Schletz; 1940–), German actress
Gale Sondergaard (1899–), actress, A-1936
Stephen Sondheim (1930–), composer and lyricist, T
Ann Sothern (Harriette Lake; 1909–), actress
E. A. Sothern (1826–81), British actor, T
E. H. Sothern (1859–1933), actor, T, son of E. A. Sothern, husband of Julia Marlowe
Sissy Spacek (1950–), actress, A-1980
Sam Spiegel (1901–), producer
Dusty Springfield (Mary O'Brien; 1939–), singer
Bruce Springsteen (1949–), singer
Robert Stack (1919–), actor
Jo Stafford (1918–), singer
Sylvester Stallone (1946–), actor and screenwriter
Terrence Stamp (1940–), British actor
Arnold Stang (1925–), comedian
Kim Stanley (Patricia Reid; 1925–), actress
Barbara Stanwyck (Ruby Stevens; 1907–), actress
Jean Stapleton (Jeanne Murray; 1923–), actress
Maureen Stapleton (1925–), actress, T, A-1981
Kay Starr (1924–), singer
Ringo Starr (Richard Starkey; 1940–), British singer, musician (Beatles)
Tommy Steele (1936–), British singer
Mary Steenburgen (1952–), actress, A-1980
Rod Steiger (1925–), actor, A-1967
David Steinberg (1942–), comedian
Jan Sterling (1923–), actress
Cat Stevens (Steven Georgion; 1947–), rock singer
Connie Stevens (Concetta Ingolia; 1938–), actress and singer
George Stevens (1904–75), director, A-1951, 1956
Stella Stevens (1938–), actress
James Stewart (1908–), actor, A-1940
Rod Stewart (1945–), rock singer
Stephen Stills (1945–), rock musician
Fred Stone (1873–1959), comedian, T
Lewis Stone (1879–1953), actor
Sly Stone (1944–), rock singer
Three Stooges: Curly Howard (1893?–1947), Shemp Howard (1895?–1955), Moe Howard (1897–75), Larry Fine (1902–75), comedy team
Larry Storch (1925–), comedian
Gale Storm (1922–), actress
Beatrice Straight (1918—), actress, A-1976
Lee Strasberg (1901–82), director, T
Susan Strasberg (1938–), actress, daughter of Lee
Charles E. (Tom Thumb) Stratton (1838–1883), midget
Peter Strauss (1947–), actor
Meryl Streep (1949–), actress, A-1979, 1982
Barbra Streisand (1942–), singer and actress, A-1968
Elaine Stritch (1922–), actress
Hunt Stromberg (1894–1968), producer
Sally Struthers (1948–), actress
Preston Sturges (1898–1959), producer
Jules Styne (1905–), British-born composer, T
Margaret Sullavan (1911–60), actress, T
Barry Sullivan (Patrick Barry; 1912–), actor
Ed Sullivan (1902–74), columnist and TV personality
Donna Summer (1948–), rock singer
Slim Summerville (1892–1946), comedian and director
David Susskind (1920–), producer and TV personality
Donald Sutherland (1934–), Canadian-born actor
Gloria Swanson (Josephine Swenson; 1899–1983), actress
John Cameron Swayze (1906–), newscaster
Nita Talbot (1930–), actress
Norma Talmadge (1897–1957), silent-film actress
William Talman (1917–68), actor
Russ Tamblyn (1935–), actor
Akim Tamiroff (1899–1972), Russian-born actor
Jessica Tandy (1909–), British-born actress, wed to Hume Cronyn
Norman Taurog (1899–), director, A-1930–31
Elizabeth Taylor (1932–), actress, A-1960, 1966
James Taylor (1948–), singer and musician
Laurette Taylor (Laurette Cooney; 1884–1946), actress, T
Robert Taylor (Spangler Brough; 1911–69), actor
Rod Taylor (1929–), Australian-born actor
Jack Teagarden (1905–64), jazz trombonist and singer
Shirley Temple (1928–), child star in 1930s, A-1934
Alec Templeton (1910–63), musician
Ellen Terry (1848–1928), British actress, T
Terry-Thomas (Thomas Terry Hoar-Stevens; 1911–), British comedian
Irving Thalberg (1899–1936), producer
Phyllis Thaxter (1921–), actress
Danny Thomas (Amos Jacobs; 1914–), comedian
Marlo Thomas (1938–), actress, daughter of Danny
Richard Thomas (1951–), actor
Sada Thompson (1929–), actress
Dame Sybil Thorndike (1882–1976), British actress
Gene Tierney (1920–), actress
Pamela Tiffin (1943–), actress
Burr Tillstrom (1917–), puppeteer
Tiny Tim (Herbert Khaury; 1923–), singer
Ann Todd (1909–), British actress
Michael Todd (1907–58), film producer
Richard Todd (1919–), British actor

SHOW BUSINESS PERSONALITIES *(continued)*
Thelma Todd (1908–35), comedienne
Lily Tomlin (1939–), comedienne
Franchot Tone (1906–68), actor
Regis Toomey (1902–), actor
Mel Torme (1925–), singer
Rip Torn (1931–), actor
Audrey Totter (1923–), actress
Lee Tracy (1898–1968), actor
Spencer Tracy (1900–67), actor, A-1937, 1938
Mary Travers (1936–), singer
John Travolta (1953–), actor
Arthur Treacher (1894–1975), British actor
Sir Herbert Beerbohm Tree (1853–1917), British actor
Claire Trevor (1909–), actress, A-1948
François Truffaut (1932–), French director
Forrest Tucker (1919–), actor
Sophie Tucker (Sophia Abuza; 1884–1966), singer
Sonny Tufts (Bowen Charleston Tufts; 1911–70), actor
Ike (1934–) and **Tina Turner** (1941–), singing duo
Lana Turner (Julia Turner; 1920–), actress
Ben Turpin (1847–1940), comedian
Rita Tushingham (1940–), British actress
Twiggy (Leslie Hornsby; 1949–), British actress
Conway Twitty (1933–), country music singer
Cicely Tyson (1933–), actress
Leslie Uggams (1943–), singer and actress
Liv Ullman (1938–), Norwegian actress
Myoshi Umeki (1929–), Japanese actress, A-1957
Peter Ustinov (1921–), British actor and director, A-1960, 1964
Brenda Vaccaro (1939–), actress
Roger Vadim (1927–), French director
Jerry Vale (1931–), singer
Caterina Valente (1931–), singer
Karen Valentine (1947–), actress
Rudolph Valentino (Rodolpho d'Antonguolla; 1895–1926), Italian born actor
Rudy Vallee (Hubert Vallee; 1901–), singer and actor
Frankie Valli (1937–), singer
Lee Van Cleef (1925–), actor
Mamie Van Doren (1933–), actress
Dick Van Dyke (1925–), actor
Jo Van Fleet (1922–), actress, A-1955
Vivian Vance (1912–79), actress
Trish Vandevere (1945–), actress
Sarah Vaughan (1922–), singer
Robert Vaughn (1933–), actor
Gwen Verdon (1925–), singer and dancer, T
Ben Vereen (1946–), dancer
Martha Vickers (1925–71), actress
King Vidor (1895–1982), director
Bobby Vinton (1935–), singer
Jon Voight (1939–), actor, A-1978
Joseph von Sternberg (1894–1969), Austrian-born director
Erich Von Stroheim (1885–1957), Austrian-born actor, director
Max Von Sydow (1929–), Swedish actor
Lindsay Wagner (1949–), actress
Robert Wagner (1930–), actor, wed to Natalie Wood
Christopher Walken (1943–), actor, A-1978
Clint Walker (1927–), actor
Nancy Walker (Ann Swoyer; 1922–), comedienne
Robert Walker (1919–51), actor
Mike Wallace (1918–), television newscaster
Eli Wallach (1915–), actor
James Wallack (1795–1864), British-American actor, T
Lester Wallack (1820–1888), actor, T, son of James
Fats Waller (1904–43), jazz pianist and singer
Hal B. Wallis (1898–), producer
Ray Walston (1917–), actor
Barbara Walters (1931–), television commentator
Walter Wanger (1894–1968), producer
David Warfield (1866–1951), actor, T
Andy Warhol (1927–), producer and director
Fred Waring (1900–), musician and bandleader
Jack L. Warner (1892–1978), producer (Warner Brothers)
Dionne Warwick (1940–), singer
Ethel Waters (1900–77), actress, T
Muddy Waters (McKinley Morganfield; 1915–83), country music singer
David Wayne (Wayne McKeekan; 1916–), actor
John Wayne (Marion Morrison; 1907–79), actor, director, producer, A-1969
Dennis Weaver (1924–), actor
Fritz Weaver (1926–), actor
Clifton Webb (Webb Hollenbeck; 1896–1966), actor, T
Jack Webb (1920–82), actor, director, and producer
Joe Weber (1867–1942) and **Lew Fields** (1867–1941), vaudeville comedians, T
Margaret Webster (1905–72), theatrical producer, T
Johnny Weissmuller (1904–), actor (Tarzan), Olympic swimmer
Raquel Welch (Raquel Tejada; 1942–), actress
Tuesday Weld (Susan Ker Weld; 1943–), actress
Lawrence Welk (1903–), musician and bandleader
Orson Welles (1915–), actor, producer, director, T, E
Oskar Werner (Josef Schliessmayer; 1922–), actor
Lina Wertmuller (1926–), film director
Adam West (William Anderson; 1929–), actor
Mae West (1892–1980), actress, T
Wheeler and Woolsey: Bert Wheeler (1895–1968), Robert Woolsey (1889–1938), comedy team
Barry White (1944–), singer
Pearl White (1889–1938), actress, queen of silent serials
Paul Whiteman (1890–1967), jazz bandleader
Margaret Whiting (1924–), singer
James Whitmore (1920–), actor
Richard Widmark (1915–), actor
Cornel Wilde (1918–), actor, producer, and director
Billy Wilder (1906–), Austrian-born producer and director, A-1945, 1960
Gene Wilder (Jerry Silberman; 1935–), actor
Michael Wilding (1912–79), actor
Andy Williams (1930–), singer
Bert Williams (1877–1922), comedian, T
Billy Dee Williams (1937–), actor
Cindy Williams (1948–), actress
Esther Williams (1923–), actress, swimming champion
Hank Williams (1923–53), country music singer
Paul Williams (1940–), songwriter
Robin Williams (1953–), television actor, "Mork"
Nicol Williamson (1936–), Scottish-born actor
Chill Wills (1903–78), actor
Meredith Willson (1902–), musician
Don Wilson (1900–82), radio and television announcer
Flip Wilson (1933–), comedian
Julie Wilson (1924–), singer
Marie Wilson (1916–72), actress
Nancy Wilson (1937–), singer
Paul Winchell (1924–), ventriloquist
William Windom (1923–), actor
Paul Winfield (1941–), actor
Debra Winger (1953–), actress
Henry Winkler (1945–), actor
Jonathan Winters (1925–), comedian
Shelley Winters (Shirley Schrift; 1922–), actress, A-1959, 1965
Robert Wise (1914–), director, A-1961, 1965
Jane Withers (1926–), actress, child star in 1930s
Stevie Wonder (Steveland Hardaway; 1950–), singer and composer
Anna May Wong (1902–60), Chinese-American actress
Natalie Wood (Natasha Gurdin; 1938–81), actress
Peggy Wood (1892–1978), actress, T
Joanne Woodward (1930–), actress, A-1957
Monty Woolley (1888–1963), actor
Jo Anne Worley (1937–), comedienne
Irene Worth (1916–), actress, T
Fay Wray (1907–), actress
Theresa Wright (1918–), actress, A-1942
Earl Wrightson (1916–), singer
Jane Wyatt (1912–), actress
William Wyler (1902–81), director, A-1942, 1946, 1959
Jane Wyman (Sarah Jane Fulks; 1914–), actress, A-1948
Tammy Wynette (Wynette Pugh; 1942–), singer
Ed Wynn (Isaiah Leopold; 1886–1966), comedian, T
Keenan Wynn (1916–), actor, son of Ed Wynn
Dana Wynter (1930–), British actress
Glenn Yarborough (1930–), singer
Peter Yarrow (1938–), folk singer
Susannah York (1942–), British actress
Alan Young (1919–), British-born actor
Gig Young (Byron Barr; 1917–78), actor, A-1969
Loretta Young (Gretchen Belzer; 1913–), actress, A-1947
Neil Young (1945–), rock musician
Robert Young (1907–), actor
Roland Young (1887–1953), British-born actor
Henny Youngman (1906–), comedian
Darryl Zanuck (1902–79), producer
Florenz Ziegfeld (1869–1932), showman, T
Efrem Zimbalist Jr. (1923–), actor
Fred Zinnemann (1907–), Austrian-born director, A-1953, 1966
Adolph Zukor (1873–1976), Hungarian-born producer, brought first major movie to U.S. (1912), A-1948

History

HOW TIME FLIES!

Today's headlines soon become history as time slips by with frightening rapidity. In the following tables, events are recalled that happened 10, 25, 50, 100, and 200 years ago.

EVENTS OF 10 YEARS AGO—1974

First political kidnapping in U.S. occurs on *Feb. 4*, as Patricia Hearst, 19-year-old granddaughter of publisher William Randolph Hearst, is taken from her apartment in Berkeley, Calif., by members of Symbionese Liberation Army; she later joins captors in terrorist activities and eludes FBI for 19 months until surrendering on *Sept. 18, 1975*; jury finds her guilty of bank robbery in 1976; sentenced to seven years in prison.

***Skylab* space mission ends** on *Feb. 8*; U.S. crew was in space for record 84 days, traveling 34,500,000 miles in 1,214 revolutions around Earth.

United States resumes diplomatic relations with Egypt on *Feb. 28*, after 7-year hiatus.

Turkish DC-10 airliner crashes in forest near Paris, France, on *March 3*, after cargo door falls off; 346 killed.

East and West Germany agree, on *March 7*, to establish permanent diplomatic missions in each other's capitals.

French President Georges Pompidou dies on *April 2*; Valéry Giscard d'Estaing elected to succeed him on *May 19*.

Tornadoes in South and Midwest kill 329 on *April 3–4*, as they sweep through 13 states; damage estimated at $540,000,000.

Military coup in Portugal on *April 25*, ends 40-year dictatorship; coup leader Gen. Antonio de Spinola becomes president; colonies given independence; military junta replaces Spinola with Gen. Francisco da Costa Gomes on *Sept. 30*

Impeachment hearings against President Richard M. Nixon begin on *May 9*, by Judiciary Committee of House of Representatives; on *July 30*, committee recommends three articles of impeachment to full House.

India becomes sixth nuclear nation of world with atomic test explosion on *May 18*.

Argentine President Juan Perón dies on *July 1*; succeeded by his wife and Vice President, Isabel, who becomes first woman president in Western Hemisphere.

War in Cyprus rages on *July 15–Aug. 16*; Greek-led national guard overthrows government; Turkey intervenes on *July 20*, landing 40,000 troops and enlarging Turkish-held portion of island.

President Nixon must turn over White House tapes and documents to special Watergate prosecutor, U.S. Supreme Court rules on *July 24*.

President Nixon resigns on *Aug. 9* to avoid impeachment; becomes first U.S. president to resign his office.

Gerald R. Ford becomes 38th president of U.S. on *Aug. 9*.

President Ford grants full pardon on *Sept. 8* to former President Nixon, preventing any prosecution of him in Watergate cover-up.

Conditional amnesty plan for Vietnam War draft evaders and deserters announced on *Sept. 16* by President Ford.

Presidential election campaign public financing law signed on *Oct. 15* by President Ford.

Democracy restored in Greece on *Nov. 17*, with first free national election in 10 years.

President Ford meets Soviet leader Leonid Brezhnev at Vladivostok on *Nov. 23–24*; leaders agree in principle to "put cap on arms race."

Nelson A. Rockefeller becomes Vice President of U.S. on *Dec. 19*; is confirmed by majority vote of both houses of Congress under provisions of 25th Amendment; U.S. has nonelected President and Vice President for first time in history.

EVENTS OF 25 YEARS AGO—1959

Fidel Castro overthrows Cuban dictator Fulgencio Batista on *Jan. 1*, after 3-year civil war; Castro becomes premier on *Feb. 16*.

Alaska becomes 49th state on *Jan. 3*.

First seven astronauts named by National Aeronautic and Space Administration (NASA) on *April 8*, after officials tell Congress its space program should have man on Moon by 1969.

Two monkeys sent into space aboard Jupiter spacecraft on *May 28*; animals travel to altitude of 300 miles and return unharmed.

St. Lawrence Seaway formally opens on *June 25*, linking Atlantic Ocean with Great Lakes; President Eisenhower and Queen Elizabeth II of Britain attend ceremonies.

Postmaster General Arthur E. Summerfield bars D.H. Lawrence's novel *Lady Chatterley's Lover* from the mails on *June 11*; ruling overturned by federal court on *July 21*.

U.S. steelworkers strike on *July 15–Nov. 7*, halting 87% of nation's steel production.

First atomic merchant ship, *Savannah*, launched on *July 21*, at Camden, N.J.

***Explorer 6* transmits first picture** of world from outer space on *Aug. 7*.

Hawaii becomes 50th state on *Aug. 21*.

Summit meeting at Camp David, Md., on *Sept. 15–27*, between President Eisenhower and Soviet Premier Nikita Khrushchev calls for "peaceful coexistence."

Antarctica Treaty signed on *Dec. 1* by U.S. and 11 nations; guarantees continent's neutrality.

President Dwight Eisenhower makes 11-nation goodwill tour on *Dec. 3–21*; most extensive foreign tour ever made by American President to date.

QUICK QUIZ: What are the duties of the National Security Council? See page 971.

EVENTS OF 50 YEARS AGO—1934

Export-Import Bank created on *Feb. 2*, to encourage flow of overseas commerce by financing trade with other nations.

King Albert I of Belgium killed on *Feb. 17* while mountain climbing in Belgium.

Crop Loan Act passed by Congress on *Feb. 23*, to provide $40,000,000 to Farm Credit Administration to make loans for planting and harvesting.

Congress passes Philippines Independence Bill on *March 24*, providing that, upon approval by Philippine legislature, independence to be proclaimed in 1946; Philippine legislature approves act on *May 1*.

First washing machine installed for public use on *April 18*, in Fort Worth, Tex.

U.S. and 12 other nations sign antiwar agreement on *April 27*; had been reached at Pan American Conference in Montevideo, Uruguay, in December 1933.

Securities and Exchange Commission (SEC) created on *June 6* to regulate stock market.

Federal Communications Commission (FCC) set up on *June 19*, to regulate telegraph, radio and cable communications.

Railroad Retirement Act of 1934 declared unconstitutional on *June 27* by Supreme Court.

Federal Housing Authority established on *June 28* to insure loans made by banks and other lending institutions for construction or improvement of family homes and farms.

President Roosevelt travels through Panama Canal on *July 11*.

U.S. formally ends military occupation of Haiti on *Aug. 1* in ceremony at Port-au-Prince.

Adolf Hitler becomes president of Germany on *Aug. 2*, after death of Hindenburg.

United Textile Workers strike *Sept. 1–Oct. 3*; one million U.S. workers idle.

Ship *Morro Castle* burns off New Jersey coast on *Sept. 8*, killing 137, during trip from Cuba.

Hurricane devastates Honshu, Japan, on *Sept. 21*, killing 4,000.

Coal-mine explosion in Wrexham, Wales, on *Sept. 22*, kills 265.

King Alexander of Yugoslavia assassinated in Marseille, France, on *Oct. 9*, by Macedonian revolutionary; League of Nations averts war between Yugoslavia and Hungary.

Union Pacific train reaches New York City on *Oct. 25*, 57 hours after leaving Los Angeles, setting new record.

Nebraska becomes first state to establish unicameral legislature, on *Nov. 6*.

Congressional elections on *Nov. 6*, give Democrats gain of 9 seats in House and 9 seats in Senate.

EVENTS OF 100 YEARS AGO—1884

***The Adventures of Huckleberry Finn*, by Mark Twain, published** on *Jan. 1*.

Steamer *City of Columbus* wrecked, on *Jan. 18*, off Gay Head Light, Mass., killing 103.

Explosion in Pocahontas, Va., coal mine on *March 13*, kills 112.

James G. Blaine chosen at convention in Chicago, on *June 3–6*, to be Republican Party candidate for President; vice-presidential nominee is John A. Logan.

Survivors of Arctic expedition rescued on *June 22*, as Captain Winfield Scott Schley's expedition locates survivors of A.W. Greely Arctic expedition that started out in 1881; only 7 of original 26 men are alive, including A.W. Greely.

Bureau of Labor Statistics established on *June 27*, as part of Department of Interior, to collect data on labor in the U.S.

Democratic Convention, meets in Chicago on *July 8–11*; nominates Grover Cleveland as its candidate for President; running mate is Thomas B. Hendricks.

Cornerstone of pedestal for Statue of Liberty laid on *Aug. 5* on Bedloe's Island in New York Harbor.

World time conference meets on *Oct. 1-Nov. 1*, in Washington, D.C.; recommends that meridian of Greenwich, England, be used as basis for counting mean time and longitude.

Naval War College founded on *Oct. 6*, at Newport, Rhode Island, to give postgraduate training to naval officers.

First transparent paper strip photographic film patented on *Oct. 14* by George Eastman, in Rochester, N.Y.

Grover Cleveland elected President of U.S. on *Nov. 4*, with 4,879,507 votes; opponent James G. Blaine receives 4,850,293; Cleveland becomes first Democratic president in nearly 25 years.

First press syndicate, McClure's Syndicate, founded on *Nov. 8*.

Construction of Washington Monument completed on *Dec. 6*.

EVENTS OF 200 YEARS AGO—1784

Treaty of Paris, ending War of Independence, ratified by Congress on *Jan. 4*.

China trade begins with voyage *on Feb. 22–Aug. 30*, of *Empress of China*.

Thomas Jefferson proposes territorial plan on *March 1* to divide western lands into 10 states; report adopted on *April 23* and, though never put into effect, becomes basis for Northwest Ordinance of 1787.

John Jay becomes secretary of foreign affairs on *May 7*, replacing Robert Livingston. Treasury Board is created on *May 28* to replace Office of Superintendent of Finance.

Settlers from western North Carolina convene on *Aug. 23* to plan new state called Franklin; area again comes under jurisdiction of North Carolina in 1888, after four years of nominal statehood under John Sevier.

Pennsylvania *Packet and Daily Advertiser* begins publication on *Sept. 21*; becomes first successful daily newspaper in U.S.

First Russian settlement in Alaska established on *Sept. 22* at Three Saints Bay, on Kodiak Island.

Congress meets on *Nov. 1*, at Trenton, N.J.; votes on *Dec. 10* to move capital; appoints commissioners on *Dec. 23* to lay out federal district on banks of Delaware River; agreement reached to move capital to New York until federal city is ready.

James Madison issues *Remonstrance Against Religious Assessments* on *Dec. 24*; arguing for separation of church and state in America.

KEY EVENTS IN WORLD HISTORY

Many of the important events and developments in world history from the time of the first civilizations are arranged in chronological order on the following pages.

For other important events, see the tables: *How Time Flies!*, pages 283–284; *Key Events in American History*, pages 303–311; *Important Dates in the History of American Women*, page 980; *History of the Middle East*, page 418; *History of the United Nations*, page 420; *Highlights of the Vietnam War*, page 677; and *World in Review*, pages 7–31.

DEVELOPMENT OF EARLY CIVILIZATIONS: 12,000–550 B.C.

c.12,000 B.C. Domestication of dogs: Evidence of dogs kept as household pets found in cave dwellings near Kirkuk, Iraq, in 1975.

c.9000–8000 B.C. End of Ice Age: Glaciers began receding in Europe, Asia, and North America.

c.8000–6000 B.C. Cultivation of grain: Wheat and barley grown for flour to make bread in Middle East; grain farming spreads to Greece about 6000 B.C.

c.7000–6000 B.C. Farm villages and towns develop in Middle East: Remains of villages of this period found in Iran, Turkey, and Israel.

c.4500–3100 B.C. Egyptians build villages along Nile River; begin to use hieroglyphics (picture writing); earliest recorded date believed 4241 B.C., marking beginning of Egyptian calendar; copper and glass come into use.

c.4000–3000 B.C. Sumerians build cities in valleys of Tigris and Euphrates rivers (now in Iraq); develop cuneiform writing; use wheel and bronze.

c.3100–2890 B.C. Egyptian kingdom formed by King Mena (or Menes) and successors of first dynasty; kings buried in stone tombs.

c.3100–2100 B.C. Elamites build city of Susa, now in western Iran; men ride horses.

c.3000–1720 B.C. Seafaring Phoenicians from city of Byblos (now in Lebanon) begin trading with Egypt and other areas around Mediterranean Sea.

c.3000–1450 B.C. Minoans develop city of Knossos on island of Crete; use earliest form of written Greek.

c.2900–1460 B.C. Hittites build city of Hattusas (now Bogazkoy) in eastern Turkey.

c.2650–2500 B.C. Great pyramids built by Egyptians as tombs for kings, including Great Pyramid of Giza for King Cheops.

c.2500–1500 B.C. Indus River valley people build cities of Harappa and Mohenjo-Daro (now in Pakistan); use script writing.

c.2360–2305 B.C. King Sargon I of Akkad conquers Sumerians in what is now Iraq.

c.2130–2112 B.C. Sumerian King Ur-Nammu builds ziggurat (tower) at city of Ur (in Iraq).

c.1813–1783 B.C. Assyrians rise to power with cities of Ashur, Nineveh, and Kalhu (in Iraq).

c.1800 B.C. Stonehenge monument of huge blocks of sandstone built in England.

c.1800 B.C. Father of Hebrews and Arabs, Abraham, begins journey from birthplace Ur, eventually leading his people to Egypt.

c.1792–1750 B.C. Babylonian King Hammurabi the Great issues code of laws; Babylonian scholars use advanced mathematics.

c.1766–1123 B.C. Chinese civilization develops under Shang dynasty of kings along Hwang Ho (Yellow River); script writing used; bronze tools and weapons made.

c.1650–1125 B.C. Mycenaean civilization in Greece centers on city of Mycenae; mythology of Greek gods develops.

c.1531 B.C. Hittites conquer Babylonians, destroying Babylon.

c.1500 B.C. Aryans from central Asia destroy Indus River valley civilization in Pakistan.

c.1457 B.C. Egyptians extend empire to include Syria as Thutmose III defeats Hittites.

c.1379–1362 B.C. Worship of single god, Aton, ordered by Egyptian Pharaoh Akhenaton; after his death, Egyptians resume worship of many gods.

c.1375–1335 B.C. Hittite King Suppiluliumas drives Egyptians out of Syria and Palestine; Hittites begin using some iron weapons.

c.1350 B.C. British Isles said to have been visited by Phoenicians, trading for tin used in making bronze.

c.1250–1232 B.C. Moses leads Israelites out of Egypt, giving them Ten Commandments of God; Israelites take southern Palestine from Phoenicians (Canaanites).

c.1200–100 B.C. Olmec civilization develops in southern Mexico; Olmecs build stone monuments, use picture writing.

c.1194–1184 B.C. Trojan War: Greeks of Mycenae capture city of Troy (now in Turkey).

c.1122–256 B.C. Chinese kings of Chou dynasty develop advanced civilization using mathematics, astronomy, silk textiles, copper coins, and some iron tools and weapons.

c.1116–1078 B.C. Assyrian King Tiglath-pileser I conquers Hittites; rules most of Middle East.

c.1100 B.C. End of Mycenaean civilization in Greece; Mycenae destroyed by invasion of Dorians from north.

c.1078–935 B.C. Assyria and Babylonia fall to invasion of Aramaeans and Chaldeans from north and east.

c.1000 B.C. Israel's first king, Saul, killed in battle with Philistines; succeeded by King David, who defeats Philistines and makes Jerusalem capital of Israel; about this time Hebrew elders begin to put Old Testament books of Bible into writing, based on oral traditions.

c.1000–950 B.C. Spain colonized by Phoenicians with settlement at Cádiz.

c.961–922 B.C. King Solomon of Israel constructs Jewish temple and palace in Jerusalem.

c.935–913 B.C. Assyrian King Assurdan II reestablishes dominance of Assyrians in what is now Iraq.

c.814–750 B.C. Phoenicians found Carthage in North Africa (now Tunisia).

c.800–700 B.C. Greek poet Homer believed to have composed *Iliad* and *Odyssey.*

c.800–300 B.C. Hinduism develops in India, with worship of many gods; society divides into caste system.

c.776 B.C. First Olympic Games held by Greeks to honor god Zeus.

c.753 B.C. Rome founded by twin brothers Romulus and Remus, according to legend.

c.745–728 B.C. Assyrian Empire extended to include Babylonia, Syria, and Palestine by King Tiglath-pileser III.

c.736–715 B.C. Greek Spartans under King Theopompus conquer Messenians of southwestern Greece.

c.725–722 B.C. Destruction of Israel as nation for next 2,600 years: Assyrian King Sargon II subdues rebelling Israelites, enslaving 27,000.

c.715 B.C. Egypt conquered by Ethiopia.

c.683–682 B.C. City-state Athens abolishes hereditary monarchy, establishing rule by archons chosen annually by council of nobles.

c.680–547 B.C. King of Lydia rules in what is now Turkey, with capital at Sardis (near present-day Izmir); first Western people to use coins as money; last king is Croesus.

c.663 B.C. Assyria conquers Egypt, driving out last Ethiopian pharaoh, Tanutamon.

c.660 B.C. Japanese Emperor Jimmu Tenno founds first dynasty, according to legend.

c.658–675 B.C. Byzantium (now Istanbul, Turkey) founded by Greek colonists.

c.626–561 B.C. Chaldeans of Babylonia conquer Assyrians; rebuild Babylon as capital of new Babylonian empire; construct hanging gardens of Babylon.

c.600 B.C. Southern France colonized by Greeks at Massalia (now Marseille).

c.587–582 B.C. Jews taken in captivity to Babylon: Babylonian King Nebuchadnezzar II captures Jerusalem; destroys Solomon's temple, ending kingdom of Judah.

QUICK QUIZ: About how many metric tons of potatoes are produced each year? See page 200.

KEY EVENTS IN WORLD HISTORY *(continued)*

c.563–483 B.C. **Buddha** (Prince Siddartha Gautama) founds Buddhism in Nepal and India.
c.551–479 B.C. **Confucius** develops philosophy-religion of Confucianism in China, providing rules of morals and ethics.
c.550 B.C. **Taoism** founded in China by Lao Tzu, according to legend.

RISE OF ANCIENT PERSIAN EMPIRE TO FALL OF ROME: 550 B.C.–A.D. 476

c.550–530 B.C. **Persian Empire** founded by Cyrus the Great, who conquers Lydians and Babylonians to control most of Middle East.
c.550–500 B.C. **Carthage grows as military power:** Phoenician colony of Carthage in what is now Tunisia becomes major power in western Mediterranean Sea.
c.550–100 B.C. **City of Teotihuacán develops in Mexico:** City grows to cover about 3 square miles.
c.539–516 B.C. **Jews freed from captivity** as Persians conquer Babylon; Solomon's temple rebuilt in Jerusalem with aid from Persians.
c.530–486 B.C. **Persian Empire extended** to include Egypt and Pakistan under leadership of Cambyses and Darius I.
c.510–506 B.C. **Democracy begins in Athens** with government controlled by 500-man legislative council; Athens fights off attempt by Sparta's King Cleomenes to restore aristocrats.
c.509 B.C. **Romans establish republic;** overthrow Etruscan King Tarquin the Proud.
c.499–478 B.C. **Greeks preserve independence** by defeating invasions of Persian armies of Darius I and Xerxes I.
c.460–429 B.C. **Age of Pericles in Athens:** Art, science, and democracy flourish under leadership of Pericles; Parthenon is built.
c.447–445 B.C. **First history published in Greece:** Greek historian Herodotus writes 9-volume history of known world after travel through Persian empire.
c.431–404 B.C. **Spartans defeat Athens** in Peloponnesian War; force Athens to surrender navy and tear down fortified walls.
c.404–399 B.C. **Egypt regains independence** from Persia under Pharaoh Amyrtaeus of Sais.
338 B.C. **Greece conquered** by King Philip II of Macedonia, defeating allied armies of Thebes and Athens in Battle of Chaeronea.
336–323 B.C. **Alexander the Great** of Macedonia consolidates rule of Greece, destroying Thebes; conquers Persian Empire, Egypt, and Pakistan; makes Babylon his capital.
c.321–184 B.C. **Northern India united** under Maurya dynasty founded by Emperor Chandragupta.
305–64 B.C. **Seleucid Empire** rules Middle East; founded by Seleucus I, one of Alexander's generals, who builds new capital cities of Antioch in Syria and Seleucia in Iraq.
305–30 B.C. **Egypt ruled by Greek dynasty** founded by Ptolemy I, one of Alexander's generals; capital Alexandria becomes center of Greek learning with great library.
279 B.C. **Gauls** from northern Europe invade Macedonia, Greece, and found kingdom of Galatia in what is now Turkey.
276–167 B.C. **Macedonia and Greece** ruled by kings of Antigonid dynasty, descended from Antigonus, one of Alexander's generals.
264–146 B.C. **Punic Wars** fought between Roman republic and Carthage, ending with destruction of Carthage, Roman dominance of Mediterranean Sea, and establishment of Roman provinces in North Africa and Spain.
c.250–139 B.C. **Greeks found and rule kingdom of Bactria** in what is now Afghanistan; capital at Kabul.
c.221–210 B.C. **Great Wall of China** built by Chinese Emperor Shih Huang Ti, who centralizes rule of China, founds Ch'in dynasty; books written on silk scrolls.
c.165 B.C. **Jews revolt** (under leadership of Judas Maccabeus) against Seleucids; found independent kingdom of Judea.
c.146–121 B.C. **Roman armies conquer** Macedonia, Greece, Turkey, Balearic Islands, and southern France.
c.108 B.C. **Korea** conquered by China.
c.105 B.C. **Paper** invented in China.
c.100 B.C. **India invaded by Scythians** from central Asia, founding Kushana dynasty.
c.100 B.C.–A.D. 200 **Mayan civilization** develops in Central America.
c.66–62 B.C. **Seleucid Empire conquered** by Roman general Pompey; Syria and Judea become provinces of Rome.
58–44 B.C. **Roman general Julius Caesar** conquers all of France (Gaul); invades Germany, Britain, and Egypt; makes himself dictator of Rome until assassinated (March 15, 44 B.C.) by senators led by Cassius and Brutus.
44–30 B.C. **Civil war among Roman generals:** Won by Julius Caesar's heir Octavian (Gaius Octavius), who in Battle of Actium (Sept. 2, 31 B.C.) defeats fleet of Roman general Mark Antony and Queen Cleopatra of Egypt; Octavian makes Egypt possession of Rome, following suicides of Antony and Cleopatra.
27 B.C.–A.D. 14 **Roman Empire** established and ruled by Octavian, who takes title *Emperor Augustus*; art and science flourish during reign, known as *Augustan Age*; Roman literature develops with Virgil, Horace, Ovid, Livy.
c.5 B.C.–A.D. 30 **Jesus Christ** lives in Roman province of Judea, founding Christian religion; sentenced to death by crucifixion by Roman governor Pontius Pilate.

—All dates following in chronology are A.D.

25–57 **Chinese Emperor Kuang Wu Ti** founds Eastern Han dynasty; Buddhism introduced to China; Vietnam conquered by Chinese army.
43–122 **England conquered** by Roman army; Emperor Hadrian builds wall between England and Scotland in 122–127.
64 **Persecution of Christians** begun by Roman Emperor Nero, who accuses them of starting fire that destroys much of Rome; St. Peter and St. Paul are believed to have been executed in 67 or 68.
70 **Romans destroy Jewish temple** in Jerusalem; outlaw Jewish priesthood; disperse many Jews throughout Roman Empire as punishment for Jewish revolt against Roman rule.
71–80 **Colosseum** built in Rome.
c.78–96 **Kushan Empire** in Afghanistan and northern India ruled by King Kanishka, who sends Buddhist missionaries to China.
98–117 **Roman Emperor Trajan** extends Roman Empire to include Arabia, Iraq, Armenia, and what is now Romania and Hungary.
117–138 **Roman Emperor Hadrian** codifies laws of Rome; establishes postal system throughout empire; constructs many buildings, including Parthenon in Rome.
132–135 **New revolt by Jews** in Jerusalem leads to final Diaspora (dispersion) of Jews.
c.224–226 **Persian Empire reestablished** by Ardashir I, founding dynasty of Persian shahs called *Sassanids,* who rule until 642.
c.250–800 **Mayan civilization** in Central America develops writing, astronomy, and mathematics; builds great pyramids.
251–270 **Plague** kills about one-fourth of people throughout Roman Empire; German tribes invade empire from north.
306–337 **Roman Emperor Constantine I** builds new capital at Constantinople (previously Byzantium, now Istanbul); becomes Christian; issues Edict of Milan (c.313), legalizing Christianity throughout Roman Empire.
313 **Koreans win independence** from China.
c.320 **Gupta dynasty** founded in northern India by Chandragupta I.
c.376 **Huns** (Mongols) from central Asia establish Hunnic Empire in what is now Hungary.
380 **Christianity made official religion** of Roman Empire by Emperor Theodosius the Great.
395 **Roman Empire permanently divided:** western empire ruled from Rome; eastern empire ruled from Constantinople.
395–476 **Western Roman Empire disintegrates** under series of weak emperors; Visigoths led by Alaric capture and sack Rome in 410; Huns led by Attila ravage Rome's provinces in 435–453; Rome again sacked in 455 by Vandals led by Genseric; in 476 last Roman emperor of west, Romulus Augustus, overthrown by Odoacer, leader of German Heruli.

BYZANTINE EMPIRE, ARAB EMPIRE, AND EUROPEAN MIDDLE AGES: 481–1294

481 Kingdom of Franks established by Clovis I in northern France and southern Germany with capital at Paris.

484–490 Hephthalites, or White Huns, invade Persia and India: Asian tribesmen loot wealthy cities; dominate region until defeated in India in 528 and in Afghanistan in 557.

493 Ostrogoth Kingdom of Italy established by Theodoric the Great.

c.500–542 King Arthur and Knights of Round Table rule in England, according to legend.

502–549 Buddhism becomes official religion in China: Emperor Liang Wu-ti adopts Buddhism; persecutes Taoists.

527–565 Byzantine Empire (Eastern Roman Empire) reaches height under Macedonian Emperor Justinian I the Great; conquers North Africa, Italy, and southeastern Spain.

c.550 Silk manufacture begins in Byzantine Empire after Christian missionaries to China smuggle out silkworm eggs and mulberry seeds.

568–586 Visigoths conquer Spain: Byzantine armies driven out of Spain by Visigoth King Leovigild.

c.587 Japanese Emperor Yomei converts to Buddhism.

589 Chinese Empire reunited by armies of Sui dynasty; Great Wall of China rebuilt.

590–640 Papal States founded in Italy: Pope Gregory takes charge of government as well as religious affairs in central and southern Italy.

c.597–605 English King Ethelbert I converts to Christianity; St. Augustine becomes first archbishop of Canterbury (Ethelbert's capital).

622–632 Mohammed founds Islamic religion; launches holy war by Arabs on nonbelievers.

630–648 Chinese armies conquer Turkestan (now part of Soviet Union).

634–644 Arab Empire expands by conquest of Iraq, Syria, Iran, Palestine, and Egypt by Muslim armies of caliph Omar.

661–680 Arab armies of caliph Muawiya make new conquests, adding North Africa, Afghanistan, Pakistan, and Turkestan to Arab Empire.

675–681 Slavic tribes invade Balkan region.

711–732 Spain and southern France invaded and conquered by Arabs and Berbers from Africa.

712–756 Chinese culture rises to new heights under Emperor Hsuan Tsung; porcelain made; paper printed with wooden blocks; mechanical clock invented.

768–814 Charlemagne, king of Franks, expands empire by conquest of Germany and northern Italy; attempts to revive Western Roman Empire by having Pope Leo III crown him emperor in 800.

c.787–794 Danish and Norse Vikings raid England and Scotland.

c.820–1431 Cambodia (Khmer) rules southeast Asia from magnificent capital at Angkor Thom.

841–856 Danish Vikings raid France, sacking Paris in 845 and 856.

c.855–879 Russian nation founded by Vikings under Prince Rurik, establishing capital at Novgorod.

866 Normandy region of France colonized by Viking Northmen (Normans).

867 Christianity splits Rome and Constantinople as Eastern Orthodox Church rejects control by Roman Catholic pope.

878 Alfred the Great prevents Danish Vikings from conquering all of England.

912–961 Muslim Spain becomes Europe's main center of learning and science under caliph AbdarRahman III.

962 Holy Roman Empire founded by Otto I, king of Germany since 936, crowned by Pope John XII.

976–1025 Byzantine Empire's power revived by Emperor Basil II, conquering Bulgaria and Armenia.

981 Greenland colonized by Norse Vikings.

987 Hugh Capet elected king of France, founding Capetian dynasty that rules until 1328.

c.1000 North America discovered by Norse Vikings, who call it *Vinland.*

1003–14 England conquered by Denmark's King Sven.

1055 Seljuk Turks from central Asia under Tughril Beg capture Baghdad, capital of Arab Empire.

1066 England invaded by Normans led by William the Conqueror, who defeats King Harold II at Battle of Hastings (Oct. 14).

1068–84 Southern Italy conquered by Normans led by Robert Guiscard; Rome sacked in 1084.

1071–85 Seljuk Turks extend empire, conquering Asiatic Turkey and Syria.

1096–99 First Crusade: Answering call by Pope Urban III to rescue Holy Land from control of Muslims, about 30,000 French and Italian crusaders invade Seljuk Turkish Empire, capturing Jerusalem and Turkey; establish Latin States of the Crusaders in Middle East.

c.1100 Timbuktu founded in West Africa, becoming center of learning for black Muslims.

1106 Northern France invaded and conquered by England's King Henry I, imprisoning his brother, who had been ruler of Normandy.

1147–49 Second Crusade: Because Muslims had reconquered most of Asiatic Turkey, new crusade is organized by kings of France and Germany, but is defeated by Turks.

c.1150–67 Universities of Paris and Oxford founded in France and England.

1167–71 Ireland claimed by England's King Henry II as Normans colonize Ireland.

1175–1206 Central India conquered by Muslim ruler of Persia.

1187 Jerusalem captured by Saladin, Muslim sultan of Syria and Egypt.

1189–92 Third Crusade: Kings of England, France, and Germany lead armies in unsuccessful effort to recapture Jerusalem; however, agreement is made with Saladin to let Christians visit Jerusalem.

c.1200–1438 Inca civilization develops in Peru; builds great cities and road system.

c.1200–1450 Mayan civilization in Central America ruled from Mayapán in Yucatán, following overthrow of rulers of Chichén-Itzá.

1202–04 Northern France recovered by France's King Philip II from England's King John.

1202–04 Fourth Crusade: Setting off to invade Arab Egypt, French knights divert to attack Byzantine Empire; capture Constantinople and massacre its people; Roman Catholics replace Greeks on throne of Byzantine Empire.

1203–23 Denmark raids and conquers many coastal areas of Baltic Sea.

1206–27 Genghis Khan leads Mongols in conquest of northern China and central Asia.

1212 Children's Crusade: Thousands of French and German children march toward Holy Land but die or are enslaved along way.

1215 (June 15–19) Magna Carta (Great Charter) agreed to by England's King John; sets first limits on monarch's absolute power by requiring assent of barons to special taxes.

1218–21 Fifth Crusade: Crusaders invade Egypt but are driven off.

1228–29 Sixth Crusade: Holy Roman Emperor Frederick II leads Teutonic Knights to Holy Land; acquires Jerusalem from sultan of Egypt, crowning himself its king.

1230–55 Mali Empire founded in West Africa by King Sundiata.

1237–41 Mongol armies conquer Russia and devastate Hungary; for next two centuries Russian princes pay tribute to Mongol Golden Horde that occupies southern Russia.

1244 Jerusalem recaptured by Muslims.

1245–65 Seljuk Turkish Empire destroyed by Mongols, who conquer Iran, Iraq, and Syria, sacking Baghdad in 1258.

1248–54 Seventh Crusade: France's King Louis IX leads attack on Egypt; captured by Muslims and held captive until ransom is paid.

1260–94 Kublai Khan rules China and Mongol Empire from Pacific Ocean to Mediterranean Sea, with capital at Peking; builds roads, canals, hospitals; encourages art and science.

1261 Greek rule of Byzantine Empire restored by Greek army that overthrows Roman Catholic Emperor Baldwin II.

1265 First English parliament meets under leader-

QUICK QUIZ: Henry Cavendish discovered what chemical element? See page 732.

KEY EVENTS IN WORLD HISTORY *(continued)*

ship of Simon de Montfort.

1269–73 Gunpowder explosives first used in war: Chinese defenders of cities in Yangtze River Valley use explosives against Mongol invaders.

1270 Eighth Crusade: Kings of England and France attack Carthage in North Africa; French King Louis IX dies of plague; nothing accomplished.

1271–95 Marco Polo of Venice travels throughout Mongol Empire; upon return writes book describing wonders of Chinese civilization.

1272–1307 Great Britain unified for first time as English King Edward I conquers Wales and Scotland.

1276–78 Austria conquered by Holy Roman Emperor Rudolf I, founder of Hapsburg dynasty that rules Austria until 1918.

1281 Typhoon saves Japan from Mongol invasion; invading army of 150,000 Mongols halted when typhoon wrecks their fleet.

1287 Mongols conquer Burma: Capital city Pagan looted; Burma made part of Kublai Khan's empire.

1291 Last Christian crusaders driven from Middle East by Muslims.

1294 First Roman Catholic missionary travels to China: Franciscan friar Giovanni di Monte Covino reaches Peking; made first archbishop of China in 1307.

RENAISSANCE, EXPLORATION, AND REFORMATION: 1300–1599

c.1300 European Renaissance begins in Florence, Italy, with painter Giotto and writers Dante, Petrarch, and Boccaccio.

1300–26 Ottoman Turkish Empire founded by Osman I: Launches holy war against non-Muslims in Middle East.

1307–08 William Tell helps Switzerland win independence from Austria, legend says.

1312–37 Mali Empire reaches height in Africa under King Mansa Musa; said to have visited Cairo with caravan of 100 camels, each carrying 300 pounds of gold, and 500 slaves, each carrying staff made of gold.

1314 Scotland wins independence from England as Robert Bruce defeats English army at Battle of Bannockburn (June 24).

1325–1519 Mexico ruled by Aztecs from capital city of Tenochtitlán (now Mexico City).

1326–61 Ottoman Turkish Empire under Sultan Orkhan I conquers northeastern Greece.

1337–1453 Hundred Years War: English and French kings fight for control of France; by 1453 England holds only French city of Calais, but English claim throne of France until 1801.

1340–41 Portuguese explorers first visit Canary Islands off coast of northwest Africa.

1346 (Aug. 26) England's King Edward III wins Battle of Crécy over French, proving superiority of longbowmen over armored knights and crossbowmen of France; cannon fired by gunpowder possibly introduced then.

1347–52 Black Death (bubonic plague) sweeps across Europe, killing about one-fourth of estimated 100 million population.

1361–89 Ottoman Turkish Empire expands under Sultan Murad I with conquest of most of what is now Yugoslavia and Bulgaria.

1368–98 Ming dynasty founded in China by Emperor Hung-wu, whose armies drive Mongols into central Asia.

1369–1405 Mongol ruler Tamerlane conquers Afghanistan, Iran, Iraq, eastern Turkey, and northern India.

c.1376–82 Bible translated into English by John Wycliffe and his followers.

1378–1417 Rival popes in Rome and at Avignon, France, contend for control of Roman Catholic Church.

1381 Peasant Revolt in England led by Wat Tyler unsuccessfully demands end to feudal system of forced labor and high land rents.

1387–1412 Denmark, Norway, and Sweden united under Queen Margrethe of Denmark.

1399 Revolt in England: King Richard II imprisoned for reasserting absolute power; parliament elects Henry IV to throne.

c.1400–1500 Muslim Arabs conquer islands of Indonesia, Malaya, and southern Philippines.

1414–17 Roman Catholics reunified with election of Pope Martin V; Council of Constance condemns and executes as heretics John Huss (Jan Hus) and Jerome of Prague for questioning validity of various church doctrines.

1418–60 Portugal's Prince Henry the Navigator sponsors exploration of Africa's coast.

c.1422–26 Technical improvements in arts: Oil painting developed by Flemish artist Jan Van Eyck; bronze statues cast by Florentine sculptor Donatello; perspective used to show depth by Florentine painter Masaccio.

1427–31 Azores Islands discovered by Portuguese explorer Diogo de Sevilla.

1429 (May 7) Joan of Arc, 17, leads French army at Battle of Orléans, forcing English to lift siege of city; saves France from being conquered; burned as witch by English at Rouen on May 31, 1431.

1453 (May 29) Byzantine Empire comes to end as Ottoman Turks capture Constantinople.

c.1454 Johann Gutenberg invents printing with movable metal type at Mainz, Germany.

1455–85 Wars of the Roses: Civil war in England between rival families of York and Lancaster for throne of England; ends with marriage of King Henry VII (of Lancaster) to Elizabeth (of York), founding Tudor dynasty.

1462–1505 Ivan III the Great rules Russia as first czar; ends payment of tribute to Mongols; seizes part of Lithuania from Poland.

1479 Spain unified by joint rule of Queen Isabella of Castile and King Ferdinand II of Aragon; they complete conquest of Moorish Spain with capture of Granada in 1492.

1487–88 Portuguese explorer Bartolomeu Dias sails around southern tip of Africa.

1492–93 Christopher Columbus makes first voyage of discovery to America; lands at Bahamas island of San Salvador on Oct. 12, 1492; discovers Cuba; establishes settlement on Santo Domingo.

1493 Line of Demarcation established by Pope Alexander VI to prevent disputes between Portugal and Spain; gives Africa and Brazil to Portugal, rest of Americas to Spain.

c.1495–1519 Leonardo da Vinci paints Renaissance masterpieces *Last Supper* and *Mona Lisa*; produces many other works of art, science, and engineering in Italy.

1497–99 Portuguese explorer Vasco da Gama sails around Africa to India and back; gives Portugal opportunity to establish monopoly on trade in spices from Far East to Europe.

1501 First black slaves in America brought to Spanish colony of Santo Domingo.

1505–15 Portugal fortifies India's southwest coast; destroys Arab ships in Arabian Gulf to cut off Arab trade with Far East; establishes Goa in India as capital of Portuguese possessions in Asia.

1506–1626 St. Peter's Church built in Rome; designed and decorated by such Renaissance artists and architects as Donato Bramante, Michelangelo, Raphael, Leonardo da Vinci, and Gian Lorenzo Bernini.

1512–20 Ottoman Turks conquer Syria, Arabia, and Egypt under leadership of Sultan Selim I.

1513 (Sept. 9) Scotland's King James IV invades England; defeated and killed at Battle of Flodden Field.

1517 (Oct. 31) Reformation begins in Germany as Martin Luther posts on door of church in Wittenberg his *Ninety-Five Theses,* denouncing abuses by Roman Catholic Church.

1519–21 Spanish conquistador Hernándo Cortés conquers Mexico; defeats Aztec Indians at their capital, Tenochtitlán; sends back treasures of gold to Spain.

1519–22 First voyage around world: Begun in 1519 by Spanish explorer Ferdinand Magellan, killed in Philippines in 1521; one of his ships, under command of Juan Sebastián del Cano, continues around world to Spain, arriving in 1522.

1520–23 Sweden declares independence from Denmark; leader of revolt takes throne as King Gustavus I.

1520–66 Ottoman Turkish Empire expands with conquests of Yugoslavia, Hungary, Iraq, Iran, Arabia, and North Africa by Sultan Suleiman I the Magnificent.

1521 Martin Luther excommunicated by Pope Leo X; declared outlaw punishable by death by Holy Roman Emperor Charles V; before Luther's death, in 1546, thousands in Europe turn to Protestantism.

1526 (Aug. 29) Hungary conquered by Turks: In Battle of Mohács, armies of Sultan Suleiman I defeat Hungarian King Lajos II; over 100,000 Hungarian Christians enslaved by Turks.
1526–30 Mogul Empire in India founded by Babar, descendant of Gengis Khan.
1527–46 Mayan civilization of Yucatán conquered by Spaniards, who burn Mayan bark-cloth books, calling them "works of the Devil."
1529 (April 22) Portugal and Spain divide Eastern Hemisphere: Sign Treaty of Saragossa establishing boundary between possessions in Far East, recognizing Portugal's control of Indonesia and Spain's possession of Philippines and Pacific Islands.
1530–31 Schmalkaldic League formed by German states and cities ruled by Protestants.
1531 Commercial tobacco farming begun in America: Rising demand for tobacco in Spain, where it had been introduced by Christopher Columbus, causes colonists in what is now Dominican Republic to begin raising tobacco for export.
1531–35 Inca empire of Peru conquered by Spanish conquistador Francisco Pizarro, who loots their gold and sends it to Spain.
1534 Reformation begins in England as King Henry VIII makes himself head of church after being excommunicated for divorcing Catherine of Aragon.
1534–64 Presbyterian Protestantism, developed by John Calvin in Switzerland, gains English Puritans and French Huguenots as adherents.
1536–40 Denmark, Norway, and Sweden adopt Lutheranism as national religion.
1538 First university in Americas founded in Santo Domingo (now Dominican Republic).
1542 First European visits Japan; believed to be Portuguese explorer Antonio da Mota.
1542–51 Roman Catholicism introduced to India and Japan by Jesuit missionary St. Francis Xavier.
1543 Theory that Earth revolves around Sun published by Polish scholar Nicolaus Copernicus; later suppressed by Roman Catholic Church as denial of biblical teaching.
1546–55 Schmalkaldic War: Holy Roman Emperor Charles V tries to force Protestant states and cities of Germany to return to Roman Catholicism; Peace of Augsburg in 1555 gives Lutherans freedom of worship.
1547–84 Russia's Czar Ivan IV the Terrible conquers Tatars (Mongols) to acquire Volga River region, but loses western Russia to Poland and Sweden.
c.1550 Muskets first developed in Spain.
1553–58 Roman Catholicism restored in England by Queen Mary I; about 300 Protestant leaders burned at stake, including Archbishop of Canterbury Thomas Cranmer.
1558–1603 England ruled by Queen Elizabeth I, who restores Protestantism, establishes Church of England (Episcopalian), and persecutes Roman Catholics, Unitarians, and radical Puritans; Renaissance reaches height in England with such writers as William Shakespeare, Edmund Spenser, and Christopher Marlowe.
1562–68 British slave trade begins with voyages of John Hawkins carrying slaves from Africa to Spanish colonies in Caribbean.
1562–98 Religious wars in France rage between Roman Catholics and Protestants (Huguenots); Roman Catholics slaughter thousands of Huguenots (Protestants) in St. Bartholomew's Day Massacre on Aug. 24, 1572; fighting ends with Edict of Nantes on April 15, 1598, giving Huguenots political rights but not full freedom of worship.
1568–1648 Protestant Netherlands wins independence from Catholic Spain in series of revolts; Renaissance reaches height in Netherlands with work of such Dutch masters as Peter Paul Rubens, Anthony Van Dyck, Franz Hals, and Rembrandt van Rijn.
1568–82 Central Japan unified by warrior-dictator Oda Nobunaga; Nagasaki becomes important port for trade with Portugal.
1571 (Oct. 7) Turkish fleet defeated by Spanish and Italian fleets in Mediterranean Sea in Battle of Lepanto, ending threat of further Turkish expansion.
1571 Manila founded by Spanish colonists in Philippines.
1571–1603 Muslim Empire of Kanem in central Africa reaches height of power under King Idris III, who rules from walled capital of N'gazargamu; wealth comes from slaves captured in south and sold in North Africa.
1574 Colony of Angola founded by Portuguese in Africa at mouth of Congo River.
1577–80 Sir Francis Drake of England sails around world after looting Spanish ships along South American coast.
1580 Spain conquers Portugal, placing Spanish Hapsburg ruler on throne.
1587 (Feb. 8) Mary Queen of Scots beheaded after being found guilty of plotting to kill England's Queen Elizabeth I.
1588 (July 31–Aug. 8) Defeat of Spanish Armada: King Philip II of Spain sends armada of 130 ships to invade England and restore Roman Catholicism; Spaniards defeated by English fleet of about 200 ships led by Adm. Lord Howard; many Spanish ships driven on Irish coast in storm.
1589–1610 France's King Henry IV comes to throne as Protestant but converts to Roman Catholicism in 1593 in effort to end religious wars; founds Bourbon dynasty that rules France to 1792.
1597 Christian persecution begins in Japan; Japan's dictator Hideyoshi executes nine Portuguese and Spanish missionaries.
1598–1605 Serfdom established in Russia by Czar Boris Godunov.
c.1599 Renaissance reaches height in Spain with work of painter El Greco, novelist Miguel de Cervantes, playwright Lope de Vega.

EUROPE'S MONARCHS MANEUVER FOR POWER AND TERRITORY: 1600–1757

1600 English East India Company founded to establish English colonies and expand trade.
1602 Dutch East India Company established to manage Netherlands' colonization and trade.
1605 (Nov. 5) Gunpowder plot: In retaliation for their persecution, English Roman Catholics try to blow up England's parliament and King James I; plot uncovered and leader Guy Fawkes hanged.
1607 First permanent English colony in North America founded at Jamestown, Virginia.
1608 French colony of Quebec established in Canada by explorer Samuel de Champlain.
1611 Protestant colony of Northern Ireland founded by England's King James I.
1611 King James Version of Bible published in England after translation by group of scholars appointed by King James I.
1611–32 Sweden becomes powerful under Gustavus II Adolphus, winning wars with Russia, Poland, and Holy Roman Empire.
1612 England establishes colony in India at Surat after defeating Portuguese fleet.
1612–14 Bermuda colonized by English.
1618–48 Thirty Years War: Protestants in Holy Roman Empire rebel against oppression by Roman Catholics; Denmark, Sweden, and France invade Germany; great loss of life and property hinders Germany's development for next two centuries.
1619–23 Dutch found Batavia (now Jakarta) on Java as center of Far Eastern spice trade; massacre English traders in East Indies.
1623–51 Japanese isolation for next two centuries begun by shogun Iemitsu; foreign traders expelled, except for few Chinese and Dutch; Christianity ruthlessly stamped out.
1627–44 Manchus invade and conquer China, founding Manchu, or Ch'ing, dynasty that rules until 1912.
1632–52 Taj Mahal built in India by Shah Jahan.
1633 Italian astronomer Galileo tried by Roman Catholic court; forced to recant belief in Copernican theory.
1634 Dutch capture Curaçao in Caribbean Sea; Peter Stuyvesant becomes first governor.
1635 French settlers colonize Guadeloupe in Caribbean Sea.
1637 First public opera house opened in Venice, Italy: New art form of musical dramas had previously been performed only in palaces of nobility.
1637 Africa's Gold Coast (Ghana) seized by Dutch from Portugal as base for slave trade.
1640 Portugal regains independence in revolt against Spanish rulers.

QUICK QUIZ: Who made the first flight over the North Pole? See page 330.

KEY EVENTS IN WORLD HISTORY *(continued)*

1642–49 Puritan revolution in England: Puritan general Oliver Cromwell leads supporters of parliament in defeating royalist armies; King Charles I convicted of treason and beheaded on Jan. 30, 1649; Cromwell rules as military dictator, suppressing Church of England and decreeing Puritanical laws.

1642–59 France attacks Spain, taking Spain's northeastern provinces.

1648 Bahamas settled by British colonists from Bermuda; islands become haven for pirates.

1650–52 Tea and coffee introduced in England: Beverages quickly win popularity with opening of public coffeehouses.

1652 (April 7) Dutch establish colony in South Africa: Settlement at Cape Town becomes supply station for Dutch ships sailing on East Indies route around Africa.

1652–74 England and Netherlands fight three naval wars, ending with Englarrd winning command of seas; Netherlands gives up colony of New Netherland (New York) to England in exchange for Surinam in South America.

1655 British capture Jamaica from Spain in Caribbean Sea.

1656 Dutch capture Sri Lanka: Take main Portuguese settlement at Colombo.

1660 Monarchy restored in England as Charles II becomes king; Church of England reestablished; other Protestant faiths and Roman Catholicism suppressed.

1661 Palace of Versailles construction begun by France's King Louis XIV.

1665–66 Plague and fire devastate London; about 75,000 persons die of plague; fire (Sept. 2–6, 1666) destroys much of London.

1682–99 War between Austria and Ottoman Turks: Vienna withstands 2-month siege by Turks; Austria captures Hungary from Turks.

1685 Protestantism outlawed in France as Edict of Nantes of 1598 is revoked; thousands of Protestants flee to other countries.

1687 (Sept. 26) Parthenon in Athens demolished: In war fought in Greece between Turks and Venetians, artillery of Venetians hits ancient temple, exploding gunpowder stored there by Turks.

1687–88 Thailand drives out foreigners: Thai people force English traders and French missionaries to leave country, closing it to foreign influence for next two centuries.

1688–89 Glorious Revolution in England: Fearing King James II plans to restore Roman Catholicism, parliamentary leaders ask Dutch Prince William of Orange to protect Protestants; when William lands with army, James flees to France; monarchy given to William and his wife, who then rule as King William III and Queen Mary II; parliament adopts Bill of Rights (Dec. 16, 1689) to protect citizens from government.

1688–97 War of the League of Augsburg (called King William's War in America): France invades Germany, attacks English colonies in America; England, Netherlands, Spain, Sweden, and German states fight against France; Treaty of Ryswick (Sept. 30, 1697) ends war with few territorial changes.

1689–1725 Czar Peter I the Great rules Russia; carries out reforms to westernize nation; establishes Russia as major military power, defeating Sweden in Great Northern War in 1700–21.

1690 (July 11) Battle of the Boyne: England's King William III defeats rebellion in Ireland led by former King James II.

1698 First practical steam engine invented by Thomas Savery in England; used to pump water from mines and to pump water supply for homes; begins era of Industrial Revolution.

1698 Arab sultan of Oman seizes control of east coast of Africa from Portuguese.

1701 Kingdom of Prussia founded in eastern Germany by King Frederick I.

1701–14 War of the Spanish Succession (called Queen Anne's War in America): France's King Louis XIV preserves his grandson on throne of Spain as King Philip V; fights against alliance of England, Netherlands, Austria, and Savoy (Sardinia); at war's end France and Spain promise not to unite as single monarchy; Austria wins control of Luxembourg and Belgium; France gives England northeastern Canada (Acadia); Spain gives England Gibraltar and 30-year contract to supply slaves to Spain's American colonies.

1707 (May 1) United Kingdom of Great Britain: Parliaments of the Kingdom of England and Wales and of the Kingdom of Scotland each pass Act of Union, forming one government under Queen Anne.

1717–20 War of the Quadruple Alliance: Spain invades and captures Sardinia and Sicily; alliance of Britain, France, Netherlands, and Austria defeats Spain; Sardinia given independence under prince of Savoy.

1721–42 British cabinet system of government established as Sir Robert Walpole serves as chief minister of George I and George II.

1733–35 War of the Polish Succession: Russia and Austria fight against France, Spain, and Sardinia, winning right to place weak kings on Polish throne, paving way for partition.

1736–39 Ottoman Turks win most of Yugoslavia in war with Austria and Russia.

1738–40 Persians led by Nadir Shah invade and conquer northern India, forcing Mogul emperor to pay tribute to remain on throne.

1740–48 War of the Austrian Succession (called King George's War in America): Austria and Britain fight against France, Spain, Prussia, and German states that refuse to recognize Maria Theresa's claim to throne of Holy Roman Empire; at war's end she and husband, Francis I, retain throne but give up province of Silesia to Prussia.

1741–43 Sweden attacks Russia but is defeated; forced to give Russia control of Finland.

1756–63 Seven Years War (called French and Indian War in America): Britain and Prussia defeat France, Austria, Spain, and Russia; France loses colonial empire in North America and India to Britain; Prussia retains Silesia; Spain cedes Florida to Britain in exchange for Cuba.

1757 (June 23) Britain wins control of Bengal in India: under leadership of Robert Clive, 3,200 troops of English East India Company defeat 50,000 Indian soldiers in Battle of Plassey.

SOCIAL, POLITICAL, AND INDUSTRIAL REVOLUTIONS: 1760–1850

1762 ***The Social Contract*** by Jean Jacques Rousseau influences leaders of American and Franch revolutions with idea government requires contract between ruler and governed.

1764–69 Machines to spin yarn invented in England by James Hargreaves and Richard Arkwright, initiating first textile factories.

1768–74 War between Russia and Ottoman Turks: Russia conquers Crimean peninsula.

1768–82 Improved steam engine to operate machinery developed by James Watt.

c.1770–1830 German literature and music enriched by writers Goethe and Schiller and composers Bach, Mozart, and Beethoven.

1772 (June 22) Slavery ruled illegal in Britain by Chief Justice William Lord Mansfield, but ruling does not affect status of slaves in colonies.

1772–95 Partition of Poland: In three steps in 1772, 1793, and 1795, Austria, Russia, and Prussia divide land and people of Poland, ending its independence.

1775–83 American Revolutionary War: France, Spain, and Netherlands aid Americans in defeating Britain; in Treaty of Paris, Britain recognizes U.S. independence, gives up Tobago and Senegal to France, and Minorca and Florida to Spain.

1782 Thailand wins independence from Burma.

1787 Freetown, Sierra Leone, founded by British abolitionists as haven for freed slaves.

1788 (Jan. 26) Sydney, Australia, settled by British colonists.

1789 (April 30) George Washington takes office as first U.S. President under Constitution.

1789 (July 14) Storming of Bastille: Paris mob captures prison, symbol of royal power.

1789–99 French Revolution: Assembly adopts constitution limiting powers of king and nobles in 1789–90; republic declared on Sept. 21, 1792; King Louis XVI beheaded on Jan. 21, 1793; Reign of Terror with thousands guillotined in 1793–95; rule by 5-man directory in 1795–99.

1790 First American textile factory opened by Samuel Slater in Pawtucket, R.I.

1791–1803 Revolt by slaves in Haiti overthrows French rule.

1792–97 War of the First Coalition: In effort to restore nobility in France, coalition of Austria, Prussia, Britain, Netherlands, Spain, and Sardinia fight against France; at war's end France controls northern Italy, Netherlands, Belgium, Switzerland, and southern Germany.
1794 Polish revolt led by Tadeusz Kosciuszko; defeated by Russia and Prussia.
1795–96 Britain takes advantage of France's conquest of Netherlands to take over Dutch colonies in Sri Lanka and South Africa.
1795–99 France ruled by directory: New constitution gives 5-man directory dictatorial power over France.
1798 Mass production of muskets with interchangeable parts developed by U.S. inventor Eli Whitney.
1798 Prediction that world population would outstrip food supply published by English economist Thomas Malthus in *Essay on the Principle of Population.*
1798–99 Egypt invaded and conquered by French troops led by Napoleon Bonaparte.
1798–1800 U.S. and France fight naval war.
1798–1802 War of the Second Coalition: Britain, Austria, Russia, Portugal, and Ottoman Turks fight against France; French armies win in Europe but are driven out of Egypt.
1799 (Nov. 9) Napoleon Bonaparte becomes dictator of France, naming himself first consul.
1800 China bans imports of opium: Decree by Emperor Chia-ch'ing has reverse of intended effect as corrupt officials accept bribes by foreign traders who increase flow of opium into China.
1801 (Jan. 1) United Kingdom of Great Britain and Ireland estalished with one monarch, one parliament, and one Protestant Episcopal Church; Catholics excluded from voting.
1804 (Jan. 1) Haiti declares independence from France; first black nation to gain freedom from European colonial rule.
1804 Napoleon I becomes emperor of France, placing crown on own head (Dec. 2).
1804–13 Russia defeats Persia, taking control of Georgia between Black and Caspian seas.
1805 (Oct. 21) Battle of Trafalgar: British fleet under Horatio Lord Nelson wins command of seas, defeating Napoleon's combined French-Spanish fleet at Strait of Gibraltar, enabling Britain to blockade Napoleonic France.
1805–09 Napoleon I conquers continental Europe.
1806 (Aug. 6) Holy Roman Empire ends, Austria having lost German states to Napoleon.
1810–15 Unsuccessful revolutions in Mexico and Venezuela put down by Spanish troops.
1811 (Aug. 14) Paraguay declares independence from Spain; becomes dictatorship in 1814 under José Rodríguez de Francia.
1812 Napoleon meets disaster in Russia: After occupying Moscow, which was burned, lack of supplies forces Napoleon to retreat in winter; most of army of 600,000 desert or die.
1812–14 War of 1812: U.S. fights Britain.
1813–14 War of Liberation of Europe: Allies (Britain, Austria, Russia, Prussia, Sweden, and Portugal) defeat Napoleon, capturing Paris, March 31, 1814; Napoleon abdicates and is exiled to island of Elba off coast of Italy.
1814–24 France restores Bourbon monarchy under King Louis XVIII.
1815 Napoleon I escapes from Elba; defeated by Allies led by Duke of Wellington at Battle of Waterloo in Belgium (June 18); exiled to island of St. Helena in South Atlantic.
1815 Congress of Vienna: Victorious Allies redraw map of Europe, returning France to pre-Napoleonic borders; Switzerland guaranteed perpetual neutrality; Sweden acquires Norway; Russia gets Poland; Netherlands obtains Belgium; Britain receives Malta, protectorate over Ionian Islands, and several French and Dutch colonies.
1816–24 South American nations win independence from Spain with patriot armies led by José de San Martín and Simón Bolívar.
1820–23 Revolt in Spain: Troops refuse to go to America to reconquer Spain's colonies; put down by intervention of French army.
1821 (Feb. 24) Mexico declares independence from Spain; ruled as monarchy by Gen. Agustín de Iturbide as Emperor Agustín I (1822–23); becomes republic on Oct. 4, 1824.
1821–31 Greece wins independence from Ottoman Turkish Empire.
1822 Liberia (then called Monrovia) established in Africa by American Colonization Society as settlement for freed American slaves.
1822 (Sept. 7) Brazil declares independence from Portugal as constitutional monarchy under Emperor Pedro I, son of Portugal's king.
1823 (July 1) United Provinces of Central America declare independence from Mexico with Manuel José Arce as first president.
1823 (Dec. 2) Monroe Doctrine issued by U.S., warning Europe against interfering in Western Hemisphere.
1825 (Sept. 27) First public railroad using steam locomotive completed in England.
1825–28 Uruguay wins independence as result of war between Argentina and Brazil.
1825–28 Russia defeats Persia and wins control of Armenia and Caspian Sea.
1828–29 Russia defeats Ottoman Turks, occupying Bulgaria and Romania.
1829 Britain grants Roman Catholics right to vote and hold public office.
1830 (July 5) France invades Algeria; takes 40 more years to conquer interior of Algeria.
1830 (July 28) Revolution in France: Charles X overthrown; replaced by Louis Philippe.
1830 (Aug. 25) Belgium begins revolt against Netherlands; national congress chooses Leopold I as king in 1831; Dutch refuse to recognize independence until 1839.
c.1830–1910 Russian literature and music reach golden age with such writers as Gogol, Turgenev, Dostoyevsky, Tolstoy, and Chekhov, and such composers as Glinka, Borodin, Mussorgsky, Tchaikovsky, and Rimsky-Korsakov.
1832–33 Egypt's ruler Mohammed Ali conquers Syria and southern Turkey, defeating Ottoman Turkish main army; intervention by Britain, France, and Russia prevents overthrow of Ottoman Empire.
1833 (Aug. 23) Britain abolishes slavery in colonies; pays compensation to owners of 700,000 slaves freed.
1837–38 Egypt captures most of Arabia from Ottoman Turkish Empire.
1838–40 Antarctica proven to be continent by U.S. Navy Lt. Charles Wilkes.
1838–41 Costa Rica, El Salvador, Guatemala, Honduras, and Nicaragua become independent.
1839–40 War between Egypt and Ottoman Turkish Empire: Turks defeated in attack on Syria and forced to surrender fleet to Egypt; intervention by Britain forces Egypt to return Turkish fleet and give up claims to Syria.
1839–42 Opium War between Britain and China: China seizes illegally smuggled opium; Britain retaliates with attacks on cities; China forced to give Hong Kong to Britain and to open other ports to trade.
1840 (Jan. 22) New Zealand settled by British.
1840 (May 6) First postage stamps issued by Britain; U.S. follows on July 1, 1847.
1844 (Feb. 27) Dominican Republic wins independence in revolt from Haiti.
1845–47 Irish potato famine and typhus kill about 750,000; about 2 million others emigrate from Ireland to U.S. and other countries.
1846–48 Mexican War: U.S. defeats Mexico.
1847 (July 26) Liberia declares independence; first black colony in Africa to gain freedom.
1848 ***Communist Manifesto*** published in Germany by Karl Marx and Friedrich Engels, calling for workers to overthrow middle class.
1848 Switzerland becomes federal union: New constitution provides centralized national government.
1848 (Feb. 24) Revolution in France: Monarchy overthrown, establishing republic; voters on Dec. 10 elect as president Prince Louis Napoleon, nephew of Napoleon I.
1848–49 Revolutions put down by royal troops in Austria, Hungary, Czechoslovakia, Germany, and Italy.
1850–64 T'ai P'ing rebellion in China: Rebel believers in Chinese form of Puritan Protestantism win control of central provinces; subdued by Manchus with aid of foreign mercenaries; about 20 million die in fighting.

QUICK QUIZ: Who was the first American in space? See page 758.

KEY EVENTS IN WORLD HISTORY *(continued)*

ITALIAN AND GERMAN UNIFICATION AND COLONIAL EXPANSION: 1852–1914

1852 (Dec. 2) France restores monarchy: President Louis Napoleon becomes Emperor Napoleon III.
1853 France annexes New Caledonia: Penal colony established in Pacific island possession.
1853–56 Crimean War: Begins as dispute over control of Christian holy places in Jerusalem; Russia attacks Ottoman Turkish Empire; Britain and France come to aid of Turks; Russia defeated in battles on Crimean peninsula; Florence Nightingale establishes modern nursing, supervising British army hospitals; in Treaty of Paris, Russia agrees to remove forts and warships from Black Sea.
1854 Japan forced to open two ports to trade by U.S. Commodore Matthew C. Perry; in following two years Britain, Russia, and Netherlands obtain similar treaties.
1854 Slavery abolished in Venezuela: Government pays compensation to former owners; freed slaves denied civil rights.
1855 Thailand opens ports to foreign trade: Britain persuades King Rama IV to allow imports for first time since 1600s.
1855–68 Ethiopia unified: Emperor Theodore brings local chiefs under control, establishing centralized government for nation, then called Abyssinia.
1856 Persia invades Afghanistan, but Britain intervenes to force Persian withdrawal and recognition of Afghanistan's independence.
1856–70 Christians persecuted in Korea with execution of missionaries.
1857–58 Britain takes over government of India from British East India Company after exiling last Mogul emperior of India.
1857–58 Second Opium War in China: Britain and France force China to legalize opium imports and open more ports to foreign trade.
1858 France conquers Cochin China (South Vietnam), occupying Saigon.
1858 (Aug. 5) First transatlantic telegraph cable completed by Cyrus W. Field; Britain's Queen Victoria exchanges greetings with U.S. President James Buchanan.
1859 Theory of evolution published by Charles Darwin in *On the Origin of Species by Means of Natural Selection.*
1859–61 Unification of Italy: Sardinia annexes most of northern Italy, defeating Austrian troops with aid of France in 1859–60; army of "red shirts" led by Giuseppi Garibaldi conquers Sicily and southern Italy in 1860–61, whose people vote to unite with northern Italy; on March 17, 1861, independent kingdom of Italy is proclaimed under King Victor Emmanuel II, who had ruled Sardinia since 1849.
1860 (Oct. 12) British and French troops capture Peking, China: Because Chinese government reneges on observing terms of treaties, foreign troops seize capital, burning royal palace.
1861 (March 3) Serfdom abolished in Russia by Czar Alexander II.
1861–65 Civil War in United States.
1863 Cambodia made French protectorate.
1863 (June 7) Mexico City captured by French troops.
1863–65 Japan's emperor orders expulsion of all foreign traders, but bombardment of Japan by U.S., British, French, and Dutch warships forces him to approve foreign trade treaties.
1864 Austria and Prussia fight Denmark, taking Danish provinces.
1864 (April 10) Mexican monarchy established by French with Austrian Archduke Maximilian as emperor of Mexico.
1865–70 Paraguayan War: Argentina, Brazil, and Uruguay invade Paraguay; about three-fourths of nation's people killed or flee to other countries; about one-fourth of Paraguay's land taken by its neighbors.
1865–76 Russia conquers Turkestan east of Caspian Sea.
1866 Seven Weeks War: Austria defeated by Prussia and Italy, both of which gain territory at Austria's expense.
1867 Malaysian Straits Settlement becomes British colony.
1867 (June 19) Mexican Emperor Maximilian executed; Mexicans restore republic.
1867 (July 1) Dominion of Canada established by Britain with confederation of Ontario, Quebec, New Brunswick, and Nova Scotia.
1867 (Sept. 9) Luxembourg becomes independent neutral nation.
1868 Japan's Emperor Mutsuhito assumes direct rule, ending 700 years of feudal rule by shoguns (military dictators); capital moved to Tokyo.
1869 (Nov. 17) Suez Canal opens.
1870 (Oct. 2) Italy annexes Rome and Papal States from pope, making Rome capital of Italy.
1870–71 Franco-Prussian War: Prussians force surrender of Emperor Napoleon III at Battle of Sedan, Sept. 2, 1870; after four-month siege, capture Paris, Jan. 28, 1871; force France to pay indemnity of 5 billion francs; France again becomes republic.
1871 (Jan. 18) New German Empire proclaimed by Kaiser Wilhelm I, who had ruled as king of Prussia since 1861.
1873–74 France conquers Tonkin (North Vietnam), capturing Hanoi.
1874 Britain conquers Ashanti kingdom in Ghana, later establishing Gold Coast colony.
1874 Britain annexes Fiji.
1875–79 Egypt takes Red Sea coastal area (Eritrea) from Ethiopia.
1877–78 Russia attacks Ottoman Turkish Empire; threat of British intervention prevents Russian capture of Constantinople; Turks grant independence to Romania, Montenegro, and Serbia; Russia occupies Bulgaria.
1878 Berlin Congress of European powers settles issues remaining from Russia's defeat of Ottoman Turks; Britain acquires Cyprus; France gains Tunisia; Austria obtains Bosnia and Herzegovina (now in Yugoslavia).
1879–84 War of the Pacific: Chile defeats Peru and Bolivia, taking Bolivia's entire coast and Peru's southern region.
1880 France founds Brazzaville, Congo, making region French protectorate.
1881–82 Persecution of Jews begins in Russia, forcing many to flee to other lands.
1882 Italy invades Red Sea coast of Ethiopia in region that later became Italian colony of Eritrea.
1882 (May 20) Triple Alliance defense pact signed by Germany, Austria, and Italy.
1882 (Sept. 13) Britain invades Egypt: Establishes military occupation.
1883 Germany begins settlement of Southwest Africa.
1883–96 France conquers Madagascar, exiling Queen Ranavalona III to island of Réunion.
1884 Eastern New Guinea divided between Britain and Germany (Dutch keep western New Guinea).
1884–85 France forces China to recognize French protectorate over Indochina.
1884–88 France and Britain take control of Somalia coast of East Africa.
1885 Serbia attacks Bulgaria, but is defeated as Bulgarians take eastern region of Serbia.
1885 Germany takes Marshall and Solomon islands in Pacific and Tanganyika in Africa.
1885 (Jan. 26) Massacre in Khartoum: British Gen. Charles Gordon and his troops slain by Sudanese.
1885 (May 2) Congo Free State (now Zaire) established by Belgium's King Leopold II.
1885–86 British troops conquer Burma.
1885–96 Britain takes control of Kenya in East Africa.
1885–98 French troops gain control of most of West Africa, defeating local rulers.
1889 Brazil becomes republic with overthrow of Emperor Pedro II by conservatives angered by his abolition of slavery in 1888.
1889 Eiffel Tower completed in Paris; at 954 feet, then highest structure in world.
1890 Zanzibar made British protectorate.
1894 (Jan. 4) France and Russia agree to defense alliance if attacked by Germany, Austria, or Italy.
1894 Uganda made British protectorate.
1894–95 War between China and Japan: Japan wins control of Korea, Formosa (now Taiwan), and Pescadores Islands.
1895–96 Italian troops invade Ethiopia but are defeated, forcing Italy to recognize Ethiopia's independence.

1896 First modern Olympic Games held at Athens, Greece.
1896–98 Sudan conquered by British troops.
1897 Germany seizes Chinese city of Tsingtao, forcing China to sign 99-year lease on port.
1897 Greece attacks Ottoman Turkish Empire but is defeated, losing territory to Turks.
1898 Spanish-American War: U.S. ends Spanish rule of Cuba, Puerto Rico, and Philippines.
1898 (Aug. 12) Hawaii annexed by U.S.
1898–1902 Rebellion in Philippines put down by U.S. troops, establishing American rule.
1899 Nigeria made British protectorate.
1899 Persian Gulf Arab Sheikdoms made British protectorate.
1899 Open Door for China notes sent to world powers by U.S. Secretary of State John Hay, obtaining assurances that leased Chinese ports would be open to U.S. trade.
1899 First Hague Peace Conference: Adopts rules of war and treatment of war prisoners; establishes permanent court of arbitration to settle international disputes.
1899–1902 Boer War in South Africa: Britain defeats Dutch settlers in South Africa to annex previously independent republics of Orange Free State and South African Republic.
1900 Psychoanalysis as treatment of mental disease promoted by publication of Sigmund Freud's *The Interpretation of Dreams.*
1900–01 Boxer War in China: China attempts to end its exploitation by killing foreigners and destroying foreign installations; U.S., Russian, British, French, and German troops subdue Chinese, capturing and looting Peking on Aug. 14, 1900, and forcing China to pay for damages to foreign property.
1901 (Jan. 1) Commonwealth of Australia established by Britain.
1902 Russia forces China to turn over control of Manchuria (northern China).
1902 Australia grants women right to vote in federal elections.
1902 Cuba gains independence with election of first president; U.S. troops withdraw.
1902 (Jan. 20) Britain and Japan sign defense treaty: Britain recognizes Japan's right to control Korea.
1903 (Nov. 3) Panama declares independence from Colombia; U.S. obtains rights to Canal Zone to build Panama Canal.
1904–05 Russo-Japanese War: Japan attacks and defeats Russia, winning Russian ports in China, control of Korea, and southern Sakhalin Island; Russia withdraws from Manchuria.
1905 Physics revolutionized by Albert Einstein's theory of relativity, quantum theory, and formula for relationship of mass and energy ($E = mc^2$).
1905 Russian czar's troops crush revolt led by V.I. Lenin, but continued turmoil forces czar to agree to establishment of nation's first parliament, called Duma.
1905 (June 7) Norway declares independence from Sweden.
1906 (May 3) British-controlled Egypt takes Sinai peninsula from Ottoman Turkish Empire.
1906–09 U.S. troops occupy Cuba to put down rebellion by opponents of President Tomás Estrada Palma.
1907 Second Hague Peace Conference: World powers agree on detailed rules of war.
1907 Morocco invaded and occupied by French troops.
1907 Japan makes Korea protectorate: Japanese troops occupy nation, force abdication of Korea's emperor.
1908 Austria annexes Bosnia and Herzogovina: Take Balkan regions from Ottoman Turkish Empire.
1908 (Oct. 5) Bulgaria declares independence from Ottoman Turkish Empire.
1908 (Oct. 7) Crete unites with Greece.
1909 (April 6) North Pole reached by American explorers Robert E. Peary and Matthew Henson.
1910 (May 31) Union of South Africa established by Britain from former Boer states.
1910 (Oct. 5) Portugal becomes republic with overthrow of monarchy.
1911 (Dec. 16) South Pole first reached by Norwegian explorer Roald Amundsen.
1911–1912 China becomes republic with overthrow of Manchu emperor.
1911–1912 Italy invades and takes Libya from Ottoman Turkish Empire.
1911–1917 Russia invades and takes control of Persia.
1912 (April 14–15) British ocean liner ***Titanic*** strikes iceberg and sinks in Atlantic Ocean on maiden voyage; 1,517 lives lost.
1912 (Nov. 28) Albania declares independence from Ottoman Turkish Empire, becoming kingdom under Prince Wilhelm of Wied in 1914.
1912–1913 First Balkan War: Bulgaria, Serbia, Montenegro, and Greece join in defeating Ottoman Turkish Empire; division of spoils by great powers dissatisfies victors, leading to second Balkan War.
1913 (June 29–Aug. 10) Second Balkan War: Serbia, Greece, Montenegro, Romania, and Ottoman Turks join in defeating Bulgaria, taking some of territory Bulgaria had been awarded in first Balkan War.
1914 (April 21–Nov. 23) U.S. Marines occupy Veracruz, Mexico, intervening in civil war to protect American interests.

PERIOD OF WORLD WAR I THROUGH WORLD WAR II: 1914–1945

1914 (June 28) Assassination of Austria's Archduke Francis Ferdinand and his wife at Sarajevo in Austrian province of Bosnia: Austria believes Serbians responsible, issuing ultimatum to Serbia that leads to World War I.
1914 (July 28) World War I begins as Austria-Hungary declares war on Serbia; Germany declares war on Russia on Aug. 1, invades Luxembourg on Aug. 2, declares war on France on Aug. 3, and invades neutral Belgium on Aug. 4, causing Britain to declare war on Germany the same day; later, Central Powers of Germany and Austria are aided by Ottoman Turkish Empire and Bulgaria, while 24 other nations join as Allies to defeat them.
1914 (Aug. 15) Panama Canal opens.
1914 (Aug. 26–30) Battle of Tannenberg: Germans defeat Russian army in east Prussia, eliminating threat of Russian invasion.
1914 (Sept. 6–8) Battle of the Marne: Germans advance to within 15 miles of Paris, but French-British counterattack forces them to pull back; Western Front stabilizes with neither side being able to make breakthrough.
1915 (May 7) British ocean liner ***Lusitania*** **sunk** by German submarine with loss of 1,198 lives.
1915 (July 3) U.S. Marines land in Haiti to preserve order; remain until 1934.
1916 (March 15) U.S. troops invade Mexico in pursuit of Mexican revolutionary Francisco (Pancho) Villa; withdraw on Feb. 5, 1917.
1916 (April 24–29) Easter Rebellion in Ireland put down by British troops; 15 Irish leaders executed, others imprisoned.
1916 (Nov. 29) U.S. Marines land in Dominican Republic; remain until 1924.
1916–28 Civil war rages in China.
1917 Russian Revolution: Riots and revolt by troops bring abdication of Czar Nicholas II on March 15; Bolsheviks (Communists) overthrow moderate provisional government on Nov. 6, making V.I. Lenin dictator.
1917 (April 6) U.S. declares war on Germany.
1917 (Dec. 6) Finland declares independence from Russia.
1918 (March 3) Russia withdraws from World War I; signs Treaty of Brest-Litovsk with Central Powers, giving up claims to Finland, Latvia, Estonia, Lithuania, Poland, and other territories.
1918 (July 16) Murder of Czar Nicholas II and his family by Bolsheviks (Communists).
1918 (Oct. 28) Czechoslovakia declares independence.
1918 (Nov. 3) Poland proclaims independence.
1918 (Nov. 9) Germany's Kaiser Wilhelm II abdicates; flees to Netherlands.
1918 (Nov. 11) Armistice ends World War I; fighting stops at 11 A.M. on Western Front.
1918–19 Flu epidemic around world kills estimated 5–20 million persons.

QUICK QUIZ: Which planet is nearest to the Sun? See page 755.

KEY EVENTS IN WORLD HISTORY *(continued)*

1918–20 Russian Civil War: Fighting rages across Russia between Communists (Reds) and anti-Communists (Whites); U.S., British, and French troops intervene on side of Whites but are withdrawn in 1919.

1919 (May 16–27) First transatlantic airplane flight: U.S. Navy NC-4 flying boat with 5-man crew flies from Newfoundland to Lisbon, Portugal.

1919 (June 28) Treaty of Versailles signed, setting peace terms with Germany and establishing League of Nations; U.S. Senate later refuses to ratify treaty or join League.

1919 (Sept. 10) Treaty of Saint-Germain signed, setting peace terms for Austria and recognizing independence of Czechoslovakia, Hungary, Poland, and Yugoslavia.

1920 (Aug. 10) Treaty of Sèvres signed, setting World War I peace terms with Ottoman Turkish Empire; Turkish nationalists object to severity of treaty and refuse to accept it.

1920 (Nov. 15) League of Nations holds first meeting at Geneva, Switzerland.

1920 (Dec. 17) Japan receives mandate over Caroline, Marshall, and Mariana islands in Pacific Ocean.

1920 (Dec. 23) Britain divides Ireland into northern and southern parts, each with own parliament.

1920–23 Greece attacks Turkish nationalists, but is driven out of Turkey; victorious Turkish nationalists get Allies to sign Treaty of Lausanne modifying World War I penalties.

1921 (Feb. 20) Riza Khan Pahlevi seizes control of Iran: After ruling as dictator for four years, makes himself shah in 1925.

1921 (Dec. 6) Irish Free State formed in southern Ireland as self-governing dominion of British Empire; Northern Ireland remains part of United Kingdom.

1922 (Feb. 6) Washington naval arms limitation treaty signed, setting size of navies of U.S., Britain, France, Italy, and Japan, and requiring scrapping of many warships.

1922 (Feb. 28) Egypt regains sovereignty under King Fuad I as Britain ends protectorate, but British troops remain in Egypt.

1922 (Oct. 31) Benito Mussolini becomes premier of Italy; *Il Duce,* as he is called by Fascist followers, becomes dictator on Nov. 25.

1922 (Nov. 1) End of Ottoman Turkish Empire: Turkish nationalist leader Mustapha Kemal (Kemal Atatürk) abolishes sultanate and (in 1923) becomes first president.

1923 French troops occupy Germany's Ruhr area: France acts after Germany defaults on war reparations.

1923 (Nov. 8–11) Munich beer-hall putsch: Unsuccessful attempt by Nazi leader Adolf Hitler to overthrow state government of Bavaria; imprisoned, Hitler writes *Mein Kampf,* blueprint for new German empire.

1924 (Jan. 21) Death of Lenin: Joseph Stalin wins struggle for power, ruling as Soviet dictator until his death in 1953.

1926 (Jan. 8) Independent Kingdom of Hejaz and Nejd (now Saudi Arabia) proclaimed by King Ibn Saud.

1927 (Dec. 14) Iraq granted independence by Britain, but British troops remain in nation.

1928 Nationalist government of China established by Chiang Kai-shek with capital at Nanking after long civil war.

1928 (April 9) Turkey disestablishes Islam as state religion.

1928 (Aug. 27) Kellogg-Briand Pact signed, outlawing war, but provides no means of enforcement.

1929 (June 7) Vatican City becomes independent nation with signing of Lateran treaties between Italy and Roman Catholic Church.

1929–40 Worldwide Great Depression brings severe unemployment and economic chaos.

1930 (April 22) London naval treaty signed, providing further reductions in size of navies of U.S., Britain, and Japan.

1931 British Commonwealth of Nations established, giving dominions such as Australia and Canada complete independence with only formal allegiance to crown.

1931 (April 14) Spain becomes republic with overthrow of King Alfonso XIII.

1931–33 Japan invades and conquers Manchuria (northern China).

1932–35 Chaco War: Paraguay and Bolivia fight over possession of oil-rich Chaco region; treaty in 1938 awards two-thirds of region to Paraguay.

1933 (Jan. 30) Adolf Hitler becomes chancellor of Germany; *Der Führer,* as he is called by followers, becomes dictator on March 23.

1934–36 Italian-Ethiopian War: Italy invades and conquers Ethiopia.

1935 (March 16) Rearmament of Germany ordered by Hitler, renouncing Versailles Treaty's ban on German armament.

1936 (Oct. 27) Berlin-Rome Axis formed as Germany and Italy agree on working partnership; Japan later joins Axis powers with pact on Sept. 27, 1940.

1936 (Dec. 10) Britain's King Edward VIII abdicates to marry American-born divorcée.

1936–38 Soviet trials and executions of hundreds of Communist and military leaders strengthen Stalin's hold on dictatorship.

1936–39 Spanish Civil War: Army revolt led by Gen. Francisco Franco restores monarchy; Italy and Germany support Franco while Soviet Union aids Spanish republicans; about 1 million die in three years of fighting; Franco establishes himself as dictator.

1937–45 War between Japan and China: Japan attacks China, taking most of coastal region by 1938; China's government retreats inland, continuing fight through World War II.

1938 (March 12–13) Austria invaded and annexed by Germany.

1938 (Sept. 29) Munich agreement: Britain, France, and Italy agree to let Germany partition Czechoslovakia.

1938 (Oct. 1) Germany annexes Sudetenland, about one-third of Czechoslovakia's area.

1939 (March 15) Most of remainder of Czechoslovakia taken by Germany.

1939 (April 7) Albania annexed by Italy.

1939 (Aug. 24) Germany and Soviet Union sign 10-year peace pact; agreement frees Hitler to start World War II.

1939 (Sept. 1) World War II begins as Germany invades Poland without warning; Britain and France declare war on Germany on Sept. 3; Soviet Union invades Poland on Sept. 17; Hitler and Stalin partition Poland on Sept. 29.

1939–40 Russo-Finnish War: Soviet Union invades Finland, forcing nation to give up about one-tenth of its territory.

1939–45 German slave labor and extermination of Jews: Germany enslaves millions of conquered people, forcing them to work for German war effort; Hitler's Nazis kill about 60% of Europe's 10 million Jews.

1940 (April 9–May 3) Norway and Denmark conquered by Germany.

1940 (May 10–June 22) German blitzkrieg conquers Luxembourg, Netherlands, Belgium, and France; about 340,000 British and French troops escape to Britain in Dunkirk evacuation, May 28–June 4.

1940 (July 21) Estonia, Latvia, and Lithuania annexed by Soviet Union.

1940–41 Germany conquers Romania, Bulgaria, Yugoslavia, and Greece.

1941 (June 22) German troops invade Soviet Union, but meet stiff resistance and bog down in winter of 1941–42.

1941 (Dec. 7) Japan makes surprise air attacks on U.S. and British bases in Pacific, bringing U.S. into World War II.

1942–45 War in Africa and Europe: Under command of Gen. Dwight D. Eisenhower, Allied forces defeat Axis troops in Africa by May 1943, invade Italy on Sept. 3, 1943, and land in France on June 6, 1944; Russian troops advance across eastern Europe in 1944–45, while Eisenhower's armies liberate western Europe and roll across Germany; German military leaders sign unconditional surrender on May 7, 1945; fighting ends at 12:01 A.M. on May 9.

1942–45 War in Pacific: U.S. Navy's defeat of Japanese fleet at Battle of Midway on June 4–7, 1942, marks turning point of war in Pacific; U.S. begins offensive with landing of Marines on Guadalcanal in Solomon Islands on Aug. 7, 1942; series of amphibious landings in 1943–45 capture Japanese island strongholds from Gilbert Islands to Okinawa; on Oct. 19, 1944, U.S. troops under Gen. Douglas MacArthur land in Philippines; atomic bombs dropped on Japan on Aug. 6 and 9, 1945, bring Japan's capitulation on Aug. 14, with formal surrender signed on Sept. 2.

END OF COLONIAL EMPIRES, COLD WAR, AND ENERGY PROBLEMS: 1945–1983

1945–48 Communist Iron Curtain: After World War II Soviet Union keeps its troops in eastern European nations it had "liberated" from Germany; Latvia, Estonia, and Lithuania incorporated into Soviet Union; British leader Winston Churchill warns on March 5, 1946, "an Iron Curtain has descended across Europe"; communist governments establish dictatorships In Yugoslavia, Albania, Bulgaria, Romania, Poland, East Germany, Hungary, and Czechoslovakia, all as satellites of Soviet Union.

1945–49 Indonesian War for Independence: Indonesian nationalists declare independence on Aug. 17, 1945; Dutch troops fight rebels in effort to reimpose colonial rule until Netherlands finally recognizes independence of Indonesia on Dec. 27, 1949.

1945–54 Indochina War: Nationalist leaders in 1945 declare independence in Cambodia (March), Laos (April), and Vietnam (September); France determines to reimpose colonial rule; for over eight years French troops supplied by U.S. battle guerrillas aided by Soviet Union and communist China; French will to fight breaks after Battle of Dien Bien Phu when after 55-day siege French army of 10,000 surrenders on May 7, 1954; at conference in Geneva, France agrees on July 21, 1954, to end fighting, recognizing independence of North and South Vietnam; earlier, in 1953, independence to Laos (Oct. 22) and Cambodia (Nov. 9) granted by France.

1946 (Jan. 1) Japan's Emperor Hirohito disclaims his divinity, ending his worship as god.

1946 (Jan. 10) UN General Assembly meets for first time; delegates of 51 nations hold meeting in London.

1946 (March 22) Transjordan (now Jordan) granted independence by Britain.

1946 (June 2) Italy votes to become republic, ending monarchy.

1946 (July 4) Philippines granted independence by United States.

1946 (Oct. 16) Ten Nazi leaders hanged as war criminals after 10-month trial at Nuremberg; chief Hitler aide Hermann Goering kills himself a few hours before execution.

1946 (Nov. 3) Japan adopts new constitution under guidance of Allied Supreme Commander Gen. Douglas MacArthur, giving all emperor's power to parliament.

1946–49 Civil War in Greece: Greece votes to restore monarchy on Sept. 1, 1946; communist guerrillas supported by Soviet Union begin struggle to overthrow government; Truman Doctrine announced by U.S. in 1947 provides aid to Greek government, enabling it to defeat guerrillas by October 1949.

1947 (Aug. 15) India and Pakistan granted independence within British Commonwealth.

1948 (Jan. 4) Burma granted independence.

1948 (Feb. 4) Ceylon (now Sri Lanka) given independence by Britain.

1948 (April 3) European Recovery Program (Marshall Plan) enacted by U.S. at urging of President Truman to provide aid to European nations to save them from communism; over $12 billion given in four years.

1948 (April 30) Organization of American States (OAS) Charter signed at Bogotá, Colombia (effective Dec. 13, 1951).

1948 (Dec. 23) Seven wartime Japanese leaders hanged for war crimes, including former Japanese prime minister Hideki Tojo.

1948–49 First Arab-Israeli War: Israel proclaims independence on May 14, 1948, upon withdrawal of British troops from Palestine; six Arab nations attack Israel; U.S. supports Israel with military supplies; UN mediation brings truce in 1949; over 900,000 Arabs flee Israel.

1948–49 Berlin blockade and Berlin airlift: Soviet Union blockades roads to West Berlin beginning on June 24; U.S. starts airlift, delivering over 2 million tons of supplies in next 16 months to prevent city from falling to communists; blockade ends on May 12, 1949.

1949 (April 4) NATO treaty signed to provide military defense of western Europe.

1949 (April 18) Ireland declares independence from Britain.

1949 (Aug. 29) Soviet Union test-explodes its first atomic bomb, setting off fears in West that communists would launch surprise A-bomb attack to destroy U.S. and western Europe.

1949 (Dec. 7) Communists win control of mainland China after 3-year civil war.

1950–53 Korean War: Begins on June 25, 1950; North Korea invades South Korea; UN calls for aid to South Korea; U.S. begins sending troops on June 27; 15 other UN nations send troops; Gen. Douglas MacArthur becomes UN supreme commander; over 1 million die in war, including 54,000 U.S. servicemen; ends with truce signed on July 27, 1953.

1950–53 Communist atomic spy ring: Members arrested in Britain and U.S. in 1950, convicted in 1951; U.S. citizens Julius and Ethel Rosenberg executed for treason on June 19, 1953.

1951 (Sept. 8) Japanese peace treaty signed in San Francisco by 49 nations: treaty goes into effect on April 28, 1952.

1951 (Dec. 24) Libya becomes independent kingdom.

1953 (June 18) Egypt becomes republic ruled by military junta.

1954–62 Algerian War of Independence: Arab nationalists attack French outposts in November 1954; over 500,000 French troops fight for 7 years to maintain colonial rule; France agrees to Algeria's independence (effective July 3, 1962).

1955 (March 25) East Germany granted full sovereignty by Soviet Union.

1955 (May 5) West Germany becomes independent under Chancellor Konrad Adenauer.

1955 (July 27) Austria regains independence as peace treaty guaranteeing its neutrality becomes effective (signed May 15).

1956 (Oct. 23–Nov. 4) Hungarian Revolution: Revolt overthrows communist government but is suppressed by Soviet army; about 150,000 Hungarians flee to U.S. and other nations.

1956 (Oct. 29–Nov. 6) Second Arab-Israeli War: Israel with support of France and Britain attacks Egypt; Suez Canal seized; U.S. and Soviet Union condemn action; UN arranges cease-fire on Nov. 6; British and French troops withdraw on Dec. 22; Israel withdraws from Egypt on March 1, 1957.

1956–77 End of French colonial empire: Begins with Indochina War of 1945–54, in which Laos, Cambodia, and Vietnam win independence, but accelerates as following nations gain independence: 1956, Morocco, Tunisia; 1958, Guinea; 1960, Cameroon, Togo, Malagasy, Dahomey, Niger, Upper Volta, Ivory Coast, Chad, Central African Republic, Congo, Gabon, Senegal, Mali, Mauritania; 1962, Algeria, after 7 years of war; 1977, Djibouti.

1956–81 Breakup of British Empire: Begins in 1947–48 with independence of India, Pakistan, Ceylon, and Burma, but accelerates as following nations gain independence: 1956, Sudan; 1957, Ghana, Malaysia; 1960, Somalia, Cyprus, Nigeria; 1961, Sierra Leone, South Africa, Kuwait, British Cameroons, Tanganyika; 1962, Jamaica, Trinidad and Tobago, Uganda; 1963, Zanzibar, Kenya; 1964, Malawi, Malta, Zambia; 1965, Gambia, Maldive Islands; 1966, Guyana, Botswana, Lesotho, Barbados; 1967, South Yemen; 1968, Mauritius, Swaziland; 1970, Tonga, Fiji; 1971, Bahrain, Qatar, United Arab Emirates; 1973, Bahamas; 1974, Grenada; 1976, Seychelles; 1978, Solomons, Tuvalu, Dominica; 1979, St. Lucia, St. Vincent, Kiribati; 1980, Vanuatu, Zimbabwe; 1981, Antigua, Belize.

1957 (Jan. 5) Eisenhower Doctrine proposed for U.S. to send troops to aid any Middle East nation to fight communist aggression; approved by U.S. Senate resolution on March 7.

1957 (Oct. 4) First man-made satellite orbits Earth: *Sputnik I* launched by Soviet Union.

1958 (Jan. 1) European Common Market begins, including Belgium, France, West Germany, Italy, Luxembourg, and Netherlands.

1958 (July 15) U.S. troops land in Lebanon under Eisenhower Doctrine; withdraw Oct. 25.

1958 (May 31) France's Gen. Charles de Gaulle becomes premier with emergency powers; becomes president on Jan. 8, 1959.

1959 (Jan. 1) Fidel Castro overthrows Cuban dictator Fulgencio Batista after 3-year civil war.

QUICK QUIZ: What is the world's tallest building? See page 931.

KEY EVENTS IN WORLD HISTORY *(continued)*

1959 (June 26) St. Lawrence Seaway formally opens, linking Atlantic Ocean and Great Lakes.

1960 Communist China and Soviet Union split in controversy over communist ideology.

1960 Soviet Premier Khrushchev cancels Paris summit meeting with President Eisenhower after Soviet Union shoots down U.S. U-2 spy plane and U.S. admits sending regular spy flights over Soviet territory.

1960 OPEC (Organization of Petroleum Exporting Countries) holds first meeting, forcing Standard Oil of New Jersey to retract an announced decrease in oil prices; OPEC's charter members were Iran, Iraq, Kuwait, Qatar, and Saudi Arabia.

1960 (Feb. 13) France becomes atomic power, exploding first A-bomb in desert of Algeria.

1960 (June 23) U.S.-Japanese mutual security treaty becomes effective.

1960–62 Belgium ends its African colonial empire, giving independence to Belgian Congo (now Zaire) on June 30, 1960, and to Rwanda and Burundi in 1962.

1960–67 Revolts in Congo (now Zaire): Immediately after Congo receives independence from Belgium, fighting breaks out as provinces of Katanga and Kasai seek independence; UN sends troops to aid government, 1960–64; rebellion ends in November 1967.

1961 (Jan. 3) U.S. breaks diplomatic relations with Cuba over refusal by Fidel Castro's government to pay for confiscated U.S. property.

1961 (April 12) First man orbits Earth in space: Soviet cosmonaut Maj. Yuri Gagarin.

1961 (April 17–20) Cuba defeats U.S.-supported Bay of Pigs invasion: Cuban troops overwhelm force of 1,600 Cuban exiles trained by U.S. CIA.

1961 (May 31) South Africa becomes independent republic: Severs ties with British Commonwealth of Nations because of criticism of its racial policies.

1961 (Aug. 13) Berlin Wall built by Soviet Union to prevent escape of East Germans to West Berlin.

1961 (Dec. 18–19) India seizes Portuguese colonies of Goa, Damao, and Diu.

1962 (Jan. 1) Western Samoa granted independence by New Zealand.

1962 (May 31) Israel executes Hitler aide Adolf Eichmann, convicted of directing World War II German extermination of Jews.

1962 (Oct. 20–Nov. 22) China invades India, but ends fighting on Nov. 22 and withdraws.

1962 (Oct. 22–28) Cuban missile crisis: U.S. blockades Cuba, forcing Soviet Union to withdraw nuclear missiles from island.

1963 (Jan. 22) France and Germany sign treaty of friendship, ending 400 years of conflict.

1964 (March 27) UN troops land in Cyprus to prevent fighting between Greeks and Turks.

1964–73 U.S. intervention in Vietnam War: U.S. begins bombing of North Vietnam on Aug. 5, 1964, in retaliation for reported attack on U.S. destroyers; on Aug. 7, U.S. Congress votes President authority "to prevent further aggression"; first U.S. ground combat authorized on June 28, 1965; over 541,000 U.S. troops fighting in Vietnam by 1969; U.S. begins withdrawing in 1969; cease-fire begins on Jan. 28, 1973; last U.S. troops leave Vietnam on March 29, 1973.

1966 (July 1) France withdraws from NATO.

1967 (June 5–10) Third Arab-Israeli War: Israel launches surprise attack; captures Egypt's Sinai peninsula to east bank of Suez Canal; takes Jordan territory west of Jordan River; seizes Golan Heights from Syria; additional 750,000 Arab refugees displaced.

1967–70 Nigerian Civil War: Attempted secession of eastern region of Biafra put down.

1968 (Aug. 20–21) Invasion of Czechoslovakia by about 650,000 troops of Soviet Union and Warsaw Pact nations ousts liberal communist regime.

1968–74 African drought south of Sahara: thousands of persons and millions of cattle die.

1970 (Sept. 4) Chile elects communist as president, first to head any nation as result of free election; later overthrown in military revolt, Sept. 11, 1973.

1970 (Dec. 12–20) Riots in Poland put down by Soviet troops, but bring resignation of communist dictator Wladyslaw Gomulka.

1971 (Feb. 11) Seabed treaty outlawing installation of atomic weapons on ocean floor signed by U.S., Soviet Union, Britain, and others; effective on May 18, 1972.

1971 (March 25–Dec. 16) Bangladesh wins independence from Pakistan in civil war.

1971 (Oct. 25) Communist China admitted to UN as U.S. ends 22 years of opposition.

1972 (Sept. 29) China and Japan end state of war that began in 1937.

1973 (Jan. 1) European Common Market adds Britain, Denmark, and Ireland.

1973 (June 1) Greece ends monarchy as military dictator deposes King Constantine II.

1973 (June 16–24) End of Cold War between U.S. and Soviet Union seen in spirit of détente at summit meeting of President Nixon and Soviet leader Leonid I. Brezhnev in U.S.

1973 (July 17) Afghanistan becomes republic as military officers depose king.

1973 (Aug. 15) All U.S. combat operations end in Southeast Asia by congressional order.

1973 (Oct. 6–24) Fourth Arab-Israeli War: Egypt and Syria launch surprise attack on Israel; Israel counterattacks, crossing Suez Canal into Egypt and invading Syria; UN cease-fire ends fighting on Oct. 24.

1973 (Oct. 17) Oil embargo begun by Arab nations against U.S., Netherlands, and other nations in effort to force support of Arab policies against Israel; causes energy shortages; Arabs end embargo in 1974 (with U.S. on March 18).

1974 (May 18) India becomes sixth nuclear nation with atomic test explosion.

1974 (July 15–Aug. 16) War in Cyprus: Civil war begins as Greek-led national guard overthrows government; on July 20, Turkey intervenes, landing 40,000 troops, enlarging Turkish-held portion of island.

1974 (Nov. 17) Democracy restored in Greece with first free national election in 10 years.

1974–76 End of Portugal's dictatorship and colonial empire in Africa: Military coup on April 25, 1974, overthrows 40-year dictatorship in Portugal; colonies given independence; socialists win parliamentary elections in 1976.

1974–76 Worldwide inflation and recession rage when Organization of Petroleum Exporting Countries (OPEC) raises crude-oil prices nearly 500% above 1973 levels.

1975 (April 17) Cambodia falls to communists; red troops capture Phnom Penh.

1975 (April 30) South Vietnam surrenders to communists; Saigon captured by North Vietnamese troops, ending 16-year Vietnam War.

1975 (Aug. 1) Helsinki Pact signed by U.S., Canada, Soviet Union, and 32 European nations guaranteeing national boundaries.

1975 (Nov. 6) Invasion of Spanish Sahara by thousands of unarmed Moroccans; Spain agrees to give up region to Morocco and Mauritania.

1975–76 Civil war rages in Lebanon between rightist Christians and leftist Muslims; ends when Syrian army occupies nation.

1975–76 Communists win civil war in Angola with aid of Cuban troops and Soviet arms.

1976 (March 23) International Bill of Rights goes into effect with ratification by 35 nations.

1976 (July 28) Earthquake devastates Tientsin-Tangshan area of China; 655,237 reported dead.

1977 (Sept. 7) U.S. and Panama sign treaties to turn Canal over to Panama on Dec. 31, 1999.

1977 (Nov. 19) Egypt's President Sadat becomes first Arab national leader to visit Israel, launching drive to achieve peace in Middle East.

1978 (Oct. 23) China and Japan sign treaty: End 40 years of hostility with peace pact.

1979 (Jan. 16) Revolt overthrows shah of Iran, who flies to exile; Muslim leader Ayatollah Ruhollah Khomeini creates Islamic state with himself as ruler for life.

1979 (March 26) Egypt-Israel peace treaty signed at White House after mediation by President Carter; goes into effect on April 25.

1979 (Dec. 27) Soviet troops invade Afghanistan; overthrow communist ruler, replacing him with pro-Soviet leader; guerrillas fight Soviet troops.

1979–81 U.S.-Iranian crisis: Iranians capture U.S. embassy in Teheran on Nov. 4, 1979; hold 52 Americans hostage until Jan. 20, 1981.

1980–83 Iraq-Iran War in Middle East: Iraq attacks Iran on Sept. 22, 1980, seeking control of Shatt Al Arab waterway at head of Persian Gulf.

1982 (April 2–June 14) Falkland Islands War: Britain defeats Argentine invasion of British colony.

1983 For events of 1983, see pages 7–31.

KINGS, QUEENS, AND RULERS

AUSTRIA [1]

Hapsburg Dynasty

Franz II [2] 1792–1835
Ferdinand I 1835–1848
Franz Josef I 1848–1916
Karl I 1916–1918

First Republic, 1918–1938
Part of Germany, 1938–1945
Second Republic, 1945–

BELGIUM

House of Coburg

Leopold I 1831–1865
Leopold II 1865–1909
Albert I 1909–1934
Leopold III 1934–1951
Baudouin 1951–

BRITAIN

Saxons and Danes

Egbert 827–839
Ethelwulf 839–858
Ethelbald 858–860
Ethelbert 860–866
Ethelred II 866–871
Alfred the Great 871–901
Edward the Elder 901–925
Athelstan 925–940
Edmund 940–946
Edred 946–955
Edwy 955–959
Edgar 959–975
Edward the Martyr 975–978
Ethelred II 978–1016
Edmund Ironside 1016
Canute the Dane 1016–1035
Harold I 1035–1040
Hardicanute 1040–1042
Edward the Confessor 1042–1066
Harold II 1066

Norman

William I 1066–1087
William II 1087–1100
Henry 1100–1135
Stephen 1135–1154

Plantagenet

Henry II 1154–1189
Richard I 1189–1199
John 1199–1216
Henry III 1216–1272
Edward I 1272–1307
Edward II 1307–1327
Edward III 1327–1377
Richard II 1377–1399

Lancaster

Henry IV 1399–1413
Henry V 1413–1422
Henry VI 1422–1461, 1470–1471

York

Edward IV 1461–1470, 1471–1483
Edward V 1483
Richard III 1483–1485

Tudor

Henry VII 1485–1509
Henry VIII 1509–1547
Edward VI 1547–1553
Jane (14 days) 1553
Mary I 1553–1558
Elizabeth I 1558–1603

Stuart

James I 1603–1625
Charles I 1625–1649

Commonwealth

Long Parliament 1649–1653

Protectorate

Oliver Cromwell 1653–1658
Richard Cromwell 1658–1659

Stuart Restoration

Charles II 1660–1685
James II 1685–1688

Orange

William III 1689–1702
and Mary II 1689–1694

Stuart

Anne 1702–1714

Hanover

George I 1714–1727
George II 1727–1760
George III 1760–1820
George IV 1820–1830
William IV 1830–1837
Victoria 1837–1901

Saxe-Coburg–Gotha

Edward VII 1901–1910

Windsor

George V 1910–1936
Edward VIII (325 days) 1936
George VI 1936–1952
Elizabeth II 1952–

BULGARIA

Saxe-Coburg–Gotha

Ferdinand I [3] 1908–1918
Boris III 1918–1943
Simeon II 1943–1946

Communist state, 1946–

CHINA

Hsia Dynasty, c.2200–1766 B.C.
Shang Dynasty, c.1766–1123 B.C.
Chou Dynasty, c.1122–256 B.C.
Ch'in Dynasty, 221–207 B.C.
Han Dynasty, 202 B.C.–A.D. 220
Disorder, 220–589
T'ang Dynasty, 618–907
Sung Dynasty, 960–1279
Yuan Dynasty, 1260–1368
Ming Dynasty, 1368–1644
Manchu (Ch'ing) Dynasty

Shun-chih 1644–1661
K'ang-hsi 1661–1722
Yung-cheng 1723–1735
Chien-lung 1736–1796
Chia-ch'ing 1796–1820
Tao-kuang 1821–1851
Hsien-feng 1851–1862
T'ung-chih 1862–1875
Kuang-hsü 1875–1908
Hsüan-t'ung 1909–1912

Republic, 1912–1949

Sun Yat-sen 1912
Yüan Shih-k'ai 1912–1916
Chiang Kai-shek 1928–1949

Communist state, 1949–

DENMARK

Waldemarian Dynasty

Waldemar the Great 1157–1182
Knut VI 1182–1202
Waldemar II 1202–1241
Eric Plowpenny 1241–1250
Abel 1250–1252
Kristoffer 1252–1259
Eric V 1259–1286
Eric VI 1286–1319
Kristoffer II 1320–1332
Waldemar IV 1340–1375
Olaf [4] 1376–1387
Margrethe I [5] 1387–1412
Eric [5] 1412–1439
Kristoffer [5] 1439–1448

House of Oldenburg

Kristian I of Oldenburg [5] 1448–1481
Hans [5] 1481–1513
Kristian II [5] 1513–1523
Frederik I [6] 1523–1533
Kristian III [6] 1534–1559
Frederik II [6] 1559–1588
Kristian IV [6] 1588–1648
Frederik III [6] 1648–1670
Kristian V [6] 1670–1699
Frederik IV [6] 1699–1730
Kristian VI [6] 1730–1746
Frederik V [6] 1746–1766
Kristian VII [6] 1766–1808
Frederik VI [6] 1808–1839
Kristian VIII 1839–1848
Frederik VII 1848–1863

House of Glücksborg

Kristian IX 1863–1906
Frederik VIII 1906–1912
Kristian X 1912–1947
Frederik IX 1947–1972
Margrethe II 1972–

EGYPT [7]

Protodynastic Period

Dynasty I .... c. 3110–2884 B.C.
Mena (Menes) .... c. 3110–3080 B.C.
Dynasty II .... c. 2883–2811 B.C.

Old Kingdom

Dynasty III .... c. 2664–2180 B.C.
Djoser .... c. 2663–2645 B.C.
Dynasty IV .... c. 2614–2502 B.C.
Snefru .... c. 2614–2591 B.C.
Khufu (Cheops) .... c. 2590–2568 B.C.
Menkaure .... c. 2534–2508 B.C.
Dynasty V .... c. 2501–2342 B.C.
Userkaf .... c. 2501–2491 B.C.
Sahure .... c. 2490–2476 B.C.
Unis .... c. 2371–2342 B.C.
Dynasty VI .... c. 2341–2180 B.C.
Teti .... c. 2341–2328 B.C.
Pepi I .... c. 2327–2278 B.C.
Pepi II .... c. 2272–2182 B.C.

First Intermediate Period

Dynasty VII .... c. 2180–2175 B.C.
Dynasty VIII .... c. 2174–2155 B.C.
Dynasty IX .... c. 2154–2100 B.C.
Dynasty X .... c. 2100–2052 B.C.
Dynasty XI .... c. 2134–1999 B.C.
Mentuhotep II .... c. 2061–2011 B.C.

[1] From 1273 members of the Hapsburg dynasty ruled Austria as part of the German Holy Roman Empire; see list under *Germany*. [2] Franz II took title emperor of Austria in 1804 and gave up title Holy Roman emperor in 1806. [3] Ruled as prince from 1887 to 1908. [4] King of Denmark and Norway after 1380. [5] Ruler of Denmark, Norway, and Sweden. [6] Ruler of Denmark and Norway. [7] Listing does not include lesser-known Egyptian rulers.

EGYPT *(continued)*

Middle Kingdom

Dynasty XII . . . . c. 1991–1786 B.C.
Amenemhet I . . . . . c. 1991–1962 B.C.
Senusert I . . . . c. 1971–1928 B.C.
Amenemhet II . . . . c. 1929–1895 B.C.
Senusert II . . . . c. 1897–1879 B.C.
Amenemhet . . . . . . c. 1842–1797 B.C.

Second Intermediate Period

Dynasty XIII . . . . c. 1785–1660 B.C.
Dynasty XIV . . . . c. 1715–1650 B.C.
Dynasty XV . . . . c. 1652–1544 B.C.
Dynasty XVI . . . . c. 1650–1550 B.C.
Dynasty XVII . . . . c. 1600–1554 B.C.

New Kingdom

Dynast XVIII . . . . c. 1554–1529 B.C.
Ahmose . . . . c. 1554–1529 B.C.
Amenhotep I . . . . . . c. 1529–1509 B.C.
Thutmose I . . . . c. 1509–1497 B.C.
Thutmose II . . . . . . c. 1497–1490 B.C.
Hatshepsut . . . . c. 1489–1469 B.C.
Thutmose III . . . . . . c. 1490–1436 B.C.
Amenhotep II . . . . . c. 1438–1412 B.C.
Thutmose IV . . . . . . c. 1412–1403 B.C.
Amenhotep III . . . . c. 1403–1366 B.C.
Akhenaton . . . . c. 1366–1349 B.C.
Tutankhamen . . . . . c. 1339–1335 B.C.
Horemheb . . . . c. 1335–1304 B.C.
Dynasty XIX . . . . c. 1304–1192 B.C.
Ramses I . . . . c. 1304–1303 B.C.
Seti I . . . . c. 1303–1290 B.C.
Ramses II . . . . c. 1290–1223 B.C.
Merneptah . . . . c. 1223–1211 B.C.
Dynasty XX . . . . c. 1192–1190 B.C.
Ramses III . . . . c. 1190–1158 B.C.

Late Dynastic Period

Dynasty XXI . . . . c. 1075–940 B.C.
Smendes . . . . c. 1075–1048 B.C.
Dynasty XXII . . . . c. 940–730 B.C.
(Libyan kings)
Dynasty XXIII . . . . c. 761–715 B.C.
Dynasty XXIV . . . . c. 725–710 B.C.
Dynasty XXV . . . . c. 736–657 B.C.
(Ethiopian kings)
Dynasty XXVI . . . . c. 664–525 B.C.
Necho I . . . . c. 664–663 B.C.
Psamtik I . . . . c. 663–609 B.C.
Necho II . . . . c. 609–594 B.C.

Ruled by Persian Empire

Dynasty XXVII . . . . c. 525–404 B.C.

Independence regained

Dynasty XXVIII . . . . c. 404–399 B.C.
Amyrtaeus . . . . c. 404–399 B.C.
Dynasty XXIX . . . . c. 399–378 B.C.
Dynasty XXX . . . . c. 378–341 B.C.

Persian rule restored

Dynasty XXXI . . . . c. 341–332 B.C.

Conquest by Alexander the Great and rule by Greeks, 332–30 B.C.

Ptolemy I Soter . . . . . c. 305–283 B.C.
Ptolemy II . . . . c. 285–246 B.C.
Ptolemy III . . . . c. 246–221 B.C.
Cleopatra . . . . c. 47–30 B.C.

Conquest by Romans, 30 B.C.

Conquest by Arabs, 639–642

Fatimid Caliphate of Egypt

Al-Mahdi 909–934
Al-Qaim 934–945
Al-Mansur 945–952
Al-Aziz 952–975
Al-Hakim 996–1021
Az-Zahir 1021–1036
Al-Mustansir 1036–1094
Al-Mustadi 1094–1101
Al-Amir 1101–1130
Al-Hafiz 1130–1149
Az-Zafir 1149–1154
Al-Faiz 1154–1160
Al-Adid 1160–1171

Ayyubid Caliphate, 1171–1250

Salah al-Din (Saladin) 1171–1193

Mameluke Sultans, 1250–1517

Ottoman Turkish conquest and rule, 1517–1914

British protectorate, 1914–1922

Independent monarchy restored

Fuad I 1922–1936
Faruk I 1936–1952
Faruk II 1952–1953

Republic, 1953–

FRANCE

Carolingian Dynasty

Charlemagne 768–814
Louis I the Pious 814–840
WEST FRANCIA
Charles the Bald 840–877
Louis II 877–879
Louis III 879–882
Carloman 879–884
Eudes 888–898
Charles the Simple 893–923
Rudolph 923–936
Louis IV 936–954
Lothair 954–986
Louis V 986–987
MIDDLE KINGDOMS
Lothair, Emperor 840–855
Louis (Italy), Emperor 855–875
Charles (Provence), King 855–863
Lothair II (Lorraine), King 855–869

Capetian Kings

Hugh Capet 987–996
Robert II 996–1031
Henri I 1031–1060
Philippe I 1060–1108
Louis VI 1108–1137
Louis VII 1137–1180
Philippe II (August) 1180–1223
Louis VIII 1223–1226
Louis IX 1226–1270
Philippe III 1270–1285
Philippe IV 1285–1314
Louis X 1314–1316
Jean I 1316
Philippe V 1316–1322
Charles IV 1322–1328

House of Valois

Philippe VI 1328–1350
Jean II 1350–1364
Charles V 1364–1380
Charles VI 1380–1422
Charles VII 1422–1461
Louis XI 1461–1483
Charles VIII 1483–1498
Louis XII 1498–1515
François I 1515–1547
Henri II 1547–1559
François II 1559–1560
Charles IX 1560–1574
Henri III 1574–1589

Bourbon Dynasty

Henri IV 1589–1610
Louis XIII 1610–1643
Louis XIV 1643–1715
Louis XV 1715–1774
Louis XVI 1774–1792

First Republic, 1792–1799

Napoleon Bonaparte

First Consul 1799–1804
Napoleon I, Emperor 1804–1814
Hundred Days 1815

Bourbon Restoration

Louis XVIII 1814–1824
Charles X 1824–1830
Louis Philippe 1830–1848

Second Republic, 1848–1852

Napoleon III, Emperor, 1852–1870

Third Republic, 1870–1940

Pétain regime, 1940–1944

Provisional government, 1944–1946

Fourth Republic, 1946–1958

Fifth Republic, 1958–

Charles de Gaulle 1958–1969
Georges Pompidou 1969–1974
Valéry Giscard d'Estaing . . . 1974–1981
François Mitterrand 1981–

GERMANY [1]

Carolingian Dynasty

Charlemagne 768–814
Louis (Ludwig I) the Pious 814–840
Lothair I 840–855
Ludwig II the German 843–876
Karl II the Bald 875–877
Karl III the Fat 876–887
Arnulf 887–899
Ludwig III the Child 899–911

Franconian House

Konrad I 911–918

Saxon House

Heinrich I the Fowler 919–936
Otto I the Great 936–973
Otto II 973–983
Otto III 983–1002
Heinrich II the Saint 1002–1024

Franconian (Salian) House

Konrad II 1024–1039
Heinrich III 1039–1056
Heinrich IV 1056–1106
Heinrich V 1106–1125
Lothair II 1125–1137

Hohenstaufen House

Konrad III 1138–1152
Friedrich I Barbarossa 1152–1190
Heinrich VI 1190–1197
Philipp of Swabia 1198–1208
Otto IV of Brunswick 1198–1215
Friedrich II 1215–1250
Konrad IV 1250–1254

Great Interregnum, 1254–1273

Rulers of Various Houses

Rudolf I of Hapsburg 1273–1291
Adolf of Nassau 1292–1298
Albrecht I of Austria 1298–1308

[1] Most rulers of Germany were Holy Roman emperors from 800 through Franz II in 1792.

GERMANY *(continued)*

Heinrich VII of Luxembourg	1308–1313
Ludwig IV of Bavaria	1314–1347
Friedrich of Austria	1314–1326
Karl IV of Luxembourg	1346–1378
Wenzel of Bohemia	1378–1400
Ruprecht of Palatinate	1400–1410
Sigismund of Luxembourg	1411–1437

Hapsburg Dynasty

Albrecht II	1438–1439
Friedrich III	1440–1493
Maximilian I	1493–1519
Karl V (of Spain)	1519–1556
Ferdinand I	1556–1564
Maximilian II	1564–1576
Rudolf II	1576–1612
Matthias	1612–1619
Ferdinand II	1619–1637
Ferdinand III	1637–1657
Leopold I	1657–1705
Josef I	1705–1711
Karl VI	1711–1740
Maria Theresia	1740–1780
Franz I	1745–1765
Josef II	1765–1790
Leopold II	1790–1792
Franz II[2]	1792–1806

Hohenzollern Dynasty

Friedrich I[3]	1701–1713
Friedrich Wilhelm I[3]	1713–1740
Friedrich II the Great[3]	1740–1786
Friedrich Wilhelm II[3]	1786–1797
Friedrich Wilhelm III[3]	1797–1840
Friedrich Wilhelm IV[3]	1840–1861
Wilhelm I[4]	1861–1888
Friedrich III	1888
Wilhelm II	1888–1918

Weimar Republic, 1918–1933

Third Reich (Nazi Dictatorship)

Adolf Hitler	1933–1945

Allied occupation, 1945–1952

Division into Federal Republic of Germany (West) and German Democratic Republic (East), 1949–

GREECE

Danish House

Otto I	1832–1862
George I	1863–1913
Constantine I	1913–1917
Alexander I	1917–1920
Constantine I	1920–1922
George II	1922–1923

First Greek Republic, 1924–1935

Monarchy restored, 1935–1973

George II	1935–1947
Paul I	1947–1964
Constantine II	1964–1973

Second Greek Republic, 1973–

HUNGARY

Arpád Dynasty

St. István I	997–1038
Peter Orseolo	1038–1046
András I	1047–1060
Béla I	1061–1063
Solomon	1063–1074
Geza I	1074–1077
St. László	1077–1095
Coloman	1095–1116
István II	1116–1131
Béla II	1131–1141
Geza II	1141–1161
István III	1161–1173
István IV	1162–1163
Béla III	1173–1196
Emeric I	1196–1204
László III	1204–1205
András II	1205–1235
Béla IV	1235–1270
István V	1270–1272
László IV	1272–1290
András III	1290–1301
Carobert	1308–1342
Lajos I the Great	1342–1382
Maria	1382–1395
Sigismund	1387–1437
Albrecht	1437–1439
Ulászló I	1439–1444
László V	1444–1457
Mátyás Hollos	1458–1490
Ulászló II	1490–1516
Lajos II	1516–1526

Hungary Partitioned and Ruled by Turkey and Austria, 1526–1918

Revolution and Disorder, 1918–1920

Regency, Admiral Nicholas Horthy, 1920–1945

Communist state, 1945–

INDIA

Mogul Emperors

Babar	1526–1530
Humayun	1530–1556
Akbar the Great	1556–1605
Jahangir	1605–1627
Shah Jahan	1628–1658
Aurangzeb	1658–1707
Bahadur Shah I	1707–1712
Jahandar Shah	1712–1713
Farruk-Siar	1713–1719
Mohammed Shah	1719–1748
Ahmed	1748–1754
Alamgir	1754–1759
Shah Alam	1759–1806
Mohammed Akbar II	1806–1837
Bahadur Shah II	1837–1857

British rule, 1857–1947

British dominion, 1947–1950

Republic, 1950–

IRAN (PERSIA)

Achaemenid Empire

Cyrus II	559–530 B.C.
Cambyses II	530–522 B.C.
Smerdis	522 B.C.
Darius I	522–486 B.C.
Xerxes I	486–465 B.C.
Artaxerxes I	465–424 B.C.
Xerxes II	424–423 B.C.
Sogdianus	424–423 B.C.
Darius II	423–404 B.C.
Artaxerxes II	404–359 B.C.
Artaxerxes III	359–338 B.C.
Arses	338–336 B.C.
Darius III	336–330 B.C.

Conquest by Alexander the Great and rule by Seleucid Greeks, 331–187 B.C.

Parthian Empire, c.171 B.C.–A.D. 224

Sasanian Empire, c.224–651

Rule by Arabs, 651–892

Samanid Dynasty, 892–999

Ghaznavid Dynasty, 999–1037

Conquest and rule by Seljuk Turks, 1037–1157

Disorder, 1157–1260

Conquest and rule by Mongol Il-khans, 1260–1353

Conquest by Mongol Timur (Tamerlane) and rule by Timurid Dynasty, 1369–1469

Safavid Dynasty

Ismail I	1502–1524
Tahmasp I	1524–1576
Ismail II	1576–1578
Mohammed Khudabanda	1578–1587
Abbas I	1587–1629
Safi I	1629–1642
Abbas II	1642–1667
Suleiman	1667–1694
Husain	1694–1722
Tahmasp II	1722–1731
Abbas III	1731–1736

Nadir Shah, 1736–1747

Zand Dynasty, 1750–1794

Kajar Dynasty

Aga Mohammed	1794–1797
Fath Ali	1797–1835
Mohammed	1835–1848
Nasir ud-Din	1848–1896
Muzaffar ud-Din	1896–1907
Mohammed Ali	1907–1909
Ahmed Mirza	1909–1925

Pahlevi Dynasty

Riza Shah Pahlevi	1925–1941
Mohammed Riza Pahlevi	1941–1979

Republic, 1979–

ISLAMIC ARAB EMPIRE

Mohammed	622–632
Abu Bakr	632–634
Omar	634–644
Othman	644–656
Ali	656–661

Omayyad Caliphate

Muawiya I	661–680
Yasid I	680–682
Muawiya II	683
Marwan I	684–685
Abdalmalik	685–705
Walid I	705–715
Sulaiman	715–717
Omar ibn Abdul-Aziz	717–720
Yazid II	720–724
Hisham	724–743
Walid II	743–744
Yazid III	744
Ibrahim	744
Marwan II	744–750

Abbasid Caliphate

Abu-l-Abbas al-Saffah	750–754
Al-Mansur	754–775
Al-Mahdi	775–785
Al-Hadi	785–786
Harun Al-Rashid	786–809
Al-Amin	809–813
Al-Mamun	813–833
Al-Mu'tasim	833–842
Al-Wathiq	842–847
Al-Mutawakkil	847–861

[1] Most rulers of Germany were Holy Roman emperors from 800 through Franz II in 1792. [2] After giving up title Holy Roman emperor in 1806, he continued to rule Austria until 1835. [3] King of Prussia. [4] Emperor of Germany after 1871.

ISLAMIC ARAB EMPIRE *(cont.)*

Al-Muntasir 861–862
Al-Musta'in 862–866
Al-Mu'tazz 866–869
Al-Muqtadi 869–870
Al-Mu'tamid 870–892
Al-Mu'tadid 892–902
Al-Muqtafi 902–908
Al-Muqtadir 908–932
Al-Qahir 932–934
Al-Radi 934–940
Al-Muttaqi 940–944
Al-Mustaqfi 944–946
Al-Muti 946–974
Al-Ta'i 974–991
Al-Qadir 991–1031
Al-Qa'im 1031–1075
Al-Muqtadi 1075–1094
Al-Mustazhir 1094–1118
Al-Mustarshid 1118–1135
Al-Rashid 1135–1136
Al-Muqtafi 1136–1160
Al-Mustanjid 1160–1170
Al-Mustadi 1170–1180
Al-Nasir 1180–1225
Al-Zahir 1225–1226
Al-Mustansir 1226–1242
Al-Musta'sim 1242–1258

Mongols destroy Baghdad and overthrow Arab Empire, 1258

ITALY

Vittorio Emanuele II 1849–1878
Umberto I 1878–1900
Vittorio Emanuele III 1900–1946
Umberto II 1946

Fascist Dictatorship

Benito Mussolini 1922–1943

Italian Republic, 1946–

JAPAN

Legendary period, 660 B.C.–A.D. 710

Emperor Jimmu Tenno 660–585 B.C.

Nara Period, 710–784
Heian Period, 794–1185
Kamakura Period, 1185–1333
Ashikaga Period, 1336–1568
Unification Period, 1568–1603

Tokugawa Shoguns

Ieyasu 1603–1605
Hidetada 1605–1623
Iemitsu 1623–1651
Ietsuna 1651–1680
Tsunayoshi 1680–1709
Ienobu 1709–1713
Ietsugu 1713–1716
Yoshimune 1716–1745
Ieshige 1745–1760
Ieharu 1760–1786
Matsudaira Sadanobu 1787–1793
Ienari 1793–1838
Ieyoshi 1838–1853
Iesada 1853–1858
Iemochi 1858–1866
Yoshinobu 1866–1867

Meiji Era

Emperor Mutsuhito 1867–1912

Taisho Era

Emperor Yoshihito 1912–1926

Showa Era

Emperor Hirohito 1926–

JORDAN

Abdullah 1946–1951
Talal 1951–1952
Hussein 1952–

LIECHTENSTEIN

Prince Johann II 1858–1929
Prince Franz I 1929–1938
Prince Franz Josef II 1938–

LUXEMBOURG

Duke Adolf of Nassau 1890–1905
William 1905–1912
Marie Adelaide 1912–1919
Charlotte 1919–1961
Prince Jean 1961–

NETHERLANDS

Houses of Orange and Nassau

Willem I (the Silent) 1581–1584
Maurice of Nassau 1584–1625
Frederik Heinrich 1625–1647
Willem II 1647–1650
Jan de Witt 1650–1672
Willem III [1] 1672–1702
Willem IV 1711–1751
Willem V 1751–1795

Batavian Republic, 1795–1806

French rule, 1806–1813

Louis Bonaparte 1806–1810

House of Orange-Nassau

Willem I 1813–1840
Willem II 1840–1849
Willem III 1849–1890
Wilhelmina 1890–1948
Juliana 1948–1980
Beatrix 1980–

NORWAY [2]

Harold I Fairhair 872–930
Haakon I the Good 935–961
Harold II Graycloak 961–970
Haakon, Jarl 970–995
Olav I Trygvesson 995–1000
Olav II (Saint Olav) 1016–1028
Magnus I the Good 1035–1047
Harold III Hardruler 1046–1066
Olav III the Quiet 1066–1093
Magnus II Bareleg 1093–1103
Sverre 1184–1202
Haakon IV the Old 1217–1263
Magnus V Lawmender 1263–1280
Erik II Priest-Hater 1280–1299
Haakon V 1299–1319

Governed by rulers of Denmark or Sweden, 1319–1905

Independence restored

Haakon VII 1905–1957
Olav V 1957–

POLAND

Piast Dynasty

Mieszko I .... c. 960–992
Boleslaw I the Brave 992–1025
Mieszko II 1025–1034
Kazimierz I 1038–1058
Boleslaw II the Bold 1058–1079
Wladyslaw I 1079–1102
Boleslaw III 1102–1138
Wladyslaw II 1138–1146
Boleslaw IV 1146–1173
Mieszko III 1173–1177
Kazimierz II the Just 1177–1194
Leszek I the White 1194–1227
Boleslaw V the Chaste 1227–1279
Lezek II the Black 1279–1288
Przemyslaw II 1290–1296

Rule by Bohemia

Wenceslaus I 1300–1305

Piast Dynasty restored

Wladyslaw IV 1305–1333
Kazimierz III the Great 1333–1370

Elected Monarch

Louis of Anjou 1370–1382

Jagiellonian Dynasty

Jadwiga 1384–1399
Wladyslaw V Jagiello 1386–1434
Wladyslaw VI 1434–1444
Kazimierz IV 1447–1492
Jan I 1492–1501
Aleksandr I 1501–1506
Zygmunt I 1506–1548
Zygmunt II 1548–1572

Elected Monarchs

Henri of Valois 1573–1574
Stefan Bathory 1575–1586
Zygmunt III 1587–1632
Wladyslaw VII 1632–1648
Jan II Kazimierz 1648–1668
Michal Wisniowiecki 1669–1673
Jan III Sobieski 1674–1696
Augustus II 1697–1704
Stanislaw Leszczynski 1704–1709
Augustus II 1709–1733
Stanislaw Leszczynski 1733–1734
Augustus III 1734–1763
Stanislaw Poniatowski 1764–1795

Partition among Austria, Russia, and Prussia, 1795–1918

Republic of Poland, 1918–1939

Partition between Germany and Soviet Union, 1939–1945

Soviet occupation, 1945–1948

Communist state, 1948–

PORTUGAL

Burgundian Dynasty

Afonso Henriques 1139–1185
Sancho I 1185–1211
Afonso II 1211–1223
Sancho II 1223–1245
Afonso III 1245–1279
Diniz 1279–1325
Afonso IV 1325–1357
Pedro I 1357–1367
Fernando I 1367–1383

Avis Dynasty

João I 1385–1433
Duarte I 1433–1438
Afonso V 1438–1481
João II 1481–1495
Manuel I 1495–1521

[1] Willem III also ruled as King William III of England and Scotland in 1689–1702. [2] Does not include claimants to Norway's throne during many periods of civil war.

João III 1521–1557
Sebastião I 1557–1578
Henrique 1578–1580
Spanish rule, 1580–1640
House of Braganza
João IV 1640–1656
Afonso VI 1656–1667
Pedro II 1667–1706
João V 1706–1750
José Manuel 1750–1777
House of Coburg-Braganza
Maria I and Pedro III 1777–1786
Maria I 1786–1816
João VI 1816–1826
Pedro IV 1826
Maria II 1826–1828
Miguel 1828–1833
Maria II 1833–1853
Pedro V 1853–1861
Luis I 1861–1889
Carlos I 1889–1908
Manuel II 1908–1910
1st Portuguese Republic, 1910–1928
Fascist Dictatorship
Antonio Salazar 1928–1968
Marcelo Caetano 1968–1974
2d Portuguese Republic, 1974–

ROMANIA

Carol I 1881–1914
Ferdinand I 1914–1927
Michael 1927–1930
Carol II 1930–1940
Michael 1940–1947
Communist state, 1947–

RUSSIA

Grand Princes of Moscow
Vsevolod III 1176–1212
Yuri II 1212–1216
Konstantin 1216–1219
Yuri II 1219–1238
Yaroslav II 1238–1246
Andrei II 1246–1252
Aleksandr Nevski 1252–1263
Yaroslav III 1263–1272
Vasili 1272–1277
Dmitri 1277–1294
Andrei III 1294–1304
Mikhail 1304–1319
Yuri III 1319–1325
Dmitri 1325–1326
Aleksandr 1326–1328
Ivan I 1328–1340
Simeon 1340–1353
Ivan II 1353–1359
Dmitri Donskoi 1359–1389
Vasili I 1389–1425
Vasili II 1425–1462
Czars of Russia
Ivan III the Great 1462–1505
Vasili III 1505–1533
Ivan IV the Terrible 1533–1584
Fedor I 1584–1598
Boris Godunov 1598–1605
Fedor II 1605
Dmitri I 1605–1606
Vasili IV 1606–1610
Romanov Dynasty
Mikhail 1613–1645
Aleksei 1645–1676
Fedor III 1676–1682
Ivan V 1682–1689
Peter I the Great 1682–1725
Ekaterina Alekseevna I 1725–1727
Peter II Alekseevich 1727–1730
Anna Ioannovna 1730–1740
Ivan VI 1740–1741
Elizaveta Petrovna 1741–1762
Peter III Fedorovich 1762
Ekaterina Alekseevna II (the Great) 1762–1796
Pavel Petrovich 1796–1801
Aleksandr I Pavlovich 1801–1825
Nikolai I Pavlovich 1825–1855
Aleksandr II Nikolaevich 1855–1881
Aleksandr III Aleksandrovich 1881–1894
Nikolai II Aleksandrovich 1894–1917
Provisional Government
Aleksandr Kerensky 1917
Bolshevik Revolution, 1917
Soviet Union, 1917–
V.I. Lenin 1917–1924
Joseph Stalin 1924–1953
Georgi Malenkov 1953–1955
Nikita S. Khrushchev 1955–1964
Leonid I. Brezhnev 1964–

SAUDI ARABIA

Ibn Saud 1932–1953
Saud 1953–1964
Faisal 1964–1975
Khalid 1975–

SPAIN

Houses of Aragon and Castile
Fernando II of Aragon and Isabel I of Castile 1479–1504
Fernando II and Felipe I 1504–1506
Fernando II and Carlos II 1506–1516
Spanish Hapsburgs
Carlos I (as Holy Roman Emperor, Karl V) 1516–1556
Felipe II 1556–1598
Felipe III 1598–1621
Felipe IV 1621–1665
Carlos II 1665–1700
Spanish Bourbons
Felipe V 1700–1746
Fernando VI 1746–1759
Carlos III 1759–1788
Carlos IV 1788–1808
French King of Spain
Joseph Bonaparte 1808–1813
1st Bourbon Restoration
Fernando VII 1813–1833
Isabel II 1833–1868
House of Savoy
Amadeo I 1868–1873
1st Spanish Republic, 1873–1875
2d Bourbon Restoration
Alfonso XII 1875–1885
Alfonso XIII 1886–1931
2d Spanish Republic, 1931–1939
Fascist Dictatorship
Francisco Franco 1939–1975
3d Bourbon Restoration
Juan Carlos I 1975–

SWEDEN

House of Vasa
Gustaf I 1523–1560
Eric XIV 1560–1568
Johan III 1568–1592
Sigismund 1592–1599
Karl IX 1604–1611
Gustaf II Adolf 1611–1632
Christina 1644–1654
Karl X Gustaf 1654–1660
Karl XI 1660–1697
Karl XII 1697–1718
Ulrika Eleonora 1718–1720
Fredrik I 1720–1751
Adolf Fredrik 1751–1771
Gustaf III 1771–1792
Gustaf IV Adolf 1792–1809
Karl XIII 1809–1818
House of Bernadotte
Karl XIV Johan 1818–1844
Oskar I 1844–1859
Karl XV 1859–1872
Oskar II 1872–1907
Gustaf V 1907–1950
Gustaf VI Adolf 1950–1973
Karl XVI Gustaf 1973–

TURKEY

Seljuk Sultans
Tughril I 1055–1063
Alp Arslan 1063–1072
Malik Shah I 1073–1092
Mahmud 1092–1094
Barkyaruk 1094–1104
Malik Shah II 1104
Seljuk Turkish Empire divided 1104
Ottoman Sultans
Osman c.1299–1326
Orkhan 1326–1359
Murad I 1359–1389
Bajazet I 1389–1403
Suleiman I 1403–1411
Musa 1411–1413
Mohammed I 1413–1421
Murad II 1421–1451
Mohammed II 1451–1481
Bajazet II 1481–1512
Selim I 1512–1520
Suleiman II 1520–1566
Selim II 1566–1574
Murad III 1574–1595
Mohammed III 1595–1603
Ahmed I 1603–1617
Mustafa I 1617–1618
Osman II 1618–1622
Mustafa I 1622–1623
Murad IV 1623–1640
Ibrahim 1640–1648
Mohammed IV 1648–1687
Suleiman III 1687–1691
Ahmed II 1691–1695
Mustafa II 1695–1703
Ahmed III 1703–1730
Mahmud I 1730–1754
Osman III 1754–1757
Mustafa III 1757–1774
Abdul-Hamid I 1774–1789
Selim III 1789–1807
Mustafa IV 1807–1808
Mahmud II 1808–1839
Abdul-Medjid I 1839–1861
Abdul-Aziz 1861–1876
Murad V 1876
Abdul-Hamid II 1876–1909
Mohammed V 1909–1918
Mohammed VI 1918–1922
Republic, 1923–

ROMAN AND BYZANTINE EMPERORS AND EMPRESSES

Octavian, the grandnephew and adopted son of Julius Caesar, founded the Roman Empire. He became emperor in 27 B.C., called himself Augustus, and took complete control of military and governmental powers. At the death of Theodosius the Great in 395, the empire was divided into east and west.

The large-scale barbarian invasions of the 400s caused the empire in the west to crumble. In 476 Odoacer, a German leader, entered Rome and forced Emperor Romulus Augustulus to abdicate.

In the east the Roman Empire continued to exist for nearly 10 more centuries under Greek rulers as the Byzantine Empire.

Where dates overlap in the following list, the title of emperor was shared.

ROMAN EMPERORS

Augustus	27 B.C.-A.D. 14
Tiberius	14–37
Caligula	37–41
Claudius	41–54
Nero	54–68
Galba	68–69
Otho	69
Vitellius	69
Vespasian	69–79
Titus	79–81
Domitian	81–96
Nerva	96–98
Trajan	98–117
Hadrian	117–138
Antoninus Pius	138–161
Marcus Aurelius	161–180
Lucius Verus	161–169
Commodus	180–192
Pertinax	193
Didius Julianus	193
Septimius Severus	193–211
Geta	209–211
Caracalla	211–217
Macrinus	217–218
Heliogabalus (Elagabalus)	218–222
Alexander Severus	222–235
Maximinus Thrax	235–238
Gordian I Africanus	238
Gordian II	238
Balbinus	238
Pupienus Maximus	238
Gordian III Pius	238–244
Philip the Arab	244–249
Decius	249–251
Hostilian	251
Gallus	251–253
Aemilian	253
Valerian	253–259
Gallienus	259–268
Claudius II Gothicus	268–270
Quintillus	270
Aurelian	270–275
Tacitus	275–276
Florian	276
Probus	276–282
Carus	282–283
Carinus	283–285
Numerian	283–284
Diocletian	284–305
Maximian	286–305; 306–308
Constantius I Chlorus	305–306
Galerius	305–311
Severus	306–307
Maxentius	306–312
Maximinus Daia	308–313
Licinius	311–324
Constantine I the Great	311–337
Constantine II	337–340
Constans	337–350
Constantius II	337–361
Julian the Apostate	361–363
Jovian	363–364
Valentinian I (in the West)	364–375
Valens (in the East)	364–378
Gratian (in the West)	375–383
Valentinian II (in the West)	375–392
Theodosius I the Great	379–395
Magnus Maximus	383–388
Eugenius	392–394

ROMAN EMPERORS IN WEST

Honorius	395–423
Constantius III	421
Johannes	423–425
Valentinian III	425–455
Petronius Maximus	455
Avitus	455–456
Majorian	457–461
Libius Severus	461–465
Anthemius	467–472
Olybrius	472
Glycerius	473
Julius Nepos	473–475
Romulus Augustulus	475–476

ROMAN EMPERORS IN EAST

Arcadius	395–408
Theodosius II	408–450
Marcian	450–457
Leo I	457–474
Leo II	473–474
Zeno	474–491

BYZANTINE RULERS IN EAST

Anastasius I	491–518
Justin I	518–527
Justinian the Great	527–565
Justin II	565–578
Tiberius II	578–582
Maurice	582–602
Phocas I	602–610
Heraclius I	610–641
Constantine III	641
Heracleon	641
Constans II	641–668
Constantine IV	668–685
Justinian II	685–695
Leontius	695–698
Tiberius II	698–705
Justinian II	705–711
Philippicus	711–713
Anastasius II	713–715
Theodosius III	715–717
Leo III	717–741
Constantine V	741–775
Leo IV	775–780
Constantine VI	780–797
Irene	797–802
Nicephorus I	802–811
Stauracius	811
Michael I	811–813
Leo V	813–820
Michael II	820–829
Theophilus I	829–842
Michael III	842–867
Basil I	867–886
Leo VI	886–912
Alexander II	912–913
Constantine VII	912–959
Romanus I	920–944
Romanus II	959–963
Basil II	963–1025
Nicephorus II	963–969
John I	969–976
Constantine VIII	1025–1028
Zoë	1028–1050
Romanus III	1028–1034
Michael IV	1034–1041
Michael V	1041–1042
Constantine IX	1042–1055
Theodora	1055–1056
Michael VI	1056–1057
Isaac I	1057–1059
Constantine X	1059–1067
Romanus IV	1068–1071
Michael VII	1071–1078
Nicephorus III	1078–1081
Alexius I	1081–1118
Andronicus I	1183–1185
Isaac II	1185–1195
Alexis III	1195–1203
Isaac II	1203–1204
Alexius IV	1203–1204
Alexius V	1204

LATIN RULERS

Baldwin I	1204–1205
Henry	1205–1216
Peter of Courtenay	1216–1217
Yolande	1217–1219
Robert of Courtenay	1219–1228
Baldwin II	1228–1261
John of Brienne	1231–1237

NICAEAN EMPERORS

Theodore I	1204–1222
John III	1222–1254
Theodore II	1254–1258
John IV	1258–1261

PALEOLOGI EMPERORS

Michael VIII	1259–1282
Andronicus II	1282–1328
Michael IX	1295–1320
Andronicus III	1328–1341
John V	1341–1347
John VI	1347–1354
John V	1355–1376
Andronicus IV	1376–1379
John V	1379–1391
John VII	1390
Manuel II	1391–1425
John VIII	1425–1448
Constantine XI	1448–1453

KEY EVENTS IN AMERICAN HISTORY

Presented here in chronological order are many of the important events in American history from the time of the early explorers to the present day. For the convenience of the reader, the table of events has been divided into 10 broad periods of history.

PERIOD OF EXPLORATION AND COLONIZATION: 1000–1763

c.1000 **Norse Vikings** discover North America; Leif Ericson lands at Vinland (probably Newfoundland).

1492 (Oct. 12) **Christopher Columbus** discovers America for Spain; after sailing 33 days out of sight of land, goes ashore on San Salvador (Watling) Island in Bahamas, believing he has reached East Indies.

1492 (Dec. 26) **First Spanish settlement** in Western Hemisphere founded by Columbus at La Navidad in what is now Haiti; later destroyed by Indians.

1496 **First Permanent Spanish city** in Western Hemisphere founded by Bartholomew Columbus: Santo Domingo, now in Dominican Republic.

1497 (June 24) **English claim for North America** established by John Cabot, landing on either Newfoundland or Nova Scotia.

1508 **First Spanish settlement in Puerto Rico** founded by Juan Ponce de León.

1513 (April 2) **Florida discovered** and claimed for Spain by Juan Ponce de León.

1513 (Sept. 25) **Pacific Ocean discovered** and all lands bordering it claimed for Spain by Vasco de Balboa, after crossing Isthmus of Panama.

1524 **French claim for North America** established by Giovanni da Verrazano; explored Atlantic coast and sailed into New York harbor.

1538 **First university in Western Hemisphere,** University of St. Thomas Aquinas, founded in Santo Domingo, now in Dominican Republic.

1540–42 **Francisco Vásquez de Coronado** explores American southwest, going as far north as Kansas and claiming region for Spain.

1541 (May 8) **Mississippi River discovered** by Spanish explorer Hernando de Soto near present-day Memphis, Tenn.

1562 **First French settlement** in what is now the U.S. founded by Jean Ribaut; called Charlesfort, on Port Royal Sound in South Carolina; later abandoned.

1564 (June) **First French colony** in Florida founded by René de Laudonnière; called Fort Caroline, near present-day Jacksonville; later destroyed by Spaniards.

1565 (Sept. 8) **First permanent European settlement** in what is now continental U.S. established at St. Augustine, Fla., by Pedro Menéndez de Avilés of Spain.

1585 **First English colony** settled on Roanoke Island, N.C.; survived only 10 months.

1587 (Aug. 18) **First English child,** Virginia Dare, born in what is now U.S., in second Roanoke settlement—the "Lost Colony."

1607 (May 14) **First permanent English settlement** in what is now U.S. established at Jamestown, Va.

1609 **Hudson River explored** and claimed for Dutch by explorer Henry Hudson.

1610 **Santa Fe** established as capital of Spanish colony of New Mexico, oldest capital city in U.S.

1614 **New Netherland (New York) founded** by Dutch with building of fort at what is now Albany, N.Y.

1619 **First black slaves** in North America arrive at Jamestown in Dutch ship.

1619 (July 30) **First legislature,** Virginia's House of Burgesses, convenes at Jamestown.

1620 (Nov. 21) **Mayflower Compact** signed by Pilgrims aboard *Mayflower* in Provincetown, Mass., harbor.

1620 (Dec. 26) **Pilgrims land** to found colony at Plymouth, Mass.

1626 **Manhattan Island, N.Y.,** bought by Dutch from Indians for about $24.

1628 (Sept. 6) **Puritans land at Salem** founding Massachusetts Bay Colony (royal charter granted March 14, 1629); Boston founded in 1630.

1634 (March 25) **Maryland founded** with landing of English Roman Catholics led by Gov. Leonard Calvert, brother of Lord Baltimore.

1636 **Providence, R.I., founded** by Roger Williams to provide religious freedom for all faiths.

1636 (Oct 28) **Harvard College founded** in Massachusetts; first institution of higher learning in U.S.

1638 **First printing press** in English colonies set up by Stephen Day at Cambridge, Mass.; publishes first book, *Bay Psalm Book,* in 1640.

1639 (Jan. 24) **Fundamental Orders of Connecticut** adopted; provides for elected governor and legislature.

1649 (April 21) **Maryland's Toleration Act** passed, granting religious freedom to all Christian faiths.

1660 (Dec. 1) **First Navigation Act** passed by British parliament to regulate colonial trade.

1664 (Sept. 8) **New Amsterdam (now New York City) captured** by British from Dutch.

1670 (April) **Colony of South Carolina begun** with settlement established at Charleston.

1673 (July 17) **Père Jacques Marquette and Louis Joliet** explore Mississippi River as far south as Arkansas for France.

1675–78 **King Philip's War** fought between colonists and Indians in Massachusetts.

1676 (Sept. 19) **Nathaniel Bacon** burns Jamestown in rebellion against Virginia's British governor.

1677 **First charter separating church and state** framed for Quaker colony of West Jersey.

1681 (March 14) **Pennsylvania** proprietary charter granted William Penn by Charles II.

1682 (April 9) **Sieur de La Salle** paddles down Mississippi River to its mouth, claiming Louisiana for France.

1684 (Oct. 18) **Massachusetts Bay Colony** charter annulled by British court.

1685–89 **Dominion of New England created** by Britain's King James II to include all New England colonies plus New York, New Jersey, and Pennsylvania; rebellions by colonists and overthrow of James II in England ends scheme.

1689 (April 18) **Rebellion in Boston** overthrows British royal governor of New England, Sir Edmund Andros.

1689 (Aug. 1) **Protestant rebellion in Maryland** overthrows governor of Roman Catholic proprietors; Maryland restored to Baltimore family proprietors in 1715 after their conversion to Protestantism.

1689–91 **Rebellion in New York:** Jacob Leisler overthrows British governor and establishes elective assembly; arrested for treason and hanged in 1691.

1689–97 **King William's War** fought by British and French in New York, New England, and Canada.

1691 (Oct. 17) **New Massachusetts royal charter** issued, incorporating Plymouth Colony and Maine into Massachusetts.

1692 **Witch trials in Salem, Mass.,** result in execution of 14 women and 6 men; 55 more plead guilty and accuse others.

1702–13 **Queen Anne's War,** in which British fight against French and Spaniards in New England, Florida, and South Carolina; France loses Hudson Bay region, Newfoundland, and Nova Scotia to Britain.

1704 (April 24) **First successful newspaper** in colonies established: *Boston News-Letter.*

1721 (May 29) **South Carolina** formally incorporated as royal colony.

1729 (July 25) **North Carolina** becomes royal colony under British king.

1732 (June 9) **Royal charter for Georgia** granted to James Edward Oglethorpe.

1735 (Aug. 4) **Freedom of the press trial** of John Peter Zenger ends as jury acquits him of libel, asserting that truth is not libelous.

1739–42 **War of Jenkins' Ear** fought between Georgia colonists and Spaniards in Florida.

1744–48 **King George's War** fought between British and French colonists; ends with no changes in territory by either side.

1749 (May 19) **Ohio Company** granted charter by

QUICK QUIZ: Scarlett O'Hara is a character in what famous book? See page 93.

KEY EVENTS IN AMERICAN HISTORY *(continued)*

King George II to settle Ohio Valley.

1753 George Washington sent to Ohio Valley by Virginia's Gov. Robert Dinwiddie to warn French to leave.

1754 (May 28) French defeated by 22-year-old Lt. Col. George Washington in first skirmish of French and Indian War, at Great Meadows, Pa.; Washington surrenders Fort Necessity to French on July 4.

1755 (July 9) British Maj. Gen. Edward Braddock killed and his army routed by French near Fort Duquesne (Pittsburgh), Pa.; Braddock's aide, Col. George Washington, escapes capture.

1759 (Sept. 18) French surrender Quebec to British.

1761 (Feb. 24) Massachusetts patriot James Otis in court suit denounces several warrants, known as writs of assistance, used by British customs officers.

1763 Indian Chief Pontiac kills hundreds of settlers along frontier in 7 months of warfare.

1763 (Feb. 10) Treaty of Paris ends French and Indian War; France loses to Britain all lands east of Mississippi River and Canada; Spain gives up Florida to Britain in exchange for Cuba.

ERA OF THE AMERICAN REVOLUTION: 1763–1783

1763 (Oct. 7) British government orders all settlers out of Ohio Valley and forbids settlement west of Appalachian Mountains.

1765 (March 22) Stamp Act passed by British parliament levying direct taxes on American colonists for first time.

1765 (March 24) Quartering Act passed by British parliament requires American colonists to provide living quarters and supplies for British troops.

1765 (Oct. 7–25) Stamp Act Congress held in New York City with delegates from nine colonies protesting British taxation without representation.

1766 (March 18) Repeal of Stamp Act approved by British parliament and king, bowing to American refusal to import taxed goods.

1766 (March 18) Declaratory Act passed by British parliament asserting its right to make laws binding on American colonists "in all cases whatsoever."

1767 Daniel Boone makes first journey over Appalachians into Kentucky.

1767 (June 29) Townshend Acts passed by British parliament, putting new import duties on glass, lead, paint, paper, and tea used by American colonists.

1767–69 Nonimportation by colonists of taxes goods cuts British trade by about 50%.

1770 (March 5) Boston Massacre: British troops fire on crowd of patriots protesting quartering of soldiers in Boston; 5 colonists killed and 8 wounded.

1770 (April 12) Repeal of Townshend Acts taxes, except those on tea, approved by King George.

1771 (May 16) Battle of Alamance fought in North Carolina between militia, led by Gov. William Tryon, and western Regulators, protesting lack of representation in legislature.

1772 (June 9) British customs schooner *Gaspée* burned by patriots near Providence, R.I.

1772 (Nov. 2) Committee of Correspondence elected by Boston town meeting with James Otis as chairman to circulate patriotic information.

1773 (May 10) Tea Act passed by British parliament giving East India Company right to undersell American tea merchants.

1773 (Dec. 16) Boston Tea Party: Sons of Liberty dressed as Indians dump tea from East India Company ships into Boston Harbor.

1774 (March 31) Boston Port Bill passed by British parliament closing Boston Harbor to trade in retaliation for Boston Tea Party.

1774 (May 20) Massachusetts Government Act: British parliament puts limits on powers of Massachusetts legislature and forbids town meetings without consent of governor.

1774 (May 20) Quebec Act approved by British parliament extends Canada's boundaries to Ohio River, ignoring claims to region by Connecticut, Massachusetts, and Virginia.

1774 (Sept. 5–Oct. 26) First Continental Congress meets in Philadelphia with delegates from 12 colonies, protesting British measures and calling for boycott on imports of all British goods.

1775 (March 30) New England Restraining Act passed by British parliament and approved by king forbids colonies of New England from trading with any other nation than Britain or its colonies in West Indies.

1775 (April 19) Battles of Lexington and Concord signal beginning of American Revolution.

1775 (June 15) George Washington elected commander in chief of Continental Army by Second Continental Congress.

1775 (June 17) Battle of Bunker Hill won by British at Boston, but more than twice as many British troops are killed and wounded than are Americans.

1775 (Aug. 23) Britain's King George III declares American colonies in open rebellion; follows on Dec. 23 with decree forbidding all trade with colonies.

1776 (Jan. 9) Thomas Paine publishes *Common Sense,* rallying Americans to cause of independence.

1776 (March 4–17) British troops evacuate Boston, sailing to Halifax, Nova Scotia.

1776 (June 1–28) Charleston, S.C., successfully beats off British attack.

1776 (July 2) British army of 10,000 lands on Staten Island for invasion of New York.

1776 (July 4) Declaration of Independence adopted by Continental Congress.

1776 (Sept. 15) British take New York City: After being defeated by British troops in Battle of Long Island on Aug. 27, George Washington decides to evacuate New York City, fighting rearguard action while withdrawing.

1776 (Oct. 28) Battle of White Plains, N.Y.: Washington's troops inflict heavy casualties on British army.

1776 (Dec. 26) Battle of Trenton, N.J.: Washington crosses Delaware River for surprise attack, capturing 918 Hessians with loss of only 5 Americans.

1777 (June 14) U.S. flag design resolved by Congress: "thirteen stripes, alternate red and white; that the Union be thirteen stars, white in a blue field."

1777 (July 2–8) Vermont becomes first state to abolish slavery and provide universal male suffrage in its constitution.

1777 (Sept. 11) Battle of Brandywine, Pa.: British defeat Washington's army, opening way for capture of Philadelphia on Sept. 26.

1777 (Sept. 19 and Oct. 17) Battles of Saratoga: First major American victory in Revolutionary War; Gen. Horatio Gates' American troops defeat invasion from Canada by British Gen. John Burgoyne south of Saratoga, N.Y.; Burgoyne surrenders entire army of about 5,000.

1778 (Feb. 6) France signs treaty of alliance with U.S. to defeat Britain.

1778 (June 18–28) British army evacuates Philadelphia, marches across New Jersey, fighting Battle of Monmouth against Washington's troops.

1778 (Dec. 29) British capture Savannah, Ga.

1779 (Sept. 23) John Paul Jones, commanding *Bonhomme Richard,* captures British 44-gun frigate *Serapis* in sea battle; replies "I have not yet begun to fight" when asked to surrender.

1780 (May 12) British capture Charleston, S.C., after 4-week siege; 5,500 American troops surrender.

1780 (Aug. 16) Battle of Camden, S.C.: British defeat American Gen. Horatio Gates; about half of American army of 4,000 are killed or captured.

1780 (Sept. 25) Maj. Gen. Benedict Arnold defects to British when his plans to surrender West Point go awry; British spy Maj. John André hanged on Oct. 2 at Tappan, N.Y.

1781 (March 1) Articles of Confederation ratified providing new U.S. national government.

1781 (Oct. 19) Surrender at Yorktown, Va., of 8,000-man British army of Gen. Charles Cornwallis after 10-day siege by American and French forces.

1783 (Sept. 3) Peace treaty signed with Britain ending Revolutionary War; effective on May 12, 1784.

EARLY YEARS OF THE NEW U.S. GOVERNMENT: 1787–1819

1787 (Feb. 4) Shays' Rebellion of dissident farmers put down by Massachusetts militia.

1787 (May 25–Sept. 17) U.S. Constitution written by Constitutional Convention presided over by George Washington at Philadelphia.

1787 (July 13) Northwest Ordinance passed by Con-

gress of the Confederation, providing government and prohibiting slavery in territory north of Ohio River.
1787 (Dec. 7) Delaware becomes first state to ratify new U.S. Constitution.
1788 (June 21) U.S. Constitution goes into effect as New Hampshire becomes 9th state to ratify.
1789 (April 1–6) First U.S. Congress begins session in New York City.
1789 (April 30) Inauguration of George Washington as 1st President of the United States at Federal Hall in New York City.
1789 (Sept. 26) John Jay becomes 1st Chief Justice of the United States.
1790 First U.S. census shows population of 3,929,625, including 697,624 slaves.
1790 Capital of United States moved to Philadelphia from New York City.
1790 (May 29) Rhode Island joins Union as 13th state.
1791 (Feb. 25) Bank of the United States chartered.
1791 (March 4) Vermont becomes 14th state.
1791 (Dec. 15) Bill of Rights Amendments to U.S. Constitution become effective.
1791–94 Two political parties form: Democratic-Republicans led by Thomas Jefferson, and Federalists headed by Alexander Hamilton.
1792 (June 1) Kentucky becomes 15th state.
1793 (April 22) Neutrality proclamation issued by President Washington in war between Britain and France growing out of French Revolution.
1793 (Oct. 28) Eli Whitney files patent claim for his invention of cotton gin.
1794 Whisky Rebellion in western Pennsylvania by farmers protesting federal tax on whisky.
1796 (June 1) Tennessee becomes 16th state.
1796 (Sept. 17) Farewell Address by George Washington, declining third term as President.
1797 (March 4) John Adams inaugurated as 2d President of the United States.
1798 (Jan. 8) Amendment 11 to U.S. Constitution proclaimed: Provides that state cannot be sued by citizen of another state or country.
1798 (June 25) Alien Act authorizes President to expel aliens suspected of treasonable activities.
1798 (July 2) George Washington commissioned as commanding general of U.S. Army to prepare for possible war with France.
1798 (July 14) Sedition Act provides fines and jail terms for persons publishing "false, scandalous and malicious" writing about the President or U.S. government.
1798 (Nov. 16) Kentucky Resolution by Thomas Jefferson adopted by state legislature declaring Alien and Sedition Acts unconstitutional.
1798 (Nov. 20) In undeclared naval war with France, French capture U.S. schooner *Retaliation* (former French *La Croyable*); sea battles continue into 1800.
1798 (Dec. 24) Virginia Resolution by James Madison passed by state legislature declaring Alien and Sedition Acts unconstitutional.
1800 (Nov. 1) President John Adams moves into White House in Washington, D.C.
1800 (Nov. 21) Congress meets in Washington, D.C., for first time.
1801 (March 4) Thomas Jefferson inaugurated as 3d President of the United States after constitutional crisis caused by tie in electoral votes between Jefferson and Aaron Burr.
1801–05 Tripoli War between U.S. and North African pirates; ends when U.S. agrees to pay tribute.
1802 (March 16) U.S. Military Academy at West Point established by act of Congress.
1803 (Feb. 24) Supreme Court first declares act of Congress unconstitutional in *Marbury* v. *Madison.*
1803 (March 1) Ohio becomes 17th state.
1803 (April 30) Louisiana Purchase: U.S. pays about $15 million to France for vast territory nearly doubling size of U.S.
1804 (July 11) Vice President Aaron Burr fatally wounds Alexander Hamilton in duel at Weehawken, N.J.
1804 (Sept. 25) Amendment 12 to U.S. Constitution proclaimed: Provides that President and Vice President should be voted on separately by electors to prevent recurrence of tie vote between Jefferson and Burr in election of 1800.
1804–06 Lewis and Clark explore Missouri River and Pacific Northwest.
1807 (Aug. 17) Robert Fulton's steamboat *Clermont* begins first successful voyage up Hudson River.
1807 (Sept. 1) Aaron Burr acquitted of treason in jury trial on charges of plotting to build western empire.
1807 (Dec. 22) Embargo Act stops all U.S. trade with foreign nations to avoid conflict with Britain and France during Napoleonic wars.
1808 (Jan. 1) Importation of slaves forbidden by act of Congress urged by President Jefferson.
1809 (March 4) James Madison inaugurated as 4th President of the United States.
1810 (Oct. 27) Annexation of West Florida from Spain proclaimed by President Madison.
1811 (Nov. 7) Battle of Tippecanoe: Gen. William Henry Harrison defeats Shawnee Prophet in major Indian fight in Indiana Territory.
1812 (April 30) Louisiana becomes 18th state.
1812 (June 18) Declaration of war on Britain approved by Congress after many incidents of British interference with U.S. ships.
1812 (Aug. 16) Detroit surrendered by Gen. William Hull to Canadian-Indian army.
1813 (Sept. 10) Battle of Lake Erie: Capt. Oliver Perry defeats British lake squadron; reports, "We have met the enemy and they are ours."
1814 (March 27) Battle of Horseshoe Bend: Gen. Andrew Jackson defeats Creek Indians (in what is now Alabama).
1814 (Aug. 24–25) Washington, D.C., captured and burned by British.
1814 (Dec. 24) Treaty of Ghent signed to end War of 1812, with no gains for either side.
1815 (Jan. 8) Battle of New Orleans: Gen. Andrew Jackson severely defeats larger British army; unaware that peace treaty had already been signed.
1815 Barbary pirate states of North Africa defeated by U.S. fleet led by Capt. Stephen Decatur, ending U.S. tribute to pirates.
1816 (April 10) Second Bank of the United States chartered.
1816 (Dec. 11) Indiana becomes 19th state.
1817 (March 4) James Monroe inaugurated as 5th President of the United States.
1817 (April 29) Disarmament of Great Lakes and Canadian border initiated by Rush-Bagot Agreement between U.S. and Britain.
1817 (Dec. 10) Mississippi becomes 20th state.
1818 (April–May) East Florida captured from Spain by troops under Gen. Andrew Jackson in First Seminole War.
1818 (Oct. 20) Northern boundary of Louisiana Purchase set at 49th parallel in agreement by U.S. and Britain; ratified Jan. 19, 1819.
1818 (Dec. 3) Illinois becomes 21st state.
1819 Panic of 1819 causes many bank failures.
1819 (Feb. 22) Adams-Onís Treaty signed; Spain gives up East Florida and all lands east of Mississippi River for $5 million.
1819 (Dec. 14) Alabama becomes 22d state.

FROM MISSOURI COMPROMISE THROUGH CIVIL WAR: 1820–1865

1820 (March 3) Missouri Compromise approved by Congress to exclude slavery from territory north of 36°30′ latitude, with exception of Missouri to be admitted as slave state.
1820 (March 15) Maine becomes 23d state.
1821 (Aug. 10) Missouri becomes 24th state.
1823 (Dec. 2) Monroe Doctrine warns European nations against interference in Western Hemisphere.
1825 (March 4) John Quincy Adams inaugurated as 6th President after being elected by House of Representatives because no candidate had majority of electoral votes.
1825 (Oct. 26) Erie Canal opens, connecting Hudson River with Great Lakes.
1828 Democratic Party formed.
1828 First *American Dictionary of the English Language* published by Noah Webster.
1829 (March 4) Andrew Jackson inaugurated as 7th

QUICK QUIZ: On what day of the week will Christmas fall in 1985? See page 106.

KEY EVENTS IN AMERICAN HISTORY *(continued)*

President of the United States.
1830 (May 28) Indian Removal Act gives President power to move eastern Indians to land west of the Mississippi River; in next 10 years some 70,000 Indians are forced to move west to reservations.
1831 Mechanical reaper first demonstrated by Cyrus McCormick.
1831 (Aug. 13–23) Slave uprising led by Nat Turner in Virginia; 57 whites and about 100 blacks killed; 20 blacks including Turner executed.
1832 (April 6–Aug. 2) Black Hawk War fought by settlers and Indians along upper Mississippi River.
1832 (July 10) Recharter of U.S. Bank vetoed by President Jackson, who detested bank.
1832 (Dec. 10) Nullification Proclamation issued by President Jackson warning that any effort by South Carolina to leave Union by force would be treason.
1834 Whig Party formed to oppose President Jackson.
1835–43 Seminole War fought between Indians and settlers in Florida.
1836 First state child-labor law by Massachusetts forbids employment of children under 15 in factories.
1836 (Feb. 23–March 6) Siege of the Alamo: 187 Texans and frontiersmen fight to death in San Antonio against 3,000-man Mexican army.
1836 (March 2) Texas declaration of independence adopted at Washington, Texas.
1836 (April 21) Battle of San Jacinto: Gen. Sam Houston defeats Mexicans and captures Mexican Gen. Santa Anna.
1836 (June 15) Arkansas becomes 25th state.
1836 (Oct. 22) Independent Republic of Texas installs Sam Houston as president.
1837 Panic of 1837 strikes nation with bank closings and unemployment.
1837 (Jan. 26) Michigan becomes 26th state.
1837 (March 3) Supreme Court membership increased to nine: Act of Congress adds two associate justices to Court.
1837 (March 4) Martin Van Buren inaugurated as 8th President of the United States.
1837 (Oct. 6) Samuel F. B. Morse files patent for his invention of the telegraph.
1837 (Nov. 7) Murder of abolitionist editor Elijah P. Lovejoy at Alton, Ill., by mob that also destroys his press.
1839 Process of vulcanizing rubber discovered by Charles Goodyear.
1839 Mormons settle Nauvoo, Ill.: Having been driven out of Missouri, about 10,000 Mormons travel to new home, making Nauvoo largest town in Illinois.
1840 (July 4) Independent Treasury Act gives federal government right to care for own funds.
1841 (March 4) William Henry Harrison inaugurated as 9th President of the United States.
1841 (April 6) John Tyler sworn in as 10th President two days after death of Harrison.
1841 (Aug. 9) Webster-Ashburton Treaty signed, settling dispute with Britain over boundary of Maine.
1841 (Aug. 13) Repeal of Independent Treasury Act by Whig-controlled Congress.
1845 (March 3) Florida becomes 27th state.
1845 (March 4) James K. Polk inaugurated as 11th President of the United States.
1845 (Dec. 29) Texas becomes 28th state.
1846 (April 25) Mexican troops attack U.S. soldiers stationed on Rio Grande in Texas.
1846 (May 13) Congress declares war on Mexico; House votes 174–14, Senate 40–2.
1846 (June 15) Oregon Treaty settling boundary with Canada at 49th parallel approved by Senate; becomes effective Aug. 5, 1846.
1846 (Dec. 28) Iowa becomes 29th state.
1847 Mormons found Salt Lake City and establish State of Deseret with Brigham Young as governor.
1847 (Sept. 14) Mexico City captured by U.S. troops led by Gen. Winfield Scott.
1848 (Jan. 24) Gold discovered in California by James W. Marshall at Sutter's Mill.
1848 (Feb. 2) Treaty of Guadalupe Hidalgo ends Mexican War; California and Southwest ceded to U.S. for payment of $15 million.
1848 (May 29) Wisconsin becomes 30th state.
1848 (July 19–20) First women's rights convention: Held at Seneca Falls, N.Y., under leadership of Elizabeth Cady Stanton and Lucretia Coffin Mott.
1849 (March 5) Zachary Taylor inaugurated as 12th President of the United States.
1850 (July 10) Millard Fillmore sworn in as 13th President after death of President Taylor.
1850 (Sept. 9) California becomes 31st state.
1850 (Sept. 9–20) Compromise of 1850 between slavery and antislavery forces in Congress admits California as free state.
1850 (Sept. 18) Fugitive Slave Act requires federal government to capture runaway slaves and punish persons who aid them.
1850 (Sept. 20) Slave trade abolished in District of Columbia by Congress, but slavery allowed to continue.
1852 (March 20) *Uncle Tom's Cabin* by Harriet Beecher Stowe published in Boston; over 1,200,000 copies sold during first two years.
1853 (March 4) Franklin Pierce inaugurated as 14th President of the United States.
1854 (Feb. 28) Republican Party founded at Ripon, Wis.
1854 (March 31) Japan forced to open its ports to U.S. trade by Commodore Matthew Perry.
1854 (May 30) Kansas-Nebraska Act repeals Missouri Compromise; "popular sovereignty" to decide slavery issue in Kansas and Nebraska.
1854 (June 29) Gadsden Purchase by the United States adds southern Arizona and New Mexico from Mexico for $10 million.
1855–56 Warfare in Kansas between slavery and antislavery factions.
1857 (March 4) James Buchanan inaugurated as 15th President of the United States.
1858 (May 11) Minnesota becomes 32d state.
1858 (Aug. 21–Oct. 15) Lincoln-Dougles debates in Illinois race for U.S. Senate; Lincoln loses election but becomes national figure.
1859 (Feb. 14) Oregon becomes 33d state.
1859 (Oct. 16–18) John Brown's raid seizes federal arsenal at Harpers Ferry, Va.
1859 (Dec. 2) John Brown hanged after being found guilty of trying to incite slave revolt.
1860 (Dec. 20) South Carolina secedes from Union, followed by 10 other Southern states in 1861: Miss. Jan. 9, Fla. Jan. 10, Ala. Jan. 11, Ga. Jan. 19, La. Jan. 26, Texas Feb. 23, Va. April 17, Ark. May 6, N.C. May 20, and Tenn. June 8.
1861 (Jan. 29) Kansas becomes 34th state.
1861 (Feb. 8) Confederate States of America organized in convention at Montgomery, Ala.; Jefferson Davis elected provisional president on Feb. 9.
1861 (March 4) Abraham Lincoln inaugurated as 16th President of the United States.
1861 (April 12) Civil War begins as South Carolina troops attack federal Fort Sumter at Charleston, S.C.; fort surrenders on April 14.
1862 (May 20) Homestead Act provides cheap land for settlement of West.
1863 (Jan. 1) Emancipation Proclamation issued by President Lincoln freeing slaves in areas controlled by Confederacy.
1863 (June 20) West Virginia becomes 35th state.
1863 (July 1–3) Battle of Gettysburg: Lee's invasion of Pennsylvania turned back by General Meade's Union army.
1864 (Oct. 31) Nevada becomes 36th state.
1865 (April 9) Lee surrenders at Appomattox Court House, Va., ending Civil War.
1865 (April 14) President Lincoln shot by John Wilkes Booth; dies on April 15.

FROM RECONSTRUCTION TO THE 20TH CENTURY: 1865–1900

1865 (April 15) Andrew Johnson sworn in as 17th President of the United States.
1865 (Dec. 18) Slavery abolished by 13th Amendment to U.S. Constitution.
1866–67 Ku Klux Klan organized; led by ex-Confederate Gen. Nathan B. Forrest.
1867 (March 1) Nebraska becomes 37th state.
1867 (March 2) Reconstruction Act passed over President Johnson's veto organizes Southern states into five military districts.
1867 (Oct. 18) Alaska purchased from Russia for $7.2 million.

1868 (Feb. 24) President Johnson impeached by 126–47 vote in House. After trial in Senate, key vote (May 16) is one short of two-thirds needed for conviction.
1868 (May 30) First Memorial Day honors war dead.
1868 (July 28) Citizenship granted former slaves by 14th Amendment to U.S. Constitution.
1869 First state board of health: Established by act of Massachusetts legislature.
1869 (March 4) Ulysses S. Grant inaugurated as 18th President of the United States.
1869 (May 10) First transcontinental railroad completed with driving of golden spike at Promontory Point, Utah.
1869 (Dec. 10) First law giving women right to vote and hold office in U.S. passed by Wyoming territorial legislature.
1870 First blacks in U.S. Congress: Black U.S. senator and U.S. representative sworn in.
1870 Last four Confederate States restored to Union: Georgia, Mississippi, Virginia, and Texas readmitted; previously 1 had been readmitted in 1866 and 6 in 1868.
1870 (March 30) Deprivation of voting rights because of race, color, or previous servitude prohibited by 15th Amendment to U.S. Constitution.
1871 (Oct. 8–9) Chicago fire destroys $3\frac{1}{2}$ square miles of city; kills 300; 100,000 made homeless.
1873 (Sept. 18) Panic of 1873 triggered by failure of Jay Cooke's banking firm.
1875 Whisky Ring scandals rock President Grant's administration with indictments of 239 persons.
1876 (March 2) Impeachment and resignation of Secretary of War William W. Belknap on bribery charges; Senate later votes to acquit.
1876 (March 10) Telephone invented by Alexander Graham Bell as it carries first words: "Mr. Watson, come here. I want you!"
1876 (June 25) Gen. George A. Custer's troops massacred by Sioux Indians of Chief Crazy Horse and Chief Sitting Bull at Battle of Little Bighorn in Montana.
1876 (Aug. 1) Colorado becomes 38th state.
1876 (Nov. 7) Disputed presidential election causes constitutional crisis.
1877 (March 5) Rutherford B. Hayes inaugurated as 19th President of the United States.
1877 (April 10–24) Reconstruction of South ends as federal troops withdraw from occupation.
1878 (Feb. 28) Bland-Allison Act passed over President Hayes' veto bases monetary system on gold and silver, with silver valued at ratio of 16–1.
1879 (Oct. 19–20) Incandescent electric light invented by Thomas A. Edison at Menlo Park, N.J.
1881 (March 4) James A. Garfield inaugurated as 20th President of the United States.
1881 (July 2) President Garfield shot by assassin in Washington, D.C.; dies on Sept. 19.
1881 (Sept. 20) Chester A. Arthur sworn in as 21st President of the United States.
1882 Standard Oil Trust formed by John D. Rockefeller, controlling 90% of nation's oil refining.
1883 (Jan. 16) Pendleton Act creates basis of present federal civil service system.
1883 (Nov. 18) Standard time zones established by U.S. and Canadian railroads.
1885 (March 4) Grover Cleveland inaugurated as 22d President of the United States.
1886 (May 4) Haymarket Riot: Bomb thrown during anarchist-labor demonstration in Chicago kills 7 policemen, wounds 70.
1886 (Sept. 4) Apache Indian War in Southwest ends with capture of Apache Chief Geronimo.
1886 (Dec. 8) American Federation of Labor (AFL) organized at convention in Columbus, Ohio.
1887 (Feb. 4) Interstate Commerce Act establishes federal regulation of railroads, beginning control of interstate commerce.
1889 (March 4) Benjamin Harrison inaugurated as 23d President of the United States.
1889 (April 22) Oklahoma land rush officially opens former Indian territory to settlement.
1889 (Nov. 2) North Dakota and South Dakota become 39th and 40th states.
1889 (Nov. 8) Montana becomes 41st state.
1889 (Nov. 11) Washington becomes 42d state.
1890 (July 2) Sherman Antitrust Act prohibits industrial monopolies, called trusts; leads to "trust-busting" suits.
1890 (July 3) Idaho becomes 43d state.
1890 (July 10) Wyoming becomes 44th state.
1890 (Dec. 29) Wounded Knee, S.D., massacre by federal troops of 300 captive Sioux Indians ends last Indian war in West.
1892 (July 6) Homestead Massacre: Strikers at Carnegie Steel Co. at Homestead, Pa., fire on strikebreakers, killing 7.
1893 Panic of 1893: Over 15,000 businesses bankrupted.
1893 First successful gasoline-powered automobile built in U.S. by Charles and Frank Duryea at Springfield, Mass.
1893 (March 4) Grover Cleveland inaugurated as 24th President of the United States.
1894 (April 30) Coxey's Army of about 500 unemployed men marches on Washington, D.C., to demand relief.
1894 (June 21–July 20) Pullman Strike: President Cleveland uses federal troops to restore order; federal court issues strike injunction.
1896 Segregation of blacks upheld by "separate but equal" doctrine of Supreme Court in *Plessy* v. *Ferguson* decision.
1896 (Jan. 4) Utah becomes 45th state.
1896 (Aug. 16) Klondike gold rush to Alaska begins with discovery of gold on Bonanza Creek just east of Alaska's border with Canada.
1897 (March 4) William McKinley inaugurated as 25th President of the United States.
1898 (Feb. 15) U.S. battleship *Maine* explodes in harbor of Havana, Cuba, killing 260 of crew.
1898 (April 25) U.S. declares war on Spain, demanding independence of Cuba.
1898 (Aug. 12) Hawaii annexed to U.S.
1898 (Dec. 10) Spanish-American War ends with signing of treaty; Spain frees Cuba, cedes Puerto Rico and Guam islands to U.S., and sells Philippines to U.S. for $20 million.
1899 Wake Island claimed by U.S.
1900 (March 14) Gold Standard Act establishes gold as standard for U.S. currency.

FROM TRUST-BUSTING THROUGH WORLD WAR I: 1901–1918

1901 (Sept. 6) President McKinley shot by assassin in Buffalo, N.Y.; dies on Sept. 14.
1901 (Sept. 14) Theodore Roosevelt sworn in as 26th President of the United States.
1902 First state workmen's compensation law adopted by Maryland.
1902 (March 10) Trust-busting begun by President Roosevelt with suit against J.P. Morgan's Northern Securities Co.
1902 (June 2) First statewide initiative and referendum law adopted by Oregon.
1903 First law limiting workday to 10 hours for women adopted by Oregon.
1903 (May 3) First direct-primary election law adopted by Wisconsin.
1903 (Dec. 17) First airplane flight by Orville and Wilbur Wright at Kitty Hawk, N.C.
1904 (Feb. 23) Panama Canal Zone control acquired by U.S. for $10 million from Panama with ratification of Hay–Bunau-Varilla Treaty.
1906 (April 18) San Francisco earthquake destroys 4 square miles of city; kills 700.
1906 (June 29) Panama Canal Act authorizes construction of canal with locks across Panama.
1906 (June 30) Pure Food and Drug Act provides federal regulation of food and drugs.
1906 (June 30) Meat Inspection Act provides federal regulation of interstate meat-packing industry.
1907 Panic of 1907: Stock market crash and many business failures follow collapse of Knickerbocker Trust Co. in New York.
1907 (Feb. 20) Immigration Act directed against Japanese authorizes President to exclude from U.S. immigrants from any other country.
1907 (Nov. 16) Oklahoma becomes 46th state.
1909 (Jan. 11) First inventory of U.S. natural resources submitted to President Roosevelt by National Conservation Commission.

QUICK QUIZ: Who won the men's singles tennis title at Wimbledon in 1982? See page 866.

KEY EVENTS IN AMERICAN HISTORY *(continued)*

1909 (March 4) William Howard Taft inaugurated as 27th President of the United States.

1909 First Model T car manufactured by Henry Ford using assembly line.

1911 First state welfare law for mothers with dependent children adopted by Illinois.

1911 (May 15) Standard Oil Co. of New Jersey ordered dissolved by Supreme Court in antitrust suit against Rockefeller-owned company.

1912 Massachusetts adopts first minimum-wage law.

1912 (Jan. 6) New Mexico becomes 47th state.

1912 (Feb. 14) Arizona becomes 48th state.

1913 Feb. 25) Federal income tax authorized by 16th Amendment to U.S. Constitution.

1913 (March 4) Woodrow Wilson inaugurated as 28th President of the United States.

1913 (May 31) Popular election of U.S. senators required by 17th Amendment to U.S. Constitution.

1913 (Dec. 23) Federal Reserve Act reorganizes national banking system.

1914 (Aug. 15) Panama Canal opened to first crossing by ship.

1914 (Sept. 26) Federal Trade Commission established to regulate interstate commerce.

1915 U.S. population reaches 100 million.

1916 (March 15) U.S. troops invade Mexico to pursue revolutionary Gen. Pancho Villa; withdraw on Feb. 5, 1917.

1917 (Jan. 17) Virgin Islands purchase by U.S. from Denmark for $25 million ratified; becomes effective on March 31.

1917 (Feb. 3) U.S. breaks relations with Germany because of its sinking of U.S. ships.

1917 (April 6) U.S. declares war on Germany; first U.S. troops land in France on June 26; over 2 million soldiers sent to France before armistice ends World War I on Nov. 11, 1918.

1918 First official U.S. airmail flights: Route flown between Washington, D.C., and New York City.

FROM PROHIBITION TO THE GREAT DEPRESSION: 1919–1932

1919 (Jan. 29) Prohibition of sale and manufacture of alcoholic beverages by 18th Amendment to U.S. Constitution; goes into effect Jan. 16, 1920.

1919 (Feb. 25) First state gasoline tax: Established by act of Oregon legislature.

1919 (June 28) Versailles Treaty signed embodying peace settlement for World War I and establishing League of Nations.

1919 (Oct. 2) President Wilson paralyzed by stroke, making him invalid for rest of life.

1919 (Nov. 19) Rejection of Versailles Treaty and League of Nations by U.S. Senate.

1919–20 Mass arrests of thousands of anarchists, communists, and labor agitators by agents of U.S. Department of Justice; hundreds deported to Russia.

1920 First commercial radio begun by KDKA in Pittsburgh and WWJ in Detroit.

1920 U.S. becomes urban nation: For first time more than half of U.S. population lives in urban instead of rural areas.

1920 Grand Canyon National Park established in Arizona, including much of spectacular Colorado River canyon.

1920 (Aug. 26) Women win right to vote with 19th Amendment to U.S. Constitution.

1920–21 Business recession with high unemployment and some 20,000 business failures.

1921 (March 4) Warren G. Harding inaugurated as 29th President of the United States.

1921 (May 19) Immigration quotas set: Congress acts after nearly 1 million immigrate to U.S. in year.

1921 (June 10) Budget and Accounting Act creates General Accounting Office and Bureau of the Budget.

1922 (Feb. 6) Naval arms-limitation pact signed by U.S., Britain, France, Italy, and Japan, scrapping many existing warships.

1923 (Aug. 3) Calvin Coolidge sworn in as 30th President following death on Aug. 2 of President Warren G. Harding in San Francisco.

1923 (Oct. 25) Investigation of Teapot Dome scandals of Harding administration begun by U.S. Senate, leading to conviction of many former officials for bribery and conspiracy.

1923–26 Ku Klux Klan reign of terror against minority groups reaches peak with many lynchings.

1925 Clarence Birdseye invents quick-frozen food process to preserve food.

1925 (July 21) Evolution trial: John Scopes convicted in Dayton, Tenn., of teaching evolution; defended by Clarence Darrow; prosecuted by William Jennings Bryan.

1925 (Dec. 17) Court-martial convicts Brig. Gen. William (Billy) Mitchell of unmilitary conduct in criticizing superiors for ignoring importance of military air power.

1926 (March 16) First liquid-fuel rocket successfully launched by Dr. Robert H. Goddard near Auburn, Mass.; invention later makes space travel possible.

1927 (May 21) First solo nonstop flight across Atlantic completed by Charles A. Lindbergh; lands in Paris 33½ hours after taking off from Long Island, N.Y.

1927 (Aug. 23) Sacco-Vanzetti case: Anarchists Nicola Sacco and Bartolomeo Vanzetti executed in Charlestown, Mass., for 1920 murder; protesters claim conviction was on political grounds rather than on evidence.

1928 (Aug. 27) War outlawed by Kellogg-Briand Peace Pact; signed by U.S. and France; 62 nations eventually sign.

1929 (Feb. 20) American Samoa organized as territory of United States.

1929 (March 4) Herbert Hoover inaugurated as 31st President of the United States.

1929 (Oct. 24) Great Depression triggered by stock market crash; unemployed number 12 million; more than 37,000 banks, corporations, and other businesses fail by 1931.

1932 (Feb. 2) Reconstruction Finance Corporation (RFC) established to loan $2 billion to businesses, banks, and farm credit groups.

1932 (March 1) Kidnap-murder of son of aviation hero Charles A. Lindbergh at Hopewell, N.J.; after sensational trial, Bruno Richard Hauptmann is convicted of crime and executed in April 1936.

1932 (July 22) Federal Home Loan Bank Act provides $125 million for first federal mortgage loans.

1932 (July 28) Bonus army of unemployed veterans, who had marched on Washington seeking immediate bonus payment, dispersed by federal troops and tanks.

FROM THE NEW DEAL THROUGH WORLD WAR II: 1933–1945

1933 (Feb. 6) "Lame Duck" 20th Amendment to U.S. Constitution changes date of presidential inaugurations after 1933 to January 20.

1933 (March 4) Franklin Delano Roosevelt inaugurated as 32d President of the United States.

1933 (March 6–9) Bank holiday proclaimed by President Roosevelt with all bank operations halted; only financially sound banks allowed to open after holiday; measure taken to stop hoarding of money by persons fearing bank failures.

1933 (March 9–June 16) Hundred Days special session of 73d Congress passes New Deal legislation to provide relief to banks, manufacturers, farmers, labor, and unemployed.

1933 (Dec. 5) Prohibition repealed by 21st Amendment to U.S. Constitution.

1934 "Dust bowl" created in Midwest by extended drought and lack of conservation measures.

1935 (May 27) Supreme Court declares National Recovery Act (NRA) unconstitutional.

1935 (Aug. 14) Social Security Act provides first federal-state unemployment and old-age insurance.

1935 (Aug. 31) Neutrality Act provides measures intended to keep U.S. from becoming involved in Italian-Ethiopian War.

1935 (Nov. 9) CIO labor organization formed; begins organizing unions in auto and steel industries using "sit-down" strikes.

1936 (Jan. 6) Supreme Court rules Agricultural Adjustment Act (AAA) unconstitutional.

1937 (May 1) Neutrality Act adopted to prevent U.S. involvement in Spanish civil war.

1937 (July 22) Court-packing legislation killed by U.S. Senate; had been sought by President Roosevelt to liberalize Supreme Court.

1938 (June 25) Wages and Hours Law provides mini-

mum wages of 40¢ an hour and maximum workweek of 40 hours (effective in 1940); labor by children under 16 outlawed.
1939 (April 20) First commercial TV broadcasts by Radio Corporation of America.
1939 (Aug. 2) Hatch Act forbids federal employees below policy level from taking part in political campaigns.
1939 (Sept. 5) Neutrality of U.S. in World War II proclaimed by President Roosevelt (Germany had invaded Poland on Sept. 1).
1939 (Nov. 4) New Neutrality Act permits "cash and carry" sales of arms to belligerents.
1940 (Sept. 3) U.S. gives Britain 50 destroyers in exchange for military bases in West Indies and Newfoundland.
1940 (Sept. 16) First U.S. peacetime draft for compulsory military service enacted.
1941 (March 11) Lend-Lease Act enables President to supply materials to Britain and Soviet Union.
1941 (Aug. 9–12) Atlantic Charter of postwar goals set in shipboard meetings off Newfoundland by President Roosevelt and British Prime Minister Churchill.
1941 (Dec. 7) Japanese bomb Pearl Harbor naval base in Hawaii.
1941 (Dec. 8) Declaration of war on Japan approved by Congress with only one dissenting vote.
1941 (Dec. 11) Germany and Italy declare war on U.S.
1942 (Aug. 13) Secret Manhattan Project to develop atomic bomb initiated; first nuclear chain reaction achieved by Enrico Fermi in Chicago on Dec. 2.
1944 (June 6) D-Day landing by U.S. troops on Normandy coast of German-occupied France.
1944 (June 22) GI Bill of Rights authorizes educational and other benefits for World War II veterans.
1945 (Feb. 4-11) Big Three meeting at Yalta in the Soviet Union of Roosevelt, Churchill, and Stalin sets postwar plans, including formation of United Nations.
1945 (April 12) Harry S. Truman sworn in as 33d President upon death of President Roosevelt at Warm Springs, Ga.
1945 (May 8) V-E Day, formal end of war in Europe; Germany had signed unconditional surrender on May 7.
1945 (June 26) United Nations Charter signed in San Francisco by delegates of 50 nations.
1945 (July 16) First atomic bomb successfully exploded near Alamogordo, N.M.
1945 (July 17–Aug. 2) Potsdam Conference in Germany attended by Truman, Stalin, and Churchill (succeeded by Clement Attlee) decides on four-power rule of Germany and issues surrender ultimatum to Japan.
1945 (Aug. 6) Atomic bomb dropped on Hiroshima; on Japan's refusal to surrender, another bomb is dropped on Nagasaki on Aug. 9.
1945 (Aug. 14) Japan agrees to surrender.
1945 (Sept. 2) V-J Day: formal surrender of Japan aboard battleship USS *Missouri* at Tokyo.

FROM COLD WAR TO PRESIDENT KENNEDY'S ASSASSINATION: 1946–1963

1946 (March 5) Communist "Iron Curtain" has descended across Europe, former British Prime Minister Churchill warns in commencement address at Fulton, Mo.
1946 (July 4) Philippines granted independence.
1947 (March 12) Truman Doctrine announced by President to resist Soviet aggression and subversion with aid for Greece and Turkey.
1947 (June 5) Marshall Plan proposed by Secretary of State George C. Marshall calling for U.S. aid to rebuild Europe and preserve its freedom; aid begun with enactment of European Recovery Program on April 3, 1948.
1947 (June 23) Taft-Hartley Act passed by Congress over President Truman's veto bans closed shop and places other restrictions on labor unions.
1947 (July 18) Pacific Islands Trust Territory placed under U.S. administration by UN.
1947 (July 26) Defense Department created to coordinate U.S. military services.
1948 (June) Berlin airlift begun by U.S. and Britain, carrying 2 million tons of supplies to West Berlin in 16 months to break Soviet blockade of city.
1949 (April 4) North Atlantic Treaty creating NATO defense force signed by U.S. and 11 other nations.
1949 (Oct. 21) U.S. Communist Party's 11 top leaders sentenced to prison for advocating overthrow of U.S. government.
1950 (Jan. 21) Alger Hiss, former State Department official, convicted of perjury for denying membership in communist spy ring.
1950 (June 27) Korean War: President Truman orders U.S. forces to aid South Korea, invaded by communist North Korea on June 25.
1950 (Aug. 1) Guam organized as U.S. territory.
1950 (Aug. 27) U.S. railroads seized by President Truman to prevent general strike; returned to private ownership on May 23, 1952.
1950 (Dec. 11) Supreme Court rules that under 5th Amendment no one can be forced to testify against himself.
1951 (March 1) President limited to two terms by 22d Amendment to U.S. Constitution.
1951 (April 11) Gen. Douglas MacArthur relieved of command in Korea by President Truman for disregarding orders (MacArthur had sought to extend war into communist China).
1951 (Sept. 4) First transcontinental TV broadcast by President Truman at Japanese peace-treaty conference in San Francisco.
1952 (April 8) Nation's steel mills seized by President Truman to prevent strike; ruled as unconstitutional by Supreme Court on June 2.
1952 (July 25) Puerto Rico becomes self-governing commonwealth of U.S.
1952 (Nov. 1) First hydrogen bomb exploded by U.S. at Enewetak atoll in Pacific.
1953 (Jan. 20) Dwight D. Eisenhower inaugurated as 34th President of the United States.
1953 (June 19) Execution of Julius and Ethel Rosenberg at Ossining, N.Y., convicted of giving atomic secrets to Soviet Union.
1953 (July 27) Korean War armistice signed at Panmunjom, Korea, ending fighting.
1954 (Jan. 21) First atomic-powered submarine, USS *Nautilus,* launched at Groton, Conn.
1954 (April 22–June 17) Televised public hearings of charges by Sen. Joseph McCarthy of communist subversion in U.S. Army; U.S. Senate votes to condemn McCarthy on Dec. 2.
1954 (May 17) Racial segregation in public schools banned by Supreme Court.
1954 (Sept. 8) Southeast Asia Treaty Organization (SEATO) defense pact signed by U.S.
1955 (Feb. 12) President Eisenhower sends U.S. military advisers to train South Vietnam's army in Indochina war.
1955 (July 18–23) Summit meeting of U.S., Britain, Soviet Union, and France at Geneva, Switzerland, confirms independence of East and West Germany.
1955 (Dec. 1) Bus boycott in Montgomery, Ala., begun by blacks under leadership of Rev. Martin Luther King Jr.; leads to Supreme Court ruling on Nov. 13, 1956, against segregation on buses.
1955 (Dec. 5) AFL and CIO merge, with George Meany becoming president.
1956 (June 29) Federal-Aid Highways Act provides $32.5 billion to build 41,000-mile interstate highway system over next 13 years.
1957 (Sept. 24) President Eisenhower orders federal troops to Little Rock, Ark., to protect black students desegregating high school.
1958 (Jan. 31) *Explorer I,* first U.S. space satellite, launched from Cape Canaveral, Fla.
1958 (Dec. 10) First jet service in U.S. begun by National Airlines on New York–Miami run.
1959 (Jan. 3) Alaska becomes 49th state.
1959 (July 21) First atomic merchant ship, *Savannah,* launched at Camden, N.J.
1959 (Aug. 21) Hawaii becomes 50th state.
1959 (Sept. 15–27) Summit meeting at Camp David, Md., between President Eisenhower and Soviet Premier Nikita Khrushchev calls for "peaceful coexistence."
1959 (Dec. 1) Antarctica Treaty signed by U.S. and 11 other nations guaranteeing continent's neutrality.
1960 (Jan. 19) U.S. and Japan sign mutual-defense treaty for military assistance.

QUICK QUIZ: Who is the U.S. Chief of Naval Operations? See page 461.

KEY EVENTS IN AMERICAN HISTORY *(continued)*

1960 (May 1) U.S. U-2 spy plane shot down over Soviet Union.

1960 (May 16) Summit conference in Paris broken off by Khrushchev over U-2 incident despite apology by President Eisenhower.

1961 (Jan. 3) President Eisenhower ends diplomatic relations with communist Cuba.

1961 (Jan. 20) John F. Kennedy inaugurated as 35th President of the United States.

1961 (March 1) Peace Corps created by President Kennedy to help developing nations.

1961 (April 3) Washington, D.C., residents given vote for President by 23d Amendment.

1961 (April 17) Unsuccessful Bay of Pigs invasion of Cuba led by U.S. CIA and Cuban exiles with authorization of President Kennedy.

1961 (June 3–4) Summit meeting by Kennedy and Khrushchev at Vienna, Austria, unsuccessfully discusses reunification of Germany.

1961 (Dec. 11) U.S. provides South Vietnam with armed helicopters and crews to fight communists; U.S. forces in Vietnam total 3,200.

1962 (Feb. 20) First U.S. astronaut to orbit Earth: Lt. Col. John H. Glenn Jr.

1962 (May 17) U.S. troops sent to Thailand to prevent possible communist invasion.

1962 (June 27) U.S. defense of Taiwan against attack by communist China pledged by President Kennedy.

1962 (Oct. 22–28) Cuban missile crisis: President Kennedy imposes naval and air blockade on Cuba, forcing Soviet Union to withdraw nuclear missiles.

1963 (June 17) Bible reading or prayers cannot be required in public schools, Supreme Court rules.

1963 (Aug. 28) Black equal-rights demonstration in Washington by 200,000 persons led by Rev. Martin Luther King Jr.

1963 (Aug. 30) Hot-line telephone set up between White House and Kremlin.

1963 (Sept. 14) First quintuplets in U.S. born to Mrs. Andrew Fischer in Aberdeen, S.D.

1963 (Oct. 10) Treaty bans atomic tests in atmosphere; signed by U.S., Britain, and Soviet Union.

1963 (Nov. 22) President Kennedy assassinated in Dallas, Texas, by former U.S. marine Lee Harvey Oswald.

ERA OF VIETNAM WAR, WATERGATE, AND ENERGY PROBLEMS: 1963–1983

1963 (Nov. 22) Lyndon B. Johnson sworn in as 36th President of the United States.

1964 (Feb. 4) Poll tax outlawed by 24th Amendment to U.S. Constitution.

1964 (July 2) Civil Rights Act forbids racial discrimination in hotels, motels, and restaurants, and by labor unions and businesses engaged in interstate commerce.

1964 (Aug. 7) Gulf of Tonkin Resolution gives President authority "to prevent further aggression" in Vietnam after reported North Vietnamese attack on U.S. destroyers on Aug. 2–4; first U.S. bombings of Vietnam on Aug. 5.

1964 (Aug. 20) War on Poverty program enacted.

1965 (April 28) U.S. Marines land in Dominican Republic to prevent communist takeover.

1965 (June 28) First ground combat by U.S. troops in Vietnam authorized by President Johnson; U.S. forces in Vietnam, 74,000.

1965 (Aug. 6) Voting Rights Act gives government power to force local communities to register blacks and allow them to vote.

1965 (Aug. 11–16) Riots by blacks in Watts area of Los Angeles result in 35 deaths.

1966 (May 30) First U.S. Moon landing by unmanned spaceship.

1966 (July 1) Medicare goes into effect, with medical insurance for persons 65 or older.

1967 (Jan. 27) Space Treaty signed banning military use of nuclear weapons in space.

1967 (Feb. 23) Presidential succession established by 25th Amendment to Constitution.

1967 (June 23–25) Summit meeting at Glassboro, N.J., by President Johnson and Soviet Premier Aleksei Kosygin.

1967 (July 23–30) Detroit riots by blacks put down by federal troops and National Guardsmen; 40 killed, more than 2,000 injured.

1968 U.S. population reaches 200 million.

1968 (Jan. 23) North Koreans seize USS ***Pueblo*** crew as spies; release them on Dec. 22.

1968 (April 4) Assassination of Rev. Martin Luther King Jr. in Memphis, Tenn.; followed by racial riots in more than 100 cities.

1968 (June 5) Sen. Robert F. Kennedy shot in Los Angeles; dies on June 6.

1968 (June 26) Iwo Jima and Bonin Islands returned to Japan by U.S.

1968 (July 1) Treaty on Nonproliferation of Nuclear Weapons signed by U.S., Britain, and Soviet Union; effective on March 5, 1970.

1968 (Aug. 26–30) Anti-Vietnam War demonstration during Democratic national convention in Chicago put down by police and troops.

1969 (Jan. 20) Richard M. Nixon inaugurated as 37th President of the United States.

1969 (March) U.S. troops in Vietnam reach peak level of 541,500.

1969 (June 8) Plans to reduce U.S. troops in Vietnam announced by President Nixon.

1969 (July 20) First man to walk on Moon: U.S. astronaut Neil Armstrong.

1969 (Oct. 15) Vietnam Moratorium Day brings out many antiwar demonstrators across nation.

1970 (April 30) President Nixon orders U.S. troops into Cambodia.

1970 (May 4) Four Kent State University students killed in Ohio when National Guard fires into war-protest demonstration.

1971 (March 29) Lt. William L. Calley Jr. convicted by court-martial of murder of 22 Vietnamese men, women, and children in 1968 My Lai massacre (Calley freed in 1974 after federal court overturns conviction).

1971 (April 20) Busing to achieve racially balanced schools upheld by Supreme Court.

1971 (May 2–5) Over 13,400 antiwar demonstrators arrested in Washington, D.C.

1971 (June 13) Secret Pentagon Papers study of Vietnam War begins to be published in series in *New York Times* and *Washington Post;* federal government obtains injunction on June 15 against further publication, but Supreme Court on June 30 throws out injunction.

1971 (July 5) Voting age lowered to 18 by 26th Amendment to U.S. Constitution.

1971 (Aug. 15) Freeze on wages and prices to combat inflation announced by President Nixon.

1972 (Feb. 21–28) Visit to communist China by President Nixon reverses U.S. policy on China.

1972 (May 15) Okinawa and Ryukyu Islands returned to Japan after 27-year U.S. rule.

1972 (May 15) Alabama Gov. George Wallace wounded and paralyzed from waist down in attempted assassination at Laurel, Md.; Arthur H. Bremmer convicted on Aug. 4 of attempted assassination and sentenced to 63 years in prison.

1972 (May 22–30) Summit meeting in Moscow between President Nixon and Soviet leader Leonid I. Brezhnev achieves first agreement limiting production of atomic weapons; ratified by U.S. Senate on Aug. 3.

1972 (June 17) Watergate offices of Democratic National Committee in Washington, D.C., secretly wiretapped; police arrest five men in act of burglarizing offices; on June 22, Nixon tells press conference, "There is no involvement by the White House."

1972 (June 17–23) Hurricane Agnes rakes East Coast from Florida to New York; storm and floods kill 122, cause $2.1 billion in damages.

1972 (June 19) Government practice of wiretapping without court order is illegal, Supreme Court rules.

1972 (July 31) Democratic vice-presidential candidate withdraws: Sen. Thomas F. Eagleton quits as candidate after disclosure he had been treated for psychiatric problems; former Peace Corps director Sargent Shriver chosen to succeed him on Democratic ticket on Aug. 5.

1972 (Sept. 15) First Watergate indictments: Seven persons indicted for break-in at Democratic national headquarters; later, White House counsel John Dean III tells Senate committee that President Nixon congratulated him on that day for keeping indictments from reaching higher in Nixon administration.

1972 (Nov. 7) President Nixon wins election to second term by landslide 60.7% of vote.

1973 (Jan. 28) Cease-fire ends U.S. participation in Vietnam War; last troops leave Vietnam on March 29.

1973 (Jan. 30) Watergate burglary trial ends with conviction of seven men; two were former officials of Committee to Reelect the President and one a former White House consultant.

1973 (Feb. 7) Senate Watergate investigating committee established by unanimous vote of Senate; leads to conviction of three cabinet officers and Nixon's two chief White House aides.

1973 (Feb. 27) Siege of Wounded Knee, S.D., begun by Indians protesting treatment by government; two Indians killed in gunfights with federal officers; siege ends on May 8.

1973 (May 11) Pentagon Papers espionage trial of Dr. Daniel Ellsberg dismissed by federal judge after disclosure that White House agents committed burglary in seeking evidence.

1973 (June 16–24) Summit meeting between President Nixon and Soviet leader Brezhnev in U.S. achieves nine agreements for U.S.-Soviet cooperation.

1973 (July 1) Congress orders halt to U.S. bombing of Cambodia and all U.S. military action in Indochina by Aug. 15.

1973 (July 16) Existence of White House tapes revealed: Witness tells Senate Watergate hearing that conversations in White House have been taped since 1970; after long court battle, President Nixon gives up tapes to investigators; tapes show President took part in effort to cover up Watergate scandals.

1973 (Oct. 10) Vice President Spiro Agnew resigns, accepts conviction for income-tax evasion to avoid trial on charges of accepting bribes.

1973 (Oct. 17) Arab nations cut oil exports to U.S. in retaliation for U.S. aid to Israel.

1973 (Nov. 7) Limitations on President's war-making powers voted by Congress over veto.

1973 (Nov. 25) Emergency restrictions on use of fuel and energy announced by President Nixon.

1973 (Dec. 6) Gerald R. Ford sworn in as Vice President: first Vice President appointed under 25th Amendment to U.S. Constitution.

1973 (Dec. 8) President Nixon discloses tax records; he paid less than $6,000 in income taxes for 1970–73 on income over $1 million.

1974 (Feb. 4) Nation's first political kidnapping: Patricia Hearst, 19-year-old granddaughter of publisher William Randolph Hearst, taken from apartment in Berkeley, Calif.; she later joins captors in terrorist activities and eludes FBI for 19 months until surrendering on Sept. 18, 1975; jury finds her guilty of bank robbery in 1976; sentenced to 7 years in prison.

1974 (July 24) U.S. Supreme Court rules President Nixon must turn over White House tapes and documents to special Watergate prosecutor.

1974 (Aug. 9) President Nixon resigns to avoid impeachment and removal by Congress because of role in Watergate scandals.

1974 (Aug. 9) Gerald R. Ford becomes 38th President of the United States.

1974 (Sept. 8) Full pardon granted to Nixon by President Ford.

1974 (Sept. 16) Conditional amnesty plan for Vietnam War draft evaders and deserters announced by President Ford.

1974 (Oct. 15) Presidential election campaign public financing law signed by President Ford.

1974 (Nov. 23–24) Summit meeting in Vladivostok, Soviet Union; Ford and Brezhnev agree in principle to "put cap on arms race."

1975 (Jan. 1) Watergate cover-up convictions: After 3-month trial, jury finds guilty President Nixon's top aides H.R. Haldeman and John D. Ehrlichman, and former Attorney General John N. Mitchell.

1975 (May) Unemployment rises to 9.2% with 8.5 million Americans out of work; highest unemployment rate since Great Depression.

1975 (May 7) End of Vietnam War Era announced by President Ford one week after South Vietnam surrenders to communists.

1975 (May 14–15) *Mayaguez* incident: U.S. Marines rescue U.S. freighter from Cambodians.

1975 (July 1) New York City financial crisis causes layoff of 40,000 city workers.

1975 (July 17) U.S. and Soviet spaceships link up for Apollo-Soyuz handshake in space.

1975 (Aug. 1) President Ford signs Helsinki pact endorsing post-World War II European boundaries and endorsing human rights.

1975 (Sept. 5 and 22) Two assassination attempts on President Ford made in California.

1975 (Dec. 20) Vietnam refugee program completed with resettlement of 130,000 in U.S.

1976 U.S. military service academies for first time admit women for officer training.

1976 (June 5) 300-foot-high Teton Dam collapses in Idaho; kills 69; estimated damage $1 billion.

1976 (June 20) U.S. closes last military bases in Thailand at request of Thai government.

1976 (July 4) U.S. celebrates 200th birthday with parades, picnics, fireworks, and prayers.

1976 (Sept. 23) First face-to-face presidential public debate in history held on TV between incumbent President Ford and challenger, Democratic presidential candidate Jimmy Carter.

1976 (Oct. 4) Death penalty for murder upheld by Supreme Court; lifts stay that blocked state executions for 10 years.

1977 (Jan. 20) Jimmy Carter inaugurated as 39th President of the United States.

1977 (March 1) U.S. extends coastal limit to 200 miles for control of fishing.

1977 (June 20) Trans-Alaska $7.7 billion pipeline begins carrying oil 789 miles from Prudhoe Bay oil field to Valdez, Alaska.

1977 (Sept. 7) President Carter signs Panama treaties, agreeing to turn over Panama Canal to Panama on Dec. 31, 1999; ratified April 18, 1978.

1977 (Oct. 1) U.S. Department of Energy becomes 12th cabinet-level executive department, with James R. Schlesinger as first U.S. secretary of energy.

1978 (Jan. 27) Nation's GNP (gross national product) reaches $2 trillion mark: economy first reached $1 trillion level in 1972.

1978 (June 6) California voters begin tax revolt; Referendum approves Proposition 13, cutting local property taxes in state from $12 billion to $5 billion; sets off nationwide efforts to put lids on federal, state, and local government spending.

1978 (Dec. 1) National Park System doubled: President Carter adds 56 million acres of Alaskan land, designating 17 new national monuments.

1979 (Jan. 1) U.S. and China establish diplomatic relations: For first time since communists seized power in China in 1949, U.S. and China exchange full ambassadors; at same time U.S. breaks formal relations with nationalist Chinese government on Taiwan.

1979 (Feb. 5) U.S. population reaches 220 million: Mark registered by census clock in Washington, D.C.

1979 (Feb. 12) President Carter asks for voluntary energy conservation: Cut-off of oil imports from Iran brings gasoline shortages to nation in next several months.

1979 (March 28) First major atomic accident in U.S.: Malfunction in reactor at Three Mile Island near Harrisburg, Pa., releases radioactive steam and threatens meltdown of uranium fuel rods; thousands evacuated in surrounding region.

1979 (June 8) MX missile system approved: President Carter gives go-ahead to $30 billion plan to deploy about 200 new intercontinental missiles in underground site.

1979 (June 13) Sioux Indians win $100 million in land claim: Court awards compensation for land confiscated in 1877.

1979 (Oct. 1) Panama Canal Zone returned to Panama: U.S. turns over control of 553-square-mile area that had been under American jurisdiction since 1904.

1979 (Oct. 17) U.S. Department of Education approved in legislation signed by President Carter; becomes 13th cabinet-level department of federal government; Shirley M. Hufstedler appointed as first secretary of education.

1979 (Oct 23) Emergency gasoline rationing approved: Congress gives President power to invoke rationing when necessary.

1981 (Jan. 20) Ronald Reagan inaugurated as 40th President of the United States.

1981 (Aug. 13) Reagan's New Economic Program becomes law; provides 25% income-tax cuts for 1981–84.

1982 Worst Recession since 1930s: U.S. unemployment soars to 10.8% of labor force with nearly 12 million out of work.

1983 For events of 1983, see pages 7–31.

QUICK QUIZ: Who was the second U.S. President to be assassinated? See page 361.

DECLARATION OF INDEPENDENCE

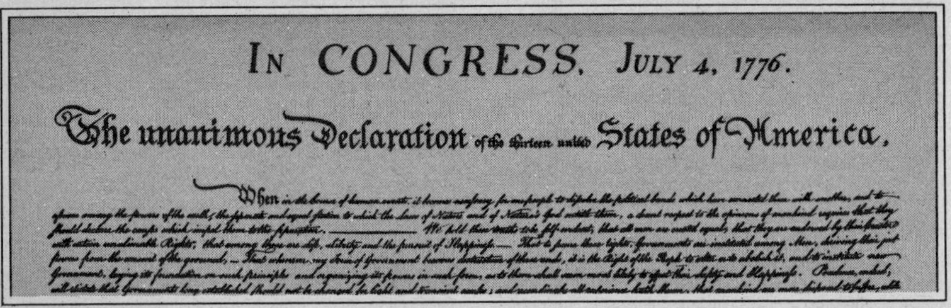
IN CONGRESS, JULY 4, 1776.

The unanimous Declaration of the thirteen united States of America,

Although the colonists had been openly fighting the British since the battles of Lexington and Concord in 1775, many members of the Continental Congress still sought a compromise. However, such patriots as John Hancock, John Adams, and Samuel Adams demanded complete independence from Britain. On June 7, 1776, Richard Henry Lee of Virginia called for a resolution on independence.

The actual drafting of the document was entrusted to Thomas Jefferson.

On July 4, 1776, Congress adopted the Declaration of Independence.

In Congress, July 4, 1776,
The unanimous Declaration of the thirteen united States of America,

When in the Course of human events, it becomes necessary for one people to dissolve the political bands which have connected them with another, and to assume among the Powers of the earth, the separate and equal station to which the Laws of Nature and of Nature's God entitle them, a decent respect to the opinions of mankind requires that they should declare the causes which impel them to the separation.

We hold these truths to be self-evident, that all men are created equal, that they are endowed by their Creator with certain unalienable Rights, that among these are Life, Liberty and the pursuit of Happiness. That to secure these rights, Governments are instituted among Men, deriving their just powers from the consent of the governed. That whenever any Form of Government becomes destructive of these ends, it is the Right of the People to alter or to abolish it, and to institute new Government, laying its foundation on such principles and organizing its powers in such form, as to them shall seem most likely to effect their Safety and Happiness. Prudence, indeed, will dictate that Governments long established should not be changed for light and transient causes; and accordingly all experience hath shown, that mankind are more disposed to suffer, while evils are sufferable, than to right themselves by abolishing the forms to which they are accustomed. But when a long train of abuses and usurpations, pursuing invariably the same Object evinces a design to reduce them under absolute Despotism, it is their right, it is their duty, to throw off such Government, and to provide new Guards for their future security.—Such has been the patient sufferance of these Colonies; and such is now the necessity which constrains them to alter their former Systems of Government. The history of the present King of Great Britain is a history of repeated injuries and usurpations, all having in direct object the establishment of an absolute Tyranny over these States. To prove this, let Facts be submitted to a candid world.

He has refused his Assent to Laws, the most wholesome and necessary for the public good.

He has forbidden his Governors to pass Laws of immediate and pressing importance, unless suspended in their operation till his Assent should be obtained; and when so suspended, he has utterly neglected to attend to them.

He has refused to pass other Laws for the accommodation of large districts of people, unless those people would relinquish the right of Representation in the Legislature, a right inestimable to them and formidable to tyrants only.

He has called together legislative bodies at places unusual, uncomfortable, and distant from the depository of their Public Records, for the sole purpose of fatiguing them into compliance with his measures.

He has dissolved Representative Houses repeatedly, for opposing with manly firmness his invasions on the rights of the people.

He has refused for a long time, after such dissolutions, to cause others to be elected; whereby the Legislative Powers, incapable of Annihilation, have returned to the People at large for their exercise; the State remaining in the mean time exposed to all the dangers of invasion from without, and convulsions within.

He has endeavoured to prevent the population of these States; for that purpose obstructing the Laws of Naturalization of Foreigners; refusing to pass others to migration hither, and raising the conditions of new Appropriations of Lands.

He has obstructed the Administration of Justice, by refusing his Assent to Laws for establishing Judiciary Powers.

He has made Judges dependent on his Will alone, for the tenure of their offices, and the amount and payment of their salaries.

He has erected a multitude of New Offices,

DECLARATION OF INDEPENDENCE *(continued)*
and sent hither swarms of Officers to harass our People, and eat out their substance.

He has kept among us, in times of peace, Standing Armies without the Consent of our legislatures.

He has affected to render the Military independent of and superior to the Civil Power.

He has combined with others to subject us to a jurisdiction foreign to our constitution, and unacknowledged by our laws; giving his Assent to their acts of pretended legislation:

For quartering large bodies of armed troops among us:

For protecting them, by a mock Trial, from Punishment for any Murders which they should commit on the Inhabitants of these States:

For cutting off our Trade with all parts of the world:

For imposing taxes on us without our Consent:

For depriving us in many cases, of the benefits of Trial by Jury:

For transporting us beyond Seas to be tried for pretended offences:

For abolishing the free System of English Laws in a neighbouring Province, and establishing therein an Arbitrary government, and enlarging its Boundaries so as to render it at once an example and fit instrument for introducing the same absolute rule into these Colonies:

For taking away our Charters, abolishing our most valuable Laws, and altering fundamentally the Forms of our Governments:

For suspending our own legislature, and declaring themselves invested with Power to legislate for us in all cases whatsoever.

He has abdicated Government here, by declaring us out of his Protection and waging War against us.

He has plundered our seas, ravaged our Coasts, burnt our towns, and destroyed the lives of our people.

He is at this time transporting large armies of foreign mercenaries to complete the works of death, desolation and tyranny, already begun with circumstances of Cruelty & perfidy scarcely paralleled in the most barbarous ages, and totally unworthy the Head of a civilized nation.

He has constrained our fellow Citizens taken Captive on the high Seas to bear Arms against their Country, to become the executioners of their friends and Brethren, or to fall themselves by their Hands.

He has excited domestic insurrections amongst us, and has endeavoured to bring on the inhabitants of our frontiers, the merciless Indian Savages, whose known rule of warfare, is an undistinguished destruction of all ages, sexes and conditions.

In every stage of these Oppressions We have Petitioned for Redress in the most humble terms: Our repeated Petitions have been answered only by repeated injury. A Prince, whose character is thus marked by every act which may define a Tyrant, is unfit to be the ruler of a free People.

Nor have We been wanting in attention to our British brethren. We have warned them from time to time of attempts by their legislature to extend an unwarrantable jurisdiction over us. We have reminded them of the circumstances of our emigration and settlement here. We have appealed to their native justice and magnanimity, and we have conjured them by the ties of our common kindred to disavow these usurpations, which, would inevitably interrupt our connections and correspondence. They too have been deaf to the voice of justice and of consanguinity. We must, therefore, acquiesce in the necessity, which denounces our Separation, and hold them, as we hold the rest of mankind, Enemies in War, in Peace Friends.

We, therefore, the Representatives of the United States of America, in General Congress, Assembled, appealing to the Supreme Judge of the world for the rectitude of our intentions, do, in the Name, and by Authority of the good People of these Colonies, solemnly publish and declare, That these United Colonies are, and of Right ought to be Free and Independent States; that they are Absolved from all Allegiance to the British Crown, and that all political connection between them and the State of Great Britain, is and ought to be totally dissolved; and that as Free and Independent States, they have full Power to levy War, conclude Peace, contract Alliances, establish Commerce, and to do all other Acts and Things which Independent States may of right do. And for the support of this Declaration, with a firm reliance on the protection of Divine Providence, we mutually pledge to each other our Lives, our Fortunes and our sacred Honor.

John Hancock

New Hampshire
Josiah Bartlett
Wm. Whipple
Matthew Thornton

Massachusetts-Bay
Saml. Adams
John Adams
Robt. Treat Paine
Elbridge Gerry

Rhode Island
Step. Hopkins
William Ellery

Connecticut
Roger Sherman
Sam'el Huntington
Wm. Williams
Oliver Wolcott

Georgia
Button Gwinnett
Lyman Hall
Geo. Walton

Maryland
Samuel Chase
Wm. Paca
Thos. Stone
Charles Carroll
of Carrollton

Virginia
George Wythe
Richard Henry Lee
Th. Jefferson
Benja. Harrison
Ths. Nelson, Jr.
Francis Lightfoot Lee
Carter Braxton

New York
Wm. Floyd
Phil. Livingston
Frans. Lewis
Lewis Morris

Pennsylvania
Robt. Morris
Benjamin Rush
Benja. Franklin
John Morton
Geo. Clymer
Jas. Smith
Geo. Taylor
James Wilson
Geo. Ross

Delaware
Caesar Rodney
Geo. Read
Tho. M'Kean

North Carolina
Wm. Hooper
Joseph Hewes
John Penn

South Carolina
Edward Rutledge
Thos. Heyward, Junr.
Thomas Lynch, Junr.
Arthur Middleton

New Jersey
Richd. Stockton
Jno. Witherspoon
Fras. Hopkinson
John Hart
Abra. Clark

QUICK QUIZ: The Dominican Republic covers two-thirds of what island? See page 541.

CONSTITUTION OF THE UNITED STATES

The Constitution of the United States embodies the fundamental principles upon which the American republic rests. A *living* instrument of government, the Constitution has been kept abreast of the times through the process of amendment, by federal laws that elaborate its clauses, and by judicial interpretation by the U.S. Supreme Court.

The original constitution of the American states, the Articles of Confederation, was ratified in 1781. Although the Articles established a kind of national unity, it did not provide for a strong central government. The individual states still held power.

When it became apparent that government under the Articles was, in the words of George Washington, "little more than the shadow without substance," agitation for a strong federal government began. This resulted in the Constitutional Convention of 1787, which met in Philadelphia to revise the Articles of Confederation.

The convention, presided over by George Washington, was torn by sharp conflict over the apportionment of power between the smaller states and the larger states.

Finally, a compromise measure won approval. This measure provided for a lower house to be elected according to population (the House of Representatives) and an upper house to be chosen by the state legislatures (the Senate). This provision for the Senate held true until 1913, when the 17th Amendment provided for the direct popular election of senators.

After the Constitution was issued, the struggle for ratification was bitter, especially over the conferring of new powers on the central government. Alexander Hamilton, John Jay, and James Madison, in a series of newspaper essays now known as the *Federalist Papers,* did much to promote the acceptance of the Constitution. Delaware, on Dec. 7, 1787, became the first state to ratify the new Constitution. On June 21, 1788, by a vote of 57 to 46, New Hampshire became the ninth state to ratify.

By the terms of the Constitution, ratification by nine states was enough for its establishment. But the government could not succeed without the addition of New York and Virginia, neither of which had ratified. On June 25, 1788, Virginia ratified, over many objections. Finally, on July 26, 1788, New York ratified, with a recommendation that a bill of rights be appended.

With 11 states having thus ratified the Constitution, the Congress of the Confederation passed a resolution on Sept. 13, 1788, to put the new Constitution into operation. On April 1–6, 1789, the first session of the 1st U.S. Congress convened. Later, North Carolina added its ratification on Nov. 21, 1789, and Rhode Island on May 29, 1790.

PREAMBLE

We the People of the United States, in Order to form a more perfect Union, establish Justice, insure domestic Tranquility, provide for the common defence, promote the general Welfare, and secure the Blessings of Liberty to ourselves and our Posterity, do ordain and establish this Constitution for the United States of America.

ARTICLE I (Legislative Branch)

Section 1. All legislative Powers herein granted shall be vested in a Congress of the United States, which shall consist of a Senate and House of Representatives.

Section 2. The House of Representatives shall be composed of Members chosen every second Year by the People of the several States, and the Electors in each State shall have the Qualifications requisite for Electors of the most numerous Branch of the State Legislature.

No Person shall be a Representative who shall not have attained to the Age of twenty five Years, and been seven Years a Citizen of the United States, and who shall not, when elected, be an Inhabitant of that State in which he shall be chosen.

Representatives and direct Taxes shall be apportioned among the several States which may be included within this Union, according to their respective Numbers, [which shall be determined by adding to the whole Number of free Persons, including those bound to Service for a Term of Years, and excluding Indians not taxed, three fifths of all other Persons.] [1] The actual Enumeration shall be made within three Years after the first Meeting of the Congress of the United States, and within every subsequent Term of ten Years, in such Manner as they shall by Law direct. The Number of Representatives shall not exceed one for every thirty Thousand, but each State shall have at Least one Representative; and until such enumeration shall be made, the State of New Hampshire shall be entitled to chuse three, Massachusetts eight, Rhode-Island and Providence Plantations one, Connecticut five, New-York six, New Jersey four, Pennsylvania eight, Delaware one, Maryland six, Virginia ten, North Carolina five, South Carolina five, and Georgia three.

When vacancies happen in the Representation from any State, the Executive Authority thereof shall issue Writs of Election to fill such Vacancies.

The House of Representatives shall chuse their speaker and other Officers; and shall have the sole Power of Impeachment.

Section 3. The Senate of the United States shall be composed of two Senators from each state, [chosen by the Legislature thereof,] [2] for six Years; and each Senator shall have one Vote.

Immediately after they shall be assembled in

[1] Changed by 14th Amendment, section 2. [2] Changed by 17th Amendment, section 1.

Consequence of the first Election, they shall be divided as equally as may be into three Classes. The Seats of the Senators of the first Class shall be vacated at the Expiration of the second Year, of the second Class at the Expiration of the fourth Year, and of the third Class at the Expiration of the sixth Year, so that one third may be chosen every second Year; [and if Vacancies happen by Resignation, or otherwise, during the Recess of the Legislature of any State, the Executive thereof may make temporary Appointments until the next Meeting of the Legislature, which shall then fill such Vacancies.] 3

No Person shall be a Senator who shall not have attained to the Age of thirty years, and been nine Years a Citizen of the United States, and who shall not, when elected, be an Inhabitant of that State for which he shall be chosen.

The Vice President of the United States shall be President of the Senate, but shall have no Vote, unless they be equally divided.

The Senate shall chuse their other Officers, and also a President pro tempore, in the Absence of the Vice President, or when he shall exercise the Office of President of the United States.

The Senate shall have the sole Power to try all Impeachments. When sitting for that Purpose, they shall be on Oath or Affirmation. When the President of the United States is tried, the Chief Justice shall preside: And no Person shall be convicted without the Concurrence of two thirds of the Members present.

Judgment in Cases of Impeachment shall not extend further than to removal from Office, and disqualification to hold and enjoy any Office of honor, Trust or Profit under the United States: but the Party convicted shall nevertheless be liable and subject to Indictment, Trial, Judgment and Punishment, according to Law.

Section 4. The Times, Places and Manner of holding Elections for Senators and Representatives, shall be prescribed in each State by the Legislature thereof; but the Congress may at any time by Law make or alter such Regulations, except as to the Places of chusing Senators.

[The Congress shall assemble at least once in every Year, and such Meeting shall be on the first Monday in December, unless they shall by Law appoint a different Day.] 4

Section 5. Each House shall be the Judge of the Elections, Returns and Qualifications of its own Members, and a Majority of each shall constitute a Quorum to do Business; but a smaller Number may adjourn from day to day, and may be authorized to compel the Attendance of absent Members, in such Manner, and under such Penalties as each House may provide.

Each House may determine the Rules of its Proceedings, punish its Members for disorderly Behaviour, and, with the Concurrence of two thirds, expel a Member.

Each House shall keep a Journal of its Proceedings, and from time to time publish the same, excepting such Parts as may in their Judgment require Secrecy; and the Yeas and Nays of the Members of either House on any question shall, at the Desire of one fifth of those Present be entered on the Journal.

Neither House, during the Session of Congress, shall without the Consent of the other, adjourn for more than three days, nor to any other Place than that in which the two Houses shall be sitting.

Section 6. The Senators and Representatives shall receive a Compensation for their Services, to be ascertained by Law, and paid out of the Treasury of the United States. They shall in all Cases, except Treason, Felony and Breach of the Peace, be privileged from Arrest during their Attendance at the Session of their respective Houses, and in going to and returning from the same; and for any Speech or Debate in either House, they shall not be questioned in any other Place.

No Senator or Representative shall, during the Time for which he was elected, be appointed to any civil Office under the Authority of the United States, which shall have been created, or the Emoluments whereof shall have been encreased during such time; and no Person holding any Office under the United States, shall be a Member of either House during his Continuance in Office.

Section 7. All Bills for raising Revenue shall originate in the House of Representatives; but the Senate may propose or concur with Amendments as on other Bills.

Every Bill which shall have passed the House of Representatives and the Senate, shall, before it become a Law, be presented to the President of the United States; If he approve he shall sign it, but if not he shall return it, with his Objections to that House in which it shall have originated, who shall enter the Objections at large on their Journal, and proceed to reconsider it. If after such Reconsideration two thirds of that House shall agree to pass the Bill, it shall be sent together with the Objections, to the other House, by which it shall likewise be reconsidered, and if approved by two thirds of that House, it shall become a Law. But in all such Cases the Votes of both Houses shall be determined by Yeas and Nays, and the Names of the Persons voting for and against the Bill shall be entered on the Journal of each House respectively. If any Bill shall not be returned by the President within ten Days (Sundays excepted) after it shall have been presented to him, the Same shall be a Law, in like Manner as if he had signed it, unless the Congress by their Adjournment prevent its Return, in which Case it shall not be a Law.

Every Order, Resolution, or Vote to which the Concurrence of the Senate and House of Representatives may be necessary (except on a question of Adjournment) shall be presented to the President of the United States; and before the Same shall take Effect, shall be approved by him, or being disapproved by him, shall be repassed by two thirds of the Senate and House of Representatives, according to the Rules and Limitations prescribed in the Case of a Bill.

Section 8. The Congress shall have Power To lay and collect taxes, Duties, Imposts and Excises, to pay the Debts and provide for the common Defence and general Welfare of the United States; but all Duties, Imposts and Excises shall be uniform throughout the United States;

To Borrow Money on the Credit of the United States;

To regulate Commerce with foreign Nations, and among the several States, and with the Indian Tribes;

3 Changed by 17th Amendment, clause 2. 4 Changed by 20th Amendment, section 2.

CONSTITUTION OF U.S. *(continued)*

To establish an uniform Rule of Naturalization, and uniform Laws on the subject of Bankruptcies throughout the United States;

To coin Money, regulate the Value thereof, and of foreign Coin, and fix the Standard of Weights and Measures;

To provide for the Punishment of counterfeiting the Securities and current Coin of the United States;

To establish Post Offices and post Roads;

To promote the Progress of Science and useful Arts, by securing for limited Times to Authors and Inventors the exclusive Right to their respective Writings and Discoveries;

To constitute Tribunals inferior to the supreme Court;

To define and punish Piracies and Felonies committed on the high Seas, and Offences against the Law of Nations;

To declare War, grant Letters of Marque and Reprisal, and make Rules concerning Captures on Land and Water;

To raise and support Armies, but no Appropriation of Money to that Use shall be for a longer Term than two Years;

To provide and maintain a Navy;

To make Rules for the Government and Regulation of the land and naval Forces;

To provide for calling forth the Militia to execute the Laws of the Union, suppress insurrections and repel Invasions;

To provide for organizing, arming, and disciplining, the Militia, and for governing such Part of them as may be employed in the Service of the United States, reserving to the States respectively, the Appointment of the Officers, and the Authority of training the Militia according to the discipline prescribed by Congress;

To exercise exclusive Legislation in all Cases whatsoever, over such District (not exceeding ten Miles square) as may, by Cession of Particular States, and the Acceptance of Congress, become the Seat of the Government of the United States, and to exercise like Authority over all Places purchased by the Consent of the Legislature of the State in which the Same shall be for the Erection of Forts, Magazines, Arsenals, dock-Yards, and other needful Buildings;—And

To make all Laws which shall be necessary and proper for carrying into Execution the foregoing Powers, and all other Powers vested by this Constitution in the Government of the United States, or in any Department or Officer thereof.

Section 9. The Migration or Importation of such Persons as any of the States now existing shall think proper to admit, shall not be prohibited by the Congress prior to the Year one thousand eight hundred and eight, but a Tax or duty may be imposed on such Importation, not exceeding ten dollars for each Person.

The Privilege of the Writ of Habeas Corpus shall not be suspended, unless when in Cases of Rebellion or Invasion the public Safety may require it.

No Bill of Attainder or ex post facto Law shall be passed.

[No Capitation, or other direct Tax shall be laid, unless in Proportion to the Census or Enumeration herein before directed to be taken.] [5]

No Tax or Duty shall be laid on Articles exported from any State.

No Preference shall be given by any Regulation of Commerce or Revenue to the Ports of one State over those of another: nor shall Vessels bound to, or from, one State, be obliged to enter, clear, or pay Duties in another.

No Money shall be drawn from the Treasury, but in Consequence of Appropriations made by Law; and a regular Statement and Account of the Receipts and Expenditures of all public Money shall be published from time to time.

No Title of Nobility shall be granted by the United States: And no Person holding any Office of Profit or Trust under them, shall, without the Consent of the Congress, accept of any present, Emolument, Office, or Title, of any kind whatever, from any King, Prince, or foreign State.

Section 10. No State shall enter into any Treaty, Alliance, or Confederation; grant Letters of Marque and Reprisal; coin Money; emit Bills of Credit; make any Thing but gold and silver Coin a Tender in Payment of Debts; pass any Bill of Attainder, ex post facto Law, or Law impairing the Obligation of Contracts, or grant any Title of Nobility.

No State shall, without the Consent of the Congress, lay any Imposts or Duties on Imports or Exports, except what may be absolutely necessary for executing its inspection Laws: and the net Produce of all Duties and Imposts, laid by any State on Imports or Exports, shall be for the Use of the Treasury of the United States; and all such Laws shall be subject to the Revision and Controul of the Congress.

No State shall, without the Consent of Congress, lay any Duty of Tonnage, keep Troops, or Ships of War in time of Peace, enter into any Agreement or Compact with another State, or with a foreign Power, or engage in War, unless actually invaded, or in such imminent Danger as will not admit of delay.

ARTICLE II (Executive Branch)

Section 1. The executive Power shall be vested in a President of the United States of America. He shall hold his Office during the Term of four Years, and, together with the Vice President,[6] chosen for the same term, be elected, as follows

Each State shall appoint, in such Manner as the Legislature thereof may direct, a Number of Electors, equal to the whole Number of Senators and Representatives to which the State may be entitled in the Congress: but no Senator or Representative, or Person holding an Office of Trust or Profit under the United States, shall be appointed an Elector.

[The Electors shall meet in their respective States, and vote by Ballot for two Persons, of whom one at least shall be an Inhabitant of the same State with themselves. And they shall make a List of all the Persons voted for, and of the Number of Votes for each; which List they shall sign and certify, and transmit sealed to the Seat of the Government of the United States, directed to the President of the Senate. The President of the Senate shall, in the Presence of the Senate and House of Representa-

[5] See also 16th Amendment. [6] Superseded by 12th Amendment.

tives, open all the Certificates, and the Votes shall then be counted. The Person having the greatest Number of Votes shall be the President, if such Number be a Majority of the whole Number of Electors appointed; and if there be more than one who have such Majority, and have an equal Number of Votes, then the House of Representatives shall immediately chuse by Ballot one of them for President: and if no Person have a Majority, then from the five highest on the list the said House shall in like Manner chuse the President. But in chusing the President, the Votes shall be taken by States, the Representation from each State having one Vote; a quorum for this Purpose shall consist of a Member or Members from two thirds of the States, and a Majority of all the States shall be necessary to a Choice. In every Case, after the Choice of the President, the Person having the greatest Number of Votes of the Electors shall be the Vice President. But if there should remain two or more who have equal Votes, the Senate shall chuse from them by Ballot the Vice President.] [7]

The Congress may determine the Time of chusing the Electors, and the Day on which they shall give their Votes: which Day shall be the same throughout the United States.

No Person except a natural born Citizen, or a Citizen of the United States, at the time of the Adoption of this Constitution, shall be eligible to the Office of President; neither shall any Person be eligible to that Office who shall not have attained to the Age of thirty five Years, and been fourteen Years a Resident within the United States.

In Case of the Removal of the President from Office, or of his Death, Resignation, or Inability to discharge the Powers and Duties of the said Office, the Same shall devolve on the Vice President, and the Congress may by Law provide for the Case of Removal, Death, Resignation or Inability, both of the President and Vice President, declaring what Officer shall then act as President, and such Officer shall act accordingly, until the Disability be removed, or a President shall be elected. [8]

The President shall, at stated Times, receive for his Services, a Compensation, which shall neither be encreased nor diminished during the Period for which he shall have been elected, and he shall not receive within that Period any other Emolument from the United States, or any of them.

Before he enter on the Execution of his Office, he shall take the following Oath or Affirmation:—"I do solemnly swear (or affirm) that I will faithfully execute the Office of President of the United States, and will to the best of my Ability, preserve, protect and defend the Constitution of the United States."

Section 2. The President shall be Commander in Chief of the Army and Navy of the United States, and of the Militia of the several States, when called into the actual Service of the United States; he may require the Opinion, in writing, of the principal Officer in each of the executive Departments, upon any Subject relating to the Duties of their respective Offices, and he shall have Power to grant Reprieves and Pardons for Offences against the United States, except in Cases of Impeachment.

He shall have Power, by and with the Advice and Consent of the Senate, to make Treaties, provided two thirds of the Senators present concur; and he shall nominate, and by and with the Advice and Consent of the Senate, shall appoint Ambassadors, other public Ministers and Consuls, Judges of the supreme Court, and all other Officers of the United States, whose Appointments are not herein otherwise provided for, and which shall be established by Law: but the Congress may by Law vest the Appointment of such inferior Officers, as they think proper, in the President alone, in the Courts of Law, or in the Heads of Departments.

The President shall have Power to fill up all Vacancies that may happen during the Recess of the Senate, by granting Commissions which shall expire at the End of their next Session.

Section 3. He shall from time to time give to the Congress Information of the State of the Union, and recommend to their Consideration such Measures as he shall judge necessary and expedient; he may, on extraordinary Occasions, convene both Houses, or either of them, and in Case of Disagreement between them, with Respect to the Time of Adjournment, he may adjourn them to such Time as he shall think proper; he shall receive Ambassadors and other public Ministers; he shall take Care that the Laws be faithfully executed, and shall Commission all the Officers of the United States.

Section 4. The President, Vice President and all civil Officers of the United States, shall be removed from Office on Impeachment for, and Conviction of, Treason, Bribery, or other High Crimes and Misdemeanors.

ARTICLE III (Judicial Branch)

Section 1. The judicial Power of the United States, shall be vested in one supreme Court, and in such Inferior Courts as the Congress may from time to time ordain and establish. The Judges, both of the supreme and inferior Courts, shall hold their Offices during good Behaviour, and shall, at stated Times, receive for their Services, a Compensation, which shall not be diminished during their Continuance in Office.

Section 2. The judicial Power shall extend to all Cases, in Law and Equity, arising under this Constitution, the Laws of the United States, and Treaties made, or which shall be made, under their Authority;—to all Cases affecting Ambassadors, other public Ministers and Consuls;—to all Cases of admiralty and maritime Jurisdiction;—to Controversies to which the United States shall be a Party;—to Controversies between two or more States; [between a State and Citizens of another State;] [9]—between Citizens of different States;—between Citizens of the same State claiming Lands under Grants of different States, and between a State, or the Citizens thereof, and foreign States, [Citizens or Subjects] [9].

In all Cases affecting Ambassadors, other public Ministers and Consuls, and those in which a State shall be Party, the Supreme Court shall have original Jurisdiction. In all the other Cases before mentioned, the supreme Court shall have appellate Jurisdiction, both as to Law and Fact, with such Exceptions, and under such Regulations as the Congress shall make.

The Trial of all Crimes, except in Cases of Impeachment, shall be by Jury; and such Trial shall be held in the State where the said Crimes shall

[7] Superseded by 12th Amendment. [8] Affected by 25th Amendment. [9] Affected by 11th Amendment.

CONSTITUTION OF U.S. *(continued)*

have been committed; but when not committed within any State, the Trial shall be at such Place or Places as the Congress may by Law have directed.

Section 3. Treason against the United States, shall consist only in levying War against them, or in adhering to their Enemies, giving them Aid and Comfort. No Person shall be convicted of Treason unless on the Testimony of two Witnesses to the same overt Act, or on Confession in open Court.

The Congress shall have Power to declare the Punishment of Treason, but no Attainder of Treason shall work Corruption of Blood, or Forfeiture except during the Life of the Person attainted.

ARTICLE IV (Relations of States)

Section 1. Full Faith and Credit shall be given in each State to the public Acts, Records, and judicial Proceedings of every other State. And the Congress may by general Laws prescribe the Manner in which such Acts, Records and Proceedings shall be proved, and the Effect thereof.

Section 2. The Citizens of each State shall be entitled to all Privileges and Immunities of Citizens in the several States.

A Person charged in any State with Treason, Felony, or other Crime, who shall flee from Justice, and be found in another State, shall on Demand of the executive Authority of the State from which he fled, be delivered up, to be removed to the State having Jurisdiction of the Crime.

No Person held to Service or Labour in one State, under the Laws thereof, escaping into another, shall in Consequence of any Law or Regulation therein, be discharged from such Service or Labour, but shall be delivered up on Claim of the Party to whom such Service or Labour may be due.

Section 3. New States may be admitted by the Congress into this Union; but no new State shall be formed or erected within the Jurisdiction of any other State; nor any State be formed by the Junction of two or more States, or Parts of States, without the Consent of the Legislatures of the States concerned as well as of the Congress.

The Congress shall have Power to dispose of and make all needful Rules and Regulations respecting the Territory or other Property belonging to the United States; and nothing in this Constitution shall be so construed as to Prejudice any Claims of the United States, or of any particular State.

Section 4. The United States shall guarantee to every State in this Union a Republican Form of Government, and shall protect each of them against invasion; and on Application of the Legislature, or of the Executive (when the Legislature cannot be convened) against domestic Violence.

ARTICLE V (Amending the Constitution)

The Congress, whenever two thirds of both Houses shall deem it necessary, shall propose Amendments to this Constitution, or, on the Application of the Legislatures of two thirds of the several States, shall call a convention for proposing Amendments, which, in either Case, shall be valid to all Intents and Purposes, as Part of this Constitution, when ratified by the Legislatures of three fourths of the several States, or by Conventions in three fourths thereof, as the one or the other Mode of Ratification may be proposed by the Congress; Provided that no Amendment which may be made prior to the Year One thousand eight hundred and eight shall in any Manner affect the first and fourth Clauses in the Ninth Section of the first Article: and that no State, without its Consent, shall be deprived of its equal Suffrage in the Senate.

ARTICLE VI (National Debts)

All Debts contracted and Engagements entered into, before the Adoption of this Constitution, shall be as valid against the United States under this Constitution, as under the Confederation.

This Constitution, and the Laws of the United States which shall be made in Pursuance thereof; and all Treaties made, or which shall be made, under the Authority of the United States, shall be the supreme Law of the Land; and the Judges in every State shall be bound thereby, any Thing in the Constitution or Laws of any State to the Contrary notwithstanding.

The Senators and Representatives before mentioned, and the Members of the several State Legislatures, and all executive and judicial Officers, both of the United States and of the several States, shall be bound by Oath or Affirmation, to support this Constitution; but no religious Test shall ever be required as a Qualification to any Office or public Trust under the United States.

ARTICLE VII (Ratification)

The ratification of the Conventions of nine States, shall be sufficient for the Establishment of this Constitution between the States so ratifying the Same.

DONE in Convention by the Unanimous Consent of the States present the Seventeenth Day of September in the Year of our Lord one thousand seven hundred and Eighty seven and of the Independence of the United States of America the Twelfth **IN WITNESS** whereof we have hereunto subscribed our Names [1]

G^{o} Washington—Presid^{t}
and deputy from Virginia

Delaware
Geo: Read
Gunning Bedford jun
John Dickinson
Richard Bassett
Jaco: Broom

Maryland
James McHenry
Dan of St Thos Jenifer
Danl Carroll

Virginia
John Blair—
James Madison Jr

North Carolina
Wm Blount
Richd Dobbs Spaight
Hu Williamson

South Carolina
J. Rutledge
Charles Cotesworth Pinckney
Charles Pinckney
Pierce Butler

Georgia
William Few
Abr Baldwin

New Hampshire
John Langdon
Nicholas Gilman

Massachusetts
Nathaniel Gorham
Rufus King

Connecticut
Wm Saml Johnson
Roger Sherman

New York
Alexander Hamilton

New Jersey
Wil: Livingston
David Brearley
Wm Paterson
Jona: Dayton

Pennsylvania
B Franklin
Thomas Mifflin
Robt Morris
Geo. Clymer
Thos FitzSimons
Jared Ingersoll
James Wilson
Gouv Morris

[1] The order of signing was geographical, beginning in the right column with New Hampshire.

AMENDMENTS TO THE CONSTITUTION

BILL OF RIGHTS

The first 10 amendments to the Constitution of the United States were ratified on Dec. 15, 1791, and form what is known as the Bill of Rights.

AMENDMENT 1 (Freedoms, Assembly, Petitions)

Congress shall make no law respecting an establishment of religion, or prohibiting the free exercise thereof; or abridging the freedom of speech, or of the press; or the right of the people peaceably to assemble, and to petition the Government for a redress of grievances.

AMENDMENT 2 (Right to Bear Arms)

A well regulated Militia, being necessary to the security of a free State, the right of the people to keep and bear Arms, shall not be infringed.

AMENDMENT 3 (Quartering of Soldiers)

No Soldier shall, in time of peace be quartered in any house, without the consent of the Owner, nor in time of war, but in a manner to be prescribed by law.

AMENDMENT 4 (Search and Arrest)

The right of the people to be secure in their persons, houses, papers, and effects, against unreasonable searches and seizures, shall not be violated, and no Warrants shall issue, but upon probable cause, supported by Oath or affirmation, and particularly describing the place to be searched, and the persons or things to be seized.

AMENDMENT 5 (Rights in Criminal Cases)

No person shall be held to answer for a capital, or otherwise infamous crime, unless on a presentment or indictment of a Grand Jury, except in cases arising in the land or naval forces, or in the Militia, when in actual service in time of War or public danger; nor shall any person be subject for the same offence to be twice put in jeopardy of life or limb; nor shall be compelled in any criminal case to be a witness against himself, nor be deprived of life, liberty, or property, without due process of law; nor shall private property be taken for public use, without just compensation.

AMENDMENT 6 (Right to Fair Trial)

In all criminal prosecutions, the accused shall enjoy the right to a speedy and public trial, by an impartial jury of the State and district wherein the crime shall have been committed, which district shall have been previously ascertained by law, and to be informed of the nature and cause of the accusation; to be confronted with the witnesses against him; to have compulsory process for obtaining witnesses in his favor, and to have the Assistance of Counsel for his defence.

AMENDMENT 7 (Rights in Civil Cases)

In Suits at common law, where the value in controversy shall exceed twenty dollars, the right of trial by jury shall be preserved, and no fact tried by a jury, shall be otherwise re-examined in any Court of the United States, than according to the rules of the common law.

AMENDMENT 8 (Bail, Fines, and Punishment)

Excessive bail shall not be required, nor excessive fines imposed, nor cruel and unusual punishments inflicted.

AMENDMENT 9 (Rights Retained by People)

The enumeration in the Constitution, of certain rights, shall not be construed to deny or disparage others retained by the people.

AMENDMENT 10 (States' Rights)

The powers not delegated to the United States by the Constitution, nor prohibited by it to the States, are reserved to the States respectively, or to the people.

AMENDMENT 11 (Lawsuits Against States)

(*Proclaimed Jan. 8, 1798*)

The Judicial power of the United States shall not be construed to extend to any suit in law or equity, commenced or prosecuted against one of the United States by Citizens of another State, or by Citizens or Subjects of any Foreign State.

AMENDMENT 12 (Presidential Elections)

(*Proclaimed Sept. 25, 1804*)

The Electors shall meet in their respective states and vote by ballot for President and Vice-President, one of whom, at least, shall not be an inhabitant of the same state with themselves; they shall name in their ballots the person voted for as President, and in distinct ballots the person voted for as Vice-President, and they shall make distinct lists of all persons voted for as President, and of all persons voted for as Vice-President, and of the number of votes for each, which lists they shall sign and certify, and transmit sealed to the seat of the government of the United States, directed to the President of the Senate;—The President of the Senate shall, in the presence of the Senate and House of Representatives, open all the certificates and the votes shall then be counted;—The person having the greatest number of votes for President, shall be the President, if such number be a majority of the whole number of Electors appointed; and if no person have such majority, then from the persons having the highest numbers not exceeding three on the list of those voted for as President, the House of Representatives shall choose immediately, by ballot, the President. But in choosing the President, the votes shall be taken by states, the representation from each state having one vote; a quorum for this purpose shall consist of a member or members from two-thirds of the states, and a majority of all the states shall be necessary to a choice.

And if the House of Representatives shall not choose a President whenever the right of choice shall devolve upon them, before the fourth day of March next following, then the Vice-President shall act as President, as in the case of the death or other constitutional disability of the President.—The person having the greatest number of votes as Vice-President, shall be the Vice-President, if such number be a majority of the whole number of Electors appointed, and if no person have a majority, then from the two highest numbers on the list, the Senate shall choose the Vice-President; a quorum

CONSTITUTIONAL AMENDMENTS *(continued)*

for the purpose shall consist of two-thirds of the whole number of Senators, and a majority of the whole number shall be necessary to a choice. But no person constitutionally ineligible to the office of President shall be eligible to that of Vice-President of the United States.

AMENDMENT 13 (Abolition of Slavery)
(*Proclaimed Dec. 18, 1865*)
Section 1. Neither slavery nor involuntary servitude, except as a punishment for crime whereof the party shall have been duly convicted, shall exist within the United States, or any place subject to their jurisdiction.
Section 2. Congress shall have power to enforce this article by appropriate legislation.

AMENDMENT 14 (Civil Rights)
(*Proclaimed July 28, 1868*)
Section 1. All persons born or naturalized in the United States, and subject to the jurisdiction thereof, are citizens of the United States and of the State wherein they reside. No State shall make or enforce any law which shall abridge the privileges or immunities of citizens of the United States, nor shall any State deprive any person of life, liberty, or property, without due process of law; nor deny to any person within its jurisdiction the equal protection of the laws.
Section 2. Representatives shall be apportioned among the several States according to their respective numbers, counting the whole number of persons in each State, excluding Indians not taxed. But when the right to vote at any election for the choice of electors for President and Vice President of the United States, Representatives in Congress, the Executive and Judicial officers of a State, or the members of the Legislature thereof, is denied to any of the male inhabitants of such State, being twenty-one years of age, and citizens of the United States, or in any way abridged, except for participation in rebellion, or other crime, the basis of representation therein shall be reduced in the proportion which the number of such male citizens shall bear to the whole number of male citizens twenty-one years of age in such State.
Section 3. No person shall be a Senator or Representative in Congress, or elector of President and Vice President, or hold any office, civil or military, under the United States, or under any State, who, having previously taken an oath, as a member of Congress, or as an officer of the United States, or as a member of any State legislature, or as an executive or judicial officer of any State, to support the Constitution of the United States, shall have engaged in insurrection or rebellion against the same, or given aid or comfort to the enemies thereof. But Congress may by a vote of two-thirds of each House, remove such disability.
Section 4. The validity of the public debt of the United States, authorized by law, including debts incurred for payment of pensions and bounties for services in suppressing insurrection or rebellion, shall not be questioned. But neither the United States nor any State shall assume or pay any debt or obligation incurred in aid of insurrection or rebellion against the United States, or any claim for the loss or emancipation of any slave; but all such debts, obligations and claims shall be held illegal and void.
Section 5. The Congress shall have power to enforce, by appropriate legislation, the provisions of this article.

AMENDMENT 15 (Black Suffrage)
(*Proclaimed March 30, 1870*)
Section 1. The right of citizens of the United States to vote shall not be denied or abridged by the United States or by any State on account of race, color, or previous condition of servitude.
Section 2. The Congress shall have power to enforce this article by appropriate legislation.

AMENDMENT 16 (Income Taxes)
(*Proclaimed Feb. 25, 1913*)
The Congress shall have power to lay and collect taxes on incomes, from whatever source derived, without apportionment among the several States, and without regard to any census or enumeration.

AMENDMENT 17 (Senatorial Election)
(*Proclaimed May 31, 1913*)
The Senate of the United States shall be composed of two Senators from each State, elected by the people thereof, for six years; and each Senator shall have one vote. The electors in each State shall have the qualifications requisite for electors of the most numerous branch of the State legislatures.

When vacancies happen in the representation of any State in the Senate, the executive authority of such State shall issue writs of election to fill such vacancies: Provided, That the legislature of any State may empower the executive thereof to make temporary appointments until the people fill the vacancies by election as the legislature may direct.

This amendment shall not be so construed as to affect the election or term of any Senator chosen before it becomes valid as part of the Constitution.

AMENDMENT 18 (Prohibition of Liquor)
(*Proclaimed Jan. 29, 1919*)
(*Repealed by 21st Amendment*)
Section 1. After one year from the ratification of this article the manufacture, sale, or transportation of intoxicating liquors within, the importation thereof into, or the exportation thereof from the United States and all territory subject to the jurisdiction thereof for beverage purposes is hereby prohibited.
Section 2. The Congress and the several States shall have concurrent power to enforce this article by appropriate legislation.
Section 3. This article shall be inoperative unless it shall have been ratified as an amendment to the Constitution by the legislatures of the several States, as provided in the Constitution, within seven years from the date of the submission hereof to the States by the Congress.

AMENDMENT 19 (Woman Suffrage)
(*Proclaimed Aug. 26, 1920*)
The right of citizens of the United States to vote shall not be denied or abridged by the United States or by any State on account of sex.

Congress shall have power to enforce this article by appropriate legislation.

AMENDMENT 20 (Terms of Office)
(*Proclaimed Feb. 6, 1933*)
Section 1. The terms of the President and Vice-

EARLY CAPITALS OF THE UNITED STATES: 1774 to 1789

The Continental Congress and its successor, the Congress of the Articles of Confederation, met in eight different cities as the seat of the national government during and after the American Revolution.

Philadelphia, Pennsylvania:
Sept. 5, 1774, to Oct. 26, 1774
May 10, 1775, to Dec. 12, 1776
Baltimore, Maryland:
Dec. 20, 1776, to March 4, 1777
Philadelphia, Pennsylvania:
March 5, 1777, to Sept. 18, 1777
Lancaster, Pennsylvania:
Sept. 27, 1777 (one day only)
York, Pennsylvania:
Sept. 30, 1777, to June 27, 1778
Philadelphia, Pennsylvania:
July 2, 1778, to June 21, 1783
Princeton, New Jersey:
June 30, 1783, to Nov. 4, 1783
Annapolis, Maryland:
Nov. 26, 1783, to June 3, 1784
Trenton, New Jersey:
Nov. 1, 1784, to Dec. 24, 1784
New York City, New York:
Jan. 11, 1785, to Nov. 4, 1785
Nov. 7, 1785, to Nov. 3, 1786
Nov. 6, 1786, to Oct. 30, 1787
Nov. 5, 1787, to Oct. 21, 1788
Nov. 3, 1788, to March 2, 1789

President shall end at noon on the 20th day of January, and the terms of Senators and Representatives at noon on the 3d day of January, of the years in which such terms would have ended if this article had not been ratified; and the terms of their successors shall then begin.

Section 2. The Congress shall assemble at least once in every year, and such meeting shall begin at noon on the 3d day of January, unless they shall by law appoint a different day.

Section 3. If, at the time fixed for the beginning of the term of the President, the President-elect shall have died, the Vice-President-elect shall become President. If a President shall not have been chosen before the time fixed for the beginning of his term, or if the President-elect shall have failed to qualify, then the Vice-President-elect shall act as President until a President shall have qualified; and the Congress may by law provide for the case wherein neither a President-elect nor a Vice-President-elect shall have qualified, declaring who shall then act as President, or the manner in which one who is to act shall be selected, and such person shall act accordingly until a President or Vice-President shall have qualified.

Section 4. The Congress may by law provide for the case of the death of any of the persons from whom the House of Representatives may choose a President whenever the right of choice shall have devolved upon them, and for the case of the death of any of the persons from whom the Senate may choose a Vice-President whenever the right of choice shall have devolved upon them.

Section 5. Sections 1 and 2 shall take effect on the 15th day of October following the ratification of this article.

Section 6. This article shall be inoperative unless it shall have been ratified as an amendment to the Constitution by the legislatures of three-fourths of the several States within seven years from the date of its submission.

AMENDMENT 21 (Repeal of Prohibition)

(*Proclaimed Dec. 5, 1933*)

Section 1. The eighteenth article of amendment to the Constitution of the United States is hereby repealed.

Section 2. The transportation or importation into any State, Territory, or possession of the United States for delivery or use therein of intoxicating liquors, in violation of the laws thereof, is hereby prohibited.

Section 3. This article shall be inoperative unless it shall have been ratified as an amendment to the Constitution by conventions in the several States, as provided in the Constitution, within seven years from the date of the submission hereof to the States by the Congress.

AMENDMENT 22 (Limit on Presidential Terms)

(*Proclaimed March 1, 1951*)

Section 1. No person shall be elected to the office of the President more than twice, and no person who has held the office of President, or acted as President, for more than two years of a term to which some other person was elected President shall be elected to the office of the President more than once. But this Article shall not apply to any person holding the office of President when this Article was proposed by the Congress, and shall not prevent any person who may be holding the office of President, or acting as President, during the term within which this Article becomes operative from holding the office of President or acting as President during the remainder of such term.

Section 2. This article shall be inoperative unless it

PRESIDENTS OF CONGRESS: 1774 to 1789

NAME	STATE	ELECTED	REMARKS
1. Peyton Randolph	Virginia	Sept. 5, 1774	Resigned: Speaker of Virginia legislature 1766–75
2. Henry Middleton	South Carolina	Oct. 22, 1774	Defected to British 1780
3. Peyton Randolph	Virginia	May 10, 1775	Resigned because of ill health
4. John Hancock	Massachusetts	May 24, 1775	First to sign Declaration of Independence
5. Henry Laurens	South Carolina	Nov. 1, 1777	Held prisoner by British 1780–81
6. John Jay	New York	Dec. 10, 1778	First Chief Justice of U.S. 1789–95
7. Samuel Huntington	Connecticut	Sept. 28, 1779	Governor of Connecticut 1786–96
8. Thomas McKean	Delaware	July 10, 1781	First President elected under Articles of Confederation
9. John Hanson	Maryland	Nov. 5, 1781	Gave Washington Congress' thanks for Yorktown victory
10. Elias Boudinot	New Jersey	Nov. 4, 1782	Signed peace treaty ending American Revolutionary War
11. Thomas Mifflin	Pennsylvania	Nov. 3, 1783	Governor of Pennsylvania 1790–99
12. Richard Henry Lee	Virginia	Nov. 30, 1784	U.S. Senator from Virginia 1789–92
13. John Hancock	Massachusetts	Nov. 23, 1785	Resigned without serving because of illness
14. Nathaniel Gorham	Massachusetts	June 6, 1786	Signer of U.S. Constitution
15. Arthur St. Clair	Pennsylvania	Feb. 2, 1787	Governor of Northwest Territory 1789–1802
16. Cyrus Griffin	Virginia	Jan. 22, 1788	U.S. district judge for Virginia 1789–1810

CONSTITUTIONAL AMENDMENTS *(continued)*

shall have been ratified as an amendment to the Constitution by the legislatures of three-fourths of the several States within seven years from the date of its submission to the States by the Congress.

AMENDMENT 23 (Washington, D.C., Suffrage)

(Proclaimed April 3, 1961)

Section 1. The District constituting the seat of Government of the United States shall appoint in such manner as the Congress may direct:

A number of electors of President and Vice President equal to the whole number of Senators and Representatives in Congress to which the District would be entitled if it were a State, but in no event more than the least populous State; they shall be in addition to those appointed by the States, but they shall be considered, for the purposes of the election of President and Vice President, to be electors appointed by a State; and they shall meet in the District and perform such duties as provided by the twelfth article of amendment.

Section 2. The Congress shall have power to enforce this article by appropriate legislation.

AMENDMENT 24 (Abolition of Poll Taxes)

(Proclaimed Feb. 4, 1964)

Section 1. The right of citizens of the United States to vote in any primary or other election for President or Vice President, for electors for President or Vice President, or for Senator or Representative in Congress, shall not be denied or abridged by the United States or any State by reason of failure to pay any poll tax or other tax.

Section 2. The Congress shall have power to enforce this article by appropriate legislation.

AMENDMENT 25 (Presidential Succession)

(Proclaimed Feb. 23, 1967)

Section 1. In case of the removal of the President from office or of his death or resignation, the Vice President shall become President.

Section 2. Whenever there is a vacancy in the office of the Vice President, the President shall nominate a Vice President who shall take office upon confirmation by a majority vote of both houses of Congress.

Section 3. Whenever the President transmits to the President pro tempore of the Senate and the Speaker of the House of Representatives his written declaration that he is unable to discharge the powers and duties of his office, and until he transmits to them a written declaration to the contrary, such powers and duties shall be discharged by the Vice President as Acting President.

Section 4. Whenever the Vice President and a majority of either the principal officers of the executive departments or of such other body as Congress may by law provide, transmit to the President pro tempore of the Senate and the Speaker of the House of Representatives their written declaration that the President is unable to discharge the powers and duties of his office, the Vice President shall immediately assume the powers and duties of the office as Acting President.

Thereafter, when the President transmits to the President pro tempore of the Senate and the Speaker of the House of Representatives his written declaration that no inability exists, he shall resume the powers and duties of his office unless the Vice President and a majority of either the principal officers of the executive department or of such other body as Congress may by law provide, transmit within four days to the President pro tempore of the Senate and the Speaker of the House of Representatives their written declaration that the President is unable to discharge the powers and duties of his office. Thereupon Congress shall decide the issue, assembling within forty-eight hours for that purpose if not in session. If the Congress, within twenty-one days after receipt of the latter written declaration, or, if Congress is not in session, within twenty-one days after Congress is required to assemble, determines by two-thirds vote of both houses that the President is unable to discharge the powers and duties of his office, the Vice President shall continue to discharge the same as Acting President; otherwise, the President shall resume the powers and duties of his office.

AMENDMENT 26 (18-Year-Old Suffrage)

(Proclaimed July 5, 1971)

Section 1. The right of citizens of the United States, who are eighteen years of age or older, to vote shall not be denied or abridged by the United States or by any State on account of age.

Section 2. The Congress shall have power to enforce this article by appropriate legislation.

CONSTITUTIONAL AMENDMENTS NOT RATIFIED

Six amendments submitted to the states have failed to be ratified by them.

In 1791, of the 12 proposed amendments to the Constitution, Articles III-XII were ratified and became the Bill of Rights, the first 10 amendments to the Constitution. But the proposed Articles I and II were not ratified. They would have provided that as the population grew there could be a representative in Congress for every 50,000 people and would have prevented Congress from raising its own salaries during the term in session.

The 11th Congress proposed an amendment forbidding acceptance by U.S. citizens of foreign titles "of nobility or honour."

On March 2, 1861, President James Buchanan signed a proposed amendment that would have forbidden any amendments to the Constitution giving Congress the power to abolish or interfere with slavery. It was not ratified.

Congress approved an amendment in 1924 giving it power to regulate child labor. It was not ratified.

In 1972 an equal rights for women amendment was approved by Congress but failed to be ratified by three-fourths of the states. It stated: "Equality of rights under the law shall not be denied or abridged by the United States or any state on account of sex."

An amendment to give Washington, D.C., voting representation in Congress was approved by Congress in 1978 and sent to the states for ratification.

U.S. TERRITORIAL EXPANSION

The total gross area (land and water) of the U.S. and its outlying areas was 3,623,420 square miles in the 1980 census. The table below outlines the nation's physical growth since independence was declared in 1776.

The area figures are precise determinations of specific territories first made by a special government committee in 1912 and subsequently adjusted to bring them into agreement with later remeasurements.

In 1979 the U.S. gave up claims to several Pacific islands including Canton and Enderbury, which became part of the nation Kiribati (formerly the Gilbert Islands).

On Oct. 1, 1979, the United States restored to Panama sovereignty over the 553-square-mile Panama Canal Zone that had been governed by the U.S. since 1904.

DATE	ACQUISITION	GROSS AREA (in sq. miles)	HOW ACQUIRED	ACQUISITION PRICE
—	Original territory	888,685	Treaty with Britain	—
1803	Louisiana	827,192	Purchase from France	$15,000,000
1819	Florida (and other areas)	72,003	Treaty with Spain	$ 5,000,000
1845	Texas	390,143	Independent republic annexed	—
1846	Oregon	285,580	Treaty with Britain	—
1848	Mexican cession	529,017	Conquest from Mexico	$15,000,000
1854	Gadsden Purchase	29,640	Purchase from Mexico	$10,000,000
1867	Alaska	586,412	Purchase from Russia	$ 7,200,000
1898	Hawaiian Islands	6,471	Independent republic annexed	—
1898	Puerto Rico	3,515	Conquest from Spain	—
1898	Guam	209	Conquest from Spain	—
1899	American Samoa	77	Division with Germany and Britain	—
1917	Virgin Islands	132	Purchase from Denmark	$25,000,000
1947	Trust Territory of the Pacific Islands (Marshall and Caroline Islands)	533	UN Trusteeship (to be terminated in 1981, granting Micronesia independence)	—
1978	Northern Mariana Islands	184	Conquest from Japan in World War II (achieved Commonwealth status in 1978)	—
—	All other [1]	15	—	—

[1] Includes following islands with gross areas (in square miles) as indicated: Midway (2); Wake (3); Palmyra (4); Navassa (2); Baker, Howland, and Jarvis (combined, 3); Johnston and Sand (combined, less than ½ sq. mi.); Kingman Reef (less than ½ sq. mi.).

U.S. GOVERNMENT LANDHOLDINGS, BY STATE

Source: General Services Administration, Sept. 30, 1982

STATE	TOTAL AREA Acres	FEDERALLY OWNED Acres	FEDERALLY OWNED %
U.S. TOTAL	**2,271,343,360**	**729,820,861.4**	**32.132**
Alabama	32,678,400	1,140,954.2	3.492
Alaska	365,481,600	327,028,961.7	89.479
Arizona	72,688,000	29,194,570.3	40.164
Arkansas	33,599,360	3,404,254.1	10.132
California	100,206,720	47,525,524.8	47.428
Colorado	66,485,760	23,949,523.7	36.022
Connecticut	3,135,360	9,940.3	0.317
Delaware	1,265,920	40,683.6	3.214
Dist. of Col.	39,040	12,278.5	31.451
Florida	34,721,280	3,651,653.0	10.517
Georgia	37,295,360	2,281,041.8	6.116
Hawaii	4,105,600	786,769.6	19.163
Idaho	52,933,120	34,281,911.6	64.765
Illinois	35,795,200	626,480.1	1.750
Indiana	23,158,400	528,699.8	2.283
Iowa	35,860,480	228,049.0	0.636
Kansas	52,510,720	733,155.2	1.396
Kentucky	25,512,320	1,417,715.8	5.557
Louisiana	28,867,840	1,157,436.1	4.009
Maine	19,847,680	135,882.3	0.685
Maryland	6,319,360	210,380.8	3.329
Massachusetts	5,034,880	84,801.1	1.684
Michigan	36,492,160	3,533,418.3	9.683
Minnesota	51,205,760	3,448,659.3	6.735
Mississippi	30,222,720	1,748,821.0	5.786
Missouri	44,248,320	2,253,755.4	5.093
Montana	93,271,040	27,468,335.1	29.450
Nebraska	49,031,680	696,120.9	1.420
Nevada	70,264,320	57,383,816.7	81.669
New Hamp.	5,768,960	738,417.0	12.800
New Jersey	4,813,440	146,438.3	3.042
New Mexico	77,766,400	25,862,337.1	33.256
New York	30,680,960	248,936.3	0.811
North Carolina	31,402,880	2,169,354.1	6.908
North Dakota	44,452,480	2,246,256.9	5.053
Ohio	26,222,080	351,104.9	1.339
Oklahoma	44,087,680	1,749,004.0	3.967
Oregon	61,598,720	30,102,588.0	48.869
Pennsylvania	28,804,480	695,456.9	2.414
Rhode Island	677,120	6,157.5	0.909
South Carolina	19,374,080	1,193,610.5	6.161
South Dakota	48,881,920	3,151,989.7	6.448
Tennessee	26,727,680	2,095,787.1	7.841
Texas	168,217,600	3,528,274.1	2.097
Utah	52,696,960	32,166,670.8	61.041
Vermont	5,936,640	319,530.1	5.382
Virginia	25,496,320	2,360,367.8	9.258
Washington	42,693,760	12,104,326.1	28.352
West Virginia	15,410,560	1,113,733.7	7.227
Wisconsin	35,011,200	1,896,917.3	5.418
Wyoming	62,343,040	30,610,009.1	49.099

QUICK QUIZ: How long is the pregnancy period of an elephant? See page 52.

THE STAR-SPANGLED BANNER

Oh! say, can you see, by the dawn's early light,
What so proudly we hailed at the twilight's last gleaming?
Whose broad stripes and bright stars thro' the perilous fight,
O'er the ramparts we watched, were so gallantly streaming?
And the rockets' red glare, the bombs bursting in air,
Gave proof thro' the night that our flag was still there.
Oh! say, does that star-spangled banner yet wave
O'er the land of the free and the home of the brave?

On the shore, dimly seen thro' the mist of the deep,
Where the foe's haughty host in dread silence reposes,
What is that which the breeze, o'er the towering steep,
As it fitfully blows, half conceals, half discloses?
Now it catches the gleam of the morning's first beam,
In full glory reflected, now shines on the stream,
'Tis the star-spangled banner. Oh! long may it wave
O'er the land of the free and the home of the brave!

And where is that band who so vauntingly swore,
That the havoc of war and the battle's confusion
A home and a country should leave us no more?
Their blood has washed out their foul footstep's pollution.
No refuge could save the hireling and slave
From the terror of flight or the gloom of the grave,
And the star-spangled banner in triumph doth wave
O'er the land of the free and the home of the brave.

Oh! thus be it ever when freemen shall stand
Between their loved home and the war's desolation,
Blest with vict'ry and peace may the Heav'n-rescued land
Praise the Pow'r that hath made and preserved us a nation.
Then conquer we must, when our cause it is just,
And this be our motto "In God is our trust."
And the star-spangled banner in triumph shall wave
O'er the land of the free and the home of the brave.

A naval bombardment during the War of 1812 led to the writing of the American national anthem.

Francis Scott Key, a successful Washington lawyer, visited the flagship of the British fleet in Chesapeake Bay, accompanying Col. John S. Skinner on an official mission to secure the release of a prisoner.

Detained on board the tender on which they had come out to the flagship, the two watched the bombardment of Fort McHenry at Baltimore, Md., on the night of Sept. 13–14, 1814.

Seeing the American flag still aloft at dawn, Key was inspired to write a poem.

The poem was first printed as a broadside and then, on Sept. 20, 1814, was published in the Baltimore *Patriot.* The next day, the Baltimore *American* also printed it with the title *Defence of Fort M'Henry.*

On Oct. 19, 1814, the poem was first sung in public and for the first time given the title *The Star-Spangled Banner.* As entertainment following a performance in Baltimore of the play *Count Benyowski,* the words were sung to a tune, *Anacreon in Heaven,* then widely known in America as the melody for a political song called "Adams and Liberty." Key had composed his poem in obvious imitation of this song. He borrowed not only the melody but meter and verse form as well.

President Wilson proclaimed *The Star-Spangled Banner* as the national anthem of the United States in 1916, but Congress did not confirm this action until 1931.

In Key's honor, the U.S. flag flies continuously over his grave at Frederick, Md.

There is no official act of Congress setting the exact wording of the national anthem, and several versions—differing only in detail—remain in use today.

PLEDGE OF ALLEGIANCE

I pledge allegiance to the flag of the United States of America and to the Republic for which it stands, one Nation under God, indivisible, with liberty and justice for all.

The Pledge of Allegiance to the flag was written by Francis Bellamy for the National Public School Celebration of Columbus Day in 1892. Bellamy was working for *The Youth's Companion,* a journal published in Boston. He had been appointed chairman of a committee to develop a program for the celebration of the 400th anniversary of the discovery of America.

Bellamy wrote the pledge in two hours on an August evening. It was published in *The Youth's Companion* on Sept. 8, 1892, and in the official program of the celebration. No one knows where the pledge was first used, although it is known to have been recited at the World's Columbian Exposition in Chicago on Oct. 21, 1892.

Originally, the pledge read: "I pledge allegiance to my flag and to the Republic for which it stands, one Nation indivisible, with liberty and justice for all."

In 1923, at the First National Flag Conference in Washington, D.C., the words "my flag" were changed to "the flag of the United States."

In the following year, at the Second National Flag Conference, the words "of America" were added to the phrase.

In 1954 the words "under God" were inserted.

Although the pledge became popular throughout the nation, it was not until 1942 that its words were included in federal legislation about flag use and customs. The pledge was given official congressional sanction in 1945.

HISTORY OF THE AMERICAN FLAG

Banners of the American Revolution: the Moultrie, Rhode Island, Bunker Hill, and Bennington flags.

Before American independence became a reality, there were colonial or regimental flags by the score. Many local banners carried such slogans as "Don't Tread On Me."

The Moultrie flag—the first distinctive American flag displayed in the South—flew over the fort on Sullivan's Island, outside Charleston, S.C., when a British fleet attacked on June 28, 1776. The garrison, under Col. William Moultrie, forced the British to withdraw—and the flag became known by his name. The design of this blue flag with a white crescent was suggested by the garrison's blue uniforms and the silver crescents worn by the men on their caps, inscribed with *Liberty or Death.*

Rhode Island had its own flag, carried at Brandywine, Trenton, and Yorktown. It bore an anchor, 13 stars, and the word *Hope*. Its white stars in a blue field are believed to have suggested the "starry blue field" displayed on our national flag.

Among famous New England banners was the Bunker Hill. This flag—one of the first to include the pine tree—was carried by American colonial troops at the Battle of Bunker Hill on June 17, 1775.

The Bennington flag was carried by the Green Mountain Boys at the Battle of Bennington on Aug. 16, 1777.

On Jan. 1, 1776, at a ceremony at Gen. George Washington's Prospect Hill headquarters in Cambridge (now part of Somerville), Mass., the Grand Union flag was raised as the standard of the Continental Army. It was similar to the Meteor flag of Great Britain, modified by red and white stripes signifying the 13 original colonies. Retention of the British Union in the canton, with its crosses of St. George and St. Andrew, indicated continued loyalty—as the colonists saw it—to the "mother country." This flag soon became known by various names, including the Grand Union flag, the Union flag, the Cambridge flag, and the Colours of the United Colonies.

On June 14, 1777, the Continental Congress adopted this resolution proposed by John Adams: "Resolved: that the flag of the United States be made of thirteen stripes, alternate red and white; that the Union be thirteen stars, white in a blue field representing a new constellation." Thus was born the Stars and Stripes. It appears to have been designed primarily for use at sea, not as a battle flag on land. On a voyage that began on Sept. 30, 1787, Capt. Robert Gray in the *Columbia* carried the flag around the world for the first time.

The original flag, with its 13 stripes and 13 stars, remained in use only a few years. On Dec. 26, 1793, after the admission of two new states to the Union, Stephen R. Bradley of Vermont introduced a bill in Congress "for altering the Flag of the United States." It provided, in less than four lines of print, that beginning on May 1, 1795, the Flag of the United States should be "fifteen stripes, alternate red and white, with a union of fifteen stars white in a blue field." This was passed on Jan. 13, 1794.

Peter H. Wendover, representative to Congress from New York, was responsible for the Flag Act of April 4, 1818, which is still in effect. This act specified "thirteen horizontal stripes, alternate red and white." It provided that the "union have 20 stars, white on a blue field" and "on the admission of every new state into the Union," one star would be added on the following July 4.

On June 24, 1912, President William Howard Taft issued an executive order officially prescribing the relative proportions of the flag and the arrangement of the stars.

By an executive order of President Eisenhower, dated Aug. 21, 1959, a banner with 50 stars became the official flag of the United States on July 4, 1960.

Left to right: Grand Union Flag; original Stars and Stripes; flag of 1795–1818; flag since 1960.

HONORING THE AMERICAN FLAG

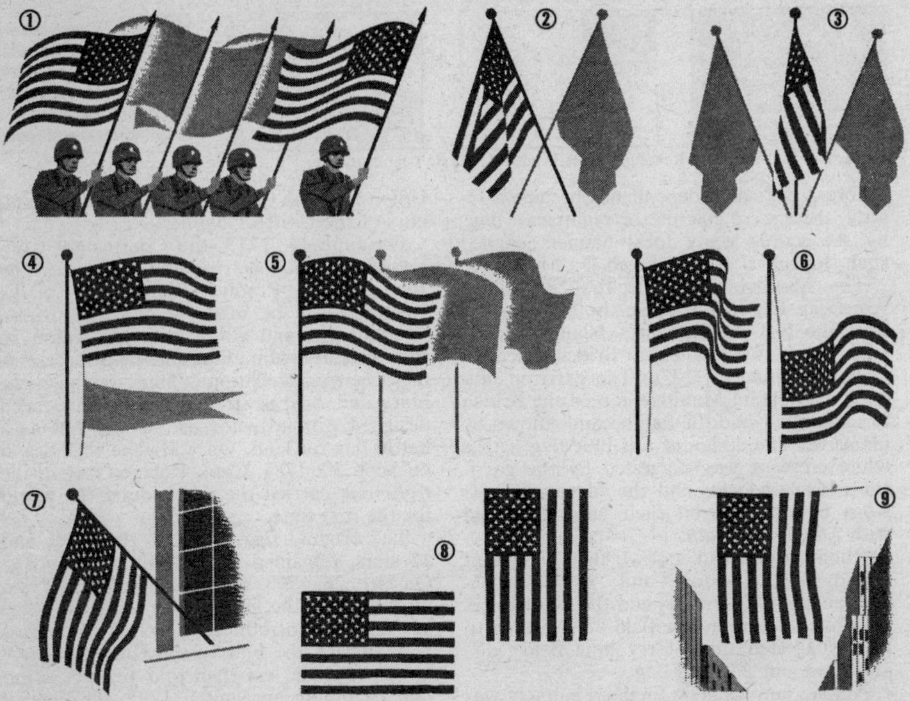

The U.S. flag code adopted by Congress provides rules for displaying and honoring the flag. The code states: "The flag represents a living country and is itself considered a living thing."

The code was amended in 1976 with Public Law 94–344 to clarify misunderstandings regarding rules that should be observed.

Below is a summary of the rules.

Raising and Lowering: The flag should be hoisted briskly and lowered ceremoniously.

When to Display: A flag made of weather-resistant material can be flown around the clock in any weather if properly illuminated.

It should be displayed especially on New Year's Day, Inauguration Day, Lincoln's Birthday, Washington's Birthday, Easter Sunday, Mother's Day, Armed Forces Day, Memorial Day, Flag Day, Independence Day, Labor Day, Constitution Day, Columbus Day, Navy Day, Veterans Day, Thanksgiving Day, Christmas Day, on other days proclaimed by the President, on the birthdays of states, and on state holidays.

Public Buildings: The flag should be displayed daily on or near the main administration building of every public institution, in or near every polling place on election days, and in or near every schoolhouse on school days.

In a Procession: When carried in a procession with another flag or flags, it should be either on the marching right (the flag's own right) or, if there is a line of other flags, in front of the center of that line (*see Figure 1 above*). It should not be carried on a parade float except flat or from a staff.

On a Vehicle: The flag should not be draped on or over any part of a vehicle, railroad train, or boat. When displayed on an automobile, the staff should be firmly clamped to the right front fender.

With Other Flags: No other flag or pennant should be placed above or, if on the same level, to the United States flag's right.

When it is displayed with another flag against a wall from crossed staffs, it should be on the right (the flag's own right) and its staff should be in front of that of the other flag *(see Figure 2)*.

The U.S. flag should be at the center and at the highest point of the group when a number of flags of states or localities or society pennants are grouped and displayed from staffs *(see Figure 3)*.

When state, city, local flags, or society pennants are flown on the same halyard with the U.S. flag, the latter should always be at the peak *(see Figure 4)*. When such other flags are flown from adjacent staffs, the U.S. flag should be hoisted first and lowered last.

When flags of two or more nations are displayed, they are to be flown from separate staffs of the same height *(see Figure 5)*. The flags should be of about equal size.

Within the United States or any U.S. territory or possession no person is permitted to display the United Nations flag or any other national or international flag equal, above, or in a position of superior prominence or honor to, or in place of, the U.S. flag. However, this does not apply to the practice at UN headquarters in New York City of displaying the flag of the UN in a position of superior prominence or honor, and other national flags in a position of equal prominence or honor.

At Half-Staff: The flag, when flown at half-staff, should first be hoisted momentarily to the peak and then lowered to one-half the distance between the top and bottom of the staff. It should be again raised to the peak before it is lowered *(see Figure 6)*.

From a Building: When displayed from a staff projecting horizontally or at an angle from the windowsill, balcony, or front of a building, the union (blue field) of the flag should be placed at the peak of the staff, unless the flag is at half-staff *(see Figure 7)*.

Not on a Staff: When the flag is displayed other than by being flown from a staff, indoors or out, it should either be displayed flat or suspended so that its folds fall freely as though it were staffed. When displayed flat (either horizontally or vertically) against a wall or window, the union should be uppermost and to the flag's own right (to the observer's left) *(see Figure 8)*.

Over a Street: When displayed over the middle of a street, the flag should be suspended vertically with the union to the north in an east-west street or to the east in a north-south street *(see Figure 9)*.

In an Auditorium: When used on a speaker's platform, the flag, if displayed flat, should be above and behind the speaker. When displayed from a staff in a church or public auditorium, the flag should hold the position of superior prominence, in advance of the audience, and in the position of honor at the clergyman's or speaker's right as he faces the audience. Any other flag so displayed should be placed at the clergyman's or speaker's left or to the right of the audience.

At an Unveiling: The flag should never be used as covering for the statue or monument.

At a Funeral: When the flag is used to cover a casket, it should be placed so that the union is at the head and over the left shoulder. It should not be lowered into the grave or allowed to touch the ground.

Saluting the Flag: During the hoisting or lowering of the flag, when it is passing in a parade or in a review, or during rendition of the national anthem, all persons present should face the flag and stand at attention.

Those in uniform should give the military salute.

When not in uniform, men should remove their hats, holding them at their left shoulder with the right hand over the heart. Men without hats should salute by placing the right hand over the heart. Aliens should stand at attention. The salute to the flag in a moving column should be made at the moment the flag passes.

Some Flag Don'ts: The flag should:

Never be dipped in salute to any person or thing.

Never be displayed with the union down *except as a signal of dire distress.*

Never touch anything beneath it, such as the ground, the floor, or water.

Never be carried flat or horizontally, but always aloft and free.

Never be used as a ceiling covering.

Never have placed upon it, nor on any part of it, nor attached to it any mark, insignia, letter, word, figure, design, picture, or drawing of any nature.

Never be used as a receptacle for receiving, holding, carrying, or delivering anything.

Never be used as wearing apparel, bedding, or drapery.

Never be festooned, drawn back, or up, in folds, but always be allowed to fall free.

Never be fastened, displayed, used or stored in such a manner as to permit it to be easily torn, soiled, or damaged in any way.

Never be used for advertising purposes in any manner whatsoever.

Never be embroidered on such articles as cushions or handkerchiefs and the like, printed or impressed on paper napkins or boxes or anything designed for temporary use and discard.

Advertising signs should not be fastened to a staff or halyard from which the flag flies.

No part of the flag should ever be used as a costume or athletic uniform. However, a flag patch may be affixed to the uniform of military personnel, firemen, policemen, and members of patriotic organizations. The lapel flag pin, being a replica, should be worn on the left lapel near the heart.

It is a federal crime to knowingly cast contempt on the flag by "publicly mutilating, defacing, defiling, burning, or trampling upon it."

QUICK QUIZ: What ballet company was founded by Sergei Diaghilev? See page 59.

FAMOUS PERSONS IN AMERICAN HISTORY

Brief biographies of famous persons in American history on the following pages include statesmen, political leaders, heroes, reformers, and others.

Biographies of *U.S. Presidents and First Ladies* appear on pages 340–387.

For biographical information on other famous Americans, see the following tables: *Authors and Writers*, pages 94–102; *Classical Musicians, Composers, Singers, and Dancers*, pages 58–63; *Show Business Personalities*, pages 271–282; *Painters, Sculptors, and Architects*, pages 64–68; *Pioneers in Medicine*, pages 452–454; *Scientists and Inventors*, pages 731–736; *Theologians and Philosophers*, pages 714–716; and obituaries of American men and women who died in 1983, pages 981–986.

Dean Gooderham Acheson (1893–1971): Played major role in developing U.S. foreign policy during and after World War II under Presidents F.D. Roosevelt and Truman; served as assistant secretary of state, 1941–45, under- secretary of state, 1945–47, secretary of state, 1949–53; became target of Sen. Joseph McCarthy (R-Wis.) and his followers, who accused Acheson of being "soft on communism" and of "coddling" communists as members of State Department; born in Middletown, Conn.

Samuel Adams (1722–1803): Patriot leader in period of American Revolution; helped organize Sons of Liberty to oppose British Stamp Act, 1765; began committee of correspondence in Massachusetts, 1772, to inform other colonies of patriot actions; organized Boston Tea Party, 1773; delegate to Continental Congress, 1774–82; voted for and signed Declaration of Independence, 1776; lieutenant governor of Massachusetts, 1789–93; governor of Massachusetts, 1793–97; born in Boston.

Jane Addams (1860–1935): Founded first settlement house (or neighborhood center) in Chicago, called Hull House, with Ellen Gates Starr, 1889; became first woman president of National Conference of Charities and Corrections, 1909; as pacifist, was president of Women's International League for Peace and Freedom, 1915–29; co-recipient of Nobel Peace Prize with Nicholas Murray Butler, 1931; born in Cedarville, Ill.

Spiro Theodore Agnew (born 1918): 39th Vice President of U.S., 1969–73; first ever forced to resign; accepted conviction for income tax evasion, 1973, to avoid prosecution on bribery charges; Republican governor of Maryland, 1967–69; nominated Richard M. Nixon for President at national convention, 1968, and became his running mate; born in Towson, Md.

Ethan Allen (1738–89): Led Vermont's Green Mountain Boys in capture of British Fort Ticonderoga, May 10, 1775, in first American victory of Revolutionary War; during Battle of Montreal in September 1775, was captured and imprisoned, 1775–78; upon return, worked to achieve recognition of Vermont's independence; born in Litchfield, Conn.

Richard Allen (1760–1831): Founded first black religious denomination in U.S., Bethel African Methodist Episcopal Church, 1794, in Philadelphia; born a slave in Philadelphia; gained freedom, 1786.

Susan Brownell Anthony (1820–1906): Early advocate of women's rights, temperance, and abolition; with Elizabeth Cady Stanton founded National Woman Suffrage Association, 1869, and was its president, 1892–1900; arrested for voting in 1872; trial brought attention to women's rights movement; born in Adams, Mass.

Johnny Appleseed (John Chapman; 1774–1845): Legendary pioneer who planted apple trees in Ohio and Indiana along route of migrating settlers during westward movement in early 1800s; born in Leominster, Mass.

Neil Alden Armstrong (born 1930): First an to set foot on Moon as commander of *Apollo 11* mission, 1969, declaring: "That's one small step for a man, one giant leap for mankind"; performed first manual docking in space with astronaut David R. Scott in *Gemini 8*, 1966; flew 78 combat missions in Korean War as Navy pilot; born near Wapakoneta, Ohio.

Benedict Arnold (1741–1801): Revolutionary War traitor; as Continental Army major general displayed heroism in American victory at Battles of Saratoga, 1777; as military commander of Philadelphia, 1778–80, was convicted by court-martial of using position for personal gain, but received only reprimand; as commander of West Point, N.Y., 1780, bargained with British to surrender fort for large bonus, but plot was uncovered by capture of British spy Maj. John André; Arnold escaped to British lines and fought against Americans for rest of Revolutionary War; born in Norwich, Conn.

John Jacob Astor (1763–1848): Became one of richest men in U.S. by monopolizing fur trade with Europe and China; established American Fur Co., 1808, and Pacific Fur Co., 1810; founded Astoria, Ore., 1811; sold fur holdings, 1834, and invested in farmland that became heart of New York City; fortune was estimated at $20 million; born in Waldorf, Germany.

Stephen Fuller Austin (1793–1836): Established first American settlement in Texas, on Brazos River, 1821; initiated demands for Texas independence from Mexico; became first secretary of state of independent Texas Republic, 1836; born in Wythe County, Va.

George Bancroft (1800–91): Historian and public official; wrote 10-volume *History of the United States*, 1834–76; as secretary of the navy, 1845–46, founded U.S. Naval Academy at Annapolis, Md.; served as U.S. minister to Britain, 1846–49, and to Germany, 1867–74; born in Worcester, Mass.

Benjamin Banneker (1731–1806): Black mathematician and astronomer; helped survey District of Columbia, 1791; published annual astronomical almanac, 1791–1802, used by abolitionists to prove blacks were as capable as whites; born in Ellicott, Md.

Henry Barnard (1811–1900): First U.S. commissioner of education, 1867–70; published *American Journal of Education*, 1855–82; did much to develop U.S. public-school system; born in Hartford, Conn.

Phineas Taylor ("P.T.") Barnum (1810–91): Showman known for his claim "There's a sucker born every minute"; opened circus *Greatest Show on Earth*, 1871; combined with major rival to form Barnum & Bailey Circus, 1881; born in Bethel, Conn.

Clara Barton (1821–1912): Known as "Angel of the Battlefield"; organized nursing services for Union Army during Civil War, 1861–65; served in Europe as nurse during Franco-Prussian War, 1870; founded American Red Cross, 1881, and was its first president, 1882–1904; initiated Red Cross help for peacetime disasters; born near Oxford, Mass.

Bernard Baruch (1870–1965): Financier and adviser to eight Presidents from Woodrow Wilson to John F. Kennedy; prepared first plan for international development and control of atomic energy as U.S. representative to UN Atomic Energy Commission, 1946; made fortune as speculator in securities; born in Camden, S.C.

Henry Ward Beecher (1813–87): Popular Protestant preacher and reformer; advocated women's rights, abolition of slavery, and civil-service reform; pastor of Plymouth Congregational Church in Brooklyn, N.Y., 1847–87; sought to reconcile evolution and religion; charged with adultery in sensational trial, 1874–75, but jury could not arrive at verdict; brother of Harriet Beecher Stowe; born in Litchfield, Conn.

Thomas Hart Benton (1782–1858): Hot-tempered Democratic U.S. senator from Missouri for 30 consecutive years, 1821–51; shot Andrew Jackson in frontier brawl in 1813 but later became Jackson's firm friend and supporter; because of personal dislike of slavery, opposed Compromise of 1850 and lost Senate seat as result; U.S. representative (D-Mo.), 1853–55; born near Hillsborough, N.C.

Billy the Kid (William H. Bonney; 1859–81): Western outlaw said to have killed 21 men, first when he was only 12; led cattle rustlers in series of slayings in New Mexico; sentenced to hang in 1881, killed two sheriff's deputies and escaped; tracked down and killed by Sheriff Pat Garrett, 1881; born in New York City.

Black Hawk (1767–1838): Indian chief of Sauk tribe; refused to honor treaty giving up lands, claiming chiefs had been made drunk before signing it; fought Black Hawk War against settlers in Illinois, 1832; Black Hawk and two sons were captured and jailed; born at Rock River, Ill.

James Gillespie Blaine (1830–93): U.S. secretary of state, 1881 and 1889–92; initiated first Pan American Conference, 1889; U.S. representative (R-Me.), 1863–76, speaker of the House, 1869–75; U.S. senator (R-Me.), 1876–81; as Republican candidate for President, 1884, was defeated largely because New York voters were angered by Blaine supporter labeling Democrats as party of "rum, Romanism and rebellion"; born in West Brownsville, Pa.

Daniel Boone (1734–1820): Pioneer frontiersman; explored Kentucky, 1767; blazed Wilderness Road through Cumberland Gap and built Boonesborough, Ky., 1775; famous as Indian fighter; born near Reading, Pa.

John Wilkes Booth (1838–65): Assassin of President Lincoln, 1865; a Shakespearean actor, he escaped after shooting Lincoln but was tracked down and killed 12 days later in barn near Port Royal, Va.; born in Bel Air, Md.

James Bowie (1796–1836): Hero of Texas War for Independence; among those who fought to death against Mexicans in Battle of the Alamo, 1836; invented frontier hunting knife, called Bowie knife; born in Burke County, Ga.

William Bradford (1590–1657): Pilgrim leader; came to America on *Mayflower* and helped found Plymouth Colony; elected colony's governor, 1621, he served for 30 of next 35 years; wrote *History of Plymouth Plantation*, 1651; born in Yorkshire, England.

Omar Nelson Bradley (1893–1981): Commander of U.S. ground forces in Normandy invasion of France, 1944; then led about 1 million U.S. troops in 12th Army Group that conquered German-occupied Europe, 1944–45; U.S. Army chief of staff, 1948–49; first chairman Joint Chiefs of Staff, 1949–53; promoted to 5-star General of the Army, 1950; wrote *A Soldier's Story*, 1951; graduated from West Point, 1915; born in Clark, Mo.

Mathew B. Brady (c.1823–96): Photographer of U.S. Civil War; took more than 3,500 photos; born in Warren County, N.Y.

Louis Dembitz Brandeis (1856–1941): Associate justice of U.S. Supreme Court, 1916–39; during most of period court was controlled by conservatives, so that Brandeis often dissented from rulings, issuing his own more liberal opinions; born in Louisville, Ky.

John Cabell Breckinridge (1821–75): 14th Vice President of U.S., 1857–61; was unsuccessful Southern Democratic candidate for President against Lincoln, 1860; served several months in 1861 as Democratic U.S. senator from Kentucky, voting against Lincoln's war measures; escaped to South to become Confederate general and then secretary of war, 1865; after war fled to Cuba, then to England, returning home in 1868; born near Lexington, Ky.

James Bridger (1804–81): Frontiersman; explored Rocky Mountains as fur trapper; was first white man to discover Great Salt Lake, 1824, and one of first to describe wonders of Yellowstone region; built Fort Bridger in Wyoming, 1843, as supply station on Oregon Trail; born in Richmond, Va.

John Brown (1800–59): Radical abolitionist; led raid on proslavery settlers at Pottawatomie Creek in Kansas, 1856, killing five; with followers, captured federal arsenal at Harpers Ferry, Va., Oct. 16, 1859, planning to use arms to start slave revolt in South; U.S. Marines led by Col. Robert E. Lee forced Brown and followers to surrender; convicted of murder and treason against Virginia, Brown was hanged on Dec. 2, 1859; born in Torrington, Conn.

QUICK-QUIZ: Which U.S. President won the 1919 Nobel Peace Prize? See page 73.

FAMOUS PERSONS IN AMERICAN HISTORY *(continued)*

Blanche Kelso Bruce (1841–98): First black to serve full term as U.S. senator (R-Miss.), 1875–81; register of U.S. treasury, 1881–85, 1897–98; born in slavery near Farmville, Va.

William Jennings Bryan (1860–1925): Three-time loser as Democratic candidate for President, 1896, 1900, 1908; as secretary of state, 1913–15, tried to keep U.S. out of World War I, resigning when President Wilson insisted on sending strong notes of protest to Germany about submarine attacks; originally won fame with "Cross of Gold" speech at Democratic convention, 1896, calling for free coinage of silver; a believer in fundamental religion, Bryan aided prosecution at Scopes evolution trial, 1925; born in Salem, Ill.

Ralph Johnson Bunche (1904–71): First black American awarded Nobel Peace Prize, 1950; UN mediator in first Arab-Israeli War, 1948–49; undersecretary of state of United Nations, 1955–71; born in Detroit, Mich.

Warren Earl Burger (born 1907): 15th Chief Justice of U.S., appointed 1969 by President Nixon; though known as conservative, surprised many by liberal rulings favoring busing to end school segregation, 1971; overturning state laws restricting abortions during first six months of pregnancy, 1973; and denying President Nixon's claim to executive privilege in Watergate investigation, 1974; judge of U.S. Court of Appeals in Washington, D.C., 1956–69; born in St. Paul, Minn.

Aaron Burr (1756–1836): 3d Vice President of U.S., 1801–05; after winning tie electoral vote for President, U.S. House of Representatives decided in favor of Thomas Jefferson; killed Alexander Hamilton in duel, 1804; tried for treason for plotting independent empire in West, but acquitted, 1807; served as U.S. senator (D-R–N.Y.), 1791–97; born in Newark, N.J.

George Bush (born 1924): 43d Vice President of U.S., 1981– ; oil company executive, 1953–66; U.S. representative (R-Tex.), 1967–71; U.S. ambassador to UN, 1971–72; chairman, Republican National Committee, 1973–74; director, CIA, 1976–77; defeated by Ronald Reagan in campaign for Republican presidential nomination, 1980; born in Milton, Mass.

Richard Evelyn Byrd (1888–1957): Made first flight over North Pole, with pilot Floyd Bennett, 1926; established "Little America" base in Antarctica, 1928–30, 1933–35; made first flight over South Pole, 1929; promoted to rear admiral in U.S. Navy, 1930; born in Winchester, Va.

Saint Frances Xavier Cabrini (1850–1917): First U.S. citizen to be made saint by Roman Catholic Church, 1946; founded Missionary Sisters of the Sacred Heart, 1880; aided poor Italians in U.S., founding orphanages, schools, and hospitals; born in Lombardy, Italy.

John Caldwell Calhoun (1782–1850): 7th Vice President of U.S., 1825–32, resigning to lead nullification fight against President Jackson; felt South Carolina could nullify federal protective tariffs that it disapproved, but wilted when Jackson threatened to use force to enforce tariff; served as secretary of war, 1817–25, and secretary of state, 1844–45; as U.S. representative (D-S.C.), 1811–17, was "war hawk" in favor of War of 1812; as U.S. senator (D-S.C.), 1832–43, 1845–50, opposed Mexican War and Compromise of 1850; born in what is now Mount Carmel, S.C.

Hattie Wyatt Caraway (1878–1950): First woman elected to U.S. Senate; was appointed U.S. senator (D-Ark.) on Nov. 13, 1931, to fill vacancy caused by death of husband, Sen. Thaddeus H. Caraway; elected to U.S. Senate on Jan. 12, 1932; reelected to full terms in 1932 and 1938; born in Bakerville, Tenn.

Benjamin Nathan Cardozo (1870–1938): Associate justice of U.S. Supreme Court, 1932–38; on principle that Constitution was flexible to permit social change, wrote ruling upholding Social Security Act, 1937; born in New York City.

Andrew Carnegie (1835–1919): Industrialist and philanthropist; starting work as telegraph messenger boy at 15, he amassed fortune estimated at $500 million; developed Carnegie Steel Company, which he sold to U.S. Steel for $225 million in 1901; contributed money to build 2,500 public libraries in English-speaking countries; endowed various foundations and institutions to promote peace and education; born in Dunfermline, Scotland.

Christopher ("Kit") Carson (1809–68): Explored West as frontiersman and fur trapper in 1820s and 1830s; guide for John C. Frémont on expeditions to Colorado, Oregon, and California, 1842–48; organized volunteer force to check Indian raids on settlers in New Mexico during Civil War; born in Madison County, Ky.

Salmon Portland Chase (1808–73): 6th Chief Justice of U.S., 1864–73; presided over Senate impeachment trial of President Johnson in 1868; as Lincoln's secretary of the treasury, 1861–64, financed Union expenses in Civil War through loans and issuing "greenbacks"; as antislavery U.S. senator from Ohio, 1849–55, 1861, fought Compromise of 1850 and Kansas-Nebraska Act; first Republican governor of Ohio, 1856–60; born in Cornish, N.H.

Cesar Estrada Chavez (born 1927): Labor organizer of migrant farm workers, especially Mexican-Americans; formed farm workers union, 1962; a believer in nonviolence, Chavez organized nationwide boycotts against grape and lettuce growers in 1960s and 1970s to force producers to agree to union contracts; born near Yuma, Ariz.

George Rogers Clark (1752–1818): Frontiersman-soldier during Revolutionary War; led about 200 militia down Ohio River and across wilderness to capture British forts at Kaskaskia, Ill., 1778, and at Vincennes, Ind., 1779; destroyed Shawnee village of Chillicothe, Ohio, 1780, putting an end to Indian raids on settlers in Kentucky; born near Charlottesville, Va.

William Clark (1770–1838): With Meriwether Lewis, explored Missouri and Columbia rivers of new Louisiana Territory, 1804–06; governor of Missouri Territory, 1813–20; younger brother of George Rogers Clark; born in Caroline County, Va.

Henry Clay (1777–1852): Whig leader; three-time loser for President, 1824, 1832, 1844; mediated Missouri Compromise of 1820 and sponsored Compromise of 1850; advocated protective tariff and federal aid for internal improvements; U.S. secretary of state, 1825–29; U.S.

senator from Kentucky, 1806–07, 1810–11, 1831–42, 1849–52; U.S. representative from Kentucky, 1811–14, 1815–21, 1823–25, also serving as Speaker of the House during most of those terms; led "war hawks" in favor of War of 1812; born in Hanover County, Va.

De Witt Clinton (1769–1828): Father of Erie Canal, linking Hudson River with Great Lakes; private secretary to uncle, New York Gov. George Clinton, 1790–95; U.S. senator (D-R–N.Y.), 1802–03; mayor of New York City, 1803–07, 1810–11, 1813–14; unsuccessful Federalist and Peace Party candidate for President, 1812; headed commission presenting plans for Erie Canal to legislature, 1815; as governor of New York, 1817–21, 1825–28, broke ground for beginning Erie Canal, 1817, and officially opened canal, 1825; born in Napanock, N.Y.

George Clinton (1739–1812): 4th Vice President of U.S., 1805–12, serving under Presidents Jefferson and Madison; first state governor of New York, 1777–95, 1801–04, elected to record seven terms; as delegate to Continental Congress, 1775–76, voted for Declaration of Independence but was unable to sign it, having been called to duty as brigadier general of militia on July 8, 1776; born in Little Britain, N.Y.

William Frederick ("Buffalo Bill") Cody (1846–1917): Frontiersman and showman; as buffalo hunter, claimed to have killed over 4,000 in 1867–68 as food for railroad construction crews; became nationally known in 1870s as result of dime novels about him written by E.Z.C. Judson (Ned Buntline); organized traveling "Wild West" show, 1883, with which he toured U.S. and Europe for rest of life; show featured markswoman Annie Oakley and, for a while, Indian Chief Sitting Bull; born in Scott County, Iowa.

Crazy Horse (c.1844–77): Sioux Indian chief who helped lead Sioux War of 1876–77, protesting federal government orders that Indians remain on reservations; defeated Gen. George Crook in Battle of Rosebud; massacred Gen. George A. Custer and troops in Battle of Little Bighorn; surrendered voluntarily but was killed while being forced into prison cell.

Davy Crockett (1786–1836): Frontiersman and congressman; served as scout for Gen. Andrew Jackson in Creek War, 1813–14, becoming colonel in Tennessee militia; represented Tennessee in Congress, first as Democrat, 1827–31, then as Whig, 1833–35; died in Battle of the Alamo, 1836; born in Greene County, Tenn.

George Armstrong Custer (1839–76): Union cavalry officer whose daring and skill won him promotion to brigadier general at age 23 during Civil War; in Battle of Little Bighorn in Montana, June 25, 1876, led U.S. cavalry attack on Sioux Indians of Crazy Horse and Sitting Bull, but he and entire column of about 225 men were slain in what became known as "Custer's Last Stand"; graduated last in his class at West Point, 1861; born in New Rumley, Ohio.

George Mifflin Dallas (1792–1864): 11th Vice President of U.S., under President Polk, 1845–49; mayor of Philadelphia, 1829; U.S. senator (D-Pa.), 1831–33; U.S. minister to Russia, 1837–39, and to Britain, 1856–61; born in Philadelphia.

Clarence Seward Darrow (1857–1938): Criminal and labor lawyer noted for his defense of underdog and unpopular causes; earned first fame for defense of labor leader Eugene V. Debs in Pullman strike of 1894; initiated use of psychiatric evidence in Leopold-Loeb murder trial, saving clients from death penalty, 1924; opposed William Jennings Bryan in Scopes trial, 1925; born in Kinsman, Ohio.

Jefferson Davis (1808–89): President of Confederate States of America during Civil War, 1861–65; imprisoned 1865–67 on charges of treason; finally released on bond signed by Horace Greeley and others and never brought to trial; served as U.S. representative (D-Miss.), 1845–46, resigning to fight as colonel in Mexican War; won acclaim in Battles of Monterrey and Buena Vista, 1846–47; U.S. senator (D-Miss.), 1847–51, opposing Compromise of 1850; U.S. secretary of war under President Pierce, 1853–57; born in Christian (now Todd) County, Ky., on June 3, 1808.

Charles Gates Dawes (1865–1951): 30th Vice President of U.S., under President Coolidge, 1925–29; co-recipient of Nobel Peace Prize in 1925 for Dawes Plan, scheduling payments of $33 billion in World War I reparations by Germany; U.S. ambassador to Britain, 1929–32; first chairman of Reconstruction Finance Corporation, 1932; born in Marietta, Ohio.

Benjamin Henry Day (1810–89): Founded New York *Sun* in 1833 as first penny newspaper hawked on streets by newsboys; circulation of 30,000 was largest of any newspaper at that time; born in West Springfield, Mass.

Stephen Day (c.1594–1668): First printer in what is now U.S.; established press in Cambridge, Mass; printed first broadside, *The Freeman's Oath*, 1639; first book, *The Bay Psalm Book*, 1640; born in Cambridge, England.

Eugene Victor Debs (1855–1926): Socialist labor leader; established American Railway Union (ARU), 1893; jailed for disobeying federal injunction against ARU boycott on moving Pullman cars to support striking Pullman workers, 1894; ran for President five times as candidate of Social Democratic (Socialist) Party, 1900–20; jailed under wartime Espionage Act, 1918–21; born in Terre Haute, Ind.

Stephen Decatur (1779–1820): U.S. Navy officer; gained first fame with daring raid in harbor of Tripoli, Libya, burning U.S. frigate *Philadelphia* that had been captured by Barbary Coast Arab pirates, 1804; in War of 1812 commanded squadron that captured British warship *Macedonian;* as commodore, 1815, led squadron to Mediterranean that forced Arab pirates to give up attacks on U.S. ships; upon return gave toast: "Our country: In her intercourse with foreign nations may she always be right; but our country, right or wrong"; born in Sinepuxent, Md.

George Dewey (1837–1917): Admiral in Spanish-American War; destroyed Spanish Pacific fleet in Manila Bay on May 1, 1898, after giving captain of lead ship of his squadron famous command: "You may fire when you are ready, Gridley"; victory assured U.S. conquest of Philippines; graduated from Annapolis, 1858; born in Montpelier, Vt.

QUICK QUIZ: What is the lowest temperature recorded in the U.S.? See page 143.

FAMOUS PERSONS IN AMERICAN HISTORY *(continued)*

John Dewey (1859–1952): Philosopher and educator; was pragmatist, believing ideas can only be judged on basis of how well they work; developed philosophy, called instrumentalism, that man can overcome obstacles by using experience and intelligence; taught at University of Chicago, 1894–1904, and at Columbia, 1904–30; opposed traditional memorization of facts, in favor of learning through activities to stimulate thought; born in Burlington, Vt.

Thomas Edmund Dewey (1902–71): Unsuccessful Republican candidate for President, 1944, 1948; three-term governor of New York, 1943–54; gained fame as district attorney and special prosecutor in New York City, convicting such gangsters as Waxey Gordon and Lucky Luciano, 1931–38; born in Owosso, Mich.

John Dickinson (1732–1808): Called "Penman of the Revolution" because of many important documents he wrote in early U.S. history; as Pennsylvania delegate to Stamp Act Congress, wrote *Declaration of Rights and Grievances of the Colonists of America*, 1765; published *Letters from a Farmer in Pennsylvania to Inhabitants of the British Colonies*, 1767; opposed and refused to sign Declaration of Independence, believing colonies should remain part of British Empire; wrote Articles of Confederation, 1776; fought in Revolutionary War, 1777–78; president of Delaware, 1781–82; president of Pennsylvania, 1782–85; presided at Annapolis Convention, 1786; delegate to Constitutional Convention, 1787; born near Trappe, Md.

Dorothea Lynde Dix (1802–87): Crusaded for building of separate hospitals for mentally ill patients, who in 1840s were confined in prisons with criminals; succeeded in getting such hospitals built in 15 states, Canada, Europe, and Japan; superintendent of nurses for Union Army during Civil War; born in Hampden, Me.

Stephen Arnold Douglas (1813–61): Unsuccessful Democratic candidate for President against Abraham Lincoln in 1860; as U.S. senator (D-Ill.), 1847–61, helped pass Compromise of 1850 and sponsored Kansas-Nebraska Act of 1854 that replaced Missouri Compromise with "popular sovereignty" in territories on slavery issue; defeated Lincoln in Illinois Senate race in 1858, featuring seven famous Lincoln-Douglas debates; born in Brandon, Vt.

Frederick Douglass (1817–95): Black abolitionist; escaped from slavery in Maryland in 1838, settling in Massachusetts; published autobiography, 1845, and fled to England until friends arranged for purchase of his freedom; founded abolitionist newspaper *North Star*, 1847; recruited black troops for Union Army during Civil War, 1861–65; U.S. minister to Haiti, 1889–91; born in Tuckahoe, Md.

W.E.B. Du Bois (1868–1963): Black civil-rights leader and scholar; helped found National Association for the Advancement of Colored People (NAACP), 1909; edited NAACP magazine *The Crisis*, 1910–34; head of sociology department, Atlanta University, 1932–44; joined Communist Party, 1961, and emigrated to Ghana, 1962; born in Great Barrington, Mass.

John Foster Dulles (1888–1959): U.S. secretary of state under President Eisenhower, 1953–59; in Cold War period, developed policy of "brinksmanship," going almost to point of war with communist nations, and threatened "massive retaliation" for communist aggressions; delegate to UN, 1945–50; U.S. senator (R-N.Y.), 1949; main author of Japanese peace treaty, 1951; born in Washington, D.C.

Eleuthère Irénée du Pont de Nemours (1771–1834): Built gunpowder plant near Wilmington, Del., 1802, providing basis for later Du Pont industrial empire developed by his descendants; learned how to make gunpowder as student of French chemist Antoine Lavoisier; born in Paris.

Amelia Earhart (1897–1937): First woman pilot to fly solo across Atlantic, 1932; first to fly solo from Hawaii to mainland, 1935; vanished in Pacific Ocean while attempting around-the-world flight, 1937; born in Atchison, Kan.

Mary Baker Eddy (1821–1910): Founded Christian Science about 1870; wrote *Science and Health*, 1875, describing belief that prayer can overcome illness; chartered Church of Christ, Scientist, 1879; established *Christian Science Monitor*, 1908; born in Bow, N.H.

Oliver Ellsworth (1745–1807): 3d Chief Justice of U.S., 1796–1800; as special envoy to Paris he negotiated treaty ending undeclared naval war between U.S. and France, 1800; as U.S. senator (Fed.-Conn.), 1789–96, largely responsible for drafting Federal Judiciary Act of 1789, laying basis for U.S. court system; Connecticut delegate to Continental Congress, 1777–84, and to Constitutional Convention, 1787; born in Windsor, Conn.

James Leonard Farmer (born 1920): Black civil-rights leader; helped found Congress of Racial Equality (CORE), 1942, to end racial discrimination by passive resistance; under his guidance as national director, CORE began lunch-counter sit-ins and freedom rides in Southern states in 1960s that often touched off mass arrests of demonstrators; assistant secretary of Health, Education, and Welfare, 1969–70; born in Marshall, Texas.

David Glasgow Farragut (1801–70): U.S. Navy admiral in Civil War; best remembered for command "Damn the torpedoes. Full steam ahead!" in his victorious attack on Mobile, Ala., in August 1864; earlier became Union hero when his fleet forced surrender of New Orleans on May 1, 1862; first U.S. Navy officer to hold ranks of rear admiral (1862), vice admiral (1864), and full admiral (1866); born near Knoxville, Tenn.

Marshall Field (1834–1906): Merchant and philanthropist; beginning as $8-a-week sales clerk, became multimillionaire developer of largest department store in Chicago; innovated marking products with firm prices; coined slogan "Give the Lady What She Wants"; gave land and millions of dollars to establish University of Chicago and Field Museum of Natural History; born in Conway Township, Mass.

Nathan Bedford Forrest (1821–77): Confederate cavalry leader in Civil War; despite lack of formal education, rose from private to lt. general; led troops in many successful raids and battles; attributed success to ability "to git thar fustest with the mostest men"; reputedly was first Grand Wizard of Ku Klux Klan; born at Chapel Hill, Tenn.

Benjamin Franklin (1706–90): Helped draft and signed Declaration of Independence, 1776, alliance with France, 1778, treaty of peace with Britain, 1783, and U.S. Constitution, 1787; edited and published *Pennsylvania Gazette,* 1729–1766, and *Poor Richard's Almanack,* 1732–57; invented Franklin stove, 1740, and proved lightning was electricity, 1752; deputy postmaster of American colonies, 1753–74; wrote Albany Plan for uniting American colonies, 1754; Pennsylvania representative in London, 1757–75; member of Continental Congress and first postmaster general, 1775–76; ambassador to France, 1776–85; governor of Pennsylvania, 1785–88; born in Boston.

John Charles Frémont (1813–90): First Republican candidate for President, 1856; led military expeditions that explored territory from Rocky Mountains to California, 1842–44; on third expedition, 1845–47, helped capture California in Mexican War and served briefly as territory's first governor; in dispute with Maj. Gen. Stephen W. Kearny, was found guilty of insubordination by court-martial and resigned from Army; gold discovered on land he owned made him millionaire overnight; upon California's admission as state, served six months as Free-Soil Democrat U.S. senator, 1850–51; major general in Union Army in West during Civil War, 1861–64; governor of Arizona Territory, 1878–81; born in Savannah.

Albert Gallatin (1761–1849): U.S. secretary of the treasury under Presidents Jefferson and Madison, 1802–14; as member of War of 1812 peace commission, negotiated Treaty of Ghent, 1814; minister to France, 1815–23, and to Britain, 1826–27; born in Geneva, Switzerland.

William Lloyd Garrison (1805–79): Abolitionist leader; published abolitionist newspaper *Liberator,* 1831–65, promising, "I will be heard!"; helped organize American Anti-Slavery Society, 1833, and served as president in 1840s and 1850s; after Civil War, crusaded for prohibition and women's rights; born in Newburyport, Mass.

Horatio Gates (c.1728–1806): Revolutionary War major general; commanded American army at Battle of Saratoga, 1777, forcing surrender of over 5,000 British troops; reputation shattered at Battle of Camden (S.C.), 1780, when his army of 4,000 was destroyed by British General Cornwallis and Gates fled in retreat; born in Maldon, England.

Henry George (1839–97): Promoted "single tax" on land use to replace all other taxes to let economic laws operate freely; published ideas in *Progress and Poverty,* 1879; twice defeated as candidate for mayor of New York City, 1886, 1897; born in Philadelphia.

Geronimo (1829–1909): Apache Indian medicine-man; his tribe raided settlers in Mexico, New Mexico, and Arizona; surrendered in 1886; imprisoned for life but allowed to make brief appearances at St. Louis World's Fair, 1904, and in Theodore Roosevelt's inaugural procession, 1905; born in southern Arizona.

Elbridge Gerry (1744–1814): 5th U.S. Vice President, 1813–14, dying in office; Massachusetts delegate to Continental Congress, 1776–85, signing both Declaration of Independence and Articles of Confederation; delegate to Constitutional Convention, 1787, but refused to sign U.S. Constitution because he disagreed with some of its provisions; Antifederalist U.S. representative from Massachusetts, 1789–93; governor of Massachusetts, 1810–12; born in Marblehead, Mass.

John Herschel Glenn Jr. (born 1921): First U.S. astronaut to orbit Earth in space, Feb. 20, 1962; U.S. Marine fighter pilot in World War II and Korean War, flying 122 combat missions; retired as astronaut, 1964; elected U.S. senator (D-Ohio), 1974; born in Cambridge, Ohio.

George Washington Goethals (1858–1928): U.S. Army engineer who directed building of Panama Canal, 1907–14; governor of Panama Canal Zone, 1914–16; born in Brooklyn, N.Y.

Barry Morris Goldwater (born 1909): Unsuccessful Republican candidate for President, 1964; called "Mr. Conservative" because of political views; U.S. senator (R-Ariz.), 1953–65, 1969– ; born in Phoenix.

Samuel Gompers (1850–1924): Labor leader who helped found and was president of American Federation of Labor (AFL), 1886–94, 1896– 1924; opposed formation of independent labor political party or union affiliations with political parties; established system of labor-management negotiations for written union contracts; born in London.

Billy (William Franklin) Graham (born 1918): Protestant evangelist; ordained as Southern Baptist minister, 1939; in four-month crusade in New York City's Madison Square Garden in 1957, nearly 2 million persons attended, resulting in more than 50,000 conversions; born near Charlotte, N.C.

Horace Greeley (1811–72): Unsuccessful Democratic and Liberal Republican candidate for President against U.S. Grant, 1872; founded and edited influential New York *Tribune,* 1841–72; helped Lincoln win Republican presidential nomination, 1860; supported abolition, prohibition, and protective tariffs; popularized phrase "Go west, young man" but did not originate it; born near Amherst, N.H.

Nathanael Greene (1742–86): Revolutionary War major general who liberated Southern states from British military occupation in series of daring battles, 1781; earlier in war, distinguished himself in Battles of Trenton, Brandywine, and Germantown; quartermaster general of Continental Army, 1778–80; born in Potowomut (now Warwick), R.I.

Alexander Meigs Haig Jr. (born 1924): U.S. secretary of state under President Reagan, 1981–82; supreme allied commander of NATO forces in Europe, 1974–78; White House chief of staff under President Nixon, 1973–74; brigade commander in Vietnam War 1966–67; graduated from West Point, 1947; born in Philadelphia, Pa.

Nathan Hale (1755–76): During Revolutionary War, while on volunteer spy mission for George Washington, was captured on Long Island, N.Y., and hanged by British, Sept. 22, 1776; remembered for heroic last words: "I only regret that I have but one life to lose for my country"; born in Coventry, Conn.

QUICK QUIZ: Who is the senior Democrat of the House of Representatives? See page 160.

FAMOUS PERSONS IN AMERICAN HISTORY *(continued)*

Alexander Hamilton (c.1757–1804): As first U.S. secretary of the treasury, 1789–95, put new government on sound financial basis; helped initiate political system of two major political parties as leader of conservative Federalists in opposition to Thomas Jefferson's liberal Democratic-Republicans; served in Revolutionary War as aide-de-camp to George Washington, 1777–81; commanded regiment at Battle of Yorktown, 1781; represented New York in Continental Congress, 1782–83; signer of U.S. Constitution, 1787; wrote most essays in *The Federalist*, urging ratification of Constitution, 1787–88; appointed major general of new U.S. Army, second in command to George Washington, 1798; killed in duel with Vice President Aaron Burr, 1804; born on island of Nevis in British West Indies.

John Hancock (1737–93): President of Continental Congress, 1775–77, 1785–86; first signer of Declaration of Independence, 1776; was joint leader with Samuel Adams of Massachusetts colonial resistance after British seized one of his merchant ships on charges of illegal trading, 1768; first state governor of Massachusetts, 1780–85, 1787–93; born in North Braintree (now Quincy), Mass.

Patrick Henry (1736–99): Virginia patriot leader; best remembered for call for colonial resistance in 1775: "I know not what course others may take; but as for me, give me liberty, or give me death!"; commanded Virginia's militia, 1775–76; delegate to Continental Congress, 1774–76; first state governor of Virginia, 1776–79, 1784–86; opposed adoption of U.S. Constitution because it lacked Bill of Rights, 1787–88; born in Hanover County, Virginia.

Oliver Wendell Holmes Jr. (1841–1935): As associate justice of U.S. Supreme Court, 1902–32, became known as "the Great Dissenter" because he disagreed so often with conservative majority; believed court should not upset social legislation unless it specifically violated Constitution; born in Boston.

J. Edgar Hoover (1895–1972): Director of Federal Bureau of Investigation (FBI), 1924–72; developed FBI into efficient crime-fighting organization free of politics; initiated services to local police, such as fingerprint file for identifying criminals; born in Washington, D.C.

Mark Hopkins (1802–87): Educator; president of Williams College, 1836–72; gained fame when President James Garfield described his effectiveness as a teacher, saying, "Give me a log hut, with only a simple bench, Mark Hopkins on one end and I on the other"; born in Stockbridge, Mass.

Samuel Houston (1793–1863): Commander of army of American settlers in Texas War of Independence, 1836; defeated Mexicans in Battle of San Jacinto, April 21, 1836; president of Texas Republic, 1836–38, 1841–44; U.S. senator (D-Texas), 1846–59; as Texas governor, 1859–61, deposed for opposition to secession; U.S. representative (D-Tenn.), 1823–27; Tennessee governor, 1827–29; born near Lexington, Va.

Charles Evans Hughes (1862–1948): 12th Chief Justice of U.S., 1930–41; fought President F.D. Roosevelt's effort at "court packing" to end court's reversals of New Deal legislation; associate justice of U.S. Supreme Court, 1910–16, resigning to run, unsuccessfully, as Republican candidate for President, 1916; secretary of state under Presidents Harding and Coolidge, 1921–25; born in Glens Falls, N.Y.

Cordell Hull (1871–1955): U.S. secretary of state, 1933–44; initiated "good neighbor" policy with Latin America, 1933; was negotiating with Japanese envoys in Washington when Pearl Harbor was bombed, 1941; developed plans for United Nations, 1944; awarded Nobel Peace Prize, 1945; U.S. representative (D-Tenn.), 1907–21, 1923–31; U.S. senator (D-Tenn.), 1931–33; born in Overton County, Tenn.

Hubert Horatio Humphrey (1911–78): 38th Vice President of U.S., under President L.B. Johnson, 1965–69; unsuccessful Democratic candidate for President, 1968; U.S. senator (D-Minn.), 1949–65, 1971–78; mayor of Minneapolis, Minn., 1945–49; born in Wallace, S.D.

Thomas Jonathan ("Stonewall") Jackson (1824–63): Confederate general; twice defeated Union Army at Bull Run, 1861, 1862; led Shenandoah Valley campaign, 1862; forced Union retreat at Chancellorsville, 1863; accidentally killed by own troops; graduated from West Point, 1846; born in Clarksburg, W.Va. (then in Va.).

Jesse Woodson James (1847–82): Western outlaw; led gang that included his brother Frank, Cole Younger, and others in bank and train robberies; killed by gang member Robert Ford for $5,000 reward; born in Clay County, Mo.

John Jay (1745–1829): lst Chief Justice of U.S., 1790–95; New York delegate to Continental Congress, 1774–79; president of Congress, 1778–79; helped negotiate and signed treaty of peace with Britain, 1783; U.S. secretary of foreign affairs, 1784–89; authored five essays in *The Federalist*, urging ratification of U.S. Constitution, 1787–88; negotiated Jay's Treaty settling outstanding disputes with Britain, 1794; governor of New York, 1795–1801; born in New York City.

John Paul Jones (1747–92): U.S. naval hero in Revolutionary War; commanded *Bonhomme Richard*, forcing surrender of more heavily armed British frigate *Serapis*, 1779; during battle, reputed to have replied to British demand for surrender: "I have not yet begun to fight!"; only Continental Navy officer to receive gold medal from Congress, 1787; rear admiral in Russian Navy, 1788–89, in war with Turks; born in Kirkcudbrightshire, Scotland.

Edward Moore ("Ted") Kennedy (born 1932): Brother of President Kennedy; U.S. senator (D-Mass.), 1962– ; unsuccessfully opposed President Carter for Democratic presidential nomination in 1980; withdrew as candidate for Democratic presidential nomination in 1972 after receiving suspended sentence for leaving scene of fatal automobile accident on Chappaquiddick Island, Mass., 1969; born in Boston, Mass.

Robert Francis Kennedy (1925–68): Brother of President Kennedy; U.S. attorney general, 1961–64; U.S. senator (D-N.Y.), 1965–68; assassinated in Los Angeles while campaigning for Democratic presidential nomination, 1968; born in Brookline, Mass.

Ernest Joseph King (1878–1956): Admiral in command of U.S. fleet during World War II, 1941–45, and chief of naval operations, 1942–45; born in Lorain, Ohio.

Martin Luther King Jr. (1929–68): Black civil-rights leader; awarded Nobel Peace Prize, 1964; ordained as Baptist minister, 1947; began nonviolent crusade for black rights with boycott of buses in Montgomery, Ala., to end racial discrimination in seating on buses, 1955; founder of Southern Christian Leadership Conference (SCLC), 1957; at demonstration of more than 200,000 persons in Washington, D.C., 1963, made address *I Have a Dream*; assassinated by white escaped convict James Earl Ray in Memphis, Tenn., on April 4, 1968; assassination caused riots in 125 cities; born in Atlanta.

Rufus King (1755–1827): Unsuccessful Federalist candidate for President, 1816; Massachusetts delegate to Congress, 1784–87; signer of U.S. Constitution, 1787; U.S. senator (Fed.-N.Y.), 1789–96, 1813–25; U.S. minister to Britain, 1796–1803, 1825–26; born in Scarboro, Me. (then part of Massachusetts).

Henry Alfred Kissinger (born 1923): U.S. secretary of state under Presidents Nixon and Ford, 1973–77, promoting policy of détente that relaxed tensions of Cold War with Soviet Union; helped restore diplomatic relations with China, 1971–72; co-winner of Nobel Peace Prize in 1973 for negotiating cease-fire that ended American participation in Vietnam War; became naturalized U.S. citizen, 1943; on faculty of Harvard University 1951–69; born in Fuerth, Germany.

Robert Marion La Follette (1855–1925): Leader of Progressive movement; U.S. senator (Prog.-Wis.), 1906–25; U.S. representative (R-Wis.), 1885–91; governor of Wisconsin, 1901–05; opposed U.S. entry into World War I, 1917; opposed U.S. participation in League of Nations or World Court, 1918–19; unsuccessful Progressive candidate for President, 1924; born in Primrose, Wis.

Alfred Mossman Landon (born 1887): Unsuccessful Republican candidate for President, 1936; as wildcat oil prospector, became millionaire by age of 40; as governor of Kansas, 1933–37, managed state finances to maintain balanced budget while other states were going deeply into debt; born in West Middlesex, Pa.

Richard Henry Lee (1732–94): Virginia delegate to Continental Congress, 1774–79; introduced resolution for Declaration of Independence on June 7, 1776; as delegate to Congress, 1784–87, opposed U.S. Constitution, promoted adoption of Bill of Rights; U.S. senator (D-R–Va.), 1789–92; born in Westmoreland County, Va.

Robert Edward Lee (1807–70): In Civil War, commanded Confederate Army of Northern Virginia, 1862–65, after declining President Lincoln's offer to command Union Army; his master strategies gave smaller Confederate forces such victories as Seven Days Battle, Second Battle of Bull Run, Fredericksburg, and Chancellorsville; defeated at Gettysburg, 1863; appointed general in chief of Confederate armies, 1865; surrendered at Appomattox Court House, 1865; president of Washington College (now Washington and Lee University), 1865–70; born in Westmoreland County, Va.

John Llewellyn Lewis (1880–1969): Labor leader; president of United Mine Workers (UMW), 1920–60; organized Committee for Industrial Organizations (CIO), 1935; after CIO unions were expelled from AFL in 1938, Lewis served as CIO president until 1942; withdrew UMW from CIO in 1942 in policy dispute; born in Lucas, Iowa.

Meriwether Lewis (1774–1809): Leader with William Clark of expedition exploring Louisiana Purchase, 1804–06; governor of Louisiana Territory, 1807–09; born in Albemarle County, Va.

Charles Augustus Lindbergh (1902–74): American hero of 1920s for his courage in making first solo flight across Atlantic Ocean, on May 20–21, 1927; called "the Lone Eagle"; became semirecluse after sensational kidnap-murder of his baby son, 1932; opposed President F.D. Roosevelt's moves toward U.S. entry in World War II, but flew 50 combat missions against Japanese as civilian; born in Detroit.

Robert R. Livingston (1746–1813): New York delegate to Continental Congress, 1775–77, 1779–81; first U.S. secretary of foreign affairs, 1781–83; as chancellor (chief judge) of New York, 1777–1801, administered presidential oath to George Washington, 1789; U.S. minister to France, 1801–04, negotiating Louisiana Purchase from France; financed Robert Fulton's steamboat, 1803–07; born in New York City.

Henry Cabot Lodge (1850–1924): U.S. senator (R-Mass.), 1893–1924; pressed for U.S. entry in World War I in 1915; organized Senate opposition to Versailles Treaty and League of Nations, 1919–20; born in Boston.

Henry Cabot Lodge Jr. (born 1902): Unsuccessful Republican candidate for Vice President in 1960 as running mate of Richard M. Nixon; U.S. ambassador to UN, 1953–60; ambassador to South Vietnam, West Germany, and Vatican, 1963–77; U.S. senator (R-Mass.), 1937–44, 1947–53; born in Nahant, Mass.

Elijah Parish Lovejoy (1802–37): Abolitionist martyr; while editor of antislavery Alton (Ill.) *Observer*, was attacked and killed by proslavery mob, 1837; born in Albion, Me.

Mary Lyon (1797–1849): Founded first women's college, Mount Holyoke Seminary (later College) in South Hadley, Mass., and served as its president, 1837–49; born in Buckland, Mass.

Douglas MacArthur (1880–1964): Commanding general of U.S. Far East forces during World War II, 1941–45; commanded occupation forces in Japan, 1945–51; supreme commander of UN forces in Korean War, 1950–51, until relieved by President Truman because of outspoken desire to invade communist China; commanded 42d Division in World War I, 1917–18; U.S. Army chief of staff, 1930–35; born in Little Rock, Ark.

Horace Mann (1796–1859): Led establishment of free public schools in U.S.; as secretary of new Massachusetts state board of education, 1837–48, set standards adopted by other states as well; founded first teacher-training school, in Lexington, Mass., 1839; U.S. representative (Whig-Mass.), 1848–53; president of Antioch College, 1853–59; born in Franklin, Mass.

George Catlett Marshall (1880–1959): Commander of all U.S. armies in World War II as chief of staff, 1939–45; as U.S. secretary of state, 1947–49, initiated Marshall Plan to rebuild Europe; awarded Nobel Peace Prize, 1953; unsuc-

QUICK QUIZ: If it is noon in New York, what time is it in Paris? See page 108.

FAMOUS PERSONS IN AMERICAN HISTORY *(continued)*
cessfully attempted to mediate civil war in China, 1946; secretary of defense under President Truman during first years of Korean War, 1950–51; born in Uniontown, Pa.

John Marshall (1755–1835): 4th Chief Justice of U.S., 1801–35; established power of Supreme Court to declare laws unconstitutional in case of *Marbury* v. *Madison*, 1803; broadened scope of federal government with doctrine of implied powers, including all those necessary to carry out specific powers mentioned in U.S. Constitution; U.S. representative (Fed.-Va.), 1799–1800; U.S. secretary of state, 1800–01; born in Germantown (now Midland), Va.

Thurgood Marshall (born 1908): First black appointed as associate justice of U.S. Supreme Court, 1967; as head of legal services of National Association for the Advancement of Colored People (NAACP), 1940–61, won major Supreme Court decisions desegregating public schools, transportation, and housing; judge of U.S. Court of Appeals, 1961–65; U.S. solicitor general, 1965–67; born in Baltimore.

Matthew Fontaine Maury (1806–76): Pioneer oceanographer; headed U.S. Navy's Depot of Charts and Instruments (later Naval Observatory and Hydrographic Office), 1842–61; developed uniform system of recording oceanographic data; joined Confederate Navy during Civil War, commanding coast and harbor defenses; professor of meteorology at Virginia Military Institute, 1868–73; born near Fredericksburg, Va.

Joseph Raymond McCarthy (1908–57): U.S. senator (R-Wis.), 1947–57; charges that communists had infiltrated U.S. government and Army bred public hysteria; tactic of making unsupported charges came to be called *McCarthyism*; U.S. Senate censured McCarthy in 1954, ending his influence; born in Grand Chute, Wis.

George Brinton McClellan (1826–85): In Civil War, commanded Union Army of Potomac, 1861–62; reorganized Union forces after Bull Run defeat, 1861; failed to capture Richmond after forcing General Lee to retreat at Antietam, Md., causing Lincoln to relieve him of command, 1862; unsuccessful Democratic candidate for President, 1864; governor of New Jersey, 1878–81; graduated second in class from West Point, 1846; born in Philadelphia.

John Cardinal McCloskey (1810–85): First American cardinal of Roman Catholic Church, 1875–85; as archbishop of New York, 1864–85, responsible for building St. Patrick's Cathedral, opened 1879; born in Brooklyn, N.Y.

George Stanley McGovern (born 1922): Unsuccessful Democratic candidate for President, 1972; during campaign called Nixon administration "most corrupt in history," but majority of voters regarded this as political oratory until full extent of Watergate scandals was revealed in 1973–74; U.S. representative (D-S.D.), 1957–61; Democratic U.S. senator from South Dakota, 1963–81; born in Avon, S.D.

George Gordon Meade (1815–72): In Civil War, commanded Union Army of the Potomac, 1863–65; defeated Confederate General Lee at Battle of Gettysburg, 1863, in turning point of war; graduated from West Point, 1835; born in Cádiz, Spain.

William ("Billy") Mitchell (1879–1936): U.S. Army general who demonstrated obsolescence of battleship by sinking several with aerial bombs in experiments in 1921–23; defying superior officers, he urged developing air force independent of U.S. Army and U.S. Navy; court-martialed and convicted of insubordination, 1925; born in Nice, France.

Walter Frederick Mondale (born 1928): 42d Vice President of U.S., 1977–81, elected as Democratic running mate of Jimmy Carter; U.S. senator (D-Minn.), 1964–77; attorney general of Minnesota, 1960–64; born in Ceylon, Minn.

John Pierpont Morgan (1837–1913): Multimillionaire banker who managed financing of many large U.S. corporations; powerful banking firm, J.P. Morgan & Company, halted gold drain on U.S. treasury by selling $62 million in bonds, 1895; organized U.S. Steel Corporation as world's largest corporation at time, 1901; helped end Panic of 1907 by loaning money to banks short of cash; born in Hartford, Conn.

Robert Morris (1734–1806): "Financier of the American Revolution"; pledged personal credit to supply Washington's army for Battles of Trenton and Princeton, 1776; appointed by Congress superintendent of finance, 1781–84; as Pennsylvania delegate to Continental Congress, 1776–78, signed Declaration of Independence and Articles of Confederation; as delegate to Constitutional Convention, signed U.S. Constitution, 1787; served Pennsylvania as U.S. senator, 1789–95; lost fortune and jailed for debt, 1798–1801; born in Liverpool, England.

Lucretia Coffin Mott (1793–1880): Abolitionist and women's rights leader; with Elizabeth Cady Stanton, organized first women's rights convention, at Seneca Falls, N.Y., 1848; aided escape of slaves through "underground railroad"; born on Nantucket, Mass.

Carry Amelia Moore Nation (1846–1911): Prohibitionist; conducted violent attacks on saloons in Kansas, using hatchet to smash liquor bottles and chop up furnishings in 1890s and early 1900s; born in Garrard County, Ky.

Chester William Nimitz (1885–1966): Admiral in command of U.S. Pacific Fleet in World War II, 1941–45; directed island-hopping campaign that led to Japan's surrender aboard his flagship, battleship USS *Missouri*, on Sept. 2, 1945; promoted to rank of 5-star fleet admiral, 1944; chief of naval operations, 1945–47; born in Fredericksburg, Texas.

Sandra Day O'Connor (born 1930); First woman appointed U.S. Supreme Court associate justice by President Reagan, 1981; Republican Arizona state senator, 1969–75, becoming first woman majority leader of any state senate, 1972–74; Arizona state court judge, 1975–81; graduated from Stanford University law school, 1952; married John Jay O'Connor 3d, 1952, having three children; born in El Paso, Texas.

James Otis (1725–83): Boston lawyer who paved way for American Revolution; his denunciation in 1761 of British writs of assistance (kind of search warrant) as illegal inspired patriots to stand up for rights; headed Massachusetts delegation to Stamp Act Congress, 1765; worked with Samuel Adams in protesting Townshend Acts and quartering of troops in Boston; born in West Barnstable, Mass.

Thomas Paine (1737–1809): Influenced adoption of Declaration of Independence by pamphlet *Common Sense,* January 1776; supported cause of freedom with series of essays, called *Crisis*, beginning in December 1776; after war, went to Europe where he wrote *The Rights of Man*, 1791–92, and *The Age of Reason*, 1794–96; returned to U.S., 1802; born in Thetford, England.

Nathaniel Brown Palmer (1799–1877): First explorer to sight Antarctica, on Nov. 18, 1820, while in command of 45-ton sloop *Hero*; first went to sea at age 14; commanded clipper ships trading with China, until retiring in 1850; born in Stonington, Conn.

George Smith Patton Jr. (1885–1945): In World War II, commanded U.S. Third Army in Europe, spearheading liberation of France, Germany, Czechoslovakia, and Austria, 1944–45; won nickname "Old Blood and Guts"; born in San Gabriel, Calif.

Robert Edwin Peary (1856–1920): First explorer to reach North Pole, April 6, 1909; promoted to rear admiral U.S. Navy, 1911, and retired; born in Cresson, Pa.

William Penn (1644–1718): Founded Pennsylvania as Quaker colony with religious freedom for other faiths, 1681; made treaty with Indians, paying for land granted to him by King Charles II, 1682; returned to England, 1684; visited Pennsylvania and wrote new constitution giving elective assembly complete lawmaking power, 1699–1701; born in London.

Frances Perkins (1882–1965): First woman member of presidential cabinet; U.S. secretary of labor under Presidents F.D. Roosevelt and Truman, 1933–45; U.S. civil service commissioner, 1946–53; born in Boston.

Matthew Calbraith Perry (1794–1858): U.S. naval officer who forced Japan to open two of its ports to U.S. trade, 1854; younger brother of Oliver Hazard Perry; born in Newport, R.I.

Oliver Hazard Perry (1785–1819): In War of 1812, commanded U.S. fleet on Lake Erie; after defeating British in Battle of Lake Erie, 1813, sent famous message: "We have met the enemy and they are ours"; born in South Kingston, R.I.

John Joseph ("Black Jack") Pershing (1860–1948): In World War I, commanding general of U.S. troops in Europe, 1917–19; U.S. Army chief of staff, 1921–24; awarded Pulitzer Prize for history in 1932 for book *My Experiences in the World War;* born near Laclede, Mo.

Charles Cotesworth Pinckney (1746–1825): Twice loser as Federalist candidate for President, 1804, 1808; also lost as President John Adams' running mate for Vice President, 1800; South Carolina delegate to Constitutional Convention and signer of U.S. Constitution, 1787; as special envoy to France, 1796, became famous for his reply to French official who asked for bribe: "It is no, no! Not a sixpence!"; major general in new U.S. Army, formed in 1798, third in command after Washington and Hamilton; born in Charleston, S.C.

Pontiac (c. 1720–69): Ottawa Indian chief who led attacks called "Pontiac's Conspiracy" on British colonial settlements west of Appalachian Mountains, 1763–66, killing hundreds of frontier families; signed peace treaty, 1766, receiving pardon by British.

Edmund Randolph (1753–1813): First U.S. attorney general under President Washington, 1789–94; U.S. secretary of state, 1794–95, resigning after being falsely charged with accepting bribe from France; as counsel, won acquittal for Aaron Burr in treason trial, 1807; as governor of Virginia, 1786–88, attended Constitutional Convention but refused to sign U.S. Constitution; born in Williamsburg, Va.

Sam Rayburn (1882–1961): Speaker of U.S. House of Representatives, 1940–47, 1949–53, 1955–61; as Texas Democrat, won election to Congress 25 consecutive times, serving 1913–61, under eight Presidents from Wilson to Kennedy; played major role in carrying out legislative programs of Presidents F.D. Roosevelt and Truman; born in Roane County, Tenn.

Paul Revere (1735–1818): Patriot and craftsman; on night of April 18–19, 1775, rode from Boston to Lexington, Mass., warning that the British were coming to arrest Samuel Adams and John Hancock for treason and to destroy patriot supplies; during Revolutionary War, made gunpowder, cannon, engraved and printed Continental currency, and served as lieutenant colonel of militia; designed many beautiful objects as silversmith; founded Revere Copper Co., at Canton, Mass., smelting copper and rolling it in sheets; born in Boston.

John Davison Rockefeller (1839–1937): Billionaire industrialist; made fortune in oil, founding Standard Oil Co., 1870; monopoly on oil broken by U.S. Supreme Court order, 1911; endowed University of Chicago, 1892, Rockefeller Institute of Medical Research, 1901, Rockefeller Foundation, 1913; born in Richford, N.Y.

Nelson Aldrich Rockefeller (1908–79): Appointed 41st Vice President of U.S. by President Ford, serving 1974–77; governor of New York four times, 1959–73; held variety of positions in federal government, 1940–45, 1953–55; unsuccessfully sought Republican presidential nomination in 1964 and 1968; grandson of John D. Rockefeller; born in Bar Harbor, Me.

Carl Schurz (1829–1906): German-American editor, statesman, general; immigrated to U.S., 1852; as leader in Wisconsin Republican Party, backed Lincoln's presidential nomination, 1860; U.S. minister to Spain, 1861–62; general in Union Army, 1862–63; editor, Detroit *Post*, 1866–67; editor-founder, St. Louis *Westliche Post*, 1867–69; U.S. senator (R-Mo.), 1869–75; as U.S. secretary of the interior, 1877–81, reformed treatment of Indians and established civil-service merit system in Interior Department; editor, New York *Evening Post*, 1881–83; chief editorial writer, *Harper's Weekly*, 1892–98; born in Liblar, Prussia.

Margaretha Meyer Schurz (1834–76): Founded first kindergarten in U.S., in Watertown, Wis., 1856; immigrated to U.S. with husband, Carl Schurz, 1852; born in Prussia.

Winfield Scott (1786–1866): General and unsuccessful Whig candidate for President in 1852; became national hero for courage displayed as fighting general in War of 1812 Battles of Chippewa and Lundy's Lane, 1814; as commanding

QUICK QUIZ: How many books were published in the U.S. in 1982? See page 88.

FAMOUS PERSONS IN AMERICAN HISTORY *(continued)*

general of U.S. Army, 1841–61, became known to troops as "Old Fuss and Feathers" because of his plumed hat; in Mexican War, commanded amphibious invasion at Veracruz, captured Mexico City, 1847; commanded Union Army at beginning of Civil War, but retired at age 75 on Nov. 1, 1861; born near Petersburg, Va.

William Henry Seward (1801–72): U.S. secretary of state under Presidents Lincoln and Andrew Johnson, 1861–69; arranged purchase of Alaska from Russia for $7.2 million, known at time as "Seward's Folly"; forced France to withdraw troops from Mexico after Civil War; first Whig governor of New York, 1839–42; as U.S. senator (Whig-N.Y.), 1849–55, (R-N.Y.), 1855–61, opposed slavery, Compromise of 1850, and Kansas-Nebraska Act; wounded by accomplice of John Wilkes Booth on night of Lincoln's assassination, 1865; born in Florida, N.Y.

Philip Henry Sheridan (1831–1888): General in Union Army in Civil War; gained fame leading successful charge on Missionary Ridge in Battle of Chattanooga, 1863; as commander of cavalry of Army of Potomac under U.S. Grant, 1864, drove Confederate troops of Gen. Jubal Early out of Virginia's Shenandoah Valley; commanding general of U.S. Army, 1884–88; believed born in Somerset, Ohio.

William Tecumseh Sherman (1820–91): Commander of Union armies of West in Civil War: captured Atlanta, Sept. 1, 1864; led "March to the Sea" across Georgia with army of over 60,000, pillaging plantations and towns, capturing Savannah, Dec. 21, 1864; marching north, accepted surrender of Confederate Gen. J.E. Johnston at Durham, N.C., April 26, 1865; famed for statement "War is hell"; commanding general of U.S. Army, 1869–1884; when asked to run for President, he said, "I will not accept if nominated and will not serve if elected"; born in Lancaster, Ohio.

Sitting Bull (c.1834–90): Sioux Indian chief; battled U.S. Army and white settlers in 1860s and 1870s in Montana and Dakotas; led followers to Canada, 1877, but returned and surrendered, 1881; on Standing Rock Reservation in South Dakota, began Ghost Dance unrest among Sioux, 1890; police and soldiers sent to arrest him killed him and a son; born in South Dakota.

Samuel Slater (1768–1835): Brought Industrial Revolution to U.S.; to monopolize textile industry, Britain had forbidden export of machines or emigration of persons familiar with them; having memorized details of machinery, Slater in disguise left Britain for U.S., 1789; with Moses Brown, built first successful cotton-spinning mill in U.S., in Pawtucket, R.I., 1790; opened own textile mills in New England; born in Belper, England.

Alfred Emanuel Smith (1873–1944): Unsuccessful Democratic presidential candidate, 1928; as first Roman Catholic to run for President, was opposed by Ku Klux Klan; also controversial because he favored repeal of prohibition; elected four times as governor of New York, serving in 1919–20; 1923–28; born in New York City.

Jedediah Strong Smith (c.1799–1831): Fur trader and explorer; in 1820s, mapped routes from Rockies to California and along Pacific coast; born in Bainbridge, N.Y.

John Smith (1580–1631): Helped found Jamestown, Va., first permanent English colony in America, 1607; captured by Indians but saved from execution by Pocahontas, daughter of chief; elected president of Virginia, 1608–09; explored and named New England, 1614; born in Willoughby, England.

Edwin McMasters Stanton (1814–69): U.S. secretary of war during and after Civil War, 1862–68; fired by President Andrew Johnson for harsh treatment of militarily occupied South, leading Stanton's Radical Republican supporters in Congress to bring about Johnson's impeachment and trial; U.S. attorney general, 1860–61; born in Steubenville, Ohio.

Elizabeth Cady Stanton (1815–1902): Leader in women's rights, abolition, and temperance movements; graduated from Troy (N.Y.) Female Seminary, 1832; married Henry B. Stanton, 1840; with Lucretia C. Mott, sponsored first U.S. women's rights convention, at Seneca Falls, N.Y., 1848; with Susan B. Anthony, organized National Woman Suffrage Association, 1869; was its first president, 1869–90; born in Johnstown, N.Y.

Alexander Hamilton Stephens (1812–83): Vice President of Confederate States of America during Civil War; represented Confederacy in peace conference with President Lincoln at Hampton Roads, Va., February 1865; U.S. representative (Whig-Ga.) 1843–52, (D-Ga.) 1852–59, 1873–82; imprisoned after Civil War; elected by Georgia to U.S. Senate, 1866, but not allowed to serve; governor of Georgia, 1882–83; born near Crawfordsville, Ga.

Thaddeus Stevens (1792–1868): Led Radical Republicans in Congress demanding harsh treatment of South after Civil War; managed impeachment of President Andrew Johnson, 1868; U.S. representative (Whig-Pa.), 1849–53, (R-Pa.), 1859–68; born in Danville, Vt.

Adlai Ewing Stevenson (1835–1914): 23d Vice President, 1893–97, under President Cleveland; U.S. representative (D-Ill.), 1875–77, 1879–81; unsuccessful Democratic candidate for Vice President, 1900, and for governor of Illinois, 1908; born in Christian County, Ky.

Adlai Ewing Stevenson (1900–65): Unsuccessful Democratic candidate for President, 1952, 1956; governor of Illinois, 1949–53; U.S. ambassador to UN, 1961–65; grandson of Vice President Adlai E. Stevenson; born in Los Angeles.

Harlan Fiske Stone (1872–1946): 11th Chief Justice of U.S., 1941–46; associate justice of Supreme Court, 1925–41; as U.S. attorney general, 1924–25, cleaned up Justice Department from effects of Teapot Dome scandals; supported New Deal legislation while on Supreme Court; born in Chesterfield, N.H.

James Ewell Brown ("Jeb") Stuart (1833–64): Confederate cavalry general in Civil War; called "eyes of the army" by General Lee; daringly circled entire Union Army to gather information; killed in battle for Richmond at Yellow Tavern, Va.; graduated from West Point, 1854; born in Patrick County, Va.

Peter Stuyvesant (c.1610–72): Last Dutch governor of New Netherland (now New York), 1647–64; captured New Sweden (now Delaware, New Jersey, and part of Pennsylvania), 1655; ruled as dictator, forbidding sale of liquor to

Indians, tolerating no religions other than Dutch Reformed; surrendered colony to British, Sept. 6, 1664; lost leg in military expedition against Caribbean island of St. Martin, 1644; born in Scherpenzeel, Netherlands.

Roger Brooke Taney (1777–1864): 5th Chief Justice of U.S., 1836–64; ruling in Dred Scott case, 1857, that Congress could not outlaw slavery in U.S. territories invalidated Missouri Compromise and Compromise of 1850, helping to bring on Civil War; served under President Jackson as attorney general, 1831–33, and as secretary of the treasury, 1833–34; because he opposed Second Bank of the U.S., Senate refused to confirm him as secretary of the treasury, 1834, and as associate justice of Supreme Court, 1835; born in Calvert County, Md.

Samuel Jones Tilden (1814–86): Democratic candidate for President, 1876; won majority of popular vote but Republican-controlled election commission awarded presidency to Rutherford B. Hayes; led reform group ousting corrupt Tweed ring from control of New York City government, 1872; governor of New York, 1875–76; founded New York Public Library with bequest; born in New Lebanon, N.Y.

Harriet Tubman (c.1820–1913): Black abolitionist; escaped slavery in Maryland, 1849; during 1850s helped hundreds of slaves escape to North on "underground railroad"; born in Dorchester County, Md.

Nat Turner (1800–31): Led slave uprising in Virginia in August 1831, killing about 60 whites; Turner and about 100 other blacks captured and killed; uprising led to severe slave restrictions in South; born in Southampton County, Va.

Cornelius Vanderbilt (1794–1877): Multimillionaire steamship and railroad magnate; quit school at 11; began operating sailboat ferry between Staten Island and New York City at 16; in 1850s began operating steamship service to Europe and San Francisco; formed New York Central Railroad, becoming its first president, 1867; donated $1 million to Central University in Nashville, Tenn., which changed its name to Vanderbilt University; fortune estimated at $100 million; born on Staten Island, N.Y.

Lillian D. Wald (1867–1940): Social worker; established city-wide visiting-nurse service in connection with New York City's Henry Street Settlement, which she founded and headed, 1895–1933; started first public-school nurse program, 1902; militantly campaigned against sweatshops and child labor; born in Cincinnati.

Earl Warren (1891–1974): 14th Chief Justice of U.S., 1953–69; liberal rulings included outlawing racial segregation in public schools (1954), liberalizing definition of obscenity (1957), banning required prayers or religious services in public schools (1962), establishing "one man, one vote" rule (1962), increasing freedom of press by limiting news media's liability for libel (1964), and improving legal protection of persons accused of crimes (1966); headed Warren Commission investigating assassination of President Kennedy, 1963–64; Republican governor of California, 1943–53; unsuccessful Republican candidate for Vice President, 1948; unsuccessful candidate for Republican presidential nomination, 1952; born in Los Angeles.

Booker Taliaferro Washington (1856–1915): Black educator and reformer; born a slave at Hales Ford, Va.; attended Hampton Institute, 1872–75; taught there, 1878–81; first president of Tuskegee Institute, Ala., 1881–1915; opposed political action for black civil rights; counseled blacks to work hard and acquire education; wrote *Up From Slavery*, 1901.

Daniel Webster (1782–1852): U.S. secretary of state, 1841–43, 1850–52; negotiated Webster-Ashburton Treaty settling Maine boundary dispute with Britain, 1842; unsuccessful Whig candidate for President, 1836; opposed War of 1812 and supported protective tariffs as Federalist U.S. representative from New Hampshire, 1813–17, and as U.S. representative from Massachusetts, 1823–27; as U.S. senator (Whig-Mass.), 1827–41, 1845–50, opposed Mexican War and supported Compromise of 1850; born in Salisbury (now Franklin), N.H.

Charles Wilkes (1798–1877): Discovered and named Antarctic continent on Jan. 30, 1840, while leading exploration mission for U.S. Navy; as rear admiral during Civil War, instigated Trent affair when he removed two Confederate commissioners from British ship, causing protest; born in New York City.

Emma Hart Willard (1787–1870): Established first college-level school for women in U.S.—Troy (N.Y.) Female Seminary, 1821; wrote poem "Rocked in the Cradle of the Deep," 1830; born in Berlin, Conn.

Frances Elizabeth Caroline Willard (1839–98): Educator and temperance reformer; president, Evanston (Ill.) College for Ladies, 1871–73; dean of women, Northwestern University, 1873–74; president, Woman's Christian Temperance Union (WCTU), 1879–98; founder and president of first international women's organization, World Woman's Christian Temperance Union, 1883; born in Churchville, N.Y.

Roger Williams (c.1603–83): Founder of Rhode Island; banished by Puritans from Massachusetts for belief in religious freedom and separation of church and state, 1635; founded first settlement at Providence, R.I., 1636; obtained charter for colony of Rhode Island, 1644; president of Rhode Island, 1654–57; born in London.

Wendell Lewis Willkie (1892–1944): Unsuccessful Republican candidate for President, 1940; president of electric utility company, 1933–40; wrote *One World*, 1943, promoting global unity; born in Elwood, Ind.

John Winthrop (1588–1649): Led Puritans to found Massachusetts Bay Colony and Boston, 1630; served as governor all but four years during 1630s and 1640s, sternly prohibiting practice of religions other than Congregationalist faith he established; born in Edwardstone, England.

John Witherspoon (1723–94): Only clergyman to sign Declaration of Independence; New Jersey delegate to Continental Congress, 1776–82; president, College of New Jersey (now Princeton University), 1768–94; Presbyterian pastor of Paisley, Scotland, 1757–68; born in Yester, Scotland.

QUICK QUIZ: Who is the director of the National Symphony Orchestra? See page 57.

PROFILES OF OUR PRESIDENTS AND FIRST LADIES

The President and Vice President of the United States are the only officials elected by the American people as a whole.

The nation has had 40 Presidents, but only 39 men have been Chief Executive. One of them, Grover Cleveland, served nonconsecutive terms and thus was both the 22d and 24th President. Ronald Reagan became the 40th President upon taking office in 1981.

The U.S. presidency is a unique institution. Few other democratic nations have a single leader perform both the symbolic role of chief of state and at the same time the job of administering the government.

The President is simultaneously chief of state, chief executive, chief legislator, party leader, chief diplomat, and commander in chief of the armed forces. The action of the President in any one role materially affects the others, because the President is the mainspring of the governmental system.

The manner in which the President exercises his several functions generally determines his place in history.

The President may supply creative leadership and seek positively to change the shape of public opinion. Or he may assume the role of a charismatic leader by inspiring the people to greater heights of action. But the President must assume the ultimate responsibility for the nation's successes and failures during his administration.

The highlights of the Presidents' lives, including information on the women who served as First Lady, appear below and on the following pages.

GEORGE WASHINGTON

1st President
(1789–97)

As commander of the Continental forces during the Revolutionary War and as the first President of the United States, George Washington became "father of his country."

In the eight years of his presidency the nation's basic institutions were established. Washington's personal qualities were remarkable.

Thomas Jefferson wrote that "his integrity was the most pure, his justice the most flexible, I have ever known. He was, indeed, in every sense of the word, a wise, a good and a great man."

EARLY LIFE

Washington was the son of Augustine Washington, a moderately wealthy planter, and his second wife, Mary Ball. He was born on the family's Virginia estate (now known as Wakefield) on Feb. 22, 1732. His father died in 1743. George's half-brother Lawrence then became head of the family. George displayed an early talent for mathematics, and at the age of 15 began earning small fees by surveying. In 1748 he assisted George Fairfax in making an extensive survey of Thomas Lord Fairfax's lands in the wilderness country west of Virginia's Blue Ridge Mountains.

In 1751–52 he accompanied Lawrence, who was suffering from tuberculosis, to Barbados. There George survived a case of smallpox, becoming immune to the disease that was to plague his troops during the Revolutionary War. Lawrence died soon after returning to his Mount Vernon home. George inherited part of his estate. At 20 he obtained a commission as major in the militia.

Washington first gained public notice in 1753 when he was entrusted with a dangerous mission before the French and Indian War. He volunteered to deliver a message from Virginia Gov. Robert Dinwiddie to the French in Ohio country, warning them to leave the British-claimed territory. His two-and-a-half-month journey took him across hundreds of miles of unmapped wilderness to the shore of Lake Erie. When he returned he was commissioned lieutenant colonel.

Washington was then sent back to the frontier in command of a militia unit. In May 1754 he fought the first skirmish of the French and Indian War. He built Fort Necessity near present-day Uniontown, Pa., but was forced to surrender it to the French on July 4, 1754.

A year later, as aide-de-camp to British Gen. Edward Braddock in the disastrous expedition against Fort Duquesne, Washington established his reputation as a military leader by rallying the survivors for an orderly retreat. In 1758, commanding colonial forces supporting British regulars, he distinguished himself anew in the final capture of the French fort.

Washington, not yet 27, retired to private life when peace returned. A tall, well-built man, he was amiable, just, and immensely vital. In 1759 he married Mrs. Martha Custis, a wealthy widow with two children. He then settled down to the life of a Virginia gentleman on his plantation, Mount Vernon.

Washington was a member of the Virginia House of Burgesses (1759–74), where he became a leader in opposing British colonial policy. He served in 1774–75 as a delegate to the Continental Congress.

COMMANDER OF THE CONTINENTAL ARMY

After the Revolution began, Washington became commander of the Continental Army, largely through the efforts of John Adams. Washington took command on July 3, 1775. His troops, unorganized and poorly disciplined, were mostly militia. Short terms of enlistment during the first years of the war kept his armies in a continuous state of disbandment and retraining.

Congress failed to provide essential equipment, supplies, and soldiers' pay. Washington was also beset with the jealousies and intrigues of insubordinate officers.

Washington's strategy was successful in forcing the British evacuation of Boston in March 1776. He was then compelled by Congress to defend New York City. Due to the poor condition of his men and the tactical error of deploying part of his forces to Brooklyn, Washington met defeat.

But he rescued his army in a withdrawal that eventually carried them to southeastern Pennsylvania.

From there, on Christmas night 1776, he and his men crossed the Delaware, a masterful move that led to the rout of the British at Trenton and Princeton.

Washington's efforts to defend Philadelphia ended in defeat at Brandywine in September 1777 and at Germantown in October.

Washington and his 9,000 men wintered at Valley Forge, Pa., 1777–78. Seldom have a general and his army endured such extended deprivation and misery.

Washington's essential greatness matched every problem and intrigue, however, and in the spring he emerged with increased powers from Congress and a well-trained force (despite 3,000 desertions).

When the British evacuated Philadelphia to return to New York, Washington attacked the British column in the Battle of Monmouth on June 28, 1778. But the battle was lost by the cowardice of one of his officers, Maj. Gen. Charles Lee.

Three years later Charles Lord Cornwallis and his English army were trapped at Yorktown, Va., by Washington with the support of French land and sea forces. Cornwallis surrendered on Oct. 19, 1781, virtually ending the Revolutionary War.

In 1783 Washington retired from the Army and returned to Mount Vernon.

He and other patriots, becoming dissatisfied with the weakness of the government under the Articles of Confederation, joined to reorganize it. In 1787 he presided over the Constitutional Convention, which wrote the Constitution of the United States.

FIRST PRESIDENT OF THE UNITED STATES

After the new government was organized, Washington was unanimously chosen as the first President. He took office on April 30, 1789, in New York City.

Washington's own views were Federalist. But in staffing his administration he was above partisanship. It was mainly his capacity for conciliation that kept the American Revolution free of terrorism, purges, and arbitrary seizures of power that have marked other revolutions.

He brought both Alexander Hamilton and Thomas Jefferson, leaders of opposing factions, into his cabinet.

Washington's poise, prestige, and dignity made the new government of the United States respected at home and abroad.

While President, Washington traveled extensively throughout the country.

Factions developed into political parties, and the strain put upon Washington as conciliator led to his refusal to accept a third term.

In public life Washington combined modesty with self-assurance. In his first inaugural address he acknowledged "deficiencies" in natural endowments and administrative experience. Characteristically, he set about overcoming them by study, as he had fitted himself for managing his plantations by studying agriculture.

Many precedents were set during his terms of office. The "advise and consent" role of the Senate evolved into the right of that body to approve or disapprove the President's actions but never to give him formal advice beforehand.

Chief among the vigorously debated issues of his administration were taxation and banking policies, the assumption of state debts, and the

WASHINGTON'S PRESIDENTIAL ADMINISTRATION

Congresses in Session:
1st, 2d, 3d, 4th

Vice President:
John Adams, 1789–97

Secretary of the Treasury:
Alexander Hamilton, 1789–95
Oliver Wolcott Jr., 1795–97

Secretary of State:
Thomas Jefferson, 1789–93
Edmund Randolph, 1794–95
Timothy Pickering, 1795–97

Secretary of War:
Henry Knox, 1789–95
Timothy Pickering, 1795–96
James McHenry, 1796–97

Attorney General:
Edmund Randolph, 1789–94
William Bradford, 1794–95
Charles Lee, 1795–97

Postmaster General:
Samuel Osgood, 1789–91
Timothy Pickering, 1791–95
Joseph Habersham, 1795–97

PRESIDENTIAL ELECTION OF 1789

Nominations: Washington, the most popular man in the nation, was chosen by the Continental Congress. **Campaign Issues:** In this first U.S. presidential election party division was at a minimum, for only those who supported the new Constitution took part. **Remarks:** Most of the 11 states that had recently ratified the Constitution had their state legislatures choose presidential electors. New York failed to do so. Rhode Island and North Carolina had not yet ratified the new United States Constitution.

PRESIDENTIAL CANDIDATES	PARTY	ELECTORAL VOTES
George Washington	None	69
John Adams	None	34
John Jay	None	9
Other candidates	None	26
Votes not cast	—	4

PRESIDENTIAL ELECTION OF 1792

Nominations: Washington and Adams, the incumbents, received the nomination of those who advocated a strong central government. Clinton was chosen by Antifederalist congressional leaders. **Campaign Issues:** The fiscal policy and strong centralization advocated by Alexander Hamilton, then secretary of the treasury and a staunch Federalist, provided the issues. **Remarks:** Washington's popularity could not be eclipsed. The Antifederalists had merely hoped to elect Clinton as Vice President.

PRESIDENTIAL CANDIDATES	PARTY	ELECTORAL VOTES
George Washington	Federalist	132
John Adams	Federalist	77
George Clinton	Antifederalist	50
Thomas Jefferson	—	4
Aaron Burr	—	1

QUICK QUIZ: What type of painting is Jackson Pollock known for? See page 66.

GEORGE WASHINGTON *(continued)*
jurisdiction of federal courts. During his second administration he was severely criticized by the Jeffersonians, especially for Jay's Treaty with England. In the war between England and France, Washington proclaimed neutrality and urged it as basic U.S. policy. In his Farewell Address, he warned against "entangling alliances."

Washington died on Dec. 14, 1799. Over 178 years later, on March 13, 1978, in accord with a resolution of Congress, the U.S. Army promoted Washington to General of the Armies of the United States to preserve his seniority.

Martha Dandridge (Custis) Washington was born in 1731. At 18 she married Daniel Parke Custis, a wealthy plantation owner who died in 1757. She married Washington two years later, on Jan. 6, 1759.

The Washingtons had no children of their own, but Washington adopted Martha's two children, John Parke Custis and Martha Parke Custis.

Besides wealth and beauty Mrs. Washington was noted for her common sense, charm, and aristocratic graciousness She was a devoted wife. She died in 1802 and was buried beside her husband at Mount Vernon.

JOHN ADAMS

2d President (1797–1801)

The second President, John Adams disliked political parties and had a stormy term of office marred by factional intrigues. Although considered aloof, he was praised for his abilities even by those who disliked him.

Adams was born on Oct. 30, 1735, in Braintree (later Quincy), Mass., the son of John and Susanna (Boylston) Adams. He graduated from Harvard at 20, taught school for a time, and was admitted to the bar in 1758.

He was an outspoken opponent of the Stamp Act, arguing against the principle of taxation without representation. He gained fame as a defense attorney for the British soldiers accused of murder in the Boston Massacre of 1770.

Becoming a zealous advocate of independence, Adams was sent by Massachusetts to the Continental Congress. There he distinguished himself as a forceful leader. He proposed George Washington as commander in chief of the Continental Army and promoted adoption of the Declaration of Independence. In 1777 Adams presented the resolution establishing the design of the U.S. flag.

He next had a successful career as a diplomat for the embattled new nation. In 1777 he was sent as a commissioner to join Benjamin Franklin in France. In 1780–81 he persuaded the Netherlands to recognize the United States and lend it money. In 1782 he returned to France and helped draw up the Treaty of Paris to end the Revolutionary War. As the first U.S. envoy to Britain in 1785, Adams and his wife were met with hostility.

In 1789 he was chosen Vice President—in his opinion, "the most insignificant office that ever the invention of man contrived or his imagination conceived." A Federalist, he served under Washington for two terms.

In the 1796 presidential election, Adams won by only three electoral votes. The runner-up, Democratic-Republican leader Thomas Jefferson, became Vice President.

The United States fought an undeclared naval war with France during his administration. He did not wholeheartedly endorse the despotic Alien and Sedition Acts of 1798, but he signed them. These acts, aimed essentially at Thomas Jefferson and other critics of the Federalists, earned him the hatred of the Jeffersonians.

Defeated by Jefferson for reelection in 1800, Adams did not attend the inauguration of his successor. He retired to Quincy, issuing political statements and writing.

Later, he carried on a long correspondence with his former rival, Jefferson.

By extraordinary coincidence, both Adams and Jefferson died on the 50th anniversary of the Republic they had done so much to establish—July 4, 1826.

Abigail Smith Adams (1744–1818) was the daughter of a minister. She and Adams were married on Oct. 25, 1764. Lively and intelligent, she was one of the most distinguished First Ladies. The Adamses had two daughters and three sons—one, John Quincy Adams, became the sixth President.

On Nov. 1, 1800, the Adamses became the first presidential family to live in the White House, although at the time it was called the Executive Mansion and had not yet been painted white.

JOHN ADAMS' PRESIDENTIAL ADMINISTRATION

Congresses in Session: 5th, 6th
Vice President:
Thomas Jefferson, 1797–1801
Secretary of State:
Timothy Pickering, 1797–1800
John Marshall, 1800–01

Secretary of the Treasury:
Oliver Wolcott Jr., 1797–1800
Samuel Dexter, 1801
Secretary of War:
James McHenry, 1797–1800
Samuel Dexter, 1800

Attorney General:
Charles Lee, 1797–1801
Postmaster General:
Joseph Habersham, 1797–1801
Secretary of the Navy:
Benjamin Stoddert, 1798–1801

PRESIDENTIAL ELECTION OF 1796

Nominations: Congressional leaders of the two parties chose their respective candidates. **Campaign Issues:** Foreign policy dominated the campaign; the Federalists supported closer ties with England, while the Democratic–Republicans sought France's friendship. **Remarks:** Because of a split in the Federalist Party—between Hamilton and Adams—many Federalist electors gave their second vote to Jefferson.

PRESIDENTIAL CANDIDATES	PARTY	ELECTORAL VOTES
John Adams	Federalist	71
Thomas Jefferson	Dem.-Rep.	68
Thomas Pinckney	Federalist	59
Aaron Burr	Dem.-Rep.	30
Other candidates	—	48

THOMAS JEFFERSON

3d President
(1801–09)

Jefferson was rivaled among Americans only by Benjamin Franklin in the range of his interests, the quality of his intellectual contribution, and his faith in human progress.

As President he sought to curb the growing power of the U.S. Supreme Court, in which he felt the Federalists were attempting to entrench their philosophy. Jefferson believed that the federal government should be concerned mostly with foreign affairs, leaving the states free to administer local matters.

The son of Peter and Jane (Randolph) Jefferson, he was born on April 13, 1743, at Shadwell, the family estate in Virginia. His father, a tobacco plantation owner and a surveyor, died when Jefferson was 14. The boy took over management of Shadwell. He graduated from the College of William and Mary at 19 and was admitted to the bar in 1767. Five years later he married and settled at Monticello, a mansion he had personally designed.

He entered politics by winning election to Virginia's House of Burgesses in 1769 at the age of 26. There he became acquainted with Patrick Henry and other patriot leaders.

Jefferson was one of the organizers of the Virginia branch of the Committees of Correspondence, the chief medium of revolutionary agitation in the colonies.

His brilliantly written pamphlet *A Summary View of the Rights of British America* called attention to his logic, legal knowledge, and literary gifts.

He was chosen to write the Declaration of Independence in June 1776 at the Second Continental Congress, which he attended as an alternate. John Adams, who also was on the committee to write the Declaration, said he deferred to Jefferson because "I had a great opinion of the elegance of his pen."

He returned to Virginia to carry out some of his political and social principles in the newly established state. Serving in its legislature (1776–79) and as its governor (1779–81), he removed feudal vestiges from the landholding system. He framed a statute on religious freedom that became a model for the rest of the country. His proposals for public education, public libraries, and a liberal university, although not then adopted, anticipated later developments.

In 1784 Jefferson served on a special diplomatic assignment in Europe, and in 1785 he succeeded Benjamin Franklin as minister to France. His absence until October 1789 prevented him from directly participating in drafting the U.S. Constitution, but his pressure contributed to the addition of the first 10 amendments, the Bill of Rights.

Jefferson entered President Washington's cabinet as secretary of state in 1790. At first he subordinated his views to preserve the unity of the new nation, backing the trade and banking measures of Secretary of the Treasury Alexander Hamilton. However, he soon became convinced that Hamilton and his group—the Federalist Party—sought to establish a monarchy, or at least an oligarchy of wealth. Jefferson opposed this and began rallying like-minded men, who came to call themselves Republicans—a group from which the present Democratic Party traces

JEFFERSON'S PRESIDENTIAL ADMINISTRATION

Congresses in Session:
7th, 8th, 9th, 10th

Vice President:
Aaron Burr, 1801–05
George Clinton, 1805–09

Secretary of State:
James Madison, 1801–09

Secretary of the Treasury:
Samuel Dexter, 1801
Albert Gallatin, 1801–09

Secretary of War:
Henry Dearborn, 1801–09

Secretary of the Navy:
Robert Smith, 1801–09

Attorney General:
Levi Lincoln, 1801–05
Robert Smith, 1805
John Breckinridge, 1805–07
Caesar Rodney, 1807–09

Postmaster General:
Joseph Habersham, 1801
Gideon Granger, 1801–09

PRESIDENTIAL ELECTION OF 1800

Nominations: Jefferson and Adams were the acknowledged leaders of their parties. **Campaign Issues:** Both parties debated an undeclared naval war with France and Federalist repression of opponents through the Alien and Sedition Acts. **Remarks:** Electoral voting caused a tie between Jefferson and Burr. The House of Representatives decided the contest. On the 36th ballot Jefferson was chosen President.

PRESIDENTIAL CANDIDATES	PARTY	ELECTORAL VOTES
Thomas Jefferson	Dem.–Rep.	73
Aaron Burr	Dem.–Rep.	73
John Adams	Federalist	65
Charles C. Pinckney	Federalist	64
John Jay	Federalist	1

PRESIDENTIAL ELECTION OF 1804

Nominations: At the first regular political caucuses, the congressional delegates of both parties unanimously nominated their respective candidates. **Campaign Issue:** Debate centered on the territorial expansion of the United States through the Louisiana Purchase, which had been achieved in the preceding year. **Remarks:** This was the first presidential election carried out under the 12th Amendment to the Constitution of the United States.

PRESIDENTIAL CANDIDATES	PARTY	ELECTORAL VOTES
Thomas Jefferson	Dem.–Rep.	162
Charles C. Pinckney	Federalist	14

VICE-PRESIDENTIAL CANDIDATES	PARTY	ELECTORAL VOTES
George Clinton	Dem.–Rep.	162
Rufus King	Federalist	14

QUICK QUIZ: Was the 1982 crime rate higher in Chicago or Detroit? See page 171.

THOMAS JEFFERSON *(continued)*
its origin. Jefferson and Hamilton became openly antagonistic. Washington was unable to reconcile them. In 1793 Jefferson left the cabinet.

He spent the next two years remodeling his Monticello home and experimenting with scientific agriculture. He was also active in building up the Democratic-Republican Party. He became its presidential nominee in 1796. He lost by only three electoral votes to Washington's Vice President, John Adams.

As runner-up Jefferson became Vice President in 1797 under a constitutional provision then in effect. He opposed Federalist policies, particularly the Alien and Sedition Acts that were aimed at the Antifederalists. In protest against the repressive acts, Jefferson drafted the Kentucky Resolutions, the earliest statement of the states' rights interpretation of the Constitution.

Jefferson and his party were convinced that Adams and the Federalists wanted to go to war against the revolutionary government of France.

In 1800 the Democratic-Republicans nominated Jefferson and Aaron Burr. They easily triumphed over John Adams and the Federalists. However, Burr and Jefferson received the same number of electoral votes, and the choice of President was left to the House of Representatives. Burr tried to win the presidency. But after a long deadlock Jefferson was elected, largely because Alexander Hamilton advised Federalist congressmen to support Jefferson.

The chief foreign problem throughout Jefferson's two terms was maintaining neutrality in the conflict between England and France, both of which preyed upon U.S. shipping. Seeking to bring pressure by withholding needed goods, Jefferson sponsored acts suspending trade, especially the Embargo Act of 1807. These finally became effective, causing loss and suffering to many citizens and arousing such protest that Jefferson relaxed enforcement attempts.

One of Jefferson's major achievements was the acquisition in 1803 of the Louisiana Territory from France for $15 million. This new territory doubled the size of the U.S. In the interest of exploration and settlement, Jefferson sponsored the Lewis and Clark Expedition that blazed the pioneer trail to the Pacific Northwest.

Jefferson ordered the arrest of former Vice President Burr for treason in 1807. He regarded Burr's acquittal by Chief Justice John Marshall as a personal affront.

Jefferson retired in 1809 but remained active. He kept up a voluminous correspondence with many public figures, including his former adversary John Adams. Jefferson was instrumental in founding the University of Virginia. He also designed its buildings and served as rector in 1819–26, helping the university become one of the most advanced institutions of its time.

Jefferson died on July 4, 1826, within a few hours of his presidential predecessor and friend, John Adams—on the 50th anniversary of the Declaration of Independence. His epitaph expressed the accomplishments for which he most wanted to be remembered: "Here was buried Thomas Jefferson, author of the Declaration of American Independence, of the Statute of Virginia for Religious Freedom, and father of the University of Virginia."

Martha Wayles (Skelton) Jefferson (1748–82) became Jefferson's wife in 1772 but died 10 years later. He did not remarry after her death. Only two of their six children survived to maturity: Martha and Mary (Maria). Jefferson had been a widower for about 18 years when he became President. Both his daughters served as his official hostesses, aided by Dolley Madison, wife of his secretary of state.

JAMES MADISON

4th President
(1809–17)

Physically small and unimpressive, Madison stood about five feet six inches tall and weighed perhaps only about 100 pounds. But he was a formidable figure in the founding period of the nation.

He was the father of the Constitution, a founder of the Democratic-Republican Party, a congressman, author of the Virginia Resolutions and of much of the *Federalist Papers*, and the fourth President of the United States.

The first of nine children of James and Nelly (Conway) Madison, he was born on March 16, 1751, in Port Conway, Va. Much of his early education was at home. He later attended the College of New Jersey (now Princeton), from which he graduated at 20. Like George Washington and others of the Virginia planter aristocracy, he supported the agitation against British colonial administration.

Madison's profound knowledge of government was first proved in 1776 when he helped draft a constitution for Virginia. In 1776 and 1777 he was a member of the executive council directing Virginia's participation in the Revolutionary War.

As a delegate to the Continental Congress for four years, Madison grew increasingly apprehensive as he watched the Congress flounder under the ineffective Articles of Confederation. After much thought he became convinced of the need for a strong national government.

In 1786 he was instrumental in the calling of a constitutional convention. At the convention in 1787 he became the leading spokesman for a strong federal government. Madison's political knowledge and persuasive logic helped secure adoption of the Constitution. The notes he kept on the sessions are the main reference source on the debates during the convention.

Madison fought for ratification of the Constitution by the states. In his own state he overcame the opposition of Patrick Henry. In the national campaign his contributions to the brilliant *Federalist Papers*, along with those of Hamilton and John Jay, had a powerful effect.

Elected to the House of Representatives in the newly established Congress (where he served for four terms), Madison led in winning passage of the Bill of Rights and in creation of the executive departments.

During Washington's presidency, Madison became a steadfast enemy of Hamilton and an ardent supporter of his friend Thomas Jefferson. It was during this time that he became one of the principal organizers of the opposition party, the Democratic-Republicans.

When John Adams became President in 1797, Madison retired to Montpelier, his Virginia plantation. In 1798 Madison framed the Virginia Resolutions, protesting the repressive Alien and Sedition Acts inspired by Hamilton. By asserting the right of individual states to decide on the constitutionality of the acts, these resolutions (along with the Kentucky Resolutions penned by Jefferson) became the theoretical base for the states' rights doctrine.

When Jefferson became President in 1801, Madison was named secretary of state. He worked closely with Jefferson in negotiations for the purchase of the Louisiana Territory and in keeping the United States out of the Napoleonic wars in Europe. In 1808, following the tradition of Washington, Jefferson declined a third term. Madison became the successful candidate of the Democratic-Republicans.

He began his administration by following Jefferson's policy of neutrality in the Napoleonic wars. Finally, however, he was bullied by the "war hawks," led by John C. Calhoun and Henry Clay, into the indecisive War of 1812 against England, which began as a protest against Britain's blockade of U.S. ships trading with France.

To pay war bills and rehabilitate the economy, Madison resorted to such Federalist measures as the funding of the national debt, establishment of a national bank, and a protective tariff.

The war, which Federalist opponents called "Mr. Madison's war," went badly. New England merchants and industrialists openly opposed American participation. Even friends and supporters of his administration became discouraged by repeated setbacks suffered by American forces. Even so, Madison won reelection in 1812.

In 1814 a British fleet entered Chesapeake Bay. British troops landed in Maryland and proceeded to defeat the American militia assigned to defend Washington, D.C., at the Battle of Bladensburg on Aug. 24, 1814. The enemy set fire to the Capitol, the White House, and other public buildings, while Madison and other members of the government fled to safety. Dolley Madison saved a painting of George Washington as she fled.

The Treaty of Ghent, signed on Dec. 24, 1814, ended the war. But because of slow communications, the Battle of New Orleans was fought two weeks later, on Jan. 8, 1815.

After the war the westward movement began in earnest. Steamboat navigation opened on the Mississippi River.

In 1817 Madison retired once more to Montpelier. Besides being a gentleman farmer, he wrote extensively, succeeded Thomas Jefferson as rector of the University of Virginia in 1826, and was a delegate to the Virginia Constitutional Convention of 1829.

Madison died at Montpelier on June 28, 1836.

Dolley Payne (Todd) Madison (1768–1849), a 26-year-old widow and the daughter of a North Carolina planter, became Madison's wife in 1794, when he was 43. An attractive, vivacious, intelligent woman, Dolley Madison was a popular First Lady. After her husband's death she was voted an honorary seat in the House of Representatives by a unanimous congressional resolution.

MADISON'S PRESIDENTIAL ADMINISTRATION

Congresses in Session:
11th, 12th, 13th, 14th

Vice President:
George Clinton, 1809–12
Elbridge Gerry, 1813–14

Secretary of War:
William Eustis, 1809–13
John Armstrong, 1813–14
James Monroe, 1814–15
William Crawford, 1815–17

Secretary of State:
Robert Smith, 1809–11
James Monroe, 1811–17

Secretary of the Navy:
Paul Hamilton, 1809–12
William Jones, 1813–14
Benjamin Crowninshield, 1815–17

Postmaster General:
Gideon Granger, 1809–14
Return J. Meigs Jr., 1814–17

Secretary of the Treasury:
Albert Gallatin, 1809–14
George Campbell, 1814
Alexander Dallas, 1814–16
William H. Crawford, 1816–17

Attorney General:
Caesar Rodney, 1809–11
William Pinkney, 1811–14
Richard Rush, 1814–17

PRESIDENTIAL ELECTION OF 1808

Nominations: Congressional caucuses nominated respective party candidates. **Campaign Issue:** Jefferson's Embargo Act. **Remarks:** A faction of the Democratic–Republicans supported Clinton for President.

PRESIDENTIAL CANDIDATES	PARTY	ELECTORAL VOTES
James Madison	Dem.–Rep.	122
Charles C. Pinckney	Federalist	47
George Clinton	Dem.–Rep.	6
Votes not cast	—	1

VICE-PRESIDENTIAL CANDIDATES	PARTY	ELECTORAL VOTES
George Clinton	Dem.–Rep.	113
Rufus King	Federalist	47
Other candidates	—	15
Votes not cast	—	1

PRESIDENTIAL ELECTION OF 1812

Nominations: A congressional caucus nominated the Democratic–Republican ticket. **Campaign Issue:** The War of 1812.

Remarks: This was the first presidential election carried out while the nation was formally at war.

PRESIDENTIAL CANDIDATES	PARTY	ELECTORAL VOTES
James Madison	Dem.–Rep.	128
DeWitt Clinton	Federalist	89
Votes not cast	—	1

VICE-PRESIDENTIAL CANDIDATES	PARTY	ELECTORAL VOTES
Elbridge Gerry	Dem.–Rep.	131
Charles J. Ingersoll	Federalist	86
Votes not cast	—	1

QUICK QUIZ: What is the chemical composition of the Earth? See page 177.

JAMES MONROE

5th President
(1817–25)

Although he did not rank in imagination or in brilliance with the Democratic-Republican Presidents who served before him, Monroe has been judged an abler administrator of his high office than either Jefferson or Madison.

The fourth Virginian to become Chief Executive, he was born in Westmoreland County on April 28, 1758. He was the son of Spence and Elizabeth (Jones) Monroe, landowning farmers.

Monroe left the College of William and Mary in 1776 to become a lieutenant in a Virginia regiment, saw action in several Revolutionary War battles, and achieved the rank of major. When the war ended he studied law under Thomas Jefferson.

In 1782 he was elected to the Virginia legislature. Then for three years he served in the Continental Congress, where he opposed a centralized federal government.

Under the new government Monroe served in the U.S. Senate and became a leading spokesman for Jefferson and the Democratic-Republicans.

Monroe was minister to France (1794–96). Because of his enthusiastic support of the French Revolution, he was the only ambassador of a foreign power invited to sit in the revolutionary legislature.

In 1799 Monroe was elected governor of Virginia. Jefferson sent him to assist Robert Livingston in 1803 during the Louisiana Purchase negotiations, which were virtually completed by the time he arrived.

As Madison's secretary of state (1811–17), Monroe also served a short-term appointment as secretary of war.

In 1816 Monroe obtained his party's presidential nomination and was easily elected.

Because of political calm, the first years of his administration were known as the Era of Good Feelings. He made a long tour of the Northern states in 1817 and a similar journey through the Southern states in 1819. Monroe was reelected in 1820 without opposition, winning all but one electoral vote.

The good feelings, however, were only apparent. Seething dissensions erupted in North-South disputes over extension of slavery into new states to be formed from the territories. The conflict was temporarily eased in 1820 by the first Missouri Compromise. Maine was admitted as a free state and Missouri as a slave state. A boundary was drawn between future free and slave states in the Louisiana Territory.

Other events in Monroe's presidency included the acquisition of Florida (1819); recognition of the Latin American republics (1822); and promulgation of the Monroe Doctrine (1823) to protect the Western Hemisphere. In 1822 Liberia was founded in Africa as a colony for freed American slaves with its capital, Monrovia, named for Monroe.

At the end of his term Monroe retired to his home in Loudoun County, Va. He served as regent of the University of Virginia in 1826 and presided over the Virginia Constitutional Convention in 1829. He died on July 4, 1831, and was buried in New York City. In 1858 his body was removed to Richmond, Va.

Elizabeth Kortright Monroe (1768–1830) married Monroe in 1786. The daughter of a New York businessman, she bore him a son (who died in infancy) and two daughters.

Their home, near Jefferson's Monticello in Virginia, was called Ash Lawn.

MONROE'S PRESIDENTIAL ADMINISTRATION

Congresses in Session:
15th, 16th, 17th, 18th

Vice President:
Daniel Tompkins, 1817–25

Secretary of State:
John Quincy Adams, 1817–25

Secretary of the Treasury:
William H. Crawford, 1817–25

Secretary of War:
John Calhoun, 1817–25

Attorney General:
Richard Rush, 1817
William Wirt, 1817–25

Secretary of the Navy:
Benjamin Crowninshield, 1817–18
Smith Thompson, 1818–23
Samuel Southard, 1823–25

Postmaster General:
Return J. Meigs Jr., 1817–23
John McLean, 1823–25

PRESIDENTIAL ELECTION OF 1816

Nominations: A congressional caucus nominated the Democratic–Republican ticket. **Campaign Issue:** None. The Democratic–Republican Party by this time had adopted most of the Federalist program. **Remarks:** This was the last election in which the Federalist Party nominated candidates for the offices of President and Vice President.

PRESIDENTIAL CANDIDATES	PARTY	ELECTORAL VOTES
James Monroe	Dem.–Rep.	183
Rufus King	Federalist	34
Votes not cast	—	4

VICE-PRESIDENTIAL CANDIDATES	PARTY	ELECTORAL VOTES
Daniel D. Tompkins	Dem.–Rep.	183
John E. Howard	Federalist	22
Other candidates	—	12
Votes not cast	—	4

PRESIDENTIAL ELECTION OF 1820

No one contested Monroe's second term because of his popularity. The Federalist Party was dead. William Plumer of New Hampshire voted against Monroe allegedly because he believed only Washington's election should be unanimous.

PRESIDENTIAL CANDIDATES	PARTY	ELECTORAL VOTES
James Monroe	Dem.–Rep.	231
John Quincy Adams	Independent	1
Votes not cast	—	3

VICE-PRESIDENTIAL CANDIDATES	PARTY	ELECTORAL VOTES
Daniel D. Tompkins	Dem.–Rep.	218
Other candidates	—	14
Votes not cast	—	3

JOHN QUINCY ADAMS

6th President (1825–29)

A high-minded man with little popular support and no political party, John Quincy Adams entered the presidency with gloomy prospects. He was charged with stealing the White House from the popular Andrew Jackson by making a political bargain with Henry Clay.

As President, Adams alienated politicians by advocating a professional civil service free of patronage. And the one important act passed by Congress with Adams' approval—raising the protective tariff rates—angered farmers.

Born on July 11, 1767, in Braintree (now Quincy), Mass., Adams was the eldest son of President John Adams.

At the age of 10 he went to France with his father. He was educated in France and the Netherlands during his father's diplomatic service. At the age of 14 he went to Moscow where he served for two years as the private secretary of American ambassador Francis Dana. He graduated from Harvard in 1787 and was admitted to the bar in 1790.

Adams served as minister to the Netherlands (1794–97) under President Washington and as minister to Prussia (1797–1801) during his father's administration.

As a Massachusetts state senator in 1802, he demonstrated his disregard for partisan politics, though he was the son of a Federalist President and was elected by the Federalists.

Elected to the U.S. Senate in 1803, he acted so independently that the Federalists maneuvered him out of office in 1808.

In 1809 he was sent as minister to Russia, where he was held in esteem. He was in Russia during Napoleon's invasion in 1812. While there he was named and confirmed to the U.S. Supreme Court, but turned down the appointment.

In 1814 Adams negotiated the Treaty of Ghent, which ended the War of 1812.

As Monroe's secretary of state (1817–25) Adams gained great respect. He negotiated the 1819 treaty with Spain that added Florida to the United States, negotiated with Britain for the settlement of a U.S.-Canadian border dispute, and firmly dealt with Russian plans to penetrate America's West Coast. But Adams won his greatest praise as the chief architect of the Monroe Doctrine.

None of the candidates for the presidency in 1824—Adams, Jackson, William H. Crawford, Henry Clay—ran with a political party designation. Jackson received the most electoral votes but not the required majority, so the election had to be decided in the House of Representatives. Because Clay had the fewest electoral votes, he was dropped from consideration by the House. After a private meeting with Adams, Clay threw his support to Adams. In turn, Adams made Clay his secretary of state.

In 1828, running on the National Republican ticket, Adams was defeated by Andrew Jackson in his bid for reelection.

He was elected to Congress in 1830, where for 17 years he distinguished himself by his untiring and conscientious service.

In Congress, he actively opposed the extension of slavery, the annexation of Texas, and war with Mexico. He succeeded in 1844 in ending the "gag rules" in congressional debate on slavery.

Adams also sponsored the advancement of science. The Smithsonian Institution owes its development largely to him.

At the age of 80 Adams suffered a stroke while at his desk in the House of Representatives. He died two days later, on Feb. 23, 1848.

Louisa Catherine Johnson Adams (1775–1852), daughter of an American diplomat, married Adams in London in 1797. She made the White House a center for cultured and animated social life during his tenancy. The couple had three sons and a daughter. Their youngest son, Charles Francis Adams, served as U.S. minister to Britain during the Civil War.

JOHN QUINCY ADAMS' PRESIDENTIAL ADMINISTRATION

Congresses in Session:
19th, 20th
Vice President:
John Calhoun, 1825–29
Secretary of State:
Henry Clay, 1825–29

Secretary of the Treasury:
Richard Rush, 1825–29

Secretary of War:
James Barbour, 1825–28
Peter Porter, 1828–29

Attorney General:
William Wirt, 1825–29
Secretary of the Navy:
Samuel Southard, 1825–29
Postmaster General:
John McLean, 1825–29

PRESIDENTIAL ELECTION OF 1824

Nominations: The disintegration of the Democratic-Republican Party led to presidential nominations by state legislatures. There were several "favorite son" candidates. **Campaign Issues:** The candidates supported domestic improvements and a higher protective tariff.

Remarks: No candidate received a majority of the electoral vote. The House of Representatives finally chose Adams after Clay was eliminated because he had the fewest electoral votes. Before 1824, records of popular votes are virtually nonexistent. State legislatures usually chose the presidential electors.

PRESIDENTIAL CANDIDATES	PARTY	ELECTORAL VOTES	POPULAR VOTE Total	Percentage	VICE-PRESIDENTIAL CANDIDATES AND ELECTORAL VOTES		PARTY
John Quincy Adams....	None	84	108,740	30.6	John C. Calhoun...	182	None
Andrew Jackson.......	None	99	153,544	43.1	Nathan Sanford...	30	None
William H. Crawford....	None	41	46,618	13.1	Nathaniel Macon..	24	None
Henry Clay............	None	37	47,136	13.2	Other candidates..	25	—

QUICK QUIZ: What is the meaning of the word *eutrophication*? See page 194.

ANDREW JACKSON

7th President
(1829–37)

Although a man of personal dignity, Andrew Jackson was feared by many established citizens of his day as a dangerous upstart and the one who brought "rabble" into the White House. A leader of the movement toward increased popular participation in government, he came to symbolize the democratic sentiments of the period. Jackson's administration, which strengthened the role of the Executive Office, has been ranked as one of the most important in U.S. history.

The first "log cabin" President, Jackson was born on March 15, 1767, in Waxhaw Settlement on the border between North and South Carolina. He was the son of Irish immigrants Andrew and Elizabeth (Hutchinson) Jackson. His father died shortly before Andrew was born.

At 13 he and his brother were imprisoned by the British during the Revolutionary War. The boys caught smallpox and were released to the care of their mother. His brother and mother both died.

The orphaned Andrew Jackson lived with relatives and friends. He was admitted to the North Carolina bar in 1787 at the age of 20.

In 1788 Jackson moved west to Nashville, which later became the capital of Tennessee. He prospered in law and land speculation.

In 1797–98 Jackson served briefly in Congress, first in the House and then in the Senate. Before the War of 1812, he spent six years as a judge of the Tennessee superior court.

In 1802 Jackson was elected major general of the Tennessee state militia, a position considered next in importance to the governorship.

In the War of 1812, troops under his command crushed the Creek Indians, allies of the British, in the Battle of Horseshoe Bend in Alabama and forced them to make peace. This brought him the rank of major general in the U.S. Army. In one campaign he captured British strongholds in Florida. He then was given command of an expedition against a British army marching on New Orleans. Although outnumbered at that battle, he gained the victory that made him a national hero — even though the Battle of New Orleans was of no real military importance, having taken place a few weeks after Britain and the U.S. had signed the Treaty of Ghent, ending the War of 1812.

Jackson had acquired the reputation for personal toughness symbolized by his nickname "Old Hickory." According to some sources his duels and brawls numbered nearly 100.

JACKSON'S PRESIDENTIAL ADMINISTRATION

Congresses in Session:
21st, 22d, 23d, 24th

Vice President:
John Calhoun, 1829–32
Martin Van Buren, 1833–37

Secretary of State:
Martin Van Buren, 1829–31
Edward Livingston, 1831–33
Louis McLane, 1833–34
John Forsyth, 1834–37

Secretary of the Treasury:
Samuel Ingham, 1829–31
Louis McLane, 1831–33
William J. Duane, 1833
Roger Taney, 1833–34
Levi Woodbury, 1834–37

Attorney General:
John Berrien, 1829–31
Roger Taney, 1831–33
Benjamin Butler, 1833–37

Secretary of War:
John Eaton, 1829–31
Lewis Cass, 1831–36
Benjamin Butler, 1836–37

Secretary of the Navy:
John Branch, 1829–31
Levi Woodbury, 1831–34
Mahlon Dickerson, 1834–37

Postmaster General:
John McLean, 1829
William Barry, 1829–35
Amos Kendall, 1835–37

PRESIDENTIAL ELECTION OF 1828

Nominations: The Tennessee legislature nominated Jackson for the presidency. Adams was the incumbent. **Campaign Issues:** Jackson and his followers charged that the government was in the hands of an "aristocratic minority." His supporters charged the election of 1824 had been stolen from him by Adams. **Remarks:** Jackson was a popular hero.

PRESIDENTIAL CANDIDATES	PARTY	ELECTORAL VOTES	POPULAR VOTE Total	Percentage	VICE-PRESIDENTIAL CANDIDATES AND ELECTORAL VOTES		PARTY
Andrew Jackson ...	Democratic	178	647,286	56.0	John C. Calhoun ...	171	Democratic
John Quincy Adams	Natl. Rep.	83	508,064	44.0	Richard Rush	83	Natl. Rep.
					William Smith	7	Democratic

PRESIDENTIAL ELECTION OF 1832

Nominations: The modern political convention system dates from Sept. 26, 1831. Wirt was nominated on the first ballot by the Anti-Masonic Party. The National Republican Party convention met in Baltimore, Dec. 12–15, 1831, and chose Clay and Sergeant. At the Democratic Party convention in Baltimore, May 21–23, 1832, Jackson unanimously received the nomination. The Independents nominated Floyd and Lee. **Campaign Issue:** The Democrats fought the rechartering of the Second Bank of the United States. **Remarks:** The Anti-Masonic Party was the first legitimate third party.

PRESIDENTIAL CANDIDATES	PARTY	ELECTORAL VOTES	POPULAR VOTE Total	Percentage	VICE-PRESIDENTIAL CANDIDATES AND ELECTORAL VOTES		PARTY
Andrew Jackson ...	Democratic	219	687,502	52.2	Martin Van Buren ..	189	Democratic
Henry Clay	Natl. Rep.	49	530,189	40.2	John Sergeant	49	Natl. Rep.
John Floyd	Independent	11	—	—	Henry Lee	11	Nullifiers
William Wirt	Anti-Masonic	7	101,051	7.6	Amos Ellmaker	7	Anti-Masonic
Votes not cast	—	2	—	—	William Wilkins	30	Independent
					Votes not cast.....	2	—

In 1818 he was ordered to punish some Seminole Indians who had been raiding across the Alabama-Georgia border. He crossed over into Spanish Florida, captured Pensacola, and ordered executed two British subjects accused of inciting the raids. His unauthorized move involved the U.S. in serious trouble with both Spain and Britain, but when Florida became U.S. territory he was named its first governor—an appointment Jackson considered vindication.

The greatest popular hero of his time, a man of action, and an expansionist, Jackson by 1821 was being actively promoted as Monroe's successor in the White House.

In 1824 Jackson was nominated for the presidency by one of the four factions into which the ruling Democratic-Republicans had split.

Jackson won a plurality of the electoral votes, but not the required majority. The election was thrown into the House of Representatives, where supporters of one of the candidates, Henry Clay, gave their votes to John Quincy Adams, who became President. The angry Jacksonians called this "bargain and corruption."

In the election of 1828 Jackson easily defeated Adams' bid for reelection.

Jackson strengthened the authority of the presidency, taking leadership from most members of his official cabinet. His "kitchen cabinet"—an unofficial group of favorite advisers—wielded great influence. Party loyalty was intense. Members were rewarded with government posts in the spoils system.

In the nullification crisis of 1832, when South Carolina declared null and void the Tariff Act of that year, Jackson took a strong pro-Union stand. He indicated he would use troops if the state tried to secede, warning: "Our Federal Union, it must be preserved." However, he felt that the South had a real grievance and ordered a compromise tariff act.

In other respects Jackson supported the doctrine of states' rights, especially when he fought against the Bank of the United States. He finally removed the funds from this national bank and deposited them in chosen state banks.

Jackson probably could have won a third term in 1836, but instead he chose to put Vice President Martin Van Buren, a New York party politician, into the White House.

Jackson retired to The Hermitage, his Tennessee estate, but his voice was heard throughout Van Buren's administration. Because Van Buren opposed the annexation of Texas, Jackson helped James Polk win the presidency in 1844. Jackson died on June 8, 1845.

Rachel Donelson (Robards) Jackson (1767–1828), a divorcée, married Jackson in 1791. A mistake in her divorce proceedings made it necessary for them to be remarried three years later. This long-lived "scandal" made Jackson the butt of slurs, one of which led to a duel in which he killed his opponent. The Jacksons had no children of their own, but they adopted the son of Mrs. Jackson's brother. He was named Andrew Jackson Jr.

Mrs. Jackson died just before her husband became President. Her niece, Emily Donelson, and Jackson's daughter-in-law, Sarah Yorke Jackson, served as White House hostesses.

MARTIN VAN BUREN

8th President
(1837–41)

Political skill and native intelligence earned Martin Van Buren the nickname "Red Fox." As a Jacksonian Democrat he proclaimed himself a champion of the people.

But he lost popular support in the financial panic of 1837 by opposing federal aid to alleviate distress. He resisted the extension of slavery, and his stand against the annexation of Texas probably cost him the Democratic nomination in 1844.

The son of Abraham Van Buren, a farmer and innkeeper, and Maria (Hoes) Van Alen Van Buren, he was born on Dec. 5, 1782, in Kinderhook, N.Y. As a boy he waited on tables in his father's tavern. Though he never attended college, he trained in law offices and was admitted to the bar in 1803.

Van Buren's first public office was surrogate of Columbia County, N.Y., in 1808. He served as a state senator (1812–20) and during that time was state attorney general (1816–19).

As a U.S. senator (1821–28) he was inconsistent on the issues of states' rights and slavery. Van Buren was far more important as a political leader than as a legislator. He became one of the principal figures in a powerful political clique known as the Albany Regency. He swung his support to Andrew Jackson.

He won election as governor of New York in 1828, but resigned after serving only two months to accept appointment by Jackson as U.S. secretary of state.

Probably the most influential of Jackson's advisers, Van Buren was nominated for Vice President by the Democratic Party in 1832 and was elected along with President Jackson.

In 1836, supported by Jackson, he was chosen as Democratic candidate for President and was swept into office.

To combat the Panic of 1837, Van Buren called a special session of Congress. He asked for the establishment of an independent treasury system so that the government could control the money collected from taxes rather than deposit it in private banks. He also proposed that the government issue paper money in the form of treasury notes. However, Congress did not pass the Independent Treasury Act until July 1840.

As a friend of labor, he reduced the workday for federal employees to 10 hours.

His opponents criticized Van Buren for spending government money to install the first hot-water tank in the White House to warm his bathwater.

QUICK QUIZ: Which 10 nations were the leading exporters in 1982? See page 198.

MARTIN VAN BUREN *(continued)*
Van Buren was defeated in his campaign for reelection as President in 1840. He then was denied renomination as his party's candidate in 1844, largely because he had angered Andrew Jackson by opposing the annexation of Texas.

Running on the antislavery Free Soil Party ticket in 1848, Van Buren failed to receive a single electoral vote.

Bitterly disappointed, he retired to his home in Kinderhook, where he died on July 24, 1862. **Hannah Hoes Van Buren** (1783–1819), who became his wife in 1807, was his boyhood sweetheart. They had four sons. She died while Van Buren was New York's attorney general. He never remarried. His daughter-in-law Angelica Singleton Van Buren served as White House hostess during his presidency.

VAN BUREN'S PRESIDENTIAL ADMINISTRATION

Congresses in Session:
25th, 26th

Vice President:
Richard M. Johnson, 1837–41

Secretary of State:
John Forsyth, 1837–41

Secretary of the Treasury:
Levi Woodbury, 1837–41

Secretary of War:
Joel Poinsett, 1837–41

Secretary of the Navy:
Mahlon Dickerson, 1837–38
James Paulding, 1838–41

Attorney General:
Benjamin Butler, 1837–38
Felix Grundy, 1838–40
Henry Gilpin, 1840–41

Postmaster General:
Amos Kendall, 1837–40
John Niles, 1840–41

PRESIDENTIAL ELECTION OF 1836

Nominations: At the Democratic convention in Baltimore, May 20–22, 1836, Van Buren was backed by Jackson and was nominated unanimously. The Whigs, who held no national convention, nominated several strong sectional candidates.
Campaign Issues: The campaign centered on Andrew Jackson, his policies, and when Van Buren should succeed him.
Remarks: This was the only election in which none of the vice-presidential candidates received the required majority vote. The U.S. Senate chose Richard M. Johnson, who had been Van Buren's running mate, over Francis Granger.

PRESIDENTIAL CANDIDATES	PARTY	ELECTORAL VOTES	POPULAR VOTE Total	POPULAR VOTE Percentage	VICE-PRESIDENTIAL CANDIDATES AND ELECTORAL VOTES		PARTY
Martin Van Buren . .	Democratic	170	765,483	50.9	Richard M. Johnson	147	Democratic
William H. Harrison	Whig	73	550,816	36.6	Francis Granger . . .	77	Whig
Hugh L. White	Whig	26	146,107	9.7	John Tyler	47	Democratic
Daniel Webster	Whig	14	41,201	2.7	William Smith	23	Independent
W.P. Mangum	Anti-Jackson	11	—	—			

WILLIAM HENRY HARRISON

9th President
(1841)

The Whigs in 1840 presented Harrison, their presidential candidate, as a cider-drinking, homespun, log-cabin-born, hardworking plow pusher. This was a fable, but it helped make the hero of the Battle of Tippecanoe an easy victor over Martin Van Buren.

What sort of a President Harrison would have been will never be known because of his early death after taking office.

Harrison's administration augured well because of the distinguished cabinet he assembled, which included Daniel Webster as secretary of state. However, Harrison died of pneumonia on April 4, 1841, a month after his inauguration—the first U.S. Chief Executive to die in the White House.

Harrison's birthplace actually was a brick mansion at "Berkeley," his family's estate in Charles City County, Va. He was born on Feb. 9, 1773, the son of Benjamin and Elizabeth (Bassett) Harrison. His father, a wealthy planter, had been one of the signers of the Declaration of Independence.

He was privately tutored and then attended

HARRISON'S PRESIDENTIAL ADMINISTRATION

Congresses in Session:
27th

Vice President:
John Tyler, 1841

Secretary of State:
Daniel Webster, 1841

Secretary of the Treasury:
Thomas Ewing, 1841

Secretary of War:
John Bell, 1841

Attorney General:
John Crittenden, 1841

Postmaster General:
Francis Granger, 1841

Secretary of the Navy:
George Badger, 1841

PRESIDENTIAL ELECTION OF 1840

Nominations: The Whigs met in Harrisburg, Pa., in December 1839, choosing Harrison and Tyler. The Democrats met in Baltimore in May 1840, and chose Van Buren without dissent. The Liberty Party met in Albany in April 1840, nominating James G. Birney and Thomas Earle—the first effort by the abolitionists to win national political power.

PRESIDENTIAL CANDIDATES	PARTY	ELECTORAL VOTES	POPULAR VOTE Total	POPULAR VOTE Percentage	VICE-PRESIDENTIAL CANDIDATES AND ELECTORAL VOTES		PARTY
William H. Harrison	Whig	234	1,274,624	53.1	John Tyler	234	Whig
Martin Van Buren . .	Democratic	60	1,127,781	46.9	Richard M. Johnson	48	Democratic
James G. Birney . . .	Liberty	—	7,053	—	Thomas Earle	—	Liberty
					L.W. Tazewell	11	Independent
					James K. Polk	1	Democratic

Hampden-Sydney College. He went on to study medicine briefly in Philadelphia under Dr. Benjamin Rush, a signer of the Declaration of Independence.

In 1791 Harrison joined the Army. He resigned his commission in 1798 to become secretary of the Northwest Territory. In 1799, at the age of 26, he became its first delegate to Congress. There his proposal to divide the territory into Ohio and Indiana was approved.

As governor of Indiana Territory (1800–12), Harrison induced the Indians to cede vast tracts of land.

When the Shawnee Indians attacked encroaching settlers in 1811, Harrison led an expedition that defeated the Indians in the Battle of Tippecanoe. Harrison won national fame with the battle and settled the territory's claim to 3 million acres of Indian land.

In the War of 1812 he was appointed supreme commander of the Army of the Northwest. Marching into Canada, he defeated the British and their Indian allies at the Battle of the Thames River on Oct. 5, 1813.

After resigning from the Army, he became a farmer at North Bend, Ohio. He then entered politics, winning election as a U.S. congressman (1817–19), state senator (1819–25), and U.S. senator from Ohio (1825–28). President John Quincy Adams appointed him as minister to Colombia (1828–29).

In 1834 Harrison was given the lucrative post of court clerk in Hamilton County, Ohio.

Dissident Whigs nominated Harrison for President in 1836. He came in second in a field of five, losing to Martin Van Buren.

In 1840 the Whig Party nominated him with John Tyler as his running mate. This second campaign, a successful one against Van Buren, is memorable for its slogan "Tippecanoe and Tyler too" and for its demagogy.

Anna Tuthill Symmes Harrison (1775–1864), the 20-year-old daughter of a well-to-do Ohio landowner, married Harrison in 1795. They had 10 children. A grandson, Benjamin Harrison, became the 23d U.S. President.

JOHN TYLER

10th President
(1841–45)

Tyler was the first Vice President to succeed to the presidency because of the death of the incumbent, William Henry Harrison.

Never did a President prove more disappointing to the party that had placed him in office.

An ex-Democrat and a cultured Virginian, Tyler was nominated to run on Harrison's ticket as Vice President to attract Southern votes.

But when he became President, Tyler soon showed that all he had in common with Whig regulars was his antagonism to Jacksonian Democrats.

Tyler was born on March 29, 1790, in Charles City County, Va., the son of a prominent lawyer-politician. He graduated from the College of William and Mary at 17, was admitted to the bar at 19, and entered politics at 21 as a member of Virginia's state legislature. He served in Congress and as governor of Virginia before being elected Vice President. Exactly one month after taking office he succeeded Harrison, who died on April 4, 1841.

Within five months Tyler had twice vetoed a keystone measure of the Whigs—a bill to reestablish the national bank. As a result, his entire cabinet resigned, with the exception of Daniel Webster, secretary of state. Webster negotiated the Webster-Ashburton Treaty in 1842, settling a serious Canadian boundary dispute. Tyler was denounced by the Whigs and had few friends among the Democrats.

Despite strong opposition, Tyler advanced the annexation of Texas, which had won its independence from Mexico and was applying for statehood. An antislavery bloc in the Senate delayed ratification of the annexation treaty, but Tyler outmaneuvered them. Three days before his term ended, an annexation resolution was passed.

Whigs turned their backs on Tyler in 1844, choosing Clay as their presidential nominee. Tyler remained in virtual retirement for years, but in 1861 he presided over an unsuccessful Washington conference called to avert civil war. He then threw his support to the Confederacy. Tyler died on Jan. 18, 1862, in Richmond, Va.

Letitia Christian Tyler (1790–1842), who married Tyler in 1813, was an invalid when he became President. She died during his second year in office.

Julia Gardiner Tyler (1820–89), who was 30 years his junior, became his second wife in 1844. The first President to marry while in office, Tyler had 15 children, eight by his first wife. All but one lived to maturity. The last died in 1947.

TYLER'S PRESIDENTIAL ADMINISTRATION

Congresses in Session:
27th, 28th

Vice President:
Vacant

Secretary of State:
Daniel Webster, 1841–43
Abel Upshur, 1843–44
John Calhoun, 1844–45

Postmaster General:
Francis Granger, 1841
Charles Wickliffe, 1841–45

Secretary of the Treasury:
Thomas Ewing, 1841
Walter Forward, 1841–43
John Spencer, 1843–44
George Bibb, 1844–45

Secretary of War:
John Bell, 1841
John Spencer, 1841–43
James Porter, 1843–44
Williams Wilkins, 1844–45

Attorney General:
John Crittenden, 1841
Hugh Legaré, 1841–43
John Nelson, 1843–45

Secretary of the Navy:
George Badger, 1841
Abel Upshur, 1841–43
David Henshaw, 1843–44
Thomas W. Gilmer, 1844
John Mason, 1844–45

QUICK QUIZ: What is the order of the U.S. presidential succession? See page 250.

JAMES KNOX POLK

11th President (1845–49)

At the 1844 Democratic convention a deadlock was broken when James K. Polk, supported by Andrew Jackson, was proposed as the nominee who could unite the opposing factions. His selection on the ninth ballot made him the first "dark horse" presidential candidate. As Jackson's protégé, Polk was called "Young Hickory" by his supporters.

An avowed expansionist in the age of "manifest destiny," Polk campaigned on promises of annexing Texas and expanding the Oregon Territory in the northwest. He narrowly defeated Whig candidate Henry Clay.

Born on Nov. 2, 1795, in Mecklenburg County, N.C., he was the son of Samuel Polk, a well-to-do farmer, and Jane Knox Polk. The family moved to Tennessee in 1806. Polk graduated from the University of North Carolina in 1818 and began to practice law in Columbia, Tenn., two years later.

He entered politics as a Jacksonian Democrat. His fiery campaigning won him the nickname "Napoleon of the Stump" and got him elected to the Tennessee legislature.

He then served seven consecutive terms in Congress (1825–39). He became chairman of the powerful Ways and Means Committee and then majority leader of the Democratic Party. During his last four years in Congress he was Speaker of the House. In 1839 he was elected governor of Tennessee, serving until 1841.

After Polk took office as President in 1845, he sent a personal emissary, John Slidell, to Mexico to try to buy New Mexico and California. When the Mexican government refused to receive Slidell, Polk sent troops under Gen. Zachary Taylor to the disputed Rio Grande boundary. Mexican troops attacked, and Polk claimed war had begun "by act of Mexico."

Congress declared war on Mexico on May 13, 1846. A succession of American victories culminated in the capture of the Mexican capital.

The Mexican War ended with the Treaty of Guadalupe Hidalgo, signed Feb. 2, 1848. Mexico accepted payment of $15 million for territory that was to become California, New Mexico, Arizona, Nevada, Utah, and parts of Colorado and Wyoming—the largest accession of territory since the Louisiana Purchase. Polk blocked the Wilmot Proviso, an attempt to exclude slavery from the new acquisitions.

In the meantime he had negotiated a Canadian boundary agreement with Britain in the Oregon Treaty of June 15, 1846. Ignoring his campaign slogan—"54°40′ or Fight!"—Polk accepted the 49th parallel as the boundary with Canada.

Polk also tried to purchase Cuba from Spain for $100 million, but his offer was rejected.

Life in the White House was straitlaced during the Polk administration. Polk was a pious Methodist, and his wife was a strict Presbyterian. They banned dancing, card playing, and alcoholic beverages from the White House. And they installed the first gas lighting, replacing candles and oil lamps.

During the negotiations that led to Texas joining the Union and becoming the 28th state in 1845, Sam Houston remarked that the only thing wrong with Polk was that he drank too much water.

Former President John Quincy Adams wrote of Polk: "He has no wit, no literature, no point of argument, no gracefulness of delivery, no elegance of language, no philosophy, no pathos, no felicitous impromptus; nothing that can constitute an orator, but confidence, fluency, and labor."

Under constant harassment in Congress, not only from the Whig opposition but from resentful Northern Democrats, Polk labored strenuously to the detriment of his health. He refused renomination and died on June 15, 1849.

Sarah Childress Polk (1803–91) married Polk in 1824. They had no children of their own, but Mrs. Polk later adopted a daughter.

POLK'S PRESIDENTIAL ADMINISTRATION

Congresses in Session:
29th, 30th

Vice President:
George Dallas, 1845–49

Secretary of State:
James Buchanan, 1845–49

Secretary of the Treasury:
Robert Walker, 1845–49

Secretary of War:
William Marcy, 1845–49

Secretary of the Navy:
George Bancroft, 1845–46
John Mason, 1846–49

Attorney General:
John Mason, 1845–46
Nathan Clifford, 1846–48
Isaac Toucey, 1848–49

Postmaster General:
Cave Johnson, 1845–49

PRESIDENTIAL ELECTION OF 1844

Nominations: At the Whig convention in Baltimore, May 1, 1844, Clay was chosen on the first ballot by acclamation. On the third ballot Frelinghuysen received 155 out of 275 votes, and then his vice-presidential nomination was made unanimous. The Democrats met in Baltimore, May 27–30, 1844. Although Van Buren had a majority of the votes, he could not obtain the necessary two-thirds majority. On the ninth ballot Polk was nominated. Dallas received the vice-presidential nomination on the second ballot, after Silas Wright had declined the nomination. The Liberty Party met in Buffalo, N. Y., Aug. 30, 1843, and unanimously nominated its candidates, Birney and Morris. **Campaign Issues:** Foreign and domestic issues included whether Texas should be annexed to the U.S. as a slave state, whether the tariff should be lowered, and what steps should be taken to settle the Oregon boundary dispute with Britain.

PRESIDENTIAL CANDIDATES	PARTY	ELECTORAL VOTES	POPULAR VOTE Total	Percentage	VICE-PRESIDENTIAL CANDIDATES
James K. Polk	Democratic	170	1,338,464	49.6	George M. Dallas
Henry Clay	Whig	105	1,300,097	48.1	Theodore Frelinghuysen
James G. Birney.......	Liberty	—	62,300	2.3	Thomas Morris

ZACHARY TAYLOR

12th President
(1849–50)

Taylor's path to the White House was paved during the Mexican War, some two years before the 1848 Whig convention nominated him. In May 1846, soon after two victories by General Taylor's forces, it was predicted he would be elected President. Taylor scoffed at the idea, but within two years the nonpolitical hero accepted the Whig presidential nomination.

Zachary Taylor was born on Nov. 24, 1784, in Orange County, Va., while his family was on its way to a new home in Kentucky. His parents were Richard and Sarah Dabney Strother Taylor.

In 1808 he was commissioned a first lieutenant in the Army. Following his victory over the Seminoles at Lake Okeechobee, Fla., Taylor was promoted to brigadier general in 1837. He earned the nickname "Old Rough and Ready" in the Florida campaign.

In 1845 he was given command of the army in Texas. During the Mexican War he was at times defiant to the point of insubordination. An armistice Taylor granted after seizing Monterrey in 1846 created serious friction with President Polk, who thought the terms were too lenient. Taylor ignored orders to hold his position. Instead, in February 1847 he led his troops a few miles south, where he defeated numerically superior Mexican forces at Buena Vista. Taylor returned home to national acclaim.

Although a slaveholder and a conservative, Taylor was under the influence of Sen. William H. Seward (New York), leader of the antislavery Whigs. Taylor campaigned on his war record.

Taylor became the first person to win the presidency without having been previously elected to public office. Because March 4 fell on Sunday, Taylor postponed his inauguration to March 5.

Taylor's call in 1850 for admission to statehood of antislavery California alienated his Southern Whig supporters.

When Southern leaders threatened to drive federal troops from New Mexico to prevent it from becoming an antislavery state, Taylor warned he would take command of the Army.

Sen. Henry Clay offered the Compromise of 1850 in an effort to placate both North and South. President Taylor probably would have vetoed the Compromise, but he died of cholera on July 9, 1850.

Margaret Mackall Smith Taylor (1788–1852) married Taylor in 1810. They had six children.

TAYLOR'S PRESIDENTIAL ADMINISTRATION

Congress in Session: 31st
Vice President: Millard Fillmore, 1849–50
Secretary of State: John Clayton, 1849–50
Secretary of the Treasury: William M. Meredith, 1849–50
Secretary of War: George Crawford, 1849–50
Attorney General: Reverdy Johnson, 1849–50
Postmaster General: Jacob Collamer, 1849–50
Secretary of the Navy: William B. Preston, 1849–50
Secretary of the Interior: Thomas Ewing, 1849–50

PRESIDENTIAL ELECTION OF 1848

Nominations: The Democratic convention in Baltimore, May 22–26, 1848, chose Lewis Cass on the fourth ballot. Butler was chosen on the second ballot with 169 out of 253 votes cast. The Whig convention in Philadelphia, June 7–9, 1848, chose Taylor by a majority vote on the fourth ballot. Fillmore was chosen on the second ballot. The Free Soil Party convention in Buffalo, N.Y., Aug. 9–10, 1848, unanimously nominated Van Buren and Adams.

PRESIDENTIAL CANDIDATES	PARTY	ELECTORAL VOTES	POPULAR VOTE Total	Percentage	VICE-PRESIDENTIAL CANDIDATES
Zachary Taylor	Whig	163	1,360,967	47.3	Millard Fillmore
Lewis Cass	Democratic	127	1,222,342	42.5	William O. Butler
Martin Van Buren	Free Soil	—	291,263	10.1	Charles Francis Adams

MILLARD FILLMORE

13th President
(1850–53)

Fillmore took office on July 10, 1850, the day after President Taylor died. During his administration he sought to preserve the Union by conciliating the South. But the nation had become too deeply divided on the slavery issue, and his attempt to carry out the Compromise of 1850 alienated both sides. In particular, his strict enforcement of the Fugitive Slave Law of 1850 aroused the wrath of the antislavery wing of the Whig Party.

Two measures he did not initiate are also associated with Fillmore's administration. One was the dispatch of Commodore Perry to Japan to open that country's ports to U.S. trade. The other was the reorganization of the postal department to provide cheaper mail rates.

Fillmore was born on Jan. 7, 1800, in Locke, N.Y., the son of Nathaniel Fillmore, a farmer, and Phoebe Millard Fillmore.

As a youth he worked at odd jobs to earn a living, and was largely self-educated. He read law in his spare time, winning admission to the bar in 1823. After practicing briefly in East Aurora, N.Y., he moved to Buffalo.

Fillmore's political career began in 1828 when he was elected to the New York assembly. He went on to serve four terms in Congress, beginning in 1833. A Whig, he became chairman of the

QUICK QUIZ: What is the highest point in Europe? See page 178.

MILLARD FILLMORE *(continued)*
powerful House Ways and Means Committee in 1841–43.

Defeated as the Whig candidate for governor of New York in 1844, Fillmore became state comptroller.

Because of the strong stand Fillmore had taken against the extension of slavery into the territories, Henry Clay backed him for the vice presidency on the successful Whig ticket in 1848. His position was intended to offset the supposed proslavery sympathies of presidential candidate Zachary Taylor.

Fillmore lost the Whigs' support in 1852, and their presidential nomination went to Gen. Winfield Scott, who favored a more radical antislavery program.

Fillmore attempted to regain the presidency in 1856 when he accepted the presidential nomination of the anti-Catholic, antiforeigner American (Know-Nothing) Party. In the election he won only eight electoral votes. Fillmore died in Buffalo, N.Y., on March 8, 1874.

Abigail Powers Fillmore (1798–1853), daughter of a Baptist clergyman, married Fillmore in 1826. They had two children. She was too ill to preside at White House functions. During her tenancy the first cooking stove was installed in the White House kitchen, replacing fireplace cookery. She died a month after Fillmore completed his presidential term.

Caroline Carmichael (McIntosh) Fillmore (1813–81), a wealthy widow, became Fillmore's second wife in 1858.

FILLMORE'S PRESIDENTIAL ADMINISTRATION

Congresses in Session:
31st, 32d

Vice President:
Vacant

Secretary of State:
Daniel Webster, 1850–52
Edward Everett, 1852–53

Secretary of the Treasury:
Thomas Corwin, 1850–53

Secretary of War:
Charles Conrad, 1850–53

Postmaster General:
Nathan Hall, 1850–52
Samuel Hubbard, 1852–53

Attorney General:
John J. Crittenden, 1850–53

Secretary of the Navy:
William Graham, 1850–52
John Kennedy, 1852–53

Secretary of the Interior:
T.M.T. McKennan, 1850
Alexander Stuart, 1850–53

FRANKLIN PIERCE

14th President
(1853–57)

Pierce began his presidency under an emotional strain. Shortly before his term began, he and his wife saw their only surviving son killed in a train wreck. Mrs. Pierce, who disliked both Washington and her husband's involvement in politics, became withdrawn and was infrequently seen in public.

A Northern Democrat, Pierce misjudged the nation's growing animosity to slavery. In the presidential election campaign, he had promised to prevent slavery from becoming a divisive political issue. But his willingness to aid Southern Democrats in the extension of slavery to new states added new fuel to the flames of the slavery controversy.

Born on Nov. 23, 1804, in Hillsboro, N.H., he was the son of Anna Kendrick Pierce and Benjamin Pierce, a Revolutionary War general and twice New Hampshire governor. He attended Bowdoin College and was admitted to the bar in 1827.

Pierce entered politics as a Jacksonian Democrat and served two terms as a congressman in 1833–37. In 1836, at 32, he became one of the youngest men elected to the U.S. Senate. He resigned eight years later because of his wife's ill health. Pierce practiced law in Concord, N.H., and became leader of the state's Democratic Party. He served as a brigadier general of New England volunteers in the Mexican War.

Pierce was chosen president of the New Hampshire constitutional convention in 1850.

A delegate to the Democratic convention in 1852, Pierce emerged as a dark-horse presidential contender. His nomination on the 49th ballot broke a hopeless deadlock among the front-runners. As a Northerner with pro-South sympathies, he was deemed acceptable to both sides. Pierce went on to defeat the Whig candidate, Winfield Scott, his Mexican War commander.

Believing that conciliation of the South would preserve the Union, he endorsed the Southern doctrine that the constitutional provisions on

PIERCE'S PRESIDENTIAL ADMINISTRATION

Congresses in Session
33d, 34th

Vice President:
William King, 1853

Secretary of State:
William Marcy, 1853–57

Secretary of the Treasury:
James Guthrie, 1853–57

Secretary of War:
Jefferson Davis, 1853–57

Attorney General:
Caleb Cushing, 1853–57

Postmaster General:
James Campbell, 1853–57

Secretary of the Navy:
James Dobbin, 1853–57

Secretary of the Interior:
Robert McCleland, 1853–57

PRESIDENTIAL ELECTION OF 1852

Nominations: At the Whig convention in Baltimore, June 17–20, 1852, Scott received a majority on the 53d ballot. The Democratic convention in Baltimore, June 1–5, 1852, deadlocked between James Buchanan and Lewis Cass. Pierce was entered as a dark horse on the 35th ballot and won on the 49th ballot. **Campaign Issues:** Personalities.

PRESIDENTIAL CANDIDATES	PARTY	ELECTORAL VOTES	POPULAR VOTE Total	POPULAR VOTE Percentage	VICE-PRESIDENTIAL CANDIDATES
Franklin Pierce	Democratic	254	1,601,117	50.9	William R. King
Winfield Scott	Whig	42	1,385,453	44.1	William A. Graham
John P. Hale	Free Soil	—	155,825	5.0	George Julian

property rights meant a guarantee of slavery.

He helped push through the Kansas-Nebraska Act in 1854 that repealed the Missouri Compromise of 1820, giving settlers in the Kansas Territory the opportunity to vote on the slavery issue. Guerrilla warfare broke out between opposing forces in "Bleeding Kansas," heightening national tensions in 1855–56.

In his expansionist drive Pierce made premature and unsuccessful attempts to buy Alaska from Russia and to annex Hawaii. Another failure was the Ostend Manifesto of 1854. Issued by the American ministers to England, France, and Spain, it proposed annexation of Cuba, presumably as a slave state. Although repudiated by the State Department and the Senate, it raised protests both at home and abroad.

Pierce was more successful with two other enterprises in foreign policy. The Gadsden Purchase for $10 million from Mexico of the southern parts of Arizona and New Mexico was ratified by the Senate on June 29, 1854. That same year Commodore Matthew C. Perry signed a treaty that opened Japan's ports to shippers.

Pierce had expected to be renominated by the 1856 Democratic national convention. Instead, he was humiliatingly rejected because of his support of the Kansas-Nebraska Act.

At the end of his term Pierce toured Europe and then returned to Concord.

In 1860 Pierce supported Jefferson Davis, his former secretary of war, as the man the Democrats should nominate for President. His opposition to the Civil War and to Lincoln's administration increased his unpopularity. He died in obscurity on Oct. 8, 1869.

Jane Means Appleton Pierce (1806–63), Pierce's wife, was the daughter of a president of Bowdoin College. None of the couple's three sons survived to maturity. While she was First Lady, the White House was equipped for the first time with a coal-burning furnace for central heating.

JAMES BUCHANAN

15th President
(1857–61)

Buchanan was the last President chosen because it was believed he would compromise and keep the slavery issue from tearing apart the nation.

He was born on April 23, 1791, in Cove Gap, Pa., the son of James and Elizabeth (Speer) Buchanan. After attending Dickinson College, he was admitted to the bar in 1812. He then built up a lucrative law practice in Lancaster, Pa.

Buchanan served in his state's legislature in both houses of Congress (first as a Federalist, then as a Jacksonian Democrat), as Polk's secretary of state, and as minister to England and Russia. In England he was involved in the notorious Ostend Manifesto proposing annexation of Cuba, even as a slave state. This permanently discredited Buchanan among large groups in the North.

In 1844, 1848, and 1852 Buchanan sought the Democratic presidential nomination.

In 1856 he became the Democratic candidate and defeated John C. Frémont, first candidate of the new Republican Party, as well as Millard Fillmore, candidate of the Whig and American (Know-Nothing) parties. He was the fourth President to enter office with less than a majority of the popular vote.

To meet the growing North-South crisis, Buchanan could only propose preservation of the "sacred balance" between the regions. He avowed personal disapproval of slavery, yet recommended the admission of Kansas as a slave state.

He deplored secession but took no steps to check it by garrisoning federal forts in the South. Even when a U.S. ship was fired on by South Carolina shore batteries, he took no action.

Buchanan's moderate views were disliked and mistrusted by extremists both in the North and in

BUCHANAN'S PRESIDENTIAL ADMINISTRATION

Congresses in Session:
35th, 36th

Vice President:
John C. Breckinridge, 1857–61

Secretary of State:
Lewis Cass, 1857–60
Jeremiah S. Black, 1860–61

Secretary of the Treasury:
Howell Cobb, 1857–60
Philip F. Thomas, 1860–61
John A. Dix, 1861

Secretary of War:
John Floyd, 1857–61
Joseph Holt, 1861

Secretary of the Navy:
Isaac Toucey, 1857–61

Attorney General:
Jeremiah Black, 1857–60
Edwin M. Stanton, 1860–61

Postmaster General:
Aaron Brown, 1857–59
Joseph Holt, 1859–61
Horatio King, 1861

Secretary of the Interior:
Jacob Thompson, 1857–61

PRESIDENTIAL ELECTION OF 1856

Nominations: The Republican convention was held in Philadelphia, June 17–19, 1856. On the first official ballot Frémont got 520 out of 558 votes. Dayton's nomination came on the first ballot. At the Democratic convention in Cincinnati, June 2–6, 1856, Buchanan was chosen on the 17th ballot. The vice-presidential nomination of Breckinridge was unanimous. **Campaign Issue:** Slavery in the Kansas-Nebraska territories was the main issue.

PRESIDENTIAL CANDIDATES	PARTY	ELECTORAL VOTES	POPULAR VOTE Total	Percentage	VICE-PRESIDENTIAL CANDIDATES
James Buchanan	Democratic	174	1,832,955	45.3	John C. Breckinridge
John C. Frémont	Republican	114	1,339,932	33.1	William L. Dayton
Millard Fillmore	American	8	871,731	21.6	Andrew J. Donelson

QUICK QUIZ: When were the first Nobel Prizes awarded? See page 70.

JAMES BUCHANAN *(continued)*

the South. He did not seek renomination.

In the last months of his administration, seven Southern states seceded and formed the Confederate States of America.

When he was 27, Buchanan had been engaged to Ann Caroline Coleman of Lancaster, but she broke the engagement because she believed he only wanted her fortune. So Buchanan became the first bachelor President.

Buchanan's niece Harrict Lane served as White House hostess during his administration.

Seven years after leaving office, Buchanan died in Lancaster on June 1, 1868.

ABRAHAM LINCOLN

16th President
(1861–65)

When Lincoln became President, the nation was divided. In the four months between his election as President and the time he took office, seven Southern states had seceded from the Union and formed the Confederate States of America with Jefferson Davis as President.

On April 12, 1861, Fort Sumter in South Carolina was bombarded by the Confederates, and the Civil War began. Lincoln became the leader of the people of the North.

EARLY YEARS

Lincoln's father, Thomas, was a farmer and carpenter who moved his family from Kentucky to Indiana to Illinois. Abraham was born in a log cabin in Hardin County, Ky., on Feb. 12, 1809. His mother, Nancy Hanks Lincoln, died when he was nine, and his father married Mrs. Sarah Bush Johnston, a widow.

Providing for himself at an early age, Lincoln did handyman jobs, split rails, clerked in a store, surveyed land, delivered merchandise downstream on flatboats to New Orleans, and put his hand to other tasks. In 1831 he settled in the little village of New Salem, Ill., near Springfield. There he became a partner in a grocery store that failed. His partner's death left him with a burden of debts—all of which he eventually paid.

Lincoln grew into a tall, gaunt, muscular man six feet four inches tall, with a ruggedly homely face. Possessed of great physical strength, he often put down bullies. This, along with his talent for pointed storytelling, brought him popularity in the frontier villages where he spent his young manhood.

When Lincoln answered a call for volunteers in the Black Hawk War, he was unanimously elected captain by the men of the New Salem troop. By 1834 he had gathered such a following that he was elected, as a Whig, to the Illinois legislature, where he achieved prominence during his four terms. He was admitted to the bar in 1836 and moved to nearby Springfield. He built up a prosperous law practice in a succession of partnerships, the last with William H. Herndon, who later became his biographer.

Lincoln reentered politics in 1846, again as a Whig, and was overwhelmingly elected to Congress. There his opposition to the Mexican War cost him the backing of expansionist-minded constituents. He served only one term.

In 1854, however, he was goaded out of retirement by indignation over the Kansas-Nebraska Act favoring the extension of slavery, which had been sponsored by Illinois Democratic Sen. Stephen A. Douglas. Lincoln ran for the Senate on the Whig ticket but was defeated. The next year he joined the newly formed Republican Party. He was among the candidates for its vice-presidential nomination, polling an impressive though not winning vote.

In 1858 Lincoln became his party's candidate for U.S. senator. One of the ringing phrases in his acceptance speech, "A house divided against itself cannot stand," helped spread his renown. His debates with Douglas, his Democratic opponent, drew nationwide attention. Lincoln asserted he was not an abolitionist, but that he regarded slavery as an injustice and an evil. He was adamantly opposed to its extension. Although Douglas won the close election, Lincoln, through his masterful exposition, had made his mark and had become widely known.

At the Republican convention in 1860, William H. Seward was the leading contender. But there was an early swing to Lincoln, who was nominated on the third ballot. With the Democrats split between Northern and Southern wings, Republican victory was inevitable. After Lincoln's election, the Southern states began seceding from the Union.

CIVIL WAR PRESIDENT

From the beginning of hostilities Lincoln faced staggering difficulties, but he attacked the vast problems with vigor and surpassing skill. Lincoln pressed onward with the war, but even when prosecuting Southern sympathizers in the North—for which he was criticized—he sought to temper punishment with mercy.

On April 14, 1861, two days after the Confederate attack on Fort Sumter, Lincoln called for 75,000 volunteers to fight the rebels. He also ordered a blockade of Southern ports to cut them off from supplies the South needed.

Hopes by Northerners for a quick victory were dashed by the Union defeat in the First Battle of Bull Run in Virginia on July 21, 1861.

Lincoln was beset not only by the difficulties of the war but by opposition from men on his own side. Radical abolitionists condemned him as weak. Conservatives accused him of dictatorship. Jealousies and hatreds caused continual friction in his cabinet. In the midst of all this strife Lincoln continued his course with wisdom and patience, sometimes standing nearly alone.

Lincoln had offered command of the Union Army to Gen. Robert E. Lee. But Lee turned the appointment down, deciding to help his native state of Virginia by accepting command of Confederate forces. Lee inflicted a series of defeats on Northern troops while Lincoln searched for a Union general who could fight.

The dubious Northern victory at Antietam in

1862 gave Lincoln the opportunity to make a great stroke by issuing the Emancipation Proclamation, which proclaimed freedom for slaves in Confederate-controlled states.

The proclamation caused renewed enthusiasm for the war. But the fighting progressed without a decisive success until the Confederacy's defeat in 1863 at Gettysburg, Pa., where Lincoln later delivered his famous Gettysburg Address.

In 1864, after Ulysses S. Grant became commander of the Union Army and William T. Sherman took Atlanta, Lincoln's perseverance seemed vindicated.

With victory clearly in sight, the Republican Party, which had been on the point of abandoning him, rallied to Lincoln. He was renominated and reelected in 1864, defeating former Union army commander George McClellan.

In his celebrated second inaugural address, Lincoln outlined his postwar program. He would show "malice toward none" and grant "charity for all." His policy would be based on peace without retribution.

A month after Lincoln's second inauguration Lee surrendered on April 9, 1865, to Grant at Appomattox Court House, Va.

But Lincoln's dream of restoring the Union in harmony was brought to an abrupt end on April 14, 1865, when actor John Wilkes Booth, a Southern fanatic, shot him at Ford's Theater in Washington. Lincoln died the next day.

Mary Todd Lincoln (1818–82) of Kentucky became Lincoln's wife in 1842 after a troubled courtship. Their marriage was not an easy one, but Mrs. Lincoln served capably as White House hostess. Because she had several relatives in the Confederate Army, her loyalty to the North was questioned.

The Lincolns had four sons: Robert Todd Lincoln (1843–1926), Edward Baker Lincoln (1846–50), William Wallace Lincoln (1850–62), and Thomas "Tad" Lincoln (1853–71).

Only one son, Robert Todd Lincoln, lived to manhood, becoming secretary of war under Presidents Garfield and Arthur.

One of their sons died at the age of four in Springfield, another in the White House at the age of 12.

The first two deaths of her sons, her husband's assassination while at her side, and the death of their youngest son at age 18 in 1871 are said to have affected Mrs. Lincoln's mind. She was temporarily committed to a private sanatorium in Batavia, Ill., in 1875.

LINCOLN'S PRESIDENTIAL ADMINISTRATION

Congresses in Session:
37th, 38th, 39th

Vice President:
Hannibal Hamlin, 1861–65
Andrew Johnson, 1865

Secretary of State:
William Seward, 1861–65

Secretary of the Treasury:
Salmon Chase, 1861–64
William Fessenden, 1864–65
Hugh McCulloch, 1865

Secretary of War:
Simon Cameron, 1861–62
Edwin McM. Stanton, 1862–65

Secretary of the Navy:
Gideon Welles, 1861–65

Attorney General:
Edward Bates, 1861–64
James Speed, 1864–65

Postmaster General:
Montgomery Blair, 1861–64
William Dennison, 1864–65

Secretary of the Interior:
Caleb Smith, 1861–63
John Usher, 1863–65

PRESIDENTIAL ELECTION OF 1860

Nominations: The Democrats met in Charleston, S.C., April 23–May 3, 1860. They failed to choose a candidate, and many Southerners bolted the party. The convention reassembled in Baltimore on June 18 and met through June 23. Finally, after more Southerners had left, Douglas was nominated. The vice-presidential nominee, Benjamin Fitzpatrick of Alabama, declined the honor, and the party national committee chose Johnson. Many of the "bolters," who called themselves National Democrats, met in Baltimore, June 23, 1860, and chose Breckinridge and Lane. The Republicans met in Chicago, May 16–18, 1860. Sen. William H. Seward of New York was favored to win the nomination. On the third ballot Lincoln received a majority, and the nomination was then made unanimous. Hamlin was chosen on the second ballot. The Constitutional Union Party met in Baltimore, May 9–10, 1860, choosing former Secretary of War John Bell as their candidate. **Campaign Issues:** The campaign centered on slavery and the status of the Union.

PRESIDENTIAL CANDIDATES	PARTY	ELECTORAL VOTES	POPULAR VOTE Total	Percentage	VICE-PRESIDENTIAL CANDIDATES
Abraham Lincoln	Republican	180	1,865,593	39.8	Hannibal Hamlin
John C. Breckinridge	Southern Democratic	72	848,356	18.1	Joseph Lane
Stephen A. Douglas	Democratic	12	1,382,713	29.5	Herschel V. Johnson
John Bell	Constitutional Union	30	592,906	12.6	Edward Everett

PRESIDENTIAL ELECTION OF 1864

Nominations: The Republicans, who had been joined by the prowar Democrats (Johnson was one), met as the National Union Party in Baltimore, June 7–8, 1864. Lincoln on a roll-call vote on the first ballot received all but 22 votes (which went to U.S. Grant), and his nomination was then made unanimous. By the end of the first ballot, after switching had taken place, Johnson had received 494 out of 500 votes and the vice-presidential nomination. The Democratic convention met in Chicago, Aug. 29–31, 1864, and McClellan, the former Union Army commanding general who had been dismissed by Lincoln, was chosen on the third ballot. Pendleton was selected as the vice-presidential candidate on the first ballot. **Campaign Issue:** Democrats criticized Lincoln's conduct of the Civil War.

PRESIDENTIAL CANDIDATES	PARTY	ELECTORAL VOTES	POPULAR VOTE Total	Percentage	VICE-PRESIDENTIAL CANDIDATES
Abraham Lincoln	Republican	212	2,206,938	55.0	Andrew Johnson
George McClellan	Democratic	21	1,803,787	45.0	George Pendleton
Votes not cast	—	81	—	—	—

QUICK QUIZ: What was the average cost per gallon of gasoline in the U.S. in 1968? See page 255.

ANDREW JOHNSON

17th President
(1865–69)

Succeeding to the presidency on the death of Lincoln, Andrew Johnson was a Southerner and a Democrat. The political split that developed between Johnson and the powerful Radical Republicans led to the first effort to remove a President of the United States by impeachment.

Born on Dec. 29, 1808, in Raleigh, N.C., Johnson was the son of Jacob and Mary McDonough Johnson. His father died when Andrew was three. At the age of 13 Johnson was apprenticed to a tailor. In 1826 he moved to Greeneville, Tenn.

EARLY CAREER

Unable to write or do arithmetic when he married at the age of 18, Johnson learned how with the help of his wife. He prospered as a tailor, and his shop became well known. Many other craftsmen, as well as laborers and farmers, met there to discuss community and general public affairs. The best debater in Greeneville, Johnson was frequently in the public eye.

At 19 Johnson won office as town alderman, and at 21 became mayor of Greeneville. He next served six years in the state legislature. He was elected to the U.S. House of Representatives (1843–53), governor of Tennessee (1853–57), and to the U.S. Senate (1857–62).

Although a slaveowner, Johnson vigorously opposed secession. Alone among Southern senators, he did not resign when secession began. In 1862 Lincoln appointed him military governor of Tennessee, and by 1864 Johnson had organized a loyal government there. For this achievement he was named Lincoln's running mate on the Republican ticket in 1864.

At the inauguration, March 4, 1865, when he was sworn in as Vice President, Johnson seemed to be drunk. President Lincoln cut off criticism with the remark, "He ain't no drunkard."

When he assumed the presidency on April 15, 1865, Johnson reverted to his earlier Democratic positions on tariffs, banking, internal improvements, and other issues, in opposition to the Republican Party. But the chief issue in his conflict with the Radical Republicans was their harsh Reconstruction policy.

Johnson intended to follow Lincoln's program of reconciliation with the South. He extended full amnesty to participants in the secession. But he opposed extension of full civil rights to Negroes on constitutional grounds and, in general, manifested Southern sympathies. Political attacks on Johnson became increasingly harsh.

When Congress passed a series of acts over his veto, including the Civil Rights Act of 1866, he appealed to the electorate in the congressional elections. Baited by mobs and slandered by the press, he lashed out at his political enemies in such harsh terms that he did great harm to his own cause. The Radicals won, and the conflict between Congress and the President intensified.

Although the problems of the postwar South dominated Johnson's administration, there were successes in foreign affairs, notably the 1867 purchase of Alaska from Russia negotiated by Secretary of State William Seward for the price of $7,200,000.

PRESIDENTIAL IMPEACHMENT

In 1867 Congress passed, over Johnson's veto, the Tenure of Office Act, which forbade the removal of any official appointed with the confirmation of the Senate. Johnson believed the act was unconstitutional (and 59 years later the U.S. Supreme Court upheld his judgment). He defied Congress by firing Secretary of War Edwin M. Stanton, replacing him with Gen. Ulysses S. Grant, who gave the office back to Stanton in February 1868. Johnson fired Stanton again, appointing Lorenzo Thomas to the post.

The Radical Republicans, led by Thaddeus Stevens, brought impeachment charges against Johnson for violation of the Tenure of Office Act. This first try failed, but on Feb. 24, 1868, the House passed a resolution of impeachment by a vote of 126 to 47.

On March 5, 1868, the Senate was organized as a court to hear the charges. The Senate on May 16 voted 35 to 19 against President Johnson, one vote shy of the required two-thirds majority needed to convict him. The vote that saved him was cast by Edmund G. Ross, a freshman Radical Republican senator from Kansas.

Despite a series of disappointments that might have deterred another man, Johnson continued his political activity. He sought and failed to win the nomination for President on the Democratic ticket in 1868, for U.S. senator in 1869, and for representative in 1872. But in 1874 he became the first former President to be elected to the U.S. Senate. A few months after reentering the Senate to represent Tennessee, he died on July 31, 1875.

Eliza McCardle Johnson (1810–76) married Andrew Johnson in 1827 when she was 16. She helped him learn to write and do arithmetic. They had three sons and two daughters. She was an invalid during her husband's term. Their daughter Martha served as the President's chief White House hostess.

ANDREW JOHNSON'S PRESIDENTIAL ADMINISTRATION

Congresses in Session:
39th, 40th

Vice President:
Vacant

Secretary of State:
William Seward, 1865–69

Secretary of the Treasury:
Hugh McCulloch, 1865–69

Attorney General:
James Speed, 1865–66
Henry Stanbery, 1866–68
William Evarts, 1868–69

Postmaster General:
William Dennison, 1865–66
Alexander Randall, 1866–69

Secretary of the Navy:
Gideon Welles, 1865–69

Secretary of War:
Edwin M. Stanton, 1865–67, 1868
Ulysses S. Grant, 1867–68
Lorenzo Thomas, 1868
John Schofield, 1868–69

Secretary of the Interior:
John P. Usher, 1865
James Harlan, 1865–66
Orville Browning, 1866–69

ULYSSES SIMPSON GRANT

18th President
(1869–77)

Grant's administrations were characterized by bitter politics and notorious corruption. A punitive Reconstruction policy gave supremacy to Northern bankers, speculators, and industrialists. It also encouraged the "carpetbaggers" who moved south to exploit both recently freed slaves and the defeated whites, helping to prolong the sectional division of the country between North and South.

Grant allowed himself to become the dupe of the "robber barons" of his time and of the shady politicians associated with them. During his two terms scandals were exposed involving cabinet members, his own secretary, and a number of congressmen. His administrations were characterized by bitter politics and corruption.

EARLY CAREER

He was born on April 27, 1822, in Point Pleasant, Ohio, the son of Jesse Root and Hannah (Simpson) Grant. He switched his given names, Hiram Ulysses, when still a boy. Then "Hiram" became "Simpson" through a clerical error when he applied for admission to West Point. Grant accepted the name change. He graduated in 1843, served with distinction in the Mexican War, and was promoted twice.

In 1854 Grant was forced to resign from the Army because of excessive drinking. He unsuccessfully tried farming, real estate, and storekeeping.

The Civil War proved his opportunity. Responding to President Lincoln's call for volunteers, he was eventually given command of a detachment of Illinois trainees. He showed outstanding ability in minor military actions and was promoted to brigadier general.

After training and mobilizing a force of 17,000 men, he conducted a bold operation against two

GRANT'S PRESIDENTIAL ADMINISTRATION

Congresses in Session:
41st, 42d, 43d, 44th
Vice President:
Schuyler Colfax, 1869–73
Henry Wilson, 1873–75
Secretary of State:
Elihu B. Washburne, 1869
Hamilton Fish, 1869–77
Postmaster General:
John Creswell, 1869–74
James W. Marshall, 1867
Marshall Jewell, 1874–76
James Tyner, 1876–77

Secretary of the Treasury:
Alexander T. Stewart, 1869
George Boutwell, 1869–73
William Richardson, 1873–74
Benjamin Bristow, 1874–76
Lot Morrill, 1876–77

Attorney General:
Ebenezer Hoar, 1869–70
Amos Akerman, 1870–71
George Williams, 1871–75
Edwards Pierrepont, 1875–76
Alphonso Taft, 1876–77

Secretary of War:
John Rawlins, 1869
William T. Sherman, 1869
William Belknap, 1869–76
Alphonso Taft, 1876
James Cameron, 1876–77
Secretary of the Navy:
Adolph Borie, 1869
George Robeson, 1869–77
Secretary of the Interior:
Jacob Cox, 1869–70
Columbus Delano, 1870–75
Zachariah Chandler, 1875–77

PRESIDENTIAL ELECTION OF 1868

Nominations: The Republican convention met in Chicago, May 20–21, 1868, and chose Grant. The Democratic Party met in New York City, July 4–9, 1868, nominated Seymour on the 22d ballot, and declared the nomination unanimous. **Campaign Issues:** A paramount issue was Reconstruction of the Confederate states, with the Republicans in favor of harsh measures. **Remarks:** Mississippi, Texas, and Virginia did not participate in the presidential election.

PRESIDENTIAL CANDIDATES	PARTY	ELECTORAL VOTES	POPULAR VOTE		VICE-PRESIDENTIAL CANDIDATES
			Total	Percentage	
Ulysses S. Grant	Republican	214	3,013,421	52.7	Schuyler Colfax
Horatio Seymour	Democratic	80	2,703,829	47.3	Francis P. Blair Jr.
Votes not cast	—	23	—	—	—

PRESIDENTIAL ELECTION OF 1872

Nominations: Liberal Republicans, who had defected from the Republican Party because they were dissatisfied with Grant, met in Cincinnati, May 1, 1872, and nominated Greeley and Brown on the sixth ballot. Democrats, meeting in Baltimore, July 9–10, 1872, accepted Greeley and Brown on the first ballot. The Republican convention in Philadelphia, June 5–6, 1872, chose Grant and Wilson. **Campaign Issues:** Besides Reconstruction and the "bloody shirt" (as vengeance against the South was called), other important issues were corruption in government and the desirability of issuing paper money, which many debtors thought would aid them. Republicans ridiculed Greeley as a lifelong opponent of Democrats who now ran on their ticket. **Remarks:** Greeley died after the election but before the Electoral College met. His electoral votes went to: Thomas A. Hendricks (42); Benjamin G. Brown (18); Charles J. Jenkins (2); David Davis (1); and 3 Greeley votes were not counted. Congress rejected Greeley votes from Arkansas, Louisiana, and Georgia.

PRESIDENTIAL CANDIDATES	PARTY	ELECTORAL VOTES	POPULAR VOTE		VICE-PRESIDENTIAL CANDIDATES	ELECTORAL VOTES
			Total	Percentage		
Ulysses S. Grant	Republican	286	3,596,745	55.6	Henry Wilson	286
Horace Greeley	Democratic–Liberal Rep.	—	2,843,446	44.0	Benjamin G. Brown	47
Charles O'Connor	Straight Dem.	—	29,489	0.4	John Quincy Adams	—
Other candidates	—	63	—	—	Other candidates	—
Votes not cast	—	17	—	—	Votes not cast	—

QUICK QUIZ: How old must a person be to be elected U.S. senator? See page 159.

ULYSSES S. GRANT *(continued)*
Confederate strongholds, Fort Henry and Fort Donelson, on the Tennessee and Cumberland rivers. It was the first major Union victory. From that time on, his military career was an almost continuous succession of triumphs, the most brilliant being the capture of Vicksburg in 1863, which cleared the Mississippi down to the sea and split the Confederacy in two.

Satisfied that he had at last found his general, Lincoln in 1864 put Grant in supreme command of the Union armies.

Grant pushed the Confederate Army south into Virginia while Gen. William T. Sherman advanced from the west to Atlanta, Ga. On April 9, 1865, Grant accepted the surrender of Gen. Robert E. Lee at Appomattox Court House, Va. His surrender terms to Lee and his treatment of the defeated Confederates were compassionate and magnanimous.

18th PRESIDENT OF THE UNITED STATES

A national hero, Grant was the Republican choice in the presidential election of 1868. He was nominated on the first ballot and easily won the presidency. At 46 he was the youngest man to become President to that time. His first term was tinged with scandal when his brother-in-law conspired with New York financier Jay Gould to corner the gold market.

In 1869 Grant approved a treaty with the Dominican Republic to annex that country. But the Senate rejected the treaty.

Grant's renomination for a second term was unanimous, and he was reelected by another landslide. His second term was wracked with scandals, leading to the resignations of two of his cabinet officers and the conviction of many government officials.

In 1880 his backers, the Stalwarts, led by Sen. Roscoe Conkling, failed to obtain Grant's nomination for a third term.

Moving to New York City, among his new financier associates, Grant invested his funds in a fraudulent banking firm. When it went bankrupt in 1884, Congress granted him some relief by reappointing him general at full pay and later by adding retirement pay.

Determined to provide for his family, Grant set to work on his memoirs. Although suffering from cancer of the throat, he kept on indomitably, finishing the two-volume book four days before his death. He died on July 23, 1885, and is interred in New York City.

Julia Dent Grant (1826–1902) was the daughter of a judge in St. Louis, Mo., and a sister of one of Grant's West Point classmates. She and Grant were married in 1848. They had three sons and a daughter, all surviving to maturity. As First Lady she was admired for her graces.

RUTHERFORD BIRCHARD HAYES

19th President
(1877–81)

The election of 1876 pitted Hayes, the Republican nominee, against Samuel J. Tilden, the Democratic candidate. It was a significant election, marking the political reentry of the South into the Union and the resurgence of the Democrats. The Republicans lost decisively in the congressional elections, and Hayes received nearly 250,000 fewer popular votes than Tilden.

A special electoral commission with a Republican majority gave the office to Hayes by a margin of only one electoral vote.

Hayes was born on Oct. 4, 1822, in Delaware, Ohio. He was the son of Rutherford Hayes, a storekeeper, and Sophia Birchard Hayes. Young Hayes attended Kenyon College and Harvard.

He practiced law in Lower Sandusky and then in 1849 moved to Cincinnati. From 1858 to 1861 he served as Cincinnati solicitor.

At the outbreak of the Civil War, Hayes enlisted and was commissioned a major. He was wounded four times, rising in rank to major general.

Elected to Congress in 1865 as a Republican, Hayes supported the Radicals' Reconstruction program. In 1867 he was elected governor of Ohio and served three terms.

HAYES' PRESIDENTIAL ADMINISTRATION

Congresses in Session:
45th, 46th
Vice President:
William Wheeler, 1877–81
Secretary of War:
George McCrary, 1877–79
Alexander Ramsey, 1879–81
Secretary of State:
William Evarts, 1877–81
Secretary of the Treasury:
John Sherman, 1877–81
Postmaster General:
David Key, 1877–80
Horace Maynard, 1880–81
Attorney General:
Charles Devens, 1877–81
Secretary of the Navy:
Richard Thompson, 1877–80
Nathan Goff Jr., 1881
Secretary of the Interior:
Carl Schurz, 1877–81

PRESIDENTIAL ELECTION OF 1876

Nominations: The Republican convention in Cincinnati, June 14–16, 1876, nominated Hayes on the seventh ballot. Wheeler was nominated by acclamation. The Democrats, meeting in St. Louis, June 27–29, 1876, nominated Tilden on the second ballot. **Campaign Issues:** Reconstruction and corruption in government. **Remarks:** An electoral commission composed of eight Republicans and seven Democrats awarded disputed votes to Hayes.

PRESIDENTIAL CANDIDATES	PARTY	ELECTORAL VOTES	POPULAR VOTE Total	Percentage	VICE-PRESIDENTIAL CANDIDATES
Rutherford B. Hayes	Republican	185	4,036,572	48.0	William A. Wheeler
Samuel J. Tilden	Democratic	184	4,284,020	51.0	Thomas A. Hendricks
Peter Cooper	Greenback	—	81,737	1.0	Samuel F. Carey

Facing a hostile Democratic majority in Congress, Hayes could not obtain passage of his legislative program.

His most outstanding act, withdrawal of the last federal troops from the South, antagonized extremists in his party. His efforts to reform the civil service also angered Republican bosses.

The economic depression during Hayes' administration brought the first nationwide strike by rail workers in 1877. When strike riots broke out in several states, Hayes sent in federal troops.

In an effort to halt Indian wars in the West, Hayes banned sale of firearms to Indians.

Hayes declined renomination and devoted his last years to education and philanthropy. He died in Fremont, Ohio, on Jan. 17, 1893.

Lucy Ware Webb Hayes (1831–89), who married Hayes in 1852, was the first college graduate to become First Lady.

Mrs. Hayes, a cheerful woman, was nicknamed "Lemonade Lucy" because she served only soft drinks in the White House. Both she and Hayes were total abstainers. Hayes' last executive order as President was to ban the sale of whisky on army posts. The Hayes' family life—they had eight children—was a happy one.

Hayes installed the first telephone in the White House, in 1877.

JAMES ABRAM GARFIELD

20th President
(1881)

The second U.S. President killed by an assassin, Garfield served too short a time for anyone to know what sort of Chief Executive he might have been.

Born on Nov. 19, 1831, in Orange Township, Ohio, Garfield was the son of Abram and Eliza Ballou Garfield. He was left fatherless at two and spent his early years in poverty. He worked as a farmer and carpenter to support his mother. At 18 he entered Western Reserve Eclectic Institute (now Hiram College). He went on to Williams College, graduating in 1856. Garfield then returned to Hiram, where he became its president. He was also a lay preacher of the Disciples of Christ. He became a state senator in 1859 and was admitted to the bar in 1860.

During the Civil War he began service as an officer of an Ohio volunteer regiment. He was promoted to the rank of major general because of his bravery at the Battle of Chickamauga.

On his election to Congress in 1863 he resigned from the Army to take his seat in the House, where he served until 1880. He was a staunch advocate of Radical Reconstruction.

Garfield was one of the members of the electoral commission that awarded the presidential election of 1876 to Hayes. He then served as Republican minority leader of the House during Hayes' administration.

As leader of the Ohio delegation to the Republican national convention in 1880, Garfield was present at his own presidential nomination as a dark-horse candidate. Top runners at the convention that year were ex-President Grant and James G. Blaine. Up to the 34th ballot Garfield never drew more than two votes, but on the 36th ballot he won the nomination. Grant and his political sponsor, Sen. Roscoe Conkling of New York, were disgruntled. An effort was made to appease them by giving second place on the ticket to Chester Arthur, one of the Stalwarts—as Grant's supporters called themselves.

One of President Garfield's immediate problems on beginning his administration was the open break forced by Senator Conkling over the distribution of political spoils. Garfield was a brilliant orator and a man of integrity and charm. His conflict with Conkling and the political machine remained unresolved, however.

Before Garfield could make his mark as President, he was killed. Charles Guiteau, a disappointed office seeker who proclaimed himself a Stalwart, shot him on July 2, 1881. Garfield lingered until his death on Sept. 19, 1881.

Lucretia Rudolph Garfield (1832–1918), his wife, had been a schoolmate. They were married in 1858. The Garfields had seven children, two of whom died in childhood.

GARFIELD'S PRESIDENTIAL ADMINISTRATION

Congress in Session:
47th
Vice President:
Chester A. Arthur, 1881
Secretary of State:
James Blaine, 1881
Secretary of the Treasury:
William Windom, 1881
Secretary of War:
Robert Todd Lincoln, 1881
Attorney General:
Wayne MacVeagh, 1881
Postmaster General:
Thomas James, 1881
Secretary of the Navy:
William Hunt, 1881
Secretary of the Interior:
Samuel Kirkwood, 1881

PRESIDENTIAL ELECTION OF 1880

Nominations: The Republicans met in Chicago, June 2–8, 1880, and on the 36th ballot Garfield received the nomination. Arthur was chosen as the vice-presidential candidate on the first ballot. The Democrats met in Cincinnati, June 22–24, 1880, and nominated Hancock and English. **Campaign Issues:** The parties based their campaigns on the personalities of their candidates. Republicans favored high tariffs and Democrats opposed them.

PRESIDENTIAL CANDIDATES	PARTY	ELECTORAL VOTES	POPULAR VOTE Total	Percentage	VICE-PRESIDENTIAL CANDIDATES
James A. Garfield	Republican	214	4,453,295	48.5	Chester A. Arthur
Winfield S. Hancock	Democratic	155	4,414,082	48.1	William English
James B. Weaver	Greenback	—	308,578	3.4	B. J. Chambers
Neal Dow	Prohibition	—	10,305	—	H. A. Thompson

QUICK QUIZ: How many people live in the Phoenix, Ariz., metropolitan area? See page 113.

CHESTER ALAN ARTHUR

21st President
(1881–85)

Chester Arthur became President on Sept. 20, 1881, after the death of President Garfield from wounds by an assassin. A New York Republican machine politician, Arthur had been given the vice-presidential nomination in 1880 to appease supporters of ex-President Grant, who had hoped for a third-term nomination. Members of Arthur's Republican clique were called Stalwarts. Those who supported Garfield were called Half-Breeds.

Arthur was born on Oct. 5, 1829, in Fairfield, Vt., the son of William Arthur, a clergyman, and Malvina Stone Arthur. He graduated from Union College in 1848 and began teaching while studying law. Arthur was admitted to the New York bar in 1854 and developed a successful law practice. An abolitionist, Arthur took many cases defending fugitive slaves and other blacks.

He helped organize the New York militia during the Civil War and then served as quartermaster general.

In 1871 President Grant rewarded him with the post of collector of the New York Custom House, a much-sought political prize. He administered the office with personal honesty but, in the style of the time, openly dispensed political patronage to members of the powerful New York Republican machine. In 1879 President Hayes, a fellow Republican determined to reform civil service, removed Arthur from office.

As President, Arthur was stigmatized as a machine politician of dubious integrity and nicknamed "the Gentleman Boss" for his courtly manners and his taste for fine foods and expensive clothes. He had the White House redecorated in *art nouveau* style by New York designer Louis Tiffany, and he installed an elevator.

To the dismay of his political associates, Arthur's presidential administration proved honest and efficient. Arthur supported the Civil Service Reform Act of 1883, which limited the spoils system. He fought the passage of the Chinese Exclusion Act. He prosecuted corruption in the postal service, and he aided the passage of a new protective tariff.

A little more than a year after Arthur succeeded to office, his kidney trouble was diagnosed as Bright's disease. Only one or two of his closest friends were permitted to know the seriousness of his ailment. He thus lived throughout his term in the White House with the secret knowledge that he was a dying man. It is believed for this reason alone he refused to seek the 1884 nomination, to the bewilderment of his supporters.

Arthur returned to New York City and resumed his law practice. He died there on Nov. 18, 1886, a year after leaving office.

Ellen Lewis Herndon Arthur (1837–80) married Arthur in 1859 but died before he became President. Arthur's vivacious sister, Mary (Mrs. John McElroy), served as official White House hostess during his term.

ARTHUR'S PRESIDENTIAL ADMINISTRATION

Congresses in Session:
47th, 48th

Vice President:
Vacant

Secretary of State:
James G. Blaine, 1881
Frederick Frelinghuysen, 1881–85

Secretary of War:
Robert Todd Lincoln, 1881–85

Secretary of the Treasury:
William Windom, 1881
Charles Folger, 1881–84
Walter Q. Gresham, 1884
Hugh McCulloch, 1884–85

Postmaster General:
Thomas L. James, 1881
Timothy Howe, 1881–83
Walter Q. Gresham, 1883–84
Frank Hatton, 1884–85

Attorney General:
Wayne MacVeagh, 1881
Benjamin Brewster, 1881–85

Secretary of the Navy:
William Hunt, 1881–82
William Chandler, 1882–85

Secretary of the Interior:
Samuel Kirkwood, 1881–82
Henry Teller, 1882–85

GROVER CLEVELAND

22d and 24th President
(1885–89, 1893–97)

The first Democrat elected President after the Civil War, Grover Cleveland won office as a champion of honesty and reform. Cleveland became the only President to serve two nonconsecutive terms, losing a bid for reelection in 1888 and then regaining the office in the election of 1892.

The son of Richard Falley and Ann Neal Cleveland, Stephen Grover Cleveland was born on March 18, 1837, in Caldwell, N.J. The family moved to upstate New York when Cleveland was a child. His father, a Presbyterian minister, died when the boy was 16. He worked in a store in Clinton, N.Y., and later taught school. After deciding to move west as a pioneer, he stopped in Buffalo to visit an uncle and settled there. He clerked in a law office, becoming a lawyer in 1859.

Cleveland began his political career as a Democrat. After filling minor posts, he was elected sheriff of Erie County, N.Y. (1871–73). While sheriff he sprang the trap to hang two convicted murderers, giving him the later distinction of being the only President to have hanged a man. Cleveland was elected mayor of Buffalo in 1882. Known as the "veto mayor," he drove corruption from his administration and acquired renown for honesty and efficiency.

He then was elected governor of New York (1883–84). As governor he fought the corruption of New York's Democratic Tammany machine. He cooperated with Republican reformer Theodore Roosevelt, who was then in the state legislature.

During the mud-slinging presidential campaign of 1884, opponents disclosed Cleveland had fathered an illegitimate child. Voters gave him extra points for refusing to deny the story, which was true. A further attack on the Democrats as the party of "rum, Romanism, and rebellion" boomeranged, costing Republican candidate James G. Blaine the Roman Catholic vote. Cleveland also received support from reform-minded Republicans, known as Mugwumps.

In his first term as President, Cleveland faced an unyielding Republican majority in the Senate. This opposition kept him from carrying through any planned policy.

Among the few significant acts of Cleveland's first term were his appointment of an Interstate Commerce Commission and passage of the Interstate Commerce Act of 1887.

Although he was forced to temper with expediency his own instinct for civil-service reform, he was adamant against graft, extravagance, and excessive tariffs.

In the presidential election of 1888 Cleveland won a plurality of the popular vote over Republican Benjamin Harrison, but he lost the electoral vote by a substantial margin.

During the period between his two administrations, Cleveland practiced law in New York City.

He helped the Democrats win control of Congress in the 1890 elections by his attacks on extravagant spending by the Republicans.

In 1892 Cleveland regained the White House for a second term, becoming the only defeated President ever to be reelected.

Inheriting the financial panic of 1893, he forced repeal of the Sherman Silver Purchase Act and sponsored issuance of government bonds to protect the gold reserve. By these measures he alienated the Populists and the silver advocates among the Democrats.

Determined to prevent interruption of postal service because of the 1894 strike of Pullman workers in Chicago, he sent federal troops to restore order. His action was against the wishes of the Democratic governor of Illinois and alienated organized labor.

Cleveland also felt that tendencies toward

CLEVELAND'S ADMINISTRATION AS 22d PRESIDENT

Congresses in Session:
49th, 50th
Vice President:
Thomas Hendricks, 1885
Secretary of State:
Thomas Bayard, 1885–89
Secretary of War:
William Endicott, 1885–89
Secretary of the Treasury:
Daniel Manning, 1885–87
Charles Fairchild, 1887–89
Attorney General:
Augustus Garland, 1885–89
Secretary of the Navy:
William Whitney, 1885–89
Postmaster General:
William Vilas, 1885–88
Don Dickinson, 1888–89
Secretary of the Interior:
Lucius Lamar, 1885–88
William Vilas, 1888–89
Secretary of Agriculture:
Norman Colman, 1889

PRESIDENTIAL ELECTION OF 1884

Nominations: The Republicans met in Chicago, June 3–6, 1884, and Blaine was nominated on the fourth ballot, receiving 541 of 813 votes. The Democrats met in Chicago, July 8–11, 1884, and on the second ballot Cleveland received 683 of 820 votes before the nomination was made unanimous. **Campaign Issues:** Charges that Cleveland had fathered an illegitimate child and that Blaine's vote in Congress had been bought several times.

PRESIDENTIAL CANDIDATES	PARTY	ELECTORAL VOTES	POPULAR VOTE Total	POPULAR VOTE Percentage	VICE-PRESIDENTIAL CANDIDATES
Grover Cleveland	Democratic	219	4,879,507	48.5	Thomas A. Hendricks
James G. Blaine	Republican	182	4,850,293	48.2	John A. Logan
Benjamin F. Butler	Greenback	—	175,370	1.7	A.M. West
John P. St. John	Prohibition	—	150,369	1.5	William Daniel

CLEVELAND'S ADMINISTRATION AS 24th PRESIDENT

Congresses in Session:
53d, 54th
Vice President:
Adlai E. Stevenson, 1893–97
Secretary of the Treasury:
John Carlisle, 1893–97
Secretary of War:
Daniel Lamont, 1893–97
Secretary of State:
Walter Gresham, 1893–95
Richard Olney, 1895–97
Attorney General:
Richard Olney, 1893–95
Judson Harmon, 1895–97
Secretary of the Navy:
Hilary Herbert, 1893–97
Postmaster General:
Wilson Bissell, 1893–95
William Wilson, 1895–97
Secretary of the Interior:
Hoke Smith, 1893–96
David Francis, 1896–97
Secretary of Agriculture:
Julius Morton, 1893–97

PRESIDENTIAL ELECTION OF 1892

Nominations: The Republicans met in Minneapolis, June 7–10, 1892. Harrison received 535⅙ votes on the first roll call with 369⅙ against him. The Democrats met in Chicago, June 21–23, 1892. Cleveland received 617⅓ votes, barely more than the two-thirds necessary for the nomination. The Populists met in Omaha, July 2–5, 1892, where Weaver won the nomination on the first ballot. **Campaign Issues:** Discontent among farmers and tariff reform, the Democrats favoring a lower tariff. Populists drew off many votes from the Republicans.

PRESIDENTIAL CANDIDATES	PARTY	ELECTORAL VOTES	POPULAR VOTE Total	POPULAR VOTE Percentage	VICE-PRESIDENTIAL CANDIDATES
Grover Cleveland	Democratic	277	5,555,426	46.0	Adlai E. Stevenson
Benjamin Harrison	Republican	145	5,182,690	43.0	Whitelaw Reid
James B. Weaver	Populist	22	1,029,846	8.5	James G. Field
Other candidates	—	—	285,297	2.5	—

QUICK QUIZ: When were the words "under God" added to the Pledge of Allegiance? See page 324.

GROVER CLEVELAND *(continued)*
U.S. imperialism were beginning to grow. He refused to permit aid to a rebel movement in Cuba and prevented the annexation of Hawaii. Almost the only popular act of Cleveland's second term was his invocation of the Monroe Doctrine in 1895, which led Britain to arbitrate a boundary dispute with Venezuela.

Cleveland's personal fortitude was manifested by the manner with which he underwent major surgery in 1893. Stricken by a cancerous growth on his jaw, he accepted the advice of friends and was operated on in secret to prevent public alarm. The operation, necessitating removal of his upper left jaw, was performed aboard a yacht.

Blaming Cleveland for the continuing depression, voters elected a Republican majority to Congress in the 1894 elections. Cleveland was further humiliated in 1896 when the Democratic convention refused him a third term.

After leaving the White House, Cleveland retired to Princeton, N.J.. He participated little in public life. In 1901 he became a trustee of Princeton University. He later became a spokesman for insurance companies against government regulation.

Cleveland died on June 24, 1908, at his home in Princeton.

Frances Folsom Cleveland (1864–1947) became the bachelor President's wife in 1886. She was the 21-year-old daughter of his late law partner, as well as Cleveland's ward. Cleveland became the only President to be married in a White House wedding. Immensely popular, Mrs. Cleveland officiated at White House functions with poise and skill. The Clevelands' second child, Esther, born in 1893, was the first child of a President to be born in the White House.

BENJAMIN HARRISON

23d President
(1889–93)

A grandson of President W. H. Harrison, Benjamin Harrison campaigned in 1888 to the tune of "Grandfather's Hat Fits Ben." The Republicans stirred anti-British sentiment against President Cleveland by tricking the British ambassador into endorsing him. Although Harrison defeated Cleveland with a majority of the electoral votes, he received 90,728 fewer popular votes.

A comparatively colorless President, Harrison followed regular Republican policies. He supported the McKinley protective tariff and the lavishly liberal Disability Pension Act. An outstanding event of his administration was the formation of what was later to become the Pan American Union.

The Sherman Antitrust Act was passed to counteract popular feeling that the Republicans were the party of "big business." This proved insufficient to win popular support, and the congressional elections of 1890 gave the Democrats control of the House.

Harrison was born on Aug. 20, 1833, at North Bend, Ohio. He was the son of Rep. John Scott Harrison and Edith Erwin Harrison.

He graduated from Miami (Ohio) University, passed the bar in 1853, and began law practice in Cincinnati. In 1854 he moved to Indianapolis, where he became a reporter for the Indiana supreme court.

When the Civil War began Harrison helped recruit a regiment of volunteers, of which he became a colonel in 1862. Achieving an outstanding war record, he attained the rank of brigadier general.

After the war, he built a prosperous practice as a corporation lawyer. From 1881 to 1887 Harrison served as U.S. senator from Indiana.

During his administration, President Harrison installed the first electric lights in the White House, replacing gas lighting.

HARRISON'S PRESIDENTIAL ADMINISTRATION

Congresses in Session:
51st, 52d

Vice President:
Levi Morton, 1889–93

Secretary of State:
James Blaine, 1889–92
John Foster, 1892–93

Secretary of the Treasury:
William Windom, 1889–91
Charles Foster, 1891–93

Secretary of War:
Redfield Proctor, 1889–91
Stephen Elkins, 1891–93

Attorney General:
William Miller, 1889–93

Postmaster General:
John Wanamaker, 1889–93

Secretary of the Navy:
Benjamin Tracy, 1889–93

Secretary of the Interior:
John Noble, 1889–93

Secretary of Agriculture:
Jeremiah Rusk, 1889–93

PRESIDENTIAL ELECTION OF 1888

Nominations: The Democrats met in St. Louis, June 5–7, 1888, and nominated Cleveland by acclamation. Thurman was a unanimous vice-presidential choice on the first roll-call vote. The Republicans met in Chicago, June 19–25, 1888. On the eighth ballot Harrison received 544 of 830 votes. Morton won the vice-presidential nomination with 592 votes on the first ballot. **Campaign:** Cleveland had approved restoring the Confederate battle flags to the South, and the Republicans made much of this. Also, a Republican politician managed to get the British ambassador to write in a letter that Cleveland would best serve the interests of Britain, arousing anti-British sentiment. **Remarks:** Opposed by New York's Tammany machine, Cleveland lost that state's 36 electoral votes, throwing the election to Harrison.

PRESIDENTIAL CANDIDATES	PARTY	ELECTORAL VOTES	POPULAR VOTE Total	POPULAR VOTE Percentage	VICE-PRESIDENTIAL CANDIDATES
Benjamin Harrison	Republican	233	5,447,129	47.9	Levi P. Morton
Grover Cleveland	Democratic	168	5,537,857	48.6	Allen G. Thurman
Clinton B. Fisk	Prohibition	—	249,506	2.2	John A. Brooks
Alson J. Streeter	Union Labor	—	146,935	1.3	C.E. Cunningham

Defeated by Cleveland in his bid for reelection in 1892, Harrison resumed his law practice. He also served as counsel for Venezuela in the Venezuela-British boundary dispute. In 1899 he represented the U.S. at the Hague Peace Conference.

He died in Indianapolis on March 13, 1901.

Caroline Lavinia Scott Harrison (1832–92), his first wife, was proficient in music and painting and brought cultural distinction to her role as First Lady. The Harrisons had two children. Mrs. Harrison became ill in 1891, dying a few months before Harrison's term ended.

Mary Scott Lord (Dimmick) Harrison (1858–1948), was Harrison's second wife. They married in 1896 and had one child. A niece of his first wife, she had served as White House hostess during her aunt's illness.

WILLIAM McKINLEY

25th President
(1897–1901)

McKinley's assassination in the first year of the 20th century marked the closing of an era. He was the last President to have served in the Civil War, and the last to embark on a war of territorial expansion—the Spanish-American War. The Western frontier had been tamed. A new industrial society was being created, and with it came a change from the 19th century pattern of life.

McKinley was born on Jan. 29, 1843, in Niles, Ohio, the son of William and Nancy (Allison) McKinley.

In 1861, at 18, he enlisted as a private in the Civil War. As a mess sergeant he received a battlefield commission for serving hot food to troops under fire. He later rose to major.

After the Civil War he passed the bar in 1867, establishing a law practice in Canton, Ohio.

After serving two years as a county prosecuting attorney, McKinley was elected to Congress in 1876. Except for one term, he remained there until 1891. While a House member he sponsored the restrictive McKinley Tariff Act of 1890 that pleased financial and business interests.

With the backing of Mark Hanna, a wealthy Ohio industrialist, McKinnley won election and reelection as governor of Ohio (1892–96). In the panic of 1893, he gained popularity by providing free food for the Ohio unemployed.

Through Hanna's astute management, McKinley won the Republican presidential nomination in 1896. The party platform emphasized higher tariffs and an expansionist foreign policy.

During McKinley's administration tariffs

McKINLEY'S PRESIDENTIAL ADMINISTRATION

Congresses in Session:
55th, 56th, 57th

Vice President:
Garret Hobart, 1897–99
Theodore Roosevelt, 1901

Secretary of State:
John Sherman, 1897–98
William Day, 1898
John Hay, 1898–1901

Secretary of the Treasury:
Lyman Gage, 1897–1901

Secretary of War:
Russell Alger, 1897–99
Elihu Root, 1899–1901

Attorney General:
Joseph McKenna, 1897–98
John Griggs, 1898–1901
Philander Knox, 1901

Postmaster General:
James Gary, 1897–98
Charles Smith, 1898–1901

Secretary of the Navy:
John Long, 1897–1901

Secretary of the Interior:
Cornelius Bliss, 1897–98
Ethan Hitchcock, 1898–1901

Secretary of Agriculture:
James Wilson, 1897–1901

PRESIDENTIAL ELECTION OF 1896

Nominations: The Republicans met in St. Louis, June 16–18, 1896, and McKinley with 661½ of 907 votes was nominated on the first ballot. The Democrats met in Chicago, July 7–11, 1896, and Bryan was nominated on the fifth ballot with 652 of 768 votes. The Populists supported Bryan. The National Democrats were so-called Gold Democrats, conservatives who opposed Bryan. **Campaign Issues:** The Democrats came out for "free and unlimited coinage of silver."

PRESIDENTIAL CANDIDATES	PARTY	ELECTORAL VOTES	POPULAR VOTE Total	Percentage	VICE-PRESIDENTIAL CANDIDATES
William McKinley	Republican	271	7,102,246	51.0	Garret Hobart
William Jennings Bryan ...	Democrat	176	6,492,559	46.7	Arthur Sewall Thomas E. Watson
John M. Palmer	Natl. Dem.	—	133,148	1.0	Simon Buckner
Other candidates	—	—	182,250	1.3	—

PRESIDENTIAL ELECTION OF 1900

Nominations: The Republicans, meeting in Philadelphia, June 19–21, 1900, made McKinley's nomination unanimous. The Democrats, meeting in Kansas City, Mo., July 4–6, 1900, chose Bryan unanimously on the first ballot. **Campaign:** Democrats accused McKinley of imperialism in Cuba and the Philippines and of being the tool of big business.

PRESIDENTIAL CANDIDATES	PARTY	ELECTORAL VOTES	POPULAR VOTE Total	Percentage	VICE-PRESIDENTIAL CANDIDATES
William McKinley	Republican	292	7,218,491	51.7	Theodore Roosevelt
William Jennings Bryan ...	Democrat	155	6,356,734	45.5	Adlai E. Stevenson
John G. Woolley	Prohibition	—	208,914	1.5	Henry B. Metcalf
Other candidates	—	—	189,126	1.3	—

QUICK QUIZ: What are hominoids? See page 181.

WILLIAM McKINLEY *(continued)*
were raised and Hawaii was annexed.

The Caribbean took the spotlight after Cubans rebelled against Spain in 1895. Ruthless Spanish repression followed, and U.S. property losses on the island were substantial. An unexplained explosion on the U.S. battleship *Maine* in Havana harbor (Feb. 15, 1898) was the final push needed to bring about war.

At McKinley's request, Congress declared war on Spain on April 25, 1898. The war lasted just four months. With U.S. victory, Cuba was placed under American military rule, and Puerto Rico, the Philippines, and Guam became U.S. possessions.

In 1900 McKinley was reelected. Less than a year later, he was shot by Leon Czolgosz, an anarchist, in Buffalo, N.Y., on Sept. 6, 1901. He died eight days later, on Sept. 14.

Ida Saxton McKinley (1847–1907) married McKinley in 1871. They had two daughters, both of whom died in childhood. She was an epileptic and an invalid during her husband's administration. But she insisted on accompanying McKinley everywhere and was with him in Buffalo where he was assassinated.

THEODORE ROOSEVELT

26th President
(1901–09)

Roosevelt entered the White House at the age of 42—the youngest man ever to attain the presidency. His vivid personality and his enthusiasm immediately made him a popular incumbent. His intellectual interests elevated the overall tone of American politics, although his glorification of military power and force drew considerable criticism.

Neither Republican boss Mark Hanna nor President McKinley had wanted Roosevelt as the vice-presidential candidate. Hanna's reaction on learning of McKinley's death was reportedly, "Now look, that damned cowboy is President of the United States."

EARLY LIFE

The first son of Theodore and Martha Bulloch Roosevelt, he was born on Oct. 27, 1858, in New York City. The scion of a wealthy family, he was educated by private tutors, traveled widely, graduated from Harvard (1880), and attended Columbia Law School.

As a youth Roosevelt's health was poor. His efforts to build up his physical strength by "roughing it" helped make him a sportsman, hunter, horseman, rancher, and explorer.

At the same time he retained wide cultural interests and was a prolific author, writing his first book in 1882, *The Naval War of 1812.*

POLITICAL AND MILITARY CAREER

Throughout his life, Roosevelt's major interest was politics, which he entered as a "young insurgent" Republican advocating reforms. Roosevelt served in the New York legislature from 1881 to 1884.

At the 1884 Republican presidential convention he opposed the nomination of James G. Blaine because of Blaine's connection with a stock-rigging scandal. This cost Roosevelt the support of the New York Republican boss, Thomas Platt. In turn, when Roosevelt, a loyal Republican, campaigned for Blaine, he lost the support of the young insurgents of his party.

Considering his political career at an end, and bereaved by the deaths of his mother and his wife on the same day in 1884, Roosevelt retired for the next two years to his North Dakota ranch. There he acquired many picturesque Western mannerisms of speech and gesture. He wrote many magazine articles about life in the West.

In 1886 Roosevelt was called back to New York City to run for mayor against powerful Democratic candidates. Although he was defeated, he attracted so much attention that President Harrison appointed him to the U.S. Civil Service Commission (1889–95), on which he became the dominant figure.

A reform mayor of New York City appointed Roosevelt head of the Board of Police Commissioners in 1895. Roosevelt proceeded vigorously to clean up the corruption-ridden police force. However, his zealous enforcement of Sunday blue laws, closing saloons, angered many of the city's residents.

In 1897 President McKinley reluctantly appointed him assistant secretary of the navy. In this post, anticipating war with Spain, he was instrumental in placing the Navy on a war footing.

At the outbreak of the Spanish-American War he resigned as assistant secretary of the navy. Then, with Leonard Wood, he organized the volunteer cavalry regiment known as the Rough Riders.

On July 1, 1898, Col. Roosevelt led the Rough Riders in a charge up Cuba's San Juan Hill, an event he always continued to regard as "the great day of my life."

Roosevelt returned from Cuba a military hero. New York's "Boss" Platt, though personally averse to him, supported him for the governorship of New York. Roosevelt won and served from 1899 to 1901.

His administration as governor of New York antagonized Platt and the other Republican bosses. It was in his relations with the New York Republican political machine that he first used the term that became one of his trademarks: "Speak softly and carry a big stick, you will go far."

In 1900 New York Republican leaders decided to dispose of Roosevelt, for at least the next four years, by backing his nomination for Vice President. The McKinley-Roosevelt slate was easily elected.

26th PRESIDENT OF THE UNITED STATES

Roosevelt served only a few months as Vice President before the assassination of McKinley made him President on Sept. 14, 1901.

This was the era of "muckraking" and reform,

and Roosevelt embodied the period. He strengthened government controls over big business through a reinvigorated Interstate Commerce Commission, directed "trust-busting" actions against big corporations, and supported passage of the Meat Inspection Act and the Pure Food and Drug Act. He also advocated conservation of forestlands and irrigation of wastelands.

Roosevelt's "big stick" policy toward Latin America contributed to anti-American feeling. When Colombia refused to give him permission to build a canal across its province Panama, Roosevelt backed a revolution in Panama. He immediately recognized the rebel regime, secured from it the desired agreement, and began construction of the canal. In 1906 he visited Panama—the first President to travel outside the U.S. while in office.

Through his mediation the Russo-Japanese War was ended in 1905 at the Portsmouth (N.H.) Peace Conference.

He helped avert war between France and Germany over Morocco by sponsoring the Algeciras Conference.

His advocacy of the Hague Tribunal raised hopes for international peace.

For his activities to improve international relations, he became in 1906 the first American awarded the Nobel Peace Prize.

Roosevelt was the first President to ride in a gasoline-powered automobile (Aug. 22, 1902). He also was the first to fly in an airplane (Oct. 11, 1910), a year after leaving the White House.

LATER ACTIVITIES

At the close of his second term Roosevelt chose as his successor William Howard Taft, his secretary of war. Roosevelt successfully backed Taft at the 1908 Republican convention and in the ensuing campaign.

After leaving the White House, Roosevelt went off on exploring and big-game expeditions and a tour of European capitals.

On his return in 1910, he broke with Taft. At the 1912 Republican convention Roosevelt sought the nomination for a third term. When Taft was selected, Roosevelt took the progressive Republicans out of the party. He organized them into a new Progressive, or "Bull Moose," Party. He then ran as the Progressive Party's presidential candidate.

During the ensuing campaign, a would-be assassin fired a shot that struck Roosevelt shortly before he was to make an address in Milwaukee, Wis., on Oct. 14, 1912. Although the bullet penetrated Roosevelt's chest, he insisted on completing his speech before going to a hospital.

The split in the Republican Party in 1912 enabled the Democratic candidate, Woodrow Wilson, to win. Roosevelt came in second, with Taft a poor third.

In addition to politics, Roosevelt engaged in what would have been separate careers for other men—exploration and writing. A former "River of Doubt" in the Brazilian jungle, which he traced to its outlet, was given the name Rio Roosevelt. He wrote nearly 40 books.

Roosevelt was deeply disappointed when President Wilson refused his offer to organize and lead a division of volunteers to fight in France in World War I.

On Jan. 6, 1919, Roosevelt died in his sleep.

Alice Hathaway Lee Roosevelt (1861–84) was his first wife. She died two days after the birth of their daughter, Alice.

Edith Kermit Carow Roosevelt (1861–1948) became Roosevelt's second wife in 1886. They had four sons and one daughter. One son died in action during World War I and two others died in World War II. As First Lady, Edith Roosevelt made the White House the social center of Washington.

THEODORE ROOSEVELT'S PRESIDENTIAL ADMINISTRATION

Congresses in Session:
57th, 58th, 59th, 60th

Vice President:
The vice-presidential office remained vacant during Roosevelt's first administration.
Charles Fairbanks, 1905–09

Secretary of State:
John Hay, 1901–05
Elihu Root, 1905–09
Robert Bacon, 1909

Secretary of War:
Elihu Root, 1901–04
William Taft, 1904–08
Luke Wright, 1908–09

Secretary of the Treasury:
Lyman Gage, 1901–02
Leslie Shaw, 1902–07
George Cortelyou, 1907–09

Attorney General:
Philander Knox, 1901–04
William Moody, 1904–06
Charles Bonaparte, 1906–09

Secretary of the Navy:
John Long, 1901–02
William Moody, 1902–04
Paul Morton, 1904–05
Charles Bonaparte, 1905–06
Victor Metcalf, 1906–08
Truman H. Newberry, 1908–09

Postmaster General:
Charles E. Smith, 1901–02
Henry Payne, 1902–04
Robert Wynne, 1904–05
George Cortelyou, 1905–07
George Meyer, 1907–09

Secretary of the Interior:
Ethan Hitchcock, 1901–07
James Garfield, 1907–09

Secretary of Agriculture:
James Wilson, 1901–09

Secretary of Commerce and Labor:
George Cortelyou, 1903–04
Victor Metcalf, 1904–06
Oscar Straus, 1906–09

PRESIDENTIAL ELECTION OF 1904

Nominations: Republicans met in Chicago, June 21–23, 1904, and chose Roosevelt unanimously. Democrats met in St. Louis, July 6–9, 1904, and nominated Parker on the first ballot.

Remarks: Roosevelt received a larger percentage of the popular vote than any previous President since tabulation of the vote had begun in 1824.

PRESIDENTIAL CANDIDATES	PARTY	ELECTORAL VOTES	POPULAR VOTE Total	POPULAR VOTE Percentage	VICE-PRESIDENTIAL CANDIDATES
Theodore Roosevelt	Republican	336	7,628,461	56.4	Charles W. Fairbanks
Alton B. Parker	Democratic	140	5,084,223	37.6	Henry G. Davis
Eugene V. Debs	Socialist	—	402,283	3.0	Benjamin Hanford
Other candidates	—	—	407,968	3.0	—

QUICK QUIZ: What is the average July temperature in Stockholm, Sweden? See page 149.

WILLIAM HOWARD TAFT

27th President
(1909–13)

The weightiest President, William Howard Taft stood six feet two inches tall and weighed over 300 pounds. An easygoing man, Taft presided over a prosperous nation more concerned with industrial growth than world affairs. He became the only President to later serve on the Supreme Court.

Taft was born on Sept. 15, 1857, in Cincinnati, Ohio, the son of Alphonso and Louise Maria Torrey Taft. His father had served as secretary of war and attorney general under President Grant. As a youth, "Willie," as he was called, won a reputation to be feared as a wrestler and boxer. Taft graduated from Yale in 1878 and from Cincinnati Law School in 1880.

EARLY CAREER

After practicing law in Cincinnati, he served successively as assistant prosecutor, assistant county solicitor, and superior court judge. He then received federal appointments as solicitor general of the U.S. (1890–92), U.S. circuit judge (1892–1900), president of the Philippine Commission (1900–01), and governor of the Philippines (1901–04).

President Roosevelt, his close friend, appointed him secretary of war (1904–08) and entrusted him with special missions to Cuba, Panama, the Philippines, and Japan.

Roosevelt chose Taft as his successor, and the Republicans nominated him as their presidential candidate in the election of 1908. Taft defeated Democrat William Jennings Bryan, who was making his third try for the White House.

PRESIDENTIAL ADMINISTRATION

Never having been elected to office before running for President, Taft had difficulty dealing with politicians and acting as leader of the Republican Party.

As President, Taft continued Roosevelt's policies, but the emphasis became more conservative. Republicans who favored progressive policies grew increasingly restive.

During his administration Arizona and New Mexico were admitted to the Union, bringing the number of U.S. states to 48.

Taft sought to conciliate the progressives by approving laws to institute postal savings and the parcel post. He also endorsed constitutional amendments authorizing direct election of senators and enactment of a federal income tax. Both were ratified by the states and were proclaimed in 1913. Taft also approved the Paine-Aldrich Act, which reduced duties on imports and opened the door to free trade with the Philippines.

These bids failed to placate the progressives, however. Led by Theodore Roosevelt, they bolted the Republican Party when it renominated Taft in 1912. They organized their own party, with Roosevelt as their candidate. The bitter split gave the election to the Democratic candidate, Gov. Woodrow Wilson of New Jersey.

Taft came in third, after Roosevelt. He was not unhappy, however, at the prospect of private life. Soon after Wilson's election he wrote, "The nearer I get to the inauguration of my successor the greater the relief I feel."

In his retirement Taft taught at Yale. During World War I he served as co-chairman of the National War Labor Board. He was among the Republicans who advocated U.S. entry into the League of Nations.

In 1921 he was appointed Chief Justice of the United States by President Harding, serving on the Supreme Court until a few weeks before his death, on March 8, 1930. He was the first President buried in Arlington National Cemetery.

Helen Herron Taft (1861–1943), his wife, was the daughter of a Cincinnati judge. She was a musician, and her White House musicales were highly regarded. She was ill during part of her husband's administration, so her sister, Mrs. Louise More, presided in her place.

The Tafts' children carried on the distinction of the family: Robert Alphonso was an influential senator. Charles Phelps was the first layman president of the Federal Council of Churches of Christ in America. Mrs. Helen Herron Taft Manning won note as an educator.

TAFT'S PRESIDENTIAL ADMINISTRATION

Congresses in Session:
61st, 62d
Vice President:
James Sherman, 1909–12
Secretary of State:
Philander Knox, 1909–13
Secretary of the Treasury:
Franklin MacVeagh, 1909–13

Secretary of War:
Jacob Dickinson, 1909–11
Henry Stimson, 1911–13
Attorney General:
George Wickersham, 1909–13
Secretary of the Interior:
Richard Ballinger, 1909–11
Walter Fisher, 1911–13

Postmaster General:
Frank Hitchcock, 1909–13
Secretary of the Navy:
George von L. Meyer, 1909–13
Secretary of Agriculture:
James Wilson, 1909–13
Secretary of Com. and Labor:
Charles Nagel, 1909–13

PRESIDENTIAL ELECTION OF 1908

Nominations: Republicans met in Chicago, June 16–19, 1908, and on the first ballot ratified by acclamation Roosevelt's choice of Taft as his successor. Democrats, meeting in Denver, July 8–10, 1908, selected Bryan on the first ballot.

Campaign: Roosevelt campaigned for Taft. Republicans promised tariff revision. Democrats called for lower tariffs, stringent antitrust enforcement, and relaxation of federal injunctions against labor strikes.

PRESIDENTIAL CANDIDATES	PARTY	ELECTORAL VOTES	POPULAR VOTE Total	POPULAR VOTE Percentage	VICE-PRESIDENTIAL CANDIDATES
William H. Taft	Republican	321	7,675,320	51.6	James S. Sherman
William Jennings Bryan	Democratic	162	6,412,294	43.1	John W. Kern
Eugene V. Debs	Socialist	—	420,793	2.8	Benjamin Hanford
Other candidates	—	—	379,833	2.5	—

WOODROW WILSON

28th President (1913-21)

An idealist, Wilson carried out many liberal domestic reforms, establishing new government controls on business to prevent abuses of workers. He then led the nation into World War I "to make the world safe for democracy." His greatest disappointment came when an isolationist U.S. Senate rejected U.S. participation in the postwar League of Nations he had conceived to preserve world peace.

EARLY CAREER

Thomas Woodrow Wilson was born in Staunton, Va., on Dec. 29, 1856, the son of Joseph Ruggles Wilson, a Presbyterian minister, and Janet "Jessie" Woodrow Wilson. He graduated from the College of New Jersey (later Princeton) in 1879 and attended the University of Virginia Law School in 1881. Admitted to the Georgia bar in 1882, he practiced law for a year in Atlanta.

Deciding to become an educator, he took his Ph.D. at Johns Hopkins. Wilson then taught history and political science at Bryn Mawr and Wesleyan. In 1890 he joined Princeton's faculty. Twelve years later he became president of Princeton University, a post he held for eight years. He initiated many educational reforms and became a popular public speaker.

Wilson was nominated and elected Democratic governor of New Jersey in 1910. Despite resistance from regular Democrats, Wilson forced many progressive policies through the state legislature.

28th PRESIDENT OF THE UNITED STATES

At the 1912 Democratic national convention Wilson won the nomination on the 46th ballot. A split in the Republican Party was instrumental in sending him to the White House with a huge electoral-vote majority but less than 42% of the popular vote.

Wilson's first term was notable for its vigor. He became the first President to initiate frequently scheduled press conferences to keep the people informed on government activities. Liberal measures, carried out under the slogan "the New Freedom," included the Federal Reserve Act, which centralized the banking system of the country; the Keating-Owen Child Labor Act; the

WILSON'S PRESIDENTIAL ADMINISTRATION

Congresses in Session:
63d, 64th, 65th, 66th

Vice President
Thomas Marshall, 1913–21

Secretary of State:
William J. Bryan, 1913–15
Robert Lansing, 1915–20
Bainbridge Colby, 1920–21

Secretary of the Treasury:
William McAdoo, 1913–18
Carter Glass, 1918–20
David Houston, 1920–21

Secretary of War:
Lindley Garrison, 1913–16
Newton Baker, 1916–21

Attorney General:
James McReynolds, 1913–14
Thomas Gregory, 1914–19
A. Mitchell Palmer, 1919–21

Postmaster General:
Albert Burleson, 1913–21

Secretary of the Navy:
Josephus Daniels, 1913–21

Secretary of the Interior:
Franklin Lane, 1913–20
John Payne, 1920–21

Secretary of Agriculture:
David Houston, 1913–20
Edwin Meredith, 1920–21

Secretary of Commerce:
William Redfield, 1913–19
Joshua Alexander, 1919–21

Secretary of Labor:
William Wilson, 1913–21

PRESIDENTIAL ELECTION OF 1912

Nominations: Republicans met in Chicago, June 18–22, 1912. Taft won, but 344 delegates did not vote. Sherman died during the campaign and was replaced by Butler. The Progressive ("Bull Moose") Party, in Chicago, Aug. 5–7, 1912, nominated Roosevelt by acclamation. The Democrats, meeting in Baltimore, June 25–July 2, 1912, took 46 ballots to decide on Wilson. **Campaign:** The Republican split between Roosevelt and Taft gave Wilson an easy victory.

PRESIDENTIAL CANDIDATES	PARTY	ELECTORAL VOTES	POPULAR VOTE Total	Percentage	VICE-PRESIDENTIAL CANDIDATES
Woodrow Wilson	Democratic	435	6,296,547	41.9	Thomas R. Marshall
Theodore Roosevelt	Progressive	88	4,118,571	27.4	Hiram Johnson
William H. Taft	Republican	8	3,486,720	23.2	James S. Sherman / Nicholas M. Butler
Eugene V. Debs	Socialist	—	901,255	6.0	Emil Seidel
Other candidates	—	—	235,025	1.5	—

PRESIDENTIAL ELECTION OF 1916

Nominations: The Republican convention in Chicago, June 7–10, 1916, chose Hughes on the third ballot when he received 949½ votes of 986. The Democratic convention in St. Louis, June 14–16, 1916, renominated its previous ticket by acclamation, with only one delegate opposed to Wilson. **Remarks:** Hughes went to bed before the California returns had come in, believing he had won a close election. By morning the West Coast results showed Wilson the winner.

PRESIDENTIAL CANDIDATES	PARTY	ELECTORAL VOTES	POPULAR VOTE Total	Percentage	VICE-PRESIDENTIAL CANDIDATES
Woodrow Wilson	Democratic	277	9,127,695	49.4	Thomas R. Marshall
Charles E. Hughes	Republican	254	8,533,507	46.2	Charles W. Fairbanks
Allan L. Benson	Socialist	—	585,113	3.2	George R. Kirkpatrick
Other candidates	—	—	233,909	1.2	—

QUICK QUIZ: When did Clarence Birdseye invent his quick-frozen food process? See page 308.

WOODROW WILSON *(continued)*
Farm Loan Act; the Clayton Antitrust Act; the Adamson Eight-Hour Law, reducing the working hours of trainmen; the La Follette Seamen's Act; and a lowered tariff.

To promote tariff reform, Wilson became the first President since John Adams to address Congress personally on the subject.

Wilson also favored equal rights for women. He welcomed the election in 1916 of America's first congresswoman, Jeannette Rankin of Montana. He aided the passage of the 19th Amendment, enfranchising women. Wilson also created a precedent by appointing the first woman to a subcabinet post, Annette Abbott Adams as assistant attorney general.

Opposed to prohibition, he vetoed the Volstead Act. Congress overrode his veto.

He disappointed many liberals by maintaining the "big stick" policy toward Latin America. On March 15, 1916, he sent U.S. troops into Mexico in pursuit of the revolutionary Pancho Villa. The United States purchased the Virgin Islands from Denmark in 1915 for $25 million.

The war in Europe that began in 1914 overshadowed all other foreign problems. Wilson sought to maintain U.S. neutrality, but went further in his warnings to Germany than Secretary of State William Jennings Bryan considered proper for a neutral. Bryan resigned after Wilson insisted on sending strong notes to Germany protesting the U-boat sinking of the *Lusitania* on May 7, 1915.

Under the slogan "He kept us out of war," Wilson barely won reelection in 1916 over Republican Charles Evans Hughes, who had resigned from the Supreme Court to run.

When Germany announced in 1917 that it would resume all-out submarine operations to impose its own blockade against the Allies, Wilson took America into the world conflict with public opinion behind him. Congress declared war on Germany on April 6, 1917.

Wilson's conduct of the war was vigorous. His stated war objectives were to "make the world safe for democracy" and to promote the "ultimate peace of the world." His program was embodied in the famous "Fourteen Points" of Jan. 8, 1918. These called for open diplomacy, adjustment of colonial claims, self-determination of peoples, and formation of a "general association of nations."

After the Allies achieved victory on Nov. 11, 1918, Wilson went to France to attend the Versailles Peace Conference. There he met fierce resistance from Lloyd George, Georges Clemenceau, and other European premiers, who made secret agreements among themselves.

Wilson finally agreed to what he considered the best treaty obtainable, acceptable chiefly because it provided for the League of Nations.

Wilson had broken irreconcilably at Versailles with his longtime friend and closest adviser Col. Edward M. House, whom he had once described as his "second personality."

En route home in 1919 he became the first President to make a radio broadcast when he addressed U.S. troops from shipboard.

Wilson was dismayed upon his return home when the League was attacked by various senators. Despite opposition led by Henry Cabot Lodge, the Senate might have ratified the Versailles treaty if reservations protecting U.S. sovereignty had been incorporated. But Wilson refused to compromise.

While stumping the country to gain support for the treaty, Wilson became ill.

A stroke on Oct. 2, 1919, paralyzed Wilson's left side. For months he was seen by only a few people. Many believed Mrs. Wilson was acting in his stead.

Although repudiated at home, Wilson was eulogized abroad. He was awarded the Nobel Peace Prize for 1919.

Nearly three years after completing his term of office, Wilson died in Washington, D.C., on Feb. 3, 1924. Entombed in the National Cathedral, he became the only President buried in Washington, D.C.

Ellen Louise Axson Wilson (1860–1914) married Wilson in 1885. They had three daughters. Mrs. Wilson died during her husband's second year in office.

Edith Bolling Galt Wilson (1872–1961), a widow, became his second wife in 1915.

WARREN GAMALIEL HARDING

29th President
(1921–23)

Harding was a handsome man who looked like the romantic ideal of a statesman. But he was ill equipped for the presidency. His administration is remembered for the Teapot Dome scandal and other corruption, although these did not become public until after his death.

Harding was born on Nov. 2, 1865, on a farm near what is now Blooming Grove, Ohio, the son of Dr. George Tryon and Phoebe Dickerson Harding.

He graduated from Ohio Central College, worked as a teacher, and studied law.

In 1884 he and two friends invested $300 to buy the bankrupt Marion (Ohio) *Star*. As its editor and eventual full owner, he became influential in local affairs and active in Republican politics.

Harding was elected a state senator (1898–1902) and lieutenant governor (1904–06). He failed in two subsequent tries for the Ohio governorship.

Harding received national attention in 1912 when he made the address nominating President Taft for a second term at the Republican national convention.

Under the guidance of Harry M. Daugherty, an able machine politician, he was elected to the U.S. Senate in 1914.

When the Republican national convention in 1920 reached a deadlock between the two main contenders for the presidential nomination, Daugherty arranged a deal in a "smoke-filled" hotel room that won Harding the nomination.

He was elected by a landslide after a "front-porch" campaign that had "back to normalcy" as its major slogan.

During his administration the nation suffered a deep postwar depression. Taxes were reduced and tariffs were raised. Immigration was restricted for the first time with quotas.

In foreign relations, Harding called the Washington Disarmament Conference in 1921–22 that put limits on the size of navies.

While Harding was returning home from a trip to Alaska, he became ill, dying in San Francisco on Aug. 2, 1923.

Harding's wife refused to let doctors perform an autopsy, leading to later speculation that he may have been poisoned. She also burned his papers and correspondence, so no one has ever been able to learn how much Harding knew about the corruption of his associates.

After Harding's death, Senate investigations revealed many scandals of his administration. These included custodianship of alien property, sale of government-owned cargo ships, mismanagement of the Veterans Bureau, corruption of the Justice Department under Attorney General Daugherty, and the leasing of naval oil reserves (Teapot Dome) to private oil interests for a bribe.

Two of his cabinet members, Daugherty and Secretary of the Interior Albert B. Fall, were indicted and tried. Fall was sent to prison, but Daugherty was freed by a hung jury.

Mrs. Florence Kling DeWolfe Harding (1860–1924), a divorcée, became his wife in 1891. They had no children. After Harding's death, gossip alleged that he had carried on several illicit romances.

HARDING'S PRESIDENTIAL ADMINISTRATION

Congresses in Session:
67th, 68th

Vice President:
Calvin Coolidge, 1921–23

Secretary of State:
Charles Evans Hughes, 1921–23

Secretary of the Interior:
Albert Fall, 1921–23
Hubert Work, 1923

Secretary of the Treasury:
Andrew Mellon, 1921–23

Secretary of War:
John Weeks, 1921–23

Attorney General:
Harry Daugherty, 1921–23

Postmaster General:
Will Hays, 1921–22
Hubert Work, 1922–23
Harry New, 1923

Secretary of the Navy:
Edwin Denby, 1921–23

Secretary of Agriculture:
Henry C. Wallace, 1921–23

Secretary of Commerce:
Herbert Hoover, 1921–23

Secretary of Labor:
James Davis, 1921–23

PRESIDENTIAL ELECTION OF 1920

Nominations: The Republican convention, in Chicago, June 8–12, 1920, deadlocked in voting on the two main contenders, Gen. Leonard Wood and Illinois Gov. Frank Lowden, but finally selected Harding on the 10th ballot. The Democrats, in San Francisco, June 28–July 6, 1920, were deadlocked until the 44th ballot. Cox then received 732½ votes, or 3½ more than the necessary 729, but a motion was carried to make the nomination unanimous. **Campaign:** Democrats attempted to make approval of the League of Nations an issue. Harding called for a return to "normalcy."

PRESIDENTIAL CANDIDATES	PARTY	ELECTORAL VOTES	POPULAR VOTE Total	POPULAR VOTE Percentage	VICE-PRESIDENTIAL CANDIDATES
Warren G. Harding	Republican	404	16,143,407	60.4	Calvin Coolidge
James M. Cox	Democratic	127	9,130,328	34.2	Franklin D. Roosevelt
Eugene V. Debs	Socialist	—	919,799	3.4	Seymour Stedman
Other candidates	—	—	540,371	2.0	—

CALVIN COOLIDGE

30th President
(1923–29)

Coolidge had qualities and a program that appealed to the Americans of his day, a period of almost wild national prosperity. Spare of words, his nickname was "Silent Cal." He was straightforward and honest, and helped liquidate the scandals of the Harding administration. His program included economy in government, tax cuts, and reduction of the national debt.

Born on July 4, 1872, at Plymouth, Vt., he was the son of John Calvin Coolidge, a storekeeper and justice of the peace, and Victoria Josephine Moor Coolidge.

He graduated from Amherst in 1895 and was admitted to the bar two years later.

In many ways the antithesis of the back-slapping politician, Coolidge nonetheless rose swiftly in public life. He held minor offices in Northampton, Mass., where he had practiced law. He served in the state legislature (1912–15), as lieutenant governor (1916–18), and then as governor of Massachusetts (1919–20).

As governor he won national fame in 1919 when he sent state militia to break a strike by Boston police.

The 1920 Republican convention chose Coolidge as Harding's running mate. He became President on Harding's death, and in 1924 he was elected to a full term.

During Coolidge's administration speakeasies flourished in the cities despite efforts by government agents to enforce the national prohibition on sales of alcoholic beverages. Gangsters controlled the flow of illegal alcoholic beverages, leading to frequent gang wars.

Women's fashions changed drastically as "flappers" wore short skirts.

The Ku Klux Klan terrorized minority groups.

In 1927 the nation waited breathlessly as Charles A. Lindbergh made his dramatic solo flight across

QUICK QUIZ: About how many people will live on the Earth in the year 2000? See page 192.

CALVIN COOLIDGE *(continued)*

the Atlantic from New York to Paris.

The Kellogg-Briand Peace Pact in 1928 outlawed war (but made no provision for enforcement).

Coolidge probably could have won another term, but he refused to seek renomination in 1928 in his famous laconic message, "I do not choose to run."

On his retirement Coolidge occupied himself mainly with writing newspaper and magazine articles and with his autobiography. The former President died on Jan. 5, 1933, in Northampton.

Grace Anna Goodhue Coolidge (1879–1957), who married Coolidge in 1905, was a graduate of the University of Vermont. She was highly regarded for her gracious and cultured manner. However, White House social activities were curtailed during Coolidge's administration by the deaths of the younger of their two sons (at 16) and of the President's father.

COOLIDGE'S PRESIDENTIAL ADMINISTRATION

Congresses in Session:
68th, 69th, 70th

Vice President:
Charles Dawes, 1925–29

Secretary of State:
Charles Hughes, 1923–25
Frank Kellogg, 1925–29

Secretary of the Treasury:
Andrew Mellon, 1923–29

Postmaster General:
Harry New, 1923–29

Secretary of War:
John Weeks, 1923–25
Dwight Davis, 1925–29

Attorney General:
Harry Daugherty, 1923–24
Harlan Stone, 1924–25
John Sargent, 1925–29

Secretary of Agriculture:
Henry C. Wallace, 1923–24
Howard M. Gore, 1924–25
William Jardine, 1925–29

Secretary of the Navy:
Edwin Denby, 1923–24
Curtis Wilbur, 1924–29

Secretary of the Interior:
Hubert Work, 1923–28
Roy O. West, 1928–29

Secretary of Commerce:
Herbert Hoover, 1923–28
William Whiting, 1928–29

Secretary of Labor:
James Davis, 1923–29

PRESIDENTIAL ELECTION OF 1924

Nominations: The Republicans, meeting in Cleveland, June 10–12, 1924, chose Coolidge on the first ballot with 1,065 of 1,109 votes. Dawes was chosen after Frank Lowden had declined the vice-presidential nomination given him on the second ballot. The Democrats met in New York City in the longest of nominating conventions—it lasted from June 24 to July 9, 1924, with 60 candidates nominated for the presidency. Southern Democrats fought against the nomination of New York Gov. Al Smith, a Roman Catholic. On the 103d ballot Davis finally received the nomination. **Campaign Issues:** The main issues were the Harding administration scandals. **Remarks:** The Progressive Party was formed as a result of left-wing dissatisfaction with the major candidates as well as with the contemporary social scene.

PRESIDENTIAL CANDIDATES	PARTY	ELECTORAL VOTES	POPULAR VOTE Total	Percentage	VICE-PRESIDENTIAL CANDIDATES
Calvin Coolidge	Republican	382	15,718,211	54.0	Charles G. Dawes
John W. Davis	Democratic	136	8,385,283	28.8	Charles W. Bryan
Robert M. LaFollette	Progressive	13	4,831,289	16.6	Burton K. Wheeler
Other candidates	—	—	155,883	0.5	—

HERBERT CLARK HOOVER

31st President
(1929–33)

While campaigning for the presidency in August 1928, Hoover said, "We are nearer to the final triumph over poverty than ever before in the history of any land. The poorhouse is vanishing from among us. We have not yet reached the goal, but we shall soon be in sight of the day when poverty will be banished from this nation." There seemed little reason then for Americans to disagree with this rosy appraisal of the nation's future, and Hoover was elected by a landslide.

Less than a year later, however, the stock market crashed, beginning the Great Depression.

Hoover was born on Aug. 10, 1874, in West Branch, Iowa, the son of Jesse Clark Hoover, a blacksmith, and Hulda Randall Minthorn Hoover. He graduated from Stanford University in 1895.

Hoover became a mining engineer, prospector, and businessman, accumulating a fortune through wide-ranging operations that took him all over the world. Because of his Quaker beliefs, he worked as organizer of relief operations during World War I. His administration of relief agencies attracted worldwide attention and respect.

In 1921 Hoover was appointed secretary of commerce by President Harding. He reorganized and expanded the department, sponsored conferences on unemployment, initiated programs to conserve fisheries, and constructed public works.

Chosen the Republican presidential nominee in 1928, Hoover won election in a campaign marred by bigotry directed at the Democratic candidate, Alfred E. Smith, because of his Roman Catholic religion.

The Great Depression deepened throughout Hoover's administration. To counter it he called for an extensive public-works program to restore business and employment.

In an effort to revive the economy, Hoover established the Reconstruction Finance Corporation, set up the Home Loan Bank, expanded the Farm Loan Bank, and supported legislation to relieve states and municipalities unable to bear the burden of the economic crisis. These measures proved ineffective, however, and Hoover's popularity waned drastically.

In foreign affairs he faced the problems of Japanese aggression in China, disarmament, and uncollected war debts.

In the presidential election of 1932, Hoover was defeated by Franklin D. Roosevelt.

In 1946 President Truman appointed Hoover coordinator of food supplies to dozens of countries devastated by World War II.

His long life in public service was further extended in 1947–49 and again in 1953–55, when he headed the Hoover Commission to reorganize the federal government.

Hoover died on Oct. 20, 1964, at the age of 90. **Lou Henry Hoover** (1875–1944), who was his college sweetheart, married Hoover in 1899. They had two sons. She was a charming White House hostess.

HOOVER'S PRESIDENTIAL ADMINISTRATION

Congresses in Session:
71st, 72d

Vice President:
Charles Curtis, 1929–33

Secretary of State:
Frank B. Kellogg, 1929
Henry Stimson, 1929–33

Secretary of the Treasury:
Andrew Mellon, 1929–32
Ogden Mills, 1932–33

Secretary of War:
James Good, 1929
Patrick Hurley, 1929–33

Attorney General:
William D. Mitchell, 1929–33

Postmaster General:
Walter Brown, 1929–33

Secretary of the Navy:
Charles Francis Adams, 1929–33

Secretary of the Interior:
Ray Lyman Wilbur, 1929–33

Secretary of Agriculture:
Arthur Hyde, 1929–33

Secretary of Commerce:
Robert Lamont, 1929–32
Roy D. Chapin, 1932–33

Secretary of Labor:
James Davis, 1929–30
William Doak, 1930–33

PRESIDENTIAL ELECTION OF 1928

Nominations: The Republicans met in Kansas City, Mo., June 12–15, 1928. On the first ballot, Hoover received 837 of 1,089 votes. The Democrats, meeting in Houston, Texas, June 26–29, 1928, chose Smith on the first ballot with $849\frac{2}{3}$ of $1,097\frac{1}{2}$ votes. **Campaign Issues:** Smith's Catholicism, prohibition, and farm relief.

PRESIDENTIAL CANDIDATES	PARTY	ELECTORAL VOTES	POPULAR VOTE Total	Percentage	VICE-PRESIDENTIAL CANDIDATES
Herbert C. Hoover	Republican	444	21,391,993	58.2	Charles Curtis
Alfred E. Smith	Democratic	87	15,016,169	40.9	Joseph T. Robinson
Norman M. Thomas	Socialist	—	267,385	0.7	James Maurer
Other candidates	—	—	69,180	0.2	—

FRANKLIN DELANO ROOSEVELT

32d President
(1933–45)

Few people in the nation ever were neutral about Franklin Roosevelt. His followers loved him and his opponents hated him with remarkable vigor.

His secretary of the interior, Harold L. Ickes, said that Roosevelt seemed "either to inspire a mad devotion that can see no flaw or to kindle a hatred of an intensity that will admit of no virtue."

Roosevelt was a tradition breaker from the time he was selected as the Democrats' standard-bearer in 1932. He upset custom by flying to the national political convention to accept its nomination in person.

Taking office at the height of a national economic crisis, Roosevelt soon brought hope to a discouraged nation with his concern for the "forgotten man" and his promise of a "New Deal" for Americans.

EARLY POLITICAL CAREER

Roosevelt was born on Jan. 30, 1882, at Hyde Park, N.Y. His parents were James and Sara Delano Roosevelt, a wealthy and socially prominent family.

He graduated from Harvard in 1904 and married his cousin Eleanor Roosevelt the following year. He attended Columbia Law School and was admitted to the bar in 1907.

After practicing law for four years, he won a Democratic seat in the New York state senate (1911–12). He established himself as leader of the reform Democrats by opposing a Tammany nominee for the U.S. Senate.

In 1912 he campaigned for Woodrow Wilson, who appointed him assistant secretary of the navy (1913–20).

The Democratic Party chose Roosevelt as their vice-presidential candidate in the unsuccessful 1920 election campaign against Harding.

In 1921 he was stricken with polio that permanently crippled him from the waist down. But by indomitable effort he learned to walk again using leg braces and crutches.

Roosevelt was urged to resume his political career by his wife and New York's Gov. Alfred E. Smith. At 46 he won election in 1928 as New York's governor, while the national Democratic ticket headed by Smith went down to defeat.

As governor, Roosevelt achieved renown for his competence. The stock market crash of 1929 brought with it the Great Depression. Roosevelt, advised by a small group of intellectuals and experts called the "Brain Trust," undertook extensive relief measures.

Roosevelt also struck at corruption in New York City politics, forcing the resignation of Mayor James J. Walker.

32d PRESIDENT OF THE UNITED STATES

Roosevelt was chosen by the Democrats in 1932 to oppose President Hoover, whose administration had seen the start of this period of disaster and despair. Roosevelt was elected by a wide margin and buoyantly set out to create a peaceful social revolution.

The new Congress, overwhelmed by the magnitude of the Depression and by the forceful personality of Roosevelt, surrendered much power to

QUICK QUIZ: What country is the world's largest producer of petroleum? See page 258.

FRANKLIN D. ROOSEVELT *(continued)*
the President. He immediately launched a series of emergency measures to reorganize industry and agriculture—under government controls—and to revive the faltering economy by a great expenditure of public funds.

Between March 9 and June 16, 1933, in the famous "hundred days" session, Congress enacted, under Roosevelt's guidance, more decisive legislation than in any previous congressional session in history.

This vast and many-faceted New Deal program encountered bitter opposition. Roosevelt's critics accused him of having too many radical schemes for social betterment. Among conservatives he was disparagingly referred to as "that man in the White House."

Nonetheless, in 1936 Roosevelt was reelected

FRANKLIN D. ROOSEVELT'S PRESIDENTIAL ADMINISTRATION

Congresses in Session:
73d, 74th, 75th, 76th, 77th, 78th, 79th
Vice President:
John Garner, 1933–41
Henry A. Wallace, 1941–45
Harry Truman, 1945
Secretary of State:
Cordell Hull, 1933–44
Edward Stettinius Jr., 1944–45
Secretary of War:
George Dern, 1933–36
Harry Woodring, 1936–40
Henry Stimson, 1940–45
Secretary of the Treasury:
William Woodin, 1933–34
Henry Morgenthau Jr., 1934–45
Attorney General:
Homer Cummings, 1933–39
Frank Murphy, 1939–40
Robert Jackson, 1940–41
Francis Biddle, 1941–45
Postmaster General:
James Farley, 1933–40
Frank Walker, 1940–45
Secretary of Agriculture:
Henry A. Wallace, 1933–40
Claude Wickard, 1940–45
Secretary of Commerce:
Daniel Roper, 1933–38
Harry Hopkins, 1938–40
Jesse Jones, 1940–45
Henry A. Wallace, 1945
Secretary of Labor:
Frances Perkins, 1933–45
Secretary of the Navy:
Claude Swanson, 1933–40
Charles Edison, 1940
Frank Knox, 1940–44
James Forrestal, 1944–45
Secretary of the Interior:
Harold Ickes, 1933–45

PRESIDENTIAL ELECTION OF 1932

Nominations: The Republicans held their convention in Chicago, June 14–16, 1932. On the first ballot Hoover received 1,126½ of 1,150 votes. The Democrats met in Chicago, June 27–29, 1932. Roosevelt on the fourth ballot received 945 of 1,148½ votes. **Campaign Issues:** The major issues dealt with methods of meeting and alleviating the economic depression. **Remarks:** Roosevelt broke tradition by flying to Chicago to accept the nomination.

PRESIDENTIAL CANDIDATES	PARTY	ELECTORAL VOTES	POPULAR VOTE Total	Percentage	VICE-PRESIDENTIAL CANDIDATES
Franklin D. Roosevelt.....	Democratic	472	22,809,638	57.4	John Nance Garner
Herbert C. Hoover	Republican	59	15,758,901	39.7	Charles Curtis
Norman M. Thomas	Socialist	—	881,951	2.2	James Maurer
Other candidates	—	—	278,534	0.7	—

PRESIDENTIAL ELECTION OF 1936

Nominations: The Republicans convened in Cleveland, June 9–12, 1936. Landon was the only candidate placed in nomination, although 19 votes went to Senator Borah. The Democrats, meeting in Philadelphia, June 23–27, 1936, renominated Roosevelt by acclamation. **Remarks:** Roosevelt won 60.8% of the vote, a record to that time.

PRESIDENTIAL CANDIDATES	PARTY	ELECTORAL VOTES	POPULAR VOTE Total	Percentage	VICE-PRESIDENTIAL CANDIDATES
Franklin D. Roosevelt.....	Democratic	523	27,752,869	60.8	John Nance Garner
Alfred M. Landon	Republican	8	16,674,655	36.5	Frank Knox
William Lemke...........	Union	—	882,479	1.9	Thomas C. O'Brien
Other candidates	—	—	318,502	0.8	—

PRESIDENTIAL ELECTION OF 1940

Nominations: The Republicans met in Philadelphia, June 24–28, 1940. Willkie won on the sixth ballot. The Democrats met in Chicago, July 15–18, 1940. Roosevelt was nominated by acclamation. **Campaign Issues:** American neutrality and the effects of New Deal reforms. **Remarks:** Roosevelt broke tradition by running for a third term.

PRESIDENTIAL CANDIDATES	PARTY	ELECTORAL VOTES	POPULAR VOTE Total	Percentage	VICE-PRESIDENTIAL CANDIDATES
Franklin D. Roosevelt.....	Democratic	449	27,307,819	54.8	Henry A. Wallace
Wendell L. Willkie	Republican	82	22,321,018	44.8	Charles L. McNary
Other candidates	—	—	218,312	0.4	—

PRESIDENTIAL ELECTION OF 1944

Nominations: The Republicans convened in Chicago, June 26–28, 1944. Dewey was the only presidential candidate nominated. The Democrats, at their convention in Chicago, July 19–21, 1944, gave Roosevelt 1,086 of 1,176 votes on first ballot. **Remarks:** Democrats campaigned on the basis that leadership should not be changed in the middle of a war.

PRESIDENTIAL CANDIDATES	PARTY	ELECTORAL VOTES	POPULAR VOTE Total	Percentage	VICE-PRESIDENTIAL CANDIDATES
Franklin D. Roosevelt.....	Democratic	432	25,606,585	53.5	Harry S. Truman
Thomas E. Dewey	Republican	99	22,014,745	46.0	John W. Bricker
Other candidates	—	—	200,612	0.5	—

by an awesome majority over his Republican opponent, Alfred M. Landon, who won only the electoral votes of Maine and Vermont.

The Supreme Court's action in declaring unconstitutional several New Deal measures slowed the pace of reform. In 1937 Roosevelt attempted to "pack the court," but was unable to reorganize it to his advantage. He failed, too, in attempting to "purge" members of Congress who had opposed New Deal measures.

By 1938 the international skies were black with the shadow of impending war. As the power of Nazi Germany grew, Roosevelt spoke out against aggression and international greed. In 1939 he personally appealed for peace to the German and Italian dictators, Hitler and Mussolini.

Roosevelt was bitterly opposed by isolationist and conservative forces. In the 1940 presidential election an acrimonious issue was made of his breaking the third-term tradition. Although Roosevelt's majority was reduced, he decisively defeated the Republican candidate, Wendell Willkie.

The history of Roosevelt's third term is that of World War II.

The Japanese attack on Pearl Harbor, Hawaii, on Dec. 7, 1941 finally drew the U.S. directly into the conflict. War production multiplied beyond the most optimistic estimates.

In the European-African theater, U.S. Gen. Dwight D. Eisenhower was made supreme commander. U.S. forces landed in North Africa and followed with the invasion of Sicily, Italy, and finally Normandy.

In the Pacific the U.S. Navy carried marines and soldiers in a series of amphibious operations against Japanese-held islands. U.S. superiority in the air brought the war to Japan itself.

In the election of 1944 Roosevelt won an unprecedented fourth term with Harry Truman as his Vice President.

Roosevelt participated in a series of conferences with Winston Churchill, Joseph Stalin, and other Allied leaders to discuss plans for the postwar world. He planned to lay the foundations of lasting peace through formation of the United Nations.

On April 12, 1945, however, Roosevelt died of a massive cerebral hemorrhage before the war had been won.

Anna Eleanor Roosevelt Roosevelt (1884–1962), his wife, was the niece of Theodore Roosevelt as well as a distant cousin of her husband. As a young woman she had been a volunteer social worker. She continued her civic activities after her marriage, even though she bore five sons and one daughter.

Mrs. Roosevelt also gave her husband substantial assistance in his political career. During her husband's administrations she established a precedent as a First Lady famous in her own right. In doing so, she subjected herself to controversy and criticism. She traveled widely, making numerous speeches and reporting her observations in the press.

After Roosevelt's death she devoted herself to humanitarian causes. From 1949 to 1952 she was a U.S. delegate to the United Nations.

HARRY S. TRUMAN

33d President
(1945–53)

Unexpectedly finding himself at the helm of the world's first atomic power, President Truman used the A-bomb to bring World War II to a quick conclusion. He then magnanimously extended American help both to friends and former foes in rebuilding their war-devastated economies. Under his leadership the United States became the protector of the free world from communist subversion and aggression in the postwar years. His accomplishments were hailed in these words by British leader Winston Churchill: "You, more than any other man, have saved Western Civilization."

EARLY LIFE

Truman was born on May 8, 1884, in Lamar, Mo., the son of John Anderson Truman, a farmer, and Martha Ellen Young Truman. He began working in a local drugstore at the age of 11 and graduated from high school at 17. He clerked and farmed until World War I, when he helped organize a field artillery unit. He rose to major by the end of the war.

Civilian life seemed bleak to Truman after the failure of his haberdashery business in Kansas City in 1921. However, he had attracted the notice of the local Democratic boss, Thomas Pendergast, who helped him win election as a Jackson County official. During this time Truman studied law.

Elected U.S. senator from Missouri in 1934, Truman served for 10 years as a sometime supporter of the New Deal. He became a national figure as chairman of the Special Senate Committee to Investigate the National Defense Program (the Truman Committee). His fair and energetic inquiry into inefficiency and bungling on war-production contracts won wide praise.

In 1944 Truman was elected Vice President as Franklin D. Roosevelt's running mate.

33d PRESIDENT OF THE UNITED STATES

When Roosevelt died on April 12, 1945, Truman became the first President to take office in the midst of a war.

He was immediately confronted with the problems of ending World War II and preparing for postwar readjustment. Germany surrendered in May. After Truman authorized the atomic bombing of Hiroshima and Nagasaki, Japan capitulated in August.

Nominated in 1948 as the Democratic presidential candidate, he upset all those who had forecast his certain defeat by the Republican nominee, Thomas E. Dewey. By his vigorous railroad "whistle-stop" campaigning, he not only countered a nationwide Republican swing but overcame splits in his own party. On the right, Sen. J.

QUICK QUIZ: Can you name three books written by Ernest Hemingway? See page 97.

HARRY S. TRUMAN *(continued)*
Strom Thurmond of South Carolina led a new States' Rights (Dixiecrat) Party of Southern Democrats antagonized by Truman's advocacy of civil rights for blacks. On the left, Henry A. Wallace led "progressive" groups at odds with Truman's anti-Soviet stand.

In his postwar domestic policy Truman faced strong congressional opposition from a coalition of Republicans and Southern Democrats.

The conservative coalition in Congress overrode his veto of the Labor-Management Relations Act (Taft-Hartley Law), enacted the McCarran-Walter Immigration Bill over his opposition, withheld support from his efforts to initiate government-sponsored health insurance, frustrated his attempts to maintain price controls, and blocked his civil-rights program.

In domestic affairs, however, he did achieve public housing projects, an increase in the minimum wage, civilian control of nuclear energy, and desegregation of the armed forces.

In foreign affairs, threatening communist advances in 1946–47 in Europe and the Middle East resulted in the Cold War. Congress backed Truman's foreign policy, which concentrated on containing communism.

The establishment of the UN was affirmed in 1945. Congress fully supported the "Truman Doctrine" in 1947, a program of economic and military assistance to nations threatened by communism. This was expanded later in 1947 by the Marshall Plan (European Recovery Program), and was supplemented by the Point Four Program in 1949 for aid to developing nations.

A victory in the Cold War was achieved in 1948–49 when an Anglo-American airlift frustrated the communists' Berlin blockade.

To safeguard Western Europe from possible communist attack, Truman pushed through the formation in 1950 of the North Atlantic Treaty Organization (NATO), an anticommunist military alliance.

The Cold War turned hot when communist North Korea attacked South Korea in 1950. Truman sent in U.S. troops under command of World War II hero Gen. Douglas MacArthur. But their advance to the Yalu River on the Chinese border brought China into the field, and the conflict became a stalemate. In 1951 Truman raised a storm of controversy when he relieved MacArthur of his Far Eastern command for failure to obey orders.

President Truman made the first coast-to-coast TV broadcast when he opened the Japanese Peace Conference in San Francisco in 1951.

The final years of his administration were shadowed by the stalemated Korean War, unsubstantiated charges by Sen. Joseph R. McCarthy of communist infiltration in the Department of State and the U.S. Army, plus partisan claims that U.S. failure to support Gen. Chiang Kai-shek had lost China to the communists.

Refusing to consider renomination in 1952, Truman went into retirement, giving much time to writing and to the establishment of the Harry S. Truman Library at Independence, Mo., where his official papers are housed. Truman died in his 88th year on Dec. 26, 1972, in Kansas City, Mo.

Elizabeth Virginia "Bess" Wallace Truman, (1885–1982), was a high school classmate who married Truman in 1919. She was retiring in nature and avoided publicity. Their daughter, Margaret, was a concert singer. During most of Truman's administration, he and his wife lived in Blair House, across the street from the White House, while the Executive Mansion was completely rebuilt with a steel framework.

TRUMAN'S PRESIDENTIAL ADMINISTRATION

Congresses in Session:
79th, 80th, 81st, 82d

Vice President:
Alben Barkley, 1949–53

Secretary of State:
Edward R. Stettinius Jr., 1945
James Byrnes, 1945–47
George Marshall, 1947–49
Dean Acheson, 1949–53

Secretary of the Treasury:
Henry Morgenthau Jr., 1945
Fred Vinson, 1945–46
John Snyder, 1946–53

Secretary of War:
Henry L. Stimson, 1945
Robert Patterson, 1945–47
Kenneth Royal, 1947

Secretary of Defense:
James Forrestal, 1947–49
Louis Johnson, 1949–50
George Marshall, 1950–51
Robert Lovett, 1951–53

Attorney General:
Francis Biddle, 1945
Tom Clark, 1945–49
J. Howard McGrath, 1949–52
James McGranery, 1952–53

Postmaster General:
Frank C. Walker, 1945
Robert Hannegan, 1945–47
Jesse Donaldson, 1947–53

Secretary of the Navy:
James Forrestal, 1945–47

Secretary of the Interior:
Harold Ickes, 1945–46
Julius Krug, 1946–49
Oscar Chapman, 1949–53

Secretary of Agriculture:
Claude R. Wickard, 1945
Clinton Anderson, 1945–48
Charles Brannan, 1948–53

Secretary of Commerce:
Henry A. Wallace, 1945–46
W. Averell Harriman, 1946–48
Charles Sawyer, 1948–53

Secretary of Labor:
Frances Perkins, 1945
Lewis Schwellenbach, 1945–48
Maurice Tobin, 1948–53

PRESIDENTIAL ELECTION OF 1948

Nominations: Republicans met in Philadelphia, June 21–25, 1948, and on the third ballot gave Dewey a unanimous vote. Democrats convened in Philadelphia, July 12–14, 1948. Truman won on the first ballot. **Campaign Issues:** Truman capitalized on attacking the "do-nothing" Republican-controlled 80th Congress, winning a surprising upset victory.

PRESIDENTIAL CANDIDATES	PARTY	ELECTORAL VOTES	POPULAR VOTE Total	Percentage	VICE-PRESIDENTIAL CANDIDATES
Harry S. Truman	Democratic	303	24,105,812	49.5	Alben W. Barkley
Thomas E. Dewey	Republican	189	21,970,065	45.1	Earl Warren
J. Strom Thurmond	States' Rights	39	1,169,063	2.4	Fielding L. Wright
Henry A. Wallace	Progressive	—	1,157,172	2.4	Glenn Taylor
Other candidates	—	—	285,495	0.6	—

DWIGHT DAVID EISENHOWER

34th President
(1953–61)

The victorious commander of allied forces that defeated Germany in World War II, "Ike" Eisenhower was sought as a presidential candidate by both major political parties. At first he rejected the overtures. But he finally succumbed, resigning from the Army in 1952 to become the Republican presidential nominee. He chose as his running mate Sen. Richard M. Nixon.

With the campaign slogan "I like Ike," the hero general easily defeated his Democratic opponent, Gov. Adlai E. Stevenson of Illinois, both in 1952 and 1956.

As President, Eisenhower quickly settled the Korean War. Then, after a brief recession, the nation enjoyed a high level of prosperity, clouded only by fears of a possible atomic war with the Soviet Union.

The Space Age began as the Soviets and the U.S. first launched satellites into orbit in 1957–58. Alaska and Hawaii were admitted to the Union as the 49th and 50th states in 1959.

Eisenhower was born on Oct. 14, 1890, in Denison, Texas, the son of David Jacob and Ida Elizabeth Stover Eisenhower. When he was a child his family moved to Abilene, Kan.

MILITARY CAREER

Eisenhower graduated from West Point in 1915 as a U.S. Army second lieutenant.

In World War I, Eisenhower was commanding officer of a training camp for the new U.S. Army tank corps, near Gettysburg, Pa. After the war he was posted, successively, to the Panama Canal Zone, the office of the assistant secretary of war, and from 1935 to 1940 to the Philippines. There he learned to fly in 1939, later making him the first President to hold a pilot's license.

During World War II, Eisenhower commanded U.S. forces in the North African landings, and in 1943 became chief of Allied forces in North Africa. After directing the invasions of Sicily and Italy, he was appointed supreme commander of Allied Expeditionary Forces.

In 1944 Eisenhower was made a 5-star general. His genial nature helped achieve essential cooperation among the Allied forces in the Normandy invasion and in the momentous battle that won victory in Europe in 1945.

After the war, he became Army chief of staff. He wrote *Crusade in Europe* (1948), an account of World War II.

Eisenhower resigned from the Army to become president of Columbia University (1948–50), but donned his uniform again to accept appointment as Supreme Commander of Allied Forces in

EISENHOWER'S PRESIDENTIAL ADMINISTRATION

Congresses in Session:
83d, 84th, 85th, 86th

Vice President:
Richard M. Nixon, 1953–61

Secretary of State:
John Foster Dulles, 1953–59
Christian Herter, 1959–61

Secretary of the Treasury:
George Humphrey, 1953–57
Robert Anderson, 1957–61

Postmaster General:
Arthur Summerfield, 1953–61

Secretary of Defense:
Charles Wilson, 1953–57
Neil McElroy, 1957–59
Thomas Gates Jr., 1959–61

Attorney General:
Herbert Brownell Jr., 1953–57
William Rogers, 1957–61

Secretary of the Interior:
Douglas McKay, 1953–56
Frederick Seaton, 1956–61

Secretary of Agriculture:
Ezra Taft Benson, 1953–61

Secretary of Commerce:
Sinclair Weeks, 1953–58
Lewis Strauss, 1958–59
Frederick Mueller, 1959–61

Secretary of Labor:
Martin Durkin, 1953
James Mitchell, 1953–61

Secretary of Health, Education, and Welfare
Oveta Culp Hobby, 1953–55
Marion Folsom, 1955–58
Arthur Flemming, 1958–61

PRESIDENTIAL ELECTION OF 1952

Nominations: The Republicans met in Chicago, July 7–11, 1952. Despite opposition by conservative Sen. Robert A. Taft (R-Ohio), Eisenhower received 845 of 1,206 votes on the first ballot, and his nomination was made unanimous. The Democrats convened in Chicago, July 21–26, 1952. Stevenson won on the third ballot. **Campaign Issues:** Conduct of the Korean War, the stalemate in the Cold War, corruption in the Democratic administration, and McCarthyism. **Remarks:** Stevenson was the first presidential nominee since Garfield to be drafted by his party.

PRESIDENTIAL CANDIDATES	PARTY	ELECTORAL VOTES	POPULAR VOTE Total	POPULAR VOTE Percentage	VICE-PRESIDENTIAL CANDIDATES
Dwight D. Eisenhower	Republican	442	33,936,234	55.1	Richard M. Nixon
Adlai E. Stevenson	Democratic	89	27,314,992	44.4	John J. Sparkman
Other candidates	—	—	290,959	0.5	—

PRESIDENTIAL ELECTION OF 1956

Nominations: The Democrats met in Chicago, Aug. 13–17, 1956. On the first ballot Stevenson had 905½ of 1,372 votes, and his nomination was made unanimous. The Republicans, meeting in San Francisco, Aug. 20–23, 1956, renominated Eisenhower by acclamation. **Campaign Issues:** Conduct of the Cold War, atomic testing, and Eisenhower's health.

PRESIDENTIAL CANDIDATES	PARTY	ELECTORAL VOTES	POPULAR VOTE Total	POPULAR VOTE Percentage	VICE-PRESIDENTIAL CANDIDATES
Dwight D. Eisenhower	Republican	457	35,590,472	57.4	Richard M. Nixon
Adlai E. Stevenson	Democratic	73	26,022,752	42.0	Estes Kefauver
Other candidates	—	1	414,000	0.6	—

QUICK QUIZ: Who is president pro tempore of the Senate? See page 159.

DWIGHT D. EISENHOWER *(continued)*
Europe (1951–52). There he organized the NATO (North Atlantic Treaty Organization) defense forces.

34th PRESIDENT OF THE UNITED STATES

During the presidential election campaign of 1952, Eisenhower had pledged to personally go to Korea to end the war there.

After winning the election, Eisenhower flew to Korea. He brought the war to an end six months after taking office.

In domestic affairs President Eisenhower restricted the role of the federal government. However, he approved extension of Social Security to millions of self-employed Americans, increased aid to farmers, and raised the minimum hourly wage to $1. He initiated construction of the 42,500-mile Interstate Highway System.

In 1956 Eisenhower refused to aid a revolt in Hungary that was crushed by Soviet troops. He also denounced an attempt by Britain, France, and Israel to seize the Suez Canal from Egypt, forcing them to withdraw their troops.

In 1957 he used federal troops to back up the Supreme Court's 1954 ruling that public schools must be racially integrated.

The President promulgated the "Eisenhower Doctrine" in 1957, promising military and economic aid to any Middle Eastern nation resisting communist subversion. The following year U.S. Marines were sent to aid Lebanon.

Late in his second term the President was embarrassed by a scandal involving his confidential aide, Sherman Adams.

President Eisenhower was frustrated in his efforts to achieve better relations with Soviet leaders by the revelation of U-2 espionage flights over the Soviet Union.

During his administration Eisenhower suffered several serious illnesses.

After leaving Washington he retired to his farm in Gettysburg, Pa., but he remained active, campaigning for Republican candidates, writing books, and commenting on national issues.

He died on March 28, 1969, and was buried in Abilene, Kan.

Mary "Mamie" Geneva Doud Eisenhower (1896–1979) became his wife in 1916. She was a reserved and unassuming White House hostess who avoided unnecessary publicity. The Eisenhowers had two sons: Doud Dwight, who died when he was 3, and John Sheldon Doud Eisenhower, who was born in 1923.

JOHN FITZGERALD KENNEDY

35th President
(1961–63)

The youngest elected President at 43, John F. Kennedy inspired the confidence of American youth. His inaugural address touched a national urge to aid mankind with its appeal: "Ask not what your country can do for you; ask what you can do for your country."

Before Kennedy had achieved most of his planned goals for the nation, he became the fourth U.S. President to be assassinated.

EARLY YEARS

Kennedy was born on May 29, 1917, in Brookline, Mass., the son of Joseph P. Kennedy, a prominent and wealthy businessman, and Rose Fitzgerald Kennedy, daughter of a former mayor of Boston.

Kennedy studied briefly at Princeton and the London School of Economics. He graduated from Harvard with honors in 1940, and in the same year published his first book, the bestselling *Why England Slept*.

During World War II, Kennedy commanded a Navy PT-boat in the Pacific. In action off the Solomon Islands, his boat was sunk by an enemy destroyer. He became a hero to his crew by his courage in securing their rescue.

He was elected to Congress in 1946 and was

KENNEDY'S PRESIDENTIAL ADMINISTRATION

Congresses in Session:
87th, 88th
Vice President:
Lyndon B. Johnson, 1961–63
Secretary of State:
Dean Rusk, 1961–63
Secretary of the Treasury:
C. Douglas Dillon, 1961–63
Secretary of Defense:
Robert S. McNamara, 1961–63
Attorney General:
Robert F. Kennedy, 1961–63
Postmaster General:
J. Edward Day, 1961–63
John A. Gronouski Jr., 1963
Secretary of the Interior:
Stewart L. Udall, 1961–63
Secretary of Agriculture:
Orville L. Freeman, 1961–63
Secretary of Commerce:
Luther H. Hodges, 1961–63
Secretary of Labor:
Arthur J. Goldberg, 1961–62
W. Willard Wirtz, 1962–63
Secretary of Health, Education, and Welfare:
Abraham A. Ribicoff, 1961–62
Anthony J. Celebrezze, 1962–63

PRESIDENTIAL ELECTION OF 1960

Nominations: Democrats met in Los Angeles, July 11–15, 1960. Kennedy was nominated on the first ballot. Republicans, meeting in Chicago, July 25–28, 1960, nominated Nixon on the first ballot. **Campaign Issues:** The Democrats charged there was a "missile gap," that U.S. prestige was declining abroad, and that the Soviets had forged ahead militarily. **Remarks:** Unpledged Alabama and Mississippi electors cast their votes for Sen. Harry F. Byrd (D-Va.).

PRESIDENTIAL CANDIDATES	PARTY	ELECTORAL VOTES	POPULAR VOTE Total	POPULAR VOTE Percentage	VICE-PRESIDENTIAL CANDIDATES
John F. Kennedy	Democratic	303	34,227,096	49.5	Lyndon B. Johnson
Richard M. Nixon	Republican	219	34,108,546	49.4	Henry Cabot Lodge
Unpledged electors	—	15	638,822	0.9	—
Other candidates	—	—	138,559	0.2	—

reelected with ease in 1948 and 1950. In 1952, despite the Republican landslide, Kennedy ran against and defeated the incumbent U.S. senator, Henry Cabot Lodge (R-Mass.).

In 1954–55 Kennedy underwent operations to repair a spinal injury, suffered during the war. While recuperating, he wrote *Profiles in Courage*, for which he won a 1957 Pulitzer Prize.

In 1958 Kennedy was overwhelmingly reelected to the Senate.

The Massachusetts senator then began a campaign for the 1960 Democratic presidential nomination. Several important primary victories in 1960 helped ensure his nomination at the convention. Kennedy chose Sen. Lyndon B. Johnson of Texas as his running mate.

Kennedy campaigned against his Republican opponent, Richard M. Nixon, partly on the issue that the country's prestige had declined greatly during the Eisenhower administration. His cause was helped by his performance in a series of TV debates with Nixon.

Kennedy won the election in the closest presidential race of the 20th century. He became the first President who was a Roman Catholic, and the first President born in the 20th century.

35th PRESIDENT OF THE UNITED STATES

The Kennedy administration's program, called the New Frontier, pressed for U.S. aid to education, enlargement of civil rights, aid to economically depressed areas, medical care for the aged, and an accelerated space program. Major accomplishments in foreign affairs were the establishment of the Peace Corps, the Alliance for Progress with Latin American countries, and the nuclear test-ban treaty.

In 1961, when the CIA-led anti-Castro invasion of communist Cuba at the Bay of Pigs failed, Kennedy and the nation suffered deep humiliation.

Confidence in American power was restored in 1962 when the President's order of a naval blockade of Cuba compelled the Soviet Union to dismantle its missile bases in Cuba and remove its bombing planes from the island.

Deeply concerned with culture, Kennedy did much to foster public interest in literature and the arts. The White House guest list included many scientists, writers, artists, and musicians.

The march toward the New Frontier was brutally halted when Kennedy was assassinated in Dallas, Texas, on Nov. 22, 1963, by Lee Harvey Oswald, a former U.S. marine who believed in communism. Kennedy was buried in Arlington National Cemetery.

Jacqueline Lee Bouvier Kennedy, born in 1929, married Kennedy in 1953. As First Lady she redecorated the White House interior. She was noted for her charm and command of foreign languages. Widespread admiration was evoked by her courage at the time of her husband's death (she was at his side when he was killed). The Kennedys had three children: Caroline Bouvier, born in 1957; John Fitzgerald, born in 1960; and Patrick Bouvier, who died two days after his birth in 1963.

Five years after Kennedy's death, she married Greek ship-owner Aristotle Onassis in 1968. She was again widowed when Onassis died in 1975.

LYNDON BAINES JOHNSON

Within hours after Kennedy's death, Johnson was sworn in as President. He entered office with the handicap of having to take over from a man who had won adulation for himself and a new respect abroad for the nation.

36th President (1963–69)

Johnson's years as President increasingly filled with controversy over the Vietnam War, but both friends and foes agreed he was a persuasive man and a brilliant politician.

Johnson was born on Aug. 27, 1908, on a ranch near Stonewall, Texas, the son of Samuel Ealy Johnson, a schoolteacher and state legislator, and Rebekah Baines Johnson. He graduated from Southwest Texas State College in 1930 and then taught school. In 1932 he became secretary to a Texas congressman. An ardent New Dealer, he was named National Youth Administration director for Texas in 1935.

Johnson was elected to Congress in 1937 to fill an unexpired term, and he held the seat until 1948. He served on active duty in the U.S. Navy in 1941–42 and then returned to Congress. In 1948 he won the Democratic nomination for U.S. senator from Texas by a scant 87 votes.

In the Senate he became Democratic whip in 1951 and Senate minority leader in 1953. Democrats won control of the Senate in 1954 and Johnson, elected to a second term, became majority leader, a post he held until 1960—despite suffering a serious heart attack in 1955. As majority leader Johnson was a powerful figure.

In 1960, after a vain try for the presidential nomination, Johnson accepted second place on the Kennedy ticket. By keeping the Southern states within the party, Johnson made a major contribution in the Democrats' victory.

In filling out the remaining 14 months of Kennedy's term, President Johnson used his legislative skill to win congressional passage of his slain predecessor's program, especially in his skillful handling of the Civil Rights Act of 1964 and the Economic Opportunity Act, which declared "war on poverty."

In the 1964 election Johnson won over Sen. Barry Goldwater, the Republican candidate, by the largest percentage of the popular vote ever recorded. He strove tirelessly to push through Congress his social reform program that he called the Great Society.

Drawing on his experience as Senate leader, Johnson succeeded in getting his massive domestic program passed. In a whirlwind of activity he initiated tax cuts, gained passage of a voting rights act, instituted the Medicare plan, obtained increased federal aid for education, and approved a new immigration law.

QUICK QUIZ: Where is the driest spot on Earth? See page 178.

LYNDON B. JOHNSON *(continued)*

During 1965 Johnson dispatched U.S. troops to fight communist forces trying to take over South Vietnam. At the same time he spurred intensified diplomatic efforts aimed at negotiating settlement of the war.

By 1967 President Johnson's popularity took a downward turn as the Vietnam conflict intensified. According to public-opinion polls, Americans were dissatisfied with the President's handling of the war and deeply concerned about urban riots, rising taxes, and inflation.

On March 31, 1968, Johnson announced he would not run for a second full term. His last year in office was one of still more tragedy: the assassination on April 4 of the respected black leader and Nobel Peace Prize-winner Dr. Martin Luther King Jr.; the resultant city riots; the assassination of Sen. Robert F. Kennedy in June; and the strife-blemished Democratic convention in August.

After leaving the presidency in 1969, Johnson retired to his ranch near Johnson City, Texas. He died there at the age of 64 on Jan. 22, 1973. **Claudia "Lady Bird" Alta Taylor Johnson,** his wife, was born in 1912. They were married in 1934 and had two daughters: Lynda Bird (born in 1944) and Luci Baines (born in 1947). As First Lady, Mrs. Johnson spearheaded projects to beautify the national environment.

JOHNSON'S PRESIDENTIAL ADMINISTRATION

Congresses in Session:
88th, 89th, 90th
Vice President:
Hubert H. Humphrey, 1965–69
Secretary of State:
Dean Rusk, 1963–69
Secretary of the Treasury:
C. Douglas Dillon, 1963–65
Henry H. Fowler, 1965–68
Joseph W. Barr, 1968–69
Secretary of Defense:
Robert S. McNamara, 1963–68
Clark M. Clifford, 1968–69
Secretary of the Interior:
Stewart L. Udall, 1963–69
Attorney General:
Robert F. Kennedy, 1963–64
Nicholas deB. Katzenbach, 1964–66
Ramsey Clark, 1967–69
Secretary of Agriculture:
Orville L. Freeman, 1963–69
Secretary of Commerce:
Luther H. Hodges, 1963–64
John T. Connor, 1965–67
A. B. Trowbridge, 1967–68
C. R. Smith, 1968–69
Secretary of Labor
W. Willard Wirtz, 1963–69
Postmaster General:
John A. Gronouski Jr., 1963–65
Lawrence F. O'Brien, 1965–68
W. Marvin Watson, 1968–69
Secretary of Health, Education, and Welfare:
Anthony J. Celebrezze, 1963–65
John W. Gardner, 1965–68
Wilbur J. Cohen, 1968–69
Secretary of Housing and Urban Development:
Robert C. Weaver, 1965–68
Robert C. Wood, 1968–69
Secretary of Transportation
Alan S. Boyd, 1966–69

PRESIDENTIAL ELECTION OF 1964

Nominations: Republicans met in San Francisco, July 13–16, 1964, and chose Goldwater on the first ballot. Democrats met in Atlantic City, N.J., Aug. 24–27, 1964, and nominated President Johnson by acclamation. **Campaign Issues:** Direct issues concerned the Vietnam War, some of the Great Society programs of the incumbent administration, and the far right-wing support that was attracted by Goldwater. **Remarks:** President Johnson received the largest popular-vote majority and greatest percentage of the total vote than ever before won by a presidential candidate.

PRESIDENTIAL CANDIDATES	PARTY	ELECTORAL VOTES	POPULAR VOTE Total	Percentage	VICE-PRESIDENTIAL CANDIDATES
Lyndon B. Johnson.......	Democratic	486	43,129,484	61.1	Hubert H. Humphrey
Barry Goldwater	Republican	52	27,178,188	38.5	William E. Miller
Other candidates	—	—	336,838	0.4	—

RICHARD MILHOUS NIXON

37th President
(1969–74)

Richard Nixon became the first President to resign, giving up his administration when it became clear he was about to be impeached and convicted by Congress as a result of his misuse of presidential power in the Watergate scandals. Many of his closest associates were convicted and jailed in the affair. His administration was further stained by the resignation and conviction for income tax evasion of Vice President Spiro Agnew, who avoided trial on charges of accepting bribes.

Despite Nixon's misuse of power, he was acclaimed for achievements in the area of foreign affairs. He brought an end to U.S. participation in the Vietnam War—the longest and costliest war in U.S. history. And he moved boldly to end the Cold War with communist China and the Soviet Union.

He was born on Jan. 9, 1913, in Yorba Linda, Calif., the son of Francis Anthony and Hannah Milhous Nixon, a devout Quaker. When he was nine years old the family moved to Whittier, Calif.

Nixon graduated from Whittier College and the Duke University Law School. During World War II he worked in the Office of Price Administration and then served as a naval officer in the Pacific.

EARLY POLITICAL CAREER

In 1946 Republicans in Nixon's California congressional district were seeking a candidate for Congress. Nixon gained their endorsement and was elected.

National fame came quickly. Serving on the House Un-American Activities Committee, Nixon pressed an investigation of charges that Alger Hiss, a former State Department official, had supplied secret documents to the Soviets. His adroit questioning discredited Hiss, who later was convicted of perjury. The case established Nixon as an articulate foe of communism. He was elected to the Senate in 1950, but by then his use of the communist issue against political opponents was provoking criticism.

In 1952 Dwight Eisenhower chose Nixon as his running mate. During the campaign Nixon was accused of accepting large sums of money from wealthy contributors. Eisenhower told him he must come "clean as a hound's tooth," so Nixon went on TV to explain. His emotional "Checkers" speech—he referred in it to a dog of that name that he had accepted as a gift—turned the issue to his advantage, and the Eisenhower-Nixon ticket was elected.

Many Vice Presidents have languished in obscurity, but not the energetic Nixon. Eisenhower had little interest in partisan politics, and Nixon welcomed the chance to speak and campaign nationally. When Eisenhower became ill on three separate occasions, Nixon acted in his behalf with confidence and restraint.

After the Republican slate was reelected in 1956, Nixon became the almost unanimous choice of his party for the presidential nomination in 1960.

Nixon narrowly lost the 1960 presidential election to Sen. John F. Kennedy when the more articulate Kennedy gained votes in a series of TV debates with him.

He ran for governor of California in 1962 and lost. Blaming biased journalists, he announced his retirement from politics and said angrily, "You won't have Nixon to kick around anymore."

But in 1968 he was awarded the Republican presidential nomination on the first ballot. The Democrats were bitterly divided over U.S. involvement in Vietnam.

Nixon won with less than a majority of the popular vote in one of the closest elections in American history. He defeated the Democratic candidate, Vice President Hubert H. Humphrey, by less than 1% of the vote.

FIRST TERM AS PRESIDENT

As President, Nixon cut U.S. troop strength in

NIXON'S PRESIDENTIAL ADMINISTRATION

Congresses in Session:
91st, 92d, 93d
Vice President:
Spiro T. Agnew, 1969–73
Gerald R. Ford, 1973–74
Secretary of State:
William P. Rogers, 1969–73
Henry A. Kissinger, 1973–74
Secretary of the Treasury:
David M. Kennedy, 1969–71
John B. Connally Jr., 1971–72
George P. Shultz, 1972–74
William E. Simon, 1974
Secretary of Defense:
Melvin R. Laird, 1969–73
Elliot L. Richardson, 1973
James R. Schlesinger, 1973–74
Attorney General:
John N. Mitchell, 1969–72
Richard G. Kleindienst, 1972–73
Elliot L. Richardson, 1973
William B. Saxbe, 1974
Secretary of the Interior:
Walter J. Hickel, 1969–71
Rogers C. B. Morton, 1971–74
Secretary of Agriculture:
Clifford M. Hardin, 1969–71
Earl L. Butz, 1971–74
Postmaster General:
(abolished as cabinet post, 1971)
Winton M. Blount, 1969–71
Secretary of Transportation:
John A. Volpe, 1969–73
Claude S. Brinegar, 1973–74
Secretary of Commerce:
Maurice H. Stans, 1969–72
Peter G. Peterson, 1972–73
Frederick B. Dent, 1973–74
Secretary of Labor:
George P. Shultz, 1969–70
James D. Hodgson, 1970–73
Peter J. Brennan, 1973–74
Secretary of Health, Education, and Welfare:
Robert H. Finch, 1969–70
Elliot L. Richardson, 1970–73
Caspar W. Weinberger, 1973–74
Secretary of Housing and Urban Development:
George W. Romney, 1969–73
James T. Lynn, 1973–74

PRESIDENTIAL ELECTION OF 1968

Nominations: Republicans in Miami Beach, Fla., Aug. 5–8, 1968, named Nixon on the first ballot. Agnew's nomination was made unanimous. The Democratic convention in Chicago, Aug. 26–29, was marred by violence both in and out of the convention hall. Humphrey and Muskie were each a first-ballot choice. **Campaign Issues:** The war in Vietnam. **Remarks:** Nixon's popular vote share—43.4%—was the lowest for a winning presidential candidate since Wilson's election in 1912. Earlier concern proved groundless that the electoral votes cast for third-party candidate Gov. George C. Wallace of Alabama might be enough to throw the election into the House of Representatives.

PRESIDENTIAL CANDIDATES	PARTY	ELECTORAL VOTES	POPULAR VOTE Total	Percentage	VICE-PRESIDENTIAL CANDIDATES
Richard M. Nixon	Republican	301	31,785,480	43.4	Spiro T. Agnew
Hubert H. Humphrey	Democratic	191	31,275,165	42.7	Edmund S. Muskie
George C. Wallace	American	46	9,906,473	13.5	Curtis E. LeMay
Others	—	—	244,444	0.4	—

PRESIDENTIAL ELECTION OF 1972

Nominations: Democrats met in Miami Beach, Fla., July 13–14, and named Sen. George McGovern of South Dakota and Sen. Thomas F. Eagleton of Missouri. When the press revealed Eagleton had received psychiatric treatment, McGovern asked him to withdraw. Sargent Shriver, brother-in-law of President Kennedy, replaced Eagleton on Aug. 8. Republicans met in Miami Beach, Aug. 22–23, nominating Nixon and Agnew for a second term. **Campaign Issues:** War in Vietnam, welfare reform. **Remarks:** One Virginia elector switched his vote from Nixon to a minor-party candidate.

PRESIDENTIAL CANDIDATES	PARTY	ELECTORAL VOTES	POPULAR VOTE Total	Percentage	VICE-PRESIDENTIAL CANDIDATES
Richard M. Nixon	Republican	520	47,169,911	60.7	Spiro T. Agnew
George McGovern	Democratic	17	29,170,383	37.5	Sargent Shriver
John G. Schmitz	American	0	1,098,482	1.4	Thomas J. Anderson
Other candidates	—	1	278,778	0.4	—

QUICK QUIZ: What is the life expectancy for a woman in Morocco? See page 471.

RICHARD NIXON *(continued)*
Vietnam from 550,000 to 27,000 by December 1972, but he increased U.S. air and naval power in Southeast Asia. In 1972, after North Vietnam invaded in force, Nixon ordered mining of the North Vietnamese ports and air attacks on land supply routes from China.

Antiwar protests were widespread but ineffective. The fatal shooting of four students by Ohio National Guardsmen during a demonstration at Kent State University in 1970 was the darkest hour of the Vietnam controversy.

The U.S. economy, plagued by government budgetary deficits, sagged in 1970. The President found it impossible to control inflation.

Many white parents opposed court-ordered busing of their children to achieve racial balance in public schools, and Nixon unsuccessfully sought a legal means of limiting such busing.

Environmentalists applauded his moves to eliminate water and air pollution, but they worked through Congress to block his plan to construct a supersonic transport plane that critics considered ecologically harmful.

President Nixon moved dramatically to end the Cold War with communist China and the Soviet Union. With U.S. support, the UN in 1971 admitted communist China and expelled the nationalist Chinese of Taiwan. In February 1972 Nixon became the first U.S. President ever to visit China while in office.

The President flew to Moscow in May 1972 for a summit meeting with leaders of the Soviet Union. Several agreements were signed, the most important being the strategic arms limitation (SALT) treaties, setting limits on the production and deployment of atomic weapons.

In the 1972 election campaign for a second term, the President sought the support of young voters going to the polls for the first time since a 1971 constitutional amendment lowered the voting age to 18. During the campaign Nixon supporters raised an unprecedented $60 million for expenses, leading to abuses later revealed in the Watergate investigations in 1973–74.

Twelve days before the election, presidential adviser Henry Kissinger, who had been conducting secret negotiations in Paris with the North Vietnamese, announced "peace is at hand."

A record of over 77 million voters cast ballots, giving the President a landslide victory over his Democratic opponent, Sen. George McGovern of South Dakota.

When Vietnam truce negotiations broke down late in 1972, Nixon ordered heavy bombing of North Vietnam until the communists returned to the talks.

SECOND TERM AND RESIGNATION

In his inaugural address in January 1973, the President promised to work for a "peace which can endure for generations to come." A week later, on Jan. 28, 1973, a Vietnam cease-fire agreement was signed in Paris, enabling all U.S. troops to be withdrawn from Vietnam by March 29. However, U.S. planes continued to bomb communist forces in Cambodia. Despite Nixon's opposition, the Democrat-controlled Congress forced an end to all U.S. military action in Southeast Asia on Aug. 15, 1973. Two years later communist military forces took over the governments of South Vietnam, Laos, and Cambodia.

Just as President Nixon seemed about to lead the nation into a new era of peace and harmony, the Watergate scandals engulfed his administration.

The affair had begun when police on June 17, 1972, arrested five men who had broken into and installed wiretapping devices in the headquarters of the Democratic National Committee at the Watergate office building in Washington, D.C.

A Senate investigation in 1973 revealed evidence that the Watergate break-in was only part of a pattern of crimes by Nixon aides in 1972 aimed at ensuring his reelection. Nixon denied he was involved in the scandals.

On Oct. 10, 1973, Vice President Agnew resigned and accepted conviction for income tax evasion to avoid being tried on charges of accepting bribes. For the first time in the nation's history Amendment 25 to the U.S. Constitution was used as President Nixon appointed Gerald R. Ford to succeed Agnew.

President Nixon ordered the firing of special Watergate prosecutor Archibald Cox on Oct. 30, 1973, because Cox had refused to drop a court suit against the President calling for the release of White House tapes and documents relating to the Watergate scandals.

A resulting public outcry caused the House of Representatives to institute hearings to determine if Nixon should be impeached.

Nine months later, in July 1974, the House Judiciary Committee voted to recommend Nixon's impeachment on three counts: obstructing justice in covering up the Watergate scandals, violating his presidential oath of office, and defying the committee's subpoenas for evidence.

Also in July 1974 the Supreme Court by a unanimous decision ordered the President to turn over evidence subpoenaed by the new Watergate special prosecutor, Leon Jaworski.

The White House on Aug. 5, 1974, made public some of the evidence ordered released by the Supreme Court. It showed that President Nixon had obstructed the FBI investigation of the Watergate break-in to protect associates and to ensure his reelection. Republican leaders told Nixon they could not prevent his impeachment and conviction.

President Nixon resigned on Aug. 9, 1974, and retired. He was succeeded by Ford.

A month later, on Sept. 8, 1974, President Ford granted Nixon a "full, free and absolute pardon for all offenses" during his administration, thus eliminating the possibility of his indictment or trial for his role in the scandals.

In subsequent months three cabinet officers, Nixon's two top White House aides, and many other administration officials and election campaign supporters were convicted on charges growing out of the scandals.

Thelma Catherine Patricia Ryan Nixon, born in 1912, was a popular White House hostess. She revealed considerable skill in person-to-person diplomacy during her trips abroad. She and Nixon were married in 1940 and had two daughters. Tricia Nixon (1946–) married Edward Cox in the White House in 1971. Julie Nixon (1948–) married President Eisenhower's grandson David Eisenhower in 1968.

GERALD RUDOLPH FORD

38th President
(1974–77)

The first nonelected President, Gerald R. Ford became Chief Executive when Richard Nixon resigned to avoid impeachment and conviction by Congress in the Watergate scandal. Ford had been appointed Vice President 10 months earlier, following the resignation of Spiro T. Agnew.

As President, Ford was confronted with the worst recession since the Great Depression of the 1930s. Ford served as President only 29 months, losing his bid for a full term to Democratic candidate Jimmy Carter.

EARLY LIFE

Ford was born on July 14, 1913, in Omaha, Neb. The son of Dorothy Gardner King and Leslie King, a wool trader, he was named Leslie Lynch King at birth. His parents were divorced in 1915. He and his mother returned to her parents' home in Grand Rapids, Mich., where she soon met and married Gerald Rudolf Ford, a young paint salesman. The boy was adopted by his stepfather and renamed Gerald Rudolph Ford Jr.

Ford went to the University of Michigan on an athletic scholarship, playing center on the Michigan football team.

Upon graduation he accepted an offer to become assistant football line coach and boxing coach at Yale University so that he could attend the Yale law school. After receiving his law degree in 1941 he returned to Grand Rapids.

After the United States entered World War II, Ford joined the U.S. Navy in April 1942, receiving a commission as an ensign. He served aboard the light aircraft carrier USS *Monterey* in the Pacific fighting against Japan, attaining the rank of lieutenant commander.

CONGRESSMAN AND VICE PRESIDENT

Upon his return to Grand Rapids in 1946, Jerry Ford resumed his law practice. At the age of 35 he won election in 1948 as U.S. representative from Michigan's 5th District.

For the next quarter of a century Ford won 12 more elections to Congress, each time by a large majority. A conservative Republican, Ford followed the party line in Congress.

When Vice President Agnew resigned in October 1973 to avoid being tried on charges of bribery, President Nixon nominated Ford to fill the vacancy. After lengthy hearings, Ford was sworn in as Vice President on Dec. 6, 1973—the first to attain the office under Amendment 25 to the U.S. Constitution.

During his eight months as Vice President, Ford toured the country speaking in 40 states in an effort to preserve confidence in the national government while Congress was holding hearings to consider the possible impeachment of President Nixon in the Watergate scandals.

PRESIDENTIAL ADMINISTRATION

Ford became President following Nixon's resignation on Aug. 9, 1974. Calling on the nation to "bind up the internal wounds of Watergate," he promised "openness and candor."

Ford's popularity took a nose dive when without consulting Congress he pardoned Nixon on Sept. 8, 1974, and eight days later announced a program of conditional amnesty for Vietnam War draft evaders and military deserters.

In the early months of Ford's administration skyrocketing inflation, caused largely by price increases for foreign oil, gripped the economy. Ford attacked inflation as "our domestic public enemy No. 1," urging consumers to buy less.

As consumers slowed their purchases, the automobile industry was hit first by a drop in sales and began closing plants in November and December 1974. The recession deepened in 1975 with unemployment soaring to more than 8.2 million persons or 8.9% of the work force in May—the highest unemployment rate since the Great Depression. To help stimulate the economy, Ford asked Congress early in 1975 to reduce income taxes. At the same time he submitted a $350 billion federal budget, and had a record deficit of more than $66 billion.

Ford asserted his conservative leadership by repeatedly vetoing spending measures passed by the Democratic-controlled Congress. Most of his 66 vetoes were upheld because of disunity in the Democratic Party. However, Congress overrode his veto 12 times—more than for any President since Andrew Johnson.

U.S. prestige in international affairs suffered in the spring of 1975 as South Vietnam and Cambodia surrendered to communist troops. When victorious Cambodian communists seized the U.S.

FORD'S PRESIDENTIAL ADMINISTRATION

Congresses in Session:
93d, 94th

Vice President:
Nelson A. Rockefeller, 1974–77

Secretary of State:
Henry A. Kissinger, 1974–77

Secretary of Defense:
James R. Schlesinger, 1974–75
Donald H. Rumsfeld, 1975–77

Secretary of Commerce:
Frederick B. Dent, 1974–75
Rogers C. B. Morton, 1975–76
Elliot L. Richardson, 1976–77

Secretary of the Treasury:
William E. Simon, 1974–76

Attorney General:
William B. Saxbe, 1974–75
Edward H. Levi, 1975–77

Secretary of the Interior:
Rogers C. B. Morton, 1974–75
Stanley K. Hathaway, 1975
Thomas S. Kleppe, 1975–77

Secretary of Labor:
Peter J. Brennan, 1974–75
John T. Dunlop, 1975–76
William J. Usery Jr., 1976–77

Secretary of Agriculture:
Earl L. Butz, 1974–76
John A. Knebel, 1976–77

Secretary of Health, Education, and Welfare:
Caspar W. Weinberger, 1974–75
F. David Mathews, 1975–77

Secretary of Housing and Urban Development:
James T. Lynn, 1974–75
Carla Anderson Hills, 1975–77

Secretary of Transportation:
Claude S. Brinegar, 1974–75
William T. Coleman Jr., 1975–77

QUICK QUIZ: What is the chief industry of the Bahamas? See page 491.

GERALD FORD *(continued)*
freighter *Mayaguez* in May, President Ford moved quickly to reaffirm American power by sending U.S. Marines to recapture the ship.

Ford continued Nixon's policy of détente with the Soviet Union. He held his first summit meeting with Soviet leader Leonid Brezhnev at Vladivostok on Nov. 23-24, 1974, but achieved no substantive new agreements.

President Ford had further meetings with Brezhnev at Helsinki, Finland, in 1975, where he signed the Helsinki Pact that formally recognized the European border changes imposed by the Soviet Union after World War II and guaranteed human rights for the peoples of Europe.

During Ford's administration, Secretary of State Henry Kissinger used "shuttle diplomacy" involving countless jet airplane flights to cool tense international situations.

Women made two separate attempts to assassinate President Ford in September 1975. On Sept. 5, Secret Service men grabbed a pistol from the hand of Lynette Alice Fromme, 27, as she pointed it at Ford from a crowd in Sacramento, Calif. She was a follower of convicted murderer Charles Manson. On Sept. 22, Sara Jane Moore, 45, a civil-rights activist, fired a pistol at Ford as he left a San Francisco hotel, but an alert bystander deflected her aim. Both women were sentenced to life imprisonment.

At the beginning of the 1976 presidential election campaign, public opinion polls showed the Democratic nominee Jimmy Carter the clear favorite with a 10% popularity lead over Ford. To combat this advantage, Ford challenged Carter to a series of TV debates, the first in history between a President and an opponent for the office.

In the national election in November, Ford lost to Carter in a close vote.

Elizabeth Bloomer (Warren) Ford (1918–), his wife, was a former professional dancer. They were married on Oct. 15, 1948, and had four children: Michael Gerald, John Gardner, Steven Meigs, and Susan Elizabeth. She strongly supported adoption of the women's equal rights amendment to the U.S. Constitution.

JIMMY CARTER

39th President (1977–81)

Defeating President Ford in the closely contested 1976 election, Jimmy Carter became the first former governor of a state of the Old Confederacy to be elected President since James Polk in 1844. His achievement was possible because his advancement of civil rights won him the support of Northern liberals and blacks.

Because of Carter's weak leadership as President, U.S. prestige declined abroad, while at home the nation slid into an economic recession with high rates of inflation and unemployment. As a result, he was soundly defeated by Ronald Reagan in the election of 1980, becoming the first Democratic President to lose a bid for a second term since 1888.

EARLY LIFE

James Earl Carter Jr. was born on Oct. 1, 1924, in Plains, Ga., the first future President to be born in a hospital. He was the eldest son of James Earl and Lillian Gordy Carter. His father was a struggling farmer and storekeeper. His mother worked as a community nurse. Carter later attributed much of his success to his remarkable mother, who at the age of 68 in 1966 joined the Peace Corps and spent two years helping lepers in India.

After graduation from high school at 16 in 1941, Carter attended Georgia Southwestern College and Georgia Tech before appointment to the U.S. Naval Academy in 1943. Graduating from Annapolis in 1946, he ranked 59th in a class of 820.

As a naval officer Carter spent several years on submarine duty and did postgraduate work in nuclear physics at Union College in Schenectady, N.Y. He helped commission one of the nation's earliest atomic submarines.

After his father's death in 1953, Carter resigned from the U.S. Navy to return to his Georgia home. Over the next 10 years he became wealthy as a peanut farmer and wholesaler.

GOVERNOR AND PRESIDENTIAL CANDIDATE

Carter won election to the Georgia senate in 1962, serving two terms until 1966 when he made an unsuccessful bid for the Democratic nomination for governor. Stung by his loss to racial segregationist Lester G. Maddox, Carter campaigned across Georgia for four years, winning election as governor in 1970.

At his inauguration as governor in January 1971, Carter became a national celebrity as the first chief executive of a Southern state to declare: "The time for racial discrimination is over." As governor he promoted civil rights for blacks and reformed the state bureaucracy, cutting state departments and agencies from 300 to 22.

Carter announced his candidacy in December 1974 for the Democratic presidential nomination. His vigorous campaign culminated in a first-ballot win at the party's national convention in New York City in July 1976.

PRESIDENTIAL ADMINISTRATION

The 1976 election campaign was highlighted by three face-to-face TV debates with President Ford, the Republican nominee. Carter's success in the debates contributed to his victory in the November election. Perhaps of even greater importance was voter mistrust of the Republican Party because of the Watergate scandals. Voters also believed Carter would restore integrity to the federal government.

In his inaugural address on Jan. 20, 1977, the soft-spoken Carter pledged his administration to "the affirmation of our nation's continuing moral strength and our belief in an undiminished, ever-expanding American dream."

In his first major act he pardoned about 10,000 draft evaders of the Vietnam War.

To improve relations with Latin America, his

administration negotiated treaties to give up U.S. control of the Panama Canal in 1999, winning Senate ratification in 1978 despite conservative opposition.

Carter achieved his greatest triumph in international relations as a mediator with the leaders of Egypt and Israel, reconciling differences to enable them to sign a peace treaty in 1979. Later in 1979, he signed a new SALT II treaty with the Soviet Union, but failed to obtain Senate ratification.

In the 1976 presidential election campaign Carter had promised to reorganize the federal government to make it more efficient. Congress gave him the power to do so in April 1977. A major accomplishment was the reform of the Civil Service system in 1978 to allow greater latitude in the promotion and discharge of the 2.8 million federal employees. A new Department of Energy was created in 1977 and a separate Department of Education in 1980.

Confronted by a growing energy crisis from the nation's dependence on foreign oil, Carter urged strong measures to reduce the use of oil and gas as fuel. He called for a multibillion-dollar effort to develop new energy sources, financing the program with a tax on windfall profits of the major oil companies. Congress adopted much of his program in 1980.

The soaring price of oil, caused by the international OPEC cartel of oil-exporting nations, weakened the U.S. economy. A huge trade deficit caused the U.S. dollar to fall in value.

Although Carter had promised to balance the federal budget, government deficit spending grew year by year. The nation fell into recession in 1980 with high rates of unemployment and inflation.

When Soviet troops invaded Afghanistan in December 1979 to prop up a puppet communist government, President Carter sought to punish the Soviet Union with economic sanctions and a boycott of the summer Olympic Games held in Moscow.

The nation suffered humiliation in foreign affairs after anti-American Iranian militants captured the U.S. embassy in Teheran on Nov. 4, 1979, holding more than 50 Americans prisoner for more than a year while the Carter administration was unable to free them.

Carter had to fight for the Democratic nomination for a second term, overcoming efforts by Sen. Edward Kennedy (D-Mass.) to oust him.

In the 1980 election campaign he sought to portray his Republican opponent Ronald Reagan as a racist and a warmonger. But in a face-to-face TV debate with Reagan in October, viewers judged the President the loser and voted him out of office in November. He retired to Plains, Ga., to write his memoirs.

Rosalynn Smith Carter (born Aug. 18, 1927) married Carter on July 7, 1946. They had four children: John William in 1947, James Earl III ("Chip") in 1950, D. Jeffrey in 1952, and Amy Lynn in 1967. Mrs. Carter worked tirelessly in Carter's election campaigns and aided him as a trusted adviser in public office.

CARTER'S PRESIDENTIAL ADMINISTRATION

Congresses in Session:
95th, 96th
Vice President:
Walter F. Mondale, 1977–81
Secretary of State:
Cyrus R. Vance, 1977–80
Edmund S. Muskie, 1980–81
Secretary of the Treasury:
W. Michael Blumenthal, 1977–79
G. William Miller, 1979–81
Secretary of Defense:
Harold Brown, 1977–81
Attorney General:
Griffin B. Bell, 1977–79
Benjamin R. Civiletti, 1979–81
Secretary of the Interior:
Cecil D. Andrus, 1977–81
Secretary of Agriculture:
Robert S. Bergland, 1977–81
Secretary of Commerce:
Juanita M. Kreps, 1977–79
Philip Klutznick, 1979–81
Secretary of Labor:
F. Ray Marshall, 1977–81
Secretary of Health, Education, and Welfare:
Joseph A. Califano Jr., 1977–79
Patricia Roberts Harris, 1979
Secretary of Health and Human Services:
Patricia Roberts Harris, 1979–81
Secretary of Housing and Urban Development:
Patricia Roberts Harris, 1977–79
Moon Landrieu, 1979–81
Secretary of Transportation:
Brock Adams, 1977–79
Neil E. Goldschmidt, 1979–81
Secretary of Energy:
James R. Schlesinger, 1977–79
Charles W. Duncan Jr., 1979–81
Secretary of Education:
Shirley M. Hufstedler, 1979–81

PRESIDENTIAL ELECTION OF 1976

Nominations: Democrats met in New York City on July 12–15, 1976. Carter easily won the Democratic presidential nomination on the first ballot with 2,238.5 votes to 769.5 for other candidates. Mondale received the Democratic vice-presidential nomination on the first ballot, 2,817 to 191. Republicans met in Kansas City, Mo., on Aug. 16–19, 1976. Ford narrowly won the Republican presidential nomination on the first ballot, defeating Ronald Reagan, 1,187 to 1,070. Dole was selected as the GOP vice-presidential nominee on the first ballot, 1,921 to 338. **Campaign Issues:** Democrats denounced Ford's pardon of President Nixon and promised programs to end high levels of unemployment, to reduce taxes for low-income families, and to reorganize the federal government bureaucracy. **Remarks:** McCarthy, a liberal Democrat running as an independent, won enough votes in four states (Iowa, Maine, Oklahoma, and Oregon) to throw their 26 electoral votes to Ford. For the first time, an incumbent President debated his challenger face to face.

PRESIDENTIAL CANDIDATES	PARTY	ELECTORAL VOTES	POPULAR VOTE Total	Percentage	VICE-PRESIDENTIAL CANDIDATES
Jimmy Carter	Democratic	297	40,825,839	50.02	Walter F. Mondale
Gerald R. Ford	Republican	240	39,147,770	47.97	Robert Dole
Eugene J. McCarthy	Independent	0	680,390	0.83	—
Roger Lea MacBride	Libertarian	0	171,627	0.21	David Bergland
Lester G. Maddox	American I.	0	168,264	0.21	William Dyke
Other candidates	—	1	609,456	0.75	—

QUICK QUIZ: Why do many wealthy persons choose to live in Monaco? See page 609.

RONALD REAGAN

A conservative Republican, Ronald Reagan won the White House in an electoral landslide over President Jimmy Carter, promising to lift the country out of economic stagnation and restore the U.S. to world leadership.

40th President
(1981–)

The nation plunged into its worst recession in 1981–82 since the Great Depression. However, by 1983 the nation's economy was beginning to recover with reduced inflation and a falling rate of unemployment.

A former movie actor, Reagan was only the 9th President to reach the office by defeating an incumbent Chief Executive. At 69 he was the oldest to be elected to a first term, the first who had been a labor-union leader, and the first who ever had been divorced.

EARLY LIFE

Ronald Wilson Reagan was born in Tampico, Ill., on Feb. 6, 1911. He was the second son of Nelle Wilson Reagan and John Edward Reagan. His brother Neil was two years older. The Reagans moved to Dixon, Ill., where the father earned a meager living as a shoe salesman.

The future President, nicknamed "Dutch" by his father, was popular in high school, being elected president of the student body.

Working his way through school by washing dishes, Reagan graduated in 1932 from Eureka (Ill.) College, where he played football, captained the swimming team, and acted in plays. He then was a radio sports announcer in Des Moines, Ia., until 1937.

MOVIE STAR, GOVERNOR, AND PRESIDENT-ELECT

Having always wanted to become a professional actor, he leaped at the offer of a Hollywood movie contract in 1937. In his acting career he appeared in some 50 movies and many TV shows. An active member of the Screen Actors Guild, he headed the labor union in 1947–52 and 1959–60.

He married movie star Jane Wyman on Jan. 25, 1940. They had two children, Maureen (born 1941), and an adopted son Michael (born 1945). They were divorced in 1948.

After winning acclaim for his speeches in support of Barry Goldwater in the 1964 presidential campaign, he turned to a new career in politics.

Reagan won election as governor of California in 1966 and reelection in 1970. During his administration in 1967–75 state taxes were reformed, ending deficit spending and rebating $4.7 billion to property-tax payers. He also slowed the growth of state government and social welfare.

Reagan was an unsuccessful candidate for the Republican presidential nomination in 1968 and 1976. But in 1980 he defeated all opponents in the state primaries and was nominated at the GOP convention. He then triumphed over Carter.

40TH PRESIDENT OF THE U.S.

At the presidential inauguration on Jan. 20, 1981, Reagan and other dignitaries dressed formally, in contrast to the informality of the ceremony four

REAGAN'S PRESIDENTIAL ADMINISTRATION

Congresses in Session:
97th, 98th
Vice President:
George Bush, 1981–
Secretary of State:
Alexander M. Haig Jr., 1981–82
George P. Shultz, 1982–
Secretary of the Treasury:
Donald T. Regan, 1981–
Secretary of Defense:
Caspar W. Weinberger, 1981–
Attorney General:
William French Smith, 1981–
Secretary of the Interior:
James G. Watt, 1981–83
William P. Clark, 1983–
Secretary of Agriculture:
John R. Block, 1981–
Secretary of Commerce:
Malcolm Baldrige, 1981–
Secretary of Labor:
Raymond J. Donovan, 1981–
Secretary of Health and Human Services:
Richard S. Schweiker, 1981–83
Margaret M. Heckler, 1983–
Secretary of Housing and Urban Development:
Samuel R. Pierce Jr., 1981–
Secretary of Transportation:
Andrew L. Lewis Jr., 1981–82
Elizabeth Dole, 1983–
Secretary of Energy:
James B. Edwards, 1981–82
Donald P. Hodel, 1982–
Secretary of Education:
Terrel H. Bell, 1981–

PRESIDENTIAL ELECTION OF 1980

Nominations: Republicans met in Detroit, Mich., on July 14–17. Reagan, who had defeated nine other contenders in state primaries, received the nomination on the first ballot on July 16 with 1,939 of the convention's 1,994 votes. At the last minute Reagan failed to persuade former President Ford to join the ticket as vice-presidential candidate. He then named Bush as his choice of running mate, and the delegates ratified the decision on July 17. The Democratic National Convention met in New York City on Aug. 11–14. Carter had battled Sen. Edward Kennedy (D–Mass.) for the nomination in state primaries, winning a majority of the delegates. Although Kennedy formally withdrew as a candidate shortly after the convention opened, the party remained divided. Carter won renomination on the first ballot with 2,123 votes to Kennedy's 1,150.5. Mondale again was chosen as the vice-presidential candidate. **Campaign:** Both candidates stressed their differences in personalities rather than issues. Reagan was judged winner in a TV debate with Carter on Oct. 28, giving him momentum to win an electoral landslide a week later. **Remarks:** Rep. John B. Anderson (R–Ill.) waged a liberal independent campaign for the presidency, winning over 6% of the popular vote.

PRESIDENTIAL CANDIDATES	PARTY	ELECTORAL VOTES	POPULAR VOTE Total	Percentage	VICE-PRESIDENTIAL CANDIDATES
Ronald Reagan	Republican	489	43,898,770	50.75	George Bush
Jimmy Carter	Democratic	49	35,480,948	41.02	Walter Mondale
John B. Anderson	Independent	0	5,719,222	6.61	Patrick Lucey
Ed Clark	Libertarian	0	920,049	1.06	David Koch
Barry Commoner	Citizens	0	232,533	0.27	LaDonna Harris
Other candidates	—	0	245,329	0.29	—

years earlier when Carter took office. In his inaugural address, Reagan emphasized his plans for a "new beginning" for the national economy.

"These United States are confronted with an economic affliction of great proportions," he said, "Our present troubles parallel and are proportionate to the intervention and intrusion in our lives that result from unnecessary and excessive growth of government.

"It is time to reawaken this industrial giant," he said, "to get government back within its means and to lighten our punitive tax burden."

The President also declared: "It is my intention to curb the size and influence of the federal establishment and to demand recognition of the distinction between the powers granted to the federal government and those reserved to the states or to the people."

Within minutes after taking office, President Reagan ordered a freeze on the hiring of civilian employees by all departments and agencies of the federal government. At his first cabinet meeting, he established as the first priority the need to "get control of the federal budget." He gave his budget director, David A. Stockman, the task of recommending where specific cuts should be made.

Although Reagan's election victory over Carter had helped Republicans win control of the U.S. Senate, Democrats still held the majority in the House of Representatives. Thus, faced with a divided Congress, he knew that to get his program enacted he must persuade the public to bring pressure to bear on their representatives.

Less than three weeks after his inauguration, President Reagan addressed the nation on TV on Feb. 5, 1981 declaring that the U.S. was confronted with "the worst economic mess since the Great Depression." He called for the cooperation of Congress to adopt his economic plan.

He unveiled details of his "Program for Economic Recovery" in an address on Feb. 18, 1981, to a joint meeting of Congress. He asked for a $41.4 billion reduction in the budget for 1982 and income tax cuts spread over the next three years. Many of his proposed reductions in government expenses pared social programs benefiting the poor.

President Reagan narrowly escaped death on March 30, 1981, when he was severely wounded by a would-be assassin, John Hinckley Jr. A jury found Hinckley not guilty by reason of insanity on June 21, 1982, and he was confined to a mental institution.

Over the next several months Reagan demonstrated great skill in persuading reluctant members of Congress to support his program, which came to be termed "Reaganomics." And on Aug. 13, 1981, he signed the economic legislation into law.

However, the United States was hard hit by a worldwide recession in 1981–1982 with unemployment rising to more than 10%—the highest since the Great Depression of the 1930s. The President's economic program was credited with bringing down the rate of inflation from more than 13% in 1981 to about 5% in 1982. But reduced revenues for the federal government and increased spending brought the greatest U.S. budget deficits in history—reaching more than $200 billion in 1983.

A decline in President Reagan's popularity was reflected in losses by Republican congressional and gubernatorial candidates in the 1982 mid-term elections. Although the Republicans managed to hang onto their 54–46 majority in the U.S. Senate, they lost 26 seats in the U.S. House of Representatives as the Democrats increased their majority to 269–166. In elections for governors, the GOP had a net loss of 7, giving the Democrats 34 governorships to 16 for the Republicans.

The nation's economy began to turn around in 1983 as consumer spending and industrial production rose, inflation held to a low rate, and unemployment fell.

Marking his first 1,000 days in office in October 1983, the President declared:

"We're witnessing an industrial renaissance, and this is only Act I. Good things are happening in America. The quality of life is improving. The voices of common sense are finally getting through. . . .Our critics may never be satisfied with anything we do, but I can only say those who created the worst economic mess in postwar history should be the last people crying wolf 1,000 days into our administration when so many trends that were headed the wrong way are headed back in the right direction."

The President pressed forward on the deployment of new nuclear cruise missiles in Western Europe in 1983. In reaction the Soviet Union broke off talks that had been seeking an agreement on reducing the number of intermediate-range atomic warheads. See page 31.

Seeking to prevent an expansion of communist influence in the Western Hemisphere, President Reagan used U.S. troops to oust a communist government on the island of Grenada in 1983 (see page 29) and actively opposed leftist forces in Central America (see page 421).

In the Middle East, the Reagan administration tried unsuccessfully to achieve a peaceful solution to problems in the region (see page 419). Diplomatic efforts were overshadowed in 1983 by the terrorist bombings in Lebanon of the U.S. embassy in April (see page 15) and the headquarters of French and U.S. peacekeeping forces in October (see page 27).

After reaching the age of 72 in 1983, President Reagan began wearing a hearing aid. His physician said the hearing impairment dated to the 1930s when a pistol was discharged close to Reagan's right ear while he was acting in a movie.

The President's popularity as rated by the Gallup Poll reached a low ebb in January 1983 when only 35% of those questioned approved his handling of the office and 56% disapproved. However, 10 months later, in October 1983, his popularity was on the upswing with the figures having changed to 48% approving and 42% disapproving. Polls indicated the President was likely to win reelection to a second term in 1984. See pages 245–248.

Nancy Davis Reagan (born July 6, 1923), a movie actress, became Reagan's second wife on March 4, 1952. They had two children: Patricia (born 1953), a songwriter, and Ronald Prescott (born 1958), a ballet dancer. As First Lady she supervised extensive redecoration of the White House.

U.S. VICE PRESIDENTS

The Vice President of the United States holds the second most important office in the executive branch of the U.S. government. The Vice President automatically becomes Chief Executive if the President dies, resigns, or is removed from office. If the President cannot perform his duties because of illness or some other reason, the Vice President becomes *acting President* until the President can resume his office.

The only official duty that the U.S. Constitution provides for the Vice President is that of being president of the U.S. Senate. As such he presides over Senate sessions and can vote only to break a tie. The President may assign other responsibilities to the Vice President.

The Vice President receives an annual salary of about $91,000, an expense allowance of $10,000, and about $400,000 for administrative and clerical help. The Vice President and his family also are provided with an official residence in Washington, D.C., called Admiral's House.

Thirteen of the 43 Vice Presidents became President—eight because of the death of a President, one because of the resignation of a President, and four by being elected President in their own right. Seven died in office.

NAME AND POLITICAL PARTY	YEARS IN OFFICE AND AGE AT INAUGURATION	SERVED UNDER PRESIDENT	BIRTHPLACE AND DATE	DEATH DATE	HIGHLIGHTS OF CAREER
1. John Adams [1] (Federalist)	1789–1797 (53)	Washington	Braintree, Mass. Oct. 30, 1735	July 4, 1826	Delegate to Continental Congress 1774–77; Commissioner to France 1778–79; wrote Massachusetts constitution 1779; diplomat in Europe 1780–88; 2d President 1797–1801
2. Thomas Jefferson [1] (Democratic-Republican)	1797–1801 (53)	J. Adams	Albemarle County, Va. April 13, 1743	July 4, 1826	Delegate to Continental Congress 1775–76; wrote Declaration of Independence 1776; Governor of Virginia 1779–81; delegate to Congress 1783–84; Secretary of State 1789–93; 3d President 1801–09
3. Aaron Burr (Democratic-Republican)	1801–1805 (45)	Jefferson	Newark, N.J. Feb. 6, 1756	Sept. 14, 1836	Attorney general N.Y. 1789–90; U.S. Senator 1791–97; killed Alexander Hamilton in duel 1804; organized expedition against Spanish colonies and Mexico; indicted for treason but acquitted 1807
4. George Clinton [2] (Democratic-Republican)	1805–1812 (65)	Jefferson and Madison	Little Britain, N.Y. July 26, 1739	April 20, 1812	Delegate to Continental Congress 1775–76; brig. general of militia 1776–77; Governor of New York 1777–95, 1801–04
5. Elbridge Gerry [2] (Democratic-Republican)	1813–1814 (68)	Madison	Marblehead, Mass. July 17, 1744	Nov. 23, 1814	Delegate to Congress 1776–85; delegate to Constitutional convention 1787; U.S. Representative (R-Mass.) 1789–93; Governor of Massachusetts 1810–12
6. Daniel D. Tompkins (Democratic-Republican)	1817–1825 (42)	Monroe	Scarsdale, N.Y. June 21, 1774	June 11, 1825	N.Y. State Supreme Court 1804–07; Governor of N.Y. 1807–17; put through state law ending slavery in New York
7. John C. Calhoun [3] (Democratic)	1825–1832 (42)	J. Q. Adams and Jackson	Abbeville District, S.C. March 18, 1782	March 31, 1850	First Vice President to resign; U.S. Rep. (D-S.C.) 1811–17; Secretary of War 1817–25; U.S. Senator (D-S.C.) 1832–43, 1845–50; Secretary of State 1844–45
8. Martin Van Buren [1] (Democratic)	1833–1837 (50)	Jackson	Kinderhook, N.Y. Dec. 5, 1782	July 24, 1862	U.S. Senator (D-N.Y.) 1821–28; Governor of New York 1829; Secretary of State 1829–31; minister to Britain 1831–32; 8th President 1837–41
9. Richard M. Johnson (Democratic)	1837–1841 (56)	Van Buren	Beargrass, Ky. Oct. 17, 1780	Nov. 19, 1850	Only Vice President ever elected by U.S. Senate; U.S. Rep. (D-Ky.) 1807–19, 1829–37; U.S. Senator (D-Ky.) 1819–29
10. John Tyler [4] (Whig)	1841 (50)	W. H. Harrison	Charles City Co., Va. March 29, 1790	Jan. 18, 1862	U.S. Rep. (D-R-Va.) 1816–21; Governor of Virginia 1825–27; U.S. Senator (D-Va.) 1827–36; 10th President 1841–45
11. George M. Dallas (Democratic)	1845–1849 (52)	Polk	Philadelphia, Pa. July 10, 1792	Dec. 31, 1864	Mayor of Philadelphia 1829; U.S. Senator (D-Pa.) 1831–33; minister to Russia 1837-39; minister to Britain 1856–61
12. Millard Fillmore [4] (Whig)	1849–1850 (49)	Taylor	Locke, N.Y. Jan. 7, 1800	March 8, 1874	U.S. Rep. (W-N.Y.) 1833–35, 1837–43; 13th President 1850–53

[1] Elected President. [2] Died in office. [3] Resigned as Vice President. [4] Succeeded to presidency on death of President.

U.S. VICE PRESIDENTS *(continued)*

NAME AND POLITICAL PARTY	YEARS IN OFFICE AND AGE AT INAUGURATION	SERVED UNDER PRESIDENT	BIRTHPLACE AND DATE	DEATH DATE	HIGHLIGHTS OF CAREER
13. William R. King 2 (Democratic)	1853 (66)	Pierce	Sampson County, N.C. April 7, 1786	April 18, 1853	U.S. Rep. (D-R-N.C.) 1811–16; U.S. Senator (D-Ala.) 1819–44, 1848–52; minister to France 1844–46; took vice-presidential oath in Havana, Cuba; died only a month later
14. John C. Breckinridge (Democratic)	1857–1861 (36)	Buchanan	Lexington, Ky. Jan. 15, 1821	May 17, 1875	Youngest Vice President; U.S. Rep. (D-Ky.) 1851–55; U.S. Senator (D-Ky.) 1861; Confederate general 1861–64; Confederate secretary of war 1865
15. Hannibal Hamlin (Republican)	1861–1865 (51)	Lincoln	Paris Hill, Me. Aug. 27, 1809	July 4, 1891	U.S. Rep. (D-Me.) 1843–47; U.S. Senator (D-Me.) 1848–57; Governor of Maine 1857; U.S. Senator (R-Me.) 1857–61, 1869–81; minister to Spain 1881–82
16. Andrew Johnson 4 (Democratic)	1865 (56)	Lincoln	Raleigh, N.C. Dec. 29, 1808	July 31, 1875	U.S. Rep. (D-Tenn.) 1843–53; Governor of Tennessee 1853–57, 1862–64; U.S. Senator (D-Tenn.) 1857–62, 1874–75; 17th President 1865–69
17. Schuyler Colfax (Republican)	1869–1873 (45)	Grant	New York, N.Y. March 23, 1823	Jan. 13, 1885	U.S. Rep. (R-Ind.) 1855–69; Speaker of House 1863–69
18. Henry Wilson 2 (Republican)	1873–1875 (61)	Grant	Farmington, N.H. Feb. 16, 1812	Nov. 22, 1875	Born Jeremiah Jones Colbaith; U.S. Senator (Free Soil-Mass.) 1855–73
19. William Wheeler (Republican)	1877–1881 (57)	Hayes	Malone, N.Y. June 30, 1819	June 4, 1887	U.S. Rep. (R-N.Y.) 1861–63, 1869–77
20. Chester Arthur 4 (Republican)	1881 (51)	Garfield	Fairfield, Vt. Oct. 5, 1829	Nov. 18, 1886	Collector, Port of New York 1871–79; 21st President 1881–85
21. Thomas A. Hendricks 2 (Democratic)	1885 (65)	Cleveland	Zanesville, Ohio Sept. 7, 1819	Nov. 25, 1885	U.S. Rep. (D-Ind.) 1851–55; U.S. Senator (D-Ind.) 1863–69; Governor of Indiana 1872
22. Levi P. Morton (Republican)	1889–1893 (64)	Harrison	Shoreham, Vt. May 16, 1824	May 16, 1920	Wall Street banker; U.S. Rep. (R-N.Y.) 1879–81; minister to France 1881–85; Governor of New York 1889–93
23. Adlai E. Stevenson (Democratic)	1893–1897 (57)	Cleveland	Christian County, Ky. Oct. 23, 1835	June 14, 1914	U.S. Rep. (D-Ill.) 1875–77, 1879–81; Assistant Postmaster General 1885–89
24. Garret A. Hobart 2	1897–1899 (52)	McKinley	Long Branch, N.J. June 3, 1844	Nov. 21, 1899	Member New Jersey legislature 1872–81; member Republican National Committee 1884–96
25. Theodore Roosevelt 4 (Republican)	1901 (42)	McKinley	New York, N.Y. Oct. 27, 1858	Jan. 6, 1919	Police Commissioner, New York City 1895–97; Assistant Secretary of Navy 1897–98; colonel in Spanish–American War 1898; Governor of New York 1899–1900
26. Charles W. Fairbanks (Republican)	1905–1909 (52)	T. Roosevelt	Unionville Center, Ohio May 11, 1852	June 4, 1918	U.S. Senator (R-Ind.) 1897–1905
27. James Sherman 2 (Republican)	1909–1912 (53)	Taft	Utica, N.Y. Oct. 24, 1855	Oct. 30, 1912	Mayor of Utica, N.Y., 1884; U.S. Rep. (R-N.Y.) 1887–91, 1893–1909
28. Thomas R. Marshall (Democratic)	1913–1921 (58)	Wilson	North Manchester, Ind. March 14, 1854	June 1, 1925	Governor of Indiana 1909–13
29. Calvin Coolidge 4 (Republican)	1921–1923 (48)	Harding	Plymouth, Vt. July 4, 1872	Jan. 5, 1933	Massachusetts lieutenant governor 1916–18; Governor of Massachusetts 1919–20; 30th President 1923–29
30. Charles G. Dawes (Republican)	1925–1929 (59)	Coolidge	Marietta, Ohio Aug. 27, 1865	April 23, 1951	U.S. Comptroller of Currency 1898–1901; director Bureau of the Budget 1921–24; won Nobel Peace Prize in 1925 for German reparations plan; ambassador to Britain 1929–32; Chicago banker 1932–51
31. Charles Curtis (Republican)	1929–1933 (69)	Hoover	N. Topeka, Kan. Jan. 25, 1860	Feb. 8, 1936	U.S. Rep. (R-Kan.) 1893–1907; U.S. Senator (R-Kan.) 1907–13, 1915–29; majority leader U.S. Senate 1924–29
32. John N. Garner (Democratic)	1933–1941 (64)	F. Roosevelt	Red River Co., Tex. Nov. 22, 1868	Nov. 7, 1967	U.S. Rep. (D-Tex.) 1903–33; Speaker of House 1931–33
33. Henry A. Wallace (Democratic)	1941–1945 (52)	F. Roosevelt	Adair County, Iowa Oct. 7, 1888	Nov. 18, 1965	Secretary of Agriculture 1933–40; Secretary of Commerce 1945–46

1 Elected President. 2 Died in office. 3 Resigned as Vice President. 4 Succeeded to presidency on death of President.

U.S. VICE PRESIDENTS *(continued)*

NAME AND POLITICAL PARTY	YEARS IN OFFICE AND AGE AT INAUGURATION	SERVED UNDER PRESIDENT	BIRTHPLACE AND DATE	DEATH DATE	HIGHLIGHTS OF CAREER
34. Harry S. Truman [4] (Democratic)	1945 (60)	F.D. Roosevelt	Lamar, Mo. May 8, 1884	Dec. 26, 1972	U.S. Senator (D-Mo.) 1935–45; 33d President 1945–53
35. Alben W. Barkley (Democratic)	1949–1953 (71)	Truman	Lowes, Graves County, Ky. Nov. 24, 1877	April 30, 1956	U.S. Rep. (D-Ky.) 1913–27; U.S. Senator (D-Ky.) 1927–49, 1955–56; majority leader U.S. Senate 1937–47
36. Richard M. Nixon [1] (Republican)	1953–1961 (40)	Eisenhower	Yorba Linda, Cal. Jan. 9, 1913	—	U.S. Rep. (R-Calif.) 1947–50; U.S. Senator (R-Calif.) 1950–53; 37th President 1969–74
37. Lyndon B. Johnson [4] (Democratic)	1961–1963 (52)	Kennedy	Stonewall, Tex. Aug. 27, 1908	Jan. 22, 1973	U.S. Rep. (D-Tex.) 1937–48; U.S. Senator (D-Tex.) 1949–60; majority leader U.S. Senate 1955–60; 36th President 1963–69
38. Hubert H. Humphrey Jr. (Democratic)	1965–1969 (53)	L.B. Johnson	Wallace, S.D. May 27, 1911	Jan. 13, 1978	Mayor of Minneapolis 1945–48; U.S. Senator 1949–65, 1971–78; proposed first medical care for aged bill; helped pass civil rights bills
39. Spiro T. Agnew [3] (Republican)	1969–1973 (50)	Nixon	Baltimore, Md. Nov. 9, 1918	—	Governor of Maryland 1967–69; forced to resign as Vice President and convicted of income tax evasion 1973
40. Gerald R. Ford [4] (Republican)	1973–1974 (60)	Nixon	Omaha, Neb. July 14, 1913	—	U.S. Rep. (R-Mich.) 1949–73; minority leader U.S. House 1965–73; 38th President 1974–77
41. Nelson Rockefeller [5] (Republican)	1974–1977 (66)	Ford	Bar Harbor, Me. July 8, 1908	Jan. 26, 1979	Assistant Secretary of State 1944–45; Under Secretary Health, Education, and Welfare 1953–54; Governor N.Y. 1958–73
42. Walter F. Mondale (Democratic)	1977–1981 (49)	Carter	Ceylon, Minn. Jan. 5, 1928	—	Attorney general of Minnesota 1960–64; U.S. Senator (D-Minn.) 1964–77
43. George Bush (Republican)	1981– (56)	Reagan	Milton, Mass. June 12, 1924	—	U.S. Rep. (R-Tex.) 1967–71; ambassador to UN 1971–72; director CIA 1976–77

PRESIDENTS ELECTED WITH MINORITY OF POPULAR VOTE

ELECTION	PRESIDENT	PARTY	POPULAR VOTE	ELECTION	PRESIDENT	PARTY	POPULAR VOTE
1824	John Quincy Adams	Independent	30.60%	1888	Benjamin Harrison	Republican	47.90%
1844	James K. Polk	Democrat	49.56%	1892	Grover Cleveland	Democrat	46.04%
1848	Zachary Taylor	Whig	47.31%	1912	Woodrow Wilson	Democrat	41.85%
1856	James Buchanan	Democrat	45.30%	1916	Woodrow Wilson	Democrat	49.40%
1860	Abraham Lincoln	Republican	39.79%	1948	Harry S. Truman	Democrat	49.51%
1876	Rutherford B. Hayes	Republican	47.94%	1960	John F. Kennedy	Democrat	49.50%
1880	James A. Garfield	Republican	48.50%	1968	Richard M. Nixon	Republican	43.40%
1884	Grover Cleveland	Democrat	48.50%				

UNCOMPLETED TERMS OF PRESIDENTS

PRESIDENT	UNCOMPLETED TERM	SUCCESSOR
William H. Harrison [2]	March 4, 1841–April 4, 1841	John Tyler
Zachary Taylor [2]	March 5, 1849–July 9, 1850	Millard Fillmore
Abraham Lincoln [6]	March 4, 1865–April 15, 1865 (second term)	Andrew Johnson
James A. Garfield [6]	March 4, 1881–Sept. 19, 1881	Chester A. Arthur
William McKinley [6]	March 4, 1901–Sept. 14, 1901 (second term)	Theodore Roosevelt
Warren G. Harding [2]	March 4, 1921–Aug. 2, 1923	Calvin Coolidge
Franklin D. Roosevelt [2]	Jan. 20, 1945–April 12, 1945 (fourth term)	Harry S. Truman
John F. Kennedy [6]	Jan. 20, 1961–Nov. 22, 1963	Lyndon B. Johnson
Richard M. Nixon [3]	Jan. 20, 1973–Aug. 9, 1974 (second term)	Gerald R. Ford

VETOES BY THE PRESIDENTS *

PRESIDENT	VETOES Regular	Pocket	PRESIDENT	VETOES Regular	Pocket	PRESIDENT	VETOES Regular	Pocket	PRESIDENT	VETOES Regular	Pocket
Washington	2	–	Polk	2	1	Arthur	4	8	Hoover	21	16
Adams	–	–	Taylor	–	–	Cleveland [7]	304	110	F. Roosevelt	372	263
Jefferson	–	–	Fillmore	–	–	B. Harrison	19	25	Truman	180	70
Madison	5	2	Pierce	9	–	Cleveland [8]	42	128	Eisenhower	73	108
Monroe	1	–	Buchanan	4	3	McKinley	6	36	Kennedy	12	9
J. Q. Adams	–	–	Lincoln	2	4	T. Roosevelt	42	40	L. Johnson	16	14
Jackson	5	7	A. Johnson	21	8	Taft	30	9	Nixon	27	16
Van Buren	–	1	Grant	45	48	Wilson	33	11	Ford	55	11
W. Harrison	–	–	Hayes	12	1	Harding	5	1	Carter	18	13
Tyler	6	4	Garfield	–	–	Coolidge	20	30	Reagan [9]	15	7

[1] Elected President. [2] Died in office. [3] Resigned. [4] Succeeded to presidency. [5] Appointed Vice President. [6] Assassinated. [7] 1st term. [8] 2d term. [9] To Dec. 12, 1983. * Source: U.S. Senate Library.

Home and Family

HIGHLIGHTS: 1983

CHANGING HOMES AND FAMILIES

The U.S. Census Bureau in a 236-page study released in 1983 reported on the changes that have occurred in American homes and families in the years from 1970 through 1982. The study was based on a nationwide sample of about 60,000 households adjusted to information from the 1980 census.

In the late 1970s, nonfamily households accounted for most of the increase in the number of households, but, the Census Bureau said, now there are indications that family households have once again become the major component of household increase. Between 1975 and 1980, there was a net increase of 9.7 million households, and the majority of these were people living alone. Between 1980 and 1982, however, nonfamily households accounted for only 47% of the 2.8 million households added over the two-year period. The rates of change for families maintained by men or women with no spouses present have been largely responsible for this shift in family and nonfamily household growth patterns.

Nonfamily households had the same 47% net household increase during the 1970–75 period as during the 1980–82 period. Persons living alone also accounted for almost the same percentage in both periods. The major difference between the two periods has been the change in the percentage of net household increase for married-couple families (whose share declined from 29% of the total to 19%) and families maintained by male or female householders with no spouse present—a share that increased from 24% to 35%.

The Census Bureau said that the median age of women heading families without a husband declined by 7 years, from 48.6 in 1970 to 41.5 in 1982.

The number of households has increased to 83,527,000 from 63,401,000—a gain of 31%. Families account for 73.1%, or 61,019,000, of the households. The remaining 22,508,000 are classified as nonfamily households—largely men or women living alone.

Almost two-thirds of the net increase in family households since 1980 has been due to a growth in the number of families that are not maintained by married couples, the Census Bureau reported. Families maintained by women with no husbands present accounted for 73% of the increase in families.

Over the past 12 years, the number of families maintained by women has increased by 3.9 million, from 5.5 million in 1970 to 9.4 million in 1982. Compared with their 1970 counterparts, the women maintaining families in 1982 were generally several years younger, much more likely either to have never married or to be divorced, and slightly more likely to be black or of Spanish origin. The households were more likely to include children and occasionally a non-relative, but such families were smaller in size in 1982 than in 1970.

The total number of married-couple families increased 11% to 49,630,000 from 44,728,000. The majority of these families had no children under 18—a total of 25,165,000, representing a 31% increase from 19,196,000 such families in 1970.

The number of married-couple families with children under 18 declined 4.2% to 24,465,000 from 25,532,000. And the number of married-couple families with 3 or more children fell 42.5% to 5,359,000 from 9,325,000.

Many more women were living alone—an increase of 112% from 7,319,000 to 11,872,000. While the number of men living alone increased 133% from 3,532,000 to 7,482,000.

The number of families headed by a woman with no husband rose 71% to 9,403,000 from 5,500,000. The majority of such families, 5,868,000, had children under 18—an increase of 105% since 1970 when there were only 2,858,000 families headed by a woman with children. The largest percentage increase came with a 167% rise in the number of families headed by an unmarried woman with one child—a number that rose from 1,008,000 to 2,691,000.

The number of families headed by a man with no wife increased 62% from 1,228,000 to 1,986,000. A father without a wife takes care of children under 18 in some 679,000 of these families.

HIGHEST HOME VALUE

The U.S. Census Bureau reported that the metropolitan area with the highest median home value is Stamford, Conn., at $138,000.

CONSUMERS AND CONSUMERISM: 1983

PRICES SLASHED FOR CONSUMER ELECTRONICS

To the delight of many consumers, price wars in the fields of home computers, videocassette recorders (VCRs), and video games abounded during 1983, despite increased sales of most items.

According to figures from the Electronic Industries Association, 1,902,615 VCRs were sold during the first half of 1983, compared with 882,433 during the same period in 1982, a 116% increase. Industry analysts predicted that at least 8 million homes would have VCRs by the end of 1983. However, increased retail competition and lower production costs resulted in lowering of prices.

The growing use of VCRs prompted a lawsuit that has gone to the Supreme Court. In 1981 the U.S. Court of Appeals for the Ninth Circuit ruled that the use of home video recorders to tape copyrighted television programs violates copyright laws. If the Supreme Court agrees, copyright holders, such as the studios that produce movies for television, stand to receive royalties. This could be accomplished by adding a royalty surcharge to the prices of VCRs and blank videotapes.

Although sales of home computers remained strong in 1983, competition among the manufacturers caused price wars in that field. Several of the major makers, including Mattel and Warner Communications (which produces Atari) reported huge losses. Osborne Computer went to bankruptcy court in September. Then, at the end of October, Texas Instruments announced it was discontinuing production of its home computer, leaving more than one million purchasers adrift. They would find it difficult to get their machines repaired and to find new programs, since software manufacturers are likely to stop producing programs for an obsolete machine.

IBM announced on Nov. 1 its anxiously awaited PCjr (known as Peanut), a scaled-down version of its best-selling personal business computer. However, the smaller machine was not to be delivered to consumers until early in 1984.

Coleco's Adam, a $600 home-computer package complete with printer, was introduced in May, but bugs in the system delayed its delivery to stores until late autumn.

By the end of 1983 it was evident that the boom in video game sales had ended. Sales of game cartridges plummeted, and revenues from arcade games were down significantly. By the end of the third quarter Atari reported losses of $536 million, and Mattel's electronic division reported a $201 million deficit. To encourage sales of game cartridges, prices were slashed so that even if sales increased,

CONSUMER PRICE INDEX: 1940–1983

Source: U.S. Department of Labor, Bureau of Labor Statistics

The Consumer Price Index of the U.S. Department of Labor is based on the amount of goods and services a consumer could buy for $1 in 1967, so the Index for all items in 1967 is 100. It shows you would have spent 42¢ in 1940 or $2.89 in 1982 for goods and services that cost $2.99 in 1983.

YEAR	ALL ITEMS	MEDICAL CARE	FOOD	APPAREL AND UPKEEP	HOUSING	TRANSPORTATION	PERSONAL CARE	READING AND ENTERTAINMENT	ALL SERVICES
1940	42.0	36.8	35.2	42.8	52.4	42.7	40.2	46.1	43.6
1945	53.9	42.1	50.7	61.5	59.1	47.8	55.1	62.4	48.7
1950	72.1	53.7	74.5	79.0	72.8	68.2	68.3	74.4	58.9
1955	80.2	64.8	81.6	84.1	82.3	77.4	77.9	76.7	70.5
1960	88.7	79.1	88.0	89.6	90.2	89.6	90.1	87.3	83.8
1964	92.9	87.3	92.4	92.7	93.8	94.3	94.5	95.0	90.2
1965	94.5	89.5	94.4	93.7	94.9	95.9	95.2	95.9	92.2
1966	97.2	93.4	99.1	96.1	97.2	97.2	97.1	97.5	95.8
1967	100.0	100.0	100.0	100.0	100.0	100.0	100.0	100.0	100.0
1968	104.2	106.1	103.6	105.4	104.2	103.2	104.2	104.7	105.2
1969	109.8	113.4	108.9	111.5	110.8	107.2	109.3	108.7	112.5
1970	116.3	120.6	114.9	116.1	118.9	112.7	113.2	113.4	121.6
1971	121.3	128.4	118.4	119.8	124.3	118.6	116.8	119.3	128.4
1972	125.3	132.5	123.5	122.3	129.2	119.9	119.8	122.8	133.3
1973	133.1	137.7	141.4	126.8	135.0	123.8	125.2	125.9	139.1
1974	147.7	150.5	161.7	136.2	150.6	137.7	137.3	133.8	152.1
1975	161.2	168.6	175.4	142.3	166.8	150.6	150.7	144.4	166.6
1976	170.5	197.1	180.8	147.6	177.2	165.5	160.5	151.2	180.4
1977	181.5	202.4	188.0	154.2	186.5	177.2	172.1	167.7	172.2
1978	195.4	219.4	211.4	159.6	202.8	185.5	182.0	176.6	210.9
1979	217.4	239.7	234.5	166.6	227.6	212.0	195.8	188.5	234.2
1980	246.8	265.9	254.6	178.4	263.3	249.7	213.1	205.3	270.3
1981	272.3	294.5	274.6	186.9	293.5	280.0	239.1	221.4	305.7
1982	288.6	328.7	285.7	191.8	314.6	291.5	248.1	235.5	333.3
1983*	301.8	361.2	292.6	200.4	326.4	303.7	263.0	247.5	349.0

* 1983 data for September.

manufacturers profits would be low. It was widely believed that video game consoles had been displaced by the more popular-priced home computers.

MESH PLAYPENS CAN BE DANGEROUS

In March, the Consumer Product Safety Commission (CPSC) warned parents that dropside mesh playpens and portable mesh cribs, used with a side left down, can pose a safety hazard to infants. When one side of the playpen or crib is down, the mesh forms a loose pocket that leaves a gap between the edge of the floor board and the mesh side. An infant could fall or roll into the pocket and suffocate.

The commission reported that three infants died of suffocation in 1983 in mesh playpens and portable cribs. In each incident, an infant was left unattended in a crib or playpen with one of the dropsides in the down position. After falling off the edge of the mattress pad, the infant's head or chest was compressed between the floor board and the mesh side so the child could not breathe. At least eight other children have died in similar accidents since 1973, with seven of the deaths involving infants six weeks of age or younger.

An estimated 6.5 million mesh playpens and 925,000 cribs are thought to be in use.

CPSC PLANS 1984 PROGRAMS

The Consumer Product Safety Commission (CPSC) announced the selection of its priority projects for fiscal year 1984.

Because residential fires are responsible for about 5,600 deaths annually, the CPSC plans to investigate whether toxic gases other than carbon monoxide play an important role in these deaths, of which 70% are believed caused by inhalation. The commission will review literature to determine more definitively what is known about toxic gases given off by various materials and expand laboratory testing to determine the relative toxicity of gases given off when such materials burn.

Also in 1984 the commission will work with voluntary standards committees to improve the safety of gas-fired heating systems.

The CPSC also will focus attention on safety for older consumers. It will study the special circumstances and life-styles of persons 65 and over which make them particularly vulnerable to injury. The research will seek to reduce the incidence of falls, fires, and scalds, as well as study the effects of indoor air pollution.

In May the CPSC celebrated its 10th anniversary. The commission was established May 13, 1973, to protect the consumer from "unreasonable risk of injury" from consumer products. It has jurisdiction over more than 15,000 generic products that are not overseen by another government agency (such as boats, planes, foods, drug, and automobiles).

FDA APPROVES USE OF SWEETENER

In July the Food and Drug Administration (FDA) approved the use of aspartame, a concentrated low-calorie sweetener, in carbonated soft drinks.

Approved as an additive for dry foods in 1981 under the name NutraSweet, aspartame is 180 times as sweet as sugar. Its maker, G. D. Searle & Co., expects aspartame to eventually eclipse saccharin in the artificial sweetener market. In August, the Coca Cola Co. announced it would use aspartame in its Diet Coke.

Controversy raged concerning the safety of aspartame because of questions about its shelf life and safety. However, FDA spokesmen said they felt their scientists had adequately answered all questions on safety of the product and the FDA would stand by its approval.

$5.25 BILLION SPENT ON SNACK FOOD IN 1982

The Potato Chip/Snack Food Association reported that in 1982 Americans consumed an average eight pounds of snack food, with 4.2 pounds of that in potato chips. Potato chips comprised 42% of the snack-food industry and garnered sales of $2.20 billion. Corn and/or tortilla chips were second in popularity, comprising 23% of the market and $1.19 billion in sales. Salted nuts were third in popularity, with 18% of the market and sales of $927 million. Cheese and corn curls, salted meat snacks, and pretzels each cornered 5% of the market. Popcorn totaled 2% of the snack food market.

HOT TUBS CAN CAUSE INFECTION

Researchers at St. Joseph Hospital in Denver, Colo., reported in the October *Journal of the American Medical Association* that hot tubs and whirlpool baths are ideal settings for bacterial growth and can easily become contaminated if the filtering system is faulty or there is insufficient chlorine in the water.

The Denver researchers reported three cases of urinary tract infection, which they linked to hot tub use. They advised that, although further study was indicated, consumers should be especially careful in monitoring hot tub and whirlpool sanitation.

CONSUMER HOTLINE PHONE NUMBERS

Here are three toll-free federal hotline numbers you may need to use.

Product Safety: To inquire about or report on the safety of products, phone 800-638-2772.

Solar Energy: To get information about solar-energy systems for heating and cooling, phone 800-523-2929.

Auto Recall: To find out if your car has been recalled by the manufacturer for the repair of defects, phone 800-424-9393.

CONSUMER DIRECTORY

U.S. Government Hotlines

The following U.S. government telephone hotlines were in effect at the time the Almanac went to press. Toll-free numbers may be changed, however, and if you have difficulty reaching any of the following, we suggest you dial 800-555-1212 to obtain the correct number.

Most of these toll-free numbers are not available in Alaska and Hawaii.

Abuse, Waste, and Fraud Hotline **800-424-5454**
To report federal abuse, waste, and fraud.

ACTION **800-424-8580**
Information for potential volunteers.

Auto Recall Hotline **800-424-9393**
To find out if your car has been recalled.

Basic Education Grants Program **800-638-6700**
General information on education grants.

Conservation and Renewable Energy Inquiry and Referral Service **800-523-2929**
Information on energy and conservation.

Consumer Product Safety Commission .. **800-638-2772**
To inquire about or report on safety of products.

Department of Energy Hotline **800-342-3722**
Receives consumer complaints on gas and heating oil supplies and prices.

Export-Import Bank **800-424-5201**
Export information for small businesses.

Fair Housing and Equal Opportunity ... **800-424-8590**
For housing and discrimination problems.

Federal Crime Insurance **800-638-8780**
Information on insurance in high-risk areas.

Federal Election Commission **800-424-9530**
Regulates campaign financing.

Library of Congress **800-424-8567**
National Library Service for the Blind and Handicapped.

National Runaway Switchboard **800-621-4000**
Advice for runaways and parents.

National Solar Heating and Cooling Information Center **800-523-2929**
Information on solar installations.

Social Welfare Fraud Hotline **800-368-5779**
For abuses in Medicare, Medicaid, Social Security.

Tax Hotline **800-555-1212**
Phone to get your state's toll-free IRS number.

VD Hotline (Operation Venus) **800-227-8922**
General information on venereal disease.

Veterans' Information **800-555-1212**
Phone to get your state's toll-free VA number.

CONSUMER ORGANIZATIONS

The following consumer organizations are among those actively working for and with consumers at

Association of Community Organizations for Reform Now (ACORN): Works for advancement of low-to-moderate-income people.
628 Barrone St., New Orleans, LA 70113 or
523 W. 15th St., Little Rock, AR 72202

Center for Community Change: Provides technical assistance to community organizations on housing, manpower, economic development, and other grass-roots concerns.
1000 Wisconsin Ave., NW, Washington, D.C. 20007

Center for Science in the Public Interest: Research and education activities focus on nutrition, food programs, and the food industry.
1755 S St., NW, Washington, D.C. 20009

Common Cause: Nonpartisan public-affairs lobbying organization concerned mainly with government reform and accountability.
2030 M Street, NW, Washington, D.C. 20036

Community Nutrition Institute: Resource center on food and nutrition policy issues; provides technical assistance to community programs.
1146 19th St., NW, Washington, D.C. 20036

Congress Watch: Lobbying arm of Public Citizen; active in many areas of national energy and consumer legislation policymaking.
133 C St., SE, Washington, D.C. 20003

Consumer Coalition for Health: Coalition of national and local organizations and individuals across the country that develops programs designed to increase public awareness of health-planning issues.
1511 K St., NW, Suite 220, Washington, D.C. 20005

Consumer Federation of America: Federation of 225 national, state, and local nonprofit groups that advocates consumer interests on food, energy, credit and banking and health issues.
1012 14th St., NW, Washington, D.C. 20005

Consumers Union of the U.S., Inc.: Independent nonprofit product-testing organization that conducts research and prepares education materials on wide variety of consumer concerns.
256 Washington St., Mt. Vernon, NY 10550

Cooperative League of the U.S.A.: National organiza-

national, state and local levels to affect public policy as it relates to inflation.

tion of cooperatives of all types; lobbies, conducts research, publishes educational materials, including "how-to" pamphlets on broad range of subjects such as farm/rural issues, housing, and health.
1828 L St., NW, Washington, D.C. 20036.

Energy Action Committee: Nonprofit public-interest organization that monitors government and industry actions in the energy field.
1523 L St., NW, Washington, D.C. 20005

Environmental Action Foundation: Education and research organization; publishes information on citizen action in environmental areas including solid waste, electric-utility rate structure and reform, and transportation.
724 Dupont Circle Building, Washington, D.C. 20036

Environmental Defense Fund: Nationwide legal-action organization working to protect the public interest in environmental quality, energy, conservation, public health, and consumer welfare.
1525 18th St., NW, Washington, D.C. 20036

Food Research and Action Center: Provides legal assistance, organizing aid, training, and information to low-income people and others working to expand and improve federal food programs.
2011 Eye St., NW, Washington, D.C. 20006

Gray Panthers: National activist organization that lobbies, advocates in court, and organizes around issues involving health care, nursing homes, age discrimination, and housing.
3700 Chestnut St., Philadelphia, PA 19104

Health Research Group: Ralph Nader-affiliated consumer advocacy organization working on consumer-health issues.
2000 P St., NW, Washington, D.C. 20036

National Consumers League: Sponsors variety of consumer-education programs and lobbies for consumer rights.
1028 Connecticut Ave., NW, Washington, D.C. 20036

The National Commission on Neighborhoods: Presidential advisory group investigates causes of neighborhood decline.
2000 K St., NW, Suite 350, Washington, D.C. 20006

ADDRESSES OF FEDERAL CONSUMER OFFICES

When corresponding with a federal consumer office, be sure to include photocopies all documents pertinent to your request or complaint.

ADVERTISING
Director, Bureau of Consumer Protection, Federal Trade Commission, Washington, D.C. 20580.

AIR TRAVEL
Routes and Service: Director, Office of Consumer Protection, Civil Aeronautics Board, Washington, D.C. 20428.

Safety: Community and Consumer Liaison Division, Federal Aviation Administration, APA–430, Washington, D.C. 20591.

ALCOHOLISM, DRUG ABUSE, AND MENTAL ILLNESS
Office of Public Affairs, Alcohol, Drug Abuse, and Mental Health Service, 5600 Fishers Lane, Rockville, MD 20857.

BANKS
Federal Credit Unions: National Credit Union Administration, Washington, D.C. 20456.

Federally Insured Savings and Loans: Consumer Division, Office of Community Investment, Federal Home Loan Bank Board, Washington, D.C. 20552.

Federal Reserve Banks: Office of Saver and Consumer Affairs, Federal Reserve System, Washington, D.C. 20551.

National Banks: Consumer Affairs, Office of the Comptroller of the Currency, Washington, D.C. 20219.

State Chartered Banks: Office of Bank Customer Affairs, Federal Deposit Insurance Corporation, Washington, D.C. 20429.

BOATING
Chief, Information and Administrative Staff, U.S. Coast Guard, Washington, D.C. 20590.

BUS TRAVEL
Consumer Affairs Office, Interstate Commerce Commission, Washington, D.C. 20423.

BUSINESS
General: Office of the Ombudsman, Department of Commerce, Washington, D.C. 20230.

Women: Director, Women-in-Business and Consumer Affairs, Small Business Administration, 1441 L St., NW, Washington, D.C. 20416.

CHILD ABUSE
National Center on Child Abuse and Neglect, P.O. Box 1182, Washington, D.C. 20013.

CREDIT
Director, Bureau of Consumer Protection, Federal Trade Commission, Washington, D.C. 20580.

CUSTOMS
Public Information Division, U.S. Customs, Washington, D.C. 20229.

DISCRIMINATION
U.S. Commission on Civil Rights, 1121 Vermont Ave., Washington, D.C. 20425.

Equal Employment Opportunity Commission, 2401 E St., NW, Washington, D.C. 20506.

DRUGS AND COSMETICS
Consumer Inquiry Section, Food and Drug Administration, 5600 Fishers Lane, Rockville, MD 20857.

ELDERLY
Administration on Aging, Washington, D.C. 20201.

ENERGY
General: Director, Office of Consumer Affairs, Department of Energy, Washington, D.C. 20585.

Energy Efficiency: Information Office, National Bureau of Standards, Washington, D.C. 20234.

ENVIRONMENT
Office of Public Awareness, Environmental Protection Agency, Washington, D.C. 20460.

FISH AND WILDLIFE
Fish and Wildlife Service, Office of Public Affairs, Washington, D.C. 20240.

FOOD
Assistant Secretary for Food and Consumer Services, U.S. Department of Agriculture, Washington, D.C. 20250.

Consumer Inquiry Section, Food and Drug Administration, 5600 Fishers Lane, Rockville, MD 20857.

FRAUD
Director, Bureau of Consumer Protection, Federal Trade Commission, Washington, D.C. 20580.

HANDICAPPED
Director, Division of Public Information, Office of Human Development Services, Department of Health and Human Services, Washington, D.C. 20201.

IMMIGRATION AND NATURALIZATION
Information Services, Immigration and Naturalization Service, 425 Eye St., NW, Washington, D.C. 20536.

JOB SAFETY
Office of Information, Occupational Safety and Health Administration, Department of Labor, Washington, D.C. 20210.

MAIL ORDERS
Federal Trade Commission, Office of the Secretary, Washington, D.C. 20580.

MAIL SERVICE
Consumer Advocate, U.S. Postal Service, Washington, D.C. 20260.

MEDICAID AND MEDICARE
Health Care Financing Administration, in the Department of Health and Human Services, Washington, D.C. 20201.

MEDICAL RESEARCH
Division of Public Information, National Institutes of Health, 9000 Rockville Pike, Bethesda, MD 20014.

Center for Disease Control, Attention, Public Inquiries, Atlanta, GA 30333.

MOVING COMPANIES, INTERSTATE
Consumer Assistance Office, Interstate Commerce Commission, Washington, D.C. 20423.

PARKS AND RECREATION AREAS
National Forests: Forest Service, U.S. Department of Agriculture, Washington, D.C. 20250.

National Parks and Historic Sites: National Park Service, Washington, D.C. 20240.

PASSPORTS
Passport Office, Department of State, 1425 K St., NW, Washington, D.C. 20524.

PATENTS AND TRADEMARKS
Patents: Commissioner, Patent Office, Department of Commerce, Washington, D.C. 20231.

Trademarks: Commissioner, Trademark Office, Department of Commerce, Washington, D.C. 20231.

PENSIONS
Office of Communications, Pension Benefit Guaranty Corporation, 2020 K St., NW, Washington, D.C. 20006.

Labor Management Standards Administration, Department of Labor, Washington, D.C. 20210.

RADIO AND TELEVISION BROADCASTING AND INTERFERENCE
Consumer Assistance Office, Federal Communications Commission, Washington, D.C. 20554.

STOCKS AND BONDS
Office of Consumer Affairs, Securities and Exchange Commission, Washington, D.C. 20549.

WAGES AND WORKING CONDITIONS
Employment Standards Administration, Department of Labor, Washington, D.C. 20210.

WARRANTIES
Division of Special Statutes, Federal Trade Commission, Washington, D.C. 20580.

NUTRITION

A basic knowledge of good nutrition is essential for maintaining health. Poor diet in early life may impair both mental and physical development and in later years contribute to heart disease, strokes, and other disorders. Eating wisely also helps to keep desirable body weights.

There are at least 50 known nutrients necessary for health—vitamins, minerals, amino acids (protein), fatty acids, and glucose. No single food can adequately supply all of them. Hence, everyone should eat a varied menu taken from the four basic food groups below:

(1) **The meat group** includes not only beef, pork, lamb, and the like, but also poultry, fish, eggs, dried peas and beans, and nuts. All of these are high in protein.

(2) **The dairy group,** rich in calcium and proteins, includes milk and milk products.

(3) **The cereal group,** which supplies carbohydrates and some protein, consists of breakfast foods and breadstuffs made from oats, barley, wheat, and corn.

(4) **The fruit and vegetable group,** high in vitamins and minerals, includes fruits, berries, leafy and other green vegetables, and the "yellow" vegetables, such as carrots, squash, sweet potatoes, and the like.

A good diet should include two to four servings daily from each of the four groups. Avoid excessive use of sugar and fats.

RECOMMENDED DAILY DIETARY ALLOWANCES

Source: *Recommended Dietary Allowances,* revised 1980, National Academy of Sciences

	Age (years)	Weight (kg)	Weight (lbs)	Height (cm)	Height (in)	Energy (calories)	Protein (grams)	WATER-SOLUBLE VITAMINS: Ascorbic Acid *	Folacin †	Niacin *	Riboflavin *	Thiamin *	Vitamin B_6 *	Vitamin B_{12} †
Infants . .	0.0-0.5	6	13	60	24	kg x 115	kg x 2.2	35	30	6	0.4	0.3	0.3	0.5
	0.5-1.0	9	20	71	28	kg x 105	kg x 2.0	35	45	8	0.6	0.5	0.6	1.5
Children .	1-3	13	29	90	35	1,300	23	45	100	9	0.8	0.7	0.9	2.0
	4-6	20	44	112	44	1,700	30	45	200	11	1.0	0.9	1.3	2.5
	7-10	28	62	132	52	2,400	34	45	300	16	1.4	1.2	1.6	3.0
Boys	11-14	45	99	157	62	2,700	45	50	400	18	1.6	1.4	1.8	3.0
	15-18	66	145	176	69	2,800	56	60	400	19	1.7	1.4	2.0	3.0
Men	19-22	70	154	177	70	2,900	56	60	400	18	1.7	1.5	2.2	3.0
	23-50	70	154	178	70	2,700	56	60	400	16	1.6	1.4	2.2	3.0
	51+	70	154	178	70	2,400	56	60	400	15	1.4	1.2	2.2	3.0
Girls	11-14	46	101	157	62	2,200	46	50	400	14	1.3	1.1	1.8	3.0
	15-18	55	120	163	64	2,100	46	60	400	14	1.3	1.1	2.0	3.0
Women .	19-22	55	120	163	64	2,100	44	60	400	13	1.3	1.1	2.0	3.0
	23-50	55	120	163	64	2,000	44	60	400	13	1.2	1.0	2.0	3.0
	51+	55	120	163	64	1,800	44	60	400	13	1.2	1.0	2.0	3.0
Pregnant mothers						+300	+30	+20	+400	+2	+0.3	+0.4	+0.6	+1.0
Nursing (lactating) mothers						+500	+20	+40	+100	+5	+0.5	+0.5	+0.5	+1.0

	Age (years)	Weight (kg)	Weight (lbs)	Height (cm)	Height (in)	Energy (calories)	Protein (grams)	FAT-SOLUBLE VITAMINS: Vitamin A (RE) [1]	Vitamin D [2]	Vitamin E [2]	MINERALS: Calcium *	Phosphorus *	Iodine †	Iron *	Magnesium *	Zinc *
Infants .	0.0-0.5	6	13	60	24	kg x 115	kg x 2.2	420	400	3	360	240	40	10	50	3
	0.5-1.0	9	20	71	28	kg x 105	kg x 2.0	400	400	4	540	360	50	15	70	5
Children	1-3	13	29	90	35	1,300	23	400	400	5	800	800	70	15	150	10
	4-6	20	44	112	44	1,700	30	500	400	6	800	800	90	10	200	10
	7-10	28	62	132	52	2,400	34	700	400	7	800	800	120	10	250	10
Boys . . .	11-14	45	99	157	62	2,700	45	1,000	400	8	1,200	1,200	150	18	350	15
	15-18	66	145	176	69	2,800	56	1,000	400	10	1,200	1,200	150	18	400	15
Men . . .	19-22	70	154	177	70	2,900	56	1,000	300	10	800	800	150	10	350	15
	23-50	70	154	178	70	2,700	56	1,000	200	10	800	800	150	10	350	15
	51+	70	154	178	70	2,400	56	1,000	200	10	800	800	150	10	350	15
Girls . . .	11-14	46	101	157	62	2,200	46	800	400	8	1,200	1,200	150	18	300	15
	15-18	55	120	163	64	2,100	46	800	400	8	1,200	1,200	150	18	300	15
Women	19-22	55	120	163	64	2,100	44	800	300	8	800	800	150	18	300	15
	23-50	55	120	163	64	2,000	44	800	200	8	800	800	15	18	300	15
	51+	55	120	163	64	1,800	44	800	200	8	800	800	150	10	300	15
Pregnant mothers						+300	+30	+200	+200	+2	+400	+400	+25	30+ [3]	+150	+25
Nursing (lactating) mothers						+500	+20	+400	+200	+3	+400	+400	+50	30+ [3]	+150	+50

* In milligrams. † In micrograms. [1] In retinol equivalents. [2] In International units. [3] Supplemental iron recommended.

CALORIES AND WEIGHT

The weight of an adult man or woman reflects the extent to which he or she balances the intake of energy in food with the expenditure of energy in activity and growth.

Weight will stay the same when the number of calories brought into the body by food equals the number of calories used by the body. Similarly, the body loses weight when it receives fewer calories from food than it uses. It gains weight when it receives more calories than are used.

Weight can be controlled by regulating either the amount of food eaten or the extent of physical activity, or both, so that the balance of calories is in the desired direction.

Overweight is a problem shared by more than 60 million Americans of all ages. There are a number of available low-caloric, nutritionally sound diets which, if faithfully followed, will take off excess pounds and help to keep them off. However, it is wise for anyone planning to lose more than a few pounds to consult a doctor.

DESIRABLE WEIGHTS FOR MEN AGE 25–59[1]
Weight in pounds according to frame (in indoor clothing)

HEIGHT[2] Feet	Inches	SLENDER FRAME	MEDIUM FRAME	LARGE FRAME
5	2	128-134	131-141	138-150
5	3	130-136	133-143	140-153
5	4	132-138	135-145	142-156
5	5	134-140	137-148	144-160
5	6	136-142	139-151	146-164
5	7	138-145	142-154	149-168
5	8	140-148	145-157	152-172
5	9	142-151	148-160	155-176
5	10	144-154	151-163	158-180
5	11	146-157	154-166	161-184
6	0	149-160	157-170	164-188
6	1	152-164	160-174	168-192
6	2	155-168	164-178	172-197
6	3	158-172	167-182	176-202
6	4	162-176	171-187	181-207

DESIRABLE WEIGHTS FOR WOMEN AGE 25–59[1]
Weight in pounds according to frame (in indoor clothing)

HEIGHT[2] Feet	Inches	SLENDER FRAME	MEDIUM FRAME	LARGE FRAME
4	10	102-111	109-121	118-131
4	11	103-113	111-123	120-134
5	0	104-115	113-126	122-137
5	1	106-118	115-129	125-140
5	2	108-121	118-132	128-143
5	3	111-124	121-135	131-147
5	4	114-127	124-138	134-151
5	5	117-130	127-141	137-155
5	6	120-133	130-144	140-159
5	7	123-136	133-147	143-163
5	8	126-139	136-150	146-167
5	9	129-142	139-153	149-170
5	10	132-145	142-156	152-173
5	11	135-148	145-159	155-176
6	0	138-151	148-162	158-179

[1] Men wearing five pounds of clothing; women wearing three. [2] In shoes with one-inch heels.

AVERAGE HEIGHTS AND WEIGHTS OF BOYS AND GIRLS

PHYSICAL GROWTH OF BOYS
(from age 1 month to 18 years; without clothing)

AGE (Month or year)	AVERAGE HEIGHT		AVERAGE WEIGHT	
	Centimeters	Inches	Kilograms	Pounds
1 mo.	54.6	21.5	4.29	9.5
3 mo.	61.1	24.1	5.98	13.2
6 mo.	67.8	26.7	7.85	17.3
9 mo.	72.3	28.5	9.18	20.2
12 mo.	76.1	30.0	10.15	22.4
18 mo.	82.4	32.4	11.47	25.3
2 yrs.	86.8	34.2	12.34	27.2
3 yrs.	94.9	37.4	14.62	32.2
4 yrs.	102.9	40.5	16.69	36.8
5 yrs.	109.9	43.3	18.67	41.2
6 yrs.	116.1	45.7	20.69	45.6
7 yrs.	121.7	47.9	22.85	50.4
8 yrs.	127.0	50.0	25.30	55.8
9 yrs.	132.2	52.1	28.13	62.0
10 yrs.	137.5	54.1	31.44	69.3
11 yrs.	143.3	56.4	35.30	77.8
12 yrs.	149.7	58.9	39.78	87.7
13 yrs.	156.5	61.6	44.95	99.1
14 yrs.	163.1	64.2	50.77	111.9
15 yrs.	169.0	66.5	56.71	125.0
16 yrs.	173.5	68.3	62.10	136.9
17 yrs.	176.2	69.4	66.31	146.2
18 yrs.	176.8	69.6	68.88	151.9

PHYSICAL GROWTH OF GIRLS
(from age 1 month to 18 years; without clothing)

AGE (Month or year)	AVERAGE HEIGHT		AVERAGE WEIGHT	
	Centimeters	Inches	Kilograms	Pounds
1 mo.	53.5	21.1	3.98	8.8
3 mo.	59.5	23.4	5.40	11.9
6 mo.	65.9	25.9	7.21	15.9
9 mo.	70.4	27.7	8.56	18.9
12 mo.	74.3	29.3	9.53	21.0
18 mo.	80.9	31.9	10.82	23.8
2 yrs.	86.8	34.2	11.80	26.0
3 yrs.	94.1	37.0	14.10	31.0
4 yrs.	101.6	40.0	15.96	35.2
5 yrs.	108.4	42.7	17.66	38.9
6 yrs.	114.6	45.1	19.52	43.0
7 yrs.	120.6	47.5	21.84	48.1
8 yrs.	126.4	49.8	24.84	54.8
9 yrs.	132.2	52.0	28.46	62.7
10 yrs.	138.3	54.4	32.55	71.8
11 yrs.	144.8	57.0	36.95	81.5
12 yrs.	151.5	59.6	41.53	91.6
13 yrs.	157.1	61.9	46.10	101.6
14 yrs.	160.4	63.1	50.28	110.8
15 yrs.	161.8	63.7	53.68	118.3
16 yrs.	162.4	63.9	55.89	123.2
17 yrs.	163.1	64.2	56.69	125.0
18 yrs.	163.7	64.4	56.62	124.8

Sources: Metropolitan Life Insurance Company; National Academy of Sciences.

CALORIE COUNT AND MAIN NUTRIENTS OF BASIC FOODS

Source: U.S. Department of Agriculture. T = trace.

In nutrition *calorie* expresses the energy-producing value of food. For the average American adult, energy is expended at about the following rates: running, 19.4 calories per minute; swimming, 11.2 calories per minute; bicycle riding, 8.2 calories per minute; walking, 5.2 calories per minute; and repose, 1.3 calories per minute.

Energy values in excess of those used for physical activities are stored in the body in the form of fat.

KINDS OF FOOD	AMOUNT	FOOD ENERGY (Calories)	PROTEIN (Grams)	FAT (Grams)	CARBOHYDRATES (Grams)
BEVERAGES, MILK, FATS					
Beer	12 oz.	150	1	0	14
Butter or margarine (1/4 lb.)	1/2 cup	815	1	92	T
Butter or margarine	1 pat	25	T	4	T
Buttermilk	1 cup	100	8	2	12
Club soda (unsweetened)	12 oz.	0	0	0	0
Cocoa	1 cup	245	10	12	27
Cola beverages	12 oz.	145	0	0	37
Cream, half-and-half	1 tbsp.	20	T	2	1
Cream, sour	1 tbsp.	25	T	3	1
Fats, vegetable	1 tbsp.	110	0	13	0
Gin, rum, vodka, whisky	1 1/2 oz.	110	0	0	T
Ginger ale	12 oz.	115	0	0	29
Lard	1 tbsp.	115	0	13	0
Malted milk	1 cup	235	11	10	27
Milk, skim	1 cup	85	8	T	12
Milk, whole	1 cup	150	8	8	11
Oils, salad or cooking	1 tbsp.	120	0	14	0
Root beer	12 oz.	150	0	0	39
Soda, fruit-flavored	12 oz.	170	0	0	45
Wine, table	3 1/2 oz.	85	T	0	4
BREADS, CEREALS, DESSERTS, PASTAS, SNACKS					
Bagel (egg)	1	165	6	2	28
Biscuit	1	105	2	5	13
Bread:					
Raisin	1 slice	65	2	1	13
Rye	1 slice	60	2	T	13
White	1 slice	70	2	1	13
Whole-wheat	1 slice	60	3	1	12
Breakfast cereals:					
Bran flakes	1 cup	105	4	1	28
Corn flakes, plain	1 cup	95	2	T	21
Oatmeal	1 cup	130	5	2	23
Puffed rice	1 cup	60	1	T	13
Puffed wheat	1 cup	55	2	T	12
Shredded wheat	1 piece	90	2	1	20
Brownie with nuts	1	95	1	6	10
Cakes (pieces):					
Angel food	1	135	3	T	32
Cupcake (iced)	1	130	2	5	21
Devil's food (iced)	1	235	3	8	40
Fruitcake	1	55	1	2	9
Gingerbread	1	175	2	4	32
Sponge	1	195	5	4	36
White (iced)	1	250	3	8	45
Candy:					
Caramel	1 oz.	115	1	3	22
Chocolate—milk	1 oz.	145	2	9	16
Chocolate—nuts	1 oz.	160	5	12	11
Fudge, plain	1 oz.	115	1	3	21
Gumdrops	1 oz.	100	T	T	25
Marshmallows	1 oz.	90	1	T	23
Mints, uncoated	1 oz.	105	T	1	25
Chocolate, baking	1 oz.	145	3	15	8
Chocolate, semisweet	1 oz.	145	1	10	16
Chocolate topping	1 oz.	125	2	5	20
Corn muffin	1	125	3	4	19

KINDS OF FOOD	AMOUNT	FOOD ENERGY (Calories)	PROTEIN (Grams)	FAT (Grams)	CARBOHYDRATES (Grams)
Crackers, graham	4	110	2	2	20
Crackers, saltine	4	50	1	1	8
Custard, baked	1 cup	305	14	15	29
Danish pastry (4 1/4" diam.)	1	275	5	15	30
Doughnut	1	205	3	11	16
Fig bar	1	50	1	1	11
Gelatin dessert	1 cup	140	4	0	34
Honey	1 tbsp.	65	T	0	17
Ice cream	1 cup	270	5	14	32
Ice milk	1 cup	185	5	6	29
Jams and preserves	1 tbsp.	55	T	T	14
Macaroni, plain	1 cup	190	7	1	39
Macaroni w/cheese	1 cup	430	17	22	40
Muffin	1	120	3	4	17
Noodles	1 cup	200	7	2	37
Pancake (4" diam.)	1	50	2	2	9
Pies (1/7 wedges of 9" pie.):					
Apple	1	345	3	15	51
Lemon meringue	1	305	4	12	45
Mince	1	365	3	16	56
Pecan	1	495	6	27	61
Pizza, cheese (1/8 piece)	1	145	6	4	22
Popcorn, plain	1 cup	25	1	T	5
Popcorn, buttered	1 cup	40	1	2	5
Popcorn, caramel	1 cup	135	2	1	30
Popsicle	1	70	0	0	18
Pretzel, thin twisted	1	25	1	T	8
Pudding, chocolate	1 cup	385	8	12	67
Pudding, tapioca	1 cup	220	8	8	28
Roll, frankfurter	1	120	3	2	21
Sherbet	1 cup	260	2	2	59
Spaghetti, plain	1 cup	155	5	1	32
Spaghetti, tomato & cheese	1 cup	260	9	9	37
Sugar, white granular	1 tbsp.	45	0	0	12
Syrup	1 tbsp.	60	0	0	15
Waffle (7" diam.)	1	205	7	8	27
Whipped cream	1 tbsp.	10	T	1	T
FRUITS AND FRUIT JUICES					
Apple, raw (2 3/4 in. dia.)	1	80	T	1	20
Apple juice	1 cup	120	T	T	30
Applesauce, sweetened	1 cup	230	T	T	61
Apricots, raw	3	55	1	T	14
Apricots, canned in syrup	1 cup	220	2	T	57
Apricots, dried, uncooked	1 cup	340	7	1	86
Avocado, raw	1	370	5	37	13
Banana, raw	1	100	1	T	26
Blackberries, raw	1 cup	85	2	1	19
Blueberries, raw	1 cup	90	1	1	22
Cantaloupe, raw	1/2	80	2	T	20
Cherries, canned	1 cup	105	2	T	26
Cranberry juice, canned	1 cup	165	T	T	42
Cranberry sauce, sweet	1 cup	405	T	1	104
Dates, pitted	1 cup	490	4	1	130
Fruit cocktail, canned	1 cup	195	1	T	50
Grapefruit, raw	1/2	50	1	T	13
Grapefruit, canned	1 cup	180	2	T	45
Grapefruit juice	1 cup	95	1	T	23

KINDS OF FOOD	AMOUNT	FOOD ENERGY (Calories)	PROTEIN (Grams)	FAT (Grams)	CARBOHYDRATES (Grams)
Grape juice, bottled	1 cup	165	T	T	42
Grapes, raw	1 cup	70	1	1	16
Lemon, raw	1	20	1	T	6
Lemonade	1 cup	105	T	T	28
Limeade	1 cup	100	T	T	27
Orange, raw	1	65	1	T	16
Orange juice	1 cup	110	2	T	26
Peach, raw	1	40	1	T	10
Peaches, canned in syrup	1 cup	200	T	T	51
Pear, raw	1	100	1	1	25
Pears, canned in syrup	1 cup	195	T	T	50
Pineapple, raw, diced	1 cup	80	1	T	21
Pineapple, canned in syrup	1 cup	190	1	T	49
Pineapple juice	1 cup	140	1	T	34
Plum, raw	1	30	T	T	8
Prunes, cooked	1 cup	255	2	1	67
Prune juice	1 cup	195	1	T	49
Raisins (½ oz. package)	1 pkg.	40	T	T	11
Raspberries, red, raw	1 cup	70	1	2	17
Rhubarb, cooked with sugar	1 cup	380	1	T	97
Strawberries, raw	1 cup	55	1	1	13
Watermelon, wedge 4" x 8"	1	110	2	1	27
MEAT, CHEESE, EGGS, POULTRY, FISH					
Bacon (slices)	2	85	4	8	T
Beef, dried or chipped	2½ oz.	145	24	4	T
Beef, hamburger	3 oz.	235	20	17	0
Beef, roast (lean only)	3 oz.	210	25	12	0
Beef, steak, broiled	3 oz.	220	24	13	0
Beef potpie (4¼" diam.)	1	515	21	30	39
Bologna (slices)	2	170	6	16	1
Cheese:					
American	1 oz.	105	6	9	T
American spread	1 oz.	82	5	6	2
Blue or Roquefort	1 oz.	105	6	8	1
Cheddar	1 oz.	115	7	9	1
Cottage	1 cup	235	28	10	6
Cream	1 oz.	100	2	10	1
Parmesan	1 oz.	130	12	9	1
Yogurt	1 cup	140	8	7	11
Chicken, broiled	3 oz.	115	20	3	0
Chicken, fried	3 oz.	215	26	10	2
Chicken potpie (9" diam.)	⅓	545	23	31	42
Chili con carne w/beans	1 cup	340	19	16	31
Corned beef (canned)	3 oz.	185	22	10	0
Egg, scrambled in fat	1	95	6	7	1
Egg, whole (boiled)	1	80	6	6	T
Fish and seafood:					
Clams, raw	3 oz.	65	11	1	2
Fish sticks	3 oz.	150	15	9	6
Haddock, fried	3 oz.	140	17	5	5
Lobster, canned	3 oz.	80	16	1	T
Oysters, raw	1 cup	160	20	4	8
Salmon, canned	3 oz.	120	17	5	0
Sardines, canned	3 oz.	175	20	9	0
Tuna, canned	3 oz.	170	25	7	0
Ham, baked	3 oz.	185	25	8	0
Hot dog (frankfurter)	2 oz.	170	7	16	1
Lamb, chop (broiled)	3.1 oz.	360	18	32	0
Lamb, leg (roasted)	3 oz.	235	22	16	0
Liver, beef (fried)	3 oz.	195	22	9	5
Luncheon ham (canned)	slice	175	9	15	1
Pork, chop	2.7 oz.	305	19	25	0
Pork, roast	3 oz.	310	21	24	0
Pork, sausage links	2	120	4	12	T
Salami	3 oz.	450	20	40	T
Veal, cutlet	3 oz.	185	23	9	0
Veal, roast	3 oz.	230	23	14	0

KINDS OF FOOD	AMOUNT	FOOD ENERGY (Calories)	PROTEIN (Grams)	FAT (Grams)	CARBOHYDRATES (Grams)
VEGETABLES AND NUTS					
Almonds, shelled, chopped	1 cup	775	24	70	25
Asparagus	1 cup	30	3	T	5
Beans, green	1 cup	30	2	T	7
Beans, lima	1 cup	260	16	1	49
Beans, navy	1 cup	210	14	1	38
Beans and pork (canned)	1 cup	310	16	7	48
Beets	1 cup	55	2	T	12
Broccoli	1 cup	40	5	T	7
Brussels sprouts	1 cup	55	6	1	10
Cabbage, cooked	1 cup	30	2	T	6
Cabbage, raw	1 cup	15	1	T	4
Carrot, raw (7" long)	1	30	1	T	7
Carrots, cooked	1 cup	50	1	T	11
Cashew nuts	1 cup	785	24	64	41
Cauliflower, cooked	1 cup	31	3	T	6
Celery, diced, raw	1 cup	20	1	T	5
Coconut, grated	1 cup	275	3	28	8
Collards	1 cup	65	7	1	10
Corn, canned (whole kernel)	1 cup	175	5	1	43
Corn, sweet	1 ear	70	2	1	16
Cucumber, peeled	1	20	1	T	5
Lettuce, iceberg (head)	1	70	5	T	16
Mushrooms, raw	1 cup	20	2	T	3
Onion, cooked	1 cup	60	3	T	14
Onion, raw (2½" diam.)	1	40	2	T	10
Parsnips	1 cup	100	2	1	23
Peanut butter	1 tbsp.	95	4	8	3
Peanuts, roasted	1 cup	840	38	72	27
Peas, green, canned	1 cup	150	8	1	29
Pecan halves	1 cup	810	11	84	17
Pepper, green, raw	1 pod	15	1	T	4
Pickle, sweet	1	20	T	T	5
Potato, baked	1	145	4	T	33
Potato, boiled	1	105	3	T	23
Potato, french-fry pieces	10	135	2	7	18
Potato, mashed	1 cup	135	4	2	27
Potato chips	10	115	1	8	10
Radishes, raw	10	10	T	T	2
Rice, cooked	1 cup	225	4	T	50
Sauerkraut, canned	1 cup	40	2	T	9
Spinach	1 cup	40	5	T	6
Sweet potato, baked	1	160	2	1	37
Tomato, raw (3" diam.)	1	40	2	T	9
Tomato catsup	1 tbsp.	15	T	T	4
Tomato juice	1 cup	45	2	T	10
Tomatoes, canned	1 cup	50	2	T	10
Turnip greens	1 cup	30	3	T	5
Turnips, diced	1 cup	35	1	T	8
Walnuts, black	1 cup	785	26	74	19
SALAD DRESSINGS, SAUCES, AND SOUPS					
Barbecue sauce	1 cup	230	4	17	20
Bean with pork soup	1 cup	170	8	6	22
Beef broth	1 cup	30	5	0	3
Bouillon cube	1	5	1	T	T
Cream of chicken soup	1 cup	180	7	10	15
Cream of mushroom soup	1 cup	215	7	14	16
Cream of tomato soup	1 cup	175	7	7	23
Salad dressings:					
Blue cheese	1 tbsp.	75	1	8	1
French	1 tbsp.	65	T	6	3
Mayonnaise	1 tbsp.	100	T	11	T
Thousand Island	1 tbsp.	80	T	8	2
Tartar sauce	1 tbsp.	75	T	8	1
Tomato soup	1 cup	90	2	3	16
Vegetarian soup	1 cup	80	2	2	13
White sauce	1 cup	405	10	31	22

FOOD IS THE SOURCE OF HEALTH

Source: U.S. Departments of Agriculture and Health and Human Services; *Food Is More Than Just Something To Eat*

In this land of plenty, millions of Americans aren't eating wisely.

The problem is not that Americans haven't enough to eat, but that they eat too many of the wrong things or too little of the right.

Food is what you eat; nutrition is how your body uses food. And if you aren't eating foods to meet your bodily needs, you may be suffering from poor nutrition. Some of the damages caused by severe malnutrition may be irreversible.

FOOD IS THE BASIS OF LIFE

Food is the source of health and well-being, gives you the energy you need for everyday living, affects your weight and height and even your strength to a great extent.

In other words, everything in life begins with food, and there is much to the saying "You are what you eat."

Food contains protein, carbohydrates, fats, vitamins, minerals, and water. All of these are nutrients; that is, they nourish the body.

The important thing to remember is that no single food does everything and all foods have something to offer. A variety of different types of food will provide all the nutrients most of us need.

PROTEIN

After water and possibly fat, protein is the most plentiful substance in the body. The substances, called enzymes, which control the processes that keep the body working are made of protein.

Protein is also part of the hemoglobin molecule in red blood cells that carries oxygen into the system.

The antibodies in the bloodstream that fight off disease and infection are also protein.

Another important use of protein in the body is for building the muscle tissue that holds the bone structure together and provides the strength to move and work. *Most Americans get more than enough protein.*

Where is protein found? Meat, poultry, fish, milk, cheese, and eggs provide good quantities of it. Bread and cereal are also important sources.

And such vegetables as soybeans, chickpeas, dry beans, and peanuts are also good sources of protein. You do not have to load up on meat, poultry, or eggs to get enough protein in your diet.

Combining cereal or vegetable foods with a little milk, cheese, or other animal protein can provide good protein in your diet.

For example, eat cereal with milk, rice with fish, spaghetti with meatballs, or simply drink a glass of milk during a meal. All these combinations provide the high-quality protein the body needs.

FATS

Fats provide energy and add flavor and variety to foods. They make meals more satisfying.

Fats carry vitamins A, D, E, and K and are essential parts of the structure of the cells that make up the body's tissues.

Our body fat protects vital organs by providing a cushion around them.

Fats are plentiful in butter, margarine, shortening, salad oils, cream, most cheeses, mayonnaise, salad dressings, nuts, and bacon.

CARBOHYDRATES

Carbohydrates are starches and sugars found in cereal grains, fruits, vegetables, and sugar added to foods for sweetening.

Carbohydrates are the major source of energy in the diet. Wheat, oats, corn, and rice—and the foods made from them, such as bread, spaghetti, macaroni, noodles, or grits—provide starch along with other important nutrients. So do potatoes, sweet potatoes, and vegetables such as peas, dry beans, peanuts, and soybeans.

Most of the other vegetables contain smaller amounts of carbohydrates.

Carbohydrates in vegetables are usually in the form of starch; in fruits they occur as sugar. Candies, jams, molasses, and syrups are primarily sugar.

WATER

Water is a vitally important nutrient. Water stands next to air in importance to life. You can get along for days, even weeks, without food but you can live only a few days without water.

Water is necessary for all the processes of digestion.

Nutrients are dissolved in water so they may pass through the intestinal wall and into the bloodstream for use throughout the body.

Water carries waste out of the body and also helps to regulate body temperature.

The body's most obvious source of water is the water a person drinks, but some is produced by the body's burning of food for energy. Coffee and tea are mostly water, and so are fruit juices and milk.

Soup is a source of water, and so are many fruits and vegetables. Even meat can be up to 80% water.

MINERALS

The most abundant mineral in the body is calcium and, except for iron, it is the most likely to be inadequate in the diets of many age groups.

From the age of 9, the diets of girls and women may lack as much as 25% to 30% of the calcium they need.

Almost all calcium, and most phosphorus, which works closely with calcium in the body, is in bones and teeth.

The other minerals play a vital role in tissue and body fluids. Soft tissue, or muscle, especially has a high phosphorus content. Calcium is required for blood to clot and for the heart to function normally. The nervous system does not work properly when calcium levels in the blood are below normal.

People who buy from the milk counter are stocking up on calcium supplies.

In the U.S. we rely on milk as a basic source of calcium. Two cups of milk, or an equivalent amount of cheese or other dairy products except butter, go a long way toward supplying all the calcium needed for the day.

But milk is not the only source. Dark-green leafy vegetables like collards, mustard greens, or turnip greens provide some calcium, and salmon and sardines supply useful amounts of it if the very tiny bones are eaten.

IRON

Iron is another essential mineral. Women of childbearing age require more iron than men do.

The diets of infants and pregnant women may need special attention to see that they contain the iron needed.

Unfortunately, only a few foods provide iron in very useful amounts. However, liver, heart, kidney, and most lean meats are generously supplied with it. So are shellfish, particularly oysters.

Whole-grain and enriched breads and cereals can provide 20% to 25% or more of the daily iron need.

Dark-green leafy vegetables are also sources of iron.

IODINE

The most important fact about iodine is that a deficiency of it can cause goiter—a swelling of the thyroid gland. The most practical ways to be sure of getting enough iodine are to use iodized salt regularly and to add seafood to the diet whenever possible.

OTHER ESSENTIAL ELEMENTS

Calcium, iron, and iodine are not the only minerals you need. Most of the others—zinc, copper, sodium, potassium, magnesium, and phosphorus—are widely available in so many foods that a little variety in selecting groceries takes care of them easily. Magnesium, for example, is abundant in nuts, whole-grain products, dry beans, and dark-green vegetables.

Phosphorus shows up in the same foods that supply you with protein and calcium, although leafy vegetables contain little phosphorus.

FLUORINE

Fluorine—an element that helps protect teeth from decay—is not so readily found in food. Many metropolitan areas add minute amounts of fluorine to local sources of drinking water.

VITAMINS

Scientists know of a dozen or more vitamins that you must have to enjoy good health. Ordinarily, you can get them from a well-chosen assortment of everyday foods.

A few of these vitamins are of great importance, and you should know what foods provide them.

VITAMIN A

Vitamin A plays a very important role in eye function, and in keeping the skin and mucous membranes resistant to infection.

Although vitamin A occurs only in foods of animal origin, the deep-yellow and dark-green vegetables and fruits supply a material—carotene—that your body can turn into vitamin A.

Vegetables and fruits can easily supply all the vitamin A you need. Such items as collards, turnip greens, kale, carrots, squash, and sweet potatoes can more than take care of daily needs; yellow peaches, apricots, cantaloupe, and papayas also help.

Many people, however, do not regularly eat these foods.

Liver is an excellent source of vitamin A. A 2-ounce serving of cooked beef liver provides more than 30,000 international units of the vitamin. That amounts to six times more vitamin A than you would need during the day. Kidney is also an excellent source of vitamin A.

There are plenty of other sources of vitamin A. Whole milk is a source, but skim milk doesn't have any vitamin A unless it is fortified—that is, vitamin A has been added to it.

Cheese made from whole milk, and margarine enriched with vitamin A, both supply this vitamin.

THE B VITAMINS

Three of the best-known vitamins—riboflavin, thiamin, and niacin—release the

FOOD IS THE SOURCE OF HEALTH *(continued)*

energy in food. They also have a role in the nervous system, keep the digestive system working calmly, and help maintain healthy skin.

Vitamin B_2 (riboflavin) is easy to find and extremely important to your diet. It is plentifully supplied by meats, milk, whole-grain or enriched breads, and cereals.

Organ meats (liver, kidney, etc.) also supply this vitamin.

A lack of thiamin (vitamin B_1) causes beriberi. Fortunately, this disease is now almost nonexistent in the U.S., although it is still detected in some alcoholics.

Thiamin is abundant in only a few foods. Lean pork is one. Dry beans and peas, some organ meats, and some nuts supply some thiamin.

Whole-grain and enriched cereals and breads are also dependable sources of the vitamin.

Niacin can be found in whole-grain and enriched cereals, meat and meat products, and peas and beans.

Other B vitamins such as B_6, B_{12}, and folacin are needed to maintain normal hemoglobin, the substance in blood that carries oxygen to the tissues. The signs of B_{12} deficiency include soreness of the mouth and tongue, numbness and tingling in the hands and legs, anemia, and loss of coordination.

Folacin is available in many foods but in small quantities.

VITAMIN C

Vitamin C, ascorbic acid, is not completely understood, but it is considered important in helping to maintain the cementing material that holds body cells together.

The citrus-fruit juice you may have for breakfast can give you more than half of the vitamin C needed for the day.

In fact, unless good foods are consciously avoided, the rest of the fruits and vegetables eaten during the day will help to provide the vitamin C required.

Potatoes and sweet potatoes provide helpful amounts of vitamin C, and so do tomatoes and peppers. In addition, green vegetables such as broccoli, turnip greens, raw cabbage, and collards make a contribution of vitamin C.

VITAMIN D

Although few foods contain vitamin D, it is readily available in milk fortified with it. Sunlight enables the body to produce vitamin D if it shines directly on the skin.

Vitamin D is important in building strong bones and teeth and is needed throughout the growth period.

Without vitamin D the body cannot absorb the calcium supplied by food. For this reason milk is often fortified with vitamin D.

Adults rarely need more vitamin D than they get in food and from the sun. However, infants and young children sometimes do not get enough.

A disease called rickets results from a lack of vitamin D. Children who suffer from this disease have absorbed too little calcium. Their bodies cannot form strong and rigid bones, and consequently they may have enlarged joints, bowed legs, knock-knees, or beaded ribs.

On the other hand, too much vitamin D can be dangerous. This causes a calcium overload in the blood and tissues. Infants given too much vitamin D may develop calcium deposits in the kidneys and end up with permanent kidney damage.

VITAMIN E

Vitamin E is known to be essential, but its exact role in the body is not fully understood by scientists.

Vitamin E is abundant in vegetable oils and margarine and is contained in such foods as wheat germ and lettuce.

A diet usually does not lack in vitamin E if it regularly includes fruits, vegetables, vegetable oil, milk, meat, and eggs.

VITAMIN K

Vitamin K is essential for the manufacture of a substance that helps blood to clot. Vitamin K is widely distributed in a variety of foods such as the green and leafy vegetables, tomatoes, cauliflower, egg yolks, soybean oil, and any kind of liver.

NUTRIENTS AND ENERGY

Almost all foods provide energy—some more than others.

This energy is measured in calories. Foods that are rich in fats, starches, or sugars contain large amounts of calories—or energy.

Fat is the most concentrated source of energy. Ounce for ounce, it provides more than twice as much energy as protein or the carbohydrates.

Foods that contain a lot of water, like watermelon and cucumbers, have few calories because water, which makes up most of their weight, provides no calories and therefore no energy.

When you eat a diet that furnishes more energy—or calories—than you need, the excess supply is stored in the body as fat. And when you continue to overeat you become overweight or fat.

When you eat less calories than the body uses, you lose weight.

HOW TO STRETCH YOUR FOOD DOLLAR

You can save a great deal of money on food if you shop carefully and cautiously.

Here are some general rules for feeding your family at less cost.

1. Learn the facts about basic nutrition. Then you will know how much protein your family needs each day and what foods provide it. You will also understand how to meet the daily minimum requirements of vitamins and minerals. See pages 398–402.

2. Plan the week's menu ahead of time. If you shop only once or twice a week instead of every day, you will spend less. Impulse buying of exotic foods will be kept to a minimum.

3. Shop around for the best prices. Special sale prices in one store can be attractive enough to make you overlook the fact that the prices of staples, bread, and milk are higher than those in another store.

4. Watch for specials and sales. Read supermarket advertisements in the newspapers on Wednesday and Thursday. These advertisements offer bargains from 6% to 34% below regular prices. It often pays to buy in quantity if the items will keep.

5. Privately labeled foods in supermarket chains usually cost less. They are often as good as well-known brands.

6. Learn how to store foods properly. Waste through spoilage can be a constant drain on your food budget. For example, use frozen foods as quickly as possible, and do not let them thaw before putting them in your freezer. Remove the store wrappings from meat and store it in a covered dish. If you freeze meat, wrap it *tightly* in foil or other material to prevent freezer burn.

7. Save on meat costs. Remember that all meat has about the same nutritional value. Lamb chops, T-bone steak, and veal cost more because they are tender and may have superior flavor.

But there are some meats with a high initial cost that, because they have little waste, are good buys—for example, canned ham and round steak. Chicken is one of the best buys in the market.

Most seafood has risen in price. Substitute cheese and egg dishes once or twice a week. Dry beans and peas are also rich in protein.

8. Stretch food by using leftovers. Think in terms of double-duty foods, especially meats. Steaks and chops are usually good for one meal only. On the other hand, leftovers from roasts, chicken, turkey, and ham can be made into a wide variety of dishes.

You can grind leftover meats for hash and casseroles, and cut up leftover poultry, meats, and vegetables for pies, stews, salads, or soups. The stripped carcass of a roasted chicken or turkey and the bones from a beef roast or smoked ham can be boiled to make a rich soup stock.

9. Do not avoid unfamiliar foods, especially meats, that are on sale, just because you don't know how to cook them. Consult a reputable cookbook that tells you how to prepare such cuts as lamb's breast, beef and lamb kidneys, tripe, and the like.

10. Be aware of the high cost of convenience foods. These include TV dinners, frozen pasta and Chinese dishes, and frozen vegetables prepared with butter sauce and other garnishes. A package of frozen green beans with mushrooms may cost from 11 to 15 cents more than one of plain green beans.

11. Buying staples in large quantities is usually economical if you have sufficient storage space. Sugar, flour, cereals, rice, potatoes, and canned foods are often better bargains in large quantities. Buying milk in a two-quart container costs less than two separate containers. Do not overlook the various brands of powdered milk, which offer substantial savings.

12. If you live in or near a large city, discuss the idea of a cooperative food-buying plan with your friends and neighbors. A dozen or more families can band together to purchase food supplies wholesale from city markets and meat warehouses at savings up to 40%. In order to do this you must have a central place, such as a garage or basement, in which to store the items. The plan also requires some bookkeeping as well as purchasing and distributing work.

TOO MUCH SALT CAN KILL

The average American eats from 2 to 2½ teaspoons of salt each day—or about 8½ pounds a year, according to the Food and Drug Administration (FDA). Only about one-third comes from sprinkling salt on your food, about one-third occurs naturally in the food you eat, and about one-third comes as flavoring in processed foods in your diet.

However, the National Research Council of the National Academy of Sciences estimates that an "adequate and safe intake" should be only about one-fourth of the amount normally consumed.

Too much salt in the diet can be especially dangerous to the 10% to 30% of persons who have inherited a tendency to develop high blood pressure, according to studies sponsored by the FDA. High blood pressure often leads to stroke, heart disease, and kidney failure.

PLANTING AND GROWING GARDEN ANNUALS

Source: U.S. Department of Agriculture

Most garden annuals, plants that live only one year, should be planted outdoors only after the last frost of spring.

To find the approximate date of the last frost in your area, see the table *Freeze Dates and Growing Season for Gardeners* on pages 406–409.

PLANT	WHEN TO PLANT SEEDS	EXPOSURE	GERMINATION TIME (days)	PLANT SPACING (inches)	REMARKS
Ageratum	After last frost	Semishade or full sun	5	10 to 12	Pinch tips to encourage branching; remove dead flowers.
Balsam	After last frost	Sun	10	12 to 14	
Calendula	Early spring or late fall	Shade or sun	10	8 to 10	
Calliopsis	After last frost	Shade or sun	8	10 to 14	
China aster	After last frost	Shade or sun	8	10 to 12	Start early in cold frame; resow for prolonged blooming.
Cockscomb	After last frost	Shade or sun	10	10 to 12	
Coleus	Sow indoors any time; outdoors after last frost	Sun or partial shade	10	10 to 12	
Cornflower	Early spring	Partial shade	5	12 to 14	
Cosmos	After last frost	Sun	5	10 to 12	
Dahlia	After last frost	Sun	5	12 to 14	For best blooms, sow several weeks before other annuals.
Forget-me-not	Spring or summer; shade in summer	Partial shade	10	10 to 12	
Four-o'clock	After last frost	Sun	5	12 to 14	Store roots; plant next year.
Globe amaranth	Early spring	Sun	15	10 to 12	
Impatiens	Indoors any time; outdoors after last frost	Partial or deep shade	15	10 to 12	
Larkspur	South late fall; North early spring	Sun	20	6 to 8	Hard to transplant; grow in peat pots.
Lupine	Early spring or late fall	Sun	20	6 to 8	
Marigold	After last frost	Sun	5	10 to 14	High fertility delays bloom.
Morning glory	After last frost	Sun	5	24 to 36	Reseeds itself.
Nasturtium	After last frost	Sun	8	8 to 12	For best flowers, grow in soil of low fertility.
Pansy	Spring or summer; shade in summer	Sun or shade	10	6 to 8	Does best in cool season.
Petunia	Early spring indoors	Sun	10	12 to 14	Transplant outdoors early summer; keep cool.
Pink	Early spring through summer; shade in summer	Sun or shade	5	8 to 12	Start early in spring indoors; keep cool; remove dead flowers.
Poppy	Early spring through summer; shade in summer	Sun	10	6 to 10	Difficult to transplant; start in peat pots; make successive plantings.
Portulaca	After last frost or in late fall	Sun	10	10 to 12	
Salpiglossis	Early spring	Sun	15	10 to 12	Needs supports; avoid cold.
Scabiosa	Spring or summer; shade in summer	Sun	10	12 to 14	Remove old flowers.
Scarlet sage	Spring or summer; shade in summer	Sun	15	8 to 12	
Snapdragon	Spring or late fall	Sun	15	6 to 10	Start cool; pinch tips to encourage branching.
Spider plant	Early spring, spring, or fall	Sun	10	12 to 14	Reseeds freely; pinch to keep plant short; water and fertilize freely.
Stock	After last frost	Sun	5	6 to 10	
Strawflower	Early spring	Sun	5	10 to 12	
Summer cypress	Early spring	Sun	15	18 to 24	
Sunflower	After last frost	Sun	5	12 to 14	
Sweet alyssum	Early spring	Sun	5	10 to 12	Damps off easily; sow in hills; do not thin.
Sweetpea	Early spring or late summer through late fall	Sun	15	6 to 8	Select heat-resistant types.
Verbena	After last frost	Sun	20	18 to 24	Pinch to encourage branching.
Vinca	After last frost	Sun	15	10 to 12	Avoid overwatering.
Zinnia	After last frost	Sun	5	8 to 12	Thin after plants begin to bloom; remove poor-flowering plants.

PLANTING AND GROWING VEGETABLES

Source: U.S. Department of Agriculture

Home-grown vegetables picked at the peak of their maturity have a tasty quality seldom found in those bought in a store.

Vegetable gardening requires labor and time. But vegetables grown at home can save on grocery bills as well as provide an enjoyable hobby.

Be cautious about how large a garden you plant the first time. A small well-kept garden will give you more enjoyment than a large neglected one.

Even though you live in a one-room apartment, you can have a vegetable garden in containers on a windowsill or balcony.

If you use plastic containers, allow for drainage by boring several small holes in the side of the container near the bottom. Put about half an inch of coarse gravel in the bottom of the container before filling it with soil.

The inexperienced gardener should choose only a few crops to plant the first year.

When you buy seeds for your garden, check to make sure they are stamped with this year's date. Old seed germinates poorly.

You can get a jump on the growing season by planting your seeds indoors, and then transplanting the plants to your garden when the weather is warmer.

The vegetables suggested in the table below all can be grown in a minigarden. Vegetables such as corn and potatoes take a great deal of space in order to provide a worthwhile harvest.

The approximate date of the last spring frost in your area can be found in the table *Freeze Dates and Growing Season for Gardeners* on pages 406–409.

VEGETABLE	PLANTING			GROWING	COMMENTS
	Weeks before frost-free date	Depth of seeds	Space between plants	Days from seed to harvest	
Beets	2 to 4 weeks	½ in.	2 to 3 in.	50 to 60 days	Tolerate partial shade; thin plants when 6 to 8 inches high.
Cabbage	4 to 6 weeks	½ in.	12 to 18 in.	65 to 120 days	Tolerates partial shade; can also be set out for a fall crop.
Carrots	2 to 4 weeks	½ in.	2 to 3 in.	65 to 80 days	Tolerate partial shade; for several harvests make plantings at 3-week intervals until 3 months before fall freezing date.
Chives	4 to 6 weeks	½ in.	2 to 3 in.	60 to 70 days	Grow in partial shade; bulbs should be divided occasionally so they do not get too thick.
Cucumbers	1 week after frost-free date	½ in.	18 in.	70 to 80 days	Need full sunlight and hot weather; start seeds indoors 3 weeks before time to set out.
Eggplant	See comments	½ in.	18 in.	100 to 140 days	Start seeds indoors 8 to 9 weeks before planting outdoors; set out on frost-free date in warm soil; needs full sunlight; cover plants during cool weather.
Leaf lettuce	4 to 6 weeks	¼ in.	4 to 6 in.	30 to 35 days	Tolerates partial shade and temperatures as low as 28°F.; make several later plantings for summer lettuce.
Mustard greens	2 to 4 weeks	¼ in.	4 to 5 in.	35 to 40 days	Make plantings at 10-day intervals for successive crops; tolerate partial shade.
Onions	4 to 6 weeks	1 to 1½ in.	2 to 3 in.	100 to 120 days	Green onions grow in partial shade; mature bulbs need full sun; onions need lots of water.
Parsley	4 to 6 weeks	¼ in.	6 to 8 in.	80 to 85 days	Does well in partial shade; start seeds indoors, soaking them overnight before planting; keep soil moist to help seeds germinate.
Peppers	1 week after frost-free date	½ in.	14 to 18 in.	110 to 120 days	Require full sunlight and hot weather; start seeds indoors 5 to 6 weeks before outdoor planting.
Radishes	2 to 4 weeks	½ in.	1 in.	22 to 35 days	Do well in partial shade; cannot withstand heat; make several plantings at 1-week intervals.
Summer squash	See comments	1 to 2 in.	18 in.	50 to 60 days	Plant on frost-free date; does best in full sunlight; plant bush types.
Tomatoes	See comments	½ in.	14 to 18 in.	55 to 100 days	Start seeds 5 to 7 weeks before transplanting on frost-free date; require full sunlight and warm weather.
Turnips	4 to 6 weeks	½ in.	3 to 4 in.	30 to 80 days	Tolerate partial shade; thin when plants are large enough to use for greens, leaving others to mature as vegetables.

FREEZE DATES AND GROWING SEASON FOR GARDENERS

Gardeners and farmers need to know the approximate date they can expect the last freezing day in the spring so they can schedule when to set out plants susceptible to frost. The length of the growing season—the time until the first freezing day in the fall—helps determine what kinds of flowers or vegetables can be grown in a certain climate.

Information in the following table comes from the *Annual Summary of Climatological Data,* National Oceanic and Atmospheric Administration.

LOCATION	LAST SPRING FREEZE	GROWING SEASON	FIRST FALL FREEZE
ALABAMA			
Athens	March 25	27 weeks	Oct. 3
Birmingham	March 23	33 weeks	Nov. 8
Gadsden	March 22	33 weeks	Nov. 12
Haleyville	April 9	25 weeks	Oct. 3
Huntsville	March 30	31 weeks	Oct. 31
Jasper	April 10	25 weeks	Oct. 3
Mobile	Feb. 27	39 weeks	Dec. 1
Montgomery	Feb. 28	37 weeks	Nov. 13
Ozark	Feb. 27	37 weeks	Nov. 13
Pittsview	April 10	25 weeks	Oct. 5
Selma	Feb. 27	37 weeks	Nov. 13
Tuscaloosa	April 10	25 weeks	Oct. 3
ALASKA			
Adak	May 31	20 weeks	Oct. 24
Anchorage	May 15	18 weeks	Sept. 16
Fairbanks	May 21	14 weeks	Aug. 30
Juneau	April 22	26 weeks	Oct. 21
Ketchikan	March 31	32 weeks	Nov. 12
Kodiak	May 22	19 weeks	Oct. 2
Seward	April 26	22 weeks	Sept. 29
Sitka	May 25	18 weeks	Oct. 3
Valdez	May 26	15 weeks	Sept. 12
Wrangell	April 23	23 weeks	Oct. 4
ARIZONA			
Bisbee	April 16	24 weeks	Oct. 31
Flagstaff	June 9	17 weeks	Sept. 16
Mesa	Feb. 9	44 weeks	Dec. 15
Nogales	May 21	19 weeks	Oct. 31
Phoenix	Jan. 3	49 weeks	Dec. 15
Prescott	May 21	19 weeks	Oct. 30
Scottsdale	Feb. 21	41 weeks	Dec. 10
Tombstone	March 10	37 weeks	Nov. 29
Tucson	April 4	33 weeks	Nov. 24
Winslow	April 22	27 weeks	Oct. 25
ARKANSAS			
Arkadelphia	April 9	31 weeks	Nov. 13
El Dorado	March 24	34 weeks	Nov. 14
Fayetteville	April 17	26 weeks	Oct. 16
Fort Smith	April 9	31 weeks	Nov. 14
Helena	April 6	32 weeks	Nov. 15
Hot Springs	March 26	33 weeks	Nov. 15
Jonesboro	March 25	30 weeks	Oct. 22
Little Rock	April 6	33 weeks	Nov. 15
Mammoth Spring	April 17	26 weeks	Oct. 16
Pine Bluff	March 24	34 weeks	Nov. 15
Texarkana	March 24	34 weeks	Nov. 15
CALIFORNIA			
Bakersfield	Feb. 7	46 weeks	Dec. 23
Barstow	April 10	33 weeks	Nov. 24
Death Valley	Jan. 5	51 weeks	none
El Centro	Feb. 6	44 weeks	Dec. 11
Eureka	Feb. 23	43 weeks	Dec. 23
Fairmont	April 19	31 weeks	Nov. 23
Fresno	Feb. 23	40 weeks	Dec. 1
Los Angeles	none	52 weeks	none
Modesto	Feb. 7	46 weeks	Dec. 23
Oakland	none	52 weeks	none
Palmdale	May 19	24 weeks	Oct. 31

LOCATION	LAST SPRING FREEZE	GROWING SEASON	FIRST FALL FREEZE
CALIFORNIA *(continued)*			
Paradise	March 3	42 weeks	Dec. 22
Red Bluff	Feb. 22	40 weeks	Nov. 30
Sacramento	Feb. 8	46 weeks	Dec. 24
San Bernardino	Jan. 3	51 weeks	Dec. 26
San Diego	none	52 weeks	none
San Francisco	Jan. 8	50 weeks	Dec. 25
San Jose	Jan. 9	46 weeks	Nov. 28
San Rafael	none	51 weeks	Nov. 30
Santa Rosa	March 9	37 weeks	Nov. 26
Stockton	Feb. 9	42 weeks	Nov. 28
Woodland	March 9	37 weeks	Nov. 23
COLORADO			
Aspen	June 8	12 weeks	Sept. 3
Boulder	April 30	19 weeks	Sept. 12
Burlington	April 22	28 weeks	Nov. 2
Colorado Springs	May 8	21 weeks	Oct. 4
Del Norte	June 3	17 weeks	Sept. 28
Denver	April 16	29 weeks	Oct. 30
Durango	June 9	15 weeks	Sept. 23
Grand Junction	April 15	29 weeks	Nov. 5
Greeley	April 16	24 weeks	Sept. 28
Lakewood	June 8	15 weeks	Sept. 12
Manassa	June 10	12 weeks	Sept. 3
Pueblo	April 22	27 weeks	Oct. 31
CONNECTICUT			
Bridgeport	April 10	24 weeks	Oct. 18
Danbury	May 8	20 weeks	Sept. 24
Hartford	April 22	24 weeks	Oct. 15
Middletown	May 8	20 weeks	Sept. 24
New Haven	April 10	24 weeks	Oct. 19
Norfolk	May 8	20 weeks	Sept. 24
Stamford	May 8	20 weeks	Sept. 24
Storrs	May 2	22 weeks	Oct. 4
Westbrook	May 9	21 weeks	Oct. 3
DELAWARE			
Bridgeville	April 20	24 weeks	Oct. 4
Dover	April 7	26 weeks	Oct. 3
Georgetown	May 8	26 weeks	Oct. 4
Middletown	April 20	24 weeks	Oct. 3
Milford	May 8	25 weeks	Oct. 3
Wilmington	April 7	26 weeks	Oct. 3
DIST. OF COLUMBIA			
Washington	May 8	20 weeks	Sept. 24
FLORIDA			
Fort Lauderdale	none	52 weeks	none
Fort Myers	none	52 weeks	none
Gainesville	Feb. 27	40 weeks	Dec. 2
Jacksonville	Feb. 27	39 weeks	Nov. 14
Key West	none	52 weeks	none
Miami	none	52 weeks	none
Orlando	Feb. 26	51 weeks	none
St. Augustine	Feb. 27	42 weeks	Dec. 18
St. Petersburg	none	52 weeks	none
Tallahassee	Feb. 28	38 weeks	Nov. 25
Tampa	Feb. 27	51 weeks	none
Tavernier	none	52 weeks	none
Titusville	Feb. 26	51 weeks	none

LOCATION	LAST SPRING FREEZE	GROWING SEASON	FIRST FALL FREEZE
GEORGIA			
Albany	March 1	37 weeks	Nov. 13
Athens	April 2	31 weeks	Nov. 7
Atlanta	March 24	33 weeks	Nov. 12
Augusta	March 16	34 weeks	Nov. 12
Brunswick	Feb. 28	40 weeks	Dec. 4
Cartersville	April 25	23 weeks	Oct. 3
Columbus	Feb. 28	37 weeks	Nov. 15
Gainesville	April 7	28 weeks	Oct. 22
Macon	March 15	35 weeks	Nov. 16
Moultrie	Feb. 28	37 weeks	Nov. 13
Rome	April 10	30 weeks	Oct. 3
Savannah	Feb. 26	39 weeks	Nov. 26
Valdosta	Feb. 28	37 weeks	Nov. 13
HAWAII			
Honolulu	none	52 weeks	none
Kailua	none	52 weeks	none
IDAHO			
Boise	May 6	20 weeks	Oct. 12
Idaho Falls	May 31	15 weeks	Sept. 13
Lewiston	April 13	28 weeks	Oct. 6
Oakley	June 8	18 weeks	Oct. 13
Pocatello	May 16	17 weeks	Sept. 13
Potlatch	June 9	9 weeks	Aug. 13
Twin Falls	May 16	20 weeks	Oct. 5
ILLINOIS			
Chicago	April 29	21 weeks	Oct. 12
Decatur	April 24	23 weeks	Oct. 2
Joliet	May 7	20 weeks	Sept. 23
Marion	April 18	24 weeks	Oct. 3
Moline	April 21	25 weeks	Oct. 14
Mount Vernon	April 17	24 weeks	Oct. 3
Olney	April 17	24 weeks	Oct. 3
Peoria	April 16	29 weeks	Oct. 21
Quincy	April 9	25 weeks	Oct. 2
Rockford	May 2	22 weeks	Oct. 9
Springfield	April 9	25 weeks	Oct. 2
Urbana	April 24	23 weeks	Oct. 2
INDIANA			
Bloomington	April 10	25 weeks	Oct. 3
Columbus	May 8	21 weeks	Oct. 2
Crawfordsville	May 8	21 weeks	Oct. 2
Evansville	April 7	28 weeks	Oct. 23
Fort Wayne	April 26	25 weeks	Oct. 17
Greencastle	May 7	21 weeks	Oct. 2
Hobart	May 10	19 weeks	Sept. 23
Indianapolis	April 23	25 weeks	Oct. 22
New Castle	May 8	20 weeks	Sept. 23
Scottsburg	May 7	21 weeks	Oct. 2
South Bend	May 2	24 weeks	Sept. 18
IOWA			
Cedar Rapids	May 6	20 weeks	Sept. 22
Davenport	April 24	23 weeks	Oct. 2
Des Moines	April 30	27 weeks	Oct. 10
Mason City	May 6	17 weeks	Sept. 3
Oskaloosa	April 24	22 weeks	Sept. 22
Pocahontas	May 6	20 weeks	Sept. 22
Sioux City	April 16	23 weeks	Sept. 22
Waterloo	May 6	22 weeks	Oct. 3
KANSAS			
Atchison	April 8	30 weeks	Nov. 6
Concordia	April 17	27 weeks	Oct. 21
Dodge City	April 16	26 weeks	Oct. 15
Fort Scott	April 5	31 weeks	Nov. 6
Goodland	May 3	23 weeks	Oct. 11
Healy	April 16	20 weeks	Sept. 3
Hill City	April 16	26 weeks	Sept. 13
Lawrence	April 5	31 weeks	Nov. 6
Lincoln	April 16	26 weeks	Oct. 15
Mankato	April 16	26 weeks	Oct. 15

LOCATION	LAST SPRING FREEZE	GROWING SEASON	FIRST FALL FREEZE
KANSAS *(continued)*			
Topeka	April 15	24 weeks	Oct. 1
Wichita	April 15	29 weeks	Nov. 6
KENTUCKY			
Ashland	May 8	20 weeks	Sept. 23
Danville	April 10	25 weeks	Oct. 3
Frankfort	May 8	26 weeks	Oct. 3
Lexington	April 25	23 weeks	Oct. 2
Louisville	April 9	28 weeks	Oct. 21
Middlesboro	May 7	26 weeks	Oct. 3
Owensboro	April 9	25 weeks	Oct. 3
Somerset	April 25	23 weeks	Oct. 3
LOUISIANA			
Alexandria	Feb. 27	40 weeks	Dec. 1
Bastrop	March 24	37 weeks	Nov. 15
Baton Rouge	Feb. 22	39 weeks	Nov. 22
Lafayette	Feb. 26	40 weeks	Dec. 1
Lake Charles	Feb. 22	39 weeks	Nov. 26
Monroe	Feb. 26	37 weeks	Nov. 14
Natchitoches	Feb. 26	37 weeks	Nov. 15
New Orleans	Feb. 27	39 weeks	Nov. 27
Shreveport	Feb. 26	37 weeks	Nov. 15
MAINE			
Augusta	May 5	20 weeks	Sept. 24
Bangor	May 6	20 weeks	Sept. 25
Bar Harbor	May 5	24 weeks	Oct. 19
Caribou	May 18	18 weeks	Sept. 22
Houlton	May 29	16 weeks	Sept. 19
Lewiston	May 2	23 weeks	Oct. 14
Portland	May 12	12 weeks	Sept. 27
MARYLAND			
Annapolis	March 26	28 weeks	Oct. 5
Baltimore	April 15	27 weeks	Oct. 21
Bittinger	May 8	20 weeks	Sept. 23
Boonsboro	April 20	27 weeks	Sept. 24
La Plata	May 8	21 weeks	Oct. 3
Salisbury	April 11	25 weeks	Oct. 4
MASSACHUSETTS			
Amherst	May 8	20 weeks	Sept. 24
Boston	April 8	30 weeks	Nov. 7
Chester	May 26	15 weeks	Sept. 5
Hyannis	May 2	24 weeks	Oct. 19
Milton	April 26	25 weeks	Oct. 21
Provincetown	April 20	25 weeks	Oct. 14
Springfield	April 26	23 weeks	Oct. 4
Stockbridge	May 21	18 weeks	Sept. 24
Woods Hole	April 25	30 weeks	Nov. 22
Worcester	April 26	24 weeks	Oct. 15
MICHIGAN			
Alpena	May 12	20 weeks	Oct. 4
Bad Axe	May 8	21 weeks	Oct. 2
Detroit	April 23	26 weeks	Oct. 21
Escanaba	May 7	20 weeks	Sept. 22
Grand Rapids	April 25	24 weeks	Oct. 12
Lansing	May 7	22 weeks	Oct. 8
Marquette	May 2	25 weeks	Oct. 26
Midland	May 8	20 weeks	Sept. 22
Muskegon	May 10	24 weeks	Oct. 2
Sault Ste. Marie	May 18	19 weeks	Sept. 29
Traverse City	May 10	19 weeks	Sept. 23
MINNESOTA			
Albert Lea	May 13	19 weeks	Sept. 21
Baudette	May 25	17 weeks	Sept. 21
Duluth	May 22	18 weeks	Sept. 24
Fergus Falls	May 15	16 weeks	Sept. 3
Rochester	May 8	20 weeks	Sept. 28
St. Cloud	May 25	20 weeks	Sept. 30
St. Paul	April 29	24 weeks	Oct. 13

FREEZE DATES AND GROWING SEASON FOR GARDENERS *(continued)*

LOCATION	LAST SPRING FREEZE	GROWING SEASON	FIRST FALL FREEZE
MINNESOTA *(continued)*			
Stillwater	May 23	17 weeks	Sept. 22
Tyler	May 7	20 weeks	Sept. 22
MISSISSIPPI			
Aberdeen	March 22	34 weeks	Nov. 15
Biloxi	Feb. 27	35 weeks	Nov. 28
Greenville	March 24	34 weeks	Nov. 15
Grenada	April 7	32 weeks	Nov. 15
Hattiesburg	Feb. 28	37 weeks	Nov. 13
Jackson	March 18	34 weeks	Nov. 8
McComb	March 22	34 weeks	Nov. 13
Meridian	March 19	34 weeks	Nov. 7
Tupelo	April 10	25 weeks	Oct. 3
MISSOURI			
Butler	April 17	29 weeks	Nov. 6
Cape Girardeau	April 9	25 weeks	Oct. 3
Columbia	April 9	28 weeks	Oct. 24
Dexter	April 9	31 weeks	Nov. 14
Festus	April 24	22 weeks	Sept. 23
Jefferson City	April 24	23 weeks	Oct. 2
Joplin	March 25	32 weeks	Nov. 6
Kansas City	April 5	31 weeks	Nov. 6
Poplar Bluff	April 10	28 weeks	Oct. 21
St. Joseph	April 13	28 weeks	Oct. 22
St. Louis	April 15	28 weeks	Oct. 20
Springfield	April 9	29 weeks	Oct. 25
MONTANA			
Bigfork	May 17	17 weeks	Sept. 13
Billings	May 16	19 weeks	Sept. 27
Butte	June 10	12 weeks	Sept. 2
Goldbutte	May 23	14 weeks	Sept. 1
Great Falls	May 16	19 weeks	Sept. 29
Havre	May 9	20 weeks	Sept. 23
Helena	May 12	19 weeks	Sept. 23
Miles City	April 25	22 weeks	Oct. 5
Missoula	May 15	19 weeks	Sept. 13
Shonkin	June 1	14 weeks	Sept. 2
NEBRASKA			
Dalton	May 22	15 weeks	Sept. 3
Grand Island	May 1	23 weeks	Oct. 11
Imperial	April 16	24 weeks	Sept. 30
Lincoln	April 23	23 weeks	Oct. 1
North Platte	May 12	16 weeks	Sept. 3
Omaha	April 16	29 weeks	Oct. 20
Scottsbluff	May 12	16 weeks	Sept. 3
NEVADA			
Carson City	June 8	14 weeks	Sept. 12
Eureka	June 8	10 weeks	Aug. 20
Las Vegas	March 4	39 weeks	Nov. 30
NEW HAMPSHIRE			
Bethlehem	May 21	18 weeks	Sept. 24
Concord	May 17	18 weeks	Sept. 24
Hanover	May 5	20 weeks	Sept. 24
Lebanon	May 20	18 weeks	Sept. 24
Monroe	May 21	18 weeks	Sept. 24
Woodstock	May 20	18 weeks	Sept. 24
NEW JERSEY			
Atlantic City	April 10	27 weeks	Oct. 19
Jersey City	April 10	27 weeks	Oct. 19
Moorestown	May 8	21 weeks	Oct. 3
Newark	April 7	29 weeks	Nov. 2
Sandy Hook	April 10	32 weeks	Nov. 23
Trenton	April 10	27 weeks	Oct. 19

LOCATION	LAST SPRING FREEZE	GROWING SEASON	FIRST FALL FREEZE
NEW MEXICO			
Alamogordo	April 5	30 weeks	Nov. 4
Albuquerque	April 5	30 weeks	Oct. 31
Carlsbad	March 25	32 weeks	Nov. 5
Gallup	June 10	16 weeks	Sept. 28
Mescalero	May 22	21 weeks	Oct. 15
San Mateo	May 21	23 weeks	Sept. 27
Santa Fe	April 27	27 weeks	Oct. 30
Taos	June 9	16 weeks	Sept. 27
NEW YORK			
Albany	April 27	23 weeks	Oct. 13
Buffalo	May 8	21 weeks	Oct. 3
Cooperstown	May 20	18 weeks	Sept. 23
Glens Falls	May 5	20 weeks	Sept. 23
New York City	April 10	27 weeks	Oct. 19
Plattsburgh	May 5	20 weeks	Sept. 24
Rochester	April 25	25 weeks	Oct. 20
Scarsdale	May 8	22 weeks	Oct. 8
Syracuse	April 28	24 weeks	Oct. 16
Utica	May 5	20 weeks	Sept. 24
NORTH CAROLINA			
Asheville	April 12	28 weeks	Oct. 24
Boone	May 7	21 weeks	Oct. 3
Charlotte	April 2	31 weeks	Nov. 4
Greensboro	April 15	29 weeks	Nov. 1
Greenville	March 27	27 weeks	Oct. 4
Hatteras	March 15	39 weeks	Dec. 10
Lenoir	April 7	21 weeks	Oct. 3
Raleigh	April 5	30 weeks	Nov. 1
Wilmington	March 17	35 weeks	Nov. 16
Winston-Salem	April 11	25 weeks	Oct. 3
NORTH DAKOTA			
Bismarck	May 11	19 weeks	Sept. 22
Fargo	May 12	19 weeks	Sept. 26
Grand Forks	May 15	16 weeks	Sept. 1
Minot	May 17	18 weeks	Sept. 21
Sheyenne	May 15	16 weeks	Sept. 1
Washburn	May 24	22 weeks	Sept. 28
OHIO			
Akron	April 30	24 weeks	Oct. 22
Cadiz	May 7	21 weeks	Oct. 1
Carpenter	May 7	20 weeks	Sept. 23
Cincinnati	April 10	28 weeks	Oct. 25
Cleveland	May 7	21 weeks	Oct. 3
Columbus	April 16	27 weeks	Oct. 31
Dayton	April 19	28 weeks	Oct. 26
Kenton	May 7	20 weeks	Sept. 23
Mansfield	May 9	22 weeks	Oct. 6
Oberlin	May 10	19 weeks	Sept. 23
Toledo	April 27	23 weeks	Sept. 24
Youngstown	May 8	21 weeks	Oct. 3
Zanesville	May 7	20 weeks	Sept. 23
OKLAHOMA			
Ada	April 5	32 weeks	Nov. 15
Beaver	April 17	26 weeks	Oct. 15
Chattanooga	April 5	32 weeks	Nov. 15
Clinton	April 4	32 weeks	Nov. 12
McAlester	April 5	32 weeks	Nov. 14
Meeker	April 6	32 weeks	Nov. 14
Oklahoma City	April 1	32 weeks	Nov. 7
Ponca City	April 5	31 weeks	Nov. 6
Tulsa	March 30	31 weeks	Nov. 1
Tuskahoma	April 9	27 weeks	Oct. 16
OREGON			
Astoria	April 13	36 weeks	Dec. 22

LOCATION	LAST SPRING FREEZE	GROWING SEASON	FIRST FALL FREEZE
OREGON *(continued)*			
Baker	June 8	14 weeks	Sept. 13
Beulah	May 30	17 weeks	Sept. 27
Eugene	April 9	29 weeks	Oct. 31
Medford	April 30	24 weeks	Oct. 17
Pendleton	April 17	25 weeks	Oct. 24
Portland	March 18	36 weeks	Nov. 28
Salem	April 14	26 weeks	Oct. 28
PENNSYLVANIA			
Allentown	April 23	25 weeks	Oct. 17
Altoona	May 11	19 weeks	Sept. 23
Erie	April 20	27 weeks	Nov. 1
Harrisburg	April 15	27 weeks	Oct. 24
Philadelphia	April 11	27 weeks	Oct. 19
Pittsburgh	April 10	25 weeks	Oct. 4
Scranton	May 5	20 weeks	Sept. 23
Williamsport	April 29	24 weeks	Oct. 14
RHODE ISLAND			
Block Island	April 26	25 weeks	Oct. 21
Kingston	May 9	21 weeks	Oct. 1
Newport	April 26	25 weeks	Oct. 19
Providence	April 14	28 weeks	Oct. 26
SOUTH CAROLINA			
Charleston	Feb. 19	42 weeks	Dec. 10
Columbia	March 30	31 weeks	Nov. 3
Greenville	March 25	32 weeks	Nov. 6
Ridgeland	April 10	25 weeks	Oct. 4
Sumter	March 18	29 weeks	Oct. 4
SOUTH DAKOTA			
Aberdeen	May 31	19 weeks	Sept. 15
Deadwood	June 1	13 weeks	Sept. 2
Dupree	May 24	18 weeks	Sept. 28
Huron	May 6	20 weeks	Sept. 29
Pierre	May 15	19 weeks	Sept. 28
Rapid City	May 23	18 weeks	Sept. 28
Sioux Falls	May 6	22 weeks	Oct. 3
TENNESSEE			
Bristol	April 20	26 weeks	Oct. 15
Chattanooga	April 3	32 weeks	Nov. 9
Cleveland	April 25	26 weeks	Oct. 21
Jackson	April 9	31 weeks	Nov. 14
Knoxville	March 22	34 weeks	Nov. 15
Memphis	April 3	30 weeks	Oct. 31
Nashville	April 9	31 weeks	Nov. 14
Waverly	April 25	23 weeks	Oct. 2
TEXAS			
Abilene	April 5	33 weeks	Nov. 25
Amarillo	April 16	29 weeks	Oct. 30
Austin	March 3	39 weeks	Nov. 28
Corpus Christi	None	52 weeks	None
Dallas	March 16	36 weeks	Nov. 21
Del Rio	Feb. 12	43 weeks	Dec. 9
El Paso	March 11	35 weeks	Nov. 13
Houston	Feb. 5	44 weeks	Dec. 11
San Angelo	March 24	33 weeks	Nov. 13
San Antonio	Feb. 26	39 weeks	Nov. 26
Texarkana	March 25	34 weeks	Nov. 15
Victoria	Feb. 25	41 weeks	Dec. 5
Waco	March 24	36 weeks	Nov. 29
UTAH			
Bonanza	June 10	13 weeks	Sept. 12
Cedar City	June 8	16 weeks	Sept. 28
Emery	June 10	13 weeks	Sept. 12
Ogden	May 20	20 weeks	Oct. 6
Milford	May 21	18 weeks	Sept. 26

LOCATION	LAST SPRING FREEZE	GROWING SEASON	FIRST FALL FREEZE
UTAH *(continued)*			
Park Valley	June 9	14 weeks	Sept. 13
Saint George	March 6	38 weeks	Nov. 24
Salt Lake City	April 28	27 weeks	Nov. 5
VERMONT			
Burlington	May 10	21 weeks	Oct. 3
Montpelier	May 5	20 weeks	Sept. 24
Newport	May 20	18 weeks	Sept. 24
Rutland	May 7	20 weeks	Sept. 24
Woodstock	May 21	18 weeks	Sept. 23
VIRGINIA			
Appomattox	April 11	25 weeks	Oct. 3
Elkwood	May 8	20 weeks	Sept. 24
Lexington	May 7	21 weeks	Oct. 3
Lynchburg	April 11	25 weeks	Oct. 3
Norfolk	March 22	34 weeks	Nov. 21
Richmond	April 11	31 weeks	Oct. 18
Roanoke	April 15	27 weeks	Oct. 22
Winchester	May 8	20 weeks	Sept. 24
Wytheville	May 8	20 weeks	Sept. 24
WASHINGTON			
Aberdeen	April 13	36 weeks	Dec. 22
Cougar	April 8	37 weeks	Dec. 23
Olympia	April 14	25 weeks	Oct. 6
Pullman	May 16	19 weeks	Sept. 27
Spokane	May 16	20 weeks	Oct. 5
Tacoma	March 8	38 weeks	Nov. 29
Vancouver	April 13	29 weeks	Oct. 5
Walla Walla	April 21	24 weeks	Oct. 9
Winthrop	May 20	17 weeks	Sept. 13
Yakima	May 13	22 weeks	Oct. 1
WEST VIRGINIA			
Beckley	May 7	20 weeks	Sept. 24
Bluefield	April 10	25 weeks	Oct. 2
Charleston	May 7	21 weeks	Oct. 2
Clarksburg	May 8	20 weeks	Sept. 24
Elkins	May 10	23 weeks	Oct. 5
Franklin	May 8	20 weeks	Sept. 23
Lewisburg	May 8	20 weeks	Sept. 24
Martinsburg	May 8	20 weeks	Sept. 24
Morgantown	May 7	20 weeks	Sept. 24
Parkersburg	April 10	25 weeks	Oct. 3
WISCONSIN			
Antigo	May 26	14 weeks	Sept. 1
Beloit	May 7	20 weeks	Sept. 22
Cumberland	May 13	19 weeks	Sept. 22
Green Bay	April 10	23 weeks	Sept. 21
LaCrosse	April 25	25 weeks	Oct. 16
Madison	April 25	25 weeks	Oct. 16
Milwaukee	May 10	19 weeks	Sept. 22
Platteville	May 7	20 weeks	Sept. 22
Stevens Point	May 13	19 weeks	Sept. 22
Superior	May 26	17 weeks	Sept. 22
West Bend	May 10	19 weeks	Sept. 22
WYOMING			
Buffalo	May 16	17 weeks	Sept. 13
Casper	May 22	18 weeks	Sept. 28
Cheyenne	May 18	19 weeks	Sept. 27
Clark	June 1	13 weeks	Sept. 2
Dillinger	June 11	12 weeks	Sept. 4
Grass Creek	June 1	11 weeks	Aug. 18
Lander	May 20	18 weeks	Sept. 23
Laramie	June 9	12 weeks	Sept. 2
Morrisey	May 14	17 weeks	Sept. 13
Sheridan	May 21	17 weeks	Sept. 18
Wamsutter	June 8	12 weeks	Sept. 3

CALENDAR OF TRADITIONAL RETAIL SALES IN STORES

Source: Citibank

MONTH	ITEMS ON SALE
January	Storewide clearances; beds; cars; Christmas cards; clothing and accessories; cosmetics; decorating accessories; decorations (Christmas); diamonds; fabrics; floor coverings; furniture; furs; infant needs; linens; lingerie; luggage; major appliances (end of month); notions; radios; stationery; television sets; tires; wrappings.
February	Storewide sales on Lincoln's and Washington's birthdays; cars; decorating accessories; fabrics; floor coverings; furniture; furs; major appliances; menswear, women's coats; women's stockings.
March	China and glassware; housewares.
April	Storewide sales after Easter; children's clothing; diamonds; fabrics; fashion clearances; lingerie; sleepwear; women's coats.
May	Storewide sales on Memorial Day; clothing for men, women, and children; decorating accessories; diamonds; housewares; infant needs; linens; luggage.
June	Floor coverings; furniture and beds; lingerie; men's clothing; sleepwear; stockings; summer sportswear (mid-month).
July	Fabrics; furniture and beds; garden equipment and garden furniture (end of month); jewelry; linens; major appliances (end of month); storm windows; summer fashion clearances (men's, women's, and children's); tires.
August	Cars; furniture and beds; furs; garden equipment and garden furniture; infant needs; linens; major appliances; rugs; stationery; women's accessories.
September	Labor Day sales on tires and special items; cars (end of model year).
October	Storewide sales on Columbus Day; cars (old models); children's clothing; infant needs; women's coats.
November	Storewide sales on Election Day and Veterans Day; furs; women's coats.
December	After-Christmas sales on cards, decorations, and wrappings; infant needs; women's coats.

WEDDING ANNIVERSARY GIFTS

ANNIVERSARY	GIFTS
First	Paper, plastics, clocks
Second	Cotton, china
Third	Leather, crystal, glass
Fourth	Fruit, flowers, silk, appliances
Fifth	Wood, silverware
Sixth	Iron, candy, sugar, wood
Seventh	Wood, copper, brass, desk sets
Eighth	Bronze, pottery, appliances, linen
Ninth	Leather, willow, pottery, glass
Tenth	Tin, aluminum, diamond jewelry
Eleventh	Steel, fashion jewelry
Twelfth	Silk, linen, pearl, colored gems
Thirteenth	Lace, textiles, furs
Fourteenth	Gold jewelry, ivory, agate
Fifteenth	Crystal, glass, watches
Sixteenth	Silver hollowware
Seventeenth	Furniture
Eighteenth	Porcelain
Nineteenth	Bronze
Twentieth	China, platinum, furniture
Twenty-fifth	Silver
Thirtieth	Pearl, diamond
Thirty-fifth	Coral, jade
Fortieth	Ruby, garnet
Forty-fifth	Sapphire, tourmaline
Fiftieth	Gold
Fifty-fifth	Emerald, turquoise
Sixtieth	Diamond
Seventy-fifth	Diamond, gold

BIRTHSTONES AND FLOWERS

MONTH	BIRTHSTONE AND MEANING	FLOWER
January	Garnet—constancy, fidelity	Carnation or Snowdrop
February	Amethyst—sincerity	Violet or Primrose
March	Aquamarine or Bloodstone—courage, truthfulness	Jonquil or Violet
April	Diamond—innocence	Daisy or Sweet Pea
May	Emerald—happiness, success	Hawthorn or Lily of the Valley
June	Pearl, Alexandrite, or Moonstone—health	Rose or Honeysuckle
July	Ruby—contentment	Larkspur or Water Lily
August	Peridot or Sardonyx—felicity	Gladiolus or Poppy
September	Sapphire—love, wisdom	Morning Glory or Aster
October	Opal or Tourmaline—hope	Calendula or Cosmos
November	Topaz—fidelity	Chrysanthemum
December	Turquoise or Zircon—prosperity, success	Narcissus, Holly, or Poinsettia

HOW TO REMOVE COMMON STAINS

Knowing how to remove stains from fabrics can save dollars. Act quickly. Do not permit fresh stains to dry and become set. Because there are so many washable synthetic fibers on the market, it is wise to save the garment tags on which washing or dry-cleaning instructions are given. There are four principal types of stain removers:

1. Absorbents include cornstarch, cornmeal, chalk, fuller's earth, and paper towels. Use them to blot grease and liquids from fabrics.

2. Washing agents include detergents, soaps, borax, washing soda, and ammonia. Detergents (dry or liquid) remove most nongreasy and some greasy stains. Borax, washing soda, and ammonia loosen dirt and grease from fabrics. Mild soap is often safer than detergents on delicate materials.

3. Chemical solvents such as acetone, rubbing alcohol, and turpentine remove many nongreasy stains. Dry-cleaning solutions and "spot lifters" are effective in removing grease stains from both washables and dry-clean-only fabrics, but be certain to follow directions on the label.

4. Bleaches, to be used only on washables, include hydrogen peroxide, liquid or dry chlorine bleach, and dry oxygen bleach. Chlorine bleach is safe only for cottons and linens. It will damage other fabrics. Oxygen bleach is less effective than chlorine, but it is safe for most washables.

Many stains can be removed at home by following these simple rules:

Blood. While stain is fresh, sponge or soak with cold water (*never* warm or hot) until stain is light brown. Wash in warm suds. Soak stubborn stains in a weak solution of bleach, and then relaunder.

Candle wax. Scrape off excess and press stain between white blotters with a hot iron. Rub spot with lard or turpentine and wash.

Chewing gum. Rub with a piece of ice until gum hardens and can be lifted off. Then sponge with dry-cleaning fluid.

Chocolate or cocoa. Soak in cool water. Rub on detergent. Wash in hot suds with bleach. Treat any remaining stain with a weak solution of bleach or hydrogen peroxide. Then relaunder in hot suds.

Coffee and tea. Pour boiling water through fabric. Then wash in hot suds with bleach.

Egg. Scrape off excess. Soak fabric in cool water with bleach, then wash in warm suds.

Fruits and berries. Sponge peach, pear, cherry, and plum stains at once with cool water and rub with glycerine. After 2 hours apply a few drops of vinegar, then launder.

Grass and foliage. Scrub with hot water and suds. If needed, use a mild bleach. Then wash promptly in warm suds.

Grease, oil, tar, butter. Apply dry-cleaning fluid. Rub on detergent. Launder. Dry. Soak in weak bleach solution. Relaunder.

Ice cream. Sponge with cool water to remove sugar and protein, then with warm suds to remove grease.

Lipstick. Soften with glycerine, then wash in hot suds.

Mildew. Soak in suds and hang out with stain exposed to sunlight. If spots persist, rub with lemon juice and salt, then bleach in the sun.

Paint. If oil-based paint, use lots of hot suds for fresh stains. For stains that have set, apply turpentine, kerosene, or lard, and then wash in hot suds. Water-emulsion paint that is still wet usually comes out in hot suds.

Pet stains. When these occur on rugs or upholstery, sponge with cold water. Make a solution of one-fourth cup of white vinegar to a quart of water, and sponge again. Allow the solution to work for 15 minutes. Then wash the stain with cool detergent suds and rinse.

Rust. Place the stained portion over a pot of boiling water and pour lemon juice on the fabric. Rinse and then launder.

Wine. Once a wine stain has set, it is very hard to remove. Cover wet stains generously with salt, which will absorb the color. Then launder in warm suds.

BIRTH DATES FOR ASTROLOGY'S SIGNS OF THE ZODIAC

BIRTH DATES	SIGN NAME	SYMBOL	ASTROLOGICAL PERSONALITY TRAITS
Mar. 21–Apr. 19	Aries, or Ram	♈	Active, dynamic, charming, diplomatic, restless
Apr. 20–May 20	Taurus, or Bull	♉	Amusing, honest, affectionate, methodical
May 21–June 20	Gemini, or Twins	♊	Intellectual, magnetic, changeable, sensitive
June 21–July 22	Cancer, or Crab	♋	Managerial, overly serious, artistic, extroverted
July 23–Aug. 22	Leo, or Lion	♌	Generous, sympathetic, imaginative, impulsive
Aug. 23–Sept. 22	Virgo, or Virgin	♍	Independent, kind, sincere, reliable, emotional
Sept. 23–Oct. 22	Libra, or Scales	♎	Practical, poised, attractive, loyal, quick-tempered
Oct. 23–Nov. 21	Scorpio, or Scorpion	♏	Inventive, intuitive, dynamic, obstinate, selfish
Nov. 22–Dec. 21	Sagittarius, or Archer	♐	Trustworthy, outgoing, moody, prideful, bright
Dec. 22–Jan. 19	Capricorn, or Goat	♑	Calm, pleasant, serious, mild-mannered, reliable
Jan. 20–Feb. 18	Aquarius, or Water Bearer	♒	Changeable, indolent, expressive, altruistic
Feb. 19–Mar. 20	Pisces, or Fishes	♓	Faithful, perceptive, reserved, imaginative, jealous

STATE MARRIAGE LAWS

STATE	RELATIVES ONE CANNOT MARRY[1]	MINIMUM AGE WITH PARENT CONSENT[2] Male	Female	BLOOD TEST REQUIRED	COMMON-LAW MARRIAGE RECOGNIZED	WAIT BETWEEN APPLICATION AND LICENSE	TIME LICENSE IS VALID
Alabama	ABE	14	14	Yes	Yes	None	30 days
Alaska	—	16	16	Yes	No	3 days	90 days
Arizona	F	16	16	Yes	No	None	NSP[23]
Arkansas	F	17	16	Yes	No	3 days	60 days
California	—	—[3]	—[3]	Yes	No	None	90 days
Colorado	—	16	16	Yes	Yes	None	30 days
Connecticut	AB	16	16	Yes	No	4 days	65 days
Delaware	F	18	16	Yes	No	None	30 days
Florida	—	16	16	Yes	No[7]	3 days	30 days
Georgia	ABEILC	16	16	Yes	Yes	3 days	30 days
Hawaii	—	16	16	Yes	No	None	30 days
Idaho	F	16	16	Yes	Yes	None[21]	NSP[23]
Illinois	F	16	16	Yes	No[8]	None	60 days
Indiana	F	17	17	Yes	No[9]	3 days	60 days
Iowa	ABEFIJ	16	16	Yes	Yes	3 days	20 days
Kansas	F	18[4]	18[4]	Yes	Yes	3 days	NSP[23]
Kentucky	FH	18[4]	18[4]	Yes	No	3 days	30 days
Louisiana	F	18	16	Yes	No	None	30 days
Maine	ABEIJKM	16	16	Yes	No	5 days	60 days
Maryland	BIJKLM	16	16	No	No	2 days	6 months
Massachusetts	ABEIL	18[4]	18[4]	Yes	No	3 days	60 days
Michigan	F	18	16	Yes	No[10]	3 days	33 days
Minnesota	F	16	18	No	No[11]	5 days	6 months
Mississippi	ABEFI	—[3]	—[3]	Yes	No[12]	None[25]	NSP[23]
Missouri	F	15	15	Yes	No[13]	3 days	NSP[23]
Montana	F	16	16	Yes	Yes	None	180 days
Nebraska	F	17	17	Yes	No[14]	2 days	NSP[23]
Nevada	F	16	16	No	No[19]	None	NSP[23]
New Hampshire	AEF	14	13	Yes	No	5 days	90 days
New Jersey	—	16	16	Yes	No[15]	3 days	30 days
New Mexico	—	16	16	Yes	No	None	NSP[23]
New York	—	16	14[5]	Yes	No[20]	None	60 days
North Carolina	O	16	16	Yes[6]	No	None	NSP[23]
North Dakota	F	16	16	Yes	No	None	60 days
Ohio	F	18	16	Yes	Yes	5 days	60 days
Oklahoma	F	16	16	Yes	Yes	None[22]	30 days
Oregon	F	17	17	Yes	No	7 days	30 days
Pennsylvania	ABEF	16	16	Yes	Yes	3 days	60 days
Rhode Island	BIMQ	18	16	Yes	Yes	None[26]	3 months
South Carolina	ABEIJKM	16	14	No	Yes	24 hours	NSP[23]
South Dakota	ABF	16	16	Yes	No[16]	None	20 days
Tennessee	ABCN	16	16	Yes	No	None[22]	30 days
Texas	—	14	14	Yes	Yes	None	21 days[24]
Utah	F	14	14	Yes	No	None	30 days
Vermont	—	14[5]	14[5]	Yes	No	None	60 days
Virginia	—	16	16	Yes	No	None	60 days
Washington	F	17	17	No	No	3 days	30 days
West Virginia	FO	18	16	Yes	No	3 days	60 days
Wisconsin	G	16	16	Yes	No[17]	5 days	30 days
Wyoming	F	16	16	Yes	No	None	NSP[23]
Dist. of Columbia	ABEIJKM	16	16	Yes	Yes	3 days	NSP[23]

[1] In every state it is illegal to marry a sister, brother, half sister, half brother, mother, father, daughter, son, granddaughter, grandson, grandmother, grandfather, great-grandmother, great-grandfather, aunt, uncle, niece, or nephew. Many states also prohibit other marriages as indicated by these capital letters: **A** stepparent; **B** stepchild; **C** stepgrandchild; **D** Half niece or half nephew; **E** son-in-law or daughter-in-law; **F** first cousin; **G** first cousin, except female 55 or older; **H** first cousin once removed; **I** father-in-law or mother-in-law; **J** spouse of grandchild; **K** spouse of grandparent; **L** stepgrandparent; **M** spouse's grandparent or grandchild; **N** great-uncle, great-aunt, grandnephew, or grandniece; **O** double first cousin; **P** grandnephew or grandniece; **Q** marriages between Jews permitted by their religion are recognized; **R** any relative by adoption; **S** spouse's niece, spouse's grandchild, brother or sister by adoption. [2] Without parental consent, minimum age for marriage is 18, with these exceptions: Mississippi, 17 for men, 15 for women; Nebraska, 19. [3] No minimum age with parental consent and court order. [4] Marriage below 18 must have court approval and parental consent. [5] With court permission. [6] Physical exam also required. [7] Unless before 1968. [8] Unless before June 30, 1905. [9] Unless before 1958. [10] Unless before 1957. [11] Unless before April 26, 1941. [12] Unless before April 5, 1956. [13] Unless before March 31, 1921. [14] Unless before 1923. [15] Unless before Dec. 1, 1939. [16] Unless before July 1, 1959. [17] Unless before 1917. [18] But both parties guilty of misdemeanor. [19] Unless before March 29, 1943. [20] Unless before April 29, 1933. [21] Except 3-day wait if both parties under 18. [22] Except 3 days if either is under 18. [23] No statutory provision. [24] After medical exam. [25] Except 3 days if either is under 21. [26] Except 5-day waiting period for female nonresident.

MARRIAGES AND DIVORCES

Source: U.S. Public Health Service

The divorce rate in the United States decreased slightly in 1982 to 5.1 per 1,000 population compared with 5.3 in 1981. The divorce rate has more than doubled since the 1960s, increasing from 2.2 per 1,000 in 1962.

The number of marriages increased in 1982 for the seventh consecutive year, while the rate increased to 10.8 per 1,000 population. The total number of marriages exceeded the number of divorces by 1,315,000.

STATE	MARRIAGES		MARRIAGE RATE [2]		DIVORCES		DIVORCE RATE [2]	
	1982 [1]	1970	1982 [2]	1970	1982 [1]	1970	1982 [1]	1970
UNITED STATES	**2,495,000**	**2,158,802**	**10.8**	**10.6**	**1,180,000**	**708,000**	**5.1**	**3.5**
Alabama	48,545	46,959	12.3	13.6	25,217	15,109	6.4	4.4
Alaska	6,330	3,390	14.5	11.2	3,629	1,695	8.3	5.6
Arizona	29,084	18,508	10.2	10.4	20,168	12,714	7.1	7.2
Arkansas	28,000	23,307	12.2	12.1	15,716	9,310	6.9	4.8
California	230,694	172,388	9.3	8.6	138,435	112,942	5.6	5.7
Colorado	35,340	24,988	11.6	11.3	17,189	10,400	5.6	4.7
Connecticut	26,861	24,929	8.5	8.2	10,870	5,812	3.4	1.9
Delaware	4,826	4,254	8.0	7.8	3,214	1,732	5.3	3.2
Florida	115,414	69,249	11.1	10.2	71,483	37,208	6.9	5.5
Georgia	71,704	63,896	12.7	13.9	32,091	18,649	5.7	4.1
Hawaii	13,368	10,599	13.4	13.8	4,290	2,589	4.3	3.4
Idaho	13,964	10,915	14.5	15.3	6,323	3,612	6.6	5.1
Illinois	106,881	115,478	9.3	10.4	50,247	36,450	4.4	3.3
Indiana	56,393	55,202	10.3	10.6	40,333 [3]	15,153	7.5 [3]	N.A.
Iowa	27,447	24,648	9.4	8.7	10,934	7,188	3.8	2.5
Kansas	26,660	22,421	11.1	10.0	12,717	8,785	5.3	3.9
Kentucky	35,141	36,269	9.6	11.3	16,768	10,664	4.6	3.3
Louisiana	44,284	35,416	10.2	9.7	13,229 [3]	5,065	3.3 [3]	N.A.
Maine	12,536	10,975	11.1	11.0	5,830	3,853	5.1	3.9
Maryland	47,467	52,237	11.1	13.3	14,974	9,252	3.5	2.4
Massachusetts	50,565	47,403	8.7	8.3	20,779	10,994	3.6	1.9
Michigan	84,045	89,694	9.2	10.1	38,228	29,993	4.2	3.4
Minnesota	37,432	31,280	9.1	8.2	14,397	8,290	3.5	2.2
Mississippi	27,645	26,328	10.8	11.9	13,264	8,211	5.2	3.7
Missouri	54,798	50,149	11.1	10.7	27,223	17,852	5.5	3.8
Montana	8,169	6,919	10.2	10.0	4,630	3,047	5.8	4.4
Nebraska	14,081	15,666	8.9	10.6	6,508	3,712	4.1	2.5
Nevada	109,190	97,605	123.9	199.7	12,248	9,138	13.9	18.7
New Hampshire	10,016	10,006	10.5	13.6	5,032	2,433	5.3	3.3
New Jersey	60,582	56,625	8.1	7.9	28,643	10,834	3.9	1.5
New Mexico	17,453	12,422	12.8	12.2	9,576	4,375	7.0	4.3
New York	162,486	161,246	9.2	8.9	62,585	26,404	3.5	1.5
North Carolina	51,023	48,291	8.5	9.5	29,715	13,702	4.9	2.7
North Dakota	6,166	5,340	9.2	8.6	2,212	985	3.3	1.6
Ohio	102,075	90,056	9.5	8.5	53,911	39,302	5.0	3.7
Oklahoma	47,930	39,004	15.1	15.2	23,926	16,842	7.5	6.6
Oregon	24,057	17,302	9.1	8.3	16,545	9,583	6.2	4.6
Pennsylvania	92,622	94,516	7.8	8.0	38,523	22,622	3.2	1.9
Rhode Island	7,881	7,531	8.2	7.9	3,618	1,687	3.8	1.8
South Carolina	53,507	57,887	16.7	22.3	13,677	5,829	4.3	2.3
South Dakota	8,343	11,034	12.1	16.6	2,572	1,357	3.7	2.0
Tennessee	58,542	45,361	12.6	11.6	29,970	16,623	6.4	4.2
Texas	205,353	139,491	13.4	12.5	101,580	51,530	6.6	4.6
Utah	18,702	11,692	12.0	11.0	8,347	3,912	5.4	3.7
Vermont	5,690	4,524	11.0	10.2	2,627	1,028	5.1	2.3
Virginia	62,265	51,964	11.3	11.2	26,262	11,879	4.8	2.6
Washington	46,972	41,313	11.1	12.1	27,772	17,887	6.5	5.2
West Virginia	16,467	15,948	8.5	9.1	10,352	5,584	5.3	3.2
Wisconsin	42,959	34,415	9.0	7.8	17,278	8,930	3.6	2.0
Wyoming	6,685	4,495	13.3	13.5	3,912	1,797	7.8	5.4
District of Columbia	5,698	7,267	9.0	9.6	3,418	2,268	5.4	3.0

[1] Provisional 1982 data. [2] Per 1,000 population. [3] Final 1978 data. N.A. = Not available.

HOW TO RID YOUR HOME OF HOUSEHOLD PESTS

Despite modern building methods and pesticide techniques, certain insects and rodents are still household problems.

There are only two ways in which they can be controlled: systematic and thorough housekeeping and the use of the proper pesticide at the right time.

Housekeepers are concerned chiefly with *insecticides* to control insects and *rodenticides* to kill rats and mice.

Insecticides come in the form of surface sprays, dusts, liquids, and pastes for crawling insects and space sprays or aerosols for flying insects.

Rodenticides are usually small poisoned pellets put out to be eaten by both rats and mice.

Below is a list of 10 insects and rodents that can be eliminated in the home with pesticides. Termite infestation is such a complex problem that it should be referred to an expert exterminator.

Ants. If you can find the ant nest by following the insects' line of march, treat it with a liquid or spray insecticide containing diazinon, malathion, carbaryl, baygon, or dursban.

Apply the substance to surfaces on which the ants crawl, and treat cracks or openings they may be using to enter the room or house.

Bedbugs. Spray the bed slats, springs, and frame. Cover the mattress completely with spray, but do not soak it.

Products used on mattresses should not contain more than 1% malathion.

Clothes Moths and Carpet Beetles. Preventive measures should be taken against clothes moths before storing woolens. Have the garments dry-cleaned. Place paradichlorobenzene crystals or naphthalene flakes or balls in the garment bags or other containers before sealing. It is best to store furs at a commercial storage company.

To get rid of carpet beetles, vacuum rugs, upholstered furniture, draperies, and the surrounding floors. Spray rugs and other woolen or mohair fabrics with a stainless insecticide containing methoxychlor, cythion, or diazinon.

Cockroaches. Preparations containing diazinon, malathion, ronnel, dursban, or ficam will control all types of cockroaches, although some may have developed resistance to certain compounds. Apply the insecticide to places where cockroaches hide and breed—under kitchen sinks, in cracks around or beneath cupboards, places where pipes pass along a wall, behind loose baseboards or moldings, and on the undersides of tables and chairs. Powered insecticide may be applied after spraying. Severe infestations should be handled by an exterminator.

Cockroaches seek warmth, moisture, and food. They hide during the day in sheltered, dark places in the home, and come out at night to forage. They feed on garbage as well as human food.

Cockroaches may transmit some diseases caused by food-poisoning organisms, and they may also damage fabrics and books.

Fleas. These insects bite humans as well as dogs and cats. The first method for keeping fleas from infesting the home is to shampoo your pet, then apply a spray, dip, or powder containing organophosphates, carbamates, or pyrethrins.

Thoroughly vacuum carpets, floors, and upholstered furniture.

Use a carbaryl flea powder to treat lint-collecting areas and on rugs where the pet rests. Consult labels of insecticide-bearing flea collars.

House Flies. You can help keep your home free of flies by installing tight-fitting screens in windows and doors.

Because flies breed in decaying organic matter, promptly dispose of garbage, pet droppings, and the like. If flies have invaded your home in large numbers, use a household or aerosol spray especially prepared for flying insects.

Mice and Rats. The first steps in keeping out these rodents are to seal holes in walls, floors, and foundations and to make certain that food is not left where they can get to it. If you have only a few mice, place snap traps along walls and holes. Bait the traps with peanut butter, bacon, cheese, or soft candy. A pet cat is often a deterrent to mice.

Rats are a more serious problem, as they ruin property, carry disease, and bite when cornered. Poisoned bait is the best weapon against them, although traps will get rid of some of them. If rats are a neighborhood problem, community action must be taken and pest-control operators called in.

Mosquitoes. Check for larvae (wigglers) in any potential breeding areas such as filled vases, rain barrels, fish tanks, and the like. Screens will help keep out adult mosquitoes. They may be exterminated with a spray designed to kill flying insects.

Pantry Pests. Some types of insect larvae, popularly called "weevils," may infest dry food products such as cornmeal, flour, and cereals. Before buying such foods, examine the packages for tears or cracks. Keep your pantry shelves clean of spilled food particles, and store dry foods in metal or glass containers having tight-fitting lids.

International Relations

A little girl crying outside her tent in a camp for Nicaraguan refugees at Jacaliapa, Honduras, represents the suffering of 7.5 million refugees throughout the world, forced to flee from their homes by wars, revolutions, and civil strife in Central America, Afghanistan, Africa, Southeast Asia, India, Sri Lanka, and other areas.

HIGHLIGHTS: 1983

Many articles dealing with international relations may be found throughout the *1984 Reader's Digest Almanac and Yearbook.*

While millions of persons in the U.S. and Western Europe took part in demonstrations aimed at halting the nuclear arms race, the United States continued to expand its military budget in 1983 to develop and deploy new weapons systems as a deterrent to Soviet military power. See pages 459–461.

At the same time, representatives of the U.S. and the Soviet Union met throughout much of the year in diplomatic talks that failed to find any common ground on which to agree to reduce the growing stockpiles of nuclear weapons. See page 31.

UNITED STATES AID TO OTHER NATIONS

Source: U.S. Department of Commerce

The United States has supplied other nations with more than $284 billion in military assistance, economic and technical aid, and loans since the end of World War II.

Over $88 billion of this foreign aid has been in the form of loans, some $74 billion of which has been repaid. The figures in this table are for July 1, 1945, to Jan. 1, 1982.

NATION	TOTAL AID BY U.S.	LOANS REPAID TO U.S.	LOANS STILL OWED TO U.S.[1]
Afghanistan	$ 581,000,000	$ 55,000,000	$ 128,000,000
Albania	20,000,000	—	—
Algeria	1,065,000,000	135,000,000	874,000,000
Angola	69,000,000	9,000,000	43,000,000
Argentina	1,403,000,000	1,007,000,000	282,000,000
Australia	1,201,000,000	1,004,000,000	204,000,000
Austria	1,353,000,000	146,000,000	56,000,000
Bahamas	59,000,000	56,000,000	3,000,000
Bangladesh	1,683,000,000	173,000,000	795,000,000
Belgium	2,249,000,000	305,000,000	108,000,000
Benin	49,000,000	**	23,000,000
Bolivia	1,013,000,000	157,000,000	344,000,000
Botswana	110,000,000	—	23,000,000
Brazil	6,079,000,000	2,625,000,000	2,333,000,000
Britain	10,548,000,000	3,962,000,000	2,182,000,000
Burma	232,000,000	22,000,000	38,000,000
Cambodia	2,278,000,000	79,000,000	209,000,000
Cameroon	195,000,000	20,000,000	100,000,000
Canada	833,000,000	440,000,000	384,000,000
Central Africa	17,000,000	—	3,000,000
Chad	76,000,000	—	—
Chile	2,713,000,000	1,579,000,000	651,000,000
Colombia	2,019,000,000	659,000,000	880,000,000
Congo	15,000,000	1,000,000	1,000,000
Costa Rica	324,000,000	79,000,000	105,000,000
Cuba	60,000,000	3,000,000	36,000,000
Cyprus	183,000,000	22,000,000	7,000,000
Czechoslov.	199,000,000	8,000,000	5,000,000
Denmark	1,065,000,000	128,000,000	71,000,000
Dominican R.	880,000,000	190,000,000	336,000,000
Ecuador	548,000,000	173,000,000	142,000,000
Egypt	6,962,000,000	597,000,000	5,037,000,000
El Salvador	420,000,000	47,000,000	199,000,000
Ethiopia	704,000,000	78,000,000	123,000,000
Finland	255,000,000	192,000,000	52,000,000
France	11,063,000,000	2,676,000,000	−195,000,000
Gabon	37,000,000	16,000,000	10,000,000
Germany, E.	17,000,000	—	—
Germany, W.	5,207,000,000	1,501,000,000	−977,000,000
Ghana	494,000,000	127,000,000	206,000,000
Greece	5,702,000,000	929,000,000	764,000,000
Guatemala	535,000,000	69,000,000	136,000,000
Guinea	209,000,000	27,000,000	98,000,000
Guyana	119,000,000	11,000,000	73,000,000
Haiti	355,000,000	27,000,000	79,000,000
Honduras	376,000,000	52,000,000	165,000,000
Hungary	61,000,000	32,000,000	12,000,000
Iceland	105,000,000	54,000,000	16,000,000
India	13,798,000,000	3,945,000,000	3,721,000,000
Indonesia	4,068,000,000	805,000,000	2,222,000,000
Iran	3,261,000,000	1,513,000,000	393,000,000
Iraq	107,000,000	26,000,000	1,000,000
Ireland	243,000,000	155,000,000	70,000,000
Israel	20,339,000,000	2,031,000,000	7,438,000,000
Italy	7,031,000,000	1,256,000,000	447,000,000
Ivory Coast	153,000,000	31,000,000	93,000,000
Jamaica	235,000,000	75,000,000	190,000,000
Japan	7,679,000,000	3,538,000,000	−152,000,000
Jordan	2,476,000,000	233,000,000	643,000,000
Kenya	426,000,000	51,000,000	185,000,000
Korea, South	15,861,000,000	2,144,000,000	3,205,000,000
Kuwait	$ 50,000,000	$ 50,000,000	$ —
Laos	2,552,000,000	—	**
Lebanon	383,000,000	84,000,000	121,000,000
Lesotho	110,000,000	—	—
Liberia	545,000,000	156,000,000	131,000,000
Libya	231,000,000	7,000,000	**
Madagascar	39,000,000	2,000,000	10,000,000
Malawi	64,000,000	1,000,000	33,000,000
Malaysia	301,000,000	184,000,000	45,000,000
Mali	156,000,000	1,000,000	6,000,000
Malta	85,000,000	1,000,000	5,000,000
Mauritania	85,000,000	1,000,000	5,000,000
Mauritius	27,000,000	**	9,000,000
Mexico	2,578,000,000	1,301,000,000	1,071,000,000
Morocco	1,655,000,000	439,000,000	641,000,000
Nepal	275,000,000	2,000,000	3,000,000
Netherlands	2,719,000,000	613,000,000	−12,000,000
New Zealand	240,000,000	148,000,000	87,000,000
Nicaragua	475,000,000	61,000,000	258,000,000
Niger	135,000,000	**	9,000,000
Nigeria	403,000,000	40,000,000	86,000,000
Norway	1,672,000,000	419,000,000	102,000,000
Oman	48,000,000	4,000,000	42,000,000
Pakistan	6,784,000,000	893,000,000	2,930,000,000
Panama	557,000,000	156,000,000	188,000,000
Paraguay	226,000,000	53,000,000	48,000,000
Peru	1,816,000,000	883,000,000	430,000,000
Philippines	3,857,000,000	821,000,000	736,000,000
Poland	3,104,000,000	1,456,000,000	971,000,000
Portugal	2,003,000,000	765,000,000	648,000,000
Romania	441,000,000	299,000,000	131,000,000
Saudi Arabia	349,000,000	290,000,000	−10,000,000
Senegal	227,000,000	9,000,000	26,000,000
Sierra Leone	105,000,000	19,000,000	29,000,000
Singapore	294,000,000	60,000,000	231,000,000
Somalia	277,000,000	6,000,000	65,000,000
Soviet Union	1,437,000,000	762,000,000	249,000,000
Spain	3,807,000,000	1,131,000,000	1,333,000,000
Sri Lanka	527,000,000	58,000,000	310,000,000
Sudan	399,000,000	40,000,000	181,000,000
Suriname	11,000,000	6,000,000	**
Sweden	174,000,000	53,000,000	34,000,000
Swaziland	32,000,000	—	7,000,000
Switzerland	101,000,000	47,000,000	54,000,000
Syria	309,000,000	27,000,000	202,000,000
Taiwan	7,305,000,000	791,000,000	1,677,000,000
Tanzania	338,000,000	11,000,000	110,000,000
Thailand	2,581,000,000	216,000,000	300,000,000
Togo	59,000,000	4,000,000	3,000,000
Trinidad-Tob.	253,000,000	36,000,000	183,000,000
Tunisia	1,143,000,000	190,000,000	418,000,000
Turkey	9,682,000,000	1,007,000,000	2,871,000,000
Uganda	71,000,000	1,000,000	10,000,000
Upper Volta	186,000,000	**	1,000,000
Uruguay	279,000,000	72,000,000	88,000,000
Venezuela	853,000,000	549,000,000	219,000,000
Vietnam	23,992,000,000	459,000,000	101,000,000
Yemen	138,000,000	—	4,000,000
Yugoslavia	3,821,000,000	964,000,000	933,000,000
Zaire	1,389,000,000	253,000,000	770,000,000
Zambia	275,000,000	53,000,000	195,000,000

[1] A negative credit indicates an excess of principal payments over new credits utilized. ** Less than $500,000.

HIGHLIGHTS: 1983 *(continued)*

As the U.S. continued to seek a diplomatic solution to problems in the Middle East (see page 419), many Americans died in Lebanon when terrorists bombed the U.S. embassy (see page 15) and the headquarters of U.S. and French peacekeeping forces (see page 27).

The U.S. landed troops in Grenada, ending the use of that Caribbean island nation as a military base for the Soviet Union and Cuba. See page 29.

In an effort to end Soviet and Cuban influence in Central America, the U.S. sought to overthrow the procommunist government of Nicaragua while providing military aid to the pro-American governments of El Salvador, Honduras, and Guatemala. See page 421.

The U.S. denounced the Soviet Union for callous disregard of human life when its military forces shot down an unarmed South Korean airliner that had strayed over Soviet air space. See page 25.

As most of the world continued to suffer from the effects of the economic recession of 1981–83, President Reagan met with leaders of other industrial nations in an economic summit conference. See page 17.

SOVIETS SEEK NEW PRESS CURBS

When the 22d General Conference of the United Nations Educational, Scientific, and Cultural Organization (UNESCO) convened in Paris in October, the Soviet Union urged the organization to develop a blacklist of news media to be banned from operating in member countries.

The Soviets asked members to "ban the mass media for building up world tension and disseminating tendatious and slanderous messages that sow the seeds of alienation and enmity."

The U.S., which provides the money for 25% of UNESCO's budget, threatened to cut off the funds if the proposal is adopted.

CHINESE-SOVIET TALKS CONTINUE

A third round of talks was held in Peking in October by representatives of China and the Soviet Union in an effort to find ways to normalize diplomatic relations. After being unable to reach agreement, the participants adjourned to March 1984.

China has demanded that Moscow remove its troops from Afghanistan, end military aid to Vietnam's forces in Cambodia, and reduce its military forces along the boundary between the Soviet Union and China.

COULD THEY DO BETTER?

Former President Gerald Ford invited other former heads of government to a conference in Vail, Colo., in August to discuss international affairs. Those attending were Helmut Schmidt, former chancellor of West Germany; Valéry Giscard d'Estaing, former president of France; James Callaghan, former prime minister of Britain; and Malcolm Fraser, former prime minister of Australia.

All agreed they could handle the world's problems better than their successors.

SMALL WARS AND INSURGENCIES

Although the world is generally considered to be enjoying peace, the inability of government leaders to settle disputes by any means short of battle was amply demonstrated.

The troops of at least 39 of the world's nations engaged in fighting in 1983 in small wars, border fighting, guerrilla warfare, or other incidents.

These included armed forces of Afghanistan, Angola, Britain, Burma, Cambodia, Chad, China, Colombia, Cuba, El Salvador, Ethiopia, France, Grenada, Guatemala, Honduras, India, Iran, Iraq, Israel, Italy, Laos, Lebanon, Libya, Malaysia, Morocco, Mozambique, Namibia, Nicaragua, Nigeria, Peru, Somalia, Soviet Union, Sri Lanka, Syria, Thailand, United States, Vietnam, Zaire, and Zimbabwe.

U.S. FREEZES FUNDS TO UN

Congress decided to freeze U.S. contributions to the UN at $363 million. The decision came in a conference committee as a compromise between the House, which had voted to increase appropriations for the UN, and the Senate, which had approved cutting funds to the UN by $500 million over the next four years.

UN-DIPLOMATIC COMMENTS

After the Soviets shot down a South Korean airliner in September, the governors of New York and New Jersey refused to give Soviet Foreign Minister Andrei Gromyko permission to land his Soviet airliner at a New York metropolitan area airport.

A Soviet UN delegate declared the UN should consider moving elsewhere.

Responding, U.S. UN delegate Charles Lichenstein said, "We will put no impediment in your way, and we will be at dockside bidding you a farewell as you set off into the sunset."

President Reagan defended Lichenstein's comment, adding that the UN should split its meetings between New York and Moscow so delegates would have "an opportunity to see two ways of life."

New York's Mayor Edward Koch, when asked if he thought the UN should remain in New York, commented, "The UN is a cesspool" and "every country needs a cesspool."

The Soviet news agency Tass called Koch's remark a "slanderous attack unprecedented in its rudeness."

HISTORY OF THE MIDDLE EAST

The strategic importance of the Middle East, linking the continents of Europe, Asia, and Africa, has caused the region to be the scene of bloody wars since the dawn of history.

3200–2800 B.C. Egyptians in Africa and Sumerians in Mesopotamia (Iraq) separately invent writing and begin recorded history.

3000–539 B.C. Egypt contends with Sumeria, Babylonia, and Assyria for control of Middle East.

539–333 B.C. Persia (Iran) conquers Assyria and Egypt, establishing Persian rule of region.

333–30 B.C. Alexander the Great of Macedonia conquers Persia and Egypt; Greek rulers govern region.

30 B.C.–A.D. 260 Rome conquers and rules Middle East.

260–637 Wars between Persia and Roman Empire (later Byzantine Empire) for control of region.

637–1055 Arabs conquer and rule Middle East.

1055 Turks conquer Middle East; region ruled as part of Ottoman Empire until World War I.

1859–69 Suez Canal constructed, linking Mediterranean Sea with Red Sea and Indian Ocean.

1878 Britain takes control of Cyprus.

1882 British troops occupy Egypt to protect British interests in Suez Canal.

1896 Zionist movement founded by Theodor Herzl, calling for Jewish state in former homeland of Palestine.

1897–1914 About 50,000 Jews migrate to Palestine to escape persecution in Europe.

1901 Iranian oil fields discovered.

1902–25 Ibn Saud conquers most of Arabia; proclaims himself king of Hejaz and Nejd in 1927; changes country's name to Saudi Arabia in 1932.

1914 Egypt declared protectorate by Britain.

1916–18 Lawrence of Arabia, British Col. T.E. Lawrence, leads Arabs seeking independence in attacks on Turks.

1917 Balfour Declaration by Britain promises help in establishing "national home" for Jews in Palestine without violating rights of Arab majority (Arabs accounted for about 90% of Palestine's 700,000 population).

1918 Turkey defeated by British troops with aid of Arabs in World War I, dismembering Ottoman Empire.

1920 Britain given mandate over Palestine by League of Nations.

1920 France given mandate over Syria and Lebanon by League of Nations.

1921 Arab emirate of Transjordan (later Jordan) founded under British control.

1921 Arab kingdom of Iraq established under British control, with Faisal I as king.

1921 Arabs in Palestine riot, protesting increased Jewish immigration; Britain issues proposed Palestine constitution, but Arabs refuse to take part in elections.

1922 (Feb. 28) Britain formally ends protectorate over Egypt, but British troops remain.

1922–23 Turkey's sultanate abolished; republic proclaimed by Kemal Ataturk, president (1923–38).

1926 Lebanon republic founded under French control.

1929 Arabs attack and kill Jews in Jerusalem, Palestine, in dispute over use of Wailing Wall.

1930 Iraq granted independence by Britain.

1933–45 Tens of thousands of Jews migrate to Palestine to escape Nazi Holocaust in which 6 million European Jews were killed.

1935 Saudi Arabia's major oil fields discovered.

1935 Persia's name changed to Iran by Reza Shah Pahlevi, army officer who deposed previous shah in 1925.

1937 British commission recommends partition of Palestine between Arabs and Jews.

1939 (May 23) British parliament approves plan to create independent Palestine state within 10 years with safeguards to protect rights of Jewish minority; Jewish immigration to Palestine to be banned after 1941.

1941 Syria and Lebanon granted independence by Free French leaders after fall of France early in World War II.

1945 Arab League created by Egypt, Iraq, Jordan, Lebanon, Saudi Arabia, Syria, and Yemen to coordinate Arab interests.

1945–48 Thousands of displaced European Jews immigrate to Palestine despite efforts of British to stop them.

1946 British and French troops withdraw from Syria.

1946 (April 25) Kingdom of Transjordan (later Jordan) becomes independent, but British officers control army.

1947 (Oct. 26) British troops withdraw from Iraq.

1947 (Nov. 29) UN General Assembly votes to partition Palestine into Arab and Jewish states; Arabs reject plan.

1948 (May 14) Israel declares its independence as a Jewish state simultaneously with Britain ending its mandate.

1948–49 First Arab-Israeli War: All of Israel's Arab neighbors attack and attempt to destroy new nation, but Israel with help of arms from U.S. is able to drive back Arab forces.

1949 About 1 million Arab refugees who had fled from Israel settle in camps in Arab nations, creating major problem in succeeding decades.

1956 (June 13) British withdraw troops from Egypt after 74 years of occupation.

1956 (July 26) Egypt nationalizes Suez Canal, seizing it from British and French owners.

1956 (Oct. 29–Nov. 6) Second Arab-Israeli War: with support of Britain and France, Israel attacks Egypt and drives to Suez Canal.

1956 (Nov. 15) UN peace-keeping force sent to Suez Canal.

1957 (March 1) Israel withdraws from Egyptian territory.

1958 (July 15) U.S. Marines land in Lebanon, carrying out "Eisenhower Doctrine" to prevent communist takeover of government; troops withdrawn in November.

1958–61 Syria and Egypt unite to form United Arab Republic, finally dissolved by Syria.

1960 Britain grants independence to Cyprus.

1964 UN sends peace-keeping force to Cyprus to prevent outbreak of war between Greece and Turkey over island.

1964 Palestine Liberation Organization founded by Arab nations to conduct terrorist raids on Israel.

1967 (May 18) Egypt demands and obtains immediate withdrawal of UN forces from its borders with Israel.

1967 (June 5–10) Third Arab-Israeli War: Israel attacks Egypt, Syria, and Jordan; captures all of Jerusalem and Jordanian land west of Jordan River, all of Egypt's Sinai Peninsula, and Syria's Golan Heights; an additional 750,000 Arabs flee from territories, adding to refugee problem.

1973 (Oct. 6–24) Fourth Arab-Israeli War: Egypt and Syria, supported with military supplies from Soviet Union, attack Israel; Israel fights back, aided by arms from U.S., driving across Suez Canal into Egypt and pushing beyond Golan Heights into Syria.

1974 Truce agreements negotiated with Egypt and Syria by U.S. Secretary of State Henry Kissinger.

1974 Turkish troops invade Cyprus after Greek-led revolt overthrows island's government.

1975–76 Civil War in Lebanon with leftist Muslims and Palestinian Arabs fighting against rightist Christians; ends after Syria sends in army to impose peace.

1977 (Nov. 19–21) Egypt's President Sadat visits Israel in effort to achieve lasting peace agreement.

1979 (Jan. 16) Muslim revolt overthrows Shah of Iran, making country Islamic republic.

1979 (March 26) Peace treaty signed by Egypt and Israel: Goes into effect April 25; other Arab countries angered, breaking relations with Egypt; Israel withdraws from Egypt's Sinai region on April 25, 1982.

1979 (Dec. 27) Soviet troops invade Afghanistan; set up puppet communist government.

1981 (Dec. 14) Israel annexes Syria's Golan Heights, seized in 1967 war.

1982 (June 6) Israeli troops invade Lebanon; capture Beirut; expel PLO.

1983 For 1983 events, see pages 8–30.

TURMOIL IN THE MIDDLE EAST

FOCUS

Wide World

U.S. Marine stands guard against snipers in sandbagged bunker in Lebanon near Beirut's international airport.

Throughout the year Middle East developments focused on Lebanon. The U.S. became deeply involved because of the presence in Beirut of U.S. troops that had landed in Lebanon in August 1982 as part of a multinational peacekeeping force. Muslim terrorists protesting the U.S. presence killed 17 Americans and 46 others in a bombing of the U.S. embassy in Beirut in April. See page 15.

After months of negotiations mediated by the U.S., Israel and Lebanon reached agreement on May 17 that Israel would remove its 30,000 troops from Lebanon. However, the agreement was contingent on the simultaneous withdrawal from Lebanon of Soviet-supported Syrian forces.

After Syria refused to agree to such a proposal, President Reagan in July accused the Syrians of seeking the partition of Lebanon so that they "could grab off some territory for themselves."

Fighting began to escalate between Lebanese government troops and Muslim guerrillas backed by Syria. Two U.S. Marines were killed by mortar fire on Aug. 29, the first American combat fatalities in the fighting. Their deaths prompted Congress to invoke the War Powers Act in September, setting an April 1985 limit for the continued presence of American troops in Lebanon without further congressional approval.

Israel withdrew its troops to southern Lebanon on Sept. 3.

A new shock to the American public came when terrorists killed 240 U.S. Marines in a bombing of headquarters of the U.S. peacekeeping force in October. See page 27.

Syria also sought to take control of the Palestine Liberation Organization (PLO) movement from PLO leader Yasir Arafat.

HISTORY OF THE UNITED NATIONS

1941 (June 12) Inter-Allied Declaration signed in London by all nations then at war with Germany to work for "a world in which, relieved of the menace of aggression, all may enjoy economic and social security."

1941 (Aug. 14) Atlantic Charter issued by U.S. President Franklin D. Roosevelt and British Prime Minister Winston Churchill detailing eight points to "base their hopes for a better future for the world."

1942 (Jan. 1) Declaration by United Nations signed by 26 nations in Washington approving basic points of Atlantic Charter; first official use of name "United Nations."

1943 (Oct. 30) Moscow Declaration on General Security signed by Britain, China, Soviet Union, and United States, recognizing "the necessity of establishing at the earliest practicable date a general international organization, based on the principle of sovereign equality."

1944 (Aug. 21) Dumbarton Oaks Conference in Washington, D.C., at which for three months representatives of 39 nations discuss proposals for establishing United Nations organization, agreeing on Security Council as executive branch of UN.

1945 (June 26) UN Charter approved by delegates of 50 nations at international conference in San Francisco.

1945 (Oct. 16) Food and Agriculture Organization of United Nations established to improve consumption, production, and distribution of food throughout world.

1945 (Oct. 24) UN Charter goes into effect upon ratification by majority of nations, including Britain, China, France, Soviet Union, and United States. Day celebrated annually as United Nations Day.

1946 (Jan. 10) UN General Assembly begins first meeting in London with delegates of 51 nations as members. Trygve Lie of Norway is elected first secretary-general of UN.

1946 (June 25) International Bank for Reconstruction and Development begins operations to assist nations by government loans.

1946 (Nov. 4) UNESCO, United Nations Educational, Scientific, and Cultural Organization, formed to promote international cooperation in solving such problems as illiteracy.

1946 (Dec. 14) Gift of $8,500,000 from U.S. millionaire John D. Rockefeller Jr. accepted by UN to buy 18 acres in New York City as site of permanent headquarters.

1947 (April 4) International Civil Aviation Organization established to develop international standards and regulations for civil aviation.

1948 (April 7) World Health Organization established to promote world health.

1948 (Sept. 17) UN peace negotiator Count Folke Bernadotte of Sweden assassinated in Jerusalem while trying to arrange truce in fighting between Arabs and Israelis.

1948 (Dec. 10) Universal Declaration of Human Rights adopted by UN General Assembly.

1949 (Jan. 1) Cease-fire between India and Pakistan obtained by UN to end two years of fighting over control of Kashmir.

1949 (Feb.–July) Cease-fire agreements arranged between Israel and Arab states by UN negotiator Ralph J. Bunche.

1949 (Dec. 27) Netherlands grants independence to Indonesia after conference arranged by UN to settle fighting.

1950 (March 23) World Meteorological Organization established to promote international reporting and observation of weather.

1950 (June 27) UN Security Council calls for member nations to send troops to aid South Korea, which had been attacked by communist North Korea. Soviet Union was boycotting meetings of Security Council at this time and so could not veto measure. Troops of U.S. and 15 other nations dispatched to aid South Korea.

1953 (July 27) UN signs truce with North Korea, ending over three years of fighting.

1956 (Nov. 7) UN obtains cease-fire in Suez Canal fighting between Egypt and Israeli-British-French forces; sends UN Emergency Force to supervise truce.

1957 (July 29) International Atomic Energy Agency created to promote peaceful uses of atomic energy.

1961 (Sept. 13) UN troops begin fighting in Congo (now Zaire) to restore order in civil war.

1961 (Sept. 18) UN Secretary-General Dag Hammarskjold killed in air crash in Africa while on Congo peace mission.

1961 (Nov. 3) U Thant of Burma elected as UN's third secretary-general to succeed Dag Hammarskjold.

1964 (March 4) UN peacekeeping force sent to Cyprus to prevent fighting between Turkish and Greek forces.

1966 (Dec. 16) UN Security Council asks member nations to stop trading with Rhodesia because of its policies against blacks.

1967 (June 10) UN negotiates truce in Six-Day Israeli-Arab War.

1971 (Oct. 25) Communist China admitted to UN and nationalist China expelled by 76–35 vote of General Assembly.

1971 (Dec. 13) UN General Assembly votes 79 to 7 with 36 abstentions for Israel to restore to Arab countries territories acquired by force.

1972 Kurt Waldheim appointed UN secretary-general on resignation of U Thant.

1973 (Oct. 22) Cease-fire in 17-day-old Middle East War ordered by UN Security Council.

1973 (Oct. 25) UN peacekeeping force sent to Middle East to prevent further fighting between Arab nations and Israel.

1974 Special session of UN General Assembly establishes emergency relief fund for poor nations of world.

1975 International Women's Year declared by UN to promote women's equality.

1977 (Nov. 4) Mandatory embargo on military supply shipments to South Africa ordered by UN; first such action against UN member.

1978 UN 6,100-man peacekeeping force stationed in southern Lebanon: Bring withdrawal of Israeli troops that invaded in March.

1983 UN membership reaches 158 with admission of St. Christopher and Nevis.

1983 For other 1983 events, see pages 7–30.

U.S. POLICY IN CENTRAL AMERICA

FOCUS

Masked El Salvador soldier prepares to go into battle against rebel guerrillas in nation's Morazon province. Extra bullets for his American-made M16 rifle form his hatband.

Wide World

President Reagan intensified efforts in 1983 to reduce Soviet influence in Central America and the Caribbean area.

"The national security of all the Americas is at stake in Central America," the President declared in an address to a joint meeting of Congress on April 27. "If we cannot defend ourselves there, we cannot expect to prevail elsewhere. Our credibility would collapse, our alliances would crumble, and the safety of our homeland would be put at jeopardy."

The U.S. State Department declared the region's "strategic importance is measured by the fact that nearly half of our foreign trade, including petroleum, passes through the Panama Canal and the Caribbean Sea."

The most dramatic implementation of U.S. strength in the region came on Oct. 25 when U.S. armed forces landed on the island of Grenada, ousting government leaders friendly to the Soviet Union and Cuba. See page 29.

U.S. Navy task forces operating offshore of Nicaragua gave a clear signal to the pro-communist government of that nation that a similar action might be undertaken there to prevent continued Nicaraguan support of rebels fighting against the pro-American government of El Salvador.

The U.S. stepped up military aid to Nicaragua's pro-American neighbors and to guerrillas fighting to overthrow Nicaragua's government.

Mexico, Panama, Venezuela, and Colombia, called the Contadora Group, attempted to mediate conflicts in the region, calling for a peace treaty to be signed by Nicaragua, El Salvador, Guatemala, Honduras, and Costa Rica.

UNITED NATIONS HEADQUARTERS

The present site of the United Nations headquarters is an 18-acre tract along the East River in midtown Manhattan. Purchased with an $8.5 million gift from John D. Rockefeller Jr., the site is now international territory.

The UN's address is United Nations, NY 10017.

In November 1947 the world body approved a design submitted by an international consulting board under the direction of Wallace K. Harrison, an American architect.

The United States loaned the organization $65 million, and construction began in September 1948. Total cost was $73 million.

The General Assembly met at "United Nations, New York" for the first time in October 1952. (Interim business had been conducted from temporary quarters at Hunter College in New York City and at Lake Success, N.Y.)

The present headquarters comprise three interconnected buildings and a library, surrounded by plazas, gardens, and lawns.

The Secretariat building is a 30-story rectangular column, sheathed in glass and marble. The Secretariat building contains offices and working space for the headquarters staff.

The General Assembly building faces a landscaped plaza to the north. It is a sloping, doubly concave structure, topped by a shallow dome.

The General Assembly Hall, in which representatives of all the member nations convene in formal session at least once a year, is 165 feet long, 115 feet wide, and three stories high. Seats for delegates and alternates are arranged in curved rows on the floor, facing the officials' podium, and flanked by seats for advisers and observers. In the rear are places for alternate delegates, representatives' guests, and the press. Public galleries overlook the hall.

Translation and press booths line the walls of the General Assembly Hall. All 2,098 seats are equipped with earphones, enabling participants and spectators to listen to proceedings in any of the UN's five official languages: Chinese, English, French, Spanish, and Russian.

The UN buildings and grounds are decorated by works of art donated by various nations.

Buildings are open to the public from 9 A.M. to 5:30 P.M. daily, except Christmas and New Year's Day. An international staff of guides conducts tours of the headquarters between 9:00 A.M. and 4:45 P.M. daily. About one million persons take the tours each year.

UNITED STATES MISSION TO THE UNITED NATIONS

Jeane J. Kirkpatrick, *Ambassador Extraordinary and Plenipotentiary*, Permanent Representative to the United Nations

Jose Sorzano, *Ambassador*, U.S. Deputy Permanent Representative to the United Nations

William C. Sherman, *Ambassador*, Representative on the Security Council

Alan Keyes, *Ambassador*, Representative, Economic and Social Council

Charles Lichenstein, *Ambassador*, Alternate Representative for Special Political Affairs

MEMBERSHIP IN PRINCIPAL UNITED NATIONS BODIES: 1984

SECURITY COUNCIL

Fifteen members: Five (indicated by *) are designated in the Charter as permanent. Ten are elected by the General Assembly for 2-year terms, ending December 31 of the year indicated.

Britain *	France *	Netherlands (1984)	Peru (1985)	Ukraine (1985)	Upper Volta (1985)
China *	India (1985)	Nicaragua (1984)	Soviet Union *	United States *	Zimbabwe (1984)
Egypt (1985)	Malta (1984)	Pakistan (1984)			

ECONOMIC AND SOCIAL COUNCIL

The General Assembly elects 54 members for 3-year terms, ending Dec. 31 of year indicated.

Algeria (1985)	Congo (1985)	Lebanon (1985)	Poland (1986)	Suriname (1985)
Argentina (1986)	Costa Rica (1986)	Liberia (1984)	Portugal (1984)	Swaziland (1984)
Austria (1984)	Djibouti (1985)	Luxembourg (1985)	Qatar (1984)	Sweden (1986)
Benin (1984)	Ecuador (1985)	Malaysia (1985)	Romania (1984)	Thailand (1985)
Botswana (1985)	Finland (1986)	Mali (1984)	Rwanda (1986)	Tunisia (1984)
Brazil (1985)	France (1984)	Mexico (1985)	St. Lucia (1984)	Uganda (1986)
Britain (1986)	Germany, East (1985)	Netherlands (1985)	Saudi Arabia (1985)	United States (1985)
Bulgaria (1985)	Germany, West (1985)	New Zealand (1985)	Sierra Leone (1985)	Venezuela (1984)
Canada (1986)	Greece (1984)	Nicaragua (1983)	Somalia (1986)	Yugoslavia (1986)
China (1986)	Indonesia (1986)	Pakistan (1984)	Soviet Union (1986)	Zaire (1986)
Colombia (1984)	Japan (1986)	Papua New Guinea (1986)	Sri Lanka (1986)	

INTERNATIONAL COURT OF JUSTICE (WORLD COURT)

Fifteen members, elected by the General Assembly and the Security Council to 9-year terms ending February 5 of the year indicated.

Taslim O. Elias, Nigeria, President	1985
Manfred Lachs, Poland	1985
Hermann Mosler, West Germany	1985
Shigeru Oda, Japan	1985
Abdullah Fikri al-Khani, Syria	1985
Steven M. Schwebel, United States	1988
Roberto Ago, Italy	1988
Abdullah Ali El-Erian, Egypt	1988
José Sette Câmara, Brazil	1988
Platon Morozov, Soviet Union	1988
Nagendra Singh, India	1991
José María Ruda, Argentina	1991
Robert Y. Jennings, Britain	1991
Guy Ladreit de Lacharrière, France	1991
Keba Mbaye, Senegal	1991

THE 158 MEMBERS OF THE UNITED NATIONS

When the UN charter went into effect on Oct. 24, 1945, there were 51 members. Among them were Belorussia and Ukraine, two of the 15 states or republics of the Soviet Union.

New members of the UN must first be passed on by the UN Security Council, and therefore may be vetoed by any of the five permanent members. Membership then must be approved by a vote of the UN General Assembly.

Some nations are *not* members of the UN, such as: Andorra, Bophuthatswana, Ciskei, North Korea, South Korea, Liechtenstein, Monaco, Namibia, Nauru, San Marino, Switzerland, Taiwan, Tonga, Transkei, and Tuvalu.

MEMBER	SINCE	MEMBER	SINCE	MEMBER	SINCE
Afghanistan	1946 (Nov. 19)	Germany, East	1973 (Sept. 18)	Panama	1945 (Nov. 13)
Albania	1955 (Dec. 14)	Germany, West	1973 (Sept. 18)	Papua New Guinea	1975 (Oct. 10)
Algeria	1962 (Oct. 8)	Ghana	1957 (March 8)	Paraguay	1945 (Oct. 24)
Angola	1976 (Dec. 1)	Greece	1945 (Oct. 25)	Peru	1945 (Oct. 31)
Antigua	1981 (Nov. 11)	Grenada	1974 (Sept. 17)	Philippines	1945 (Oct. 24)
Argentina	1945 (Oct. 24)	Guatemala	1945 (Nov. 21)	Poland	1945 (Oct. 24)
Australia	1945 (Nov. 1)	Guinea	1958 (Dec. 12)	Portugal	1955 (Dec. 14)
Austria	1955 (Dec. 14)	Guinea-Bissau	1974 (Sept. 17)	Qatar	1971 (Sept. 21)
Bahamas	1973 (Sept. 18)	Guyana	1966 (Sept. 20)	Romania	1955 (Dec. 14)
Bahrain	1971 (Sept. 21)	Haiti	1945 (Oct. 24)	Rwanda	1962 (Sept. 18)
Bangladesh	1974 (Sept. 17)	Honduras	1945 (Dec. 17)	St. Christopher and	
Barbados	1966 (Dec. 9)	Hungary	1955 (Dec. 14)	Nevis	1983 (Sept. 23)
Belgium	1945 (Dec. 27)	Iceland	1946 (Nov. 19)	St. Lucia	1979 (Sept. 18)
Belize	1981 (Sept. 25)	India	1945 (Oct. 30)	St. Vincent	1980 (Sept. 16)
Belorussia	1945 (Oct. 24)	Indonesia	1950 (Sept. 28)	São Tomé and Príncipe	1975 (Sept. 16)
Benin	1960 (Sept. 20)	Iran	1945 (Oct. 24)	Saudi Arabia	1945 (Oct. 24)
Bhutan	1971 (Sept. 21)	Iraq	1945 (Dec. 21)	Senegal	1960 (Sept. 28)
Bolivia	1945 (Nov. 14)	Ireland	1955 (Dec. 14)	Seychelles	1976 (Sept. 28)
Botswana	1966 (Oct. 17)	Israel	1949 (May 11)	Sierra Leone	1961 (Sept. 27)
Brazil	1945 (Oct. 24)	Italy	1955 (Dec. 14)	Singapore	1965 (Sept. 21)
Britain	1945 (Oct. 24)	Ivory Coast	1960 (Sept. 20)	Solomons	1978 (Sept. 19)
Bulgaria	1955 (Dec. 14)	Jamaica	1962 (Sept. 18)	Somalia	1960 (Sept. 20)
Burma	1948 (April 19)	Japan	1956 (Dec. 18)	South Africa	1945 (Nov. 7)
Burundi	1962 (Sept. 18)	Jordan	1955 (Dec. 14)	Soviet Union	1945 (Oct. 24)
Cambodia	1955 (Dec. 14)	Kenya	1963 (Dec. 16)	Spain	1955 (Dec. 14)
Cameroon	1960 (Sept. 20)	Kuwait	1963 (May 14)	Sri Lanka	1955 (Dec. 14)
Canada	1945 (Nov. 9)	Laos	1955 (Dec. 14)	Sudan	1956 (Nov. 12)
Cape Verde	1975 (Sept. 16)	Lebanon	1945 (Oct. 24)	Suriname	1975 (Dec. 4)
Central Africa	1960 (Sept. 20)	Lesotho	1966 (Oct. 17)	Swaziland	1968 (Sept. 24)
Chad	1960 (Sept. 20)	Liberia	1945 (Nov. 2)	Sweden	1946 (Nov. 19)
Chile	1945 (Oct. 24)	Libya	1955 (Dec. 14)	Syria	1945 (Oct. 24)
China	1945 (Oct. 24)	Luxembourg	1945 (Oct. 24)	Tanzania	1961 (Dec. 14)
Colombia	1945 (Nov. 5)	Madagascar	1960 (Sept. 20)	Thailand	1946 (Dec. 16)
Comoros	1975 (Nov. 12)	Malawi	1964 (Dec. 1)	Togo	1960 (Sept. 20)
Congo	1960 (Sept. 20)	Malaysia	1957 (Sept. 17)	Trinidad-Tobago	1962 (Sept. 18)
Costa Rica	1945 (Nov. 2)	Maldives	1965 (Sept. 21)	Tunisia	1956 (Nov. 12)
Cuba	1945 (Oct. 24)	Mali	1960 (Sept. 28)	Turkey	1945 (Oct. 24)
Cyprus	1960 (Sept. 20)	Malta	1964 (Dec. 1)	Uganda	1962 (Oct. 25)
Czechoslovakia	1945 (Oct. 24)	Mauritania	1961 (Oct. 27)	Ukraine	1945 (Oct. 24)
Denmark	1945 (Oct. 24)	Mauritius	1968 (April 24)	United Arab Emirates	1971 (Dec. 9)
Djibouti	1977 (Sept. 20)	Mexico	1945 (Nov. 7)	United States	1945 (Oct. 24)
Dominica	1978 (Dec. 18)	Mongolia	1961 (Oct. 27)	Upper Volta	1960 (Sept. 20)
Dominican Republic	1945 (Oct. 24)	Morocco	1956 (Nov. 12)	Uruguay	1945 (Dec. 18)
Ecuador	1945 (Dec. 21)	Mozambique	1975 (Sept. 16)	Vanuatu	1981 (Sept. 15)
Egypt	1945 (Oct. 24)	Nepal	1955 (Dec. 14)	Venezuela	1945 (Nov. 15)
El Salvador	1945 (Oct. 24)	Netherlands	1945 (Dec. 10)	Vietnam	1977 (Sept. 20)
Equatorial Guinea	1968 (Nov. 12)	New Zealand	1945 (Oct. 24)	Western Samoa	1976 (Dec. 15)
Ethiopia	1945 (Nov. 13)	Nicaragua	1945 (Oct. 24)	Yemen, North	1947 (Sept. 30)
Fiji	1970 (Oct. 13)	Niger	1960 (Sept. 20)	Yemen, South	1967 (Dec. 14)
Finland	1955 (Dec. 14)	Nigeria	1960 (Oct. 7)	Yugoslavia	1945 (Oct. 24)
France	1945 (Oct. 24)	Norway	1945 (Nov. 27)	Zaire	1960 (Sept. 20)
Gabon	1960 (Sept. 20)	Oman	1971 (Oct. 7)	Zambia	1964 (Dec. 1)
Gambia	1965 (Sept. 21)	Pakistan	1947 (Sept. 30)	Zimbabwe	1980 (Aug. 25)

UN SECRETARIES-GENERAL

The secretary-general is the UN's chief administrative officer. Since its beginning in 1945 the United Nations has had five secretaries-general:

Trygve Lie (1896–1968) of Norway served from Feb. 1, 1946, until he resigned in September 1952 during his second term in office.

Dag Hammarskjöld (1905–61) of Sweden, named in April 1953, was serving a second term when he died in a plane crash while on a UN mission in the Congo on Sept. 18, 1961.

U Thant (1909–74) of Burma was appointed in 1962 and resigned in 1972.

Kurt Waldheim (1918–) of Austria served from 1972 to 1981.

Javier Pérez de Cuellar (1920–) of Peru took office on Jan. 1, 1982.

PRINCIPAL ORGANS OF THE UNITED NATIONS

GENERAL ASSEMBLY

The General Assembly is the main deliberative organ of the United Nations. Including representatives from all UN member nations, it discusses and makes recommendations on matters within the scope of the organization's Charter. It also approves the UN budget and apportions expenses among the members. A president, elected at the beginning of each session, presides.

The General Assembly convenes annually on the third Tuesday in September. Each member nation has one vote and is permitted to send up to 5 representatives to each session. On ordinary matters, decisions are carried by a simple majority of members present and voting; on more important matters, by a two-thirds majority.

The General Assembly works through 7 main committees: Political and Security; Special Political Committee; Economic and Financial; Social, Humanitarian, and Cultural; Trusteeship; Administrative and Budgetary; and Legal.

SECURITY COUNCIL

The UN Security Council has primary responsibility for maintaining peace and security. The Council has 5 permanent members—Britain, China, France, the Soviet Union, and the United States—and 10 nonpermanent members elected to 2-year terms by the General Assembly. The Security Council is organized to function continuously. Each member has one vote. Decisions on procedural matters are carried by a majority of 9 members. However, on important matters, the 9 affirmative votes must include concurrence of the 5 permanent members. This is known as the "veto" privilege. Abstention does not constitute a veto.

The Security Council is empowered to investigate any situation that might lead to friction between two or more countries. All UN members are pledged to carry out its decisions, as well as to make available to the Council assistance and facilities—including armed forces—for maintenance of international peace. A country that is a member of the United Nations, but not of the Security Council, may participate in its discussions when that nation's interests are specially affected. Nonmembers can be invited to participate in Security Council discussions of disputes to which they are parties. A member that is a party to a dispute may not vote.

The Disarmament Commission includes all UN member nations. It prepares proposals for regulation, limitation, and reduction of armed forces and armaments; for elimination of all weapons adaptable to mass destruction; and for international control of atomic energy to ensure its use for peaceful purposes.

The Military Staff Committee is composed of the chiefs of staff of the 5 permanent members—Britain, China, France, the Soviet Union, and the United States—or their representatives. It advises and assists the Security Council on such questions as the Council's military requirements for the maintenance of peace, the strategic direction of armed forces placed at its disposal, and the regulation of armaments.

ECONOMIC AND SOCIAL COUNCIL

The UN Economic and Social Council examines and makes recommendations on international economic, social, cultural, educational, and health issues. The Council comprises 54 members, 18 of whom are elected each year to 3-year terms by the General Assembly. It is aided by separate regional commissions for Europe, Asia and the Far East, Latin America, and Africa.

TRUSTEESHIP COUNCIL

The UN Trusteeship Council is the principal organ assisting the General Assembly in supervision and administration of trust territories. It comprises member nations administering trust territories, permanent members of the Security Council not administering trust territories, and as many other members (elected to 3-year terms by the General Assembly) as are required to provide an equal number of administering and nonadministering members.

Originally, 11 territories were placed under the trusteeship system; 10 have become independent or joined other independent states. The onc still under UN trusteeship is the Trust Territory of the Pacific Islands (Micronesia), under U.S. administration.

INTERNATIONAL COURT OF JUSTICE

The International Court of Justice, or *World Court*, is the judicial organ of the UN. It sits at The Hague, in the Netherlands. Fifteen judges are elected to 9-year terms by the General Assembly and the Security Council, voting independently. Every UN member has automatic access to the Court and is pledged to comply with its decisions. The Court has jurisdiction over all cases specifically referred to it, and over all matters specially provided for in the Charter or in treaties and conventions in force. The Court renders legal opinions on matters referred to it by the General Assembly, Security Council, and specialized agencies authorized by the General Assembly.

UN SPECIALIZED AGENCIES AND AUTONOMOUS BODIES

Food and Agriculture Organization of the United Nations (FAO)
Headquarters: Rome, Italy
Established Oct. 16, 1945, to promote development of agriculture and good nutrition

General Agreement on Tariffs and Trade (GATT)
Headquarters: Geneva, Switzerland
Established Jan. 1, 1948, to provide international trade and tariff standards

Intergovernmental Maritime Consultative Organization (IMCO)
Headquarters: London, England
Established March 17, 1958, to promote international cooperation in maritime navigation

International Atomic Energy Agency (IAEA)
Headquarters: Vienna, Austria
Established July 29, 1957, to promote development of nuclear power for peaceful purposes

International Bank for Reconstruction and Development (World Bank)
Headquarters: Washington, D.C.
Established Dec. 27, 1945, to assist reconstruction and development of member states

International Civil Aviation Organization (ICAO)
Headquarters: Montreal, Quebec
Established April 4, 1947, to study international civil aviation problems and set standards

International Development Association (IDA)
Headquarters: Washington, D.C.
Established Sept. 24, 1960, for the purpose of making loans to less-developed countries

International Finance Corporation (IFC)
Headquarters: Washington, D.C.
Established July 20, 1956, to further economic development by encouraging private enterprise

International Fund for Agricultural Development (IFAD)
Headquarters: Rome, Italy.
Established Dec. 29, 1977, to help developing countries obtain investments to aid agricultural production

International Labor Organization (ILO)
Headquarters: Geneva, Switzerland
Established April 11, 1919, for the purpose of improving labor conditions and living standards through international action

International Monetary Fund (IMF)
Headquarters: Washington, D.C.
Established Dec. 27, 1945, for the purpose of promoting international monetary cooperation

International Telecommunication Union (ITU)
Headquarters: Geneva, Switzerland
Founded at Paris May 17, 1865, to establish international regulations for telegraph, telephone, and radio services

United Nations Capital Development Fund (UNCDF)
Headquarters: New York City.
Established Dec. 13, 1966, to provide grants and loans to developing countries

United Nations Children's Fund (UNICEF)
Headquarters: United Nations, N.Y.
Established Dec. 11, 1946, to aid the world's children by helping solve problems of health, hunger, and education

United Nations Conference on Trade and Development (UNCTAD)
Headquarters: Geneva, Switzerland
Established Dec. 30, 1964, to encourage economic growth in countries dependent on international trade

United Nations Development Program (UNDP)
Headquarters: Geneva, Switzerland
Established Nov. 22, 1966, to assist economic growth of developing nations

United Nations Disaster Relief Office (UNDRO)
Headquarters: Geneva, Switzerland
Established Dec. 14, 1971, to help coordinate aid in disaster areas

United Nations Educational, Scientific, and Cultural Organization (UNESCO)
Headquarters: Paris, France
Established Nov. 4, 1946, for the purpose of promoting international collaboration in education, science, and culture

United Nations Environment Program (UNEP)
Headquarters: Nairobi, Kenya
Established Dec. 15, 1972, as an outgrowth of the Stockholm Conference on the Human Environment, to identify major international environmental problems, monitoring the environment through the "Earthwatch" system

United Nations Fund for Population Activities (UNFPA)
Headquarters: United Nations, N.Y.
Established July 1967, to study and assist in population and family-planning problems

United Nations Industrial Development Organization (UNIDO)
Headquarters: Vienna, Austria
Established Nov. 17, 1966, to promote industrial growth in developing countries

United Nations Institute for Training and Research (UNITAR)
Headquarters: United Nations, N.Y.
Established Dec. 11, 1963, to carry out research and training programs to help developing nations

United Nations Office of High Commissioner for Refugees (UNHCR)
Headquarters: Geneva, Switzerland
Established Dec. 3, 1949, to protect the rights of refugees in foreign countries

United Nations Relief and Works Agency for Palestine Refugees in the Near East (UNRWA)
Headquarters: Vienna, Austria, and Amman, Jordan
Established Dec. 8, 1949, to aid refugees from Arab-Israeli War of 1948

United Nations Research Institute for Social Development (UNRISD)
Headquarters: Geneva, Switzerland
Established July 1, 1964, to research social problems related to economic growth

United Nations University (UNU)
Headquarters: Tokyo, Japan
Established Dec. 11, 1972, to provide a worldwide network of institutions of higher education

Universal Postal Union (UPU)
Headquarters: Bern, Switzerland
Established July 1, 1875, to promote cooperation in international postal services

World Food Council (WFC)
Headquarters: Rome, Italy
Established Dec. 17, 1974, on recommendation of World Food Conference to coordinate international efforts to feed hungry persons and to assist agricultural development of poor nations

World Health Organization (WHO)
Headquarters: Geneva, Switzerland
Established April 7, 1948, to promote world health through advisory and technical services

World Intellectual Property Organization (WIPO)
Headquarters: Geneva, Switzerland
Established April 26, 1970; affiliated with UN in 1974; promotes the protection of such intellectual properties as rights to literary, artistic, and scientific works

World Meteorological Organization (WMO)
Headquarters: Geneva, Switzerland
Established April 4, 1951, to promote international cooperation in weather observation

INTERNATIONAL ORGANIZATIONS AND ALLIANCES

Agency for the Prohibition of Nuclear Weapons in Latin America (OPANAL)
Headquarters: Mexico City. Established Sept. 2, 1969, to prevent introduction of nuclear weapons in Latin America. *Members:* Bahamas, Barbados, Bolivia, Brazil, Chile, Colombia, Costa Rica, Dominican Republic, Ecuador, El Salvador, Grenada, Guatemala, Haiti, Honduras, Jamaica, Mexico, Nicaragua, Panama, Paraguay, Peru, Suriname, Trinidad-Tobago, Uruguay, Venezuela.

Andean Pact
Established Oct. 16, 1969, to end trade barriers among member nations and create a common market. *Members:* Bolivia, Colombia, Ecuador, Peru, Venezuela.

ANZUS Pact
Defense alliance established April 29, 1952. *Members:* Australia, New Zealand, U.S.

Arab League
Established March 22, 1945; headquarters in Tunis, Tunisia; fosters cooperation among Arab nations. *Members:* Algeria, Bahrain, Djibouti, Egypt (suspended), Iraq, Jordan, Kuwait, Lebanon, Libya, Mauritania, Morocco, Oman, Palestinians (PLO), Qatar, Saudi Arabia, Somalia, Sudan, Syria, Tunisia, United Arab Emirates, North Yemen, South Yemen.

Association of Southeast Asian Nations (ASEAN)
Established Aug. 9, 1967, to stimulate economic growth of region. *Members:* Indonesia, Malaysia, Philippines, Singapore, Thailand.

Caribbean Community and Common Market (CARICOM)
Established Aug. 1, 1973, to coordinate economic and foreign policies. *Members:* Antigua, Bahamas, Barbados, Belize, Dominica, Grenada, Guyana, Jamaica, Montserrat, St. Kitts-Nevis, St. Lucia, St. Vincent, Trinidad-Tobago.

Central African Customs and Economic Union (UDEAC)
Established Jan. 1, 1966, to aid economic, social, technical, and cultural development of members. *Members:* Cameroon, Central Africa, Congo, Gabon.

Central American Common Market (CACM)
Established June 3, 1961, to form a common market. *Headquarters:* Guatemala City. *Members:* Costa Rica, El Salvador, Guatemala, and Nicaragua.

Colombo Plan
Headquarters: Colombo, Sri Lanka. Established July 1, 1951, to aid development of members: Afghanistan, Australia, Bangladesh, Bhutan, Britain, Burma, Cambodia, Canada, Fiji, India, Indonesia, Iran, Japan, South Korea, Laos, Malaysia, Maldives, Nepal, New Zealand, Pakistan, Papua New Guinea, Philippines, Singapore, Sri Lanka, Thailand, United States, Vietnam.

Conference on Security and Cooperation in Europe (CSCE—Helsinki Pact)
Formed in 1975 by signing of Helsinki Agreement to cooperate in economics, peacekeeping, and promotion of human rights. *Members:* Austria, Belgium, Britain, Bulgaria, Canada, Cyprus, Czechoslovakia, Denmark, East Germany, Finland, France, Greece, Hungary, Iceland, Ireland, Italy, Liechtenstein, Luxembourg, Malta, Monaco, Netherlands, Norway, Poland, Portugal, Romania, San Marino, Soviet Union, Spain, Sweden, Swit- zerland, Turkey, United States, Vatican, West Germany, Yugoslavia.

Council for Mutual Economic Assistance (COMECON)
An economic organization of communist-bloc nations, founded Jan. 25, 1949, with headquarters in Moscow. *Members:* Bulgaria, Cuba, Czechoslovakia, East Germany, Hungary, Mongolia, Poland, Romania, Soviet Union, Vietnam. *Associate Member,* Yugoslavia.

Council of Europe
Headquarters: Strasbourg, France. Established Aug. 3, 1949, to promote unity, economic progress, and social progress among members. *Members:* Austria, Belgium, Britain, Cyprus, Denmark, France, West Germany, Greece, Iceland, Ireland, Italy, Liechtenstein, Luxembourg, Malta, Netherlands, Norway, Portugal, Spain, Sweden, Switzerland, Turkey.

Economic Community of West African States (ECOWAS)
Established by treaty signed May 28, 1975, at Lagos, Nigeria, to provide economic cooperation among members: Benin, Cape Verde, Gambia, Ghana, Guinea, Guinea-Bissau, Ivory Coast, Liberia, Mali, Mauritania, Niger, Nigeria, Senegal, Sierra Leone, Togo, Upper Volta.

European Economic Community (EEC)
European Common Market, established Jan. 1, 1958; also includes European Coal and Steel Community (ECSC), European Atomic Energy Community (EURATOM), and European Parliament. *Members:* Belgium, Britain, Denmark, France, West Germany, Greece, Italy, Ireland, Luxembourg, Netherlands.

European Free Trade Association (EFTA)
Established May 3, 1960, for free trade among members. *Members:* Austria, Iceland, Norway, Portugal, Sweden, Switzerland. *Associate member:* Finland.

Gulf Cooperation Council
Established May 26, 1981, to strengthen security and stability in the Persian Gulf oil-producing area. *Members:* Bahrain, Kuwait, Oman, Qatar, Saudi Arabia, United Arab Emirates.

Latin American Free Trade Association (LAFTA)
Founded June 2, 1961, with headquarters in Montevideo. *Members:* Argentina, Bolivia, Brazil, Chile, Colombia, Ecuador, Mexico, Paraguay, Peru, Uruguay, and Venezuela.

Nordic Council
Established Feb. 12, 1953, as an interparliamentary union to promote cooperation of Scandinavian nations in nonmilitary matters. *Members:* Denmark, Finland, Iceland, Norway, Sweden.

North Atlantic Treaty Organization (NATO)
Defense alliance, established Sept. 17, 1949. *Headquarters:* Brussels. *Members:* Belgium, Britain, Canada, Denmark, France, West Germany, Greece, Iceland, Italy, Luxembourg, Netherlands, Norway, Portugal, Spain, Turkey, United States.

Organization for Economic Cooperation and Development (OECD)
Established Sept. 30, 1961, to promote economic cooperation among members: Australia, Austria, Belgium, Britain, Canada, Denmark, Finland, France, West Germany, Greece, Iceland, Ireland, Italy, Japan, Luxembourg, Netherlands, New Zealand, Norway, Portugal, Spain, Sweden, Switzerland, Turkey, United States, Yugoslavia.

Organization of African Unity (OAU)
Established May 25, 1963, OAU promotes the unity and development of members: Algeria, Angola, Benin, Botswana, Burundi, Cameroon, Cape Verde, Central Africa, Chad, Comoros, Congo, Djibouti, Egypt, Equatorial Guinea, Ethiopia, Gabon, Gambia, Ghana, Guinea, Guinea-Bissau, Ivory Coast, Kenya, Lesotho, Liberia, Libya, Madagascar, Malawi, Mali, Mauritania, Mauritius, Morocco, Mozambique, Niger, Nigeria, Rwanda, São Tomé and Príncipe, Senegal, Seychelles, Sierra Leone, Somalia, Sudan, Swaziland, Tanzania, Togo, Tunisia, Uganda, Upper Volta, Zaire, Zambia, Zimbabwe.

Organization of American States (OAS)
Headquarters: Washington, D.C. Formerly the Pan American Union, the OAS was organized Dec. 31, 1951, for defense and cooperation. *Members:* Antigua, Argentina, Barbados, Bolivia, Brazil, Chile, Colombia, Costa Rica, Cuba, Dominica, Dominican Republic, Ecuador, El Salvador, Grenada, Guatemala, Haiti, Honduras, Jamaica, Mexico, Nicaragua, Panama, Paraguay, Peru, St. Lucia, St. Vincent, Suriname, Trinidad-Tobago, United States, Uruguay, Venezuela.

Organization of Eastern Caribbean States (OECS)
Established June 18, 1981. Headquarters: Castries, St. Lucia. *Members:* Antigua, Dominica, Grenada, Monserrat, St. Kitts, St. Lucia, St. Vincent.

Organization of Petroleum Exporting Countries (OPEC)
Established Nov. 14, 1960, to control production and pricing of crude oil. *Members:* Algeria, Ecuador, Gabon, Indonesia, Iran, Iraq, Kuwait, Libya, Nigeria, Qatar, Saudi Arabia, United Arab Emirates, Venezuela.

South Pacific Forum
Headquarters: Suva, Fiji. Established August 1971 to promote economic and political cooperation. *Members:* Australia, Cook Islands, Fiji, Kiribati, Nauru, New Zealand, Niue, Papua New Guinea, Solomon Islands, Tonga, Tuvalu, Vanuatu, Western Samoa.

Southern African Development Coordination Conference
Established April 1, 1980, to promote regional economic cooperation and reduce dependence on South Africa. *Members:* Angola, Botswana, Lesotho, Malawi, Mozambique, Swaziland, Tanzania, Zambia, Zimbabwe.

Warsaw Treaty Organization
Headquarters: Moscow. Military alliance of communist states, established June 5, 1955. *Members:* Bulgaria, Czechoslovakia, East Germany, Hungary, Poland, Romania, Soviet Union.

Language

NEW WORDS

The American language is growing at a rapid rate as dozens of new words come into use each year. These words come from a wide variety of fields including science, technology, politics, economics, and education. Each specialized group coins new words, and some of these spread quickly, especially when they are picked up by newspapers and the television and radio media. Others may become popular only in one city or geographic region.

Words new in 1983 and in recent years are listed below:

acid fog—fog laden with sulfuric acid droplets released by industrial or oil-refining operations

AIDS—*a*cquired *i*mmune *d*eficiency *s*yndrome, fatal disorder of body's immune system thought to be transmitted mainly by sexual contact or contaminated blood for transfusions

algeny—upgrading of existing organisms and design of wholly new ones with intent of perfecting their performance (term coined by Joshua Lederberg, Nobel laureate in physics)

apple green—very hard bullet coated with tough light-green plastic capable of penetrating bullet-proof vest

artificial intelligence—theory that human intelligence may be simulated by computer programmed to make responses outside realm of conventional logic

aseptic packaging—method of packaging fruit juices, milk, and other beverages in specially treated containers of paper, polyethylene, and aluminum foil that require no refrigeration; contents and containers are sterilized separately and have shelf life of about six months

aspartame—sweetener many times sweeter than sugar; made from two amino acids, L-aspartic acid and L-phenylalanine, found in protein-bearing foods such as bananas and beans

block modeling—computer programming technique that evaluates how persons relate to each other in group situation, especially as employees within corporation

boll weevil—nickname for conservative Democratic legislator who joins in support of conservative Republican measure; see also *gypsy moth*

Bone Valley—five-county area in central Florida where phosphate is mined and turned into fertilizer

boomerang divorce—divorce after which couple continue living together

buydown—arrangement whereby buyer or seller pays bank or other lender specified amount in exchange for reduced interest on mortgage for home or condominium over first few years

CAD/CAM—application of computer technology to design and manufacturing, especially in electronics and engineering industries (acronym for *c*omputer-*a*ided *d*esign and *c*omputer-*a*ided *m*anufacturing)

celebrity rot—decline in aging entertainer's ability to perform as well as in younger years

cellular radio—radiotelephone system for automobiles; city or metropolitan region is divided into small area "cells," each with low-power transmitter; as car moves along, call is switched automatically from cell to cell without interruption

co-generation—production of power by combined combustion of fuels, offering higher efficiency than conventional methods by recycling exhaust fumes and excess steam

computer literacy—ability to understand terminology and use of computers

condop—building in which residential tenants form one cooperative unit and commercial tenants another unit

copycat syndrome—irrational tendency to commit antisocial or criminal act in imitation of others who have done so

debt-equity swap—exchange by one company of newly issued stock (equity) for another firm's outstanding bonds (debt) that offer high long-term interest

dense pack—military defensive strategy based on dense concentration of missiles; if area is attacked by enemy missiles, exploding warheads from first strike would create enough radiation and debris to deflect or destroy successive missiles; see also *pindown*

derelict art—sculptured works of art made of trash, driftwood, and other found materials, usually displayed on vacant land

disk camera—camera using film disk that rotates automatically after each exposure, replacing conventional cartridge of rolled film

domestic-content bill—legislation requiring that products, such as cars, manufactured in U.S. have specified percentage of domestic parts and labor

double depression—in psychiatry, new episode of depression affecting person afflicted with chronic depression

dowry death—in India, murder of wife by husband or members of his family for failure by her family to provide specified dowry

dry painting—see *powder coating*

dumb terminal—electronic device for entering input and displaying output of computer but unable to perform computer operations independently

dust children—in Southeast Asia, children of Asian mothers and American or European servicemen

ecocide—destruction of natural environment by massive use of herbicides, especially as wartime tactic

electronic cottage—concept of enabling workers to perform services at home linked to employer

NEW WORDS *(continued)*

by electronic communication equipment

ergonomics—science of designing equipment for maximum user comfort; also known as human-factors engineering

ethnotherapy—psychological counseling to aid troubled members of ethnic groups overcome feelings of inadequacy

feet people—refugees traveling overland on foot, as from war-torn countries in Central America to the United States

flat tax—fixed rate of income tax for all persons, eliminating exemptions and deductions from internal-revenue code

flexible benefits—program by which employees of company may select wage and fringe benefits to suit special needs

Flexibook—book with strong pliable cover combining durability of hardcover with economy of paperback

flip tax—transfer tax or fee levied on sale by owners of cooperative apartments in formerly rental building

floppy disk—magnetic memory disk for storage and retrieval of computer data; made of thin, flexible ("floppy") Mylar plastic; disk permanently kept in envelope for protection against fingerprints or scratches

Fluosol-DA—blood substitute for anemic surgery patients requiring transfusions; contains substances (perfluorochemicals) that can carry large amounts of oxygen

footprint—area of major destruction produced by nuclear weapon

fragile X chromosome—human sex chromosome with easily breakable arms; in males, broken X chromosome is thought responsible for mental retardation

fugitive air emission—pollutant inadvertently released into atmosphere

gender gap—real or supposed difference in attitude or character between men and women

gentrification—upgrading of property values in town or city district by widespread renovation of deteriorated residential or commercial buildings

giveback—in labor-management affairs, return by workers of benefits or contractual arrangements in exchange for job security or other consideration

golden parachute—corporate contract with provision for cash settlement to executive released in takeover by another firm

grant lands—designated areas granted by state or federal authority to private companies for exploitation of natural resource, such as oil or gas, with exemption from paying production royalties

green vote—voters concerned with environmental issues, considered as bloc

greeny—slang for environmentalist or conservationist

GRF—growth hormone *r*eleasing *f*actor, substance in brain vital in controlling release of hormone responsible for growth in humans and animals

GRID—*g*ay-*r*elated *i*mmune *d*eficiency, disease mainly affecting homosexual men and associated with certain types of anemia, cancer, and fungal infections; see also *AIDS*.

gypsy moth—nickname for Republican legislator who shifts allegiance from national-party platform to support measure that reflects needs of local constituency; see also *boll weevil*

gypsy scholar—university graduate with doctorate in humanities or social science who moves from school to school in quest of regular appointment

hacker—one who explores resources of home computer for fun or profit

heavy breather—popular romantic fiction, especially in paperback or magazine

high-definition television—TV system offering images with refined clarity by use of frames providing more than double usual number of lines

high technology—advanced technology characterized by sophisticated concepts and devices, as in microelectronics, space research, genetic engineering, word processing, etc.

honeybee—nickname for conservative Republican legislator who would "sweeten the pot" in support of Reaganomics by such measures as flat tax and stricter revenue collection; see also *yellowjacket*

hybridoma—cell formed by fusion of two different cells, used in cancer research

imagery rehearsal—sports training technique in which athlete reviews own best performances in effort to regain optimum physical and mental condition prior to next competition

impact player—in football, offensive back capable of changing course of game by running, pass catching, or kick returning

inference reader—brokerage specialist who studies economic, political, and social conditions to determine their implications for investment

infill—construction of building on vacant lot in mainly built-up area

jock couture—athletic apparel, such as warmup suits and sweatshirts, considered as fashion

level billing—system of billing for utility service in which estimated charges for year are spread evenly in equal monthly payments

lymphokine—hormone-like substance secreted by mass of fused cells (hybridoma) that can simulate immune response to infection; produced in laboratory for cancer research

membrane keyboard—keyboard for computer terminal, appliance, etc., consisting of three sheets of flexible plastic: keys printed on top layer, when activated, plunge through middle spacer and make contact with bottom layer, completing electrical circuit

merit shop—in construction industry, system of awarding subcontracts to lowest qualified bidders whether unionized or not

microscape—artistic rendering of high-technology object using camera aided by microscope

misery index—combined rate of inflation and unemployment at any given time

Nameonics—trademark for advertising technique of using product name in catchy phrases; derived from "mnemonics" system of improving memory

new federalism—program that selectively would reduce or eliminate role of federal government in state or local affairs

oncogene—type of gene found in all cells capable of turning normal cell into cancerous one

Orthotron—physical-therapy device that concentrates on rehabilitation of muscles around joint after injury to knee, ankle, or shoulder

outro—part of radio or television broadcast in which announcer or commentator signs off

PET—acronym for *p*ositron *e*mission *t*omography, technique for scanning brain to study disorders by injecting solution carrying radioactive isotope in bloodstream whose emissions are converted by computer to show areas of greatest activity

pindown—military offensive strategy in which exploding warheads many miles above enemy missile site would spread enough heat and radiation to destroy missiles being fired; see also *dense pack*

pixel—abbreviation of "picture element," smallest unit that can be lighted on computer display screen

PMS—premenstrual syndrome, state of mental instability affecting some women before onset of menstrual period

powder coating—paint applied as powder by spray gun to appliance, electrical equipment, or other objects; spraying gives each particle electrical charge for even deposit and exact thickness; also called *dry painting*

quango—in Britain, government-funded but privately managed foundation for sponsoring and funding overseas cultural tours and promotions; acronym for quasi-governmental nongovernmental organ

Reaganomics—economic program of Reagan administration offering individuals incentives to work, save, and invest by lowering income taxes and reducing government spending

Reaganville—camp of makeshift dwellings for homeless people to dramatize effects of Reaganomics; coined by analogy to *Hoovervilles* of depression years

refusenik—Soviet Jew whose request for exit visa is denied by government

reprography—reproduction of printed or other graphic materials

satietin—protein in human blood that sends message to brain that hunger has been satisfied

SCID—*s*evere *c*ombined *i*mmunodefiency *d*isease, inherited defect in body's ability to combat viruses and bacteria

Silicon Valley—area around San Francisco Bay, California, with high concentration of advanced-technology electronics firms

sliver—in real estate, tall narrow building looming over adjacent structures

smart bomb—radioactively tagged antibodies produced by mass of fused cells (hybridoma) that can seek out and destroy cancer cells without damage to nearby healthy tissues

space junk—debris in outer space, fallen from or jettisoned by spacecraft or other launched objects

squeal rule—proposed legislation that would require government-sponsored clinic offering birth-control prescriptions to persons under 18 to inform parents of action taken

starch blocker—diet pill that supposedly curbs action of starch-digesting enzyme amylase, enabling user to consume carbohydrates without gaining weight

Steel Valley—area of industrial suburbs southeast of Pittsburgh, Pa., along Monongahela River, with high concentration of steel mills

sticker shock—extreme dismay at unexpected high price tag on consumer product, especially on automobile

structural unemployment—loss of employment due to changes in job requirements and character of labor force

technology pull—influence exerted by new developments in technology toward reexamination of traditional solutions to problems

technology transfer—securing of advanced, often classified, technological systems, materials, or equipment of one nation by another by covert means

teletext—system that enables TV viewer to choose pages of text to be displayed on TV screen

tevatron—atom smasher capable of speeding electrons to energy level of 1,000 billion electron volts, or TeV

transdermal medication—procedure for administering medicine through skin: patch with microscopic membrane applied to skin allows measured release of medicine for circulation in bloodstream

transposon—gene or group of genes capable of moving from one cell to another and transferring genetic instructions; thought to be responsible for transmittal of bacterial or viral diseases

ultralight—very light, open-sided, single-seat aircraft made of metal tubing, wire, and fabric and powered by small engine

underground economy—economic activity by persons whose incomes from services, sales, or trading are unreported

unfolding house—prefabricated house assembled and folded at factory for delivery and setting up at buyer's lot

urban amenity zone—area in city designed to attract private enterprise by provision of improved housing, transportation, and shopping facilities

variable rate mortgage—mortgage with interest rate that can be adjusted in relation to changing economic conditions

videotex—two-way system of communication between customer and outside service source, using telephone to make requests and television to receive responses

wealthfare—preferential consideration enabling corporations and wealthy persons to use exemptions, shelters, credits, or other benefits to minimize or avoid normal income-tax obligations

wimp—slang for obnoxious or ineffectual person

yellow rain—yellow powder released by plane in chemical warfare; derived from highly toxic fungi, it causes convulsions, hemorrhaging, and agonizing death within minutes of exposure

yellow snow—yellowish dustlike particles from acid-bearing paper in library books

yellowjacket—nickname for conservative Republican legislator who supports Reaganomics but urges more severe budget cuts; see also *honeybee*

zero-discount note—corporate note selling at discount and paying full amount at maturity but offering no interest payments

HOW TO WRITE A REPORT

Preparing a report is a time-consuming, mentally taxing task. It can also be absorbing and rewarding. Involved are eight essential steps.

1. Choose and analyze a subject. Select a subject in which you are interested. It is difficult to write effectively unless you are concerned with your material.

Choose a subject about which sufficient information is available to you in the form of printed materials or from experts who can be reached.

Select a subject about which you can arrive at a conclusion or a set of conclusions. An effective report is a group of facts that *prove* or *disprove* a specific statement, theory, or idea about a particular subject.

2. Make a careful investigation. In gathering material for a report, start by reading a good résumé of the subject. Most often you should start with an encyclopedia article. If your topic is not covered in a general or special-subject encyclopedia, you may find the needed summary in a magazine article or in a chapter from a book.

Find the books that can help you. Begin your search in the card catalog of your library for books mentioned in the bibliography following the résumé article you have read.

Search for recently written material. Examine recent issues of the *Reader's Guide to Periodical Literature.* You can then compare what is listed there with entries in the *International Index to Periodicals* and *Bulletin of the Public Affairs Information Service* (P.A.I.S.). In addition, you might consult entries in the *Art Index, Agricultural Index, Education Index, Applied Science and Technology Index,* and *Business Periodical Index.*

If necessary, write or telephone people who can provide information.

3. Take notes on your findings. Take notes on 3-by-5-inch cards, which can be easily shuffled into place according to the subject outline. Place no more than one note on a card; *never* use both sides of the card.

Each book or other source used should be entered on a separate card *in full bibliographical detail,* giving full name of the author, title, place of publication, publisher, and date.

You will then have two files of cards: (1) a master file that will include *all* bibliographical details on each book or article used, and (2) a file containing notes taken for the body of your paper.

Notes must be *legible* to avoid misinterpretation later, and must be *full* so that repeated trips to the library to verify them will not be necessary.

Distinguish between fact and opinion in the notes made. They all should be worded so that there will be no confusion later as to what *you* wrote or thought and what the *author* meant.

4. Prepare an outline. No one can write an effective report without some sort of outline.

An outline need not be detailed or elaborate. Only a few minutes may be needed to prepare a rough "sketch" outline that may pay big dividends.

You will probably make a number of tentative outlines as your work proceeds. When you are ready to state conclusions and have some idea of the framework of the entire structure, you can rearrange your notes under the outline headings.

5. Write a first draft. Prepare a first draft as a working copy. You can then make changes in sequence, strengthen your beginning, eliminate overlapping details, or make your discussion more effective.

Write in a clear, straightforward manner. A research paper need not be stiff, overly formal, or pedantic. It can be enlivened by touches of humor.

You must avoid *plagiarism*. You must *not* copy the words written by someone else unless you put them in quotation marks and name their source. Unless the idea and the phrasing are your own, refer the reader in a footnote to the source for your statement.

6. Add footnotes or explanatory comments. The purpose of a footnote is to name the authority for some fact or to develop some point referred to in the body of a paper.

7. Prepare a bibliography. In a report a bibliography is an alphabetical, sometimes classified, list containing the names of all works quoted from or generally used in preparation. The bibliography should be placed at the end of the report on a separate page.

Unless instructed otherwise, arrange items in the bibliography alphabetically by last names of the authors. List titles by the same author alphabetically. Citing the publisher's name is optional, but the place and date of publication are usually given.

8. Revise and proofread with care. The final version of a report must be carefully prepared. It should be as nearly letter-perfect as possible. To make sure of this, read slowly through the text to correct spelling and punctuation. Larger errors involving revision or addition may necessitate redoing a page.

Check your footnotes and bibliography.

If time permits, lay the paper aside for at least one day. Then reread it with fresh eyes. You may be surprised at how many errors and lapses you discover.

HOW TO PREPARE A SPEECH

So you were asked to speak at the next club meeting. And you were so flattered that you accepted. But now the time is rapidly approaching when you must make your appearance, and you haven't yet prepared your speech. Worried? Here are some tips that can help you overcome your stage fright.

1. Choose a topic to interest your audience. Who are the people you are speaking to? What are their interests? Write out what you believe is a fair profile of your audience. What is their average age? Will there be more men than women, or vice versa? What are their occupations? What common bond or interest brings them together as a group? Once you know your audience you should be ready to make a list of topics that might interest them.

2. Make sure your topic fits the occasion. What is the purpose of the meeting? If it is a Little League dinner celebrating the end of the season, you certainly shouldn't give a speech on *How to Pot Geraniums*, even if you happen to be the world's greatest authority on that subject.

3. Try to make your topic timely. If the meeting is a week before Christmas, you shouldn't try to speak on the events leading up to the Declaration of Independence. Think ahead to what events are going to take place at the time of the meeting or soon after. What can you talk about that will relate to those events?

4. Make sure your topic fits the time allowed. How long is your speech supposed to be? If you have only been allowed five minutes, don't choose such a broad topic that it can't possibly be discussed thoroughly within that period. For example, *The History of Space Exploration* would require much more than five minutes. So reduce your topic to *Man's First Walk on the Moon* to fit the time allowed.

5. Stimulate your audience to action. After the audience has heard your speech, what do you want them to do? If you want them to stop littering the streets with waste paper, then you must make them want to use the litter baskets. Even if you are giving a purely informative speech, such as *The History of the Bill of Rights*, you should try to get your audience to go out and read more about the subject because of the interest you have evoked by your speech. So in planning your topic, consider what you are going to ask your audience to do about it.

6. Be specific with your topic. Avoid a generalized topic, narrowing it to a specific aspect of the subject. For example, *Baseball* is too broad a subject for a good speech. Instead, talk on a specific aspect of baseball, such as *Four Ways to Hit More Home Runs* or *How One Boy Learned What Team Spirit Means.*

7. Choose a topic you are interested in. Avoid choosing a topic that you yourself find uninteresting. Otherwise, how can you possibly excite your audience about it?

8. Prepare your speech in three parts. Your speech should be divided into three main parts: (1) the introductory remarks, (2) the main body of the speech, and (3) the conclusion.

As you gather materials for your speech and make notes, arrange them into these three parts.

9. Wake up the audience at the outset. The introductory remarks, the first part of your speech, must catch the attention of the audience and make them want to listen to you. You may want to ask a question: "How many of you ever hit a home run?" or "Which one of you threw this gum wrapper on the floor?" Or you may wish to open with a startling statement: "Look down the row you are sitting in. At least one of the people you see will die of a heart attack within the next two years."

10. Avoid jokes unless you are a practiced storyteller. If you have tried telling jokes to your family and friends, and have received only weak smiles in return, avoid trying to open your speech with a joke.

If you are determined to use a joke, practice it on strangers. If they don't laugh, discard it.

11. Limit the main points you want to make. As you prepare the main body of your speech, limit yourself to making only two, three, or four main points. Organize your speech so that it will be clear to the audience exactly what are the main points you are trying to get across. Many speakers ramble on from one topic to another, and at the end the members of the audience ask each other, "What was he trying to say?"

12. Use specific examples. Back up each point with at least one specific example.

13. Avoid technical vocabulary. Although you are an authority on your subject, your audience is not. Make sure that the vocabulary you use is simplified so your audience can understand you. If you have to use a technical term, define it for the audience.

14. Conclude with a climax. The conclusion should be the best part of the speech and the part the audience remembers longest. You should summarize your main points and make your audience want to act on what you have said.

PUNCTUATE IT RIGHT!

Too much punctuation may be as confusing as too little. If a sentence is so complicated that no amount of punctuation seems adequate, the writer should reorganize it.

PERIOD (.)

The period is used at the end of sentences, after an indirect question, and after a polite request resembling a question. It is also the end mark for initials and certain abbreviations.

Here are examples of sentences that end with a period.

Declarative: *Mrs. Morris placed the book on the table.*

Imperative: *Do it today. Sit down.*

Indirect Question: *The members of the committee asked when the meeting would take place.*

Polite Request: *Will you open the door for me, please.*

QUESTION MARK (?)

The question mark signifies that the sentence asks a question: *What time is it? Am I late?*

Sometimes a sentence consists of several questions, each of which should end with a question mark. However, the separate questions within the sentence do not begin with a capital, since they are part of the sentence: *Who will attend the conference? the president? the vice president? the secretary?*

EXCLAMATION POINT (!)

The exclamation point at the end of a statement denotes strong emotion or a sense of urgency. Often this may be a phrase or even a single word: *What a show! Hurrah! Please hurry!*

An interjection such as *Oh!* or *Ah!* at the beginning of a sentence is usually followed by a comma, and the sentence is ended with an exclamation point: *Oh, what a day this has been!*

COMMA (,)

Here are examples of sentence structure that call for the comma:

Series: The comma separates various elements in a series—either words, phrases, or clauses—when there are at least three units: *The dog jumped up, barked ferociously, bared his teeth, and took off after the rabbit.*

Style adopted by some newspapers, magazines, and publishing firms does not require the comma before the conjunction in a series, as in: *The flag is red, white and blue.*

When *et cetera,* or its abbreviation *etc.*, ends a series it should be preceded by a comma. A comma should also follow *etc.* when it is not the last word in a sentence: *She stopped off to get some fruit, vegetables, etc., on the way home.*

Introductory Elements: When the main clause of the sentence comes first, there is no need for a comma in the sentence: *Take along a few magazines when you visit him.*

An introductory phrase containing a verb usually should be followed by a comma: *After making the survey, the committee published its report.*

If the introductory phrase is very short or does not contain a verb, it need not be followed by a comma unless the phrase is parenthetical or explanatory: *After much debate the meeting was adjourned.* But: *On the contrary, I believe the President was absolutely right.*

A comma sets off an introductory *yes* or *no*: *No, we shall not be ready on time.*

A parenthetical expression (word, phrase, or clause) that can be omitted without drastically changing the meaning of the sentence should be set off by commas: *The king, who was ill, was not present.*

Quotations: Use the comma before direct quotations, unless they are very long—usually a paragraph or more. In such cases a colon should be used: *She asked, "Is the train on time?"*

Appositives: A comma or commas should set off an identifying or explanatory word or phrase (called an *appositive*) which helps to make the meaning of the sentence clearer: *Mr. Jones, our grocer, traveled last summer to Canada, his native country.*

Contrasting Expressions: Use a comma to separate contrasting expressions—word, phrase, or clause: *We shall leave today, not tomorrow.*

Parallel Adjectives: Commas should separate parallel adjectives: *The tall, thin, scowling man made a poor impression.*

Conjunctions: The comma should be used before a conjunction (*but, and, or,* etc.) that connects two independent clauses: *John played shortstop, and he filled in a few times when the regular catcher was hurt.*

If the clauses are short and uncomplicated the comma may be omitted: *We were drenched but Mother didn't scold us.*

When two verbs have the same subject, the connecting conjunction is not usually preceded by a comma: *It snowed all morning but stopped at noon.*

Numbers and Dates: Use the comma with numbers in the thousands: *1,792 new cars.* Omit the comma in a date using only month and year: *April 1970.* But do use commas with the day of the month: *April 2, 1970.*

SEMICOLON (;)

The semicolon separates two independent clauses when the conjunction is omitted: *We are enclosing an envelope for your convenience; it requires no postage.*

Compound Sentences: The semicolon separates members of a compound sentence when the clauses are connected by such words as *however, nevertheless, consequently, thus: The team was undefeated; however, three games ended in ties.*

When part of a compound sentence contains a comma, the semicolon must be used to separate the members: *If nominated, he will run; but his chances seem rather slim.*

Series: Phrases or clauses in a series are separated by the semicolon when one or more contain a comma: *Our profits for the three years were unusually high: 1974, $2,345,000; 1975, $2,070,400; 1976, $2,545,000.*

COLON (:)

The colon generally indicates that a list, example, or strong assertion will follow: *Johnny had three jobs to do: clean the garage, mow the lawn, and sweep the back porch.*

The colon is also used after the salutation of a formal letter (*Dear Sir*:); between elements of a biblical citation (*Exodus 16:1–4*); after the name of the speaker in a play (*Hamlet: To be, or not to be: that is the question*); and to separate hours and minutes when time is expressed in figures (*We shall be there at 3:30* P.M.).

APOSTROPHE (')

The apostrophe commonly forms the possessive of nouns and pronouns. (However, personal pronouns such as *mine, yours, theirs* do not take the apostrophe.) With words ending in an *s*, use *'s* with one-syllable words, but use only an apostrophe with words of two or more syllables unless the *s* is not sounded: *James's, Adams', Arkansas's.*

Be careful not to use an apostrophe in the plurals of proper nouns where no possessive is intended: *We are going to see the Smiths and the Jeffersons* (not *Smith's* or *Smiths', Jefferson's* or *Jeffersons'*).

Contractions: An apostrophe is also used to show that one or more letters have been omitted from a word, or that numerals have been omitted from a number: *it's*—it is; *can't*—cannot; *'29*—1929.

QUOTATION MARKS (" ") (' ')

Double quotation marks (" ") are required at the beginning and end of a word or words spoken in direct discourse: *Roy said, "I'm reading a good book."*

If a direct quotation is interrupted by one or more words, double quotation marks are placed around the quoted matter only, and not around the interrupting words: *"Hurry along," said the coach, "or the game will not start on time."*

Double quotation marks set off words or phrases the writer does not wish to claim as his or her own: *Let my opponent produce his "incontrovertible evidence."*

Single quotation marks (' ') enclose a quotation within a quotation: *Jack remarked, "I believe that Patrick Henry said, 'Give me liberty or give me death.' "*

Enclose in double quotation marks the titles of essays, magazine articles, lectures, term papers, and book chapters.

HYPHEN (-)

Use the hyphen for end-of-line word divisions and in compound words.

Words may be divided at the end of a line *only* between syllables. (If in doubt as to how to divide a word, check your dictionary.) Never divide one-syllable words.

Compound Words: When two or more words precede a noun and form a single idea modifying the noun, they should be hyphenated: *He spoke in a matter-of-fact tone.*

Prefixes: Hyphens are sometimes used to separate prefixes from words where the meaning might otherwise be distorted: *The upholsterer re-covered the chair. Mr. Aiken recovered his stolen property.*

The hyphen is generally used when words are compounded with the prefix *self: self-satisfied; self-sufficient.*

The hyphen is also used to separate a prefix from a proper noun: *anti-American.*

Numbers: Hyphens are used in all numbers from *twenty-one* to *ninety-nine*, and in fractions: *one-half, three-quarters.*

DASH (—)

A word of caution against confusing the hyphen (-) and the dash (—). The hyphen connects. The dash often separates. The dash may be used in place of the comma and parentheses in handling appositive and parenthetical expressions. It is also used to mark intentional repetition and interruption: *Exercise every day—I mean every day.*

PARENTHESES [( )]

Parentheses marks are used to enclose words that give additional information but have little, if any, direct connection with the main thought expressed. They should be used sparingly: *If we win the contest (and I feel certain we shall), we shall compete in the finals.*

Parentheses are widely used to enclose references to statements, authors, and so forth: We are using the book *Effective Business English* (Jones and Smith).

FORMS OF ADDRESS

Many people either may meet or have the occasion to write letters to persons of importance—high government officials, congressmen, judges, officers of the armed services, clergymen, physicians, and college professors. There are certain proper forms of address that should be used.

PRESIDENT OF THE UNITED STATES

Address Business: The President
The White House
Washington, D.C. 20500
Social: The President
and Mrs. . . .
The White House
Washington, D.C. 20500
Salutation Formal: Sir:
Informal: My Dear Mr. President:
Closing Formal: I have honor to remain,
Most respectfully yours,
Informal: Very respectfully yours,
In conversation: Mr. President *or* Sir

CHIEF JUSTICE OF THE UNITED STATES

Address Business: The Chief Justice
The Supreme Court
Washington, D.C. 20543
Social: The Chief Justice
and Mrs. . . .
Home address
Salutation Formal: Sir:
Informal: My Dear Mr. Chief Justice:
Closing Formal: Very truly yours,
Informal: Sincerely yours, *or*
Faithfully yours,
In conversation: Mr. Chief Justice *or* Sir

ASSOCIATE JUSTICE OF THE SUPREME COURT

Address Business: Mr. Justice . . .
The Supreme Court
Washington, D.C. 20543
Social: Mr. Justice . . .
and Mrs. . . .
Home address
Salutation Formal: Sir:
Informal: My Dear Mr. Justice . . . :
Closing Formal: Very truly yours,
Informal: Sincerely yours,
In conversation: Mr. Justice *or* Mr.
Justice . . . *or* Sir

CABINET OFFICER

Address Business: The Honorable . . .
The Secretary of the
Treasury *or* The
Attorney General
Washington, D.C.
Social: The Honorable . . .
The Secretary of the Treasury *or* The Attorney
General and Mrs. . . .
Home address
Salutation Formal: Sir: *or* Dear Sir:
Informal: My Dear Mr. Secretary:
or My Dear Mr. Attorney
General:
Closing Formal: Very truly yours,
Informal: Sincerely yours,
In conversation: Mr. Secretary *or*
Mr. Attorney General
or . . . Sir.

UNITED STATES SENATOR

Address Business: The Honorable . . .
United States Senate
Washington, D.C. 20510
Social: The Honorable . . .
and Mrs. . . .
Home address
Salutation Formal: Sir: *or* Madam:
Informal: My Dear Senator . . . :
Closing Formal: Very truly yours,
Informal: Sincerely yours,
In conversation: Senator *or* Senator . . .
or Sir *or* Madam

UNITED STATES REPRESENTATIVE

Address Business: The Honorable . . .
United States House of
Representatives
Washington, D.C. 20515
Social: The Honorable . . .
and Mrs. . . .
Home address
or (for a woman member)
Mr. and Mrs. . . .
Salutation Formal: Sir: *or* Madam:
Informal: My Dear Mr. (or
Mrs.) . . . :
Closing Formal: Very truly yours,
Informal: Sincerely yours,
In conversation: Mr. . . . *or* Mrs. . . . *or*
Sir *or* Madam

STATE SENATORS AND REPRESENTATIVES

Address like U.S. senators and representatives.

AMBASSADOR OF THE UNITED STATES

Address Business: The Honorable . . .
The Ambassador of the
United States
American Embassy
Address
Social: The Honorable . . .
and Mrs. . . .
Home address
or (for a woman ambassador) Mr. and Mrs. . . .
Salutation Formal: Sir: *or* Madam:
Informal: My Dear Mr. (*or* My Dear
Madam) Ambassador:
Closing Formal: Very truly yours,
Informal: Sincerely yours,
In conversation: My Dear Mr. (*or* Madam)
Ambassador *or* Sir (*or*
Madam)

CONSUL OF THE UNITED STATES

Address Business: Mr. . . .
American Consul
Address
Social: Mr. and Mrs. . . .
Home Address
Salutation Formal: Sir: *or* My Dear Sir:
Informal: Dear Mr. . . .
In conversation: Mr. . . .
Title of Introduction: Mr. . . .

AMBASSADOR OF A FOREIGN COUNTRY

Address	Business:	His Excellency, . . . The Ambassador of . . . Washington, D.C.
	Social:	His Excellency, . . . The Ambassador of . . . Home address
Salutation	Formal:	Excellency:
	Informal:	My Dear Mr. Ambassador:
Closing	Formal:	Very truly yours,
	Informal:	Sincerely yours,
	In conversation:	Mr. Ambassador *or* Excellency *or* Sir

GOVERNOR OF A STATE

Address	Business:	The Honorable . . . Governor of . . . (capital city, state)
	Social:	The Honorable . . . and Mrs. . . . Home address
Salutation	Formal:	Sir:
	Informal:	Dear Governor . . . :
Closing	Formal:	Very truly yours,
	In conversation:	Governor . . . *or* Sir

MAYOR

Address	Business:	His (*or* Her) Honor the Mayor City Hall Address
	Social:	His Honor the Mayor and Mrs. *or* (*for woman mayor*) Mr. and Mrs. Home address
Salutation	Formal:	Sir: *or* Madam:
	Informal:	Dear Mayor . . . :
Closing	Formal:	Very truly yours,
	In conversation:	Mr. (*or* Madam) Mayor

JUDGE

Address	Business:	The Honorable . . . Justice Appellate Division Supreme Court of the State of . . . Address
	Social:	The Honorable . . . and Mrs. . . . Home address
Salutation	Formal:	Sir: *or* Madam:
	Informal:	Dear Judge . . .
Closing	Formal:	Very truly yours,
	In conversation:	Mr. (*or* Madam) Justice

PROTESTANT CLERGYMAN

Address	Business:	The Reverend . . . *or* (if he holds the degree) The Reverend . . . , D.D.
	Social:	The Reverend . . . and Mrs. . . . Home address
Salutation	Formal:	Sir: *or* My Dear Sir:
	Informal:	Dear Mr. (*or* Dr.) . . . :
Closing	Formal:	Sincerely yours, *or* Faithfully yours,
	In conversation:	Mr. (*or* Dr.) . . . (*never* Reverend . . .)

RABBI

Address	Business:	Rabbi . . . *or* (if he holds the degree) Dr. . . . , D.D. Address of his synagogue
	Social:	Rabbi (*or* Dr.) and Mrs. . . . Home address
Salutation	Formal:	Dear Sir:
	Informal:	Dear Rabbi (*or* Dr.) . . .
Closing	Formal:	Sincerely yours,
	Informal:	Sincerely yours,
	In conversation:	Rabbi (*or* Dr.)

CATHOLIC PRIEST

Address	Business:	The Reverend . . . (and the initials of his order, if needed) Address of his church
Salutation	Formal:	Reverend Father:
	Informal:	Dear Father . . . :
Closing	Formal:	I remain, Reverend Father, yours faithfully,
	Informal:	Faithfully yours,
	In conversation:	Father *or* Father . . . *or* Your Reverence

OFFICERS OF THE ARMED SERVICES

(Commander or higher in the Navy; captain or higher in the Air Force, Army, and Marines)

Address	Business:	Admiral . . . , USN *or* Colonel . . . , USMC *or* General . . . , USA *or* USAF (plus any title) Address of base, ship, or government department
	Social:	Admiral (*or* Colonel *or* General) and Mrs. . . . Home address
Salutation	Formal:	Sir:
	Informal:	My Dear Admiral (*or* Colonel *or* General) . . . :
Closing	Formal:	Very truly yours,
	Informal:	Sincerely yours,

PHYSICIAN

Address	Business:	. . . , M.D. Office address
	Social:	Dr. and Mrs. . . . Home address
Salutation	Formal:	Dear Sir:
	Informal:	Dear Dr. . . . :
Closing	Formal:	Very truly yours,
	Informal:	Sincerely yours,

COLLEGE (OR UNIVERSITY) PROFESSOR

Address	Business:	Professor *or* (if he holds the Ph.D. degree) Dr. *or* Mr. . . . Office address
	Social:	Professor (*or* Dr. *or* Mr.) and Mrs. . . .
Salutation	Formal:	Dear Sir:
	Informal:	Dear Professor (*or* Dr. *or* Mr.) . . .
Closing	Formal:	Very truly yours,
	Informal:	Sincerely yours,
	In conversation:	Professor (*or* Dr.) . . . (within the college); Mr. . . . (elsewhere)

SPELL IT RIGHT!

Here are five tips to better spelling:

1. Keep a list of your spelling errors and study them.
2. Learn to spell the most commonly misspelled words. (See opposite page.)
3. Use newly acquired words and make them a part of your oral and written vocabulary.
4. When in doubt as to the correct spelling of a word, consult your dictionary.
5. Study the following rules. These will help you overcome many of the most common spelling pitfalls.

Which is it: -ant or **-ent? -ance** or **-ence?** If you know that a word ends in *-ant,* related words will always end in *-ance* and *-ancy.* And if a word ends in *-ent,* related words will end in *-ence* and *-ency.*

Here are 8 representative *-ant, -ance, -ancy* words: *acceptance, assistant, attendant, insurance, maintenance, relevancy, resistant, tolerant.* In the *-ent, -ence, -ency* group the following 12 words are troublesome to many people: *apparent, coincident, conference, confident, consistency, correspondent, dependent, existence, occurrence, persistent, reference, superintendent.*

Which is it: -cede, -ceed, or **sede?** There is only one word that ends in *-sede: supersede.* Only three words end in *-ceed: proceed* (but *procedure*), *exceed, succeed.* All other words with this phonetic sound end in *-cede: precede, recede, secede.*

Which is it: ie or **ei?** After *c,* when the sound is long *e,* the *e* usually precedes the *i* (ei): *ceiling, deceive, receipt, receive.*

After most other letters, the *i* precedes the *e* (ie): *achieve, believe, grief, lien, siege, thief.*

When the sound is not long *e,* and especially if the sound is long *a,* the *e* precedes the *i* (ei): *sleigh, veil, weigh.*

Which is it: -ary or **-ery?** Because the word endings *-ary* and *-ery* sound alike, they can cause spelling problems. However, one fact will solve most of the problems. More than 300 words end in *-ary;* only a few words end in *-ery.* If you learn these few you will conquer the difficulty: *artillery, bakery, brewery, celery, cemetery, confectionery, distillery, dysentery, millinery, monastery, refinery, stationery* (writing paper).

Which is it: -ar, -er, or **-or?** Here are two tips on *-ar, -er,* and *-or* words. First, the ending *-ar* is not common. All you need do is to learn a few common *-ar* words such as *beggar, cedar, collar, dollar, liar, registrar, scholar,* and *similar.*

The more confusing endings are *-er* and *-or.* So here's a second tip: For simple, common words *-er* is usually the right ending. The Latin *-or* goes with advanced words.

In American English *-re* is not a common ending. Learn the correct spelling of these six *-re* words: *acre, lucre, macabre, massacre, mediocre, ogre.*

Which is it: -al, -el, or **-le?** No good rule has ever been devised to help you decide whether a word ends in *-al, -el,* or *-le.* Pronunciation will not help you either, because all three sound alike when spoken.

You must try to memorize the spelling of words with these endings. When in doubt, consult your dictionary.

Which is it: -able or **-ible?** Two points about *-able* and *-ible* simplify the decision as to which spelling is correct:

1. *-able* is the basic form. Many more words end in *-able* than in *-ible.*
2. An *a* for an *a* and an *i* for an *i*: If the adjective is closely related to a noun that ends in *-ation,* the adjective is almost certain to end in *-able.* If a related noun ends in *-ion* instead of *-ation,* the adjective is pretty sure to end in *-ible.*

Which is it: c or **ck?** If a word ends in a *c,* you must add a *k* before a suffix beginning with *e, i,* or *y* to keep the *c* hard: *frolic* becomes *frolicking; mimic* becomes *mimicking; panic* becomes *panicking; picnic* becomes *picnicking* and *picnicker; traffic* becomes *trafficking* and *trafficker.*

The final -e rule: A final silent *e* is usually dropped before a suffix beginning with a vowel (like *-able, -ion, -ing*): *blam(e)able, confus(e)ion, hop(e)ing.* But a final silent *e* is retained before a consonant: *blameworthy, hopeless.*

Which is it: -efy or **-ify?** The ending *-ify* is much more common than *-efy.* In fact, words ending in *-efy* may be considered exceptions. Here are some *-efy* words (the exceptions): *liquefy, putrefy, rarefy, stupefy.*

Which is it: -ise, -ize, or **-yze?** The usual suffix is *-ize,* and *-yze* and *-ise* are rather rare exceptions. Only two common words end in *-yze: analyze* and *paralyze.* Only about 30 common words end in *-ise: advertise, comprise, despise, exercise,* among them.

Which is it: -ly or **-ally ?** When the original ends in *-ic,* the adverb-making suffix sometimes is *-ally* instead of *-ly,* as in *artistically* and *fantastically.* One common word ending in *-ic* that is made into an adverb by adding only *-ly* is *public;* the adverb is *publicly.*

When is a final y changed to i ? If a word ends in *y* preceded by a consonant (any letter other than *a, e, i, o, u*), change the *y* to an *i* when you add a suffix. Here are some examples: *ally* becomes *allies* and *allied; city* becomes *cities; duty* becomes *duties* and *dutiful.*

SPELLING DEMONS

SIXTH GRADE SPELLING DEMONS

Here are some of the words most frequently misspelled by sixth-graders. Many adults still misspell some of them. Check yourself to see if you need to relearn any of these words.

accommodate	athletics	challenge	February	Halloween	separate
across	balloon	coming	forth	minute	similar
already	bicycle	deceive	fourth	missile	sincerely
arithmetic	business	describe	good night	niece	surprise
athlete	ceiling	description	grammar	really	writing

HIGH SCHOOL SPELLING DEMONS

Here are some of the words taken from school and job-placement tests most frequently misspelled by high school seniors and graduates. How many of them do you find troublesome?

absence	conscious	dispensable	guidance	occasion	receive
absurd	convenient	embarrass	humorous	occurred	recommend
accidentally	correspondence	environment	immediately	omitted	repetition
advertisement	criticize	escape	independent	opportunity	restaurant
all right	definite	exaggerate	irresistible	parallel	rhythm
amateur	dependent	existence	laboratory	performance	schedule
attendance	descend	experience	lightning	permanent	success
believe	desperate	fascinate	losing	prejudice	tragedy
committee	develop	foreign	necessary	privilege	villain
condemn	difference	government	neighbor	professor	weird

CIVIL SERVICE WORDS

Since many people who take Civil Service exams are high school graduates, the words most frequently misspelled are much the same as those on high school lists. Civil Service spelling tests also show 24 more demons related to government and office work.

accident	enforcement	monetary	simplified
auxiliary	expedient	municipal	society
career	federal	personnel (*vs.* personal)	supervisor
clerical	filing (*vs.* filling)	president	technical
county (*vs.* country)	legality	responsibility	tendency
comptroller	mechanism	salary	yield

COLLEGE WORDS

This list contains words most often misspelled by students who have had two years of college. Demons from the high school list above are not repeated although many of those words continue to be misspelled by college and university students.

achieve	competition	desirable	exercise	noticeable	pronunciation
aggravate	conscientious	despair	grievance	occurrence	responsibility
appearance	convenience	dining	knowledge	permissible	superintendent
argument	council	disappear	maintenance	precede	supersede
athlete	definitely	enforcement	marriage	procedure	usage
cemetery	descend	exceed	mischievous	proceed	wholly

ADULT SPELLING DEMONS

Many business excutives and professionals with college degrees still have spelling problems. Here are some words they misspell most often, not repeating demons from the above lists.

accessible	assistant	coolly	incidentally	irritable	perseverance
acquainted	burglar	drunkenness	insistent	license	recognize
analyze	campaign	envelope	intercede	mortgage	seize

HOW DO THE EXPERTS DO?

Editors, writers, and English teachers are especially good spellers. The following list consists of 60 everyday words most often misspelled by such experts. How many can you spell correctly?

abscess	chrysanthemum	fission	inoculate	phlegm	sacrilegious
accelerator	connoisseur	fricassee	liquefy	picnicking	sheriff
aggressor	demagogue	fuselage	millennium	poliomyelitis	sieve
allotted	desiccate	gaiety	millionaire	prairie	subpoena
annihilate	dilapidated	gynecologist	miscellaneous	prescription	tariff
assassin	discriminate	harebrained	moccasin	propeller	tonsillitis
besiege	dissipate	hippopotamus	paraffin	questionnaire	tyranny
broccoli	ecstasy	hypocrisy	paralyze	raspberry	vacillate
catalyst	effervescent	immaculate	penitentiary	requiem	vengeance
category	exhilarate	innocuous	perspiration	rhinoceros	zephyr

WAYS TO BUILD YOUR VOCABULARY

Building a large vocabulary—understanding and using a wide variety of words—is important for success in almost any field. To build such a vocabulary sometimes requires bone-hard work.

Each person has three vocabularies.

First, there is an *active,* or *speaking,* vocabulary—the words we use every day in speaking.

Second, there is our *writing* vocabulary. It contains some words we do not use in speech.

Third, each person has a *recognition,* or *reading,* vocabulary, the largest of the three. Through this recognition vocabulary we can understand speakers and read books, magazines, and newspapers.

Consistent effort is needed to move words from our recognition to our active vocabulary.

Here are seven commonsense, time-tested suggestions for building your vocabulary:

1. Make friends with your dictionary. The most important element in vocabulary growth is the *will* to learn new words and to learn how to use them.

All reading and listening should lead straight to a good dictionary. You should actually *study* each word you look up. It requires only a moment to learn the spelling, pronunciation, or one meaning of a word. But hasty examination will prevent your mastering the word and adding it to your active vocabulary.

Equip yourself with a large dictionary that contains 100,000 words or more. It is unwise to buy a "cheap" dictionary when an excellent one can be purchased for only a few dollars more.

2. Learn a few basic word elements. Numerous word elements rarely appear independently but do form parts of longer words. Such elements, known as "combining forms," may be illustrated by "graph," as in *photograph, lithography, telegraph, phonograph, geography*; and "micro," as in *microphone, microscope, microcosm,* and *microfilm.*

3. Learn the meanings of common prefixes. A prefix is a letter of the alphabet (or a group of letters) put before a word to add to or qualify meaning. Understanding the meaning (or meanings) of constantly appearing prefixes, such as *anti-*, *post-*, and *pre-*, will build your vocabulary by making large numbers of words instantly recognizable and usable

4. Learn the meaning of common suffixes. A suffix is an element that is placed after a word or word root to make a term of different meaning or use, such as *-ful, -less, -ly,* or *-some.*

5. Make a study of synonyms. A synonym is a word having the same meaning, or nearly the same meaning, as another. A study of synonyms for the word "old" might add these words, among others, to your vocabulary: *aged, immemorial, ancient, aboriginal, hoary, antique, elderly, patriarchal, passé, venerable, antediluvian,* and *antiquated.*

6. Make a study of antonyms. An antonym is a word that is opposite in meaning to another word: *small* and *little* are antonyms of "large"; *happy* is an antonym of "sad."

Learning the opposite, or negative, of one or more of the meanings of another word will not be so valuable as studying synonyms, but the effort is worthwhile. Seeking antonyms for the verb *praise* may add these words, among others, to your vocabulary: *abuse, blame, censure, condemn, deprecate, disparage, impugn, inveigh against, lampoon, stigmatize, vilify.* The word *join,* for example, has such opposites as *cleave, disconnect, sever, separate,* and *sunder.*

These opposite meanings are not all-inclusive: A word may be an antonym of another only in a limited meaning. For example, one antonym of *man* (*woman*) concerns sex; another (*child*), age; another (*animal*), biology; another (*God*), religion. Like synonyms, antonyms must be selected carefully and used with exactness.

7. Use your vocabulary. How to use words exactly and emphatically is the most important phase of the problem of vocabulary building. It is indeed necessary to increase your vocabulary and not use words incorrectly. But the mere size of your vocabulary is not always a test of speaking or writing ability. Nor does it follow that if you stick to the principles of correct usage you will write effectively. Much dull and feeble speech and writing is correct, but correctness alone is a negative virtue. Using words clearly, exactly, strongly—that is most important and most difficult to do.

Who is the best conversationalist you know? What are the characteristics of his or her language? If you reply honestly, you will probably select a person whose speech seems *forceful* or *vivid* to you, someone who talks clearly, someone whose conversation is *smooth, logical, precise, animated.* Few will select a person whose talk is merely *correct.* Rarely will any comment be made on the niceties of conventional grammar, on violations of established usage, on subject-verb agreement, or on the right case of pronouns. True, the person you choose may use correct English—more often than not he or she will—but your remarks will not be "He uses correct English" nearly so often as "He's interesting to listen to."

Medicine and Health

Barbara McClintock, an 81-year-old New York genetic research scientist, was awarded the 1983 Nobel Prize for Medicine. Her studies in the 1940s and 1950s of mutations of corn led to the discovery of "jumping genes" and a greater understanding of cancer.

Wide World

HIGHLIGHTS: 1983

SOARING HEALTH COSTS

An average of $1,365 was spent for health care in 1982 for every man, woman, and child in the U.S. according to figures released by the Department of Health and Human Services in August 1983. This was more than three times the per capita amount spent just 10 years earlier in 1972—$437.77.

Altogether health-care costs in 1982 were $322.4 billion, an amount equal to 10.5% of the Gross National Product (GNP). They increased 12.5% over the expenditure of $286.6 billion in the previous year—three times the growth rate of the GNP.

Medicare and Medicaid payments by the federal and state governments were $83 billion in 1982, an increase of 14.9% over 1981.

The $135.5 billion spent for hospital care also represented a 14.9% increase over the previous year.

The spending for the services of physicians increased 12.8% to $61.8 billion.

Nursing-home care cost $27.3 billion and the services of dentists were $19.5 billion.

Some $22.4 billion was spent for drugs and medical supplies, with an additional $5.7 billion for eyeglasses and medical appliances.

EFFORTS TO CUT COSTS

Because governments and insurance companies pay most of the costs of health care in the U.S., doctors and hospitals have been able

HIGHLIGHTS: 1982 *(continued)*

to increase the amount they charge at a much higher rate than average price increases for other services and commodities.

Despite opposition from doctors and hospitals, the state of California embarked on a program in 1982 to cut health-care costs by introducing a system of competitive pricing.

Public-health officials believe the new system will save the state some $400 million in health-care costs in 1984.

Under the California system, the state contracts with hospitals on a competitive bidding basis to provide health services for indigent patients at a flat daily fee, without regard to the type of treatment they require.

In addition, private insurance companies in California can offer group health insurance at lower rates by contracting with physicians and hospitals to provide lower-cost medical services to their policy holders.

MYSTERIOUS AIDS DISEASE

The mysterious fatal disease AIDS (acquired immune deficiency syndrome) continued to spread in 1983 with doctors unable to determine either its cause or cure.

The U.S. Centers for Disease Control (CDC) in Atlanta had received reports on 2,678 cases of AIDS disease up to Nov. 7, 1983. In 1,102 cases the patients died. None of the remaining patients with AIDS have been cured.

The disease seemed to be spreading. New cases of AIDS were reported at a rate of about 50 a week during the second half of 1983, compared with 24 per week in January 1983 and 11 per week in July 1982.

Dr. James W. Curran, head of the AIDS task force of CDC, said that 71% of the AIDS victims were promiscuous homosexual men. Other groups identified by CDC at high risk in developing the disease were addicts who inject drugs intravenously, Haitians, hemophiliacs, and the children of AIDS victims.

CDC defines a case of AIDS as "a reliably diagnosed disease that is at least moderately indicative of an underlying cellular immunodeficiency in a person who has had no known cause of underlying cellular immunodeficiency or any other underlying reduced resistance reported to be associated with that disease."

CDC doctors believe that AIDS is transmitted sexually or by its introduction into the blood stream by hypodermic needles or transfusions.

The CDC said no AIDS cases have been documented among nurses, doctors, or laboratory workers caring for AIDS patients or processing laboratory specimens.

"To date," the CDC reported, "no person-to-person transmission has been identified other than through intimate contact or blood transfusion."

CDC doctors said research indicates that a period from a few months to two years may elapse from the time a victim is exposed to the disease and the time that the symptoms become recognizable as AIDS.

Because no specific test is known to detect AIDS, the Public Health Service asked all members of high-risk groups to cease donating blood or plasma for use by other persons.

The Public Health Service made the following recommendations for controlling the spread of the disease:

"1. Sexual contact should be avoided with persons known or suspected to have AIDS. Members of high-risk groups should be aware that multiple sexual partners increase the probability of developing AIDS.

"2. As a temporary measure, members of groups at increased risk for AIDS should refrain from donating plasma and/or blood. This recommendation includes all individuals belonging to such groups, even though many individuals are at little risk of AIDS. Centers collecting plasma and/or blood should inform potential donors of this recommendation. The Food and Drug Administration (FDA) is preparing new recommendations for manufacturers of plasma derivatives and for establishments collecting plasma or blood. This is an interim measure to protect recipients of blood products and blood until specific laboratory tests are available.

"3. Studies should be conducted to evaluate screening procedures for their effectiveness in identifying and excluding plasma and blood with a high probability of transmitting AIDS. These procedures should include specific laboratory tests as well as careful histories and physicial examinations.

"4. Physicians should adhere strictly to medical indications for transfusions, and autologous blood transfusions are encouraged.

"5. Work should continue toward development of safer blood products for use by hemophilia patients."

In addition the Public Health Service said, "As long as the cause remains unknown, the ability to understand the natural history of AIDS and to undertake preventive measures is somewhat compromised. However, the above recommendations are prudent measures that should reduce the risk of acquiring and transmitting AIDS."

The New York Academy of Sciences held a four-day meeting in November of medical researchers studying AIDS. Those present were in general agreement that they should search for a single virus or infectious agent that transmits AIDS. However, Dr. Joseph A. Sonnabend, editor of the AIDS research journal, said he believed the disease might be caused by the body being subjected to many types of infections rather than a single one.

LOOKING INSIDE THE BODY

A new method to look inside the body began to be used for research in more and more hospitals. The technique, called NMR (nuclear magnetic resonance), eliminates the use of X rays with their potential danger of excessive radiation. An NMR scanner costs about $1.5 million.

Some researchers believe that the use of NMR to look inside the living body and see how it functions will revolutionize treatment in most fields of medicine.

NMR uses a powerful magnetic field and radio waves instead of X rays to photograph the interior of the body. The technique depends on computer enhancement developed by the National Aeronautics and Space Agency (NASA) to improve the quality of photographs transmitted by radio from space satellites and space probes.

In NMR a patient is placed inside a large magnetic coil, and the magnetic field is turned on. The magnetic field affects the atoms in certain molecules and causes them to align with the magnetic field lines. (Similar to iron filings lining up on a sheet of paper held over a magnet.) A field of radio energy is beamed through the patient, causing a slightly different alignment. When the radio waves are turned off, the molecules oscillate, emitting weak radio signals that provide a photographic image of the inside of the body.

NMR can be used with a patient repeatedly with no known side effects. This is unlike X rays, which have the potential of causing genetic damage or cancer.

VISITING THE DOCTOR

Americans make an average of 2.6 office visits to physicians each year, according to results from a 1981 survey made by the U.S. Public Health Service's National Center for Health Statistics.

Women make about 60% of the visits to doctors' offices, with those 65 and older averaging 4.5 visits per year.

Young men aged 15 to 24 have the fewest doctor visits, averaging only 1.3 each year.

With a total of 585,177,000 office visits each year, physicians with general or family practices accounted for nearly one-third—189,966,000. Surgeons had 31.4% of the visits, and doctors with medical specialities received 31.3%. Psychiatrists had only 2.7% of all office visits.

Almost two-thirds of the visits, 64.2%, were made by a patient returning for further help with a medical problem the doctor already was treating.

The single most common reason for an office visit was to receive a general medical examination, accounting for 30,222,000 visits. Second was for a prenatal examination, 23,501,000, and third was a postoperative visit, 18,071,000.

Among the patients visiting doctors' offices the most common diagnosis was of respiratory diseases, such as a common cold, which accounted for 12.5%. The second most common were diseases of the circulatory system, 10%, and third were diseases of the nervous system and sense organs, 9.7%.

In 60.5% of all office visits, the physician prescribed medication. The most common drugs used were antibiotics, prescribed 13.7% of the time. Second were analgesic and antipyretic drugs, such as aspirin, prescribed 9% of the time.

Some 73% of the visits lasted less than 15 minutes, not counting time spent by the patient waiting in the reception room.

SWEETS CAUSE SLEEP

Researchers at Boston University School of Medicine reported that increasing the amount of sugar in the diet makes children and adults sleepy, rather than aggressive or hyperactive.

The researchers suggested that a nursing mother with a baby who has difficulty falling asleep should eat a candy bar before the evening feeding.

GENE-SPLICE TEST DELAYED

The first field test of a gene-engineered organism had been approved by the National Institutes of Health to take place In October. However, the test was delayed indefinitely by the University of California because of threatened court suits by opponents of gene-splicing.

The test was to have been conducted at Tule Lake, Calif., by spraying a potato field with gene-engineered bacteria believed capable of making the plants resistant to frost damage.

Opponents had announced that they planned to ask a federal court for a restraining order to prevent the experiment. They claimed the frost-preventing bacteria might cause unknown danger to the environment if they escaped from the potato field. They said the bacteria might make other plants resistant to frost, change their growing season, and affect animals and insects dependent upon them.

Meanwhile, scientists at the Lawrence Berkeley Laboratory in California announced that they had identified for the first time the five genes that regulate photosynthesis.

James E. Hearst, a chemistry professor who headed the research team, said the discovery opened the door to new ways to produce energy and practical applications for increasing food production.

RISING HEALTH COSTS IN THE U.S.: 1935–1990

Source: Health Care Financing Administration, Dept. of Health and Human Services, by fiscal years

YEAR	TOTAL SPENT	AV. SPENT PER PERSON	HOSPITAL CARE	PHYSICIANS' SERVICES	DENTISTS' SERVICES	MEDICINES AND SUPPLIES
1935	$ 3,600,000,000	$ 29.49	$ 700,000,000	$ 1,000,000,000	$ 500,000,000	$ 600,000,000
1940	$ 3,978,000,000	$ 29.62	$ 1,011,000,000	$ 973,000,000	$ 419,000,000	$ 637,000,000
1950	$ 12,662,000,000	$ 81.86	$ 3,851,000,000	$ 2,747,000,000	$ 961,000,000	$ 1,726,000,000
1960	$ 26,895,000,000	$ 146.30	$ 9,062,000,000	$ 5,684,000,000	$ 1,977,000,000	$ 3,657,000,000
1965	$ 41,749,000,000	$ 210.98	$ 13,878,000,000	$ 8,473,000,000	$ 2,809,000,000	$ 5,180,000,000
1968	$ 56,169,000,000	$ 284.64	$ 20,999,000,000	$ 11,104,000,000	$ 3,673,000,000	$ 6,421,000,000
1970	$ 74,663,000,000	$ 357.90	$ 27,756,000,000	$ 14,340,000,000	$ 4,750,000,000	$ 7,996,000,000
1971	$ 83,284,000,000	$ 394.23	$ 30,817,000,000	$ 15,918,000,000	$ 5,068,000,000	$ 8,579,000,000
1972	$ 93,493,000,000	$ 437.77	$ 34,938,000,000	$ 17,162,000,000	$ 5,625,000,000	$ 9,335,000,000
1973	$103,161,000,000	$ 478.34	$ 38,681,000,000	$ 19,075,000,000	$ 6,531,000,000	$10,056,000,000
1974	$116,379,000,000	$ 534.63	$ 44,780,000,000	$ 21,245,000,000	$ 7,366,000,000	$10,999,000,000
1975	$132,720,000,000	$ 603.57	$ 52,106,000,000	$ 24,932,000,000	$ 8,237,000,000	$11,940,000,000
1976	$149,655,000,000	$ 674.14	$ 59,888,000,000	$ 27,565,000,000	$ 9,448,000,000	$13,022,000,000
1977	$169,248,000,000	$ 754.81	$ 67,761,000,000	$ 31,852,000,000	$10,535,000,000	$14,066,000,000
1978	$189,325,000,000	$ 835.57	$ 75,700,000,000	$ 35,807,000,000	$11,779,000,000	$15,413,000,000
1979	$214,612,000,000	$ 936.92	$ 85,665,000,000	$ 40,692,000,000	$13,502,000,000	$17,186,000,000
1980	$249,000,000,000	$1,075.00	$100,400,000,000	$ 46,800,000,000	$15,400,000,000	$19,300,000,000
1981	$286,600,000,000	$1,225.00	$118,000,000,000	$ 54,800,000,000	$17,300,000,000	$21,400,000,000
1982	$322,400,000,000	$1,365.00	$135,500,000,000	$ 61,800,000,000	$19,500,000,000	$22,400,000,000
1985*	$456,000,000,000	$1,930.00	$191,597,000,000	$ 87,385,200,000	$27,573,000,000	$31,673,600,000
1990*	$756,000,000,000	$3,200.00	$317,667,820,000	$144,884,660,000	$45,716,034,000	$52,514,828,000

* Estimates

DANGEROUS DISEASES IN THE UNITED STATES: 1965–1981

Source: U.S. Centers for Disease Control

	1970		1975		1979		1980		1981	
	Cases	Rate [1]	Cases	Rate [1]	Cases	Rate [1]	Cases	Rate [1]	Cases	Rate [1]
Amebiasis	2,888	1.42	2,775	1.30	4,107	1.90	5,271	2.38	6,632	2.96
Anthrax	2	0.00	2	0.00	—	0.00	1	0.00	—	0.00
Aseptic meningitis	6,480	3.18	4,475	2.10	8,754	4.05	8,028	3.61	9,547	4.16
Botulism	12	0.01	20	0.01	45	0.02	89	0.04	103	0.04
Brucellosis (undulant fever)	213	0.10	310	0.15	215	0.10	183	0.08	185	0.08
Chicken pox	—	—	154,248	72.38	199,081	102.93	190,894	96.69	200,766	100.48
Diphtheria	435	0.21	307	0.14	59	0.03	3	0.00	5	0.00
Encephalitis, primary [2]	1,580	0.78	4,064	1.91	1,504	0.68	1,362	0.60	1,478	0.64
Encephalitis, postinfectious	370	0.18	237	0.11	84	0.04	40	0.02	38	0.02
Hepatitis A	56,797	27.87	35,855	16.82	30,407	13.82	29,087	12.84	25,802	11.25
Hepatitis B	8,310	4.08	13,121	6.16	15,452	7.02	19,015	8.39	21,152	9.22
Hepatitis, unspecified	—	—	7,158	3.36	10,534	4.79	11,894	5.25	10,975	4.79
Leprosy	129	0.06	162	0.08	185	0.08	223	0.10	256	0.11
Leptospirosis	47	0.02	93	0.04	94	0.04	85	0.04	82	0.04
Malaria	3,051	1.50	373	0.18	894	0.11	2,062	0.91	1,388	0.61
Measles (rubeola)	47,351	23.23	24,374	11.44	13,597	6.18	13,506	5.96	3,124	1.36
Meningococcal infections	2,505	1.23	1,478	0.69	2,724	1.24	2,840	1.25	3,525	1.54
Mumps	104,953	55.55	59,647	27.99	14,225	6.55	8,576	3.86	4,941	2.20
Pertussis (whooping cough)	4,249	2.08	1,738	0.82	1,623	0.74	1,730	0.76	1,248	0.54
Poliomyelitis, total	33	0.02	8	0.00	34	0.02	9	0.00	6	0.00
Paralytic	31	0.02	8	0.00	26	0.01	8	0.00	6	0.00
Psittacosis	35	0.02	49	0.02	137	0.06	124	0.05	124	0.05
Rabies in man	2	0.00	2	0.00	4	0.00	—	0.00	2	0.00
Rheumatic fever, acute [3]	3,227	2.45	2,854	2.01	629	0.44	432	0.30	264	0.17
Rubella (German measles)	56,552	27.75	16,652	7.81	11,795	5.36	3,904	1.72	2,077	0.91
Rubella, congenital [4]	77	0.04	30	0.01	62	0.03	50	0.01	19	0.01
Salmonellosis	22,096	10.84	22,612	10.61	33,138	15.06	33,715	14.88	39,990	17.44
Shigellosis (dysentery)	13,845	6.79	16,584	7.78	20,135	9.15	19,041	8.41	19,859	8.66
Tetanus	148	0.07	102	0.05	81	0.04	95	0.04	72	0.03
Trichinosis	109	0.05	252	0.12	157	0.07	131	0.06	206	0.10
Tuberculosis [5]	37,137	18.22	33,989	15.95	27,669	12.57	27,749	12.25	27,373	11.94
Tularemia	172	0.08	129	0.06	196	0.09	234	0.10	288	0.13
Typhoid fever	346	0.17	375	0.18	528	0.24	510	0.23	584	0.25
Typhus fever, flea-borne	27	0.01	41	0.02	69	0.03	81	0.04	61	0.03
Typhus fever, tick-borne	380	0.19	844	0.40	1,070	0.49	1,163	0.52	1,192	0.52
Venereal diseases										
Syphilis	91,382	45.30	80,356	37.70	67,049	30.68	68,832	30.39	72,799	31.98
Gonorrhea	600,072	297.47	999,937	469.19	1,004,058	459.49	1,004,029	443.27	990,864	435.24

1 Rate per 100,000 population. 2 Includes indeterminate category. 3 Not all states reporting. 4 Data prior to 1974 not comparable to later data. 5 Rate per 1,000 live births.

MAJOR CONTAGIOUS DISEASES

DISEASE	CAUSE	INCUBATION	SYMPTOMS	DURATION	DANGERS	PREVENTION
Chicken pox or varicella	Virus; contact with infected person; breathing infectious droplets	10 to 20 days	Fever; loss of appetite; red itchy rash; pus forms crusts	About 2 weeks	Scratching rash can cause infection and scars	None; having chicken pox causes future immunity
Common cold	Viruses; contact with infected person; breathing infectious droplets	18 to 48 hours	Stuffy or runny nose; headache; sore throat; coughing	Several days to several weeks	Can weaken resistance to other diseases	None; improve general physical condition by drinking orange juice and taking vitamins
Diphtheria	Bacillus; contact with infected person	2 to 5 days	Like cold; high fever; gray membrane in throat	Several weeks	Can be fatal without medical treatment	Immunization; begin at age 2 months
Flu or influenza	Viruses; contact with infected person; breathing infectious germs	1 to 4 days	Fever; chills; aches and pains; weakness	Few days to few weeks	Can lead to fatal pneumonia	Immunization against certain strains of viruses
Measles or rubeola	Virus; contact with infected person	2 to 3 weeks	Fever as high as 106°; pink rash	Several weeks	Weakens resistance to diseases	Immunization; begin at age 1 year
Mono, mononucleosis, or glandular fever	Virus; direct contact with infected person, such as kissing	Few days to few weeks	Fever; fatigue; headache; swollen glands in neck	Usually 3 to 6 weeks	Can lead to hepatitis	None
Mumps or parotitis	Virus; contact with saliva of infected person	2 to 3 weeks	Painful swelling of face and neck; fever up to 104°	Usually 2 to 3 weeks	Can lead to other serious diseases	Immunization; especially important for men; begin at age 1 year
Pinworms or seatworms	Parasitic worm; contact with worm eggs	Few days	Itching around rectum; mild stomach pain	Not limited	Go to doctor for treatment	None; eggs are not killed by disinfectants and stay alive in dust
Pneumonia	Bacteria; viruses; foreign matter in lungs	Variable	Chills; chest pain; hard dry cough	Several weeks	Cause of many deaths	None; especially dangerous to pre-school children and elderly persons
Polio, poliomyelitis, or infantile paralysis	Virus; not known how it spreads	Few days to few weeks	Fever; headache; vomiting; drowsiness; stiff neck and back	No known cure	Can cause death or paralysis	Immunization; important for persons of all ages; begin at age 2 months
Rubella, German measles, or three-day measles	Virus; contact with victim	2 to 3 weeks	Mild fever; sore throat; rash	Few days	In pregnant woman causes birth defects in baby	Immunization; important for women before pregnancy; begin at age 1 year
Scarlet fever or scarlatina	Streptococcus bacteria	2 to 5 days	Vomiting; headache; fever; bright red rash; very red tongue	Several weeks	Can lead to kidney disease	None; having scarlet fever usually causes future immunity
Smallpox	Virus; breathing infectious droplets; contact with victim's belongings	10 to 14 days	Fever; headache; nausea; red pus-filled spots	Several weeks	Causes death or leaves deep scars	Vaccination; very important for all persons
Tetanus or lockjaw	Bacteria invade body through wounds	Few days to few weeks	Muscle spasms; locking of jaw muscles	Variable	Causes death unless treated	Immunization; germs live in dust, so any dirt in wound can cause disease
Tuberculosis, TB, or consumption	Bacteria in air, in dust, in unpasteurized milk	Variable	Persistent cough; fatigue; loss of weight	Several years	Causes death unless treated	None; do not drink unpasteurized milk; keep away from persons who have tuberculosis
Whooping cough or pertussis	Bacteria; very contagious	1 to 2 weeks	Like heavy cold; vomiting; deep cough	Several weeks	Causes death unless treated	Immunization; especially important for infants

HEART AND ARTERY DISEASE: NO. 1 KILLER

Source: American Heart Association; U.S. Department of Health and Human Services

Nearly 1,000,000 Americans die each year of heart and artery diseases—over twice as many as die of cancer and about 20 times as many as are killed in automobile accidents. An estimated 42.8 million Americans have various forms of heart and artery disease, and the economic cost of cardiovascular disease amounts to about $64.4 billion annually.

CORONARY HEART DISEASE

Coronary heart disease is the most frequent and dangerous form of heart disease among adults, afflicting about 4.6 million. It causes over 60% of heart-disease deaths in persons between the ages of 45 and 64. Coronary heart disease usually develops as a result of the buildup of cholesterol and other fatty substances in the arteries that supply the heart with blood.

WATCH YOUR BLOOD PRESSURE!

The most prevalent cause of heart and artery diseases is high blood pressure, also called *hypertension.*

Over 37 million Americans have high blood pressure, which can lead to hardening of the arteries (arteriosclerosis), coronary heart attacks, and stroke.

High blood pressure usually can be brought under control once it has been diagnosed. But often by the time it has been discovered, damage already has been done to the heart and to the arteries.

Consequently it is very important for persons of all ages to have their blood pressure checked regularly by a doctor.

Normal blood pressure for adults aged 18 to 45 is 120/80. The first number is the *systolic* pressure, when the heart is contracting. The second number is the *diastolic* pressure, when the heart is relaxed and filling. Systolic pressures over 140 and diastolic pressures over 90 often require treatment.

TREATMENT OF HIGH BLOOD PRESSURE

High blood pressure cannot be cured. However, it can be brought under control, so that it may not cause damage to the heart and other body systems. Therefore, the person who has high blood pressure often must continue treatment for the disease for the rest of his life.

The usual treatment for mild cases of high blood pressure is a change of diet to reduce the amount of sodium taken into the body. Because table salt is the commonest source of sodium in food, the diet usually calls for eating salt-free foods.

For severe cases of high blood pressure a doctor usually prescribes antihypertensive drugs.

A wide range of antihypertensive drugs can be used to bring down the blood pressure. Often a doctor and patient have to work together for some time to find which of these drugs can control the patient's blood pressure with the fewest undesirable side effects.

PREVENTING HIGH BLOOD PRESSURE

Although doctors do not know all the causes of high blood pressure, they do know that overweight people and cigarette smokers have a tendency to high blood pressure. Emotions and worry also can cause blood pressure to rise, so regular relaxation and adequate sleep and rest are desirable for all persons.

STROKE

About 164,000 persons die each year as a result of a *stroke,* a medical condition occurring when the brain receives an insufficient supply of blood. Most major strokes result from *cerebral thrombosis,* a blood clot formed in a major artery; *cerebral hemorrhage,* when an artery in the brain ruptures; or *cerebral embolism,* when a clot forms in another part of the body, then moves to clog an artery that supplies the brain.

RHEUMATIC HEART DISEASE

In children, when a streptococcal sore throat is not properly treated, rheumatic fever may result, damaging the heart. Over 2 million adult Americans have rheumatic heart disease.

The heart disease that results from rheumatic fever causes about 8,000 deaths a year, usually after the age of 21. This highlights the importance of taking your child to a doctor when he develops a bad sore throat, so that it can be correctly treated to avoid rheumatic fever.

CONGENITAL HEART DEFECTS

About 25,000 babies each year are born with a heart defect, the leading cause of heart-disease deaths among infants. About 6,500 people, primarily babies and older children, die each year from these congenital heart defects. Many of the defects can be corrected by surgery if detected early enough.

PULMONARY HEART DISEASES

These are heart diseases of the right ventricle of the heart, which pumps all of the blood through the vessels of the lungs. These diseases may develop as a result of chronic bronchitis or emphysema.

FIRST AID FOR EMERGENCIES

BASIC MEASURES, INCLUDING BURNS

Do NOT move an injured person, especially if the injuries have been caused by a fall, crash, or other violence. *Only* move an injured person to save him from further danger.

Act fast if the victim is in danger of dying of bleeding, suffocation, burns, or shock. If breathing stops, a person may die within three minutes.

Keep the victim lying quietly. Keep him warm with blankets, but do not overheat him.

If the victim has vomited—and there is no danger of the neck being broken—turn his body and head to one side to prevent choking.

Call a doctor. Ask what steps to take until the doctor can get there.

Examine the person gently. Do NOT pull clothing away from burns.

Do NOT wash third-degree burns. Cover them immediately with sterile dressing. (Third-degree burns are those destroying tissue in the deepest layer of the skin.)

Always expect shock and be ready to treat shock (see advice in second column).

Reassure the victim while keeping yourself calm.

Do NOT give liquids to an unconscious or semiconscious person. Fluids may enter his windpipe and cause suffocation.

Do NOT try to awaken an unconscious person by slapping, shaking, or shouting.

Do NOT give alcohol to a badly injured person.

USE PRESSURE TO STOP BLEEDING

Stop the bleeding by direct pressure on or around the wound. If the wound is very wide, you may have to press directly *in* the wound to stop the bleeding.

Apply constant pressure. Do NOT release the pressure every few seconds to see if the bleeding has stopped.

Raise wounded arms or legs, if there are no other complicating injuries. Raising the injured limb as high as possible causes less blood to flow into it.

If bleeding does not stop from pressure, an artery or vein may be cut. Apply pressure on arteries to cut off the flow of blood from the heart to the wound:

For a hand wound, press your thumbs hard on the inside of the wrist.

For an arm wound, press your fingers on the inside of the arm just below the armpit.

For a leg wound, press the heel of the palm of your hand against the inside of the leg just below the groin.

For a face wound, press your fingers under the side of the jaw.

For a scalp wound, press against the side of the head just in front of the ear.

For a neck or head wound, press on the neck just below and forward of the ear.

A tourniquet may be used to stop bleeding from a severe arm or leg wound when other measures have failed. Place the tourniquet just above the wound. If the wound is in or just below a joint area, place the tourniquet immediately above the joint. Make sure the tourniquet is at least 2″ wide. Tighten it *only enough* to stop the bleeding. The tourniquet should NOT be loosened except on advice of a physician. Note time it was applied and attach note to patient.

MOUTH-TO-MOUTH RESUSCITATION

Remove any obstruction to breathing from inside the victim's mouth, such as food, gum, or mud.

Place victim on back with mouth up.

Pull victim's jaw open and forward, and continue to hold it this way throughout resuscitation.

Pinch victim's nose closed.

Blow into the victim's mouth. Then remove your mouth and listen for an outward rush of air from the victim. If there is none, again check the victim's mouth for obstructions.

Continue blowing into the victim's mouth. *For an adult,* blow 12 deep breaths each minute. *For a child,* blow 20 shallow breaths each minute.

CLOSED-CHEST HEART MASSAGE

Start massage IMMEDIATELY after the heart stops.

Place one hand on top of the other on victim's chest at bottom of breastbone.

Apply pressure with heel of bottom hand, pushing downward about 2 inches.

Repeat the pressure 60 times a minute.

HOW TO HELP A POISON VICTIM

Dilute the poison by having the victim drink water or milk. The first minute may be the most critical.

Induce vomiting, if the victim is conscious, by placing a finger down the victim's throat.

Do NOT induce vomiting if the victim is unconscious or if the victim has swallowed acid, ammonia, cleaning fluid, drain cleaner, lye, or a petroleum product, such as gasoline.

Call a doctor *after* you have diluted the poison. Otherwise the victim may die while you are phoning.

Save the poison container and remaining poison. Take both with you when you take the victim to a hospital or to a doctor.

EMERGENCY TREATMENT FOR SHOCK

When a person goes into shock, he becomes pale and his skin feels cold and clammy. He breathes rapidly.

Raise the victim's feet higher than his head, unless he has a head injury.

Keep the victim warm with blankets, but too much heat can be harmful.

Give the victim a nonalcoholic drink containing sugar or salt, if the victim is fully conscious.

Do NOT give any liquid if the victim is unconscious or has a possible abdominal injury.

Talk reassuringly to the victim and hold his hand.

HOW TO HELP A CHOKING VICTIM

Stand behind the person. Hug the person by wrapping your arms around his waist. Let his head and upper body hang forward.

Clench one of your hands as a fist. Grasp the wrist of that hand with your other hand, so the fist is against the victim's stomach, just below the ribs and above the navel.

With all your strength, pull your fist into the victim's stomach with a quick upward jerk. Repeat until the food is forced out of the victim's throat.

GROWTH OF THE AMERICAN LIFE SPAN

Source: U.S. Public Health Service

YEAR	LIFE SPAN (in yrs.)	YEAR	LIFE SPAN (in yrs.)	YEAR	LIFE SPAN (in yrs.)	YEAR	LIFE SPAN (in yrs.)	YEAR	LIFE SPAN (in yrs.)	YEAR	LIFE SPAN (in yrs.)
1900	47.3	1935	61.7	1958	69.6	1965	70.2	1971	71.1	1977	73.2
1910	50.0	1940	62.9	1960	69.7	1966	70.1	1972	71.1	1978	73.3
1915	54.5	1945	65.9	1961	70.2	1967	70.5	1973	71.3	1979	73.8
1920	54.1	1950	68.2	1962	70.0	1968	70.2	1974	71.9	1980	73.6
1925	59.0	1955	69.6	1963	69.6	1969	70.4	1975	72.5	1981	74.1
1930	59.7	1957	69.5	1964	70.2	1970	70.9	1976	72.8	1982	74.5

LIFE EXPECTANCY BY AGE, SEX, AND RACE*

Source: U.S. Public Health Service

AGE	AVERAGE YEARS OF LIFE REMAINING								
	TOTAL POPULATION			WHITE POPULATION			OTHER POPULATION		
	Both Sexes	Male	Female	Both Sexes	Male	Female	Both Sexes	Male	Female
Under 1 year	74.5	70.8	78.2	75.1	71.4	78.7	70.9	66.5	75.2
1– 5 years	74.3	70.7	78.0	74.8	71.3	78.4	71.0	66.7	75.3
5–10 years	70.5	66.8	74.1	71.0	67.4	74.5	67.2	62.9	71.5
10–15 years	65.6	61.9	69.2	66.1	62.5	69.6	62.4	58.1	66.6
15–20 years	60.7	57.1	64.3	61.2	57.6	64.7	57.5	53.2	61.7
20–25 years	56.0	52.4	59.4	56.4	53.0	59.8	52.7	48.5	56.8
25–30 years	51.3	47.9	54.6	51.7	48.4	55.0	48.1	44.1	52.0
30–35 years	46.6	43.2	49.7	47.0	43.7	50.1	43.6	39.7	47.3
35–40 years	41.9	38.6	44.9	42.2	39.1	45.3	39.1	35.4	42.6
40–45 years	37.2	34.0	40.2	37.5	34.4	40.5	34.6	31.1	38.0
45–50 years	32.6	29.6	35.5	32.9	29.9	35.8	30.4	27.0	33.6
50–55 years	28.3	25.3	31.0	28.5	25.6	31.3	26.3	23.2	29.3
55–60 years	24.2	21.4	26.7	24.4	21.6	26.9	22.7	19.8	25.4
60–65 years	20.3	17.7	22.6	20.4	17.8	22.8	19.2	16.6	21.7
65–70 years	16.8	14.4	18.8	16.8	14.5	18.8	16.2	13.8	18.2
70–75 years	13.6	11.6	15.2	13.6	11.6	15.2	13.3	11.4	15.0
75–80 years	10.7	9.1	11.9	10.7	9.0	11.9	10.9	9.2	12.2
80–85 years	8.2	7.0	9.0	8.2	6.9	9.0	8.6	7.2	9.6
85 or older	6.2	5.2	6.7	6.1	5.2	6.6	6.6	5.3	7.5

* Data for 1982.

LEADING CAUSES OF DEATH AMONG AMERICANS

Source: U.S. Public Health Service

CAUSE OF DEATH	NUMBER OF DEATHS 1982	NUMBER OF DEATHS 1970	DEATH RATE PER 100,000 1982	DEATH RATE PER 100,000 1970
Heart & artery diseases	813,980	800,818	351.6	394.2
Chronic heart diseases	266,920	344,175	115.2	169.4
Sudden heart attack	295,010	357,241	127.4	175.8
Arteriosclerosis	26,550	31,682	11.5	15.6
Rheumatic fever	6,690	14,889	2.9	7.3
Hypertensive heart	23,700	14,991	10.2	7.3
Hypertension	7,830	8,273	3.4	4.1
Cancer	435,550	330,730	188.1	162.8
Lungs	116,270	69,517	50.2	34.2
Digestive organs	112,180	94,703	48.5	46.6
Genital organs	47,690	41,190	20.6	20.3
Breast	37,500	29,917	16.2	14.7
Urinary organs	18,730	15,514	8.1	7.6
Leukemia	17,130	14,492	7.4	7.1
Mouth and pharynx	8,430	7,612	3.6	3.7
Other cancer	77,620	57,785	33.5	28.4
Stroke	159,630	207,166	68.9	101.9
Cerebral thrombosis	28,680	57,845	12.4	28.5
Cerebral hemorrhage	20,210	41,379	8.7	20.4
Other cerebrovascular diseases	110,740	107,942	47.8	53.1
Accidents	95,680	114,638	41.3	56.4
Motor vehicle	46,630	54,633	20.1	26.9
All other accidents	49,050	60,006	21.2	29.5
Violent deaths	50,180	40,328	21.6	19.9
Suicides	27,860	23,480	12.0	11.6
Homicides	22,320	16,848	9.6	8.3
Pneumonia	49,690	59,032	21.5	29.0
Diabetes	33,220	38,324	14.3	18.9

CAUSE OF DEATH	NUMBER OF DEATHS 1982	NUMBER OF DEATHS 1970	DEATH RATE PER 100,000 1982	DEATH RATE PER 100,000 1970
Ill-defined conditions	29,880	25,781	12.9	12.7
Cirrhosis of the liver	27,250	31,399	11.8	15.5
Infant mortality	20,760	43,205	9.0	21.3
Injuries in birth	6,040	22,801	2.6	11.2
Other infant diseases	14,720	20,404	6.4	10.0
Nephritis and nephrosis	18,390	8,877	7.9	4.4
Emphysema	13,110	16,824	5.7	8.3
Congenital defects	12,710	22,721	5.5	11.2
Blood poisoning	11,340	3,535	4.9	1.7
Peptic ulcer	7,240	8,607	3.1	4.2
Benign tumors	6,840	4,828	3.0	2.4
Hernia and intestinal obstructions	4,960	7,235	2.1	3.6
Bronchitis	3,550	7,156	1.5	3.5
Anemias	3,130	3,427	1.4	1.7
Asthma	3,060	2,322	1.3	1.1
Gallstones	2,900	3,973	1.3	2.0
Nutritional deficiencies	2,440	2,470	1.1	1.2
Kidney infections	2,190	8,190	0.9	4.0
Tuberculosis	1,980	5,217	0.9	2.6
Meningitis	1,220	1,701	0.5	0.8
Hepatitis, infectious	840	1,014	0.4	0.7
Influenza	770	3,707	0.3	1.8
Appendicitis	520	1,397	0.2	0.7
Prostate disease	470	2,168	0.2	0.5
Intestinal infection	340	2,567	0.1	1.3
Complications of pregnancy	330	803	0.1	0.4

U.S. BIRTHS AND DEATHS

Source: U.S. Public Health Service

The U.S. birthrate increased to 16.0 births per 1,000 people in 1982, compared with 15.9 in 1981. An estimated 3,704,000 live births occurred during the year. The death rate decreased to 8.6 deaths per 1,000 population. Altogether some 2,818,000 persons were added to the population in 1982 by natural increase—the difference between the number of births and the number of deaths.

AREA	BIRTHS		BIRTHRATE[2]		DEATHS		DEATH RATE[2]	
	1982[1]	1970	1982[1]	1970	1982[1]	1970	1982[1]	1970
UNITED STATES	**3,704,000**	**3,731,386**	**16.0**	**18.4**	**1,986,000**	**1,921,031**	**8.6**	**9.5**
New England	167,082	200,048	13.4	16.9	113,224	115,567	9.1	9.8
Maine	16,425	17,750	14.5	17.9	10,045	11,053	8.9	11.1
New Hampshire	13,849	13,188	14.6	17.9	7,416	7,356	7.8	10.0
Vermont	7,772	8,354	15.1	18.8	4,472	4,449	8.7	10.0
Massachusetts	75,908	94,618	13.1	16.6	56,629	57,258	9.8	10.1
Rhode Island	13,003	15,648	13.6	16.5	9,089	9,492	9.5	10.0
Connecticut	40,125	50,490	12.7	16.7	25,573	25,939	8.1	8.6
Middle Atlantic	508,456	630,460	13.8	16.9	351,718	383,205	9.5	10.3
New York	249,171	317,714	14.1	17.4	166,761	188,026	9.4	10.3
New Jersey	96,401	120,242	13.0	16.8	66,025	68,183	8.9	9.5
Pennsylvania	162,884	192,504	13.7	16.3	118,932	126,996	10.0	10.8
East North Central	640,201	754,174	15.4	18.7	354,415	376,814	8.5	9.4
Ohio	163,767	199,696	15.2	18.7	93,647	100,453	8.7	9.4
Indiana	83,453	99,306	15.3	19.1	46,843	48,556	8.6	9.3
Illinois	180,423	205,472	15.8	18.5	97,688	110,680	8.5	10.0
Michigan	135,585	171,922	14.9	19.4	74,537	76,334	8.2	8.6
Wisconsin	76,973	77,778	16.2	17.6	41,700	40,791	8.8	9.2
West North Central	284,485	284,170	16.4	17.4	157,250	164,232	9.1	10.1
Minnesota	66,645	68,456	16.1	18.0	33,342	33,888	8.1	8.9
Iowa	45,631	48,290	15.7	17.1	26,792	29,387	9.2	10.4
Missouri	78,843	80,902	15.9	17.3	48,925	51,851	9.9	11.1
North Dakota	13,608	10,902	20.3	17.6	5,685	5,613	8.5	9.1
South Dakota	12,665	11,690	18.3	17.6	6,515	6,566	9.4	9.9
Nebraska	26,849	25,726	16.9	17.3	14,681	15,039	9.3	10.1
Kansas	40,244	38,204	16.7	17.0	21,310	21,888	8.8	9.7
South Atlantic	563,477	574,244	14.7	18.7	335,068	289,916	8.8	9.5
Delaware	9,510	10,502	15.8	19.2	5,131	4,916	8.5	9.0
Maryland	57,063	68,864	13.4	17.6	33,313	32,832	7.8	8.4
District of Columbia	18,638	15,230	29.5	20.1	8,462	8,851	13.4	11.7
Virginia	77,783	86,424	14.2	18.6	41,291	39,015	7.5	8.4
West Virginia	28,203	30,964	14.5	17.8	19,137	20,063	9.8	11.5
North Carolina	86,692	98,184	14.4	19.3	48,968	44,737	8.1	8.8
South Carolina	49,418	52,160	15.4	20.1	24,364	22,780	7.6	8.8
Georgia	91,924	96,880	16.3	21.1	44,610	41,819	7.9	9.1
Florida	144,246	115,036	13.8	16.9	109,792	74,903	10.5	11.0
East South Central	235,436	248,310	15.9	19.4	134,113	128,478	9.1	10.0
Kentucky	57,055	60,212	15.6	18.7	32,797	33,277	8.9	10.3
Tennessee	71,744	72,182	15.4	18.4	43,251	38,157	9.3	9.7
Alabama	61,040	66,832	15.5	19.4	35,101	33,743	8.9	9.8
Mississippi	45,597	49,084	17.9	22.1	22,964	23,301	9.0	10.5
West South Central	489,907	385,792	19.5	20.0	202,458	175,207	8.1	9.1
Arkansas	34,166	35,492	14.9	18.5	21,995	20,664	9.6	10.7
Louisiana	85,100	74,374	19.5	20.4	36,071	33,445	8.3	9.2
Oklahoma	55,494	44,890	17.5	17.5	28,533	26,763	9.0	10.5
Texas	315,147	231,036	20.6	20.6	115,859	94,335	7.6	8.4
Mountain	231,226	171,554	19.3	20.7	82,997	66,343	6.9	8.0
Montana	14,222	12,622	17.8	18.2	6,545	6,602	8.2	9.5
Idaho	19,351	14,486	20.1	20.3	6,611	6,155	6.9	8.6
Wyoming	10,050	6,502	20.0	19.6	3,018	2,937	6.0	8.8
Colorado	55,116	41,570	18.1	18.8	20,184	17,433	6.6	7.9
New Mexico	23,711	22,098	17.4	21.8	8,260	7,434	6.1	7.3
Arizona	52,565	37,672	18.4	21.3	22,613	14,865	7.9	8.4
Utah	43,188	27,032	27.8	25.5	8,997	7,061	5.8	6.7
Nevada	13,023	9,572	14.8	19.6	6,769	3,856	7.7	7.9
Pacific	573,350	482,634	17.3	18.2	254,551	221,269	7.7	8.3
Washington	66,327	60,748	15.6	17.8	33,472	29,954	7.9	8.8
Oregon	42,129	35,166	15.9	16.8	21,648	19,516	8.2	9.3
California	435,019	362,756	17.6	18.2	192,171	166,338	7.8	8.3
Alaska	11,068	7,528	25.3	25.1	1,770	1,438	4.0	4.8
Hawaii	18,807	16,436	18.9	21.4	5,490	4,023	5.5	5.2

[1] Provisional 1981 data. [2] Per 1,000 population.

ALCOHOLISM—NO. 1 DRUG PROBLEM

Source: National Institute on Alcohol Abuse and Alcoholism

What is the No. 1 dangerous drug problem in the United States? Heroin addiction? Wrong.

Alcohol is the drug that dwarfs all others in its grip on many Americans, in the toll of agony, in illness, in economic loss, in disrupted families, and in neglected children.

Alcohol is believed to be a major factor in causing heart disease, birth defects leading to mental retardation, and cancer.

Alcohol is a mood-altering drug that consumed in moderate amounts can produce euphoria. But alcohol also depresses the central nervous system, so that the initial "lift" wears off as intoxication deepens. Large amounts of alcohol over a long period of time produce anxiety. Like other dangerous drugs, it may induce psychological and physical dependence. This dependence, an illness, is called *alcoholism*.

ARE YOU ON ROAD TO ALCOHOLISM?

If your answers are "Yes" to the following questions, you should beware that you are on the way to becoming an alcoholic.

1. Do you plan on having a drink at a certain time of the day?
2. Do you look forward more and more to having a drink as the day wears on?
3. Do you like to get high on alcohol and stay that way?
4. Are you disappointed when you go to a party where drinks are not served?
5. Do you worry about always having a supply of your favorite alcoholic beverage on hand at home?
6. Do you avoid the company of people who don't drink?
7. Do you like to have a drink or two if you are feeling depressed?
8. Do you have a drink or two if you don't feel up to par physically?

DANGERS OF ALCOHOLISM

Some 100 million Americans consume alcoholic beverages. Experts estimate that about 13.3 million of this group are alcoholics, including 3.3 million youths aged 14 to 17. About one-fourth of alcoholics are women. The vast majority of alcoholics are in their mid-30s, with good jobs, homes, and families.

■ Alcoholism costs Americans $43 billion a year in lost work, medical expenses, auto accidents and related problems.

■ As many as 95,000 deaths a year can be blamed on drinking.

■ An alcoholic is 2 to 6 times more likely to die of disease, accident, or violence than the average person.

■ 36% of high school students get drunk at least four times a year. About 1 in 20 get drunk at least once a week.

■ 26% of the admissions to state and county mental institutions are persons with alcohol-related problems.

■ Between 30% and 40% of delinquent children come from alcoholic homes.

■ Drivers and pedestrians who drink cause more than 800,000 crashes and 25,000 traffic deaths in the United States each year.

■ 24% of alcoholics die in accidents, falls, fires, and suicides.

■ 33% of those who take their own lives are alcoholics—a suicide rate 58 times higher than for the rest of the population.

FREE INFORMATION

The National Clearinghouse for Alcohol Information, Box 2345, Rockville, Md. 20852, supplies answers to specific questions on alcoholism.

HOW TO HELP AN ALCOHOLIC

If a friend or relative drinks too much, here are some ways to help:

1. Do not attempt to punish, threaten, bribe, preach, or act like a martyr.
2. Try to remain calm and honest in talking with the person about his or her behavior.
3. Do not try to shield the person from the consequences by covering up or making excuses for his or her behavior.
4. Do not hide or dump bottles, or try to shelter the problem drinker from situations where alcohol is served.
5. Let him or her know that you are reading about and learning more about alcoholism.
6. Do not argue with an alcoholic while he or she is drunk.
7. Talk about the situation with someone you trust who knows about alcoholism.
8. Do not take over the alcoholic's responsibilities, leaving him or her with no sense of importance or dignity.
9. Explain the nature of alcoholism as an illness to children in the alcoholic's family.
10. Do not drink with the problem drinker.
11. Refuse to ride with the alcoholic person if he or she insists on driving while drunk.
12. Do not, above all, accept personal guilt for the alcoholic person's behavior.
13. Be patient and live one day at a time. Recovery from alcoholism does not occur overnight. Try to accept setbacks and relapses with calm and understanding.
14. Help guide the alcoholic to obtain professional help.

CANCER FACTS THAT CAN SAVE YOUR LIFE

Source: American Cancer Society

Cancer will eventually strike 3 in 8 of all Americans now living, according to present rates—about 67 million persons, affecting about 3 of every 4 families.

During the year about 855,000 Americans will be diagnosed as having cancer. About 450,000 will die, at a rate of over 1,230 a day. Some 350,000 will be saved from cancer during the year, but about 148,000 or more will die needlessly because their cancers will not have been detected soon enough.

BREAST CANCER

Breast cancer is the leading cause of cancer deaths in women today. About 115,000 cases of breast cancer will occur during the year, and over 37,300 will die.

If breast cancer is detected before it has spread to other parts of the body, the victim has an 87% chance of surviving 5 or more years. But if it has already spread to the axillary lymph nodes, the patient's chance of recovery drops to only 47%.

Every woman should follow a monthly program of breast self-examination. If you are a woman and you do not understand this simple self-examination procedure, go to your physician or to a health clinic at once and have it explained to you. Then follow up by carrying out your own monthly examination. If you feel a lump or thickening of the tissue in one of your breasts, do not delay going to a physician.

LUNG CANCER

Lung cancer is the leading cause of cancer deaths in men today. About 83,000 men and about 34,000 women will die of lung cancer during the year.

Unlike breast cancer, lung cancer is not easy to detect in its early stages. As a result only about 1 out of 10 victims of lung cancer can be saved from death.

If you have a nagging cough or hoarseness, see your doctor before it is too late.

But the best way to avoid lung cancer is prevention. Medical researchers believe that most lung cancer is caused by smoking or by breathing pollutants in the air.

COLON–RECTUM CANCER

About 59,400 people will die this year from colon-rectum cancer. Many of these deaths could have been prevented if the cancer had been detected earlier.

The best way to save your life from this cancer is by an annual medical examination that includes a proctoscopic examination of the rectum every 3 to 5 years after age 50.

FREE PHONE INFORMATION

For toll-free phone information about cancer, from the National Cancer Institute, dial 1-800-462-7255.

An annual at-home detection test, the stool guaiac slide test, is recommended after 50.

ORAL CANCER

Cancer of the mouth and throat strikes about 27,500 Americans each year, and about 40% survive five years after diagnosis.

If you have a mouth sore that does not heal quickly or have difficulty in swallowing, see a physician with no further delay.

SKIN CANCER

About 7,400 Americans die each year from skin cancer. Medical researchers stress that most cases of skin cancer can be prevented if you will resist overexposure to the sun.

Examine your skin regularly. If you have a skin sore that does not heal quickly, or if a mole or wart begins to increase in size, report it to your physician immediately.

UTERINE CANCER

Some 55,000 American women each year contract uterine cancer, and 9,700 die.

The increasing awareness by women of the need for regular pelvic examinations by a physician and the use of the Pap test for detection of uterine cancer have caused deaths from this type of cancer to decline by 70% in the past 40 years.

If you are a woman, help save your life by having an annual pelvic examination and a Pap test at least every three years.

LEUKEMIA AND LYMPHOMAS

Cancer of the blood and the lymph system strikes about 65,000 Americans each year, and over 38,300 die of the diseases each year.

Acute leukemia mainly strikes children and is treated by drugs that extend life up to 10 years. Chronic leukemia mainly affects adults, who treated by drugs can lead nearly normal lives for many years.

CANCER'S 7 WARNING SIGNALS

If you detect one of these signals, see your doctor.

- **Change in bowel or bladder habits**
- **A sore that does not heal**
- **Unusual bleeding or discharge**
- **Thickening or lump in breast or elsewhere**
- **Indigestion or difficulty in swallowing**
- **Obvious change in wart or mole**
- **Nagging cough or hoarseness**

DRUGS COMMONLY ABUSED AND MISUSED

Sources: U.S. Bureau of Narcotics and Dangerous Drugs and National Institute on Drug Abuse

How can you guard your children from drug abuse and misuse? Learn more about drugs.

Even before your son or daughter goes to school, you should teach that *any* drug is harmful if misused. You should make sure your child understands that, even when the doctor gives a prescription, harm may result if more than the prescribed amount is taken.

DRUG NAME	SLANG OR TRADE NAMES	HOW USED	EFFECTS AND SYMPTOMS	DANGERS
Amphetamines, other stimulants	Pep pills, eye-openers, lid poppers, uppers, wake-ups, truck drivers, dexies, browns, bennies, cartwheels, greenies, footballs, jolly beans	Swallowed, sometimes injected	Talkativeness, hyperactivity, bright shiny eyes, dilated pupils, irritability, loss of appetite, restlessness, increased sweating	Death from overdose, psychological dependence, psychosis
Barbiturates, sleeping pills, other depressants	Barbs, blues, seccy, seggy, phennies, red devils, reds and blues, tooies, nimbles, double trouble, yellow jackets, blue devils, blue birds, nimby, goofballs, candy, peanuts	Swallowed, sometimes injected	Drowsiness, sluggishness, faulty judgment, slurred speech, irrational behavior, constricted eye pupils, increased sweating, excessive laughter, confusion, depression, poor coordination	Death from overdose, (especially if taken with alcohol), death from withdrawal, convulsions, physical dependence
Cocaine	Coke, happy dust, joy powder, snow, the leaf, bernies, Bernice, C, gold dust, heaven dust, star dust, white girl	Sniffed, injected	Hallucinations, dilated eye pupils, tremors, euphoria, talkativeness, anxiety, loss of appetite, irritability, restlessness, hyperactivity	Death from overdose, convulsions, psychological dependence, paranoia
Codeine	Schoolboy	Swallowed, injected	Drowsiness, constricted eye pupils, slurred speech; on withdrawal—anxiety, tremors, nausea, cramps, diarrhea	Death from overdose, physical dependence, psychological dependence
DMT, Dimethyl-tryptamine	Businessman's special, 45-minute psychosis	Smoked, injected	Hallucinations, irrational behavior, rambling speech, dilated eye pupils, euphoria	Psychological dependence
Heroin	Horse, junk, skag, snow, stuff, big Harry, H, hard stuff, white stuff, joy powder, the thing	Injected, sniffed	Drowsiness, anxiety, constricted eye pupils, loss of appetite, constipation	Death from overdose, convulsions, physical dependence
Hydromorphone	Lords, Dilaudid	Swallowed, injected	Euphoria, constricted eye pupils, slurred speech	Death from overdose, physical dependence
LSD, Lysergic Acid Diethylamide	Acid, cubes, sugar, sugar lump, Big D, the chief, royal blue, blue acid, pearly gates	Swallowed, injected	Hallucinations, tremors, euphoria, increased sweating, dilated eye pupils, rambling speech, distortion of space and time	Psychosis, possible chromosome damage, psychological dependence
Marijuana, hashish, hash oil	Pot, grass, reefers, roach, bone, hay, hemp, tea, Acapulco gold, love weed, joint, muggles, pod, straw, Texas tea, hash, boo, red, Mary Jane, stick	Smoked, swallowed	Hallucinations, talkativeness, irritability and restlessness, inflamed eyes, increased appetite, reduced motivation, impulsive behavior	Psychological dependence
Meperidine	Demerol, Dolantol, Isonipecaine, Pethidine	Swallowed, injected	Drowsiness, anxiety, euphoria, constricted eye pupils, loss of appetite, poor reflexes	Death from overdose, physical dependence
Methadone	Dolophine, dolls, dollies, amidone	Injected, swallowed	Impaired coordination, loss of appetite, euphoria, anxiety	Death from overdose, physical dependence
Methamphetamine	Speed, meth, Methedrine, splash, crystal bombita, Doe	Swallowed, injected	Abnormal alertness, loss of appetite, aggressiveness, depression, distortion of time and space	Death from overdose, psychosis, paranoia, psychological dependence
Methaqualone	Quaalude, Rorer, Sopor, Parest, Optimil, Somnafac	Swallowed	Drunken euphoria, loss of coordination, convulsions during withdrawal	Death from overdose, physical dependence
Morphine	Morph, dreamer, melter, monkey, Miss Emma, tab	Injected	Sleepiness, poor coordination, loss of appetite, hallucinations	Physical dependence
Peyote, Psilocybin	Mesc, mescal beans, mushrooms, cactus	Swallowed	Hallucinations, irrational behavior, nausea, rambling speech, hyperactivity	Psychotic reactions, psychological dependence
Phencyclidine	PCP, Angeldust	Swallowed, smoked with marijuana, snorted	Estrangement from surroundings, hallucinations, bizarre behavior	Death from overdose, schizophrenia, memory problems

QUESTIONS AND ANSWERS ABOUT DRUG ABUSE

MARIJUANA

What are the effects of smoking a marijuana cigarette? The psychological effects include illusions and distortions of hearing, vision, and the sense of time. The feeling from smoking marijuana often is one of a passive euphoria, or "high," and sometimes the person may tend to withdraw into himself.

How long do the effects of marijuana last? A few inhalations of strong marijuana can intoxicate a person for several hours.

Does the heavy use of marijuana affect a young person's personality development? Heavy, chronic marijuana use has been associated with the *amotivational syndrome,* a loss of desire to work and to compete.

Is marijuana an addicting drug? Chronic users become psychologically dependent upon the drug, according to researchers.

Is there anything in marijuana that leads to other drugs? Marijuana users are more likely to experiment with other types of drugs than those who have never used it. However, nothing in marijuana itself produces a need to use other drugs.

HALLUCINOGENS

What are hallucinogens? Also called *psychedelics* and *psychotomimetics,* they are drugs capable of provoking alterations of sensation. LSD is one of the most potent and a widely studied of the hallucinogens.

What is LSD? LSD (lysergic acid diethylamide) is derived from lysergic acid, which comes from ergot, a fungus growth on rye. One ounce of LSD is enough to provide 300,000 average doses, each of which is a tiny speck whose effect lasts from 8 to 12 hours.

Is LSD an addicting drug? Although a person may use LSD habitually, the user does not experience physical withdrawal symptoms if it is suddenly discontinued.

What are the effects of LSD? LSD basically causes changes in sensation. Hallucinations can occur, and the sense of time and of self is altered. Emotional variations may range from bliss to sheer horror. In the parlance of the LSD user a "good trip" consists of pleasant imagery and feelings. In a "bad trip" or "bummer," perceived images arouse dread and horror.

Is LSD dangerous? Clinical reports on the illicit use of LSD have warned of the following dangers: (1) *Panic*—the user may grow frightened because he cannot "turn off" the drug's action. (2) *Flashbacks*—a flashback is a recurrence of some of the features of the LSD state days or months after the last dose, causing the user to believe he is losing his mind. (3) *Accidental death*—because LSD users may feel invulnerable, some have walked into traffic or jumped from high windows.

Does LSD cause mental problems? There is no doubt that it can bring about acute and sometimes long-lasting mental problems in susceptible persons.

NARCOTICS

What is a narcotic? A narcotic or analgesic is a drug that relieves pain and induces sleep.

Which narcotics are abused? Heroin accounts for about 90% of the illegal opiates in use. Paregoric and cough medicines containing codeine are also abused.

What are the effects of heroin? When sniffed, injected under the skin ("skin popping"), or shot directly into a vein, heroin causes a dreamlike state of great well-being. As tolerance to the drug develops, however, the physically dependent person cannot reach the same "high" as easily, requiring more and more heroin.

What are withdrawal symptoms like? Some 12 to 16 hours after the last injection, the addict gets chills, muscle aches and jerks, and severe abdominal discomfort. Frightful hallucinations may develop.

Why is heroin addiction dangerous? Users may contract hepatitis from dirty needles. An overdose, resulting in death, occurs when a user has lost or has never developed tolerance to strong heroin. If the addict should obtain such a dose, death may occur minutes after injection.

What are the social problems in addiction? The life of the addict is centered around obtaining money to buy heroin. The user may steal from family members, commit burglaries and muggings, and deal in heroin. Female addicts often turn to prostitution.

STIMULANTS

What are stimulants? Stimulants are drugs, usually amphetamines, that increase alertness. They are used in medicine to relieve depression. A powerful stimulant contained in coca leaves is cocaine, or coke. The use of cocaine causes insomnia and loss of appetite. An overdose of cocaine causes convulsions and death.

What is amphetamine abuse? When amphetamines are taken in large quantities, an ecstatic "high" occurs that may last a few hours. The user talks a lot, is restless and anxious, and has little desire for food and sleep. In a heavy user, withdrawal causes lethargy, fatigue, and sometimes depression.

SEDATIVES OR SLEEPING PILLS

What are sedative drugs? Sedative drugs are used in medicine to reduce tension and anxiety, to treat certain psychosomatic disorders, and to induce sleep.

Are sedatives addicting? Yes. Tolerance to large doses of barbiturates develops, and sudden withdrawal can cause severe convulsions.

Why are large amounts of sedatives dangerous? Accidental deaths are not uncommon, because a person who takes sleeping pills regularly may repeat the prescribed dosage several times without realizing it. The consumption of just a few sleeping pills with an alcoholic drink can cause sudden death.

PIONEERS IN MEDICINE

The symbol (N) indicates scientist was awarded Nobel Prize: see pages 70–77. For deaths in 1983, see pages 981–986.

Alfred Adler (1870–1937), Austrian psychiatrist: founded first child psychology clinic (1920).

Fred H. Albee (1876–1945), American orthopedic surgeon: made first practical bone grafts.

Karl Ernest von Baer (1792–1876), German biologist: founded science of embryology.

Sir Frederick G. Banting (1891–1941), Canadian physician: with C. H. Best, discovered insulin (1921) for treatment of diabetes. (N)

Christiaan N. Barnard (1922–), South African surgeon: performed first successful human heart transplant (1967).

George Wells Beadle (1903–), American geneticist: discovered that genes control chemical processes in living cells. (N)

William Beaumont (1785–1853), American physician: made first experiments on live patient to understand digestive process (published 1833).

Emil von Behring (1854–1917), German physiologist: discovered diphtheria and tetanus antitoxins (1890). (N)

Martinus Willem Beijerinck (1851–1931), Dutch botanist: discovered and named the *virus* (1895).

Hans Berger (1873–1941), German neuropsychiatrist: developed first electroencephalograph (1929) to measure brain waves.

Albert C. T. Billroth (1829–94), German surgeon: discovered bacteria cause infections in wounds.

Elizabeth Blackwell (1821–1910), first American woman physician: founded women's medical college in New York (1857).

Alfred Blalock (1899–1964), American surgeon: with Helen Taussig, developed corrective heart surgery for "blue babies" (1944).

Konrad Emil Bloch (1912–), German-American biochemist: discovered how living cells make cholesterol. (N)

Richard Bright (1789–1858), British physician: defined nephritis or Bright's disease (1827).

Robert Brown (1773–1858), British physician: discovered nucleus in living cells (1831).

Sir David Bruce (1855–1931), British surgeon: isolated germs causing Malta fever and sleeping sickness.

Albert Léon Calmette (1863–1933), French bacteriologist: co-discoverer of BCG vaccine, introduced in 1921 for prevention of tuberculosis.

Alexis Carrel (1873–1944), French surgeon: first kept tissues alive outside the body. (N)

Ferdinand J. Cohn (1828–98), German biologist: first to prove bacteria are plants.

Carl Ferdinand Cori (1896–) and his wife **Gerty Theresa Radnitz Cori** (1896–1957), Czech-American physiologists: discovered how enzymes change starch into sugar. (N)

Francis H. C. Crick (1916–), British biologist and physicist: helped develop radar in World War II; co-discoverer (1953) of structure of DNA, basic substance in genes responsible for heredity. (N)

George Washington Crile (1864–1943), American surgeon: contributed to surgical treatment of high blood pressure, nerve-block anesthesia, and blood transfusion.

Harvey Cushing (1869–1939), American surgeon: developed brain surgery techniques.

Michael Ellis De Bakey (1908–), American surgeon: developed artificial heart; first person to surgically repair weakened blood vessels.

George F. Dick (1881–1967), American physician: with his wife, Gladys Dick, isolated germ causing scarlet fever (1923).

Carl Djerassi (1923–), Austrian-American chemist: developed first practical birth-control pills (1954).

Edward Adelbert Doisy (1893–), American chemist: discovered vitamin K, isolated female sex hormone. (N)

Gerhard Domagk (1895–1964), German physician: discovered first sulfa drug (1932). (N)

Charles Richard Drew (1904–50), American black surgeon: developed blood and plasma banks (1940).

Paul Ehrlich (1854–1915), German bacteriologist: developed blood count (1897), chemotherapy to kill germs with drugs (1904), and Salvarsan drug for treatment of syphilis (1909). (N)

Christiaan Eijkman (1858–1930), Dutch physician: discovered rice hulls contain substance that prevents the disease beriberi (1900), leading others to discover vitamins.

Willem Einthoven (1860–1927), Dutch physiologist: developed electrocardiograph (1903). (N)

John Franklin Enders (1897–), American bacteriologist: developed measles vaccine (1963). (N)

Carlos Juan Finlay (1833–1915), Cuban physician: identified mosquito that carries yellow fever (1900).

Sir Alexander Fleming (1881–1955), British bacteriologist: discovered penicillin (1928). (N)

Sigmund Freud (1856–1939), Austrian psychiatrist: founded psychoanalysis; devised new theory about mental disorders.

Casimir Funk (1884–1967), Polish biochemist: discovered and named vitamins (1912).

Galen (c.130–200), Greek-Roman physician: systematized medical knowledge of his time.

Joseph Goldberger (1874–1929), Hungarian-American physician: discovered cure for pellagra (1915).

Camillo Golgi (1844–1926), Italian physician: developed way of staining tissues with silver nitrate for microscopic study (1873). (N)

Camille Guérin (1872–1961), French bacteriologist: co-discoverer of BCG vaccine, introduced in 1921 for prevention of tuberculosis.

Samuel F. C. Hahnemann (1755–1843), German physician: founded homeopathic medicine.

Stephen Hales (1677–1761), British physiologist: first to measure blood pressure (1705).

Bernard Naftali Halpern (1904–78), French physician: discovered antihistamine drugs.

William Harvey (1578–1657), English physician: discovered circulation of blood (1628).

Sir Walter Norman Haworth (1883–1950), British chemist: first to make vitamin C. (N)

Hermann L. F. von Helmholtz (1821–94), German physiologist: invented ophthalmoscope (1846), measured nerve impulses.

Philip Showalter Hench (1896–1965), American physician: co-discoverer of use of ACTH for treatment of rheumatic diseases. (N)

Hippocrates (c.460–377 B.C.), Greek physician

and the "father of medicine": first to base medical treatment on scientific observation.

Chevalier Jackson (1865–1958), American surgeon: developed lighted esophagoscope.

Edward Jenner (1749–1823), British physician: developed vaccination against smallpox (1796).

Carl Gustav Jung (1875–1961), Swiss psychiatrist: founded analytical psychology.

Paul Karrer (1889–1971), Swiss chemist: did valuable research on vitamins A, E, K, and the carotenes. (N)

Edward Calvin Kendall (1886–1972), American biochemist: discovered thyroxine, hormone of thyroid gland (1914); discovered cortisone (1936), used to treat arthritis and other diseases. (N)

Shibasaburo Kitasato (1852–1931), Japanese bacteriologist: isolated tetanus germ (1889) and bubonic plague bacillus (1894).

Edwin Klebs (1834–1913), German-American bacteriologist: discovered pneumonia bacillus (1875) and, with Friedrich Löffler, diphtheria bacillus (1884).

Robert Koch (1843–1910), German physician: established science of bacteriology; discovered microorganisms causing anthrax (1876), tuberculosis (1882), and cholera (1884). (N)

Emil Theodor Kocher (1841–1917), Swiss surgeon: performed first goiter operation to remove enlarged thyroid gland (1878). (N)

Arthur Kornberg (1918–), American biochemist: co-discoverer of synthetic nucleic acids, key substance in heredity; developed nucleic acid that reproduces itself (1967). (N)

Hans Adolf Krebs (1900–81), German biochemist: discovered citric-acid cycle in sugar metabolism (1953), called Krebs cycle. (N)

Richard Kuhn (1900–67), German chemist: discovered vitamin B_2, riboflavin. (N)

René Théophile Hyacinthe Laënnec (1781–1826), French physician: invented stethoscope (1816).

Karl Landsteiner (1868–1943), Austrian-American physician: discovered main blood types (1900), polio virus (1908); with A. S. Wiener, discovered Rh blood factor (1940). (N)

Charles L. A. Laveran (1845–1922), French physician: discovered parasite causing malaria (1880). (N)

Anton van Leeuwenhoek (1632–1723), Dutch biologist: perfected single-lens microscope; first to describe bacteria, protozoa, and blood cells.

Sir Joseph Lister (1827–1912), British surgeon: introduced antisepsis in surgery (1865).

Friedrich Löffler (1852–1915), German bacteriologist: with Edwin Klebs, discovered diphtheria bacillus (1884); with Paul Frosch, discovered virus causing hoof-and-mouth disease in cattle (1897).

Crawford Williamson Long (1815–78), American physician: first to use ether as anesthetic in surgery (1842).

Feodor Lynen (1911–79), German chemist: helped discover how body uses and makes cholesterol and fatty acids. (N)

John James Rickard Macleod (1876–1935), British physiologist: co-discoverer of insulin (1921). (N)

Marcello Malpighi (1628–94), Italian physician: discovered capillary blood vessels.

Sir Patrick Manson (1844–1922), British physician: discovered parasite causing elephantiasis (1877); called "father of tropical medicine."

William Worral Mayo (1819–1911) and sons, **William James Mayo** (1861–1939) and **Charles Horace Mayo** (1865–1939), American surgeons: founded Mayo Clinic in Rochester, Minn. (1889).

Elmer Verner McCollum (1879–1967), American biochemist: invented alphabet system of naming vitamins (1915).

Ephraim McDowell (1771–1830), American surgeon: performed first successful removal of tumor from ovary (1809).

Sir Peter Brian Medawar (1915–), British zoologist: proved organs and tissues transplantable between unrelated animals (1953). (N)

Charles Frederick Menninger (1862–1953) and sons, **Karl Augustus Menninger** (1893–) and **William Claire Menninger** (1899–1966), American psychiatrists: founded Menninger Clinic in Topeka, Kan. (1919).

Franz Mesmer (1734–1815), Austrian physician: pioneered hypnotism in medicine (1778).

Elie Metchnikoff (1845–1916), Russian biologist: developed theory that white blood cells attack disease germs. (N)

George Minot (1885–1950), American physician: discovered liver-extract treatment for pernicious anemia (1926). (N)

Egas Moniz (1874–1955), Portuguese neurologist: developed prefrontal lobotomy as surgical treatment of severe mental illness. (N)

Thomas Hunt Morgan (1866–1945), American biologist: advanced knowledge of heredity by discovering that genes transmit inherited characteristics (1926). (N)

Giovanni Battista Morgagni (1682–1771), Italian physician: pioneered use of autopsies to study causes of diseases.

William T. G. Morton (1819–68), American dentist: first to use ether as anesthetic in dentistry (1846).

Florence Nightingale (1820–1910), British nurse: founder of nursing as profession.

Hideyo Noguchi (1876–1928), Japanese bacteriologist: developed skin test for diagnosis of syphilis; discovered parasite of yellow fever.

Sir William Osler (1849–1919), Canadian physician: developed method of teaching new doctors as interns in hospital wards.

George Nicholas Papanicolaou (1883–1962), American physician: devised "Pap" smear test for cancer detection.

Philippus Aureolus Paracelsus (1493–1541), Swiss physician: introduced use of specific chemicals as treatment for specific illnesses.

Ambroise Paré (1510–90), French surgeon: introduced use of artificial limbs.

Louis Pasteur (1822–95), French bacteriologist: first to prove bacteria cause disease; developed pasteurization to kill bacteria with heat (1864); developed vaccine for rabies (1885).

Ivan Petrovich Pavlov (1849–1936), Russian physiologist: proved nerves control flow of digestive juices; pioneered in study of conditioned reflexes. (N)

Walter Reed (1851–1902), U.S. Army surgeon: helped discover cause of yellow fever.

Tadeus Reichstein (1897–), Swiss chemist: discovered how to make ascorbic acid, vitamin C (1933); isolated cortisone (1936). (N)

PIONEERS IN MEDICINE *(continued)*

Howard Taylor Ricketts (1871–1910), American pathologist: identified microorganisms (named *rickettsia* after his death) that cause Rocky Mountain spotted fever and typhus.

Sir Ronald Ross (1857–1932), British physician: proved *Anopheles* mosquito carries malaria (1898).

Benjamin Rush (1745–1813), American physician and signer of Declaration of Independence: established first free U.S. medical clinic at Philadelphia (1786).

Albert Sabin (1906–), Russian-American bacteriologist: developed oral polio vaccine (1957).

Jonas Salk (1914–), American physician: developed first successful vaccine for polio (1953).

Frederick Sanger (1918–), British chemist: helped determine structure of insulin. (N)

Béla Schick (1877–1967), Hungarian-American pediatrician: devised test for susceptibility to diphtheria (1913).

Theodor Schwann (1810–82), German physiologist and histologist: discovered that cell is fundamental unit of life (1839).

Ignaz Philipp Semmelweiss (1818–65), Hungarian physician: pioneered use of antiseptic methods in childbirth (1860).

Sir James Young Simpson (1811–70), British physician: first to use chloroform as anesthetic in childbirth (1847).

Lazzaro Spallanzani (1729–99), Italian biologist: proved bacteria float in air and heating kills bacteria.

Wendell M. Stanley (1904–71), American biochemist: proved viruses are solid particles that contain protein (1935). (N)

Andrew Taylor Still (1828–1917), American founder of osteopathic medicine: organized osteopathic college, Kirksville, Mo., in 1892.

James Batcheller Sumner (1887–1955), American biochemist: first to isolate pure crystals of an enzyme (1926). (N)

Albert Szent–Gyorgyi (1893–), Hungarian-American biochemist: discovered actin, a muscle protein. (N)

Helen Taussig (1898–), American pediatrician: with A. Blalock, developed corrective heart surgery for "blue babies" (1944).

Max Theiler (1899–1972), South African physician: discovered vaccine against yellow fever (1937). (N)

Andreas Vesalius (1514–64), Flemish physician: wrote first comprehensive textbook on human anatomy (1543).

Rudolf Virchow (1821–1902), German physician: pioneered scientific study of diseases, or *pathology* (1850s).

Selman A. Waksman (1888–1973), U.S. microbiologist: discovered streptomycin (1943). (N)

August von Wassermann (1866–1925), German physiologist and bacteriologist: developed blood test for diagnosing syphilis (1906).

James Dewey Watson (1928–), American biochemist: co-discoverer of molecular structure of DNA (1953). (N)

Maurice H. F. Wilkins (1916–), British biophysicist: first to explain structure of deoxyribonucleic acid (DNA). (N)

Daniel Hale Williams (1856–1931), American black physician: first surgeon to repair pericardium, sac around the heart (1893).

Alexandre E. J. Yersin (1863–1943), Swiss-French bacteriologist: independently discovered bubonic plague bacillus (1894).

MAJOR ADVANCES IN MEDICINE AND DRUGS

1628	Blood circulation described
1676	Bacteria and blood cells discovered
1707	Pulse rate measured
1733	Blood pressure measured
1794	Therapeutic oxygen inhalation
1796	Smallpox vaccine
1820	Quinine, for malaria
1839	Iodine, as antiseptic
1842	Ether, as surgical anesthetic
1844	Nitrous oxide, anesthetic
1847	Chloroform, anesthetic
1864	Pasteurization developed
1865	Phenol (carbolic acid), for surgical asepsis
1869	Chloral hydrate, sedative
1876	Anthrax bacteria discovered
1878	First operation to remove goiter
1882	Tuberculosis bacteria discovered
1884	Cholera bacteria discovered
1884	Cocaine, as local anesthetic
1885	Rabies immunization
1890	Diphtheria antitoxin
1890	Tetanus antitoxin
1894	Thyroid extract, for goiter
1895	Viruses discovered
1895	X rays discovered
1897	Blood count developed
1898	Radium discovered
1899	Aspirin, an analgesic
1900	Blood types discovered
1903	Barbitol (veronal), barbiturate
1904	Chemotherapy first used

1909	Salvarsan, for syphilis
1912	Phenobarbital, sedative
1913	Niacin, antipellagra vitamin
1913	Vitamin A
1914	Blood storage developed
1920	Cod liver oil (vitamin D)
1921	Insulin, a pancreatic hormone, to control diabetes mellitus
1921	BCG tuberculosis vaccine
1923	Scarlet-fever germ isolated
1926	Gene theory of heredity
1926	Thiamine, a vitamin
1926	Liver extract, for anemia
1927	Ephedrine, a stimulant and nasal decongestant
1928	Vitamin C (ascorbic acid) isolated
1929	Cyclopropane, an anesthetic
1932	Curare (arrow poison) alkaloids, for tetanus and spastic disorders
1933	Whooping-cough vaccine
1935	Sulfa drugs proved effective
1935	Amphetamine, a stimulant
1935	Blood bank developed
1936	Cortisone discovered
1937	Yellow-fever vaccine
1937	Antihistamines, to control allergic reactions and motion sickness
1937	Heparin, an anticoagulant
1940	Rh blood factor
1941	Penicillin, first antibiotic, proved effective
1941	Fluorides, for prevention of dental caries

1943	Streptomycin, a broad-spectrum antibiotic
1943	ACTH, a pituitary hormone
1945	Methadone, a synthetic narcotic for control of drug addiction
1946	Iodine^{131}, for exophthalmic goiter and diagnosis of thyroid disorders
1948	Aureomycin, antibiotic
1948	Vitamin B_{12}, for pernicious anemia
1950	First successful human organ transplant operation with kidney
1952	Isoniazid, a synthetic chemical effective against tuberculosis
1953	Salk polio vaccine
1953	DNA structure discovered
1954	Reserpine, a tranquilizer obtained from rauwolfia
1954	Enovid, first birth-control pill
1957	Growth (pituitary) hormone, for dwarfism
1957	Sabin oral polio vaccine
1963	Measles vaccine
1967	First successful human heart transplant operation
1968	First synthesis of an enzyme
1969	Rubella vaccine
1970	L–Dopa, for Parkinsonism; first gene synthesized
1977	Ara–A, first antivirus drug, proved effective
1978	Pneumonia vaccine
1981	First vaccine produced by gene-splicing

MEDICAL TERMS AND WHAT THEY MEAN

abasia—inability to walk from lack of muscular coordination; caused by damage to brain or nervous system

abdomen—region of body below chest and above pelvis; muscular wall of diaphragm separates abdominal cavity from chest; abdomen contains digestive, excretory, and sex organs

abortion—induced or natural loss or destruction of fertilized ovum or fetus before birth

abrasion—skin scrape with bleeding; can become infected unless cleaned and treated

abscess—area of infection in which pus forms, usually caused by bacteria

acetanilid—drug used to reduce fever and pain

Achilles tendon—thick tendon at back of ankle connecting calf muscles in leg to heel bone

acidosis—condition caused by lack of alkali in blood; symptoms include weakness, drowsiness

acne—pimples and blackheads caused by skin pores becoming blocked; may come from improper diet or lack of cleanliness

acromegaly—abnormal enlargement of hands, feet, or features of face; results from excess of growth hormones

ACTH—hormone produced by pituitary gland; has been used to relieve pain in treatment of various diseases

addiction—craving for certain foods or drugs, such as alcohol or habit-forming narcotics

Addison's disease—debilitating disease that causes weakness, darkening of skin, low blood pressure; results from insufficient hormone production by cortex of adrenal glands

adenoids—glandular tissue at upper part of throat, behind nose; excessive growth or infection of adenoids causes breathing difficulty

adrenalin—hormone secreted by adrenal glands; stimulates heart to beat faster, increasing blood pressure, and enabling muscles to work faster and harder

agoraphobia—fear of large open spaces

allergen—allergy-producing substance

allergy—unusual reaction of body to substances normally having no adverse effect on most other persons

allopathy—medical treatment to create effects opposed to those of specific disease

alopecia—loss of hair, usually hereditary

amblyopia—dimness of vision; may be hereditary or caused by improper diet or excessive use of tobacco or alcohol

amnesia—temporary or permanent loss of memory

analgesic—medicine that relieves pain; aspirin is one of commonest analgesics

androgen—male sex hormone that determines such characteristics as deep voice and beard

anemia—blood disorder with reduced hemoglobin or red cells; symptoms: paleness, constant tiredness

aneurysm—abnormal weakening of artery wall, forming pulsating blood-filled sac; rupture of weakened artery wall can cause death

angina pectoris—pain in chest, shoulder, neck, or left arm, generally caused by *arteriosclerosis*

anodontia—failure of teeth to grow in; may be hereditary or glandular malfunction

anorexia nervosa—disorder marked by intentional starvation and severe weight loss; typically involves eating binges followed by self-induced vomiting; mainly affects young women with abnormal fear of obesity

antacid—remedy for upset stomach; baking soda is common antacid

antibiotic—medicine produced by microorganisms, such as molds; antibiotics prevent growth and reproduction of certain disease germs; common antibiotics include penicillin, streptomycin, Aureomycin, Chloromycetin

antibody—natural substance in body that protects against disease or infection

anticoagulant—substance that slows clotting of blood; example: heparin

antidote—remedy to counteract poison

antigen—substance that stimulates production of *antibodies* when it enters body; examples: bacteria, pollen, viruses

antihistamine—medicine used to counteract symptoms of hay fever, allergies, and common cold; may cause drowsiness

antitoxin—type of *antibody*, acts against poison (toxin) that enters body; antitoxins produced in the blood of animals used to treat such diseases as *tetanus*

anxiety—in psychiatry, irrational worry or fear in absence of obvious danger

aphasia—loss or impairment of ability to speak, write, or understand others; caused by brain damage, often after *stroke*

aphonia—loss of voice or ability to speak louder than whisper; may be caused by excessive use of voice, brain damage, or cancer of larynx (voice box)

aphrodisiac—substance supposed to stimulate sexual powers

apoplexy—stroke caused by blockage of blood vessel in brain by blood clot

appendicitis—inflammation and swelling of appendix; if not surgically removed, it may rupture and cause death; symptom: pain around navel, spreading to lower right of abdomen

arteriosclerosis—hardening of arteries; caused by accumulation of calcium and cholesterol on artery walls; brings about clots in blood that may cause stroke in brain or heart attack

artery—vessel carrying blood from heart to parts of body

arthritis—disease affecting joints and supporting tissues; causes swelling, pain; can cripple hands, arms, and legs

asepsis—absence of germs, achieved by use of germ-killing antiseptics and sterilization

asphyxia—suffocation from lack of oxygen

asthma—chronic disease of bronchial tubes; causes breathing difficulty

atherosclerosis—accumulation of fatty deposits on artery walls, causing arteriosclerosis

athlete's foot—contagious infection of foot; caused by fungus in wet, warm places

autism—mental disorder in which child or adult ignores others, lives in own dream world

bacitracin—antibiotic used as treatment for skin infections

bedsore—ulcer of skin caused by lying in bed in same position for long time

benign—not harmful in itself and likely not to

MEDICAL TERMS *(continued)*

recur after being removed, as a tumor

biopsy—removal of bit of tissue from living body for microscopic examination; used in diagnosing such diseases as *cancer* and *cirrhosis*

blood poisoning—presence in bloodstream of bacteria from infection; symptoms include weakness, chills, fever; fatal if not treated

blood pressure—force of blood against artery walls; normal blood pressure for adults aged 18 to 45 is 120/80; first number is *systolic* pressure caused by heart contracting; second number is *diastolic* pressure when heart relaxes; high blood pressure can cause stroke or heart attack

blood types—four main types of blood: O, A, B, and AB based on substances found in red blood cells and *plasma*; before *transfusions*, blood types must be determined for correct matching; *Rh factor* also important in classifying blood; only O-type can be given to anyone

body temperature—normal heat of body; averages 98.6° F. (37° C.); temperature over 100° F. (37.8° C.) in adult indicates fever

boil—pus-filled infection on skin caused by bacteria; never open boil yourself because pus can get into bloodstream, causing *blood poisoning*

botulism—bacterial infection from improperly canned, bottled, or preserved food

bronchitis—inflammation of respiratory passages; caused by viral infection, smoking, air pollution

bubonic plague—acute contagious disease usually transmitted to people by fleas of rats; in past has caused widespread epidemics, killing millions of persons; symptoms appear suddenly: chills, fever, vomiting, delerium

bursitis—painful inflammation at joint caused by irritation of bursa (liquid-filled sac at joint)

cancer—group of diseases characterized by abnormal cell growth, crowding out healthy tissue and interfering with vital function of affected organs; malignant tumors develop

carcinogen—cancer-causing substance

carcinoma—cancer that originates in skin or mucous membranes

cardiac—pertaining to heart

caries—bacterial decay of tooth or bone

cataract—clouded condition in lens of eye, resulting in blurred vision; can be corrected by surgery

cauterize—to destroy abnormal or infected tissue by applying hot iron, laser beam, or other means

cerebral hemorrhage—bleeding inside brain from ruptured blood vessel; symptoms: headache, nausea, unconsciousness, paralysis

cerebral palsy—disorders caused by damage to brain before, during, or after birth

chemotherapy—use of chemicals and drugs to treat or to prevent disease

chicken pox—contagious disease; symptoms: fever, eruptions on skin; lasts about two weeks

cholera—acute epidemic disease; spread by polluted water, contaminated food, insects; symptoms: vomiting, diarrhea

cholesterol—substance in fats and oils, main material of *gallstones*; contributes to hardening of arteries; high cholesterol diet may help cause heart disease

chorea—involuntary twitching, once called "St. Vitus's dance"; often associated with *rheumatic fever*

chromosome—part of every plant or animal cell; carries genes determining physical characteristics of specific plant or animal

chronic—lasting long time without rapid change for better or worse

cirrhosis—chronic disease of liver; often associated with alcoholism

claustrophobia—fear of confined space

coagulant—substance that speeds up clotting of blood

congenital—existing at birth

conjunctivitis—inflammation of conjunctiva (mucous membrane covering eyeball and inner part of eyelids); also called pinkeye

contraception—prevention of pregnancy by use of methods of birth control

coronary thrombosis—blocking of artery supplying blood to heart muscles; common cause of heart attacks

cystic fibrosis—incurable hereditary disease of childhood; sweat glands and mucus-secreting glands do not function properly, involving lungs and pancreas

cystitis—bladder infection or inflammation

cystoscope—hollow tube with lights and mirrors used to examine interior of bladder

depilatory—agent for removing unwanted hair

diabetes—noncontagious disease in which pancreas does not produce enough insulin or body does not use insulin properly; symptoms: thirst, excessive urination

edema—excessive water and salt in tissues, causing swelling

electrocardiograph—instrument that records electrical current produced by action of heart muscle; resulting electrocardiogram (EKG) shows wave pattern traced on paper; used to diagnose heart ailments

electroencephalograph—instrument that records electrical impulses in brain (brain waves); resulting electroencephalogram (EEG) used in diagnosing brain disorders

embolism—blocking of blood vessel by loose blood clot, air bubble, or other material; can cause *stroke*

emphysema—incurable respiratory disorder; air sacs in lungs lose elasticity, causing impaired breathing, heart strain; contributing factors: smoking, air pollution

encephalitis—acute inflammation of brain; commonly known as "sleeping sickness" because main symptom is sleepiness; caused by virus carried by mosquitoes and ticks

endocarditis—inflammation of heart lining

enteritis—inflammation of intestine

epilepsy—chronic disorder of nervous system; causes periodic convulsions and unconsciousness; caused by brain injury or brain infection

erysipelas—also called "St. Anthony's fire"; skin disease; symptoms: hot red patches on skin, fever, headache, nausea

estrogens—female hormones responsible for regulating female sex functions

fluoridation—addition of fluoride salts to drinking water to reduce tooth decay

food poisoning—acute illness caused by eating contaminated food; symptoms: pain in abdomen, vomiting, diarrhea

frostbite—injury to skin, ears, nose, toes, or fingers from cold; body tissues freeze without pain when exposed to cold; may cause *gangrene*; any pressure on frozen toes or fingers may cause permanent injury; do not massage frozen parts; professional treatment necessary

gallstone—solid rocklike mass that forms in gallbladder; can cause inflammation of gallbladder; symptoms: pain in upper abdomen, fever, vomiting, tiredness; treated by surgery

gamma globulin—protein in blood *plasma*; contains numerous kinds of *antibodies*; used as serum to produce immunity for diseases such as measles

gangrene—death of body tissues in part of body; may be caused by infection or frostbite; severe cases require surgery

gastritis—inflammation of stomach lining

German measles—also called rubella; contagious virus infection; symptoms: swollen lymph glands, 3-day rash; if contracted during early pregnancy, can cause miscarriage or birth defects; vaccine available

gingivitis—inflammation of gums around teeth; symptom: bleeding gums; can lead to *pyorrhea*

glaucoma—disorder of eyes marked by increased pressure within eyeballs; symptoms: pain in eyes, blurred vision, appearance of halos around electric lights

gonorrhea—highly contagious bacterial infection; usually transmitted during sexual intercourse; readily cured in early stages by professional treatment

gout—high level of uric acid in tissues and joints, causing sharp pain

hallucination—vivid perception of something not present in reality

hallucinogen—substance that produces *hallucinations*; includes such drugs as marijuana, mescaline, LSD

hematoma—swelling under skin, caused by ruptured blood vessel

hemophilia—hereditary disorder affecting males; blood clots too slowly to prevent excessive bleeding from minor injuries

hemorrhage—heavy bleeding from blood vessel

hemorrhoids—enlarged veins in region of anus, usually painful; also known as "piles"

hepatic—pertaining to liver

hepatitis—inflammation of liver; usually caused by virus; contagious; symptoms: loss of appetite, fever, pain in upper right abdomen

hernia—abnormal protrusion of organ through tissue wall surrounding it; corrected by surgery

herpes—viral infection of genital skin from sexual contact with infected person

hyperglycemia—condition caused by too much sugar in blood; symptom of diabetes

hypertension—high blood pressure

hypochondria—excessive concern with one's health; person exaggerates trivial symptoms or suffers imaginary ailments; type of *neurosis*

hypoglycemia—deficiency of glucose in blood; may be caused by insulin injection

hysterectomy—removal by surgery of uterus, and in some cases ovaries, Fallopian tubes, and cervix

immunization—procedure for protection against disease; introduces or induces production of antibodies, usually by inoculation; natural immunity may be developed to specific disease after contracting it and recovering

interferon—protein substance produced in body cells of humans and other mammals that stops growth of viral infections in uninfected cells; subject of research as possible drug to use in treating or preventing cancer

intrauterine device (IUD)—contraceptive device inserted into uterus; common types include spirals or loops of flexible plastic

leukemia—type of cancer affecting blood-forming tissues; produces abnormally large number of white blood cells; symptoms: fever, loss of appetite

lumbago—pain in lumbar region of lower back; may be due to *arthritis*

malignant—likely to grow or spread, as a tumor

mastectomy—surgical removal of breast tissue, usually to treat breast cancer

measles—also called rubeola; acute virus disease, sometimes followed by complications; vaccine should be given at age 1 year

meningitis—contagious disease causing inflammation of membrane covering brain and lung; symptoms: headache, vomiting, fever, spasms pulling head back; in infants, spots on skin

metabolism—total of processes by which food, water, and oxygen are converted into living tissue, energy, and waste

metastasis—transfer of disease from one part of body to another by germs or by abnormal cells transported in blood or lymph

mononucleosis—contagious disease producing abnormally large number of monocytes (type of white blood cell); sometimes called "kissing disease" because of way it can be transmitted; symptoms: chills, fever, sore throat, tiredness

multiple sclerosis—progressive disease forming hardened patches on nerve sheaths in brain and spinal cord, preventing nerves from responding normally; symptoms: unsteady balance, jerky movements of arms and legs, stiff muscles

mumps—acute contagious disease, usually of childhood; causes swelling of salivary glands; vaccine available

muscular dystrophy—hereditary disease causing muscles to weaken and deteriorate; mostly affects boys

nephritis—inflammation of kidneys

neuralgia—severe pain along a nerve in the face, mouth, or throat

neuritis—inflammation of nerve causing pain in any part of body

neurology—study or treatment of disorders of nervous system

neurosis—emotional disturbance produced by unresolved and unconscious conflicts; often accompanied by *anxiety* and depression

nyctophobia—fear of darkness

oral contraception—method of birth control by taking pills containing sex hormones

osteo—pertaining to bones

ovulation—release of egg cell from ovary

pacemaker—nerve and muscle cells in heart that establish and regulate heart rhythm; when natural pacemaker does not function properly, artificial pacemaker may be implanted to stimulate heart with small electrical impulses

palsy—type of paralysis and disorder marked by

MEDICAL TERMS *(continued)*

constant trembling of parts of body; injury or disorder of nervous system impairs ability to control voluntary muscles

Pap test—quick, painless test to detect some types of cancer, especially of cervix; women over 30 should have Pap test annually

paranoia—mental disorder characterized by delusions of persecution or power

Parkinsonism—chronic, slowly progressive disorder that affects part of brain controlling voluntary movement; also known as Parkinson's disease

phlebitis—inflammation of vein forming blood clot, commonly in leg

phobia—extreme fear, usually so overpowering as to prevent person from functioning normally

phobophobia—fear of fear

physical therapy—treatment of injury, disability, or physical defect by massage, heat, exercise, or other external means

placebo—harmless substance given to humor patient; used in research as control to check effectiveness of drug

plasma—liquid part of blood; used rather than whole blood for some transfusions; can be used in transfusing persons of any *blood type*

platelets—part of blood that causes blood to clot; person with deficiency of platelets may bleed excessively from minor injuries

pleurisy—inflammation of pleura (double membrane that covers each lung and lines chest cavity)

pneumonia—acute infection of lungs; tiny air sacs become filled with fluid; breathing impaired

polyp—growth in mucous membrane, as in nasal passage, vocal cord, or alimentary tract

postpartum—postnatal; occurring after delivery of baby

prosthesis—artificial substitute for part of body, ranging from denture to artificial leg

psoriasis—skin disease marked by red patches

psychiatry—study, diagnosis, and treatment of mental illness and personality disorders

psychoanalysis—technique developed by Sigmund Freud to bring back repressed memories and understand unconscious impulses

psychology—science of study of mind, especially concerned with behavior

psychosis—severe mental disorder, often involving disintegration of personality

psychosomatic—denoting disorders, such as ulcers and migraine headaches, that may be completely or partly due to emotional causes

psychotherapy—treatment of emotional and mental disorders largely through discussion of them

pyorrhea alveolaris—disease forming pus at roots of teeth; tissue of gums shrinks; teeth become loose, causing loss of teeth

rabies—disease usually transmitted by bite of animal; symptoms: muscle spasms, convulsions, periodic rage and calm, spasms of throat when attempting to drink; death follows within 2 to 3 days after appearance of symptoms

renal—pertaining to kidneys

Rh factor—inherited substance in red blood cells; if present, as in most persons, blood is Rh positive; if absent, blood is Rh negative; person with Rh negative blood never should receive transfusion of Rh positive blood

rheumatic fever—bacterial disease of children and young adults; usually follows untreated streptococcus infections; symptoms: fever, swollen joints, nosebleed; may cause heart damage

ringworm—fungus infection of skin

rubella—German measles

schizophrenia—serious mental disorder characterized by delusions, retreat from reality, and possible deterioration of personality

sciatica—severe pain in sciatic nerve, affecting buttocks, thigh, leg, and foot

shock—signs and symptoms associated with failure or collapse of circulatory system; may follow extensive surgery, severe injury, or heavy bleeding; requires emergency medical treatment

silicosis—chronic disease of lungs from long exposure to mines or silica (sand and stone) products

sphygmomanometer—instrument used to measure blood pressure

streptococcus—type of bacteria that causes scarlet fever and strep throat

stroke—damage to brain from blocked or ruptured artery; symptoms: unconsciousness, paralysis of one side of body; high blood pressure and hardening of arteries are underlying causes

syphilis—contagious bacterial disease transmitted in sexual intercourse; can cause brain disease, blindness, heart disease; treated with penicillin

tendinitis—painful inflammation of tendon, commonly in shoulder

thrombosis—blocking of blood vessel by blood clot; can cause gangrene, stroke, or heart attack

toxic shock syndrome—systemic bacterial infection associated with prolonged use of menstrual pads or diaphragm

toxin—poisonous substance produced by germs, chemicals, and some plants and animals

trachoma—highly contagious virus disease of eyelids; can lead to blindness if untreated; widespread in tropical areas

transfusion—injection of blood or blood parts into person's circulatory system

trauma—injury caused to organ by blow or wound; in *psychiatry*, grave emotional shock that may have lasting effect on personality

trichinosis—disease caused by eating undercooked pork; parasitic roundworms invade blood and body organs; symptoms: fever, nausea, vomiting, diarrhea, abdominal pain

tuberculosis—chronic communicable disease; attacks lungs and other body parts

tumor—abnormal tissue growth on or in body; may be *benign* or *malignant*

ulcer—inflamed open sore on skin or on mucous membrane lining stomach, small intestine, or other body cavity

uremia—toxic condition of blood caused by wastes normally removed by kidneys and excreted in urine

vaccine—preparation containing bacteria or viruses treated to give immunity against specific diseases

venereal disease—infection transmitted mainly by sexual intercourse, such as *syphilis* and *gonorrhea*

Wassermann test—method of determining presence of syphilis

zoophobia—fear of animals

National Defense

Wide World

"The World After Nuclear War," a two-day conference held by scientists in Washington, D.C., in October 1983, presented reports on how the world environment would be affected by nuclear war. Led by Cornell astronomer Carl Sagan and Stanford biologist Paul Ehrlich, the scientists described the devastation that would be caused if 40% of the world's stockpile of nuclear weapons were set off with 5,000 megatons of explosions (equivalent to 400,000 Hiroshimas). The scientists said such a nuclear war would create clouds of dust blocking most sunlight from reaching the Earth, resulting in a continuous winter in which survivors would die of cold and starvation.

HIGHLIGHTS: 1983

NUCLEAR FREEZE MOVEMENT

While U.S. and Soviet diplomats discussed limitations on nuclear arms (see page 31), millions of ordinary citizens in many countries took part in demonstrations that called for the superpowers to stop adding to the stockpile of nuclear weapons.

Public debate on the issue was stimulated when 100 million TV viewers on Nov. 20 watched the ABC film "The Day After" that depicted the nuclear destruction of Kansas City in an atomic war and its horrifying effects on the survivors.

The U.S. House of Representatives voted 278–149 on May 4 approving a resolution to make an immediate freeze on the production and deployment of all nuclear weapons a major objective of U.S.-Soviet disarmament talks.

HIGHLIGHTS: 1983 *(continued)*

However, the U.S. Senate tabled the resolution by a 58–40 vote on Oct. 31.

The Soviet Union has promoted such a nuclear armaments freeze. However, the Reagan administration has opposed it on grounds that it would give the Soviet Union a strategic advantage because of the larger number of nuclear weapons already existing in the Soviet arsenal. Proponents of the nuclear freeze have argued that each side already has more than enough nuclear weapons to destroy civilization and most of mankind.

After two years of debate, Roman Catholic bishops of the U.S. voted, 238–9, on May 3 in Chicago to approve a 150-page pastoral letter that denounced "the concept of nuclear war as a viable strategy for self-defense."

The bishops' letter, condemning the use of nuclear weapons for any purpose, made these recommendations:

"1. Support for immediate, bilateral, verifiable agreements to halt the testing, production, and deployment of new nuclear weapons systems.

"2. Support for negotiated bilateral deep cuts in the arsenals of both superpowers.

"3. Support for early and successful conclusion of negotiations of the comprehensive test ban treaty.

"4. Removal by all parties of short-range nuclear weapons which multiply dangers disproportionate to their deterrent value.

"5. Removal by all parties of nuclear weapons from areas where they are likely to be overrun in the early stages of war, thus forcing rapid and uncontrollable decisions on their use.

"6. Strengthening of command and control over nuclear weapons to prevent inadvertent and unauthorized use."

The Roman Catholic bishops of France took a divergent view in a "Win the Peace" document approved 93–8 on Nov. 8 in Paris.

ARMED FORCES MONTHLY BASIC PAY SCALES[1]

COMMISSIONED OFFICERS' PAY GRADES

YEARS	O-1[2]	O-2[2]	O-3[2]	O-4	O-5	O-6	O-7	O-8	O-9	O-10[3]
0-2	$1,143.00	$1,316.40	$1,509.90	$1,624.50	$1,927.50	$2,409.90	$3,251.40	$3,912.90	$4,320.30	$4,874.40
2+	1,189.80	1,437.60	1,687.80	1,978.20	2,263.50	2,647.80	3,472.50	4,030.20	4,433.40	5,046.00
3+	1,437.60	1,727.10	1,804.20	2,110.50	2,419.50	2,821.20	3,472.50	4,125.90	4,527.60	5,046.00
4+	1,437.60	1,785.30	1,996.50	2,110.50	2,419.50	2,821.20	3,472.50	4,125.90	4,527.60	5,046.00
6+	1,437.60	1,822.80	2,091.90	2,149.20	2,419.50	2,821.20	3,627.90	4,125.90	4,527.60	5,046.00
8+	1,437.60	1,822.80	2,167.50	2,244.60	2,419.50	2,821.20	3,627.90	4,433.40	4,642.80	5,239.50
10+	1,437.60	1,822.80	2,284.20	2,397.30	2,493.30	2,821.20	3,838.50	4,433.40	4,642.80	5,239.50
12+	1,437.60	1,822.80	2,397.30	2,532.30	2,627.10	2,821.20	3,838.50	4,642.80	4,836.00	5,640.60[3]
14+	1,437.60	1,822.80	2,456.40	2,647.80	2,802.90	2,916.90	4,030.20	4,642.80	4,836.00	5,640.60[3]
16+	1,437.60	1,822.80	2,456.40	2,763.90	3,012.60	3,378.30	4,433.40	4,836.00	5,239.50	6,044.10[3]
18+	1,437.60	1,822.80	2,456.40	2,840.40	3,185.70	3,551.10	4,737.90	5,046.00	5,239.50	6,044.10[3]
20+	1,437.60	1,822.80	2,456.40	2,840.40	3,282.00	3,627.90	4,737.90	5,239.50	5,640.60[3]	6,448.50[3]
22+	1,437.60	1,822.80	2,456.40	2,840.40	3,396.60	3,838.50	4,737.90	5,449.50	5,640.60[3]	6,448.50[3]
26+	1,437.60	1,822.80	2,456.40	2,840.40	3,396.60	4,163.10	4,737.90	5,449.50	6,044.10[3]	6,850.80[3]

WARRANT OFFICERS' PAY GRADES

YEARS	W-1	W-2	W-3	W-4
0-2	$1,020.30	$1,224.60	$1,398.00	$1,538.10
2+	1,169.70	1,324.50	1,516.50	1,650.00
3+	1,169.70	1,324.50	1,516.50	1,650.00
4+	1,267.20	1,363.20	1,535.70	1,687.80
6+	1,324.50	1,437.60	1,554.00	1,764.60
8+	1,381.50	1,516.50	1,667.70	1,842.30
10+	1,437.60	1,573.80	1,764.60	1,919.70

WARRANT OFFICERS' PAY GRADES

YEARS	W-1	W-2	W-3	W-4
12+	$1,497.30	$1,631.40	$1,822.80	$2,053.80
14+	1,554.00	1,687.80	1,880.40	2,149.20
16+	1,611.30	1,746.90	1,936.80	2,224.80
18+	1,667.70	1,804.20	1,996.50	2,284.20
20+	1,727.10	1,861.50	2,073.90	2,358.30
22+	1,727.10	1,936.80	2,149.20	2,437.20
26+	1,727.10	1,936.80	2,224.80	2,627.10

ENLISTED PAY GRADES

YEARS	E-1	E-2	E-3	E-4	E-5	E-6	E-7	E-8	E-9[4]
0-2	$596.40	$668.70	$695.10	$738.00	$791.10	$901.20	$1,047.60	—	—
2+	596.40	668.70	732.90	779.10	861.00	982.50	1,130.70	—	—
3+	596.40	668.70	762.60	824.70	902.70	1,023.60	1,173.00	—	—
4+	596.40	668.70	792.90	888.90	942.00	1,067.10	1,213.80	—	—
6+	596.40	668.70	792.90	924.00	1,003.80	1,106.40	1,255.50	—	—
8+	596.40	668.70	792.90	924.00	1,044.60	1,146.90	1,295.10	$1,500.60	—
10+	596.40	668.70	792.90	924.00	1,086.30	1,188.90	1,336.80	1,543.20	$1,788.90
12+	596.40	668.70	792.90	924.00	1,126.20	1,250.10	1,378.20	1,583.70	1,829.70
14+	596.40	668.70	792.90	924.00	1,146.90	1,289.40	1,440.60	1,625.10	1,871.10
16+	596.40	668.70	792.90	924.00	1,146.90	1,331.10	1,481.40	1,668.00	1,914.00
18+	596.40	668.70	792.90	924.00	1,146.90	1,351.20	1,523.10	1,706.40	1,956.60
20+	596.40	668.70	792.90	924.00	1,146.90	1,351.20	1,542.90	1,748.40	1,994.70
22+	596.40	668.70	792.90	924.00	1,146.90	1,351.20	1,646.40	1,851.00	2,099.70
26+	596.40	668.70	792.90	924.00	1,146.90	1,351.20	1,851.00	2,057.70	2,303.70

1 Pay scale effective Jan. 1, 1984. 2 Officers in the first 3 pay grades who have had 4 years of enlisted service receive some additional pay. 3 Monthly basic pay is limited to $5,499.90 by Level V of the Executive Schedule. 4 Highest-ranking enlisted person in each service receives $2,800.20.

The French bishops supported the use of nuclear weapons for defense and condemned the Soviet Union for seeking "conquest of the world" by use of all means, including "even the aspiration of people for peace."

$250 BILLION DEFENSE BUDGET

Both houses of Congress approved on Nov. 18 a $250 billion appropriation for national defense in 1984. The measure was passed by the House 311–99 and by the Senate 75–6.

The appropriation, the largest in U.S. history, provided an increase in military spending of about 3% over inflation. President Reagan had asked for about $10 billion more.

The measure gave a go-ahead to funding of the controversial MX "Peacekeeper" missiles and B-1 bombers. Some $24 million was allocated to aid rebels fighting against the government of Nicaragua. However, Congress turned down a request for funds to develop nerve-gas weapons.

Congress approved the spending of about $20 billion for production of 100 B-1 intercontinental bombers. The first eight of the huge planes are under construction, and 10 more will be started in 1984. New technology is being used to reduce the ability of Soviet radar to detect the B-1.

Some $2.1 billion was allocated for production of the first 21 intercontinental MX missiles. In all 100 of the missiles, each carrying 10 nuclear warheads, are to be deployed in underground silos in southeastern Wyoming and western Nebraska by 1989. The schedule calls for the first 10 of the missiles to be operational by 1986. The first MX missile was successfully tested in June 1983 with the 70-foot missile speeding some 4,000 miles from Vandenberg Air Force Base in California to a target in the Marshall Islands.

DRAFT REGISTRATION UPHELD

The U.S. Court of Appeals in San Francisco decided, 2–1, on July 19 to overturn a lower-court ruling that had thrown out an indictment of a 21-year-old who had refused to register for the draft. The lower court had ruled that President Carter's 1980 proclamation of the draft registration was invalid because it did not provide a 30-day waiting-period before going into effect. However, the appeals court decided that the waiting-period rule did not apply to presidential proclamations.

Some 10.4 million men have registered for the draft since July 1980. But an estimate 410,000 young men have failed to register and are subject to prosecution.

JOINT CHIEFS OF STAFF

The Joint Chiefs of Staff of the U.S. armed forces was established within the Department of Defense in 1947. The position of Chairman of the Joint Chiefs of Staff was created in 1949.

CHAIRMAN

Gen. John W. Vessey Jr., USA (July 1, 1982–Current)

Gen. David C. Jones, USAF (June 1978–June 1982)
Gen. George S. Brown, USAF (July 1974–June 1978)
Adm. Thomas H. Moorer, USN (July 1970–July 1974)
Gen. Earle G. Wheeler, USA (July 1964–July 1970)
Gen. Maxwell D. Taylor, USA (Oct. 1962–July 1964)
Gen. Lyman L. Lemnitzer, USA (Oct. 1960–Sept. 1962)
Gen. Nathan F. Twining, USAF (Aug. 1957–Sept. 1960)
Adm. Arthur W. Radford, USN (Aug. 1953–Aug. 1957)
Gen. of the Army Omar N. Bradley, USA (Aug. 1949–Aug. 1953)

CHIEF OF STAFF, UNITED STATES ARMY

Gen. John A. Wickham Jr. (June 1983–Current)

Gen. Edward Charles Meyer (June 1979–June 1983)
Gen. Bernard W. Rogers (Sept. 1976–June 1979)
Gen. Frederick C. Weyand (Oct. 1974–Sept. 1976)
Gen. Creighton W. Abrams (Oct. 1972–Sept. 1974)
Gen. William C. Westmoreland (July 1968–June 1972)
Gen. Harold K. Johnson (July 1964–July 1968)
Gen. Earle G. Wheeler (Oct. 1962–July 1964)
Gen. George H. Decker (Sept. 1960–Sept. 1962)
Gen. Lyman L. Lemnitzer (July 1959–Sept. 1960)
Gen. Maxwell D. Taylor (June 1955–June 1959)
Gen. Matthew B. Ridgway (Aug. 1953–June 1955)
Gen. J. Lawton Collins (Aug. 1949–Aug. 1953)
Gen. Omar N. Bradley (Feb. 1948–Aug. 1949)
Gen. of the Army Dwight D. Eisenhower (Nov. 1945–Feb. 1948)

CHIEF OF NAVAL OPERATIONS

Adm. James D. Watkins (July 1, 1982–Current)

Adm. Thomas B. Hayward (July 1978–June 1982)
Adm. James J. Holloway III (June 1974–June 1978)
Adm. Elmo R. Zumwalt Jr. (July 1970–June 1974)
Adm. Thomas H. Moorer (Aug. 1967–June 1970)
Adm. David L. McDonald (Aug. 1963–Aug. 1967)
Adm. George W. Anderson (Aug. 1961–July 1963)
Adm. Arleigh A. Burke (Aug. 1955–Aug. 1961)
Adm. Robert B. Carney (Aug. 1953–Aug. 1955)
Adm. William M. Fechteler (Aug. 1951–Aug. 1953)
Adm. Forrest P. Sherman (Nov. 1949–July 1951)
Adm. Louis E. Denfield (Dec. 1947–Nov. 1949)
Fleet Adm. Chester W. Nimitz (Dec. 1945–Dec. 1947)

CHIEF OF STAFF, UNITED STATES AIR FORCE

Gen. Charles A. Gabriel (July 1, 1982–Current)

Gen. Lew Allen Jr. (July 1978–June 1982)
Gen. David C. Jones (July 1974–June 1978)
Gen. George S. Brown (July 1973–July 1974)
Gen. John D. Ryan (Aug. 1969–July 1973)
Gen. John P. McConnell (Feb. 1965–Aug. 1969)
Gen. Curtis E. LeMay (June 1961–Jan. 1965)
Gen. Thomas D. White (July 1957–June 1961)
Gen. Nathan F. Twining (June 1953–June 1957)
Gen. Hoyt S. Vandenberg (April 1948–June 1953)
Gen. Carl Spaatz (Sept. 1947–April 1948)

COMMANDANT OF THE MARINE CORPS

Gen. Robert H. Barrow (July 1979–Current)

Gen. Louis H. Wilson Jr. (July 1975–July 1979)
Gen. R.E. Cushman Jr. (Jan. 1972–July 1975)
Gen. Leonard F. Chapman Jr. (Jan. 1968–Dec. 1971)
Gen. Wallace M. Greene Jr. (Jan. 1964–Dec. 1967)
Gen. David M. Shoup (Jan. 1960–Dec. 1963)
Gen. Randolph McC. Pate (Jan. 1956–Dec. 1959)
Gen. Lemuel C. Shepherd (Jan. 1952–Dec. 1955)

U.S. MILITARY FORCES ACTIVE STRENGTH

Source: U.S. Department of Defense

MILITARY PERSONNEL	1970	1975	1980	1981	1982	1983
Army	1,322,548	784,333	774,607	776,303	779,870	774,723
Navy	692,660	539,100	527,296	546,526	551,428	554,885
Marine Corps	259,737	195,951	187,647	191,492	194,409	192,429
Air Force	791,349	612,751	559,282	569,616	584,041	593,253
Totals	3,066,294	2,132,136	2,048,832	2,083,940	2,109,748	2,115,290

U.S. MILITARY STRENGTH ABROAD

Source: U.S. Department of Defense

PLACE	NUMBER OF U.S. MILITARY PERSONNEL		
	1982	1981	1980
West Germany	242,985	248,481	250,912
Japan	48,496	48,865	42,240
South Korea	38,882	38,801	37,608
Afloat, W. Europe	32,252	39,718	20,334
Afloat, Pacific	23,214	16,164	17,748
Afloat, various areas	21,905	17,236	24,908
Philippines	15,123	14,500	14,552
Italy	13,430	13,118	12,193
Panama	9,182	9,186	8,891
Spain	9,014	8,886	8,786
Guam	8,969	8,788	9,103
Turkey	5,083	5,133	5,017
Puerto Rico	3,922	3,531	3,547
Greece	3,499	3,427	3,310
Iceland	3,124	2,916	2,858

PLACE	NUMBER OF U.S. MILITARY PERSONNEL		
	1983	1982	1981
Netherlands	2,616	2,528	2,431
Belgium	2,303	2,289	2,119
Cuba (Guantánamo)	2,322	2,264	2,128
Bermuda	1,850	1,351	1,336
Portugal/Azores	1,582	1,473	1,395
Egypt	1,365	1,191	179
Diego Garcia	1,186	1,860	1,459
Australia	685	660	643
Canada	660	628	645
Saudi Arabia	627	598	763
Greenland	330	314	304
Honduras	255	24	19
Other places	2,119	2,371	3,337
TOTAL	511,914	510,449	490,988

U.S. AIR FORCE ACTIVE AIRCRAFT

Source: U.S. Department of Defense

	1960	1970	1975	1980	1981	1982	1983 *	1984 *
U.S. Air Force total	**15,312**	**11,245**	**7,239**	**7,034**	**7,092**	**7,194**	**7,305**	**7,301**
Bomber	2,193	570	498	414	412	411	363	332
Tanker	1,230	663	657	529	534	539	544	550
Fighter/Attack/Interceptor	3,922	3,404	2,299	2,769	2,850	2,925	3,026	3,055
Reconnaissance/Electronic Warfare	685	1,017	494	354	344	363	392	412
Cargo/Transport	2,549	1,854	927	836	835	832	828	849
Search and Rescue (Fixed Wing)	129	87	44	35	36	37	35	36
Helicopter (including Rescue)	372	457	269	230	230	230	238	237
Special Research	2	—	—	—	—	—	—	—
Trainer	3,914	2,625	1,861	1,678	1,644	1,660	1,664	1,638
Utility/Observation	316	568	189	189	207	197	215	192
Support of allied nations	—	**948**	**243**	—	—	—	—	—
Air National Guard	**2,269**	**1,900**	**1,647**	**1,560**	**1,636**	**1,665**	**1,656**	**1,670**
Air Force Reserve	**770**	**420**	**448**	**474**	**452**	**455**	**458**	**456**
Other non-Air Force agencies	361	212	—	—	—	—	—	—
Total active Air Force aircraft	**18,712**	**14,725**	**9,577**	**9,069**	**9,180**	**9,314**	**9,419**	**9,427**

U.S. NAVY AND MARINE CORPS STRENGTH

Source: U.S. Department of Defense

	1968	1972	1976	1980	1982	1983 *	1984 *
TOTAL U.S. FLEET	**957**	**645**	**484**	**479**	**513**	**506**	**526**
Strategic Forces	**51**	**50**	**50**	**48**	**39**	**40**	**41**
FBM Submarines (SSBN)	41	41	41	40	33	34	35
Support (AS, TAK)	10	9	9	8	6	6	6
Battle Forces	**756**	**520**	**367**	**384**	**420**	**414**	**424**
Carriers (CV, CVN, CVS)	23	17	13	13	13	13	13
Battleships (BB)	1	—	—	—	—	—	1
Cruisers (CG, CAG, CGN, CA, CC)	34	28	26	26	27	28	29
Destroyers (DD, DDR, DDG)	221	131	69	80	84	68	68
Frigates (FF, FFG)	50	66	64	71	82	89	95
Submarines (SS, SSN, SSG, SSGN)	105	94	74	79	96	99	98
Patrol Combatants	6	16	8	3	4	6	6
Amphibious Warfare Ships	157	77	62	63	59	58	58
Mine Warfare	84	31	3	3	3	3	3
Mobile Logistics Ships	75	60	48	46	51	52	48
Support Forces	**100**	**69**	**63**	**41**	**43**	**43**	**49**
Mobilization Forces	**50**	**6**	**4**	**6**	**11**	**9**	**12**
Auxiliaries and Sealift	**59**	**19**	**14**	**15**	**27**	**27**	**34**
Mobilization Forces, secondary	**39**	**49**	**57**	**44**	**33**	**26**	**24**
U.S. Navy Aircraft, operating	**7,103**	**5,658**	**4,931**	**4,436**	**4,528**	**4,994**	**5,057**
Marine Corps Divisions	**4**	**3**	**3**	**3**	**3**	**3**	**3**

* Planned strength.

WORLD MILITARY EXPENDITURES AND SIZE OF ARMED FORCES

Source: U.S. Arms Control and Disarmament Agency, data for 1980, except otherwise footnoted.

NATIONS	MILITARY EXPENDITURES	ARMED FORCES
WORLD TOTAL	$656,700,000,000	26,587,000
Afghanistan	69,000,000[1]	110,000[1]
Albania	167,000,000[4]	52,000
Algeria	796,000,000	101,000
Angola	82,000,000[2]	53,000
Argentina	2,894,000,000	160,000
Australia	3,279,000,000	70,000
Austria	913,000,000	41,000
Bahrain	55,000,000	2,000
Bangladesh	153,000,000	121,000
Barbados	2,000,000	1,000
Belgium	4,174,000,000	88,000
Benin	24,000,000	7,000
Bolivia	96,000,000[4]	24,000
Botswana	24,000,000	3,000
Brazil	2,308,000,000	455,000
Britain	22,889,000,000	323,000
Bulgaria	3,743,000,000	162,000
Burma	228,000,000	212,000
Burundi	22,000,000	8,000
Cambodia	67,000,000[2]	70,000[1]
Cameroon	86,000,000	14,000
Canada	4,520,000,000	79,000
Cape Verde	3,000,000	4,000
Central Africa	12,000,000	5,000
Chad	27,000,000[4]	9,000[3]
Chile	567,000,000	115,000
China	47,000,000,000	4,500,000
Colombia	350,000,000	65,000
Congo	48,000,000	14,000
Cuba	1,140,000,000	375,000
Cyprus	32,000,000	9,000
Czechoslovakia	6,122,000,000	212,000
Denmark	1,732,000,000	35,000
Dominican Republic	95,000,000	23,000
Ecuador	185,000,000	35,000
Egypt	1,362,000,000	340,000
El Salvador	85,000,000	8,000
Equatorial Guinea	5,000,000[2]	2,000[4]
Ethiopia	427,000,000	240,000
Fiji	9,000,000	1,000
Finland	781,000,000	40,000
France	25,552,000,000	495,000
Gabon	11,000,000	2,000
Germany, East	8,314,000,000	231,000
Germany, West	27,721,000,000	495,000
Ghana	46,000,000	20,000
Greece	2,432,000,000	182,000
Guatemala	65,000,000	15,000
Guinea	18,000,000[2]	18,000
Guinea–Bissau	8,000,000	12,000
Guyana	21,000,000	7,000
Haiti	18,000,000	7,000
Honduras	43,000,000	12,000
Hungary	2,542,000,000	119,000
India	4,521,000,000	1,268,000
Indonesia	1,594,000,000	250,000
Iran	11,342,000,000[1]	280,000
Iraq	2,671,000,000[4]	220,000
Ireland	291,000,000	15,000
Israel	5,051,000,000	165,000
Italy	8,937,000,000	366,000
Ivory Coast	116,000,000	11,000
Jamaica	17,000,000	2,000
Japan	10,885,000,000	239,000
Jordan	399,000,000	70,000
Kenya	253,000,000	16,000
Korea, North	1,300,000,000	716,000
Korea, South	3,846,000,000	639,000

NATIONS	MILITARY EXPENDITURES	ARMED FORCES
Kuwait	$1,315,000,000	10,000
Laos	N.A.	46,000
Lebanon	98,000,000[3]	9,000[3]
Liberia	15,000,000	5,000
Libya	523,000,000	53,000
Luxembourg	55,000,000	1,000
Madagascar	125,000,000	28,000
Malawi	25,000,000	6,000
Malaysia	1,110,000,000	82,000
Mali	33,000,000	8,000
Malta	6,000,000	1,000
Mauritania	86,000,000	11,000
Mauritius	2,000,000	0
Mexico	627,000,000	110,000
Morocco	1,142,000,000	117,000
Mozambique	78,000,000[1]	27,000
Nepal	17,000,000	25,000
Netherlands	5,472,000,000	115,000
New Zealand	455,000,000	13,000
Nicaragua	49,000,000	50,000
Niger	17,000,000	6,000
Nigeria	2,266,000,000	222,000
Norway	1,558,000,000	37,000
Oman	1,179,000,000	14,000
Pakistan	1,265,000,000	549,000
Panama	24,000,000	11,000
Papua New Guinea	30,000,000	4,000
Paraguay	49,000,000	15,000
Peru	900,000,000	150,000
Philippines	808,000,000	156,000
Poland	9,546,000,000	421,000
Portugal	852,000,000	60,000
Qatar	555,000,000	5,000
Romania	3,757,000,000	215,000
Rwanda	21,000,000	6,000
Saudi Arabia	16,740,000,000	50,000
Senegal	66,000,000	14,000
Sierra Leone	11,000,000	4,000
Singapore	620,000,000	57,000
Somalia	93,000,000	54,000
South Africa	2,043,000,000	78,000
Soviet Union	207,400,000,000	4,300,000
Spain	3,656,000,000	342,000
Sri Lanka	27,000,000	18,000
Sudan	260,000,000	68,000
Swaziland	9,000,000	3,000
Sweden	3,710,000,000	68,000
Switzerland	2,284,000,000	19,000
Syria	2,205,000,000	250,000
Taiwan	2,086,000,000[1]	465,000
Tanzania	248,000,000	57,000
Thailand	1,000,000,000	250,000
Togo	25,000,000	8,000
Trinidad–Tobago	16,000,000	2,000
Tunisia	116,000,000	29,000
Turkey	3,546,000,000	567,000
Uganda	176,000,000	6,000
United Arab Emirates	1,658,000,000	30,000
UNITED STATES	143,981,000,000	2,075,000
Upper Volta	35,000,000	8,000
Uruguay	130,000,000	29,000
Venezuela	671,000,000	58,000
Vietnam	N.A.	650,000
Yemen	325,000,000	30,000
Yemen, Southern	126,000,000	20,000
Yugoslavia	3,484,000,000	258,000
Zaire	199,000,000	42,000
Zambia	130,000,000	15,000
Zimbabwe	380,000,000	24,000

[1] 1978 data. [2] 1975 data. [3] 1977 data. [4] 1979 data. N.A.=Not Available.

U.S. ARMED FORCES IN MAJOR CONFLICTS

Source: U.S. Department of Defense

The military services of the U.S. have taken part in nine major wars in which nearly 650,000 American military personnel were killed in action.

More American men and women served in the armed services in World War II than in any other war—over 16 million. More were killed or wounded in that war than in any other—more than 1 million.

The Continental Army was first formed by order of the Continental Congress on June 15, 1775, with George Washington as commander in chief. A Continental Navy was formed by the Continental Congress on Dec. 22, 1775, with the appointment of Esek Hopkins as its commander. Various congressional committees and boards maintained civilian control over the armed forces during the early part of the Revolutionary War.

The first secretary of war, Maj. Gen. Benjamin Lincoln, was appointed by Congress on Oct. 30, 1781.

The Department of Defense, created by Congress in 1949, provides civilian administration of the armed services. The secretary of defense is a cabinet-level officer.

WARS	BRANCH OF SERVICE	NUMBER SERVING	MILITARY CASUALTIES Total	Deaths in Action	Other Deaths	Nonfatal Wounds
Revolutionary War 1775–1783	**Total**	**184,000 to 250,000**	**10,623**	**4,435**	—	**6,188**
	Army	—	10,048	4,044	—	6,004
	Navy	—	456	342	—	114
	Marines	—	119	49	—	70
War of 1812 1812–1815	**Total**	**286,730**	**6,765**	**2,260**	—	**4,505**
	Army	—	5,950	1,950	—	4,000
	Navy	—	704	265	—	439
	Marines	—	111	45	—	66
Mexican War 1846–1848	**Total**	**78,718**	**17,435**	**1,733**	**11,550**	**4,152**
	Army	—	17,373	1,721	11,550	4,102
	Navy	—	4	1	—	3
	Marines	—	58	11	—	47
Civil War 1861–1865	**Union Forces**	**2,213,363**	**646,392**	**140,414**	**224,097**	**281,881**
	Army	2,128,948	639,568	138,154	221,374	280,040
	Navy }	84,415	6,233	2,112	2,411	1,710
	Marines }		591	148	312	131
	Confederate Forces [1]	**600,000 to 1,500,000**	**159,821 to 164,821 +**	**74,524**	**85,297 to 90,297**	—
Spanish-American War 1898	**Total**	**306,760**	**4,108**	**385**	**2,061**	**1,662**
	Army	280,564	4,024	369	2,061	1,594
	Navy	22,875	57	10	—	47
	Marines	3,321	27	6	—	21
World War I 1917–1918	**Total**	**4,734,991**	**320,518**	**53,402**	**63,114**	**204,002**
	Army	4,057,101	300,041	50,510	55,868	193,663
	Navy	599,051	8,106	431	6,856	819
	Marines	78,839	12,371	2,461	390	9,520
World War II 1941–1945	**Total**	**16,112,566**	**1,076,245**	**291,557**	**113,842**	**670,846**
	Army	11,260,000	884,135	234,874	83,400	565,861
	Navy	4,183,466	100,392	36,950	25,664	37,778
	Marines	669,100	91,718	19,733	4,778	67,207
Korean War 1950–1953	**Total**	**5,720,000**	**157,530**	**33,629**	**20,617**	**103,284**
	Army	2,834,000	114,729	27,704	9,429	77,596
	Navy	1,177,000	6,077	458	4,043	1,576
	Marines	424,000	29,272	4,267	1,261	23,744
	Air Force	1,285,000	7,452	1,200	5,884	368
Vietnam War 1961–1973	**Total**	**8,744,000**	**211,005**	**47,253**	**10,449**	**153,303**
	Army	4,368,000	134,921	30,867	7,252	96,802
	Navy [2]	1,842,000	6,694	1,605	911	4,178
	Marines	794,000	66,141	13,066	1,683	51,392
	Air Force	1,740,000	3,249	1,715	603	931

1 Other deaths include 26,000 to 31,000 Confederates who died in Union prisons. 2 Includes small number of Coast Guard casualties.

Nations of the World

United Press Int.

Guerrillas blew up the approach to the Urbina Bridge in El Salvador on Sept. 4, cutting the main highway between San Miguel and the Honduran border. Pedestrians use ropes to pull themselves up the ramp to cross the bridge.

HIGHLIGHTS: 1983

NEW NATIONS

St. Christopher and Nevis, a former British colony in the Caribbean, declared its independence on Sept. 19. Commonly known as St. Kitts, the country is one of the world's 10 smallest nations. See page 637.

Brunei, a small British protectorate on the island of Borneo in the South China Sea, received its independence on Jan. 1, 1984. See page 511.

The Turkish Cypriot state on the northern coast of Cyprus in the Mediterranean Sea declared its independence on Nov. 15. However, the UN Security Council, which has tried to mediate differences between Greek and Turkish Cypriots on the island, passed a resolution calling the declaration of independence illegal and asking that it be rescinded. See page 535.

Three nations that have been part of the U.S. Trust Territory of the Pacific since the end of World War II moved closer to independence in 1983. The three, Belau, Micronesia, and the Marshalls, each held referendums in which voters approved self-government under compacts of free association with the U.S. The compacts must be ratified by the U.S. Congress and the

HIGHLIGHTS: 1983 *(continued)*

United Nations to become effective. See pages 495–496, 604–605, and 608–609.

WARS AND CIVIL WARS

Tens of thousands of persons died in wars and civil wars that raged in many parts of the world during the year.

After the Marxist prime minister of Grenada was slain during a coup led by rivals within his government, the U.S. intervened on Oct. 25, landing armed forces to protect Americans on the Caribbean island. See page 29.

The United States was caught in the middle of the continuing civil war in Lebanon. Americans suffered many casualties when terrorists blew up the U.S. embassy in April (see page 15) and headquarters of the U.S. and French peacekeeping forces in October (see page 27).

The largest war, between Iraq and Iran in the Middle East, entered its fourth year. As France began supplying Iraq with Exocet missiles, Iran threatened to cut off all oil shipments out of the Persian Gulf if Iraq used the missiles to attack its oil fields. The U.S. warned Iran that it would use force to keep the waterway open.

Thousands died in El Salvador as civil war continued between leftist guerrillas and government forces supported by the U.S. Accusing the leftist government of Nicaragua with supplying military aid to the Salvadorian guerrillas, the U.S. aided guerrillas seeking to topple the Nicaraguan government. The U.S. also conducted large-scale military exercises in cooperation with neighboring Honduras, bringing charges from Nicaragua that the U.S. was planning an armed invasion. See pages 544–545, 568, and 618.

Fighting brought deaths to thousands in Afghanistan as Soviet troops sought to exterminate rebels opposed to the communist government. See pages 482–483.

Jungle warfare continued in Cambodia as Soviet-supported Vietnamese troops fought government-in-exile forces of Prince Sihanouk and Pol Pot that were aided by the U.S. and China. See page 515.

In the African nation Chad, Libyan-backed rebels captured large areas in the northeastern part of the country. However, France and Zaire sent troops to aid Chad's forces, halting the rebel advances. See page 522.

In India's state of Assam fighting between Muslims and Hindus brought death to thousands. See page 573.

Riots and fighting in Sri Lanka between Tamil and Sinhalese forces resulted in hundreds of deaths and made thousands homeless. See page 654.

ELECTIONS AND COUPS

Argentina, still suffering the consequences of its disastrous war with Britain over the Falkland Islands, moved toward reestablishment of democracy as the military government permitted the first free presidential election in 10 years. See page 488.

Still riding a wave of popularity for winning the Falkland Islands War against Argentina, Britain's Conservative Prime Minister Margaret Thatcher achieved a landslide victory in parliamentary elections in June. See page 508.

After 13 years as prime minister of Austria, 72-year-old Bruno Kreisky resigned after his Socialist Party lost its parliamentary majority in an election in May. He was succeeded by 54-year-old Fred Sinowatz as head of a coalition government.

West Germany's conservative Chancellor Helmut Kohl consolidated his position by leading the Christian Democrats to victory in a March election—giving the socialists their worst defeat in 20 years.

Italy swore in its first socialist prime minister, 49-year-old Bettino Craxi, to head a coalition government after a parliamentary election in June that saw the socialists win seats from both leading parties, the Christian Democrats and the Communists. See page 584.

In Israel Yitzhak Shamir, 68, who had been foreign minister, became prime minister after the resignation of ailing 70-year-old Menachem Begin, who had held the office for six years. See page 581.

In Australia the Labor Party regained control of the government in an election in March. Robert Hawke, 52, became prime minister. See page 490.

In Guatemala Gen. Oscar Mejia Victores, who had been minister of defense, in August overthrew President Efrain Rios Montt, a general who had seized power 15 months earlier. See page 565.

In Iceland 54-year-old Steingrimur Hermannsson became prime minister at the head of a coalition cabinet after none of the country's six political parties won a majority in an election in April. See page 570.

In the Maldives, a tiny Indian Ocean island nation, President Maumoon Abdul Gayoom was reelected by the national legislature.

POPULATIONS[1] OF CONTINENTS

Africa	518,433,000
North America	252,963,000
South America	404,020,000
Asia	2,732,390,000
Europe	490,814,000
Australia and Oceania	24,020,900

[1] January 1984 population estimates.

LARGEST NATIONS IN AREA

RANK	NATION	AREA (sq. mi.)	LOCATION
1	Soviet Union	8,649,538	Europe–Asia
2	Canada	3,849,670	North America
3	China	3,692,950	Asia
4	United States	3,618,770	North America
5	Brazil	3,286,488	South America
6	Australia	2,967,909	South Pacific
7	India	1,269,346	Asia
8	Argentina	1,068,301	South America
9	Sudan	967,500	Africa
10	Algeria	919,595	North Africa

SMALLEST NATIONS IN AREA

RANK	NATION	AREA (sq. mi.)	LOCATION
178	Vatican City	0.17	Europe
177	Monaco	0.58	Europe
176	Nauru	8.00	South Pacific
175	Tuvalu	10.00	South Pacific
174	San Marino	23.60	Europe
173	Liechtenstein	61.00	Europe
172	Marshall Islands	70.00	South Pacific
171	St. Christopher-Nevis	101.00	Caribbean
170	Maldives	115.00	Indian Ocean
169	Malta	122.00	Mediterranean

LARGEST NATIONS IN POPULATION

RANK	NATION	POPULATION[1]	LOCATION
1	China	1,048,210,000	Asia
2	India	748,210,000	Asia
3	Soviet Union	273,405,000	Europe–Asia
4	United States	235,311,000	North America
5	Indonesia	162,604,000	Asia
6	Brazil	132,184,000	South America
7	Japan	119,565,000	Asia
8	Bangladesh	96,707,700	Asia
9	Pakistan	91,260,300	Asia
10	Nigeria	86,528,100	Africa

SMALLEST NATIONS IN POPULATION

RANK	NATION	POPULATION[1]	LOCATION
178	Vatican City	1,006	Europe
177	Tuvalu	8,060	South Pacific
176	Nauru	8,154	South Pacific
175	Belau	14,007	South Pacific
174	San Marino	22,177	Europe
173	Liechtenstein	26,668	Europe
172	Monaco	27,610	Europe
171	Marshall Islands	35,707	South Pacific
170	Andorra	38,249	Europe
169	St. Christopher-Nevis	44,932	Caribbean

178 NATIONS OF THE WORLD: LOCATION, AREA, POPULATION, CAPITALS

NATION	LOCATION	AREA In Sq. Mi.	Rank	POPULATION[1] Total	Rank	Per Sq. Mi.	CAPITAL
WORLD	—	57,506,000	—	4,699,790,000	—	81.7	New York (UN)
Afghanistan	Asia	250,000	40	14,162,700	51	56.6	Kabul
Albania	Europe	11,100	126	2,880,750	107	259.5	Tiranë
Algeria	North Africa	919,595	10	20,973,000	35	22.8	Algiers
Andorra	Europe	175	163	38,249	170	218.6	Andorra la Vella
Angola	Africa	481,354	21	7,666,110	70	15.9	Luanda
Antigua	Caribbean	171	164	78,511	165	459.1	St. John's
Argentina	South America	1,068,301	8	29,284,300	28	27.4	Buenos Aires
Australia	South Pacific	2,967,909	6	15,398,300	47	5.2	Canberra
Austria	Europe	32,374	106	7,595,290	71	234.6	Vienna
Bahamas	Caribbean	5,380	139	225,247	153	41.9	Nassau
Bahrain	Asia	258	159	407,267	140	1,578.5	Manama
Bangladesh	Asia	55,598	87	96,707,700	8	1,739.4	Dhaka
Barbados	Caribbean	166	166	253,561	151	1,527.4	Bridgetown
Belau	South Pacific	191	162	14,007	175	73.3	Koror
Belgium	Europe	11,781	123	9,882,750	61	838.9	Brussels
Belize	Central America	8,867	132	155,131	157	17.5	Belmopan
Benin	Africa	43,484	95	3,755,090	98	86.4	Porto Novo
Bhutan	Asia	18,147	115	1,402,060	126	77.3	Thimphu
Bolivia	South America	424,165	26	5,960,060	84	14.1	La Paz; Sucre
Bophuthatswana	Africa	17,010	116	1,417,520	125	83.3	Mmabatho
Botswana	Africa	231,805	43	1,038,860	129	4.5	Gaborone
Brazil	South America	3,286,488	5	132,184,000	6	40.2	Brasilia
Britain	Europe	94,515	73	56,019,900	15	592.7	London
Brunei	SE Asia	2,226	147	209,567	154	94.1	Bandar Seri Begawan
Bulgaria	Europe	42,823	98	8,956,900	67	209.2	Sofia
Burma	Asia	261,218	39	37,536,400	24	143.7	Rangoon
Burundi	Africa	10,747	128	4,481,770	94	417.0	Bujumbura
Cambodia	SE Asia	69,898	83	6,051,050	82	86.6	Phnom Penh
Cameroon	Africa	183,569	49	9,447,270	65	51.5	Yaoundé
Canada	North America	3,849,670	2	24,789,600	31	6.4	Ottawa
Cape Verde	Africa	1,557	149	298,496	147	191.7	Praia
Central Africa	Africa	240,535	42	2,566,060	112	10.6	Bangui
Chad	Africa	495,755	19	5,021,030	91	10.1	N'Djaména
Chile	South America	292,258	36	11,562,400	55	39.6	Santiago
China	Asia	3,692,950	3	1,048,210,000	1	283.8	Peking
Ciskei	Africa	3,205	145	694,718	135	216.8	Bisho
Colombia	South America	439,737	24	27,955,600	29	63.6	Bogotá
Comoros	Indian Ocean	694	153	391,759	141	564.5	Moroni
Congo	Africa	132,047	56	1,710,710	120	13.0	Brazzaville
Costa Rica	Central America	19,575	113	2,633,040	110	134.5	San José
Cuba	Caribbean	44,218	94	9,977,140	59	225.6	Havana
Cyprus	Mediterranean	3,572	144	657,276	137	184.0	Nicosia
Czechoslovakia	Europe	49,371	91	15,443,900	46	312.8	Prague

[1] Jan. 1, 1984, population estimates.

LOCATION, AREA, POPULATION, CAPITALS *(continued)*

NATION	LOCATION	AREA In Sq. Mi.	Rank	POPULATION[1] Total	Rank	Per Sq. Mi.	CAPITAL
Denmark	Europe	16,629	117	5,112,420	90	307.4	Copenhagen
Djibouti	Africa	8,494	133	321,253	146	37.8	Djibouti
Dominica	Caribbean	290	155	73,925	166	254.9	Roseau
Dominican Republic	Caribbean	18,816	114	6,001,540	83	319.0	Santo Domingo
Ecuador	South America	109,484	66	9,491,020	64	86.7	Quito
Egypt	Africa	386,900	28	45,948,200	20	118.8	Cairo
El Salvador	Central America	8,124	134	4,748,720	93	584.5	San Salvador
Equatorial Guinea	Africa	10,831	127	268,265	149	24.8	Malabo
Ethiopia	Africa	471,778	23	31,447,600	27	66.7	Addis Ababa
Fiji	SE Asia	7,056	135	678,888	136	96.2	Suva
Finland	Europe	130,120	57	4,856,700	92	37.3	Helsinki
France	Europe	211,208	46	54,741,500	16	259.2	Paris
Gabon	Africa	103,347	69	942,343	132	9.1	Libreville
Gambia	Africa	4,361	140	646,356	138	148.2	Banjul
Germany, East	Europe	41,768	100	16,738,000	43	400.7	East Berlin
Germany, West	Europe	95,976	71	61,481,000	12	640.6	Bonn
Ghana	Africa	92,100	74	13,572,200	53	147.4	Accra
Greece	Europe	50,944	89	9,984,910	58	196.0	Athens
Grenada	Caribbean	133	168	111,727	161	840.1	St. George's
Guatemala	Central America	42,042	99	6,384,290	78	151.9	Guatemala City
Guinea	Africa	94,926	72	5,503,860	87	58.0	Conakry
Guinea-Bissau	Africa	13,948	121	846,653	133	60.7	Bissau
Guyana	South America	83,000	78	836,521	134	10.1	Georgetown
Haiti	Caribbean	10,714	130	5,155,670	89	481.2	Port-au-Prince
Honduras	Central America	43,277	96	4,359,320	95	100.7	Tegucigalpa
Hungary	Europe	35,919	104	10,666,700	56	297.0	Budapest
Iceland	North Atlantic	39,768	101	237,308	152	6.0	Reykjavík
India	Asia	1,269,346	7	748,210,000	2	589.4	New Delhi
Indonesia	SE Asia	782,662	13	162,604,000	5	207.8	Jakarta
Iran	Asia	636,296	16	43,142,800	21	67.8	Teheran
Iraq	Asia	167,925	52	14,737,800	49	87.8	Baghdad
Ireland	Europe	27,136	110	3,555,360	102	131.0	Dublin
Israel	Asia	10,715	129	5,349,110	88	525.7	Jerusalem
Italy	Europe	116,304	64	56,860,300	14	488.9	Rome
Ivory Coast	Africa	124,504	62	8,998,730	66	72.3	Abidjan
Jamaica	Caribbean	4,244	142	2,336,560	115	550.6	Kingston
Japan	Asia	145,809	55	119,565,000	7	820.0	Tokyo
Jordan	Asia	37,738	103	2,558,420	113	67.8	Amman
Kenya	Africa	224,961	45	17,805,600	42	79.1	Nairobi
Kiribati	South Pacific	278	156	60,484	168	217.6	Bairiki, Tarawa
Korea, North	Asia	46,540	92	18,963,000	40	407.5	Pyongyang
Korea, South	Asia	38,025	102	41,578,200	22	1,093.4	Seoul
Kuwait	Asia	6,880	136	1,700,730	121	247.2	Kuwait
Laos	SE Asia	91,429	76	3,668,920	100	40.1	Vientiane
Lebanon	Asia	4,015	143	2,591,460	111	645.4	Beirut
Lesotho	Africa	11,720	124	1,450,070	123	123.7	Maseru
Liberia	Africa	43,000	97	2,124,710	116	49.4	Monrovia
Libya	Africa	679,362	15	3,586,110	101	5.3	Tripoli
Liechtenstein	Europe	61	173	26,668	173	437.2	Vaduz
Luxembourg	Europe	998	151	367,652	143	368.4	Luxembourg-Ville
Madagascar	Indian Ocean	226,658	44	9,516,710	63	42.0	Antananarivo
Malawi	Africa	45,747	93	6,718,590	74	146.9	Lilongwe
Malaysia	SE Asia	127,317	59	15,171,700	48	119.2	Kuala Lumpur
Maldives	Indian Ocean	115	170	170,424	155	1,482.0	Male
Mali	Africa	478,767	22	7,474,940	72	15.6	Bamako
Malta	Mediterranean	122	169	362,817	144	2,973.9	Valletta
Marshalls	South Pacific	70	172	35,707	171	510.1	Majuro
Mauritania	Africa	397,955	27	1,607,030	122	4.0	Nouakchott
Mauritius	Indian Ocean	790	152	1,015,440	130	1,285.4	Port-Louis
Mexico	North America	761,605	14	75,701,800	11	99.4	Mexico City
Micronesia	South Pacific	271	157	84,840	164	313.1	Kolonia
Monaco	Europe	0.58	177	27,610	172	47,603.4	Monaco-Ville
Mongolia	Asia	604,250	17	1,834,520	119	3.0	Ulaanbaatar
Morocco	Africa	275,117	38	22,208,400	34	80.7	Rabat
Mozambique	Africa	309,496	34	13,214,900	54	42.7	Maputo
Namibia	Africa	318,261	32	1,094,290	128	3.4	Windhoek
Nauru	South Pacific	8	176	8,154	176	1,019.3	Yaren
Nepal	Asia	54,362	88	16,286,500	44	299.6	Kathmandu
Netherlands	Europe	15,770	120	14,403,000	50	913.3	Amsterdam; The Hague

[1] Jan. 1, 1984, population estimates.

LOCATION, AREA, POPULATION, CAPITALS *(continued)*

NATION	LOCATION	AREA In Sq. Mi.	Rank	POPULATION[1] Total	Rank	Per Sq. Mi.	CAPITAL
Nicaragua	Central America	50,193	90	2,863,000	109	57.0	Managua
Niger	Africa	489,191	20	6,089,720	81	12.4	Niamey
Nigeria	Africa	356,669	30	86,528,100	10	242.6	Abuja
Norway	Europe	125,182	61	4,131,570	96	33.0	Oslo
Oman	Asia	82,030	79	992,631	131	12.1	Muscat
Pakistan	Asia	310,404	33	91,260,300	9	294.0	Islamabad
Panama	Central America	29,762	108	1,996,610	118	67.1	Panama City
Papua New Guinea	South Pacific	178,260	50	3,306,610	104	18.5	Port Moresby
Paraguay	South America	157,048	53	3,143,250	105	20.0	Asunción
Peru	South America	496,225	18	19,422,500	38	39.1	Lima
Philippines	SE Asia	115,830	65	53,528,200	17	462.1	Manila
Poland	Europe	120,725	63	36,720,600	25	304.2	Warsaw
Portugal	Europe	35,553	105	9,611,932	62	270.4	Lisbon
Qatar	Asia	4,247	141	271,573	148	63.9	Doha
Romania	Europe	91,699	75	22,642,900	33	246.9	Bucharest
Rwanda	Africa	10,169	131	5,715,990	86	562.1	Kigali
St. Christopher and Nevis	Caribbean	101	171	44,932	169	444.9	Basseterre
St. Lucia	Caribbean	238	160	119,659	160	502.8	Castries
St. Vincent	Caribbean	150	167	130,063	158	867.1	Kingstown
San Marino	Europe	23.6	174	22,177	174	939.7	San Marino
São Tomé–Príncipe	South Atlantic	372	154	88,488	163	237.9	São Tomé
Saudi Arabia	Asia	830,000	12	10,621,900	57	12.8	Riyadh
Senegal	Africa	75,750	80	6,438,140	76	85.0	Dakar
Seychelles	Indian Ocean	171	165	65,360	167	382.2	Victoria
Sierra Leone	Africa	27,699	109	3,753,530	99	135.7	Freetown
Singapore	SE Asia	224	161	2,518,130	114	11,241.7	Singapore
Solomons	South Pacific	11,500	125	258,074	150	22.4	Honiara
Somalia	Africa	246,201	41	6,310,950	79	25.6	Mogadishu
South Africa	Africa	434,674	25	25,227,800	30	58.0	Cape Town; Pretoria
Soviet Union	Europe–Asia	8,649,538	1	273,405,000	3	31.6	Moscow
Spain	Europe	194,897	48	36,156,079	23	185.5	Madrid
Sri Lanka	Indian Ocean	25,332	111	15,788,900	45	623.3	Colombo
Sudan	Africa	967,500	9	20,885,700	36	21.6	Khartoum
Suriname	South America	63,037	86	356,201	145	5.7	Paramaribo
Swaziland	Africa	6,704	137	610,747	139	91.1	Mbabane; Lobamba
Sweden	Europe	173,732	51	8,331,000	68	48.0	Stockholm
Switzerland	Europe	15,941	119	6,405,260	77	401.8	Bern
Syria	Asia	71,498	82	9,905,810	60	138.5	Damascus
Taiwan	Asia	13,892	122	18,980,600	39	1,366.3	Taipei
Tanzania	Africa	364,900	29	20,854,900	37	57.2	Dodoma; Dar es Salaam
Thailand	SE Asia	198,457	47	51,476,800	18	259.4	Bangkok
Togo	Africa	21,925	112	2,867,090	108	130.8	Lomé
Tonga	South Pacific	270	158	104,290	162	386.3	Nukualofa
Transkei	Africa	16,070	118	3,345,670	103	208.2	Umtata
Trinidad–Tobago	Caribbean	1,981	148	1,099,390	127	555.0	Port-of-Spain
Tunisia	Africa	63,170	85	7,017,650	73	111.1	Tunis
Turkey	Europe–Asia	301,382	35	47,713,500	19	158.3	Ankara
Tuvalu	South Pacific	10	175	8,060	177	806.0	Fongafale
Uganda	Africa	91,134	77	14,027,800	52	153.9	Kampala
United Arab Emirates	Asia	32,278	107	1,448,060	124	44.9	Abu Dhabi
UNITED STATES	North America	3,618,770	4	235,311,000	4	65.0	Washington, D.C.
Upper Volta	Africa	105,869	67	6,648,420	75	62.8	Ouagadougou
Uruguay	South America	68,037	84	2,920,410	106	42.9	Montevideo
Vanuatu	South Pacific	5,700	138	128,727	159	22.6	Port Vila
Vatican City	Europe	0.17	178	1,006	178	5,917.6	—
Venda	Africa	2,510	146	379,929	142	151.4	Thohoyandou
Venezuela	South America	352,145	31	18,274,000	41	51.9	Caracas
Vietnam	SE Asia	127,242	60	57,668,100	13	453.2	Hanoi
Western Samoa	South Pacific	1,097	150	160,725	156	146.5	Apia
Yemen, North	Asia	75,290	81	5,822,130	85	77.3	Sana
Yemen, South	Asia	128,560	58	2,116,470	117	16.5	Aden
Yugoslavia	Europe	98,766	70	22,918,000	32	232.0	Belgrade
Zaire	Africa	905,568	11	31,706,500	26	35.0	Kinshasa
Zambia	Africa	290,586	37	6,309,020	80	21.7	Lusaka
Zimbabwe	Africa	150,804	54	7,905,410	69	52.4	Harare (Salisbury)

[1] Jan. 1, 1984, population estimates.

VITAL STATISTICS, EDUCATION, COMMUNICATIONS

NATION	VITAL STATISTICS					COMMUNICATIONS				
	Birth Rate[1]	Death Rate[1]	Infant Deaths[2]	Life Expectancy Men/Women	Urban Pop.	Literacy Rate[3]	Phones[1]	Radio Sets[1]	TV Sets[1]	News-papers[4]
WORLD	29.0	12.0	98.0	55.0	83.6%	—	191	—	—	—
Afghanistan	45.2	21.1	184.6	40.0/41.0	14.5%	12%	3	6	0.7	4
Albania	33.3	8.1	86.8	64.9/67.0	33.8%	75%	5	75	1.9	54
Algeria	47.4	14.2	86.3	54.4/56.3	52.0%	35%	25	168	39	22
Andorra	17.4	4.6	—	—	37.0%	100%	435	219	113	250
Angola	47.6	23.1	24.1	39.5/42.6	16.6%	15%	5	18	—	17
Antigua	16.5	5.6	31.5	60.5/64.3	33.8%	88%	92	225	207	80
Argentina	25.2	8.9	40.8	65.2/71.4	80.4%	85%	103	838	176	154
Australia	15.3	7.3	11.0	70.8/77.8	86.0%	98.5%	526	770	383	336
Austria	12.0	12.2	13.9	68.9/76.1	51.9%	98%	398	352	282	351
Bahamas	21.6	4.7	31.9	64.0/69.3	57.9%	93%	344	475	—	118
Bahrain	34.4	6.3	35.5	64.1/68.1	78.1%	40%	210	342	257	21
Bangladesh	46.8	18.7	132.0	45.8/46.6	10.1%	24%	1	8	0.5	5
Barbados	17.0	8.5	25.1	62.7/67.4	3.7%	90%	219	524	200	85
Belau	21.1	4.3	46.4	—	63.6%	45%	86	—	—	—
Belgium	12.7	11.6	11.2	68.6/75.1	94.6%	97%	468	452	293	228
Belize	38.7	5.3	33.7	45.0/49.0	59.0%	80%	43	449	—	41
Benin	48.8	19.1	109.6	44.3/47.5	13.9%	20%	3	58	0.1	0.3
Bhutan	42.7	20.6	—	44.0/42.5	4.1%	5%	1	9	—	—
Bolivia	46.6	18.0	77.3	46.5/50.9	41.7%	62%	26	92	18	39
Bophuthatswana	43.0	14.0	100.0	55.7/62.7	12.1%	—	9	—	—	—
Botswana	50.7	17.5	—	46.7/50.0	16.1%	32%	11	82	—	21
Brazil	33.3	9.1	24.2	57.6/61.1	63.5%	83%	63	295	126	45
Britain	13.3	11.8	12.0	70.0/76.2	77.7%	99%	497	931	394	410
Brunei	27.8	3.6	20.0	61.9/62.1	—	—	—	164	122	—
Bulgaria	14.3	10.7	19.9	68.7/73.9	62.1%	95%	141	314	196	234
Burma	38.6	14.3	247.5	51.0/54.1	20.0%	75%	4	21	—	10
Burundi	42.0	20.4	150.0	40.0/43.0	2.2%	15%	1	34	—	0.3
Cambodia	30.9	29.4	127.0	29.0/31.4	10.3%	48%	1	14	4.2	10
Cameroon	42.3	19.4	137.2	44.4/47.6	28.0%	50%	2	91	—	3
Canada	15.5	7.1	10.9	70.2/77.5	75.5%	98%	671	1,104	466	241
Cape Verde	27.6	9.4	104.9	58.3/62.0	19.7%	37%	6	129	—	—
Central Africa	44.3	22.5	190.0	33.0/36.0	26.6%	20%	2	36	—	0.3
Chad	44.1	24.1	160.0	29.0/35.0	18.4%	15%	1	23	—	0.4
Chile	21.5	6.8	14.7	61.3/67.6	81.1%	90%	50	297	112	87
China	21.3	7.4	55.0	66.0/68.6	25.5%	75%	28	16	3.4	8
Ciskei	—	—	—	—	—	—	—	—	—	—
Colombia	32.1	8.2	39.5	60.0/64.5	59.5%	81%	60	114	76	48
Comoros	47.3	18.6	51.7	44.4/47.6	20.3%	20%	3	114	—	—
Congo	44.6	19.0	180.0	44.4/47.6	29.7%	50%	10	61	2.2	1
Costa Rica	29.2	4.2	24.2	66.3/70.5	43.8%	90%	104	82	73	70
Cuba	14.7	5.6	19.3	68.5/71.8	60.3%	96%	33	263	114	91
Cyprus	19.6	9.1	17.2	71.9/74.9	42.2%	86%	179	483	161	108
Czechoslovakia	16.2	12.1	16.6	67.1/74.1	66.7%	99%	206	291	256	304
Denmark	11.2	10.9	8.8	71.3/77.4	82.6%	99%	636	377	358	367
Djibouti	42.0	7.6	—	—	—	5%	12	138	32	307
Dominica	21.4	5.3	19.6	57.0/59.2	—	80%	56	426	—	88
Dominican Republic	36.7	9.0	37.2	57.2/58.6	39.8%	68%	29	41	57	42
Ecuador	41.6	10.4	70.9	59.5/61.8	43.1%	81%	33	279	49	49
Egypt	41.0	11.0	73.5	51.6/53.8	44.2%	44%	12	132	32	79
El Salvador	39.2	7.4	53.0	56.6/60.4	40.1%	63%	16	340	62	51
Equatorial Guinea	42.3	19.4	53.2	44.4/47.6	35.1%	20%	5	253	2.8	4
Ethiopia	49.8	25.2	84.2	37.5/40.6	13.6%	15%	3	7	0.8	2
Fiji	28.6	4.2	9.9	69.5/73.1	37.2%	80%	73	485	—	87
Finland	13.1	9.4	7.7	68.8/77.2	59.7%	99%	496	525	316	480
France	14.8	10.1	10.0	69.9/78.0	73.0%	99%	459	337	292	205
Gabon	31.2	21.3	229.0	25.0/45.0	32.0%	40%	12	176	16	—
Gambia	47.5	22.9	165.0	39.4/42.6	18.2%	15%	5	109	—	21
Germany, East	14.6	14.2	12.1	68.8/74.7	76.2%	99%	189	376	309	517
Germany, West	10.0	11.5	13.5	69.0/75.6	38.4%	99%	463	370	337	423
Ghana	48.4	17.2	156.0	46.7/50.0	31.4%	30%	6	106	4.4	42
Greece	15.9	8.7	18.7	70.1/73.6	64.8%	95%	289	307	147	107
Grenada	24.5	6.8	15.4	60.1/65.6	14.8%	—	54	303	—	31
Guatemala	42.1	10.3	70.2	53.7/55.5	36.8%	47%	16	40	19	39
Guinea	46.1	20.7	216.0	41.9/45.1	11.2%	20%	2	25	—	4
Guinea-Bissau	40.0	23.0	47.1	39.4/42.6	18.1%	5%	5	36	—	11
Guyana	28.3	7.3	45.9	59.0/63.0	29.6%	86%	33	358	—	77

[1] Per 1,000 population. [2] Per 1,000 live births. [3] Percent of population over age 15 who can read and write.
[4] Daily newspaper circulation per 1,000 population.

NATION	VITAL STATISTICS					COMMUNICATIONS				
	Birth Rate [1]	Death Rate [1]	Infant Deaths [2]	Life Expectancy Men/Women	Urban Pop.	Literacy Rate [3]	Phones [1]	Radio Sets [1]	TV Sets [1]	News-papers [4]
Haiti	41.8	15.7	—	49.1/52.2	27.5%	23%	7	21	3	7
Honduras	47.1	11.8	26.9	55.4/58.9	31.4%	60%	10	49	14	63
Hungary	13.9	13.6	23.1	66.7/73.6	53.1%	97%	118	243	249	242
Iceland	19.8	6.6	5.4	73.4/79.3	87.4%	99%	475	579	270	557
India	16.8	5.1	122.0	67.3/75.0	21.9%	36%	4	24	1.0	20
Indonesia	33.2	14.1	134.0	47.5	18.2%	60%	2	40	2.3	18
Iran	42.5	11.5	108.1	57.6/57.4	48.8%	50%	32	63	54	15
Iraq	47.0	13.0	30.6	53.6/56.7	63.7%	40%	26	157	47	22
Ireland	21.9	9.7	11.2	68.8/73.5	52.2%	98%	187	371	223	229
Israel	24.1	6.7	14.1	71.5/75.0	87.9%	88%	313	212	153	208
Italy	11.2	9.7	14.3	69.7/75.9	48.0%	95%	337	240	231	97
Ivory Coast	47.5	18.2	138.0	44.4/47.6	32.4%	22%	12	120	51	7
Jamaica	26.7	5.8	16.2	62.7/66.6	37.1%	82%	60	332	77	59
Japan	13.7	6.2	7.4	73.5/78.9	75.9%	99%	494	777	245	569
Jordan	46.9	10.5	14.9	52.6/52.0	59.8%	70%	22	174	53	29
Kenya	53.8	14.4	51.4	46.9/51.2	9.9%	40%	12	35	3.9	10
Kiribati	21.9	6.5	48.9	56.9/59.0	29.7%	90%	12	198	—	—
Korea, North	32.5	8.3	—	60.5/64.6	14.7%	85%	—	40	—	20
Korea, South	25.3	8.1	5.0	62.7/69.1	57.3%	90%	90	151	48	197
Kuwait	41.5	4.8	39.1	66.4/71.5	22.1%	60%	153	409	425	159
Laos	44.1	20.3	123.0	42.1/45.0	14.7%	28%	2	83	—	3
Lebanon	30.1	8.7	13.6	63.2/67.1	60.1%	86%	112	648	194	92
Lesotho	36.7	14.5	114.4	49.2/51.4	1.0%	55%	3	23	—	1
Liberia	49.8	20.9	159.2	45.8/44.0	27.6%	18%	5	177	11	6
Libya	47.4	12.7	130.0	53.8/57.0	29.8%	35%	20	46	56	26
Liechtenstein	14.3	6.7	10.8	—	28.6%	100%	770	481	231	477
Luxembourg	11.6	11.5	11.5	66.8/72.8	67.9%	98%	548	512	245	358
Madagascar	46.0	25.0	102.0	37.5/38.3	14.1%	53%	5	135	1	9
Malawi	48.5	25.1	130.0	40.9/44.2	8.5%	25%	3	43	—	5
Malaysia	30.0	5.7	26.7	67.1/72.7	28.8%	48%	44	150	64	87
Maldives	44.4	13.9	120.0	—	11.3%	36%	5	28	—	—
Mali	49.4	22.2	120.0	40.6/43.8	16.8%	9%	7	14	—	0.5
Malta	15.4	9.1	15.5	69.4/73.4	94.3%	87%	262	433	230	195
Marshalls	35.2	3.0	24.2	—	—	—	—	—	—	—
Mauritania	50.2	22.3	187.0	40.6/43.8	22.8%	17%	1	69	—	0.2
Mauritius	26.4	7.2	33.0	60.7/65.3	43.0%	60%	40	196	73	79
Mexico	38.3	7.8	44.1	62.8/68.0	66.0%	74%	75	288	108	85
Micronesia	28.6	4.4	28.0	—	—	—	16	—	—	—
Monaco	20.6	21.1	1.9	—	100.0%	99%	1,607	360	680	432
Mongolia	37.1	8.3	—	60.5/64.6	51.0%	95%	25	92	3.1	69
Morocco	45.4	13.6	149.0	53.8/57.0	40.6%	28%	11	108	39	21
Mozambique	44.8	19.0	19.1	44.4/47.6	7.0%	20%	43	25	0.1	4
Namibia	43.5	15.1	—	50.0/52.5	—	—	57	—	—	—
Nauru	19.8	4.5	19.0	44.0	—	99%	220	463	—	—
Nepal	43.7	20.7	169.0	44.0/42.5	4.0%	20%	2	18	—	3
Netherlands	12.8	8.1	8.7	72.4/78.9	88.1%	99%	509	308	293	325
New Zealand	16.9	8.2	12.6	69.0/75.5	83.0%	98%	568	888	278	345
Nicaragua	46.6	12.2	101.7	51.2/54.6	53.1%	87%	22	262	40	69
Niger	51.4	22.4	200.0	40.6/43.8	8.2%	8%	1	39	0.1	1
Nigeria	49.8	17.8	180.0	37.2/36.7	22.8%	30%	2	74	6	9
Norway	12.5	10.0	8.8	72.3/78.7	43.7%	99%	453	327	288	456
Oman	48.9	18.6	138.0	46.2/48.4	5.3%	50%	14	—	—	—
Pakistan	36.0	12.0	124.0	53.7/48.8	25.5%	24%	4	66	9	14
Panama	31.4	6.0	21.3	64.3/67.5	51.2%	82%	99	152	117	79
Papua New Guinea	42.5	15.7	159.0	50.5/50.0	12.6%	32%	16	52	—	6
Paraguay	36.7	7.6	38.6	61.9/66.4	39.6%	74%	18	63	19	39
Peru	38.6	11.6	70.3	52.6/55.5	67.4%	50%	28	145	49	51
Philippines	36.2	8.6	56.8	59.1/62.4	31.8%	83%	11	45	21	18
Poland	19.5	9.8	21.2	67.3/75.0	57.7%	98%	95	240	216	237
Portugal	16.3	9.4	26.0	65.1/72.9	26.4%	70%	138	160	122	54
Qatar	29.9	9.4	138.0	54.8/58.3	72.8%	25%	261	476	302	33
Romania	18.6	9.9	31.6	67.4/72.1	48.6%	98%	51	145	163	181
Rwanda	51.0	22.0	127.0	44.3/47.5	3.5%	25%	1	32	—	0.1
St. Christopher-Nevis	24.4	10.7	49.5	58.0/62.0	—	89%	—	299	63	22
St. Lucia	31.5	7.2	33.0	55.1/58.5	—	80%	71	752	16	35
St. Vincent	35.1	7.1	38.1	58.5/59.7	—	80%	46	300	7	—
San Marino	13.6	7.5	3.5	—	74.4%	97%	257	381	41	65
São Tomé–Príncipe	41.9	9.6	49.7	33.8	20.5%	10%	10	247	—	—
Saudi Arabia	45.9	14.4	152.0	51.5/54.6	14.0%	25%	53	37	38	11

[1] Per 1,000 population. [2] Per 1,000 live births. [3] Percent of population over age 15 who can read and write.
[4] Daily newspaper circulation per 1,000 population.

VITAL STATISTICS, EDUCATION, COMMUNICATIONS *(continued)*

NATION	VITAL STATISTICS					COMMUNICATIONS				
	Birth Rate [1]	Death Rate [1]	Infant Deaths [2]	Life Expectancy Men/Women	Urban Pop.	Literacy Rate [3]	Phones [1]	Radio Sets [1]	TV Sets [1]	News-papers [4]
Senegal	47.8	22.1	92.9	40.6/43.8	31.7%	10%	8	54	0.4	5
Seychelles	27.6	7.0	26.6	64.6/71.1	26.1%	60%	111	317	—	56
Sierra Leone	45.5	19.2	136.3	44.3/47.5	13.9%	15%	5	22	6	10
Singapore	17.3	5.2	13.2	65.1/70.0	100.0%	84.2%	291	179	212	249
Solomons	36.1	13.0	52.4	—	9.1%	60%	11	68	—	—
Somalia	46.2	19.9	177.0	40.9/44.1	20.2%	10%	2	23	—	1
South Africa	37.9	10.3	117.0	58.9/61.7	47.9%	75%	121	96	69	66
Soviet Union	18.3	10.3	27.7	64.0/74.0	62.3%	99.8%	89	473	303	251
Spain	15.1	7.7	11.1	70.4/76.2	64.2%	97%	310	258	253	128
Sri Lanka	28.5	6.6	37.1	64.8/66.9	22.4%	87%	6	47	—	42
Sudan	45.8	18.4	93.6	45.5/47.5	20.4%	20%	3	74	6	1
Suriname	28.0	7.9	30.4	62.5/66.7	37.8%	80%	61	394	105	74
Swaziland	47.5	19.1	149.0	44.3/47.5	7.9%	35%	22	151	0.9	15
Sweden	11.7	11.0	6.7	72.5/78.7	82.7%	99%	796	390	374	526
Switzerland	11.6	9.3	8.5	70.3/76.2	54.6%	99%	725	355	312	395
Syria	46.4	8.9	12.6	54.5/58.6	47.9%	50%	25	224	45	12
Taiwan	26.0	5.0	25.0	70.0	77.0%	90%	177	103	79	99
Tanzania	46.3	15.8	162.5	48.8/52.2	13.3%	61%	6	28	0.3	10
Thailand	32.3	8.9	16.6	53.6/58.7	13.2%	82%	11	128	17	21
Togo	47.8	18.9	127.0	31.6/38.5	15.2%	18%	3	208	0.6	3
Tonga	13.0	1.9	20.5	—	21.8%	95%	23	211	—	—
Transkei	—	—	—	55.7/62.7	7.1%	—	6	—	—	—
Trinidad-Tobago	25.7	6.5	26.4	64.1/68.1	49.4%	95%	70	263	133	171
Tunisia	36.0	11.1	125.0	57.4/58.4	40.1%	62%	30	141	48	44
Turkey	39.6	14.6	153.0	53.7	44.6%	62%	42	97	70	41
Tuvalu	22.3	6.5	48.9	56.9/59.0	29.7%	49%	0.5	0.5	—	—
Uganda	44.7	14.4	160.0	50.8/54.3	7.1%	25%	3	19	5	2
United Arab Emirates	30.5	7.3	138.0	59.6/63.5	57.0%	25%	200	316	—	8
UNITED STATES	15.8	8.7	12.6	69.5/77.2	73.5%	99%	837	2,040	635	282
Upper Volta	47.8	22.1	182.0	32.1/31.1	3.7%	7%	1	16	1	0.2
Uruguay	18.6	10.6	37.4	65.5/71.6	83.0%	94%	99	566	126	267
Vanuatu	45.0	20.0	—	—	23.1%	20%	25	170	—	—
Vatican City	0.0	11.4	0.0	—	100.0%	100%	—	—	—	250
Venda	—	—	—	—	—	—	—	—	—	—
Venezuela	36.9	6.1	33.1	65.0/69.7	76.1%	78%	85	407	127	176
Vietnam	40.1	14.3	42.8	51.1/54.3	24.2%	78%	1	121	26	5
Western Samoa	36.9	6.7	40.0	60.8/65.2	21.3%	90%	37	329	13	1
Yemen	48.6	24.1	22.7	40.4/42.2	5.8%	15%	1	18	0.2	10
Yemen, South	47.6	20.9	22.7	43.0/45.1	33.3%	25%	6	54	18	1
Yugoslavia	17.0	9.0	32.8	65.4/70.2	38.6%	85%	96	209	189	103
Zaire	46.2	18.7	104.0	44.4/47.6	30.3%	40%	1	101	0.3	9
Zambia	49.2	17.2	259.0	46.7/50.0	40.4%	28%	11	22	11	19
Zimbabwe	47.3	13.6	122.0	51.8/55.3	19.6%	30%	30	39	10	16

[1] Per 1,000 population. [2] Per 1,000 live births. [3] Percent of population over age 15 who can read and write. [4] Daily newspaper circulation per 1,000 population.

NATIONS OF THE WORLD: MONEY, ECONOMY, TRANSPORTATION

NATION	MONETARY UNIT		ECONOMIC INDICATORS				TRANSPORTATION	
		Value [1]	Gross Domestic Product Annual [1]	Per Capita [1]	Cost of Living	Electric Power [2]	Highways [3]	Rail-roads [4]
Afghanistan	afghani	2 ¢	$3,400,000,000	$ 230	118 [5]	49	3,000	9.6
Albania	lek	14 ¢	2,150,000,000	830	—	1,611	1,287	277
Algeria	dinar	21 ¢	42,900,000,000	2,142	258 [9]	440	45,070	3,908
Andorra	Fr. franc	13 ¢	—	—	—	3,800	96	—
	Sp. peseta	⅔ ¢						
Angola	kwanza	3½ ¢	3,900,000,000	591	—	210	8,577	3,189
Antigua	E.C. dollar	37 ¢	124,500,000	1,640	333 [5]	780	240	78
Argentina	New peso	8 ¢	130,000,000,000	4,160	315,807 [5]	1,260	47,550	39,738
Australia	dollar	91 ¢	152,571,000,000	10,240	328 [5]	6,662	243,750	42,855
Austria	schilling	6 ¢	67,760,656,000	9,023	207 [5]	5,525	21,812	6,497
Bahamas	dollar	$1.00	1,400,000,000	6,000	216 [6]	3,500	1,350	—
Bahrain	dinar	$2.65	3,592,000,000	6,315	—	13,786	93	—
Bangladesh	taka	4 ¢	9,300,000,000	102	455 [6]	27	4,076	4,085
Barbados	dollar	50 ¢	819,402,920	3,270	478 [5]	1,315	1,450	—
Belau	dollar	$1.00	—	—	—	—	—	—

[1] In $U.S. [2] Kilowatt hours per capita. [3] Paved kilometers. [4] Total kilometers. [5] 100 = 1970 prices. [6] 100 = 1972 prices. [7] 100 = 1979 prices. [8] $100 = 1976 prices.

NATION	MONETARY UNIT		ECONOMIC INDICATORS				TRANSPORTATION	
		Value [1]	Gross Domestic Product Annual [1]	Per Capita [1]	Cost of Living	Electric Power [2]	Highways [3]	Railroads [4]
Belgium	franc	2¢	$ 87,501,600,000	$ 8,779	238 [5]	5,160	49,280	4,130
Belize	dollar	50¢	135,000,000	1,000	—	310	340	—
Benin	CFA franc	⅕¢	976,740,000	284	142 [5]	2	705	579
Bhutan	ngultrum	11¢	113,000,000	100	—	8	418	—
Bolivia	peso	⅕¢	7,000,000,000	1,217	741 [5]	300	1,400	3,651
Bophuthatswana	S. Af. rand	90¢	15,168,000	110	—	—	—	—
Botswana	pula	92¢	998,900,000	1,067	183 [8]	450	1,105	726
Brazil	cruzeiro	⅒¢	295,300,000,000	2,360	4,901 [9]	1,160	83,965	24,600
Britain	pound	$1.45	376,533,000,000	6,722	438 [5]	4,900	339,483	17,664
Brunei	dollar	50¢	2,300,000,000	10,985	—	1,646	1,090	13
Bulgaria	lev	$1.04	69,687,500,000	7,780	—	4,304	4,291	4,341
Burma	kyat	12¢	5,900,000,000	180	275 [5]	55	3,200	4,353
Burundi	franc	1¢	1,200,000,000	238	367 [5]	.05	300	—
Cambodia	—	—	500,000,000	50	—	19	2,622	612
Cameroon	CFA franc	⅕¢	8,400,000,000	669	243 [5]	180	2,682	1,173
Canada	dollar	80¢	303,324,000,000	12,236	271 [5]	15,900	189,800	67,067
Cape Verde	escudo	1½¢	142,000,000	473	437 [5]	30	—	—
Central Africa	CFA franc	⅕¢	605,900,000	285	134 [8]	30	454	—
Chad	CFA franc	⅕¢	500,000,000	109	—	15	242	—
Chile	peso	2¢	24,472,000,000	2,178	552,122 [5]	1,070	9,365	8,293
China	yuan	51¢	249,200,000,000	242	—	300	262,000	52,500
Ciskei	S. Af. rand	90¢	—	—	—	—	—	—
Colombia	peso	1¢	37,967,000,000	1,396	1,093 [5]	825	9,160	3,436
Comoros	CFA franc	⅕¢	92,400,000	240	—	10	295	—
Congo	CFA franc	⅕¢	1,824,000,000	939	269 [5]	85	555	800
Costa Rica	colón	2½¢	4,980,000,000	2,109	728 [5]	835	2,425	790
Cuba	peso	$1.16	13,900,000,000	1,372	—	1,015	9,000	14,725
Cyprus	pound	$2.38	2,181,856,500	3,995	106 [6]	1,700	4,580	—
Czechoslovakia	koruna	8¢	137,200,000,000	8,970	113 [5]	4,993	60,300	13,131
Denmark	krone	10¢	61,000,000,000	11,920	315 [5]	4,175	64,551	5,758
Djibouti	franc	½¢	331,000,000	1,070	—	725	279	97
Dominica	E.C. dollar	37¢	65,000,000	883	300 [5]	200	360	—
Dominican Rep.	peso	$1.00	7,910,300,000	1,412	137 [7]	515	5,800	1,600
Ecuador	sucre	2¢	13,261,000,000	1,507	117 [12]	350	11,925	1,121
Egypt	pound	$1.43	35,108,359,000	775	310 [5]	531	12,300	4,857
El Salvador	colón	40¢	3,514,000,000	667	135 [11]	260	1,500	602
Eq. Guinea	ekuele	⅓¢	100,000,000	417	—	100	331	—
Ethiopia	birr	48¢	4,243,800,000	135	262 [5]	25	3,650	1,089
Fiji	dollar	85¢	823,565,000	1,279	310 [5]	537	390	644
Finland	markka	17¢	49,295,000,000	10,106	358 [5]	8,500	31,000	6,071
France	franc	12¢	813,500,000,000	14,970	319 [5]	5,200	803,000	36,500
Gabon	CFA franc	⅕¢	3,718,000,000	2,974	316 [5]	890	459	970
Gambia	dalasi	38¢	198,000,000	330	333 [5]	65	431	—
Germany, East	mark	42¢	162,900,000,000	9,731	—	6,273	47,475	14,248
Germany, West	mark	37¢	657,192,140,000	10,648	183 [5]	6,000	169,568	32,555
Ghana	cedi	37¢	10,156,400,000	896	6,388 [5]	280	6,084	985
Greece	drachma	1¢	37,300,000,000	3,755	572 [5]	2,840	16,090	2,476
Grenada	E.C. dollar	37¢	97,000,000	870	100 [13]	239	600	—
Guatemala	quetzal	$1.00	9,310,000,000	1,209	185 [8]	235	1,740	909
Guinea	syli	4¢	1,490,000,000	264	—	95	4,780	1,610
Guinea–Bissau	peso	2½¢	200,000,000	333	—	40	418	—
Guyana	dollar	33¢	507,000,000	603	323 [5]	600	550	110
Haiti	gourde	20¢	2,015,000,000	365	316 [5]	51	600	88
Honduras	lempira	50¢	2,707,000,000	708	258 [5]	195	1,700	751
Hungary	forint	3¢	20,900,000,000	4,180	174 [5]	2,437	25,000	7,864
Iceland	króna	4¢	2,461,100,000	10,634	2,640 [5]	15,450	166	—
India	rupee	10¢	156,870,000,000	222	258 [5]	180	514,250	60,693
Indonesia	rupiah	⅒¢	75,000,000,000	480	192 [7]	95	26,583	6,964
Iran	rial	1¢	66,500,000,000	1,621	411 [5]	580	19,000	4,601
Iraq	dinar	$3.22	31,300,000,000	2,300	152 [10]	742	6,490	1,700
Ireland	pound	$1.14	16,741,800,000	4,814	508 [5]	3,115	87,422	2,675
Israel	shekel	1¢	21,742,500,000	5,404	15,457 [5]	3,705	4,459	767
Italy	lira	1/16¢	356,669,000,000	6,178	513 [5]	3,220	260,500	20,085
Ivory Coast	CFA franc	⅕¢	9,800,000,000	1,153	364 [5]	245	3,461	657
Jamaica	dollar	32¢	2,983,000,000	1,340	593 [5]	871	12,600	370
Japan	yen	½¢	1,134,200,000,000	8,894	255 [5]	4,435	474,434	29,711
Jordan	dinar	$2.68	4,837,800,000	1,567	207 [8]	467	4,837	817
Kenya	shilling	8¢	6,501,100,000	380	335 [9]	100	6,425	2,040
Kiribati	Austr. dollar	91¢	36,000,000	630	—	102	483	—

[1] In U.S. dollars. [2] Kilowatt hours per capita. [3] Paved kilometers. [4] Total kilometers. [5] 100 = 1970 prices. [6] 100 = 1977 prices. [7] 100 = 1978 prices. [8] 100 = 1975 prices. [9] 100 = 1972 prices. [10] 100 = 1973 prices. [11] 100 = 1979 prices. [12] 100 = 1981 prices. [13] 100 = 1980 prices.

MONEY, ECONOMY, TRANSPORTATION *(continued)*

NATION	MONETARY UNIT		ECONOMIC INDICATORS				TRANSPORTATION	
		Value [1]	Gross Domestic Product Annual [1]	Per Capita [1]	Cost of Living	Electric Power [2]	Highways [3]	Railroads [4]
Korea, North	won	$1.06	$ 14,100,000,000	$ 750	—	1,800	304	4,535
Korea, South	won	1/10 ¢	71,670,000,000	1,794	586 [5]	1,024	9,290	—
Kuwait	dinar	$3.42	24,282,000,000	16,518	133 [7]	6,687	2,255	—
Laos	kip	3 ¢	290,000,000	90	457 [5]	223	1,300	—
Lebanon	pound	20 ¢	4,100,000,000	1,169	—	827	6,270	378
Lesotho	maloti	91 ¢	540,000,000	355	307 [5]	36	320	1.6
Liberia	U.S. dollar	$1.00	715,000,000	384	260 [5]	1,140	804	499
Libya	dinar	$3.37	25,000,000,000	7,900	167 [5]	1,805	10,800	—
Liechtenstein	Swiss franc	48 ¢	292,000,000	14,000	147 [5]	2,110	131	19
Luxembourg	Belg. franc	2 ¢	4,635,006,700	10,785	225 [5]	2,700	4,981	592
Madagascar	franc	1/5 ¢	3,324,700,000	351	316 [5]	65	4,694	884
Malawi	kwacha	88 ¢	1,225,000,000	230	295 [5]	60	1,940	754
Malaysia	ringgit	43 ¢	29,110,000,000	2,006	194 [5]	592	15,900	1,678
Maldives	rupee	14 ¢	67,000,000	424	—	57	—	—
Mali	franc	1/10 ¢	1,150,000,000	163	439 [5]	20	1,670	642
Malta	pound	$2.31	1,217,000,000	3,797	225 [5]	1,380	1,179	—
Marshalls	dollar	$1.00	—	—	—	—	—	—
Mauritania	ouguiya	2 ¢	800,000,000	536	135 [8]	95	1,350	650
Mauritius	rupee	9 ¢	1,020,000,000	1,016	444 [5]	415	1,636	—
Mexico	peso	3/4 ¢	161,883,000,000	2,203	850 [11]	870	95,990	14,210
Micronesia	dollar	$1.00	—	—	—	—	—	—
Monaco	French franc	13 ¢	—	—	—	—	—	1.6
Mongolia	tugrik	31 ¢	1,200,000,000	380	—	1,060	700	1,585
Morocco	dirham	15 ¢	15,151,000,000	669	192 [6]	242	24,700	2,625
Mozambique	metical	3 ¢	2,710,000,000	220	196 [5]	870	4,593	3,436
Namibia	S. Af. rand	90 ¢	1,712,000,000	1,695	—	830	4,079	2,340
Nauru	Austr. dollar	91 ¢	155,400,000	21,400	—	3,333	27	—
Nepal	rupee	7 ¢	2,467,650,000	108	146 [6]	23	1,751	73
Netherlands	guilder	33 ¢	138,433,000,000	9,613	151 [8]	4,340	92,525	9,645
New Zealand	dollar	66 ¢	26,735,692,000	7,984	435 [5]	9.2	46,716	4,716
Nicaragua	córdoba	10 ¢	2,880,000,000	1,085	258 [6]	490	1,655	344
Niger	CFA franc	1/5 ¢	1,997,100,000	350	352 [5]	20	3,001	—
Nigeria	naira	$1.45	74,428,500,000	1,059	248 [8]	80	30,019	3,505
Norway	krone	13 ¢	58,579,000,000	13,915	283 [5]	24,300	17,699	8,514
Oman	rial	$2.90	6,227,800,000	6,000	—	1,412	2,200	—
Pakistan	rupee	7½ ¢	27,878,854,000	316	373 [7]	215	23,500	8,815
Panama	balboa	$1.00	3,839,600,000	3,840	220 [5]	990	2,715	192
Papua New Guin.	kina	$1.16	2,286,200,000	650	252 [7]	408	640	—
Paraguay	guarani	4/5 ¢	5,932,000,000	1,765	387 [5]	340	1,370	970
Peru	sol	1/25 ¢	20,999,000,000	1,118	4,064 [5]	805	6,030	2,192
Philippines	peso	7 ¢	39,184,400,000	772	173 [13]	368	20,000	3,510
Poland	zloty	1 ¢	170,000,000,000	4,670	134 [5]	3,175	65,000	27,236
Portugal	escudo	2/5 ¢	23,608,357,000	2,490	270 [9]	1,910	49,537	3,602
Qatar	riyal	28 ¢	6,000,000,000	22,472	100 [14]	11,446	442	—
Romania	lei	6 ¢	50,200,000,000	2,228	—	3,048	29,228	11,110
Rwanda	franc	1 ¢	1,388,000,000	270	265 [5]	30	460	—
St. Christopher-Nevis	EC dollar	37 ¢	51,100,000	1,135	—	615	300	57
St. Lucia	EC dollar	37 ¢	1,307,037,000	1,071	437 [5]	240	500	—
St. Vincent	EC dollar	37 ¢	73,444,000	547	—	173	300	—
San Marino	It. lira	1/16 ¢	—	—	—	—	104	—
São Tomé–Prínc.	dobra	2 ¢	40,000,000	490	—	170	—	—
Saudi Arabia	riyal	29¢	121,000,000,000	14,578	229 [5]	1,667	16,500	575
Senegal	CFA franc	1/5 ¢	2,215,400,000	424	325 [5]	180	3,461	1,033
Seychelles	rupee	15 ¢	128,000,000	1,330	158 [10]	2,270	145	—
Sierra Leone	leone	78 ¢	1,326,000,000	350	461 [5]	60	1,225	84
Singapore	dollar	47 ¢	14,196,000,000	5,743	127 [13]	2,944	2,006	38
Solomons	dollar	87 ¢	93,900,000	320	161 [13]	106	241	—
Somalia	shilling	7 ¢	411,000,000	187	217 [10]	16	2,335	—
South Africa	rand	83 ¢	69,665,000,000	2,733	319 [5]	3,840	80,296	35,434
Soviet Union	ruble	$1.39	1,587,000,000,000	5,942	101 [5]	5,018	386,000	142,000
Spain	peseta	2/3 ¢	188,309,000,000	4,948	543 [5]	3,840	63,042	16,282
Sri Lanka	rupee	4 ¢	5,298,701,200	339	301 [5]	116	24,300	1,496
Sudan	pound	77 ¢	8,870,000,000	370	385 [5]	70	1,576	5,516
Suriname	guilder	56 ¢	1,080,000,000	3,042	278 [5]	3,370	2,210	166
Swaziland	emilangeni	92 ¢	385,100,000	686	357 [5]	200	510	292
Sweden	krona	13 ¢	98,680,000,000	11,773	294 [5]	11,280	51,899	12,518
Switzerland	franc	46 ¢	100,500,000,000	15,698	192 [5]	7,630	62,145	5,157

[1] In U.S. dollars. [2] Kilowatt hours per capita. [3] Paved kilometers. [4] Total kilometers. [5] 100 = 1970 prices. [6] 100 = 1974 prices. [7] 100 = 1971 prices. [8] 100 = 1975 prices. [9] 100 = 1976 prices. [10] 100 = 1977 prices. [11] 100 = 1972 prices. [12] 100 = 1979 prices. [13] 100 = 1978 prices. [14] 100 = 1981 prices.

MONEY, ECONOMY, TRANSPORTATION *(continued)*

NATION	MONETARY UNIT		ECONOMY INDICATORS				TRANSPORTATION	
		Value [1]	Gross Domestic Product Annual [1]	Per Capita [1]	Cost of Living	Electric Power [2]	Highways [3]	Rail-roads [4]
Syria	pound	25 ¢	$ 16,200,000,000	$ 1,735	337 [10]	487	12,051	1,543
Taiwan	NT dollar	2 ½ ¢	46,700,000,000	2,600	—	900	12,243	2,785
Tanzania	shilling	8 ¢	4,800,000,000	260	464 [5]	70	3,588	3,555
Thailand	baht	4 ⅓ ¢	36,286,000,000	748	297 [5]	327	16,244	3,897
Togo	CFA franc	⅕ ¢	812,500,000	317	233 [5]	20	1,320	442
Tonga	dollar	$1.11	39,000,000	400	339 [5]	78	177	—
Transkei	S. Af. rand	90 ¢	180,000,000	90	—	—	788	209
Trinidad–Tobago	dollar	42 ¢	6,807,000,000	6,190	433 [5]	1,579	3,600	—
Tunisia	dinar	$1.47	8,826,400,000	1,292	155 [7]	448	9,970	2,089
Turkey	lira	½ ¢	53,785,000,000	1,152	2,831 [5]	537	36,670	8,446
Tuvalu	Austr. dollar	96 ¢	1,200,000	180	—	333	—	—
Uganda	shilling	1 ¢	765,000,000	56	486 [5]	65	1,934	1,216
United Arab Emir.	dirham	27 ¢	36,000,000,000	28,000	135 [5]	8,528	780	—
UNITED STATES	dollar	$1.00	3,025,700,000,000	12,974	248 [5]	10,277	6,303,770	262,323
Upper Volta	CFA franc	⅕ ¢	1,100,000,000	177	127 [5]	20	967	1,689
Uruguay	peso	3 ¢	9,395,000,000	3,201	20,747 [5]	1,690	6,700	2,795
Vanuatu	vatu	1 ¢	—	—	—	163	240	—
Vatican City	It. lira	1/14 ¢	—	—	—	—	—	—
Venda	S. Af. rand	90 ¢	—	—	—	—	—	—
Venezuela	bolívar	8 ¢	69,367,000,000	4,716	286 [5]	2,500	22,780	173
Vietnam	dong	10 ¢	8,400,000,000	153	—	72	5,471	2,587
Western Samoa	tala	$1.22	70,000,000	451	185 [6]	282	375	—
Yemen, North	rial	22 ¢	3,800,000,000	502	187 [5]	53	467	—
Yemen, South	dinar	$2.90	792,000,000	310	171 [5]	252	322	—
Yugoslavia	dinar	1 ¢	66,300,000,000	2,900	1,040 [5]	2,771	56,655	9,465
Zaire	zaïre	3 ¢	7,500,000,000	271	1,813 [5]	1,475	2,654	5,254
Zambia	kwacha	83 ¢	3,400,000,000	575	323 [5]	1,690	5,565	2,027
Zimbabwe	dollar	$1.01	7,380,000,000	919	259 [5]	1,110	12,243	2,785

[1] In U.S. dollars. [2] Kilowatt hours per capita. [3] Paved kilometers. [4] Total kilometers. [5] 100 = 1970 prices. [6] 100 = 1973 prices. [7] 100 = 1977 prices.

SELECTED DEPENDENCIES, TERRITORIES, COLONIES, AND POSSESSIONS

NAME	CONTROLLED BY	LOCATION	AREA (sq. mi.)	POPULATION [1] Total	Per sq. mi.	CAPITAL
Andamans–Nicobars	India	Bay of Bengal	3,203	219,714	68.6	Port Blair
Anguilla	Britain	Caribbean	35	6,801	194.3	The Valley
Azores	Portugal	Atlantic Ocean	902	262,628	291.2	Ponta Delgada
Balearic Islands	Spain	Mediterranean	1,936	663,630	342.8	Palma
Bermuda	Britain	North Atlantic	20	54,811	2,740.6	Hamilton
Canary Islands	Spain	Atlantic Ocean	2,808	1,353,680	482.1	Las Palmas, Santa Cruz
Cayman Islands	Britain	Caribbean	100	20,754	207.5	George Town
Channel Islands	Britain	English Channel	75	130,621	1,741.6	St. Peter Port, St. Helier
Christmas Island	Australia	South Pacific	52	3,485	67.0	Flying Fish Cove
Cook Islands	New Zealand	South Pacific	90	17,606	195.6	Avarua
Corsica	France	Mediterranean	3,367	204,232	60.7	Ajaccio, Bastia
Faeroe Islands	Denmark	North Atlantic	540	45,334	84.0	Tórshavn
Falkland Islands	Britain	South Atlantic	4,700	1,993	0.42	Stanley
Galápagos Islands	Ecuador	Pacific	3,028	6,000	2.0	Baquerizo Moreno
Gibraltar	Britain	Europe	2.3	26,479	11,512.6	Gibraltar
Greenland	Denmark	North Atlantic	16,629	52,341	3.1	Godthaab (Nuuk)
Guadeloupe	France	Caribbean	687	311,057	452.8	Basse-Terre
Guiana, French	France	South America	35,135	78,322	2.2	Cayenne
Hong Kong	Britain	SE Asia	403	5,353,150	13,283.3	Victoria
Lakshadweep	India	Arabian Sea	12.4	42,952	3,463.9	Kavaratti
Macau	Portugal	SE Asia	6.2	307,063	49,526.3	Macau
Madeira	Portugal	Atlantic Ocean	307	272,340	888.1	Funchal
Mahore	France	Indian Ocean	144	56,476	392.2	Dzaoudzi
Man, Isle of	Britain	Irish Sea	227	68,846	303.3	Douglas
Martinique	France	Caribbean	425	301,626	709.7	Fort-de-France
Montserrat	Britain	Caribbean	38	12,891	339.2	Plymouth
Netherlands Antilles	Netherlands	Caribbean	371	249,240	671.8	Willemstad, Curaçao
New Caledonia	France	South Pacific	7,374	142,767	19.4	Nouméa
Polynesia, French	France	South Pacific	1,544	158,016	102.3	Papeete, Tahiti
Réunion	France	Indian Ocean	970	513,134	529.0	Saint-Denis
Saint Pierre–Miquelon	France	North Atlantic	93	6,096	65.5	St. Pierre
Samoa, American	U.S.	South Pacific	77	37,151	399.5	Pago Pago
Sardinia	Italy	Mediterranean	9,301	1,613,820	173.5	Cagliari
Sicily	Italy	Mediterranean	9,926	4,906,200	494.3	Palermo
Turks and Caicos	Britain	Caribbean	166	8,311	50.1	Cockburn Town
Virgin Islands, British	Britain	Caribbean	59	12,579	213.2	Road Town
Wallis and Futuna	France	South Pacific	106	11,110	104.8	Matu Utu

[1] Jan. 1, 1983, population estimates.

NORTH AMERICA

SOUTH AMERICA
CUBA
DOM. REP.
JAMAICA
HAITI
PUERTO RICO
CARIBBEAN SEA
ST. CHRISTOPHER AND NEVIS
ANTIGUA
GUADELOUPE
GRENADA
ST. GEORGE'S
BARBADOS
ST. LUCIA
ST. VINCENT
TRINIDAD-TOBAGO
NETHERLANDS ANTILLES
PANAMA CANAL
Barranquilla
Maracaibo
CARACAS
PORT OF SPAIN
Orinoco R.
GUYANA
GEORGETOWN
SURINAM
PARAMARIBO
GUYANE (Fr.)
CAYENNE
VENEZUELA
Medellín
BOGOTÁ
Cali
COLOMBIA
QUITO
ECUADOR
Guayaquil
AMAZON BASIN
Amazon R.
Manaus
Belém
Fortaleza
Natal
Recife
PERU
ANDES
Trujillo
BRAZIL
Callao
LIMA
Cuzco
LAKE TITICACA
LA PAZ
MATO GROSSO
Salvador
Arequipa
BOLIVIA
Cochabamba
Oruro
SUCRE
BRASÍLIA
Belo Horizonte
PARAGUAY
Antofagasta
DESERT OF ATACAMA
MOUNTAINS
CHACO
São Paulo
Rio de Janeiro
Santos
CHILE
ASUNCIÓN
Tucumán
Paraná R.
Porto Alegre
PACIFIC OCEAN
Santa Fe
Córdoba
Valparaíso
SANTIAGO
PAMPAS
Rosario
URUGUAY
JUAN FERNÁNDEZ
BUENOS AIRES
MONTEVIDEO
Concepción
ARGENTINA
Mar del Plata
ATLANTIC OCEAN
Puerto Montt
PATAGONIA
STRAIT OF MAGELLAN
FALKLAND ISLANDS (Brit.)
Punta Arenas
TIERRA DEL FUEGO
CAPE HORN
MILES 0 200 400 600 800 1000

EUROPE
MILES 0 100 200 300 400 500
REYKJAVIK
ICELAND
NORWEGIAN SEA
FAEROE IS. (DEN.)
SHETLAND IS.
ORKNEY IS.
HEBRIDES
NORTH SEA
SCOTLAND
NORTHERN IRELAND
Glasgow
Edinburgh
Belfast
IRELAND
DUBLIN
Limerick
Cork
BRITAIN (UNITED KINGDOM)
Liverpool
Manchester
Birmingham
WALES
Cardiff
ENGLAND
LONDON
ENGLISH CHANNEL
CHANNEL IS.
ATLANTIC OCEAN
BAY OF BISCAY
Trondheim
Bergen
NORWAY
OSLO
SWEDEN
STOCKHOLM
Goteborg
Malmo
DENMARK
COPENHAGEN
GULF OF BOTHNIA
FINLAND
HELSINKI
Leningrad
Tallinn
BALTIC SEA
Riga
MOSCOW
Vilnius
SOVIET UNION (U.S.S.R.)
Kiev
WARSAW
Lodz
POLAND
Krakow
NETHERLANDS
AMSTERDAM
The Hague
Hamburg
BERLIN
EAST GERMANY
Leipzig
Dresden
BELGIUM
BRUSSELS
BONN
LUXEMBOURG
PRAGUE
CZECHOSLOVAKIA
Seine R.
PARIS
Nantes
Strasbourg
WEST GERMANY
Munich
Rhine R.
Danube R.
VIENNA
Odessa
FRANCE
BERNE
LIECHTENSTEIN
SWITZ.
ALPS
AUSTRIA
BUDAPEST
HUNGARY
ROMANIA
Lyon
Rhone R.
Bordeaux
Trieste
Milan
Venice
BUCHAREST
BLACK SEA
Marseille
Nice
MONACO
Florence
SAN MARINO
ADRIATIC SEA
BELGRADE
YUGOSLAVIA
BULGARIA
SOFIA
Porto
PYRENEES
ANDORRA
SPAIN
PORTUGAL
LISBON
MADRID
Barcelona
CORSICA
ITALY
ROME
ALBANIA
TIRANA
Istanbul
TURKEY
Valencia
SARDINIA
BALEARIC IS.
Naples
TYRRHENIAN SEA
GREECE
AEGEAN SEA
ATHENS
IONIAN SEA
Seville
GIBRALTAR (Brit.)
SICILY
MALTA
CRETE
MEDITERRANEAN SEA
AFRICA

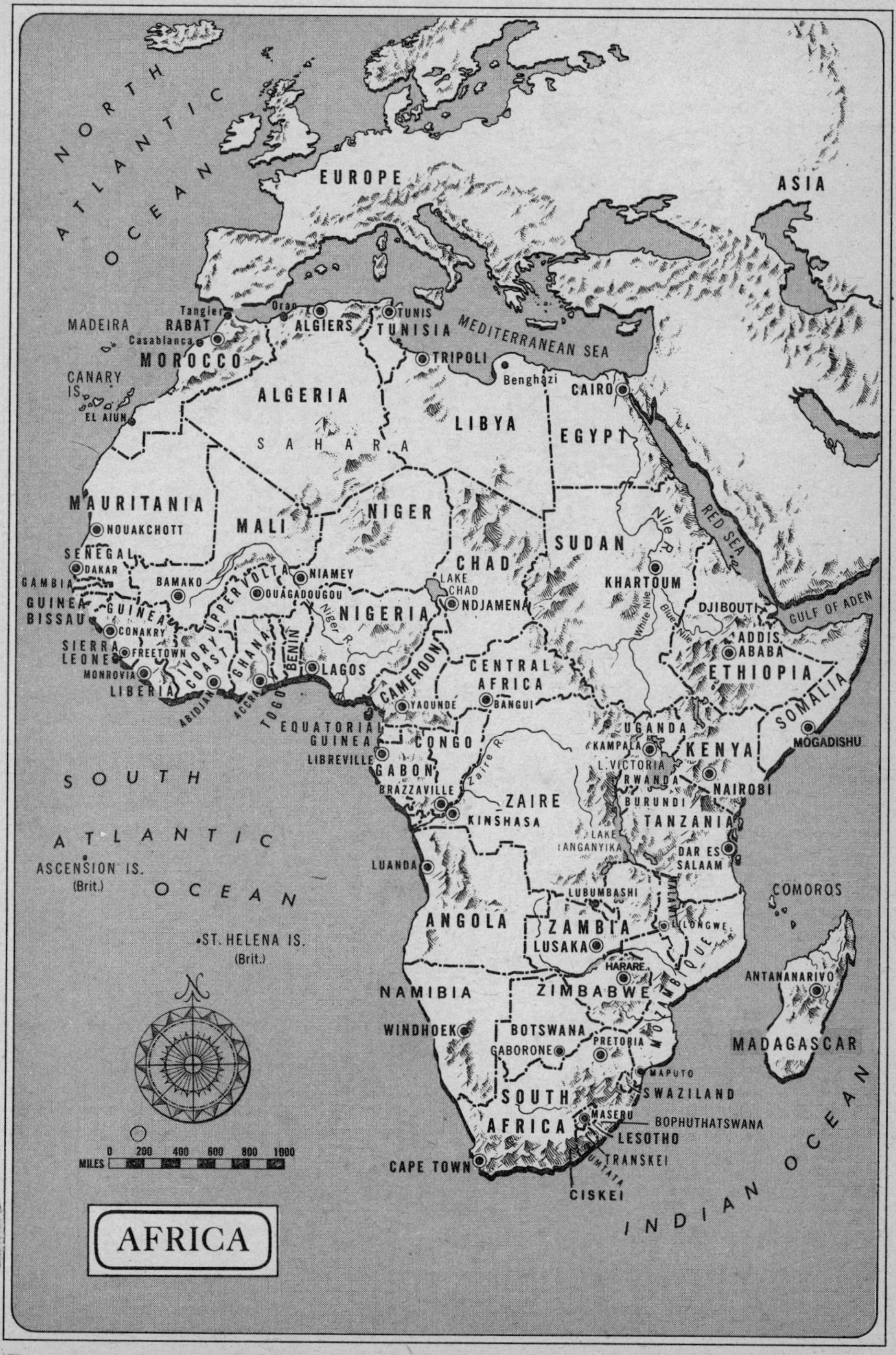
NORTH ATLANTIC OCEAN
EUROPE
ASIA
MADEIRA
Tangier
RABAT
Casablanca
Oran
ALGIERS
TUNIS
TUNISIA
MEDITERRANEAN SEA
MOROCCO
TRIPOLI
Benghazi
CANARY IS.
EL AIUN
ALGERIA
LIBYA
CAIRO
EGYPT
SAHARA
MAURITANIA
NOUAKCHOTT
MALI
NIGER
SUDAN
RED SEA
Nile R.
SENEGAL
DAKAR
GAMBIA
BAMAKO
UPPER VOLTA
NIAMEY
OUAGADOUGOU
CHAD
LAKE CHAD
NDJAMENA
KHARTOUM
GUINEA BISSAU
GUINEA
CONAKRY
NIGERIA
Niger R.
DJIBOUTI
GULF OF ADEN
White Nile
Blue Nile
ADDIS ABABA
ETHIOPIA
SIERRA LEONE
FREETOWN
MONROVIA
LIBERIA
IVORY COAST
ABIDJAN
GHANA
ACCRA
TOGO
BENIN
LAGOS
CAMEROON
YAOUNDE
CENTRAL AFRICA
BANGUI
SOMALIA
MOGADISHU
EQUATORIAL GUINEA
CONGO
UGANDA
KAMPALA
KENYA
L. VICTORIA
LIBREVILLE
GABON
Zaire R.
RWANDA
NAIROBI
BRAZZAVILLE
ZAIRE
BURUNDI
KINSHASA
TANZANIA
LAKE TANGANYIKA
DAR ES SALAAM
SOUTH ATLANTIC OCEAN
ASCENSION IS. (Brit.)
LUANDA
COMOROS
LUBUMBASHI
MALAWI
ANGOLA
ZAMBIA
LILONGWE
ST. HELENA IS. (Brit.)
LUSAKA
MOZAMBIQUE
HARARE
ANTANANARIVO
NAMIBIA
ZIMBABWE
WINDHOEK
BOTSWANA
PRETORIA
MADAGASCAR
GABORONE
MAPUTO
SWAZILAND
SOUTH AFRICA
MASERU
BOPHUTHATSWANA
LESOTHO
TRANSKEI
CAPE TOWN
UMTATA
CISKEI
MILES 0 200 400 600 800 1000
INDIAN OCEAN
AFRICA

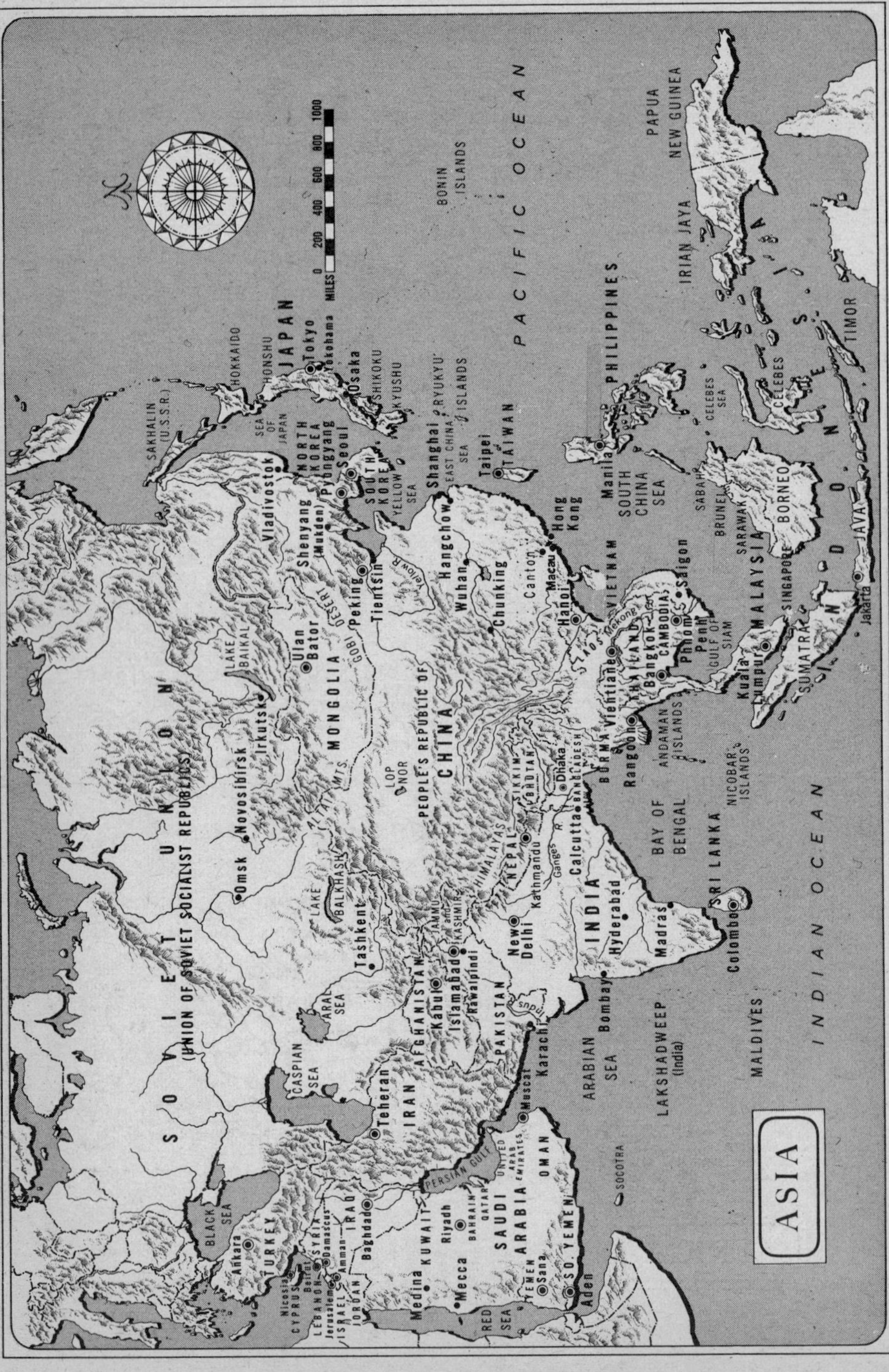
ASIA
SOVIET UNION
(UNION OF SOVIET SOCIALIST REPUBLICS)
MONGOLIA
PEOPLE'S REPUBLIC OF CHINA
JAPAN
NORTH KOREA
SOUTH KOREA
TAIWAN
PHILIPPINES
VIETNAM
LAOS
THAILAND
CAMBODIA
BURMA
MALAYSIA
INDONESIA
INDIA
NEPAL
BHUTAN
SIKKIM
BANGLADESH
SRI LANKA
PAKISTAN
AFGHANISTAN
IRAN
IRAQ
SYRIA
TURKEY
LEBANON
ISRAEL
JORDAN
CYPRUS
KUWAIT
SAUDI ARABIA
BAHRAIN
QATAR
UNITED ARAB EMIRATES
OMAN
YEMEN
SO. YEMEN
PAPUA NEW GUINEA
IRIAN JAYA
BORNEO
SUMATRA
JAVA
CELEBES
TIMOR
SABAH
SARAWAK
BRUNEI
SINGAPORE
JAMMU
KASHMIR
MALDIVES
LAKSHADWEEP (India)
SAKHALIN (U.S.S.R.)
HOKKAIDO
HONSHU
SHIKOKU
KYUSHU
RYUKYU ISLANDS
BONIN ISLANDS
ANDAMAN ISLANDS
NICOBAR ISLANDS
SOCOTRA
PACIFIC OCEAN
INDIAN OCEAN
ARABIAN SEA
BAY OF BENGAL
SOUTH CHINA SEA
EAST CHINA SEA
YELLOW SEA
SEA OF JAPAN
CELEBES SEA
GULF OF SIAM
PERSIAN GULF
RED SEA
BLACK SEA
CASPIAN SEA
ARAL SEA
LAKE BALKHASH
LAKE BAIKAL
LOP NOR
GOBI DESERT
ALTAI MTS.
HIMALAYAS
Ganges R.
Indus R.
Yellow R.
Mekong R.
Tokyo
Yokohama
Osaka
Vladivostok
Pyongyang
Seoul
Shanghai
Taipei
Shenyang (Mukden)
Peking
Tientsin
Ulan Bator
Hangchow
Wuhan
Chunking
Canton
Macau
Hong Kong
Manila
Hanoi
Saigon
Vientiane
Bangkok
Phnom Penh
Rangoon
Kuala Lumpur
Jakarta
Dhaka
Calcutta
Kathmandu
New Delhi
Hyderabad
Madras
Bombay
Colombo
Karachi
Islamabad
Rawalpindi
Kabul
Tashkent
Omsk
Novosibirsk
Irkutsk
Teheran
Baghdad
Damascus
Beirut
Amman
Jerusalem
Nicosia
Ankara
Riyadh
Mecca
Medina
Muscat
Sana
Aden
MILES 0 200 400 600 800 1000

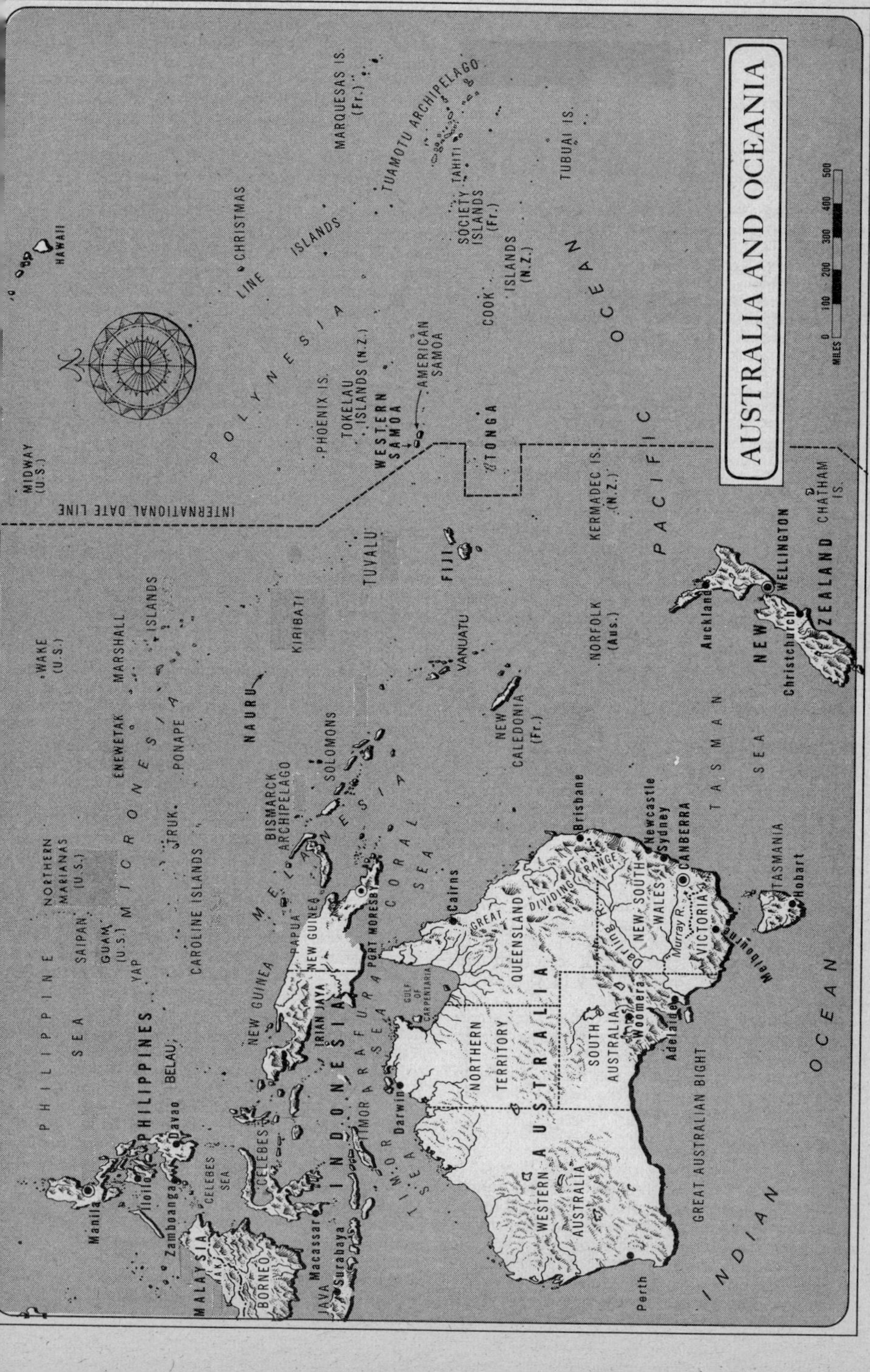
AUSTRALIA AND OCEANIA
MILES 0 100 200 300 400 500
INTERNATIONAL DATE LINE
P A C I F I C O C E A N
I N D I A N O C E A N
TASMAN SEA
CORAL SEA
ARAFURA SEA
TIMOR SEA
PHILIPPINE SEA
CELEBES SEA
GREAT AUSTRALIAN BIGHT
GULF OF CARPENTARIA
POLYNESIA
MICRONESIA
MELANESIA
MIDWAY (U.S.)
HAWAII
CHRISTMAS
LINE ISLANDS
MARQUESAS IS. (Fr.)
TUAMOTU ARCHIPELAGO
TAHITI
SOCIETY ISLANDS (Fr.)
TUBUAI IS.
COOK ISLANDS (N.Z.)
AMERICAN SAMOA
WESTERN SAMOA
TOKELAU ISLANDS (N.Z.)
PHOENIX IS.
TONGA
KERMADEC IS. (N.Z.)
CHATHAM IS.
NEW ZEALAND
WELLINGTON
Auckland
Christchurch
FIJI
TUVALU
KIRIBATI
WAKE (U.S.)
MARSHALL ISLANDS
ENEWETAK
PONAPE
NAURU
VANUATU
NORFOLK (Aus.)
NEW CALEDONIA (Fr.)
SOLOMONS
BISMARCK ARCHIPELAGO
TRUK
CAROLINE ISLANDS
NORTHERN MARIANAS (U.S.)
SAIPAN
GUAM (U.S.)
YAP
BELAU
PHILIPPINES
Manila
Iloilo
Zamboanga
Davao
MALAYSIA
BORNEO
CELEBES
Macassar
JAVA
Surabaya
INDONESIA
IRIAN JAYA
NEW GUINEA
PAPUA NEW GUINEA
PORT MORESBY
AUSTRALIA
WESTERN AUSTRALIA
NORTHERN TERRITORY
SOUTH AUSTRALIA
QUEENSLAND
NEW SOUTH WALES
VICTORIA
TASMANIA
GREAT DIVIDING RANGE
Darling R.
Murray R.
Perth
Darwin
Cairns
Brisbane
Newcastle
Sydney
CANBERRA
Melbourne
Hobart
Adelaide
Woomera

AFGHANISTAN

Official Name: Democratic Republic of Afghanistan.
Area: 250,000 square miles (647,497 sq. km.).
Population: 14,162,700.
Chief Cities: Kabul, capital, 318,094; Kandahar, 243,103; Herat, 162,946.
Largest Metropolitan Area: Kabul, 749,000.
Government: Soviet-controlled communist state.
President: Babrak Karmal (since 1979).
Prime Minister: Ali Kishtmand (since 1981).
Flag: Black, red, and green stripes; emblem has star above rising sun and open book.
Languages: Pushtu (50%), Persian or Dari (35%), Turkic (11%).
Ethnic Groups: Pushtuns (50%), Tajiks (25%), Uzbeks (9%), Hazaras (9%).
Religion: Sunni Muslim (87%), Shia Muslim (12%), other (1%).
Leading Industries: Agriculture (sheep, goats, fruits, wheat, cotton, nuts, vegetables); mining (natural gas, copper, iron); manufacturing (fur and leather products, carpets, textiles, food processing).
Foreign Trade: *Major exports*—fruits and nuts, natural gas, karakul skins, raw cotton, carpets, wool; *major imports*—petroleum products, sugar, tea, machinery, textiles.
Places of Interest: Kabul museum and bazaar; Khyber Pass; ancient ruins of Balkh; Blue Mosque at Mazar-i-Sharif; Paghman summer resort; largest Buddha statue in world (180 ft. high) in Valley of the Gods at Bamian; temples of Herat.

AFGHANISTAN TODAY

A landlocked country of southwest Asia, Afghanistan was torn by civil war in 1980–83 as Muslim guerrillas fought against Soviet troops supporting the puppet communist national government.

One of the world's poor nations, Afghanistan has difficulty raising enough food to meet the needs of its population. The mountainous terrain prevents most land from being farmed. Most farmers have just enough land to raise crops for their families. Only about 1 person in 27 goes to school, and no more than 1 in 10 can read and write. Most live and dress as they have for hundreds of years.

The country has substantial mineral resources of coal, gas, and petroleum, but these have been mined only to a limited degree.

The Soviet Union lies to the north, China to the northeast, Pakistan to the east and south, and Iran to the west.

EARLY HISTORY

In ancient times the region was called *Bactria.* It was the home of the two-humped Bactrian camel, still used as a beast of burden in Afghanistan.

Persian rulers of Bactria were overthrown by Alexander the Great in the 300s B.C. Then the country was overrun by a series of overlords, including Greeks, Turks, and Arabs.

The invading Mongol hordes of Genghis Khan in the 1200s and Tamerlane in the 1300s were followed by the Mogul emperors of India.

Afghanistan achieved independence under the leadership of Ahmad Shah Durrani, who became shah (king) in 1747.

British efforts to control India and central Asia led to the First Afghan War (1832–42). Afghan resistance caused the British to withdraw temporarily.

British fear of expanding Russian influence in central Asia brought on the Second Afghan War (1878–79), won by Britain. Abdur Rahman became king in 1881, agreeing to let Britain manage foreign affairs. His grandson, Amanullah Shah, brought about the Third Afghan War (1919), in which Afghanistan won independence.

Amanullah's cousin, Sardar Mohammad Nadir Shah, became king in 1929. He was assassinated in 1933 and was succeeded by his son Mohammad Zahir Shah.

On July 17, 1973, while King Mohammad Zahir was visiting Italy, his brother-in-law Prime Minister Mohammad Daoud overthrew the government. Daoud proclaimed a republic with himself as president and prime minister.

The opening of the Trans-Asia Highway across Afghanistan from Istanbul to Calcutta in the mid-1970s brought auto tourists from Europe.

COMMUNIST STATE

Using Soviet-built tanks and fighter planes, Afghan troops led by Col. Abdul Qader, deputy commander of the air force, overthrew the government on April 27, 1978. President Daoud and 30 members of his family were executed.

The rebels established a communist government under domination of the pro-Soviet People's Democratic Party (PDP). The rebels released from prison the head of the PDP, 61-year-old novelist Noor Mohammad Taraki, and made him president. Moscow poured in millions of dollars of aid to Taraki's government and sent in "military advisers." Muslim tribesmen rebelled against the communist central government.

In a bloody palace coup on Sept. 14, 1979, U.S.-educated Prime Minister Hafizullah Amin took over the government, making himself president. Former President Taraki and many of his supporters were killed during the takeover.

The Soviet Union invaded Afghanistan with about 85,000 troops beginning on Christmas 1979. Amin was executed on Dec. 27 and was replaced by Babrak Karmal, an Afghan communist in exile under Soviet protection.

U.S. President Carter led Western powers in denouncing the Soviet action. On Jan. 4, 1980, he reduced U.S. grain sales to the Soviet Union and led a boycott of Moscow's Olympic Games.

Fighting spread throughout the country in 1980–83 as Muslims opposed the Soviet occupation. An estimated 2.8 million Afghans fled to neighboring Pakistan and Iran. Although Soviet troops managed to control the main cities and highways, Muslim guerrillas dominated the countryside. An estimated million Afghans died in the fighting and in executions by the Soviet regime.

Major fighting between guerrillas and Soviet troops occurred in 1982 in the Panjshir Valley, about 60 miles north of Kabul. Guerillas repeatedly attacked government buildings in Kabul, including the Soviet embassy.

An explosion in a Soviet-built 1.7-mile-long highway tunnel in Salang Pass in the Hindu Kush mountains on Nov. 3, 1982, was reported to have killed about 1,100 person, including several hundred Soviet troops.

The UN General Assembly for the third year in a row appealed 114–21 to the Soviet Union on Nov. 29, 1982, to withdraw its troops from Afghanistan.

Covert U.S. military aid to the Afghan rebels was said to have been stepped up to the level of about $50 million a year in 1983. U.S. intelligence sources said casualties among Soviet forces had reached 15,000 in 1983.

U.S. Secretary of State George Shultz traveled to Pakistan in July 1983 for consultations concerning Pakistan's negotiations with the Soviet Union to obtain the withdrawal of Soviet troops from Afghanistan. Shultz visited Afghan refugee camps near the Khyber Pass, telling them, "Fellow fighters for freedom, we are with you!"

Abdul Rasool Sayaf, leader of the Afghan Mujahedeen guerrillas, claimed that in fighting in July 1983 northwest of Kabul the rebels killed 1,500 Soviet and government troops, destroyed 40 tanks, and shot down three Soviet planes.

Deposed King Mohammad Zahir, 68, announced in Rome on Aug. 22, 1983, that he was resuming political activity to help in the fight against the communists.

Western diplomats reported that more than 100 were killed in Herat in August 1983 in a clash between rival factions of government troops and police.

In September 1983 guerrillas took control of the roads in the eastern province of Paktia, cutting off food and water supplies for Soviet and government troops in the town of Urgun.

ALBANIA

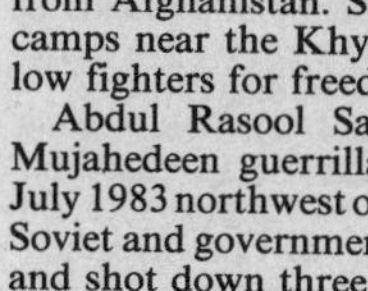

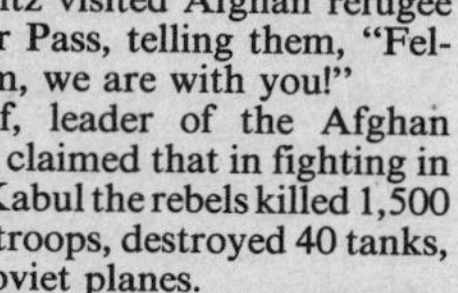

Official Name: People's Socialist Republic of Albania.
Area: 11,100 square miles (28,748 sq. km.).
Population: 2,880,750.
Capital: Tirana (Tiranë), 169,300.
Government: One-party communist state.
Heads of Government: First Secretary of Albanian Workers Party (AWP), Enver Hoxha (took office in 1946); Prime Minister, Adil Carcani (since 1982); President of the Presidium, Ramiz Alia (since 1982).
Legislature: *National Assembly,* 250 members.
Flag: Red field with centered black two-headed eagle topped by gold-edged red star.
Language: Albanian (Gheg and Tosk dialects).
Main Ethnic Group: Albanians (96%).
Religions: Abolished in 1967, but Albanians are believed to be 70% Muslim and 30% Christian.
Leading Industries: Agriculture (corn, wheat, goats, sheep, cattle, cotton, sugar beets, tobacco, vegetables); mining (chrome, copper, nickel, petroleum, bitumen); manufacturing (food processing, textiles, chemicals, metalwork).
Foreign Trade: *Major exports*—metal ores, petroleum, bitumen, tobacco; *major imports*—machinery, iron and steel, coke, sugar, wheat, processed food.
Places of Interest: 15th century Mesi Bridge near Shkodër; various mosques; old quarter and Venetian clock tower in Tirana.

ALBANIA TODAY

About the size of Maryland, Albania is the poorest nation of Europe. Fearful of foreign domination, Albania's communist dictatorship has largely isolated the country. The U. S. has had no diplomatic relations with Albania since 1939.

Two-thirds of the Albanian people live on state-owned farms or in small villages, making their living by raising crops or livestock. Few Albanians had any education before World War II, but the government reports that today 3 out of 4 Albanians can read and write. The government closed 2,169 churches and mosques in 1967, proclaiming Albania "the first atheist state in the world." Since then the government has carried on an active campaign against all religions.

The Adriatic Sea lies to the west, Yugoslavia to the northeast, and Greece to the southeast.

EARLY HISTORY

Once part of the kingdom of Illyria and then of the Roman and Byzantine empires, Albania was later invaded by Slavic tribes and was absorbed in the 800s by Bulgaria.

The country became a target of Ottoman Turkish expansion in the late 1300s. The Turks controlled Albania from 1478 (when they completed its conquest) until 1912 (when the Albanians won independence).

Italian, Greek, French, and Serbo-Montenegrin forces occupied the land during World War I. The Albanians eventually expelled all foreign troops and also successfully resisted Yugoslav and Greek encroachments.

Ahmed Zogu emerged from Albania's internal political struggle to seize power in 1925. At first he proclaimed a republic with himself as president, but in 1928 he made himself King Zog I. He ruled as a dictator until the spring of 1939, when Italy invaded and annexed the country.

A COMMUNIST NATION

Following Italy's World War II surrender in 1943, German troops replaced the Italians. The Nazis withdrew at the end of 1944, leaving Albania to the communist-led National Liberation Front headed by Enver Hoxha. He set up a communist state in 1946.

With over 750,000 Albanians living in neighboring Yugoslavia, fear of that country has been a constant factor in Albania.

When Stalin expelled Yugoslavia from the Cominform in 1948, Albania sided with Moscow. After Stalin's death in 1953, Hoxha continued to follow a hard "Stalinist" line.

SPLIT WITH MOSCOW

When communist China split with the Soviet Union over ideology in 1960, Albania sided with China. The Soviets broke diplomatic relations with Albania in 1961 and then cut off all military

QUICK QUIZ: What is the salary of the President of the U.S.? See page 970.

ALBANIA *(continued)*
and economic aid. The vacuum was filled by China, which provided hundreds of industrial and military experts and financed industrial projects.

Albania played a conspicuous role in the expulsion of nationalist China (Taiwan) from the United Nations in 1971.

Albania isolated itself from its neighbors from 1946 until 1971, when diplomatic relations were finally resumed with Greece and Yugoslavia.

An attempted coup in 1973 brought a purge of hundreds of officials.

A new constitution in 1976 made it illegal to accept loans or aid from capitalist nations.

Albania lost its last powerful friend when China on July 13, 1978, cut off aid to the Balkan nation after having supplied about $5 billion over the past 24 years. Chinese technicians withdrew from Albania, and Albanian students left China. The break came after Albania sided with Vietnam in that country's dispute with China.

In August 1978 Albania launched a propaganda barrage, declaring China had tried to force Albania to join Yugoslavia and Romania in a military alliance. The government said 15 senior army officers were executed in 1975 for plotting with China to end Albania's sovereignty.

Mehemet Shehu, 68, who had been prime minister since 1954, was officially reported to have killed himself on Dec. 17, 1981. But Western officials believed he was killed in a dispute with Hoxha.

Hoxha declared Shehu had been unmasked as a foreign agent. He then purged most other top officials in 1982, naming Ramiz Alia to replace Haxhi Leshi, who had been the country's president for 29 years.

The government said it had "liquidated" an armed invasion on Sept. 25, 1982. Leka I, son of King Zog, claimed credit for the invasion.

ALGERIA

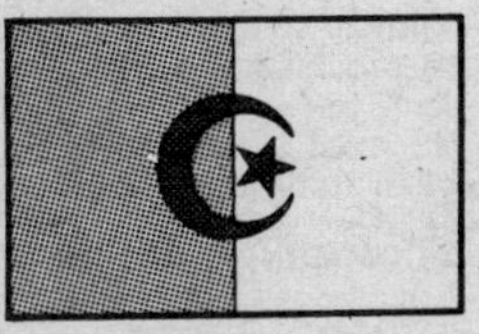

Official Name: Democratic and Popular Republic of Algeria.
Area: 919,595 square miles (2,381,741 sq. km.).
Population: 20,973,000.
Chief Cities: Alger (Algiers), capital, 903,530; Ouahran (Oran), 327,493; Constantine, 243,558; Annaba (Bône), 152,006.
Largest Metropolitan Area: Algiers, 2,000,000.
Government: Socialist military junta.
President: Chadli Benjedid (since 1979).
Prime Minister: Mohamed Benahmed Abdelghani (since 1979).
Legislature: *National Assembly,* 261 members.
U.S. Ambassador to Algeria: Michael H. Newlin
Algerian Ambassador to U.S.: Layachi Yaker.
Languages: Arabic (80%), Berber (18%), French (1%), other (1%).
Flag: Green and white bar, with centered red crescent enclosing red star.
Principal Ethnic Group: Arabic-Berber (98%).
State Religion: Islam (99%).
Leading Industries: Mining (petroleum, gas, iron ore, phosphates, lead, zinc, mercury); agriculture (wheat, barley, oats, wine grapes, citrus fruits, olives, vegetables, figs, dates, tobacco, livestock); manufacturing (oil refining, chemicals, iron and steel, fertilizers, textiles, transportation equipment); tourism.
Foreign Trade: *Major exports*—crude petroleum, wine, citrus fruits; *major imports*—grain, food, manufactured goods, machinery.
Places of Interest: Sahara Desert; Atlas Mountains. *In Algiers:* Court of the Great Mosque; the Casbah; government buildings. *In Constantine:* Perregaux Bridge; Muslim College.

ALGERIA TODAY

Although Algeria ranks as the world's 10th- largest country in area, 34 other nations have larger populations. This disparity between population and area exists because the sandy wastelands of the Sahara Desert cover seven-eighths of Algeria. The country imports about 60% of its food.

Most Algerians live on the narrow strip of fertile land along the Mediterranean coast between Morocco to the west and Tunisia to the east. The majority farm crops or raise livestock. Only about 1 in 4 can read and write. Over half of the people are under the age of 20 with a life expectancy of 53 years.

Few Algerians live in the Sahara, but large petroleum and natural-gas deposits found there have made Algeria one of the world's important producers of oil and natural gas. The country has 6% to 7% of the world's reserves of oil and gas. Revenues from oil and gas pay for much of Algeria's industrial development.

EARLY HISTORY

The Phoenician colony of Carthage in nearby Tunisia controlled the Algerian coast from about 800 to 146 B.C.

After crushing Carthage, Rome governed the coastal areas and parts of the interior.

Islam was introduced by Arab invaders in the 600s A.D. Berber Muslim rulers united Algeria with Morocco and Spain.

A Turkish pirate, Barbarossa, helped Algeria expel Spanish invaders in the 1500s. He then declared himself sultan. Thus Algeria came under the rule of the Ottoman Empire.

In the 1700s and 1800s Algeria fought wars with the U.S. as a Barbary Coast pirate state.

FRENCH RULE

France invaded Algeria in 1830. Northern Algeria was made an integral part of France in 1848.

Fierce Berber resistance delayed French control of the Sahara region for many years.

On Nov. 1, 1954, the National Liberation Front (FLN) began a war for independence. Thousands died as a 500,000-man French army tried to put down the revolt. The war ended with a cease-fire on March 18, 1962.

INDEPENDENCE

France granted independence to Algeria on July 3, 1962. A power struggle among FLN leaders was resolved when Ahmed Ben Bella gained control in August 1962. A new constitution was approved in 1963, and Ben Bella was elected Algeria's first president.

On June 19, 1965, a military coup led by Col. Houari Boumediene overthrew Ben Bella, and he was imprisoned for 15 years. All political parties except the FLN were outlawed. Boumediene implemented a socialist program.

Algeria joined with other Arab nations in halting oil shipments to the United States and other nations in the energy crisis of 1973–74.

Diplomatic relations with the United States, broken in 1967 as a result of the third Arab-Israeli war, were resumed on Nov. 12, 1974.

Algeria broke relations with Morocco and Mauretania in 1976 when those countries took possession of Spain's former colony, the Spanish Sahara. Algerian troops aided guerrillas seeking independence for the region.

Algerians voted on Nov. 19, 1976, ratifying a new constitution. All persons 18 or over could vote, with women allowed to cast ballots for the first time.

The nation's economy soared with rising oil prices in the 1970s. The U.S. replaced France as Algeria's main trading partner.

Algerians took a major step toward democracy on Feb. 24, 1977, when for the first time in 14 years they elected a 261-member parliament.

The 46-year-old Boumediene died on Dec. 27, 1978. The FLN chose as his successor 49-year-old Col. Chadli Benjedid, who was formally elected president on Feb. 7, 1979, in a national election in which he was the only candidate.

A severe earthquake destroyed the town of Al Asnam on Oct. 10, 1980, killing about 2,950 persons and leaving 300,000 homeless.

Algerian diplomats played a major role in negotiations that brought the release in 1981 of 52 American hostages held prisoner for over a year in Iran.

Algeria's 5-year plan for 1980–84 stressed expansion of private enterprise and decreased reliance on government-owned industries.

ANDORRA

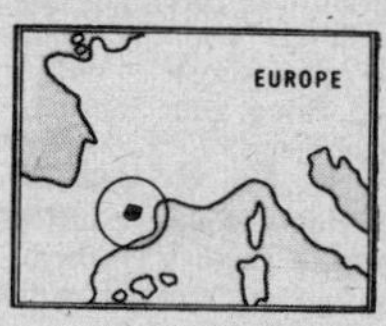

Official Name: Principality of Andorra.
Area: 175 square miles (453 sq. km.).
Population: 38,249.
Capital: Andorra la Vella, 19,764.
Government: Parliamentary principality.
Chiefs of State: President of France and bishop of Urgel (Spain).
Legislature: *General Council of the Valleys, 24 members.*
Flag: Blue, yellow, and red bars, with coat of arms in yellow bar.
Languages: Catalan (official), Spanish, French.
Principal Ethnic Group: Catalan.
Official Religion: Roman Catholicism (99%).
Leading Industries: Tourism; agriculture (sheep, cattle, oats, barley, tobacco); manufacturing (electricity, cigarettes, handicrafts, matches, postage stamps, anisette, footwear); mining (iron ore, lead).
Places of Interest: Pyrenees Mountains; Engolasters Lake; Valira River; Les Escaldes thermal springs; Our Lady of Meritxell shrine and government building at Andorra la Vella.

ANDORRA TODAY

Located high in the Pyrenees Mountains between Spain and France, Andorra is a 700-year-old nation with a land area smaller than the city of Chicago. Isolated from the wars and political turmoil of Europe, the people of Andorra lead peaceful lives. Winters in Andorra are cold with much snow, while summer weather is usually mild.

Over 7 million tourists visit Andorra each year to buy products cheaply and to enjoy winter skiing. Andorra has over 250 hotels and restaurants. Smuggling of goods between Spain and France is a thriving industry because Andorra is a free port. Thus, manufactured goods cost less there than in Spain or France.

The land is rugged and mountainous. Little of it can be farmed for crops. Most of the farmers, therefore, raise sheep or cattle.

HISTORY

Tradition says that Charlemagne granted the Andorrans a charter for their support after driving the Muslim Moors from Andorra in the 800s. The bishop of Urgel and the count of Foix were established as co-princes of Andorra in 1278. The rights of the latter passed to the kings, and later the presidents, of France.

Women first won the right to vote in 1970.

An influx of foreign residents in the 1960s and 1970s gave foreigners about a 2 to 1 majority over native-born Andorrans.

With prosperity brought by the booming tourist industry in the 1970s and 1980s, Andorrans debate whether they should change their constitution, which limits the vote to heads of families who are third-generation residents. This gives the right to vote to only about 10% of the population.

ANGOLA

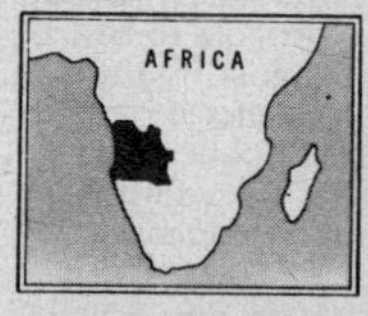

Official Name: People's Republic of Angola.
Area: 481,354 square miles (1,246,700 sq. km.).
Population: 7,666,110.
Capital: Luanda, 475,328.
Government: Communist state.
President: José Eduardo dos Santos (since 1979).
Flag: Red stripe over black stripe; yellow symbol represents socialism, industry, and agriculture.
Languages: Portuguese, Bantu.
Ethnic Groups: Ovimbundu (33%), Bakongo (25%), Kimbundu (25%), Chokwe (8%), Portuguese and Cunhama (9%).
Religions: Animism, Roman Catholicism, Protestant.
Leading Industries: Mining (diamonds, iron ore, petroleum); agriculture (coffee, cotton, sisal, corn, livestock); manufacturing (chemicals, tobacco products, food processing).
Foreign Trade: *Major exports*—coffee, petroleum, diamonds, iron ore; *major imports*—food, raw materials,

QUICK QUIZ: What was the most popular TV series in the 1982–83 season? See page 268.

ANGOLA *(continued)*
consumer goods.
Places of Interest: Government buildings in Luanda; Matala Dam on the Cunene River.

ANGOLA TODAY

Almost twice as large as Texas, Angola was the last major European colony in Africa to gain independence, after nearly five centuries of Portuguese domination.

Aided by the Soviet Union and Cuba, communists won control of the country in a civil war in 1975–76. However, some 30,000 Cuban troops based in Angola continue to battle anticommunist guerrillas in southern Angola.

A small part of Angola, called Cabinda, lies north of the Congo (Zaire) River, separated from Angola proper by a strip of land that is Zaire's only outlet to the Atlantic Ocean. Cabinda has major oil reserves.

The U.S. does not officially recognize the communist government of Angola. But U.S. oil companies aid the development of the nation's petroleum resources.

Like most other developing countries, Angola has many severe problems. Although the country has rich mineral resources of diamonds, iron ore, and petroleum, most of the people are uneducated Bantu tribesmen.

Few Angolans can read and write. Most food is imported. Many Angolans work on huge coffee plantations that provide the country's second major export after minerals.

Northern Angola is forested and has hot tropical temperatures from November to April. Southern Angola is a dry semidesert.

HISTORY

Portuguese explorer Diogo Cão landed at the mouth of the Congo River in 1483, establishing Portugal's control of Angola. The Dutch occupied Angola's ports briefly from 1641 to 1648. From the 1500s to the 1800s Portugal shipped an estimated 3 million slaves from Angola to Brazil.

Guerrilla warfare began in Angola in 1961 as the black majority sought independence. For more than 13 years 50,000 Portuguese soldiers fought the guerrillas. In 1974 Portugal's revolutionary government promised Angola independence.

Civil war raged throughout 1975 as rival political groups battled for control of Angola. With independence on Nov. 11, 1975, Portuguese troops withdrew. The U.S. Congress in 1976 forbade sending military aid to the anticommunists.

By mid-February 1976, the Marxist Popular Movement for the Liberation of Angola (MPLA) led by Agostinho Neto won control, aided by Soviet weapons and Cuban troops. South Africa, which had intervened on the side of the anticommunists, withdrew its troops on March 27, 1976.

President Neto died of cancer in Moscow on Sept. 10, 1979. The ruling Marxist party chose as his successor Soviet-educated Deputy Prime Minister José Eduardo dos Santos, 37.

The government executed by firing squad in August 1980 more than 20 persons accused as anticommunist guerrillas. In retaliation the guerrillas bombed government petroleum facilities at the port of Lobito.

In 1981–82 South African troops supported by planes and tanks drove deep into southern Angola to destroy Namibian guerrilla bases. South Africa reported killing hundreds of guerrillas and Angolan troops, including two Soviet military advisers. The South Africans also captured one Soviet soldier.

Jonas Savimbi, leader of the rebel Union for the Total Independence of Angola (UNITA), which is supplied by South Africa, controls much of the southern third of the country.

UNITA rebels aided by South African bombers captured the strategic town of Cangamba in mid-August 1983, driving closer to the important trans-Angolan railway.

ANTIGUA

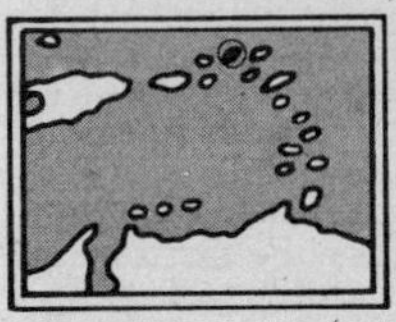

Official Name: Antigua and Barbuda.
Area: 171 square miles (442 sq. km.).
Islands: Antigua (108 sq. mi.), Barbuda (62 sq. mi.), Redona (1 sq. mi.).
Population: 78,511.
Capital: St. John's, 21,814.
Government: Parliamentary democracy.
Prime Minister: Vere Cornwall Bird (since 1976).
Parliament: House of Representatives, 17 members.
U.S. Ambassador to Antigua: Milan Bish.
Antiguan Ambassador to U.S. Edmund Hawkins Lake.
Flag: Yellow sun rising against black sky and over blue water; red triangles at lower corners; white triangle in bottom center.
Language: English.
Principal Ethnic Group: Blacks of African descent.
Main Religion: Christianity, majority Anglican.
Leading Industries: Tourism, agriculture (cotton, vegetables, fruits, livestock), fishing, manufacturing (rum distilling, clothing, food processing).
Foreign Trade: *Major exports*—clothing, rum, lobsters; *major imports*—food, fuel, machinery.
Places of Interest: Beaches; in St. John's, cathedral from 1683, government buildings, shops; Shirley Heights and Nelson's Dockyard at English Harbor.

ANTIGUA TODAY

One of the 10 smallest nations in population, Antigua includes three islands and several islets in the Caribbean Sea. The main islands are Antigua, Barbuda, and Redonda.

The year-round warm climate and sandy beaches attract many northern visitors, making tourism the leading money-producing industry.

The main agricultural crop for export is cotton, but the islanders grow many vegetables and fruits for local consumption. Fishing also is an important food source, as well as providing some export income.

Although most Antiguans are poor, almost all can read and write because education is compulsory through the elementary grades. About two-thirds of the people are under the age of 25.

The U.S. maintains military facilities in Antigua under a lease that provides about 5% of the country's national budget.

HISTORY

Discovered by Christopher Columbus in 1493, Antigua was named after the Church of Santa Maria de la Antigua in Seville, Spain.

The Spanish and French made early unsuccessful attempts to settle the islands, being driven off by the fierce Carib Indians. But British settlers led by Sir Thomas Warner succeeded in establishing a colony in 1632 that remained part of the British empire for the next three centuries.

Until slavery was abolished in 1834, many African slaves were imported to work on sugar plantations, which throughout most of the colonial period made up the leading industry.

From 1871 to 1956 Antigua was governed as part of the Federation of the Leeward Islands. As a separate colony it was joined to the British Federation of the West Indies from 1958 to 1962.

Britain gave Antigua complete control of its internal affairs in 1967 with status as an associated state in the British Commonwealth of Nations.

The country's two main political parties are the Antigua Labour Party (ALP) and the Progressive Labour Movement (PLM).

The PLM under Prime Minister George Walter governed until losing an election in 1976 to the ALP, whose leader, Vere Cornwall Bird, became prime minister.

Bird led his ALP party to another election victory on April 24, 1980, winning 13 of the 17 seats in the House of Representatives.

INDEPENDENCE

Britain granted Antigua its independence on Nov. 1, 1981. The 71-year-old Bird became the independent nation's first prime minister.

The government spent more than $1,000,000 for its independence celebration. It lifted a 15% sales tax on paint, encouraging merchants in St. John's to repaint shops and offices in a rainbow of colors. A new parliament building and a new airport terminal were dedicated as part of the festivities. Britain's Princess Margaret represented the crown during the ceremonial lowering of the British Union Jack and the raising of Antigua's new flag.

Representatives of the 1,500 residents of the tiny island of Barbuda refused to sign the final independence agreement, insisting that they will seek to secede from Antigua to establish Barbuda's own sovereignty.

ARGENTINA

Official Name: Republic of Argentina.
Area: 1,068,301 square miles (2,766,889 sq. km.).
Population: 29,284,300.
Chief Cities: Buenos Aires, capital, 2,983,000; Córdoba, 781,565; Rosario, 750,455; La Plata, 391,247; Tucumán, 321,567.
Largest Metropolitan Area: Buenos Aires, 9,910,000.
Government: Democratic republic.
President: Raúl Alfonsín (since 1983).
Congress: *Chamber of Deputies,* 254 members; *Senate,* 46 members.
U.S. Ambassador to Argentina: Frank V. Ortiz Jr.
Argentinian Ambassador to U.S.: Lucio Garcia del Solar.
Flag: Blue, white, and blue stripes; golden sun in white stripe has 32 rays.
Official Language: Spanish.
Main Ethnic Group: Spanish ancestry.
Official Religion: Roman Catholicism (94%).
Leading Industries: Manufacturing (steel, food processing, textiles, chemicals, vehicles, machinery, petroleum refining); agriculture (cattle, sheep, hogs, corn, wheat, cotton, citrus fruits, rye, alfalfa); mining (petroleum, gas, coal, iron ore, salt, uranium).
Foreign Trade: *Major exports*—meat, corn, wheat, hides and skins, wool, Quebracho extract, linseed; *major imports*—nonelectric machinery, iron, steel, motor vehicles, paper and paperboard.
Places of Interest: Iguassú Falls; Nahuel Huapi National Park; Lake Traful; Mar del Plata beach resort; colonial buildings in La Plata; Mendoza; Córdoba; Salta. *In Buenos Aires:* Paleimo Park; Casa Rosada (Government House); National Historical Museum; cathedral.

ARGENTINA TODAY

The world's eighth-largest country in area, Argentina has many natural resources. Its people enjoy high standards of living and education.

The nation's economy suffered a severe decline in 1982 after Argentina lost the Falkland Islands war with Britain.

Argentina shares with Chile the majestic mountain peaks of the Andes range. Mt. Aconcagua, near the Chilean border, is the highest peak in the Western Hemisphere. In the east are the fertile plains of the Pampa, home of the Argentine cowboy, the gaucho. To the northeast lie subtropical deltas, dense forests, and grassy savannas. In the north are dry lowlands. South of the Pampa lies uninhabited Patagonia.

EARLY HISTORY

The Spanish navigator Juan Díaz de Solís discovered Argentina in 1516.

In 1810 revolutionists seeking independence from Spain overthrew the viceroyalty and set up a governing junta in Buenos Aires. Other Argentine provinces joined, led by Gen. José de San Martín, and in 1816 declared independence.

PERONISM

An army colonel, Juan Perón, became Argentina's president in 1946 and ruled dictatorially for a decade, welding a coalition between the army and labor unions. In 1955 anti-Peronists overthrew Perón. He fled and later settled in Spain.

A series of provisional, military-dominated governments then succeeded each other.

The 77-year-old Perón returned from exile in 1973 and was elected president. His third wife, Isabel Martínez de Perón, became vice president.

Upon Perón's death on July 1, 1974, his 43-year-old widow succeeded him as president, becoming the first woman to head a national government in the Western Hemisphere.

Commanders of the armed forces overthrew

QUICK QUIZ: Herman Wouk won a Pulitzer Prize for what novel? See page 102.

ARGENTINA *(continued)*

and imprisoned Mrs. Perón in a bloodless coup on March 24, 1976. Martial law was proclaimed and the nation's congress was dismissed. Mrs. Perón was inprisoned until July 1981, when she was allowed to fly to exile in Spain.

MILITARY RULE

The commander in chief of the army, Lt. Gen. Rafael Videla, was sworn in as Argentina's 39th president on March 29, 1976.

The military junta arrested some 6,000 to 30,000 persons in 1976–79 in an effort to end terrorist activities. Thousands disappeared, never to be seen again. In 1983 the military government announced that all were dead.

The United States reduced military aid to Argentina in 1977 because of the military regime's violation of human rights.

To reinstitute "civilian" government, President Videla on Aug. 1, 1978, resigned from the army. However, he remained responsible to the military junta of heads of the armed forces.

The junta chose Gen. Roberto Eduardo Viola, 56, retired commander of the armed forces, to replace Videla. Viola was sworn in as president on March 29, 1981.

The military junta stepped up activities against opponents in 1981. Dozens of human-rights activists were arrested, although the winner of the 1980 Nobel Peace Prize, human-rights leader Adolfo Pérez Esquivel, was not jailed.

Inflation of consumer prices continued at a rate of about 100% in 1981. During the first half of the year, the peso fell in value on international markets by more than 75%, while the nation's annual foreign-trade deficit mounted to more than $2.4 billion.

After Viola became ill in November, the junta replaced him as president on Dec. 22, 1981, with Gen. Leopoldo Galtieri, 55, commander of the army.

In an attempt to divert the people from criticism of the government, the military junta on April 2, 1982, made a surprise invasion of Britain's Falkland Islands colony, which Argentinians call the Malvinas. After a short but fierce war (see page 15), Argentine troops surrendered on June 14. President Galtieri was forced to resign three days later. He was replaced by Maj. Gen. Reynaldo Bignone.

In the months following Argentina's defeat, inflation soared to 450%. The number of strikes and demonstrations increased as politicians called for free elections to end military rule.

Inflation continued at an annual rate of more than 900% in 1983. The government on June 1 issued new currency. Each new peso was worth 10,000 pesos of the previous currency.

As the nation teetered on the edge of bankruptcy, unable to afford payments on its $40 billion foreign debt, the military permitted the first free elections in 10 years on Oct. 30, 1983.

Raúl Alfonsín, 56, a former congressman who had repeatedly denounced the military junta, won the presidency in a surprise victory, capturing 52% of the vote. His moderate, middle-class Radical Civic Union gave the Peronist Party its first defeat in a national election in four decades, winning a majority of seats in the lower house of the new Congress. Alfonsín took office as president on Dec. 10, 1983.

AUSTRALIA

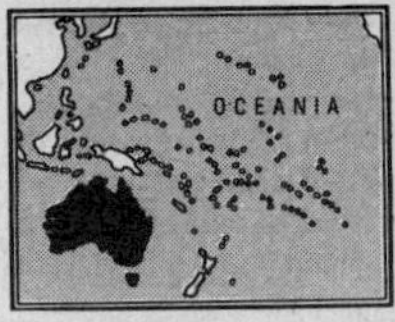

Official Name: Commonwealth of Australia.
Area: 2,967,909 square miles (7,686,848 sq. km.).
Population: 15,398,300.
Chief Metropolitan Areas: Canberra, capital, 246,100; Sydney, 3,280,900; Melbourne, 2,803,600; Brisbane, 1,086,500; Adelaide, 952,700; Perth, 918,000; Newcastle, 402,300; Wollongong, 231,000; Hobart, 170,900; Gold Coast, 164,100; Geelong, 142,100.
Government: Federal parliamentary state.
Prime Minister: Robert Hawke (since 1983).
Chief of State: Queen Elizabeth II.
Parliament: *Senate*, 64 members; *House of Representatives*, 124 members.
U.S. Ambassador to Australia: Robert Dean Nesen.
Australian Ambassador to U.S.: Sir Robert Cotton.
Flag: Blue field with red, white, and blue Union Jack in upper left and large white seven-pointed star below; five smaller white stars on right represent Southern Cross.
Official Language: English.
Principal Ethnic Group: British descent.
Main Religions: Anglicanism (38%), Roman Catholicism (23%), Methodism (11%), Presbyterianism (10%).
Leading Industries: Manufacturing (steel, aluminum, vehicles, textiles, machines); agriculture (cattle, sheep, hogs, wheat, oats, fruits, vegetables); mining (bauxite, iron ore, coal, tin, copper, zinc, lead, gold, uranium); fishing.
Foreign Trade: *Major exports*—coal, wool, petroleum, wheat, meat, sugar, metal ores; *major imports*—machinery, transport equipment, electrical machinery, textiles, drugs and chemicals.
Places of Interest: Great Barrier Reef off Queensland coast; Botany Bay; Blue Mountains, with Jenolan Caves; Mount Kosciusko National Park; Parliament House and St. Paul's Cathedral in Melbourne; St. James' Church, Opera House, and Australian Museum in Sydney; Canberra; Shepparton resort in Victoria; Ballarat, reconstructed village of 1850s; 12,000-year-old rock paintings in Queensland.

AUSTRALIA TODAY

The only nation to cover an entire continent, Australia is the world's sixth-largest country. It is a federation of six states.

The land is rich in natural resources, and the people, mostly of British descent, enjoy one of the highest standards of living in the world. Most

STATES AND MAINLAND TERRITORIES

	Area[1]	Population[2]	Capital
New South Wales	309,499	5,216,070	Sydney
Queensland	666,875	2,405,340	Brisbane
South Australia	379,924	1,291,290	Adelaide
Tasmania	26,178	422,112	Hobart
Victoria	87,877	3,841,710	Melbourne
Western Australia	975,101	1,284,200	Perth
Capital Territory	927	230,035	Canberra
Northern Territory	519,771	136,752	Darwin

[1] In square miles. [2] Jan. 1984 estimate.

Australians live along the east coast.

However, Australia is sparsely settled in relation to its size. Nearly as large as the United States, it has only about one-fifteenth as many people. Government encouragement of immigration has helped double the population in the past four decades.

Transportation is a major problem because there are few highways or railroads. Air travel is the only way to reach many parts of the interior.

Bordering the narrow eastern coastal plain is the Great Dividing Range, which extends from Queensland to the south of New South Wales. The highest peak, Mt. Kosciusko in New South Wales, is only 7,310 feet. Much of the interior is barren desert. Major rivers include the Murray and its tributary, the Darling. Northern Australia has a tropical climate.

DISCOVERY AND COLONIZATION

Aborigines were the continent's only inhabitants when Capt. James Cook took formal possession of the east coast for Britain in 1770.

The first European settlement was a British penal colony established in 1788 at Port Jackson (the port of Sydney).

Many of the early settlers were convicts or soldiers. As the number of free settlers increased, the practice of transporting convicts from Britain was curtailed and finally was discontinued altogether in 1868.

Gold strikes in the colonies of Victoria and New South Wales in 1851 brought thousands of new settlers. By 1859 six colonies, including the island of Tasmania, had been organized.

FORMATION OF THE COMMONWEALTH

A constitution drafted in 1897–98 was approved by the colonists and the British parliament. The Commonwealth of Australia came into being in 1901. The parliament of the federal government met in Melbourne until moved to Canberra in 1927. Australian soldiers fought with distinction on the side of the Allies in both world wars.

PRIME MINISTERS OF AUSTRALIA

1901–03	Edmund Barton	Protectionist
1903–04	Alfred Deakin	Protectionist
1904	John C. Watson	Labor
1904–05	George H. Reid	Free trade
1905–08	Alfred Deakin	Protectionist
1908–09	Andrew Fisher	Labor
1909–10	Alfred Deakin	Fusion
1910–13	Andrew Fisher	Labor
1913–14	Joseph Cook	Liberal
1914–15	Andrew Fisher	Labor
1915–17	William M. Hughes	Labor
1917–23	William M. Hughes	Nationalist
1923–29	Stanley M. Bruce	Nationalist
1929–32	James Scullin	Labor
1932–39	Joseph A. Lyons	United
1939	Earle Page	Country
1939–41	Robert G. Menzies	United
1941	Arthur Fadden	Country
1941–45	John Curtin	Labor
1945	Francis M. Forde	Labor
1945–49	Ben Chifley	Labor
1949–66	Robert G. Menzies	Liberal
1966–67	Harold E. Holt	Liberal
1967–68	John McEwen	Country
1968–71	John G. Gorton	Liberal
1971–72	William McMahon	Liberal
1972–75	Edward Gough Whitlam	Labor
1975–83	Malcolm Fraser	Liberal
1983–	Robert Hawke	Labor

EXPANDING INDUSTRIAL NATION

Australia began the century as an agricultural country but by the end of World War II had become an industrial one.

A surprise victory by the Labor Party in a national election in December 1972 ended 23 years of coalition rule. The head of the Labor Party, Edward Gough Whitlam, became prime minister and immediately launched a series of liberal reforms in domestic and foreign policies.

In a general election on May 18, 1974, Prime Minister Whitlam's Labor Party won a 5-vote majority in the House of Representatives. In the Senate, Labor tied with the Liberal-Country coalition, each receiving 29 seats.

In October-November 1975 a coalition of the Liberal and National Country parties forced a governmental crisis by blocking appropriations in the Senate because Whitlam refused to call new national elections. On Nov. 11 Governor-General Sir John Kerr removed Prime Minister Whitlam from office and appointed opposition leader Malcolm Fraser to succeed him as head of a coalition cabinet. In national elections on Dec. 13, 1975, Fraser's coalition parties won majorities in both houses of parliament.

Parliament in August 1977 passed legislation outlawing strikes by public employees and giving the government the right to dismiss strikers.

In August 1977 Prime Minister Fraser lifted a ban on mining and exporting uranium imposed by the Labor government in 1972. Australian uranium deposits, valued at about $150 billion, account for 20% of the known reserves of non-communist nations.

Fraser called early parliamentary elections on Dec. 10, 1977, in which his conservative coalition surprised political forecasters by winning a larger majority than in the 1975 election.

A large-scale diamond rush developed in northwestern Australia after the discovery in July 1978 of major deposits of the valuable gems. Some 20 mining companies quickly staked claims.

Labor unrest grew in Australia in 1979 as a result of government efforts to prevent unauthorized strikes. When the government arrested 10 union leaders for failing to obtain police permits before addressing meetings, 200 unions called a 24-hour general strike on June 21, 1979, that shut down most industry.

Prime Minister Fraser's government reacted strongly in 1980 against the Soviet Union's invasion of Afghanistan, substantially increasing spending on national defense and offering the U.S. a naval base at Cockburn Sound near Perth.

Fraser's conservative coalition won parliamentary elections on Oct. 18, 1980, but with a sharply reduced majority.

Australia experienced an economic boom in 1981 with unemployment falling to 5.1%. Increased exports of coal, petroleum, and other mining products led a greater growth rate than in

QUICK QUIZ: How many U.S. military personnel were killed in World War II? See page 464.

any other major industrial nation.

A gold rush developed after a prospector in 1980 discovered north of Melbourne a 60-pound gold nugget that sold for $1 million. This was followed in 1981 with two discoveries by other prospectors of gold nuggets valued at $100,000.

A severe drought struck Australia in 1982–83, cutting farm production and causing food prices to soar. The government provided economic assistance to hard-hit farmers. The drought was broken by heavy rains in May and June 1983.

Confidence in the government was shaken in 1982 by a royal commission report that millions of dollars in taxes had been lost because of incompetence and deception by government employees.

The Labor Party regained control of the government in an election on March 5, 1983, winning a majority of 25 seats in the lower house of parliament. Labor leader Robert Hawke, 52, replaced Fraser as prime minister.

Faced with recession, an unemployment rate of more than 10%, and an inflation rate of more than 11%, the government devalued the Australian dollar by 10% immediately after the election.

Hawke's government approved plans in July 1983 for a $300 million communications satellite system. The first of three satellites would be launched by the U.S. space shuttle in July 1985.

AUSTRALIAN DEPENDENCIES

AUSTRALIAN CAPITAL TERRITORY

Area: 927 square miles (2,400 sq. km.).
Capital: Canberra, 246,100.
The Capital Territory is bordered on all sides by New South Wales. The land was transferred to the commonwealth for the seat of government in 1911. Residents are represented in parliament by one elected member. The federal minister for the interior supervises general administration.

NORTHERN TERRITORY

Area: 519,771 square miles (1,346,200 sq. km.).
Population: 136,752.
Capital: Darwin, 61,412.
The Northern Territory is largely a tableland that rises to a maximum elevation of 1,200 feet from the 1,040-mile-long coastline. There are large areas of fine pasturelands, especially in the north and northeast, but much of the interior is desert, especially in the west.

Products include manganese, gold, sorghum, beef, and pearl shell.

South Australia formally transferred the territory to the federal government in 1911.

In an election on Aug. 13, 1977, voters gave a majority of seats in the new 19-member legislative assembly to the Liberal-Country Party, which had promised to win statehood for the territory.

AUSTRALIAN ANTARCTIC TERRITORY

Area: 2,360,000 square miles (6,112,372 sq. km.).
Australia claimed the area in 1936.

CHRISTMAS ISLAND

Area: 52 square miles (135 sq. km.).
Population: 3,485.
Christmas Island is in the Indian Ocean, 220 miles south of Java Head. Sovereignty was transferred to Australia from Singapore in 1958. About 60% of its people are Chinese. The island's only economic activity is phosphate extraction and export.

COCOS (KEELING) ISLANDS

Area: 5.4 square miles (14 sq. km.).
Population: 558.
Capital: Bantam.
The territory, two atolls comprising 27 small coral islands, lies in the Indian Ocean, about 1,400 miles south of Sri Lanka. The Cocos Islands were discovered in 1609 by Capt. William Keeling. The islands were given to the Clunies-Ross family by Queen Victoria in 1886. Australia reached agreement in 1978 to purchase the islands for $7.2 million from the Clunies-Ross family.

HEARD AND McDONALD ISLANDS

Area: 142 square miles (368 sq. km.).
The islands, in the Indian Ocean about 2,500 miles southwest of Perth, were transferred to Australia by Britain in 1947. The territory is governed under the laws of the Australian Capital Territory and is uninhabited.

LORD HOWE ISLAND

Area: 7 square miles (17 sq. km.).
Population: 300.
Lord Howe Island, the most southerly island known to have coral reefs, is situated in the Tasman Sea, 436 miles northeast of Sydney. It was discovered in 1788. It is a dependency of New South Wales.

MACQUARIE ISLAND

Macquarie, about 1,000 miles southeast of Hobart, has been a dependency of Tasmania since the 1800s. It is uninhabited except for a federal government weather and research base.

NORFOLK ISLAND

Area: 15 square miles (40 sq. km.).
Population: 1,800.
Capital: Kingston.
Norfolk Island, situated in the Tasman Sea, 1,035 miles northeast of Sydney, was discovered by Capt. James Cook in 1774. It has been a distinct settlement since 1856, when 194 descendants of the *Bounty* mutineers were taken from Pitcairn to Norfolk Island as a result of an offer made to them by Queen Victoria of Britain. The descendants of these people make up about one-fourth of the population.

Among the crops produced are bean seeds, maize, pineapples, citrus fruits, potatoes, onions, and other vegetables.

The scenic beauty and climate attract many visitors, making tourism a major industry.

AUSTRIA

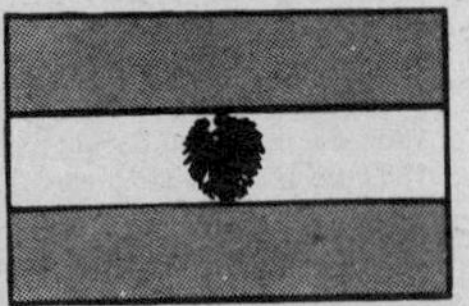

Official Name: Republic of Austria.
Area: 32,374 square miles (83,849 sq. km.).
Population: 7,595,290.

Largest Cities: Wien (Vienna), capital, 1,592,800; Graz, 250,893; Linz, 208,000; Salzburg, 139,000; Innsbruck, 120,355.
Government: Federal republic.
Chancellor: Fred Sinowatz (since 1983).
President: Rudolf Kirchschläger (since 1974).
Legislature: *Bundesrat,* 58 members; *Nationalrat,* 183 members.
U.S. Ambassador to Austria: Helene von Damm.
Austrian Ambassador to U.S.: Thomas Klestil.
Flag: Red, white, and red stripes, with coat of arms in center.
Official Language: German.
Main Ethnic Group: German descent (98%).
Religions: Roman Catholic (90%), Protestant (6%).
Leading Industries: Manufacturing (steel, chemicals, machinery, consumer products); agriculture (livestock, dairy products, barley, oats, corn, sugar beets, potatoes); tourism; mining (magnesite, graphite, iron ore, lignite).
Foreign Trade: *Major exports*—iron and steel, machinery, yarn and fabrics, lumber; *major imports*—automobiles, coal, petroleum products.
Places of Interest: Danube River; Vienna Woods; Mozart's birthplace at Salzburg and the Salzburg Music Festival; Tyrol; Innsbruck old quarters; Graz. *In Vienna:* Schönbrunn Palace; St. Stephen's Cathedral; State Opera House; Spanish Riding School; UN City.

AUSTRIA TODAY

Austria's major problem is its location between the communist powers of eastern Europe and the West. Defeated as an ally of Germany in World Wars I and II, Austria today is about the size of the state of Maine—only a remnant of an empire that once dominated central Europe. Austria endeavors to maintain its neutrality by constitutional law. It takes part in no military alliances and has no foreign military bases.

Other than fearing the consequences of a war between East and West, the Austrians are contented and prosperous. Most live in cities, working in business and industry.

Thousands of tourists visit Austria each year for winter sports in the snow-covered Alps, to attend music festivals, to go to art museums, or to view the scenic attractions along the beautiful Danube River.

EARLY HISTORY

From prehistoric times Austria has been a crossroads of Europe. Rome conquered the territory between 16 and 9 B.C. From the end of the Roman Empire until 803, when it became part of Charlemagne's empire, it was overrun by Germanic tribes. In the 900s Austria was added to the Holy Roman Empire.

By 1273 the Austrian lands had come under the control of the House of Hapsburg, which ruled until 1918. With one brief interruption, the Hapsburgs were rulers of the Holy Roman Empire from 1438 until 1806, when it was dissolved by Napoleon.

By the end of the 1400s the Hapsburg territories ranged from the plains north of the Danube to the Adriatic. They formed a multinational empire with the German-speaking lands (in substance, the future Austrian republic) in the center. To the north, east, and south were Czech, Hungarian, Italian, Polish, Ruthenian, Romanian, Slovak, and southern Slav territories.

The cultural development of present-day Austria was strongly influenced both by its German ethnic, social, and political composition and by ties to Slavic and Romance peoples and to the Magyars (Hungarians).

An Austrian empire was officially established in 1804. By 1815 Austria became the leading power in the German confederation and in the Holy Alliance. Austria's skillful foreign minister, Prince Klemens von Metternich, acted as chief arbiter of Europe. Revolutions in Hungary, Bohemia, and Vienna brought an end to the Age of Metternich in 1848.

Hungary forced Emperor Franz Josef I to accord it equal rights in a dual monarchy, forming the Austro-Hungarian Empire in 1867.

The assassination on June 28, 1914, of Archduke Franz Ferdinand, the emperor's nephew and heir, triggered World War I. Defeat of Austria and Germany by the Allies ended the Austro-Hungarian Empire in 1918. Austria became a republic.

FEDERAL REPUBLIC OF AUSTRIA

In the 1920s Austria suffered economic collapse and social and political unrest. Austrian Nazis assassinated Chancellor Engelbert Dollfuss in 1934 but failed in an attempted coup. In March 1938 Adolf Hitler annexed Austria to Germany.

After World War II Austria was divided into four occupation zones. The Soviet Union refused to end the occupation until Oct. 25, 1955, when Austria was finally reestablished as an independent republic obligated to remain neutral. The country was then permitted to join the UN.

After parliamentary elections in March 1970, Chancellor Bruno Kreisky formed Austria's first socialist government since World War II.

Upon the death in 1974 of Franz Jonas, who had been president since 1965, Rudolf Kirchschläger, a socialist, was elected president. He was reelected in 1980. Kreisky's Socialist Party won a parliamentary majority in national elections on Oct. 5, 1975.

In a national referendum on Nov. 5, 1978, voters turned down by ½% the nation's first atomic power plant. Chancellor Kreisky had supported use of the $530 million facility, which had been ready to start operation.

Kreisky led his Socialist Party to victory in national parliamentary elections on May 6, 1979, increasing its majority to 96 seats in the lower house.

In Vienna the city's first subway system began operating in 1981. The $1 billion subway project had been under construction since 1969.

The government permitted 90-year-old former Empress Zita to return for a visit in May 1982 after 64 years of exile. However, she continued to refuse to give up her claim to the Austrian throne.

In a national election on April 24, 1983, the Socialist Party lost its majority control of parliament. Fred Sinowatz, 54, who had been the 72-year-old Kreisky's first deputy, became chancellor, heading a coalition cabinet of socialists and members of the conservative Freedom Party.

QUICK QUIZ: What horse won the Kentucky Derby in 1979? See page 832.

BAHAMAS

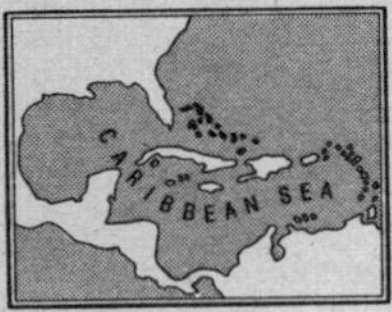

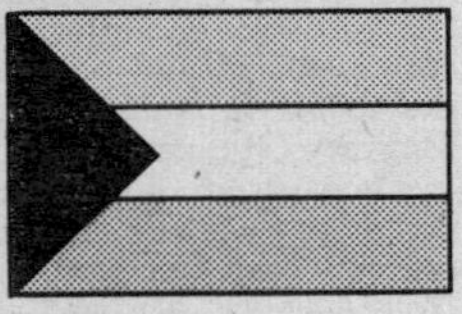

Official Name: Commonwealth of The Bahamas.
Area: 5,380 square miles (13,935 sq. km.).
Population: 225,247.
Capital: Nassau, 3,233 (metropolitan area, 101,503).
Government: Parliamentary state.
Prime Minister: Lynden O. Pindling (since 1968).
Chief of State: Queen Elizabeth II, represented by Governor-General Gerald C. Cash (since 1976).
Legislature: *House of Assembly,* 43 members; *Senate,* 16 members.
U.S. Ambassador to Bahamas: Lev E. Dobriansky.
Bahamian Ambassador to U.S.: Reginald L. Wood.
Flag: Black triangle and three stripes, with aquamarine stripes at top and bottom and gold band in middle.
Language: English.
Main Ethnic Group: Black (85%).
Chief Religions: Anglicanism, Roman Catholicism, Methodism, Baptist.
Leading Industries: Tourism; banking; fishing; petroleum refining; agriculture (fruits, vegetables); cement; salt; chemicals.
Foreign Trade: *Major exports*—petroleum products, tomatoes, salt, rum, seafood, cement, pulpwood; *major imports*—food, manufactured products.
Places of Interest: San Salvador (Watling) Island, believed to have been Christopher Columbus' first landing place in New World; Exuma Cays National Land and Sea Park, 176-square-mile preserve for sea life; gambling casinos at Freeport on Grand Bahama Island; resort hotels; swimming beaches. *In Nassau:* Fort Fincastle, the Bahamian Museum, Fort Charlotte, Seafloor Aquarium.

BAHAMAS TODAY

An island country off the east coast of Florida, the Bahamas attract about 2 million American tourists each year. Money spent by the tourists represents over three-fourths of the Bahamas' income.

Since 1955 gambling has been legalized in the Freeport area of Grand Bahama Island, only a few minutes flight from Florida. Many gambling casinos and resort hotels have been built.

The islands' second major industry is banking. Because of the nation's low taxation, many foreign corporations had established headquarters there. But in 1976 the government imposed taxes on corporations that were not 60% Bahamian owned. As a result many corporations moved to other tax havens.

The government seeks to diversify the islands' economy by encouraging new industries and better utilization of the natural resources.

A large oil refinery completed in the late 1960s at Freeport caused a 70% increase in the value of the nation's exports and made petroleum products the Bahamas' leading export commodity. In addition, the Freeport area has seen the development of cement, pharmaceutical, and light manufacturing plants.

Before the development of the tourist industry and oil refining, the islands depended largely on fishing and agriculture.

The more than 700 islands that make up the Bahamas extend over about 90,000 square miles. They lie in a band 500 miles long and 200 miles wide, starting about 50 miles east of Florida.

Only about 40 of the largest islands are inhabited. Most of the rest are little more than small sandy or rocky beaches.

The largest, Andros Island, lies about midway between Florida and Cuba. The capital, Nassau, is on New Providence Island. The closest large island to the United States is Grand Bahama Island whose largest city is Freeport. Other major islands include Acklins, Cat, Eleuthera, Great Abaco, Great Exuma, Great Inagua, Little Abaco, and San Salvador.

DISCOVERY AND COLONIZATION

The Bahamas were the first land discovered by Christopher Columbus in the New World in 1492 when he landed on San Salvador (or Watling) Island. Although Columbus claimed the islands for Spain, the Spaniards made no effort to colonize them.

British colonists began developing the islands after Charles I granted the Bahamas to Sir Robert Heath in 1626.

The Bahamas became a crown colony of Britain in 1717.

The first royal governor, Capt. Woodes Rogers, devoted his efforts to rooting out the pirates. The motto of the islands, part of the Great Seal of the Bahamas, became *Expulsis Piratis Restituta Commercia,* or "Pirates Expelled, Commerce Restored."

During the American Revolution, the islands were the scene of one of the first operations of the new U.S. Continental Navy, when its first commander, Esek Hopkins, led a raid in 1776. U.S. Marines landed and carried off cannon and gunpowder. Many British Loyalists fled from the United States to settle in the Bahamas.

In the 1920s American bootleggers used the Bahamas as a smuggling base as did drug smugglers in the 1960s–1980s.

The Bahamas were granted complete internal self-government in 1964.

The islands were governed until 1967 by the white-dominated United Bahamian Party.

Widespread government scandals involving payoffs for gambling licenses in the late 1960s led to victory in the election of 1967 by the black-led Progressive Liberal Party (PLP). PLP leader Lynden O. Pindling became prime minister. Pindling's PLP again won election in 1972.

INDEPENDENCE

The Bahamas received full independence from Britain on July 10, 1973, retaining their status as a member of the Commonwealth of Nations. Pindling continued in office as the sovereign nation's first prime minister. On Aug. 1, 1973, the first Bahamian took office as governor-general—Sir Milo Butler.

In August 1975 the government banned fishing for lobsters in the Bahama Banks to the south and east of the islands. The action hurt the Florida fishing industry.

In the first national election since independence, on July 19, 1977, Pindling's PLP party won a landslide victory, taking 30 of the seats in the 38-member assembly.

In the 1970s–1980s the islands became the main transshipment point for illegal drugs being smuggled into the United States. Smugglers hide their boats by day among the islands' thousands of cays and then run their cargoes overnight to the coast of Florida. With only a handful of police boats to search among the hundreds of islands, the government has expressed helplessness in trying to halt the smuggling.

An influx of about 25,000 illegal immigrants from Haiti in the 1970s–1980s strained the nation's economy.

In a general election on June 10, 1982, Pindling's PLP party won another five-year term in office, capturing 32 assembly seats to 11 for the opposition Free National Movement (FNM).

Pindling denied a report broadcast in the U.S. by NBC in September 1983 that charged the prime minister and members of his cabinet received as much as $100,000 a month in bribes paid by drug smugglers.

BAHRAIN

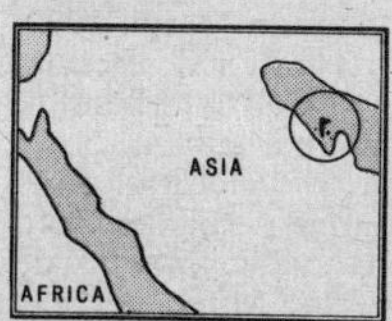

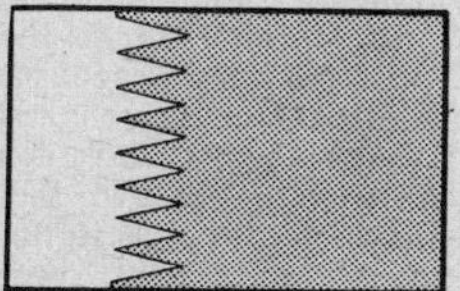

Official Name: State of Bahrain.
Area: 258 square miles (668 sq. km.).
Population: 407,267.
Capital: Manama, 88,785.
Government: Arab emirate.
Chief of State: Emir Isa bin Salman Al Khalifa (reigned since 1961).
Premier: Khalifa bin Salman Al Khalifa (appointed in 1970).
U.S. Ambassador to Bahrain: Donald Charles Leidel.
Bahrainian Ambassador to U.S.: Abdulaziz Abdulrahman Buali.
Flag: Red flag with broad white serrated band in hoist.
Languages: Arabic (official), Persian, English.
Main Ethnic Group: Arab (80%).
Religion: Islam.
Leading Industries: Petroleum mining and refining; aluminum refining; construction; ship repairs; fishing; agriculture (dates, vegetables, livestock).
Foreign Trade: *Major export*—petroleum products; *major imports*—consumer goods, automobiles, machinery, food, oil-industry equipment.
Places of Interest: Ancient burial mounds in uplands; oil refineries; royal residences.

BAHRAIN TODAY

Bahrain is an island nation in the Persian Gulf, important as an oil-refining and trading center. Its 33 islets halfway down the gulf, off Saudi Arabia, form an archipelago 30 miles long and 10 miles wide. Bahrain enjoys a temperate climate and splendid offshore fishing.

About 70% of Bahrain's biennial government budget of over $1.7 billion derives from oil income. The government uses the revenues to provide free education and health services, to subsidize housing, and to develop industries.

Bahrain collects no customs duties on goods passing through the country, promoting use of port facilities by export-import companies.

HISTORY

From the mid-1500s Bahrain was occupied successively by the Portuguese, Persians, and Omanese. In 1783 it was taken over by the Atabi Arabs from the mainland, founders of the present ruling dynasty. In 1820 the sheik signed a general treaty of peace with Britain. Bahrain became a British protectorate in 1861.

Oil deposits were discovered in 1932, the first in the Arabian peninsula. One of the largest oil refineries in the Middle East, with a capacity of 200,000 barrels a day, was built at Sitrah. More than half the oil refined comes by pipeline from Saudi Arabia.

Iran abandoned its long-standing claim to Bahrain in 1970, paving the way for the termination of the British protectorate.

To help diversify the nation's economy, an international consortium in 1971 completed the largest aluminum smelter in the Middle East.

Emir Al Khalifa declared the country independent on Aug. 15, 1971, and proclaimed the nation's first constitution in 1973. Leftists won control of the 30-member national assembly. Then the emir ended the nation's experiment with democracy on Aug. 26, 1975, dissolving the assembly.

Since 1974 Bahrain has enjoyed a construction boom, especially in housing and new hotels. To hold inflation down, the government began in 1977 to subsidize the cost of food.

Bahrain's banking industry flourished in the 1970s–80s as some 40 international banks transferred operations from Lebanon after that country was devastated by civil war. Bahrain levies no taxes on the banks.

Bahrain did not renew the U.S. Navy's lease on port facilities when it expired in June 1977, ending the stigma of being an Arab country with a U.S. military base. However, arrangements were made to continue to service the U.S. Middle Eastern fleet.

In May 1982, 73 radical Muslims were convicted of attempting to overthrow the royal government in December 1981. Evidence indicated the plot had been backed by the revolutionary government of Iran, which claims Bahrain as part of its territory.

The emir of Bahrain visited President Reagan in Washington, D.C., in July 1983 for discussions on ways to achieve peace in the Middle East.

Bahrain's weather service reported on Aug. 11, 1983, that for the first time in 81 years rain had fallen on the island during the month of August.

The U.S. in September 1983 agreed to sell $180 million worth of jet fighter planes to Bahrain for delivery in 1986. The planes would be the nucleus of the island nation's first air force.

Linking Bahrain to the Saudi Arabian mainland for the first time, a $1 billion 15-mile highway causeway is scheduled for completion by 1986. Saudi Arabia financed the construction.

QUICK QUIZ: Who was the female U.S. figure skating champion in 1983? See page 858.

BANGLADESH

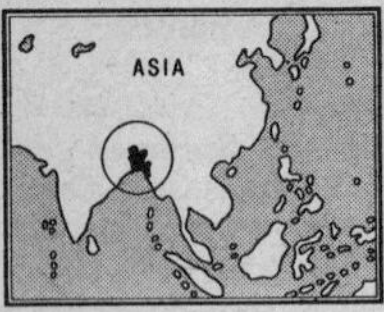

Official Name: People's Republic of Bangladesh.
Area: 55,598 square miles (143,998 sq. km.).
Population: 96,707,700.
Chief Metropolitan Areas: Dacca, capital, 1,730,253; Chittagong, 889,760; Khulna, 437,304; Narayanganj, 186,769.
Government: Martial law.
Head of Government: Lt. Gen. H.M. Ershad (since 1982).
U.S. Ambassador to Bangladesh: Jane A. Coon.
Bangladesh Ambassador to U.S.: Humayun Rasheed Choudhury.
Flag: Off-centered brilliant orange circle on field of brilliant bottle green.
Languages: Bengali (official), English.
Main Ethnic Group: Bengali (98%).
Chief Religions: Islam (85%), Hinduism (14%).
Leading Industries: Agriculture (rice, jute, cattle, sugarcane, tobacco, cotton, tea); food processing; jute processing; manufacturing (rope, textiles, chemicals, paper); fishing.
Foreign Trade: *Major exports*—jute, animal hides, leather, fish, tea; *major imports*—food, coal, machines, vehicles, textiles.
Places of Interest: Bay of Bengal; Chittagong; Cox's Bazaar beach resort. *In Dacca:* Lal Bagh fort; tomb of Bibi Peri; Bara Katra caravansary; Husaini Dalan monument; Tejgaon Church; Shrine of Ba Yazid.

BANGLADESH TODAY

The eighth-largest country in the world in population, Bangladesh also is one of the most poverty-stricken. Although Bangladesh covers an area only about the size of Wisconsin, it has about as many people as live in all the states west of the Mississippi River. And four or more babies are born every minute—about 6,000 a day. However, 2 of every 5 babies die within their first month.

With so many people to feed and so little land on which to grow food, the Bangladeshis constantly verge on starvation even when the rice harvest is good. Most Bangladeshis cannot read and write.

Food shortages and poor sanitation contribute to continual epidemics of cholera and other diseases. Cyclones and tidal waves from the Bay of Bengal have repeatedly flooded low-lying areas, killing tens of thousands of persons.

Jute, a fiber used in making burlap bags, is Bangladesh's most important export.

EARLY HISTORY

Located in the northeastern corner of India at the mouth of the Ganges River, Bangladesh was known for many years as East Bengal. In the 1200s Turkish Muslims conquered the area, converting the population to Islam. In the 1500s it became part of the Mogul empire. In the 1700s and 1800s the region became part of Britain's colonial empire in India.

When the British gave up colonial rule of India in 1947, the subcontinent was divided into Muslim Pakistan and Hindu India. East Bengal became East Pakistan, although separated from West Pakistan by 1,000 miles of Indian territory.

In November 1970 about 300,000 Bengalis drowned in a massive tidal wave during a cyclone.

Sheik Mujibur (Mujib) Rahman led his Awami Party to victory in the East Pakistan parliamentary elections of December 1970, giving strong support to a Bengali separatist movement. When the Pakistan government refused to let the new parliament meet in March, the Bengalis began a civil disobedience demonstration.

Gen. Agha Yahya Khan, president of Pakistan, led his army in a bloody repression of East Bengal on March 25, 1971. Mujib was arrested and tried for treason. The Bengalis fought back in a civil war that produced thousands of casualties plus nearly 9 million refugees who fled to India. In support of Bangladesh independence, India entered the war on Dec. 3, 1971, and in 13 days defeated Pakistan.

INDEPENDENCE

Bangladesh became an independent nation on Dec. 16, 1971. Released from prison in January 1972, Mujib returned to become Bangladesh's first prime minister. Indian troops withdrew in March 1972.

In March 1973, in the first national election, Mujib's Awami League party won all but a handful of the 315 seats in the national parliament.

Mujib became president with dictatorial powers on Jan. 26, 1975, a day after parliament had amended the constitution to enable him to do so. A month later, on Feb. 24, Mujib decreed Bangladesh a one-party state.

On Aug. 15, 1975, Mujib and members of his family were slain by rebelling army officers. Khandaker Moshtaque Ahmed, the commerce minister, seized power, becoming the nation's president. However, on Nov. 5, 1975, he was overthrown in another coup and imprisoned.

Maj. Gen. Ziaur (Zia) Rahman, commander of the army, took control of the government in November 1975, invoking martial law. The former chief justice of the supreme court, Abu Sadat Mohammed Sayem, was named president.

On April 21, 1977, Zia took over the position of president in addition to his posts as chief martial-law administrator and head of the army.

Over 230 persons were killed on Oct. 2, 1977, in an unsuccessful coup by lower-echelon army and air force officers. Subsequently, the government convicted more than 400 persons of taking part in the rebellion, and 92 were sentenced to death. On Oct. 14 President Zia banned the three main political parties for inciting violence.

The government ended restrictions on political activities in April 1978 in preparation for the nation's first presidential election on June 3. Zia won the election by a majority of nearly 4 to 1.

In the first parliamentary election in six years, on Feb. 18, 1979, President Zia's Bangladesh National Party (BNP) won two-thirds of the elective seats. Seven weeks later, on April 7, Zia ended martial law, restoring civilian rule.

President Zia was slain on May 30, 1981, in an attempted coup by military officers. The coup leader Maj. Gen. Mohammas Abdul Manzoor and two of his aides were killed by loyal troops, and 12 other officers later were sentenced to be hanged. They were executed on Sept. 23, 1981.

BANGLADESH *(continued)*

Vice President Abdus Sattar, 75, became acting president. He was elected president in a national vote on Nov. 15, 1981, with a 3 to 1 lead over his major opponent

Army commander Lt. Gen. Hussain Mohammed Ershad, 52, seized control of the government on March 24, 1982. He suspended the constitution and imposed martial law. President Sattar was placed under house arrest and more than 600 persons were jailed, including many former government officials who were charged with corruption. Ershad appointed a retired judge, Ahsanuddin Chowdhury, 68, as a figurehead president.

Relations with India deteriorated in 1983 after that country announced plans to build a $500 million barbed-wire fence along the 1,000-mile boundary between the two to prevent Bangladeshis from illegally immigrating to India. India estimated that about 40,000 Bangladeshis had illegally moved to India in 1982.

Ershad lifted a ban on political activities in November 1983. At the same time he set May 1984 for a presidential election to be followed by parliamentary elections in November 1984.

BARBADOS

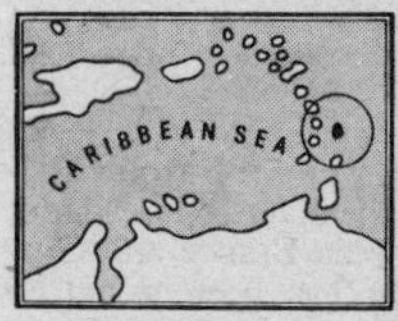

Official Name: Barbados.
Area: 166 square miles (431 sq. km.).
Population: 253,561.
Capital: Bridgetown, 100,000 (metropolitan area).
Government: Parliamentary democracy.
Prime Minister: J.M.G. Adams (since 1976).
Chief of State: Queen Elizabeth II.
Legislature: *Senate,* 21 members; *House of Assembly, 27 members.*
U.S. Ambassador to Barbados: Milan Bish.
Barbadian Ambassador to U.S.: Peter Douglas Laurie.
Flag: Blue, gold, and blue bars, with black trident in gold bar.
Official Language: English.
Main Ethnic Groups: Blacks (80%), mixed (15%).
Principal Religion: Anglicanism (70%).
Leading Industries: Tourism; agriculture (sugarcane, corn, yams, fruits); sugar refining; manufacturing (rum, molasses, soap); fishing.
Foreign Trade: *Major exports*—raw sugar, seafood, molasses, rum; *major imports*—petroleum, meat, dairy products, automobiles, steel.
Places of Interest: Deep-sea fishing ports and marinas; beach resorts; Andromeda Gardens at Bathsheba; Welchman Hall Gully gardens; sugar farms; old plantation homes. *In Bridgetown:* St. Michael's Anglican Cathedral; Sam Lord's Castle.

BARBADOS TODAY

A prosperous Caribbean island nation with a stable democratic government, Barbados has an economy based on tourism and sugar.

Barbados is the most densely populated island in the West Indies. But a determined family-planning program has succeeded in reducing the population growth rate to less than 1%.

The island has many resort hotels for tourists attracted to Barbados by the year-round warm weather and the hundreds of miles of swimming beaches.

Barbados lies on the eastern edge of the Lesser Antilles, with its eastern coast facing the Atlantic Ocean and its western coast on the Caribbean Sea. The generally flat land rises to a central high point of 1,104 feet at Mt. Hillaby.

HISTORY

Barbados was claimed for England by Capt. John Powell in 1625 and was settled in 1627. Its parliament, founded in 1639, is the third oldest in the Americas (after Bermuda's and Virginia's).

The slaves who were imported to work the extensive sugar plantations were freed in 1834. However, the plantation owners retained political control of the island.

Political control by whites was broken only after universal suffrage was achieved in 1951, largely as a result of the efforts of a black attorney, Sir Grantley Adams.

The country has two major political parties. Adams' Barbados Labour Party (BLP) headed the government from 1954 to 1961. The Democratic Labour Party (DLP) led by Errol Barrow won majority control of parliament in 1961.

Barbados received independence from Britain on Nov. 30, 1966. Barrow became the independent nation's first prime minister. His DLP party won national elections in 1966 and 1971.

In an election upset, the BLP party won a majority in the national assembly on Sept. 2, 1976. BLP leader J.M.G. (Tom) Adams, son of Sir Grantley Adams, became prime minister.

During the next several years the nation prospered, with annual increases of 5% or more in the GNP. Tourism expanded and by 1979 Barbados enjoyed a surplus in its balance of trade.

Adams led his party to another victory in a national election on June 18, 1981, winning 17 of the 27 seats in the House of Assembly.

BELAU

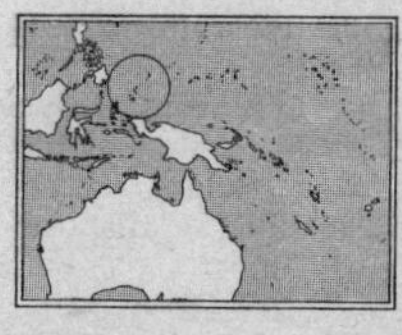

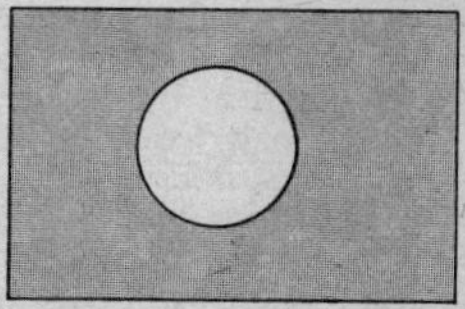

Official Name: Republic of Belau.
Area: 190.66 square miles (494 sq. km.)
Population: 13,495.
Capital: Koror, 7,685.
Government: Self-governing republic.
President: Haruo I. Remeliik (since 1981).
Legislature: 38 members.
Flag: Light blue field with yellow disk in middle representing the Moon.
Languages: Micronesian dialects, English.
Main Religion: Christian.
Chief Ethnic Group: Micronesian.
Leading Industries: Fishing; agriculture (coconut

QUICK QUIZ: What Mexican city developed in 550–100 B.C.? See page 286.

BELAU *(continued)*
palms, fruits, vegetables, poultry, hogs).
Foreign Trade: *Major export*—copra; *major imports*—consumer goods.

A poor island nation in the western Pacific Ocean, Belau includes 350 islands with a land area about the size of New Orleans but with only a fortieth as many people as that city.

The main islands are Babeldaob (Babelthuap), 153.2 sq. mi.; Peleliu (Beleliou), 4.5 sq. mi.; Koror, 3.6 sq. mi.; and Angaur, 3.3 sq. mi.

The economy depends largely on U.S. aid for imported consumer goods. But most Belauans live on the abundance of fish, fruits, and vegetables.

Rain forests cover much of Babeldaob.

Micronesia lies to the north and east. The Philippines are to the west. Indonesia and Papua New Guinea are to the south.

People came from Asia thousands of years ago, evidenced by ancient ruins.The first European to visit Papua was the Spanish explorer Ruy López de Villalobos in 1543.

Germany bought the islands from Spain in 1899, but lost them to Japan in World War I.

The island of Koror became Japan's main administrative center for its Pacific islands.

In World War II, U.S. Marines landed on Peleliu and Angaur in September 1944, capturing them after heavy fighting. After the war Belau became part of the UN Trust Territory of the Pacific Islands.

Moving toward self-government, Belauans voted on July 12, 1978, to separate from Micronesia. After several attempts, a constitution was approved in a referendum on July 9, 1980.

Haruo I. Remeliik was elected on Nov. 4, 1980, the first president of Belau.

Belau became self-governing when the constitution went into effect on Jan. 1, 1981.

The U.S. and Belau signed a compact of free association on Aug. 26, 1982, giving the U.S. national defense rights in the islands for 50 years in return for $1 billion in aid during the period.

In a plebiscite on Feb. 10, 1983, about 60% of Belau's 7,000 voters approved autonomy under the compact with the U.S. However, a constitutional amendment to permit transit and storage of nuclear weapons by the U.S. did not receive a required 75% voter approval.

To resolve the issue, the U.S. and Belau signed a new treaty on July 1, 1983, that would permit U.S. nuclear ships to enter Belau's waters but would prohibit storage, testing, or disposal of nuclear armaments.

The treaties will become effective after formal ratification by the U.S. and Belau congresses.

BELGIUM

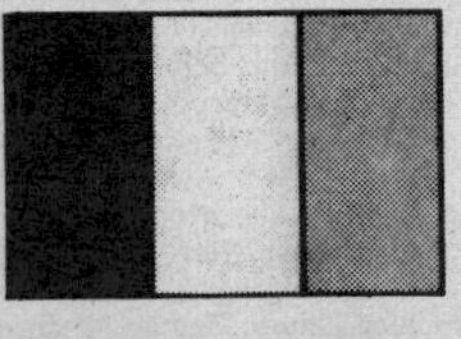

Official Name: Kingdom of Belgium.
Area: 11,781 square miles (30,513 sq. km.).
Population: 9,882,750.
Chief Cities: Bruxelles (Brussels), capital, 785,969; Ghent, 242,609; Charleroi, 223,071; Liège, 222,160; Antwerp, 195,689; Bruges, 118,384.
Largest Metropolitan Area: Brussels, 1,008,715.
Government: Constitutional monarchy.
Prime Minister: Wilfried Martens (since 1981).
King: Baudouin (since 1951).
Parliament: *Senate,* 181 members; *Chamber of Representatives,* 212 members.
U.S. Ambassador to Belgium: Geoffrey Swaebe.
Belgian Ambassador to U.S.: Raoul Shoumaker.
Flag: Bars of black, yellow, and red.
Official Languages: Flemish (Dutch) and French.
Chief Ethnic Groups: Flemish (Dutch-speaking; 56%), Walloon (French-speaking; 32%).
Main Religion: Roman Catholicism (75%).
Leading Industries: Manufacturing (steel, textiles, machinery, chemicals); agriculture (wheat, oats, rye, barley, cattle, poultry, horses, sugar beets, vegetables); mining (coal, zinc, lead, copper).
Foreign Trade: *Major exports*—iron and steel, transport equipment, textile yarn and fabrics, cut diamonds, glassware, chemical products, nonferrous metals; *major imports*—motor vehicles, copper, wool, machinery, iron ore, cotton, wheat, petroleum products.
Places of Interest: Ardennes Forest; Meuse Valley; cathedrals, palaces, and museums in Brussels; cathedral and Rubens' house in Antwerp; Bruges city canals; Mons churches; Ypres war memorials; Ghent; Liège; Ostend seaside resort; Industrial Exhibition Halls and Palace of Fine Arts at Charleroi; Grottoes of Han at Han-sur-Lesse; Namur resort.

BELGIUM TODAY

A small industrial nation in western Europe, Belgium is a little larger than the state of Maryland. Because of its location between France and Germany, Belgium historically has been a battleground for its more powerful neighbors.

Belgium's highly industrialized economy prospered after the establishment of the European Common Market in 1958. But because the country has few natural resources, Belgium suffered economically from the skyrocketing prices of petroleum in the 1970s–80s.

A parliamentary democracy whose king is a figurehead, Belgium has had difficulty in achieving internal political harmony. The root of the nation's domestic problems lies in the country's division into three language regions, each having its own goals. The Dutch-speaking Flemish people live in Flanders, the northern part of the country along the border with the Netherlands. French-speaking Walloons live in the southern Ardennes region along the border with France. Brussels, in the central plain between the two, is a bilingual political battleground.

Because of the conflicting regional and language-group interests, the people of Belgium divide their votes among six or more political parties none of which is able to win a majority of seats in the parliament. As a result, coalition governments representing two or more parties join forces to run Belgium's government. When the parties to the coalition disagree, the government falls.

EARLY HISTORY

The country was part of the Roman province of *Belgica* and later part of Charlemagne's empire. Under Burgundian rule since the mid-1300s, Belgium became a hereditary possession of the Germanic Hapsburg dynasty by marriage in 1477.

Hapsburg King Felipe II of Spain gained control of Belgium in 1555 when his father, Karl V, divided his kingdom. In 1568 the Low Countries (modern Belgium, the Netherlands, and Luxembourg) revolted against King Felipe. The northern provinces won their independence, but Belgium was reconquered by Spain.

France took Belgium in 1797 and held it until Napoleon's final defeat at the Battle of Waterloo, fought in Belgium in 1815.

The victorious powers of the Napoleonic wars again united Belgium with the Netherlands and Luxembourg under Dutch King Willem I to form a buffer state against France.

INDEPENDENCE

When the Belgians revolted in 1830, England and France imposed an armistice, dissolved the unitary kingdom, and guaranteed Belgium's independence and neutrality.

The new state chose Leopold of Saxe-Coburg as its king in 1831. Upon his death in 1865 he was succeeded by his son Leopold II, whose encouragement of rapid industrialization and colonial acquisition brought prosperity. He established the African Congo as a private colony, but it was transferred to the state in 1908.

BELGIUM IN WORLD WARS I AND II

Albert I, nephew of Leopold II, succeeded to the throne in 1909.

Disregarding Belgium's neutrality, Germany invaded Belgium in 1914, crossing it to attack France. In protest Britain immediately declared war on Germany. King Albert's small army was quickly overpowered by the Germans.

After World War I Belgium ended its status of guaranteed neutrality and entered into a defensive alliance with France. King Albert died in 1934 and was succeeded by Leopold III.

With the resurgence of Germany under Hitler, Belgium withdrew from alliance with France in 1936 and declared a policy of independent neutrality. When the Germans invaded Belgium in 1940, King Leopold, as chief of his country's army, resisted for 18 days. He then surrendered and refused to accompany his government to London. The cabinet declared the surrender illegal.

POSTWAR BELGIUM

Leopold's unpopularity caused a long political crisis after the liberation of Belgium in 1944. Leopold finally gave up the throne to his son Baudouin, who became king on July 17, 1951.

Belgium gave up its colonial empire, granting independence to the Congo (now Zaire) in 1960.

A government crisis was brought about by the resignation of Prime Minister Gaston Eyskens in November 1972. It ended in January 1973 with the formation of a coalition government under Prime Minister Edmond Leburton, the first socialist to head the government since 1958.

Leburton's coalition government collapsed early in 1974. In elections in March the moderate Social Christians won the largest bloc, 72 seats, in the Chamber of Deputies. Their leader, Dutch-speaking Leo Tindemans, became premier.

In a national election on April 17, 1977, the Social Christians won the largest number of seats, 80, in the 212-member chamber of deputies.

Tindemans began a new term as prime minister in June 1977, forming a coalition government of four parties that agreed to constitutional revisions to solve Belgium's regional problems.

Paul vanden Boeynants, leader of the French-speaking members of the Social Christian Party, became prime minister on Oct. 20, 1978, after Tindemans resigned when parliament turned down his regionalization plan to settle the country's language conflict. Boeynants previously served as prime minister in 1966–68.

A new parliamentary election was held on Dec. 17, 1978. Boeyants resigned the following day, declaring the election had decided nothing, although his Social Christian Party had gained 2 seats, increasing its plurality to 82.

After months of negotiations, Wilfried Martens, leader of the Flemish Social Christians, became prime minister on April 3, 1979.

The parliament approved legislation on Aug. 5, 1980, granting partial autonomy to Dutch-speaking Flanders and French-speaking Wallonia. Each region was given the power to elect its own assembly to control local matters.

Faced with a worsening economic situation, Prime Minister Martens announced plans in March 1981 to suspend the indexing of wages to inflation. In the subsequent uproar by labor unions, he was forced to resign.

Mark Eyskens, finance minister in Martens' cabinet, became prime minister on April 6, 1981, heading a new coalition of Socialists and Christian Democrats. In parliamentary elections on Nov. 8, 1981, Christian Democrats and Socialists tied with 61 seats each while right-wing Liberals won 52. Politicians began a search for a coalition to form the nation's 32d government since 1945.

Wilfried Martens again became prime minister on Dec. 17, 1981, after putting together a right-center cabinet from a four-party coalition.

As unemployment rose to more than 20% in steelmaking centers, parliament in February 1982 voted Martens the power to issue economic austerity measures by decree.

The government arrested an official of the foreign ministry in August 1983 for selling documents revealing Western technology secrets to the Soviet Union. Six Soviet and Romanian diplomats were expelled. An electronics company in Brussels had provided the cover for the spy ring.

The nation's 800,000 government employes went on strike for two weeks in September 1983, shutting down all public services in protest against the government's refusal to grant them wage increases.

BELIZE

Official Name: Belize.
Area: 8,867 square miles (22,965 sq. km.).

QUICK QUIZ: What nation conquered Russia and Turkey in the 1200s? See page 287.

BELIZE *(continued)*

Population: 155,131.
Chief Cities: Belmopan, capital, 3,000; Belize, 39,050.
Government: Parliamentary democracy.
Prime Minister: George C. Price (since 1964).
Belize Ambassador to U.S.: Henry Edney Conrad Cain.
U.S. Ambassador to Belize: Malcom R. Barnebey.
Flag: Blue field with red stripes at top and bottom; coat of arms in center.
Parliament: *National Assembly,* 18 members; *Senate,* 8 members.
Languages: English (official), Spanish, Mayan.
Chief Ethnic Groups: Black (51%), mestizo (22%), Indian (19%), other (8%).
Main Religion: Christianity, majority Roman Catholic.
Leading Industries: Agriculture (sugarcane, citrus fruits, bananas, livestock), fishing, manufacturing (sugar refining, clothing, cigarettes).
Foreign Trade: *Major exports*—sugar, molasses, bananas, clothing, citrus fruits, lobsters; *major imports*—food, fuel, consumer goods, vehicles, machinery.
Places of Interest: Ancient Mayan ruins of Xunantunich and Altun Ha; government buildings in planned city, Belmopan; Carib Indian village of Hopkins; Mayan Indian village of San Jose.

BELIZE TODAY

Somewhat larger than Massachusetts, Belize is a poor English-speaking Central American country, once known as British Honduras.

Agriculture has been the mainstay of the country's economy with sugar and molasses, made from sugarcane, its chief export. However, because much of the country's fertile cropland remains undeveloped, Belize must import about 25% its food needs.

The country pins its hope for the future on geologic surveys that indicate large petroleum reserves lying beneath its soil.

A spectacular barrier reef lies along the east coast that faces the Caribbean Sea. Rainfall ranges from 69 to 156 inches a year.

Mexico is to the north and Guatemala to the west and south.

HISTORY

The Mayan Indian civilization flourished in what is now Belize for many centuries, leaving behind the ruins of great temples.

The first European settlers were shipwrecked British seamen, who founded the town of Belize in 1638.

Britain defeated a Spanish attack on the colony in 1798, but it was not formally named as the colony of British Honduras until 1840.

Britain gave the colony complete control of its internal affairs in 1964. George C. Price, leader of the People's United Party (PUP), became the chief minister. He remained in power in the following decades as his party won each successive election through the most recent in 1979.

For many years neighboring Guatemala claimed Belize as rightfully its territory. In 1975 and 1977 British troops were sent to the colony to protect it from threatened Guatemalan invasions.

Britain granted Belize independence on Sept. 21, 1981. Price became the first prime minister of the sovereign nation.

Neighboring Guatemala refused to give Belize diplomatic recognition, and in 1982–83 renewed its territorial claims.

The government opened its doors to refugees from El Salvador and Haiti in 1983, offering 50-acre plots of land to each family along with financial aid to help them become independent farmers in the largely unpopulated interior.

The nation's first election since independence was scheduled for 1984. Price's People's United Party was expected to win handily.

BENIN

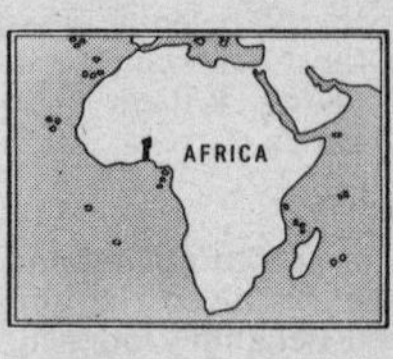

Official Name: People's Republic of Benin.
Area: 43,484 square miles (112,622 sq. km.).
Population: 3,755,090.
Chief Cities: Porto Novo, official capital, 104,000; Cotonou, political capital, 178,000.
Government: One-party communist state.
President and Premier: Mathieu Kerekou (seized power in 1972).
Benin Ambassador to U.S.: Guy-Landry Hazoume.
U.S. Ambassador to Benin: George E. Moose.
Parliament: *Revolutionary National Assembly,* 365 members.
Flag: Green field with red star in upper hoist corner.
Official Language: French.
Ethnic Groups: Fons or Dahomey (50%), Samba, Baroba, Chabe.
Religions: Animism (65%), Roman Catholicism (15%), Islam (13%).
Leading Industries: Agriculture (corn, rice, manioc, beans, palm products, peanuts, yams, cotton, kapok, tobacco, cashew nuts); manufacturing and processing (cotton ginning, palm-kernel oil, textiles, beer, soap, cement).
Foreign Trade: *Major exports*—palm products, raw cotton, peanuts; *major imports*—fabrics, motor vehicles, petroleum products, iron and steel.
Places of Interest: Pendjari Game Preserve; national park of the "W"; Cotonou floating fishing village; Porto Novo Ethnographic Museum; Abomey historical museum; Temple of the Serpents in Ouidah.

BENIN TODAY

A small, densely populated West African nation, Benin (formerly called Dahomey) is a poverty-stricken communist one-party state.

About the size of Tennessee, Benin is largely dependent on agriculture for its economy. Cotton and palm-kernel oil account for about three-fourths of the country's exports.

What little manufacturing and processing industry Benin has is concerned mostly with the ginning of cotton and the production of palm products. The government opened the nation's largest single industrial plant in 1975, a textile mill employing 2,000.

About 9 out of every 10 Beninese farm for their living. Few can read and write.

Most of the country's foreign trade passes through the port of Cotonou, Benin's largest city, which lies on the 75-mile-long coastline. Most government operations are located in Cotonou, the unofficial political capital.

Long beaches, a tradition of hospitality to visitors, and unspoiled wildlife reserves provide the potential for a tourist industry.

Togo lies to the west, with Upper Volta and Niger to the north, and Nigeria to the east.

EARLY HISTORY AND FRENCH RULE

Benin's earliest known settlers, the Adja, established a kingdom near the coast before the 1100s. The kingdom of Benin grew to control the interior region in the 1300s to 1400s. Both Benin and the adjacent kingdom of Dahomey were subject to the larger empire of Oyo. At annual festivals the kings sacrificed hundreds of their subjects to tribal gods.

In 1485 Portuguese traders reached the area. Dahomey and Benin soon became centers of the African slave trade.

In 1822 King Gezo of Dahomey, leading an army of female warriors, ended Oyo supremacy.

French influence began in 1851. After several attacks by tribesmen on French coastal trading posts between 1889 and 1891, France established a protectorate. In 1904 Dahomey became a territory of French West Africa.

The people of Dahomey were given French citizenship in 1946 and the opportunity to take part in local assemblies. In 1958 Dahomey received a large measure of self-government.

INDEPENDENCE

The country was granted independence on Aug. 1, 1960. Hubert Maga (from the north), the first president, was deposed in October 1963 by Col. Christophe Soglo, a southerner. In December 1967 Soglo was deposed in a bloodless coup led by Lt. Col. Alphonse Alley. His regime was overthrown by the army in December 1969.

Maga again became president in May 1970 and was peacefully succeeded in May 1972 by Justin Ahomadegbé Tometin. On Oct. 26, 1972, an army coup overthrew the government, and Mathieu Kerekou was installed as president and premier.

A severe drought in 1972–74 set back the nation's already poor economy.

In November 1974 Kerekou proclaimed that the country would thenceforth be a Marxist-Leninist state. The government then nationalized banks, insurance companies, and manufacturing and processing plants.

Kerekou renamed the country the *People's Republic of Benin* on Nov. 30, 1975.

An armed force landed by transport plane at Cotonou on Jan. 16, 1977, and then escaped after an unsuccessful attempt to overthrow Kerekou. The Beninese leader blamed "French imperialists" aided by Morocco, Gabon, Togo, Ivory Coast, and Senegal.

The UN Security Council, after an investigation and lengthy debate, condemned the raid but avoided naming those responsible.

To provide a broader base for his Marxist-Leninist government, Kerekou established a one-party Revolutionary National Assembly that began meeting in February 1980.

When Nigeria expelled illegal aliens in 1983, tens of thousands of the refugees settled in Benin, adding a new burden to the nation's declining economy.

BHUTAN

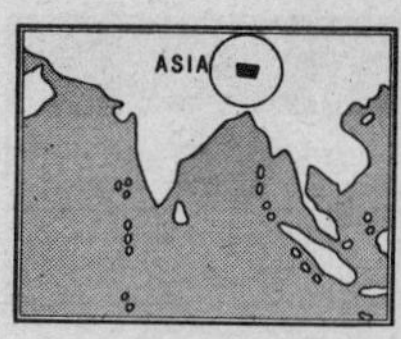

Official Name: Kingdom of Bhutan.
Area: 18,147 square miles (47,000 sq. km.).
Population: 1,402,060.
Capital: Thimphu, 8,922.
Government: Constitutional monarchy.
King: Jigme Singye Wangchuk (reigned since 1972).
Legislature: *National Assembly (Tsongdu),* not more than 150 members.
Flag: Yellow triangle above orange one, divided diagonally; white dragon in center.
Official Language: Druk-ke.
Religions: Buddhism (75%), Hinduism (25%).
Ethnic Groups: Bhotia (60%), Nepalese (25%), Lepcha and Santal (15%).
Leading Industries: Agriculture (rice, corn, wheat, barley, yaks, fruits); forestry; handicrafts; mining (dolomite, coal).
Foreign Trade: *Major exports*—postage stamps, rice, dolomite, handicrafts, fruits; *major imports*—kerosene, sugar, textiles.
Places of Interest: Royal residences in Punakka and Thimphu; fortified town of Wangdu Phodrang; 16th century bridge over Sankosh River; Buddhist monasteries.

Bhutan, a small country in the eastern Himalayan hill area, is bordered on the north by the Tibet region of China and on the south by India.

The terrain varies from the icy 24,000-foot peaks of the Himalaya to the steamy jungles of the southern lowland. Between these extremes lie eight fertile valleys.

Most Bhutanese farm or raise yaks. Few know how to read and write. They produce enough food to support themselves without importing food products.

The country's major source of revenue for foreign trade is money received from about 1,500 tourists yearly. India provides about $10 million a year in aid.

Bhutan's early history is obscure. About 1630 a refugee Dukpa Lama from Tibet became the first Dharma Raja, with both spiritual and temporal powers. In the following centuries Bhutan was beset by internal rivalry among powerful penlops (governors).

After a war in 1865 the British annexed part of southern Bhutan and in 1910 assumed control of Bhutan's foreign relations.

A hereditary monarchy was established in 1907. A government council selected Sir Ugyen Wangchuk as the country's first maharaja. He was succeeded in 1927 by his son, and in 1952 by his grandson Jigme Dorji Wangchuk.

India in 1949 returned part of the lands previously annexed by Britain.

Jigme Singye Wangchuck, 16, succeeded to the throne upon the death of his father in 1972. The new king, the fourth of his line, was crowned at Thimphu on June 2, 1974.

QUICK QUIZ: What was the result of the Schmalkaldic War of 1546–55? See page 289.

BOLIVIA

Official Name: Republic of Bolivia.
Area: 424,165 square miles (1,098,581 sq. km.).
Population: 5,960,060.
Chief Cities: La Paz, administrative capital, 654,713; Sucre, legal capital, 106,590; Santa Cruz, 237,128; Cochabamba, 194,156; Oruro, 124,091.
Government: Democracy.
President: Hernán Siles Zuazo (since 1982).
U.S. Ambassador to Bolivia: Edwin Gharst Corr.
Bolivian Ambassador to U.S.: Mariano Baptista Gumucio.
Flag: Stripes of red, gold, and green, with coat of arms on center stripe.
Official Languages: Spanish, Quechua, Aymará.
Ethnic Groups: Indian (65%), Cholo (mixed Indian-European descent, 25%), Spanish descent (10%).
Official Religion: Roman Catholicism (95%).
Leading Industries: Agriculture (potatoes, corn, sugarcane, cassava, cotton, barley, rice, wheat, coffee, bananas, llamas, alpacas); mining (tin, petroleum, natural gas, lead, zinc, copper, tungsten, bismuth, antimony, gold, sulfur, silver, iron ore); manufacturing (textiles, handicrafts, food processing).
Foreign Trade: *Major exports*—tin, antimony, tungsten, zinc, silver, lead, oil, natural gas; *major imports*—flour, motor vehicles.
Places of Interest: Lake Titicaca; Chacaltaya ski resort; San Francisco Church and Tiwanaci ancient ruins in La Paz.

BOLIVIA TODAY

A landlocked South American country, Bolivia has extensive natural resources. However, Bolivians have benefited little from them because of two disastrous wars and many revolutions.

Over half the people are Indians, who live in thatched mud huts and raise just enough food to feed their families. Corn and potatoes are the staples. Few Indians have gone to school, and most cannot read and write. Many work in the country's tin mines and oil fields.

Bolivia is divided into three regions. Two bleak Andean ranges that flank a high plateau (Altiplano) stretch along the Chilean border in the west. The valleys (Yungas) scar the eastern slopes of the Andes. The tropical plains (Llanos and Chaco) are in the east.

SPANISH CONQUEST

Pre-Inca ruins, such as those at Tiahuanaco, indicate the existence of an early Indian civilization in Bolivia. About 1200 the country came under the rule of the Incas. The Spanish conquest of the Inca empire brought the subjugation of the Bolivian region by 1538.

INDEPENDENCE

Called Upper Peru under Spanish rule, Bolivia was one of the first colonies to rebel. Its War of Independence lasted from 1809 to 1825.

Bolivia became an independent republic on Aug. 6, 1825. It was named for its liberator, Gen. Simón Bolívar.

For most of its independent history, Bolivia has endured factional strife and military dictators. It lost much of its territory in wars.

In 1879 Chile seized Bolivia's only access to the ocean, the mineral-rich Atacama Desert.

From 1932 to 1935 Bolivia fought the bloody Chaco War with Paraguay, losing much land and suffering a humiliating defeat.

The Movement of the National Revolution (MNR), which seized power in 1952, gave equality to the Indian masses, began land reforms, and nationalized big foreign mining companies.

MILITARY RULE

In 1964 Vice President René Barrientos Ortuño overthrew the government. He died in a plane crash in April 1969, and Vice President Luis Siles Salinas was named president.

Siles was ousted by a military coup on Sept. 26, 1969. Gen. Alfredo Ovando Candia assumed the presidency. Ovando was forced to resign on Oct. 6, 1970. Gen. Juan José Torres, a leftist, became president.

Col. Hugo Banzer Suárez overthrew Torres in August 1971, becoming president. All strikes and union activities were outlawed.

Bolivia held its first presidential election in a dozen years on July 9, 1978, but fraud was so prevalent that a court annulled the results.

Air Force Gen. Juan Pereda Asbún seized power on July 21, 1978, deposing Banzer and making himself president. Four months later, on Nov. 24, 1978, Army Gen. David Padilla Arancibia ousted Pereda.

Bolivia made a new effort to return to democracy with a national election held on July 1, 1979, for a new congress and a civilian president. None of the eight presidential candidates received a majority. Congress decided on Aug. 6, 1979, to give the presidency on an interim basis to Walter Guevara Arze, 68, a former foreign minister.

Conservative Col. Alberto Natusch Busch overthrew Guevara on Nov. 1, 1979. When the people of La Paz demonstrated against him, Natusch's troops and planes fired into the crowds, killing about 60 persons.

Natusch agreed to step down on Nov. 16, and the president of Congress, Lydia Gueiler Tejada, 51, was chosen by that body as the nation's interim president.

In a national election on June 29, 1980, Hernán Siles Zuazo, a leftist who had been president in 1956–60, won a plurality in the race for president against 13 other candidates.

Army commander Gen. Luis García Metza Tejada overthrew the government on July 17, 1980, to prevent Siles Zuazo from taking office. He launched a campaign of terror against opponents, arresting and killing hundreds. The U.S. cut off all military and economic aid.

The U.S. continued to withhold aid in 1981 on evidence that President Garcia Metza and other high military officers were receiving millions of dollars in payoffs from the country's $1.5 billion illegal traffic in cocaine.

On Aug. 4, 1981, Gen. Garcia Metza resigned. A month later the junta named a new president, Gen. Celso Torrelio Villa.

President Celso Torrelio restored rights to political parties and labor unions and granted amnesty to exiles. But he was unable to cope with the deteriorating economy. The junta replaced him on July 21, 1982, with Gen. Guido Vildoso Calderón.

DEMOCRACY RESTORED

With inflation running at an annual rate of 150%, President Vildoso on Sept. 14, 1982, decreed stiff austerity measures that increased prices and held down wages. Labor unions immediately called a general strike, declaring workers would not return to their jobs until Vildoso resigned. On Sept. 27 the military junta gave in to the unions, ordering the nation's congress to reconvene.

Congress voted 113–29 to restore the presidency to 69-year-old Siles Zuazo, recalling him from exile in Peru.

After being sworn into office on Oct. 10, 1982, President Siles Zuazo immediately fired the commanders of the armed forces, naming as commander in chief Gen. Alfredo Villaroel Barja, a moderate who had formerly served as defense minister.

The president also appointed two communists as members of his cabinet.

In February 1983 the government expelled to France Nazi war criminal Klaus Barbie, whom France had sought to extradite since 1972.

The worst drought in the nation's history in 1983 destroyed most of the crops of subsistence farmers, bringing great hardship. The nearly bankrupt government struggled to import millions of dollars of food to prevent mass starvation.

BOPHUTHATSWANA

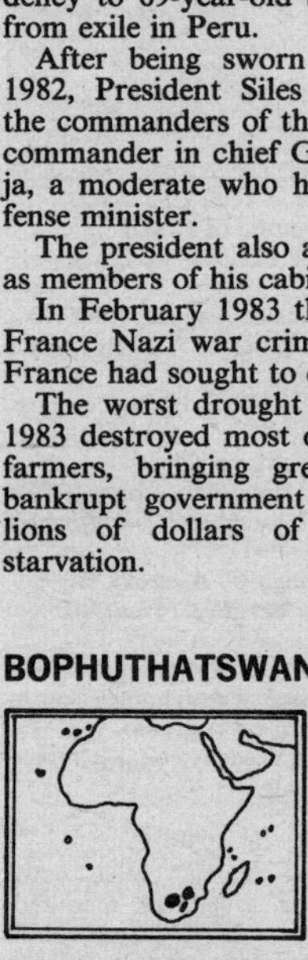

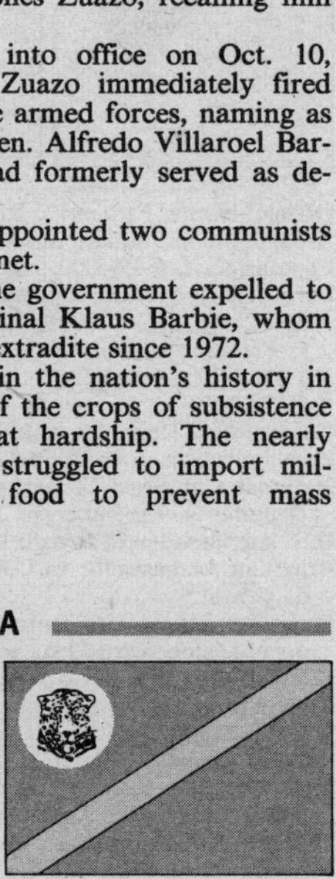

Official Name: Republic of Bophuthatswana.
Area: 17,010 square miles (44,055 sq. km.).
Population: 1,417,520.
Leading Cities: Mmabatho, capital, 5,000; GaRankuwa, 72,518; Mabopane, 64,854; Mafikeng, 10,000.
Government: Republic.
President: Chief Lucas M. Mangope (since 1977).
National Assembly: 96 members (48 elected).
Flag: Dark blue background divided by diagonal orange bar; leopard's head in white circle in upper hoist corner.
Official Languages: Tswana, English, Afrikaans.
Chief Ethnic Group: Tswana (Western Sotho of Bantus).
Main Religion: Animism.
Leading Industries: Tourism, agriculture (wheat, corn, peanuts, vegetables, alfalfa, cotton, cattle, sheep, goats); manufacturing (food processing, pottery, furniture, textiles, plastics); mining (platinum, asbestos, iron ore, chrome, vanadium, diamonds).
Foreign Trade: *Major exports*—asbestos, chrome, diamonds, iron ore, manganese, platinum; *major imports*—consumer goods, food.
Places of Interest: *In Mmabatho:* government buildings; Sun City, casino-resort complex.

BOPHUTHATSWANA TODAY

Although declared an independent nation by South Africa, Bophuthatswana has failed to gain recognition as sovereign by any other country.

Given its freedom as part of South Africa's apartheid policy of separating the races, Bophuthatswana is made up of six areas separated by land that remains part of South Africa. Two regions lie along the border of Botswana.

Bophuthatswana is the main source of platinum for Western industrial countries.

A substantial part of the nation's income derives from South African tourists who flock to Bophuthatswana's casino-resort Sun City, enjoying entertainment by such stars as Frank Sinatra and Liza Minnelli who refuse to appear in South Africa.

HISTORY

The Bantu-speaking Sotho tribes, from which the Tswana are descended, migrated to southern Africa in the 900s to 1600s. About 75 Tswana tribes developed, often warring with each other.

In the 1820s and 1830s life in the region was disrupted by invasions of tribes driven from the coastal areas by European colonists.

In 1961 a Tswana territorial authority was established. Eleven years later, on June 1, 1972, the territory was given self-government.

In the first national election, on Oct. 4, 1972, the Bophuthatswana National Party (BNP) won 20 of the 24 elective seats. BNP leader Chief Lucas M. Mangope became chief minister of the Bophuthatswana government.

Bophuthatswana was granted independence on Dec. 6, 1977, by South Africa, which at the same time deprived the 1 million Tswana who live and work in South Africa of South African citizenship.

Chief Mangope became Bophuthatswana's first president, his party having won control of the national assembly in an election held on Aug. 24, 1977. During the election campaign, Chief H.T.R. Masseloane's National Party opposed independence for Bophuthatswana.

A new capital, Mmabatho, was built in 1977, just outside the South African city of Mafeking.

South Africa on Sept. 19, 1980, transferred the city of Mafeking to Bophuthatswana, which changed the name to Mafikeng.

BOTSWANA

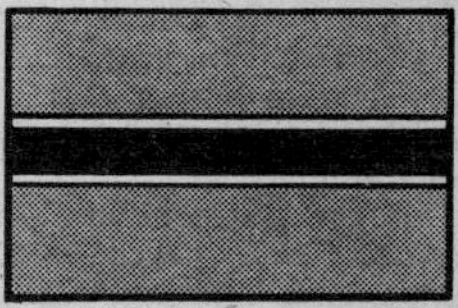

Official Name: Republic of Botswana.
Area: 231,805 square miles (600,372 sq. km.).
Population: 1,038,860.
Capital: Gaborone, 60,000.
Government: Parliamentary democracy.
President: Quett Masire (since 1980).
Legislature: *National Assembly*, 36 members.
U.S. Ambassador to Botswana: Theodore C. Maino.

QUICK QUIZ: What was achieved by the Battle of Trafalgar in 1805? See page 291.

BOTSWANA *(continued)*

Botswana Ambassador to U.S.: Moteane J. Melamu.
Flag: Wide light-blue bands separated from a central black band by narrow white stripes.
Languages: English (official), Bantu (Tswana).
Main Ethnic Group: Tswana (98%).
Religion: Animism (85%).
Leading Industries: Agriculture (cattle, corn, sorghum); mining (diamonds, copper, nickel, manganese, coal); tourism; food processing.
Foreign Trade: *Major exports*—meat, hides, diamonds, copper, nickel, manganese; *major imports*—grains, fuels, motor vehicles, textiles, clothing.
Places of Interest: Kalahari Desert; Okavango swamps; Makarikari salt pans; game and bird sanctuaries; Gaborone gambling casino; Stone Age rock paintings on cliffs of Tsodilo Hills.

BOTSWANA TODAY

The southern African country of Botswana is one of the few nations on the continent that has maintained a multiparty democracy since attaining independence. However, Botswana remains economically dependent on South Africa.

With about the same area and climate as Texas, Botswana has specialized for many years in cattle raising. Most of the people follow a tribal way of life that has changed little in hundreds of years.

Tourists from Zimbabwe and South Africa visit Botswana to gamble at the casino in Gaborone and to hunt, fish, bird-watch, and photograph at the parks in the Okavango delta region, the Chobe game park, and the Khutse game reserve.

Most of Botswana's exports and imports pass through South Africa and parts of Bophuthatswana, which lie to the south. Zambia and Zimbabwe border Botswana on the northeast. Namibia is to the west and north.

The Kalahari Desert covers much of the south. The Okavango River forms an extensive swamp in the northwest.

HISTORY

Under Khama the Great and other chiefs, the Bechuana (Tswana) people sought British protection against the Transvaal Boers in the 1880s. Britain established the Bechuanaland Protectorate in 1885. In 1909–55 it was threatened by incorporation into South Africa.

In 1948 the country was thrown into turmoil when Oxford-educated Seretse Khama, heir to the throne of the leading Bamandwato tribe, married a white English girl, Ruth Williams. He was forced by the British to live in exile. When he renounced his claim to the chieftainship, he was allowed to return to Bechuanaland in 1956.

Organizing the Bechuanaland Democratic Party, Khama helped lead his people to self-government.

In the first general election, in 1965, his party won an overwhelming majority, and Khama became chief minister.

The nation achieved full independence on Sept. 30, 1966, and was renamed Botswana. Sir Seretse Khama was elected by the national assembly as the first president of the new republic. He was reelected in 1969, 1974, and 1979 when his Botswana Democratic Party (BDP) again won parliamentary elections.

The discovery of substantial mineral deposits in Botswana in the 1970s stimulated its impoverished economy. British and American interests developed a diamond mine at Orapa. A large copper-nickel mine began production at Selbi-Pikwe in 1975. The country's GNP grew at an annual rate of about 20%.

Upon the death of Sir Seretse Khama in 1980, he was succeeded as president by Dr. Quett Masire, who had served as vice president.

Drought destroyed about 75% of the nation's crops in 1981–82. President Masire appealed for international aid to prevent starvation.

BRAZIL

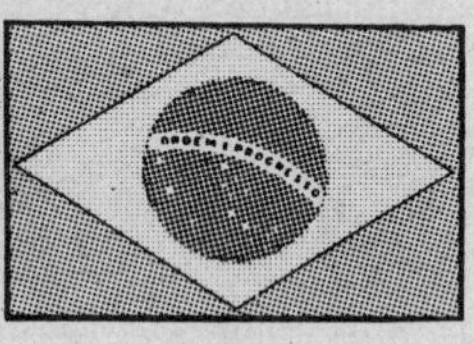

Official Name: Federative Republic of Brazil.
Area: 3,286,488 square miles (8,511,965 sq. km.).
Population: 126,457,000.
Largest Metropolitan Areas: Brasília, capital, 1,306,400; São Paulo, 8,732,000; Rio de Janeiro, 5,539,100; Belo Horizonte, 1,937,200; Salvador, 1,501,700; Recife, 1,432,800; Fortaleza, 1,306,800; Pôrto Alegre, 1,221,000.
Government: Republic under military rule.
President: Gen. João Baptista Figueiredo (since 1979).
National Congress: *Senate,* 67 members; *Chamber of Deputies,* 479 members.
U.S. Ambassador to Brazil: Diego C. Asencio.
Brazilian Ambassador to U.S.: Sergio Correa Affonso da Costa.
Flag: Green field with centered yellow diamond enclosing blue globe with 22 stars (five of which form Southern Cross) and motto "Ordem e Progresso."
Main Ethnic Groups: European descent (62%), mixed European-Indian-black (26%).
Official Language: Portuguese.
Main Religion: Roman Catholicism (93%).
Leading Industries: Agriculture (cattle, coffee, corn, rice, sugarcane, rubber, cocoa, soybeans); manufacturing (steel, automobiles, plastics, paper, alcohol, chemicals, machinery, consumer goods); mining (iron ore, manganese, gold, uranium, diamonds, coal, petroleum, bauxite, nickel); construction.
Foreign Trade: *Major exports*—industrial products, cocoa, coffee, soybeans, sugar, iron ore, manganese; *major imports*—petroleum, wheat, machinery.
Places of Interest: Brasília; Rio de Janeiro; Christ of Corcovado statue; Amazon River; Iguassú Falls; Portuguese colonial sites at Salvador; Ouro Preto, Congonhas, Sabara—the "Cities of Gold"; Ipiranga Museum and Monument at São Paulo; St. John del Rey gold mine; Copacabana and Santos beach resorts; scenic highway between São Paulo and Santos.

BRAZIL TODAY

The world's fifth-largest country in area, Brazil also is the seventh largest in population. As such, it faces many major problems.

Brazil's government is dominated by military leaders who prevent constitutional democracy from functioning and restrict freedom in the name of national security and stability. A high percentage of Brazilians live in poverty in the cities and in rural areas.

Brazil has made tremendous strides in industrial

izing its economy. By the 1980's exports of industrial products exceeded those of agricultural products. However, this was accomplished at the expense of political and civil liberties.

Almost as large as the United States, but with half as many people, Brazil has huge undeveloped areas in the interior along the Amazon River. The Amazon basin accounts for 60% of Brazil's area but contains only 8% of its population. The government has made a concerted effort to open up and settle the western region. One of the keys to this program has been the construction of a $100 million 3,500-mile Trans-Amazon Highway, begun in 1970. The highway created boom towns along its route, just as the coming of the railroads once brought boom towns in the western U.S. Settlers are given interest-free loans to start farms.

The same spirit of lawlessness and treatment of Indians that marked the American West is prevalent on the new Brazilian frontier. Indians wearing war paint have attacked settlers and highway construction crews invading their territory. In turn the Indians often have been mistreated and killed with little provocation. Only about 100,000 Indians survive of the 1 to 5 million who once lived in Brazil.

The country has vast natural resources, but must import about 80% of the oil it uses.

GEOGRAPHY

Occupying almost half the South American continent, Brazil is bordered on the north by French Guiana, Suriname, Guyana, Venezuela, and Colombia. Peru and Bolivia lie to the west. Paraguay and Argentina are to the southwest and Uruguay to the south.

A tropical climate prevails in the Amazon River basin in the north. Over half the country's area consists of highlands between 650 and 3,000 feet above sea level, where the climate is temperate. Brazil's major waterways are the Amazon, the second-longest river in the world, the Paraná, and the São Francisco.

PORTUGUESE DISCOVERY AND COLONIZATION

In 1500 Pedro Alvares Cabral, a Portuguese admiral, claimed the region for his country. In 1532 Martim Afonso de Sousa founded the first colony at São Vicente and introduced sugarcane cultivation. When Brazil became the major source of sugar in the 17th century, many Negro slaves were imported.

Between 1693 and 1700 mineral wealth was discovered in central Brazil, and the region flourished for a century as a major world supplier of gold and diamonds. By 1763 Rio de Janeiro had replaced Salvador as the colony's capital. In 1808, after Napoleon's capture of Lisbon, Portugal's royal family fled to Brazil. Rio became the seat of the Portuguese empire.

BRAZILIAN EMPIRE

King João VI returned to Portugal in 1821, leaving his son, Dom Pedro, as regent. In 1822, acceding to widespread demands for liberty, Dom Pedro became Pedro I, emperor of an independent Brazil. His popularity diminished, and in 1831 he abdicated in favor of his son Pedro de Alcântara (Pedro II), who governed until 1889. The progressive rule of Pedro II laid the foundation of modern Brazil.

Foreign demand for rubber stimulated the growth of such cities as Belém and Manaus.

The abolition of slavery in 1888 fanned rebellion as the owners of plantations supported the republican movement.

REPUBLIC OF BRAZIL

In 1889 a bloodless revolt established the United States of Brazil, with Manuel Deodoro da Fonseca as first president.

By 1914 Brazil had gained political stability and international recognition. The country's rubber monopoly ended, however, with the development of plantations in Southeast Asia.

In 1930 a revolution brought Getúlio Vargas to the presidency. His regime degenerated into a dictatorship and was overthrown in 1945. Vargas became president again in 1950, this time by popular vote, but he committed suicide in 1954.

Juscelino Kubitschek, elected president in 1955, initiated heavy construction programs and industrial expansion. He created a new capital, Brasília, in the country's wilderness to encourage development of the interior.

Jânio Quadros, elected president in 1960 by the largest plurality vote in Brazil's history, failed to stem an economic crisis. He resigned after seven months. João Goulart, the vice president, took over in 1961. His 30-month regime was marked by strikes, riots, and inflation.

MILITARY RULE

A military uprising forced Goulart into exile in 1964. Marshal Humberto de Alencar Castello Branco became interim president. In 1966 Marshal Artur da Costa e Silva became president.

Faced with growing opposition, President Costa e Silva arrested opposition political leaders. He dissolved the national assembly, suspended constitutional rights, imposed strict censorship, and seized total power on Dec. 13, 1968. He suffered a stroke and died in December 1969.

Military leaders named Gen. Emilio Garrastazú Médici to the presidency on Oct. 7, 1969. He set up ambitious economic and social goals. Prosperity made him popular.

Gen. Ernesto Geisel was sworn in as president on March 15, 1974, having been chosen to succeed Médici by the military leadership.

Work got under way in 1976 on the world's biggest hydroelectric project—the Itaipu Dam on the Paraná River, which will cost about $9 billion by the time it is completed in the 1980s.

The military government's emphasis on industrialization caused the nation's gross national product to increase fivefold during the 1970s—from about $40 billion to $236 billion by 1980.

Because the U.S. State Department criticized human-rights practices in Brazil, the government in March 1977 canceled its 25-year-old military assistance treaty with the U.S. and rejected $50 million in American military aid for 1978.

In 1977 President Geisel extended his own term of office by an additional year to six years

QUICK QUIZ: When was serfdom abolished in Russia? See page 292.

BRAZIL *(continued)*
and made it possible for a simple majority in congress to approve a constitutional amendment instead of the previous two-thirds majority.

Despite the opposition of Roman Catholic leaders, the Brazilian congress passed legislation in 1977 legalizing divorce in what is the world's largest Roman Catholic country.

President Carter visited Brazil on March 29–30, 1978, receiving a rather cool reception from the nation's military leaders who still resented criticisms by the U.S. government about their restrictions on human rights for Brazilians.

However, during the next several months the government relaxed several of its limitations on human rights. For the first time in a decade, unions were allowed to strike against private employers. In June the government ended its prepublication censorship of newspapers, but continued controls on radio and TV broadcasting.

Gen. João Baptista de Figueiredo, chief of the national intelligence service, was elected president by a special 592-member electoral college in 1978. He took office on March 15, 1979, pledging to return the country to full civilian control at the end of his 6-year term.

The government announced plans in 1979 to reduce dependency on imported petroleum by investing $5 billion through 1985 to produce alcohol fuel from sugarcane and other farm crops. Plans called for auto manufacturers to produce nearly 2 million cars to use 100% alcohol as fuel, while other automobiles would use a gasohol mixture including 20% alcohol.

President Figueiredo signed an amnesty on Aug. 28, 1979, that permitted an estimated 5,000 political exiles to return to Brazil in the following months. The amnesty excluded about 200 persons accused of acts of political violence. The government announced it had freed its last political prisoner on Oct. 8, 1980.

Rightist terrorists opposed to the government's liberalization policies and especially to the lack of censorship of leftist publications stepped up bombing attacks in 1980, killing scores of liberal leaders and known criminals.

The nation's first nuclear electric-power reactor began operation in 1981 with a capacity of 625 megawatts. A second reactor nearly twice as large is scheduled for completion in 1987.

Brazil and the Soviet Union signed a 5-year $6 billion trade pact on July 15, 1981, with Brazilian grain and other farm products being exchanged for Soviet petroleum, machinery, and technical aid.

The discovery of gold at Serra Pelada in northern Brazil in 1978 brought a gold rush of thousands of prospectors to that region. In 1981–82 mines in the area produced $180 million in gold. A miner in July 1982 found a 7.5-kilogram nugget worth $100,000.

Development progressed in the 1980s on what is believed to be the world's largest mineral deposit, discovered in 1968 at Carajas in northern Brazil. It contains an estimated 18 billion tons of high-grade iron ore as well as large amounts of copper, managanese, nickel, and copper. Government plans call for investment of $61 billion in development of the Carajas project, an amount equal to the national debt. Shipment of 35 million tons of ore a year was expected by 1987.

A major step toward a return to democracy was taken on Nov. 15, 1982, with the first secret-ballot election of state and local officials since 1962. Government-backed candidates won a majority of the offices, with the opposition divided among four main parties.

The nation's economy deteriorated in the 1980s. The government found it increasingly difficult to meet payments on its huge foreign debt of about $92 billion. In an effort to stem inflation, running at an annual rate of 130%, the government on July 14, 1983, ordered salary increases limited to 80% of the inflation rate. Food shortages, caused by five years of drought in northeastern Brazil, brought widespread hunger. Food riots in major cities in 1983 were marked by the looting of supermarkets and grocery stores.

BRITAIN

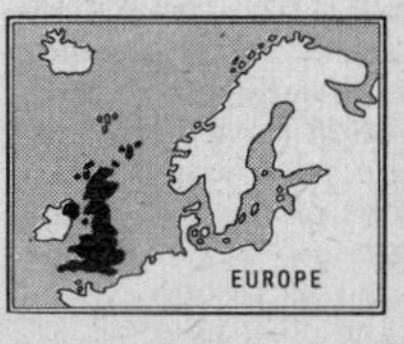

Official Name: United Kingdom of Great Britain and Northern Ireland.
Area: 94,515 square miles (244,794 sq. km.).
Population: 56,019,900.
Largest Metropolitan Areas: London, capital, 7,167,600; Manchester, 2,389,260; Birmingham, 2,358,980; Leeds, 1,735,700; Glasgow, 1,727,625; Liverpool, 1,226,310.
Government: Constitutional monarchy.
Prime Minister: Margaret Thatcher (since 1979).
Queen: Elizabeth II (since 1952).
Parliament: *House of Lords,* 1,173 members; *House of Commons,* 650 members.
U.S. Ambassador to Britain: Charles H. Price.
British Ambassador to U.S.: Sir Oliver Wright.
Flag: The Union Jack, combination of red-on-white crosses of England's St. George and Ireland's St. Patrick, with white-on-blue cross of Scotland's St. Andrew.
Main Religions: Anglicanism (66%), Roman Catholicism (9%), Presbyterianism (2%).
Languages: English (official), Gaelic, Irish, Welsh.
Leading Industries: Manufacturing (steel, machinery, cement, paper, electricity, motor vehicles, chemicals, aluminum, textiles, consumer goods); agriculture (sheep, cattle, dairy products, poultry, barley, potatoes, sugar beets, wheat, oats, fruits, vegetables); mining (coal, iron ore, natural gas, tin, petroleum); tourism; fishing.
Foreign Trade: *Major exports*—machinery, motor vehicles, metals and metal products, chemicals and drugs, textiles; *major imports*—food products, raw materials and fuels, machinery, motor vehicles, petroleum.
Places of Interest: *England*—Windsor Castle; Hampton Court; Shakespeare country around Stratford; Brighton; Lake District; Stonehenge; Devon and Cornwall; Oxford and Cambridge university towns; cathedral towns; Bath. *In London*—Westminster Abbey; Tower of London; Buckingham Palace; British Museum; Museum of London. *Wales*—Tintern Abbey; Caernarvon Castle. *Scotland*—Edinburgh; Scottish Highlands; the Trossachs. *Northern Ireland*—Giant's Causeway; County Fermanagh.

BRITAIN TODAY

An island kingdom that once was the most powerful nation in the world, Britain faces many serious economic problems. With the loss of the bulk of its worldwide empire in the past three decades, Britain today is a nation only half as large as its ancient rival France.

Britain is a union of England, Scotland, Wales, and Northern Ireland. A scattering of islands and small territories around the world still are British colonies and dependencies. But most of Britain's former colonies have been granted complete independence. Many, such as Australia and Canada, retain ties through membership in the British Commonwealth of Nations.

Britain was the birthplace of the Industrial Revolution in the mid-1700s and became the world's first industrial nation. But with the loss of the captive markets of its major colonies, Britain has been unable to compete successfully in today's free-for-all foreign trade. As recently as 1958 Britain ranked second only to the United States in world trade, but today it stands fifth in the value of its exports behind the U.S., West Germany, Japan, and France.

The British people also have seen a decline in their standard of living. The per capita gross domestic product has fallen to about half that of the United States. Because Britain must import much of the food its people eat and many of the raw materials its factories process, the nation has been hard hit by worldwide inflation. The average Briton has to pay taxes equal to about a third of his income.

The idea that many problems might be solved by membership in the European Common Market, accomplished in 1973, has proved illusory. However, a bright hope for Britain's future developed in the 1970s–1980s as offshore oil discoveries promised petroleum self-sufficiency.

EARLY HISTORY

A people called the Iberians are thought to have inhabited Britain during the Stone Age. Sometime before the 500s B.C. Celtic tribes from northern Europe began a centuries-long series of invasions. Troops under Julius Caesar landed in Britain in 55 B.C. By A.D. 142 Rome held all the land to the River Clyde, where Hadrian's Wall was put up to keep out the Picts of Scotland. The Romans introduced Christianity.

As their empire declined, the Romans withdrew their legions, and Germanic invaders from northern Europe—Angles, Saxons, and Jutes—took their place in Britain. Driving the Britons west to Wales and Cornwall, they formed the kingdoms of Kent, Essex, Wessex, Sussex, East Anglia, Mercia, and Northumbria in the south and east between 500 and 800.

Late in the 700s Danish Vikings began to harass the Anglo-Saxon kingdoms. In the 860s the Danes invaded the island. By 1016 Canute, a Dane, was king of England, and Anglo-Saxon rule was over, except for a brief period under Edward the Confessor.

MIDDLE AGES

In 1066 a Norman duke, William the Conqueror, led the last successful invasion of Britain. He became William I (1066–87) of England when his Norman troops beat a force of Anglo-Saxons under Harold at Hastings. William imposed a feudal system.

The first Plantagenet ruler, Henry II (1154–89), began the conquest of Ireland.

Feudal nobles forced King John (1199–1216) to approve the Magna Carta in 1215, the first step toward the parliamentary system.

Edward I (1272–1307), who completed the conquest of Wales in 1282, enlarged parliament, increasing its powers. In 1296 he conquered Scotland, but the defeat of his son Edward II (1307–27) at Bannockburn by Robert the Bruce in 1314 restored Scottish independence, which England recognized by treaty in 1328. Longstanding English claims to French territory and commercial rivalry with France precipitated the Hundred Years War (1338–1453). In 1346 Edward III (1327–77) invaded Normandy. He crushed the French at Crécy in 1346. Ten years later his son Edward, the Black Prince, won a second victory for England at Poitiers.

The war continued under Henry IV (1399–1413), Britain's first ruler of the Lancastrian line. Henry V (1413–22) routed the French at Agincourt (1415) and was acknowledged heir to the throne of France. After Henry's death the French rallied under Joan of Arc. The French victory at Orléans was the first of a series which, in time, left England only the port of Calais.

At the end of the Hundred Years War the rival families of York and Lancaster began a bloody struggle for the English throne: the Wars of the Roses (1455–85). Henry Tudor, a Lancastrian, ended the wars by defeating Richard III (1483–85) of York at Bosworth Field in 1485, and founded the Tudor dynasty as Henry VII (1485–1509).

REFORMATION

Henry VIII (1509–47) broke with the pope when denied the right to divorce the first of his six wives. He then claimed supreme authority over the Catholic Church in England. Under Henry, the Church of England emerged as Anglican Protestant. His eldest daughter, Mary (1553–58), restored Catholicism as the state religion, but supremacy of the Protestant Church of England was permanently reestablished by another of Henry's daughters, Elizabeth I (1558–1603).

BUILDING A COLONIAL EMPIRE

Elizabeth's reign was one of the glories of English history. The defeat of the Spanish Armada in 1588 made England a major naval power. The previous year Mary Stuart, Queen of Scots, a Catholic rival for the throne, had been executed. Men of daring such as Sir Walter Raleigh and Sir Francis Drake staked out an overseas empire. Men of genius such as William Shakespeare and Francis Bacon brought a flowering of English arts and science.

Elizabeth was succeeded by James VI of Scotland, the Protestant son of Mary Stuart. Ruling over Scotland and England as James I (1603–25), he established the first English colonies in North

QUICK QUIZ: When did Finland declare independence from Russia? See page 293.

BRITAIN *(continued)*
America at Jamestown and Plymouth.

COMMONWEALTH AND RESTORATION

Conflict with parliament arose from James' belief in the divine right of kings. His son Charles I (1625–49) aggravated the conflict. Civil war broke out in 1642 between his supporters and the Puritan partisans of parliament. Oliver Cromwell led the Puritans to victory, and King Charles was captured and beheaded in 1649.

England, now a commonwealth, was governed by parliamentary committee until 1653, when Cromwell dismissed parliament and ruled as Lord Protector, or dictator.

In 1660, two years after Cromwell's death, the monarchy was restored with the popular reign of Charles II (1660–85), a Stuart. The austere Puritan social code was replaced by a renewed sense of freedom. Political and religious strife returned when Charles was succeeded by his brother James II (1685–88), who reasserted the discredited divine right of kings and plotted to restore Roman Catholicism. James was deposed in 1688, without bloodshed, in the "Glorious Revolution." His Protestant daughter Mary and her husband, William of Orange, the ruler of Holland, were invited to govern England. The rule of William III (1689–1702) and Mary II (1689–94) ushered in a period of political stability. The Bill of Rights was passed and political parties were established.

CREATING THE UNITED KINGDOM

Under Queen Anne (1702–14), last of the Protestant Stuarts, the Act of Union (1707) created the United Kingdom of Great Britain by uniting Scotland with England and Wales.

Anne's death brought her German cousin George I (1714–27), the first of the Hanover line, to the throne. Like him, his son and successor George II (1727–60) spoke little English. The parliament became more powerful than the king. Under George II Britain added to its empire, chiefly at the expense of Bourbon France, emerging from the Seven Years War (1756–63) in possession of India and of North America from the Atlantic coastline to the Mississippi River.

King George III (1760–1820) dismissed William Pitt the Elder, the prime minister responsible for Britain's colonial successes. He then attempted to impose his own views on parliament. In the American Revolution (1775–83) all the North American colonies except Canada were lost. Following the defeat of Napoleon (1815) by an army under the command of the Duke of Wellington, Britain acquired new colonies in the Mediterranean, the Caribbean, Africa, and Asia.

INDUSTRIAL REVOLUTION

The Industrial Revolution, which began in the mid-1700s, gave Britain the world's first industrial economy. But the factory system brought many abuses to workers.

The first of a series of reforms, in 1832, extended the right to vote to the middle classes and made parliament more truly representative. In the following year child-labor and factory-inspection laws were passed, and slavery was abolished in the colonies. Repeal of the Corn Laws in 1846 was intended to lower the price of grain for ordinary consumers. Prime Minister Benjamin Disraeli's Reform Bill of 1867 extended voting privileges to many factory laborers. Prime Minister William Gladstone's Reform Bill of 1884 established universal male suffrage.

Many of these reforms occurred during the long reign of Queen Victoria (1837–1901), which also witnessed the transfer of India from rule by the British East India Company to the British crown (1859) and the annexation of South Africa after the Boer War (1899–1902). The globe-girdling British Empire, rich, stable, and prosperous, was at the peak of its power.

WORLD WARS I AND II

Britain allied itself with its traditional enemy, France, in 1904. Ten years later Britain and France fought World War I against the empires of Germany and Austria-Hungary. Under Prime Minister David Lloyd George, Britain emerged victorious. To its empire were added former German colonies in Africa and the Middle East.

World War I marked the end of British expansion. Ireland's rebellion (1916–21) brought division of the island into the Irish Free State and Northern Ireland.

Britain granted independence in 1931 to Australia, Canada, Ireland, New Zealand, and South Africa, which became the first members of the British Commonwealth of Nations.

In 1936 Edward VIII abdicated to marry an American divorcée, a marriage disapproved of by the Church of England and the cabinet. His brother became king as George VI.

Hoping to avoid another war, Neville Chamberlain's government adopted a policy of appeasement toward Nazi Germany. But when Hitler's troops invaded Poland in 1939, Britain immediately declared war on Germany.

During World War II the British people rallied under the inspired leadership of Prime Minister Winston Churchill, holding out against intensive air attacks by Nazi bombers.

SOCIALIST BRITAIN

In July 1945 the socialist Labour Party, led by Clement Attlee, won an overwhelming electoral victory. In the next six years the Labour Party nationalized such basic industries as coal mines, steel mills, the railways, and the Bank of England. An extensive social-welfare program included socialized medicine.

The Labour government in 1947 granted independence within the Commonwealth to India and Pakistan, heralding the end of Britain's empire. In the following decades most of Britain's remaining colonies received independence.

Churchill returned to power in 1951–55.

King George VI died in 1952. His daughter became Queen Elizabeth II.

The Labour Party won elections in 1964, making Harold Wilson prime minister. Conservatives led by Edward Heath won control in June 1970.

Britain joined the European Economic Community (the Common Market) on Jan. 1, 1973.

Britain was hard hit by the Arab oil embargo that began in October 1973. A parliamentary election called for Feb. 28, 1974, resulted in neither the Conservative nor Labour Party receiving a majority, although Labour won a plurality. Wilson again became prime minister.

Prime Minister Wilson called new parliamentary elections on Oct. 10, 1974, in which his Labour Party won a firm majority in the House of Commons for the next five years.

Because many Britons blamed the slumping economy on membership in the European Common Market, the Labour government held an unprecedented national referendum on the issue on June 5, 1975, in which 67.2% of the people supported continued British participation.

On March 16, 1976, Wilson announced his retirement. Foreign Minister James Callaghan was sworn in as prime minister on April 5.

Reflecting Britain's declining prestige, the value of the pound dropped as low as $1.57 late in October 1976—35% lower than its value of $2.40 in 1975.

Racial tensions caused by an influx of some 2 million black and Asian immigrants in the 1960s and 1970s brought race riots in 1977.

FIRST WOMAN PRIME MINISTER

The nation's continuing inflation and a wave of strikes for large wage increases brought increasing disenchantment with Callaghan's government. On March 28, 1979, he became the first prime minister in 55 years to be forced out of office by a parliamentary no-confidence vote.

In a national election on May 3, 1979, the Conservative Party won a landslide victory with a 43-seat majority in the House of Commons. Conservative leader Margaret Thatcher, 53, became Britain's first woman prime minister, promising to move the nation away from socialism.

The Conservatives cut government spending in 1979 by about $9 billion, reduced government controls on business, and announced plans for income tax cuts and restrictions on labor unions.

Increasing production of petroleum from the North Sea enabled Britain to reduce its imports of foreign oil in 1979–81.

For the first time in 10 years the nation achieved a favorable balance of trade in 1981.

Unemployment and racial bigotry were blamed for a series of riots by teenagers that broke out in the slums of London, Liverpool, and 30 other industrial cities in July 1981.

The pomp and ceremony of the wedding of Prince Charles, the heir to the throne, on July 29, 1981, helped heal the nation's tensions. On June 21, 1982, he and Princess Diana had their first child, Prince William, who became second in line for the throne.

Britons were shocked in 1982 by two incidents concerning the royal family. On July 9 an intruder exposed lax security at Buckingham Palace by climbing a drainpipe, entering the queen's bedroom, sitting on her bed, and carrying on a conversation with her for about 10 minutes before being carted off to jail. In October Prince Andrew, 22, third in line to the throne, was revealed to be holidaying in the Caribbean with actress Kathleen (Koo) Stark, who had appeared nude in movies. After newspapers had nicknamed the prince "Randy Andy," he cut his vacation short on orders of his mother, Queen Elizabeth.

When Argentine troops seized the British colony of the Falkland Islands on April 2, 1982, Britons rallied behind the government's determination to recapture the lost possession. A British fleet and troops dispatched to the islands engaged in a short, hard-fought war, forcing the Argentinians to surrender on June 14.

Prime Minister Thatcher, whose popularity soared as a result of the victory in the Falkland War, stuck resolutely to economic austerity. When railroad engineers struck for two weeks in 1982 demanding a higher wage increase than the 3% offered by the government, Mrs. Thatcher ended the walkout by threatening to fire all 24,000 strikers. Wage-increase limits of 3% for public employees also were ordered for 1983 by

BRITISH COMMONWEALTH OF NATIONS

The Commonwealth of Nations is an association of countries and dependencies that formerly were part of the British Empire. Independent members voluntarily maintain trade and military ties.

INDEPENDENT MEMBERS

Antigua	Gambia	Nauru	Sri Lanka
Australia	Ghana	New Zealand	Swaziland
Bahamas	Grenada	Nigeria	Tanzania
Bangladesh	Guyana	Papua New Guinea	Tonga
Barbados	India	Saint Christopher and Nevis	Trinidad-Tobago
Belize	Jamaica	Saint Lucia	Tuvalu
Botswana	Kenya	Saint Vincent	Uganda
Britain	Kiribati	Seychelles	Vanuatu
Brunei	Lesotho	Sierra Leone	Vanuatu
Canada	Malawi	Singapore	Western Samoa
Cyprus	Malaysia	Solomons	Zambia
Dominica	Malta		Zimbabwe
Fiji	Mauritius		

BRITISH COLONIES AND DEPENDENCIES

Anguilla	Gibraltar
Bermuda	Hong Kong
British Antarctic Territory	Isle of Man
British Indian Ocean Territory	Montserrat
British Virgin Islands	Pitcairn Islands
Cayman Islands	Saint Helena
Channel Islands	Turks and Caicos
Falkland Islands	

PRIME MINISTERS OF BRITAIN

1902-05	Arthur J. Balfour	Conservative
1905-08	Henry Campbell-Bannerman	Liberal
1908-16	Herbert H. Asquith	Liberal
1916-22	David Lloyd George	Liberal
1922-23	Andrew Bonar Law	Conservative
1923-24	Stanley Baldwin	Conservative
1924	J. Ramsay MacDonald	Labour
1924-29	Stanley Baldwin	Conservative
1929-35	J. Ramsay MacDonald	Labour
1935-37	Stanley Baldwin	Conservative
1937-40	Neville Chamberlain	Conservative
1940-45	Winston Churchill	Conservative
1945-51	Clement R. Attlee	Labour
1951-55	Winston Churchill	Conservative
1955-57	Anthony Eden	Conservative
1957-63	Harold Macmillan	Conservative
1963-64	Alexander Douglas-Home	Conservative
1964-70	Harold Wilson	Labour
1970-74	Edward Heath	Conservative
1974-76	Harold Wilson	Labour
1976-79	James Callaghan	Labour
1979-	Margaret Thatcher	Conservative

QUICK QUIZ: Who led monarchist forces in the Spanish Civil War of the 1930s? See page 294.

BRITAIN *(continued)*
the Thatcher cabinet.

Britain's economy showed continued signs of beginning to recover in 1982, although unemployment reached 14% with 3.34 million jobless—the highest rate in western Europe. The inflation rate dropped to about 7% by year's end, and bank loan rates fell a similar amount.

Confidence in British security was shaken in 1982 with the arrest and conviction of Geoffrey Prime, a British translator working for British intelligence, who admitted he had spied for the Soviet Union for 14 years, passing along many military secrets of Britain and the U.S.

In a national election on June 9, 1983, Prime Minister Thatcher's Conservative Party won the largest landslide victory since the Labour Party defeated Winston Churchill in 1945. She became the first prime minister since 1900 to win two consecutive elections with margins large enough to ensure a full 5-year term. The conservatives took 397 seats in parliament, the Labour Party 209, and minor parties 44.

Britain's economy began to recover in 1983. Unemployment declined slightly in August for the first time in four years although more than 3 million, or 12.7% of the work force, still did not have jobs. The annual inflation rate fell to about 4%, its lowest level in about 15 years. Gross national product was expected to rise about 2% for the year.

THE FOUR COUNTRIES OF THE UNITED KINGDOM

ENGLAND

Area: 50,331 square miles (130,357 sq. km.).
Population: 46,347,800.
Capital: London, 7,167,600 (metropolitan area).
Members in House of Commons: 516.

England is the largest of the four countries of the United Kingdom. It covers the southeastern three-fifths of the island of Great Britain. Its explorers and colonists spread the English language to all parts of the world and made London the capital of a worldwide empire. The history of England is detailed on preceding pages.

WALES

Area: 8,016 square miles (20,761 sq. km.).
Population: 2,807,390.
Capital: Cardiff, 278,900.
Members in House of Commons: 36.

Wales is the third largest of the four countries of the United Kingdom.

Wales has huge reserves of coal that helped make Britain a leading industrial power.

When the Germanic Angles and Saxons conquered England in the 400s, the original Britons escaped to Wales, the mountainous western part of the island of Great Britain. They preserved the independence of Wales until William the Conqueror proclaimed himself Lord of Wales in 1071.

English King Edward I claimed control of Wales in 1284. He started naming the heir to the English throne the Prince of Wales in 1301.

In 1536 Henry VIII of England united the two countries, giving the Welsh seats in the English parliament and making English the country's official language. In 1976 the Welsh language was returned to equal status with English in the schools. Bilingual road signs replaced English-only signs.

Nationalist demands for home rule suffered a setback on March 1, 1979, when voters rejected a plan for limited self-government.

SCOTLAND

Area: 30,410 square miles (78,762 sq. km.).
Population: 5,130,030.
Capital: Edinburgh, 463,923.
Largest Metropolitan Area: Glasgow, 1,727,625.
Members in House of Commons: 71.

Scotland is the second largest of the four countries of the United Kingdom. A mountainous country, Scotland covers the northern third of the island of Great Britain.

When the Roman general Agricola conquered Scotland in A.D. 80, he called the country *Caledonia* and the people *Picts*, meaning painted, because they painted their bodies. In the 500s a Celtic tribe from Ireland, called the *Scots*, invaded and conquered Scotland.

In succeeding centuries English kings endeavored to make Scotland part of England, but the Scots resisted. In 1603 the Scottish king James VI inherited the English throne upon the death of Queen Elizabeth I. He became James I of England but ruled Scotland as a separate country.

During the reign of Queen Anne, the Scottish parliament voted in 1707 to unite with England and Wales to form the United Kingdom.

The discovery of oil and gas fields offshore from eastern Scotland in 1973–74 brought an economic boom. It also stimulated demands by Scottish nationalists for home rule and for Scotland to be given a major share of the oil revenues.

But a plan for home rule was defeated in a referendum on March 1, 1979, when fewer than 40% of Scotland's registered voters cast ballots in favor of the measure.

NORTHERN IRELAND

Area: 5,463 square miles (14,148 sq. km.).
Population: 1,546,480.
Capital: Belfast, 297,983.
Members in House of Commons: 17.

The smallest of the four countries of the United Kingdom, Northern Ireland is the northeastern tip of the island of Ireland. About two-thirds of the people are Protestants and one-third Roman Catholics.

Because of Irish revolts against attempted English domination, England's King James I in 1603 forced Irish Roman Catholics in Northern Ireland to give up their land to English and Scottish Protestants whose descendants still constitute a majority in Northern Ireland.

In 1801 the British parliament united all of Ireland with the United Kingdom. After a revolt in Ireland during World War I, Britain separated Northern Ireland from the rest of Ireland in 1920. The Protestant majority of Northern Ireland chose to remain part of the United Kingdom.

Seeking to unite all of Ireland, the outlawed Irish Republican Army (IRA) has carried on a campaign of assassinations and bombings against the Northern Ireland Protestants and British soldiers stationed in the country since 1969. Protestant extremists have retaliated.

On May 1, 1975, voters elected 78 members to a convention given the task of devising a government acceptable to both Protestants and Catholics. But the convention disbanded on March 3, 1976, after 10 months of futile efforts to write a new constitution. Britain announced it would continue direct rule of Northern Ireland.

On Aug. 27, 1979, the IRA shocked the world by assassinating the senior statesman of the royal family, Earl Mountbatten of Burma, 79.

Ten imprisoned IRA dissidents died in 1981 in a hunger strike in which they had tried to win status as political prisoners.

Under British guidance a new 78-member assembly was elected on Oct. 20, 1982, but the assembly was boycotted by Catholics.

In the 14-year period 1969–83 terrorists killed over 2,300 persons.

BRITISH DEPENDENCIES

ANGUILLA

Area: 35 square miles (91 sq. km.).
Population: 6,801.
Capital: The Valley.

One of the northernmost Caribbean islands, Anguilla lies about 160 miles east of Puerto Rico and about 60 miles north of St. Kitts. Fishing is the main industry.

The island first became a British colony about 1650. After being ruled from St. Kitts for two centuries, Anguillans revolted on May 30, 1967, demanding self-government. Two years later the islanders declared independence and announced the severing of all ties with Britain. British paratroops and London police invaded the island on March 19, 1969, and put down the revolt.

On Feb. 10, 1976, Britain granted Anguilla a constitution as a separate self-governing dependency. The People's Progressive Party led by Ronald Webster won 6 of the 7 seats in the national assembly elected on March 15, 1976.

When Webster lost a confidence vote in the assembly in 1977, the British governor-general named Emile Gumbs as chief minister.

Webster regained power as chief minister in 1980 when his Anguilla United Movement won 6 of the 7 elective seats in the legislative assembly. His party won another general election on June 22, 1981.

BERMUDA

Area: 20 square miles (53 sq. km.).
Population: 54,811.
Capital: Hamilton, 2,060.

Situated in the Atlantic Ocean some 580 miles east of Cape Hatteras, N.C., Bermuda consists of 150 coral islands, 20 inhabited.

Discovered in 1503 by the Spaniard Juan de Bermúdez, the islands were settled in 1612 by a group of Englishmen who had been shipwrecked while on their way to Virginia. The crown acquired the islands from a chartered company in 1684. Bermuda has the oldest British colonial legislature in the world. The crown-appointed governor is assisted by a 9-member executive council, an appointed legislative council of 11 members, and a 40-member house of assembly.

In 1968 Bermuda was granted internal autonomy. The governing, mainly white, United Bermuda Party (UBP) won control of the government, defeating the black Progressive Labour Party.

Rioting broke out in December 1977, and British troops were flown in to restore order.

Led by Premier John David Gibbons, the UNP retained control of the government in an election on Dec. 9, 1980. Gibbons resigned on Jan. 15, 1982. He was succeeded as premier and head of the UNP by John W. Swan, 46.

BRITISH ANTARCTIC TERRITORY

Area: 2,025 square miles (5,245 sq. km.), excluding Graham Land.

The British Antarctic Territory was formed in 1962 to include the South Shetland Islands (1,785 square miles), the South Orkney Islands (240 square miles), and Graham Land (the British territory on Palmer Peninsula, Antarctica, 473,000 square miles).

BRITISH INDIAN OCEAN TERRITORY

Area: 30 square miles (78 sq. km.).
Population: 2,000.

Situated in the Indian Ocean about 700 miles south of India, the territory consists only of the Chagos Archipelago, or Oil Islands. The three main inhabited islands are Diego Garcia, Peros Banhos, and Salomon. The people fish and raise coconuts for a living. The U.S. Navy built a major base on Diego Garcia in the 1970s.

From 1965 to 1976 the territory included the Aldabra Islands, Desroches Island, and the Farquhar Group, all of which were transferred to the administration of Seychelles in 1976.

BRITISH VIRGIN ISLANDS

Area: 59 square miles (153 sq. km.).
Population: 12,579.
Capital: Road Town, 2,260.

The British Virgin Islands consist of 36 islands and islets in the Caribbean east of Puerto Rico. Almost all the people are of African descent. Britain obtained the islands in 1666.

About 90% of the people live on the largest island, Tortola.

The climate is subtropical with winter temperatures ranging from 67° to 82°F.

Livestock raising, farming, fishing, and tourism all contribute to the economy.

CAYMAN ISLANDS

Area: 100 square miles (259 sq. km.).
Population: 20,754.
Capital: Georgetown, 3,975.

The Cayman Islands consist of Grand Cayman, the principal island, Little Cayman, and Cayman Brac. They lie in the Caribbean Sea some 200 miles northwest of Jamaica. About a third of the people are European, a fifth black, and the rest of mixed races. Tourism is the chief industry.

Noted for their underwater beauty, the islands are visited by about 20,000 scuba divers each year.

Although discovered by Columbus in 1503, the islands were never settled by the Spanish. Spain ceded the islands to Britain in the Treaty of Madrid in 1670. They were colonized by British from Jamaica and were its dependency until

QUICK QUIZ: When were the Rosenbergs executed as communist spies? See page 295.

BRITISH DEPENDENCIES *(continued)*

1959. In 1962 they became a separate colony.

CHANNEL ISLANDS

Area: 75 square miles (194 sq. km.).
Population: 130,621.
Capitals: St. Helier, Jersey, 26,351; St. Peter Port, Guernsey, 16,800.

Lying in the English Channel near the French coast, the main Channel Islands are Jersey, Guernsey, Alderney, and Sark.

The islands were acquired by the Duke of Normandy in the 900s and became part of Britain after the Norman Conquest (1066). In World War II they were occupied by Germany.

The islands ship large quantities of vegetables, fruits, and flowers to the English market. Jersey and Guernsey cattle are raised.

FALKLAND ISLANDS

Area: 4,700 square miles (12,173 sq. km.).
Population: 1,993.
Capital: Stanley, 1,098.

Situated in the South Atlantic some 480 miles northeast of Cape Horn, the Falklands crown colony has two principal islands, East Falkland and West Falkland. They are mostly hilly moorlands with a cool, rainy, and windy climate. The people are Christians of British stock.

An English navigator, John Davis, sighted the islands in 1592, but the first settlement was made by the French in 1764 on East Falkland. The British settled West Falkland in 1765, but both colonies were later abandoned. In 1820 Argentina colonized East Falkland. The British recaptured it in 1832–33. South Georgia, a whaling settlement 800 miles to the east, and the South Sandwich Islands are part of the colony. The main industry is sheep farming.

Argentina, which calls the islands the *Malvinas,* invaded and captured the colony on April 2, 1982. After a short but bloody war, Britain recaptured the islands, forcing Argentine troops to surrender on June 14.

Britain began construction in 1983 of a $300 million airport to accommodate jet airliners.

GIBRALTAR

Area: 2.3 square miles (6 sq. km.).
Population: 26,479.
Capital: Gibraltar.

The Rock of Gibraltar, towering 1,400 feet high, is a peninsula jutting into the Mediterranean from Spain's southwest coast.

The Moors settled Gibraltar in 711, naming it Jebel-al-Tarik (Mount of Tarik). The Spanish took it in 1309, lost it again to the Moors, and regained it in 1462. The English won possession in 1704 and have maintained it since, although besieged many times by the Spanish and French. Spain renewed its claim after World War II.

In a referendum on Sept. 10, 1967, the people of Gibraltar voted overwhelmingly to keep their special ties with Britain.

In 1969 the border was sealed by the Spanish government. Britain and Spain reached agreement on April 10, 1980, to reopen the border. Later, Spain refused to honor the agreement.

However, on Dec. 15, 1982, Spain ended the 13-year blockade.

HONG KONG

Area: 403 square miles (1,045 sq. km.).
Population: 5,353,150.
Chief Cities: Victoria, capital, 633,138; New Kowloon, 1,478,581; Kowloon, 716,272.

Hong Kong lies on the China coast, 91 miles southeast of Canton. It includes Hong Kong Island (29 square miles), the mainland peninsula of Kowloon (3.5 square miles), the New Territories (369.5 square miles) between Kowloon and China, and over 230 offshore islets. The climate is subtropical.

Hong Kong harbor is one of the world's busiest. Victoria, the administrative capital, rises sharply from the waterfront and extends halfway up Victoria Peak. Kowloon and New Kowloon are crowded commercial and industrial centers.

More than 98% of the people are of Chinese descent. English and Chinese are both official languages.

China ceded Hong Kong Island to Britain in 1842 following British occupation during the Opium War. Kowloon became part of the colony in 1860. China leased the New Territories to Britain in 1898 for 99 years.

The colony's location, its deep, sheltered harbor, abundant labor supply, and free-port economy have made it an important center of trade, commerce, and industry. The largest industry is textile manufacturing. Much food, raw material, and water come from communist China. The colony is also an international banking center.

In the 1970s and 1980s Hong Kong had one of the most rapidly growing economies in the world.

On a visit to China in September 1982, British Prime Minister Margaret Thatcher opened negotiations on the future of Hong Kong after Britain's lease on the New Territories expires in 1997. China's communist leaders declared they intend to take sovereignty of the entire colony.

Negotiations on Hong Kong's future continued in 1983 between Chinese and British diplomats.

ISLE OF MAN

Area: 221 square miles (572 sq. km.).
Population: 68,846.
Capital: Douglas, 19,897.

The Isle of Man lies in the north Irish Sea midway between Britain and Northern Ireland.

Inhabited since Neolithic times, Man was ruled by the Vikings until about 800, by the Norwegians until 1266, and by the Scots until the 1300s, when it passed to the earls of Salisbury and Derby. It came under the direct administration of the British crown in 1765.

Tourism, dairying, fishing, quarrying, and agriculture support the economy.

MONTSERRAT

Area: 38 square miles (98 sq. km.).
Population: 12,891.
Capital: Plymouth, 1,267.

Montserrat was discovered in the Caribbean by Christopher Columbus in 1493 and named after a monastery in Spain. First settlers were English and Irish colonists from the nearby island of St. Kitts in 1632. The French disputed British control of the island, holding it briefly in 1782–83.

Montserrat became self-governing in 1960.

Tourism, construction, and agriculture are the main industries. Cotton is the main export.

PITCAIRN ISLANDS

Area: 18.5 square miles (48 sq. km.).
Population: 48.
Capital: Adamstown.

Pitcairn is a volcanic, mountainous Pacific island about 1,200 miles southeast of Tahiti. Its area is 1.75 sq. mi., but the colony also includes three uninhabited islands: Henderson (12 sq. mi.), Ducie (2.5 sq. mi.), and Oeno (2 sq. mi.).

Pitcairn was discovered by the British in 1767 and settled in 1790 by mutineers off H.M.S. *Bounty* and some Tahitian women.

SAINT HELENA

Area: 47 square miles (122 sq. km.).
Population: 4,925.
Capital: Jamestown, 1,475.

A mountainous island in the South Atlantic Ocean about 1,200 miles west of Africa, St. Helena was discovered by the Portuguese in 1502 and claimed by the Dutch in 1633. The British East India Company took the island in 1659. The Dutch unsuccessfully attempted to regain it in 1673. Napoleon I was exiled on the island from 1815 to 1821. In 1834 it became a crown colony.

Ascension Island (34 sq. mi. [88 sq. km.]; population: 1,146), about 700 miles northwest of St. Helena, was annexed in 1922.

Tristano da Cunha (40 sq. mi. [104 sq. km.]; population: 292) and the uninhabited islands of Gough, Nightingale, and Inaccessible became dependencies of St. Helena in 1938. The four islands lie about 1,500 miles southwest of St. Helena. Tristan da Cunha was evacuated after a volcanic eruption in 1961, but its people returned in 1963.

TURKS AND CAICOS ISLANDS

Area: 166 square miles (430 sq. km.).
Population: 8,311.
Capital: Cockburn Town, Grand Turk, 2,287.

The Turks and Caicos lie east of Cuba. The only regularly inhabited of the eight Turk Islands are Grand Turk and Salt Cay. South and North Caicos are the most important of the Caicos group. The population is mostly black.

Though discovered by Juan Ponce de León in 1512, the islands were uninhabited until Bermudians arrived to gather salt in 1678. Administered as part of Jamaica until 1962, the islands are administered by a crown-appointed governor and a partly elected state council. Salt, crayfish, and sisal are exported. Britain promised independence whenever the islanders want it.

To encourage tourism, the government completed construction of a new $7 million airport in 1983.

BRUNEI

Official Name: Brunei Darus Salam.
Area: 2,226 square miles (5,765 sq. km.).
Population: 209,567.
Capital: Bandar Seri Begawan, 36,987.
Government: Monarchy.
Head of Government: Sultan Sir Hassanal Bolkiah (since 1968).
Legislative Council: 21 members (10 elected).
Flag: White and black diagonal stripes on yellow field; state arms in center.
Languages: Malay (official), English.
Main Ethnic Groups: Malay (65%), Chinese (25%).
Official Religion: Islam.
Leading Industries: Petroleum mining; agriculture (rubber, rice, coconuts, fruits, vegetables, livestock); fishing; forestry.
Foreign Trade: *Major exports*—petroleum, rubber, natural gas; *major imports*—machinery, transportation equipment, food, beverages, tobacco, chemicals, drugs.
Places of Interest: Kampong Ayer, water village, where about 20,000 people live in houses built on stilts over the Brunei River; markets and government buildings in Bandar Seri Begawan.

BRUNEI TODAY

Somewhat larger than Delaware, Brunei lies on the northwest South China Sea coast of the island of Borneo. The country is made up of two heavily forested parks that are bordered by and separated from each other by Malaysia's state of Sarawak.

Brunei is one of the richest small countries of the world, receiving most of its income from the export of oil. Although many of the people still live in waterside houses built on stilts, most have a color TV set in the living room.

Ruled as an absolute monarchy by a sultan, the government spends a high percentage of its income on armaments to equip its small army with such modern weapons as guided missiles and helicopters.

About half the Bruneians can read and write. Many live as subsistence farmers or fishermen. Chinese, who make up about a fourth of the population, are largely merchants and traders.

The government provides free health care, inexpensive housing, and interest-free loans for cars and TV sets. And there is no income tax.

HISTORY

Once a powerful state controlling Borneo and other islands, the sultan of Brunei lost all but the present territory in the mid-1800s.

Brunei became a protectorate of Britain by a treaty in 1888 under which Britain took control of the nation's defense and foreign affairs.

The discovery of petroleum deposits in 1929 laid the basis for the nation's later prosperity.

Japan occupied Brunei during World War II.

When the nation of Malaysia was formed in 1963 by consolidating British colonies in the region, Brunei refused to join.

Sir Omar Ali Saifuddin, who had been sultan since 1950, abdicated in 1967. His son, Hassanal Bolkiah, was crowned as Brunei's 29th sultan on Aug. 1, 1968.

As Britain sought to divest itself of its worldwide empire, the sultan reluctantly signed an agreement on Jan. 7, 1979, to accept full independence in five years.

Although Brunei became independent on Jan. 1, 1984, it retained the appearance of a British colony, with Britons holding most important civil service posts in the government.

QUICK QUIZ: What was Albert Billroth's contribution to medicine? See page 452.

BULGARIA

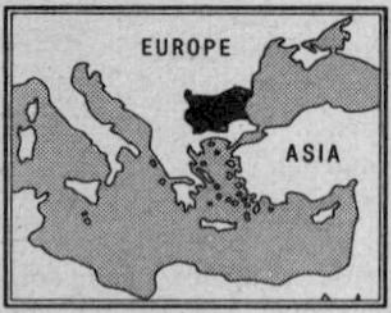

Official Name: People's Republic of Bulgaria.
Area: 42,823 square miles (110,912 sq. km.).
Population: 8,956,900.
Chief Cities: Sofia, capital, 1,014,059; Plovdiv, 328,031; Varna, 275,375; Ruse, 167,667; Bourgas, 162,185.
Government: Communist state.
Head of Government: First Secretary of the Communist Party, Todor Zhivkov (since 1954).
Prime Minister: Grisha Filipov (since 1981).
Legislature: *National Assembly,* 400 members.
U.S. Ambassador to Bulgaria: Jack Richard Perry.
Bulgarian Ambassador to U.S.: Stoyan I. Zhulev.
Flag: Stripes of white, green, and red, with national coat of arms in top left-hand corner.
Main Language: Bulgarian.
Ethnic Groups: Bulgarian (85%), Turk (9%).
Principal Religion: Eastern Orthodox.
Leading Industries: Manufacturing (machinery, food and tobacco processing, metals, leather goods, lumber, textiles, chemicals, fertilizers); agriculture (livestock, wheat, grapes, roses, tobacco, barley, tomatoes, mushrooms, sugar beets).
Foreign Trade: *Major exports*—food, tobacco, metals, textiles, machinery, rose oil, wine, leather; *major imports*—grain, clothing, oil, gas, steel, wood.
Places of Interest: Shipka Pass; Kazanluk, in Valley of Roses; Varna Black Sea resort; Old Plovdiv; Rila Monastery; Veliko Turnovo. *In Sofia:* Alexander Nevsky Memorial Church; Boyana Church; Georgi Dimitrov mausoleum; Park of Liberty; museums.

BULGARIA TODAY

Bulgaria is a communist nation on the Black Sea northeast of Greece. A mountainous country about the size of Tennessee, Bulgaria has changed from an agricultural to an industrial nation in the decades since World War II. The major industries are food processing and the production of chemicals and machinery.

However, about a third of the Bulgarians still depend on farming for their living. A leading tobacco-grower, Bulgaria makes many of the cigarettes smoked in the Soviet Union.

Western police officials have accused the Bulgarian government of being deeply involved in the smuggling of drugs, arms, and tobacco to western Europe, using the revenues to finance terrorist activities.

The Balkan Mountains cross Bulgaria from east to west between the Danubian tableland in the north and the Thracian Plain in the south. The Danube flows along Bulgaria's northern boundary, and the Maritsa River drains the Thracian Plain region.

EARLY HISTORY

Bulgaria, part of ancient Thrace and Moesia, was settled by Slavic tribes in the 500s A.D. The Bulgars, a Turkic-speaking people, crossed the Danube, conquered the Slavs, and, led by Khan Asparukh, founded the first Bulgarian empire in 681.

Under the leadership of Krum (802?–814), the Bulgars expanded and consolidated their empire. Krum's forces captured Sofia and killed the Byzantine emperor Nicephorus I. Under Boris I the Bulgars adopted Christianity (865). The first Bulgarian empire fell in 1018, when it was annexed by the Byzantine empire. The second empire, founded in 1186, lasted until the Ottoman Turks subdued the Bulgars in 1396.

TURKISH RULE

For nearly 500 years the Turks held Bulgaria. A revolt in 1876 was savagely put down by the Turks in the "Bulgarian Massacres." Russia intervened, defeated the Turks, and created an expanded, pro-Russian Bulgaria.

Other European powers, particularly Britain and Austria-Hungary, feared Russian penetration into the Balkans. At their insistence Russia was forced to accept a treaty revision at the Congress of Berlin (1878). Northern Bulgaria was made a principality under Ottoman control. Alexander of Battenberg was its first prince.

Eastern Rumelia, south of the Balkan Mountains, was annexed by Bulgaria in 1885. His successor, Prince Ferdinand of Saxe-Coburg-Gotha, came to power in 1887.

INDEPENDENT KINGDOM

In 1908 Ferdinand proclaimed full independence and assumed the title of czar.

Bulgaria sided with Germany in World War I. In 1918 Ferdinand abdicated in favor of his son Boris III. Bulgaria lost much territory as the result of the peace treaty.

Bulgaria backed the Axis powers in World War II. Boris died in 1943. His 6-year-old son was named King Simeon II.

COMMUNIST RULE

Soviet troops seized the country in 1944. A Soviet-supervised election overthrew the monarchy, and Simeon II went into exile. A communist state was organized in 1945 under the leadership of Prime Minister Georgi Dimitrov.

After Dimitrov's death in 1949, his brother-in-law Vulko Chervenkov became dictator. In 1954 he gave up his position as head of the Communist Party to Todor Zhivkov.

To encourage foreign investment the government in 1980 began permitting foreign companies to own up to 90% of joint ventures.

The nation celebrated its 1300th anniversary in 1981 with a series of cultural events.

In an effort to reduce the high cost of imported fuel, the government pressed ahead in the 1980s to build more nuclear power plants.

The government established in 1982 what it called the New Economic Mechanism (NEM) in which each enterprise must not pay more in wages and salaries than its revenues after expenses.

A diplomatic crisis developed between Bulgaria and Italy in 1982 after Italian police arrested a Bulgarian official suspected of directing the attempt to assassinate Pope John Paul II in 1981.

Bulgaria protested the arrest in New York on Sept. 23, 1983, of Bulgarian official Penyu Kostadinov on charges of nuclear espionage.

BURMA

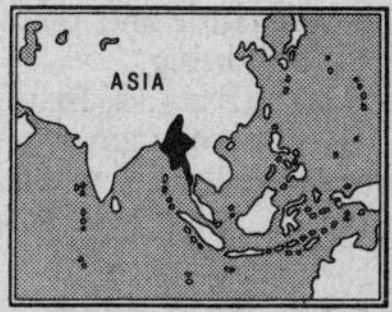

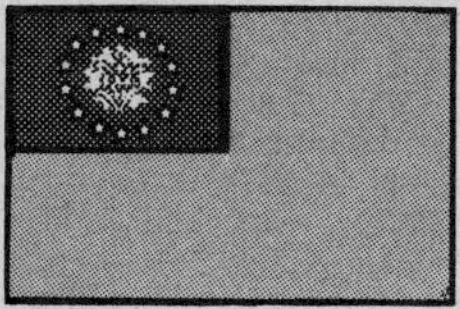

Official Name: Socialist Republic of the Union of Burma.
Area: 261,218 square miles (676,552 sq. km.).
Population: 37,536,400.
Chief Cities: Rangoon, capital, 2,276,000; Mandalay, 458,000; Karbe, 253,600; Moulmein, 188,000.
Government: One-party republic.
Head of Government: Gen. U Ne Win, Chairman of Burmese Socialist Program Party (since 1962).
President: U San Yu (since 1981).
Prime Minister: U Maung Maung Kha (since 1977).
Legislature: *National Assembly,* 475 members.
U.S. Ambassador to Burma: Daniel A. O'Donohue.
Burmese Ambassador to U.S.: U Kyee Myint.
Flag: Red field with blue rectangle in upper hoist corner containing gear wheel and rice encircled by 14 white stars representing Burma's states.
Languages: Burmese (official), English.
Main Ethnic Groups: Burman (65%), Shan (11%), Karen (7%), Kachin (6%), Chin (2%).
Religion: Buddhism (85%).
Leading Industries: Agriculture (rice, tobacco, sugarcane, rubber, jute, peanuts); forestry and lumber; mining (petroleum, natural gas, lead, zinc, tungsten, nickel); manufacturing (food processing, textiles, construction materials).
Foreign Trade: *Major exports*—rice, teak, jute, rubber; *major imports*—textile yarn and fabrics, nonelectric machinery, vehicles, chemicals.
Places of Interest: Inle Lake; Sagaing Hills. *In Rangoon:* Shwedagon and Sule pagodas; national museum. *In Pegu:* Shwemaudaw Pagoda and 181-foot-long Shwethalyaung (Reclining Buddha). *In Pagan:* Over 2,500 monuments in ancient royal capital.

BURMA TODAY

About the size of Texas, Burma is a Southeast Asian nation that for nearly two decades rejected most contact with the outside world. An isolationist socialist-military regime allowed the country's once prosperous economy to stagnate.

Nearly all of its people are poor with an average income of less than $180 per year. Only about 7 in 10 can read and write.

Burma was relatively unaffected by the soaring oil prices of the 1970s because it is nearly self-sufficient in petroleum. However, inflation was fueled by a thriving black market in consumer goods smuggled in from Thailand to avoid the government's ban on luxury imports.

The country has fertile plains and delta in the south and central area. Uplands form a protective arc of hills across the northern frontiers with Bangladesh, India, China, Laos, and Thailand.

BRITISH RULE

Conflict between the British and the Burmese for influence over states bordering Burma brought about an Anglo-Burmese war (1824–26), as a result of which the British gained control of part of lower Burma. A second Anglo-Burmese war in 1852 and a third in 1885 ended Burma's independence. Grafted onto India as a province, Burma was governed from New Delhi.

Under British rule Burma became the world's largest exporter of rice—"the rice bowl of Asia."

In 1937 Burma was separated from India.

In 1942 the Japanese, aided by Burmese nationalists, expelled the British from most of Burma. British rule was restored in 1946.

INDEPENDENCE

The independent Union of Burma was formed on Jan. 4, 1948. U Nu was named premier. He led the country for most of its first 10 years.

In the late 1950s U Nu's party split into rival groups. Fearing the outbreak of civil war, he asked the head of the armed forces, Gen. U Ne Win, to take charge of the government temporarily in 1958. When U Nu's party won the parliamentary election in 1960, Ne Win stepped aside and U Nu again became premier.

When civil war threatened in 1962, Ne Win again took over the government and established a socialist military dictatorship. U Nu was imprisoned, and then exiled from 1966 to 1980.

Under Ne Win the government took over ownership of most businesses and industries. Foreign private investment and aid were rejected.

A new constitution was adopted on Jan. 4, 1974, creating a one-party state under Ne Win's Burmese Socialist Program Party (BSPP).

Sporadic fighting has gone on along Burma's borders for more than three decades. In northeast Burma communist rebels hold an estimated 7,000 square miles along the Chinese border. Altogether some 20 different ethnic groups carry on warfare against the government.

The government on Sept. 1, 1976, ended martial law that had been imposed in 1974. About 1,600 persons were ordered released from prison, and sentences were reduced for 3,300 others.

Prime Minister U Sein Win resigned on March 29, 1977, after he and other cabinet members were criticized for failure to follow the nation's economic plan.

U Sein Win was replaced as prime minister by 57-year-old U Maung Maung Kha.

A bumper rice crop in 1978–79 stimulated a spurt in growth in Burma's economy, permitting the export of about 700,000 tons of rice.

Ne Win's regime became disenchanted with communist domination of the third-world movement and announced its official withdrawal in 1979. Subsequently a more friendly relationship developed with Western nations. U.S. economic aid to Burma resumed in 1980.

A 475-member parliament was chosen in a one-party election on Oct. 4, 1981.

Citing illness, the 70-year-old Ne Win resigned as president and was succeeded on Nov. 9, 1981, by U San Yu, 63, a retired general. However, Ne Win remained in charge of the government as chairman of the BSPP party.

Burma broke relations on Nov. 4, 1983, with North Korea, which it accused of a terrorist bombing on Oct. 9 at Rangoon that killed four visiting South Korean officials and 15 other persons.

QUICK QUIZ: What was the name of the treaty that ended the French and Indian War? See page 304.

BURUNDI

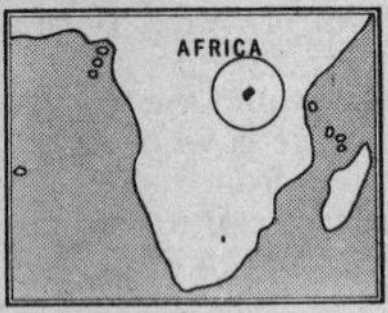

Official Name: Republic of Burundi.
Area: 10,747 square miles (27,834 sq. km.).
Population: 4,481,770.
Capital: Bujumbura, 78,810.
Government: One-party dictatorship.
President: Jean-Baptiste Bagaza (since 1976).
U.S. Ambassador to Burundi: James R. Bullington.
Burundi Ambassador to U.S.: Simon Sabimbona.
Flag: White diagonal cross, with red quarters on top and bottom and green quarters to left and right; centered white circle bears three red stars edged in green.
Official Languages: Kirundi, French.
Ethnic Groups: Hutu (85%), Tutsi (14%), Twa (1%).
Religions: Roman Catholicism (50%), animism (40%), Protestantism (10%).
Leading Industries: Agriculture (coffee, cotton, tea, peanuts, cattle); food processing; fishing; mining.
Foreign Trade: *Major exports*—coffee, cotton, tea, hides; *major imports*—clothing, textiles, motor vehicles, flour, petroleum products.
Places of Interest: Lake Tanganyika; Ruvuvu River, source of Nile; Bujumbura.

BURUNDI TODAY

About the size of Maryland in area and population, Burundi is one of the poorest countries of Africa. It has few natural resources. Even its soil is mostly eroded and unfertile. Coffee accounts for about 90% of Burundi's exports.

Most people lead primitive tribal lives, raising beans, corn, and yams, or fishing in Lake Tanganyika. Few can read or write.

The country has few villages or towns. Most Burundians live with members of their own extended families in rural compounds called *rugos.*

A land of grassy plains, forests, and rocky hills, Burundi has a hot equatorial climate in its lowlands. But its upland regions have cool nights with an occasional frost. The White Nile River has its southernmost source in Burundi.

Landlocked Burundi has no railroads and less than 200 miles of paved roads. Rwanda lies to the north, Tanzania to the east and south, and Zaire to the west. Burundi's border with Zaire runs down the middle of Lake Tanganyika.

HISTORY

Tall Watutsi (Tutsi) warriors dominated the shorter Bahutu (Hutu) for centuries under an absolute monarch call the *mwami.*

Burundi was absorbed by German East Africa in 1898. Then it was mandated to Belgium after World War I as part of Ruanda-Urundi.

On July 1, 1962, Urundi was granted independence as a monarchy, renamed Burundi.

Mwami (king) Mwambutsa IV was deposed on July 8, 1966, by his son, who became Ntare V.

Prime Minister Michel Micombero overthrew Ntare V on Nov. 28, 1966, and proclaimed Burundi a republic. Micombero, a Tutsi, named himself president. He ruled as dictator by decree.

The Hutu majority revolted in April 1972 and May 1973. An estimated 150,000 Hutu and tens of thousands of Tutsi died in the fighting.

The Minority Rights Group (MRG), a British organization, accused Micombero's government in 1976 of having systematically killed all Hutus who had more than a high school education.

Lt. Col. Jean-Baptiste Bagaza led a military coup on Nov. 1, 1976, that overthrew Micombero. A Belgian-educated political scientist, Bagaza said he would try to end tribal strife.

President Bagaza established "civilian government" in 1980, making the Central Committee of Burundi's sole political party the main legislative body to approve his decrees and dissolving his military junta of army officers.

CAMBODIA

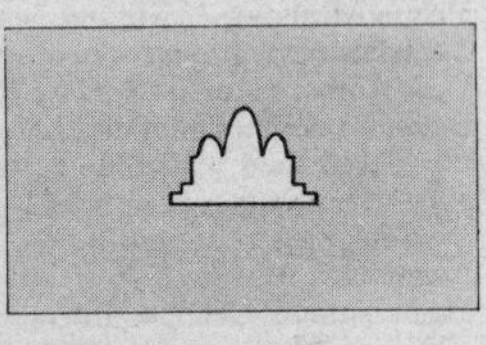

Official Name: Democratic Kampuchea.
Area: 69,898 square miles (181,035 sq. km.).
Population: 6,051,050.
Capital: Phnom Penh, 150,000.
Government: One-party communist state, supported by Vietnamese troops.
President: Heng Samrin (since 1979).
Prime Minister: Chan Sy (since 1982).
Flag: Red field with Angkor Wat pagoda in yellow.
Official Language: Khmer.
Main Ethnic Groups: Khmer (85%), Chinese (6%).
Religion: Buddhism (85%).
Leading Industries: Agriculture (rubber, rice, corn); fishing; forest products.
Foreign Trade: *major export*—rubber; *major imports*—food, fuel, machinery.
Places of Interest: Angkor Wat ruins and other ornamental monuments, temples, and palaces covering over 60 square miles, located at Siemreap. *In Phnom Penh:* national museum; royal palace; Silver Pagoda; floating villages on Mekong River.

CAMBODIA TODAY

A devastated country of Southeast Asia, Cambodia was ruined in the 1970s–1980s by wars and by the repressive measures of its communist leaders. Millions of Cambodians—half the population—died or fled to neighboring countries.

The communist government is a puppet of Vietnam, kept in power with an occupation army of about 180,000 Vietnamese troops. Opponents of the regime have waged guerrilla warfare since 1979, supported by China and other nations.

Most Cambodians are farmers. Before the disasters of the 1970s–1980s, the country exported large amounts of rice, corn, and rubber.

Mountains along the border with Thailand rise sharply from the Gulf of Thailand coast, drop to a plains region, and ascend again in the north. Much of the best land for rice farming lies in the central basin along the Mekong River and around Tonle Sap (Great Lake).

About the size of Oklahoma, Cambodia lies

south of Thailand. Laos is to the northeast. Vietnam lies to the east and south.

EARLY HISTORY

About A.D. 100 the Kingdom of Funan was established in southern Cambodia. Three centuries later an Indian Brahman took control of Funan. Indian influences shaped the country's customs, alphabet, and legal code.

The Khmer Empire was established in northern Cambodia in 802. It conquered Funan and most of Southeast Asia. A vast complex of shrines and temples was built at its capital, Angkor.

After disintegration of the Khmer Empire in the 1400s, Cambodia was dominated alternately by the Thais and the Vietnamese. In the 1700s Thailand annexed three of Cambodia's provinces.

France established a protectorate over Cambodia in 1863. It later became part of French Indochina.

Anti-French sentiment spread during World War II, when Vichy France bowed to Japan's demands for Cambodian bases. King Norodom Sihanouk, who had become monarch in 1941 at the age of 18, cooperated with Japan.

France granted Cambodia independence under King Sihanouk within the French Union on Nov. 9, 1953. Sihanouk abdicated in favor of his parents in 1955. He then became premier. Cambodia left the French Union in 1955, declaring its complete independence. In 1960 Prince Sihanouk was installed as chief of state.

Beginning in 1963, Sihanouk permitted North Vietnamese and Vietcong troops to build up military bases along Cambodia's border. The communists armed the Khmer Rouge, Cambodia's Communist Party, and staged border raids into South Vietnam. The U.S. Air Force at President Nixon's direction secretly began bombing communist forces in Cambodia in 1969.

In March 1970 Cambodian Premier Lon Nol overthrew Sihanouk, who fled to communist China. Relations with Hanoi were severed in May. On April 30 the U.S. and South Vietnam sent 20,000 troops into Cambodia to destroy communist bases. American troops were withdrawn on June 29, but South Vietnamese forces remained and the U.S. continued bombing communist forces in Cambodia.

On Oct. 9, 1970, Lon Nol proclaimed the nation a republic named the *Khmer Republic.* In elections on June 4, 1972, Lon Nol became the nation's first elected president.

President Nixon announced on March 27, 1973, that U.S. planes would continue to bomb communist troops in Cambodia until the communists agreed to a cease-fire. But the U.S. Congress, angered because Nixon had not consulted it, passed legislation that ended all U.S. military action in Indochina on Aug. 15, 1973.

The communists closed Phnom Penh's major supply route, the Mekong River, in February 1975. The U.S. then initiated an airlift to supply government forces fighting around the capital. Communist troops pressed their offensive on Phnom Penh, and on April 1 President Lon Nol fled from Cambodia, leaving the government in the hands of Premier Long Boret. On April 12 the U.S. ambassador and his staff flew out of Phnom Penh, and the U.S. airlift ended.

COMMUNIST AND VIETNAMESE RULE

Refusing attempts by Premier Long Boret to negotiate a cease-fire, Khmer Rouge troops captured Phnom Penh on April 16, 1975, ending the war. Communist firing squads executed Long Boret and other officials and generals of the former government.

Hundreds of thousands died when communists forced city dwellers to march into the countryside and work as farm laborers.

The Khmer Rouge announced on April 25, 1975, that Prince Norodom Sihanouk would be chief of state for life. But Sihanouk resigned on April 2, 1976, and went into seclusion. Khieu Samphan then took the title of president, but the government was controlled by Pol Pot as secretary-general of the Cambodian Communist Party.

The communists changed the country's official name to *Democratic Kampuchea.* However, the government was the reverse of "democratic." Thousands of opponents were tortured and executed, some for nothing more than criticizing the quantity or quality of their food rations. Few foreigners were allowed to remain in the country.

In April 1978 President Carter denounced Cambodia as "the worst violator of human rights in the world today." Officials estimated that about 2.5 million Cambodians had been killed by the Pol Pot government.

Vietnam launched a full-scale invasion of Cambodia on Dec. 25, 1978, and two weeks later captured Phnom Penh on Jan. 7, 1979.

Pol Pot and members of his government fled to the jungles, carrying on guerrilla warfare.

Soviet-supported Vietnam set up a new government with Heng Samrin as president.

Prince Sihanouk escaped from Cambodia in January 1979, appearing at a special meeting of the UN Security Council, where he denounced the Vietnamese invasion. Later Sihanouk quit his role as a representative of the Pol Pot government, condemning it for the atrocities committed against Cambodians.

International agencies mounted a huge relief effort in 1979–80 to prevent Cambodians from starving because continued fighting prevented the growing of rice. The U.S. provided over $150 million in food and aid for relief.

About 500,000 Cambodian refugees fled to Thailand in 1978–80.

Khieu Samphan, prime minister of the Pol Pot government, called Western news correspondents to his jungle headquarters in August 1980 to announce that the Khmer Rouge had decided to reject communism as a philosophy.

In an agreement signed in Kuala Lumpur, Malaysia, on June 22, 1982, Prince Sihanouk became president of a Cambodian government-in-exile, bringing together three major groups opposing the Vietnamese-backed regime of Heng Samrin. Most posts in the Sihanouk government went to leaders of the former Pol Pot regime. The U.S., China, and anticommunist nations of Asia supported the Sihanouk government, while the Soviet Union backed the Vietnam puppet regime.

QUICK QUIZ: When was the King James Bible first published in England? See page 289.

CAMEROON

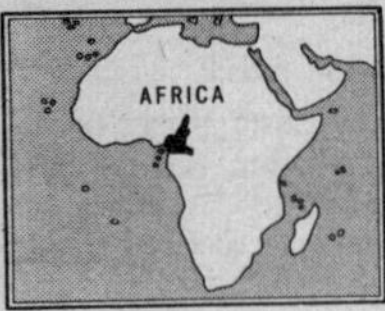

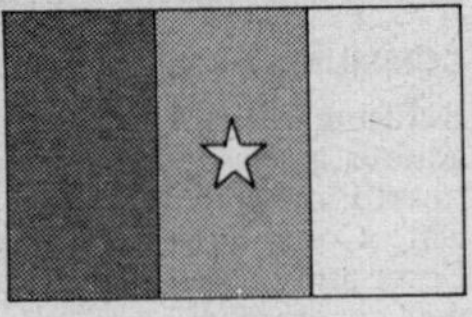

Official Name: United Republic of Cameroon.
Area: 183,569 square miles (475,442 sq. km.).
Population: 9,447,270.
Chief Cities: Yaoundé, capital, 250,000; Douala, 350,000; Nkongsamba, 100,000.
Government: One-party republic.
President: Paul Biya (since 1982).
Prime Minister: Bello Bouba Maigari (since 1982).
National Assembly: 120 members.
U.S. Ambassador to Cameroon: Myles Frechette.
Cameroonian Ambassador to U.S.: Paul Pondi.
Flag: Tricolor of green, red, and yellow bars, with yellow star centered on red bar.
Official Languages: French and English.
Main Ethnic Group: Over 200 Bantu tribes.
Religions: Animism (40%), Islam (25%), Roman Catholicism (20%).
Leading Industries: Mining (petroleum); agriculture (cocoa, coffee, cotton, bananas, cattle, rice, sugarcane, palm oil); forestry; manufacturing (food processing, aluminum, textiles, jute bags, soap).
Foreign Trade: *Major exports*—petroleum, cocoa, coffee, cotton, wood, prawns, aluminum; *major imports*—machinery, textiles, transport equipment, consumer goods, alumina, chemicals.
Places of Interest: Bamiléké Plateau; Waza Forest and wildlife preserve; Bamoun country; beaches.

CAMEROON TODAY

Cameroon is a prosperous West African oil-exporting country that is making progress in its efforts to leap from primitive to modern times.

Somewhat larger than California, Cameroon has not experienced the political unrest that has set back many of its neighbors.

While establishing extensive preserves to protect its wildlife, Cameroon has moved ahead to improve agricultural production.

About four-fifths of the Cameroonians live in the French-speaking eastern part of the country. Altogether there are over 200 tribes that speak 24 different African languages.

The people are poor, and the majority still follow a primitive tribal culture. But Cameroon boasts that a higher proportion of its children are in school or have graduated from school than in any other African nation.

By encouraging foreign investment, Cameroon has been able to build hydroelectric power plants and railroads to develop its large deposits of bauxite, thus becoming the largest aluminum-producing nation in Africa. Cameroon also is one of the world's important producers of cocoa.

Southern Cameroon rises eastward from the coastal plains to a densely wooded plateau about 1,000 feet high. In the central interior region is the Adamaoua Plateau, 2,500 to 4,500 feet above sea level. The principal rivers are the Benoué and the Sanaga.

Mount Cameroon, the highest point in the country, rises to 13,350 feet on the Atlantic coastline northeast of Douala.

Nigeria lies to the north. Chad and Central Africa are to the east. Congo, Gabon, and Equatorial Guinea are to the south.

EARLY HISTORY

The Portuguese visited the area in the 1400s but made no permanent settlements. From the 1500s to the 1800s the Cameroon coast was a regular source of supply for the slave trade of Spain, Britain, and the Netherlands.

Germany established a protectorate in 1884. British and French armies invaded the German protectorate in 1914. After World War I the western part of Cameroon was turned over to Britain. The remainder, about four-fifths of the total territory, was ceded to France.

During World War II French Cameroon was seized by the Free French, who made it a training base for troops.

The French and British Cameroons became United Nations trusteeships in 1946. The Cameroonians were granted limited self-government by the administering European powers.

INDEPENDENCE

The French Cameroon assembly voted for full independence in 1957. France and the UN concurred, and the Republic of Cameroon became independent on Jan. 1, 1960.

Plebiscites were held in British Cameroons in 1961. The northern region chose to unite with Nigeria. The southern region elected to join with Cameroon. The northern region of British Cameroons became part of Nigeria on June 1, 1961.

The southern region, newly named West Cameroon, joined East Cameroon, formerly French Cameroon, on Oct. 1, 1961, forming the new Federal Republic of Cameroon. West Cameroon and East Cameroon each had its own parliament.

Ahmadou Ahidjo was chosen as first president of the federal republic in 1961. He was re-elected without opposition to new 5-year terms in 1965, 1970, 1975, and 1980. All political parties in the country were consolidated into one party, the National Cameroonian Union (UNC), in 1966.

After Cameroon had functioned for 11 years as a federal government, President Ahidjo proposed that the separate state governments be abolished. In a referendum on May 20, 1972, the people approved Ahidjo's proposal, changing from a federal to a unitary state.

The Trans-Cameroon Railway was completed in 1974, linking Douala and Ngaoundere.

Offshore oil wells began production in 1977, and by 1981 were pumping about 100,000 barrels a day. An oil refinery built in 1975–81 made the nation self-sufficient in petroleum products. Huge natural-gas reserves held promise of increased prosperity in the future. The government receives 60% of the revenues from oil and gas produced by foreign companies.

Paul Biya, 49, who had been prime minister, was sworn in as president on Nov. 6, 1982, following the resignation because of illness of President Ahidjo.

The nation's fifth 5-year development plan for 1981–86 calls for the expenditure of $7.6 billion to improve agriculture and industry while further utilizing Cameroon's natural resources.

CANADA

Official Name: Canada.
Area: 3,849,670 square miles (9,970,610 sq. km.).
Population: 24,789,600.
Chief Cities: Ottawa, capital, 295,163; Montreal, 980,354; Toronto, 599,217; Calgary, 592,743; Winnipeg, 564,473; North York, 559,521; Edmonton, 532,246; Scarborough, 443,353.
Largest Metropolitan Areas: Toronto, 2,998,947; Montreal, 2,828,349; Vancouver, 1,268,183; Ottawa, 717,978; Edmonton, 657,057; Winnipeg, 584,842.
Government: Federal parliamentary state.
Prime Minister: Pierre Trudeau (since 1980).
Chief of State: Queen Elizabeth II, represented by Governor-General Edward Schreyer (since 1979).
Parliament: *Senate,* 102 members (appointed); *House of Commons,* 282 members (elected to 5-year terms).
U.S. Ambassador to Canada: Kenneth Curtis.
Canadian Ambassador to U.S.: Allan E. Gotlieb.
Flag: Red maple leaf on white field, with red bars at each side.
Official Languages: English and French.
Ethnic Backgrounds: British (44%); French (30%); native Indian and Eskimo (1%); other (25%).
Main Religions: Roman Catholicism (46%), United Church of Canada (18%), Anglicanism (12%).
Leading Industries: Manufacturing (steel, paper, electricity, aluminum, food processing, vehicles); mining (petroleum, copper, zinc, iron, lead, natural gas, asbestos, nickel, salt); agriculture (cattle, hogs, poultry, dairy products, wheat, barley, potatoes, corn, rapeseed, tobacco); forestry; fishing; tourism.
Foreign Trade: *Major exports*—manufactured goods, newsprint, wood, wood pulp, wheat, natural gas; *major imports*—motor vehicles and parts, chemical products, tools, machinery, aircraft, petroleum, communications equipment.
Places of Interest: Banff National Park, Alta.; Barkerville (gold-rush town), B.C.; Bell Homestead, Brantford, Ont.; Calgary Stampede, Alta.; Citadel, Quebec City, Que.; CN Tower, Toronto, Ont.; Fort Macleod Mounted Police Museum, Alta.; Fortress of Louisbourg, N.S.; Gaspé Peninsula, Que.; Man and His World exhibition, Montreal, Que.; L'Anse aux Meadows (Viking site), Nfld.; Niagara Falls, Ont.; parliament buildings, Ottawa, Ont.; parks, Vancouver, B.C.; Royal Botanical Gardens, Hamilton, Ont.

CANADA TODAY

The second-largest nation in the world in land area, Canada is rich in natural resources. But Canada, like Australia, is underpopulated. Only 7% of the land is under cultivation, and only about 27% of its area is used for production of lumber or paper. The difficulties in transporting oil to the east coast from its large but dwindling western reserves explain Canada's unique position as both a leading oil exporter and an increasingly dependent oil importer.

One of Canada's major problems has been in maintaining its identity as a nation in relation to the more powerful United States, which lies to the south and is Canada's best foreign-trade customer. U.S. investments are important to Canada's economy. Investment proposals by foreign companies are subject to screening under the Foreign Investment Review Act (1973) to assure that they benefit Canada.

Another major problem is the division of the nation into two language groups: French-speaking, mainly in Quebec, and English-speaking, throughout most of the rest of Canada.

GEOGRAPHY

Canada is a federation of 10 provinces and two territories.

Most of the country's population is concentrated in the southeastern region in Ontario and Quebec near the Great Lakes and the St. Lawrence River.

To the east of this region is the Atlantic coastal area of New Brunswick, Newfoundland, Nova Scotia, and Prince Edward Island.

The Canadian Shield, a vast, U-shaped, rocky expanse, surrounds Hudson Bay. Thousands of lakes are scattered over this area. To the north are the Hudson Bay lowlands. Farther north is Canada's Arctic Archipelago, which includes Baffin, Victoria, and Ellesmere islands.

Canada's interior plains stretch to the west of the Shield.

The far west is mountainous. Major mountain systems are the Canadian Rockies, the Cascades, and the Coast Mountains. Vancouver Island and the Queen Charlotte Islands lie in the Pacific Ocean near the west coast.

Canada has more lakes than any other country in the world. Among the largest are Great Bear Lake, Great Slave Lake, and Lake Winnipeg. Major rivers include the St. Lawrence, Yukon, Fraser, Columbia, Mackenzie, Peace, and Slave. The southeast and far west have generally tem-

CANADA'S PROVINCES AND TERRITORIES

NAME	AREA Sq. Mi.	Sq. Km.	Rank	POPULATION Number	Rank	ADMISSION Date	Rank	CAPITAL
Alberta	255,287	661,190	5	2,476,910	4	1905 (Sept. 1)	8	Edmonton
British Columbia	365,947	947,800	4	2,903,420	3	1871 (July 20)	6	Victoria
Manitoba	250,947	649,950	7	1,028,900	5	1870 (July 15)	5	Winnipeg
New Brunswick	28,355	73,440	10	707,256	8	1867 (July 1)	1	Fredericton
Newfoundland	156,649	405,720	9	573,570	9	1949 (Mar. 31)	10	St. John's
Nova Scotia	21,425	55,490	11	858,439	7	1867 (July 1)	1	Halifax
Ontario	412,581	1,068,580	3	8,827,250	1	1867 (July 1)	1	Toronto
Prince Edward Island	2,185	5,660	12	124,735	10	1873 (July 1)	7	Charlottetown
Quebec	594,860	1,540,680	2	6,538,750	2	1867 (July 1)	1	Quebec
Saskatchewan	251,866	652,330	6	993,550	6	1905 (Sept. 1)	8	Regina
Northwest Territories	1,322,910	3,426,320	1	47,415	11	—	—	Yellowknife
Yukon Territory	186,661	483,450	8	23,878	12	—	—	Whitehorse

QUICK QUIZ: When did the first regular jet air service begin in the U.S.? See page 309.

CANADA *(continued)*

perate climates with mild winters and warm summers. Seasonal variations are more extreme in the interior plains, where summers are dry and hot and winters are cold. To the north, summers are short and winters are long and very cold. The northern part of the Canadian Shield and areas northward have an Arctic climate. Rainfall ranges from 2.40 in. (6.1 cm.) a year at Eureka in the Arctic to 115.39 in. (293.1 cm.) at Estevan Point, British Columbia.

DISCOVERY AND COLONIZATION

The Vikings explored the coast of Newfoundland about A.D. 1000, but their colonies did not survive. In 1497 Canada was claimed for England by John Cabot, an Italian-born explorer in the service of Henry VII. In 1524 Giovanni da Verrazano explored the coast, and in 1534 Jacques Cartier erected a cross at Gaspé and claimed the land for the king of France. There followed visits by British and French explorers.

The first permanent settlement was established by the Frenchmen Samuel de Champlain and the Sieur de Monts at Port Royal in Nova Scotia (1605). They founded Quebec in 1608.

In 1610–11 Henry Hudson explored Hudson Bay and James Bay.

The struggle between the British and French became intense after Britain established its first settlement in Nova Scotia in 1623. Port Royal and Quebec were captured by Sir David Kirke in 1628 and 1629, respectively, but were returned to the French in 1632. The French gradually pushed westward in search of furs, following such explorers as Nicolet, La Salle, Brulé, Joliet, and Marquette. The French settlement in Acadia was captured by an expedition from New England in 1654 but was restored to the French in 1655.

The colony of New France, centered on the St. Lawrence River, grew steadily to a population of more than 12,400 by 1692.

The French and Indian Wars with Britain in the early 1700s culminated in the defeat of the French on the Plains of Abraham and the surrender of Quebec in 1759. New France was ceded to the British by the Treaty of Paris in 1763.

PRIME MINISTERS OF CANADA

1867–1873	Sir John A. Macdonald	Conservative
1873–1878	Alexander Mackenzie	Liberal
1878–1891	Sir John A. Macdonald	Conservative
1891–1892	Sir John J. C. Abbott	Conservative
1892–1894	Sir John S. D. Thompson	Conservative
1894–1896	Sir Mackenzie Bowell	Conservative
1896	Sir Charles Tupper	Conservative
1896–1911	Sir Wilfrid Laurier	Liberal
1911–1917	Sir Robert L. Borden	Conservative
1917–1920	Sir Robert L. Borden	Unionist
1920–1921	Arthur Meighen	Unionist
1921–1926	W. L. Mackenzie King	Liberal
1926	Arthur Meighen	Conservative
1926–1930	W. L. Mackenzie King	Liberal
1930–1935	Richard B. Bennett	Conservative
1935–1948	W. L. Mackenzie King	Liberal
1948–1957	Louis S. St. Laurent	Liberal
1957–1963	John G. Diefenbaker	Prog. Cons.
1963–1968	Lester B. Pearson	Liberal
1968–1979	Pierre E. Trudeau	Liberal
1979–1980	Joe Clark	Prog. Cons.
1980–	Pierre E. Trudeau	Liberal

BRITISH RULE

The Quebec Act of 1774 provided for preservation of the French-Canadian language, religion, and culture. During and after the American Revolution, Canada became a haven for Americans loyal to England.

The Constitutional Act of 1791 created a division between Upper Canada (later Ontario) and Lower Canada (later Quebec), making a total of six colonial units with Nova Scotia, New Brunswick (separated from Nova Scotia in 1784), Newfoundland and Ile St. Jean (renamed Prince Edward Island in 1798).

Westward expansion brought settlement of Manitoba in 1812 on land obtained from the Hudson's Bay Company. Many battles of the War of 1812 between Britain and the U.S. were fought in Canada. Grain and timber began to replace fur and fish in importance. New methods of transport appeared with the building of canals in the 1820s and railways in the 1840s.

Rebellions in Upper and Lower Canada led to Lord Durham's report (1839) that set forth the principles of responsible cabinet government. Upper and Lower Canada were reunited in 1841.

DOMINION OF CANADA

Following conferences at Charlottetown and Quebec, the British North America Act of 1867 created the Dominion of Canada with the four provinces of Quebec, Ontario, Nova Scotia, and New Brunswick. The Hudson's Bay Company territories in the Northwest were surrendered to Canada in 1869. The province of Manitoba was established in 1870, British Columbia in 1871, Prince Edward Island in 1873, Alberta and Saskatchewan in 1905, and Newfoundland in 1949. Canada entered the 20th century with a population of more than 5 million and a railway system linking its coasts.

After confederation the Canadian government recognized the need to develop all aspects of nationhood. Participation on the side of Britain in World War I led to strong nationalism.

CANADA AS A WORLD POWER

The Statute of Westminster in 1931 established the political equality of Canada with Britain in the Commonwealth of Nations. Thereafter Canada moved quickly to develop an autonomous role in the world. Canada declared war on Germany on Sept. 10, 1939, a week after Britain.

Since World War II Canada has taken a leading part in world affairs as a "middle power." It has played a significant role in the UN and NATO.

Lester Bowles Pearson, leader of the Liberal Party, was prime minister from April 1963 to April 1968.

Pierre Elliott Trudeau, a French-Canadian lawyer who had been minister of justice, succeeded Pearson in 1968. Trudeau called for elections on June 25, 1968. The decisive Liberal victory gave Canada its first majority government since 1962.

The 1970s recession was slower in hitting Canada than other industrial nations partly because of its oil export income.

Following the lead of Britain earlier in the month, Canadians turned conservative at parliamentary elections held on May 22, 1979. The Pro-

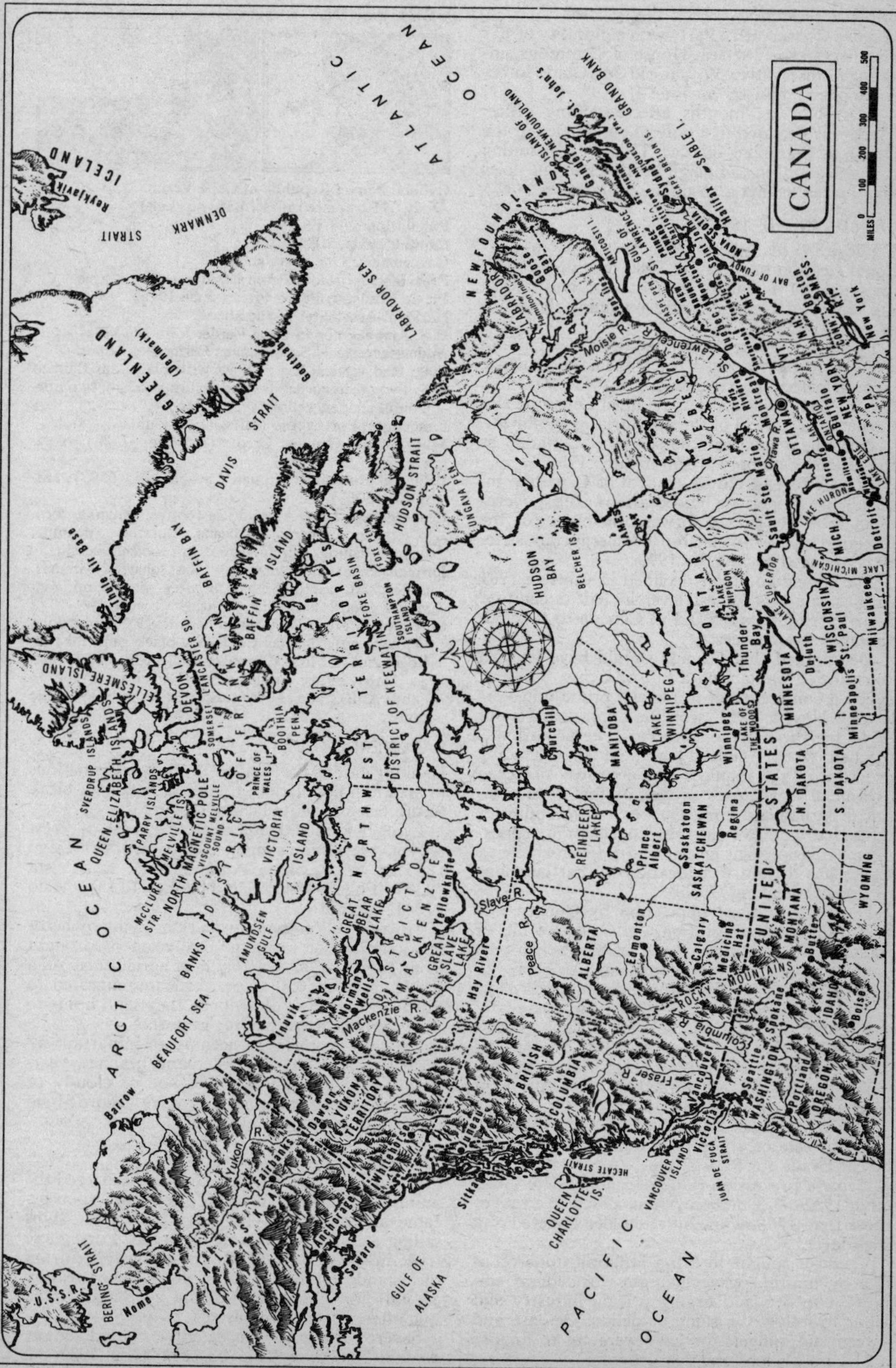
CANADA
MILES 0 100 200 300 400 500
ARCTIC OCEAN
ATLANTIC OCEAN
PACIFIC OCEAN
GREENLAND (Denmark)
ICELAND
Reykjavik
DENMARK STRAIT
DAVIS STRAIT
BAFFIN BAY
LABRADOR SEA
Thule Air Base
Godthab
ELLESMERE ISLAND
QUEEN ELIZABETH ISLANDS
SVERDRUP ISLANDS
PARRY ISLANDS
MELVILLE IS.
DEVON I.
LANCASTER SD.
SOMERSET I.
BAFFIN ISLAND
NORTH MAGNETIC POLE
VISCOUNT MELVILLE SOUND
McCLURE STR.
BANKS I.
VICTORIA ISLAND
PRINCE OF WALES I.
BOOTHIA PEN.
AMUNDSEN GULF
BEAUFORT SEA
DISTRICT OF FRANKLIN
NORTHWEST TERRITORIES
DISTRICT OF KEEWATIN
DISTRICT OF MACKENZIE
FOXE BASIN
FOXE PEN.
SOUTHAMPTON ISLAND
HUDSON STRAIT
UNGAVA PEN.
HUDSON BAY
BELCHER IS.
JAMES BAY
GREAT BEAR LAKE
GREAT SLAVE LAKE
Yellowknife
Norman Wells
Mackenzie R.
Inuvik
Hay River
Slave R.
Peace R.
Churchill
REINDEER LAKE
LAKE WINNIPEG
Winnipeg
LAKE OF THE WOODS
MANITOBA
SASKATCHEWAN
Saskatoon
Prince Albert
Regina
ALBERTA
Edmonton
Calgary
Medicine Hat
BRITISH COLUMBIA
ROCKY MOUNTAINS
Columbia R.
Fraser R.
Vancouver
Victoria
VANCOUVER ISLAND
QUEEN CHARLOTTE IS.
HECATE STRAIT
JUAN DE FUCA STRAIT
YUKON TERRITORY
Dawson
Whitehorse
Yukon R.
ALASKA
Fairbanks
Anchorage
Seward
Juneau
Sitka
Nome
Barrow
BERING STRAIT
U.S.S.R.
GULF OF ALASKA
ONTARIO
LAKE NIPIGON
Thunder Bay
LAKE SUPERIOR
Sault Ste. Marie
LAKE HURON
LAKE MICHIGAN
LAKE ONTARIO
LAKE ERIE
Toronto
Hamilton
OTTAWA
Ottawa R.
Montreal
Trois Rivieres
Quebec
QUEBEC
St. Lawrence R.
Moisie R.
LABRADOR
Goose Bay
NEWFOUNDLAND
ISLAND OF NEWFOUNDLAND
St. John's
Gander
GRAND BANK
ANTICOSTI I.
GULF OF ST. LAWRENCE
GASPE PEN.
NEW BRUNSWICK
PRINCE EDWARD ISLAND
NOVA SCOTIA
Halifax
SABLE I.
CAPE BRETON IS.
ST. PIERRE AND MIQUELON (FR.)
BAY OF FUNDY
ME.
VT.
N.H.
MASS.
Boston
CONN.
R.I.
NEW YORK
New York
Buffalo
PA.
MICH.
Detroit
WISCONSIN
Milwaukee
MINNESOTA
Duluth
St. Paul
Minneapolis
N. DAKOTA
S. DAKOTA
MONTANA
Butte
WYOMING
IDAHO
Boise
WASHINGTON
Seattle
Spokane
OREGON
Portland
UNITED STATES

CANADA *(continued)*
gressive Conservative Party won a plurality of 137 members in the 282-seat House of Commons, enabling Conservative 39-year-old Joe Clark to become prime minister on June 4.

Less than six months after attaining office, Clark was defeated in a vote of confidence in the House of Commons on Dec. 13, 1979, for failing to make good on campaign promises to cut taxes and instead asking a gasoline tax increase.

CANADA IN THE 1980s

Trudeau led his Liberal Party to victory in a national election on Feb. 18, 1980, winning a clear majority of 146 seats to the Conservatives' 103 in the House of Commons and regaining the office of prime minister.

Efforts by Quebec's premier René Lévesque to win sovereignty for his French-speaking province were defeated in a referendum on May 20, 1980. But in 1981 Quebec voters retained Lévesque and his party in control of the provincial government.

Parliament adopted the song "O Canada" as the official national anthem in June 1980.

In an effort to reduce control of Canadian industry by American corporations, the government in 1981 pressed forward on plans for the foreign share of ownership of energy industries to be reduced to 50% by 1990.

The Canadian dollar declined in value in 1981 to 80 cents—its lowest level in half a century. American tourists flocked to Canada to take advantage of low prices.

Determined that Canada should have its own constitution containing a bill of rights, Trudeau called a conference of provincial prime ministers and on Nov. 5, 1981, won the approval of 9 out of 10 for the new constitution. The accord was reached when Trudeau accepted an amending procedure that requires the approval of seven provincial legislatures as well as that of the national parliament. Only Quebec's prime minister refused to approve the new constitution, opposing a provision that guaranteed English-speaking Canadians a right to education in that language in French-speaking Quebec.

Despite continued opposition by Quebec, the new Canadian constitution, embodying a bill of rights and severing the power of the British parliament to amend the constitution, was approved 246–24 by Canada's house of commons on Dec. 2, 1981. The following week it was passed by the senate. In March 1982 the British parliament gave the document its formal approval. Then on April 17, 1982, Queen Elizabeth formally proclaimed the Canadian constitution in ceremonies held in Ottawa.

The government announced on Oct. 13, 1982, a record sale of 8.3 million tons of grain to the Soviet Union for $1.5 billion.

Canada's recession-ridden economy deteriorated in 1982–83. Unemployment soared to a rate of more than 12%, while inflation also hovered at a high level.

Trudeau sought to bring inflation under control by limiting wage increases for federal employees to 6% and urging private industry and labor to follow the same guideline. Defense and foreign aid budgets for 1983 were cut to finance a $1.1 billion jobs creation program.

CAPE VERDE

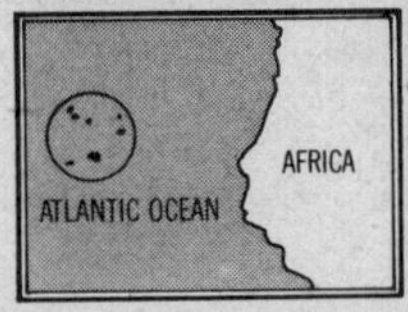

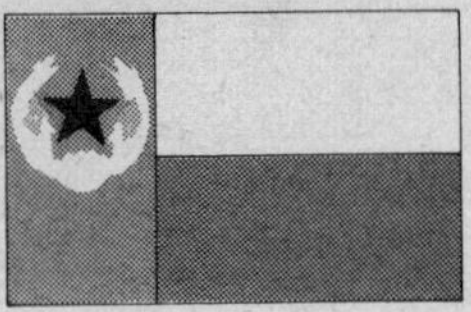

Official Name: Republic of Cape Verde.
Area: 1,750 square miles (4,352 sq. km.).
Population: 298,496.
Capital: Praia, 20,000.
Government: One-party state.
President: Aristedes Pereira (since 1975).
Prime Minister: Pedro Pires (since 1975).
National Assembly: 56 members.
U.S. Ambassador to Cape Verde: John M. Yates.
Ambassador to U.S.: Jose Luis Fernandes Lopes.
Flag: Red vertical bar at hoist with black star flanked by two green cornstalks and yellow seashell; two horizontal stripes, yellow over green.
Languages: Portuguese (official), Crioulo.
Main Ethnic Groups: Creole (mulatto—71%), black (28%).
Principal Religions: Roman Catholicism (65%), animism (30%).
Leading Industries: Agriculture (coffee, bananas, corn, vegetables, sugarcane, beans, potatoes, peanuts, fruits); fishing; shipping; tourism; food processing.
Foreign trade: *Major exports*—tuna, lobsters, bananas, coffee, salt, peanuts; *major imports*—petroleum, consumer goods, corn, rice, sugar.
Places of Interest: White sand beaches; 9,281-foot Pico volcano and Chã das Caldeiras, black sand lake on Fogo; ruins of first European settlement on São Tiago; 15th century capital city of Ribeira Grande on Santo Antão, ancient fortress, tiled cathedral, Gothic tombs.

CAPE VERDE TODAY

Ranking among the smallest of the world's nations in area and population, Cape Verde faces a bleak future because of its lack of resources.

Lying about 400 miles off the coast of West Africa, the nation's main islands are São Tiago (383 sq. mi.), Santa Antão (301), Boa Vista (239), Fogo (184), São Nicolau (132), Maio (104), and Sal (83).

Most Cape Verdeans make their living by herding livestock or farming. But years of drought from 1968 to 1982 severely hurt agriculture. As a result about 40,000 Cape Verdeans migrated to Portugal to find work. Money they send home to their families helps pay for imports.

Tourism promises to become an important industry because of the white sand beaches, year-round mild climate, and absence of cloudy or rainy weather. Some islands have recorded no rainfall in more than 11 years.

HISTORY

Portuguese explorer Diogo Gomes discovered the uninhabited islands in 1460. The islands soon became an important provisioning stop for ships sailing around Africa and to Brazil. Portuguese trade in slaves from Guinea was controlled from the islands for hundreds of years. The wealthy capital city of Ribeira Grande on Santo Antão was often attacked by pirates.

Severe droughts repeatedly caused many deaths: 20,000 in 1900–03, 25,000 in 1920–22,

20,000 in 1940–43, and 3,000 in 1946–48.

After more than five centuries of Portuguese rule the islands were granted independence on July 5, 1975.

Aristedes Pereira, leader of the nation's only political party, the African Party for the Independence of Guinea-Bissau and Cape Verde (PIAGC), became Cape Verde's first president.

CENTRAL AFRICA

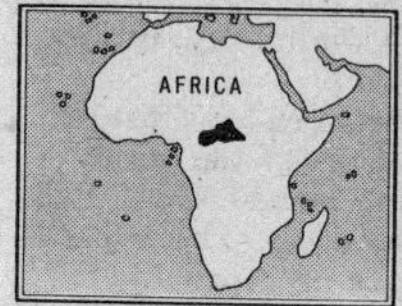

Official Name: Central African Republic.
Area: 240,535 square miles (622,984 sq. km.).
Population: 2,566,060.
Chief Cities: Bangui, capital, 187,000.
Government: Military junta.
Head of State: Gen. André Kolingba (since 1981).
U.S. Ambassador to Central Africa: Edmund DeJarnette.
Ambassador to U.S.: Christian Lingama-Toleque.
Flag: Blue, white, green, and yellow stripes crossed by vertical red bar; gold star in upper hoist corner.
Languages: French (official), Sangho.
Ethnic Groups: Banda (29%), Baya (28%), Mandia (24%), Ubangi (14%), Sara (5%).
Religions: Protestantism (40%), Roman Catholicism (28%), animism (24%), Islam (8%).
Leading Industries: Agriculture (cattle, cotton, coffee, bananas, rubber, mangoes, manioc); mining (diamonds, uranium); manufacturing (textiles, food processing); forestry and lumbering.
Foreign Trade: *Major exports*—diamonds, cotton, coffee, wood; *major imports*—textile and leather machinery, textiles.
Places of Interest: Game reserves in north; Bangui.

CENTRAL AFRICA TODAY

Although nearly as large as Texas, Central Africa is a poor, landlocked country that has few resources. Nine out of ten of the people raise crops and livestock, mostly to feed their families. The country's only two important cash crops are coffee and cotton.

Large tropical forests provide the potential for a substantial lumber industry, but the lack of good transportation facilities makes the export of large amounts of lumber difficult.

The country's best hope for improving its economic situation seems to lie in the development of its mining industry. Gem and industrial diamonds account for over half the value of the country's exports. In the 1970s the French Atomic Energy Commission cooperated in the development of mining and refining facilities to work a large deposit of uranium found in the eastern part of the country. France is the nation's main trading partner.

The nation stretches north to Chad, east to the Sudan, south to Congo and Zaire, and west to Cameroon. The terrain is chiefly rolling plateau, becoming tropical forest in the south and hilly savanna in the north.

From October to June the weather is dry and hot; temperatures exceed 110 ° F. in the daytime and range from 55 ° to 70 ° F. at night. From June through September temperatures range from 75 ° to 110 ° F. Tornadoes and floods are frequent.

HISTORY

In 1889 the French established an outpost at Bangui. In 1894 the area between the Ubangi and Shari rivers was made a French territory. It was united with Chad in 1905 to form the Ubangi-Shari-Chad Colony. In 1910 the colony became part of French Equatorial Africa. Chad was detached from Ubangi-Shari in 1920.

The first representative assembly was created in 1945. A year later Ubangi-Shari received representation in the French parliament.

As the Central African Republic, the country was proclaimed autonomous within the French Community in 1958. Its first president, Barthelemy Boganda, was killed in a plane crash in 1959.

The nation won full independence on Aug. 13, 1960. David Dacko, Boganda's nephew and leader of the African Social Evolution Party (MESAN), was elected president in 1960 and 1964. He outlawed opposition parties.

Col. Jean-Bédel Bokassa ousted Dacko by a military coup on Jan. 1, 1966. He dissolved the national assembly and abolished the constitution. Suspected political opponents were jailed without trial, tortured, and often beaten to death. He also was said to practice cannibalism.

Bokassa renamed the country the *Central African Empire* on Dec. 4, 1976, and crowned himself as Emperor Bokassa I in a ceremony at the Bangui sports stadium.

When schoolboys demonstrated against a government decree ordering them to buy uniforms from a shop partly owned by one of Bokassa's three wives, Bokassa ordered them arrested and about 100 were killed on April 18–19, 1979. Despite Bokassa's denials of involvement, an international investigative team reported that the emperor personally killed 39 of the students. In reaction to the incident, the U.S. cut off $2.5 million annual foreign aid.

Former President Dacko, 49, who had acted as an adviser to Bokassa, overthrew the emperor on Sept. 20, 1979, reestablishing a republic with himself as president. The coup was accomplished with the aid of French troops. Bokassa was in Libya at the time of the coup and remained abroad.

In an election on March 15, 1981, Dacko announced he had defeated other candidates by winning 50.23% of the vote.

Gen. André Kolingba, chief of staff of the army, seized power on Sept. 1, 1981, making himself head of state. He established a 22-man military junta to govern the country with himself as chairman. Political parties and the constitution were suspended.

Ange Patasse, a cabinet minister under Emperor Bokassa, tried to oust Kolingba on March 3, 1982. Loyalist troops put down the coup, and Patasse took refuge in the French embassy.

After severe drought devastated crops in 1983, Kolingba called for "urgent and massive" international assistance.

QUICK QUIZ: Who holds the National League record for stolen bases in a season? See page 777.

CHAD

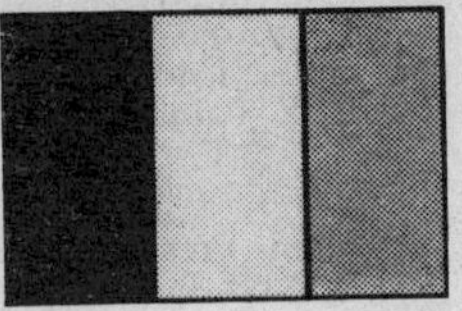

Official Name: Republic of Chad.
Area: 495,755 square miles (1,284,000 sq. km.).
Population: 5,021,030.
Capital: N'Djaména, 179,000.
Government: Rule by decree.
President: Hissen Habré (since 1982).
U.S. Ambassador to Chad: Jay P. Moffat.
Chad Ambassador to U.S.: Mahamat Ali Adoum.
Flag: Blue, yellow, red bars.
Languages: French (official), Arabic, Sara.
Ethnic Groups: Arab, Bantu, Sudanese.
Religions: Animism (50%), Islam (45%), Roman Catholicism (5%).
Leading Industries: Agriculture (cotton, cattle, millet, sorghum, rice, sweet potatoes); mining (natron); manufacturing (textiles, food processing).
Foreign Trade: *Major exports*—cotton, cattle; *major imports*—petroleum products, machinery, motor vehicles.
Places of Interest: Lake Chad; Sahara Desert.

CHAD TODAY

Chad is almost as large as the combined area of California, Arizona, New Mexico, and Nevada, but about half the country is covered by the wasteland of the Sahara Desert.

One of the world's poorest countries, Chad has been made even poorer by many years of civil war.

The nation's economy is almost entirely dependent upon agriculture and foreign aid. Most of the people of the northern part of the country are Muslim nomads who tend flocks of sheep, goats, and cattle, and live mostly on milk and dates. The people of southern Chad are mostly black farmers who grow grain crops, especially millet and sorghum. Their diet is largely gruel and beer.

Animosity between the Arabs of northern Chad and the blacks of southern Chad has existed for hundreds of years. The Arabs call southern Chad *Dar al-Abib*, meaning "Territory of Slaves," because it was the region where the Arabs frequently captured blacks for slaves.

The northern Sahara region of Chad is a dry barren land relieved only by occasional oases. Chad's central area is semidesert with some tropical trees and grazing land.

Lake Chad, on the western border, is a broad body of water surrounded by huge marshes.

Landlocked Chad is bordered by Libya on the north, Sudan to the east, Central Africa to the south, Cameroon and Nigeria to the southwest, and Niger to the west.

EARLY HISTORY OF CHAD

In the 700s A.D. peoples from the upper Nile built walled city-states on the eastern shores of Lake Chad. Saharan Berbers forged these states into a centralized kingdom called *Kanem*, which later was absorbed into the empire of Bornu in what is now Nigeria.

British explorers first entered the area in 1822. The French pushed northward into Chad in the 1890s, killing Rabeh, a military adventurer who had devastated the Muslim states (1892–98).

The French created the Military Territory of Chad in 1900. Chad was united in 1906 with Ubangi-Shari (now Central Africa). In 1910 it became a part of French Equatorial Africa.

Chad was detached from Ubangi-Shari in 1920. It became an autonomous state in 1958.

INDEPENDENCE

Chad won independence on Aug. 11, 1960, remaining within the French Community. François Tombalbaye, became president.

A civil war began in 1965 between Muslim northerners and Christian-led blacks of the south. In June 1973 Tombalbaye imprisoned Gen. Félix Malloum, commander of the army. The army attacked the presidential palace on April 13, 1975, killing Tombalbaye. Malloum became ruler.

The government agreed to a cease-fire on Jan. 22, 1978, with Arab rebel leader Hissen Habré. On Aug. 29, 1978, the ruling military junta was dissolved. Malloum became president and Habré became prime minister.

Civil war broke out anew in February 1979 between troops of Malloum and Habré. French paratroops flew into N'Djaména to rescue about 4,000 westerners from the fighting.

After a cease-fire was negotiated with the assistance of Nigeria, President Malloum resigned on March 23, 1979, and flew to exile in Nigeria.

A new government was formed on Aug. 21, 1979, with Muslim guerrilla leader Goukouni Oueddei as president.

New fighting began on March 22, 1980, between troops of Goukouni and Habré. Most Europeans and the U.S. embassy staff were evacuated. In May 1980 France withdrew its last 1,100 troops. An estimated 100,000 Chadians fled to neighboring countries.

Libya intervened in the civil war in 1980 on the side of President Goukouni, invading Chad with about 4,000 troops. The Libyans won control of the capital, N'Djaména on Dec. 15.

Habré and his supporters retreated to eastern Chad, where they continued guerrilla warfare in 1981–82, supported by Sudan and Egypt.

On Jan. 6, 1981, Libyan leader Col. Mu'ammar al-Qadhafi announced that Libya and Chad would be merged as one nation. However, responding to pressure from other African nations, Libya withdrew its army in November 1981. It was replaced by a peacekeeping force of African troops under auspices of the Organization for African Unity (OAU).

On June 7, 1982, rebel forces of Muslim former Prime Minister Habré captured the capital without opposition by OAU forces. President Goukouni fled. Habré consolidated his rule over most of the country, being sworn in as president on Oct. 21, 1983.

The civil war resumed with new intensity in the spring of 1983 in northern Chad. Backed by Libyan troops, forces of former President Goukouni captured much of northeastern by July. To counter Libya, the U.S. airlifted military supplies and advisers to aid Habre. France sent about 2,500 troops and 10 fighter planes. And Zaire provided about 2,700 troops. The civil war quieted to a stalemate by September.

CHILE

Official Name: Republic of Chile.
Area: 292,258 square miles (756,945 sq. km.).
Population: 11,562,400.
Chief Cities: Santiago, capital, 3,853,275; Viña del Mar, 272,814; Valparaíso, 266,280; Concepción, 198,824; Talcahuano, 185,744; Antofagasta, 161,226.
Government: Military dictatorship.
President: Gen. Augusto Pinochet Ugarte (seized power in 1973).
U.S. Ambassador to Chile: James David Theberge.
Chilean Ambassador to U.S.: José Miguel Barros.
Flag: Stripes of white and red; union is blue square with five-pointed white star.
Language: Spanish.
Principal Ethnic Group: Mestizo (mixed Spanish- Indian ancestry).
Main Religions: Roman Catholicism (official, 67%), Protestantism (9%).
Leading Industries: Mining (copper, iron ore, sodium nitrate, coal); manufacturing (steel, textiles, food processing, consumer goods); agriculture (wheat, sugar beets, livestock, potatoes, corn, beans).
Foreign Trade: *Major exports*—copper, iron ore, nitrates, coal; *major imports*—electrical machinery, chemical products, cereals, crude petroleum.
Places of Interest: Chilean lake country; Valparaíso; Indian ruins of Antofagasta province; Villarrica mountain area; Viña del Mar beach resort. *In Santiago:* Santa Lucia and San Cristóbal hills; presidential palace, cathedral; historical museum and national library; Forestal and President Balmaceda parks.

CHILE TODAY

A long narrow country, Chile stretches 2,650 miles along the western coast of South America. It averages only 110 miles in width and is 221 miles across at its widest point.

For many years Chile was one of the few Latin American countries where the government was regularly chosen by constitutional free elections and human rights were respected. But today Chile is ruled by a military dictatorship that has suspended all civil liberties. The change came in September 1973 when the armed forces overthrew the country's elected Marxist president because they feared he was leading Chile to become a satellite of the Soviet Union.

Although rich in natural resources and one of the world's leading producers of copper, Chile has lagged in developing improved farming methods and manufacturing industries. As a result it must import much of its food and consumer products.

Chileans are better educated and have a higher standard of living than their neighbors in Peru and Bolivia. About three-fourths of the people live in cities.

A land of dramatic contrasts, Chile is hemmed by natural frontiers of desert, mountains, and ocean. Its white deserts in the north, especially the Atacama Desert, are among the driest regions in the world. They are rich in nitrate, copper, and other mineral deposits. In the east are the immense Andes Mountains. Mt. Aconcagua, in Argentina near the Chilean border, is 22,834 feet high—the loftiest peak in the Western Hemisphere. The Andes decrease in height as they run south to Chile's beautiful lake country. About 30 rivers drain into the Pacific from the Andes. To the west, a lower coastal range runs along the ocean.

A fertile central valley, about 600 miles long and 45 miles wide, is the center of Chile's agriculture and industry and the home of 90% of the population. Chile has many earthquakes.

EARLY HISTORY

Led by Pedro de Valdivia, the Spanish conquistadores founded Santiago in 1541 and later established other settlements in the central region. During Chile's colonial period, which was marked by savage Indian wars and internal dissension, the country was essentially a neglected land of pioneers.

On Sept. 18, 1810, Chile declared its independence from Spain. A 7-year war followed in which Chilean patriots led by Bernardo O'Higgins won the country's freedom.

The constitution of 1833, chiefly the work of Diego Portales, paved the way for parliamentary government. It lasted until 1925 with few amendments. The years 1841 to 1961 were marked by political reform and material progress.

Chile won the "War of the Pacific" against Bolivia and Peru in 1884, acquiring the northern desert regions with their mineral wealth.

In 1920, when employment and political unrest had brought Chile to the verge of revolution, Arturo Alessandri was elected president with the support of the working and middle classes. He was ousted by a military coup in 1924, but was recalled in 1925. Alessandri introduced labor reforms and a new constitution. Conservative opposition led to his second ouster in 1925 and to the 6-year military dictatorship of Col. Carlos Ibáñez, which in turn collapsed in 1931.

Constitutional government was restored with Alessandri again elected to the presidency in 1932.

In 1938 a "Popular Front" of Democrats, Radicals, Socialists, and Communists carried Pedro Aguirre Cerda into the presidency. Various coalitions of the center and left parties held power to the end of the decade.

Chile established traditions of constitutional democracy with the successive elections to the presidency of Juan Antonio Ríos in 1942, of Gabriel Gonzáles Videla in 1946, of former dictator Carlos Ibáñez in 1952, of Jorge Alessandri in 1958, and of Eduardo Frei in 1964.

MARXIST REGIME

In a presidential election in September 1970, Salvador Allende Gossens, head of Chile's Socialist Party, was the candidate of a leftist Popular Unity (UP) coalition that included the Communists. He won by a narrow plurality, with 36.3% of the vote in a three-way race. Congress

QUICK QUIZ: What is the largest single religion in the U.S.? See page 709.

CHILE *(continued)*
confirmed his election after amending the constitution to guarantee continued democratic government. Allende was the first avowed Marxist to be freely elected as president of a nation.

Former U.S. President Richard Nixon revealed in 1976 that he had ordered the CIA to try to prevent Allende from becoming Chile's president. The CIA was unsuccessful in attempts to foment a military coup.

President Allende established diplomatic relations with communist states. He expropriated many banks, vital industries, and farm estates. His government nationalized foreign-owned businesses, among them properties of four U.S. corporations—Anaconda, Kennecott, Cerro, and ITT.

Chile's economic situation worsened as wage increases led to increased demands for consumer goods, while curbs on profits and declining productivity reduced total output.

MILITARY DICTATORSHIP

On Sept. 11, 1973, military forces led by the commander of the army, Gen. Augusto Pinochet Ugarte, surrounded and bombarded the presidential palace. Allende died during the coup.

The country was placed under strict military rule. Some 2,500 or more of Allende's followers were summarily executed. Many were imprisoned in military camps without trial—estimates of those jailed ranged from 10,000 to more than 80,000. The UN and the World Council of Churches helped more than 6,000 foreign refugees leave the country. About 30,000 Chileans were exiled.

In 1975 the U.S. Congress cut off military aid to Chile because of human-rights violations.

Shifting to a free-market economy in 1975, the government reduced tariffs and sold off to private enterprise 400 state-owned businesses. An economic boom resulted with gross national product growing at an annual rate of about 8.5% in 1976–81.

Relations between the U.S. and Chile worsened in 1978–79 when the U.S. formally demanded the extradition of Gen. Juan Manuel Contreras Sepulveda, former head of the secret police, and two of his associates on charges of plotting and carrying out the assassination in Washington D.C., in 1976 of Orlando Letelier, a critic of the Pinochet government. But after Chile's supreme court refused U.S. requests for extradition of the three officers on Oct. 1, 1979, the U.S. did not retaliate as it previously had threatened.

Although strikes had been outlawed since 1973, the government announced new decrees in July 1979 banning labor unions from any activity that affected the public interest.

The military government launched new crackdowns on opponents in 1980, arresting and imprisoning them without trial.

A national referendum on Sept. 12, 1980, approved a new constitution to continue Pinochet in power until 1989.

The U.S. sought to restore better relations with Chile in 1981. On Feb. 20, U.S. President Reagan revoked economic sanctions that had been imposed by President Carter in 1979.

Although the government's free economy had brought inflation under control, reducing it from a rate of 600% in 1978 to 10% in 1981, Chile was hit hard in 1982–83 by falling copper prices and the world recession. Unemployment rose to 25%, and many businesses went bankrupt.

President Pinochet on Sept. 11, 1982, declared that he would restore democracy with a congressional election in 1990 and a free presidential election in 1997.

As Pinochet celebrated 10 years of military rule in 1983, a rising tide of protest called for a return to democracy. Beginning in May, opponents organized monthly antigovernment demonstrations. Dozens of demonstrators were killed and hundreds were arrested when police and soldiers broke up these protests. In an effort to appease opponents, the government permitted about 2,000 political exiles to return. However, on Aug. 6 the nation's five leading political parties formed a coalition Democratic Alliance that urged Pinochet's resignation. The government agreed to talks with coalition leaders, indicating willingness to relax banned political activities.

CHILE'S DEPENDENCIES

EASTER ISLAND

Area: 63 square miles (163 sq. km.).
Population: 2,000.
Capital: Hanga Roa.

Easter Island (or Rapa Nui) is a volcanic island in the South Pacific about 2,350 miles west of Chile. It is famed for its hieroglyphics and large stone heads carved from volcanic stone.

The people of Easter Island are of Polynesian origin and raise yams, taro roots, bananas, potatoes, and sugarcane. The island is governed by Valparaíso province.

JUAN FERNANDEZ

Area: 57 square miles (148 sq. km.).
Population: 615.

The Juan Fernández group includes two major islands: Robinson Crusoe (36 sq. mi.) and Alexander Selkirk (21 sq. mi.). They are the largest of several volcanic islands in the group, which is located about 400 miles west of Valparaíso. Lobster fishing is the main industry.

The islands are believed to have been discovered by a Spanish explorer, possibly before 1572. The English author Daniel Defoe is believed to have based his story *Robinson Crusoe* on the four-years the Scottish castaway Alexander Selkirk spent on Más Atierra (the original name of Robinson Crusoe Island).

CHILEAN ANTARCTIC TERRITORY

Area: 482,625 square miles (1,249,993 sq. km.).
Population: 200.

Chile claimed the Palmer Peninsula section of Antarctica in 1940 and has established four bases there. Parts of the territory also are claimed by Britain and Argentina.

DIEGO RAMIREZ ISLANDS

This group of uninhabited islands is situated 60 miles southwest of Cape Horn.

SALAY GOMEZ ISLAND, SAN AMBROSIO ISLAND, AND SAN FELIX ISLAND

These islands are small, uninhabited Pacific Ocean possessions of Chile.

CHINA

Official Name: People's Republic of China.
Area: 3,692,950 square miles (9,564,701 sq. km.).
Population: 1,048,210,000.
Chief Metropolitan Areas: Peking (Beijing), capital, 8,626,050; Shanghai, 10,820,000; Tientsin (Tianjin), 4,280,000; Shenyang, 2,411,000; Wuhan, 2,146,000; Chungking (Chongqing), 2,121,000; Canton (Guangzhou), 1,840,000; Harbin, 1,552,000; Dairen-Port Arthur (Dalian-Lushun), 1,508,000; Nanking (Nanjing), 1,419,000; Sian (Xian), 1,310,000; Tsingtao (Qingdao), 1,121,000; Chengtu (Chengdu), 1,107,000; Taiyuan, 1,020,000.
Government: One-party communist state.
Heads of Government: Deng Xiaoping, Chairman of the Communist Party's advisory commission (since 1977); Hu Yaobang, secretary-general of the Communist Party (since 1981); Zhao Ziyang, prime minister (since 1980); Li Xiannian, state president (since 1983).
Legislature: *National People's Congress,* 3,221 members.
U.S. Ambassador to China: Arthur W. Hummel Jr.
Chinese Ambassador to U.S.: Zhang Wenjin.
Flag: Red field, with gold star in upper hoist corner; four smaller gold stars form arc on right.
Official Language: Chinese
Main Ethnic Group: Han Chinese (94%).
Religions: Confucianism, Buddhism, and Taoism.
Leading Industries: Agriculture (rice, cotton, sugarcane, sugar beets, jute and hemp, livestock, tobacco, vegetables, corn, tea, wheat, potatoes, soybeans); fishing; manufacturing (steel, machinery, fertilizer, vehicles, chemicals, textiles); mining (coal, petroleum, natural gas, iron ore, other minerals).
Foreign Trade: *Major exports*—petroleum, agricultural products, iron and steel, textiles, tin, consumer products; *major imports*—machinery, grain.
Places of Interest: Great Wall of China; waterfalls in the Kweichow Mountains; Gobi Desert; Shanghai; Hangchow. *In Peking:* former Imperial Palace; Temple of Heaven complex; Summer Palace; city gate.

CHINA TODAY

China has the largest population of any country in the world—about five times that of the United States. Even so, it is not as crowded as other large countries of Asia, such as Bangladesh and India, because it has the third-largest area after the Soviet Union and Canada.

To hold down population growth, the government penalize parents who have more than one child.

Many of China's problems stem from trying to change in only a few decades from a largely agricultural country into a modern industrial nation. Its problems have been similar to those of the Soviet Union in the 1920s and 1930s.

To speed industrialization, the communist government since 1980 has encouraged the development of more than 2.6 million privately-owned small businesses.

The nation's science and technology have enabled it to build and test atomic and hydrogen bombs and launch space satellites and intercontinental ballistic missiles.

About one-fifth of China, mainly in the east, is a region of lowlands. The rest consists of great plateaus, plains, and massive mountains. The diverse regions range from areas of tropical abundance to barren deserts, and from dense evergreen forests to depleted woodlands.

The principal mountain systems are the Altai in the northwest, the Himalaya in the southwest, the Tien Shan range in the far west, and the Kunlun range in the east.

The country's chief waterways include the Yangtze River, over 3,600 miles long, in central China; the Yellow River, the chief waterway of northern China; the Amur, on the northeastern border; and the Min, Si, and headwaters of the Mekong and Red rivers in the south.

EARLY HISTORY

The story of the Hsia, traditionally China's first dynasty, is largely legendary. The recording of history began only during the subsequent Shang dynasty (about 1766–1123 B.C.).

The Chou dynasty (about 1122–256 B.C.), ruled during a classical era that produced the philosophers Confucius and Lao-tzu.

The Ch'in dynasty (221–207 B.C.) gave China its name and its first emperor, ended feudalism,

CHINA'S PROVINCES AND REGIONS

NAME[1]	AREA Sq. Mi.	Sq. Km.	POPULATION[3]
Anhwei (Anhui)	54,016	139,900	49,665,724
Chekiang (Zhejiang)	39,305	101,800	38,884,603
Fukien (Fujian)	47,529	123,100	25,931,106
Heilungkiang (Heilongjiang)	178,997	463,600	32,665,546
Honan (Henan)	64,479	167,000	74,422,739
Hopei (Hebei)	78,263	202,700	53,005,875
Hunan (Hunan)	81,275	210,500	54,008,851
Hupeh (Hubei)	72,394	187,500	47,084,150
Inner Mongolia[2] (Nei Monggol)	454,635	1,177,500	18,510,000
Kansu (Gansu)	141,506	366,500	19,569,261
Kiangsi (Jiangxi)	63,630	164,800	33,184,827
Kiangsu (Jiangsu)	39,460	102,200	60,521,114
Kirin (Jilin)	72,200	187,000	22,560,053
Kwangsi-Chuang[2] (Guangxi Zhuang)	85,097	220,400	36,420,960
Kwangtung (Guangdong)	89,344	231,400	59,299,220
Kweichow (Guizhou)	67,182	174,000	28,552,997
Liaoning (Liaoning)	57,915	150,000	35,721,693
Ningsia Hui[2] (Ningxia Hui)	25,637	66,400	3,895,578
Shansi (Shanxi)	60,657	157,100	25,291,389
Shantung (Shandong)	59,189	153,300	74,419,054
Shensi (Shaanxi)	75,600	195,800	28,904,423
Sinkiang-Uighur[2] (Xinjiang Uygur)	635,833	1,646,800	13,081,681
Szechwan (Sichuan)	219,692	569,000	99,713,310
Tibet[2] (Xizang)	471,662	1,221,600	1,892,393
Tsinghai (Qinghai)	278,380	721,000	3,895,706
Yunnan (Yunnan)	168,418	436,200	32,553,817

[1] Pinyin spellings in parentheses. [2] Autonomous region. [3] 1982 census.

QUICK QUIZ: Who is the patron saint of fishermen? See page 708.

RULING DYNASTIES OF CHINA

c.2200–1766 B.C. Legendary Hsia dynasty: Stone Age civilization; used painted, then black, pottery.
c.1766–1123 B.C. Shang (or Yin) dynasty: Bronze Age civilization; writing developed.
c.1122–256 B.C. Chou dynasty: Advanced feudal society.
221–207 B.C. Ch'in dynasty: First emperors with centralized government; Great Wall built.
202 B.C.–A.D. 220 Han dynasty: Science and arts flourished; paper invented.
220–589 Six dynasties: China divided among local feudal rulers; invasions by Huns and Turks.
589–618 Sui dynasty: Empire reunited; Buddhism flourished; poetry and sculpture outstanding.
618–907 T'ang dynasty: Printing on paper and mechanical clocks invented.
907–959 Five dynasties: Anarchy prevailed.
960–1279 Sung dynasty: Advanced civilization; magnetic compass invented; gunpowder used in warfare.
1260–1368 Yuan dynasty of Mongol rulers, founded by Kublai Khan; extensive public works; advancements in science and arts; novel developed in literature.
1368–1644 Ming dynasty: Mongols driven out of China; many cultural achievements.
1644–1912 Manchu (or Ch'ing) dynasty: European colonial incursions, ended with establishment of republic.

CHINA *(continued)*

and centralized the government. Roads, canals, and much of the Great Wall were constructed.

The Han dynasty (202 B.C.–A.D. 220) was noted for its artistry and territorial expansion.

Under the Sung dynasty (960–1279) many innovations occurred, including gunpowder for military use, printing, the magnetic compass, and a new literary form, the novel.

The Mongols, under Genghis Khan, invaded and by 1215 had taken northern China. Genghis' grandson Kublai Khan founded the Yuan dynasty and completed the conquest of the Sung.

The Mongols were ousted in 1368 by the founders of the Ming dynasty.

European penetration began in 1557 when the Portuguese established a colony at Macao.

MANCHU DYNASTY

The Manchus, meanwhile, were advancing from the north. They took Peking in 1644. Their dynasty, the Ch'ing, ruled until 1911.

China's vast riches increasingly lured European and American traders. China forbade the import of opium, but foreign traders smuggled in huge quantities of the narcotic. This precipitated the first Opium War (1839–42). China was forced to open five ports to British trade and to cede Hong Kong.

In the second Opium War (1856–60), the British and French joined forces. Ports were opened from the Yangtze north to Manchuria.

The U.S. sought equal trading rights, calling in 1900 for an Open Door policy to give all nations the right to trade in Chinese ports. The Boxer Rebellion of 1900 marked a desperate popular attempt to eliminate foreign domination.

NATIONALIST CHINA

A revolution in 1911 led by Dr. Sun Yat-sen forced the abdication of the boy emperor Hsüan-t'ung (P'u-i) on Feb. 12, 1912. Sun was named provisional president of the new Republic of China, but soon resigned. His successor's dictatorial rule brought another revolt led by Sun in 1913. It failed and Sun was exiled.

Sun created the Kuomintang (Nationalist) Party, returning to China in 1917. Civil war began. Sun died in 1925, but the Kuomintang army went on under Chiang Kai-shek to defeat the central and northern warlords. In 1928 his government received foreign recognition. Chiang continued to fight the communists, forcing them into the 6,000-mile Long March to the northwest, where they settled in Shensi province in 1935.

Japan invaded Manchuria in 1931, setting up a puppet state called *Manchukuo* with China's former emperor P'u-i as the figurehead ruler.

Japan launched full-scale war on China in 1937. World War II brought Allied aid to China.

COMMUNIST RULE BY MAO

After World War II Chiang received U.S. support and supplies, but by 1949 communists had won control of the mainland. Chiang and his supporters fled to the island of Taiwan.

The *People's Republic of China* was declared by the communists on Oct. 1, 1949, under leadership of Mao Tse-tung (Mao Zedong) as chairman of the Communist Party and Chou En-lai (Zhou Enlai) as prime minister. Agriculture was collectivized and industry was nationalized.

In 1950 China intervened in the Korean War on the side of the North Koreans. Also in 1950 China conquered Tibet. In 1962 an undeclared border war was waged with India.

In 1960 China split with the Soviet Union in a continuing controversy over ideology.

China became a nuclear power with its first explosion of an atomic bomb in 1964. It exploded its first hydrogen bomb in 1967.

Influenced by his wife Jiang Qing, Mao launched the Great Proletarian Cultural Revolution in 1966 to purge her opponents from power.

The chief target of the revolution was the Communist Party establishment led by Liu Shao-chi, who was chairman of the party in 1959–66.

China veered toward anarchy as millions of zealous pro-Mao Red Guard students seized power in provincial capitals.

By the end of 1968 the Cultural Revolution appeared to be over, with the expulsion of Liu Shao-chi from the party in October.

In the summer of 1971, Defense Minister Lin Biao, who had been believed to be Mao's hand-picked successor, was accused of plotting to assassinate Mao. He fled in a plane that crashed in Mongolia in September, killing all occupants.

China's seat in the United Nations from 1949 to 1971 was held by Taiwan (Chiang's Republic of China). Admission of mainland China was repeatedly voted down, because of U.S. opposition. But in 1971 the U.S. reversed its position. Then the UN General Assembly voted to admit the Peking government and to expel Taiwan.

A weeklong visit by President Nixon to China in February 1972 demonstrated easing relations.

Climaxing a 6-day visit to Peking on Sept. 29, 1972, Japan's Premier Kakuei Tanaka agreed to establish diplomatic relations.

In mid-February 1973, U.S. Secretary of State Henry Kissinger visited Peking where he had cordial talks with Chairman Mao and Premier Chou that resulted in the establishment of "liaison offices"—one step below formal diplomatic recognition.

China launched a New Cultural Revolution under the leadership of Chairman Mao in February 1974. The new campaign was directed at "reactionaries" who clung to the beliefs of the ancient philosopher Confucius.

A new constitution was adopted in 1975 which made the chairman of the Communist Party, Mao Tse-tung, commander of the armed forces.

Communists supported by China conquered Cambodia, South Vietnam, and Laos in 1975, turning those Southeast Asian countries into communist states.

In September 1975 China established diplomatic relations with the European Common Market.

U.S. President Gerald Ford and First Lady Betty Ford visited China on Dec. 2–5, 1975, meeting with Chairman Mao and other leaders.

The 77-year-old Chou En-lai, who had served as prime minister of China since it was taken over by the communists, died on Jan. 8, 1976. He was succeeded as prime minister by Hua Guofeng.

Chou's chosen successor, Deputy Prime Minister Deng Xiaoping, was stripped of all offices and branded a reactionary. In April 1976 riots broke out in Peking and other cities when the people believed Chou's memory was being degraded.

Major earthquakes in July 1976 caused severe damage to the industrial region of Tientsin and Tangshan. Some 242,000 persons were killed.

CHINA UNDER HUA AND DENG

After ruling China for nearly 27 years, 82-year-old Mao died on Sept. 9, 1976. More than 750,000 Chinese attended a memorial for Mao on Sept. 18, which was presided over by his successor, Hua Guofeng, who became chairman of the Communist Party as well as prime minister.

Mao's widow, Jiang Qing, and three other members of the Communist Party's politburo were arrested in October 1976. They were branded as a radical "Gang of Four" who were trying to take over China. In following months there were reports that over a million of their followers were arrested and over 7,000 killed.

The 74-year-old Deng was restored as deputy prime minister in July 1977, and it soon became clear he had taken charge of running the government. His previous downfall was officially blamed on the discredited "Gang of Four."

Well known as a pragmatist, Deng told the Chinese Communist Party's 11th congress in August 1977: "The minimum requirement for a communist is to be an honest person. There must be less empty talk and more hard work."

A concerted campaign was launched to discredit the supposed infallibility of Chairman Mao. Chinese officials openly spoke of the last years of his reign as "10 lost years." Hundreds of thousands of persons who had been purged during Mao's "cultural revolutions" were restored to official positions.

Obviously envious of the economic prosperity of neighboring Japan, China signed a $20 billion trade pact with Japan on Feb. 16, 1978. This was followed on Aug. 12 with the signing of a treaty of peace and friendship with Japan. Ratification documents were exchanged on Oct. 23, 1978, bringing a formal end to four decades of war between China and Japan.

China actively began encouraging Western tourists to visit the country in 1978, ending its reclusiveness of three decades.

A new constitution was approved on March 5, 1978, by the national legislature, restoring rights to citizens and to ethnic groups.

China and the U.S. established formal diplomatic relations on Jan. 1, 1979, as the U.S. ended diplomatic ties with the Taiwan government. In late January and early February 1979, Deng made a 9-day visit to the U.S., the first by a Chinese communist leader. He and President Carter signed agreements to strengthen relations.

On July 7, 1979, China and the U.S. signed a comprehensive trade agreement giving China most-favored-nation trade status. The pact was approved by the U.S. Congress on Jan. 24, 1980. Within a year the U.S. became China's second most important trading partner, after Japan.

CHINA IN THE 1980s

Angered by what it regarded as the mistreatment of ethnic Chinese by the Vietnamese government and by Vietnam's overthrow of the pro-Chinese government of Cambodia, China "punished" its neighbor to the south with a large-scale four-week border war from Feb. 17 to March 15, 1979.

Avowedly to prepare for younger leadership of the nation, Hua and Deng resigned their government posts in September 1980, but Deng retained control of the government through his Communist Party position.

Zhao Ziyang, 61, was appointed prime minister on Sept. 7, 1980, to manage the day-to-day affairs of the government. Zhao promised to carry on the economic reforms initiated by Deng and make China a "modernized, highly democratic and civilized socialist state" within two decades.

A meeting of the National People's Congress in September 1980 ratified the changes in leadership. It approved an amendment to the constitution abolishing the right of people to air dissenting views in critical wall posters. The congress also ratified a law designed to reduce the birthrate by raising the minimum age for marriage to 22 for men and 20 for women. The Communist Party called on its 38 million members to have no more than one child per family.

The U.S. and China signed new agreements on Sept. 17, 1980, paving the way for scheduled airline service and mutual use of each other's ports by merchant ships.

Drought and floods cut China's food production in 1980, causing it to sign a 4-year agreement with the U.S. on Oct. 22, 1980, to buy 6 to 8 million tons of grain annually.

Mao's widow, Jiang Qing, and nine of her associates in the "Gang of Four" were brought to trial in televised proceedings that began on Nov. 20, 1980, and concluded with their sentencing more than two months later on Jan. 25, 1981. They were found guilty of persecuting more than 725,000 persons, of whom nearly 35,000 died, during the Cultural Revolution. The 67-year-old Jiang Qing was given a suspended death sentence,

CHINA *(continued)*
later commuted to life imprisonment.

Deng made his supreme position clear in 1981 at a meeting of the Communist Party's Central Committee. Mao's self-chosen successor, Hua, was demoted and replaced as chairman by a protégé of Deng—Hu Yaobang. At the same time Deng took control of the armed forces, making himself chairman of the party's military commission, a post previously held by Hua.

China began construction in 1982 of its first full-scale nuclear power plant near Shanghai. It is scheduled to begin operation in 1988, producing 600 megawatts of electricity. Seeking to become a major oil-exporting nation to improve its economy, China contracted with U.S. and Japanese firms in 1982–83 to search for petroleum in its offshore waters.

After spending some 33 years in prison, more than 4,000 Chinese nationalists were freed in a government amnesty announced in March 1982.

Strained relations between the U.S. and China eased with agreement on a joint communiqué issued on Aug. 17, 1982, in which the U.S. pledged to limit sales of arms to Taiwan, and China agreed to use peaceful means in seeking political reunification of the island with mainland China.

The 12th Communist Party Congress held in September 1982 reaffirmed 78-year-old Deng Xiaoping's leadership, electing him chairman of a newly created advisory commission. It endorsed his plans to quadruple China's industrial production by the year 2000. To further discredit Mao, his handpicked successor Hua was ousted as a member of the politburo.

A new constitution was adopted on Dec. 4, 1982. It stresses the importance of human rights, but denies workers the right to strike. To reduce population growth, the constitution requires all married couples to practice birth control.

China and the Soviet Union conducted talks in 1983 on the resumption of normal relations. However, China demanded that to do so the Soviet Union must end its occupation of Afghanistan and stop supporting Vietnamese occupation of Cambodia.

New economic reforms were introduced in February 1983. Shops and factories no longer were required to turn over all profits to the government. Instead, taxes on businesses were established, permitting remaining profits to be used by managers for investment or for employee benefits.

The government harshly cracked down on career criminals in 1983. In sports stadiums before cheering crowds, public executions were conducted of hundreds of murderers, rapists, robbers, and embezzlers.

The U.S. in June 1983 relaxed its ban on the sale of computers and other high-technology equipment to China.

A year-long trade dispute was settled on July 30, 1983, with agreement that China can increase its exports of textiles to the U.S. China had boycotted the import of U.S. farm products because of U.S. restrictions on textile imports.

Warming U.S.-Chinese relations were furthered by announcement in October 1983 that Prime Minister Zhao Ziyang would visit Washington in January 1984 and President Reagan would go to China in April.

CISKEI

Official Name: Ciskei.
Area: 3,205 square miles (8,300 sq. km.).
Population: 694,718.
Capital: Bisho.
Government: One-party state.
Head of State: Chief Lennox L. Sebe (since 1973).
Parliament: National Assembly, 22 members.
Flag: A crane, symbol of courage and energy, centered on white diagonal stripe; blue triangles in upper left and lower right corners.
Language: Xhosa.
Principal Ethnic Group: Ciskei Xhosa.
Main Religions: Christianity, animism.
Leading Industries: Agriculture (cattle, sheep, corn, tea, coffee, nuts), fishing, forestry.
Foreign Trade: *Major exports*—livestock, meat, wool, hides; *major imports*—food, fuel.

About two-thirds the size of Connecticut, Ciskei is the fourth of South Africa's black homelands to be granted "independence." As with its sister states, none of the world's nations except South Africa recognizes its sovereignty.

Although larger than about a fourth of the world's independent nations both in area and population, Ciskei is poorer than most because it has no known valuable resources other than its land. South Africa subsidizes about 75% of its national budget.

Most of the people live by subsistence farming. But large quantities of food must be imported. About two-thirds of the income of the people comes from money sent home by Ciskei's men who work in other parts of South Africa.

Ciskei borders the Indian Ocean on South Africa's southeastern coast. Lying west of the Great Kei River, it is adjacent to another "independent" black homeland, Transkei, whose people speak the same Xhosa language. Two South African towns are just outside Ciskei's border—East London and King William's Town.

Granted partial self-government in 1971, Ciskei held its first general election in February 1973. The Ciskeian National Independence Party, led by Chief Lennox L. Sebe, won every seat in the national assembly, soundly defeating the Ciskeian National Party, led by Chief J. Mabandla. Mabandla's party had favored merging Ciskei with neighboring Transkei.

Ciskei was declared a self-governing territory on Aug. 1, 1973.

Chief Sebe placed his brother, Gen. Charles Sebe, in charge of security police and stifled all opposition.

In a referendum held on Dec. 4, 1980, 97% of the people of Ciskei voted in favor of independence. A year later, on Dec. 4, 1981, South Africa granted Ciskei its "sovereignty" with Chief Sebe as head of the government.

On July 19, 1983, Chief Sebe jailed his powerful brother and many of his associates on charges of corruption.

COLOMBIA

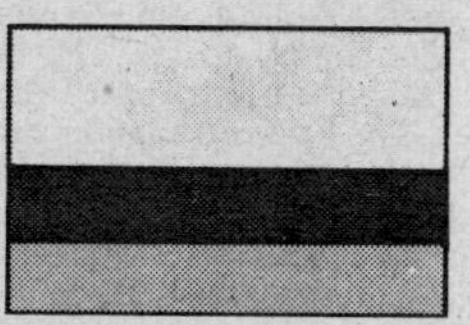

Official Name: Republic of Colombia.
Area: 439,737 square miles (1,138,914 sq. km.).
Population: 27,955,600.
Largest Cities: Bogotá, capital, 4,324,000; Medellín, 1,589,000; Cali, 1,382,000; Barranquilla, 891,000; Cartagena, 453,000; Bucaramanga, 424,000.
Government: Democracy.
President: Belisario Betancur (since 1982).
Parliament: *Senate,* 114 members; *House of Representatives,* 199 members.
U.S. Ambassador to Colombia: Lewis Arthur Tambs.
Colombian Ambassador to U.S.: Alvaro Gomez Hurtado.
Flag: Tricolor with wide yellow stripe atop narrower blue and red stripes.
Official Language: Spanish.
Main Ethnic Groups: Mestizo (mixed Indian-Spanish, 58%), European descent (20%), mulatto (14%).
Principal Religion: Roman Catholicism (95%).
Leading Industries: Agriculture (corn, rice, cassava, sugar, coffee, cattle, bananas, tobacco, cotton, wheat, potatoes); mining (oil, natural gas, gold, silver, platinum, emeralds, coal, iron, nickel); manufacturing (textiles, steel, chemicals).
Foreign Trade: *Major exports*—coffee, petroleum, coal, bananas, cotton, beef, sugar; *major imports*—machinery, motor vehicles, consumer goods.
Places of Interest: Island of San Andrés; Zipaquira underground Salt Mine Cathedral; Guatavita Lake; San Agustín Archaeological Park. *In Bogotá:* Plaza Bolívar; Gold Museum; national museum; Museum of July 20th, 1810; colonial buildings; planetarium; museum of modern art.

COLOMBIA TODAY

Colombia is a South American nation larger than Texas and California combined. With a wealth of natural resources, Colombia is an important petroleum producer and contains 60% of South America's coal reserves. It is second only to Brazil in coffee production.

Colombia also has prospered as one of the main sources of marijuana and cocaine smuggled into the U.S.

Colombia is one of the few South American nations governed by freely elected civilians.

Most Colombians are poor. Many farm workers, eke out a subsistence for their families by growing corn and beans.

An intensive family-planning program reduced the population growth rate from 3.2% in 1965 to 2.1% by the 1980s.

Government-owned oil refineries and hydroelectric plants have been developed to speed industrialization. The government welcomes foreign investors and protects their interests.

Since the 1940s leftist guerrillas have ambushed government troops, carried out political kidnappings, and conducted other acts of terrorism. The government also carries on an unceasing war against drug smugglers.

Colombia has coastlines on the Caribbean to the north and the Pacific to the west. Called the "Gateway to South America," the country is bordered on the northwest by Panama, on the northeast by Venezuela, on the southeast by Brazil, and on the south by Peru and Ecuador.

Three ranges of the Andes Mountains cross Colombia, roughly paralleling the Pacific coast. The Magdalena and Cauca rivers converge in the north and empty into the Caribbean.

SPANISH COLONIZATION

Spanish explorers who came to Colombia in 1499 found some gold and jewels. The Colimas Indians of the Cauca Valley were especially noted for their works of gold. Over 15,000 gold objects of pre-Spanish art are preserved today in Bogotá's Gold Museum.

Permanent colonization on the isthmus began after 1514. The region—including portions of present-day Panama, Venezuela, Ecuador, and most of Colombia—was called New Granada, a Spanish colony for three centuries.

INDEPENDENCE

The colonists began their struggle for independence from Spain on July 20, 1810. In 1819 Simón Bolívar became president of the republic of Gran Colombia. By 1830 Venezuela and Ecuador had declared themselves separate states. The remaining territory became the republic of New Granada, which assumed its present name, Colombia, in 1866.

Two political parties developed: Conservatives, favoring centralized government and close ties with the church, and Liberals, advocating a loose federal government and separation of church and state. Their rivalry caused nearly a hundred civil wars by 1899, when the War of a Thousand Days took 100,000 lives.

In 1903 Colombia refused to ratify the leasing of territory to the U.S. to build a canal, and Panama declared itself independent.

An undeclared civil war, called *La Violencia,* between Conservatives and Liberals in 1948–57 resulted in an estimated 300,000 deaths.

Constitutional amendments adopted in 1957 established a unique system that required the presidency to alternate between the Liberal and Conservative parties until 1974.

RETURN TO TWO-PARTY DEMOCRACY

In the first major two-party national election in more than two decades, on April 21, 1974, Alfonso López Michelsen, the Liberal Party candidate, was elected president. His term was marred by widespread political corruption.

In a closely contested election on June 4, 1978, Liberal candidate Julio César Turbay Ayala defeated Conservative Belisario Betancur, 2,506,228 to 2,358,644, to win a 4-year term as president.

Guerrillas of the Movement of April 19 (M-19) took the embassy of the Dominican Republic on Feb. 27, holding hostage 58 persons, including ambassadors of the U.S. and 13 other countries. Colombian troops besieged the embassy for two months until April 27 when the guer-

COLOMBIA *(continued)*
rillas were allowed to fly to Cuba.

The army claimed a major victory over the M-19 guerrilla movement in March 1981, killing 16 and capturing 75. However, the guerrilla leader Jaime Bateman Cayón remained at large.

The government invested billions of dollars in developing 15 major hydroelectric projects in an effort to add 8,623 megawatts to the nation's power system by the end of 1991.

In congressional elections on March 14, 1982, the governing Liberal Party won majorities in both houses of congress.

However, a split in the Liberal Party enabled Betancur, 59, to defeat former President Alfonso Lopez in a presidential election on May 30, 1982, with 3.2 million votes to 2.8 million, ending eight years of Liberal Party government. Betancur pledged to end the state of siege in effect for more than three decades to fight the guerrillas, and less than a month later the government did so.

Sworn in as Colombia's 73d president on Aug. 7, 1982, Betancur offered amnesty to guerrillas. He faced major problems with inflation at a rate of about 30% and unemployment nearing 10%.

Although hundreds of guerrillas accepted the amnesty and put down their arms, fighting, killing, and kidnapping continued in 1983.

A major earthquake nearly destroyed the provincial capital Popayan on March 31, 1983, killing 157 persons and making 70,000 homeless.

COMOROS

Official Name: Federal and Islamic Republic of the Comoros.
Area: 694 square miles (1,797 sq. km.).
Population: 391,759.
Capital: Moroni, Grande Comore, 12,000.
Government: Political-military directorate.
President: Ahmed Abdallah (since 1978).
Prime Minister: Ali Mroudjae (since 1981).
Parliament: Federal Assembly, 39 elected members.
U.S. Ambassador to Comoros: Robert B. Keating.
Comoros Ambassador to U.S.: Ali Mlahaili.
Flag: Green field with white crescent and four white stars in center.
Languages: Arabic and Swahili.
Main Ethnic Group: Antalaotra (mixed Arab-Malay-African ancestry).
Principal Religion: Islam.
Leading Industries: Agriculture (coconuts, coffee, sisal, vanilla, cocoa, sugarcane, cassava, sweet potatoes, vegetables, mangoes, bananas, goats, cattle); fishing; manufacturing (food processing, soap, lumber).
Foreign Trade: *Major exports*—copra, vanilla, spices, cocoa; *major imports*—food, consumer goods.
Places of Interest: Kartala volcano (7,746 feet) on Grande Comore; swimming beaches; fishing villages.

COMOROS TODAY

Lying between the east coast of Africa and the island of Madagascar, Comoros is one of the smallest and poorest nations in the world.

The main islands of Comoros are: Grande Comore, 443 sq. mi.; Anjouan, 164 sq. mi.; and Moheli, 81 sq. mi. The Comoros island Mahore (Mayotte) remains a French dependency.

The Comoro islanders make their living mainly by farming and fishing. Many work on the large plantations that produce vanilla, coffee, coconuts, sisal, cocoa, spices, and plants from which are made essential oils used in perfumes. Families grow their own food on small farms that provide sweet potatoes, cassava, fruits, and vegetables. However, much food has to be imported.

Few people can read and write, and only 3 of every 10 children attend school.

The islands have a hot climate the year round. The dry season, from May to October, has temperatures that fall to about 70° F. in the evening. In the wet season, from November to April, the temperature rarely falls below 80° F.

There are many tropical storms. Reservoirs catch water during the rainy season, but deep wells must be sunk to supplement the supply of drinking water in the dry season.

The mountainous islands are of volcanic origin. The highest volcano is 7,746-foot Kartala on Grande Comore.

HISTORY

The islands became part of the East African empire of the sultan of Oman in the 800s. They appeared on Portuguese sailing charts by 1527.

France acquired rights to Mahore from the local chiefs, making it a colony in 1843. A protectorate was extended over all the Comoros in 1886. On July 25, 1912, France made all the Comoros a colony. From 1914 they were administered from Madagascar.

France gave the Comoros the status of an overseas territory on Jan. 1, 1947. Local self-government developed with a 30-member assembly.

The islands were granted complete internal self-government in 1960. In a referendum on Dec. 22, 1974, 95% of the people voted for immediate independence.

The Comoros national assembly declared independence from France on July 6, 1975, and elected Ahmed Abdallah as president.

The residents of Mahore appealed to France to preserve their colonial status. When French troops withdrew from most of the Comoros in July, some remained on Mahore as a sign of continued French protection.

On Aug. 3, 1975, President Abdallah was overthrown in a bloodless coup led by Ali Soilih, head of the National United Front. He nationalized all French-owned property and tried to create a Chinese Maoist state. His youthful followers persecuted conservatives and attempted to stamp out the Islamic religion. France terminated its annual $18.5 million aid.

The people of Mahore voted almost unanimously on Feb. 8, 1976, to remain a dependency of France. See page 553.

A military coup on May 13, 1978, overthrew Soilih. He was killed while trying to escape.

Former president Abdallah was restored to power, winning election as president without opposition on Oct. 22, 1978. He proclaimed that people were again free to practice religions of their choice.

CONGO

Official Name: People's Republic of the Congo.
Area: 132,047 square miles (342,000 sq. km.).
Population: 1,710,710.
Largest Metropolitan Areas: Brazzaville, capital, 136,200; Pointe-Noire, 115,000.
Government: Marxist military junta.
President: Denis Sassou-Nguessou (since 1979).
Prime Minister: Col. Louis-Sylvain Goma (since 1975).
U.S. Ambassador to Congo: Kenneth Lee Brown.
Congo Ambassador to U.S.: Nicolas Mondjo.
Flag: Red field with green wreath, yellow star, hammer, and hoe in upper corner.
Languages: French (official), Lingala, Kikongo.
Main Ethnic Groups: Bakongo (45%), Bateke (20%), M'Bochi (10%).
Religions: Animism (48%); Roman Catholicism (47%); Islam (5%).
Leading Industries: Agriculture (corn, bananas, cassava, rice, peanuts, goats, poultry, palm nuts, sugarcane, tobacco, coffee, cocoa); forestry and lumbering; manufacturing (cement, textiles, food processing, tobacco products, soap, sugar, palm oil); mining (petroleum, potash).
Foreign Trade: *Major exports*—wood, sugar, palm nuts, coffee, cocoa, peanuts, tobacco; *major imports*—machinery, vehicles.
Places of Interest: Mayombé Mountains; rain forest; Bateke Plateau; Brazzaville.

CONGO TODAY

Ruled by a Marxist military junta, Congo is a hot African country that straddles the equator. It is about the size of New Mexico both in area and population. Thick tropical forests cover much of the country. Income from offshore oil fields provides about 70% of the government's income. Congo's Atlantic coast port of Pointe-Noire is a major shipping center.

The majority of Congolese make their living by subsistence agriculture. But about 4 out of 10 people live in cities and towns, employed in businesses and services. As a result a higher percentage of the people can read and write and have a somewhat better standard of living than those in many other black countries of Africa.

A narrow, treeless coastal plain is bordered by the Mayombé Mountains, which run parallel to the coastline. To the north is a grassy plateau region, and to the east the Niari River valley.

The Congo (Zaire) and Ubangi rivers form the eastern border with Zaire. Gabon and Cameroon lie to the east and Central Africa to the north.

EARLY HISTORY

A large Congo empire reached the peak of its power during the 1500s. In the preceding century the Portuguese were the first European explorers of the coastal areas of the Congo, discovering the mouth of the Congo River in 1484.

Beginning in the 1600s French traders, interested in slaves and ivory, began to establish trading centers. By 1785 at least a hundred French ships a year visited the region.

Exploration of the interior was undertaken by the French beginning in the 1870s. The Congress of Berlin in 1885 recognized French claims to the area.

The colony was first called *French Congo* and was later renamed *Middle Congo.* In 1910 Middle Congo, Gabon, and Ubangi-Shari were combined as French Equatorial Africa. By 1956 Middle Congo had gained local autonomy, and in 1958 the colony's voters approved making it the autonomous *Congo Republic.*

INDEPENDENCE

On Aug. 15, 1960, the Congo Republic became fully independent. Fulbert Youlou was elected first president, with the support of all parties. On Aug. 13–15, 1963, Youlou was toppled by a revolt. In December 1963 a new constitution was approved. Alphonse Massamba-Débat was elected to a 5-year term as president.

On Aug. 3, 1968, four days after President Massamba-Débat had dissolved the national assembly, the army seized power. Massamba-Débat was forced to resign on Sept. 5.

Maj. Marien Ngouabi, head of the army, declared himself president on Jan. 1, 1969.

Ngouabi proclaimed a new constitution on Jan. 3, 1970, establishing a one-party Marxist communist state. The official name of the Congo was changed to the *People's Republic of the Congo.* A Marxist Congolese Labor Party (CLP) was created with Ngouabi as its leader.

An offshore oil field began production in 1972, contributing to an improvement in the economy. However, the fields were expected to be depleted by the late 1980s.

Ngouabi was slain on March 18, 1977, by assassins who escaped. Four days later the Roman Catholic archbishop of Brazzaville, Emile Cardinal Biayenda, was murdered in reprisal by members of Ngouabi's family.

The ruling military junta executed former President Massamba-Débat on March 25, 1977, after announcing that he had confessed to plotting Ngouabi's assassination. Sixteen other persons also were executed for complicity.

Col. Joachim Yhombi Opango, 38, was made president on April 13, 1977, by the military junta. Two days later he abolished the national assembly and made the military junta supreme.

Diplomatic relations between Congo and the United States were restored on June 7, 1977, after a 12-year break that had begun in 1965.

The Marxist military junta announced on Feb. 8, 1979, that Col. Denis Sassou-Nguessou had become head of state, replacing President Opango, who was imprisoned on charges of treason. The new leader previously had been minister of defense.

Congo experienced an economic boom in the 1980s with increased revenues from oil production. President Sassou-Nguessou encouraged U.S. oil companies and other foreign investors to aid in promoting "Marxist-capitalism."

The nation's 5-year plan for 1982–87 emphasized road building and industrial development.

QUICK QUIZ: What is the length of the St. Lawrence River? See page 187.

COSTA RICA

Official Name: Republic of Costa Rica.
Area: 19,575 square miles (50,700 sq. km.).
Population: 2,633,040.
Chief Cities: San José, capital, 236,747.
Largest Metropolitan Area: San José, 395,401.
Government: Democratic republic.
President: Luis Alberto Monge (since 1982).
Parliament: *Legislative Assembly,* 57 members.
U.S. Ambassador to Costa Rica: Curtin Winsor Jr.
Costa Rican Ambassador to U.S.: Soto Harrison.
Flag: Stripes top to bottom of blue, white, red, white, blue; national crest in white oval on red stripe.
Official Language: Spanish.
Ethnic Groups: Spanish descent and mestizo (97%), black (2%), Indian (1%).
Official Religion: Roman Catholicism (97%).
Leading Industries: Agriculture (coffee, bananas, cattle, cocoa, maize, pineapples, sugarcane, tobacco, rice, potatoes); food processing; manufacturing (textiles, clothing, footwear, cigarettes, furniture, construction materials); mining (gold, salt).
Foreign Trade: *Major exports*—coffee, bananas, beef, sugar, cocoa; *major imports*—paper products, machinery, iron and steel, pharmaceuticals, petroleum, chemicals, food, manufactured goods.
Places of Interest: Irazú Volcano; Arenal and Poas volcanoes; Osa Peninsula, national biological preserve; basalt balls near Palmar Monte; Valley of Orosi; Puntarenas. *In San José:* Canvillo Park; national museum; national palace; national theater.

COSTA RICA TODAY

About the size of West Virginia in area and population, Costa Rica has a more stable democratic government than other Central American countries.

In the early 1980s the economy floundered with high unemployment and inflation. Bananas and coffee remained the most important products, but other agricultural and manufacturing products account for more than 40% of the exports.

The development of bauxite mining and the manufacture of aluminum as well as an expanding tourist industry provide the best opportunities for future economic growth.

Costa Rica's traditional foreign policy has been one of nonintervention in the affairs of neighboring Central American countries. The country has been an active participant in the Organization of American States (OAS).

Many Americans retire to Costa Rica because the government collects no tax on the income of retirees and allows them to import automobiles and household goods duty free.

Costa Rica lies entirely within the tropical zone, but its climate, flora, and living conditions are tempered by the altitude.

The capital, San José, is located in a fertile central valley.

Most Costa Ricans live at altitudes of 3,000 to 4,000 feet. At these heights the climate is springlike throughout the year.

Costa Rica has several active volcanoes, two of which, Irazú, 11,260 ft., and Arenal, 5,092 ft., erupted in the 1960s.

Nicaragua lies to the north; Panama to the east.

HISTORY

The country was discovered and probably named by Columbus during his voyage of 1502. Spain ignored its small colony because of the scarcity of minerals, and the province grew slowly.

Costa Rica, along with the rest of Central America, declared independence from Spain without violence on Sept. 15, 1821. In 1824 it became a state in the Federal Republic of Central America. When that government failed in 1838, Costa Rica resumed independence.

An invasion led by the American military adventurer William Walker was put down in 1856 by a united Costa Rican people.

The 1890s saw the arrival of the great fruit companies and the construction of a railroad from the Caribbean to the city of San José.

Since independence Costa Rica's political life has been characterized by a series of smooth, democratic changes of government. Only for three periods (1870–82, 1917–19, and 1948) was the country ruled by dictatorship. Gen. Tomás Guardia seized power in 1870 and ruled by dictatorial means for a dozen years until his death in 1882.

A second military rule, established by Gen. Federico Tinoco in 1917, was overthrown by a popular revolt in 1919. After the restoration of democratic government in 1919, Costa Rica enjoyed a long period of political stability.

In 1948 the national assembly declared invalid the presidential election of Otilio Ulate. Col. José Figuéres Ferrer, a supporter of Ulate, led a revolt and temporarily seized power. He then turned over the presidency to Ulate in 1949.

Figuéres himself was chosen president in the 1953 election, serving until 1958. Figuéres staged an impressive political comeback in the February 1970 presidential election.

Daniel Oduber Quirós, candidate of the ruling National Liberation Party (PLN), was elected president on Feb. 3, 1974, with 42.5% of the popular vote.

Rodrigo Carazo Odio, leader of the opposition Unity Party, won a 4-year term as president in a national election on Feb. 5, 1978. He defeated the governing PLN candidate Luis Alberto Monge with 51% to 43% of the vote.

In 1979 the government permitted Nicaragua's Sandinista rebels to use Costa Rican border areas as bases in their successful civil war that overthrew Nicaragua's Somoza dictatorship. In addition Costa Rica provided camps for an estimated 100,000 Nicaraguan refugees.

Falling coffee prices in 1981–82 brought the worst economic crisis since the Great Depression. In 1981 the government defaulted on payments of its foreign debt of $3.2 billion.

Luis Alberto Monge, 56, a social democrat and former labor organizer, took office as president on May 8, 1982, after his National Liberation Party soundly defeated the governing Unity Party in national elections in February. He immediately imposed austerity measures to reduce imports and attempt to revive the economy.

CUBA

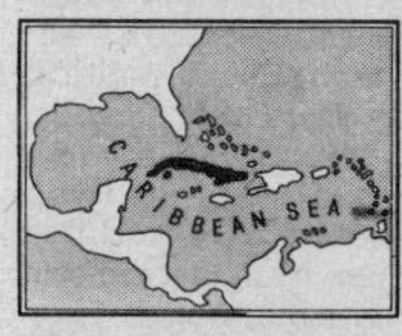

Official Name: Republic of Cuba.
Area: 44,218 square miles (114,524 sq. km.).
Population: 9,977,140.
Chief Cities: Havana (La Habana), capital, 1,008,500; Santiago de Cuba, 315,801; Camagüey, 221,826; Holguín, 151,938; Guantánamo, 148,833; Santa Clara, 146,651.
Largest Metropolitan Area: Havana, 1,861,442.
Government: One-party communist state.
President: Fidel Castro Ruz (since 1959).
Legislature: *Council of Ministers,* 23 members.
U.S. Diplomatic Representative to Cuba: Lyle Franklin Lane.
Cuban Diplomatic Representative to U.S.: Ramón Sánchez Parodi.
Flag: Alternate blue and white stripes; red triangle at hoist bears five-pointed white star.
Official Language: Spanish.
Ethnic Groups: Spanish descent (75%), mixed (13%), black (12%).
Main Religion: Roman Catholicism (85%).
Leading Industries: Agriculture (sugarcane, tobacco, bananas, pineapples, citrus fruits, cattle, rice, cotton, coffee, cocoa, vegetables); fishing; manufacturing (sugar refining, textiles, rum, tobacco products, oil refining, cement, machine parts); mining (nickel, iron, chromite, copper, manganese, clay, petroleum).
Foreign Trade: *Major exports*—sugar, inorganic chemicals, tobacco, nickel; *major imports*—crude petroleum, wheat, tractors, cotton fabrics, nonelectrical machinery.
Places of Interest: Morro Castle fortress in Havana Harbor; Guantánamo U.S. Naval Base; Bay of Pigs; Isle of Pines (Isle of Youth); Santa Maria Beach; Hanabanilla Mountain and Lake Resort.

CUBA TODAY

The communist government of this Caribbean island has survived for more than two decades largely because of billions of dollars of aid each year from the Soviet Union. It has alienated the governments of many South and Central American nations by supporting revolutionary terrorists and guerrillas. Thousands of Cuban troops have been sent to Africa to help communists control Ethiopia and Angola.

U.S. officials have accused Cuba of aiding the smuggling of drugs into the U.S. to pay for subversive activities in Latin America.

All power rests with President Fidel Castro. Radio and television speeches and mass meetings have replaced parliamentary deliberations. Political opponents are subject to summary trial by a revolutionary tribunal.

The Castro regime has made sweeping economic changes aimed at increasing Cuba's production and replacing capitalism with a controlled communist economy. All land, industries, and businesses have been placed under state control.

The largest island in the Caribbean Sea, Cuba lies 90 miles south of Key West, Fla. Jamaica is about 100 miles to the southeast. Windward Passage separates Cuba's eastern tip from Haiti.

The island is about 745 miles long and 60 miles wide. Its nearly 2,500-mile-long coast has many bays, inlets, coral reefs, and marshes.

There are three mountainous regions. The rugged Sierra Maestra in the easternmost province, Oriente, rise to 6,542 feet. The lower Sierra de los Organos are in the west. The Sierra de Trinidad stand in central Cuba. Tropical forests cover the mountains.

Several small islands lie off the coast. The largest is the Isle of Pines, renamed the Isle of Youth by Castro in 1978. The island is said to be the setting of Robert Louis Stevenson's *Treasure Island.*

Cuba's largest river, the Cauto, winds across the southeastern corner of the island.

The climate of Cuba remains hot throughout the year with an average of 70° F. in the winter and 81° F. in the summer. About 54 inches of rain fall annually.

SPANISH RULE

Discovered by Columbus on his first voyage to America in 1492, Cuba remained under Spanish rule until 1898. During the early colonial period Havana served as the last port visited by ships carrying treasure back to Spain.

In 1762 the British captured Havana. Their occupation lasted only a year.

In 1868 Carlos Manuel de Céspedes and other patriots issued a proclamation calling for revolt against Spain. The civil conflict lasted 10 years before being crushed.

Patriot and writer José Marti formed the Cuban Revolutionary Party while in exile in the United States. His call to arms in 1895 sparked a new civil war. He was killed in battle the same year, but the revolt continued.

INDEPENDENCE

After the U.S. battleship *Maine* was blown up in Havana harbor in 1898, the United States declared war on Spain. Spain was defeated by U.S. forces in the Spanish-American War, and Cuba became independent. Cuba's constitution was adopted in 1901. The island remained under U.S. occupation until 1902, when Tomás Estrada Palma became the republic's first president.

Cuba was ostensibly free, but the U.S. government had insisted that it ratify the Platt Amendment, giving the United States the right to intervene in Cuban affairs. In addition, U.S. companies owned or controlled about half of Cuba's economic resources.

In a 1903 treaty, Cuba gave the U.S. perpetual rights to a naval base at Guantánamo Bay.

In 1906 President Estrada Palma, unable to suppress a revolt by the opposition Liberal Party, called in U.S. troops. A U.S. military governor took over for the next two years and four months. U.S. Marines also intervened briefly in 1912 and 1917. Beginning in 1920 a U.S. supervisor was imposed on the Cuban government for several years.

The Platt Amendment was abrogated by President Franklin D. Roosevelt in 1934.

CUBA *(continued)*

With the post-World War I economic decline, Cuba fell victim to increasing unemployment and poverty. President Gerardo Machado y Morales, inaugurated in 1925, established dictatorial rule. He was ousted in 1933 by the democratic opposition, which in turn fell victim in 1934 to a coup led by Fulgencio Batista y Zaldívar, then an army sergeant. Batista ruled through puppet presidents until 1940, when he proclaimed a new constitution and was elected president. He was supported by the communists, to whom he gave control of the trade-union movement. His candidate lost the 1944 election. In 1952 Batista again seized power through an army coup. In 1953 a raid on an army barracks by rebels led by Fidel Castro resulted in about 100 deaths. Castro was captured, but he was released from prison in 1955 under a general amnesty and left Cuba.

COMMUNIST TAKEOVER OF CUBA

In December 1956 Castro launched an uprising. The rebellion spread. On Jan. 1, 1959, Batista fled the country.

Once in power, Castro failed to implement his promise to restore the democratic constitution. He made Cuba a police state, arresting thousands of opponents. Many Cubans fled to the United States. U.S.-owned property, valued at about $1.8 billion, was seized and nationalized in 1960.

The United States retaliated by halting purchases of Cuban sugar and beginning a trade boycott. On Jan. 3, 1961, the United States broke diplomatic relations.

On April 17, 1961, an invasion force of Cuban exiles, trained and equipped by the American CIA, landed at the Bay of Pigs with the intention of launching a rebellion against the Castro government. The invaders were quickly overwhelmed, and many were captured.

Castro announced on May 1, 1961, that Cuba would become a one-party communist state.

At the urging of the United States, the Organization of American States (OAS) voted in January 1962 by a slim majority to exclude Cuba from further participation in OAS activities.

The U.S. and the Soviet Union came close to war in 1962 when the Soviets secretly began to install atomic missiles on Cuban soil. Faced with a naval blockade of Cuba ordered by President Kennedy in October 1962, the Soviets removed their missiles.

Because of Cuba's support of a communist guerrilla movement in Venezuela, the OAS voted on July 26, 1964, to brand Cuba an aggressor, to break all diplomatic ties, and to suspend all trade except for food and medical supplies.

CUBA IN THE 1970s–1980s

The United States and Cuba on Feb. 15, 1973, signed an agreement to prevent the hijacking of planes and boats between the two countries. Between 1961 and 1973 some 85 airplanes had been hijacked in the U. S. and flown to Cuba.

The U.S. joined 15 Latin American nations on July 29, 1975, in voting to end the OAS sanctions against Cuba.

In the first nationwide vote since the revolution, 5.5 million Cubans went to the polls on Feb. 15, 1976, to give 97.7% approval to a new constitution formalizing Communist Party rule.

Castro said in 1977 that he had released all but 2,000 to 3,000 of the more than 15,000 political prisoners arrested in the early years of his regime.

The United States took several major steps toward restoration of normal relations with Cuba in 1977. In March restrictions were lifted on the spending of U.S. dollars by Americans in Cuba, and American tourists again began visiting the island on Caribbean cruises. On Sept. 1, 1977, Cuba and the United States exchanged diplomatic representatives, calling them "counselors" rather than ambassadors. Restoration of full diplomatic relations hinged on settlement of the U.S. claim of $1.8 billion for American property confiscated by Castro's government and of Cuba's demand that the U.S. withdraw from its naval base at Guantánamo Bay.

The U.S. State Department warned Cuba on Nov. 17, 1977, that its buildup of 27,000 troops in Angola, Ethiopia, and 14 other African countries "will have an impact on the pace and even the possibility of normalizing relations."

There were repeated angry exchanges between Castro and U.S. President Carter in 1978 over the use of Cuban troops in Africa. On May 13 Carter said U.S.-Cuban relations could not improve so long as Cuba disregarded human rights by holding thousands of political prisoners.

In August 1978 Cuba agreed to release 480 Cuban-Americans who had been prevented for 17 years from emigrating to the U.S.

Revelation in August 1979 that a brigade of 3,000 Soviet troops had been stationed in Cuba since 1962 brought U.S. protests.

Castro sought to enhance his leadership among developing nations by hosting a meeting of heads of state of about 60 countries in Cuba in 1979.

Disease struck Cuba's two most important export crops, sugar and tobacco, in 1980, causing an economic slump that increased unemployment and caused shortages in consumer goods.

In the first wage increase in 15 years, agricultural workers had their monthly pay raised to $115 on July 1, 1980.

To help relieve the bad economic conditions, Castro allowed about 126,000 persons to leave the country in 1980, most of whom made their way to the U.S.

In a gesture of friendship toward the United States, the Cuban government on Oct. 27, 1980, freed 33 American prisoners, five of whom were fugitives from U.S. criminal indictments.

The Cuban economy suffered in 1982 from a drop in world sugar prices to record lows. As a result, Castro's government was unable to meet payments on about $1.3 billion in foreign debts.

Demanding that Cuba stop supplying arms to the leftist government of Nicaragua and to guerrillas fighting in El Salvador, the U.S. tightened the economic screws by barring tourist and business travel to Cuba after May 15, 1982. This action cut off Cuba's main source of American currency.

U.S. relations with Cuba worsened in 1983 after U.S. troops landed on Grenada, defeating Cuban troops that supported the communist government of that island nation and ousting Cuban and Soviet diplomats. See page 29.

CYPRUS

Official Name: Republic of Cyprus.
Area: 3,572 square miles (9,251 sq. km.).
Population: 657,276.
Capital: Nicosia, 125,100.
Government: Republic.
President: Spyros Achilles Kyprianou (since 1977).
Legislature: *House of Representatives,* 50 members.
U.S. Ambassador to Cyprus: Raymond C. Ewing.
Cyprus Ambassador to U.S.: Andreas J. Jacovides.
Flag: White field with outline map of Cyprus in gold above crossed green olive branches.
Languages: Greek, Turkish, English.
Chief Ethnic Groups: Greek (80%), Turkish (18%).
Main Religions: Greek Orthodox (80%), Islam (18%).
Leading Industries: Agriculture (grapes, wheat, barley, citrus fruits, potatoes, vegetables); tourism; mining (asbestos, copper, iron, chromium); food processing (wine, olive oil); manufacturing (textiles, shoes, furniture).
Foreign Trade: *Major exports*—minerals, fruits, vegetables, nuts, wine, cheese, clothing; *major imports*—machinery, textiles, motor vehicles, petroleum products, medicines, food, consumer goods.
Places of Interest: National museum, Nicosia; Kourion museum and sanctuary, Episkopi; medieval castle, Kolossi; Temple of Aphrodite, Kouklia; archaeological sites at Larnaca, Episcopi, Paphos, Politico, and Kakopetria; Mt. Olympus; Tomb of St. Lazarus, Larnaca; beach resorts.

CYPRUS TODAY

Cyprus is a prosperous, sunny island in the Mediterranean about 44 miles south of Turkey and 64 miles west of Syria. Although Cyprus is about the size of Puerto Rico, it has only one-fifth as large a population.

The island has been divided into two separate states since 1974. Greek Cypriots rule 64% of the island as the government officially recognized by the U.S. and Britain. The northern 36% of the island is governed by Turkish Cypriots.

More than half the people make their living as farmers. Grapes, olives, oranges, lemons, and grapefruit are among the important products.

Over 500,000 tourists each year enjoy the warm climate and pleasant swimming beaches.

EARLY HISTORY

Cyprus was inhabited as long ago as 6000 B.C. By 2200 B.C. it was the major source of the ancient world's copper. About 1500 B.C. Greeks began to colonize the island. For centuries Cyprus was ruled variously by Egyptians, Assyrians, Persians, Greeks, Romans, and Byzantines. Christianity was brought by the Apostles Paul and Mark. King Richard I of England took the island from its Byzantine rulers in 1191. It was annexed by Venice in 1489 and fell under Ottoman Turkish rule in 1571.

The Congress of Berlin in 1878 placed Cyprus under Britain, which annexed the island in 1914 and made it a crown colony in 1925.

The Greek Cypriot movement for *enosis* (union with Greece) was resisted by the Turkish Cypriots and the British. It flared in violence in 1931 and again in 1954. In 1955 a Greek ex-army officer, Col. George Grivas, launched a terrorist campaign for enosis. The campaign intensified in 1956, when the British deported Greek Orthodox Archbishop Makarios III.

INDEPENDENCE AND CIVIL WAR

Britain granted independence to Cyprus on Aug. 16, 1960, with Archbishop Makarios as president.

In 1963 an attempt by Makarios to give the Greek Cypriots control of the government precipitated civil war. A UN peacekeeping force arrived in 1964 to keep Greeks and Turks apart.

Makarios began a third 5-year term as president on Feb. 8, 1973, after elections were canceled because no opposition candidate had registered. Grivas, leader of the forces calling for union with Greece, had ordered his followers to boycott the elections, as had the Turkish Cypriots.

The Cyprus national guard led by Greek army officers on July 15, 1974, overthrew Makarios, who escaped capture and fled to Malta. Five days later some 40,000 Turkish troops invaded Cyprus to protect Turkish Cypriots.

Amid fears of war between Greece and Turkey, the UN ordered a cease-fire on July 22, 1974. Fighting continued sporadically. About 180,000 Greeks had been driven from their homes.

On Dec. 7, 1974, President Makarios returned from his temporary exile and resumed control.

Antagonism between Greece and Turkey over Cyprus continued in 1975–76 to threaten disruption of the NATO military alliance. Greek Cypriots blamed the U.S. for the Turkish invasion.

Turkey proclaimed the Turkish-held northern part of Cyprus an autonomous state on Feb. 13, 1975. Rauf Denktash became its acting president. Denktash won the first presidential election held by the Turkish state on June 20, 1976.

Archbishop Makarios in 1976 rejected Turkish proposals for a federation of the separate Greek and Turkish states. He died on Aug. 3, 1977, and was succeeded as president by Spyros Kyprianou.

After about 1,500 Turkish troops were withdrawn from the island in May 1979, UN Secretary-General Kurt Waldheim succeeded in getting the nation's Greek and Turkish leaders to meet for discussions about settlement of their differences. But no results were achieved.

In a parliamentary election on May 24, 1981, communists won the largest number of votes, 32.8%. The pro-Western Democratic Rally received 31.9%. But the balance of power continued to be held by the centrist Democratic Party of President Kyprianou that won only 20%.

In alliance with the communist AKEL Party, Kyprianou won election to a five-year term as president on Feb. 13, 1983, with 56.54% of the vote.

Turkish Cypriots declared the northern part of the island an independent republic on Nov. 15, 1983. The UN Security Council adopted a resolution calling the act "legally invalid."

QUICK QUIZ: How many nuclear reactors generated power in 1983? See page 257.

CZECHOSLOVAKIA

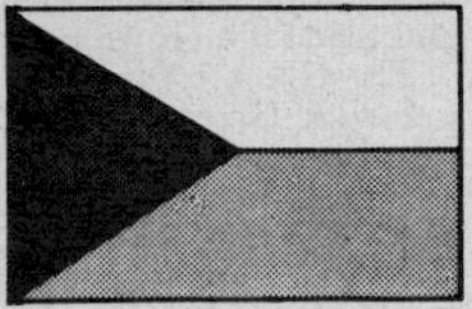

Official Name: Czechoslovak Socialist Republic.
Area: 49,371 square miles (127,869 sq. km.).
Population: 15,443,900.
Chief Cities: Praha (Prague), capital, 1,193,135; Bratislava, 381,476; Brno, 376,001; Ostrava, 326,716.
Government: Communist state.
Heads of Government: Gustav Husák, president (since 1975) and first secretary of the Czechoslovak Communist Party (since 1969); premier, Lubomír Strougal (since 1970).
Federal Assembly: *Chamber of the Nations, 75 Czechs and 75 Slovaks; Chamber of the People,* 200 members.
U.S. Ambassador to Czechoslovakia: William H. Luers.
Czechoslovakian Ambassador to U.S.: Stanislav Suja.
Flag: White over red stripe with blue triangle at hoist.
Official Languages: Czech and Slovak.
Chief Ethnic Groups: Czech (65%), Slovak (30%).
Main Religions: Roman Catholicism (77%), Protestantism (20%).
Leading Industries: Manufacturing (steel, coke, iron, cement, fertilizers, textiles, chemicals, vehicles, weapons); agriculture (potatoes, sugar beets, wheat, barley, oats, rye, corn, cattle, dairy products, hogs, sheep); mining (coal, iron ore, uranium, mercury, antimony, magnesium).
Foreign Trade: *Major exports*—motor vehicles, iron and steel, footwear, metalworking machinery, railway vehicles, coal; *major imports*—metal scrap, crude petroleum, agricultural machinery, cotton, motor vehicles.
Places of Interest: High Tatras Mountains; Carlsbad and Marienbad resorts; Primate's Castle in Bratislava; Spílberk Castle in Brno; Capuchin Monastery; Košice; Olomouc. *In Prague:* Hradčany Castle; Charles Bridge; St. Vitus Cathedral; Old Town Square.

CZECHOSLOVAKIA TODAY

Czechoslovakia is a communist industrial nation about the size of the state of New York.

Many of the country's problems stem from rivalry by its two major ethnic groups: a Czech majority and a Slovak minority.

Struggles between the Czechs and Slovaks contributed to political instability that enabled communists to take over after World War II.

Efforts by Czech leaders to liberalize the communist state in 1968 were smashed by an invasion of tanks and troops of the Soviet Union and its eastern European satellites.

One of the world's 10 leading steelmaking nations, Czechoslovakia supplies the Soviet Union and other communist nations with such products as machinery, chemicals, and textiles. However, about half the people are farmers.

GEOGRAPHY

Landlocked in central Europe, Czechoslovakia is bordered on the north by Poland, on the east by the Soviet Union, and on the south by Hungary and Austria. West Germany lies to the southwest, and East Germany to the northwest.

The Carpathian Mountains and the Sudeten range form a natural boundary in the north, as do the Erzgebirge (Ore Mountains) in the northwest and the Bohemian Forest in the west. From these northern heights the country slopes to an area of hills, lowlands, and plains.

The country's three main regions are Bohemia in the west, central Moravia, and eastern Slovakia.

The Moravian Gate cuts across the country from north to south, a natural line of travel along the Oder and Morava rivers. Other principal rivers are the Danube, the Elbe, and the Moldau (Vltava).

EARLY HISTORY

The first known settlers of the Czech lands of Bohemia and Moravia were Celts, followed by Germanic tribes about 100 B.C. Slovak settlers from the east displaced both the Celtic and Germanic peoples by the 400s A.D., and Slavs spread into Slovakia by the 500s. Christianity was introduced by the 800s.

The kingdom of Bohemia emerged under "Good King Wenceslas" in the 900s, but was soon absorbed into the Holy Roman Empire. The Thirty Years War (1618–48) began between the Catholic Hapsburg emperor and the Protestant Czech nobility.

As part of the Austrian Empire for 300 years until 1918, the country was superficially Germanized, with Czech used only as the language of the peasants. Between 1848 and 1914 the refusal of the Germans, particularly in Bohemia, to grant the Czechs equality contributed to the collapse of the Austro-Hungarian Empire in World War I.

FIRST CZECHOSLOVAK REPUBLIC

On Oct. 28, 1918, the first Czechoslovak Republic came into being. It included formerly Austrian Bohemia and Moravia, which were mainly Czech, and formerly Hungarian Slovakia. Ruthenia, which was mainly Ukrainian, was added in 1919. Tomáš G. Masaryk became the first president. Eduard Beneš succeeded him in 1935.

The first Czechoslovak Republic enjoyed the benefits of a liberal, democratic constitution, internationally respected leadership, and economic advantages because most of Austria-Hungary's industries were in territory incorporated into Czechoslovakia. However, ethnic-group differences resulted in serious problems.

The large German minority living in the Sudeten border districts of Bohemia demanded union with Hitler's Germany. In September 1938 the Munich Pact, signed by Czechoslovakia's allies Britain and France, awarded the Sudetenland to Germany. Czechoslovakia was not consulted.

In March 1939 Hitler occupied the rest of Bohemia as well as Moravia.

Beneš established a Czech government-in-exile in London during World War II.

COMMUNIST TAKEOVER

After Germany's defeat in 1945, Beneš returned to Prague and resumed the presidency of Czechoslovakia. In the 1946 elections the communists emerged as the strongest among many minority parties. Klement Gottwald, the communist leader, headed a coalition cabinet.

A Moscow-directed coup in February 1948 and the threat of Soviet invasion forced the democratic Prague government to surrender all power to the communist minority. Beneš resigned in June 1948. Gottwald became president.

The Soviet subjection of Czechoslovakia shocked the free world and is often regarded as the start of the Cold War. The event led to the formation of the Western NATO military alliance, which was soon matched by the Warsaw Pact of communist countries.

For the next two decades Czech life was marked by political purges, rigid censorship, concentration camps, and suppression of freedoms. In the late 1950s purge trials took the lives of many Czech leaders. Czechoslovakia's economy and living standards declined steadily.

Gottwald was succeeded as president in 1953 by Antonín Zapotocký. In 1957 Communist Party head Antonín Novotny took over the presidency.

PERIOD OF LIBERALIZATION

During the first half of 1968 old-guard Stalinists were replaced in the Czech government by younger, more moderate men. Antonín Novotny was deposed as secretary of the Communist Party and replaced by Alexander Dubček. Ludvík Svoboda became president. A new cabinet pledged liberal political and economic reforms.

The press, radio, theater, and all other media became increasingly outspoken, subjecting the past history of the regime to criticism.

In mid-July 1968 Dubček refused demands by Moscow and the Warsaw Pact nations that the new leaders of Czechoslovakia slow the pace of liberalization.

SOVIET INVASION

On Aug. 21, 1968, Soviet, East German, Polish, Hungarian, and Bulgarian troops, led by Soviet tanks and planes, suddenly invaded and occupied Czechoslovakia.

In mid-April 1969 Dubček was ousted as party secretary and succeeded by Gustav Husák.

As a warning to other communist states, the Kremlin announced the "Brezhnev doctrine," asserting the right of the Soviet Union to intervene forcibly in any "socialist" country it considered menaced from within or without.

Political purge trials continued to 1973. Supporters of the liberal Dubček were charged with antigovernment activities. The trials all ended with convictions and prison terms.

The first direct word from Dubček on the results of his ouster came in a letter smuggled into Italy in 1974 in which he described himself as "dishonored and defenseless."

When Dubček wrote a letter of complaint about being harassed by the secret police in 1975, he was denounced as a traitor by Husák, who said Dubček could leave Czechoslovakia if he did not like living there.

COMMUNIST CONSOLIDATION

Soviet communist leader Leonid I. Brezhnev visited Prague in February 1973 during the country's celebration of the 25th anniversary of communist rule. He declared that the situation in Czechoslovakia had "returned to normal" and that the role of the Communist Party had been "consolidated." As part of the celebration, President Svoboda declared an amnesty for the 50,000 persons who fled the country after the 1968 invasion. But few took the opportunity to return.

Through agreement with the Vatican, the first Roman Catholic bishops in 25 years were appointed in Czechoslovakia in 1973.

The Czechoslovakian federal assembly ratified a treaty with West Germany in July 1974, normalizing relations between the two nations for the first time since World War II.

When Svoboda became too ill to continue in office, Husák took over the title of president in 1975 while retaining his position as head of the Communist Party.

Early in January 1977 a group of Czech intellectuals calling themselves "Charter 77" issued a manifesto declaring that their nation's government was violating the human-rights covenants of the 1975 Helsinki agreement by depriving the people of freedom of speech, freedom of religion, and many other civil rights. The statement was signed by 242 prominent writers, artists, scientists, and others.

On Jan. 26, 1977, the U.S. State Department officially charged Czechoslovakia with violating the Helsinki pact by arresting and harassing human-rights activists.

The government in October 1977 tried and convicted three of the signers of Charter 77 and a fourth dissident for "antistate activities." Two were sent to jail for terms of 3 and 3½ years. The other two received suspended sentences.

The communist government moved to collectivize in 1978 the remaining privately owned farms, which had continued to provide about half the nation's fruits and vegetables.

When Brezhnev visited Czechoslovakia on May 30, 1978, police arrested many persons suspected of being human-rights activists to prevent any embarrassing demonstrations.

On Aug. 21, 1978, on the 10th anniversary of Soviet occupation, a few students gathered at the statue of St. Wenceslas in Prague. Riot police in armored trucks stood ready, but no large-scale demonstrations developed.

Reflecting worldwide inflation, the government raised prices in July 1979 by 50% to 100%.

Six Czech human-rights activists, including the playwright Vaclav Havel, were tried and convicted of subversion on Oct. 22–23, 1979. The six were given jail terms up to 5 years.

Apprehension about the actions of the Solidarity movement in neighboring Poland caused a new government crackdown in 1981 with arrests of dozens of Czech human-rights activists. Many were exiled.

The U.S., Britain, and France returned to Czechoslovakia in 1982 some 18.4 metric tons of gold that had been seized by the Nazis in World War II and then captured by the Allies. The gold was returned after the Czech government agreed to pay compensation for property nationalized after the communists took power.

QUICK QUIZ: Who was the first U.S. President to die in the White House? See page 350.

DENMARK

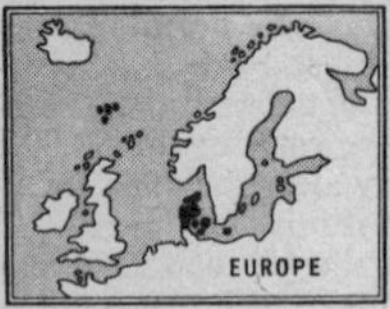

Official Name: Kingdom of Denmark.
Area: 16,629 square miles (43,069 sq. km.).
Population: 5,112,420.
Chief Cities: Kobenhaven (Copenhagen), capital, 502,416; Arhus, 246,111; Odense, 167,911; Alborg, 154,605; Frederiksberg, 101,899.
Largest Metropolitan Area: Copenhagen, 1,391,634.
Government: Constitutional monarchy.
Prime Minister: Poul Schluter (since 1982).
Queen: Margrethe II (since 1972).
Legislature: *Folketing,* 179 members.
U.S. Ambassador to Denmark: Terence A. Todman.
Danish Ambassador to U.S.: Otto Rose Borch.
Flag: White Latin cross on red field.
Official Language: Danish.
Principal Ethnic Group: Danes (98%).
Official Religion: Evangelical Lutheranism (97%).
Leading Industries: Manufacturing (electronic equipment, machinery, furniture, engines, chemicals, food processing, ships); tourism; agriculture (dairy products, hogs, poultry, cattle, barley, rye, potatoes, oats, wheat); fishing; mining (iron ore).
Foreign Trade: *Major exports*—manufactured goods, bacon, butter; *major imports*—machinery, motor vehicles, steel, petroleum.
Places of Interest: Silkeborg lakes; Kronborg (Hamlet's) Castle at Elsinore; Hans Christian Andersen's House at Odense; Egeskov Castle at Funen; Old Town Museum at Arhus; ancient town of Ribe; Ebeltoft. *In Copenhagen:* Little Mermaid statue; Christiansborg Palace; zoo; Tivoli amusement park.

DENMARK TODAY

Once the homeland of a Viking empire that stretched from England to Russia, Denmark today is a small industrial country in Europe. It ranks as one of the 10 leading fishing nations.

The Danes enjoy a high standard of living and have strong democratic traditions. More than half the people make their living from service industries, many in the tourist industry.

The government provides free medical care and extensive social-welfare benefits, supporting the programs with high taxation.

Denmark has many political parties reflecting a variety of political views. Usually no one party can command majority support.

The homeland of Denmark is slightly smaller than the combined areas of Vermont and New Hampshire, but the island of Greenland, an integral part of Denmark since 1953, is bigger than Alaska and Texas combined.

The country's only land connection with the European continent is its 42-mile southern boundary with West Germany.

On the north Denmark faces the Skagerrak. On the east are the Kattegat, the Sound, and the Baltic Sea. The North Sea lies to the west.

Denmark consists of the peninsula of Jutland and 483 neighboring islands, of which 97 are inhabited. The five largest islands are Fyn (Funen), Lolland, Bornholm, Falster, and Zealand (Sjaelland), where Copenhagen is located.

The countryside is predominantly rolling flatlands. The climate is moderate.

EARLY HISTORY

In the Viking Age (about A.D. 790–1030) Danish Vikings raided France and invaded England. Harold Bluetooth became a Christian in 960. He fell in battle (985) against his son Sweyn Forkbeard. Sweyn held parts of Norway and all of England. His son Canute the Great ruled over a huge northern empire that included England.

In 1397 Norway and Sweden joined Denmark in the Union of Kalmar under Danish Queen Margrethe I, who reigned from 1387 to 1412. A Swedish revolt in 1523 ended the union, but Norway remained united with Denmark until 1814. The Lutheran creed was adopted in 1536. In 1660 Frederik III established royal absolutism.

In the Napoleonic wars, Frederik VI allied with the French. By the Treaty of Kiel (1814) Denmark had to give up Norway to Sweden.

CONSTITUTIONAL MONARCHY

Under Frederik VII (1848–63) liberal trends brought domestic reforms. Absolutism was abolished. A liberal constitution was adopted in 1849.

An uprising in the duchies of Schleswig and Holstein led to two wars with Prussia in 1848–49 and 1864. At the conclusion of the last war, Denmark had to cede the duchies.

Denmark was neutral during World War I, but the nation's economy was disrupted by the Allied blockade. A plebiscite was held in 1920 in the northern parts of Schleswig, and the mainly Danish-speaking areas were returned to Denmark.

Nazi Germany invaded Denmark and occupied the country in 1940–45.

POSTWAR DENMARK

After World War II Denmark joined the United Nations, NATO, and the inter-Scandinavian Nordic Council.

The Social Democrats were ousted from the government by a centrist coalition in January 1968, but they returned to power in October 1971 with Jens Otto Krag as prime minister.

King Frederik IX died on Jan. 14, 1972. His eldest daughter was crowned the next day as Queen Margrethe II, the first woman to sit on the throne of Denmark in over five centuries.

Social Democrat Anker Jorgensen succeeded Krag as prime minister in October 1972.

Denmark's entry into the European Common Market on Jan 1, 1973, opened new opportunities for the expansion of the economy.

After parliamentary elections in December 1973, Poul Hartling, leader of the Liberal Party, formed a new minority government.

In an election on Jan. 9, 1975, the Social Democrats won and Jorgensen again became prime minister.

In a national referendum on Sept. 19, 1978, Danes approved a constitutional amendment lowering the voting age and the age to stand for parliament to 18.

Dependent on imports of petroleum, Denmark suffered in the 1970s and early 1980s from inflation, a growing foreign-trade deficit, and unemployment. The government's social programs caused a rising national debt.

Although unable to win a majority in parliamentary elections in 1977, 1979, and 1981, Jorgensen continued as prime minister, forming minority coalition cabinets. However, when parliament rejected his proposals for tough economic measures to bring inflation under control, he left office, resigning on Sept. 2, 1982.

Poul Schluter, 53, Denmark's first conservative prime minister in 81 years, was sworn in on Sept. 10, 1982, heading a coalition government.

Schluter's austerity program was narrowly approved by parliament on Oct. 16, 1982. It froze wages, ended pay raises linked to inflation, and cut social welfare and unemployment benefits.

DENMARK'S OVERSEAS AREAS

GREENLAND (Kâlatdlit-Numât)

Area: 840,000 square miles (2,175,600 sq. km.).
Population: 52,341.
Capital: Godthaab (Nuuk), 3,585.
Languages: Greenlandic (official) and Danish.

Greenland, the world's largest island (1,660 miles long, with a maximum width of 650 miles), is considered part of North America.

The ice cap that covers 84% of the island has an average thickness of nearly 5,000 feet, but may be over 14,000 feet thick in some areas.

Most Greenlanders are of mixed Eskimo and European ancestry.

The main industry is fishing.

Greenland was first colonized about A.D. 981 by Eric the Red. The early colonists died out in the 1400s when the climate turned colder. Modern colonization by Europeans was begun in 1721 by Hans Egede, a Norwegian missionary. Greenland became a possession of Denmark in 1380.

An offer to buy Greenland by U.S. Secretary of State James F. Byrnes in 1946 was rejected by Denmark. The U.S. maintains two air bases and several early-warning radar stations in Greenland.

Denmark granted self-government on May 1, 1979. Greenlandic (Eskimo) replaced Danish as the official language. Denmark retained control of foreign relations and continued to provide about $250 million in annual aid.

In a referendum on Feb. 23, 1982, Greenlanders voted 52% to 46% to withdraw from the European Common Market in order to be able to charge other nations for fishing rights.

FAEROE ISLANDS

Area: 540 square miles (1,399 sq. km.).
Population: 45,334.
Capital: Tórshavn, 10,726.

The Faeroe Islands lie in the Atlantic between Scotland's Shetland Islands and Iceland.

Seventeen of the 19 islands are inhabited. The capital, Tórshavn, is located on Streymoy, the largest island. The main industry of the Faeroes is fishing. The principal language is Faeroese.

Celts were the earliest known inhabitants, but in the 700s Norsemen settled the islands.

With Norway the Faeroes came under the Danish crown in 1380. The islands obtained home rule in 1948. The popularly elected parliament (the Lagting) meets in Tórshavn. Two Faeroese representatives sit in the Danish parliament.

DJIBOUTI

Official Name: Republic of Djibouti.
Area: 8,494 square miles (22,000 sq. km.).
Population: 321,253.
Capital: Djibouti, 62,000.
Government: One-party republic.
President: Hassan Gouled Aptidon (since 1977).
Legislature: *Assembly,* 65 deputies.
U.S. Ambassador to Djibouti: Alvin P. Adams Jr.
Djiboutian Ambassador to U.S.: Salah Hadji Farah Dirir.
Flag: Light green stripe over light blue with red star on white triangle.
Languages: Arabic (official), Somali, Afar, French.
Main Ethnic Groups: Issa (Somali; 45%), Afar (45%).
Religion: Islam.
Leading Industries: Service (port facilities, transportation, ship repairs); commerce; agriculture (cattle, sheep, goats, donkeys, dates); mining (salt); processing (hides, skins); handicrafts.
Foreign Trade (excluding transit shipments to and from Ethiopia): *Major exports*—hides, skins, cattle; *major imports*—food, textiles, consumer goods.
Places of Interest: Free-port shops in Djibouti; beach resorts; Lake Assal (512 feet below sea level).

DJIBOUTI TODAY

A little larger than Massachusetts, Djibouti is an East African country that was known as *French Somaliland* and later as *Afars and Issas* (the names of its two main tribes). It owes its existence as a nation largely to its location at the southern entrance to the Red Sea, making it an important stopping place for vessels traveling through the Suez Canal.

Most Djiboutians live in and around Djibouti, the port city and capital. They work mainly in service industries connected with the extensive shipping trade. The bulk of Ethiopia's exports and imports flow through the port.

Most of the country's land away from the coast is barren and desolate with little or no vegetation other than thorn bushes. Only about 10% of the land can provide pasture for livestock. Nomadic tribesmen lead poverty-stricken lives tending herds of goats, sheep, camels, and cattle.

Mountains near the northern coast of the Gulf of Tadjoura rise to a height of 5,426 feet.

The country has a hot climate with little rainfall. Temperatures average above 90°F. from May to October, often soaring above 110°F.

EARLY HISTORY

In early times Muslim Arabs and Persians established trading posts on the Gulf of Tadjoura. Camel caravans from Ethiopia brought gems, ostrich feathers, coffee, and slaves that were carried by ship to the Arab and Persian empires. The local people converted to Islam and were ruled by Muslim sultans.

QUICK QUIZ: How can a bill become law after it is vetoed by the President? See page 157.

DJIBOUTI *(continued)*

The French purchased from the local sultan an anchorage at Obock on the north coast of the Gulf of Tadjoura in 1862.

When the British claimed what is now northern Somalia in the 1880s, the French took possession of the area around the Gulf of Tadjoura, naming the colony French Somaliland in 1888.

Leonce Lagarde, the first governor of French Somaliland, began construction of Djibouti in 1888. The city quickly became a thriving seaport and was made the capital in 1892.

Completion of a 486-mile railroad between Djibouti and Addis Ababa on June 7, 1917, brought the area increased prosperity.

In World War II the colony was administered by the pro-Nazi Vichy government of France from 1940 to 1942. But an allied blockade of Djibouti forced the colony to come over to the side of the Free French.

STEPS TOWARD INDEPENDENCE

In a referendum in September 1958 the people voted by a narrow margin to accept the status of an overseas territory with representation in France's parliament.

When Somalia (former British and Italian Somalilands) became independent in 1960, agitation for joining French Somaliland to the new nation was begun by the Somalis. Subsequently, the French expelled thousands of Somalis from the territory of French Somaliland.

In a new referendum in March 1967 on the issue of independence, 60% of the voters chose to maintain dependency with France.

The name of the territory was changed on July 5, 1967, to the *French Territory of Afars and Issas.* The pro-French political party of the Afars won control of the territory's government in elections in 1963, 1968, and 1973 with their leader, Ali Aref Bourhan, chosen as president of the executive council.

The French government announced on Dec. 31, 1975, that it planned to grant Afars and Issas independence but would maintain troops in the country to protect French interests.

The people of the territory voted on May 8, 1977, in favor of independence. At the same time they elected a national assembly from a single list of 65 candidates that had previously been agreed to by the four main political parties.

INDEPENDENCE

Djibouti was granted its independence by France on June 27, 1977. Hassan Gouled Aptidon, leader of the Issas majority in the legislature, was chosen by his fellow representatives as the nation's first president.

Gouled declared the new nation would remain neutral in the undeclared war between its larger neighbors, Somalia and Ethiopia, both of which promised to respect Djibouti's independence.

About 30,000 refugees from the Somali-Ethiopian war and drought in 1979–80 increased hardship in poverty-stricken Djibouti.

Gouled was reelected president in June 1981, winning 84% of the vote as the sole candidate.

In October 1981 the national assembly voted to make Gouled's Popular Assembly for Progress the nation's only legal political party.

DOMINICA

Official Name: Commonwealth of Dominica.
Area: 290 square miles (751 sq. km.).
Population: 73,925.
Capital: Roseau, 16,000.
Government: Parliamentary republic.
Prime Minister: Eugenia Charles (since 1980).
President: Jenner Armour (since 1979).
Legislature: *House of Assembly,* 21 members.
U.S. Ambassador to Dominica: Milan D. Bish.
Ambassador to U.S.: Franklin Baron.
Flag: Dark green field with parrot on red disk in center; tricolor cross of yellow, white, and black bars.
Languages: English (official), French patois.
Chief Ethnic Group: Black
Principal Religion: Roman Catholicism.
Leading Industries: Agriculture (bananas, citrus fruits, coconuts, cocoa); manufacturing (food processing, floor mats); mining (pumice); tourism.
Foreign Trade: *Major exports*—bananas, citrus fruits, copra, cocoa; *major imports*—food, tobacco, clothing, machinery, petroleum.
Places of Interest: Black volcanic sand beach; scenic mountain rivers; tropical forests; hot mineral springs; Carib Indian reserve.

The Caribbean island of Dominica lies between the French islands of Guadeloupe to the north and Martinique to the south. Tourism and raising bananas and citrus fruits are the main industries.

Sparsely populated compared with most other Caribbean islands, mountainous Dominica has preserved much of its natural tropical beauty. The island is about 20 miles long and 16 miles wide. The highest point is Morne Diablotins (4,747 ft.).

The island was discovered on Nov. 3, 1493, by Christopher Columbus. Settlement began with French colonists in 1632. Dominica was taken by Britain in 1759, recaptured by France in 1778, and restored to Britain in 1783. It became self-governing on March 1, 1967.

Britain granted Dominica independence on Nov. 3, 1978, with Patrick R. John as the first prime minister. He was forced to resign after one person was killed and eight were wounded on May 29, 1979, when soldiers fired into a crowd demonstrating against restrictive labor legislation he had proposed.

Two hurricanes struck the island in 1979, leaving thousands homeless.

In the first national election since independence, on July 21, 1980, the Dominica Freedom Party won 17 of the 21 seats in parliament. Its leader, Eugenia Charles, 61, became prime minister—the first woman head of government in the Caribbean. In one of her first acts, she disbanded the nation's 99-man army.

About a dozen gunmen attempted to overthrow the government on Dec. 19, 1981, but were thwarted by loyal police. Five months later a court acquitted former Prime Minister John of plotting the attempted coup.

DOMINICAN REPUBLIC

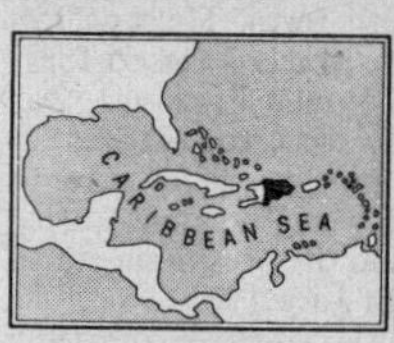

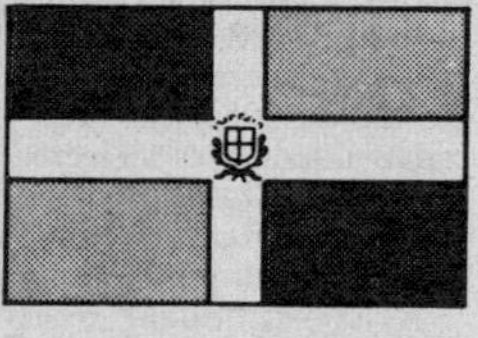

Official Name: Dominican Republic.
Area: 18,816 square miles (48,734 sq. km.).
Population: 6,001,540.
Chief Cities: Santo Domingo, the capital, 673,470; Santiago de los Caballeros, 155,000.
Largest Metropolitan Area: Santo Domingo, 817,645.
Government: Republic.
President: Salvador Jorge Blanco (since 1982).
National Congress: *Senate,* 27 members; *Chamber of Deputies,* 91 members.
U.S. Ambassador to Dom. Rep.: Robert L. Yost.
Dominican Republic Ambassador to U.S.: Carlos Despradel.
Flag: White cross bearing national coat of arms; two red and two blue quarters.
Languages: Spanish (official), French, English.
Ethnic Groups: Mulatto (73%), Spanish descent (16%), black (11%).
Official Religion: Roman Catholicism (97%).
Leading Industries: Agriculture (sugarcane, tobacco, vegetables, coffee, cocoa, bananas, rice, corn, cattle, poultry); food processing (sugar, molasses, rum); tourism; manufacturing (textiles, cement, bottles, paper, matches, tobacco products); mining (bauxite, gold, silver, iron ore, salt, gypsum).
Foreign Trade: *Major exports*—sugar, gold, silver, nickel, coffee, cacao, bauxite, tobacco, *major imports*—petroleum, iron and steel, machinery, chemical and pharmaceutical products, foodstuffs.
Places of Interest: *In Santo Domingo:* Basilica Santa Maria la Menor, with the Columbus Tomb and Cross; Alcázar de Colón, built by Columbus' son; viceregal museum; Tower of Homage; national capitol; Plaza de la Cultura.

DOMINICAN REPUBLIC TODAY

The Dominican Republic is a Caribbean island nation about twice the size of New Hampshire.

About 200,000 American visitors a year come to enjoy the nation's beaches and resorts.

Dominicans have a much lower standard of living than the people of nearby Puerto Rico. Most are farm workers. About a third of the people cannot read and write. Many Dominicans live close to starvation the year round.

Dependent on oil imports for its energy needs, the nation suffered in the 1970s and 1980s from high inflation and unemployment.

The Dominican Republic covers the eastern two-thirds of the island of Hispaniola. It has a 193-mile border on the west with Haiti. The Mona Passage separates it from Puerto Rico.

The climate is mildly tropical and humid. Temperatures range from 72° to 83° F., but the winters are colder in the mountain areas.

HISTORY

Columbus discovered the island in 1492, claimed it for Spain, and named it Las Española (Hispaniola). Santo Domingo, founded in 1496, was the first permanent European settlement in the Western Hemisphere.

In 1697 Spain was forced by the Treaty of Ryswick to cede to France the western third of the island now known as Haiti. France acquired the rest of Hispaniola in 1795.

With British aid the Dominicans revolted against French rule in 1809, proclaiming the first Dominican Republic. The 1814 Treaty of Paris returned the country to Spanish rule.

In 1822 it was overrun and annexed by Haiti.

Led by Juan Pablo Duarte, the Dominicans rebelled, drove out the Haitians, and once again proclaimed a republic on Feb. 27, 1844.

In 1870 the Dominicans approved a treaty that would have annexed the republic to the United States, but the U.S. Senate refused to ratify it.

In 1904 several foreign powers threatened to intervene to collect their debts. To forestall such a move, the U.S. in 1905 took over the administration of Dominican customs. In 1916 the U.S. occupied the republic and established a military government that ruled until 1924. The U.S. retained customs control until 1941.

From 1930 the Dominican Republic was governed by dictator Gen. Rafael Leonidas Trujillo Molina, until his assassination in 1961.

Joaquín Balaguer, a conservative, who had been appointed by Trujillo, continued to rule.

At the nation's first free elections in four decades, on Dec. 20, 1962, leftist Juan Bosch of the Dominican Revolutionary Party (PR) won the presidency. He took office in February 1963 but was overthrown seven months later by a military coup. A junta took control.

In 1965 civil war broke out as left-wing forces tried to restore Bosch to power. Fearing a communist takeover, U.S. President Johnson sent in 28,000 U.S. Marines in April. About 3,000 Dominicans were killed before the revolt was put down. The last U.S. troops were withdrawn in 1966.

Balaguer defeated Bosch in a presidential election in 1966. He was reelected in 1970 and 1974.

Antonio Guzmán Fernandez of the leftist Dominican Revolutionary Party defeated Balaguer in a presidential election on May 16, 1978.

The country was devastated on Aug. 31, 1979, by hurricane David that killed 1,380 persons, injured 4,000, and left 200,000 without homes. Property damage was estimated at $837 million.

In an election of May 16, 1982, Salvador Jorge Blanco, 56, of the governing Dominican Revoluntionary Party, defeated 13 other presidential candidates with a plurality of 46.7%.

President Guzmán, 71, who had not been a candidate in the election, killed himself on July 3, 1982, apparently because he learned that aides had betrayed him with extensive corruption that was only revealed in the weeks after his death. Vice President Jacobo Majluta Azar served as president until the inauguration of Jorge Blanco.

President Jorge Blanco in his inaugural address on Aug. 16, 1982, described the nation as "financially bankrupt," outlining a program of increased taxes and reduced government spending to bring under control unemployment (30%) and inflation (12%).

QUICK QUIZ: How many cases of polio were reported in the U.S. in 1982? See page 442.

ECUADOR

Official Name: Republic of Ecuador.
Area: 109,484 square miles (283,561 sq. km.).
Population: 9,491,020.
Chief Cities: Quito, capital, 807,665; Guayaquil, 1,116,280.
Government: Democratic republic.
President: Osvaldo Hurtado Larrea (since 1981).
Congress: 71 members.
Ambassador to U.S.: Ricardo Crespo Zaldumbide.
U.S. Ambassador to Ecuador: Samuel F. Hart.
Flag: Yellow, blue, and red stripes, with national coat of arms at center.
Languages: Spanish (official), Quechua, Jivaro.
Ethnic Groups: Mestizo (55%), Indian (25%), black (10%), Spanish descent (10%).
Official Religion: Roman Catholicism (95%).
Leading Industries: Agriculture (bananas, cocoa, coffee, sugarcane, cattle, dairying); mining (petroleum, gold, copper, sulfur, natural gas); manufacturing (textiles, cement, lumber, tobacco products, sugar); fishing.
Foreign Trade: *Major exports*—petroleum, bananas, coffee, cocoa, sugar, seafood; *major imports*—machinery, vehicles, paper, textiles, consumer goods.
Places of Interest: Andes Mountains; Panecillo; Cotopaxi Volcano; Equatorial Monument; Valley of Chillos; Guayas River; Galápagos Islands; Playas beach resort; Guayaquil; Quito.

ECUADOR TODAY

About the size of Nevada, Ecuador is an oil-exporting nation. Petroleum provides about two-thirds of its foreign-exchange income. However, most Ecuadoreans remain poor.

Ecuador is so named because the equator passes through the country. Colombia lies to the north and Peru to the south.

The Pacific coast region is a rich agricultural belt in which most of Ecuador's export crops are grown. Two parallel ranges of the Andes run north-south in mid-country.

About three-fourths of Ecuador is covered by forests. Climate varies with the region. Most of the northern coast is a wet, tropical forest. The southern coastal area, including Guayaquil, is cooled by the Peru Current.

HISTORY

The small tribes of Indians who first inhabited Ecuador were conquered near the end of the 1400s by Incas from the south. The Incas ruled until the Spanish conquest in 1534.

Ecuador won independence from Spain on May 24, 1822. It then became part of Simón Bolívar's Gran Colombia. When that confederation was dissolved in 1830, Ecuador became a separate, independent nation. The country's first and second presidents were conservative Juan José Flores and liberal Vicente Rocafuerte.

From 1830 to 1948 Ecuador had 62 presidents, dictators, and juntas.

More stable government began in 1948 with the election of Galo Plaza Lasso, the first freely elected president to serve his full term. He was followed in 1952 by liberal José María Velasco Ibarra. A conservative, Camilo Ponce Enríquez, was elected in 1956. In 1960 Velasco, running as an independent, was reelected, but he was forced into exile in 1961 by a leftist coup. Vice President Carlos Julio Arosemena Monroy held the presidency until ousted by a military junta in July 1963.

A constitutional assembly elected in 1966 chose a provisional president, Otto Arosemena Gómez. In June 1968 Velasco was again elected. He assumed dictatorial powers in June 1970. On Feb. 15, 1972, he was overthrown by a military junta, and Gen. Guillermo Rodríguez Lara assumed the presidency.

Ecuador became an oil-exporting nation with completion in August 1972 of a pipeline from oil fields in the Amazon basin across the Andes mountains to the Pacific coast.

The government took over 25% of the production of U.S.-owned oil companies in 1974.

A military junta headed by Vice Adm. Alfredo Poveda Burbano deposed Rodríguez in 1976.

Under pressure from the U.S. to restore political democracy, the military junta took steps in 1978 to establish civilian rule.

On Jan. 15, 1978, voters approved a new constitution that would give illiterates the vote.

The first presidential election in 10 years was held on July 16, 1978. The most popular politician, Assad Bucaram, a populist former mayor of Guayaquil, was not allowed to run by the military junta because he was born in Lebanon.

Jaime Roldós Aquilera, Bucaram's 38-year-old nephew-in-law, won a runoff presidential election on April 29, 1979, with 68% of the popular vote.

Democratic civilian rule was restored on Aug. 10, 1979, when the military junta turned the government over to Roldós.

Ecuadorian troops clashed with Peruvian forces along a disputed border in January 1981.

President Roldós, his wife, his defense minister, and six others were killed in a plane crash on May 24, 1981. He was succeeded by 41-year-old Vice President Osvaldo Hurtado Larrea, head of the moderate Popular Democracy Party.

Torrential rains in the winter of 1982–83 brought the worst flooding in 50 years, causing 30 deaths and $100 million in damage.

Lower oil prices in 1982–83 forced the government to take severe economic austerity measures that caused strikes and demonstrations.

General elections for president and members of Congress were called for Jan. 29, 1984.

GALAPAGOS ISLANDS

Area: 3,028 square miles (7,842 sq. km.).
Population: 6,000.
Capital: Baquerizo Moreno.

This Ecuadorian territory—60 volcanic islands in the Pacific about 650 miles west of Ecuador—was declared a national park in 1936 to protect its unique wildlife.

The British scientist Charles Darwin studied the animal life of the islands in 1835 as he was developing his theory of evolution.

The Galápagos tortoises, with a life span of over 200 years, are believed to be the world's longest-living animals.

EGYPT

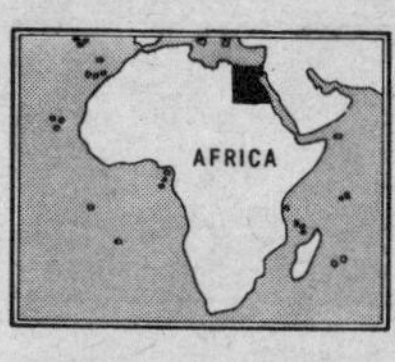

Official Name: Arab Republic of Egypt.
Area: 386,900 square miles (1,002,066 sq. km.).
Population: 45,948,200.
Chief Cities: Cairo, capital, 5,074,016; Alexandria, 2,317,705; Giza, 1,246,713; Shubra El-Khema, 393,700; El-Mahalla El-Kubra, 292,853; Tanta, 284,636; Port Said, 262,760; Mansura, 257,866.
Government: Strong-president parliamentary republic.
President: Hosni Mubarak (since 1981).
Legislature: *National Assembly,* 392 members.
U.S. Ambassador to Egypt: Nicholas A. Veliotes.
Egyptian Ambassador to U.S.: Ashraf A. Ghorbal.
Flag: Red, white, and black stripes, with gold hawk emblem in white stripe.
Languages: Arabic (official), English.
Ethnic Groups: Egyptian, Copt, Bedouin, Nubian.
Main Religions: Islam (85%), Coptic Christian (15%).
Leading Industries: Agriculture (cotton, rice, corn, wheat, barley, beans, sugarcane, poultry, cattle); manufacturing (textiles, chemicals, steel, machinery, electrical equipment, food processing); tourism; mining (iron ore, petroleum, uranium, phosphate).
Foreign Trade: *Major exports*—petroleum, cotton, textiles; *major imports*—machinery, wheat, transport equipment, iron and steel, tea.
Places of Interest: Pyramids and Sphinx at Giza; Nile River; Abu Simbel temples; Aswan Dam; Alexandria; Luxor and Karnak temples, Valley of the Kings, Queen Hatshepsut Temple, and Memmon Colossi at Luxor. *In Cairo:* Citadel; Mohammed Ali Mosque; Coptic churches.

EGYPT TODAY

Egypt is the largest and most powerful of the Arab countries of the Middle East. Petroleum is its major export, but it has limited oil reserves. With few other natural resources than its soil and electric power generated by the Nile River, Egypt relies on other nations for aid in developing its industries. The U.S. provides over $2 billion in military and economic aid annually.

Most Egyptians live a hand-to-mouth existence as farmers and livestock herdsmen. Only 4 of 10 Egyptians can read and write.

Antiquated farming methods prevent Egypt from growing enough food to feed its people.

Four wars with Israel in 1948–73 cost Egypt the lives of 100,000 soldiers and left it with huge foreign debts.

The northward-flowing Nile River divides eastern and western Egypt. The vast, rainless Sahara covers most of Egypt.

Lower Egypt in the north includes the Nile Delta, 8,500 square miles of rich cropland.

The productive portion of Upper Egypt in the south consists of a narrow strip of irrigated land about 20 miles wide that follows the course of the Nile River from Cairo to the Sudan.

Libya lies to the west, Sudan to the south, and Israel to the east.

EARLY HISTORY

The earliest Egyptian dynasty united the kingdoms of Upper and Lower Egypt about 3200 B.C. The great pyramids were built as tombs for kings about 2650–2500 B.C.

Egypt fell under Persian control in 525 B.C. Greek rule by the Macedonians under Alexander the Great and the Ptolemy dynasty followed. Then came Roman rule. The present culture of Egypt was basically set by the Muslim conquest of A.D. 640 that brought the Islamic religion.

After the breakup of the Abbasid empire in the 800s, Egypt was ruled by local caliphs and sultans.

The Ottoman Turks conquered Egypt in 1517 and held it for nearly 300 years.

Napoleon invaded Egypt in 1798. After French withdrawal, a soldier named Mohammed Ali seized power. Under his rule Egypt remained part of the Ottoman Empire.

France and Britain exerted increasing influence on Egyptian affairs after completion of the Suez Canal in 1869. A nationalist revolt in 1882 caused Britain to send troops to protect British interests. Britain made Egypt a protectorate in 1914.

INDEPENDENT MONARCHY

In 1922 Britain granted Egypt its independence under the former sultan as King Fuad I. However, Britain kept troops in Egypt to protect the Suez Canal.

Upon Fuad's death in 1936, his son Faruk succeeded him.

In World War II Egypt was a crucial base for the Allies in North Africa.

Egypt took the major part in the Arab-Israeli war of 1948. The defeat of Egyptian forces and corruption brought decline in royal prestige. In 1952 Faruk was exiled after a military coup.

ARAB REPUBLIC OF EGYPT

Egypt became a republic on June 18, 1953. Gen. Mohammed Naguib was the first president.

Col. Gamal Abdel Nasser ousted Naguib in November 1954, making himself dictator.

Nasser had his greatest success in the second Arab-Israeli War in 1956 when he turned a military defeat at the hands of Britain, France, and Israel into a political victory—retaining control of the Suez Canal, which he had seized.

In 1958 Nasser established a federation with Syria called the United Arab Republic (U.A.R.). The federation collapsed in 1961.

Israel attacked Egypt on June 5, 1967, in the third Arab-Israeli War, capturing the Sinai Peninsula.

During the next three years, Egypt rebuilt its armed forces with Soviet assistance.

Anwar al-Sadat became president after Nasser died of a heart attack on Sept. 28, 1970.

Relations with the Soviet Union became strained. In mid-1972 President Sadat ordered the withdrawal of Soviet military personnel.

Egypt and Syria attacked Israel in October 1973 in a fourth war, which lasted 18 days. Israel counterattacked, making new territorial gains.

U.S.-Egyptian diplomatic relations, broken in 1967, resumed in 1974.

In March 1976 Sadat abrogated the 1971 treaty

QUICK QUIZ: What are *cardiomyopathies*? See page 444.

EGYPT *(continued)*

of friendship and cooperation with the Soviet Union. The following month he canceled the Soviet navy's right to use Egyptian ports.

The development of new oil fields enabled Egypt to become an oil-exporting nation in 1977.

In a dramatic reversal of policy, Sadat initiated a drive to achieve peace in the Mideast by visiting Israel in November 1977. After months of negotiation, Sadat and Israeli Prime Minister Menachem Begin signed a peace treaty on March 26, 1979. Eighteen Arab League countries denounced the treaty, ordering an economic boycott of Egypt and breaking diplomatic relations with Sadat's government. Egyptians voted 99% approval of the treaty on April 19, 1979.

The first multiparty parliamentary elections since 1952 were held on June 7 and 14, 1979, with Sadat's party winning a landslide victory by capturing 330 of the 372 contested seats.

EGYPT IN THE 1980s

Egyptian voters in 1980 approved constitutional amendments Sadat had proposed. Among the amendments, Sadat was given an unlimited term as president, Islamic law was made the basis for legislation, and a multiparty political system was institutionalized.

The government announced in 1980 the discovery of the largest uranium deposit in the Middle East. Plans were made to develop three mines to exploit the deposits.

In February 1980 Egypt and Israel established formal diplomatic relations for the first time.

A $140 million tunnel under the Suez Canal was completed in 1980, connecting Cairo by highway to Israel and Jordan.

The U.S. and Egypt signed an agreement on June 29, 1981, enabling Egypt to acquire two nuclear reactors to generate electricity.

Throughout the first eight months of 1981 Egypt experienced a growing wave of riots and protests led by fanatic Muslims and Christian Copts. On Sept. 3, Sadat cracked down on the religious fundamentalists, arresting more than 1,500.

Charging that the Soviet Union had been inciting "sedition and conflicts among Egyptians" as part of a "hostile plot," Sadat on Sept. 15, 1981, expelled the Soviet ambassador, his staff, and over a thousand Soviet technicians.

Less than a month later, Sadat was assassinated on Oct. 6, 1981, while reviewing a military parade near Cairo. Five radical Muslims convicted of the crime were executed on April 15, 1982. Another 17 received prison terms.

Hosni Mubarak, former head of the air force chosen by Sadat as his vice president, succeeded to the presidency. He declared he would carry on Sadat's policies to seek peace in the Mideast.

In accordance with the 1979 peace treaty, Egypt reoccupied its Sinai region after withdrawal of Israelis on April 25, 1982.

Sadat's 57-year-old millionaire half-brother, Ismat, and his three sons were arrested on Oct. 29, 1982, charged with defrauding home buyers of millions of dollars. Found guilty in 1983, they were sentenced to a year in prison. Three cabinet ministers were forced to resign in 1983 because of disclosures at the Sadat trial.

EL SALVADOR

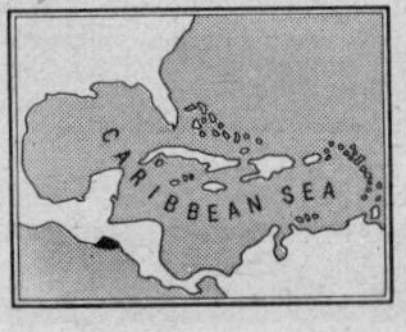

Official Name: Republic of El Salvador.
Area: 8,124 square miles (21,041 sq. km.).
Population: 4,748,720.
Capital: San Salvador, 335,930.
Heads of government: President of constituent assembly, Roberto d'Aubuisson (since 1982); provisional president, Alvaro Alfredo Magaña (since 1982).
Government: Provisional.
U.S. Ambassador to El Salvador: Thomas Pickering.
El Salvador Ambassador to U.S.: Ernesto Rivas-Gallont.
Flag: Blue, white, and blue stripes, with nation's coat of arms in center.
Official Language: Spanish.
Main Ethnic Groups: Mestizo (89%), Indian (10%).
Religion: Roman Catholicism (98%).
Leading Industries: Agriculture (coffee, cotton, corn, millet, sugarcane, henequen, beans, cattle, sheep, goats); mining (gold, silver); food processing; manufacturing (textiles, steel, cement, consumer goods); fishing (shrimp).
Foreign Trade: *Major exports*—coffee, cotton, sugar, shrimp, textiles; *major imports*—crude petroleum, iron and steel, fertilizers, medicines, paper.
Places of Interest: San Salvador; Izalco Volcano; El Tazumal ruins at Chalchuapa; Santa Ana Cathedral; Ilopango and Coatepeque lakes.

EL SALVADOR TODAY

About the size of Massachusetts, El Salvador is the most densely populated country in Central America. Coffee accounts for over half the country's exports.

El Salvador has been wracked by civil war since the 1970s, with thousands killed each year. More are killed in assassinations and massacres than in military fighting. Leftist guerrillas seeking to overthrow the government are supported by the pro-Soviet regime in Nicaragua. Trying to prevent a communist takeover, the U.S. provides substantial military and economic aid to El Salvador.

The majority of people work as farm laborers, barely earning food and shelter. Only about half of all Salvadorans can read and write.

Most of the people live in the central plateau between volcanic mountain ranges.

EARLY HISTORY

Before the Spanish conquest, El Salvador, called *Cuscatlán* (Land of Jewels), was the home of the Aztec-related Pipil Indians and probably an Aztec colony. Spanish conquistador Pedro de Alvarado conquered El Salvador in 1525.

Subsequently, Spain neglected the area in favor of wealthier territories.

San Salvador declared independence from Spain on Sept. 22, 1821, becoming part of the United Provinces of Central America.

INDEPENDENCE

The country became separately independent in 1838. Since then its history has been beset by internal strife and military dictatorship.

In the 1950s and 1960s some 300,000 Salvadorans migrated to sparsely populated neighboring Honduras in search of jobs and land. On July 14, 1969, El Salvador's army invaded Honduras. A cease-fire was arranged after five days, but the war took at least 1,000 lives and left bitter feelings on both sides. Troops of El Salvador and Honduras again clashed along their jungle frontier in July 1976.

The National Conciliation Party (PCN), controlled by the armed forces, governed from 1961.

Gen. Carlos Humberto Romero became president in 1977. Military officers overthrew him in a bloodless coup on Oct. 15, 1979. A military-civilian junta took control.

Under U.S. pressure to end dominance of the nation by wealthy families, the junta in 1980 announced a land-reform program and nationalization of banks and financial institutions.

The nation's leading spokesman for human rights, Roman Catholic Archbishop Oscar Arnulfo Romero, was slain by rightist terrorists while conducting mass on March 14, 1980. About 30 persons were killed when battling broke out at his funeral.

The junta appointed José Napoléon Duarte as president on Dec. 13, 1980—the first civilian head of government in 49 years.

On evidence that Cuba and Nicaragua were supplying arms to leftist guerrillas, the U.S. on Jan. 16, 1981, resumed sale of arms to El Salvador that had been suspended for three years. In mid-1981, 55 U.S. military trainers were sent to El Salvador, but with orders not to engage in combat.

In a free election supervised by international observers on March 28, 1982, voters chose members of a new constitutent assembly. Ultra-rightist Roberto d'Aubuisson became president of the constituent assembly. The assembly chose Alvaro Alfredo Magaţa, an economist, as the nation's provisional president.

The constituent assembly in May 1982 suspended the government's land-reform program.

The civil war continued to rage in 1983, with the number of deaths estimated at over 45,000 since 1979. Guerrillas assassinated the deputy commander of U.S. military advisers, Lt. Cmdr. Albert A. Schaufelberger 3d, on May 25, 1983.

In an effort to intimidate Nicaragua from continuing aid to the guerrillas, the U.S. carried out massive military exercises in 1983 with fleets off the country's Atlantic and Pacific coasts.

A government peace mission met with guerrilla leaders in Colombia in 1983, trying to get them to cease fighting and take part in elections scheduled for 1984. However, the leftists refused, claiming the elections would be rigged.

President Reagan asked for $206.3 million in aid for El Salvador in 1984. However, the U.S. Congress, angered by the Salvadoran government's disregard of human rights, restricted the amount of aid to be given if trials were not held for suspects in the 1980 slayings of 4 U.S. churchwomen and 2 U.S. labor organizers.

A presidential election was scheduled for March 25, 1984.

EQUATORIAL GUINEA

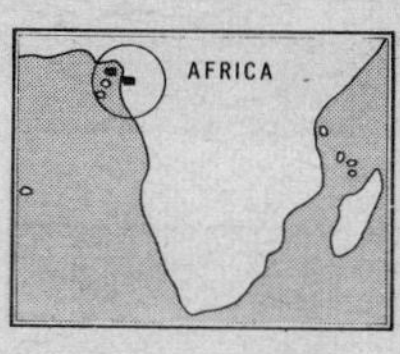

Official Name: Republic of Equatorial Guinea.
Area: 10,831 square miles (28,051 sq. km.).
Population: 268,265.
Capital: Malabo, 37,237.
Government: Military dictatorship.
President: Col. Teodoro Obiang Nguema (since 1979).
National Assembly: 60 members.
U.S. Ambassador: Hume A. Horan.
Equatorial Guinean Ambassador to U.S.: Florencio Maye Ela.
Flag: Green, white, and red stripes, with blue triangle at hoist; coat of arms centered in white stripe.
Languages: Spanish (official), tribal dialects.
Chief Ethnic Group: Fang (75%).
Main Religion: Roman Catholicism (60%).
Leading Industries: Agriculture (cocoa, coffee, bananas, oil palms, sisal, cattle, vegetables, fruits); forestry and lumbering; food processing.
Foreign Trade: *Major exports*—cocoa, coffee, wood; *major imports*—food, tobacco, textiles.
Places of Interest: Swimming beaches; tropical islets.

Somewhat smaller than Maryland, Equatorial Guinea has two widely separated provinces:

(1) The western Africa mainland area of Río Muni (10,046 sq. mi.) is a forested region with about three-fourths of the population.

(2) The island of Bioko (formerly Fernando Po) (785 sq. mi.) lies about 20 miles off the coast of Cameroon. It also controls the smaller island of Pagalu (formerly Annobíon), over 200 miles to the southwest.

The farms and plantations of the offshore island of Bioko grow cocoa. Exports of coffee and okume wood, used in the production of plywood, come from Río Muni.

Bioko, discovered by the Portuguese in 1471, was ceded to Spain in 1778. Río Muni was awarded to Spain by the Treaty of Berlin (1885).

The two areas were joined as the colony of Spanish Guinea.

On Oct. 12, 1968, Equatorial Guinea became independent with Francisco Macias Nguema as its first president. He established a one-party dictatorship. In 1976 he Africanized his name by changing it to *Masie* and dropped "Francisco."

During Masie's 11-year reign about one-third of the population, some 100,000, fled to exile, and an estimated 40,000 were tortured and killed.

Col. Teodoro Obiang Nguema, 33, a nephew of the dictator, overthrew Masie on Aug. 3, 1979. The former ruler was captured, tried for genocide, and executed with 6 aides on Sept. 29, 1979.

The U.S., which had broken diplomatic relations in 1976, resumed friendly relations in 1980.

Voters approved a new constitution on Aug. 15, 1982, to keep President Obiang in office until 1989. A one-party legislative assembly was elected on Aug. 28, 1983.

QUICK QUIZ: What nation was the first to win independence in the 1980s? See page 673.

ETHIOPIA

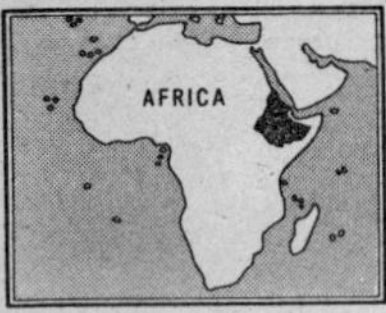

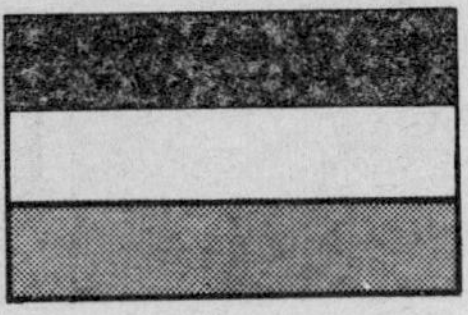

Official Name: Ethiopia.
Area: 471,778 square miles (1,221,900 sq. km.).
Population: 31,447,600.
Chief Cities: Addis Ababa, capital, 1,277,159; Asmara (Āsmera), 443,060.
Government: Communist military junta.
Dictator: Mengistu Haile Mariam (since 1977).
Flag: Green, yellow, and red stripes.
Languages: Amharic (official), Gallinya, Tigrinya, Arabic.
Main Ethnic Groups: Galla (40%), Amhara (25%), Tigre (12%), Sidama (9%), Somali (2%).
Leading Religions: Islam (40%), Ethiopian Orthodox Christian (35%), animism (20%).
Leading Industries: Agriculture (coffee, cotton, cattle, grains, fruits, vegetables, sugarcane); manufacturing (processing farm products, textiles, cement); mining (gold, platinum).
Foreign Trade: *Major exports*—coffee, cereal, oilseeds, hides and skins; *major imports*—petroleum products, vehicles, machinery, steel, textiles.
Places of Interest: Addis Ababa; Gondar fortress city; Lake Tana; Blue Nile Falls; Lalībela churches carved out of solid rock; ruins at Axum (Āksum); Asmara; Harar; Āwash Game Reserve; beach resorts.

ETHIOPIA TODAY

Ethiopia is a large but poor communist-ruled African country. Almost twice as large as Texas, Ethiopia has the third-largest African population after Nigeria and Egypt. Coffee accounts for more than half the nation's exports.

About 6,000 Soviet and 12,000 Cuban troops aid the government in fighting rebels.

Ethiopians are divided among more than 40 different tribes. Most are farmers or cattle-raising herdsmen who lead primitive lives unaffected by modern technology. They have a life expectancy of only 40 years.

Ethiopia is a land of geographical contrasts. Snow-capped Ras Dashan, the highest mountain, rises to 15,158 feet. The Great Rift Valley slices through the plateau region that makes up about two-thirds of the land. Lake Tana is the headwater of the Blue Nile River.

The Red Sea lies to the north, Djibouti and Somalia to the east, Kenya to the south, and Sudan to the west.

EARLY HISTORY

Menelik, the legendary first son of Solomon and the Queen of Sheba, is said to have founded the Ethiopian empire about 1000 B.C. Semitic tribes from Arabia arrived in the 900s to 600s B.C. Christianity was introduced in the 300s A.D.

About A.D. 1260 a new Ethiopian dynasty came to power that allegedly returned the throne to the line of Solomon. By 1855 authority was centralized under Emperor Theodore II.

Menelik II became emperor of Ethiopia in 1889. Italy's army invaded the country in 1895 but was defeated the next year at Aduwa.

Ras Tafari Makonnen, a favorite grandnephew of Menelik II, had Menelik's daughter Judith crowned empress in 1916 with himself as regent.

On the death of the empress in 1930, Ras Tafari became emperor as Haile Selassie I.

In 1935 the Italians invaded and conquered the country, forcing the emperor to flee to Britain in 1936. With British help in World War II, Haile Selassie regained his throne in 1941.

Ethiopia obtained its Red Sea coastline in 1952 when Eritrea, with UN approval, federated with Ethiopia. Eritrea became a province in 1962, but at the same time Eritrean nationalists began a civil war for independence.

A drought in the Tigre and Wallo regions caused 100,000 to 500,000 Ethiopians to die of starvation in 1973–74.

REVOLUTIONARY ETHIOPIA

On June 29, 1974, Ethiopian troops seized control of the government, declaring a "war on feudalism." They arrested 200 former cabinet members and advisers to the emperor.

The army deposed Haile Selassie on Sept. 12, 1974, ending his 58 years of rule. He died a prisoner in 1975. The junta officially abolished the Ethiopian monarchy on March 21, 1975.

A 120-man military committee known as the *Dergue* took power, headed by Lt. Gen. Aman Michael Andom. General Aman, an Eritrean, was himself arrested and killed by the junta on Nov. 24, 1974. On the same day 59 nobles and former officials were executed, including two former premiers. Leadership of the junta was taken over by Gen. Teferi Bante as chairman.

The communist military rulers announced on April 21, 1976, the establishment of a commission to prepare the way for formation of a Soviet-style "People's Democratic Republic."

Chief of state Gen. Teferi Bante was too slow on the draw on Feb. 3, 1977, when a shoot-out developed at a meeting of the military junta. When the smoke cleared, Teferi and 10 other junta members were dead. Lt. Col. Mengistu Haile Mariam emerged as dictator.

A reign of terror inspired by Mengistu swept Ethiopia in 1977–78. An estimated 5,000 persons were killed.

Ethiopia expelled 300 U.S. officials in April 1977 and closed U.S. aid agencies. Western news correspondents also were expelled.

Full-scale war developed with Somalia in 1977 as Somalis sought to take the southeastern Ogaden region from Ethiopia. On Sept. 14, 1977, the Somalis captured the Ethiopian city of Jijiga, about 100 miles from the Somali border.

But in 1978, with some $1 billion in Soviet arms flown in by airlift, with about 16,000 Cuban troops, and with a Soviet general and 1,500 Soviet "military advisers," the Ethiopians succeeded in driving the Somalis back and recapturing Jijiga on March 5. Fighting with Somali guerrillas in the Ogaden continued intermittently in 1979–82.

In the northeast, an estimated 100,000 Ethiopian troops launched a counteroffensive in May 1978 against Eritrean rebels supplied by Arab nations. On July 27 Ethiopia broke the 10-month siege by the rebels of the major city of Asmara. In August the Ethiopian government announced that 33,000 of its troops had been killed or wounded fighting the Eritreans.

The government reported nine assassination attempts on the life of Mengistu in 1978. Many members of the ruling military junta were executed.

Mengistu flew to Moscow in 1978, where on Nov. 20 he signed a 20-year treaty of friendship with the Soviet Union.

The U.S. recalled its ambassador in 1980 at the request of the Mengistu government.

Amnesty International estimated in 1981 that from 10,000 to 40,000 political prisoners remained in Ethiopia's jails.

Ethiopia had one of the worst droughts in its history in 1983. An estimated 1 million persons faced starvation. In July the U.S. increased emergency food aid to Ethiopia from $2.3 million to $5.3 million.

The 21-year-old civil war in Eritrea continued in 1983 with rebels claiming the killing of 1,300 Ethiopian soldiers in August.

FIJI

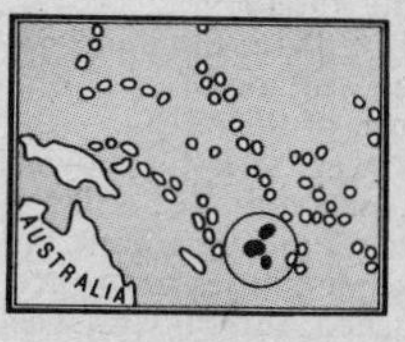

Official Name: Dominion of Fiji.
Area: 7,056 square miles (18,274 sq. km.).
Population: 678,888.
Capital: Suva, 63,628.
Government: Parliamentary democracy.
Prime Minister: Ratu Sir Kamisese K.T. Mara (since 1970).
Governor-General: Ratu Sir George Cakobau (since 1973).
Parliament: *Senate,* 22 members; *House of Representatives,* 52 members.
U.S. Ambassador to Fiji: Fred J. Eckert.
Fijian Ambassador to U.S.: Ratu Jone Filipe Radrodro.
Flag: Azure blue with Fiji shield centered on right; Union Jack in upper hoist quarter.
Languages: English (official), Fijian, Hindustani.
Main Ethnic Groups: Indian (50%), Fijian (45%).
Religions: Christianity (41%), Hinduism (35%), Islam (12%).
Leading Industries: Agriculture (sugarcane, coconuts, rice, bananas, cocoa, tobacco, fruits, vegetables, poultry); mining (gold); tourism; food processing; forestry and lumbering; fishing; manufacturing (cement, consumer goods).
Foreign Trade: *Major exports*—sugar, coconut products, gold; *major imports*—machinery, manufactured goods, foodstuffs.
Places of Interest: Beach resorts; native villages; volcanic islands. *In Suva:* Fiji Museum, Botanical Gardens; University of the South Pacific.

FIJI TODAY

The South Pacific nation of Fiji has many economic problems that stem from poor roads, lack of cheap electric power, the difficulties of farmers obtaining land, and the lack of technicians and managers for industry. Asian Indians make up a majority of the population.

Fiji's economy depends on four principal industries—sugar, copra, gold mining, and tourism.

Sugarcane, the main crop, is almost entirely raised by Asian Indian farmers, descendants of plantation laborers imported in the 1870s.

Industrial development and tourism are becoming increasingly important. Many new hotels have been built. Fiji is an important port of call for cruise ships. More than 130,000 tourists visit each year.

The native Fijians, a mixture of Melanesians and Polynesians, own about 83% of the land, which is held in trust for them by a government agency. The protective land-tenure system has limited development. Asian Indians can lease the land only for periods of 10 years at a time.

About 100 of Fiji's 844 islands are inhabited. The two main islands are Viti Levu (4,011 sq. mi.) and Vanua Levu (2,137 sq. mi.). Suva, the capital, is located on Viti Levu.

Most of Fiji's larger islands are mountainous and volcanic, with rugged, craggy interiors. Mount Victoria, on Viti Levu, is the highest mountain (about 4,300 feet). Fertile river deltas thick with mangroves intersect the coastal plains. Most of the smaller islands are of limestone and coral, their cliffs rising steeply to flat tops with little vegetation. The climate is warm and humid. A 300-mile arc of coral, the Great Sea Reef, protects the western archipelago.

EARLY HISTORY

Discovered by the Dutch explorer Abel Tasman in 1643, the Fiji islands were visited by British Capt. James Cook in 1774. Later, trading vessels came for sandalwood.

For many years the region was known as the "Cannibal Islands" because of the reputation of the Fijians as fearsome man-eaters.

Tribal wars for island supremacy were climaxed in 1855 by the victory of the chief of Bau, with the help of neighboring Tonga.

Fiji remained under Tonga's domination for the next 20 years.

Attempts at confederation failed, and tribal chiefs asked the British to intervene. From 1874 British governors administered the islands.

Local government was introduced in 1876.

INDEPENDENCE

Britain granted Fiji independence on Oct. 10, 1970—the 96th anniversary of the cession of the islands to Queen Victoria. Ratu Sir Kamisese K.T. Mara became the newly independent nation's first prime minister.

The country's two main political parties are the Alliance Party, which has governed since 1967, and the opposition National Federation Party (NFP), made up largely of Asian Indians.

Fiji sent half of its army, 500 men, to Lebanon in 1978 as part of the UN peace-keeping force in that country.

Mara's governing Alliance Party again won a general election in July 1982, but with a majority reduced to 28 seats in the lower house.

One of the few nations without broadcast TV, the government began in 1982 to provide community centers with equipment to show videotaped programs.

QUICK QUIZ: What is the name of the U.S. ambassador to the United Nations? See page 422.

FINLAND

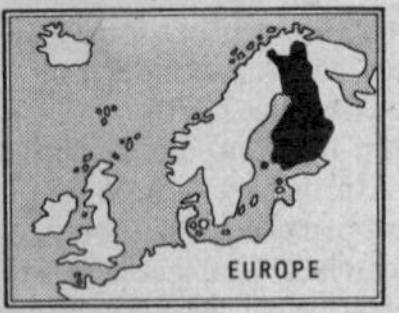

Official Name: Republic of Finland.
Area: 130,120 square miles (337,009 sq. km.).
Population: 4,856,700.
Chief Cities: Helsinki, capital, 484,311; Tampere, 165,701; Turku, 164,245; Espoo, 131,735.
Largest Metropolitan Area: Helsinki, 888,970.
Government: Multiparty parliamentary democracy.
President: Mauno Koivisto (since 1982).
Prime Minister: Kalevi Sorsa (since 1982).
Parliament: 200 members.
U.S. Ambassador to Finland: Keith Foote Nyborg.
Finnish Ambassador to U.S.: Richard Bertil Muller.
Flag: Light blue cross on a white field.
Official Languages: Finnish, Swedish.
Ethnic Groups: Finnish (94%), Swedish (6%).
Main Religions: Lutheran (97%), Russian Orthodox (1%).
Leading Industries: Manufacturing (paper, furniture, machinery, electrical products, vehicles, chemicals, textiles, ships, ceramics, furs); forestry and lumbering; agriculture (dairy products, poultry, cattle, wheat, rye, potatoes); mining (copper, zinc, iron).
Foreign Trade: *Major exports*—paper, wood, machinery, ships, chemicals, furs; *major imports*—petroleum, machinery, electronics, food, aircraft.
Places of Interest: *In Helsinki:* Temple Square underground church, Mannerheim's house, cathedral, Finlandia Hall, Suomenlinna island fortress. *In Järvenpää:* Jean Sibelius' house. *In Vuokatti:* Kainuu Nature and Play Park. Savonlinna Opera Festival in July; inland waterway cruises; Lapland.

FINLAND TODAY

Somewhat smaller than Montana, Finland lies northwest of the Soviet Union. After having fought three wars with its huge neighbor in this century, Finland today walks a tightrope of neutrality to preserve its democratic freedom.

Finland is one of the world's leading producers of newsprint. Like most industrialized nations of the West, Finland has struggled in the 1970–80s to cope with the problems of inflation.

About one-third its hardworking people live in cities, making their living from manufacturing and service industries. The others live in small towns or on farms. The people enjoy a much higher standard of living than that of the neighboring Soviet Union. Finland has no illiteracy.

The U.S. maintains an exchange program with Finland financed in part from a trust fund established in 1976 from Finland's final repayment of its post-World War I debt to the U.S.

GEOGRAPHY AND CLIMATE

More than 60,000 lakes dot Finland's forested landscape. Northern Finland above the Arctic Circle forms part of Lapland. It has many low mountains. In the central and southern regions the land is mainly low-lying and undulating.

July temperatures in Helsinki rarely go above 75° F. In February, winter temperatures range from 12° F. to –30° F.

Norway lies to the north, Sweden and the Gulf of Bothnia to the west, the Gulf of Finland and the Baltic Sea to the south, and the Soviet Union to the east.

EARLY HISTORY

The Finns' ancestors came into the land from the south through Estonia and Russia about 2,000 years ago.

By the 700s the Finns had taken the country from the Lapps.

From the 1100s Sweden controlled the region. In 1809 Czar Alexander I joined Finland to the Russian Empire as an autonomous grand duchy. In 1863 the Finnish legislature met for the first time since the Russian annexation.

INDEPENDENCE

During Russia's communist revolution the Finns declared their independence on Dec. 6, 1917. After a war of independence Finland adopted a republican constitution on July 17, 1919.

The Soviet Union invaded Finland in 1939–40. The Finns put up stiff resistance, but were forced to cede one-tenth of their land.

Finland began a second war with the Soviet Union in June 1941. The Soviets mounted a fierce offensive in 1944 that made Finland accept an armistice in September. The boundaries and peace terms of 1940 were reestablished, and Finland was forced to pay huge war reparations.

A friendship treaty with the Soviet Union in 1948 accepted the principle of Finnish neutrality, but provided for Soviet military assistance if Finland is attacked.

Under the leadership of Presidents J. K. Paasikivi (1944–56) and Urho Kekkonen (1956–81), Finland pursued a policy of cooperation with the Soviet Union as well as friendship with the West.

Parliament in 1973 approved an agreement for free trade in industrial products with the Common Market nations. In 1974 free-trade agreements also were made with Bulgaria and Hungary.

In parliamentary elections on March 18–19, 1979, voters shifted to the right as the largest party, the Social Democrats, lost 2 seats for a total of 52. The Conservative Party gained 12 seats for a total of 47, making it the second strongest. The remaining 101 seats were split among smaller parties. Women candidates won 26% of the seats.

Social Democrat Mauno Koivisto, president of the Bank of Finland, became prime minister on May 26, 1979, heading a left-center cabinet.

The nation experienced an economic boom in 1979–80 with foreign trade expanding by 21% during the two-year period.

Prime Minister Koivisto became acting president on Sept. 11, 1981, when 81-year-old President Kekkonen became ill.

The 57-year-old Kovisto easily won a presidential election in 1982.

Kalevi Sorsa, 51, also a Social Democrat, succeeded Kovisto as prime minister.

Sorsa's centrist coalition government increased its parliamentary majority in a national election on March 20–21, 1983.

FRANCE

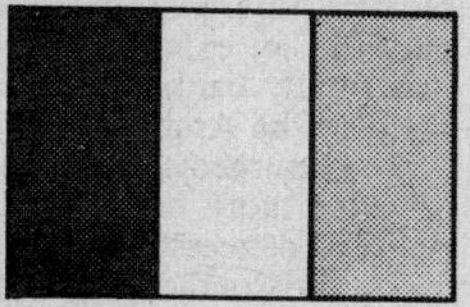

Official Name: French Republic.
Area: 211,208 square miles (547,026 sq. km.).
Population: 54,741,500.
Chief Cities: Paris, capital, 2,317,227; Marseille, 914,356; Lyon, 462,841; Toulouse, 383,176; Nice, 346,620; Nantes, 263,689; Strasbourg, 257,303; Bordeaux, 226,281; Saint-Étienne, 221,775.
Largest Metropolitan Area: Paris, 8,612,531.
Government: Presidential-parliamentary democracy.
President: François Mitterrand (since 1981).
Prime Minister: Pierre Mauroy (since 1981).
Parliament: *Senate,* 283 members; *National Assembly,* 491 members.
U.S. Ambassador to France: Arthur A. Hartman.
French Ambassador to U.S.: Bernard Vernier-Palliez.
Flag: Tricolor of blue, white, and red bars.
Official Language: French.
Main Religions: Roman Catholicism (90%), Islam (4%), Protestantism (2%), Judaism (1%).
Leading Industries: Manufacturing (steel, paper, electricity, aluminum, cement, automobiles, aircraft, chemicals, textiles, perfume, furniture); food processing; tourism; construction; agriculture (cattle, sheep, dairy products, poultry, hogs, sugar beets, corn, wheat, oats, barley, potatoes, grapes, fruits, vegetables); mining (iron ore, bauxite, uranium, salt, coal, natural gas, petroleum); fishing.
Foreign Trade: *Major exports*—automobiles, iron and steel, alcoholic beverages, petroleum products, clothing; *major imports*—crude petroleum, fruits, office machines, chemicals, copper.
Places of Interest: Angoulême; Avignon; Bourges; Brittany peninsula; Carcassonne; Chartres; the château country (Loire Valley); Clermont-Ferrand; Colmar; Dijon; Grasse; Grenoble; Nîmes; Pau; Rheims; the Riviera; Rouen; Strasbourg; Vienne. *In Paris:* Nôtre-Dame, Ste. Chapelle, the Madeleine, Tuileries gardens, the Louvre, Arc de Triomphe, Montmartre, Sorbonne, Luxembourg Palace and Gardens, Hôtel des Invalides, Opéra, Panthéon, Eiffel Tower. *Near Paris:* Fontainebleau, Versailles.

FRANCE TODAY

About a third larger than California, France has more land than any other nation in western Europe. However, France ranks fourth in population after West Germany, Italy, and Britain.

France is a leading producer of bauxite, cement, electric power, steel, and uranium.

For hundreds of years France fought wars with Germany, Britain, Austria, and Italy to establish itself as a world power. With the rise of the United States and the Soviet Union as superpowers, France has had difficulty reconciling itself to a secondary role in world politics.

To enhance its status and military independence, France developed its own atomic weapons. Like China, France test-explodes them in the atmosphere in defiance of world opinion.

Although France granted independence in the past quarter of a century to most of its former colonies, many of these new nations continued as members of the French Community. This organization preserves use of the French franc as its money and establishes economic and military links. France also maintains control over a scattering of its former colonial possessions as overseas departments and territories, described at the end of this article.

France is a highly industrialized nation. But about half its people continue to live on farms or in rural villages. With a long tradition of democracy and freedom, the people take a vigorous part in their government.

GEOGRAPHY AND CLIMATE

France is bordered on the north by Belgium, Luxembourg, and West Germany; on the east by Switzerland and Italy; and on the south by Monaco, Spain, and Andorra.

The land is varied and rich. In the southwest the Pyrenees rise along the Spanish border. In the east are the rugged peaks of the Alps and the Jura Mountains, and the wooded mountains of the Vosges range and the Ardennes plateau.

Four major river systems water the country. The Seine rises in the Plateau de Langres and flows northwest through the Paris Basin to the English Channel. The Loire, flowing from the Massif Central, courses westward to the Atlantic. The Garonne runs northwest from the Pyrenees to the Atlantic estuary of the Gironde. The Rhone-Saône system flows from the Alps into the Mediterranean. The Rhine River runs along the Franco-German frontier.

The country has four distinct climatic regions. The dry Mediterranean south has hot summers and mild winters. The central and eastern uplands are moist and seasonably varied. The oceanic west and northwest have cool temperatures and considerable rainfall. The mountainous regions in the southwest and southeast have cold winters, often with heavy snowstorms.

EARLY HISTORY

France was a crossroads of migrant agricultural peoples for hundreds of years. Conquering Celtic invaders brought a degree of order among the quarreling inhabitants, imposed their language to some extent, and gave the area the name *Gaul.*

Greek settlers began colonizing southern France about 600 B.C.

Roman armies in the 100s B.C. conquered part of Gaul. Julius Caesar subjugated the rest of the region in 58–44 B.C. A Latin tongue took root, and a network of military roads brought some degree of unity. Christianity was introduced.

When the Roman Empire weakened after the 200s A.D., a northern tribe, the Salian Franks, subdued much of the country.

After making an alliance with the Roman Catholic Church, Clovis, a leader of the Franks, extended Frankish rule and Christianity by force of arms in the 400s. Clovis founded the Merovingian dynasty.

MIDDLE AGES

Beset by Muslim invaders moving up from Spain,

QUICK QUIZ: Name the world's largest nation in area? See page 467.

FRANCE *(continued)*

the Frank leader Charles Martel defeated the Arab cavalry at the Battle of Tours in 732, preventing a Muslim conquest of France.

Charlemagne was Charles Martel's grandson. A militant imperialist and ally of the church, he was crowned emperor of the Western Roman Empire on Christmas Day in the year 800. Under Charlemagne, France was only part of a vast Frankish domain.

Following Charlemagne's death the empire fell apart from Viking invasions and regional revolts.

In 987 a fresh beginning was made with the election to the throne of Hugh Capet, duke of Francia. The Capetians, as the new ruling group was known, allied themselves with the church and the growing urban classes to extend their rule slowly over all of France.

For more than 300 years the Capetians wore down the feudal forces in France. They disciplined the bishops, created the beginnings of a central administrative system, crusaded against infidels and heretics, and warded off the English. Their line ended in 1328.

In the Hundred Years War (1337–1453) with England, France was devastated. At the Battle of Orléans on May 7, 1429, Joan of Arc inspired the French army to rout the English, leading to ultimate French victory.

KINGDOM OF FRANCE

In the late 1550s the Reformation swept through France, pitting Catholic against Protestant. Civil war followed.

A strong central government with a high degree of religious tolerance was now considered necessary to save the nation. A Protestant, the Bourbon Prince Henri of Navarre, took the throne. Embracing Catholicism himself and granting religious freedom to the Protestants (Huguenots) in the Edict of Nantes (1598), he became the most popular king France ever had. Although the wealthy urban classes enjoyed power, France was still a feudal monarchy.

The assassination of Henri in 1610 left the royal government open to challenges from both nobles and bourgeoisie. In this struggle Henri's successors were supported by two great statesmen, Cardinals Richelieu and Mazarin, who were enemies of the nobles, of Protestantism, and of urban democratic tendencies. Guiding France through the perils of the Thirty Years War (1618–48), the cardinals put down internal revolt (the Fronde of 1648–53), continued the colonial expansion begun in the previous century, and helped project the Bourbon house in the person of Louis XIV (1643–1715) to the peak of France's power.

Louis XIV and his lieutenants held the nobility in check, helped industry expand, and systematically eliminated old provincial, municipal, and religious liberties. Royal control was absolute.

Warlike and authoritarian, Louis made France the greatest of Europe's powers, but he also brought the country to economic ruin.

The reign of Louis XV was marked by opposition at home, the loss of empire abroad (Canada fell to England in 1763), and a dazzling display of art and literature. This was the great age of the Enlightenment, and France was the intellectual capital of Europe.

FRENCH REVOLUTION

The French state, however, was insolvent, and the farmers suffered from landlords seeking higher revenues in an expanding economy. The monarchy was finally bankrupted, in part through involvement in the American Revolution.

The bourgeois creditors of the state refused to advance more credit unless they got social and political concessions from the crown.

The aristocracy was determined to reverse the trend toward absolute monarchy and to regain its former authority.

The common people of rural France waited for some royal action that would ease their lot.

Nobles and bourgeois joined forces to compel Louis XVI to summon the States-General, which had not met since 1614. Then the struggle for power became more complex.

The middle-class representatives of the common people challenged the aristocracy in 1789. They rallied the king temporarily to their side. Within months, following riots against crown and nobility, they seized control of the state.

The revolutionary government overturned the social and political structure of France, launched the egalitarian creed throughout Europe, and reduced the church to a department of state. Finally the revolutionaries executed the king, who had turned against them and had hoped to be rescued by other European monarchs.

The strains of war and resultant unrest at home precipitated a bloody reign of terror that set the stage for the rise of Napoleon.

NAPOLEONIC ERA

By 1799, after a decade of domestic turmoil, the epochal French Revolution ended in military dictatorship. Young, brilliant, ambitious Gen. Napoleon Bonaparte seized total power.

Napoleon crowned himself emperor of the French in 1804. At home he squashed political conflict and restricted the powers of the church.

France reached its height of power as Napoleon won victory after victory until he controlled most of Europe.

After Napoleon's disastrous defeat in Russia in 1812, his conquests were stripped away by the victory of an allied coalition in 1814.

Napoleon returned from exile in 1815 to rally France again, but was routed at Waterloo.

The former emperor was imprisoned on St. Helena, where he died in 1821.

RESTORATION OF MONARCHY

The unpopular Bourbons were restored under Louis XVIII in 1814 by allied arms, but the old order never returned.

In 1830 Charles X was driven out by the revolt of the middle and lower classes in the cities.

His successor, Louis Philippe, was ousted in the 1848 revolution.

SECOND REPUBLIC AND NAPOLEON III

The Second Republic, founded in 1848, was undermined by clashes between the new French factions. The republic then was eliminated by its elected president, Louis Napoleon Bonaparte.

Like his uncle, France's new ruler established a dictatorship to end political quarrels and to preserve the social order. Proclaimed Emperor

Napoleon III in 1852, he presided until 1870.

The regime enriched the industrial and commercial classes but won no loyalty from them.

Napoleon III expanded the empire in Southeast Asia but was unsuccessful in Mexico. He helped bring about the unification of Italy but was defeated in a war with Germany (Prussia).

THIRD REPUBLIC AND WORLD WARS I AND II

Out of defeat by Germany (1870–71) another republic was born. It accepted severe peace terms, mastered the revolt of the Paris commune, and by 1875 had all but banished the ghost of monarchy.

The Third Republic had a conservative parliamentary government. It expanded the school system and extended its empire in Africa and Asia. It made an ally of Russia in 1894 and of Britain in 1904.

Like much of armed and divided Europe, France took up arms in 1914 hoping to win security. It also hoped to recover Alsace-Lorraine, surrendered to Germany in 1871.

France emerged victorious but exhausted from World War I.

France reacted to Hitler's invasion of Poland by declaring war on Germany in 1939. It suffered swift and total defeat in 1940. World War I hero Marshal Henri Philippe Pétain established a government in southern France at Vichy that collaborated with the Nazis.

A Free French movement led by Gen. Charles de Gaulle from abroad condemned the government at Vichy, won over the loyalty of much of the empire, and fought on the side of the Allies. After liberation, France was ruled by de Gaulle until he resigned in 1946.

FOURTH REPUBLIC

For 12 years the unstable Fourth Republic struggled to modernize the economy and cope with nationalist movements in the crumbling empire, while French prestige sank in the world.

The regime collapsed in 1958 when faced with a French army rebellion in Algeria.

To avoid civil war, Paris called de Gaulle from retirement. The nation gave him a mandate to rule and to prepare a new constitution.

FIFTH REPUBLIC

General de Gaulle in September 1958 established a Fifth Republic with himself as a strong president. He governed by decree when necessary.

Driving forcefully toward the leadership of western Europe, de Gaulle granted independence to Algeria. He prevented Britain from joining the European Common Market. And in 1968 he withdrew French military forces from NATO as a protest against U.S. foreign policy.

The regime concentrated on foreign affairs and building atomic weapons while social and economic problems continued to await solution.

In May 1968 a student revolt and a nationwide general strike brought the republic close to anarchy. De Gaulle, however, appealed for law and order, promising reforms. His government received an overwhelming endorsement in general elections on June 23, 1968.

In April 1969, however, de Gaulle resigned after a proposed constitutional reform was defeated in a nationwide referendum.

Georges Pompidou was elected president in 1969 to succeed de Gaulle. Pompidou reversed de Gaulle's policy of opposing Britain's entry into the European Common Market. On July 5, 1972, he named Pierre Messmer, as prime minister.

The French government caused a storm of world criticism by test-exploding atomic weapons at Mururoa Atoll in the South Pacific Ocean in the summers of 1973 and 1974. The International Court of Justice, acting on complaints by Australia and New Zealand, ordered France to cancel the tests. The French government, however, proceeded with the explosions.

The death of President Pompidou on April 2, 1974, brought new national elections.

FRANCE UNDER GISCARD d'ESTAING

Valéry Giscard d'Estaing, a conservative who had served as minister of finance, won the presidency in the runoff election on May 19, 1974.

President Giscard d'Estaing appointed Jacques Chirac, Pompidou's former minister of the interior, as premier on May 27, 1974.

Giscard d'Estaing quickly established himself as more liberal than his Gaullist predecessors. He added a woman to the cabinet, lowered to 18 the age for voting and attaining full legal rights of an adult, and increased the minimum wage for workers. Unemployed workers were guaranteed a year's pay.

Raymond Barre, an economist, became prime minister on Aug. 25, 1976, after Chirac resigned.

President Giscard D'Estaing's center-right coalition won a resounding victory in the elections on March 19, 1978, capturing 290 of the 491 seats in the national assembly.

France was particularly hard hit by soaring fuel prices in the 1970s. To help reduce dependency on imported fuel, the government ordered a speed-up in the construction and planning of nuclear power plants.

The government announced on June 26, 1980, the successful test of a neutron bomb, a type of atomic bomb designed to kill enemy soldiers while limiting damage to surrounding structures.

FRANCE TURNS TO SOCIALISM

In the first round of a presidential election held on April 26, 1981, President Giscard d'Estaing won a plurality of 28% of the vote against the nine other candidates. But a close second was socialist candidate François Mitterrand with 26%.

A televised debate between the two leading candidates highlighted a three-week runoff campaign that followed. Mitterrand emphasized his plans to nationalize banks and the nation's leading industries.

Mitterrand's victory in the May 10, 1981, election with 55% of the vote caused panic selling of stocks by investors in the French financial markets. After his inauguration on May 21, 1981, he appointed Pierre Mauroy as prime minister. In elections in June 1981, the socialists won a majority in parliament. The first leftist cabinet for France since 1958 included four communists.

QUICK QUIZ: What is the only nation to cover an entire continent? See page 488.

FRANCE *(continued)*

The first major legislation adopted by the socialist parliament on July 15, 1981, was a plan to decentralize the nation's government by restoring power to elected local governments, eliminating the veto powers of appointed regional and departmental prefects.

The death penalty was abolished by parliament in September 1981, bringing to an end the work of the guillotine.

Faced with unemployment that had risen to more than 2 million (10% of the work force), the government, on Feb. 1, 1982, reduced the workweek to 39 hours from 40 and increased vacation time to 5 weeks. The socialists promised to cut the workweek to 35 hours by 1985.

Beginning on Feb. 13, 1982, the socialist government began nationalizing about 30% of the nation's industry, including 39 banks, 5 industrial groups, 2 steel companies, 2 financial holding concerns, and companies in the armaments and aerospace industries. The government paid some $8 billion in bonds to stockholders of the companies.

France suffered a huge trade deficit in 1982, causing the value of the French franc to fall to a low of $0.14—compared with $0.24 in 1980. To preserve the franc's value, the government obtained a $4 billion loan from an international group of banks on Oct. 27, 1982.

With inflation running at a rate of about 14%, the government on June 12, 1982, froze wages and prices, a move opposed by labor unions. Faced with a wave of strikes, the freeze was lifted on Nov. 1. However, severe restrictions were placed on wage and price increases.

By mid-1983 public-opinion polls showed that more than half the people were dissatisfied with Mitterrand's government. Unemployment stood at about 9% of the work force and inflation continued at a high rate. Industries nationalized by the socialists had lost $2.5 billion in two years.

CORSICA

Area: 3,367 square miles (8,722 sq. km.).
Population: 204,232.
Cities: Ajaccio, capital, 40,834; Bastia, 49,375.

Called *Corse* in French, the mountainous Mediterranean island of Corsica is nearly three times as large as the state of Rhode Island. It lies about 100 miles southeast of France.

Corsica is separated from the Italian island of Sardinia by an 8-mile-wide strait. It is best known as the birthplace of Napoleon I.

Most of the people make their living farming and raising livestock. Great herds of sheep graze on the mountain slopes, providing the island's two most profitable products, wool and cheese.

Prehistoric people lived on the island at least as early as 2000 B.C., leaving large stone monuments.

Greeks from Phocaea, in what is now Turkey, established a colony on Corsica about 560 B.C. These invaders were followed by Carthaginians, Romans, Vandals, and Arabs. The Italian cities of Pisa and Genoa drove out the Arabs in the 1000s A.D. and then fought each other for control of the island for several centuries.

France invaded and conquered Corsica in 1768, and the following year Napoleon was born there. British forces landed on the island in the 1790s and during the Napoleonic wars. But Corsica was restored to France in 1815.

France granted Corsica limited autonomy in 1982. In the first election for a 61-member regional assembly on Aug. 8, 1982, no party won a majority. A moderate leftist, Prosper Alfonsi, was elected first president of the assembly.

Nationalists seeking complete independence continued terrorist bombing attacks in 1982–83.

THE FRENCH COMMUNITY

Independent nations that once were part of the French colonial empire and present dependencies of France are bound together by economic and military agreements, although not by a formal international organization.

INDEPENDENT MEMBERS

Central Africa	Djibouti	Gabon
Chad	France	Senegal

OVERSEAS DEPARTMENTS OF FRANCE

French Guiana	Martinique	Réunion	St. Pierre and Miquelon
Guadeloupe	Mahore		

OVERSEAS TERRITORIES OF FRANCE

French Polynesia	New Caledonia
French Southern and Antarctic Territories	Wallis and Futuna Islands

ASSOCIATES BY SPECIAL AGREEMENTS

Algeria	Ivory Coast	Niger
Benin	Mali	Togo
Cameroon	Mauritania	Upper Volta

FRANCE'S DEPENDENCIES

FRENCH GUIANA (GUYANE)

Area: 35,135 square miles (91,000 sq. km.).
Population: 78,322.
Capital: Cayenne, 38,901.

Located on the northern coast of South America, French Guiana is bordered on the north by the Atlantic Ocean, on the east and south by Brazil, and on the west by Suriname.

Most French Guianese are blacks. About 7 in 10 are literate in the French language.

Guiana's farmers raise cattle, bananas, pineapples, sugarcane, fruits, and vegetables. Gold is mined, but large deposits of bauxite have not been developed.

France began to colonize Guiana in 1635 but did not establish firm control until 1677. For nearly a century (1852–1947) French convicts were sent to Guiana's penal colony, Devil's Island. The territory's borders were settled in 1854. It became an overseas department of France in 1946 with representation in France's parliament.

In the 1960s France built its main space- research center at the former prison camp at Kourou. In 1975 the French government began investing $160 million to develop paper manufacturing to utilize the area's forests.

FRENCH POLYNESIA

Area: 1,544 square miles (4,000 sq. km.).
Population: 160,163.
Capital: Papeete, Tahiti, 85,000.

The nearly 130 islands of French Polynesia are scattered over a vast area of the South Pacific.

For administrative purposes, the islands have been divided into five groups: the *Windward*

Islands, including Tahiti and Moorea; the *Leeward Islands, including Raiatea and Bora-Bora (the Windward and Leeward islands make up the Society Islands); the Tuamotu and Gambier Islands;* the *Austral Islands;* and the *Marquesas Islands.*

Most of the people are French-speaking Christian Polynesians.

Exports include copra, vanilla, coffee, and phosphates.

Tourism is an important revenue source.

The Society Islands were discovered and claimed for England in 1767, but French claims were established a year later. In 1842 France declared a protectorate, and in 1880 the islands became a French colony.

The Tuamotu Islands were discovered by Spain in 1606. They became a French protectorate in 1844 and were annexed in 1881.

The Gambier Islands, discovered by the British in 1797, were annexed by France in 1881.

The Austral Islands came under French control in 1880.

The southern Marquesas were discovered by Spain in 1595, and the northern Marquesas were sighted by an American in 1791. In 1842 French sovereignty over the Marquesas was recognized by local chieftains.

The islands of French Polynesia were grouped into a single colony in 1903. They became an overseas territory of France in 1946.

France's nuclear-testing center, on Mururoa (720 miles southeast of Tahiti), began operating in 1966, when France exploded its first atomic bomb. In 1968 France's first hydrogen bomb was detonated near Mururoa.

GUADELOUPE AND DEPENDENCIES

Area: 687 square miles (1,779 sq. km.).
Population: 311,057.
Capital: Basse-Terre, 20,000.
Largest City: Point-à-Pitre, 70,000.

Guadeloupe is located in the Leeward Islands of the Lesser Antilles in the eastern Caribbean Sea. It consists of two islands, Basse-Terre and Grande-Terre, separated by a narrow channel, the Rivière Salée. Volcanic Basse-Terre lies to the west, while the flat island of Grande-Terre is to the east.

Most of the French-speaking inhabitants of Guadeloupe are of black or mixed descent.

The economy is based on tourism and farming. The main crops are sugarcane, bananas, and pineapples.

Guadeloupe's dependencies include the islands of Marie Galante, Les Saintes, Désirade, and St. Barthélemy. About two-thirds of the island of St. Martin, located about 110 miles northeast of Guadeloupe, is administered by Guadeloupe. The other third is the Dutch St. Maarten.

Columbus discovered Guadeloupe in 1493, and France founded the first permanent colony in 1635. Except for British occupation in the 1700s and during the Napoleonic wars, Guadeloupe remained French. It became an overseas department of France in 1946.

The people enjoy the same social-welfare benefits as the people of France, including family allowances and medical aid.

Guadeloupe has become a popular winter resort for Americans and Canadians. Its climate is warm the year round with mean temperatures of 74 ° F. in January and 87 ° F. in August.

More than 72,000 persons evacuated the southern half of the island of Basse-Terre before the 4,813-foot La Soufrière volcano exploded on Aug. 30, 1976, throwing out lava and rocks.

MAHORE

Area: 144 square miles (375 sq. km.).
Population: 56,476.
Capital: Dzaoudzi.

The island of Mahore (formerly Mayotte) lies in the Mozambique Channel off the coast of Africa about midway between Madagascar and Mozambique. It is the southernmost of the Comoro Islands and the only one whose people chose to remain a French dependency when the Comoros declared their independence.

The majority of the people earn their living by farming or fishing. Their most important export products are essential oils, used in perfume making, and spices. The economy depends on subsidies from France to import food and necessities.

France obtained the right from the local chiefs to use Mahore as a military base in 1840–41. Mahore was made a French colony in 1843. French settlers began cultivating sugarcane plantations on the island. By 1912 France had taken over all the Comoros as a colony administered from Madagascar. The islands became an overseas territory of France in 1958 and were granted internal self-government in 1960.

When the other Comoros declared their independence in July 1975, the people of Mahore refused to go along and repelled an attempted invasion by the new Comoros government. On Feb. 8, 1976, Mahore voted 99% in favor of remaining a French dependency. In a vote on April 11, 1976, the islanders chose by an 80% majority to become an overseas department of France.

MARTINIQUE

Area: 425 square miles (1,100 sq. km.).
Population: 301,626.
Capital: Fort-de-France, 97,814.

Martinique is situated in the Windward Islands of the Lesser Antilles in the eastern Caribbean Sea. The island's terrain is generally mountainous, and the highest peak is volcanic Mt. Pelée (4,583 feet).

The people are French-speaking and mostly of black or mixed descent. Sugar, pineapples, bananas, and rum are the main products.

Famed for the beauty of its forested mountains and sandy beaches, Martinique has been called the *Pearl of the Antilles.* The island has a thriving tourist industry, as many visitors come to enjoy the warm climate that averages from 76 ° to 81 ° F. the year round.

Columbus discovered Martinique in 1502. France settled the island in 1635. Britain occupied the island in 1762–63 and 1794–1815.

An eruption of Mt. Pelée on May 8, 1902, destroyed the city of St. Pierre, killing about 40,000 persons.

QUICK QUIZ: Katharine Hepburn and Henry Fonda won Oscars for what 1981 film? See page 265.

FRENCH DEPENDENCIES *(continued)*

Martinique became an overseas department of France in 1946. It is represented in the French parliament by two senators and three deputies.

NEW CALEDONIA

Area: 7,374 square miles (19,103 sq. km.).
Population: 142,767.
Capital: Nouméa, 74,335.

New Caledonia is a territory of France that includes several island groups in the South Pacific. The island of New Caledonia itself has an area of 6,530 square miles.

Main dependencies of New Caledonia include: the *Loyalty Islands* (area 756 sq. mi.), a chain of islands that lie about 78 miles to the east; the *Chesterfield Islands,* uninhabited coral islets about 400 miles to the northwest; the *Isle of Pines,* about 30 miles to the southeast.

Located about 750 miles east of Australia, the island is mountainous and covered with lush vegetation. Nearly half the people are Melanesian. About 40% are European, mostly French.

Mining is the most important industry. New Caledonia has large reserves of nickel, iron, manganese, and chrome.

The French explorer Louis Antoine de Bougainville sailed near New Caledonia in 1768. Capt. James Cook gave the island its name, landing there on Sept. 4, 1774. The island was annexed by France in 1853 and was used as a penal colony from 1864 to 1894. Following occupation by U.S. forces in World War II, the island became an overseas territory of France in 1946.

A French-appointed governor heads the island's administration. He is assisted by a council of government chosen by the popularly elected territorial assembly. In 1979 France sent 100 riot police to cope with increased violence by nationalists demanding independence.

Parties calling for independence won control of the territorial assembly in June 1982.

RÉUNION

Area: 970 square miles (2,512 sq. km.).
Population: 532,015.
Capital: Saint-Denis, 109,072.

Réunion is located in the Indian Ocean about 450 miles east of the island of Madagascar. The island has one active and nine inactive volcanoes. The people are descendants of French settlers, blacks, Malays, Indochinese, and Malabar Indians.

The island has a prosperous economy based largely on growing sugarcane. All children attend school, and most people read and write French. About 25% of the people are of French descent. Portuguese explorers visited Réunion in the 1500s. The island was claimed for France in 1638 and settled in 1665. Until 1793 Réunion was called Bourbon Island. In 1946 it became an overseas department of France.

SAINT PIERRE AND MIQUELON

Area: 93 square miles (242 sq. km.).
Population: 6,096.
Capital: Saint Pierre, 4,287.

Saint Pierre and Miquelon lie in the Atlantic Ocean about 15 miles southwest of Newfoundland. There are two main islands—Saint Pierre (10 sq. mi.) and Miquelon (83 sq. mi.). The southern part of Miquelon sometimes is considered to be a separate island called Lauglade.

Most of the people are descendants of early Basque and French settlers and are Roman Catholics. Fishing is the main industry. The soil is so rocky and the climate so cold that no food crops can be grown.

The Portuguese explorer Faguendez visited Saint Pierre and Miquelon in 1520. The islands were claimed for France in 1535 by Jacques Cartier. The first French settlement was founded in 1604. The islands were ceded to Britain in 1713, restored to France in 1763, retaken by Britain from 1778 to 1783 and during the Napoleonic wars, and finally returned to the French in 1816. In 1935 the islands were granted local autonomy. They were made a department of France in 1976.

SOUTHERN AND ANTARCTIC TERRITORIES

Area: 1,138,616 square miles (439,622 sq. km.).
Population: 180.
Capital: Port aux Français, Kerguélen.

The French Southern and Antarctic Territories consists of two archipelagos, two islands, and an area on the Antarctic continent.

Kerguélen Archipelago, a large subantarctic island and 300 smaller islands in the South Indian Ocean, was discovered by Yves Joseph de Kerguélen-Trémarec in 1772. Research stations, a hospital, and a military camp are located there.

Crozet Archipelago, 5 large and 15 small islands in the South Indian Ocean about 800 miles west of Kerguélen, was also discovered in 1772. A meteorological station was built there in 1964.

Saint Paul is a tiny, uninhabited island in the Indian Ocean northeast of Kerguélen.

New Amsterdam Island, located about 50 miles north of Saint Paul, has research stations and a hospital.

Terre Adélie, situated on the Antarctic continent, was discovered on Jan. 19, 1840, by Dumont d'Urville. Nearby Commonwealth Bay is said to be the windiest place in the world, with wind speeds reaching 200 mph.

WALLIS AND FUTUNA

Area: 106 square miles (274 sq. km.).
Population: 11,110.
Capital: Mata Utu, Uvéa, 6,000.

Wallis and Futuna are two small groups of Pacific islands located about 250 miles west of Samoa. The Wallis Islands consist of Uvéa and about 20 smaller islands. The islands of Futuna and Alofi make up the Hoorn (or Horne) Islands, located about 125 miles west of the Wallis Islands. Most of the population is Polynesian, and the main economic activities are copra production and fishing.

Dutch navigators discovered the Hoorn Islands in 1617. The Wallis Islands were sighted in 1767 by the English explorer Samuel Wallis. France established a protectorate over the islands in 1887–88.

In 1961 Wallis and Futuna became an overseas territory of France. The islands are governed by a French administrator with the assistance of a territorial council consisting of the kings of each of the three main islands and three appointed members.

GABON

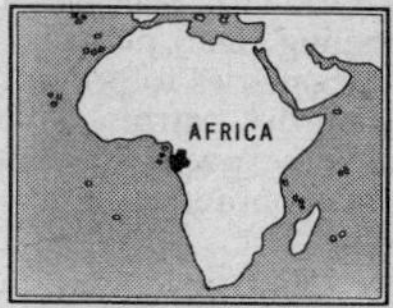

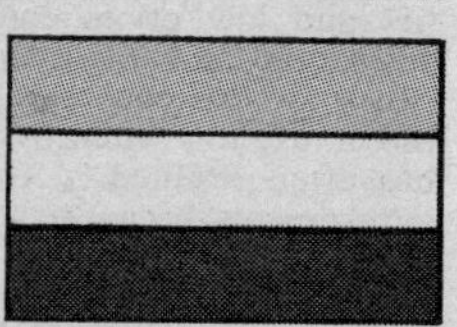

Official Name: Gabonese Republic.
Area: 103,347 square miles (267,667 sq. km.).
Population: 942,343.
Capital: Libreville, 57,000.
Government: One-party state.
President: Omar Bongo (since 1967).
Premier: Léon Mebiame (since 1975).
National Assembly: 47 members.
U.S. Ambassador to Gabon: Arthur T. Tienken.
Ambassador to U.S.: Abdoulaye Mocktar-Mbingt.
Flag: Stripes of green (top), yellow (middle), and blue (bottom).
Official Language: French.
Chief Ethnic Groups: Fang (32%), Eshira (19%), Adouma (12%), Okande (5%).
Religions: Christianity (46%), animism, Islam.
Leading Industries: Mining (petroleum, manganese, uranium, iron ore, lead, zinc, copper, diamonds); forestry and lumbering; agriculture (cocoa, coffee, vegetables, fruits); construction; fishing.
Foreign Trade: *Major exports*—petroleum, wood, manganese, uranium; *major imports*—petroleum products, iron and steel, trucks, agricultural machinery, clothing.
Places of Interest: Dense hardwood forests; Crystal Mountains; Mt. Iboundji; Libreville; Lambaréné, site of Dr. Albert Schweitzer's hospital; national parks.

GABON TODAY

Gabon, about the size of Colorado, is a prosperous oil-exporting country of West Africa.

Rich in natural resources, Gabon is one of the world's leading producers of uranium, with about 1,000 tons exported to France each year.

Gabon also has large deposits of petroleum, manganese, and iron ore. Oil accounts for about three-fourths of its export income. Its forests support a thriving lumber industry, and its rivers provide substantial hydroelectric potential.

The government has offered encouragement to foreign investors to develop the natural resources, and has worked hard to improve port and transportation facilities.

Its people have a higher per capita income than any other African nation. The nation's prosperity nearly eliminated unemployment. But most of the people do not have enough education to handle high-paying jobs in industry. Only about 1 person in 5 can read and write.

Disease and malnutrition give the Gabonese one of the lowest life expectancies in the world, with the average man dying by the age of 25.

An equatorial country in western Africa, Gabon has a hot and humid climate. Much of the land is covered by dense tropical rain forests. The country's major waterway is the Ougooé River.

During the rainy season, from February to June, more than 100 inches of rain fall in Libreville. The heavy rains make jungle roads impassable, so the country relies on aircraft for interior travel.

The coastal lowlands extend 20 to 125 miles into the interior and adjoin a 60-mile-wide belt of rocky cliffs.

Equatorial Guinea and Cameroon lie to the north, and Congo to the east and south.

EARLY HISTORY

Portuguese exploration began about 1470, followed by the British, Dutch, Spanish, and French during the centuries of slave trading.

In 1839 French explorer Edouard Bouet-Willaumez signed a treaty of peace with "King" Denis of Gabon. Denis, a notorious African slave trader, turned over part of northern Gabon to France in return for protection.

The capital, Libreville (place of liberation), was founded in 1849 when the French captured a slave ship and released its captives at the mouth of the Como River.

Control by France gradually expanded, and the colony of Gabon was established in 1885. Gabon became one of the four territories of French Equatorial Africa in 1910.

Dr. Albert Schweitzer established the first hospital in the region in 1913 at Lambaréné.

Gabon was granted internal self-government in 1957. Leon M'ba became chief minister.

INDEPENDENCE

Gabon was proclaimed fully independent on Aug. 17, 1960. Leon M'ba was elected president.

M'ba was reelected in March 1967, but died in office that November. Vice President Albert-Bernard Bongo became president.

Bongo declared Gabon a one-party state in March 1968, dissolving the powerful Gabonese Democratic bloc and creating a new party, the Gabonese Democratic Party (PDG). He was reelected president in 1973 without opposition.

Gabon became a full member of the Organization of Petroleum Exporting Countries (OPEC) in 1975. Symbolizing his nation's closer relations with the Arab oil producers, President Bongo changed his French given name of Albert-Bernard to the Arabic name *Omar.*

Work began in 1975 on the 600-mile Trans-Gabon Railway from Libreville to the interior cities of Mékambo and Franceville. The first 115-mile section of the railroad opened to regular traffic in 1979. The line, planned for completion in 1985, will permit expansion of uranium and iron mining.

Bongo expelled 10,000 Benin workers from Gabon by airlift in July 1978. The action came after Benin's ruler Mathieu Kerekou accused Gabon of attempting to overthrow him.

As host to a 1977 conference of the Organization of African Unity (OAU), Gabon borrowed more than $2 billion to prepare for the meeting. As a result, the government had to use nearly half its revenues in 1979–80 in paying off interest and part of the debt. An austerity program caused a decline of about 20% in the gross national product.

However, new oil finds in 1979 indicated petroleum production could be increased in the 1980s with consequent growth in the economy.

QUICK QUIZ: What body of water separates Ireland from Great Britain? See page 579.

GAMBIA

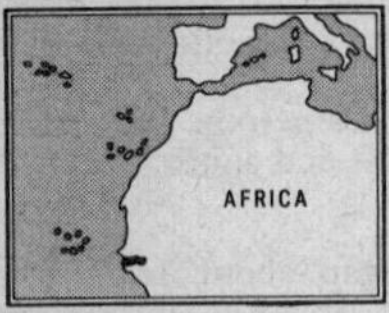

Official Name: Republic of The Gambia.
Area: 4,361 square miles (11,295 sq. km.).
Population: 646,356.
Capital: Banjul, 49,181.
Government: Presidential-parliamentary democracy.
President: Sir Dawda Kairaba Jawara (since 1970).
House of Representatives: 37 members.
U.S. Ambassador to Gambia: Sharon E. Ahmad.
Ambassador to U.S.: Lamin Abdou Mbye.
Flag: Red, blue, and green stripes from top to bottom, separated by narrow white stripes.
Official Language: English.
Chief Ethnic Groups: Mandingo (40%), Fula (13%), Wolof (12%), Serahuli (7%), Jola (7%).
Leading Religions: Islam (85%), animism, Christianity.
Leading Industries: Agriculture (peanuts, cattle, rice, palm kernels, bees, vegetables, fruits); fishing; tourism; food processing; handicrafts.
Foreign Trade: *Major exports*—peanuts, palm kernels, hides, fish, beeswax; *major imports*—textiles, food, machinery, hardware, consumer goods.
Places of Interest: Flora and fauna along the Gambia River; Banjul; beaches.

GAMBIA TODAY

Africa's smallest independent country, Gambia is a shining example of two-party democracy amid the many dictatorships of the continent.

With less area than the state of Connecticut, Gambia averages only about 20 miles in width but is about 200 miles long from east to west. It is surrounded by Senegal, except for an Atlantic shoreline of about 50 miles.

Unlike most of the small nations of Africa that quickly eradicated signs of colonialism upon attaining independence, Gambia remains proud of its British colonial heritage. Many Britons continue to work in the government offices. And the capital, Banjul, retains the appearance of a British city of the Victorian age.

The Gambia River, which extends the length of the country, provides excellent transportation. However, Gambia has few natural resources.

Most Gambians are poor tribesmen. Some are nomads who raise cattle. Many are farmers who raise just enough food to feed their families. Only about 12 persons in 100 can read and write, and only about 20,000 children go to school.

Peanuts, the only sizable cash crop, provide 95% of Gambia's exports.

The government uses much of its limited resources to promote tourism. About 50,000 visitors each year, mostly from Europe.

The village of Juffure attracts an unusual number of foreign visitors as the ancestral home of Kunta Kinte of the book *Roots* written by American author Alex Haley. President Jawara declared Juffure a national monument. The village has changed little since Kunta Kinte was stolen by slave traders in 1767.

Because Gambia has relatively low import duties and low prices compared with Senegal, a substantial amount of smuggling takes place between the two countries. Senegal tries to prevent the smuggling with roving border patrols. This has often resulted in friction between the two governments because the long border is largely unmarked.

The country is generally low-lying and flat, with elevations ranging from sea level to 120 feet. Temperatures vary from a low of 60° F. in winter to a high of 110° F. in summer. The country averages 11 hours of sunshine every day from November to May. Rainfall averages 30 to 55 inches a year, largely in June to September.

EARLY HISTORY

The Gambia River was discovered in 1456 by Portuguese explorers. It was then part of the kingdom of Mali. Portugal controlled the region until the late 1500s.

Britain and France fought for the territory and the moderately profitable slave trade until the 1800s.

After 1815 France controlled Saint-Louis and Gorée islands.

The British established the first permanent settlement at Bathurst (now Banjul) in 1816. Gambia was administered through a governor-general in Sierra Leone in 1821–43 and 1866–88. It was a separate colony between 1843 and 1866 and returned to crown-colony status in 1888. The country's present boundaries were established by agreement with France in 1889.

Sir Dawda K. Jawara was elected prime minister in 1962. Under his leadership Gambia was granted full internal self-government in 1963.

INDEPENDENCE

Gambia received independence from Britain on Feb. 18, 1965.

The nation became a republic within the British Commonwealth of Nations with a new constitution promulgated on April 24, 1970. It took the official name *Republic of the Gambia.* Jawara became the nation's first president.

One of the few African countries with a multiparty political system, Gambia held its first national elections in March 1972. Jawara was elected to a 5-year term as president. His People's Progressive Party (PPP) won 28 seats in the house of representatives, and the opposition United Party won 3 seats. Four representatives are appointed by the tribal chiefs.

While President Jawara was attending the wedding of Britain's Prince Charles in London, a communist-led rebellion attempted to overthrow the government on July 30, 1981.

At Jawara's request, Senegal sent troops that defeated the rebels and freed 135 hostages, including the president's senior wife. About 500 persons were killed in a week of fighting.

Gambia joined with Senegal in a confederation called *Senegambia* that became effective on Feb. 1, 1982.

Each nation retained its sovereignty but agreed to develop joint policies for defense, foreign affairs, finance, and customs.

The 58-year-old Jawara was reelected to his third five-year term as president on May 5, 1982.

GERMANY, EAST

Official Name: German Democratic Republic.
Area: 41,768 square miles (108,178 sq. km.).
Population: 16,738,000.
Chief Cities: East Berlin, capital, 1,145,743; Leipzig, 563,388; Dresden, 516,284; Karl-Marx-Stadt, 316,937; Magdeburg, 288,725; Halle, 232,217.
Government: One-party communist state.
Heads of Government: First Secretary of Communist Party, Erich Honecker (since 1971); President, Willi Stoph (appointed in 1973); Premier, Horst Sindermann (since 1973).
Legislature: *Volkskammer,* 500 members.
U.S. Ambassador to East Germany: Herbert Stuart Okun.
East German Ambassador to U.S.: Gerhard Herder.
Flag: Black, red, and gold stripes, with centered coat of arms.
Official Language: German.
Principal Ethnic Group: German (99.8%).
Main Religions: Protestantism (59%), Roman Catholicism (8%).
Leading Industries: Manufacturing (steel, chemicals, textiles, cement, machinery, electronic computers, consumer products); agriculture (dairy products, cattle, poultry, potatoes, sugar beets, wheat, rye, barley, oats); construction; mining (lignite, potash, coal, iron ore, copper, uranium, cobalt).
Foreign Trade: *Major exports*—machinery, coal briquettes, chemicals; *major imports*—coal, crude petroleum, coke, machinery, wheat, iron ore.
Places of Interest: East Berlin's Brandenburg Gate; Dresden's Frauenkirche; Jena's Goethe monument; Leipzig. *In Potsdam:* state buildings; Karl-Marx-Stadt.

EAST GERMANY TODAY

The communist leaders of East Germany look enviously at the booming industrial production of neighboring West Germany, while the people look equally enviously at the freedom and higher standard of living across the border. Although forbidden to watch TV broadcasts from West Germany, most East Germans do so in the privacy of their homes.

A repressive communist police state, East Germany guards its borders with barbed wire and machine guns to prevent its people from escaping to the West. Even so several thousand each year do escape, although dozens are killed by guards and land mines. About 5,000 people who unsuccessfully try to escape are imprisoned. Some 1,000 to 1,500 are permitted to leave each year for ransom payments of about $20,000 apiece by the West German government.

The government owns and controls all industrial and agricultural facilities. It emphasizes heavy industry at the expense of consumer goods.

GEOGRAPHY AND CLIMATE

The sandy Baltic coast in the north has hills and lakes. The central region has fertile plains as well as the Harz Mountains. The Thuringian Forest range dominates the southern region. In the southeast the Erzgebirge range forms a natural frontier with Czechoslovakia. The principal rivers are the Elbe, Saale, Havel, and Spree.

Winter temperatures average at freezing or below, while summer temperatures rise to an average of about 64 ° F.

West Germany lies to the west and south, Poland and Czechoslovakia are to the east, and the Baltic Sea is to the north.

COMMUNIST STATE

East Germany and East Berlin came under Soviet occupation at the end of World War II. For the earlier history of Germany see article *Germany, West,* on the following pages.

The Soviet Union turned its occupied zone into the *German Democratic Republic* (*GDR*) on Oct. 7, 1949. This followed the creation of the Federal Republic of Germany (West Germany) three weeks earlier by the Allies.

As head of the Communist Party, Walter Ulbricht dominated the GDR from its formation.

The Western powers refused to recognize the new government of East Germany, but all Soviet-bloc countries extended recognition immediately.

Soviet troops effectively crushed an anticommunist revolt in East Germany in June 1953.

Between 1949 and 1961 some 3.5 million East Germans escaped to West Germany.

In August 1961 the East German government constructed a wall of barbed wire and concrete around the western sector of Berlin to stop the flow of East Germans into West Berlin.

DEVELOPMENTS IN 1970s–1980s

Erich Honecker succeeded Ulbricht as communist ruler in 1971.

After long negotiations, East and West Germany began to relax relations in 1972. A treaty establishing diplomatic relations between the two states was signed on Dec. 21, 1972. Ratification by the parliaments of both states was completed in six months, and the pact went into effect on June 21, 1973.

The new understanding opened the door to UN membership for both Germanys in September 1973, and brought about diplomatic recognition by the U.S. and other Western nations.

Amnesty International reported in October 1977 that from 100,000 to 200,000 East Germans had asked permission to emigrate but had been refused. The report said thousands of them had been jailed as political prisoners.

New restrictive laws went into effect Aug. 1, 1979, providing long jail terms for anyone taking part in an antigovernment demonstration or for passing on any information damaging to the government to "foreign organizations." Security was further tightened in 1981–82.

The government marked the 20th anniversary of the building of the Berlin Wall with a huge military parade on Aug. 13, 1981, at which Honecker declared it had "saved peace in Europe." An estimated 185,000 East Germans escaped over the wall in those two decades.

QUICK QUIZ: What is the real name of entertainer Danny Kaye? See page 277.

GERMANY, WEST

Official Name: Federal Republic of Germany.
Area: 95,976 square miles (248,577 sq. km.).
Population: 61,481,000.
Chief Cities: Bonn, capital, 286,184; West Berlin, 1,902,750; Hamburg, 1,653,043; Munich, 1,299,693; Cologne (Köln), 976,136; Essen, 652,501; Frankfurt am Main, 628,203; Dortmund, 609,454; Düsseldorf, 594,770; Stuttgart, 581,989.
Government: Parliamentary democracy.
Chancellor: Helmut Kohl (since 1982).
President: Karl Carstens (since 1979).
Legislature: *Bundesrat,* 41 members; *Bundestag,* 498 members.
U.S. Ambassador to W. Germany: Rozanne L. Ridgway.
West German Ambassador to U.S.: Peter Hermes.
Flag: Black, red, and gold stripes.
Language: German.
Principal Ethnic Group: German (99%).
Leading Religions: Protestantism (47%), Roman Catholicism (45%).
Leading Industries: Manufacturing (steel, cement, paper, aluminum, electricity, machinery, motor vehicles, chemicals, textiles); agriculture (dairy products, cattle, hogs, poultry, potatoes, sugar beets, rye, wheat, oats, barley, vegetables, fruits); mining (coal, lignite, zinc, natural gas, gold, salt, petroleum); construction.
Foreign Trade: *Major exports*—automobiles, organic chemicals, plastics, scientific instruments; *major imports*—crude petroleum, fresh fruits, foodstuffs, copper, petroleum products, clothing, automobiles.
Places of Interest: The Alps; Black Forest; Harz Mountains; Weser Hills; Rhine and Danube rivers; Heidelberg; Bremen; Bayreuth; Berchtesgaden; Goethe's house and museum in Frankfurt; Germanic National Museum in Nuremberg; Hamburg botanical gardens and flower park; Cologne Cathedral; Charlemagne's throne in Aachen; Passau medieval town. *In Berlin:* Wall between West and East Berlin; Grünewald Hunting Lodge; Kaiser Wilhelm Memorial Church; Hansa Quarter; Dahlem Museum.

WEST GERMANY TODAY

West Germany is smaller than Oregon, but it has risen from destruction and defeat in World War II to become the leading industrial nation of western Europe. The main competitor of the U.S. and Japan in world trade, West Germany ranks among the world's leading producers of steel, cement, aluminum, electricity, coal-lignite, gold, paper, natural gas, and zinc.

West Germany has the largest population of any country of western Europe. It is also the most crowded of the major European nations because of land lost by World War II. As a result West Germany depends heavily on imports to feed its population.

Although ruled for hundreds of years by kings, emperors, and dictators, the West German people in the generations since World War II have developed a stable, democratic government that has become a beacon of freedom for refugees from communist eastern Europe. Ancient enmities with France and Britain have been healed.

West Germany today plays an important role in cooperative international organizations, such as NATO, the European Common Market, and the United Nations.

GEOGRAPHY AND CLIMATE

Wide lowlands extend from the Netherlands to East Germany in the north.

The upland regions of the central German mountains stretch from the Rhine to the East German border.

The wide valley and gorge of the Rhine cross the southeastern part of West Germany.

Mountains and plateaus range across southern Germany, with the Black Forest in the west, the Bavarian Forest in the east, and the Bavarian Alps in the far south.

The Rhine River, whose two main tributaries are the Mosel and the Main, empties into the North Sea. To the east are the Ems, Weser, and Elbe rivers, all with important ports on their estuaries. To the south the Danube flows eastward for about 400 miles.

Lake Constance, lying on the Swiss and Austrian borders, is the largest lake.

The average temperature ranges from below 21° F. in the mountains during the winter to about 68° F. in the valleys during the summer. Rain, falling throughout the year, varies from 20 to 78 inches, depending on the region and altitude. Snow may reach a depth of 6 feet in some areas during January and February.

West Germany is bordered on the north by Denmark; on the east by East Germany and Czechoslovakia; on the south by Austria and Switzerland; and on the west by France, Luxembourg, Belgium, and the Netherlands.

EARLY HISTORY

The Teutons and the Cimbri are thought to be among the earliest Germanic tribes. Roman records report their defeat by the general Marius in 102–101 B.C. Germanic tribes that included the Alemanni, Burgundians, Franks, Lombards, Ostrogoths, and Visigoths advanced south as the Roman Empire weakened and collapsed.

Charlemagne, the Germanic leader of the Franks who was crowned Roman emperor in A.D. 800, extended his sovereignty over most of Germany.

MIDDLE AGES

Powerful feudal princes divided Germany at a time when it was being invaded by Slavs, Norsemen, and Magyars.

Otto I, Saxon king of the Germans, created the Holy Roman Empire. He was crowned its first emperor in Rome in 962. However, rivalry among the feudal states in Germany and the struggle for supremacy between the emperors and the popes rendered the empire a loose and ineffective federation with little central authority.

The empire was strengthened under the Hohenstaufens, who subdued many of the large duchies. In 1180 Friedrich I Barbarossa dismembered Saxony, the last remaining great duchy.

His grandson Friedrich II was king of Sicily. He also became king of the Germans (1212) and emperor of the Holy Roman Empire (1220–

1250). Friedrich II ruled from Sicily, paying little attention to German problems. By the end of his reign the French monarchy and Italian city-states had begun their ascendancy.

REFORMATION

The weakness of the Holy Roman Empire became particularly evident when Germany found itself the center of the Reformation, the religious schism initiated by Martin Luther in 1517.

The Roman Catholic German emperor could not enforce his own religious policies or halt the conversion to Protestantism of many nobles.

The empire was torn by the Thirty Years War (1618–48). The Treaty of Westphalia in 1648 elevated the territorial sovereignty of the states above that of the empire.

PRUSSIA AND AUSTRIA COMPETE

Prussia grew into the only German state that could challenge Austria. When Friedrich the Great defeated Austria in 1740, Prussia joined the ranks of the great European powers.

Napoleon's rise to power in Europe brought an end to the Holy Roman Empire.

At the Congress of Vienna (1814–15) the German states were reduced in number, and a national structure was formed through the German Confederation, with Prussia and Austria as the dominant states. Austria, however, gained control of the confederation.

In 1848 liberal revolutions in Germany failed to unify the nation. The Prussian monarchy tried its own scheme of unification, but in 1850 Austria checked Prussian ambitions by threatening war.

GERMAN EMPIRE

In 1862 Prime Minister Otto von Bismarck of Prussia resolved to eliminate Austrian influence over Germany.

Bismarck achieved his goal with victory over Austria in the Austro-Prussian War (1866). Prussia went on to win the Franco-Prussian War of 1870–71 and was able to unify Germany under Emperor Wilhelm I in 1871. Bismarck became Germany's first chancellor.

From 1871 to 1914 the German Empire expanded rapidly. Its economy flourished. The acquisition of colonies and construction of a navy enhanced its power and prestige.

In 1888 Wilhelm II became emperor and two years later dismissed Bismarck as chancellor.

The rulers of Germany and Austria seized upon the assassination of the heir to the Austrian throne in 1914 as an opportune occasion to defeat or at least to divide their enemies.

Europe was thus plunged into World War I, which ended with Germany's defeat.

WEIMAR REPUBLIC

With the German defeat the Weimar Republic replaced the empire. At its inception the republic was saddled with the humiliating Treaty of Versailles (1919). Germany lost its overseas possessions and had to pay heavy reparations.

In the late 1920s the worldwide depression hit the German economy particularly hard, causing massive unemployment and social chaos.

HITLER'S NAZI GERMANY

By 1932 Adolf Hitler's National Socialist (Nazi) Party was the largest in the Reichstag. He became chancellor in January 1933. Within the year Hitler assumed dictatorial powers.

Hitler launched a campaign to eliminate all Jews from Germany. The official policy of anti-Semitism culminated during World War II in the "final solution" to the "Jewish problem"—the extermination of an estimated 6 million Jews in death camps.

In violation of the Versailles Treaty, Hitler remilitarized the Rhineland in 1936, annexed Austria in March 1938, and seized the Sudetenland of Czechoslovakia in September 1938.

In March 1939 Germany took over the rest of Czechoslovakia and demanded Danzig and the Polish Corridor that separated most of Germany from East Prussia.

World War II began when Germany invaded Poland on Sept. 1, 1939. The Nazis enjoyed spectacular successes up to 1941, but beginning with the invasion of Russia in that year, the tide gradually turned.

The war ended in May 1945 with Germany's unconditional surrender after Hitler's suicide.

ALLIED OCCUPATION

At conferences in Yalta and Potsdam the U.S., Britain, and the Soviet Union decided to divide Germany into four occupation zones, with Berlin under four-power control.

The Soviet Union, however, embarked on its own policy, and efforts to govern Germany through the Allied Control Commission collapsed.

In 1948–49 East Germany cut off land access to Berlin from West Germany. The U.S., Britain, and France organized an airlift to supply Berlin. As a result, the East Germans restored land access.

On Sept. 21, 1949, the democratic *Federal Republic of Germany* was granted self-government. It was created out of the U.S., British, and French zones of Germany. Theodor Heuss was elected president, and the Bundestag chose Konrad Adenauer as chancellor.

INDEPENDENCE FOR WEST GERMANY

West Germany was granted full independence on May 5, 1955, by the U.S., Britain, and France. The United States gave West Germany over $5 billion in aid to rebuild its industries and become a bulwark against the Soviet Union.

Under Adenauer the country achieved economic recovery and political stability.

Adenauer's foreign policy was built on cooperation with the United States, support of NATO, and reconciliation with France. In 1955 West Germany was allowed to rearm under supervision of NATO members. It established diplomatic relations with the Soviet Union. Efforts to reunite East and West Germany were defeated by Cold War tensions.

In 1961 East Germany built the Berlin Wall between the east and west sectors of Berlin to try to prevent East Germans from escaping.

Adenauer retired in 1963. Ludwig Erhard, who as economics minister had been largely responsible for Germany's "economic miracle," became

QUICK QUIZ: What monetary unit is used in Finland? See page 473.

GERMANY, WEST *(continued)*

chancellor. Erhard continued the foreign and domestic policies of Adenauer.

Erhard was succeeded in 1966 by Kurt Georg Kiesinger, who governed until 1969 with a coalition of Christian Democrats and Social Democrats. The Allies gave up their last occupation rights in May 1968.

OSTPOLITIK OF CHANCELLOR BRANDT

Following the parliamentary elections on Sept. 28, 1969, a coalition of Social Democrats and Free Democrats was formed under Chancellor Willy Brandt, who had been foreign minister in the Kiesinger cabinet.

The German political scene under Brandt was dominated by his *Ostpolitik,* a drive to normalize relations with the communist bloc, including East Germany. *Ostpolitik* led to treaties with the Soviet Union and Poland in 1970 that recognized the inviolability of postwar borders. The Bundestag ratified the treaties on May 17–19, 1972.

The first formal treaty between West and East Germany was ratified and went into effect Oct. 17, 1972. The treaty relaxed some border traffic regulations, enabling more West Germans to visit East Germany. Brandt then went on to win a November election with his coalition parties receiving over 54% of the popular vote.

A week after Brandt's reelection, his government signed a new and more important treaty with East Germany on Dec. 21, 1972, establishing diplomatic relations between the two. The treaty was ratified and went into effect on June 21, 1973. The two Germanys then were admitted to the UN in September 1973.

REGIME OF CHANCELLOR SCHMIDT

New leaders were chosen in 1974 for both of Germany's top political posts. Chancellor Brandt resigned suddenly on May 6, accepting complete responsibility for "negligence" in having employed a communist East German spy as his assistant for party affairs. Brandt designated 55-year-old Helmut Schmidt, his finance minister, as his successor. Schmidt's elevation as West Germany's fifth chancellor was ratified on May 16 by a 267 to 225 vote of the Bundestag. A day before, 54-year-old Walter Scheel, vice chancellor and foreign minister since 1969, was elected to the ceremonial office of president.

Chancellor Schmidt's coalition of the Social Democratic Party (SPD) and Free Democratic Party (FDP) won a close election over the Christian Democratic Party (CDU) on Oct. 3, 1976.

Terrorists of the left, attempting to bring anarchy to West Germany, stepped up their attacks in 1977. On Sept. 5 the terrorists kidnapped and later killed one of the nation's leading industrialists, Hanns-Martin Schleyer. Four of the gang hijacked a Lufthansa Boeing 737 airliner at Majorca on Oct. 13, 1977. The terrorists took the airliner on a 6,000-mile four-day flight to Somalia, killed the pilot en route, and threatened to kill the remaining passengers and crew by blowing up the plane.

Chancellor Schmidt's government won widespread acclaim when a 60-man West German commando unit made a daring raid on the hijacked airliner at Mogadishu, Somalia, on Oct.

CHANCELLORS OF WEST GERMANY

1949–63	Konrad Adenauer	Christian Democrat
1963–66	Ludwig Erhard	Christian Democrat
1966–69	Kurt Georg Kiesinger	Christian Democrat
1969–74	Willy Brandt	Social Democrat
1974–82	Helmut Schmidt	Social Democrat
1982–	Helmut Kohl	Christian Democrat

18, 1977, freeing the 86 hostages while killing three of the hijackers and wounding the fourth.

Schmidt and Soviet Leader Leonid I. Brezhnev signed on May 6, 1978, a 25-year economic cooperation agreement. As the Soviet Union's largest trading partner among Western nations, West Germany sells more than $5 billion in exports to the Soviet Union annually.

Karl Carstens, 64, speaker of the Bundestag and a former member of the Nazi Party, was elected president to succeed Scheel by an electoral assembly on May 23, 1979. As the Christian Democratic candidate, Carstens won by a vote of 528 to 431.

Parliament in 1979 lifted the statute of limitations that would have prevented the continued prosecution in the 1980s of former Nazis.

West Germany and East Germany continued to strengthen ties in 1980 with agreement on a $282 million pact to improve road, rail, and waterway links between the two nations.

In a national election on Oct. 5, 1980, Chancellor Schmidt's coalition strengthened its majority control of the lower house of parliament, winning 53.5% of the vote and gaining 16 seats. He had been opposed by the conservative governor of Bavaria, Franz Josef Strauss.

The growth of West Germany's economy ground almost to a halt in 1981 as the country's balance-of-trade deficit soared to $15 billion.

Ignoring U.S. sanctions against the Soviet Union, Schmidt's government in 1982 arranged $1.6 billion in credit to help build the Soviet Union's natural-gas pipeline from Siberia to western Europe.

CHRISTIAN DEMOCRATS REGAIN POWER

With the nation hurting from the worldwide recession, squabbling on economic issues developed among the members of Schmidt's coalition. The Free Democratic Party decided to switch its support from Schmidt. On Oct. 1, 1982, the Bundestag voted 256 to 235 to oust Schmidt.

Helmut Kohl, 52, head of the conservative Christian Democrats, became chancellor. In presenting his program to the Bundestag on Oct. 13, 1982, he said he planned to revive the nation from its "worst economic crisis" by cutting social-welfare benefits, encouraging private investment, and restricting immigration. He said he planned to strengthen relations with the U.S. Kohl promised a national election in March 1983.

Unemployment rose to a peak of more than 10% early in 1983 and then began to decline as the recession eased.

The main issue in a parliamentary election on March 6, 1983, was whether the government should approve the stationing of new U.S. missiles in West Germany. Kohl's pro-American conservative coalition won an increased majority, while the socialists who opposed deployment of the missiles suffered their worst defeat in more than 20 years.

GHANA

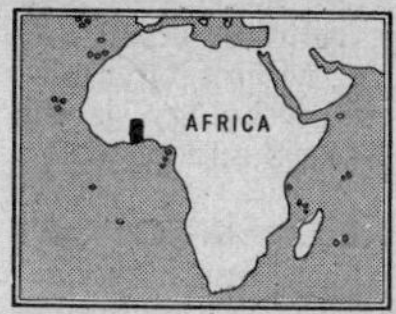

Official Name: Republic of Ghana.
Area: 92,100 square miles (238,537 sq. km.).
Population: 13,572,200.
Chief Cities: Accra, capital, 564,194; Kumasi, 260,286; Sekondi-Takoradi, 91,874.
Largest Metropolitan Area: Accra, 738,498.
Government: Leftist military-civilian junta.
Head of Government: Jerry J. Rawlings (since 1981).
U.S. Ambassador to Ghana: Robert E. Fritts.
Ghanian Ambassador to U.S.: Eric Kwamena Otoo.
Flag: Red, gold, and green stripes, with black star in gold stripe.
Languages: English (official), Akan, Ewe, Ga, Hausa.
Main Ethnic Group: Black.
Religions: Animism (45%), Christianity (43%), Islam (12%).
Leading Industries: Agriculture (cocoa, coffee, palm kernels, corn, rice, peanuts, rabbits, tobacco, rubber, cassava, sweet potatoes, tomatoes, cotton, vegetables, fruits); forestry and lumbering; mining (gold, diamonds, manganese, bauxite); manufacturing (electricity, aluminum, steel, tires, vehicle assembly, oil refining); fishing (tuna).
Foreign Trade: *Major exports*—cocoa, aluminum, petroleum, tuna, wood, gold, diamonds, manganese; *major imports*—auto parts, automobiles, food, medicines, textile machinery.
Places of Interest: Cape Coast Castle; Boti Waterfall; Elmina resort; national museum, Accra; Kumasi Cultural Center; Bolgatanga market; Mole Game Reserve at Damongo; Aburi Botanical Garden; Paga crocodile pond; Dawhenya irrigation project.

GHANA TODAY

About the size of Illinois and Indiana combined, Ghana is the world's leading grower of cacao beans, from which cocoa and chocolate are made.

Most Ghanaians are poor. Only about 1 in 4 can read and write.

In the west a forested belt extends north from the coast into the hilly Ashanti region.

The climate is hot and humid in the south, and warm and humid in the north. A rainy season lasts from May to September.

Upper Volta lies to the north, Togo to the east, and Ivory Coast to the west.

EARLY HISTORY

The ancient Ghana empire flourished from the 300s to the 1000s.

The Portuguese came in 1470, developing gold mining and slave trading. The first British trading visit to the area was by Thomas Windham in 1553.

After Britain declared the slave trade illegal in 1807, all Europeans except the British withdrew.

From 1826 to 1900 the British fought a long series of campaigns against the Ashantis of the interior. The coastal region was annexed by Britain as the Gold Coast Colony in 1874.

The Gold Coast became one of the most politically advanced African colonies. Blacks were admitted into the government in 1942.

The Convention People's Party (CPP), founded by Kwame Nkrumah, won legislative elections in 1951, and for the first time the black majority had power.

INDEPENDENCE

On March 6, 1957, Ghana (as the Gold Coast was renamed) became the first black African colony granted independence by Britain.

In 1960 Ghana became a republic. Nkrumah, a communist, was elected president. He then established a one-party dictatorship.

In 1966 while in Peking, Nkrumah was deposed by a military coup. A military junta headed by Gen. A.A. Afrifa ruled until 1969.

Ghana's first free general elections since 1956 were held Aug. 29, 1969. The Progress Party of Kofi Busia, leader of the opposition to Nkrumah, won a majority of seats in the national assembly.

On Jan. 13, 1972, a military coup, led by Col. Ignatius Kutu Acheampong, overthrew Busia.

Lt. Gen. Fred W.K. Akuffo seized power in a bloodless coup on July 5, 1978.

Petroleum was discovered in commercial amounts in 1978.

Flight Lt. Jerry J. Rawlings, 31, led a coup that overthrew the government on June 4, 1979. Declaring a "moral revolution," Rawlings arrested dozens of officials on charges of corruption. Eight were executed, including three former heads of state, Akuffo, Acheampong, and Afrifa.

After a new constitution similar to that of the U.S. was drawn up, Rawlings ordered the first multiparty elections since 1969. Ghanaians elected a national assembly and chose as president Dr. Hilla Limann, 52, an economist.

The nation's economy declined in 1980–81 because of crop failures. President Limann appealed in 1981 to foreign governments and private investors for more economic aid.

Rawlings overthrew Limann's government on Dec. 31, 1981, declaring it had brought Ghana "total economic ruin." He suspended the constitution and appointed a seven-man leftist military-civilian council to help him rule. Several hundred persons were killed in the uprising. Limann and more than 200 former officials were imprisoned. Many Ghanaians fled to neighboring countries.

An admirer of Libyan strong man Col. Mu'ammar al-Qadhafi, Rawlings reestablished diplomatic relations with Libya that had been broken by Limann in 1980. Libya sent financial aid and food to Rawlings' government. Soviet-bloc nations also promised economic help.

Rawlings froze prices in an effort to bring under control inflation that had been running at an annual rate of 116%.

When three justices of Ghana's supreme court were slain in 1982, other judges went on strike. In 1983, Rawlings abolished the entire judicial system.

Ghana's economy deteriorated further in 1983 as the government tried to cope with an influx of more than 500,000 poverty-stricken Ghanians expelled from Nigeria. The World Bank and the International Monetary Fund approved a $300 million loan to aid economic recovery.

QUICK QUIZ: What is the main export of Niger? See page 619.

GREECE

Official Name: Hellenic Republic.
Area: 50,944 square miles (131,944 sq. km.).
Population: 9,984,910.
Chief Cities: Athinai (Athens), capital, 867,023; Thessaloniki (Salonika), 345,799; Piraiéus (Piraeus), 187,362; Péristéri, 118,413.
Largest Metropolitan Area: Athens, 2,101,103.
Government: Parliamentary democracy.
Prime Minister: Andreas Papandreou (since 1981).
President: Constantine Karamanlis (since 1980).
Parliament: 300 members.
Greek Ambassador to U.S.: Nicholas Karandreas.
U.S. Ambassador to Greece: Monteagle Stearns.
Flag: White cross on blue field in upper hoist corner; blue and white stripes.
Language: Greek.
Chief Ethnic Group: Greek (97%).
Main Religion: Greek Orthodox (98%).
Leading Industries: Manufacturing (textiles, chemicals, steel, tobacco products, aluminum, consumer products); agriculture (tobacco, cotton, wheat, raisins, currants, olives, grapes, fruits, vegetables); shipping; tourism; mining (petroleum, bauxite, iron, zinc, lead, lignite, chrome, nickel).
Foreign Trade: *Major exports*—tobacco, currants, raisins, grapes; *major imports*—machinery, transport equipment, iron and steel, crude petroleum.
Places of Interest: Mount Olympus; Pindus Mountains; islands of Corfu, Rhodes, Cyclades, Mykonos, and Crete—Minoan ruins; Temple of Apollo in Corinth; Delphi ruins; Temple of Poseidon in Sounion. *In Athens:* Parthenon, Acropolis, and Acropolis Museum; temples of Nike, Theseus, Zeus.

GREECE TODAY

Although ancient Greece was the birthplace of democracy, modern Greece has experienced only a few brief periods of democratic government. Civilian government, civil rights, and political democracy were restored only 10 years ago.

The U.S. maintains four military bases in Greece.

The people of Greece have one of the lowest standards of living in western Europe. About 4 out of 10 are farmers, barely making a living for their families. But most people are educated. Only about 1 in 10 cannot read and write.

Greece has lacked basic mineral and energy resources to become a leading industrial nation. Manufacturing provides only about one-fifth of the national income. As a result, Greece has a huge annual trade deficit with the cost of imports three times that of exports. Petroleum from deposits in the Aegean Sea fill only about one-fifth of Greece's requirements.

The tourism and shipping industries provide a major share of the money Greece uses to import needed petroleum and manufactured products.

Hundreds of thousands of visitors each year are attracted by the Acropolis, the Parthenon, and other ruins of ancient Greece. Others come to Greece to enjoy the blue skies and warm beaches of the Greek isles.

Greece is a mountainous and heavily wooded country. The Pindus range, running north and south, is the most important. Mount Olympus, home of the gods in Greek mythology, is the highest peak (9,551 feet). Valleys and plains lie between the mountains.

The main rivers are in the north and have their origins in other countries. None is navigable. Southern Greece includes the Peloponnesian peninsula and some 437 offshore islands, the largest of which is Crete.

Greece, the southernmost country of the Balkan peninsula, is bordered on the north by Albania, Yugoslavia, and Bulgaria; on the east by Turkey and the Aegean Sea; on the south by the Mediterranean Sea; and on the west by the Ionian Sea.

EARLY HISTORY

Neolithic man lived in Greece at least as early as 4000 B.C. Beginning about 2000 B.C., successive waves of Greek-speaking Achaeans, an Indo-European people, migrated into the area, supplanting the existing cultures.

By 1100 B.C. two major civilizations had flourished and vanished. The Minoan civilization was centered on the island of Crete and later influenced the mainland from the south. The Mycenaean civilization, generally less advanced than the Minoan, was on the mainland.

ANCIENT GREEK EMPIRE

Greek city-states began to develop about 1000 B.C. They were sufficiently well established by 800 B.C. to become the source of democracy and of colonization efforts. By 600 B.C. colonies founded from the city-states were located on islands in the Ionian, Aegean, and Mediterranean seas, in Asia Minor, on the African coast, and as far west as France and Spain.

Ancient Greek civilization reached its zenith in the 400s B.C., when Athens was the center of a vast overseas empire.

After the death of Alexander the Great in 323 B.C., Greek power disintegrated. By 146 B.C. Greece had become a province of the new Mediterranean power, the Roman Empire.

BYZANTINE AND TURKISH RULE

After Roman Emperor Constantine moved the capital of the empire in A.D. 330 to Constantinople (now Istanbul, Turkey), the Grecian influence was strongly felt.

While Rome languished under barbarian control, Constantinople and Greece were the centers of a thriving Byzantine Greek civilization.

In the Fourth Crusade, Constantinople was sacked by crusaders en route to the Holy Land (1204). The Greeks won it back in 1261.

Constantinople fell to the Turks in 1453. Greece then became a Turkish province in 1460.

INDEPENDENT MONARCHY

After almost four centuries of subjugation by the Turks, a war of independence was begun by the Greeks on March 25, 1821. Supported by Britain, France, and Russia, the revolt was ultimately successful, and in July 1832 the sultan recognized the independence of Greece.

Prince Otto of Bavaria was made king of

Greece in 1833. He was overthrown in 1862 and was succeeded by Prince William George of Denmark, who became George I.

Greece unsuccessfully attempted to enlarge its territory in the Greco-Turkish war of 1897.

In the early 1900s the Greeks fought with neighboring Slavs and Turks in an effort to reclaim national territory. In the two Balkan wars (1912 and 1913), Greece obtained Epirus, parts of Thrace and Macedonia, and Crete.

Greece fought on the side of the Allies in World War I and was rewarded with territory from Bulgaria and Turkey.

The people voted for a monarchy in 1920 and for a republic in 1924. King George II, who was dethroned in 1924, returned in 1935 following a plebiscite. On Aug. 4, 1936, the crown accepted Gen. Ioannis Metaxas as dictator.

Metaxas headed the resistance when Italy invaded Greece in 1940. Greece was occupied by Italy and Germany in 1941–44.

After World War II, five years of civil war ensued between the government and communist guerrillas. U.S. aid under the Truman Doctrine helped bring final defeat of the communists in 1949. About 120,000 Greeks were killed in the fighting.

King George II died in 1947 and was succeeded by his brother Paul I. Upon Paul's death in 1964, his son Constantine II came to the throne.

A political crisis developed in 1965 between the king and Prime Minister George Papandreou over the issue of an investigation of a secret organization within the army (ASPIDA). In June 1965 Papandreou resigned. A period of unstable governments ensued.

MILITARY RULE

A military coup took place on April 21, 1967. A military junta took control, naming Col. George Papadopoulos as premier and defense minister.

On Dec. 13, 1967, King Constantine unsuccessfully attempted a countercoup. In its aftermath, he and the royal family fled to Rome.

After oil deposits were discovered in the Aegean Sea in 1973, disputes developed with Turkey over rights to the fuel resource.

Papadopoulos deposed the exiled king on June 1, 1973. He decreed Greece a republic and took the title of president.

On Nov. 25, 1973, military leaders overthrew Papadopoulos. Brig. Gen. Dimitrios Ioannides seized control of the government.

The Greek military junta supported the overthrow of the government of Archbishop Makarios on Cyprus in July 1974. When Turkey invaded Cyprus and threatened war if Greece intervened, the military junta collapsed.

DEMOCRATIC REPUBLIC

Constantine Karamanlis, a conservative former premier in 1955–63 who had been living in France, was called home and sworn in as premier on July 24, 1974.

Premier Karamanlis ordered a general amnesty for political prisoners. He restored freedom of the press and freedom of speech.

Anti-American demonstrations broke out in August 1974 as Greeks blamed the U.S. for failing to prevent Turkey's invasion of Cyprus. Karamanlis withdrew Greek forces from the NATO alliance, but applied for readmission in 1976.

The first free parliamentary elections in 10 years were held on Nov. 17, 1974. Karamanlis' New Democracy Party won a sweeping victory, capturing more than two-thirds of the 300 seats.

In a referendum held on Dec. 8, 1974, voters overwhelmingly rejected a return to monarchy.

A new constitution was adopted in June 1975, establishing a parliamentary republic. Parliament elected Constantine Tsatsos, 76, as president.

After a month-long trial former President Papadopoulos and two other leaders of the 1967 coup were sentenced to death for treason on Aug. 23, 1975. But the Greek cabinet commuted the sentences to life imprisonment.

To overcome dependence on imported oil, the government announced plans in 1978 to build 18 new hydroelectric generating plants, 10 new lignite-fired generators, and one 600-megawatt nuclear power plant, all to be completed by 1987.

Having led Greece back to democracy, the 73-year-old Karamanlis decided in 1980 to turn leadership of his party over to younger men and accepted parliamentary election to the less demanding post as the nation's president. Foreign minister George John Rallis, 62, was chosen on May 8 to succeed Karamanlis as prime minister.

After a military coup in Turkey, that country agreed to Greece's readmission to NATO, which was achieved on Oct. 20, 1980.

Although Greece joined the European Community (Common Market) on Jan. 1, 1981, the nation's economy did not immediately benefit from the expanded trade opportunities.

In a landslide victory in elections on Oct. 18, 1981, socialists won a majority of 174 of parliament's 300 seats to 113 for Prime Minister Rallis' New Democracy Party.

Socialist Andreas Papandreou, 62, a former American economics professor who gave up U.S. citizenship to enter Greek politics, became prime minister on Oct. 21, 1981.

Because Greece's economy declined in 1981–83 as a result of the worldwide recession, the socialist government postponed plans for nationalization of industries. Instead, it concentrated on social reforms, passing laws in 1982 that legalized civil marriage and ended criminal prosecution of adultery. Other laws were drawn to separate the government from the Greek Orthodox Church, to expropriate hundreds of thousands of acres of church land, to permit divorce without church sanction, to break the communist hold on labor unions, and to emancipate women.

Elected on a platform calling for Greece's withdrawal from NATO and the closing of U.S. military bases in Greece, Papandreou reversed himself by agreeing in 1983 to permit the U.S. bases to continue to operate at least until 1988. At the same time the U.S. promised Greece about $500 million in annual military aid.

However, Papandreou broke ranks with other Western leaders in 1983 by refusing to condemn the Soviet Union for shooting down a South Korean airliner and by campaigning for postponement of the deployment of new U.S. missiles in Europe.

QUICK QUIZ: Mauritius was the home of what extinct animal? See page 606.

GRENADA

Official Name: State of Grenada.
Area: 133 square miles (344 sq. km.).
Population: 111,727.
Capital: St. George's, 7,303.
Government: Transitional.
Head of Government: Governor General Sir Paul Scoon (since 1983).
Flag: Red border with yellow stars above and below green and yellow triangles; red circle with yellow star in center; nutmeg on green triangle.
Official Language: English.
Main Ethnic Group: Black.
Principal Religions: Roman Catholic, Anglican.
Leading Industries: Tourism; agriculture (nutmegs, cocoa, bananas, fruits, vegetables, sugarcane, cotton, spices); fishing; food processing.
Foreign Trade: *Major exports*—nutmegs, cocoa beans, mace, bananas; *major imports*—petroleum, food, consumer goods.
Places of Interest: *In St. George's: Fort George, government buildings, shops; Sauteurs; Grenville; island of Carricou; beaches.*

GRENADA TODAY

A Caribbean island nation, Grenada is one of the smallest nations in the world.

Part of the Windward Islands chain, the mountainous island of Grenada lies less than 100 miles off the coast of Venezuela. The country also includes part of the small Grenadines islands to the north.

The source of much of the world's nutmeg, the island displays a nutmeg on its national flag.

HISTORY

Settled by French colonists in the 1600s, Grenada became a British possession in 1763.

Grenada was granted self-government in 1967. Prime Minister Eric M. Gairy's United Labor Party won elections in 1967 and 1972.

The nation achieved full independence within the British Commonwealth of Nations on Feb. 7, 1974, with Gairy continuing as prime minister.

A coup in which two persons were killed overthrew Gairy's dictatorial rule on March 13, 1979, while Gairy was visiting the U.S. The head of the Marxist New Jewel Movement, Maurice Bishop, 33, whose father was killed by Gairy's secret police in 1974, became prime minister. Bishop suspended the constitution and set up a governing 14-member Marxist revolutionary council.

On Oct. 15, 1979, Bishop's government shut down the only opposition newspaper.

Construction moved forward in 1980–83 on an international airport, largely financed by Cuba, which was expected to use it as a military base.

Bishop was slain on Oct. 19, 1983, by his Marxist associates in a coup that began six days earlier.

The U.S. landed troops on Oct. 25, 1983, defeating a Cuban military garrison and arresting the coup leaders. See page 29.

GUATEMALA

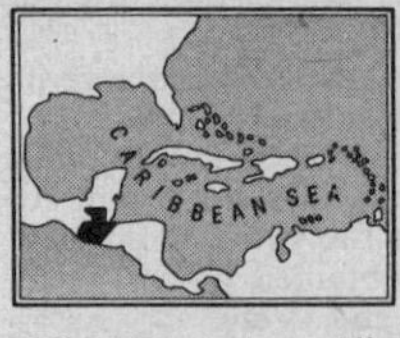

Official Name: Republic of Guatemala.
Area: 42,042 square miles (108,889 sq. km.).
Population: 6,384,290.
Capital: Guatemala City, 793,336.
Government: Martial-law dictatorship.
President: Gen. Oscar Mejia Victores (since 1983).
U.S. Ambassador to Guatemala: Frederic L. Chapin.
Guatemalan Ambassador to U.S.: Jorge Luis Zelaya Coronado.
Flag: Blue, white, and blue bars, with national coat of arms in center.
Languages: Spanish (official), Maya.
Main Ethnic Groups: Maya-Quiché Indians (55%), mestizo (42%).
Religion: Roman Catholicism (92%).
Leading Industries: Agriculture (coffee, cotton, bananas, sugarcane, cattle, corn, rice, beans, wheat, spices, tobacco); manufacturing (tobacco products, chemicals, textiles, plastics, tires, chemicals, consumer goods); food processing; construction; mining (nickel, petroleum); fishing (shrimp).
Foreign Trade: *Major exports*—coffee, cotton, bananas, sugar, beef, wood, chicle; *major imports*—iron and steel, textiles, pharmaceuticals, vehicles, petroleum, food, consumer goods.
Places of Interest: National palace at Guatemala City; Mayan ruins at Tikal, Uaxactum, Piedras Negras, Zaculeu; Spanish ruins at Antigua Guatemala.

GUATEMALA TODAY

About the size of Tennessee, Guatemala is a poor Central American nation dominated by its generals. Thousands of persons are killed or disappear each year in a civil war between the military regime and rebel guerrillas.

The U.S. is Guatemala's main trading partner, buying about a fourth of its exports.

Guatemala's economy depends largely on agriculture. Coffee makes up about half the country's exports, followed in importance by cotton, bananas, and sugar.

Most Guatemalans are poor farmers.

The country has a 50-mile coastline on the Caribbean and a 200-mile coast on the Pacific. The land ranges from a coastal plain to mountainous areas.

There are 30 volcanoes, 8 of which are active.

Mexico lies to the west and north. Belize is to the northeast. Honduras lies to the east and El Salvador to the southeast.

EARLY HISTORY

Guatemala was part of the territory occupied originally by the Mayas, whose influence and power began to decline in the 1100s.

From 1524 to 1821 Central America from Yucatán to Panama was ruled by the Spanish.

By the mid-1700s Antigua, the capital, was one of the great cities of the New World, comparable to Mexico City and Lima. Severe earthquakes in 1773 destroyed the city, and the capital was moved to Guatemala City.

INDEPENDENCE

Guatemala declared its independence from Spain on Sept. 15, 1821. It was briefly annexed by Mexico, and then was a member of the Central American Federation until 1838. Since then it has been ruled largely by military dictators with a few brief periods of representative government.

Guatemala suffered a major disaster on Feb. 4, 1976, when a devastating earthquake destroyed much of the capital city and scores of other towns and villages. Some 22,934 persons were killed.

Petroleum in commercial quantities was discovered in 1976, but reserves are limited.

The U.S. suspended military aid in 1977 because of the government's human-rights violations.

The nation's congress chose Gen. Romeo Lucas García as president in 1978.

Amnesty International in 1981 accused President Lucas of personally directing a campaign of torture and murder against opponents that resulted in more than 3,000 deaths in 1980.

Religious leaders estimated 11,000 Guatemalans were killed in 1981 in the civil war.

In a presidential election on March 7, 1982, the ruling party's candidate, Gen. Angel Anibal Guevara, was declared the winner, although the results were generally regarded as fraudulent.

Before Guevara could take office, Gen. Efrain Rios Montt, a born-again Christian, overthrew the government on March 23, 1982.

Gen. Rios Montt decreed martial law on July 1, 1982, declaring, "It is time to do what God orders" in warring against guerrillas. Thousands of Guatemalans fled to neighboring countries.

In October 1982 Amnesty International reported that Gen. Rios Montt's forces had "massacred more than 2,600 Indians and peasants" in the summer campaign.

Gen. Oscar Mejia Victores, 53, the minister of defense, overthrew Montt on Aug. 8, 1983. He promised restoration of civilian rule by 1985.

GUINEA

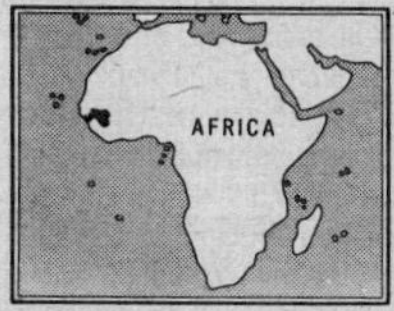

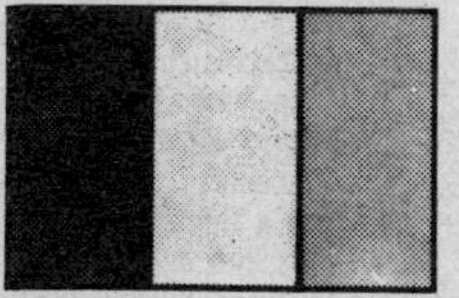

Official Name: Republic of Guinea.
Area: 94,926 square miles (245,857 sq. km.).
Population: 5,503,860.
Capital: Conakry, 197,267.
Government: One-party communist state.
President: Ahmed Sékou Touré (since 1958).
Premier: Lansana Beavogui (took office in 1972).
National Assembly: 75 members.
U.S. Ambassador to Guinea: James D. Rosenthal.
Guinean Ambassador to U.S.: Mamady L. Conde.
Flag: Red, yellow, and green bars.
Languages: French (official), Fulani, Malinké, Susu.
Principal Religion: Islam.
Main Ethnic Groups: Fulani (Hamitic; 28%), Malinké (17%), Susu (9%).
Leading Industries: Agriculture (rice, palm kernels, tea, bananas, coffee, yams, pineapples, peanuts, manioc, millet, corn, vegetables, fruits, livestock); mining (bauxite, diamonds, gold, iron); manufacturing (bauxite refining); fishing.
Foreign Trade: *Major exports*—alumina, pineapples, bananas, palm kernels, coffee; *major imports*—machinery, metals, food, transport equipment.
Places of Interest: Mount Nimba National Reserve; national museum in Conakry.

GUINEA TODAY

About the size of Oregon, Guinea is a communist police state and one of Africa's poorest countries. Most of the people live in thatched mud huts in tribal villages, growing enough food to feed their families and little else. Few adults can read or write, and few children go to school.

However, Guinea has large deposits of bauxite, iron, gold, and diamonds, as well as the potential for hydroelectric development.

The coastal plain ascends to a mountainous region called Futa Jallon. Interior Guinea is a rolling plain, partly woodland and partly grassy savanna, averaging about 1,000 feet in height. In the forested highlands Mt. Nimba rises to 5,748 feet. The Niger, the Senegal, and the Gambia rivers flow from the Futa Jallon.

The climate is humid and tropical. Temperatures range from 60° to 100° F. Annual rainfall has measured 168 inches at Conakry.

Guinea is bordered on the north by Guinea-Bissau, Senegal, and Mali; on the east by Mali and Ivory Coast; and on the south by Liberia and Sierra Leone.

HISTORY

The empires of Ghana and the Malinkés dominated Guinea in medieval times.

Portuguese explorers and slave traders came to the Guinea coast in the 1400s.

The Treaty of Paris of 1814 secured French rights in Guinea. In 1849 a French protectorate was declared.

Guinea declared itself independent on Oct. 2, 1958, with Ahmed Sékou Touré as its first president.

Touré—an avowed Marxist—turned to the Soviet Union and communist China for help. Guinea remained nonaligned, however, and has since received assistance from Western nations.

In November 1970 Guinea defeated an anti-regime invasion by land and sea, allegedly backed by Portugal. Some 92 persons were sentenced to death for treason (34 in absentia).

Guinea's export revenues rose nearly 800% from 1972 to 1976 as two large bauxite mining developments got into production.

The International League for Human Rights appealed to the UN in 1977 to intervene in Guinea to halt what it called a "reign of terror" by Touré in which thousands of Guineans were imprisoned and tortured and from which more than 2 million fled to other countries.

Touré visited President Carter in Washington, D.C., in 1979 and President Reagan in 1982 seeking increases in U.S. economic aid.

Amnesty International in October 1982 called on Touré to account for 2,800 Guineans who disappeared in the 1970s.

QUICK QUIZ: What U.S. magazine has the largest circulation? See page 688.

GUINEA-BISSAU

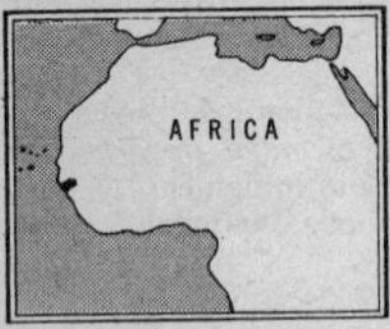

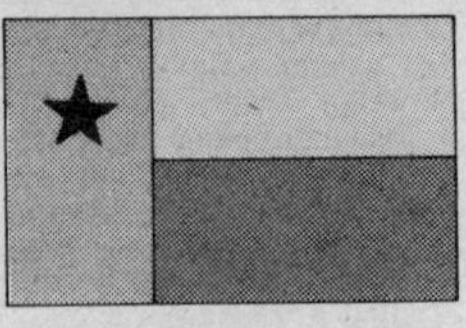

Official Name: Republic of Guinea-Bissau.
Area: 13,948 square miles (36,125 sq. km.).
Population: 846,653.
Capital: Bissau, 60,000.
Government: One-party socialist state.
Head of Government: João Bernardo Veira (since 1980).
National People's Assembly: 150 members.
U.S. Ambassador to Guinea-Bissau: Wesley W. Egan Jr.
Ambassador to U.S.: Inacio Semedo Jr.
Flag: Red vertical bar at hoist with black star; two horizontal stripes, yellow above green.
Languages: Portuguese, Fulani, Malinké, Felup, Papel, Balanta, Mandyako.
Main Ethnic Group: Bantu (97%).
Principal Religions: Animism (66%), Islam (30%).
Leading Industries: Agriculture (rice, millet, palm kernels, peanuts, cattle); fishing; forestry.
Foreign Trade: *Major exports*—peanuts, palm kernels, shrimp; *major imports*—food, consumer goods.
Places of Interest: Bissau; islands of the Bijagos archipelago; Boloma, capital until 1948.

About the size of Massachusetts and Connecticut combined, Guinea-Bissau was the first of Portugal's African colonies to win independence.

One of the poorest countries of Africa, Guinea-Bissau has an economy that depends on farming, fishing, livestock raising, and lumbering. It spends four times more for imports than it receives from exports. Most Guinea-Bissauans live in tribes whose way of life has changed little in thousands of years.

A tropical country with a hot humid climate the year round, Guinea-Bissau has an Atlantic coastline indented by many rivers. Much of the coast is low and swampy. Inland hills rise to about 800 feet. Many people live in the offshore islands of the Bijagos archipelago. Senegal is to the north and Guinea to the south.

The Portuguese explorer Nuno Tristão first visited the area in 1446. The region became a center for the Portuguese slave trade.

Called Portuguese Guinea for over 500 years of Portuguese rule, the area was made an overseas province in 1951. An independence movement began in 1959 with guerrilla warfare that raged for the next 15 years.

The African Independence Party (PAIGC) declared independence on Sept. 24, 1973, with Luis Cabral as president. Portugal recognized Guinea-Bissau's independence on Sept. 10, 1974.

Prime Minister João Bernardo Veira overthrew and imprisoned Cabral in 1980, accusing him of directing the murder of hundreds of opponents.

In May 1981 Veira ended the government monopoly on rice, permitting small merchants to resume buying and selling the food staple.

In the 1970s and 1980s the government sought assistance from wealthier countries to develop rice farming to become self-sufficient in food production. Mineral exploration was begun seeking bauxite and petroleum deposits.

GUYANA

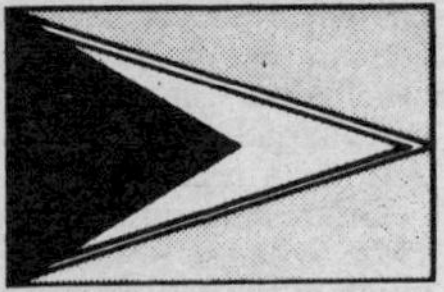

Official Name: Cooperative Republic of Guyana.
Area: 83,000 square miles (214,969 sq. km.).
Population: 873,950.
Capital: Georgetown, 72,049.
Government: Marxist socialist republic.
President: Forbes Burnham (since 1980).
National Assembly: 53 members.
U.S. Ambassador to Guyana: Gerald E. Thomas.
Guyanese Ambassador to U.S.: Cedric Hilburn Grant.
Flag: Green field with black-edged red triangle superimposed on white-edged yellow triangle.
Languages: English (official), East Indian dialects.
Main Ethnic Groups: East Indian (55%), black (35%).
Principal Religions: Christianity (57%), Hinduism (33%), Islam (9%).
Leading Industries: Mining (bauxite, petroleum, gold, diamonds); agriculture (rice, sugarcane, palm kernels, coffee, fruits, vegetables); food processing; fishing; forestry and lumbering.
Foreign Trade: *Major exports*—sugar, bauxite, alumina, rice, gold, diamonds, shrimp; *major imports*—machinery, petroleum, textiles, motor vehicles, wheat.
Places of Interest: Kaieteur Waterfall; St. George's Cathedral and Guyana Museum in Georgetown; Bartica area; Rupununi savanna country.

Guyana is the only South American country with a British cultural background. The Marxist socialist government operates most industry, including the profitable bauxite mines.

About the size of Idaho, the country is largely covered by a thick, uninhabited tropical forest. Most Guyanese live in the narrow plain along the Atlantic coast.

By 1620 the Dutch had partially settled the country. The three colonies of Berbice, Demerara, and Essequibo were ceded to Britain in 1814 and united as British Guiana in 1831. Britain granted independence on May 26, 1966.

In 1964 elections Forbes Burnham of the People's National Congress became prime minister. He was reelected in 1968 and 1973.

Guyana became a republic on Feb. 23, 1970.

A national referendum on July 10, 1978, gave the government the right to change the constitution without holding national votes.

World attention focused on Guyana in 1978 when members of an American religious cult murdered a visiting U.S. congressman on Nov. 18. The cult's founder, the Rev. Jim Jones, and over 900 followers committed mass suicide.

Burnham became president on Oct. 6, 1980, under a new constitution that gave the office strengthened powers as chief executive.

Burnham was declared winner of a presidental election on Dec. 15, 1980. However, international observers reported that the election was conducted with "massive and blatant fraud."

In August 1981 the U.S. refused to give a $20 million loan to aid Guyana's rice production.

Petroleum was discovered in April 1982 in the region near the border with Brazil.

HAITI

Official Name: Republic of Haiti.
Area: 10,714 square miles (27,750 sq. km.).
Population: 5,155,670.
Capital: Port-au-Prince, 790,900.
Government: Dictatorship.
President: Jean-Claude Duvalier (since 1971).
National Assembly: 58 members.
U.S. Ambassador to Haiti: Clayton E. McManaway Jr.
Haitian Ambassador to U.S.: Fritz N. Cineas.
Flag: Black and red bars; centered white rectangle contains emblems of war around palm tree.
Languages: French (official), Creole.
Ethnic Groups: Black (95%), Mulatto (5%).
Religions: Roman Catholicism (official; 80%), voodooism.
Leading Industries: Agriculture (coffee, sisal, sugar cane, rice, cocoa, poultry, vegetables, fruits); food processing; mining (copper, bauxite); tourism; manufacturing (textiles, soap, cement, assembly plants); fishing.
Foreign Trade: *Major exports*—coffee, sugar, sisal; *major imports*—cotton textiles, foodstuffs, petroleum, machinery.
Places of Interest: Sans Souci Palace ruins and King Henri Christophe fortress La Citadelle; Toussaint L'Ouverture Monument in Cap-Haïtien; national museum in Port-au-Prince; vacation resorts at Pétionville and Kenscoff.

HAITI TODAY

About the size of Maryland, Haiti is a poor, overpopulated Caribbean nation. It has been ruled as a police state by the Duvalier family for over two decades.

Only about 1 in 5 Haitians can read and write. Some farm only to raise their own food. Others work on coffee or sugar plantations. About half the people are unemployed.

About two-thirds of the government's national budget comes from foreign loans and aid by the U.S. and other nations. The U.S. has provided over $250 million in aid in the past three decades.

Development of the island's resources has been hampered by corruption and by the lack of highways. About two-thirds of the country is too mountainous to be farmed.

During the Duvalier regimes an estimated 300,000 to 400,000 Haitians have made their way to new homes in the U.S.

Haiti occupies the western third of the island of Hispaniola, which it shares with the Dominican Republic to the east.

EARLY HISTORY

The island of Hispaniola was discovered for Spain by Christopher Columbus in 1492.

Having killed most of the Arawak natives by 1533, the Spanish settled mainly on the eastern side of the island in the vicinity of Santo Domingo. The western area became a base for French and English pirates.

By the Treaty of Ryswick (1697) Spain ceded the western region, now Haiti, to France. French settlers imported many slaves.

The French Revolution, which began in 1789, sparked black slave rebellions in which most of the white colonists were killed or fled.

In 1792 French troops were sent to crush the revolt but were defeated by a self-educated, freed slave, Pierre-Dominique Toussaint L'Ouverture. Agreeing in 1799 to govern for France, Toussaint occupied Santo Domingo in the eastern part of the island, abolished slavery, and gave the island a constitution. In 1802, however, France's new ruler, Napoleon Bonaparte, sent troops to restore French authority. Toussaint, captured by treachery, died in a French prison.

INDEPENDENT KINGDOM

The French troops were decimated by disease and by clashes with blacks led by Jean-Jacques Dessalines. The army withdrew in 1803, and in 1804 Dessalines declared Haiti's independence. Dessalines ruled as a despot under the title of Emperor Jacques I until his assassination in 1806.

The country then divided, with the north ruled autocratically by Henri Christophe, a black who proclaimed himself King Henri I. A republic in the south and west was governed by a mulatto, Alexandre Pétion, until his death in 1818. His successor, was Jean Pierre Boyer. Following the suicide of King Henri in 1820, the entire island was united in 1822 when Boyer's forces conquered Santo Domingo. A year after Boyer's ouster in 1843, Santo Domingo gained independence as the Dominican Republic. From 1843 to 1915, Haiti was ruled by 22 dictators.

HAITI IN THE 1900s

In 1905 the U.S. took Haiti's customs into receivership, and 10 years later the U.S. seized full control. The U.S. withdrew its troops in 1934, but retained financial control until 1947.

François "Papa Doc" Duvalier became dictator after being elected president in 1957. His regime, faced by economic decline and political unrest, became repressive, with all opposition held in check by secret-police terror. The economy of Haiti stagnated.

Duvalier died on April 21, 1971, and was succeeded by his 19-year-old son, Jean-Claude "Baby Doc" Duvalier, as president for life.

The Duvalier fortune, acquired during more than two decades of rule, is unofficially estimated at over $400 million.

Duvalier cracked down on opponents in 1979, launching a new wave of arrests. Political opponents were given long jail terms.

About 30,000 Haitians fled to the United States in 1980 and were granted political asylum.

U.S. President Reagan on Sept. 29, 1981, ordered the Coast Guard to intercept and turn back to Haiti boats carrying illegal immigrants bound for the United States.

In 1983, for the first time in 26 years, municipal elections were held. The Duvalier candidate for mayor was defeated in the nation's largest city, Cap Haitien.

QUICK QUIZ: Which nation of the world is the most highly industrialized? See page 598.

HONDURAS

Official Name: Republic of Honduras.
Area: 43,277 square miles (112,088 sq. km.).
Population: 4,359,320.
Chief Cities: Tegucigalpa, capital, 273,894; San Pedro Sula, 150,991.
Government: Democratic republic.
President: Roberto Suazo Córdova (since 1982).
Congress: 78 members.
U.S. Ambassador to Honduras: John Negroponte.
Honduran Ambassador to U.S.: Juan Agurcia Ewing.
Flag: Stripes of blue, white, and blue, with five blue stars in center.
Official Language: Spanish.
Main Ethnic Groups: Mestizo (90%), African (5%), Indian (4%).
Main Religion: Roman Catholicism (90%).
Leading Industries: Agriculture (bananas, coffee, cattle, corn, beans, rice, sugarcane, tobacco, vegetables, fruits); forestry and lumbering; manufacturing (textiles, detergents, cement, paper, chemicals, food products, clothing); mining (gold, silver, copper, lead, zinc).
Foreign Trade: *Major exports*—bananas, coffee, meat, sugar, lumber, silver, tobacco; *major imports*—petroleum products, paper and paperboard, textile yarn and fabrics, electrical machinery.
Places of Interest: Tegucigalpa; Mayan ruins at Copán; Comayagua and Trujillo ancient cities; Bay Islands; Yojoa Lake; San Fernando Castle at Omoa; La Ceiba, Puerto Cortés, Tela beaches.

HONDURAS TODAY

About the size of Tennessee, Honduras is a poor Central American country. Banana-growing is its most important industry.

About two-thirds of the people are impoverished farm workers. Over half cannot read or write.

Development of the country has been hampered because there are few roads and highways. Much of the eastern part of Honduras can only be reached by airplanes or coastal boats.

Narrow lowlands along the Gulf of Fonseca and the Caribbean coast fringe this mountainous land, whose northern peaks exceed 7,500 feet.

The climate varies from wet and tropical on the coastal plains to dry and cool in the highlands. The capital, Tegucigalpa (elevation 3,500 feet), has a continual springlike climate. The wet season is May to November.

Rainfall averages 100 inches annually on the northern coast and 30 inches in the south.

Nicaragua lies to the south, El Salvador to the southwest, and Guatemala to the west.

EARLY HISTORY

A center of Mayan civilization before A.D. 900, Honduras was discovered by Columbus in 1502 on his fourth voyage to the New World.

Attracted by exaggerated tales of gold and silver in Honduras, adventurers made the country's early days a chronicle of revolution and intrigue. Rival Spanish factions from Mexico, Guatemala, and Panama struggled for control. Invaders included Hernán Cortés, who in 1524 made a historic march from Mexico to impose his rule on the region. In 1538 Honduras became a part of Guatemala.

On Sept. 15, 1821, Honduras and the other Central American provinces declared their independence from Spain. They were annexed by Mexico, but broke away within a year.

From 1823 to 1838 Honduras joined its neighbors in the United Provinces of Central America.

Honduras declared its independence as a republic on Nov. 5, 1838.

U.S. Marines were sent to the country several times between 1912 and 1925 to preserve order.

HONDURAS IN THE 1970s–1980s

On Dec. 4, 1972, Gen. Oswaldo López Arellano, who had ruled as dictator in 1963–71, overthrew the government and made himself president.

In 1972 the U.S. gave up to Honduras its claim to the Swan Islands, about 100 miles off the Caribbean coast.

Hurricane Fifi devastated Honduras with 110-mph winds and tidal waves on Sept. 18–19, 1974, killing 2,000 persons and destroying property and banana crops worth $500 million.

In March 1975 army officers forced President López to give up command of the armed forces to Col. Juan Melgar Castro.

Early in April 1975 the U.S. Securities and Exchange Commission (SEC) accused a U.S. firm, United Brands, of concealing from its stockholders the payment of a $1.25 million bribe to an unnamed "high" Honduran official to reduce banana export taxes. When López refused to cooperate with investigators, the junta deposed him, making Colonel Melgar president on April 22. Melgar ruled as dictator by decree.

The new government promised to expropriate 1.5 million acres of land for distribution to 120,000 landless farm families.

In 1975 tens of thousands of peasants demonstrated, urging a speed-up in land reforms. Soldiers killed about 15 peasants to halt a mass march on the capital. Gunfights broke out between landowners and peasants.

Gen. Policarpo Paz Garcia, commander of the armed forces, and two other generals overthrew Melgar on Aug. 7, 1978. Fulfilling a promise to restore civilian government, Paz Garcia called an election on April 20, 1980, for a 71-member assembly that wrote a new constitution.

After 18 years of military rule, Hondurans elected a civilian government on Nov. 29, 1981. The right-of-center Liberal Party won the presidency and a majority in the new 78-member congress.

Roberto Suazo Córdova, 55, a physician, was sworn in as president on Jan. 27, 1982. He faced severe problems. The country was nearing economic collapse with declining export income.

Honduras became a refuge in the 1980s for tens of thousands of Nicaraguans, Salvadorans, and Guatemalans fleeing civil wars.

Fearing an invasion by troops of the leftist government of Nicaragua, Honduras beefed up its armed forces in 1982–83 with U.S. assistance. Border clashes occurred and many observers believed full-scale war might erupt.

HUNGARY

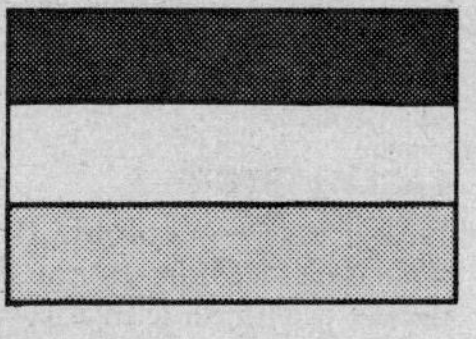

Official Name: Hungarian People's Republic.
Area: 35,929 square miles (93,030 sq. km.).
Population: 10,666,700.
Chief Cities: Budapest, capital, 2,058,000; Miskolc, 206,000; Debrecen, 191,000; Szeged, 171,000.
Government: One-party communist state.
Heads of Government: János Kádár, first secretary, Hungarian Socialist Workers Party (since 1956); Gyorgy Lazar, prime minister (since 1975); president of the presidential council, Pál Losonczi (took office in 1967).
National Assembly: 352 members.
U.S. Ambassador to Hungary: Nicolas Salgo.
Hungarian Ambassador to U.S.: Venceo Hazi.
Flag: Red, white, and green tricolor.
Official Language: Hungarian.
Main Ethnic Group: Magyar (96%).
Religions: Roman Catholicism (67%), Protestantism (25%), Unitarianism, Judaism (8%).
Leading Industries: Manufacturing (steel, cement, textiles, chemicals, machinery, transportation equipment); agriculture (corn, wheat, sugar beets, potatoes, fruits, vegetables, livestock); mining (bauxite, coal, natural gas); tourism.
Foreign Trade: *Major exports*—transport equipment, machinery, bauxite, wheat, corn, meat, steel; *major imports*—petroleum, coke, textile fibers.
Places of Interest: Visegrad fortress on the Danube Bend; Lake Balaton; Eger fortress; Esztergom Palace and Cathedral; Tihanyi and Pannonhalma abbeys; Heviz thermal spa; Hortebagy Horse Show. *In Budapest:* The Citadel; Matthias Church; opera house.

HUNGARY TODAY

About the size of Indiana, Hungary is a communist country in eastern Europe.

Hungarians enjoy a higher standard of living than the people of neighboring communist nations because of an innovative economic system that enables managers and workers to make profits. Small businesses and small farms are operated privately for a profit. The government encourages foreign investments in joint ventures.

The Danube River forms over one-third the length of the northern border with Czechoslovakia, and then veers south through Budapest and into Yugoslavia. Plains lie to the east and west of the Danube. The Tisza is Hungary's second most important river.

The uplands in the northeast occupy about one-third of the land area. The highest mountain is Kekes (3,300 feet). Lake Balaton, in west central Hungary, is the country's largest lake.

Hungary has hot summers (average July temperature 71 °F.) and cold winters (average January temperature 31 °F.). Rainfall averages 25 inches a year. Summer droughts are frequent.

Austria lies to the west, Czechoslovakia to the north, the Soviet Union to the northeast, Romania to the east, and Yugoslavia to the south.

EARLY HISTORY

Hungary was founded in the 800s A.D. by Arpád, a semilegendary chief of the Magyars.

In 1001 Hungary was unified under István (Stephen) I. For Christianizing his people, he was canonized as St. István in 1087.

Nobles forced András II to sign in 1222 the Golden Bull, the "Magna Carta of Hungary."

The country fell into anarchy after András III died in 1301.

Mátáyas Hollos (Matthias Corvinus), elected king in 1458, restored Hungary to an era of glory.

By 1526 Hungary fell under Turkish domination. But at the end of the 1600s the Austrian Hapsburg armies expelled the Turks and took control of Hungary. Resistance against Austria was led by Francis II Rákoczy, one of Hungary's national heroes, but by 1711 he had been defeated.

A rebellion exploded in 1848 led by Louis Kossuth, who declared Hungary an independent republic in 1849. With Russian assistance, Austria put down the revolt.

Following Austria's defeat by the Prussians in 1866, Hungarian nationalism was recognized by creation of the Austro-Hungarian dual empire.

INDEPENDENCE

Hungary declared itself an independent republic on Nov. 16, 1918. In March 1919 the communist dictator Béla Kun took over the government. Romanian troops intervened, and Kun fled. In November a new government was established with Adm. Nicholas Horthy as regent and head of state. His authoritarian regime lasted 25 years.

During World War II German troops occupied the country and in 1944 arrested Horthy. Soviet troops took Hungary in February 1945.

Hungary's last free election, held in November 1945, gave anticommunists a majority. A Hungarian republic was proclaimed in 1946 with Zoltan Tildy as president.

COMMUNIST RULE

Tildy was ousted in 1948 by a Soviet-assisted communist coup. A Soviet-style *Hungarian People's Republic* came into being on Aug. 20, 1949.

After Stalin's death in 1953 Premier Imre Nagy relaxed controls, but two years later he and his cabinet were ousted for "anti-Marxism."

In October 1956 a revolt erupted in Budapest. Imre Nagy again became premier. He announced that free multiparty elections would be held. Two days later Soviet troops intervened. Communist rule was forcibly restored under János Kádár. Thousands of Hungarians fled as refugees to other countries. Nagy was executed.

For a dozen years Hungary remained one of the most repressive communist police states. But most freedom of expression was restored by the 1980s.

In 1968 Hungary and the United States formally resumed full diplomatic relations.

Kádár's government introduced the New Economic Mechanism (NEM) in 1968, which allows profits at various levels.

On Jan. 6, 1978, U.S. Secretary of State Cyrus R. Vance returned to Hungary the country's

QUICK QUIZ: When was the Bank of the United States first chartered? See page 305.

HUNGARY *(continued)*
most treasured symbol, the 10-century-old crown of St. István (Stephen). The crown had been turned over to the U.S. for safekeeping in World War II. Many Hungarian-Americans protested giving the crown to communists.

Hungary received most-favored nation trade status with the U.S. in a pact approved by the U.S. Congress in 1978.

Hungary took a major step toward capitalism with a law that went into effect on Jan. 1, 1982, permitting the establishment of privately owned profit-making firms with up to 30 employees. Many government-owned small businesses, such as restaurants, were leased to private managers.

Hungary raised food prices by about 20% in 1982 to bring them in line with world prices.

ICELAND

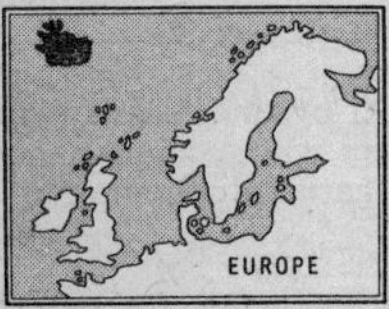

Official Name: Republic of Iceland.
Area: 39,768 square miles (103,000 sq. km.).
Population: 237,308.
Capital: Reykjaví, 83,376.
Government: Parliamentary republic.
President: Vigdis Finnbogadottir (since 1980).
Prime Minister: Steingrimur Hermannsson (since 1983).
Parliament *(Althing):* Upper House, 20 members; Lower House, 40 members.
U.S. Ambassador to Iceland: Marshall Brement.
Icelandic Ambassador to U.S.: Hans G. Andersen.
Flag: White-bordered red cross on blue field.
Official Language: Icelandic.
Principal Ethnic Group: Norwegian descent (99%).
Official Religion: Evangelical Lutheranism.
Leading Industries: Fishing and fish processing; manufacturing (electricity, metal products, clothing, furniture, fertilizer, cement); construction; agriculture (cattle, sheep, hay, vegetables); mining (diatomite).
Foreign Trade: *Major exports*—frozen fish, salted fish, herring meal fodder, herring oil, aluminum; *major imports*—ships and boats, petroleum products, aircraft, cord nets and netting.
Places of Interest: Surtsey Island; Golden Fall; Great Geyser; Myvatn; Mt. Hekla. *In Reykjaví:* hot spring reservoirs that heat city; Lutheran Cathedral.

ICELAND TODAY

About the size of Kentucky, Iceland is an island in the North Atlantic. It lies just south of the Arctic Circle, 200 miles southeast of Greenland.

The sparsely settled island has few mineral resources. Fishing has been developed as Iceland's most profitable industry. The island's hydroelectric potential has been tapped to create an aluminum manufacturing industry. The geothermal energy of hot springs and volcanoes is used to heat homes as well as greenhouses where vegetables are raised. The U.S. maintains a large NATO air base at Keflavík.

The people have achieved a high standard of living, but depend on imports of oil and manufactured goods.

Iceland has many active volcanoes. The highest peak, Hvannadalshnúkur, rises 6,952 feet. Huge glaciers cover much of the interior. But the Gulf Stream provides a relatively mild coastal climate.

EARLY HISTORY

Norse settlers colonized the island about A.D. 870. The *Althing,* established in 930, is the oldest active parliament in the world.

Iceland came under Norwegian control in 1262 and became part of the Danish-Norwegian state in 1381.

Jón Sigurdsson, an Icelandic statesman, helped win a constitution and limited home rule in 1874. With the 1918 Act of Union, the country obtained full self-government under the Danish crown.

INDEPENDENCE

On June 17, 1944, while Denmark was occupied by Germany, Iceland declared its independence. Under the terms of a 1951 agreement, the U.S. is responsible for the island's defense.

Asgeir Ásgeirsson was president from 1952 to 1968. He was succeeded by Kristján Eldjárn, president from 1968 to 1980.

A major issue in 1974 national elections was continued U.S. operation of the NATO air base at Keflavík, opposed by leftists and supported by conservatives. The leftist parties lost their majority in parliament. Geir Hallgrimsson became prime minister with a conservative coalition that rescinded leftist plans to close the U.S. base.

Iceland on Oct. 15, 1975, banned foreign fishing within 200 miles of its coastline. The resulting "cod war" with Britain was settled in 1977 when all British trawlers were excluded from Iceland's 200-mile zone pending agreement with the European Common Market.

A strike for higher pay by 12,000 government employees in October 1977 isolated Iceland for about two weeks. The walkout cut off flights in and out of the country.

In a national election on June 25, 1978, socialists and communists made substantial gains at the expense of the governing conservative-center coalition, causing Prime Minister Hallgrimsson to resign.

Olafur Johannesson, of the centrist Progressive Party, became prime minister after forming a coalition cabinet on Aug. 31, 1978.

Unable to reduce the nation's 55% inflation rate, Johannesson's coalition government collapsed and new elections were held on Dec. 2–3, 1979. Results were inconclusive.

After two months of wrangling, Gunnar Thoroddsen, 69, of the Independence Party formed a coalition cabinet. He became prime minister on Feb. 8, 1980, with Johannesson as foreign minister.

Iceland became the first European country to elect a woman as ceremonial head of state on June 29, 1980, when voters chose Vigdis Finnbogadottir, 50, as the nation's president.

A national election on April 23, 1983, divided the national legislature's seats among six parties. Steingrimur Hermannsson, 54, head of the Progressive Party became prime minister in coalition with the Independence Party.

INDIA

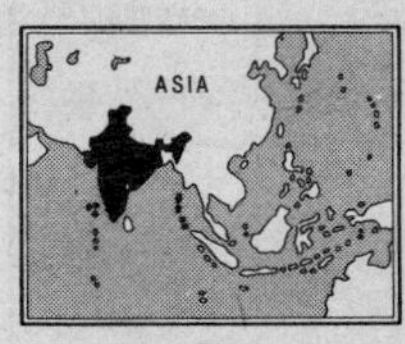

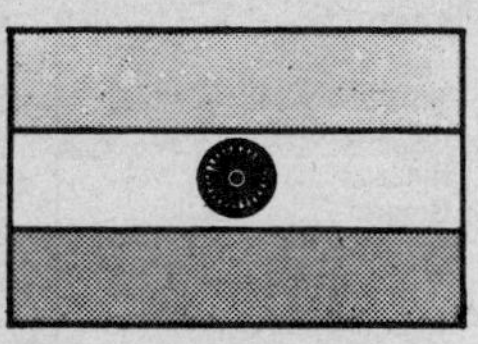

Official name: Republic of India.
Area: 1,269,346 square miles (3,287,590 sq. km.).
Population: 748,210,000.
Chief Cities: New Delhi, capital, 301,801; Bombay, 5,970,575; Delhi, 3,287,883; Calcutta, 3,148,746; Madras, 2,469,449; Hyderabad, 1,607,396; Ahmedabad, 1,585,544; Bangalore, 1,540,741; Kanpur, 1,154,388.
Largest Metropolitan Areas: Calcutta, 8,297,000; Bombay, 7,605,000; Delhi, 4,891,000; Madras, 3,169,930.
Government: Parliamentary republic.
President: Zail Singh (since 1982).
Prime Minister: Indira Gandhi (since 1980).
U.S. Ambassador to India: Harry G. Barnes Jr.
Indian Ambassador to U.S.: K. R. Narayanan.
Parliament: *Rajya Sabha* (Council of States), 240 members; *Lok Sabha* (House of the People), 545 members.
Flag: Deep saffron, white, and green stripes, with centered 24-spoke Wheel of Asoka in blue.
Official Languages: Hindi, English, Assamese, Bengali, Gujarati, Kannada, Kashmiri, Malayallam, Marathi, Oriya, Punjabi, Sanskrit, Tamil, Telegu, Urdu.
Main Ethnic Groups: Aryan in the north (72%), Dravidian in the south (25%).
Chief Religions: Hinduism (84%), Islam (10%).
Leading Industries: Agriculture (sugarcane, pepper, tea, peanuts, rice, jute, bananas, tobacco, cotton, wheat, vegetables, cattle); manufacturing (steel, machinery, cement, motor vehicles, sugar refining, textiles, jute products, handicrafts); construction; tourism; mining (petroleum, iron ore, coal, chrome, thorium, nickel, copper, lead, zinc, bauxite, natural gas, manganese).
Foreign Trade: *Major exports*—jute, tea, iron ore, leather, cotton; *major imports*—wheat, fertilizer, chemicals, machinery, steel, petroleum.
Places of Interest: Taj Mahal in Agra; Ganges River; Khajuraho temples; Ajanta and Ellora temple caves; Red Fort and Qutb Minar tombs and mosques in Delhi; Amber Palace in Jaipur; ancient temples in Madras; Srinagar in the Vale of Kashmir; Dal Lake.

INDIA TODAY

India is the second most heavily populated country in the world, next to China. Although India has less than one-third the area of the U.S., it has about three times as many people. And the population increases at the rate of 25 babies born each minute—over 13 million a year.

India's people are among the poorest in the world. Many nearly starve year after year. Almost half the people earn less than $7.50 a month. Only 1 person in 4 can read and write.

Rich in natural resources, India ranks among the world's leading nations in production of coal, electricity, forestry products, iron, and natural rubber.

In the north the Himalaya mountains—rising to the highest elevations in the world—serve as a barrier between India and China. The area's three great rivers—Indus, Ganges, and Brahmaputra—start in the Himalaya.

The lowlands of India stretch eastward for 2,000 miles from the Indus River delta to the delta of the Ganges and the Brahmaputra. Centered in the peninsula, the Deccan Plateau is surrounded by hills and mountains. Beyond the Eastern Ghat mountain range are the plains of the Coromandel Coast on the Bay of Bengal.

The coasts and the Ganges delta are hot and humid. In the far west are the semiarid steppes and the barren Thar Desert, while in the north the climate changes from near tropical to arctic as the land rises in the Himalaya.

EARLY HISTORY

About 3000 B.C. civilization developed in the Indus Valley. About 1500 B.C. Aryans invaded the country and absorbed this civilization. The following 2,000 years saw Hinduism and the caste system come into being. The first important Aryan kingdom, Magadha, during the reign of Bimbisara (542–490 B.C.), heard the teachings of Jainism and Buddhism from the mouths of their founders.

Alexander the Great invaded in 327–325 B.C., but his armies were overcome by Chandragupta, who founded the Maurya empire.

Asoka (273–236 B.C.) unified northern India and established Buddhism as the state religion.

The Gupta dynasty reached its height under Samudragupta (about A.D. 340–380).

In the 1000s the Muslim Mahmud of Ghanzi invaded India and extended his empire to the Ganges and the deserts of Rajputana.

The greatest Mogul emperor, Akbar (reigned 1556–1605), extended his rule from northern India well into the Deccan. His policy of religious toleration was not continued by his successors.

European colonization of India began with the arrival of Vasco da Gama in 1498.

By the mid-1800s Britain had won control of most of India. British domination and rising internal strife led to the Sepoy Mutiny of 1857, a rebellion by native troops. In 1877 Queen Victoria was crowned empress of India.

After World War I the nationalist movement came under the sway of Mohandas K. (Mahatma) Gandhi. He organized a series of passive-resistance campaigns.

INDEPENDENCE

Britain partitioned the peninsula in 1947 into Hindu India and Muslim Pakistan. On Aug. 15, India was granted independence. Jawaharlal Nehru became India's first prime minister.

Partition led to religious riots, killings, and a crisscrossing migration of millions of people. Gandhi attempted to stop the religious violence, but on Jan. 30, 1948, he was assassinated.

India fought Pakistan for control of Kashmir in 1948–49 and again in 1965.

On Jan. 26, 1950, India became a parliamentary republic in the British Commonwealth.

Chinese troops invaded Kashmir and northeastern India on Oct. 20, 1962. After stiff Indian resistance, the Chinese withdrew a month later.

QUICK QUIZ: What was the former name of Djibouti? See page 539.

INDIA *(continued)*

Nehru died in 1964, and Lal Bahadur Shastri succeeded him as prime minister.

When Shastri died suddenly, Mrs. Indira Gandhi, Nehru's daughter, was chosen prime minister on Jan. 19, 1966, and won general elections in 1967 and 1971.

DEVELOPMENTS IN THE 1970s

A flood of 9 million Bengali refugees poured into India after the outbreak of civil war in east Pakistan (now Bangladesh) in March 1971. In support of the rebels, India invaded the province on Dec. 3. Pakistan surrendered 13 days later.

India, on May 18, 1974, became the first of the world's underdeveloped nations to explode an atomic device.

In 1975 India annexed the independent nation of Sikkim, making it India's 22d state.

When a court ruled that Mrs. Gandhi was guilty of violating election laws, she declared a state of emergency on June 26, 1975, suspended civil liberties, and imposed censorship. Mrs. Gandhi had 28,836 political opponents arrested and jailed "to save India from anarchy."

In 1976 India resumed full diplomatic relations with China for the first time since 1961, and with Pakistan for the first time since 1971.

In an effort to reduce the population growth rate, the government in 1976 raised the minimum age for marriage to 21 for men and 18 for women and launched a vigorous sterilization program.

Mrs. Gandhi put through constitutional amendments, in December 1976, that gave her dictatorial powers. But a month later she relaxed her 19-month-old arbitrary rule and called a general election.

Mrs. Gandhi and her Congress Party were overwhelmingly defeated in the election held on March 16–20, 1977. The opposition Janata Party captured a majority of 298 seats in the 542-member Lok Sabha.

Morarji Ranchhodji Desai, 81, leader of the Janata Party became prime minister. He had been imprisoned for 18 months by Mrs. Gandhi during her emergency rule, after having served as her deputy prime minister in 1967–69.

Desai freed the remaining 17,000 political prisoners and restored human rights.

Desai, who had criticized Mrs. Gandhi as being pro-Soviet, declared India would observe "true nonalignment" in international affairs.

Neelam Sanjiva Reddy, 64, was chosen unanimously as president of India in July 1977.

Relations between the U.S. and India improved in 1978 with a visit to India by President Carter on Jan. 1–3, and a return visit by Desai to the White House in June. In April Carter overruled objections by the Nuclear Regulatory Commission to let 8 tons of enriched uranium be sold to India for use in generating electric power.

PRIME MINISTERS OF INDIA

1947–64	Jawaharlal Nehru	Congress
1964–66	Lal Bahadur Shastri	Congress
1966–77	Indira Gandhi	Congress
1977–79	Morarji Desai	Janata
1979–80	Charan Singh	Janata-Secular
1980–	Indira Gandhi	Congress (I)

INDIA'S 22 STATES

STATE	AREA (sq. mi.)	CAPITAL
Andhra Pradesh	106,855	Hyderabad
Assam	30,318	Shillong
Bihar	67,134	Patna
Gujarat	75,670	Ahmadabad
Haryana	17,074	Chandigarh
Himachal Pradesh	21,495	Simla
Jammu and Kashmir *	85,806	Srinagar
Karnataka	74,044	Bangalore
Kerala	15,005	Trivandrum
Madhya Pradesh	170,982	Bhopal
Maharashtra	118,828	Bombay
Manipur	8,632	Imphal
Meghalaya	8,683	Shillong
Nagaland	6,381	Kohima
Orissa	60,171	Bhubaneswar
Punjab	19,445	Chandigarh
Rajasthan	132,130	Jaipur
Sikkim	2,744	Gangtok
Tamil Nadu	50,220	Madras
Tripura	4,045	Agartala
Uttar Pradesh	133,674	Lucknow
West Bengal	33,920	Calcutta

* Disputed by Pakistan.

Although the caste system was officially abolished upon independence, many riots occurred in 1978–80 as untouchable activists sought to end discrimination.

Mrs. Gandhi began efforts to make a political comeback after being ousted from the Congress Party on Jan. 3, 1978. She set up her own political party and won election to parliament in November 1978. But in December 1978 she was ousted from parliament and jailed for one week for having harassed officials in 1975.

The worst floods of the century struck West Bengal in September 1978. Over 1,200 persons drowned as rivers overflowed.

Because of a split in his Janata Party, the 83-year-old Desai resigned as prime minister on July 15, 1979. He was succeeded by his deputy prime minister, Charan Singh, 77, whose defection to form the Janata-Secular Party had helped cause the fall of Desai's cabinet. When Singh was unable to put together a coalition majority government, President Reddy dissolved parliament on Aug. 22, 1979, and ordered new elections.

INDIA IN THE 1980s

Indira Gandhi's new Congress (I) Party won a landslide victory in elections in January 1980, capturing four-fifths of the seats in parliament. The 62-year-old Mrs. Gandhi resumed office as prime minister on Jan. 14, 1980.

Strengthening her socialist government's control over business, Mrs. Gandhi nationalized six of India's largest banks by decree in April 1980. India put a space satellite into orbit on July 18, 1980, the sixth nation to do so. The achievement demonstrated India's ability to develop long-range ballistic missiles for use in war. In another move to strengthen the nation's military might, the government contracted with the Soviet Union in May 1980 for $1.6 billion in weapons.

To bolster U.S. relations with India, President Carter overruled the U.S. Nuclear Regulatory Commission in 1980 to permit the export of 38 tons of enriched uranium for use in generating electric power. The action was taken despite India's refusal to guarantee that the atomic fuel would not be used for weapons.

Mrs. Gandhi had promised during her election campaign that she would not reinstate dictatorial rule, but on Sept. 23, 1980, she decreed a law giving the government power to imprison anyone for a year without trial. Several hundred persons were arrested under the new law in the next several weeks.

At Prime Minister Gandhi's urging parliament adopted a law in September 1981 that gave the government sweeping powers to arrest without warrant strikers in essential services, such as transportation and communications.

Zail Singh, 67, a Sikh, was elected in 1982 as the nation's 7th president. He was sworn in to the largely ceremonial office on July 25.

Sikhs demanding autonomy for their home state Punjab attacked India's parliament building on Oct. 11, 1982, killing 5 persons and injuring 100. Subsequently, about 25,000 Sikhs were arrested after riots in Punjab.

Prime Minister Gandhi and President Zia of Pakistan conferred in New Delhi on Nov. 1, 1982, in the first such meeting between leaders of the two nations in 10 years.

India's hopes of becoming self-sufficient in petroleum by the 1990s were buoyed in 1982 as production from its offshore Bombay High oil field reached 240,000 barrels a day. Plans call for 600,000 barrels a day by 1985 and double that amount by 1990.

An estimated 5,000 persons were killed and 250,000 made homeless in massacres and fighting between Hindus and Muslims in February and March 1983 in the state of Assam. An election campaign in the state touched off the violence.

India's first commercial satellite was launched into orbit on Aug. 31, 1983, by the U.S. space shuttle. It will provide telecommunications, weather forecasting, and TV broadcasting.

Prime Minister Gandhi dismissed the state government of Punjab on Oct. 6, 1983, instituting direct rule from New Delhi to end strife between Hindus and Sikhs in which about 200 persons had been killed since 1980.

INDIA'S TERRITORIES

In addition to those below, India also administers the cities of Chandigarth and Delhi as territories.

ANDAMAN AND NICOBAR ISLANDS

With an area of 3,203 sq. mi., the islands lie in the Bay of Bengal. Port Blair, the capital is 780 miles southeast of Calcutta. The Andamans include 5 large islands designated the Great Andamans, an island to the south called Little Andaman, and more than 200 islets. The Nicobars, 75 miles to the south, consist of 19 islands, 12 inhabited.

The Negrito people of the Andamans lead a tribal life in the interior—hunting, fishing, and avoiding contact with civilization. Most of the Andaman islanders are Indians, with some Burmese Karennis. The Nicobarese are of Mongoloid stock.

The Andamans were first settled as a penal colony by the British in 1858. In World War II the Japanese occupied them in 1942. Britain settled the Nicobars in 1869.

ARUNACHAL PRADESH

The mountainous 32,270 sq. mi. region on the border with China and Burma formerly was known as the North East Frontier Agency.

Most of the people are Mongol tribesmen.

The northern boundary with the Tibet region of China, called the McMahon Line, was established by Britain in 1914. China invaded the North East Frontier Agency briefly in 1962.

The region was renamed and made a union territory of India on Jan. 21, 1972.

DADRA AND NAGAR HAVELI

These 190 sq. mi. former colonies of Portugal lie north of Bombay, India. More than a third of the region is covered with teak forests.

Portugal obtained the region in 1780. In 1954 Indian nationalists invaded. It was made a union territory of India on Aug. 11, 1961.

GOA, DAMAN, AND DIU

The 1,472 sq. mi. territory encompasses what once was Portuguese India. It includes three widely separated former Portuguese colonies on India's west coast: Goa, Daman, and Diu.

Goa was captured in March 1510 by Afonso de Albuquerque and became the capital of Portugal's empire in Asia. The Portuguese acquired Damão (now Daman) in 1531 and Diu in 1534.

On Dec. 18, 1961, Indian troops invaded and captured all three colonies. The colonies were made a union territory of India in March 1962.

In 1974–75 many Roman Catholics traveled to Goa for an exposition in which the body of missionary St. Francis Xavier was displayed in a glass coffin in the Se Cathedral. The fact that his body has not decomposed since his death in 1522 is regarded as a miracle by Catholics.

LAKSHADWEEP

With an area of 12.4 sq. mi., the 27 islands in the territory lie in the Arabian Sea 200 miles west of Kerala. They include the Laccadives and Amindivis. The largest is Minicoy.

MIZORAM

The 8,142 sq. mi. Mizoram territory borders on Bangladesh and Burma. During British rule of India efforts were made to stamp out headhunting among the Lushai tribes that live in the evergreen forests covering Mizoram's hills.

Until it was made a union territory on Jan. 21, 1972, Mizoram was known as the Mizo Hills district of Assam.

PONDICHERRY

The 185 sq. mi. Pondicherry administers four widely separated former French colonies in India. *Pondicherry* itself lies on India's east coast, south of the city of Madras. The district of *Karikal* is a coastal enclave 90 miles south of Pondicherry. The district of *Yanam* lies about 400 miles to the north of Pondicherry. *Mahé,* the fourth district, stands on India's west coast, a few miles north of the city of Calicut.

Settled by the French in 1674. Pondicherry was ceded to India on May 28, 1956. It was made a union territory on Aug. 16, 1962.

QUICK QUIZ: One furlong equals how many miles? See page 720.

INDONESIA

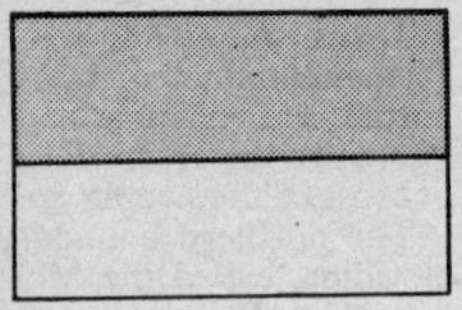

Official Name: Republic of Indonesia.
Area: 788,662 square miles (2,027,087 sq. km.)
Population: 162,604,000.
Chief Cities: Jakarta, capital, 4,576,009; Surabaya, 1,556,255; Bandung, 1,201,730; Semarang, 646,590; Medan, 635,562; Palembang, 582,961.
Government: Military-controlled republic.
President: General Suharto (took office in 1967).
Parliament: *People's Representation Council,* 460 members.
U.S. Ambassador to Indonesia: John H. Holdridge.
Indonesian Ambassador to U.S.: A. Hasnan Habib.
Flag: Red stripe above white stripe.
Languages: Indonesian (official), English.
Ethnic Groups: Malay (95%), Chinese, Papuan, Arab.
Leading Religions: Islam (90%), Christianity (4%), Hinduism (3%), Buddhism (1%).
Leading Industries: Agriculture (rice, corn, sugarcane, tea, coffee, rubber, tobacco, cassava, coconuts, peanuts, spices, vegetables, fruits); manufacturing (textiles, assembly of motor vehicles, food processing, cement, consumer goods); mining (petroleum, tin, bauxite, coal, natural gas, copper, diamonds, gold, silver, sulfur, nickel, manganese); fishing; forestry and lumbering.
Foreign Trade: *Major exports*—crude petroleum and products, rubber, coffee, tin, spices, timber; *major imports*—rice, cotton, machinery, flour, consumer goods.
Places of Interest: Botanical gardens of Bogor; Puncak resort area; Tangkubanperahu Volcano; Borobudur Temple on Java; Bali; Sumatra; Beautiful Indonesia in Miniature, near Jakarta.

INDONESIA TODAY

Indonesia includes 13,677 islands between the mainland of Southeast Asia and Australia. The islands stretch 3,300 miles from east to west—nearly as far as from New York to Paris.

Once known as the *East Indies,* Indonesia has the fifth-largest population in the world, after China, India, the Soviet Union, and the United States. Indonesia's islands cover an area about five times larger than that of California. However, its people cannot raise enough farm products to feed themselves. So Indonesia is one of the largest importers of rice.

The government imposes strict censorship on news and holds thousands of political prisoners.

Transportation is one of the country's major problems. Boats and planes must be used for travel between islands. The larger islands are mountainous and heavily forested with relatively few paved roads.

Indonesia has many natural resources. It is one of the world's leading nations in the production of natural rubber, petroleum, and tin. However, Indonesia's industrial production remains underdeveloped. Its gross national product is only about one-twentieth that of Japan.

Indonesians are among the poorest people in the world. Less than half can read and write. About two-thirds do not get enough to eat daily. About one-fourth of the workers are unemployed.

With annual revenues of more than $20 billion from oil exports, Indonesia has pressed forward to make greater use of the islands' natural resources. New highways have been built, port facilities have been improved, and many electric-power projects have been constructed.

The islands of Indonesia have many mountains and volcanoes. The highest, Jaya in Irian Jaya (western New Guinea), rises to 16,500 feet. Mt. Kerinci on Sumatra is 12,467 feet high.

Indonesia straddles the equator, so the coastal lowland areas have a hot, tropical climate the year round. The interior upland regions of the larger islands enjoy a cooler climate.

EARLY HISTORY

Migrants from the Asian mainland populated Indonesia between 2500 and 1000 B.C.

In the precolonial period Indian cultural influence was dominant. The great Shrivijaya maritime empire, with its capital in southern Sumatra, was a renowned center of Buddhist learning. About A.D. 800 the Sailendra dynasty built the great Buddhist temple Borobudur in central Java.

From the 1100s, Arab traders spread the Islamic religion. In the 1300s Hinduism was ascendant in the powerful, Java-based Majapahit empire.

Western dominance began in 1511 when the Portuguese landed at Malacca, on the Malayan peninsula, "in search of Christians and spices."

NETHERLANDS EAST INDIES

By 1623 the Netherlands East India Company was able to establish a monopoly. The Dutch government revoked the company's charter in 1790 and assumed full administration of the islands 10 years later.

Independence movements began in the early 1900s. The first successful mass organization was Sarakat Islam (Islamic Association). Immediately after World War I the organization's Marxist faction founded the Indonesian Communist Party. Tension mounted between the communist and noncommunist branches. In 1921 the communists were expelled from the Islamic Association.

The Indonesian Nationalist Party was formed in 1927 by Sukarno and Mohamad Hatta. The Dutch exiled Sukarno and other nationalist leaders to remote island outposts.

Japanese occupation of the islands during World War II further stimulated the nationalist movement.

INDEPENDENCE

With Japan's defeat, Sukarno and Hatta declared the independence of the Republic of Indonesia on Aug. 17, 1945. For the next four years the Indonesians battled to keep the Dutch from resuming colonial rule.

The UN succeeded in getting both sides to end the conflict. Sukarno was elected president on Dec. 16, 1949. Eleven days later, on Dec. 27, the Netherlands formally recognized Indonesia's independence.

The first elections to the nation's parliament, held in 1955, sharpened party cleavages and indicated strength for the Communist Party.

Tensions developed between President Sukarno and Vice President Hatta, due partly to Sukarno's tolerance of the communists and his antagonism to the Muslim Masjumi Party, favored by Hatta. In 1956 the vice president resigned.

Sukarno became dictator, declaring martial law in 1957.

In 1960 diplomatic relations with the Netherlands were severed, and Indonesian troops began infiltration of Netherlands New Guinea (Irian Jaya). The Netherlands turned the region over to the United Nations in 1962. The UN placed the territory under Indonesia's jurisdiction in May 1963.

Sukarno strongly opposed the formation of Malaysia in 1963, and openly waged war against that nation.

After the failure of an attempted communist coup on Oct. 1, 1965, anticommunist rioting swept the country with 100,000 to 400,000 persons killed.

Lt. Gen. Suharto emerged as the strong man of a new regime. He ordered the army to eliminate all traces of the Communist Party. An estimated 500,000 persons were jailed.

In March 1967 the national assembly formally revoked Sukarno's governing authority and appointed Suharto as acting president. In March 1968 Suharto was elected to a 5-year term as president by the assembly. Sukarno was arrested in 1969 and died in June 1970.

INDONESIA'S 27 PROVINCES (by island groups)

	AREA (sq. mi.)	CAPITAL
Borneo (Kalimantan)	208,286	
Central Kalimantan	—	Palangkaraya
East Kalimantan	—	Samarinda
South Kalimantan	—	Banjarmasin
West Kalimantan	—	Pontianak
Celebes (Sulawesi)	69,255	
Central Sulawesi	—	Palu
North Sulawesi	—	Manado
South Sulawesi	—	Ujungpandang
Southeast Sulawesi	—	Kendari
Java (Jawa)	48,763	
Central Jawa	—	Semarang
East Jawa	—	Surabaya
Jakarta	—	Jakarta
Yogyakarta	—	Yogyakarta
West Jawa	—	Bandung
Lesser Sunda Islands (Nusa Tenggara)	36,179	
Bali	—	Denpasar
East Nusa Tenggara	—	Kupang, Timor
West Nusa Tenggara	—	Mataram, Lombok
Loro Sae (East Timor)	—	Dili
Moluccas (Maluku)	28,766	Ambon
Sumatra (Sumatera)	165,000	
Aceh	—	Banda Aceh
Bengkulu	—	Bengkulu
Jambi	—	Jambi
Lampung	—	Tandjungkarang-Telukbetung
North Sumatera	—	Medan
Riau	—	Pekanbaru
South Sumatera	—	Palembang
West Sumatera	—	Padang
West New Guinea (Irian Jaya)	151,789	Kotabaru

DEVELOPMENTS IN THE 1970s–1980s

In 1971 elections Suharto's Golkar Party won 73% of the seats in parliament.

The People's Consultative Assembly, a 960-member presidential electoral body, unanimously reelected President Suharto to a second 5-year term on March 22, 1973.

In August 1975 a civil war broke out in the Portuguese colony on the island of Timor, the western half of which already was part of Indonesia. Indonesian troops intervened in the fighting. Indonesia formally incorporated the former Portuguese colony on July 17, 1976, making it the nation's 27th province, Loro Sae. However, guerrilla fighting against Indonesian troops continued into the 1980s.

Indonesia in 1976 became the fourth nation to own its own space satellite communications system. The satellites link 40 earth stations.

The U.S. Securities and Exchange Commission (SEC) charged in February 1977 that dozens of U.S. corporations had been shaken down for $1.11 million by the former head of Indonesia's government-owned oil company. In April 1977 the official, Gen. Ibnu Sutowo, was placed under house arrest along with other close associates.

The first national election in six years was held on May 2, 1977. However, the government censored the topics that could be discussed, preventing corruption from becoming an issue. Opposition candidates were screened. The ruling Golkar Party won 62% of the vote.

A national assembly reelected Suharto to a third 5-year term as president on March 22, 1978.

In October 1977 Amnesty International reported that Indonesia still was holding about 100,000 political prisoners, disputing a claim by the Indonesian government that only 30,000 remained in prison. From December 1977 through 1979 the government released 31,226 political prisoners.

Opposition to President Suharto's military government was aired in 1980 with publication of charges that he and other high officials enriched themselves with multimillion dollar kickbacks.

The government's third 5-year plan for 1979–84 called for an annual economic growth rate of 6.5%, down from the 7.5% rate of 1974–79.

Indonesia's economy was stimulated in 1979–81 by rising oil prices that contributed to a 60% increase in export income and an annual trade surplus of more than $2 billion.

Galunggung volcano on Java began erupting on April 5, 1982. About 30,000 villagers were forced to abandon their homes as subsequent eruptions turned the region around the volcano into a wasteland. About 30 persons died.

A drought in the summer of 1982 hurt rice production, causing food shortages.

President Suharto visited the U.S. in October 1982, conferring with President Reagan.

Suharto was elected by the national assembly to a fourth 5-year term in March 1983.

Falling oil prices hurt Indonesia's economy in 1982–83, causing the government to cut back planned public-works projects by $21 billion.

QUICK QUIZ: What are Kenya's major exports? See page 589.

IRAN

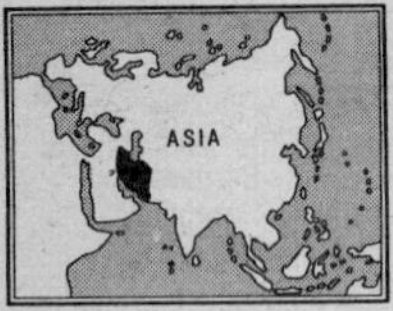

Official Name: Islamic Republic of Iran.
Area: 636,296 square miles (1,648,000 sq. km.).
Population: 43,142,800.
Chief Cities: Teheran, capital, 4,496,159; Esfahan, 671,825; Mashdad, 670,180; Tabriz, 598,576.
Government: Islamic dictatorship.
Head of State: Ayatollah Ruhollah Khomeini (since 1979).
President: Hojatolislam Ali Khamenei (since 1981).
Prime Minister: Mir Hussein Moussavi (since 1981).
Parliament: *Majlis,* 270 members.
Flag: Stripes of green (*top*), white, and red; word "Allah" in red on white center stripe.
Main Languages: Iranian, Kurdish, Arabic, Turkic, English, French.
Chief Ethnic Groups: Iranian, Turk, Kurd, Arab, Armenian.
Main Religion: Islam (98%).
Leading Industries: Mining (petroleum, natural gas, coal, salt, chromite, lead, copper, iron ore); agriculture (sheep, cattle, goats, wheat, sugar beets, barley, rice, cotton, tea, tobacco); manufacturing (oil refining, steel, electrical equipment, cement, textiles, sugar, flour, furniture, building materials); fishing.
Foreign Trade: *Major exports*—petroleum, carpets and rugs, cotton textiles; *major imports*—machinery, iron and steel, pharmaceuticals and medicinal products, wheat.
Places of Interest: Elburz Mountains; Caspian shore resorts; gold-domed mosque in shrine city of Meshed; Mt. Damavaud; ruins of Persepolis and royal tombs; Sepah Mosque and Golestan Palace Museum in Teheran; Shiraz; Esfahan.

IRAN TODAY

About five times the size of California, Iran is an oil-rich nation in the Middle East wracked by revolution and war. It is ruled by radical-conservative Islamic religious leaders who use torture and execution against opponents.

The majority of people are very poor. Only about 1 in 4 can read and write.

Most of Iran is a plateau averaging 4,000 feet above sea level. The Elburz and Zagros mountains cover extensive areas. Large sections of the interior are desert. Rainfall is generally meager.

Iran is bordered on the north by the Soviet Union. Afghanistan and Pakistan lie to the east, and Iraq and Turkey to the west.

EARLY HISTORY

The early inhabitants of present-day Iran, the Elamites, developed a high degree of civilization by about 3100 B.C. Two Aryan tribes, the Medes and the Persians, settled in the area about 900 B.C. The Medes ruled what is now western Iran. The Persians controlled an area extending northeast from the Persian Gulf.

The powerful Persian ruler Cyrus (559–530 B.C.) brought the Medes under his control. He then conquered Babylonia, founding the Persian Empire that eventually encompassed Egypt and eastern Greece. Persian power was crushed in 331 B.C. by Alexander the Great. Alexander's empire crumbled after his death, and his successors battled for supremacy. Most of Persia went to Seleucus I, the Greek ruler of Syria who had been one of Alexander's generals. The Seleucid dynasty tried to follow the Persian pattern of government, but its hold was weak. Parthian rule succeeded the Seleucids. A stronger, more energetic dynasty, the Sassanian, overthrew the Parthians in A.D. 224 and built a flourishing empire that successfully opposed Rome.

Arabs invaded Persia and crushed the Sassanian dynasty about 651. Islam became the dominant religion. Turkish invasions and settlement followed in the 900s. The land later fell to the Mongol invaders, Genghis Khan in the 1200s and Tamerlane in the 1300s.

Native Iranian rule was restored by the Safavid rulers (1502–1736). The dynasty reached its peak during the regime of Shah Abbas I (1587–1629).

A Turkish general, Nadir Shah, ruled in 1736–47, raiding and looting India.

The Zand dynasty (1750–94) restored order before being overthrown by Aga Mohammed Khan, whose Kajar dynasty lasted until 1925. Persia's borders shrank steadily. Land was lost to the Afghans, and in 1813 and 1828 Caucasian territories were taken over by Russia, which exploited the oil deposits.

In 1906 the shah approved formation of a parliament, or Majlis, and the constitution it enacted. In 1907 an Anglo-Russian pact divided Persia into spheres of influence, but the treaty was annulled after World War I.

MODERN EMPIRE OF IRAN

In 1921 a coup directed by army officer Reza Khan resulted in a military dictatorship. Four years later Reza Khan deposed the shah and adopted the title Reza Shah Pahlevi.

He undertook reforms in all aspects of Persian life, and in 1935 officially changed the country's name to Iran. In 1935 Teheran University was opened. In 1937 women were unveiled. In 1938 the first railroad was built.

The shah's friendly relations with Germany, however, led to the occupation of Iran by British and Russian troops in 1941. The shah abdicated in favor of his son, Mohammed Reza Pahlevi.

In 1945 the Soviets, who had occupied northern Iran, refused to evacuate their troops. But promised U.S. aid under the Truman Doctrine led to the withdrawal of the Soviet troops.

When militant nationalist Mohammed Mossadegh, leader of the extremist National Front, became premier in 1951, he promptly seized control of the Anglo-Iranian Oil Company. The British retaliated with a blockade.

With aid by the U.S., royalists overthrew Mossadegh in 1953, and the shah regained absolute power.

The shah announced on March 16, 1973, the nationalization of the oil industry.

The shah decreed Iran a one-party state on March 2, 1975, establishing the National Resurrection Party. The shah's secret police imprisoned, tortured, and killed his opponents.

Riots in Iran grew in intensity throughout 1978,

organized by Muslim extremists who objected to the shah's efforts to modernize Iran.

After the U.S. advised him not to call out his army against the rebels, the shah flew to exile on Jan. 16, 1979, and died in Egypt in 1980.

ISLAMIC STATE

The uprising against the shah had been directed from abroad by Ayatollah Ruhollah Khomeini, a Muslim religious leader who had been exiled by the shah 15 years earlier. Khomeini returned to Iran on Feb. 1, 1979. The shah's prime minister resigned on Feb. 11 and fled to exile. Terror swept Iran as Khomeini's militia arrested and executed hundreds of former officials and military officers. On March 30–31, 1979, a national referendum approved establishment of an Islamic republic.

Khomeini's government nationalized banks, insurance companies, and most remaining heavy industry in June and July 1979.

Khomeini ordered Iranian women to give up smoking and wear the Muslim veil.

An uprising by Kurds seeking independence in western Iran brought heavy fighting in 1979–82.

Relations between the U.S. and Iran reached a crisis after President Carter permitted the exiled shah to enter the U.S. in 1979 for medical treatment. Iranian terrorists seized the U.S. embassy in Teheran on Nov. 4, 1979, holding over 50 Americans hostage. The Iranian government refused to negotiate release of the hostages, and a U.S. attempt to free them by military force failed in April 1980. The U.S. broke diplomatic relations with Iran on April 7, 1980. With the help of Algerian diplomats, the U.S. hostages were finally freed on Jan. 20, 1981.

In a national referendum on Dec. 2–3, 1979, Iranians approved a new constitution that made Khomeini leader of Iran for life.

Abol Hasan Bani-Sadr was elected as Iran's first president on Jan. 25, 1980. Mohammed Ali Rajai became prime minister.

Border clashes between Iran and Iraq escalated into a full-scale war on Sept. 22, 1980, with each inflicting severe damage to the other.

On June 21, 1981, Khomeini dismissed President Bani-Sadr, who fled into exile, replacing him with Rajai as president.

About 1,800 of Bani-Sadr's supporters were executed. In turn, the underground People's Mujahedeen killed about 1,000 prominent Khomeini followers. President Rajai and his prime minister were assassinated on Aug. 30, 1981.

Khomeini chose as the new president a fundamentalist clergyman, Hojatolislam Ali Khamenei, who was formally elected on Oct. 2, 1981.

By mid-1982 Iran was receiving about $2 billion a month from the sale of oil to Japan, the U.S., and other Western countries.

Sadegh Ghotbzadeh, 46, Iran's foreign minister during the U.S. hostage crisis, was executed on Sept. 15, 1982, for trying to overthrow Khomeini.

The stalemated Iraq-Iran war entered its fourth year in 1983. Khomeini declared that Iran would cut off all oil shipments in the Persian Gulf if Iraq attacked its oil fields. The U.S. warned Iran that it would use military force to keep the strategic waterway open.

IRAQ

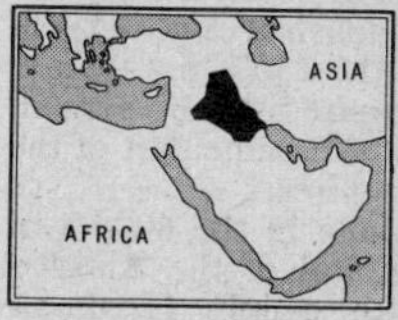

Official Name: Republic of Iraq.
Area: 167,925 square miles (434,924 sq. km.).
Population: 14,737,800.
Chief Cities: Baghdad, capital, 1,490,759; Basra, 310,950; Mosul, 264,146; Kirkuk, 175,303; Najaf, 134,027; Hilla, 84,704.
Largest Metropolitan Area: Baghdad, 1,657,424.
Government: One-party socialist-military state.
President: Saddam Hussein (since 1979).
Legislature: *National Assembly,* 250 members.
Flag: Red, white, and black stripes, with three green stars in center stripe.
Languages: Arabic (official), Kurdish.
Main Ethnic Groups: Arab (75%), Kurd (20%).
Chief Religion: Islam (95%).
Leading Industries: Mining (petroleum); agriculture (sheep, dates, wheat, barley, rice, cotton, cattle, goats, camels); food processing; manufacturing (textiles, cement, leather products).
Foreign Trade: *Major exports*—petroleum, dates, cement, wool; *major imports*—motor vehicles, sugar, textiles.
Places of Interest: Ruins of Babylon, Hanging Gardens, throne room of "writing on the wall," Lion of Babylon; Agarguf ruins; Arch of Ctesiphon. *In Baghdad:* Iraq Museum; mosques; tomb of Sitt Zubaidah.

IRAQ TODAY

A little larger than California, Iraq ranks among the leading oil-producing nations of the world, but its petroleum facilities were damaged in a war with Iran in 1980–83.

Most of the people are poor, and only about 4 out of 10 can read and write. The majority are farmers or nomadic herdsmen. The most important cash crop of the farmers is dates, of which Iraq is the world's leading exporter.

The leftist military government runs the country as a police state. Iraq broke diplomatic relations with the United States in 1967 because of U.S. aid to Israel in the Arab-Israeli war in June of that year. But the U.S. maintains a diplomatic mission at the Belgian embassy, and U.S. companies carry on foreign trade with Iraq.

The Tigris and Euphrates rivers flow across Iraq from northwest to southeast. They join to form the Shatt Al Arab that empties into the Persian Gulf.

The northern climate is temperate, but the plains suffer heat and strong northeasterly winds during the summer. Temperatures may reach 120 °F. between May and October. Winters are damp, with average temperatures of 50 °F.

ANCIENT MESOPOTAMIA

Archaeological excavations have established that cultures existed in this region, once known as Mesopotamia, for more than 10,000 years.

QUICK QUIZ: What are San Marino's two main sources of income? See page 639.

IRAQ *(continued)*

The written history of the area began about 4000 B.C. when the Sumerians established city- states in southern Mesopotamia. In the 2300s B.C. Sumer was absorbed into a huge empire ruled by Sargon, king of Akkad. The area later became part of the Assyrian and Babylonian empires.

Arabs overran Mesopotamia in the 600s A.D. Baghdad was made the capital of the Abbasid caliphate in 762. The fifth caliph, Harun-al-Rashid, figured in the stories of *the Thousand and One Nights.*

Mongol conquerors devastated the country in 1258 and again in 1401. Baghdad was captured in 1534 by the Ottoman Turks, and Mesopotamia stayed under Turkish control until World War I.

KINGDOM OF IRAQ

During World War I, Britain, with the help of Hussein, the sharif of Mecca, gained control of the country, known since 1918 as Iraq.

The League of Nations in 1920 made Iraq a mandated territory under British administration. Britain arranged for Faisal I, the son of Hussein, to become king of Iraq. In 1932 the League of Nations mandate was ended, and Iraq joined the League as an independent nation.

Upon Faisal's death in 1933, he was succeeded by his son Ghazi, who was killed in an auto accident in 1939. The throne was inherited by Ghazi's three-year-old son Faisal II.

A pro-Axis government, briefly in power in 1941, collapsed under British military pressure.

Led by pro-Western statesman Nuri es-Said, Iraq in 1955 joined Turkey, Iran, Pakistan, and Britain in the Baghdad Pact defense treaty.

REPUBLIC OF IRAQ

On July 14, 1958, Gen. Abdul Karim Kassem overthrew the regime. He killed Nuri es-Said and young King Faisal II, establishing the Republic of Iraq. Kassem withdrew Iraq from the Baghdad Pact in 1959.

A military coup on Feb. 8, 1963, overthrew Kassem. He and many Iraqi communists were executed. The Arab Socialist Baath Party took control with Abdul Salam Arif as president. Iraq became a one-party military-socialist state.

In April 1966 Abdul Salam Arif died in a helicopter crash. He was succeeded as president by his elder brother, Abdul Rahman Arif.

President Arif, who was held responsible for Iraq's defeat in the 1967 war with Israel, was ousted by a bloodless military coup on July 17, 1968. The leader of the coup, former premier Ahmed Hassan al-Bakr, took over as president and formed a new government.

DEVELOPMENTS IN THE 1970s–1980s

A lengthy rebellion of the Kurdish minority in the Zagros Mountains against the Iraqi government temporarily ended in March 1970 when the Baathist regime agreed to grant autonomy to the Kurds within four years.

Iraq joined in the October 1973 Middle East War between the Arab nations and Israel and cut off oil shipments to the U.S. for several months.

Angered at not being given independence, the Kurds took up arms in March 1974, receiving military support from Iran.

In an agreement with Iraq on March 5, 1975, Iran stopped providing supplies to the Kurdish rebels, after which the revolt collapsed.

Iraq completed nationalizing its entire oil industry in December 1975.

The International League for Human Rights reported to the UN in 1977 that the Iraqi government was systematically destroying the Kurds. Refugees said in July 1977 that scores of Kurdish villages had been destroyed and thousands of Kurds were pressed into forced labor, clearing a strip 20 kilometers (12.4 miles) wide along the border facing Iran and Turkey.

The government executed 21 communists in May 1978 and imprisoned 10 others after discovery of a plot to overthrow the government by infiltrating the military forces.

Iraq's relations with the Soviet Union noticeably cooled after exposure of the plot. The government, which had been dependent on Soviet weapons for two decades, began buying arms from France and other Western nations.

The government began a $36 million project in 1978 to excavate and restore the ancient city of Babylon, which stands about 55 miles south of Baghdad. Archaeologists estimated the project would not be completed before the 1990s.

After 11 years as president, the 68-year-old Bakr resigned on July 16, 1979, because of illness. He was succeeded by Gen. Saddam Hussein, 42, who had been vice chairman of the Revolutionary Command Council.

Within two weeks of taking over as president, Hussein arrested scores of officials, charging them with plotting to overthrow him. A firing squad executed 21 of the plotters on Aug. 8, 1979, including five members of the Revolutionary Command Council. A special court had condemned them to death and sentenced 33 others to prison terms for the coup attempt.

In the first national election in 20 years, on June 20, 1980, voters chose the 250 members of a new parliament from among 800 candidates approved by the country's only political party, the Arab Baath Socialist Party.

Ayatollah Khomeini, ruler of neighboring Iran, called in 1980 for the overthrow of Hussein by the Shiite Muslims, who make up the majority of Iraq's population.

In retaliation, Hussein launched a full-scale war with Iran beginning on Sept. 22, 1980, as Iraq claimed control of the Shatt Al Arab waterway that previously had been shared with Iran.

Israeli warplanes bombed a nuclear reactor near Baghdad on June 7, 1981, claiming Iraq intended to use it to produce atomic bombs.

After initially invading Iran in 1980, Iraq withdrew its troops in June 1982. In turn, Iran invaded Iraq in July 1982. Observers estimated from 100,000 to 250,000 troops had been killed in the first three years of the war.

When Iraq threatened in 1983 to use French Exocet missiles to destroy Iranian oil facilities, Iran warned it would retaliate by cutting off all shipping in the Persian Gulf.

Iraq's economy suffered in 1983 as Saudi Arabia and other Arab supporters cut aid in half—from about $12 billion to $6 billion. Iraq's revenues from oil exports fell from $25 billion in 1980 to less than $7 billion in 1983.

IRELAND

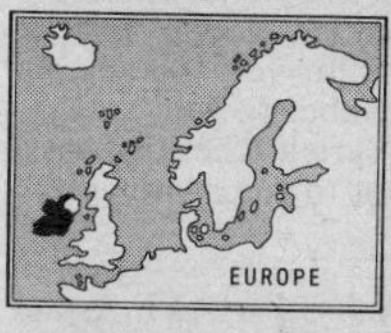

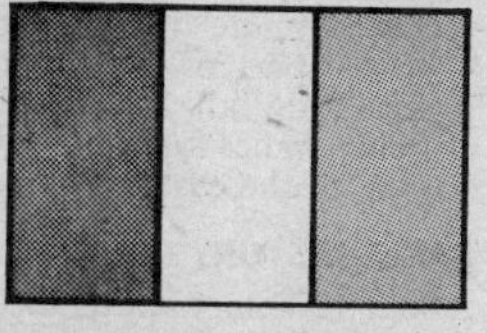

Official Name: Ireland (*Eire* in Gaelic).
Area: 27,136 square miles (70,283 sq. km.).
Population: 3,555,360.
Chief Cities: Dublin, capital, 566,034; Cork, 128,235.
Largest Metropolitan Area: Dublin, 650,153.
Government: Parliamentary republic.
Prime Minister: Garret FitzGerald (since 1982).
President: Patrick Hillery (since 1976).
Parliament: *Seanad Eireann* (Senate), 60 members; *Dáil Eireann* (House), 166 members.
U.S. Ambassador to Ireland: Robert Francis Kane.
Irish Ambassador to U.S.: Tadhg O'Sullivan.
Flag: Green, white, and orange bars.
Official Languages: Irish (Gaelic) and English.
Leading Ethnic Group: Irish.
Main Religions: Roman Catholicism (94%), Anglicanism (4%).
Leading Industries: Manufacturing (electronics, brewing, distilling, food processing, textiles, paper, machinery, chemicals, vehicle assembly); agriculture (sheep, cattle, horses, hay, potatoes, turnips, sugar beets, barley, wheat, oats, rye); fishing; tourism.
Foreign Trade: *Major exports*—machinery, textiles, chemicals, meat, dairy products; *major imports*—machinery, iron and steel, textiles, petroleum.
Places of Interest: Blarney Castle near Cork; Great Rock of Cashel; Killarney lakes; River Shannon; Galway castles; Limerick; Waterford; Kennedy family home and memorial park at Dunganstown. *In Dublin:* Castle; St. Patrick's Cathedral; Daniel O'Connell Monument; Phoenix Park; Abbey Theatre.

IRELAND TODAY

Somewhat larger than the state of West Virginia, the Republic of Ireland covers five-sixths of the island of Ireland. It shares the island with Northern Ireland, which is part of Britain's United Kingdom. Ireland is separated from the island of Great Britain by the narrow Irish Sea.

Although industrialization proceeded rapidly in the 1960s–80s, about half the people live on farms or in small villages. Because it must import more than it can export, Ireland depends on income from tourism to make up the difference.

Coastal highlands and a central plain give a saucer shape to the island.

Mild winds from Europe and warm, damp air from the Gulf Stream combine to give the country a temperate climate. Temperatures average 40°F. in the winter and 60°F. in the summer.

EARLY HISTORY

Prehistoric people lived in Ireland as early as 6000 B.C. They were conquered by Celtic tribes from Britain and Europe about 400 B.C.

St. Patrick brought Christianity in A.D. 432.

In the 700s to 1000s Norse Vikings established seaports in Ireland.

King Henry II of England forced Irish nobles to recognize his overlordship in 1171.

To stem rising rebellion after the Reformation in the 1500s, Britain gave confiscated Irish lands to pro-British Irish and English Protestants. In the 1700s Irish Catholics lost all legal rights.

In 1801 the Act of Union created the United Kingdom of Great Britain and Ireland.

In the 1840s the country was devastated by a great potato famine. A million Irish died in five years, and 1.6 million emigrated.

Sinn Fein, the political arm of the secret Irish Republican Army (IRA), instigated the 1916 Easter Rebellion in Dublin. In the 1919 general elections Sinn Fein won enough seats to set up its own parliament (Dáil Eireann) in Dublin, while the IRA waged guerrilla warfare against Britain.

The Irish Free State was established in 1922 as a British dominion.

Eamon De Valera led Sinn Fein extremists in a fight for full independence. In 1937 a new constitution changed the country's name to *Eire*. De Valera was named prime minister.

INDEPENDENT REPUBLIC OF IRELAND

John A. Costello, head of the Fine Gael Party, became prime minister in 1948. On April 18, 1949, he declared Ireland an independent republic.

De Valera, of the Fianna Fáil Party, returned to power as prime minister in 1951–54 and 1957–59. He then served as president in 1959–73.

In parliamentary elections on Feb. 28, 1973, a coalition of the Fine Gael and smaller Labor Party won a narrow victory. Liam Cosgrave of the Fine Gael became prime minister.

Cosgrave acknowledged officially for the first time in March 1974 that Northern Ireland was part of Britain's United Kingdom.

The Fianna Fail Party won a surprise victory in a national election on June 16, 1977, taking 84 seats in the 148-member Dáil Eireann. John Lynch, head of Fianna Fail, became prime minister in July. He had promised tax cuts and called for the British to leave Northern Ireland.

Charles J. Haughey, 54, succeeded Lynch as prime minister and head of Fianna Fail on Dec. 11, 1979. In an election on June 11, 1981, none of the parties won a majority.

Garret FitzGerald, head of the Fine Gael Party, became prime minister on June 30, 1981, with the aid of minor parties.

Haughey again became prime minister after his party won a narrow victory in a general election on Feb. 18, 1982. However, the economy grew worse with unemployment rising to 12% and inflation to 20%.

After a national election on Nov. 24, 1982, FitzGerald again became prime minister, heading a coalition government with the small Labor Party. He established an austerity budget for 1983 that cut government spending and raised taxes.

The discovery of oil off Ireland's southeast coast, announced on Aug. 2, 1983, spurred hopes that the country, which spends $1 billion each year on oil imports, might become self-sufficient in oil by the 1990s.

An anti-abortion amendment to the constitution was adopted by a national referendum on Sept. 7, 1983, with a 2 to 1 vote.

See also *Northern Ireland,* page 511.

QUICK QUIZ: What college football team was undefeated in 1980 and 1982? See page 814.

ISRAEL

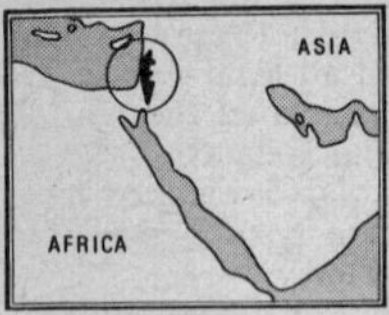

Official Name: State of Israel.
Area: 10,715 sq. mi. (27,752 sq. km.).
Population: 5,349,110.
Chief Cities: Jerusalem, capital, 376,000; Tel Aviv–Yafo (Jaffa), 343,300; Haifa, 227,800; Ramat Gan, 120,900; Bat Yam, 124,100; Holon, 121,200.
Largest Metropolitan Area: Tel Aviv–Yafo, 1,219,900.
Government: Parliamentary republic.
Prime Minister: Yitzhak Shamir (since 1983).
President: Chaim Herzog (since 1983).
Parliament: *Knesset,* 120 members.
U.S. Ambassador to Israel: Samuel W. Lewis.
Israeli Ambassador to U.S.: Meir Rosenne.
Flag: White field bearing blue Star of David between two blue stripes.
Languages: Hebrew, Arabic, English.
Main Ethnic Groups: Jewish (85%), Arab (15%).
Leading Religions: Judaism (official–85%), Islam, Christianity.
Leading Industries: Manufacturing (food processing, textiles, clothing, aircraft, chemicals, metal products, vehicle assembly, machinery, cut diamonds, cement); agriculture (poultry, dairy products, citrus fruits, grapes, wheat, sugar beets, cotton, olives, figs, vegetables); mining (potash, petroleum, phosphates, bromine, natural gas); construction.
Foreign Trade: *Major exports*—diamonds, citrus fruits, textile yarn and thread, potassic fertilizers; *major imports*—diamonds, crude petroleum, ships and boats, meat, corn.
Places of Interest: Many Old and New Testament sites; ruins of Masada on Dead Sea; Mt. Carmel in Haifa; Nazareth; Bethlehem; Capernaum; Sodom; King Solomon's copper mines. *In Jerusalem:* Wailing Wall; Dome of the Rock; Church of the Holy Sepulchre.

ISRAEL TODAY

About the size of New Jersey, Israel is a small Middle Eastern nation on the east coast of the Mediterranean Sea. It is the only nation in the world in which Judaism is the official religion. Most of the people are or descend from Jewish immigrants to their biblical homeland.

Surrounded by Arab nations that wanted to destroy the Jewish state, Israel fought four wars for its existence since declaring its independence in 1948. The nation remained continually on the alert against attack from its neighbors, spending two-thirds of its national budget for military preparedness.

The nation has few natural resources, and much of the land is desert. However, with hard work and over $2 billion annual aid from the U.S., Israel has developed an industrial economy.

Israeli pioneers have reclaimed large desert areas for farming and citrus-fruit orchards.

Israel's people enjoy a much higher standard of living than Arabs in neighboring countries. Most Israelis live in cities and make their living from manufacturing or service industries.

The northern part of the country is hilly, with valleys and plains. South of this region is a narrow coastal plain. In the south is the Negev Desert.

The climate ranges from moderate in the northern part of the country to very hot in the desert. Rain falls from September to May.

Lebanon lies to the north, Syria to the northeast, Jordan to the east, and Egypt to the southwest.

EARLY HISTORY

About 1000 B.C. scattered Hebrew tribes in Israel (then called Canaan) banded together under King Saul to fight invading Philistines.

Political unity was achieved under King David, who established the capital at Jerusalem. His son and successor, Solomon, built the Temple and made Jerusalem the cultural and religious capital of Israel about 961–922 B.C.

After Solomon's death the kingdom split into two quarrelsome parts, Judah and Israel. Both soon fell to Assyrian conquerors, who enslaved about 27,000 Israelites in 722 B.C.

In Judah the Assyrians were followed by Egyptians and Babylonians, who exiled the ruling class of Judah in 587–582 B.C. Although the exiles were soon allowed to return, the area was repeatedly overrun by conquerors—Persians, Greeks, Seleucids, Romans, Byzantines, Arabs, Crusaders, and Turks. In 1516 the region became part of the Ottoman Empire.

In the 1890s Zionism, an international movement, was founded by Theodor Herzl to restore Palestine to the Jews. Many European Jews left their homes to settle in Palestine.

In World War I the region fell into British hands. Anxious for Jewish help, England in 1917 issued the Balfour Declaration, promising a national home for the Jews.

As Jews fled to Israel in the 1930s and 1940s to escape Nazi German persecution, an Arab rebellion caused Britain to limit Zionist immigration during and after World War II.

INDEPENDENT ISRAEL

In 1947 the United Nations agreed to divide Palestine into two independent states, one Jewish and one Arab, with Jerusalem serving as an international or neutral zone.

The plan was accepted by the Jews. On May 14, 1948, they proclaimed Israel's independence when the British withdrew.

On the same day Egypt, Iraq, Jordan, Lebanon, Syria, and Saudi Arabia attacked Israel. Armistices were concluded in 1949.

SECOND ARAB–ISRAELI WAR

In 1956 an Egyptian-Syrian-Jordanian military alliance threatened Israel with hostile encirclement. At the same time Egypt's expropriation of the Suez Canal Company alienated Britain and France. While an Anglo-French attack knocked out the Egyptian air force, Israeli forces quickly overran Egypt's Sinai region.

Combined pressure from the U.S. and the Soviet Union in the UN caused Israel's eventual withdrawal. A UN emergency force was stationed along the Egyptian-Israeli border.

THIRD ARAB–ISRAELI WAR

Israeli armed forces launched air and land strikes on Egypt, Jordan, and Syria on June 5, 1967.

In six days Israeli forces captured Jerusalem, the Sinai peninsula, the West Bank of the Jordan, the Gaza strip, and Golan Heights of Syria. A cease-fire began on June 11, 1967.

About 2 million Arabs displaced from their homes by the Arab-Israeli wars lived in refugee camps in Arab countries. In 1964 the militant Palestine Liberation Organization (PLO) was formed by the refugees to create an armed force that would compel Israel to give up land for an independent Arab Palestine. In the years that followed, the PLO carried out terrorist attacks on Israel, and Israelis retaliated with raids on PLO installations in Lebanon and elsewhere.

FOURTH ARAB–ISRAELI WAR

Egypt and Syria launched a new war on Israel on two fronts on Oct. 6, 1973, during Yom Kippur. Other Arab nations soon joined the war.

After heavy fighting, Israeli troops were advancing in Syria and Egypt when the UN Security Council ordered a cease-fire on October 22. Three days later the UN sent a peacekeeping force to the Middle East to prevent further fighting.

The war resulted in a worldwide fuel crisis when Arab oil-producing nations cut off oil shipments for six months to the United States, Japan, and other nations that had aided Israel.

AN UNEASY PEACE

In a national election on May 17, 1977, the right-wing Likud Party won an upset victory, capturing a plurality of 41 seats to Labor's 34 in the Knesset. Remaining seats in the 120-member parliament were split among 10 other parties.

Menachem Begin, 63, leader of the Likud Party, became prime minister on June 21, 1977. Considered one of Israel's founding fathers, Begin had headed the guerrilla army called Irgun Zvai Leumi in the 1940s that killed many British soldiers in an effort to drive Britain out of Palestine.

Events took a dramatic turn on Nov. 19–21, 1977, when Egyptian President Sadat flew to Israel to address the Israeli parliament at the invitation of Prime Minister Begin, breaking the 30-year deadlock in which Arab leaders had refused to meet face to face with Israeli officials.

Begin returned Sadat's visit in December 1977, becoming the first Israeli prime minister to travel to Egypt. Formal peace negotiations began in January 1978.

Fears of a new Mideast war rose in March 1978 when Israel invaded southern Lebanon to destroy Palestinian terrorists. After the UN sent a 4,000-man peacekeeping force to the area, Israeli troops withdrew from Lebanon by June.

Culminating more than a year of negotiations spearheaded by U.S. President Carter, Israel and Egypt signed a peace treaty in Washington, D.C., on March 26, 1979. Upon ratification, the treaty became effective on April 25, 1979.

Israel began withdrawing from Egypt's Sinai peninsula on May 25, 1979, turning over the town of El Arish to Egyptian control. The first Israeli ships were allowed to sail through Egypt's Suez Canal on May 29.

Meanwhile, Israel continued steps toward absorbing former Jordanian territories on the West Bank of the Jordan River, establishing new settlements there in 1979–82 in disregard of protests from Arab nations, the UN, and the U.S.

ISRAEL'S PRIME MINISTERS

1948–63	David Ben-Gurion	Mapai Workers' Party
1963–69	Levi Eshkol	Mapai Workers' Party
1969–74	Golda Meir	Labor Party
1974–77	Yitzhak Rabin	Labor Party
1977	Shimon Peres	Labor Party
1977–83	Menachem Begin	Likud Party
1983–	Yitzhak Shamir	Likud Party

Israel and Egypt restored formal diplomatic relations with the exchange of ambassadors on Feb. 26, 1980. However, negotiations with Egypt broke down in 1980 on providing Arab autonomy in the West Bank and Gaza areas.

The Israeli parliament on July 30, 1980, formally made the Arab eastern part of Jerusalem part of the nation's capital.

Israel dispatched its warplanes on June 7, 1981, to destroy a nuclear plant in Iraq, claiming it was going to be used to produce atomic weapons.

In an election on June 30, 1981, Begin's party won a plurality of one seat over Labor.

Israel's parliament on Dec. 14, 1981, formally annexed the Golan Heights area taken from Syria in 1967. The annexation emphasized Israel's determination not to give up the area in any further peace negotiations with Arab states.

However, Israel made good on its peace treaty obligations by returning the Sinai region to Egypt on April 25, 1982, even though Israeli troops had to forcibly eject thousands of Israeli settlers from the area. An 11-nation 3,000-man military force, about half from the U.S., took up peacekeeping positions along the new Sinai border. The U.S. also completed two new $1.1-billion air bases for Israel in the Negev desert to compensate for facilities given up in the evacuation of the Sinai.

Israeli troops invaded Lebanon on June 6, 1982, to end use of that country as a PLO military base. In fierce battles, Israel quickly defeated the PLO and the Syrian occupation army. The world was horrified in September 1982 by the massacre of more than 700 Palestinians in Israeli-occupied Beirut. Defense Minister Ariel Sharon and three generals were forced to resign after an investigation found the army leaders indirectly responsible for the massacre.

Chaim Herzog, 64, of the Labor Party began a 5-year term as the nation's president on May 5, 1983, after being elected by parliament to the largely ceremonial office.

The economy worsened in 1983 as inflation rose to an annual rate of about 150%. With the world's highest per capita foreign debt, the government used a third of its budget to pay interest on the $21.5 billion it owes.

The ailing 70-year-old Begin resigned on Sept. 15, 1983.

Yitzhak Shamir, 68, foreign minister under Begin, became prime minister on Oct. 10, 1983. The new government immediately devalued currency by 23% and raised food prices by 50%.

See also page 419.

QUICK QUIZ: What nation is called "the Switzerland of Africa"? See page 657.

ITALY

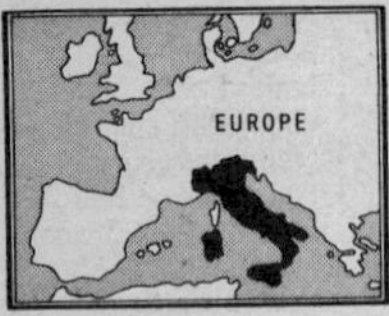

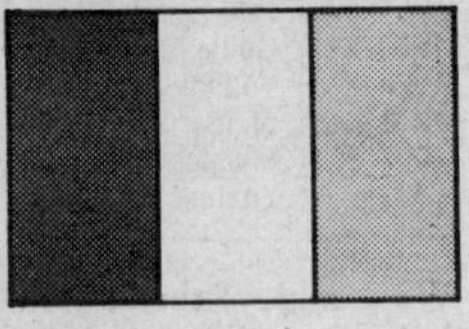

Official Name: Italian Republic.
Area: 116,304 square miles (301,225 sq. km).
Population: 56,860,300.
Chief Cities: Roma (Rome), capital, 2,897,505; Milano (Milan), 1,706,268; Napoli (Naples), 1,225,227; Torino (Turin), 1,181,567.
Government: Parliamentary republic.
Prime Minister: Bettino Craxi (since 1983).
President: Alessandro Pertini (since 1978).
Parliament: *Senate,* 322 members; *Chamber of Deputies,* 630 members.
U.S. Ambassador to Italy: Maxwell M. Rabb.
Italian Ambassador to U.S.: Rinaldo Petrignani.
Flag: Green, white, and red bars.
Official Language: Italian.
Main Ethnic Group: Italian.
Official Religion: Roman Catholicism (99%).
Leading Industries: Manufacturing (steel, automobiles, chemicals, electricity, office machines, electronic equipment, appliances, machinery, clothing, shoes, publishing); food processing; tourism; agriculture (sheep, goats, cattle, wheat, potatoes, corn, rice, grapes, olives, barley, oats, tobacco, fruits, vegetables); mining (natural gas, petroleum, mercury, sulfur, marble, asbestos, bauxite).
Foreign Trade: *Major exports*—automobiles, petroleum products, clothing, shoes, office machines, citrus fruits, vegetables; *major imports*—petroleum, machinery, food, scrap iron and steel, coal, cotton.
Places of Interest: Renaissance art galleries in Florence; Isle of Capri; St. Mark's Square in Venice; La Scala opera house in Milan; Adriatic coast resorts; Dolomite winter-sports at Trentino; Naples; Genoa; Sicily; Sardinia. *In Rome:* St. Peter's Basilica; Vatican; Sistine Chapel; Colosseum; Pantheon.

ITALY TODAY

About the size of Florida and Georgia combined, Italy has few natural resources. Lack of such mineral resources as iron ore, coal, and petroleum has handicapped Italy's industrial growth. However, it is among the world's leading producers of cement, electricity, natural gas, and steel.

Almost a third of Italy is mountainous and unable to be farmed. This along with backward farming methods combine to limit food production, making Italy dependent on imports to feed its people.

Italy's government lacks stability because no party has a majority of seats in the parliament. The conservative Christian Democrats control only a few more seats than the Communist Party.

In the 1970s–1980s leftist and rightist terrorist groups defied government authority with thoûsands of kidnappings, bombings, and killings.

Only the Po River valley, the coastal plains, and lowland relieve the mountainous landscape of Italy. Alpine ranges in the north include the Maritime, Graian, Pennine, Bergamasque, Dolomites, and Carnic mountains. Below them lies the great fertile basin of the Po Valley, Italy's agricultural and industrial core.

From the valley's lower limits rise the rugged Apennine chain. It runs down the length of the peninsula and leaps the Strait of Messina to cover much of northern Sicily.

Southern Italy and Sicily are in the midst of an earthquake belt that has given rise to Europe's three best-known active volcanoes; Vesuvius (4,190 feet), Etna (10,958 feet), and Stromboli (3,308 feet).

Italy's largest and most famous lakes—Maggiorè, Como, and Garda—are all located in the Alps. The country's most important rivers are the Po and the Adige in the north, and the Arno and the Tiber in the central region.

EARLY HISTORY

The earliest known settlers—Latins, Sabines, Umbrians, and Ligurians—took over large areas in the northern part of the peninsula. They were displaced in the 800s B.C.. by the Etruscans. Greeks and Phoenicians began their expansion into Sicily and the southern part of the peninsula about the 700s B.C..

Rome, the home of the Latins, lay between the Etruscan and Greek settlements. The Roman republic annexed the Etruscan kingdom in the 400s B.C. and united most of Italy by 270 B.C.

The Punic Wars (264–146 B.C.) between Rome and Carthage ended with Carthage destroyed and Rome the dominant power in the Mediterranean region. During the next century the Romans expanded into Gaul (France) and Britain.

ROMAN EMPIRE

In 27 B.C. Rome became an empire with Augustus as its first emperor. Early in the 300s A.D. Emperor Constantine accepted Christianity, and churches spread throughout Italy and all of the Roman Empire. At the same time, Constantine moved the imperial capital to Constantinople (now Istanbul).

Rome subsequently declined, and fell in 476 to German tribes.

The Ostrogoths and Lombards occupied the peninsula in the 500s, but in 774 their kingdom was absorbed by the Frankish empire headed by Charlemagne. During the 900s the powerful German king Otto I extended his rule into the Italian peninsula. In 962 he was crowned emperor of the Holy Roman Empire by the pope.

ITALIAN CITY-STATES

From the 900s to the 1300s the Italian city-states, the popes, and the Holy Roman emperors vied for power. Towns were divided and most noble families backed one of the two opposition parties: the papal Guelphs and the imperial Ghibellines. After the 1200s the Italian cities of Venice, Bologna, and Florence emerged as autonomous centers of political power and of learning. By the 1500s the Italian Renaissance had breathed new life into European art and learning.

Invasions by France, Spain, and Austria during the 1500s and 1600s divided the Italian states and brought most of them under foreign rule. In the early 1800s Austria became the dominant power in the Italian peninsula. Sporadic attempts to drive out the Austrians were effectively checked. Failing to achieve their goals in the revolutions of 1848 and 1849, nationalist leaders such as Giuseppe

Garibaldi and Giuseppe Mazzini turned for help to Piedmont, the only Italian state to gain a liberal constitution, and to its able prime minister, Count Camillo Cavour. With the aid of France, Piedmont drove out the Austrians in 1859.

INDEPENDENT KINGDOM AND FASCIST RULE

Cavour succeeded in uniting most of the Italian states in the Kingdom of Italy, proclaimed on March 17, 1861, under the rule of Victor Emmanuel II of Savoy. The entire Italian peninsula was unified by 1870 with Rome as the capital.

Although at first neutral in World War I, promises of territories and concessions induced Italy to enter the war on the Allied side.

Fascist leader Benito Mussolini seized control in 1923. His dictatorship soon controlled all aspects of Italian life. Mussolini set out to assert Italy's power by the conquest of Ethiopia in 1935–36 and by annexing Albania in 1939.

Italy entered World War II on the side of Germany on June 11, 1940. Italian defeats aroused popular discontent with the fascist regime. In July 1943 King Victor Emmanuel III ordered Mussolini's arrest. The new government concluded an armistice with the Allies, who had already begun to invade Sicily. But German forces took control of northern and central Italy. The Allies entered Rome on June 4, 1944. Mussolini was executed by Italian partisans in April 1945. A formal peace treaty was signed between Italy and the Allies on Feb. 10, 1947.

ITALIAN REPUBLIC

A popular referendum on June 2, 1946, ended Italy's monarchy. The Italian Republic officially came into being on Jan. 1, 1948.

Alcide de Gasperi, leader of the Christian Democratic Party, headed Italy's postwar government in 1945–53.

The declining influence of the Roman Catholic Church in Italy was demonstrated when Italians voted 3 to 2 on May 12, 1974, in favor of the nation's 1970 divorce law.

Italy and Yugoslavia agreed on a draft treaty on Oct. 1, 1975, bringing final settlement of their 30-year Trieste dispute. The treaty formally gave the area south of Trieste to Yugoslavia.

The wave of terror by which the anarchist Red Brigades sought to disrupt Italy reached a peak in 1978 with the kidnapping and murder of former Prime Minister Aldo Moro. The terrorists killed Moro's five bodyguards to capture him on March 16. Nearly two months later Moro was slain and his body left in Rome on May 9.

Giovanni Leone, who had served as Italy's president since 1971, resigned on June 15, 1978, after newspaper charges of tax fraud in relation to $1.6 million in bribes allegedly paid by the U.S. Lockheed corporation to Italian officials.

Socialist Alessandro Pertini, 81, who was jailed for 11 years by Mussolini, was chosen president by a special electoral assembly on July 8, 1978.

New parliamentary elections were held June 3–4, 1979. Christian Democrats retained their plurality in the 630-seat lower house, losing only 1 seat and holding 262. The communists lost 27 seats, ending with 201 as the second-largest party.

ITALY'S PRIME MINISTERS SINCE 1945

1945–53	Alcide de Gasperi	1968–70	Mariano Rumor
1953–54	Giuseppe Pella	1970–72	Emilio Colombo
1954–55	Mario Scelba	1972–73	Giulio Andreotti
1955–57	Antonio Segni	1973–74	Mariano Rumor
1957–58	Adone Zoli	1974–76	Aldo Moro
1958–59	Amintore Fanfani	1976–79	Giulio Andreotti
1959–60	Antonio Segni	1979–80	Francesco Cossiga
1960–63	Amintore Fanfani	1980–81	Arnaldo Forlani
1963–64	Giovanni Leone	1981–82	Giovanni Spadolini
1964–68	Aldo Moro	1982–83	Amintore Fanfani
1968	Giovanni Leone	1983–	Bettino Craxi

Christian Democrat Francesco Cossiga, 51, a former minister of interior, was sworn in as prime minister on Aug. 5, 1979.

ITALY IN THE 1980s

In one of the worst terrorist incidents neofascists killed 84 persons in the bombing of the railway station in Bologna on Aug. 2, 1980.

After 13 years of work and an expenditure of about $375 million, a 9-mile subway line was opened in Rome in Feb. 16, 1980, designed to serve commuters from southeastern suburbs.

Prime Minister Cossiga survived a vote of confidence in July 1980 after he had been accused of aiding the son of a fellow legislator to escape from arrest as a terrorist. But on Sept. 27 he was defeated and forced to resign when he lost by one vote on an austerity program that had sought to overcome the rising inflation rate by increasing taxes.

Arnaldo Forlani, president of the Christian Democratic Party, was invited by President Pertini on Oct. 2, 1980, to become prime minister.

A major earthquake struck southern Italy on Nov. 23–24, 1980, destroying 133 towns and villages, killing more than 3,000 persons, and leaving over 300,000 homeless.

Revelation in 1981 that many high government officials belonged to an illegal secret Masonic lodge engaged in criminal activities caused Prime Minister Forlani to resign on May 26.

After a month-long government crisis, Giovanni Spadolini, 56, head of the small Republican Party, became prime minister with a coalition cabinet on June 28, 1981. He was the first non-Christian Democrat to hold the office since Italy became a republic.

Spadolini announced a rigorous economic program, calling for $8 billion cuts in spending for social programs and aid to local governments.

Italy's Marxist Red Brigade terrorists kidnapped U.S. Brig. Gen. James L. Dozier on Dec. 17, 1981, in Verona. Forty-two days later he was rescued unhurt by police who stormed a Red Bridgade hideaway in Padua on Jan. 28, 1982. Seventeen of the kidnappers were sentenced to jail terms of 2 to 27 years.

Spadolini resigned in November 1982 when he lost the support of socialists in parliament.

Christian Democrat Amintore Fanfani, 74, who had headed the government in the 1950s–1960s, became prime minister in December 1982.

In a general election on June 26–27, the nation's leading political party, the Christian Democrats, suffered a crushing defeat as its share of

QUICK QUIZ: Who was the first U.S. President to resign his office? See page 380.

ITALY *(continued)*
parliamentary votes fell from 38.3% to 32.9%. The communist share fell slightly to 29.9, while socialists made substantial gains, rising from 9.8% to 11.4%.

Bettino Craxi, 49, became Italy's first socialist prime minister on Aug. 4, 1983, heading a five-party coalition cabinet that included the Christian Democrats. Craxi sought to cut government spending in an effort to improve Italy's economy, which in 1983 had 10% unemployment and an inflation rate of nearly 16%.

ITALY'S SEMIAUTONOMOUS ISLANDS

SARDINIA

Area: 9,194 square miles (23,812 sq. km.)
Population: 1,641,990.
Capital: Cagliari, 236,931.

About the size of New Hampshire, Sardinia is the second-largest island in the Mediterranean after Sicily. It lies about 100 miles west of Italy. It is separated only by a narrow strait from the French island of Corsica to the north.

Thousands of stone monuments built by prehistoric Stone Age people dot the countryside.

In about the 800s B.C. Phoenicians established trading colonies on the coast. They were followed by Carthaginians, Romans, Vandals, and the Greek Byzantine Empire.

In the 1000s A.D. Arab rulers of Spain took control of the island. The Italian city-states of Pisa and Genoa contended for mastery of the island in the 1100s and 1200s. In the 1300s it passed to rule by Spain. In 1718 it was awarded to the rulers of Savoy in northern Italy, who became kings of Sardinia until 1861, when they became rulers of Italy. In 1948 Sardinia was granted semiautonomous status.

SICILY

Area: 9,817 square miles (25,426 sq. km.).
Population: 5,099,750.
Chief Cities: Palermo, capital, 662,567; Catania, 398,642; Messina, 261,332; Siracusa (Syracuse), 118,025.

The largest island in the Mediterranean Sea, Sicily has been a stepping-stone between Italy and Africa throughout its history.

The island lies southwest of the toe of Italy's boot, separated from the mainland by the 2- to 10-mile-wide Strait of Messina.

Because of its year-round warm climate, the island attracts many tourists during the winter.

Peoples called the Sicani and Siculi lived on the island in prehistoric times. Greeks began colonies in the 700s B.C., making Syracuse a major center. Carthage won control in the 300s B.C.

The Romans took Sicily in 211 B.C., making it their first overseas province. It fell to the Byzantine Empire in A.D. 535. Arabs from Africa conquered Sicily in the 800s. Normans under Roger I captured Sicily in the 1000s. It came under the rule of German kings in the 1100s and was the seat of the Holy Roman Empire under Frederick II in 1215–1250. French, Spanish, Austrian, and Italian rulers contended for Sicily for the next 600 years.

In 1861 Sicily became part of the new Kingdom of Italy. The island was granted semiautonomous status on May 15, 1946.

IVORY COAST

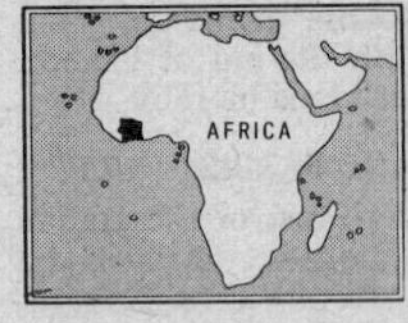

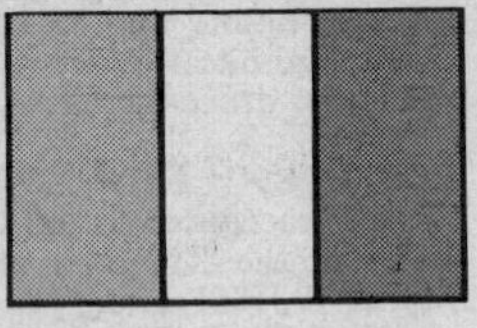

Official Name: Republic of the Ivory Coast.
Area: 124,504 square miles (322,463 sq. km.).
Population: 8,998,730.
Capital: Abidjan, 282,000.
Government: One-party republic.
President: Félix Houphouët-Boigny (since 1960).
National Assembly: 147 members.
U.S. Ambassador to Ivory Coast: Robert H. Miller.
Ivory Coast Ambassador to U.S.: Rene Anamy.
Flag: Tricolor of orange, white, and green bars.
Languages: French (official), Baoulé, Dioula, Mandingo, Mande.
Main Ethnic Group: Black.
Religions: Animism (64%), Islam (24%), Christianity (12%).
Leading Industries: Agriculture (coffee, cocoa, cotton, bananas, pineapples, coconuts, rubber, sugar); forestry and lumbering; food processing; tourism; manufacturing (textiles, shoes, consumer products); mining (petroleum, diamonds, iron ore).
Foreign Trade: *Major exports*—cocoa, coffee, petroleum, wood, palm oil, cotton, pineapples, sugar; *major imports*—cotton fabrics, automobiles, tractors.
Places of Interest: Abidjan plateau; Ebrié lagoon; Banco National Park; Grand Bassam; Dabou; Bingerville; Bouaké; beach resorts.

IVORY COAST TODAY

A little larger than New Mexico, the Ivory Coast is a prosperous West African country. Ivorians enjoy a standard of living much higher than those of their neighbors.

Benefiting from a stable government since becoming independent in 1960, Ivory Coast has maintained a steady pace of economic growth. It has used foreign aid and loans to diversify its agriculture so that coffee, cocoa, and wood each provide a major share of export income.

The country's valuable resources include petroleum, iron ore, and timber.

From the coast the land slopes gradually to a height of about 1,400 feet in the north. The narrow 340-mile coastline—flat and sandy in the east—becomes more indented and rocky in the west. Beyond the coast is a vast forest region occupying nearly one-third of the country. In the northwest mountain ranges reach 5,000 feet.

The coastal region has a tropical climate with year-round temperatures of 73° to 80° F. Annual rainfall of 80 to 120 inches falls mostly from mid-May to mid-July.

Liberia and Guinea lie to the west, Mali and Upper Volta to the north, and Ghana to the east.

EARLY HISTORY

Before its organization as a French colony, the area that is now the Ivory Coast had no political or cultural unity. Several traditional kingdoms existed in parts of the country, while in others political organization rarely exceeded the village level.

French explorers reached the region in 1483, beginning the lucrative ivory trade from which the area later derived its name.

French missionaries, landing at Assinie in 1687, were the first white settlers. The settlement was soon abandoned, however, and the Ivory Coast remained relatively free of European influence until the 1800s, thus avoiding being drawn into the slave trade.

French interest was reasserted in 1842 with the establishment of a protectorate over the coastal area. Thereafter, mostly as a result of private initiative, French influence was carried to the interior.

In 1893 the territory was declared a colony. Treaties with local chieftains strengthened France's hold, but major military action was necessary to establish effective control.

Complete French control of the Ivory Coast was finally achieved in 1917.

The French began to develop the country in the 1920s. Yet the colonial administration, based on government by decree, was little changed until the creation of the French Union in 1946. At that time some political rights were extended to native Africans.

Over the next 10 years the Parti Démocratique de Côte d'Ivoire (PDCI), under the leadership of Félix Houphouët-Boigny, emerged as the dominant political force. Most of its opposition had been eliminated by 1956, the year internal autonomy was granted.

INDEPENDENCE

The Ivory Coast became an autonomous state within the French Community in 1958. Two years later, on Aug. 7, 1960, it proclaimed its independence as a republic.

Houphouët-Boigny became president after winning 98% of the votes in an election in November 1960. He was reelected in 1965, 1970, 1975, and 1980.

Since independence the economic development of the nation has proceeded rapidly, spurred in large part by the unusually liberal terms offered to foreign investors. The government has maintained strong ties with France, the United States, and West Germany.

In 1972 Ivory Coast was among seven French-speaking states that set up a West African Economic Community (CEAO) to promote trade among its members.

France's President Giscard d'Estaing visited in 1978, praising the country for having "proved it is possible to escape from the curse of underdevelopment in the framework of a free economy."

Production of petroleum began in 1980 from fields discovered in 1978–80. By 1983 Ivory Coast became an oil-exporting nation.

In a step toward democracy, the nation held its first national election with a choice of candidates in November 1980.

The government announced in 1983 that planning was under way to move the nation's capital to the inland city Yamoussoukro, the birthplace of President Houphouët-Boigny.

Drought and falling cocoa and coffee prices hurt the nation's economy in 1982–83.

JAMAICA

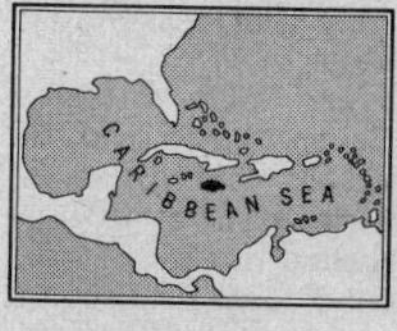

Official Name: Jamaica.
Area: 4,244 square miles (10,991 sq. km.).
Populaton: 2,336,560.
Capital: Kingston, 111,879.
Government: Parliamentary democracy.
Prime Minister: Edward P. G. Seaga (since 1980).
Chief of State: Governor-general Florizel Glasspole (appointed in 1973).
Parliament: *Senate,* 21 members; *House of Representatives,* 60 members.
U.S. Ambassador to Jamaica: William A. Hewitt.
Jamaican Ambassador to U.S.: Keith Johnson.
Flag: Gold cross with green field in top and bottom quarters; black to left and right.
Official Language: English.
Main Ethnic Groups: Black (76%), mulatto (15%).
Leading Religions: Anglicanism (20%), Baptist (19%), Church of God (12%), Roman Catholicism (7%).
Leading Industries: Agriculture (sugarcane, bananas, cattle, hogs, poultry, cocoa, coconuts, fruits, vegetables); mining (bauxite, gypsum); tourism; manufacturing and processing (alumina, rum, molasses, cement, chemicals, petroleum products, consumer products); fishing.
Foreign Trade: *Major exports*—alumina, bauxite, sugar, bananas; *major imports*—crude petroleum, automobiles.
Places of Interest: Kingston; Port Royal; Montego Bay; Ocho Rios resort; Negril Beach; Port Antonio; Royal Botanical Gardens at Hope.

JAMAICA TODAY

About the size of Connecticut, Jamaica is the world's second-largest producer of bauxite (aluminum ore).

The mining of bauxite, the processing of alumina, sugar, and tourism support the economy of the British Commonwealth nation.

Sugar and other agricultural products for many years provided the bulk of the island's income, but today farm products account for less than a fifth of Jamaica's exports. The decreasing importance of agriculture brought many families to the cities, causing serious unemployment.

The island of Jamaica lies in the Caribbean, about 90 miles south of Cuba. A limestone-based plateau, its average elevation is about 1,500 feet. Alluvial coastal deposits surround a mountainous interior dominated in the east by the Blue Mountains, which rise to 7,402 feet.

EARLY HISTORY

Jamaica was discovered by Columbus in 1494. It was settled 15 years later by Spaniards, who introduced the cultivation of sugarcane. The native Arawaks, unaccustomed to hard labor, soon died out. Then the Spaniards imported Africans to work the plantations.

At war with Spain, England captured Jamaica in 1655. The Spaniards left after freeing their

QUICK QUIZ: What U.S. state has the second-largest population? See page 874.

JAMAICA *(continued)*

slaves, who took to the hills and harassed the settlers. The former slaves, called Maroons, were finally granted land and freedom in 1739.

The island became a base for pirates, who grew rich plundering Spanish galleons. Port Royal, the capital, acquired a reputation for wickedness.

The English imported African slaves to raise sugarcane. Slavery was abolished in 1838.

Jamaica became a crown colony in 1866. It was granted full internal autonomy in 1953.

In 1958 Jamaica joined with several other British Caribbean possessions in a West Indian Federation. Three years later Jamaica withdrew.

INDEPENDENCE

On Aug. 6, 1962, Jamaica was granted full independence, with Sir Alexander Bustamante, a labor leader, as the first prime minister. Hugh Shearer became prime minister in 1967.

The ruling Jamaica Labour Party lost in general elections on Feb. 29, 1972, to the People's National Party. The PNP leader, Michael Manley, became the prime minister. Manley, a socialist, led the government in acquiring majority control of the island's sugar industry in 1974 and its bauxite mines in 1975.

Manley, an admirer of Cuba's Fidel Castro, said he hoped to preside over "the most peaceful and constitutional revolution in history."

The government began a land-reform program that from 1973 to 1975 allocated land to 11,000 small farmers and farm cooperatives in an effort to increase food production.

Thousands of unemployed persons were hired by the government at $26 a week to clean streets and improve the island's appearance in what was called the Crash Work Program. A national minimum wage of $20 for a 40-hour week was adopted in 1975.

Despite claims by the opposition that Prime Minister Manley would soon turn Jamaica into "another Cuba," his PLP party won a landslide victory in an election on Dec. 15, 1976, taking 48 of the 60 seats in the house of representatives.

The island's economy declined year after year during the late 1970s with 1 worker in 3 unemployed by the 1980s while prices rose at an annual rate of more than 30%.

The U.S. and other Western nations reduced economic aid as Manley's government leaned closer to communism.

In a bitter 9-month election campaign in 1980 some 450 persons were killed.

The pro-Western Jamaica Labor Party (JLP) won a surprise landslide victory on Oct. 30, 1980, capturing 51 of the 60 seats in parliament's lower house. Its leader, Edward P. G. Seaga, 50, was sworn in as prime minister on Nov. 1.

As one of his first acts as prime minister, Seaga expelled Cuba's ambassador. He then broke diplomatic relations on Oct. 29, 1981.

Seaga promised to restore Jamaica's economy in the 1980s by revitalizing the tourist industry while turning from socialism to free enterprise. For the first time in eight years, the gross national product rose in 1981 and the unemployment rate declined. Inprovement continued in 1982–83.

For results of parliamentary elections on Dec. 15, 1984, see page 30.

JAPAN

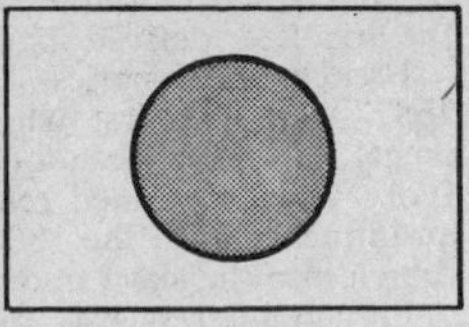

Official Name: Japan.
Area: 145,809 square miles (377,644 sq. km.).
Population: 119,565,000.
Chief Cities: Tokyo, capital, 8,448,382; Yokohama, 2,763,270; Osaka, 2,682,221; Nagoya, 2,089,332; Kyoto, 1,467,700; Kobe, 1,372,086; Sapporo, 1,371,108; Kitakyushu, 1,068,415; Fukuoka, 1,070,951; Kawasaki, 1,043,674.
Largest Metropolitan Area: Tokyo, 11,687,222.
Government: Constitutional monarchy.
Prime Minister: Yasuhiro Nakasone (since 1982).
Emperor: Hirohito (since 1926).
Diet: *House of Councillors,* 252 members; *House of Representatives,* 511 members.
U.S. Ambassador to Japan: Michael J. Mansfield.
Japanese Ambassador to U.S.: Yoshio Okawara.
Flag: Red sun on white field.
Official Language: Japanese.
Principal Ethnic Group: Japanese.
Main Religions: Shintoism and Buddhism.
Leading Industries: Manufacturing (shipbuilding, textiles, aluminum, electricity, electrical and electronic equipment, steel, cement, paper, consumer goods); shipping; agriculture (rice, barley, tea, poultry, wheat, soybeans, sweet potatoes, sugar beets, vegetables, fruits); fishing; forestry; mining (coal, manganese, zinc, copper, lead, sulfur); tourism.
Foreign Trade: *Major exports*—ships and boats, electrical and electronic products, steel, synthetic fabrics, automobiles; *major imports*—crude petroleum, wood, iron ore, cotton.
Places of Interest: Mt. Fuji; Fuji-Hakone-Izu National Park; Nikko National Park and resort; Lake Chuzenji; Island of Hokkaido; Kyoto; Osaka; Kobe; Nagoya; Hiroshima; Nagasaki; Tanegashima Island space center. *In Tokyo:* Tokyo Tower atop Kasumigaseki Building; Imperial Palace; Hibiya and Meiji parks; Shiba Zojo-ji Temple; Great Buddha at Kamakura.

JAPAN TODAY

Although smaller than Montana, Japan is the third most important industrial nation in the world after the United States and the Soviet Union. It is the major competitor of the United States in world trade. Because Japan lacks the three most important minerals needed for industrialization—iron, petroleum, and coking coal, it must import raw materials from other countries.

Japan also lacks sufficient hydroelectric potential to power its industries and light its cities, so it has become a leading developer of atomic electric generating plants. It plans to decrease dependence on foreign oil imports to 50% of energy needs by the 1990s.

Japan is so mountainous that only 19% of its

AREA OF JAPAN'S MAIN ISLANDS

	SQ. MI.	SQ. KM.	LARGEST CITY
Honshu	87,805	227,414	Tokyo
Hokkaido	30,144	78,073	Sapporo
Kyushu......	14,114	36,555	Kitakyushu
Shikoku	7,049	18,257	Matsuyama

land is suitable for farming. By use of up-to-date scientific methods Japanese farmers attain the world's highest crop yields per acre, but even so the country must import about 35% of its food.

About three-fourths of the Japanese people live in and around the cities. Consequently Japan has many problems of urban pollution and urban transit. Most Japanese are well educated. Their standard of living is at about the same level as that of Americans.

Stretching in a 1,500-mile arc from north to south are four main islands: Hokkaido, Honshu, Shikoku, and Kyushu; and nearly 3,000 smaller islands, mostly tiny islets. Japan has 192 volcanoes, 40 of them still active. Dormant Mt. Fuji (12,388 feet) is the tallest.

JAPAN'S PRIME MINISTERS SINCE 1945

1945–46	Kijuro Shidehara	Nonpartisan
1946–47	Shigeru Yoshida	Coalition
1947–48	Tetsu Katayama	Socialist
1948	Hitoshi Ashida	Democratic
1948–54	Shigeru Yoshida	Democratic-Liberal
1954–56	Ichiro Hatoyama	Democratic
1956–57	Tanzan Ishibashi	Liberal Democratic
1957–60	Nobusuke Kishi	Liberal Democratic
1960–64	Hayato Ikeda	Liberal Democratic
1964–72	Eisaku Sato	Liberal Democratic
1972–74	Kakuei Tanaka	Liberal Democratic
1974–76	Takeo Miki	Liberal Democratic
1976–78	Takeo Fukuda	Liberal Democratic
1978–80	Masayoshi Ohira	Liberal Democratic
1980–82	Zenko Suzuki	Liberal Democratic
1982–	Yasuhiro Nakasone	Liberal Democratic

EARLY HISTORY

Japanese myths say Jimmu Tenno, descendant of the sun goddess and ancestor of the present emperor, founded the empire about 660 B.C.

Anthropologists believe Chinese colonists about 200 B.C. brought China's ideographic script as well as its philosophy, literature, arts, and sciences to Japan. Buddhism was officially introduced in the 500s A.D.

Under the empress Suiko (593–628) a constitution and an official calendar were adopted.

In the 1100s power fell into the hands of the Minamoto, whose leader, Yoritomo, set up a military government in 1192 at Kamakura. For 700 years military governors, called *shoguns,* ruled Japan in the emperor's name.

China's Mongol ruler Kublai Khan twice launched invasions of Japan in 1274 and 1281, but each time the Mongols were driven off.

Portuguese navigators, arriving in 1542, were the first Europeans seen in Japan. They brought with them the first firearms. In 1549 St. Francis Xavier introduced Christianity.

By 1601 Ieyasu Tokugawa, a warrior, had unified Japan. He was appointed shogun in 1603 and established the Tokugawa shogunate that ruled until 1868. Ieyasu's center of government was Edo, the present Tokyo. After Ieyasu's death in 1616 a policy of national isolation was adopted. Christians were executed. Society became ossified under the ruling lords into four classes: *samurai* (warriors), merchants, artisans, and peasants. For the next two centuries Japan remained isolated from the world, permitting only the Dutch to conduct foreign trade.

JAPAN'S GROWTH AS A MILITARY POWER

U.S. Commodore Matthew C. Perry forced Japan to open its ports to trade with a treaty concluded on March 3, 1854. The first Japanese ambassador arrived in Washington in 1860.

Ruling power was restored to the emperor in 1868, and the capital was moved from Kyoto to Tokyo. This development was known as the Meiji Restoration. Feudalism was abolished. In 1889 the emperor granted a new constitution, establishing a bicameral parliament.

Japan took Formosa (now Taiwan) and the Pescadores from China in the Sino-Japanese War of 1894–95. After forming an alliance with Britain in 1902, Japan defeated Russia in the Russo-Japanese War of 1904–05. It gained the Liaotung peninsula in Manchuria and half of Sakhalin Island. Korea was annexed in 1910.

As a reward for supporting the Allies in World War I, Japan received a mandate over the northern Pacific islands formerly held by Germany. At the Washington Naval Conference of 1922, Japan was recognized as the third-leading naval power.

Universal manhood suffrage was introduced in 1925. Hirohito became emperor in 1926.

Japan's military leaders invaded and occupied China's province of Manchuria in 1931, and they ended Japan's parliamentary government in 1932.

Beginning in 1937 Japan waged an undeclared war with China. Japan signed a military alliance in 1939 with Nazi Germany and Fascist Italy. The defeat of France by Germany in 1940 enabled Japan to gain a foothold in Indochina.

JAPAN'S DEFEAT IN WORLD WAR II

In an attempt to halt Japanese aggression in Asia, the U.S. began to reduce its shipments of oil and steel to Japan. On Dec. 7, 1941, Japan launched a surprise attack on Pearl Harbor, Hawaii, nearly wiping out the entire U.S. fleet. The U.S. immediately declared war.

After 1944 Japan's losses grew swiftly and steadily, culminating in the atomic bombing of Hiroshima and Nagasaki by the U.S. on Aug. 6 and 9, 1945.

Japan capitulated on Aug. 14, 1945, and the formal surrender was signed on September 2. The country was demilitarized and occupied by U.S. forces. A new constitution, adopted in 1946, established a parliamentary government.

A Japanese peace treaty was signed in San Francisco on Sept. 8, 1951, by Japan and 48 other nations, including the U.S. Japan signed a bilateral security treaty with the U.S. the same day.

JAPAN'S RECOVERY AS A WORLD POWER

Japan regained full independence on April 28, 1952, when the peace treaty became effective.

The United States returned the Bonin Islands and Iwo Jima to Japan in 1968 and the Ryukyu Islands in May 1972, while retaining military installations on Okinawa.

Ending an era of conflict that had begun in 1937, Japan and China reestablished diplomatic relations in 1972.

QUICK QUIZ: How many members comprise the Federal Trade Commission? See page 975.

JAPAN *(continued)*

In a national election for the house of representatives on Dec. 5, 1976, the ruling Liberal Democratic Party lost its majority, winning only 249 of the 511 seats. However, 9 independent members joined the party to keep it in power.

The U.S. and Japan reached agreement in September 1977 enabling Japan to open the Tokai Mura atomic fuel reprocessing plant north of Tokyo to produce fuel for its increasing number of atomic power stations.

A dispute within the ruling party over economic policies resulted in Masayoshi Ohira, 68, replacing Takeo Fukuda as prime minister on Dec. 7, 1978.

Prime Minister Ohira traveled to Washington, D.C., in May 1979 for meetings with President Carter to discuss the growing trade gap between the two nations.

President Carter returned Ohira's visit in June 1979 when he attended a two-day economic conference in Tokyo that included the leaders of Britain, Canada, France, Italy, and West Germany.

In a parliamentary election on Oct. 7, 1979, the governing Liberal Democratic Party lost ground after Prime Minister Ohira called for higher taxes during the campaign. The party won 249 seats, 1 less than in 1976. It retained its governing majority in the lower house by a slim 2 votes.

Japan's economy slowed in 1979–80, registering a trade deficit of more than $9 billion in 1979, largely because of rising prices of oil imports.

On May 16, 1980, Ohira's government was defeated by a no-confidence vote, 243–187, the first such loss by a Japanese prime minister in 27 years. After scheduling national elections, the 70-year-old Ohira died of a heart attack on June 12, 1980, at the height of the political campaign.

The governing Liberal Democratic Party in the election on June 22, 1980, strengthened its leadership with clear majorities in both the lower and upper houses of parliament.

Zenko Suzuki, a former cabinet minister, became prime minister on July 17, 1980. He said Japan should build its armed forces without relying entirely on the U.S.-Japanese military alliance.

Yasuhiro Nakasone, 64, became prime minister on Nov. 26, 1982, after winning a mail-in vote by more than a million members of the Liberal Democratic Party. He said he would endeavor to improve trade relations with the U.S.

Prime Minister Nakosone won endorsement by voters in an election on June 26, 1983, as his Liberal Democratic Party increased its majority in the upper house of parliament.

In a sensational trial in 1983 Kakuei Tanaka, widely regarded as Japan's behind-the-scenes political boss, was convicted and sentenced to four years in prison for taking $2.1 million in bribes to arrange airline purchases of Lockheed aircraft while he was prime minister in 1972–74.

Japan achieved an estimated foreign trade surplus of $30 billion in 1983 largely from sales to the U.S. In an effort to ease strained economic relations with the U.S., the government announced in October 1983 that it would begin reducing tariffs on 1,268 categories of products in 1984, three years earlier than previously planned.

President Reagan visited Japan on Nov. 9-12, 1983.

For results of parliamentary election on Dec. 18, 1984, see page 30.

JORDAN

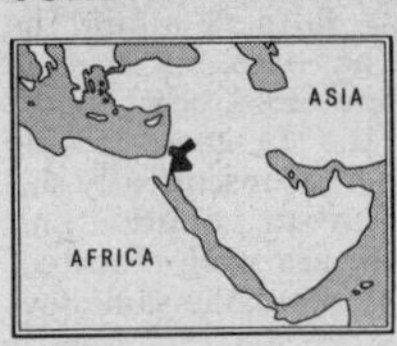

Official Name: Hashemite Kingdom of Jordan.
Area: 37,738 square miles (97,740 sq. km.).
Population: 2,558,420.
Chief Cities: Amman, capital, 711,850; Zarka, 263,400; Irbid, 136,770.
Government: Absolute monarchy.
King: Hussein (reigned since 1952).
Prime Minister: Mudar Badran (since 1980).
Parliament: *Senate,* 30 members; *House of Representatives,* 60 members.
U.S. Ambassador to Jordan: Richard N. Viets.
Jordanian Ambassador to U.S.: Ibrahim Izziddin.
Flag: Black, white, and green stripes, with seven-pointed white star in red triangle on left.
Languages: Arabic (official), Circassian.
Main Ethnic Group: Arab (95%).
Religions: Islam (95%), Christianity (5%).
Leading Industries: Agriculture (wheat, barley, figs, olives, grapes, tobacco, sheep, goats, poultry, fruits, vegetables); mining (phosphate); manufacturing (cement, textiles, chemicals, petroleum refining, food processing); tourism.
Foreign Trade: *Major exports*—phosphates, tomatoes; *major imports*—motor vehicles, crude petroleum, sugar, rice, textiles, machinery, weapons, consumer goods.
Places of Interest: Citadel Hill and Roman theater in Amman; Petra, city of red rock; Greco-Roman ruins at Jerash; Crusader architecture at Kerak; Aqaba seaport; Azraq National Park; Wadi Rum Valley; forts and palaces.

JORDAN TODAY

A little larger than Indiana, Jordan lacks the petroleum resources that have vitalized the economies of other formerly poor Arab nations.

However, Jordan has received over $2 billion in economic aid from the U.S. since World War II. The Arab nation has used this aid wisely in developing its agriculture and the mining of its phosphate deposits. Irrigation projects have opened new farmland.

About half of the people are Arab refugees made homeless by the Arab-Israeli wars.

EARLY HISTORY

Jordan includes the biblical lands of Gilead, Ammon, Bashan, Edom, and Moab. The later Nabataean kingdom was annexed to the Roman Empire in A.D. 106. Arabs conquered the land in the 600s. After the Crusades it fell to the Mamelukes of Egypt, then in the 1500s to the Ottoman Turks. It remained part of their empire until British armies took the area in 1917–18.

Called Transjordan, the region became a British mandate in 1920. The British placed Abdullah ibn Hussein on the throne as emir in 1921.

INDEPENDENCE

Britain ended its mandate and on May 25, 1946, recognized Abdullah as king of independent Transjordan (renamed Jordan in 1950).

In 1948 Jordan joined the Arab states in attacking the newly independent state of Israel. Jordan's British-led troops captured Jerusalem on May 15, 1948. After concluding an armistice with Israel in 1949, Abdullah annexed the Palestine area west of the Jordan River.

Abdullah was assassinated in 1951 and was succeeded by his son Talal, who was in turn deposed by parliament in 1952 because of mental illness. Talal's son Hussein became king in 1952 and was formally crowned on May 2, 1953.

Because Britain sided with Israel in the second Arab-Israeli war, in 1956, Jordan ordered Britain to remove its troops that had remained stationed in the country since 1946.

In the third Arab-Israeli war, in 1967, Israel defeated Jordan, capturing Arab Jerusalem and all of Jordan's territory west of the Jordan River.

After that war Palestine Arab guerrillas in Jordan continued attacks on Israel until King Hussein agreed to a new Arab-Israeli cease-fire on Aug. 7, 1970. This prompted the guerrillas to focus attention on their cause with a series of dramatic skyjackings. The Jordanian army persuaded Hussein to attack the Palestinians. A brief civil war erupted.

Although Jordan did not directly attack Israel in the fourth Arab-Israeli war, in October 1973, it sent troops to assist Syria.

In 1975 King Hussein, bowing to a decision by other Arab nations, gave up his claims to the west bank of the Jordan to the Palestine Liberation Organization (PLO), which hopes to establish an Arab Palestine state. Hussein's action brought him improved status with other Arab leaders and an influx of financial aid from oil-rich Arab nations.

King Hussein in February 1976 convened the nation's parliament that had been elected in 1967. It adopted a constitutional amendment enabling the king to postpone indefinitely any new parliamentary election.

In May 1976 the king revealed a $2 billion development plan designed to increase the nation's economic growth at a rate of 12% a year.

King Hussein denied reports published in American newspapers in February 1977 that he had received millions of dollars in payments from the CIA over the past 20 years.

Hussein met with PLO leader Yasir Arafat in March 1977 for the first time since the Jordanian army fought the Palestinians in 1970. The two discussed plans for a future Palestinian state on the west bank of the Jordan River.

The 41-year-old Hussein celebrated his silver jubilee as monarch in 1977, having ruled longer than any other contemporary Arab leader.

On June 15, 1978, Hussein married Elizabeth Halaby, 26, daughter of an American businessman. As queen she adopted the Arabic name Noor al-Hussein, meaning "Light of Hussein."

Hussein refused invitations to join peace negotiations in 1978–80 between Israel and Egypt.

In the Iraq-Iran war in 1980–83 Jordan supported Iraq. Jordan's port of Aqaba on the Red Sea became the main base for ships of the Soviet Union and other nations that brought war supplies to Iraq.

KENYA

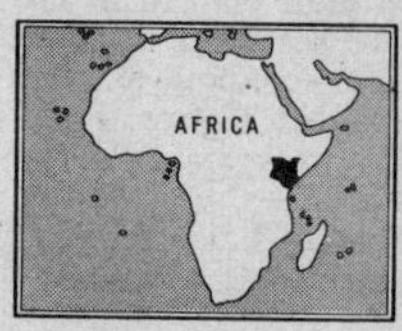

Official Name: Republic of Kenya.
Area: 224,961 square miles (582,646 sq. km.).
Population: 17,805,600.
Chief Metropolitan Areas: Nairobi, capital, 818,000; Mombasa, 391,000.
Government: One-party republic.
President: Daniel arap Moi (since 1978).
National Assembly: 170 members.
U.S. Ambassador to Kenya: Gerald Thomas.
Kenyan Ambassador to U.S.: Peter Mbogua.
Flag: Black, red, and green bands separated by white stripes; red, black, and white shield over crossed white spears in center.
Languages: English and Swahili (official), Arabic.
Main Ethnic Groups: Kikuyu (20%), Luo (15%), Baluhya (13%), Kamba (11%), Kisii (6%), Meru (5%).
Religions: Animism (38%), Protestantism (37%), Roman Catholicism (22%), Islam (3%).
Leading Industries: Agriculture (coffee, tea, cattle, sugar cane, dairy products, poultry, pyrethrum [flower used in insecticides], sisal, corn, fruits, vegetables); tourism; manufacturing (processing farm products, oil refining, consumer goods); forestry and lumbering; mining (copper).
Foreign Trade: *Major exports*—coffee, tea, sugar, sisal; *major imports*—crude petroleum, motor vehicles, agricultural machinery.
Places of Interest: Rift Valley; Treetops Hotel, west of Mt. Kenya; national museum in Nairobi; Nairobi, Tsavo, Aberdare, Lake Nakuru national parks; Masai Mara, Amboseli, and Samburu game reserves.

KENYA TODAY

About as large as Arizona and New Mexico combined, Kenya has few important natural resources. Although the country's economy depends largely on agriculture, only about 12% of the land can be farmed and about 6% used for grazing livestock. Kenya's major exports are coffee and tea.

About three-fourths of the people depend on agriculture for a living. Only about 1 Kenyan in 5 can read and write, and many children never attend school.

Because Kenya must import all the petroleum it needs for energy, the nation was hard hit by soaring oil prices of the 1970s–1980s. About one-third of its income from foreign trade goes to the purchase of petroleum, severely limiting the amount of money that can be used in development projects to broaden the base of the economy.

The single most important contribution to cash income is tourism, which brings more than 300,000 visitors each year. The nation's leading tourist attractions are the national park sanctuaries for lions, elephants, leopards, cheetahs, giraffes, zebras, gazelles, and other wild animals.

The country is noted for its topographic variety. The low-lying coast rises gently to a dry coast-

QUICK QUIZ: What nations are members of the Andean Pact? See page 426.

KENYA *(continued)*
al plain that gives way to a high plateau in the southwest (10,000 feet above sea level at some points). Most of the people and economic activity are located in the plateau area. Mt. Kenya, a perpetually snow-clad 17,058-foot peak, stands in the semidesert northern region.

The Great Rift Valley includes Lake Turkana (formerly Rudolf), the country's largest lake.

EARLY HISTORY

Throughout the Middle Ages Kenya attracted Indian Ocean trade.

In 1498 Portuguese explorers arrived and established trading posts, but they were driven out by the Arabs in 1729. From 1740 Arabs ruled the Kenyan coast from Zanzibar.

In 1887 the British East Africa Company leased the Kenyan coast from the sultan of Zanzibar. Kenya became a British protectorate in 1895. It was organized as a crown colony in 1920.

Jomo Kenyatta, as secretary of an association of the Kikuyu tribe, began campaigning in 1928 for land reform and political rights for Africans. When his campaign was ignored, Kenyatta organized a group called the Mau Mau that began a rebellion in 1952.

During the next eight years over 12,000 persons died in the fighting. The British jailed Kenyatta from 1954 to 1961.

Britain agreed in 1960 to grant self-government to the black majority. Although Kenyatta's party, the Kenyan African National Union (KANU), won an election in February 1961, its members refused to take office until Kenyatta was released from confinement in August. KANU won another election in May 1963.

INDEPENDENCE

Kenya was granted independence by Britain on Dec. 12, 1963, with Kenyatta as prime minister. Exactly one year later Kenya became a republic in the British Commonwealth of Nations with Kenyatta taking office as president.

In the spring of 1966 Ogingo Odinga, the nation's vice president, broke with Kenyatta and formed an opposition party, the Kenya People's Union (KPU).

Odinga was put under house arrest on Oct. 27, 1969, following an antigovernment demonstration by the KPU. Three days later the KPU was banned, leaving KANU the only legal political party in Kenya. On Nov. 11, 1969, Kenyatta was reelected to a second term.

The Kenyan government began a campaign to Africanize the country in March 1968. In the next six years thousands of Asian shopkeepers and businessmen were forced to leave Kenya.

The nation was hard hit by drought in 1974. Some 250,000 cattle—90% of the herds of the Masai tribes—were reported to have died.

Although Kenya is a one-party state, voters chose between rival KANU candidates in the 1974 parliamentary election. The voters defeated four of Kenyatta's cabinet ministers.

In July 1976 President Idi Amin of neighboring Uganda threatened to bomb Kenya. His threats came because Kenya had allowed Israel's planes to land for refueling after the daring July 4 raid on Uganda to rescue hostages held by Arab hijackers. Kenya called on its nationals to leave Uganda as war threatened. However, friendly relations were reestablished in August.

Because Kenyatta was in his eighties, concern rose in the 1970s as to what would happen to the nation when he died. When politicians attempted to hold public meetings on the subject they were warned by the attorney general in October 1976 that it was a crime punishable by death even to imagine the death of the president. No more meetings were held.

Tanzania closed its border with Kenya on Feb. 3, 1977, in a dispute over the shutting down of an airline that had been jointly operated by Kenya, Tanzania, and Uganda. Kenyan officials said it was an effort to prevent the people of socialist Tanzania from coming to Kenya to see the economic growth possible under free enterprise.

In an effort to preserve Kenya's wildlife, which attracts thousands of tourists each year, the government announced on May 19, 1977, a ban on the killing of elephants, rhinoceroses, leopards, zebras, and other wild animals. The move was applauded by conservationists but was deplored by Kenya's 300 or more professional hunters, who were told to convert hunting trips for tourists into photographic safaris.

Kenyatta died in his sleep on Aug. 22, 1978. He was believed to be about 89, but had no record of his birth. Hundreds of thousands of Kenyans lined the route of his funeral procession that included representatives of 82 nations.

Daniel arap Moi, 54, who had served as vice president under Kenyatta, succeeded to the presidency without opposition. He was formally inaugurated as president on Oct. 14, 1978. He was elected to 5-year terms in 1979 and 1983.

A former school headmaster, President Moi made one of his first decrees the abolition of school fees. He also ordered free milk served at schools and promised to increase the number of teachers and other school personnel by 10%.

To emphasize his belief in human rights, President Moi on Dec. 12, 1978, released all 16 prisoners who had been jailed by the Kenyatta regime for political reasons.

Kenya and the U.S. reached agreement on June 27, 1980, for American ships, planes, and troops to use Kenya's ports and bases in return for increased economic and military aid.

Kenya officially became a one-party state on June 9, 1982, when parliament unanimously approved a constitutional amendment making the ruling Kenya African National Union (KANU) the only legal party.

An attempt to overthrow the government was put down by police on Aug. 1, 1982, with 145 persons killed and several hundred wounded. The nation's 2,100-man air force was disbanded and its members jailed for taking part in the rebellion. Universities also were closed because of student support for the rebellion.

Kenya's fourth 5-year plan, for 1979–83, provided for major investments to be directed to increase the income levels of the poor by aiding small farmers and by providing greater employment opportunities in the cities. One of the major projects enabled the resettlement of farmers on unused or mismanaged land to increase the country's agricultural output.

KIRIBATI

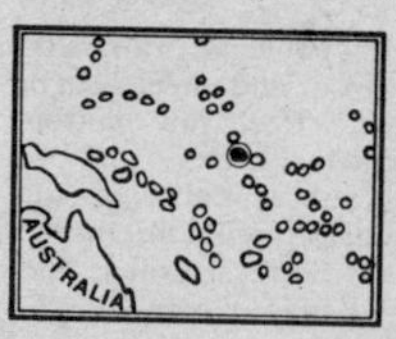

Official Name: Republic of Kiribati.
Area: 278 square miles (720 sq. km.).
Population: 60,484.
Capital: Bairiki, Tarawa, 10,616.
Government: Democratic republic.
President: Ieremia Tabai (since 1979).
National Assembly: 35 members.
U.S. Ambassador to Kiribati: Fred J. Eckert.
Kiribati Ambassador to U.S.: Atanraoi Baiteke.
Flag: Bird flying over rising gold sun in red sky; white and blue wavy stripes.
Languages: English and Gilbertese.
Main Ethnic Group: Micronesians.
Major Religion: Christianity.
Leading Industries: Agriculture (coconuts, breadfruit, pandanus, bananas, pawpaws); fishing (tuna, shrimp); handicrafts.
Foreign Trade: *Major exports*—copra from coconuts, shrimp, handicrafts, postage stamps; *major imports*—food, fuel, clothing, lumber, consumer goods.
Places of Interest: Island villages, beaches.

Formerly known as the British colony of the Gilbert Islands, Kiribati includes 33 islands scattered across about 2 million square miles of the central and south Pacific Ocean.

The islands stretch about 3,000 miles from Ocean Island (Banaba) in the west to the southern Line Islands in the east.

The islands have almost no natural resources. Even the sandy soil is of poor quality for growing crops. The national economy is largely dependent on aid from Britain.

The first Europeans to sight the islands were Spanish navigators in the 1500s and 1600s.

The first European settlers in 1837 were deserters from whaling ships. From the 1850s to the 1870s trading ships visited the islands, kidnapping islanders to work as laborers on plantations elsewhere in the South Pacific.

Christianity was brought to the islands with the arrival in 1857 of American missionaries.

In 1892 a British protectorate was declared for the Gilberts and the neighboring Ellice Islands (now Tuvalu). In 1916 Britain made the Gilbert and Ellice Islands a colony.

The islands were occupied by Japan in World War II, but they were recovered by the Allies in a fierce battle on Tarawa on Nov. 20–23, 1943, in which 4,690 Japanese troops and 1,087 U.S. Marines were killed.

Britain granted independence to Kiribati on July 12, 1979.

Ieremia (Jeremiah) Tabai, 29, was chosen in 1979 as Kiribati's first president.

In a treaty with the U.S. signed in September 1979, Kiribati received sovereignty over 14 islands in the Phoenix and Line groups, including Canton and Enderbury islands.

KOREA, NORTH

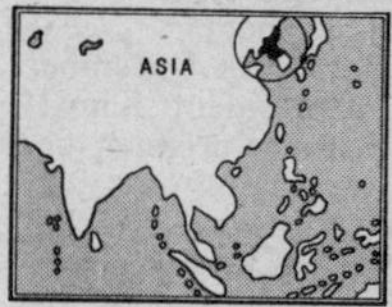

Official Name: Democratic People's Republic of Korea.
Area: 46,540 square miles (120,538, sq. km.).
Population: 20,902,300.
Chief Cities: Pyongyang, the capital, 653,100; Chongjin, 184,300; Hungnam, 143,600; Kaesong, 139,900.
Government: One-party communist state.
President: Kim Il Sung (ruler since 1948).
Prime Minister: Li Jong Ok (since 1977).
Supreme People's Assembly: 541 members.
Flag: Large red center stripe bordered by thin white stripes and wider blue stripes; white circle enclosing red 5-pointed star on center stripe near hoist.
Language: Korean.
Main Ethnic Group: Korean.
Major Religions: Confucianism, Buddhism.
Leading Industries: Manufacturing (machines, electricity, chemicals, steel, textiles, cement, petroleum refining, aluminum); agriculture (rice, corn, vegetables); mining (coal, iron ore, graphite, petroleum, lead, nickel, tungsten, zinc).
Foreign Trade: *Major exports*—food products, minerals; *major imports*—oil, wheat, machines.
Places of Interest: Diamond Mountains; Buddhist monasteries; Mt. Kwanmo; Pyongyang.

NORTH KOREA TODAY

About the size of Mississippi, North Korea is a communist police state.

With economic and technical assistance from the Soviet Union and China, the country has developed heavy industry to produce machinery. It is among the world's leading nations in mining coal, lead, and zinc.

About half the people work and live on collective farms. The most important crop is rice.

The Korean peninsula is mountainous. The highest peak is Mt. Paektu (9,003 feet).

COMMUNIST RULE

Korea's history (see Korea, South) is regionally inseparable until 1945. With the Japanese defeat at the end of World War II, the 38th parallel was established as an administrative convenience, not as a political dividing line. Americans accepted the surrender of Japanese forces in the south, and Soviet forces did the same in the north.

The Soviet Union set up the communist government of North Korea on Sept. 9, 1948. Kim Il Sung, a guerrilla in Manchuria before he fled to the Soviet Union in 1941, was made head of the government.

On June 25, 1950, the North Korean army invaded South Korea. The U.S. and 15 other United Nations members sent military forces to aid South Korea. Communist China entered the conflict in support of North Korea. A cease-fire agreement was reached in July 1953, and Korea was again divided at the 38th parallel.

On Jan. 23, 1968, the North Koreans cap-

QUICK QUIZ: In what year was the UN Charter approved? See page 420.

KOREA, NORTH *(continued)*
tured the USS *Pueblo* and imprisoned the crew for nearly a year before releasing them.

A new constitution was adopted in December 1972, establishing the office of president. Kim Il Sung, who had ruled for 24 years as premier, became president.

In 1974–75 South Koreans discovered that North Korea had made extensive new preparations for war, digging highway-wide tunnels under defenses at the 38th parallel.

North Korea established a 200-mile economic sea limit on Aug. 1, 1977, banning Japanese fishermen from an area extending all the way to Japan itself.

At the same time it forbade all foreign military craft from coming closer than 50 miles of its coast without permission.

A recession and failure to meet economic goals by its heavy industry forced North Korea to default in 1977 on its estimated $2 billion in foreign debts, causing Japan, Switzerland, Sweden and other creditors to cut off further loans.

In September 1979 the U.S. disclosed discovery of a new North Korean tunnel, the fourth found since 1974, that had been dug under the demilitarized zone to prepare for a sneak attack on South Korea.

To ensure that his 39-year-old son Kim Jong Il would succeed him as ruler, 68-year-old President Kim Il Sung in 1980 named his son to the influential post of secretary of the country's Communist Party.

The U.S. accused North Korea in August 1981 of firing a missile at an American reconnaissance plane. North Korea denied having tried to shoot down the plane.

KOREA, SOUTH

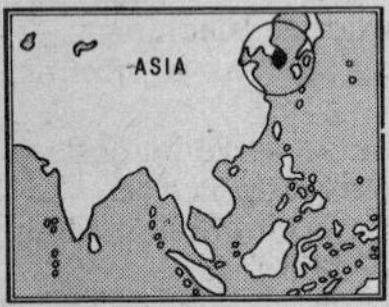

Official Name: Republic of Korea.
Area: 38,025 square miles (98,484 sq. km.).
Population: 41,578,200.
Chief Cities: Seoul, capital, 8,366,756; Pusan, 3,160,276; Taegu, 1,607,458; Inchon, 1,084,730.
Largest Metropolitan Area: Seoul, 8,366,756.
Government: Martial law.
President: Chun Doo Hwan (since 1980).
Prime Minister: Kim Sang Hyup (since 1982).
National Assembly: 276 members.
U.S. Ambassador to South Korea: Richard L. Walker.
South Korean Ambassador to U.S.: Byong Hion Lew.
Flag: White field with circular emblem divided in half by curved line (red top and blue bottom); black bar design in each corner.
Language: Korean.
Principal Ethnic Group: Korean.
Religions: Confucianism, Shamanism, Christianity, Buddhism, Chodokyo.
Leading Industries: Agriculture (rice, wheat, barley, beans, cotton, livestock, poultry); manufacturing (steel, textiles, cement, electricity, plastics, clothing, plywood, electronics, chemicals); fishing; forestry and lumbering; mining (coal, iron ore, tungsten, graphite).
Foreign Trade: *Major exports*—plywood, raw silk, cotton fabrics, electronics, iron and steel; *major imports*—transport equipment, rice, raw cotton, wheat, crude petroleum, textile machinery.
Places of Interest: Restored ancient capital, Kyongju; Cheju Island. *In Seoul:* National museum in Duksoo Palace; Changduk Palace and Secret Garden; Kyungbok Palace; Pagoda Park; Kings' Tomb.

SOUTH KOREA TODAY

About the size of Indiana, South Korea is a small Asian country that won its independence from Japan after World War II. In the 1950s the U.S. and the United Nations helped South Korea preserve its independence during the Korean War, in which communist North Korea and China attempted to overrun the country.

South Korea had one of the most rapidly expanding economies in the world in the 1960s–80s. Its gross national product grew from $2.27 billion in 1962 to an estimated $65 billion in 1981. However, most of the people are poor.

Although South Korea is a constitutional republic, the country has been ruled since it was created by dictators with little regard for human rights.

The U.S. maintains armed forces in South Korea to protect it from attack by North Korea.

The mountainous peninsula has many harbors along the west coast. Summers are hot and humid. Winters are cold and dry.

EARLY HISTORY

According to Korean legend, Tangun founded Korean civilization about 4,300 years ago. Korea's recorded history began in the 1100s B.C. when a Chinese prince, Ki-tze, founded a colony at Pyongyang. Chinese influence remained until about 100 B.C., when three warring tribes (Silla, Koguryo, and Paekche) came to power.

Silla kings with their capital at Kyongju united the country in A.D. 668. A new kingdom, Koryo, ruled the Korean peninsula in 935–1392. In the 1200s the Mongols conquered the land. In 1637 Korea fell to the Manchu rulers of China. Because of its isolation, Korea became known as the Hermit Kingdom.

In 1876 Korea was forced by Japan to open its ports to outside trade. Six years later Korea signed a commercial treaty with the U.S. In 1895 Japan won a war against the Chinese in Korea. Russia tried to acquire Korea but was defeated by Japan in 1905.

In 1910 Japan formally annexed Korea as a colony. The Koreans opposed Japanese rule. In 1919 a government-in-exile was formed in Shanghai under Syngman Rhee.

In 1945, near the end of World War II, Soviet troops entered the northern part of Korea. A month later, American forces landed in the south. The U.S. and Soviet Union agreed on a purely administrative dividing line across Korea—the 38th parallel.

INDEPENDENT SOUTH KOREA

On Aug. 15, 1948, a separate pro-Western government was established for South Korea. Syngman Rhee became president.

U.S. troops were withdrawn by June 1949.

On June 25, 1950, the North Korean army invaded South Korea. The U.S. and UN came to the support of South Korea, and 16 member nations sent troops. Communist China entered the war on the side of North Korea in 1951. A cease-fire was achieved in July 1953. Korea remained divided at the 38th parallel.

President Rhee served from 1948 to 1960, when charges of election-rigging led to his resignation and subsequent exile. New elections were held, but on May 16, 1961, the government was ousted by a military junta headed by Gen. Park Chung Hee. In 1963 he was elected president.

In 1972 President Park imposed martial law on South Korea and changed the constitution to permit his reelection. In 1975 he made it a crime for anyone to criticize the constitution or the government to foreigners.

President Park in February 1977 announced that a new capital would be built about 60 miles south of Seoul.

U.S. President Jimmy Carter announced plans in 1977 for a gradual withdrawal of American troops from South Korea.

President Park was reelected to a fourth term on July 6, 1978, by a special 2,583-member electoral assembly.

In a parliamentary election on Dec. 12, 1978, the opposition New Democratic Party (NDP) won 34% of the vote to 32% by President Park's Democratic Republican Party (DRP). However, 15 independent members joined with the governing party to give it a majority of 86 to the NDP's 68 among the elected members. Park's control of parliament was augmented by the appointment of 77 additional members.

For the first time in almost six years, South Korean and North Korean officials met in 1979 at Panmunjom in a series of sessions to discuss possible reunification of Korea.

U.S. President Carter visited South Korea from June 29 to July 1, 1979. After returning to the United States, he announced on July 20 that the withdrawal of the remaining 32,000 U.S. combat troops in South Korea would be postponed.

President Park was assassinated on Oct. 26, 1979, by Kim Jae Kyu, head of the Korean central intelligence agency, who was arrested and executed. Martial law was imposed throughout the nation with army chief of staff Gen. Chung Seung Hwa in charge. Prime Minister Choi Kyu Han became president.

Younger military officers overthrew Gen. Chung on Dec. 12, 1979. Maj. Gen. Chun Doo Hwan emerged as the new military strong man.

In the following months tens of thousands of opponents to the regime were imprisoned without trial. Former presidential candidate Kim Dae Jung, the most prominent spokesman for democracy, was arrested, tried by a military court, and was sentenced to death. However, he later was freed and allowed to visit the U.S. for medical treatment.

Chun made himself president in September 1980. Under a new constitution, he then had himself sworn in to a seven-year term on March 3, 1981. In carefully controlled parliamentary elections on March 25, 1981, President Chun's party easily won a substantial majority.

The Soviet Union on Sept. 1, 1983, shot down a South Korean airliner that had strayed over its territory, killing all 269 aboard. See page 25.

A bomb explosion in Rangoon, Burma, on Oct. 9, 1983, killed 17 South Korean officials, including four cabinet ministers. North Korean terrorists were blamed for the slayings.

President Reagan visited South Korea on Nov. 12–14, 1983, reaffirming U.S. friendship.

KUWAIT

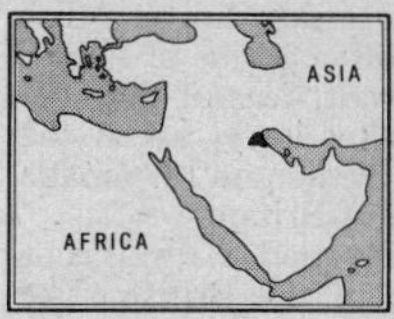

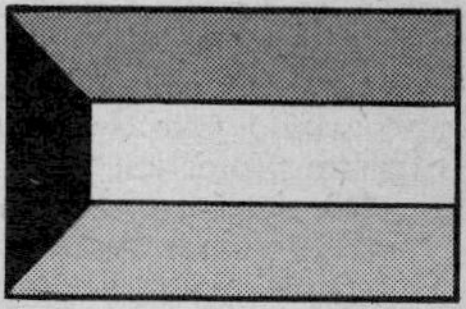

Official Name: State of Kuwait.
Area: 6,880 square miles (17,818 sq. km.).
Population: 1,700,730.
Chief Cities: Kuwait, capital, 700,000; Hawalli, 106,542; Salmiyyah, 38,791.
Government: Monarchy (emirate).
Emir: Sheik Jabir al-Ahmad al-Sabah (since 1977).
Prime Minister and Crown Prince: Sheik Saad al-Abdullah Al-Sabah (since 1977).
National Assembly: 66 members (50 elected).
U.S. Ambassador to Kuwait: Francois M. Dickman.
Kuwaiti Ambassador to U.S.: Saud Nasir al-Sabah.
Flag: Green, white, and red stripes, with black trapezoid at flagstaff.
Languages: Arabic (official), Persian, English.
Main Ethnic Group: Arab (85%).
Religion: Islam (99%).
Leading Industries: Mining (petroleum, natural gas); construction; manufacturing and processing (electricity, desalinization of seawater, oil refining, ammonia, fertilizer, cement, consumer products); shipping; fishing; agriculture (sheep, goats, wheat, dates, vegetables).
Foreign Trade: *Major export*—petroleum; *major imports*—food, oil refinery equipment, automobiles, trucks, machinery, consumer goods.
Places of Interest: Oil wells; modern city of Kuwait; royal residences; seaport of Mina al-Ahmad.

KUWAIT TODAY

About the size of New Jersey, Kuwait is one of the most prosperous countries in the world. The Middle East's third-largest producer of oil, Kuwait has about one-quarter of the world's oil reserves. Its people pay no taxes.

Kuwait has given and loaned billions of dollars to poorer Arab states, has invested billions in the United States and other industrial countries, and has purchased planes and other equipment for Arab states opposing Israel.

The government also has used its oil wealth to give free medical services, education, a 124-acre amusement park, and other benefits to everyone in Kuwait. Local telephone service is also free, and almost every family owns at least one car and one TV set.

The government holds down food costs by

QUICK QUIZ: What U.S. state had the lowest crime rate in 1982? See page 170.

KUWAIT *(continued)*
subsidizing food imports.

Abundant natural gas provides energy for Kuwait's expanding industries. The nation's capital is a thriving modern city on Kuwait Bay.

EARLY HISTORY

Kuwait was founded about 1740 by Arab nomads who migrated from northern Arabia to the Persian Gulf coast. Sabah Abu Abdullah founded an emirate there in 1756. Under his successors, Kuwait's population grew to several thousand.

The British came to Kuwait's aid when it was threatened in the first half of the 1800s by the Wahabi of Arabia, a puritanical Muslim sect that waged holy war against all other forms of Islam.

In 1897 the emir of Kuwait, fearful that the Turks would take over his territory, asked the British for protection. An agreement in 1899 made Kuwait a quasi-protectorate of Britain.

In 1919 Saudi Arabia invaded Kuwait but was repelled with the help of the British. The Saudis placed a land blockade on Kuwait that lasted 20 years, although in 1922 the two governments established the Neutral Zone in which they shared sovereignty until 1966, when the zone was partitioned between them.

With the discovery of oil in Kuwait in 1938, and its development after 1945, Iraq decided in 1952 to renew an ancient claim to Kuwait. This was promptly rejected by the British.

INDEPENDENCE

By mutual consent the British protectorate was revoked on June 19, 1961, and Kuwait became a fully independent nation.

Several hundred thousand Arab refugees from the Arab-Israeli wars (1948–73) were allowed to settle in Kuwait.

Kuwait and Saudi Arabia signed an agreement on Dec. 18, 1969, dividing a previous 2,000-square-mile Neutral Zone between them and establishing a new boundary.

Iraqi troops invaded Kuwait on March 20, 1973, near the Persian Gulf, claiming the boundary between the countries had never been settled. After Saudi Arabia sent more than 15,000 troops to assist Kuwait, Iraq withdrew.

In 1975 the government bought complete control of the oil and gas industry from the U.S. and other foreign owners. Its gross national product doubled from 1974 to 1975, reaching more than $10.6 billion a year.

Sheik Sabah, who had ruled since 1965, dissolved the elected parliament and ended freedom of the press on Aug. 29, 1976, in a dispute with Palestinian radicals.

Sheik Jabir al-Ahmad al-Sabah became emir on Dec. 31, 1977, after Sheik Sabah died.

A new conservative national assembly was elected on Feb. 23, 1981. About 90% of the 42,000 registered voters went to the polls. Only male Kuwaitis over 21 were eligible to register, about 90,000 altogether.

Parliament rejected a proposal in January 1982 that would have given women the right to vote. But later in the month, as hundreds of women demonstrated in the streets, the legislators legalized abortion, making Kuwait the first Persian Gulf Arab state to do so.

LAOS

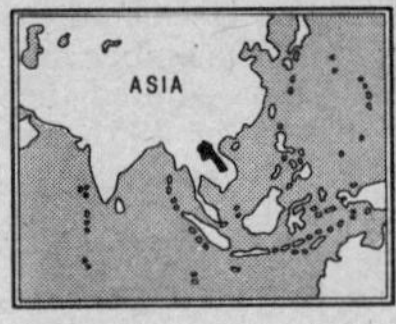

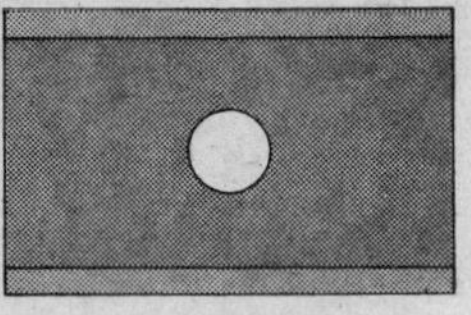

Official Name: Lao People's Democratic Republic.
Area: 91,429 square miles (236,800 sq. km.).
Population: 3,668,920.
Chief Cities: Vientiane, capital, 132,253; Luang Prabang, 42,000.
Government: Communist one-party state.
President: Prince Souphanouvong (since 1975).
Prime Minister: Kaysone Phomvihan (since 1975).
Flag: Narrow red stripes top and bottom; wide blue stripe in middle with large white circle.
Languages: Lao (official), French.
Main Ethnic Group: Lao.
Religions: Buddhism and animism.
Leading Industries: Agriculture (rice, coffee, tea, cattle, fruits, vegetables, corn, cotton, tobacco); mining (tin, iron ore); fishing; manufacturing (textiles, handicrafts); forestry and lumbering.
Foreign Trade: *Major exports*—tin, teak, coffee; *major imports*—rice and other foods, petroleum, transport equipment, consumer goods.
Places of Interest: Annamite Cordillera; former royal palace, wats (temples) and pagodas. *In Vientiane:* Shrine of That Luang; Luang Prabang.

LAOS TODAY

Somewhat smaller than Oregon, Laos is a mountainous Southeast Asian country ruled by communists. The government relies heavily on foreign aid from the Soviet Union and Vietnam.

One of the poorest and most underdeveloped nations of the world, Laos must import food and other goods its people need to survive.

Most Laotians are poverty-stricken rice farmers. Few can read or write.

Over 80% of the country is rugged jungle terrain. The flatlands are mostly in the valleys of the Mekong River and its tributaries.

EARLY HISTORY

First settled in the 1100s by refugee Thai tribes from China, Laotian territory was the seat of the Buddhist kingdom of Lan Xang, founded in 1353 by King Fa Ngum. In 1707 the kingdom split into two regions: Luang Prabang in the north and Vientiane in the south.

France made Laos a protectorate in 1893.

Japanese forces invaded Laos in 1941. Just before Japan's World War II surrender in September 1945, King Sisavang Vong of Luang Prabang proclaimed himself king of all Laos. On Oct. 12, 1945, nationalists of the Free Laos movement declared the country independent. French troops reoccupied Laos in May 1946.

Laos became an associated state in the French Union on July 19, 1949. France granted Laos full independence on Oct. 22, 1953.

A communist movement, the Pathet Lao, was created by Prince Souphanouvong in 1950. Three years later Vietnamese communists invaded Laos to assist the Pathet Lao. The conference at Geneva in 1954 that ended the Indochina War brought a cease-fire to Laos.

In 1957 Laos' premier, Prince Souvanna Phouma, and his half-brother, Prince Souphanouvong, formed a coalition government. Sri Savang Vatthanna became king on Nov. 4, 1959, after the death of his father, King Sisavang Vong.

Civil war with the communist Pathet Lao again broke out in 1960. The U.S. supported government troops.

On Feb. 8, 1971, South Vietnam forces, with U.S. air support, drove into Laos to cut the Ho Chi Minh Trail, a road used by North Vietnam.

The Laotian government signed a cease-fire agreement with the Pathet Lao, ending 10 years of war at noon on Feb. 22, 1973.

COMMUNIST TAKE-OVER OF LAOS

After North Vietnam conquered South Vietnam, the Pathet Lao on Dec. 3, 1975, forced King Sri Savang Vatthanna to abdicate. Prince Souphanouvong became the first president of Laos. The new premier was Kaysone Phomvihan, secretary-general of the Laotian Communist Party.

The government arrested hundreds of former political leaders in April 1976 in what was called a "cultural revolution."

In March 1977 the government reported that it had arrested 69-year-old former King Sri Savang Vatthanna, his wife, and children, sending them to a "reeducation center" to be taught to grow vegetables and learn Marxist-Leninist principles.

A severe drought in 1977 caused an estimated 60% loss in the rice crop. The government appealed to other countries to send rice to save the Laotian people from starvation.

France broke diplomatic relations with Laos on Aug. 22, 1978, after the Laotian government expelled French diplomats on charges they were aiding guerrillas in attacks on the communists.

An American congressional delegation that visited Laos in August 1978 received the bodies of four U.S. pilots, the first information on 230 servicemen missing in action in Laos.

As an ally of Vietnam and the Soviet Union, Laos sent troops to aid Vietnam in its 1979 conquest of Cambodia.

Thousands of Lao people fled from the country to neighboring Thailand in 1979–83, adding to the estimated 200,000 Laotian refugees who had left the country in 1975–78 to escape the repression of the communist regime.

LEBANON

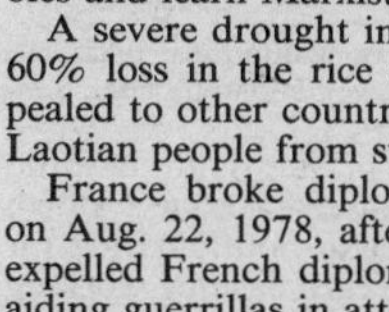

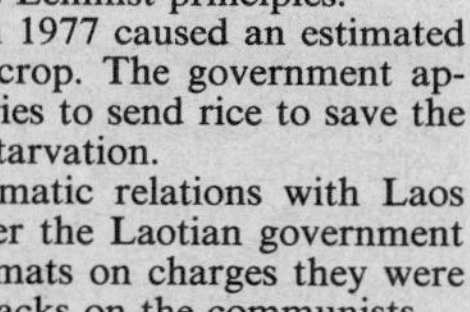

Official Name: Republic of Lebanon.
Area: 4,015 square miles (10,400 sq. km.).
Population: 2,591,460.
Chief Cities: Beirut (Bayrūt), capital, 474,870; Tripoli, 127,611.
Largest Metropolitan Area: Beirut, 938,940.
Government: Parliamentary republic.
President: Amin Gemayel (since 1982).
Prime Minister: Shafiq al-Wazzan (since 1980).
Chamber of Deputies: 99 members.
U.S. Ambassador to Lebanon: Reginald Bartholomew.
Lebanese Ambassador to U.S.: Abdallah Bouhabib.
Flag: Red, white, and red stripes, with green cedar tree in white stripe.
Languages: Arabic (official), French, English, Armenian.
Principal Ethnic Groups: Arab (94%), Armenian (6%).
Religions: Christianity (50%), Islam (50%).
Leading Industries: Trade and banking; manufacturing (oil refining, textiles, food processing, cement, tobacco products); agriculture (sheep, poultry, fruits, vegetables, grapes, figs, wheat, cotton); tourism.
Foreign Trade: *Major exports*—apples, pears, quinces, eggs, dried beans, wool; *major imports*—animals, automobiles, wheat, beans, gasoline.
Places of Interest: Baalbeck temple; ruins at Anjar and Byblos; Tyre excavations; Beit-Eddine Palace; Castle of the Sea at Saida (Sidon); Jeita Grotto; Beirut Museum; Tripoli citadel.

LEBANON TODAY

Smaller than Connecticut, Lebanon is a Middle Eastern Arab nation torn by fighting among Christian rightists, Muslim leftists, and troops of Syria and Israel. The battles wrecked the nation's cities and destroyed Lebanon's previously prosperous economy.

With a population almost evenly divided between Christians and Muslims, Lebanon before the civil war had achieved political stability by traditionally choosing a Christian as president and a Muslim as prime minister. Unlike the people in other Arab countries, most Lebanese could read and write and took an active part in elective politics.

The Lebanon Mountains dominate the country's landscape. To the west is a narrow coastal plain where the largest cities are located.

The Mediterranean coast has a mild climate the year round. But the mountain regions have heavy snows that attract skiing enthusiasts.

EARLY HISTORY

In ancient times the Phoenicians, who lived in what is now Lebanon, spread civilization throughout the Mediterranean as seafaring traders and colonizers. The Phoenician city-state of Tyre reached its peak of prosperity about 1000 B.C.

Persians, Assyrians, Babylonians, Egyptians, and Greeks under Alexander the Great fought in turn for the area. In time it came under Roman rule along with Syria. A Christian sect, the Maronites, settled in Lebanon, making it mainly Christian.

After centuries of warfare and invasion, the Middle East was unified under the Ottoman Empire in the 1500s. Egyptian occupation in 1832 increased tension between the Christian Maronites and the Islamic Druses. Fearing annihilation, the Maronites appealed for help.

European powers in 1864 forced the Turks to agree to a pro-Christian government for the province of Mount Lebanon that was created.

After World War I France received a mandate over Lebanon. It became a republic in 1926.

Lebanon declared its independence on Nov. 26, 1941, but France refused to recognize Lebanon's

QUICK QUIZ: Who was the first Speaker of the House of Representatives? See page 166.

LEBANON *(continued)*

sovereignty until Nov. 27, 1943. French troops withdrew in December 1946.

During the Arab-Israeli wars of 1948–1973, many Palestinian refugees settled in Lebanon. The Palestine Liberation Organization (PLO) made Lebanon a base for attacks on Israel.

CIVIL WAR

A civil war began on April 13, 1975, among rightist Christians, leftist Muslims, and PLO guerrillas. With the acquiescence of the U.S. and Israel, 30,000 Syrian troops intervened in April 1976. The Syrian army took control of Beirut on Nov. 15, 1976, putting an end to the heaviest fighting that had killed about 60,000.

Israeli troops invaded southern Lebanon on March 14, 1978, destroying PLO strongholds, but withdrew in June after a UN peacekeeping force arrived in the area.

After new border fighting between Israel and the PLO, Israel invaded Lebanon on June 6, 1982, and quickly overran much of the country, defeating PLO and Syrian forces. In August 1982 U.S. Marines and troops of Italy and France supervised the evacuation of 14,000 PLO guerrillas from Beirut.

With Israeli troops holding southern Lebanon and Syrian forces occupying the northern and eastern parts, parliament on Aug. 23, 1982, elected a new president, Bashir Gemayel, 34, leader of the rightist Christian militia. Most Muslim members boycotted the election.

Before he could take office, the president-elect and 25 others were slain in a bomb explosion at his Christian Phalangist Party headquarters on Sept. 14, 1982. Believing the PLO responsible for the bombing, the Phalangists took revenge with a massacre of over 700 Palestinians in Beirut on Sept. 16–18.

A week later parliament elected Gemayel's brother, Amin Gemayel, 40, as the nation's president. He took office on Sept. 23.

At the request of Gemayel's government on Sept. 24, 1982, the U.S., Italy, France, and Britain brought in troops to establish an international peacekeeping force in Beirut.

Terrorists bombed the U.S. embassy in Beirut on April 18, 1983, killing 17 Americans and scores of Lebanese. See page 15.

The U.S. sought to have Israel, Syria, and the PLO withdraw their troops from the country. After months of negotiation, Israel and Lebanon signed an agreement on May 17, 1983, providing that Israel would remove its troops when Syria and the PLO also did so. However, the agreement became meaningless when Syria and the PLO refused to participate.

Israel unilaterally pulled back its troops on Sept. 4, 1983, to the Awwali River in southern Lebanon, about 25 miles north of the Israeli border. Lebanese government troops sought to establish control over areas around Beirut abandoned by the Israelis. But they met stiff resistance from PLO and Muslim Druse militiamen. To support the Lebanese army, the U.S. began on Sept. 17 to use its warships to bombard guerrillas.

On Oct. 23, 1983, terrorists almost simultaneously bombed headquarters of the U.S. and French peacekeeping forces, killing 240 U.S. marines and sailors and 58 French troops. See page 27.

LESOTHO

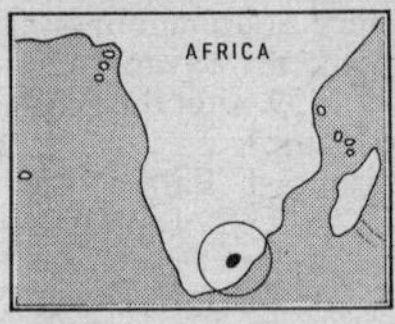

Official Name: Kingdom of Lesotho.
Area: 11,720 square miles (30,355 sq. km.).
Population: 1,450,070.
Capital: Maseru, 75,000.
Government: Dictatorship.
Prime Minister: Leabua Jonathan (since 1965).
King: Motlotlehi Moshoeshoe II (since 1966).
Parliament: *National Assembly,* 60; *Senate,* 33.
U.S. Ambassador to Lesotho: Keith Lepham Brown.
Lesotho Ambassador to U.S.: 'M'alineo N. Tau.
Flag: Parallel bars of green and red at hoist, with white conical Basuto hat on blue field.
Official Languages: English and Sesotho.
Ethnic Groups: Sotho (85%), Nguini (15%).
Religions: Christianity (70%), animism (30%).
Leading Industries: Agriculture (corn, wheat, sorghum, peas, beans, sheep, cattle); mining (diamonds); manufacturing (carpets, candles, fertilizer, pottery, jewelry).
Foreign Trade: *Major exports*—wool, cattle, mohair, diamonds; *major imports*—food, machinery, vehicles, consumer goods.
Places of Interest: Drakensberg Mountains; bushmen cave and cliff paintings in Cave Sandstone area; Sehlabathebe National Park.

A little larger than the state of Maryland, Lesotho has few known natural resources. About a fourth of the country's men travel to South Africa for several months each year to earn cash by working in the mines. Otherwise most of the people live in tribal villages, farming for a living. Heavily dependent on foreign aid, Lesotho imports food and goods worth 12 times its exports.

Lesotho is a rugged, mile-high plateau country nestled amid the 11,000-foot peaks of the Drakensberg Mountains. Only about 10% of the land can be farmed. Temperatures average 45° F. in July and 70° F. in January.

Formerly called *Basutoland,* Lesotho is landlocked by South Africa on three sides and by Transkei to the south.

The Basotho nation came into being in 1818 under the leadership of Moshesh I. In 1867 the Basotho requested British protection against Boer advances from South Africa, and in 1868 Britain annexed Basutoland. Internal self-government was introduced in 1959.

Independence was granted on Oct. 4, 1966, with Leabua Jonathan as prime minister.

The country's first election since independence was held on Jan. 31, 1970. Jonathan declared the results invalid and suspended the constitution.

Jonathan ruled as dictator by decree. In April 1973 he established an appointed national assembly. Opponents tried to overthrow Jonathan's rule in January 1975. A court found 18 persons guilty of treason in the coup attempt.

Guerrilla warfare against Chief Jonathan's dictatorship intensified in 1979–83.

South African troops raided Lesotho in 1982 and 1983 to kill guerrillas.

LIBERIA

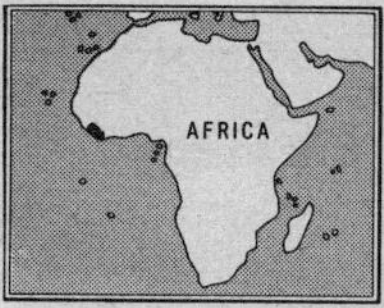

Official Name: Republic of Liberia.
Area: 43,000 square miles (111,369 sq. km.).
Population: 2,124,710.
Capital: Monrovia, 96,226.
Government: Military dictatorship.
President: Samuel Kanyon Doe (since 1980).
Military Junta: People's Redemption Council (PRC), 22 members.
U.S. Ambassador to Liberia: William Swing.
Liberian Ambassador to U.S.: Joseph Saye Guannu.
Flag: Alternating stripes of red and white, with blue square containing white star in upper hoist corner.
Religions: Animism (75%), Islam (15%), Christianity (10%).
Main Ethnic Group: Black.
Languages: English (official), many tribal languages.
Leading Industries: Agriculture (rice, cassava, coffee, sugarcane, tobacco, cocoa, rubber, palm kernels, citrus fruits, vegetables); mining (iron ore, diamonds, gold); shipping; manufacturing (soap, plastics, paint, paper products, textiles, building materials, fertilizer, tobacco products); forestry and lumbering; tourism.
Foreign Trade: *Major exports*—iron ore, rubber, diamonds, coffee, cacao; *major imports*—machinery, transport equipment, manufactured goods.
Places of Interest: Atlantic coast beaches and resorts; Providence Island; Monrovia; Lake Piso; Bong mine; Totota Zoo; LAMCO mining site.

LIBERIA TODAY

About the size of Ohio, Liberia is one of the world's 10 leading producers of iron ore and natural rubber. Most Liberians lead a tribal life in the country's tropical forests.

The government is heavily dependent on aid from the U.S. and Israel.

One of Liberia's most pressing problems as it seeks to become an industrial nation is to improve and expand its educational system to provide skilled workers and technicians and managers. Only about 1 in 4 Liberians can read and write. The majority of the people speak tribal dialects.

The world's largest merchant fleet sails under the Liberian flag—over 2,200 ships. Most are owned by Americans, Greeks, and other foreigners who register the ships in Liberia to avoid strict control. Ship registration fees make up about 8% of Liberia's gross national product.

Liberia lies on the west coast of Africa. Guinea is to the north, Ivory Coast to the east, and Sierra Leone to the northwest.

LIBERIA'S HISTORY

The colony of Liberia was founded for liberated American slaves in 1822 by the National Colonization Society, a white abolitionist group whose agents governed the area until 1847.

The Republic of Liberia was established on July 26, 1847, becoming the first black African colony to gain independence.

Beginning in 1926, Liberia encouraged American companies to develop rubber plantations that became a mainstay of the economy.

Huge iron-ore deposits were discovered in 1955 at Mt. Nimba on the border with Guinea. Shipments from the mines began in 1963. Iron ore accounts for over half of the nation's exports.

From 1877 to 1980 the True Whigs governed as the country's only political party. William V. S. Tubman, was president of Liberia from 1943 until his death on July 23, 1971. He was succeeded by William R. Tolbert Jr.

Master Sgt. Samuel K. Doe, 28, led a coup on April 12, 1980, in which President Tolbert and 27 others were killed. Doe made himself president, forming a 17-member military junta called the People's Redemption Council (PRC) to run the government under martial law. On April 22 the new rulers publicly executed 13 of the leading officials of Tolbert's government.

Doe had five members of his junta executed by firing squad on Aug. 14, 1981, accusing them of plotting his overthrow.

President Doe declared in 1982 that he would return the nation to civilian rule in 1985. He visited the White House in August 1982 to demonstrate his friendship for the United States.

LIBYA

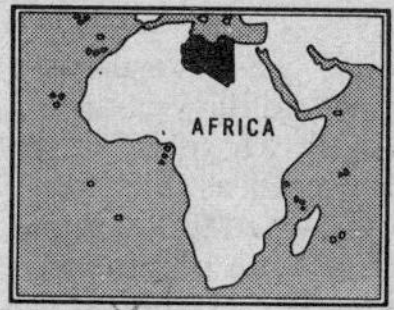

Official Name: Socialist People's Libyan Arab Jamahiriya.
Area: 679,362 square miles (1,759,540 sq. km.).
Population: 3,586,110.
Chief Cities: Tripoli, capital, 213,506; Benghazi, 137,295.
Government: Socialist military dictatorship.
Head of State: Col. Mu'ammar al-Qadhafi (since 1969).
Flag: Green field.
Languages: Arabic (official), Berber.
Main Ethnic Groups: Arab and Berber.
Official Religion: Islam (97%).
Leading Industries: Mining (petroleum); agriculture (cattle, sheep, goats, peanuts, olives, grapes, dates, barley, wheat); construction; manufacturing (petroleum products, textiles, tobacco products).
Foreign Trade: *Major exports*—petroleum, hides and skins, peanuts; *major imports*—machinery, clothing, automobiles, wheat flour.
Places of Interest: Marble arch of Marcus Aurelius in Tripoli; 2d century amphitheater at Sabratha; ancient city of Leptis; Cyrene archaeological site.

LIBYA TODAY

Over twice as large as Texas, Libya is largely covered by the hot, nearly uninhabited Sahara Desert. Most Libyans live along the 1,100-mile Mediterranean coast. Yet oil fields in the Sahara make Libya a leading oil-producing nation.

The socialist military dictator who rules Libya

QUICK QUIZ: Where is the nation of Andorra located? See page 485.

LIBYA *(continued)*

gives the people little voice in their government.

The government uses much of its oil riches to purchase jet fighter planes and other military equipment, and to finance terrorists.

Egypt and Sudan lie to the east, Tunisia and Algeria to the west, and Niger and Chad to the south.

EARLY HISTORY

Beginning about 630 B.C. Greeks colonized northeastern Libya, called Cyrenaica. About the same time Phoenicians colonized northwestern Libya, or Tripolitania, which became part of the state of Carthage. In the 1st century B.C. both became part of the Roman Empire.

In A.D. 642–643 Libya was conquered by Arabs, who converted the local Berber peoples to Islam.

Libya became part of the Ottoman Turkish Empire in 1551. Ottoman rule ended when Italy invaded Libya in 1911, making it a colony.

The Muslim leader Mohammed Idris fought Italian rule from 1916 until British troops captured Libya during World War II in October 1942. The country remained under British administration as a UN trust until 1951.

INDEPENDENCE

Libya became independent on Dec. 24, 1951, with Idris as king. The discovery of oil in 1959 brought wealth.

The 79-year-old King Idris was overthrown on Sept. 1, 1969, in a bloodless military coup led by Col. Mu'ammar al-Qadhafi. He proclaimed the country a republic with himself as dictator.

Libya nationalized foreign-owned oil companies in 1973–74 and joined the Arab oil embargo of countries that had befriended Israel in the Arab-Israeli war in 1973.

The Libyan leader completed publication of his 2-volume *Green Book* in 1978 in which he described a utopian "new socialist society."

A Libyan mob attacked and burned the U.S. embassy in Tripoli on Dec. 2, 1979. Four months later, in May 1980, the U.S. withdrew all diplomats but did not break diplomatic relations.

The Libyan government paid $220,000 to the U.S. President Carter's brother Billy in 1980 in an effort to influence U.S. government policies.

Libyan tanks and troops intervened in the civil war in neighboring Chad in 1980–81, occupying that nation's capital.

Accusing Libya of international terrorism, the U.S. on May 6, 1981, ordered Libya's diplomats in Washington to leave the country.

Two Libyan fighter planes were shot down by U.S. Navy jets on Aug. 19, 1981, when they attacked the American planes off Libya's coast.

American CIA officials confirmed in 1981 that former CIA agents hired by Qadhafi had duped the U.S. Army into letting Green Berets go to Libya to train terrorists.

After the U.S. government revealed Qadhafi had hired assassins to kill President Reagan and other high U.S. officials, President Reagan on Dec. 10, 1981, asked the 2,500 Americans working in Libya to leave the country and invalidated U.S. passports for travel to Libya.

On March 10, 1982, the U.S. banned oil imports from and high-technology exports to Libya.

LIECHTENSTEIN

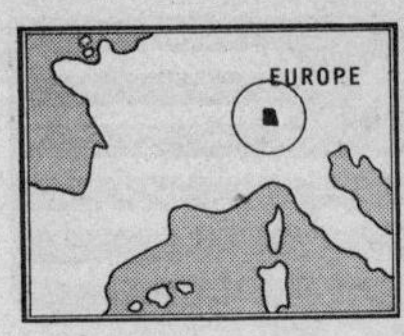

Official Name: Principality of Liechtenstein.
Area: 61 square miles (157 sq. km.).
Population: 26,668.
Capital: Vaduz, 4,000.
Government: Constitutional principality.
Prime Minister: Hans Brunhart (since 1978).
Chief of State: Prince Franz Josef II (since 1938).
Legislature: *Diet,* 15 members.
Flag: Blue and red, with gold crown in blue stripe.
Language: German.
Principal Ethnic Group: German.
Religion: Roman Catholicism (92%).
Leading Industries: Manufacturing (precision instruments, textiles, ceramics, pharmaceuticals, false teeth, food processing); banking; tourism; agriculture (cattle, dairy products, grapes, corn, potatoes, wheat, vegetables).
Foreign Trade: *Major exports*—textiles, pottery, instruments, pharmaceuticals, postage stamps; *major imports*—food, manufactured goods.
Place of Interest: Mt. Naafkopf; medieval village of Vaduz and the prince's 700-year-old castle; ski resort at Malbun.

Liechtenstein is the most highly industrialized country in the world, with only 3% of the people dependent on farming for their living. Its prosperous people enjoy a high standard of living.

Because of low taxes, about 50,000 foreign businesses have headquarters in Liechtenstein.

Thousands of tourists visit each year. There are many hotels and ski resorts.

The sale of postage stamps provides a large share of the government's annual budget.

Covering an area smaller than Cleveland, Ohio, Liechtenstein is bordered by Austria on the east and Switzerland on the north, south, and west. Warm winds protect the country from temperature extremes. Summers are cool and winters are cold with much snow.

The barony of Schellenberg and the county of Vaduz, founded in 814, were bought by Johann Adam von Liechtenstein in 1699 and 1712. The Holy Roman emperor joined the two areas to create the principality of Liechtenstein in 1719.

Following French and Russian invasions during the Napoleonic wars, Liechtenstein joined the German Confederation in 1815. Ties with Austria developed, leading to withdrawal from the confederation in 1866. It remained neutral in both World War I and World War II.

Since 1924 Switzerland has administered the principality's defense, foreign affairs, and customs.

In 1973 a national referendum was held in which the all-male electorate voted 2,128 to 1,675 against giving women the right to vote.

The nation in 1978 celebrated the 40th anniversary of rule by 72-year-old Franz Josef II.

In national elections in 1978 and 1982, the Patriotic Union Party won control of parliament. The party's leader, Hans Brunhart, served as prime minister from 1978.

LUXEMBOURG

Official Name: Grand Duchy of Luxembourg.
Area: 998 square miles (2,586 sq. km.).
Population: 367,652.
Capital: Luxembourg-Ville, 78,400.
Government: Constitutional grand duchy.
Prime Minister: Pierre Werner (since 1979).
Chief of State: Grand Duke Jean (since 1964).
Legislature: *Council of State,* 21 members; *Chamber of Deputies,* 59 members.
U.S. Ambassador to Luxembourg: John E. Dolibois.
Luxembourgian Ambassador to U.S.: Paul Peters.
Flag: Red, white, and light blue stripes.
Languages: French, German, Luxembourgish.
Principal Ethnic Group: Gallo-Germanic.
Religion: Roman Catholicism (97%).
Leading Industries: Manufacturing (steel, machinery, rubber, chemicals, wine, fertilizer); mining (iron ore); trade and banking; agriculture (grapes, poultry, hogs, cattle, dairy products, sheep, oats, potatoes, wheat, vegetables).
Foreign Trade: *Major exports*—iron and steel; *major imports*—coal, petroleum.
Places of Interest: Grand ducal palace; national museum; Cathedral of Notre Dame; Citadel of St. Espirit; Quirinus rock chapel; Chervaux and Vianden castles.

Somewhat smaller than Rhode Island, Luxembourg is one of the world's 20 most important steel-producing nations.

Luxembourg has the highest per capita usage of electricity among industrialized nations—50% greater than that of the United States.

Lowlands rise gradually from the Luxembourg-Lorraine iron-mining basin in the southwest to the Ardennes Plateau in the north.

Belgium lies to the west, France to the south, and West Germany to the east.

Luxembourg began as a feudal domain in A.D. 963. In 1308 the count of Luxembourg became Holy Roman Emperor Henry VII, and in 1354 Luxembourg was raised to a duchy.

After 1443 it was governed by the rulers of the Netherlands. Luxembourg was granted autonomy in 1839, but Dutch kings continued to rule.

In 1867 the Treaty of London declared Luxembourg an independent, neutral state. It became a parliamentary democracy under a constitution adopted in 1868. At the death of Dutch King Willem III in 1890, the grand duchy went to Duke Adolf of Nassau.

Luxembourg was occupied by German troops in both world wars.

Grand Duke Jean became the country's ruler on Nov. 12, 1964, when his mother, Grand Duchess Charlotte, abdicated.

In a national election on June 10, 1979, the opposition Christian Social Party won a plurality of 24 seats. Christian Social leader Pierre Werner became prime minister, forming a coalition cabinet with the Liberal Party.

MADAGASCAR

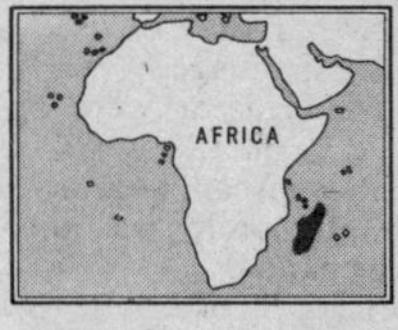

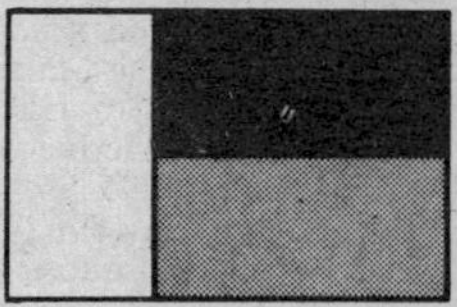

Official Name: Democratic Republic of Madagascar.
Area: 226,658 square miles (587,041 sq. km.).
Population: 9,576,710.
Capital: Antananarivo (Tananarive), 347,466.
Government: One-party Marxist socialist state.
President: Didier Ratsiraka (since 1975).
Prime Minister: Desire Rakotoarijaona (since 1977).
Parliament: *National People's Assembly,* 137 members.
U.S. Ambassador: Robert B. Keating.
Ambassador to U.S.: Leon Maxime Rajaobelina.
Flag: White bar; stripes of red over green.
Official Languages: Malagasy and French.
Main Ethnic Group: Merina (Malayo-Polynesian descent).
Religions: Christianity (40%), animism, Islam.
Leading Industries: Agriculture (coffee, cotton, cloves, vanilla, tobacco, rice, sugar, sisal, cattle); mining (chromite, graphite, mica); food processing; manufacturing (leather products, textiles, paper, consumer goods, tobacco products); fishing.
Foreign Trade: *Major exports*—chromite, graphite, coffee, vanilla, cloves, meat, sugar, sisal; *major imports*—machinery, electrical equipment, chemicals, rice, textiles, trucks, petroleum.
Places of Interest: Antananarivo marketplaces.

MADAGASCAR TODAY

Although larger than Texas, Madagascar is an underdeveloped island nation with few known natural resources.

The country's revolutionary socialist government rules through a one-party parliamentary system. Banks, insurance companies, mines, and shipping have been nationalized.

Once an exporter of rice, the nation has become a rice importer as its economy has declined.

The former French colony depends heavily on economic aid from France.

Most of the people are poor farmers. Only 4 in 10 persons can read and write.

Madagascar, the world's fourth-largest island, lies in the Indian Ocean about 250 miles east of the African coast of Mozambique. Its west coast is deeply indented and bordered by a gradually rising plain leading to a central plateau. The highest mountain, 9,450-foot Mt. Tsaratanana, stands in the north.

EARLY HISTORY

Immigration to Madagascar from the southwest Pacific began before the Christian era and continued until the 1400s. These immigrants, later known as Merinas, settled mainly in the central highlands. The coastal regions were colonized by immigrants from Africa and Arabia. In the 1500s and 1600s the Merina kingdom became the strongest on the island and later imposed its rule over most of Madagascar.

In the 1800s King Radama I (reigned 1810–

QUICK QUIZ: What travel documents do you need for a visit to Ghana? See page 960.

MADAGASCAR *(continued)*

28) allowed English and French missionaries to open churches and schools, and they devised a written form of the Malagasy language.

French efforts to take Madagascar were opposed by the Merina rulers in the wars of 1883–85 and 1895–96. Madagascar became a French colony in 1896. The monarchy was abolished and the last queen was exiled.

In 1947 an armed uprising broke out. Between 60,000 and 90,000 people were killed before it was crushed by French troops in 1947.

Madagascar was granted self-government as the autonomous Malagasy Republic within the French Community on Oct. 14, 1958.

INDEPENDENCE

Madagascar attained full independence on June 26, 1960. Philibert Tsiranana, head of the dominant Social Democratic Party, became president. He was reelected president in 1965 and 1972. During his administration French settlers continued to dominate the economy.

After a week of student riots and a general strike, President Tsiranana turned over his powers to the army chief, Maj. Gen. Gabriel Ramanantsoa, on May 18, 1972.

At a national referendum in October 1972 the voters approved extending military rule for five years, ousting Tsiranana from the government.

On Feb. 5, 1975, Lt. Col. Richard Ratsimandrava became the new military government leader. Six days later, on Feb. 11, Ratsimandrava was assassinated in an ambush in Antananarivo.

On Feb. 13–14, 1975, government troops stormed military police barracks and socialist headquarters, killing 21 persons and arresting 297, including former President Tsiranana.

About two-thirds of the 140,000 French settlers fled from Madagascar in 1975, leaving the nation short of managers and technicians.

The new government forced the United States and France to close military bases.

Didier Ratsiraka, a former naval officer, who had served as foreign minister since 1972, was chosen president and head of the 19-member military junta on June 15, 1975.

At a referendum on Dec. 21, 1975, the people approved a new constitution written by Ratsiraka and elected him to a 7-year term as president.

In an election on June 30, 1977, the 137 members of the national assembly were elected to 5-year terms. All were selected by the single political party, the National Front for the Defense of the Malagasy Socialist Revolution.

After riots in which up to 1,000 Comoros immigrants were killed in northwestern Madagascar, the Comoros government in 1977 undertook to repatriate the remaining 25,000 or more Comorians living in Madagascar.

Three persons were killed and 150 were arrested in two days of riots on May 29–30, 1978, by students protesting lowered educational standards. Additional riots occurred in 1981 and 1982.

Because of the declining economy, the government was unable to meet interest payments on its foreign debt of $1 billion in 1982, and foreign commercial banks refused to make further loans.

Ratsiraka won a 7-year term as president in an election on Nov. 7, 1982, receiving 80% of the vote.

MALAWI

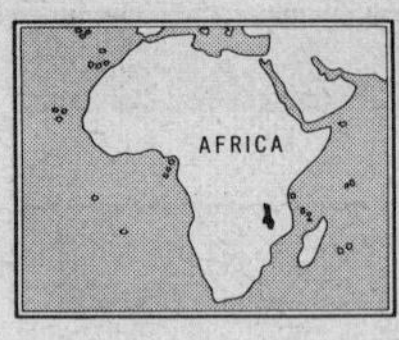

Official Name: Republic of Malawi.
Area: 45,747 square miles (118,484 sq. km.).
Population: 6,718,590.
Chief Cities: Lilongwe, capital, 130,000; Balantyre-Limbe, 219,000.
Government: One-party republic.
President: Hastings Kamuzu Banda (since 1966).
National Assembly: 107 members.
U.S. Ambassador to Malawi: John A. Burroughs Jr.
Malawi Ambassador to U.S.: Nelson T. Mizere.
Flag: Black, red, and green stripes, with red rising sun on black stripe.
Official Languages: Chichewa and English.
Main Ethnic Groups: Chewa, Nyanja.
Religions: Animism (67%), Christianity, Islam.
Leading Industries: Agriculture (cotton, peanuts, coffee, tea, tobacco, maize, cattle, sorghum, sugar, millet); fishing; food processing; construction.
Foreign Trade: *Major exports*—sugar, tobacco, tea, peanuts, cotton; *major imports*—machinery, consumer products, motor vehicles, petroleum.
Places of Interest: Lake Malawi; Mlanje Mountains; Great Rift Valley; public gardens at Lilongwe; Blantyre-Limbe tea estates.

MALAWI TODAY

About the size of Pennsylvania, Malawi has few resources other than farm and grazing land. Lake Malawi (formerly Lake Nyasa) covers about 20% of the country's area, and much of the rest is too mountainous to be farmed.

Most of the people live in tribal villages, seldom seeing any money from one year to the next. They live by fishing and farming. Only about 1 in 7 persons can read and write.

Long and narrow, Malawi is a landlocked country in southeast Africa. Lake Malawi extends along the eastern border with Tanzania and Mozambique. Zambia is to the west.

Lake Malawi drains south into the Shire River. The steep cliffs of the Rift Valley rise to the west.

EARLY HISTORY

For several centuries Lake Malawi attracted Bantu tribes from the northwest. The Malawi kingdom was established in the region in the 1300s. By the 1600s the Malawi people had fallen under dominance of the Yao tribes, who sold the Malawi as slaves to Arab traders.

The Scottish missionary-explorer David Livingstone became the first European to reach Lake Malawi, on Sept. 16, 1859. He and Scottish missionaries who followed him fought the Arab slave trade.

Britain established a protectorate in 1891, calling the area *Nyasaland.*

Resentful of mistreatment by British plantation owners, Malawi tribesmen led by John Chilembwe staged an unsuccessful uprising in 1915.

In 1953 Nyasaland was forced by the British into federation with North and South Rhodesia.

The Nyasaland African Congress (NAC), founded in 1944, opposed the federation. The NAC gained strength in 1958 when its leaders recalled Dr. Hastings Kamuzu Banda from 40 years of study abroad.

The British, faced with rising protests, outlawed the NAC in 1959 and imprisoned Banda and 1,200 of his followers. Other followers, however, built up the Malawi Congress Party (MCP). They persuaded the British to release Banda in 1960.

In elections in August 1961 Banda won control of the territorial government. The federation was dissolved on Dec. 31, 1963.

INDEPENDENCE

Under Banda's leadership, Nyasaland became the independent state of Malawi within the British Commonwealth of Nations on July 6, 1964. A coup in 1964 proved unsuccessful, and Banda was able to resolve dissension within his party.

Malawi became a republic on July 6, 1966, with Banda as its first president.

Since 1967 a program of persecution has been carried on against the Jehovah's Witnesses sect, whose members refuse to salute the Malawi flag. The government banned the group and placed about 30,000 in prison camps. In December 1975 officials of the sect protested their members were being beaten, tortured, and raped.

In 1970 Banda was acclaimed president for life by a convention of the Malawi Congress Party, the only authorized political party in the country.

In ruling his country Banda brooks no opposition. When one of his cabinet ministers, Aleke Banda, mentioned himself as a possible successor to the president in an article published in Zambia, he was dismissed in March 1973 from both the cabinet and the party.

Malawi passed a law in 1974 banning miniskirts, with a penalty of six months in prison for any woman baring her knees.

The government moved its capital in 1975 from Zomba to the new centrally located city of Lilongwe to encourage opening up the interior of the country. The capital was developed at a cost of more than $250 million by a profit-making corporation. Lilongwe's extensive public gardens employ 2,000 workers.

Some $68 million was budgeted by the gov- ernment in 1976 for expenditure on agricultural development and hydroelectric power projects. Wages and prices were controlled by the government in an effort to reduce inflation.

The former head of the secret police, Martin Gwede, and the former head of the MCP party, Albert Andrew Muwalo Nqumayo, were convicted of treason on Feb. 14, 1977, and sentenced to death for plotting to overthrow President Banda.

On July 4, 1977, Banda released most of the remaining 2,000 political prisoners he had jailed.

The first general election in 17 years was held on June 29, 1978. Although all candidates were members of the MCP party, several contested for 47 of the 87 seats in the national assembly. A national election was held on June 29, 1983, for an expanded 107-member parliament. Candidates were not permitted to campaign before the election.

MALAYSIA

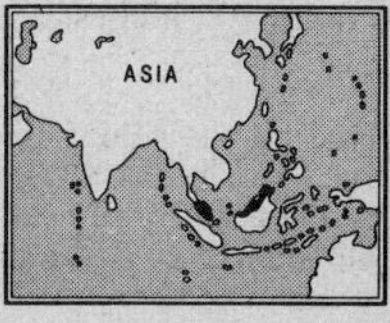

Official Name: Malaysia.
Area: 127,317 square miles (329,749 sq. km.).
Population: 15,171,700.
Chief Cities: Kuala Lumpur, capital, 451,977; George Town, 269,603; Ipoh, 247,953; Johore Bahru, 136,234; Klang, 113,611.
Government: Constitutional monarchy.
Prime Minister: Datuk Seri Mahathir Mohamad (since 1981).
King: Sultan Ahmad Shah of Pahang (since 1979).
Parliament: *Senate* (Dewan Negara), 58 members; *House of Representatives* (Dewan Ra'ayat), 154.
U.S. Ambassador to Malaysia: Thomas P. Shoesmith.
Malaysian Ambassador to U.S.: Zain Azraai.
Flag: Red and white stripes with blue field containing gold crescent and 14-pointed gold star.
Languages: Malay and English (both official), Chinese, Tamil.
Main Ethnic Groups: Malay (44%), Chinese (36%), Indian and Pakistani (10%).
Religions: Islam, Buddhism, Christianity, Hinduism.
Leading Industries: Agriculture (rubber, rice, palm kernels, tea, peppers, coconuts); mining (tin, petroleum, iron ore, natural gas, bauxite); forestry and lumbering; manufacturing (steel, automobiles, electronics, petroleum products, rubber products, palm oil, chemicals, textiles); fishing; tourism.
Foreign Trade: *Major exports*—petroleum, rubber, lumber, palm oil, tin, iron ore; *major imports*—machinery, rice, textiles.
Places of Interest: Batu Cave; Cameron Highlands; Malaysia National Park. *In Kuala Lumpur:* National museum; national mosque; houses on stilts.

MALAYSIA TODAY

Although about the size of New Mexico, Malaysia has over 10 times as many people.

The nation has two parts separated by 400 miles of the South China Sea. West Malaysia lies on a peninsula in Southeast Asia just south of Thailand. East Malaysia covers the northern coast of the island of Borneo.

Malaysia is an oil-exporting nation and the world's leading producer of tin and natural rubber.

Because Malaysia has abundant natural resources, it has a stronger economy and more industry than most other nations of Southeast Asia. But about 1 in 3 Malaysians are poor farm workers who cannot read and write.

Malaysia's king is elected for a 5-year term by the sultans of the nine states of West Malaysia from among their own members.

About 80% of West Malaysia is covered by mountains and tropical forests. Most of the people live along the more than 1,200 miles of coast.

The East Malaysian states of Sarawak and Sabah lie on the island of Borneo. The nation's highest mountain, Mt. Kinabalu (13,455 feet), stands in Sabah.

The climate along the coasts is hot, but it

QUICK QUIZ: What nation boasts the world's largest merchant fleet? See page 956.

MALAYSIA *(continued)*

becomes cool in the hills and mountains of the interior. Annual rainfall averages 100 inches.

EARLY HISTORY

Portuguese traders first arrived on the Malay peninsula in 1511. In 1786 the British East India Company leased the island of Penang. By the early 1900s Britain controlled all the Malay states as colonies or protectorates.

In 1946 the Union of Malaya was formed, uniting Penang and Malacca with the nine Malay states. The union became the Federation of Malaya in 1948.

Communist insurrections erupted in 1948. The guerrilla terrorism in the countryside finally was brought under control in 1959.

INDEPENDENT MALAYSIA

The Federation of Malaya was granted independence by Britain on Aug. 31, 1957, with Tunku Abdul Rahman as prime minister.

Malaysia became an independent constitutional monarchy on Sept. 16, 1963. It incorporated the former Federation of Malaya and the former British colonies of Singapore, Sarawak, and North Borneo (Sabah). Singapore was expelled and given its separate independence in 1965.

The worst racial rioting in Malaysia's history broke out May 13, 1969, in Kuala Lumpur. Violent strife between Malays and Chinese brought the assumption of emergency powers by a National Operations Council under Deputy Prime Minister Tun Abdul Razak.

On Jan. 12, 1970, the government announced the formation of a 65-member national consultative council to avert a recurrence of racial strife.

Tun Abdul Razak became prime minister upon Rahman's retirement in September 1970.

Offshore oil strikes made in 1973 went into production in 1975, boosting the economy.

Razak died of leukemia on Jan. 14, 1976. He was succeeded as prime minister on the following day by his brother-in-law Datuk Hussein Onn.

Prime Minister Datuk Hussein's National Front coalition won a comfortable two-thirds majority in parliamentary elections held in 1978.

MALAYSIA IN THE 1980s

Prime Minister Hussein resigned because of illness in July 1981. He was succeeded by Datuk Seri Mahathir Mohamad.

Prime Minister Mahathir's governing party won 132 of the seats in the 154-member parliament in an election on April 24, 1982.

The prospering economy, which grew at an average rate of 8% a year in the 1970s, slowed somewhat in the 1980s, but still outperformed that of most other nations with a growth rate of 5% in 1982.

The number of Malaysians living at the poverty level declined from 49.3% in 1970 to 29.2% in 1980. The government plans to reduce this to 16.7% in 1990 and eliminate poverty altogether by 2000.

An $18.6 billion 5-year plan for 1981–85 emphasizes private investment in the development of heavy industry, including a liquid natural-gas plant and a project to make the nation self-sufficient in producing fertilizer.

MALDIVES

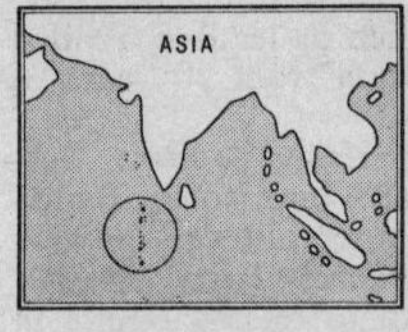

Official Name: Republic of Maldives.
Area: 115 square miles (298 sq. km.).
Population: 170,424.
Capital: Malé, 29,555.
Government: Republic ruled by decree.
President: Maumoon Abdul Gayoom (since 1978).
Legislature: *Majlis,* 48 members.
U.S. Ambassador to Maldives: John Hathaway Reed.
Maldivian Ambassador to U.S.: Abdul Sattar.
Flag: Red field with green panel containing white crescent.
Languages: Divehi (official), Arabic.
Ethnic Groups: Sinhalese, Arab, Dravidian.
Official Religion: Sunni Islam.
Leading Industries: Fishing; agriculture (coconuts, corn, millet, pumpkins, sweet potatoes, fruits); tourism; shipping; handicrafts, rope making.
Foreign Trade: *Major exports*—fish, rope, copra, ambergris, lace, shells, handicrafts; *major imports*—grain, drugs, textiles, consumer goods.
Places of Interest: Plants and animals of the various islands; Malé; beach resorts.

One of the 10 smallest and poorest nations in the world, the Maldives have a land area smaller than the city of Philadelphia. Only a few Maldivians can read and write.

The 2,000 or more Maldive islands string out over 550 miles of the Indian Ocean. The largest has an area of about 5 square miles. About 215 are inhabited. The climate is hot and humid.

Almost all the men of the Maldives fish for a living. Dried fish is the country's main export, with Sri Lanka the main customer. Rice, the main staple of the islanders, must be imported.

About 50,000 tourists visit the islands each year. A tourist who breaks the law is subject to punishment by banishment to an uninhabited isle with no food other than what he can catch from the sea or pick from coconut palms.

The islands were ruled as a sultanate by members of the Didi clan from about 1100 until 1968. Arab traders visited in 1153, converting the people to Islam. In the 1600s the Maldives came under the protection of Sri Lanka (Ceylon), then under Dutch rule.

The Maldives became a protectorate of Britain in December 1887. Britain established an air base in 1939 on Gan, an island in Addu, the southernmost atoll, but closed it in 1976.

The Maldives were granted full independence on July 26, 1965. The nation was a constitutional monarchy until Nov. 11, 1968, when Sultan Mohammed Farid Didi I was deposed. A republic was proclaimed under President Amir Ibrahim Nasir, the sultan's prime minister in 1956–68.

President Nasir suspended the constitution and imposed rule by decree on March 6, 1975. Nasir resigned because of illness in 1978.

Without opposition Maumoon Abdul Gayoom was elected president by the national legislature in 1978 and 1983.

MALI

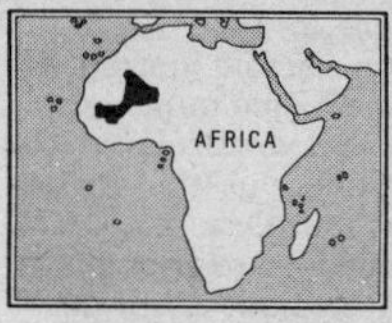

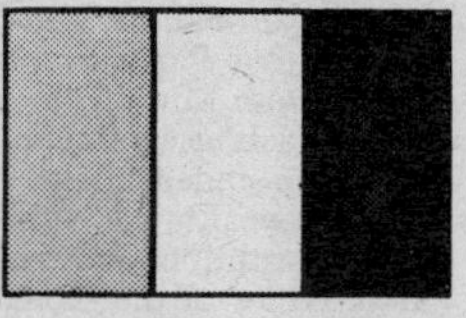

Official Name: Republic of Mali.
Area: 478,767 square miles (1,240,000 sq. km.).
Population: 7,474,940.
Capital: Bamako, 404,022.
Government: Military dictatorship.
President: Col. Moussa Traoré (since 1968).
U.S. Ambassador to Mali: Parker W. Borg.
Mali Ambassador to U.S.: Lassana Keita.
Flag: Bars of green, yellow, and red.
Languages: French (official), Bambra.
Ethnic Groups: Mande (50%), Peul (17%), Voltaic (12%), Songhai (6%), Tuareg and Moors (5%).
Main Religion: Islam (90%).
Leading Industries: Agriculture (cattle, cotton, rice, peanuts, sorghum, millet, goats, sheep); fishing; mining (gold); manufacturing (textiles, cigarettes, matches, baskets, food processing).
Foreign Trade: *Major exports*—cotton, peanuts, fish, livestock; *major imports*—textiles, food, machinery, motor vehicles, petroleum products.
Places of Interest: Cliff-dwelling Dogon tribes near Sangha; Bamako; Timbuktu; Lake Débo.

MALI TODAY

A little larger than the combined areas of Texas and California, Mali is one of the most poverty-stricken nations in the world. Ironically, the country counts among its mineral resources bauxite, uranium, iron ore, copper, manganese, phosphate, and gold. Currently only gold is mined, and that in small quantities, because the primitive transportation system of the landlocked country cannot handle large ore shipments. The military government hopes to find foreign investors willing to develop the minerals and the necessary transportation and communications facilities.

Meanwhile, most of the people farm crops or herd livestock, barely raising enough food to feed their families.

Mali is bordered by Senegal, Mauritania, Algeria, Niger, Upper Volta, Ivory Coast, and Guinea. The greater part of the country spreads north, east, and west of the great bend of the Niger River, while a rather small area lies south of the Niger.

The northern half of Mali is covered by the Sahara Desert. To the south is semidesert, and in the far southwest are savanna lands. The country generally has a hot climate with little rainfall.

EARLY HISTORY

For many years Mali was part of the empire of Ghana. As Islam expanded in the western Sahara, Almoravid Berbers from Mauritania launched a *jihad,* or holy war, against peoples to the south. In 1076 Abu Bakr overthrew Ghana. Although in 1087 the Soninke leaders of Ghana recovered their independence for a century, their great empire had been disrupted.

In the 1000s the small Malinke state of Kangaba, south of Ghana, also embraced Islam and began to annex nearby kingdoms. The emperor Sundiata Keita conquered Ghana in 1235 and established the Muslim empire of Mali, which became the richest and most powerful of the western Sudanese empires.

Under the leadership of Mansa Musa (1307–32), Mali reached its peak as a center of Muslim trade and learning. The empire disintegrated after his death.

The Songhai controlled the next great Islamic empire, with its center at Gao, until 1591, when the Moroccans defeated the Songhai at Tondibi and became the new rulers.

French troops conquered the region in 1881 to 1898. It became known as the territory of *French Soudan* in the colony of French West Africa, which was established in 1904.

INDEPENDENT REPUBLIC OF MALI

The French Soudan was granted self-government in 1958 as a member state in the French Community. In 1959 the colony, renamed the *Sudanese Republic,* joined Senegal in the Mali Federation, which became independent on June 20, 1960. The federation dissolved on Aug. 20, 1960.

The former French Soudan proclaimed itself the *Republic of Mali* on Sept. 22, 1960, and withdrew from the French Community.

Modibo Keita, head of the Sudanese Union Party, became Mali's first president. Keita socialized Mali's economy, and formed close ties with the Soviet Union and communist China. These moves had a disastrous effect on Mali's economy and caused a split in the Sudanese Union Party among pro-Soviet, pro-Chinese, and pro-French factions. In 1967 Keita tried to appease the pro-French faction by reestablishing economic ties with France.

Keita took steps to strengthen his power in late 1967 and 1968. He dissolved the national assembly and began ruling by decree.

Mali's army, fearing the growing role of Keita's Chinese-trained militia, overthrew and imprisoned Keita on Nov. 19, 1968.

Lt. Moussa Traoré became president, and Capt. Yoro Diakité was named premier. Following an attempt to reinstate Keita on Aug. 13, 1969, Traoré assumed the premiership. For attempting a coup in 1971, Diakité was sentenced to life imprisonment in 1972.

Six years of drought from 1969 to 1974 killed up to 100,000 people and about three-fourths of the cattle in the nation. Many of the 700,000 Tuareg nomads of northern Mali migrated to other countries.

President Traoré invoked emergency powers in 1977 after demonstrations in May at the funeral of former President Keita, who died after being imprisoned since the 1968 coup.

Traoré arrested several cabinet members in February 1978, charging them with treason and fraud of more than $1.2 million in distribution of grain to drought victims.

New drought in 1980–81 brought appeals from President Traoré for aid to save his people from famine.

QUICK QUIZ: What is Greenland's main industry? See page 539.

MALTA

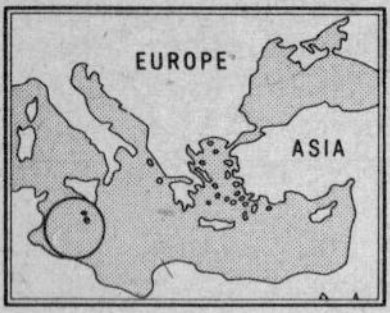

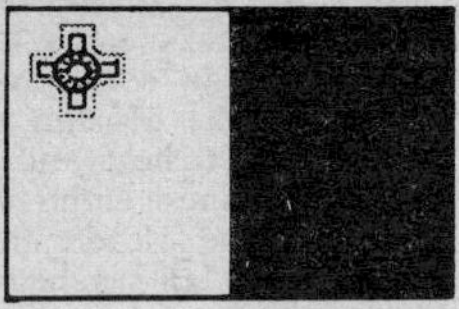

Official Name: Republic of Malta.
Area: 122 square miles (316 sq. km.).
Population: 362,817.
Cities: Valletta, capital, 14,048; Sliema, 22,000.
Government: Parliamentary republic.
Prime Minister: Dom Mintoff (since 1971).
President: Agatha Barbara (since 1982).
House of Representatives: 65 members.
U.S. Ambassador to Malta: James M. Rentschler.
Maltese Ambassador to U.S.: Leslie Agius.
Flag: White and red bars, with George Cross in silver on white bar.
Languages: Maltese, English.
Official Religion: Roman Catholicism (99%).
Ethnic Groups: Arab, Italian, English.
Leading Industries: Shipbuilding and ship repairs; tourism; agriculture (poultry, dairy products, flowers, vegetables, fruits); manufacturing (textiles, yarn, clothing, electronic equipment, food processing).
Foreign Trade: *Major exports*—cotton yarn, textiles, cut flowers, ships and boats, wine; *major imports*—food, petroleum, automobiles, consumer products.
Places of Interest: Valletta; Hypogeum underground Neolithic temple at Paola; cave of Ghar Dalam; Blue Grotto at Zurrieq; cathedral museum at Mdina.

MALTA TODAY

With a land area about as large as Kansas City, Mo., the island nation of Malta has only one major resource—its strategic location. It lies at the geographic center of the Mediterranean Sea, about 60 miles south of Sicily.

The socialist government depends on foreign aid to develop industries in an effort to become a "nonaligned" neutral nation.

The government also seeks to expand tourism to exploit Malta's year-round sunny climate and many historic monuments and buildings.

Malta includes two main islands, Malta and Gozo, and the small island of Comino.

EARLY HISTORY

Malta's strategic position has attracted successive waves of invaders. Phoenicians, Greeks, Carthaginians, Romans, Byzantines, and Arabs occupied the islands. In 1090 Malta was seized by the Normans.

In 1530 the Holy Roman emperor Charles V awarded Malta to the Knights of St. John of Jerusalem, who beat off repeated Turkish attacks.

Napoleon seized control in 1798. The Maltese rose against the French and, with the help of Britain, evicted them two years later.

In 1814 Malta became a British colony.

Maltese courage while under siege during World War II was rewarded in 1942, when the George Cross was bestowed on Malta itself—the first time an entire people had been so honored.

INDEPENDENT MALTA

Malta became independent on Sept. 21, 1964. The country was governed from 1964 to 1971 by the conservative Nationalist Party, led by Prime Minister Giorgio Borg Olivier.

In a national election held in June 1971, the Malta Labor Party won by a narrow margin. Its leader, Dom Mintoff, became prime minister.

Malta's house of representatives declared the nation an independent republic in the British Commonwealth of Nations on Dec. 13, 1974. The constitution was amended to restrict political activities of the Roman Catholic Church.

Mintoff's socialist policies narrowly received voter approval in an election on Sept. 18, 1976, when the Labor Party won a majority of 34 seats in the 65-member House of Representatives.

For nearly two centuries Malta's economy had been dependent on jobs and money provided by British military bases located there. But the socialist government refused to renew leases on the bases. On April 1, 1979, the British military presence in Malta ended after 179 years.

Libya promised aid to Malta to make up for the loss of income from Britain.

After receiving aid from Libya for several years, Malta expelled Libyan advisers in August 1980 in a dispute over rights to offshore oil.

Malta and Italy signed an agreement on Sept. 15, 1980, under which Italy promised to protect Malta's neutrality.

China provided foreign aid of about $50 million and a corps of workers in 1980 to build a drydock capable of handling 300,000-ton tankers.

Mintoff's government established diplomatic relations with the Soviet Union in 1981 and agreed to allow the Soviets to use the former British naval base as an oil-storage depot for their ships.

In an election on Dec. 12, 1981, Mintoff's socialist Labor Party narrowly kept control of the house of representatives by 34 seats to 31, even though the opposition Nationalist Party won a majority of votes, 114,132 to 109,990. Nationalist members boycotted sessions of the new house until March 29, 1983, charging that gerrymandering of election districts had robbed them of victory.

Agatha Barbara, 59, former minister of education, was chosen by the house of representatives on Feb. 16, 1982, as the nation's president, the first woman to hold the ceremonial office.

Mintoff pushed through legislation on June 29, 1983, permitting the government to confiscate property of the Roman Catholic Church, the largest landowner in Malta.

MARSHALLS

Official Name: Republic of the Marshall Islands.
Area: 69.84 square miles (181 sq. km.).
Population: 34,401.
Capital: Majuro, 11,898.
Government: Self-governing republic.
President: Amata Kabua (since 1979).
Legislature: *Nitijela,* 33 members.
Flag: Blue field with white star in upper hoist corner; diagonal widening stripes, red over white.

Languages: Marshallese, English.
Main Religion: Christian.
Chief Ethnic Group: Micronesian.
Leading Industries: Fishing; agriculture (coconut palms, fruits, vegetables, poultry, hogs).
Foreign Trade: *major export*—copra; *major imports*—food, consumer goods.

One of the 10 smallest countries in the world both in population and land area, the Marshalls include 34 atolls and 1,225 islands. The land area and population are about equal to those of the city of Palm Springs, Calif.

Major atolls include Kwajalein, 6 sq. mi.; Alinglapalap, 5.7 sq. mi.; Arno, 5 sq. mi.; Jaluit, 4.4 sq. mi.; Majuro, 3.5 sq. mi.; Enewetak, 2.5 sq. mi.; Namu, 2.4 sq. mi.; and Bikini, 2.3 sq. mi.

The Marshalls' economy depends heavily on U.S. payments for use of a $1 billion military base on Kwajelein atoll to test and recover missiles fired 4,200 miles from California.

The Marshalls lie about 2,000 miles southwest of Hawaii. Micronesia is to the west and Kiribati is to the south.

The first European to visit the islands was Spanish explorer Alvaro de Saavedra in the 1520s. British sea captain John Marshall came to the islands in 1788, giving them his name.

Germany established a protectorate in 1886 and bought the islands from Spain in 1899.

During World War I Japanese forces occupied the Marshalls. In 1920 Japan was given a League of Nations mandate over the islands.

In World War II, the U.S. captured the Marshalls in February 1944, killing about 8,000 Japanese troops with a loss of about 300 Americans.

In 1947 the Marshalls became part of the U.S. Trust Territory of the Pacific Islands.

From 1946 to 1958 the U.S. tested 64 nuclear weapons at Bikini and Enewetak atolls, after relocating residents of those islands.

After a massive cleanup of radioactive waste at Bikini and Enewetak, islanders were allowed to return to the two atolls in 1970–80. However, when it was discovered that Bikini still gave off dangerous radiation in 1978, those who had returned to that atoll were again forced to move.

The Marshalls became self-governing in 1979. A constitution was approved in a referendum on March 1, and the 33 members of the first constitutional legislature, the Nitijela, were elected on April 10. The legislature chose Amata Kabua, 50, a tribal chief, as the nation's first president.

President Kabua signed an agreement with the U.S. on Oct. 20, 1982, granting the U.S. military rights to Kwajalein atoll for 30 years in return for economic aid of about $750 million.

Hundreds of Marshall islanders filed court suits in 1981–83 totaling over $4 billion for damages from American nuclear tests in the 1940s to 1960s.

The U.S. agreed on June 25, 1983, to pay residents of the islands $183.7 million over a 15-year period to compensate for the nuclear tests.

In a referendum on Sept. 7, 1983, the Marshall islanders approved by a margin of 4 to 1 the compact of free association with the U.S. The agreement must be ratified by the U.S. Congress and by the United Nations.

MAURITANIA

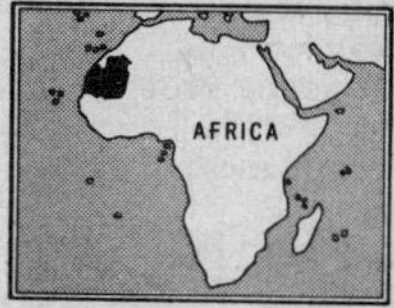

Official Name: Islamic Republic of Mauritania.
Area: 397,955 square miles (1,030,700 sq. km.).
Population: 1,607,030.
Capital: Nouakchott, 134,986.
Government: Military junta.
President: Lt. Col. Mohammed Khouna Ould Haidala (since 1980).
U.S. Ambassador to Mauritania: Edward L. Peck.
Mauritanian Ambassador to U.S.: Abdellah Ould Daddah.
Flag: Gold star and crescent on green field.
Languages: French (official), Arabic.
Ethnic Groups: Arab-Berber (80%), black (20%).
Religion: Islam.
Leading Industries: Agriculture (cattle, sheep, goats, horses, millet, dates, gum arabic, vegetables, fruits); mining (iron ore, copper, gold, salt); fishing.
Foreign Trade: *Major exports*—iron ore, copper, livestock, gum arabic, fish, salt, dates; *major imports*—food, vehicles, petroleum, machinery, textiles.
Places of Interest: Kédia d'Idjit Mountains; iron mines; Nouakchott; Port-Etienne.

MAURITANIA TODAY

Larger than Texas and California combined, Mauritania depends on the export of iron ore and copper for most of the cash income that has enabled it to obtain a few benefits of modern civilization. European companies share profits from the mining operations with the government.

Most Mauritanians live as they have for hundreds of years—the Arabs and Berbers as nomadic herdsmen and the black tribesmen as subsistence farmers and livestock raisers. Few can read and write, and only about 10% of the children attend school.

Most of the country is desert. The Senegal River on the southern border is the only waterway. Mauritania's climate is mostly hot and dry.

MAURITANIA'S HISTORY

In Roman times *Mauretania* was the name of a vast kingdom that included western Algeria, Morocco, and part of what is now Mauritania.

In the 1000s A.D. Berber invasions into the present-day Mauritania area pushed the black African inhabitants southward. The area became the base for holy wars in which the Muslims conquered Morocco, Algeria, Spain, and Ghana.

The French began invading Mauritania in 1904. Mauritania became part of French West Africa in 1920 and was administered from Saint-Louis along with Senegal.

In 1958 it became the self-governing Islamic Republic of Mauritania within the French Community.

Mauritania was granted full independence on Nov. 28, 1960, under President Mokhtar Ould Daddah, who previously had been prime minister. He was reelected to 5-year terms as president in 1966, 1971, and 1976.

QUICK QUIZ: When was the first women's rights convention held in the U.S.? See page 980.

MAURITANIA *(continued)*

Mauritania's 1961 constitution was amended in 1964 to establish a single-party system.

Six years of drought and famine brought the nation to the verge of disaster in 1974.

In November 1974 the government nationalized the iron-mining industry.

Mauritania joined with Morocco in 1976 in partitioning the former Spanish Sahara. Mauritanian troops clashed with those of the Algerian-backed Polisario guerrillas who sought independence for the Western Sahara.

Army Chief of Staff Lt. Col. Mustapha Ould Salek overthrew and imprisoned President Daddah and his cabinet on July 9, 1978.

Prime Minister Ahmed Ould Bousseif and 11 other persons were killed in a plane crash in the Atlantic Ocean off Senegal on May 27, 1979. A week later on June 3, President Salek resigned and was replaced by Lt. Col. Mohammed Mahmoud Ould Luly. Lt. Col. Mohammed Khouna Ould Haidala was appointed prime minister.

A peace agreement was signed with the Polisario guerrillas on Aug. 5, 1979, in which Mauritania gave up its claims to the Western Sahara region. Mauritania also ended its military alliance with Morocco.

Haidala overthrew Luly on Jan. 4, 1980, making himself president.

Although the military junta outlawed slavery in a decree of July 1980, the Anti-Slavery Society of London estimated in 1981 that about 100,000 black Mauritanians remained in slavery to Muslim Moors.

MAURITIUS

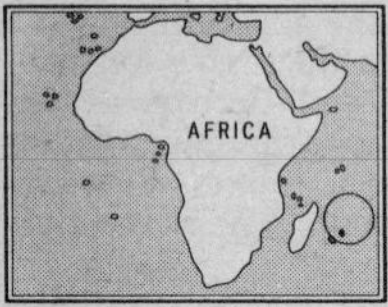

Official Name: Mauritius.
Area: 790 square miles (2,045 sq. km.).
Population: 1,015,440.
Capital: Port-Louis, 144,412.
Government: Parliamentary state.
Prime Minister: Aneerood Jugnauth (since 1982).
Legislative Assembly: 70 members.
Ambassador to U.S.: Chitmansing Jesseransing.
U.S. Ambassador to Mauritius: George Andrews.
Flag: Red, blue, yellow, and green stripes.
Languages: English (official), Creole, Hindi, Urdu, French.
Main Ethnic Groups: Asian Indian descent (67%), Creole (28%), Chinese descent (3%).
Chief Religions: Hinduism (47%), Christianity (34%), Islam (16%).
Leading Industries: Agriculture (sugarcane, rice, tea, tobacco, aloe, potatoes, onions, vegetables, fruits, livestock, poultry); food processing; fishing.
Foreign Trade: *Major exports*—sugar, molasses, tea; *major imports*—rice, wheat, cotton fabrics, petroleum products, fertilizers, machinery, consumer goods.
Places of Interest: Pamplemousses Garden; Nicolière Reservoir; Plaine Champagne; Black River gorges; Grand Bassin Lake; Morne Brabant; Mahebourg Naval Museum; Blue Bay Beach; Belle Mare.

MAURITIUS TODAY

About two-thirds the size of Rhode Island, Mauritius has no important mineral deposits. The economy depends almost entirely on sugar, which accounts for more than 90% of its exports. Tea and molasses are also exported. Tourism is being developed as a source of foreign exchange.

Mauritius was the home of the flightless dodo bird until it became extinct in the 1600s.

An island of volcanic origin, Mauritius lies in the Indian Ocean about 500 miles east of Madagascar. The island of Mauritius itself has an area of 720 square miles. The nation also includes several smaller islands, including Rodriguez (42 sq. mi.), Agalega, and Cargados Carajos. On Mauritius a plain rises toward a central plateau of about 2,200 feet before dropping to the southern and western coasts.

HISTORY OF MAURITIUS

Although Mauritius was probably visited by Arabs, Malays, and Portuguese, the first colonists were the Dutch in 1589. They named the island after their ruler, Prince Maurice of Nassau. A Dutch settlement, established in 1638, was abandoned in 1710.

The French claimed the island in 1713, but it was taken by the British in 1810. It was formally ceded to Britain by the Treaty of Paris in 1814. The island was administered jointly with Seychelles until 1903.

In 1965 the British detached the island of Diego Garcia from Mauritius control and leased it to the U.S. as a military base for intercontinental bombers. The 1,200 residents of the island were relocated to other islands.

Parliamentary elections in 1967 were won by a coalition that included the island's Labor Party and parties representing Muslims and Hindus.

Mauritius was granted full independence as a parliamentary state within the British Commonwealth of Nations on March 12, 1968. It was admitted to UN membership in April 1968.

Sir Seewoosagur Ramgoolam, who had headed the colonial government since 1947 as leader of the Labor Party, became prime minister upon independence in 1968.

As president of the Organization of African Unity (OAU), Prime Minister Ramgoolam helped lead the drive for black majority rule in South Africa, even though South Africa is one of Mauritius' main trading partners.

In a national election on Dec. 20, 1976, the Marxist Militant Mauritian Movement (MMM) party won 34 seats in the 70-member national assembly, but the other parties joined in a coalition that kept Ramgoolam as prime minister.

The Marxist MMM in a landslide election victory on June 12, 1982, ended 35 years of governing by the pro-Western 81-year-old Ramgoolam. The new prime minister, Aneerood Jugnauth, 52, formed a leftist coalition cabinet that included the MMM.

When the MMM withdrew from the cabinet coalition, Jugnauth called new elections on Aug. 21, 1983. He formed a new socialist party and arranged a coalition with two minor parties. Jugnauth's coalition decisively defeated the MMM to win a majority of 41 seats to the MMM's 19.

MEXICO

Official Name: United Mexican States.
Area: 761,605 square miles (1,972,547 sq. km.).
Population: 75,701,800.
Chief Cities: Mexico City, capital, 9,191,295; Netzahualcoyotl, 2,331,151; Guadalajara, 1,906,145; Monterrey, 1,064,629; Puebla de Zaragoza, 710,833; Juárez, 625,040; León, 624,816; Tijuana, 566,344; Acapulco, 462,144; Chihuahua, 385,953; Mexicali, 348,528.
Largest Metropolitan Area: Mexico City, 14,750,182.
Government: Federal republic.
President: Miguel de la Madrid Hurtado (since 1982).
National Congress: *Senate,* 64 members; *Chamber of Deputies,* 400 members.
U.S. Ambassador to Mexico: John Gavin.
Mexican Ambassador to U.S.: Jorge Espinosa de los Reyes.
Flag: Green, white, and red bars; coat of arms in white bar—brown eagle on cactus devouring green serpent (representing Aztec legend), encircled by laurel wreath.
Official Language: Spanish.
Main Ethnic Groups: Mestizo (mixed Spanish-Indian descent), (60%), American Indian (30%).
Religion: Roman Catholicism (97%).
Leading Industries: Trade and services; manufacturing (steel, petroleum products, cement, automobiles, fertilizers, textiles, paper, aluminum, electricity); tourism; agriculture (sugarcane, coffee, cattle, cotton, wheat, rice, maize, fruits, vegetables); mining (petroleum, natural gas, coal, iron ore, copper, manganese, zinc, lead); fishing; construction.
Foreign Trade: *Major exports*—petroleum, cotton, sugar, coffee, shrimp, zinc, lead, copper; *major imports*—food, machinery, consumer goods.
Places of Interest: Mayan archaeological ruins on Yucatán peninsula; Aztec ruins and pyramids near Mexico City; Popocatépetl, Parícutin, Ixtaccíhuatl and Citlaltépetl volcanoes; Sierra Madre mountains; Acapulco; Guadalajara; Oaxaca. *In and near Mexico City:* Cathedral of Zócalo; University of Mexico; national palace; Chapultepec Park; Xochimilco floating gardens; National Museum of Anthropology.

MEXICO TODAY

With huge oil reserves and one of the most stable governments in Latin America, Mexico has hopes of becoming a major industrial nation.

Because one-third of the people still depend on agriculture for their living, Mexico has been a leader in the "green revolution" that encourages farmers to use more productive seed, hybrids, and fertilizers. The government has spent millions of dollars on irrigation projects to reclaim unproductive land. However, many Mexicans still live at a subsistence level. About 1 in 3 cannot read and write.

In an effort to encourage decentralization of manufacturing, the government gives tax reductions to industries locating in rural areas.

Mexico is about one-fourth the size of the U.S., which lies to the north. Guatemala and Belize lie to the south.

The land is dominated by a high central plateau running north and south, enclosed by the mountain ranges of the Sierra Madre. The longest river is the Rio Grande.

Climate ranges from subtropical in the coastal zones to extreme cold in the mountains.

EARLY HISTORY

Indian civilizations developed in Mexico more than 2,000 years ago.

The Maya Indians in the Yucatán peninsula mastered the arts of construction and stonecarving, built cities, developed a calendar, and studied astronomy. The Nahuatl culture, established much later in the central plains, included the Toltecs and the Aztecs.

Mexico came under Spanish rule after conquistador Hernán Cortés landed at Veracruz in 1519 and conquered the highly civilized Aztecs.

INDEPENDENCE

A drive for independence began on Sept. 16, 1810, led by Miguel Hidalgo, a Mexican priest. Independence from Spain was finally achieved in 1821 under the leadership of Agustín de Iturbide and Vicente Guerrero. Iturbide became emperor in 1822, but was deposed in 1823.

Gen. Antonio López de Santa Anna ruled in the 1830s and 1840s. The territory of Texas seceded in 1836 and joined the U.S. in 1844.

STATES OF MEXICO

NAME	AREA (sq. mi.)	CAPITAL	NAME	AREA (sq. mi.)	CAPITAL
Aguascalientes	2,158	Aguascalientes	Morelos	1,908	Cuernavaca
Baja California Norte	27,071	Mexicali	Nayarit	10,665	Tepic
Baja California Sur	28,447	La Paz	Nuevo León	24,925	Monterrey
Campeche	21,666	Campeche	Oaxaca	36,820	Oaxaca
Chiapas	28,528	Tuxtla	Puebla	13,096	Puebla
Chihuahua	95,401	Chihuahua	Querétaro	4,544	Querétaro
Coahuila	58,522	Saltillo	Quintana Roo	16,228	Chetumal
Colima	2,106	Colima	San Luis Potosí	24,266	San Luis Potosí
Durango	46,196	Durango	Sinaloa	22,429	Culiacán
Federal District	579	Mexico City	Sonora	71,403	Hermosillo
Guanajuato	11,810	Guanajuato	Tabasco	9,522	Villahermosa
Guerrero	24,631	Chilpancingo	Tamaulipas	30,822	Ciudad Victoria
Hidalgo	8,103	Pachuca	Tlaxcala	1,511	Tlaxcala
Jalisco	30,941	Guadalajara	Veracruz	28,114	Jalapa
México	8,286	Toluca	Yucatán	16,749	Mérida
Michoacán	23,114	Morelia	Zacatecas	28,973	Zacatecas

QUICK QUIZ: Deaths by what type of cancer have declined by 70% in the past 40 years? See page 449.

MEXICO *(continued)*

After the Mexican War (1846–48), Mexico was forced to cede half its territory to the U.S.

In 1861, during a period of internal disorder, French troops captured the capital and crowned Austrian Archduke Maximilian as emperor. After the French withdrew, the forces of Benito Juárez regained control, and in 1867 Maximilian was executed. Mexico again became a republic.

Gen. Porfirio Díaz seized power in 1876 and ruled as dictator. He was overthrown in 1911 by a liberal revolt led by Francisco Madero.

Liberal factions disputed, and leaders such as Francisco Villa and Emiliano Zapata rose and fell. A violent anticlerical movement persecuted the Roman Catholic Church.

A reform constitution was adopted in 1917. A succession of leaders attempted to bring stability to the political and governmental structure. Most notable of the leaders were Álvaro Obregón and Plutarco Elías Calles.

From 1934 to 1940 the liberal regime of Lázaro Cárdenas instituted widespread reforms.

In 1938 Mexico became the first noncommunist country to nationalize its petroleum industry, taking over all foreign-owned oil companies. Pemex, a government corporation, was established to manage the petroleum holdings.

PRESIDENTS AND RULERS OF MEXICO

YEARS	NAME	PARTY
1821–22	Agustín de Iturbide, president	
1822–23	Agustín de Iturbide, emperor	
1824–28	Gen. Guadalupe Victoria	
1828–29	Vicente Guerrero	C
1829–32	Gen. Anastasio Bustamante	C
1833–36	Gen. Antonio López de Santa Anna	C
1837–41	Gen. Anastasio Bustamante	C
1841–44	Gen. Antonio López de Santa Anna	C
1844–46	José Joaquin Herrera	M
1846	Mariano Paredes	C
1846–47	Gen. Antonio López de Santa Anna	C
1848–51	José Joaquín Herrera	M
1851–53	Mariano Arista	M
1853–55	Gen. Antonio López de Santa Anna	C
1855	Juan Álvarez	L
1855–58	Ignacio Comonfort	L
1858–72	Benito Juárez	L
1864–67	Maximilian, emperor	
1872–76	Sebastián Lerdo de Tejada	L
1876–80	Gen. Porfirio Díaz	L
1880–84	Manuel González	L
1884–1911	Gen. Porfirio Díaz, dictator	
1911–13	Francisco Madero	L
1913–14	Gen. Victoriano Huerta, dictator	
1914–20	Venustiano Carranza	L
1920–24	Álvaro Obregón	L
1924–28	Plutarco Elías Calles	L
1929	Emilio Portes Gil	PNR
1929–32	Pascual Órtiz Rubio	PNR
1932–34	Abelardo Rodríguez	PNR
1934–40	Lázaro Cárdenas	PNR
1940–46	Gen. Manuel Ávila Camacho	PRM
1946–52	Miquel Alemán Valdéz	PRI
1952–58	Adolfo Ruiz Corines	PRI
1958–64	Adolfo López Mateos	PRI
1964–70	Gustavo Díaz Ordaz	PRI
1970–76	Luís Echeverrá Álvarez	PRI
1976–82	José López Portillo	PRI
1982–	Miguel de la Madrid Hurtado	PRI

C = Conservative; M = Moderate; L = Liberal; PNR = National Revolutionary Party; PRM = Party of the Mexican Revolution; PRI = Institutional Revolutionary Party.

POLITICAL STABILITY

Mexican affairs since 1940 have been marked by political stability with the dominance of the Institutional Revolutionary Party (PRI) during the presidency of Gen. Manuel Ávila Camacho (1940–46) and his successors.

Mexico became an oil exporter after major oil finds in the 1970s–1980s.

José López Portillo, 55, who had served as minister of finance, was elected president on July 4, 1976, as the PRI candidate.

President López Portillo declared on Sept. 1, 1979, that Mexico's energy needs were secure for 60 years with proven reserves of oil and natural gas at the equivalent of nearly 46 billion barrels and potential reserves of 200 billion barrels.

In 1982 Mexico became the United States' second-largest supplier of foreign oil at a rate of more than 530,000 barrels a day.

A decline in oil prices and the worldwide recession drove Mexico into a severe economic crisis in 1982. The peso was devaluated twice, reducing its value in U.S. dollars to one-third that at the beginning of 1982.

President López Portillo nationalized the Mexico's banks on Sept. 1, 1982, and at the same time imposed restrictions to prevent pesos from being converted into U.S. dollars. He ordered Mexicans owning an estimated $23 billion in property in the U.S. to sell it immediately and return the money to Mexico. Some $5 billion in American bank accounts in Mexico was converted to pesos.

To aid Mexico in the payment of its debts, the U.S. government in 1982 paid $1 billion in advance on orders for petroleum and granted credits of $1 billion to buy U.S. farm products.

Miguel de la Madrid Hurtado, 47, became president on Dec. 1, 1982, having won election on July 4 as candidate of the ruling party.

De la Madrid adopted austerity economic policies in 1983 that brought some reduction from 1982's annual inflation rate of 100%. Mexico's workers were forced to accept a reduced standard of living as the government allowed wage increases of only 25% in January and 15.6% in July.

Devaluation of the peso brought an influx of bargain-hunting American tourists in 1983. Tourist dollars and strong oil exports gave Mexico a foreign exchange surplus, enabling the government to reschedule payments on its $83 billion foreign debt.

President de la Madrid declared war on corrupt public officials. Centerpiece of his crackdown was the jailing of Jorge Díaz Serrano, charged with enriching himself with $34 million while heading the government oil company, Pemex.

MICRONESIA

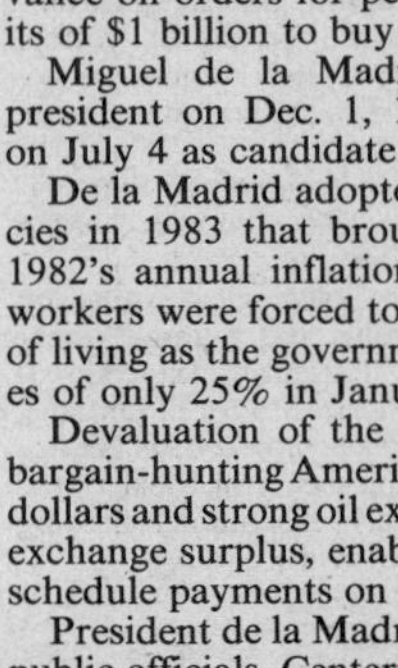

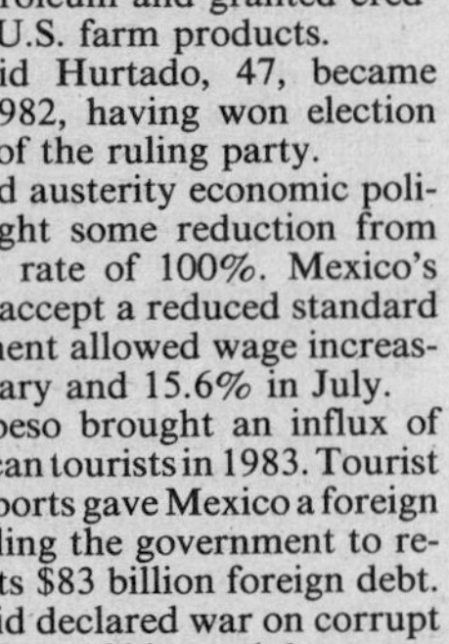

Official Name: Federated States of Micronesia.
Area: 270.79 square miles (701 sq. km.)
Population: 84,840.
Capital: Kolonia, Ponape, 5,550.
Government: Self-governing republic.

President: Tosiwo Nakayama (since 1979).
Congress: 14 members.
Flag: Medium blue field with four white stars arranged in circle in center.
Languages: Micronesian dialects, English.
Chief Ethnic Group: Micronesian.
Main Religion: Christian.
Leading Industries: Fishing; agriculture (coconut palms, fruits, vegetables, poultry, hogs); mining (bauxite, phosphates).
Foreign Trade: *Major exports*—copra, bauxite, phosphates; *major imports*—food, consumer goods.
Places of Interest: Sunken Japanese warships in Truk lagoon; "Venice" ruins of ancient civilization on Ponape.

Although Micronesia covers a vast area of the central Pacific Ocean, its land area is only about as large as the city of Columbus, Ohio. Its population is only one-seventh of that city's.

Micronesia includes some 607 islands and islets. Among its largest islands and atolls are Ponape, 129 sq. mi.; Kosrae, 42.3 sq. mi.; Yap, 38.7 sq. mi.; Truk, 38.6 sq. mi.; and Ulithi, 1.8 sq. mi.

The government is a federation of four states: Yap, Ponape, Kosrae, and Truk.

Many Micronesians lead a traditional way of life, living on tropical fruits, vegetables, and fish. However, the islanders are dependent on aid from the U.S. for modern consumer goods.

The Marshalls lie to the northeast. Guam and the Marianas are to the north. Palau (Belau) is to the southwest.

The islands are believed to have been settled by peoples from Asia about 4,000 years ago. A prehistoric civilization developed on Ponape with cities built on canals like those of Venice.

Spain claimed the islands in the 1500s as part of its Pacific empire, but did not colonize them. Named Carolina after Spain's King Charles II, the group became known for many centuries as the Caroline Islands.

The expanding German empire bought the islands from Spain in 1899, but lost them to Japan during World War I.

Truk and Yap served as important Japanese military bases in World War II. Neutralizing Truk and Yap by air bombardment, the U.S. captured Ulithi atoll on Sept. 23, 1944, and made it a major naval supply base. After the war, the islands became part of the U.S. Trust Territory of the Pacific Islands.

In a referendum on a constitution for the Federated States of Micronesia on July 12, 1978, the Marshalls and Palau voted to separate.

Micronesia became self-governing on May 10, 1979, with the swearing-in of the 14 members of the unicameral legislature. Having been chosen by the legislature, Tosiwo Nakayama of Truk took office as president on May 15.

The U.S. and Micronesia signed a compact of free association on Oct. 1, 1982, in which American aid and grants of about $1 billion over 15 years were promised in return for military rights in specific islands.

In a referendum on June 21, 1983, Micronesian voters approved the compact by 79% to 21%. It must be ratified by the U.S. Congress and the United Nations before it becomes effective.

MONACO

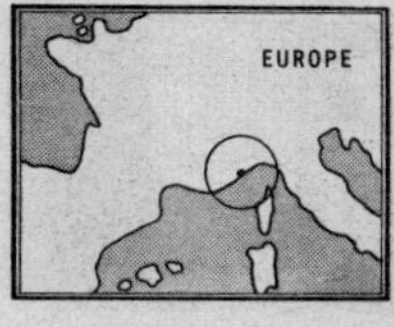

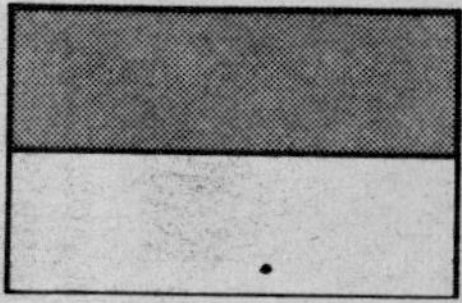

Official Name: Principality of Monaco.
Area: 0.58 square miles (1.49 sq. km.).
Population: 27,610.
Capital: Monaco-Ville, 25,000.
Government: Constitutional principality.
Chief of State: Prince Rainier III (since 1949).
Head of Government: Minister of State André Saint-Mleux (since 1972).
National Council: 18 members.
Flag: Red stripe over white stripe.
Main Ethnic Groups: French (58%), Italian (17%), Monegasque (15%).
Languages: French (official), English, Italian, Monegasque.
Official Religion: Roman Catholicism (95%).
Leading Industries: Tourism and gambling, chemicals, food products, plastics, instruments.
Places of Interest: Royal palace; oceanographic museum; garden; Monte Carlo Casino.

Less than half as large as New York City's Central Park, Monaco is the second-smallest nation in the world after Vatican City. It is surrounded by France except for its coast on the Mediterranean Sea. Tourists provide more than half of Monaco's income, much from the Monte Carlo gambling casino founded in 1863.

Because Monaco has no income tax and no direct corporation tax, many wealthy persons and foreign corporations locate there.

Rocky cliffs overhang sandy beaches of the Riviera coast. Two peninsulas enclose an excellent harbor. Winters are mild, and summer temperatures are moderated by sea breezes.

Monaco was probably settled by Phoenicians. In 1215 the Genoese built a fortified castle on the site of present-day Monaco. In 1297 control passed to the Grimaldi family of Genoa. Monaco was a Spanish protectorate from 1524 to 1641, a French protectorate from 1641 to 1793, and part of France from 1793 to 1814. Following Napoleon's defeat, the Treaty of Vienna (1815) established Monaco as a protectorate of Sardinia. In 1861 France assumed the protectorate.

The last absolute monarch, Prince Albert, reigned from 1889 to 1922. He provided the first constitution in 1911 and signed a treaty in 1918 establishing French protection of Monaco.

Louis II ruled from 1922 until 1949, when he was followed by his grandson Prince Rainier III.

In 1956 Prince Rainier married American movie star Grace Kelly, who died on Sept. 14, 1982, after an auto accident.

Prince Rainier in 1962 announced a new constitution giving women the right to vote and abolishing the death penalty.

In a national election on Jan. 15, 1978, the National and Democratic Union (UND) won all 18 seats in the National Council.

QUICK QUIZ: Is a royalty payment taxable on the U.S. income tax return? See page 914.

MONGOLIA

Official Name: Mongolian People's Republic.
Area: 604,250 square miles (1,565,000 sq. km.).
Population: 1,834,520.
Capital: Ulaanbaatar, 418,700.
Government: One-party communist state.
Chief of State: Yumjaagiyn Tsedenbal, chairman, Presidium of Great People's Khural, and first secretary of Communist Party (since 1952).
Premier: Jambyn Batmonh (since 1974).
Legislature: *People's Great Khural,* 354 members.
Flag: Red, blue, and red bars, with national "soyombo" emblem in gold below five-pointed gold star.
Official Language: Mongolian.
Main Ethnic Groups: Mongolian (90%), Turk (7%).
Religion: Buddhism.
Leading Industries: Agriculture (cattle, horses, sheep, goats, camels, dairy products, wheat, hay, potatoes, vegetables); manufacturing (processing agricultural products); mining (coal, petroleum, copper, molybdenum, gold, fluorspar).
Foreign Trade: *Major exports*—livestock, butter, wool and hair, hides, furs; *major imports*—machinery, petroleum, cloth, building materials.
Places of Interest: Khangai Mountains; Erdeni-Dzuu monastery, ruins of ancient Mongol capital. *In Ulaanbaatar:* government buildings, opera house.

MONGOLIA TODAY

Over twice as large as Texas but with fewer people than live in the Houston metropolitan area, Mongolia is a sparsely populated communist country. Landlocked between the Soviet Union to the north and China to the east, west, and south, Mongolia allies itself with the Soviet Union. Its 1,500-mile border with China's Inner Mongolia is heavily fortified.

Mongolia is a large plateau, with an average elevation of 3,000 to 4,000 feet. In the southeast is the vast Gobi Desert. The climate is generally dry, with cold winters and hot summers.

Forests in the northern mountains, hills, and highland steppes give way gradually to lower steppe grasslands, semidesert country, and barren desert. The principal rivers are the Selenga, Orkhon, and Kerulen.

HISTORY OF MONGOLIA

In the 1200s Genghis Khan established the Mongolian Empire, with its capital at Karakorum. After 1368 Mongolia fell under the rule of China.

The revolution in China in 1911 led to Mongolia's autonomy.

Russian-supported Mongolian communists took over the government in July 1921. The Jebtsun Damba Khutukhtu remained as titular leader until his death in 1924, when the *Mongolian People's Republic* was established. Khorloin Choybalsan (1895–1952) became head of the communist government. Since 1952 Yumjaagiyn Tsedenbal has ruled.

The government ended private ownership of livestock in 1958, establishing collectivized herds and farms.

Mongolia and the Soviet Union agreed to a joint project in 1973 to exploit huge copper and molybdenum deposits northwest of Ulaanbaatar.

Mongolia in 1983 ordered about 8,000 Chinese living in the country either to work on state farms or be expelled, declaring that they were "shirkers." China protested that those being deported were allowed to take nothing with them except the clothes they were wearing.

MOROCCO

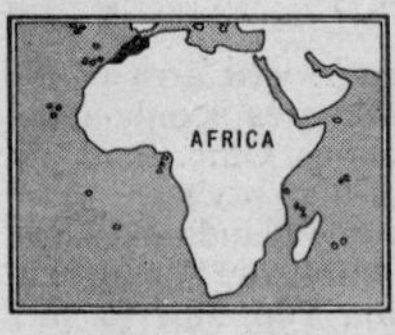

Official Name: Kingdom of Morocco.
Area: 275,117 square miles (712,550 sq. km.).
Population: 22,208,400.
Chief Cities: Rabat, capital, 435,510; Casablanca, 1,371,330; Marrakech, 330,400; Fez, 321,460; Meknès, 244,520, Tangier (Tanger), 185,850.
Largest Metropolitan Area: Casablanca, 1,753,400.
Government: Constitutional monarchy.
King: Hassan II (reigned since 1961).
Prime Minister: Muhammad Karim Lamrani (since 1983).
Parliament: 264 members.
U.S. Ambassador to Morocco: Joseph Verner Reed Jr.
Moroccan Ambassador to U.S.: Ali Bengelloun.
Flag: Red field with green five-pointed star.
Languages: Arabic (official), Berber dialects, French, Spanish.
Main Ethnic Groups: Arab, Berber, black.
Official Religion: Islam (98%).
Leading Industries: Agriculture (poultry, goats, cattle, citrus fruits, olives, raisins, barley, wheat, corn, potatoes, grapes, vegetables); forestry and lumbering; mining (phosphates, manganese, cobalt, iron ore, lead, zinc, petroleum); fishing; tourism; manufacturing (food processing, textiles, leather, cement, wine, paint).
Foreign Trade: *Major exports*—phosphates, fruits, tomatoes, preserved fish, manganese; *major imports*—machinery, fuels, food, consumer goods.
Places of Interest: Tombs of the Merinides princes and 1,000-year-old university in Fez; Bahia Palace and tombs of the Saadians in Marrakech; the Casbah in Tangier; Mohammed V Mausoleum in Rabat; Casablanca.

MOROCCO TODAY

Almost as large as Texas, Morocco has a wide variety of mineral resources, but only phosphates and manganese are mined and exported in large quantities. These two minerals account for over half of the country's exports. Otherwise, Morocco depends on tourism and agriculture as the mainstays of its economy. Government planning calls for improved tourist facilities, new irrigation projects, and training of more skilled workers.

The country prospered in the 1970s–80s because of high demand and high prices for phosphates for fertilizer.

But most Moroccans are poor, and only 1 in 4 can read and write. Many still wear the traditional costume of a long hooded robe called a *djellaba* and pointed slippers called *babouche.* Many of the women wear veils.

Algeria lies to the east, the Mediterranean Sea to the north, the Atlantic Ocean to the west, and Mauritania to the south.

Two small Spanish overseas provinces are in Morocco: Ceuta, on the northernmost tip, and Melilla, on the northeastern coast.

The northern coastal plain along the Mediterranean Sea includes the Rif Mountains, rising to 7,000 feet above sea level.

The Atlas Mountains, with peaks as high as 13,600 feet, extend in three parallel ranges from the Atlantic coast in the southwest to Algeria and the Mediterranean Sea in the northeast.

In the south and east semiarid steppes stretch into the Sahara Desert.

Rain (about 40 inches annually) and mountain snow make northwestern Morocco the best-watered country of North Africa.

The U.S. and Morocco have had a treaty of peace and friendship since 1787—the longest unbroken treaty relationship in American history.

HISTORY OF MOROCCO

Phoenician settlements existed at Melilla, Tangier, and Larache from 1100 B.C. The Romans formed northeast Morocco into the province of Mauritania Tingitana.

Arab conquest in the 600s A.D. introduced the religion of Islam. From 1064 to 1269 two great dynasties, the Almoravides and the Almohades, united Morocco and, at times, ruled all North Africa and most of Spain.

In the early 1500s Spain and Portugal took nearly all of Morocco's ports.

From the mid-1880s France, Spain, Britain, Italy, and Germany competed for influence in Morocco. In 1912 Morocco signed the Treaty of Fez, becoming a French protectorate, with Spain administering some areas.

Abdelkrim al-Khattabi, a Rif Berber chief, led a war of resistance from 1921 to 1926.

After World War II Sultan Sidi Mohammed led a nationalist movement.

Morocco was granted independence by France on March 2, 1956, with Sidi Mohammed as King Mohammed V. In 1961 he was succeeded by his son King Hassan II.

The 579-square-mile Spanish colony of Ifni on the Atlantic coast was ceded to Morocco by Spain in 1969.

A new constitution, proposed by the king and reducing his absolute power, was confirmed by a popular referendum in March 1972.

An attempt to shoot down a plane carrying the king failed in 1972. The head of the plot, Gen. Mohammed Oufkir, killed himself.

In April 1974 Morocco nationalized foreign-owned oil companies. That same year, Hassan began a campaign to force Spain to give up its overseas provinces of Ceuta and Melilla and Spanish Sahara to Morocco.

King Hassan organized a march of 350,000 unarmed Moroccans into the phosphate-rich Spanish Sahara on Nov. 6, 1975, but withdrew at the urging of the UN Security Council. On Nov. 14 Spain agreed to give up the Sahara colony. Morocco and Mauritania sent in troops and civilian officials in December.

Spain withdrew its troops from the Western Sahara, formally turning it over to Morocco and Mauritania on Feb. 26, 1976. On the following day the Saharan nationalists, called the Polisario Front, declared independence as the *Sahara Arab Democratic Republic.*

Morocco and Mauritania broke relations with Algeria on March 7, 1976. They agreed on April 14, 1976, to partition the 102,703-square-mile area. Morocco annexed the northern two-thirds and Mauritania the southern third.

On June 3, 1977, in the first freely contested national election in 14 years, independent candidates supporting King Hassan won a majority of seats in the 264-member parliament.

The U.S. gave up its last military base on Sept. 30, 1978, turning over to the Moroccan government its communications facilities at Kenitra.

After Mauritania signed a peace agreement with the Polisario guerrillas and withdrew its claims to the Western Sahara in August 1979, Morocco announced it had taken over the southern part of the region, making it the nation's 37th province. Fighting continued in 1979–83 with the Polisario guerrillas, who are supplied by Algeria and Libya.

A severe drought in 1980–82 caused a 25% drop in agricultural production.

The U.S. and Morocco signed an agreement on May 27, 1982, giving American planes the right to use the nation's air bases in an emergency. U.S. military aid to Morocco was increased from $30 to $100 million in 1983.

Morocco's 5-year plan for 1981–85 placed emphasis on energy production with $766 million to develop the nation's huge oil shale reserves and construct the first of several electric power stations fueled by oil shale.

MOZAMBIQUE

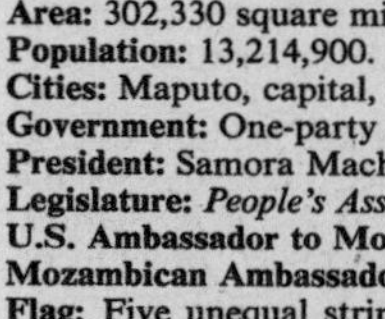

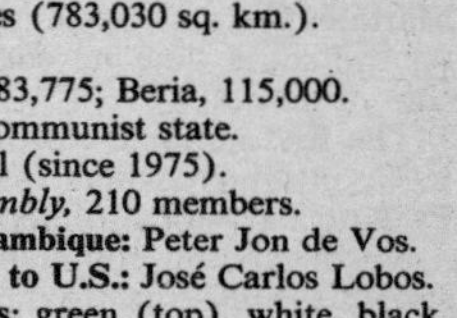

Official Name: People's Republic of Mozambique.
Area: 302,330 square miles (783,030 sq. km.).
Population: 13,214,900.
Cities: Maputo, capital, 383,775; Beria, 115,000.
Government: One-party communist state.
President: Samora Machel (since 1975).
Legislature: *People's Assembly,* 210 members.
U.S. Ambassador to Mozambique: Peter Jon de Vos.
Mozambican Ambassador to U.S.: José Carlos Lobos.
Flag: Five unequal stripes: green (top), white, black, white, and yellow; red triangle at hoist with yellow star with book, hoe, and rifle representing motto, "Study, Produce, Struggle."
Languages: Portuguese (official), tribal.
Main Ethnic Group: Black.
Religions: Animism (65%), Christianity (22%), Islam (11%).

QUICK QUIZ: A U.S. adult passport is valid for how many years? See page 958.

MOZAMBIQUE *(continued)*

Leading Industries: Agriculture (cashew nuts, cotton, sugarcane, sisal, tea, corn, sweet potatoes, peanuts, millet, manioc, palm kernels, fruits, vegetables); manufacturing (processing agricultural products, glass, paint, automobile assembly, cement, furniture); mining (coal, iron, tantalite, fluorite).

Foreign Trade: *Major exports*—cashews, cotton, sugar, tea, copra; *major imports*—machinery, textiles, vehicles, petroleum, steel.

Places of Interest: Maputo; Cabora Bassa dam on Zambesi River.

MOZAMBIQUE TODAY

Almost twice as large as California, Mozambique is a communist-ruled African nation.

The former Portuguese colony has substantial mineral resources, but the development of mining has been hindered by poor transportation.

Most of the people are poor African tribesmen who raise barely enough food to live. No more than 1 in 10 can read and write.

Although the government opposes South Africa's racial policies, it depends for most of its foreign exchange on revenues from transshipment of South African exports and money sent home by 60,000 Mozambican workers in South Africa.

The lowland climate is hot, with a rainy season from November to March.

HISTORY OF MOZAMBIQUE

Vasco da Gama visited Mozambique en route to India in 1498. Portuguese trading posts were established in the 1500s. At the end of World War I part of German East Africa was added to the colony. In 1952 the colony was made part of Portugal as an overseas province.

African nationalists began waging guerrilla war in 1964. Some 70,000 Portuguese troops fought against the guerrillas for a decade. The communist-supported nationalist group, Frelimo, operated out of headquarters in Tanzania.

After a military coup overthrew the government of Portugal, Mozambique was granted a provisional government on Sept. 20, 1974.

The huge Cabora Bassa hydroelectric dam on the Zambesi River was completed on Dec. 5, 1974. Its 3,600-megawatt capacity was planned to aid the nation's future industrial development.

Full independence was achieved on June 25, 1975, with the head of Frelimo, Samora Machel, 41, becoming the country's first president. Machel called for development of a Marxist state.

President Machel gave the capital Laurenço Marques the new name Maputo on Feb. 3, 1976. At the same time he ended the private ownership of homes.

The first national election was held on Dec. 4, 1977, in which voters ratified the choice of the Frelimo Party of 210 members of the legislature.

South African commandos raided Maputo on Jan. 30, 1981, destroying the headquarters of anti-South African guerrillas.

In March 1981 Mozambique expelled four American diplomats on charges of espionage.

Guerrillas supported by South African arms stepped up attacks in 1982–83 that were designed to disrupt railroads and hurt the economy.

Government officials reported in November 1983 that 700,000 or more persons were starving because of a prolonged drought.

NAMIBIA

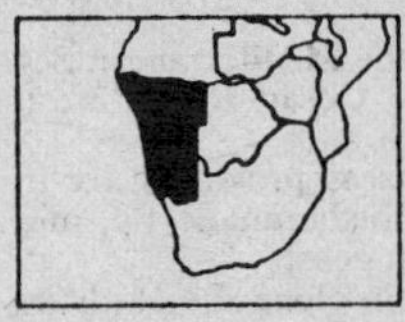

Area: 318,261 square miles (824,292 sq. km.).

Population: 1,094,290.

Capital: Windhoek, 61,369.

Government: Rule by South Africa.

Flag: Prior to independence, flag of South Africa with horizontal orange, white, and blue stripes; in center of white band are miniature reproductions of British Union Jack and flags of Orange Free State and Transvaal Republic.

Main Languages: Afrikaans, English, German.

Ethnic groups: Black (88%), white (12%).

Principal Religion: Lutheran.

Leading Industries: Agriculture (corn, millet, sorghum, livestock); mining (diamonds, copper, lead, zinc, uranium); manufacturing (food processing, textiles, clothing, ore smelting); fishing.

Foreign Trade: *Major exports*—diamonds, copper, lead, zinc, uranium, fish, cattle, karakul fur pelts; *major imports*—construction materials, fertilizer, grain, food, consumer goods.

Places of Interest: Game reserve at Etosha; karakul sheep ranches; Walvis Bay; government buildings in Windhoek; prehistoric cave paintings.

NAMIBIA TODAY

About as large as Texas and Louisiana combined, Namibia has been a center of international controversy and guerrilla warfare for more than a decade as the United Nations has sought to free it from control by South Africa.

Most Namibians live as members of tribal groups that follow ancient customs. Few can read and write.

Walvis Bay on the Atlantic coast is the country's main port. Nearly 1,500 miles of rail lines connect the port to mining and ranching areas.

As one of the world's leading diamond-mining countries, Namibia depends on diamond exports for nearly a third of its gross national product. Another third comes from the wages of Namibians who work in South Africa and send home their pay for the support of their families.

The climate is hot and dry with annual rainfall averaging only 2 inches along the coast and increasing to 22 inches inland. Walvis Bay has an average temperature of 74 °F. in its warmest month, February, and 57 ° F. during August.

Namibia is bordered on the north by Angola and Zambia, on the east by Botswana, and on the southeast and south by South Africa.

EARLY HISTORY

The earliest people to live in Namibia are believed to have been the Bushmen. Beautifully colored paintings dating from prehistoric Stone Age times decorate many caves in Namibia.

Although the coastal region was explored by the Portuguese in the late 1400s, the inhospitable desert climate and warlike tribes discouraged exploration of the interior until the 1800s.

Britain annexed Walvis Bay in 1878 and

incorporated it as part of the Cape of Good Hope Colony in 1884.

A German merchant, F.A.W. Lüderitz, purchased much of the coastal area from Hottentot tribes in the early 1800s. He placed the region, then known as *South West Africa,* under protection of the German empire in 1884. Diamonds were discovered on the southwest coast in 1908.

During World War I, South African troops invaded the region, forcing the Germans to surrender in July 1915.

South Africa remained in control of the country, receiving a League of Nations mandate for South West Africa on Dec. 17, 1920.

UNITED NATIONS–SOUTH AFRICAN DISPUTE

After World War II and the demise of the League of Nations, South Africa proposed to the United Nations in 1946 a plan to annex South West Africa. The UN rejected this proposal, insisting that South Africa submit to a trusteeship for the region.

The UN General Assembly adopted a resolution on Oct. 27, 1966, stating that South Africa had forfeited its mandatory rights. Two years later the General Assembly resolved that South West Africa would thenceforth be known as Namibia. South Africa refused to accept either resolution. In 1971 the World Court handed down an advisory opinion that South Africa had no jurisdiction over South West Africa and should withdraw its administration. South Africa rejected this opinion.

Black nationalists of the Ovambo tribes formed the South West Africa Peoples Organization (SWAPO), which has fought guerrilla warfare for the independence of Namibia since 1966. SWAPO is recognized by the UN as the authoritative representative of the Namibian people.

A constitutional conference with delegates from all ethnic groups in Namibia met in Windhoek in 1975–77 to draft a plan for a government.

On Jan. 31, 1976, the UN Security Council unanimously approved a resolution calling for UN-supervised elections in Namibia.

The UN General Assembly approved a resolution in December 1976 endorsing an "armed struggle" by blacks to win independence.

Namibians voted on Dec. 4–8, 1978, in the first multi-racial elections to choose members of an assembly to draw up a constitution. Boycotted by several political parties including SWAPO, the election was won by the South African-backed Democratic Turnhalle Alliance (DTA) that captured 41 of the 50 assembly seats. The UN refused to recognize the validity of the election.

In May 1979 the assembly was converted into a 65-man national legislature with the appointment of 15 additional delegates. In 1983 South Africa dissolved the assembly and resumed direct rule.

Throughout 1979–83 discussions were held between South African leaders and representatives of the UN in an effort to reach agreement on an acceptable plan to enable Namibia to become independent. South Africa insists it will not give independence to Namibia until Cuban troops are withdrawn from neighboring Angola.

NAURU

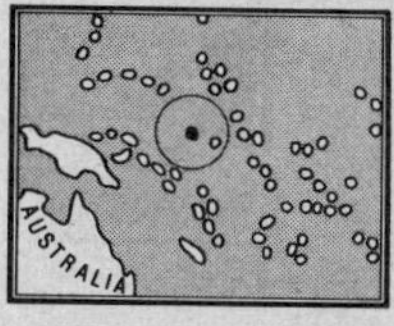

Official Name: Republic of Nauru.
Area: 8 square miles (21 sq. km.).
Population: 8,154.
Capital: Yaren.
Government: Parliamentary republic.
President: Hammer DeRoburt (since 1978).
Parliament: 18 members.
U.S. Ambassador to Nauru: Robert Dean Nesen.
Nauruan Ambassador to U.S.: T. W. Star.
Flag: Blue field halved by horizontal gold stripe, white star at lower hoist corner.
Languages: English and Nauruan.
Main Ethnic Groups: Nauruan (50%), Gilbert and Ellice islanders (27%), Chinese (16%).
Religion: Christianity.
Leading Industry: Mining (phosphates).
Foreign Trade: *Major export*—phosphates; *major imports*—food, water, consumer goods.
Places of Interest: Phosphate mines.

NAURU TODAY

The world's smallest republic, Nauru covers an area smaller than that of Sioux Falls, S.D. The island nation lies in the Pacific Ocean 2,200 miles northeast of Sydney, Australia.

The revenue from Nauru's extensive phosphate deposits has given Nauruans one of the highest per capita incomes in the world.

The people pay no taxes. The government subsidizes all imports, making food available at a nominal cost. Everyone can read and write.

To ensure Nauru's continued prosperity when the phosphate deposits run out, a substantial fund estimated at $1 billion has been established to cover long-term investments and development.

A coral reef surrounds the island and fringes a sandy beach. Beyond the island's narrow coastal belt, a coral cliff rises 100 feet above sea level.

HISTORY OF NAURU

The first European to discover Nauru was British sea captain John Fearn in 1798.

In 1888 the island was annexed by Germany, and in 1914 it was occupied by Australia.

After World War I Nauru became a mandate under Australian administration.

Japanese forces occupied Nauru in 1942–45.

In 1947 Australia placed Nauru under the UN trusteeship system.

The nation became independent on Jan. 31, 1968. Hammer DeRoburt, head chief since 1956, was chosen as its first president.

The phosphate mines were nationalized in 1970 with $20 million paid to the British owners.

Britain's Queen Elizabeth visited Nauru on Oct. 21, 1982, the first time a British monarch ever had come to the smallest member of the British Commonwealth of Nations.

QUICK QUIZ: Can you name the world's largest passenger ship? See page 957.

NEPAL

Official Name: Kingdom of Nepal.
Area: 54,362 square miles (140,797 sq. km.).
Population: 16,286,500.
Chief Cities: Kathmandu, capital, 150,402.
Government: Constitutional monarchy.
King: Birendra Bir Bikram Shah Dev (since 1972).
Prime Minister: Lokandra Chand (since 1983).
Parliament: *National Panchayat,* 135 members.
U.S. Ambassador to Nepal: Carleton S. Coon Jr.
Nepalese Ambassador to U.S.: Bhekh Bahadur Thapa.
Flag: Red bordered in blue with white moon in upper triangle and white sun below.
Languages: Nepali (official), Newari, 11 others.
Ethnic Groups: Brahman, Chetris, Gurung, Magyar, Tamang, Newar, Bhotia, Rais, Limbu, Sherpa.
Official Religion: Hinduism (90%).
Leading Industries: Agriculture (cattle, rice, corn, millet, wheat, tea, barley, opium poppies, jute, pepper, tobacco); tourism; forestry and lumbering; food processing; mining (copper, iron, mica, zinc, cobalt); manufacturing (burlap bags, textiles).
Foreign Trade: *Major exports*—farm products, timber; *major imports*—clothing, food, consumer goods.
Places of Interest: Durbar Square, Temple of Teleja, and other temples in Kathmandu; Swayambhunath Buddha; Tiger Tops resort in King Mahendra National Park; Mount Everest National Park; Langtang National Park.

About the size of Arkansas, Nepal is one of the least developed and most isolated nations in the world.

Most Nepalese are poor farmers who cannot read and write. Their average life is 42 years.

The Himalaya mountains on the northern border with China include Mt. Everest, the world's highest peak (29,028 feet).

At Kathmandu the average temperature is 86° F. in May and 35° F. in December.

The Shah dynasty of Gurkha has ruled Nepal since the 1700s. Wars with Tibet and China (1791–92) and with British India (1814–16) set its present boundaries. The Gurkha rulers were reduced to figureheads in 1847 by the Ranas, who governed as hereditary prime ministers.

In 1951 a rebellion led to the overthrow of the Rana regime. King Tribhuvan became an absolute monarch. He was followed in 1955 by King Mahendra, who died in 1972. Mahendra was succeeded by his son Birendra, whose formal coronation as king was held on Feb. 24, 1975.

In a national referendum on May 2, 1980, a majority voted to retain a partyless governmental system rather than adopt multiparty democracy.

In a national election in 1981 a new 135-member parliament was chosen. Prime Minister Surya Bahadur Thapa, who had served since 1972, continued as head of the government.

A no-confidence vote of 108–17 in parliament forced Thapa to resign on July 11, 1983. Lokandra Chand, 49, former speaker of parliament, succeeded him as prime minister on the following day.

NETHERLANDS

Official Name: Kingdom of the Netherlands.
Area: 15,770 square miles (40,844 sq. km.).
Population: 14,403,000.
Chief Cities: Amsterdam, capital, 717,748; The Hague ('s Gravenhage), seat of government, 457,564; Rotterdam, 580,791; Utrecht, 236,545.
Largest Metropolitan Area: Rotterdam, 1,016,170.
Government: Parliamentary democracy.
Queen: Beatrix (since 1980).
Prime Minister: Ruud Lubbers (since 1982).
Legislature: *First Chamber,* 75 members; *Second Chamber,* 150 members.
U.S. Ambassador to Netherlands: L. Paul Brenner III.
Netherlands Ambassador to U.S.: Jan Hendrik Lubbers.
Flag: Red, white, and blue stripes.
Official Language: Dutch.
Main Ethnic Group: Dutch (of Germanic origin).
Chief Religions: Protestantism (41%), Roman Catholicism (40%).
Leading Industries: Trade and services; manufacturing (steel, chemicals, food processing, textiles, clothing, printing, furniture, diamond cutting, leather products, electricity, ceramics); agriculture (cattle, hogs, sheep, poultry, wheat, sugar beets, potatoes, oats, flowers, vegetables); mining (natural gas, petroleum); fishing; shipping; tourism.
Foreign Trade: *Major exports*—food, machinery, chemicals, textiles, petroleum products, consumer goods, flower bulbs; *major imports*—automobiles, corn, coal, lumber, petroleum, metal ores.
Places of Interest: The Hague; Soestdijk Royal Palace near Baarn; villages around Lake Ijssel; cheese centers of Gouda and Edam; Utrecht; Rotterdam. *In Amsterdam:* Anne Frank House; botanical gardens; Artis Zoological Gardens; Rembrandt's home; Rijks Museum; monuments.

NETHERLANDS TODAY

About twice the size of New Jersey, the Netherlands is a prosperous European nation that continues to increase its area by building dikes and pumping out seawater to reclaim land covered by the Zuider Zee.

For many years the Netherlands controlled a colonial empire that stretched around the world. But today that empire has dwindled to one overseas province, the Netherlands Antilles in the Caribbean Sea (see page 618).

With a long tradition of democratic government, the Netherlands has been a leading proponent of unifying Europe. It has urged its larger neighbors to give up their nationalism and accept a democratic European parliament.

The Netherlands' most important resource is natural gas. Its Groningen natural-gas field is one of the largest energy sources in Europe, and makes the country the third most important producer of natural gas in the world.

The land is generally low and flat, with the exception of a few rolling hills along the southeastern border.

At least 25% of the country's area lies below sea level and must be protected by dikes. Irrigation is provided by an extensive system of canals.

The climate is moderate, with few extremes. Summer temperatures rarely exceed 75° F., but winters are damp and cold.

Dutch flowers, particularly tulips and hyacinths, are world renowned.

The Netherlands is bordered on the east by West Germany and on the south by Belgium.

EARLY HISTORY

The Batavi, the Frisii, and other Germanic and Celtic tribes first settled the marshy Rhine and Meuse delta areas of the Low Countries. Julius Caesar conquered the region about 55 B.C. The Romans developed the canals and dikes.

The area became part of Charlemagne's empire in the 700s. Following collapse of the empire, principalities in Holland and Utrecht and the cities of Amsterdam, Haarlem, and Groningen rose to importance during the Middle Ages.

The dukes of Burgundy extended control over the area in the 1300s and 1400s. In 1515 Karl V of the House of Hapsburg inherited the Burgundian lands. He abdicated in 1555 in favor of his son King Felipe II of Spain. Felipe's suppression of religious, political, and economic freedoms was met with fierce resistance.

INDEPENDENT NETHERLANDS REPUBLIC

In 1568 the Netherlands' 80-year war of liberation broke out. It was led by Willem the Silent, prince of Orange. Under his leadership the seven northern provinces united in 1581 as the *Republic of the United Netherlands.* They continued the fight even after the southern provinces gave in to Spanish rule. The struggle was not resolved until the Treaty of Westphalia (1648), ending the Thirty Years War, recognized the Netherlands Republic as independent from Spain.

By the end of the 1600s the Netherlands had become the world's greatest maritime and commercial power, with colonies in Asia and the Americas. During the 1700s colonial rivalry with England, France, and Spain resulted in the loss of colonies and a decline in power. The Netherlands aided the American colonists with loans in the Revolutionary War (1775–83).

In 1795 French troops invaded and founded the Republic of Batavia, which in 1806 became the Napoleonic Kingdom of Holland.

KINGDOM OF THE NETHERLANDS

After Napoleon's defeat in 1815, the Congress of Vienna restored the nation's independence as the *Kingdom of the United Netherlands,* comprising the Netherlands and what is now Belgium, under Willem I of the House of Orange.

During the reign of Willem I (1813–40) the country again became a maritime and commercial power. In 1830 the Belgians revolted and formed a separate kingdom.

Reforms under Willem II (1840–48) and Willem III (1849–90) led to internal prosperity.

The Netherlands remained neutral until World War II, when the country was overrun by German troops. After enduring ruthless suppression by the Nazis, the country was liberated in 1945.

Queen Wilhelmina, after 58 years of rule, abdicated in 1948 to her daughter Juliana.

After four years of periodic fighting and negotiations, Indonesia was granted independence in 1949. The Dutch were forced to give up Netherlands New Guinea to Indonesia in 1962.

Thousands of persons immigrated to the Netherlands from Surinam in 1974–75 before that former South American colony was granted its independence on Nov. 25, 1975.

The government began construction in 1976 on a $1.5 billion, 5.6-mile dam across the Eastern Scheldt estuary. To be completed by 1985, the dam will have openings to admit small ships and to preserve marine ecology.

In the late 1970s the economy developed what was called the "Dutch disease." Income from the nation's huge gas reserves was spent to expand social welfare benefits instead of developing industry. Dutch products became uncompetitive and unemployment rose.

In a national election on May 25, 1977, Prime Minister Joop den Uyl's socialist Labor Party won a plurality of 53 seats. The Christian Democrats won 49 and the Liberals 28.

After months of haggling, a new center-right coalition government was formed on Dec. 19, 1977, with Andreas A.M. van Agt, head of the Christian Democratic Party, as prime minister.

NETHERLANDS IN THE 1980s

Having reigned since 1948, the 71-year-old Juliana abdicated on April 30, 1980. Her 42-year-old daughter Beatrix became queen.

In national elections on May 26, 1981, no party won a parliamentary majority, but conservative Christian Democrats achieved a plurality of 48 seats. The Labor Party was second with 44.

During the next year van Agt remained head of the government, but repeatedly was forced to form new cabinets because of disharmony among the political parties.

Queen Beatrix visited the U.S. in April 1982 to celebrate 200 years of close friendship between the U.S. and the Netherlands, which helped finance the American Revolution.

In a general election on Sept. 8, 1982, the socialist Labor Party opposed the deployment of 48 U.S. cruise missiles in the Netherlands and demanded that the government provide jobs for the nation's 550,000 unemployed. The conservative Christian Democratic Party favored the deployment of the missiles and called for cuts in welfare and unemployment benefits to curb government spending. The Labor Party gained a plurality of 47 seats in the lower house of parliament, the conservative Christian Democrats held onto 45, and the Liberals were third with 36. While politicians maneuvered to establish a majority coalition, van Agt, 51, resigned on Oct. 13, 1982, saying, "I have used up much of my vitality."

Ruud Lubbers, 43, a millionaire economist and new head of the conservative Christian Democrats, became the youngest prime minister in the nation's history on Nov. 5, 1982, forming a coalition cabinet with the Liberal Party. He promised heavy cuts in government spending.

QUICK QUIZ: Where will the 1988 summer Olympic Games be held? See page 836.

NETHERLANDS ANTILLES

Area: 371 square miles (961 sq. km.).
Population: 249,240.
Capital: Willemstad, Curaçao, 149,091.
Main Islands: Curaçao (173 sq. mi.), Bonaire (95 sq. mi.), Aruba (69 sq. mi.), St. Maarten (southern half of St. Martin, 17 sq. mi.), St. Eustatius (21 sq. mi.), Saba (5 sq. mi.).

The last remnant of the Dutch empire, these Caribbean islands divide into two groups. The Windward Islands (Curaçao, Aruba, and Bonaire) lie about 15 to 40 miles off the northwestern coast of Venezuela. The Leeward Islands (St. Maarten [part of St. Martin Island, shared with Guadeloupe], Saba, and St. Eustatius) are about 220 miles east of Puerto Rico.

The Windward Islands are volcanic-based, partly coral, semiarid, and covered with desert-like vegetation. The smaller Leeward Islands are hilly and fertile. The Antilles' temperature ranges between 77° and 87° F.

About 85% of the people are mestizo, a mixture of black, Indian, Spanish, and Dutch ancestry. Most are Christians. The people speak Dutch (official), Papiamento, and English.

Aruba and Curaçao, with some of the world's largest oil refineries, have a prosperous economy based largely on the petroleum industry.

The Antilles' year-round warm climate and unique blend of Dutch, African, and Spanish cultures draw large numbers of tourists, providing a major source of revenue.

Aruba is noted for its many miles of fine swimming beaches and Curaçao for its shops filled with imported goods. Washington National Park on Bonaire is a bird sanctuary with many flamingos. Scuba divers enjoy exploring the coral reefs off Bonaire.

After oil refining and tourism, the mining of phosphates provides the largest share of the islands' income. The Netherlands Antilles has one of the higher per capita incomes in the Caribbean.

Curaçao, the largest island in the Antilles, was discovered in 1499 by the explorers Alonso de Ojeda and Amerigo Vespucci.

Along with Aruba and Bonaire, Curaçao was captured by the Dutch in 1634, and Peter Stuyvesant became Curaçao's first governor. Britain occupied Curaçao during the Napoleonic wars, but it was restored to the Netherlands in 1816.

Curaçao was the center of the Dutch slave trade in the Caribbean area until the government freed slaves in 1863.

The Netherlands Antilles became a coequal part of the Kingdom of the Netherlands in December 1954. The Netherlands Antilles is divided into four territories: Aruba, Bonaire, Curaçao, and the Windward Islands. Each has its own elected council that governs local affairs.

A 21-member unicameral legislature enacts laws for the entire Netherlands Antilles.

Racial rioting in 1969 severly hurt the islands' tourism industry, which did not recover until the late 1970's.

The people of Aruba voted in March 1977 in favor of independence from the Netherlands Antilles. However, the Dutch government refused. Discussion continued in 1979–83 about eventual independence for the Antilles.

NEW ZEALAND

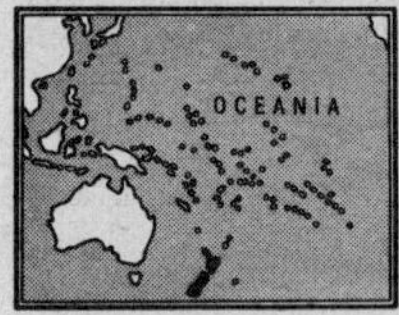

Official Name: Dominion of New Zealand.
Area: 103,736 square miles (268,675 sq. km.).
Population: 3,202,330.
Chief Cities: Wellington, capital, 137,600; Christchurch, 171,300; Auckland, 147,600; Manukau, 143,500.
Largest Metropolitan Areas: Auckland, 750,600.
Government: Parliamentary democracy.
Prime Minister: Robert D. Muldoon (since 1975).
Chief of State: Queen Elizabeth II, represented by Governor-General Sir Denis Blundell (since 1976).
House of Representatives: 92 members.
U.S. Ambassador to New Zealand: H. Monroe Browne.
Ambassador to U.S.: Lancelot R. Adams-Schneider.
Flag: Blue field with British Union Jack at upper hoist corner; four red stars outlined in white represent Southern Cross constellation.
Languages: English (official), Maori.
Ethnic Groups: European (92%), Maori (8%).
Main Religions: Anglicanism (34%), Presbyterianism (22%), Roman Catholicism (15%), Methodism (7%).
Leading Industries: Trade and services; manufacturing (food processing, machinery, clothing, furniture, cement, fertilizers); agriculture (sheep, cattle, dairy products, wheat, barley, oats, corn, fruits, vegetables); forestry and lumbering; fishing; mining (gold, coal, petroleum, natural gas); tourism.
Foreign Trade: *Major exports*—wool, lamb and mutton, butter; *major imports*—automobiles, petroleum and petroleum products, cotton fabrics, agricultural machinery.
Places of Interest: Tongariro and Egmont national parks; Franz Josef and Fox glaciers; Milford Sound fjords; Hanmer (thermal) Springs resort; Glowworm Grotto at Waitomo; Mt. Cook ski resort.

NEW ZEALAND TODAY

About the size of Colorado, New Zealand is a mountainous island nation some 1,200 miles southeast of Australia. Most of its people are of British descent, and they preserve British traditions. New Zealand also administers several island dependencies (see next page).

Despite expansion of the nation's manufacturing industry, agricultural products account for 95% of New Zealand's exports.

New Zealand has one of the most comprehensive social-welfare programs of any nation, including old-age pensions, free hospital care for everyone, and compensation for all accidents, no matter what their cause.

Most New Zealanders take a summer vacation from mid-December to mid-January.

The nation includes two principal islands, North Island (44,035 sq. mi.) and South Island (58,305 sq. mi.), separated by Cook Strait. Other islands are Steward Island, off the southern tip of South Island, and the Chatham Islands, about 500 miles east of South Island.

The Southern Alps run the length of South Island and contain several glaciers. The highest of these mountains is 12,349-foot Mt. Cook.

The majority of people live in the narrow coastlands in the eastern part of North Island. This island has many active volcanoes, including 9,175-foot Mt. Ruapehu.

The climate ranges from year-round warm temperatures at the northern tip of North Island to cold winters in August on South Island.

EARLY HISTORY

The race of Polynesians called Maoris came to New Zealand from Southeast Asia at least as early as 1350. When the Dutch explorer Abel J. Tasman discovered the islands in 1642, the unfriendly Maoris prevented him from landing. In 1769 Capt. James Cook of England visited the islands, and in the 1790s several small English whaling settlements were established. In the early 1800s whaling, sealing, and a little primitive agriculture were the only activities carried on by the few settlers, some of whom were navy deserters and escaped convicts from Australia.

In 1840 the New Zealand Company organized the first large migration to the islands and established a settlement at Wellington. In that year the Maoris granted sovereignty over New Zealand to the British crown. In 1845–48 and 1860–70 Maori uprisings were suppressed by military force.

The first real stimulus to New Zealand's settlement was the discovery of gold on South Island in 1861. Development of an export trade in butter and meat, primarily to Britain, was accelerated by refrigerated ships after 1882.

Parliamentary democracy was well established by 1890. New Zealand became a self-governing dominion on Sept. 26, 1907.

INDEPENDENT NEW ZEALAND

In 1947 New Zealand was the last dominion to ratify the 1931 Statute of Westminster, granting independence to members of the British Commonwealth.

The conservative National Party headed the government for 12 years from 1960 to 1972, winning elections in 1960, 1963, 1966, and 1969.

In national elections held on Nov. 25, 1972, the Labour Party won a surprise victory, and its leader, Norman Eric Kirk, became prime minister. Previously, the Labour Party had governed New Zealand in 1935–49 and 1957–60. Kirk died of a heart attack in 1974, and Wallace Rowling, 46, became prime minister.

New Zealand placed new restrictions on immigration in 1974 to limit newcomers to 12,000 to 15,000 persons a year.

Discovery of a large offshore gas field in 1975 promised to reduce New Zealand's dependency on imported oil in the 1980s.

In elections on Nov. 29, 1975, the National Party defeated Labour. Its leader, Robert D. Muldoon, became prime minister.

Muldoon's party won a national election on Nov. 25, 1978, but with a reduced majority of 49 seats to the opposition's 43.

The government expelled the Soviet Union's ambassador on Jan. 25, 1980, on charges of contributing a large sum of money to the New Zealand Communist Party.

A national election on Nov. 28, 1981, further reduced Muldoon's party to 47 seats.

An anti-American bill sponsored by the Labour Party to ban nuclear weapons from New Zealand was defeated by Muldoon by a single vote on April 29, 1982, just three weeks before the visit of a U.S. nuclear submarine.

In an effort to reduce the 15% inflation rate in 1982, the government froze wages and prices. To combat unemployment, income taxes were cut drastically for middle-income taxpayers.

NEW ZEALAND DEPENDENCIES

COOK ISLANDS

Area: 90 square miles (234 sq. km.).
Population: 17,606.
Capital: Avarua, on Rarotonga.

The Cook Islands in the South Pacific divide into two groups.

The seven Northern Group islands are low-lying, sparsely populated, scattered coral atolls.

The fertile islands in the Lower Group are more heavily populated. Rarotonga, the largest Cook island, is volcanic. Citrus fruits and juices, copra, and tomatoes are the leading exports.

Some of the islands were discovered in 1773 by Capt. James Cook, others by John Williams 50 years later. They became a British protectorate in 1888 and were annexed to New Zealand in 1901. The islands' constitution, adopted in 1965, provides for full internal self-government in association with New Zealand.

A monthly ship and a weekly airplane carry passengers, freight, and mail between New Zealand and Rarotonga. A $22 million jet airport was completed at Rarotonga in 1974 to encourage increased tourism.

NIUE

Area: 100 square miles (259 sq. km.).
Population: 3,267.
Capital: Tufukla.

Niue, part of the Cook group but separately administered since 1903, lies in the Pacific 580 miles northwest of Rarotonga. The people are Polynesian and speak Samoan. Niue became self-governing in 1974 with a prime minister and a 14-member elected assembly. The soil is fertile.

ROSS DEPENDENCY

Area: 160,000 square miles (414,398 sq. km.).

This region includes the Antarctic continent between longitude 160° E. and 150° W. and the islands south of latitude 60° S. New Zealand took jurisdiction in 1923. The region includes a whaling center and a research station.

TOKELAU

Area: 4 square miles (10 sq. km.).
Population: 1,548.

The islands, consisting of three atolls, lie about 300 miles north of Western Samoa and are administered from there. Once part of the Gilbert and Ellice Islands colony, they became a New Zealand territory in 1925. The people are Polynesian. Copra is the islands' principal export.

QUICK QUIZ: How many civilians are employed by the Department of Defense? See page 969.

NICARAGUA

Area: 50,193 square miles (130,000 sq. km.).
Population: 2,863,000.
Capital: Managua, 608,020.
Government: Martial law by junta.
Nicaraguan Ambassador to U.S.: Jose Antonio Jarquin Toledo.
U.S. Ambassador: Anthony Cecil Eden Quainton.
Flag: Blue, white, and blue stripes, with coat of arms on white stripe.
Languages: Spanish (official), English, Indian dialects.
Ethnic Groups: Mestizo (70%), European descent (17%), black (9%), Indian (4%).
Religion: Roman Catholicism (95%).
Leading Industries: Trade and services; agriculture (coffee, cotton, sugarcane, cattle, bananas, corn, tobacco, rice, beans, fruits, vegetables); mining (gold, silver, gypsum); fishing; manufacturing (food processing, textiles, clothing, footwear, tobacco products).
Foreign Trade: *Major exports*—cotton, meat, coffee, sugar, sesame, cottonseed; *major imports*—insecticides, motor vehicles, pharmaceuticals, iron and steel, petroleum, machinery.
Places of Interest: Lake Nicaragua; Mt. Momotombo and other volcanoes; earthquake ruins and rebuilding in Managua; Granada; León Cathedral; Pacific beach resorts; Great Corn Island in the Caribbean.

NICARAGUA TODAY

About the size of Iowa, Nicaragua is a poverty-stricken Central American country torn by civil war and natural disasters.

Although the nation has substantial natural resources and hydroelectric potential, these have remained largely undeveloped.

More than half of Nicaragua's fertile land remains covered by tropical forests.

Most of the people are poor. Only about half can read and write.

The nation's population, principal cities, and major industries are largely concentrated in a narrow, fertile, volcanic belt between Lakes Nicaragua and Managua and the Pacific Ocean.

The climate is warm and humid, with an average annual temperature of 81° F.

Honduras lies to the north and Costa Rica to the south.

HISTORY

Discovered by Christopher Columbus in 1502, Nicaragua was explored in 1522 and 1523 by the Spanish conquistadores Gil González Dávila and Francisco Hernández de Córdoba. The latter founded Granada and León.

Nicaragua was ruled by the captaincy-general of Guatemala until it declared independence from Spain on Sept. 15, 1821. Nicaragua belonged to the United Provinces of Central America from 1823 until it became an independent republic in 1838.

William Walker, an American military adventurer, led an expeditionary army to Nicaragua making himself president in 1856. He was expelled in 1857 and was executed in 1860 in Honduras.

Internal chaos led to the stationing of U.S. Marines in Nicaragua in 1912–25 and 1927–33.

In the 1920s and early 1930s the U.S. occupation was fought by guerrillas led by Augusto César Sandino, who was assassinated in 1934.

Gen. Anastasio Somoza seized the presidency in 1936. He ruled as dictator until his assassination in 1956. Two sons continued his dictatorship: Luis Somoza, president in 1956–63, and Anastasio Somoza Debayle, president in 1967–79.

A revolutionary movement called the Sandinistas (after the guerrilla martyr Sandino) fought the Somozas from 1962. But the Somozas merely became more powerful, amassing a fortune estimated at $900 million.

On Aug. 22, 1978, guerrillas led by Edén Pastora Gómez, known as "Commander Zero," stormed the national palace in Managua. They held the nation's congress hostage for two days until Somoza paid $500,000 ransom and freed 83 political prisoners.

The Sandinistas began a major offensive from Costa Rica on May 29, 1979, that carried them to victory. Somoza fled into exile on July 17. A 5-member Sandinista military junta took control of the government on July 20.

The civil war was estimated to have cost 50,000 lives and $1.3 billion in property damage.

The revolutionary junta expropriated the property of Somoza and his associates, which included about 30% of Nicaragua's farmland, and distributed it to landless peasants directly or as cooperatives. About 5,000 of Somoza's supporters were jailed and many were executed. Elections were promised by 1985.

The Reagan administration suspended economic aid to Nicaragua in January 1981 because of evidence the junta was aiding left-wing guerrillas in El Salvador.

The U.S. CIA began training and arming guerrilla groups that mounted border attacks from Honduras.

The nation's economy degenerated with inflation at a rate of about 50% and unemployment about 20%. On Sept. 10, 1981, the junta declared a state of economic emergency, outlawing strikes and freezing prices.

When conservative businessmen complained in October 1981 that the junta was turning the nation into a communist state, the government threw opposition leaders in prison and shut down opposition newspapers.

Despite opposition by the U.S., Nicaragua was elected 104–50 to a seat on the UN Security Council for 1983–84.

The former Sandinista leader Pastora announced on April 15, 1982, that because of the procommunist slant of the ruling junta he would lead a new guerrilla movement to overthrow it.

Attacks on oil storage depots by U.S.-trained guerrillas in 1983 forced the government to impose strict rationing on private use of gasoline.

In October 1983 the government offered to sign non-aggression treaties with the U.S. that would end Nicaraguan aid to guerrillas in El Salvador if the U.S. would agree to end military training of forces in Honduras and El Salvador.

NIGER

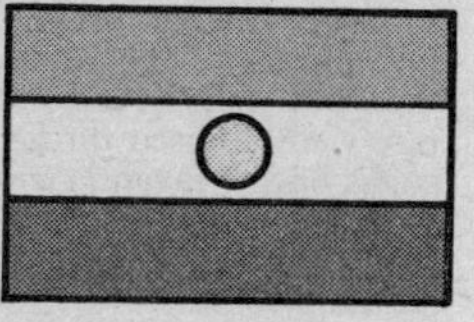

Official Name: Republic of Niger.
Area: 489,191 square miles (1,267,000 sq. km.).
Population: 6,089,720.
Capital: Niamey, 130,299.
Government: Military junta.
Chief of State and Head of Government: Lt. Col. Seyni Kountché (seized power in 1974).
Supreme Military Council: 12 members.
U.S. Ambassador to Niger: William R. Casey Jr.
Niger Ambassador to U.S.: Joseph Diatta.
Flag: Orange, white, and green stripes, with centered orange disk—the sun.
Languages: French (official), Hausa, Djerma.
Main Ethnic Groups: Hausa (50%), Djerma (23%), Fulani (15%), Tuareg (10%).
Chief Religion: Islam (85%).
Leading Industries: Mining (uranium, tin, coal, iron, phosphate); agriculture (peanuts, cotton, cattle, sorghum).
Foreign Trade: *Major exports*—uranium, peanuts, cotton, meat, hides; *major imports*—petroleum, machinery, food, consumer goods.
Places of Interest: Lake Chad; native villages.

NIGER TODAY

Although larger than Texas and California combined, Niger is a poor, landlocked African nation. The northern four-fifths of Niger is covered by the wasteland of the Sahara Desert. The climate is hot, dry, and dusty.

Most of the people are desert nomads or farmers who raise only enough food to support their families. Only about 1 in 20 can read and write. Children under 15 make up almost half the population.

Formerly a French colony, Niger maintains close relationship with France, which is its main trading partner.

High-grade uranium ore is the nation's main export. Niger also has large deposits of iron ore and phosphates, but exploitation of these important minerals is handicapped by the nation's poor transportation system. There is no railroad to the nearest port—1,000 miles away on the Atlantic coast. And there are few hard-surfaced roads for use by trucks. Consequently, much freight has to be flown in and out of the country.

Niger encourages development of the country's resources by foreign investors and does not require government participation in such projects.

Niger's main political problems result from internal antagonisms—between Arab-Berber nomads and black farmers, between Djerma-Songhai and Hausa ethnic groups, and between traditional conservatives and Western-educated young radicals.

The most fertile cropland is in the southwestern part of Niger in the 300-mile-long valley of the Niger River.

Algeria and Libya lie to the north, Chad to the east, Nigeria and Benin to the south, and Mali and Upper Volta to the west.

EARLY HISTORY OF NIGER

From the 600s until the late 1800s, portions of Niger successively belonged to the Songhai, Hausa, and Fulani empires. In the 1600s Tuareg tribes formed confederations in the north.

European explorers who first reached Niger in the 1800s found a state of chronic warfare and anarchy. French penetration began in the 1890s with the establishment of military posts along the Niger River. Through conquest and treaties with local sultans and Britain, most of the country's present boundaries were set by 1914.

In 1922 Niger became a French colony under civil administration in the French West Africa federation. Niger became autonomous in 1958.

INDEPENDENCE

France granted Niger full independence on Aug. 3, 1960. Hamani Diori was elected president in 1960 and was reelected in 1965 and 1970. He banned political parties other than his own Parti Progressiste Nigérien (PPN).

Uranium was discovered in 1955 and began to be mined in 1971, stimulating the nation's economy.

On April 15, 1974, Lt. Col. Seyni Kountché, chief of staff of Niger's 2,500-man army, overthrew Diori. He charged that Diori had failed to deal with the "catastrophic situation" of Niger's many years of drought.

In August 1975 Kountché arrested his chief aide, Vice President Sani Souna Sido, on charges of plotting against him.

Oil and phosphate deposits were discovered in 1975, but their extent remained to be determined.

In February 1976 the government made an emergency appeal to other nations for 200,000 tons of food to save 1.2 million of its people from starving. The problem was caused by the continuing drought that caused crop failures in 1974–75 and 1975–76. The government also asked for $2.7 million in economic aid to fight rats that attacked the nation's scanty remaining food supplies.

Loyal troops put down an attempt to overthrow Kountché's government on March 15, 1976. The leader of the revolt, Capt. Sidi Mohamed, and nine others were sentenced to death.

The government's 5-year plan for 1979–83 emphasized agricultural development, exploitation of mineral resources, and improvement of education and health services.

To reduce petroleum imports, Niger put into operation in 1981 a combined coal mine and 18-megawatt coal-fired electric power plant to supply electricity to uranium mines and towns in the north-central region. The plant, using coal from a large deposit found in 1971, was expected to save 25% of the nation's petroleum needs. The coal deposit was believed to contain 5 million to 15 million tons.

Although climbing uranium-ore exports made the gross national product of Niger grow at an annual rate of 10% during the late 1970s, falling uranium prices caused the nation's economy to stagnate in the 1980s.

QUICK QUIZ: Which U.S. state became the first to legalize use of marijuana? See page 879.

NIGERIA

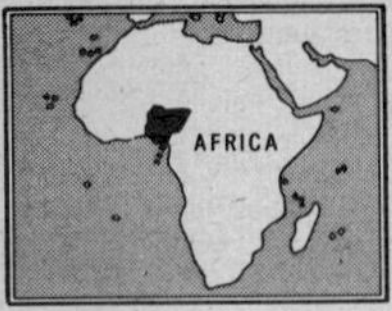

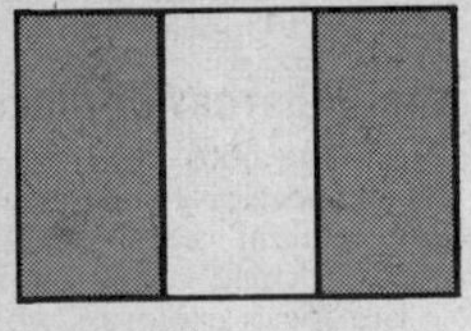

Official Name: Federal Republic of Nigeria.
Area: 356,669 square miles (923,768 sq. km.).
Population: 86,528,100.
Chief Cities: Abuja, capital, 50,000; Lagos, 1,060,848; Ibadan, 847,000; Ogbomosho, 432,000; Kano, 399,000.
Largest Metropolitan Area: Lagos, 1,476,837.
Government: Multiparty democratic republic.
President: Alhaji Shehu Shagari (since 1979).
Congress: *Senate,* 96 members; *House of Representatives,* 450.
U.S. Ambassador to Nigeria: Thomas R. Pickering.
Ambassador to U.S.: Chief Abudu Yesufu Eke.
Flag: Bars of green, white, and green.
Languages: English (official), tribal dialects.
Chief Ethnic Groups: Hausa (21%), Yoruba (20%), Ibo (17%), Fulani (8%).
Main Religions: Islam (47%), Christianity (34%), animism (19%).
Leading Industries: Mining (petroleum, natural gas, tin, coal, iron ore); agriculture (peanuts, cattle, cotton, palm kernels, cocoa, rubber, bananas, corn, yams, rice, fruits, vegetables); manufacturing (food processing, cement, petroleum products, textiles, tobacco products, consumer goods).
Foreign Trade: *Major exports*—crude petroleum, cacao, peanuts and oil, tin, palm nuts and oil, rubber, cotton; *major imports*—food, iron and steel, textiles, automobiles.
Places of Interest: Museum of Nigerian antiquities in Lagos; Muslim city of Kano; Ibadan; Benin.

NIGERIA TODAY

Nigeria is the world's richest, most heavily populated, black nation. A federation of 19 states, it is somewhat larger than Texas and Oklahoma combined. It is one of the world's 10 leading producers of petroleum, forestry products, natural rubber, and tin.

Using its oil wealth to build needed facilities of all kinds, the government has placed emphasis on improving the educational system to reduce illiteracy and enable more Nigerians to find jobs as skilled workers and managers. Additional money was spent in building and improving roads to open up interior regions.

The government also has invested large sums to create a "green revolution" to improve the country's agriculture. However, most Nigerians continue to live as subsistence farmers.

Nigeria has about 250 tribes, each with its own language. Three groups are dominant: Hausa-Fulani in the north, Yoruba in the west, and Ibo in the east.

Benin lies to the west, Niger to the north, Lake Chad to the northeast, and Cameroon to the east.

EARLY HISTORY OF NIGERIA

Nigeria's earliest known culture, Nok, flourished in 500 B.C. Later, migrants from the northeast founded the Yoruba and Edo kingdoms of Oyo and Benin and the spiritual center of Ife.

Sub-Saharan states were founded in the 600s to 700s A.D. by the Zaghawa nomads, thought to be of Berber origin. These states were the forerunners of the Kanem empire established in the 700s. Islamic traditions of the Kanem empire were diffused through the seven Hausa city-states on the savanna fringes of the Sahara.

In the 1400s and 1500s the Portuguese and then the British engaged in slave trading on the Atlantic coast.

The Hausa city-states were conquered in the early 1800s in the Islamic crusade of the Fulani warrior Usman dan Fodio.

Slavery ended after 1861 when Britain annexed Lagos as a colony.

In 1883 the Niger Coast Protectorate was declared, and in 1885 the Berlin Conference recognized Britain's claim to southern Nigeria. British troops captured the Muslim stronghold at Kano in 1903. The British created the unified colony and protectorate of Nigeria in 1914.

A nationalist movement after World War I received strong support from Ibo leaders. In 1954 Nigeria became a federation of three autonomous regions, later increased to four.

INDEPENDENCE

Nigeria was granted full independence on Oct. 1, 1960, with a constitution providing for a federal parliamentary democracy.

Through 1965 an uneasy political balance was maintained by a coalition in the federal government between the northern Hausa-Fulani and the eastern Ibo. The Yoruba of the west formed the opposition.

On Jan. 15, 1966, the Nigerian national government was ousted by a military coup attributed to young Ibo officers. The federal prime minister, Sir Abubakr Tafawa Balewa, and the premiers of the western and northern regions were among those murdered. Army Chief of Staff Maj. Gen. Johnson Aguiyi-Ironsi, an Ibo, became chief of state.

Ironsi dissolved the federation and established a unitary republic in May 1966, triggering anti-Ibo riots in the north.

A new military coup on July 29, 1966, killed Ironsi and brought to power Lt. Col. Yakubu Gowon, a northern Christian from a non-Hausa minority group. Some 30,000 Ibo were massacred, and over 1 million were driven from the north.

On May 30, 1967, the young Ibo leader Col. Odumegwu Ojukwu proclaimed the independence of the Republic of Biafra (the 29,484-square-mile former Eastern Region). Biafra's secession was resisted by federal troops who invaded Biafra on July 6, 1967. In the next 30 months tens of thousands died in battles and of starvation. On Jan. 15, 1970, Biafran leaders surrendered.

MILITARY RULE IN THE 1970s

Nigeria took over thousands of foreign-owned businesses in March 1974, as the government forbade foreign ownership of 55 kinds ranging from dry-cleaning shops to publishing houses.

The six years of drought that ended in 1974 hurt Nigeria's economy despite increased revenue from petroleum and gas.

Brig. Gen. Murtala Muhammed ousted Gowon in a bloodless coup on July 29, 1975.

On Feb. 13, 1976, Gen. Muhammed was killed in an unsuccessful coup.

Lt. Gen. Olusegun Obasanjo, commander of the army, succeeded Muhammed as head of state.

Thirty-seven persons were executed in 1976 for implication in Muhammed's assassination.

MULTIPARTY DEMOCRACY

The first nationwide elections in over 11 years were held on Aug. 31, 1977, to choose members for an assembly to write a new constitution.

U.S. President Carter toured Nigeria on March 31–April 3, 1978—the first visit by an American chief executive.

The constituent assembly presented the nation's new constitution to Obasanjo on Aug. 29, 1978. It provided for a government with a strong president elected for a 4-year term and a bicameral national congress.

Obasanjo ended the 12-year state of emergency on Sept. 21, 1978, lifting a ban on political activities in preparation for national elections.

The military government nationalized British petroleum interests in Nigeria on July 31, 1979.

In a series of elections in July and August 1979, Nigerians elected a president, members of a national congress, 19 state governors, and state legislators. Alhaji Shehu Shagari, 54, winner of the presidential election, took office on Oct. 1, 1979.

In 1980 President Shagari visited the United States to appeal for aid in improving Nigeria's farm production. His government planned a five-year $13.5 billion program to achieve food self-sufficiency.

Some 5,000 to 7,000 were killed in northern Nigeria in December 1980 in battles between the army and a fanatic Muslim sect led by Alhaji Mohammadu Marwa. He was killed in the fighting and hundreds of his followers were imprisoned. When Nigeria celebrated its 22d anniversary of independence on Oct. 1, 1982, amnesty was granted the jailed Muslim fanatics. Less than a month later they caused new riots in which 452 persons, including many police, were killed.

The government in 1982 began moving its departments from Lagos to the new capital city Abuja built in the interior at a cost of $1.3 billion. All the government ministries and institutions are scheduled to be in Abuja by 1987. Government plans for Abuja call for it to cost $15 billion and have a population of 1.6 million by the year 2000.

Nigeria's booming economy slackened in 1982 as the worldwide oil glut reduced petroleum exports. The lower oil revenues forced the government to cut back on many of its development projects.

Because of worsening economic conditions, the government in January and February 1983 expelled about 1.2 million illegal aliens who had come to Nigeria from Ghana and other West African countries. The exodus was one of the largest forced migrations in modern history.

In elections from Aug. 6 to Sept. 3, 1983, Shagari won reelection to a second four-year term and his National Party of Nigeria (NPN) took substantial majorities in both houses of parliament.

NORWAY

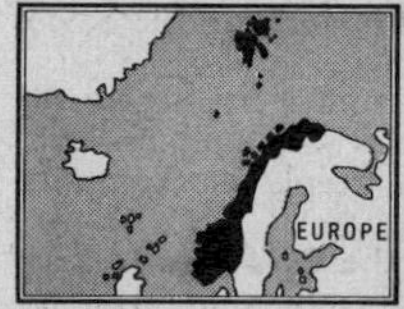

Official Name: Kingdom of Norway.
Area: 125,182 square miles (324,219 sq. km.).
Population: 4,131,750.
Chief Cities: Oslo, capital, 456,132; Bergen, 210,100; Trondheim, 134,705.
Largest Metropolitan Area: Oslo, 645,413.
Government: Constitutional monarchy.
Prime Minister: Kaare Willoch (since 1981).
King: Olav V (reigned since 1957).
Legislature: *Storting,* 155 members.
U.S. Ambassador to Norway: Mark Evans Austad.
Norwegian Ambassador to U.S.: Knut Hedemann.
Flag: Blue Latin cross bordered in white on red field.
Language: Norwegian (Bokmal and Nynorsk dialects).
Principal Ethnic Group: Norwegian.
State Religion: Lutheranism (96%).
Leading Industries: Manufacturing (aluminum, paper, chemicals, ships, furniture); trade and shipping; services; construction; mining (petroleum, natural gas, iron ore, lead, zinc, copper, molybdenum); agriculture (cattle, sheep, goats, dairy products, barley, potatoes, fruits, vegetables); fishing; forestry and lumbering.
Foreign Trade: *Major exports*—petroleum, gas, manufactured goods, shipping services, aluminum, fish, paper, pulp; *major imports*—machinery, ships, food.
Places of Interest: North Cape and "land of the midnight sun"; fjord country; old Bergen; Nidaros Cathedral at Trondheim; Stavanger Cathedral; Mai- haugen museum at Lillehammer. *In Oslo:* Akershus Castle; Vigeland sculptures, Frogner Park; museums.

NORWAY TODAY

Somewhat larger than New Mexico, Norway is an important industrial and trading nation of northern Europe. Production from huge offshore deposits of oil and gas has brought Norway increased prosperity.

Since the time of the Vikings, Norwegians have been seafarers. Norway has the world's third-largest merchant fleet, and, until surpassed by oil exports, income from shipping was Norway's largest source of foreign exchange.

Norway has experienced tremendous economic expansion, especially in mining, shipbuilding, and manufacturing industries. Growth has enabled mining and manufacturing to surpass in importance the country's traditional industries of agriculture, forestry, and fishing, bringing the Norwegian people a high standard of living.

Wealth from its offshore oil and gas fields has enabled Norway to cut income taxes, while at the same time increasing social benefits. The government placed restrictions on the production of petroleum and gas to ensure a steady income for many years into the future.

To protect its well-paid labor force from an influx of cheap labor, Norway severely limits most immigration.

Norway occupies the western and northern-

QUICK QUIZ: The U.S. had how many airports in 1983? See page 950.

NORWAY *(continued)*

most part of the Scandinavian peninsula. Sweden lies to the east and south. Finland and the Soviet Union are to the northeast.

About one-third of the country lies within the Arctic Circle. The terrain is mountainous, and the 1,700-mile coastline is deeply marked with fjords, bays, and inlets.

The warming waters of the Gulf Stream keep Norway's climate comparatively mild. The far north is the land of the midnight sun with continuous daylight from mid-May to the last of July. From late November to the end of January the sun does not rise above the horizon.

EARLY HISTORY

Hunters and fishermen lived in Norway at least 8,000 years ago. Fortified settlements began to be built about A.D. 400.

The Viking Age in which Norwegian seafarers raided and plundered along the coasts of Europe began about 900. Much of Norway was united for the first time in 900–940 by King Harold Fairhair (Harold I). Christianity was introduced by Olav I (995–1000). Olav II was killed by a peasant army in 1030, and Norway then passed under the rule of Canute the Great of England and Denmark.

The latter half of the 1100s was a period of warfare among contenders for the Norwegian throne. In the 1200's Haakon IV acquired Iceland, Greenland, the Faeroe Islands, the Shetlands, and the Orkneys.

The royal male line died out with Haakon V in 1319, so Norway entered into union with Sweden under Magnus V. Queen Margrethe I of Denmark united the three Scandinavian kingdoms in the Union of Kalmar (1397), which lasted until Sweden broke away in 1523. Union between Norway and Denmark continued until 1814, when Denmark ceded Norway to Sweden.

INDEPENDENT KINGDOM OF NORWAY

On June 7, 1905, the Norwegian parliament declared the union with Sweden dissolved. Norway became an independent kingdom under Haakon VII, a Danish prince.

Norway was neutral in World War I and sought neutrality in World War II. However, Germany invaded in April 1940, occupying the country until 1945. A puppet government was established under Vidkun Quisling, whose name became a synonym for traitor.

Olav V became king in 1957 upon the death of Haakon VII.

Odvar Nordli, head of the Labor Party, became prime minister on Jan. 12, 1976.

Norway set a 200-mile fishing and economic zone along its coast on Jan. 1, 1977, closing much of the North Sea to foreign fishermen.

Nordli's government won another four years in office in a national election on Sept. 11–12, 1977.

The government agreed in September 1980 to stockpile large amounts of military equipment and arms for use by U.S. Marines who would be flown in by airlift in the event of a war with the Soviet Union, but continued not to permit NATO troops to be stationed in Norway.

Nordli resigned because of illness on Jan. 30, 1981. He was succeeded by the nation's first woman prime minister, Gro Harlem Brundtage, 41, a physician.

In a national election on Sept. 13–14, 1981, voters ousted the socialist Labor Party, giving a majority of parliamentary seats to a coalition of conservative parties.

Economist Kaare Willoch, head of the Conservative Party, became prime minister on Oct. 13, 1981, leading the nation's first right-wing government in 12 years. He promised to cut taxes and reduce social-welfare spending.

Dependent on oil exports for 25% of its foreign exchange, Norway's economy stagnated in 1981–83 because of lower petroleum prices.

NORWEGIAN OVERSEAS AREAS

SVALBARD

Area: 23,957 square miles (62,004 sq. km.).
Population: 3,705.

Svalbard, some 400 miles north of Norway, is a barren archipelago with an Arctic climate and rich coal deposits. West Spitsbergen is the largest island. The islands first were found by Norwegians in the 1100s. The Dutch rediscovered them in 1596. From the 1600s rival claims were made by the Dutch, British, and Norwegians. In 1920 Norway's sovereignty was recognized. Svalbard officially became part of Norway in 1925.

JAN MAYEN: Island (144 sq. mi.) 300 miles north of Iceland; annexed in 1929.

BOUVET ISLAND: Uninhabited South Atlantic island (23 sq. mi.); became a dependency in 1930.

PETER I ISLAND: Uninhabited Antarctic island (96 sq. mi.); became a dependency in 1933.

QUEEN MAUD LAND: Part of Antarctic continent; claimed by Norway in 1939.

OMAN

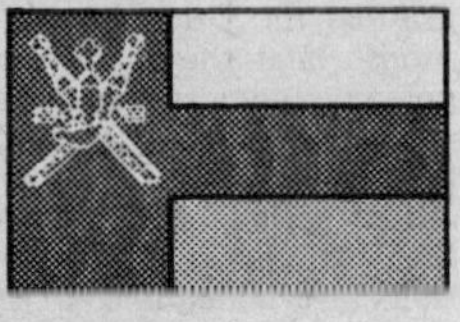

Official Name: Sultanate of Oman.
Area: 82,030 square miles (212,457 sq. km.).
Population: 992,631.
Cities: Muscat, capital, 10,000; Matrah, 70,000.
Government: Absolute monarchy.
Sultan: Qaboos Bin Said (reigned since 1970).
U.S. Ambassador to Oman: John Countryman.
Omani Ambassador to U.S.: Ali Salim Bader Al-Hinai.
Flag: Red bar with crossed white swords next to staff; white, red, and green stripes.
Official Language: Arabic.
Chief Ethnic Groups: Arab, Iranian, Baluchi.
Main Religion: Islam.
Leading Industries: Mining (petroleum, copper); construction; agriculture (dates, livestock, pomegranates, coconuts, grains, fruits, vegetables); oil refining; fishing; food processing.
Foreign Trade: *Major exports*—petroleum, dates, pomegranates, limes, fish, hides; *major imports*—food, cotton goods, rice, coffee, tea, motor vehicles, construction materials.
Places of Interest: Royal palace; ancient forts.

OMAN TODAY

About the size of Kansas, Oman is an oil-rich Arab sultanate on the Arabian Sea.

Oman has used much of its oil income of more than $2 billion a year to educate its children, to provide free outdoor color television sets for each community, to build a lavish new palace for the sultan, and to equip its army. Airports, highways, and sewerage systems have been constructed.

Because about three-fourths of the people depend on farming for their living, the government stimulated agriculture by importing new breeds of livestock and constructing model farms.

The country generally has a hot desert climate, averaging between 69° and 90° F. Average annual rainfall is less than 4 inches in Muscat.

HISTORY

Oman was an important farming and trading area with many towns and villages and an elaborate irrigation system in the 2000s B.C.

In the 600s A.D. Saudi Arabian traders spread Muslim influence to the Persian Gulf.

In the 1500s the Portuguese conquered the region now called Oman, using Muscat as a base to control Persian Gulf trade. Arabs ejected the Portuguese in 1650.

In 1696–98 Oman drove the Portuguese out of bases in East Africa, captured Mombassa in Kenya, and won control of Zanzibar.

The present Said dynasty came to power in Muscat and Oman in 1741. British influence was established with a treaty of friendship in 1798.

In the early 1800s Oman was the most powerful state in Arabia, controlling much of East Africa. But when the ruler died in 1856, his sons quarreled and then divided the empire in 1861.

Zanzibar continued to pay tribute to the sultans until its independence in 1964.

Oman had become a poor country before oil began to be produced in 1967.

In July 1970 the sultan's son, Qaboos Bin Said, overthrew his father. The new sultan changed the name of the country from Muscat and Oman to Oman. He began using the oil income for progressive economic and social reforms.

The sultan took majority control of the oil industry on Jan. 1, 1974.

After a dozen years of fighting in southern Oman, the government announced in January 1976 that rebel leaders had surrendered. The civil war had begun in 1964 as rebels sought independence for the Dhofar area. The rebels were supplied with Chinese and Soviet arms from Southern Yemen.

Britain closed its military base at Masira, Oman, on March 31, 1977, its last military outpost in the Middle East.

The U.S. on June 5, 1980, announced an agreement with Oman for use of ports and air bases by American military forces.

The country's $21.3 billion 5-year plan for 1981–85 placed emphasis on the development of companies to oversee expansion of production from agriculture and fisheries. The nation's first oil refinery began production in 1982.

PAKISTAN

Official Name: Islamic Republic of Pakistan.
Area: 310,404 square miles (803,943 sq. km.).
Population: 91,260,300.
Chief Cities: Islamabad, capital, 77,318; Karachi, 3,498,634; Lahore, 2,165,372; Shah Faisalabad (formerly Lyallpur), 822,263; Hyderabad, 628,310; Rawalpindi, 615,392.
Government: Military dictatorship.
President: Gen. Mohammad Zia ul-Haq (since 1978).
U.S. Ambassador to Pakistan: Ronald I. Spiers.
Pakistani Ambassador to U.S.: Ejaz Azim.
Flag: Green field with white crescent and star; white bar along hoist.
Chief Ethnic Groups: Punjabi (65%), Sindhi (11%), Pathan (8%).
Principal Languages: Urdu (official), English, Punjabi.
Main Religion: Islam (97%).
Leading Industries: Agriculture (wheat, cattle, sugarcane, rice, cotton, barley, corn, tobacco); manufacturing (textiles, chemicals, steel, electricity); mining (natural gas, petroleum, coal); fishing.
Foreign Trade: *Major exports*—cotton, rice, textiles; *major imports*—machinery, raw materials.
Places of Interest: Modern capital of Islamabad; Karachi museum; Shalimar Gardens, fort and Badshahi Mosque in Lahore; Peshawar museum and bazaars; Mohenjo-Daro excavations; Taxila ruins near Rawalpindi; Khyber Pass near Peshawar; Kaghan Valley; Tarbela Dam.

PAKISTAN TODAY

About as large as Texas and Louisiana combined, Pakistan has the ninth-largest population among the nations of the world.

The country is burdened by more than 2.8 million Afghan refugees from the war in Afghanistan.

Unlike most developing countries, Pakistan is self-sufficient in raising wheat to meet the food needs of its people.

Most Pakistanis are poor farm workers who earn less than $300 per year. Less than 1 in 5 can read and write.

The government owns most large basic manufacturing industries, as well as transportation, banking, and insurance.

However, the country's major export is its workers for construction projects in other Muslim countries. They send home over $2 billion in annual earnings.

Because Pakistan is an Islamic state, the oil-rich Arab nations of the Middle East have invested hundreds of millions of dollars to help develop its industrialization program. In addition, large amounts of aid have been provided by the United States, China, and other nations.

Pakistan rises from the deserts of Sind in the south and Baluchistan in the west to the forested hills in the north, and then to the

QUICK QUIZ: What national park had the most visitors in 1982? See page 940.

PAKISTAN *(continued)*

soaring Himalayas. The Indus River waters much of the eastern and central region.

The climate is hot and dry near the coast of the Arabian Sea, but is cool and temperate in the northeastern uplands.

Iran lies to the west, Afghanistan to the north, China to the northeast, and India to the east.

EARLY HISTORY

In the 700s the Islamic faith was introduced by Arab traders. In the 900s Muslim warriors swept into the subcontinent and conquered most of Pakistan. Muslim rule lasted 1,000 years, reaching its peak under the Mogul empire in the 1500s.

Portuguese traders arrived in the 1400s. By the 1800s the British East India Company had become the dominant power, with the last Mogul emperor deposed in 1859.

Under the leadership of Mohammed Ali Jinnah and Liaquat Ali Khan, the Muslim League began demanding in 1940 a separate state composed of areas where Muslims were in the majority.

INDEPENDENCE

In 1947 Britain agreed to the formation of separate Hindu and Islamic states. Pakistan came into being as an independent dominion within the British Commonwealth of Nations on Aug. 14, 1947, with Liaquat Ali Khan as prime minister and with Mohammed Ali Jinnah as governor-general. Islamic Pakistan consisted of two provinces, East and West Pakistan, separated from each other by 1,000 miles of Indian territory.

Muslim-Hindu disputes intensified after independence. States with Hindu majorities but Muslim rulers were forcibly joined to India. Kashmir, a state with a majority of Muslim residents but ruled by a Hindu minority, became the chief point of contention, and fighting over control of Kashmir broke out between Pakistan and India in 1948. The UN negotiated a cease-fire the following year, but tension remained high. Pakistani-Indian fighting resumed in September 1965. A peace accord was signed early in 1966.

Elsewhere, Pakistan faced economic and political difficulties. Following the death of Mohammed Ali Jinnah in 1948 and the assassination of Liaquat Ali Khan in 1951, the precarious control of the new government gradually disintegrated.

A new constitution went into effect on March 23, 1956, making the nation the *Islamic Republic of Pakistan*. Maj. Gen. Iskander Mirza became the first president.

By 1958 the East Pakistan provincial legislature was in turmoil. In West Pakistan the khan of Kalat moved toward secession. On Oct. 7, 1958, the commander in chief of the army, Gen. Mohammed Ayub Khan, took over the government.

Violent antigovernment riots erupted in late 1968 and early 1969.

On March 25, 1969, President Ayub resigned and turned the government over to Gen. Agha Mohammed Yahya Khan, commander in chief of the armed forces.

WAR WITH INDIA AND BANGLADESH

In general elections in March 1971 the nationalist Awami League, led by Sheik Mujibur (Mujib) Rahman, won nearly all of East Pakistan's seats, giving it a majority in the national assembly.

When President Yahya postponed convocation of the assembly, revolt swept East Pakistan. The league proclaimed the province an independent nation called *Bangladesh*. Pakistan outlawed the league and imprisoned Mujib.

The Pakistani army attempted to crush the rebellion in East Pakistan. About 9 million Bengali refugees flooded into India.

India, which sided with the rebels, began an armed invasion of Pakistan on Dec. 3, 1971. Pakistani forces surrendered on Dec. 16.

RULE BY BHUTTO IN THE 1970s

The defeated military junta in Pakistan collapsed. Zulfikar Ali Bhutto, head of the National Party, was sworn in as provisional president in late December 1971. Bhutto released Mujib, who returned to Bangladesh.

In January 1972 Pakistan withdrew from the Commonwealth of Nations because Britain had established diplomatic relations with Bangladesh.

On April 12, 1973, President Bhutto signed into law a new constitution that provided for a president and a prime minister elected by the national assembly. Bhutto gave up the presidency to become prime minister.

Bhutto's socialist government completed the nationalization of basic industries in 1974.

The government also began a program in 1974 of giving 1,350 square feet of free land to each homeless rural family.

Bhutto in August 1974 announced restoration of basic civil rights that had been suspended since 1970. But six months later, on Feb. 10, 1975, he banned the main opposition political party, the National Awami Party (NAP).

The United States ended a 10-year arms embargo against Pakistan on Feb. 23, 1975.

After six years of construction the world's second-largest dam, the $1.3 billion Tarbela Dam on the Indus River, was completed in 1976.

The government announced plans in 1976 to construct 24 nuclear power plants by 1996.

After a parliamentary election on March 7, 1977, Bhutto announced that his Pakistan People's Party had won a landslide victory, taking 133 of the 200 elective seats. Opponents declared the election had been stolen by fraud.

MILITARY RULE BY PRESIDENT ZIA

Gen. Mohammad Zia ul-Haq, 53, chief of staff of the army, seized control of the government on July 5, 1977, jailing Bhutto and his closest aides. Zia imposed martial law but freed the press, radio, and TV of censorship. He established severe Islamic punishments, including amputations of hands and public whipping, for such crimes as theft and annoying women.

Bhutto was convicted of murder in 1978. He was hanged on April 4, 1979.

When President Fazal Elahi Chaudry completed his elected 5-year term, Zia took over the presidency on Sept. 16, 1978, while retaining his titles as chief martial-law administrator and armed forces commander.

After the CIA confirmed in 1979 that Pakistan was building a secret plant to manufacture enriched uranium that could be used to make atomic weapons, the U.S. cut off economic and military aid of about $40 million a year. Zia denied Pakistan planned to build atomic weapons and appealed for restoration of U.S. aid, but he said Pakistan might explode a research device.

Relations between Pakistan and the Soviet Union worsened in 1979–80 when Zia permitted millions of Afghan tribesmen to take refuge and use Pakistan as a base for guerrilla raids against Afghanistan's communist government and troops of its Soviet ally. The influx of Afghan refugees added to Pakistan's difficult economic and social problems.

After scheduling a national election for November 1979, Zia canceled it on Oct. 16, 1979, banned political activities, and arrested hundreds of politicians, including the widow and daughter of executed former prime minister Bhutto. He also tightened martial law.

Mobs of Pakistani Muslims, inflamed by anti-American statements by Iran's Ayatollah Khomeini, attacked and burned the U.S. embassy in Islamabad on Nov. 21, 1979, killing two Americans and two Pakistani employees.

After Soviet troops invaded Afghanistan to control its communist government, the U.S. in January 1980 offered $400 million in military aid to bolster Pakistan's defenses. However, President Zia rejected the offer as "peanuts," explaining that substantially more aid was necessary. He also indicated he feared the U.S. would attach strings to the aid to try to halt Pakistan's effort to develop an atomic bomb.

In the face of the threat posed by Soviet troops on Pakistan's border with Afghanistan, the U.S. reached agreement with President Zia on Sept. 15, 1981, to provide $3.2 billion in military and economic aid over a five-year period. The U.S. promised swift delivery of 40 F16 jet fighter-bombers.

The nation's first blast furnace began producing pig iron in 1981, part of a $2.5 billion steel mill being built with Soviet help. When completed in 1985 it will be able to produce 1.1 million tons of steel annually. Imported iron ore and coal are carried from ships to the mill by a 28-mile-long conveyor belt.

China and Pakistan formally opened on Aug. 27, 1982, the 468-mile Karakoram highway link from Xinjiang, China, across the Himalayas and through Kashmir.

A wave of terrorism swept Pakistan in 1982 with attacks on government officials and acts of sabotage. The terrorists were believed led by two sons of former Prime Minister Bhutto, said to be hiding in Afghanistan under Soviet protection.

In response to the terrorism, President Zia decreed on Sept. 28, 1982, that anyone sheltering terrorists would be publicly executed.

Pakistan and India moved to improve relations with the first meeting in a decade between the leaders of the two countries that have fought each other in three wars in the past four decades. President Zia and India's Prime Minister Gandhi conferred in New Delhi on Nov. 1, 1982.

Pakistan was torn by riots throughout 1983 as opponents led demonstrations against Zia's martial law government. In discussions with political leaders Zia promised national elections in 1985.

PANAMA

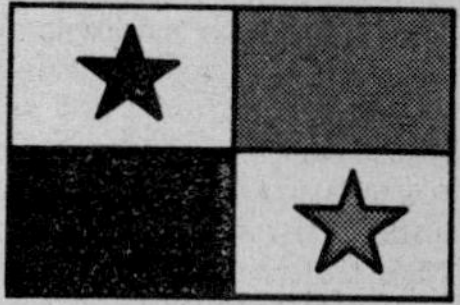

Official Name: Republic of Panama.
Area: 29,762 square miles (77,083 sq. km.).
Population: 1,996,610.
Capital: Panama City, 452,360.
Government: Republic.
President: Ricardo de la Espriella (since 1982).
Parliament: *Legislative Council*, 57 members; *National Assembly*, 505 members.
U.S. Ambassador to Panama: Everett E. Briggs.
Ambassador to U.S.: Aqualino E. Boyd.
Flag: Quarters of blue, red, and white, with blue and red stars on the two white portions.
Official Language: Spanish.
Main Ethnic Groups: Mestizo (70%), black (13%), European descent (10%), Indian (6%).
Official Religion: Roman Catholicism (93%).
Leading Industries: Agriculture (rice, bananas, corn, cocoa, abaca, tobacco, coffee, palm kernels, livestock); fishing; trade and services; manufacturing (food processing, oil refining, tobacco products, textiles, soap, cement); forestry and lumbering; mining (gold).
Foreign Trade: *Major exports*—bananas, refined petroleum, shrimp, cocoa; *major imports*—crude petroleum, motor vehicles, foodstuffs.
Places of Interest: Panama Canal; Panama City; El Valle; Darién; Contadora, Taboga, San Blas islands; Pacific coast beaches; Piñas Bay; Portobelo ruins near Colón.

PANAMA TODAY

Almost as large as South Carolina, Panama numbers among its resources large copper deposits, rich farmland, and the Panama Canal. About half the people are farmers. Most of the rest make a living directly or indirectly from the canal.

For many years U.S. control of the Panama Canal had been a major point of contention between the U.S. and Panama. Panamanians felt that their country did not receive a fair share of the profits from operation of the canal and that Panama should have sovereignty over the Panama Canal Zone. In 1979 the U.S. gave up sovereignty over the canal zone.

Panama lies between the Caribbean and the Pacific on the isthmus linking North and South America.

There are lowlands on both coasts of Panama. The eastern portion of the country is covered by rain forest. Colombia is to the east and Costa Rica to the west.

EARLY HISTORY

Panama's history has been shaped by its strategic location between two oceans. The Spanish explorer Rodrigo de Bastidas visited eastern Panama in 1501, and Columbus claimed the area for Spain in the following year. In 1513 Vasco Núñez de Balboa became the first European to cross the narrow isthmus to reach the Pacific. Occupied

QUICK QUIZ: About how many motorcycles are registered in the U.S.? See page 933.

by Spaniards, Panama served as the route for shipping Inca treasures to Spain in the 1500s and 1600s. Spanish rule was overthrown in 1821, and Panama became a province of Colombia.

The California gold rush in 1849 revived interest in Panama's geographical importance as a route from the Atlantic to the Pacific. The Panama Railroad (completed in 1855) carried gold-rush traffic across the isthmus.

French attempts during the 1880s to build a canal were unsuccessful because 20,000 workers died of yellow fever.

The U.S. bought the canal rights from France, but Colombia demanded more money.

INDEPENDENCE AND THE PANAMA CANAL

On Nov. 3, 1903, Panamanians revolted and declared independence from Colombia. President Theodore Roosevelt immediately sent U.S. Marines to protect the new government. On Nov. 18, 1903, the U.S. and Panama signed the Hay–Bunau-Varilla Treaty giving the U.S. control of the 10-mile-wide Panama Canal Zone for a payment of $10 million plus $250,000 a year.

U.S. Col. William C. Gorgas in 1904–13 wiped out the mosquitoes in Panama that caused yellow fever and malaria.

Construction of the canal began in 1907 under Col. George W. Goethals. On Aug. 15, 1914, the first ship went through the canal from the Atlantic to the Pacific. Officially opened on July 12, 1920, the canal cost about $350 million.

Brig. Gen. Omar Torrijos Herrera, commander of the national guard, seized control of the government on Oct. 11, 1968.

After 13 years of negotiations, the U.S. agreed in 1977 to treaties returning control of the canal to Panama. Ratification by the U.S. Senate was completed on April 18, 1978.

In October 1978 Torrijos stepped down as chief of state after the National Assembly elected his choice as president, Aristedes Royo.

The U.S. on Oct. 1, 1979, formally returned to Panama sovereignty over the 553-square-mile Panama Canal Zone that had been governed by the U.S. since 1904. All U.S. control over the canal will end at noon on Dec. 31, 1999.

Panamanians were given a taste of democracy for the first time in 12 years on Sept. 28, 1980, when a multiparty election was held for 19 of the 57 seats in the Legislative Council. A majority of the seats were won by the government party while many opponents boycotted the election.

Gen. Torrijos was killed in the crash of a military plane in western Panama on July 31, 1981. Military commanders said they would continue to support the civilian government established by Torrijos.

The first oil pipeline across the Isthmus of Panama, completed at a cost of $300 million, began pumping in 1982. It enables tankers too large to go through the canal to pump oil from the Pacific to the Atlantic at a rate of 800,000 barrels a day.

President Royo was ousted on July 30, 1982, by national guard commander Gen. Rubén Darío Paredes.

Ricardo de la Espriella, who had been vice president, succeeded Royo as president.

National elections were scheduled for 1984.

PAPUA NEW GUINEA

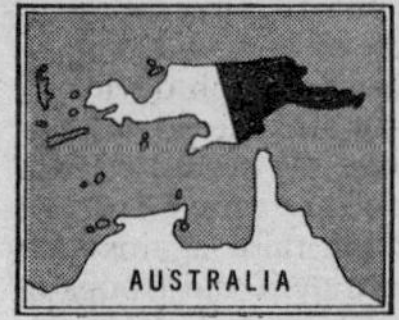

Official Name: Papua New Guinea.
Area: 178,260 square miles (461,691 sq. km.).
Population: 3,306,610.
Capital: Port Moresby, 113,449.
Government: Parliamentary state.
Prime Minister: Michael Somare (since 1982).
Parliament: *House of Assembly*, 109 members.
U.S. Ambassador: M. Virginia Schafer.
PNG Ambassador to U.S.: Kubulan Los.
Flag: Five-star constellation on lower black triangle; gold bird of paradise on upper red triangle.
Languages: English, Pidgin English, Motu, more than 700 tribal dialects.
Ethnic Groups: Melanesians, Asians, Australians..
Religions: Christianity, tribal religions.
Leading Industries: Mining (copper, gold); agriculture (cocoa, copra, rubber, tea, fruits, vegetables); forestry and lumbering; fishing; food processing.
Foreign Trade: *Major exports*—copper, gold, plywood, lumber, seafood, cocoa, rubber, tea; *major imports*—machinery, vehicles, food.
Places of Interest: Port Moresby government buildings; thatched-roof tribal villages; copper mines on island of Bougainville; Rabaul on island of New Britain; towns of Mt. Hagan, Lae, Goroka, Aitape, Wewak, Popondetta, Madang, Kerema, and Daru on mainland New Guinea.

PAPUA NEW GUINEA TODAY

Larger than California, Papua New Guinea is an island nation just north of Australia. Most of the mountainous country is covered by tropical rain forests with few roads. The extent of the country's mineral resources is unknown, but copper and gold are mined for export. Only a small portion of the nation's land is farmed.

Communication among the people is a major difficulty. More than 700 tribal dialects are spoken, with one tribe being unable to understand another. Many of the people speak Pidgin English. Few can read and write. Most people live in tribal villages leading the same primitive life as their ancestors. Wars between tribes are frequent.

The country depends heavily on over $200 million annual aid from Australia.

The country covers the eastern half of New Guinea. Its largest offshore islands are New Britain (14,600 sq. mi.), Bougainville (3,880 sq. mi.), and New Ireland (3,340 sq. mi.). The western half of New Guinea is the Indonesian province of Irian Jaya.

The coastal plain is 50 to 150 miles wide. Inland mountains tower to 14,500 feet.

The climate is hot along the coasts, with cooler temperatures in the uplands. There is much rain.

EARLY HISTORY

The people of Papua New Guinea are believed to have come to the islands from the Asian mainland thousands of years ago.

The first European known to have visited New

Guinea was the Portuguese governor of the Molucca Islands, Jorge de Meneses, in 1526.

In 1884 Britain made southeastern New Guinea a protectorate, and Germany claimed northeastern New Guinea and the offshore islands.

Southeastern New Guinea became Australia's Territory of Papua on Sept. 1, 1906. With the defeat of Germany in World War I, the League of Nations transferred administration of northeastern New Guinea and the offshore islands to Australia in 1920.

During World War II the Japanese captured northern New Guinea, but Port Moresby became an important Allied military base. The U.S. and Australia recaptured all New Guinea by 1944.

In 1949 Australia united northeastern and southeastern New Guinea under a single administration called *Papua New Guinea.*

Papua New Guinea's first house of assembly convened in 1964 with debates conducted in Pidgin English. New elections were held in 1968.

After national elections in 1972 a coalition government was formed with Michael Somare of the Pangu Party as chief minister. Australia granted complete self-government on Dec. 1, 1973.

The government in September 1974 reached an agreement with copper-mining companies to turn over about half their profits in taxes.

Nationalists on the copper-rich island of Bougainville declared their independence from Papua New Guinea on Sept. 1, 1975, naming their government the Republic of the Northern Solomons. But the rebellion was put down.

INDEPENDENCE

Australia gave Papua New Guinea complete independence on Sept. 16 1975, with Somare as the nation's first prime minister.

Papua New Guinea reached agreement with the European Economic Community (EEC) in March 1977, allowing it to export products to the EEC without having to pay tariffs.

The first national election since independence was held June 18 to July 9, 1977. Prime Minister Somare's coalition parties won a majority of 60 seats in the 109-member parliament.

Increasing unemployment and a soaring crime rate brought criticism of Somare's administration. On March 11, 1980, he lost a vote of confidence 57 to 49. He was succeeded as prime minister by Sir Julius Chan, 43, head of the opposition People's Progress Party.

A $13 million American tuna boat was confiscated in February 1982 because it violated the country's 200-mile offshore economic zone.

Eight political parties and 1,126 candidates competed for 109 parliamentary seats in a 3-week election that began on June 5, 1982. The process takes so long because of the difficulty of collecting ballots from remote areas.

Former Prime Minister Somare, 47, was returned to office on Aug. 3, 1982. His Pangu Party won a plurality of 41 seats and he was supported by smaller parties to form a majority coalition. Chan's People's Progress Party won only 10 seats with almost half his cabinet members defeated.

Somare cut the government budget in 1983, firing 10% of government workers.

PARAGUAY

Official Name: Republic of Paraguay.
Area: 157,048 square miles (406,752 sq. km.).
Population: 3,143,250.
Capital: Asunción, 463,735 (met. area, 601,645).
Government: Republic under dictatorship.
President: Gen. Alfredo Stroessner (since 1954).
Legislature: *Senate,* 30 members; *Chamber of Deputies,* 60 members.
U.S. Ambassador to Paraguay: Arthur H. Davis Jr.
Paraguayan Ambassador to U.S.: Mario Lopez Escobar.
Flag: Red, white, and blue stripes; national coat of arms in center.
Official Languages: Spanish, Guaraní.
Main Ethnic Group: Mestizo (95%).
Official Religion: Roman Catholicism (97%).
Leading Industries: Agriculture (cotton, soybeans, livestock, tobacco; wheat, corn, manioc, sweet potatoes, beans, rice, sugarcane, fruits; lumbering and forestry; food processing; manufacturing (electricity, oil refining, cement, consumer goods).
Foreign Trade: *Major exports*—cotton, meat, timber, oilseed, tobacco, quebracho extract, hides; *major imports*—machinery, food, steel, consumer goods.
Places of Interest: Guairá Falls; Port President Stroessner; San Bernardino and El Tirol tourist resorts; Jesuit missions in south. *In Asunción:* Cathedral; Pantheon of the Heroes; botanical garden.

PARAGUAY TODAY

About the size of California, Paraguay is a landlocked South American country.

The nation has no mineral resources to aid in building a modern economy. However, Paraguay enjoyed one of the highest economic growth rates in the world in the 1970s–1980s with construction of $10 billion in hydroelectric projects financed by Brazil and Argentina.

Most Paraguayans are farm and ranch workers. Most raise only enough food for their families. In the past two decades about a million persons migrated to Argentina to escape poverty and political repression.

Throughout most of its history the nation has been ruled by a succession of dictators, so that the people have grown used to lack of political freedom. Two major wars in the 1870s and 1930s contributed to the nation's poverty.

The country's only paved highway links the capital, Asunción, with Brazil. Most villages and towns have dirt streets and no sidewalks.

The Paraguay and Alto Paraná rivers are important waterways. To the west of the Paraguay River lies the arid, sparsely settled region of the Chaco Boreal.

Argentina lies to the south and west, Brazil to the northeast, and Bolivia to the northwest.

HISTORY OF PARAGUAY

Spanish conquistadores came to Paraguay in 1524, establishing Asunción in 1537 and inter-

QUICK QUIZ: Who was the first Democrat elected President after the Civil War? See page 362.

marrying with the docile Guaraní Indians. In the 1500s and 1600s Jesuit missionaries instituted a written form of the Guaraní language, still used by most Paraguayans today.

In 1721 a successful revolt led by José de Antequera enabled him to rule an independent Paraguay for about 10 years.

Paraguay declared independence from Spain on May 14, 1811. The first of three strong dictators who shaped the nation took power in 1814—José Gaspar Rodríguez Francia, who ruled until his death in 1840. Then came Carlos Antonio López (1842–62) and López's son, Francisco Solano López (1862–70).

In 1865 López plunged his country into the War of the Triple Alliance against Brazil, Argentina, and Uruguay. At the war's end in 1870 Paraguay had lost 55,000 square miles of territory and over 500,000 people.

In 1932 a territorial dispute led to a 3-year Chaco War with Bolivia. Paraguay won, although at a cost of some 40,000 men.

Higinio Morínigo established a dictatorship in 1940, but resigned in 1948. From 1949 to 1954 the country was ruled by Federico Chavez.

In 1954 Gen. Alfredo Stroessner, commander of the army, made himself dictator.

In March 1973 the British Anti-Slavery Society urged the UN Human Rights Commission to take action to prevent the extermination of the Ache Indians in Paraguay, charging that most men of the tribe had been slain and the women and children sold into slavery.

Paraguay and Brazil signed an agreement on April 26, 1973, to build a $3 billion dam and hydroelectric project at Itaipu on the Paraná River between the two countries. Two other major hydroelectric projects were undertaken jointly with Argentina, the Yacyreta Dam and the Corpus Project, costing about $7 billion.

In apparent response to U.S. President Jimmy Carter's call for human rights, the government in January 1977 freed three communists who had been jailed for 19 years. In February the government also released 11 women political prisoners and their 17 children. However, human-rights organizations said that about 350 political prisoners remained in Paraguay's jails.

Opposition political parties boycotted an election on Feb. 6, 1977, for a constituent assembly, so supporters of Stroessner won all 120 seats. The assembly met on March 7–11 to amend the constitution to enable the president to be elected to office more than twice.

Stroessner won his sixth 5-year term as president in an election on Feb. 12, 1978, receiving 86% of the vote against candidates of the Liberal and Liberal-Radical parties.

President Stroessner in 1979 provided a haven in Paraguay for deposed Nicaraguan dictator Anastasio Somoza Debayle, who had been refused admission by other nations. However, Somoza was assassinated in Asunción on Sept. 17, 1980. Stroessner's government broke diplomatic relations with Nicaragua a few days later, charging its government with complicity in the slaying.

The 70-year-old Stroessner won election in 1983 to his seventh 5-year term as president.

The Itaipu Dam, the world's largest hydroelectric project, began producing electricity in 1983.

PERU

Official Name: Republic of Peru.
Area: 496,225 square miles (1,285,216 sq. km.).
Population: 19,422,500.
Chief Cities: Lima, capital, 4,278,800; Arequipa, 455,200; Callao, 436,100; Trujillo, 386,900.
Largest Metropolitan Area: Lima, 4,278,800.
Government: Multiparty democracy.
President: Fernando Belaúnde Terry (since 1980).
Prime Minister: Fernando Schwalb (since 1982).
Congress: *Chamber of Deputies,* 180 members; *Senate,* 60 members.
U.S. Ambassador to Peru: Frank V. Ortiz Jr.
Peruvian Ambassador to U.S.: Celso Pastor de la Torre.
Flag: Red, white, and red bars, with coat of arms centered on white bar.
Official Languages: Spanish, Quechua.
Ethnic Groups: Indian (46%), mestizo (43%), European descent (11%).
Official Religion: Roman Catholicism.
Leading Industries: Agriculture (sugarcane, cotton, rice, wheat, coffee, potatoes, livestock, fruits, vegetables); mining (petroleum, iron ore, copper, gold, silver, lead, zinc, tungsten, manganese, coal); fishing; food processing; manufacturing (textiles, cement, leather products, plastics, chemicals).
Foreign Trade: *Major exports*—petroleum, copper, sugar, iron ore, silver, cotton, zinc, coffee, lead; *major imports*—machinery, food, trucks, chemicals.
Places of Interest: Inca ruins Machu Picchu and Cuzco; prehistoric ruins of Chavín de Huantar near Huarás; Lake Titicaca; El Misti Volcano. *In Lima:* Cathedral and tomb of Pizarro; Court of the Inquisition; Plaza de Armas; Torre Tagle Palace. *In Arequipa:* Cathedral; Lucioni Gardens.

PERU TODAY

Almost twice as large as Texas, Peru is a South American country enjoying the restoration of democracy after years of military rule.

Richer in natural resources than most other nations of its size, Peru is among the world's leading nations in fishing and the mining of lead and zinc. But its people have remained poor.

The Andes Mountains split the country in two. A narrow coastal desert, from 10 to 100 miles wide, extends about 1,400 miles along the Pacific coast. The temperate slopes of the Andes make up Peru's most populous region.

About half of Peru lies east of the Andes—a sparsely populated lowland area of rain forests.

Ecuador and Colombia lie on the north, Brazil and Bolivia on the east, and Chile on the south.

HISTORY OF PERU

As early as 300 B.C. the Nazca people of Peru drew on the ground hundreds of huge pictures, such as a hummingbird with a 900-foot wing-span.

The Nazca and other early cultures were absorbed by the Inca Empire in the 1400s A.D. The Incas, with their capital at Cuzco, controlled territory from Ecuador to Chile.

Drawn by the Inca treasure, Francisco Pizarro

conquered the empire in 1533. Lima, established in 1535, was for three centuries the seat of Spanish control over all Hispanic South America except Venezuela. In the 1780s Inca leader Túpac Amaru led an unsuccessful revolt against Spain.

Peru's independence was declared on July 28, 1821, by Gen. José de San Martín. Venezuela's liberator Simón Bolívar led Peru's armies in battling Spain's troops to final victory in 1826.

Peru suffered a costly defeat by Chile in the War of the Pacific in 1879–83, losing its southern provinces of Tacna, Arica, and Tarapacá. Later, in 1929, Tacna was restored to Peru.

Although military leaders and dictators have dominated Peru's government throughout most of its history, Fernando Belaúnde Terry of the Popular Action Party was elected president in a free multiparty election in 1963.

A military coup on Oct. 3, 1968, overthrew Belaúnde, who was exiled to Argentina. Gen. Juan Velasco Alvarado, army chief of staff, became president, heading a socialist military junta that nationalized privately owned property. About 17 million acres of land were distributed to 300,000 peasants. But the socialist economic policies drove the nation to the verge of bankruptcy.

Gen. Francisco Morales Bermúdez, a moderate, was named premier by Velasco on Feb. 1, 1975. Seven months later, on Aug. 29, 1975, Morales led a bloodless coup, overthrowing Velasco and making himself president. The new president dropped Marxists from the government and began turning a number of nationalized industries back to private ownership.

The nation's state of emergency was ended by President Morales on Aug. 29, 1977.

In the first free election in 15 years, Peruvians in 1978 elected a 100-member assembly that drafted a new constitution.

DEMOCRACY RESTORED

In a national election on May 18, 1980, former President Belaúnde, 68, regained the office with a 5-year term, receiving 45% of the popular vote. His Popular Action Party also won control of the Congress.

The military turned the government over to Belaúnde and the new Congress on Peru's Independence Day, July 28, 1980.

Belaúnde's government received help from international loan agencies to finance a 5-year development plan for 1981-85 to develop agriculture, transportation, and public services.

Although Peru's economy grew at a higher rate than most other South American countries in 1980–82, lower prices for oil, copper, and silver cut government revenues and forced Belaunde to reduce capital developments. About half of Peru's workers were unemployed or underemployed in 1982–83, and inflation continued at a rate of 50%.

After terrorists blacked out Lima by attacking the power plant on Aug. 19, 1982, the government declared martial law in the capital city for 60 days, imprisoning 34,000 suspected criminals.

A Maoist guerrilla group called Shining Path killed hundreds of Peruvians in 1982–83 with bombings of government buildings and attacks on remote villages.

PHILIPPINES

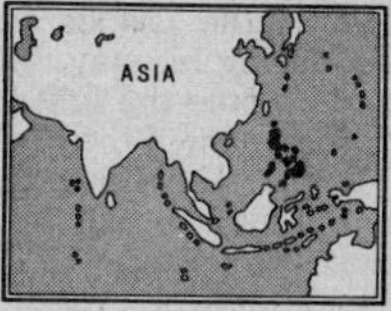

Official name: Republic of the Philippines.
Area: 115,830 square miles (300,000 sq. km.).
Population: 53,528,200.
Chief Cities: Manila, capital, 7,800,000; Davao, 515,520; Cebu, 418,517; Iloilo, 247,956; Zamboanga, 240,066.
Government: Republic under rule by decree.
President: Ferdinand Marcos (since 1965).
Prime Minister: Cesar Virata (since 1981).
National Assembly: 192 members.
U.S. Ambassador to Philippines: Michael Hayden Armacost.
Philippine Ambassador to U.S.: Benjamin T. Romualdez.
Flag: Blue and red stripes bordered by white triangle containing yellow stars and sun.
Official Languages: Filipino, English, Spanish.
Main Ethnic Group: Malayo-Polynesian (90%).
Religions: Roman Catholicism (83%), Protestantism (9%), Islam (5%), animism (3%).
Leading Industries: Agriculture (rice, abaca, coconuts, sugarcane, corn, tobacco, livestock, fruits, vegetables); food processing; manufacturing (tobacco products, textiles, clothing, automobiles, oil refining); forestry and lumbering; fishing; mining (gold, silver, copper, iron, chromite, nickel).
Foreign Trade: *Major exports*—coconut products, sugar, wood, abaca; *major imports*—food, petroleum, consumer goods.
Places of Interest: Nayong Filipino (Philippine village) and Malacanang Palace in Manila; Tagaytay Ridge overlooking Lake Taal; Pagsanjan Falls; Corregidor Island; Banawe rice terraces at Ifugao; Mayon Volcano at Legaspi; Baguio; Cebu City.

PHILIPPINES TODAY

Once called "the show window of democracy in Asia," the Philippines today is ruled as a dictatorship by Ferdinand Marcos. However, political groups may speak out against the government.

The country is among the world's leading producers of copper, gold, and natural rubber. Agriculture employs over half of the nation's workers and provides about a third of the national income. But most Filipinos are very poor.

The U.S. maintains military air and naval bases in the Philippines.

The Philippines include 7,107 islands, stretching some 1,100 miles from within 150 miles of Taiwan to less than 15 miles of Borneo.

From May to November, typhoons are a hazard. Temperatures range from hot jungles and rain forests to cool pine-clad highlands.

EARLY HISTORY

In prehistoric times the Philippines were settled by peoples who came from the islands of Indonesia and the Malay peninsula. In the 1200s the islands became part of the Indo-Malay empires. The missionary zeal of Islam swept the region in

QUICK QUIZ: What foods have high fat content? See page 400.

PHILIPPINES *(continued)*
the 1300s.

Ferdinand Magellan claimed the islands for Spain in 1521. He was slain during his stay, but one of his vessels went on to become the first to circle the earth. The islands were named the Philippines in honor of Philip (Felipe) II of Spain. In 1564 Miguel López de Legaspi arrived with soldiers instructed to Christianize the islands. In 20 years he was able to establish control over the major inhabited areas except for Muslim Mindanao and Sulu. The colony was placed under the administration of the viceroy of Mexico.

Growing Filipino nationalism, inspired by the writings of José Rizal, caused an unsuccessful revolt in 1896. Although Rizal was executed by the Spanish authorities, the rebellion continued under the leadership of Emilio Aguinaldo. The Filipino rebels declared independence in 1898.

AMERICAN RULE

After Adm. George Dewey destroyed the Spanish fleet in Manila Bay on May 1, 1898, the U.S. paid Spain $20 million for the Philippines. When U.S. rule was established, Aguinaldo angrily began fighting the U.S. troops. The battles went on for two years until Aguinaldo was captured. William Howard Taft, later President, became the first U.S. governor in 1901.

Beginning in 1907 representatives to the national legislature were elected. In 1935 the Tydings-McDuffie Act gave the islands commonwealth status with self-government.

On Dec. 8, 1941, Japan launched a surprise attack and within a month occupied Manila. Gen. Douglas MacArthur, commanding some 90,000 American and Filipino troops, was forced to retreat to Luzon. He withdrew to Australia, but U.S. troops, commanded by Gen. Jonathan Wainwright, held out on Bataan, and then on the island of Corregidor, until May 6, 1942.

On Oct. 20, 1944, a U.S. invasion force, under MacArthur's command, landed on the central Philippine island of Leyte. By July 5, 1945, the Philippines had been recaptured.

INDEPENDENCE

The United States granted the Philippines independence on July 4, 1946. The presidents of the new republic in succession were Manuel Roxas (1946–48), Elpidio Quirino (1948–53), Ramón Magsaysay (1953–57), Carlos P. Garcia (1957–61), and Diosado Macapagal (1961–65).

Ferdinand Marcos was elected president in 1965 and reelected in 1969. Claiming communist subversion threatened the Philippines, Marcos declared martial law on Sept. 21, 1972, arresting opposition leaders and newsmen.

A revolt by Muslims in the southern Philippines began in 1972, and fighting continued into the 1980s.

President Marcos enlarged Manila on Nov. 6, 1975, merging it with the former official capital Quezon City and 15 other cities and towns. Marcos appointed his wife, Imelda Marcos, as governor of Manila, succeeding the elected mayors.

A national referendum held in October 1976 ratified constitutional amendments that in effect permit President Marcos to remain in office for life with dictatorial powers.

The government signed a 5-year $500 million agreement with the U.S. on Jan. 7, 1979, that assured continued U.S. use of air and naval bases.

After $7\frac{1}{2}$ years in solitary confinement under sentence of death, the man who had been expected to become president if national elections had been held in 1973, Benigno S. Aquino Jr., was permitted to leave prison to fly to the U.S. on May 8, 1980, to undergo a heart operation.

Marcos ended martial law on Jan. 17, 1981, but retained all the repressive laws he previously had decreed. Two days later he formally gave governmental power to the National Assembly, but retained his right to legislate by decree.

A referendum, branded a fraud by opponents, approved amendments to the constitution in April 1981 to permit Marcos to serve another term as president.

Marcos won reelection on June 16, 1981, with 86% of the votes in a poll in which nonvoters were threatened with imprisonment.

Under the revised constitution, Marcos appointed his finance minister, Cesar Virata, as prime minister on July 3, 1981. Marcos indicated he might appoint his wife to the position at some future time.

Marcos fired all 14 judges on the nation's supreme court on May 10, 1982, after they were exposed in a scandal for raising the bar exam score for the son of one of the judges. But five days later he reappointed 12 of them.

For the first time in 16 years, Marcos and his wife visited Washington, D.C., on Sept. 16, 1982, where they were warmly received by President Reagan. Opponents of Marcos in the Philippines denounced Reagan for praising Marcos for "great progress" in the area of human rights, claiming 60,000 persons had died in battles with government forces in the past 10 years.

The military killed a Roman Catholic priest in 1982 for having joined guerrillas opposed to the government and put bounties on the heads of several others. Cardinal Jaime Sin, archbishop of Manila, declared on Oct. 20, 1982, that there could be a full-scale revolution unless the government permitted priests to speak out for the poor.

Marcos' chief political opponent, Benigno S. Aquino Jr., was assassinated at the Manila airport on Aug. 21, 1983, as he returned from three years of exile in the U.S.

Although Marcos denied complicity in the slaying, the incident touched off widespread demonstrations against the government. President Reagan cancelled a planned November 1983 visit to the Philippines because of the turbulence.

MAIN ISLANDS OF THE PHILIPPINES

NAME	AREA (sq. mi.)	LARGEST CITY
Luzon	47,765	Manila
Mindanao	38,344	Davao
Palawan	5,751	Puerto Princesa
Negros	5,278	Bacolod
Samar	5,185	Calbayog
Panay	4,748	Iloilo
Mindoro	3,955	Pinamalayan
Leyte	3,090	Tacloban
Cebu	1,965	Cebu
Bohol	1,590	Tagbilaran
Masbate	1,563	Masbate
Catanduanes	583	Virac

POLAND

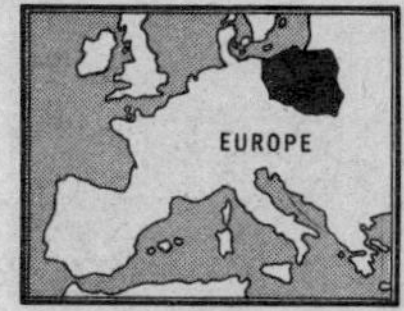

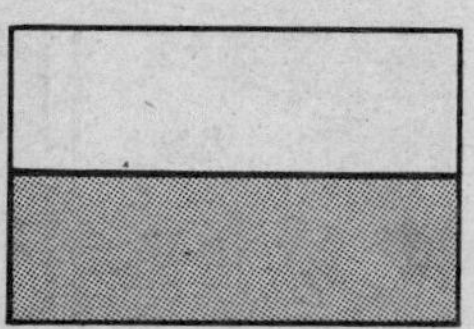

Official Name: Polish People's Republic.
Area: 120,725 square miles (312,677 sq. km.).
Population: 36,720,600.
Chief Cities: Warszawa (Warsaw), capital, 1,542,500; Lódz, 823,700; Kraków, 719,200; Wroclaw, 598,500; Poznan, 537,600; Gdansk, 448,200; Szczezecin, 383,900; Katowice, 352,300; Bydgoszecz, 342,200.
Government: Communist state.
Head of Government: Prime Minister and First Secretary of the Central Committee of the Communist Party, Gen. Wojciech Jaruzelski (since 1981).
Legislature: *Sejm,* 460 members.
U.S. Ambassador to Poland: Francis J. Meehan.
Polish Ambassador to U.S.: Romuald Spasowski.
Flag: White stripe over red stripe.
Official Language: Polish.
Principal Ethnic Group: Polish (98%).
Religion: Roman Catholicism (95%).
Leading Industries: Manufacturing (steel, electricity, cement, chemicals, ships, vehicles, machinery, textiles, paper); mining (coal, lignite, zinc, lead, natural gas, copper, sulfur); agriculture (wheat, sugar beets, potatoes, oats, barley, corn, livestock, fruits, vegetables); construction; trade and services.
Foreign Trade: *Major exports*—coal, lignite, coke, railway rolling stock, ships, cement; *major imports*—iron ore, petroleum and petroleum products, fertilizers, wheat, food.
Places of Interest: Masurian and Augustow Lake district; Baltic Sea resorts; Sudetan and Tatra Mountains; Malbork Castle near Gdansk; Kraków. *In Warsaw:* Palace of Culture and Science; Kampinos Forest National Park; Old Town; Wilanow Palace; birthplace of Chopin.

POLAND TODAY

About the size of New Mexico, Poland has ample mineral resources as well as rich farmland. It is one of the world's 10 leading producers of cement, coal, copper, electricity, steel, and zinc. But more Poles make their living from farming than from any other industry.

As with other communist nations, the standard of living of the people is substantially below that of the industrial nations of western Europe.

The communists rule Poland as a police state. However, the people are allowed greater religious freedom than in most other communist states. A person can be a member of both the Communist Party and the Roman Catholic Church.

Poland also is the only communist country in Europe where farmers still own as much as 85% of the land.

The Soviet Union maintains large armed forces in Poland.

The land is generally low and flat, about nine-tenths of it lying below 1,000 feet. Temperatures range from an average of 60° F. in summer to below 30° F. in winter. The principal rivers are the Vistula, Oder, Bug, and Warta.

The Soviet Union lies to the east, Czechoslovakia to the south, East Germany to the west, and the Baltic Sea to the north.

EARLY HISTORY

Slavic tribes in Poland were united during the 800s A.D. by the Piast dynasty. In 966 Duke Mieszko I adopted Christianity. His son, Boleslaw the Brave, became king in 1025.

A new dynasty was established in 1386 by a Lithuanian grand duke, Jagiello, who became King Wladyslaw II of Poland. The Polish-Lithuanian empire extended from the Baltic to the Black Sea. The Jagiellonian dynasty ended without heir in 1572. The throne became elective.

In 1772 Russia, Prussia, and Austria seized about one-third of Poland's territory in the *first partition.* In the *second partition* in 1793 Russia acquired Lithuania and the Ukraine from Poland while Prussia took about 22,000 square miles of western Poland. The patriot Thaddeus Kosciusko, who had served in the Continental Army during the American Revolution, led an unsuccessful Polish uprising in 1794. His defeat by the Russians led to the *third partition* in 1795–96, in which the remainder of Poland was divided among Russia, Prussia, and Austria.

After World War I a Polish republic was formed in 1918. Józef Pilsudski became the first president. The noted pianist Jan Paderewski served as prime minister. Pilsudski ruled as dictator from 1926 until his death in 1935.

In 1939 a Soviet-German pact opened the way for a new partition of Poland. The Germans attacked the country on Sept. 1, 1939, beginning World War II. Less than three weeks later the Soviets invaded from the east. The Germans murdered 6 million Poles, half of them Jews. The Russians executed 15,000 Polish army officers and deported 1.7 million Poles.

After World War II the Soviet Union annexed 70,000 square miles of Poland, but gave the new Poland 40,000 square miles of former German East Prussia, Pomerania, and Silesia.

COMMUNIST RULE

The 1945 Yalta agreement by the Allies pledged free elections in Poland. But under Soviet military occupation communists won control in national elections in 1947. Wladyslaw Gomulka headed the communist puppet government.

On December 12, 1970, strikes and riots erupted at Gdansk (formerly Danzig), Szczecin (Stettin), and other cities, in protest against food price increases. Police and troops crushed the disorders, with heavy casualties. Gomulka was replaced by Edward Gierek on Dec. 20, 1970.

On June 24, 1976, the government announced it was increasing retail food prices by as much as 100%. The next day, riots broke out in Warsaw, Radom, and Plock. That night the government backed down, canceling the price rise.

On Oct, 16, 1978, Karol Cardinal Wojtyla was elevated to pope as John Paul II—the first Polish pope. He visited Poland in June 1979, drawing huge crowds as he called on communist leaders to grant the people greater freedom.

Widespread labor unrest flared in the weeks

QUICK QUIZ: Which states do not levy personal income tax? See page 920.

POLAND *(continued)*

that followed a government order on July 1, 1980, raising meat prices 40% to 60%. The climax came during Aug. 13–31, when 17,000 workers seized a Gdansk shipyard and were supported by strikers in other cities. Under leadership of 37-year-old Lech Walesa, the strikers won written agreement from the government to permit the organization of independent labor unions.

Stanislaw Kania, 53, a former head of the secret police, replaced Gierek on Sept. 6, 1980.

The Polish government on Nov. 9, 1980, approved the charter of Walesa's Solidarity union as the first free labor union officially recognized in a communist nation.

With Soviet approval, 58-year-old Gen. Wojciech Jaruzelski ousted Kania on Oct. 18, 1981.

Solidarity leaders at a meeting in Gdansk on Dec. 12, 1981, were secretly taped while discussing a possible ouster of the communist government. Gen. Jaruzelski cracked down immediately on Dec. 13, declaring martial law. Walesa and thousands of other Solidarity activists were imprisoned. The army patrolled city streets. In the weeks that followed tens of thousands of Poles fled to western European countries as refugees. The U.S. imposed economic sanctions on the Polish and Soviet governments as a protest.

Jaruzelski controlled Poland as a rigid police state in 1982. Strikes and demonstrations called by underground Solidarity leaders were broken up by the police and the army. The Polish Communist Party ousted 50,000 of its members.

Poland's parliament on Oct. 8, 1982, banned Solidarity, replacing it with government-controlled trade unions. U.S. President Reagan reacted the next day by announcing suspension of Poland's most-favored-nation trade agreement.

However, on Oct. 26, 1982, the Polish parliament passed a new law directed against strikers, giving the government power to imprison persons who refuse to work at government-assigned jobs.

In an agreement between Jaruzelski and the Roman Catholic Church, Archbishop Josef Glemp discouraged Poles from taking part in a general strike called by underground Solidarity leaders for Nov. 10, 1982.

Solidarity leader Lech Walesa was released from imprisonment on Nov. 13, 1982, and allowed to return to his home in Gdansk.

Pope John Paul II visited his homeland again in June 1983, where he was greeted by huge peaceful demonstrations. See page 19.

The government officially ended martial law on July 22, 1983, but adopted new laws to enforce restrictions on human rights.

Riot police quelled demonstrations in many cities on Aug. 31, 1983, as workers marked the third anniversary of the founding of Solidarity.

Walesa was awarded the Nobel Peace Prize in 1983 for his work with the Solidarity union. The government press declared the award was part of an anti-Polish campaign by Western powers. Walesa donated the $190,000 award to a fund to aid individual Polish farmers.

A wave of food hoarding began after the government announced in September 1983 that food prices would be boosted by 30% to 40% on Jan. 1, 1984. Walesa called for public demonstrations against the price increases.

PORTUGAL

Official Name: Republic of Portugal.
Area: 35,553 square miles (92,082 sq. km.).
Population: 9,611,932.
Chief Cities: Lisboa (Lisbon), capital, 861,500; Pôrto, 334,100.
Largest Metropolitan Area: Lisbon, 1,611,887.
Government: Multiparty democratic republic.
President: Gen. António Ramalho Eanes (since 1976).
Prime Minister: Mario Soares (since 1983).
Assembly of the Republic: 250 deputies.
U.S. Ambassador to Portugal: Henry A. Holmes.
Portuguese Ambassador to U.S.: Leonardo Charles de Zaffiri Duarte Mathias.
Flag: Green and red bars with national coat of arms.
Official Language: Portuguese.
Principal Ethnic Group: Portuguese.
Religion: Roman Catholicism (97%).
Leading Industries: Trade and services; manufacturing (textiles, cork products, cement, petroleum refining, steel, wine, food processing; agriculture (wheat, potatoes, maize, rye, oats, olives, livestock, fruits, vegetables); forestry and lumbering; mining (coal, pyrites, copper, tungsten); fishing.
Foreign Trade: *Major exports*—wine, cork, fish, tomato paste, textiles; *major imports*—diamonds, automobiles, petroleum products, peanuts, plastics, textile machinery, sugar.
Places of Interest: Bucaco mountain and forest; Praja de Rocha beach resort; Nazaré fishing village; Azores and Madeira islands; Fatima sanctuary; Queluz; Coimbra; Pôrto. *In Lisbon:* Moorish fortress and palace; Jerónimos monastery; Monument to Christ.

PORTUGAL TODAY

Somewhat smaller than Indiana, Portugal is a poor European nation struggling to achieve a stable political democracy after half a century of fascist dictatorship.

Lying between the Atlantic on the west and Spain on the east, Portugal occupies about one-sixth of the Iberian peninsula.

Extensive plains extend from the Tagus River south to Cape Saint Vincent, Europe's southwestern tip. Portugal's highest point is the 6,532-foot Serra da Estréla, northeast of Lisbon.

Important rivers include the Douro, Tagus, Minho, and Guadiana, all originating in Spain.

The weather varies with cool summers and cold winters in the north, and a warm Mediterranean climate in the south.

EARLY HISTORY

Ancient Phoenicians, Carthaginians, and Greeks all established colonies on the coast. In 27 B.C. the Romans made the region a province called *Lusitania.* After the Romans, Visigoths controlled the region until they were defeated in 711 by the Moors.

In 1143 Portugal became an independent nation under King Afonso Henriques.

Portugal's era of glory began with the reign of João I (1385–1433). His son, Henry the Navigator, encouraged exploration that gave Portugal a huge overseas empire.

From 1580 to 1640 Spain ruled Portugal. Independence was reestablished in 1640 when the Portuguese revolted and installed João VI as king.

Napoleon's forces invaded Portugal in 1807, and the royal family fled to Brazil. King João VI returned to Portugal in 1820.

THE PORTUGUESE REPUBLIC

The monarchy was overthrown in 1910, and a republic was established. Portugal was ruled as a fascist dictatorship by António de Oliveira Salazar in 1928–68 and by Marcello Caetano in 1968–74.

On April 25, 1974, Gen. António de Spinola, a leftist, overthrew Caetano. The military junta replaced Spinola as president on Sept. 30, 1974, with Gen. Francisco da Costa Gomes.

The junta let voters go to the polls on April 25, 1975, in the first free election since 1926, choosing an assembly to draw up a constitution.

The Marxist revolutionary government in 1975 nationalized most industries and expropriated large landholdings. It also ended Portugal's 500-year-old African colonial empire.

Under a new democratic constitution, a national assembly was elected on April 25, 1976, with socialists led by Mário Soares winning a plurality of 106 of the 263 seats. Army Chief of Staff Gen. António Ramalho Eanes, 41, was elected president on June 27, 1976. Soares became prime minister.

Many persons were injured in riots in farming areas after parliament adopted a law on Aug. 11, 1977, that small farms seized in the 1975 revolution should be returned to their owners.

When Soares' coalition cabinet disintegrated in 1978, President Eanes appointed a politically independent industrialist, Alfredo Nobre da Costa, as prime minister. Seventeen days later, on Sept. 14, the national assembly rejected Nobre da Costa's program. Eanes then appointed as prime minister a law professor, Carlos da Mota Pinto, 42, whose government lasted only to June 6, 1979.

President Eanes ordered new parliamentary elections. He appointed as caretaker prime minister the nation's first woman head of state, Maria de Lurdes Pintassilgo, 49, a moderate leftist.

Portuguese voters moved toward the right in parliamentary elections held on Dec. 2, 1979, and on Oct. 5, 1980. The conservative Democratic Alliance of Francisco Sá Carneiro, who became prime minister on Jan. 3, 1980, won majorities in both elections, with 128 seats and then with 134.

Sá Carneiro was killed in a plane crash on Dec. 4, 1980. Minister of State Francisco Pinto Balsemão was named as prime minister.

In a presidential election on Dec. 7, 1980, President Eanes, supported by independents, socialists, and communists, won reelection to another 4-year term, receiving about 57% of the vote.

After leftists in the army obstructed the return to private ownership of industries nationalized during the 1970s revolution, parliament revised the constitution effective Oct. 30, 1982, eliminating the power of the military to veto legislation.

In a national election on April 25, 1983, the socialists won a plurality of 101 parliamentary seats, followed by the centrist social democrats with 75, and the communists with 41. Soares again became prime minister in June 1983, after forming a coalition with the social democrats.

In an effort to help the sagging economy, Soares adopted a tough austerity program in 1983, ending government subsidies that had held down food and energy prices.

PORTUGUESE OVERSEAS AREAS

AZORES

Area: 902 square miles (2,336 sq. km.).
Population: 262,628.
Capital: Ponta Delgada, 69,930.

Lying in the Atlantic Ocean about 750 miles west of Europe, the Azores include nine main islands and several small ones. Most people make their living as fishermen and farmers. Main exports include canned fish, pineapples, butter, and cheese.

The Azores were discovered in 1427–31 by the Portuguese explorer Diogo de Sevilla. Settled by Portuguese and Flemish colonists, the Azores became an important stop for ships during the exploration of the Americas.

The U.S. maintains an air base on Terceira Island. Portugal and the U.S. signed a treaty on June 18, 1979, providing for continued U.S. use of the air base until 1983.

On April 30, 1976, Portugal granted the Azores internal self-government with an elected assembly. Nationalists continued to demonstrate in 1977–80, calling for complete independence.

MACAU (formerly MACAO)

Area: 6.2 square miles (16 sq. km.).
Population: 307,063.
Capital: Macau City, 241,413.

Macau, at the mouth of mainland China's Pearl River, is about 40 miles from Hong Kong.

The colony consists of Macau City on Macau peninsula, and two smaller islands—Taipa and Coloane. About 99% of the people are Chinese.

Portugal colonized Macau in 1557 and paid rent to China until 1949. When Portugal began freeing its colonies in 1975, China indicated it preferred Macau's status to remain unchanged.

Macau's main income is from gambling casinos patronized by Chinese from Hong Kong, where gambling is banned.

MADEIRA

Area: 307 square miles (795 sq. km.).
Population: 272,340.
Capital: Funchal, 105,791.

Situated in the Atlantic Ocean about 600 miles southwest of Portugal, the group includes two main islands, Madeira and Pôrto Santo, and several uninhabited smaller islands.

Thousands of tourists go to Madeira each year to enjoy the beaches and tropical scenery.

The Portuguese explorer João Gonçalves Zarco first sighted the islands in 1418. Portuguese settlers colonized Madeira, importing slaves to work the plantations. On April 30, 1976, Portugal granted Madeira autonomy with an elected assembly for internal self-government.

QUICK QUIZ: What is the driving distance between Chicago, Ill., and El Paso, Tex.? See page 938.

QATAR

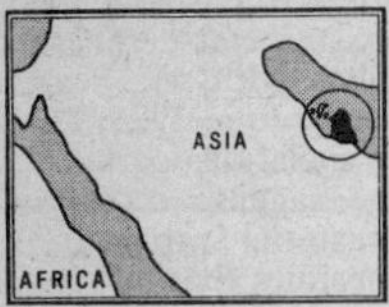

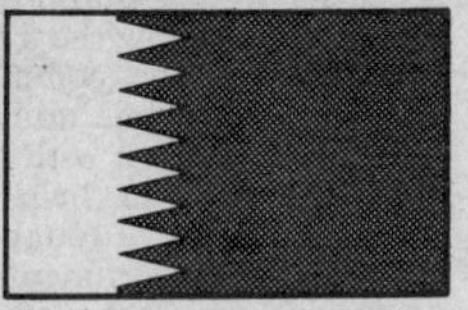

Official Name: State of Qatar.
Area: 4,247 square miles (11,000 sq. km.).
Population: 271,573.
Capital: Doha, 100,000.
Government: Absolute monarchy.
Emir: Khalifa bin Hamad al-Thani (since 1972).
U.S. Ambassador to Qatar: Charles F. Dunbar.
Ambassador to U.S.: Abdelkader Braik al-Ameri.
Flag: Maroon field; white serrated band at hoist.
Official Language: Arabic.
Main Ethnic Groups: Qatari (45%), Pakistani (35%).
Religion: Islam (98%).
Leading Industries: Mining (petroleum, natural gas); construction; manufacturing (electricity, cement, oil refining, steel); agriculture (livestock, vegetables, fruits); fishing.
Foreign Trade: *Major exports*—petroleum, gas, steel, chemicals; *major imports*—food, consumer goods.
Places of Interest: Royal residence; oil refineries.

QATAR TODAY

About the size of Massachusetts, Qatar is an oil-rich Arab country that is largely a hot, sandy desert. Most of the people live in and around the capital city of Doha.

New industries have been developed with oil revenues, including an electric power plant, a desalting plant to supply drinking water from the sea, and improved harbor facilities.

Qatar's population more than doubled in the 1970s as thousands of Pakistanis and other foreigners came to work on development projects.

The desert land has sparse vegetation, although vegetables, grain, and fruits are grown.

Qatar is a peninsula jutting into the Persian Gulf. Saudi Arabia and the United Arab Emirates border it on the south.

HISTORY

For many years Qatar was dominated by the rulers of Bahrain. In 1868 Britain undertook negotiations to end Bahrain's rule. But in 1872 the Ottoman Turks absorbed Qatar.

With the collapse of the Turkish empire in World War I, Britain in 1916 made Qatar a protectorate.

Oil was discovered in Qatar in 1940. Commercial production began in 1949.

Qatar declared its independence on Sept. 1, 1971. A treaty of friendship replaced the "special treaty" relationship with Britain.

Emir Ahmed bin Ali al-Thani ruled from 1960 to 1972. He was deposed in a bloodless coup on Feb. 22, 1972, by his cousin Sheik Khalifa bin Hamad al-Thani.

The ruler uses a substantial part of the nation's oil and gas income to develop social services, free housing for Qataris, and heavy industry, including a $300 million steel plant completed in 1978 and a $500 million petrochemical industry that began production in 1980.

ROMANIA

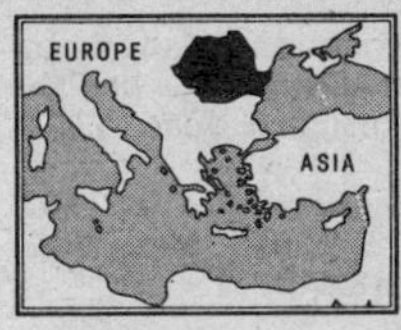

Official Name: Socialist Republic of Romania.
Area: 91,699 square miles (237,500 sq. km.).
Population: 22,642,900.
Chief Cities: Bucureşti (Bucharest), capital, 1,929,360; Braşov, 320,168; Constanta, 293,866; Cluj, 289,808.
Government: Communist state.
President: Nicolae Ceausescu (since 1974).
Prime Minister: Constantin Dascalescu (since 1982).
Grand National Assembly: 369 members.
U.S. Ambassador to Romania: David B. Funderburk.
Romanian Ambassador to U.S.: Mircea Malita.
Flag: Blue, yellow, and red bars, with national coat of arms in center.
Languages: Romanian (official), Hungarian, German.
Main Ethnic Groups: Romanian (89%), Hungarian (8%), German (2%).
Leading Religions: Eastern Orthodox (80%), Roman Catholic (9%).
Leading Industries: Manufacturing (steel, electricity, cement, chemicals, ships, machinery, furniture, paper, textiles, shoes); mining (oil, coal, natural gas, iron, salt, copper, lead, gold, silver, uranium); agriculture (livestock, poultry, dairying, grain, sugar beets, vegetables, fruits); construction; lumbering; fishing.
Foreign Trade: *Major exports*—machinery, petroleum products, chemicals, consumer goods, furniture, textiles, shoes, food products; *major imports*—petroleum, iron ore, machinery, chemicals.
Places of Interest: Danube delta; Black Sea beach resorts; monastaries in northern Moldavia; Mt. Retezat; 120 spas. *In Bucharest:* Old Court, Patriarchy, History Museum, Liberty Park, Herastrau Park, museums and art galleries.

ROMANIA TODAY

One of the least industrialized communist countries of eastern Europe, Romania depends heavily on agriculture, which long has made it one of the leading wheat- and corn-growing nations. Once a major oil-exporting country, it now imports about 40% of its petroleum needs.

Under leadership of Nicolae Ceausescu since 1965, Romania is one of the most repressive communist police states.

Romania is economically dependent on the Soviet Union as its main trading partner. However, it sometimes criticizes Soviet foreign policy.

Government economic planning has placed emphasis on the development of heavy industry. Neglect of modernizing agriculture production resulted in food shortages in the 1980s.

About the size of Oregon, Romania is a land of great geographical contrasts. The Carpathian Mountains surround the central plateau of Transylvania. Beyond are three major plateaus: Moldavia to the east, Wallachia to the south, and Dobruja on the Black Sea coast between Bulgaria and the Soviet Union.

The Soviet Union lies to the north and northeast, Bulgaria to the south, and Hungary and Yugoslavia to the west.

EARLY HISTORY

The Roman province of Dacia included most of present-day Romania in the 100s A.D. After Rome withdrew in 271, the area was overrun successively by Goths, Huns, Avars, Slavs, and Mongols.

In the 1000s Hungary took control of Transylvania, ruling it until the early 1900s.

The states of Wallachia and Moldavia were founded in the 1300s.

Prince Vlad Tepes of Wallachia, said to be the original for the fictional vampire Count Dracula, fought off Turkish invaders until he was killed when they finally conquered Wallachia in 1476. The Turks then took Moldavia in 1504.

KINGDOM OF ROMANIA

In 1859 Moldavia and Wallachia united under Prince Alexander John Cuza, with the principality taking the name *Romania* in 1862. Cuza was cast aside in 1866 in favor of Prince Karl of the house of Hohenzollern-Sigmaringen.

Romania declared independence on May 9, 1877. Prince Karl became King Carol I in 1881.

After fighting on the side of the Allies in World War I, Romania acquired Transylvania and the Banat from Hungary, Bukovina from Austria, and Bessarabia from Russia.

In June 1940 Hungary seized Transylvania, the Soviet Union annexed the northern part of Romania called Bessarabia, and Bulgaria took Dobruja in the southeast.

In September 1940 Marshal Ion Antonescu ousted King Carol II, placing his young son Michael on the throne with the help of the Iron Guard—a fascist military organization. Romania joined the Axis Powers.

In August 1944 Antonescu was overthrown by King Michael, and Romania switched to the Allied side.

COMMUNIST RULE

After the Soviet advance into the country in 1944–45, a communist-led coalition headed by Petri Groza came to power. In 1947 Michael was forced to abdicate, and Romania was declared a communist republic.

A peace treaty in 1947 restored Transylvania to Romania, but gave Bessarabia to the Soviet Union and part of Dobruja to Bulgaria.

Romania remained an obedient Soviet satellite until 1962, when the Soviet Union attempted unsuccessfully to persuade it to abandon its plan for industrialization and become an agricultural reserve for the Soviet bloc. Since then Romanian leaders Gheorghe Gheorgiu-Dej (1961–65) and Nicolae Ceausescu (since 1965) have pursued a somewhat more independent course.

While the Soviet bloc supported the Arab countries during the June 1967 Arab-Israeli war, Romania refused to condemn Israel as the aggressor and did not break relations with it.

The Ceausescu regime supported the liberalization program in Czechoslovakia, refusing to join in Warsaw Pact military action against the Dubček government in Czechoslovakia in 1968.

In 1974 Romania modified its press laws to end censorship prior to publication, putting the burden on editors to delete anticommunist ideas from articles before printing them.

Although the Soviet Union broke off trade agreements with the U.S. in a dispute over freedom of immigration, Romania negotiated a new trade agreement with the U.S. on April 2, 1975, and eased immigration restrictions.

In September 1978 the government fired several cabinet ministers and other high officials, including its UN ambassador, as a result of secret disclosures to the U.S. CIA by Romanian Lt. Gen. Ion Pacepa, No. 2 man in Romania's spy organization, who defected to the U.S. on July 29, 1978.

Ceausescu appointed his brother-in-law, Ilie Verdet, 54, as prime minister on March 30, 1979.

Increased energy usage and declining petroleum production caused Romania to become a net importer of petroleum in 1976. The government announced plans to build six nuclear power plants and turn to other energy sources to achieve energy self-sufficiency by 1990.

Increasing food shortages caused the government to decree on Oct. 17, 1981, rationing of grain products and banning their use as livestock feed. Then on Feb. 9, 1982, the government hiked food prices by 35% while raising wages only 16%.

In an attempt to divert blame for the country's declining economy from himself, Ceausescu fired Prime Minister Verdet and a dozen other high officials in May 1982, accusing them of inefficiency and corruption. Constantin Dascalescu was named the new prime minister.

In 1982 Romania began forcing emigrants to pay a departure tax of from $3,600 to $40,000 to compensate for the amount of public education they had received. However, the tax was revoked in June 1983 after the U.S. threatened to end Romania's favored-nation trade status if the tax continued.

RWANDA

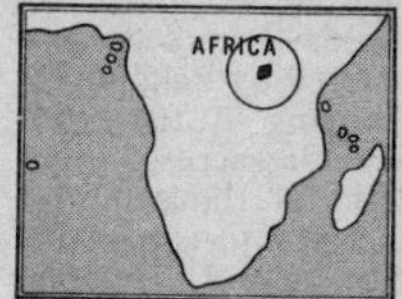

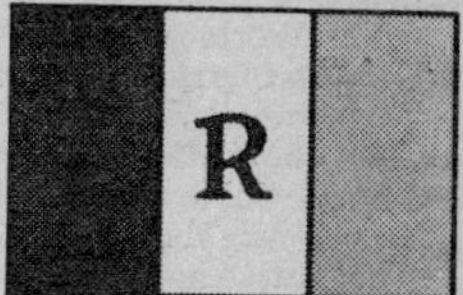

Official Name: Republic of Rwanda.
Area: 10,169 square miles (26,338 sq. km.).
Population: 5,715,990.
Capital: Kigali, 54,403.
Government: One-party dictatorship.
President: Juvenal Habyarimana (since 1973).
U.S. Ambassador to Rwanda: John Blane.
Rwandan Ambassador to U.S.: Simon Insoner.
Flag: Bars of red, yellow, and green, with black *R* in center.
Official Languages: French and Kinyarwanda.
Main Ethnic Groups: Hutu (89%), Tutsi (10%).
Religions: Christianity (60%), Islam, animism.
Leading Industries: Agriculture (coffee, cattle, pyrethrum, tea, beans, corn); manufacturing (light consumer goods); mining (tin, wolfram).
Foreign Trade: *Major exports*—coffee, tin, tea; *major imports*—textiles, oil and gasoline, food, machinery.
Places of Interest: Kigali; Gisenyi; Butare Museum; Akagera and Virungas national parks; Rusumo Falls; Gabiro guesthouse at Kibungo.

QUICK QUIZ: How many highway deaths occured in 1982? See page 934.

RWANDA *(continued)*

RWANDA TODAY

About the size of Vermont, Rwanda is one of the poorest countries in the world.

Most Rwandans live as they have for centuries, growing enough food and raising enough cattle to subsist, but not enough to afford more than a primitive existence. Only about 10% can read and write. The average Rwandan lives only to age 44.

Only a few Europeans live in Rwanda, and most of those who do supervise the tin and wolfram mines—the country's only substantial industry other than agriculture.

Violence between the Hutu and the Tutsi has continued sporadically since independence. The Tutsi government of neighboring Burundi has accused the Hutu government of Rwanda of massacring Tutsi tribesmen. In turn the Rwanda government has accused Burundi of harboring Tutsi guerrillas.

Rwanda's exports and imports travel by truck along a 1,000-mile road through Uganda to the port of Mombasa, Kenya.

The land is mountainous, with elevations ranging from 4,800 feet at Lake Kivu in the west to 14,787-foot Mt. Karisimbi in the northwest. In the east are a hilly plateau and lakes. The climate is tropical.

Uganda lies to the north, Tanzania to the east, Burundi to the south, and Zaire to the west.

EARLY HISTORY

The kingdom of Rwanda can be traced back to the 1500s. Led by a royal clan from Ethiopia, waves of Tutsi conquered the local Hutu tribes.

In 1899 Rwanda was incorporated as a colony into German East Africa.

After World War I the League of Nations mandated Rwanda and its neighbor Burundi to Belgium as the territory of Rwanda-Urundi.

After World War II, Rwanda-Urundi became a UN trust territory administered by Belgium.

In November 1959 an uprising by the Hutu against the Tutsi brought the massacre of thousands of Tutsi and the flight of thousands of others to neighboring Burundi and to Uganda.

The Tutsi king was overthrown and a republic was proclaimed in 1961.

INDEPENDENCE

Belgium granted self-government to Rwanda on Jan. 1, 1962, with Gregoire Kayibanda, head of the Parmehutu Party, as president.

Rwanda received independence on July 1, 1962. Kayibanda was reelected in 1965 and 1969.

In a bloodless coup on July 5, 1973, Defense Minister Maj. Gen. Juvenal Habyarimana overthrew Kayibanda.

Habyarimana dissolved the national assembly and ruled by decree. He made his National Revolutionary Movement for Development (MRND) the only political party in 1975. Habyarimana was elected without opposition to a 5-year term as president on Dec. 17, 1978.

Rwanda appealed for international help in 1982 when Uganda uprooted about 25,000 Rwandan immigrants, burning their homes and stealing their cattle. Thousands fled back to Rwanda, pleading for food and shelter.

ST. CHRISTOPHER AND NEVIS

Official Name: St. Christopher and Nevis.
Area: 101 square miles (262 sq. km.)
Population: 44,932.
Capital: Basseterre, 15,000.
Government: Multiparty parliamentary democracy.
Prime Minister: Kennedy Simmonds (since 1980).
National Assembly: 11 members.
U.S. Ambassador: Milan D. Bish.
Flag: Two white stars on black diagonal stripe bordered by thin yellow stripes; green triangle in upper hoist corner and red triangle at bottom.
Main Language: English.
Largest Ethnic Group: Blacks.
Chief Religion: Anglican.
Leading Industries: Agriculture (sugarcane, cotton, vegetables, fruits, livestock); tourism; manufacturing (sugar refining, brewing, electronic equipment, textiles, furniture); fishing.
Foreign Trade: *Major exports*—sugar, cotton; *major imports*—food, consumer products, petroleum.
Places of Interest: Mount Misery; Brimstone Hill fort; beach resorts.

One of the smallest countries of the world, St. Christopher and Nevis lies in the Caribbean Sea, southeast of Puerto Rico.

Usually called St. Kitts, the country consists of two volcanic islands: St. Christopher (65 sq. mi.) and Nevis (36 sq. mi.)

About a third of the people make their living from agriculture. Sugar, grown largely on St. Christopher, accounts for about two-thirds of the exports. The main crop on the island of Nevis is cotton.

Most of the people can read and write.

Christopher Columbus landed on Saint Christopher during his second voyage in 1493, and the island was named for his patron saint.

In 1623 Sir Thomas Warner established on St. Christopher the first British colony in the Caribbean. French colonists also arrived on the island in 1624. British colonists landed on Nevis in 1629.

Britain and France disputed possession of the islands until 1783 when France gave up its claim.

St. Christopher, Nevis, and the island of Anguilla became a self-governing associated state of Britain on Feb. 27, 1967. But three months later Anguilla withdrew from the state to become a separate British dependency.

In an election in February 1980, the Labor Party, which had dominated the state's politics since the 1960s, won only four seats. Dr. Kennedy Simmonds, leader of the People's Action Movement, formed a coalition with the Nevis Reform Party to achieve a one-seat majority and attain the office of prime minister.

Britain granted the nation full independence on Sept. 19, 1983. Four days later it joined the United Nations.

SAINT LUCIA

Official Name: State of St. Lucia.
Area: 238 square miles (616 sq. km.).
Population: 119,659.
Capital: Castries, 45,000.
Government: Multiparty parliamentary democracy.
Prime Minister: John Compton (since 1982).
House of Assembly: 17 members.
U.S. Ambassador to St. Lucia: Milan D. Bish.
Saint Lucian Ambassador to U.S.: Barry Bertrand Lucas Auguste.
Flag: Blue field with white, black, and yellow triangle in center.
Main Languages: English (official); French patois widely spoken.
Ethnic Groups: Black (97%), white (3%).
Principal Religion: Roman Catholicism.
Leading Industries: Agriculture (bananas, coconuts, cocoa, citrus fruits, spices); fishing; forestry; manufacturing (rum, food processing, clothing, electricity, fertilizer, batteries); tourism.
Foreign Trade: *Major exports*—bananas, coconut products, coconuts, fruits and vegetables, spices; *major imports*—flour, meat, fish, sugar, milk, alcoholic beverages, metals, lumber, fuel oil, clothing, shoes, machinery, automobiles.
Places of Interest: Fort Rodney on Pigeon Island; Morne Fortune (Lucky Hill) battlefield; beach resorts; Piton volcanoes near Soufrière.

ST. LUCIA TODAY

A volcanic Caribbean island about one-twelfth the size of Puerto Rico, St. Lucia lies closer to South America than to the United States. Its nearest neighbors are the French island of Martinique to the north, St. Vincent to the south, and Barbados to the east.

Most of the people are descendants of African slaves. Although English is generally understood, most of the people speak a French patois. Most of the islanders make their living from tourism or from agriculture. About one-third of the population live in the capital city of Castries.

The agricultural land largely is divided into small family farms of less than 5 acres. More than 10,000 families raise bananas, which account for about 80% of the island's exports. Coconuts provide the second most important export crop.

Income from tourism amounts to almost as much as receipts from exports. Over 100,000 tourists visit St. Lucia each year, about half of whom are passengers on cruise ships.

Tropical rain forests cover the steep slopes of the island's volcanoes. The highest peak is 3,117-foot Mt. Gimie. Twin volcanoes called the Pitons rise sharply from the sea near Soufrière on the southwest coast.

The island has a year-round tropical climate with an average temperature of 80°F. (26°C.). Annual rainfall of 60 to 138 inches comes mainly from May to August.

EARLY HISTORY

The earliest inhabitants of St. Lucia were the Arawak Indians from South America. They later were driven out by the fierce Carib Indians.

English colonists who tried to settle the island in 1605 and 1638 were killed or driven off by the Carib Indians. French colonists subjugated the Carib Indians in 1660.

During the next 150 years the French and English battled for possession of the island.

In 1778 some 1,300 British troops repulsed an attack by 5,000 French soldiers.

In May 1781 French Adm. Comte de Grasse unsuccessfully attacked the island with a fleet of 25 warships. However, St. Lucia was given to France in the 1783 peace treaty.

Britain took the island again in April 1796 with an assault by 12,000 troops under command of Lt. Gen. Sir Ralph Abercrombie with most of the fighting taking place on Morne Fortune (Lucky Hill) near Castries. But France again won possession in a peace treaty.

The final battle for St. Lucia took place in June 1803, during the Napoleonic wars, when British troops again stormed ashore and defeated French defenders. In the 1814 Treaty of Paris, France ceded the island to Britain.

Britain ended slavery on St. Lucia in 1834, compensating owners for freeing 13,291 slaves, who made up 80% of the island's population.

St. Lucia was administered as a separate British colony until 1838, when it was annexed to the British Windward Islands Colony.

St. Lucia received its own British governor in 1959 as part of the short-lived Federation of the West Indies.

Britain granted St. Lucia self-government on May 3, 1967. The government was controlled for 15 years by the conservative United Workers Party (UWP), which won national elections in 1964, 1968, and 1974. UWP leader John Compton served as chief minister.

INDEPENDENT NATION

Compton conducted lengthy negotiations with Britain that gained independence for St. Lucia on Feb. 22, 1979. The new nation remained part of the British Commonwealth of Nations.

The leftist St. Lucia Labour Party (SLP), campaigning for closer relations with communist nations, won a national election on July 2, 1979, capturing 12 of the 17 seats in the House of Assembly. Allan Louisy, 62, head of the SLP became prime minister.

A split in the SLP caused Louisy to be replaced as prime minister by Winston Cenac in 1981. Strikes opposing Cenac's policies forced him to resign on Jan. 16, 1982. He was succeeded by Michael Pilgrim.

John Compton again became prime minister after his pro-Western United Workers Party (UWP) won 14 of the 17 seats in the national assembly in an election on May 3, 1982.

Compton appealed to the U.S. and Britain for additional aid to help revive the ailing economy.

QUICK QUIZ: Which U.S. state has the lowest personal income per capita? See page 878.

SAINT VINCENT

Official Name: St. Vincent and the Grenadines.
Area: 150 square miles (388 sq. km.)
Population: 130,063.
Capital: Kingstown, 23,645.
Government: Multiparty parliamentary democracy.
Prime Minister: Robert Milton Cato (since 1974).
House of Assembly: 13 members.
Flag: Vertical stripes of blue, yellow, and green; green coat of arms on yellow stripe.
U.S. Ambassador to St. Vincent: Milan D. Bish.
Ambassador to U.S.: Hudson K. Tannis.
Language: English.
Main Ethnic Group: Black.
Chief Religions: Methodism, Anglicanism, Roman Catholicism.
Leading Industries: Agriculture (bananas, sweet potatoes, arrowroot, coconuts, nutmegs, peanuts, mace, cocoa, food crops); tourism; manufacturing and processing (starch, coconut oil, cigarettes, rum distilling, furniture, flour, clothing); fishing; forestry.
Foreign Trade: *Major exports*—bananas, sweet potatoes, arrowroot, coconut oil, nutmegs, peanuts; *major imports*—food, textiles, cement, lumber, petroleum products, fertilizer, automobiles.
Places of Interest: Soufrière volcano; beach resorts; in Layou, prehistoric Carib Indian altar; in Kingstown, botanic garden.

ST. VINCENT TODAY

One of the chain of Windward Islands in the eastern Caribbean Sea, St. Vincent has an area about the size of Carson City, Nev. But its population is over four times that of Carson City.

The nation also includes hundreds of islets called the Grenadines that stretch to the south.

Most Vincentians earn their living from agriculture or from industries that process farm products. About half the farmland is divided among huge plantations and the rest among small farms of 10 acres or less.

The island's fastest-growing industry is tourism. About 20,000 visitors come to St. Vincent annually to enjoy the black sand beaches, the tropical scenery, and the climate.

Although many of the people are poor, most can read and write because of the excellent school system in which primary education is free. About one-fourth of the population is made up of children who are enrolled in schools.

The island's tallest volcano, 4,048-foot Soufrière, erupts periodically. Its eruption in 1902 killed about 2,000 persons. The volcano came to life in April 1979, sending smoke thousands of feet into the air. Some 20,000 persons were evacuated from the northern part of the island around the volcano, but later returned to their homes after the volcano quieted.

St. Vincent often experiences water shortages during the dry season from January to May. In the rest of the year, annual rainfall varies from 60 inches on the coast to 150 inches in the mountains of the interior.

Temperatures seldom rise to more than 90° F. in daytime and may fall to 64° F. at night.

St. Vincent lies 21 miles south of St. Lucia and about 100 miles west of Barbados.

HISTORY

The earliest known inhabitants were the Arawak Indians, who later were killed or driven out by the warlike Carib Indians.

Christopher Columbus landed on St. Vincent on Jan. 22, 1498.

The Carib Indians remained in control of the island throughout most of the 1700s, although a few European colonists, mostly French, established some settlements.

British forces captured the island from the French in 1762. It was retaken by the French in 1779 during the American Revolution, but was restored to Britain by treaty in 1783.

In 1795–96 the British deported most of the Carib Indians to the island of Rattan in the Bay of Honduras.

From 1958 to 1962 St. Vincent was part of the Federation of the West Indies. During this period the island received internal self-government, beginning in 1960.

The island received the status of an associated state in the British Commonwealth of Nations on Oct. 27, 1969, with complete control of its own domestic affairs.

In a general election on Dec. 9, 1974, the conservative St. Vincent Labor Party (SVLP) won control of the House of Assembly with SLVP leader Robert Milton Cato as prime minister.

Responding to the rising tide of nationalism among its neighbors in the Carribean, St. Vincent was granted independence by Britain, on Oct. 27, 1979, with Cato as prime minister. Britain promised to provide $23 million in aid.

In the first national election since independence, held on Dec. 5, 1979, Cato's party won 11 of the national assembly's 13 seats.

Leftist rebels on Union Island tried to secede from St. Vincent, but were subdued in a battle with police on Dec. 8, 1979, in which one was killed and 19 arrested.

SAN MARINO

Official Name: Most Serene Republic of San Marino.
Area: 23.6 square miles (61 sq. km.).
Population: 22,177.
Capital: San Marino, 4,695.
Government: Communist-governed republic.
Chiefs of State: Co-regents chosen for 6-month terms; 11-man Congress of State (cabinet).
Legislature: *Grand and General Council,* 60 members.
Flag: White stripe over blue stripe with national coat of arms in center.
Language: Italian.
Main Ethnic Group: Sanmarinese.
Principal Religion: Roman Catholicism.

Leading Industries: Tourism; agriculture (wheat, grapes, vegetables, livestock); manufacturing (wine, textiles, leather products, ceramics).
Foreign Trade: *Major exports*—wine, textiles, ceramics, postage stamps; *major imports*—manufactured goods.
Places of Interest: Mt. Titano; Rocca medieval fortress; San Marino Cathedral; Pinacoteca di Stato Museum; Palazzo dei Valloni.

SAN MARINO TODAY

With an area only as large as Newark, N.J., San Marino is surrounded by the mountains of northeast Italy. It has two main industries—farming and tourism.

The government has two main sources of income: (1) the sale of postage stamps and (2) an annual subsidy paid by Italy.

More tourists usually visit each day in the summer than the country's entire population.

The capital city, also called San Marino, lies on the slopes of 2,425-foot Mt. Titano, about 65 miles east of Florence, Italy.

HISTORY

According to legend, San Marino was founded in the 300s by Marinus, a Christian stonecutter from Dalmatia fleeing religious persecution. The independence of San Marino was recognized in 1631 by Pope Urban VIII.

Since 1862 San Marino and Italy have had treaties regulating customs and common interests. San Marino declared war on Germany in World War I but tried to remain neutral in World War II.

A coalition of communists and socialists governed from 1945 to 1957. Women received the right to vote in 1960.

The neutrality of San Marino was confirmed in a new agreement with Italy in 1971.

In parliamentary elections on May 28, 1978, leftist parties gained seats. Although the conservative Christian Democrats retained their plurality with 26 seats, they were unable to form a coalition cabinet with the socialists after the election.

In the first papal visit in the republic's more than 1,600-year history, Pope John Paul II visited the tiny country on Aug. 29, 1982.

In general elections in 1980 and 1983 the leftist coalition retained control of the government.

SÃO TOMÉ AND PRÍNCIPE

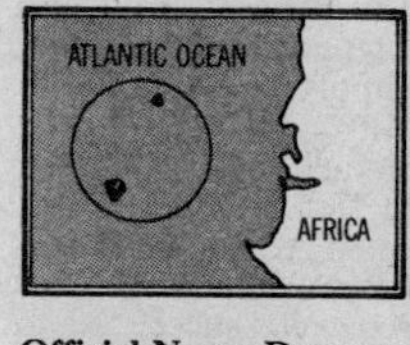

Official Name: Democratic Republic of São Tomé and Príncipe.
Area: 372 square miles (964 sq. km.).
Population: 88,488.
Capital: São Tomé, 5,714.
Government: One-party socialist state.
President: Manuel Pinto da Costa (since 1975).
Prime Minister: Miguel Trovoada (since 1975).
U.S. Ambassador to: Arthur T. Tienken.
Flag: Stripes of green, yellow, and green with red triangle at hoist; two black stars on center yellow stripe.
Language: Portuguese.
Main Ethnic Groups: Black (90%), mixed Portuguese black ancestry (7%).
Religions: Roman Catholicism, animism.
Leading Industries: Agriculture (coffee, cocoa, coconuts, palm kernels, vegetables, fruits); fishing; turtle shell products; food processing; tourism.
Foreign Trade: *Major exports*—coffee, cocoa; *major imports*—food, consumer goods.
Places of Interest: Swimming beaches; medieval plays and festivals on religious feast days; saltwater fishing; coffee plantations; volcanic craters.

SÃO TOMÉ AND PRÍNCIPE TODAY

Only one-third the size of Rhode Island, the island country of São Tomé and Príncipe lies in the Gulf of Guinea, about 125 miles off the west coast of Africa. The largest island is São Tomé (330 sq. mi.). Príncipe (42 sq. mi.) lies about 93 miles to the northeast.

Most of the people are descendants of African slaves. They make their living by farming or fishing. The main exports are coffee and cocoa.

São Tomé has 10 volcanic peaks. The highest, Pico de São Tomé, rises to 6,640 feet. Rain forests cover the mountain slopes, harboring 60 types of tropical birds.

Beaches, saltwater fishing, and a mild climate that averages 62.6° F. attract tourists.

HISTORY

São Tomé was discovered by Portuguese explorers Joáo de Santarém and Pedro Escobar on Dec. 21, 1470. Príncipe was sighted almost a month later, on Jan. 17, 1471. Neither island was inhabited.

In the late 1400s Portugal sent convicts and exiled Jews to the islands. Sugar plantations were founded, worked by slaves from Africa. São Tomé became a major slave trading port for transshipment of African slaves to the Americas. Coffee was introduced in 1800 and cocoa in 1822.

Prosperity declined after 1909 when Britain and Germany boycotted cocoa from the islands because plantation laborers continued to be treated as slaves by their Portuguese masters.

The islands were made an overseas province of Portugal in 1951.

Full independence was granted by Portugal on July 12, 1975, with Manuel Pinto da Costa as the first president. Most of the islands' 4,000 Portuguese residents returned to Portugal.

Under a constitution that became effective on Dec. 12, 1975, the socialist Movement for the Liberation of São Tomé and Príncipe (MLSTP) was designated as the only political party. The president was given absolute power to choose or dismiss a prime minister and cabinet officers.

The country depends on foreign aid and loans to make up annual trade deficits as the import costs outweigh revenues from exports. The main trading partners are Portugal and Netherlands.

The government's economic plans for the 1980s call for diversification of agriculture to end the country's dependence on food imports.

QUICK QUIZ: What are the leading industries of Maine? See page 886.

SAUDI ARABIA

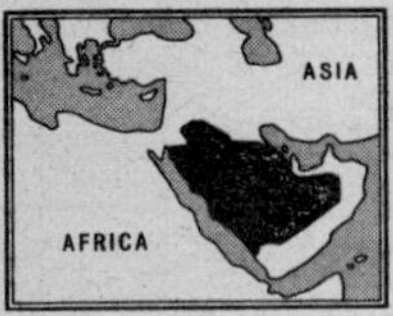

Official Name: Kingdom of Saudi Arabia.
Area: 830,000 square miles (2,149,690 sq. km.).
Population: 10,621,900.
Chief Cities: Riyadh, capital, 666,840; Jidda, 561,104; Mecca, 366,801; Taif, 204,857; Medina, 198,186.
Government: Absolute monarchy.
King and Prime Minister: Fahd ibn Abdul-Aziz (since 1982).
First Deputy Prime Minister: Crown Prince Abdullah ibn Abdul-Aziz (since 1982).
U.S. Ambassador to Saudi Arabia: Walter L. Cutler.
Saudi Arabian Ambassador to U.S.: Faisal Alhegelan.
Flag: Green, with inscription "There is no god but Allah and Mohammed is His messenger" in white Arabic characters above white sword.
Official Language: Arabic.
Principal Ethnic Group: Arab (99%).
State Religion: Islam (99%).
Leading Industries: Mining (petroleum); construction; agriculture (livestock, dates, wheat, corn, alfalfa, grapes, rice, coffee, fruits, vegetables); manufacturing (oil refining, cement, steel).
Foreign Trade: *Major export*—petroleum; *major imports*—vehicles, machinery, iron and steel.
Places of Interest: Kaaba, Islam's most sacred shrine, in Mecca; mosques and palaces; Asir Kingdom National Park.

SAUDI ARABIA TODAY

About one-fourth the size of the United States, Saudi Arabia is a desert kingdom populated by nomadic Arab tribes. But huge deposits of petroleum have changed Saudi Arabia in a few decades from a poor nation to one of the world's richest with an annual oil income of about $100 billion. It is a major source of U.S. oil imports.

The government has used much of the oil revenues to build highways and other public works. Thousands of new schools have been opened. Much money also has been given to poor Arab countries. Two new cities, each planned for a population of 250,000, have been built—Yanbu on the Red Sea and Jubail on the Persian Gulf.

Occupying most of the Arabian peninsula, Saudi Arabia stretches from the Persian Gulf in the east to the Red Sea and the Gulf of Aqaba in the west. Qatar and the United Arab Emirates lie to the east. To the north are Jordan, Iraq, and Kuwait. To the south are Oman, Southern Yemen, and Yemen.

Most of Saudi Arabia is desert. In the west is a fertile coastal plain 10 to 40 miles wide, giving way to steep mountains that rise to over 8,000 feet in the southwest. The Nejd plateau slopes eastward and is bordered by the desert areas of Nefud in the north, Dahna and Nefud Dahi in the east, and Rab al Khali in the south. In the deserts, temperatures range from 70 °to 130 ° F.

EARLY HISTORY

Historians believe Arabia was the original home of the Semitic peoples of the Middle East.

Mohammed founded the religion of Islam at Mecca and Medina about A.D. 622–632. The Muslim armies of the caliph Omar conquered most of the Middle East by 644. The Arab empire extended from Spain and North Africa to the subcontinent of India from the 700s to 1000s. Baghdad, the capital of the Arab empire, fell to the Seljuk Turks in 1055.

From the 1500s Arabia was part of the Ottoman Turkish empire.

In the 1700s Mohammed ibn Saud, the Arab ruler of Nejd, gathered a Bedouin army to gain control of Arabia. His son and successor Abdullah I was defeated by Egypt's Mohammed Ali in 1815–16.

In 1902 young Abdul Aziz ibn Saud regained control of Nejd. By 1925 he had annexed the Kingdom of Hejaz. Britain endorsed independence of his dominions in 1927.

KINGDOM OF SAUDI ARABIA

Saudi Arabia was proclaimed a unified kingdom in 1932 under King Abdul Aziz ibn Saud. Huge oil deposits were discovered in 1935.

In 1945 Saudi Arabia joined the United Nations and the Arab League, ending its isolation.

Ibn Saud was succeeded by his son Saud in 1953. But King Saud was deposed in 1964 to be followed by his younger brother Faisal.

Saudi Arabia did not join directly in the Arab-Israeli war of October 1973, but led in the 1973–74 oil embargo of the U.S. and other nations friendly to Israel.

In June 1974 the government took 60% control of foreign-owned oil companies.

King Faisal was assassinated by a nephew on March 25, 1975, and was succeeded by his half-brother Khalid Abdul-Aziz.

The discovery of new offshore oil fields in the Persian Gulf in 1975 pushed the nation's known oil reserves to about 180 billion barrels, enough to last 60 years at the present rate of production.

Saudi Arabia's royal family was shaken when several hundred rebels seized Islam's holiest shrine, the Grand Mosque, in Mecca on Nov. 20, 1979, and their leader proclaimed himself the savior of Islam. Saudi troops besieged the mosque for two weeks before forcing the rebels to surrender. About 220 persons died in the fighting, including 120 soldiers. On Jan. 9, 1980, 63 of the captured rebels were beheaded in public executions.

With the outbreak of war between Iraq and Iran in 1980, Saudi Arabia stepped up oil production to stabilize the world supply available to oil-importing nations.

Despite opposition from Israel, the U.S. agreed in 1981 to sell Saudi Arabia $8.5 billion of arms, including its most sophisticated Advanced Warning and Control System (AWACS) aircraft.

King Fahd ibn Abdul-Aziz, 60, succeeded to the throne on June 13, 1982, after the death of his half-brother, King Khalid. Friendly to the U.S., King Fahd became known as a modernist in previous government service, being credited with opening education to Saudi Arabian women.

Fahd strongly supported government plans to spend some $250 billion in a five-year plan for 1981–86 to develop heavy industry that would reduce the nation's dependence on oil revenues.

SENEGAL

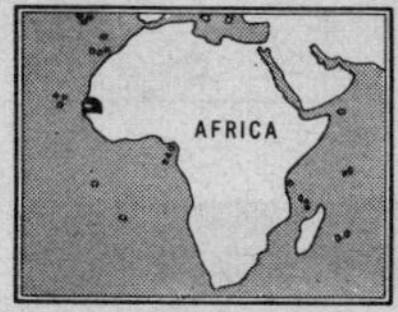

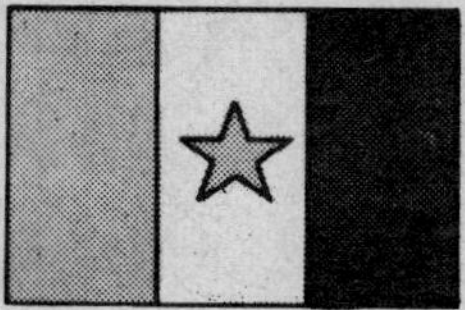

Official Name: Republic of Senegal.
Area: 75,750 square miles (196,192 sq. km.).
Population: 6,438,140.
Capital: Dakar, 798,792.
Government: Multiparty socialist republic.
President: Abdou Diouf (since 1981).
National Assembly: 120 members.
U.S. Ambassador to Senegal: Charles W. Bray III.
Senegalese Ambassador to U.S.: Abourahmane Dia.
Flag: Bars of green, gold, and red, with centered green star.
Languages: French (official), English, tribal dialects.
Main Ethnic Groups: Wolof (36%), Peuhl (18%), Serere (17%), Toucouleur (9%), Diola (9%), Mandingo (7%).
Religions: Islam (80%), animism, Christianity.
Leading Industries: Agriculture (peanuts, millet, sorghum, cotton, sugarcane, rice, livestock, vegetables, fruits); fishing; mining (phosphates); food processing; tourism; forestry.
Foreign Trade: *Major exports*—peanuts and peanut oil, phosphates, fish; *major imports*—food, consumer goods, machinery, transport equipment.
Places of Interest: Gorée Island; Niokolo-Koba national park. *In Dakar:* Native markets; French Institute of Black Africa.

SENEGAL TODAY

About the size of South Dakota, Senegal is one of the few multiparty democracies in Africa. Because Dakar was for half a century the capital of French colonies in West Africa, Senegal is more industrially developed than most other West African countries. However, its economy depends heavily on aid from France. Peanuts account for about one-third of Senegal's exports.

Most of Senegal consists of hot, dry savanna with light, low-fertility soil. Some parts of the north are semidesert. The south is forested and rises to a height of 1,315 feet. Chief rivers include the Gambia and the Senegal.

Located on the west coast of Africa's bulge into the Atlantic Ocean, Senegal lies south of Mauritania. Mali is to the east. Guinea and Guinea-Bissau are to the south. Senegal surrounds the small country of Gambia, except for that nation's outlet to the Atlantic.

The capital, Dakar, lies on Cape Verde, the westernmost part of the African continent.

EARLY HISTORY

Stone Age artifacts indicate that Senegal has been populated for thousands of years.

The name *Senegal* came from the Zenaga Berbers of Mauritania who invaded the region in the 100s, converting the Toucouleur people of the region to Islam. By the mid-1400s Portuguese explorers reached the area. They were followed by Dutch, French, and British traders.

FRENCH RULE

After the Napoleonic wars Britain recognized French claims to the area north of the Gambia River.

The French first built a fort at Dakar in 1857. French designs on the interior were long blocked by the Toucouleur empire of El Hadj Omar, which did not fall to French conquest until 1893, although by 1861 the French had absorbed western Senegal.

France agreed to give Britain control of the Gambia River in a treaty in 1889, resulting in the present-day nation of Gambia.

In 1902 Dakar became the administrative center for French West Africa.

Remaining loyal to the Vichy regime in World War II, Senegal repulsed an attempt by the Free French to take Dakar in 1940.

After the war, Senegalese leaders worked for a viable French Union, but when Guinea defected from the union in 1958, Senegal became an autonomous member of the French Community.

In 1959 the country joined with the Sudanese Republic to form the Mali Federation.

INDEPENDENCE

On Aug. 20, 1960, Senegal declared itself independent, with Léopold Sédar Senghor as the first president. It was admitted to the UN that year.

An attempt to overthrow Senghor in 1962 resulted in the imprisonment of Premier Mamadou Dia until 1974.

Throughout the 1960s and early 1970s Senghor and his ruling party forbade political opposition while winning reelection to 5-year terms in 1963, 1968, and 1973.

In February 1976 Senegal extended its territorial limits 150 miles to sea and forbade foreign fishing within 200 miles of its coast.

The constitution was amended in 1976 to allow opposition parties to exist in addition to Senghor's ruling Socialist Party.

In the nation's first multiparty election on Feb. 26, 1978, Senghor won 82% of the vote and his Socialist Party took 83 of the 100 seats in the national assembly. The opposition Democratic Party won the other 17 seats.

The 74-year-old Senghor turned the presidency over to his chosen successor, Abdou Diouf, on Jan. 1, 1981. Diouf, 45, had served as the nation's prime minister since 1970.

Work began in 1981 on a $2 billion irrigation project on the Senegal River financed by loans from Arab oil-exporting nations. The project is planned to develop a million acres of new farmland in Senegal, Mali, and Mauritania.

When communists tried to overthrow the government of neighboring Gambia in August 1981, Senegal put down the rebellion.

On Feb. 1, 1982, Senegal and Gambia formed the confederation of *Senegambia* to link their economies, national security forces, and foreign policy. But each nation retained its sovereignty.

In a free election on Feb. 27, 1983, President Diouf easily defeated four other presidential candidates, winning with about 85% of the vote. His Socialist Party captured 109 seats in the national assembly.

QUICK QUIZ: Which major league baseball park has the largest seating capacity? See page 785.

SEYCHELLES

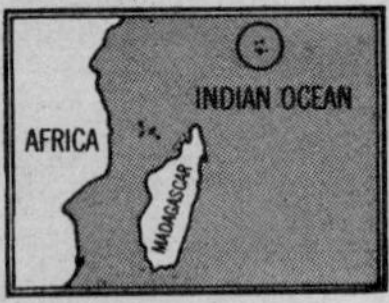

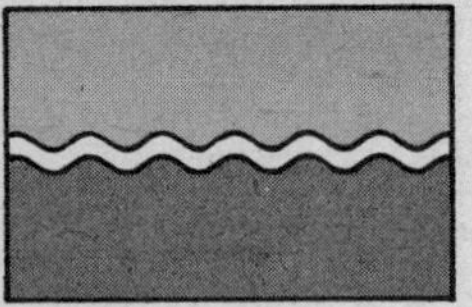

Official Name: Republic of Seychelles.
Area: 171 square miles (444 sq. km.).
Population: 65,360.
Capital: Victoria, 13,736.
Government: One-party socialist state.
President: France Albert René (since 1977).
Legislative Assembly: 23 members.
U.S. Ambassador to Seychelles: Walter C. Wallace.
Seychelles Ambassador to U.S.: Giovinella Gonthier.
Flag: Red stripe at top, wavy white band in middle, and green stripe at bottom.
Languages: English and French (official), Creole.
Main Ethnic Group: Creole (mixed French and black descent; 94%).
Principal Religion: Roman Catholicism.
Leading Industries: Agriculture (coconuts, cinnamon, vanilla, fruits, vegetables); tourism; fishing.
Foreign Trade: *Major exports*—cinnamon, coconuts; *major imports*—machinery, vehicles, food.
Places of Interest: Vallée de Mai on Praslin Island; tourist resorts; beaches; Bird Island bird sanctuary.

Seychelles is a small nation of 92 islands off the east coast of Africa. The largest islands are Mahé (55 sq. mi.) and Praslin (17 sq. mi.).

Tourism is the main industry with thousands of visitors attracted each year by the Seychelles' tropical beauty and many swimming beaches.

Other than caring for tourists, most Seychellois make their living by farming and fishing.

The climate seldom varies from a temperature of 75 °to 85 ° F. on the coast. Mountains rise to a height of 2,993 feet on Mahé. Rainfall ranges from 70 to 135 inches a year.

Arab ships visited in the 1100s. French settlers brought African slaves in the 1770s.

The British captured the islands in 1810, and the French formally gave them up in the Treaty of Paris of 1814. The islands were administered as part of the British colony of Mauritius until 1903, when they were made a separate crown colony. Islanders were first given the opportunity to vote in 1948. A U.S. space-tracking station was established on Mahé in 1963.

The conservative Seychelles Democratic Party (SDP) won elections in 1970 and 1974 with SDP leader James R. Mancham as chief minister.

Britain granted Seychelles independence on June 29, 1976, with Mancham as president.

Sixty armed rebels overthrew Mancham's government on June 5, 1977. For president they chose France Albert René, head of the Seychelles People's United Party (SPUP).

René established a one-party Marxist socialist state. However, he continued to lease land to the U.S. for the space-tracking station.

Attempted coups were put down by René's forces in November 1979, November 1981, and August 1982.

A new 23-member national assembly was chosen on May 7, 1983, in a one-party election.

SIERRA LEONE

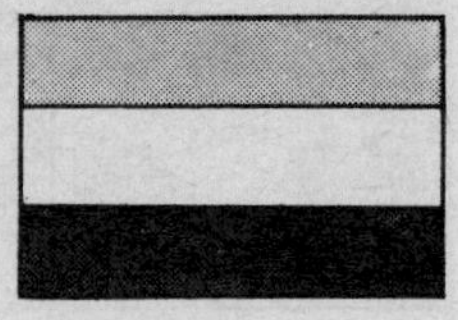

Official Name: Republic of Sierra Leone.
Area: 27,699 square miles (71,740 sq. km.).
Population: 3,753,530.
Capital: Freetown 214,443.
Government: One-party republic.
President: Siaka Stevens (since 1971).
House of Representatives: 104 members.
U.S. Ambassador to Sierra Leone: Arthur W. Lewis.
Sierra Leone Ambassador to U.S.: Dauda Sulaiman Kamara.
Flag: Stripes of green (top), white, and blue.
Languages: English (official), Krio (Pidgin English), tribal dialects.
Ethnic Groups: Mende (30%), Temne (30%), others (40%).
Religions: Animism (66%), Islam (28%), Christianity (6%).
Leading Industries: Mining (diamonds, iron, bauxite, rutile); agriculture (rice, peanuts, coffee, palm kernels, cocoa, cassava, ginger, livestock); fishing; forestry and lumbering; food processing; tourism.
Foreign Trade: *Major exports*—diamonds, iron ore, palm kernels; *major imports*—cotton fabrics, petroleum products, mining machinery, rice.
Places of Interest: Mountainous area of the Sierra Leone peninsula; Freetown; swimming beaches.

SIERRA LEONE TODAY

Although Sierra Leone has large deposits of diamonds, bauxite, and other minerals, it is a poor country. About three-fourths of the Sierra Leonians are farmers, but they do not raise even enough of their basic crop, rice, to feed everyone.

Britain is Sierra Leone's largest customer, purchasing more than half the nation's exports.

About the size of South Carolina, Sierra Leone is bordered by Guinea in the north and by Liberia in the southeast.

The peninsula in the extreme west is a hilly area. The remainder of western Sierra Leone consists of a coastal plain. Farther inland the land rises abruptly to a low plateau. Freetown, the capital, has one of the world's largest harbors.

HISTORY

The area was named *Serra Lyoa* (later corrupted to Sierra Leone)—meaning "Lion Mountains"—in the 1400s by Portuguese seamen.

In 1787 British abolitionists, in a plan to return former English and American slaves to Africa, sent a small expedition to Sierra Leone. They were driven away by the local tribal chief, but other expeditions followed. By 1792 nearly all of England's destitute blacks had been transported to Sierra Leone. They were joined by captured Maroons from Jamaica and by former slaves from other British colonies.

In 1808 the British took over the colony for use as a naval base.

During the next 60 years Sierra Leone received thousands of liberated slaves

The British expanded inland from Freetown, and in 1896 the interior was declared a protectorate. The two areas later were merged.

Sierra Leone was granted independence on April 21, 1961, remaining in the British Commonwealth of Nations.

The results of the March 17, 1967, elections gave a slight edge to the All People's Congress, led by Siaka Stevens, over the ruling Sierra Leone People's Party, led by Prime Minister Albert Margai. But army officers staged a coup, installing a military government.

A group of noncommissioned army officers ousted the military regime in 1968. Siaka Stevens was sworn in as prime minister.

In April 1971 Stevens declared Sierra Leone a republic, becoming its president.

Stevens' APC party won general elections in 1973, after the opposition party boycotted the election because of police intimidation.

On May 6, 1977, President Stevens' APC again won a general election as opposition parties charged murder and police brutality had prevented them from fully participating. He declared the country a one-party state in 1978.

Stevens hosted the organization of African Unity (OAU) conference in June 1980.

Protesting high food prices caused by a 200% inflation rate, labor unions started a general strike on Aug. 14, 1981, closing most businesses and public services. The strike ended after Stevens declared a state of emergency on Sept. 1.

The first election for the one-party parliament was held on May 1, 1982. With three candidates for each of 85 seats, 37 representatives in the previous parliament were defeated.

SINGAPORE

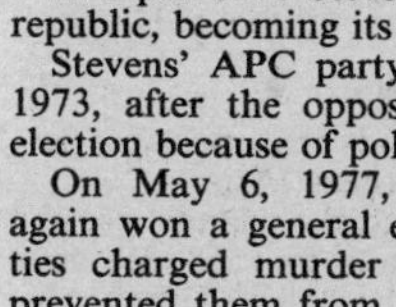

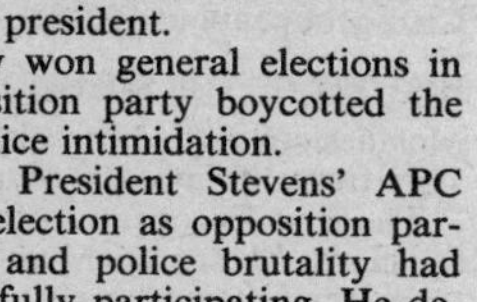

Official Name: Republic of Singapore.
Area: 224 square miles (581 sq. km.).
Population: 2,518,130.
Capital: Singapore, 2,390,800.
Government: Parliamentary state.
Prime Minister: Lee Kuan Yew (appointed in 1959).
Legislative Assembly: 75 members.
U.S. Ambassador to Singapore: Harry E.T. Thayer.
Singapore Ambassador to United States: Punch Coomaraswamy.
Flag: Red and white stripes, with white crescent and five white stars on red stripe.
Languages: Malay, Chinese, English, and Tamil.
Main Ethnic Groups: Chinese (74%), Malay (14%), Indian and Pakistani (8%).
Religions: Buddhism, Islam, Hinduism, Christianity.
Foreign Trade: *Major exports*—petroleum products, arms, rubber; *major imports*—petroleum products, rubber, crude petroleum.
Places of Interest: St. Andrew's Cathedral; Muslim Holy Sultan Mosque; Fort Canning Hill garrison; national museum; botanical gardens; various Chinese temples; Van Cleef Aquarium; House of Jade.

SINGAPORE TODAY

Singapore is a prosperous island nation with an area about the same as that of Chicago but with only about three-fourths as large a population. Its people have the highest standard of living in the Orient after Japan.

Most of the main island of Singapore is a sprawling city. Little land is available for farming, so most food is imported, as are fuel and raw materials. To reduce population growth, extra taxes are levied on couples who have more than two children. Stiff license fees on automobiles and taxicabs entering the downtown area have reduced traffic congestion.

Public opposition to the government's suppressive measures against political opponents has been blunted by Singapore's remarkable prosperity and low unemployment rate. As a regional center for banking, finance, and technology, the island nation attracts ever-larger foreign investment.

The nation's economy depends on processing, packing, and transshipping to world markets the basic products of Southeast Asia. It also distributes within the region manufactured goods from the world's industrial nations.

Singapore's oil-refinery complex, the third largest in the world, provides about one-fourth of the nation's manufacturing income. Oil-rig construction became a growth industry.

Malaysia and the United States are Singapore's major trading partners.

Singapore lies between the southern tip of Southeast Asia's Malay peninsula and Indonesia's island of Sumatra. The weather is usually hot and humid with much rain.

EARLY HISTORY

The earliest known colonizers of Singapore were Sumatrans in the 1000s.

In the 1700s Singapore became part of the Dutch colony of Johore.

In 1819 Sir Thomas Stamford Raffles, an agent of the British East India Company, set up a trading station at Singapore. Five years later the British bought the island from the Dutch. Singapore was made a part of the Straits Settlements, with Malacca and Penang in 1826. The island became a British crown colony in 1867.

Singapore was an important British naval base before World War II. In 1941 Japanese forces seized the city after a fierce battle. It was retaken, without fighting, in 1945. In 1946 Singapore was made a separate crown colony. It became a self-governing state in 1959.

In 1963 Singapore joined the Federation of Malaysia, but tensions grew between Singapore's local Chinese leaders and the Malaysians.

INDEPENDENCE

On Aug. 9, 1965, it withdrew from Malaysia and became the independent *Republic of Singapore.*

In 1971 Prime Minister Lee Kuan Yew, charging that communists were fomenting racial rioting, restricted freedom of the press.

In a war on crime, the government requires mandatory death sentences for criminals convicted of armed robbery and other crimes of violence. In 1976 the death penalty was extend-

QUICK QUIZ: What U.S. yacht won the America's Cup race in 1974 and 1977? See page 872.

ed to anyone found in possession of 15 grams of heroin or 30 grams of morphine.

In 1977 the government launched a new drive against its critics, imprisoning and fining newsmen and others who spoke out against Lee.

Prime Minister Lee's party won its sixth general election in 21 years on Dec. 23, 1980, taking all 75 parliamentary seats. But an opposition candidate won one seat in a by-election in October 1981.

Singapore's economy grew at an annual average rate of 9.4% in the 1970s. The rate rose to more than 10% in the early 1980s, but slowed to 5% in 1982.

SOLOMONS

Official Name: Solomon Islands.
Area: 11,500 square miles (29,785 sq. km.).
Population: 258,074.
Capital: Honiara, 14,942.
Government: Parliamentary democracy.
Prime Minister: Solomon Mamaloni (since 1981).
Legislative Assembly: 38 members.
U.S. Ambassador to Solomons: M. Virginia Schafer.
Solomons Ambassador to U.S.: Francis Bugotu.
Flag: Blue and green triangles divided by diagonal yellow stripe; five white stars in upper hoist corner.
Languages: English (official), Pidgin English, tribal dialects.
Main Ethnic Groups: Melanesians (93%), Polynesians (4%), Micronesians (2%), others (1%).
Leading Industries: Agriculture (coconuts and oil palms, rice, cocoa, yams, taro, cassava, vegetables, peanuts, cattle), processing (copra and palm oil), forestry (lumber), fishing, mining (gold, bauxite, copper, nickel).
Foreign Trade: *Major exports*—fish, timber, copra, cocoa, seashells, gold; *major imports*—petroleum, manufactured goods.
Places of Interest: Swimming beaches, tropical forests, shell-money manufacturing on Malaita, palm plantations, Mt. Popomanaseu on Guadalcanal.

SOLOMONS TODAY

A South Pacific nation of six large islands and many smaller ones, the Solomons lie about 1,800 miles southwest of Hawaii and some 1,100 miles northeast of Australia. The island chain extends about 900 miles in a southeasterly direction from Papua New Guinea's island of Bougainville.

Although the thatch-roofed shops of the small capital city of Honiara on Guadalcanal boast air conditioning and a plentiful supply of Japanese-made products, most of the dark-skinned Melanesian people of the Solomons follow much the same way of life their ancestors did hundreds of years ago. However, all have given up the practice of cannibalism that persisted into the early 1900s.

Most people live by raising their own fruits and vegetables and by fishing.

Dense tropical rain forests cover the mountainous islands, erasing the scars of the furious World War II battles fought between Americans and Japanese. The highest mountain, Mt. Popomanaseu, rises 7,647 feet on Guadalcanal. That 2,500-square-mile island also has extensive palm plantations and beef cattle ranches.

Altogether the Solomons have a land area somewhat larger than the state of Maryland, but stretch out over an ocean area larger than Texas. The main islands include Guadalcanal, Malaita, San Cristóbal, New Georgia, Santa Isabel, and Choiseul. Airlines provide service among the islands and to Australia and Fiji.

The nation's Shortland Islands lie just east of Bougainville, about 340 miles northwest of Honiara. The northernmost island is the coral atoll of Ontong Java, about 290 miles north of Honiara. The most southeasterly islet is Fataka in the Santa Cruz group, about 650 miles southeast of Honiara.

HISTORY OF THE SOLOMONS

Melanesians settled the islands centuries ago, possibly from Malaysia in Southeast Asia.

The first European to find the islands was the Spaniard Alvaro de Mendaña in 1568. He gave them their name because he believed they contained the lost gold mines of King Solomon. His beliefs were not completely without foundation, because in this century gold mining has become the islands' fifth-ranking export.

In the 1800s British sea captains began enslaving the islanders, taking them to Fiji and to Australia as plantation workers.

Britain established a protectorate over the main islands in 1893. In 1898–99 the Santa Cruz Islands to the southeast were added to the protectorate. In 1900 the Shortland Islands to the northwest, Ontong Java to the north, and other islands were transferred to British control by Germany in exchange for British recognition of German rights in what is now Western Samoa.

The Solomons were the scene of heavy fighting in World War II. The Japanese captured the islands in May–July 1942. The U.S. began its counteroffensive in the South Pacific with the landing of Marines on Guadalcanal on Aug. 8, 1942. Fighting in the Solomons continued until late 1943 when the Japanese finally were driven out after about 20,000 had been killed.

Britain began preparing the islands for independence in 1953 when local councils began to be set up on each of the islands. Central legislative and executive councils were established in 1960. Elections were introduced in 1964.

A new constitution was adopted in 1975, giving the islanders policy-making powers.

Britain granted the Solomons independence on July 7, 1978. Highly dependent on aid from Britain, the Solomons remained part of the British Commonwealth of Nations. Peter Kenilorea became the first prime minister.

In the nation's first election since independence in 1980, Prime Minister Kenilorea's United Party won 14 seats, the People's Alliance Party took 8, the National Democratic Party won 2, and independent candidates captured the remaining 14 parliamentary seats.

Solomon Mamaloni, head of the People's Alliance Party, was chosen prime minister in a 20–17 vote by the legislative assembly in August 1981 because of dissatisfaction with Kenilorea's administration.

SOMALIA

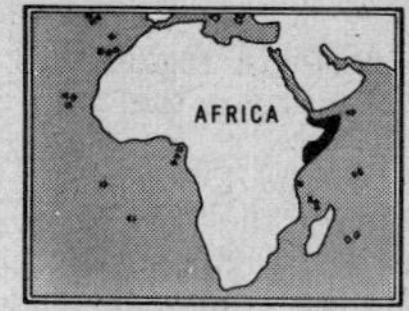

Official Name: Somali Democratic Republic.
Area: 246,201 square miles (637,657 sq. km.).
Population: 6,310,950.
Capital: Mogadishu, 230,000.
Government: One-party socialist state.
President: Maj. Gen. Mohammed Siad Barre (since 1969).
Parliament: People's Assembly, 171 members.
U.S. Ambassador to Somalia: Robert B. Oakley.
Somali Ambassador to U.S.: Mohamud Haji Nur.
Flag: Light blue field with centered white star.
Languages: Somali, Arabic.
Main Ethnic Group: Somali (mixture of Arab, Persian, and Cushitic descent).
State Religion: Islam.
Leading Industries: Agriculture (cattle, sheep, goats, camels, bananas, sorghum, corn, beans, peanuts, sugarcane, cotton); fishing; food processing; manufacturing (leather products, textiles); mining (tin).
Foreign Trade: *Major exports*—livestock, bananas, hides and skins; *major imports*—food, rice, cotton, fabrics, petroleum products, machinery, transport equipment, paper products, tea.
Places of Interest: Lac Badana National Park; Gedka-Dabley, Benadir, and Lower Juba wildlife reserves; Dallo forests; Indian Ocean resorts; Bajuni Islands.

SOMALIA TODAY

Although almost as large as Texas, Somalia is one of the world's 25 poorest countries. Most Somalis live as nomadic herdsmen, raising camels, cattle, goats, and sheep.

The country has some deposits of iron and other minerals, but there is little mining and almost no manufacturing.

Somalia's economy worsened with the influx in 1978–81 of more than a million refugees from revolution and war in Ethiopia. The UN, U.S., and international organizations sent food and economic aid while searching for some long-range solution to the massive refugee problem.

The greater part of the country is covered by the vast Ogaden plateau, mountain-bordered in the north but sloping in the south to a lowland area crossed by the Webi Shabeelle and Jubba rivers.

Kenya and Ethiopia lie to the west, and Djibouti to the northwest.

EARLY HISTORY

Somali tribes have occupied the region for more than 2,000 years. From the 900s to 1400s it was part of the Zenj empire, which was overthrown by the Portuguese in the 1500s.

In the 1600s Muscat and Oman gained control of the coastal towns. In the 1800s their authority passed to the sultan of Zanzibar.

BRITISH AND ITALIAN RULE

A British protectorate was established in the north between 1884 and 1886, and an Italian protectorate in the south in 1889. British rule was constantly threatened by Somali resistance, led by Mohammed Ibn Abdullah Hassan, who was finally defeated in 1920 by British forces.

From 1934 to 1936 Italian Somalia was a staging area for the Italian conquest of Ethiopia. During World War II Italian troops briefly occupied British Somaliland. Italian Somalia was returned to Italian control in 1950 under a 10-year UN trusteeship. In 1954 part of British Somaliland was transferred to Ethiopia.

INDEPENDENCE

British Somaliland and Italian Somalia joined on July 1, 1960, to form independent Somalia.

Large numbers of Somalis live in Ethiopia, Kenya, and adjacent areas. Pressures for a Greater Somalia have been, and remain, a source of conflict with neighbors.

Aden Abdulla Osman was president of Somalia from 1960 to 1967, when he was defeated by Abdirashid Ali Shermarke. President Shermarke was assassinated on Oct. 15, 1969.

On Oct. 21, 1969, a leftist military junta led by Maj. Gen. Mohammed Siad Barre seized power.

In 1970 the country was renamed the *Somali Democratic Republic.* All foreign banks and oil companies were nationalized. The army was equipped and trained by Soviet advisers.

The first Somali written language was introduced by the government in 1972.

The U.S. government reported in 1975 that the Soviet Union had installed atomic guided-missile facilities in Somalia. The Soviet activities were cited as a major reason for the building of a U.S. Navy base on the island of Diego Garcia in the Indian Ocean.

In June 1976 the Socialist Revolutionary Party was organized as the nation's only political party. The following month the party's 7-man central committee was made Somalia's ruling body under President Mohammed Siad Barre.

In mid-1977 Somali guerrillas began a major drive to capture the Ogaden region of Ethiopia. When the Soviet Union and Cuba aided Ethiopia, Somalia on Nov. 13, 1977, canceled its treaty of friendship with the Soviet Union and broke relations with Cuba.

An Ethiopian offensive in March 1978 forced Somali troops to withdraw from Ethiopia's northern Ogaden region. But guerrilla fighting continued into the 1980s.

The first election since Barre seized power was held on Dec. 30, 1979, with members of the national People's Assembly and local district assemblies approved from a single slate of candidates.

The U.S. and Somalia signed an agreement on Aug. 22, 1980, permitting the U.S. to use military bases in Somalia in return for economic and military aid.

Drought and floods compounded the nation's economic problems in 1981–83.

The Somali government reported in July 1983 that it had driven back Ethiopian forces that had pushed three miles inside the border.

About 2,800 U.S. troops took part in joint training exercises in Somalia in August 1983.

QUICK QUIZ: Who won the U.S. Open golf championship in 1983? See page 822.

SOUTH AFRICA

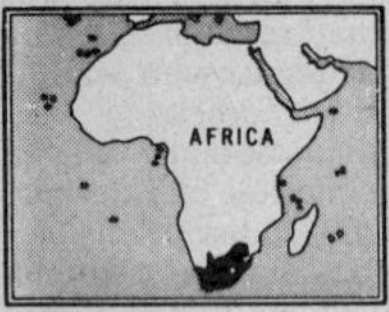

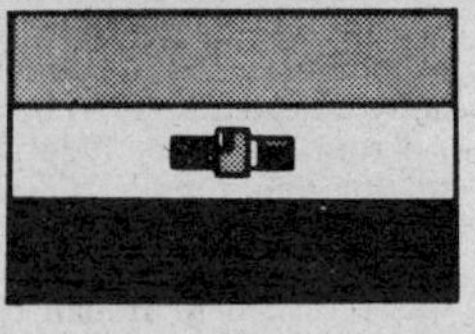

Official Name: Republic of South Africa.
Area: 434,674 square miles (1,125,800 sq. km.).
Population: 25,227,800.
Chief Metropolitan Areas: Cape Town, legislative capital, 1,490,935; Pretoria, administrative capital, 739,043; Bloemfontein, judicial capital, 198,343; Johannesburg, 1,726,073; Durban, 960,792; East Rand, 848,396; Port Elizabeth, 585,399.
Government: Parliamentary republic.
President: Marais Viljoen (since 1979).
Prime Minister: Pieter Willem Botha (since 1978).
Parliament: Senate, 51 members; House of Assembly, 165 members.
U.S. Ambassador to South Africa: Herman W. Nickel.
South African Ambassador to U.S.: Bernardus Fourie.
Flag: Orange, white, and blue stripes; in center, replicas of Union Jack, old flag of Orange Free State, and old Transvaal Vierkleur (four-color).
Languages: Afrikaans, English (both official), many black languages.
Ethnic Groups: Black (70%), white (17%), "colored" (mixed-race) (10%), Indian (Asian descent) (3%).
Main Religions: Christianity (73%), animism (13%), Hinduism (2%), Islam (1%).
Leading Industries: Trade and services; manufacturing (steel, chemicals, automobiles, textiles, metal products, machinery, consumer products); mining (diamonds, gold, coal, iron, copper, uranium, many others); agriculture (corn, sheep, dairy products, cattle, wheat, sugarcane, tobacco, fruits, vegetables); fishing.
Foreign Trade: *Major exports*—gold, metal products, food, diamonds, wool; *major imports*—automobiles, petroleum, machinery, manufactured goods.
Places of Interest: Kruger National Park; Cape Point; Kirstenbosch National Botanical Gardens; garden route tour from Cape Town to Durban; Oudtshoorn caves; Johannesburg gold mines; Kimberley diamond mine; Indian market and beaches at Durban; Zululand game reserves; Sudwala caves and adjoining Dinosaur Park.

SOUTH AFRICA TODAY

Rich in natural resources, white-ruled South Africa leads the world in gold mining and produces about a third of the world's diamonds. It also has large amounts of iron, coal, copper, tin, and uranium. It lacks only natural petroleum, but has undertaken large scale production of petroleum from coal. South Africa's farmlands produce ample amounts of wheat and other food crops to have some left over for export.

Most of the world opposes South Africa's racial segregation policies, which include barring blacks from voting in national elections.

About three times the size of California, South Africa is bordered on the northwest by Namibia (South West Africa), on the north by Botswana and Zimbabwe Rhodesia, and on the northeast by Mozambique and Swaziland. The eastern part of South Africa surrounds Lesotho, Transkei, Bophuthatswana, Ciskei, and Venda.

Most of South Africa is a plateau, with an average height of 4,000 feet. In the east the land rises steeply from fertile coastal lowlands to the Drakensberg Mountains.

In the east central and northern regions are the prairie-like veld. Cape Agulhas is the continent's southern tip.

The Orange River rises in the Drakensberg Mountains and with its tributary, the Vaal, flows westward into the Atlantic. The Limpopo River rises in the Witwatersrand in the Transvaal.

APARTHEID (SEPARATE RACIAL DEVELOPMENT)

Less than 1 person in 5 in South Africa is white. Yet whites control the government and all aspects of life by the policy of racial segregation called *apartheid*. To enforce the policy, parliament passed restrictive racial laws in the 1950s and 1960s. Some restrictions in sports and other areas were lifted in the 1970s, including removal in 1979 of the ban on black labor unions.

Police can arrest and imprison people without a court order and hold them indefinitely without letting them communicate with lawyers, families, or friends. Or they can be "banned" to their homes and denied rights of free speech. The security police are protected from court restraints, but may be prosecuted for excesses.

About two-thirds of the blacks live on tribal reserves that cover about 13% of the country's land area. Millions of blacks have been forcibly moved from white areas to nine *homelands*: Bophuthatswana, Ciskei, Gazankulu, KwaZulu, Lebowa, Qwaqwa, Swazi, Transkei, and Venda. South Africa granted sovereignty to Transkei in 1976, to Bophuthatswana in 1977, to Venda in 1979, and to Ciskei in 1981.

Other nations have refused to recognize the sovereignty of the South Africa homelands because they view the homelands program as part of the nation's apartheid policy of racial segregation. The program requires blacks who are members of tribes that have independent homelands to give up their South African citizenship, even though they live in South Africa. Thus, by the time all the homelands are "independent" most blacks would no longer be citizens of South Africa, so the whites then would be the majority of South African citizens and could validly control the government.

Wholly dependent on South Africa for their economic existence, the homelands are "landlocked islands" surrounded by South Africa.

Migrant blacks who take jobs in the cities of South Africa are forbidden to bring their wives and children with them. They and permanent black resident families live in "locations" set aside on the outskirts of cities or towns. Asians and those of mixed ancestry are similarly restricted to specific living areas. Education is segregated, except in some private schools.

Most professional and supervisory jobs are held by whites. Blacks do most unskilled and semiskilled labor on farms, in mines, in manufacturing plants, and in public service.

EARLY HISTORY

Hottentots, Bushmen, and other Africans lived in southern Africa for thousands of years, but little is known of their history other than the cave paintings they drew.

Portuguese explorer Bartolomeu Dias in 1488 became the first European to reach the Cape of Good Hope. The first permanent European settlement was made at Cape Town in 1652 by the Dutch East India Company. The Dutch were soon joined by French and German settlers. These early arrivals came to be known as *Boers.*

BRITISH RULE

Through the Napoleonic wars, Britain gained formal possession of the Cape Colony in 1814.

Because of dissatisfaction with British rule and the abolition of slavery in 1833, many Boers migrated to the interior in the Great Trek of 1835–48.

The Boers then founded the Transvaal, Natal, and the Orange Free State territories. Their migration led to war with the Zulus and other Bantu tribesmen. The Boers defeated the Zulus in 1838 at the Battle of Blood River.

Britain annexed Natal in 1843. After discovery of gold and diamonds, it annexed part of the Orange Free State in 1871 and the South Africa Republic (Transvaal) in 1877.

Boer resentment of British encroachment erupted in 1899 into the Boer War, or South African War, which the British won in 1902.

Britain formed the Union of South Africa on May 31, 1910, joining Cape Colony, Natal, the Orange River Colony (Orange Free State), and the Transvaal. The Union of South Africa gained sovereignty in 1934.

Apartheid became official policy under Prime Minister Dr. Daniel Malan, whose party won the 1948 elections.

REPUBLIC OF SOUTH AFRICA

On May 31, 1961, the country became the independent *Republic of South Africa.* Six months later it withdrew from the British Commonwealth of Nations, reacting to criticism of its racial policies.

With the growing number of independent black African nations, pressures mounted in the U.S. and UN against South Afiican apartheid. The U.S. ended the sale of all military equipment to South Africa on Dec. 31, 1963.

South Africa continued its rigid policy of apartheid under Prime Minister Hendrik F. Verwoerd, who was assassinated in 1966, and under his successor, Balthazar Johannes Vorster.

In November 1974 the UN General Assembly suspended South Africa's voting privileges in the international organization.

A wave of protest riots and strikes by black students began on June 16, 1976, in Soweto, a black suburb of Johannesburg. Over 500 were killed and nearly 4,000 injured.

The UN Security Council on Nov. 4, 1977, unanimously ordered a worldwide mandatory embargo on the shipment of military supplies to South Africa—the first such action ever taken by the UN against a member nation.

In December 1977 the UN General Assembly adopted by huge majorities resolutions calling on the UN Security Council to embargo oil shipments to South Africa and to cut off foreign investment in South African enterprises.

President Nicolaas Diederichs, 75, died on Aug. 21, 1978. A month later Vorster resigned as prime minister and was elected president by the electoral college of parliament.

Pieter Willem Botha, 62, formerly defense minister under Vorster, was chosen as prime minister on Sept. 28, 1978, by the ruling National Party.

Vorster resigned as president in June 1979 and was succeeded by Marais Viljoen, 63, who previously had been president of the senate.

As the price of gasoline rose to $2.43 a gallon in 1979, the government rushed construction of several plants to convert coal into oil. The plants are expected to provide from one-third to one-half of the country's oil needs by the late 1980s.

A flash of light detected by a U.S. satellite off the southern coast of South Africa on Sept. 22, 1979, was interpreted by some nuclear scientists as evidence South Africa had tested an atomic bomb. However, the government denied doing so.

In 1980 South Africa experienced the worst wave of racial violence since 1976. In June guerrillas bombed two of the country's new coal-to-oil conversion plants and an oil refinery. Later in the same month police fired on black demonstrators in Cape Town, killing about 30. A strike for higher pay by about 3,000 black city workers in Johannesburg in July was broken by forcibly deporting about half of them.

In an all-white parliamentary election on April 29, 1981, Prime Minister Botha's National Party won all but 35 of the 165 elected seats, seven less than in the previous election. With more than 10% of the vote having gone to far-right candidates who want stricter apartheid laws, Botha was expected to postpone promised liberal reforms of those laws.

In 1982–83 the worst drought in the nation's history reduced grain harvests by about 50%, devastating the economy in the black homelands.

A bomb planted by the outlawed black African National Congress (ANC) killed 18 persons and injured 217 at air force headquarters in Pretoria on May 20. In reprisal, the South African air force three days later bombed Maputo, the capital of neighboring Mozambique, which shelters leaders and guerrillas of the ANC. Six persons were reported killed and 40 wounded in the reprisal attack.

More than three decades of wrangling between the UN and South Africa over the status of Namibia (South West Africa) continued in the 1980s as South Africa refused to give up control of the former German colony. The UN General Assembly voted on Sept. 14, 1981, to call on all nations to impose sanctions against South Africa and give military help to guerrillas fighting for the independence of Namibia. See page 612.

Voters on Nov. 2, 1983, approved by nearly 2 to 1 a new constitution proposed by Botha to become effective in 1984. The powers of the president were greatly strengthened. The new constitution also provided for a three-house parliament—one for whites, one for Asians, and one for mixed-blood "coloreds." Blacks continued to be excluded from representation and from voting.

QUICK QUIZ: What is the largest breed of dogs registered in the U.S.? See page 856.

SOVIET UNION

Official Name: Union of Soviet Socialist Republics.
Area: 8,649,538 square miles (22,402,200 sq. km.).
Population: 273,405,000.
Chief Cities: Moskva (Moscow), capital, 8,011,000; Leningrad, 4,588,000; Kiev, 2,192,000; Tashkent, 1,816,000; Kharkov, 1,464,000; Gorki, 1,358,000; Novosibirsk, 1,328,000; Minsk, 1,295,000; Kuibyshev, 1,226,000; Sverdlovsk, 1,225,000.
Largest Metropolitan Areas: Moscow, 8,099,000; Leningrad, 4,638,000.
Government: Communist one-party state.
Head of the Soviet government: Yuri V. Andropov, general secretary of the Communist Party (since 1982), chairman of the presidium of the Supreme Soviet (since 1983).
Prime Minister: Nilolai A. Tikhonov (since 1980).
Supreme Soviet: *Soviet of the Union,* 750 members; *Soviet of Nationalities,* 750 members.
U.S. Ambassador to Soviet Union: Arthur A. Hartman.
Soviet Ambassador to U.S.: Anatoliy F. Dobrynin.
Flag: Red field with gold hammer and sickle below gold-bordered star in upper hoist corner.
Major Languages: Russian (official), Slavic (76%), Altaic (8%), other (16%).
Main Ethnic Groups: Russian (52%), Ukrainian (16%), Uzbek (5%), Belorussian (4%).
Religions: Atheism (official), Russian Orthodoxy (18%).
Leading Industries: Manufacturing (steel, cement, paper, electricity, vehicles, electronics, armaments); agriculture (wheat, livestock, corn, rye, oats, potatoes, fruits, vegetables); mining (petroleum, natural gas, coal, lignite, iron ore, diamonds, bauxite, copper, lead, zinc, salt); forestry and lumbering; fishing.
Foreign Trade: *Major exports*—equipment for industrial plants, petroleum; *major imports*—machinery, clothing, ships, raw sugar, metal ores, wheat.
Places of Interest: Lake Baikal; Black Sea resorts; Caucasus area; the Crimea; Baltic Sea area; Kiev. *In Moscow:* The Kremlin, containing Nikolai Palace (now home of Supreme Soviet), Kremlin Theater, belfry of Ivan the Terrible, Cathedral of the Archangel Michael, Patriarch's Palace; Lenin Mausoleum; St. Basil's Cathedral. *In Leningrad:* Hermitage Museum (former Winter Palace).

SOVIET UNION TODAY

As one of the world's two great superpowers, the Soviet Union competes with the United States for world leadership.

Stretching from eastern Europe across the continent of Asia, the Soviet Union has nearly two-and-a-half times the area of the U.S. and a population about 20% larger.

The Soviet Union has a communist form of government with one-party domination of political activities and state ownership of economic activities. It suppresses such civil rights as freedom of speech and freedom of the press. Refusing to work is a crime punishable by imprisonment.

Since World War II the Soviet Union and the U.S. have engaged in a costly arms race in which each nation has built atomic intercontinental missiles capable of destroying the other.

As a by-product of the armament buildup, the two superpowers competed in a space race. The Soviet Union became the first to fire a satellite into orbit around the earth in 1957 and the first to launch a cosmonaut into earth orbit in 1961. However, the United States came back to win the space race by being the first to place men on the moon in 1969.

SOVIET GOVERNMENT

Though the constitution of the Soviet government is patterned somewhat after those of Western democracies, there are no checks and balances and little real separation of powers.

The country is ruled by the Communist Party's Politburo, whose 14 members are also the chief officials of the government and of the party.

In theory, the highest legislative body is the bicameral Supreme Soviet, elected by universal suffrage from single lists of Communist Party-approved candidates. It meets twice yearly but functions as a rubber stamp. A 38-member presidium acts as a council to the president.

The Communist Party controls all levels of government and practically every phase of Soviet life. It is the only political party in the country—its power guaranteed by the constitution. Membership in the party is about 14.5 million, or 9% of the adult population.

The party's highest organ, theoretically, is its congress, which normally meets every four years to formalize broad policies of the Politburo. The congress elects a central committee to act for it between sessions.

GEOGRAPHY

The world's largest country, the Soviet Union covers nearly one-sixth of the earth's land area.

The Soviet Union extends through 11 time zones, varying widely in terrain and climate.

Its Ural Mountains are considered the dividing line between Europe and Asia. The Carpathian Mountains fringe the Soviet Union in the west. The Caucasus Mountains lie between the Black and Caspian seas. The Pamir, Tien Shan, Altai, and other ranges rise along the southern border.

The Soviet Union includes 15 Soviet states. The largest is Russia (Russian Soviet Federated Socialist Republic), with 70% of the total land area and more than half the people. Second

STATES OF THE SOVIET UNION

NAME	AREA (sq. mi.)	CAPITAL
Armenia	11,506	Yerevan
Azerbaijan	33,436	Baku
Belorussia	80,155	Minsk
Estonia	17,413	Tallinn
Georgia	26,911	Tbilisi
Kazakhstan	1,048,306	Alma-Ata
Kirghizstan	76,641	Frunze
Latvia	24,595	Riga
Lithuania	25,174	Vilnius
Moldavia	13,012	Kishinev
Russia	6,592,850	Moscow
Tadzhikistan	55,251	Dushanbe
Turkmenistan	188,456	Ashkhabad
Ukraine	233,090	Kiev
Uzbekistan	173,592	Tashkent

SOVIET UNION
MILES
0
200
400
600
800
1000
ARCTIC OCEAN
GREENLAND
SPITSBERGEN
FRANZ JOSEF LAND
NOVAYA ZEMLYA
SEVERNAYA ZEMLYA
NEW SIBERIAN IS.
TAIMYR PENINSULA
BARENTS SEA
ALASKA
INTERNATIONAL DATE LINE
BERING SEA
CHUKCHI PENINSULA
KAMCHATKA
KURILE ISLANDS
SEA OF OKHOTSK
SAKHALIN
Kolyma R.
Lena R.
Yenisey R.
Ob R.
Irtysh R.
Volga R.
Dnieper R.
Amur R.
UNION OF SOVIET SOCIALIST REPUBLICS
RUSSIAN SOVIET FEDERATED SOCIALIST REPUBLIC
URAL MTS.
Murmansk
Archangel
Perm
Nizhni Tagil
Sverdlovsk
Chelyabinsk
Magnitogorsk
Ufa
Orenburg
Kazan
Kuibyshev
Gorki
Yaroslavl
Ivanovo
Kalinin
MOSCOW
Tula
Voronezh
Saratov
Volgograd
Astrakhan
Kharkov
Dnepropetrovsk
Makeyevka
Donetsk
Rostov
Krasnodar
Kiev
Odessa
Sevastopol
Lvov
Minsk
Riga
Tallinn
Leningrad
EST.
LAT.
LITH.
BELORUSSIA
UKRAINE
MOLD.
Omsk
Novosibirsk
Tomsk
Barnaul
Novokuznetsk
Krasnoyarsk
Irkutsk
LAKE BAIKAL
Khabarovsk
Vladivostok
KAZAKHSTAN
Karaganda
LAKE BALKHASH
Alma-Ata
Frunze
KIRGHIZSTAN
TADZHIKISTAN
Dushanbe
Samarkand
Tashkent
UZBEKISTAN
TURKMENISTAN
ARAL SEA
CASPIAN SEA
CAUCASUS MTS.
GEORGIA
ARMENIA
AZERBAIJAN
Tbilisi
Yerevan
BLACK SEA
TURKEY
ANKARA
SYRIA
IRAQ
BAGHDAD
KUWAIT
SAUDI ARABIA
IRAN
TEHRAN
AFGHANISTAN
KABUL
PAK.
KASHMIR
MONGOLIA
ULAN BATOR
ALTAI MTS.
SINKIANG
Urumchi
CHINA
Lanchow
PEKING
Tientsin
Nanking
Hangchow
Shanghai
MANCHURIA
Changchun
YELLOW SEA
NORTH KOREA
PYONGYANG
SOUTH KOREA
SEOUL
SEA OF JAPAN
JAPAN
TOKYO
IRELAND
BRITAIN
LONDON
NORTH SEA
NETH.
GERMANY
BERLIN
DENMARK
NORWAY
OSLO
SWEDEN
STOCKHOLM
FINLAND
HELSINKI
POLAND
WARSAW
CZECH.
HUNG.
ROMANIA
BUCHAREST

SOVIET UNION *(continued)*

most populous is the Ukraine (Ukrainian Soviet Socialist Republic), with 20% of the people.

EARLY HISTORY OF RUSSIA

Rurik, an almost legendary Swede, is generally credited with founding the Russian state when he led his Varangian tribe into Novgorod in the year 862. Rurik's dynasty later ruled the duchy of Moscow and eventually all of Russia.

Saint Vladimir (Vladimir I, reigned 980–1015), initially a pagan, became the first Christian ruler of Kiev. Through his victories over Lithuanians, Bulgars, and the Greeks in the Crimea, he is considered the founder of the powerful Kievan state. Under Yaroslav the Wise in the 1000s, Kiev reached a peak of prosperity and culture. In 1240 Kiev fell to the Mongols, who, under Batu Khan, created an empire called the Golden Horde that ruled most of what is now the eastern and southern Soviet Union.

Northern Russia fell under domination of Moscow. Its power was solidified by Dmitri Donskoi. Under Ivan III (1462–1505), who drove out the Mongols, and Vasily III (1505–33), many principalities were brought under Russian control.

CZARIST RUSSIA

Ivan IV, known as "Ivan the Terrible," was the first ruler crowned czar (caesar) of all Russia (1547).

After the reign of Boris Godunov (1598–1605) came dynastic upheavals, civil war, and territorial losses to Sweden and Poland. Following the defeat of the Poles, the nobleman Mikhail Romanov was elected czar (1613), founding the last Russian dynasty. Peter the Great (1689–1725) opened Russia to Westernization.

Continuing Peter's expansionist and authoritarian policies, Ekaterina II (Catherine the Great; 1762–96) made Russia a leading power.

Under Aleksandr I (1801–25) more lands were added to the empire. With Napoleon's defeat on Russian soil (1812), Aleksandr became one of Europe's most powerful rulers.

The spread of liberal ideas among many of the aristocrats and educated bourgeois led to the abortive Decembrist Conspiracy (1825), an attempt to block the accession of Nikolai I.

After Britain and France defeated Russia in the Crimean War (1854–56), Czar Aleksandr II (1855–81) inaugurated a series of reforms. He freed the serfs, modernized the courts, and established provincial, county, and town self-government on a modest scale. He also extended the Russian empire in the Far East. He was assassinated in 1881 by a terrorist group.

Aleksandr III (1881–94) repudiated his father's policies and instituted a period of severe repression, especially against the Jews. He was followed by Nikolai II (1894–1917), the last czar. During Nikolai's administration, Russia was defeated in the Russo-Japanese War (1904–05). Popular discontent in 1905 forced Nikolai to accept a constitution, establishing a representative parliament, the Duma.

In World War I a poorly prepared Russia joined the Allies against the Central Powers. Russian armies suffered massive setbacks.

RUSSIAN REVOLUTION

Revolution erupted in February 1917, when troops refused to fire upon crowds milling in the streets of St. Petersburg (Leningrad) as part of a general strike. The czar abdicated, and a moderate provisional government took over, headed successively by Prince Georgi Lvov and Aleksandr Kerensky.

In November 1917 the Bolsheviks (communists), led by Vladimir Lenin and Leon Trotsky, seized power. The royal family was executed. Lenin had founded the Bolshevik Party in 1903. Although the communists represented only a small minority of the population, Lenin ruled as a dictator until his death in 1924. His government successfully fought off attempts to overthrow it during a civil war (1918–20). The Communist International (Comintern), founded in 1919, attempted through local communist parties to undermine western European governments.

STALIN'S RULE

After Lenin's death, Joseph Stalin, general secretary of the Central Committee of the Communist Party since 1922, won a bitter power struggle against Leon Trotsky (murdered in Mexico, 1940). Stalin created a brutal police state. He pushed the nation into rapid industrialization, forcibly collectivized agriculture, and expanded the secret police, censorship, forced labor, and concentration camps. In "blood purges" in the late 1930s he executed tens of thousands, mostly without trials, including surviving founding fathers of the Soviet state and a majority of the military leadership. Stalin also systematically imprisoned hundreds of thousands of people.

The Soviet Union received diplomatic recognition by a number of European governments in 1924 and by the United States in 1933. It became a member of the League of Nations in 1934.

SOVIET TERRITORIAL EXPANSION

In 1939 the Soviet Union signed a nonagression pact with Nazi Germany that preceded World War II. The Soviet Union absorbed Latvia, Lithuania, Estonia (political conquests still not recognized by the United States and many other nations), and later the eastern half of Poland. Also in 1939 Russia attacked Finland, eventually taking a large part of its eastern territory.

In 1941 Hitler launched a surprise attack on Russia, inflicting civilian and military losses of 20 million lives and driving the Soviet Union to join the Allied side. With U.S. lend-lease aid, Soviet armies drove back the Germans.

Following Allied victory, the Soviet Union imposed communist governments in eastern European countries occupied by the Red Army. By mid-1948 Poland, Czechoslovakia, Hungary, Romania, Bulgaria, East Germany, Yugoslavia, and Albania were Soviet satellites.

COLD WAR

With the breakup of the wartime alliance, mutual hostility (the Cold War) came to characterize Soviet relations with the West.

The Soviet Union's test explosion of its first atomic bomb in 1949, using secrets stolen from Britain and the U.S., brought fears that an attack on noncommunist countries might be launched without warning.

The formation of the NATO military alliance by the U.S., Canada, and western European nations in 1950 was countered by Moscow with the Warsaw Pact alliance of its satellites.

After Stalin's death in 1953, Georgi M. Malenkov became chairman of the Council of Ministers, but in 1955 he was replaced by Nikolai Bulganin. In October 1956 Soviet troops crushed a popular revolt in Hungary.

By 1956 Nikita S. Khrushchev, Communist Party first secretary, emerged as the most powerful figure in the Soviet Union. In 1963 he agreed to a limited nuclear test-ban treaty with the U.S.

The Chinese communists rejected destalinization and the "peaceful coexistence" formula. Sino-Soviet differences produced a schism that divided the communist movement throughout the world.

The Soviet Union and the United States came close to war in 1962 when Khrushchev installed atomic missiles in Cuba that could be used to attack the U.S. However, war was averted after President Kennedy imposed a naval blockade on Cuba, forcing Khrushchev to withdraw the missiles.

RULE BY LEONID BREZHNEV

In 1964 Khrushchev was abruptly removed from office, to be succeeded by Leonid Brezhnev as Communist Party first secretary and Alexei Kosygin as premier.

In August 1968 the Soviet Union and its Warsaw Pact allies (except Romania) invaded Czechoslovakia and crushed a more liberal communist government under Alexander Dub-ček. Moscow announced the "Brezhnev Doctrine," proclaiming the Soviet Union's right to intervene in any "socialist" country.

As part of his "détente" policies to ease tensions with communist regimes, President Nixon held a summit meeting with Brezhnev in Moscow on May 22–30, 1972, where they signed two agreements limiting production of nuclear weapons, as formulated during four years of SALT (Strategic Arms Limitation Talks) negotiations.

In June 1973 Brezhnev made a 9-day visit to the U.S. for a meeting with President Nixon hailed as the official end to the Cold War.

When Nobel Prize-winner Aleksandr I. Solzhenitsyn published a book, *The Gulag Archipelago, 1918–1956,* exposing the horrors of Soviet secret labor-prisons, he was arrested and exiled in 1974.

The Soviet Union began construction of a second Trans-Siberian railroad in 1974. A work force of 100,000 was employed in building the 2,000-mile line to be completed in 1985.

The Soviet government on Jan. 10, 1975, canceled its 1972 trade agreement with the U.S. because of requirements by the U.S. Congress that the Soviet Union relax its restrictive emigration.

In May 1977 the 70-year-old Brezhnev ousted 74-year-old Nikolai V. Podgorny from the presidency. He then took the title of president, becoming the first Soviet ruler to hold titles as both head of the party and chief of state.

A new "hot line" communication system using space satellites to carry messages between the White House and the Kremlin went into service on Jan. 16, 1978. It replaced a land cable "hot line" that had been installed in 1963.

In 1979 the Soviet government eased restrictions on the emigration of Jews, permitting a record 51,000 to leave the country and bringing to about 240,000 the number allowed to leave during the 1970s. But in the 1980s Jewish emigration was reduced to a trickle.

Seven years of negotiations between the U.S. and the Soviet Union for a new pact limiting strategic arms resulted in a SALT II treaty signed by Brezhnev and President Carter on June 18, 1979. But deteriorating relations with the U.S. prevented U.S. Senate ratification of the treaty.

The Soviet Union invaded Afghanistan in December 1979, setting up a puppet communist government loyal to Moscow. Soviet troops battled Afghan guerrillas opposed to the communists.

On Jan. 4, 1980, U.S. President Carter denounced the Soviet actions in Afghanistan, cut grain sales to the Soviet Union, and suspended the sale of high-technology equipment such as computers. He also organized a partial boycott of summer Olympic Games in Moscow.

On Jan. 22, 1980, Andrei D. Sakharov, Nobel Prize-winning father of the Soviet hydrogen bomb, was arrested and exiled without trial to the city of Gorki for having criticized the Soviet invasion of Afghanistan.

Nikolai A. Tikhonov, 75, was appointed prime minister on Oct. 23, 1980, succeeding Kosygin.

After the Soviet Union pressured its puppet government in Poland to crackdown on that country's Solidarity labor union in December 1981, President Reagan imposed new trade sanctions on both the Soviet Union and Poland.

Soviet military forces remained bogged down in Afghanistan in 1981–83 in their effort to suppress anticommunist guerrillas.

RULE BY YURI V. ANDROPOV

After the death of the 75-year-old Brezhnev on Nov. 10, 1982, the new head of the Communist Party was Yuri V. Andropov, 68, former head of the KGB, the Soviet secret police and spy network.

Seven months later, on June 16, 1983, Andropov consolidated his power by taking the titular role of president of the Soviet Union (chairman of the presidium of the Supreme Soviet).

The Soviet Union agreed in July 1983 to buy 9 million tons of corn, wheat, and soybeans from the U.S. over the next five years.

Throughout 1983 U.S. and Soviet negotiators attempted to reach agreement on a pact that would control the deployment of nuclear arms in Europe. See pages 13 and 31.

U.S. President Reagan and other world leaders denounced the Soviet Union for its immorality after a Soviet fighter plane shot down a South Korean airliner that had strayed over Soviet territory on Sept. 1, 1983, killing all 269 persons aboard. See page 25.

Reports persisted that Andropov was in failing health, suffering from Parkinson's disease as well as heart and kidney ailments. He appeared to have lost much weight. He trembled as he walked or stood to speak. Andropov ceased attending public functions after August 1983, leading to speculation he might be replaced.

QUICK QUIZ: Who was the No. 1 NFL draft choice in 1983? See page 808.

SPAIN

Official Name: Spanish State.
Area: 194,897 square miles (504,782 sq. km.).
Population: 36,156,079.
Chief Cities: Madrid, capital, 3,200,067; Barcelona, 1,742,354; Valencia, 739,724; Seville, 607,228; Zaragoza, 569,565; Bilbao, 438,035; Málaga, 427,756.
Government: Parliamentary monarchy.
King: Juan Carlos I (since 1975).
Prime Minister: Felipe González Márquez (since 1982).
Legislature *(Cortes): Congress of Deputies,* 350 members; *Senate,* 248 members.
U.S. Ambassador to Spain: Thomas O. Enders.
Spanish Ambassador to U.S.: Gabriel Manueco de Lecea.
Flag: Wide yellow stripe in center with narrow red stripes at top and bottom.
Official Language: Castilian Spanish.
Ethnic Groups: Spanish-Castilian, Basque, Catalan, Galician, Andalusian.
Main Religion: Roman Catholicism.
Leading Industries: Trade and services; manufacturing (steel, ships, automobiles, textiles, cement, paper, cork products, consumer goods); agriculture (livestock, wheat, sugar beets, potatoes, barley, olives, grapes, fruits, vegetables); tourism; mining (lead, coal, iron, petroleum, uranium); forestry and lumbering; fishing.
Foreign Trade: *Major exports*—Shoes, textiles, automobiles, citrus fruits, olive oil, wine; *major imports*—crude petroleum, corn, soybeans, meat.
Places of Interest: *In Madrid:* Prado Museum, royal palace, nearby El Escorial palace and monastery. *In Toledo:* cathedral, Sto. Tomé Church. *In Barcelona:* Sagrada Familia Church, Gothic Quarter, cathedral. *In Seville:* Giralda tower and cathedral, Alcázar palaces. *In Granada:* Alhambra Moorish palace-citadel. *In Cordoba:* Great Mosque; Costa del Sol resort area. *In Segovia:* Roman aqueduct.

SPAIN TODAY

Larger than California both in area and population, Spain is the fifth most important industrial nation of western Europe. It is among the leading producers of cement, fish, and uranium.

Although Spain has experienced substantial economic growth with the aid of large loans and grants from the U.S., it has a per capita income about half that of West Germany.

The U.S. maintains three air bases and a naval base in Spain.

Over 30 million tourists visit Spain each year because of its mild climate and many historical and cultural attractions.

The rugged Pyrenees mountains and the republic of Andorra on the north separate Spain from France. Portugal lies to the west. Gibraltar stands at the southern tip of Spain.

The nation is divided into 17 autonomous regions, which each elect their own local parliaments.

Spain has six mountain ranges, grazing lands, a vast central plateau, plains, and rocky coastlines. The most important rivers are the Ebro, Douro, Tagus, Guadalquivir, and Guadiana.

EARLY HISTORY

In the 800s B.C. Phoenician traders settled on the southwest coast. Carthaginians colonized the Mediterranean east coast and the Balearic Islands, where Greeks also planted colonies.

In the 200s B.C. the Carthaginians conquered most of Iberia but subsequently were defeated by the Romans. Christianity was established in the 200s and 300s A.D. Then hordes of Germanic tribes began sweeping into the peninsula in 409.

In the 700s Spain was conquered by Muslim Berbers (Moors). Under Abd-ar-Rahman III (891–961) Muslim Spain reached its apex.

The Moors lost their last stronghold (Granada) in 1492, when it fell to the forces of Fernando V and Isabel I, rulers of Castile and Aragon. In that same year Columbus made his first voyage of discovery to America.

Spain's "golden century" was the 1500s, under rule by the Hapsburg dynasty. The country acquired a huge overseas empire. Spain ruled the seas and had the strongest military force in Europe. But incessant wars with England, the Netherlands, and France squandered Spain's resources.

Napoleon forced King Carlos IV to abdicate in 1808 and installed Joseph Bonaparte as king. By 1814 British forces under the Duke of Wellington succeeded in driving out the French. Colonial rebellions and the Spanish-American War (1898) brought an end to most of Spain's overseas empire.

A military dictatorship led by Primo de Rivera took power in 1923 under the Bourbon king Alfonso XIII. De Rivera was ousted in 1930.

CIVIL WAR AND FRANCISCO FRANCO

A republican victory at the polls in 1931 brought an end to the monarchy. A Popular Front (republicans, socialists, communists, and syndicalists) won elections in February 1936.

Gen. Francisco Franco began a revolt on July 18, 1936, taking command of the Spanish army in Morocco. He led an invasion of Spain and began three years of devastating civil war.

The defending Loyalists (republicans) were backed by the Popular Front, the Basques, and the Catalans. Franco received substantial aid from Nazi Germany and Fascist Italy. The Loyalists were aided by the Soviet Union. By 1939 Franco defeated the republican forces.

Spain was ruled as a harsh dictatorship by Franco for 36 years in 1939–75. He headed the only legal political party, the National Movement.

During World War II Spain favored the Axis Powers but remained technically neutral.

Franco announced in 1969 that Prince Juan Carlos de Borbón y Borbón would be his successor and heir to the Spanish throne.

CONSTITUTIONAL MONARCHY RESTORED

Juan Carlos was proclaimed king on Nov. 22, 1975, two days after Franco's death. He dedicated himself to restore political liberties.

Spain gave up its last large overseas colony on Feb. 26, 1976, turning over the 102,703-square-mile Spanish Sahara on the west coast of Africa to Morocco and Mauritania.

The parliament lifted Franco's ban on political parties in June 1976.

King Juan Carlos I dismissed Franco's last prime minister, Carlos Arias Navarro, on July 2, 1976, replacing him with Adolfo Suárez Gonzáles, head of the National Movement Party.

In 1977 Spain restored diplomatic relations with the Soviet Union for the first time since 1939.

The first free national election since the Spanish civil war was held on June 15, 1977, to elect a new two-house parliament to replace the unicameral *Cortes* of the Franco years. A coalition of center-right parties led by Prime Minister Suárez won the election.

A national referendum on Dec. 6, 1978, approved by a vote of 87.7% a new democratic constitution to replace the dictatorial "Fundamental Laws" of Generalissimo Franco. King Juan Carlos signed the constitution on Dec. 27, 1978, making Spain a parliamentary democracy with guarantees of human rights and free enterprise. It also removed the official status of Roman Catholicism, previously the state religion.

In the first election under the new constitution on March 1, 1979, Prime Minister Suárez's centrist party, the Union of the Democratic Center (UCD), won control of parliament.

SPAIN IN THE 1980s

Prime Minister Suárez resigned on Jan. 29, 1981. He was succeeded by Deputy Prime Minister Leopoldo Calvo Sotelo, 54, a former industrialist.

Rightist army and national police officers attempted a coup on Feb. 23, 1981, as civil guards seized the parliament building, holding the members hostage. However, King Juan Carlos saved Spain's fledgling democracy by going on TV to denounce the rebels and to order the army to support the government. Three leaders of the revolt later were sentenced to 30 years in prison.

The Franco government's ban on divorce was lifted when parliament adopted a divorce law on June 22, 1981.

Ending its political and military isolation from the rest of western Europe, Spain formally joined the NATO military alliance on May 30, 1982, as its 16th member.

Recession slowed Spain's industrial growth in 1981–83, bringing both unemployment and inflation to a rate of 15%. Farmers in southern Spain suffered the worst drought in a century.

Felipe González Márquez, 40, led his Socialist Party to an overwhelming victory in the election on Oct. 28, 1982. The socialists took a clear majority of 201 members in the 350-seat congress of deputies. The main opposition, the right-wing Popular Alliance, won 106 seats in the lower house.

González, who had promised no sweeping changes, became prime minister on Dec. 2, 1982, forming the first socialist cabinet since the Spanish Civil War of 1936–39.

In the first papal visit in the history of Spain, Pope John Paul II traveled through the country for 10 days beginning on Oct. 31, 1982.

The government lifted its 13-year land blockade of the British colony Gibraltar on Dec. 14, 1982, as it sought better relations with western Europe.

González' government seized control of Spain's largest multibillion-dollar corporation, Rumasa, on Feb. 24, 1983, and five months later indicted its chairman for fraudulent bookkeeping.

The socialists consolidated their position in local elections on May 8, 1983, winning most city and regional posts with about 42% of the votes.

Prime Minister González visited the U.S. in June 1983 for talks with President Reagan in which he emphasized the need for negotiations on social issues to end civil wars in Central America.

Basque nationalists, seeking independence for their region, carried out many terrorist attacks in the 1980s against police and government officials.

SPANISH OVERSEAS AREAS

BALEARIC ISLANDS

Area: 1,936 square miles (5,014 sq. km.).
Population: 663,630.
Capital: Palma, 267,081.

The Balearic Islands *(Islas Baleares)* lie in the Mediterranean Sea off the east coast of Spain. The largest islands are Majorca *(Mallorca),* 1,400 sq. mi.; Minorca *(Menorca),* 266 sq. mi.; Ibiza *(Iviza),* 209 sq. mi.; and Formentera, 32 sq. mi. The year-round warm climate makes the islands a popular tourist resort area.

Many Stone Age monuments built by prehistoric people dot the countryside of Majorca and Minorca. The islands were colonized by Phoenicians and Carthaginians. Fought over for centuries by contending powers, the islands came under the rule of Spanish kings in the 1200s. Limited local autonomy was granted on June 30, 1978.

CANARY ISLANDS

Area: 2,808 square miles (7,273 sq. km.).
Population: 1,353,680.
Capitals: Las Palmas de Gran Canaria, 328,187; Santa Cruz de Tenerife, 157,791.

The 13 Canary Islands lie off the northwest coast of Morocco in the Atlantic Ocean. The largest islands are Tenerife, 795 sq. mi.; Fuerteventura, 668 sq. mi.; and Grand Canary, 592 sq. mi. The islands have many mountains and volcanoes, the highest of which is snow-capped 12,198-foot Pico de Teide on Tenerife.

The warm subtropical climate of the Canaries attracts over a million tourists each year.

The islands received their name from the Latin word for dog, *canis,* because of the fierce dogs found there. Songbirds called canaries were first discovered in these islands by ancient Phoenician traders. The French explorer Jean de Béthencourt conquered the islands in 1402–04, making himself king. Spain gained sovereignty over the Canaries in 1479. The islands were divided into two provinces by Spain on Sept. 21, 1927.

CEUTA AND MELILLA

Area: 12 square miles (31 sq. km.).
Population: 176,211.

These two city enclaves stand on the Mediterranean coast of Morocco. Both are governed as parts of Spain. Ceuta was built on the site of a Phoenician colony and may have been the location of one of the ancient Pillars of Hercules. It was seized from the Arabs by Portugal in 1415 and passed into Spanish hands in 1580. Melilla has been Spanish since 1496. Morocco pressed claims for the cities in the 1970s–1980s.

QUICK QUIZ: How many U.S. military personnel were stationed in Spain in 1983? See page 462.

SRI LANKA

Official Name: Democratic Socialist Republic of Sri Lanka.
Area: 25,332 square miles (65,610 sq. km.).
Population: 15,788,900.
Chief Cities: Colombo, capital, 616,000; Dahiwala–Mt. Lavinia, 169,000; Jaffna, 118,000.
Government: Presidential-parliamentary democracy.
President: Junius Richard Jayewardene (since 1978).
Prime Minister: Ranasinghe Premadasa (since 1978).
Legislature: *National State Assembly,* 169 members.
U.S. Ambassador to Sri Lanka: John Hathaway Reed.
Sri Lanka Ambassador to U.S.: H.E. Ernest Corea.
Flag: Yellow border around maroon rectangle with bo leaves in each corner; yellow sword-carrying lion in center; green and orange bars at hoist.
Languages: Sinhalese (official), English, Tamil.
Main Ethnic Groups: Sinhalese (72%), Tamil (20%), Moors (7%), others (1%).
Principal Religions: Buddhism (67%), Hinduism (17%), Christianity (8%), Islam (7%).
Leading Industries: Agriculture (tea, rubber, coconuts, rice, cocoa, corn, spices, fruits, vegetables); forestry and lumbering; fishing; manufacturing (cement, textiles); mining (gems, salt, graphite).
Foreign Trade: *Major exports*—tea, rubber, coconut products; *major imports*—wheat, rice, food, fertilizer, machinery, textiles, petroleum products, sugar, flour, transportation equipment.
Places of Interest: Gal Oya Valley, Wilpattu, Ruhunu national parks; ruins at Anuradhapura and Polonnaruwa; Fortress in the Sky at Sigiriya; Buddhist Temple of the Tooth at Kandy; Bentota, Ambalangoda, Mt. Lavinia beach resorts. *In Colombo: Pettah (Old Town); Colombo Museum; Victoria Park.*

SRI LANKA TODAY

An island-nation about the size of West Virginia, Sri Lanka lies in the Indian Ocean only 18 miles off India's southern coast. Unlike many other developing nations, Sri Lanka has maintained a democratic government since gaining independence in 1948. Although the majority of people are poor, 9 out of 10 can read and write.

Sri Lanka has few natural resources. Because much of the land is used to raise tea, rubber, and coconuts for export, Sri Lanka does not grow enough food to feed its people.

Hostility between the island's two major ethnic groups, the Buddhist Sinhalese majority and the Hindu Tamil minority, repeatedly flares in violent riots.

The island's highest point is Pidurutalagala (8,281 feet), but most of Sri Lanka has elevations of 1,000 feet or less.

EARLY HISTORY

Formerly called *Ceylon,* Sri Lanka was settled in the 500s B.C. by Sinhalese from northern India, conquering the ancient Veddas. In 483 B.C. Vijaya, an Indian prince, established the first Sinhalese kingdom, with the capital at Anuradhapura. Buddhism was introduced in the 200s B.C.

Rajaraja I, ruler of the Tamil kingdom of Chola in southern India, extended his domain to Ceylon in the 1000s A.D. Polonnaruwa became the capital of Chola.

During the "Golden Age of Lanka" in the mid-1100s, the Sinhalese under King Prakrama Bahu I ruled the whole island.

The first Western conquerors were Portuguese, who began to introduce Christianity in 1505. They were followed by the Dutch in the 1600s. In 1796 the British took over. Britain conquered the last free Ceylonese kingdom, Kandy, in 1815.

In 1931 Ceylon became the first Asian country to extend voting rights to women.

INDEPENDENCE

On Feb. 4, 1948, Ceylon became independent as a British dominion. Don Stephen Senanayake, the first prime minister, was succeeded in 1952 by his son Dudley. In elections that year his United National Party (UNP) retained power.

The Sri Lanka Freedom Party (SLEP) won the 1956 elections. S.W.R.D. Bandaranaike, who became prime minister, was assassinated in 1959.

New elections held in 1960 made Bandaranaike's widow, Sirimavo Bandaranaike, the world's first woman prime minister.

From 1965 to 1970 Senanayake returned as prime minister of a pro-Western government.

Mrs. Bandaranaike again became prime minister in 1970, forming a leftist coalition government.

On May 22, 1972, the nation became a republic within the British Commonwealth of Nations.

J.R. Jayewardene, a 70-year-old Buddhist nicknamed "Yankee Dick" because of his pro-Western capitalist views, became prime minister in 1977. His UNP party had overwhelmingly defeated Mrs. Bandaranaike's leftist SLEP party in parliamentary elections on July 21.

Parliament amended the constitution in October 1977 to establish a strong presidential-parliamentary system similar to that of France. Jayewardene became president on Feb. 3, 1978. A new constitution was proclaimed on Sept. 7, 1978, strengthening the presidency.

The government began construction in March 1980 of the huge Victoria Reservoir on the Mahaweli River in the north-central part of the island. The 5-year hydroelectric project, which will help relieve the nation's dependence on imported petroleum, was financed in large part by about $250 million in aid from Britain.

The success of Jaywardene's private enterprise policies brought prosperity as the gross national product soared 25% from 1980 to 1981.

The 76-year old President Jayewardene was rewarded with a full six-year term in the nation's first presidential election on Oct. 20, 1982, receiving about 53% of the vote.

After Tamil guerrillas ambushed and killed 13 Sinhalese soldiers on July 23, 1983, severe rioting broke out throughout the country. More than 380 persons were killed and over 100,000 were made homeless in several weeks of rioting, looting, and arson. Communist leaders accused of fomenting the riots were arrested. Political parties promoting an independent Tamil nation were banned. Thousands of Tamil refugees fled from southern Sri Lanka to Tamil regions in the north.

SUDAN

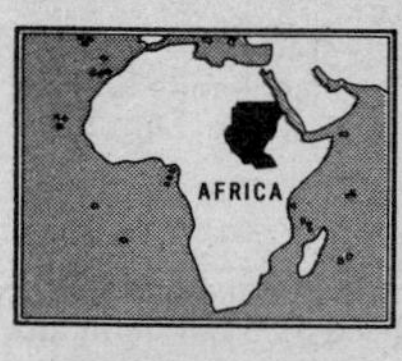

Official Name: Democratic Republic of the Sudan.
Area: 967,500 square miles (2,505,813 sq. km.).
Population: 20,885,700.
Chief Cities: Khartoum, capital, 261,840; Omdurman, 258,532; Khartoum North, 127,672; Port Sudan, 110,091.
Government: One-party republic.
President: Maj. Gen. Gaafar Muhammed Nimeiri (seized power in 1969).
Legislature: *National Assembly,* 151 members.
U.S. Ambassador to Sudan: Hume A. Horan.
Sudanese Ambassador to U.S.: Omer Salih Eissa.
Flag: Green triangle; red, white, and black stripes.
Official Language: Arabic.
Main Ethnic Groups: Arab (70%), black (23%).
Principal Religions: Islam (70%), animism (25%), Christianity (5%).
Leading Industries: Agriculture (livestock, cotton, sorghum, wheat, sesame, peanuts, castor beans, fruits, vegetables); food processing; mining (petroleum); manufacturing (textiles, handicrafts).
Foreign Trade: *Major exports*—cotton, sesame, peanuts; *major imports*—fertilizers, sugar, wheat, flour, machinery, petroleum, chemicals.
Places of Interest: Archaeological ruins along Nile; Nubian Desert; Dindar National Park.

SUDAN TODAY

About one-fourth the size of the United States, Sudan is the largest country in Africa. But it also is one of the 25 poorest countries. Although its major resource is soil, Sudan must import much of the food its people need.

New strains were put on the economy in 1978–80 as half a million refugees came to Sudan from wars and revolutions in Chad, Ethiopia, Uganda, and Zaire.

The nation has foreign debts of about $8 billion dollars and spends about $1 billion more on imports than it receives each year for exports.

Despite government development of huge irrigation projects, agricultural production declined in the 1970s–1980s. Most Sudanese live by subsistence farming or by herding livestock. Only about 1 person in 10 can read and write.

The Nile River flows north through the Sudan plain. A rain forest in the south gives way to savanna grasslands in the central region and to a desert in the north.

Egypt lies to the north; the Red Sea and Ethiopia to the east; Kenya, Uganda, and Zaire to the south; and Central Africa, Chad, and Libya to the west.

EARLY HISTORY

Ancient Egypt established outposts in the Sudan from which developed the kingdom of Kush. In A.D. 350 Kush was destroyed by the Aksumites from Ethiopia. In the 500s Christian missionaries established states that coexisted with Muslim-Arab Egypt for over 600 years. By the 1300s Arabs had taken over Christian Nubia and settled in the Sudan, where they introduced Islam.

In 1820–21 troops of the Ottoman viceroy of Egypt, Mohammed Ali, imposed Turko-Egyptian rule over northern Sudan. Southern Sudan was conquered by Egypt in 1863–79.

The Sudanese revolted, under the leadership of Mohammed Ahmed, the Mahdi. His forces massacred a British army led by Gen. Charles Gordon at Khartoum on Jan. 26, 1885, drove out the Egyptians, and established an independent, theocratic Mahdist state. British Gen. Herbert Kitchener invaded the Sudan in 1898, ending Mahdist rule. From 1899 to 1956 Britain and Egypt controlled Sudan.

INDEPENDENCE

On Jan. 1, 1956, Sudan gained independence from Britain and Egypt as a republic. Two years later army officers seized control.

A popular revolution in 1964 reestablished civilian rule. The assembly elected in 1965 was controlled by Mohammed Ahmed Mahgoub.

In May 1969 the Mahgoub regime was ousted in a military coup. Maj. Gen. Gaafar Muhammed Nimeiri became president.

In October 1971 Nimeiri was elected president in a national referendum. He then dissolved the military revolutionary council and announced creation of a new political party, the Sudanese Socialist Union (SSU).

An uprising by blacks in the south against government Arabization policies raged from 1955 until a cease-fire was achieved in 1972. The civil war cost perhaps 500,000 lives.

In May 1977 Sudan expelled Soviet military advisers and turned to the U.S. for aid.

Nimeiri granted amnesty to political prisoners in 1977–78 and encouraged opponents to return to Sudan from exile.

The first major oil find in Sudan was made in July 1979 at Abu Jabra by the American Chevron company, bringing in a 500-barrel-a-day well.

The government announced on March 16, 1981, it had thwarted the 15th attempted coup since Nimeiri took power. A general and several other military officers were arrested for the plot.

On March 22, 1981, Sudan broke ranks with other Arab nations to restore diplomatic relations with Egypt that had been severed in 1979 because of Egypt's peace treaty with Israel.

Believing that the leader of Libya was involved in plotting to overthrow him, Nimeiri expelled all Libyan diplomats from Sudan on June 25, 1981.

Sudan and Egypt signed a pact in October 1982 to coordinate political and economic policies.

Nimeiri was reelected without opposition to a third six-year term as president in April 1983.

A mutiny by an army unit in southern Sudan on May 15, 1983, was put down by loyal troops in fighting that claimed 78 lives.

Under an Islamic penal code adopted in September 1983, thieves are punished by having a hand chopped off. All alcoholic drinks are prohibited.

President Nimeiri freed all 13,000 prisoners from Sudan's jails to give them a new chance under the new penal code.

QUICK QUIZ: What nation of today was once known as Mesopotamia? See page 578.

SURINAME

Official Name: Republic of Suriname.
Area: 63,037 square miles (163,265 sq. km.).
Population: 356,201.
Capital: Paramaribo, 150,000.
Government: Socialist-military state.
Head of Military Junta: Lt. Col. Dési Bouterse (since 1981).
Prime Minister: Errol Alibux (since 1983).
U.S. Ambassador: Robert Werner Duemling.
Suriname's Ambassador to U.S.: H.A.F. Heidweiller.
Flag: Stripes of green, white, red, white, and green with yellow star centered on red stripe.
Languages: Dutch (official), English, Sranang Tongo.
Main Ethnic Groups: Asian Indian descent (37%), Creole (mixed black-European descent) (31%), Javanese descent (13%), Bush Negro (8%).
Principal Religions: Hinduism (26%), Islam (26%), Roman Catholicism (21%), Protestantism (18%).
Leading Industries: Mining (bauxite); agriculture (rice, bananas, coconuts, fruits, vegetables); manufacturing (aluminum, electricity, food processing, clothing); forestry and lumbering; fishing.
Foreign Trade: *Major exports*—bauxite, aluminum, alumina; *major imports*—food, machinery, petroleum, steel, cotton, grain, consumer goods.
Places of Interest: *In Paramaribo:* colonial buildings, oriental bazaars; swimming beaches; jungle villages; sport fishing and hunting; river canoeing.

SURINAME TODAY

Somewhat larger than the state of Georgia, Suriname is the smallest and newest of South America's independent nations.

The former Dutch colony's most important resource is bauxite, the ore from which aluminum is made. The country's rivers produce electricity to power aluminum-making plants.

Farms grow ample quantities of rice, the people's major food staple.

Most of Suriname's farms are along the northern coast at the mouths of the Suriname, Saramacca, Coppername, and Nickerie rivers. The center of the country is heavily forested. The southern three-fourths of the land is a hilly, largely uninhabited area that rises to 4,120 feet in the Wilhelmina Mountains.

The country has a hot tropical climate that averages 79 ° F. the year round. There are two rainy seasons—from November to February and from March through July.

Suriname lies on the northeast coast of South America. Guyana is to the west, Brazil to the south, and French Guiana to the east.

EARLY HISTORY

The first European settlement was established in 1651 by Lord Willoughby of England. He encouraged experienced colonists to emigrate from other settlements in the Americas. Among them were Portuguese Jews from Brazil, who built the first synagogue in the Western Hemisphere in 1665.

After the English captured New York from the Dutch, the Treaty of Breda was signed in 1667 by which the Dutch received Suriname in exchange for giving up claims to New York.

During the 1700s and early 1800s the colony, known as *Dutch Guiana,* changed hands several times but ended in possession of the Dutch by the Vienna treaty of 1815.

INDEPENDENCE

The Netherlands granted Suriname independence on Nov. 25, 1975, and promised $1.5 billion in aid for 1976–86.

On Nov. 1, 1977, Prime Minister Henck Arron's National Party Combination (NPK) won the first parliamentary election since independence.

An army coup overthrew Arron on Feb. 25, 1980. The military made Henk Chin A Sen, a civilian, prime minister.

In a second military coup, on Aug. 13, 1980, the sergeants who had headed the junta were arrested. The new junta named Chin A Sen as president.

Lt. Col. Dési Bouterse, head of the military junta, ousted Chin A Sen on Feb. 5, 1982.

A revolt by right-wing army forces on March 14, 1982, failed to overthrow Bouterse.

Bouterse approved a new constitution on March 25, 1982, proclaiming Suriname a socialist state.

Fifteen prominent Surinamers were arrested by the military on Sunday morning Dec. 8, 1982, charged with plotting the overthrow of the military government. All were slain later in the day "while trying to escape," according to the official announcement.

Outraged by the incident, the Netherlands and the U.S. suspended economic aid to Suriname.

Bourtese arrested his second in command, Maj. Roy Horb, on Jan. 31, 1983, along with several cabinet ministers, charging they were planning to overthrow him. Four days later Horb was found hanged in his jail cell.

SWAZILAND

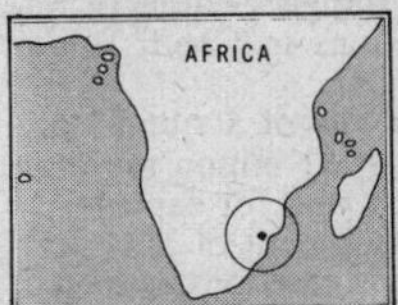

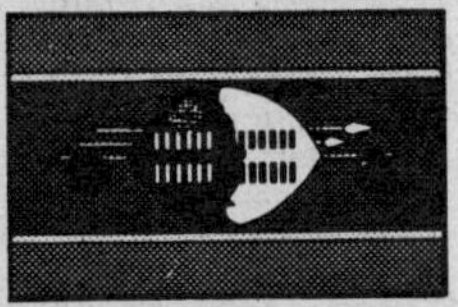

Official Name: Kingdom of Swaziland.
Area: 6,704 square miles (17,363 sq. km.).
Population: 610,747.
Capital: (administrative) Mbabane, 20,800; (traditional) Lobamba.
Government: Absolute monarchy.
Regent: Queen Mother Ntombi (since 1983).
Prime Minister: Prince Bhekimpi Dlamini (since 1983).
Crown Prince: Makhosetive (since 1983).
Parliament: 50 members.
U.S. Ambassador to Swaziland: Robert H. Phinny.
Swazi Ambassador to U.S.: Lawrence Mfama Mncina.
Flag: Stripes of blue, yellow, red, yellow, and blue, with black and white Swazi shield of Emasotsha regiment.
Languages: siSwati and English (both official), Zulu.
Main Ethnic Groups: Swazi, Zulu.
Religions: Christianity (60%), animism (40%).
Leading Industries: Agriculture (cattle, goats, poultry, sugarcane, rice, citrus fruits, cotton, maize, sorghum, tobacco, pineapples); forestry and lumbering; mining

(iron, coal, asbestos); manufacturing (food processing, chemicals, machinery, consumer goods); tourism.
Foreign Trade: *Major exports*—iron ore, sugar, wood products, asbestos, coal, canned fruits; *major imports*—food, clothing, vehicles, machinery, petroleum.
Places of Interest: Mountain scenery in the west; hot springs at Mbabane; game preserves.

SWAZILAND TODAY

Once dependent on subsistence farming for its economy, Swaziland became one of the most prosperous small nations of Africa during the 1970s. British and South African investors helped develop iron mines, sugar refineries, a pulp paper mill, and sugar, pineapple, and orange plantations. An east-west railroad also was built across the country to carry exports to the port of Maputo, Mozambique.

Called "the Switzerland of Africa," Swaziland attracts over 100,000 tourists each year to its gambling casinos, fine hotels, golf courses, and game preserves.

Despite efforts to develop a diversified economy, about three-fourths of Swaziland's people live by raising cattle and corn. Only about 1 Swazi in 3 can read and write.

Somewhat larger than Connecticut, Swaziland is bordered on the north, west, and south by South Africa and on the east by Mozambique. Three topographical regions extend from north to south: a mountainous region in the west averages between 3,500 and 4,500 feet above sea level; a middle plateau; and a low plain in the east, averaging about 1,000 feet.

HISTORY

The Swazi settled in northern Zululand about 1750. They had their first formal relations with Britain in the 1840s when they sought help against the Zulus. Mineral rights were granted to the Europeans by the Swazi, and in 1894 South Africa assumed responsibility for the protection and administration of the country.

After the Boer War, Swaziland was administered by the British governor of the Transvaal. In 1907 a British resident commissioner was appointed. Sobhuza II became king in 1921.

Political parties were formed in the 1960s that demanded independence from British rule. In 1964 the first election was held in which the Swazi could vote. The king's political party, Imbokodvo, won all 24 seats in the national assembly.

Swaziland became independent on Sept. 6, 1968. King Sobhuza II in 1973 scrapped the constitution prepared by the British and took over absolute power. He outlawed political parties and political meetings.

The 83-year-old King Sobhuza died on Aug. 21, 1982, a year after celebrating the diamond jubilee of his rule. He was believed to have had as many as 100 wives and about 600 children. The king's senior wife, Dzewile, became regent.

The royal council of elders, called the Liqoqo, announced in August 1983 that 15-year-old Prince Makhosetive had been chosen to succeed as king when he reaches his majority. His mother, Queen Ntombi, replaced Queen Dzeliwe as regent, with the title Indlovukazi, or Great She-Elephant.

SWEDEN

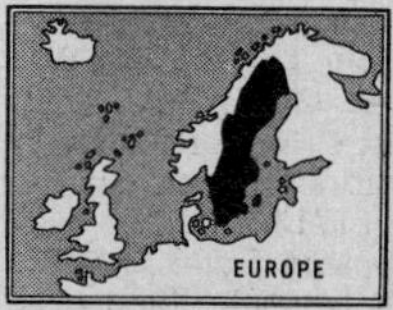

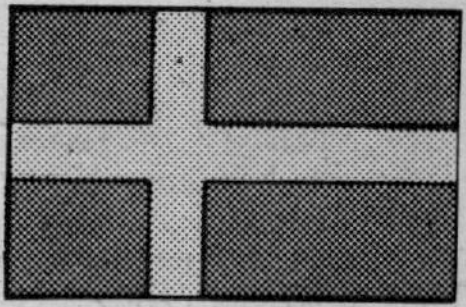

Official Name: Kingdom of Sweden.
Area: 173,732 square miles (449,964 sq. km.).
Population: 8,331,100.
Chief Cities: Stockholm, capital, 649,384; Göteborg, 434,699; Malmö, 235,111; Uppsala, 145,032; Norrkoping, 119,993; Västerås, 117,257; Örebro, 116,877; Linköping, 111,866; Jönköping, 107,652.
Largest Metropolitan Area: Stockholm, 1,384,310.
Government: Parliamentary monarchy.
Prime Minister: Olaf Palme (since 1982).
King: Karl XVI Gustaf (since 1973).
Legislature: *Riksdag,* 349 members.
U.S. Ambassador to Sweden: Franklin S. Forsberg.
Swedish Ambassador to U.S.: Count Wilhelm Wachtmeister.
Flag: Light blue field with yellow cross.
Official Language: Swedish.
Main Ethnic Group: Swedes.
State Religion: Evangelical Lutheranism (95%).
Leading Industries: Trade and services; manufacturing (paper, electricity, steel, metal products, machinery, automobiles, aircraft, consumer goods); mining (iron, coal, copper, lead, zinc, manganese); agriculture (dairy products, cattle, hay, sugar beets, barley, oats, wheat, potatoes, fruits, vegetables); forestry; lumbering; fishing.
Foreign Trade: *Major exports*—machinery and transport equipment, manufactured goods, paper, wood pulp, wood, iron ore; *major imports*—machinery and transport equipment, manufactured goods, fuels.
Places of Interest: "Land of the Midnight Sun"—Lapland; Gotland Island; Lake Siljan; "The Crystal Land"—glassworks near Kalmar; Göta Canal; New Älvsborg Fortress in Göteborg. *In Stockholm:* Drottningholm Palace; Royal Warship Wasa Museum.

SWEDEN TODAY

About twice as large as Minnesota, Sweden has a higher standard of living than the United States and the world's longest life expectancy.

Sweden has one of the most extensive social-welfare programs in the world, paid with taxes that absorb about 70% of the national income.

The south has a temperate climate with about a two-month winter and four-month summer. The long, cold winter in the north lasts more than seven months.

Norway lies to the west and Finland to the northeast. Sweden's largest islands are Gotland and Oland in the Baltic Sea.

EARLY HISTORY

Tacitus, the Roman historian, first mentioned the Swedes (Suiones) about A.D. 100. In the 800s their semilegendary chieftain Rurik is said to have founded Russia. By the 900s Swedish influence extended south to the Black Sea. Warfare against Norsemen and Danes went on for centuries. In 1397 all the Scandinavian crowns were united under Queen Margrethe I of Denmark.

QUICK QUIZ: How many times did Sam Rayburn (D–Tex.) win election to Congress? See page 337.

SWEDEN *(continued)*

Sweden became an independent kingdom in 1523, when the Swedes elected Gustaf I as ruler. By the time of its involvement in the Thirty Years War (1618–48), Sweden, under Gustaf II Adolf (1611–32), was the foremost Protestant power.

Sweden became a constitutional monarchy under Queen Ulrika Eleonora (1718–20).

Sweden warred with Napoleon I and lost Finland to Russia (1809). Napoleon's brilliant marshal Jean Baptiste Jules Bernadotte was elected by the *Riksdag* to succeed the childless Karl XIII. Bernadotte ascended the throne in 1818 as Karl XIV, founding the present Swedish dynasty.

The last war in Swedish history was fought in 1814, when Bernadotte enforced the Treaty of Kiel's award of Norway to Sweden. Norway remained in union with Sweden until 1905.

With neutrality as its foreign policy, Sweden remained uninvolved in both world wars.

The Social Democratic Party was dominant in 1932–76, except for a short period in 1936.

A coalition of opposition parties defeated the socialists after 44 years of rule in national elections on Sept. 19, 1976. Thorbjorn Falldin, head of the Center Party, became prime minister.

Liberal leader Ola Ullsten became prime minister on Oct. 13, 1978, after Falldin's coalition collapsed.

In a national election on Sept. 16, 1979, the governing nonsocialist parties won a one-seat majority in parliament with 175 members to 174 for the socialists and communists. Falldin again became prime minister in October.

SWEDEN IN THE 1980s

In Sweden's first nationwide strike-lockout in 70 years, about 1 million workers were idled for 10 days on May 2–11, 1980. The dispute was settled when management negotiators accepted government urging to grant a 7% wage increase.

A nationwide referendum on March 23, 1980, decided 3 to 2 favor of an ambitious program to double the number of Sweden's nuclear electric generating plants to reduce oil imports.

By a 1-vote margin parliament adopted on Sept. 6, 1980, the highest value-added tax (sales tax) in Europe—a record 23.46%.

Socialist Olof Palme, 55, who previously had served as prime minister in 1969–76, was restored to the office on Oct. 7, 1982, two weeks after his Social Democratic Party won control of parliament in a general election.

A day after taking office, Palme ordered an economic austerity program, devaluing the krona 16% and establishing a general price freeze. He told the nation that taxes also had to be increased to meet the rising expenses of government.

After counting 40 violations of Swedish territorial waters in a year by what were believed to be Soviet submarines, the government recalled its ambassador to Moscow in protest in April 1983. Three months later, on July 1, 1983, new orders were issued to the Swedish navy to attack such intruders without warning.

Over 75,000 persons paraded through Stockholm on Oct. 5, 1983, in the largest political demonstration in the nation's history. They protested heavier taxes on business to be used to purchase stock in the businesses by labor unions.

SWITZERLAND

Official Name: Swiss Confederation.
Area: 15,941 square miles (41,288 sq. km.).
Population: 6,405,260.
Chief Cities: Bern, capital, 142,900; Zurich, 377,300; Basel, 183,200; Geneva, 152,700; Lausanne, 131,000.
Largest Metropolitan Area: Zurich, 709,300.
Government: Federal republic of 23 cantons.
Executive: *Federal Council,* 7 members elected by Federal Assembly. President chosen annually.
Federal Assembly: *Council of States,* 46 members; *National Council,* 200 members.
U.S. Ambassador to Switzerland: John Davis Lodge.
Swiss Ambassador to U.S.: Anton Hegner.
Flag: White cross on red field.
Languages: German (65%), French (18%), Italian (12%), Romansch (1%), other (4%).
Main Religions: Roman Catholicism (49.4%), Protestantism (47.8%).
Leading Industries: Manufacturing (machinery, electrical equipment, watches, precision instruments, chocolate, cheese, chemicals, textiles, electricity, consumer products); tourism; banking, trade, and services; agriculture (dairy products, cattle, goats, hogs, sheep, sugar beets, grains, potatoes, grapes, fruits, vegetables); forestry and lumbering; mining (salt, building stone).
Foreign Trade: *Major exports*—watches, instruments, cheese, chocolate, textile machinery, organic chemicals, medical supplies, metalworking machine tools; *major imports*—iron and steel, automobiles, petroleum, clothing.
Places of Interest: Swiss National Park; Alps; Lake Lucerne; Interlaken, Gstaad, St. Moritz resorts; Rhone Valley. *In Zurich:* Grossmünster Cathedral; churches. *In Geneva:* Ariana Park, UN headquarters in Europe. *In Basel:* Art museum; 11th century cathedral. *In Bern:* Clock tower; the Bear Pit; town hall, Gothic cathedral and rose gardens. *In Lucerne:* Lion Monument; Wagner's home, Tribschen.

SWITZERLAND TODAY

About twice the size of New Jersey, Switzerland has enjoyed peace and neutrality for more than a century and a half. It is a leading center for banking and finance and a favorite meeting place for diplomats. Its people enjoy one of the world's highest standards of living.

About half the country's income comes from manufacturing. Most of the rest comes from service industries, particularly those accommodating the many tourists who visit Switzerland each year to enjoy the mountain scenery or take part in winter sports.

Lacking coal and oil to develop an industrialized economy, the Swiss use their mountain rivers to provide electric power for factories.

Only about a fourth of the land can be used for crops, so much food must be imported.

In a $3 billion civil-defense program begun in 1962, underground nuclear shelters will be provided for the entire population by the year 2000.

Swiss citizens have more of a voice in their

laws than those of other countries, voting in national referendums up to four times each year to approve or reject proposed laws. A petition with only 50,000 signatures can force a referendum.

Switzerland is bordered on the north by West Germany, on the east by Austria and Liechtenstein, on the south by Italy, and on the west by France.

Two mountain systems cover most of the country—the Alps in the south and the Jura in the west and northwest. In the central Alps rise the Rhine, the Rhone, and the Ticino rivers. The highest peak is 15,203-foot Monte Rosa.

HISTORY

The Helvetians, who lived in the northern foothills of the Alps, were conquered by the Romans in 58 B.C. After A.D. 401, the area was dominated by a succession of rival neighbors.

In the 800s the area was part of the Empire of Charlemagne. As the Carolingian Empire fell into decay, the Hapsburg, Zähringer, and Savoy dynasties made encroachments.

In 1291 a defensive league against the Hapsburgs was formed by the cantons of Unterwalden, Uri, and Schwyz (from which the country takes its name). This marks the beginning of the *Swiss Confederation,* the nation's present official name.

By 1513 the confederation had grown to 13 largely autonomous cantons. The Treaty of Westphalia, which in 1648 ended the Thirty Years War, recognized Swiss independence.

In 1798 French revolutionary forces invaded Switzerland and formed the Helvetic Republic. Napoleon's Act of Mediation in 1803 restored the old confederation, but under French dominance.

NEUTRAL SWITZERLAND

In 1815 the Treaty of Paris and the Congress of Vienna guaranteed Switzerland's perpetual neutrality.

Switzerland's 23 cantons are governed today under a constitution adopted in 1874.

Since 1959 a coalition of four major parties has controlled the government.

In February 1971, Swiss women for the first time won the right to vote in federal elections.

In a national referendum on March 1, 1980, Swiss voters rejected by about 4 to 1 a proposal to sever ties between government and religion. The proposal would have ended the practice of supporting religious sects with government taxes.

By a 3–2 margin, Swiss voters on June 14, 1981, approved a constitutional amendment guaranteeing equal rights to women.

The Swiss government began taking steps in 1982 to join the United Nations, assuring the public that UN membership would not affect the nation's neutrality. A public referendum on the issue was planned for 1984.

The government closed the Soviet Union's Novosti news agency in Bern on April 29, 1983, and expelled its bureau chief, charging the Soviets with infiltrating antinuclear peace groups to stimulate demonstrations that threatened the national security.

In national elections on Oct. 23, 1983, the four-party governing coalition retained power, Communists lost two of their three seats in the lower house.

SYRIA

Official Name: Syrian Arab Republic.
Area: 71,498 square miles (185,180 sq. km.).
Population: 9,905,810.
Chief Cities: Damascus, capital, 1,156,000; Aleppo, 919,244; Homs, 325,724; Lattakia, 204,000; Hama, 197,804.
Government: Republic.
President: Hafez al-Assad (since 1971).
Prime Minister: Abdul Rauf al-Kasm (since 1980).
Legislature: *People's Council,* 195 members.
U.S. Ambassador to Syria: Robert P. Paganelli.
Syrian Ambassador to U.S.: Dr. Rafic Jouejati.
Flag: Red, white, and black stripes, with two green stars in center stripe.
Languages: Arabic (official), Armenian, Kurdish, French, English.
Ethnic Groups: Arab (90%), Kurd, Armenian, Turkmen, Circassian.
Main Religions: Islam (86%), Christianity (13%).
Leading Industries: Agriculture (livestock, cotton, wheat, barley, sugar beets, fruits, vegetables); mining (petroleum, phosphates); construction; manufacturing (textiles, cement, ceramics, food processing, oil refining, electricity); trade and services; tourism.
Foreign Trade: *Major exports*—cotton, barley, wool, wheat; *major imports*—iron and steel, machinery, petroleum products, weapons.
Places of Interest: Palmyra monuments; Krak des Chevaliers (Crusaders Castle) in Homs district; Aleppo; waterwheels at Hama. *In Damascus:* Omayyad Mosque; Azem Palace; Hamidieh Bazaar; biblical street called Straight.

SYRIA TODAY

A militant Arab state, Syria has taken part in five wars with its neighbor Israel. Its leaders refuse to negotiate peace until Israel gives back all territory it won in those wars.

Syria's socialist government has nationalized most industry and expropriated and redistributed most large landholdings. The country is dependent on more than $1 billion a year in aid from wealthy Arab oil countries. It also is supplied with arms by the Soviet Union.

Western Syria consists of a narrow Mediterranean coastal plain and the Alawite and Anti-Lebanon mountains and plateau. A fertile region in the north gives way to a central steppe area and a desert region in the south. The main rivers are the Euphrates, Khabur, and Barada.

Somewhat larger than North Dakota, Syria lies at the eastern end of the Mediterranean Sea. Turkey is on the north, Iraq on the east and southeast, Jordan on the south, Israel on the southwest, and Lebanon on the west.

EARLY HISTORY

Ancient Syria was the home of the Amorites, Canaanites, Phoenicians, and Hebrews. It was conquered by several waves of foreign invaders—

QUICK QUIZ: James Bridger was the first white man to discover what lake? See page 329.

SYRIA *(continued)*

Aramaeans, Assyrians, Babylonians, and Persians. Syria was unified after its conquest by Alexander the Great in 332 B.C. It passed to the Romans in 63 B.C. and to the Byzantines in A.D. 395.

In the 600s Syria fell to the Arabs, who introduced the Arabic language and culture. From 661 to 750, under the Damascus caliphate of the Omayyads, Syria controlled a vast Islamic domain.

From 1516 to World War I Syria was part of the Ottoman Turkish Empire.

From 1920 to 1946 France controlled Syria as a League of Nations mandate.

INDEPENDENCE

Syria gained independence as a republic on April 17, 1946.

From 1958 to 1961 Syria was part of the United Arab Republic (Egypt and Syria) under the presidency of Egypt's President Nasser.

Syrian troops participated in four Arab-Israeli wars (1948, 1956, 1967, 1973).

A military coup in February 1968 installed Nureddin al-Attassi as head of state. His regime received substantial military equipment from the Soviet Union. In November 1970, however, he was ousted by rightist military officers, who made Hafez al-Assad president in 1971.

In 1972 Syria nationalized all properties of the Western-owned Iraq Petroleum Company.

Syria joined Egypt in attacking Israel in October 1973. After the UN-ordered cease-fire on October 24, artillery duels and border clashes between Syria and Israel continued into 1974. Finally, on May 31, 1974, Syria signed a U.S.-negotiated pact with Israel for mutual withdrawal of their armed forces.

In 1974 the U.S. and Syria resumed diplomatic relations, broken since 1967.

Syria sent troops and tanks into Lebanon on May 31, 1976, and within six months ended the civil war in that country. Syrian troops remained in Lebanon to police the peace.

On Feb. 8, 1978, Assad was elected without opposition to a second 7-year term as president.

Syria and Iraq broke diplomatic relations in August 1980 after Iraq expelled Syrian diplomats for stocking their Baghdad embassy with arms.

Syria and Libya announced on Sept. 10, 1980, that the two nations would merge. When war broke out between Iraq and Iran later in the month, Libya and Syria aided Iran. But leaders of the two nations were unable to work out details for the merger in a meeting three months later.

On Oct. 8, 1980, Syria and the Soviet Union signed a 20-year military and economic treaty.

Muslim fanatics seeking to overthrow the government waged a campaign of terrorism in 1978–82. When the radical Muslim Brotherhood began a revolt in the city of Hama in February 1982, government troops stormed the city. An estimated 6,000 persons were killed. Bulldozers were used to level entire neighborhoods.

The Syrian army in Lebanon lost huge amounts of Soviet-supplied arms to the Israelis who invaded that country in 1982.

Syria refused requests by Lebanon in 1983 that it withdraw its troops (see page 419).

The Soviet Union in 1983 sent 5,000 troops to aid Syria with SS21 missiles capable of devastating Israel's cities.

TAIWAN

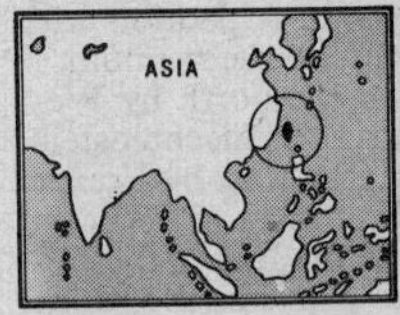

Official Name: Republic of China.
Area: 12,456 square miles (32,260 sq. km.).
Population: 18,980,600.
Chief Cities: Taipei, capital, 1,769,568; Kaohsiung, 1,000,000; Taichung, 575,000; Tainan, 550,000.
Government: One-party parliamentary republic.
President: Chiang Ching-kuo (took office in 1978).
Prime Minister: Sun Yun-hsuan (since 1978).
Legislature: *Legislative Yüan,* about 430 members.
Flag: Red field bearing blue rectangle, upper left, that contains 12-pointed white sun.
Languages: Chinese (Peking dialect; official), English, Japanese, Hokkien, Hakka.
Ethnic Groups: Han Chinese, 98% (Taiwanese 80%, mainlanders 18%), aborigines (2%).
Religions: Confucianism, Taoism, Buddhism, Christianity.
Leading Industries: Manufacturing (electronics, textiles, chemicals, fertilizer, cement, glass, plastics, aircraft); agriculture (poultry, hogs, rice, sugarcane, tea, fruits, vegetables); forestry and lumbering; tourism; fishing; mining (coal, natural gas, sulfur).
Foreign Trade: *Major exports*—textiles, electronic equipment, plywood, canned food; *major imports*—machinery, iron and steel, raw cotton, soybeans, motor vehicles, wheat, petroleum.
Places of Interest: Sun-Moon Lake; Fo Kuang Mountain temple; Taroko Gorge. *In Taipei:* national palace museum; botanical gardens; temples; Grass Mountain resort area; 75th Buddha, near Changhua. *In Tainan:* forts and temples.

TAIWAN TODAY

About twice the size of Hawaii, Taiwan has achieved a strong and prosperous economy in the more than three decades since the government of nationalist China retreated to the island. Its people enjoy one of the highest standards of living in the Far East.

With a variety of major public works and industrial projects under way, the government hopes to move from the status of a developing nation to that of a developed nation. Projects include improved port facilities, railroad and highway construction, airport development, and the building of a steel mill, shipyards, and petrochemical plants.

Tourism is a major industry with about 1.5 million visitors each year.

While Taiwan's economy has grown, its influence in world politics has diminished because of the insistence of its leaders that it represents the legal government of mainland China. As a result many nations, including the U.S., officially have broken diplomatic relations with Taiwan, and it has lost its seat in the UN. But most of these nations continue to trade with Taiwan. The U.S. sells more than half a billion dollars of arms to Taiwan each year.

The authoritarian government controls communication with strict censorship and prevents expression of political opposition.

Taiwan (formerly called *Formosa*) is an island about 100 miles from the China mainland. It measures some 240 miles north to south, and 85 miles at its greatest width.

The Pescadores (Penghu Islands), an island group belonging to Taiwan, lie about 25 miles from the southwest coast. Matsu and Quemoy (Kinmen), two small island groups controlled by Taiwan, are just off the mainland coast.

Mountains cover about two-thirds of Taiwan. Their eastern slope is rugged and sparsely settled, while the western slope is fertile and has one of the world's greatest population densities. The highest mountain, Yü Shan, rises to 13,110 feet.

The U.S. government has emphasized that it does not intend to build up Taiwan's armies for an invasion of communist-governed mainland China.

HISTORY OF TAIWAN

Chinese immigration to Taiwan began as early as the T'ang dynasty (618–907). In 1628 Dutch forces defeated Spaniards for control of Taiwan. After the Manchu conquest of the island in 1683, Taiwan was administered as part of China. In 1895 it was ceded to Japan following the Sino-Japanese War. Uprisings continued for decades.

After World War II, Japan surrendered Taiwan to China in 1945. Japan renounced all claims to Taiwan in 1951.

In 1949 the advancing communist forces of Mao Tse-tung forced President Chiang Kai-shek's nationalist government to flee from the mainland to Taiwan. Communist China's plans to invade the island were blocked in 1950 when President Harry S. Truman sent the U.S. Seventh Fleet to patrol Taiwan Strait.

The U.S. signed an agreement in 1955 to defend Taiwan and the Pescadores from any attack by Communist China.

In October 1971 the UN General Assembly with U.S. support voted for Red China's admission but, despite U.S. objections, expelled Taiwan. President Nixon declared that U.S.-Taiwan alliances would be maintained.

In 1972, at the age of 85, Chiang Kai-shek turned over the running of the government to his eldest son, Chiang Ching-kuo, as premier.

After Chiang Kai-shek died in 1975, Premier Chiang became head of the ruling Nationalist Party (Kuomintang). The 65-year-old Chiang was elected president without opposition by the national assembly on March 21, 1978. Two months later he was sworn into the office that had been held by his father for three decades. He apppointed Sun Yun-hsuan as prime minister.

To extend diplomatic recognition to China, the U.S. ended formal relations with Taiwan on Jan. 1, 1979. President Carter also abrogated the 1955 mutual defense pact with Taiwan, effective Dec. 31, 1979. However, the U.S. continued to maintain unofficial diplomatic relations with Taiwan through the American Institute.

In an effort to strengthen relations with China, President Reagan agreed on Aug. 17, 1982, to "gradually reduce" U.S. arms sales to Taiwan in return for China's assurance that it would not use military force to take Taiwan.

TANZANIA

Official Name: United Republic of Tanzania.
Area: 364,900 square miles (945,087 sq. km.).
Population: 20,854,900.
Capital: Official capital, Dodoma, 60,000; actual capital, Dar es Salaam, 757,346.
Government: One-party socialist republic.
President: Julius Kambarage Nyerere (since 1961).
Prime Minister: Edward Sokoine (since 1983).
Legislature: *National Assembly* (mainland), 219 members; House of Representatives (Zanzibar), 40 members.
U.S. Ambassador to Tanzania: David Charles Miller Jr.
Tanzanian Ambassador to U.S.: Benjamin W. Mkapa.
Flag: Green triangle (upper left) and blue triangle (lower right) separated by diagonal gold-bordered black stripe.
Languages: Swahili (official), English.
Main Ethnic Group: Black.
Principal Religions: Islam (35%), Christianity (35%); animism (30%).
Leading Industries: Agriculture (livestock, cotton, coffee, sisal, cloves, coconuts, tea, tobacco, cashews, sugarcane); mining (diamonds, gold, tin, gemstones); manufacturing (food processing, oil refining, textiles, cement, consumer goods); tourism.
Foreign Trade: *Major exports*—cotton, coffee, sisal, diamonds, cloves; *major imports*—corn, machinery, transport equipment, steel, crude petroleum.
Places of Interest: Mt. Kilimanjaro; Ngorongoro Crater; nine national parks; five game preserves; Olduvai Gorge; Amboni Caves; Pemba and Mafia islands; Dar es Salaam; former sultan's palace, Zanzibar.

TANZANIA TODAY

Although more than twice as large as California, Tanzania is one of the poorest African nations. It is a federation of a mainland area formerly called Tanganyika and the island of Zanzibar.

Tanzania is one of the world's leading diamond-mining nations. But its economy is largely based on agriculture.

Most Tanzanians scratch out a bare living, raising corn, beans, and cassava. About two-thirds can read and write.

Mainland Tanzania is largely an infertile plateau, 1,000 to 4,000 feet high, bisected from north to south by the Great Rift Valley. On the more fertile margins of the plateau are Lakes Victoria, Tanganyika, and Malawi. Mt. Kilimanjaro (19,340 feet), the highest mountain in Africa, is in the northeast.

Tanzania is bordered on the south by Zambia, Malawi, and Mozambique; on the west by Rwanda, Burundi, and Zaire; and on the north by Kenya and Uganda.

EARLY HISTORY OF TANZANIA

Archaeological discoveries at Olduvai Gorge indicate that manlike creatures lived in the area 3 million years ago. Ancient Greek mariners

QUICK QUIZ: Does a banana have more or fewer calories than an avocado? See page 399.

TANZANIA *(continued)*

called the coast *Azania.*

Zanzibar and various coastal cities, especially Kilwa, were colonized from the Persian Gulf area, probably in the 700s. A series of autonomous Muslim city-states flourished with a Swahili language and culture.

In the 1500s the Portuguese destroyed the Muslim city-states and then controlled the coast until ousted by Arabs from Oman in the 1700s.

European colonization led to establishment in 1890 of a British protectorate in Zanzibar and to German colonization of Tanganyika, as the mainland area was called. German control ended after World War I when Britain took over Tanganyika under a League of Nations mandate.

INDEPENDENCE

The Tanganyika African National Union (TANU), headed by Julius Nyerere, led Tanganyika to independence on Dec. 9, 1961. Zanzibar became independent in December 1963.

On April 26, 1964, Tanganyika and Zanzibar united with Nyerere as president. The new country was named the *United Republic of Tanzania* in October 1964.

The socialist government nationalized clove plantations in Zanzibar in 1964 and took over many major companies in 1967 and 1968.

Nyerere was unopposed in reelections in 1970, 1975, and 1980.

With massive economic and technical aid from China, a 1,162-mile railroad was built in 1970–76 from Dar es Salaam to Kapiri Mposhi, Zambia.

Centrally located Dodoma has been named the official capital, but few government offices have been transferred there from Dar es Salaam pending completion of a $550 million construction program by 1985.

President Nyerere reported that by mid-1975 over 9 million Tanzanians had been moved into more than 6,900 socialist collective villages. The government in 1976 moved thousands of unemployed from Dar es Salaam to the countryside.

President Nyerere uses the Swahili word *ujamaa,* meaning "familyhood," to describe the village socialism he fosters. He explains that familyhood calls for sharing.

Full-scale war began in 1978 after Ugandan President Idi Amin announced on Nov. 1 that his troops had annexed 710 square miles of Tanzanian territory. Tanzania fought back, invaded Uganda, and drove Amin into exile, capturing Uganda's capital on April 11, 1979. Victorious Tanzanian troops began withdrawing from Uganda in July 1979. Tanzania's economy suffered because of the estimated $500 million cost of the war.

Zanzibar was granted autonomy in 1979 with a separate constitution. In the first Zanzibar election since 1964, its people chose a 40-member House of Representatives on Jan. 7, 1980, from among 80 candidates nominated by the only political party, Chama Cha Mapinduzi (CCM). Aboud Jumbe was elected president of Zanzibar on Oct. 26, 1980.

Hard hit by drought in 1980–83, Tanzania appealed for aid to prevent starvation. The U.S. and other nations responded with 260,000 tons of grain.

THAILAND

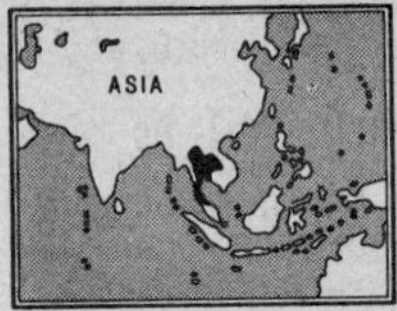

Official Name: Kingdom of Thailand.
Area: 198,457 square miles (514,000 sq. km.).
Population: 51,476,800.
Chief Cities: Bangkok, capital, 4,178,000; Thonburi, 627,989.
Government: Monarchy controlled by military.
King: Phumiphon Adunyadet (reigned since 1950).
Prime Minister: Prem Tinsulanonda (since 1980).
Parliament: *House of Representatives,* 324 elected members; *Senate,* 225 appointed members.
U.S. Ambassador to Thailand: John Gunther Dean.
Thailand Ambassador to U.S.: Kasem S. Kasemsri.
Flag: From top to bottom, five stripes: red, white, blue (double width), white, and red.
Official Language: Thai.
Main Ethnic Groups: Thai (75%), Chinese (14%).
Principal Religions: Buddhism (96%), Islam (4%).
Leading Industries: Agriculture (rice, corn, sugarcane, rubber, cotton, livestock, poultry); mining (tin, gems, tungsten); forestry and lumbering; fishing; manufacturing (food processing, cement, paper).
Foreign Trade: *Major exports*—rice, corn, rubber, tin, tapioca products, kenaf; *major imports*—machinery, textiles, petroleum.
Places of Interest: Chiangmai; Ayutthaya palaces and temples; Lop Buri ruins; old city of Nakhon Pathom. *In Bangkok:* Grand Palace; Emerald Buddha Temple; Temple of Dawn; rose garden; floating market.

THAILAND TODAY

Larger than California, Thailand is a noncommunist country in Southeast Asia. The word *Thai* means "free," and the Thais, unlike their neighbors, have maintained independence from both European colonialism and communist expansion.

Thailand is one of the world's leading producers of natural rubber and tin. The Thai government has done little to foster the development of industry or manufacturing. The economy depends on rice farming and U.S. aid.

The country has four main regions. The north is a forest highland area. A series of mountain ranges in the northwest rise to more than 8,500 feet in Inthanon Peak. The central plains are a fertile lowland with silt accumulations from the Chao Phraya River, which flows into the Gulf of Siam. The most fertile region is the Bangkok Delta, known as the rice basket or heartland of the country. To the northeast rises a dry upland area, ending at the Mekong River on the border with Laos. Peninsular Thailand, reaching to Malaysia, is a mountainous ridge.

Laos lies to the east, Cambodia and Malaysia to the south, and Burma to the west.

EARLY HISTORY OF THAILAND

Archaeological discoveries indicate that an early civilization developed in the 4000s B.C. in Thailand. By 3600 B.C. it had become the first culture in history to use bronze.

But the ancestors of the present-day Thai people, who lived in what is now China's

Yunnan province, only began migrating to the region about 1,000 years ago. They established a kingdom at Sukhothai in the 1200s.

The Thai capital was moved in the 1300s to Ayutthaya on the Chao Phraya River north of present-day Bangkok.

In 1782 the Chakkri dynasty was established with its capital at Bangkok. That dynasty has continued to reign to the present time.

Modernization began under the enlightened rule of King Mongkut (Rama IV, 1851–68) and his son Chulalongkorn (Rama V, 1868–1910), who abolished slavery. The Western powers acquired extensive extraterritorial privileges, which they retained until 1937.

CONSTITUTIONAL MONARCHY

In 1932 a coup by young radicals forced King Prajadipok (Rama VII, 1925–35), to give up his absolute powers and accept a constitution.

During World War II Japan occupied Thailand. After the war King Phumiphon Adunyadet (Rama IX) became ruler in 1946 while still a student in Switzerland. He returned to Thailand in 1950.

A military coup brought Field Marshal Sarit Thanarat to power in 1957. Upon Sarit's death in 1963, Lt. Gen. Thanom Kittikachorn became premier.

During the Vietnam War, the U.S. built some 93 military installations including a dozen air bases from which B-52s bombed communist forces in Cambodia, Laos, and Vietnam. Some 48,000 U.S. servicemen were stationed in Thailand. Subsidized with $50 million a year by the U.S., Thailand sent 11,000 troops to fight in Vietnam from 1968 to 1972.

In October 1973, college students led mobs that overthrew Thanom. A democratic constitution was adopted on Oct. 7, 1974. Free national elections were held on Jan. 26, 1975.

Kukrit Pramoj became premier on March 13, 1975. He immediately called on the U.S. to withdraw its remaining military personnel.

After communists took over Cambodia, Laos, and South Vietnam in 1975, hundreds of thousands of refugees fled to Thailand.

In elections on April 4, 1976, Kukrit Pramoj lost his seat in parliament. His 71-year-old brother Seni Pramoj became prime minister.

A right-wing military junta led by Defense Minister Adm. Sa-ngad Chaloryu seized power on Oct. 6, 1976.

The junta chose a civilian judge, Thanin Kraivichien, as prime minister on Oct. 8, 1976.

Gen. Kriangsak Chamanand, supreme commander of the military forces, led a bloodless coup on Oct. 20, 1977, that overthrew Prime Minister Thanin. Kriangsak became prime minister on Nov. 11, 1977.

A new constitution adopted in December 1978 ensured continued control by the military.

In the first national election under the new constitution on April 22, 1979, the Social Action Party of former prime minister Kukrit Pramoj won the largest number of elected seats in parliament. However, Prime Minister Kriangsak remained in power.

THAILAND IN THE 1980s

Soaring oil prices brought antigovernment demonstrations in Bangkok in 1980, causing Kriangsak to resign as prime minister on Feb. 29.

Gen. Prem Tinsulanonda, 59, succeeded Kriangsak.

Vietnamese troops invaded Thailand on June 23, 1980, and again on Jan. 3, 1981, in pursuit of Cambodian guerrillas, but withdrew in the face of Thai military resistance.

In what became known as the "April Fool's coup," army generals seized control of Bangkok on April 1–3, 1981, in an attempt to overthrow Prime Minister Prem. However, the royal family fled from the capital with Prem and broadcast appeals in his behalf. The rebel officers then surrendered and later were pardoned.

Thousands of industrial workers were dismissed from their jobs when the government established a $2.75 per hour minimum wage on Oct. 1, 1981.

A 265-mile undersea pipeline was completed in 1981, bringing to the mainland natural gas from large deposits discovered in the Gulf of Thailand.

In a parliamentary election on April 18, 1983, none of the 15 political parties won a majority. Prem remained prime minister, heading a coalition cabinet.

The government reported in 1983 that it was helping care for over 350,000 refugees from Cambodia, Laos, and Vietnam. An appeal was issued to Western nations to let more cf the refugees immigrate from Thailand.

The nation's five-year plan for 1981–86 calls for the development of iron and steel mills and other heavy industry fueled by natural gas.

TOGO

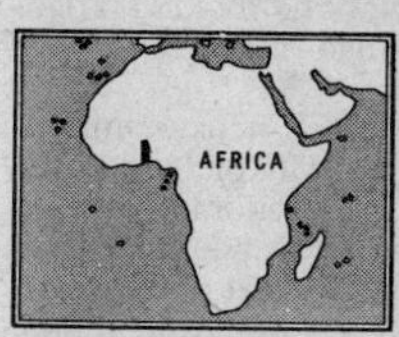

Official Name: Republic of Togo.
Area: 21,925 square miles (56,785 sq. km.).
Population: 2,867,090.
Capital: Lomé, 148,156.
Government: One-party dictatorship.
President: Gen. Gnassingbe Eyadema (since 1967).
U.S. Ambassador to Togo: Howard Kent Walker.
Togo Ambassador to U.S.: Yao Grunitzky.
Parliament: General Assembly.
Flag: Green and yellow stripes, with white star centered in red square at upper hoist corner.
Languages: French (official), tribal dialects.
Main Ethnic Groups: Hamitic and Bantu tribes.
Religions: Animism (75%), Christianity (20%), Islam (5%).
Leading Industries: Agriculture (cocoa, coffee, palm kernels, corn, peanuts, cotton, manioc, millet, sorghum, livestock, fruits, vegetables); mining (phosphates); manufacturing (textiles, food processing, construction materials); fishing.
Foreign Trade: *Major exports*—phosphates, cocoa, coffee, palm nuts, cotton, peanuts, fish, manioc flour

QUICK QUIZ: What is the birthstone of a person born in July? See page 410.

TOGO *(continued)*
and starch: *major imports*—manufactured goods, machinery, transport equipment, food, cotton fabrics, tobacco.
Places of Interest: Togo Mountains; native villages; Lomé.

TOGO TODAY

Togo is a hot tropical country of West Africa, about the size of West Virginia. Its most important resource, other than its farmland, is a huge deposit of phosphates. Otherwise the country's economy depends mostly on subsistence farming and fishing.

To balance the annual budget, the government counts on foreign aid each year.

The people are poor. Most struggle for their existence by raising food on plots of land owned in common by several families. Some work on large plantations that grow coffee for export. Few children go to school. The hard life of the people of Togo results in one of the lowest life-expectancy rates in the world, with the average Togolese living only to the age of 40.

The government has endeavored to diversify the economy with the construction of roads, hotels, and industrial plants.

Togo is a narrow country about 75 miles wide and 360 long. Upper Volta lies on the north, Dahomey on the east, and Ghana on the west.

Because of coastal sandbars and lagoons, there is no good harbor. Inland the terrain is hilly and mountainous.

HISTORY OF TOGO

As a nation Togo has little precolonial history. The colony of Togoland, created by Germany in 1885, consisted of today's Togo in the east and part of present-day Ghana in the west.

In 1922 the League of Nations divided Togoland into French and British mandates, with Togo going to the French.

The United Nations assumed trusteeship of the territory in 1946. In a 1956 plebiscite the Togolese voted 3 to 1 for autonomy, and in April 1960 Togo became an independent state.

Sylvanus Olympio, a man of great ability, was president of Togo until his assassination in the military coup of 1963. His successor was Nicolas Grunitzky, appointed by the military.

In January 1967 Grunitzky was ousted by Gen. Gnassingbe Eyadema, who became president on April 14.

To get a larger share of the profits from the mining of phosphate, the government nationalized the phosphate industry on Feb. 4, 1975.

The government began an active campaign in 1976–77 to obtain the 11,200-square-mile area of the former colony of British Togoland, which was absorbed by Ghana in 1957.

As head of the only political party, the Togolese People's Rally, Eyadema was reelected to a 7-year term on Dec. 30, 1979. A one-party general assembly also was elected.

In 1980 Amnesty International protested Eyadema's imprisonment without trial of opponents.

To lure more tourists, Togo in May 1981 became the first African country to eliminate visa requirements for U.S. and Canadian visitors.

Falling commodity prices caused severe governmental finance problems in the 1980s.

TONGA

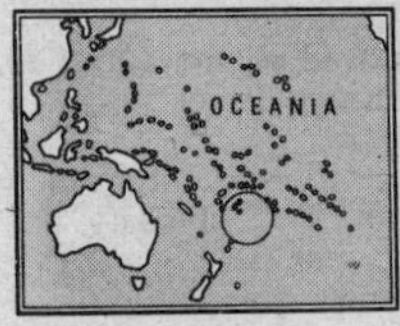

Official Name: Kingdom of Tonga.
Area: 270 square miles (699 sq. km.).
Population: 104,290.
Capital: Nuku'alofa, 22,000.
Government: Constitutional monarchy.
King: Taufa'ahau Tupou IV (reigned since 1965).
Prime Minister: Prince Tu'ipelehake (since 1965).
Legislative Assembly: 23 members.
Tonga Ambassador to U.S.: 'Inoke Faletau
U.S. Ambassador to Tonga: Fred J. Eckert.
Flag: Red field with red cross on white square in upper hoist corner.
Language: Tongan (official), English.
Main Ethnic Group: Tongan (98%).
Religions: Methodism (60%), Mormonism (20%), other Christian denominations (20%).
Leading Industries: Agriculture (bananas, coconuts, fruits, vegetables); fishing; food processing.
Foreign Trade: *Major exports*—bananas, coconut products; *major imports*— textiles, food, timber, steel.
Places of Interest: Royal palace and chapel; terraced tombs; blow holes; sacred flying foxes; Nuku'alofa.

TONGA TODAY

The South Pacific island kingdom of Tonga has a land area about equal to the city of Dallas, Texas, but only about one-eighth as many people. Two-thirds of Tonga's people live on the largest island, Tongatapu, which covers about 99 square miles.

The government owns all the land. But each man, upon reaching the age of 16, is entitled to rent an *api* of 8.25 acres for farming and a village plot of 0.375 acre on which to build a house. Most Tongans live by raising tropical fruits and vegetables and catching fish to feed their families.

An archipelago of 150 islands and islets, Tonga lies east of Fiji and south of Western Samoa. The islands stretch across about 500 miles of ocean from north to south.

HISTORY OF TONGA

Tonga's hereditary monarchs date at least from the 1000s A.D. In the 1200s the power of the Tonga monarchy extended as far as Hawaii.

One of the islands was discovered by the Dutch in 1616, and others by Capt. James Cook in 1773 and 1777. Cook called them the Friendly Islands because of their good-natured inhabitants.

The famous mutiny aboard the British ship *Bounty* took place in 1789 in waters off Tonga.

British missionaries arrived in 1797.

The present dynasty was founded by the Christian king George Tupou I in 1845.

A British protectorate was proclaimed in 1900.

On June 4, 1970, Tonga was granted independence with membership in the British Commonwealth of Nations.

A hurricane and tidal wave on March 3, 1982, destroyed many villages, killing six persons, and leaving thousands homeless.

TRANSKEI

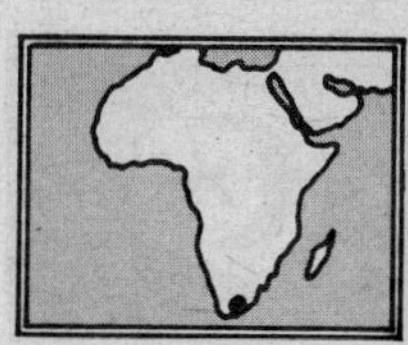

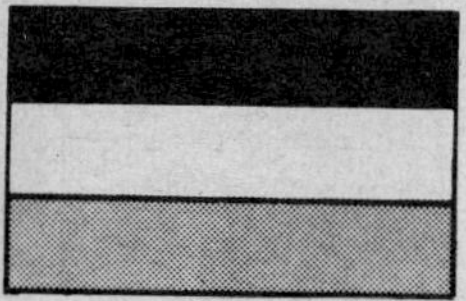

Official Name: Republic of Transkei.
Area: 16,070 square miles (41,620 sq. km).
Population: 3,345,670.
Capital: Umtata, 30,000.
Government: Parliamentary republic.
Prime Minister: Chief George Matanzima (since 1979).
President: Chief Kaiser Matanzima (since 1979).
Flag: Stripes of red (top), white, and green (bottom).
National Assembly: *The Bunga,* 150 members (75 tribal chiefs and 75 elected members).
Chief Languages: Xhosa (official), English, Afrikaans, Sesotho.
Principal Ethnic Group: Xhosa-speaking Bantus.
Main Religions: Methodist (60%), animism (40%).
Leading Industries: Agriculture (cattle, sheep, corn, tea, coffee, nuts); manufacturing (electricity, food processing, textiles); fishing; forestry; tourism.
Foreign Trade: *Major exports*—livestock, meat products, wool, hides; *major imports*—petroleum products, consumer goods, vehicles, machinery.
Places of Interest: Wild Coast nature area between Kei and Umtamvuna rivers; Magwa Falls; beaches.

A poor south African nation about twice the size of New Jersey, Transkei is completely dependent on South Africa. It has a 168-mile coastline on the Indian Ocean, with a harbor at Port St. Johns.

The small capital city of Umtata boasts a twin-tower 14-story government building. But most of the people live in tribal villages.

Cattle and corn are the main products. When in need of cash money, the men go to South Africa to work in the mines. Polygamy is legal.

The climate is mild. Winters are cool and dry with an occasional frost. Summers are warm to hot with about 25 inches of rain.

South Africa borders Transkei on the west and the northeast. Lesotho lies to the north.

Britain annexed the region in 1872–94.

South Africa gave Transkei independence as a republic on Oct. 26, 1976. Chief Kaiser Matanzima, head of the Transkei National Independence Party, became the first prime minister.

With Transkei's independence, 1.5 million Xhosa tribesmen living outside Transkei automatically lost their South African citizenship and became citizens of Transkei. Other nations refused to grant Transkei diplomatic recognition, claiming it was a puppet of South Africa.

Chief Botha Sigcau, the country's president since 1976, died on Dec. 1, 1978. Chief Kaiser Matanzima gave up the office of prime minister in February 1979 to accept election as president. He appointed his brother, George Matanzima, as prime minister.

In an effort to demonstrate Transkei's sovereignty, Chief Matanzima broke diplomatic relations with South Africa on April 10, 1978. Relations were restored on Feb. 7, 1980.

TRINIDAD-TOBAGO

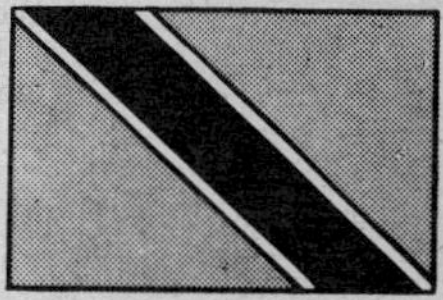

Official Name: Republic of Trinidad and Tobago.
Area: 1,981 square miles (5,130 sq. km.).
Population: 1,099,390.
Capital: Port of Spain, 11,032.
Government: Parliamentary republic.
Prime Minister: George M. Chambers (since 1981).
President: Sir Ellis Clarke (since 1976).
Parliament: *Senate,* 31 appointed members; *House of Representatives,* 36 elected members.
U.S. Ambassador to Trinidad-Tobago: Melvin H. Evans.
Trinidad-Tobago Ambassador to U.S.: James O'Neil-Lewis.
Flag: Red field crossed diagonally by white-bordered black stripe.
Languages: English (official), Spanish.
Main Ethnic Groups: Black (43%), Asian Indian (40%).
Principal Religions: Roman Catholicism (32%), Protestantism (29%), Hinduism (20%), Islam (6%).
Leading Industries: Mining (petroleum, natural gas); manufacturing (oil refining, chemicals, textiles, cement, food processing); agriculture (sugarcane, cocoa, coconuts, fruits, vegetables); tourism; fishing.
Foreign Trade: Major exports—petroleum, sugar, cocoa, natural asphalt, chemicals; major imports—steel, food, chemicals, machinery, vehicles.
Places of Interest: *On Trinidad:* The Saddle; Caroni Bird Sanctuary; Maracas Bay; Pitch Lake; Port of Spain. *On Tobago:* Bird of Paradise Sanctuary; Man O'War Bay; Pigeon Point; Coral Sea Gardens; Turtle Beach.

TRINIDAD-TOBAGO TODAY

The mining and refining of petroleum are the largest industries of Trinidad-Tobago. Oil products make up about 85% of the country's exports. Huge natural gas reserves promise a source of power for developing industry.

Other important industries are the raising of sugarcane and the refining of sugar. Many islanders work in the cane fields.

The revenues from oil and sugar provide the islanders with one of the highest per capita incomes in the Caribbean. However, unemployment stands at about 10%.

The warm climate, ocean beaches, and mountain scenery of Trinidad and Tobago make the islands a popular winter vacation spot for tourists from the United States. Calypso, the steel band, and limbo all originated in Trinidad. These are featured in the colorful celebrations and carnival leading up to Ash Wednesday each year. Tourists enjoy seeing the bird of paradise and scarlet ibis in bird sanctuaries.

The islands of Trinidad and Tobago lie about 20 miles apart in the Caribbean Sea off Venezuela's northeast coast.

Trinidad, the largest island, has an area of 1,864 square miles. It has three mountain ranges, which run roughly east to west. Mountains in the northern range rise to 3,085 feet. Small streams flow to the sea through gently rolling flatlands between the mountains.

Tobago (116 sq. mi.) is generally more rugged than Trinidad. It has a central volcanic core that ascends to 1,890 feet.

Daily high temperatures average 92 °F. throughout the year.

EARLY HISTORY

The islands were discovered by Columbus in 1498, bringing them under Spanish rule.

During the 1600s and 1700s cocoa and sugar plantations were established with slave labor imported from Africa. In 1783 the Spanish government offered free land grants that attracted many non-Spanish settlers, especially French.

Trinidad was captured by the British in 1797 during a war with France. It was officially ceded to Britain in 1802, when it became a crown colony. Tobago was acquired by Britain in 1814 and was made a crown colony in 1877. Trinidad and Tobago were joined as a single colony in 1889.

Slaves on Trinidad were emancipated in 1833. To replace these plantation workers, the British brought in 150,000 Hindus and Muslims from India between 1845 and 1917.

INDEPENDENCE

Under the leadership of Dr. Eric Williams, the islands won independence on Aug. 31, 1962. Williams became the nation's first prime minister.

Black-power demonstrations marked by arson and looting shook the country in the first months of 1970. They reached a climax in a mutiny staged by half of the 800-man army. The government suppressed the rebellion in three days.

Offshore oil and gas fields discovered in 1972–75 brought Trinidad-Tobago sudden wealth as it joined the rolls of the oil-exporting nations. The oil revenues made it possible for the government to cut personal income taxes, to increase social-welfare benefits, and at the same time to subsidize food prices to prevent inflation from soaring.

To stabilize its currency the government in May 1976 tied its money to that of the United States at a rate of $1 U.S. to $1.20 of Trinidad-Tobago currency.

Trinidad-Tobago became a republic within the British Commonwealth on Aug. 1, 1976. Sir Ellis Clarke, who had served as governor-general, was chosen as the first president.

Prime Minister Williams' PNM party won its fifth 5-year term in national elections in 1976.

The main political party, the People's Nationalist Movement (PNM), draws its strength primarily from blacks, who make up 43% of the population. The chief opposition is the leftist United Labor Front (ULF).

After the death of the 69-year-old Williams on March 29, 1981, George M. Chambers succeeded him as prime minister.

Chambers led the PNM party to victory in a parliamentary election on Nov. 9, 1981, winning 26 of the 36 seats in the lower house.

The government sought to diversify industry in the 1980s, promoting use of its extensive natural-gas reserves.

TUNISIA

Official Name: Republic of Tunisia.
Area: 63,170 square miles (163,610 sq. km.).
Population: 7,017,650.
Chief Cities: Tunis, capital, 468,997; Bizerte, 95,023; Sousse, 82,666; Sfax, 79,595.
Government: Republic.
President: Habib Bourguiba (since 1957).
Prime Minister: Muhammed Mzali (since 1980).
Legislature: *National Assembly,* 136 members.
U.S. Ambassador to Tunisia: Walter Leon Cutler.
Tunisian Ambassador to U.S.: Habib Ben Yahia.
Flag: Red field with white circle containing red crescent and star.
Languages: Arabic (official), French.
Main Ethnic Group: Arab-Berber (98%).
Official Religion: Islam.
Leading Industries: Agriculture (olives, grapes, wheat, fruits, vegetables); manufacturing (oil refining), chemicals, textiles, wine, electricity, cement, consumer products); mining (petroleum, natural gas, phosphates, iron, zinc, lead); tourism; fishing.
Foreign Trade: *Major exports*—crude oil, olive oil, phosphates, citrus fruits, iron, wine, lead; *major imports*—wheat, motor vehicles, textile yarn and thread, vegetable oils, sulfur, wood.
Places of Interest: Roman ruins; beach resorts; Djerba Island; ancient city of Kairouan; fortified city of Monastir; Bardo Museum and Belvédère Park in Tunis; site of ancient Carthage; national parks.

TUNISIA TODAY

Helped by about $1 billion in aid from the United States since World War II, Tunisia has developed a diversified economy that is no longer solely dependent on agriculture.

While its richer North African neighbors Algeria and Libya have turned to state-controlled socialism, Tunisia has relied on private enterprise to develop its economy. Tourism has become the main industry.

However, not enough new industries have been developed to provide jobs for the many Tunisians who leave their farms each year to seek a better life in the cities. Many young people educated in Tunisia's colleges and universities must go to Europe to obtain well-paying jobs.

Most of the people are poor. About half earn a living as farmers. Only about 4 of 10 Tunisians can read and write.

Somewhat larger than the state of Georgia, Tunisia lies on the Mediterranean coast of Africa between Algeria in the west and Libya in the southeast.

The east-west Atlas mountain range divides Tunisia into two main regions. North of the mountains is the relatively well-watered, fertile Tell zone with groves of olive trees and pastures for livestock. To the south are a semiarid plain and plateau that extend into the Sahara Desert.

The majority of people live in the coastal plain bordering the Mediterranean Sea. Nomadic tribes live in the southern region.

EARLY HISTORY OF TUNISIA

Tunisia was the center of ancient Carthage and later, from the 100s B.C., of a Roman province.

Tunisia was occupied by the Vandals in the 400s A.D. and recovered by the Byzantine Empire in the 500s. The country was finally conquered by the Arabs in the 600s.

During the Middle Ages it was the center from which Arab power and Islam spread south and west and also north across the Mediterranean. In 1535 Carthage was captured by the Holy Roman Emperor Karl V. The ruling dynasty turned for help to the Turks, who expelled the Spaniards in 1574 and made Tunisia a Turkish province.

Britain, France, and Italy assumed financial control of Tunisia in 1869. Tunisia became a French protectorate in 1883.

After the fall of France in World War II, Tunisia remained loyal to the Vichy government. The country became a central theater of the war in North Africa.

Habib Bourguiba, leader of the Neo-Destour Party, led the struggle for independence from France in the 1940s and 1950s.

INDEPENDENCE

On March 20, 1956, France granted Tunisia independence as a monarchy.

Tunisia's constituent assembly abolished the monarchy on July 25, 1957, establishing a republic with Habib Bourguiba as president. He won election without opposition in 1959, 1964, and 1969. The national assembly elected Bourguiba president for life in 1974.

Floods struck Tunisia in March 1973, leaving 53,000 homeless and 119 dead or missing.

To clarify the line of succession, Bourguiba changed the constitution in 1973. It provides that on his death he will be succeeded as head of the government by the prime minister. Then a presidential election will be held within 45 days.

Guerrillas crossed into Tunisia from Algeria on Jan. 27, 1980, attacking the mining city of Gafsa. Forty-five persons were killed and over 100 injured before most of the guerrillas were captured. The Tunisian government claimed Libya had trained the guerrillas and had planned to invade Tunisia to support the attackers. Thirteen of the captured guerrillas were hanged on April 17, 1980, and others were sentenced to prison. Tunisia expelled Libya's ambassador and recalled its own ambassador.

Bourguiba named former education minister Muhammed Mzali, 54, as prime minister on April 23, 1980, replacing ailing 69-year-old Hedi Nouira, who had held the office since 1970.

On July 19, 1981, Bourguiba ended an 18-year ban on the Communist Party.

In the first multiparty election in 25 years of independence, Tunisians chose members of a new national assembly on Nov. 1, 1981. Bourguiba's party won a majority.

Tunisia and Libya restored friendly relations on Feb. 28, 1982, with the signing of a reconciliation agreement providing for cooperation in foreign relations and economic affairs.

Two women were appointed to the nation's cabinet for the first time in 1983.

TURKEY

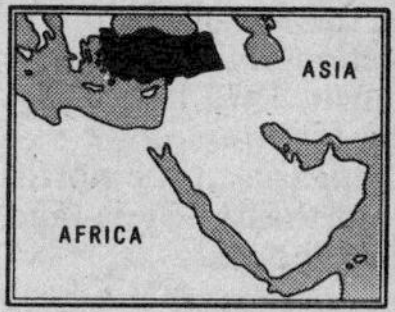

Official Name: Republic of Turkey.
Area: 301,382 square miles (780,576 sq. km.).
Population: 47,713,500.
Chief Cities: Ankara, capital, 2,106,076; Istanbul, 2,822,579; Izmir, 730,692; Adana, 586,254; Bursa, 404,345; Gaziantep, 363,322; Eskisehir, 295,428.
Largest Metropolitan Area: Istanbul, 3,864,493.
Government: Republic with strong president.
President: Gen. Kenan Evren (since 1982).
Prime Minister: Turgat Ozal (since 1983).
National Assembly: 400 elected members.
U.S. Ambassador to Turkey: Robert Strausz-Hupe.
Turkish Ambassador to U.S.: Sukru Elekdag.
Flag: White star and crescent on red field.
Languages: Turkish (official), Kurdish.
Main Ethnic Groups: Turk (90%), Kurd (7%).
Religion: Islam (98%).
Leading Industries: Manufacturing (steel, textiles, electricity, tobacco products, food processing, consumer products); agriculture (wheat, barley, corn, cotton, sugar beets, livestock, tobacco, fruits, vegetables); mining (coal, lignite, iron, petroleum); services; fishing.
Foreign Trade: *Major exports*—cotton, tobacco; *major imports*—petroleum, motor vehicles, machinery.
Places of Interest: Bosporus bridge; Black Sea and Mediterranean resorts; Göreme Valley; ruins of Troy; ancient city of Sardis; Temple of Diana at Ephesus; tomb of Antiochus I on Mt. Nimrud; Ankara; Izmir. *In Istanbul:* Topkapi Palace; Grand Bazaar; St. Sofia; the Blue Sofia; the Blue Mosque.

TURKEY TODAY

Larger than Texas, Turkey was for 1,600 years the seat of empires that dominated southeastern Europe and the Middle East. Today Turkey's largest city, Istanbul (once called Constantinople), stands on the southeastern tip of Europe, but 97% of Turkey lies in Asia.

The country's strategic position on the Soviet Union's southwestern frontier makes Turkey a key member of the NATO military alliance. The U.S. uses 12 military bases in Turkey.

Turkey is a developing country striving to become an industrial nation. The people of Turkey are poorer than those of neighboring countries. About half cannot read or write. Hundreds of thousands of Turkish workers have gone to West Germany and other European nations to find work. The money they send home to their families has been an important part of the foreign exchange used in developing new industries in Turkey. In addition the U.S. has given and loaned Turkey about $8 billion in economic and military assistance in the past three decades.

Lacking most important industrial natural resources, Turkey pins hopes for the future on developing oil wells in the adjacent Aegean Sea in areas disputed with Greece.

Turkey controls the only outlet for Soviet

QUICK QUIZ: What are the characteristics of a person born under the sign of Leo? See page 411.

TURKEY *(continued)*

ships from the Black Sea to the Mediterranean Sea, including the Bosporus, the Sea of Marmara, and the Dardanelles. Completion of the huge Bosporus bridge across the strait in 1973 linked European and Asian Turkey by highway.

Greece lies to the west, Bulgaria to the north, the Soviet Union to the northeast, Syria and Iraq to the south, and Iran to the east.

EARLY HISTORY

In about 600 B.C. Greeks founded the city of Byzantium (now Istanbul) on hills strategically commanding the Bosporus. Roman legions captured Byzantium in A.D. 196.

In A.D. 330 the Christian emperor Constantine moved his capital from Rome to Byzantium, renamed Constantinople. The Byzantine Empire ruled eastern Europe and the Middle East for more than 1,000 years.

In 1453 the Turks, led by Ottoman Sultan Mohammed II, ended the Byzantine Empire with the capture of Constantinople. Islam supplanted Christianity. The Ottoman Empire dominated the Middle East until the early 1900s.

Turkey entered World War I on the German side. After Turkey's surrender in 1918, Sultan Mohammed VI, last of the Ottoman rulers, accepted the Treaty of Sèvres (1920), which reduced the empire to a minor state.

REPUBLIC OF TURKEY

A Turkish national resistance movement, led by Mustafa Kemal (later called Kemal Ataturk), rejected the Sèvres settlement. Ataturk declared the sultan deposed in 1922 and repulsed a Greek offensive in the west.

A republic, with Kemal Ataturk as president, was proclaimed in 1923. The Treaty of Lausanne (1923) established the present Turkish boundaries. The next year Ataturk introduced a new constitution that set up a national legislative assembly. Ataturk abolished Islam as the state religion, replaced Islamic law with European law. He moved the capital to Ankara.

Former Premier Ismet Inonu became president after Ataturk's death in 1938. Turkey did not declare war on Germany and Japan until 1945. Ataturk's successors remained in power until 1950, when Celal Bayar, leader of the Democratic Party, won the presidency. He appointed Adnan Menderes as premier.

In May 1960 an army revolt overthrew the elected government. Menderes was sentenced to death and hanged in 1961. In the same year a new constitution was adopted restoring parliamentary democracy.

Gen. Cemal Gursel, head of a faction favoring strict adherence to the principles of Ataturk, won the presidency in 1961. Gursel died in 1966. Gen. Cevdet Sunay succeeded him.

TURBULENT 1970s–1980s

In 1973 parliament elected Adm. Fahri Koruturk to a 7-year term as president.

Throughout the 1970s neither of the country's leading political parties was able to hold a clear majority in parliament. Conservative Suleyman Demirel, head of the Justice Party, and Bulent Ecevit, leader of the socialist Republican People's Party (RPU), alternated in serving as prime minister.

The Greek-led overthrow of the Cyprus government in July 1974 caused Turkey to invade the island with 40,000 troops.

The U.S. cut off arms shipments to Turkey on Feb. 5, 1975, because Turkey had used NATO arms in its invasion of Cyprus. In retaliation, Turkey took over U.S. military bases.

In a national parliamentary election on June 5, 1977, the socialist RPU won the largest number of seats, 213, but not a clear majority. RPU leader Ecevit again became prime minister, but after 10 days in office he was defeated in a confidence vote, 229 to 217. He regained the office in January 1978.

Threatening to change the East-West balance of power in the Middle East unless the U.S. ended its arms ban on Turkey, Ecevit visited Moscow and signed pacts on June 23, 1978, that pledged nonaggression and expanded trade with the Soviet Union. The U.S. Congress repealed its ban on arms sales to Turkey in September 1978. The Turkish government agreed in October to let the U.S. reopen four military bases.

Lacking petroleum resources of its own, Turkey was especially hard hit by soaring oil prices in the 1970s–1980s. The country's economy reached a state of crisis in 1979 with inflation at a rate of 70% and an estimated 25% of its workers unemployed. In an effort to temporarily ease the crisis, the government obtained agreement from the International Monetary Fund in 1980 for loans of $1.16 billion.

The U.S. and Turkey signed a 5-year agreement on March 29, 1980, providing continued use by the U.S. of 12 military bases. In return, the U.S. promised $2.5 billion in economic and military aid to Turkey over the period of the agreement.

After his conservative party won all five seats at stake in parliamentary by-elections, Demirel became prime minister on Nov. 12, 1979.

Violence between terrorists of the left and right increased during the first 9 months of 1980 with some 2,000 persons killed.

Promising to end the violence, Gen. Kenan Evren, chief of the armed forces, led a bloodless coup on Sept. 12, 1980. All political activity was banned until 1983. Demirel, Ecevit, and other political leaders were repeatedly arrested and jailed for short periods.

Evren became chief of state as head of a military junta called the National Security Council. The junta appointed a retired admiral, Bulent Ulusu, as prime minister. In all, some 56,000 persons were arrested in the following weeks.

Gen. Evren assured the U.S. and other NATO allies of continued cooperation. He said democratic government would be restored by 1984.

The 65-year-old Evren became president for a 7-year term after voters on Nov. 7, 1982, approved a new constitution that formalized the military rule in effect since 1980. The constitution gave the president wide powers.

Three political parties competed in an election on Nov. 6, 1983, to choose the 400 members of a new national assembly. The conservative Motherland Party won a 212-seat majority. Its leader, Turgut Ozal, 56, an electronic engineer, became prime minister.

TUVALU

Official Name: Tuvalu.
Area: 10 square miles (26 sq. km.).
Population: 8,060.
Capital: Fongafale on Funafuti, 826.
Government: Parliamentary state.
Prime Minister: Tomasi Puapua (since 1982).
Chief of State: Queen Elizabeth II of Britain.
Tuvalu Ambassador to U.S.: Ionatana Ionatana.
U.S. Ambassador to Tuvalu: Fred J. Eckert.
Parliament: 12 members.
Flag: British blue ensign with nine yellow stars representing the nation's islands.
Languages: Tuvaluan, English.
Main Ethnic Group: Tuvaluans of Polynesian descent.
Principal Religion: Christianity, largely Protestant.
Leading Industries: Agriculture (coconuts, pulaka or taro, pandanus fruit, bananas, pawpaws); fishing.
Foreign Trade: *Major export*—copra from coconuts; *major imports*—food, fuel.
Places of Interest: villages; beaches.

One of the smallest of the world's nations, Tuvalu encompasses nine tropical islands in the South Pacific, about 600 miles north of Fiji. The group formerly was the Ellice Islands.

The Tuvaluans lead a simple existence, living in thatched huts on a diet of tropical fruits, vegetables, and fish. The only export is copra from coconuts, which provides money to import additional food, fuel, and manufactured goods. Islanders receive an elementary education.

The islands are scattered over an area of about half a million square miles of ocean. Stretching about 450 miles from northwest to southeast. The nine islands are: Nanumea, Nanumanga, Niutao, Nui, Vaitupu, Nukufetau, Funafuti, Nukulaelae, and Niulakita.

All the islands are coral atolls, rising no more than 15 feet above sea level.

In prehistoric times, Polynesians from Samōa settled the islands.

The first European explorer to visit was the Spanish navigator Alvaro de Mendaña, who discovered Nui in 1568 and Niulakita in 1595.

In the mid-1800's "blackbirders" raided the islands, carrying off as slaves all but about 3,000 of an estimated population of 20,000.

In 1892 Britain established a protectorate over Tuvalu, then called the Ellice Islands, governing them from the Gilbert Islands, which lie to the northwest. Britain created the Gilbert and Ellice Islands colony in 1916. During World War II the islands were occupied by Japanese troops in 1942–43, until driven out by U.S. forces.

The islanders voted in 1974 to separate from the Gilberts, becoming the separate territory of Tuvalu on Jan. 1, 1976. Britain granted Tuvalu complete independence on Oct. 1, 1978.

Queen Elizabeth II of Britain visited Tuvalu in October 1982.

UGANDA

Official Name: Republic of Uganda.
Area: 91,134 square miles (236,036 sq. km.).
Population: 14,027,800.
Capital: Kampala, 330,700.
Government: Democratic republic.
President: Milton Obote (since 1980).
Prime Minister: Otema Alimadi (since 1980).
National Assembly: 146 elected members.
Ambassador to U.S.: John Wycliffe Lwamafa.
U.S. Ambassador to Uganda: Allen Clayton Davis.
Flag: Black, yellow, and red stripes, with crested crane on white circle in center.
Languages: English (official), Luganda, Swahili.
Main Ethnic Group: Black.
Religions: Christianity (50%), animism (35%), Islam (15%).
Leading Industries: Agriculture (coffee, cotton, tea, tobacco, peanuts, livestock, fruits, vegetables); manufacturing (food, copper smelting, textiles, cement, shoes, fertilizer); mining (copper, tin).
Foreign Trade: *Major exports*—coffee, cotton, copper, tea; *major imports*—petroleum products, machinery, cotton fabrics, vehicles.
Places of Interest: Lake Victoria; "Mountains of the Moon" in the Ruwenzori Range; Queen Elizabeth and Kidepo Valley national parks; Kabalega Falls; wildlife preserves; Kampala.

UGANDA TODAY

Somewhat smaller than Oregon, Uganda is a poor African country struggling to regain stability after a decade of repressive dictatorship and war.

Dependent largely on agriculture, forestry, and fishing to support its economy, Uganda has few mineral resources other than copper and tin. Only about 1 out of 5 Ugandans can read and write.

Although the equator runs through the southern part of the country, the high altitude gives Uganda a moderate climate.

The Ruwenzori Mountains are in the west with Mt. Margherita rising to 16,763 feet on the Zaire border.

Lake Victoria is in the southeast.

Kenya lies to the east, Sudan to the north, Zaire to the west, and Tanzania and Rwanda to the south.

EARLY HISTORY

Powerful kingdoms began to develop in the lakes area south of the Nile during the 1400s or early 1500s.

Bunyoro was the most powerful of the southern kingdoms until the 1800s. Then a succession of able rulers made Buganda the leading kingdom. The first visitors were Arab and Swahili ivory and slave traders.

Britain and Germany agreed in 1890 that Britain should control the region. In 1894 Britain established a protectorate over Buganda

QUICK QUIZ: Can you name three nations that are not members of the UN? See page 423.

UGANDA *(continued)*
that was later extended to the rest of Uganda.

INDEPENDENCE

Uganda gained its independence on Oct. 9, 1962, remaining a member of the British Commonwealth of Nations. In 1963 King Mutesa of Buganda became Uganda's first president with Milton Obote as prime minister.

In February 1966 Obote suspended the constitution, and the king fled to Britain. Obote then made himself president.

On Jan. 25, 1971, while Obote was abroad, Gen. Idi Amin seized power.

In 1972 Amin expelled about 60,000 British Asians, seizing their businesses and property.

The United States, Britain, Canada, and other countries cut off financial aid and technical assistance in 1973. The U.S. closed its embassy in Uganda in November 1973.

Israeli commandos attacked Uganda's Entebbe airport on July 3–4, 1976, freeing over 100 hostages held by Palestinian airplane hijackers.

The human-rights organization Amnesty International reported that during Amin's first six years in office he had been responsible for killing as many as 300,000 persons.

Amin began a war with neighboring Tanzania in 1978, announcing on Nov. 1 that his troops had annexed 710 square miles of Tanzania.

Determined to destroy the Ugandan dictator, Tanzania resisted the invasion and then counterattacked, routing Amin's forces and capturing Uganda's capital, Kampala, on April 11, 1979. Amin escaped into exile.

A provisional government approved by Tanzania was sworn in on April 13, 1979, with a former college teacher, Yusufu Kironde Lule, as president. On June 20, 1979, the legislature ousted Lule as president, giving the office to Godfrey L. Binaisa, a former attorney general under Obote.

When President Binaisa tried to dismiss his army chief of staff, Brig. Gen. David Oyite Ojok, he was overthrown on May 12, 1980. A 6-man military junta took over the government with the consent of Tanzania.

In a national election on Dec. 10–11, 1980, former President Milton Obote's Ugandan People's Congress won a majority of the 126 elective seats in the national assembly. Obote was sworn in as president on Dec. 15 and a few days later appointed former foreign minister Otema Alimadi as prime minister.

Throughout 1981–83 Uganda was torn by antigovernment guerrilla terrorists and retaliatory summary executions and massacres of suspected guerrillas by government troops. About 120,000 Ugandans fled to refuge in Zaire.

The UN high commissioner for refugees reported in October 1982 that about 100,000 Rwandan refugees were being evicted by the Ugandans and their property confiscated.

The army conducted a major drive in 1983 against guerrillas in the Luwero district near Kampala. About 100,000 people fled from their homes during the military drive and were housed in refugee camps.

President Obote freed 2,100 prisoners on Oct. 9, 1983, in celebration of Uganda's 21st anniversary of independence.

UNITED ARAB EMIRATES

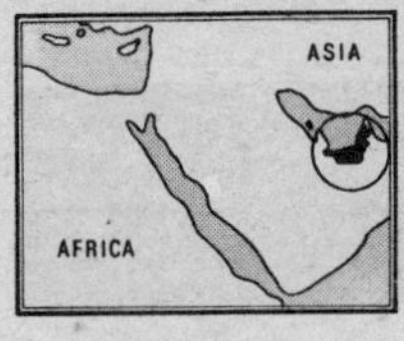

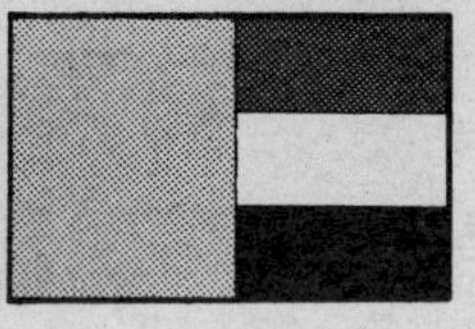

Official Name: United Arab Emirates.
Area: 32,278 square miles (83,600 sq. km.).
Population: 1,448,060.
Largest Cities: Abu Dhabi, capital, 85,000; Dubai, 60,000.
Government: Confederation of monarchies.
President: Sheik Zayid bin Sultan al Nuhayan, ruler of Abu Dhabi (since 1971).
Prime Minister and Vice President: Sheik Rashid bin Said al Maktum, ruler of Dubai (since 1979).
Legislature: *National Assembly,* 40 members.
U.S. Ambassador to United Arab Emirates: George Quincey Lumsden.
United Arab Emirates Ambassador to U.S.: Ahmad Salem Al-Mokarrab.
Flag: Red bar at hoist; stripes of green, white, and black.
Languages: Arabic (official), Persian, English.
Main Ethnic Group: Arab (72%).
Principal Religion: Islam (90%).
Leading Industries: Mining (petroleum, natural gas); manufacturing (petroleum refining, gas liquefaction, aluminum, chemicals, fertilizer, cement, plastics); agriculture (dates, sheep, goats, tobacco, fruits).
Foreign Trade: *Major exports*—petroleum, natural gas; *major imports*—manufactured goods, machinery, vehicles, construction materials.
Places of Interest: Oil refineries; royal residences; national zoo at Al Ain; beaches.

UNITED ARAB EMIRATES TODAY

About the size of the state of Maine, the country is mostly a desert with temperatures of 120° F. in the shade. Until oil began to be produced in 1962, the sheikdoms were very poor. But in the 1980s oil income soared over $20 billion a year.

The government receives 60% of all oil produced. Much of the income is spent for welfare projects, port improvements, water de- salinization, oil refineries, and industrial plants. Free education, health care, and phone service are provided by the government. There are no income taxes. Foreign immigrants make up about 85% of the population.

The United Arab Emirates (UAE) is a confederation of seven Arab sheikdoms on the Persian Gulf. The sheikdoms are: Abu Dhabi, Dubai, Sharjah, Ajman, Ras al-Khaimah, Umm al-Qaiwain, and Fujairah.

Saudi Arabia and Qatar lie to the west. Oman is to the east.

EARLY HISTORY

The coastal area was ruled by Portugal in the 1500s to 1600s and then by Iran. The Iranians were expelled in 1783 by an Arab tribe.

Known as the *Trucial States,* the Persian Gulf sheikdoms subsequently were called the Pirate Coast, a base of operation for over 800 Arab pirate ships as well as European marauders.

From 1806 onward, the Persian Gulf states gradually came under British protection. Piracy was brought to an end in 1853 when sheiks signed the Perpetual Maritime Truce, which was arranged and supervised by Britain.

Between 1880 and 1916 the sheiks of the Persian Gulf states concluded protective treaties with Britain. Economic development began after oil was discovered in Abu Dhabi in 1958.

After Britain announced in 1967 that it would withdraw its military forces from the Persian Gulf area by the end of 1971, the sheikdoms set up a provisional government.

INDEPENDENCE

On Dec. 2, 1971, six of the sheikdoms proclaimed themselves the independent United Arab Emirates with Sheik Zayid of Abu Dhabi as president. A seventh sheikdom joined the union on Feb. 1, 1972.

The country also has large natural-gas deposits, and in 1974–75 huge plants were built on Das Island to liquefy 3 million tons of gas a year for shipment to Japan.

In December 1976 Sheik Zayid was elected to a second 5-year term as president by the rulers of the other emirates. They also agreed to turn over to his control the military forces.

In the 1970s and 1980s the government spent huge sums to build industries to support the country when its oil reserves are exhausted. A port with berths for 66 large ships was built at Jebel Ali, in Dubai, along with a steel fabrication unit, power plant and associated desalination units, an aluminum smelter, and a liquid petroleum facility.

UPPER VOLTA

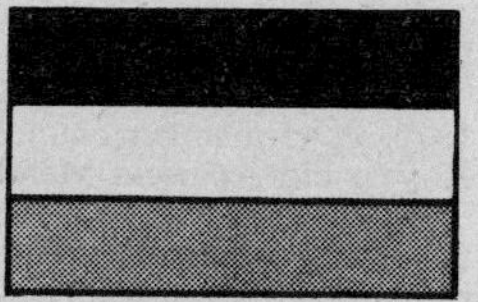

Official Name: Republic of Upper Volta.
Area: 105,869 square miles (274,200 sq. km.).
Population: 6,648,420.
Capital: Ouagadougou, 200,000.
Government: Military junta.
Head of State: Capt. Thomas Sankara (since 1983).
U.S. Ambassador to Upper Volta: Julius W. Walker Jr.
Ambassador to U.S.: Tiemoko Marc Garango.
Flag: Black, white, and red stripes.
Official Language: French.
Main Ethnic Groups: Mossi (67%), Bobo (15%).
Principal Religion: Animism.
Leading Industries: Agriculture (cattle, poultry, millet, sorghum, corn, cotton, sugar, peanuts, fruits, vegetables); fishing; forestry and lumbering; manufacturing (electricity, bicycles, food processing, textiles, plastics, soap); mining (manganese).
Foreign Trade: *Major exports*—livestock, meat, peanuts, cotton; *major imports*—petroleum products, textiles, clothing, machinery.
Places of Interest: Spiked mosque at Bobo Dioulasso; Ouagadougou.

UPPER VOLTA TODAY

About the size of Colorado, Upper Volta is one of the world's 10 poorest countries, depending on aid from France and other countries.

Most of the people consider themselves lucky if they can get enough food to keep from starving. Only about 1 person in 10 can read and write. Most live by farming or herding cattle.

A landlocked country, Upper Volta covers a plateau 650 to 1,000 feet high. The main rivers are the Black, White, and Red Volta rivers.

Much of the fertile land in the valleys remains fallow because people fear the river-blindness disease carried by black flies along the rivers.

Mali lies to the northwest, Niger to the northeast, and Ivory Coast, Ghana, Togo, and Dahomey to the south.

HISTORY OF UPPER VOLTA

By the 1300s the Mossi people of the area were raiding the wealthy trading cities on the Niger River and beyond. They organized the state of Ouagadougou, Yatenga, and Fada-n-Gurma. They later founded the Dagomba state.

The French claimed the region in 1896. At first Upper Volta was included in the Ivory Coast colony. In 1919 it was detached. In 1933 the territory was divided among the Ivory Coast, Niger, and French Sudan colonies.

France granted independence to the Republic of Upper Volta on Aug. 5, 1960. Maurice Yaméogo, the only candidate for the presidency, was elected.

In January 1966, following antigovernment riots, Lt. Col. Aboubakar Sangoulé Lamizana seized power. President Yaméogo, who had been reelected several days earlier, was imprisoned.

New elections held in 1970 were won by the Democratic Union. Its leader, Gerard Kango Ouedraogo, was named premier in February 1971.

On Feb. 8, 1974, Lamizana, with the help of the army, threw out the elected government of Premier Ouedraogo and again took control.

Like other African nations bordering the Sahara Desert, Upper Volta suffered six years of drought in 1969–74 that destroyed cattle and crops, bringing widespread famine.

Lamizana restored multiparty democracy in 1978. In parliamentary elections on April 30, 1978, Ouedraogo's Democratic Union won a majority of 28 seats in the national assembly. In a presidential election in May Lamizana defeated Macaire Ouedraogo, a banker, by a margin of 56% to 44% for a 5-year term.

Pope John Paul II visited Upper Volta on May 10, 1980, as part of a 6-nation African tour. He appealed to the world for more aid to help the poor country.

After striking unions paralyzed the country for several months, Col. Saye Zerbo, a former foreign minister, led a coup that overthrew the government on Nov. 25, 1980. He headed a military junta that banned all political activity.

Maj. Jean-Baptist Ouedraogo made himself president in a military revolt on Nov. 7, 1982.

Supplied with arms by Libya, Marxist Capt. Thomas Sankara, 35, overthrew Ouedraogo on Aug. 5, 1983, in a coup in which 13 persons were killed. Sankara had been dismissed as prime minister and jailed by Ouedraogo three months earlier.

QUICK QUIZ: When did Algeria win independence from France? See page 484.

URUGUAY

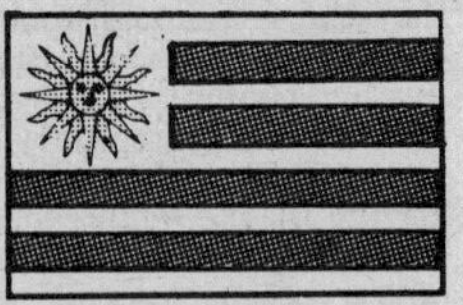

Official Name: Oriental Republic of Uruguay.
Area: 68,037 square miles (176,215 sq. km.).
Population: 2,920,410.
Capital: Montevideo, 1,173,254.
Government: Military junta.
President: Gregorio Alvarez (since 1981).
U.S. Ambassador to Uruguay: Thomas Aranda Jr.
Ambassador to U.S.: Alejandro Vegh Villegas.
Flag: Blue stripes on white field, with golden sun in upper hoist corner.
Language: Spanish.
Ethnic Groups: European descent (85%), mestizo (10%), mulatto and black (5%).
Principal Religions: Roman Catholicism (66%), Protestantism (2%), Judaism (2%).
Leading Industries: Agriculture (cattle, sheep, hogs, rice, wheat, corn, fruits, vegetables); manufacturing (food processing, electricity, leather products, glass, ceramics, furniture, clothing); forestry and lumbering; tourism; fishing; construction.
Foreign Trade: *Major exports*—meat, wool, leather, fish, rice, shoes, glass, ceramics, cement; *major imports*—petroleum, machinery, motor vehicles and aircraft, chemicals, iron and steel.
Places of Interest: Santa Teresa National Park; beach resorts; Pan de Azúcar (Sugar Loaf peak); Castle of Piria; Lobos Island. *In Montevideo:* Plaza Independencia; town hall (*cabildo*); legislative palace.

URUGUAY TODAY

About the size of Missouri, Uruguay is a small South American country with few natural resources. Uruguay's economy depends primarily upon tourism, banking, and livestock raising.

Because Uruguay is poor in natural mineral resources, it has lagged in the development of manufacturing. The government owns and operates basic industries.

Austerity in spending and reduced taxes on imports have held inflation to a lower rate than in neighboring countries.

With a highly educated population, Uruguay for many years was considered the most outstanding example of political democracy in South America. However, a stagnating economy, inflation, government spending, and a leftist guerrilla movement caused the military in 1973 to force the nation to abandon democracy and civil rights.

Brazil lies to the northeast and Argentina to the west.

EARLY HISTORY OF URUGUAY

Spaniards explored the Río de la Plata as early as 1515, but permanent settlement did not occur until 1624. Uruguay's native Charrúa Indians, who strenuously resisted Spanish occupation, were killed off or absorbed by the 1830s. Portuguese from Brazil fortified the present site of Montevideo in 1717, but the Spaniards later drove them off, and Uruguay became part of the Spanish viceroyalty centered in Argentina. Montevideo was permanently settled in 1726.

A war of independence, led by José Gervasio Artigas, began in 1810. Portuguese forces captured Montevideo in 1820, and for five years Uruguay was part of Brazil.

INDEPENDENCE

In 1825 the "Thirty-three Immortals," led by Juan Antonio Lavalleja, declared Uruguay's independence. On Aug. 25, 1828, Uruguay was established as an independent buffer state between Brazil and Argentina. A constitution was adopted in 1830. Fructuoso Rivera became president.

The following decades were marked by internal strife, disputes with Brazil and Argentina, and violent changes of government.

José Batlle y Ordóñez, a liberal, served two terms as president (1903–07, 1911–15). He launched social, economic, and political reforms.

From 1952 to 1966 Uruguay was governed by a council. In November 1966 the people elected as president Oscar Daniel Gestido of the liberal Colorado Party. He died in 1967 and was succeeded by Vice President Jorge Pacheco Areco.

Strikes and unrest brought periods of limited martial law in 1968 and 1969. Terrorist activities included abductions of foreign diplomats by leftist urban guerrillas called *Tupamaros.*

URUGUAY IN THE 1970s–1980s

In 1971 conservative Juan M. Bordaberry was elected president after a 79-day recount.

The army, air force, and navy rebelled in February 1973, demanding an important voice in running the country. In June 1973 Bordaberry ended 40 years of democratic government in Uruguay. All political activities were banned.

Military leaders ousted Bordaberry on June 12, 1976. A 45-member council in July 1976 elected 72-year-old Aparicio Méndez as president.

When President Méndez took office on Sept. 1, 1976, he immediately banned the political rights of all Uruguayans who had held office in the past 10 years. Only officeholders in the existing government were exempted.

In March 1977 the government said it would reject all U.S. aid because of American criticism.

The $1 billion Salto Grande Dam on the Uruguay River, constructed by Argentina and Uruguay in 1974–81, was expected to stimulate industrial development with its hydroelectric 1.8 billion kilowatt capacity.

Permitted to vote for the first time in 7 years on Nov. 30, 1980, Uruguayans turned down, 58% to 42%, a new constitution that would have given the military continuing control of the government.

The junta appointed former army commander in chief Gen. Gregorio Alvarez to succeed Méndez as president on Sept. 1, 1981.

The three main political parties were permitted to resume activities in 1982 in preparation for general elections promised for November 1984.

When the parties held elections on Nov. 28, 1982, to choose convention delegates, opponents of the military regime won over 80% of the votes.

After leaders of the parties refused to accept amendments to the constitution proposed by the junta, the government announced on Aug. 2, 1983, a new ban on political activity.

VANUATU

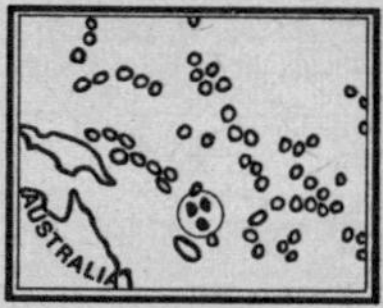

Official Name: Republic of Vanuatu.
Area: 5,700 square miles (14,763 sq. km.).
Population: 128,727.
Capital: Vila, Efate, 3,072.
Government: Democratic parliamentary republic.
President: George Sokomanu (since 1980).
Prime Minister: Rev. Walter Lini (since 1980).
Representative Assembly: 39 members.
Flag: Emblem of crossed mele leaves surrounded by yellow hog tusk on black triangle at hoist; red upper panel and green lower panel separated by thin black and yellow stripes.
Languages: English and French (official), Bislama (New Hebrides pidgin), Melanesian languages.
Chief Ethnic Group: Melanesian (92%).
Main Religions: Christianity, animism.
Leading Industries: Agriculture (coconuts, cocoa, coffee, cattle, taros, yams); fishing; food processing; mining (manganese); tourism; handicrafts.
Foreign Trade: *Major exports*—copra, fish, manganese, meat; *major imports*—food, petroleum, machinery; consumer goods.
Places of Interest: Swimming beaches; tropical rain forests; villages; volcanoes.

VANUATU TODAY

The first nation to win independence in the 1980s, Vanuatu had been jointly ruled by Britain and France for 74 years as the condominium of New Hebrides.

A group of more than 70 islands and islets in the southwest Pacific Ocean, Vanuatu has an area nearly as large as Hawaii. The main islands are Espiritu Santo, Malekula, Efate, Erromango, Tanna, Ambrym, Pentecost, Maevo, Aoba, and Aneityum. The island chain stretches about 500 miles from the Torres Islands in the north to Aneityum in the south.

Vanuatu lies about 1,000 miles northeast of Australia, 600 miles west of Fiji, and 250 miles northeast of New Caledonia.

The larger islands are covered by thick rain forests. Active volcanoes stand on several islands, including Ambrym and Tanna. The highest peak, Tabwemasana, on Espiritu Santo Island, is 6,160 feet high.

Most Vanuatuans are dark-skinned Melanesians, whose ancestors were cannibals less than a century ago. Most make their living from agriculture or fishing. Only about 1 person in 10 can read and write.

Because the value of imports are three times that of exports, Vanuatu depends heavily on economic aid from Britain and France.

Tourism is a growing industry. Some 40,000 cruise-ship passengers visit each year. Several hotels are located at Vila on Efate Island and at Luganville on Espiritu Santo. Commercial airlines provide two flights a week to and from Australia.

The climate is generally hot, humid, and rainy. Annual rainfall averages 91 inches.

EARLY HISTORY

The Portuguese explorer Pedro Fernándes de Queirós discovered the islands in 1606, naming the main one Australia del Espiritu Santo. British explorer Capt. James Cook gave the islands the name New Hebrides in 1774.

During the early 1800s French and British missionaries, planters, and traders settled in the islands. The native Melanesians suffered depredations by "blackbirder" ships that shanghaied them to work as laborers on plantations in Fiji.

Britain and France agreed in 1887 to jointly administer the islands.

ANGLO-FRENCH CONDOMINIUM

The government of the New Hebrides was established as an Anglo-French condominium by the London Convention of Oct. 20, 1906. This agreement was replaced by the Anglo-French Protocol of Aug. 6, 1914, which was ratified in 1922.

The islands were placed under joint administration of British and French commissioners.

During World War II the U.S. constructed a huge air and naval base at Esperitu Santo that was used as a staging facility for the invasions of Japanese-held Guadalcanal, Tarawa, and other islands in the south Pacific. The U.S. built 17 airstrips and many miles of roads on the islands.

From 1957 to 1975 an appointed advisory council, including the French and British resident commissioners, controlled local government.

The advisory council was replaced in 1976 with a 42-member representative assembly, including 29 elected members.

The first general election, in November 1975, was won by the Vanu aku Party (VAP), which captured 21 seats. However, disagreements among the political parties, which represent French, British, and local interests, delayed formation of a unified government until Dec. 22, 1978.

Parliamentary elections in November 1979 were won by the VAP, whose leader, Rev. Walter Lini, an Anglican priest, became chief minister.

INDEPENDENCE

France and Britain granted Vanuatu independence as a republic on July 30, 1980, with Lini as the sovereign nation's first prime minister. George Sokomanu, who had served as Lini's deputy chief minister, was chosen as Vanuatu's first president by vote of a special electoral college.

One of the first acts of the new government was to ask a force of 200 British and French troops to temporarily remain in occupation of the island of Espiritu Santo, where rebels armed with bows and arrows threatened to secede from Vanuatu as the separate nation of Vemarana.

The French and British troops were replaced in mid-August by 150 soldiers loaned by Papua New Guinea. On Aug. 31, 1980, they captured rebel Jimmy Stevens and about 70 of his followers, ending the rebellion. Stevens was sentenced to 14 years in prison.

In the first election since independence in November 1983, Prime Minister Lini's party won a 13-seat majority in the assembly.

QUICK QUIZ: What is the only official duty of the U.S. Vice President? See page 388.

VATICAN CITY

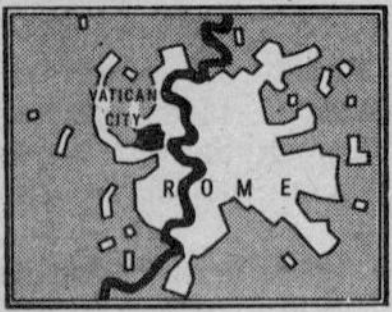

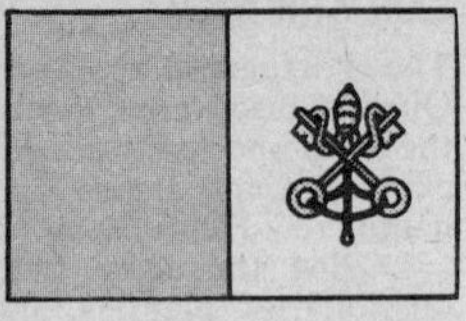

Official Name: State of the Vatican City.
Area: 0.17 sq. mi. (109 acres) (0.44 sq. km.).
Population: 1,006.
Government: Ecclesiastical state.
Pope: John Paul II (since 1978).
Flag: Yellow and white bars; crossed keys of St. Peter under papal tiara on white bar.
Languages: Latin (official), Italian.
Official Religion: Roman Catholicism (100%).
Places of Interest: St. Peter's Basilica; Vatican museums, including the Sistine Chapel.

VATICAN CITY TODAY

The world's smallest sovereign nation, Vatican City lies entirely within the Italian city of Rome. It occupies a small triangle on the west bank of the Tiber River. Vatican City also has jurisdiction over several churches and palaces in Rome and nearby Castel Gandolfo.

The government is an absolute monarchy with all powers vested in the pope of the Roman Catholic Church. He in turn delegates most of these powers, including diplomatic relations with other nations, to a secretary of state that he appoints. The government is often called merely the *Vatican.* The pope's court is known as the *Holy See.*

The government's security force consists of 75 Swiss guards. The official radio station is Radio Vatican. The official newspaper is *l'Osservatore Romano.* The state has its own postal and telephone systems. Most citizens are Vatican employees, who can buy tax-free food and goods.

Through the pope, the Vatican affects the lives of more than half a billion Roman Catholics throughout the world.

HISTORY

For many centuries after the fall of the Roman Empire, popes ruled Rome and central Italy, which were called the *Papal States.* With the unification of Italy in 1861, most of the Papal States except Rome were added to the new kingdom of Italy. In 1870 the Italian king took Rome from the pope, annexing it to Italy and making it his capital. Then, for more than half a century, Pope Pius IX and his successors refused to acknowledge Italy's sovereignty and regarded themselves as prisoners in Vatican City.

Treaties called the Lateran Accords signed on Feb. 11, 1929, by Italy and the Vatican established the independence and sovereignty of Vatican City. The accords were brought up to date with revisions in 1976–77, ending Roman Catholicism's status as the official religion of Italy and reducing the pope's authority over education and marriage in Italy.

Britain and the Vatican resumed full diplomatic relations in 1982 some 450 years after they were broken by Britain's King Henry VIII in 1532.

See also the list of popes on page 713.

VENDA

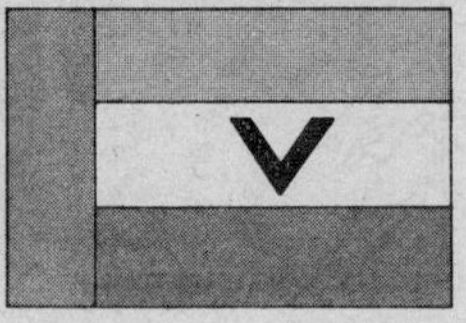

Official Name: Republic of Venda.
Area: 2,510 square miles (6,500 sq. km.).
Population: 379,929.
Capital: Thohoyandou.
Government: Parliamentary republic.
Prime Minister: Chief Patrick Mphephu (since 1973).
Flag: Blue stripe at hoist; green, yellow and brown horizontal stripes; brown V on yellow stripe.
Parliament: Legislative Assembly, 84 members (42 elected and 42 tribal chiefs).
Chief Languages: Venda (official), English, Afrikaans.
Principal Ethnic Group: Venda-speaking Bantus.
Main Religions: Christianity, animism.
Leading Industries: Agriculture (cattle, sheep, corn); personal services; forestry; mining (graphite).
Foreign Trade: *Major exports*—agricultural products; *major imports*—petroleum products, consumer goods, vehicles, machinery.

One of the black homelands established by South Africa as part of its apartheid policy of separation of the races, Venda is a small country about the size of Delaware.

Granted independence by South Africa, Venda has been unable to gain recognition for its sovereignty from other nations.

Most of the people live on the food they raise, seldom seeing any money except what they receive from relatives working in South Africa.

The country is divided into two parts, both surrounded by South Africa. Although Venda lies close to the southern border of Zimbabwe, a South African defense zone separates Venda from Zimbabwe. South Africa's Kruger Game Park lies between Venda and Mozambique to the east.

The Venda people, a division of the Bantus, are believed to have come to their present homeland from Zimbabwe. Stone structures made by the Venda resemble ancient ruins in Zimbabwe.

Chief Patrick Mphephu became chief minister of Venda when it was granted internal self-government in 1973. In elections that year his Venda National Party won only 5 of the 18 elective seats in the legislative assembly, but he was made chief minister by the vote of tribal chiefs who were automatically assembly members.

In a new election in 1978, Mphephu retained power, again with the vote of the nonelected chiefs, even though his party won only 11 of the 42 elective seats in the new legislature.

When the Venda Independence Party of Baldwin Mudau challenged his leadership in 1978, Mphephu ordered the arrest of about 50 of its members. The Independence Party had won 31 of the elective seats in the legislature.

South Africa granted Venda independence on Sept. 13, 1979, while continuing to provide about $35 million annual aid to support its economy. The UN Security Council denounced Venda's independence as a "totally invalid" effort "to perpetuate" South African apartheid.

VENEZUELA

Official Name: Republic of Venezuela.
Area: 352,145 square miles (912,050 sq. km.).
Population: 18,274,000.
Chief Cities: Caracas, capital, 1,662,627; Maracaibo, 874,000; Valencia, 488,000; Barquisimeto, 474,000; Maracay, 333,000; Barcelona–Puerto La Cruz, 267,000; San Cristóbal, 264,000; Ciudad Guayana, 199,001; Cabimas, 173,000.
Largest Metropolitan Area: Caracas, 2,849,191.
Government: Republic.
President: Luis Herrera Campíns (since 1979).
Congress: *Senate,* 49 members; *Chamber of Deputies,* 200 members.
U.S. Ambassador to Venezuela: George W. Landau.
Venezuelan Ambassador to U.S.: Marcial Perez Chiriboga.
Flag: Yellow, blue, and red stripes, with seven white stars in semicircle in center; national coat of arms in upper hoist corner.
Official Language: Spanish.
Ethnic Groups: Mestizo (70%), mulatto (13%), European descent (10%), black (5%), Indian (2%).
Religions: Roman Catholicism (96%), Protestantism (2%), Judaism (0.1%).
Leading Industries: Manufacturing (steel, motor vehicles, ships, oil refining, chemicals, food processing, textiles, cement); mining (petroleum, iron, diamonds, manganese); services; agriculture (livestock, coffee, cocoa, corn, rice, sugar, tobacco, cotton, fruits, vegetables); tourism; forestry and lumbering.
Foreign Trade: *Major exports*—petroleum and petroleum products, iron ore, coffee, cocoa; *major imports*—machinery, steel, automobiles, wheat.
Places of Interest: Angel Falls; Mt. Avila; Margarita Island; Lake Maracaibo; Bavarian village of Colonía Tovar; beach resorts; home of Simón Bolívar in Caracas; Spanish colonial buildings in Merida.

VENEZUELA TODAY

Larger than California, Oregon, and Washington combined, Venezuela is the most prosperous country in South America.

Venezuela is a leading oil-exporting nation. It also is one of the world's 10 most important producers of iron ore. Oil and iron ore account for about 98% of the value of the country's annual exports, although these industries employ only about 2% of Venezuela's workers. A fifth of the people are farmers.

Caracas, the capital, resembles Los Angeles or Miami with many skyscrapers and freeways.

The government's vigorous support of education has nearly wiped out illiteracy.

Venezuela has a 1,750-mile coastline on the Caribbean Sea. Its beaches and resorts attract many tourists. Colombia lies to the west, Brazil to the south, and Guyana to the east.

EARLY HISTORY

Columbus discovered the Orinoco River in 1498.

PRESIDENTS SINCE 1958

1958–1964	Rómulo Betancourt	Democratic Action
1964–1969	Raúl Leoni	Democratic Action
1969–1974	Rafael Caldera	Christian Social
1974–1979	Carlos Andrés Pérez	Democratic Action
1979–1984	Luis Herrera Campíns	Christian Social

German adventurers followed, but organization of the country was undertaken by Spain. Caracas was founded in 1567.

In 1811 Francisco de Miranda led a revolt against Spanish leaders. Independence was declared on July 5, 1811. Simón Bolívar completed the struggle for independence in 1821. Bolívar's dream of a Greater Colombia to include Venezuela was realized briefly, but after his death in 1830 Venezuela became independent. Dictator followed dictator in succeeding decades.

A revolution in 1945 brought to power a liberal democratic government headed by Rómulo Betancourt. In 1947 Rómulo Gallegos won a free presidential election but was ousted by a military coup in 1948. Marcos Pérez Jiménez became president and dictator in 1953.

DECADES OF DEMOCRACY

After the overthrow of Pérez Jiménez in 1958, Rómulo Betancourt of the Democratic Action Party was elected president. During his administration a new constitution was adopted limiting the presidency to one 5-year term.

Betancourt began a land-reform program that redistributed millions of acres of land to more than 100,000 small farmers.

After Venezuela broke relations with Cuba in 1961, Cuban-supported communist guerrillas tried to overthrow Betancourt.

Rafael Caldera of the Christian Social Party won the 1968 presidential election. At his inauguration in March 1969 a milestone was achieved as he became the first president in Venezuelan history to peacefully take over the government from an opposition party.

On Jan. 1, 1975, the government nationalized U.S.-owned iron mines, and on Jan. 1, 1976, nationalized the petroleum industry, paying the foreign owners with government bonds.

Work began in 1977 on a new $2 billion subway system for Caracas. It opened on Jan. 2, 1983.

Luis Herrera Campíns became president on March 12, 1979. As candidate of the Christian Social Party, he had won an upset victory in a national election on Dec. 3, 1978, that ousted the governing Democratic Action Party from office. President Herrera criticized the outgoing regime for having run up a national debt of more than $11 billion despite Venezuela's huge income from petroleum exports.

The nation's 5-year plan for 1981–85 calls for the investment of more than $64 billion dollars in housing, electric power, industry, agriculture, education, and other areas. Some $19 billion would be used largely to develop the huge oil reserves north of the Orinoco River, estimated as five times larger than those of Saudi Arabia.

A presidential election was held on Dec. 4, 1983 (for results, see page 30).

QUICK QUIZ: What is the world's most populous metropolitan area? See page 110.

VIETNAM

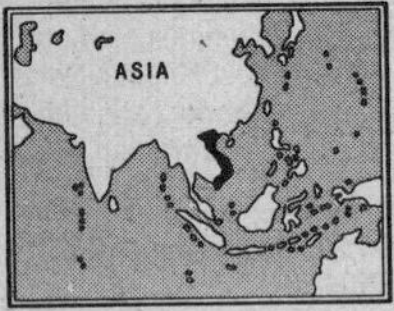

Official Name: Socialist Republic of Vietnam.
Area: 127,242 square miles (329,556 sq. km.).
Population: 57,668,100.
Chief Cities: Hanoi, capital, 414,620; Ho Chi Minh City (Saigon), 1,825,297; Danang, 492,194; Nhatrang, 216,227; Quinhon, 213,757; Hué, 209,043; Haiphong, 182,490.
Government: One-party communist state.
Government Leaders: Le Duan, secretary-general of the Communist Party (since 1960); prime minister, Pham Van Dong (since 1955); Truong Chinh (since 1981), head of state council.
Legislature: *National Assembly,* 496 members.
Flag: Gold star centered on red field.
Languages: Vietnamese (official), French, Chinese.
Main Ethnic Groups: Kinh (87%), Chinese (6%).
Principal Religions: Buddhism (70%), Roman Catholicism (10%).
Leading Industries: Agriculture (rice, poultry, rubber, tea, livestock, coffee, tobacco, sugarcane, corn, manioc, fruits, vegetables); manufacturing (food processing, textiles, cement, fertilizer, consumer products); fishing; forestry and lumbering; mining (coal, phosphates, iron, bauxite, gold, petroleum, chrome, zinc, tungsten).
Foreign Trade: *Major exports*—coal, rubber; *major imports*—food, petroleum, machinery, vehicles.
Places of Interest: Hanoi, government buildings; Ho Chi Minh City (Saigon), gardens, zoos, museums.

VIETNAM TODAY

Although somewhat smaller than Montana, Vietnam has the third-largest population of any communist nation after China and the Soviet Union.

Wars from the 1940s to 1970s devastated many of Vietnam's cities, towns, and villages, leaving behind countless problems.

About half of Vietnamese adults cannot read and write. In the area of health, diseases that have been eliminated in more developed countries kill from one-third to one-half of Vietnamese babies before they reach the age of six.

The nation's economy depends largely on agriculture, but cannot supply enough food for the people. Most Vietnamese earn their living as rice farmers. However, Vietnam has the potential for substantial industrial development with ample mineral resources that include coal and iron ore.

Vietnam is a long, narrow country that extends for about 1,000 miles from north to south. Northern Vietnam is hilly and mountainous while southern Vietnam is the low, flat delta of the Mekong River. Tropical forests cover much of the country.

The country has a year-round warm and wet tropical climate. Mountain regions are cool from about October to March. Heavy rains fall from May to September.

China lies to the north. Laos and Cambodia are to the west. The Gulf of Tonkin and the South China Sea are to the east.

EARLY HISTORY

Vietnamese legend attributes the founding of the nation more than 4,000 years ago to King Hung.

China's Han dynasty conquered Vietnam in 111 B.C. For more than 1,000 years China ruled northern Vietnam. A revolt by the Vietnamese threw off Chinese rule in A.D. 939.

Meanwhile, in southern Vietnam a kingdom called Champa had been founded by an Indonesian people. Champa carried on trade with India for many centuries and was influenced by Hindu art and religion.

Vietnam's emperor Le Thanh-Ton conquered Champa in 1471, unifying the region. But by the early 1600s Vietnam again had become divided with the kingdoms of Tonkin in the north and Cochin China in the south.

European traders began visiting the region in the 1500s.

FRENCH CONTROL

In the late 1700s French military officers helped Prince Nguyen Anh of Cochin China win control of the entire country. In 1802 he established himself as Emperor Gia-Long with his capital at Hué. His descendants continued to rule for the next century and a half.

By the mid-1800s French missionaries had converted about 2 million Vietnamese to Roman Catholicism. Fearing the foreign influence of the Christians, the government began a campaign of persecution, killing many of them.

France's Emperor Napoleon III demanded in 1858 that Vietnamese Emperor Tu-Duc stop the persecution of Christians. Then France, in 1859, began its conquest of the country, first capturing Saigon with the aid of Spain.

France made southern Vietnam (Cochin China) a colony in 1867. After much fighting, France established a protectorate over all of Vietnam on June 6, 1884.

By 1893 France also had won control of Cambodia and Laos. It then incorporated these countries with Vietnam into the Indochinese Union, headed by a French governor-general. Vietnam was divided into three parts: Tonkin in the north, Annam in the center, and Cochin China in the south.

During the next half century Indochina became France's most prosperous colony. Hanoi became the capital of French Indochina.

In the 1930s Vietnamese aspirations for independence were spurred by the Indochinese Communist Party founded by Ho Chi Minh, who had been educated in France.

After the defeat of France by Germany in World War II, the Vichy French colonial administration gave Japan complete control of Indochina. Ho Chi Minh organized Vietnamese patriots into the Vietminh movement, which carried out guerrilla attacks on the Japanese.

INDOCHINA WAR

When Japan surrendered to the U.S. in World War II in August 1945, the Vietminh seized control of Hanoi and forced Emperor Bao Dai to abdicate. Ho Chi Minh declared Vietnam an independent republic on Sept. 2, 1945.

France tried to reassert its control of Vietnam, establishing a separate regime in Cochin

China (southern Vietnam) in June 1946. Fighting soon began between the French troops and the Vietminh. The Indochina War dragged on for eight years, ending with French defeat in 1954 and a peace settlement at Geneva.

The nation was divided at the 17th parallel into North Vietnam (capital at Hanoi) and South Vietnam (capital at Saigon). The settlement provided that elections should be held in 1956 to vote on reuniting the country. However, the U.S. and South Vietnam refused to sign the Geneva agreement and repudiated a unification referendum. The U.S. signed a defense treaty with South Vietnam in 1954.

VIETNAM WAR

In South Vietnam, Emperor Bao Dai was ousted in October 1955 by his prime minister, Ngo Dinh Diem, who declared the nation a republic with himself as its first president. Communists began guerrilla warfare against South Vietnam.

The U.S. sent constantly increasing supplies and military advisers to South Vietnam.

In the belief Diem was incapable of winning the war, the U.S. government encouraged a coup in 1963 in which Diem was assassinated.

After attacks by North Vietnamese patrol craft on U.S. destroyers in the Gulf of Tonkin in 1964, the U.S. Congress gave President Lyndon Johnson authority to use any means to prevent further aggression by North Vietnam.

U.S. troops began combat operations in Vietnam in 1965. Within four years more than 500,000 U.S. servicemen were fighting against North Vietnamese troops and guerrillas.

Meanwhile, Nguyen Van Thieu had been elected president of South Vietnam in 1967.

Ho Chi Minh, the leader of North Vietnam, died in September 1969. He was succeeded as president by Ton Duc Thang, who died in 1980.

Antiwar sentiment in the U.S. caused President Richard Nixon to begin withdrawing U.S. forces from Vietnam in 1969. A cease-fire agreement became effective on Jan. 28, 1973. All U.S. forces left by March 29, 1973.

Over 57,000 Americans died in the war.

North Vietnam launched a new offensive in March 1975. South Vietnam's defenses quickly collapsed. The war ended on April 30, 1975, with South Vietnam's unconditional surrender.

UNIFIED COMMUNIST VIETNAM

The communists quickly moved to unify Vietnam. Hanoi became the capital for the entire country. Saigon was renamed Ho Chi Minh City.

On July 2, 1976, the national assembly approved unification and elected North Vietnam leaders as heads of the new state.

American and Vietnamese diplomats met in Paris on Nov. 12, 1976, for the first talks since the end of the Vietnam War. The meetings, which continued intermittently into 1977, sought to settle problem issues and lead to the establishment of regular diplomatic relations.

Letters made public in 1977 showed that President Nixon secretly had promised North Vietnam

HIGHLIGHTS OF THE INDOCHINA AND VIETNAM WARS: 1945–1975

1945 (Sept. 2) Independence of Democratic Republic of Vietnam proclaimed by communist Ho Chi Minh.

1946 (March 6) France recognizes Ho's government, granting internal self-rule to Vietnam.

1946 (June 1) After disputes with Ho, France declares southern Vietnam independent, calling it Cochin China.

1946 (Dec. 19) War begins with surprise attack by troops of Ho Chi Minh launched on French military bases.

1954 (May 7) French army surrenders fortress of Dien Bien Phu after 55-day siege by North Vietnamese.

1954 (July 21) Truce signed, ending 8-year Indochina War; nation divided into North and South Vietnam.

1954 (Aug. 11) Peace agreement signed in Geneva, Switzerland, providing referendum in 1956 to decide government of unified Vietnam. United States and South Vietnam refuse to sign agreement.

1954 (Sept. 8) Southeast Asia Collective Defense Treaty signed by U.S. and seven other nations pledging joint action to protect South Vietnam and other nations in area.

1964 (Aug. 2–4) U.S. destroyers in Gulf of Tonkin attacked by North Vietnamese torpedo boat.

1964 (Aug. 5) Retaliatory bombing of North Vietnam by U.S. planes ordered by President Johnson.

1964 (Aug. 7) Congress votes Gulf of Tonkin Resolution, giving President authority "to prevent further aggression."

1965 (June 28) First U.S. combat operations on ground authorized by President Johnson.

1968 (Jan. 30) Tet offensive, biggest communist attack of war begun, directed at Saigon.

1968 (March 16) My Lai massacre of 100 to 400 Vietnamese civilians by U.S. troops led by Lt. William L. Calley Jr.

1968 (May 13) Peace talks begin in Paris between U.S. and North Vietnam as war rages.

1969 (March) U.S. troops fighting in Vietnam reach peak level of 541,500.

1969 (June 8) President Nixon announces U.S. will begin to withdraw troops.

1969 (Nov. 15) About 300,000 antiwar demonstrators march on Washington.

1970 (April 30–June 30) U.S. troops enter Cambodia to destroy North Vietnamese supply bases.

1972 (April 2) North Vietnamese troops invade South Vietnam in major new offensive.

1972 (May 8) Mining of North Vietnam's ports and bombing of supply routes to China ordered by Nixon.

1972 (August) Last U.S. combat troops leave Vietnam.

1972 (Oct. 26) Peace Negotiator Henry Kissinger reports U.S. and North Vietnam are in substantial agreement on 9-point plan; expresses belief "peace is at hand."

1972 (Dec. 13) U.S. suspends Kissinger-Tho talks, claiming North Vietnamese have changed their position on previously agreed-upon points.

1972 (Dec. 18) President Nixon orders heaviest bombing of war on North Vietnam; 28 U.S. planes lost in 13 days.

1973 (Jan. 27) Truce agreements formally signed in Paris by U.S., North Vietnam, South Vietnam, and Vietcong.

1973 (Jan. 28) Cease-fire begins in Vietnam at 8 A.M.

1973 (March 29) Last U.S. military personnel leave.

1973 (April 1) Last of 590 U.S. prisoners of war released.

1975 (March 10) North Vietnamese troops begin offensive on provincial capital of Ban Me Thuot.

1975 (March 16) South Vietnam orders withdrawal of troops from northern and central provinces; withdrawal quickly turns into headlong retreat.

1975 (April 21) South Vietnam's President Nguyen Van Thieu resigns and flees to safety in Taiwan a few days later.

1975 (April 29) U.S. ambassador and 1,000 Americans evacuate Saigon by helicopter as communist troops attack city's outskirts.

1975 (April 30) Unconditional surrender of South Vietnam announced by President Duong Van Minh.

QUICK QUIZ: What is the No. 1 dangerous drug problem in the U.S.? See page 448.

VIETNAM *(continued)*

$4.75 billion in postwar aid when the communists agreed to a Vietnam War cease-fire in 1973.

The U.S. Congress passed legislation in July 1977 forbidding the expenditure of funds for aid to Vietnam.

In September 1977 Vietnam was admitted to membership in the United Nations after the U.S. withdrew its objections.

Relations worsened between the U.S. and Vietnam in February 1978 when the U.S. government expelled Vietnam's UN representative Dinh Ba Thi for participation in espionage in the U.S. with an American and a Vietnamese refugee.

The Vietnamese government announced in March 1978 that it was banning all private business and confiscating the property of capitalists.

The government announced in May 1978 that it had resettled some 1.3 million persons from cities into previously uninhabited forest areas. In all, the government's plan calls for more than 10 million persons to be moved to sparsely settled regions during a 20-year period.

Vietnam signed an alliance with the Soviet Union on Nov. 3, 1978, which the Chinese denounced as directed against them.

Soviet-equipped Vietnamese troops launched an offensive on Dec. 25, 1978, against the Chinese-supported regime of Pol Pot in Cambodia. In a lightning drive the Vietnamese army captured the Cambodian capital Phnom Penh on Jan. 7, 1979, and set up a new government allied with Vietnam. However, Pol Pot's forces took to the jungles and fought a guerrilla war against the 200,000 Vietnamese troops in Cambodia. Vietnamese troops invaded Thailand in June 1980, claiming the Thais were aiding Pol Pot's troops, but withdrew after a day's fighting.

Vowing that Vietnam needed to be "punished," China invaded northern Vietnam on Feb. 17, 1979, with about 200,000 troops. In a hard-fought four-week war, the Chinese destroyed Vietnamese cities and towns within about 40 miles of the Chinese border. After withdrawing its troops on March 15, China announced that it had inflicted about 50,000 casualties on the Vietnamese while claiming Chinese forces suffered 20,000.

In 1978–79 hundreds of thousands of refugees left Vietnam, becoming known as "boat people" because of the leaky boats in which they escaped. Evidence mounted that Vietnam was extorting millions of dollars from the refugees to allow them to leave. After protests by neighboring countries about the burden of caring for them, an international conference of 65 nations was called in Geneva, Switzerland, in July 1979. At the conference, the Vietnamese government promised to try to stem the flow of refugees.

Truong Chinh, 73, chairman of the 5-member state council, became head of state in 1981 when a new constitution went into effect.

The U.S. government in 1981–83 refused to consider establishing diplomatic relations until the Vietnamese government accounts for the fate of some 2,500 American military personnel missing since the end of the Vietnam War.

The government announced in October 1983 the resettlement of 97,000 city dwellers on state-run rubber and coffee plantations.

WESTERN SAMOA

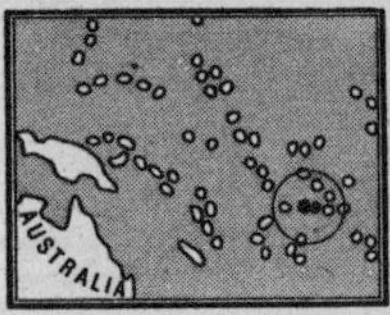

Official Name: Western Samoa.
Area: 1,097 square miles (2,842 sq. km.).
Population: 160,725.
Capital: Apia, 32,616.
Government: Parliamentary democracy.
Chief of State: Malietoa Tanumafili II (since 1963).
Prime Minister: Tofilau Eti (since 1982).
Legislature: *Legislative Assembly,* 47 members.
U.S. Ambassador: W. Monroe Browne.
Western Samoan Ambassador to U.S.: Iulia Toma.
Flag: Red field with blue rectangle in upper hoist corner; five white stars represent Southern Cross.
Official Languages: Samoan and English.
Main Ethnic Group: Samoan (89%).
Religions: Congregationalism (50%), Methodism (20%), Roman Catholicism (20%).
Leading Industries: Agriculture (bananas, coconuts, cocoa, poultry, fruits, vegetables); fishing; forestry and lumbering; manufacturing (food processing, handicrafts); tourism.
Foreign Trade: *Major exports*—copra, cocoa, bananas; *major imports*—food, manufactured goods.
Places of Interest: Home of Robert Louis Stevenson; Mt. Vaea on Upolu Island.

About the size of Rhode Island, the Pacific islands of Western Samoa have an economy that depends mostly on agriculture and fishing.

The nation's major exports are bananas, copra, and cocoa. Tourism also brings cash.

The Samoans live in tribal villages, following social customs that have survived for many centuries. There are no political parties. Most Samoans are Christians.

Halfway between Honolulu and Sydney, Western Samoa has two principal islands (Savai'i and Upolu) and seven small islands. About 113 inches of rain falls from October to March.

The first Europeans to sight the islands were the Dutch in 1772. English missionaries arrived in 1830, in the midst of a long struggle among the native chiefs that ended in 1889 when Samoa was declared neutral and independent. Malietoa Laupepa was recognized as king.

In 1900 Eastern Samoa was annexed by the U.S. and Western Samoa by Germany.

From 1919 to 1962 New Zealand administered Western Samoa.

The country was granted independence by New Zealand on Jan. 1, 1962. Malietoa Tanumafili II became chief of state in 1963. Western Samoa became a member of the British Commonwealth of Nations in 1970 and the UN in 1976.

A modern airport and a highway were completed in the mid-1970s.

A strike by some 4,000 government employees for higher wages that began on April 6, 1981, cut off all but emergency services for 90 days.

The nation's supreme court in September 1982 nullified the election seven months earlier of Vaai Kolone as prime minister because of fraud in the voting.

YEMEN, NORTH

Official Name: Yemen Arab Republic.
Area: 75,290 square miles (195,000 sq. km.).
Population: 5,822,130.
Chief Cities: Sana, capital, 134,588; Taiz, 40,000; Hodeida, 40,000.
Government: Military-controlled republic.
President: Lt. Col. Ali Abdullah Saleh (since 1978).
Prime Minister: Abdel Karim Iryani (since 1980).
Constituent People's Assembly: 99 members.
U.S. Ambassador to North Yemen: David E. Zweifel.
Yemen Ambassador to U.S.: Mohamed Ahmed Al-Eryani.
Flag: Red, white, and black stripes, green star.
Language: Arabic.
Main Ethnic Group: Arab.
Official Religion: Islam.
Leading Industries: Agriculture (wheat, sorghum, coffee, cattle, sheep, qat, cotton, fruits); manufacturing (handicrafts, textiles, cement, cigarettes, nails, shoes).
Foreign Trade: *Major exports*—qat, coffee, cotton; *major imports*—food, machinery, vehicles.
Places of Interest: Dhafar antiquities; Throne of Belgis and ruins of Marib Dam at Marib; Al-Janad Mosque; Salah Palace in Taiz.

North Yemen is about the size of South Dakota. Its government, which fosters private enterprise, remains in a state of cold war with its Marxist neighbor South Yemen.

The country has a cooler climate, more rain, and greater possibilities for agriculture development than other areas of the Arabian peninsula.

In North Yemen's interior, mountains rise to a height of more than 12,000 feet. Hills and mountainsides have been terraced by the farmers.

Most of the people are poor. Over a million Yemeni men work in Saudi Arabia, sending home about $2 billion to their families each year

Saudi Arabia lies to the north, South Yemen to the south, and the Red Sea to the west.

North Yemen contained the biblical kingdom of Sheba. The area was ruled by the Himyarites from 115 B.C. to A.D. 525. Yemenis claim to have built the first skyscraper 2,000 years ago, the 20-story Palace of Ghamdan at Sana.

About 885 the Zaidi founded the Rassid dynasty of imams (rulers). Two successive periods of Egyptian control began in the 1200s. In 1517 the Turks occupied the region. After Turkey's defeat in World War I, Yemen was ruled by the Hamid al-Din dynasty of imams.

In 1962 Imam Ahmed's death and the succession of his son Muhammad Badr were followed by a republican revolution led by Col. Abdullah al-Sallal and supported by Egyptian troops. The Yemen Arab Republic was established on Sept. 26, 1962. Republican control soon was established in the coastal Tihama area, while royalist Imani forces held the highlands.

Egypt, the Soviet Union, and communist China supported the republicans in the ensuing civil war, while Saudi Arabia backed the royalists.

Republican forces broke a siege of Sana by royalist troops in 1968. The 8-year civil war came to an end in 1970 with agreement to include royalist leaders in future cabinets.

Col. Ibrahim al-Hamdi, deputy commander of the army, overthrew the government in a bloodless coup on June 13, 1974.

President Hamdi and his brother Lt. Col. Abdullah al-Hamdi were assassinated on Oct. 11, 1977. Lt. Col. Ahmed Hussein al-Ghashmi, Hamdi's second in command, took control.

President Ghashmi was assassinated on June 24, 1978, by a bomb carried by a South Yemen envoy, who also was killed. He was succeeded by 36-year-old Lt. Col. Ali Abdullah Saleh.

Nine high-ranking army officers were reported killed in another unsuccessful coup on Oct. 15, 1978. Twenty-one persons, including a former cabinet minister, were executed for the plot.

Soviet-supplied South Yemen troops invaded North Yemen on Feb. 23, 1979. Reacting to this attempted communist expansion in the Middle East, the U.S. announced on March 9 it was rushing $390 million in arms to North Yemen to aid its army. On March 16 the two nations agreed to a truce, and South Yemen withdrew its troops.

An earthquake destroyed many villages on Dec. 13, 1982, killing more than 2,000 persons.

YEMEN, SOUTH

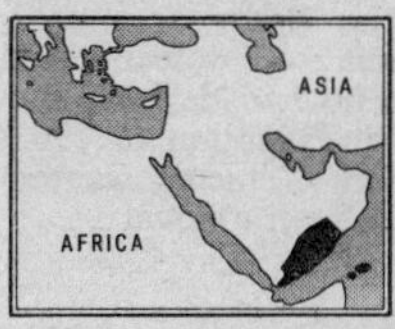

Official Name: People's Democratic Republic of Yemen.
Area: 128,560 square miles (332,968 sq. km.).
Population: 2,116,470.
Capital: Aden, 271,590.
Government: One-party Marxist state.
Chief of State and Prime Minister: Nasir Muhammad al Hasani (since 1980).
People's Supreme Assembly: 111 members.
Flag: Red, white, and black stripes with light blue triangle containing red star at hoist.
Languages: Arabic (official), English.
Main Ethnic Group: Arab (90%).
Religion: Islam.
Leading Industries: Agriculture (cotton, livestock, coffee, sorghum, sesame, millet, tobacco, fruits); oil refining; manufacturing (soap, cigarettes, handicrafts); fishing; mining (salt).
Foreign Trade: *Major exports*—petroleum products, cotton, cottonseed, salt, hides and skins, coffee; *major imports*—food, building materials, automobiles, machinery, manufactured goods, crude oil.
Places of Interest: Ancient ruined cities; Socotra Island; biblical valley of Hadhramant at Shibam.

SOUTH YEMEN TODAY

South Yemen is the only Arab Marxist nation. About the size of Nevada, it is a desert country at

QUICK QUIZ: Who has the title "Great She–Elephant"? See page 657.

YEMEN, SOUTH *(continued)*

the southern end of the Arabian peninsula. The main industry is the refining of petroleum at the port city and capital of Aden.

Most of the people are poor farmers or nomadic livestock herders. Only about 1 person in 10 can read and write. With few natural resources, the country depends on foreign aid largely from communist nations.

South Yemen has a hot dry climate. Summer temperatures soar above 130 ° F.

Extending the length of the Arabian Sea coast is a low, rugged plain. The interior contains a series of increasingly higher ridges that merge into a rugged highland plateau fragmented by a series of deep, dry valleys (wadis).

EARLY HISTORY

South Yemen was included in the Minaean, Sabaean, and Himyarite kingdoms of Arabia that flourished from about 1200 to 50 B.C.

The spread of Judaism and Christianity to southern Yemen in the 500s A.D. brought about religious rivalry. Abyssinian and Persian occupation followed.

By 885 the highland areas of southern Yemen belonged to the Islamic rulers of Yemen. The coastal area recognized the Baghdad caliphate, and was later ruled by Egyptians and Turks.

The British captured Aden in 1839, making it part of the British Empire for more than a century. Aden increased in importance after the opening of the Suez Canal in 1869.

In 1962 Aden joined the British-sponsored Federation of South Arabia to protect itself from Yemeni republicans who had deposed the imam. A United Nations investigation in 1963 indicated that most southern Yemenis wanted union with Yemen and British withdrawal.

INDEPENDENCE

In September 1967, as British troops withdrew from all parts of the country except Aden, the National Liberation Front (NLF) took charge. In November fierce street battles broke out in Aden, and Britain decided to withdraw its military forces.

South Yemen became independent on Nov. 30, 1967. The moderate government of President Qahtan al-Shaabi resigned on June 22, 1969, and was replaced by a Marxist regime.

South Yemen broke diplomatic relations with the United States on Oct. 24, 1969.

On June 26, 1978, President Salim Rubayya Ali of South Yemen was overthrown and executed by his Marxist colleagues. Ali Nasir Muhammad al Hasani, who had been prime minister since 1972, succeeded to the presidency.

Six months later, on Dec. 28, 1978, Abd al-Fattah Ismail, secretary-general of the Marxist National Front, took over the presidency.

An invasion of North Yemen in a 3-week war from Feb. 23 to March 16, 1979, ended with a truce negotiated by other Arab countries.

South Yemen signed a 20-year friendship pact with the Soviet Union in October 1979.

On April 21, 1980, Prime Minister Muhammad overthrew Ismail, taking over as chief of state. Seeking better international relations, he went to Saudi Arabia in June 1980 for the first official visit since South Yemen's independence.

YUGOSLAVIA

Official Name: Socialist Federal Republic of Yugoslavia.
Area: 98,766 square miles (255,804 sq. km.).
Population: 22,918,000.
Chief Cities: Beograd (Belgrade), capital, 746,105; Zagreb, 566,224; Skoplje, 312,980; Sarajevo, 243,980; Ljubljana, 173,853.
Largest Metropolitan Area: Belgrade, 774,744.
Government: One-party communist republic.
President: Chosen annually from among 8-member presidency committee.
Prime Minister: Milka Planinc (since 1982).
Legislature: *Assembly—Federal Council,* 220 delegates; *Council of the Republics and Provinces,* 58 delegates.
U.S. Ambassador to Yugoslavia: David Anderson.
Yugoslavian Ambassador to U.S.: Budomir Loncar.
Flag: Red star outlined in gold, centered on stripes of blue, white, and red.
Languages: Serbo-Croatian, Slovenian, Macedonian, Hungarian, Albanian.
Main Ethnic Groups: Serb (40%), Croat (22%), Slovene and Bosnian (8%), Macedonian (6%), Albanian (6%), Montenegrin and Hungarian (2%), Turk (1%).
Principal Religions: Eastern Orthodox (41%), Roman Catholicism (32%), Islam (12%).
Leading Industries: Agriculture (wheat, potatoes, corn, barley, tobacco, sugar beets, fruits, vegetables, livestock); manufacturing (steel, cement, chemicals, food processing, fertilizer, textiles); mining (bauxite, lignite, zinc, lead, petroleum, natural gas, iron, coal, copper, gold); forestry and lumbering; tourism.
Foreign Trade: *Major exports*—timber, nonferrous metals, livestock and meat, machinery, metal products; *major imports*—machinery, metal products, chemicals, textiles, petroleum.
Places of Interest: Mountain and coastal resorts; Roman, Byzantine, Serbian, and Turkish antiquities at Skoplje; Plitvice lakes; Postoina caves; Dubrovnik; Split; Opatija; Ljubljana; Zagreb. *In Belgrade:* national museum; Museum of Modern Art; Kalemegdan citadel (now a museum).

YUGOSLAVIA TODAY

About the size of Wyoming, Yugoslavia is a communist nation in southeastern Europe. It is among the world's leading producers of bauxite, lead, and lignite.

The country's main problem in international relations has been to maintain independence from the Soviet Union and play a leading role among the nonaligned nations of the world.

About two-thirds of the people speak the Serbo-Croatian language.

The two largest ethnic groups, the Serbs and Croatians, have feuded with each other for hundreds of years.

The remaining third of the population includes large minority groups of Slovenes, Macedonians, Albanians, Bosnian Muslims, Montenegrins, Hungarians, and Turks.

In an effort to give these various ethnic groups local self-government, Yugoslavia is divided into six republics and two autonomous provinces within Serbia (Kosovo and Vojvodina).

Croatian nationalists, many living in exile, continue to work for independence of a Croatian state, sometimes carrying out bombings and airplane hijackings to call attention to their cause.

Although Yugoslavia has made progress toward industrialization through use of its wealth of natural resources, almost three-fourths of the people still live on farms and in villages. However, Yugoslavs enjoy more consumer goods then most other communist nations of Europe.

The nation's official name is the *Socialist Federal Republic of Yugoslavia.*

The Danube River and its tributaries drain Yugoslavia's fertile lowland area in the north and northeast. Yugoslavia's coastline along the Adriatic Sea is about 1,000 miles long. About two-thirds of the country is covered by mountain ranges that run northwest to southeast a few miles inland from the Adriatic coast. The climate is similar to that of the U.S. east coast.

Yugoslavia is bounded on the north by Italy, Austria, and Hungary; on the east by Romania and Bulgaria; and on the south by Greece and Albania.

EARLY HISTORY

The various parts of Yugoslavia had never been united under one government before 1918:

Serbia was under Turkish domination from 1371 to 1878. After the Balkan Wars of 1912–13, Serbia became independent and acquired Macedonia, an ancient kingdom that had been under Turkish control.

Montenegro, under Turkish rule for centuries, became independent in 1878.

Slovenia, passing to Austrian Hapsburg rule in 1335, was under their domination until 1918.

Croatia was part of Hungary from the 1000s and then was ruled by Austria-Hungary from 1867. It became part of Serbia after World War I.

Bosnia and Herzegovina became Turkish possessions in the 1500s and were annexed by Austria in 1908.

The 1914 assassination by Serbian nationalists in Sarajevo, Bosnia, of Austria's Archduke Franz Ferdinand led to World War I. The collapse of the Austro-Hungarian and Turkish empires opened the way for unification of the Balkan Slavs.

King Peter I of Serbia became the ruler of the new Kingdom of the Serbs, Croats, and Slovenes in 1918, but his son Alexander ruled as regent until Peter's death in 1921.

King Alexander declared himself absolute ruler in 1929 and changed the kingdom's name to Yugoslavia. In 1934 Alexander was assassinated. His heir, Peter II, succeeded under the regency of Prince Paul.

Yugoslavia attempted to remain neutral in World War II, but Germany invaded the country on April 6, 1941, and defeated its army in two weeks. King Peter II fled to London.

Several resistance movements emerged. The most important were the royalist Chetniks, led by a Serb general, Draja Mikhailovich, and the pro-Soviet partisans led by the Croat communist Josip Broz Tito. Both guerrilla armies fought against the Germans and each other.

By 1944 Britain and the U.S. switched support to Tito, who also received military aid from the Soviet Union.

REPUBLICS OF YUGOSLAVIA

REPUBLIC	CAPITAL	AREA
Bosnia and Herzegovina	Sarajevo	19,741 sq. mi.
Croatia	Zagreb	21,829 sq. mi.
Macedonia	Skoplje	9,928 sq. mi.
Montenegro	Titograd	5,333 sq. mi.
Serbia	Belgrade	34,116 sq. mi.
Slovenia	Ljubljana	7,819 sq. mi.

COMMUNIST RULE

A leftist coalition headed by Tito declared a republic on Nov. 29, 1945. Tito became president. Mikhailovich was captured, tried as a war criminal, and executed on July 17, 1946.

Although the Communist Party ruled the country, it resisted Soviet efforts to penetrate and control Yugoslavia. Matters came to a head in January 1948 when the recently created Communist Information Bureau (Cominform), dominated by Moscow, expelled Yugoslavia, charging it with "revisionism." This break forced Tito to draw closer to the West.

After the death of Stalin in 1953, however, diplomatic and trade relations with the Soviet Union were resumed. A dramatic visit to Yugoslavia by Soviet leader Nikita Khrushchev in 1955 restored cooperative relations.

A meeting between President Tito and Chancellor Willy Brandt of West Germany in 1973 worked out differences between the two nations regarding reparations Yugoslavia claimed for damages during World War II.

To combat low productivity, the government for the first time in 1975 gave the managers of communist businesses the right to fire workers who fail to meet production goals.

In January 1976 the U.S. resumed selling arms to Yugoslavia. American military aid had been suspended since 1961.

At a meeting between Soviet leader Leonid Brezhnev and Tito in Yugoslavia in November 1976, the Yugoslav president turned down Soviet requests for closer military cooperation.

After a protracted illness, Tito died on May 4, 1980, three days short of his 88th birthday.

In March and April 1981 riots in the southern region of Kosovo left 9 dead and about 200 injured. The agitation was fomented by Albanian nationalists seeking unification of the region with Albania.

Milka Planinc, 58, was elected by parliament as prime minister on May 16, 1982, becoming the first woman to head the nation's government. She formerly had been leader of the Communist Party in Croatia.

Prime Minister Planinc was faced with difficult economic problems in meeting $5.3 billion in annual payments on the nation's $20 billion foreign debt.

The government announced that recession had caused a 10% decline in the nation's standard of living in 1983.

QUICK QUIZ: What drug was first discovered by Gerhard Domagk? See page 452.

ZAIRE

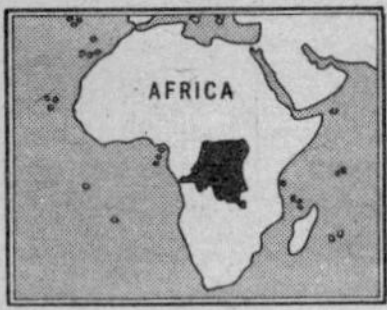

Official Name: Republic of Zaire.
Area: 905,568 square miles (2,345,409 sq. km.).
Population: 31,706,500.
Chief Cities: Kinshasa, capital, 2,008,352; Kananga, 601,239; Luluabourg, 506,033; Lubumbashi, 403,623; Mbuji-Mayi, 336,654; Kisangani, 310,705.
Government: One-party dictatorship.
President: Mobutu Sese Seko (seized power in 1965).
Prime Minister: Joseph Nsigna (since 1981).
Legislature: *National Assembly,* 420 members.
U.S. Ambassador to Zaire: Peter D. Constable.
Zairian Ambassador to U.S.: Kasongo Mutuale.
Flag: Green field with yellow circle in center showing arm carrying torch.
Languages: French (official), tribal dialects.
Main Ethnic Group: Bantu (80%).
Religions: Animism (50%), Christianity (50%).
Leading Industries: Agriculture (coffee, cocoa, tea, rubber, palm kernels, cotton, sugarcane, livestock, fruits, vegetables); mining (copper, petroleum, zinc, tin, cobalt, diamonds, gold); forestry and lumbering; manufacturing (food processing, textiles, clothing, cement, consumer goods).
Foreign Trade: *Major exports*—copper, diamonds, cobalt, coffee, tin, palm oil; *major imports*—food, motor vehicles, cotton fabrics, petroleum products.
Places of Interest: Boyoma Falls, Point Kalina, Cristal Mountains—all on Zaire River. *In Kinshasa:* Botanical and zoological gardens; Museum of Native Life; St. Anne's Cathedral; Pioneers and Stanley monuments.

ZAIRE TODAY

About one-fourth the size of the United States, Zaire is rich in natural resources. The country's economy has suffered because of low copper prices since the mid-1970s.

Zaire is the world's largest producer of cobalt and industrial diamonds and the sixth most important copper-mining country. It ranks eighth in tin-ore mining and ninth in natural rubber. Offshore oil wells began production in 1975. In addition its rivers provide potential for hydroelectric power. Hopeful of becoming the leading industrial nation of Africa, the government has sought loans and investments from both communist and noncommunist nations.

As with most other African countries, a problem equal to the lack of capital is the scarcity of educated skilled workers. Most of the people belong to the more than 200 Bantu tribes that live in the tropical forests or on the upland plains. Few can read and write. The tribesmen support themselves with primitive subsistence farming that has changed little in hundreds of years. But Zaire also must import much food.

The third-largest nation in Africa, Zaire derives its name from the Zaire (Congo) River, whose course lies within the country's borders. Except for a narrow corridor on the northern bank of the Zaire River, the country is landlocked.

Much of the central Zaire River basin area, comprising nearly half the country, is densely forested. The land in the higher regions to the north and south is savanna or bush country. Southeast of the central plateau the elevation gradually rises to 6,000 feet, and to the east mountain ranges reach a height of 16,763 feet at the crest of Margherita Peak.

In the lower western and central regions the climate is tropically hot and humid. The climate in the higher eastern elevations is more temperate. South of the equator rains are heavy and frequent from fall to late spring. North of the equator the season of heaviest rainfall is from April to November.

Congo lies to the west; Central Africa and Sudan to the north; Uganda, Rwanda, Burundi, and Tanzania to the east; and Zambia and Angola to the south.

EARLY HISTORY

Pygmies or Bushmen probably first occupied the Zaire basin. They were later displaced by migrants (mostly Bantu), who settled the area in the 600s and 700s and established kingdoms. The kingdom of Kongo (Congo) gave its name to the river and to the French and Belgian colonial territories carved from the basin.

Henry Stanley of Britain explored the Congo River in 1877. His reports sparked the interest of King Leopold II of Belgium, who in 1878 formed a company to exploit the region.

The Congress of Berlin in 1885 recognized Leopold's claims, and he became absolute monarch of the Congo Free State.

International protests over reported abuse of the Congolese population forced Leopold to cede his private state to Belgium. It became the colony of Belgian Congo in 1908.

INDEPENDENCE

Belgium granted the country independence on June 30, 1960. Parliament chose Joseph Kasavubu as president and Patrice Lumumba as premier. Almost immediately the country was swept by disorders. Belgian troops intervened to protect Belgian nationals. The gravest challenge was the secession of the richest province, Katanga, led by Moïse Tshombe.

When rivalry between Kasavubu and Lumumba crippled the government, Col. Joseph-Désiré Mobutu (now Mobutu Sese Seko), head of the army, supported Kasavubu. Lumumba was jailed but escaped, and then was murdered.

In January 1963 the central government, with UN military aid, took over Katanga province.

Tshombe was invited in 1964 to return from exile to become premier. Fighting intensified in Katanga. In October 1965 Kasavubu replaced Tshombe as premier with Evariste Kimba.

Mobutu, now a general, proclaimed himself president and assumed total power on Nov. 24, 1965. Kimba and other opponents were hanged.

In 1973–74 Zaire confiscated stores and plantations owned by foreigners, and in January 1975 nationalized all industries, building trades, and distribution services.

On March 8, 1977, Katangan rebels invaded Zaire's eastern province of Shaba from Angola. They were defeated in May after Morocco sent 1,500 troops to aid Zaire.

In May 1978 Katangan rebels again invaded Zaire from Angola. Capturing the copper-mining town of Kolwezi, they massacred about 200 whites. French and Belgian paratroops drove out the invaders.

The human rights organization Amnesty International issued a report on May 20, 1980, accusing Mobutu's regime of executing and starving to death hundreds of political prisoners.

The longest and most powerful electric power line in the world was constructed in 1974–81 from the Inga Dam in western Zaire across 1,100 miles of jungle to the copper-mining center of Kolwezi.

Prime Minister Nguza Karl-i-Bond fled to exile in Europe where he resigned on April 16, 1981. He accused Mobutu of taking more than $150 million in government funds for personal use.

Low world-market prices for copper, Zaire's main export product, have crippled the nation's economy since the mid-1970s. Unable to meet payments on its debts of about $6 billion, the government was forced by its foreign creditors to adopt stringent financial measures. The International Monetary Fund on June 22, 1981, granted Zaire a 3-year credit of $1.2 billion.

Israel and Zaire reached agreement in January 1983 on a 5-year military pact to strengthen Zaire's defenses.

Zaire devalued its currency by 80% on Sept. 12, 1983, increasing the price of imports by 80%.

ZAMBIA

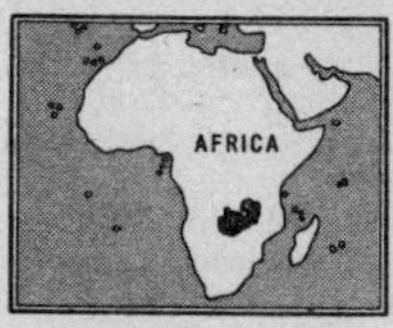

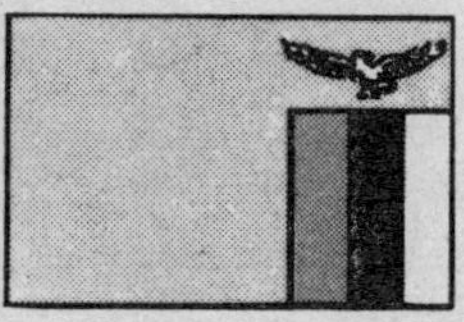

Official Name: Republic of Zambia.
Area: 290,586 square miles (752,614 sq. km.).
Population: 6,309,020.
Chief Cities: Lusaka, capital, 559,000; Kitwe, 325,000; Ndola, 307,000; Chingola, 183,000.
Government: One-party republic.
President: Kenneth D. Kaunda (took office in 1964).
Prime Minister: Nalumino Mundia (since 1981).
Legislature: *National Assembly,* 136 members.
U.S. Ambassador to Zambia: Nicholas Platt.
Zambian Ambassador to U.S.: Putteho Muketoi Ngonda.
Flag: Green field with red, black, and orange bars on right surmounted by eagle.
Languages: English (official), tribal languages, including Bemba, Tnga, Nyanja.
Main Ethnic Group: Black (99%).
Religions: Animism (70%), Christianity (30%).
Leading Industries: Agriculture (corn, tobacco, peanuts, cotton, livestock, fruits, vegetables); mining (copper, cobalt, zinc, lead, coal); manufacturing (textiles, food processing, tobacco products).
Foreign Trade: *Major exports*—copper, lead, zinc, cobalt; *major imports*—machinery, vehicles.
Places of Interest: Victoria Falls; Lake Tanganyika; Zambezi River; Luangwa Valley and Kafue national parks; Lusaka; Maramba Cultural Center and national museum in Livingstone.

ZAMBIA TODAY

Somewhat larger than Texas, Zambia has an abundance of natural resources. It is one of the world's largest producers of copper. It is also an important source of cobalt, zinc, and lead.

The Zambian government obtained a majority interest in previously foreign-owned mining industries in 1970, agreeing to compensate the owners out of future earnings. Since then, the government has financed large-scale agricultural and industrial development projects.

Although Zambia's per capita national income is three to four times that of many of Africa's black nations, most Zambians still are poor farmers who barely raise enough food to live. Only about half the people can read and write.

Most of the country is a plateau of flat, wooded grassland broken by scrub-covered hills and by valleys of the Zambezi and Luangwa rivers.

Landlocked Zambia is surrounded by Zaire, Tanzania, Malawi, Mozambique, Zimbabwe (Rhodesia), Botswana, Namibia, and Angola.

HISTORY

In the 1400s Bantu tribesmen moved into the area from the north.

In the early 1800s Nguni-speaking Africans and Swahili-speaking slave traders arrived.

Explorer David Livingstone first saw Victoria Falls in 1855.

British developer Cecil Rhodes in 1888 obtained mineral rights. The region became known as *Northern Rhodesia*. The British South African Company, developing the copper resources, governed the territory.

In 1924 Northern Rhodesia became a British protectorate. In 1953 Britain founded the Federation of Rhodesia and Nyasaland, transferring control to white-ruled Southern Rhodesia (now Zimbabwe). The federation was dissolved in 1963. Northern Rhodesia then proceeded toward independence under African majority rule.

Zambia, as the new republic was named, became independent within the British Commonwealth of Nations on Oct. 24, 1964. Kenneth Kaunda was elected as Zambia's first president.

A new constitution adopted in 1973 made Kaunda's United National Independence Party (UNIP) the nation's only political party.

On July 1, 1975, President Kaunda decreed the nationalization of privately owned land, movie theaters, private hospitals, and newspapers.

Completion of the 1,162-mile TanZam Railway in 1976, linking Zambia's copper mines with the Tanzanian port of Dar es Salaam, promised increased economic growth.

Faced with a worsening economy, Zambia lifted its trade embargo on neighboring Zimbabwe on Oct. 6, 1978, in order to use its rail lines for trade with Mozambique and South Africa.

Strikes by miners at government-owned copper mines in 1981 prompted Kaunda to arrest four top union leaders in July. The union leaders likened themselves to those of Poland's Solidarity movement in opposing the government's adherence to a one-party socialist state.

Kaunda won reelection as president without opposition on Oct. 27, 1983.

QUICK QUIZ: What is the meaning of the term *aphasia*? See page 455.

ZIMBABWE

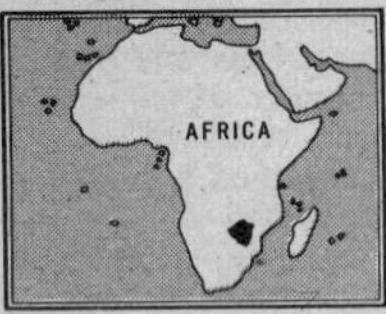

Official Name: Republic of Zimbabwe.
Area: 150,804 square miles (390,580 sq. km.).
Population: 7,905,410.
Chief Cities: Harare (Salisbury), capital, 633,000; Bulawayo, 366,000.
Government: Parliamentary democracy.
Prime Minister: Robert Mugabe (since 1980).
President: Rev. Canaan Banana (since 1980).
Parliament: *House of Assembly,* 100 members (80 black, 20 white); *Senate,* 40 members.
U.S. Ambassador to Zimbabwe: Robert V. Keeley.
Zimbabwe Ambassador to U.S.: Edmond O. Z. Chipamaunga.
Flag: Zimbabwe bird on red star in white triangle at hoist; stripes, top to bottom, of green, gold, red, black, red, gold, and green.
Languages: English (official), Shona, Ndebele.
Main Ethnic Groups: Blacks (96%), European descent (4%).
Religions: Animism, Anglicanism, Presbyterianism, Roman Catholicism.
Leading Industries: Agriculture (corn, tobacco, sugarcane, cotton, wheat, tea, millet, sorghum, livestock, vegetables, fruits); mining (coal, chrome, asbestos, gold, copper); manufacturing (electricity, clothing, chemicals, steel, vehicles, petroleum products).
Foreign Trade: *Major exports*—maize, tobacco, asbestos, copper, clothing, meat; *major imports*—textiles, fertilizers, automobiles, petroleum, tobacco.
Places of Interest: Victoria Falls; Wankie National Park; Inyanga and Vumba mountains; Mana pools; Harare (Salisbury); Bulawayo; Zimbabwe ruins.

ZIMBABWE TODAY

Formerly called Rhodesia, Zimbabwe won international recognition as an independent nation in 1980. After 15 years in which a white minority resisted world pressure and guerrilla warfare to retain control of the government, a peaceful transition to black majority rule was achieved.

The new black government pledged itself to protect the rights of whites, who have enjoyed a standard of living comparable to that of Americans. At the same time it sought massive international aid to improve the lot of blacks, most of whom live as tribal subsistence farmers. Fewer than 1 black in 3 can read and write.

One of the leading gold-mining countries, Zimbabwe lies between the Limpopo and Zambezi rivers. Mt. Inyangani, on the eastern border, rises to 8,514 feet. Zambia is on the north, Mozambique on the east, South Africa on the south, and Botswana on the west.

EARLY HISTORY

The name Zimbabwe comes from the stone ruins of a city built by a black civilization in the 1000s to 1400s.

In the 1890s the British South Africa Company of Cecil Rhodes acquired the area.

In 1923 the British government took over the region, calling the colony Southern Rhodesia.

Britain refused independence to Southern Rhodesia in 1964 unless representative government was assured for the black majority.

In the 1965 elections the Rhodesia Front, representing white nationalism, won an overwhelming victory, retaining in office Ian Smith, who had been prime minister since 1964.

INDEPENDENCE

On Nov. 11, 1965, Southern Rhodesia declared independence from Britain. Britain and other nations refused to grant diplomatic recognition because the all-white government restricted the rights of blacks. The United Nations in 1966 called for a trade embargo on Rhodesia. The U.S. joined in the trade boycott.

All ties between Britain and Rhodesia were severed on March 2, 1970, when the government proclaimed itself the *Republic of Rhodesia.*

Black guerrillas fought government troops and civilians from 1965 to 1979.

On March 3, 1978, the Rhodesian government signed an agreement with leaders of the United African National Council (UANC) providing for a transitional government leading to black majority rule. The head of the UANC, American-educated Methodist Bishop Abel Muzorewa, joined Smith's government.

In a national election on April 17–21, 1979, 1.7 million blacks voted for the first time, giving 51 parliamentary seats to Muzorewa's UANC party. On May 29, 1979, Muzorewa became the nation's first black prime minister.

Under the leadership of Lord Carrington, Britain's foreign minister, Muzorewa and guerrilla leaders signed a peace agreement on Dec. 21, 1979, after a conference in London. A cease-fire went into effect on Dec. 28, 1979.

In an election on Feb. 27–29, the Zanu-Patriotic Front party of former guerrilla leader Robert Mugabe won control of parliament with 57 of the 80 seats reserved for blacks.

Britain formally recognized independence for the Republic of Zimbabwe on April 18, 1980, with Mugabe, a Marxist socialist, as prime minister. Mugabe formed a coalition government that included Joshua Nkomo, a former guerrilla leader who was Mugabe's main rival.

Despite Mugabe's assurances of protection, whites continued to leave the country, some 90,000 emigrating in 1980–83.

To display opposition to South Africa's apartheid policy, Zimbabwe broke diplomatic relations on Sept. 3, 1980. But because of economic dependence on South Africa, trade relations continued.

On Feb. 17, 1982, Mugabe dismissed Nkomo from his cabinet, accusing him of plotting to overthrow the government. Later, Mugabe announced that he planned to convert Zimbabwe into a one-party state and to eliminate private enterprise. After Nkomo's ouster from the cabinet, the nation experienced increasing violence between Mugabe's armed forces and Nkomo's followers. Several foreign tourists were kidnapped and killed.

Faced with a deteriorating economy, Mugabe in 1983 cut social programs and increased taxes.

Former prime minister Bishop Abel Muzorewa was imprisoned on Oct. 31, 1983, on charges of "clandestine" activities after he returned from a visit to Israel.

Newspapers and Magazines

Wide World

A child peers from behind a post at a refugee camp in El Salvador in photo by *Dallas Times-Herald* photographer James B. Dickman. It is part of a series that won him the 1983 Pulitzer Prize for feature photography.

HIGHLIGHTS: 1983

NEWSPAPERS SHOW GAINS

Daily newspaper circulation in the U.S. reached an all-time high of 62,487,177 for the six-month period ending Sept. 30, 1982, a gain of 1.7% in average circulation over the same period in 1981. There were 1,711 daily newspapers at the end of 1982, a loss of 19 from the year before.

Other figures compiled by the *Editor & Publisher International Yearbook* in 1983 showed a total of 434 morning newspapers, with a circulation of 33,275,087. The number of newspapers that publish all day increased from 30 to 33 during 1972, but the number of afternoon papers dropped from 1,352 to 1,310.

Sunday newspapers continued to show increases as circulation jumped to 56,260,764 for the 768 Sunday editions.

USA TODAY TOPS MILLION CIRCULATION

The nation's newest general-interest daily newspaper, *USA TODAY*, announced in April that it had reached an audited average daily net paid circulation of 1,109,587. The figure, certified for the week ending April 15 by the independent auditing firm of Price Waterhouse & Co., made *USA TODAY* the third-largest circulation daily newspaper in the nation, after the *Wall Street Journal* and *New York Daily News.*

The paper began publication in September 1982 and quickly became popular, with special praise from readers for its extensive sports coverage. The paper's generous use of color pictures, maps, and charts, as well as its full-page weather forecasting contributed to its quick acceptance by readers.

USA TODAY has been criticized for its preponderance of news capsules, rather than in-depth articles. In an interview marking the paper's first anniversary in September 1983, editor John C. Quinn defended its journalistic style, saying, "Life is a lot of little paragraphs." Allen H. Neuharth, president of the Gannett Company, which owns the paper, said that although the first year's losses were substantial, he hoped it would be profitable by 1987.

HITLER DIARIES FOUND TO BE FAKES

In April the West German magazine *Stern* announced the discovery of previously unknown diaries of Adolf Hitler. The 60

HIGHLIGHTS: 1983 *(continued)*

volumes were said to cover the years 1932–45 and were reported to have been the object of a 3-year search by *Stern* reporter Gerd Heidemann, 51, of Hamburg.

The diaries supposedly were on board a plane that crashed near Bornersdorf, East Germany, at the end of World War II. *Stern* claimed its investigators located the grave of the pilot and found the diaries in a nearby hayloft.

Heidemann arranged the sale to *Stern* through Konrad Fischer, a Stuttgart dealer in Nazi memorabilia, also known as Konrad Kujau. *Stern* reportedly paid more than $3 million for the books, then sold the publishing rights to the *Times of London* for $400,000.

Both publications claimed to have verified the authenticity of the diaries, but upon publication of the first excerpts on April 25, world skepticism resulted in closer examination.

On May 6 the West German government announced that the volumes were forgeries on the basis of chemical tests proving the type of paper used had not been available until 1955, ten years after Hitler's death. Authorities also claimed that much of the editorial content apparently had been taken from a book, *Hitler: Speeches and Proclamations—1932–1945,* which had been put together and published privately by Max Domarus in 1963.

Fraud charges were filed against both Kujau and Heidemann, who also had been fired from the magazine. Red-faced *Stern* officials quickly reorganized their editorial staff.

CHICAGO SUN-TIMES SOLD

Australian newspaper executive Rupert K. Murdoch announced Nov. 1 that he had purchased the *Chicago Sun-Times* and its Field Newspaper Syndicate for $90 million from Marshall Field 5th and his half-brother, Frederick, who are dissolving family-owned Field Enterprises. Murdoch outbid *Sun-Times* publisher James Hoge and a group of Chicago investors.

The new owner, whose other newspaper acquisitions include the *New York Post, Boston Herald, San Antonio Express,* and *The Village Voice,* said he would try to maintain the "high standards" of the *Sun-Times.*

WASHINGTON POST LIBEL VERDICT REVERSED

On May 2, 1983, a federal judge in Washington, D.C., overturned a 1982 libel verdict against the *Washington Post* and threw out a jury award of $2.05 million to the president of the Mobil Oil Corporation.

In the 1982 trial, Mobil president William P. Tavoulareas convinced a jury that an article printed on Nov. 30, 1979, alleging he had used his considerable influence and money to help establish his son, Peter, in a shipping business, was published with the reporters' knowledge that it was false.

In the May decision, Judge Oliver Gasch said he found no evidence of "actual malice."

Wide World

Hans Booms, president of the West German Federal Archives, holds up a volume of the alleged Hitler diaries at a press conference on May 6. His office, in cooperation with the West German Federal Criminal Office, established that the diaries were fakes. Booms also holds the book, *Hitler: Speeches and Proclamations—1932–1945,* by Max Domarus, from which the diaries allegedly were copied.

NEWSPAPER AND MAGAZINE AWARDS: 1983

In addition to awards listed below, see the Pulitzer Prizes on pages 78–85.

NEWSPAPER GUILD HEYWOOD BROUN AWARD

The annual Heywood Broun Award of the Newspaper Guild is named after the Guild's founder and first president.

Stephen R. Morin, of the *Providence (R.I.) Journal Bulletin,* received a check and citation for a series of articles about abused children.

GEORGE POLK AWARDS

The George Polk Awards, sponsored by Long Island University (New York) to honor the memory of a CBS correspondent killed in Greece in 1948, included:

Foreign Reporting: Thomas L. Friedman and David K. Shipler, *New York Times,* for coverage of the war in Lebanon.

National Reporting: Richard Halloran, *New York Times,* for series of articles on the Pentagon's strategy for a nuclear war.

Regional Reporting: Jim Henderson, *Dallas Times Herald,* for "Racism in the South," a series of articles documenting conditions persisting for blacks today, particularly in rural areas.

Local Reporting: David Johnston and Joel Sappell, *Los Angeles Times,* for series of investigative reports on activities of the Public Disorders Intelligence Division of the Los Angeles Police Department.

Metropolitan Reporting: Doug Cumming, *Providence Journal Bulletin,* for series "Ticket to Ride, the Commuter Airlines," that examines emergence of new air carriers as result of federal deregulation of airline industry.

Magazine Reporting: Roger Rosenblatt, *Time Magazine,* for "Children of War," a portrait of youngsters in five war-torn nations.

Financial Reporting: Phillip L. Zweig, *American Banker,* for reports on the collapse of Penn Square Bank."

Criticism: Stanley Kauffman, *New Republic,* for his film reviews.

News Photography: Robby Castro, Associated Press, for his photograph of an Israeli soldier extending a canteen to a wounded Syrian soldier in Lebanon.

Special Award: Rod Nordland, *Philadelphia Inquirer,* for articles depicting the plight of people of East Timor, Vietnam, and Cambodia.

U.S. DAILY NEWSPAPERS

Source: *Editor & Publisher*

YEAR	NO.	CIRCULATION	YEAR	NO.	CIRCULATION
1945	1,749	48,384,188	1973	1,774	63,147,280
1950	1,772	53,829,000	1974	1,768	61,877,197
1955	1,760	56,147,000	1975	1,756	60,655,431
1960	1,763	58,882,000	1976	1,762	60,977,011
1965	1,751	60,358,000	1977	1,753	61,495,140
1968	1,752	62,535,000	1978	1,756	61,989,997
1969	1,758	62,060,000	1979	1,763	62,223,040
1970	1,748	62,108,000	1980	1,745	62,201,840
1971	1,749	61,743,141	1981	1,730	61,432,434
1972	1,761	62,510,242	1982	1,711	62,487,177

OVERSEAS PRESS CLUB AWARDS

The annual awards presented by the Overseas Press Club for distinguished reporting and interpretation of foreign affairs included:

Daily Newspaper or Wire Service Reporting from Abroad: Walter Wisniewski and Jack Redden, United Press International, for "Massacre in Beirut."

Daily Newspaper or Wire Service Interpretation of Foreign Affairs (Bob Considine Memorial Award): Joseph Kingsbury Smith, Hearst Newspapers, for "Exclusive Interview with Yuri Andropov."

Robert Capa Gold Medal for Photography: Harry Mattison, *Time Magazine,* for "El Salvador."

Photographic Reporting from Abroad: Eli Reed, *San Francisco Examiner,* for photographs of Central America.

Magazine Photographic Reporting from Abroad: Bill Pierce, *Time Magazine,* for his entitled photographs.

Magazine Reporting from Abroad: *Newsweek,* for "Mideast Coverage."

Magazine Interpretation of Foreign Affairs: *Time Magazine,* for "After Brezhnev."

Cartoon on Foreign Affairs: Richard Locher, *Chicago Tribune,* for editorial cartoons.

Business News Reporting from Abroad: Larry Gurwin, *Institutional Investor,* for "Death of a Banker."

International Reporting (Any Media) Demonstrating Concern for Humanity: Walt Bogdanich, Joe Frolik, and Christopher Jensen, *The Plain Dealer,* for "In the Name of Charity."

NATIONAL MAGAZINE AWARDS

Sponsored by the American Society of Magazine Editors and administered by the Columbia University Graduate School of Journalism:

General Excellence: "To *Life* for its . . . varied and skillful blend of words and pictures, which captures the world in all its anguish, splendor and humor. . . ."

General Excellence: "To *Science '82* for its superior combination of versatility, good writing and editing, and effective graphics."

General Excellence: "To *Harper's* for exploring subjects of serious intellectual content and lasting value, and writing about them with skepticism, verve, and humor."

General Excellence: "To *Louisiana Life* for its masterful weave of design and content, and writing that is graceful and exuberant."

Essays and Criticism: "To *The American Lawyer* for "Headnotes" by Steven Brill."

Fiction: "To *North American Review* for . . . combining good literature with fascinating social comment."

Reporting Excellence: "To *Institutional Investor* for "Drysdale: What Really Happened?"

Public Service: "To *Foreign Affairs* for "Nuclear Weapons and the Atlantic Alliance."

Single-Topic Issue: "To *IEEE Spectrum* for "Technology in War and Peace."

Service to the Individual: "To *Sunset* for "Fish Market Revolution."

U.S. DAILY NEWSPAPER CIRCULATION LEADERS: 1982

NEWSPAPER (M) Morning (E) Evening (A) All-day	CIRCULATION Daily	Weekend or Sunday	NEWSPAPER (M) Morning (E) Evening (A) All-day	CIRCULATION Daily	Weekend or Sunday
New York Daily News (M)	1,544,101	1,986,151	Milwaukee Journal (E)	307,112	517,505
Wall Street Journal (M)	1,925,722	—	Atlanta Journal (M)	210,793	507,089
New York Times (M)	905,675	1,498,873	Houston Chronicle (A)	419,869	502,654
Los Angeles Times (M)	1,052,637	1,306,002	Miami Herald (M)	416,512	502,093
Chicago Tribune (A)	758,255	1,101,615	Cleveland Plain Dealer (M)	457,531	482,038
Philadelphia Inquirer (M)	561,018	1,031,321	St. Louis Post-Dispatch (E)	235,521	438,857
Washington (D.C.) Post (M)	726,009	971,957	Houston Post (M)	376,455	436,659
New York Post (A)	960,120	618,278	Portland Oregonian (A)	308,164	403,385
Detroit News (A)	642,531	843,580	Arizona Republic (M)	264,379	398,734
Detroit Free Press (M)	631,989	771,083	Dallas News (M)	317,279	389,855
Boston Globe (A)	510,978	750,308	Kansas City Star (M)	284,966	387,235
San Francisco Chronicle (M)	537,621	680,843	Baltimore Sun (M)	183,188	377,183
Chicago Sun-Times (M)	651,579	677,681	Des Moines Register (M)	265,914	371,542
Pittsburgh Press	259,850	606,053	Indianapolis Star (M)	225,148	370,356
Newark (N.J.) Star Ledger (M)	424,224	604,986	Denver Post (M)	256,257	358,265
Minneapolis Tribune (M)	362,505	577,645	Dallas Times Herald (A)	269,409	355,753
Newsday, Garden City, N.Y. (E)	515,728	576,906	Rocky Mountain News (M)	321,693	346,886
U.S.A. Today (M)	531,438	—	Seattle Times (A)	253,969	340,444

CANADIAN DAILY NEWSPAPER CIRCULATION LEADERS: 1982

Toronto Star (A)	486,265	791,564	Winnipeg Free Press (E)	177,863	237,749
Toronto Sun (M)	252,394	425,838	Ottawa Citizen (E)	178,609	224,898
Toronto Globe and Mail (M)	330,364	—	Edmonton Journal (E)	172,570	213,916
Le Journal de Montreal (M)	297,836	309,630	Calgary Herald (E)	149,837	184,156
Montreal, The Gazette (M)	203,485	277,044	Vancouver Province (M)	131,658	160,580
Montreal, La Presse (E)	182,065	275,018	Hamilton Spectator (E)	147,227	147,227
Vancouver Sun (E)	228,185	272,186	Quebec, La Soleil (E)	119,185	133,415

NEW U.S. DAILY NEWSPAPERS: 1982-83

Jenkintown (PA) Montgomery County Record
Kialua-Kona (HI) West Hawaii Today
Lihue (HI) Garden Island
Murfreesboro (TN) Morning Press
Pinole (CA) West County Times
Washington (D.C.) Times
Washington (D.C.) U.S.A. Today

MERGED AND SUSPENDED U.S. DAILY NEWSPAPERS: 1982-83

Beverly (MA) Times merged with Peabody (MA) Times
Buffalo (NY) Courier-Express (suspended)
Cleveland (OH) Press (suspended)
Des Moines (IA) Tribune merged with Des Moines Register
Duluth (MN) Herald merged with Duluth News-Tribune
Geneva (OH) Star-Beacon (suspended)
Lexington (KY) Herald merged with Lexington Leader
Little Falls (MN) Transcript merged with St. Cloud Times
Macon (GA) Telegraph merged with The (Macon) News
Minneapolis (MN) Star merged with Minneapolis Tribune
Monroeville (PA) Tribune merged with Greensburg Tribune Review
Oakland (CA) East Bay Today merged with Oakland Tribune
Orland (CA) Register (suspended)
Portland (OR) Journal merged with Portland Oregonian
Sarasota (FL) Journal merged with Sarasota Herald-Tribune
Spartanburg (SC) Herald merged with Spartanburg Journal
Springfield (OH) Sun merged with Springfield News
Sylacauga (AL) Advance merged with Talladega Home
Tampa (FL) Tribune merged with Tampa Times
Waseca (MN) Journal (suspended)
White Plains (NY) Today (suspended)

U.S. MAGAZINE CIRCULATION LEADERS: 1982

Source: Magazine Publishers Association

MAGAZINE	CIRCULATION	MAGAZINE	CIRCULATION	MAGAZINE	CIRCULATION
Reader's Digest	17,900,290	Penthouse	3,775,016	Popular Science	1,858,649
TV Guide	17,003,698	Newsweek	3,024,503	The Workbasket	1,774,258
National Geographic	10,613,599	Scholastic Magazine	2,948,221	Parents	1,647,258
Modern Maturity	8,328,199	Cosmopolitan	2,926,060	The Elks Magazine	1,638,386
Better Homes & Gardens	8,088,226	People	2,671,045	Popular Mechanics	1,612,351
		Prevention	2,555,030	Mechanix Illustrated	1,600,433
AARP News Bulletin	7,723,715	American Legion Magazine	2,533,358	True Story	1,592,529
Family Circle	7,400,984			Outdoor Life	1,537,015
Woman's Day	6,932,355	Sports Illustrated	2,360,025	Seventeen	1,523,594
McCall's	6,267,469	Globe	2,206,717	Boys' Life	1,467,365
Good Housekeeping	5,489,934	Senior Scholastic Unit.	2,163,070	Changing Times	1,459,281
Ladies Home Journal	5,134,649	U.S. News & World Report	2,157,978	Life	1,456,937
National Enquirer	5,119,382	Southern Living	2,141,289	Sunset	1,429,685
Playboy	4,501,324	Glamour	2,119,242	Adventure Road	1,423,524
Time	4,464,228	Field & Stream	2,035,211	Ebony	1,416,027
The Star	4,008,247	Smithsonian	1,954,750	Motorland	1,353,820
Redbook	3,864,417	V.F.W. Magazine	1,879,699		

People in the News

United Press Int'l.

Samantha Smith, 11, looks over a Bulgarian newspaper sent to her in July because it contained a story about her upcoming visit to the Soviet Union at the invitation of Soviet President Yuri V. Andropov. The Manchester, Maine, sixth-grader had written to Andropov earlier in the year asking why the Soviet Union wanted to conquer the world. She received a personal reply from Andropov saying the Soviets wanted peace and inviting her and her parents to visit. The Smith family spent two weeks in July touring the Soviet Union, but did not meet Andropov, though they were accorded red-carpet treatment. Samantha came home convinced the Soviet people want peace.

WOMEN IN THE NEWS

French author and philosopher **Simone de Beauvoir** received the 1983 Sonning Prize for European culture. . . . First Lady **Nancy Reagan** presented to actress **Shelley Bruce,** 17, the 1983 Courage Award from the Volunteer Crusade Leaders of the American Cancer Society. The teenage actress, known for her role as Annie on Broadway, was treated for leukemia.

Barbara Bush wife of Vice President George Bush, received the Woman of Achievement award in June from the Girls Club of New York. . . . In March, Mrs. Bush was named Woman of the Year by the Women's National Republican Club. . . . **Barbara Sinatra,** wife of singer Frank Sinatra, received the fifth annual Scopus Award from the Palm Springs, Calif., chapter of American Friends of Hebrew University for her fund-raising efforts for the American Cancer Society, Hadassah, and the world Mercy fund.

In May, **Katharine Fanning,** editor and publisher of the *Anchorage* (Alaska) *Daily News,* became the first woman editor of the *Christian Science Monitor*. . . . **Dana Connors,** 22, daughter of actor Mike Connors, was named queen of the 1983 Shenandoah Apple Blossom Festival in Winchester, Va. . . . **Lorene Alison Stokes,** daughter of Rep. Louis Stokes (D-Ohio) became the first black queen of the International Azalea Festival in Norfolk, Va.

The National Mother's Day Committee named nine women to receive Outstanding Mothers Awards in 1983. They included **Sen. Paula Hawkins** (R-Fla.), actresses **Ellen Burstyn** and **Joan Bennett,** TV reporter **Carol Martin,** singer **Barbara Mandrell,** writer **Cathy Spellman, Dr. Adelaide Scanlon,** musician **Eugenia Zukerman,** and **Matilda Cuomo,** wife of New York **Gov. Mario Cuomo.**

Editors of *Harper's Bazaar* chose as America's ten most beautiful women actresses **Karen Allen, Rachel Ward, Joan Collins, Jaclyn Smith, Jane Seymour, Jennifer Beals, Victoria Principal, Twiggy,** singer **Crystal Gayle,** and model **Shari Belafonte-Harper**. ... Puppeteer **Shari Lewis** received the Kennedy Center award for excellence for her work with children and young people. ... Actress **Bette Davis** received the Defense Department's Distinguished Public Service Medal for her "dedicated, continuing support of the American armed forces."

Fashion designer **Richard Blackwell** issued his 23d list of the Worst Dressed Women in January. Heading the list was Britain's **Princess Diana,** followed by actresses **Bonnie Franklin** and **Victoria Principal,** singer **Bette Midler,** actress **Charlene Tilton, Christina Onassis, Princess Yasmin Khan,** golfer **Jan Stephenson,** and TV star **Cathy Lee Crosby.** Tied for tenth were Houston **Mayor Kathy Whitmire** and **Dustin Hoffman** in his title role in the film *Tootsie.*

Singer **Diana Ross** received the Woman of the Year award from the Children's Diabetes Foundation. ... U.S. Treasurer **Angela Buchanan,** after giving birth to a son in January, became the first woman to hold the position and give birth while in office. She later resigned her office and was succeeded by **Katharine D. Ortega.** ... President Reagan signed a bill in February naming the Old Post Office building complex as the Nancy Hanks Center, in memory of the late Nancy Hanks, former chairman of the National Endowment for the Arts.

Actress-singer **Olivia Newton-John** was chosen 1983 Style Maker of the Year by the National Hairdressers and Cosmetologists Association. ... Actress **Lynda Carter** was honored as Hispanic Woman of the Year by the Hispanic Women's Council at a dinner in Beverly Hills, Calif.

Actress and model **Brooke Shields** entered Princeton University in September with pleas than she be treated "like any other student." The 18-year-old was assigned to a double room in a dormitory with another freshman from Pennsylvania as her roommate.

LIFE AMONG THE ENTERTAINERS

Actor **Laurence Olivier** was honored in April by the Film Society of Lincoln Center for his 50 years of acting. Film luminaries **George C. Scott, Jean Simmons, Christopher Plummer, Maureen Stapleton, Charlton Heston,** and **Tony Curtis** were among the many who paid tribute to the 75-year-old Lord Olivier. ... In March film director, writer, actor **John Huston,** received the American Film Institute's

Shirley Temple, 55, and Buddy Ebsen, 75, who appeared together in *Captain January* in 1936, renew acquaintance on ABC-TV's *Good Morning America,* as part of the show's week-long series of movie reunions.

United Press Int'l.

Life Achievement Award.

The Harvard Hasty Pudding Club named *E.T.* director **Steven Spielberg** its Man of the Year, while actress and singer **Julie Andrews** was named Woman of the Year by the same organization.

Art director **Gene Allen,** co-winner of a 1964 Oscar for art direction for *My Fair Lady,* was elected president of the Academy of Motion Picture Arts and Sciences in August. . . . Actresses **Marie Windsor** and **Beverly Garland** were honored with stars in the Hollywood Walk of Fame. . . . **Frank Sinatra** received a lifetime gold union card from the Las Vegas Bartender's Union at Caesar's Palace, as well as a special bar stool inscribed with his name. . . . In January, Sinatra was honored as Convention Man of the Year, also in Las Vegas.

In February, singer **Liza Minnelli** broke a lifelong custom and publicly sang two songs made famous by her late mother, **Judy Garland,** at an 80th birthday tribute to her father, director **Vincente Minnelli.** . . . Musicians **Isaac Stern** and **Zubin Mehta** received the Joseph Prize for Human Rights at the annual B'nai B'rith Anti-Defamation League dinner.

Singer **Eddie Fisher,** 54, was inducted into the George C. Thomas Junior High School's Hall of Fame, his alma mater. The Philadelphia school's list of graduates also includes singers **Fabian** and **James Darren.** . . . Fisher's ex-wife **Debbie Reynolds** received a standing ovation in March when she appeared on stage in *Woman of the Year,* arriving directly from her hospital bed only three days after she collapsed on stage from exhaustion. In August, their daughter, actress **Carrie Fisher,** married songwriter **Paul Simon.** Simon and partner **Art Garfunkel** toured together during the summer for the first time in 13 years.

Country music star **Willie Nelson** received a lifetime achievement award from the Songwriters Hall of Fame in March. Inducted into the hall of fame were **Neil Sedaka, Stevie Wonder, John Kander, Fred Ebb, Hugh Martin,** and **Ralph Blane.** . . . At the National Film Society's "Hollywood on Broadway" convention in September, **James Cagney** received the Golden Screen award, **Joan Bennett** and **Sylvia Sidney** received Artistry in Cinema awards, **Mildred Natwick** received the Classic Screen award, and **Gwen Verdon** was honored with the third annual Ellie award, named for Eleanor Powell.

Five artists received 1983 Kennedy Center Honors awards for lifetime achievement in December. They included singer **Frank Sinatra,** actor **James Stewart,** director **Elia Kazan,** composer and music critic **Virgil Thomson,** and dancer and choreographer **Katherine Dunham.** . . . Composer **Andrew Lloyd Webber,** 35, paid $2 million for London's Palace theater in hopes of restoring the 92-year-old landmark in London's West End section.

United Press Int'l.

Jane Powell stands next to Roseland Ballroom's "Wall of Fame" as she prepares to donate to the New York ballroom's permanent display the shoes she wore when she danced with Fred Astaire in *Royal Wedding.*

Male stars **Tom Selleck, Sylvester Stallone, Patrick Duffy, George Hamilton,** and **Rick Springfield** won "Best-Looking Hair" awards in Redken Laboratories first national men's hair-styling poll of more than 20,000 hair stylists and barbers around the nation. . . . *M*A*S*H* stars **Alan Alda, Mike Farrell,** and **William Christopher** attended a ceremony at the Smithsonian's National Museum of American History in July in which two sets and various memorabalia and photos were presented to the museum as part of an exhibition called "*M*A*S*H:* Binding Up the Wounds," in honor of the popular TV series.

Soon after they met on the set of the TV mini-series *The Thorn Birds,* actress **Rachel Ward** and Australian actor **Bryan Brown** were married in England. . . . Actor and director **Michael Landon** married **Cindy Clerico,** a former makeup artist he met on the set of *Little House on the Prairie.* . . . Actor **Harrison Ford** married screenwriter **Melissa**

Matheson. . . . Actor **Richard Dreyfuss** married TV actress and producer **Jeramie Rain.** . . . **Richard Burton** took former British TV production assistant **Sally Hay** as his fifth wife. . . . Comedian **Jerry Lewis** married dancer **Sandee Pitnick** less than two months after successfully undergoing double heart bypass surgery. . . . Actor **John Schneider** married former Miss America **Tawny Godin Little.**

Actress **Terry Moore,** who claimed she had legally married **Howard Hughes** aboard ship in 1949 and that her marriage was never dissolved, reached a settlement of "not more than eight figures" with the family of the late billionaire. Although she lost in several courts, the case was on appeal before the Nevada Supreme Court when the settlement was reached.

A Santa Monica, Calif., jury decided in March that late comedian **Groucho Marx** was defrauded by companion **Erin Fleming** during their six-year relationship. Jurors awarded $221,000 in compensatory damages and $250,000 in punitive damages to Bank of America, executor of the Marx estate. During the 10-week trial, a parade of friends of the late Marx testified that there was love between him and Miss Fleming, but the jury upheld the bank's charge that she had "exerted undue influence" on the elderly comedian to obtain money and gifts.

Isaac Dworetsky, a World War II bomber pilot who earned a straight A average while holding down two jobs, tips his cap after receiving a standing ovation for his speech as class valedictorian on June 11 at Bronx (N.Y.) Community College.

Wide World

STATESMEN, POLITICIANS, OTHERS

President Reagan presented the Presidential Medal of Freedom to 12 Americans in February. The recipients included choreographer **George Balanchine**, novelist and playwright **Clare Booth Luce,** historian **James Burnham,** president of Howard University **James Cheek,** evangelist **Billy Graham,** historian **Dumas Malone,** song stylist **Mabel Mercer,** aerospace pioneer **Simon Ramo,** former **Sen.** (R-N.Y.) **Jacob K. Javits,** architect **R. Buckminster Fuller,** philosopher **Eric Hoffer,** and University of Alabama football coach **Paul W. (Bear) Bryant.** The award to Bryant, who died Jan. 26, 1983, was presented posthumously. **Eric Hoffer** died in May 1983, and **R. Buckminster Fuller** died July 1.

The International Platform Association elected five new members to its Orators Hall of Fame in July. Honorees were **William Jennings Bryan, Gen. Douglas MacArthur,** Illinois **Gov. Adlai Stevenson, President John F. Kennedy,** and former Israeli foreign minister **Abba Eban.**

A survey of historians rated five U.S. Presidents as failures, according to **Prof. Robert K. Murray** of Pennsylvania State University. He announced in February that 970 historians who responded to his questionnaire concluded that the nation's greatest leaders were **Abraham Lincoln, Franklin D. Roosevelt, George Washington** and **Thomas Jefferson** but that at the bottom of the list were **Warren G. Harding, Ulysses S. Grant, Richard M. Nixon, Andrew Johnson,** and **James Buchanan.**

Readers of *US* magazine chose **Princess Diana** of Wales and **Pope John Paul II** the world's best-liked man and woman. . . . The American Optometric Association declared that the most distinctive eyes of 1983 belonged to **Lucille Ball, William F. Buckley Jr., Rodney Dangerfield, Lena Horne, Angela Lansbury, Dolly Parton, Vincent Price, Sissy Spacek, Donald Sutherland,** and **Ben Vereen.**

The Lefthanders International Organization named actress **Goldie Hawn** as Lefthander of the Year as well as Lefthanded Female Entertainer of the Year. **Michael Landon** was named Lefthanded Male Entertainer of the Year and singer **Crystal Gayle** as Lefthanded Musician of the Year. Also

Wide World

Wearing the traditional high hats of chimney sweeps, Mike Warren, *left*, of Elgin, Ill., and Fred Toldo, of Mystic, Conn., get together at the convention of the National Chimney Sweep Guild at St. Louis, Mo., in April. Warren, 14, was the youngest member of the organization, while Toldo, 66, was the oldest sweep attending the meeting.

among lefthanders honored were **Vice President George Bush** as Public Figure of the Year.

Producer-director **Sir Richard Attenborough** and **Dr. Martin Luther King Sr.** were named 1983 recipients of the Martin Luther King Jr. Nonviolent Peace Prize in January. ... **Blake Giddens,** 14, of Alamogordo, N.M., won the 56th Annual Scripps-Howard National Spelling Bee in Washington, D.C., in June, by correctly spelling *ratatouille* and *Purim.*

John F. Kennedy Jr., son of the late President, graduated from Brown University in June. He was awarded a bachelor's degree in history. ... **Ron Reagan,** son of **President Reagan,** resigned from the Joffrey Ballet Company in January in order to pursue other interests.

The ten sexiest men in America, according to the September issue of *Playgirl* magazine, are entertainers **Bob Hope, David Bowie, Ted Danson, Eddie Murphy,** newscaster **Frank Gifford, Vice President George Bush,** music director **Zubin Mehta,** New Jersey **Sen. Bill Bradley,** and Los Angeles Dodger **Greg Brock.** ... *Playboy Fashion Magazine's* third annual best-dressed included **Sen. John Heinz** (R-Pa.), actors **John Forsythe, Tom Selleck,** and **Harrison Ford,** boxer **Gerry Cooney,** comedian **Bill Cosby,** TV personalities **Doc Severinsen** and **Bryant Gumbel,** author **John Irving,** and Britain's **Prince Andrew.**

Britain's **Prince William** celebrated his first birthday June 21, but without the presence of his parents. **Prince Charles** and **Princess Diana** were on a trip in Canada on the big day, but planned to have a big celebration on their return in early July. Earlier in the year, the baby prince accompanied his parents on a five-week tour of Australia and New Zealand.

Five years after they took part in a civil ceremony, **Prince** and **Princess Michael of Kent** renewed their wedding vows in a Catholic service on July 29. **Prince Michael,** brother to the **Duke of Kent,** married the **Baroness Marie-Christine von Reibnitz** in Vienna, Austria, in 1978, but although the bride's previous marriage had been annulled, dispensation from the church was withheld because Prince Michael intended to have the children brought up as members of the Church of England so they would not forfeit their right of succession to the British throne. The recognition of the marriage came after the birth of two children and a five-year campaign by the princess to have her marriage sanctioned by the Roman Catholic Church.

On the 50th anniversary of the inauguration of **President Franklin D. Roosevelt,** the Roosevelt Freedom Medal was awarded to five honorees at a ceremony at St. James Church in Hyde Park, N.Y., where Roosevelt served as senior deacon. Awards were presented March 4 to former New York **Gov. W. Averell Harriman,** former **Sen. Jacob Javits, Coretta Scott King,** former Secretary of Defense **Robert S. McNamara,** and civil-rights authority **Joseph L. Rauh Jr.**

Poets **Anthony Hecht** of Rochester, N.Y., and **John Hollander** of New Haven, Conn., were awarded Yale University's Bollingen Prize in Poetry for 1983. . . . **Jaroslav Pelikan,** Sterling professor of history at Yale University, was selected by the National Endowment for the Humanities to deliver the 1983 Jefferson Lecture in the Humanities. The lectureship, along with a $10,000 stipend, is the highest honor conferred by the federal government for outstanding achievement in the humanities. . . . The **Rev. Aloysius Schwartz,** 53, an American priest who ran a home for orphans in South Korea after the Korean War, was named winner of the 1983 Magasaysay Award for International Understanding. . . . South African black leader **Nelson Mandela** and **King Juan Carlos** of Spain were named to receive the first $25,000 Simón Bolívar Prize by UNESCO on July 24. . . . **James Schuyler** won the $10,000 Academy of American Poets Fellowship for "distinguished poetic achievement."

The American Institute for Public Service honored nine people for their achievements in public service in July. Those receiving the 11th annual Jefferson Awards were actor **Kirk Douglas,** Federal Reserve Board chairman **Paul A. Volcker,** actress **Helen Hayes, Jan Scruggs,** founder of the Vietnam Veterans Memorial Fund, **Dean Crisp** of Ashevill, N.C., **Darlene Handley** of Chicago, Ill., **Dr. Robert Kustra** of Franklin, Wis., **Candy Lightner** of Fair Oaks, Calif., and **Tony Messineo** of St. Louis, Mo.

Walter H. Annenberg, former ambassador to Britain, was awarded the Ralph Lowell Medal, public television's highest honor, for giving $150 million to the Corporation for Public Broadcasting to support a national effort to produce college-level courses on radio and television.

Thirteen-year-old **Jason Hardman** of Elsinore, Utah, received a certificate of appreciation and plaque when he met with **President Reagan, Sen. Orrin Hatch** (R-Utah), **Rep. Howard Nielson** (R-Utah) and **Eleanor Hashim**, chairman of the National Commission on Library and Information Science on Aug. 4. When he was 10, Jason got tired of having to bicycle six miles each week to the closest library, in Monroe, Utah, so he successfully led a campaign to establish a 20,000-volume library in Elsinore.

The Capitol Hill Toastmasters Club named House Majority Leader **Jim Wright** (D-Tex.) its Speaker of the Year. . . . **Sen. Claiborne Pell** (D-R.I.), **Rep. Henry A.**

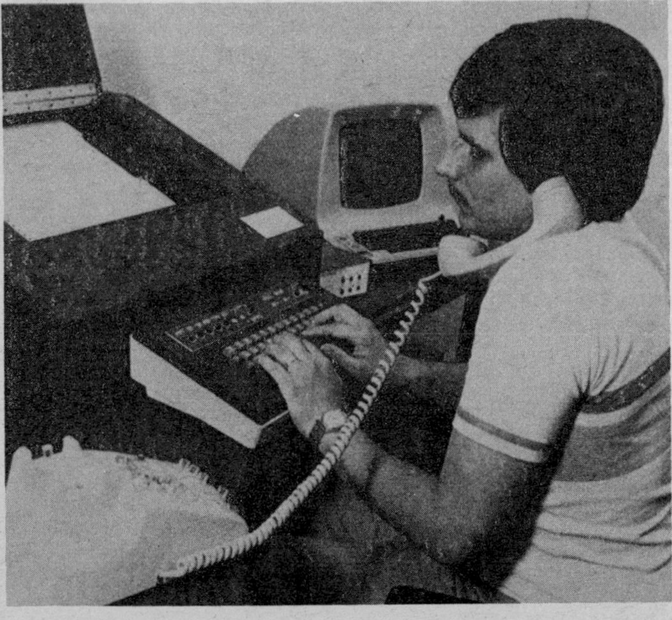

Wide World

Totally blind since the age of 8, Dexter Orange, 21, sits at a Braille computer terminal as he processes information at his job as a computer programmer at the Tallahassee, Fla., Public Service Commission. Orange graduated in April from Florida State University as the top student in the computer science program and the only student to maintain a straight A average.

United Press Int'l.

Singer Perry Como, 71, admires a bust of himself during a special program at New York City's Rainbow Grill in June. The program celebrated Como's 40th anniversary with RCA Records and his 50th year in show business.

Waxman (D-Calif.), **J.C. Turner,** president of International Union of Operating Engineers, and **Molly Sinclair** of the *Washington Post* received outstanding consumer service awards in June from the Consumer Federation of America.

Ray and **Chloris Grewe** of Portland, Ore., watched proudly as their three children, **Kent,** 26, **Scott,** 27, and **Kathy,** 28, all graduated in June from the School of Medicine at Oregon Health Services University in Portland. . . . **Thomas Edward Kill** of Seattle, Wash., went to court in August to change his name to **Thomas Edward Jirgensohn** since he plans to become a doctor and feared his name would frighten prospective patients away.

Jonathan LaSalle, 35, spoke to the governor of California on March 24, after waiting for 475 days. He had walked into the state capitol in December 1981 and asked to speak to then **Gov. Edmund G. Brown** about a civil service job he had lost. When told the governor was not available, LaSalle said he would wait. He spent the next 474 days sitting in front of the governor's office. Finally, he was allowed to meet with the present governor, **George D. Deukmejian,** at which time he promised to cease his vigil. . . . The North Miami Senior High School journalists, gathered for their annual banquet at a Miami, Fla., restaurant in May, got a surprise guest speaker. Also in the restaurant was former **President Richard M. Nixon,** who agreed to address the group after a request by the school principal, **Nicholas Borota.**

Keith Russel Finch, 16, of Blacksburg, Va., won the championship of the American Legion's 46th annual National High School oratorical contest in April. His rhetoric in defense of the U.S. Constitution brought him the honor and a $16,000 scholarship. . . . **Jimmy Tirikos,** 13, of Ashland, Mass., saved the life of his 19-month-old brother **Nicholas** by following phone instructions by a firefighter on how to administer mouth-to-mouth resuscitation. After finding the baby unconscious in the family swimming pool in June, Jimmy grabbed him and called the fire department. Firefighter **Jack Healy** calmed him down and gave him clear directions. The baby recovered.

Supreme Court **Justice William J. Brennan,** 76, married his secretary of 26 years, **Mary Fowler,** 68, in March. . . . Budget Director **David Stockman** married IBM sales executive **Jennifer Blei** in February.

Jeane Kirkpatrick, U.S. ambassador to the UN, received the National Service Medal from the Freedoms Foundation at Valley

Forge in June. . . . Archaeologist **Alfred Friendly Sr.** was made an honorary lifetime member of the Turkish Historical Society in June for his contributions to the archaeological excavations at Side, on Turkey's Mediterranean coast.

Barbara and **Arthur Johnson** of Nashville, Tenn., welcomed a third child, a daughter, on Jan. 22. Astonishingly, their two older children were also born on that same date—a son in 1973 and a daugher in 1978—at perfect five-year intervals. . . . **Annette Barrious,** 23, of Santa Paula, Calif., won a slot machine jackpot worth $1,065,358 at Caesar's Palace hotel in Las Vegas, Nev., while on her honeymoon in August. . . . **Debbie Fuhrman** and **George Stickles** of Dallas, Tex., were married in February by computer. Using the computer operation CompuServ, the bride and groom typed their vows into the nationwide system. The vows appeared on screens of subscribers across the nation, including the bride's sister in California and mother in Arizona. Selected guests had been issued a special code that allowed them to type in comments when the preacher (also linked by computer from a different location in Dallas) asked if anyone had any objections to the marriage. It was thought to be the first electronic wedding in the U.S.

THE GOLDEN YEARS

Entertainer **Bob Hope** celebrated his 80th birthday with the taping of a 3-hour TV show entitled *Happy Birthday, Bob,* which included tributes from **President Reagan** and a variety of show-business personalities. He also got a plaque and birthday cake from the U.S. Senate, which passed a resolution honoring him. . . . Also celebrating his 80th birthday in May was **Dr. Benjamin Spock,** who spent the day at his solar-heated home in Arkansas.

John Ficklin, 64, retired after 44 years of service in the White House. He began as a part-time pantry man in 1939 and retired as maitre d'hotel in June, after serving nine Presidents. . . . Former Secretary of State **Henry Kissinger** celebrated his 60th birthday at a party for 350 at a New York hotel in May.

Philosopher **Mortimer J. Adler** received a bachelor of arts degree from Columbia University 60 years after he was denied it because he failed to pass a required swimming test. Although he had completed the four-year curriculum in three years in 1923, he was denied the degree. In May, Columbia agreed to waive the requirement. . . . **Thomas Small,** 89, became the oldest person to earn a degree at Harvard University. It took him nearly 20 years to obtain a master of liberal arts in June.

Chicago newspaper columnist **Irv Kupcinet** celebrated the 40th anniversary of his "Kup" column in January. . . . **Jerome Fanciulli,** 94, the only surviving charter member, helped celebrated the 75th anniversary of the National Press Club in Washington, D.C., in March.

United Press Int'l.

Comedian Milton Berle, 75, *left,* puckers up to George Burns, 87, after the May 2 taping of the *Parade of Stars* benefit for the Actors Fund of America. It was Burns' first visit to the Palace Theater in New York since 1931, when he and late wife, Gracie Allen, reigned as king and queen of vaudeville.

Postal Service

A special $9.35 postage stamp for use principally on Express Mail Next Day Service was issued in August to emphasize the increased use of the Express Mail Service. The service, which provides overnight delivery of items weighing up to 70 pounds, is available from more than 3,500 post offices and thousands of designated collection boxes. The flat postage rate for up to two pounds is $9.35. The new stamp could be used for other items sent via the U.S. Mail, but was expected to be used with the smaller packages. The third flight of the space shuttle *Challenger,* launched on Aug. 30, carried a payload of envelopes specially cacheted with the new stamp.

U.S. Postal Service

HIGHLIGHTS: 1983

Postmaster General William F. Bolger announced on Nov. 1 that he would ask the Postal Rate Commission for a 15% increase in the price of mailing a first-class letter, from 20 cents to 23 cents. The Postal Service also would request increases in other mail rates, including raising the price of mailing a post card to 15 cents from other mail rates.

Bolger said the increases, to be effective in October 1984, were needed to prevent an $800 million loss in fiscal 1984. In September, Bolger had estimated a net operating profit of $500 million for fiscal 1983.

The 1982 fiscal year saw a net income of $802 million, and an increase in volume to a record 114 billion pieces of mail.

The U.S. Postal Service put simplified parcel mailing regulations into effect on Feb. 27. Under the new regulations, parcels weighing up to 70 pounds and measuring up to 108 inches in length and girth combined, can be mailed from any post office to any destination within the United States. These standards apply regardless of whether the package is shipped by Express Mail, Priority Mail, parcel post, or another fourth-class service. Previously, most post offices in the nation's 6,200 largest cities could not accept parcels weighing more than 40 pounds or measuring more than 84 inches.

The Postal Service entered the age of automation on April 6 by unveiling equipment that can electronically process and sort up to 10,000 letters per work hour. The new machines, optical character readers (OCRs) and bar code sorters (BCSs) were to be installed in 118 postal facilities by October 1984. Initially, the machines were to be used to sort first-class mail bearing the 5-digit ZIP code, but would be adapted to process letters bearing the expanded ZIP-4 codes.

Postmaster General Bolger explained that the optional scanning equipment would read the addresses on the face of an envelope, compare the ZIP code with the city and state to verify its accuracy, and convert the ZIP code into a series of bar-half-bar codes printed on the lower right corner of the envelope. At the destination post office, the bar codes would be read by bar code sorters to automatically sort the letters down to the carrier route level and, in some instances, down to a particular office building or firm.

Bolger said the program, which will cost about $690 million, will produce annual savings of approximately $600 million.

TIPS ON USING THE POSTAL SERVICE

The U.S. Postal Service tries to meet your needs as a sender and receiver of mail by providing a variety of services. Some services and regulations that may be unfamiliar to you are described below.

MINIMUM AND MAXIMUM SIZES

The Postal Service will not handle cards or letters less than 3½ inches high and 5 inches long unless they are more than ¼ inch thick. Cards less than seven-thousandths of an inch thick also are prohibited.

Cards or letters more than 6 inches high or 11½ inches wide are subject to a surcharge, as is letter mail of odd shapes in which the length is more than 1.3 times the height or less than 2.5 times the height.

E-COM

Electronic Computer-Originated Mail (E-COM) service is available from 25 specially equipped post offices. E-COM allows volume mailers to electronically transmit computer messages for delivery as First-Class mail. E-COM messages are limited to two pages. They cost 26¢ for the first page and 5¢ for the second. The mailer must also pay a $50 annual fee.

EXPRESS MAIL

If you send a letter or package up to 70 pounds by Express Mail, the U.S. Postal Service *guarantees* to return your money if it is not delivered within the time stated.

The Express Mail customer can choose one of four delivery options: (1) custom designed service, (2) next-day service, (3) same-day airport service, and (4) international service.

FORWARDING MAIL TO A NEW ADDRESS

If you move to a new address, you can obtain a "Change of Address Kit" from your local post office.

The kit contains change of address cards for you to send to magazines, charge accounts, and friends. There is also a change of address form with which to notify your local post office as to when you plan to move and your new address. Postal workers will forward mail to your new address for one year.

ADDRESS CORRECTION SERVICE

If one of your friends or correspondents moves and neglects to notify you of the new address, the Postal Service may be able to help you obtain the new address.

Mail a letter to your friend at the old address, and mark on the envelope "Address Correction Requested."

If your friend has notified the post office of his new address, the post office will then forward your letter to the new address and return to you a form containing your friend's new address with a charge of 25¢.

If the post office cannot determine the new address of your friend, it will merely return your letter at no charge.

PACKAGING FOR SECURE DELIVERY

The way you package a parcel sent by mail can affect the condition in which the contents arrive at their destination.

Packages containing breakable items should be marked "Fragile" above the address and below the postage. Those containing food that can spoil should be marked "Perishable." Before sealing the carton, place a list of the contents, your address, and the address of the person to whom it is being sent *inside* the package.

Wrap your package in paper at least as strong as that used for large grocery bags.

Use tape to seal all openings in the wrapping, including those at each end of the parcel.

Reinforce the package by using nylon filament tape instead of twine, running it completely around the length and the width of the parcel.

ZIP CODES

If you put the correct ZIP Code on the address of all mail that you send, the post office can deliver it more quickly. The ZIP Codes for many cities and towns are listed on pages 114–137.

Here is how ZIP Code works. The first digit of every five-digit ZIP Code designates a national area, from "0" in the Northeast states to "9" in the Western states.

The first three digits together stand for one of 552 large cities or sectional centers. The last two digits designate a delivery area or post office within the sectional center.

In the nine-digit ZIP Code the last four digits indicate the exact block or building. It is voluntary, and called "ZIP PLUS 4."

The *National Zip Code and Post Office Directory* lists the names of all the post offices and the five-digit codes for every postal delivery zone in the United States.

You can use the directory at your local post office or buy it there for $9; or (if you turn in the front cover of a prior issue) for $8. You also can obtain a copy of the directory by sending $9 to:

Superintendent of Documents
Government Printing Office
Washington, D.C. 20420

U.S. POSTAL RATES AND FEES

DOMESTIC MAIL	RATE
First Class:	
1st ounce	20¢
2d to 12th ounces	17¢ per ounce
Over 12 ounces	See Priority Mail table on page 700
Postal and postcards	13¢
Double postcards	13¢ each half
Business reply letters:	
with advance deposit	5¢
without advance deposit	18¢
Second Class (newspapers, periodicals):	
Mailed singly by public	19¢ for 1 oz.; 35¢ for 2 oz.; each additional oz. 10¢
Bulk rates:	
In county per pound	4.1¢
In county per piece	2.6¢
Outside county	Consult postmaster
£8**Third Class:**	
Mailed singly (circulars, books, catalogs, merchandise, etc., weighing less than one lb. each)	37¢ up to 2 ounces 71¢ up to 4 ounces 85¢ up to 6 ounces 95¢ up to 8 ounces $1.05 up to 10 ounces $1.15 up to 12 ounces $1.25 up to 14 ounces $1.35 up to 15.9 ounces
Keys and identification devices	55¢ up to 2 ounces
Bulk rates	Consult postmaster
Fourth Class:	
Parcel Post	See table on page 700
Books and records rate:	
1st pound	63¢
2d to 7th pounds	23¢ per pound
Over 7 pounds	14¢ for each additional pound
Library rate:	
1st pound	32¢
2d to 7th pounds	12¢
Over 7 pounds	7¢
Special Delivery (fee in addition to postage):	
1st class	$2.10 to $3.00
2d, 3d, and 4th class	$2.35 to $3.40
Certified Mail:	
Regular delivery	75¢ plus postage
Money Orders (for safe transmission of money):	
Amount $0.01 to $500	75¢ to $1.55
Special Handling (fee in addition to postage; 3d and 4th class only):	75¢ for first 10 lbs. $1.30 over 10 lbs.
Restricted delivery (not available for mail insured for $20 or less):	Additional $1.00 fee
Special Services:	
Address Correction	25¢
Certificate of mailing	40¢
Insurance (in addition to postage):	
Liability up to $20	45¢
Liability up to $50	85¢
Liability up to $100	$1.25
Liability up to $150	$1.70
Liability up to $200	$2.05
Liability up to $300	$3.45
Liability up to $400	$4.70

DOMESTIC MAIL *(continued)*	RATE
Registered Mail (in addition to postage):	
Value $0.00 to $25,000	$3.30 to $11.10
Return Receipts for certified, registered, or insured (not available for mail insured for $20 or less):	
Requested at time of mailing:	
Showing to whom and date delivered	Additional 60¢ fee
Also showing address where delivered	Additional 70¢ fee
Requested after mailing to show to whom and date delivered	Additional $3.75 fee
C.O.D. Mail:	
Up to limit of $400	$1.20 to $3.60
INTERNATIONAL MAIL	**RATE**
Mail to Canada or Mexico:	
Surface Mail—1 ounce	20¢
Surface Mail—2d to 12th ounce	17¢ per ounce
Surface Mail—over 12 ounces (Max. weights: Canada, 60 lbs.; Mexico, 4 lbs.)	Use 8th zone Priority Mail rates (see page 696)
Postal and postcards (surface)	13¢
Small packets of merchandise or samples, or printed matter:	
up to 2 ounces	37¢
over 2 oz. to 4 oz.	71¢
over 4 oz. to 6 oz.	85¢
over 6 oz. to 8 oz.	95¢
over 8 oz. to 10 oz.	$1.14
over 10 oz. to 12 oz.	$1.36
over 12 oz. to 14 oz.	$1.58
over 14 oz. to 1 lb.	$1.81
Mexico only, up to 2 lbs.	$2.76
Mail to Other Countries:	
Surface rates—1 ounce	23¢
over 1 oz. to 2 oz.	37¢
over 2 oz. to 4 oz.	71¢
over 4 oz. to 8 oz.	95¢
over 8 oz. to 1 lb.	$1.81
over 1 lb. to 2 lbs.	$2.76
over 2 lbs. to 4 lbs.	$3.86
Air letters: (To Central America, Colombia, Venezuela, Caribbean islands, Bahamas, Bermuda, and St. Pierre and Miquelon)	35¢ per ½ oz. up to 2 oz.; 30¢ for each additional ½ oz.
Air letters: (To all other countries)	40¢ per ½ oz. up to 2 oz.; 35¢ each additional ½ oz.
Aerogrammes (folded as envelope and sent by air)	30¢ each
Postal and postcards—surface	19¢
Postal and postcards—airmail	28¢
Small packets of merchandise or samples, 1 or 2 lbs. maximum—surface:	
up to 2 oz.	37¢
over 2 oz. to 4 oz.	71¢
over 4 oz. to 8 oz.	95¢
over 8 oz. to 1 lb.	$1.81
over 1 lb. to 2 lbs.	$2.76

U.S. FOURTH CLASS (PARCEL POST)

Weight in pounds up to	Zone Local	Up to 150 miles 1-2	150–300 miles 3	300–600 miles 4	600–1,000 miles 5	1,000–1,400 miles 6	1,400–1,800 miles 7	Over 1,800 miles 8
2	$1.52	$1.55	$1.61	$1.70	$1.83	$1.99	$2.15	$2.48
3	1.58	1.63	1.73	1.86	2.06	2.30	2.55	3.05
4	1.65	1.71	1.84	2.02	2.29	2.61	2.94	3.60
5	1.71	1.79	1.96	2.18	2.52	2.92	3.32	4.07
6	1.78	1.87	2.07	2.33	2.74	3.14	3.64	4.54
7	1.84	1.95	2.18	2.49	2.89	3.38	3.95	5.02
8	1.91	2.03	2.30	2.64	3.06	3.63	4.27	5.55
9	1.97	2.11	2.41	2.75	3.25	3.93	4.63	6.08
10	2.04	2.19	2.52	2.87	3.46	4.22	5.00	6.62
11	2.10	2.28	2.60	3.00	3.68	4.51	5.38	7.15
12	2.17	2.36	2.66	3.10	3.89	4.80	5.75	7.69
13	2.21	2.41	2.72	3.19	4.02	4.96	5.95	7.97
14	2.26	2.46	2.78	3.28	4.13	5.12	6.14	8.24
15	2.31	2.51	2.83	3.36	4.25	5.26	6.32	8.48
16	2.35	2.56	2.89	3.44	4.35	5.40	6.49	8.72
17	2.40	2.59	2.94	3.51	4.45	5.53	6.65	8.94
18	2.44	2.64	2.99	3.59	4.55	5.65	6.80	9.15
19	2.48	2.68	3.04	3.66	4.64	5.77	6.94	9.35
20	2.52	2.72	3.10	3.73	4.73	5.89	7.09	9.55
21	2.56	2.76	3.14	3.79	4.82	6.00	7.22	9.73
22	2.60	2.81	3.20	3.86	4.90	6.10	7.35	9.91
23	2.64	2.84	3.26	3.92	4.99	6.21	7.48	10.08
24	2.68	2.93	3.36	4.02	5.07	6.31	7.60	10.24
25	2.72	3.00	3.47	4.15	5.14	6.40	7.75	10.40
26	2.76	3.04	3.56	4.27	5.27	6.58	8.02	10.56
27	2.79	3.08	3.65	4.40	5.44	6.79	8.28	10.71
28	2.83	3.13	3.70	4.47	5.59	7.00	8.53	10.85
29	2.87	3.17	3.75	4.53	5.76	7.17	8.64	10.99
30	2.90	3.21	3.80	4.59	5.84	7.27	8.75	11.13
31	2.97	3.25	3.85	4.65	5.91	7.36	8.86	11.29
32	3.01	3.30	3.90	4.71	5.98	7.44	8.96	11.41
33	3.05	3.34	3.95	4.76	6.05	7.53	9.06	11.53
34	3.08	3.38	4.00	4.82	6.12	7.61	9.16	11.76
35	3.12	3.42	4.04	4.88	6.19	7.69	9.26	12.07
36	3.16	3.44	4.08	4.93	6.25	7.78	9.36	11.88
37	3.20	3.50	4.14	4.98	6.32	7.86	9.45	12.20
38	3.23	3.54	4.18	5.04	6.39	7.93	9.54	12.51
39	3.27	3.58	4.23	5.09	6.45	8.01	9.63	12.82
40	3.31	3.62	4.27	5.14	6.51	8.09	9.72	13.08
41	3.34	3.66	4.32	5.19	6.58	8.16	9.81	13.20
42	3.38	3.70	4.36	5.24	6.64	8.24	9.90	13.31
43	3.42	3.74	4.40	5.29	6.70	8.31	9.98	13.42
44	3.46	3.78	4.45	5.34	6.76	8.38	10.14	13.53
45	3.49	3.81	4.49	5.39	6.82	8.45	10.36	13.64
46	3.53	3.85	4.53	5.44	6.88	8.52	10.58	13.74
47	3.56	3.89	4.58	5.49	6.94	8.66	10.80	13.85
48	3.60	3.93	4.62	5.54	6.99	8.83	11.02	13.95
49	3.64	3.97	4.66	5.59	7.05	9.01	11.24	14.05
50	3.67	4.01	4.71	5.64	7.13	9.18	11.46	14.15
51	3.71	4.04	4.75	5.69	7.27	9.36	11.68	14.25
52	3.74	4.08	4.79	5.79	7.40	9.53	11.90	14.35
53	3.78	4.12	4.83	5.90	7.54	9.71	12.12	14.44
54	3.82	4.16	4.87	6.00	7.67	9.88	12.34	14.54
55	3.85	4.19	4.94	6.11	7.81	10.06	12.56	14.76
56	3.89	4.23	5.02	6.21	7.94	10.23	12.78	15.02
57	3.92	4.27	5.11	6.32	8.08	10.41	13.00	15.28
58	3.96	4.32	5.19	6.42	8.21	10.58	13.22	15.54
59	3.99	4.39	5.28	6.53	8.35	10.76	13.44	15.80
60	4.03	4.46	5.36	6.63	8.48	10.93	13.66	16.06
61	4.06	4.53	5.45	6.74	8.62	11.11	13.88	16.32
62	4.10	4.60	5.53	6.84	8.75	11.28	14.10	16.58
63	4.13	4.67	5.62	6.95	8.89	11.46	14.32	16.84
64	4.17	4.74	5.70	7.05	9.02	11.63	14.54	17.10
65	4.20	4.81	5.79	7.16	9.16	11.81	14.76	17.36
66	4.24	4.88	5.87	7.26	9.29	11.98	14.98	17.62
68	4.31	5.02	6.04	7.47	9.56	12.33	15.42	18.14
70	4.38	5.16	6.21	7.68	9.83	12.68	15.86	18.66

U.S. PRIORITY MAIL (over 12 oz.)

Weight in pounds up to	Local / Local 1–2–3	300–600 miles 4	600–1,000 miles 5	1,000–1,400 miles 6	1,400–1,800 miles 7	Over 1,800 miles 8
1	$2.24	$2.24	$2.24	$2.34	$2.45	$2.58
1.5...	2.30	2.42	2.56	2.72	2.87	3.07
2	2.54	2.70	2.88	3.09	3.30	3.57
2.5...	2.78	2.98	3.21	3.47	3.73	4.06
3	3.01	3.25	3.53	3.85	4.16	4.56
3.5...	3.25	3.53	3.85	4.22	4.59	5.05
4	3.49	3.81	4.18	4.60	5.02	5.55
4.5...	3.73	4.09	4.50	4.97	5.45	6.05
5	3.97	4.37	4.83	5.35	5.88	6.54
6	4.44	4.92	5.47	6.10	6.74	7.53
7	4.92	5.48	6.12	6.86	7.60	8.52
8	5.39	6.03	6.77	7.61	8.46	9.51
9	5.87	6.59	7.42	8.36	9.32	10.51
10	6.35	7.15	8.07	9.12	10.18	11.50
11	6.82	7.70	8.71	9.87	11.04	12.49
12	7.30	8.26	9.36	10.62	11.89	13.48
13	7.77	8.81	10.01	11.38	12.75	14.47
14	8.25	9.37	10.66	12.13	13.61	15.46
15	8.73	9.93	11.31	12.88	14.47	16.45
16	9.20	10.48	11.95	13.63	15.33	17.44
17	9.68	11.04	12.60	14.39	16.19	18.43
18	10.15	11.59	13.25	15.14	17.05	19.42
19	10.63	12.15	13.90	15.89	17.91	20.42
20	11.11	12.71	14.55	16.65	18.77	21.41
21	11.58	13.26	15.19	17.40	19.63	22.40
22	12.06	13.82	15.84	18.15	20.48	23.39
23	12.53	14.37	16.49	18.91	21.34	24.38
24	13.01	14.93	17.14	19.66	22.20	25.37
25	13.49	15.49	17.79	20.41	23.06	26.36
26	13.96	16.04	18.43	21.16	23.92	27.35
27	14.44	16.60	19.08	21.92	24.78	28.34
28	14.91	17.15	19.73	22.67	25.64	29.33
29	15.39	17.71	20.38	23.42	26.50	30.33
30	15.87	18.27	21.03	24.18	27.36	31.32
31	16.34	18.82	21.67	24.93	28.22	32.31
32	16.82	19.38	22.32	25.68	29.07	33.30
33	17.29	19.93	22.97	26.44	29.93	34.29
34	17.77	20.49	23.62	27.19	30.79	35.28
35	18.25	21.05	24.27	27.94	31.65	36.27
36	18.72	21.60	24.91	28.69	32.51	37.26
37	19.20	22.16	25.56	29.45	33.37	38.25
38	19.67	22.71	26.21	30.20	34.23	39.24
39	20.15	23.27	26.86	30.95	35.09	40.24
40	20.63	23.83	27.51	31.71	35.95	41.23
41	21.10	24.38	28.15	32.46	36.81	42.22
42	21.58	24.94	28.80	33.21	37.66	43.21
43	22.05	25.49	29.45	33.97	38.52	44.20
44	22.53	26.05	30.10	34.72	39.38	45.19
45	23.01	26.61	30.75	35.47	40.24	46.18
46	23.48	27.16	31.39	36.22	41.10	47.17
47	23.96	27.72	32.04	36.98	41.96	48.16
48	24.43	28.27	32.69	37.73	42.82	49.15
49	24.91	28.83	33.34	38.48	43.68	50.15
50	25.39	29.39	33.99	39.24	44.54	51.14
51	25.86	29.94	34.63	39.99	45.40	52.13
52	26.34	30.50	35.28	40.74	46.25	53.12
53	26.81	31.05	35.93	41.50	47.11	54.11
54	27.29	31.61	36.58	42.25	47.97	55.10
55	27.77	32.17	37.23	43.00	48.83	56.09
56	28.24	32.72	37.87	43.75	49.69	57.08
58	29.19	33.83	39.17	45.26	51.41	59.06
60	30.15	34.95	40.47	46.77	53.13	61.05
62	31.10	36.06	41.76	48.27	54.84	63.03
64	32.05	37.17	43.06	49.78	56.56	65.01
66	33.00	38.28	44.35	51.28	58.28	66.99
68	33.95	39.39	45.65	52.79	60.00	68.97
70	34.91	40.51	46.95	54.30	61.72	70.96

POSTAL SERVICE ADDRESS ABBREVIATIONS

STATES AND TERRITORIES

Alabama	AL	Georgia	GA	Maryland	MD	New Mexico	NM	South Dakota	SD
Alaska	AK	Guam	GU	Massachusetts	MA	New York	NY	Tennessee	TN
Arizona	AZ	Hawaii	HI	Michigan	MI	North Carolina	NC	Texas	TX
Arkansas	AR	Idaho	ID	Minnesota	MN	North Dakota	ND	Utah	UT
California	CA	Illinois	IL	Mississippi	MS	Ohio	OH	Vermont	VT
Canal Zone	CZ	Indiana	IN	Missouri	MO	Oklahoma	OK	Virginia	VA
Colorado	CO	Iowa	IA	Montana	MT	Oregon	OR	Virgin Islands	VI
Connecticut	CT	Kansas	KS	Nebraska	NE	Pennsylvania	PA	Washington	WA
Delaware	DE	Kentucky	KY	Nevada	NV	Puerto Rico	PR	West Virginia	WV
District of Columbia	DC	Louisiana	LA	New Hampshire	NH	Rhode Island	RI	Wisconsin	WI
Florida	FL	Maine	ME	New Jersey	NJ	South Carolina	SC	Wyoming	WY

OTHER POSTAL SERVICE ADDRESS ABBREVIATIONS

Academy	ACAD	Central	CTL	Fort	FT	Junction	JCT	Parkway	PKY	Spring	SPG
Airport	ARPRT	Church	CHR	Fountain	FTN	Lake	LK	Place	PL	Square	SQ
Alley	ALY	Circle	CIR	Freeway	FWY	Lane	LN	Plaza	PLZ	State	ST
Annex	ANX	City	CY	Gateway	GTWY	Light	LGT	Point	PT	Station	STA
Avenue	AVE	College	CLG	Great	GR	Little	LTL	Prairie	PR	Street	ST
Bayou	BYU	Court	CT	Grove	GRV	Lower	LWR	Ridge	RDG	Terrace	TER
Beach	BCH	Creek	CRK	Harbor	HBR	Manor	MNR	River	RIV	Tower	TWR
Boulevard	BLVD	Crossing	XING	Heights	HTS	Meadows	MDWS	Road	RD	Trail	TRL
Bluff	BLF	Drive	DR	High	HI	Memorial	MEM	Rural	R	Trailer	TRLR
Branch	BR	East	E	Highway	HWY	Middle	MDL	Saint	ST	Turnpike	TPKE
Bridge	BRG	Estates	EST	Hill	HL	Mission	MSN	Sainte	ST	Upper	UPR
Brook	BRK	Expressway	EXPY	Hospital	HOSP	Mount	MT	San	SN	Union	UN
Camp	CP	Extension	EXT	House	HSE	Mountain	MTN	Santa	SN	University	UNIV
Cape	CPE	Ferry	FRY	Institute	INST	National	NAT	School	SCH	Valley	VLY
Causeway	CWSY	Field	FLD	Island	IS	North	N	Seminary	SMNRY	Village	VLG
Center	CTR	Forest	FRST	Isle	IS	Park	PK	South	S	West	W

AIR PARCEL POST RATES FROM THE U.S. TO OTHER COUNTRIES

Air parcel post service is available to most countries of the world. Insured parcels must be sealed. To most countries the greatest length of a package allowed is 3½ feet, and the greatest length and girth combined is 6 feet. To some countries, parcels may measure 4 feet in length if not more than 16 inches in girth. Consult your local post office.

Country	First 4 oz.	Added 4 oz.[1]	Max. insurance	Max. weight in lbs.
Afghanistan	$5.40	$1.10	No	22
Albania	4.60	.90	No	22
Algeria	5.40	1.10	No	44
Andorra	3.80	.70	$ 420	44
Angola	6.20	1.30	No	22
Antigua	3.00	.50	$ 100	22
Argentina	5.40	1.10	$ 210	44
Aruba	3.00	.50	$ 210	44
Australia	5.40	1.10	$ 420	44
Austria	3.80	.70	$ 420	44
Azores	4.60	.90	$ 420	22
Bahamas	3.00	.50	$ 126	22
Bahrain	5.40	1.10	$ 100	22
Balearic Islands	4.60	.90	$ 210	22
Bangladesh	6.20	1.30	$ 200	22
Barbados	3.80	.70	$ 100	22
Belgium	6.20	1.30	$ 210	44
Belize	3.00	.50	No	22
Benin	5.40	1.10	No	44
Bermuda	3.00	.50	No	33
Bolivia	3.80	.70	No	44
Botswana	6.20	1.30	No	22
Brazil	6.20	1.30	No	44
Britain	4.60	.90	$1,200	44
Brunei	5.40	1.10	No	22
Bulgaria	5.40	1.10	No	22
Burma	5.40	1.10	No	22
Burundi	6.20	1.30	No	22
Cameroon	4.60	.90	No	22

Country	First 4 oz.	Added 4 oz.[1]	Max. insurance	Max. weight in lbs.
Canada	—	—	$ 400	35
Canary Islands	$4.60	$0.90	$ 210	22
Cape Verde	5.40	1.10	$ 21	22
Central Africa	6.20	1.30	No	44
Chad	5.40	1.10	No	44
Chile	5.40	1.10	No	22
China[2]	5.40	1.10	$ 420	44
Colombia	3.80	.70	$ 210	44
Comoros	6.20	1.30	No	44
Congo	5.40	1.10	No	44
Corsica	6.20	1.30	$ 420	44
Costa Rica	3.00	.50	No	44
Curacao	3.00	.50	$ 210	44
Cyprus	5.40	1.10	$ 213	44
Czechoslovakia	4.60	.90	$ 200	44
Denmark	3.80	.70	$ 420	44
Djibouti	6.20	1.30	$ 420	44
Dominica	3.00	.50	$ 100	22
Dominican Republic	3.00	.50	No	44
Ecuador	3.80	.70	$ 50	44
Egypt	4.60	.90	$ 210	44
El Salvador	3.00	.50	No	44
Equatorial Guinea	5.40	1.10	No	44
Ethiopia	5.40	1.10	$ 210	44
Faeroe Islands	4.60	.90	$ 395	44
Falkland Islands	5.40	1.10	No	22
Fiji	3.80	.70	$ 126	22
Finland	5.40	1.10	$ 420	44
France	6.20	1.30	$ 420	44

[1] Additional 4 ounces or fraction up to 5 pounds. [2] Mail must be addressed to the "People's Republic of China."

AIR PARCEL POST RATES TO OTHER COUNTRIES *(continued)*

Country	First 4 oz.	Added 4 oz.[1]	Max. insurance	Max. weight in lbs.
French Guiana	$4.60	$ .90	No	44
French Polynesia	5.40	1.10	$ 420	44
Gabon	5.40	1.10	No	44
Gambia	3.80	.70	No	22
Germany, East	4.60	.90	$ 210	22
Germany, West	4.60	.90	$ 420	44
Ghana	5.40	1.10	$ 80	22
Gibraltar	5.40	1.10	$ 50	22
Greece	4.60	.90	$ 210	44
Greenland	5.40	1.10	$ 420	44
Grenada	3.80	.70	$ 100	22
Guadeloupe	3.00	.50	No	44
Guatemala	3.00	.50	$ 100	44
Guinea	3.80	.70	No	44
Guinea–Bissau	3.80	.70	$ 210	22
Guyana	3.80	.70	$ 210	22
Haiti	3.00	.50	No	44
Honduras	3.80	.70	No	22
Hong Kong	4.60	.90	$ 420	22
Hungary	4.60	.90	$ 420	44
Iceland	5.40	1.10	$ 210	44
India	5.40	1.10	$ 210	22
Indonesia	6.20	1.30	No	22
Iran	5.40	1.10	$ 210	44
Iraq	5.40	1.10	No	44
Ireland	4.60	.90	$1,000	22
Israel	4.60	.90	No	33
Italy	4.60	.90	$ 210	44
Ivory Coast	5.40	1.10	No	44
Jamaica	3.00	.50	No	22
Japan	6.20	1.30	$ 420	22
Jordan	4.60	.90	No	22
Kenya	5.40	1.10	No	22
Kiribati	3.80	.70	No	44
Korea, South	5.40	1.10	$ 210	22
Kuwait	4.60	.90	$ 210	44
Laos	6.20	1.30	No	22
Lebanon	4.60	.90	No	11
Lesotho	6.20	1.30	No	22
Liberia	3.80	.70	$ 105	22
Libya	4.60	.90	No	44
Liechtenstein	3.80	.70	$ 420	44
Luxembourg	3.80	.70	$ 210	44
Macau	4.60	.90	$ 126	22
Madagascar	4.60	.90	No	44
Madeira Islands	3.80	.70	$ 420	22
Malawi	5.40	1.10	No	22
Malaysia	5.40	1.10	$ 105	22
Maldives	5.40	1.10	No	22
Mali	4.60	.90	No	44
Malta	4.60	.90	No	22
Martinique	3.00	.50	No	44
Mauritania	5.40	1.10	No	44
Mauritius	6.20	1.30	No	22
Mexico	3.00	.50	No	44
Monaco	6.20	1.30	$ 420	44
Montserrat	3.00	.50	$ 100	44
Morocco	4.60	.90	No	44
Mozambique	6.20	1.30	No	22
Namibia	6.20	1.30	No	22
Nauru	4.60	.90	$ 210	22
Nepal	5.40	1.10	No	22
Netherlands	4.60	.90	$ 420	44
Netherlands Antilles	3.00	.50	$ 210	44
Nevis	3.00	.50	$ 100	22
New Calendonia	5.40	1.10	$ 420	44
New Zealand	5.40	1.10	$ 210	22
Nicaragua	3.80	0.70	$ 210	44
Niger	$5.40	$1.10	No	44
Nigeria	4.60	.90	No	22
Norway	5.40	1.10	$ 420	44
Oman	5.40	1.10	$ 100	22
Pakistan	5.40	1.10	$ 210	22
Panama	3.00	.50	No	44
Papua New Guinea	5.40	1.10	$ 105	22
Paraguay	4.60	.90	No	44
Peru	3.80	.70	No	44
Philippines	5.40	1.10	$ 210	44
Pitcairn Islands	3.80	.70	No	22
Poland	4.60	.90	No	44
Portugal	3.80	.70	$ 420	22
Qatar	4.60	.90	$ 100	22
Réunion	6.20	1.30	No	44
Romania	4.60	.90	No	22
Rwanda	5.40	1.10	No	22
Saba	3.00	.50	$ 210	44
St. Helena	3.80	.70	No	22
St. Kitts	3.00	.50	$ 100	22
St. Lucia	3.00	.50	$ 100	22
St. Pierre & Miquelon	3.00	.50	No	44
St. Vincent	3.00	.50	$ 100	22
San Marino	4.60	.90	$ 120	44
Santa Cruz Islands	3.80	.70	No	22
Saudi Arabia	4.60	.90	No	22
Senegal	5.40	1.10	No	44
Seychelles	5.40	1.10	No	22
Sierra Leone	4.60	.90	No	22
Singapore	5.40	1.10	$ 100	22
Solomons	4.60	.90	No	22
Somalia	5.40	1.10	No	22
South Africa	6.20	1.30	No	22
Soviet Union	6.20	1.30	$ 210	22
Spain	4.60	.90	$ 210	22
Sri Lanka	5.40	1.10	$ 210	22
Sudan	5.40	1.10	No	22
Suriname	3.80	.70	$ 100	44
Swaziland	5.40	1.10	No	22
Sweden	5.40	1.10	$ 420	44
Switzerland	3.80	.70	$ 420	44
Syria	4.60	.90	$ 210	44
Taiwan	4.60	.90	$ 210	44
Tanzania	6.20	1.30	No	22
Thailand	5.40	1.10	$ 126	22
Togo	5.40	1.10	No	44
Tonga	3.80	.70	No	22
Trinidad–Tobago	3.80	.70	$ 153	22
Tristan da Cunha	3.80	.70	No	22
Tunisia	4.60	.90	No	44
Turkey	4.60	.90	$ 210	44
Turks and Caicos Is.	3.00	.50	No	22
Tuvalu	3.80	.70	No	22
Uganda	5.40	1.10	No	22
United Arab Emirates	5.40	1.10	$ 100	22
Upper Volta	4.60	.90	No	44
Uruguay	3.80	.70	No	44
Vanuatu	3.80	.70	No	44
Vatican City	4.60	.90	No	44
Venezuela	3.80	.70	No	44
Wallis and Futuna	5.40	$1.10	$ 420	44
Western Samoa	3.80	.70	$ 210	22
Yemen, North	5.40	1.10	No	44
Yemen, South	5.40	1.10	No	44
Yugoslavia	4.60	.90	$ 210	44
Zaire	5.40	1.10	No	44
Zambia	6.20	1.30	No	22
Zimbabwe	6.20	1.30	No	22

[1] Additional 4 ounces or fraction up to 5 pounds.

Religion

Wide World

Pope John Paul II signs a new code of canon law at a formal ceremony on Jan. 25. Incorporating many changes brought about by the Second Vatican Council, the new code took effect on Nov. 27. It marked the first revision in canon law since 1917. Resulting from 17 years of work by a Vatican commission, the new code was signed on the 24th anniversary of the decision by Pope John XXIII to summon an ecumenical council to modernize church doctrine. The new code decentralizes church authority by widening the powers of bishops and the role of lay persons. It also lessens the severity of punishments for violations of church code.

HIGHLIGHTS: 1983

PRESBYTERIAN CHURCHES MERGE

Ending a North-South split dating from 1861, the United Presbyterian Church in the U.S.A. and the Presbyterian Church in the U.S. merged, on June 10, 1983, to become the Presbyterian Church (U.S.A.)

The 830,000-member Presbyterian Church in the U.S., headquartered in Atlanta, had been separated from the larger, 2.4 million-member Northern body during the Civil War.

After the delegates to the General Assemblies of the two churches voted their denominations out of existence, a parade down Peachtree Street in Atlanta celebrated formation of the new Presbyterian body.

On June 11 the delegates elected the Rev. John Randolph Taylor, 54, of Charlotte, N.C., to be the reunited church's first moderator. Chosen by overwhelming majority on the first ballot, for a term of one year, Taylor had been co-chairman of the committee that drafted the plan of reunion. He expressed hope that the new church would be receptive to change and ask, "What is the best way to be . . . in the 20th century?" He also outlined a program combining evangelism and social action.

Still to be decided during the first year of the church's existence was the thorny issue of where to locate its main headquarters. The Northern wing has been headquartered in New York City and the Southern denomination in Atlanta.

REFORM JEWS CHANGE RULES

In March the Central Conference of American Rabbis, the national organization for reform rabbis, voted to change the rule governing who is considered Jewish.

A resolution approved at the annual convention of reform rabbis of North America, at Los Angeles, Calif., declared that "the child of one Jewish parent is under the presumption of Jewish descent." Previously, Reform Judaism, considered the most liberal of the three major branches of Judaism, had recognized young children of a Jewish father and non-Jewish mother as Jews if they were raised as such, but formal conversion was required when they reached adulthood.

Jewish law has always accorded the status of Jew to a child of a Jewish mother and non-Jewish father. However, the Committee on

HIGHLIGHTS: 1983 *(continued)*

Patrilineal Descent, which drew up the resolution, reported that Jewish fathers felt discriminated against in modern times, with mixed marriages on the rise.

The resolution also required that the presumption of Jewish status must be established through "appropriate and timely public and formal acts of identification with the Jewish faith and people." A child might affirm his Jewish identity by the study of Torah, bar mitzvah, or confirmation. An adult might fulfill the requirement by intensive Jewish study.

Though not binding on individual rabbis, the resolution was intended to assure acceptance in the Reform Jewish community in the U.S. and Canada of those children of mixed marriages who desire to live as Jews.

SOLZHENITSYN WINS TEMPLETON PRIZE

Soviet exile Aleksandr I. Solzhenitsyn received the 1983 Templeton Foundation Prize for Progress in Religion. The award, begun in 1972 by American financier John M. Templeton, called Solzhenitsyn a "pioneer in the renaissance of religion in atheist nations" and a "living symbol of the continuing vitality of the Orthodox tradition of spirituality."

In a speech in London accepting the $170,000 award in May, Solzhenitsyn warned against the predominance of atheism and self-destruction and urged mankind to continue to reach "for the warm hand of God, which we have so rashly and self-confidently pushed away."

The Soviet writer was exiled in 1974 after writing a book describing the horrors of Soviet secret labor-prisons. He currently lives a semireclusive life in rural Vermont.

Other winners of the Templeton Prize have included evangelist Billy Graham and Mother Theresa of India.

TRAVELS OF POPE JOHN PAUL II

Saying he had come to "share the pain" in a region that was "crying out" for an end to strife and hate, Pope John Paul II traveled to eight Caribbean nations on March 2–9. He began the weeklong visit in Costa Rica, where he declared that peace and social justice was attainable if "each people can confront its problems in a climate of sincere dialogue without alien interference."

The next day he addressed the judges of the Inter-American Court of Human Rights in San Jose, Costa Rica, only hours after Guatemala had ignored Vatican appeals and executed six men previously convicted of subversive acts by a secret tribunal. The Vatican denounced the executions in a strongly worded statement.

In Nicaragua on March 4, the pope said that five priests who held government posts there were "acting outside or against the will of the bishops" and thus questioning the unity of the church.

After a visit to Panama on March 5, the pontiff arrived in strife-torn El Salvador on March 6. There he called for "authentic dialogue" between the factions in an effort to end the three-year-old civil war.

In Guatemala on March 7, the pope issued a plea for Indian rights and called for an end to political violence. He arrived in Honduras on March 8, warning lay preachers against becoming instruments of radical political groups.

John Paul II concluded his Central American trip in Haiti on March 9, where he issued a strong appeal to the Haitian Catholic Church to push for social justice and human rights.

The pope visited his native Poland June 16–23, receiving a tumultuous welcome. See page 19.

On Aug. 14–15 the pope paid a visit to the shrine at Lourdes, France, where in 1858 Marie Bernarde Soubirous, 14, reported seeing the Virgin Mary appear 18 times. More than 60,000 persons come to Lourdes each year to drink the water in the hope of a miraculous cure for their illnesses or afflictions. The pontiff held an open-air mass in the grotto where the young French peasant girl beheld the Virgin Mary.

In the first papal visit to Austria in two centuries, John Paul II appealed to the U.S. and Soviet Union to negotiate for peace in good faith. Also, during the Sept. 10–14 visit, the pope stressed a warning against abortion.

CHURCH COUNCIL SEES ACCORD ON UNITY

The sixth assembly of the World Council of Churches meeting in Vancouver, Canada, in August endorsed a landmark "Lima Agreement" that could lead to closer ties among all branches of Christianity.

The agreement was named for the city in Peru where theologians from divergent churches hammered out an accord in 1982 defining three key elements of Christianity—baptism, holy communion, and ministry.

The 300 member churches were to study the agreement and report back at the 1984 convention as to whether they can accept the definitions set forth. It was hoped that the accord would resolve theological differences and bind the various branches of Christianity closer together.

MAJOR WORLD RELIGIONS

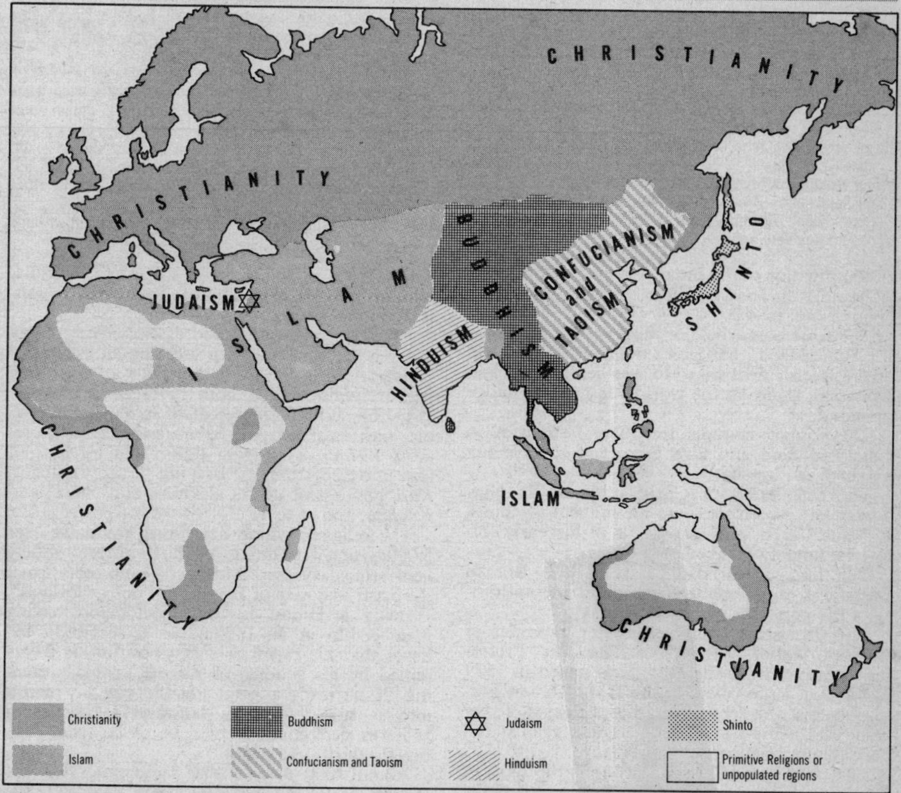

This map gives a general idea of the areas where the world's major religions have exerted their strongest direct influence. Not shown are North and South America, where the Christian religion has been predominant.

Throughout history man has turned to religion to find meaning for life and to explain the unknown.

Man's awareness of God, or of some supernatural power or powers, has impelled belief in a sacred, transcendent order that deals with human experience in the world or beyond it.

The nine largest world religions are: Buddhism, Christianity, Confucianism, Hinduism, Islam, Judaism, Shinto, Sikhism, and Taoism.

BUDDHISM

Adherents Worldwide: About 245 million, chiefly in Southeast Asia, Sri Lanka, Korea, China, Japan, and Tibet.
Adherents in U.S.: About 60,000.
Chief Scripture: The Pali Canon.
Dates from: The time of Prince Siddhartha Gautama, the Buddha (about 2,500 years ago).

Buddhism teaches that the way beyond sorrow and suffering is a middle path between striving and spiritual contemplation. Its ethical system is based upon compassion and elimination of self-interest. Its theology accepts the rebirth of persons through the transmigration of souls.

An object of Buddhist life is to achieve nirvana, blissful detachment from the world, through which the cycle of rebirth stops.

Early Buddhism was close to Hinduism, but eventually split into several branches. The main branches include: Mahayana Buddhism, which stresses salvation and contemplation; and Hinayana, which preserves the monastic tradition of the early believers. Zen Buddhism is a Japanese type of Mahayana. The Lamaism of Tibet is a combination of Buddhism and the primitive beliefs of the region.

Buddhism has long ceased to be an important influence on the Indian subcontinent, the area where it originated. About A.D. 1000 many areas in southern Asia that were formerly Buddhist fell to the influence of Islam.

Buddhist precepts have influenced some Western philosophers, most notably Arthur Schopenhauer (1788–1860).

The Buddhist Churches of America were incorporated under that name in 1942.

MAJOR WORLD RELIGIONS *(continued)*

CHRISTIANITY

Adherents Worldwide: About 1 billion (including 565 million Roman Catholics, 324 million Protestants, and 92 million Eastern Orthodox).
Church Members in U.S.: About 133 million.
Chief Scripture: The Bible (the Old Testament and the New Testament).
Dates from: The time of Jesus Christ (about 2,000 years ago).
Major Holidays: Christmas (Dec. 25), the Epiphany (Jan. 6), All Saints' Day (Nov. 1); Ash Wednesday, Palm Sunday, Good Friday, Easter Sunday, Ascension Day, and Pentecost; dates vary annually.

A continuation of the Judaic tradition, Christianity began with Jesus of Nazareth, who lived from about 5 B.C. to A.D. 30.

The Christian article of faith is that Jesus was the Son of God, that He came to save the world and was crucified, that He was resurrected and will come again on the world's last day to judge mankind.

The primary commandments of Jesus were to believe in God and love Him, and to love thy neighbor as thyself.

The foundation of Christianity is the New Testament, which recounts the life and teachings of Jesus Christ, and the works of his early followers, notably St. Paul.

The largest Christian body is the Roman Catholic Church, centralized under the authority of the pope, the bishop of Rome.

The Protestant churches are the products of the Reformation of the 1500s. The term "Protestant" derives from the *protestatio* issued in 1529 by the Lutheran rulers in the Holy Roman Empire against the repressive Diet of Speyer. It became the name for all who argued against the papal claim of universal supremacy.

The third great Christian group is the Eastern Orthodox, arising mainly from the ancient political split of the Roman Empire into East and West. The patriarch of Constantinople (in Istanbul) is first in honor among all the Orthodox leaders, and most of the churches consider him the spiritual leader of Eastern Orthodoxy. Over 3.8 million Americans belong to various branches of Eastern Orthodoxy.

CONFUCIANISM

Adherents Worldwide: About 275 million, mainly in China and Taiwan.
Chief Scripture: The Analects.
Dates from: The time of Confucius (about 2,500 years ago).

Confucianism is primarily a body of ethics, and can be considered an institutional religion only in that it requires sacrifices to the gods and ancestors. However, Confucianism does not restrict itself to any formalized theology.

Confucians generally conduct their lives according to five cardinal virtues: kindness, righteousness, decorous behavior, wisdom, and uprightness. Confucius taught that the chief ethic was benevolence, and one of his prime precepts was "Treat inferiors with propriety."

The basis of Confucianism derives from the Analects of Confucius and the writings of Mencius, a sage of the 4th century B.C. Confucius was the foremost philosopher of China.

With the overthrow of China's monarchy in 1911–12, Confucianism waned. In the 1970s the communist government of China launched a campaign to wipe out Confucianism.

HINDUISM

Adherents: Over 500 million live in India or in Indian communities in other lands.
Chief Scriptures: The Veda, a huge body of sacred texts, including the Upanishads (Secret Doctrines), Bhagavad-Gita (Song of the Blessed One), and many other writings.
Dates from: Prehistoric times, although the earliest writings date from about 1000 B.C.

The religion of the majority of people of India, Hinduism holds that divinity, or *ātman*, is contained in all beings.

Hinduism interprets God as embodying many different personalities, representing all aspects of reality. Among the most important of these deities are: *Siva*, a god both of creation and destruction, usually represented as a dancing figure with an extra pair of arms; *Brahma*, a creator; *Vishnu*, a sleeping figure who dreams of the universe, thereby keeping it in existence; *Kali*, goddess of death, sickness, and chaos; and *Krishna*, god of love.

The religion, which developed gradually over 5,000 years, has not given birth to any widely held ethical system. Although some sects exist, the great majority of Hindus are not sectarians.

Being a Hindu is contingent upon having membership in an Indian caste. A Hindu believes that his caste, or social position, is determined by his actions, or *Karma*, in his present life. If he leads a good life, he will be reborn into a superior caste. However, if his soul achieves perfection, he will be saved from continual rebirth and death.

About 1000 B.C., at the same time that the earliest of the Vedas were being recorded, the caste system began to become important in the Hindu social structure. The Brahman caste became the high priests of Hinduism about 800 B.C., a position that they hold to the present time.

Since India won independence in 1947, the government has tried to end the caste system. Most of today's Hindus worship according to the Puranic creed, a theological school that stabilized about A.D. 1500.

ISLAM

Adherents Worldwide: About 700 million.
Adherents in U.S.: About 2 million.
Chief Scripture: The Koran.
Dates from: The time of Mohammed (about 1,400 years ago).
Major Holidays: Eid-al-Fitr (after fasting month of Ramadan) and Eid-al-Azha (feast of sacrifice on last day of Hajj).

Islam, an Arabic word meaning "submission to Allah (God)," is based on the revelations of Allah to Mohammed, who was born in Mecca (now in Saudi Arabia) and who lived from about A.D. 570 to 632. Among Muslims, Mohammed is believed to have been a descendant of Abraham, the founder of Judaism.

Mohammed received the revelations of Allah

compiled in the Koran, and provided explanations of Koranic teachings in the Sunna.

The main Islamic article of faith is a simple one: "There is no god but God (Allah), and Mohammed is His messenger." In addition, the followers of Islam have other major articles of faith: recitation of five daily prayers; observance of Ramadan (a monthlong period of fasting and self-examination); giving of alms (zakat); and, if possible, a pilgrimage to Mecca, the birthplace of Mohammed. The most important religious service is held at midday each Friday.

Islam divides into four interpretations: Hanafi, Shafai, Hanbali, and Maliki.

In the century after the death of Mohammed, Arab Muslim armies conquered the Middle East, North Africa, Spain, and southern France.

Although Muslim influence was prevented from spreading farther into Europe after Charles Martel's Christian military victory at Tours in 732, Islam continued its eastern growth. It served as a unifying force among the many Arab tribes.

Islam's missionary organization, the Ahmadiyya movement, was founded in 1889 by Hazrat Ahmad (1835–1908). It brought Islam to the U.S. in 1920. Today a majority of persons in 57 nations are Muslims.

JUDAISM

Adherents Worldwide: About 15 million.
Adherents in U.S.: About 5.9 million.
Chief Scriptures: The Torah (Old Testament) and the Talmud.
Dates from: The time of Abraham (about 1800 B.C.).
Major Holidays: Pesach (Passover), Shavuot (Pentecost), Sukkot (Tabernacles), Rosh Hashanah (New Year), Yom Kippur (Day of Atonement), Hanukkah (Festival of Lights); dates vary annually.

Judaism recognizes one God, sometimes called *Elohim* or *Jehovah.*

The basic prayer of Judaism, called the Shema, begins: "Hear, O Israel, the Lord our God, the Lord is one."

The Jewish Sabbath is from sunset Friday to sunset Saturday.

Beginning with the patriarch Abraham, the Jews have had many great leaders and prophets, including Moses, who freed his people from Egyptian bondage in the 1200s B.C. and received the Ten Commandments and the Torah as a constitution for a new nation.

The ancient city of Jerusalem once was, and again is, central to Judaism. However, in ancient times Jerusalem was repeatedly destroyed and rebuilt. About A.D. 135 the Romans put down a Jewish revolt and forced the Jews to leave the Holy Land in what is called the *Diaspora.*

For many centuries Jews were persecuted by Christians in the belief they were responsible for the death of Jesus Christ. About 6 million Jews were slaughtered by Germans and others during World War II.

The Zionist movement for a Jewish homeland, which began in the 1800s, bore fruit in 1948, when the Jewish state of Israel was created in Palestine.

In the United States and in much of Europe, Jewish congregations are classified as Orthodox, Conservative, or Reform, depending on their degree of adherence to ancient religious customs and dietary laws.

SHINTO

Adherents Worldwide: About 63 million, all of whom are Japanese.
Chief Scripture: None.
Dates from: Antiquity; originated with the beginnings of the Japanese culture.

Shinto is a set of rituals and customs involving pilgrimages, festivals, and worship of a great host of gods. It is a folk religion, limited strictly to the Japanese people, and thus without any universal prophetic message. The word *shin-to* means "way of the gods."

The highest deity is the sun goddess, known as the Ruler of Heaven.

Gods are worshiped through the sacrifice of rice and rice wine (sake).

Shinto did not evolve an ethical system of its own, but gradually borrowed ethical principles from Buddhism and Confucianism.

From about the 500s A.D., the emperor of Japan was considered the chief Shinto priest and had the immortal status of a deity. In the 1800s a state form of Shinto was organized in coordination with Japan's newly awakened imperialism. This militaristic form of Shinto disappeared after World War II, when Emperor Hirohito disavowed his divinity. Many of today's Shinto sects stress world peace and brotherhood.

SIKHISM

Adherents Worldwide: About 8 million.
Chief Scripture: Granth Sahib.
Dates from: About A.D. 1500.

Most of the people who follow the religion of Sikhism live in the state of Punjab in northwestern India. The religion combines the beliefs of Islam and Hinduism.

Sikhism was founded by Guru Nanak (1469–1539). He taught that there was a single God, rejecting the many deities of Hinduism and the worship of idols. He attempted to eliminate the caste system of Hinduism, uniting his followers into one class.

The sacred writings of Sikhism began to be compiled by Guru Arjan (1563–1606), who also built the Sikhs' sacred city of Amritsar.

TAOISM

Adherents Worldwide: About 30 million.
Chief Scripture: Tao-te ching.
Dates from: About 2,600 years ago, founded by Lao-tzu.

Tao in Chinese means "path," and the basis of early Taoism is the allowance of the affairs of men to take the path of nature. The religion stresses quietism, contemplation, and the elimination of all striving and strong passions.

After the 500s A.D., Taoism took on aspects of Confucianism and Buddhism. Taoist monasteries were established throughout China.

Taoism developed beliefs concerning an afterlife, which included a heaven and hell, as well as a cosmology that divided all reality into male and female principles, or *yang* and *yin*. In its later development, Taoism became concerned with magic and also provided the basis for many secret societies.

PATRON SAINTS

Since the early days of Christianity certain saints and angels have been regarded as patrons of specific occupations, groups, localities, and nations.

SUPPLIANTS	SAINTS
Accountants	St. Matthew
Actors	St. Genesius
Advertisers	St. Bernardine of Siena
Altar boys	St. John Berchmans
Anesthetists	St. René Goupil
Archers	St. Sebastian
Architects	St. Thomas, apostle; St. Barbara
Art	St. Catherine of Bologna
Artists	St. Luke
Astronomers	St. Dominic
Athletes	St. Sebastian
Authors	St. Francis de Sales
Aviators	Our Lady of Loreto; St. Thérèse of Lisieux; St. Joseph of Cupertino
Bakers	St. Elizabeth of Hungary; St. Nicholas
Bankers	St. Matthew
Barbers	Sts. Cosmas and Damian; St. Louis
Barren women	St. Anthony of Padua; St. Felicitas
Beggars	St. Alexius
Blacksmiths	St. Dunstan
Blind	St. Odilia; St. Raphael
Bookkeepers	St. Matthew
Booksellers	St. John of God
Boy Scouts	St. George
Brewers	St. Augustine of Hippo; St. Luke; St. Nicholas of Myra
Bricklayers	St. Stephen
Brides	St. Nicholas of Myra
Builders	St. Vincent Ferrer
Butchers	St. Anthony of Egypt; St. Hadrian; St. Luke
Cabinetmakers	St. Anne
Canada	St. Joseph; St. Anne
Cancer patients	St. Peregrine
Carpenters	St. Joseph
Children	St. Nicholas of Myra
China	St. Joseph
Choir boys	St. Dominic Savio
Comedians	St. Vitus
Confessors	St. Alphonsus Liguori; St. John Nepomucene
Cooks	St. Lawrence; St. Martha
Dairy workers	St. Brigid
Deaf	St. Francis de Sales
Denmark	St. Ansgar; St. Canute
Dentists	St. Apollonia
Dying	St. Joseph; St. Barbara
Ecology	St. Francis of Assisi
Editors	St. John Bosco
Emigrants	St. Frances Xavier Cabrini
Engineers	St. Ferdinand III
England	St. George
Ethiopia	St. Frumentius
Eye Sufferers	St. Lucy
Falsely accused	St. Raymund Nonnatus
Farmers	St. George; St. Isidore
Firemen	St. Florian
Fishermen	St. Andrew
Florists	St. Dorothy; St. Thérèse of Lisieux
France	St. Joan of Arc; St. Thérèse; Our Lady of Assumption
Funeral dirs.	St. Dismas; St. Joseph of Arimathea
Gardeners	St. Dorothy; St. Adelard; St. Tryphon; St. Fiacre; St. Phocas
Germany	St. Boniface; St. Michael
Glassworkers	St. Luke
Gravediggers	St. Anthony, abbot
Greece	St. Nicholas; St. Andrew
Grocers	St. Michael
Headaches	St. Teresa of Avila
Heart Patients	St. John of God
Housewives	St. Anne
Hunters	St. Hubert; St. Eustachius
India	Our Lady of Ass'pt'n
Infantrymen	St. Maurice
Innkeepers	St. Amand
Invalids	St. Roch
Ireland	St. Patrick; St. Brigid; St. Columba
Italy	St. Francis of Assisi; St. Catherine of Siena
Japan	St. Peter Baptist
Jewelers	St. Eligius
Journalists	St. Francis de Sales
Jurists	St. Catherine of Alexandria; St. John Capistrano
Laborers	St. Isidore; St. James; St. John Bosco
Lawyers	St. Ivo; St. Genesius; St. Thomas More
Librarians	St. Jerome
Maids	St. Zita
Mentally ill	St. Dympna
Merchants	St. Francis of Assisi; St. Nicholas of Myra
Messengers	St. Gabriel
Metal workers	St. Eligius
Mexico	Our Lady of Guad'l'pe
Miners	St. Barbara
Mothers	St. Monica
Motorcyclists	Our Lady of Grace
Motorists	St. Christopher; St. Frances of Rome
Mountaineers	St. Bernard, Menthon
Musicians	St. Gregory the Great; St. Cecilia; St. Dunstan
Norway	St. Olaf
Nurses	St. Camillus de Lellis; St. John of God; St. Agatha; St. Alexius; St. Raphael
Orators	St. John Chrysostom
Orphans	St. Jerome Aemilian
Painters	St. Luke
Paratroopers	St. Michael
Pawnbrokers	St. Nicholas
Pharmacists	Sts. Cosmas and Damian; St. James the Greater
Philosophers	St. Justin; St. Catherine of Alexandria
Physicians	St. Pantaleon; Sts. Cosmas and Damian; St. Luke, St. Raphael
Pilgrims	St. Alexius; St. James
Plasterers	St. Bartholomew
Poets	St. David; St. Cecilia
Poison sufferers	St. Benedict
Poland	St. Casimir; St. Stanislaus of Kracow; Our Lady of Czestochowa
Policemen	St. Michael
Poor	St. Lawrence; St. Anthony of Padua
Possessed	St. Bruno; St. Denis
Postal workers	St. Gabriel
Preg. mothers	St. Margaret; St. Raymund Nonnatus; St. Gerard Majella
Priests	St. Jean-Baptiste Vianney
Printers	St. John of God; St. Augustine of Hippo; St. Genesius
Prisoners	St. Dismas; St. Barbara; St. Joseph Cafasso
Public relations	St. Bernardino, Siena
Radio workers	St. Gabriel
Rheumatics	St. James the Greater
Sailors	St. Cuthbert; St. Brendan; St. Eulalia; St. Christopher; St. Peter Gonzales; St. Erasmus
Scholars	St. Brigid
Scientists	St. Albert
Scotland	St. Andrew; St. Columba
Sculptors	St. Claude
Searchers for lost articles	St. Anthony of Padua
Secretaries	St. Genesius
Servants	St. Martha; St. Zita
Shoemakers	Sts. Crispin and Crispinian
Sick	St. Michael; St. John of God; St. Camillus de Lellis
Singers	St. Gregory; St. Cecilia
Skaters	St. Lidwina
Skiers	St. Bernard
Social workers	St. Louise de Marillac
Soldiers	St. Hadrian; St. George; St. Ignatius; St. Sebastian; St. Martin of Tours; St. Joan of Arc
Spain	St. James; St. Teresa
Stenographers	St. Genesius; St. Cassian
Students	St. Thomas Aquinas; St. Catherine of Alexandria
Sweden	St. Bridget; St. Eric
Tailors	St. Homobonus
Tax collectors	St. Matthew
Taxi drivers	St. Fiacre
Teachers	St. Gregory the Great; St. Catherine of Alexandria; St. John Baptist de la Salle
TV workers	St. Gabriel
Throat sufferers	St. Blaise
Travelers	St. Christopher; St. Anthony of Padua; St. Nicholas of Myra; St. Raphael
United States	Immaculate Concept.
Wales	St. David
Women in labor	St. Anne
Young girls	St. Agnes

U.S. RELIGIOUS DENOMINATIONS

Church membership in the United States increased in 1982 to 138,452,614 from a total of 134,816,943, according to the National Council of Churches of Christ.

Some 59.7% of the U.S. population belonged to an organized religion in 1982, and there were 339,053 churches.

Roman Catholicism remained the largest single religion in the U.S. Its 51,207,579 members in 1982 represented an increase of 757,737 since 1981.

Because of space limitations, only U.S. religious denominations reporting 16,000 or more members are listed in the following table.

Adventist: Advent Christian Church: Organized, 1860; address, P.O. Box 23152, Charlotte, NC 28212; churches, 364; membership, 29,838.

Adventist: Seventh-day Adventists: Organized, 1863; address, 6840 Eastern Ave. N.W., Washington, DC 20012; churches, 3,769; membership, 588,536.

Baha'i Faith: Founded in Iraq, 1863; address, National Spiritual Assembly, 536 Sheridan Rd., Wilmette, IL 60091; assemblies, 130.

Baptist: American Baptist Association: Organized, 1905; address, 4605 N. State Line Ave., Texarkana, TX 75501; churches, 1,641; membership, 225,000.

Baptist: American Baptist Churches in the U.S.A.: Organized, 1907; address, Valley Forge, PA 19481; churches, 5,817; membership, 1,607,541.

Baptist: Baptist General Conference: Organized, 1879; address, 2002 S. Arlington Heights Rd., Arlington Heights, IL 60005; churches, 715; membership, 127,662.

Baptist: Baptist Missionary Association of America: Organized, 1950; address, 721 Main St., Little Rock, AR 72201; churches, 1,390; membership, 228,381.

Baptist: Conservative Baptist Association of America: Organized, 1947; address, 25 W. 560 Geneva Rd., Box 66, Wheaton, IL 60187; churches, 1,125; membership, 225,000.

Baptist: Free Will Baptists: Organized, 1727; address, 1134 Murfreesboro Rd., Nashville, TN 37217; churches, 2,479; membership, 216,848.

Baptist: General Association of Regular Baptist Churches: Organized, 1932; address, 1300 N. Meacham Rd., Schaumberg, IL 60195; churches, 1,571; membership, 300,839.

Baptist: General Baptists, General Association of: Founded in England, 1607; address, 100 Stinson Drive, Poplar Bluff, MO 63901; churches, 870; membership, 75,028.

Baptist: National Baptist Convention of America: Organized, 1880; address, 2823 N. Houston, Fort Worth, TX 76106; churches, 11,398; membership, 2,668,799.

Baptist: National Baptist Convention, United States of America, Inc.: Organized, 1880; address, 915 Sprain St., Baton Rouge, LA 70802; churches, 26,000; membership, 5,500,000.

Baptist: National Primitive Baptist Convention, Inc.: Organized, 1907; address, P.O. Box 2355, Tallahassee, FL 32301; churches, 606; membership, 250,000.

Baptist: North American Baptist Conference: 1 S. 210 Summit Ave., Oakbrook Terrace, IL 60181; churches, 260; membership, 43,146.

Baptist: Primitive Baptists: Address, S. Second St., Thornton, AR 71766; churches, 1,000; membership, 72,000.

Baptist: Progressive National Baptist Convention, Inc.: Organized, 1961; address, 601 50th St., N.E., Washington, DC 20019; churches, 655; membership, 521,692.

Baptist: Southern Baptist Convention: Formed, 1845; address, 460 James Robertson Pkwy.,

50 LARGEST U.S. RELIGIOUS DENOMINATIONS

DENOMINATION	MEMBERSHIP
Roman Catholic Church	51,207,579
Southern Baptist Convention	13,782,644
United Methodist Church	9,519,407
Judaism	5,921,205
National Baptist Convention, U.S.A., Inc.	5,500,000
The Church of God in Christ	3,709,661
Church of Jesus Christ of Latter-day Saints	3,490,000
Presbyterian Church (U.S.A.)	3,202,392
Lutheran Church in America	2,921,829
Episcopal Church	2,767,440
National Baptist Convention of America	2,668,799
Lutheran Church—Missouri Synod	2,636,715
American Lutheran Church	2,346,207
African Methodist Episcopal Church	2,210,000
Islam	2,000,000
Greek Orthodox Archdiocese	1,950,000
(Pentecostal) Assemblies of God	1,788,394
United Church of Christ	1,726,244
American Baptist Churches in the U.S.A.	1,607,541
Churches of Christ	1,600,222
Christian Church (Disciples of Christ)	1,173,135
African Methodist Episcopal Zion Church	1,134,176
Christian Church and Churches of Christ	1,063,254
Orthodox Church in America (Russian)	1,000,000
Christian Methodist Episcopal Church	786,707
Seventh-day Adventists	588,536
Jehovah's Witnesses	588,503
Progressive National Baptist Convention, Inc.	521,692
Church of the Nazarene	492,203
United Pentecostal Church, Intl.	465,000
Church of God (Cleveland, Tenn.)	456,797
Armenian Church of America (Eastern Orthodox)	450,000
Salvation Army	414,999
Wisconsin Evangelical Lutheran Synod	410,288
Reformed Church in America	345,762
General Assn. of Regular Baptist Churches	300,839
Polish National Catholic Church of America	282,411
National Primitive Baptist Convention	250,000
Baptist Missionary Association of America	228,381
American Baptist Association	225,000
Conservative Baptist Association of America	225,000
Free Will Baptists	216,848
Christian Reformed Church	215,411
(Pentecostal) Church of God in Christ, Intl.	200,000
Christian and Missionary Alliance	195,042
Reorganized Church of Jesus Christ of Latter Day Saints	190,087
National Council of Community Churches	190,000
Church of God (Anderson, Ind.)	178,581
Church of the Brethren	170,267
The Antiochian Orthodox Christian Archdiocese	152,000

U.S. RELIGIOUS DENOMINATIONS *(continued)*
Nashville, TN 37219; churches, 36,022; membership, 13,782,644.

Baptist: United Free Will Baptist Church: Organized, 1870; address, Kinston College, 1000 University St., Kinston, NC 28501; churches, 836; membership, 100,000.

Bible Way Church of Our Lord Jesus Christ World Wide, Inc.: Established, 1957; address, 1100 New Jersey Ave., N.W., Washington, DC 20001; churches, 350; membership, 30,000.

Brethren: Church of the Brethren: Founded in Germany, 1708; address, 1451 Dundee Ave., Elgin, IL 60120; churches, 1,064; membership, 170,267.

Brethren: Fellowship of Grace Brethren Churches: Separated from Church of the Brethren in 1882; address, Box 544, Winona Lake, IN 46590; churches, 284; membership, 42,023.

Brethren in Christ Church: Founded, 1778; address, P.O. Box 245, Upland, CA 91786; churches, 167; membership, 16,201.

Buddhist Churches of America: Founded, 1899; 1710 Octavia St., San Francisco, CA 94109; churches, 60; membership, 60,000.

Christadelphians: Organized, 1844; address, 1002 Webster Lane, Des Plaines, IL 60016; churches, 850; membership, 15,800.

Christian and Missionary Alliance: Organized, 1887; address, 350 N. Highland Ave., Nyack, NY 10960; churches, 1,436; membership; 195,042.

Christian Church (Disciples of Christ): Organized, 1832; address, Box 1986, 222 S. Downey Ave., Indianapolis, IN 46206; churches, 4,296; membership, 1,173,135.

Christian Churches and Churches of Christ: Founded, early 1800s; address, Box 39456, Cincinnati, OH 45231; churches, 5,605; membership, 1,063,254.

Christian Science: Church of Christ, Scientist: Founded, 1879; address, Christian Science Center, Boston, MA 02115; branches, 3,000.

Church of God: Organized, about 1880; address, Box 2420, Anderson, IN 46018; churches, 2,275; membership, 178,581.

Church of God: General Conference of Churches of God: Organized, 1825; address, Room 200, 900 S. Arlington Ave., Harrisburg, PA 17109; churches, 344; membership, 34,638.

Church of the Nazarene: Organized, 1908; address, 6401 The Paseo, Kansas City, MO 64131; churches, 4,853; membership, 484,276.

Churches of Christ: No general organization higher than local congregation; churches, 12,700; membership, 1,600,000.

Community Churches, National Council of: Organized, 1950; 900 Ridge Rd., Homewood, IL 60430; churches, 185; membership, 190,000.

Congregational Christian Churches, National Association of: Organized, 1955; address, P.O. Box 1620, Oak Creek, WI 53154; churches, 442; membership, 107,300.

Congregational Christian Conference, Conservative: Founded, 1948; address, 2849 N. Rice St., Ste. 204, St. Paul, MN 55113; churches, 138; membership, 25,011.

Eastern Orthodox: Albanian Orthodox Archdiocese in America: Established, 1908; address, 529 E. Broadway, S. Boston, MA 02127; churches, 16; membership, 40,000.

Eastern Orthodox: American Carpatho-Russian Orthodox Greek Catholic Church: Organized, 1938; address, Johnstown, PA 15906; churches, 70; membership, 100,000.

Eastern Orthodox: Antiochian Orthodox Christian Archdiocese of All North America: Established, 1975; address, 358 Mountain Rd., Englewood, NJ 07631; churches, 110; membership, 152,000.

Eastern Orthodox: Armenian Apostolic Church of America: Established, 1887; address, 138 E. 39th St., New York, NY 10016; churches, 29; membership, 125,000.

Eastern Orthodox: Armenian Church of America, Diocese of the: Established, 1889; address, 630 Second Ave., New York, NY 10016; churches, 66; membership, 450,000.

Eastern Orthodox: Bulgarian Eastern Orthodox Church: Founded, 1907; address, 550 A W. 50th St., New York, NY 10019; churches, 13; membership, 86,000.

Eastern Orthodox: Coptic Orthodox Church: Founded, ancient Egypt; address, 427 West Side Ave., Jersey City, NJ 07304; churches, 25; membership, 100,000.

Eastern Orthodox: Greek Orthodox Archdiocese of North and South America: Founded, 1864; address, 8–10 East 79th St., New York, NY 10021; churches, 535; membership, 1,950,000.

Eastern Orthodox: Holy Apostolic and Catholic Church of the East (Assyrian): Founded, 37 A.D.; address, 7444 N. Kildare, Skokie, IL 60076; churches, 12; membership, 30,000.

Eastern Orthodox: Orthodox Church in America (formerly Russian Orthodox Greek Catholic Church of America): Established, 1792; address, P.O. Box 675, Syosset, NY 11791; churches, 440; membership, 1,000,000.

Eastern Orthodox: Romanian Orthodox Episcopate of America: Organized, 1929; address, 2522 Grey Tower Rd., Jackson, MI 49201; churches, 34; membership, 40,000.

Eastern Orthodox: Russian Orthodox Church in the U.S.A., Patriarchal Parishes of the: Address, 15 E. 97th St., New York, NY 10029; churches, 41; membership, 51,500.

Eastern Orthodox: Russian Orthodox Church Outside Russia: Organized, 1920; address, 75 E. 93d St., New York, NY 10028; churches, 81; membership, 55,000.

Eastern Orthodox: Serbian Eastern Orthodox Church in the U.S.A. and Canada: Organized, 1921; address, P.O. Box 519, Libertyville, IL 60048; churches, 77; membership, 95,000.

Eastern Orthodox: Syrian Orthodox Church of Antioch: Organized, 1957; address, 49 Kipp Ave., Lodi, NJ 07644; churches, 13; membership, 30,000.

Eastern Orthodox: Ukrainian Orthodox Church in the U.S.A.: Organized, 1919; address, South Bound Brook, NJ 08880; churches, 107; membership, 87,745.

Eastern Orthodox: Ukrainian Orthodox Church in America (Ecumenical Patriarchate): Organized, 1928; address, 90–34 139th St., Jamaica, NY 11435; churches, 28; membership, 25,000.

Episcopal Church: Became autonomous from the Anglican Church of England in 1789; address, 815 Second Avenue, New York, NY 10017; churches, 7,234; membership, 2,767,440.

Evangelical Congregational Church: Formed, 1928; 100 W. Park Ave., Myerstown, PA 17067; churches, 160; membership, 27,405.

Evangelical Covenant Church of America: Organized, 1885; address, 5101 N. Francisco Ave., Chicago, IL 60625; churches, 542; membership, 79,523.

Evangelical Free Church of America: Organized, 1880s; address, 1515 E. 66th St., Minneapolis, MN 55423; churches, 805; membership, 103,900.

Evangelical Presbyterian Church: Founded, 1981; address, 2312 Monroe St., Dearborn, MI 48124; churches, 35; membership, 19,000.

Evangelistic: Christian Congregation, Inc.: Incorporated, 1887; address, 804 W. Hemlock St., La Follette, TN 37766; churches, 1,426; membership, 100,245.

Evangelistic: Missionary Church: Formed by merger of United Missionary Church and Missionary Church Association, 1969; address, 3901 S. Wayne Ave., Fort Wayne, IN 46807; churches, 289; membership, 24,742.

Free Christian Zion Church of Christ: Organized, 1905; address, 1315 Hutchinson Street, Nashville, AR 71852; churches, 742; membership, 22,260.

Independent Fundamental Churches of America: Organized, 1930; address, 1860 Mannheim Rd., Box 250, Westchester, IL 60153; churches, 1,019; membership, 120,446.

Islam: Address, Islamic Center, 2551 Massachusetts Ave., N.W., Washington, DC 20008.

Jehovah's Witnesses: Organized, 1870s; 25 Columbia Heights, Brooklyn, NY 11201; congregations, 7,590; membership, 588,503.

Judaism: First congregation in America, 1654; total membership, 5,921,205.

Judaism (Conservative): United Synagogue of America: Address, 155 Fifth Ave., New York, NY 10010; congregations, 800.

Judaism (Orthodox): Union of Orthodox Jewish Congregations of America: Address, 116 E. 27th St., New York, NY 10016; congregations, 3,000.

Judaism (Reform): Union of American Hebrew Congregations: Address, 838 Fifth Ave., New York, NY 10021; congregations, 700.

Lutheran: American Lutheran Church: Organized, 1960; address, 422 S. 5th St., Minneapolis, MN 55415; churches, 4,865; membership, 2,346,207.

Lutheran: Evangelical Lutheran Churches, Association of: Organized, 1976; address, 12015 Manchester Rd., Ste. 80LL, St. Louis, MO 63131; churches, 270; membership, 109,434.

Lutheran: Evangelical Lutheran Synod: Organized, 1853; address, Bethany Lutheran College, Mankato, MN 56001; churches, 108; membership, 19,795.

Lutheran Church in America: Organized, 1962; address, 231 Madison Ave., New York, NY 10016; churches, 5,801; membership, 2,921,829.

Lutheran Church—Missouri Synod: Organized, 1847; address, 1333 S. Kirkwood Rd., St. Louis, MO 63122; churches, 5,701; membership, 2,636,715.

Lutheran: Wisconsin Evangelical Lutheran Synod: Organized, 1850; address, 3512 W. North Ave., Milwaukee, WI 53208; churches, 1,139; membership, 407,043.

Mennonite: General Conference of Mennonite Brethren Churches: Established in America, 1874; address, Hillsboro, KS 67063; churches, 127; membership, 17,813.

Mennonite: Old Order Amish Church: address, Raber's Bookstore, Baltic, OH 43804; churches, 535; membership, 80,250.

Mennonite Church: Established in America, 1683; address, 528 E. Madison St., Lombard, IL 60148; churches, 1,151; membership, 99,651.

Mennonite Church, The General Conference: Organized, 1860; address, 722 Main Street, Newton, KS 67114; churches, 218; membership, 36,644.

Methodist: African Methodist Episcopal Church: Founded, 1787; address, 1002 Kirkwood Ave., Nashville, TN 37203; churches, 6,200; membership, 2,210,000.

Methodist: African Methodist Episcopal Zion Church: Founded, 1796; address, P.O. Box 30714, Charlotte, NC 28230; churches, 6,020; membership, 1,134,176.

Methodist: Christian Methodist Episcopal Church: Organized, 1870; address, P.O. Box 74, Memphis, TN 38101; churches, 2,883; membership, 786,707.

Methodist: Free Methodist Church of North America: Organized, 1860; address, 901 College Ave., Winona Lake, IN 46590; churches, 1,010; membership, 69,949.

Methodist: Reformed Zion Union Apostolic Church: Organized, 1869; address, 416 South Hill Ave., South Hill, VA 23970; churches, 50; membership, 16,000.

Methodist: United Methodist Church: Formed, 1968; address, 601 W. Riverview Ave., Dayton, OH 45406; churches, 38,417; membership, 9,519,407.

Metropolitan Community Churches, Universal Fellowship of: Founded, 1968; address, 5300 Santa Monica Blvd., #304, Los Angeles, CA 90029; churches, 180; membership, 30,000.

Moravian Church in America: Established, 1735; address, P.O. Box 1245, 69 W. Church St., Bethlehem, PA 18018; churches, 151; membership, 54,355.

Mormon: Church of Jesus Christ of Latter-day Saints: Organized, 1830; address, 50 East North Temple St., Salt Lake City, UT 84150; churches, 7,686; membership, 3,490,000.

New Apostolic Church of North America: Established, 1863; address, 3753 N. Troy St., Chicago, IL 60618; churches, 396; membership, 28,733.

Old Roman Catholic Church (English Rite): Established in America, 1916; address, 4200 N. Kedvale Ave., Chicago, IL 60641; churches, 139; membership, 61,570.

Pentecostal: Apostolic Overcoming Holy Church of God: Organized, 1916; address, 1120 N. 24th St., Birmingham, AL 35234; churches, 300; membership, 75,000.

Pentecostal: Assemblies of God: Founded, 1914; address, 1445 Boonville Avenue, Springfield, MO 65802; churches, 9,930; membership, 1,788,394.

Pentecostal: Church of God: Organized, 1903; 2504 Arrow Wood Dr., S.E., Huntsville, AL 35803; churches, 2,035; membership, 75,890.

Pentecostal: Church of God (Cleveland, Tenn.): Organized, 1886; address, Keith St. at 25th

U.S. RELIGIOUS DENOMINATIONS *(continued)*
N.W., Cleveland, TN 37311; churches, 5,281; membership, 456,797.
Pentecostal: Church of God in Christ: Organized, 1895; address, 938 Mason St., Memphis, TN 38126; churches, 9,982; membership, 3,709,661.
Pentecostal: Church of God in Christ, International: Organized, 1969; address, 170 Adelphi St., Brooklyn, NY 11025; churches, 300; membership, 200,000.
Pentecostal: Church of God of Prophecy: Organized, 1886; Bible Pl., Cleveland, TN 37311; churches, 1,977; membership, 72,977.
Pentecostal: Church of Our Lord Jesus Christ of the Apostolic Faith, Inc.: Organized, 1919; address, 2081 Seventh Ave., New York, NY 10027; churches, 155; membership, 45,000.
Pentecostal: Full Gospel Fellowship of Churches and Ministers, Int'l.: Founded, 1962; address, 1545 W. Mockingbird Lane, Ste. 1012, Lock Box 209, Dallas, TX 75235; churches, 420; membership, 65,000.
Pentecostal: International Church of the Foursquare Gospel: Organized, 1927; address, Angelus Temple, 1100 Glendale Boulevard, Los Angeles, CA 90026; churches, 714; membership, 89,215.
Pentecostal: Open Bible Standard Churches, Inc.: Formed, 1935; address, 2020 Bell Ave., Des Moines, IA 50315; churches, 277; membership, 46,907.
Pentecostal: The (Original) Church of God, Inc.: Organized, 1886; address, P.O. Box 3086, Chattanooga, TN 37404; churches, 70; membership, 20,000.
Pentecostal Church of God of America, Inc.: Organized, 1919; address, Messenger Plaza, 211 Main St., Joplin, MO 64801; churches, 1,118; membership, 83,860.
Pentecostal Holiness Church, Int'l.: Organized, about 1895; address, P.O. Box 12609, Oklahoma City, OK 73157; churches, 2,340; membership, 86,103.
Pentecostal: United Holy Church of America, Inc.: Organized, 1886; address, P.O. Box 19846, Philadelphia, PA 19143; churches, 470; membership, 28,980.
Pentecostal: United Pentecostal Church International: Formed, 1945; address, 8855 Dunn Rd., Hazelwood, MO 63042; churches, 2,849; membership, 465,000.
Plymouth Brethren: Organized, 1820s; address, P.O. Box 294, Wheaton, IL 60187; churches, 1,100; membership, 98,000.
Polish National Catholic Church of America: Organized, 1897; address, 529 E. Locust St., Scranton, PA 18505; churches, 162; membership, 282,411.
Presbyterian: Associate Reformed Presbyterian Church (General Synod): Reorganized, 1935; address, 1 Cleveland St., Greenville, SC 29601; churches, 156; membership, 31,518.
Presbyterian Church (U.S.A.): Established, 1706; merger, 1983; addresses: 475 Riverside Dr., N.Y., NY 10027, 341 Ponce de Leon Ave. N.E., Atlanta, GA 30365; churches, 13,042; membership, 3,202,392.
Presbyterian Church in America: Established, 1973; address, Box 312, Brevard, NC 28712; churches, 698; membership, 136,582.
Presbyterian: Cumberland Presbyterian Church: Organized, 1810; address, 1978 Union Ave., Memphis, TN 38104; churches, 833; membership, 97,599.
Presbyterian: Orthodox Presbyterian Church: Organized, 1936; address, 7401 Old York Rd., Philadelphia, PA 19126; churches, 157; membership, 17,108.
Presbyterian: Second Cumberland Presbyterian Church in U.S.: Organized, 1869; address, 226 Church St.; Huntsville, AL 35801; churches, 121; membership, 30,000.
Quaker: Evangelical Friends Alliance: Formed, 1965; address, 29 N. Garland Ave., Colorado Spgs., CO 80909; churches, 217; membership, 24,095.
Quaker: Friends General Conference: Organized, 1900; address, 1520-B Race St., Philadelphia, PA 19102; churches, 233; membership, 26,184.
Quaker: Friends United Meeting: Organized, 1965; address, 101 Quaker Hill Dr., Richmond, IN 47374; churches, 532; membership, 60,084.
Reformed Church in America: Established 1628 as the Reformed Protestant Dutch Church; address, 475 Riverside Dr., New York, NY 10115; churches, 910; membership, 345,762.
Reformed Churches: Christian Reformed Church: Founded, 1857; address, 2850 Kalamazoo Ave., S.E., Grand Rapids, MI 49508; churches, 634; membership, 215,411.
Reorganized Church of Jesus Christ of Latter Day Saints: Reorganized, 1860; address, The Auditorium, P.O. Box 1059, Independence, MO 64051; churches, 1,056; membership, 190,087.
Roman Catholic Church: Established in Maryland, 1634; address, 1312 Massachusetts Ave. N.W., Washington, DC 20005; parishes, churches, and missions, 24,277; membership, 51,207,579.
Salvation Army: Established, 1880; address, 120–130 W. 14th St., New York, NY 10011; churches, 1,062; membership, 414,999.
Scientology, Church of: Founded, 1950; address, 5930 Franklin Ave., Los Angeles, CA 90028; churches, 47.
Triumph the Church and Kingdom of God in Christ (International): Founded, 1902; address, Rt. 4, Box 77056, Birmingham, AL 35228; churches, 475; membership, 54,307.
Unitarian Universalist Association: Universalists organized, 1793; Unitarians organized, 1825; merger, 1961; address, 25 Beacon Street, Boston, MA 02108; churches, 935; membership, 131,844.
United Brethren in Christ: Founded, 1800; address, 302 Lake St., Huntington, IN 46750; churches, 258; membership, 27,154.
United Church of Christ: Union, 1957, of the Evangelical and Reformed Church and the Congregational Christian Churches; 105 Madison Ave., New York, NY 10016; churches, 6,443; membership, 1,726,244.
Volunteers of America: Founded, 1896; address, 3939 North Causeway Boulevard, Ste. 202, Metairie, LA 70002; churches, 607; membership, 36,634.
Wesleyan Church: Union, 1968, of the Pilgrim Holiness Church and Wesleyan Methodist Church; address, P.O. Box 2000, Marion, IN 46952; churches, 1,711; membership, 103,712.

ROMAN CATHOLIC POPES

POPE	REIGN
St. Peter	d.67
St. Linus	67–76
St. Cletus or Anacletus	76–88
St. Clement I	88–97
St. Evaristus	97–105
St. Alexander I	105–15
St. Sixtus I	115–25
St. Telesphorus	125–36
St. Hyginus	136–40
St. Pius I	140–55
St. Anicetus	155–66
St. Soter	166–75
St. Eleutherius	175–89
St. Victor I	189–99
St. Zephyrinus	199(?)–217
St. Callistus I	217–22
St. Urban I	222–30
St. Pontian	230–35
St. Anterus	235–36
St. Fabian	236–50
St. Cornelius	251–53
St. Lucius I	253–54
St. Stephen I	254–57
St. Sixtus II	257–58
St. Dionysius	259–68
St. Felix I	269–74
St. Eutychian	275–83
St. Caius	283–96
St. Marcellinus	296–304
St. Marcellus I	308–09
St. Eusebius	309 or 310
St. Miltiades	311–14
St. Sylvester I	314–35
St. Marcus	336
St. Julius I	337–52
Liberius	352–66
St. Damasus I	366–84
St. Siricius	384–99
St. Anastasius I	399–401
St. Innocent I	401–17
St. Zosimus	417–18
St. Boniface I	418–22
St. Celestine I	422–32
St. Sixtus III	432–40
St. Leo I	440–61
St. Hilarius	461–68
St. Simplicius	468–83
St. Felix III (II)[1]	483–92
St. Gelasius I	492–96
Anastasius II	496–98
St. Symmachus	498–514
St. Hormisdas	514–23
St. John I	523–26
St. Felix IV (III)	526–30
Boniface II	530–32
John II	533–35
St. Agapetus I	535–36
St. Silverius	536–37
Vigilius	537(?)–55
Pelagius I	556–61
John III	561–74
Benedict I	575–79
Pelagius II	579–90
St. Gregory I	590–604
Sabinianus	604–06
Boniface III	607
St. Boniface IV	608–15
St. Deusdedit or Adeodatus I	615–18
Boniface V	619–25
Honorius I	625–38
Severinus	640
John IV	640–42
Theodore I	642–49
St. Martin I	649–55
St. Eugene I	654–57
St. Vitalian	657–72
Adeodatus II	672–76
Donus	676–78
St. Agatho	678–81
St. Leo II	682–83
St. Benedict II	684–85
John V	685–86
Conon	686–87
St. Sergius I	687–701
John VI	701–05
John VII	705–07
Sisinnius	708
Constantine	708–15
St. Gregory II	715–31
St. Gregory III	731–41
St. Zacharias	741–52
Stephen II	752
Stephen II (III)	752–57
St. Paul I	757–67
Stephen III (IV)	768–72
Adrian I	772–95
St. Leo III	795–816
Stephen IV (V)	816–17
St. Paschal	817–24
Eugene II	824–27
Valentine	827
Gregory IV	827–44
Sergius II	844–47
St. Leo IV	847–55
Benedict III	855–58
St. Nicholas I	858–67
Adrian II	867–72
John VIII	872–82
Marinus I	882–84
St. Adrian III	884–85
Stephen V (VI)	885–91
Formosus	891–96
Boniface VI	896
Stephen VI (VII)	896–97
Romanus	897
Theodore II	897
John IX	898–900
Benedict IV	900–03
Leo V	903
Sergius III	904–11
Anastasius III	911–13
Lando	913–14
John X	914–28
Leo VI	928
Stephen VII (VIII)	928–31
John XI	931–35
Leo VII	936–39
Stephen VIII (IX)	939–42
Marinus II	942–46
Agapetus II	946–55
John XII[2]	955–64
Leo VIII[2]	963–65
Benedict V[2]	964–66
John XIII	965–72
Benedict VI	973–74
Benedict VII	974–83
John XIV	983–84
John XV	985–96
Gregory V	996–99
Sylvester II	999–1003
John XVII	1003
John XVIII	1004–09
Sergius IV	1009–12
Benedict VIII	1012–24
John XIX	1024–32
Benedict IX[3]	1032–44 1045, 1047–48
Sylvester III[3]	1045
Gregory VI[3]	1045–46
Clement II[3]	1046–47
Damasus II	1048
St. Leo IX	1049–54
Victor II	1055–57
Stephen IX (X)	1057–58
Nicholas II	1059–61
Alexander II	1061–73
St. Gregory VII	1073–85
Victor III	1086–87
Urban II	1088–99
Paschal II	1099–1118
Gelasius II	1118–19
Callistus II	1119–24
Honorius II	1124–30
Innocent II	1130–43
Victor IV	1138
Celestine II	143–44
Lucius II	1144–45
Eugene III	1145–53
Anastasius IV	1153–54
Adrian IV	1154–59
Alexander III	1159–81
Lucius III	1181–85
Urban III	1185–87
Gregory VIII	1187
Clement III	1187–91
Celestine III	1191–98
Innocent III	1198–1216
Honorius III	1216–27
Gregory IX	1227–41
Celestine IV	1241
Innocent IV	1243–54
Alexander IV	1254–61
Urban IV	1261–64
Clement IV	1265–68
Gregory X	1271–76
Innocent V	1276
Adrian V	1276
John XXI	1276–77
Nicholas III	1277–80
Martin IV	1281–85
Honorius IV	1285–87
Nicholas IV	1288–92
St. Celestine V	1294
Boniface VIII	1294–1303
Benedict XI	1303–04
Clement V	1305–14
John XXII	1316–34
Benedict XII	1334–42
Clement VI	1342–52
Innocent VI	1352–62
Urban V	1362–70
Gregory XI	1370–78
Urban VI	1378–89
Boniface IX	1389–1404
Innocent VII	1404–06
Gregory XII	1406–15
Martin V	1417–31
Benedict XIV	1425–30
Eugene IV	1431–47
Nicholas V	1447–55
Callistus III	1455–58
Pius II	1458–64
Paul II	1464–71
Sixtus IV	1471–84
Innocent VIII	1484–92
Alexander VI	1492–1503
Pius III	1503
Julius II	1503–13
Leo X	1513–21
Adrian VI	1522–23
Clement VII	1523–34
Paul III	1534–49
Julius III	1550–55
Marcellus II	1555
Paul IV	1555–59
Pius IV	1559–65
St. Pius V	1566–72
Gregory XIII	1572–85
Sixtus V	1585–90
Urban VIII	1590
Gregory XIV	1590–91
Innocent IX	1591
Clement VIII	1592–1605
Leo XI	1605
Paul V	1605–21
Gregory XV	1621–23
Urban VIII	1623–44
Innocent X	1644–55
Alexander VII	1655–67
Clement IX	1667–69
Clement X	1670–76
Innocent XI	1676–89
Alexander VIII	1689–91
Innocent XII	1691–1700
Clement XI	1700–21
Innocent XIII	1721–24
Benedict XIII	1724–30
Clement XII	1730–40
Benedict XIV	1740–58
Clement XIII	1758–69
Clement XIV	1769–74
Pius VI	1775–99
Pius VII	1800–23
Leo XII	1823–29
Pius VIII	1829–30
Gregory XVI	1831–46
Pius IX	1846–78
Leo XIII	1878–1903
St. Pius X	1903–14
Benedict XV	1914–22
Pius XI	1922–39
Pius XII	1939–58
John XXIII	1958–63
Paul VI	1963–78
John Paul I	1978
John Paul II	1978–

[1] The presence of antipopes (not listed here) sometimes places question on a pope's number. In all such cases, the alternate number is cited on this list in parentheses. [2] John XII was deposed in 963 by a church council. If this deposition was invalid, Leo was an antipope. If the deposition was valid, Leo was the legitimate pope and Benedict an antipope. [3] Benedict IX was deposed on three different occasions (in 1044, 1046, and 1048). If the depositions were illegitimate, Sylvester III, Gregory VI, and Clement II were antipopes.

THEOLOGIANS AND PHILOSOPHERS

Peter Abelard (1079–1142), French philosopher and theologian who used a dialectic method in an effort to support Christian dogma. He is best known for his tragic romance with Héloïse, an abbess, and their exchange of love letters.

Aristotle (384–322 B.C.), Greek philosopher whose writings have greatly influenced Western thought. His philosophy became dominant in the 13th century when it was largely adopted by the Christian scholastic philosophers.

Asoka (died 232 B.C.), Indian emperor who galvanized growth of Buddhism in Asia by making it India's state religion and by sending Buddhist missionaries to distant countries. Asoka thus transformed Buddhism from a local religion to a faith of world importance.

Averroës (1126–98), Islamic Spanish philosopher whose studies and interpretations of Aristotle's thought exerted considerable influence on European philosophy and Christian theology, including that of Thomas Aquinas.

Karl Barth (1886–1968), Swiss Protestant theologian whose views stress the importance of Christian revelation and tend to favor the theology of the prescientific age.

Henri Bergson (1859–1941), French philosopher of Jewish origin but inclined toward Christian mysticism, who stressed the importance of intuition in the perception of reality.

George Berkeley (1685–1753), Anglo-Irish clergyman and philosopher who saw an ordered coherence in the world as proof of God's existence. He spent three years in America attempting to establish a college to train missionaries to convert the Indians.

Bernard of Clairvaux (1090–1153), French abbot whose mystical teachings exerted a powerful influence on Christianity throughout western Europe.

John Biddle (1615–62), English theologian who founded Unitarianism, a Christian denomination that affirms the existence of God but denies the Holy Trinity.

Jakob Böhme or **Boehme** (1575–1624), German theosophist and mystic whose writings were concerned with the necessity of evil because of the dualism of the divine nature of God. One of his works was declared heretical.

Dietrich Bonhoeffer (1906–45), German theologian and Lutheran pastor who advocated a secularized reinterpretation of Christianity. His anti-Hitler sentiments resulted in his execution by the Nazis.

Martin Buber (1878–1965), Jewish mystical philosopher who was influenced by the Christian existentialism of Kierkegaard. In turn, Buber exerted influence on modern Christian thought in the form of a highly personalized ("I-Thou") approach to God and the world.

Buddha (Siddhartha Gautama; c. 563–483 B.C.), Indian nobleman who founded Buddhism, one of the major Asian religions. He renounced sensual pleasures and advocated total spiritual detachment from the world.

Rudolf Karl Bultmann (1884–1976), German Protestant existentialist theologian and scholar who attempted to distinguish between what he interpreted as the mythical and the historical elements in the New Testament.

John Calvin (1509–64), French theologian who was one of the most important figures of the Reformation. His doctrines are central to the Presbyterian and Reformed churches.

Chuang-tse (369?–275? B.C.), Chinese Taoist philosopher whose writings are among the most important in Taoist literature.

Clement of Alexandria (150?–215?), Greek Christian theologian who was possibly the first to attempt to reconcile Platonistic and Stoic thought with Christian belief and ethics.

Confucius (c. 551–479? B.C.), Chinese philosopher whose ethical precepts, the *Analects*, set forth standards of personal behavior with a view toward social harmony in an ideal state.

Thomas Cranmer (1489–1556), English churchman who was archbishop of Canterbury and a supporter of Henry VIII against Rome. He contributed to the preparation of the Book of Common Prayer.

René Descartes (1596–1650), French philosopher and scientist whose method of achieving certitude began with the assertion of self (*cogito ergo sum*) and proceeded to attempt a rational proof of God's existence.

Jonathan Edwards (1703–58), American theologian whose preaching, based largely on the thought of Calvin, Berkeley, and Locke, exerted a powerful influence on colonial America.

Ralph Waldo Emerson (1803–82), American essayist, poet, and philosopher whose belief in a mystical unity of nature (transcendentalism) has been an important influence in American thought.

Gamaliel II (1st century A.D.), Jewish teacher and an innovator of Jewish prayers and rituals in the wake of the upheaval following the Roman destruction of Jerusalem. He was a grandson of Gamaliel, cited in the New Testament (Acts 5:33–39).

Georg Wilhelm Friedrich Hegel (1770–1831), German idealist philosopher whose dialectical interpretation of history influenced such diverse thinkers as Marx, Kierkegaard, and Dewey.

Martin Heidegger (1889–1976), German philosopher whose writing, an extension of the phenomenological school of Edmund Husserl, interprets "being" as the continual, elusive process of "becoming." His major work, *Being and Time* (1927), has influenced existentialism.

Theodor Herzl (1860–1904), Hungarian Jewish religious leader, considered the father of modern Zionism. Primarily a writer, his best-known work is the pamphlet *Der Judenstaat* (The Jewish State). He convened the first Zionist Congress at Basel, Switzerland, in 1897.

Hillel (1st century B.C.), Jewish scholar and one of the leading figures in the compilation of Talmudic law. He laid the foundation of a systematic legal interpretation of Hebrew writings. Although born in Babylonia, he went to Palestine, the center of Judaism, at age 40 and was elected leader of the Sanhedrin.

Richard Hooker (1554?–1600), English theologian whose writings constitute a major influence on Anglican theological concepts and ecclesiastical organization.

John Huss or Jan Hus (1369?–1415), Bohemian religious reformer whose denunciation of abuses of the Catholic hierarchy ultimately led to his martyrdom. He is considered a forerunner of the Protestant Reformation and is regarded as a Czech national hero.

William Ralph Inge (1860–1954), English theologian who was influential as a teacher at Cambridge and Oxford universities. His writings explore the mystical aspects of Christianity.

Jesus Christ (c. 5 B.C.–A.D. 30), founder of Christianity. The books of the New Testament tell about his life on earth, his teachings, the miracles that he performed, and his trial, crucifixion, and resurrection. His disciples and followers spread Christianity throughout the Roman Empire.

Immanuel Kant (1724–1804), German philosopher who ranks among the greatest figures in the history of Western thought. His *Critique of Pure Reason* (1781) denies that God's existence can be verified by rational proofs.

Sören Kierkegaard (1813–55), Danish philosopher whose belief in the superiority of subjective over objective truth led him to conclude that adherence to Christian belief is of less value than the acting out of a Christian life. He is considered the father of existentialism.

John Knox (1513?–72), Scottish religious leader who founded Scottish Presbyterianism. He was closely associated with John Calvin.

Lao-tzu (604–531 B.C.), Chinese philosopher who is considered the founder of the Taoist religion. His only known writing is a treatise on the origins of the universe, entitled *Tao Teh King*.

Hugh Latimer (1485?–1555), English bishop whose staunch faithfulness to Protestantism led to his martyrdom by Queen Mary I.

John Locke (1632–1704), English philosopher who believed that all ideas originate from sensory perception. This set the foundation for the empirical school of philosophy. His belief in man's tendency toward social good influenced modern democratic thought.

Martin Luther (1483–1546), German leader of the Protestant Reformation whose rebellion against abuses of the Roman Catholic Church marked a major turning point in Europe's social and religious history. Founder of the Lutheran Church, his teachings have been a major influence on all of Protestantism.

Maimonides (Moses ben Maimon; 1135–1204), Jewish philosopher and physician who organized Jewish oral law into concepts that were understandable to the layman. His most important work is *Moreh Nevukhim* (Guide for the Perplexed).

Jacques Maritain (1882–1973), French Catholic philosopher who attempted to reconcile Aquinas' teachings with contemporary thought.

Cotton Mather (1663–1728), American Puritan clergyman who exercised great influence through his preaching and writings in colonial New England. He was among the chief investigators of suspected witchcraft in Salem, Mass.

Increase Mather (1639–1723), American clergyman and a leading advocate of Puritan theocracy. He was the father of Cotton Mather.

Philipp Melanchthon (1497–1560), German theologian and humanist who was an associate of Martin Luther and an important voice in the Reformation.

Mencius or **Meng-tse** (372–289 B.C.), Chinese religious reformer and sage who influenced a resurgence of Confucian thought during his lifetime, and who was later venerated in Confucian temples.

Moses Mendelssohn (1729–86), German Jewish philosopher who espoused reforms of Jewish ritual law, thus pioneering a faith adaptable to modern needs.

Mohammed (570?–632), Arab prophet of the religion of Islam. Incorporating Jewish and Christian beliefs with his own distinctive theology, he is believed by his Muslim followers to be the last great prophet of the Jewish and Christian traditions and successor to Jesus. He wrote the Koran as the revelations of Allah (God).

John Courtney Murray (1904–67), American Catholic theologian and scholar who was a leader in the liberal Catholic movement.

Nestorius (died after 451), Middle Eastern theologian who founded the Nestorian Church, an early Christian heretical sect.

John Henry Newman (1801–90), English Roman Catholic cardinal and a leader of the Oxford Movement, a major reorganizational effort within the Anglican Church. His decision to become a Roman Catholic stirred controversy within England's church circles; he justified his action in *Apologia pro Vita Sua*.

Helmut Richard Niebuhr (1894–1962), American Protestant theologian who attempted to reconcile Christian doctrine with the dominant ideas of the 20th century.

Reinhold Niebuhr (1892–1971), American Protestant theologian who wrote extensively on the social aspects of modern Christian life.

Friedrich Wilhelm Nietzsche (1844–1900), German moral philosopher who viewed his contemporary Christian civilization as decadent and looked forward to an era when a new breed of men would revivify the civilization.

Matthew Parker (1504–75), English religious leader who, as archbishop of Canterbury, led the Anglican Church in a middle course between Roman Catholicism and Protestantism.

Blaise Pascal (1623–62), French religious thinker and scientist who stressed that faith was the ultimate bridge between man and God.

Philo Judaeus (20? B.C.–A.D. 50?), Jewish Alexandrian philosopher whose teachings regarding God's perfection and total transcendence over man had a marked influence on early Christian writings. His thought amounts to a fusion of Platonic philosophy with the doctrines of Hebrew scriptures.

Plato (427?–347? B.C.), Greek philosopher and disciple of Socrates. Plato's writings have had immense influence on the religious and secular thought of Western civilization.

Plotinus (205–270), Alexandrian philosopher of the Neoplatonist school whose thought influenced early Christian doctrine.

Nicholas Ridley (1500?–55), English church reformer who took part in compiling the Book of Common Prayer. A staunch adherent of Anglicanism, he was martyred, along with Hugh Latimer, by Queen Mary I.

THEOLOGIANS AND PHILOSOPHERS *(continued)*

Saint Thomas Aquinas (1225–74), Italian theologian and philosopher who ranks as the most influential figure in medieval philosophy. He formulated the official Roman Catholic philosophy, most explicitly in *Summa Theologica.*

Saint Augustine (354–430), Latin bishop and doctor of the Christian church, considered by many to be the founder of a formalized Christian theology. His books include the *Confessions,* a spiritual autobiography; and *City of God*, a defense of Christian beliefs.

Saint Thomas à Becket (1118?–70), archbishop of Canterbury. A defender of church rights against lay power, he quarreled with Henry II and was murdered in Canterbury Cathedral by the king's knights.

Saint Francis of Assisi (1182–1226), Italian friar and preacher who founded the Franciscan order in 1209. His monastic rule demanded poverty, and the members of his order lived by begging. According to legend he experienced the miracle of the stigmata in 1224.

Saint John of the Cross (San Juan de la Cruz; 1542–91), Spanish mystic and poet. With St. Theresa of Ávila he founded the Discalced Carmelites. His works include three great mystical poems: *The Dark Night of the Soul, The Flame of Divine Love*, and *The Spiritual Canticle.*

Saint Ignatius Loyola (1491–1556), Spanish Catholic founder of the Jesuit order.

Saint John Nepomucene Neuman (1811–60), first American man canonized by Roman Catholic Church (1977). Born in Bohemia (now Czechoslovakia), he came to U.S. in 1836. He was vicar of the Redemptionists order, 1847–52, and then served as bishop of Philadelphia, 1852–60, expanding parochial school enrollment from 500 to 9,000.

Saint Patrick (389?–461?), patron saint of Ireland who converted the Irish people to Christianity and established churches.

Saint Paul (died A.D. 67?), an organizer of the Christian church. Jewish by birth, he tried to stamp out the Christian movement in Jerusalem, but he was converted on the way to Damascus. He made several missionary journeys and founded churches to which he sent letters (the Pauline epistles of the New Testament).

Saint Peter (died A.D. 67?), one of Jesus' disciples, helped organize the early Christian church. He is regarded as the first pope by the Roman Catholic Church.

Saint Elizabeth Ann Seton (1774–1821), first person born in U.S. canonized a saint by Roman Catholic Church (1975). Founded Sisters of Charity in 1809. Pioneered parochial education and charitable institutions in U.S.

Saint Theresa of Ávila (1515–82), Spanish Roman Catholic nun of the Carmelite order. Both a vigorous administrator and author of religious tracts, she exerted great influence on the 16th century Catholic Reformation.

Girolamo Savonarola (1452–98), Italian Catholic reformer and religious leader of Florence whose attacks against the papacy ultimately led to his execution.

Friedrich Daniel Ernst Schleiermacher (1768–1834), German theologian who claimed that religion and philosophy do not contradict each other, but that religion should be purged of metaphysical overtones.

Arthur Schopenhauer (1788–1860), German philosopher whose writings utilized the philosophy of Kant and showed influences of Buddhism in negation of the individual will. His major work is *The World as Will and Representation* (1818).

Albert Schweitzer (1875–1965), Alsatian theologian and medical missionary who established a hospital for African natives in Lambaréné, Gabon. His ethical principle, Reverence for Life, requires a respect for all living creatures.

Joseph Smith (1805–44), American religious leader who founded the Church of Jesus Christ of the Latter-day Saints (Mormons), published the *Book of Mormon* in 1830.

Baruch Spinoza (1632–77), Dutch Jewish rationalist philosopher. He believed God to be identical with nature and thus conceived of man as an extension, or attribute, of divinity.

Emanuel Swedenborg (1688–1772), Swedish theologian and scientist who wrote extensively on physiology before writing religious tracts. His religious thinking became most widely known after his death.

Jeremy Taylor (1613–67), Anglican bishop and religious writer whose finely styled prose was widely popular in the 1600s.

William Temple (1881–1944), archbishop of Canterbury considered the leading influence in forming the British Council of Churches and the World Council of Churches.

Thomas à Kempis (1379?–1471), German monk and devotional writer. He probably wrote *The Imitation of Christ*, still widely read.

Paul Johannes Tillich (1886–1965), German-American existentialist theologian who incorporated psychology into his theological system.

William Tyndale (1494?–1536), English Protestant martyr whose scriptural translations later formed the basis of the King James Bible.

Vardhamana (called **Mahavira;** 500s B.C.), Indian prophet. He founded Jainist religion in reaction against certain Hindu beliefs and practices. Jainism emphasizes man's need to transcend all of his passions.

John Wesley (1703–91), English Anglican minister who founded the Methodist Church. In 1784 he ordained the first American Methodist bishops.

William of Ockham (1285?–1347), English scholastic philosopher who drew a sharp distinction between the realms of philosophy and theology to avoid purported contradictions.

John Wyclif or **Wycliffe** (1330?–84), English ecclesiastical reformer and forerunner of the Reformation. He insisted on the supremacy of scripture over the authority of the church.

Brigham Young (1801–77), American Mormon preacher who led his sect in its migration west.

Zoroaster or **Zarathustra** (628?–551? B.C.), ancient Persian religious teacher and prophet. He founded Zoroastrianism, which disappeared only with rise of Islam in 600s A.D. Zoroastrianism introduced the idea of an ultimate resurrection of the dead.

Huldreich Zwingli (1484–1531), Swiss religious leader who was major figure behind Protestant Reformation in Switzerland.

Science and Invention

Sylvia Earle, a marine biologist and oceanic explorer, poses with the diving suit she wore while setting a women's depth record of 1,250 feet for a walk on the ocean floor. The suit was part of an exhibition called "Exploring the Deep Frontier" at the American Museum of Natural History in New York. Miss Earle is a curator at the California Academy of Sciences.

United Press Int'l.

HIGHLIGHTS: 1983

In addition to the 1983 developments in science and invention included in this section, see also the separate sections *Awards, Climate and Weather, Earth, Ecology and Environment, Energy and Resources, Medicine and Health,* and *Space and Astronomy.*

NEW STANDARD OF MEASUREMENT

The General Conference on Weights and Measures, meeting in Paris, France, in October 1983 adopted a new worldwide standard of measurement based on the speed of light.

The length of one meter now is defined as the distance that light travels through a vacuum in one 299,792,458th of a second.

Since 1960 the length of a meter had been defined as the wavelength of orange light given off by the gas krypton 86. Before 1960 the length of a standard meter had been

HIGHLIGHTS: 1983 *continued*

marked out on a platinum-iridium bar held for safekeeping by the International Bureau of Weights and Measures in a vault at Sevres, France.

CHEMICAL ELEMENT 109 CREATED

A new artificially created element has been added to the growing list of different kinds of matter known to man. Unnamed, except for its atomic number 109, the new element was first created on Aug. 29, 1982, at a laboratory in Darmstadt, West Germany.

Physicists Gottfried Munzenberg and Peter Armbruster were credited with discovery of the new radioactive element that is heavier than any of the 92 elements that occur naturally.

The element existed for only one 5,000th of a second after being detected by bombarding bismuth metal with a stream of iron atoms.

PLASTIC AUTOMOBILE ENGINE TESTED

As scientists have discovered new ways to improve plastics by rearranging their molecules to increase their strength and resistance to heat, plastics have replaced the use of metals and glass in one consumer product after another, such as toothpaste tubes and ketchup bottles.

Now the use of steel in automobile engines may become the next to go. A New Jersey inventor, Matty Holtzberg, has built such engines at his Polimotor Research Center under contract to the Ford Motor Company. The engines will be tested in racing cars in 1984.

As well as being much lighter than its metal counterpart, the plastic engine would be economical to produce because it would not require the massive machine tools needed to shape metal.

DISKS FOR AROMATIC MOODS

Instead of music or computer programs, new disks and a disk player introduced by the Charles of the Ritz Company in 1983 provide 40 different scents that the firm claims can produce different moods in your home.

The disk player costs about $20, and a disk that can be used 150 times costs about $5. The scent from one play of a disk lasts about an hour. Among the different scents offered were ocean breeze, after-dinner mints, English garden, men's world, and seduction.

NEW MICROSCOPES TO EXPLORE ATOMS

Two huge electron microscopes that can look into solid materials and display their atoms were unveiled in September 1983 at the new $7.5 million federally financed National Microscopy Center at the Lawrence Berkeley Laboratories in Berkeley, Calif.

The two microscopes are the ARM (atomic resolution microscope) and the HVEM (high voltage electron microscope). They were manufactured in Japan by the Japanese Electron Optical Laboratory.

Each microscope is housed in its own three-story building. The first floor of each building is filled with a cushion of springs and rubber tubes that prevent vibration. The second floor of each is a "lens" to focus electrons on the material being examined. The top floor of each holds an accelerator to produce a high-speed stream of electrons to magnify the image.

Earlier electron microscopes could provide glimpses of atoms only with computer-aided enhancement. However, the new ARM can show the atoms of materials directly as well as show the relationship of adjacent atoms.

The new microscopes were expected to make it possible for scientists to improve the qualities of alloys and other materials that combine atoms of several elements.

WORLD'S BIGGEST ATOM SMASHER PLANNED

Plans for the world's largest and most powerful atom smasher moved forward in 1983.

The federal Department of Energy announced on Oct. 21, 1983, that specific construction plans for the $2 billion SSC (superconducting super-collider) would be decided within 12 months. Some $18 million was allocated for research on the project in 1984.

Some of the funds for the SSC were to come from money previously budgeted for a smaller atom smasher, the CBA (colliding beam accelerator), that had been under construction at the Brookhaven National Laboratory on Long Island, N.Y. The CBA project was cancelled in mid-1983 because scientists decided that by the time it was completed in the late 1980s it would be too small to compete with larger atom smashers being built in Europe and the Soviet Union.

The SSC, planned for completion in the 1990's, would be about 50 times more powerful than any other high-energy accelerator now in existence. It would have a circumference of 60 to 120 miles and would generate up to 50 trillion electron-volts with which to smash atoms to discover new insights into the forces and subatomic particles that make up matter.

The most powerful atom smasher currently in operation is the $130 million Tevatron at Fermi National Laboratory in Batavia, Ill., which began functioning in July 1983. The Tevatron, with a track 4 miles in circumference, has reached energy of 512 billion electron volts, the highest ever recorded. It is expected to nearly double that energy output in 1984.

Colorado, Utah, New Mexico, Arizona, and California are among the states being considered by the Department of Energy as a site for the huge SSC project.

EXPANDING BACKLOG OF PATENTS

Although the U.S. Patent Office increased its staff of examiners by nearly 25% in 1983, the backlog of patents awaiting approval continued to grow. At the end of 1982 the backlog stood at 216,509, but as new applications continued to pour in at a rate of about 500 per day the backlog grew to some 232,000 by September.

VIDEODISKS OVERTAKE VIDEOTAPES

The Electronic Industries Association reported that a survey of manufacturers indicates that for the first time more videodisks than videotapes will be sold in 1984.

The trade association predicted that 13 million disks will be sold compared with 10 million tapes. The report said that about 1,000 different titles are now available on videodisks, which sell for about half the price of videotapes.

TREES WARN EACH OTHER OF DANGER

Two University of Washington scientists reported that their experiments show that trees send out signals to each other when attacked by swarms of insects.

The scientists, Gordon H. Orians and David F. Rhoades, conducted experiments in which they placed swarms of tent caterpillars in trees to discover what defense mechanisms the trees have.

In their report to the National Science Foundation, which funded the project, they said they found that the trees produce chemicals to make their leaves inedible to the insects.

In addition, the scientists said nearby trees that had not yet been attacked also began producing the protective chemicals, indicating that somehow they had been warned by their neighbors.

U.S. RACES TO DEVELOP SUPERCOMPUTER

In a race with Japan to develop a fifth-generation supercomputer, the Department of Defense named Lynn Conway, manager of the Knowledge Systems Area of Xerox Corporation's Palo Alto Research Center, to head research for the project.

The first generation of computers used vacuum tubes, the second transistors, the third microchips, and the fourth chips with VSLI (very large scale integrated circuits).

An electrical engineer, Conway was one of the pioneers in the development of VSLI.

The Defense Department has asked for $145 million in 1984–85 for research on the supercomputer project, to be administered by the Information Processing Techniques Office of the Defense Advanced Research Projects Agency.

Earlier in 1983, a consortium of 12 U.S. computer companies formed a research arm to ensure U.S. technological superiority. The research organization, called Microelectronics and Computer Technology Corp. (MCC), is to be headed by Bobby Inman, former deputy director of the CIA. MCC announced in May that its headquarters would be located in Austin, Texas. It will spend about $150 million a year on research.

Japan has allocated $200 million for a 10-year supercomputer research project.

NEW SUBATOMIC PARTICLES DISCOVERED

An international team of 126 research scientists detected three subatomic particles in 1983 that had been sought for many years.

The scientists used the CERN atom smasher of the European Laboratory for Particle Physics near Geneva, Switzerland, which can accelerate a beam of protons to 270 million electron volts.

The particles discovered were called W positive, W negative, and Z zero. The particles carry what physicists call "weak force," one of the three basic forces of nature.

SCIENCE AWARDS

President Reagan in April presented the Department of Energy's highest award to two nuclear scientists. Each received a gold medal and $25,000. They were:

Herbert Anderson of Santa Fe, N.M., who was cited for "pioneer collaboration with Enrico Fermi in demonstrating the emission of neutrons in fission."

Seth Neddermeyer of Seattle, Wash., cited for participating in the discovery of the positron and for his share in the discovery of the muon, the first of the subatomic particles.

The National Medal of Science was presented by President Reagan to 11 scientists and engineers in May. They included Edward Teller, father of the hydrogen bomb; Philip W. Anderson, for studies of condensed matter; Seymour Benzer, research on genes; Glenn W. Burton, contributions to biology; Mildred Cohn, research on enzymatic catalysis; F. Albert Cotton, discoverer of multiple metal bonds; Edward Heinemann, designer of military aircraft; Donald L. Katz, chemical engineering research; Yoichiro Nambu, study of elementary particles; Gilbert Stork, discovery of synthetic reactions; Charles H. Townes, study of electromagnetic radiations; and Marshall Stone, for synthesis of analysis, algebra, and topology.

LENGTH AND DISTANCE: U.S. MEASURES (AND METRIC EQUIVALENTS)

1 mil = 0.001 inch = 0.0254 millimeter
1 inch (in.) = 25.4 millimeters = 2.54 centimeters
1 foot (ft.) = 12 inches = ⅓ yard = 0.00018939 mile = 30.48 centimeters =0.3048 meter
1 yard (yd.) = 3 feet = 36 inches = 0.9144 meter
1 rod (rd.) = 16½ feet = 5½ yards = 5.0292 meters
1 furlong (fur.) = ⅛ mile = 40 rods = 220 yards = 660 feet = 201.168 meters
1 statute mile (mi.) = 8 furlongs = 320 rods = 1,760 yards = 5,280 feet = 1.609344 kilometers = 0.86897624 nautical mile
1 league (land) = 3 statute miles = 4.8280 kilometers

NAUTICAL MEASURES OF LENGTH AND DISTANCE

1 span = 9 inches = 22.86 centimeters
1 fathom (fm.) = 8 spans = 72 inches = 6 feet = 1.8288 meters
1 cable = 120 fathoms = 240 yards = 720 feet = 219.4560 meters
1 league (nautical) = 3 nautical miles = 5,556 meters = 3.452338 statute miles
1 nautical mile (or international mile) (mi.) = 2,025.37182852 yards = 6,076.11548556 feet = 1,852 meters = 1.852 kilometers = 1.150779448 statute miles = 1′ (minute) latitude
1 ° (degree) **latitude** = 60 nautical miles

SURVEYOR'S (or GUNTER'S) CHAIN MEASURES

1 link (li.) = 7.92 inches = 0.201168 meter
1 chain (ch.) = 100 links = 66 feet = 20.1168 meters
1 furlong (fur.) = 10 chains = 40 rods = 660 feet = 201.168 meters
1 statute mile = 80 chains = 8 furlongs = 5,280 feet = 1.609344 kilometers

ENGINEER'S CHAIN MEASURES

1 link (li.) = 1 foot = 0.3048 meter
1 chain (ch.) = 100 links = 100 feet = 30.48 meters
1 statute mile = 52.8 chains = 5,280 feet = 1.609344 kilometers

AREA: U.S. MEASURES (AND METRIC EQUIVALENTS)

1 square inch (sq. in.) = 6.45160 square centimeters = 0.00694444 square foot
1 square foot (sq. ft.) = 144 square inches = 929.0304 square centimeters
1 square yard (sq. yd.) = 1,296 square inches = 9 square feet = 0.83612736 square meter
1 square rod (sq. rd.) = 30¼ square yards = 272¼ square feet = 25.29285264 square meters
1 acre (A.) = 160 square rods = 4,840 square yards = 43,560 square feet = 0.40468564224 hectare
1 square mile (sq. mi.) = 640 acres = 27,878,400 sq. ft. = 2.589988110336 square kilometers

SURVEYOR'S MEASURES OF LAND AREA

1 square link (sq. li.) = 62.7264 square inches = 404.68564 square centimeters
1 square pole (sq. p.) = 625 square links = 30¼ square yards = 25.29285264 square meters
1 square chain (sq. ch.) = 16 square poles = 484 square yards = 404.68564224 square meters
1 acre (A.) = 10 square chains = 4,840 square yards = 43,560 square feet = 0.40468564324 hectare
1 section (sec.) = 640 acres = 1 square mile = 2.589988110336 square kilometers
1 township (tp.) = 36 sections = 36 square miles = 93.23957 square kilometers

WEIGHT OR MASS: U.S. MEASURES (AND METRIC EQUIVALENTS)

AVOIRDUPOIS UNITS OF WEIGHT

Everyday weights are measured in avoirdupois units in the United States. When necessary to distinguish these units from other measuring units, such as fluid ounces or troy ounces, use the abbreviation **avdp.**

1 grain (gr.) = 0.00228571 ounce = 0.00208333 troy ounce = 64.79891 milligrams = 0.00017361 troy pound
1 dram (dr.) = 27¹¹⁄₃₂ grains = 27.34375 grains = 1.7718449 grams
1 ounce (oz.) = 16 drams = 437½ grains = 0.9114583 troy ounce = 0.9114583 apothecaries' ounce = 0.0625 pound = 0.07595486 troy pound = 28.349523125 grams
1 pound (lb.) = 16 ounces = 256 drams = 7,000 grains = 1.215278 troy pound = 1.215278 apothecaries' lbs. = 453.59237 grams = 0.45359237 kilogram
1 hundredweight (cwt.) = 100 pounds = 0.05 ton = 45.359237 kilograms
1 ton (designated as **short** ton or **net** ton) = 2,000 pounds = 0.8928571 long ton (or gross ton) = 907.18474 kilograms = 0.90718474 metric ton

BRITISH UNITS OF AVOIRDUPOIS WEIGHT

1 stone = 14 pounds = 6.35029318 kilograms
1 hundredweight = 112 pounds = 50.80234544 kilograms
1 ton (designated as **long** ton or **gross** ton) = 2,240 pounds = 1.12 short tons = 1,016.0469088 kilograms

TROY UNITS OF WEIGHT

Gems and precious metals are measured using troy weight.

1 grain = 0.0022857 avdp. ounce = 64.79891 milligrams
1 carat = 3.086 grains = 0.00705 avdp. ounce = 200 milligrams = 0.2 gram
1 assay ton (AT) = 29,166⅔ milligrams (same as number of troy ounces in short ton)
1 pennyweight (dwt.) = 24 grains = T0.05485715 avdp. ounce = 1.55517384 grams
1 ounce = 480 grains = 20 pennyweights = 1.097143 avdp. ounces = 31.1034768 grams
1 pound = 5,760 grains = 240 pennyweights = 12 troy ounces = 0.8228571 avdp. pound = 13.16571 avdp. ounces = 373.2417216 grams = 0.3732417216 kilogram
1 short ton = 2,000 avdp. pounds = 29,166⅔ troy ounces

APOTHECARIES' UNITS OF WEIGHT

1 grain = 0.0022857 avdp. ounce = 64.79891 milligrams
1 scruple = 20 grains = 0.04571429167 avdp. ounce = **1.29584782 grams**
1 dram =60 grains = 3 scruples = 0.137142875 avdp. ounce = 3.8879346 grams
1 ounce = 480 grains = 24 scruples = 8 drams = 1.097143 avdp. ounces = 31.1034768 grams
1 pound = 5,760 grains = 288 scruples = 96 drams = 12 apothecaries' ounces = 13.16571 avdp. ounces = 373.2417216 grams = 0.3732417216 kilogram

VOLUME AND CAPACITY: U.S. MEASURES (AND METRIC EQUIVALENTS)

1 **cubic inch** (cu. in.) = 16.387064 cubic centimeters = 0.5541126 fluid ounce = 0.016387064 liter

1 **cubic foot** = 1,728 cubic inches = 957.5065 fluid ounces = 0.028316846592 cubic meter = 29.92208 fluid quarts = 7.480519 U.S. gallons = 28.316846592 liters = 6.228822724 British imperial gallons

1 **cubic yard** (cu. yd.) = 46,656 cubic inches = 27 cubic feet = 0.764554857984 cubic meter = 201.9740 U.S. gallons = 168.1782135 British imperial gallons = 764.554857984 liters

MEASURES OF VOLUME-MASS

1 **cubic foot of seawater** = 64 pounds

1 **cubic foot of fresh water** = 62.428 pounds at 39.2° F.

1 **cubic foot of ice** = 56 pounds

1 **measurement ton** = 40 cubic feet = 1 freight ton

1 **displacement ton** = 35 cubic feet of seawater = 1 long ton

1 **register ton** = 100 cubic feet = 2.8316846592 cubic meters

HOUSEHOLD MEASURES OF LIQUID CAPACITY

1 **teaspoon** = $\frac{1}{3}$ tablespoon = $\frac{1}{6}$ fluid ounce = 80 drops = 4.928921667 milliliters

1 **tablespoon** = 3 teaspoons = $\frac{1}{2}$ fluid ounce = 240 drops = 14.786765 milliliters

1 **fluid ounce** (fl. oz.) = 2 tablespoons = 6 teaspoons = 29.57353 milliliters = 1.8046875 cubic inches

1 **gill** (gi.) = $\frac{1}{2}$ cup = 4 fluid ounces = 7.21875 cubic inches = 118.29411825 milliliters = 1,920 minims

1 **cup** = 16 tablespoons = 8 fluid ounces = 14.4375 cubic inches = 236.58824 milliliters

1 **pint** (pt.) = 2 cups = 4 gills = 16 fluid ounces = 28.875 cubic inches = 0.473176473 liter

1 **quart** (qt.) = 2 pints = 4 cups = 32 fluid ounces = 57.75 cubic inches = 0.832672482 British quart = 0.946352946 liter = 0.03342014 cubic foot

1 **British imperial quart** = 1.20095 U.S. quarts = 69.355 cubic inches = 1.1365248824 liters

1 **gallon** (gal.) = 4 quarts = 8 pints = 16 cups = 128 fluid ounces = 231 cubic inches = 3,785.411784 milliliters = 0.832672482 British imperial gallon = 3.785411784 liters

1 **British imperial gallon** = 1.20095 U.S. gallons = 160 British fluid ounces = 277.42 cubic inches = 4.546099295 liters

1 **barrel (liquids)** = 31.5 U.S. gallons = 4.21 cubic feet = 119.2404712 liters

1 **barrel (petroleum)** = 42 U.S. gallons = 0.1589872949 cubic meter = 5.6145852 cubic feet = 158.9872949 liters

APOTHECARIES' MEASURES OF LIQUID CAPACITY

1 **minim (or drop)** (min.) = $\frac{1}{60}$ fluid dram = $\frac{1}{480}$ fluid ounce = 0.0020833 fluid ounce = 0.0037597656 cubic inch = 0.06161152 milliliter

1 **British fluid drachm** = 0.961 U.S. fluid dram = 0.216734 cubic inch = 3.55164 milliliters

1 **fluid dram** (fl. dr.) = 60 minims = $\frac{1}{8}$ fluid ounce = 0.125 fluid ounce = 0.225585937 cubic inch = 3.69669125 cubic centimeters = 3.69669125 milliliters

1 **British fluid ounce** = 0.961 U.S. fluid ounce = 1.733875 cubic inches = 28.41312 milliliters

1 **fluid ounce** (fl. oz.) = 8 fluid drams = $\frac{1}{16}$ fluid pint = 1.8046875 cubic inches = 29.57353 cubic centimeters = 29.57353 milliliters = 1.041 British fluid ounces

1 **pint** = 128 fluid drams = 16 fluid ounces = 7,680 minims = 28.875 cubic inches = 473.176473 cubic centimeters = 473.176473 milliliters = 0.473176473 liter

1 **quart** = 2 pints = 32 fluid ounces = 256 fluid drams = 57.75 cubic inches = 946.352946 cubic centimeters = 0.946352946 liter = 0.832672482 British quart

1 **gallon** = 4 quarts = 8 pints = 128 fluid ounces = 231 cubic inches = 3,785.411784 cubic centimeters = 3.785411784 liters = 0.832672482 British gallon

CUSTOMARY DRY MEASURES OF CAPACITY

1 **pint** = 33.6003125 cubic inches = 550.61047 cubic centimeters = 0.55061047 liters

1 **quart** = 2 pints = 67.200625 cubic inches = 1,101.22094 cubic centimeters = 1.10122094 liters = 0.969 British dry quart

1 **British imperial dry quart** = 1.032 U.S. dry quarts = 69.355 cubic inches = 1.1365 liters

1 **peck** (pk.) = 8 quarts = 16 pints = 0.25 bushel = 537.605 cubic inches = 8,809.7675 cubic centimeters = 8.8097675 liters

1 **bushel** (bu.), **U.S. struck measure** = 4 pecks = 32 dry quarts = 64 dry pints = 2,150.42 cubic inches = 35.23907 liters

1 **British imperial bushel** = 1.032 U.S. struck measure bushels = 2,219.36 cubic inches = 36.368735 liters

1 **bushel, U.S. heaped measure** = $1\frac{1}{4}$ struck measure bushels = 1.278 struck measure bushels = 2,747.715 cubic inches = 45.035527 liters

1 **barrel** (bbl.), **cranberries** = 5,286 cubic inches = $86\frac{45}{64}$ dry quarts = 2.709 struck measure bushels

1 **barrel** (bbl.), **standard** (other fruits and vegetables and dry commodities) = 7,056 cubic inches = 105 dry quarts = 3.281 struck measure bushels = 0.115627 cubic meter

LENGTH: METRIC MEASURES AND EQUIVALENTS

1 **nanometer** (nm.) = 0.00000003937008 inch

1 **micron** (m.) = 1,000 nanometers = 0.00003937008 inch

1 **millimeter** (mm.) = 0.03937008 inch

1 **centimeter** (cm.) = 10 millimeters = 0.3937008 inch

1 **decimeter** (dm.) = 100 millimeters = 10 centimeters = 3.937008 inches

1 **meter** (m.) = 1,000 millimeters = 100 centimeters = 10 decimeters = 39.37008 inches = 3.280840 feet = 1.093613 yards = 0.54680665 fathom = 0.00062137 statute mile = 0.00053996 nautical mile

1 **decameter** (dam.) = 10 meters = 32.80840 feet = 10.93613 yards = 393.7008 inches = 0.0062137 mile

1 **hectometer** (hm.) = 10 decameters = 100 meters = 328.0840 feet = 109.3613 yards

1 **kilometer** (km.) = 1,000 meters = 100 decameters = 10 hectometers = 3,280.83990 feet = 1,093.61330 yards = 0.621371192 statute mile = 0.53995680 nautical mile

AREA: METRIC MEASURES AND EQUIVALENTS

1 **square millimeter** (mm.^{2}) = 0.0015500031 square inch
1 **square centimeter** (cm.^{2}) = 100 square millimeters = 0.15500031 square inch = 0.001076391 square foot
1 **square decimeter** (dm.^{2}) = 100 square centimeters = 15.500031 square inches = 0.1076391 square foot
1 **square meter** (m.^{2}) = 1,000,000 square millimeters = 10,000 square centimeters = 100 square decimeters = 10.76391045 square feet = 1.19599005 square yards
1 **are** (a.) = 100 square meters = 119.599005 square yards = 0.02471053815 acre
1 **hectare** (ha.) = 10,000 square meters = 100 ares = 2.471053815 acres
1 **square kilometer** (km.^{2}) = 1,000,000 square meters = 100 hectares = 247.1053815 acres = 0.38610216 square statute mile = 0.29155335 square nautical mile

VOLUME: METRIC MEASURES AND EQUIVALENTS

1 **cubic millimeter** (mm.^{3}) = 0.001 cubic centimeter = 0.00006102374 cubic inch
1 **cubic centimeter** (cm.^{3}) = 1,000 cubic millimeters = 0.06102374 cubic inch = 0.00026417205 U.S. gallon
1 **cubic decimeter** (dm.^{3}) = 1,000 cubic centimeters = 1 liter = 61.02374 cubic inches = 0.03531467 cubic foot
1 **stere** (s) = 1 cubic meter
1 **cubic meter** (m.^{3}) = 1,000,000 cubic centimeters = 1,000 cubic decimeters = 35.31467 cubic feet = 1.30795059 cubic yards = 264.17205 U.S. gallons
1 **cubic decameter** (dam.^{3}) = 1,000 cubic meters = 1,307.9506 cubic yards
1 **cubic hectometer** (hm.^{3}) = 1,000 cubic decameters = 1,307,950.6 cubic yards

CAPACITY: METRIC MEASURES AND EQUIVALENTS

1 **milliliter** (ml.) = 0.001 liter = 0.03381402 fluid ounce = 16.23073 minims = 0.06102374 cubic inch
1 **centiliter** (cl.) = 10 milliliters = 0.01 liter = 0.3381402 fluid ounce = 0.6102374 cubic inch
1 **deciliter** (dl.) = 100 milliliters = 10 centiliters = 3.381402 fluid ounces = 6.102374 cubic inches
1 **liter** (l.) = 1,000 milliliters = 10 deciliters = 33.81402 fluid ounces = 1 cubic decimeter = 61.02374 cubic inches = 1.056688 fluid quarts = 0.26417205 U.S. gallon = 0.90808298 dry quart
1 **decaliter** (dal.) = 10 liters = 2.6417205 U.S. gallons
1 **hectoliter** (hl.) = 100 liters = 10 decaliters = 26.417205 U.S. gallons = 2.837759 U.S. bushels = 3.531467 cubic feet
1 **kiloliter** (kl.) = 1,000 liters = 10 hectoliters = 35.31467 cubic feet = 264.17205 U.S. gallons

WEIGHT: METRIC MEASURES AND EQUIVALENTS

1 **microgram** (µg.) = 0.000001 gram = 0.00001543236 grain
1 **milligram** (mg.) = 1,000 micrograms = 0.001 gram = 0.01543236 grain
1 **centigram** (cg.) = 10 milligrams = 0.01 gram = 0.1543236 grain = 0.003527396 avdp. ounce
1 **decigram** (dg.) = 10 centigrams = 0.1 gram = 1.543236 grains = 0.03527396 avdp. ounce
1 **gram** (g.) = 1,000 milligrams = 10 decigrams = 15.43236 grains = 0.03527396 avdp. ounce
1 **decagram** (dag.) = 10 grams = 0.3527396 avdp. ounce
1 **hectogram** (hg.) = 100 grams = 10 decagrams = 3.527396 avdp. ounces
1 **kilogram** (kg.) = 1,000 grams = 10 hectograms = 35.27396 avdp. ounces = 32.15075 troy ounces = 2.204623 avdp. pounds = 2.679229 troy pounds
1 **quintal** (q.) = 100 kilograms = 220.4623 avdp. pounds
1 **metric ton** (M.T.) = 1,000 kilograms = 2,204.623 advp. pounds = 1.1023113 short tons = 0.9842065 long ton

HOW TO CONVERT UNITS OF MEASURE BY MULTIPLICATION

U.S. MEASURE	MULTIPLY BY	TO GET METRIC	METRIC MEASURE	MULTIPLY BY	TO GET U.S.
LENGTH AND DISTANCE					
inches	× 25.4	= millimeters	**millimeters**	× 0.03937008	= inches
inches	× 2.54	= centimeters	**centimeters**	× 0.3937008	= inches
feet	× 0.3048	= meters	**meters**	× 3.280840	= feet
yards	× 0.9144	= meters	**meters**	× 1.093613	= yards
miles	× 1.609344	= kilometers	**kilometers**	× 0.62137	= miles
AREA OR SURFACE					
square inches	× 6.4516	= square centimeters	**square centimeters**	× 0.1550003	= square inches
square feet	× 0.09290304	= square meters	**square meters**	× 10.76391	= square feet
square yards	× 0.83612736	= square meters	**square meters**	× 1.195990	= square yards
acres	× 0.40468564224	= hectares	**hectares**	× 2.47105	= acres
square miles	× 2.58998811	= square kilometers	**square kilometers**	× 0.386102	= square miles
VOLUME					
cubic inches	× 16.387064	= cubic centimeters	**cubic centimeters**	× 0.06102374	= cubic inches
cubic feet	× 0.028316846592	= cubic meters	**cubic meters**	× 35.31467	= cubic feet
cubic yards	× 0.764554857984	= cubic meters	**cubic meters**	× 1.3079506	= cubic yards
CAPACITY					
fluid ounces	× 29.57353	= milliliters	**milliliters**	× 0.03381402	= fluid ounces
liquid pint	× 0.473176473	= liters	**liters**	× 2.113376	= liquid pints
liquid quart	× 0.946352946	= liters	**liters**	× 1.056688	= liquid quarts
gallons	× 3.785411784	= liters	**liters**	× 0.26417205	= gallons
bushels	× 35.23907	= liters	**liters**	× 0.02837759	= bushels
WEIGHT					
grains	× 0.06479891	= grams	**grams**	× 15.43236	= grains
ounces avdp.	× 28:349523125	= grams	**grams**	× 0.03527396	= ounces avdp.
pounds avdp.	× 0.45359237	= kilograms	**kilograms**	× 2.204623	= pounds avdp.
tons	× 0.90718474	= metric tons	**metric tons**	× 1.1023113	= tons

TIME MEASUREMENTS

1 **microsecond** = 0.000001 second
1 **second** = 1,000,000 microseconds = 0.016667 minute = 0.00027778 hour = 0.00069444 day = 15" longitude
1 **minute** = 60 seconds = 0.0166667 hour = 0.00069444 day = 15′ longitude
1 **hour** = 3,600 seconds = 60 minutes = 15° longitude = 0.04166667 day
1 **day** = 24 hours = 1,440 minutes = 86,400 seconds = 360° longitude
1 **mean solar day** (1 rotation of Earth with respect to Sun) = 24 hours, 3 minutes, 56.55536 seconds = 1.00273791 rotations with respect to vernal equinox = 1.0027378118868 rotations of Earth with respect to stars

1 **sidereal month** = 27.321661 days = 27 days, 7 hours, 43 minutes, 11.5 seconds
1 **synodical month** = 29.530588 days = 29 days, 12 hours, 44 minutes, 2.8 seconds
1 **calendar year** = 31,536,000 seconds = 525,600 minutes = 8,760 hours = 365 days
1 **solar year** = 31,556,925.975 seconds = 525,948.766 minutes = 8,765.8128 hours = 365 days, 5 hours, 48 minutes, 46 seconds
1 **light-year** = 5,880,000,000,000 statute miles = 9,460,000,000,000 kilometers = 5,110,000,000,000 nautical miles

SPEED: U.S. AND METRIC MEASURES

1 **foot per minute** = 0.01666667 foot per second = 0.00508 meter per second
1 **yard per minute** = 3 feet per minute = 0.05 foot per second = 0.03409091 statute mile per hour = 0.02962419 knot = 0.01524 meter per second
1 **statute mile per hour** = 88 feet per minute = 29.333 yards per minute = 1.466667 feet per second = 1.609344 kilometers per hour = 0.86897624 knot = 0.44704 meter per second
1 **knot** = 101.26859143 feet per minute = 6,076.11548556 feet per hour = 33.75619714 yards per minute = 1.852 kilometers per hour = 1.68780986 feet per second = 1.15077945 statute miles per hour = 0.51444444 meter per second
1 **meter per second** = 196.85039340 feet per minute = 65.6167978 yards per minute = 3.6 kilometers per hour = 3.28083990 feet per second = 2.23693632 statute miles per hour = 1.94384449 knots

1 **kilometer per hour** = 0.53995680 knot = 0.62137119 statute mile per hour
Speed of light (in vacuum) = 186,282 statute miles per second = 161,875 nautical miles per second = 299,792 kilometers per second = 983.570 feet per microsecond
Speed of light (in air) = 186,230 statute miles per second = 299,708 kilometers per second = 161,829 nautical miles per second = 983.294 feet per microsecond
Speed of sound (in air at 60° F. at sea level) = 1,116.99 feet per second = 761.59 statute miles per hour = 661.80 knots = 340.46 meters per second
Speed of sound (in salt water at 60° F.) = 4,945.37 feet per second = 3,371.85 statute miles per hour = 2,930.05 knots = 1,507.35 meters per second

SPECIAL UNITS OF MEASUREMENT

Ampere: Unit of electric current. A potential difference of 1 volt across a resistance of 1 ohm produces a current of 1 ampere.
Bale: Bale of cotton weighs 500 pounds gross or 480 pounds net.
Board Foot: Volume of 1-inch-thick, 1-foot-square board, rough sawn.
BTU: British thermal unit, equal to 252 calories; amount of heat needed to increase temperature of 1 pound of pure water by 1° F.
Calorie: Amount of heat needed to increase the temperature of 1 gram of pure water by 1° C.
Carat: Used to indicate purity of gold alloys, on a scale of 24: 14 carats means 14 parts gold to 10 parts alloy.
Cord: Equals 128 cubic feet of firewood (4 ft. × 4 ft. × 8 ft.).
Decibel: Unit of relative loudness in acoustics.
Hand: Unit used in measuring height of horses; equals 4 inches.
Hertz: Modern unit in electronics, equivalent to and replacing the former "cycles per second"; abbreviated as *hz.*
Horsepower: Standard theoretical unit of the time rate of work or power. It is equal to the work done in lifting 550 pounds 1 foot in 1 second; equals 745.7 watts.
Joule: Unit of energy measurement equal to 0.24 calorie or 10 million ergs.
Kilowatt-hour: Equal to consumption of 1,000 watts of power over a period of 1 hour.
Ohm: Unit of electrical resistance. A circuit in which a potential difference of 1 volt produces a current of 1 ampere has a resistance of 1 ohm.
Pi (π): Ratio (3.14159 . . .) of the circumference of circle to its total diameter.
Pica: In typography, equals 12 points; about 1/6 inch; 0.166044 inch; 4.2175176 millimeters.
Point: In typography, about 1/72 inch; 0.013837 inch; 0.3514598 millimeter.
Quire: Either 24 or 25 sheets of paper of uniform size and quality; equal to 1/20 of a ream.
Ream: Twenty quires or 480 uniform sheets of paper, except newsprint or book paper (equal to 500 sheets), or a "perfect ream" of 516.
Roentgen: Dosage unit of radiation exposure produced by X rays and gamma rays, alpha, beta, and neutron; it applies to biological effects only.
Talent: Ancient unit of coin and weight equal to about 3,600 shekels as a weight, and about 3,000 shekels as silver or gold revenue. Hebrew gold *shekel* probably weighed about 252 grains troy, or slightly over 1/2 ounce.
Volt: Unit of electromotive force, or potential difference; potential difference of 1 volt across a resistance of 1 ohm produces a current of 1 ampere.
Watt: Power expended by current of 1 ampere across potential difference of 1 volt equals 1 watt.

TEMPERATURE CONVERSION TABLE *

Source: Ever Ready Thermometer Company

The numbers in boldface type in the center columns—the key to the table—refer to the temperature in either Celsius (formerly centigrade) or Fahrenheit degrees. Thus, for example, +30 in the center column, if chosen to represent 30 ° Fahrenheit, will convert to –1.1 ° Celsius, the figure found to the left of the column. If, on the other hand, it is made to represent 30 ° Celsius, it will convert to 86.0 ° Fahrenheit, the figure to the right of the column.

For degrees of temperature not included in this table, the following formulas provide the necessary conversion:

F° = (C° < 1.8) + 32 or C° = (F°–32) < 5÷9

DEGREES C.	**DEGREES**	DEGREES F.	DEGREES C.	**DEGREES**	DEGREES F.	DEGREES C.	**DEGREES**	DEGREES F.
–34.4	**–30**	–22.0	–9.4	**+15**	+59.0	+15.6	**+60**	+140.0
–33.9	**–29**	–20.2	–8.9	**+16**	+60.8	+16.1	**+61**	+141.8
–33.3	**–28**	–18.4	–8.3	**+17**	+62.6	+16.7	**+62**	+143.6
–32.8	**–27**	–16.6	–7.8	**+18**	+64.4	+17.2	**+63**	+145.4
–32.2	**–26**	–14.8	–7.2	**+19**	+66.2	+17.8	**+64**	+147.2
–31.7	**–25**	–13.0	–6.7	**+20**	+68.0	+18.3	**+65**	+149.0
–31.1	**–24**	–11.2	–6.1	**+21**	+69.8	+18.9	**+66**	+150.8
–30.6	**–23**	–9.4	–5.5	**+22**	+71.6	+19.4	**+67**	+152.6
–30.0	**–22**	–7.6	–5.0	**+23**	+73.4	+20.0	**+68**	+154.4
–29.4	**–21**	–5.8	–4.4	**+24**	+75.2	+20.6	**+69**	+156.2
–28.9	**–20**	–4.0	–3.9	**+25**	+77.0	+21.1	**+70**	+158.0
–28.3	**–19**	–2.2	–3.3	**+26**	+78.8	+21.7	**+71**	+159.8
–27.8	**–18**	–0.4	–2.8	**+27**	+80.6	+22.2	**+72**	+161.6
–27.2	**–17**	+1.4	–2.2	**+28**	+82.4	+22.8	**+73**	+163.4
–26.7	**–16**	+3.2	–1.7	**+29**	+84.2	+23.3	**+74**	+165.2
–26.1	**–15**	+5.0	–1.1	**+30**	+86.0	+23.9	**+75**	+167.0
–25.6	**–14**	+6.8	–0.6	**+31**	+87.8	+24.4	**+76**	+168.8
–25.0	**–13**	+8.6	0.0	**+32**	+89.6	+25.0	**+77**	+170.6
–24.4	**–12**	+10.4	+0.6	**+33**	+91.4	+25.6	**+78**	+172.4
–23.9	**–11**	+12.2	+1.1	**+34**	+93.2	+26.1	**+79**	+174.2
–23.3	**–10**	+14.0	+1.7	**+35**	+95.0	+26.7	**+80**	+176.0
–22.8	**–9**	+15.8	+2.2	**+36**	+96.8	+27.2	**+81**	+177.8
–22.2	**–8**	+17.6	+2.8	**+37**	+98.6	+27.8	**+82**	+179.6
–21.7	**–7**	+19.4	+3.3	**+38**	+100.4	+28.3	**+83**	+181.4
–21.1	**–6**	+21.2	+3.9	**+39**	+102.2	+28.9	**+84**	+183.2
–20.6	**–5**	+23.0	+4.4	**+40**	+104.0	+29.4	**+85**	+185.0
–20.0	**–4**	+24.8	+5.0	**+41**	+105.8	+30.0	**+86**	+186.8
–19.4	**–3**	+26.6	+5.5	**+42**	+107.6	+30.6	**+87**	+188.6
–18.9	**–2**	+28.4	+6.1	**+43**	+109.4	+31.1	**+88**	+190.4
–18.3	**–1**	+30.2	+6.7	**+44**	+111.2	+31.7	**+89**	+192.2
–17.8	**0**	+32.0	+7.2	**+45**	+113.0	+32.2	**+90**	+194.0
–17.2	**+1**	+33.8	+7.8	**+46**	+114.8	+32.8	**+91**	+195.8
–16.7	**+2**	+35.6	+8.3	**+47**	+116.6	+33.3	**+92**	+197.6
–16.1	**+3**	+37.4	+8.9	**+48**	+118.4	+33.9	**+93**	+199.4
–15.6	**+4**	+39.2	+9.4	**+49**	+120.2	+34.4	**+94**	+201.2
–15.0	**+5**	+41.0	+10.0	**+50**	+122.0	+35.0	**+95**	+203.0
–14.4	**+6**	+42.8	+10.6	**+51**	+123.8	+35.6	**+96**	+204.8
–13.9	**+7**	+44.6	+11.1	**+52**	+125.6	+36.1	**+97**	+206.6
–13.3	**+8**	+46.4	+11.7	**+53**	+127.4	+36.7	**+98**	+208.4
–12.8	**+9**	+48.2	+12.2	**+54**	+129.2	+37.2	**+99**	+210.2
–12.2	**+10**	+50.0	+12.8	**+55**	+131.0	+37.8	**+100**	+212.0
–11.7	**+11**	+51.8	+13.3	**+56**	+132.8	+38.3	**+101**	+213.8
–11.1	**+12**	+53.6	+13.9	**+57**	+134.6	+38.9	**+102**	+215.6
–10.6	**+13**	+55.4	+14.4	**+58**	+136.4	+39.4	**+103**	+217.4
–10.0	**+14**	+57.2	+15.0	**+59**	+138.2	+40.0	**+104**	+219.2

* Absolute zero is –273.15 ° C. or –459.67 ° F.

KELVIN SCALE

The British physicist Lord Kelvin (1824–1907) devised a temperature scale based on thermodynamic laws. Known also as the absolute scale, Kelvin's system became a fundamental temperature scale used in scientific measurement. Absolute temperatures are used in formulas derived from the laws governing the behavior of gases, which expand and contract in volume at high and low temperatures. According to the kinetic molecular theory, absolute zero is the point at which the molecules of substances have no heat energy. Absolute zero, –273.15 ° on the Celsius scale, is 0 ° Kelvin. Thus degrees Kelvin are equivalent to degrees of Celsius plus 273.15. The freezing point of water (0 ° Celsius and 32 ° Fahrenheit) is 273.15 ° Kelvin. The conversion formulas are: K ° = C ° + 273.15 or K ° = (F °–32) < (5 ÷ 9) + 273.15

MATHEMATICAL TABLES

NAMES OF LARGE NUMBERS

NAME	EQUIVALENT	Number of Zeros	Power of 10	NAME	EQUIVALENT	Number of Zeros	Power of 10
million	1,000 thousands	6	10^{6}	**duodecillion**	1,000 undecillions	39	10^{39}
billion	1,000 millions	9	10^{9}	**tredecillion**	1,000 duodecillions	42	10^{42}
trillion	1,000 billions	12	10^{12}	**quattuordecillion**	1,000 tredecillions	45	10^{45}
quadrillion	1,000 trillions	15	10^{15}	**quindecillion**	1,000 quattuordecillions	48	10^{48}
quintillion	1,000 quadrillions	18	10^{18}	**sexdecillion**	1,000 quindecillions	51	10^{51}
sextillion	1,000 quintillions	21	10^{21}	**septendecillion**	1,000 sexdecillions	54	10^{54}
septillion	1,000 sextillions	24	10^{24}	**octodecillion**	1,000 septendecillions	57	10^{57}
octillion	1,000 septillions	27	10^{27}	**novemdecillion**	1,000 octodecillions	60	10^{60}
nonillion	1,000 octillions	30	10^{30}	**vigintillion**	1,000 novemdecillions	63	10^{63}
decillion	1,000 nonillions	33	10^{33}	**googol**	—	100	10^{100}
undecillion	1,000 decillions	36	10^{36}				

ROMAN NUMERALS

I	**1**	**V**	**5**	**IX**	**9**	**XIII**	**13**	**XVII**	**17**	**XXX**	**30**	**LXX**	**70**	**D**	**500**
II	**2**	**VI**	**6**	**X**	**10**	**XIV**	**14**	**XVIII**	**18**	**XL**	**40**	**LXXX**	**80**	**M**	**1,000**
III	**3**	**VII**	**7**	**XI**	**11**	**XV**	**15**	**XIX**	**19**	**L**	**50**	**XC**	**90**	$\overline{\textbf{V}}$	**5,000**
IV	**4**	**VIII**	**8**	**XII**	**12**	**XVI**	**16**	**XX**	**20**	**LX**	**60**	**C**	**100**	$\overline{\textbf{X}}$	**10,000**

DECIMAL EQUIVALENTS OF FRACTIONS

.015625 = 1/64	.171875 = 11/64	.350000 = 7/20	.531250 = 17/32	.687500 = 11/16	.857143 = 6/7
.031250 = 1/32	.187500 = 3/16	.359375 = 23/64	.546875 = 35/64	.700000 = 7/10	.859375 = 55/64
.046875 = 3/64	.200000 = 1/5	.375000 = 3/8	.550000 = 11/20	.703125 = 45/64	.875000 = 7/8
.050000 = 1/20	.203125 = 13/64	.390625 = 25/64	.555555 = 5/9	.714286 = 5/7	.888889 = 8/9
.062500 = 1/16	.218750 = 7/32	.400000 = 2/5	.562500 = 9/16	.718750 = 23/32	.890625 = 57/64
.078125 = 5/64	.222222 = 2/9	.406250 = 13/32	.571429 = 4/7	.734375 = 47/64	.900000 = 9/10
.083333 = 1/12	.234375 = 15/64	.416667 = 5/12	.578125 = 37/64	.750000 = 3/4	.906250 = 29/32
.093750 = 3/32	.250000 = 1/4	.421875 = 27/64	.583333 = 7/12	.765625 = 49/64	.916667 = 11/12
.100000 = 1/10	.265625 = 17/64	.428571 = 3/7	.593750 = 19/32	.777778 = 7/9	.921875 = 59/64
.109375 = 7/64	.281250 = 9/32	.437500 = 7/16	.600000 = 3/5	.781250 = 25/32	.950000 = 19/20
.111111 = 1/9	.285714 = 2/7	.444444 = 4/9	.609375 = 39/64	.796875 = 51/64	.953125 = 61/64
.125000 = 1/8	.296875 = 19/64	.450000 = 9/20	.625000 = 5/8	.800000 = 4/5	.968750 = 31/32
.140625 = 9/64	.300000 = 3/10	.453125 = 29/64	.640625 = 41/64	.812500 = 13/16	.984375 = 63/64
.142857 = 1/7	.312500 = 5/16	.468750 = 15/32	.650000 = 13/20	.828125 = 53/64	
.150000 = 3/20	.328125 = 21/64	.484375 = 31/64	.656250 = 21/32	.833333 = 5/6	
.156250 = 5/32	.333333 = 1/3	.500000 = 1/2	.666667 = 2/3	.843750 = 27/32	
.166667 = 1/6	.343750 = 11/32	.515625 = 33/64	.671875 = 43/64	.850000 = 17/20	

COMMON AREA FORMULAS

FIGURE	FORMULA	MEANING OF LETTERS
Rectangle	$A = ab$	a = base, b = height
Square	$A = a^2$	a = one side
Triangle	$A = \frac{ab}{2}$	a = base, b = height
Parallelogram	$A = ab$	a = base, b = height
Regular pentagon	$A = 1.720a^2$	a = one side
Regular hexagon	$A = 2.598a^2$	a = one side
Regular octagon	$A = 4.828a^2$	a = one side
Circle	$A = \pi r^2$	π = 3.1416, r = radius

COMMON VOLUME FORMULAS

FIGURE	FORMULA	MEANING OF LETTERS
Cube	$V = a^3$	a = one side
Pyramid	$V = \frac{ah}{3}$	a = area of base h = height
Cylinder	$V = \pi r^2 h$	π = 3.1416 h = height r = radius of base
Cone	$V = \frac{\pi r^2 h}{3}$	π = 3.1416 r = radius of base h = height
Sphere	$V = 4\frac{\pi r^3}{3}$	π = 3.1416 r = radius

MULTIPLES OF PI

No.	Value	No.	Value
1π	3.1416	$\frac{1}{\pi}$	0.3183
2π	6.2832	$1/2\pi$	1.5708
3π	9.4248	$1/3\pi$	1.0472
4π	12.5664	$1/4\pi$	0.7854
5π	15.7080	$1/5\pi$	0.6283
6π	18.8496	$1/6\pi$	0.5236
7π	21.9912	$1/7\pi$	0.4488
8π	25.1328	$1/8\pi$	0.3927
9π	28.2744	$1/9\pi$	0.3491
π^2	9.8696	$\sqrt{\pi}$	1.7725

GEOMETRY OF REGULAR POLYGONS

		If length of side = 1, then:			If Radius
No. of Sides	Name of Polygon	Area =	Radius of Circumscribed Circle =	Radius of Inscribed Circle =	of Circumscribed Circle = 1, then Side =
3	triangle	0.433013	0.5773	0.2887	1.7321
4	square	1.000000	0.7071	0.5000	1.4142
5	pentagon	1.720477	0.8056	0.6882	1.1756
6	hexagon	2.598076	1.0000	0.8660	1.0000
7	heptagon	3.633912	1.1524	1.0383	0.8677
8	octagon	4.828427	1.3066	1.2071	0.7653
9	nonagon	6.181824	1.4619	1.3737	0.6840
10	decagon	7.694209	1.6180	1.5388	0.6180

POWERS OF 10

$10^1 = 10$
$10^2 = 100$
$10^3 = 1{,}000$
$10^4 = 10{,}000$
$10^5 = 100{,}000$
$10^6 = 1{,}000{,}000$
$10^7 = 10{,}000{,}000$
$10^{-1} = 0.1$
$10^{-2} = 0.01$
$10^{-3} = 0.001$
$10^{-4} = 0.0001$
$10^{-5} = 0.00001$
$10^{-6} = 0.000001$
$10^{-7} = 0.0000001$

THE CHEMICAL ELEMENTS

At one time a chemical element could be defined as a substance that could not be broken down into two or more different kinds of matter. But in the late 1930s and early 1940s, scientists found that atoms of elements could be broken apart into subatomic particles. Ever since, scientists have had to qualify their definition of an element as a substance that cannot be broken down into anything else *by ordinary chemical means.*

The ancients and medieval alchemists are usually credited with the discovery of 12 elements, including gold, silver, tin, carbon, sulfur, iron, copper, zinc, arsenic, mercury, lead, and bismuth.

The concept of an "element" was not really developed until about 200 years ago. In 1789 the French scientist Antoine Lavoisier proposed a definition of an "element" and listed 23 of what scientists now regard as true chemical elements.

Alessandro Volta's discoveries concerning electric current (about 1800) led to Sir Humphry Davy's discovery of 6 new elements in the early 1800s.

In the 1860s and 1870s almost 30 new elements were discovered because of the new technique of spectroscopy and the arrangement of known elements into a periodic table with elements grouped according to their atomic numbers and atomic weights. Finally, the advent of atom smashers led to the discovery of more than a dozen elements with atomic numbers above uranium.

The atomic number of an element tells the number of protons (positively charged particles) it contains in its nucleus.

SYMBOL, NAME, AND ATOMIC NUMBER			ATOMIC WEIGHT[1]	DATE OF DISCOVERY AND DISCOVERER	
H	Hydrogen	1	1.00797	1766	H. Cavendish, Britain
He	Helium	2	4.0026	1868	In the sun: P. Janssen, France
				1895	On the earth: W. Ramsay, Britain; N. Langlet and P. T. Cleve, Sweden
Li	Lithium	3	6.939	1817	J. A. Arfvedson, Sweden
Be	Beryllium	4	9.01218	1798	L. N. Vauquelin, France
B	Boron	5	10.811	1808	H. Davy, Britain; J. L. Gay-Lussac and L. J. Thénard, France
C	Carbon	6	12.01115	—	Ancient
N	Nitrogen	7	14.0067	1772	D. Rutherford, Britain
O	Oxygen	8	15.9994	1774	J. Priestley, Britain
F	Fluorine	9	18.9984	1886	H. Moissan, France
Ne	Neon	10	20.179	1898	W. Ramsay and M. W. Travers, Britain
Na	Sodium	11	22.98977	1807	H. Davy, Britain
Mg	Magnesium	12	24.312	1808	H. Davy, Britain
Al	Aluminum	13	26.98154	1825	H. C. Oersted, Denmark
Si	Silicon	14	28.86	1823	J. J. Berzelius, Sweden
P	Phosphorus	15	30.97376	1669	H. Brand, Germany
S	Sulfur	16	32.064	—	Ancient
Cl	Chlorine	17	35.453	1774	K. W. Scheele, Sweden
A	Argon	18	39.948	1894	W. Ramsay and J. Rayleigh, Britain
K	Potassium	19	39.102	1807	H. Davy, Britain
Ca	Calcium	20	40.08	1808	H. Davy, Britain
Sc	Scandium	21	44.9559	1879	L. F. Nilson, Sweden
Ti	Titanium	22	47.90	1791	W. Gregor, Britain
V	Vanadium	23	50.9414	1830	N. G. Sefström, Sweden
Cr	Chromium	24	51.996	1797	L. N. Vauquelin, France
Mn	Manganese	25	54.938	1774	K. W. Scheele and J. G. Gahn, Sweden
Fe	Iron	26	55.847	—	Ancient
Co	Cobalt	27	58.9332	1735	G. Brandt, Sweden
Ni	Nickel	28	58.70	1751	A. F. Cronstedt, Sweden
Cu	Copper	29	63.546	—	Ancient
Zn	Zinc	30	65.37	1746	A. Marggraf, Germany
Ga	Gallium	31	69.72	1875	L. de Boisbaudran, France
Ge	Germanium	32	72.59	1886	C. A. Winkler, Germany
As	Arsenic	33	74.9216	—	Medieval
Se	Selenium	34	78.96	1817	J. J. Berzelius, Sweden
Br	Bromine	35	79.904	1826	A. J. Balard, France
Kr	Krypton	36	83.80	1898	W. Ramsay and M. W. Travers, Britain
Rb	Rubidium	37	85.4678	1861	R. W. Bunsen and G. R. Kirchhoff, Germany
Sr	Strontium	38	87.62	1790	A. Crawford, Scotland
Y	Yttrium	39	88.905	1794	J. Gadolin, Finland
Zr	Zirconium	40	91.22	1789	M. H. Klaproth, Germany
Nb	Niobium	41	92.9064	1801	C. Hatchett, Britain
Mo	Molybdenum	42	95.94	1778	K. W. Scheele, Sweden
Tc	Technetium	43	97[2]	1937	E. Segre and C. Perrier, Italy
Ru	Ruthenium	44	101.07	1844	K. Klaus, Estonia

SYMBOL, NAME, AND ATOMIC NUMBER			ATOMIC WEIGHT[1]	DATE OF DISCOVERY AND DISCOVERER	
Rh	Rhodium	45	102.9055	1803	W. H. Wollaston, Britain
Pd	Palladium	46	106.4	1803	W. H. Wollaston, Britain
Ag	Silver	47	107.868	—	Ancient
Cd	Cadmium	48	112.40	1817	F. Stromeyer, Germany
In	Indium	49	114.82	1863	F. Reich and H. T. Richter, Germany
Sn	Tin	50	118.69	—	Ancient
Sb	Antimony	51	121.75	—	Ancient
Te	Tellurium	52	127.60	1782	M. von Reichenstein, Austria
I	Iodine	53	126.9044	1811	B. Courtois, France
Xe	Xenon	54	131.30	1898	W. Ramsay and M. W. Travers, Britain
Cs	Cesium	55	132.9054	1860	R. Bunsen and G. R. Kirchhoff, Germany
Ba	Barium	56	137.34	1808	H. Davy, Britain
La	Lanthanum	57	138.9055	1839	C. G. Mosander, Sweden
Ce	Cerium	58	140.12	1803	J. J. Berzelius and W. von Hisinger, Sweden; M. H. Klaproth, Germany
Pr	Praseodymium	59	140.9077	1885	C. A. von Welsbach, Austria
Nd	Neodymium	60	144.24	1885	C. A. von Welsbach, Austria
Pm	Promethium	61	145 [2]	1945	J. A. Marinsky, L. E. Glendenin, and C. D. Coryell, U.S.
Sm	Samarium	62	150.35	1879	L. de Boisbaudran, France
Eu	Europium	63	151.96	1896	E. A. Demarcay, France
Gd	Gadolinium	64	157.25	1880	J. C. de Marignac, Switzerland
Tb	Terbium	65	158.9254	1843	C. G. Mosander, Sweden
Dy	Dysprosium	66	162.50	1886	L. de Boisbaudran, France
Ho	Holmium	67	164.9304	1878	J. L. Soret, Switzerland
Er	Erbium	68	167.26	1843	C. G. Mosander, Sweden
Tm	Thulium	69	168.9342	1879	P. T. Cleve, Sweden
Yb	Ytterbium	70	173.04	1878	J. de Marignac, Switzerland
Lu	Lutetium	71	174.97	1907	G. Urbain, France
Hf	Hafnium	72	178.49	1923	G. von Hevesy, Sweden; D. Coster, Netherlands
Ta	Tantalum	73	180.9479	1802	A. G. Ekeberg, Sweden
W	Tungsten	74	183.85	1783	J. J. d'Elhuyar and D. F. d'Elhuyar, Spain
Re	Rhenium	75	186.207	1925	W. Noddack and I. E. Tacke, Germany
Os	Osmium	76	190.2	1804	S. Tennant, Britain
Ir	Iridium	77	192.22	1804	S. Tennant, Britain
Pt	Platinum	78	195.09	1735	A. De Ulloa, Spain
Au	Gold	79	196.9665	—	Ancient
Hg	Mercury	80	200.59	—	Ancient
Tl	Thallium	81	204.37	1861	W. Crookes, Britain
Pb	Lead	82	207.19	—	Ancient
Bi	Bismuth	83	208.9804	—	Medieval
Po	Polonium	84	210 [2]	1898	M. Curie and P. Curie, France
At	Astatine	85	210 [2]	1940	E. G. Segre, D. R. Corson, and K. R. MacKenzie, U.S.
Rn	Radon	86	222 [2]	1900	F. E. Dorn, Germany
Fr	Francium	87	223 [2]	1939	M. Perey, France
Ra	Radium	88	226 [2]	1898	M. Curie and P. Curie, France
Ac	Actinium	89	227 [2]	1899	A. L. Debierne, France
Th	Thorium	90	232.0381	1828	J. J. Berzelius, Sweden
Pa	Protactinium	91	231.0359	1917	O. Hahn and L. Meitner, Germany; J. Cranston and F. Soddy, Britain
U	Uranium	92	238.029	1789	M. H. Klaproth, Germany
Np	Neptunium	93	237 [2]	1940	E. McMillan and P. Abelson, U.S.
Pu	Plutonium	94	244 [2]	1940	G. T. Seaborg, E. M. McMillan, A. C. Wahl, and J. W. Kennedy, U.S.
Am	Americium	95	243 [2]	1945	G. T. Seaborg, R. A. James, S. G. Thompson, and A. Ghiorso, U.S.
Cm	Curium	96	247 [2]	1944	G. T. Seaborg, R. A. James and A. Ghiorso, U.S.
Bk	Berkelium	97	247 [2]	1949	S. G. Thompson, A. Ghiorso and G. T. Seaborg, U.S.
Cf	Californium	98	251 [2]	1950	S. G. Thompson, K. Street Jr., A. Ghiorso, and G. T. Seaborg, U.S.
E	Einsteinium	99	254 [2]	1952	A. Ghiorso et al., U.S.
Fm	Fermium	100	257 [2]	1953	A. Ghiorso et al., U.S.
Mv	Mendelevium	101	258 [2]	1955	A. Ghiorso, B. Harvey, G. Choppin, S. G. Thompson, G. T. Seaborg, U.S.
No	Nobelium	102	255 [2]	1958	A. Ghiorso, T. Sikkeland, J. Walton, and G. T. Seaborg, U.S.
Lr	Lawrencium	103	260 [2]	1961	A. Ghiorso, A. E. Larsh, R. M. Latimer, and T. Sikkeland, U.S.
Rf	Kurchatovium / Rutherfordium	104	A257 [2]	1964 / 1969	G. N. Flerov et al., U.S.S.R. / A. Ghiorso et al., U.S. — Soviet claim disputed by U.S.
Ha	Bohrium / Hahnium	105	A261 [2]	1968 / 1970	G. N. Flerov et al., U.S.S.R. / A. Ghiorso et al., U.S. — Soviet claim disputed by U.S.
	Unnamed	106	263 [2]	1974 / 1974	G. N. Flerov et al., U.S.S.R. / G. T. Seaborg, A. Ghiorso, et al., U.S. — Soviet claim disputed by U.S.
	Unnamed	107	—	1981	Peter Ambruster, Gottfried Munzenberg, West Germany
	Unnamed	108	—	—	Not yet seen.
	Unnamed	109	—	1982	Peter Ambruster, Gottfried Munzenberg, West Germany

[1] The standard for chemical atomic weights (adopted in 1961) is that of carbon—12.011. [2] Most stable known isotope.

GREAT INVENTIONS

The origins of many great inventions are shrouded in the distant past. The inventors of writing, the wheel, and fire making will forever remain anonymous. And subsequent development of innovations such as the abacus, the windmill, gunpowder, the cannon, and the concrete arch must be attributed to countries or civilizations rather than to any particular individual or group of individuals.

Abacus: Uncertain; possibly by Babylonians as long ago as 3,500 years. In various forms it was known and used by ancient Chinese, Hindus, Egyptians, and Greeks
Adding machine (first commercially successful): William Burroughs, United States (1888)
Adding machine (simple): Blaise Pascal, France (1642)
Addressograph: J. S. Duncan, United States (1893)
Air brake, Westinghouse: George Westinghouse, U.S. (1868)
Air conditioning: Willis H. Carrier, United States (1902)
Air pump: Otto von Guericke, Germany (1654)
Airplane (first successful heavier-than-air): Orville and Wilbur Wright, United States (1903)
Airship (nonrigid): Henri Giffard, France (1852)
Aluminum (processing): Charles M. Hall, United States (1886); Paul Héroult, France (1886)
Atomic bomb: International team of scientists, U.S. (1945)
Atomic pile (self-sustaining nuclear chain reaction): Enrico Fermi and staff, United States (1942)
Automatic pilot (airplane): William Green, U.S. (1929)
Automobile: Karl Benz, Germany (1885)
Bakelite (plastic): Leo H. Baekeland, United States (1909)
Balloon (hot air): Jacques and Joseph Montgolfier, France (1783)
Barbed wire: Joseph F. Glidden, United States (1873)
Barometer: Evangelista Torricelli, Italy (1643)
Bessemer steel process: Henry Bessemer, England (1856)
Bicycle: Baron Karl Drais von Sauerbronn, Germany (1816–18)
Bifocal lens: Benjamin Franklin, United States (1780)
Bottle-making machine (automatic): M. J. Owens, U.S. (1898)
Braille printing: Louis Braille, France (1829)
Bridge, suspension (chain): James Finley, U.S. (1800)
Bridge, suspension (wire cable): John A. Roebling, U.S. (1845)
Bunsen burner: Robert Wilhelm von Bunsen, Germany (1855)
Camera (camera obscura): Europe (early 1500s)
Camera (photographic): Joseph Niepce, France (1826)
Camera (Kodak): George Eastman, United States (1888)
Canning (food): Nicolas Appert, France (1809)
Cannon (iron): Germans, Germany (c.1320)
Car (steam-driven): Nicolas Cugnot, France (c.1769)
Carburetor: Gottlieb Daimler, Germany (1892)
Carpet sweeper: M. R. Bissell, United States (1876)
Cash register: James Ritty, United States (1879)
Cathode-ray tube: Sir William Crookes, Britain (1878)
Cellophane: Jacques E. Brandenberger, Switzerland (1908)
Celluloid: Alexander Parkes, Britain (1855)
Cement: Joseph Aspdin, England (1824)
Chronometer: John Harrison, England (1759)
Clock (mechanical): I-Hsing and Liang Ling-Tsan, China (725)
Clock (pendulum): Christiaan Huygens, Netherlands (1656)
Compass (mariner's): Arabs (800s)
Computer (analog): Vannevar Bush, United States (1930)
Computer (digital): Howard Aiken, United States (1944)
Cotton gin: Eli Whitney, United States (1793)
Cream separator: Carl Gustaf de Laval, Sweden (1876)
Cyclotron: Ernest O. Lawrence, United States (1930)
Cylinder lock: Linus Yale, United States (1860)
Daguerreotype: Louis J. M. Daguerre, France (1839)
Diesel engine: Rudolf Diesel, Germany (1892)
Disc brake: Frederick W. Lanchester, Britain (1902)
Dynamite: Alfred B. Nobel, Sweden (1867)
Electric fan: Schuyler S. Wheeler, United States (1886)
Electric flat iron: H. W. Seeley, United States (1882)
Electric generator (disk): Michael Faraday, England (1831)
Electric generator (coil): Hippolyte Pixii, France (1832)
Electric motor (A.C.): Nikola Tesla, United States (1888)
Electric motor (D.C.): Zenobe Gramme, Belgium (1873)
Electric power generating plant (commercial): Thomas A. Edison, United States (1882)
Electrocardiograph: Willem Einthoven, Netherlands (1903)
Electroencephalograph: Hans Berger, Germany (1929)
Electromagnet: Joseph Henry, United States; William Sturgeon, England (1824)
Electroplating: George and Henry Elkington, Britain (1840)
Elevator (safety): Elisha G. Otis, United States (1852)
Engraving (half-tone process): Frederick E. Ives, U.S. (1878)
Flush toilet: Joseph Brahmah, Britain (1778)
Frequency modulation (FM): Edwin H. Armstrong, U.S. (1933)
Frozen food (retail): Clarence Birdseye, U.S. (1917–29)
Gas lighting: William Murdock, Scotland (1792)
Gasoline (antiknock tetraethyl lead): Thomas Midgley, United States (1921)
Geiger counter: Hans Geiger, Germany (1908)
Glider: Sir George Cayley, England (1804)
Gunpowder: Chinese, China (800s)
Gyrocompass: Elmer A. Sperry, United States (1911)
Gyroscope: G. C. Bohnenberger, Germany (1810)
Helicopter: Igor Sikorsky, United States (1939)
Holography: Dennis Gabor, England (1948)
Hydroplane: Glenn H. Curtiss, United States (1911)
Ice-making machine: John Gorrie, United States (1851)
Internal-combustion engine (first workable): Jean Joseph E. Lenoir, France (1860)
Internal-combustion engine (high-speed): Gottlieb Daimler, Germany (1885); Karl Benz, Germany (1885)
Jet aircraft engine: Sir Frank Whittle, England (1930)
Jet airplane: Ernst Heinkel Co., Germany (1939).
Kaleidoscope: Sir David Brewster, Britain (1817)
Kerosene (coal oil): Abraham Gesner, Canada (1852)
Knitting machine: William Lee, England (1589)
Lamp (arc): Humphry Davy, England (1809)
Lamp (arc, commercial): Paul Jablochkov, Russia (1876)
Lamp (carbon-filament electric): Joseph W. Swan, England (1850)
Lamp (incandescent carbon-filament electric): Thomas A. Edison, United States (1879)
Lamp (incandescent drawn tungsten-filament electric): William D. Coolidge, United States (1910)
Lamp (miner's safety): Humphry Davy, England (1815)
Lamp (neon): Georges Claude, France (1915)
Lamp (oil with glass chimney): Aimé Argand, Switzerland (1784)
Laser: Gordon Gould, United States (1957)
Lathe: Greeks, Greece (c.1500 b.c.)
Lever: Archimedes, Greece (200s b.c.)
Lightning rod: Benjamin Franklin, Pennsylvania (1752)
Linoleum: Frederick Walton, England (1860)
Lithography: Aloys Senefelder, Bohemia (1798)
Lock (cylinder): Linus Yale Jr., United States (1861)
Locomotive (steam): Richard Trevithick, Wales (1804)
Locomotive (electric): Werner von Siemens, Germany (1879)
Loom (power): Edmund Cartwright, England (1786)
Machine gun: Richard J. Gatling, United States (1862)
Mass spectrograph: F. Aston, Britain (1919)
Match (book): Joshua Pusey, United States (1892)
Match (friction): John Walker, England (1827)
Match (safety): Gustave E. Pasch, Sweden (1844)
Microcomputer (silicon chip): Michael J. Cochrane, Gary W. Boone, U.S. (1971)
Micrometer: William Gascoigne, Britain (1636)
Microphone: Alexander Graham Bell, United States (1875–76)
Microscope (compound): Hans and Zacharias Janssen, Netherlands (1590)

Microscope (electron): Ernst Ruska, Germany (1933)
Microscope (field ion): Erwin W. Mueller, U.S. (1936)
Microwave oven: Percy L. Spencer, United States (1945)
Milking machine: Anna Baldwin, U.S. (1878)
Motion pictures (camera): Thomas A. Edison, U.S. (1891)
Motion picture (peep show): Thomas A. Edison, U.S. (1894)
Motion picture (projected): Auguste Marie Louis Nicolas Lumière and Louis Jean Lumière, France (1895)
Motor scooter: Greville Bradshaw, England (1919)
Motorcycle: Gottlieb Daimler, Germany (1885)
Music synthesizer: Robert A. Moog, U.S. (1967)
Nylon: Wallace H. Carothers, United States (1935)
Oil well (modern): Edwin Drake, United States (1859)
Outboard engine: Ole Evinrude, United States (1909)
Parachute: André-Jacques Garnerin, France (1797)
Parking meter: Carlton C. Magee, United States (1935)
Patent leather: Seth Boyden, United States (1819)
Pen (ball-point): John Loud, United States (1888)
Pen (fountain): Lewis Waterman, United States (1884)
Pen (lever-fill): W. A. Sheaffer, United States (1913)
Phonograph (cylinder): Thomas A. Edison, U.S. (1877)
Phonograph (disk): Emile Berliner, United States (1890–94)
Photoelectric cell: G. R. Carey, United States (1875)
Photoengraving: William Fox Talbot, England (1852)
Photography (color): Gabriel Lippmann, France (1891)
Photography (on celluloid film): Rev. Hannibal W. Goodwin, United States (1887)
Photography (on transparent paper strip film): George Eastman, United States (1884)
Photography (on metal): Joseph Niepce, France (1826)
Photography (on paper): William Fox Talbot, England (1839)
Pipeline (oil): Samuel van Syckel, United States (1865)
Plastic (celluloid): John W. Hyatt, United States (1869)
Plow (steel): John Deere, United States (1837)
Polaroid Land camera: Edwin Land, United States (1947)
Porcelain: Chinese, China (700s A.D.)
Potter's wheel: Asia Minor (c.6500 B.C.)
Printing (movable type): Pi Sheng, China (c. 1045); Johann Gutenberg, Germany (c. 1454)
Printing (offset): Ira Rubel, United States (1905)
Printing (rotary): Richard Hoe, United States (1846)
Radar: Albert H. Taylor and Leo C. Young, United States (1922)
Radio (wireless): Guglielmo Marconi, Italy (1895)
Radio (transatlantic): Guglielmo Marconi, Italy (1901)
Radio (voice): Valdemar Poulsen, Denmark (1904)
Radio (automobile): William P. Lear, U.S. (1926)
Radio tube diode: John A. Fleming, England (1904)
Radio tube triode: Lee De Forest, United States (1906)
Railroad (steam): George Stephenson, England (1825)
Railway car coupling: Eli H. Jannery, United States (1868)
Railway sleeping coach: George M. Pullman, U.S. (1859)
Raincoat (waterproof): Charles Macintosh, Scotland (1819)
Rayon: Hilaire Chardonnet, France (1884)
Razor (electric): Col. Jacob Schick, United States (1931)
Razor (safety): King C. Gillette, United States (1895)
Reaping machine: Cyrus H. McCormick, United States (1831)
Record (long playing): Peter Goldmark, United States (1948)
Recording (magnetic tape): J. A. O'Neill, United States (1927)
Recording (magnetic wire): Valdemar Poulsen, Denmark (1898)
Revolver: Samuel Colt, United States (1835)
Rifle (automatic): John Moses Browning, United States (1917)
Rifle (repeating): O. F. Winchester, United States (1860)
Rocket (liquid-fuel): Robert H. Goddard, U.S.; Hermann Oberth, Germany; Konstantin E. Tsiolkovsky, Soviet Union (1920s)
Rocket (military): Sir William Congreve, Britain (1808)
Rubber (latex foam): Dunlop Rubber Co., England (1928)
Rubber (vulcanized): Charles Goodyear, United States (1839)
Rubber tire (pneumatic): John B. Dunlop, Britain (1888)
Rubber tire (solid): Thomas Hancock, England (1846)
Rudder (ship): Vikings (1100s)
Safety pin: Walter Hunt, United States (1849)
Screw propeller: John Ericsson, United States (1837)
Self-starter (internal-combustion engine): Charles F. Kettering, United States (1911)
Sewing machine: Barthélemy Thimonnier, France (1841); Elias Howe, U.S. (1846)
Sewing machine (foot-operated): Isaac Singer, U.S. (1851)
Sewing machine (electric): Singer Sewing Machine Co., United States (1889)
Sextant: John Hadley, England; Thomas Godfrey, U.S. (1730)
Ship (seagoing): Egyptians or Phoenicians (2500 B.C.)
Ship (steam): J. C. Périer, France (1775)
Ship (steam, commercial): Robert Fulton, U.S. (1807)
Ship (turbine): Sir Charles Parsons, Britain (1894)
Slot machine: Charles Fey, U.S. (1895)
Spectacles (curved glass): Salvino D'Armato, Italy (1285)
Spectroscope: Joseph von Fraunhofer, Germany (1814)
Spinning frame: Sir Richard Arkwright, England (1769)
Spinning jenny: James Hargreaves, England (1770)
Spinning mule: Samuel Crompton, England (1779)
Stainless steel: Harry Brearley, England (1913)
Steam engine (no moving parts): Thomas Savery, England (1698)
Steam engine (piston): Thomas Newcomen, England (c.1712)
Steam engine (condenser): James Watt, Scotland (1769)
Steam shovel: William S. Otis, U.S. (1838)
Steel production: Henry Bessemer, England (1856)
Stethoscope: René Laënnec, France (1816)
Stirrups (metal): China (500s A.D.)
Stove (coal): Jordan L. Mott, United States (1833)
Stove (Franklin): Benjamin Franklin, United States (1740)
Stove (gas): Robert W. Bunsen, Germany (1855)
Stove (electric): W. S. Hadaway, United States (1896)
Submarine: David Bushnell, United States (1776)
Submarine (nuclear-powered, *Nautilus*): Government scientists, United States (1955)
Tank (armored): Sir Ernest Swinton, England (1914)
Telegraph (electric): Samuel F. B. Morse, U.S. (1832–37)
Telegraph (visual semaphore): Claude Chappe, France (1793)
Telephone: Alexander Graham Bell, United States (1875–76)
Telescope (simple): Hans Lippershey, Netherlands (1608)
Telescope (refracting): Galileo Galilei, Italy (1609)
Telescope (reflecting): Isaac Newton, England (1668)
Telescope (radio): Karl Jansky, United States (1931)
Television (electronic): Vladimir K. Zworykin, United States (1923)
Television (mechanical): John L. Baird, Scotland (1926)
Thermometer: Galileo Galilei, Italy (1593)
Thermometer (improved): Gabriel D. Fahrenheit, Germany (1714)
Thermos bottle: Sir James Dewar, Britain (1892)
Torpedo (self-propelled): Robert Whitehead, Scotland (1866)
Tractor (steam): Nicolas Cugnot, France (1769)
Tractor (track-type): Benjamin Holt, United States (1906)
Tram (railed): Mine rail tracks, Alsace (1550)
Transformer: Otto Bláthy, Hungary (1884)
Transistor: John Bardeen, William Shockley, and Walter Brattain, United States (1947)
Tungsten filament: Irving Langmuir, United States (1915)
Typesetting machine (Linotype): Ottmar Mergenthaler, United States (1884)
Typesetting machine (Monotype): Tolbert Lanston, United States (1885)
Typewriter: Christopher L. Sholes, Carlos Glidden, U.S. (1867)
Vacuum cleaner: I. W. McGaffey, United States (1869)
Vacuum tube (triode): Lee De Forest, United States (1906)
Washing machine (manual): Hamilton E. Smith, U.S. (1858)
Washing machine (electric): Alva J. Fisher, U.S. (1907)
Watch (mainspring): Peter Henlein, Germany (c.1500)
Watch (self-winding): Louis Recordon, Britain (1780)
Welder (electric): Elihu Thomson, United States (1877)
Wheel (solid): Sumerians (c.3300 B.C.)
Wheel (spoked): Egypt (c.1900 B.C.)
Windmill: Iran (corn-grinding mills; c.600 A.D.)
Xerography: Chester Carlson, United States (1937–48)
X ray: Wilhelm Roentgen, Germany (1895)
Zipper: Whitcomb L. Judson, United States (1891)
Zipper (meshed-tooth): Gideon Sundback, United States (1913)

HOW TO PROTECT YOUR INVENTION

What Can Be Patented? If you have invented something that you wish to patent, it would have to meet the statutory standard that it be "any new and useful process, machine, manufacture, or composition of matter, or any new and useful improvements thereof." This includes practically everything made by man and the processes for making them.

Patents may also be granted on new life forms, on any distinct and new variety of plant, other than a tuber-propagated plant, which is asexually reproduced, or any new, original, and ornamental design for an article of manufacture.

What Cannot Be Patented? A patent may *not* be granted on a useless invention, on a method of doing business, on mere printed matter, or on a device or machine that will not operate. Furthermore, even if your invention is novel or new, a patent may not be obtained if your invention would have been obvious to a person having ordinary skill in the same area at the time of your invention. And a patent may not be obtained if the invention was in public use or on sale in the U.S. for more than one year prior to the filing of your patent application, or the invention has been patented or described in a printed publication anywhere in the world more than a year before your U.S. patent application is filed. Finally, you may not receive a patent for an invention useful only in applying nuclear material for military purposes.

Applying for a Patent. If your invention appears worthy of a patent, the law gives you the privilege of preparing your own application. But since the law is complicated, you would be wise to consult an expert—a registered patent attorney or agent.

Your application will include a claim or claims describing the scope of your invention.

Patentability (novelty and unobviousness) is judged by the claims.

After a patent is granted, questions of patent validity and infringement are determined by a court on the basis of the claims.

Obviously you cannot know that your invention is unique unless you have done some research. The Patent and Trademark Office has a Public Search Room at its offices (2021 Jefferson Davis Highway, Arlington, Va.). Here you can conduct your own search, or employ a patent attorney to do so.

Once the search is done and it appears that your invention may be unique and patentable, your attorney will prepare a final draft of your application. The original should be signed by you and sent to the Commissioner of Patents and Trademarks, Washington, D.C. 20231. There is a basic filing fee of $150 for the small inventor and $300 for a large corporation. Small additional amounts are charged if claims exceed a certain number.

Patent Rights. If you are to receive a utility patent, there is a basic $250 fee for the small inventor and $500 for a large corporation.

After payment, you will receive your patent, which gives you "the right to exclude others from making, using, or selling" the invention for a period of 17 years from the date of the patent. Payment of periodic maintenance fees is required to assure a full 17-year term. Information from your patent will also be published in the Patent and Trademark Office's *Official Gazette.*

The entire process, from application to grant, currently averages 24 months.

Patent Laws. Your right to be granted a patent—the exclusive privilege to control something that you have invented and to share in any compensation that your invention brings—is derived from Article I, Section 8, of the United States Constitution. The first U.S. patent law was passed by Congress in 1790. In 1836 the patent laws were revised, the office of Commissioner of Patents was established, and Patent No. 1, the first numbered patent, was issued to Sen. John Ruggles of Maine on July 13, 1836. The Patent and Trademark Office was transferred to the Interior Department in 1849 and to the Commerce Department in 1925.

Trademarks and Service Marks. A trademark is a word, name, symbol, or device used to indicate the source of goods being sold. It distinguishes these goods from other similar goods.

Trademark rights may be used to prevent others from using a confusingly similar mark. But trademark rights do NOT prevent others from making the same kind of goods or selling similar goods using a nonconfusing mark.

A *service mark* is similar to a trademark but is used in the sale or advertising of services rather than goods.

Trademarks or service marks used in interstate or foreign commerce may be registered in the Patent and Trademark Office.

You can obtain more information about trademarks by writing to Commissioner of Patents and Trademarks, Washington, D.C. 20231.

WHAT IS A COPYRIGHT?

A copyright protects an author or artist from having others make copies of his work without permission.

Plays, articles, books, musical compositions, pictures, computer programs, and forms of art can be protected by copyright.

A copyright protects the *form* of the expression, rather than the subject matter. For example, you might copyright your written description of how an automobile works. This copyright would prevent others from copying *your* description without your permission. But it would NOT prevent others from writing their own descriptions of how an automobile works.

Under a revised copyright law effective on Jan. 1, 1978, works copyrighted on or after that date are protected for the life of the author and for 50 years after the author's death.

Copyrights are registered in the Copyright Office in the Library of Congress.

You can obtain more information about copyrights or copyright forms by writing to Register of Copyrights, Library of Congress, Washington, D.C. 20559, or by phoning (202)287–9100.

SCIENTISTS AND INVENTORS

Scientists who have won Nobel Prizes are indicated below by (N). Their prize-winning achievements are listed on pages 70–77. For deaths of scientists and inventors in 1983, see pages 981–986.

Jean Louis Agassiz (1807–73), Swiss-American biologist and geologist: proved glaciers once covered much of the Earth.

Howard Hathaway Aiken (1900–73), American mathematician: designed world's first large-scale digital computer, the Mark I, for International Business Machines Corp. (1944).

André Marie Ampère (1775–1836), French physicist and mathematician: developed laws of electromagnetism, using electric currents; *ampere*, unit to measure flow of electric current, named after him.

Carl D. Anderson (1905–), American physicist: discovered *positron*, or anti-electron, a unit of matter (1932). (N)

Sir Edward Victor Appleton (1892–1965), British physicist: discovered Appleton layer of free electrons in ionosphere that bounces radio waves back to Earth, leading to development of radar. (N)

Archimedes (287–212 B.C.), Greek mathematician and engineer: father of experimental science; discovered laws of lever, pulley, displacement, and buoyancy; invented catapult and Archimedean screw, a kind of pump.

Aristarchus (200s B.C.) Greek astronomer: first to say Earth revolves around Sun, but theory disregarded for hundreds of years.

Aristotle (384–322 B.C.) Greek philosopher: father of objective science; developed syllogism in logic; made first scientific study of biology.

Sir Richard Arkwright (1732–92), British inventor: developed water-powered spinning machine (1769), starting Industrial Revolution.

Edwin Howard Armstrong (1890–1954), American electrical engineer: invented FM (frequency modulation) radio, eliminating static (1933).

Francis W. Aston (1877–1945), British physicist: invented mass spectrograph (1919). (N)

Amedeo Avogadro (1776–1856), Italian physicist: developed Avogadro's law of gases (1811); differentiated molecules and atoms; provided basis for determining correct atomic weights.

Roger Bacon (1214?–94), English philosopher and scientist: pioneered in controlled experiments and observation of phenomena; introduced gunpowder formula to Europe (1242).

Leo Hendrik Baekeland (1863–1944), Belgian-American chemist: invented Bakelite, first artificial resin plastic (1909).

Adolf von Baeyer (1835–1917), German chemist: developed synthetic dyes. (N)

John Bardeen (1908–), American physicist: co-inventor of transistor (1947). (N)

Nikolai G. Basov (1922–), Russian physicist: developed masers (1955), using molecular energy to amplify radio waves. (N)

Antoine Henri Becquerel (1852–1908), French physicist: co-discoverer with Curies of natural radioactivity. (N)

Alexander Graham Bell (1847–1922), American scientist: invented telephone (1875–76).

Karl Benz (1844–1929), German engineer: invented first gasoline-powered automobile (1885).

Friedrich Bergius (1884–1949), German chemist: converted coal dust to oil. (N)

Jöns Jakob Berzelius (1779–1848), Swedish chemist: developed system still used to write chemical symbols and formulas; discovered elements selenium (1817), silicon (1823), thorium (1828); co-discovered cerium (1803).

Sir Henry Bessemer (1813–98), British inventor: developed Bessemer process for converting pig iron into steel (1856).

Clarence Birdseye (1886–1956), American inventor: invented fast-frozen food processing (1925) and dehydrated food processing (1949).

Max Bodenstein (1871–1942), German chemist: first described chain reactions (1916) in chemical processes.

Niels Bohr (1885–1962), Danish physicist: described atom as miniature solar system with electrons in orbits around nucleus (1913). (N)

William Cranch Bond (1789–1859) and his son **George Phillips Bond** (1825–65), American astronomers: took first photograph of star (1850); discovered dark ring of Saturn and Saturn's eighth moon.

Max Born (1882–1970), German physicist: pioneered research in quantum mechanics. (N)

Carl Bosch (1874–1940), German chemist: developed commercial process using Friedrich Bergius' discovery to convert coal into oil. (N)

Johann Friedrich Böttger (1682–1719), German chemist: first European to discover how to make porcelain (1708).

Nathaniel Bowditch (1773–1838), American astronomer and mathematician: wrote *The American Practical Navigator* (1799).

Seth Boyden (1788–1870), American inventor: developed patent-leather process (1819).

Robert Boyle (1627–91), Irish alchemist and chemist: proved air, earth, fire, and water were not elements as alchemists had believed; developed Boyle's law of gases.

James Bradley (1693–1762), English astronomer: discovered aberration of light.

Sir William Henry Bragg (1862–1942) and his son **Sir William Lawrence Bragg** (1890–1971), British physicists: developed X-ray spectrometer to explore atomic structures. (N)

Tycho Brahe (1546–1601), Danish astronomer: proved changes occur in stars with discovery of new star (1572); proved comets originate in outer space (1577).

Jacques Edwin Brandenberger (1872–1954), Swiss chemist: invented cellophane (1908).

Walter Houser Brattain (1902–), American physicist: co-inventor of transistor (1947). (N)

John Moses Browning (1855–1926), American inventor: designed Browning machine gun (1890) and Browning automatic rifle (1917).

Robert Wilhelm Bunsen (1811–99), German chemist: developed electrolytic cell to produce magnesium (1852), Bunsen burner (1855).

William Burroughs (1855–98), American inventor: first reliable adding machine (1889).

Vannevar Bush (1890–1974), American electrical engineer: invented first analog computer, called differential analyzer, in 1930, used in World War II to aim antiaircraft guns.

Melvin Calvin (1911–), American chemist:

SCIENTISTS AND INVENTORS *(continued)*
discovered how plants make food by photosynthesis. (N)

Georg Cantor (1845–1918), German mathematician: developed theory of sets (1870s).

Chester F. Carlson (1906–68), American physicist: invented xerography method of electrostatic printing in 1937–48.

Wallace H. Carothers (1896–1937), American chemist: developed nylon (1935).

Rachel Carson (1907–64), American biologist: her book *Silent Spring* warned of dangers to wildlife by misuse of insecticides.

Edmund Cartwright (1743–1823), English clergyman and inventor: invented first successful steam-powered loom to weave cloth (1786).

George Washington Carver (1859?–1943), American botanist and chemist: invented hundreds of products made from peanuts, sweet potatoes, pecans, and other farm crops.

Henry Cavendish (1731–1810), English physicist and chemist: discovered hydrogen (1766); demonstrated water is compound of oxygen and hydrogen.

Sir James Chadwick (1891–1974), British physicist: discovered neutron (1932). (N)

Owen Chamberlain (1920–), American physicist: co-discoverer of antiproton (1955). (N)

Hilaire Chardonnet (1839–1924), French chemist: invented rayon (1884).

Rudolf J. E. Clausius (1822–88), German physicist: discovered thermodynamics laws (1850).

Sir John Douglas Cockcroft (1897–1967), British physicist: with Ernest T. S. Walton, first to split atoms by bombardment with protons. (N)

Samuel Colt (1814–62), American inventor: developed first successful revolver (1835).

Arthur Holly Compton (1892–1962), American physicist: helped prove quantum theory with discovery of Compton effect in which X rays act as atomic particles; helped develop atomic bomb. (N)

Sir William Congreve (1772–1828), British inventor: developed military rockets (1808), used by British Army against Napoleon and against Americans in War of 1812.

Peter Cooper (1791–1883), American inventor: built *Tom Thumb*, first U.S. steam locomotive used on commercial railroad (1830).

Nicolaus Copernicus (1473–1543), Polish astronomer: revolutionized astronomy by demonstrating that Earth moves around Sun instead of being the stationary center of universe.

Frederick Gardener Cottrell (1877–1948), American chemist: invented first electrical precipitator to reduce pollution from industrial smokestacks (1910).

Bernard Courtois (1777–1838), French chemist: discovered element iodine (1811).

Jacques-Yves Cousteau (1910–), French inventor: developed Aqua-Lung (1943) for skin divers to breathe underwater.

Sir William Crookes (1832–1919), British chemist: discovered element thallium (1861); invented a cathode-ray tube, the radiometer, and the spinthariscope.

Pierre Curie (1859–1906) and his wife **Marie Sklodowska Curie** (1867–1934), French chemists and physicists: discovered radioactive elements radium and polonium (1898). (N)

John Dalton (1766–1844), English chemist: developed atomic theory (1803); made first table of atomic weights.

Charles Robert Darwin (1809–82), British naturalist: wrote *On the Origin of Species* (1859), his theory of evolution.

Leonardo da Vinci (1452–1519), Italian artist and scientist: drew sketches and plans for many devices invented hundreds of years later, including helicopter, machine gun, parachute.

Sir Humphry Davy (1778–1829), English chemist: discovered elements potassium and sodium (1807); invented electric arc (1808); discovered elements barium, calcium, and magnesium (1808); invented miner's safety lamp (1815).

Louis Victor de Broglie (1892–), French physicist: developed wave mechanics (1923).

Lee De Forest (1873–1961), American inventor: developed triode vacuum tube (1906), making possible long-distance radio and TV.

Willem de Sitter (1872–1934), Dutch astronomer: first proposed theory of expanding universe (1917).

John Deere (1804–86), American inventor: invented first steel plow (1837).

Arthur Jeffrey Dempster (1886–1950), American physicist: discovered uranium 235 (in 1935), basic material used in atomic bombs.

René Descartes (1596–1650), French philosopher and mathematician: developed analytical geometry (1637).

Joseph Dixon (1799–1869), American inventor: made lead pencils from graphite (1827).

Amos E. Dolbear (1837–1910), American physicist and inventor: invented "talking machine" (1864), 12 years before Bell patented telephone; produced first radio waves (1882).

Charles E. Duryea (1861–1938) and **J. Frank Duryea** (1869–1967), brothers, American inventors: built first successful gasoline-powered automobile in U.S. (1893).

James Buchanan Eads (1820–87), American engineer: developed armored warships (1862).

George Eastman (1854–1932), American inventor: developed first Kodak camera using roll film (1888); began mass-producing cameras at $1 each (1900).

Sir Arthur Stanley Eddington (1882–1944), British astronomer: discovered relationship between mass and brightness in stars; discovered deflection of light by Sun's gravitational field (1919).

Harold Eugene Edgerton (1903–). American electrical engineer: invented photographic electronic flash equipment (1931).

Thomas Alva Edison (1847–1931), American inventor: among his more than 1,100 inventions were phonograph (1877), electric light (1879), stencil duplicating process for mimeograph machines (1887), and motion-picture projector (1889).

Albert Einstein (1879–1955), German-American physicist: developed theory of relativity (1905) and unified field theory (1929); his theories made possible development of atomic bombs and atomic energy.

John Ericsson (1803–89), Swedish-American engineer: invented first successful propeller with blades for use on ships (1837).

Euclid (c.300 B.C.), Greek mathematician: compiled first geometry textbook.

Oliver Evans (1755–1819), American inventor: built first steam-powered land vehicle in U.S. (1805).

Gabriel Daniel Fahrenheit (1686–1736), German physicist: developed scale of temperatures.

Thaddeus Fairbanks (1796–1886), American inventor: platform weighing scale (1831).

Michael Faraday (1791–1867), English chemist and physicist: discovered electromagnetic induction (1831), leading to development of electric generators and motors; formulated laws of electrolysis.

Philo Taylor Farnsworth (1906–71), American inventor: patented image dissector (1928), electronic device basic to television.

Pierre de Fermat (1601–65), French mathematician: introduced theory of mathematical probability and modern theory of numbers.

Enrico Fermi (1901–54), Italian-American physicist: split the atom in nuclear fission (1934); produced first atomic chain reaction (1942); helped develop atomic bomb. (N)

Cyrus West Field (1819–92), American businessman: laid first successful telegraph cable across Atlantic (1858); laid new cable in 1866.

John Fitch (1743–98), American inventor: built first successful steamboat (1787).

Henry Ford (1863–1947), American inventor and businessman: introduced moving assembly line to produce "Model T" Fords (1913).

Jean B. L. Foucault (1819–68), French physicist: proved light travels more slowly in water (1850); used pendulum to prove rotation of Earth (1851); built first gyroscope (1852).

Benjamin Franklin (1706–90), American statesman and scientist: proved lightning is electricity (1752); invented lightning rod (1752) and bifocal glasses (1780).

R. Buckminster Fuller (1895–1983), American inventor: designed Dymaxion prefabricated metal home in 1927; invented geodesic dome of triangular elements in 1960s.

Robert Fulton (1765–1815), American artist and inventor: built *Clermont*, first commercially successful steamboat in U.S. (1807).

Galileo Galilei (1564–1642), Italian physicist and astronomer: discovered law of pendulum (1584), law of falling bodies (1589), four moons of Jupiter (1610); proved Copernican theory of astronomy.

Richard Jordan Gatling (1818–1903), American inventor: developed first practical machine gun in U.S. (1862).

Karl Friedrich Gauss (1777–1855), German mathematician: helped develop modern number theory and laws of electromagnetism.

Joseph Louis Gay-Lussac (1778–1850), French chemist and physicist: made discoveries about gases; co-discovered element boron (1808),

Hans Geiger (1882–1947), German physicist: invented Geiger counter (1908).

Josiah Willard Gibbs (1839–1903), American mathematician and physicist: founder of physical chemistry and thermodynamics; member American Hall of Fame.

Donald Arthur Glaser (1926–), American physicist: invented bubble chamber (1953), device used to study subatomic particles. (N)

Carlos Glidden (1834–77), American co-inventor of typewriter (1867).

Robert Hutchings Goddard (1882–1945), American physicist: built first successful liquid-fueled rocket (1926), making space travel possible.

Charles Goodyear (1800–60), American inventor: discovery of vulcanization process (1839) initiated rubber industry.

John Gorrie (1803–55), American physician: invented first ice-making machine (1851).

Gordon Gould (1920–), American physicist: invented first practical ruby laser (1957).

Thomas Graham (1805–69), Scottish chemist: pioneer in physical chemistry; stated how gases mix in Graham's law of diffusion (1833).

Otto von Guericke (1602–86), German scientist: invented 34-foot-high water barometer; invented air pump (1650).

Johann Gutenberg (1395?–1468?), German inventor: invented metal type molding of letters, making mass printing possible (c. 1455).

Fritz Haber (1868–1934), German chemist: developed process for making synthetic ammonia (1913) for fertilizers and explosives. (N)

Otto Hahn (1879–1968), German chemist: co-discoverer of element protactinium (1917); with Fritz Strassman, split nucleus of uranium atom (1938). (N)

George Ellery Hale (1868–1938), American astronomer: invented spectroheliograph (1889) for photographing Sun; founded three major observatories, Yerkes (1895), Mt. Wilson (1904), and Mt. Palomar (1928).

Charles Martin Hall (1863–1914), American chemist: discovered how to make aluminum from bauxite (1886), working independently of **Paul Héroult** (1863–1914), French chemist who discovered same process in same year.

Edmund Halley (1656–1742), English astronomer: developed star catalog for Southern Hemisphere; correctly forecast return of Halley's comet in 1910.

James Hargreaves (1722?–78), English inventor: developed first spinning jenny to spin many threads at same time (1770).

Werner Heisenberg (1901–76), German physicist: founded study of subatomic particles (1927). (N)

Hermann L. F. von Helmholtz (1821–94), German physicist: developed law of conservation of energy; invented ophthalmoscope (1851).

Sir William Herschel (1738–1822), British astronomer: first person to discover a planet since prehistoric times when he sighted Uranus in 1781; discovered infrared radiation (1800).

Heinrich Rudolf Hertz (1857–94), German physicist: discovered electromagnetic waves (1887), making possible radio and TV.

Georg von Hevesy (1885–1966), Hungarian chemist: co-discoverer of hafnium (1923). (N)

Hipparchus (100s B.C.), Greek astronomer: made first catalog of stars; discovered changes of equinoxes.

John Philip Holland (1840–1914), Irish-American inventor: built first practical submarine for U.S. Navy (1898).

Elias Howe (1819–67), American inventor: built first practical sewing machine (1846).

James Hutton (1726–97), Scottish geologist: founded modern geology with theory that rocks were formed by lava from volcanoes (1785).

SCIENTISTS AND INVENTORS *(continued)*

Christian Huygens (1629–95), Dutch scientist: developed telescope lens (1655) with which he discovered Saturn's ring and one of Saturn's moons; discovered wave theory of light; invented micrometer to measure small objects; invented pendulum clock (1673).

Joseph M. Jacquard (1752–1834), French inventor: invented automatic pattern loom (1801–04).

Karl Guthe Jansky (1905–50), American engineer: discovered radio waves from outer space (1932), leading to radio astronomy.

Thomas Jefferson (1743–1826), American President and inventor: among his many inventions were swivel chair and dumbwaiter.

Charles Francis Jenkins (1867–1934), American inventor: developed phantascope (1891–94), first successful motion-picture projector.

J. Hans Jensen (1906–), German physicist: discovered nuclear shell structure of atomic nuclei. (N)

Frédéric Joliot (1900–58) and his wife **Irène Joliot-Curie** (1897–1956), French physicists: produced isotopes by high-energy bombardment of elements (1934). (N)

James Prescott Joule (1818–89), English physicist: determined relationship between heat and mechanical energy (conservation of energy).

Lord Kelvin (William Thomson; 1824–1907), British physicist: invented Kelvin temperature scale for use with gas thermometers, with absolute zero equal to –273 ° C.

Johannes Kepler (1571–1630), German astronomer and mathematician: wrote laws of motion of the planets.

Donald William Kerst (1911–), American physicist: developed betatron (1940), an atomic accelerator.

Charles Franklin Kettering (1876–1958), American inventor: invented automobile self-starter (1911) and other auto improvements.

Chevalier de Lamarck (1744–1829), French naturalist: founder of invertebrate paleontology; concluded plants and animals change to adapt to their environments; made first efforts to scientifically forecast weather.

Edwin Herbert Land (1909–), American inventor: invented polarized plastic sheets (1928); developed polaroid camera that takes and prints pictures in a few seconds (1947); invented self-developing color film (1963).

Marquis de Laplace (1749–1827), French astronomer and mathematician: described origin of solar system from a nebula (1796).

Antoine Laurent Lavoisier (1743–94), French chemist: gave first scientific explanation of fire as union of material with oxygen (1777); proved law of conservation of matter; wrote first modern textbook of chemistry (1789).

Ernest Orlando Lawrence (1901–58), American physicist: invented cyclotron (1930) and bevatron (1954), atomic particle accelerators; produced first man-made mesons (1948). (N)

Nicolas Leblanc (1742–1806), French physician: discovered process for making soda from common salt (1790).

Gottfried Wilhelm von Leibniz (1646–1716), German mathematician: developed theories of differential and integral calculus; invented an early type of calculating or adding machine.

Jean Joseph Etienne Lenoir (1822–1900), French inventor: invented first internal-combustion engine, using illuminating gas as fuel (1860); built vehicle using his engine (1863).

Willard Frank Libby (1908–80), American chemist: discovered carbon 14 (radiocarbon) in 1947; developed method of using it to date prehistoric plant and animal fossils. (N)

Carolus Linnaeus (1707–78), Swedish botanist: established present-day scientific method of naming and classifying plants and animals.

Hendrick Antoon Lorentz (1853–1928), Dutch physicist: developed electron theory. (N)

Sir Bernard Lovell (1913–), British astronomer: built first completely directional radio telescope, at Jodrell Bank, England.

Archibald M. Low (1888–1956), British physicist: demonstrated principles of television (1914); invented radio control systems for torpedoes and rockets.

Percival Lowell (1855–1916), American astronomer: predicted discovery of Pluto (1905).

Guglielmo Marconi (1874–1937), Italian electrical engineer: invented first practical radio system (1895); sent first transatlantic radio signal (1901). (N)

Sir Hiram Stevens Maxim (1840–1916), British-American inventor: invented first completely automatic machine gun (1889).

James Clerk Maxwell (1831–79), British mathematician and physicist: developed mathematical descriptions of electricity and magnetism; predicted (1864) electromagnetic waves.

Julius Robert von Mayer (1814–78), German physician and physicist: independently discovered law of conservation of energy (1842).

Maria Goeppert Mayer (1906–72), German-American physicist: independently developed theory of structure of atomic nuclei. (N)

Cyrus Hall McCormick (1809–84), American inventor: invented reaping machine to harvest wheat (1831).

Lise Meitner (1878–1968), Austrian physicist: co-discoverer of element protactinium (1917); mathematically determined energy released by nuclear fission, helping lead to atomic bomb.

Gregor Johann Mendel (1822–84), Austrian monk and botanist: developed theory of heredity and founded science of genetics.

Dmitri Ivanovich Mendeleev (1834–1907), Russian chemist: developed periodic table of elements, predicting elements not yet discovered.

Ottmar Mergenthaler (1854–99), German-American inventor: invented Linotype typesetting machine (1883).

Charles Messier (1730–1817), French astronomer: made first star catalog of northern sky (1784).

Julius Lothar Meyer (1830–95), German chemist: demonstrated relationship of atomic weights to properties of elements (1869).

Albert Abraham Michelson (1852–1931), German-American physicist: with Edward W. Morley, disproved that substance called ether fills vacuums (1887); invented interferometer (1880); made first accurate measurements of diameter of a star (1920) and speed of light (1926). (N)

Robert Andrews Millikan (1868–1953), American physicist: measured electric charge of electron and intensity of cosmic rays. (N)

Samuel Finley Breese Morse (1791–1872), American artist and inventor: invented electric telegraph (1832–37).

Paul Mueller (1899–1965), Swiss chemist: discovered power of DDT insecticide (1939). (N)

Walther Hermann Nernst (1864–1941), German chemist: developed third law of thermodynamics. (N)

Simon Newcomb (1835–1909), American astronomer: computed new, more accurate, tables of orbits of Moon and planets.

Thomas Newcomen (1663–1729), English inventor: with Thomas Savery, built first piston steam engine (c.1712).

Sir Isaac Newton (1642–1727), English scientist and mathematician: described basic laws of gravity and motion (1687); invented calculus, new branch of mathematics (independently of Leibniz); invented reflecting telescope.

Joseph Nicéphore Niepce (1765–1833), French scientist: made first crude photograph (1826), using process called *heliography.*

Alfred Otto Carl Nier (1911–), American physicist: separated from uranium the isotope U-235, basic atomic material (1940).

Alfred Bernhard Nobel (1833–96), Swedish chemist: invented dynamite (1867); established Nobel prizes to encourage peace and progress.

Robert N. Noyce (1927–), American physicist: developed electronic integrated circuit on silicon chip, making possible development of microcomputers and hand-held calculators.

Hans Christian Oersted (1777–1851), Danish physicist: discovered magnetic field surrounds any wire carrying electricity (1819); made first aluminum (1825).

Ransom Eli Olds (1864–1950), American inventor: first to use assembly line to mass-produce automobiles (1901).

J. Robert Oppenheimer (1904–67), American physicist: directed construction of first atomic bombs (1943–45).

Elisha Graves Otis (1811–61), American inventor: invented safety elevator (1852), steam plow (1857), bake oven (1858).

Blaise Pascal (1623–62), French mathematician and scientist: formulated Pascal's law, explaining pressures of liquid; invented theory of probability; invented adding machine (1642).

Linus Carl Pauling (1901–), American chemist: built accurate models of molecules; led scientists in trying to ban atomic testing. (N)

Karl Pearson (1857–1936), British mathematician: founded science of statistics.

Sir William Henry Perkin (1838–1907), British chemist: made synthetic aniline dye (1856).

Auguste Piccard (1884–1962), Swiss physicist: invented stratosphere balloon to ascend to high altitudes (1931); invented bathyscaph to descend to depths of ocean (1953).

Max Planck (1858–1947), German physicist: revolutionized physics with quantum theory of energy (1901). (N)

Joseph Priestley (1733–1804), British clergyman and chemist: discovered hydrochloric acid (1772), laughing gas (1772), sulfur dioxide (1774), oxygen (1774).

Alexander M. Prokhorov (1916–), Russian physicist: with Nikolai Basov, discovered masers (1955), a means of amplifying radio waves with molecular energy.

Ptolemy (100s A.D.), Greek astronomer and geographer: his theory of Earth being motionless at center of universe was accepted for 1,500 years; his miscalculation of size of Earth led Columbus to believe he had reached Asia when he discovered Americas.

Michael Idvorsky Pupin (1858–1935), Hungarian-American physicist: invented 34 devices to improve telephone, telegraph, and radio.

Pythagoras (500s B.C.), Greek philosopher and mathematician: believed Earth was round and had motions, but his ideas were discounted for hundreds of years.

Isidor Isaac Rabi (1898–), Austrian-American physicist: supervised U.S. development of radar (1940–45); developed data on magnetic properties of atomic nuclei. (N)

Sir William Ramsay (1852–1916), British chemist: co-discoverer of elements argon (1894), helium (1895), and krypton, neon, xenon (all 1898). (N)

Ira Remsen (1846–1927), American physician and chemist: founded *American Chemical Journal* (1879), first scientific journal in U.S.

David Rittenhouse (1732–96), American astronomer: accurately measured Earth's distance from Sun (1769); built accurate model of solar system (1770).

James Ritty (1836–1918), American inventor: invented first practical cash register (1879).

Wilhelm Conrad Roentgen (1845–1923), German physicist: discovered X rays (1895). (N)

Henry Augustus Rowland (1848–1901), American physicist: determined value of *ohm*, unit for measuring resistance to electric current.

Bertrand Arthur William Russell (1872–1970), English mathematician and philosopher: coauthor of *Principia Mathematica,* landmark in symbolic logic.

Ernest Rutherford (1871–1937), British physicist: called father of nuclear physics; stated theory of atomic transmutation (1902); described nuclear structure of atom (1911); produced protons by bombarding nitrogen atoms with alpha particles (1919). (N)

Andrei Dmitriyevich Sakharov (1921–): Soviet physicist: developed first hydrogen bomb for Soviet Union in 1950s; became outspoken critic of communist restrictions on human rights. (N)

Carl Wilhelm Scheele (1742–86), German-Swedish chemist: discovered oxygen (1774), chlorine (1774), and molybdenum (1778).

Erwin Schrödinger (1887–1961), Austrian physicist: provided mathematical basis for quantum theory with Schrödinger equation. (N)

Glenn Theodore Seaborg (1912–), American chemist: co-discoverer of six elements—plutonium (1940), curium (1944), americium (1945), berkelium (1949), californium (1950), mendelevium (1955); chairman, U.S. Atomic Energy Commission (1961–71).

Alois Senefelder (1771–1834), German inventor: invented lithography (1798).

Harlow Shapley (1885–1972), American astronomer: developed new information about Milky Way.

William Shockley (1910–), American physicist: co-discoverer of transistor (1947). (N)

SCIENTISTS AND INVENTORS *(continued)*

Christopher Latham Sholes (1819–90), American inventor: co-invented typewriter (1867–68).

Sir Charles William Siemens (1823–83), German-British inventor: invented furnace (1856) that led to open-hearth steelmaking process.

Igor I. Sikorsky (1889–1972), Russian-American aircraft designer: designed and built first four-engine plane (1913) and first successful single-rotor helicopter (1939).

Isaac Merrit Singer (1811–75), American inventor: invented improvements on early sewing machines to make them practical (1851).

Frederick Soddy (1877–1956), British chemist: coined term *isotopes* for atoms of same element that have different weights. (N)

Elmer Ambrose Sperry (1860–1930), American inventor: invented gyrocompass (1911), leading to automatic pilots for aircraft.

Hermann Staudinger (1881–1965), German chemist: his exploration of giant molecules led to development of many plastics. (N)

Charles Proteus Steinmetz (1865–1923), German-American mathematician and engineer: solved problems of using alternating current in generating and transmitting electricity.

George Stephenson (1781–1848), British inventor: built one of first practical locomotives, *Puffing Billy* (1814); his locomotive *The Rocket* (1829) reached speed of 30 mph.

Fritz Strassmann (1902–), German chemist: co-discoverer of method of splitting uranium atom (1938).

Theodor Svedberg (1884–1971), Swedish chemist: invented ultracentrifuge. (N)

Richard L. M. Synge (1914–), British biochemist: invented partition chromatography, method of analyzing tiny samples. (N)

Leo Szilard (1898–1964), Hungarian-American physicist: helped develop nuclear reactor (1942).

Edward Teller (1908–), American physicist: developed hydrogen bomb (1952).

Nikola Tesla (1856–1943), Slavic-American electrical engineer: invented alternating-current electric motor (1888).

Thales (c.640–c.546 B.C.), Greek philosopher: pioneered scientific method of observation; used geometry to predict eclipse of Sun.

Sir Joseph John Thomson (1856–1940), British physicist: discovered electron (1897). (N)

Clyde William Tombaugh (1906–), American astronomer: discovered planet Pluto (1930).

Evangelista Torricelli (1608–47), Italian mathematician and physicist: invented mercury barometer (1643).

Charles Hard Townes (1915–), American physicist: pioneered in development of laser-maser principle (1953–58). (N)

John Tyndall (1820–93), British scientist: discovered Tyndall effect in scattering of light passing through small particles; described effects of *Penicillium* mold slowing growth of bacteria (1876) half a century before its value in medicine was recognized.

Harold Clayton Urey (1893–1981), American chemist: discovered heavy hydrogen (1932), used in development of atomic energy. (N)

Jacobus Henricus Van't Hoff (1852–1911), Dutch chemist: pioneered in stereochemistry, study of internal molecular structure. (N)

Alessandro Volta (1745–1827), Italian physicist: invented electric battery (1800); electromagnetic unit, *volt*, named after him.

Wernher Von Braun (1912–77), German-American rocket engineer: developed V-2 guided missile rocket for Germany in World War II; developed Jupiter and Saturn rockets for U.S. space program.

John Von Neumann (1903–57), Hungarian-American mathematician: wrote *The Mathematical Foundations of Quantum Mechanics* (1944); helped develop high-speed electronic computers.

Ernest T. S. Walton (1903–), British physicist: co-developer of first nuclear accelerators (1932). (N)

Sir Robert Alexander Watson-Watt (1892–1973), British electronics engineer and inventor: invented practical radar (1935).

James Watt (1736–1819), Scottish engineer: made steam engines practical with invention of separate condenser (1769); invented steam radiators for heating (1784).

Carl Auer Welsbach (1858–1929), Austrian chemist: discovered elements neodymium and praseodymium (1885); invented mantle used in gas lighting before invention of electric lights.

George Westinghouse (1846–1914), American inventor: invented railroad air brake (1868).

Sir Charles Wheatstone (1802–75), British physicist and inventor: independently invented electric telegraph (1837).

Alfred North Whitehead (1861–1947), British mathematician and philosopher: coauthor of *Principia Mathematica.*

Eli Whitney (1765–1825), American inventor: invented cotton gin to remove seeds from cotton (1793); introduced use of interchangeable parts, enabling mass production of guns (1798).

Sir Frank Whittle (1907–), British inventor: invented turbojet engine for airplanes (1930).

Norbert Wiener (1894–1964), American mathematician: devised mathematical theory of cybernetics (1948); helped develop high-speed electronic computers.

Eugene Paul Wigner (1902–), Hungarian-American physicist: made many contributions to development of atomic energy. (N)

Charles T. R. Wilson (1869–1959), British physicist: invented Wilson cloud chamber (1912), device to make visible tracks of high-speed atomic particles. (N)

Friedrich Wöhler (1800–82), German chemist: first to synthesize organic compounds from inorganic material (1828).

Jethro Wood (1774–1834), American inventor: invented cast-iron plow (1819).

Wilbur Wright (1867–1912) and his brother **Orville Wright** (1871–1948), American inventors: invented first successful airplane (1903).

Hideki Yukawa (1907–81), Japanese physicist: developed theory showing existence of meson (1935), discovered next year. (N)

Richard Zsigmondy (1865–1929), Austrian chemist: invented ultramicroscope, aiding in research in colloid chemistry. (N)

Vladimir Kosma Zworykin (1889–1982), Russian-American physicist and electronics engineer: invented iconoscope TV camera tube (1923) and kinescope TV picture tube (1929); perfected electron microscope (1939).

Social Welfare

HIGHLIGHTS: 1983

Major changes in the Social Security program were signed into law by President Reagan on April 20, 1983, under the Social Security Amendments of 1983 act.

The cost-of-living adjustment (COLA), which previously would have been received in July 1983, was deferred to January 1984. Future COLAs will be effective on a calendar-year basis.

Mandatory social security coverage was extended, as of January 1984, to the President, Vice President, members of Congress, federal judges, most federal political appointees, all newly hired federal civilian employees, and all employees of nonprofit organizations.

Up to 50% of social security benefits will be included in the taxable income of those whose incomes, including nontaxable interest income and half of their social security benefits, exceed $25,000 annually if they are single and $32,000 if married and filing a joint tax return.

The age of eligibility for full benefits will be gradually increased from age 65 to age 67 over the period 2000 to 2027. This change will affect persons born in 1938 or later.

The delayed retirement credit (currently 3% per year) payable to persons who postpone retirement past the full-benefit retirement age (now 65), will be gradually increased, beginning with people who reach age 62 after 1986.

Changes were also made in the method by which Medicare makes payments to hospitals. For hospital fiscal years beginning on or after Oct. 1, 1983, such facilities would no longer be reimbursed on a reasonable-cost basis for their inpatient operating costs, but would be paid an amount determined by type of illness.

Social security tax rates for the self-employed will increase to equal the combined employer-employee rate. The rise will be partially offset by income tax credits and, after 1989, by tax deductions.

SOCIAL WELFARE EXPENDITURES: 1950–1980

Source: Social Security Bulletin, data for fiscal years

From 1979 to 1980 social-welfare expenditures rose by 3.9%, and in 1980 equaled 19% of the total U.S. gross national product.

Combined federal, state, and local government expenditures for social-welfare programs are shown in millions of dollars (add 000,000).

	1950	1960	1965	1970	1975	1979	1980
TOTAL	**$23,508.4**	**$52,293.3**	**$77,175.3**	**$145,855.7**	**$290,047.3**	**$430,684.5**	**$493,354.5**
Social insurance	4,946.6	19,306.7	28,122.8	54,691.2	$23,013.1	$194,176.4	$229,552.3
Social security and Medicare	784.1	11,032.3	16,997.5	36,835.4	78,429.9	131,719.4	152,110.4
Railroad retirement	306.4	934.7	1,128.1	1,609.9	3,085.1	4,310.6	4,768.7
Public employee retirement	817.9	2,569.9	4,528.5	8,658.7	20,118.6	33,929.8	39,490.2
Unemployment benefits	2,190.1	2,829.6	3,002.6	3,819.5	13,835.9	11,313.1	18,326.4
State temporary disability	72.1	347.9	483.5	717.7	990.0	1,232.2	1,379.1
Workers' compensation	625.1	1,308.5	1,859.4	2,950.4	6,479.1	11,518.8	13,253.4
Public aid	2,496.2	4,101.1	6,283.4	16,487.7	41,326.4	63,955.1	72,385.1
Public assistance	2,490.2	4,041.7	5,874.9	14,433.5	27,378.5	40,008.6	45,474.0
Supplemental security income	—	—	—	—	6,091.6	7,532.3	8,226.5
Food stamps	—	—	—	576.9	4,693.9	6,478.1	9,083.3
Health and medical programs	2,063.5	4,463.8	6,246.4	9,906.8	17,707.5	25,387.9	28,118.8
Hospital and medical care	1,222.3	2,853.3	3,452.3	5,313.4	9,407.0	11,314.9	12,202.8
Maternal and child health	29.8	141.3	227.3	431.4	545.5	760.0	798.0
Medical research	69.2	448.9	1,165.2	1,635.4	2,646.0	4,647.0	5,218.0
School health	30.6	101.0	142.2	246.6	321.0	520.0	569.0
Other public health	350.8	401.2	671.0	1,348.0	2,919.0	6,025.0	6,848.0
Veterans' programs	6,865.7	5,479.2	6,031.0	9,078.0	17,018.8	20,601.6	21,465.5
Pensions and compensation	2,092.1	3,402.7	4,141.4	5,393.8	7,578.5	10,578.2	11,306.0
Health and medical	748.0	954.0	1,228.7	1,784.0	3,516.8	5,700.9	6,203.9
Education	2,691.6	490.6	40.9	1,018.5	4,433.8	2,794.1	2,400.7
Life insurance	475.7	494.1	434.3	502.3	566.0	638.2	664.5
Education	6,674.1	17,626.2	28,107.9	50,845.5	80,863.2	109,261.5	170,587.6
Elementary and secondary	5,596.2	15,109.0	22,357.7	38,632.3	59,774.6	77,714.6	86,773.0
Higher	914.7	2,190.7	4,826.4	9,907.1	16,384.2	24,129.8	26,090.7
Vocational and adult	160.8	298.0	853.9	2,144.4	4,441.3	7,029.4	7,375.2
Housing	14.6	176.8	318.1	701.2	3,171.7	6,225.8	7,209.1
Other social welfare	447.7	1,139.4	2,065.7	4,145.2	6,946.6	11,076.2	14,036.1
Vocational rehabilitation	30.0	96.3	210.5	703.8	1,036.4	1,309.2	1,125.1
Institutional care	145.5	420.5	789.5	201.7	296.1	444.0	482.4
Child nutrition	160.2	398.7	617.4	896.0	2,517.6	4,374.6	5,289.3
Child welfare	104.9	211.5	354.3	585.3	597.0	800.0	800.0

YOUR SOCIAL SECURITY BENEFITS

Source: Social Security Administration

For most Americans, social security provides a partial replacement of income when family earnings drop or stop because of retirement, disability, or death.

The average monthly benefit paid to a retired worker with no dependents in June 1983 was $412. The maximum benefit for a single worker retiring in 1983 was $709.50, and for a married worker with nonworking spouse, $1,063.

In addition, social security's Medicare program helps pay hospital and medical bills for most persons 65 and over and for some younger disabled persons.

Almost every American is covered by social security. Today about 1 of every 6 Americans receives a monthly social security benefit check.

SOCIAL SECURITY NUMBER AND RECORD

You should have a social security card that contains your number, your name, and your signature. *You keep this same social security identification number all your life.*

If you do not have a social security number, you should apply for one at once at any local social security office.

You must have a social security number when you obtain a job. Even if you do not work, you need a social security number of your own for such purposes as identification on tax forms or in case you ever have to apply for public assistance.

Make sure your employer has your correct social security number. If your employer does not use your correct number, you may not receive credit under social security.

Once you have a social security number, the Social Security Administration will maintain a separate earnings record in your name for the rest of your life. This record keeps track of the credits you accumulate toward social security benefits. Information in your social security record is confidential and cannot be disclosed without authorization.

All wage earners and persons who are self-employed should check on their social security earnings record *every three years.* To do so, you should obtain a "Request for Statement of Earnings" form from any local social security office. After you fill out the form and mail it in, the Social Security Administration will send back a report that shows what earnings have been accumulated.

Before you or your family can get monthly cash social security benefits, you or your spouse (or one of your parents, if you are a child) must have credit for a certain amount of work under social security. The exact amount of work credit required depends on your age and the type of benefit.

SOCIAL SECURITY TAXES

If you are employed, your employer deducts social security taxes from your paycheck and matches them with an equal contribution. The self-employed pay taxes at the combined employer-employee rate, partially offset by an income-tax credit.

The money collected in social security taxes is maintained in separate trust funds by

GROWTH OF SOCIAL SECURITY: 1940–1982

Source: Social Security Administration, data for fiscal years

YEAR	PENSION PAYMENT EXPENDITURES			BENEFICIARIES		AVERAGE MONTHLY BENEFITS			
	Total	Retirement & Survivors	Disability	Retirement & Survivors	Disability	Retired Worker	Retired Couple	Widow or Widower	Disabled Worker
1940	$ 23,500,000	$ 15,805,000	—	222,488	—	$ 22.60	$ 34.73	$ 20.28	—
1945	247,800,000	239,834,000	—	1,288,107	—	24.19	37.01	20.19	—
1950	928,400,000	727,266,000	—	3,477,243	—	43.86	67.46	36.54	—
1955	4,855,300,000	4,333,147,000	—	7,960,616	—	61.90	94.97	48.69	—
1960	11,080,500,000	10,269,709,000	$ 528,304,000	14,157,138	687,451	74.04	112.76	57.68	$ 89.31
1965	18,093,700,000	15,225,894,000	1,392,190,000	19,127,716	1,739,051	83.92	127.55	73.75	97.76
1967	21,154,300,000	18,885,714,000	1,860,789,000	21,564,773	2,140,214	85.37	129.61	74.99	98.43
1968	24,667,300,000	20,737,093,000	2,088,352,000	22,225,263	2,335,134	98.86	150.07	86.43	111.86
1969	26,459,600,000	23,732,010,000	2,443,437,000	22,826,514	2,487,548	100.40	152.28	87.27	112.74
1970	31,569,800,000	26,266,928,000	2,778,118,000	23,563,634	2,664,995	118.10	179.29	101.71	131.29
1971	36,865,100,000	31,101,018,000	3,381,448,000	24,361,500	2,930,008	132.17	200.52	113.17	146.52
1972	41,275,200,000	34,540,813,000	4,045,895,000	25,204,542	3,271,486	162.35	246.44	137.66	179.32
1973	51,130,500,000	42,169,744,000	5,161,840,000	26,309,163	3,558,982	166.40	251.18	156.35	183.00
1974	58,194,100,000	47,848,838,000	6,158,569,000	26,941,483	3,911,334	188.20	283.96	176.03	205.70
1975	66,585,700,000	54,838,818,000	7,629,796,000	25,732,311	4,352,200	207.18	312.37	192.33	225.89
1976	75,332,100,000	62,140,449,000	9,222,211,000	28,399,725	4,623,827	224.86	338.99	207.13	245.17
1977	84,263,800,000	71,270,519,000	11,135,237,000	29,228,350	4,854,206	242.98	366.05	221.95	265.19
1978	92,530,700,000	78,524,090,000	12,213,895,000	29,718,195	4,868,576	263.19	439.00	238.84	288.25
1979	103,967,300,000	87,591,968,000	13,428,454,000	30,347,848	4,777,218	294.27	442.63	266.87	322.03
1980	120,117,557,000	104,560,850,000	15,437,473,000	30,843,914	4,682,172	341.41	513.36	311.16	370.74
1981	136,266,778,000	119,413,467,000	16,853,311,000	31,474,000	4,456,000	385.97	580.72	346.08	413.15
1982	152,054,034,000	134,654,629,000	17,399,405,000	31,804,000	3,973,000	419.25	631.74	375.28	440.60

the U.S. Treasury. The funds can be used only for payment of social security benefits and expenses.

RETIREMENT BENEFITS

If you have enough work credits you can retire with benefits as early as the age of 62, but if you do you will receive for the rest of your life only 80% of the monthly benefits to which you would be entitled if you waited until you were 65 to retire.

The size of the monthly benefits you will collect when you retire at age 65 depends on your covered earnings under social security over a period of years.

You must include in taxable income for federal income tax purposes up to half of your social security benefits if your income, including nontaxable interest and half your social security benefits, exceeds $25,000 a year if single and $32,000 if married and filing jointly.

The government will deposit your benefits directly in your bank account if you wish.

A retired worker 65 to 69 can earn up to $6,960 without losing any social security benefits. For every $2 earned above that amount the retiree loses $1 of benefits. Beginning in 1990, benefits for persons who reach the normal retirement age will be reduced $1 for each $3 of excess earnings.

A person who is 70 may earn any amount without losing benefits, starting with the month in which he or she is 70.

There is a special rule that generally applies only in the first year of retirement: Even though earnings may exceed the annual exempt amount, a benefit can be paid for any *month* a person performs little or no work. More information on this can be obtained at any social security office.

A worker who delays retirement past 65 will have his or her benefits increased. For persons who reached age 62 before 1979, the credit is $\frac{1}{12}$ of 1% for each month in which he or she does not collect benefits from 65 to 70.

For persons who reach 62 after 1978 and before 1987 the credit is 3% for each year ($\frac{1}{4}$% for each month).

The credit will gradually increase, reaching 8% a year ($\frac{2}{3}$ of 1% for each month) for persons who reach 62 after 2004.

Your social security retirement benefits will be automatically increased whenever the Consumer Price Index rises by 3% or more over a comparable measuring period of the previous year.

If you plan to retire in the next few years and wish to estimate your retirement income, consult officials at your local social security office and they will assist you.

DISABILITY BENEFITS

If you have enough work credits and become disabled by accident or illness so that your physical or mental condition prevents you from working before you reach 65, social security provides income protection. The disability must have lasted or be expected to last at least a year.

Your checks can start for the sixth full month of your disability.

You will receive checks monthly as long as you are disabled and continue to be unable to work.

The amount of the monthly benefit for disability depends on the worker's age and covered earnings under social security.

An insured worker's unmarried child 18 or older who becomes severely disabled before reaching 22 can receive monthly checks as long as the disability continues.

SOCIAL SECURITY TAXES

Source: Social Security Administration

In the more than four decades that the Social Security System has existed, payroll taxes to support it have increased dramatically from the maximum of $30 paid yearly by an employee in 1937.

YEARS	MAXIMUM TAXABLE WAGE	EMPLOYEE TAXES[1]		SELF-EMPLOYED TAX	
		Rate	Maximum Tax	Rate	Maximum Tax
1937–49	$3,000	1.00%	$ 30.00	—	—
1950	3,000	1.50%	45.00	—	—
1951–53	3,600	1.50%	54.00	2.25%	$ 81.00
1954	3,600	2.00%	72.00	3.00%	108.00
1955–56	4,200	2.00%	84.00	3.00%	126.00
1957–58	4,200	2.25%	94.50	3.375%	141.75
1959	4,800	2.50%	120.00	3.75%	180.00
1960–61	4,800	3.00%	144.00	4.50%	216.00
1962	4,800	3.125%	150.00	4.70%	225.60
1963–65	4,800	3.625%	174.00	5.40%	259.20
1966	6,600	4.20%	277.20	6.15%	405.90
1967	6,600	4.40%	290.40	6.40%	422.40
1968	7,800	4.40%	343.20	6.40%	499.20
1969–70	7,800	4.80%	374.40	6.90%	538.20

YEARS	MAXIMUM TAXABLE WAGE	EMPLOYEE TAXES[1]		SELF-EMPLOYED TAX	
		Rate	Maximum Tax	Rate	Maximum Tax
1971	$7,800	5.20%	$ 405.60	7.50%	$ 585.00
1972	9,000	5.20%	468.00	7.50%	675.00
1973	10,800	5.85%	631.80	8.00%	864.00
1974	13,200	5.85%	772.20	7.90%	1,042.80
1975	14,100	5.85%	824.85	7.90%	1,113.90
1976	15,300	5.85%	895.05	7.90%	1,208.70
1977	16,500	5.85%	965.25	7.90%	1,303.50
1978	17,700	6.05%	1,070.85	8.10%	1,433.70
1979	22,900	6.13%	1,403.77	8.10%	1,854.90
1980	25,900	6.13%	1,587.67	8.10%	2,097.90
1981	29,700	6.65%	1,975.05	9.30%	2,762.10
1982	32,400	6.70%	2,170.80	9.35%	3,029.40
1983	35,700	6.70%	2,391.90	9.35%	3,337.95
1984	37,800	7.0%	2,646.00	11.30%	4,271.40

[1] Payroll taxes deducted from wages are equally matched by employers.

And the disabled worker's spouse can receive checks if 62 or older or if caring for children who are under 16 or disabled.

Total monthly benefits to the family of a disabled worker who first becomes entitled to disability benefits after June 1980 are limited to the *lower* of 85% of the worker's average earnings before becoming disabled or 150% of the worker's disability benefit.

SURVIVORS' BENEFITS

Like life insurance, social security provides monthly benefits for the family of a worker who dies.

A lump-sum payment of $255 can be made for burial expenses.

The dependents of a deceased worker who are eligible for monthly cash benefits include:

1. Unmarried children under 18 (or 19 if full-time high school students).
2. Unmarried son or daughter 18 or over who was severely disabled before 22 and continues to be disabled.
3. Widow or widower 60 or older.
4. Widow or widower under 60, or surviving divorced spouse, if caring for worker's child under 16 (or disabled) who is getting a benefit based on the deceased worker's earnings.
5. Widow or widower 50 or older who becomes disabled not later than seven years after worker's death, or within seven years after ceasing to receive checks for care of deceased worker's children.
6. Dependent parents 62 or older.
7. Unmarried divorced spouse 60 or older (50 if disabled), if marriage to insured worker lasted 10 years before divorce.
8. Grandchildren, under certain conditions.

The monthly payments to these survivors may range from 50% to 100% of the amount the worker would receive at 65 as retirement benefits.

APPLYING FOR SOCIAL SECURITY BENEFITS

Before you or your family can get any social security checks, you must apply for them at a social security office. When you apply, you should have with you:
1. Social security number: Your own social security card or a record of your number. If your claim is on another person's record, you will need that person's social security number.
2. Proof of your age: A birth certificate or a baptismal certificate that records birth date.
3. Your marriage certificate, if applying for spouse's benefits, or widow's or widower's benefits.
4. Your children's birth certificates, if applying for children's benefits.
5. Your Form W-2 for the previous year, or copies of your last two federal income tax returns if you are self-employed.
6. Proof of your dependence for support on the insured worker, if you are applying for benefits as a dependent parent.

If you do not have these proofs, do not delay applying. When you apply, a social security official will tell you about alternate means of proof that you can obtain.

RIGHT OF APPEAL

If you believe that a decision made on your claim is not correct, you may ask the Social Security Administration to reconsider it. Employees of any social security office will explain how you may appeal and will help you get your claim reconsidered or request a hearing.

FOOD STAMPS

The Food Stamp Program helps low-income people buy more food.

Food stamps are available to all low-income persons who qualify, *not* just those receiving public assistance or social security benefits.

Unemployed families and working families with low incomes also may qualify.

The number of food-stamp recipients dropped by about 725,000 in 1982.

To find out whether or not you are eligible for food stamps, inquire at your local food stamp or welfare office. Eligibility depends on your household's income and assets.

Families whose gross incomes are more than 130% of the poverty level are ineligible for food stamps.

Food stamps can be used at any approved supermarket or grocery store for the purchase of any food item.

FOOD STAMP PROGRAM
Source: U.S. Department of Agriculture

YEAR	NUMBER OF PARTICIPANTS	TOTAL BENEFITS	AV. MONTHLY BENEFITS PER PERSON
1962	143,000	$ 13,153,000	$ 7.67
1965	424,000	32,494,000	6.38
1966	864,000	64,781,000	6.25
1967	1,447,000	105,455,000	6.08
1968	2,211,000	172,985,000	6.52
1969	2,878,000	228,587,000	6.63
1970	4,340,000	550,806,000	10.55
1971	9,368,000	1,522,904,000	13.55
1972	11,103,000	1,794,875,000	13.48
1973	12,190,000	2,102,133,000	14.60
1974	12,896,000	2,725,988,000	17.62
1975	17,063,000	4,386,144,000	21.43
1976	18,557,008	5,310,133,000	23.85
1977	17,085,000	5,077,357,000	24.77
1978	16,044,000	5,165,209,000	26.83
1979	17,770,000	6,478,066,000	30.55
1980	22,000,000	8,717,000,000	34.40
1981	22,425,000	10,623,000,000	39.48
1982	21,700,000	10,200,000,000	39.18

MEDICARE AND MEDICAID

Medicare includes separate social security hospital and medical insurance programs administered by the Health Care Financing Administration of the Department of Health and Human Services.

Medicaid, on the other hand, is a health assistance program for about 23 million low-income people, especially for those receiving welfare or Supplementary Security Income.

MEDICARE HOSPITAL INSURANCE

Persons 65 and older eligible for social security or rail retirement benefits automatically receive free Medicare hospital insurance. Others 65 and older can purchase hospital insurance by paying a monthly premium of $155.

Younger persons can receive Medicare if they have been entitled for 24 months to disability benefits under social security, somewhat longer under railroad retirement, or, under certain conditions, if they need continuing hemodialysis treatment for kidney disease or a kidney transplant.

Anyone 65 or over, or anyone under 65 entitled to Medicare hospital insurance, may enroll for medical insurance.

A person who is not already receiving social security benefits should check with the local social security office about Medicare 3 months before the 65th birthday.

The Medicare hospital insurance provides:

Hospitalization: Coverage of up to 90 days of hospital benefits in a period of time called a "benefit period." A benefit period begins when you enter the hospital and ends when you have been out of a hospital or skilled nursing facility for 60 days in a row.

The patient pays the first $356 of costs during the first 60 days of inpatient hospital care, and then pays $89 for each day of hospitalization from 61 to 90 days.

If all 90 days are used up, a "lifetime reserve" can be drawn on for up to 60 more days of benefits. During these additional days, the Medicare beneficiary pays $178 a day of the hospital expenses.

After each "benefit period," the 90 days of hospital benefits are renewed but "lifetime reserve" days are not renewable.

Subject to those limitations, hospital insurance covers (1) the cost of a semiprivate room (two to four patients to a room), a private room only if medically necessary (if the patient elects a private room, he pays the difference); (2) board; (3) hospital services except private-duty nursing; (4) the services of interns or residents in approved teaching programs; and (5) drugs and medical supplies used by the patient in the hospital.

The same coverage extends to hospitalization in tuberculosis or psychiatric institutions. There is a lifetime limit of 190 days of coverage for treatment in a psychiatric hospital.

Skilled Nursing Facility: Up to 100 days if medically necessary, in a skilled nursing facility after at least 3 days of hospitalization.

The patient pays $44.50 for each day in excess of 20 days, up to the limit of 100 days. Subject to that limitation, insurance covers cost of a semiprivate room, board, general nursing (but not private-duty nursing), prescribed drugs, and therapy by employees of the skilled nursing facility.

Home Health Services: All covered home visits by nurses or therapists of an approved home health agency when recommended by an attending physician.

MEDICARE MEDICAL INSURANCE

A person who enrolls when first eligible pays $14.60 a month for coverage by Medicare medical insurance. The person also pays the first $75 of covered medical expenses each year. Medicare then pays 80% of approved charges for covered services received for the rest of the year.

The medical insurance covers physicians' and surgeons' services and medical and health services such as diagnostic tests, surgical dressings, certain ambulance services, hospital outpatient charges, and home health services.

Payments for home health services are 100% of reasonable costs.

MEDICARE AND MEDICAID: 1970–1982

Source: Health Care Financing Administration

YEAR	MEDICARE PAYMENTS			NUMBER OF MEDICARE BILLS PAID		MEDICAID
	Total	Hospital	Medical	Hospital	Medical	Expenditures
1970	$ 7,099,000,000	$ 5,124,000,000	$1,975,000,000	7,512,000	39,695,000	$ 4,516,000,000
1973	9,583,000,000	7,057,000,000	2,526,000,000	8,295,000	43,508,000	8,714,000,000
1974	12,418,000,000	9,099,000,000	3,318,000,000	9,562,000	67,995,000	9,737,000,000
1975	15,588,000,000	11,315,000,000	4,273,000,000	10,318,000	83,106,000	12,086,000,000
1976	18,420,000,000	13,340,000,000	5,080,000,000	11,170,000	87,116,000	13,977,000,000
1977	21,774,000,000	15,737,000,000	6,038,000,000	11,478,000	111,723,000	16,355,000,000
1978	24,934,000,000	17,682,000,000	7,252,000,000	12,264,000	112,660,000	18,168,000,000
1979	29,331,000,000	20,623,000,000	8,708,000,000	12,775,000	142,725,000	20,582,000,000
1980	35,700,000,000	25,064,000,000	10,635,000,000	13,660,000	154,388,000	24,041,000,000
1981	43,455,000,000	30,342,000,000	13,113,000,000	14,694,000	169,540,000	28,432,000,000
1982	51,086,000,000	35,631,000,000	15,455,000,000	16,619,000	187,700,000	29,906,000,000

VETERANS' BENEFITS

Source: Veterans Administration

Almost 100 million Americans are potentially eligible for veterans' benefits and services, including 30 million living veterans, their 66 million family members, and 4 million survivors of deceased veterans.

The federal government spends more than $22 billion yearly for veterans' benefits.

To find out about your own eligibility for specific veterans' benefits, contact your local Veterans Administration (VA) office. Consult your telephone directory for the number to call. Toll-free special telephone service is available for calls to the VA.

Veterans with dishonorable discharges are *not* eligible for most benefits described here.

HOSPITALIZATION

Veterans with service-connected disabilities have priority for treatment at Veterans Administration hospitals.

However, if beds are available, needed hospitalization is provided for (1) any war veteran who is 65 or older, or (2) any younger veteran who cannot pay the cost of hospitalization.

AUTOMOBILES FOR THE DISABLED

The VA will pay up to $4,400 toward the purchase of a car plus the cost of adaptive equipment for a veteran whose service-connected disability resulted in loss of use of one or both hands or feet or severe permanent impairment of vision in both eyes.

CLOTHING ALLOWANCE

An annual clothing allowance of $327 can be paid to any veteran entitled to receive compensation for a service-connected disability for which he or she wears or uses a prosthetic or orthopedic appliance that tends to wear out clothing.

PENSIONS AND DISABILITY COMPENSATION

The VA has two basic programs providing monthly cash benefits to veterans and their survivors.

Disability Compensation. Veterans with service-connected disabilities receive monthly payments ranging from $62 to $3,461, depending on the extent of their disability. Additional allowances are paid for dependents if the veteran's disability is rated at 30% or more.

Veterans' Pensions. Needy war veterans 65 or older (or younger war veterans totally disabled by nonservice injury or illness) are eligible for monthly pension payments.

The size of the pension depends on the amount of the veteran's additional yearly income. Eligible veterans are guaranteed an annual income level of $5,328 if they are single. Those with one dependent receive a pension to bring their income level to $6,980, and this is increased by $903 for each additional dependent.

Death Benefits. Dependents of a veteran who dies of service-connected injuries or illness are eligible for substantial benefits. Lesser amounts are payable to needy dependents of veterans who die of a nonservice related cause.

ALCOHOL AND DRUG TREATMENT

All veterans who have not been dishonorably discharged can receive treatment for alcohol and drug dependency.

MEDICAL AND DENTAL TREATMENT

Veterans can receive free medical and dental treatment for service-connected disabilities.

Medical aid also covers the purchase of needed prosthetic appliances and aids for the blind, including a trained guide dog.

EDUCATIONAL BENEFITS

Veterans with service between Feb. 1, 1955, and Dec. 31, 1976, can receive up to 45 months of GI Bill payments for attending school or on-the-job training. Eligibility expires 10 years after discharge.

VETERANS' BENEFITS: 1940–1983

Source: U.S. Veterans Administration

YEAR	Compensation & Pensions	Education & Readjustment Benefits	Medical Care & Administrative Expenses
1940	$ 429,153,465	—	$ 94,456,620
1945	771,796,517	—	159,559,021
1950	2,223,092,285	$2,792,589,648	901,988,427
1955	2,681,726,077	707,946,023	869,576,297
1960	3,367,449,929	514,175,433	1,086,674,142
1963	3,868,465,721	95,565,684	1,246,430,391
1964	3,959,187,575	68,827,751	1,291,950,776
1965	4,107,721,052	49,392,151	1,358,410,178
1966	4,391,943,303	42,097,184	1,406,735,536
1967	4,494,130,947	297,601,153	1,518,644,942
1968	4,611,180,743	461,506,628	1,620,046,513
1969	4,939,409,724	678,903,395	1,735,043,428
1970	5,357,407,811	1,018,861,723	2,007,783,909
1971	5,839,390,281	1,631,738,617	2,256,979,848
1972	6,167,996,446	1,935,797,731	2,650,982,373
1973	6,568,081,137	2,696,239,516	2,966,237,960
1974	6,734,790,004	3,268,556,875	3,290,194,883
1975	7,551,176,877	4,529,227,472	3,919,256,993
1976	8,242,088,546	5,543,354,200	4,446,765,605
1977	9,038,803,014	3,891,448,932	5,072,993,821
1978	9,630,679,653	3,336,611,015	5,683,811,346
1979	10,540,134,325	2,800,897,985	6,205,941,745
1980	11,256,935,680	2,383,912,487	6,646,752,559
1981	12,492,329,634	2,332,820,985	7,199,253,633
1982	13,347,772,503	2,001,298,853	8,008,923,888
1983	13,423,350,065*	1,884,556,591*	N.A.

* Estimates. N.A. = Not Available.

A single veteran with a full-time course of study at an approved institution receives $342 per month.

On-the-job payments for a single trainee start at $249 for the first 6 months.

A separate voluntary contributory program is available for veterans who entered active duty on or after Jan. 1, 1977.

Another separate program is available for disabled veterans.

The children and spouse of a veteran who died or was totally service-disabled also are eligible for educational benefits. Eligibility for children extends until they are 26 years old. Eligibility for a spouse extends for 10 years from the time the veteran became totally disabled or died.

About 6.5 million Vietnam-era veterans—almost 66%—have participated.

Only 50.5% of World War II veterans took advantage of the GI Bill.

LOANS FOR HOMES, MOBILE HOMES

Veterans, service personnel on active duty, and certain unmarried surviving spouses of veterans may apply for home loans guaranteed or insured by the VA. The VA guarantee may be 60% of the loan amount or $27,500, whichever is less, for conventionally built homes. The maximum guarantee for manufactured or mobile homes is 50% or $20,000, whichever is less.

There is no time limit on using this loan privilege. Such loans often can be arranged with no down payment by the borrower. Veterans also have preferences for FHA insured loans.

Since 1944 the VA has provided, guaranteed, or insured over 10.9 million loans with a value of more than $200 billion.

GRANTS FOR "SPECIALLY ADAPTED" HOMES

Certain disabled veterans, who are generally confined to a wheelchair, may be entitled to a grant of up to $32,500 to construct a new house or to remodel an existing house to meet their needs. Others may receive smaller grants for adaptation of living quarters.

In addition the VA provides up to $40,000 mortgage life insurance on such a home.

GI INSURANCE

Up to $10,000 of Service-Disabled Veterans Insurance (S-DVI) can be issued to veterans separated on or after April 25, 1951, with a service-connected disability. Application must be made within one year of notice granting such a disability.

Dividends are paid on government life insurance policies prefixed with the letters K, V, RS, W, J, JR, and JS. On all but K, dividends may purchase paid-up insurance additions.

Most VA policies waive premiums if the insured becomes totally disabled for 6 or more consecutive months prior to the 65th birthday. Some policies have riders providing income in cases of total disability.

VA programs include Servicemen's Group Life Insurance (SGLI), Veterans Group Life Insurance (VGLI), and Veterans Mortgage Life Insurance (VMLI).

SGLI provides up to $35,000 group life insurance to active-duty service personnel, ready reservists, and retired reservists. Upon separation from active duty veterans may convert their SGLI to VGLI.

VGLI provides up to $35,000 group life insurance for a 5-year term. At the end of the term, VGLI may be converted to an individual policy with a participating commercial insurance company.

VMLI provides up to $40,000 of mortgage life insurance protection to disabled veterans with specially adapted housing.

BURIAL BENEFITS

The VA will pay up to $150 toward the burial plot of war veterans or certain peace-time veterans. If the eligible veteran was receiving pension or compensation funds at the time of death, up to $300 is payable toward funeral expenses.

When a veteran dies, his or her family usually is also eligible for a $255 lump-sum death payment from Social Security.

An American flag to drape the casket of a veteran can be obtained from a local VA office or from most local post offices. After the funeral, the flag is given to the next of kin.

A headstone or a small allowance for its purchase will be supplied for the burial place of a deceased veteran.

Burial space will be provided for a deceased veteran in a national cemetery as well as for the veteran's spouse, minor children, and, under special conditions, adult unmarried children. Special restrictions apply to burial in Arlington National Cemetery.

When a member of the armed forces dies on active duty and the body is not recovered, the family may obtain a headstone or marker for placement in a private cemetery or in the memorial section of a national cemetery.

REEMPLOYMENT AND UNEMPLOYMENT

Veterans with 5 years or less of military service have their job rights protected in their previous employment and acquire seniority for the time in military service. The veteran must apply for reemployment within 90 days after discharge. Veterans seeking a job can apply for unemployment benefits from the state immediately upon discharge.

UNEMPLOYMENT INSURANCE

If you have lost your job through no fault of your own, you may be eligible to receive weekly unemployment insurance payments while looking for new employment.

You should apply for the benefits at your local state employment office.

FEDERAL–STATE UNEMPLOYMENT INSURANCE

About 87.6 million workers in the United States are covered by federal-state unemployment insurance.

The federal and state governments collect payroll taxes from employers at a rate of 3.5% of up to the first $7,000 of each worker's wages to pay the benefits.

In a few states employees also pay a small tax to the unemployment fund.

Because each state has its own laws regarding unemployment insurance, the benefits vary from state to state. Depending on how much you previously were earning, your benefits may range from a low of $5 weekly in some states to a high of $196 a week in another. The average amount received is about $106 a week.

Regular benefits end after 26 to 36 weeks of unemployment.

INELIGIBILITY

You cannot collect unemployment insurance if you voluntarily quit your last job or if you were fired because of misconduct. Most states also will not pay unemployment benefits to workers who are unemployed because of a labor dispute.

While collecting unemployment benefits, you lose your eligibility if you refuse to take a suitable job that is offered you.

If you believe you are being unfairly denied unemployment benefits, each state has a procedure by which you can appeal the decision to a review tribunal.

OTHER UNEMPLOYMENT COMPENSATION

The federal government funds separate unemployment compensation plans for federal civilian employees and for military personnel who cannot find jobs after they have been discharged. And the federal government also administers a separate unemployment insurance program for railroad workers.

Some corporations and labor unions also have programs that pay an unemployed worker extra benefits over those received from the regular state plan.

HISTORY

The first state unemployment insurance law was adopted by Wisconsin in 1932.

When the federal government enacted the Social Security Act of 1935, it instituted the present system of unemployment insurance in which the federal government collects payroll taxes and makes money available to states whose unemployment compensation laws meet federal standards.

FEDERAL–STATE UNEMPLOYMENT INSURANCE: 1940–1982

Source: U.S. Department of Labor

Year	Average Weekly Benefit	Average Weekly Beneficiaries	Total Benefits Paid	Number of First Payments	Weeks Compensated	Claimants Exhausting Benefits	Funds Available for Benefits at End of Year
1940	$ 10.56	982,392	$ 518,700,000	5,220,073	51,084,375	2,596,128	$ 1,817,108,000
1945	18.77	464,996	445,866,000	2,861,190	24,179,769	254,271	6,914,009,000
1950	20.76	1,304,991	1,373,114,000	5,211,883	67,859,529	1,853,336	6,972,295,000
1955	25.04	1,099,466	1,350,268,000	4,507,894	56,099,729	1,272,232	8,263,850,000
1960	32.87	1,640,429	2,726,656,000	6,753,387	85,630,399	1,603,372	6,643,257,000
1964	35.96	1,372,695	2,522,100,000	5,497,903	71,380,122	1,370,857	7,296,220,000
1965	37.19	1,131,025	2,166,004,000	4,813,229	58,813,298	1,085,977	8,357,350,000
1966	39.76	895,133	1,771,298,000	4,140,026	46,546,925	780,700	9,828,244,000
1967	41.25	1,017,356	2,092,338,000	4,628,083	52,902,523	867,403	10,778,138,000
1968	43.43	935,930	2,031,617,000	4,197,699	48,668,357	848,179	11,717,246,000
1969	46.17	922,503	2,127,877,000	4,213,803	47,948,702	811,532	12,637,508,000
1970	50.34	1,516,500	3,848,467,000	6,401,782	78,857,992	1,295,319	11,895,901,000
1971	54.02	1,813,700	4,957,026,000	6,540,358	94,312,380	2,006,700	9,703,424,000
1972	56.76	1,562,706	4,470,969,000	5,703,866	81,260,712	1,809,450	9,422,799,000
1973	59.00	1,369,669	4,007,562,000	5,328,998	71,222,809	1,495,092	10,933,767,000
1974	64.25	1,880,833	5,974,922,000	7,729,590	97,803,299	1,926,147	10,593,936,000
1975	70.23	3,371,246	11,754,684,646	11,160,042	175,304,812	4,195,023	4,522,933,588
1976	75.16	2,450,476	8,974,546,269	8,560,107	127,424,765	3,270,042	3,361,647,042
1977	78.79	2,188,672	8,357,160,144	7,985,099	113,244,354	2,850,136	4,387,301,806
1978	83.67	1,946,073	8,214,290,495	7,580,045	101,195,817	2,032,776	9,307,267,000
1979	89.67	2,036,552	9,263,468,406	8,077,727	106,307,994	2,044,131	12,459,909,222
1980	98.87	2,739,773	14,485,642,608	10,002,397	149,130,050	3,076,957	11,463,586,659
1981	106.48	2,605,617	14,113,804,758	9,399,675	136,013,195	2,990,817	12,017,254,000
1982	119.34	3,559,459	20,404,462,000	11,648,448	185,387,401	4,174,709	7,984,273,000

WORKERS' COMPENSATION

State workers' compensation laws cover about 89 of every 100 civilian workers, providing cash benefits and medical payments to workers and their survivors for work-related deaths, injuries, and illnesses.

Each state has its own workers' compensation laws, so benefits vary considerably from state to state. Employers are held responsible for work-related injuries and occupational diseases regardless of fault. Employers are required to purchase insurance with private insurance companies, pay premiums into a state insurance fund, or qualify as self-insurers.

Cash benefits to the worker and his or her family may be paid in weekly payments or a lump-sum settlement. In addition, hospital and other medical expenses are paid. Generally the weekly benefits amount to two-thirds of the worker's average weekly wages, ranging from $112 to $996 per week.

A disabled worker or survivor can collect workers' compensation payments in addition to those provided by federal social security, although a social security offset exists that is based on the worker's average weekly wage.

You can find out more about your coverage by talking to your employer or writing to your state compensation agency.

You or your family will not automatically receive these benefits if you are injured or are killed at work. You or your family must file a claim for the benefits with your employer or the appropriate state agency.

WORKERS' COMPENSATION: 1940–1981
Source: Social Security Administration

YEAR	TOTAL BENEFITS	CASH BENEFITS	MEDICAL
1940	$ 256,000,000	$ 161,000,000	$ 95,000,000
1945	408,000,000	283,000,000	125,000,000
1950	615,000,000	415,000,000	200,000,000
1955	916,000,000	591,000,000	325,000,000
1960	1,295,000,000	860,000,000	435,000,000
1964	1,707,000,000	1,142,000,000	565,000,000
1965	1,814,000,000	1,214,000,000	600,000,000
1966	2,000,000,000	1,320,000,000	680,000,000
1967	2,189,000,000	1,439,000,000	750,000,000
1968	2,376,000,000	1,546,000,000	830,000,000
1969	2,634,000,000	1,714,000,000	920,000,000
1970	3,031,000,000	1,981,000,000	1,050,000,000
1971	3,563,000,000	2,433,000,000	1,130,000,000
1972	4,061,000,000	2,811,000,000	1,250,000,000
1973	5,103,000,000	3,623,000,000	1,480,000,000
1974	5,781,000,000	4,021,000,000	1,760,000,000
1975	6,598,000,000	4,568,000,000	2,030,000,000
1976	7,584,000,000	5,204,000,000	2,380,000,000
1977	8,630,000,000	5,950,000,000	2,680,000,000
1978	9,793,000,000	6,813,000,000	2,980,000,000
1979	12,027,000,000	8,507,000,000	3,520,000,000
1980	13,562,000,000	9,632,000,000	3,930,000,000
1981	14,955,000,000	10,555,000,000	4,400,000,000

PENSION AND RETIREMENT BENEFIT PLANS

Because social security payments amount to only a fraction of the annual amount earned before retirement, most retired persons must supplement their social security benefits with additional income if they are to maintain their accustomed standard of living.

Most commonly such supplemental income, often with benefits larger than those of social security, comes from pension and retirement benefit plans.

Pension plans may be provided to their employees by federal, state, or local governments, by private businesses, or by the individuals themselves.

The first pensions by the U.S. government were established for disabled veterans of the American Revolution in legislation by Congress in 1792. The first local government pensions were established by New York City in 1859 for its police. The first pension plan by a U.S. business came in 1875 by the American Express Company. Columbia University adopted the first American college pension plan for professors in 1892. The following year Chicago established the first pension plan for public school teachers. Pensions for federal Civil Service employees were first adopted by Congress in 1920.

Private pension and retirement plans are regulated by the federal government under the Employee Retirement Income Security Act (ERISA) of 1974. These plans are administered by the Office of Pension and Welfare Benefit Programs of the U.S. Department of Labor and the Internal Revenue Service. ERISA also established the Pension Benefit Guaranty Corporation, which insures certain types of private pension plans.

Private companies can establish a variety of retirement plans in which they do not have to pay taxes on the money contributed. Individuals receiving benefits under such plans only have to pay income taxes on retirement income which is attributable to contributions made by their employers.

Under the Economic Tax Recovery Act of 1981, government workers, workers in private industry covered by a tax-qualified retirement plan, and self-employed workers can set up their own individual retirement account (IRA). Employees can receive tax deductions for amounts they pay into employer-sponsored retirement plans or into an individual retirement plan (IRA).

Nearly 52 million U.S. workers participate in about 600,000 private pension plans.

PUBLIC ASSISTANCE—SSI AND AFDC

The federal government pays monthly checks to people in financial need who are 65 or older or who are blind or disabled.

The Supplemental Security Income (SSI) program began in 1974, replacing earlier federal-state public assistance programs for the aged, blind, and disabled.

The federal government also pays a major share of the welfare benefits to needy families with children under the state-administered program called Aid to Families with Dependent Children (AFDC).

MONTHLY INCOME FLOOR

The SSI program, administered by the Social Security Administration, establishes a basic nationwide monthly benefit standard for persons in financial need who are 65 or over, or blind, or disabled.

This basic monthly payment automatically rises to keep pace with the cost of living. Such an automatic increase of 3.5% went into effect on Jan. 1, 1984, raising the SSI monthly payment to $314.00 for individuals and $472.00 for couples.

Monthly checks sent by the federal government make up the difference between a person's low income and the basic payment.

Benefits for eligible recipients are higher in some states because those states add to the federal payments.

INELIGIBILITY

Supplemental Security Income payments may be suspended, reduced, or terminated in any of the following circumstances:

1. An increase in income or resources.
2. Confinement in a public institution.
3. Refusal to accept or undergo treatment for drug addiction or alcoholism.
4. Absence from the U.S. for 30 or more consecutive days.
5. Refusal to accept vocational rehabilitation services without good cause.
6. Loss of U.S. citizenship or of permission to live in the U.S.
7. Failure to apply for or obtain benefits under other programs that may be payable to the recipient.
8. Termination of blindness or disability.
9. Death of a person getting SSI payments.

A recipient must be given written notice of any proposed change in his payments and has 60 days to appeal the action.

WELFARE—AFDC

The nation's largest cash-assistance welfare program—Aid to Families with Dependent Children (AFDC)—was not included in the SSI program. It is operated by the states with federal help. In this program about 10.5 million needy parents and children received about $12.9 billion in support payments in 1982.

Because most of the persons receiving this assistance are families deserted by fathers, the government has made an effort to find the missing fathers, getting them to provide $3.84 billion in 1976–82.

AFDC grants average $282.05 a month per family.

PUBLIC ASSISTANCE, AFDC, AND SSI: 1940–1982

Source: Social Security Administration

YEAR	FEDERAL PAYMENTS					RECIPIENTS OF BENEFITS			
	Total [1]	Old-age	Blind	Disabled	AFDC [2]	Old-age	Blind	Disabled	AFDC [2]
1940	$1,020,115,000	$472,778,000	$21,735,000	—	$ 133,770,000	2,070,000	73,400	—	1,222,000
1945	990,700,000	725,683,000	26,515,000	—	149,667,000	2,056,000	71,500	—	943,000
1950	2,372,200,000	1,453,917,000	52,567,000	$ 8,042,000	551,653,000	2,786,000	97,500	69,000	2,233,000
1955	2,525,600,000	1,487,991,000	67,804,000	134,630,000	617,841,000	2,538,000	104,100	241,000	2,192,000
1960	3,276,700,000	1,626,021,000	86,080,000	236,402,000	1,000,784,000	2,305,000	106,900	369,000	3,073,000
1965	4,025,900,000	1,594,183,000	77,308,000	416,765,000	1,660,186,000	2,087,000	85,100	557,000	4,396,000
1966	4,305,507,000	1,630,131,000	84,708,000	487,212,000	1,863,925,000	2,073,000	83,700	588,000	4,666,000
1967	4,931,681,000	1,698,145,000	86,950,000	573,575,000	2,266,400,000	2,073,000	82,700	646,000	5,309,000
1968	5,672,143,000	1,673,191,000	87,828,000	655,792,000	2,849,298,000	2,027,000	80,700	702,000	6,086,000
1969	6,866,956,000	1,746,714,000	91,300,000	786,757,000	3,563,427,000	2,074,000	80,600	803,000	7,313,000
1970	8,864,400,000	1,866,087,000	97,496,000	975,504,000	4,852,964,000	2,082,000	81,000	935,000	9,659,000
1971	10,814,400,000	1,919,693,000	100,691,000	1,185,314,000	6,203,528,000	2,024,000	80,300	1,068,000	10,653,000
1972	11,066,700,000	1,893,982,000	104,736,000	1,392,896,000	6,909,260,000	1,934,000	79,800	1,168,000	11,065,000
1973	11,397,200,000	1,749,324,000	102,978,000	1,566,140,000	7,212,035,000	1,820,000	77,900	1,275,000	10,815,000
1974	14,059,500,000	2,414,034,000	125,791,000	2,556,988,000	7,916,563,000	2,285,909	74,616	1,635,539	11,006,000
1975	16,312,600,000	2,516,515,000	132,155,000	3,335,028,000	9,210,995,000	2,307,105	74,489	1,932,681	11,383,000
1976	17,496,900,000	2,472,571,000	134,060,000	3,345,778,000	10,140,543,000	2,147,697	76,366	2,011,876	11,184,000
1977	18,221,100,000	2,363,887,000	142,138,000	3,628,060,000	10,603,820,000	2,050,921	77,362	2,109,409	10,761,000
1978	18,575,700,000	2,342,080,000	148,027,000	3,881,531,000	10,730,415,000	1,967,900	77,135	2,171,890	11,050,270
1979	19,198,436,000	2,420,720,000	162,444,000	4,285,559,000	10,658,500,000	1,871,716	77,250	2,200,609	10,210,000
1980 [3]	21,463,955,000	2,781,228,000	200,616,000	5,357,412,000	12,031,000,000	1,807,776	78,401	2,255,840	10,674,000
1981 [3]	21,660,034,000	2,697,680,000	202,119,000	5,456,897,000	13,066,600,000	1,678,090	78,570	2,262,215	11,079,000
1982 [3]	21,260,561,000	2,698,708,000	212,691,000	5,794,097,000	12,945,065,000	1,548,741	77,356	2,231,493	10,491,400

[1] Total includes general assistance federal payments. The total also includes state payments under the Supplemental Security Income program after 1973. [2] Aid to Families with Dependent Children. [3] Estimates.

Space and Astronomy

As seen from above, the space shuttle *Challenger* glides in orbit high above the Earth with its cargo bay doors open in this unusual photograph. The photo was taken in June with a camera mounted on the SPAS satellite, which was placed in orbit above the shuttle and later recovered by the space-shuttle crew.

HIGHLIGHTS: 1983

FOUR SPACE SHUTTLE FLIGHTS

The U.S. space-shuttle program made four successful scheduled flights in 1983.

The space shuttle *Challenger* made its first flight on April 4 to April 9, after being delayed two months because of flaws discovered in its engines. Four astronauts went aloft: Paul Weitz, commander; Col. Karol Bobko, pilot; and two mission specialists, Story Musgrave and Donald Peterson. In the first walk in space by Americans in nine years, Musgrave and Peterson spent four hours outside the shuttle, demonstrating that the shuttle has the capacity to repair orbiting satellites. The major payload item launched by this flight was a two-and-a-half-ton communications satellite. The rocket engines on the satellite failed to place it in the correct orbit, but ground controllers later were able to correct its position.

HIGHLIGHTS: 1983 *(continued)*

The first American woman astronaut, Sally K. Ride, a physicist mission specialist, was a member of the crew of the second *Challenger* mission on June 18 to June 24. Others were Capt. Robert Crippen, commander; Capt. Frederick Hauck, pilot; and mission specialists Norman Thagard and John Fabian. The mission launched two communications satellites into orbit: the Canadian *Anik C* and the Indonesian *Palpa B.* The astronauts successfully demonstrated the ability to recover a satellite from orbit so that it could be refueled or repaired. In the test they launched and recovered five times a small satellite called SPAS, using a long robotic mechanical arm for the retrievals.

The first black American astronaut, Lt. Col. Guion S. Bluford II, served as a mission specialist on *Challenger*'s third flight on Aug. 30 to Sept. 5. Others in the crew were Capt. Richard Truly, commander; Cmdr. Daniel Brandenstein, pilot; and mission specialists William Thornton and Lt. Cmdr. Dale Gardner. The mission launched Insat-1B, a weather-communications satellite for India. The shuttle also carried into space 260,000 envelopes carrying the Postal Services Express Mail $9.35 stamp, which were to be sold to collectors with profits being divided between NASA and the Postal Service.

The third mission came close to disaster when the protective lining on one of *Challenger*'s rocket engines burned nearly through during its firing. Cmdr. Brandenstein, pilot of the flight, said if the engine had burned for only a few more seconds it would have meant "curtains" for the crew.

FIRST SPACELAB FLIGHT

The fourth space-shuttle flight of 1983 was launched on Nov. 28. On this mission the space shuttle was transformed into an orbiting scientific laboratory by carrying aloft in its cargo bay the huge reusable $1.1 billion Spacelab built by the European Space Agency (ESA). The shuttle had a crew of six, enabling scientists to man the Spacelab around the clock on a 24-hour schedule during the nine-day flight. The space shuttle *Columbia,* last used for a flight in November 1982, was specially modified to carry the Spacelab and the larger crew. Scientists from 14 nations provided the 71 experiments to be carried out during the mission. These encompassed investigations in five broad science and technology disciplines, including astronomy, solar physics, space plasma physics, atmospheric physics, and the life sciences.

The crew for the flight: John Young, commander; Brewster Shaw, pilot; and mission specialists Owen Garriott, Robert Parker, Ulf Merbold, and Byron K. Lichtenberg. Merbold, representing the Max-Planck Institute of Stuttgart, West Germany, and Lichtenberg of the Massachusetts Institute of Technology were the first nonprofessional astronauts carried into space on a shuttle mission.

POSSIBLY ANOTHER SOLAR SYSTEM

Although astronomers believe there must be other solar systems in the universe, none has

---

SCHEDULE OF SHUTTLE FLIGHTS

1984 (May 7)—Materials Science Laboratory: Experiments with materials at zero gravity.
1984 (June 4)—Large Format Camera-1: To photograph Earth with high-precision camera.
1984 (Aug. 30)—Shuttle Radar Laboratory: Mapping Earth's surface with radar and film.
1984 (Oct. 24)—Materials Science Laboratory: Experiments with materials at zero gravity.
1984 (Nov. 22)—Spacelab: Experiments on the growing of crystals and actions of fluids in space.
1985 (March 29)—Spacelab: Sky survey using X-ray telescope, infrared telescope, and cosmic-ray detector.
1985 (Nov. 26)—Materials Science Laboratory: More research on materials used in space.
1985 (Dec. 18)—Space Life Science Laboratory: Research on safety, well-being, and productivity of humans in space.
1986 (March 6)—Astro-1: Study of Halley's Comet using ultraviolet telescopes.
1986 (April 1)—Shuttle Radar Laboratory: Mapping Earth's surface.
1986 (July 9)—Materials Science Laboratory: Research on materials used in space.
1986 (Nov. 26)—Astro 2: Further study of Halley's Comet.
1986 (Dec. 10)—Environmental Observation Mission: To measure long-term changes in energy radiated by the Sun.
1987 (Jan. 16)—Office of Aeronautics and Space Technology: Tests of solar arrays.
1987 (Jan. 31)—Materials Science Laboratory: Research on materials in space.
1987 (April 7)—Shuttle Radar Laboratory: Mapping Earth's surface.
1987 (May 12)—Materials Science Laboratory: Research on materials in space.
1987 (May 27)—International Microgravity Laboratory: Study of gravity.
1987 (July 23)—Astro-3: Continuing study of Halley's Comet.
1987 (Oct. 1)—Office of Aeronautics and Space Technology: Study of solar arrays.
1987 (Oct. 23)—Materials Science Laboratory: Research on materials in space.
1987 (Nov. 14)—Environmental Observation Mission: Study of solar energy.
1987 (Dec. 1)—Shuttle Radar Laboratory: Mapping Earth's surface.
1988 (March 18)—Shuttle High Energy Astrophysics Laboratory: Study of celestial X-ray sources.
1988 (May 3)—Materials Science Laboratory: Research on materials in space.
1988 (June 2)—Space Life Sciences Laboratory: Research on effects of space on humans.
1988 (Sept. 17)—Space Plasma Laboratory: Research in space plasma processes.
1990—Solar Optical Telescope: Study of heating and energy balance of Sun.
1990—Shuttle Infrared Telescope Facility: Study of celestial objects with infrared telescope.

The $80 million Infrared Astronomical Satellite (IRAS) was placed in orbit about 560 miles above the Earth on Jan. 25, 1983. A joint project of NASA, Britain, and the Netherlands, the telescope monitored infrared radiation, or heat radiation, providing much new information about distant objects in space.

NASA

yet been proven to actually exist. However, in August NASA scientists reported that the Infrared Astronomical Satellite (IRAS), launched in January 1983, had discovered what may be a solar system around the star Vega, about 150 million miles from Earth. One of the brightest stars, Vega is believed to have formed only about 1 billion years ago, making it only about one-fourth as old as the Sun.

NASA scientists H. H. Aumann and Fred Gillett said that the radiation from Vega indicates that a ring of large particles apparently extends out from the star to a distance of 7.4 billion miles, about the same distance the solar system extends from the Sun. The scientists said the materials surrounding Vega have a mass comparable to those of the solar system. However, the scientists could not determine whether any of the particles around Vega were as large as a planet.

HOW DID THEY GET HERE?

NASA scientists reported in March that meteorites found in Antarctica are believed to be pieces of rock from Mars and from the Moon. Donald Bogard, curator of the National Repository for Antarctic Meteorites in Houston, said two meteorites were identified as being from Mars because they contained rare gases found in the atmosphere of that planet. The rocks also had a composition similar to rocks found on the surface of Mars by two *Viking* spacecraft that landed there.

The meteorite identified as being from the Moon was one of 375 meteorites found in Antarctica in 1982. Dr. William Cassidy of the University of Pittsburgh, who led the expedition that collected the meteorites, said the Moon meteorite, named ALHA 81005, was exactly like sample rocks brought back from the Moon by U.S. astronauts.

DISTANCES OF THE STARS

We live some 93 million miles from the nearest star, our Sun.

Light from the Sun takes over 8 minutes to reach Earth, even though it travels at some 186,282 miles a second.

Other distances in our solar system are so immense that the Astronomical Unit (AU) is used to measure them—one AU is the average Earth-Sun distance.

The AU is too small, however, to measure the distances to stars other than our Sun. Instead, the light-year unit is used. A light-year is the distance light travels in a year—about 6 *trillion* miles.

Thus the next nearest star to Earth—a double one named Rigil Centaurus (Alpha Centauri A) and a companion—is 4.3 light-years distant, as shown below.

The table shows some other stars known to be located within a distance of 17 light-years. Also indicated are the spectral types of these stars and their luminosity, or brightness.

Beyond these "nearby" stars lie other stars in our galaxy, the Milky Way. Containing billions of stars, the Milky Way is a great disk about 100,000 light-years in diameter.

The nearest galaxies to the Earth are the Magellanic Clouds, at a distance of about 170,000 light-years.

STAR	SPECTRAL TYPE	DISTANCE IN LIGHT-YEARS	BRIGHTNESS (Sun = 1.0)
Sun	G2	—	1.0
Alpha Cen A*	G2	4.3	1.3
Barnard's*	M5	5.9	0.00044
Wolf 359	M6	7.6	0.00002
Lalande 21185*	M2	8.1	0.0052
Sirius A*	A1	8.6	23.0
Luyten 726-8A*	M6	8.9	0.00006
Ross 154	M5	9.4	0.0004
Ross 248	M6	10.3	0.00011
Epsilon Eri	K2	10.7	0.30
Luyten 789-6	M6	10.8	0.00012
Ross 128	M5	10.8	0.00033
61 Cygni A*	K5	11.2	0.083
Epsilon Ind	K5	11.2	0.13
Procyon A*	F5	11.4	7.6
Sigma 2398 A*	M3.5	11.5	0.0028
Groombridge 34A*	M1	11.6	0.0058
Lacaille 9352	M2	11.7	0.012
Tau Ceti	G8	11.9	0.44
BD + 5° 1668	M4	12.2	0.0014
Lacaille 8760	M1	12.5	0.025
Kapteyn's	M0	12.7	0.0040
Kruger 60 A*	M4	12.8	0.0017
Ross 614 A*	M5	13.1	0.0004
BD-12° 4523	M5	13.1	0.0013
van Maanen's	white dwarf F	13.9	0.00017
Wolf 424 A*	M6	14.1	0.0014
CD-37° 15492	M3	14.5	0.0058
Groombridge 1618	M0	15.0	0.040
CD-46° 11540	M4	15.1	0.0030
CD-49° 13515	M3	15.2	0.0058
CD-44° 11909	M5	15.3	0.00063
Luyten 1159-16	M7	15.4	0.00023
Lalande 25372	M3.5	15.7	0.0076
AOe 17415-6*	M3.5	15.7	0.0044
CC 658	white dwarf	15.8	0.0008
Ross 780	M5	15.8	0.0016
Omicron^2 Eri A*	K0	15.9	0.33
BD + 20° 2465*	M4.5	16.1	0.0036
Altair	A7	16.6	10.0
70 Oph. A*	K1	16.7	0.44
AC + 79° 3888	M4	16.8	0.0009
BD + 43° 4305*	M5	16.9	0.0021
Stein 2051A*	M5	17.0	0.0008

* These stars are binary or larger multiples—that is, they have one or more smaller stars associated with them.

STAR COLORS AND TEMPERATURES

The floods of radiation given off by stars range the whole electromagnetic spectrum from gamma rays and X rays through light and heat to radio waves.

These radiations come from nuclear-fusion reactions maintained by the great pressures and temperatures deep within the stars. The calculated temperature of the center of the Sun is about 25,000,000°F. At such extremes, hydrogen atoms will fuse into helium atoms with a loss in total mass and the release of tremendous quantities of energy.

Stars vary greatly in color and temperature as well as in size. Astronomers analyze the radiations from stars with many instruments, including the spectroscope, which divides light into a color spectrum. The spectra of stars indicate their temperatures. The standard spectral classification of stars is given in the capital letters in the following table, with the color and approximate surface temperatures of stars in these classes.

The stars that fall into intermediate positions are indicated by a range of numbers from 0 to 9 with each letter. Our Sun, for example, has the spectral classification of G2 and a surface temperature of about 10,440°F.

SPECTRAL CLASSIFICATION	COLOR SCALE	STAR SURFACE TEMPERATURE (° Fahrenheit)
O	Blue	63,000
B	Bluish	45,000
A	White	19,800
F	Yellowish	13,500
G Dwarf	Yellow	10,440
G Giant	Yellow	9,540
K Dwarf	Orange	8,820
K Giant	Orange	7,200
M Dwarf	Orange-red	6,120
M Giant	Orange-red	5,400
S	Red	4,680
N	Red	4,680
R	Red	4,140

SKY-WATCHER'S CALENDAR: 1984

Source: *Astronomical Phenomena*, U.S. Naval Observatory

The calendar below lists various astronomical phenomena that will occur in 1984.

Evening and Morning Stars. The planets in the western sky shortly after sunset are *evening stars*, and those seen in the eastern sky shortly before sunrise are *morning stars*.

Occultation. When the Moon passes between the Earth and one of the planets or bright stars, this phenomenon is called *occultation*. The occultation of Venus by a crescent moon is depicted on the flags of many Islamic countries.

Meteor Showers. Meteors, or shooting stars, are visible on almost any night of the year, but at certain times the Earth encounters large numbers of meteors all moving together along the same orbit. These groups of meteors are named for the constellations from which they seem to radiate.

Meteors are pieces of rock or metal traveling in orbit around the Sun. Scientists estimate that about 1,000 tons of meteorites fall on the Earth every day.

Comets are bodies traveling around the Sun in greatly elongated orbits. Most comets can only be seen with telescopes, but from time to time a comet develops a tail of gas or dust that reflects the light from the Sun.

Conjunction of Planets. The orbits of the planets work out so that from time to time the planets appear to pass quite close to each other or to the Sun.

JANUARY

1–May 3 Saturn seen as morning star.
1–May 9 Venus seen as morning star.
1–May 11 Mars seen as morning star.
1–June 29 Jupiter seen as morning star.
2–3 Quadrantid meteor shower at maximum: About 110 meteors per hour visible, seeming to radiate from handle of Big Dipper.
7 Comet Taylor makes closest approach to Sun in its 7-year orbit.
18 (9:05 A.M. EST) Full Moon.
25 (4:00 A.M. EST) 1.6° south of Moon.
25 (8:00 P.M. EST) Saturn 0.2° north of Moon.
26 (9:00 P.M. EST) Venus 0.8° north of Jupiter.

FEBRUARY

16 (7:41 P.M. EST) Full Moon.
19 Comet Smirnova-Chernykh makes closest approach to Sun in its 8.5-year orbit.
20 Comet Crommelin makes closest approach to Sun in its 27.4-year orbit.
22 (4:00 A.M. EST) Saturn 0.3° north of Moon.
24 (5:00 A.M. EST) Uranus 0.2° north of Moon.
26 (3:00 A.M. EST) Jupiter 2° north of Moon.

MARCH

17 (5:10 A.M. EST) Full Moon.
20 Spring equinox: Spring begins at 5:25 A.M. EST.
27 Comet Encke makes closest approach to Sun in its 3.3-year orbit.

APRIL

2 (7:00 P.M. EST) Mercury 6° north of Moon.
15 (2:11 P.M. EST) Full Moon.
16 (8:00 P.M. EST) Saturn 0.6° north of Moon.
18 (10:00 P.M. EST) Uranus 0.6° north of Moon.
21 (4:00 A.M. EST) Jupiter 3° north of Moon.
21–22 Lyrid meteor shower at maximum: About 20 to 30 per hour seem to radiate from constellation Lyra.
29 (2:00 A.M. EST) Daylight-saving time begins: Set clocks ahead 1 hour.
29 (8:00 P.M. EST) Mercury 0.7° north of Venus.

MAY

3–4 Eta Aquarids meteor shower at maximum: About 20 per hour seem to radiate from constellation Aquarius.
3–Oct. 25 Saturn seen as evening star.
11–Dec. 31 Mars seen as evening star.
14 (4:00 A.M. EDT) Saturn 0.5° north of Moon.
14 (12:29 P.M. EDT) Full Moon.
14–15 Penumbral eclipse of Moon: Seen in most of North America; begins at 10:41 P.M. EDT, May 14; middle of eclipse at 12:40 A.M. EDT, May 15; ends at 2:38 A.M. EDT, May 15.
19 (7:00 A.M. EDT) Mars at closest point to Earth.
30 Annular eclipse of Sun: Seen in most of North America; central eclipse begins at 10:57 A.M. EDT; middle of eclipse at 12:53 P.M. EDT; central eclipse ends at 2:32 P.M. EDT.
31 Comet Wolf makes closest approach to Sun in its 8.2-year orbit.

JUNE

13 (10:42 A.M. EDT) Full Moon.
13 Penumbral eclipse of Moon: Not visible in U.S.
14 (12:00 midnight EDT) Neptune 3° north of Moon.
21 Summer solstice: Summer begins at 1:02 A.M. EDT.
29–Dec. 31 Jupiter seen as evening star.

JULY

9 Comet Faye's closest approach to Sun in 7.3-year orbit.
11 (7:00 P.M. EDT) Jupiter 3° north of Moon.
12 (10:20 P.M. EDT) Full Moon.
22–Dec. 31 Venus seen as evening star.
27–28 Delta Aquarids meteor shower at maximum: About 35 per hour seem to radiate from constellation Aquarius.
28 Comet Tuttle-Giacobini-Kresák makes closest approach to Sun in its 5.6-year orbit.

AUGUST

3 (8:00 P.M. EDT) Saturn 0.3° north of Moon.
6 (12:00 midnight EDT) Uranus 0.5° north of Moon.
7 (9:00 P.M. EDT) Jupiter 2° north of Moon.
11 (11:43 A.M. EDT) Full Moon.
12 Perseid meteor shower at maximum: About 70 per hour seem to radiate from constellation Perseus.
31 (5:00 A.M. EDT) Saturn 0.5° north of Moon.

SEPTEMBER

2 (3:00 A.M. EDT) Mars 1.7° south of Moon.
2 (6:00 A.M. EDT) Uranus 0.8° north of Moon.
4 (1:00 A.M. EDT) Jupiter 3° north of Moon.
10 (3:01 A.M. EDT) Full Moon.
22 Comet Wolf-Harrington makes closest approach to Sun in its 6.5-year orbit.
22 Autumn equinox: Autumn begins at 4:33 P.M. EDT.
26 (8:00 P.M. EDT) Venus 2° south of Moon.
30 (8:00 P.M. EDT) Mars 0.3° north of Moon.

OCTOBER

8 Comet Neujmin 1 makes closest approach to Sun in its 18.2-year orbit.
9 (7:58 P.M. EDT) Full Moon.
13 (7:00 P.M. EDT) Mars 1.9° south of Jupiter.
20–21 Orionid meteor shower at maximum: About 30 per hour seem to radiate from constellation Orion.
26 (8:00 P.M. EDT) Venus 0.3° south of Moon.
27 (2:00 A.M. EDT) Uranus 1.3° north of Moon.
28 (2:00 A.M. EDT) Daylight-saving time ends: Set clocks back 1 hour.
29 (12:00 midnight EST) Jupiter 3° north of Moon.
29 (7:00 P.M. EST) Venus 1.5° south of Uranus.

NOVEMBER

8 (12:43 P.M. EST) Full Moon.
8 Penumbral Eclipse of Moon: Visible in extreme northwestern North America.
16–17 Leonid meteor shower at maximum: About 10 per hour seem to radiate from constellation Leo.
22 Total Eclipse of Sun: Seen only in Australia and South Pacific Ocean.
25 (8:00 P.M. EST) Venus 1.6° north of Moon.
28–Dec. 31 Saturn seen as morning star.

DECEMBER

1 Comet Arend-Rigaux makes closest approach to Sun in its 6.8-year orbit.
7 Comet Schaumasse makes closest approach to Sun in its 8.3-year orbit.
8 (5:53 A.M. EST) Full Moon.
13–14 Geminid meteor shower at maximum: About 55 per hour seem to radiate from constellation Gemini.
21 Winter solstice: Winter begins at 11:23 A.M. EST.
21–22 Ursid meteor shower at maximum: About 10 per hour seem to radiate from vicinity of North Star.
25 (9:00 P.M. EST) Venus 3° north of Moon.
26 (2:00 A.M. EST) Mercury 3° north of Uranus.

SUNRISE AND SUNSET CALENDAR: 1984

Tables on this and the opposite page enable you to find the times for sunrise and sunset. Suggestions for using the tables follow.

CONVERTING TIME TO A.M. AND P.M.

The times used in the table are based on a 24-hour clock. The time 0 00 is midnight and 12 00 is noon. The times from 0 01 to 11 59 are morning or A.M., and the times from 12 01 to 23 59 are afternoon and evening or P.M.

To convert the times shown to those commonly used with a 12-hour clock, subtract 12 hours from all times from 13 00 to 23 59. Thus 14 12 would be the same as 2:12 P.M., or 20 23 would be 8:23 P.M.

LATITUDE AND LONGITUDE

To use the table below to find the time of sunrise or sunset, you need to know the latitude and longitude of the place where you live. The latitude and longitude of more than 300 cities are listed on pages 138–140. Use the latitude and longitude of your nearest city listed.

The table below shows the time of events in northern latitudes—those north of the equator. For your convenience a state or city is named in each of the latitude columns. Thus 20 ° N. latitude passes through the state of Hawaii; New Orleans is close to the line of 30 ° N. latitude; and so on.

CONVERT MEAN TIME TO REAL TIME

The times given in the table are for local *mean* time. This is the time on the standard time meridian that passes through your time zone. The standard time meridians (longitude) are Atlantic 60 °, Eastern 75 °, Central 90 °, Mountain 105 °, Pacific 120 °, and Alaska-Hawaii 150 °.

To convert mean time to real local time, find out the longitude of the place where you live. For each degree of longitude that your home is east of the standard time meridian, subtract 4 minutes from the mean time shown in the table. For each degree of longitude west, add 4 minutes. For example, if you live at 78 ° longitude, you are 3 ° west of the Eastern Standard Time meridian (78 ° – 75 ° = 3 ° west). Therefore, add 12 min- utes to the times shown (3 ° × 4 min. = 12 min.). Thus, for the place where you live a mean time 7 07 shown in the table actually should be changed to 7 19 (7 07 + 0 12 = 7 19).

INTERPOLATING TIME FOR YOUR LATITUDE

Because the times in the table are given for specific degrees of latitude and it is unlikely that your home lies exactly on one of these parallels, it is necessary also to correct the times by interpolating for your own latitude.

Suppose, for example, that your home has a latitude of 38 °. This falls between the 35 ° and 40 ° columns shown in the table. The difference between 35 ° and 40 ° is 5 ° (40 ° – 35° = 5 °), and the difference between 35 ° and 38 ° is 3 ° (38 ° – 35 ° = 3 °). To correct the times for your latitude, you would have to subtract 3/5 of the difference between the times shown for 35 ° and 40 °. For example, in the sunrise table for May 6, the difference in time between 35 ° and 40 ° is 10 minutes (5 04 – 4 54 = 10 min.). Three-fifths of 10 minutes is 6 minutes (10 × 3/5 = 6). So you would subtract 6 minutes from the time shown for 35 ° to obtain the local mean time for the place where you live (5 04 – 6 min. = 4 58). Note: If the time at the higher latitude is *later* (instead of earlier), you would *add* the difference (rather than subtract).

STANDARD AND DAYLIGHT TIMES

The times given in the sunrise and sunset table are for the local standard time zone where you live. During those periods of the year in which you use daylight time, add 1 hour to the time shown in a table to change it to daylight time.

CALCULATING SUNRISE AND SUNSET

Using the suggestions above, correct the times shown in the sunrise and sunset table:

(1) Interpolate them for your latitude.
(2) Convert them from mean time to real time (based on your longitude).
(3) If you are using daylight time, add 1 hour.

SUNRISE AND SUNSET: 1984

Source: U.S. Naval Observatory.

DATE	TIME OF SUNRISE						TIME OF SUNSET					
	20 ° N. Latitude (Hawaii)	30 ° N. Latitude (New Orleans)	35 ° N. Latitude (Albuquerque)	40 ° N. Latitude (Philadelphia)	48 ° N. Latitude (Seattle)	60 ° N. Latitude (Alaska)	20 ° N. Latitude (Hawaii)	30 ° N. Latitude (New Orleans)	35 ° N. Latitude (Albuquerque)	40 ° N. Latitude (Philadelphia)	48 ° N. Latitude (Seattle)	60 ° N. Latitude (Alaska)
	h m	h m	h m	h m	h m	h m	h m	h m	h m	h m	h m	h m
Jan. 19 ...	6 38	6 56	7 07	7 19	7 43	8 43	17 43	17 25	17 15	17 03	16 39	15 39
Jan. 23 ...	6 38	6 55	7 05	7 16	7 39	8 35	17 46	17 29	17 19	17 07	16 45	15 49
Jan. 27 ...	6 37	6 53	7 03	7 14	7 35	8 27	17 48	17 32	17 23	17 12	16 51	15 59
Jan. 31 ...	6 36	6 51	7 00	7 10	7 30	8 18	17 51	17 36	17 27	17 17	16 57	16 09
Feb. 4 ...	6 35	6 49	6 57	7 07	7 25	8 09	17 53	17 39	17 31	17 22	17 04	16 20
Feb. 8 ...	6 33	6 46	6 54	7 02	7 19	7 59	17 55	17 42	17 35	17 27	17 10	16 31
Feb. 12 ...	6 31	6 43	6 50	6 58	7 13	7 48	17 57	17 46	17 39	17 31	17 16	16 41
Feb. 16 ...	6 29	6 40	6 46	6 53	7 06	7 38	17 59	17 49	17 43	17 36	17 23	16 52
Feb. 20 ...	6 27	6 36	6 42	6 48	6 59	7 27	18 01	17 52	17 47	17 41	17 29	17 02
Feb. 24 ...	6 24	6 32	6 37	6 42	6 52	7 15	18 03	17 55	17 50	17 45	17 35	17 12
Feb. 28 ...	6 21	6 28	6 32	6 36	6 45	7 04	18 04	17 58	17 54	17 50	17 42	17 23
Mar. 3 ...	6 18	6 24	6 27	6 30	6 37	6 52	18 06	18 01	17 58	17 54	17 48	17 33
Mar. 7 ...	6 15	6 19	6 22	6 24	6 29	6 40	18 07	18 03	18 01	17 59	17 54	17 43

DATE	TIME OF SUNRISE						TIME OF SUNSET					
	20° N. Latitude (Hawaii)	30° N. Latitude (New Orleans)	35° N. Latitude (Albuquerque)	40° N. Latitude (Philadelphia)	48° N. Latitude (Seattle)	60° N. Latitude (Alaska)	20° N. Latitude (Hawaii)	30° N. Latitude (New Orleans)	35° N. Latitude (Albuquerque)	40° N. Latitude (Philadelphia)	48° N. Latitude (Seattle)	60° N. Latitude (Alaska)
	h m	h m	h m	h m	h m	h m	h m	h m	h m	h m	h m	h m
Mar. 11...	6 12	6 15	6 16	6 18	6 21	6 29	18 09	18 06	18 04	18 03	18 00	17 53
Mar. 15...	6 08	6 10	6 11	6 11	6 13	6 16	18 10	18 08	18 08	18 07	18 06	18 03
Mar. 19...	6 05	6 05	6 05	6 05	6 05	6 04	18 11	18 11	18 11	18 11	18 11	18 12
Mar. 23...	6 01	6 00	5 59	5 59	5 57	5 52	18 12	18 13	18 14	18 15	18 17	18 22
Mar. 27...	5 58	5 55	5 54	5 52	5 48	5 40	18 13	18 16	18 17	18 19	18 23	18 32
Mar. 31...	5 54	5 51	5 48	5 46	5 40	5 28	18 14	18 18	18 21	18 23	18 29	18 42
Apr. 4...	5 51	5 46	5 43	5 39	5 32	5 16	18 15	18 21	18 24	18 27	18 35	18 52
Apr. 8...	5 48	5 41	5 37	5 33	5 24	5 04	18 16	18 23	18 27	18 31	18 40	19 01
Apr. 12...	5 44	5 36	5 32	5 27	5 16	4 52	18 17	18 25	18 30	18 36	18 46	19 11
Apr. 16...	5 41	5 32	5 27	5 21	5 09	4 40	18 19	18 28	18 33	18 40	18 52	19 21
Apr. 20...	5 38	5 28	5 22	5 15	5 01	4 29	18 20	18 30	18 37	18 44	18 58	19 31
Apr. 24...	5 35	5 24	5 17	5 09	4 54	4 17	18 21	18 33	18 40	18 48	19 03	19 41
Apr. 28...	5 33	5 20	5 12	5 04	4 47	4 06	18 23	18 35	18 43	18 52	19 09	19 51
May 2...	5 30	5 16	5 08	4 59	4 40	3 55	18 24	18 38	18 46	18 56	19 15	20 01
May 6...	5 28	5 13	5 04	4 54	4 34	3 44	18 25	18 41	18 50	19 00	19 20	20 11
May 10...	5 26	5 10	5 00	4 50	4 28	3 34	18 27	18 43	18 53	19 04	19 26	20 20
May 14...	5 24	5 07	4 57	4 46	4 22	3 24	18 29	18 46	18 56	19 08	19 31	20 30
May 18...	5 23	5 05	4 54	4 42	4 17	3 15	18 30	18 48	18 59	19 11	19 36	20 39
May 22...	5 22	5 03	4 52	4 39	4 13	3 07	18 32	18 51	19 02	19 15	19 41	20 48
May 26...	5 21	5 01	4 50	4 36	4 09	2 59	18 33	18 53	19 05	19 18	19 45	20 57
May 30...	5 20	5 00	4 48	4 34	4 06	2 52	18 35	18 55	19 07	19 21	19 50	21 04
June 3...	5 20	4 59	4 47	4 32	4 03	2 46	18 37	18 58	19 10	19 24	19 53	21 11
June 7...	5 20	4 58	4 46	4 31	4 02	2 42	18 38	18 59	19 12	19 27	19 57	21 17
June 11...	5 20	4 58	4 45	4 31	4 00	2 38	18 39	19 01	19 14	19 29	19 59	21 22
June 15...	5 20	4 58	4 45	4 30	4 00	2 36	18 41	19 03	19 16	19 31	20 01	21 25
June 19...	5 21	4 59	4 46	4 31	4 00	2 35	18 42	19 04	19 17	19 32	20 03	21 27
June 23...	5 22	5 00	4 47	4 32	4 01	2 36	18 42	19 05	19 18	19 33	20 04	21 28
June 27...	5 23	5 01	4 48	4 33	4 02	2 38	18 43	19 05	19 18	19 33	20 04	21 27
July 1...	5 24	5 02	4 50	4 35	4 04	2 42	18 43	19 05	19 18	19 33	20 03	21 25
July 5...	5 25	5 04	4 52	4 37	4 07	2 47	18 44	19 05	19 17	19 32	20 02	21 21
July 9...	5 27	5 06	4 54	4 39	4 10	2 53	18 43	19 04	19 16	19 31	20 00	21 16
July 13...	5 28	5 08	4 56	4 42	4 14	3 00	18 43	19 03	19 15	19 29	19 57	21 10
July 17...	5 30	5 10	4 59	4 45	4 18	3 08	18 42	19 02	19 13	19 27	19 53	21 03
July 21...	5 31	5 12	5 01	4 49	4 23	3 16	18 41	19 00	19 11	19 24	19 49	20 55
July 25...	5 33	5 15	5 04	4 52	4 27	3 25	18 40	18 58	19 08	19 20	19 45	20 47
July 29...	5 34	5 17	5 07	4 56	4 32	3 34	18 38	18 55	19 05	19 17	19 40	20 37
Aug. 2...	5 36	5 20	5 10	4 59	4 37	3 43	18 36	18 52	19 02	19 13	19 34	20 28
Aug. 6...	5 37	5 22	5 13	5 03	4 43	3 53	18 34	18 49	18 58	19 08	19 28	20 17
Aug. 10...	5 38	5 24	5 16	5 07	4 48	4 02	18 32	18 46	18 54	19 03	19 22	20 07
Aug. 14...	5 40	5 27	5 19	5 11	4 53	4 12	18 29	18 42	18 49	18 58	19 15	19 56
Aug. 18...	5 41	5 29	5 22	5 14	4 59	4 22	18 26	18 38	18 45	18 52	19 08	19 44
Aug. 22...	5 42	5 31	5 25	5 18	5 04	4 31	18 23	18 34	18 40	18 47	19 00	19 33
Aug. 26...	5 43	5 34	5 28	5 22	5 10	4 41	18 20	18 29	18 35	18 41	18 53	19 21
Aug. 30...	5 44	5 36	5 31	5 26	5 15	4 50	18 17	18 25	18 29	18 35	18 45	19 09
Sept. 3...	5 45	5 38	5 34	5 30	5 21	5 00	18 13	18 20	18 24	18 28	18 37	18 57
Sept. 7...	5 46	5 40	5 37	5 33	5 26	5 09	18 10	18 15	18 18	18 22	18 29	18 45
Sept. 11...	5 46	5 42	5 40	5 37	5 32	5 19	18 06	18 10	18 13	18 15	18 21	18 33
Sept. 15...	5 47	5 44	5 43	5 41	5 37	5 28	18 03	18 05	18 07	18 09	18 12	18 21
Sept. 19...	5 48	5 47	5 46	5 45	5 43	5 37	17 59	18 00	18 01	18 02	18 04	18 09
Sept. 23...	5 49	5 49	5 49	5 48	5 48	5 47	17 55	17 55	17 55	17 55	17 56	17 56
Sept. 27...	5 50	5 51	5 52	5 52	5 54	5 56	17 52	17 50	17 50	17 49	17 47	17 44
Oct. 1...	5 51	5 53	5 55	5 56	5 59	6 06	17 48	17 45	17 44	17 42	17 39	17 32
Oct. 5...	5 52	5 56	5 58	6 00	6 05	6 15	17 45	17 41	17 38	17 36	17 31	17 20
Oct. 9...	5 53	5 58	6 01	6 04	6 11	6 25	17 41	17 36	17 33	17 29	17 23	17 08
Oct. 13...	5 54	6 01	6 04	6 08	6 16	6 35	17 38	17 31	17 28	17 23	17 15	16 57
Oct. 17...	5 55	6 03	6 08	6 13	6 22	6 45	17 35	17 27	17 22	17 17	17 08	16 45
Oct. 21...	5 57	6 06	6 11	6 17	6 28	6 55	17 32	17 23	17 18	17 12	17 00	16 34
Oct. 25...	5 58	6 09	6 15	6 21	6 34	7 05	17 29	17 19	17 13	17 06	16 53	16 22
Oct. 29...	6 00	6 12	6 18	6 26	6 40	7 15	17 27	17 15	17 09	17 01	16 46	16 12
Nov. 2...	6 02	6 15	6 22	6 30	6 47	7 25	17 25	17 12	17 05	16 56	16 40	16 01
Nov. 6...	6 04	6 18	6 26	6 35	6 53	7 35	17 23	17 09	17 01	16 52	16 34	15 51
Nov. 10...	6 06	6 21	6 30	6 39	6 59	7 46	17 22	17 07	16 58	16 48	16 28	15 41
Nov. 14...	6 08	6 24	6 34	6 44	7 05	7 56	17 20	17 04	16 55	16 44	16 23	15 32
Nov. 18...	6 11	6 28	6 37	6 49	7 11	8 06	17 20	17 03	16 53	16 41	16 19	15 24
Nov. 22...	6 13	6 31	6 41	6 53	7 17	8 15	17 19	17 01	16 51	16 39	16 15	15 16
Nov. 26...	6 16	6 34	6 45	6 58	7 22	8 25	17 19	17 00	16 49	16 37	16 12	15 10
Nov. 30...	6 18	6 38	6 49	7 02	7 28	8 33	17 19	17 00	16 49	16 36	16 10	15 04
Dec. 4...	6 21	6 41	6 52	7 06	7 32	8 41	17 20	17 00	16 48	16 35	16 08	14 59
Dec. 8...	6 23	6 44	6 56	7 09	7 37	8 48	17 21	17 00	16 48	16 35	16 07	14 56
Dec. 12...	6 26	6 46	6 59	7 13	7 41	8 54	17 22	17 01	16 49	16 35	16 07	14 54
Dec. 16...	6 28	6 49	7 01	7 15	7 44	8 58	17 24	17 02	16 50	16 36	16 07	14 53
Dec. 20...	6 30	6 51	7 04	7 18	7 47	9 02	17 25	17 04	16 52	16 38	16 09	14 54
Dec. 24...	6 32	6 53	7 06	7 20	7 48	9 03	17 27	17 06	16 54	16 40	16 11	14 56
Dec. 28...	6 34	6 55	7 07	7 21	7 50	9 04	17 30	17 09	16 56	16 42	16 14	15 00
Jan. 1 (85)	6 35	6 56	7 08	7 22	7 50	9 02	17 32	17 11	16 59	16 45	16 17	15 05
Jan. 5 (85)	6 36	6 57	7 09	7 22	7 50	9 00	17 35	17 14	17 02	16 49	16 22	15 11

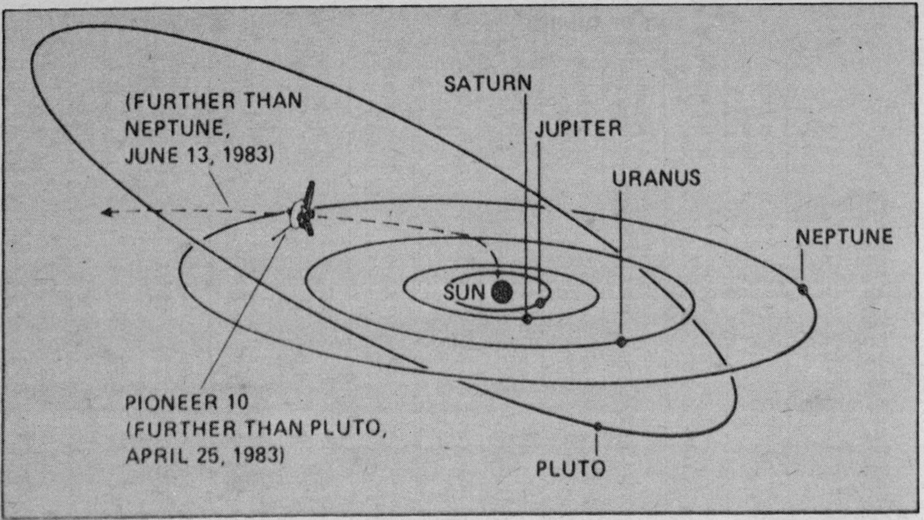

NASA

On June 13, 1983, the spacecraft *Pioneer 10* became the first man-made object to leave the solar system. The spacecraft took more than 11 years since its launch on March 2, 1972, to travel 2.8 million miles to the outer limit. Scientists said they believe *Pioneer 10* will continue speeding through space for billions of years—long after mankind and the Earth itself have ceased to exist. They saw little chance it would strike another object.

EXPLORING THE SOLAR SYSTEM

The solar system includes the Sun and all the celestial objects that orbit it—planets, asteroids, meteors, comets, dust, gas, and man-made satellites. The nine planets in order of distance from the Sun are Mercury, Venus, Earth, Mars, Jupiter, Saturn, Uranus, Neptune, and Pluto.

Since the advent of the Space Age, space probes have been sent to the Sun and the planets, greatly expanding knowledge about man's neighbors in space.

THE SUN

One of the many stars in the Milky Way galaxy, the Sun has a surface temperature of about 11,000° F. The main form of energy radiating from this sphere of seething gas is light. Other radiations include gamma rays, X rays, infrared rays, cosmic rays, and radio waves. The Sun also sprays out what is known as the *solar wind,* a continuous flow of charged particles, protons and electrons.

The Sun is essentially a huge ball of hydrogen. In its interior, where temperatures approach 25,000,000° F., this element is converted into helium, releasing immense quantities of energy.

The Sun has polar caps, as have Earth and Mars. However, with a temperature of about 1,800,000° F., the caps are not frozen ice.

The atmosphere of the Sun consists of several layers of gases. The layer next to the surface, about 10,000 miles thick, is called the *chromosphere.* Enveloping this layer are the inner and outer *coronas.* You can see the corona during a total solar eclipse.

A giant ring of microscopic dust that is 600,000 miles wide encircles the Sun at a distance of 900,000 miles from the surface.

A ring of gas and dust also is believed to encircle the entire solar system at a distance of 9.3 billion miles from the Sun.

Sunspots are dark, turbulent regions often seen within larger, brighter areas known as *flocculi* on the surface of the Sun. The presence of a sunspot is frequently accompanied by a surge of energy called a *solar flare.* They often disrupt radio communications.

FACTS ABOUT THE SUN

Distance from Earth: Closest, 91.4 million miles; farthest, 94.5 million miles; average, 92.9 million miles.

Diameter: About 864,000 miles, or more than 109 times the width of Earth.

Source of life on Earth: All life on Earth depends on heat and light from the Sun. Sunlight travels at the speed of light, reaching Earth about 8 minutes and 20 seconds after being radiated from the Sun.

Speed: The Sun travels around the center of the Milky Way at about 150 miles per second, taking 225 million years to make one orbit around the galaxy.

Rotation: The Sun revolves on its axis from west to east, like Earth. It makes a complete revolution in about 30 days. Because the Sun is a ball of gases, its equator rotates faster than its polar regions.

Age: About 4.6 billion years. This means that in the lifetime of the Sun, it has only revolved around the center of the Milky Way galaxy 20 times. Thus, if we consider that one revolution is the equivalent of one year in the Sun's life, the Sun would be only 20 years old.

MERCURY

Mercury is the planet nearest the Sun. It is also the smallest and fastest.

Because Mercury orbits between Earth and the Sun, it is seen in phases like those of the Moon. Its eccentric orbit makes it appear largest when in the crescent phases and much smaller when it is full. It has many craters, like those of the Moon and Mars.

A very hot planet, Mercury has an atmosphere made up largely of the gas helium.

VENUS

Venus is the planet closest to Earth. After the Sun and Moon, it is the brightest object in our view.

The diameter of Venus is only about 400 miles less than that of the Earth.

Venus revolves about the Sun in a nearly circular orbit at a distance of 67,200,000 miles. When Venus is closest to Earth, it is about 26,000,000 miles away.

The U.S. and the Soviet Union have sent

NATURAL SATELLITES OF THE PLANETS

PLANETS AND SATELLITES [1]	AVERAGE DISTANCE FROM PLANET (in miles)	DIAMETER (in miles)	PERIOD OF REVOLUTION AROUND PLANET days	hrs.	mins.	APPARENT MAGNITUDE	DISCOVERER AND DATE
EARTH							
Moon	238,866	2,057.6	27	7	43	−12.7	—
MARS							
Phobos	5,825	5	0	57	39	11.5	Asaph Hall, 1877
Deimos	14,580	3	1	6	18	12.5	Asaph Hall, 1877
JUPITER							
XVI Metis	79,500	25	0	7	4	—	Stephen P. Synnott, 1980
XV Adresta	79,500	19–25	0	7	8	—	Voyager 1, 1979
V Amalthea	112,779	149	0	11	57	13.0	Edward Barnard, 1892
XIV Thebe	137,000	43–50	0	16	16	—	Stephen P. Synnott, 1980
I Io	262,219	2,256	1	18	28	5.5	Galileo, 1610
II Europa	417,189	1,942	3	13	14	5.8	Galileo, 1610
III Ganymede	665,489	3,278	7	3	43	5.1	Galileo, 1610
IV Callisto	1,170,663	2,994	16	16	32	6.3	Galileo. 1610
XIII Leda	6,893,492	4	239	—	—	20.0	Charles Kowal, 1974
VI Himalia	7,137,691	106	251	—	—	14.0	Charles Perrine, 1904
VII Elara	7,299,247	50	260	—	—	18.0	Charles Perrine, 1905
X Lysithea	7,370,084	9	264	—	—	19.0	Seth Nicholson, 1938
XII Ananke (R)	13,204,137	3.7–17	631	—	—	19.0	Seth Nicholson, 1951
XI Carme (R)	14,005,706	5–25	692	—	—	19.0	Seth Nicholson, 1938
VIII Pasiphae (R)	14,608,436	5–28.5	739	—	—	18.5	P.J. Melotte, 1908
IX Sinope (R)	14,707,856	3.7–22	758	—	—	19.0	Seth Nicholson, 1914
SATURN [2]							
XIV 1980 S27	85,540	19	0	14	20	—	Voyager 1, 1980
XIII 1980 S26	86,590	136	0	14	43	—	Voyager 1, 1980
XV Atlas	88,050	120	0	14	20	—	Voyager 1, 1980
XI 1980 S3	94,089	55x25	0	14	43	—	Pioneer 11, 1980
X 1980 S1	94,120	60x55	0	15	5	—	Voyager 1, 1980
I Mimas	115,300	242	0	22	37	12.1	Sir William Herschel, 1789
II Enceladus	147,900	310	1	8	53	11.8	Sir William Herschel, 1789
III Tethys	183,100	652	1	21	18	10.3	Giovanni Cassini, 1684
XVII 1980 S25	183,100	19–25	1	21	18	—	Univ. of Arizona, 1980
XVI 1980 S13	183,100	19–25	1	21	18	—	French astronomers, 1980
XII 1980 S6	234,920	100	2	17	44	—	Voyager 1, 1980
IV Dione	234,600	696	2	17	44	10.4	Giovanni Cassini, 1684
V Rhea	327,600	951	4	12	25	9.8	Giovanni Cassini, 1672
VI Titan	759,100	3,194	15	23	20	8.4	Christian Huygens, 1655
VII Hyperion	921,100	180	21	7	40	14.2	G.P. & W.C. Bond, 1848
VIII Iapetus	2,212,100	895	79	22	6	11.0	Giovanni Cassini, 1671
IX Phoebe (R)	8,047,000	136	550	10	50	16.5	William Pickering, 1898
URANUS							
V Miranda	80,700	124	1	9	56	16.9	Gerard Kuiper, 1948
I Ariel	119,100	826	2	12	29	14.0	William Lassell, 1851
II Umbriel	165,900	690	4	3	28	15.0	William Lassell, 1851
III Titania	272,100	994	8	16	56	13.8	Sir William Herschel, 1787
IV Oberon	363,900	1,013	13	11	7	14.0	Sir William Herschel, 1787
NEPTUNE							
Triton (R)	219,500	1,988	5	21	3	13.6	William Lassell, 1846
Nereid	3,461,000	200?	359	10	—	19.7	Gerard Kuiper, 1949
PLUTO							
Charon	11,800	1,250	6	9	17	17.0	James W. Christy, 1978

[1] An (R) following a satellite's name indicates it revolves retrograde to planet's rotation. [2] Four to six additional small moons of Saturn were discovered in 1982.

EXPLORING THE SOLAR SYSTEM *(continued)*

many unmanned spaceships to explore the planet, whose surface is obscured from view by a heavy cloud layer. Using radar to penetrate the clouds, the spaceships have discovered that the surface is much more rugged than that of Earth, with higher mountains and deeper canyons.

Incapable of supporting life as known on Earth, Venus has a surface temperature of 869 ° F. that seems to be evenly distributed in all regions. Huge thunderstorms apparently rage continually.

Although the clouds have winds of 100 to 200 mph, winds at the surface of the planet were measured at only 10 mph.

Sulfur gases in the planet's atmosphere seem to burn and glow continuously from the intense heat, turning the sky orange.

MARS

Mars is half again as far from the Sun as is Earth, and thus is colder. Its summer noon temperature reaches only about 80 ° F. at its equator.

The planet takes 1.88 years to orbit the Sun, so its seasons are about twice as long as those on Earth. It is inclined 24 ° to its orbit, nearly the same as is Earth.

A day on Mars is just slightly longer than Earth's—24 hours and 37 minutes. The planet, which is 4,218 miles in diameter, has about 11% of Earth's mass and is of lower density—an object of 100 pounds on Earth would weigh a mere 38 pounds on Mars.

Circling Mars are two small satellites, Phobos (*fear*) and Deimos (*panic*). Deimos orbits Mars once a day, but Phobos makes almost three daily revolutions.

Two U.S. *Viking* spacecraft landed on Mars in 1976, sending back the first photos and data from the surface of the planet.

The *Viking I* lander reported in July 1976 that the Martian atmosphere is composed of 95% carbon dioxide, 2% to 3% nitrogen, 1% to 2% argon-40, and 0.3% oxygen.

The planet's low atmospheric pressure prevents water from remaining on the surface, except as ice in the northern polar region.

There are regions of quite different geological character on Mars: vast valleys and "stream" channels, towering mountains, and some densely cratered Moon-like areas. The 1972 photo map of Mars, produced from *Mariner 9* data, revealed such remarkable features as Nix Olympica, a volcanic mountain 300 miles wide and 10½ miles high. The photos also showed channels apparently once cut by rivers of water on the planet's surface.

Mars is best seen when opposite the Sun in the sky. Because of the motion of Mars and Earth about the Sun, this point at "opposition" occurs every two years and two months.

ASTEROIDS

About 20,000 to 30,000 asteroids, or minor planets, circle the Sun, mostly in orbits that lie between those of Mars and Jupiter. The first and largest asteroid, Ceres, was discovered on Jan. 1, 1801, by Italian astronomer Giuseppe Piazzi.

All the asteroids are smaller than the Moon. Diameters of the larger asteroids include: Ceres, 600 miles; Pallas, 350 miles; Vesta, 310 miles; Hygeia, 240 miles; Interamnia, 200 miles; and Davida, 170 miles.

Some scientists believe that asteroids and comets are pieces of a large planet that exploded about 6 million years ago.

JUPITER

The largest planet, Jupiter has a volume that would engulf 1,347 Earths. Its mass is twice that of the rest of the planets combined.

Scientists believe there is a possibility that some forms of life exist in Jupiter's atmosphere, which has zones of water vapor at temperatures comparable to those on Earth.

Jupiter rotates once in somewhat less than 10 hours. Because of this rapid rotation—fastest of all the planets—Jupiter is oblate, its poles are flattened, and its equator bulges. Jupiter has 16 moons. Ganymede, the larg-

PLANETS OF OUR SOLAR SYSTEM

PLANET	DIAMETER (in miles)	MASS (Earth = 1)	DENSITY (water = 1)	GRAVITY (Earth = 1)	ESCAPE VELOCITY (in miles per sec.)	INCLINATION OF AXIS	ALBEDO OR REFLECTIVITY	SPEED IN SOLAR ORBIT (in miles per sec.)
MERCURY	3,100	0.056	5.13	0.36	2.6	unknown	0.056	29.8
VENUS	7,519	0.815	5.26	0.87	6.4	6 °	0.76	21.8
EARTH	7,926	1.00	5.52	1.00	7.0	23 ° 27′	0.36	18.5
MARS	4,218	0.108	3.94	0.38	3.1	24 °	0.16	15.0
JUPITER	88,732	317.9	1.33	2.61	37.9	3 ° 1′	0.73	8.1
SATURN	74,316	95.2	0.69	0.90	23.0	26 ° 7′	0.76	6.0
URANUS	29,200	14.6	1.56	1.07	13.7	97 ° 9′	0.93	4.2
NEPTUNE	27,700	17.3	2.27	1.41	15.5	28 ° 8′	0.84	3.4
PLUTO	1,900	0.06 ?	4.00 ?	0.3 ?	unknown	unknown	0.14 ?	3.0

PLANETARY EXPLORATION BY U.S. SPACECRAFT

PLANET	DISTANCE [1]	SPACECRAFT	ENCOUNTER
Venus	26,000,000	Mariner 2	Flyby: Dec. 14, 1962; returns surface temperature measurements
		Mariner 5	Flyby: Oct. 19, 1967; closes within 2,480 miles of planet
		Mariner 10	Flybys: March 29, 1974; Sept. 21, 1974; March 16, 1975
		Pioneer Venus 1	Eight-month orbiting of planet, beginning Dec. 5, 1978
		Pioneer Venus 2	Five probes sent into Venus' atmosphere on Dec. 9, 1978
Mars	35,000,000	Mariner 4	Flyby: July 14, 1965; sends first close photos from 6,118 miles
		Mariner 6	Flyby: July 31, 1969
		Mariner 7	Flyby: Aug. 5, 1969
		Mariner 9	Orbited Mars from Nov. 13, 1971, to Oct. 27, 1972
		Viking 1	Lander 1 touched down on planet's surface on July 20, 1976; sends first photos from surface of Mars
		Viking 2	Lander 2 touched down on Sept. 3, 1976; analysis of soil samples failed to prove or disprove existence of microbial life
Mercury	48,000,000	Mariner 10	Flybys: March 29, 1974; Sept. 21, 1974; March 16, 1975
Jupiter	366,000,000	Pioneer 10	Flyby: Dec. 4, 1973
		Pioneer 11	Flyby: Dec. 5, 1974
		Voyager 1	Flyby: March 5, 1979; discovered ring around planet and 3 new moons
		Voyager 2	Flyby: July 9, 1979
		Galileo	Planned probe in 1989
Saturn	743,000,000	Pioneer 11	Flyby: Sept. 1, 1979; discovered new 11th moon and new rings
		Voyager 1	Flyby: Nov. 12, 1980; discovered new moons and many rings
		Voyager 2	Flyby: Aug. 25, 1981
Uranus	1,606,000,000	Voyager 2	Flyby: scheduled Jan. 24, 1986

[1] Minimum distance from Earth in miles.

est, is bigger than Mercury.

Approaching Jupiter from space, an observer would see a huge yellowish globe striped with multicolored dark and light bands—all in a kind of mottled motion that reveals a turbulent cloud layer.

The planet also is surrounded by a thin ring of rock and dust particles.

The smooth surface of the planet is a gigantic sea of compressed hydrogen and helium. Jupiter has a central rocky core surrounded by liquid metallic hydrogen at a temperature of 54,000° F., about six times the heat of the surface of the Sun. Because of its internal heat, Jupiter gives off more heat than it receives from the Sun.

Clouds of methane, ammonia, water, and other compounds float in bands around the planet, whipped along by winds of 200 mph.

Hydrogen makes up more than 76% of Jupiter's mass. Helium is about 22%.

Photos sent back by space probes indicate Jupiter's Great Red Spot—an oval about 30,000 miles long and 7,000 miles wide—is a huge hurricane-like storm.

SATURN

Over 700,000,000 miles from Earth, Saturn is yellowish overall and has atmospheric bands across its face. It is girdled by many glittering rings in the plane of its equator. These rings extend about 286,000 miles from the planet.

Most experts think the rings are probably bits of ice-covered rock, between dust and gravel in size—or perhaps chunks of water ice itself. The rings are incredibly thin for their span and are so tenuous that stars can be seen through them. Their thickness is at most a few thousand feet.

Saturn, second-largest planet in the solar system, is so gaseous that it is also the least dense. If there were a celestial sea of water to dunk it in, it would float.

PERIOD OF ROTATION				PERIOD OF REVOLUTION (in Earth days)	UNIT SOLAR RADIATION AVAILABLE (Earth=1)	AVERAGE DISTANCE FROM SUN (in million miles)	MINIMUM DISTANCE FROM EARTH (in million miles)	AVERAGE TRAVEL TIME FROM EARTH	PLANET
days	hrs.	min.	sec.						
58.65	—	—	—	88 days	6.7	36.0	48	115 days	MERCURY
243.10	—	—	—	116.8 days	1.9	67.2	26	146 days	VENUS
—	23	56	4	365.26 days	1.00	92.9	—	—	EARTH
—	24	37	23	687 days	0.43	141.5	35	237 days	MARS
—	9	55	33	11.86 years	0.04	483.4	366	2.6 years	JUPITER
—	10	39	26	29.46 years	0.01	886.0	743	5.6 years	SATURN
—	12	18	—	84.01 years	0.0031	1,782.0	1,606	15 years	URANUS
—	18	12	—	164.8 years	0.001	2,792.0	2,678	30 years	NEPTUNE
6.387	—	—	—	247.7 years	0.0006	3,675.0	2,650	30 years	PLUTO

EXPLORING THE SOLAR SYSTEM *(continued)*

The planet has possibly as many as 23 moons. The largest of these moons—Titan, with a diameter of 3,194 miles—has an atmosphere, largely of nitrogen. Its surface is concealed by clouds. Its surface temperature is believed to be about −288 °F.

URANUS

The pale green planet Uranus orbits 1.79 billion miles from the Sun. About 29,200 miles in diameter, Uranus has its axis inclined 8° from the orbital plane. An observer living at one of the poles would see a "midnight Sun" for about 42 years and live in darkness the next 42 years.

Uranus has nine rings encircling it, like those of Saturn but smaller.

Uranus has 5 moons. Like the other giant planets, it is rich in light elements, especially hydrogen and helium. But it is denser than Jupiter and Saturn.

NEPTUNE

The bluish green hue of Neptune, a near twin of Uranus, stems from the methane in its atmosphere. Astronomers discovered two faint rings around the planet in 1982. It has two moons. One, Triton, is remarkably similar to Earth's moon. At 2.8 billion miles from the Sun, a spacecraft orbiting Neptune would chill to −370 °F. if it were not heated. Since Neptune's discovery in 1846, it has made less than three-quarters of one revolution of the Sun.

PLUTO

At 3.7 billion miles from the Sun, Pluto is cold and dark. Its diameter is only about one-third that of the Earth. Pluto is made up of frozen methane and water.

Its orbit about the Sun departs by 17° from the plane of the other planets' orbits.

Charon, a moon circling around Pluto, was discovered on June 22, 1978, by U.S. astronomer James W. Christy.

HIGHLIGHTS OF SPACE EXPLORATION

The Space Age was inaugurated by the Soviet Union on Oct. 4, 1957, when it launched *Sputnik I*, the first man-made satellite to orbit Earth.

Four months later, on Jan. 31, 1958, the United States launched *Explorer I* as part of the first U.S. satellite program, Project Vanguard, initiated as part of the 1957–58 International Geophysical Year (IGY). *Vanguard I*, the project's second satellite, launched March 17, 1958, was the first with solar-powered batteries.

The U.S. space program had begun on Nov. 7, 1957, when President Eisenhower created a Scientific Advisory Committee, headed by Massachusetts Institute of Technology president, Dr. James R. Killian. In March 1958 the Killian Committee recommended creation of a civilian space agency. Congress passed the National Aeronautics and Space Act of 1958.

Two months later, on October 1, the National Aeronautics and Space Administration (NASA) was born. Its nucleus was the National Advisory Committee for Aeronautics (NACA), which for 43 years had been active in U.S. aeronautical research.

President John F. Kennedy said in a historic address to Congress on May 25, 1961:

"I believe that this Nation should commit itself to achieving the goal, before this decade is out, of landing a man on the Moon and returning him safely to Earth."

This goal was achieved with man's first walk on the Moon in July 1969.

The NASA program has been marred by only one major tragedy. On Jan. 27, 1967, a fire erupted inside an *Apollo* spacecraft during ground testing, resulting in the death of three astronauts—Lt. Col. Virgil I. Grissom, USAF; Lt. Col. Edward H. White II, USAF; and Lt. Comdr. Roger B. Chaffee, USN.

1957 (Oct. 4) First man-made satellite: *Sputnik I* orbited by Soviet Union.

1958 (Jan. 31) First U.S. satellite successfully launched: *Explorer I* remains in orbit until March 31, 1970, circling Earth 58,408 times and traveling 2.67 billion miles.

1958 (Oct. 11) First NASA launch: *Pioneer I* reaches altitude of 70,717 miles. The 84-pound spacecraft had a life of only 43 hours.

1959 (Feb. 17) First weather satellite: *Vanguard II* is first satellite to send weather information back to Earth.

1959 (Aug. 2) First TV photo of Earth from space: Transmitted by Explorer 6 as it orbits Earth.

1959 (Sept. 12) First space probe to strike Moon: *Luna 2* launched by Soviet Union.

1959 (Oct. 4) First photos of far side of Moon: Soviet Unions *Luna 3* spacecraft accomplishes feat.

1960 (March 11) Interplanetary radiation measured: *Pioneer 5* launched to measure radiation en route to Venus.

1960 (April 1) First meteorological satellite: *Tiros I* begins series of 10 consecutive successful research missions, providing 22,952 cloud-cover photos.

1960 (Aug. 12) First passive communications satellite: 100-foot balloon, *Echo I*, inflated in orbit.

1961 (April 12) First manned orbital flight: Soviet Union sends Yuri A. Gagarin on 1 hr. 48-min. flight aboard *Vostok I* for one orbit around Earth.

1961 (May 5) First American in space: Astronaut Alan B. Shepard Jr. takes 14.8-min. suborbital flight aboard *Freedom 7*.

1961 (July 21) Second U.S. suborbital flight: Astronaut Virgil I. Grissom makes 15-min., 118-mile-high, 303-mile-long flight in *Liberty Bell 7*.

1961 (Aug. 6–7) First long-duration orbital flight: Soviet Union launches Gherman S. Titov into space aboard *Vostok II*; flight takes 25 hrs. 18 min., includes 17.5 orbits.

1962 (Feb. 20) First American in orbit: Astronaut John H.

Glenn Jr. in *Friendship 7 (Mercury-Atlas 6)* flies 81,000 miles, orbiting Earth 3 times in 4 hrs. 55 min.

1962 (April 23) First U.S. probe to strike Moon: *Ranger IV* fails to televise pictures to Earth.

1962 (March 7) First scientific observatory spacecraft: *OSO 1* placed in orbit with 13 experiments to study Sun.

1962 (April 26) First international satellite: *Ariel-1* carries British experiments.

1962 (May 24) Second U.S. manned orbital flight: Astronaut M. Scott Carpenter pilots *Aurora 7* in 3 orbits of Earth; overshoots landing area by 250 miles.

1962 (July 10) First privately financed satellite: *Telstar I* carries out series of communication transmission tests, including TV, telephone, data, and photo facsimile.

1962 (Aug. 11) Third Soviet manned orbital flight: *Vostok III* carries cosmonaut Andrian G. Nikolayev on 64 orbits around Earth.

1962 (Aug. 12) Fourth Soviet manned orbital flight: *Vostok IV* carries cosmonaut Pavel R. Popovich on 48 orbits; comes within 3 miles of *Vostok III* on first orbit.

1962 (Oct. 3) Third U.S. manned orbital flight: Astronaut Walter M. Schirra Jr. makes nearly 6 orbits, traveling 160,000 miles in 9 hrs. 13 min. in *Sigma 7.*

1963 (May 15–16) Final flight of Mercury Project: Astronaut Gordon Cooper in *Faith 7* orbits Earth 22 times in 34 hrs. 20 min.

1963 (June 14) Fifth Soviet manned orbital flight: *Vostok V* carries cosmonaut Valery F. Bykovsky on 81 Earth orbits.

1963 (June 16) First woman in space: Valentina V. Tereshkova pilots Soviet craft, *Vostok VI,* on 48 Earth orbits.

1963 (July 26) First satellite communication between U.S. and Africa: *Syncom 2* communications satellite placed in stationary orbit over Brazil.

1964 (Jan. 25) First joint U.S.-Soviet Union space experiment: *Echo 2* passive communications satellite orbited.

1964 (July 20) First successful electric rocket engine tested in space: Used aboard U.S. *Sert I* spacecraft.

1964 (July 28–31) Spacecraft photographs Moon: *Ranger 7* sends back 4,316 clear photos before crashing onto lunar surface.

1964 (Sept. 5) Orbiting Geophysical Observatory program: *OGO 1* placed in orbit for space experiments.

1964 (Oct. 12) First 3-man orbital flight: Soviet cosmonauts Konstantin Feoktistov, Vladimir Komarov, and Boris Yegorov fly 16 orbits in *Voshkod I.*

1964 (Nov. 28) First close photos of Mars: *Mariner 4* launched on 228-day, 325-million-mile flight to Mars, sending back first close photos of planet.

1965 (March 18) First space walk: Aleksei A. Leonov leaves *Voshkod II* spacecraft for 10 minutes; fellow cosmonaut Pavel I. Belyayev also aboard Soviet craft in 17 orbits.

1965 (March 23) First maneuvering of manned spacecraft in orbit: Second phase of U.S. manned space program begun with 3-orbit flight of *Gemini 3* by astronauts Virgil I. (Gus) Grissom and John W. Young.

1965 (April 6) First commercial communications satellite: *Early Bird (Intelsat 1)* placed in synchronous equatorial orbit over Atlantic Ocean.

1965 (June 3–7) First U.S. space walk: *Gemini 4* orbits Earth 62 times with astronauts James A. McDivitt and Edward H. White; White leaves spaceship for first U.S. walk in space.

1965 (Aug. 21–29) Third Gemini flight: Astronauts L. Gordon Cooper and Charles Conrad Jr. make 120 orbits around Earth during 8-day mission in Gemini 5.

1965 (Dec. 4–18) Fourth Gemini flight: 14-day endurance mission flown by astronauts Frank Borman and James A. Lovell Jr. in *Gemini 7,* making 206 Earth orbits.

1965 (Dec. 15) First rendezvous by spacecraft: *Gemini 6,* piloted by astronauts Walter Schirra Jr. and Thomas P. Stafford, rendezvous within 6 feet of *Gemini 7* in orbit.

1966 (Feb. 3) Weather satellite system inaugurated: U.S. Weather Bureau's satellite information system becomes operational with launch of 305-pound *ESSA-1.*

1966 (March 16–17) First space docking experiment: Performed by astronauts Neil Armstrong and David R. Scott in *Gemini 8* with Gemini unmanned target vehicle.

1966 (April 3) First spacecraft orbits Moon: Soviet *Luna 10* was launched on March 31.

1966 (May 30–June 2) First U.S. unmanned space landing on Moon: Spacecraft *Surveyor I* makes soft landing on Moon's Ocean of Storms; sends back 11,327 photos.

1966 (June 3–6) Longest spacewalk: Astronauts Thomas P. Stafford and Eugene A. Cernan launched on 3-day flight aboard *Gemini 9;* Cernan. performs longest spacewalk to date—more than 2 hours.

1966 (July 18–21) First successful docking of spacecraft: *Gemini 10,* piloted by astronauts John W. Young and Michael Collins, overtakes and docks with Gemini vehicle.

1966 (Aug. 10) First U.S. spacecraft orbits Moon: Unmanned *Lunar Orbiter 1* takes first photos of Earth as seen from vicinity of Moon.

1966 (Nov. 11–15) Final Gemini mission: Astronauts James A. Lovell Jr. and Edwin A. Aldrin Jr. in *Gemini 12* successfully docked with target vehicle in Earth orbit; Aldrin performed two walks in space.

1967 (Jan. 27) Disaster in Apollo flight experiment: Three astronauts training as crew for first Apollo mission killed when fire sweeps through vehicle during ground test.

1967 (April 23) Soviet cosmonaut killed: Vladimir M. Komarov killed as *Soyuz I* crashes after reentry.

1967 (Aug. 1) Mapping of Moon completed by spacecraft: U.S. *Lunar Orbiter 5* launched, completing mapping mission preparatory to manned Apollo flights to Moon.

1967 (Sept. 7–9) First successful U.S. biological research spacecraft: *Biosatellite 2* carries radiation and general biological experiments into orbit around Earth.

1967 (Sept. 8–11) Spacecraft explores possible landing sites for Apollo mission: *Surveyor 5* lands on Moon, takes photos of potential landing areas and begins chemical analysis of Moon's surface.

1967 (Nov. 9) First Apollo unmanned flight test: *Saturn V* 3-stage launch vehicle sent aloft and brought back to Earth at lunar-return velocity.

1968 (Jan. 7–10) Laser beam from Earth received on Moon: Unmanned *Surveyor 7* receives light signal from Earth while returning TV pictures of Moon's surface and performing digging experiments.

1968 (July 4) Astonomy research craft launched: *Radio Astronomy Explorer Satellite* provides data on new elements and distant regions of universe.

1968 (Oct. 11–22) First manned Apollo flight: Mission lasts 10 days and 20 hours orbiting Earth with *Apollo 7* manned by astronauts Walter M. Schirra Jr., Donn F. Eisele, and R. Walter Cunningham; crew seen by home TV viewers in first telecast from space.

1968 (Oct. 26–30) First Soviet manned rendezvous: Cosmonaut Georgi T. Beregovoi pilots *Soyuz 3* to rendezvous with unmanned *Soyuz 2.*

1968 (Dec. 21–27) First manned Moon-orbiting mission: Astronauts Frank Borman, James A. Lovell, and William Anders in *Apollo 8* orbit Moon 10 times.

1969 (Jan. 14) Soviet docking in space: Cosmonaut Vladimir A. Shatalov pilots *Soyuz 4* to docking with *Soyuz 5.*

1969 (March 3–13) First manned flight of Lunar Module: Astronuats James A. McDivitt, David R. Scott, and Russell L. Schweickart pilot *Apollo 9;* first manned flight of lunar hardware in Earth orbit tests human reactions to space and weightlessness.

1969 (May 18–26) Second manned Moon-orbiting mission: *Apollo 10,* crewed by astronauts Eugene A. Cernan, John W. Young, and Thomas P. Stafford, circles Moon 31 times; *Lunar Module* (LM) flown to within 47,000 feet of Moon's surface; first live color TV pictures sent from space.

1969 (July 20) First astronauts land on Moon: Launched on July 16, *Apollo 11* manned by astronauts Neil A. Armstrong, Edwin E. Aldrin Jr. and Michael Collins; Armstrong and Aldrin become first men to walk on Moon; President Nixon congratulates astronauts in first telephone call to Moon; astronauts remain on Moon for more than 21 hours;

return to Earth on July 24.

1969 (Oct. 11–18) Three Soviet spacecraft orbit simultaneously: *Soyuz 6, Soyuz 7,* and *Soyuz 8* launched a day apart to perform experiments in welding metals and tests for building orbiting space laboratory.

1969 (Nov. 14–24) Second Moon-landing flight: *Apollo 12* flown by astronauts Charles Conrad Jr., Richard E. Gordon Jr., and Alan L. Bean; Conrad and Bean stay on Moon for 32 hours.

1970 (April 13) Accident in space aborts Moon flight: *Apollo 13* launched on April 11, manned by astronauts James A. Lovell, John L. Swigert Jr., and Fred W. Haise Jr. Rupture of oxygen tank forces crew to take emergency action, returning to Earth on April 17.

1970 (Dec. 12) First American spacecraft launched with foreign crew: *Explorer 42* launched into equatorial orbit from San Marco platform off coast of Kenya by Italian crew.

1971 (Jan. 31–Feb. 9) Third successful lunar landing mission: *Apollo 14* manned by astronauts Alan B. Shepard Jr., Stuart A. Roosa, and Edgar D. Mitchell; Shepard and Mitchell stay on Moon for over 33 hours.

1971 (April 22–24) Soviet spacecraft links up with orbiting space station: Cosmonauts Vladimir A. Shatalov, Aleksei S. Yeliseyev, and Nikolai Rukavishnikov, aboard *Soyuz 10,* link up with orbiting space station, *Salyut,* for 5½ hours.

1971 (June 6–30) Soviet cosmonauts die after link-up with *Salyut I* space station: Cosmonauts Georgi T. Dobrovolsky, Vladislav N. Volkov, and Viktor I. Patsayev aboard *Soyuz 11*, docked with space station and orbited with *Salyut* for 23 days; crew died during reentry from failure of pressurization.

1971 (July 26–Aug. 7) Fourth lunar landing mission: *Apollo 15* flown by astronauts David R. Scott, James B. Irwin, and Alfred M. Worden; Scott and Irwin became first to use *Lunar Roving Vehicle* (LRV) to travel over 17 miles exploring Moon's surface.

1971 (Nov. 13) First close photos of Mars' moons: *Mariner 9,* launched May 30, in Mars' orbit, takes first close photos of moons Deimos and Phobos and of Mars dust storm.

1972 (March 2) *Pioneer 10* launched to explore distant planets: Unmanned spacecraft is first powered completely by nuclear energy; after photographing Jupiter and Saturn, it left the solar system on June 13, 1983.

1972 (April 16–27) *Apollo 16* mission to Moon: Fifth lunar landing flight manned by astronauts John W. Young, Thomas K. Mattingly II, and Charles M. Duke Jr.; Young and Duke remained on Moon for 71 hours.

1972 (Dec. 7–19) Final Apollo flight to Moon: *Apollo 17* flown by astronauts Eugene A. Cernan, Ronald B. Evans, and Harrison H. Schmidt; Cernan and Schmidt stay on Moon more than 3 days.

1973 (April 6) *Pioneer 11* sent to explore planets: Flyby of Jupiter occurs on Dec. 5, 1974; flyby of Saturn on Sept. 1, 1979, discovers new 11th moon and new rings.

1973 (May 14) *Skylab* becomes first U.S. space station: Orbits 268.7 miles above Earth.

1973 (May 25–June 22) First manned *Skylab* expedition: Astronauts Charles Conrad Jr., Joseph P. Kerwin, and Paul J. Weitz, aboard *Skylab 2,* rendezvous with *Skylab 1,* repair it, and conduct experiments during 28-day mission.

1973 (July 28–Sept. 25) Second manned *Skylab* expedition: Astronauts Alan L. Bean, Jack R. Lousma, and Owen K. Garriott, launched aboard *Skylab 3,* spend over 59 days in space.

1973 (Sept. 27–29) First Soviet manned flight after 2-year hiatus: Cosmonauts Vasily G. Lazarev and Oleg K. Makharov pilot *Soyuz 12* on 2-day test flight.

1973 (Nov. 3) First probe to fly past two planets: *Mariner 10* sends photos and data from Venus on Feb. 5, 1974, and photos and data from Mercury on March 29 and Sept. 21, 1974, and March 16, 1975.

1973 (Nov. 16) to 1974 (Feb. 8) Final *Skylab* mission: Astronauts Gerald Carr, Edward Gibson, and William Pogue remain in space more than 84 days, after launch aboard *Skylab 4.*

1973 (Dec. 18–26) Soviet cosmonauts grow nutritive protein samples: Tests done by Pyotr Klimuk and Valentin Lebedev aboard *Soyuz 13.*

1974 (July 3–19) *Soyuz 14* launched: Cosmonauts spend two weeks on board space sation *Salyut 3.*

1975 (Jan. 11–Feb. 9) Soviets set endurance record: Cosmonauts Aleksei Gubarev and Georgi Crechko remain 30 days aboard *Salyut 4* space station, after launch in spaceship *Soyuz 17.*

1975 (July 17) First international rendezvous and docking in space: U.S astronauts Thomas P. Stafford, Vance D. Brand, and Donald K. Slayton dock their *Apollo* spacecraft with Soviet *Soyuz 19,* manned by cosmonauts Aleksei Leonov and Valeri Kubasov; crews exchange visits.

1975 (Aug. 20) First U.S. attempt to softland spacecraft on other planet: *Viking 1* reaches Mars July 20, 1976, and begins relaying first analysis of surface material on another planet.

1975 (Sept. 9) *Viking 2 launched:* Sister ship to *Viking 1* lands on Mars on Sept. 3, 1976.

1976 (July 6–Aug. 24) Soviet *Soyuz 21* launched: Cosmonauts Boris Volynov and Vitaly Zhobolov spend 50 days aboard *Salyut 5* space station, launched June 22.

1977 (Aug. 12) Orbiting astronomical observatory launched: *HEAO–1* maps X-rays and gamma rays.

1977 (Aug. 20) *Voyager 2* launched to study distant planets: Flyby of Jupiter occurs July 9, 1979; on flyby of Saturn Aug. 25, 1981, sends back more than 18,000 photos; scheduled to encounter Uranus in January 1986 and Neptune in August 1989.

1977 (Sept. 5) *Voyager 1* sets off to investigate Jupiter and Saturn: Jupiter flyby March 5, 1979, discovers ring around planet and 3 new moons; Saturn flyby on Nov. 12, 1980, discovers additional new moons and rings.

1978 (May 20) *Pioneer-Venus 1* to study Venus: Begins orbiting planet Dec. 5, 1978.

1978 (June 26) First ocean-monitoring satellite: U.S. SEASAT-1 launched.

1978 (Aug. 8) Multiprobe spacecraft to study Venus: *Pioneer-Venus 2* sent into Venus' atmosphere on Dec. 9, 1978.

1979 (July 11) *Skylab* falls out of orbit: 77-ton spacecraft, launched May 14, 1973, scatters debris over desert area of Western Australia.

1980 (April 9–Oct. 11) Soviets set new endurance record: Cosmonauts Leonid Popov and Valery Ryumin spend 185 days aboard the *Salyut 6* space station and the spaceships *Soyuz 35* and *Soyuz 37.*

1981 (April 12–14) Reusable space shuttle *Columbia:* Makes first successful flight, orbiting Earth 36.5 times; manned by astronauts John W. Young and R. L. Crippen.

1981 (Nov. 12–14) Second space shuttle flight: Astronauts Joe H. Engle and Richard H. Truly pilot *Columbia* for 36.5 orbits.

1982 (March 22–30) Third space shuttle flight: Astronauts Jack Lousma and Gordon A. Fullerton pilot *Columbia* for 129 orbits.

1982 (April 19) Soviets launch new *Salyut 7* space station: replaces *Salyut 6*, which burns on reentry July 30.

1982 (May 13–Dec. 10) Soviets set new endurance record: Cosmonauts Lt. Col. Anatoly Berezovnoy and Valentin Lebedov spend record 211 days in space, living aboard *Salyut 7* orbiting space station.

1982 (June 24–July 2) French astronaut visits *Salyut 7:* Col. Jean-Loup Chrétien becomes first noncommunist to fly in Soviet spacecraft.

1982 (June 27–July 4) Final *Columbia* test flight: Astronauts Thomas K. Mattingly II and Henry W. Harstfield Jr. pilot shuttle for 112 orbits in fourth and final test flight.

1982 (Aug. 19–27) Second woman flies in space: Soviet cosmonaut Svetlana Savitskaya travels aboard *Soyuz T–7* and visits orbiting *Salyut 7.*

1982 (Nov. 11–16) Space shuttle *Columbia* completes first operational flight: 4-man crew launches satellites.

1983 For space events of the year, see pages 8–30 and 747–750.

FACTS ABOUT THE MOON

More has been learned about the Moon than any other of the Earth's neighbors in space because of the Apollo program that enabled men to walk on the Moon and bring back hundreds of pounds of rocks. Following are some of the important facts we now know about the Moon.

Age of the Moon: Over 4.6 billion years. Moon rocks brought back by the astronauts have been dated as old as 4.6 billion years.

Composition of the Moon: The content of rocks on the Moon is much different from that of the Earth. The Moon has only an estimated 8.5% iron, while the Earth is about 36% iron. The Moon has proportionately three times as much uranium as the Earth, but only about one-third the Earth's percentage of gold and only about half the proportion of potassium.

Diameter of the Moon: 2,160 miles, about the distance from San Francisco to Chicago.

Circumference of the Moon: 6,785 miles, about the distance from Chicago to Athens, Greece.

Surface area: 14,650,000 square miles, about four times the area of the United States.

Mass: 81,000 trillion tons.

Gravity: One-sixth that of the Earth. A man who weighs 180 pounds on Earth weighs only 30 pounds when on the surface of the Moon.

Sidereal month (period of Moon's revolution around Earth in relation to the stars): 27 days, 7 hours, 43 minutes, 11.5 seconds.

Synodic month (period of Moon's revolution around Earth in relation to Sun): 29 days, 12 hours, and 44 minutes.

Average speed traveling around the Earth: 2,287 miles an hour.

Distance from the Earth: *Closest,* 221,456 miles; *farthest,* 252,711 miles, *mean distance,* 238,875 miles.

Length of a day on the Moon: 14 Earth days.

Distance traveled in orbit each year: 1,500,000 miles.

Temperature at noon on the Moon: 243 ° F., hot enough to boil water.

Temperature at midnight on the Moon: –297 ° F., cold enough to freeze carbon dioxide into dry ice.

Escape velocity from the Moon: 1.5 miles per second, or about 5,400 miles an hour.

CALENDAR OF PHASES OF THE MOON: 1984

Source: *Astronomical Phenomena,* U.S. Naval Observatory; all times are Eastern Standard Time (EST)

NEW MOON		FIRST QUARTER		FULL MOON		LAST QUARTER	
Day	Time	Day	Time	Day	Time	Day	Time
Jan. 2	12:16 A.M.	Jan. 11	4:48 A.M.	Jan. 18	9:05 A.M.	Jan. 24	11:48 P.M.
Feb. 1	6:46 P.M.	Feb. 9	11:00 P.M.	Feb. 16	7:41 P.M.	Feb. 23	12:12 P.M.
Mar. 2	1:31 P.M.	Mar. 10	1:27 P.M.	Mar. 17	5:10 A.M.	March 24	2:58 A.M.
April 1	7:10 A.M.	April 8	11:51 P.M.	April 15	2:11 P.M.	April 22	7:26 P.M.
April 30	10:45 P.M.	May 8	6:50 A.M.	May 14	11:29 P.M.	May 22	12:45 P.M.
May 30	11:48 A.M.	June 6	11:42 A.M.	June 13	9:42 A.M.	June 21	6:10 A.M.
June 28	10:18 P.M.	July 5	4:04 P.M.	July 12	9:20 P.M.	July 20	11:01 P.M.
July 28	6:51 A.M.	Aug. 3	9:33 P.M.	Aug. 11	10:43 A.M.	Aug. 19	2:40 P.M.
Aug. 26	2:25 P.M.	Sept. 2	5:30 A.M.	Sept. 10	2:01 A.M.	Sept. 18	4:31 A.M.
Sept. 24	10:11 P.M.	Oct. 1	4:52 P.M.	Oct. 9	6:58 P.M.	Oct. 17	4:14 P.M.
Oct. 24	7:08 A.M.	Oct. 31	8:07 A.M.	Nov. 8	12:43 P.M.	Nov. 16	1:59 A.M.
Nov. 22	5:57 P.M.	Nov. 30	3:00 A.M.	Dec. 8	5:53 A.M.	Dec. 15	10:25 A.M.
Dec. 22	6:47 A.M.	Dec. 30	12:27 A.M.	—	—	—	—

PHASES OF THE MOON

The Moon shines only by reflected light. Its phases, or apparent changes in shape, result from the varying part of the sunlit hemisphere of the Moon visible to observers on Earth. Its lighted portion varies in shape because of the relative positions of the Moon, the Sun, and the Earth.

At New Moon, when the Moon is on the line between the Sun and the Earth, eclipses of the Sun by the Moon may occur if the Moon is properly positioned.

The Moon moves on in its orbit of the Earth from west to east. It passes through its waxing Crescent phase into First Quarter when it is at Half Moon.

Through the waxing Gibbous phase, it comes then to Full Moon, on the opposite side of the Earth from the Sun, when the Earth's shadow may be cast across the Moon in lunar eclipses.

The Moon moves on through waning Gibbous into Last Quarter. It then passes through the waning Crescent phase into New Moon again.

Occasionally the unlit portion of the Moon facing the Earth glows in "earthshine" (sunlight reflected from the Earth to the Moon and back again). Certain parts of the Moon, such as the bright crater Aristarchus, are especially reflective.

The worst storms have been found to be significantly related to lunar phases. Such storms are more likely to occur, in the long run, from 1 to 3 days after New Moon and from 3 to 5 days after Full Moon. Similar relationships between storms and the phases of the Moon have been reported in many parts of the world.

The magnetic disturbances that sometimes disrupt radio communications, and the beginning of hurricanes in the Caribbean, have been found to be similarly related to lunar positions. The way in which these effects are produced is still a mystery.

THE CONSTELLATIONS

When you look up on a clear night at the stars, many of them appear to be clustered in groups called constellations.

Ancient observers gave 48 constellations names suggested by the patterns of their stars.

Usually the stars forming these apparent groups are entirely unrelated and are located at greatly varying distances, although all the stars visible to the naked eye are in our own Milky Way galaxy.

Modern astronomers recognize 88 constellations, including most of the ancient ones.

Strict boundaries for the constellations were established by the International Astronomical Union in 1928.

The constellation boundaries are used as reference areas for locating, naming, and classifying the stars, and for roughly fixing the positions of comets, meteors, and other celestial bodies viewed in the sky.

The table names the constellations. Those marked with an asterisk (*) are not visible from midnorthern latitudes.

LATIN NAME	ENGLISH	LATIN NAME	ENGLISH	LATIN NAME	ENGLISH
Andromeda	Chained Maiden	Boötes	Herdsman	Carina *	Keel
Antila	Air Pump	Caelum	Chisel	Cassiopeia	Lady in Chair
Apus *	Bird of Paradise	Camelopardalis	Giraffe	Centaurus *	Centaur
Aquarius	Water Bearer	Cancer	Crab	Cepheus	King
Aquila	Eagle	Canes Venatici	Hunting Dogs	Cetus	Whale
Ara *	Altar	Canis Major	Great Dog	Chamaeleon *	Chameleon
Aries	Ram	Canis Minor	Small Dog	Circinus *	Compasses
Auriga	Charioteer	Capricornus	Sea Goat	Columba	Dove

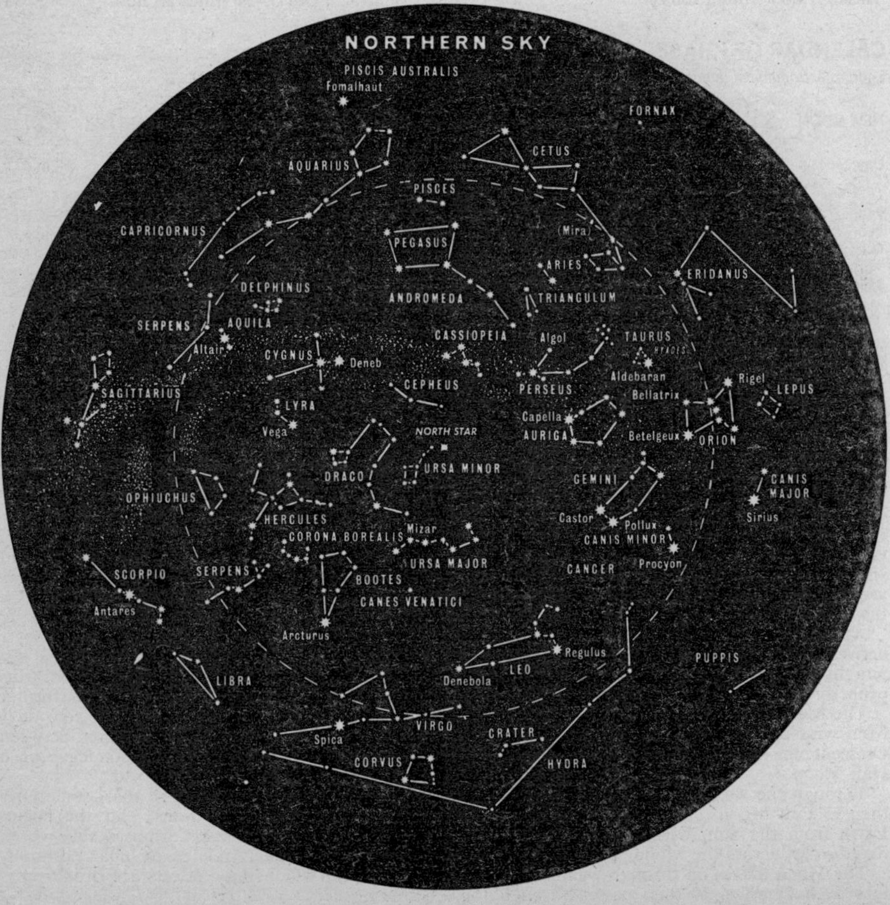

LATIN NAME	ENGLISH	LATIN NAME	ENGLISH	LATIN NAME	ENGLISH
Coma Berenices . . .	Berenice's Hair	Leo Minor	Small Lion	Pyxis	Compass
Corona Australis . .	Southern Crown	Lepus	Hare	Reticulum *	Net
Corona Borealis . . .	Northern Crown	Libra	Scales	Sagitta	Arrow
Corvus	Crow	Lupus *	Wolf	Sagittarius	Archer
Crater	Cup	Lynx	Lynx	Scorpius	Scorpion
Crux *	(Southern) Cross	Lyra	Lyre	Sculptor	Sculptor
Cygnus	Swan	Mensa *	Table (Mountain)	Scutum	Shield
Delphinus	Dolphin	Microscopium	Microscope	Serpens	Serpent
Dorado *	Swordfish	Monoceros	Unicorn	Sextans	Sextant
Draco	Dragon	Musca *	Fly	Taurus	Bull
Equuleus	Little Horse	Norma *	Square	Telescopium *	Telescope
Eridanus	River Eridanus	Octans *	Octant	Trianguium	Triangle
Fornax	Furnace	Ophiuchus	Serpent Bearer	Triangulum Australe*	Southern Triangle
Gemini	Twins	Orion	Hunter	Tucana *	Toucan
Grus *	Crane	Pavo *	Peacock	Ursa Major	Great Bear
Hercules	Hercules	Pegasus	Pegasus	Ursa Minor	Small Bear
Horologium *	Clock	Perseus	Champion	Vela *	Sails
Hydra	Sea Serpent	Phoenix *	Phoenix	Virgo	Virgin
Hydrus *	Water Snake	Pictor *	Painter's (Easel)	Volans *	Flying Fish
Indus *	Indian	Pisces	Fishes	Vulpecula	Fox
Lacerta	Lizard	Piscis Austrinus . . .	Southern Fish		
Leo	Lion	Puppis	Poop (Stern)		

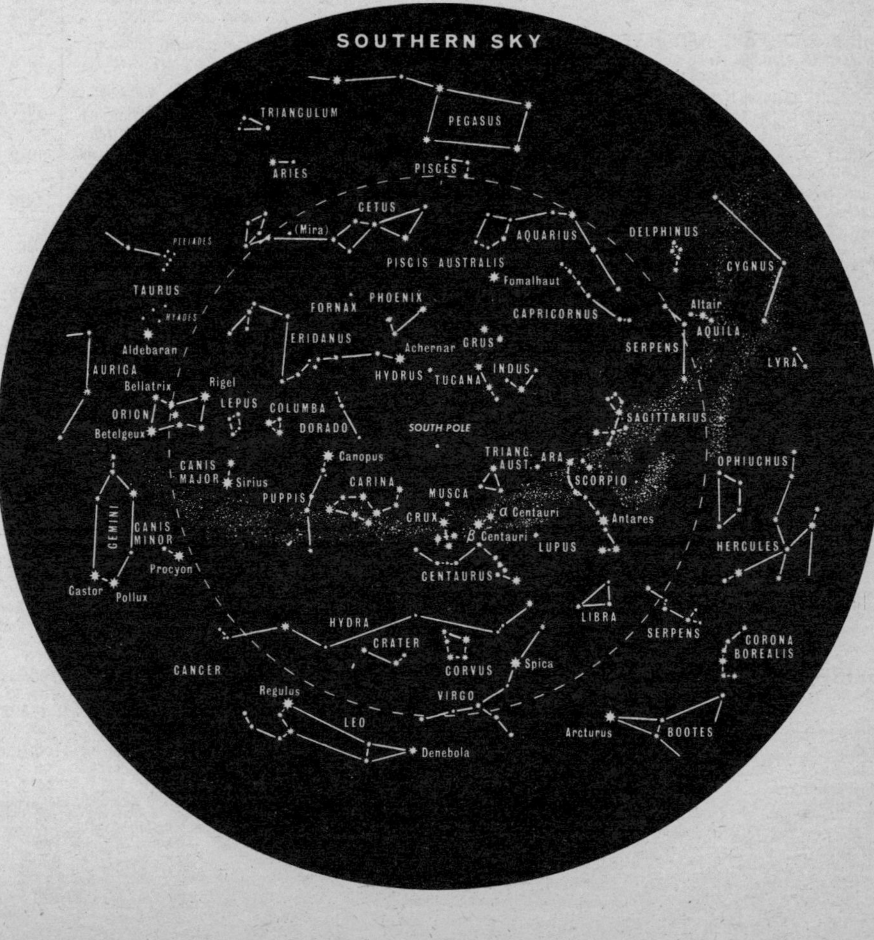

ASTRONOMICAL TELESCOPES

A *refractor* telescope uses a lens to collect light from a distant object and bring it to a focus. A *reflector* telescope uses a concave mirror for the same purpose.

Because lenses fail to bring all colors to the same focus, most large astronomical telescopes built in the past 50 years are reflectors.

Today, visual observations are rarely made with astronomical telescopes, for photographs can record objects much fainter than the eye can see. Large telescopes thus are used as cameras or to collect light for analysis in other ways.

Radio telescopes are used to study radio waves coming from celestial objects.

LARGE REFRACTING TELESCOPES

Source: U. S. Naval Observatory

DIAMETER OF LENS	OBSERVATORY AND LOCATION	YEAR
40.0 in. (1.02 m.)	Yerkes Observatory, Williams Bay, Wisconsin	1897
36.0 in. (0.91 m.)	Lick Observatory, Mt. Hamilton, California	1888
32.7 in. (0.83 m.)	Paris Observatory, Meudon, France	1889
32.0 in. (0.81 m.)	Astrophysical Observatory, Potsdam, East Germany ..	1899
30.0 in. (0.76 m.)	Allegheny Observatory, Pittsburgh, Pennsylvania .	1914
29.1 in. (0.74 m.)	Nice Observatory at Mont Gros, Nice, France	1886

LARGE RADIO AND RADAR TELESCOPES

Source: U.S. National Radio Astronomy Observatory

SIZE	OBSERVATORY	YEAR
27 x 82 ft., 23 mi. (36 km.)[1]	National Radio Astronomy Observatory, Socorro, N.M.	1980
16,000 ft. (4.9 km.)[1]	Mullard Observatory, Cambridge, England	1972
2.05 mi. (3.3 km.)[1] interferometer.	Clark Lake Radio Obs., Borrego Springs, Calif.	1975
1.86 mi. (3 km.)[2]	CSIRO, Culgoora, Australia ..	1967
1.86 mi. (3 km.)[1]	Netherlands Foundation for Radio Astronomy, Westerbork, Neth.	1973
1.44 mi. (2.3 km.)[1] interferometer.	U. of Tokyo Observatory, Nobeyama, Japan	1970
1,890 ft. (576 m.)[3]	Special Astrophysical Obs., Zelenchukskaya, USSR ...	1976
1,837 ft. (560 m.)[1]	U. of Tokyo Observatory, Nobeyama, Japan	1983
1,000 ft. (305 m.)[3]	Arecibo Obs., Puerto Rico ...	1974[5]
1,000 ft. (305 m.)[3]	Radio Astronomy Station, Nançay, France	1964
328 ft. (100 m.)[3].	Max Planck Institute, Effelsberg, West Germany	1970
300 ft. (91.4 m.)[3]	National Radio Astronomy Obs., Green Bank, W. Va. .	1963
250 ft. (76.2 m.)[3]	Nuffield Laboratories, Jodrell Bank, England	1971[5]
210 ft. (64 m.)[3] ..	NASA, Goldstone, California.	1966

LARGE REFLECTING TELESCOPES

Source: U.S. Naval Observatory

DIAMETER OF MIRROR	OBSERVATORY AND LOCATION	YEAR
236 in. (6 m.)....	Special Astrophysical Obs., Zelenchukskaya, USSR ...	1976
200 in. (5.08 m.) .	Hale Observatory, Palomar Mountain, California	1948
175 in. (4.5 m.) .. (6 x 72 in. mirrors)	Multiple Mirror Telescope, Mt. Hopkins, Arizona	1979
158 in. (4 m.)....	Kitt Peak National Observatory, Tucson, Arizona	1973
158 in. (4 m.)....	Cerro Tololo Inter-American Observatory, Chile	1974
153 in. (3.9 m.) ..	Anglo-Australian Telescope, Siding Spring, Australia ...	1975
150 in. (3.8 m.)[6] .	British Infrared Telescope, Mauna Kea, Hawaii	1978
144 in. (3.66 m.) .	Canada-France-Hawaii Telescope, Mauna Kea, Hawaii.	1979
142 in. (3.6 m.) ..	European Southern Observatory, La Silla, Chile	1976
138 in. (3.5 m.) ..	Max Planck Institute of Astrophysics, W. Germany	UC
126 in. (3.20 m.)[6]	NASA-U. of Hawaii, Mauna Kea, Hawaii	1979
120 in. (3.05 m.) .	Lick Observatory, Mt. Hamilton, California	1959
107 in. (2.72 m.) .	McDonald Observatory, Fort Davis, Texas	1968
102 in. (2.59 m.) .	Crimean Astrophysical Obs., Simferopol, USSR	1960
100 in. (2.54 m.) .	Hale Observatory, Mt. Wilson, California	1917
100 in. (2.54 m.) .	Carnegie Institution, Las Campanas, Chile.........	1976
98 in. (2.49 m.)...	Isaac Newton Telescope, La Palma, Canary Islands .	1979

1 Baseline interferometer. 2 Diameter, radioheliograph. 3 Diameter, single antenna for centimeter wavelengths and longer. 4 Diameter, single antennas for millimeter wavelengths. 5 Upgraded. 6 Infrared telescope. UC=under construction.

BRIGHTEST STARS

STARS	GREEK LETTER AND CONSTELLATION	APPARENT MAGNITUDE	ABSOLUTE MAGNITUDE	DISTANCE IN LIGHT-YEARS
Sun	Sun	–26.73	4.84	—
Sirius	Alpha Canis Majoris	– 1.42	1.45	8.7
Canopus	Alpha Carinae	– 0.72	–3.10	98
Rigil Kentaurus	Alpha Centauri A	– 0.01	4.39	4.3
Arcturus	Alpha Boötis	– 0.06	–0.3	36
Vega	Alpha Lyrae	0.04	0.5	26.5
Capella	Alpha Aurigae	0.05	–0.6	45
Rigel	Beta Orionis	0.14	–7.1	900
Procyon	Alpha Canis Minoris	0.37	2.7	11.3
Betelgeuse	Alpha Orionis	0.41	–5.6	520

Sports and Games

Wide World

Australia II, foreground, became the first challenger to win the prestigious America's Cup in the 132 years of competition for yachting's most coveted prize. On Sept. 26, *Australia II* crossed the finish line 41 seconds ahead of the U.S. entry *Liberty,* at Newport R.I., for its fourth victory in the best-of-seven series. Skippered by John Bertrand, *Australia II* had to overcome a 3–1 deficit and win three consecutive races to win the cup. In the final race, *Liberty,* with Dennis Conner at the helm, led at the start and was leading by 57 seconds at the fourth mark, when *Australia II* pulled ahead for good. During the Cup trials in the summer, officials of the New York Yacht Club, which sponsors the races, objected to the Australian yacht's controversial winged keel, but withdrew its objections Aug. 26. Many observers felt the success of *Australia II* was due to the keel design, which allowed her to turn faster and point closer to the wind.

SPORTS AND GAMES: CONTENTS

MAJOR U.S. SPORTS AWARDS

ATHLETE OF THE YEAR (Associated Press)

YEAR	MALE ATHLETE	SPORT	YEAR	FEMALE ATHLETE	SPORT
1940	Tommy Harmon	Football	1940	Alice Marble	Tennis
1941	Joe DiMaggio	Baseball	1941	Betty Hicks Newell	Golf
1942	Frank Sinkwich	Football	1942	Gloria Callen	Swimming
1943	Gunder Haegg	Track	1943	Patty Berg	Golf
1944	Byron Nelson	Golf	1944	Ann Curtis	Swimming
1945	Byron Nelson	Golf	1945	Babe Didrikson Zaharias	Golf
1946	Glenn Davis	Football	1946	Babe Didrikson Zaharias	Golf
1947	Johnny Lujack	Football	1947	Babe Didrikson Zaharias	Golf
1948	Lou Boudreau	Baseball	1948	Fanny Blankers-Koen	Track
1949	Leon Hart	Football	1949	Marlene Bauer	Golf
1950	Jim Konstanty	Baseball	1950	Babe Didrikson Zaharias	Golf
1951	Dick Kazmaier	Football	1951	Maureen Connolly	Tennis
1952	Bob Mathias	Track and Football	1952	Maureen Connolly	Tennis
1953	Ben Hogan	Golf	1953	Maureen Connolly	Tennis
1954	Willie Mays	Baseball	1954	Babe Didrikson Zaharias	Golf
1955	Hopalong Cassady	Football	1955	Patty Berg	Golf
1956	Mickey Mantle	Baseball	1956	Pat McCormick	Diving
1957	Ted Williams	Baseball	1957	Althea Gibson	Tennis
1958	Herb Elliott	Track	1958	Althea Gibson	Tennis
1959	Ingemar Johansson	Boxing	1959	Maria Bueno	Tennis
1960	Rafer Johnson	Decathlon	1960	Wilma Rudolph	Track
1961	Roger Maris	Baseball	1961	Wilma Rudolph	Track
1962	Maury Wills	Baseball	1962	Dawn Fraser	Swimming
1963	Sandy Koufax	Baseball	1963	Mickey Wright	Golf
1964	Don Schollander	Swimming	1964	Mickey Wright	Golf
1965	Sandy Koufax	Baseball	1965	Kathy Whitworth	Golf
1966	Frank Robinson	Baseball	1966	Kathy Whitworth	Golf
1967	Carl Yastrzemski	Baseball	1967	Billie Jean King	Tennis
1968	Denny McLain	Baseball	1968	Peggy Fleming	Ice Skating
1969	Tom Seaver	Baseball	1969	Debbie Meyer	Swimming
1970	George Blanda	Football	1970	Chi Cheng	Track
1971	Lee Trevino	Golf	1971	Evonne Goolagong	Tennis
1972	Mark Spitz	Swimming	1972	Olga Korbut	Gymnastics
1973	O.J. Simpson	Football	1973	Billie Jean King	Tennis
1974	Muhammad Ali	Boxing	1974	Chris Evert	Tennis
1975	Fred Lynn	Baseball	1975	Chris Evert	Tennis
1976	Bruce Jenner	Track	1976	Nadia Comaneci	Gymnastics
1977	Steve Cauthen	Horse Racing	1977	Chris Evert	Tennis
1978	Ron Guidry	Baseball	1978	Nancy Lopez	Golf
1979	Willie Stargell	Baseball	1979	Tracy Austin	Tennis
1980	U.S. Olympic Team	Hockey	1980	Chris Evert	Tennis
1981	John McEnroe	Tennis	1981	Tracy Austin	Tennis
1982	Wayne Gretzky	Hockey	1982	Mary Decker Tabb	Track

JAMES E. SULLIVAN MEMORIAL TROPHY (Amateur Athletic Union)

1933	Glenn Cunningham	Track	1958	Glenn Davis	Track (Sprinter)
1934	Bill Bonthron	Track	1959	Parry O'Brien	Track (Shot Put)
1935	Lawson Little	Golf	1960	Rafer Johnson	Track (Decathlon)
1936	Glenn Morris	Track (Decathlon)	1961	Wilma Rudolph	Track (Sprinter)
1937	Don Budge	Tennis	1962	Jim Beatty	Track
1938	Don Lash	Track	1963	John Pennel	Track (Pole Vaulter)
1939	Joe Burk	Rowing	1964	Don Schollander	Swimming
1940	Greg Rice	Track	1965	Bill Bradley	Basketball
1941	Les MacMitchell	Track	1966	Jim Ryun	Track (Mile Runner)
1942	Cornelius Warmerdam	Track (Pole Vaulter)	1967	Randy Matson	Track (Shot Put)
1943	Gil Dodds	Track	1968	Debbie Meyer	Swimming
1944	Ann Curtis	Swimming	1969	Bill Toomey	Track (Decathlon)
1945	Doc Blanchard	Football	1970	John Kinsella	Swimming
1946	Arnold Tucker	Football	1971	Mark Spitz	Swimming
1947	Jack Kelly Jr.	Rowing	1972	Frank Shorter	Track (Distance Runner)
1948	Bob Mathias	Track (Decathlon)	1973	Bill Walton	Basketball
1949	Dick Button	Figure Skating	1974	Rick Wohlhuter	Track
1950	Fred Wilt	Track	1975	Tim Shaw	Swimming
1951	Bob Richards	Track (Pole Vaulter)	1976	Bruce Jenner	Track
1952	Horace Ashenfelter	Track (Distance Runner)	1977	John Naber	Swimming
1953	Sammy Lee	Diving	1978	Tracy Caulkins	Swimming
1954	Mal Whitfield	Track (Runner)	1979	Kurt Thomas	Gymnastics
1955	Harrison Dillard	Track (Sprinter)	1980	Eric Heiden	Speed skating
1956	Pat McCormick	Diving	1981	Carl Lewis	Track
1957	Bobby Joe Morrow	Track (Sprinter)	1982	Mary Decker Tabb	Track

PEOPLE IN SPORTS

U.S. skier Phil Mahre races to victory during second run of Aspen World Cup Giant Slalom on March 7. He clocked 1:15.89 for a total of 2:31.49 to win, assuring him his third consecutive World Cup Championship. He accumulated 248 points for the season, defeating his closest challenger, Sweden's Ingemar Stenmark, who had won the championship in 1976–78. See page 859 for other skiing highlights.

Joan Benoit, 25, of Boston, Mass., set a new world record for the women's marathon at the Boston Marathon April 18. Her time of 2:22.42 was nearly three minutes faster than the previous record of 2:25.29 set by New Zealand's **Allison Roe** in 1981. Ironically, that record was tied by Norway's **Grete Waitz** the day before, on April 17, in the London Marathon. . . . The overall winner of the Boston race was **Greg Meyer,** of Wellesley, Mass., with a time of 2:09.00.

Rod Dixon, of New Zealand, won the New York Marathon, Oct. 23, after taking the lead from Britain's **Geoff Smith** only in the last mile. Dixon ran the race in 2:08:59, the second-fastest New York marathon in history, and only nine seconds ahead of Smith's second-place finish. . . . **Grete Waitz,** of Norway, won her fifth New York women's marathon with a time of 2:27:00.

Ron Tabb, of Eugene, Ore., won the first Australian marathon, June 12 in Sydney, with a time of 2:10.53. **Annick Loir-Lebreton,** of France, won the women's division in 2:37.46.8.

More than 50 leading women runners from 20 nations, including **Mary Decker** and **Grete Waitz,** filed a sex discrimination suit in August against the International Olympic Committee, the Los Angeles Olympic Organizing Committee, and other international track authorities. The suit asks that 5,000- and 10,000-meter runs for women be included in the 1984 Olympic Games in Los Angeles. A women's marathon and 3,000-meter run have been added to the 1984 women's competition, but the female runners feel they need long-distance events, as are on the men's program.

Two brothers from Keswick, Cumbria, England, completed a record run across the Himalayas in 101 days in June. **Richard,** 29, and **Adrian Crane,** 27, arrived in Rawalpindi, Pakistan, June 28, after a journey that included crossing 64 passes and climbing a total of 300,000 feet—equal to more than 10 times the height of Mt. Everest. The greatest distance they covered in one day was 52 miles. Overall, they were on the move for more than 700 hours. The brothers were attempting to raise money for Intermediate Technology, an organization working for improvement in the Third World.

Ferdie Adoboe, 19, of Ghana, a student at the University of Massachusetts, set a world record running a 100-yard dash backward in 12.8 seconds in July. . . . **Harold Johnson,** 34, of Santa Monica, Calif., won the second annual Manhattan Island Marathon Swim on July 24, finishing the 28.5-mile course in 8 hours, 15 minutes, 45 seconds. **Julie Billingsley,** 24, of Washington, D.C., was the first woman to cross the finish line at 8:33.39.

Samantha Druce, 12, became the youngest

PEOPLE IN SPORTS *(continued)*

person to swim the English Channel on Aug. 19. Another 12-year-old, **Alison Wetherly,** gained the honor on Aug. 18 but lost it the next day because Samantha is 43 days younger than Alison. . . . **Alison Streeter,** 18, became the first British woman to swim the Channel both ways on Aug. 4. The round-trip swim took 21 hours and 16 minutes.

French diver **Philippe Jeantot,** 31, won the BOC Challenge, setting a new world record in the first single-handed sailing race around the world. Jeantot, in a 56-foot aluminum cutter, the *Crèdit Agricole,* circumnavigated the globe in 159 days, 2 hours, 26 minutes. He crossed the finish line in Newport, R.I., on May 9, after a 27,550-mile journey that began Aug. 28, 1982. The previous record for solo global sailing was 169 days, 4 hours, 11 minutes, set by **Alain Colas** of France, in 1973–74.

British adventurer **Peter Bird,** 36, barely missed in his attempt to become the first man to row alone across the Pacific Ocean. On June 15, he was forced to ask the Australian Navy to rescue him from stormy seas just 33 nautical miles short of his goal of completing the 8,990-mile journey from San Francisco, Calif., to Australia. His 39-foot boat *Hele on Britannia,* broke up as it was being towed to a Queensland naval base. He began his 10-month voyage in August 1982.

Frenchman **Laurent Fignon,** 22, won the 70th Tour de France bicycling race on July 24, finishing the 22-stage event in 105 hours, 7 minutes, 52 seconds. . . . In June, **Patricia Kimmel,** 12, of Cumberland, Md., won the girls' division of the 60th Annual National Marbles Tournament. **Kerry Acord,** 11, of Mount View, W.Va., won the boys' championship. . . . **Bill Kennedy,** 21, of Libertyville, Ill., set a new record for marathon bowling in August, when he rolled 911 games, knocking down 112,402 pins in 161 hours.

The East Marietta, Ga., team won the Little League World Series in Williamsport, Pa., on Aug. 27, defeating the team from the Dominican Republic, 3–1. . . . A team from Culver City, Calif., won the Babe Ruth World Series Championship in Frederick, Md., on the same day, with a 16–11 victory over the Nashville, Tenn., team.

Belgian mountain climber **Jean Bourgeois,** 44, turned up safe in Katmandu, Nepal, on Jan. 14, two weeks after he disappeared and was given up for dead on Mt. Everest. Bourgeois fell Dec. 30, 1982, while climbing with an 11-man French team, and a search for him was abandoned Jan. 2. Having only a vague recollection of the accident, Bourgeois said he had walked for nearly three days after his fall and found himself in a Tibetan village on Jan. 1. He encountered some Chinese on Jan. 4, who brought him to the Nepal border, giving him bus fare to Katmandu.

George Meehan, 30, of Kent, England, ended what is believed the longest walk of all time on Sept. 18. His 19,000-mile walk from the southern tip of South America to the Beaufort Sea, in northern Alaska, began on Jan. 26, 1977, and took 2,426 days.

Tom McEvoy, of Grand Rapids, Mich., won the World Championship of Poker in Dublin, Ireland, in September. . . . **Angel Cordero Jr.,** 40, became the fourth jockey in Thoroughbred racing history to win 5,000 races when he rode three winners at New York's Belmont Park on June 29. . . . **George Anctil,** 94, of Duluth, Minn., hit his fourth hole-in-one on June 1, the oldest man to hit a hole-in-one on a regulation course, according to *Golf Digest.*

In February, **Albert McReynolds,** 36, was awarded $250,000 from a tackle manufacturer for catching a 78½-pound striped bass off Atlantic City, N.J., in September 1982. . . . In May **Jimmy Crisp,** of Seymour, Mo., won the Western Bass U.S. Invitational Tournament at Table Rock Lake in Kimberling City, Mo. He won $100,000 for his five-fish total weight of 25.18 pounds. . . . **Larry Pease,** 65, and **Phil Reilly,** 66, each received $500,000 for catching one of five tagged fish during a fish derby in Puget Sound in August.

Stephanie Shinn, 13, of Moses Lake, Wash., set a world record by staying aloft for 1 hour, 11 minutes in a small-class hot-air balloon in May. . . . Jockey **Jill Kaenel** celebrated her 16th birthday by winning one race and coming in third in two others at Pimlico Race Course in April.

Rodney Barton, sophomore at Arizona State University, won the men's singles title in the National Collegiate Badminton Championships in Washington, D.C., in April. . . . **Claire Allison,** of the University of Wisconsin, won the women's singles title.

Chinese tennis player **Hu Na** was granted political asylum by the U.S. in April, touching off a political conflict between the U.S. and China. Hu Na had defected in July 1982.

On Jan. 18, the family of Olympic star **Jim Thorpe** formally received the gold medals for pentathlon and decathlon won at the 1912 Olympics and taken away after disclosure that he had been paid to play baseball at an earlier time. At a Los Angeles ceremony, **Antonio Samaranch,** president of the International Olympic Committee, presented the gold medals to Thorpe's children. Thorpe died in 1953.

Walter Poenisch, 69, accepted a $15,000 settlement of a $1.5 million lawsuit against three defendants, including swimmer **Diana Nyad,** who accused him of faking a world record swim from Cuba to Florida in 1978.

AWARDS AND HONORS

The Women's Sports Foundation, in September, named tennis ace **Martina Navratilova** its professional sportswoman of the year, and runner **Mary Decker** its amateur sportswoman of the year. . . .The foundation's Women's Sports Hall of Fame chose swimmer **Donna De Varona,** figure skater **Tenley Albright,** skier **Andrea Mead Lawrence,** field athlete **Helen Stephens,** and diver **Micki King Hogue** for induction in 1983.

President Reagan awarded the Presidential Citizens Medal posthumously to Kansas City Chiefs running back **Joe Delaney** in July. Delaney drowned on June 9 while trying to save three children from drowning in Monroe, La. Two of the children died, but one scrambled to safety.

Baltimore Orioles owner **Edward Bennett Williams** received the Torch of Learning Award of the American Friends of the Hebrew University. . . .On July 6 the U.S. Postal Service issued a 20-cent commemorative stamp honoring baseball star **Babe Ruth**. . . .Boston Red Sox player **Carl Yastrzemski,** who retired from baseball after the 1983 season, was awarded an honorary docorate in physical education from Providence College in May.

Jacquelyn and **John Hernandez** of San Francisco, parents of St. Louis Cardinals first baseman **Keith Hernandez,** were named 1983 Baseball Parents of the Year in April by the Little League Baseball Association.

Tennis ace **Chris Evert Lloyd** was elected president of the Women's Tennis Association (WTA) in August. . . .**Martina Navratilova** was voted Player of the Year by the WTA, and **Carling Bassett** was named Most Impressive Newcomer. . . .**Mary Decker** received the Tanqueray Achievement Award as the world's top female distance runner in May. In March, she received the Jesse Owens International award as the top amateur athlete in the world. . . .Sportswriter **Shirley Povich** received the Red Smith award from the Associated Press in June in honor of his 60-year career with the *Washington Post.*

Drivers **Duke Nalon, Harlan Fengler, Gil Anderson,** and **Clif Durant,** car builder **Frank Kurtis,** driver-mechanic **Myron Stevens,** and carburetor designer **Ed Winfield** were elected to the Auto Racing Hall of Fame in April. . . .The Professional Bowlers Association (PBA) Hall of Fame added tournament director **Harry Golden** and national titleist **Bill Allen** to its membership in May. . . .In March, the PBA named **Sam Zurich,** 26, of Huntington, N.Y., to receive its 17th annual Steve Nagy Sportsmanship Award.

World Tennis magazine selected **Billie Jean King** and **Rod Laver** as the most significant players in the past 30 years. . . .Chicago Cubs broadcaster **Jack Brickhouse** was inducted into the Hall of Fame of the National Sportscasters and Sportswriters Association in April.

Former basketball stars **Bill Bradley, Dave DeBusschere, Jack Twyman,** coach **Dean Smith,** and, posthumously, referee **Lloyd Keith** and AAU president **Lou Wilke,** were inducted into the Naismith Memorial Basketball Hall of Fame in May. . . .Milwaukee Brewers first baseman **Cecil Cooper** won the 13th annual Roberto Clemente Award for "best exemplifying the game."

Former hockey players **Bobby Hull, Stan Mikita,** and **Ken Dryden** were elected to the Hockey Hall of Fame in June. . . .The Track Hall of Fame announced election of five new members in April. They were former track and field stars **Lee Evans, Mildred McDaniel,** and the late **Archie Hahn,** former U.S. Olympic team coach **Dr. LeRoy Walker,** and **Tom Botts,** University of Missouri coach in 1941–72.

U.S. Postal Service

The U.S. Postal Service issued a block of four 35-cent international airmail stamps on Nov. 4, 1983, commemorating the 1984 Olympic Games. Tickets to the 1984 Summer Games, to be held at Los Angeles, went on sale June 15, through a nationwide mail-order system. Order forms were available at Sears, Roebuck and Co. outlets and some New York and California banks. The 1984 Games are to be orchestrated by the Los Olympic Organizing Committee, Los Angeles, CA 90084.

AUTOMOBILE RACING

United Press Int'l.

Pace car, *right*, pulls down pit road at start of Indianapolis 500-mile race on May 29, 1983. Tom Sneva, won the race, averaging 162.117 mph, second fastest in Indy 500 history. Al Unser Sr. was second by only 11.1 seconds, despite efforts of his son Al Unser Jr., who intentionally blocked Sneva for several laps while his father was ahead, hoping Sneva would fall further behind. Sneva finally passed during lap 191. Unser Jr., who finished in 10th place, was penalized two laps for passing during a caution period.

WINNERS OF THE INDIANAPOLIS 500

YEAR	WINNER	CAR	AVG. SPEED
1911	Ray Harroun	Marmon	74.590
1912	Joe Dawson	National	78.720
1913	Jules Goux	Peugeot	75.930
1914	Rene Thomas	Delage	82.470
1915	Ralph De Palma	Mercedes	89.840
1916	Dario Resta	Peugeot	84.000[1]
1919	Howard Wilcox	Peugeot	88.050
1920	Gaston Chevrolet	Monroe	88.620
1921	Tommy Milton	Frontenac	89.620
1922	Jim Murphy	Murphy Special	94.480
1923	Tommy Milton	H.C.S. Special	90.950
1924	L. L. Corum, Joe Boyer	Duesenberg Special	98.230
1925	Peter De Paolo	Duesenberg Special	101.130
1926	Frank Lockhart	Miller Special	95.904[2]
1927	George Souders	Duesenberg	97.545
1928	Louis Meyer	Miller Special	99.482
1929	Ray Keech	Simplex Special	97.585
1930	Billy Arnold	Hartz-Miller	100.448
1931	Louis Schneider	Bowes Special	96.629
1932	Fred Frame	Miller Special	104.144
1933	Louis Meyer	Miller Special	104.162
1934	Bill Cummings	Miller Special	104.863
1935	Kelly Petillo	Gilmore Special	106.240
1936	Louis Meyer	Ring Free Special	109.069
1937	Wilbur Shaw	Shaw-Gilmore Spcl.	113.580
1938	Floyd Roberts	Burd Piston Reg. Special	117.200
1939	Wilbur Shaw	Boyle Special	115.035
1940	Wilbur Shaw	Boyle Special	114.277
1941	Mauri Rose, Floyd Davis	Noc-Out Hose Clamp Special	115.117
1946	George Robson	Thorne Eng. Special	114.820
1947	Mauri Rose	Blue Crown Special	116.338
1948	Mauri Rose	Blue Crown Special	119.814
1949	Bill Holland	Blue Crown Special	121.327
1950	Johnny Parsons	Wynn's Special	124.002[3]
1951	Lee Wallard	Balanger Special	126.244
1952	Troy Ruttman	Agajanian Special	128.922
1953	Bill Vukovich	Fuel Injection Special	128,740
1954	Bill Vukovich	Fuel Injection Special	130.840
1955	Bob Sweikert	John Zink Special	128.209
1956	Pat Flaherty	John Zink Special	128.490
1957	Sam Hanks	Belond Exhaust Spcl.	135.601
1958	Jimmy Bryan	Belond AP Special	133.791
1959	Rodger Ward	Leader Card 500	135.857
1960	Jim Rathman	Ken-Paul Special	138.767
1961	A. J. Foyt	Bowes Seal Special	139.130
1962	Rodger Ward	Leader Card 500	140.293
1963	Parnelli Jones	Agajanian-Willard Spcl.	143.137
1964	A. J. Foyt	S.T.W. Offenhauser	147.350
1965	Jim Clark	Lotus-Ford	150.686
1966	Graham Hill	Lotus-Ford	144.317
1967	A. J. Foyt	Coyote Ford	151.207
1968	Bobby Unser	Eagle-Offenhauser	152.882
1969	Mario Andretti	Hawk-Ford	156.867
1970	Al Unser	Lola-Ford	155.749
1971	Al Unser	P.J. Colt-Ford	157.735
1972	Mark Donohue	McLaren-Offenhauser	162.962*
1973	Gordon Johncock	McLaren-Offenhauser	158.589[4]
1974	Johnny Rutherford	McLaren-Offenhauser	158.589
1975	Bobby Unser	Eagle-Offenhauser	149.213[5]
1976	J. Rutherford	McLaren-Offenhauser	148.725[6]
1977	A. J. Foyt	Coyote Foyt	161.331
1978	Al Unser	Lola-Cosworth	161.363
1979	Rick Mears	Penske-Cosworth	158.899
1980	J. Rutherford	Chaparral-Cosworth	142.862
1981	Bobby Unser	Penske-Cosworth	139.084
1982	Gordon Johncock	Wildcat-Cosworth	162.026
1983	Tom Sneva	March-Cosworth	162.117

* Track record. [1] 300 miles. [2] 400 miles. [3] 345 miles. [4] 332.5 miles. [5] 435 miles. [6] 255 miles.

U.S. AUTO CLUB NATIONAL CHAMPIONS (Indy-type cars)

1910	Ray Harroun	**1925**	Peter De Paolo	**1946–48**	Ted Horn	**1967**	A. J. Foyt
1911	Ralph Mulford	**1926**	Harry Hartz	**1949**	Johnnie Parsons	**1968**	Bobby Unser
1912	Ralph De Palma	**1927**	Peter De Paolo	**1950**	Henry Banks	**1969**	Mario Andretti
1913	Earl Cooper	**1928–29**	Louis Meyer	**1951**	Tony Bettenhausen	**1970**	Al Unser
1914	Ralph De Palma	**1930**	Billy Arnold	**1952**	Chuck Stevenson	**1971–72**	Joe Leonard
1915	Earl Cooper	**1931**	Louis Schneider	**1953**	Sam Hanks	**1973**	Roger McCluskey
1916	Dario Resta	**1932**	Bob Carey	**1954**	Jimmy Bryan	**1974**	Bobby Unser
1917	Earl Cooper	**1933**	Louis Meyer	**1955**	Bob Sweikert	**1975**	A. J. Foyt
1918	Ralph Mulford	**1934**	Bill Cummings	**1956–57**	Jimmy Bryan	**1976**	Gordon Johncock
1919	Howard Wilcox	**1935**	Kelly Petillo	**1958**	Tony Bettenhausen	**1977–78**	Tom Sneva
1920	Gaston Chevrolet	**1936**	Mauri Rose	**1959**	Rodger Ward	**1979**	A. J. Foyt
1921	Tommy Milton	**1937**	Wilbur Shaw	**1960–61**	A. J. Foyt	**1980**	Johnny Rutherford
1922	James Murphy	**1938**	Floyd Roberts	**1962**	Rodger Ward	**1981–82**	George Snider
1923	Eddie Hearne	**1939**	Wilbur Shaw	**1963–64**	A. J. Foyt	**1982–83**	Tom Sneva
1924	James Murphy	**1940–41**	Rex Mays	**1965–66**	Mario Andretti		

GRAND PRIX WORLD CHAMPIONS (Formula 1 cars)

1963	Jim Clark, Britain	**1970**	Jochen Rindt, Austria	**1977**	Niki Lauda, Austria
1964	John Surtees, Britain	**1971**	Jackie Stewart, Britain	**1978**	Mario Andretti, United States
1965	Jim Clark, Britain	**1972**	Emerson Fittipaldi, Brazil	**1979**	Jody Scheckter, South Africa
1966	Jack Brabham, Australia	**1973**	Jackie Stewart, Britain	**1980**	Alan Jones, Australia
1967	Denis Hulme, New Zealand	**1974**	Emerson Fittipaldi, Brazil	**1981**	Nelson Piquet, Brazil
1968	Graham Hill, Britain	**1975**	Niki Lauda, Austria	**1982**	Keke Rosberg, Finland
1969	Jackie Stewart, Britain	**1976**	James Hunt, Britain	**1983**	Nelson Piquet, Brazil

SPORTS CAR CLUB OF AMERICA (SCCA) CAN-AM CHALLENGE

YEAR	SERIES WINNER	CAR	YEAR	SERIES WINNER	CAR
1971	Peter Revson	McLaren M8F-Chevy	**1978**	Alan Jones	Lola T-333CS-Chevy
1972	George Follmer...	Porsche 917/10-Porsche (T)	**1979**	Jacky Ickx	Lola T-333CS-Chevy
1973	Mark Donohue ...	Porsche 917/30-Porsche (T)	**1980**	Patrick Tambay ..	Lola T-530-Chevy
1974	Jackie Oliver.....	Shadow DN4-Dodge	**1981**	Geoff Brabham...	V.D.S.-001
1975–76	Not Held		**1982**	Al Unser Jr.......	Galles GR3
1977	Patrick Tambay ..	Lola T-333CS-Chevy	**1983**	Jacques Villeneuve	Frissbee & Galles GR3

WINSTON CUP GRAND NATIONAL CHAMPIONS OF NASCAR (National Association for Stock Car Auto Racing)

YEAR	CHAMPION	CAR	YEAR	CHAMPION	CAR	YEAR	CHAMPION	CAR
1949	Red Byron	Oldsmobile	**1958-59**	Lee Petty	Olds./Plym.	**1970**	Bobby Isaac	Dodge
1950	Bill Rexford	Oldsmobile	**1960**	Rex White	Chevrolet	**1971-72**	Richard Petty	Plym./Dodge
1951	Herb Thomas	Plymouth-Hudson	**1961**	Ned Jarrett	Chevrolet	**1973**	Benny Parsons	Chevrolet
1952	Tim Flock	Hudson	**1962-63**	Joe Weatherly	Pontiac-Merc.	**1974-75**	Richard Petty	Dodge
1953	Herb Thomas	Hudson	**1964**	Richard Petty	Plymouth	**1976-78**	Cale Yarborough	Chev./Olds.
1954	Lee Petty	Chrysler	**1965**	Ned Jarrett	Ford	**1979**	Richard Petty	Olds./Chev.
1955	Tim Flock	Chrysler	**1966**	David Pearson	Dodge	**1980**	Dale Earnhardt	Chevrolet
1956	Buck Baker	Chrysler-Dodge	**1967**	Richard Petty	Plymouth	**1981-82**	Darrell Waltrip	Buick
1957	Buck Baker	Chevrolet	**1968-69**	David Pearson	Ford	**1983**	Bobby Allison	Buick

WINNERS OF THE DAYTONA 500 (Stock Cars)

YEAR	WINNER	CAR	SPEED (mph)	YEAR	WINNER	CAR	SPEED (mph)
1964	Richard Petty	Plymouth .	154.334	**1974**	Richard Petty	Dodge	140.894
1965[1]	Fred Lorenzen.....	Ford	141.539	**1975**	Benny Parsons	Chevrolet .	153.649
1966[2]	Richard Petty	Plymouth .	160.627	**1976**	David Pearson.....	Mercury ..	152.181
1967	Mario Andretti.....	Ford	146.926	**1977**	Cale Yarborough...	Chevrolet .	153.218
1968	Cale Yarborough...	Mercury ..	143.251	**1978**	Bobby Allison	Ford	159.730
1969	Lee Roy Yarborough	Ford	157.950	**1979**	Richard Petty	Oldsmobile	143.997
1970	Pete Hamilton	Plymouth .	149.601	**1980**	Buddy Baker	Oldsmobile	177.602
1971	Richard Petty	Plymouth .	144.462	**1981**	Richard Petty	Buick.....	169.651
1972	A. J. Foyt	Mercury ..	161.550	**1982**	Bobby Allison	Buick.....	153.991
1973	Richard Petty	Dodge	157.205	**1983**	Cale Yarborough...	Pontiac ...	155.979

[1] 332.5 miles (rain). [2] 495 miles (rain).

WORLD SPEED RECORDS (One Mile)

YEAR	DRIVER	CAR	SPEED (mph)	YEAR	DRIVER	CAR	SPEED (mph)
Gasoline-engine cars				**Gasoline-engine cars**			
1898	Chasseloup Laubat..	Jeantaud.......	39.24	**1935**	Sir Malcolm Campbell	Bluebird Special	301.13
1904	Henry Ford	Ford..........	91.37	**1939**	John R. Cobb	Railton	368.90
1910	Barney Oldfield	Benz	131.72	**1947**	John R. Cobb	Railton-Mobil ...	394.19
1919	Ralph De Palma.....	Packard	149.88	**1964**	Donald Campbell....	Bluebird	403.10
1920	Tommy Milton	Duesenberg	155.05	**1965**	Bob Summers	Goldenrod	409.23
1927	H. O. D. Seagrave ...	Sunbeam	203.79	**Jet- or rocket-powered cars**			
1928	Ray Keech..........	White Triplex ...	207.55	**1963**	Craig Breedlove.....	Spirit of America	407.45
1929	H. O. D. Seagrave ...	Irving Napier ...	231.45	**1964**	Art Arfons..........	Green Monster..	536.71
1931	Sir Malcolm Campbell	Napier-Campbell	246.09	**1965**	Craig Breedlove.....	Spirit of America	600.60
1932	Sir Malcolm Campbell	Napier-Campbell	253.96	**1970**	Gary Gabelich	Blue Flame	622.41
1933	Sir Malcolm Campbell	Napier-Campbell	272.11	**1983**	Richard Noble	Thrust 2	633.468

BASEBALL

Wide World

Philadelphia Phillies runner Joe Morgan slides safely into second base under the tag attempt by Baltimore Orioles shortstop Cal Ripken Jr. during the second World Series game at Baltimore on Oct. 12. Baltimore won the game, 4–1, and went on to win the Series, 4 games to 1. Ripken was named the American League's most valuable player.

The American League Baltimore Orioles defeated the National League Philadelphia Phillies 4 games to 1 to win the World Series on Oct. 16. The two teams had never met before in a World Series.

Philadelphia won the first game at Baltimore by a score of 2–1. Baltimore right fielder Jim Dwyer hit a home run to give the Orioles a 1–0 lead in the bottom of the first inning. Then Philadelphia second baseman Joe Morgan hit a home run in the sixth inning to tie the game. The game-winning homer was hit by Phillies center fielder Garry Maddox in the eighth inning.

Baltimore took the second game, 4–1, at Baltimore on Oct. 12 on the strength of a three-run fifth inning. Left fielder John Lowenstein led off with a home run, then three straight hits came off the bats of second baseman Rich Dauer, third baseman Todd Cruz, and catcher Rick Dempsey.

In the third game at Philadelphia on Oct. 14 Philadelphia's Joe Morgan and Gary Matthews each hit solo home runs, assuring Baltimore's 3–2 victory.

The fourth game, at Philadelphia, saw a seesaw battle that resulted in a 5-4 victory for Baltimore. In that game, each team had 10 hits, with Baltimore's offense assisted by second baseman Rich Dauer's three hits and three runs batted in.

In the fifth and final game, on Oct. 16 at Philadelphia, Baltimore walloped the Phillies, 5–0. Orioles first baseman Eddie Murray hit two home runs, and catcher Rick Dempsey slammed one. Dempsey was named the most valuable player of the series, batting .385. He hit one home run and four doubles, setting a record for extra-base hits in a five-game World Series.

In the National League playoff series, Philadelphia swept the Los Angeles Dodgers, 3 games to 1. Baltimore subdued the Chicago White Sox by the same margin in the American League.

At the end of the regular season, Atlanta Braves outfielder Dale Murphy was named Most Valuable Player of the National League for the second consecutive year, becoming the fourth player in history to win back-to-back awards. During the 1983 season he batted .302 and led the league in runs batted in, with 131. He also hit 36 home runs and stole 30 bases.

The American League's Most Valuable Player was Cal Ripken Jr., the Baltimore shortstop. After winning Rookie of the Year honors in 1982, he became the first major league player to win the MVP award in his second season. Ripken batted .318 with 102 runs batted in and 27 home runs.

The American League's Rookie of the Year was Chicago White Sox outfielder Ron Kittle. He finished the season with a .254 batting average, driving in 100 runs and slugging 35 home runs. He also struck out 150 times, leading the league in strikeouts.

New York Mets outfielder Darryl Strawberry was the National League's Rookie of the Year. He batted .257 with 74 runs batted in and 26 home runs.

Chicago White Sox pitcher LaMarr Hoyt was voted the Cy Young Award as the best pitcher in the American League. The right-hander won 24 games and lost 10 during the regular season, with an earned-run average of 3.66. In 260 innings pitched, he walked 31 and struck out 148 batters.

The Cy Young Award for best pitcher in the National League went to Philadelphia left-hander John Denny, who helped pitch his team into the World Series. Denny finished the regular season with a 19–6 record and an earned-run average of 2.37. In 242 innings pitched, he gave up 53 walks and struck out 139 batters.

At the end of the regular season, Philadelphia southpaw pitcher Steve Carlton entered the major league record books by compiling a career total of 3,709 strikeouts. It was a seesaw battle during the season against Houston Astros right-hander Nolan Ryan, who finished the season with a career total of 3,692 strikeouts. The old record was 3,508 strikeouts by Walter Johnson, during 1907–27.

Wide World

Chicago White Sox second baseman Julio Cruz (16) dives up and over Baltimore Oriole Al Bumbry to make the tag in the sixth inning of the first game of the American League playoff at Baltimore on Oct. 5. Chicago won the game, 2–1, but lost the next three in a row as Baltimore took the American League pennant. The Orioles went on to win the World Series against the Philadelphia Phillies 4 games to 1.

WORLD SERIES BOX SCORES: 1983

GAME 1: PHILADELPHIA 2, BALTIMORE 1

	1	2	3	4	5	6	7	8	9	R	H	E
Philadelphia	0	0	0	0	0	1	0	1	0	2	5	0
Baltimore	1	0	0	0	0	0	0	0	0	1	5	1

Pitchers: Philadelphia—Denny (winner, 7⅔), Holland (1⅓); Baltimore—McGregor (loser, 8), Stewart (⅔), T. Martinez (⅓); Home runs: Dwyer, Morgan, Maddox; Attendance at Baltimore Oct. 11: 52,204.

GAME 2: BALTIMORE 4, PHILADELPHIA 1

	1	2	3	4	5	6	7	8	9	R	H	E
Philadelphia	0	0	0	1	0	0	0	0	0	1	3	0
Baltimore	0	0	0	0	3	0	1	0	x	4	9	1

Pitchers: Baltimore—Boddicker (winner, 9); Philadelphia—Hudson (loser, 4⅓), Hernandez (⅔), Andersen (2), Reed (1). Home runs: Lowenstein; Attendance at Baltimore Oct. 12: 52,132.

GAME 3: BALTIMORE 3, PHILADELPHIA 2

	1	2	3	4	5	6	7	8	9	R	H	E
Baltimore	0	0	0	0	0	1	2	0	0	3	6	1
Philadelphia	0	1	1	0	0	0	0	0	0	2	8	2

Pitchers: Baltimore—Flanagan (4), Palmer (winner, 2), Stewart (2), T. Martinez (save, 1); Philadelphia—Carlton (loser, 6⅔), Holland (2⅓); Home runs: Matthews, Morgan, Ford; Attendance at Philadelphia Oct. 14: 65,792.

GAME 4: BALTIMORE 5, PHILADELPHIA 4

	1	2	3	4	5	6	7	8	9	R	H	E
Baltimore	0	0	0	2	0	2	1	0	0	5	10	1
Philadelphia	0	0	0	1	2	0	0	0	1	4	10	0

Pitchers: Baltimore—Davis (winner, 5), Stewart (2⅓), T. Martinez (save, 1⅔); Philadelphia—Denny (loser, 5⅓), Hernandez (⅓), Reed (1⅓), Andersen (2); Home runs: None; Attendance at Philadelphia Oct. 15: 66,947.

GAME 5: BALTIMORE 5, PHILADELPHIA 0

	1	2	3	4	5	6	7	8	9	R	H	E
Baltimore	0	1	1	2	1	0	0	0	0	5	5	0
Philadelphia	0	0	0	0	0	0	0	0	0	0	5	1

Pitchers: Baltimore—McGregor (winner, 9); Philadelphia—Hudson (loser, 4), Bystrom (1), Hernandez (3), Reed (1); Home runs: Murray (2), Dempsey; Attendance at Philadelphia Oct. 16: 67,064.

WORLD SERIES RESULTS: 1903–1983

YEAR	WINNERS	LOSERS	GAMES
1903 [1]	Boston (A)	Pittsburgh	5–3
1904	Not played		–
1905	New York (N)	Philadelphia (A)	4–1
1906	Chicago (A)	Chicago (N)	4–2
1907 [2]	Chicago (N)	Detroit (A)	4–0
1908	Chicago (N)	Detroit (A)	4–1
1909	Pittsburgh (N)	Detroit (A)	4–3
1910	Philadelphia (A)	Chicago (N)	4–1
1911	Philadelphia (A)	New York (N)	4–2
1912 [2]	Boston (A)	New York (N)	4–3
1913	Philadelphia (A)	New York (N)	4–1
1914	Boston (N)	Philadelphia (A)	4–0
1915	Boston (A)	Philadelphia (N)	4–1
1916	Boston (A)	Brooklyn (N)	4–1
1917	Chicago (A)	New York (N)	4–2
1918	Boston (A)	Chicago (N)	4–2
1919 [1]	Cincinnati (N)	Chicago (A)	5–3
1920 [1]	Cleveland (A)	Brooklyn (N)	5–2
1921 [1]	New York (N)	New York (A)	5–3
1922 [2]	New York (N)	New York (A)	4–0
1923	New York (A)	New York (N)	4–2
1924	Washington (A)	New York (N)	4–3
1925	Pittsburgh (N)	Washington (A)	4–3
1926	St. Louis (N)	New York (A)	4–3
1927	New York (A)	Pittsburgh (N)	4–0
1928	New York (A)	St. Louis (N)	4–0
1929	Philadelphia (A)	Chicago (N)	4–1
1930	Philadelphia (A)	St. Louis (N)	4–2
1931	St. Louis (N)	Philadelphia (A)	4–3
1932	New York (A)	Chicago (N)	4–0
1933	New York (N)	Washington (A)	4–1
1934	St. Louis (N)	Detroit (A)	4–3
1935	Detroit (A)	Chicago (N)	4–2
1936	New York (A)	New York (N)	4–2
1937	New York (A)	New York (N)	4–1
1938	New York (A)	Chicago (N)	4–0
1939	New York (A)	Cincinnati (N)	4–0
1940	Cincinnati (N)	Detroit (A)	4–3
1941	New York (A)	Brooklyn (N)	4–1
1942	St. Louis (N)	New York (A)	4–1
1943	New York (A)	St. Louis (N)	4–1
1944	St. Louis (N)	St. Louis (A)	4–2
1945	Detroit (A)	Chicago (N)	4–3
1946	St. Louis (N)	Boston (A)	4–3
1947	New York (A)	Brooklyn (N)	4–3
1948	Cleveland (A)	Boston (N)	4–2
1949	New York (A)	Brooklyn (N)	4–1
1950	New York (A)	Philadelphia (N)	4–0
1951	New York (A)	New York (N)	4–2
1952	New York (A)	Brooklyn (N)	4–3
1953	New York (A)	Brooklyn (N)	4–2
1954	New York (N)	Cleveland (A)	4–0
1955	Brooklyn (N)	New York (A)	4–3
1956	New York (A)	Brooklyn (N)	4–3
1957	Milwaukee (N)	New York (A)	4–3
1958	New York (A)	Milwaukee (N)	4–3
1959	Los Angeles (N)	Chicago (A)	4–2
1960	Pittsburgh (N)	New York (A)	4–3
1961	New York (A)	Cincinnati (N)	4–1
1962	New York (A)	San Francisco (N)	4–3
1963	Los Angeles (N)	New York (A)	4–0
1964	St. Louis (N)	New York (A)	4–3
1965	Los Angeles (N)	Minnesota (A)	4–3
1966	Baltimore (A)	Los Angeles (N)	4–0
1967	St. Louis (N)	Boston (A)	4–3
1968	Detroit (A)	St. Louis (N)	4–3
1969	N.Y. Mets (N)	Baltimore (A)	4–1
1970	Baltimore (A)	Cincinnati (N)	4–1
1971	Pittsburgh (N)	Baltimore (A)	4–3
1972	Oakland (A)	Cincinnati (N)	4–3
1973	Oakland (A)	N.Y. Mets (N)	4–3
1974	Oakland (A)	Los Angeles (N)	4–1
1975	Cincinnati (N)	Boston (A)	4–3
1976	Cincinnati (N)	New York (A)	4–0
1977	New York (A)	Los Angeles (N)	4–2
1978	New York (A)	Los Angeles (N)	4–2
1979	Pittsburgh (N)	Baltimore (A)	4–3
1980	Philadelphia (N)	Kansas City (A)	4–2
1981	Los Angeles (N)	New York (A)	4–2
1982	St. Louis (N)	Milwaukee (A)	4–3
1983	Baltimore (A)	Philadelphia (N)	4–1

[1] A nine-game World Series was scheduled. [2] One tie game played.

PENNANT WINNERS—MAJOR LEAGUE BASEBALL

NATIONAL LEAGUE

YEAR	CLUB	W	L	PCT.	MANAGER
1912	New York	103	48	.682	John McGraw
1913	New York	101	51	.664	John McGraw
1914	Boston	94	59	.614	G. Stallings
1915	Philadelphia	90	62	.592	P. Moran
1916	Brooklyn	94	60	.610	W. Robinson
1917	New York	98	56	.636	John McGraw
1918	Chicago	84	45	.651	F. Mitchell
1919	Cincinnati	96	44	.686	P. Moran
1920	Brooklyn	93	61	.604	W. Robinson
1921	New York	94	59	.614	John McGraw
1922	New York	93	61	.604	John McGraw
1923	New York	95	58	.621	John McGraw
1924	New York	93	60	.608	John McGraw
1925	Pittsburgh	95	58	.621	W. McKechnie
1926	St. Louis	89	65	.578	R. Hornsby
1927	Pittsburgh	94	60	.610	O. Bush
1928	St. Louis	95	59	.617	W. McKechnie
1929	Chicago	98	54	.645	Joe McCarthy
1930	St. Louis	92	62	.597	C. Street
1931	St. Louis	101	53	.656	C. Street
1932	Chicago	90	64	.584	C. Grimm
1933	New York	91	61	.599	Bill Terry
1934	St. Louis	95	58	.621	Frank Frisch
1935	Chicago	100	54	.649	C. Grimm
1936	New York	92	62	.597	Bill Terry
1937	New York	95	57	.625	Bill Terry
1938	Chicago	89	63	.586	C. Hartnett
1939	Cincinnati	97	57	.630	W. McKechnie
1940	Cincinnati	100	53	.654	W. McKechnie
1941	Brooklyn	100	54	.649	Leo Durocher
1942	St. Louis	106	48	.688	W. Southworth
1943	St. Louis	105	49	.682	W. Southworth
1944	St. Louis	105	49	.682	W. Southworth
1945	Chicago	98	56	.636	C. Grimm
1946	St. Louis	98	58	.628	E. Dyer
1947	Brooklyn	94	60	.610	B. Shotton
1948	Boston	91	62	.595	W. Southworth
1949	Brooklyn	97	57	.630	B. Shotton
1950	Philadelphia	91	63	.591	E. Sawyer
1951	New York	98	59	.624	Leo Durocher
1952	Brooklyn	96	57	.627	C. Dressen
1953	Brooklyn	105	49	.682	C. Dressen
1954	New York	97	57	.630	Leo Durocher
1955	Brooklyn	98	55	.641	Walt Alston
1956	Brooklyn	93	61	.604	Walt Alston
1957	Milwaukee	95	59	.617	F. Haney
1958	Milwaukee	92	62	.597	F. Haney
1959	Los Angeles	88	68	.564	Walt Alston
1960	Pittsburgh	95	59	.617	D. Murtaugh
1961	Cincinnati	93	61	.604	F. Hutchinson
1962	San Fran.	103	62	.624	A. Dark
1963	Los Angeles	99	63	.611	Walt Alston
1964	St. Louis	93	69	.574	J. Keane
1965	Los Angeles	97	65	.599	Walt Alston
1966	Los Angeles	95	67	.586	Walt Alston
1967	St. Louis	101	60	.627	A. Schoendienst
1968	St. Louis	97	65	.599	A. Schoendienst
1969	N.Y. Mets	100	62	.617	Gil Hodges
1970	Cincinnati	102	60	.630	S. Anderson
1971	Pittsburgh	97	65	.599	D. Murtaugh
1972	Cincinnati	95	59	.617	S. Anderson
1973	N.Y. Mets	82	79	.509	Yogi Berra
1974	Los Angeles	102	60	.630	Walt Alston
1975	Cincinnati	108	54	.667	S. Anderson
1976	Cincinnati	102	60	.630	S. Anderson
1977	Los Angeles	98	64	.605	T. Lasorda
1978	Los Angeles	95	67	.586	T. Lasorda
1979	Pittsburgh	98	64	.605	Chuck Tanner
1980	Philadelphia	91	71	.562	Dallas Green
1981	Los Angeles	63	47	.573	T. Lasorda
1982	St. Louis	92	70	.568	W. Herzog
1983	Philadelphia	90	72	.556	Paul Owens

AMERICAN LEAGUE

YEAR	CLUB	W	L	PCT.	MANAGER
1912	Boston	105	47	.691	J. Stahl
1913	Philadelphia	96	57	.627	Connie Mack
1914	Philadelphia	99	53	.651	Connie Mack
1915	Boston	101	50	.669	W. Carrigan
1916	Boston	91	63	.591	W. Carrigan
1917	Chicago	100	54	.649	C. Rowland
1918	Boston	75	51	.595	E. Barrow
1919	Chicago	88	52	.629	W. Gleason
1920	Cleveland	98	56	.636	Tris Speaker
1921	New York	98	55	.641	M. Huggins
1922	New York	94	60	.610	M. Huggins
1923	New York	98	54	.645	M. Huggins
1924	Washington	92	62	.597	S. Harris
1925	Washington	96	55	.636	S. Harris
1926	New York	91	63	.591	M. Huggins
1927	New York	110	44	.714	M. Huggins
1928	New York	101	53	.656	M. Huggins
1929	Philadelphia	104	46	.693	Connie Mack
1930	Philadelphia	102	52	.662	Connie Mack
1931	Philadelphia	107	45	.704	Connie Mack
1932	New York	107	47	.695	Joe McCarthy
1933	Washington	99	53	.651	Joe Cronin
1934	Detroit	101	53	.656	G. Cochrane
1935	Detroit	93	58	.616	G. Cochrane
1936	New York	102	51	.667	Joe McCarthy
1937	New York	102	52	.662	Joe McCarthy
1938	New York	99	53	.651	Joe McCarthy
1939	New York	106	45	.702	Joe McCarthy
1940	Detroit	90	64	.584	D. Baker
1941	New York	101	53	.656	Joe McCarthy
1942	New York	103	51	.669	Joe McCarthy
1943	New York	98	56	.636	Joe McCarthy
1944	St. Louis	89	65	.578	J. Sewell
1945	Detroit	88	65	.575	S. O'Neill
1946	Boston	104	50	.675	Joe Cronin
1947	New York	97	57	.630	S. Harris
1948	Cleveland	97	58	.626	Lou Boudreau
1949	New York	97	57	.630	Casey Stengel
1950	New York	98	56	.636	Casey Stengel
1951	New York	98	56	.636	Casey Stengel
1952	New York	95	59	.617	Casey Stengel
1953	New York	99	52	.656	Casey Stengel
1954	Cleveland	111	43	.721	Al Lopez
1955	New York	96	58	.623	Casey Stengel
1956	New York	97	57	.630	Casey Stengel
1957	New York	98	56	.636	Casey Stengel
1958	New York	92	62	.597	Casey Stengel
1959	Chicago	94	60	.610	Al Lopez
1960	New York	97	57	.630	Casey Stengel
1961	New York	109	53	.673	Ralph Houk
1962	New York	96	66	.593	Ralph Houk
1963	New York	104	57	.646	Ralph Houk
1964	New York	99	63	.611	Yogi Berra
1965	Minnesota	102	60	.630	Sam Mele
1966	Baltimore	97	63	.606	H. Bauer
1967	Boston	92	70	.568	R. Williams
1968	Detroit	103	59	.636	M. Smith
1969	Baltimore	109	53	.673	Earl Weaver
1970	Baltimore	108	54	.667	Earl Weaver
1971	Baltimore	101	57	.639	Earl Weaver
1972	Oakland	93	62	.600	Dick Williams
1973	Oakland	94	68	.580	Dick Williams
1974	Oakland	90	72	.556	Alvin Dark
1975	Boston	95	65	.594	Darrell Johnson
1976	New York	97	62	.610	Billy Martin
1977	New York	100	62	.617	Billy Martin
1978	New York	100	63	.613	Bob Lemon
1979	Baltimore	102	57	.642	Earl Weaver
1980	Kansas City	97	65	.599	Jim Frey
1981	New York	59	48	.551	Bob Lemon
1982	Milwaukee	95	67	.586	Harvey Kuenn
1983	Baltimore	98	64	.605	Joe Altobelli

SELECTED WORLD SERIES BASEBALL RECORDS: 1903–1983

TEAM RECORDS:

World championships won	New York Yankees (AL)—22; St. Louis Cardinals (NL)—8
Played in most World Series	New York Yankees (AL)—33 times from 1921 through 1981
Games won	New York Yankees (AL)—109
Played in most World Series, National League	Giants, New York/San Francisco (NL)—15 times from 1905 through 1962 (14 times representing New York and once San Francisco)
Hits by one team, one game	New York Giants (NL) and St. Louis Cardinals (NL), tie—20. The Giants made 20 hits against the Yankees in the Oct. 7, 1921, World Series game; the Cardinals did the same against the Boston Red Sox in the Oct. 10, 1946, series game
Batting average, highest	New York Yankees (AL)—.338 in the seven-game series against the Pittsburgh Pirates in 1960
Batting average, lowest, one series	Los Angeles Dodgers (NL)—.142 against Baltimore pitchers in 1966
Runs batted in, one series	New York Yankees (AL)—54 runs in seven games in 1960
Runs, one series	New York Yankees (AL)—55 in seven-game series against Pittsburgh Pirates (NL) in 1960
Home runs, one series	New York Yankee batters (AL)—12 home runs in seven games against the Brooklyn Dodgers in 1956
Home runs, one game	New York Yankee batters (AL)—5 home runs against St. Louis Cardinal pitching in a game played Oct. 9, 1928
Doubles, one series	St. Louis Cardinals (NL)—19 doubles against the Boston Red Sox in 1946; the Philadelphia Athletics (AL) also scored 19 series doubles against the Chicago Cubs in 1910
Bases on balls received, one series	New York Yankee batters (AL)—38 times against Brooklyn Dodger pitching in seven games in 1947
Strike outs, one series	Oakland A's batters (AL)—62 times against New York Mets pitching in seven games in 1973
Double plays, one series	Brooklyn Dodgers (NL)—12, in a seven-game series against the New York Yankees in 1955
Triple plays, one series	Cleveland Indians (AL)—1. The only World Series triple play was an unassisted one made by Cleveland 2d baseman Billy Wambsganss in the 1920 series against Brooklyn
Fielding record, one series	New York Yankees (AL)—1.000 (no errors) in the 1937 World Series against the New York Giants; Baltimore Orioles (AL)—1.000 (no errors) in the 1966 World Series against Los Angeles

INDIVIDUAL RECORDS:

Home runs, one game	Babe Ruth, New York Yankees (AL)—3 home runs on Oct. 6, 1926, and again on Oct. 9, 1928; Reggie Jackson, New York Yankees (AL)—3 consecutive home runs on Oct. 18, 1977
Home runs in single World Series	Reggie Jackson, New York Yankees (AL)—5 against Los Angeles Dodgers (NL) in 1977
Home runs in World Series, lifetime	Mickey Mantle, New York Yankees (AL)—18
Batting average, lifetime, 20 or more games	Lou Brock, St. Louis (NL)—.391, in three World Series: 1964, 1967, 1968 (21 games, 87 at-bats, 34 hits)
Hits, lifetime	Yogi Berra, New York Yankees (AL)—71, between 1947 and 1963
Hits, game	Paul Molitor, Milwaukee Brewers (AL)—5 on Oct. 12, 1982
Batting average in single World Series by regular starting player	Babe Ruth, New York Yankees (AL)—.625, in the 1928 series against the St. Louis Cardinals (four games)
Game-winning home runs, one series	Casey Stengel, New York Giants (NL)—won two games with home runs in 1923 series; Rudy York of Boston Red Sox (AL) also won two games with home runs in 1946 series
Game-winning home runs, lifetime	Hank Greenberg, Detroit Tigers (AL)—won three series games with home runs: in 1935 against Chicago Cubs; in 1940 against Cincinnati Reds; and in 1945 against Chicago Cubs
Runs batted in, one game	Bobby Richardson, New York Yankees (AL)—6 on Oct. 8, 1960, against the Pittsburgh Pirates (NL)
Runs, in one series	Reggie Jackson, N.Y. Yankees (AL)—10 in 1977
Runs, lifetime	Mickey Mantle, N.Y. Yankees (AL)—42 in 12 series, 65 games (1951–64)
Errors, one game	Willie Davis, Los Angeles Dodgers (NL)—three errors, all in the same inning against the Baltimore Orioles on Oct. 6, 1966
Played in most World Series	Yogi Berra, New York Yankees (AL)—14 times from 1947 to 1963
Played on most championship teams	Yogi Berra, New York Yankees (AL)—10 times
Pitching no-hitter, one game	Don Larsen, New York Yankees (AL)—won a perfect no-hitter against the Brooklyn Dodgers, Oct. 8, 1956. He faced the minimum 27 batters, threw 97 pitches, and allowed no base runners
Pitcher with most World Series wins, lifetime	Whitey Ford, New York Yankees (AL)—10, between 1950 and 1964
Pitcher with most strikeouts, one game	Bob Gibson, St. Louis Cardinals (NL)—17, against the Detroit Tigers in the first game of the 1968 World Series
Pitching consecutive scoreless innings	Whitey Ford, New York Yankees (AL)—33 ⅔ innings, during the 1960, 1961, and 1962 series

INDIVIDUAL MAJOR LEAGUE BASEBALL RECORDS: 1900–1983

BATTING	AMERICAN LEAGUE	NATIONAL LEAGUE
Games, career	3,308—Carl Yastrzemski, Boston (1961–83)	3,298—Hank Aaron (1954–76) *
Years leading league	12—Ty Cobb, Detroit (1907–15, 1917–19)	8—Honus Wagner, Pittsburgh (1900, 1903–04, 1906–09, 1911)
Batting average, career	.367—Ty Cobb, Detroit (1905–26), Philadelphia (1927–28)	.359—Rogers Hornsby, St. Louis, N.Y., Boston, Chicago (1915–32)
Batting average, season	.422—Napoleon Lajoie, Phila. (1901)	.424—Rogers Hornsby, St. Louis (1924)
Games, consecutive	2,130—Lou Gehrig, New York (1925–39)	1,207—Steve Garvey, San Diego (1975–83)
Runs scored, career	2,244—Ty Cobb, Detroit, Phil. (1905–28)	2,174—Hank Aaron (1954–76) *
Runs scored, season	177—Babe Ruth, New York (1921)	158—Chuck Klein, Philadelphia (1930)
Runs scored, game	6—John Pesky, Boston (1946)	6—Mel Ott, New York (1934, 1944); Frank Torre, Milwaukee (1957)
Runs batted in, career	2,209—Babe Ruth, Boston (1914–19), New York (1920–34), Boston (NL) (1935) *	2,297—Hank Aaron, Milw. (NL), Atlanta (NL), Milw. (AL) (1954–76) *
Runs batted in, season	184—Lou Gehrig, New York (1931)	190—Hack Wilson, Chicago (1930)
Runs batted in, game	11—Tony Lazzeri, New York (1936)	12—Jim Bottomley, St. Louis (1924)
Hits, career	4,191—Ty Cobb, Detroit, Philadelphia	3,869—Pete Rose, Cincinnati, Philadelphia (1963–82)
Hits, season	257—George Sisler, St. Louis (1920)	254—Frank O'Doul, Philadelphia (1929); Bill Terry, New York (1930)
Games batted safely, consecutive	56—Joe DiMaggio, New York (1941)	44—Pete Rose, Cincinnati (1978)
Long hits (doubles, triples, home runs) career	1,356—Babe Ruth, Boston, New York, Boston (NL) (1914–35) *	1,477—Hank Aaron, Milw. (NL), Atlanta (NL), Milw. (AL) (1954–76) *
Long hits, season	119—Babe Ruth (1921)	107—Chuck Klein, Philadelphia (1930)
Slugging average, career	.690—Babe Ruth (1914–35) *	.578—Rogers Hornsby (1915–32)
Home runs, career	714—Babe Ruth (1914–35) *	755—Hank Aaron, Milw. (NL), Atlanta (NL), Milw. (AL) (1954–76) *
Home runs, season (162 games, Maris; 154 games, Ruth)	61—Roger Maris, N.Y. (1961) 60—Babe Ruth, N.Y. (1927)	56—Hack Wilson, Chicago (1930) 54—Ralph Kiner, Pittsburgh (1949)
Home runs, game	4—Lou Gehrig, New York (1932)	4—Chuck Klein, Philadelphia (1936)
Home runs, grand slam, career	23—Lou Gehrig, New York (1925–39)	18—Willie McCovey, San Fran., San Diego, Oakland, San Fran. (1959–80)
Home runs, grand slam, season	5—Jim Gentile, Baltimore (1961)	5—Ernie Banks, Chicago (1955)
Strikeouts, career	2,106—Reggie Jackson, K.C., Oakland, Baltimore, N.Y., Calif. (1967–83)	1,936—Willie Stargell, Pittsburgh (1962–82)
Games, no strikeouts, consecutive	115—Joe Sewell, Cleveland (1929)	77—Lloyd Waner, Pittsburgh, Boston, Cincinnati (1941)
Stolen bases, career	892—Ty Cobb, Detroit, Philadelphia (1905–28)	938—Lou Brock, Chicago, St. Louis, (1961–79)
Stolen bases, season	130—Rickey Henderson, Oakland (1982)	118—Lou Brock, St. Louis (1974)
Stolen bases, game	6—Eddie Collins, Philadelphia (1912)	5—Dennis McGann, N.Y. (1904)
Stealing home, career	35—Ty Cobb, Detroit, Philadelphia	27—George Burns, N.Y., Cincinnati, Philadelphia (1911–25)
Stealing home, season	7—Rod Carew, Minnesota (1969)	7—Pete Reiser, Brooklyn (1946)

PITCHING	AMERICAN LEAGUE	NATIONAL LEAGUE
Games pitched, career	899—Sparky Lyle, Boston, N.Y., Texas, Chicago (1967–82)	846—ElRoy Face, Pittsburgh (1953, 1955–68), Montreal (1969)
Games pitched, season	90—Mike Marshall, Minn. (1979)	106—Mike Marshall, L.A. (1974)
Games started, career	666—Walter Johnson, Wash. (1907–27)	665—Warren Spahn (1942–65)
Games started, season	51—Jack Chesbro, N.Y. (1904)	48—Joe McGinnity, N.Y. (1903)
Games completed, career	531—Walter Johnson, Wash. (1907–27)	437—Grover Alexander (1911–29)
Games completed, season	48—Jack Chesbro, N.Y. (1904)	45—Victor Willis, Boston (1902)
Earned run average, career (2,000 or more innings)	2.37—Walter Johnson, Wash. (1907–1927)	2.33—James L. Vaughn, Chicago (1913–21)
Earned run average, season	1.01—Hubert Leonard, Boston (1914)	1.12—Bob Gibson, St. Louis (1968)
Games won, career	416—Walter Johnson, Wash. (1907–27)	373—Grover Alexander, Christy Mathewson, N.Y., Cin. (1900–16)
Games won, season	41—Jack Chesbro, N.Y. (1904)	37—Christy Mathewson (1908)
Games won, consecutive	17—John Allen, Cleveland (1936–37); Dave McNally, Baltimore (1968–69)	24—Carl Hubbell, New York (1936–37)
Shutout games, career	113—Walter Johnson, Wash. (1907–27)	90—Grover Alexander (1911–29)
Shutout games, season	13—John Coombs, Philadelphia (1910)	16—Grover Alexander (1916)
Shutout innings, consecutive	56—Walter Johnson, Wash. (1913)	58—Don Drysdale, Los Angeles (1968)
No-hit games, career	4—Nolan Ryan, California, 1973 (2), 1974 (1), 1975 (1) †	4—Sandy Koufax, Los Angeles (1962–65)
Strikeouts, 9-inning game	19—Nolan Ryan, Calif. (1974)	19—Steve Carlton, St. Louis (1969); Tom Seaver, New York (1970)
Strikeouts, season	383—Nolan Ryan, California (1973)	382—Sandy Koufax, Los Angeles (1965)
Strikeouts, career	3,508—Walter Johnson, Wash. (1907–27)	3,709—Steve Carlton, St. L., Phil. (1965–83)
Won-lost percentage, season, 16 or more decisions	.938—John Allen, Cleveland (1937), won 15, lost 1	.947—ElRoy Face, Pittsburgh (1959), won 18, lost 1

* Career total includes play in both leagues. † Fifth no-hitter for Houston (NL), Sept. 26, 1981.

POSTSEASON BASEBALL PLAYOFFS: 1970–1983

NATIONAL LEAGUE

1970	Cincinnati defeated Pittsburgh, 3 games to 0
1971	Pittsburgh defeated San Francisco, 3 games to 1
1972	Cincinnati defeated Pittsburgh, 3 games to 2
1973	New York defeated Cincinnati, 3 games to 2
1974	Los Angeles defeated Pittsburgh, 3 games to 1
1975	Cincinnati defeated Pittsburgh, 3 games to 0
1976	Cincinnati defeated Philadelphia, 3 games to 0
1977	Los Angeles defeated Philadelphia, 3 games to 1
1978	Los Angeles defeated Philadelphia, 3 games to 1
1979	Pittsburgh defeated Cincinnati, 3 games to 0
1980	Philadelphia defeated Houston, 3 games to 2
1981	Los Angeles defeated Montreal, 3 games to 2
1982	St. Louis defeated Atlanta, 3 games to 0
1983	Philadelphia defeated Los Angeles, 3 games to 1

AMERICAN LEAGUE

1970	Baltimore defeated Minnesota, 3 games to 0
1971	Baltimore defeated Oakland, 3 games to 0
1972	Oakland defeated Detroit, 3 games to 2
1973	Oakland defeated Baltimore, 3 games to 2
1974	Oakland defeated Baltimore, 3 games to 1
1975	Boston defeated Oakland, 3 games to 0
1976	New York defeated Kansas City, 3 games to 2
1977	New York defeated Kansas City, 3 games to 2
1978	New York defeated Kansas City, 3 games to 1
1979	Baltimore defeated California, 3 games to 1
1980	Kansas City defeated New York, 3 games to 0
1981	New York defeated Oakland, 3 games to 0
1982	Milwaukee defeated California, 3 games to 2
1983	Baltimore defeated Chicago, 3 games to 1

POSTSEASON PLAYOFF GAMES: 1983

NATIONAL LEAGUE: Philadelphia won National League Pennant, 3 games to 1.

GAME 1: PHILADELPHIA 1, LOS ANGELES 0										R	H	E
Philadelphia	1	0	0	0	0	0	0	0	0	1	5	1
Los Angeles	0	0	0	0	0	0	0	0	0	0	7	0

Pitchers: Philadelphia—Carlton (winner, $7\frac{2}{3}$), Holland (save, $1\frac{1}{3}$); Los Angeles—Reuss (loser, 8), Niedenfuer (1).
Home runs: Schmidt.
Attendance at Los Angeles Oct. 4: 55,967.

GAME 2: LOS ANGELES 4, PHILADELPHIA 1										R	H	E
Philadelphia	0	1	0	0	0	0	0	0	0	1	7	2
Los Angeles	1	0	0	0	2	0	0	1	x	4	6	1

Pitchers: Los Angeles—Valenzuela (winner, 8), Niedenfuer (save, 1); Philadelphia—Denny (loser, 6), Reed (2).
Home run: Matthews.
Attendance at Los Angeles Oct. 5: 55,967.

GAME 3: PHILADELPHIA 7, LOS ANGELES 2										R	H	E
Los Angeles	0	0	0	2	0	0	0	0	0	2	4	0
Philadelphia	0	2	1	1	2	0	1	0	x	7	9	1

Pitchers: Philadelphia—Hudson (winner, 9); Los Angeles—Welch (loser, $1\frac{1}{3}$), Pena ($2\frac{2}{3}$), Honeycutt ($\frac{1}{3}$), Beckwith ($1\frac{2}{3}$), Zachry (2).
Home runs: Marshall, Matthews.
Attendance at Philadelphia Oct. 7: 53,490.

GAME 4: PHILADELPHIA 7, LOS ANGELES 2										R	H	E
Los Angeles	0	0	0	1	0	0	0	1	0	2	10	0
Philadelphia	3	0	0	0	2	2	0	0	x	7	13	1

Pitchers: Philadelphia—Carlton (winner, 6), Reed ($1\frac{1}{3}$), Holland ($1\frac{2}{3}$); Los Angeles—Reuss (loser, 4), Beckwith ($\frac{2}{3}$), Honeycutt ($1\frac{1}{3}$), Zachry (2).
Home runs: Matthews, Baker, Lezcano.
Attendance at Philadelphia Oct. 8: 64,494.

AMERICAN LEAGUE: Baltimore won American League Pennant, 3 games to 1.

GAME 1: CHICAGO 2, BALTIMORE 1										R	H	E
Chicago	0	0	1	0	0	1	0	0	0	2	7	0
Baltimore	0	0	0	0	0	0	0	0	1	1	6	1

Pitchers: Chicago—Hoyt (winner, 9); Baltimore—McGregor (loser, $6\frac{2}{3}$), Stewart ($\frac{1}{3}$), T. Martinez (2).
Home runs: None.
Attendance at Baltimore Oct. 5: 51,289.

GAME 2: BALTIMORE 4, CHICAGO 0										R	H	E
Chicago	0	0	0	0	0	0	0	0	0	0	5	2
Baltimore	0	1	0	1	0	2	0	0	x	4	6	0

Pitchers: Baltimore—Boddicker (winner, 9); Chicago—Bannister (loser, 6), Barojas (1), Lamp (1).
Home run: Roenicke.
Attendance at Baltimore Oct. 6: 52,347.

GAME 3: BALTIMORE 11, CHICAGO 1										R	H	E
Baltimore	3	1	0	0	2	0	0	1	4	11	8	1
Chicago	0	1	0	0	0	0	0	0	0	1	6	1

Pitchers: Baltimore—Flanagan (winner, 5), Stewart (save, 4); Chicago—Dotson (loser, 5), Tidrow (3), Koosman ($\frac{1}{3}$), Lamp ($\frac{2}{3}$).
Home run: Murray.
Attendance at Chicago Oct. 7: 46,635.

GAME 4: BALTIMORE 3, CHICAGO 0											R	H	E
Baltimore	0	0	0	0	0	0	0	0	0	3	3	9	0
Chicago	0	0	0	0	0	0	0	0	0	0	0	10	0

Pitchers: Baltimore—Davis (6), T. Martinez (winner, 4); Chicago—Burns (loser, $9\frac{1}{3}$), Barojas (0), Agosto ($\frac{1}{3}$), Lamp ($\frac{1}{3}$).
Home run: Landrum.
Attendance at Chicago Oct. 8: 45,477.

TEAM BATTING—MAJOR LEAGUE BASEBALL REGULAR SEASON: 1983

NATIONAL LEAGUE

Club	PCT.	G	AB	R	H	HR
Atlanta	.272	162	5,472	746	1,489	130
St. Louis	.270	162	5,550	679	1,496	83
Montreal......	.264	163	5,611	677	1,482	102
Pittsburgh	.264	162	5,531	659	1,460	121
Chicago	.261	162	5,512	701	1,436	140
Houston	.257	162	5,502	643	1,412	97
San Diego.....	.250	163	5,527	653	1,384	93
Los Angeles ...	.250	163	5,440	654	1,358	146
Philadelphia...	.249	163	5,426	696	1,352	125
San Francisco .	.247	162	5,369	687	1,324	142
New York	.241	162	5,444	575	1,314	112
Cincinnati.....	.239	162	5,333	623	1,274	107

AMERICAN LEAGUE

Club	PCT.	G	AB	R	H	HR
Toronto	.277	162	5,581	795	1,546	167
Milwaukee	.277	162	5,621	764	1,556	132
Detroit	.274	162	5,592	789	1,530	156
New York	.273	162	5,631	770	1,535	153
Kansas City ...	.271	163	5,598	696	1,515	109
Boston	.270	162	5,590	724	1,512	142
Baltimore	.269	162	5,546	799	1,492	168
Cleveland	.265	162	5,476	704	1,451	86
Chicago	.262	162	5,484	800	1,439	157
Oakland	.262	162	5,516	708	1,447	121
Minnesota	.261	162	5,601	709	1,462	141
California	.260	162	5,640	722	1,467	154
Texas	.255	163	5,610	639	1,429	106
Seattle	.240	162	5,335	558	1,280	111

1983 FINAL STANDINGS—MAJOR LEAGUE BASEBALL

NATIONAL LEAGUE

EASTERN DIVISION	WON	LOST	PCT.	G.B.[1]
Philadelphia[2]	90	72	.556	—
Pittsburgh	84	78	.519	6
Montreal	82	80	.506	8
St. Louis	79	83	.488	11
Chicago	71	91	.438	19
New York	68	94	.420	22

WESTERN DIVISION	WON	LOST	PCT.	G.B.[1]
Los Angeles	91	71	.562	—
Atlanta	88	74	.543	3
Houston	85	77	.525	6
San Diego	81	81	.500	10
San Francisco	79	83	.488	12
Cincinnati	74	88	.457	17

AMERICAN LEAGUE

EASTERN DIVISION	WON	LOST	PCT.	G.B.[1]
Baltimore[2]	98	64	.605	—
Detroit	92	70	.568	6
New York	91	71	.562	7
Toronto	89	73	.549	9
Milwaukee	87	75	.537	11
Boston	78	84	.481	20
Cleveland	70	92	.432	28

WESTERN DIVISION	WON	LOST	PCT.	G.B.[1]
Chicago	99	63	.611	—
Kansas City	79	83	.488	20
Texas	77	85	.475	22
Oakland	74	88	.457	25
California	70	92	.432	29
Minnesota	70	92	.432	29
Seattle	60	102	.370	39

[1] Games behind. [2] League pennant winner.

1983 TEAM-BY-TEAM VICTORIES—MAJOR LEAGUE BASEBALL

To determine a team's regular-season wins read horizontally. To determine a team's regular-season losses read down the proper column. For postseason playoff results, see page 778.

NATIONAL LEAGUE

EASTERN DIVISION	Phil.	Pitt.	Mon.	St.L.	Chi.	N.Y.	Atl.	Cin.	Hou.	L.A.	S.D.	S.F.	TOTAL WINS
Philadelphia	–	11	10	14	13	12	5	6	8	1	5	5	90
Pittsburgh	7	–	10	10	9	9	6	6	6	6	9	6	84
Montreal	8	8	–	9	11	8	5	8	4	5	8	8	82
St. Louis	4	8	9	–	8	12	5	6	10	3	6	8	79
Chicago	5	9	7	10	–	9	7	4	5	6	5	4	71
New York	6	9	10	6	9	–	4	5	3	5	6	5	68

WESTERN DIVISION	L.A.	Atl.	Hou.	S.D.	S.F.	Cin.	Chi.	Mon.	N.Y.	Phil.	Pitt.	St.L.	TOTAL WINS
Los Angeles	–	11	12	6	5	11	6	7	7	11	6	9	91
Atlanta	7	–	11	9	9	12	5	7	8	7	6	7	88
Houston	6	7	–	11	12	13	7	8	9	4	6	2	85
San Diego	12	9	7	–	11	9	7	4	6	7	3	6	81
San Francisco	13	9	6	7	–	8	8	4	7	7	6	4	79
Cincinnati	7	6	5	9	10	–	8	4	7	6	6	6	74

AMERICAN LEAGUE

EASTERN DIVISION	Balt.	Det.	N.Y.	Tor.	Mil.	Bos.	Clev.	Cal.	Chi.	K.C.	Min.	Oak.	Sea.	Tex.	TOTAL WINS
Baltimore	–	5	6	7	11	8	6	7	7	8	8	8	8	9	98
Detroit	8	–	5	6	6	9	8	8	4	7	9	6	8	8	92
New York	7	8	–	7	9	6	7	7	4	6	8	8	7	7	91
Toronto	6	7	6	–	5	6	9	8	7	6	7	6	8	8	89
Milwaukee	2	7	4	8	–	9	10	6	8	6	8	6	5	8	87
Boston	5	4	7	7	4	–	7	6	6	5	5	8	7	7	78
Cleveland	7	5	6	4	3	6	–	4	4	7	6	7	8	3	70

WESTERN DIVISION	Chi.	K.C.	Tex.	Oak.	Cal.	Min.	Sea.	Balt.	Bos.	Clev.	Det.	Mil.	N.Y.	Tor.	TOTAL WINS
Chicago	–	9	8	8	10	8	12	5	6	8	8	4	8	5	99
Kansas City	4	–	8	7	7	6	8	4	7	5	5	6	6	6	79
Texas	5	5	–	11	7	8	7	3	5	9	4	4	5	4	77
Oakland	5	6	2	–	8	9	9	4	4	5	6	6	4	6	74
California	3	6	6	5	–	6	6	5	6	8	4	6	5	4	70
Minnesota	5	7	5	4	7	–	9	4	7	6	3	4	4	5	70
Seattle	1	5	6	4	7	4	–	4	5	4	4	7	5	4	60

1983 LEADING BASEBALL BATTERS[1]

AMERICAN LEAGUE
(Close of regular season)

PLAYER—CLUB	PCT.	AB	R	H	HR	RBI
Boggs, Boston	.361	582	100	210	5	74
Carew, California	.339	472	66	160	2	44
Whitaker, Detroit	.320	643	94	206	12	72
Trammell, Detroit	.319	505	83	161	14	66
Ripken, Baltimore	.318	663	121	211	27	102
Moseby, Toronto	.315	539	104	170	18	81
McRae, Kansas City	.311	589	84	183	12	82
Brett, Kansas City	.310	464	90	144	25	93
Simmons, Milwaukee	.308	600	76	185	13	108
Yount, Milwaukee	.308	578	102	178	17	80

NATIONAL LEAGUE
(Close of regular season)

PLAYER—CLUB	PCT.	AB	R	H	HR	RBI
Madlock, Pittsburgh	.323	473	68	153	12	68
L. Smith, St. Louis	.321	492	83	158	8	45
Cruz, Houston	.318	594	85	189	14	92
Hendrick, St. Louis	.318	529	73	168	18	97
Knight, Houston	.304	507	43	154	9	70
Murphy, Atlanta	.302	589	131	178	36	121
Moreland, Chicago	.302	533	76	161	16	70
Pena, Pittsburgh	.301	542	51	163	15	70
Oliver, Montreal	.300	614	70	184	8	84
Dawson, Montreal	.299	633	104	189	32	113

[1] Based on 502 or more plate appearances.

1983 LEADING BASEBALL PITCHERS[1]

AMERICAN LEAGUE

PITCHER—CLUB	ERA	W	L	IP	H	BB	SO
Honeycutt, Texas	2.42	14	8	174.2	168	37	56
Boddicker, Baltimore	2.77	16	8	179.0	141	52	120
Stieb, Toronto	3.04	17	12	278.0	223	93	187
Hough, Texas	3.18	15	13	252.0	219	95	152
McGregor, Baltimore	3.18	18	7	260.0	271	45	86
Dotson, Chicago	3.23	22	7	240.0	209	106	137
Haas, Milwaukee	3.27	13	3	179.0	170	42	75
Young, Seattle	3.27	11	15	203.2	178	79	130
Zahn, California	3.33	9	11	203.0	212	51	81
Morris, Detroit	3.34	20	13	293.2	257	83	232

NATIONAL LEAGUE

PITCHER—CLUB	ERA	W	L	IP	H	BB	SO
Hammaker, San Fran.	2.25	10	9	172.1	147	32	127
Denny, Philadelphia	2.37	19	6	242.2	229	53	139
Welch, Los Angeles	2.65	15	12	204.0	164	72	156
Soto, Cincinnati	2.70	17	13	273.2	207	95	242
Pena, Los Angeles	2.75	12	9	177.0	152	51	120
Reuss, Los Angeles	2.94	12	11	223.1	233	50	143
Ryan, Houston	2.98	14	9	196.1	134	101	183
McMurtry, Atlanta	3.08	15	9	224.2	204	88	105
Rhoden, Pittsburgh	3.09	13	13	244.1	256	68	153
Carlton, Philadelphia	3.11	15	16	283.2	277	84	275

[1] 162 or more innings pitched.

STAR BASEBALL PITCHERS OF THE PAST

PITCHERS	CAREER	YEARS	G	IP	W	L	PCT	H	R	ER	SO	BB	ERA
Grover Cleveland Alexander	1911–1930	20	696	5,189	373	208	.642	4,868	1,851	—	2,198	951	2.56
Charles (Chief) Bender	1903–1925	16	459	3,026	212	128	.624	2,653	989	—	1,720	705	2.46
Mordecai (Three-finger) Brown	1903–1916	14	481	3,168	239	130	.631	2,707	863	—	1,381	674	2.03
Jack Chesbro	1899–1909	11	392	2,886	198	127	.609	2,602	1,202	—	1,276	674	2.68
John Clarkson	1882–1894	12	517	4,514	327	176	.650	4,384	—	—	2,013	1,192	—
Stan Coveleski	1912–1928	14	450	3,083	216	142	.603	3,055	1,244	N.A.	981	802	2.87
Jerome (Dizzy) Dean	1930–1947	12	317	1,966	150	83	.644	1,921	776	663	1,155	458	3.04
Urban (Red) Faber	1914–1933	20	669	4,087	254	212	.545	4,104	1,794	1,420	1,471	1,213	3.15
Bob Feller	1936–1956	18	570	3,828	266	162	.621	3,271	1,557	1,384	2,581	1,764	3.25
Whitey Ford	1950–1967	16	498	3,171	236	106	.690	2,766	1,107	967	1,956	1,086	2.74
James (Pud) Galvin	1879–1892	14	675	5,959	361	309	.539	6,334	—	—	1,786	744	—
Vernon (Lefty) Gomez	1930–1943	14	368	2,503	189	102	.649	2,290	1,091	929	1,468	1,095	3.34
Clark Griffith	1891–1914	21	416	3,370	240	140	.632	3,372	—	—	962	800	—
Burleigh Grimes	1916–1934	19	615	4,178	270	212	.560	4,406	2,043	1,636	1,512	1,295	3.52
Robert (Lefty) Grove	1925–1941	17	616	3,940	300	141	.680	3,849	1,594	1,339	2,266	1,187	3.06
Jesse J. (Pop) Haines	1918–1937	19	555	3,207	210	158	.571	3,460	1,556	1,298	981	871	3.64
Waite Hoyt	1918–1938	21	674	3,762	237	182	.566	4,037	1,781	1,500	1,206	1,003	3.59
Carl Hubbell	1928–1943	16	535	3,591	253	154	.622	3,461	1,380	1,188	1,677	725	2.98
Walter Johnson	1907–1927	21	802	5,924	416	279	.599	4,920	1,902	N.A.	3,508	1,353	2.17
Tim Keefe	1880–1893	14	599	5,050	344	225	.605	4,452	—	—	2,542	1,225	—
Sandy Koufax	1955–1966	12	397	2,325	165	87	.655	1,754	806	713	2,396	817	2.76
Bob Lemon	1941–1958	18	460	2,849	207	128	.618	2,559	1,185	1,024	1,277	1,251	3.23
Ted Lyons	1923–1946	21	594	4,162	260	230	.531	4,489	2,056	1,696	1,073	1,121	3.67
Richard (Rube) Marquard	1908–1925	18	536	3,307	201	177	.532	3,233	1,443	—	1,593	858	3.08
Christy Mathewson	1900–1916	17	635	4,781	373	188	.655	4,203	1,613	—	2,505	837	2.13
Joe McGinnity	1899–1908	10	467	3,455	247	145	.630	3,236	1,442	—	1,058	803	2.66
Charles (Kid) Nichols	1890–1906	15	582	5,067	360	202	.641	4,854	—	—	1,866	1,245	2.95
Herb Pennock	1912–1934	22	617	3,558	240	162	.597	3,900	1,693	1,403	1,227	916	3.55
Eddie Plank	1901–1917	17	623	4,503	326	192	.629	3,898	1,470	—	2,257	1,042	2.34
Charles (Hoss) Radbourne	1880–1891	12	517	4,543	308	191	.617	4,500	2,300	—	1,746	856	—
Eppa Rixey	1912–1933	21	692	4,494	266	251	.515	4,633	1,986	1,572	1,350	1,082	3.15
Robin Roberts	1948–1966	19	676	4,689	286	245	.539	4,582	1,962	1,774	2,357	902	3.40
Charles (Red) Ruffing	1924–1947	22	624	4,342	273	225	.548	4,294	2,117	1,833	1,987	1,541	3.80
Warren Spahn	1942–1965	21	750	5,246	363	245	.597	4,830	2,016	1,798	2,583	1,434	3.08
Arthur (Dazzy) Vance	1915–1935	16	442	2,967	197	140	.585	2,809	1,246	1,066	2,045	840	3.24
George (Rube) Waddell	1897–1910	13	407	2,958	191	142	.574	2,480	1,104	—	2,310	771	2.16
Ed Walsh	1904–1917	14	431	2,968	195	126	.607	2,335	877	—	1,731	620	1.82
Mickey Welch	1880–1892	13	565	4,783	308	209	.596	4,648	2,548	—	1,841	1,305	—
Early Wynn	1939–1963	23	691	4,566	300	244	.551	4,291	2,037	1,796	2,334	1,775	3.54
Denton T. (Cy) Young	1890–1911	22	906	7,377	511	313	.620	7,078	3,168	—	2,819	1,209	2.63

BATTING CHAMPIONS—MAJOR LEAGUE BASEBALL

NATIONAL LEAGUE

1915	Larry Doyle, New York	.320
1916	Hal Chase, Cincinnati	.339
1917	Edd Roush, Cincinnati	.341
1918	Zack Wheat, Brooklyn	.335
1919	Edd Roush, Cincinnati	.321
1920	Rogers Hornsby, St. Louis	.370
1921	Rogers Hornsby, St. Louis	.397
1922	Rogers Hornsby, St. Louis	.401
1923	Rogers Hornsby, St. Louis	.384
1924	Rogers Hornsby, St. Louis	.424
1925	Rogers Hornsby, St. Louis	.403
1926	Gene Hargrave, Cincinnati	.353
1927	Paul Waner, Pittsburgh	.380
1928	Rogers Hornsby, Boston	.387
1929	Lefty O'Doul, Philadelphia	.398
1930	Bill Terry, New York	.401
1931	Chick Hafey, St. Louis	.349 [1]
1932	Lefty O'Doul, Brooklyn	.368
1933	Chuck Klein, Philadelphia	.368
1934	Paul Waner, Pittsburgh	.362
1935	Arky Vaughan, Pittsburgh	.385
1936	Paul Waner, Pittsburgh	.373
1937	Joe Medwick, St. Louis	.374
1938	Ernie Lombardi, Cincinnati	.342
1939	Johnny Mize, St. Louis	.349
1940	Debs Garms, Pittsburgh	.355
1941	Pete Reiser, Brooklyn	.343
1942	Ernie Lombardi, Boston	.330
1943	Stan Musial, St. Louis	.357
1944	Dixie Walker, Brooklyn	.357
1945	Phil Cavarretta, Chicago	.355
1946	Stan Musial, St. Louis	.365
1947	Harry Walker, St. Louis–Philadelphia	.363
1948	Stan Musial, St. Louis	.376
1949	Jackie Robinson, Brooklyn	.342
1950	Stan Musial, St. Louis	.346
1951	Stan Musial, St. Louis	.355
1952	Stan Musial, St. Louis	.336
1953	Carl Furillo, Brooklyn	.344
1954	Willie Mays, New York	.345
1955	Richie Ashburn, Philadelphia	.338
1956	Hank Aaron, Milwaukee	.328
1957	Stan Musial, St. Louis	.351
1958	Richie Ashburn, Philadelphia	.350
1959	Hank Aaron, Milwaukee	.355
1960	Dick Groat, Pittsburgh	.325
1961	Roberto Clemente, Pittsburgh	.351
1962	Tommy Davis, Los Angeles	.346
1963	Tommy Davis, Los Angeles	.326
1964	Roberto Clemente, Pittsburgh	.339
1965	Roberto Clemente, Pittsburgh	.329
1966	Matty Alou, Pittsburgh	.342
1967	Roberto Clemente, Pittsburgh	.357
1968	Pete Rose, Cincinnati	.335
1969	Pete Rose, Cincinnati	.348
1970	Rico Carty, Atlanta	.366
1971	Joe Torre, St. Louis	.363
1972	Billy Williams, Chicago	.333
1973	Pete Rose, Cincinnati	.338
1974	Ralph Garr, Atlanta	.353
1975	Bill Madlock, Chicago	.354
1976	Bill Madlock, Chicago	.339
1977	Dave Parker, Pittsburgh	.338
1978	Dave Parker, Pittsburgh	.334
1979	Keith Hernandez, St Louis	.344
1980	Bill Buckner, Chicago	.324
1981	Bill Madlock, Pittsburgh	.341
1982	Al Oliver, Montreal	.331
1983	Bill Madlock, Pittsburgh	.323

AMERICAN LEAGUE

1915	Ty Cobb, Detroit	.369
1916	Tris Speaker, Cleveland	.386
1917	Ty Cobb, Detroit	.383
1918	Ty Cobb, Detroit	.382
1919	Ty Cobb, Detroit	.384
1920	George Sister, St. Louis	.407
1921	Harry Heilmann, Detroit	.394
1922	George Sisler, St. Louis	.420
1923	Harry Heilmann, Detroit	.403
1924	Babe Ruth, New York	.378
1925	Harry Heilmann, Detroit	.393
1926	Heinie Manush, Detroit	.378
1927	Harry Heilmann, Detroit	.398
1928	Goose Goslin, Washington	.379
1929	Lew Fonseca, Cleveland	.369
1930	Al Simmons, Philadelphia	.381
1931	Al Simmons, Philadelphia	.390
1932	Dale Alexander, Detroit–Boston	.367
1933	Jimmy Foxx, Philadelphia	.356
1934	Lou Gehrig, New York	.363
1935	Buddy Myer, Washington	.349
1936	Luke Appling, Chicago	.388
1937	Charley Gehringer, Detroit	.371
1938	Jimmy Foxx, Boston	.349
1939	Joe DiMaggio, New York	.381
1940	Joe DiMaggio, New York	.352
1941	Ted Williams, Boston	.406
1942	Ted Williams, Boston	.356
1943	Luke Appling, Chicago	.328
1944	Lou Boudreau, Cleveland	.327
1945	George Sternweiss, New York	.309
1946	Mickey Vernon, Washington	.353
1947	Ted Williams, Boston	.343
1948	Ted Williams, Boston	.369
1949	George Kell, Detroit	.343 [2]
1950	Billy Goodman, Boston	.354
1951	Ferris Fain, Philadelphia	.344
1952	Ferris Fain, Philadelphia	.327
1953	Mickey Vernon, Washington	.337
1954	Bobby Avila, Cleveland	.341
1955	Al Kaline, Detroit	.340
1956	Mickey Mantle, New York	.353
1957	Ted Williams, Boston	.388
1958	Ted Williams, Boston	.328
1959	Harvey Kuenn, Detroit	.353
1960	Pete Runnels, Boston	.320
1961	Norm Cash, Detroit	.361
1962	Pete Runnels, Boston	.326
1963	Carl Yastrzemski, Boston	.321
1964	Tony Oliva, Minnesota	.323
1965	Tony Oliva, Minnesota	.321
1966	Frank Robinson, Baltimore	.316
1967	Carl Yastrzemski, Boston	.326
1968	Carl Yastrzemski, Boston	.301
1969	Rod Carew, Minnesota	.332
1970	Alex Johnson, California	.329
1971	Tony Oliva, Minnesota	.337
1972	Rod Carew, Minnesota	.318
1973	Rod Carew, Minnesota	.350
1974	Rod Carew, Minnesota	.364
1975	Rod Carew, Minnesota	.359
1976	George Brett, Kansas City	.333
1977	Rod Carew, Minnesota	.388
1978	Rod Carew, Minnesota	.333
1979	Fred Lynn, Boston	.333
1980	George Brett, Kansas City	.390
1981	Carney Lansford, Boston	.336
1982	Willie Wilson, Kansas City	.332
1983	Wade Boggs, Boston	.361

[1] In 1931 Hafey compiled an average of .3489. Bill Terry of New York was second with .3486, and Jim Bottomley of St. Louis was third with .3482. [2] In 1949 Kell compiled .3429. Ted Williams of Boston was second with .3427.

HOME RUN CHAMPIONS—MAJOR LEAGUE BASEBALL

NATIONAL LEAGUE YEAR	PLAYER AND CLUB	HOME RUNS	AMERICAN LEAGUE YEAR	PLAYER AND CLUB	HOME RUNS
1919	Cliff Cravath, Philadelphia	12	1919	Babe Ruth, Boston	29
1920	Fred Williams, Philadelphia	15	1920	Babe Ruth, New York	54
1921	George Kelly, New York	23	1921	Babe Ruth, New York	59
1922	Rogers Hornsby, St. Louis	42	1922	Kenneth R. Williams, St. Louis	39
1923	Fred Williams, Philadelphia	41	1923	Babe Ruth, New York	41
1924	Jacques Fournier, Brooklyn	27	1924	Babe Ruth, New York	46
1925	Rogers Hornsby, St. Louis	39	1925	Bob Meusel, New York	33
1926	Hack Wilson, Chicago	21	1926	Babe Ruth, New York	47
1927	H. Wilson, Chi.; F. Williams, Phil.	30	1927	Babe Ruth, New York	60
1928	H. Wilson, Chi.; J. Bottomley, St. L.	31	1928	Babe Ruth, New York	54
1929	Chuck Klein, Philadelphia	43	1929	Babe Ruth, New York	46
1930	Hack Wilson, Chicago	56	1930	Babe Ruth, New York	49
1931	Chuck Klein, Philadelphia	31	1931	B. Ruth and L. Gehrig, N.Y.	46
1932	C. Klein, Phil.; M. Ott, N.Y. (tie)	38	1932	Jimmy Foxx, Philadelphia	58
1933	Chuck Klein, Philadelphia	28	1933	Jimmy Foxx, Philadelphia	48
1934	M. Ott, N.Y.; R. Collins, St. L. (tie)	35	1934	Lou Gehrig, New York	49
1935	Wally Berger, Boston	34	1935	J. Foxx, Phil.; H. Greenberg, Det.	36
1936	Mel Ott, New York	33	1936	Lou Gehrig, New York	49
1937	M. Ott, N.Y.; J. Medwick, St. L.	31	1937	Joe DiMaggio, New York	46
1938	Mel Ott, New York	36	1938	Hank Greenberg, Detroit	58
1939	Johnny Mize, St. Louis	28	1939	Jimmy Foxx, Boston	35
1940	Johnny Mize, St. Louis	43	1940	Hank Greenberg, Detroit	41
1941	Dolph Camilli, Brooklyn	34	1941	Ted Williams, Boston	37
1942	Mel Ott, New York	30	1942	Ted Williams, Boston	36
1943	Bill Nicholson, Chicago	29	1943	Rudy York, Detroit	34
1944	Bill Nicholson, Chicago	33	1944	Nick Etten, New York	22
1945	Tommy Holmes, Boston	28	1945	Vern Stephens, St. Louis	24
1946	Ralph Kiner, Pittsburgh	23	1946	Hank Greenberg, Detroit	44
1947	R. Kiner, Pitt.; J. Mize, N.Y.	51	1947	Ted Williams, Boston	32
1948	R. Kiner, Pitt.; J. Mize, N.Y.	40	1948	Joe DiMaggio, New York	39
1949	Ralph Kiner, Pittsburgh	54	1949	Ted Williams, Boston	43
1950	Ralph Kiner, Pittsburgh	47	1950	Al Rosen, Cleveland	37
1951	Ralph Kiner, Pittsburgh	42	1951	Gus Zernial, Chicago–Phil.	33
1952	R. Kiner, Pitt.; H. Sauer, Chi.	37	1952	Larry Doby, Cleveland	32
1953	Eddie Mathews, Milwaukee	47	1953	Al Rosen, Cleveland	43
1954	Ted Kluszewski, Cincinnati	49	1954	Larry Doby, Cleveland	32
1955	Willie Mays, New York	51	1955	Mickey Mantle, New York	37
1956	Duke Snider, Brooklyn	43	1956	Mickey Mantle, New York	52
1957	Hank Aaron, Milwaukee	44	1957	Roy Sievers, Washington	42
1958	Ernie Banks, Chicago	47	1958	Mickey Mantle, New York	42
1959	Eddie Mathews, Milwaukee	46	1959	R. Colavito, Clev.; H. Killebrew, Wash.	42
1960	Ernie Banks, Chicago	41	1960	Mickey Mantle, New York	40
1961	Orlando Cepeda, San Francisco	46	1961	Roger Maris, New York	61
1962	Willie Mays, San Francisco	49	1962	Harmon Killebrew, Minnesota	48
1963	H. Aaron, Mil.; W. McCovey, S.F.	44	1963	Harmon Killebrew, Minnesota	45
1964	Willie Mays, San Francisco	47	1964	Harmon Killebrew, Minnesota	49
1965	Willie Mays, San Francisco	52	1965	Tony Conigliaro, Boston	32
1966	Hank Aaron, Atlanta	44	1966	Frank Robinson, Baltimore	49
1967	Hank Aaron, Atlanta	39	1967	Carl Yastrzemski, Boston	44
				Harmon Killebrew, Minnesota	44
1968	Willie McCovey, San Francisco	36	1968	Frank Howard, Washington	44
1969	Willie McCovey, San Francisco	45	1969	Harmon Killebrew, Minnesota	49
1970	Johnny Bench, Cincinnati	45	1970	Frank Howard, Washington	44
1971	Willie Stargell, Pittsburgh	48	1971	Bill Melton, Chicago	33
1972	Johnny Bench, Cincinnati	40	1972	Dick Allen, Chicago	37
1973	Willie Stargell, Pittsburgh	44	1973	Reggie Jackson, Oakland	32
1974	Mike Schmidt, Philadelphia	36	1974	Dick Allen, Chicago	32
1975	Mike Schmidt, Philadelphia	38	1975	Reggie Jackson, Oakland	36
				George Scott, Milwaukee	36
1976	Mike Schmidt, Philadelphia	38	1976	Graig Nettles, New York	32
1977	George Foster, Cincinnati	52	1977	Jim Rice, Boston	39
1978	George Foster, Cincinnati	40	1978	Jim Rice, Boston	46
1979	Dave Kingman, Chicago	48	1979	Gorman Thomas, Milwaukee	45
1980	Mike Schmidt, Philadelphia	48	1980	Ben Oglivie, Milwaukee	41
				Reggie Jackson, New York	41
1981	Mike Schmidt, Philadelphia	31	1981	Four-way tie[1]	22
1982	Dave Kingman, N.Y. Mets	37	1982	Reggie Jackson, California	39
				Gorman Thomas, Milwaukee	39
1983	Mike Schmidt, Philadelphia	40	1983	Jim Rice, Boston	39

[1] Tony Armas, Oakland; Eddie Murray, Baltimore; Dwight Evans, Boston; Bobby Grich, California.

RUNS-BATTED-IN LEADERS — MAJOR LEAGUE BASEBALL

NATIONAL LEAGUE

1914	Sherwood Magee, Philadelphia	101
1915	Cliff Cravath, Philadelphia	118
1916	Hal Chase, Cincinnati	84
1917	Heinie Zimmerman, New York	100
1918	Fred Merkle, Chicago	71
1919	Henry (Hi) Myers, Brooklyn	72
1920	G. Kelly, N.Y.; R. Hornsby, St. Louis	94
1921	Rogers Hornsby, St. Louis	126
1922	Rogers Hornsby, St. Louis	152
1923	Irish Meusel, New York	125
1924	George Kelly, New York	136
1925	Rogers Hornsby, St. Louis	143
1926	Jim Bottomley, St. Louis	120
1927	Paul Waner, Pittsburgh	131
1928	Jim Bottomley, St. Louis	136
1929	Hack Wilson, Chicago	159
1930	Hack Wilson, Chicago	190
1931	Chuck Klein, Philadelphia	121
1932	Frank Hurst, Philadelphia	143
1933	Chuck Klein, Philadelphia	120
1934	Mel Ott, New York	135
1935	Wally Berger, Boston	130
1936	Joe Medwick, St. Louis	138
1937	Joe Medwick, St. Louis	154
1938	Joe Medwick, St. Louis	122
1939	Frank McCormick, Cincinnati	128
1940	Johnny Mize, St. Louis	137
1941	Dolph Camilli, Brooklyn	120
1942	Johnny Mize, New York	110
1943	Bill Nicholson, Chicago	128
1944	Bill Nicholson, Chicago	122
1945	Dixie Walker, Brooklyn	124
1946	Enos Slaughter, St. Louis	130
1947	Johnny Mize, New York	138
1948	Stan Musial, St. Louis	131
1949	Ralph Kiner, Pittsburgh	127
1950	Del Ennis, Philadelphia	126
1951	Monte Irvin, New York	121
1952	Hank Sauer, Chicago	121
1953	Roy Campanella, Brooklyn	142
1954	Ted Kluszewski, Cincinnati	141
1955	Duke Snider, Brooklyn	136
1956	Stan Musial, St. Louis	109
1957	Hank Aaron, Milwaukee	132
1958	Ernie Banks, Chicago	129
1959	Ernie Banks, Chicago	143
1960	Hank Aaron, Milwaukee	126
1961	Orlando Cepeda, San Francisco	142
1962	Tommy Davis, Los Angeles	153
1963	Hank Aaron, Milwaukee	130
1964	Ken Boyer, St. Louis	119
1965	Deron Johnson, Cincinnati	130
1966	Hank Aaron, Atlanta	121
1967	Orlando Cepeda, St. Louis	111
1968	Willie McCovey, San Francisco	105
1969	Willie McCovey, San Francisco	126
1970	Johnny Bench, Cincinnati	148
1971	Joe Torre, St. Louis	137
1972	Johnny Bench, Cincinnati	125
1973	Willie Stargell, Pittsburgh	119
1974	Johnny Bench, Cincinnati	129
1975	Greg Luzinski, Philadelphia	120
1976	George Foster, Cincinnati	121
1977	George Foster, Cincinnati	149
1978	George Foster, Cincinnati	120
1979	Dave Winfield, San Diego	118
1980	Mike Schmidt, Philadelphia	121
1981	Mike Schmidt, Philadelphia	91
1982	Al Oliver, Montreal	109
1983	Dale Murphy, Atlanta	121

AMERICAN LEAGUE

1914	Sam Crawford, Detroit	112
1915	Sam Crawford, Detroit	116
1916	Wally Pipp, New York	99
1917	Robert Veach, Detroit	115
1918	G. Burns, Phil.; R. Veach, Det.	74
1919	Babe Ruth, Boston	112
1920	Babe Ruth, New York	137
1921	Babe Ruth, New York	170
1922	Ken Williams, St. Louis	155
1923	Tris Speaker, Cleveland; Babe Ruth, N.Y.	130
1924	Goose Goslin, Washington	129
1925	Bob Meusel, New York	138
1926	Babe Ruth, New York	145
1927	Lou Gehrig, New York	175
1928	Babe Ruth and Lou Gehrig, N.Y.	142
1929	Al Simmons, Philadelphia	157
1930	Lou Gehrig, New York	174
1931	Lou Gehrig, New York	184
1932	Jimmy Foxx, Philadelphia	169
1933	Jimmy Foxx, Philadelphia	163
1934	Lou Gehrig, New York	165
1935	Hank Greenberg, Detroit	170
1936	Hal Trosky, Cleveland	162
1937	Hank Greenberg, Detroit	183
1938	Jimmy Foxx, Boston	175
1939	Ted Williams, Boston	145
1940	Hank Greenberg, Detroit	150
1941	Joe DiMaggio, New York	125
1942	Ted Williams, Boston	137
1943	Rudy York, Detroit	118
1944	Vern Stephens, St. Louis	109
1945	Nick Etten, New York	111
1946	Hank Greenberg, Detroit	127
1947	Ted Williams, Boston	114
1948	Joe DiMaggio, New York	155
1949	Ted Williams, Vern Stephens, Boston	159
1950	Vern Stephens, Walt Dropo, Boston	144
1951	Gus Zernial, Chicago-Philadelphia	129
1952	Al Rosen, Cleveland	105
1953	Al Rosen, Cleveland	145
1954	Larry Doby, Cleveland	126
1955	R. Boone, Det.; J. Jensen, Bost.	116
1956	Mickey Mantle, New York	130
1957	Roy Sievers, Washington	114
1958	Jackie Jensen, Boston	122
1959	Jackie Jensen, Boston	112
1960	Roger Maris, New York	112
1961	Roger Maris, New York	142
1962	Harmon Killebrew, Minnesota	126
1963	Dick Stuart, Boston	118
1964	Brooks Robinson, Baltimore	118
1965	Rocky Colavito, Cleveland	108
1966	Frank Robinson, Baltimore	122
1967	Carl Yastrzemski, Boston	121
1968	Ken Harrelson, Boston	109
1969	Harmon Killebrew, Minnesota	140
1970	Frank Howard, Washington	126
1971	Harmon Killebrew, Minnesota	119
1972	Dick Allen, Chicago	113
1973	Reggie Jackson, Oakland	117
1974	Jeff Burroughs, Texas	118
1975	George Scott, Milwaukee	109
1976	Lee May, Baltimore	109
1977	Larry Hisle, Minnesota	119
1978	Jim Rice, Boston	139
1979	Don Baylor, California	139
1980	Cecil Cooper, Milwaukee	122
1981	Eddie Murray, Baltimore	78
1982	Hal McRae, Kansas City	133
1983	Cecil Cooper, Milwaukee	126

PITCHERS WITH LOWEST EARNED RUN AVERAGE (ERA)[1]

YEAR	NATIONAL LEAGUE PITCHER AND CLUB	INNINGS	ERA	AMERICAN LEAGUE PITCHER AND CLUB	INNINGS	ERA
1952	Hoyt Wilhelm, New York	159	2.43	Allie Reynolds, New York	244	2.07
1953	Warren Spahn, Milwaukee	266	2.10	Eddie Lopat, New York	178	2.43
1954	John Antonelli, New York	259	2.29	Mike Garcia, Cleveland	259	2.64
1955	Bob Friend, Pittsburgh	200	2.84	Billy Pierce, Chicago	206	1.97
1956	Lew Burdette, Milwaukee	256	2.71	Whitey Ford, New York	226	2.47
1957	John Podres, Brooklyn	196	2.66	Bobby Shantz, New York	173	2.45
1958	Stu Miller, San Francisco	182	2.47	Whitey Ford, New York	219	2.01
1959	Sam Jones, San Francisco	271	2.82	Hoyt Wilhelm, Baltimore	226	2.19
1960	Mike McCormick, San Francisco	253	2.70	Frank Baumann, Chicago	185	2.68
1961	Warren Spahn, Milwaukee	263	3.01	Dick Donovan, Washington	169	2.40
1962	Sandy Koufax, Los Angeles	184	2.54	Hank Aguirre, Detroit	216	2.21
1963	Sandy Koufax, Los Angeles	311	1.88	Gary Peters, Chicago	243	2.33
1964	Sandy Koufax, Los Angeles	223	1.74	Dean Chance, Los Angeles	278	1.65
1965	Sandy Koufax, Los Angeles	336	2.04	Sam McDowell, Cleveland	274	2.17
1966	Sandy Koufax, Los Angeles	323	1.73	Gary Peters, Chicago	204	2.03
1967	Phil Niekro, Atlanta	207	1.96	Joe Horlen, Chicago	258	2.06
1968	Bob Gibson, St. Louis	304	1.12	Luis Tiant, Cleveland	258	1.60
1969	Juan Marichal, San Francisco	299	2.10	Dick Bosman, Washington	193	2.19
1970	Tom Seaver, New York	291	2.81	Diego Segui, Oakland	162	2.56
1971	Tom Seaver, New York	286	1.76	Vida Blue, Oakland	312	1.82
1972	Steve Carlton, Philadelphia	346	1.98	Luis Tiant, Boston	179	1.91
1973	Tom Seaver, New York	290	2.07	Jim Palmer, Baltimore	296	2.40
1974	Buzz Capra, Atlanta	217	2.28	Jim (Catfish) Hunter, Oakland	318	2.49
1975	Randy Jones, San Diego	285	2.24	Jim Palmer, Baltimore	323	2.09
1976	John Denny, St. Louis	207	2.52	Mark Fidrych, Detroit	250⅓	2.34
1977	John Candelaria, Pittsburgh	231	2.34	Frank Tanana, California	241	2.54
1978	Craig Swan, New York	207	2.43	Ron Guidry, New York	274	1.74
1979	James Richard, Houston	292	2.71	Ron Guidry, New York	236	2.78
1980	Don Sutton, Los Angeles	212	2.21	Rudy May, New York	175	2.47
1981[3]	Nolan Ryan, Houston	149	1.69	Steve McCatty, Oakland	186	2.32
1982	Stephen Rogers, Montreal	277	2.40	Rick Sutcliffe, Cleveland	216	2.96
1983	Atlee Hammaker, San Francisco	172	2.25	Rick Honeycutt, Texas	174	2.42

PITCHERS WITH HIGHEST WON-LOST PERCENTAGES[2]

YEAR	NATIONAL LEAGUE PITCHER AND CLUB	GAMES Won	GAMES Lost	PCT.	AMERICAN LEAGUE PITCHER AND CLUB	GAMES Won	GAMES Lost	PCT.
1952	Hoyt Wilhelm, New York	15	3	.833	Bobby Shantz, Philadelphia	24	7	.774
1953	Carl Erskine, Brooklyn	20	6	.769	Eddie Lopat, New York	16	4	.800
1954	John Antonelli, New York	21	7	.750	Sandy Consuegra, Chicago	16	3	.842
	Hoyt Wilhelm, New York	12	4	.750				
1955	Don Newcombe, Brooklyn	20	5	.800	Tommy Byrne, New York	16	5	.762
1956	Don Newcombe, Brooklyn	27	7	.794	Whitey Ford, New York	19	6	.760
1957	Bob Buhl, Milwaukee	18	7	.720	Dick Donovan, Chicago	16	6	.727
1958	Warren Spahn, Milwaukee	22	11	.667	Tom Sturdivant, New York	16	6	.727
	Lew Burdette, Milwaukee	20	10	.667	Bob Turley, New York	21	7	.750
1959	Elroy Face, Pittsburgh	18	1	.947	Bob Shaw, Chicago	18	6	.750
1960	Lindy McDaniel, St. Louis	12	4	.750	Jim Coates, New York	13	3	.813
1961	Johnny Podres, Los Angeles	18	5	.783	Whitey Ford, New York	25	4	.862
1962	Bob Purkey, Cincinnati	23	5	.821	Ray Herbert, Chicago	20	9	.690
1963	Ron Perranoski, Los Angeles	16	3	.842	Whitey Ford, New York	24	7	.774
1964	Sandy Koufax, Los Angeles	19	5	.792	Wally Bunker, Baltimore	19	5	.792
1965	Sandy Koufax, Los Angeles	26	8	.765	Jim Grant, Minnesota	21	7	.750
1966	Juan Marichal, San Francisco	25	6	.806	Dave Boswell, Minnesota	12	5	.706
1967	Nelson Briles, St. Louis	14	5	.736	Joel Horlen, Chicago	19	7	.730
1968	Steve Blass, Pittsburgh	18	6	.750	Dennis McLain, Detroit	31	6	.843
1969	Bob Moose, Pittsburgh	14	3	.824	Jim Palmer, Baltimore	16	4	.800
1970	Wayne Simpson, Cincinnati	14	3	.824	Dave McNally, Baltimore	24	9	.727
1971	Tug McGraw, New York	11	4	.733	Dave McNally, Baltimore	21	5	.807
1972	Gary Nolan, Cincinnati	15	5	.750	Jim Hunter, Oakland	21	7	.750
1973	George Stone, New York	12	3	.800	Roger Moret, Boston	13	2	.866
1974	Tommy John, Los Angeles	13	3	.813	Bill Champion, Milwaukee	11	4	.733
1975	Al Hrabosky, St. Louis	13	3	.813	Roger Moret, Boston	14	3	.824
1976	Richard Rhoden, Los Angeles	12	3	.800	Bill Campbell, Minnesota	17	5	.773
1977	John Candelaria, Pittsburgh	20	5	.800	Don Gullett, New York	14	4	.778
1978	Gaylord Perry, San Diego	21	6	.778	Ron Guidry, New York	25	3	.893
1979	James Bibby, Pittsburgh	12	4	.750	Ron Davis, New York	14	2	.875
1980	Jerry Reuss, Los Angeles	18	6	.750	Steve Stone, Baltimore	25	7	.781
1981[3]	Tom Seaver, Cincinnati	14	2	.875	Ron Guidry, New York	11	5	.688
1982	Phil Niekro, Atlanta	17	4	.810	Jim Palmer, Baltimore	15	5	.750
1983	John Denny, Philadelphia	19	6	.760	Richard Dotson, Chicago	22	7	.759

[1] Must have pitched 162 innings. [2] Must have been involved in 15 won-lost decisions. [3] Strike shortened season.

MAJOR LEAGUE BASEBALL PARKS

TEAM	STADIUM	SEATING CAPACITY	DISTANCE FROM HOME PLATE (in feet) Right Field	Center Field	Left Field
NATIONAL LEAGUE					
Atlanta Braves	Atlanta Stadium	52,934	330	402	330
Chicago Cubs	Wrigley Field	37,272	353	400	355
Cincinnati Reds	Riverfront Stadium	52,392	330	404	330
Houston Astros	The Astrodome	45,000	340	406	340
Los Angeles Dodgers	Dodger Stadium	56,000	330	400	330
Montreal Expos	Olympic Stadium	58,838	325	404	325
New York Mets	Shea Stadium	55,300	338	410	338
Philadelphia Phillies	Veterans Stadium	66,507	330	408	330
Pittsburgh Pirates	Three Rivers Stadium	54,598	335	400	335
St. Louis Cardinals	Busch Memorial Stadium	50,222	330	414	330
San Diego Padres	Jack Murphy Stadium	51,319	330	405	330
San Francisco Giants	Candlestick Park	58,000	335	400	335
AMERICAN LEAGUE					
Baltimore Orioles	Memorial Stadium	53,208	309	405	309
Boston Red Sox	Fenway Park	33,465	302	390	315
California Angels	Anaheim Stadium	67,335	370	404	370
Chicago White Sox	Comiskey Park	43,651	341	401	341
Cleveland Indians	Cleveland Stadium	74,208	320	400	320
Detroit Tigers	Tiger Stadium	52,687	325	440	340
Kansas City Royals	Royals Stadium	40,635	330	410	330
Milwaukee Brewers	County Stadium	53,192	362	402	362
Minnesota Twins	Hubert H. Humphrey Metrodome	55,122	367	408	385
New York Yankees	Yankee Stadium	57,545	353	417	387
Oakland Athletics	Oakland Coliseum	50,219	330	397	330
Seattle Mariners	The Kingdome	59,438	316	410	316
Texas Rangers	Arlington Stadium	41,284	330	380	330
Toronto Blue Jays	Exhibition Stadium	43,737	330	400	330

MAJOR LEAGUE BASEBALL ATTENDANCE FIGURES AT HOME PARKS

NATIONAL LEAGUE CLUB	TOTAL 1983 ATTENDANCE	RECORD SEASON Attendance	Year	NATIONAL LEAGUE CLUB	TOTAL 1983 ATTENDANCE	RECORD SEASON Attendance	Year
Atlanta	2,119,935	2,119,935	1983	New York	1,112,774	2,697,479	1970
Chicago	1,479,717	1,674,993	1969	Philadelphia	2,128,339	2,775,011	1979
Cincinnati	1,190,419	2,629,708	1976	Pittsburgh	1,225,916	1,705,828	1960
Houston	1,351,962	2,278,217	1980	St. Louis	2,317,914	2,317,914	1983
Los Angeles	3,510,313	3,608,881	1982	San Diego	1,539,815	1,670,107	1978
Montreal	2,320,651	2,320,651	1983	San Francisco	1,251,530	1,795,356	1960

AMERICAN LEAGUE CLUB	TOTAL 1983 ATTENDANCE	RECORD SEASON Attendance	Year	AMERICAN LEAGUE CLUB	TOTAL 1983 ATTENDANCE	RECORD SEASON Attendance	Year
Baltimore	2,042,071	2,042,071	1983	Milwaukee	2,397,131	2,397,131	1983
Boston	1,782,285	2,353,114	1979	Minnesota	858,939	1,483,547	1967
California	2,555,016	2,807,360	1979	New York	2,257,976	2,627,417	1980
Chicago	2,132,821	2,132,821	1983	Oakland	1,294,941	1,735,489	1982
Cleveland	768,941	2,620,627	1948	Seattle	813,537	1,338,523	1977
Detroit	1,829,636	2,031,847	1968	Texas	1,363,469	1,519,671	1979
Kansas City	1,963,875	2,288,714	1980	Toronto	1,930,415	1,930,415	1983

ALL-STAR BASEBALL GAME RESULTS

YEAR	WINNING LEAGUE	SCORE	YEAR	WINNING LEAGUE	SCORE	YEAR	WINNING LEAGUE	SCORE	YEAR	WINNING LEAGUE	SCORE
1933	American	4–2	1947	American	2–1	1960	National	5–3	1971	American	6–4
1934	American	9–7	1948	American	5–2		National	6–0	1972	National	4–3
1935	American	4–1	1949	American	11–7	1961	National	5–4	1973	National	7–1
1936	National	4–3	1950	National	4–3		Tie game	1–1	1974	National	7–2
1937	American	8–3	1951	National	8–3	1962	National	3–1	1975	National	6–3
1938	National	4–1	1952	National	3–2		American	9–4	1976	National	7–1
1939	American	3–1	1953	National	5–1	1963	National	5–3	1977	National	7–5
1940	National	4–0	1954	American	11–9	1964	National	7–4	1978	National	7–3
1941	American	7–5	1955	National	6–5	1965	National	6–5	1979	National	7–6
1942	American	3–1	1956	National	7–3	1966	National	2–1	1980	National	4–2
1943	American	5–3	1957	American	6–5	1967	National	2–1	1981	National	5–4
1944	National	7–1	1958	American	4–3	1968	National	1–0	1982	National	4–1
1945	No game		1959	National	5–4	1969	National	9–3	1983	American	13–3
1946	American	12–0		American	5–3	1970	National	5–4			

BASEBALL HALL OF FAME

PITCHERS	CAREER	Won	Lost
Grover Alexander	1911–1930	373	208
Charles (Chief) Bender	1903–1925	212	128
Mordecai (Three-finger) Brown	1903–1916	239	130
Jack Chesbro	1899–1909	199	128
John Clarkson	1882–1894	328	175
Stan Coveleski	1912–1925	216	142
W. A. Cummings	1872–1877	146	92
Jerome (Dizzy) Dean	1930–1947	150	83
Urban (Red) Faber	1914–1933	253	211
Bob Feller	1936–1956	266	162
Edward (Whitey) Ford	1950–1967	236	106
James (Pud) Galvin	1876–1892	365	309
Bob Gibson	1959–1975	251	174
Vernon (Lefty) Gomez	1930–1942	189	95
Clark Griffith	1891–1914	237	140
Burleigh Grimes	1916–1934	270	212
Robert (Lefty) Grove	1925–1941	300	141
Jesse J. (Pop) Haines	1920–1937	210	158
Waite Hoyte	1919–1938	237	182
Carl Hubbell	1928–1943	253	154
Walter Johnson	1907–1927	416	279
Addie Joss	1902–1910	159	96
Tim Keefe	1880–1893	346	225
Sandy Koufax	1955–1966	165	87
Bob Lemon	1946–1958	207	128
Ted Lyons	1923–1946	260	230
Juan Marichal	1960–1975	243	142
Richard (Rube) Marquard	1908–1925	201	177
Christy Mathewson	1900–1916	373	188
Joe McGinnity	1899–1908	247	142
Charles (Kid) Nichols	1890–1906	360	202
Leroy (Satchel) Paige	1948–1952	28	31
Herb Pennock	1912–1934	241	163
Eddie Plank	1901–1917	325	190
Charles (Hoss) Radbourne	1880–1891	308	191
Eppa Rixey	1912–1933	266	251
Robin Roberts	1948–1966	286	245
Charles (Red) Ruffing	1924–1947	273	225
Amos Rusie	1889–1901	243	160
Warren Spahn	1940–1967	363	245
A. G. Spalding	1871–1877	252	68
Arthur (Dazzy) Vance	1915–1935	197	140
George (Rube) Waddell	1897–1910	193	140
Ed Walsh	1904–1917	195	126
John Ward	1878–1894	158	102
Mickey Welch	1880–1892	309	211
Early Wynn	1939–1963	300	244
Denton T. (Cy) Young	1890–1911	511	315

CATCHERS	CAREER	AVERAGE
Lawrence (Yogi) Berra	1946–1965	.285
Roger Bresnahan	1897–1915	.279
Roy Campanella	1948–1957	.276
Gordon (Mickey) Cochrane	1925–1937	.320
Bill Dickey	1928–1946	.313
William (Buck) Ewing	1880–1897	.311
Charles (Gabby) Hartnett	1922–1941	.297
Mike Kelly	1878–1893	.315
Connie Mack	1886–1896	.249
Wilbert Robinson	1886–1902	.280
Ray Schalk	1912–1929	.253

FIRST BASEMEN	CAREER	AVERAGE
Adrian (Cap) Anson	1876–1897	.339
Jake Beckley	1888–1907	.309
Sunny Jim Bottomley	1922–1935	.310
Dennis (Dan) Brouthers	1879–1896	.348
Frank Chance	1898–1914	.297
Charles Comiskey	1882–1894	.269
Roger Connor	1880–1897	.317
Jimmy Foxx	1925–1945	.325
Henry (Lou) Gehrig	1923–1939	.340
Henry (Hank) Greenberg	1933–1947	.313
George Kelly	1915–1932	.297
Buck Leonard	1930–1944	(Negro leag.)
Johnny Mize	1936–1953	.312
George Sisler	1915–1930	.340
Bill Terry	1923–1936	.341

SECOND BASEMEN	CAREER	AVERAGE
Eddie Collins	1906–1930	.333
Johnny Evers	1902–1919	.270
Frank Frisch	1919–1937	.316
Charley Gehringer	1924–1942	.321
Billy Herman	1931–1947	.304
Rogers Hornsby	1915–1937	.359
Napoleon Lajoie	1896–1916	.339
Jackie Robinson	1947–1956	.311

THIRD BASEMEN	CAREER	AVERAGE
Frank (Home Run) Baker	1908–1922	.307
Jimmy Collins	1895–1908	.294
William (Judy) Johnson	1918–1938	.340
George Kell	1943–1957	.306
Eddie Mathews	1952–1968	.271
John McGraw	1891–1906	.334
Brooks Robinson	1955–1977	.267
Harold (Pie) Traynor	1920–1937	.320

SHORTSTOPS	CAREER	AVERAGE
Luke Appling	1930–1950	.310
Dave Bancroft	1915–1929	.279
Ernie Banks	1953–1971	.274
Lou Boudreau	1938–1952	.295
Joe Cronin	1926–1945	.302
Travis Jackson	1922–1937	.291
Hugh Jennings	1891–1918	.314
Walter (Rabbit) Maranville	1912–1935	.258
Joe Sewell	1920–1933	.312
Joe Tinker	1902–1916	.264
John (Honus) Wagner	1897–1917	.329
Roderick (Bobby) Wallace	1894–1918	.267
George Wright	1876–1882	.251

OUTFIELDERS	CAREER	AVERAGE
Henry Aaron	1954–1976	.305
Earl Averill	1929–1941	.318
James (Cool Papa) Bell	1921–1950	(Negro leag.)
Jesse Burkett	1890–1905	.342
Max Carey	1910–1929	.285
Oscar Charleston	1915–1944	(Negro leag.)
Fred Clarke	1894–1915	.315
Roberto Clemente	1955–1972	.317
Ty Cobb	1905–1928	.367
Earl B. Combs	1924–1935	.325
Sam Crawford	1899–1917	.309
Hazen (Kiki) Cuyler	1921–1938	.321
Ed Delahanty	1888–1903	.346
Martin Dihigo	1923–1950	.320
Joe DiMaggio	1936–1951	.325
Hugh Duffy	1888–1906	.330
Elmer Flick	1898–1910	.315
Josh Gibson	1929–1946	(Negro leag.)
Leon (Goose) Goslin	1921–1938	.316
Billy Hamilton	1888–1901	.344
Harry Heilmann	1914–1932	.342
Harry Hooper	1909–1925	.281
Monte Irvin	1930s–40s	(Negro leag.)
Al Kaline	1953–1974	.297
Willie Keeler	1892–1910	.345
Joe Kelley	1892–1910	.321
Ralph Kiner	1946–1955	.279
Chuck Klein	1928–1944	.320
Fred Lindstrom	1924–1936	.311
John Henry Lloyd	1905–1931	.362
Mickey Mantle	1951–1968	.298
Henry (Heinie) Manush	1923–1939	.330
Willie Mays	1951–1973	.302
Thomas McCarthy	1884–1896	.294
Joe Medwick	1932–1948	.324
Stan Musial	1941–1963	.331

BASEBALL HALL OF FAME *(continued)*

OUTFIELDERS *(continued)*

James O'Rourke	1876–1894	.315
Mel Ott	1926–1947	.304
Edgar (Sam) Rice	1915–1934	.322
Frank Robinson	1956–1976	.294
Edd Roush	1913–1931	.323
George (Babe) Ruth	1914–1935	.342
Al Simmons	1924–1944	.334
Duke Snider	1947–1964	.295
Tris Speaker	1907–1928	.344
Sam Thompson	1885–1898	.336
Lloyd Waner	1927–1945	.316
Paul Waner	1926–1945	.333
Zack Wheat	1909–1927	.317
Ted Williams	1939–1960	.344
Lewis R. (Hack) Wilson	1923–1934	.319
Ross Youngs	1917–1926	.322

OTHERS ELECTED FOR MERITORIOUS SERVICE

Walter Alston, manager, Brooklyn, Los Angeles (1954–76)
Edward G. Barrow, American League executive
Morgan G. Bulkeley, first National League president
Alexander J. Cartwright, organized first baseball club
Henry Chadwick, wrote first baseball rule book
Albert B. (Happy) Chandler, baseball commissioner, 1946–51
Charles A. Comiskey, player, manager, and executive
John (Jocko) Conlan, National League umpire (1941–65)
Tom Connolly, American League umpire for 52 years
Billy Evans, umpire and later general manager of Cleveland Indians and Boston Red Sox
Andrew (Rube) Foster, founder of Negro National League
Ford C. Frick, National League president (1934–51) and baseball commissioner (1951–65)
Warren Giles, president of the National League (1951–69)
Will Harridge, president of the American League (1931–58)
Bucky Harris, player and manager (1919–47)
Cal Hubbard, American League umpire (1936–52)
Miller Huggins, managed N.Y. Yankees to six pennants
Ban Johnson, first American League president
Bill Klem, National League umpire for 46 years
Kenesaw M. Landis, baseball's first commissioner
Al Lopez, catcher 1928–47; manager, Cleveland Indians 1951–57, Chicago White Sox 1957–65, 1968–69
Leland MacPhail, manager, Cincinnati, Brooklyn, N.Y. Yankees (1933–47); introduced night games (1935)
Joe McCarthy, managed N.Y. Yankees to nine pennants and won seven World Series
Bill McKechnie, managed three different clubs to pennants
Branch Rickey, executive of three National League clubs
Casey Stengel, manager N.Y. Yankees and N.Y. Mets
George Weiss, general manager of N.Y. Yankees and Mets
Harry Wright, National League manager for 30 years
Tom Yawkey, owner of Boston Red Sox (1933–76)

CY YOUNG AWARD (Top Major League Pitchers)

NATIONAL LEAGUE

1973	Tom Seaver, New York
1974	Mike Marshall, Los Angeles
1975	Tom Seaver, New York
1976	Randy Jones, San Diego
1977	Steve Carlton, Philadelphia
1978	Gaylord Perry, San Diego
1979	Bruce Sutter, Chicago
1980	Steve Carlton, Philadelphia
1981	Fernando Valenzuela, Los Angeles
1982	Steve Carlton, Philadelphia
1983	John Denny, Philadelphia

AMERICAN LEAGUE

1973	Jim Palmer, Baltimore
1974	Jim (Catfish) Hunter, Oakland
1975	Jim Palmer, Baltimore
1976	Jim Palmer, Baltimore
1977	Sparky Lyle, New York
1978	Ron Guidry, New York
1979	Mike Flanagan, Baltimore
1980	Steve Stone, Baltimore
1981	Rollie Fingers, Milwaukee
1982	Pete Vuckovich, Milwaukee
1983	LaMarr Hoyt, Chicago

LEADING HOME RUN HITTERS—LIFETIME TOTALS

PLAYER	HR	PLAYER	HR	PLAYER	HR	PLAYER	HR
Hank Aaron	755	Willie McCovey	521	Carl Yastrzemski *	452	Rocky Colavito	374
Babe Ruth	714	Ernie Banks	512	Billy Williams	426	Gil Hodges	370
Willie Mays	660	Eddie Matthews	512	Duke Snider	407	Ralph Kiner	369
Frank Robinson	586	Mel Ott	511	Al Kaline	399	Tony Perez *	368
Harmon Killebrew	573	Lou Gehrig	493	Johnny Bench *	389	Joe DiMaggio	361
Mickey Mantle	536	Reggie Jackson *	478	Frank Howard	382	Johnny Mize	359
Jimmy Foxx	534	Stan Musial	475	Orlando Cepeda	379	Yogi Berra	358
Ted Williams	521	Willie Stargell	475	Norm Cash	377	Lee May	354

* Active player in 1983 season.

STAR BASEBALL HITTERS OF THE PAST

PLAYER AND TEAM(S)	YEARS	GAMES	AT BAT	RUNS	HITS	BAT. AV.
Ty Cobb, Detroit, Philadelphia (AL)	1905–28	3,033	11,429	2,244	4,191	.367
Rogers Hornsby, St. Louis, N.Y., Boston, Chicago (NL)	1915–32	2,259	8,173	1,579	2,930	.359
Tris Speaker, Bost., Clev., Wash., Phil. (AL)	1907–28	2,789	10,208	1,881	3,515	.344
Ted Williams, Boston (AL)	1939–60	2,292	7,706	1,798	2,654	.344
Babe Ruth, Boston, New York (AL), Boston (NL)	1914–35	2,503	8,399	2,174	2,873	.342
Harry Heilmann, Detroit (AL), Cincinnati (NL)	1914–32	2,146	7,787	1,291	2,660	.342
Bill Terry, New York (NL)	1923–36	1,721	6,428	1,120	2,193	.341
Lou Gehrig, New York (AL)	1923–39	2,164	8,001	1,888	2,721	.340
George Sisler, mainly with St. Louis (AL)	1915–30	2,055	8,267	1,284	2,812	.340
Napoleon Lajoie, mainly with Philadelphia (AL)	1896–1916	2,475	9,589	1,503	3,251	.339
Eddie Collins, Philadelphia, Chicago (AL)	1906–30	2,826	9,952	1,818	3,313	.333
Paul Waner, Pitt., Brooklyn, Boston (NL), N.Y. (AL)	1926–45	2,549	9,459	1,626	3,152	.333
Stan Musial, St. Louis (NL)	1941–63	3,026	10,972	1,949	3,630	.331
Jimmy Foxx, Phil., Boston (AL), Chicago, Phil, (NL)	1925–45	2,317	8,134	1,751	2,646	.325
Joe DiMaggio, New York (AL)	1936–51	1,736	6,821	1,390	2,214	.325
Joe Medwick, St. Louis, Brooklyn, N.Y., Boston (NL)	1932–48	1,984	7,635	1,198	2,471	.324
Charley Gehringer, Detroit (AL)	1924–42	2,323	8,858	1,773	2,838	.321
Chuck Klein, Philadelphia, Chicago, Pittsburgh (NL)	1928–44	1,753	6,486	1,168	2,076	.320
Frank Frisch, New York, St. Louis (NL)	1919–37	2,311	9,112	1,532	2,880	.316
Hank Aaron, Milw. (NL), Atlanta (NL), Milw. (AL)	1954–76	3,298	12,364	2,174	3,771	.305
Willie Mays, N.Y. (NL), San. Fran. (NL), N.Y. (NL)	1951–73	2,992	10,881	2,062	3,283	.302
Mickey Mantle, New York (AL)	1951–68	2,401	8,102	1,677	2,415	.298

BASEBALL MOST VALUABLE PLAYER AWARDS

NATIONAL LEAGUE

YEAR	PLAYER	CLUB
1948	Stan Musial	St. Louis
1949	Jackie Robinson	Brooklyn
1950	Jim Konstanty	Philadelphia
1951	Roy Campanella	Brooklyn
1952	Hank Sauer	Chicago
1953	Roy Campanella	Brooklyn
1954	Willie Mays	New York
1955	Roy Campanella	Brooklyn
1956	Don Newcombe	Brooklyn
1957	Hank Aaron	Milwaukee
1958	Ernie Banks	Chicago
1959	Ernie Banks	Chicago
1960	Dick Groat	Pittsburgh
1961	Frank Robinson	Cincinnati
1962	Maury Wills	Los Angeles
1963	Sandy Koufax	Los Angeles
1964	Ken Boyer	St. Louis
1965	Willie Mays	San Francisco
1966	Roberto Clemente	Pittsburgh
1967	Orlando Cepeda	St. Louis
1968	Bob Gibson	St. Louis
1969	Willie McCovey	San Francisco
1970	Johnny Bench	Cincinnati
1971	Joe Torre	St. Louis
1972	Johnny Bench	Cincinnati
1973	Pete Rose	Cincinnati
1974	Steve Garvey	Los Angeles
1975	Joe Morgan	Cincinnati
1976	Joe Morgan	Cincinnati
1977	George Foster	Cincinnati
1978	Dave Parker	Pittsburgh
1979	Willie Stargell	Pittsburgh
	Keith Hernandez	St. Louis
1980	Mike Schmidt	Philadelphia
1981	Mike Schmidt	Philadelphia
1982	Dale Murphy	Atlanta
1983	Dale Murphy	Atlanta

AMERICAN LEAGUE

YEAR	PLAYER	CLUB
1948	Lou Boudreau	Cleveland
1949	Ted Williams	Boston
1950	Phil Rizzuto	New York
1951	Yogi Berra	New York
1952	Bobby Shantz	Philadelphia
1953	Al Rosen	Cleveland
1954	Yogi Berra	New York
1955	Yogi Berra	New York
1956	Mickey Mantle	New York
1957	Mickey Mantle	New York
1958	Jackie Jensen	Boston
1959	Nellie Fox	Chicago
1960	Roger Maris	New York
1961	Roger Maris	New York
1962	Mickey Mantle	New York
1963	Elston Howard	New York
1964	Brooks Robinson	Baltimore
1965	Zoilo Versalles	Minnesota
1966	Frank Robinson	Baltimore
1967	Carl Yastrzemski	Boston
1968	Dennis McLain	Detroit
1969	Harmon Killebrew	Minnesota
1970	Boog Powell	Baltimore
1971	Vida Blue	Oakland
1972	Dick Allen	Chicago
1973	Reggie Jackson	Oakland
1974	Jeff Burroughs	Texas
1975	Fred Lynn	Boston
1976	Thurman Munson	New York
1977	Rod Carew	Minnesota
1978	Jim Rice	Boston
1979	Don Baylor	California
1980	George Brett	Kansas City
1981	Rollie Fingers	Milwaukee
1982	Robin Yount	Milwaukee
1983	Cal Ripken Jr.	Baltimore

BASEBALL ROOKIE OF THE YEAR AWARDS

NATIONAL LEAGUE

YEAR	PLAYER AND POSITION	CLUB
1955	Bill Virdon, outfielder	St. Louis
1956	Frank Robinson, outfielder	Cincinnati
1957	John Sanford, pitcher	Philadelphia
1958	Orlando Cepeda, first baseman	San Francisco
1959	Willie McCovey, first baseman	San Francisco
1960	Frank Howard, outfielder	Los Angeles
1961	Billy Williams, outfielder	Chicago
1962	Ken Hubbs, second baseman	Chicago
1963	Pete Rose, second baseman	Cincinnati
1964	Dick Allen, third baseman	Philadelphia
1965	Jim Lefebvre, second baseman	Los Angeles
1966	Tommy Helms, third baseman	Cincinnati
1967	Tom Seaver, pitcher	New York
1968	Johnny Bench, catcher	Cincinnati
1969	Ted Sizemore, second baseman	Los Angeles
1970	Carl Morton, pitcher	Montreal
1971	Earl Williams, catcher	Atlanta
1972	Jon Matlack, pitcher	New York
1973	Gary Matthews, outfielder	San Francisco
1974	Bake McBride, outfielder	St. Louis
1975	John Montefusco, pitcher	San Francisco
1976	Pat Zachry, pitcher	Cincinnati
	Butch Metzger, pitcher	San Diego
1977	Andre Dawson, outfielder	Montreal
1978	Bob Horner, third baseman	Atlanta
1979	Rick Sutcliffe, pitcher	Los Angeles
1980	Steve Howe, pitcher	Los Angeles
1981	Fernando Valenzuela, pitcher	Los Angeles
1982	Steve Sax, second baseman	Los Angeles
1983	Darryl Strawberry, outfielder	New York

AMERICAN LEAGUE

YEAR	PLAYER AND POSITION	CLUB
1955	Herb Score, pitcher	Cleveland
1956	Luis Aparicio, shortstop	Chicago
1957	Tony Kubek, infielder	New York
1958	Albie Pearson, outfielder	Washington
1959	Bob Allison, outfielder	Washington
1960	Ron Hansen, shortstop	Baltimore
1961	Don Schwall, pitcher	Boston
1962	Tom Tresh, outfielder-shortstop	New York
1963	Gary Peters, pitcher	Chicago
1964	Tony Oliva, outfielder	Minnesota
1965	Curt Blefary, outfielder	Baltimore
1966	Tommie Agee, outfielder	Chicago
1967	Rod Carew, second baseman	Minnesota
1968	Stan Bahnsen, pitcher	New York
1969	Lou Piniella, outfielder	Kansas City
1970	Thurman Munson, catcher	New York
1971	Chris Chambliss, first baseman	Cleveland
1972	Carlton Fisk, catcher	Boston
1973	Al Bumbry, outfielder	Baltimore
1974	Mike Hargrove, first baseman	Texas
1975	Fred Lynn, outfielder	Boston
1976	Mark Fidrych, pitcher	Detroit
1977	Eddie Murray, DH, outfielder	Baltimore
1978	Lou Whitaker, second baseman	Detroit
1979	Alfredo Griffin, shortstop	Toronto
	John Castino, third baseman	Minnesota
1980	Joe Charboneau, outfielder	Cleveland
1981	Dave Righetti, pitcher	New York
1982	Cal Ripken Jr., shortstop	Baltimore
1983	Ron Kittle, outfielder	Chicago

BASKETBALL

COLLEGE BASKETBALL: 1982–1983

North Carolina State University upset top-ranked University of Houston, 54–52, at Albuquerque, N.M., on April 4, 1983, to capture the 45th annual NCAA basketball tournament.

The North Carolina State Wolfpack was ranked 16th in the nation at the end of the regular season, with a 20–10 record. After winning the Atlantic Coast Conference tournament, the Wolfpack edged Pepperdine, 69–67, Nevada-Las Vegas, 71–70, and trounced Utah, 75–56, in the regional semifinals. The Wolfpack then went on to edge Virginia, 63–62, in the West regional final. In the national semifinal, the team defeated Georgia, 67–60.

In the title game, North Carolina State led 33–25 at the half. Houston recovered in the second half to lead 42–35, but the game was tied at 52–52 with 1:59 remaining. At 44 seconds to go, the Wolfpack began to work the ball around Houston's basket to use up the clock, until senior guard Dereck Whittenburg attempted a 30-foot jump shot with nine seconds left. The ball dropped short of the basket, but sophomore forward Lorenzo Charles grabbed it in midair and dunked it with one second left to go, giving the Wolfpack a 2-point victory.

Houston, with a 27–2 record, entered the tournament as the top-ranked team. Coach Guy Lewis' Cougars reached the final game by a series of impressive victories. They defeated Maryland, 60–50, Memphis State, 70–63, Villanova, 89–71, and Louisville, 94–81.

Houston's sophomore center, Akeem Abdul Olajuwon from Nigeria, was named most valuable player of the NCAA tournament, with 20 points, 18 rebounds, and 7 blocked shots in the title game.

Fresno State soundly defeated DePaul University, 69–60, to win the 46th National Invitation Tournament (NIT) at Madison Square Garden in New York City on March 30. In the title game, Fresno State had only a 3-point lead with 1:40 left to go, but clinched the victory by making eight consecutive free throws. The Bulldogs finished the tournament with an overall 25–10 record.

Fresno State's junior forward Ron Anderson was named most valuable player of the tournament. He scored 14 points and pulled down 8 rebounds.

At the end of the regular season, Associated Press sportswriters ranked the top teams: (1) Houston, (2) Louisville, (3) St. John's N.Y., (4) Virginia, (5) Indiana, (6) Nevada-Las Vegas, (7) UCLA, (8) North Carolina, (9) Arkansas, (10) Missouri.

In women's basketball the University of Southern California edged defending champion Lousiana Tech, 69–67, to win the NCAA division 1 championship at Norfolk, Va., on April 2.

ALL-AMERICA COLLEGE BASKETBALL TEAMS: 1982–1983

Source: Associated Press

FIRST TEAM: Ralph Sampson, Virginia; Wayman Tisdale, Oklahoma; Dale Ellis, Tennessee; Patrick Ewing, Georgetown; Michael Jordan, North Carolina.

SECOND TEAM: Keith Lee, Memphis State; Derek Harper, Illinois; Clyde Drexler, Houston; Steve Stipanovich, Missouri; Darrell Walker, Arkansas.

THIRD TEAM: John Pinone, Villanova; Antoine Carr, Wichita State; Sam Perkins, North Carolina; Kenny Fields, UCLA; Ennis Whatley, Alabama.

Houston center Akeem Abjul Olajuwon takes down rebound during NCAA championship game in Albuquerque, N.M., on April 4, as North Carolina State center Cozell McQueen looks on. North Carolina State won, 54–52.

Wide World

NATIONAL COLLEGIATE ATHLETIC ASSOCIATION TOURNAMENT

YEAR	CHAMPION	COACH	YEAR	CHAMPION	COACH
1939	Oregon	Howard Hobson	1960	Ohio State	Fred Taylor
1940	Indiana	Branch McCracken	1961–62	Cincinnati	Edward Jucker
1941	Wisconsin	Harold Foster	1963	Loyola (Chicago)	George Ireland
1942	Stanford	Everett Dean	1964	UCLA	John Wooden
1943	Wyoming	Everett Shelton	1965	UCLA	John Wooden
1944	Utah	Vadal Peterson	1966	Texas Western	Donald Haskins
1945–46	Oklahoma A & M	Henry Iba	1967–73	UCLA	John Wooden
1947	Holy Cross	Alvin Julian	1974	North Carolina State	Norm Sloan
1948–49	Kentucky	Adolph Rupp	1975	UCLA	John Wooden
1950	City College (N.Y.)	Nat Holman	1976	Indiana	Bobby Knight
1951	Kentucky	Adolph Rupp	1977	Marquette	Al McGuire
1952	Kansas	Forest C. Allen	1978	Kentucky	Joe B. Hall
1953	Indiana	Branch McCracken	1979	Michigan State	Jud Heathcote
1954	La Salle	Kenneth Loeffler	1980	Louisville	Denny Crum
1955–56	San Francisco	Phil Woolpert	1981	Indiana	Bobby Knight
1957	North Carolina	Frank McGuire	1982	North Carolina	Dean Smith
1958	Kentucky	Adolph Rupp	1983	North Carolina State	Jim Valvano
1959	California	Pete Newell			

NCAA 45th ANNUAL BASKETBALL CHAMPIONSHIP TOURNAMENT: 1983

NATIONAL FINALS
Championship:
N. Carolina St. 54, Houston 52
Played at Albuquerque, N.M., on April 4, 1983

NATIONAL SEMIFINALS
N. Carolina St. 67, Georgia 60
Houston 94, Louisville 81

REGIONAL FINALS
East:
Georgia 82, North Carolina 77
Mideast:
Louisville 80, Kentucky 68
Midwest:
Houston 89, Villanova 71
West:
N. Carolina St. 63, Virginia 62

REGIONAL SEMIFINALS
N. Carolina State 75, Utah 56
Houston 70, Memphis State 63
North Carolina 64, Ohio State 51
Georgia 70, St. John's 67
Kentucky 64, Indiana 59
Louisville 65, Arkansas 63
Villanova 55, Iowa 54
Virginia 95, Boston Coll. 92

NCAA OUTSTANDING PLAYER AWARD

1955 Bill Russell, San Francisco	1962 Paul Hogue, Cincinnati	1971 vacated	1979 Earvin Johnson, Mich. St.
1956 Hal Lear, Temple	1963 Art Heyman, Duke	1972–73 Bill Walton, UCLA	1980 Darrell Griffith, Louisville
1957 Wilt Chamberlain, Kansas	1964 Walt Hazzard, UCLA	1974 David Thompson, NCS	1981 Isiah Thomas, Indiana
1958 Elgin Baylor, Seattle	1965 Bill Bradley, Princeton	1975 Rick Washington, UCLA	1982 James Worthy, North Carolina
1959 Jerry West, W. Va.	1966 Jerry Chambers, Utah	1976 Kent Benson, Indiana	1983 Akeem Abdul Olajuwon, Houston
1960 Jerry Lucas, Ohio St.	1967–69 Lew Alcindor, UCLA	1977 Butch Lee, Marquette	
1961 Jerry Lucas, Ohio St.	1970 Sidney Wicks, UCLA	1978 Jack Givens, Kentucky	

NATIONAL INVITATION TOURNAMENT

YEAR	CHAMPION	COACH	YEAR	CHAMPION	COACH
1946	Kentucky	Adolph Rupp	1965	St. John's (N.Y.)	Joe Lapchick
1947	Utah	Vadal Peterson	1966	Brigham Young	Stanley Watts
1948	St. Louis	Edward Hickey	1967	Southern Illinois	Jack Hartman
1949	San Francisco	Pete Newell	1968	Dayton	Don Donoker
1950	City College (N.Y.)	Nat Holman	1969	Temple	Harry Litwack
1951	Brigham Young	Stanley Watts	1970	Marquette	Al McGuire
1952	La Salle	Kenneth Loeffler	1971	North Carolina	Dean Smith
1953	Seton Hall	John Russell	1972	Maryland	Lefty Driesell
1954	Holy Cross	Lester Sheary	1973	Virginia Tech	Don DeVoe
1955	Duquesne	Donald Moore	1974	Purdue	Fred Schaus
1956	Louisville	Bernard Hickman	1975	Princeton	Pete Carril
1957	Bradley	Chuck Orsborn	1976	Kentucky	Joe Hall
1958	Xavier of Ohio	James McCafferty	1977	St. Bonaventure (N.Y.)	Jim Satalin
1959	St. John's (N.Y.)	Joe Lapchick	1978	Texas	Abe Lemons
1960	Bradley	Chuck Orsborn	1979	Indiana	Bobby Knight
1961	Providence College	Joe Mullaney	1980	Virginia	Terry Holland
1962	Dayton	Tom Blackburn	1981	Tulsa	Nolan Richardson
1963	Providence College	Joe Mullaney	1982	Bradley	Dick Versace
1964	Bradley	Chuck Orsborn	1983	Fresno State	Boyd Grant

NATIONAL INVITATION TOURNAMENT WINNERS: 1983

CHAMPIONSHIP
Fresno St. 69, DePaul 60

NATIONAL SEMIFINALS
Fresno St. 86, Wake For. 62
DePaul 68, Nebraska 58

QUARTERFINALS
Fresno St. 76, Ore. St. 67
DePaul 75, Mississippi 67
Neb. 67, Tex. Christian 57
Wake For. 78, S. Car. 61

SECOND ROUND
Fresno St. 72, Mich. St. 58
DePaul 65, Northwestern 63
Mississippi 65, S.Fla. 57
Nebraska 85, Iona 73
S. Car. 75, Va. Tech. 68
Texas Christian 78, Arizona State 76
Wake For. 75, Vanderbilt 68
Ore. St. 88, N. Orleans 71

FIRST ROUND
Fresno St. 71, Texas-El Paso 64
S. Fla. 81, Fordham 69
Miss. 87, Ala. St. 75
Virginia Tech 85, William & Mary, 79
Ore. St. 77, Idaho 59
Iona 90, St. Bonav. 76
Van. 79, E. Tenn. St. 74
Arizona St. 87, Fullerton St. 83
DePaul 76, Minnesota 73
Tex. Christ. 64, Tulsa 62
Mich. St. 72, Bowling Green 71
Nebraska 72, Tulane 65
Northwestern 71, Notre Dame 57
New Orleans 99, La. State 94
S. Car. 100, Old Dominion 90
Wake Forest 78, Murray State 80

BEST WON-LOST BASKETBALL RECORDS[1]: 1982–1983

TEAM	TOTAL WON	TOTAL LOST	PCT.
Houston	31	3	.912
Nevada-Las Vegas	28	3	.903
Wichita State	25	3	.893
Louisville	32	4	.889
Arkansas	26	4	.867
Tennessee-Chattanooga	26	4	.867
Virginia	29	5	.853
St. John's (N.Y.)	28	5	.848
St. Peter's	22	5	.815
Indiana	24	6	.800
Arkansas-Little Rock	23	6	.793
UCLA	23	6	.793
Alabama State	22	6	.786
Boston College	25	7	.781
North Carolina	28	8	.778
Illinois State	24	7	.774
Oklahoma State	24	7	.774
Virginia Commonwealth	24	7	.774

TEAM SCORING LEADERS[1]: 1982–1983

TOP OFFENSIVE TEAMS	GAMES	POINTS FOR	AVERAGE
Boston College	32	2,697	84.3
Syracuse	31	2,612	84.3
South Carolina State	28	2,353	84.0
Alabama State	28	2,352	84.0
Houston	34	2,800	82.4
Oklahoma	33	2,717	82.3
Wichita State	28	2,304	82.3
Virginia	34	2,785	81.9
Alcorn State	32	2,621	81.9
Indiana State	28	2,288	81.7
Long Island	29	2,369	81.7

TOP DEFENSIVE TEAMS	GAMES	POINTS AGAINST	AVERAGE
Princeton	29	1,507	52.0
Fresno State	35	1,880	53.7
James Madison	31	1,670	53.9
Notre Dame	29	1,619	55.8
Arkansas	29	1,651	56.9
Wyoming	29	1,657	57.1
St. Peter's	27	1,557	57.7
Texas-El Paso	29	1,673	57.7
Montana	29	1,679	57.9
William & Mary	29	1,680	57.9
Houston Baptist	29	1,682	58.0

INDIVIDUAL SCORING LEADERS[1]

PLAYER AND SCHOOL	GAMES	POINTS	AVG.
H. Kelly, Texas Southern	29	835	28.8
J. Malone, Miss. State	29	777	26.8
C. Yates, George Mason	27	723	26.8
C. Bradley, South Florida	32	855	26.7
J. Jakubick, Akron	29	774	26.7
G. Goorjian, Loyola (Calif.)	23	601	26.1
A. Hughes, Loyola (Ill.)	29	744	25.7
W. Tisdale, Oklahoma	33	810	24.5
K. Lyons, North Texas St.	30	728	24.3
W. Jackson, Centenary	29	697	24.0
M. McLaughlin, Cen. Mich.	27	648	24.0

INDIVIDUAL REBOUND LEADERS[1]

PLAYER AND SCHOOL	GAMES	REBOUNDS	AVG.
X. McDaniel, Wichita State	28	403	14.4
F. Giles, S. Carolina State	28	360	12.9
M. Cage, San Diego State	28	354	12.6
M. Halsel, Northeastern	28	350	12.5
J. Cross, Maine	26	310	11.9
S. Green, Nevada-Las Vegas	31	368	11.9
H. Kelly, Texas Southern	29	340	11.7
R. Sampson, Virginia	33	386	11.7
A. Olajuwon, Houston	34	388	11.4
S. Mosley, Nevada-Reno	29	325	11.2
G. Foster, FDU-Teaneck	29	324	11.2

INDIVIDUAL SINGLE GAME HIGHS[1]

PLAYER AND SCHOOL (AGAINST OPPONENT)	POINTS
H. Kelly, Texas Southern (Jarvis Christian)	60
W. Tisdale, Oklahoma (Abilene Christian)	51
K. Lyons, North Texas St. (La. Tech)	47

PLAYER AND SCHOOL (AGAINST OPPONENT)	REBOUNDS
C. Scurry, Long Island (Marist)	26
F. Giles, S. Carolina State (Del. State)	24
R. McKinstry, Evansville (Oral Roberts)	23

COLLEGE BASKETBALL CONFERENCE CHAMPIONS[2]: 1982–1983

CONFERENCE	CHAMPION	WON	LOST
Atlantic Coast	North Carolina*	12	2
	Virginia*	12	2
Atlantic Ten East	Rutgers*	11	3
Atlantic Ten West	West Virginia	10	4
	St. Bonaventure*	10	4
Big East	St. John's	12	4
	Boston College*	12	4
	Villanova*	12	4
Big Eight	Missouri*	12	2
Big Sky	Weber State	10	4
	Nevada-Reno*	10	4
Big Ten	Indiana	13	5
East Coast East	LaSalle	7	2
	American*	7	2
	Hofstra*	7	2
East Coast West	Rider*	10	3
ECAC North Atlantic	Boston University	8	2
	New Hampshire*	8	2
ECAC Metro North	Long Island*	11	3
ECAC Metro South	Robert Morris	12	2
ECAC South	William & Mary*	9	0
Ivy	Princeton	12	2
Metro	Louisville	12	0
Metro Atlantic	Iona*	8	2
Mid-American	Bowling Green*	15	3
Mid-Continent	Western Illinois	9	3
Mid-Eastern	Howard*	11	1
Midwestern City	Loyola (Ill.)*	12	2
Missouri Valley	Wichita State*	17	1
Ohio Valley	Murray State*	11	3
Pacific Coast	Nevada-Las Vegas	15	1
Pacific Ten	UCLA	15	3
Southeastern	Kentucky*	13	5
Southern	Tenn.-Chattanooga	15	1
Southland	Lamar	9	3
Southwest	Houston	16	0
Southwestern	Alabama State*	12	2
	Texas Southern*	12	2
Sun Belt	Va. Commonwealth*	12	2
	Old Dominion	12	2
Trans-America	Ark.-Little Rock*	12	2
West Coast	Pepperdine	10	2
Western Athletic	Utah	11	5
	Texas-El Paso	11	5
	Brigham Young	11	5

[1] Source: NCAA, statistics include playoff games. [2] End of regular season. * Lost conference postseason tournament.

PROFESSIONAL BASKETBALL: 1982–1983

Wide World

Philadelphia 76er Moses Malone (2) evades Los Angeles Laker Kareem Abdul-Jabbar (33) as he goes up for two points during fourth game of NBA championship series at Los Angeles on May 31.

The Philadelphia 76ers humiliated the Los Angeles Lakers, 4 games to 0, to win the National Basketball Association (NBA) championship at Los Angeles, on May 31. The 76ers thus completed the best postseason by any NBA team ever, with a 12–1 record. They swept New York, 4 games to 0, in the conference semifinal, and defeated Milwaukee, 4 games to 1, in the Eastern conference title series.

Philadelphia completed the regular season with the best record in the NBA, winning 65 and losing 17, for .793. Los Angeles had the second-best record with 58 wins and 24 losses, for .707.

Los Angeles, the 1981–1982 NBA champion, defeated Portland, 4 games to 1, in the conference semifinal, and San Antonio, 4 games to 1, for the Western conference title.

Philadelphia center Moses Malone was named most valuable player of the final series, averaging 25.8 points and 18.0 rebounds a game. For the second consecutive year, Malone was voted by NBA players as the season's most valuable player. In the regular season, he averaged 24.5 points per game and led the league in rebounds with 15.3 per game.

Alex English of Denver won his first NBA scoring title with an average of 28.4 points per game. Runner-up was teammate Kiki Vandeweghe, who had 26.7 per game.

San Antonio's Artis Gilmore's .626 field-goal percentage made him the league's most accurate shooter for the third consecutive year. The top free-thrower was Calvin Murphy of Houston, who had a .920 average.

Terry Cummings of San Diego, named rookie of the year, finished the regular season with a 23.7 average.

In team statistics, the Denver Nuggets led the league in offense, with 123.2 points per game. Los Angeles was second, with 115.0.

East defeated West, 132–123, in the 33d annual NBA All-Star game, on Feb. 13. Philadelphia forward Julius Erving, who scored 25 points, was named most valuable player of the game, held at Los Angeles, Calif.

A strike set for April 1 was averted on March 31, when the NBA and the NBA Players Association agreed on a new 4-year contract, giving the players 53% of the NBA's gross revenues, beginning in the 1984–85 season. The new contract also provided for minimum and maximum payrolls for the teams. A new minimum individual salary was set at $65,000.

NATIONAL BASKETBALL ASSOCIATION FINAL STANDINGS: 1982–1983

TEAM	WON	LOST	PCT.	TEAM	WON	LOST	PCT.
Atlantic Division				**Midwest Division**			
Philadelphia 76ers	65	17	.793	San Antonio Spurs	53	29	.646
Boston Celtics	56	26	.683	Denver Nuggets	45	37	.549
New Jersey Nets	49	33	.598	Kansas City Kings	45	37	.549
New York Knickerbockers	44	38	.537	Dallas Mavericks	38	44	.463
Washington Bullets	42	40	.512	Utah Jazz	30	52	.366
				Houston Rockets	14	68	.171
Central Division				**Pacific Division**			
Milwaukee Bucks	51	31	.622	Los Angeles Lakers	58	24	.707
Atlanta Hawks	43	39	.524	Phoenix Suns	53	29	.646
Detroit Pistons	37	45	.451	Seattle Supersonics	48	34	.585
Chicago Bulls	28	54	.341	Portland Trail Blazers	46	36	.561
Cleveland Cavaliers	23	59	.280	Golden State Warriors	30	52	.366
Indiana Pacers	20	62	.244	San Diego Clippers	25	57	.305

NBA INDIVIDUAL SCORING LEADERS: 1982–1983

PLAYER AND TEAM	G[1]	FG[2]	FT[3]	PTS[4]	AVG[5]	PLAYER AND TEAM	G[1]	FG[2]	FT[3]	PTS[4]	AVG[5]
English, Denver	82	959	406	2,326	28.4	Bird, Boston	79	747	351	1,867	23.6
Vandeweghe, Denver..	82	841	489	2,186	26.7	Thomas, Detroit	81	725	368	1,854	22.9
Tripucka, Detroit	58	565	392	1,536	26.5	Moncrief, Milwaukee ..	76	606	499	1,712	22.5
Gervin, San Antonio ..	78	757	517	2,043	26.2	Griffith, Utah	77	752	167	1,709	22.2
Malone, Philadelphia ..	78	654	600	1,908	24.5	King, New York........	68	603	280	1,486	21.9
Aguirre, Dallas	81	767	429	1,979	24.4	Abdul-Jabbar, L.A......	79	722	278	1,722	21.8
Carroll, Golden State..	79	785	337	1,907	24.1	Paxson, Portland	81	682	388	1,756	21.7
Free, Cleveland	73	649	430	1,743	23.9	Issel, Denver..........	80	661	400	1,726	21.6
Theus, Chicago	82	749	434	1,953	23.8	Short, Golden State ...	67	589	255	1,437	21.4
Cummings, San Diego.	70	684	292	1,660	23.7	M. Johnson, Milwaukee	80	723	264	1,714	21.4

1 Games. 2 Field Goals. 3 Free Throws 4 Total Points. 5 Average per Game.

NATIONAL BASKETBALL ASSOCIATION TEAM STATISTICS: 1982–1983

TEAM	GAMES	SCORING AVERAGE			FIELD GOALS			FREE THROWS		
		For	Against	Difference	Made	Attempts	Pct.	Made	Attempts	Pct.
Denver	82	123.2	97.5	+2.5	3,951	7,999	.494	2,179	2,696	.808
Los Angeles.....	82	115.0	99.3	−0.1	3,964	7,512	.528	1,495	2,031	.736
San Antonio	82	114.3	102.0	+5.1	3,697	7,340	.504	1,887	2,468	.765
Kansas City.....	82	113.8	102.2	+4.4	3,719	7,485	.497	1,839	2,530	.727
Dallas..........	82	112.7	102.6	−1.0	3,674	7,550	.487	1,852	2,462	.752
Detroit	82	112.7	103.0	+2.8	3,623	7,602	.477	1,921	2,588	.742
Boston	82	112.1	104.4	+7.7	3,711	7,547	.492	1,730	2,348	.737
Philadelphia	82	112.1	104.6	−7.4	3,600	7,212	.499	1,966	2,650	.742
Chicago	82	111.0	105.3	+2.1	3,537	7,373	.480	1,983	2,690	.737
Seattle	82	110.0	106.7	+5.4	3,597	7,277	.494	1,796	2,459	.730
Utah	82	109.0	106.8	+3.2	3,525	7,342	.480	1,844	2,440	.756
Indiana.........	82	108.7	109.5	+5.5	3,707	7,723	.480	1,447	1,910	.758
Golden State....	82	108.6	110.7	+3.7	3,627	7,508	.483	1,620	2,199	.737
San Diego	82	108.6	110.9	−11.6	3,625	7,634	.475	1,589	2,195	.724
Portland........	82	107.4	112.3	−3.6	3,459	7,124	.486	1,855	2,512	.738
Phoenix	82	107.0	112.3	+1.5	3,555	7,158	.497	1,626	2,189	.743
Milwaukee	82	106.6	113.1	−0.4	3,486	7,133	.489	1,731	2,299	.753
New Jersey	82	105.8	113.1	−0.4	3,510	7,140	.492	1,622	2,301	.705
Atlanta	82	101.6	113.2	−4.2	3,352	7,146	.469	1,586	2,111	.751
New York.......	82	100.0	113.4	−4.8	3,272	6,793	.482	1,621	2,282	.710
Houston........	82	99.3	114.5	−5.9	3,338	7,446	.448	1,402	1,934	.725
Washington.....	82	99.2	115.9	−4.9	3,306	7,059	.468	1,452	2,059	.705
Cleveland	82	97.1	122.6	+0.6	3,252	6,995	.465	1,430	1,983	.721

NATIONAL BASKETBALL ASSOCIATION CHAMPIONS:

REGULAR SEASON									PLAYOFF CHAMPIONSHIP
Year	Eastern Conference	Won	Lost	Pct.	Western Conference	Won	Lost	Pct.	Winner
1966	Philadelphia	55	25	.687	Los Angeles.........	45	35	.562	Boston over Los Angeles (4–3)
1967	Philadelphia	68	13	.840	St. Louis............	56	26	.683	Philadelphia over San Fran. (4–2)
1968	Philadelphia	62	20	.756	San Francisco	44	37	.643	Boston over Los Angeles (4–2)
1969	Baltimore............	57	25	.695	Los Angeles.........	55	27	.671	Boston over Los Angeles (4–3)
1970	New York............	60	22	.732	Atlanta	48	34	.585	New York over Los Angeles (4–3)
1971*	New York (Atlantic) ..	52	30	.634	Milwaukee (Midwest).	66	16	.805	Milwaukee over Baltimore (4–0)
	Baltimore (Central) ..	42	40	.512	Los Angeles (Pacific).	48	34	.585	
1972	Boston (Atlantic)	56	26	.683	Los Angeles (Pacific).	69	13	.841	Los Angeles over New York (4–1)
	Baltimore (Central) ..	38	44	.463	Milwaukee (Midwest).	63	19	.768	
1973	Boston (Atlantic)	68	14	.829	Milwaukee (Midwest).	60	22	.732	New York over Los Angeles (4–1)
	Baltimore (Central) ..	52	30	.634	Los Angeles (Pacific).	60	22	.732	
1974	Boston (Atlantic)	56	26	.683	Milwaukee (Midwest).	59	23	.720	Boston over Milwaukee (4–3)
	Washington (Central)	47	35	.573	Los Angeles (Pacific).	47	35	.573	
1975	Boston (Atlantic)	60	22	.732	Chicago (Midwest) ...	47	35	.573	Golden St. over Washington (4–0)
	Washington (Central)	60	22	.732	Golden State (Pacific)	48	34	.585	
1976	Boston (Atlantic)	54	28	.659	Milwaukee (Midwest).	38	44	.463	Boston over Phoenix (4–2)
	Cleveland (Central) ..	49	33	.598	Golden State (Pacific)	59	23	.720	
1977	Philadelphia (Atlantic)	50	32	.610	Denver (Midwest)....	50	32	.610	Portland over Philadelphia (4–2)
	Houston (Central) ...	49	33	.598	Los Angeles (Pacific).	53	29	.646	
1978	Philadelphia (Atlantic)	55	27	.671	Denver (Midwest)....	48	34	.585	Washington over Seattle (4–3)
	San Antonio (Central)	52	30	.634	Portland (Pacific)....	58	24	.707	
1979	Washington (Atlantic)	54	28	.659	Kansas City (Midwest)	48	34	.585	Seattle over Washington (4–1)
	San Antonio (Central)	48	34	.585	Seattle (Pacific)	52	30	.634	
1980	Boston (Atlantic)	61	21	.744	Milwaukee (Midwest).	49	33	.598	Los Angeles over Philadelphia (4–2)
	Atlanta (Central)	50	32	.610	Los Angeles (Pacific).	60	22	.732	
1981	Boston (Atlantic)	62	20	.756	San Antonio (Midwest)	52	30	.634	Boston over Houston (4–2)
	Milwaukee (Central) .	60	22	.732	Phoenix (Pacific)	57	25	.695	
1982	Boston (Atlantic)	63	19	.768	San Antonio (Midwest)	48	34	.585	Los Angeles over Philadelphia (4–2)
	Milwaukee (Central) .	55	27	.671	Los Angeles (Pacific).	57	25	.695	
1983	Philadelphia (Atlantic)	65	17	.793	San Antonio (Midwest)	53	29	.646	Philadelphia over Los Angeles (4–0)
	Milwaukee (Central) .	51	31	.622	Los Angeles (Pacific).	58	24	.707	

* In 1970–71 the NBA reorganized into four conferences: Atlantic, Central, Midwest, and Pacific.

NATIONAL BASKETBALL ASSOCIATION INDIVIDUAL AWARDS

MOST VALUABLE PLAYER (PODOLOFF CUP) AND ROOKIE OF THE YEAR

YEAR	MVP	ROOKIE OF THE YEAR
1961	Bill Russell, Boston	Oscar Robertson, Cinn.
1962	Bill Russell, Boston	Walt Bellamy, Chicago
1963	Bill Russell, Boston	Terry Dischinger, Chicago
1964	Oscar Robertson, Cinn.	Jerry Lucas, Cinn.
1965	Bill Russell, Boston	Willis Reed, New York
1966	Wilt Chamberlain, Phil.	Rick Barry, San Francisco
1967	Wilt Chamberlain, Phil.	Dave Bing, Detroit
1968	Wilt Chamberlain, Phil.	Earl Monroe, Baltimore
1969	Wes Unseld, Baltimore	Wes Unseld, Baltimore
1970	Willis Reed, N.Y.	Abdul-Jabbar, Milw.
1971	Abdul-Jabbar, Milw.	Dave Cowens, Boston Geoff Petrie, Portland (tie)
1972	Abdul-Jabbar, Milw.	Sidney Wicks, Portland
1973	Dave Cowens, Boston	Bob McAdoo, Buffalo
1974	Abdul-Jabbar, Milw.	Ernie DiGregorio, Buffalo
1975	Bob McAdoo, Buffalo	Keith Wilkes, Golden State
1976	Abdul-Jabbar, L.A.	Alvan Adams, Phoenix
1977	Abdul-Jabbar, L.A.	Adrian Dantley, Buffalo
1978	Bill Walton, Portland	Walter Davis, Phoenix
1979	Moses Malone, Houston	Phil Ford, Kansas City
1980	Abdul-Jabbar, L.A.	Larry Bird, Boston
1981	Julius Erving, Phil.	Darrell Griffith, Utah
1982	Moses Malone, Houston	Isiah Thomas, Detroit
1983	Moses Malone, Phil.	Terry Cummings, San Diego

NBA LEADERS IN REBOUNDS: 1982–1983

PLAYER AND TEAM	GAMES	NUMBER	AVG.
Malone, Philadelphia	78	1,194	15.3
Williams, New Jersey	82	1,027	12.5
Laimbeer, Detroit	82	993	12.1
Gilmore, San Antonio	82	984	12.0
Sikma, Seattle	75	858	11.4
Roundfield, Atlanta	77	880	11.4
Robinson, Cleveland	77	856	11.1
Ruland, Washington	79	871	11.0
Bird, Boston	79	870	11.0
Cummings, San Diego	70	744	10.6

NBA LEADERS IN ASSISTS: 1982–1983

PLAYER AND TEAM	GAMES	NUMBER	AVG.
E. Johnson, Los Angeles	79	829	10.5
Moore, San Antonio	77	753	9.8
Green, Utah	78	697	8.9
Drew, Kansas City	75	610	8.1
Johnson, Washington	68	549	8.1
Williams, Seattle	80	643	8.0
Williams, Kansas City	72	569	7.9
Thomas, Detroit	81	634	7.8
Nixon, Los Angeles	79	566	7.2
Davis, Dallas	79	565	7.2

NATIONAL BASKETBALL ASSOCIATION PLAYOFFS: 1983

Championship Series:
Philadelphia defeated Los Angeles, 4 games to 0.
Conference Finals:
Philadelphia defeated Milwaukee, 4 games to 1.
Los Angeles defeated San Antonio, 4 games to 1.

Conference Semifinals:
Philadelphia defeated New York, 4 games to 0.
Los Angeles defeated Portland, 4 games to 1.
San Antonio defeated Denver, 4 games to 1.
Boston defeated Washington, 4 games to 1.

NATIONAL BASKETBALL ASSOCIATION SCORING LEADERS

SEASON	PLAYER AND TEAM	G[1]	FG[2]	FT[3]	TP[4]	AVG[5]
1951–52	Paul Arizin, Philadelphia Warriors	66	548	578	1,674	25.4
1952–53	Neil Johnston, Philadelphia Warriors	70	504	556	1,564	22.3
1953–54	Neil Johnston, Philadelphia Warriors	72	591	577	1,759	24.4
1954–55	Neil Johnston, Philadelphia Warriors	72	521	589	1,631	22.7
1955–56	Bob Pettit, St. Louis Hawks	72	646	557	1,849	25.7
1956–57	Paul Arizin, Philadelphia Warriors	71	613	591	1,817	25.6
1957–58	George Yardley, Detroit Pistons	72	673	655	2,001	27.8
1958–59	Bob Pettit, St. Louis Hawks	72	719	667	2,105	29.2
1959–60	Wilt Chamberlain, Philadelphia Warriors	72	1,065	577	2,707	37.6
1960–61	Wilt Chamberlain, Philadelphia Warriors	79	1,251	531	3,033	38.4
1961–62	Wilt Chamberlain, Philadelphia Warriors	80	1,597	835	4,029	50.4
1962–63	Wilt Chamberlain, San Francisco Warriors	80	1,463	660	3,586	44.8
1963–64	Wilt Chamberlain, San Francisco Warriors	80	1,204	540	2,948	36.5
1964–65	Wilt Chamberlain, Philadelphia 76ers	73	1,063	408	2,534	34.7
1965–66	Wilt Chamberlain, Philadelphia 76ers	79	1,074	501	2,649	33.5
1966–67	Rick Barry, San Francisco Warriors	78	1,011	753	2,775	35.6
1967–68	Dave Bing, Detroit Pistons	79	835	472	2,142	27.1
1968–69	Elvin Hayes, San Diego Rockets	82	930	467	2,327	28.4
1969–70	Jerry West, Los Angeles Lakers	74	831	647	2,309	31.2
1970–71	Lew Alcindor (Kareem Abdul-Jabbar), Milwaukee Bucks	82	1,063	470	2,596	31.7
1971–72	Kareem Abdul-Jabbar, Milwaukee Bucks	81	1,159	504	2,822	34.8
1972–73	Nate Archibald, Kansas City–Omaha Kings	82	1,028	603	2,719	34.0
1973–74	Bob McAdoo, Buffalo Braves	74	901	459	2,261	30.6
1974–75	Bob McAdoo, Buffalo Braves	82	1,095	641	2,831	34.5
1975–76	Bob McAdoo, Buffalo Braves	78	934	559	2,427	31.1
1976–77	Pete Maravich, New Orleans Jazz	73	886	501	2,273	31.1
1977–78	George Gervin, San Antonio Spurs	82	864	504	2,232	27.2
1978–79	George Gervin, San Antonio Spurs	80	947	471	2,365	29.6
1979–80	George Gervin, San Antonio Spurs	78	1,024	505	2,585	33.1
1980–81	Adrian Dantley, Utah Jazz	80	909	632	2,452	30.7
1981–82	George Gervin, San Antonio	79	993	555	2,551	32.3
1982–83	Alex English, Denver Nuggets	82	959	406	2,326	28.4

[1] Games. [2] Field Goals. [3] Free Throws. [4] Total Points. [5] Average per Game.

BICYCLING

UNITED STATES BICYCLING CHAMPIONS

Source: U.S. Cycling Federation and *Velo-news*

SENIOR MEN BICYCLING CHAMPIONS

	ROAD	SPRINT	4,000-METER PURSUIT	POINTS RACE	1,000 METERS
1975	John Howard	Steve Woznick	Ron Skarin	—	Steve Woznick
1976	Wayne Stetina	Les Barczewski	Leonard Nitz	—	Bob Vehe
1977	Wayne Stetina	Les Barczewski	Paul Deem	Nelson Saldana	Jerry Ash
1978	Dale Stetina	Les Barczewski	Dave Grylls	Ron Skarin	Jerry Ash
1979	Steve Wood	Les Barczewski	Dave Grylls	Gus Pipenhagen	Jerry Ash
1980	Dale Stetina	Mark Gorski	Leonard Nitz	Scott Hembree	Brent Emery
1981	Tom Broznowski	Les Barczewski	Leonard Nitz	John Beckman	Brent Emery
1982	Greg Demgen	Mark Gorski	Leonard Nitz	John Beckman	Leonard Nitz
1983	Thurlow Rogers	Mark Gorski	Leonard Nitz	Brent Emery	Mark Whitehead

SENIOR WOMEN BICYCLING CHAMPIONS / JUNIOR MEN BICYCLING CHAMPIONS

	SENIOR WOMEN BICYCLING CHAMPIONS			JUNIOR MEN BICYCLING CHAMPIONS	
	ROAD	SPRINT	3,000-METER PURSUIT	ROAD	TRACK
1975	Linda Stein	Sue Novara	Mary Jane Reoch	Larry Shields	Kurtis Miller
1976	Connie Carpenter	Sheila Young	Connie Carpenter	Larry Shields	Chris Springer
1977	Connie Carpenter	Sue Novara	Connie Carpenter	Greg LeMond	Chris Springer
1978	Barbara Hintzen	Sue Novara	Mary Jane Reoch	Jeff Bradley	Eric Baltes
1979	Connie Carpenter	Sue Novara	Connie Carpenter	Greg LeMond	Mark Whitehead
1980	Beth Heiden	Sue Novara	Elizabeth Davis	Sterling McBride	John Butler
1981	Connie Carpenter	Sheila Young	Rebecca Twigg	Mike Jensen	Russ Dalbey
1982	Sue Novara-Reber	Connie Paraskevin	Rebecca Twigg	Roy Knickman	Dave Lettieri
1983	Rebecca Twigg	Connie Paraskevin	Cindy Olavarri	Roy Knickman	Roy Knickman

BOWLING

U.S. MEN'S OPEN CHAMPIONSHIP (Bowling Proprietors Association of America)

1956	Bill Lillard	1962–63	Dick Weber	1969	Billy Hardwick	1974	Larry Laub	1979	Joe Berardi
1957–58	Don Carter	1964	Bob Strampe	1970	Bobby Cooper	1975	Steve Neff	1980	Steve Martin
1959	Billy Welu	1965–66	Dick Weber	1971	Mike Limongello	1976	Paul Moser	1981	Marshall Holman
1960	Harry Smith	1967	Les Schissler	1972	Don Johnson	1977	Johnny Petraglia	1982	Dave Husted
1961	Bill Tucker	1968	Jim Stefanich	1973	Mike McGrath	1978	Nelson Burton Jr.	1983	Gary Dickinson

U.S. WOMEN'S OPEN CHAMPIONSHIP (Bowling Proprietors Association of America)

1963	Marion Ladewig	1967	Gloria Bouvia	1972	Lorrie Koch	1976	Patty Costello	1980	Pat Costello
1964	La Verne Carter	1968–69	D. Fothergill	1973	Millie Martorella	1977	Betty Morris	1981	Donna Adamek
1965	Ann Slattery	1970	Mary Baker	1974	Pat Costello	1978	Donna Adamek	1982	Shinobu Saitoh
1966	Joy Abel	1971	Paula Sperber	1975	Paula Sperber	1979	Diana Silva	1983	Dana Miller

AMERICAN BOWLING CONGRESS ALL-EVENTS CHAMPIONSHIP

1954	Brad Lewis	1960	Vince Lucci	1966	John Wilcox	1972	Mac Lowry	1978	Chris Cobus
1955	Fred Bujack	1961	Luke Karan	1967	Gary Lewis	1973	Ron Woolet	1979	Bob Busacchi
1956	Bill Lillard	1962	Billy Young	1968	Vince Mazzanti	1974	Bob Hart	1980	Steve Fehr
1957	Jim Spalding	1963	Bus Oswalt	1969	Edward Jackson	1975	Bobby Meadows	1981	Rod Toft
1958	Al Faragalli	1964	Les Zikes	1970	Mike Berlin	1976	Jim Lindquist	1982	Rich Wonders
1959	Ed Lubanski	1965	Tom Hathaway	1971	Al Cohn	1977	Bud Debenham	1983	Tony Cariello

WOMEN'S INTERNATIONAL BOWLING CONGRESS ALL-EVENTS CHAMPIONSHIP

1952	Virginia Turner	1959	Pat McBride	1966	Kate Helbig	1973	Toni Calvary	1980	Cheryl Robinson
1953	Doris Knechtges	1960	Judy Roberts	1967	Carol Miller	1974	Judy Soutar	1981	Virginia Norton
1954	Anne Johnson	1961	Evelyn Teal	1968	Susie Reichley	1975	Virginia Park	1982	Aleta Rzepecki
1955	Marion Ladewig	1962	Flossie Argent	1969	Helen Duval	1976	Betty Morris	1983	Virginia Norton
1956	Doris Knechtges	1963	Helen Shablis	1970	D. Fothergill	1977	Akiko Yamaga		
1957	Anita Cantaline	1964	Jean Havlish	1971	Lorrie Koch	1978	Annese Kelly		
1958	Mae Ploegman	1965	D. Zimmerman	1972	Millie Martorella	1979	Betty Morris		

AMERICAN BOWLING CONGRESS MASTERS CHAMPIONSHIP

1955	Buzz Fazio	1961	Don Carter	1967	Lou Scalia	1973	Dave Soutar	1979	Doug Myers
1956	Dick Hoover	1962	Bill Golembiewski	1968	Pete Tountas	1974	Paul Colwell	1980	Neil Burton
1957	Dick Hoover	1963	Harry Smith	1969	Jim Chestney	1975	Ed Ressler	1981	Randy Lightfoot
1958	Tom Hennessey	1964	Billy Welu	1970	Don Glover	1976	Nelson Burton Jr.	1982	Joe Berardi
1959	Ray Bluth	1965	Billy Welu	1971	Jim Godman	1977	Earl Anthony	1983	Mike Lastowski
1960	Bill Golembiewski	1966	Bob Strampe	1972	Bill Beach	1978	Frank Ellenburg		

AMERICAN BOWLING CONGRESS SINGLES CHAMPIONSHIP

1964	Jim Stefanich	1968	Wayne Kowalski	1972	Bill Pointer	1976	Mike Putzer	1980	Mike Eaton
1965	Ken Roeth	1969	Greg Campbell	1973	Ed Thompson	1977	Frank Gadaleto	1981	Rob Vital
1966	Don Chapman	1970	Jake Yoder	1974	Gene Krause	1978	Rich Mersek	1982	Bruce Bohm
1967	Frank Perry	1971	Al Cohn	1975	Jim Setser	1978	Rick Peters	1983	Ricky Kendrick

PROFESSIONAL BOWLERS ASSOCIATION FIRESTONE TOURNAMENT OF CHAMPIONS

1967	Jim Stefanich	1971	John Petraglia	1975	Dave Davis	1979	George Pappas	1983	Joe Bernardi
1968	Dave Davis	1972	Mike Durbin	1976	Marshall Holman	1980	Wayne Webb		
1969	Jim Godman	1973	Jim Godman	1977	Mike Berlin	1981	Steve Cook		
1970	Don Johnson	1974	Earl Anthony	1978	Earl Anthony	1982	Mike Durbin		

BOXING

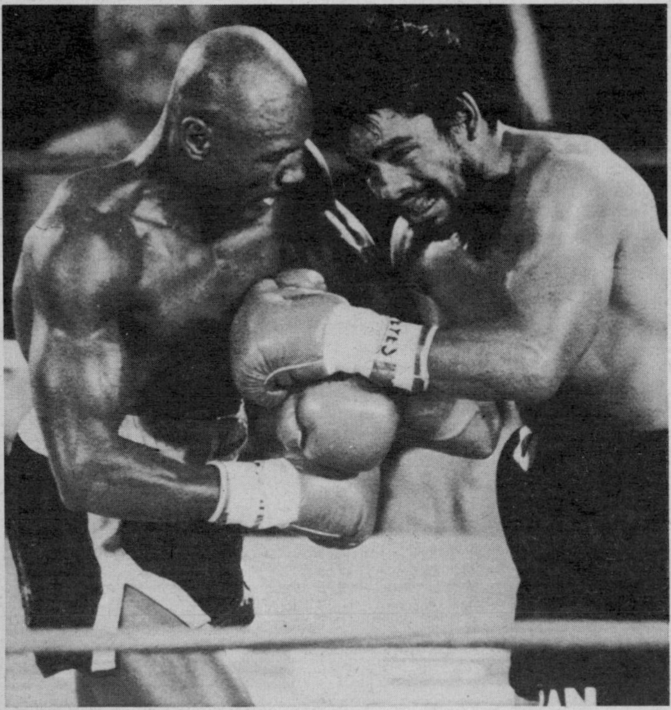

Wide World

Middleweight champion Marvelous Marvin Hagler connects with a blow to Roberto Durán of Panama, *right,* during their championship bout at Las Vegas, Nev., on Nov. 10. Hagler successfully defended his WBA and WBC middleweight championships with a unanimous decision. He dominated the 15-round bout but had to win the last two rounds on all judges' cards to win the decision after Duran seemed to have a chance in the 12th and 13th rounds.

World Boxing Council (WBC) heavyweight champion Larry Holmes announced on Dec. 11 that he was resigning the WBC heavyweight title he had held since 1978, saying he would fight as heavyweight champion of the new International Boxing Federation, formed earlier in 1983 by Bob Lee, deputy commissioner of the New Jersey State Athletic Commission.

Holmes' last fight as the WBC champion was on Nov. 25, when he scored a first-round victory over Marvis Frazier in a non-title bout at Las Vegas, Nev. Referee Mills Lane stopped the bout at 2:57 after Frazier, 23, had been knocked down a minute before. The challenger was the son of Joe Frazier, who took the championship away from Muhammad Ali in 1971.

South African-born Gerrie Coetzee became the World Boxing Association (WBA) heavyweight champion on Sept. 23, when he knocked out previously undefeated Michael Dokes in the 10th round, at Richfield, Ohio. Dokes had won the championship in December 1982, when he defeated Mike Weaver in the first round with a technical knockout.

In August unbeaten Milton McCrory, of Detroit, Mich., won a 12-round split decision over Colin Jones of Wales, to win the WBC welterweight title.

Carlos de Leon scored a unanimous decision over S.T. Gordon to win the WBC cruiserweight title in Las Vegas, Nev., in July.

Also in July, Lupe Madera won the WBA junior flyweight title when his fight against defending champion Katsuo Tokashiki was stopped on points in the fourth round.

UNITED STATES AMATEUR BOXING CHAMPIONSHIPS: 1983

Source: U.S.A. Amateur Boxing Federation, Inc.; Colorado Springs, Colo., Nov. 7–12, 1983

CLASS	CHAMPION	CLASS	CHAMPION
106 pounds	Paul Gonzales, Los Angeles, Calif.	**147 pounds**	Mark Breland, Brooklyn, N.Y.
112 pounds	Steve McCrory, Detroit, Mich.	**156 pounds**	Frank Tate, Detroit, Mich.
119 pounds	Jesse Benavides, Corpus Christi, Tex.	**165 pounds**	Michael Grogan, Atlanta, Ga.
125 pounds	Andrew Minsker, Milaukie, Ore.	**178 pounds**	Ricky Womack, Detroit, Mich.
132 pounds	Clifford Gray, Boynton Beach, Fla.	**Heavyweight**	Henry Mulligan, Hockessin, Del.
139 pounds	Zacharay Padilla, Azusa, Calif.	**Super Heavyweight**	Tyrell Biggs, Philadelphia, Pa.

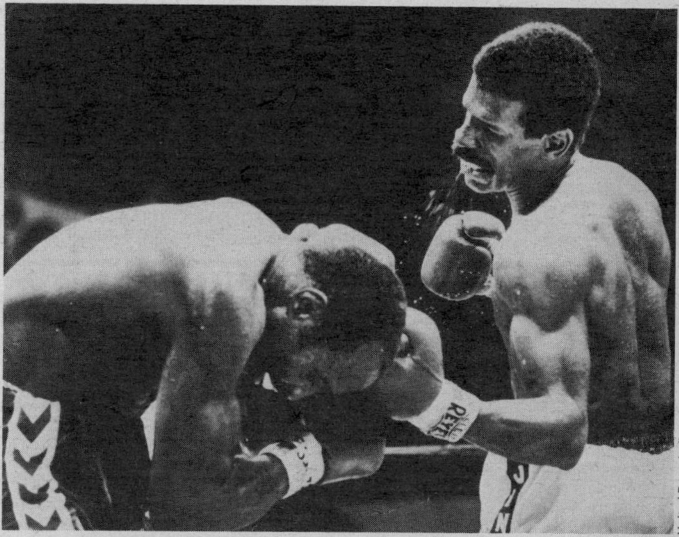

United Press Int'l.

The WBA's light heavyweight champion Michael Spinks slams a hard left to the head of the WBC's light heavyweight champion Dwight Braxton during their title unification bout at Atlantic City, N.J., on March 18. Spinks scored a unanimous 15-round decision, and became the title holder in both the WBA and WBC. Before the bout, Spinks, 26, was undefeated in 22 fights and had 18 knockouts. Braxton, 30, had a record of 19–1–1.

PROFESSIONAL BOXING CHAMPIONS BY CLASSES: 1983†

Because the two rival professional boxing associations, the WBA and the WBC, have generally managed to prevent the fighters they separately recognize as champions from meeting each other in decisive championship boxing title bouts, the table below has been prepared by the editors of *The Ring Magazine* to reflect their choice of the fighter in each division who most deserves the title of "world champion" and receives the coveted *Ring* championship belt.

CLASS AND WEIGHT	WORLD BOXING ASSOCIATION (WBA)	WORLD BOXING COUNCIL (WBC)
Heavyweight (over 195 pounds)	Gerrie Coetzee[1], South Africa	Vacant
Cruiserweight [3] (176–195 pounds)	Ossie Ocasio [2], Puerto Rico	Carlos De Leon[1], Puerto Rico
Light Heavyweight (161–175 pounds)	*Michael Spinks[1], U.S.	*Michael Spinks[1], United States
Middleweight (155–160 pounds)	*Marvin Hagler [2], United States	*Marvin Hagler [2], United States
Junior Middleweight (148–154 pounds)	Roberto Durán[1], Panama	*Thomas Hearns, United States
Welterweight (141–147 pounds)	Donald Curry[1], United States	Milton McCrory[1], United States
Junior Welterweight (136–140 pounds)	Vacant	Bruce Curry[1], United States
Lightweight (131–135 pounds)	Ray Mancini [2], United States	Edwin Rosario, Puerto Rico
Junior Lightweight (127–130 pounds)	Roger Mayweather[1], United States	Hector Comacho[1], United States
Featherweight (123–126 pounds)	*Eusebio Pedroza [2], Panama	Juan LaPorte [2], Puerto Rico
Junior Featherweight (119–122 pounds)	Leo Cruz [2], Dominican Republic	Jaime Garza[1], United States
Bantamweight (116–118 pounds)	*Jeff Chandler [2], United States	Albert Davila[1], Mexico
Junior Bantamweight (113–115 pounds)	Jiro Watanabe [2], Japan	Payao Pootarat[1], Thailand
Flyweight (109–112 pounds)	Santos Laciar [2], Argentina	*Frank Cedeño[1], Philippines
Junior Flyweight (under 109 pounds)	Lupe Madera[1], Mexico	Jung-Koo Chang[1], South Korea

† Source: *The Ring Magazine.* *Rated as World Champion by *The Ring Magazine.* [1] Won title in 1983. [2] Successfully defended title in 1983. [3] WBA calls class Junior Heavyweight (176–190 pounds).

HEAVYWEIGHT BOXING CHAMPIONS (over 175 pounds)*

CHAMPION	REIGN	CHAMPION	REIGN	CHAMPION	REIGN
John L. Sullivan	1882–92	Max Schmeling [3]	1930–32	Ingemar Johannson	1959–60
James J. Corbett	1892–97	Jack Sharkey	1932–33	Floyd Patterson	1960–62
Bob Fitzsimmons	1897–99	Primo Carnera	1933–34	Sonny Liston	1962–64
James J. Jeffries[1]	1899–1905	Max Baer	1934–35	Cassius Clay [6]	1964–70
Marvin Hart	1905–06	Jim Braddock	1935–37	Joe Frazier	1970–73
Tommy Burns	1906–08	Joe Louis [4]	1937–49	George Foreman	1973–74
Jack Johnson	1908–15	Ezzard Charles	1949–51	Muhammad Ali	1974–78
Jess Willard	1915–19	Jersey Joe Walcott	1951–52	Leon Spinks	1978
Jack Dempsey	1919–26	Rocky Marciano [5]	1952–56	Muhammad Ali	1978–79
Gene Tunney [2]	1926–28	Floyd Patterson	1956–59	Larry Holmes	1980–

* Source: *The Ring Magazine.* [1] Jeffries retired in 1905. [2] Tunney retired undefeated in 1928. [3] In 1931 the New York Boxing Commission reversed its decision in favor of Schmeling's opponent, Jack Sharkey. [4] Louis retired in 1949. [5] Marciano retired undefeated in 1956. [6] In 1967 Clay's title was declared vacant by the World Boxing Association (WBA) and the New York Athletic Commission after Clay failed to answer a draft call for military service. Clay had changed his name to Muhammad Ali in 1965.

LIGHT HEAVYWEIGHT BOXING CHAMPIONS (Up to 175 pounds)*

CHAMPION	REIGN	CHAMPION	REIGN	CHAMPION	REIGN
Jack Root	1903	Mike McTigue[1]	1927	Joey Maxim	1950–52
George Gardner	1903	Tommy Loughran	1927–29	Archie Moore	1952–62
Bob Fitzsimmons	1903–05	Jimmy Slattery	1930	Harold Johnson	1962–63
"Philadelphia" Jack O'Brien	1905–07	Maxie Rosenbloom[2]	1930–34	Willie Pastrano	1963–65
Jack Dillon	1915–16	Bob Olin	1934–35	Jose Torres	1965–66
Battling Levinsky	1916–20	John Henry Lewis	1935–38	Dick Tiger	1966–68
Georges Carpentier	1920–22	Melio Bettina[3]	1939	Bob Foster	1968–74
Battling Siki	1922–23	Billy Conn	1939–40	Vacant	1974–83
Mike McTigue	1923–25	Anton Christoforidis	1941	Michael Spinks	1983–
Paul Berlenbach	1925–26	Gus Lesnevich	1941–48		
Jack Delaney	1926–27	Freddie Mills	1948–50		

1 Delaney resigned the crown and McTigue reclaimed it in 1927. 2 Loughran resigned the title and Slattery became champion. 3 Bettina was the victor in an elimination tournament after Lewis resigned as titleholder.

MIDDLEWEIGHT BOXING CHAMPIONS (Up to 160 pounds)*

CHAMPION	REIGN	CHAMPION	REIGN	CHAMPION	REIGN
Jack Dempsey ("The Nonpareil")	1884–91	Marcel Thil	1932–37	Carmen Basilio	1957–58
		Fred Apostoli	1937–39	Sugar Ray Robinson	1958–60
Bob Fitzsimmons	1891–97	Ceferino Garcia	1939–40	Paul Pender	1960–62
Charles (Kid) McCoy	1897–98	Ken Overlin	1940–41	Dick Tiger	1962–63
Tommy Ryan	1898–1904	Billy Soose	1941	Joey Giardello	1963–65
Stanley Ketchel	1908	Tony Zale	1941–47	Dick Tiger	1965–66
Billy Papke	1908	Rocky Graziano	1947–48	Emile Griffith	1966–67
Stanley Ketchel	1908–10	Tony Zale	1948	Nino Benvenuti	1967
Frank Klaus[1]	1913	Marcel Cerdan	1948–49	Emile Griffith	1967–68
George Chip	1913–14	Jake LaMotta	1949–51	Nino Benvenuti	1968–70
Al McCoy	1914–17	Sugar Ray Robinson	1951	Carlos Monzon	1970–77
Mike O'Dowd	1917–20	Randy Turpin	1951	Rodrigo Valdez	1977–78
Johnny Wilson	1920–23	Sugar Ray Robinson	1951–52	Hugo Corro	1978–79
Harry Greb	1923–26	Bobo Olson[3]	1953–55	Vito Antuofermo	1979–80
Tiger Flowers	1926	Sugar Ray Robinson[3]	1955–57	Alan Minter	1980
Mickey Walker[2]	1926–31	Gene Fullmer	1957	Marvin Hagler	1980–
Gorilla Jones	1931–32	Sugar Ray Robinson	1957		

1 Ketchel was shot and killed in 1910. Papke reclaimed the title and Klaus defeated him in 1913 to gain the middleweight crown. 2 Walker relinquished the title in 1931. The NBA and New York State Athletic Commission each sponsored separate tournaments to determine a new champion. During the next ten years Gorilla Jones, Ben Jeby, Marcel Thil, Lou Brouillard, Vince Dundee, Teddy Yarosz, Babe Risko, Freddy Steele, Al Hostak, Solly Krieger, Fred Apostoli, Ceferino Garcia, Ken Overlin, and Billy Soose were all recognized as champions. 3 Robinson retired from the ring in 1952. Olson outpointed Randy Turpin to become champion in 1953. Robinson returned to the ring in 1955.

WELTERWEIGHT BOXING CHAMPIONS (Up to 147 pounds)*

CHAMPION	REIGN	CHAMPION	REIGN	CHAMPION	REIGN
Mysterious Billy Smith	1892–94	Jackie Fields	1932–33	Don Jordan	1958–60
Tommy Ryan	1894–98	Young Corbett 3d	1933	Benny (Kid) Paret	1960–61
Mysterious Billy Smith	1898–1900	Jimmy McLarnin	1933–34	Emile Griffith	1961
Matty Matthews	1900–01	Barney Ross	1934	Benny (Kid) Paret	1961–62
Rube Ferns	1901	Jimmy McLarnin	1934–35	Emile Griffith	1962–63
Joe Walcott	1901–04	Barney Ross	1935–38	Luis Rodriguez	1963
Dixie Kid	1904–05	Henry Armstrong	1938–40	Emile Griffith	1963–66
Honey Mellody	1906–07	Fritzie Zivic	1940–41	Curtis Cokes[4]	1966–69
Mike (Twin) Sullivan[1]	1907–10	Freddie Cochrane	1941–46	Jose Napoles	1969–70
Ted (Kid) Lewis	1915–19	Marty Servo	1946	Billy Backus	1970–71
Jack Britton	1919–22	Sugar Ray Robinson[2]	1946–51	Jose Napoles	1971–75
Mickey Walker	1922–26	Johnny Bratton	1951	John H. Stracey	1975–76
Peter Latzo	1926–27	Kid Gavilan[3]	1951–54	Carlos Palomino	1976–79
Joe Dundee	1927–29	Johnny Saxton	1954–55	Wilfred Benitez	1979
Jackie Fields	1929–30	Tony DeMarco	1955	Sugar Ray Leonard	1979–80
Young Jack Thompson	1930	Carmen Basilio	1955–56	Roberto Duran	1980
Tommy Freeman	1930–31	Johnny Saxton	1956	Sugar Ray Leonard	1980–82
Young Jack Thompson	1931	Carmen Basilio	1956–57		
Lou Brouillard	1931–32	Virgil Akins	1958		

*Source: *The Ring Magazine.* 1 Sullivan vacated his title in 1910 by becoming a middleweight. 2 Because Servo refused to fight Robinson, the New York State Commission declared his title vacant. 3 Robinson gave up the crown in 1951 after winning the middleweight title. 4 Cokes was accepted as titleholder when Griffith became middleweight champion.

LIGHTWEIGHT BOXING CHAMPIONS (Up to 135 pounds)*

CHAMPION	REIGN	CHAMPION	REIGN	CHAMPION	REIGN
George (Kid) Lavigne	1896–99	Barney Ross	1933–35	Wallace (Bud) Smith	1955–56
Frank Erne	1899–1902	Tony Canzoneri [2]	1935–36	Joe Brown	1956–62
Joe Gans	1901–08	Lou Ambers	1936–38	Carlos Ortiz	1962–65
Battling Nelson	1908–10	Henry Armstrong	1938–39	Ismael Laguna	1965
Ad Wolgast	1910–12	Lou Ambers	1939–40	Carlos Ortiz	1965–68
Willie Ritchie	1912–14	Lew Jenkins	1940–41	Teo Cruz	1968–69
Freddie Welsh	1914–17	Sammy Angott [3]	1941–42	Mando Ramos	1969–70
Benny Leonard [1]	1917–24	Ike Williams	1947–51	Ismael Laguna	1970
Jimmy Goodrich	1925	Jimmy Carter	1951–52	Ken Buchanan	1970–72
Rocky Kansas	1925–26	Lauro Salas	1952	Roberto Duran	1972–79
Sammy Mandell	1926–30	Jimmy Carter	1952–54	Alexis Arguello	1981–83
Al Singer	1930	Paddy DeMarco	1954		
Tony Canzoneri	1930–33	Jimmy Carter	1954–55		

[1] Leonard retired undefeated. [2] Ross relinquished his title. [3] Angott resigned his title in 1942. From 1943 to 1947, the NBA and the New York State Athletic Commission recognized different champions. The dispute was settled in 1947.

FEATHERWEIGHT BOXING CHAMPIONS (Up to 126 pounds)*

CHAMPION	REIGN	CHAMPION	REIGN	CHAMPION	REIGN
Torpedo Billy Murphy	1890	Benny Bass	1927–28	Kid Bassey	1957–59
Young Griffo	1890–92	Tony Canzoneri	1928	Davey Moore	1959–63
George Dixon	1892–97	Andre Routis	1928–29	Sugar Ramos	1963–64
Solly Smith	1897–98	Battling Battalino	1929–32	Vicente Saldivar	1964–67
Dave Sullivan	1898	Tommy Paul	1932–33	Johnny Famechon	1969–70
George Dixon	1898–1900	Freddie Miller	1933–36	Vicente Saldivar	1970
Terry McGovern	1900–01	Petey Sarron	1936–37	Kuniaki Shibata	1970–72
Young Corbett	1901–04	Henry Armstrong	1937–38	Clemente Sanchez	1972
Jimmy Britt	1904	Joey Archibald	1938–40	Jose Legra	1972–73
Abe Attell	1904	Harry Jeffra	1940–41	Eder Jofre	1973–74
Tommy Sullivan	1904–05	Joey Archibald	1941	Alexis Arguello	1974–77
Abe Attell	1906–12	Chalky Wright	1941–42	Danny Lopez	1978–80
Johnny Kilbane	1912–23	Willie Pep	1942–48	Salvador Sanchez	1980–82
Eugene Criqui	1923	Sandy Saddler	1948–49	Eusebio Pedroza	1982–
Johnny Dundee	1923–25	Willie Pep	1949–50		
Louis (Kid) Kaplan	1926–27	Sandy Saddler	1950–57		

BANTAMWEIGHT BOXING CHAMPIONS (Up to 118 pounds)*

CHAMPION	REIGN	CHAMPION	REIGN	CHAMPION	REIGN
Terry McGovern	1899–1900	Bud Taylor	1927–28	Jose Becerra	1959–60
Harry Harris	1901–02	Al Brown	1929–35	Eder Jofre	1961–65
Harry Forbes	1902–03	Baltazar Sangchili	1935–36	Masahiko Harada	1965–68
Frankie Neil	1903–04	Tony Marino	1936	Lionel Rose	1968–69
Joe Bowker	1904	Sixto Escobar	1936–37	Ruben Olivares	1969–70
Jimmy Walsh	1905–07	Harry Jeffra	1937–38	Jesus Castillo	1970–71
Vacant	1908–09	Sixto Escobar	1938–40	Ruben Olivares	1971–72
Johnny Coulon	1910–14	Georgie Pace	1940	Rafael Herrera	1972
Kid Williams	1914–17	Lou Salica	1940–42	Enrique Pinder	1972–73
Pete Herman	1917–20	Manuel Ortiz	1942–47	Romeo Anaya	1973
Joe Lynch	1920–21	Harold Dade	1947	Arnold Taylor	1973–74
Pete Herman	1921	Manuel Ortiz	1947–50	Soo Hwan Hong	1974–75
Johnny Buff	1921–22	Vic Toweel	1950–52	Alfonso Zamora	1975–77
Joe Lynch	1922–24	Jimmy Carruthers	1952–54	Jorge Lujan	1977–80
Abe Goldstein	1924	Robert Cohen	1954–56	Julian Solis	1980
Eddie Martin	1924–25	Mario D'Agata	1956–57	Jeff Chandler	1980–
Charley Rosenberg	1925–27	Alphonse Halimi	1957–59		

FLYWEIGHT BOXING CHAMPIONS (Up to 112 pounds)*

CHAMPION	REIGN	CHAMPION	REIGN	CHAMPION	REIGN
Jimmy Wilde	1916–23	Rinty Monaghan	1948–50	Chartchai Chionoi	1970
Pancho Villa	1923–25	Dado Marino	1950–52	Erbito Salavarria	1970–73
Fidel La Barba	1925–27	Yoshio Shirai	1952–54	Venice Borkorsor	1973
Frenchy Belanger	1927–28	Pascual Perez	1954–60	Miguel Canto	1975–79
Frankie Genaro	1928–31	Pone Kingpetch	1960–62	Chan-Hee Park	1979–80
Spider Pladner	1929	Masahiko Harado	1962–63	Shoji Oguma	1980–81
Frankie Genaro	1929–31	Pone Kingpetch	1963	Antonio Avelar	1981–82
Victor Perez	1931–32	Hiroyuki Ebihara	1963–64	Prudencio Cardona	1982
Jackie Brown	1932–35	Pone Kingpetch	1964–65	Freddy Castillo	1982
Benny Lynch	1935–38	Salvatore Burruni	1965–66	Eleoncio Mercedes	1982–83
Peter Kane	1938–41	Walter McGowan	1966	Charlie Magri	1983
Vacant	1941–42	Chartchai Chionoi	1966–69	Frank Cedeño	1983–
Jackie Paterson	1943–47	Efren Torres	1969–70		

*Source: *The Ring Magazine*

CHESS

Source: U.S. Chess Federation

The triennial World Computer Championship ended Oct. 25 in New York with a surprise victory for "Cray Blitz," running on the Cray-1 computer. The program, which won the 1982 Mississippi State championship, defeated 1980 winner "Belle" in the final round by the score of $4\frac{1}{2}$ to $\frac{1}{2}$. There were 22 entrants, representing eight nations.

The U.S. Championship tournament at Thiel College, Greenville, Pa., ended July 31 with a three-way tie between Grandmasters Walter Browne of Berkeley, Calif., Larry Christiansen of Los Angeles, Calif., and Roman Dzindzichashvili of Corona, New York. In August, Christiansen tied with Swiss Grandmaster Viktor Korchnoi to win first place in the U.S. Open championship.

International Master Leonid Bass of Milwaukee, Wis., won the 1983 National Open championship at Las Vegas, Nev., in March.

WORLD CHESS CHAMPIONS

YEARS	CHAMPION	COUNTRY	YEARS	CHAMPION	COUNTRY
1851–58	Adolph Anderssen	Germany	1948–57	Mikhail Botvinnik	Soviet Union
1858–62	Paul C. Morphy	United States	1957–58	Vassily Smyslov	Soviet Union
1862–66	Adolph Anderssen	Germany	1958–60	Mikhail Botvinnik	Soviet Union
1866–94	Wilhelm Steinitz	Austria, U.S.	1960–61	Mikhail Tal	Soviet Union
1894–1921	Emanuel Lasker	Germany	1961–63	Mikhail Botvinnik	Soviet Union
1921–27	José R. Capablanca	Cuba	1963–69	Tigran Petrosian	Soviet Union
1927–35	Alexander A. Alekhine	France	1969–72	Boris Spassky	Soviet Union
1935–37	Max Euwe	Netherlands	1972–75	Bobby Fischer	United States
1937–46	Alexander A. Alekhine	France	1975–	Anatoly Karpov	Soviet Union

FENCING

NATIONAL COLLEGIATE ATHLETIC ASSOCIATION FENCING CHAMPIONSHIPS

TEAM CHAMPIONSHIPS

1949	Army; Rutgers	1955	Columbia	1962	Navy	1969	Pennsylvania	1975	Wayne State
1950	Navy	1956	Illinois	1963	Columbia	1970	New York U.	1976	New York U.
1951–52	Columbia	1957	New York U.	1964	Princeton	1971	New York U.; Columbia	1977–78	Notre Dame
1953	Pennsylvania	1958	Illinois	1965	Columbia			1979–80	Wayne State
1954	Columbia; New York U.	1959	Navy	1966–67	New York U.	1972	Detroit	1981	Pennsylvania
		1960–61	New York U.	1968	Columbia	1973–74	New York U.	1982–83	Wayne State

FOIL CHAMPIONS

1941	Edward McNamara, Northwestern	1956	Ralph DeMarco, Columbia	1969	Norman Braslow, Pennsylvania
1942	Byron Kreiger, Wayne State	1957–58	Bruce Davis, Wayne State	1970	Walter Krause, New York U.
1947	Abraham Balk, New York U.	1959	Joe Paletta, Navy	1971–72	Tyrone Simmons, Detroit
1948	Albert Axelrod, City College, N.Y.	1960	Gene Glazer, New York U.	1973	Brooke Makler, Pennsylvania
1949	Ralph Tedeschi, Rutgers	1961–62	Herbert Cohen, New York U.	1974–76	Greg Benko, Wayne State
1950	Robert Nielsen, Columbia	1963	Jay Lustig, Columbia	1977	Pat Gerard, Notre Dame
1951	Robert Nielsen, Columbia	1964	Bill Hicks, Princeton	1978	Ernest Simon, Wayne State
1952	Harold Goldsmith, City College, N.Y.	1965	Joe Nalven, Columbia	1979	Andy Bonk, Wayne State
1953	Ed Nober, Brooklyn College	1966	Al Davis, New York U.	1980–81	Ernie Simon, Wayne State
1954	Robert Goldman, Pennsylvania	1967	Mike Gaylor, New York U.	1982	Alexander Flom, George Mason
1955	Herman Velasco, Illinois	1968	Gerard Esponda, San Francisco	1983	Paul Schmidt, Princeton

SABER CHAMPIONS

1948	James Day, Navy	1959	Al Morales, Navy	1970–72	Bruce Soriano, Columbia
1949–50	Alex Treves, Rutgers	1960	Mike Desaro, New York U.	1973	Peter Westbrook, New York U.
1951	Chambless Johnston, Princeton	1961	Israel Colon, New York U.	1974	Steve Danosi, Wayne State
1952	Frank Zimolzak, Navy	1962	Barton Nisonson, Columbia	1975	Yuri Rabinovich, Wayne State
1953	Robert Parmacek, Pennsylvania	1963	Bela Szentivanyi, Wayne State	1976	Brian Smith, Columbia
1954	Steve Sobel, Columbia	1964	Craig Bell, Illinois	1977–78	Mike Sullivan, Notre Dame
1955	Barry Pariser, Columbia	1965	Howard Goodman, New York U.	1979	Yuri Rabinovich, Wayne State
1956	Gerald Kaufman, Columbia	1966	Paul Apostol, New York U.	1980–81	Paul Friedberg, Pennsylvania
1957	Bernie Balaban, New York U.	1967–68	Todd Makler, Pennsylvania	1982	Neil Hick, Wayne State
1958	Art Schankin, Illinois	1969	Antony Kestler, Columbia	1983	John Friedberg, North Carolina

ÉPÉE CHAMPIONS

1942	Ben Burtt, Ohio State	1957	James Margolis, Columbia	1970	John Nadas, Case Western Reserve
1947	Abraham Balk, New York U.	1958–59	Roland Wommack, Navy	1971	George Szunyogh, New York U.
1948	William Bryan, Navy	1960	Gil Eisner, New York U.	1972	Ernesto Fernandez, Pennsylvania
1949	Richard C. Bowman, Army	1961	Jerry Halpern, New York U.	1973–75	Risto Hurme, New York U.
1950	Thomas Stuart, Navy	1962	Thane Hawkins, Navy	1976	Randy Eggleton, Pennsylvania
1951	Daniel Chafetz, Columbia	1963	Larry Crum, Navy	1977	Hans Wieselgren, New York U.
1952	James Wallner, New York U.	1964–65	Paul Pesthy, Rutgers	1978	Bjorne Vaggo, Notre Dame
1953	Jack Tori, Pennsylvania	1966	Bernhardt Hermann, Iowa	1979	Carlo Songini, Cleveland State
1954	Henry Kolowrat, Princeton	1967	George Masin, New York U.	1980–81	Gil Pezza, Wayne State
1955	Donald Tadrawski, Notre Dame	1968	Don Sieja, Cornell	1982	Peter Schifrin, San Jose State
1956	Kinmont Hoitsma, Princeton	1969	James Wetzler, Pennsylvania	1983	Ola Harstrom, Notre Dame

FISHING

WORLD FRESHWATER FISHING RECORDS

Source: *International Game Fish Association*

SPECIES	WEIGHT[1]	LENGTH[2]	GIRTH[2]	PLACE CAUGHT	DATE	ANGLER
Bass (largemouth)	22– 4	32 ½″	28 ½″	Montgomery Lake, Ga.	June 2, 1932	George W. Perry
Bass (redeye)	8– 3	23″	16 ½″	Flint River, Ga.	Oct. 23, 1977	David A. Hubbard
Bass (rock)	3– 0	13 ½″	10 ¾″	York River, Ont.	Aug. 1, 1974	Peter Gulgin
Bass (smallmouth)	11–15	27″	21 ⅔″	Dale Hollow Lake, Ky.	July 9, 1955	David L. Hayes
Bass (spotted)	8–15	—	—	Smith Lake, Ala.	Mar. 18, 1978	Philip C. Terry Jr.
Bass (white)	5– 9	20 ¾″	17″	Colorado River, Tex.	March 31, 1977	David S. Cordill
Bass (yellow)	2– 4	16 ¼″	12 ¾″	Lake Monroe, Ind.	Mar. 27, 1977	Donald L. Stalker
Bluegill	4–12	15″	18 ¼″	Ketona Lake, Ala.	Apr. 9, 1950	T. S. Hudson
Bowfin	21– 8	—	—	Florence, N.C.	Jan. 29, 1980	Robert L. Harmon
Buffalo (bigmouth)	70– 5	—	—	Bastrop, La.	Apr. 21, 1980	Delbert Sisk
Buffalo (smallmouth)	51	—	—	Lawrence, Kan.	May 2, 1979	Scott Butler
Bullhead (black)	8	24″	17 ¾″	Lake Waccabuc, N.Y.	Aug. 1, 1951	Kani Evans
Carp	55– 5	42″	31″	Clearwater Lake, Minn.	July 10, 1952	Frank J. Ledwein
Catfish (blue)	97	57″	37″	Missouri River, S.D.	Sept. 16, 1959	Edward B. Elliott
Catfish (channel)	58	47 ¼″	29 ⅛″	Santee-Cooper Res., S.C.	July 7, 1964	W. B. Whaley
Catfish (flathead)	91– 4	—	—	Lake Lewisville, Tex.	March 28, 1982	Mike Rogers
Catfish (white)	17– 7	—	—	Success Lake, Calif.	Nov. 15, 1981	Chuck Idell
Char (Arctic)	29–11	39 ¾″	26″	Arctic River, N.W.T.	Aug. 21, 1968	Jeanne P. Branson
Crappie (black)	6	20″	19 ½″	Seaplane Canal, La.	Nov. 28, 1969	Lettie T. Robertson
Crappie (white)	5– 3	21″	19″	Enid Dam, Miss.	July 31, 1957	Fred L. Bright
Dolly Varden	4	24 ¼″	10 ⅞″	Togiak Nat'l. Wildlife Refuge, Alaska	July 18, 1982	Jonathan Olch
Drum (freshwater)	54– 8	31 ½″	29″	Nickajack Dam, Tenn.	Apr. 20, 1972	Benny E. Hull
Gar (alligator)	279	93″	—	Rio Grande, Texas	Dec. 2, 1951	Bill Valverde
Gar (longnose)	50– 5	72 ¼″	22 ¼″	Trinity River, Texas	July 30, 1954	Townsend Miller
Grayling (Arctic)	5–15	29 ⅞″	15 ⅛″	Katseyedie R., N.W.T.	Aug. 16, 1967	Jeanne P. Branson
Kokanee	6– 9 ¾	24 ½″	14 ½″	Priest Lake, Idaho	June 9, 1975	Jerry Verge
Muskellunge	69–15	64 ½″	31 ¾″	St. Lawrence R., N.Y.	Sept. 22, 1957	Arthur Lawton
Perch (white)	4–12	19 ½″	13″	Messalonskee Lake, Me.	June 4, 1949	Mrs. Earl Small
Perch (yellow)	4– 3 ½	—	—	Bordentown, N.J.	May 1865	Dr. C. C. Abbot
Pickerel (chain)	9– 6	31″	14″	Homerville, Ga.	Feb. 17, 1961	Baxley McQuaig Jr.
Pike (northern)	46– 2	52 ½″	25″	Sacandaga Res., N.Y.	Sept. 15, 1940	Peter Dubuc
Redhorse (silver)	9–11	—	—	Winnipeg River, Canada	May 22, 1982	John D. Richards
Salmon (Atlantic)	79– 2	—	—	Tana River, Norway	1928	Henrik Henriksen
Salmon (chinook)	93	50″	39″	Alaska Kelp Bay, Alas.	June 24, 1977	Howard Rider
Salmon (chum)	27– 3	39 ⅜″	24 ½″	Raymond Cove, Alas.	June 11, 1977	Robert A. Jahnke
Salmon (coho or silver)	31	—	—	Cowichan Bay, B.C.	Oct. 11, 1947	Mrs. Lee Hallberg
Salmon (landlocked)	22– 8	36″	—	Sebago Lake, Maine	Aug. 1, 1907	Edward Blakely
Sauger	8–12	28″	15″	Lake Sakakawea, N.D.	Oct. 6, 1971	Mike Fischer
Shad (American)	9– 4	—	—	Delaware River, Pa.	Apr. 26, 1979	J. Edward Whitman
Sturgeon (white)	360	111″	86″	Snake River, Idaho	Apr. 24, 1956	Willard Cravens
Sunfish (green)	2– 2	14 ¾″	14″	Stockton Lake, Mo.	June 18, 1971	Paul M. Dilley
Sunfish (redbreast)	1– 8 ½	11″	12 ⅝″	Suwannee River, Fla.	Apr. 30, 1977	Tommy D. Cason Jr.
Sunfish (red ear)	4– 8	16 ¼″	17 ¾″	Chase City, Va.	June 19, 1970	Maurice E. Ball
Trout (brook)	14– 8	31 ½″	—	Nipigon River, Ontario	July 1916	Dr. W. J. Cook
Trout (brown)	35–15	—	—	Nahuel Huapi, Argentina	Dec. 16, 1952	Eugenio Cavaglia
Trout (cutthroat)	41	39″	—	Pyramid Lake, Nev.	Dec. 1925	John Skimmerhorn
Trout (golden)	11	28″	16″	Cook's Lake, Wyo.	Aug. 5, 1948	Charles S. Reed
Trout (lake)	65	52″	38″	Great Bear Lake, N.W.T.	Aug. 8, 1970	Lary Daunis
Trout (rainbow)[3]	42– 2	43″	23 ½″	Bell Island, Alaska	June 22, 1970	David R. White
Trout (tiger)	20–13	33 ¾″	21 ⅝″	Lake Michigan, Wis.	Aug. 12, 1978	Pete M. Friedland
Walleye	25	41″	29″	Old Hickory Lake, Tenn.	Aug. 1, 1960	Mabry Harper
Warmouth	2–2	11 ⅞″	13 ⅛″	Douglas Swamp, S.C.	May 19, 1973	Willie Singletary
Whitefish (lake)	13–15	—	—	Meaford, Ont., Canada	Apr. 19, 1981	Wayne Caswell
Whitefish (mountain)	5	19″	14″	Athabasca R., Alberta	June 3, 1963	Orville Welch

[1] In pounds and ounces. [2] In inches. [3] Also known as Steelhead or Kamloops.

AMERICAN CASTING ASSOCIATION RECORDS

Men: All Distance[1]	Steve Rajeff	1983	5,076 ft.
Men: All Accuracy[2]	Steve Rajeff	1977	593 pts.
Men: Distance Plugs[3]	Chris Korich	1983	3,347 ft.
Men: Distance Flies[3]	Steve Rajeff	1983	1,886 ft.
Men: Accuracy Plugs[4]	Steve Rajeff	1977	297 pts.
Men: Accuracy Flies[4]	Tim Rajeff	1981	300 pts.
Women: All Accuracy[2]	B. M. Sporran	1982	559 pts.
Women: Accuracy Plugs[4]	B. M. Sporran	1983	282 pts.
Women: Accuracy Flies[4]	Cecelia Ray	1981	282 pts.
Intm.: All Accuracy[2]	Steve Willson	1970	564 pts.
Intm.: Accuracy Plugs[4]	Don Lanser	1970	284 pts.
Intm.: Accuracy Flies[4]	Luke Brugnara	1978	298 pts.

[1] Total of 12 casts. [2] Of possible 600 points. [3] Total of 6 casts. [4] Of possible 300 points.

SALTWATER FISHING ALL–TACKLE RECORDS

Source: International Game Fish Association

SPECIES	WEIGHT (in lbs. and oz.)	LENGTH (in ft. and in.)	GIRTH (in inches)	WHERE CAUGHT	DATE	ANGLER
Albacore	88–2	4' 2"	37"	Canary Islands	Nov. 19, 1977	Siegfried Dickemann
Amberjack (greater)	155–10	—	—	Challenger Bank, Bermuda	June 24, 1981	Joseph Dawson
Barracuda (great)	83	6 '¼"	29"	Lagos, Nigeria	Jan. 13, 1952	K.J.W. Hackett
Bass (black sea)	8–12	—	—	Oregon Inlet, N.C.	Apr. 21, 1979	Joe W. Mizelle Sr.
Bass (giant sea)	563–8	7' 5"	72"	Anacapa Island, Calif.	Aug. 20, 1968	James D. McAdam Jr.
Bass (striped)	78–8	53"	34½"	Atlantic City, N.J.	Sept. 21, 1982	Albert R. McReynolds
Bluefish	31–12	3' 11"	23"	Hatteras Inlet, N.C.	Jan. 30, 1972	James M. Hussey
Bonefish	19	3' 3⅝"	17"	Zululand, South Africa	May 26, 1962	Brian W. Batchelor
Bonito (Atlantic)	16–12	—	—	Puerto Rico, Canary Is.	Dec. 6, 1980	Rolf Fedderies
Bonito (Pacific)	23–8	2' 11¼"	23¼"	Seychelles	Feb. 19, 1975	Mrs. Ann Cochain
Cobia	110–5	5' 3"	34"	Mombasa, Kenya	Sept. 8, 1964	Eric Tinworth
Cod, Atlantic	98–12	5' 3"	41"	Isle of Shoals, Mass.	June 8, 1969	Alphonse J. Bielevich
Conger	87–2	90"	28½"	Dartmouth, England	June 16, 1982	Peter L. King
Dolphin	87	6' 9⅔"	28"	Costa Rica	Sept. 25, 1976	Manual Salazar
Drum (black)	113–1	4' 5⅛"	43½"	Lewes, Del.	Sept. 15, 1975	Gerald M. Townsend
Drum (red)	90	4' 7½"	38¼"	Rodanthe, N.C.	Nov. 7, 1973	Elvin Hooper
Flounder	30–12	3' 2½"	30½"	Viña del Mar, Chile	Nov. 1, 1971	Augusto Núñez Moreno
Halibut (Atlantic)	250	—	—	Gloucester, Mass.	July 3, 1981	Louis P. Sirard
Jack (crevalle)	54–7	—	—	Mort Michel, Gabon	Jan. 15, 1982	Thomas F. Gibson Jr.
Jewfish	680	7' 1½"	66"	Fernandina Beach, Fla.	May 20, 1961	Lynn Joyner
Kawakawa	26	—	—	New South Wales, Australia	Jan. 26, 1980	Wally Elfring
Mackerel (king)	90	5' 11"	30"	Key West, Fla.	Feb. 16, 1976	Norton I. Thomton
Marlin (Atlantic blue)	1,282	14' 8"	76½"	St. Thomas, Virgin Is.	Aug. 6, 1977	Larry Martin
Marlin (black)	1,560	14' 6"	81"	Cabo Blanco, Peru	Aug. 4, 1953	Alfred C. Glassell Jr.
Marlin (Pacific blue)	1,376	—	—	Kona, Hawaii	May 31, 1982	Guy Wm. de Beaubien
Marlin (striped)	455–4	10' 7"	4'4"	Mayor Island, N.Z.	March 8, 1982	Bruce Jenkinson
Marlin (white)	181–14	—	—	Vitoria, Brazil	Dec. 8, 1979	Evandro Luiz Caser
Permit	51–8	3' 8¼"	35"	Lake Worth, Fla.	April 28, 1978	William M. Kenney
Pollock	46–7	4' 2½"	30"	Brielle, N.J.	May 6, 1975	James T. Holton
Pompano (African)	41–8	—	—	Fort Lauderdale, Fla.	Feb. 15, 1979	Wayne Sommers
Roosterfish	114	5' 4"	33"	LaPaz, Mexico	June 1, 1960	Abe Sackheim
Runner (rainbow)	33–10	4' 7¼"	22½"	Clarion Is., Mexico	Mar. 14, 1976	Ralph Mikkelsen
Sailfish (Atlantic)	128–1	8' 10"	34"	Luanda, Angola	Mar. 27, 1974	Harm Steyn
Sailfish (Pacific)	221	10' 9"	—	Galápagos Islands	Feb. 12, 1947	C. W. Stewart
Seabass (white)	83–12	5' 5½"	34"	San Felipe, Mexico	Mar. 31, 1953	L. C. Baumgardner
Seatrout (spotted)	16	2' 8½"	21¾"	Mason's Beach, Va.	May 28, 1977	William G. Katko
Shark (blue)	437	—	—	Catherine Bay, Australia	Oct. 2, 1976	Peter Hyde
Shark (hammerhead)	991	176"	76"	Sarasota, Fla.	May 30, 1982	Allen Ogle
Shark (porbeagle)	465	9' 3"	56"	Padstow, England	July 23, 1976	Jorge Potier
Shark (shortfin mako)	1,080	—	—	Montauk, New York	Aug. 26, 1979	James L. Melanson
Shark (thresher)	802	—	—	New Zealand	Feb. 8, 1981	Dianne North
Shark (tiger)	1,780	13' 10½"	103"	Cherry Grove, S.C.	June 14, 1964	Walter Maxwell
Shark (white)	2,664	16' 10"	114"	Ceduna, Australia	Apr. 21, 1959	Alfred Dean
Snook	53–10	—	—	Rio de Parasmina, Costa Rica	Oct. 18, 1978	Gilbert Ponzi
Swordfish	1,182	14' 11¼"	78"	Iquique, Chile	May 7, 1953	L. Marron
Tanguigue	99	—	—	Natal, South Africa	Mar. 14, 1982	Michael J. Wilkinson
Tarpon	283	7' 2⅗"	—	Lake Maracaibo, Venezuela	Mar. 19, 1956	M. Salazar
Tautog (blackfish)	21–6	2' 7½"	23½"	Cape May, N.J.	June 12, 1954	R. N. Sheafer
Trevally	116	5' 3¼"	39¾"	Pago Pago, Am. Samoa	Feb. 20, 1978	William G. Foster
Tuna (Atlantic bigeye)	375–8	—	—	Ocean City, Md.	Aug. 26, 1977	Cecil Browne
Tuna (blackfin)	42	3' 6½"	29½"	Bermuda	June 2, 1978	Alan J. Card
Tuna (bluefin)	1,496	—	—	Nova Scotia, Canada	Oct. 26, 1979	Ken Fraser
Tuna (dogtooth)	288–12	97.63	26.77	Kwan-Tall Island Cheju-Do, Korea	Oct. 6, 1982	Boo-Il Oh
Tuna (longtail)	79–2	—	—	Montague Is., Australia	Apr. 12, 1982	Tim Simpson
Tuna (Pacific bigeye)	435	7' 9"	63½"	Cabo Blanco, Peru	Apr. 17, 1957	Dr. Russel V. A. Lee
Tuna (skipjack)	41–12	—	—	Black River, Mauritius	Mar. 13, 1982	Bruno de Ravel
Tuna (southern bluefin)	348–5	—	—	New Zealand	Jan. 16, 1981	Rex Wood
Tuna (yellowfin)	388–12	7' 7¼"	62¼"	San Benedicto Is., Mexico	Apr. 1, 1977	Curt Wiesenhutter
Tunny (little)	27	3' 3"	22"	Key Largo, Fla.	Apr. 20, 1976	William E. Allison
Wahoo	149	6' 7¾"	37½"	Cat Cay, Bahamas	June 5, 1962	John Pirovano
Weakfish	19	34½"	22½"	Chesapeake Bay, Va.	May 19, 1983	Philip W. Halstead
Yellowtail	111	5' 2"	38"	New Zealand	June 11, 1961	A.F. Plim
Yellowtail (California)	71–15	—	—	Alijos Rocks, Mexico	June 24, 1979	Michael Carpenter

FOOTBALL—PROFESSIONAL FOOTBALL HIGHLIGHTS

United Press Int'l.

Georgia tailback and 1982 Heisman Trophy winner Herschel Walker makes his last collegiate appearance at the Sugar Bowl in New Orleans, La., on Jan. 1, 1983. In February Walker, a junior, turned professional and signed a multimillion-dollar contract with the New Jersey Generals of the new United States Football League. He ended the season as top rusher of the league, with 1,812 yards and 17 touchdowns.

As the National Football League (NFL) season moved to a close, division titles were won by Miami, Pittsburgh, Los Angeles Raiders, Washington, Detroit, and San Francisco. They entered the playoffs, along with wild card entries Seattle, Denver, Dallas, and the Los Angeles Rams. For results, see page 30. See page 805 for 1983–84 NFL final standings.

The premier season of the new United States Football League (USFL) got under way on March 6, with a field of 12 teams. Although home-game attendance was sparse during the four-month season, officials were optimistic that future years would see increased attendance and interest. Television ratings, however, were much better than expected.

At the end of the regular season, four teams participated in the playoffs. The Philadelphia Stars, with a 15–3 record, captured the Atlantic Division title, the Michigan Panthers (12–6) won the Central Division title, and the Oakland Invaders (9–9) won the Pacific Division title. The Chicago Blitz (12–6) gained a wild card entry.

In the semifinal playoffs on July 10, Philadelphia defeated Chicago, 44–38, and Michigan downed Oakland, 37–21.

The championship game, played before a crowd of 50,906 at Denver, Colo., saw Michigan edge Philadelphia, 24–22. Michigan quarterback Bobby Herbert was named most valuable player of the championship. He completed 20 of 39 passes for 314 yards and three touchdowns.

During the regular season, Herbert was the top passer, with 275 completions in 451 attempts, for 3,586 yards and 27 touchdowns. Philadelphia's Dave Trout was the league's top scorer, with 37 extra points and 28 field goals. New Jersey Generals star Herschel Walker took the rushing crown with 1,812 yards.

In October the USFL announced a new divisional alignment for its 1984 season, beginning on Feb. 26. Eighteen teams will be divided into two conferences, Eastern and Western, and each conference will have two divisions. Eight teams will enter the playoffs, concluding with the championship game to be played at Tampa Bay on July 15.

UNITED STATES FOOTBALL LEAGUE

1983 FINAL STANDINGS

	W	L	T	PCT.	PTS.	OP		W	L	T	PCT.	PTS.	OP
Atlantic Division													
†Philadelphia Stars	15	3	0	.833	379	204	New Jersey Generals	6	12	0	.333	314	437
Boston Breakers	11	7	0	.611	399	334	Washington Federals	4	14	0	.222	297	442
Central Division													
†Michigan Panthers	12	6	0	.667	451	337	Tampa Bay Bandits	11	7	0	.611	363	378
Chicago Blitz	12	6	0	.667	456	271	Birmingham Stallions	9	9	0	.500	343	346
Pacific Division													
†Oakland Invaders	9	9	0	.500	319	317	Denver Gold	7	11	0	.389	284	304
Los Angeles Express	8	10	0	.444	296	370	Arizona Wranglers	4	14	0	.222	261	442

UNITED STATES FOOTBALL LEAGUE TOP PLAYERS: 1983

TOP PASSERS

	ATTEMPTS	COMPLETIONS			TOUCHDOWNS		INTERCEPTIONS		RATING
		Total	Pct.	Yards	Total	Pct.	Total	Pct.	POINTS
Bobby Hebert, Michigan	451	257	57.0	3,586	27	6.0	17	3.8	49.0
Fred Besana, Oakland	550	345	62.7	3,980	21	3.8	26	2.9	45.0
Greg Landry, Chicago	334	188	56.3	2,383	16	4.8	9	2.7	43.5
Jimmy Jordan, Tampa Bay	238	145	60.9	1,831	14	5.9	14	5.9	41.0
Chuck Fusina, Philadelphia	421	238	56.5	2,718	15	3.6	10	2.4	38.0
Alan Risher, Arizona	424	236	55.7	2,672	20	4.7	16	3.8	29.0
Bobby Scott, N.J., Chicago	374	210	56.0	2,813	11	3.0	18	5.0	27.0
John Walton, Boston	589	330	56.0	3,772	20	3.4	18	3.1	27.0
Tom Ramsey, Los Angeles	307	160	52.1	1,975	13	4.2	14	4.6	25.0
Bob Lane, Birmingham	346	175	50.6	2,264	14	4.0	18	5.2	23.0
Mike Rae, Los Angeles	319	175	54.9	1,964	11	3.4	10	3.1	23.0
John Reaves, Tampa Bay	259	139	53.7	1,726	9	3.5	16	6.2	20.0

TOP RECEIVERS

	COMPLETIONS			TDs
	No.	Yards	Avg.	
Trumaine Johnson, Chi.	81	1,322	16.3	10
Danny Buggs, Tampa Bay	76	1,146	15.1	5
Ricky Ellis, Los Angeles	69	716	10.0	6
Raymond Chester, Oakland	68	951	14.0	5
E. Truvillion, Tampa Bay	66	1,080	16.4	15
A. Whittington, Oakland	66	584	8.8	2
Mark Keel, Arizona	65	802	12.3	2
Drew Taylor, Washington	64	523	8.2	2
Joey Walters, Washington	63	959	15.2	6
Jackie Flowers, Arizona	63	869	13.8	11
Neil Balholm, Arizona	63	703	11.2	5
Nolan Franz, Boston	62	848	13.7	4

TOP RUSHERS

	YARDS	AVG.	TDs
Herschel Walker, New Jersey	1,812	4.4	17
Kelvin Bryant, Philadelphia	1,442	4.5	16
Ken Lacy, Michigan	1,180	5.1	6
Tim Spencher, Chicago	1,157	3.9	6
A. Whittington, Oakland	1,043	3.7	6
Kevin Long, Chicago	1,022	3.9	12
Richard Crump, Boston	990	5.2	8
Ken Talton, Birmingham	907	4.0	5
Craig James, Washington	823	4.1	4
Harry Sydney, Denver	801	4.6	9
Billy Taylor, Washington	757	4.4	5
Calvin Murray, Arizona	699	3.9	4

TOP PUNTERS

	NO.	YARDS	AVG.
Stan Talley, Oakland	87	3,825	44.0
Jeff Partridge, Los Angeles	87	3,672	42.2
Sean Landeta, Philadelphia	86	3,601	41.9
Dario Casarino, Birm., Bos.	67	2,782	41.5
Steve Gortz, Denver	85	3,496	41.1
Dana Moore, Washington	86	3,480	40.5
Frank Corral, Chicago	74	2,989	40.4
Z. Andrusyshyn, Tampa Bay	90	3,583	39.8
Mike Mees, Arizona	52	2,059	39.6
A. Bollinger, Birmingham	51	2,008	39.4
Jim Asmus, Arizona	52	2,012	38.7

PASS INTERCEPTORS

	TOTAL	YARDS	AVG.
Luther Bradley, Chicago	12	167	13.9
Doug Greene, Washington	9	121	13.4
Mike Williams, New Jersey	8	68	8.5
Scott Woerner, Philadelphia	8	50	6.3
David Dumars, Denver	7	242	34.6
Eddie Brown, Chicago	6	88	14.7
Tommy Wilcox, Arizona	6	59	9.8
Mike Lush, Philadelphia	6	52	8.7
David Martin, Denver	6	44	7.3
Jeff George, Tampa Bay	6	33	5.5
Jeff Brown, Washington	6	27	4.5

TOP SCORERS

	TDs	X PTs	FGs	TOTAL
David Trout, Philadelphia	0	37	28	121
Tim Mazzetti, Boston	0	38	27	119
Herschel Walker, N.J.	18	2	0	110
Scott Norwood, Birmingham	0	34	25	109
Frank Corral, Chicago	0	39	22	105
Novo Bojovic, Michigan	0	49	18	103
Kelvin Bryant, Philadelphia	17	0	0	102
Z. Andrusyshyn, Tampa Bay	0	32	23	101
E. Truvillion, Tampa Bay	15	2	0	92
Kevin Shea, Oakland	0	32	19	89

PUNT RETURNS

	NO.	YARDS	AVG.
David Martin, Denver	35	380	10.9
Gordon Banks, Oakland	30	292	9.7
Anthony Carter, Michigan	40	387	9.7
Lenny Willis, Chicago	54	489	9.1
Scott Woerner, Philadelphia	43	360	8.4
Alvin Bailey, Tampa Bay	44	365	8.3
Wally Henry, Arizona	20	161	8.1
Ron Frederick, Birmingham	23	170	7.4
Eric Robinson, Washington	24	171	7.1
Thomas Lott, New Jersey	25	155	6.2

† Won division title.

SUPER BOWL GAMES: 1967–1983

1967 **Super Bowl I** The Coliseum, Los Angeles, Calif.

Green Bay (NFL)	7	7	14	7	35
Kansas City (AFL)	0	10	0	0	10

1968 **Super Bowl II** Orange Bowl Stadium, Miami, Fla.

Green Bay (NFL)	3	13	10	7	33
Oakland (AFL)	0	7	0	7	14

1969 **Super Bowl III** Orange Bowl Stadium, Miami, Fla.

New York (AFL)	0	7	6	3	16
Baltimore (NFL)	0	0	0	7	7

1970 **Super Bowl IV** Tulane Stadium, New Orleans, La.

Kansas City (AFL)	3	13	7	0	23
Minnesota (NFL)	0	0	7	0	7

1971 **Super Bowl V** Orange Bowl Stadium, Miami, Fla.

Baltimore (AFC)	0	6	0	10	16
Dallas (NFC)	3	10	0	0	13

1972 **Super Bowl VI** Tulane Stadium, New Orleans, La.

Dallas (NFC)	3	7	7	7	24
Miami (AFC)	0	3	0	0	3

1973 **Super Bowl VII** The Coliseum, Los Angeles, Calif.

Miami (AFC)	7	7	0	0	14
Washington (NFC)	0	0	0	7	7

1974 **Super Bowl VIII** Rice Stadium, Houston, Texas

Miami (AFC)	14	3	7	0	24
Minnesota (NFC)	0	0	0	7	7

1975 **Super Bowl IX** Tulane Stadium, New Orleans, La.

Pittsburgh (AFC)	0	2	7	7	16
Minnesota (NFC)	0	0	0	6	6

1976 **Super Bowl X** Orange Bowl Stadium, Miami, Fla.

Pittsburgh (AFC)	7	0	0	14	21
Dallas (NFC)	7	3	0	7	17

1977 **Super Bowl XI** Rose Bowl, Pasadena, Calif.

Oakland (AFC)	0	16	3	13	32
Minnesota (NFC)	0	0	7	7	14

1978 Super Bowl XII La. Superdome, New Orleans, La.

Dallas (NFC)	10	3	7	7	27
Denver (AFC)	0	0	10	0	10

1979 **Super Bowl XIII** Orange Bowl, Miami, Fla.

Pittsburgh (AFC)	7	14	0	14	35
Dallas (NFC)	7	7	3	14	31

1980 **Super Bowl XIV** Rose Bowl, Pasadena, Calif.

Pittsburgh (AFC)	3	7	7	14	31
Los Angeles (NFC)	7	6	6	0	19

1981 **Super Bowl XV** La. Superdome, New Orleans, La.

Oakland (AFC)	14	0	10	3	27
Philadelphia (NFC)	0	3	0	7	10

1982 **Super Bowl XVI** Pontiac Superdome, Pontiac, Mich.

San Francisco (NFC)	7	13	0	6	26
Cincinnati (AFC)	0	0	7	14	21

1983 **Super Bowl XVII** Rose Bowl, Pasadena, Calif.

Washington (NFC)	0	10	3	14	27
Miami (AFC)	7	10	0	0	17

PRO FOOTBALL SUPER BOWL RECORDS

INDIVIDUAL RECORDS

Points, lifetime: 24, Franco Harris, Pittsburgh
Touchdowns, lifetime: 4, Franco Harris, Pittsburgh
Yards gained rushing, lifetime: 354, Franco Harris, Pittsburgh
Yards gained rushing, game: 166, John Riggins, Washington vs. Miami, 1983
Longest run from scrimmage: 58 yards, Tom Matte, Baltimore vs. N.Y. Jets, 1969
Passes completed, lifetime: 61, Roger Staubach, Dallas
Yards gained passing, lifetime: 932, Terry Bradshaw, Pittsburgh
Yards gained, game: 318, Terry Bradshaw, Pittsburgh vs. Dallas, 1979
Longest pass completion: 80 yards, Jim Plunkett, Oakland vs. Philadelphia, 1981
Pass receptions, lifetime: 16, Lynn Swann, Pittsburgh
Touchdown passes, lifetime: 9, Terry Bradshaw, Pittsburgh
Touchdown passes, game: 4, Terry Bradshaw, Pittsburgh vs. Dallas, 1979
Fumbles, game: 3, Roger Staubach, Dallas, 1976

TEAM RECORDS

Games played: 5, Dallas
Games won: 4, Pittsburgh
First downs, game: 24, Cincinnati vs. San Francisco, 1982 and Washington vs. Miami, 1983
Touchdowns, game: 5, Green Bay vs. Kansas City, 1967, and Pittsburgh vs. Dallas, 1979
Field goals, game: 4, Green Bay vs. Oakland, 1968
Yards gained, game: 429, Oakland vs. Minnesota, 1977
Passes completed, game: 25, Cincinnati vs. San Francisco, 1982
Yards gained passing, game: 309, Pittsburgh vs. Los Angeles, 1980

NATIONAL FOOTBALL LEAGUE FINAL STANDINGS: 1983–1984

AMERICAN FOOTBALL CONFERENCE (AFC)

Eastern Division	W	L	T	PCT.	PTS.	OP
* Miami	12	4	0	.750	389	250
New England	8	8	0	.500	274	289
Buffalo	8	8	0	.500	283	351
Baltimore	7	9	0	.438	264	354
N.Y. Jets	7	9	0	.438	313	331
Central Division						
* Pittsburgh	10	6	0	.625	355	303
Cleveland	9	7	0	.563	356	342
Cincinnati	7	9	0	.438	346	302
Houston	2	14	0	.125	288	460
Western Division						
* L.A. Raiders	12	4	0	.750	442	338
† Seattle	9	7	0	.563	403	397
† Denver	9	7	0	.563	302	327
San Diego	6	10	0	.375	358	462
Kansas City	6	10	0	.375	386	367

* Clinched division title. † Clinched playoff spot.

NATIONAL FOOTBALL CONFERENCE (NFC)

Eastern Division	W	L	T	PCT.	PTS.	OP
* Washington	14	2	0	.875	541	332
† Dallas	12	4	0	.750	479	360
St. Louis	8	7	1	.531	374	428
Philadelphia	5	11	0	.313	233	322
N.Y. Giants	3	12	1	.219	267	347
Central Division						
* Detroit	9	7	0	.563	347	286
Green Bay	8	8	0	.500	429	439
Chicago	8	8	0	.500	311	301
Minnesota	8	8	0	.500	316	348
Tampa Bay	2	14	0	.125	241	380
Western Division						
* San Francisco	10	6	0	.625	432	293
† L.A. Rams	9	7	0	.563	361	344
New Orleans	8	8	0	.500	319	337
Atlanta	7	9	0	.438	370	389

NATIONAL FOOTBALL LEAGUE TOP PLAYERS: 1982

TOP PASSERS (108 or more attempts)

AMERICAN CONFERENCE	ATTEMPTS	COMPLETIONS Total	Pct.	Yards	AVERAGE GAIN	TOUCHDOWNS Total	Pct.	INTERCEPTIONS Total	Pct.	RATING[1]
Ken Anderson, Cincinnati	309	218	70.6	2,495	8.07	12	3.9	9	2.9	95.5
Dan Fouts, San Diego...	330	204	61.8	2,883	8.74	17	5.2	11	3.3	93.6
Richard Todd, N.Y. Jets	261	153	58.6	1,961	7.51	14	5.4	8	3.1	87.3
Steve Grogan, New Eng.	122	66	54.1	930	7.62	7	5.7	4	3.3	84.2
Terry Bradshaw, Pittsburgh	240	127	52.9	1,768	7.37	17	7.1	11	4.6	81.4
Jim Plunkett, L.A. Raiders	261	152	58.2	2,035	7.80	14	5.4	15	5.7	77.3
Bill Kenney, Kansas City	169	95	56.2	1,192	7.05	7	4.1	6	3.6	77.0
Steve DeBerg, Denver ..	223	131	58.7	1,405	6.30	7	3.1	11	4.9	67.2
NATIONAL CONFERENCE										
Joe Theismann, Wash...	252	161	63.9	2,033	8.07	13	5.2	9	3.6	91.3
Danny White, Dallas	247	156	63.2	2,079	8.42	16	6.5	12	4.9	91.1
Joe Montana, San Fran..	346	213	61.6	2,613	7.55	17	4.9	11	3.2	87.9
Jim McMahon, Chicago .	210	120	57.1	1,501	7.15	9	4.3	7	3.3	80.1
Steve Bartkowski, Atlanta	262	166	63.4	1,905	7.27	8	3.1	11	4.2	78.1
Vince Ferragamo, L.A. ..	209	118	56.5	1,609	7.70	9	4.3	9	4.3	77.7
Ron Jaworski, Phila.....	286	167	58.4	2,076	7.26	12	4.2	12	4.2	77.5
Tommy Kramer, Minn...	308	176	57.1	2,037	6.61	15	4.9	12	3.9	77.3

[1] NFL combined rating points awarded for percent of completions, TDs, interceptions, and average gain.

AMERICAN CONFERENCE

TOP RECEIVERS	COMPLETIONS No.	Yards	Avg.	TDs
Kellen Winslow, San Diego	54	721	13.4	6
Wes Chandler, San Diego.	49	1,032	21.1	9
Cris Collinsworth, Cin. ...	49	700	14.3	1
Ozzie Newsome, Cleveland	49	633	12.9	3
Dan Ross, Cincinnati	47	508	10.8	3
Todd Christensen, L.A. Raiders	42	510	12.1	4
Henry Marshall, Kansas City	40	549	13.7	3
Wesley Walker, N.Y. Jets .	39	620	15.9	6

TOP SCORERS	TDs	X PTs	FGs	TOTAL
Marcus Allen, L.A. Raiders	14	0	0	84
Rolf Benirschke, San Diego	0	32	16	80
Nick Lowery, Kansas City	0	17	19	74
Jim Breech, Cincinnati ...	0	25	14	67
Uwe von Schamann, Miami	0	21	15	66
Chris Bahr, L.A. Raiders..	0	32	10	62
Pat Leahy, New York Jets	0	26	11	59
Wes Chandler, San Diego.	9	0	0	54
Chuck Muncie, San Diego	9	0	0	54

TOP RUSHERS	YARDS	AVG.	TDs
Freeman McNeil, New York Jets	786	5.2	6
Andra Franklin, Miami	701	4.0	7
Marcus Allen, L.A. Raiders ..	697	4.4	11
Joe Cribbs, Buffalo	633	4.7	3
Anthony Collins, New England	632	3.9	1
Pete Johnson, Cincinnati	622	4.0	7
Franco Harris, Pittsburgh ...	604	4.3	2
Chuck Muncie, San Diego ...	569	4.1	8

TOP PUNTERS	NO.	YARDS	AVG.
Luke Prestridge, Denver	45	2,026	45.0
Rohn Stark, Baltimore	46	2,044	44.4
Rich Camarillo, New England	49	2,140	43.7
Jeff Gossett, Kansas City....	33	1,366	41.4
John James, Detroit-Houston	43	1,741	40.5
John Goodson, Pittsburgh ...	49	1,981	40.4
Ray Guy, Los Angeles Raiders	47	1,839	39.1
Steve Cox, Cleveland	48	1,877	39.1

PASS INTERCEPTORS	TOTAL	YARDS	AVG.
Ken Riley, Cincinnati........	5	88	17.6
Bobby Jackson, N.Y. Jets ...	5	84	16.8
Dwayne Woodruff, Pittsburgh	5	53	10.6
Donnie Shell, Pittsburgh	5	27	5.4
Tim Fox, San Diego.........	4	103	25.8
Burgess Owens, L.A. Raiders	4	56	14.0
Ken Easley, Seattle	4	48	12.0

NATIONAL CONFERENCE

TOP RECEIVERS	COMPLETIONS No.	Yards	Avg.	TDs
Dwight Clark, San Fran. ..	60	913	15.2	5
James Wilder, Tampa Bay	53	466	8.8	1
William Andrews, Atlanta.	42	503	12.0	2
Wendell Tyler, L.A. Rams.	38	375	9.9	4
Jeff Moore, San Fran.....	37	405	10.9	4
Pat Tilley, St. Louis	36	465	12.9	2
Matt Suhey, Chicago.....	36	333	9.3	0
James Lofton, Green Bay	35	696	19.9	4

TOP SCORERS	TDs	X PTs	FGs	TOTAL
Wendell Tyler, L.A. Rams.	13	0	0	78
Mark Moseley, Washington	0	16	20	76
Bill Capece, Tampa Bay ..	0	14	18	68
Jan Stenerud, Green Bay.	0	25	13	64
Eddie Lee Ivery, Green B.	10	0	0	60
Ray Wersching, San Fran.	0	23	12	59
Rafael Septien, Dallas....	0	28	10	58
Joe Danelo, N.Y. Giants ..	0	18	12	54
Wilbert Montgomery, Phila.	9	0	0	54

TOP RUSHERS	YARDS	AVG.	TDs
Tony Dorsett, Dallas	745	4.2	5
Billy Sims, Detroit	639	3.7	4
Walter Payton, Chicago	596	4.0	1
Ottis Anderson, St. Louis....	587	4.0	3
William Andrews, Atlanta....	573	4.1	5
Wendell Tyler, L.A. Rams....	564	4.1	9
John Riggins, Washington ...	553	3.1	3
George Rogers, New Orleans	535	4.4	3

TOP PUNTERS	NO.	YARDS	AVG.
Carl Birdsong, St. Louis	54	2,365	43.8
John Misko, L.A. Rams......	45	1,961	43.6
Russell Erxleben, New Orl. ..	46	1,976	43.0
Dave Jennings, N.Y. Giants...	49	2,096	42.8
Danny White, Dallas	37	1,542	41.7
Larry Swider, Tampa Bay ...	39	1,620	41.5
Bob Parsons, Chicago	58	2,394	41.3
Tom Skladany, Detroit	36	1,483	41.2

PASS INTERCEPTORS	TOTAL	YARDS	AVG.
Everson Walls, Dallas	7	61	8.7
Bobby Watkins, Detroit	5	22	4.4
Herman Edwards, Philadelphia	5	3	0.6
Terry Jackson, N.Y. Giants ..	4	75	18.8
Terry Schmidt, Chicago	4	39	9.8
Willie Teal, Minnesota	4	15	3.8
Roynell Young, Philadelphia .	4	0	0.0

STARS OF THE NATIONAL FOOTBALL LEAGUE

LEADING PASSERS

Year	Player	A[1]	C[2]	YG[3]	Year	Player	A[1]	C[2]	YG[3]
1947	Sammy Baugh, Washington	354	121	2,938	1965	Rudy Bukich, Chicago Bears	312	176	2,641
1948	Tom Thompson, Philadelphia	246	141	1,965	1966	Bart Starr, Green Bay	251	156	2,257
1949	Sammy Baugh, Washington	255	145	1,903	1967	Sonny Jurgensen, Washington	508	288	3,747
1950	Norm Van Brocklin, L.A.	233	127	2,061	1968	Earl Morrall, Baltimore	317	182	2,909
1951	Bob Waterfield, L.A.	176	88	1,556	1969	Sonny Jurgensen, Washington	442	274	3,102
1952	Norm Van Brocklin, L.A.	205	113	1,736	1970	John Brodie, San Francisco	378	223	2,941
1953	Otto Graham, Cleveland	258	167	2,722	1971	Bob Griese, Miami	263	145	2,089
1954	Norm Van Brocklin, L.A.	260	139	2,637	1972	Norm Snead, N.Y. Giants	325	196	2,307
1955	Otto Graham, Cleveland	185	98	1,721	1973	Roger Staubach, Dallas	286	179	2,428
1956	Ed Brown, Chicago Bears	168	96	1,667	1974	Ken Anderson, Cincinnati	328	213	2,667
1957	Tom O'Connell, Cleveland	110	63	1,229	1975	Ken Anderson, Cincinnati	377	228	3,169
1958	Eddie LeBaron, Washington	145	79	1,365	1976	Ken Stabler, Oakland	291	194	2,737
1959	Charley Conerly, New York	194	113	1,706	1977	Bob Griese, Miami	307	180	2,252
1960	Milt Plum, Cleveland	250	151	2,297	1978	Roger Staubach, Dallas	413	231	3,190
1961	Milt Plum, Cleveland	302	177	2,416	1979	Roger Staubach, Dallas	461	267	3,586
1962	Bart Starr, Green Bay	285	178	2,438	1980	Brian Sipe, Cleveland	554	337	4,132
1963	Y.A. Tittle, New York	367	221	3,145	1981	Ken Anderson, Cincinnati	479	300	3,754
1964	Bart Starr, Green Bay	272	163	2,144	1982	Dan Fouts, San Diego	330	204	2,889[5]

LEADING PASS RECEIVERS

Year	Player	Passes Received	Year	Player	Passes Received
1947	Jim Keane, Chicago Bears	64	1964	Johnny Morris, Chicago Bears	93
1948	Tom Fears, Los Angeles	51	1965	Dave Parks, San Francisco	80
1949	Tom Fears, Los Angeles	77	1966	Charles Taylor, Washington	72
1950	Tom Fears, Los Angeles	84	1967	Charles Taylor, Washington	70
1951	Elroy Hirsch, Los Angeles	66	1968	Clifton McNeil, San Francisco	71
1952	Mac Speedie, Cleveland	62	1969	Dan Abramowicz, New Orleans	73
1953	Pete Pihos, Philadelphia	63	1970	Dick Gordon, Chicago	71
1954	Pete Pihos, Philadelphia (tie)	60	1971	Fred Biletnikoff, Oakland	61
	Billy Wilson, San Francisco (tie)	60	1972	Harold Jackson, Philadelphia	62
1955	Pete Pihos, Philadelphia	62	1973	Harold Carmichael, Philadelphia	67
1956	Billy Wilson, San Francisco	60	1974	Lydell Mitchell, Baltimore	72
1957	Billy Wilson, San Francisco	52	1975	Chuck Foreman, Minnesota	73
1958	Ray Berry, Baltimore (tie)	56	1976	MacArthur Lane, Kansas City	66
	Pete Retzlaff, Philadelphia (tie)	56	1977	Lydell Mitchell, Baltimore	71
1959	Ray Berry, Baltimore	66	1978	Rickey Young, Minnesota	88
1960	Ray Berry, Baltimore	74	1979	Joe Washington, Baltimore	82
1961	Jim Phillips, Los Angeles	78	1980	Kellen Winslow, San Diego	89
1962	Bobby Mitchell, Washington	72	1981	Kellen Winslow, San Diego	88
1963	Bobby Joe Conrad, St. Louis	73	1982	Kellen Winslow, San Diego	54[5]

RUSHING LEADERS

Year	Player	Yards Gained	Year	Player	Yards Gained
1947	Steve Van Buren, Philadelphia	1,008	1965	Jim Brown, Cleveland	1,544
1948	Steve Van Buren, Philadelphia	845	1966	Gale Sayers, Chicago Bears	1,231
1949	Steve Van Buren, Philadelphia	1,146	1967	Leroy Kelly, Cleveland	1,205
1950	Marion Motley, Cleveland	810	1968	Leroy Kelly, Cleveland	1,239
1951	Eddie Price, New York	971	1969	Gale Sayers, Chicago	1,032
1952	Dan Towler, Los Angeles	894	1970	Larry Brown, Washington	1,125
1953	Joe Perry, San Francisco	1,018	1971	Floyd Little, Denver	1,133
1954	Joe Perry, San Francisco	1,049	1972	O.J. Simpson, Buffalo	1,251
1955	Alan Ameche, Baltimore	961	1973	O.J. Simpson, Buffalo	2,003[4]
1956	Rick Casares, Chicago Bears	1,126	1974	Otis Armstrong, Denver	1,407
1957	Jim Brown, Cleveland	942	1975	O.J. Simpson, Buffalo	1,817
1958	Jim Brown, Cleveland	1,527	1976	O.J. Simpson, Buffalo	1,503
1959	Jim Brown, Cleveland	1,329	1977	Walter Payton, Chicago	1,852
1960	Jim Brown, Cleveland	1,257	1978	Earl Campbell, Houston	1,450
1961	Jim Brown, Cleveland	1,408	1979	Earl Campbell, Houston	1,697
1962	Jim Taylor, Green Bay	1,474	1980	Earl Campbell, Houston	1,934
1963	Jim Brown, Cleveland	1,863	1981	George Rogers, New Orleans	1,674
1964	Jim Brown, Cleveland	1,446	1982	Freeman McNeil, N.Y. Jets	786[5]

SCORING LEADERS

Year	Player	Points	Year	Player	Points
1946	Ted Fritsch, Green Bay	100	1956	Bobby Layne, Detroit	99
1947	Pat Harder, Chicago Cardinals	102	1957	Sam Baker, Washington	77
1948	Pat Harder, Chicago Cardinals	110		Lou Groza, Cleveland	77
1949	Pat Harder, Chi., Gene Roberts, N.Y.	102	1958	Jimmy Brown, Cleveland	108
1950	Doak Walker, Detroit	128	1959	Paul Hornung, Green Bay	94
1951	Elroy Hirsch, Los Angeles	102	1960	Paul Hornung, Green Bay	176[4]
1952	Gordon Soltau, San Francisco	94	1961	Paul Hornung, Green Bay	146
1953	Gordon Soltau, San Francisco	114	1962	Jim Taylor, Green Bay	114
1954	Bob Walston, Philadelphia	114	1963	Don Chandler, New York	106
1955	Doak Walker, Detroit	96	1964	Lenny Moore, Baltimore	128

[1] Attempts. [2] Completions. [3] Yards gained. [4] Record. [5] Season reduced to 9 games due to strike.

SCORING LEADERS *(continued)*

		POINTS			POINTS
1965	Gale Sayers, Chicago	132	1974	Chester Marcol, Green Bay	94
1966	Bruce Gossett, Los Angeles	120	1975	O.J. Simpson, Buffalo	138
1967	Jim Bakken, St. Louis	132	1976	Toni Linhart, Baltimore	109
1968	Leroy Kelly, Cleveland	113	1977	Errol Mann, Oakland	99
1969	Fred Cox, Minnesota	117	1978	Frank Corral, Los Angeles	118
1970	Fred Cox, Minnesota	120	1979	John Smith, New England	115
1971	Garo Yepremian, Miami	121	1980	John Smith, New England	129
1972	Chester Marcol, Green Bay	125	1981	Ed Murray, Detroit	121
1973	David Ray, Los Angeles	130	1982	Marcus Allen, Los Angeles	84[1]

[1] Season reduced to 9 games due to strike.

TOP NFL COLLEGE DRAFT CHOICES: 1983

NUMBER	PLAYER	POSITION	FROM SCHOOL	TO PRO TEAM
1	John Elway	Quarterback	Stanford	Baltimore
2	Eric Dickerson	Running Back	S.M.U.	L.A. Rams
3	Curt Warner	Running Back	Penn State	Seattle
4	Chris Hinton	Guard	Northwestern	Denver
5	Billy Ray Smith	Linebacker	Arkansas	San Diego
6	Jimbo Covert	Offensive Tackle	Pitt	Chicago
7	Todd Blackledge	Quarterback	Penn State	Kansas City
8	Michael Haddix	Running Back	Miss. State	Philadelphia
9	Bruce Matthews	Offensive Tackle	U.S.C.	Houston
10	Terry Kinard	Defensive Back	Clemson	Giants
11	Tim Lewis	Defensive Back	Pitt	Green Bay
12	Tony Hunter	Tight End	Notre Dame	Buffalo

NO. 1 NFL DRAFT CHOICES: 1964–1983

YEAR	CLUB	PLAYER	POSITION	SCHOOL
1964	San Francisco 49ers (NFL)	Dave Parks	End	Texas Tech
1965	New York Jets (AFL)	Joe Namath	Quarterback	Alabama
1965	New York Giants (NFL)	Tucker Frederickson	Running Back	Auburn
1966	Miami Dolphins (AFL)	Jim Grabowski	Running Back	Illinois
1966	Atlanta Falcons (NFL)	Tommy Nobis	Line Backer	Texas
1967	Baltimore Colts	Bubba Smith	Tackle	Michigan State
1968	Minnesota Vikings	Ron Yary	Tackle	Southern California
1969	Buffalo Bills	O.J. Simpson	Running Back	Southern California
1970	Pittsburgh Steelers	Terry Bradshaw	Quarterback	Louisiana Tech
1971	New England Patriots	Jim Plunkett	Quarterback	Stanford
1972	Buffalo Bills	Walt Patulski	Defensive End	Notre Dame
1973	Houston Oilers	John Matuszak	Defensive End	Tampa
1974	Dallas Cowboys	Ed Jones	Defensive End	Tennessee State
1975	Atlanta Falcons	Steve Bartkowski	Quarterback	California
1976	Tampa Bay Buccaneers	Leroy Selmon	Defensive End	Oklahoma
1977	Tampa Bay Buccaneers	Ricky Bell	Running Back	Southern California
1978	Houston Oilers	Earl Campbell	Running Back	Texas
1979	Buffalo Bills	Tom Cousineau	Line Backer	Ohio State
1980	Detroit Lions	Billy Sims	Running Back	Oklahoma
1981	New Orleans Saints	George Rogers	Running Back	South Carolina
1982	New England Patriots	Kenneth Sims	Defensive Tackle	Texas
1983	Baltimore Colts	John Elway	Quarterback	Stanford

NATIONAL FOOTBALL LEAGUE STADIUMS

NATIONAL CONFERENCE

TEAM	STADIUM	SEATING
Atlanta Falcons	Atlanta Stadium	60,748
Chicago Bears	Soldier Field	65,793
Dallas Cowboys	Texas Stadium	65,101
Detroit Lions	Pontiac Silverdome	80,638
Green Bay Packers	Lambeau Field & Milwaukee Co. Stadium	56,189 55,958
Los Angeles Rams	Anaheim Stadium	69,007
Minnesota Vikings	Hubert H. Humphrey Metrodome	62,212
New Orleans Saints	Louisiana Superdome	71,330
New York Giants	Giants Stadium, N.J.	76,891
Philadelphia Eagles	Veterans Stadium	72,204
St. Louis Cardinals	Civic Center Busch Memorial Stadium	51,392
San Francisco 49ers	Candlestick Park	61,185
Tampa Bay Buccaneers	Tampa Stadium	72,812
Washington Redskins	Robert F. Kennedy Stadium	55,045

AMERICAN CONFERENCE

TEAM	STADIUM	SEATING
Baltimore Colts	Memorial Stadium	60,586
Buffalo Bills	Rich Stadium	80,020
Cincinnati Bengals	Riverfront Stadium	59,754
Cleveland Browns	Cleveland Stadium	80,322
Denver Broncos	Denver Mile High Stadium	75,103
Houston Oilers	Astrodome	47,690
Kansas City Chiefs	Arrowhead Stadium	78,067
Los Angeles Raiders	Los Angeles Memorial Coliseum	92,498
Miami Dolphins	Orange Bowl	75,459
New England Patriots	Sullivan Stadium, Foxboro, Mass.	61,297
New York Jets	Shea Stadium	60,372
Pittsburgh Steelers	Three Rivers Stadium	59,000
San Diego Chargers	San Diego Jack Murphy Stadium	52,675
Seattle Seahawks	Kingdome	64,757

NATIONAL FOOTBALL LEAGUE CONFERENCE CHAMPIONS

YEAR	EASTERN CONFERENCE	W	L	T	YEAR	WESTERN CONFERENCE	W	L	T
1938	New York Giants	8	2	1	1938	Green Bay Packers	8	3	0
1939	New York Giants	9	1	1	1939	Green Bay Packers	9	2	0
1940	Washington Redskins	9	2	0	1940	Chicago Bears	8	3	0
1941	New York Giants	8	3	0	1941	Chicago Bears	10	1	1
1942	Washington Redskins	10	1	1	1942	Chicago Bears	11	0	0
1943	Washington Redskins	6	3	1	1943	Chicago Bears	8	1	1
1944	New York Giants	8	1	1	1944	Green Bay Packers	8	2	0
1945	Washington Redskins	8	2	0	1945	Cleveland Rams	9	1	0
1946	New York Giants	7	3	1	1946	Chicago Bears	8	2	1
1947	Philadelphia Eagles	8	4	0	1947	Chicago Cardinals	9	3	0
1948	Philadelphia Eagles	9	2	1	1948	Chicago Cardinals	11	1	0
1949	Philadelphia Eagles	11	1	0	1949	Los Angeles Rams	8	2	2
1950	Cleveland Browns	10	2	0	1950	Los Angeles Rams	9	3	0
1951	Cleveland Browns	11	1	0	1951	Los Angeles Rams	8	4	0
1952	Cleveland Browns	8	4	0	1952	Detroit Lions	9	3	0
1953	Cleveland Browns	11	1	0	1953	Detroit Lions	10	2	0
1954	Cleveland Browns	9	3	0	1954	Detroit Lions	9	2	1
1955	Cleveland Browns	9	2	1	1955	Los Angeles Rams	8	3	1
1956	New York Giants	8	3	1	1956	Chicago Bears	9	2	1
1957	Cleveland Browns	9	2	1	1957	Detroit Lions	8	4	0
1958	New York Giants	9	3	0	1958	Baltimore Colts	9	3	0
1959	New York Giants	10	2	0	1959	Baltimore Colts	9	3	0
1960	Philadelphia Eagles	10	2	0	1960	Green Bay Packers	8	4	0
1961	New York Giants	10	3	1	1961	Green Bay Packers	11	3	0
1962	New York Giants	12	2	0	1962	Green Bay Packers	13	1	0
1963	New York Giants	11	3	0	1963	Chicago Bears	11	1	2
1964	Cleveland Browns	10	3	1	1964	Baltimore Colts	12	2	0
1965	Cleveland Browns	11	3	0	1965	Green Bay Packers	10	3	1
1966	Dallas Cowboys	10	3	1	1966	Green Bay Packers	12	2	0
1967	Dallas Cowboys	9	5	0	1967	Green Bay Packers	9	4	1
1968	Cleveland Browns	10	4	0	1968	Baltimore Colts	13	1	0
1969	Cleveland Browns	10	3	1	1969	Minnesota Vikings	12	2	0
	AMERICAN CONFERENCE [1]					NATIONAL CONFERENCE [1]			
1970	Baltimore Colts	11	2	1	1970	Dallas Cowboys	10	4	0
1971	Miami Dolphins	10	3	1	1971	Dallas Cowboys	11	3	0
1972	Miami Dolphins	14	0	0	1972	Washington Redskins	11	3	0
1973	Miami Dolphins	12	2	0	1973	Minnesota Vikings	12	2	0
1974	Pittsburgh Steelers	10	3	1	1974	Minnesota Vikings	10	4	0
1975	Pittsburgh Steelers	12	2	0	1975	Dallas Cowboys	10	4	0
1976	Oakland Raiders	13	1	0	1976	Minnesota Vikings	11	2	1
1977	Denver Broncos	12	2	0	1977	Dallas Cowboys	12	2	0
1978	Pittsburgh Steelers	14	2	0	1978	Dallas Cowboys	12	4	0
1979	Pittsburgh Steelers	12	4	0	1979	Los Angeles Rams	9	7	0
1980	Oakland Raiders	11	5	0	1980	Philadelphia Eagles	12	4	0
1981	Cincinnati Bengals	12	4	0	1981	San Francisco 49ers	13	3	0
1982	Miami Dolphins	7	2	0	1982	Washington Redskins	8	1	0

[1] NFL reorganization in 1970 (records exclude playoff games).

DIVISIONAL CHAMPIONSHIP PLAYOFF GAMES

	AMERICAN FOOTBALL CONFERENCE				NATIONAL FOOTBALL CONFERENCE			
Season	Winner	Loser	Score	Site	Winner	Loser	Score	Site
1964	Buffalo	San Diego	20–7	Buffalo	Cleveland	Baltimore	27–10	Cleveland
1965	Buffalo	San Diego	23–0	San Diego	Green Bay	Cleveland	23–12	Green Bay
1966	Kansas City	Buffalo	31–7	Buffalo	Green Bay	Dallas	34–27	Dallas
1967	Oakland	Houston	40–7	Oakland	Green Bay	Dallas	21–17	Green Bay
1968	N.Y. Jets	Oakland	27–23	New York	Baltimore	Cleveland	34–0	Cleveland
1969	Kansas City	Oakland	17–7	Oakland	Minnesota	Cleveland	27–7	Minnesota
1970	Baltimore	Oakland	21–17	Baltimore	Dallas	San Francisco	17–10	San Francisco
1971	Miami	Baltimore	21–0	Miami	Dallas	San Francisco	14–3	Dallas
1972	Miami	Pittsburgh	21–17	Pittsburgh	Washington	Dallas	25–3	Washington
1973	Miami	Oakland	27–10	Miami	Minnesota	Dallas	27–10	Dallas
1974	Pittsburgh	Oakland	24–13	Oakland	Minnesota	Los Angeles	14–10	Minnesota
1975	Pittsburgh	Oakland	16–10	Pittsburgh	Dallas	Los Angeles	37–7	Los Angeles
1976	Oakland	Pittsburgh	24–7	Oakland	Minnesota	Los Angeles	24–13	Minnesota
1977	Denver	Oakland	20–17	Denver	Dallas	Minnesota	23–6	Dallas
1978	Pittsburgh	Houston	34–5	Pittsburgh	Dallas	Los Angeles	28–0	Los Angeles
1979	Pittsburgh	Houston	27–13	Pittsburgh	Los Angeles	Tampa Bay	9–0	Tampa Bay
1980	Oakland	San Diego	34–27	San Diego	Philadelphia	Dallas	20–7	Philadelphia
1981	Cincinnati	San Diego	27–7	Cincinnati	San Francisco	Dallas	28–27	San Francisco
1982	Miami	N.Y. Jets	14–0	Miami	Washington	Dallas	31–17	Washington

PRO FOOTBALL INDIVIDUAL ALL-TIME RECORDS

The records listed on this page do not include statistics from the 1983 season unless indicated, because those figures were incomplete when the *Reader's Digest Almanac* went to press.

INDIVIDUAL RECORDS

Seasons, active player: 26, George Blanda (1949–75)
Points, lifetime: 2,002, George Blanda (1949–75), Chicago Bears, Baltimore, Houston, Oakland
Points, season: 176, Paul Hornung, Green Bay, (1960)—15 touchdowns, 41 points after touchdown, 15 field goals
Points, one game: 40, Ernie Nevers for Chicago Cardinals against Chicago Bears, Nov. 28, 1929—6 touchdowns and 4 points after touchdown
Touchdowns, lifetime: 126, Jim Brown, Cleveland (1957–65), 106 running, 20 on passes
Touchdowns, season: 24, John Riggins, Washington Redskins (1983) 24 rushing
Touchdowns, game: 6, Ernie Nevers, Chicago Cardinals against Chicago Bears, Nov. 28, 1929
Field goals, lifetime: 338, Jan Stenerud (1967–83), Kansas City, Green Bay
Field goals, season: 35, Ali Haji-Sheikh, N.Y. Giants, 1983
Field goals, one game: 7, Jim Bakken for St. Louis against Pittsburgh, Sept. 24, 1967
Field goal, longest: 63 yards, Tom Dempsey for New Orleans against Detroit, Nov. 8, 1970
Field goals, highest completion percentage, season: 95.24, Mark Moseley, Washington (1982)
Rushing—most seasons leading league: 8, Jim Brown, Cleveland (1957–61) and (1963–65)
Rushing—most yards gained lifetime: 12,312, Jim Brown, Cleveland (1957–65)
Rushing—most yards gained, season: 2,003, O. J. Simpson, Buffalo (1973)
Rushing—most yards gained, game: 275, Walter Payton for Chicago against Minnesota, Nov. 20, 1977
Run, longest from scrimmage: 99 yards for touchdown, by Tony Dorsett for Dallas Cowboys against Minnesota Vikings, Jan. 3, 1983.
Touchdowns rushing, lifetime: 106, Jim Brown, Cleveland (1957–65)
Touchdowns rushing, season: 19, Jim Taylor, Green Bay (1962)
Touchdowns rushing, game: 6, Ernie Nevers, Chicago Cardinals against Chicago Bears, Nov. 28, 1929
Passing—most seasons leading league: 6, Sammy Baugh, Washington (1937, '40, '43, '45, '47, '49)
Passes completed, lifetime: 3,686, Fran Tarkenton, N.Y. Giants (1967–71), Minnesota (1961–66; 1972–78), 6,467 attempts
Passes completed, season: 360, Dan Fouts, San Diego (1981), 609 attempts
Passes completed, game: 42, Richard Todd for New York Jets against San Francisco 49ers, Sept. 21, 1980, 59 attempts
Passes, most consecutive completed: 17, Bert Jones for Baltimore against N.Y. Jets, Dec. 15, 1974
Passing, most yards gained, career: 47,003, Fran Tarkenton, N.Y. Giants (1967–71), Minnesota (1961–66; 1972–78)
Passing, most yards gained, season: 4,802, Dan Fouts, San Diego Chargers (1981).
Touchdown passes, lifetime: 342, Fran Tarkenton, N.Y. (1967–71), Minnesota (1961–66; 1972–78)
Touchdown passes, season: 36, George Blanda, Houston (1961).
Touchdown passes, game: 7, Sid Luckman for Chicago Bears against New York, Nov. 14, 1943.
Pass receptions, lifetime: 649, Charley Taylor, Washington (1964–75, 1977)
Pass receptions, season: 101, Charlie Hennigan, Houston (1964)
Pass receptions, game: 18, Tom Fears for Los Angeles against Green Bay, Dec. 3, 1950
Pass interception return, longest: 102 yards for touchdown, Bob Smith, Detroit against Chicago Bears, Nov. 24, 1949
Punt, longest: 98 yards by Steve O'Neal for New York Jets against Denver, Sept. 21, 1969
Punting, highest average, lifetime: 45.1 yards, Sammy Baugh, Washington (1937–52)
Punting, highest average, season: 51.4 yards, Sammy Baugh, Washington (1940)
Punting, highest average, game (at least 4 punts): 61.75, Bob Cifers, Detroit against Chicago Bears, Nov. 24, 1946
Kickoff return, longest: 106 yards for a touchdown, by Al Carmichael for Green Bay against Chicago, Oct. 7, 1956.
Yards gained, lifetime: 15,459 yards, Jim Brown, Cleveland (1957–65)
Yards gained, season: 2,462, Terry Metcalf, St. Louis (1975)

NFL TOP PASSERS—LIFETIME [1]

PLAYER	YEARS	ATTEMPTS	COMPLETIONS Total	COMPLETIONS Pct.	YARDS	TOUCHDOWNS Total	TOUCHDOWNS Pct.	INTERCEPTIONS Total	INTERCEPTIONS Pct.	AVERAGE GAIN	RATING
Roger Staubach	11	2,958	1,685	57.0	22,700	153	5.2	109	3.7	7.67	83.5
Sonny Jurgenson	18	4,262	2,433	57.1	32,224	255	6.0	189	4.4	7.56	82.8
Len Dawson	19	3,741	2,136	57.1	28,711	239	6.4	183	4.9	7.67	82.6
Ken Anderson	11	3,539	2,036	57.5	25,562	160	4.5	124	3.5	7.22	80.5
Fran Tarkenton	18	6,467	3,686	57.0	47,003	342	5.3	266	4.1	7.27	80.5
Bart Starr	16	3,149	1,808	57.4	24,718	152	4.8	138	4.4	7.85	80.3
Bert Jones	9	2,464	1,382	56.1	17,663	122	5.0	97	3.9	7.17	79.1
Dan Fouts	9	3,203	1,849	57.7	24,256	145	4.5	142	4.4	7.57	78.4
Ken Stabler	11	2,938	1,779	60.6	22,280	163	5.5	171	5.8	7.58	78.3
Johnny Unitas	18	5,186	2,830	54.6	40,239	290	5.6	253	4.9	7.76	78.2
Otto Graham	6	1,565	872	55.7	13,499	88	5.6	94	6.0	8.63	78.1
Frank Ryan	13	2,133	1,090	51.1	16,042	149	7.0	111	5.2	7.52	77.7
Bob Griese	12	3,019	1,689	55.9	22,142	172	5.7	152	5.0	7.33	77.4
Norm Van Brocklin	12	2,895	1,553	53.6	23,611	173	6.0	178	6.1	8.16	75.3
Sid Luckman	12	1,744	904	51.8	14,686	137	7.9	132	7.6	8.42	75.0
Don Meredith	9	2,308	1,170	50.7	17,199	135	5.8	111	4.8	7.45	74.7
Roman Gabriel	16	4,498	2,366	52.6	29,444	201	4.5	149	3.3	6.55	74.5
Earl Morrall	21	2,689	1,379	51.3	20,809	161	6.0	148	5.5	7.74	74.2
Y. A. Tittle	15	3,817	2,118	55.5	28,339	212	5.6	221	5.8	7.42	73.8
Greg Landry	11	1,747	957	54.8	12,451	80	4.6	81	4.6	7.13	73.6

[1] Does not include 1983. Rating points awarded for percent of completions, TDs, interceptions, and average gain.

NATIONAL PROFESSIONAL FOOTBALL HALL OF FAME

Herb Adderley, def. back: Green Bay (1961–69), Dallas (1970–72)
Lance Alworth, wide receiver: San Diego (1962–70)
Doug Atkins, end: Cleveland, Chicago, New Orleans (1953–69)
Morris (Red) Badgro, end: N.Y. Yankees, N.Y. Giants, Brooklyn Dodgers (1927–36)
Cliff Battles, halfback: Boston, Washington (1932–37)
Sammy Baugh, quarterback: Washington (1937–52)
Chuck Bednarik, center: Philadelphia (1949–62)
Bert Bell, NFL commissioner (1949–59)
Bobby Bell, linebacker: Kansas City (1963–74)
Raymond Berry, end: Balt. (1955–67)
Charles W. Bidwill, owner: Chicago Cardinals (1933–47)
George Blanda, quarterback, place-kicker: Chi., Hou., Oak. (1949–76)
Jim Brown, fullback: Cleve. (1957–65)
Paul Brown, coach: Cleveland (1946–52), Cincinnati (1968–69)
Roosevelt Brown, tackle: New York Giants (1953–65)
Dick Butkus, linebacker: Chi. (1965–73)
Tony Canadeo, halfback: Green Bay (1940–52)
Joe Carr, NFL pres. (1921–38)
Guy Chamberlin, end, coach: Canton, Cleveland, Frankford, Chicago (1919–28)
Jack Christiansen, defensive back: Detroit (1951–58)
Dutch Clark, quarterback: Portsmouth, Detroit (1931–38)
George Connor, tackle, linebacker: Chicago Bears (1948–55)
Jimmy Conzelman, quarterback, coach, executive: Decatur, Rock Island, Milwaukee, Detroit, Providence, Chicago (1920–48)
Willie Davis, defensive end: Cleveland, Green Bay (1958–69)
Art Donovan, defensive tackle: Baltimore, N.Y., Dallas (1950–61)
Paddy Driscoll, quarterback, coach: Decatur, Chicago Cardinals, Chicago Bears (1920–57)
Bill Dudley, halfback: Pittsburgh, Detroit, Washington (1942–53)
Turk Edwards, tackle, Boston, Washington (1942–53)
Weeb Ewbank, coach: Baltimore (1954–62), N.Y. Jets (1963–73)
Tom Fears, end: L.A. (1948–56)
Ray Flaherty, coach: (1926–49)
Len Ford, end: Los Angeles, Cleveland (1948–58)
Danny Fortmann, M.D., guard: Chicago, N.Y. Yankees (1936–43)
Bill George, linebacker: Chicago Bears, Los Angeles (1952–66)
Frank Gifford, halfback: New York Giants (1952–60, 1962–64)
Sid Gillman, coach: Los Angeles, San Diego, Houston (1955–74)
Otto Graham, quarterback: Cleveland (1946–55)
Red Grange, halfback: Chicago Bears, N.Y. Yankees (1925–34)
Forrest Gregg, tackle: Green Bay, Dallas (1956, 1958–71)
Lou Groza, tackle, kicker: Cleveland (1946–59, 1961–67)
Joe Guyon, halfback: Canton, Cleveland, Oorang Indians, Rock Island, K.C., N.Y. (1918–27)
George Halas, end, coach, owner: Chicago Bears (1920–67)
Ed Healey, tackle: Rock Island, Chicago Bears (1920–27)
Mel Hein, center: New York Giants (1931–45)
Pete (Fats) Henry, tackle: Canton, Akron, New York, Pottsville, Pittsburgh (1920–30)
Arnie Herber, quarterback: Green Bay, New York (1930–45)
Bill Hewitt, end: Chicago, Philadelphia, Pittsburgh (1932–39, 1943)
Clarke Hinkle, fullback: Green Bay (1932–41)
Elroy (Crazylegs) Hirsch, end, halfback: Chicago Rockets, Los Angeles (1946–57)
Cal Hubbard, tackle, end: N.Y., Green Bay, Pittsburgh (1927–36)
Sam Huff, linebacker: N.Y. Giants, Washington (1956–68)
Lamar Hunt, first president of the AFL (1960)
Don Hutson, end: G.B. (1935–45)
David (Deacon) Jones, def. end: L.A., San Diego, Wash. (1961–74)
Sonny Jurgenson, quarterback: Philadelphia, Washington (1957–74)
Walter Kiesling, guard, coach: Duluth, Pottsville, Boston, Chicago Bears, Green Bay, Pittsburgh (1926–56)
Frank (Bruiser) Kinard, tackle: Brooklyn, N.Y. (1938–47)
Curly Lambeau, coach: Green Bay Packers (1919–49), Chicago Cardinals (1950–51), Washington Redskins (1952–53)
Dick (Night Train) Lane, defensive back: Los Angeles, Chicago Cardinals, Detroit (1952–65)
Yale Lary, defensive back, punter: Detroit (1952-53, 1956–64)
Dante Lavelli, end: Cleveland (1946–56)
Bobby Layne, quarterback: Chicago Bears, New York, Detroit, Pittsburgh (1948–62)
Alphonse (Tuffy) Leemans, fullback: N.Y. Giants (1937–43)
Bob Lilly, def. tackle: Dallas (1961–74)
Vince Lombardi, coach: Green Bay, Washington (1958–69)
Sid Luckman, quarterback: Chicago Bears (1939–50)
Roy (Link) Lyman, tackle: Canton, Cleveland, Frankford, Chicago Bears (1922–34)
Tim Mara, owner: New York Giants (1925–59)
Gino Marchetti, defensive end: Dallas, Baltimore (1953–66)
George Preston Marshall, owner: Boston Braves (1932), Boston Redskins (1933–36), Washington Redskins (1937–69)
Ollie Matson, halfback: Chi. Cardinals, L.A., Detroit, Phil. (1952–66)
George McAfee, halfback: Chicago Bears (1940–41, 1945–50)
Hugh McElhenny, halfback: San Francisco (1952–60)
John Blood McNally, halfback: Milwaukee, Duluth, Pottsville, Green Bay, Pittsburgh (1925–39)
Mike Michalske, guard: New York, Green Bay (1927–37)
Wayne Millner, end: Boston, Washington (1936–41, 1945)
Bobby Mitchell, wide receiver: Cleveland, Washington (1958–68)
Ron Mix, tackle: San Diego (1960–69), Oakland (1971)
Lenny Moore, running back: Baltimore (1956–67)
Marion Motley, fullback: Cleveland, Pittsburgh (1946–55)
George Musso, guard: Chi. (1933–44)
Bronko Nagurski, fullback: Chicago Bears (1930–37, 1943)
Earle (Greasy) Neale, coach: Philadelphia (1941–50)
Ernie Nevers, fullback: Duluth, Chicago Cardinals (1926–37)
Ray Nitschke, linebacker: Green Bay Packers (1958–72)
Leo Nomellini, defensive tackle: San Francisco (1953–63)
Merlin Olsen, tackle: L.A. (1962–76)
Jim Otto, center: Oak. (1960–74)
Steve Owen, tackle: K.C. (1924–25), N.Y. Giants (1926–30); coach, N.Y. Giants (1931–53)
Ace Parker, quarterback: Brooklyn Dodgers, Boston Yanks, New York Yankees (1937–46)
Jim Parker, guard, tackle: Baltimore (1957–67)
Joe Perry, fullback: San Francisco, Baltimore (1948–62)
Pete Pihos, end: Phil. (1947–55)
Hugh (Shorty) Ray, NFL official (1938–56)
Daniel F. Reeves, owner: Los Angeles Rams (1946–71)
Jim Ringo, center: Green Bay, Philadelphia (1953–67)
Andy Robustelli, end: Los Angeles, New York Giants (1951–64)
Art Rooney, owner: Pittsburgh Pirates (1933–40), Pittsburgh Steelers (1941–42, 1949–77)
Gale Sayers, running back: Chicago Bears (1965–71)
Joe Schmidt, linebacker: Detroit (1953–65)
Bart Starr, quarterback: Green Bay (1956–71)
Ernie Stautner, defensive tackle: Pittsburgh (1950–63)
Ken Strong, halfback, place-kicker: Staten Island, New York (1929–39, 1944–47)
Joe Stydahar, tackle: Chicago Bears (1936–42, 1945–46)
Jim Taylor, fullback: Green Bay, New Orleans (1958–67)
Jim Thorpe, halfback: Canton, Oorang Indians, Cleveland, Toledo, Rock Island, New York (1915–26, 1929)
Y. A. Tittle, quarterback: Baltimore, San Francisco, New York Giants (1948–64)
George Trafton, center: Decatur, Chi. Staleys, Chi. Bears (1920–32)
Charley Trippi, halfback: Chicago Cardinals (1947–55)
Emlen Tunnell, safety: New York, Green Bay (1948–61)
Clyde (Bulldog) Turner, center: Chicago Bears (1940–52)
Johnny Unitas, quarterback: Baltimore (1956–72), San Diego (1973)
Norm Van Brocklin, quarterback: Los Angeles, Phila. (1949–60)
Steve Van Buren, halfback: Philadelphia (1944–52)
Paul Warfield, wide receiver: Cleveland, Miami, WFL (1964–77)
Bob Waterfield, quarterback: Cleveland, Los Angeles (1945–52)
Bill Willis, guard: Cleve. (1946–53)
Larry Wilson, defensive back: St. Louis Cardinals (1960–72)
Alex Wojciechowicz, center: Detroit, Philadelphia (1938–50)

COLLEGE FOOTBALL HIGHLIGHTS: 1983

Two major college football teams remained undefeated during the 1983 regular season. The University of Nebraska finished with a 12–0–0 record, and the University of Texas with a 11–0–0 record. At the end of the regular season, the teams were ranked No. 1 and No. 2 respectively by both the Associated Press and United Press International.

Nebraska captured the Big Eight Conference championship for the third consecutive year and led the NCAA in rushing offense, with 4,820 yards. Second to Brigham Young in total offense, Nebraska scored 65 touchdowns and averaged 546.7 yards per game. The Cornhuskers were first in scoring offense, with 624 points, averaging 52.0 per game.

Nebraska's star running back Mike Rozier received the prestigious Heisman Trophy as the outstanding college football player in the nation. He led the NCAA Division 1A in both rushing and scoring. Rozier, a senior, ran for 2,148 yards and scored a record-tying 29 touchdowns. He was only the second player in NCAA history to gain more than 2,000 yards in a season.

Brigham Young University quarterback Steve Young was first in offense. In 11 games he passed for 3,902 yards and gained 623 yards rushing, averaging 395.1 yards per game. First in passing efficiency, he was credited with 33 touchdowns. He completed 306 passes during the season, a new major college football record.

Brigham Young led the NCAA in passing offense, gaining 4,193 yards in 11 games for an average of 381.2 yards per game. Brigham Young also led in total offense, scoring 65 touchdowns and averaging 584.2 yards per game.

As a result of its undefeated season, the University of Texas won the Southwest Conference championship for the first time since 1977. Texas was first in total defense, allowing only 2,332 yards in 11 games for an average of 212.0 per game. The team allowed only 10 touchdowns during the season. Southern Methodist University and Virginia were tied for second place in defense, each averaging 256.1 yards per game.

Arizona State's Luis Zendejas kicked 28 field goals, the best in Division 1–A. Bruce Kallmeyer of Kansas was second with 24.

The University of Illinois won the Big Ten championship and its first trip to the Rose Bowl in 20 years when it defeated the University of Michigan, 16–6, at Michigan on Oct. 29. Although there were three games to play afterward, the Michigan game was considered crucial for the championship. Illinois ended the season with a record of 10–1–0, losing only to Missouri, 28–18, during the first game of the year. Illinois was 9–0–0 in Big Ten competition. The Illini were second in rushing defense, allowing 1,034 yards in 11 games. Michigan was third in rushing defense, allowing 1,051 yards in 11 games.

For results of postseason college football bowl games in December 1982 and on January 2, 1983, see page 30.

ALL-AMERICA COLLEGE FOOTBALL TEAMS: 1983

ASSOCIATED PRESS

OFFENSIVE TEAM	POSITIONS	DEFENSIVE TEAM	POSITIONS
Irving Fryar, Nebraska	Wide Receiver	Wilbur Marshall, Florida	End
Gerald McNeil, Baylor	Wide Receiver	Ron Rivera, California	End
Gordon Hudson, Brigham Young	Tight End	Rick Bryan, Oklahoma	Tackle
Brian Blados, North Carolina	Tackle	Reggie White, Tennessee	Tackle
Bill Fralic, Pittsburgh	Tackle	William Perry, Clemson	Middle Guard
Doug Dawson, Texas	Guard	Carl Banks, Michigan	Linebacker
Terry Long, East Carolina	Guard	Ricky Hunley, Arizona	Linebacker
Tom Dixon, Michigan	Center	Jeff Leiding, Texas	Linebacker
Steve Young, Brigham Young	Quarterback	Mossy Cade, Texas	Back
Bo Jackson, Auburn	Running Back	Russell Carter, Southern Methodist	Back
Mike Rozier, Nebraska	Running Back	Jerry Gray, Texas	Back
Luis Zendejas, Arizona State	Kicker	Jack Weil, Wyoming	Punter

UNITED PRESS INTERNATIONAL

OFFENSIVE TEAM	POSITIONS	DEFENSIVE TEAM	POSITIONS
Irving Fryar, Nebraska	Wide Receiver	Fred Gilbert, Georgia	End
Gordon Hudson, Brigham Young	Tight End	Ron Faurot, Arkansas	End
Bill Fralic, Pittsburgh	Tackle	Rick Bryan, Oklahoma	Tackle
Conrad Goode, Missouri	Tackle	Reggie White, Tennessee	Tackle
Stefan Humphries, Michigan	Guard	William Perry, Clemson	Middle Guard
Dean Steinkuhler, Nebraska	Guard	Ricky Hunley, Arizona	Linebacker
Tony Slaton, Southern California	Center	Wilber Marshall, Florida	Linebacker
Steve Young, Brigham Young	Quarterback	Carl Banks, Michigan State	Linebacker
Bo Jackson, Auburn	Running Back	Russell Carter, Southern Methodist	Back
Greg Allen, Florida State	Running Back	Jerry Gray, Texas	Back
Mike Rozier, Nebraska	Running Back	Terry Hoage, Georgia	Back
Bruce Kallmeyer, Kansas	Place Kicker	Jack Weil, Wyoming	Punter

TOP-RATED COLLEGE FOOTBALL TEAMS: 1983 (end of regular season)

COACHES' POLL (UPI)

RANK	TEAM	W	L	T	POINTS
1	Nebraska	12	0	0	507
2	Texas	11	0	0	475
3	Auburn	10	1	0	435
4	Miami, Fla.	10	1	0	375
5	Illinois	10	1	0	373
6	Southern Methodist	10	1	0	345
7	Georgia	9	1	1	258
8	Michigan	9	2	0	217
9	Brigham Young	10	1	0	211
10	Iowa	9	2	0	195

WRITERS' RATINGS (AP)

RANK	TEAM	W	L	T	POINTS
1	Nebraska	12	0	0	1,077
2	Texas	11	0	0	1,028
3	Auburn	10	1	0	961
4	Illinois	10	1	0	889
5	Miami, Fla.	10	1	0	875
6	Southern Methodist	10	1	0	813
7	Georgia	9	1	1	731
8	Michigan	9	2	0	671
9	Brigham Young	10	1	0	619
10	Iowa	9	2	0	566

WON-LOST SEASON RECORDS OF MAJOR COLLEGE FOOTBALL TEAMS: 1983

TEAM	W	L	T
Air Force	9	2	0
Alabama	7	3	0
Arizona	7	3	1
Arizona State	6	4	1
Arkansas	6	5	0
Auburn	10	1	0
Army	2	9	0
Baylor	7	3	1
Boston College	9	2	0
Boston University	8	3	0
Brigham Young	10	1	0
California	5	5	1
Clemson	9	1	1
Colgate	8	3	0
Colorado State	5	7	0
Dartmouth	4	5	1
East Carolina	8	3	0
Florida	8	2	1
Florida State	6	5	0
Furman	9	1	1
Georgia	9	1	1
Grambling	8	1	2
Harvard	6	2	2
Idaho State	8	3	0
Illinois	10	1	0
Indiana	3	8	0
Iowa	9	2	0
Iowa State	4	7	0
Jackson State	8	3	0
Kansas	4	6	1
Kansas State	3	8	0
Louisiana State	4	7	0
Maryland	8	3	0
Massachusetts	3	8	0
Memphis State	6	4	1
Miami, Florida	10	1	0
Michigan	9	2	0
Michigan State	4	6	1
Minnesota	1	10	0
Mississippi	6	5	0
Mississippi State	3	8	0
Missouri	7	4	0
Navy	3	8	0
Nebraska	12	0	0
New Mexico	6	6	0
North Carolina	8	3	0
North Carolina State	3	8	0
North Texas State	8	3	0
Notre Dame	6	5	0
Ohio State	8	3	0
Oklahoma	8	4	0
Oklahoma State	7	4	0
Oregon	4	6	1
Penn State	7	4	1
Pennsylvania	6	3	1
Pittsburgh	8	2	1
Purdue	3	7	1
Rutgers	3	8	0
San Diego State	2	8	1
San Jose State	5	6	0
South Carolina	5	6	0
South Carolina State	7	3	0
Southern California	4	6	1
Southern Methodist	10	1	0
Southern Mississippi	7	4	0
Southwest Louisiana	4	6	0
Syracuse	6	5	0
Temple	4	7	0
Tennessee	8	3	0
Texas	11	0	0
Texas A & M	5	5	1
Texas Tech	3	7	1
Tulane	4	7	0
Tulsa	8	3	0
UCLA	6	4	1
Utah State	5	6	0
Virginia Tech.	9	2	0
VMI	2	9	0
Washington	8	3	0
Washington State	7	4	0
West Virginia	8	3	0
Wisconsin	7	4	0
Wyoming	7	5	0
Yale	1	9	0

HEISMAN MEMORIAL TROPHY WINNERS

The John W. Heisman Memorial Trophy is awarded annually to the nation's leading college football player. It was originated in 1935 by the Downtown Athletic Club of New York.

YEAR	PLAYER	POSITION	TEAM
1935	Jay Berwanger	Back	Chicago
1936	Larry Kelley	End	Yale
1937	Clint Frank	Quarterback	Yale
1938	Davey O'Brien	Quarterback	TCU
1939	Nile Kinnick	Back	Iowa
1940	Tom Harmon	Back	Michigan
1941	Bruce Smith	Back	Minnesota
1942	Frank Sinkwich	Back	Georgia
1943	Angelo Bertelli	Quarterback	Notre Dame
1944	Les Horvath	Quarterback	Ohio State
1945	Felix Blanchard	Back	Army
1946	Glenn Davis	Back	Army
1947	Johnny Lujack	Quarterback	Notre Dame
1948	Doak Walker	Back	So. Methodist
1949	Leon Hart	End	Notre Dame
1950	Vic Janowicz	Back	Ohio State
1951	Dick Kazmaier	Back	Princeton
1952	Billy Vessels	Back	Oklahoma
1953	Johnny Lattner	Back	Notre Dame
1954	Alan Ameche	Back	Wisconsin
1955	Howard Cassady	Back	Ohio State
1956	Paul Hornung	Quarterback	Notre Dame
1957	John Crow	Back	Texas A&M
1958	Pete Dawkins	Back	Army
1959	Billy Cannon	Back	Louisiana State
1960	Joe Bellino	Back	Navy
1961	Ernie Davis	Back	Syracuse
1962	Terry Baker	Back	Oregon State
1963	Roger Staubach	Quarterback	Navy
1964	John Huarte	Quarterback	Notre Dame
1965	Mike Garrett	Back	So. California
1966	Steve Spurrier	Quarterback	Florida
1967	Gary Beban	Quarterback	UCLA
1968	O. J. Simpson	Tailback	So. California
1969	Steve Owens	Back	Oklahoma
1970	Jim Plunkett	Quarterback	Stanford
1971	Pat Sullivan	Quarterback	Auburn
1972	Johnny Rodgers	Back	Nebraska
1973	John Cappelletti	Tailback	Penn State
1974	Archie Griffin	Tailback	Ohio State
1975	Archie Griffin	Tailback	Ohio State
1976	Tony Dorsett	Tailback	Pittsburgh
1977	Earl Campbell	Back	Texas
1978	Billy Sims	Tailback	Oklahoma
1979	Charles White	Running Back	So. California
1980	George Rogers	Running Back	So. Carolina
1981	Marcus Allen	Running Back	So. California
1982	Herschel Walker	Running Back	Georgia
1983	Mike Rozier	Running Back	Nebraska

UNDEFEATED, UNTIED MAJOR TEAMS: 1969–1983

YEAR	COLLEGE	WINS[1]
1969	Penn State	10 †
	San Diego State	10 ‡
	Texas	10 ‡
	Toledo	10 ‡
1970	Arizona State	10 †
	Dartmouth	9
	Ohio State	9 ‡
	Texas	10 ‡
	Toledo	11 ‡
1971	Alabama	11 ‡
	Michigan	11 ‡
	Nebraska	12 †
	Toledo	11 †
1972	Southern California	11 †
1973	Alabama	11 ‡
	Miami (Ohio)	10 †
	Notre Dame	10 †
	Penn State	11 †
1974	Alabama	11 ‡
	Oklahoma	11
1975	Arizona State	11 †
	Ohio State	11 ‡
1976	Pittsburgh	11 †
	Rutgers	11
	Maryland	11 ‡
1977	Texas	11 ‡
1978	Penn State	11 ‡
1979	Alabama	11 †
	Ohio State	11 ‡
	Florida State	11 ‡
	Brigham Young	11 ‡
1980	Georgia	11 †
1981	Clemson	11 †
1982	Georgia	11 ‡
1983	Nebraska	12
	Texas	11

[1] Regular season games only. Subsequent bowl win is indicated by (†), loss (‡), and tie (§).

COLLEGE RUSHING CHAMPIONS

YEAR	PLAYER, TEAM	GAMES	PLAYS	YARDS[1]
1954	Art Luppino, Arizona	10	179	1,359
1955	Art Luppino, Arizona	10	209	1,313
1956	Jim Crawford, Wyoming	10	200	1,104
1957	Leon Burton, Arizona State	10	117	1,126
1958	Dick Bass, Pacific	10	205	1,361
1959	Pervis Atkins, New Mexico State	10	130	971
1960	Bob Gaiters, New Mexico State	10	197	1,338
1961	Jim Pilot, New Mexico State	10	191	1,278
1962	Jim Pilot, New Mexico State	10	208	1,247
1963	Dave Casinelli, Memphis State	10	219	1,016
1964	Brian Piccolo, Wake Forest	10	252	1,044
1965	Mike Garrett, So. California	10	267	1,440
1966	Ray McDonald, Idaho	10	259	1,329
1967	O. J. Simpson, So. California	9	266	1,415
1968	O. J. Simpson, So. California	10	355	1,709
1969	Steve Owens, Oklahoma	10	358*	1,523
1970	Ed Marinaro, Cornell	9	285	158.3
1971	Ed Marinaro, Cornell	9	356	209.0
1972	Pete VanValkenburg, Brig. Young	10	232	138.6
1973	Mark Kellar, Northern Illinois	11	291	156.3
1974	Louie Giammona, Utah State	10	329	153.4
1975	Ricky Bell, So. California	11	357	170.5
1976	Tony Dorsett, Pittsburgh	11	338	177.1
1977	Earl Campbell, Texas	11	267	158.5
1978	Billy Sims, Oklahoma	11	231	160.2
1979	Charles White, So. California	10	293	180.3
1980	George Rogers, So. Carolina	11	297	161.9
1981	Marcus Allen, So. California	11	403	212.9*
1982	Ernest Anderson, Oklahoma St.	11	353	170.6
1983	Mike Rozier, Nebraska	12	275	179.0

COLLEGE SCORING CHAMPIONS

YEAR	PLAYER, TEAM	GAMES	TD	XPT.	FG	PTS.[2]
1954	Art Luppino, Arizona	10	24	22	0	166
1955	Jim Swink, TCU	10	20	5	0	125
1956	Clendon Thomas, Oklahoma	10	18	0	0	108
1957	Leon Burton, Arizona State	10	16	0	0	96
1958	Dick Bass, Pacific	10	18	8	0	116
1959	Pervis Atkins, N.M. State	10	17	5	0	107
1960	Bob Gaiters, N.M. State	10	23	7	0	145
1961	Jim Pilot, New Mexico State	10	21	12	0	138
1962	Jerry Logan, W. Texas State	10	13	32	0	110
1963	Cosmo Iacavazzi, Princeton	9	14	0	0	84
	Dave Casinelli, Memph. State	10	14	0	0	84
1964	Brian Piccolo, Wake Forest	10	17	9	0	111
1965	Howard Twilley, Tulsa	10	16	31	0	127
1966	Ken Hebert, Houston	10	11	41	2	113
1967	Leroy Keyes, Purdue	10	19	0	0	114
1968	Jim O'Brien, Cincinnati	10	12	31	13	142
1969	Steve Owens, Oklahoma	10	23	0	0	138
1970	Brian Bream, Air Force	10	20	0	0	12.0
	Gary Kosins, Dayton	9	18	0	0	12.0
1971	Ed Marinaro, Cornell	9	24	4	0	16.4
1972	Harold Henson, Ohio State	10	20	0	0	12.0
1973	Jim Jennings, Rutgers	11	21	2	0	11.6
1974	Bill Marek, Wisconsin	9	19	0	0	12.7
1975	Pete Johnson, Ohio State	11	25	0	0	13.6
1976	Tony Dorsett, Pittsburgh	11	22	2	0	12.2
1977	Earl Campbell, Texas	11	19	0	0	10.4
1978	Billy Sims, Oklahoma	11	20	0	0	10.9
1979	Billy Sims, Oklahoma	11	22	0	0	12.0
1980	Sammy Windner, So. Miss.	11	20	0	0	10.9
1981	Marcus Allen, So. California	11	23	0	0	12.5
1982	Greg Allen, Florida State	10	20	0	0	12.0
1983	Mike Rozier, Nebraska	12	29	0	0	14.5

* Record. [1] Beginning in 1970, ranked on per-game (instead of total) yards. [2] Beginning in 1970, ranked on per-game (instead of total) points. Source: National Collegiate Sports Services.

COLLEGE FOOTBALL PASSING CHAMPIONS[1]: 1983

Source: NCAA Statistics Service.

	GAMES	ATT.	CMP.	CMP. PCT.	INT.	INT. PCT.	YDS.	YDS./ ATT.	TD	TD PCT.	RATING POINTS
Steve Young, Brigham Young	11	429	306	71.33	10	2.33	3,902	9.10	33	7.69	168.5
Chuck Long, Iowa	10	236	144	61.02	8	3.39	2,434	10.31	14	5.93	160.4
Mike Eppley, Clemson	11	166	99	59.64	9	5.42	1,410	8.49	13	7.83	146.0
Cody Carlson, Baylor	11	180	98	54.44	7	3.89	1,617	8.98	12	6.67	144.1
Rick Neuheisel, UCLA	11	236	163	69.07	10	4.24	1,947	8.25	9	3.81	142.5
R. Cunningham, Nevada–L.V.	11	316	189	59.81	8	2.53	2,545	8.05	18	5.70	141.2
Marlon Adler, Missouri	11	175	102	58.29	13	7.43	1,603	9.16	11	6.29	141.1
Brad Baumberger, Wyoming	12	189	112	59.26	7	3.70	1,551	8.21	10	5.29	138.2
Jack Trudeau, Illinois	11	324	203	62.65	13	4.01	2,446	7.55	18	5.56	136.4
Raphel Cherry, Hawaii	11	299	170	56.86	15	5.02	2,478	8.29	18	6.02	136.3
Mike Tomczak, Ohio State	10	205	116	56.59	12	5.85	1,716	8.37	12	5.85	134.5
Ricky Turner, Washington St.	10	172	100	58.14	5	2.91	1,351	7.85	8	4.65	133.7
Doug Strang, Penn State	12	259	134	51.74	7	2.70	1,944	7.51	19	7.34	133.6
Boomer Esiason, Maryland	10	294	163	55.44	8	2.72	2,322	7.90	15	5.10	133.2

[1] Minimum of 15 attempts per game.

COLLEGE FOOTBALL NATIONAL CHAMPIONSHIP TEAMS

Various groups have picked the annual college football team champion since 1924. The Associated Press started polling sportswriters in 1936 to determine the team winner. In 1950 United Press International began to poll football coaches. The NCAA recognizes both polls.

1925	Dartmouth	1941	Minnesota	1957	Auburn (AP)	1971	Nebraska
1926	Stanford	1942	Ohio State		Ohio State (UPI)	1972	So. California
1927	Illinois	1943	Notre Dame	1958	Louisiana State	1973	Notre Dame
1928	So. California	1944	Army	1959	Syracuse	1974	Oklahoma (AP)
1929	Notre Dame	1945	Army	1960	Minnesota		So. Calif. (UPI)
1930	Notre Dame	1946–47	Notre Dame	1961	Alabama	1975	Oklahoma
1931	So. California	1948	Michigan	1962	So. California	1976	Pittsburgh
1932	Michigan	1949	Notre Dame	1963	Texas	1977	Notre Dame
1933	Michigan	1950	Oklahoma	1964–65	Alabama	1978	Alabama (AP)
1934	Minnesota	1951	Tennessee	1966	Notre Dame		So. Calif. (UPI)
1935	Southern Methodist	1952	Michigan State	1967	So. California	1979	Alabama
1936	Minnesota	1953	Maryland	1968	So. Calif. (UPI)	1980	Georgia
1937	Pittsburgh	1954	Ohio State (AP);		Ohio State (UPI)	1981	Clemson
1938	Texas Christian		UCLA (UPI)	1969	Texas	1982	Penn State
1939	Texas A & M	1955	Oklahoma	1970	Nebraska (AP)	1983	Nebraska
1940	Minnesota	1956	Oklahoma		Texas (UPI)		

COLLEGE FOOTBALL CONFERENCE CHAMPIONS

ATLANTIC COAST CONFERENCE CHAMPIONS

1955*	Maryland—Duke	1962	Duke	1969	South Carolina	1976	Maryland
1956	Clemson	1963	North Carolina State	1970	Wake Forest	1977	North Carolina
1957	North Carolina State	1964	North Carolina State	1971	North Carolina	1978	Clemson
1958	Clemson	1965	Duke	1972	North Carolina	1979	North Carolina State
1959	Clemson	1966	Clemson	1973	North Carolina State	1980	North Carolina
1960	Duke	1967	Clemson	1974	Maryland	1981–82	Clemson
1961	Duke	1968	North Carolina State	1975	Maryland	1983	Maryland

BIG EIGHT CONFERENCE CHAMPIONS

1936	Nebraska	1948	Oklahoma	1960	Missouri	1972	Oklahoma
1937	Nebraska	1949	Oklahoma	1961	Colorado	1973	Oklahoma
1938	Oklahoma	1950	Oklahoma	1962	Oklahoma	1974	Oklahoma
1939	Missouri	1951	Oklahoma	1963	Nebraska	1975*	Oklahoma—Nebraska
1940	Nebraska	1952	Oklahoma	1964	Nebraska	1976*	Oklahoma—Colorado
1941	Missouri	1953	Oklahoma	1965	Nebraska		—Oklahoma State
1942	Missouri	1954	Oklahoma	1966	Nebraska	1977	Oklahoma
1943	Oklahoma	1955	Oklahoma	1967	Oklahoma	1978*	Oklahoma—Nebraska
1944	Oklahoma	1956	Oklahoma	1968	Kansas	1979	Oklahoma
1945	Missouri	1957	Oklahoma	1969*	Missouri—Nebraska	1980	Oklahoma
1946*	Oklahoma—Kansas	1958	Oklahoma	1970	Nebraska	1981–83	Nebraska
1947*	Oklahoma—Kansas	1959	Oklahoma	1971	Nebraska		

BIG TEN CHAMPIONS

1937	Minnesota	1949*	Ohio State—Michigan	1961	Ohio State	1972–73*	Ohio St.—Michigan
1938	Minnesota	1950	Michigan	1962	Wisconsin	1974*	Ohio State—Michigan
1939	Ohio State	1951	Illinois	1963	Illinois	1975	Ohio State
1940	Minnesota	1952*	Wisconsin—Purdue	1964	Michigan	1976*	Michigan—Ohio State
1941	Minnesota	1953*	Illinois—Mich. State	1965	Michigan State	1977*	Michigan—Ohio State
1942	Ohio State	1954	Ohio State	1966	Michigan State	1978*	Michigan—
1943*	Michigan—Purdue	1955	Ohio State	1967*	Indiana—Purdue—		Michigan State
1944	Ohio State	1956	Iowa		Minnesota	1979	Ohio State
1945	Indiana	1957	Ohio State	1968	Ohio State	1980	Michigan
1946	Illinois	1958	Iowa	1969*	Michigan—Ohio State	1981*	Iowa—Ohio State
1947	Michigan	1959	Wisconsin	1970	Ohio State	1982	Michigan
1948	Michigan	1960*	Minnesota—Iowa	1971	Michigan	1983	Illinois

IVY LEAGUE CHAMPIONS

1957	Princeton	1965	Dartmouth	1970	Dartmouth	1977	Yale
1958	Dartmouth	1966*	Dartmouth—Harvard	1971*	Cornell—Dartmouth	1978	Dartmouth
1959	Pennsylvania		—Princeton	1972	Dartmouth	1979–80	Yale
1960	Yale	1967	Yale	1973	Dartmouth	1981*	Yale—Dartmouth
1961*	Columbia—Harvard	1968*	Harvard—Yale	1974*	Harvard—Yale	1982*	Harvard—
1962	Dartmouth	1969*	Dartmouth—	1975	Harvard		Dartmouth—Penn
1963*	Dartmouth—Princeton		Princeton—Yale	1976*	Yale—Brown	1983*	Harvard—Penn
1964	Princeton						

PACIFIC COAST ATHLETIC CONFERENCE CHAMPIONS

1969	San Diego State	1975	San Jose State	1978*	Utah St.—San Jose St.	1981	San Jose State
1970–71	Long Beach State	1976	San Diego State	1979	San Jose State	1982	Fresno State
1972–74	San Diego State	1977	Fresno State	1980	Long Beach State	1983	Calif. St., Fullerton

* Tie.

PACIFIC TEN CHAMPIONS

1936* Washington—So. Cal.	1949–50 California	1962 Southern California	1972 Southern California
1937 California	1951 Stanford	1963 Washington	1973 Southern California
1938* California—So. Cal.	1952 Southern California	1964* Oregon State—	1974 Southern California
1939 Southern California	1953-55 UCLA	Southern California	1975* California—UCLA
1940 Stanford	1956 Oregon State	1965 UCLA	1976 Southern California
1941 Oregon State	1957* Oregon State—Oregon	1966 Southern California	1977 Washington
1942 UCLA	1958 California	1967 Southern California	1978 Southern California
1943–45 Southern California	1959* Washington—Southern	1968 Southern California	1979 Southern California
1946 UCLA	California—UCLA	1969 Southern California	1980–81 Washington
1947 Southern California	1960 Washington	1970 Stanford	1982–83 UCLA
1948* Oregon—California	1961 UCLA	1971 Stanford	

SOUTHEASTERN CONFERENCE CHAMPIONS

1935-36 LSU	1948 Georgia	1960 Mississippi	1971-75 Alabama
1937 Alabama	1949 Tulane	1961* Alabama—LSU	1976 Georgia
1938 Tennessee	1950 Kentucky	1962 Mississippi	1977* Alabama—Kentucky
1939* Tennessee—Ga. Tech.	1951* Georgia Tech—Tenn.	1963 Mississippi	1978 Alabama
1940 Tennessee	1952 Georgia Tech	1964 Alabama	1979 Alabama
1941 Mississippi State	1953 Alabama	1965 Alabama	1980 Georgia
1942 Georgia	1954–55 Mississippi	1966* Georgia—Alabama	1981* Georgia—Alabama
1943–44 Georgia Tech	1956 Tennessee	1967 Tennessee	1982 Georgia
1945 Alabama	1957 Auburn	1968 Georgia	1983 Auburn
1946* Georgia—Tennessee	1958 LSU	1969 Tennessee	
1947 Mississippi	1959 Georgia	1970 LSU	

SOUTHERN CONFERENCE CHAMPIONS

1935-36 Duke	1948 Clemson	1961 Citadel	1971 Richmond
1937 Maryland	1949 North Carolina	1962 VMI	1972 East Carolina
1938 Duke	1950 Washington & Lee	1963 Virginia Tech	1972 East Carolina
1939 Duke	1951* Maryland—VMI	1964 West Virginia	1973 East Carolina
1940 Clemson	1952 Duke	1965 West Virginia	1974 VMI
1941 Duke	1953 West Virginia	1966* William & Mary—	1975 Richmond
1942 William & Mary	1954 West Virginia	East Carolina	1976 East Carolina
1943 Duke	1955 West Virginia	1967 West Virginia	1977* Tenn.-Chat.—VMI
1944 Duke	1956 West Virginia	1968 Richmond	1978* Tenn.-Chat.—Furman
1945 Duke	1957 VMI	1969* Davidson—	1979 Tennessee-Chat.
1946 North Carolina	1958 West Virginia	Richmond	1980–83 Furman
1947 William & Mary	1959–60 VMI	1970 William & Mary	

SOUTHWEST CONFERENCE CHAMPIONS

1937 Rice	1950 Texas	1961* Texas—Arkansas	1973 Texas
1938 TCU	1951 TCU	1962 Texas	1974 Baylor
1939 Texas A & M	1952 Texas	1963 Texas	1975* Texas A & M—
1940 Texas A & M—SMU	1953* Rice—Texas	1964–65 Arkansas	Arkansas—Texas
1941 Texas A & M	1954 Arkansas	1966 SMU	1976* Houston—Texas Tech
1942–43 Texas	1955 Texas	1967 Texas A & M	1977 Texas
1944 TCU	1956 Texas A & M	1968 Texas	1978 Houston
1945 Texas	1957 Rice	1969 Texas	1979* Arkansas—Houston
1946* Arkansas—Rice	1958 TCU	1970 Texas	1980 Baylor
1947-48 SMU	1959* Texas—TCU—Ark.	1971 Texas	1981–82 SMU
1949 Rice	1960 Arkansas	1972 Texas	1983 Texas

MISSOURI VALLEY CONFERENCE CHAMPIONS

1938 Tulsa	1952 Houston	1963* Cincinnati—Wichita	1973 North Texas
1939 Washington	1953* Okla. A&M—Detroit	1964 Cincinnati	1974–75 Tulsa
1940-43 Tulsa	1954 Wichita	1965 Tulsa	1976* Tulsa—New Mexico St.
1944 Oklahoma A & M	1955* Detroit—Wichita	1966* North Texas—Tulsa	1977 West Texas State
1945 Oklahoma A & M	1956 Houston	1967 North Texas	1978 New Mexico State
1946 Tulsa	1957 Houston	1968 Memphis State	1979 West Texas State
1947 Tulsa	1958 North Texas	1969 Memphis State	1980 Tulsa
1948 Oklahoma A & M	1959* North Texas—Houston	1970 Louisville	1981* Drake—Tulsa
1949 Detroit	1960 Wichita	1971 North Texas	1982–83 Tulsa
1950 Tulsa	1961 Wichita	1972* Louisville—West	
1951 Tulsa	1962 Tulsa	Texas—Drake	

WESTERN ATHLETIC CONFERENCE CHAMPIONS

1962–63 New Mexico	1969 Arizona State	1974 Brigham Young	1978–83 Brigham Young
1964* New Mexico—	1970 Arizona State	1975 Arizona State	
Utah—Arizona	1971 Arizona State	1976* Brigham Young—Wyo.	
1965 Brigham Young	1972 Arizona State	1977* Brigham Young—	
1966–68 Wyoming	1973* Arizona—Arizona State	Arizona State	

* Tie.

COLLEGE FOOTBALL'S MAJOR BOWL GAMES

ROSE BOWL (at Pasadena, Calif.) (played in January)

1902	Michigan 49, Stanford 0	1937	Pittsburgh 21, Washington 0	1962	Minnesota 21, UCLA 3
1916	Washington State 14, Brown 0	1938	California 13, Alabama 0	1963	So. Calif. 42, Wisconsin 37
1917	Oregon 14, Pennsylvania 0	1939	Southern California 7, Duke 3	1964	Illinois 17, Washington 7
1918	Mare Island Marines 19, Camp Lewis (Army) 7	1940	So. Calif. 14, Tennessee 0	1965	Michigan 34, Oregon State 7
1919	Great Lakes (Navy) 17, Mare Island Marines 0	1941	Stanford 21, Nebraska 13	1966	UCLA 14, Michigan State 12
1920	Harvard 7, Oregon 6	1942	Oregon State 20, Duke 16[1]	1967	Purdue 14, So. Calif. 13
1921	California 28, Ohio State 0	1943	Georgia 9, UCLA 0	1968	So. Calif. 14, Indiana 3
1922	Washington and Jefferson 0, California 0	1944	So. Calif. 29, Wash. 0[2]	1969	Ohio State 27, So. Calif. 16
1923	So. Calif. 14, Penn State 3	1945	So. Calif. 25, Tenn. 0	1970	So. Calif. 10, Michigan 3
1924	Navy 14, Washington 14	1946	Alabama 34, So. Calif. 14	1971	Stanford 27, Ohio State 17
1925	Notre Dame 27, Stanford 10	1947	Illinois 45, UCLA 14	1972	Stanford 13, Michigan 12
1926	Alabama 20, Washington 19	1948	Michigan 49, So. Calif. 0	1973	So. Calif. 42, Ohio State 17
1927	Alabama 7, Stanford 7	1949	Northwestern 20, California 14	1974	Ohio State 42, So. Calif. 21
1928	Stanford 7, Pittsburgh 6	1950	Ohio State 17, California 14	1975	So. Calif. 18, Ohio State 17
1929	Georgia Tech. 8, California 7	1951	Michigan 14, California 6	1976	UCLA 23, Ohio State 10
1930	So. Calif. 47, Pittsburgh 14	1952	Illinois 40, Stanford 7	1977	So. Calif. 14, Michigan 6
1931	Alabama 24, Washington State 0	1953	So. Calif. 7, Wisconsin 0	1978	Washington 27, Michigan 20
1932	So. Calif. 21, Tulane 12	1954	Michigan State 28, UCLA 20	1979	So. Calif. 17, Michigan 10
1933	So. Calif. 35, Pittsburgh 0	1955	Ohio State 20, So. Calif. 7	1980	So. Calif. 17, Ohio State 16
1934	Columbia 7, Stanford 0	1956	Michigan State 17, UCLA 14	1981	Michigan 23, Washington 6
1935	Alabama 29, Stanford 13	1957	Iowa 35, Oregon State 19	1982	Washington 28, Iowa 0
1936	Stanford 7, SMU 0	1958	Ohio State 10, Oregon 7	1983	UCLA 24, Michigan 14
		1959	Iowa 38, California 12	1984	See page 30.
		1960	Washington 44, Wisconsin 8		
		1961	Washington 17, Minnesota 7		

[1] Because of World War II restrictions, the 1942 Rose Bowl game was played at Duke Stadium, Durham, North Carolina. [2] The only Rose Bowl game between two Pacific Coast Conference teams.

ORANGE BOWL (at Miami, Fla.) (played in January)

1935	Bucknell 26, Miami (Fla.) 0	1951	Clemson 15, Miami 14	1968	Oklahoma 26, Tennessee 24
1936	Catholic University 20, Mississippi 19	1952	Georgia Tech 17, Baylor 14	1969	Penn State 15, Kansas 14
1937	Duquesne 13, Miss. State 12	1953	Alabama 61, Syracuse 6	1970	Penn State 10, Missouri 3
1938	Alabama Poly 6, Michigan State 0	1954	Oklahoma 7, Maryland 0	1971	Nebraska 17, LSU 12
1939	Tennessee 17, Oklahoma 0	1955	Duke 36, Nebraska 7	1972	Nebraska 38, Alabama 6
1940	Georgia Tech 21, Missouri 7	1956	Oklahoma 20, Maryland 6	1973	Nebraska 40, Notre Dame 6
1941	Miss. State 14, Georgetown 7	1957	Colorado 27, Clemson 21	1974	Penn State 16, LSU 9
1942	Georgia 40, Texas Christian 26	1958	Oklahoma 48, Duke 21	1975	Notre Dame 13, Alabama 11
1943	Alabama 37, Boston College 21	1959	Oklahoma 21, Syracuse 6	1976	Oklahoma 14, Michigan 6
1944	LSU 19, Texas A & M 14	1960	Georgia 14, Missouri 0	1977	Ohio State 27, Colorado 10
1945	Tulsa 26, Georgia Tech 12	1961	Missouri 21, Navy 14	1978	Arkansas 31, Oklahoma 6
1946	Miami (Fla.) 13, Holy Cross 6	1962	LSU 25, Colorado 7	1979	Oklahoma 31, Nebraska 24
1947	Rice 8, Tennessee 0	1963	Alabama 17, Oklahoma 0	1980	Oklahoma 24, Fla. State 7
1948	Georgia Tech 20, Kansas 14	1964	Nebraska 13, Auburn 7	1981	Oklahoma 18, Florida State 17
1949	Texas 41, Georgia 28	1965	Texas 21, Alabama 17	1982	Clemson 22, Nebraska 15
1950	Santa Clara 21, Kentucky 13	1966	Alabama 39, Nebraska 28	1983	Nebraska 21, La. State 20
		1967	Florida 27, Georgia Tech 12	1984	See page 30.

SUGAR BOWL (at New Orleans, La.) (played in January)

1936	Texas Christian 3, La. State 2	1951	Kentucky 13, Oklahoma 7	1968	LSU 20, Wyoming 13
1937	Santa Clara 21, La. State 14	1952	Maryland 28, Tennessee 13	1969	Arkansas 16, Georgia Tech 2
1938	Santa Clara 6, Louisiana State 0	1953	Georgia Tech 24, Mississippi 7	1970	Mississippi 27, Arkansas 22
1939	Texas Christian 15, Carnegie Tech 7	1954	Georgia Tech 42, West Virginia 19	1971	Tennessee 34, Air Force 13
1940	Texas A&M 14, Tulane 13	1955	Navy 21, Mississippi 0	1972	Oklahoma 40, Auburn 22
1941	Boston College 19, Tennessee 13	1956	Georgia Tech 7, Pittsburgh 0	1973	Oklahoma 14, Penn State 0
1942	Fordham 2, Missouri 0	1957	Baylor 13, Tennessee 7	1974	Notre Dame 24, Alabama 23
1943	Tennessee 14, Tulsa 7	1958	Mississippi 39, Texas 7	1975	Nebraska 13, Florida 10
1944	Georgia Tech 20, Tulsa 18	1959	Louisiana State 7, Clemson 0	1976	Alabama 13, Penn State 6
1945	Duke 29, Alabama 26	1960	Mississippi 21, LSU 0	1977	Pittsburgh 27, Georgia 3
1946	Oklahoma A & M 33, St. Mary's (Calif.) 13	1961	Mississippi 14, Rice 6	1978	Alabama 35, Ohio State 6
1947	Georgia 20, North Carolina 10	1962	Alabama 10, Arkansas 3	1979	Alabama 14, Penn State 7
1948	Texas 27, Alabama 7	1963	Mississippi 17, Arkansas 13	1980	Alabama 24, Arkansas 9
1949	Oklahoma 14, North Carolina 6	1964	Alabama 12, Mississippi 7	1981	Georgia 17, Notre Dame 10
1950	Oklahoma 35, Louisiana State 0	1965	La. State 13, Syracuse 10	1982	Pittsburgh 24, Georgia 20
		1966	Missouri 20, Florida 18	1983	Penn St. 27, Georgia 23
		1967	Alabama 34, Nebraska 7	1984	See page 30.

COTTON BOWL (at Dallas) (played in January)

1937	Texas Christian 16, Marquette 6	1942	Alabama 29, Texas A & M 21	1947	Louisiana State 0, Arkansas 0
1938	Rice 28, Colorado 14	1943	Texas 14, Georgia Tech 7	1948	So. Methodist 13, Penn State 13
1939	St. Mary's 20, Texas Tech 13	1944	Randolph Field 7, Texas 7	1949	So. Methodist 21, Oregon 13
1940	Clemson 6, Boston College 3	1945	Oklahoma A & M 34, TCU 0	1950	Rice 27, North Carolina 13
1941	Texas A & M 13, Fordham 12	1946	Texas 40, Missouri 27	1951	Tennessee 20, Texas 14

COTTON BOWL *(continued)*

1952 Kentucky 20, Texas Christian 7
1953 Texas 16, Tennessee 0
1954 Rice 28, Alabama 6
1955 Georgia Tech 14, Arkansas 6
1956 Miss. 14, Texas Christian 13
1957 Texas Christian 28, Syracuse 27
1958 Navy 20, Rice 7
1959 Air Force 0, Texas Christian 0
1960 Syracuse 23, Texas 14
1961 Duke 7, Arkansas 6
1962 Texas 12, Mississippi 7
1963 Louisiana State 13, Texas 0
1964 Texas 28, Navy 6
1965 Arkansas 10, Nebraska 7
1966 Louisiana State 14, Arkansas 7
1967 Georgia 24, So. Methodist 9
1968 Texas A & M 20, Alabama 16
1969 Texas 36, Tennessee 13
1970 Texas 21, Notre Dame 17
1971 Notre Dame 24, Texas 11
1972 Penn State 30, Texas 6
1973 Texas 17, Alabama 13
1974 Nebraska 19, Texas 3
1975 Penn State 41, Baylor 20
1976 Arkansas 31, Georgia 10
1977 Houston 30, Maryland 21
1978 Notre Dame 38, Texas 10
1979 Notre Dame 35, Houston 34
1980 Houston 17, Nebraska 14
1981 Alabama 30, Baylor 2
1982 Texas 14, Alabama 12
1983 SMU 7, Pittsburgh 3
1984 See page 30.

SUN BOWL (at El Paso, Texas)*

1937 Hardin Simmons 34, Texas Mines 6
1938 West Virginia 7, Texas Tech 6
1939 Utah 26, New Mexico 0
1940 Catholic U. 0, Arizona St. 0
1941 Western Reserve 26, Arizona St. 13
1942 Tulsa 6, Texas Tech 0
1943 2d Air Force 13, Hardin-Simmons 7
1944 Southwest. (Tex.) 7, N. Mexico 0
1945 Southwest. (Tex.) 35, U. of Mex. 0
1946 New Mexico 34, Denver 24
1947 Cincinnati 38, Virginia Tech 6
1948 Miami (O.) 13, Texas Tech 12
1949 West Virginia 21, Texas Mines 12
1950 U. Tex. El Paso 33, Georgetown 20
1951 West Texas St. 14, Cincinnati 13
1952 Texas Tech 25, Col. Pacific 14
1953 Col. Pacific 26, Miss. Southern 7
1954 U. Tex. El Paso 37, Miss. South. 14
1955 U. Texas El Paso 47, Florida St. 20
1956 Wyoming 21, Texas Tech 14
1957 Geo. Wash. 13, U. Texas El Paso 0
1958 Louisville 34, Drake 20
1959 Wyoming 14, Hardin-Simmons 6
1960 New Mexico St. 28, No. Texas St. 8
1961 New Mexico St. 20, Utah State 13
1962 Villanova 17, Wichita 9
1963 West Texas St. 15, Ohio U. 14
1964 Oregon 21, So. Methodist 14
1965 Georgia 7, Texas Tech 0
1966 U. Texas El Paso 13, TCU 12
1967 Wyoming 28, Florida St. 20
1968 U. Texas El Paso 14, Mississippi 7
1969 Auburn 34, Arizona 10
1970 Nebraska 45, Georgia 6
1971 Georgia Tech 17, Texas Tech 9
1972 LSU 33, Iowa State 15
1973 North Carolina 32, Texas Tech 28
1974 Missouri 34, Auburn 17
1975 Mississippi St. 26, N. Carolina 24
1976 Pittsburgh 33, Kansas 19
1977 Oklahoma 44, Wyoming 7
1978 Stanford 24, Louisiana State 14
1979 Texas 42, Maryland 0
1980 Washington 14, Texas 7
1981 Nebraska 31, Mississippi State 17
1982 Oklahoma 40, Houston 14
1983 N. Carolina 26, Texas 10
1984 See page 30.

GATOR BOWL (at Jacksonville, Fla.) (played in December)

1945 Wake Forest 26, S.C. 14
1946 Oklahoma 34, N.C. State 13
1947 Maryland 20, Georgia 20
1948 Clemson 24, Missouri 23
1949 Maryland 20, Missouri 7
1950 Wyoming 20, Washington & Lee 7
1951 Miami (Fla.) 14, Clemson 0
1952 Florida 14, Tulsa 13
1953 Texas Tech 35, Auburn 13
1954 Auburn 33, Baylor 13
1955 Vanderbilt 25, Auburn 13
1956 Georgia Tech 21, Pittsburgh 14
1957 Tennessee 3, Texas A & M 0
1958 Mississippi 7, Florida 3
1959 Arkansas 14, Georgia Tech 7
1960 Florida 13, Baylor 12
1961 Penn State 30, Georgia Tech 15
1962 Florida 17, Penn State 7
1963 North Carolina 35, Air Force 0
1964 Florida State 36, Oklahoma 19
1965 Georgia Tech 31, Texas Tech 21
1966 Tennessee 18, Syracuse 12
1967 Penn State 17, Fla. State 17
1968 Missouri 35, Alabama 10
1969 Florida 14, Tennessee 13
1970 Auburn 35, Mississippi 28
1971 Georgia 7, North Carolina 3
1972 Auburn 24, Colorado 3
1973 Texas Tech 28, Tennessee 19
1974 Auburn 27, Texas 3
1975 Maryland 13, Florida 0
1976 Notre Dame 20, Penn State 9
1977 Pittsburgh 34, Clemson 3
1978 Clemson 17, Ohio State 15
1979 No. Carolina 17, Michigan 15
1980 Pittsburgh 37, South Carolina 9
1981 North Carolina 31, Arkansas 27
1982 Florida St. 31, W. Va. 12
1983 See page 30.

ASTRO-BLUEBONNET BOWL (at Houston, Texas) (played in December)

1960 Texas 3, Alabama 3
1961 Kansas 33, Rice 7
1962 Missouri 14, Georgia Tech 10
1963 Baylor 14, LSU 7
1964 Tulsa 14, Mississippi 7
1965 Tennessee 27, Tulsa 6
1966 Texas 19, Mississippi 0
1967 Colorado 31, Miami (Fla.) 21
1968 SMU 28, Oklahoma 27
1969 Houston 36, Auburn 7
1970 Oklahoma 24, Alabama 24
1971 Colorado 29, Houston 17
1972 Tennessee 24, Louisiana St. 17
1973 Houston 47, Tulane 7
1974 Houston 31, N. Carolina State 31
1975 Texas 38, Colorado 21
1976 Nebraska 27, Texas Tech 24
1977 So. Calif. 47, Texas A & M 28
1978 Stanford 25, Georgia 22
1979 Purdue 27, Tennessee 22
1980 North Carolina 16, Texas 7
1981 Michigan 33, UCLA 14
1982 Arkansas 28, Florida 24
1983 See page 30.

LIBERTY BOWL (at Memphis, Tenn.) (played in December)

1960 Penn State 41, Oregon 12
1961 Syracuse 15, Miami 14
1962 Oregon State 6, Villanova 0
1963 Miss. State 16, N.C. State 12
1964 Utah 32, West Virginia 6
1965 Mississippi 13, Auburn 7
1966 Miami (Fla.) 14, Va. Tech 7
1967 N.C. State 14, Georgia 7
1968 Mississippi 34, Va. Tech 17
1969 Colorado 47, Alabama 33
1970 Tulane 17, Colorado 3
1971 Tennessee 14, Arkansas 13
1972 Georgia Tech 31, Iowa State 30
1973 No. Carolina St. 31, Kansas 18
1974 Tennessee 7, Maryland 3
1975 So. Calif. 20, Texas A & M 0
1976 Alabama 36, UCLA 6
1977 Nebraska 21, North Carolina 17
1978 Missouri 20, LSU 15
1979 Penn State 9, Tulane 6
1980 Purdue 28, Missouri 25
1981 Ohio State 31, Navy 28
1982 Alabama 21, Illinois 15
1983 See page 30.

PEACH BOWL (at Atlanta, Georgia) (played in December)

1969 West Virginia 14, South Carolina 3
1970 Arizona State 48, N. Carolina 26
1971 Mississippi 41, Georgia Tech 18
1972 North Carolina St. 49, West Va. 13
1973 Georgia 17, Maryland 16
1974 Texas Tech 6, Vanderbilt 6
1975 West Virginia 13, N.C. State 10
1976 Kentucky 21, N. Carolina 0
1977 N.C. State 24, Iowa State 14
1978 Purdue 41, Georgia Tech 21
1979 Baylor 24, Clemson 18
1980[1] Miami (Fla.) 20, Virginia 10
1981 W. Virginia 26, Florida 6
1982 Iowa 28, Tennessee 22
1983 See page 30.

FIESTA BOWL (at Tempe, Arizona) (played in December)

1971 Arizona State 45, Florida State 38
1972 Arizona State 49, Missouri 35
1973 Arizona State 28, Pittsburgh 7
1974 Okla. State 16, Brigham Young 6
1975 Arizona State 17, Nebraska 14
1976 Oklahoma 41, Wyoming 7
1977 Penn State 42, Arizona State 30
1978 UCLA 10, Arkansas 10
1979 Pittsburgh 16, Arizona 10
1980 Penn State 31, Ohio State 19
1981[2] Penn St. 26, So. California 10
1982[3] Ariz. St. 32, Oklahoma 21
1983 See page 30.

* Games for 1970–80 played in December of previous year. [1] Jan. 2, 1981. [2] Jan. 1, 1982. [3] Jan. 1, 1983.

MAJOR COLLEGE FOOTBALL RECORDS

INDIVIDUAL RECORDS

Touchdowns scored in one game: 7 by Arnold Boykin, Mississippi versus Mississippi State, Dec. 1, 1951; 11* by Philip King, Princeton versus Columbia, Nov. 4, 1890; 11 by Jefferson Fletcher, Harvard versus Exeter, Nov. 3, 1886; 11 by Henry Beecher, Yale versus Wesleyan, Oct. 30, 1886.

Touchdowns scored in one season: 29 by Lydell Mitchell, Penn State, in 1971; 38* by Mayes McLain, Haskell, in 1926.

Touchdowns scored in a career: 59 by Glenn Davis, Army, 1943–46; 59 by Tony Dorsett, Pittsburgh, in 1973—76; 72* by Willie Heston, Michigan, 1901–04; 66 by Henry Beecher, Yale, 1885–87.

Points scored in one game: 43 by Jim Brown, Syracuse versus Colgate, Nov. 17, 1956 (6 TDs, 7 PATs); 64* by Bernard Trafford, Harvard versus Wesleyan, Nov. 3, 1891 (7 TDs, 4 points each; 18 PATs, 2 points each).

Points scored in a season: 174 by Lydell Mitchell, Penn State, 1971 (29 TDs); 270* by Bernard Trafford, Harvard, 1891 (24 TDs, 4 points each; 77 PATs, 2 points each; 4 FGs, 5 points each).

Points scored in a career: 356 by Tony Dorsett, Pittsburgh, 1973–76; 730* by Knowlton Ames, Princeton, 1886–89 (62 TDs, 4 points each; 176 PATs, 2 points each; 6 FGs, 5 points each).

Yards gained in one game: 599 by Virgil Carter, Brigham Young versus U. Texas–El Paso, Nov. 5, 1966 (86 rushing, 513 passing).

Yards gained in a season: 4,627 by Jim McMahon, Brigham Young, 1979 (56 rushing, 4,571 passing).

Yards gained in a career: 9,723 by Jim McMahon, Brigham Young (1977–78, 1980–81).

Yards gained by rushing in one game: 356 by Eddie Lee Ivery, Georgia Tech versus Air Force, Nov. 11, 1978; 362* by Jim Thorpe, Carlisle versus Pennsylvania, Nov. 16, 1912 (29 rushes).

Yards gained by rushing in one season: 2,342 by Marcus Allen, Southern California, 1981 (403 rushes); 2,148 by Mike Rozier, Nebraska, 1983 (275 rushes).

Yards gained by rushing in a career: 6,082 by Tony Dorsett, Pittsburgh, 1973–76; 5,598 by Charles White, Southern California, 1977–79; 5,259 by Herschel Walker, Georgia, 1980–82.

Passes completed in one game: 45 by Sandy Schwab, Northwestern against Michigan, Oct. 23, 1982; 44 by Jim McMahon, Brigham Young, against Colorado State, Nov. 7, 1981.

Passes completed in one season: 306 by Steve Young, Brigham Young, 1983 (attempted 429).

Passes completed in a career: 820 by Ben Bennett, Duke, 1980–83 (attempted 1,375).

Passes, consecutive completed: 22 by Steve Young, Brigham Young, (last 8 versus Utah State, Oct. 30, 1982, first 14 versus Wyoming, Nov. 6, 1982).

Passes, highest percentage completed in one game (minimum 20 completed): 92.6% by Rick Neuheisel, UCLA vs. Washington, Oct. 29, 1983 (25 of 27).

Passes, highest percentage completed in a season (minimum 150 attempts): 71.3% by Steve Young, Brigham Young, 1983 (306 of 429).

Passes, highest percentage completed in a career (minimum 400 attempts): 65.2% by Steve Young, Brigham Young, 1981–83 (592 of 908).

Passing yards gained in one game: 621 by Dave Wilson, Illinois, against Ohio State, Nov. 8, 1980.

Passing yards gained in one season: 4,571 by Jim McMahon, Brigham Young, 1980.

Touchdown passes in one game: 9 by Dennis Shaw, San Diego State versus New Mexico State, Nov. 15, 1969.

Touchdown passes in a season: 47 by Jim McMahon, Brigham Young, 1980.

Touchdown passes in a career: 84 by Jim McMahon, Brigham Young, 1977–78, 1980–81.

Passes caught in one game: 22 by Jay Miller, Brigham Young versus New Mexico, Nov. 3, 1973 (263 yards).

Touchdown passes caught in one game: 6 by Tim Delaney, San Diego State versus New Mexico State, Nov. 15, 1969.

Field goals in one game: 6 by Charley Gogolak, Princeton versus Rutgers, Sept. 25, 1965 (attempted 6); 7* by Edward Robertson, Purdue versus Rose Poly, Oct. 27, 1900 (attempted 12).

Field goals, season: 28, Paul Woodside, West Virginia, 1982.

Points by kicker, game: 23 by Bobby Raymond, Florida vs. Florida State, Dec. 3, 1983.

Points by kicker, season: 112 by Luis Zendejas, Arizona St., 1983.

Field goal, longest made: 67 yards by Russell Erxleben, Texas versus Rice, Oct. 1, 1977.

Points kicked after touchdown in one game: 13 by Terry Leiweke, Houston versus Tulsa, Nov. 23, 1968 (attempted 14). 23* by Arlo Davis, Oklahoma versus Kingfisher, Sept. 29, 1917 (attempted 26).

TEAM RECORDS

Touchdowns in one game: 15 by Wyoming versus Colorado State College, Nov. 5, 1949 (9 rushing, 6 passing). 32* by Georgia Tech versus Cumberland, Oct. 7, 1916.

Touchdowns in one season: 89 by Nebraska in 1983. 144* by Harvard in 1886 (4 points each).

Points scored in one game: 103 by Wyoming versus Colorado State (0), Nov. 5, 1949. 222* by Georgia Tech versus Cumberland (0), Oct. 7, 1916.

Points scored in one season: 624 by Nebraska, 1983.

Yards gained in one game: 883 by Nebraska versus New Mexico State, Sept. 18, 1982. 1,261* by Michigan versus Buffalo, Oct. 26, 1901.

Yards gained rushing in one game: 758 by Oklahoma versus Colorado, Oct. 4, 1980. 1,261* by Michigan versus Buffalo, Oct. 26, 1901 (76 rushes).

Passes completed in one game: 47 by Wake Forest versus Maryland, Oct. 17, 1981.

Touchdown passes in one game: 10 by San Diego State versus New Mexico State, Nov. 15, 1969.

First downs in one game: 43 by Nebraska versus New Mexico State, Sept. 18, 1982 (28 by rushing, 15 passing).

Points kicked after touchdown in one game: 13 by Wyoming versus Northern Colo., Nov. 5, 1949.

Yards gained by passes in one game: 698 by Tulsa versus Idaho State, Oct. 7, 1967 (completed 39 of 62).

Yards on punt returns in one game: 319 by Texas A & M versus North Texas State, Sept. 21, 1946 (10 returns).

Yards on kickoff returns in one game: 295 by Cincinnati versus Memphis State, Oct. 30, 1971.

Average points per game in a season: 56.0 by Army in 1949 (504 points in 9 games).

Fumbles lost in a game: 10 by Wichita State versus Florida State, Sept. 20, 1969.

* Pre-1937 records: There was no general clearinghouse for national records until the NCAA took over the task in 1937. Touchdowns—TDs; points after touchdown—PATs; field goals—FGs.

GOLF

Wide World

Hal Sutton grimaces as he misses birdie putt on 9th hole during final round of 65th Professional Golf Association (PGA) championship at Pacific Palisades, Calif., on Aug. 8. Sutton defeated runner-up Jack Nicklaus by one stroke, finishing with a four-round total of 274. Sutton, 1982 Rookie of the Year, finished as leading money winner of the 1983 season. Earning $426,668, Sutton finished 12 times in the top 10. On March 28, he won the Tournament Players Championship, at Ponte Vedra, Fla., defeating John Cook by one stroke. His 72-hole total was a 5-under-par 283. Sutton was voted player of the year by golf writers, and led the tour in birdies, with 399.

No golfer won more than two events on the Professional Golf Association (PGA) tour in 1983. Hal Sutton, the leading money-winner, with earnings of $426,668, captured the PGA championship and the Tournament Players Championship.

Seve Ballesteros of Spain happily donned the prestigious green Masters jacket, when he won the Masters championship at August, Ga., on April 11, for the second time in four years. He had a 72-hole total of 280.

Larry Nelson sank a 62-foot birdie putt on the 16th green at Oakmont, Pa., on June 20, to capture the 83d U.S. Open championship. He edged 1982 winner Tom Watson by one shot, with a 4-under-par 280.

The $100,000 first prize in the World Series of Golf, at Akron, Ohio, in August, was won by Nick Price of South Africa. He defeated Jack Nicklaus by four strokes.

On Sept. 19, Fuzzy Zoeller won the $135,000 first prize at the Las Vegas Pro-Celebrity Classic, the newest and richest event on the tour. He had an 18-under-par 340 in the 90-hole event.

At Southport, England, on July 17, Tom Watson won his fifth British Open title by one stroke, with a 9-under par 275.

In women's golf, JoAnne Carner topped the list of money winners for the second consecutive year, with $291,404. In August, she successfully defended her World Championship of Women's Golf title, at Shaker Hts., Ohio, with a 6-under-par 282.

Patty Sheehan rallied with five straight birdies to win the 1983 Ladies Professional Golf Association (LPGA) championship at Mason, Ohio, with a 9-under-par 279.

Australian Jan Stephenson captured the prestigious U.S. Women's Open title, at Tulsa, Okla., on July 31. Her 6-over-par 290, was one stroke ahead of JoAnne Carner. Stephenson was only the third foreigner to win the coveted title.

U.S. PROFESSIONAL GOLF ASSOCIATION CHAMPIONS

1916	Jim Barnes	1935	Johnny Revolta	1949	Sam Snead	1962	Gary Player	1975	Jack Nicklaus
1917–18	No play	1936–37	Denny Shute	1950	Chandler Harper	1963	Jack Nicklaus	1976	Dave Stockton
1919	Jim Barnes	1938	Paul Runyan	1951	Sam Snead	1964	Bobby Nichols	1977	Lanny Wadkins
1920	Jock Hutchison	1939	Henry Picard	1952	Jim Turnesa	1965	Dave Marr	1978	John Mahaffey
1921	Walter Hagen	1940	Byron Nelson	1953	Walter Burkemo	1966	Al Geiberger	1979	David Graham
1922–23	Gene Sarazen	1941	Victor Ghezzi	1954	Chick Harbert	1967	Don January	1980	Jack Nicklaus
1924–27	Walter Hagen	1942	Sam Snead	1955	Doug Ford	1968	Julius Boros	1981	Larry Nelson
1928–29	Leo Diegel	1943	No play	1956	Jack Burke	1969	Ray Floyd	1982	Ray Floyd
1930	Tommy Armour	1944	Bob Hamilton	1957	Lionel Hebert	1970	Dave Stockton	1983	Hal Sutton
1931	Tom Creavy	1945	Byron Nelson	1958	Dow Finsterwald	1971	Jack Nicklaus		
1932	Olin Dutra	1946	Ben Hogan	1959	Bob Rosburg	1972	Gary Player		
1933	Gene Sarazen	1947	Jim Ferrier	1960	Jay Hebert	1973	Jack Nicklaus		
1934	Paul Runyan	1948	Ben Hogan	1961	Jerry Barber	1974	Lee Trevino		

U.S. WOMEN'S OPEN GOLF CHAMPIONS

1946	Patty Berg	1955	Fay Crocker	1965	Carol Mann	1976	JoAnne Carner[1]
1947	Betty Jameson	1956	Kathy Cornelius[1]	1966	Sandra Spuzich	1977–78	Hollis Stacy
1948	Babe Didrikson Zaharias	1957	Betsy Rawls	1967	Catherine Lacoste[2]	1979	Jerilyn Britz
1949	Louise Suggs	1958–59	Mickey Wright	1968	Susie Maxwell Berning	1980	Amy Alcott
1950	Babe Didrikson Zaharias	1960	Betsy Rawls	1969–70	Donna Caponi	1981	Pat Bradley
1951	Betsy Rawls	1961	Mickey Wright	1971	JoAnne Carner	1982	Janet Alex
1952	Louise Suggs	1962	Murle Lindstrom	1972–73	Susie M. Berning	1983	Jan Stephenson
1953	Betsy Rawls[1]	1963	Mary Mills	1974	Sandra Haynie		
1954	Babe Didrikson Zaharias	1964	Mickey Wright[1]	1975	Sandra Palmer		

MASTERS GOLF CHAMPIONS

1934	Horton Smith	1949	Sam Snead	1961	Gary Player	1974	Gary Player
1935	Gene Sarazen	1950	Jimmy Demaret	1962	Arnold Palmer	1975	Jack Nicklaus
1936	Horton Smith	1951	Ben Hogan	1963	Jack Nicklaus	1976	Ray Floyd
1937	Byron Nelson	1952	Sam Snead	1964	Arnold Palmer	1977	Tom Watson
1938	Henry Picard	1953	Ben Hogan	1965–66	Jack Nicklaus	1978	Gary Player
1939	Ralph Guldahl	1954	Sam Snead	1967	Gay Brewer	1979	Fuzzy Zoeller[1]
1940	Jimmy Demaret	1955	Cary Middlecoff	1968	Bob Goalby	1980	Seve Ballesteros
1941	Craig Wood	1956	Jack Burke	1969	George Archer	1981	Tom Watson
1942	Byron Nelson	1957	Doug Ford	1970	Billy Casper	1982	Craig Stadler[1]
1946	Herman Keiser	1958	Arnold Palmer	1971	Charles Coody	1983	Seve Ballesteros
1947	Jimmy Demaret	1959	Art Wall Jr.	1972	Jack Nicklaus		
1948	Claude Harmon	1960	Arnold Palmer	1973	Tommy Aaron		

PGA TOUR LEADING MONEY WINNERS

1939	Henry Picard	$10,303	1955	Julius Boros	$ 65,122	1970	Lee Trevino	$150,037
1940	Ben Hogan	10,655	1956	Ted Kroll	72,836	1971	Jack Nicklaus	244,491
1941	Ben Hogan	18,358	1957	Dick Mayer	65,835	1972	Jack Nicklaus	320,542
1942	Ben Hogan	13,143	1958	Arnold Palmer	42,407	1973	Jack Nicklaus	308,362
1944	Byron Nelson	37,968	1959	Art Wall Jr.	53,168	1974	Johnny Miller	353,201
1945	Byron Nelson	63,336	1960	Arnold Palmer	75,263	1975	Jack Nicklaus	323,149
1946	Ben Hogan	42,556	1961	Gary Player	64,540	1976	Jack Nicklaus	266,438
1947	Jimmy Demaret	27,937	1962	Arnold Palmer	81,448	1977	Tom Watson	310,653
1948	Ben Hogan	32,112	1963	Arnold Palmer	128,230	1978	Tom Watson	362,429
1949	Sam Snead	31,594	1964	Jack Nicklaus	113,285	1979	Tom Watson	462,636
1950	Sam Snead	35,759	1965	Jack Nicklaus	140,752	1980	Tom Watson	530,808
1951	Lloyd Mangrum	26,089	1966	Billy Casper	121,945	1981	Tom Kite	375,699
1952	Julius Boros	37,033	1967	Jack Nicklaus	188,988	1982	Craig Stadler	446,462
1953	Lew Worsham	34,002	1968	Billy Casper	205,169	1983	Hal Sutton	426,668
1954	Bob Toski	65,820	1969	Frank Beard	175,224			

LPGA TOUR LEADING MONEY WINNERS

1952	Betsy Rawls	$14,505	1963	Mickey Wright	$31,270	1974	JoAnne Carner	$ 87,094
1953	Louise Suggs	19,816	1964	Mickey Wright	29,800	1975	Sandra Palmer	94,805
1954	Patty Berg	16,011	1965	Kathy Whitworth	28,658	1976	Judy Rankin	150,734
1955	Patty Berg	16,492	1966	Kathy Whitworth	33,518	1977	Judy Rankin	122,890
1956	Marlene Hagge	20,235	1967	Kathy Whitworth	32,938	1978	Nancy Lopez	189,813
1957	Patty Berg	16,272	1968	Kathy Whitworth	48,380	1979	Nancy Lopez	215,987
1958	Beverly Hanson	12,640	1969	Carol Mann	49,153	1980	Beth Daniel	231,000
1959	Betsy Rawls	26,774	1970	Kathy Whitworth	30,235	1981	Beth Daniel	206,978
1960	Louise Suggs	16,892	1971	Kathy Whitworth	41,182	1982	JoAnne Carner	310,399
1961	Mickey Wright	22,236	1972	Kathy Whitworth	65,064	1983	JoAnne Carner	291,404
1962	Mickey Wright	21,641	1973	Kathy Whitworth	82,864			

[1] Won in playoff. [2] Amateur golfer.

U.S. OPEN GOLF CHAMPIONS

YEAR	CHAMPION	SCORE [1]	YEAR	CHAMPION	SCORE [1]	YEAR	CHAMPION	SCORE [1]
1895	Horace Rawlins	173	1925	Willie Macfarlane	291*	1957	Dick Mayer	282*
1896	James Foulis	152	1926	Bobby Jones [2]	293	1958	Tommy Bolt	283
1897	Joe Lloyd	162	1927	Tommy Armour	301*	1959	Billy Casper	282
1898	Fred Herd	328	1928	Johnny Farrell	294*	1960	Arnold Palmer	280
1899	Willie Smith	315	1929	Bobby Jones [2]	294*	1961	Gene Littler	281
1900	Harry Vardon	313	1930	Bobby Jones [2]	287	1962	Jack Nicklaus	283*
1901	Willie Anderson	331*	1931	Billie Burke	292*	1963	Julius Boros	293*
1902	L. Auchterlonie	307	1932	Gene Sarazen	286	1964	Ken Venturi	278
1903	Willie Anderson	307*	1933	Johnny Goodman [2]	287	1965	Gary Player	282*
1904	Willie Anderson	303	1934	Olin Dutra	293	1966	Billy Casper	278*
1905	Willie Anderson	314	1935	Sam Parks Jr.	299	1967	Jack Nicklaus	275
1906	Alex Smith	295	1936	Tony Manero	282	1968	Lee Trevino	275
1907	Alex Ross	302	1937	Ralph Guldahl	281	1969	Orville Moody	281
1908	Fred McLeod	322*	1938	Ralph Guldahl	284	1970	Tony Jacklin	281
1909	George Sargent	290	1939	Byron Nelson	284*	1971	Lee Trevino	280*
1910	Alex Smith	298*	1940	Lawson Little	287*	1972	Jack Nicklaus	290
1911	John McDermott	307*	1941	Craig Wood	284	1973	Johnny Miller	279
1912	John McDermott	294	1942–45	No match		1974	Hale Irwin	287
1913	Francis Ouimet [2]	304	1946	Lloyd Mangrum	284*	1975	Lou Graham	287*
1914	Walter Hagen	290	1947	Lew Worsham	282*	1976	Jerry Pate	277
1915	J. D. Travers [2]	297	1948	Ben Hogan	276	1977	Hubert Green	278
1916	Chick Evans Jr. [2]	286	1949	Cary Middlecoff	286	1978	Andrew North	285
1917–18	No match		1950	Ben Hogan	287*	1979	Hale Irwin	284
1919	Walter Hagen	301*	1951	Ben Hogan	287	1980	Jack Nicklaus	272
1920	Edward Ray	295	1952	Julius Boros	281	1981	David Graham	273
1921	Jim Barnes	289	1953	Ben Hogan	283	1982	Tom Watson	282
1922	Gene Sarazen	288	1954	Ed Furgol	284	1983	Larry Nelson	280
1923	Bobby Jones [2]	296*	1955	Jack Fleck	287*			
1924	Cyril Walker	297	1956	Cary Middlecoff	281			

* Tie for first place, playoff determined champion. [1] For 72 holes except for 1895-97 when 36 holes were played. [2] Amateur.

BRITISH OPEN GOLF CHAMPIONS

The oldest prestigious golf tournament, the British Open, initiated formal competition in golf in 1860. The first American champion was Jock Hutchison in 1921.

1860	Willie Park Sr.	1888	Jack Burns	1909	J. H. Taylor	1934	Henry Cotton	1960	Kel Nagle
1861–62	Tom Morris Sr.	1889	Willie Park Jr.	1910	James Braid	1935	Alf Perry	1961–62	Arnold Palmer *
1863	Willie Park Sr.	1890	John Ball	1911	Harry Vardon	1936	Alf Padgham	1963	Bob Charles
1864	Tom Morris Sr.	1891	Hugh Kirkaldy	1912	Ted Ray	1937	Henry Cotton	1964	Tony Lema *
1865	A. L. Strath	1892	H. H. Hilton	1913	J. H. Taylor	1938	R.A.Whitecombe	1965	Peter Thomson
1866	Willie Park Sr.	1893	W. Auchterlonie	1914	Harry Vardon	1939	Richard Burton	1966	Jack Nicklaus *
1867	Tom Morris Sr.	1894	J. H. Taylor	1915–19	No Play	1940–45	No play	1967	R. de Vicenzo
1868–70	Tom Morris Jr.	1895	J. H. Taylor	1920	George Duncan	1946	Sam Snead *	1968	Gary Player
1871	No play	1896	Harry Vardon	1921	Jock Hutchison *	1947	Fred Daly	1969	Tony Jacklin
1872	Tom Morris Jr.	1897	H. H. Hilton	1922	Walter Hagen *	1948	Henry Cotton	1970	Jack Nicklaus *
1873	Tom Kidd	1898	Harry Vardon	1923	Arthur Havers	1949	Bobby Locke	1971–72	Lee Trevino *
1874	Mungo Park	1899	Harry Vardon	1924	Walter Hagen *	1950	Bobby Locke	1973	Tom Weiskopf *
1875	Willie Park Sr.	1900	J. H. Taylor	1925	Jim Barnes *	1951	Max Faulkner	1974	Gary Player
1876	Bob Martin	1901	James Braid	1926	Bobby Jones *	1952	Bobby Locke	1975	Tom Watson *
1877–79	Jamie Anderson	1902	Alex Herd	1927	Bobby Jones *	1953	Ben Hogan *	1976	Johnny Miller *
1880–82	Bob Ferguson	1903	Harry Vardon	1928	Walter Hagen *	1954	Peter Thomson	1977	Tom Watson *
1883	W. L. Fernie	1904	Jack White	1929	Walter Hagen *	1955	Peter Thomson	1978	Jack Nicklaus *
1884	Jack Simpson	1905	James Braid	1930	Bobby Jones *	1956	Peter Thomson	1979	S. Ballesteros
1885	Bob Martin	1906	James Braid	1931	Tommy Armour *	1957	Bobby Locke	1980	Tom Watson *
1886	D. L. Brown	1907	Arnaud Massy	1932	Gene Sarazen *	1958	Peter Thomson	1981	Bill Rogers *
1887	Willie Park Jr.	1908	James Braid	1933	Denny Shute *	1959	Gary Player	1982–83	Tom Watson *

* American.

RYDER CUP INTERNATIONAL PROFESSIONAL GOLF MATCH

1927	United States 9½, Britain 2½	1959	United States 8½, Britain 3½
1929	Britain 7, United States 5	1961	United States 14½, Britain 9½
1931	United States 9, Britain 3	1963	United States 23, Britain 9
1933	Britain 6½, United States 5½	1965	United States 19½, Britain 12½
1935	United States 9, Britain 3	1967	United States 23½, Britain 8½
1937	United States 8, Britain 4	1969	United States 16, Britain 16 (tie)
1939–45	No matches	1971	United States 18½, Britain 13½
1947	United States 11, Britain 1	1973	United States 18, Britain 13
1949	United States 7, Britain 5	1975	United States 21, Britain 11
1951	United States 9½, Britain 2½	1977	United States 12½, Britain 7½
1953	United States 6½, Britain 5½	1979	United States 17, Britain 11
1955	United States 8, Britain 4	1981	United States 18½, Britain 9½
1957	Britain 7½, United States 4½	1983	United States 14½, Britain 13½

UNITED STATES AMATEUR GOLF CHAMPIONS: MEN

The United States Golf Association (USGA) held its first amateur men's championship in 1895. Robert T. "Bobby" Jones Jr., generally regarded as America's greatest amateur golfer, won the championship a record five times in 1924, 1925, 1927, 1928, and 1930.

1895	C. MacDonald	1915	Robert Gardner	1933	George Dunlap, Jr.	1952	Jack Westland	1968	Bruce Fleisher
1896–98	H. Whigham	1916	Chick Evans, Jr.	1934–35	Lawson Little	1953	Gene Littler	1969	Steve Melnyk
1899	H. Harriman	1917–18	No play	1936	John Fischer	1954	Arnold Palmer	1970	Lanny Wadkins
1900–01	Walter Travis	1919	Davidson Herron	1937	John Goodman	1955–56	Harvie Ward	1971	Gary Cowan
1902	Louis James	1920	Chick Evans, Jr.	1938	Willie Turnesa	1957	Hillman Robbins	1972	Vinny Giles
1903	Walter Travis	1921	Jesse Guilford	1939	Bud Ward	1958	Charles Coe	1973	Craig Stadler
1904–05	Chandler Egan	1922	Jess Sweetser	1940	Dick Chapman	1959	Jack Nicklaus	1974	Jerry Pate
1906	Eben Byers	1923	Max Marston	1941	Bud Ward	1960	Deane Beman	1975	Fred Ridley
1907–08	Jerry Travers	1924–25	Bobby Jones	1942–45	No play	1961	Jack Nicklaus	1976	Bill Sander
1909	Robert Gardner	1926	George Von Elm	1946	Ted Bishop	1962	Labron Harris Jr.	1977	John Faught
1910	William Fownes Jr.	1927–28	Bobby Jones	1947	Skee Riegel	1963	Deane Beman	1978	John Cook
1911	Harold Hilton	1929	Harrison Johnston	1948	Willie Turnesa	1964	Bill Campbell	1979	Mark O'Meara
1912	Jerry Travers	1930	Bobby Jones	1949	Charles Coe	1965	Robert Murphy Jr.	1980	Hal Sutton
1913	Jerry Travers	1931	Francis Ouimet	1950	Sam Urzetta	1966	Gary Cowan	1981	Nathaniel Crosby
1914	Francis Ouimet	1932	Ross Somerville	1951	Billy Maxwell	1967	Bob Dickson	1982–83	Jay Sigel

NATIONAL COLLEGIATE ATHLETIC ASSOCIATION GOLF CHAMPIONS

1897	Louis Bayard Jr., Princeton	1928	Maurice McCarthy, Georgetown	1957	Rex Baxter Jr., Houston
1898	James Reid Jr., Yale	1929	Tom Aycock, Yale	1958	Phil Rodgers, Houston
	James Curtis, Harvard	1930–31	George Dunlap Jr., Princeton	1959–60	Dick Crawford, Houston
1899	Percy Pyne, Princeton	1932	J. W. Fischer, Michigan	1961	Jack Nicklaus, Ohio State
1901	H. Lindsley, Harvard	1933	Walter Emery, Oklahoma	1962	Kermit Zarley, Houston
1902	Charles Hitchcock Jr., Yale	1934	Charles Yates, Georgia Tech	1963	R. H. Sikes, Arkansas
1903	F. O. Reinhart, Princeton	1935	Ed White, Texas	1964	Terry Small, San Jose State
1904	A. L. White, Harvard	1936	Charles Kocsis, Michigan	1965	Marty Fleckman, Houston
1905	Robert Abbott, Yale	1937	Fred Haas Jr., Louisiana State	1966	Bob Murphy, Florida
1906	W. E. Clow Jr., Yale	1938	John Burke, Georgetown	1967	Hale Irwin, Colorado
1907	Ellis Knowles, Yale	1939	Vincent D'Antoni, Tulane	1968	Grier Jones, Oklahoma State
1908	H. H. Wilder, Harvard	1940	Dixon Brooke, Virginia	1969	Bob Clark, Los Angeles State
1909	Albert Seckel, Princeton	1941	Earl Stewart, Louisiana State	1970	John Mahaffey, Houston
1910	Robert Hunter, Yale	1942	Frank Tatum Jr., Stanford	1971	Ben Crenshaw, Texas
1911	George Stanley, Yale	1943	Wallace Ulrich, Carleton	1972	Ben Crenshaw, Texas
1912	F. C. Davison, Harvard	1944	Louis Lick, Minnesota		Tom Kite, Texas
1913	Nathaniel Wheeler, Yale	1945	John Lorms, Ohio State	1973	Ben Crenshaw, Texas
1914	Edward Allis, Harvard	1946	George Hamer, Georgia	1974	Curtis Strange, Wake Forest
1915	Francis Blossom, Yale	1947	Dave Barclay, Michigan	1975	Jay Haas, Wake Forest
1916	J. W. Hubbell, Harvard	1948	Bob Harris, San Jose State	1976–77	Scott Simpson, USC
1917–18	No play	1949	Harvie Ward, North Carolina	1978	David Edwards, Oklahoma State
1919	A. L. Walker Jr., Columbia	1950	Fred Wampler, Purdue	1979	Gary Hallberg, Wake Forest
1920	Jess Sweetser, Yale	1951	Tom Nieporte, Ohio State	1980	Jay Don Blake, Utah State
1921	Simpson Dean, Princeton	1952	Jim Vickers, Oklahoma	1981	Ron Commans, So. California
1922	Pollack Boyd, Dartmouth	1953	Earl Moeller, Oklahoma State	1982	Billy Brown, Houston
1923–24	Dexter Cummings, Yale	1954	Hillman Robbins, Memphis State	1983	Jim Carter, Arizona State
1925–26	Fred Lamprecht, Yale	1955	Joe Campbell, Purdue		
1927	Watts Gunn, Georgia Tech	1956	Rick Jones, Ohio State		

BRITISH AMATEUR GOLF CHAMPIONS

The oldest golf tournament for amateurs is the British Amateur Tournament, played since 1885. It has been won 18 times by American amateur golfers, most recently in 1979.

1885	A. F. MacFie	1904	W. J. Travis	1925	Robert Harris	1948	Frank Stranahan*	1965	Mike Bonallack
1886–87	H. G. Hutchinson	1905	A. G. Barry	1926	Jess Sweetser*	1949	Sam McCready	1966	Bobby Cole
1888	John Ball	1906	James Robb	1927	W. Tweddell	1950	Frank Stranahan*	1967	Bob Dickson*
1889	J. E. Laidlay	1907	John Ball	1928	T. P. Perkins	1951	Dick Chapman*	1968–70	Mike Bonallack
1890	John Ball	1908	E. A. Lassen	1929	Cyril Tolley	1952	Harvie Ward*	1971	Steve Melnyk*
1891	J. E. Laidlay	1909	R. Maxwell	1930	Bobby Jones*	1953	Joseph Carr	1972	Trevor Homer
1892	John Ball	1910	John Ball	1931	E. Martin Smith	1954	Doug Bachli	1973	Dick Siderowf*
1893	P. L. Anderson	1911	H. H. Hilton	1932	J. De Forest	1955	Joseph Conrad*	1974	Trevor Homer
1894	John Ball	1912	John Ball	1933	Michael Scott	1956	John Beharrell	1975	Marvin M. Giles
1895	L. M. B. Melville	1913	H. H. Hilton	1934–35	Lawson Little*	1957	Reid Jack	1976	Dick Siderowf*
1896	F. G. Tait	1914	J. L. C. Jenkins	1936	H. Thompson	1958	Joseph Carr	1977–78	Peter McEvoy
1897	A. J. T. Allan	1915–19	No play	1937	Robert Sweeny Jr.	1959	Deane Beman*	1979	Jay Sigel*
1898	F. G. Tait	1920	Cyril J. Tolley	1938	C. R. Yates*	1961	Mike Bonallack	1980	David Evans
1899	John Ball	1921	W. I. Hunter	1939	Alex Kyle	1960	Joseph Carr	1981	Phillipe Ploujoux
1900–01	H. H. Hilton	1922	E. W. Holderness	1940–45	No play	1962	Richard Davies*	1982	Martin Thompson
1902	C. Hutchings	1923	R. Wethered	1946	James Bruen	1963	Michael Lunt	1983	Philip Parkins
1903	R. Maxwell	1924	E. W. Holderness	1947	Willie Turnesa*	1964	Gordon Clark		

* United States golfer.

U.S. AMATEUR GOLF CHAMPIONS: WOMEN

The United States Golf Association (USGA) held its first amateur women's championship in 1895. Glenna Collett Vare won the championship six times between 1922 and 1935.

1895	Mrs. C. S. Brown	**1919–20**	Alexa Stirling	**1946**	Babe Zaharias	**1964**	Barbara McIntire
1896–98	Beatrix Hoyt	**1921**	Marion Hollins	**1947**	Louise Suggs	**1965**	Jean Ashley
1899	Ruth Underhill	**1922**	Glenna Collett	**1948**	Grace Lenczyk	**1966**	JoAnne Carner
1900	Frances Griscom	**1923**	Edith Cummings	**1949**	Dorothy Porter	**1967**	Lou Dill
1901–02	Genevieve Hecker	**1924**	Dorothy Campbell Hurd	**1950**	Beverly Hanson	**1968**	JoAnne Carner
1903	Bessie Anthony	**1925**	Glenna Collett	**1951**	Dorothy Kirby	**1969**	Catherine Lacoste
1904	Georgiana Bishop	**1926**	Helen Stetson	**1952**	Jacqueline Pung	**1970**	Martha Wilkinson
1905	Pauline Mackay	**1927**	Miriam Burns Horn	**1953**	Mary Lena Faulk	**1971**	Laura Baugh
1906	Harriot Curtis	**1928–30**	Glenna Collett	**1954**	Barbara Romack	**1972**	Mary Budke
1907	Margaret Curtis	**1931**	Helen Hicks	**1955**	Patricia Lesser	**1973**	Carol Semple
1908	Kate Harley	**1932–34**	Virginia Van Wie	**1956**	Marlene Stewart	**1974**	Cynthia Rill
1909–10	Dorothy Campbell	**1935**	Glenna Collett Vare	**1957**	JoAnne Gunderson	**1975**	Beth Daniel
1911–12	Margaret Curtis	**1936**	Pamela Barton	**1958**	Anne Quast	**1976**	Donna Horton
1913	Gladys Ravenscroft	**1937**	Mrs. J. A. Page Jr.	**1959**	Barbara McIntire	**1977**	Beth Daniel
1914	Mrs. H. A. Jackson	**1938**	Patty Berg	**1960**	JoAnne Gunderson	**1978**	Cathy Sherk
1915	Mrs. C. H. Vanderbeck	**1939–40**	Betty Jameson	**1961**	Anne Quast Decker	**1979**	Carolyn Hill
1916	Alexa Stirling	**1941**	Mrs. Frank Newell	**1962**	JoAnne Gunderson	**1980–82**	Juli Simpson Inkster
1917–18	No play	**1942–45**	No play	**1963**	Anne Quast Welts	**1983**	Joanne Pacillo

CURTIS CUP INTERNATIONAL WOMEN'S GOLF TEAM MATCH

The United States has dominated this series of matches between women amateur golf teams representing the U.S. and Britain. The matches are played every two years in even years.

1932	United States 5½, Britain 3½	**1956**	Britain 5, United States 4	**1972**	United States 10, Britain 8
1934	United States 6½, Britain 2½	**1958***	Britain 4½, United States 4½	**1974**	United States 13, Britain 5
1936*	United States 4½, Britain 4½	**1960**	United States 6½, Britain 2½	**1976**	United States 11½, Britain 8½
1938	United States 5½, Britain 3½	**1962**	United States 8, Britain 1	**1978**	United States 12, Britain 6
1948	United States 6½, Britain 2½	**1964**	United States 10½, Britain 7½	**1980**	United States 13, Britain 5
1950	United States 7½, Britain 1½	**1966**	United States 13, Britain 5	**1982**	United States 14½, Britain 3½
1952	Britain 5, United States 4	**1968**	United States 10½, Britain 7½		
1954	United States 6, Britain 3	**1970**	United States 11½, Britain 6½		

* Tie.

WALKER CUP INTERNATIONAL MEN'S GOLF TEAM MATCH

The oldest international amateur golf team match, the Walker Cup competition is played between teams representing the United States and Britain. The cup was presented by G. Herbert Walker, former president of the United States Golf Association, and the first competition was held in 1922. Since 1924 the match has taken place every two years.

1922	United States 8; Britain 4	National Golf Links of America, Southampton, N.Y.
1923	United States 6; Britain 5; one match halved	St. Andrews, Scotland
1924	United States 9; Britain 3	Garden City Golf Club, Garden City, N.Y.
1926	United States 6; Britain 5; one match halved	St. Andrews, Scotland
1928	United States 11; Britain 1	Chicago Golf Club, Wheaton, Ill.
1930	United States 10; Britain 2	Royal St. George's Golf Club, Sandwich, England
1932	United States 8; Britain 1; three matches halved	The Country Club, Brookline, Mass.
1934	United States 9; Britain 2; one match halved	St. Andrews, Scotland
1936	United States 9; Britain 0; three matches halved	Pine Valley Golf Club, Clementon, N.J.
1938	Britain 7; United States 4; one match halved	St. Andrews, Scotland
1940–45	No competition because of World War II	
1947	United States 8; Britain 4	St. Andrews, Scotland
1949	United States 10; Britain 2	Winged Foot Golf Club, Mamaroneck, N.Y.
1951	United States 6; Britain 3; three matches halved	Birkdale Golf Club, Southport, England
1953	United States 9; Britain 3	Kittansett Club, Marion, Mass.
1955	United States 10; Britain 2	St. Andrews, Scotland
1957	United States 8; Britain 3; one match halved	Minikahda Club, Minneapolis, Minn.
1959	United States 9; Britain 3	Muirfield, Scotland
1961	United States 11; Britain 1	Seattle Golf Club, Seattle, Wash.
1963	United States 12; Britain 8; four matches halved	Turnberry, Scotland
1965	United States 11; Britain 11	Baltimore Country Club, Baltimore, Md.
1967	United States 13; Britain 7	Royal St. George's Golf Club, Sandwich, England
1969	United States 10; Britain 8	Milwaukee Country Club, Milwaukee, Wis.
1971	Britain 13; United States 11	St. Andrews, Scotland
1973	United States 14; Britain 10	The Country Club, Brookline, Mass.
1975	United States 15½; Britain 8½	St. Andrews, Scotland
1977	United States 16; Britain 8	Shinnecock Hills Golf Club, Southampton, N.Y.
1979	United States 15½; Britain 8½	Muirfield, Scotland
1981	United States 15; Britain 9	Pebble Beach, Calif.
1983	United States 13½; Britain 10½	Royal Liverpool Club, Hoylake, England

GYMNASTICS

The University of Nebraska won its fifth consecutive NCAA gymnastics championship, compiling 287.80 points, at State College, Pa., on April 7–9. UCLA's Peter Vidmar was named all-around champion for the second straight year. Nebraska's Scott Johnson won, or shared, the title for parallel bars, horizontal bar, and floor exercise. UCLA was second in team competition. Penn State was third.

The third NCAA women's national championships were held at Salt Lake City, Utah, on April 8–9. Utah took team honors for the third consecutive year, with team member Megan McCunniff named all-around gymnast. Arizona State University was second in team competition. California State at Fullerton was third. Elaine Alfano of Utah won the title in the vault. Jeri Cameron of Arizona State won the gold medal for the uneven bars, while teammate Kim Neal captured first place in floor exercise.

At the National Sports Festival, at Colorado Springs, Colo., on June 24–July 3, Scott Johnson of Colorado Springs tied his 1982 meet record of seven medals, this time winning five golds, a silver, and a bronze. In women's competition, Kelly Garrison of South Altus, Okla., won six medals.

At the U.S. championships, in Chicago, Ill., in June, Dianne Durham of Gary, Ind., was named all-around gymnast, the first black to win a major women's national title. Mitch Gaylord of UCLA won the men's all-around title.

Wide World

Mary Lou Retton of Fairmont, Va., vaults her way to a gold medal on Aug. 28 in the women's individual finals of the McDonald's 1983 International Gymnastics Championships at Los Angeles, Calif. Retton also won gold medals for the uneven parallel bars and floor exercise, as well as a bronze medal for the balance beam.

NATIONAL COLLEGIATE ATHLETIC ASSOCIATION GYMNASTIC CHAMPIONS

NCAA TEAM CHAMPIONS

1976 Penn State	**1978** Oklahoma	**1980-83** Nebraska
1977 Indiana St.—Oklahoma	**1979** Nebraska	

ALL-TIME INDIVIDUAL CHAMPIONS (ALL-AROUND)

1976 Peter Kormann, S. Conn.	**1978** Bart Conner, Oklahoma	**1980–81** Jim Hartung, Nebraska
1977 Kurt Thomas, Indiana St.	**1979** Kurt Thomas, Indiana St.	**1982–83** Peter Vidmar, UCLA

FLOOR EXERCISE

1979 Mike Wilson, Oklahoma	**1981** James Yuhashi, Oregon	**1983** David Branch, Arizona State
Bart Conner, Oklahoma	**1982** Steve Elliott, Nebraska	Don Hinton, Arizona State
1980 Steve Elliott, Nebraska	Jim Mikus, Nebraska	Scott Johnson, Nebraska

POMMEL HORSE (SIDE HORSE)

1977 Chuck Walter, New Mexico	**1980** David Stoldt, Illinois	**1982** Peter Vidmar, UCLA
1978–79 Mike Burke, N. Illinois	**1981** Steve Jennings, New Mexico	**1983** Doug Kieso, Northern Illinois

STILL RINGS

1976 Doug Wood, Iowa State	**1979** Kirk Mango, N. Illinois	**1982** Jim Hartung, Nebraska
1977 Doug Wood, Iowa State	**1980–81** Jim Hartung, Nebraska	Alex Schwartz, UCLA
1978 Scott McEldowney, Oregon		**1983** Alex Schwartz, UCLA

VAULTING (LONG HORSE)

1977 Steve Wejmar, Washington	**1979** Leslie Moore, Oklahoma	**1982** Randall Wickstrom, California
1978 Ron Galimore, Louisiana St.	**1980–81** Ron Galimore, Iowa State	**1983** Chris Riegel, Nebraska

PARALLEL BARS

1976 Gene Whelan, Penn State	**1978** John Corritore, Michigan	**1980–82** Philip Cahoy, Nebraska
1977 Kurt Thomas, Indiana State	**1979** Kurt Thomas, Indiana St.	**1983** Scott Johnson, Nebraska

HORIZONTAL BAR

1977 John Hart, UCLA	**1979** Kurt Thomas, Indiana St.	**1982** Bill Paul, California
1978 Mel Cooley, Washington	**1980–81** Philip Cahoy, Nebraska	**1983** Scott Johnson, Nebraska

HOCKEY

Wide World

New York Islanders goalie Bill Smith makes a reflex save during the third game of the NHL Stanley Cup series on May 14. The Islanders won the game 5–1 and went on to win the series and the Stanley Cup for the fourth consecutive year. Smith was voted the Conn Smyth trophy as most valuable player in the final series.

The New York Islanders captured their fourth consecutive NHL Stanley Cup at Uniondale, N.Y., by sweeping the Edmonton Oilers, 4–2, on May 17, 1983. The Islanders swept the championship series 4 games to 0.

In the final game, the Islanders built up a 3–0 lead by the end of the first period on the strength of three goals by Bryan Trottier, John Tonelli, and Mike Bossy, in a 1-minute, 37-second stretch. The Oilers responded in the second period with goals by Hari Kurri and Mark Messier. New York's Ken Morrow clinched the title by scoring a goal with 1:09 left to play.

Islanders' goaltender Billy Smith was voted the most valuable player of the Stanley Cup series, receiving the Conn Smythe trophy. He finished the playoffs with a 2.68 goals-against average.

The Islanders finished the playoff with a 15–5 record. In the Patrick division semifinals, they trounced Washington 3 games to 1. Then they defeated their arch rivals, the New York Rangers, 4 games to 2, for the division title. The Islanders next beat the Boston Bruins 4 games to 2 in the Prince of Wales Conference title game.

On their way to the Stanley Cup final, the Oilers humiliated Winnipeg 3 games to 0 in the Smythe division semifinal. Next, they defeated Calgary 4 games to 1 in the division final. Edmonton then beat the Chicago Black Hawks 4 games to 0 to win the Clarence Campbell Conference title.

At the end of the regular season, Edmonton's Wayne Gretzky won the Art Ross Trophy as leading scorer for the third straight year. In the 1982–83 season, Gretzky scored 71 goals and had 125 assists.

In college action, the University of Wisconsin outskated Harvard, 6–2, to win the National Collegiate Hockey Championship at Grand Forks, N.D., on March 27. It was the Badgers' fourth NCAA title. Wisconsin goalie Marc Behrend was voted the most outstanding player of the tournament.

NATIONAL COLLEGIATE ATHLETIC ASSOCIATION HOCKEY CHAMPIONSHIPS

1962	Michigan Tech over Clarkson, 7–1	1973	Wisconsin over Denver, 4–2
1963	North Dakota over Denver, 6–5	1974	Minnesota over Michigan Tech, 4–2
1964	Michigan over Denver, 6–3	1975	Michigan Tech over Minnesota, 6–1
1965	Michigan Tech over Boston College, 8–2	1976	Minnesota over Michigan Tech, 6–4
1966	Michigan State over Clarkson, 6–1	1977	Wisconsin over Michigan, 6–5
1967	Cornell over Boston U., 4–1	1978	Boston U. over Boston College, 5–3
1968	Denver over North Dakota, 4–0	1979	Minnesota over North Dakota, 4–3
1969	Denver over Cornell, 4–3	1980	North Dakota over Northern Michigan, 5–2
1970	Cornell over Clarkson, 6–4	1981	Wisconsin over Minnesota, 6–3
1971	Boston U. over Minnesota, 4–2	1982	North Dakota over Wisconsin, 5–2
1972	Boston U. over Cornell, 4–0	1983	Wisconsin over Harvard, 6–2

NATIONAL HOCKEY LEAGUE FINAL STANDINGS: 1982–1983

TEAM	WON	LOST	TIED	GOALS	POINTS
PRINCE OF WALES CONFERENCE					
Charles F. Adams Division					
Boston	50	20	10	327	110
Montreal	42	24	14	350	98
Buffalo	38	29	13	318	89
Quebec	34	34	12	343	80
Hartford	19	54	7	261	45
Lester Patrick Division					
Philadelphia	49	23	8	326	106
N.Y. Islanders	42	26	12	302	96
Washington	39	25	16	306	94
N.Y. Rangers	35	35	10	306	80
New Jersey	17	49	14	230	48
Pittsburgh	18	53	9	257	45

TEAM	WON	LOST	TIED	GOALS	POINTS
CLARENCE CAMPBELL CONFERENCE					
James Norris Division					
Chicago	47	23	10	338	104
Minnesota	40	24	16	321	96
Toronto	28	40	12	293	68
St. Louis	25	40	15	285	65
Detroit	21	44	15	263	57
Conn Smythe Division					
Edmonton	47	21	12	424	106
Calgary	32	34	14	321	78
Vancouver	30	35	15	303	75
Winnipeg	33	39	8	311	74
Los Angeles	27	41	12	308	66

NHL STANLEY CUP PLAYOFFS: 1983

Championship Series:
New York Islanders won finals and Stanley Cup, defeating Edmonton Oilers, 4 games to 0.

Conference Finals:
New York Islanders defeated Boston Bruins, 4 games to 2.
Edmonton Oilers defeated Chicago Black Hawks, 4 games to 0.

Division Finals:
New York Islanders defeated New York Rangers, 4 games to 2.
Edmonton Oilers defeated Calgary Flames, 4 games to 1.
Boston Bruins defeated Buffalo Sabres, 4 games to 3.
Chicago Black Hawks defeated Minnesota North Stars, 4 games to 1.

STANLEY CUP NHL CHAMPIONS

1893–94	Montreal A.A.A.	1912–13	Quebec Bulldogs	1932	Toronto Maple Leafs	1952	Detroit Red Wings
1895	Montreal Victorias	1914	Toronto Blueshirts	1933	New York Rangers	1953	Montreal Canadiens
1896	Winnipeg Victorias, Montreal Victorias	1915	Vancouver Mil.	1934	Chi. Black Hawks	1954–55	Detroit Red Wings
		1916	Montreal Canadiens	1935	Montreal Maroons	1956–60	Montreal Canadiens
1897–98	Montreal Victorias	1917	Seattle Met.	1936–37	Detroit Red Wings	1961	Chi. Black Hawks
1899	Montreal Shamrocks	1918	Toronto Arenas	1938	Chi. Black Hawks	1962–64	Toronto Maple Leafs
1900	Montreal Shamrocks	1919	No decision	1939	Boston Bruins	1965–66	Montreal Canadiens
1901	Winnipeg Victorias	1920–21	Ottawa Senators	1940	New York Rangers	1967	Toronto Maple Leafs
1902	Montreal A.A.A.	1922	Toronto St. Pats	1941	Boston Bruins	1968–69	Montreal Canadiens
1903–05	Ottawa Silver Seven	1923	Ottawa Senators	1942	Toronto Maple Leafs	1970	Boston Bruins
1906	Montreal Wanderers	1924	Montreal Canadiens	1943	Detroit Red Wings	1971	Montreal Canadiens
1907	Kenora Thistles, Mont. Wanderers	1925	Victoria Cougars	1944	Montreal Canadiens	1972	Boston Bruins
		1926	Montreal Maroons	1945	Toronto Maple Leafs	1973	Montreal Canadiens
1908	Montreal Wanderers	1927	Ottawa Senators	1946	Montreal Canadiens	1974–75	Philadelphia Flyers
1909	Ottawa Senators	1928	New York Rangers	1947–49	Toronto Maple Leafs	1976–79	Montreal Canadiens
1910	Montreal Wanderers	1929	Boston Bruins	1950	Detroit Red Wings	1980–83	New York Islanders
1911	Ottawa Senators	1930–31	Montreal Canadiens	1951	Toronto Maple Leafs		

NATIONAL HOCKEY LEAGUE LEADING SCORERS: 1982–1983

PLAYER	TEAM	GAMES	GOALS	ASSISTS	POINTS
Wayne Gretzky	Edmonton	80	71	125	196
Peter Stastny	Quebec	75	47	77	124
Denis Savard	Chicago	78	35	85	120
Bike Bossy	N.Y. Islanders	79	60	58	118
Marcel Dionne	Los Angeles	80	56	51	107
Barry Pederson	Boston	77	46	61	107
Mark Messier	Edmonton	77	48	58	106
Michel Goulet	Quebec	80	57	48	105
Glenn Anderson	Edmonton	72	48	56	104
Kent Nilsson	Calgary	80	46	58	104
Jari Kurri	Edmonton	80	45	59	104
Lanny McDonald	Calgary	80	66	32	98
Rick Middleton	Boston	80	49	47	96
Paul Coffey	Edmonton	80	29	67	96
Anton Stastny	Quebec	79	32	60	92
Dale Hawerchuk	Winnipeg	79	40	51	91
Steve Larmer	Chicago	80	43	47	90
Ron Francis	Hartford	79	31	59	90
Bryan Trottier	N.Y. Islanders	80	34	55	89
Stan Smyl	Vancouver	74	38	50	88
Al Secord	Chicago	80	54	32	86
Thomas Gradin	Vancouver	80	32	54	86

NATIONAL HOCKEY LEAGUE TROPHY WINNERS

ART ROSS TROPHY
(Leading scorer in regular season)

YEAR	PLAYER	GAMES PLAYED	GOALS	ASSISTS	POINTS
1953–54	Gordie Howe, Detroit	70	33	48	81
1954–55	Bernie Geoffrion, Montreal	70	38	37	75
1955–56	Jean Beliveau, Montreal	70	47	41	88
1956–57	Gordie Howe, Detroit	70	44	45	89
1957–58	Dickie Moore, Montreal	70	36	48	84
1958–59	Dickie Moore, Montreal	70	41	55	96
1959–60	Bobby Hull, Chicago	70	39	42	81
1960–61	Bernie Geoffrion, Montreal	64	50	45	95
1961–62	Bobby Hull, Chicago	70	50	34	84
1962–63	Gordie Howe, Detroit	70	38	48	86
1963–64	Stan Mikita, Chicago	70	39	50	89
1964–65	Stan Mikita, Chicago	70	28	59	87
1965–66	Bobby Hull, Chicago	65	54	43	97
1966–67	Stan Mikita, Chicago	70	35	62	97
1967–68	Stan Mikita, Chicago	72	40	47	87
1968–69	Phil Esposito, Boston	74	49	77	126
1969–70	Bobby Orr, Boston	76	33	87	120
1970–71	Phil Esposito, Boston	78	76	76	152
1971–72	Phil Esposito, Boston	76	66	67	133
1972–73	Phil Esposito, Boston	78	55	75	130
1973–74	Phil Esposito, Boston	78	68	77	145
1974–75	Bobby Orr, Boston	80	46	89	135
1975–76	Guy Lafleur, Montreal	80	56	69	125
1976–77	Guy Lafleur, Montreal	80	56	80	136
1977–78	Guy Lafleur, Montreal	78	60	72	132
1978–79	Bryan Trottier, N.Y. Islanders	76	47	87	134
1979–80	Marcel Dionne, L.A. Kings	80	53	84	137
1980–81	Wayne Gretzky, Edmonton	80	55	109	164
1981–82	Wayne Gretzky, Edmonton	80	92	120	212
1982–83	Wayne Gretzky, Edmonton	80	71	125	196

HART MEMORIAL TROPHY (Most valuable player)

1945–46	Max Bentley, Chicago
1946–47	Maurice Richard, Montreal
1947–48	Herbert O'Connor, New York
1948–49	Sid Abel, Detroit
1949–50	Chuck Rayner, New York
1950–51	Milt Schmidt, Boston
1951–53	Gordie Howe, Detroit
1953–54	Al Rollins, Chicago
1954–55	Ted Kennedy, Detroit
1955–56	Jean Beliveau, Montreal
1956–58	Gordie Howe, Detroit
1958–59	Andy Bathgate, New York
1959–60	Gordie Howe, Detroit
1960–61	Bernie Geoffrion, Montreal
1961–62	Jacques Plante, Montreal
1962–63	Gordie Howe, Detroit
1963–64	Jean Beliveau, Montreal
1964–66	Bobby Hull, Chicago
1966–68	Stan Mikita, Chicago
1968–69	Phil Esposito, Boston
1969–72	Bobby Orr, Boston
1972–73	Bobby Clarke, Philadelphia
1973–74	Phil Esposito, Boston
1974–76	Bobby Clarke, Philadelphia
1976–78	Guy Lafleur, Montreal
1978–79	Bryan Trottier, N.Y. Islanders
1979–83	Wayne Gretzky, Edmonton

VEZINA TROPHY (Best goalkeeper record)

1964–65	Terry Sawchuk and Johnny Bower, Toronto
1965–66	Lorne Worsley and Charlie Hodge, Montreal
1966–67	Denis De Jordy and Glenn Hall, Chicago
1967–68	L. Worsley, R. Vachon, Mont.
1968–69	Jacques Plante and Glenn Hall, St. Louis
1969–70	Tony Esposito, Chicago
1970–71	Ed Giacomin and
1970–71	Gilles Villemure, New York
1971–72	Tony Esposito and Gary Smith, Chicago
1972–73	Ken Dryden, Montreal
1973–74	Tony Esposito, Chicago, and Bernie Parent, Philadelphia
1974–75	Bernie Parent, Philadelphia
1975–76	Ken Dryden, Montreal
1976–79	Ken Dryden, Montreal, and Michel Larocque, Montreal
1979–80	Bob Suave and Don Edwards, Buffalo
1980–81	Richard Sevigny, Denis Herron, and Michel Larocque, Montreal
1981–82	Bill Smith, N.Y. Islanders
1982–83	Pete Peeters, Boston

CALDER MEMORIAL TROPHY (Rookie of the year)

1953–54	Camille Henry, New York
1954–55	Ed Litzenberger, Chicago
1955–56	Glenn Hall, Detroit
1956–57	Larry Regan, Boston
1957–58	Frank Mahovlich, Toronto
1958–59	Ralph Backstrom, Montreal
1959–60	Bill Hay, Chicago
1960–61	Dave Keon, Toronto
1961–62	Bobby Rousseau, Montreal
1962–63	Kent Douglas, Toronto
1963–64	Jacques Laperriere, Montreal
1964–65	Roger Crozier, Detroit
1965–66	Brit Selby, Toronto
1966–67	Bobby Orr, Boston
1967–68	Derek Sanderson, Boston
1968–69	Danny Grant, Minnesota
1969–70	Tony Esposito, Chicago
1970–71	Gil Perreault, Buffalo
1971–72	Ken Dryden, Montreal
1972–73	Steve Vickers, New York
1973–74	Denis Potvin, N.Y. Islanders
1974–75	Eric Vail, Atlanta
1975–76	Bryan Trottier, N.Y. Islanders
1976–77	Willi Plett, Atlanta
1977–78	Mike Bossy, N.Y. Islanders
1978–79	Bobby Smith, Minnesota
1979–80	Ray Bourque, Boston
1980–81	Peter Statsny, Quebec
1981–82	Dale Hawerchuk, Chicago
1982–83	Steve Larmer, Chicago

LADY BYNG MEMORIAL TROPHY (For skillful and sportsmanlike play)

1954–55	Sid Smith, Toronto
1955–56	Earl Reibel, Detroit
1956–57	Andy Hebenton, New York
1957–58	Camille Henry, New York
1958–59	Alex Delvecchio, Detroit
1959–60	Don McKenney, Boston
1960–61	Leonard Kelly, Toronto
1961–63	Dave Keon, Toronto
1963–64	Ken Wharram, Chicago
1964–65	Bobby Hull, Chicago
1965–66	Alex Delvecchio, Detroit
1966–68	Stan Mikita, Chicago
1968–69	Alex Delvecchio, Detroit
1969–70	Phil Goyette, St. Louis
1970–71	Johnny Bucyk, Boston
1971–72	Jean Ratelle, New York
1972–73	Gil Perreault, Buffalo
1973–74	Johnny Bucyk, Boston
1974–75	Marcel Dionne, Detroit
1975–76	Jean Ratelle, Boston
1976–77	Marcel Dionne, Los Angeles
1977–78	Butch Goring, Los Angeles
1978–79	Bob MacMillan, Atlanta
1979–80	Wayne Gretzky, Edmonton
1980–81	Rick Kehoe, Pittsburgh
1981–82	Rick Middleton, Boston
1982–83	Mike Bossy, N.Y. Islanders

JAMES NORRIS MEMORIAL TROPHY (Outstanding defenseman)

1959–62	Doug Harvey, Mont.-N.Y.
1962–65	Pierre Pilote, Chicago
1965–66	J. Laperriere, Montreal
1966–67	Harry Howell, New York
1967–75	Bobby Orr, Boston
1975–76	Denis Potvin, N.Y. Islanders
1976–77	Larry Robinson, Montreal
1977–79	Denis Potvin, N.Y. Islanders
1979–80	Larry Robinson, Montreal
1980–81	Randy Carlyle, Pittsburgh
1981–82	Doug Wilson, Chicago
1982–83	Rod Langway, Washington

CONN SMYTHE TROPHY (Most valuable player in the Stanley Cup playoffs)

1970–71	Ken Dryden, Montreal
1971–72	Bobby Orr, Boston
1972–73	Yvan Cournoyer, Montreal
1973–75	Bernie Parent, Philadelphia
1975–76	Reggie Leach, Philadelphia
1976–77	Guy Lafleur, Montreal
1977–78	Larry Robinson, Montreal
1978–79	Bob Gainey, Montreal
1979–80	Bryan Trottier, N.Y. Islanders
1980–81	Butch Goring, N.Y. Islanders
1981–82	Mike Bossy, N.Y. Islanders
1982–83	Billy Smith, N.Y. Islanders

NATIONAL HOCKEY LEAGUE PRINCE OF WALES TROPHY WINNERS

1925	Montreal Canadiens	1942	New York Rangers	1961	Montreal Canadiens	1971–72	Boston Bruins
1926	Montreal Maroons	1943	Detroit Red Wings	1962	Montreal Canadiens	1973	Montreal Canadiens
1927	Ottawa Senators	1944–47	Montreal Canadiens	1963	Toronto Maple Leafs	1974	Boston Bruins
1928–31	Boston Bruins	1948	Toronto Maple Leafs	1964	Montreal Canadiens	1975	Buffalo Sabres
1932	New York Rangers	1949–55	Detroit Red Wings	1965	Detroit Red Wings	1976–79	Montreal Canadiens
1933	Boston Bruins	1956	Montreal Canadiens	1966	Montreal Canadiens	1980	Buffalo Sabres
1934	Detroit Red Wings	1957	Detroit Red Wings	1967	Chicago Black Hawks	1981	Montreal Canadiens
1935	Boston Bruins	1958	Montreal Canadiens	1968	Montreal Canadiens	1982	New York Islanders
1936–37	Detroit Red Wings	1959	Montreal Canadiens	1969	Montreal Canadiens	1983	New York Islanders
1938–41	Boston Bruins	1960	Montreal Canadiens	1970	Chicago Black Hawks		

NATIONAL HOCKEY LEAGUE CLARENCE S. CAMPBELL BOWL WINNERS

1968	Philadelphia Flyers	1974–77	Philadelphia Flyers	1981	New York Islanders
1969–70	St. Louis Blues	1978–79	New York Islanders	1982–83	Edmonton Oilers
1971–73	Chicago Black Hawks	1980	Philadelphia Flyers		

NATIONAL HOCKEY LEAGUE ALL-STAR GAMES

When All-Star games began to be played in 1947, the All-Star team played the defending champion team of the previous season. Later, East Division All-Stars played West Division All-Stars in midseason. In the 1978–79 season, a team of All-Stars from the NHL opposed the best players of the Soviet Union in a three-game series. The first six players of the NHL team were selected in continent-wide voting among fans. The coach and manager chose the other players on the squad.

1948	All-Stars 3, Toronto 1	1963	All-Stars 3, Toronto 3	1977	Prince of Wales Conf. 4, C.S. Campbell Conf. 3
1949	All-Stars 3, Toronto 1	1964	All-Stars 3, Toronto 2		
1950	Detroit 7, All-Stars 1	1965	All-Stars 5, Montreal 2	1978	Prince of Wales Conf. 3, C.S. Campbell Conf. 2
1951	1st Team 2, 2d Team 2	*1967	Montreal 3, All-Stars 0		
1952	1st Team 1, 2d Team 1	1968	Toronto 4, All-Stars 3	1979	Soviet National Stars 2, NHL All-Stars 1
1953	All-Stars 3, Montreal 1	1969	East 3, West 3		
1954	All-Stars 2, Detroit 2	1970	East 4, West 1	1980	Prince of Wales Conf. 6, C.S. Campbell Conf. 3
1955	Detroit 3, All-Stars 1	1971	West 2, East 1		
1956	All-Stars 1, Montreal 1	1972	East 3, West 2	1981	C.S. Campbell Conf. 4, Prince of Wales Conf. 1
1957	All-Stars 5, Montreal 3	1973	East 5, West 4		
1958	Montreal 6, All-Stars 3	1974	West 6, East 4	1982	Prince of Wales Conf. 4, C.S. Campbell Conf. 2
1959	Montreal 6, All-Stars 1	1975	Prince of Wales Conf. 7, C.S. Campbell Conf. 1		
1960	All-Stars 2, Montreal 1			1983	C.S. Campbell Conf. 9, Prince of Wales Conf. 3
1961	All-Stars 3, Chicago 1	1976	Prince of Wales Conf. 7, C.S. Campbell Conf. 5		
1962	Toronto 4, All-Stars 1				

* Game shifted to midseason.

SELECTED NATIONAL HOCKEY LEAGUE RECORDS

TEAM RECORDS	
Most points, one season	132—Montreal Canadiens, 1976–77, won 60, lost 8, tied 12
Most wins, one season	60—Montreal Canadiens, 1976–77
Longest winning record	15 games—N.Y. Islanders, Jan. 21–Feb. 20, 1982
Most goals, one season	424—Edmonton Oilers, 1982–83
Most goals, both teams, one game	21—Jan. 10, 1920: Montreal Canadiens defeated Toronto St. Patricks, 14–7
Most penalty minutes, one team, one game	211—Minnesota North Stars, Feb. 26, 1981, against Boston.
INDIVIDUAL RECORDS	
Most seasons	26—Gordie Howe, Detroit Red Wings, 1946–47 through 1970–71; Hartford Whalers, 1979–80
Most games	1,767—Gordie Howe, Detroit Red Wings, Hartford Whalers, 1946–71, 1979–80
Most goals	801—Gordie Howe, Detroit Red Wings, Hartford Whalers, 1946–71, 1979–80
Most assists	1,049—Gordie Howe, Detroit Red Wings, Hartford Whalers, 1946–71, 1979–80
Highest goals-per-game average, career (among players with 200 or more goals)	.843—Wayne Gretzky, Edmonton Oilers, 1979–80—1982–83
Most 50-or-more goal seasons	6—Guy Lafleur, Montreal Canadiens in 11 seasons Mike Bossy, N.Y. Islanders, in 6 seasons.
Most goals, one season	92—Wayne Gretzky, Edmonton Oilers, 1981–82
Most penalty minutes, one season	472—Dave Schultz, Philadelphia Flyers, 1974–75
Longest consecutive goal-scoring streak	16 games—Harry (Punch) Broadbent, Ottawa Senators, 1921–22
Most goals, one game	7—Joe Malone, Quebec Bulldogs, Jan. 31, 1920, against Toronto St. Patricks
Most points, one game	10—Darryl Sittler, Toronto Maple Leafs, Feb. 7, 1976, against Boston; 6 goals, 4 assists

HORSE RACING

Wide World

Deputed Testamony, *right*, comes up on rail to win 108th Preakness Stakes at Pimlico Race Track on May 21.

Sunny's Halo, a 3-year-old colt trained in Arkansas by David Cross, won the 109th Kentucky Derby at Churchill Downs, Ky., by two lengths on May 7. Jockey Eddie Delahoussaye rode Sunny's Halo across the finish line in 2:02$^1/_5$.

The Preakness, run at Pimlico Race Track in Baltimore, Md., on May 21, was won by Deputed Testamony, with Donald A. Miller Jr. aboard, beating Desert Wine by nearly three lengths. The sloppy track seemed to defeat Derby winner Sunny's Halo, who finished sixth. Deputed Testamony's winning time was 1:55$^2/_5$.

Veteran jockey Laffit Pincay Jr. guided Caveat to a 3$^1/_2$-length victory over Slew o' Gold in the Belmont Stakes, in Elmont, N.Y., on June 11. The Belmont stewards posted an inquiry sign after the race and studied the films to see if Caveat had interfered with Au Point, the early leader, when Caveat brushed by him on the rail. The stewards let the results stand.

Ralph Hanover, driven by Ron Waples, won the Little Brown Jug pacing classic at Delaware, Ohio, on Sept. 22, becoming only the seventh horse in history to capture pacing's triple crown. Earlier the colt had won the Messenger Stakes and the Cane Pace, the first two legs in the triple crown.

Duenna, a filly driven by Stanley Dancer, won the Hambletonian, at The Meadowlands, in East Rutherford, N.J., on Aug. 6. Duenna was the first filly to win the race since 1966.

Tolomeo, an English horse with Irish jockey Pat Eddery aboard, won the Arlington Million race at Arlington Heights, Ill., on Aug. 28, beating John Henry by a neck to capture thoroughbred racing's richest race.

THOROUGHBRED HORSE OF THE YEAR (ECLIPSE AWARD)

YEAR	HORSE	YEAR	HORSE	YEAR	HORSE	YEAR	HORSE
1936	Granville	1949	Capot	1960	Kelso	1971	Ack Ack
1937	War Admiral	1950	Hill Prince	1961	Kelso	1972	Secretariat
1938	Seabiscuit	1951	Counterpoint	1962	Kelso	1973	Secretariat
1939–40	Challedon	1952	Native Dancer	1963	Kelso	1974	Forego
1941–42	Whirlaway	1953	Tom Fool	1964	Kelso	1975	Forego
1943	Count Fleet	1954	Native Dancer	1965	Moccasin	1976	Forego
1944	Twilight Tear	1955	Nashua	1966	Buckpasser	1977	Seattle Slew
1945	Busher	1956	Swaps	1967	Damascus	1978–79	Affirmed
1946	Assault	1957	Dedicate	1968	Dr. Fager	1980	Spectacular Bid
1947	Armed	1958	Round Table	1969	Arts and Letters	1981	John Henry
1948	Citation	1959	Sword Dancer	1970	Personality	1982	Conquistador Cielo

LEADING MONEY-WINNING RACEHORSES

Source: Thoroughbred Racing Association of North America

YEAR	HORSE	AGE (in years)	STARTS	WINS	SECONDS	THIRDS	AMOUNT WON
1950	Noor	5	12	7	4	1	$346,940
1951	Counterpoint	3	15	7	2	1	250,525
1952	Crafty Admiral	4	16	9	4	1	277,225
1953	Native Dancer	3	10	9	1	0	513,425
1954	Determine	3	15	10	3	2	328,700
1955	Nashua	3	12	10	1	1	752,550
1956	Needles	3	8	4	2	0	440,850
1957	Round Table	3	22	15	1	3	600,383
1958	Round Table	4	20	14	4	0	662,780
1959	Sword Dancer	3	13	8	4	0	537,004
1960	Bally Ache	3	15	10	3	1	455,045
1961	Carry Back	3	16	9	1	3	565,349
1962	Never Bend	2	10	7	1	2	402,969
1963	Candy Spots	3	12	7	2	1	604,481
1964	Gun Bow	4	16	8	4	2	580,100
1965	Buckpasser	2	11	9	1	0	568,096
1966	Buckpasser	3	14	13	1	0	669,078

YEAR	HORSE	AGE (in years)	STARTS	WINS	SECONDS	THIRDS	AMOUNT WON
1967	Damascus	3	16	12	3	1	$817,944
1968	Forward Pass	3	13	7	2	0	546,674
1969	Arts and Letters	3	14	8	5	1	555,604
1970	Personality	3	18	8	2	1	444,049
1971	Riva Ridge	2	9	7	0	0	503,263
1972	Droll Roll	4	8	4	1	2	471,633
1973	Secretariat	3	21	16	3	1	860,404
1974	Chris Evert	3	7	4	1	2	551,063
1975	Foolish Pleasure	3	11	5	4	1	716,278
1976	Forego	6	8	6	1	1	491,701
1977	Seattle Slew	3	7	6	0	0	641,370
1978	Affirmed	3	11	8	2	0	901,541
1979	Spectacular Bid	3	12	10	1	1	1,279,333
1980	Temperence Hill	3	17	8	3	1	1,130,452
1981	John Henry	6	10	8	0	0	1,798,030
1982	Perrault	5	8	4	1	2	1,197,400
1983	All Along	4	7	4	1	1	2,138,963

THOROUGHBRED HORSE RACING'S TRIPLE CROWN

The Triple Crown of Thoroughbred horse racing in the United States consists of winning three races for 3-year-olds: the Kentucky Derby, the Preakness Stakes, and the Belmont Stakes.

Only 11 horses have won the Triple Crown: Sir Barton in 1919, Gallant Fox in 1930, Omaha in 1935, War Admiral in 1937, Whirlaway in 1941, Count Fleet in 1943, Assault in 1946, Citation in 1948, Secretariat in 1973, Seattle Slew in 1977, and Affirmed in 1978.

KENTUCKY DERBY

The Kentucky Derby is the oldest continually run horse race in the U.S. The $1\frac{1}{4}$-mile race for 3-year-old horses is run annually at Churchill Downs in Louisville, Ky., on the first Saturday in May. From 1875 through 1895 the race was $1\frac{1}{2}$ miles. Two jockeys have won five times: Eddie Arcaro in 1938, 1941, 1945, 1948, and 1952; and Bill Hartack in 1957, 1960, 1962, 1964, and 1969.

YEAR	WINNER	PURSE	JOCKEY	TIME
1875	Aristides	$2,850	Oliver Lewis	2:37 ¾
1876	Vagrant	2,950	Bobby Swim	2:38 ¼
1877	Baden Baden	3,300	Billy Walker	2:38
1878	Day Star	4,050	J. Carter	2:37 ¼
1879	Lord Murphy	3,550	C. Shaver	2:37
1880	Fonso	3,800	George Lewis	2:37 ½
1881	Hindoo	4,410	Jimmy McLaughlin	2:40
1882	Apollo	4,560	Babe Hurd	2:40 ¼
1883	Leonatus	3,760	Billy Donohue	2:43
1884	Buchanan	3,990	Isaac Murphy	2:40 ¼
1885	Joe Cotton	4,630	Erskine Henderson	2:37 ¼
1886	Ben Ali	4,890	P. Duffy	2:36 ½
1887	Montrose	4,200	Isaac Lewis	2:39 ¼
1888	Macbeth II	4,740	G. Covington	2:38 ¼
1889	Spokane	4,970	Thomas Kiley	2:34 ½
1890	Riley	5,460	Isaac Murphy	2:45
1891	Kingman	4,680	Isaac Murphy	2:52 ½
1892	Azra	4,230	Alonzo Clayton	2:41 ½
1893	Lookout	4,090	E. Kunze	2:39 ¼
1894	Chant	4,020	Frank Goodale	2:41
1895	Halma	2,970	James Perkins	2:37 ½
1896	Ben Brush	4,850	Willie Simms	2:07 ¾
1897	Typhoon II	4,850	Buttons Garner	2:12 ½
1898	Plaudit	4,850	Willie Simms	2:09
1899	Manuel	4,850	Fred Taral	2:12
1900	Lt. Gibson	4,850	Jimmy Boland	2:06 ¼
1901	His Eminence	4,850	Jimmy Winkfield	2:07 ¾
1902	Alan-a-Dale	4,850	Jimmy Winkfield	2:08 ¾
1903	Judge Himes	4,850	Hal Booker	2:09
1904	Elwood	4,850	Frankie Prior	2:08 ½
1905	Agile	4,850	Jack Martin	2:10 ¾
1906	Sir Huron	4,850	Roscoe Troxler	2:08 ⅘
1907	Pink Star	4,850	Andy Minder	2:12 ⅗
1908	Stone Street	4,850	Arthur Pickens	2:15 ⅕
1909	Wintergreen	4,850	Vince Powers	2:08 ⅕
1910	Donau	4,850	Robert Herbert	2:06 ⅖
1911	Meridian	$4,850	George Archibald	2:05
1912	Worth	4,850	Carroll Shilling	2:09 ⅖
1913	Donerail	5,475	Roscoe Goose	2:04 ⅘
1914	Old Rosebud	9,125	John McCabe	2:03 ⅖
1915	Regret	11,450	Joe Notter	2:05 ⅖
1916	George Smith	9,750	Johnny Loftus	2:04
1917	Omar Khayyam	16,600	Charles Borel	2:04 ⅗
1918	Exterminator	14,700	Willie Knap	2:10 ⅘
1919	Sir Barton	20,825	Johnny Loftus	2:09 ⅘
1920	Paul Jones	30,375	Ted Rice	2:09
1921	Behave Yourself	38,450	Charles Thompson	2:04 ⅕
1922	Morvich	46,775	Albert Johnson	2:04 ⅗
1923	Zev	53,600	Earl Sande	2:05 ⅖
1924	Black Gold	52,775	John D. Mooney	2:05 ⅕
1925	Flying Ebony	52,950	Earl Sande	2:07 ⅗
1926	Bubbling Over	50,075	Albert Johnson	2:03 ⅘
1927	Whiskey	51,000	Linus McAtee	2:06
1928	Reigh Count	55,375	Chick Lang	2:10 ⅖
1929	Clyde Van Dusen	53,950	Linus McAtee	2:10 ⅘
1930	Gallant Fox	50,725	Earl Sande	2:07 ⅗
1931	Twenty Grand	48,725	Charles Kurtsinger	2:01 ⅘
1932	Burgoo King	52,350	Eugene James	2:05 ⅕
1933	Brokers Tip	48,925	Don Meade	2:06 ⅘
1934	Cavalcade	28,175	Mack Garner	2:04
1935	Omaha	39,525	Willie Saunders	2:05
1936	Bold Venture	37,725	Ira Hanford	2:03 ⅗
1937	War Admiral	52,050	Charles Kurtsinger	2:03 ⅕
1938	Lawrin	47,050	Eddie Arcaro	2:04 ⅘
1939	Johnstown	46,350	James Stout	2:03 ⅖
1940	Gallahadion	60,150	Carroll Bierman	2:05
1941	Whirlaway	61,275	Eddie Arcaro	2:01⅖
1942	Shut Out	64,225	Wayne D. Wright	2:04⅖
1943	Count Fleet	60,725	Johnny Longden	2:04
1944	Pensive	64,675	Con McCreary	2:04⅕
1945	Hoop Jr.	64,850	Eddie Arcaro	2:07
1946	Assault	96,400	Warren Mehrtens	2:06⅗

KENTUCKY DERBY *(continued)*

YEAR	WINNER	PURSE	JOCKEY	TIME
1947	Jet Pilot	$92,160	Eric Guerin	2:06 4/5
1948	Citation	83,400	Eddie Arcaro	2:05 2/5
1949	Ponder	91,600	Steve Brooks	2:04 1/5
1950	Middleground	92,650	Willie Boland	2:01 3/5
1951	Count Turf	98,050	Conn McCreary	2:02 3/5
1952	Hill Gail	96,300	Eddie Arcaro	2:01 3/5
1953	Dark Star	90,050	Henry Moreno	2:02
1954	Determine	102,050	Ray York	2:03
1955	Swaps	108,400	Willie Shoemaker	2:01 4/5
1956	Needles	123,450	Dave Erb	2:03 2/5
1957	Iron Liege	109,550	Bill Hartack	2:02 1/5
1958	Tim Tam	116,400	Ismael Valenzuela	2:05
1959	Tomy Lee	119,650	Willie Shoemaker	2:02 1/5
1960	Venetian Way	114,850	Bill Hartack	2:02 2/5
1961	Carry Back	120,500	John Sellers	2:04
1962	Decidedly	119,650	Bill Hartack	2:00 2/5
1963	Chateaugay	108,900	Braulio Baeza	2:01 4/5
1964	Northern Dancer	114,300	Bill Hartack	2:00
1965	Lucky Debonair	112,000	Willie Shoemaker	2:01 1/5
1966	Kauai King	$120,500	Don Brumfield	2:02
1967	Proud Clarion	119,700	Bobby Ussery	2:00 3/5
1968	Dancer's Image	122,600	Ismael Valenzuela	2:02 1/5
1969	Majestic Prince	155,700	Bill Hartack	2:01 4/5
1970	Dust Commander	128,000	Mike Manganello	2:03 2/5
1971	Canonero II	125,000	Gustavo Avila	2:03 1/5
1972	Riva Ridge	140,300	Ron Turcotte	2:01 4/5
1973	Secretariat	155,050	Ron Turcotte	1:59 2/5
1974	Cannonade	274,000	Angel Cordero Jr.	2:04
1975	Foolish Pleasure	209,600	Jacinto Vasquez	2:02
1976	Bold Forbes	165,200	Angel Cordero Jr.	2:01 3/5
1977	Seattle Slew	214,700	Jean Cruguet	2:02 1/5
1978	Affirmed	186,900	Steve Cauthen	2:01 1/5
1979	Spectacular Bid	324,900	Ron Franklin	2:02 2/5
1980	Genuine Risk	339,300	Jacinto Vasquez	2:02
1981	Pleasant Colony	317,200	Jorge Velasquez	2:02
1982	Gato del Sol	428,850	Eddie Delahoussaye	2:02 2/5
1983	Sunny's Halo	426,000	Eddie Delahoussaye	2:02 1/5

PREAKNESS STAKES (at Pimlico, Baltimore, Md., 1 3/16 miles for 3-year-olds)

YEAR	WINNER	PURSE	JOCKEY	TIME
1934	High Quest	$25,175	R. Jones	1:58 1/5
1935	Omaha	25,325	Willie Saunders	1:58 2/5
1936	Bold Venture	27,325	G. Woolf	1:59
1937	War Admiral	45,600	Charles Kurtsinger	1:58 2/5
1938	Dauber	51,875	M. Peters	1:59 4/5
1939	Challedon	53,710	G. Seabo	1:59 4/5
1940	Bimelech	53,230	F.A. Smith	1:58 3/5
1941	Whirlaway	49,365	Eddie Arcaro	1:58 4/5
1942	Alsab	58,175	B. James	1:57
1943	Count Fleet	43,190	Johnny Longden	1:57 2/5
1944	Pensive	60,075	Conn McCreary	1:59 1/5
1945	Polynesian	66,170	Wayne D. Wright	1:58 4/5
1946	Assault	96,620	Warren Mehrtens	2:01 2/5
1947	Faultless	96,005	D. Dodson	1:59
1948	Citation	91,870	Eddie Arcaro	2:02 2/5
1949	Capot	79,985	T. Atkinson	1:56
1950	Hill Prince	56,115	Eddie Arcaro	1:59 1/5
1951	Bold	83,110	Eddie Arcaro	1:56 2/5
1952	Blue Man	86,135	Conn McCreary	1:57 2/5
1953	Native Dancer	65,200	Eric Guerin	1:57 4/5
1954	Hasty Road	91,600	J. Adams	1:57 2/5
1955	Nashua	67,550	Eddie Arcaro	1:54 3/5
1956	Fabius	84,250	Bill Hartack	1:58 2/5
1957	Bold Ruler	62,250	Eddie Arcaro	1:56 1/5
1958	Tim Tam	97,900	Ismael Valenzuela	1:57 1/5
1959	Royal Orbit	$136,200	W. Harmatz	1:57
1960	Bally Ache	121,000	Bobby Ussery	1:57 3/5
1961	Carry Back	126,200	John Sellers	1:57 3/5
1962	Greek Money	135,800	J. L. Rotz	1:56 1/5
1963	Candy Spots	127,500	Willie Shoemaker	1:56 1/5
1964	Northern Dancer	124,200	Bill Hartack	1:56 4/5
1965	Tom Rolfe	128,100	Ron Turcotte	1:56 1/5
1966	Kauai King	129,000	Don Brumfield	1:55 2/5
1967	Damascus	141,500	Willie Shoemaker	1:55 1/5
1968	Forward Pass	142,700	Ismael Valenzuela	1:56 4/5
1969	Majestic Prince	129,500	Bill Hartack	1:55 3/5
1970	Personality	150,000	E. Belmonte	1:56 1/5
1971	Canonero II	137,400	Gustavo Avila	1:54
1972	Bee Bee Bee	135,300	E. Nelson	1:55 3/5
1973	Secretariat	129,900	Ron Turcotte	1:54 2/5
1974	Little Current	156,500	Miguel Rivera	1:54 3/5
1975	Master Derby	158,100	Darrel McHargue	1:56 2/5
1976	Elocutionist	129,700	John Lively	1:55
1977	Seattle Slew	138,600	Jean Cruguet	1:54 2/5
1978	Affirmed	136,200	Steve Cauthen	1:54 2/5
1979	Spectacular Bid	295,300	Ron Franklin	1:54 1/5
1980	Codex	250,600	Angel Cordero Jr.	1:54 1/5
1981	Pleasant Colony	200,800	Jorge Velasquez	1:54 3/5
1982	Aloma's Ruler	209,900	Jack Kaenel	1:55 2/5
1983	Deputed Testamony	253,700	Donald A. Miller Jr.	1:55 2/5

BELMONT STAKES (at Belmont Park, L.I., N.Y., 1 1/2 miles for 3-year-olds)

YEAR	WINNER	PURSE	JOCKEY	TIME
1936	Granville	$29,800	Willie Saunders	2:30 3/5
1937	War Admiral	38,020	Charles Kurtsinger	2:28 3/5
1938	Pasteurized	34,530	James Stout	2:29 2/5
1939	Johnstown	37,020	James Stout	2:29 3/5
1940	Bimelech	35,030	F.A. Smith	2:29 3/5
1941	Whirlaway	39,770	Eddie Arcaro	2:31
1942	Shut Out	44,520	Eddie Arcaro	2:29 1/5
1943	Count Fleet	35,340	Johnny Longden	2:28 1/5
1944	Bounding Home	55,000	G.L. Smith	2:32 1/5
1945	Pavot	52,675	Eddie Arcaro	2:30 1/5
1946	Assault	75,400	Warren Mehrtens	2:30 4/5
1947	Phalanx	78,900	R.Donoso	2:29 2/5
1948	Citation	77,700	Eddie Arcaro	2:28 1/5
1949	Capot	60,900	T. Atkinson	2:30 1/5
1950	Middleground	61,350	Willie Boland	2:28 3/5
1951	Counterpoint	82,000	D. Gorman	2:29
1952	One Count	82,400	Eddie Arcaro	2:30 1/5
1953	Native Dancer	82,500	Eric Guerin	2:28 3/5
1954	High Gun	89,000	Eric Guerin	2:30 4/5
1955	Nashua	83,700	Eddie Arcaro	2:29
1956	Needles	83,600	Dave Erb	2:29 4/5
1957	Gallant Man	77,300	Willie Shoemaker	2:26 3/5
1958	Cavan	73,430	P. Anderson	2:30 1/5
1959	Sword Dancer	93,525	Willie Shoemaker	2:28 2/5
1960	Celtic Ash	$ 96,785	Bill Hartack	2:29 3/5
1961	Sherluck	104,900	Braulio Baeza	2:29 1/5
1962	Jaipur	109,500	Willie Shoemaker	2:28 4/5
1963	Chateaugay	101,700	Braulio Baeza	2:30 1/5
1964	Quadrangle	110,850	Manuel Ycaza	2:28 2/5
1965	Hail to All	104,150	John Sellers	2:28 2/5
1966	Amberoid	117,700	Willie Boland	2:29 3/5
1967	Damascus	104,950	Willie Shoemaker	2:28 4/5
1968	Stage Door Johnny	117,700	H. Gustines	2:27 1/5
1969	Arts and Letters	104,050	Braulio Baeza	2:28 4/5
1970	High Echelon	125,000	J. L. Rotz	2:34
1971	Pass Catcher	125,000	W. Blum	2:30 2/5
1972	Riva Ridge	93,540	Ron Turcotte	2:28
1973	Secretariat	90,120	Ron Turcotte	2:24
1974	Little Current	52,564	Miguel Rivera	2:29 1/5
1975	Avatar	116,160	Willie Shoemaker	2:28 1/5
1976	Bold Forbes	117,000	Angel Cordero Jr.	2:29
1977	Seattle Slew	109,080	Jean Cruguet	2:29 3/5
1978	Affirmed	110,580	Steve Cauthen	2:26 4/5
1979	Coastal	269,000	Ruben Hernandez	2:28 3/5
1980	Temperence Hill	293,700	Eddie Maple	2:29 4/5
1981	Summing	170,580	George Martens	2:29
1982	Conquistador Cielo	159,720	Laffit Pincay Jr.	2:28 1/5
1983	Caveat	215,100	Laffit Pincay Jr.	2:27 4/5

THOROUGHBRED RACING WORLD RECORDS

Source: The American Racing Manual (Daily Racing Form)

DISTANCE	TIME	HORSE	AGE	WEIGHT	TRACK OR PLACE	DATE
1/4 mile	0:20 4/5	Big Racket	4	114	Hipodromo, Mexico City	1945 (Feb. 5)
2 1/2 furlongs	0:26 4/5	Tie Score	5	115	Hipodromo, Mexico City	1946 (Feb. 5)
3/8 mile	0:33 1/2	Atoka	6	105	Butte, Mont.	1906 (Sept. 7)
3 1/2 furlongs	0:38 2/5	Tango King	9	116	Northlands Park, Alta., Canada	1981 (Apr. 10)
1/2 mile	0:44 2/5	Western Romance	3	116	Stampede Park, Alta, Canada	1980 (Apr. 19)
4 1/2 furlongs	0:50 2/5	Kathryn's Doll	2	111	Turf Paradise, Phoenix, Ariz.	1967 (April 9)
5/8 mile	0:55 1/5	Chinook Pass	3	113	Longacres, Wash.	1982 (Sept. 17)
5 1/2 furlongs	1:01 3/5	Zip Pocket	3	129	Turf Paradise, Phoenix, Ariz.	1967 (Nov. 19)
5 3/4 furlongs	1:07 1/5	Last Freeby	4	116	Timonium, Md.	1974 (July 20)
3/4 mile [1]	1:06 1/5	Gelding [2]	3	123	Brighton, England [3]	1929 (Aug. 6)
3/4 mile	1:07 1/5	Grey Papa	6	116	Longacres, Seattle, Wash.	1972 (Sept. 4)
6 1/2 furlongs	1:13 4/5	Best Hitter	4	114	Longacres, Seattle, Wash.	1973 (Aug. 4)
7/8 mile	1:19 2/5	Rich Cream	5	115	Hollywood Park, Inglewood, Calif.	1980 (May 16)
1 mile	1:32 1/5	Dr. Fager	4	134	Arlington Heights, Ill.	1968 (Aug. 24)
1 mile, 40 yards	1:38 2/5	Impecunious	3	126	Salem Depot, N.H.	1973 (Sept. 3)
1 mile, 70 yards [1]	1:37 1/5	Aborigine	6	119	Penn National, Pa.	1978 (Aug. 20)
1 1/16 miles	1:38	Told	4	123	Penn National, Pa.	1980 (Sept. 14)
1 1/8 miles [1]	1:45 2/5	Tentam	4	118	Saratoga Springs, N.Y.	1973 (Aug. 10)
1 1/8 miles	1:45 2/5	Secretariat	3	124	Belmont Park, Elmont, N.Y.	1973 (Sept. 15)
1 3/16 miles	1:51 2/5	Toonerville	N.A.	N.A.	Hialeah, Hialeah, Fla.	1976 (Feb. 7)
1 1/4 miles [1]	1:57 3/5	King Pellinore	4	124	Santa Anita Park, Arcadia, Calif.	1976 (Oct. 10)
1 5/16 miles	2:07	Roberto	3	122	York, England	1972 (Aug. 15)
1 3/8 miles [1]	2:11	Cougar II	6	126	Hollywood Park, Inglewood, Calif.	1972 (April 29)
1 1/2 miles	2:23	John Henry	5	126	Santa Anita, Arcadia, Calif.	1980 (March 16)
1 9/16 miles	2:37 3/5	Lone Wolf	5	115	Keeneland, Lexington, Ky.	1961 (Oct. 31)
1 5/8 miles [1]	2:37 4/5	Red Reality	6	113	Saratoga Springs, N.Y.	1972 (Aug. 23)
1 5/8 miles [1]	2:37 4/5	Malwak	5	110	Saratoga Springs, N.Y.	1973 (Aug. 22)
1 mi., 5 1/2 furlongs	2:51 3/5	Distribute	9	109	River Downs, Cincinnati, Ohio	1940 (Sept. 7)
1 3/4 miles [1]	2:50 4/5	Swartz Pete	6	N.A.	Auckland, New Zealand	1966 (Jan. 1)
1 7/8 miles [1]	3:11 4/5	El Moro	8	116	Delaware Park, Wilmington, Del.	1963 (July 22)
2 miles [1]	3:15	Polazel	3	N.A.	Salisbury, England	1924 (July 8)
2 miles, 40 yards	3:29 2/5	Winning Mark	4	107	Thistledown, Cleveland, Ohio	1940 (July 20)
2 miles, 70 yards	3:30 2/5	Sun n Shine	4	113	Hawthorne, Cicero, Ill.	1974 (Oct. 19)
2 1/16 miles	3:29 3/5	Midafternoon	4	126	Jamaica, L.I., N.Y.	1956 (Nov. 15)
2 1/8 miles [1]	3:35	Centuron	5	119	Newbury, England	1923 (Sept. 29)
2 3/16 miles	3:51 1/8	Santiago	5	112	Narragansett Park, Pawtucket, R.I.	1941 (Sept. 27)
2 1/4 miles [1]	3:37 2/5	Dakota	4	116	Lingfield, England	1927 (May 27)
2 3/8 miles	4:15	Wiki Jack	4	97	Tijuana, Mexico	1925 (Feb. 8)
2 1/2 miles	4:14 3/5	Miss Grillo	6	118	Pimlico, Baltimore, Md.	1948 (Nov. 12)
2 5/8 miles [4]	4:51 2/5	Worthman	5	101	Tijuana, Mexico	1925 (Feb. 22)
2 3/4 miles	4:48 4/5	Shot Put	4	126	Washington Park, Homewood, Ill.	1940 (Aug. 14)
2 7/8 miles [5]	5:23	Bosh	5	100	Tijuana, Mexico	1925 (March 8)
3 miles	5:15	Farragut	5	113	Agua Caliente, Mexico	1941 (March 9)
3 3/8 miles	6:13	Winning Mark	4	104	Washington Park, Homewood, Ill.	1940 (Aug. 21)
4 miles	7:10 4/5	Sotemia	5	119	Churchill Downs, Louisville, Ky.	1912 (Oct. 7)

[1] Turf. [2] By Blink-Broken Tendril. [3] Downhill course. [4] Track heavy. [5] Track sloppy. [6] N.A.=Not available.

HARNESS RACING'S TRIPLE CROWN FOR 3-YEAR-OLDS

Source: The United States Trotting Association

HAMBLETONIAN [1]

YEAR	PURSE	WINNER	DRIVER	TIME	YEAR	PURSE	WINNER	DRIVER	TIME
1952	$ 87,638	Sharp Note	Bion Shively	2:02 3/5	1968	$116,190	Nevele Pride	Stanley Dancer	1:59 2/5
1953	117,118	Helicopter	Harry Harvey	2:01 3/5	1969	124,910	Lindy's Pride	Howard Beissinger	1:57 3/5
1954	106,831	Newport Dream	Del Cameron	2:02 4/5	1970	143,620	Timothy T	John Simpson Jr.	1:58 2/5
1955	86,863	Scott Frost	Joe O'Brien	2:00 3/5	1971	129,770	Speedy Crown	Howard Beissinger	1:57 2/5
1956	100,604	The Intruder	Ned Bower	2:01 2/5	1972	119,090	Super Bowl	Stanley Dancer	1:56 2/5
1957	111,126	Hickory Smoke	John Simpson	2:00 1/5	1973	144,710	Flirth	Ralph Baldwin	1:57 1/5
1958	106,719	Emily's Pride	Flave Nipe	1:59 4/5	1974	160,150	Christopher T	Billy Haughton	1:58 3/5
1959	125,283	Diller Hanover	Frank Ervin	2:01 1/5	1975	232,192	Bonefish	Stanley Dancer	1:59
1960	147,481	Blaze Hanover	Joe O'Brien	1:59 3/5	1976	263,524	Steve Lobell	Billy Haughton	1:56 2/5
1961	131,573	Harlan Dean	James Arthur	1:58 2/5	1977	284,131	Green Speed	Billy Haughton	1:55 3/5
1962	116,612	A. C.'s Viking	Sanders Russell	1:59 3/5	1978	241,280	Speedy Somolli	Howard Beissinger	1:55
1963	115,549	Speedy Scot	Ralph Baldwin	1:57 3/5	1979	300,000	Legend Hanover	George Sholty	1:56 1/5
1964	115,281	Ayers	John Simpson	1:56 4/5	1980	300,000	Burgomeister	Wm. Haughton	1:56 3/5
1965	122,245	Egyptian Candor	Del Cameron	2:03 4/5	1981	837,000	Shiaway St. Pat	Ray Remmer	2:01 1/5
1966	122,540	Kerry Way	Frank Ervin	1:58 4/5	1982	875,000	Speed Bowl	Tom Haughton	1:57
1967	122,650	Speedy Streak	Del Cameron	2:00	1983	1,080,000	Duenna	Stanley Dancer	1:57 2/5

[1] At Du Quoin, Ill., until 1981 when moved to East Rutherford, N. J.

KENTUCKY FUTURITY (at Lexington, Ky.)

YEAR	PURSE	WINNER	DRIVER	TIME	YEAR	PURSE	WINNER	DRIVER	TIME
1956	$ 53,731	Nimble Colby	Ralph Baldwin	2:02	1970	$ 76,351	Timothy T	Joe Simpson Jr	1:59⅘
1957	50,460	Cassin Hanover	Fred Egan	2:02⅕	1971	63,415	Savoir	James Arthur	1:58⅕
1958	53,330	Emily's Pride	Flave Nipe	1:59⅕	1972	56,210	Super Bowl	Stanley Dancer	1:59
1959	53,810	Diller Hanover	Ralph Baldwin	2:01⅕	1973	64,174	Arnie Almahurst	Joe O'Brien	1:59⅕
1960	64,040	Elaine Rodney	Clint Hodgins	1:58⅗	1974	100,000	Waymaker	John Simpson Jr.	1:58⅕
1961	59,330	Duke Rodney	Eddie Wheeler	1:58⅕	1975	100,000	Noble Rouge	William Herman	1:59⅗
1962	55,230	Safe Mission	Joe O'Brien	1:59⅕	1976	100,000	Quick Pay	Peter Haughton	1:59
1963	61,128	Speedy Scot	Ralph Baldwin	1:57⅕	1977	100,000	Texas	Billy Herman	1:57⅗
1964	57,096	Ayres	John Simpson	1:58⅕	1978	100,000	Doublemint	Peter Haughton	1:58⅗
1965	65,133	Armbro Flight	Joe O'Brien	1:59⅗	1979	100,000	Classical Way	John Simpson Jr.	1:57⅘
1966	61,602	Governor Armbro	Joe O'Brien	2:00⅖	1980	100,000	Final Score	Tom Haughton	1:58
1967	58,642	Speed Model	Art Hult	1:59⅕	1981	124,311	Filet of Sole	John Simpson Jr.	1:57⅗
1968	57,000	Nevele Pride	Stanley Dancer	1:57	1982	116,200	Jazz Cosmos	Mickey McNichol	1:57
1969	64,757	Lindy's Pride	Howard Beissinger	1:59	1983	150,000	Power Seat	William O'Donnell	1:54⅘

YONKERS TROT (at Yonkers, N.Y.—1 1/16-mile race before 1963, now 1 mile)

YEAR	PURSE	WINNER	DRIVER	TIME	YEAR	PURSE	WINNER	DRIVER	TIME
1962	$105,422	A. C.'s Viking	Sanders Russell	2:10⅘	1973	$ 93,242	Tamerlane	Charles Clark	2:04⅘
1963	135,127	Speedy Scot	Ralph Baldwin	2:03⅗	1974	125,822	Spitfire Hanover	Del Miller	2:05⅖
1964	116,691	Ayres	John Simpson	2:01⅗	1975	200,000	Surefire Hanover	Stanley Dancer	2:03
1965	122,236	Noble Victory	Stanley Dancer	2:02	1976	202,004	Steve Lobell	Billy Haughton	2:01⅘
1966	123,375	Polaris	George Sholty	2:06	1977	239,000	Green Speed	Billy Haughton	1:59
1967	150,000	Pomp	Harry Pownall	2:04⅘	1978	233,594	Speedy Somolli	Howard Beissinger	1:59⅗
1968	150,000	Nevele Pride	Stanley Dancer	2:03⅗	1979	237,765	Chiola Hanover	James Allen	2:04⅖
1969	100,000	Lindy's Pride	Howard Beissinger	2:03⅘	1980	263,540	Nevele Impulse	Dick Macomber	2:03⅖
1970	106,770	Victory Star	Vernon Dancer	2:03	1981	279,700	Ma Bandy	Carl Allen	2:02⅕
1971	110,795	Quick Pride	Stanley Dancer	2:02⅘	1982	415,160	Mystic Park	Frank O'Mara	2:02⅖
1972	94,097	Super Bowl	Stanley Dancer	2:02	1983	486,150	Joie De Vie	William Gilmour	2:00⅗

PACING'S TRIPLE CROWN

LITTLE BROWN JUG (at Delaware, Ohio—1 mile)

Source: United States Trotting Association.

YEAR	PURSE	WINNER	DRIVER	TIME	YEAR	PURSE	WINNER	DRIVER	TIME
1956	$ 52,666	Noble Adios	John Simpson	2:00⅘	1970	$100,110	Most Happy Fella	Stanley Dancer	1:57⅕
1957	73,528	Torpid	John Simpson	2:00⅘	1971	102,964	Nansemond	Herve Filion	1:57⅖
1958	65,252	Shadow Wave	Joe O'Brien	2:01	1972	104,916	Strike Out	Keith Waples	1:56⅗
1959	76,582	Adios Butler	Clint Hodgins	1:59⅖	1973	120,000	Melvin's Woe	Joe O'Brien	1:57⅗
1960	66,510	Bullet Hanover	John Simpson	1:58⅗	1974	132,630	Armbro Omaha	William Haughton	1:57⅗
1961	70,069	Henry T. Adios	Stanley Dancer	1:58⅘	1975	147,813	Seatrain	Ben Webster	1:56⅘
1962	75,038	Lehigh Hanover	Stanley Dancer	1:58⅘	1976	153,799	Keystone Ore	Stanley Dancer	1:56⅘
1963	68,294	Overtrick	John Patterson	1:57⅕	1977	150,000	Governor Skipper	John Chapman	1:56⅕
1964	66,590	Vicar Hanover	William Haughton	2:00⅘	1978	186,760	Happy Escort	Bill Popfinger	1:57⅖
1965	70,000	Bret Hanover	Frank Ervin	1:57	1979	226,455	Hot Hitter	Herve Filion	1:55⅗
1966	74,616	Romeo Hanover	George Sholty	1:59⅗	1980	207,361	Niatross	Clint Galbraith	1:54⅘
1967	84,778	Best of All	Jim Hackett	1:59⅕	1981	243,779	Fan Hanover	Glen Garnsey	1:56⅗
1968	104,226	Rum Customer	William Haughton	1:59⅗	1982	328,900	Merger	John Campbell	1:56⅗
1969	109,731	Laverne Hanover	William Haughton	2:00⅖	1983	358,800	Ralph Hanover	Ron Waples	1:55⅗

CANE PACE (at Yonkers, N.Y.—1 mile)

YEAR	PURSE	WINNER	DRIVER	TIME	YEAR	PURSE	WINNER	DRIVER	TIME
1964	$123,191	Race Time	George Sholty	2:01⅘	1974	$121,822	Boyden Hanover	William Herman	1:59⅘
1965	125,236	Bret Hanover	Frank Ervin	2:01	1975	200,000	Nero	Joe O'Brien	1:58⅘
1966	126,915	Romeo Hanover	William Myer	1:59⅘	1976	200,000	Keystone Ore	Stanley Dancer	1:57⅕
1967	150,000	Meadow Paige	William Haughton	2:03	1977	286,500	Jade Princess	Jack Kopas	1:59
1968	150,000	Rum Customer	William Haughton	1:59⅘	1978	307,594	Armbro Tiger	Herve Filion	1:59⅕
1969	100,000	Kat Byrd	Eldon Harner	2:02⅖	1979	336,420	Happy Motoring	Wm. Popfinger	1:57⅗
1970	102,770	Most Happy Fella	Stanley Dancer	1:58⅗	1980	321,365	Niatross	Clint Galbraith	1:57⅗
1971	106,795	Albatross	Stanley Dancer	2:00	1981	373,850	Wildwood Jeb	James Marohn	1:58⅕
1972	107,097	Hilarious Way	John Simpson Jr.	2:02⅖	1982	307,980	Cam Fella	Pat Crowe	1:57⅗
1973	101,242	Smog	Vernon Dancer	1:58⅘	1983	559,230	Ralph Hanover	Ron Waples	1:57

MESSENGER STAKE (at Westbury, L.I., N.Y.—1 mile)

YEAR	PURSE	WINNER	DRIVER	TIME	YEAR	PURSE	WINNER	DRIVER	TIME
1964	$150,960	Race Time	Ralph Baldwin	2:01⅖	1974	$151,044	Armbro Omaha	William Haughton	1:59⅗
1965	151,252	Bret Hanover	Frank Ervin	2:02	1975	154,223	Bret's Champ	William Haughton	1:59⅕
1966	169,885	Romeo Hanover	George Sholty	2:01	1976	161,290	Windshield Wiper	William Haughton	2:00
1967	178,064	Romulus Hanover	William Haughton	1:59⅒	1977	159,155	Governor Skipper	John Chapman	1:59⅕
1968	189,018	Rum Customer	William Haughton	2:01⅘	1978	167,862	Abercrombie	Glen Garnsey	1:58⅖
1969	182,976	Bye Bye Sam	Stanley Dancer	2:02⅗	1979	180,225	Hot Hitter	Henri Filion	1:59⅘
1970	123,450	Most Happy Fella	Stanley Dancer	2:00⅗	1980	173,522	Niatross	Clint Galbraith	1:59⅗
1971	114,977	Albatross	Stanley Dancer	2:00⅖	1981	224,954	Seahawk Hanover	Ben Webster	1:58
1972	154,733	Silent Majority	William Haughton	2:01⅘	1982	259,000	Cam Fella	Pat Crowe	1:59
1973	122,732	Valiant Bret	Lucien Fontaine	2:00⅗	1983	379,004	Ralph Hanover	Ron Waples	1:57

HARNESS HORSE RACING RECORDS AND CHAMPIONS

Source: United States Trotting Association

WORLD HARNESS RACE ONE-MILE RECORDS

HORSE	SEX	DRIVER	YEAR	TRACK	TIME
Trotting—Mile Track					
Lindy's Crown	Horse	Howard Beissinger	1980	Du Quoin, Ill.	1:54 4/5
Winky's Gill	Mare	Hakan Wallner	1983	Springfield, Ill.	1:55 2/5
Iris De Vandel	Gelding	Ron Turcotte	1983	E. Rutherford, N.J.	1:55 2/5
Pacing—Mile Track					
Trenton	Horse	Tom Haughton	1982	Springfield, Ill.	1:51 3/5
Three Diamonds	Mare	Bruce Riegle	1982	Lexington, Ky.	1:53 1/5
New Lew	Gelding	Lew Williams	1979	E. Rutherford, N.J.	1:54
Trotting—Five-eighths-mile Track					
Lindy's Crown	Horse	Howard Beissinger	1980	Wilmington, Del.	1:57 1/5
Keystone Sister	Mare	Del Miller	1981	Meadow Lands, Pa.	1:58
Dudate Windswept	Gelding	Stephen Guy	1978	Laurel, Md.	1:58
Pacing—Five-eighths-mile Track					
It's Fritz	Horse	Marty Allen	1983	Meadow Lands, Pa.	1:52 1/5
Toy Poodle	Mare	William Herman	1981	Wilmington, Del.	1:54 1/5
Rambling Willie	Gelding	Robert Farrington	1977	Wilmington, Del.	1:54 3/5
Trotting—Half-mile Track					
Nevele Pride	Horse	Stanley Dancer	1969	Saratoga Springs, N.Y.	1:56 4/5
Armbro Flight	Mare	Joe O'Brien	1965	Delaware, Ohio	1:59 1/5
Stately's Pride	Gelding	William Gilmour	1983	Westbury, N.Y.	1:59
Pacing—Half-mile Track					
It's Fritz	Horse	Marty Allen	1983	Louisville, Ky.	1:53 3/5
Fan Hanover	Mare	Glen Garnsey	1982	Maywood, Ill.	1:56
Majestic Charger	Gelding	William O'Donnell	1982	Freehold, N.J.	1:55 4/5

HARNESS HORSE OF THE YEAR

YEAR	HORSE	GAIT	YEAR	HORSE	GAIT	YEAR	HORSE	GAIT
1949	Good Time	pacer	1959	Bye Bye Byrd	pacer	1974	Delmonica Hanover	trotter
1950	Proximity	trotter	1960–61	Adios Butler	pacer	1975	Savoir	trotter
1951	Pronto Don	trotter	1962	Su Mac Lad	trotter	1976	Keystone Ore	pacer
1952	Good Time	pacer	1963	Speedy Scot	trotter	1977	Green Speed	trotter
1953	Hi-Lo's Forbes	pacer	1964–66	Bret Hanover	pacer	1978	Abercrombie	pacer
1954	Stenographer	trotter	1967–69	Nevele Pride	trotter	1979–80	Niatross	pacer
1955–56	Scott Frost	trotter	1970	Fresh Yankee	trotter	1981	Fan Hanover	pacer
1957	Torpid	pacer	1971–72	Albatross	pacer	1982	Cam Fella	pacer
1958	Emily's Pride	trotter	1973	Sir Dalrae	pacer	1983	Cam Fella	pacer

QUARTER HORSE RACING

Source: American Quarter Horse Association

WORLD RECORDS

DIST.	HORSE	AGE	WT.	DATE	TIME	DIST.	HORSE	AGE	WT.	DATE	TIME
440 yds.	Truckle Feature	3	120	8/26/73	0:21.02	300 yds.	Nita Boone	3	122	8/08/82	0:15.19
400 yds.	Bold Love	3	120	3/28/80	0:19.18	250 yds.	Junior Meyers	6	121	5/16/71	0:13.00
350 yds.	Van Too Too	5	118	9/03/73	0:17.24	220 yds.	Junior Meyers	4	120	8/10/69	0:11.62
330 yds.	Good N Tension	2	120	4/06/74	0:16.47						

ALL AMERICAN FUTURITY, RUIDOSO DOWNS, N.M., 2-YEAR-OLD QUARTER HORSES [5]

YEAR	WINNER	TIME	PURSE	OWNER	TRAINER	JOCKEY
1965	Savannah Jr.	0:20.30	$ 419,460	J. R. & R. E. Cates	Ted W. Wells Jr.	Jack Wallace
1966	Go Dick Go	0:20.27	$ 430,600	Joseph Leitner	Clarence V. Jay	Buddy Nesmith
1967	Laico Bird	0:20.11	$ 486,600	Floyd H. Jones Jr.	Jimmie Jones	Bobby Harmon
1968	Three Oh's	0:20.07	$ 602,000	Dr. D. G. Strole	C. W. Cascio	Jerry Nicodemus
1969	Easy Jet	0:20.49	$ 600,000	Walter Merrick	Walter Merrick	Willie Lovell
1970	Rocket Wrangler	0:20.09	$ 670,000	J. R. Adams	Charles Cascio	Jerry Nicodemus
1971	Mr. Kid Charge	0:19.65	$ 753,910	Will F. Whitehead	James Chapman	Johnny Cox
1972	Possumjet	0:20.04	$1,035,900	Jack M. Byers	Jack Byers	Pete Herrera
1973	Timeto Thinkrich	0:21.58	$1,030,000	Frank Vessels	Jerry Fisher	John Watson
1974	Easy Date	0:21.60	$1,030,000	Walter Merrick	James McArthur	Don Knight
1975	Bugs Alive in 75	0:21.98	$1,030,000	Ralph W. Shebester	J. B. Montgomery	Jerry Burgess
1976	Real Wind	0:21.70	$1,030,000	J.D. & E. Kitchens	T. A. Walker	Gary Sumpter
1977	Hot Idea	0:21.76	$ 766,000	Jackson/Bruce	G. Tefertiller	Terry Lipham
1978	Moon Lark	0:21.85	$1,000,000	Jas/Paul/Sam Howard	Jack Brooks	Jackie Martin
1979	Pie in the Sky	0:21.76	$1,000,000	Dan & Jolene Urschel	Leo Wood	Danny Cardoza
1980	Higheasterjet	0:22.15	$1,000,000	Jerry Highsmith	Johnie Goodman	Billy Hunt
1981	Special Effort	0:21.69	$1,000,000	Dan & Jolene Urschel	Johnie Goodman	Billy Hunt
1982	Mr. Master Bug	0:22:20	$2,000,000	Marvin L. Barnes	Jack Brooks	Jackey Martin
1983	On A High	0:22:04	$2,000,000	J. Rheudsal, P. Carter, B.F. Phillips Jr.	Dwayne Gilbreath	Steve Harris

[5] Previously 400 yards, the All American Futurity was changed to 440 yards in 1973.

OLYMPIC GAMES

SUMMER OLYMPIC GAMES: 1896–1988

	YEAR	PLACE	NATIONS	EVENTS	LEADING WINNERS OF GOLD MEDAL CHAMPIONSHIPS First	Second	Third
I	1896	Athens, Greece	10	42	United States (11)	Greece (8)	Germany (3½)
II	1900	Paris, France	20	60	France (28)	United States (22)	Britain (14)
III	1904	St. Louis, Mo.	10	67	United States (78)	Cuba (5) [2] Germany (5) [2]	—
—[1]	1906	Athens, Greece	21	75	France (14)	United States (12)	Greece (8) [2] Britain (8) [2]
IV	1908	London, England	22	104	Britain (56)	United States (22)	Sweden (8)
V	1912	Stockholm, Sweden	28	106	United States (25)	Sweden (23½)	Britain (10)
VI	1916	Berlin, Germany	—	—	Canceled because of World War I		
VII	1920	Antwerp, Belgium	29	154	United States (41)	Sweden (19)	Finland (15)
VIII	1924	Paris, France	44	137	United States (45)	Finland (14)	France (13)
IX	1928	Amsterdam, Neth.	46	120	United States (22)	Germany (9½)	Italy (7) [2] Switzerland (7) [2]
X	1932	Los Angeles, Calif.	37	124	United States (41)	Italy (12)	France (10)
XI	1936	Berlin, Germany	49	142	Germany (33)	United States (24)	Hungary (10)
XII	1940	Helsinki, Finland	—	—	Canceled because of World War II		
XIII	1944	Unawarded	—	—	Canceled because of World War II		
XIV	1948	London, England	59	138	United States (38)	Sweden (17)	Hungary (10)
XV	1952	Helsinki, Finland	69	149	United States (40)	Soviet Union (22)	Hungary (16)
XVI	1956	Melbourne, Australia	67	145	Soviet Union (37) [4]	United States (32)	Australia (13)
XVII	1960	Rome, Italy	84	150	Soviet Union (43)	United States (34)	Italy (13)
XVIII	1964	Tokyo, Japan	94	162	United States (36)	Soviet Union (30)	Japan (16)
XIX	1968	Mexico City, Mexico	109	172	United States (45)	Soviet Union (28)	France (10) [2] Japan (10) [2]
XX	1972	Munich, W. Germany	112	195	Soviet Union (50)	United States (33)	East Germany (20)
XXI	1976	Montreal, Canada	89	198	Soviet Union (47)	East Germany (40)	United States (34)
XXII	1980	Moscow, Soviet Union	81	203	Soviet Union (80)	East Germany (47)	Bulgaria (8)
XXIII	1984	Los Angeles, Calif.	—	—	—	—	—
XXIV	1988	Seoul, South Korea	—	—	—	—	—

WINTER OLYMPICS: 1924–1988

	YEAR	PLACE	NATIONS	EVENTS	LEADING WINNERS OF GOLD MEDAL CHAMPIONSHIPS First	Second	Third
I	1924	Chamonix, France	16	16	Norway (4)	Finland (3)	Austria (2)
II	1928	St. Moritz, Switzerland	25	15	Norway (5½)	United States (2) [2] Sweden (2) [2]	—
III	1932	Lake Placid, N.Y.	17	19	United States (6)	Norway (3)	France (1) [2] Sweden (1) [2] Finland (1) [2] Canada (1) [2] Austria (1) [2]
IV	1936	Garmisch-Partenkirchen, Germany	28	21	Norway (7)	United States (3)	Sweden (2)
V	1948	St. Moritz, Switzerland	28	24	Sweden (4) [2] Norway (4) [2]	—	United States (3) [2] Switzerland (3) [2]
VI	1952	Olso, Norway	30	23	Norway (7)	United States (4)	Finland (3) [2] Germany (3) [2]
VII	1956	Cortina, Italy	32	24	Soviet Union (6)	Austria (4)	Finland (3)
VIII	1960	Squaw Valley, Calif.	30	27	Soviet Union (6)	Germany (4)	United States (3) [2] Sweden (3) [2] Norway (3) [2]
IX	1964	Innsbruck, Austria	36	34	Soviet Union (11)	Austria (4) [2]	Germany (3) [2] France (3) [2] Finland (3) [2] Sweden (3) [2] Norway (3) [2]
X	1968	Grenoble, France	37	35	Norway (6)	Soviet Union (5)	France (4) [2] Italy (4) [2]
XI	1972	Sapporo, Japan	35	35	Soviet Union (8)	Switzerland (4) [2] Netherlands (4) [2] East Germany (4) [2]	
XII	1976	Innsbruck, Austria	37	35	Soviet Union (13)	East Germany (7)	United States (3) [2] Norway (3) [2]
XIII	1980	Lake Placid, N.Y.	38	39	Soviet Union (10)	East Germany (9)	United States (6)
XIV	1984	Sarajevo, Yugoslavia	—	—	—	—	—
XV	1988	Calgary, Canada	—	—	—	—	—

[1] Unofficial Olympics. [2] Tie. [3] Equestrian events held in Stockholm, Sweden. [4] Includes full credit for ties.

WINTER OLYMPIC GAMES FINAL MEDAL STANDINGS: 1980

NATION	GOLD	SILVER	BRONZE	TOTAL
East Germany	9	7	7	23
Soviet Union	10	6	6	22
United States	6	4	2	12
Norway	1	3	6	10
Finland	1	5	3	9
Austria	3	2	2	7
West Germany	0	2	3	5
Switzerland	1	1	3	5
Liechtenstein	2	2	1	5
Netherlands	1	2	1	4
Sweden	3	0	1	4
Italy	0	2	0	2
Canada	0	1	1	2
Britain	1	0	0	1
Hungary	0	1	0	1
Japan	0	1	0	1
Bulgaria	0	0	1	1
Czechoslovakia	0	0	1	1
France	0	0	1	1

SUMMER OLYMPIC GAMES FINAL MEDAL STANDINGS: 1980

NATION	GOLD	SILVER	BRONZE	TOTAL
Soviet Union	80	70	47	197
East Germany	47	36	43	126
Bulgaria	8	16	16	40
Hungary	7	10	15	32
Poland	3	14	14	31
Romania	6	6	13	25
Britain	5	7	9	21
Cuba	8	7	5	20
Italy	8	3	4	15
France	6	5	3	14
Czechoslovakia	2	2	9	13
Sweden	3	3	6	12
Australia	2	2	5	9
Yugoslavia	2	3	4	9
Finland	3	1	4	8
Spain	1	3	2	6
Denmark	2	1	2	5
Austria	1	3	1	5
North Korea	0	3	2	5
Brazil	2	0	2	4
Ethiopia	2	0	2	4
Mongolia	0	2	2	4
Netherlands	0	1	3	4
Mexico	0	1	3	4
Greece	1	0	2	3
Jamaica	0	0	3	3
Switzerland	2	0	0	2
Tanzania	0	2	0	2
Ireland	0	1	1	2
Belgium	1	0	0	1
India	1	0	0	1
Zimbabwe	1	0	0	1
Venezuela	0	1	0	1
Uganda	0	1	0	1
Lebanon	0	0	1	1
Guyana	0	0	1	1

SUMMER OLYMPIC WINNERS AND RECORDS

ARCHERY: MEN

Year	Winner	POINTS
1972	John Williams, United States	2,528
1976*	Darrell Pace, United States	2,571
1980	T. Poikolainen, Finland	2,455

ARCHERY: WOMEN

Year	Winner	POINTS
1972	Doreen Wilber, United States	2,424
1976*	Luann Ryon, United States	2,499
1980	K. Losaberidze, USSR	2,491

BASKETBALL: MEN

Year	Winner
1936	United States
1948	United States
1952	United States
1956	United States
1960	United States
1964	United States
1968	United States
1972	Soviet Union
1976	United States
1980	Yugoslavia

BASKETBALL: WOMEN

Year	Winner
1976	Soviet Union
1980	Soviet Union

BOXING: LIGHT FLYWEIGHT

Year	Winner
1968	Francisco Rodriguez, Venezuela
1972	Gyoergy Gedeo, Hungary
1976	Jorge Hernandez, Cuba
1980	Shamil Sabyrov, USSR

BOXING: FLYWEIGHT

Year	Winner
1904	G. Finnegan, U.S.A.
1920	F. De Genaro, U.S.A.
1924	F. La Barba, U.S.A.
1928	A. Kocsis, Hungary
1932	I. Enekes, Hungary
1936	W. Kaiser, Germany
1948	P. Perez, Argentina
1952	N. Brooks, U.S.A.
1956	T. Spinks, Britain
1960	G. Torck, Hungary
1964	F. Atzori, Italy
1968	R. Delgado, Mexico
1972	G. Kostadinov, Bulgaria
1976	Leo Randolph, U.S.A.
1980	Petar Lessov, Bulgaria

BOXING: BANTAMWEIGHT

Year	Winner
1904	O. L. Kirk, U.S.A.
1908	A. Thomas, Britain
1920	C. Walker, S. Africa
1924	W. Smith, S. Africa
1928	V. Tamagnini, Italy
1932	H. Gwynne, Canada
1936	U. Sergo, Italy
1948	T. Csik, Hungary
1952	P. Hamalainen, Finland
1956	W. Behrendt, W. Ger.
1960	O. Grigoryev, USSR
1964	T. Sakurai, Japan
1968	V. Sokolov, USSR
1972	O. Martinez, Cuba
1976	Gu Yong Jo, N. Korea
1980	Juan Hernandez, Cuba

BOXING: FEATHERWEIGHT

Year	Winner
1904	O. L. Kirk, U.S.A.
1908	R. K. Gunn, Britain
1920	P. Fritsch, France
1924	J. Fields, U.S.A.
1928	L. Van Klaveren, Neth.
1932	C. Robledo, Argentina
1936	O. Casanovas, Argentina
1948	E. Formenti, Italy
1952	J. Zachara, Czech.
1956	V. Sefronov, USSR
1960	F. Musso, Italy
1964	S. Stepashkin, USSR
1968	A. Roldan, Mexico
1972	B. Kousnetsov, USSR
1976	A. Herrara, Cuba
1980	Rudi Fink, E. Germany

BOXING: LIGHTWEIGHT

Year	Winner
1904	H. J. Spanger, U.S.A.
1908	F. Grace, Britain
1920	S. Mosberg, U.S.A.
1924	H. Nielsen, Denmark
1928	C. Orlandi, Italy
1932	L. Stevens, S. Africa
1936	I. Harangi, Hungary
1948	G. Dreyer, S. Africa
1952	A. Bolognesi, Italy
1956	R. McTaggart, Britain
1960	K. Pazdzier, Poland
1964	J. Grudzien, Poland
1968	R. Harris, U.S.A.
1972	J. Szczepanski, Poland
1976	Howard Davis, U.S.A.
1980	Angel Herrera, Cuba

* Olympic record.

BOXING: LIGHT WELTERWEIGHT

1952	C. Adkins, U.S.A.	**1960**	B. Nemecek, Czech.	**1968**	J. Kulei, Poland	**1976**	Ray Leonard, U.S.A.
1956	V. Engoibarian, USSR	**1964**	J. Kulei, Poland	**1972**	R. Seales, U.S.A.	**1980**	Patrizio Oliva, Italy

BOXING: WELTERWEIGHT

1904	A. Yong, U.S.A.	**1932**	E. Flynn, U.S.A.	**1956**	N. Linca, Romania	**1972**	E. Correa, Cuba
1920	T. Schneider, Canada	**1936**	S. Suvio, Finland	**1960**	G. Benvenuti, Italy	**1976**	J. Bachfeld, E. Germany
1924	J. Delarge, Belgium	**1948**	J. Torma, Czech.	**1964**	M. Kasprzyk, Poland	**1980**	A. Aldama, Cuba
1928	E. Morgan, N. Zealand	**1952**	Z. Chychia, Poland	**1968**	M. Wolke, E. Germany		

BOXING: LIGHT MIDDLEWEIGHT

1952	L. Papp, Hungary	**1960**	W. McClure, U.S.A.	**1968**	B. Lagutin, USSR	**1976**	J. Rybicki, Poland
1956	L. Papp, Hungary	**1964**	M. Kasprzyk, Poland	**1972**	D. Kottysch, W. Ger.	**1980**	A. Martinez, Cuba

BOXING: MIDDLEWEIGHT

1904	C. Mayer, U.S.A.	**1928**	P. Toscani, Italy	**1952**	Floyd Patterson, U.S.A.	**1968**	C. Finnegan, Britain
1908	J. Douglas, Britain	**1932**	C. Barth, U.S.A.	**1956**	G. Chatkov, USSR	**1972**	V. Lemechev, USSR
1920	H. Mallin, Britain	**1936**	J. Despeaux, France	**1960**	E. Crook, U.S.A.	**1976**	Mike Spinks, U.S.A.
1924	H. Mallin, Britain	**1948**	L. Papp, Hungary	**1964**	V. Popenchenko, USSR	**1980**	Jose Gomez, Cuba

BOXING: LIGHT HEAVYWEIGHT

1920	E. Eagan, U.S.A.	**1936**	R. Michelot, France	**1960**	Cassius Clay, U.S.A.	**1976**	Leon Spinks, U.S.A.
1924	H. Mitchell, Britain	**1948**	G. Hunter, S. Africa	**1964**	C. Pinto, Italy	**1980**	Slobodan Kacar, Yugoslavia
1928	V. Avendano, Argentina	**1952**	Norvel Lee, U.S.A.	**1968**	D. Pozdniak, USSR		
1932	D. Carstens, S. Africa	**1956**	James Boyd, U.S.A.	**1972**	M. Parlov, Yugoslavia		

BOXING: HEAVYWEIGHT

1904	S. Berger, U.S.A.	**1928**	R. Jurado, Argentina	**1952**	E. Sanders, U.S.A.	**1968**	George Foreman, U.S.A.
1908	A. Oldham, Britain	**1932**	S. Lovell, Argentina	**1956**	P. Rademacher, U.S.A.	**1972**	T. Stevenson, Cuba
1920	R. Rawson, Britain	**1936**	H. Runge, Germany	**1960**	F. De Piccoli, Italy	**1976**	T. Stevenson, Cuba
1924	O. von Porat, Norway	**1948**	R. Iglesias, Argentina	**1964**	Joe Frazier, U.S.A.	**1980**	T. Stevenson, Cuba

CANOEING: KAYAK SINGLES—WOMEN: 500 METERS

1948	K. Hoff, Denmark	2:31.9	**1960**	A. Seredina, USSR	2:08.08	**1972**	Y. Ryabchinskaya, USSR	2:03.17
1952	S. Saimo, Finland	2:18.4	**1964**	L. Khvedosiuk, USSR	2:12.87	**1976**	C. Zirzow, E. Germany	2:01.05
1956	E. Dementieva, USSR	2:18.9	**1968**	L. Pinaeva, USSR	2:11.09	**1980**	B. Fischer, E. Germany	1:57.96*

CANOEING: KAYAK PAIRS—WOMEN: 500 METERS

1960	USSR: M. Shubina, A. Seredina	1:54.76	**1972**	USSR: L. Pinaeva, E. Kuryshko	1:53.50
1964	W. Germany: R. Esser, A. Zimmerman	1:56.95	**1976**	USSR: Popova, Kreft	1:51.15
1968	W. Germany: A. Zimmermann, R. Esser	1:56.44	**1980**	E. Germany, Bischof, Genauss	1:43.88

CANOEING: KAYAK PAIRS—MEN: 500 METERS

1976	E. Germany: Mattern, Olbricht	1:35.87	**1980**	Soviet Union: Parfenovich, Chukhrai	1:32.38

CANOEING: KAYAK SINGLES—MEN: 1,000 METERS

1936	G. Hradetzky, Austria	4:22.9	**1960**	E. Hansen, Denmark	3:53.0	**1976**	R. Helm, E. Germany	3:48.20
1948	G. Fredriksson, Sweden	4:33.2	**1964**	R. Peterson, Sweden	3:57.13	**1980**	R. Helm, E. Germany	3:48.77
1952	G. Fredriksson, Sweden	4:07.9	**1968**	M. Hesz, Hungary	4:02.63			
1956	G. Fredriksson, Sweden	4:12.8	**1972***	A. Shaparenko, USSR	3:48.06			

CANOEING: CANADIAN SINGLES—MEN: 1,000 METERS

1936	F. Amyot, Canada	5:32.1	**1960**	J. Parti, Hungary	4:33.9	**1976**	M. Ljubek, Yugoslavia	4:09.51
1948	J. Holocek, Czech	5:42.0	**1964**	J. Eschert, W. Germany	4:35.14	**1980**	L. Lubenov, Romania	4:12.38
1952	J. Holocek, Czech	4:56.3	**1968**	T. Tatai, Hungary	4:36.14			
1956	L. Rottman, Romania	5:05.3	**1972***	I. Patzaichin, Romania	4:08.94			

CANOEING: KAYAK PAIRS—MEN: 1,000 METERS

1936	Austria: A. Kainz, A. Dorfner	4:03.8	**1964**	Sweden: S. Sjodelius, G. Utterberg	3:28.54
1948	Sweden: H. Berglund, L. Klingstroem	4:07.3	**1968**	USSR: A. Shaparenko, V. Morozov	3:37.54
1952	Finland: K. Wires, Y. Hietanen	3:51.1	**1972**	USSR: N. Gorbachev, V. Kratassyuk	3:31.23
1956	W. Germany: M. Scheuer, M. Miltenberger	3:49.6	**1976**	USSR: Nagorny, Romanovsky	3:29.01
1960	Sweden: G. Fredriksson, S. Sjodelius	3:34.73	**1980**	USSR: V. Parfenovich, S. Chukhrai	3:26.72*

CANOEING: CANADIAN PAIRS—MEN: 1,000 METERS

1936	Czechoslovakia: V. Syrovatka, J. Brzak	4.50.1	**1964**	USSR: A. Khimich, S. Oschepkov	4:04.65
1948	Czechoslovakia: J. Brzak, B. Kudrna	5:07.1	**1968**	Romania: I. Potzaichin, S. Covaliov	4:07.18
1952	Denmark: B. Rasch, F. Haunstoft	4:38.3	**1972**	USSR: V. Chessyunas, Y. Lobanov	3:52.60
1956	Romania: A. Dumitru, S. Ismailciuc	4:47.4	**1976**	USSR: S. Petrenko, A. Vinogradov	3:52.76
1960	USSR: L. Geyshter, S. Makarenko	4:17.9	**1980**	Romania: I. Potzaichin, T. Simionov	3:47.65*

CANOEING: KAYAK RELAY—MEN: 1,000 METERS

1960	W. Germany	7:39.43	**1968**	Norway	3:14.38	**1976***	USSR	3:06.69
1964	USSR	3:14.67	**1972**	USSR	3:14.02	**1980**	E. Germany	3:13.76

CANOEING: SLALOM—MEN: 500 METERS

KAYAK SLALOM: SINGLES		CANADIAN SLALOM: SINGLES		CANADIAN SLALOM: PAIRS	
1972	Siegbert Horn, E. Germany	**1972**	Reinhard Eiben, E. Germany	**1972**	E. Germany: W. Hofmann, R. Amend
1976	V. Diba, Romania	**1976**	A. Rogov, USSR	**1976**	USSR: Petrenko, Vinogradov
1980	V. Parfenovich, USSR	**1980**	S. Postrekhin, USSR	**1980**	Hungary: Foltan, Vaskuti

CYCLING: ROAD RACE—INDIVIDUAL: 200 KILOMETERS

1896	A. Konstantinidis, Greece	**1928**	H. Hansen, Denmark	**1956**	E. Baldini, Italy	**1976**	B. Johansson, Sweden
1906	Vast, Bardonneau (tie), France	**1932**	A. Pavesi, Italy	**1960**	V. Kapitonov, USSR	**1980**	S. Sukhoruchenkov, USSR
1912	R. Lewis, S. Africa	**1936**	R. Charpentier, France	**1964**	M. Zanin, Italy		
1920	H. Stenquist, Sweden	**1948**	J. Bayaert, France	**1968**	P. Vianelli, Italy		
1924	A. Blanchonnet, France	**1952**	A. Noyelle, Belgium	**1972**	H. Kuiper, Neth.		

* Olympic record.

SUMMER OLYMPIC WINNERS AND RECORDS *(continued)*

CYCLING: ROAD RACE—TEAM: 100 KILOMETERS

1912	Sweden	1928	Denmark	1948	Belgium	1960	Italy	1972	USSR
1920	France	1932	Italy	1952	Belgium	1964	Netherlands	1976	USSR
1924	France	1936	France	1956	France	1968	Netherlands	1980	USSR

CYCLING: INDIVIDUAL TIME TRIAL—1,000 METERS

1928	W. Falck-Hansen, Denmark	1:14.2	1952	Mockridge, Australia .	1:11.1	1968	P. Trentin, France....	1:03.91
1932	E. Gray, Australia	1:13.0	1956	L. Faggin, Italy.......	1:09.8	1972	N. Fredborg, Denmark	1:06.44
1936	A. van Vliet, Netherlands	1:12.0	1960	S. Gaiardoni, Italy....	1:07.27	1976	K.J.Gruenke, E.Germany	1:05.927
1948	J. Dupont, France....	1:13.5	1964	P. Sercu, Belgium....	1:09.59	1980*	L. Thoms	1:02.955

CYCLING: INDIVIDUAL PURSUIT—4,000 METERS

1964	J. Daller, Czechoslovakia	5:04.7	1976	G. Braun, W. Germany	4:47.61
1968	D. Rebillard, France	4:41.71	1980*	R. Dill-Bundi, Switzerland	4:35.66
1972	K. Knudsen, Norway	4:45.74			

CYCLING: TEAM PURSUIT—4,000 METERS

1920	Italy 5:20.0	1932	Italy ..4:53.0	1952	Italy 4:46.1	1964	W.Germany 4:35.6	1976	W.Germany 4:21.06
1924	Italy 5:15.0	1936	France 4:45.0	1956	Italy 4:37.4	1968	Denmark ..4:22.44	1980*	USSR 4:15.70
1928	Italy 5:01.8	1948	France 4:57.8	1960	Italy 4:30.9	1972	W.Germany 4:22.14		

CYCLING: SCRATCH SPRINT (Time for final 200 meters in seconds)

1924	L. Michard, France	12.8	1948	M. Ghella, Italy..........	12.0	1968*	D. Morelon, France.....	10.68
1928	R. Beaufrand, France	13.2	1952	E. Sacchi, Italy	12.0	1972	D. Morelon, France	—[1]
1932	J. van Edmond, Netherlands	12.2	1956	M. Rousseau, France	11.4	1976	A. Tkac, Czechoslovakia .	—[1]
1936	T. Merkens, Germany....	11.8	1964	G. Pettenella, Italy.......	13.6	1980	L. Hesslich, E. Germany ..	—[1]

CYCLING: TANDEM—2,000 METERS

1908	France	1928	Netherlands	1948	Italy	1960	Italy	1972	USSR
1920	Britain	1932	France	1952	Australia	1964	Italy		
1924	France	1936	Germany	1956	Australia	1968	France		

EQUESTRIAN: INDIVIDUAL—THREE-DAY EVENT

1912	A. Nordlander, Sweden	1936	L. Stubbendorff, Germany	1964	M. Checcoli, Italy
1920	Helmer Morner, Sweden	1948	B. Chevallier, France	1968	J. Guyon, France
1924	A. van der Voort van Zijp, Neth.	1952	H. von Blixen-Finecke, Sweden	1972	R. Meade, Britian
1928	F.P. de Mortanges, Netherlands	1956	P. Kastenman, Sweden	1976	E. Coffin, U.S.A.
1932	F. P. de Mortanges, Netherlands	1960	L. Morgan, Australia	1980	F.E. Roman, Italy

EQUESTRIAN: INDIVIDUAL—DRESSAGE

1912	C. Bonde, Sweden	1936	H. Pollary, Germany	1964	H. Chammartin, Switzerland
1920	J. Lundblad, Sweden	1948	H. Moser, Switzerland	1968	I. Kizimov, USSR
1924	E. Linder, Sweden	1952	H. St. Cyr, Sweden	1972	L. Linsenhoff, W. Germany
1928	C. von Langen, Germany	1956	H. St. Cyr, Sweden	1976	C. Stueckelberger, Switzerland
1932	R. Lesage, France	1960	S. Filatov, USSR	1980	E. Theurer, Austria

EQUESTRIAN: INDIVIDUAL—GRAND PRIX JUMPING

1912	J. Cariou, France	1936	K. Hasse, Germany	1964	P. d'Oriola, France
1920	T. Lequio, Italy	1948	H. Mariles Cortes, Mexico	1968	W.C. Steinkraus, U.S.A.
1924	A. Gemuseus, Switzerland	1952	P. d'Oriola, France	1972	G. Mancinelli, Italy
1928	F. Ventura, Czechoslovakia	1956	H. Winkler, W. Germany	1976	A. Schockemoehle, W. Germany
1932	T. Nishi, Japan	1960	R. d'Inzeo, Italy	1980	J. Kowalczyk, Poland

EQUESTRIAN: TEAM—THREE-DAY EVENT

1912	Sweden	1928	Netherlands	1948	U.S.A.	1960	Australia	1972	Britain
1920	Sweden	1932	U.S.A.	1952	Sweden	1964	Italy	1976	U.S.A.
1924	Netherlands	1936	Germany	1956	Britain	1968	Britain	1980	USSR

EQUESTRIAN: TEAM—DRESSAGE

1928	Germany	1948	France	1964	W. Germany	1976	W. Germany
1932	France	1952	Sweden	1968	W. Germany	1980	USSR
1936	Germany	1956	Sweden	1972	USSR		

EQUESTRIAN: TEAM—GRAND PRIX JUMPING

1912	Sweden	1928	Spain	1952	Britain	1964	W. Germany	1976	France
1920	Sweden	1936	Germany	1956	W. Germany	1968	Canada	1980	USSR
1924	Sweden	1948	Mexico	1960	W. Germany	1972	W. Germany		

FENCING: FOILS—MEN: INDIVIDUAL

1896	E. Gravelotte, France	1928	L. Gauldin, France	1960	V. Zhdanovich, USSR
1900	C. Coste, France	1932	G. Marzi, Italy	1964	E. Franke, Poland
1904	R. Fonst, Cuba	1936	G. Gaudini, Italy	1968	I. Drima, Romania
1912	N. Nadi, Italy	1948	J. Buhan, France	1972	W. Woyda, Poland
1920	N. Nadi, Italy	1952	C. d'Oriola, France	1976	F. dal Zotto, Italy
1924	R. Ducret, France	1956	C. d'Oriola, France	1980	V. Smirnov, USSR

* Olympic record. [1] Time not available.

FENCING: FOILS—WOMEN: INDIVIDUAL

1924	E. Osiier, Denmark	1952	I. Camber, Italy	1972	Ragno Lonzi, Italy
1928	H. Mayer, Germany	1956	G. Sheen, Britain	1976	I. Schwarczenberger, Hungary
1932	E. Preis, Austria	1960	A. Schmid, W. Germany	1980	P. Trinquet, France
1936	I. Elek, Hungary	1964	I. Rejto, Hungary		
1948	I. Elek, Hungary	1968	E. Novikova, USSR		

FENCING: FOILS—MEN: TEAM

1904	Cuba	1928	Italy	1948	France	1960	USSR	1972	Poland
1920	Italy	1932	France	1952	France	1964	USSR	1976	W. Germany
1924	France	1936	Italy	1956	Italy	1968	France	1980	France

FENCING: FOILS—WOMEN: TEAM

1960	USSR	1964	Hungary	1968	USSR	1972	USSR	1976	USSR	1980	France

FENCING: ÉPÉE—MEN: INDIVIDUAL

1900	R. Fonst, Cuba	1928	L. Gaudin, France	1960	G. Delfino, Italy
1904	R. Fonst, Cuba	1928	C. Cornaggia-Medici, Italy	1964	G. Kriss, USSR
1908	G. Alibert, France	1936	F. Riccardi, Italy	1968	G. Kulcsar, Hungary
1912	P. Anspach, Belgium	1948	L. Cantone, Italy	1972	C. Fenyvesi, Hungary
1920	A. Massard, France	1952	E. Mangiarotti, Italy	1976	A. Pusch, W. Germany
1924	C. Delporte, Belgium	1956	C. Pavesi, Italy	1980	J. Harmenberg, Sweden

FENCING: ÉPÉE—MEN: TEAM

1908	France	1924	France	1936	Italy	1956	Italy	1968	Hungary	1980	France
1912	Belgium	1928	Italy	1948	France	1960	Italy	1972	Hungary		
1920	Italy	1932	France	1952	Italy	1964	Hungary	1976	Sweden		

FENCING: SABRE—MEN: INDIVIDUAL

1896	J. Georgiadis, Greece	1928	O. Tersztyanszky, Hungary	1964	T. Pezsa, Hungary
1900	G. de la Falaise, France	1932	G. Piller, Hungary	1968	J. Pawlowski, Poland
1904	M. Diaz, Cuba	1936	E. Kabos, Hungary	1972	V. Sidiak, USSR
1908	J. Fuchs, Hungary	1948	A. Gerevich, Hungary	1976	V. Krovopuskov, USSR
1912	J. Fuchs, Hungary	1952	P. Kovacs, Hungary	1980	V. Krovopuskov, USSR
1920	N. Nadi, Italy	1956	R. Karpati, Hungary		
1924	S. Posta, Hungary	1960	R. Karpati, Hungary		

FENCING: SABRE—MEN: TEAM

1904	Cuba	1920	Italy	1932	Hungary	1952	Hungary	1964	USSR	1976	USSR
1908	Hungary	1924	Italy	1936	Hungary	1956	Hungary	1968	USSR	1980	USSR
1912	Hungary	1928	Hungary	1948	Hungary	1960	Hungary	1972	Italy		

FIELD HOCKEY—MEN

1908	Britain	1928	India	1948	India	1956	India	1964	India	1972	W. Germany	1980	India
1920	Britain	1936	India	1952	India	1960	Pakistan	1968	Pakistan	1976	New Zealand		

FIELD HOCKEY—WOMEN

1980	Zimbabwe

GYMNASTICS: ALL-AROUND—MEN: TEAM

1896	Germany	1912	Italy	1928	Switzerland	1948	Finland	1960	Japan	1972	Japan
1904	U.S.A.	1920	Italy	1932	Italy	1952	USSR	1964	Japan	1976	Japan
1908	Sweden	1924	Italy	1936	Germany	1956	USSR	1968	Japan	1980	USSR

GYMNASTICS: ALL-AROUND—WOMEN: TEAM

1928	Netherlands	1948	Czech.	1956	USSR	1964	USSR	1972	USSR	1980	USSR
1936	Germany	1952	USSR	1960	USSR	1968	USSR	1976	USSR		

GYMNASTICS: ALL-AROUND—MEN: INDIVIDUAL

1900	S. Sandras, France	1928	G. Miez, Switzerland	1960	B. Shakhlin, USSR
1904	A. Heida, U.S.A.	1932	R. Neri, Italy	1964	Y. Endo, Japan
1908	A. Braglia, Italy	1936	A. Schwarzmann, Germany	1968	S. Kato, Japan
1912	A. Braglia, Italy	1948	V. Huhtanen, Finland	1972	S. Kato, Japan
1920	G. Zampori, Italy	1952	V. Chukarin, USSR	1976	N. Andrianov, USSR
1924	L. Stukelj, Yugoslavia	1956	V. Chukarin, USSR	1980	A. Dityatin, USSR

GYMNASTICS: ALL-AROUND—WOMEN: INDIVIDUAL

1952	M. Gorokhovskaja, USSR	1960	L. Latynina, USSR	1968	V. Caslavska, Czech.	1976	N. Comaneci, Romania
1956	L. Latynina, USSR	1964	V. Caslavska, Czech.	1972	L. Turischeva, USSR	1980	Y. Davydova, USSR

GYMNASTICS: LONG HORSE—MEN

1896	K. Schumann, Germany	1948	P. Aaltonen, Finland	1964	H. Yamashita, Japan
1904	(tie) A. Heida, G. Eyser, U.S.A.	1952	V. Chukarin, USSR	1968	M. Voronin, USSR
1924	F. Kriz, U.S.A.	1956	(tie) H. Bantz, W. Germany;	1972	K. Koeste, E. Germany
1928	E. Mack, Switzerland		V. Mouratov, USSR	1976	N. Andrianov, USSR
1932	S. Guglielmetti, Italy	1960	(tie) B. Shakhlin, USSR;	1980	N. Andrianov, USSR
1936	K. Schwarzmann, Germany		T. Ono, Japan		

GYMNASTICS: LONG HORSE—WOMEN

1952	Y. Kalinthouk, USSR	1960	M. Nikolaeva, USSR	1968	V. Caslavska, Czech.	1976	N. Kim, USSR
1956	L. Latynina, USSR	1964	V. Caslavska, Czech.	1972	K. Janz, E. Germany	1980	N. Shaposhnikova, USSR

GYMNASTICS: PARALLEL BARS—MEN

1896	A. Flatow, Germany	1932	R. Neri, Italy	1956	V. Chukarin, USSR	1972	S. Kato, Japan
1904	G. Eyser, U.S.A.	1936	K. Frey, Germany	1960	B. Shakhlin, USSR	1976	S. Kato, Japan
1924	A. Guttinger, Switz.	1948	M. Reusch, Switz.	1964	Y. Endo, Japan	1980	A. Tkachyov, USSR
1928	L. Vacha, Czech.	1952	H. Eugster, Switz.	1968	A. Nakayama, Japan		

SUMMER OLYMPIC WINNERS AND RECORDS *(continued)*

GYMNASTICS: PARALLEL BARS—WOMEN

1952	M. Korondi, Hungary	1960	P. Astakhova, USSR	1968	V. Caslavska, Czech.	1976	N. Comaneci, Romania
1956	A. Keleti, Hungary	1964	P. Astakhova, USSR	1972	K. Janz, E. Germany	1980	M. Gnauck, E. Germany

GYMANASTICS: FLOOR EXERCISES—MEN

1956	V. Mouratov, USSR	1964	F. Menichelli, Italy	1972	N. Andrianov, USSR	1980	R. Bruckner, E. Germany
1960	N. Aihara, Japan	1968	S. Kato, Japan	1976	N. Andrianov, USSR		

GYMNASTICS: FLOOR EXERCISES—WOMEN

1952	A. Keleti, Hungary	1964	L. Latynina, USSR	1976	N. Kim, USSR
1956	(tie) A. Keleti, Hungary	1968	(tie) V. Caslavska, Czech.;	1980	N. Kim, USSR,
	L. Latynina, USSR		L. Petrik, USSR		N. Comaneci, Romania
1960	L. Latynina, USSR	1972	Olga Korbut, USSR		

GYMNASTICS: BALANCE BEAM—WOMEN

1952	N. Botcharova, USSR	1960	E. Bosakova, Czech.	1968	N. Kutchinskava, USSR	1976	N. Comaneci, Romania
1956	A. Keleti, Hungary	1964	V. Caslavska, Czech.	1972	Olga Korbut, USSR	1980	N. Comaneci, Romania

GYMNASTICS: POMMELED HORSE—MEN

1896	L. Zutter, Switzerland	1948	(tie) P. Aaltonen, V. Houtanen,	1964	M. Cerar, Yugoslavia
1904	A. Heida, U.S.A.		I. Savolainen, Finland	1968	M. Voronin, USSR
1924	J. Wilhelm, Switzerland	1952	V. Chukarin, USSR	1972	V. Klimenko, USSR
1928	H. Hanggi, Switzerland	1956	B. Shakhlin, USSR	1976	Z. Magyar, Hungary
1932	I. Pelle, Hungary	1960	(tie) E. Ekman, Finland;	1980	Z. Magyar, Hungary
1936	K. Frey, Germany		B. Shakhlin, USSR		

GYMNASTICS: FLYING RINGS—MEN

1986	J. Mitropoulos, Greece	1932	G. Gulack, U.S.A.	1956	A. Azarian, USSR	1972	A. Nakayama, Japan
1904	H. Glass, U.S.A.	1936	A. Hudec, Czech.	1960	A. Azarian, USSR	1976	N. Andrainov, USSR
1924	F. Martino, Italy	1948	K. Frei, Switz.	1964	T. Hayata, Japan	1980	A. Dityatin, USSR
1928	L. Stukelj, Yugoslavia	1952	G. Chaguinian, USSR	1968	A. Nakayama, Japan		

GYMNASTICS: HORIZONTAL BAR—MEN

1896	H. Weingaertner, Ger.	1932	D. Bixler, U.S.A.	1960	T. Ono, Japan	1976	M. Tsukahara, Japan
1904	(tie) A. Heida, E. Hennig,	1936	A. Saarvala, Finland	1964	B. Shakhlin, USSR	1980	S. Deltchev, Bulgaria
1904	U.S.A.	1948	J. Stalder, Switz.	1968	(tie) M. Voronin, USSR;		
1924	L. Stukelj, Yugoslavia	1952	J. Gunthard, Switz.		A. Nakayama, Japan		
1928	G. Miez, Switzerland	1956	T. Ono, Japan	1972	M. Tsukahara, Japan		

HANDBALL: TEAM (MEN)						**HANDBALL: TEAM (WOMEN)**	
1972	Yugoslavia	1976	USSR	1980	E. Germany	1980	USSR

JUDO LIGHTWEIGHT		MIDDLEWEIGHT		HEAVYWEIGHT		OPEN CLASS	
1964	T. Nakatani, Japan	1964	I. Okano, Japan	1964	I. Inokuma, Japan	1964	A. Geesink, Neth.
1972	T. Kawaguchi, Japan	1972	S. Sekine, Japan	1972	W. Ruska, Neth.	1972	W. Ruska, Neth.
1976	H. Rodriguez, Cuba	1976	I. Sonada, Japan	1976	S. Novikov, USSR	1976	H. Uemura, Japan
1980	E. Gamba, Italy	1980	J. Roethlisberger,	1980	A. Parisi, France;	1980	D. Lorenz, E. Germany
	T. Rey, France[1]		Switzerland;		R. Van de Walle,		
	N. Solodukhin, USSR[2]		S. Khabareli, USSR[3]		Belgium[4]		
WELTERWEIGHT				LIGHT HEAVYWEIGHT			
1972	**T. Nomura, Japan**	1976	V. Nevzorov, USSR	1972	S. Chochoshvily, USSR	1976	K. Ninomiya, Japan

PENTATHLON: WOMEN—INDIVIDUAL

1964	I. Press, USSR	1972	Mary Peters, Britain	1980*	O. Tkachenko, USSR
1968	I. Becker, W. Germany	1976	Sigurn Siegl, E. Germany		

MODERN PENTATHLON: MEN—INDIVIDUAL

1912	Jim Thorpe, U.S.A.	1928	S. Thofelt, Sweden	1952	L. Hall, Sweden	1968	B. Ferm, Sweden
	G. Lilliehood, Sweden	1932	J. Oxenstierna, Sweden	1956	L. Hall, Sweden	1972	A. Balczo, Hungary
1920	J. Dyrssen, Sweden	1936	G. Handrick, Germany	1960	F. Nemeth, Hungary	1976	J. Pyciak-Peciak, Poland
1924	Bo Lindman, Sweden	1948	W. Grut, Sweden	1964	F. Torok, Hungary	1980	A. Starostin, USSR

MODERN PENTATHLON: MEN—TEAM

1952	Hungary	1960	Hungary	1968	Hungary	1976	Britain
1956	USSR	1964	USSR	1972	USSR	1980	USSR

ROWING: SINGLE SCULLS—MEN

1900	H. Barrelet, France	1928	H. Pearce, Australia	1956	V. Ivanov, USSR	1976	P. Karppinen, Finland
1908	H. Blackstaffe, Britain	1932	H. Pearce, Australia	1960	V. Ivanov, USSR	1980	P. Karppinen, Finland
1912	W. Kinnear, Britain	1936	G. Schafer, Germany	1964	V. Ivanov, USSR		
1920	John Kelly, U.S.A.	1948	M. Wood, Australia	1968	J. Wienese, Neth.		
1924	J. Beresford, Britain	1952	Y. Chukalov, USSR	1972	Y. Malishev, USSR		

ROWING: DOUBLE SCULLS—MEN

1920	U.S.A.	1932	Britain	1952	Argentina	1964	USSR	1976	Norway
1924	U.S.A.	1936	Germany	1956	USSR	1968	USSR	1980	E. Germany
1928	U.S.A.	1948	Britain	1960	Czechoslovakia	1972	USSR		

ROWING: PAIRS WITHOUT COXSWAIN—MEN

1908	Britain	1928	Germany	1948	Britain	1960	USSR	1972	E. Germany
1920	Italy	1932	Britain	1952	U.S.A.	1964	Canada	1976	E. Germany
1924	Netherlands	1936	Germany	1956	U.S.A.	1968	E. Germany	1980	E. Germany

ROWING: PAIRS WITH COXSWAIN—MEN

1900	Netherlands	1928	Switzerland	1936	Germany	1952	France	1960	W. Germany	1968	Italy	1976	E. Germany
1924	Switzerland	1932	U.S.A.	1948	Denmark	1956	U.S.A.	1964	U.S.A.	1972	E. Germany	1980	E. Germany

* Olympic record. [1] Extra Lightweight. [2] Half Lightweight. [3] Half Middleweight. [4] Half Heavyweight.

ROWING: FOURS WITHOUT COXSWAIN—MEN

1908 Britain	**1928** Britain	**1936** Germany	**1952** Yugoslavia	**1960** U.S.A	**1968** E. Germany	**1976** E. Germany
1924 Britain	**1932** Britain	**1948** Italy	**1956** Canada	**1964** Denmark	**1972** W. Germany	**1980** E. Germany

ROWING: FOURS WITH COXSWAIN—MEN

1912	Germany	**1928**	Italy	**1948**	U.S.A.	**1960**	W. Germany	**1972**	W. Germany
1920	Switzerland	**1932**	Germany	**1952**	Czechoslovakia	**1964**	W. Germany	**1976**	USSR
1924	Switzerland	**1936**	Germany	**1956**	Italy	**1968**	New Zealand	**1980**	E. Germany

ROWING: EIGHTS WITH COXSWAIN—MEN

1900	U.S.A.	**1920**	U.S.A.	**1932**	U.S.A.	**1952**	U.S.A.	**1964**	U.S.A.	**1976**	E. Germany
1908	Britain	**1924**	U.S.A.	**1936**	U.S.A.	**1956**	U.S.A.	**1968**	W. Germany	**1980**	E. Germany
1912	Britain	**1928**	U.S.A.	**1948**	U.S.A.	**1960**	W. Germany	**1972**	New Zealand		

ROWING: WOMEN

SINGLE SCULLS		DOUBLE SCULLS		PAIRS WITHOUT COXSWAIN	
1976	E. Germany	**1976**	Bulgaria	**1976**	Bulgaria
1980	Romania	**1980**	USSR	**1980**	E. Germany
FOURS WITH COXSWAIN		EIGHTS WITH COXSWAIN		QUADRUPLE SCULLS WITH COXSWAIN	
1976	E. Germany	**1976**	E. Germany	**1976**	E. Germany
1980	E. Germany	**1980**	E. Germany	**1980**	E. Germany

SHOOTING: TRAPSHOOTING

1908	W.H. Ewing, Canada	72	**1952**	G. Genereux, Canada	192	**1968**	J. Brathwaite, Britain	198
1912	James Graham, U.S.A.	96	**1956**	G. Rossini, Italy	195	**1972** *	A. Scalzone, Italy	199
1920	Mark Arie, U.S.A.	95	**1960**	I. Dumitrescu, Romania	192	**1976**	D. Haldeman, U.S.A.	190
1924	G. Halasy, Hungary	98	**1964**	E. Mattarelli, Italy	198	**1980**	L. Giovannetti, Italy	198

SHOOTING: PISTOL—RAPID FIRE: 25 METERS

1936	C. van Oyen, Germany	36	**1960**	W. McMillan, U.S.A.	587	**1976** *	N. Klaar, E. Germany	597
1948	K. Takacs, Hungary	580	**1964**	P. Linnosvuop, Finland	592	**1980**	C. Ion	596
1952	K. Takacs, Hungary	579	**1968**	J. Zapedski, Poland	593			
1956	S. Petrescu, Romania	587	**1972**	J. Zapedzki, Poland	595			

SHOOTING: PISTOL—FREE: 50 METERS

1936	T. Ullmann, Sweden	539	**1960**	A. Gustchin, USSR	560	**1976**	V. Potteck, E. Germany	573
1948	C.E. Vasquez, Peru	545	**1964**	V. Markkanen, Finland	560	**1980** *	A. Melemtev, USSR	581
1952	Huelet Benner, U.S.A.	553	**1968**	G. Kosykh, USSR	562			
1956	P. Linnosvuoo, Finland	556	**1972**	R. Skanaker, Sweden	567			

SHOOTING: SMALL-BORE RIFLE—PRONE: 50 METERS

1960	P. Kohnke, W. Germany	590	**1968**	Jan Kurka, Czech.	598	**1976** *	K. Smiezek, W. Germany	599
1964	L. Hammerl, Hungary	597	**1972** *	Ho Jun Li, North Korea	599	**1980**	K. Varga, Hungary, H. Heilfort, E. Germany	599

SHOOTING: SMALL-BORE RIFLE—3-POSITION

1960	V. Shamburkin, USSR	1,149	**1968**	B. Klingner, W. Ger.	1,157	**1976**	K. Smiezek, W. Germany	599
1964	Lones Wigger, U.S.A.	1,164	**1972**	John Writer, U.S.A.	1,166	**1980** *	V. Vlasov, USSR	1,173

SHOOTING: SKEET SHOOTING

1968 *	Evgeny Petrov, USSR	198	**1976** *	J. Panacek, Czech.	198
1972	Konrad Wirnhier, W. Germany	195	**1980**	H. Rasmussen, Den.	196

SHOOTING: MOVING TARGET

1972	Lakov Zhelezniak, USSR	569
1976	A. Gazov, USSR	579
1980 *	I. Sokolov, USSR	589

SOCCER

1900	Britain	**1912**	Britain	**1928**	Uruguay	**1952**	Hungary	**1964**	Hungary	**1976**	E. Germany
1904	Canada	**1920**	Belgium	**1936**	Italy	**1956**	USSR	**1968**	Hungary	**1980**	Czech.
1908	Britain	**1924**	Uruguay	**1948**	Sweden	**1958**	Yugoslavia	**1972**	Poland		

SWIMMING: 100-METER FREESTYLE—MEN

1896	A. Hajos, Hungary	1:22.2	**1928**	John Weissmuller, U.S.A.	0:58.6	**1964**	D. Schollander, U.S.A.	0:53.40
1900	Jarvis, Britain	1:16.0	**1932**	Y. Miyazaki, Japan	0:58.2	**1968**	M. Wenden, Australia	0:52.22
1904	†de Halmay, Hungary	1:02.8	**1936**	Ferenc Csik, Hungary	0:57.6	**1972**	Mark Spitz, U.S.A.	0:51.22
1908	Charles Daniels, U.S.A.	1:05.6	**1948**	Walter Ris, U.S.A.	0:57.3	**1976** *	J. Montgomery, U.S.A.	0:49.99
1912	Duke Kahanamoku, U.S.A.	1:03.4	**1952**	Clarke Scholes, U.S.A.	0:57.4	**1980**	J. Woithe, E. Germany	0:50.40
1920	Duke Kahanamoku, U.S.A.	1:01.4	**1956**	Jon Henricks, Australia	0:55.4			
1924	John Weissmuller, U.S.A.	0:59.0	**1960**	J. Devitt, Australia	0:55.2			

SWIMMING: 100-METER FREESTYLE—WOMEN

1912	F. Durack, Australia	1:22.2	**1936**	H. Mastenbroek, Neth.	1:05.9	**1964**	Dawn Fraser, Australia	0:59.50
1920	Ethelda Bleibtrey, U.S.A.	1:13.6	**1948**	Greta Andersen, Denmark	1:06.3	**1968**	Margo Jan Henne, U.S.A.	1:00.00
1924	Ethel Lackie, U.S.A.	1:12.4	**1952**	Katalin Szoke, Hungary	1:06.8	**1972**	Sandra Neilson, U.S.A.	0:58.59
1928	Albina Osipowich, U.S.A.	1:11.0	**1956**	Dawn Fraser, Australia	1:02.0	**1976**	K. Ender, E. Germany	0:55.65
1932	Helene Madison, U.S.A.	1:06.8	**1960**	Dawn Fraser, Australia	1:01.2	**1980** *	B. Krause, E. Germany	0:54.79

SWIMMING: 400-METER FREESTYLE—MEN

1908	Henry Taylor, Britain	5:35.8	**1936**	Jack Medica, U.S.A.	4:44.5	**1968**	Michael Burton, U.S.A.	4:09.00
1912	G. Hodgson, Canada	5:24.4	**1948**	William Smith, U.S.A.	4:41.0	**1972**	B. Cooper, Australia	4:00.27
1920	Norman Ross, U.S.A.	5:26.8	**1952**	Jean Boiteux, France	4:30.7	**1976**	B. Goodell, U.S.A.	3:51.93
1924	John Weissmuller, U.S.A.	5:04.2	**1956**	Murray Rose, Australia	4:27.3	**1980** *	V. Salnikov	3:51.31
1928	A. Zorilla, Argentina	5:01.6	**1960**	Murray Rose, Australia	4:18.3			
1932	Clarence Crabbe, U.S.A.	4:48.4	**1964**	Don Schollander, U.S.A.	4:12.2			

* Olympic record. †100 yards.

SUMMER OLYMPIC WINNERS AND RECORDS *(continued)*

SWIMMING: 400-METER FREESTYLE—WOMEN

1924	Martha Norelius, U.S.A.	6:02.2	1952	V. Gyenge, Hungary	5:12.1	1972	Shane Gould, Australia	4:19.04
1928	Martha Norelius, U.S.A.	5:26.4	1956	L. Crapp, Australia	4:54.6	1976	Petra Thuemer, E. Ger.	4:09.89
1932	Helene Madison, U.S.A.	5:28.5	1960	C. von Saltza, U.S.A.	4:50.6	1980*	Ines Diers, E. Germany	4:08.76
1936	H. Mastenbroek, Neth	5:26.4	1964	Ginny Duenkel, U.S.A.	4:43.3			
1948	Ann Curtis, U.S.A.	5:17.8	1968	Deborah Meyer, U.S.A.	4:31.8			

SWIMMING: 100-METER BACKSTROKE—MEN

1908	Arno Bieberstein, Germany	1:24.6	1936	Adolf Kiefer, U.S.A.	1:05.9	1968	R. Matthes, E. Germany	0:58.7
1912	Harry Hebner, U.S.A.	1:21.2	1948	Allen Stack, U.S.A.	1:06.4	1972	R. Matthes, E. Germany	0:56.58
1920	Warren Kealoha, U.S.A.	1:15.2	1952	Y. Oyakawa, U.S.A.	1:05.4	1976*	J. Naber, U.S.A.	0:55.49
1924	Warren Kealoha, U.S.A.	1:13.2	1956	D. Thiele, Australia	1:02.2	1980	B. Baron, Sweden	0:56.53
1928	George Kojac, U.S.A.	1:08.2	1960	D. Thiele, Australia	1:01.9			
1932	M. Kiyokawa, Japan	1:08.6	1964	Event not held				

SWIMMING: 100-METER BACKSTROKE—WOMEN

1924	Sybil Bauer, U.S.A.	1:23.2	1952	J. Harrison, S. Africa	1:14.3	1972	Melissa Belote, U.S.A.	1:05.78
1928	Marie Braun, Netherlands	1:22.0	1956	J. Grinham, Britain	1:12.9	1976	U. Richter, E. Germany	1:01.83
1932	Eleanor Holm, U.S.A.	1:19.4	1960	Lynn Burke, U.S.A.	1:09.3	1980*	R. Reinisch, E. Germany	1:00.86
1936	Dina Senff, Netherlands	1:18.9	1964	Cathy Ferguson, U.S.A.	1:07.7			
1948	Karen Harup, Denmark	1:14.4	1968	Kaye Hall, U.S.A.	1:06.2			

SWIMMING: 200-METER BREASTSTROKE—MEN

1908	F. Holman, Britain	3:09.2	1936	T. Hamuro, Japan	2:41.5	1968	F. Munoz, Mexico	2:28.7
1912	W. Bathe, Germany	3:01.8	1948	Joseph Verduer, U.S.A.	2:39.3	1972	John Hencken, U.S.A.	2:21.55
1920	H. Malmroth, Sweden	3:04.4	1952	J. Davis, Australia	2:34.4	1976	D. Wilkie, Britain	2:15.11
1924	Robert Skelton, U.S.A.	2:56.6	1956	M. Furukawa, Japan	2:34.7	1980*	R. Zulpa, USSR	2:15.85
1928	Y. Tsuruta, Japan	2:48.8	1960	W. Mulliken, U.S.A.	2:37.4			
1932	Y. Tsuruta, Japan	2:45.4	1964	Ian O'Brian, Australia	2:27.8			

SWIMMING: 200-METER BREASTSTROKE—WOMEN

1924	Lucy Morton, Britain	3:33.2	1952	Eva Szekely, Hungary	2:51.7	1968	Sharon Wichman, U.S.A.	2:44.4
1928	Hilde Schrader, Germany	3:12.6	1956	U. Happe, W. Germany	2:53.1	1972	B. Whitfield, Australia	2:41.71
1932	C. Dennis, Australia	3:06.3	1960	A. Lonsbrough, Britain	2:49.5	1976	M. Koshevaia, USSR	2:33.35
1936	H. Maehata, Japan	3:03.6	1964	G. Prozumenschikova, USSR	2:46.4	1980	L. Kachushite, USSR	2:29.54
1948	Nel Vliet, Netherlands	2:57.2						

SWIMMING: 100-METER BUTTERFLY STROKE—MEN

1968	Douglas Russell, U.S.A.	0:55.9	1976	M. Vogel, U.S.A.	54.35
1972*	Mark Spitz, U.S.A.	0:54.27	1980	P. Arvidsson, Sweden	54.92

SWIMMING: 100-METER BUTTERFLY STROKE—WOMEN

1956	Shelley Mann, U.S.A.	1:11.0	1968	L. McClements, Australia	1:05.5	1976*	K. Ender, E. Germany	1:00.13
1960	Carolyn Schuler, U.S.A.	1:09.5	1972	M. Aoki, Japan	1:03.34	1980	C. Metschuck	1:00.42
1964	Sharon Stouder, U.S.A.	1:04.7						

SWIMMING: 400-METER INDIVIDUAL MEDLEY—MEN

1964	Dick Roth, U.S.A.	4:45.4	1972	G. Larsson, Sweden	4:31.98	1980*	A. Sidorenko, USSR	4:22.89
1968	Charles Hickcox, U.S.A.	4:48.4	1976	R. Strachan, U.S.A.	4:23.68			

SWIMMING: 400-METER INDIVIDUAL MEDLEY—WOMEN

1964	Donna de Varona, U.S.A.	5:18.7	1972	G. Neall, Australia	5:02.97	1980*	P. Schneider, E. Germany	4:36.29
1968	Claudia Kolb, U.S.A.	5:08.5	1976	U. Tauber, E. Germany	4:42.77			

SWIMMING: 400-METER FREESTYLE RELAY—WOMEN

1912	Britain	5:52.8	1932	U.S.A.	4:38.0	1956	Australia	4:17.1	1972	U.S.A.	3:55.19
1920	U.S.A.	5:11.6	1936	Netherlands	4:36.0	1960	U.S.A.	4:08.9	1976	U.S.A.	3:44.82
1924	U.S.A.	4:58.8	1948	U.S.A.	4:29.2	1964	U.S.A.	4:03.8	1980*	E. Germany	3:42.71
1928	U.S.A.	4:47.6	1952	Hungary	4:24.4	1968	U.S.A.	4:02.5			

SWIMMING: 400-METER MEDLEY RELAY—MEN

1960	U.S.A.	4:05.4	1968	U.S.A.	3:54.9	1976*	U.S.A.	3:42.22
1964	U.S.A.	3:58.4	1972	U.S.A.	3:48.16	1980	Australia	3:45.70

SWIMMING: 400-METER MEDLEY RELAY—WOMEN

1960	U.S.A.	4:41.1	1968	U.S.A.	4:28.3	1976	E. Germany	4:07.95
1964	U.S.A.	4:33.9	1972	U.S.A.	4:20.75	1980*	E. Germany	4:06.67

SWIMMING: 200-METER BACKSTROKE—MEN

1964	Jed Graef, Australia	2:10.3	1972	R. Matthes, E. Germany	2:02.82	1980	S. Wladar, Hungary	2:01.93
1968	R. Matthes, E. Germany	2:09.6	1976*	J. Naber, U.S.A.	1:59.19			

SWIMMING: 200-METER BACKSTROKE—WOMEN

1968	Lillian Watson, U.S.A.	2:24.8	1976	U. Richter, E. Germany	2:13.43
1972	Melissa Belote, U.S.A.	2:19.19	1980*	R. Reinisch, E. Germany	2:11.77

SWIMMING: 200-METER BUTTERFLY STROKE—MEN

1956	William Yorzyk, U.S.A.	2:19.3	1968	Carl Robie, U.S.A.	2:08.7	1980	S. Fesenko, USSR	1:59.76
1960	Michael Troy, U.S.A.	2:12.8	1972	Mark Spitz, U.S.A.	2:00.70			
1964	Kevin Berry, Australia	2:06.6	1976*	M. Bruner, U.S.A.	1:59.23			

SWIMMING: 200-METER BUTTERFLY STROKE—WOMEN

1968	Ada Kok, Netherlands	2:24.7	1976	A. Pollack, E. Germany	2:11.43
1972	Karen Moe, U.S.A.	2:15.57	1980*	I. Geissler, E. Germany	2:10.44

* Olympic record.

SWIMMING: 100-METER BREASTSTROKE—MEN

1968	Donald McKenzie, U.S.A.	1:07.7	1976*	J. Hencken, U.S.A.	1:03.11
1972	Nobutaka Taguchi, Japan	1:04.94	1980	D. Goodhew, Britain	1:03.34

SWIMMING: 100-METER BREASTSTROKE—WOMEN

1968	D. Bjedov, Yugoslavia	1:15.8	1976*	H. Anke, E. Germany	1:11.16
1972	Catherine Carr, U.S.A.	1:13.58	1980	U. Geweniger, E. Germany	1:10.22

SWIMMING: 200-METER FREESTYLE—MEN

1968	Mike Wenden, Australia	1:55.2	1976	B. Furniss, U.S.A.	1:50.29
1972	Mark Spitz, U.S.A.	1:52.78	1980*	S. Kopliakov, USSR	1:49.81

SWIMMING: 200-METER FREESTYLE—WOMEN

1968	Deborah Meyer, U.S.A.	2:10.5	1976	K. Ender, E. Germany	1:59.26
1972	Shane Gould, Australia	2:03.56	1980*	B. Krause, E. Germany	1:58.33

SWIMMING: 200-METER INDIVIDUAL MEDLEY—MEN

1968	Charles Hickcox, U.S.A.	2:12.0	1972*	Gunnar Larsson, Sweden	2:07.17

SWIMMING: 200-METER INDIVIDUAL MEDLEY—WOMEN

1968	Claudia Kolb, U.S.A.	2:24.7	1972*	Shane Gould, Australia	2:23.07

SWIMMING: 800-METER FREESTYLE—WOMEN

1968	Deborah Meyer, U.S.A.	9:24.0	1976	P. Thuemer, E. Germany	8:37.14
1972	Keena Rothhammer, U.S.A.	8:53.68	1980*	M. Ford, Australia	8:28.90

SWIMMING: 800-METER FREESTYLE RELAY—MEN

1908	Britain	10:55.6	1928	U.S.A.	9:36.2	1952	U.S.A.	8:31.1	1968	U.S.A.	7:52.3
1912	Australia	10:11.6	1932	Japan	8:58.2	1956	Australia	8:23.6	1972	U.S.A.	7:35.78
1920	U.S.A.	10:04.4	1936	Japan	8:51.5	1960	U.S.A.	8:10.2	1976*	U.S.A.	7:23.22
1924	U.S.A.	9:53.4	1948	U.S.A.	8:46.0	1964	U.S.A.	7:52.1	1980	USSR	7:23.50

SWIMMING: 1,500—METER FREESTYLE—MEN

1908	H. Taylor, Britain	22:48.4	1936	N. Terada, Japan	19:13.7	1968	Michael Burton, U.S.A.	16:38.9
1912	G. Hodgson, Canada	22:00.0	1948	James McLane, U.S.A.	19:18.5	1972	Michael Burton, U.S.A.	15:52.58
1920	Norman Ross, U.S.A.	22:23.2	1952	Ford Konno, U.S.A.	18:30.0	1976	B. Goodell, U.S.A.	15:02.40
1924	A. Charlton, Australia	20:06.6	1956	M. Rose, Australia	17:58.9	1980*	V. Salnikov, USSR	14:58.27
1928	Arne Borg, Sweden	19:51.8	1960	J. Konrads, Australia	17:19.6			
1932	K. Kitamura, Japan	19:12.4	1964	R. Windle, Australia	17:01.7			

SWIMMING: 3-METER SPRINGBOARD DIVING—MEN

1908	A. Zurner, Germany	1936	Richard Degener, U.S.A.	1968	Bernard Wrightson, U.S.A.
1912	P. Gunther, Germany	1948	Bruce Harlan, U.S.A.	1972	Vladimir Vasin, USSR
1920	Louis Keuhn, U.S.A.	1952	David Browning, U.S.A.	1976	Phil Boggs, U.S.A.
1924	Albert White, U.S.A.	1956	Robert Clotworthy, U.S.A.	1980	Aleksandr Portnov, USSR
1928	Pete Desjardins, U.S.A.	1960	Gary Tobian, U.S.A.		
1932	Michael Galitzen, U.S.A.	1964	Ken Sitzberger, U.S.A.		

SWIMMING: 3-METER SPRINGBOARD DIVING—WOMEN

1920	Aileen Riggin, U.S.A.	1948	Victoria Draves, U.S.A.	1968	Sue Gossick, U.S.A.
1924	Elizabeth Becker, U.S.A.	1952	Patricia McCormick, U.S.A.	1972	Micki King, U.S.A.
1928	Helen Meany, U.S.A.	1956	Patricia McCormick, U.S.A.	1976	Jennifer Chandler, U.S.A.
1932	Georgia Coleman, U.S.A.	1960	Ingrid Kramer, W. Germany	1980	Irina Kalinina, USSR
1936	Marjorie Gestring, U.S.A.	1964	Ingrid Engel-Kramer, W. Germany		

SWIMMING: 10-METER PLATFORM DIVING—MEN

1904	G.E. Sheldon, U.S.A.	1928	P. Desjardins, U.S.A.	1956	J. Capilla, Mexico	1976	K. Di Biasi, Italy
1908	H. Johansson, Sweden	1932	Harold Smith, U.S.A.	1960	R. Webster, U.S.A.	1980	F. Hoffmann,
1912	E. Adlerz, Sweden	1936	M. Wayne, U.S.A.	1964	R. Webster, U.S.A.		E. Germany
1920	Clarence Pinkston, U.S.A.	1948	Samuel Lee, U.S.A.	1968	K. Di Biasi, Italy		
1924	Albert White, U.S.A	1952	Samuel Lee, U.S.A.	1972	K. Di Biasi, Italy		

SWIMMING: 10-METER PLATFORM DIVING—WOMEN

1912	G. Johansson, Sweden	1936	D. Poynton-Hill, U.S.A.	1964	Lesley Bush, U.S.A.
1920	S. Fryland-Clausen, Denmark	1948	Victoria Draves, U.S.A.	1968	M. Duchkova, Czechoslovakia
1924	Caroline Smith, U.S.A.	1952	Patricia McCormick, U.S.A.	1972	Ulrika Knape, Sweden
1928	Elizabeth Pinkston, U.S.A.	1956	Patricia McCormick, U.S.A.	1976	E. Vaytsekhovskaia, USSR
1932	Dorothy Poynton, U.S.A.	1960	Ingrid Kramer, W. Germany	1980	M. Jaschke, E. Germany

TRACK AND FIELD: 100-METER DASH—MEN

1896	Thomas Burke, U.S.A.	0:12.0	1928	P. Williams, Canada	0:10.8	1964	Bob Hayes, U.S.A.	0:10.0
1900	Francis Jarvis, U.S.A.	0:10.8	1932	Eddie Tolan, U.S.A.	0:10.3	1968*	James Hines, U.S.A.	0:09.9
1904	Archie Hahn, U.S.A.	0:11.0	1936	Jesse Owens, U.S.A.	0:10.3	1972	Valery Borzov, USSR	0:10.14
1908	R. Walker, S. Africa	0:10.8	1948	H. Dillard, U.S.A.	0:10.3	1976	Hasley Crawford,	
1912	Ralph Craig, U.S.A.	0:10.8	1952	L. Remigino, U.S.A.	0:10.4		Trinidad-Tobago	0:10.06
1920	C. Paddock, U.S.A.	0:10.8	1956	Bobby Morrow, U.S.A.	0:10.5	1980	Allan Wells, Britain	0:10.25
1924	H. Abrahams, Britain	0:10.6	1960	Armin Hary, W. Germany	0:10.2			

* Olympic record.

SUMMER OLYMPIC WINNERS AND RECORDS *(continued)*

TRACK AND FIELD: 100-METER DASH—WOMEN

1928	Elizabeth Robinson, U.S.A.	0:12.2
1932	S. Walasiewicz, Poland	0:11.9
1936	Helen Stephens, U.S.A.	0:11.5
1948	F. Blankers-Koen, Neth.	0:11.9
1952	M. Jackson, Australia	0.11.5
1956	B. Cuthbert, Australia	0:11.5
1960	Wilma Rudolph, U.S.A.	0:11.0
1964	Wyomia Tyus, U.S.A.	0:11.4
1968*	Wyomia Tyus, U.S.A.	0:11.0
1972	R. Stecher, E. Germany	0:11.07
1976	A. Richter, W. Germany	0:11.08
1980	L. Kondratyeva, USSR	0:11.06

TRACK AND FIELD: 200-METER DASH—MEN

1900	W.B. Tewksbury, U.S.A.	0:22.2
1904	Archie Hahn, U.S.A.	0:21.6
1908	R. Kerr, Canada	0:22.6
1912	Ralph Craig, U.S.A.	0:21.7
1920	Allan Woodring, U.S.A.	0:22.0
1924	Jackson Scholz, U.S.A.	0:21.6
1928	P. Williams, Canada	0:21.8
1932	Eddie Tolan, U.S.A.	0:21.2
1936	Jesse Owens, U.S.A.	0:20.7
1948	Mel Patton, U.S.A.	0:21.1
1952	A. Stanfield, U.S.A.	0:20.7
1956	Bobby Morrow, U.S.A.	0:20.6
1960	Livio Berruti, Italy	0:20.5
1964	Henry Carr, U.S.A.	0:20.3
1968*	Tommie Smith, U.S.A.	0:19.0
1972	Valery Borzov, USSR	0:20.0
1976	D. Quarrie, Jamaica	0:20.23
1980	Pietro Mennea, Italy	0:20.19

TRACK AND FIELD: 200-METER DASH—WOMEN

1948	F. Blankers-Koen, Netherlands	0:24.4
1952	M. Jackson, Australia	0:23.7
1956	Betty Cuthbert, Australia	0:23.4
1960	Wilma Rudolph, U.S.A.	0:24.0
1964	Edith McGuire, U.S.A.	0:23.0
1968	I. Kirszenstein, Poland	0:22.5
1972	R. Stecher, E. Germany	0:22.4
1976*	B. Eckert, E. Germany	0:22.37
1980	B. Wockel, E. Germany	0.22.03

TRACK AND FIELD: 400-METER RACE—MEN

1896	Thomas Burke, U.S.A.	0:54.2
1900	Maxey Long, U.S.A.	0:49.4
1904	Harry Hillman, U.S.A.	0:49.2
1908	W. Halswelle, Britain	0:50.0
1912	Charles Reidpath, U.S.A.	0:48.2
1920	Bevil Rudd, S. Africa	0:49.6
1924	Eric Liddell, Britain	0:47.6
1928	Ray Barbuti, U.S.A.	0:47.8
1932	William Carr. U.S.A.	0:46.2
1936	Archie Williams, U.S.A.	0:46.5
1948	Arthur Wint, Jamaica	0:46.2
1952	G. Rhoden, Jamaica	0:45.9
1956	Charles Jenkins, U.S.A.	0:46.7
1960	Otis Davis, U.S.A.	0:44.9
1964	Mike Larrabee, U.S.A.	0:45.1
1968*	Lee Evans, U.S.A.	0:43.8
1972	Vincent Matthews, U.S.A.	0:44.66
1976	A. Juantorena, Cuba	0:44.26
1980	V. Markin, USSR	0:44.60

TRACK AND FIELD: 400-METER RACE—WOMEN

1964	Betty Cuthbert, Australia	0:52.0
1968	C. Besson, France	0:52.0
1972	M. Zehrt, E. Germany	0:51.08
1976	Irena Szcwinska, Poland	0:49.29
1980*	Marita Koch, E. Germany	0:48.88

TRACK AND FIELD: 800-METER RACE—MEN

1896	E. Flack, Australia	2:11.0
1900	A. Tysoe, Britain	2:01.4
1904	James Lightbody, U.S.A.	1:56.0
1908	Melvin Sheppard, U.S.A.	1.52.8
1912	James Meredith, U.S.A.	1:51.9
1920	Albert Hill, Britain	1.53.4
1924	Douglas Lowe, Britain	1:52.4
1928	Douglas Lowe, Britain	1:51.8
1932	T. Hampson, Britain	1:49.8
1936	John Woodruff, U.S.A.	1:52.9
1948	Mal Whitfield, U.S.A.	1:49.2
1952	Mal Whitfield, U.S.A.	1:49.2
1956	Thomas Courtney, U.S.A.	1:47.7
1960	P. Snell, New Zealand	1:46.3
1964	P. Snell, New Zealand	1:45.1
1968	R. Doubell, Australia	1:44.3
1972	David Wottle, U.S.A.	1:45.9
1976*	A. Juantorena, Cuba	1:43.50
1980	Steve Ovett, Britain	1:45.40

TRACK AND FIELD: 800-METER RACE—WOMEN

1928	L. Radke-Batschauer, Germany	2:16.8
1960	L. Shevcova, USSR	2:04.3
1964	Ann Packer, Britain	2:01.1
1968	Madeline Manning U.S.A.	2:00.9
1972	H. Falck, W. Germany	1:58.6
1976	Tatiana Kazankina, USSR	1:54.94
1980*	N. Olizarenko, USSR	1:53.50

TRACK AND FIELD: 1,500-METER RACE—MEN

1896	E. Flack, Australia	4:33.2
1900	E. Bennett, Britain	4:06.2
1904	James Lightbody, U.S.A.	4:05.4
1908	Melvin Sheppard, U.S.A.	4:03.4
1912	A. Jackson, Britain	3:56.8
1920	Albert Hill, Britain	4:01.8
1924	Paavo Nurmi, Finland	3:53.6
1928	Harri Larva, Finland	3:53.2
1932	Luigi Beccali, Italy	3:51.2
1936	Jack Lovelock, N. Zealand	3:47.8
1948	H. Ericksson, Sweden	3:49.8
1952	J. Barthel, Luxembourg	3:45.2
1956	Ron Delany, Ireland	3:41.2
1960	H. Elliott, Australia	3:35.6
1964	P. Snell, N. Zealand	3:38.1
1968*	K. Keino, Kenya	3:34.9
1972	P. Vasala, Finland	3:36.3
1976	John Walker, N. Zealand	3:39.17
1980*	Sebastian Coe, Britain	3:38.4

TRACK AND FIELD: 1,500-METER RACE—WOMEN

1972	Ludmila Bragina, USSR	4:01.4
1976	Tatiana Kazankina, USSR	4:05.48
1980*	Tatiana Kazankina, USSR	3:56.6

TRACK AND FIELD: 5,000-METER RACE—MEN

1912	H. Kolehmainen, Finland	14:36.6
1920	J. Guillemot, France	14:55.6
1924	Paavo Nurmi, Finland	14:31.2
1928	Villie Ritola, Finland	14:38.0
1932	L. Lehtinen, Finland	14:30.0
1936	G. Hockert, Finland	14:22.2
1948	G. Reiff, Belgium	14:17.6
1952	E. Zatopek, Czech.	14:06.6
1956	Vladimir Kuts, USSR	13:39.6
1960	M. Halberg, N. Zealand	13:43.4
1964	Bob Schul, U.S.A.	13:48.8
1968	M. Gammoudl, Tunisia	14:05.0
1972	L. Viren, Finland	13:26.4
1976	L. Viren, Finland	13:24.76
1980	M. Yifter, Ethiopia	13:21.0

TRACK AND FIELD: 10,000-METER RACE—MEN

1912	H. Kolehmainen, Finland	31:20.8
1920	Paavo Nurmi, Finland	31:45.8
1924	Villie Ritola, Finland	30:23.2
1928	Paavo Nurmi, Finland	30:18.8
1932	J. Kusocinski, Poland	30:11.4
1936	I. Salminen, Finland	30:15.4
1948	Emil Zatopek, Czech	29:59.6
1952	Emil Zatopek, Czech	29:17.0
1956	Vladimir Kuts, USSR	28:45.6
1960	P. Bolotnikov, USSR	28:32.2
1964	Billy Mills, U.S.A.	28:24.4
1968	N. Temu, Kenya	29:27.4
1972*	L. Viren, Finland	27:38.4
1976	L. Viren, Finland	27:40.38
1980	M. Yifter	27:42.7

* Olympic record.

TRACK AND FIELD: MARATHON—MEN

Year	Winner	Result
1896	S. Loues, Greece	2:58:50.0
1900	M. Theato, France	2:59:45.0
1904	Thomas Hicks, U.S.A.	3:28:53.0
1908	John Hayes, U.S.A.	2:55:18.4
1912	K. McArthur, S. Africa	2:36:54.8
1920	H. Kolehmainen, Finland	2:32:35.8
1924	A. Stenroos, Finland	2:41:22.6
1928	A.B. El Ouafi, France	2:32:57.0
1932	J. Zabala, Argentina	2:31:36.0
1936	K. Son, Japan	2:29:19.2
1948	D. Cabrera, Argentina	2:34:51.6
1952	E. Zatopek, Czech.	2:23:03.2
1956	A. Mimoun, France	2:25:00.0
1960	A. Bikila, Ethiopia	2:15:16.2
1964	A. Bikila, Ethiopia	2:12:11.2
1968	M. Wolde, Ethiopia	2:20:26.4
1972	Frank Shorter, U.S.A.	2:12:19.8
1976*	W. Cierpinski, E. Ger.	2:09:55.0
1980	W. Cierpinski, E. Ger.	2:11:03.0

TRACK AND FIELD: 110-METER HURDLES—MEN

Year	Winner	Result
1896	Thomas Curtis, U.S.A.	0:17.6
1900	Alvin Kraenzlein, U.S.A.	0:15.4
1904	Frederick Schule, U.S.A.	0:16.0
1908	Forrest Smithson, U.S.A.	0:15.0
1912	Frederick Kelly, U.S.A.	0:15.1
1920	E. Thomson, Canada	0:14.8
1924	Daniel Kinsey, U.S.A.	0:15.0
1928	S. Atkinson, S. Africa	0:14.8
1932	George Saling, U.S.A.	0:14.6
1936	Forrest Towns, U.S.A.	0:14.2
1948	William Porter, U.S.A.	0:13.9
1952	H. Dillard, U.S.A.	0:13.7
1956	Lee Calhoun, U.S.A.	0:13.5
1960	Lee Calhoun, U.S.A.	0:13.8
1964	Hayes Jones, U.S.A.	0:13.6
1968	W. Davenport, U.S.A.	0:13.3
1972*	Rodney Milburn, U.S.A.	0:13.24
1976	Guy Drut, France	0:13.30
1980	Thomas Munkelt, E. Germany	0:13.39

TRACK AND FIELD: 100-METER HURDLES—WOMEN

Year	Winner	Result
1972	Annelie Ehrhardt, E. Germany	0:12.59
1976	J. Schaller, E. Germany	0:12.77
1980*	V. Komisova, USSR	0:12.56

TRACK AND FIELD: 400-METER HURDLES—MEN

Year	Winner	Result
1900	W.B. Tewksbury, U.S.A.	0:57.6
1904	Harry Hilman, U.S.A.	0:53.0
1908	Charles Bacon, U.S.A.	0:55.0
1920	Frank Loomis, U.S.A.	0:54.0
1924	Morgan Taylor, U.S.A.	0:52.6
1928	Lord David Burgley, Britain	0:53.4
1932	Robert Tisdall, Ireland	0:51.8
1936	Glenn Hardin, U.S.A.	0:52.4
1948	Roy Cochran, U.S.A.	0:51.1
1952	Charles Moore, U.S.A.	0:50.8
1956	Glenn Davis, U.S.A.	0:50.1
1960	Glenn Davis, U.S.A.	0:49.3
1964	Rex Cawley, U.S.A.	0:49.6
1968	David Hemery, Britain	0:48.1
1972	J. Akii-bua, Uganda	0:47.82
1976*	Edwin Moses, U.S.A.	0:47.64
1980	Volker Beck, E. Ger.	0:48.70

TRACK AND FIELD: 3,000-METER STEEPLECHASE—MEN

Year	Winner	Result
1920	P. Hodges, Britain	10:00.4
1924	V. Ritola, Finland	9:33.6
1928	T. Loukola, Finland	9:21.8
1932	V. Iso-Hollo, Finland	10:33.4
1936	V. Iso-Hollo, Finland	9.03.8
1948	T. Sjostrand, Sweden	9:04.6
1952	H. Ashenfelter, U.S.A.	8:45.4
1956	Chris Brasher, Britain	8:41.2
1960	Z. Krzyszkowiak, Poland	8:34.2
1964	Gaston Roelants, Belgium	8:30.8
1968	Amos Biwott, Kenya	8:51.0
1972	K. Keino, Kenya	8:23.6
1976*	A. Garderud, Sweden	8:08.02
1980	B. Malinowski, Poland	8:09.70

TRACK AND FIELD: 400-METER RELAY—MEN

Year	Winner	Result
1912	Britain	0:42.4
1920	U.S.A.	0:42.2
1924	U.S.A.	0:41.0
1928	U.S.A.	0:41.0
1932	U.S.A.	0:40.0
1936	U.S.A.	0:40.0
1948	U.S.A.	0:40.3
1952	U.S.A.	0:40.1
1956	U.S.A.	0:39.5
1960	W. Germany	0:39.5
1964	U.S.A.	0:39.0
1968	U.S.A.	0:38.2
1972*	U.S.A.	0:38.19
1976	U.S.A.	0:38.33
1980	USSR	0:38.26

TRACK AND FIELD: 400-METER RELAY—WOMEN

Year	Winner	Result
1928	Canada	0:48.4
1932	U.S.A.	0:47.0
1936	U.S.A.	0.46.9
1948	Netherlands	0:47.5
1952	U.S.A.	0:45.9
1956	Australia	0:44.5
1960	U.S.A.	0:44.5
1964	Poland	0:43.6
1968	U.S.A.	0:42.8
1972	W. Germany	0:42.81
1976	E. Germany	0:42.55
1980*	E. Germany	0:41.60

TRACK AND FIELD: 1,600-METER RELAY—MEN

Year	Winner	Result
1908	U.S.A.	3:29.4
1912	U.S.A.	3:16.6
1920	Britain	3:22.2
1924	U.S.A.	3:16.0
1928	U.S.A.	3:14.2
1932	U.S.A.	3:08.2
1936	Britain	3:09.0
1948	U.S.A.	3:10.4
1952	Jamaica	3:03.9
1956	U.S.A.	3:04.8
1960	U.S.A.	3:02.2
1964	U.S.A.	3:00.7
1968*	U.S.A.	2:56.1
1972	Kenya	2:59.8
1976	U.S.A.	2:59.52
1980	USSR	3:01.1

TRACK AND FIELD: 1,600-METER RELAY—WOMEN

Year	Winner	Result
1972	E. Germany	3:23.0
1976*	E. Germany	3:19.23
1980	USSR	3:20.2

TRACK AND FIELD: 20-KILOMETER WALK—MEN

Year	Winner	Result
1956	L. Spirine, USSR	1:31:27.0
1960	V. Golubnichy, USSR	1:34:07.2
1964	Ken Matthews, U.S.A.	1:29:34.0
1968	L. Golubnichy, USSR	1:33:58.4
1972	P. Frenkel, E. Germany	1:26:42.4
1976	D. Bautista, Mexico	1:24:40.6
1980	M. Damilano, Italy	1:23:35.5

TRACK AND FIELD: 50-KILOMETER WALK—MEN

Year	Winner	Result
1932	T. Green, Britain	4:50:10.0
1936	H. Whitlock, Britain	4:30:41.4
1948	J. Ljunggren, Sweden	4:41:52.0
1952	G. Dordoni, Italy	4:28:07.8
1956	N. Read, N. Zealand	4:30:42.8
1960	D. Thompson, Britain	4:25:30.0
1964	A. Pamich, Italy	4:11:12.4
1968	C. Hohne, E. Germany	4:20:13.6
1972	B. Kannenberg, W. Ger.	3:56:11.6
1980	H. Gauder, E. Germany	3:49:24.0

TRACK AND FIELD: HIGH JUMP—MEN

Year	Winner	Result
1896	Ellery Clark, U.S.A.	5′ 11¼″
1900	Irving Baxter, U.S.A.	6′ 2⅘″
1904	Samuel Jones, U.S.A.	5′ 11″
1908	Harry Porter, U.S.A.	6′ 2¾″
1912	Almer Richards, U.S.A.	6′ 4″
1920	R. Landon, U.S.A.	6′ 4¼″
1924	Harold Osborn, U.S.A.	6′ 5 15/16″
1928	R.W. King, U.S.A.	6′ 4⅜″
1932	D. McNaughton, Can.	6′ 5⅝″
1936	C. Johnson, U.S.A.	6′ 7 15/16″
1948	J. Winter, Australia	6′ 6″
1952	Walter Davis, U.S.A.	6′ 8¼″
1956	Charles Dumas, U.S.A.	6′ 11¼″
1960	R. Shavlakadze, USSR	7′ 1″
1964	V. Brumel, USSR	7′ 1⅘″
1968	Dick Fosbury, U.S.A.	7′ 4¼″
1972	Yuri Tarmak, USSR	7′ 3¾″
1976	J. Wszola, Poland	7′ 4½″
1980*	G. Wessig, E. Germany	7′ 9″

* Olympic record.

SUMMER OLYMPIC WINNERS AND RECORDS *(continued)*

TRACK AND FIELD: HIGH JUMP—WOMEN

Year	Winner	Record
1928	E. Catherwood, Canada	5' 3"
1932	Jean Shiley, U.S.A.	5' 5 1/4"
1936	I. Csak, Hungary	5' 3"
1948	Alice Coachman, U.S.A.	5' 6 1/8"
1952	E. Brand, S. Africa	5' 5 3/4"
1956	M. McDaniel, U.S.A.	5' 9 1/4"
1960	I. Balas, Romania	6' 1/4"
1964	I. Balas, Romania	6' 2 4/5"
1968	M. Rezkova, Czech.	5' 11 3/4"
1972	U. Meyfarth, W. Germany	6' 3 1/4"
1976	R. Ackermann, W. Germany	6' 3 3/4"
1980*	S. Simeoni, Italy	6' 5 1/2"

TRACK AND FIELD: LONG JUMP—MEN

Year	Winner	Record
1896	Ellery Clark, U.S.A.	20' 10"
1900	A. Kraenzlein, U.S.A.	23' 6 7/8"
1904	Myer Prinstein, U.S.A.	24' 1 3/8"
1908	Frank Irons, U.S.A.	24' 6 1/2"
1912	A. Gutterson, U.S.A.	24' 11 1/4"
1920	W. Pettersson Sweden	23' 5 1/2"
1924	DeHart Hubbard, U.S.A.	24' 5 1/8"
1928	Edward Hamm, U.S.A.	25' 4 3/4"
1932	Edward Gordon, U.S.A.	25' 3/4"
1936	Jesse Owens, U.S.A.	26' 5 3/8"
1948	Willie Steele, U.S.A.	25' 8"
1952	Jerome Biffle, U.S.A.	24' 10"
1956	Gregory Bell, U.S.A.	25' 8 1/4"
1960	Ralph Boston, U.S.A.	26' 7 3/4"
1964	L. Davies, Britain	26' 5 7/10"
1968*	Bob Beamon, U.S.A.	29' 2 1/2"
1972	Randy Williams, U.S.A.	27' 1/2"
1976	Arnie Robinson, U.S.A.	27' 4 1/2"
1980	L. Dombroski, E. Germany	28' 1/4"

TRACK AND FIELD: LONG JUMP—WOMEN

Year	Winner	Record
1948	O. Gyarmati, Hungary	18' 8 1/4"
1952	Y. Williams, New Zealand	20' 5 3/4"
1956	E. Krzesinska, Poland	20' 9 3/4"
1960	V. Krepkina, USSR	20' 10 3/4"
1964	Mary Rand, Britain	22' 2 1/8"
1968	V. Viscopoleanu, Rom.	22' 4 1/2"
1972	Rosendahl, W. Germany	22' 3"
1976	A. Voigt, E. Germany	22' 2 1/2"
1980*	T. Kolpakova, USSR	23' 2"

TRACK AND FIELD: DISCUS THROW—MEN

Year	Winner	Record
1896	R. Garrett, U.S.A.	95' 7 1/2"
1900	R. Bauer, Hungary	118' 2 7/8"
1904	M. Sheridan, U.S.A.	128' 10 1/2"
1908	M. Sheridan, U.S.A.	134' 2"
1912	A. Taipale, Finland	145' 9/16"
1920	E. Niklander, Finland	146' 7"
1924	C. Houser, U.S.A.	151' 5 1/4"
1928	C. Houser, U.S.A.	155' 2 4/5"
1932	J. Anderson, U.S.A.	162' 4 7/8"
1936	K. Carpenter, U.S.A.	165' 7 1/2"
1948	A. Consolini, Italy	173' 2"
1952	Sim Iness, U.S.A.	180' 6 1/2"
1956	A. Oerter, U.S.A.	184' 10 1/2"
1960	A. Oerter, U.S.A.	194' 2"
1964	A. Oerter, U.S.A.	200' 1 1/2"
1968	A. Oerter, U.S.A.	212' 6 1/2"
1972	L. Danek, Czech.	211' 3"
1976*	Mac Wilkens, U.S.A.	221' 5.4"
1980	V. Rasshchupkin, USSR	218' 7"

TRACK AND FIELD: DISCUS THROW—WOMEN

Year	Winner	Record
1928	Konopacka, Poland	129' 11 7/8"
1932	L. Copeland, U.S.A.	132' 2"
1936	Mauermayer, Germany	156' 3 3/16"
1948	M. Ostermeyer, France	137' 6 1/2"
1952	N. Romaschkova, USSR	168' 8 1/2"
1956	O. Fikotova, Czech.	176' 1 1/2"
1960	N. Ponomareva, USSR	180' 8 1/4"
1964	Tamara Press, USSR	187' 10 3/4"
1968	L. Manoliu, Romania	191' 2 1/2"
1972	Faina Melnik, USSR	218' 7"
1976	E. Schlaak, E. Germany	226' 4 1/2"
1980*	E. Jahl, E. Germany	229' 6 1/2"

TRACK AND FIELD: SHOT PUT—MEN

Year	Winner	Record
1896	R. Garrett, U.S.A.	36' 9 3/4"
1900	R. Sheldon, U.S.A.	46' 3 1/8"
1904	Ralph Rose, U.S.A.	48' 7"
1908	Ralph Rose, U.S.A.	46' 7 1/2"
1912	P. McDonald, U.S.A.	50' 4"
1920	V. Porhola, Finland	48' 7 1/8"
1924	C. Houser, U.S.A.	49' 2 1/2"
1928	John Kuck, U.S.A.	52' 11/16"
1932	Leo Sexton, U.S.A.	52' 6 3/16"
1936	H. Woellke, Germany	53' 1 3/4"
1948	W. Thompson, U.S.A.	56' 2"
1952	P. O'Brien Jr., U.S.A.	57' 1 1/2"
1956	P. O'Brien Jr., U.S.A.	60' 11"
1960	W. Nieder, U.S.A.	64' 6 3/4"
1964	Dallas Long, U.S.A.	66' 8 2/3"
1968	R. Matson, U.S.A.	67' 4 3/4"
1972	W. Komar, Poland	69' 6"
1976	U. Beyer, E. Germany	69' 3/4"
1980*	V. Kiselyov, USSR	70' 1/2"

TRACK AND FIELD: SHOT PUT—WOMEN

Year	Winner	Record
1948	M. Ostermeyer, France	45' 1 1/2"
1952	G. Zybina, USSR	50' 1 1/2"
1956	T. Tishkyevich, USSR	54' 5"
1960	Tamara Press, USSR	56' 9 7/8"
1964	Tamara Press, USSR	59' 6 1/5"
1968	M. Gummel, E. Ger.	64' 4"
1972	N. Chizova, USSR	69' 0"
1976	I. Christova, Bulgaria	69' 5"
1980*	I. Slupianek, E. Germany	73' 6 1/4"

TRACK AND FIELD: JAVELIN THROW—MEN

Year	Winner	Record
1908	E. Lemming, Sweden	179' 10 1/2"
1912	E. Lemming, Sweden	198' 11 1/4"
1920	Jonni Myrra, Finland	215' 9 3/4"
1924	Jonni Myrra, Finland	206' 6 3/4"
1928	E. Lundquist, Sweden	218' 6 1/8"
1932	M. Jarvinen, Finland	238' 7"
1936	G. Stock, Germany	235' 8 5/16"
1948	T. Rautavaara, Finland	228' 10 1/2"
1952	Cy Young, U.S.A.	242' 3/4"
1956	E. Danielson, Norway	281' 2 1/4"
1960	V. Tsibulenko, USSR	277' 8 3/8"
1964	P. Nevala, Finland	271' 2 1/3"
1968	Jan Lusis, USSR	295' 7 1/4"
1972	W. Wolfermann, W. Germany	296' 10"
1976*	M. Nemeth, Hungary	310' 4"
1980	D. Kula, USSR	299' 2"

TRACK AND FIELD: JAVELIN THROW—WOMEN

Year	Winner	Record
1932	Mildred Didrikson, U.S.A.	143' 4"
1936	T. Fleischer, Germany	148' 2 3/4"
1948	H. Baume, Austria	149' 6"
1952	D. Zatopkova, Czech.	165' 7"
1956	I. Janzeme, USSR	176' 8"
1960	E. Ozolina, USSR	183' 8"
1964	M. Penes, Romania	198' 7 1/2"
1968	A. Nemeth, Hungary	198' 1/2"
1972	R. Fuchs, E. Germany	209' 7"
1976	R. Fuchs, E. Germany	216' 4"
1980*	M. Colon, Cuba	224' 5"

TRACK AND FIELD: POLE VAULT—MEN

Year	Winner	Record
1896	William Hoyt, U.S.A.	10' 9 3/4"
1900	Irving Baxter, U.S.A.	10' 9 7/8"
1904	Charles Dvorak, U.S.A.	11' 6"
1908	(tie) A. Gilbert; E. Cook Jr., U.S.A.	12' 2"
1912	Harry Babcock, U.S.A.	12' 11 1/2"
1920	Frank Foss, U.S.A.	12' 5 9/16"
1924	Lee Barnes, U.S.A.	12' 11 1/2"
1928	Sabin Carr, U.S.A.	13' 9 3/8"
1932	W. Miller, U.S.A.	14' 1 7/8"
1936	Earle Meadows, U.S.A.	14' 3 1/4"
1948	Guinn Smith, U.S.A.	14' 1 1/4"
1952	Bob Richards, U.S.A.	14' 11 1/4"
1956	Bob Richards, U.S.A.	14' 11 1/2"
1960	Don Bragg, U.S.A.	15' 5 1/8"
1964	Fred Hansen, U.S.A.	16' 8 3/4"
1968	Bob Seagren, U.S.A.	17' 8 1/2"
1972	W. Nordwig, E. Germany	18' 1/2"
1976	T. Slusarski, Poland	18' 1/2"
1980*	W. Kozakiewicz, Poland	18' 11 1/2"

* Olympic record.

TRACK AND FIELD: TRIPLE JUMP—MEN

1896	James Connolly, U.S.A.	45′	**1948**	A. Ahman, Sweden	50′ $6\frac{1}{4}$″
1900	Myer Prinstein, U.S.A.	47′ $4\frac{1}{4}$″	**1952**	A. Ferreira da Silva, Brazil	53′ $2\frac{1}{2}$″
1904	Myer Prinstein, U.S.A.	47′	**1956**	A. Ferreira da Silva, Brazil	53′ $7\frac{1}{2}$″
1908	T. Ahearne, Britain	48′ $11\frac{1}{4}$″	**1960**	J. Schmidt, Poland	55′ $1\frac{3}{8}$″
1912	G. Lindblom, Sweden	48′ $5\frac{1}{8}$″	**1964**	J. Schmidt, Poland	55′ $3\frac{2}{5}$″
1920	V. Tuulos, Finland	47′ $7\frac{1}{16}$″	**1968***	V. Saneev, USSR	57′ $\frac{3}{4}$″
1924	A. Winter, Australia	50′ $11\frac{1}{8}$″	**1972**	V. Saneev, USSR	56′ 11″
1928	M. Oda, Japan	49′ $10\frac{13}{16}$″	**1976**	V. Saneev, USSR	56′ $8\frac{3}{4}$″
1932	C. Nambu, Japan	51′ 7″	**1980**	J. Uudmae, USSR	56′ $11\frac{1}{8}$″
1936	N. Tajima, Japan	52′ $5\frac{7}{8}$″			

TRACK AND FIELD: HAMMER THROW—MEN

1900	John Flanagan, U.S.A.	167′ 4″	**1948**	I. Nemeth, Hungary	183′ $11\frac{1}{2}$″
1904	John Flanagan, U.S.A.	168′ 1″	**1952**	J. Csermak, Hungary	197′ $11\frac{3}{4}$″
1908	John Flanagan, U.S.A.	170′ $4\frac{1}{4}$″	**1956**	H. Connolly, U.S.A.	207′ $3\frac{1}{2}$″
1912	M. McGrath, U.S.A.	179′ $7\frac{1}{8}$″	**1960**	V. Rudenkov, USSR	220′ $1\frac{5}{8}$″
1920	Patrick Ryan, U.S.A.	173′ $5\frac{5}{8}$″	**1964**	R. Klim, USSR	228′ $9\frac{2}{3}$″
1924	F. Tootell, U.S.A.	174′ $10\frac{1}{4}$″	**1968**	G. Zsivotzky, Hungary	240′ 8″
1928	P. O'Callaghan, Ireland	168′ $7\frac{1}{2}$″	**1972**	A. Bondarchuk, USSR	248′ 8″
1932	P. O'Callaghan, Ireland	176′ $11\frac{1}{8}$″	**1976**	J. Sedych, USSR	254′ 4″
1936	Karl Hein, Germany	185′ $4\frac{1}{4}$″	**1980***	Y. Sedykh, USSR	268′ $4\frac{1}{2}$″

TRACK AND FIELD: DECATHLON—MEN

1912	Jim Thorpe, U.S.A.	**1936**	Glenn Morris, U.S.A.	**1964**	W. Holdorf, W. Germany
1920	H. Lovland, Norway	**1948**	Bob Mathias, U.S.A.	**1968**	Bill Toomey, U.S.A.
1924	Harold Osborn, U.S.A.	**1952**	Bob Mathias, U.S.A.	**1972**	Nikolai Avilov, USSR
1928	P. Yrjola, Finland	**1956**	Milt Campbell, U.S.A.	**1976**	Bruce Jenner, U.S.A.
1932	James Bausch, U.S.A.	**1960**	Rafer Johnson, U.S.A.	**1980**	Daley Thompson, Britain

VOLLEYBALL—MEN

1964 USSR	**1972** Japan	**1980** USSR
1968 USSR	**1976** Poland	

VOLLEYBALL—WOMEN

1964 Japan	**1972** USSR	**1980** USSR
1968 USSR	**1976** Japan	

WATER POLO—MEN

1900 Britain	**1912** Britain	**1928** Germany	**1948** Italy	**1960** Italy	**1972** USSR
1904 U.S.A.	**1920** Britain	**1932** Hungary	**1952** Hungary	**1964** Hungary	**1976** Hungary
1908 Britain	**1924** France	**1936** Hungary	**1956** Hungary	**1968** Yugoslavia	**1980** USSR

WEIGHTLIFTING: FLYWEIGHT (114.5 lbs.)

1972	Z. Smalcerz, Poland	745 lbs.	**1980***	K. Osmanoliev, USSR	540 lbs.
1976	A. Voronin, USSR	534.5 lbs.			

WEIGHTLIFTING: BANTAMWEIGHT (123 lbs.)

		POUNDS			POUNDS			POUNDS
1948	Joe DePietro, U.S.A.	677	**1960**	Charles Vinci, U.S.A.	760	**1972**	Imre Foldi, Hungary	833
1952	Ivan Udovov, USSR	694	**1964**	A. Vakhonin, USSR	788.1	**1976**	N. Nourikian, Bulgaria	578.5
1956	Charles Vinci, U.S.A.	754.5	**1968**	M.N. Seresht, Iran	808.5	**1980**	D. Nunez, Cuba	606.2

WEIGHTLIFTING: FEATHERWEIGHT (132 lbs.)

1920	L. de Haes, Belgium	485	**1948**	M. Fayad, Egypt	733	**1968**	Y. Miyake, Japan	863.5
1924	P. Gabetti, Italy	887	**1952**	R. Chimishyan, USSR	743.5	**1972**	N. Nourikian, Bulgaria	888
1928	F. Andrysek, Austria	633	**1956**	Isaac Berger, U.S.A.	776.75	**1976**	N. Kolenisnikov, USSR	628
1932	R. Suvigny, France	633	**1960**	Y. Minaev, USSR	821	**1980**	V. Mazin, USSR	639
1936	A. Teriazzo, U.S.A.	688	**1964**	Y. Miyake, Japan	876.3			

WEIGHTLIFTING: LIGHTWEIGHT (149 lbs.)

1920	A. Neyland, Estonia	567	**1936**	M. Mesbah, Egypt	755	**1964**	W. Baszanowski, Poland	953.5
1924	E. Decottignies, France	970	**1948**	I. Shams, Egypt	793	**1968**	W. Baszanowski, Poland	962.5
1928	(tie) D. Helbig, Germany;		**1952**	Tommy Kono, U.S.A.	798.75	**1972**	M. Kirzhinov, USSR	1,014
	H. Haas, Austria	710	**1956**	Igor Rybak, USSR	837	**1976**	Z. Kaczmarek, Poland	677.5
1932	R. Duverger, France	716	**1960**	V. Bushuev, USSR	876	**1980**	Y. Roussev, Bulgaria	755

WEIGHTLIFTING: MIDDLEWEIGHT (165 lbs.)

1920	B. Gance, France	540	**1948**	Frank Spellman, U.S.A.	859	**1968**	V. Kurentsov, USSR	1,045
1924	C. Galimberti, Italy	1,085	**1952**	Peter George, U.S.A.	881.5	**1972**	Y. Bikov, Bulgaria	1,069.23
1928	F. Roger, France	738	**1956**	F. Bogdanovskii, USSR	925.5	**1976**	Y. Mitkov, Bulgaria	738.5
1932	R. Ismayr, Germany	760	**1960**	A. Kurynov, USSR	964.25	**1980**	A. Zlatev, Bulgaria	792
1936	K. El Touni, Egypt	854	**1964**	H. Zdrazila, Czech	981			

WEIGHTLIFTING: LIGHT HEAVYWEIGHT (181.5 lbs.)

1920	E. Cadine, France	639	**1948**	S. Stanczyk, U.S.A.	920.00	**1968**	B. Selitsky, USSR	1,067.00
1924	C. Rigoulot, France	1,107	**1952**	T. Lomakin, USSR	920.25	**1972**	L. Jenssen, Norway	1,118.00
1928	S. Nosseir, Egypt	782	**1956**	Tommy Kono, U.S.A.	986.25	**1976**	V. Shary, USSR	803.00
1932	L. Hostin, France	804	**1960**	I. Palinski, Poland	975.25	**1980**	Y. Vardanyan, USSR	882
1936	L. Hostin, France	821	**1964**	R. Plyukfeider, USSR	1,047.20			

* Olympic record.

SUMMER OLYMPIC WINNERS AND RECORDS *(continued)*

WEIGHTLIFTING: MIDDLE HEAVYWEIGHT (198 lbs.)

1952	N. Schemansky, U.S.A.	980.75	1964	V. Golovanov, USSR	1,074.70	1976	D. Rigert, USSR	841.50
1956	A. Vorobiev, USSR	1,019.25	1968	K. Kangasniemi, Finland	1,138.50	1980	P. Baczako, Hungary	832.2
1960	A. Vorobiev, USSR	1,041.25	1972	A. Nikolov, Bulgaria	1,157.00			

WEIGHTLIFTING: 1st HEAVYWEIGHT (220 lbs.)

1980	O. Zaremba, Czechoslovakia	870.8

WEIGHTLIFTING: 2d HEAVYWEIGHT (Up to 242 lbs.)

1920	F. Bottini, Italy	595	1948	John Davis, U.S.A.	997.00	1964	L. Zhabotinsky, USSR	1,259.50
1924	G. Tonani, Italy	1,140	1952	John Davis, U.S.A.	1,013.75	1972	Yan Talts, USSR	1,278.00
1928	J. Strassberger, Germany	821	1956	Paul Anderson, U.S.A.	1,102.00	1976	V. Khristov, Bulgaria	880
1932	J. Skobia, Czechoslovakia	837	1960	Y. Vlasov, USSR	1,184.25	1980	L. Taranenko, USSR	931.4
1936	J. Manger, Germany	903	1968	L. Zhabotinsky, USSR	1,262.10			

WEIGHTLIFTING: SUPER HEAVYWEIGHT (Over 242 lbs.)

1972	Vasily Alexeev, USSR	1,411	1976	Vasily Alexeev, USSR	968	1980	S. Rakhmanov, USSR	970

WRESTLING: FREESTYLE—PAPERWEIGHT (105.5 lbs.)

1972	Roman Dmitriev, USSR	1976	K. Issaev, Bulgaria	1980	C. Pollio, Italy

WRESTLING: FREESTYLE—FLYWEIGHT (114.5 lbs.)

1948	L. Viitala, Finland	1960	A. Bilek, Turkey	1968	S. Nakata, Japan	1976	Y. Takada, Japan
1952	H. Gemici, Turkey	1964	Y. Yoshida, Japan	1972	K. Kato, Japan	1980	A. Beloglazov, USSR
1956	M. Tzalkalmanidze, USSR						

WRESTLING: FREESTYLE—BANTAMWEIGHT (125.5 lbs.)

1904	G. Mehnert, U.S.A.	1932	Robert Pearce, U.S.A.	1956	M. Dagistanli, Turkey	1972	H. Yanagida, Japan
1908	G. Mehnert, U.S.A.	1936	O. Zombori, Hungary	1960	Terrence McCann, U.S.A.	1976	V. Umin, USSR
1924	K. Pihlajamaki, Finland	1948	N. Akar, Turkey	1964	Y. Uetake, Japan	1980	S. Beloglazov, USSR
1928	K. Makinen, Finland	1952	S. Ishii, Japan	1968	Y. Uetake, Japan		

WRESTLING: FREESTYLE—FEATHERWEIGHT (136.5 lbs.)

1908	George Dole, U.S.A.	1932	H. Pihlajamaki, Finland	1956	S. Sasahara, Japan	1972	Z. Abdulbekov, USSR
1920	Charles Ackerly, U.S.A.	1936	K. Pihlajamaki, Finland	1960	M. Dagistanli, Turkey	1976	Yang Jung Mo, S. Korea
1924	Robin Reed, U.S.A.	1948	G. Bilge, Turkey	1964	O. Watanabe, Japan	1980	M. Abushev, USSR
1928	Allie Morrison, U.S.A.	1952	B. Sit, Turkey	1968	M. Kaneko, Japan		

WRESTLING: FREESTYLE—LIGHTWEIGHT (149.5 lbs.)

1908	G. de Relwyskow, Britain	1928	O. Kapp, Estonia	1952	O. Anderberg, Sweden	1968	A. Movahed, Iran
		1932	C. Pacome, France	1956	E. Habibi, Iran	1972	Dan Gable, U.S.A.
1920	K. Antilla, Finland	1936	K. Karpati, Hungary	1960	Shelby Wilson, U.S.A.	1976	P. Pinegin, USSR
1924	Russell Vis, U.S.A.	1948	C. Atik, Turkey	1964	E. Dimov, Bulgaria	1980	S. Absaidov, USSR

WRESTLING: FREESTYLE—WELTERWEIGHT (163 lbs.)

1924	H. Gehri, Switzerland	1948	Y. Dogu, Turkey	1964	I. Ogan, Turkey	1980	V. Raitchev, Bulgaria
1928	A. Haavisto, Finland	1952	William Smith, U.S.A.	1968	M. Atalay, Turkey		
1932	Jack Van Bebber, U.S.A.	1956	M. Ikeda, Japan	1972	Wayne Wells, U.S.A.		
1936	Frank Lewis, U.S.A.	1960	D. Blubaugh, U.S.A.	1976	I. Date, Japan		

WRESTLING: FREESTYLE—MIDDLEWEIGHT (180 lbs.)

1908	S. Bacon, Britain	1928	E. Kyburz, Switzerland	1952	D. Cimakuridze, USSR	1968	B. Gurevitch, USSR
1920	E. Leino, Finland	1932	I. Johansson, Sweden	1956	N. Nikolov, Bulgaria	1972	L. Tediashvili, USSR
1924	F. Haggmann, Switzerland	1936	E. Poilve, France	1960	H. Gungor, Turkey	1976	J. Peterson, U.S.A.
		1948	Glen Brand, U.S.A.	1964	P. Gardjev, Bulgaria	1980	I. Abilov, Bulgaria

WRESTLING: FREESTYLE—LIGHT HEAVYWEIGHT (198 lbs.)

1920	A. Larsson, Sweden	1936	K. Fridell, Sweden	1960	I. Atli, Turkey	1976	L. Tediashvili, USSR
1924	John Spellman, U.S.A.	1948	Henry Wittenberg, U.S.A.	1964	A. Medved, USSR	1980	S. Oganesyan, USSR
1928	T. Sjostedt, Sweden	1952	W. Palm, Sweden	1968	A. Ayuk, Turkey		
1932	Peter Mehringer, U.S.A.	1956	G. Takhti, Iran	1972	Ben Peterson, U.S.A.		

WRESTLING: FREESTYLE—HEAVYWEIGHT (220 lbs.)

1908	G.C. O'Kelly, Britain	1932	J. Richthoff, Sweden	1956	H. Kaplan, Turkey	1968	A. Medved, USSR
1920	R. Roth, Switzerland	1936	K. Palusalu, Estonia	1960	W. Dietrich, W. Germany	1972	Ivan Yarygin, USSR
1924	Harry Steele, U.S.A.	1948	G. Bobis, Hungary			1976	Ivan Yarygin, USSR
1928	J. Richthoff, Sweden	1952	A. Mekokishvili, USSR	1964	A. Ivanitsky, USSR	1980	Ilya Mate, USSR

WRESTLING: FREESTYLE—SUPER HEAVYWEIGHT (Over 220 lbs.)

1972	Aleksandr Medved, USSR	1976	Soslan Andiev, USSR	1980	S. Andiev, USSR

WRESTLING: GRECO-ROMAN—PAPERWEIGHT (105.5 lbs.)

1972	Gheorghe Berceanu, Romania	1976	A. Shumakov, USSR	1980	Z. Ushkempirov, USSR

WRESTLING: GRECO-ROMAN—FLYWEIGHT (114.5 lbs.)

1948 P. Lombardi, Italy	**1960** D. Pirvulescu, Romania	**1972** P. Kirov, Bulgaria
1952 B. Gourevitch, USSR	**1964** T. Hanahara, Japan	**1976** V. Konstantinov, USSR
1956 N. Soloviev, USSR	**1968** P. Kirov, Bulgaria	**1980** V. Blagidze, USSR

WRESTLING: GRECO-ROMAN—BANTAMWEIGHT (125.5 lbs.)

1924 E. Putsep, Estonia	**1948** K. Pettersen, Sweden	**1960** O. Karavaev, USSR	**1972** R. Kazakov, USSR
1928 K. Leucht, Germany	**1952** I. Hodos, Hungary	**1964** M. Ichiguchi, Japan	**1976** P. Ukkola, Finland
1932 J. Brendel, Germany	**1956** K. Vyropaev, USSR	**1968** J. Varga, Hungary	**1980** S. Serikov, USSR
1936 M. Lorinc, Hungary			

WRESTLING: GRECO—ROMAN—FEATHERWEIGHT (136.5 lbs.)

1912 K. Koskelo, Finland	**1932** G. Gozzo, Italy	**1956** R. Makinen, Finland	**1972** G. Markov, Bulgaria
1920 O. Friman, Finland	**1936** Y. Erkan, Turkey	**1960** M. Sille, Turkey	**1976** K. Lipien, Poland
1924 K. Anttila, Finland	**1948** M. Oktav, Turkey	**1964** I. Polyak, Hungary	**1980** S. Migiakis, Greece
1928 V. Vali, Estonia	**1952** Y. Punkin, USSR	**1968** R. Rurua, USSR	

WRESTLING: GRECO-ROMAN—LIGHTWEIGHT (149.5 lbs.)

1908 E. Porro, Italy	**1928** L. Keresztes, Hungary	**1952** C. Safin, USSR	**1968** M. Mumemura, Japan
1912 E. Vare, Finland	**1932** E. Malmberg, Sweden	**1956** K. Lehtonen, Finland	**1972** S. Khisamutdinov, USSR
1920 E. Vare, Finland	**1936** L. Koskela, Finland	**1960** A. Kordidze, USSR	**1976** S. Nalbandian, USSR
1924 O. Friman, Finland	**1948** K. Freij, Sweden	**1964** K. Ayvaz, Turkey	**1980** S. Rusu, Romania

WRESTLING: GRECO-ROMAN—WELTERWEIGHT (163 lbs.)

1932 I. Johansson, Sweden	**1952** M. Szilvasi, Hungary	**1964** A. Kolesov, USSR	**1976** A. Bykov, USSR
1936 R. Svedberg, Sweden	**1956** M. Bayrak, Turkey	**1968** R. Vesper, E. Germany	**1980** F. Kocsis, Hungary
1948 G. Andersson, Sweden	**1960** M. Bayrak, Turkey	**1972** V. Macha, Czechoslovakia	

WRESTLING: GRECO-ROMAN—MIDDLEWEIGHT (180 lbs.)

1908 F. Martenson, Sweden	**1936** I. Johansson, Sweden	**1968** L. Metz, E. Germany
1912 C. Johansson, Sweden	**1948** A. Gronberg, Sweden	**1972** C. Hegedus, Hungary
1920 C. Westergren, Sweden	**1952** A. Gronberg, Sweden	**1976** M. Petkovic, Yugoslavia
1924 E. Vesterland, Finland	**1956** G. Kartosa, USSR	**1980** G. Korban, USSR
1928 V. Kokkinen, Finland	**1960** D. Dobrev, Bulgaria	
1932 V. Kokkinen, Finland	**1964** B. Simic, Yugoslavia	

WRESTLING: GRECO-ROMAN—LIGHT HEAVYWEIGHT (198 lbs.)

1908 V. Weckmann, Finland	**1932** R. Svensson, Sweden	**1964** B. Alexandrov, Bulgaria
1912 (tie) A. Ahlgren, Sweden	**1936** A. Cadier, Sweden	**1968** B. Radev, Bulgaria
I. Boling, Finland	**1948** K. Nilsson, Sweden	**1972** V. Rezantsev, USSR
1920 C. Johansson, Sweden	**1952** K. Grondhal, Finland	**1976** V. Rezantsev, USSR
1924 C. Westergren, Sweden	**1956** V. Nikolaev, USSR	**1980** N. Nottny, Hungary
1928 I. Moustafa, Egypt	**1960** Tevik Kis, Turkey	

WRESTLING: GRECO-ROMAN—HEAVYWEIGHT (220 lbs.)

1896 K. Schumann, Germany	**1928** R. Svensson, Sweden	**1956** A. Parfenov, USSR	**1976** N. Bolboshin, USSR
1908 R. Weisz, Hungary	**1932** C. Westergren, Sweden	**1960** I. Bogdan, USSR	**1980** G. Raikov, Bulgaria
1912 Y. Saarela, Finland	**1936** K. Palusalu, Estonia	**1964** I. Kozma, Hungary	
1920 A. Lindfors, Finland	**1948** A. Kirecci, Turkey	**1968** I. Kozma, Hungary	
1924 H. Degiane, France	**1952** J. Kotkas, USSR	**1972** N. Martinescu, Romania	

WRESTLING: GRECO-ROMAN—SUPER HEAVYWEIGHT (Over 220 lbs.)

1972 Anatoly Roshin, USSR	**1976** A. Kolchinsky, USSR	**1980** A. Kolchinsky, USSR

YACHTING: FINN CLASS

1952 Denmark	**1960** Denmark	**1968** USSR	**1976** East Germany
1956 Denmark	**1964** West Germany	**1972** France	**1980** Finland

YACHTING: FLYING DUTCHMAN CLASS

1960 Norway	**1964** New Zealand	**1968** Britain	**1972** Britain	**1976** West Germany	**1980** Spain

YACHTING: TEMPEST CLASS	**YACHTING: SOLING CLASS**	**YACHTING: TORNADO CLASS**	**YACHTING: 470 CLASS**
1972 USSR	**1972** U.S.A.	**1976** Britain	**1976** West Germany
1976 Sweden	**1976** Denmark	**1980** Brazil	**1980** Brazil
	1980 Denmark		

YACHTING: STAR CLASS

1932 U.S.A.	**1948** U.S.A.	**1956** U.S.A.	**1964** Bahamas	**1972** Australia
1936 Germany	**1952** Italy	**1960** USSR	**1968** U.S.A.	**1980** USSR

YACHTING: DRAGON CLASS

1948 Norway	**1956** Sweden	**1964** Denmark	**1968** U.S.A.	**1972** Australia
1952 Norway	**1960** Greece			

WINTER OLYMPIC WINNERS AND RECORDS

BIATHLON—10 km

1980	Frank Ullrich, E. Germany	0:32:10.69

BIATHLON—20 km

1960	Klas Lestander, Sweden	1:33:21.6	1972	Magnar Solberg, Norway	1:15:55.50
1964	Vladimir Melanin, USSR	1:20:26.8	1976	Nikolai Kruglov, USSR	1:14:12.26
1968	Magnar Solberg, Norway	1:13:45.9	1980*	Anatoli Aljabiev, USSR	1:08:16.31

BIATHLON RELAY

1968	USSR	2:13.02	1972	USSR	1:51.44	1976	USSR	1:57:55.67	1980*	USSR	1:34:03.27

BOBSLED: 2-MAN BOB (winning driver)

1932	U.S.A., Hubert Stevens	8:14.74	1964	Britain, Antony Nash	4:21.90
1936	U.S.A., Ivan Brown	5:29.29	1968	Italy, Eugenio Monti	4:41.54
1948	Switzerland, F. Endrich	5:29.2	1972	W. Germany, Wolfgang Zimmerer	4:47.07
1952	W. Germany, Andreas Ostler	5:24.54	1976*	E. Germany, Meinhard Nehmer	3:40.43
1956	Italy, Dalla Costa	5:30.14	1980	Switzerland, Erich Schaerer	4:09.36

BOBSLED: 4-MAN BOB (winning driver)

1924	Switzerland, Edward Scherrer	5:45.54	1956	Switzerland, Franz Kapus	5:10.44
1928	U.S.A., William Fiske	3:20.5	1964	Canada, Victor Emery	4:14.46
1932	U.S.A., William Fiske	7:53.68	1968*	Italy, Eugenio Monti	2:17.39
1936	Switzerland, Perre Musy	5:19.85	1972	Switzerland, Jean Wicki	4:43.07
1948	U.S.A., Edward Rimkus	5:20.1	1976	E. Germany, Meinhard Nehmer	3:44.42
1952	W. Germany, Andreas Ostler	5:07.84	1980	E. Germany, Meinhard Nehmer	3:59.92

ICE HOCKEY

1920	Canada	1928	Canada	1936	Britain	1952	Canada	1960	U.S.A.	1968	USSR	1976	USSR
1924	Canada	1932	Canada	1948	Canada	1956	USSR	1964	USSR	1972	USSR	1980	U.S.A.

SKATING: FIGURE SKATING—MEN

1908	Ulrich Salchow, Sweden	1936	Karl Schafer, Austria	1964	Manfred Schnelldorfer, W. Ger.
1920	Gillis Grafstrom, Sweden	1948	Richard Button, U.S.A.	1968	Wolfgang Schwarz, Austria
1924	Gillis Grafstrom, Sweden	1952	Richard Button, U.S.A.	1972	Ondrej Nepela, Czechoslovakia
1928	Gillis Grafstrom, Sweden	1956	H.A. Jenkins, U.S.A.	1976	John Curry, Britain
1932	Karl Schafer, Austria	1960	David Jenkins, U.S.A.	1980	Robin Cousins, Britain

SKATING: FIGURE SKATING—WOMEN

1908	Madge Syers, Britain	1936	Sonja Henie, Norway	1964	Sjoukje Dijkstra, Netherlands
1920	Magda Julin-Mauroy, Sweden	1948	Barbara Ann Scott, Canada	1968	Peggy Fleming, U.S.A.
1924	Heima von Szabo-Planck, Austria	1952	Jeanette Altwegg, Britain	1972	Beatrix Schuba, Austria
1928	Sonja Henie, Norway	1956	Tenley Albright, U.S.A.	1976	Dorothy Hamill, U.S.A.
1932	Sonja Henie, Norway	1960	Carol Heiss, U.S.A.	1980	Anett Poetzsch, E. Germany

SKATING: FIGURE SKATING—PAIRS

1908	Germany: Anna Hubler, Heinrich Burger	1956	Austria: Elizabeth Schwarz, Kurt Oppelt
1920	Finland: Ludovika and Walter Jakobsson	1960	Canada: Barbara Wagner, Robert Paul
1924	Austria: Helene Engelmann, Alfred Berger	1964	USSR: Ludmila Beloussova, Oleg Protopopov
1928	France: Andrée Joly, Pierre Brunet	1968	USSR: Ludmila Beloussova, Oleg Protopopov
1932	France: Andrée and Pierre Brunet	1972	USSR: Irina Rodnina, Aleksei Ulanov
1936	Germany: Maxie Heber, Ernest Baier	1976	USSR: Irina Rodnina, Aleksandr Zaitsev
1952	W. Germany: Ria and Paul Falk	1980	USSR: Irina Rodnina, Aleksandr Zaitsev

SKATING: ICE DANCING

1976	USSR: Ludmila Pakhoma, Aleksandr Gorshkov	1980	USSR: Natalia Linichuk, Gennadi Karponosov

SKATING: SPEED SKATING—MEN: 500 METERS

1924	Charles Jewtraw, U.S.A.	0:44.0	1956	Evgeniy Grishin, USSR	0:40.20
1928	Clas Thunberg, Finland, and Bernt Evensen, Norway (tie)	0:43.4	1960	Evgeniy Grishin, USSR	0:40.20
			1964	Richard McDermott, U.S.A.	0:40.10
1932	John A. Shea, U.S.A.	0:43.4	1968	Erhard Keller, W. Germany	0:40.30
1936	Ivar Ballangrud, Norway	0:43.4	1972	Erhard Keller, W. Germany	0:39.40
1948	Finn Helgesen, Norway	0:43.1	1976	Evgeny Kulikov, USSR	0:39.17
1952	Kenneth Henry, U.S.A.	0:43.2	1980*	Eric Heiden, U.S.A.	0:38.03

SKATING: SPEED SKATING—WOMEN: 500 METERS

1932	Jean Wilson, Canada	0:58.0	1972	Anne Henning, U.S.A.	0:43.3
1960	Helga Haase, W. Germany	0:45.9	1976	Sheila Young, U.S.A.	0:42.76
1964	Lidia Skoblikova, USSR	0:45.0	1980*	Karin Enke, E. Germany	0:41.78
1968	Ludmila Titova, USSR	0:46.1			

SKATING: SPEED SKATING—MEN: 1,000 METERS

1976	Peter Mueller, U.S.A.	1:19.32	1980*	Eric Heiden, U.S.A.	1:15.18

SKATING: SPEED SKATING—WOMEN: 1,000 METERS

1932	Elizabeth Du Bois, U.S.A.	2:04.0	1972	Monika Pflug, W. Germany	1:31.40
1960	Kara Guseva, USSR	1:34.1	1976	Tatiana Averina, USSR	1:28.43
1964	Lidia Skoblikova, USSR	1:33.2	1980*	Natalia Petruseva, USSR	1:24.10
1968	Carolina Geijssen, Netherlands	1:32.60			

* Olympic record.

SKATING: SPEED SKATING—MEN: 1,500 METERS

1924	Clas Thunberg, Finland	2:20.8
1928	Clas Thunberg, Finland	2:21.1
1932	John A. Shea, U.S.A.	2:57.5
1936	Charles Mathisen, Norway	2:19.2
1948	Sverre Farstad, Norway	2:17.6
1952	Hjalmar Anderson, Norway	2:20.4
1956	Evgeniy Grishin and Y. Mikhailov, USSR (tie)	2:08.6
1960	Edgar Roadaas, Norway, and Evgeniy Grishin, USSR (tie)	2:10.4
1964	Ants Antson, USSR	2:10.3
1968	Cornelis Verkerk, Netherlands	2:03.4
1972	Ard Schenk, Netherlands	2:02.96
1976	Jan-Egil Storholt, Norway	1:59.38
1980*	Eric Heiden, U.S.A.	1:55.44

SKATING: SPEED SKATING—WOMEN: 1,500 METERS

1932	Kit Klein, U.S.A.	3:06.0
1960	Lidia Skoblikova, USSR	2:52.2
1964	Lidia Skoblikova, USSR	2:22.6
1968	Kaija Mustonen, Finland	2:22.40
1972	Dianne Holum, U.S.A.	2:20.80
1976	Galina Stepanskaya, USSR	2:16.58
1980*	Annie Borckink, Netherlands	2:10.95

SKATING: SPEED SKATING—MEN: 5,000 METERS

1924	Clas Thunberg, Finland	8:39.0
1928	Ivar Ballangrud, Norway	8:50.5
1932	Irving Jaffee, U.S.A.	9:40.8
1936	Ivar Ballangrud, Norway	8:19.6
1948	Reidar Liaklev, Norway	8:29.4
1952	Hjalmar Anderson, Norway	8:10.6
1956	Boris Shilkov, USSR	7:48.70
1960	Victor Kosichkin, USSR	7:51.30
1964	Knut Johannesen, Norway	7:38.40
1968	Fred Anton Maier, Norway	7:22.40
1972	Ard Schenk, Netherlands	7:23.60
1976	Sten Stenson, Norway	7:24.48
1980*	Eric Heiden, U.S.A.	7:02.29

SKATING: SPEED SKATING—WOMEN: 3,000 METERS

1960	Lidia Skoblikova, USSR	5:14.3
1964	Lidia Skoblikova, USSR	5:14.9
1968	Johanna Schut, Netherlands	4:56.2
1972	Stien Kaiser-Baas, Netherlands	4:52.14
1976	Tatiana Averina, USSR	4:45.19
1980*	Bjoerg Eva Jensen, Norway	4:32.13

SKATING: SPEED SKATING—MEN: 10,000 METERS

1924	Julien Skutnabb Finland	18:04.8
1928	No decision because of thawing ice	
1932	Irving Jaffee, U.S.A.	19:13.6
1936	Ivar Ballangrud, Norway	17:24.3
1948	Ake Seyffarth, Norway	17:26.3
1952	Hjalmar Anderson, Norway	16:45.8
1956	Sigvard Ericsson, Sweden	16:35.9
1960	Knut Johannesen, Norway	15:46.6
1964	Jonny Nilsson, Sweden	15:50.1
1968	Johnny Hoeglin, Sweden	15:23.6
1972	Ard Schenk, Netherlands	15:01.35
1976	Piet Kleine, Netherlands	14:50.59
1980*	Eric Heiden, U.S.A.	14:28.13

SKIING: ALPINE—MEN: DOWNHILL

1948	Henry Oreiller, France	2:55.0
1952	Zeno Colo, Italy	2:30.8
1956	Anton Sailer, Austria	2:52.2
1960	Jean Vuarnet, France	2:06.0
1964	Egon Zimmermann, Austria	2:18.16
1968	Jean-Claude Killy, France	1:59.85
1972	Bernhard Russi, Switzerland	1:51.43
1976	Franz Klammer, Austria	1:45.73
1980*	Leonhard Stock, Austria	1:45.50

SKIING: ALPINE—WOMEN: DOWNHILL

1948	Hedi Schlunegger, Switzerland	2:28.3
1952	Trude Jochum-Beiser, Austria	1:47.1
1956	Madeleine Berthod, Switzerland	1:40.7
1960	Heidi Biebl, W. Germany	1:37.6
1964	Christi Haas, Austria	1:55.3
1968	Olga Pall, Austria	1:40.8
1972*	Marie Theres Nadig, Switzerland	1:36.68
1976	Rosi Mittermaier, W. Germany	1:46.16
1980	Annemarie Moser, Austria	1:37.52

SKIING: ALPINE—MEN: GIANT SLALOM

1952	Stein Eriksen, Norway	2:25.0
1956	Anton Sailer, Austria	3:00.1
1960	Roger Staub, Switzerland	1:48.3
1964*	Francois Bonlieu, France	1:46.7
1968	Jean-Claude Killy, France	3:29.28
1972	Gustavo Thoeni, Italy	3:09.62
1976	Heini Hemmii, Switzerland	3:26.97
1980	Ingemar Stenmark, Sweden	2:40.74

SKIING: ALPINE—WOMEN: GIANT SLALOM

1952	Andrea Mead Lawrence, U.S.A.	2:06.8
1956	Ossi Reichert, W. Germany	1:56.5
1960	Yvonne Ruegg, Switzerland	1:39.9
1964	Marielle Goitschel, France	1:52.2
1968	Nancy Greene, Canada	1:51.97
1972	Marie Theres Nadig, Switzerland	1:29.90
1976*	Kathy Kreiner, Canada	1:29.13
1980	Hanni Wenzel, Liechtenstein	2:41.66

SKIING: ALPINE—MEN: SLALOM

1948	Edi Reinalter, Switzerland	2:10.3
1952	Othmar Schneider, Austria	2:00.0
1956[1]	Anton Sailer, Austria	—
1960	Ernst Hinterseer, Austria	2:08.9
1964	Josef Stiegler, Austria	2:11.13
1968	Jean-Claude Killy, France	1:39.73
1972*	Francisco Fernandez Ochoa, Spain	1:09.27
1976	Piero Gros, Italy	2:03.29
1980	Ingemar Stenmark, Sweden	1:44.26

SKIING: ALPINE—WOMEN: SLALOM

1948	Gretchen Fraser, U.S.A.	1:57.2
1952	Andrea Mead Lawrence, U.S.A.	2:10.6
1956[1]	Renee Colliard, Switzerland	—
1960	Anne Heggtveigt, Canada	1:49.6
1964	Christine Goitschel, France	1:29.8
1968	Marielle Goitschel, France	1:25.86
1972	Barbara Cochran, U.S.A.	1:31.24
1976	Rosi Mittermaier, W. Germany	1:30.54
1980*	Hanni Wenzel, Liechtenstein	1:25.09

* Olympic record. [1] Scored in points instead of time.

WINTER OLYMPIC WINNERS AND RECORDS *(continued)*

SKIING: NORDIC—WOMEN: 5 KILOMETERS

1964	Claudia Boyarskikh, USSR	17:50.5	1976	Helena Takalo, Finland	15:48.69
1968	Toini Gustafsson, Sweden	16:45.2	1980 *	Raisa Smetanina, USSR	15:06.92
1972	Galina Koulacova, USSR	17:00.50			

SKIING: NORDIC—WOMEN: 10 KILOMETERS

1952	Lydia Wideman, Finland	41:40.0	1968	Toini Gustafsson, Sweden	36:46.50
1956	Ljubavi Kazyreva, USSR	38:11.0	1972	Galina Koulacova, USSR	34:17.80
1960	Marija Gusakova, USSR	39:46.6	1976 *	Raisa Smetanina, USSR	30:13.41
1964	Claudia Boyarskikh, USSR	40:24.3	1980	Barbara Petzold, E. Germany	30:31.54

SKIING: NORDIC—WOMEN: 20-KILOMETER RELAY

1956	Finland	1:09:01.0	1964	USSR	59:20.2	1972 *	USSR	48:46.10	1980	E. Ger.	1:02:11.10
1960	Sweden	1:04:21.4	1968	Norway	57:30.00	1976	USSR	1:07:49.75			

SKIING: NORDIC—MEN: 15 KILOMETERS

1956	Hallgier Brenden, Norway	49:39.0	1972	Sven-Ake Lundback, Sweden	45:28.20
1960	Hakon Brusveen, Norway	51:55.5	1976	N. Bashukov, USSR	43:58.47
1964	Eero Maentyranta, Finland	50:54.1	1980 *	Thomas Wassberg, Sweden	41:57.63
1968	Harald Groenningen, Norway	47:54.20			

SKIING: NORDIC—MEN: 30 KILOMETERS

1956	Veikko Hakulinen, Finland	1:44:06.0	1972	Vyacheslav Vedenin, USSR	1:36:31.10
1960	Sixten Jernberg, Sweden	1:51:03.9	1976	Sergei Saveliev, USSR	1:30:29.38
1964	Eero Maentyranta, Finland	1:30:50.7	1980 *	Nikolai Zimjatov, USSR	1:27:02.80
1968	Franco Nones, Italy	1:35:39.20			

SKIING: NORDIC—MEN: 50 KILOMETERS

1924	Thorlief Haug, Norway	3:44:32.0	1960	Kalevi Hamalainen, Finland	2:59:06.30
1928	Per E. Hedlund, Sweden	4:52:03.0	1964	Sixten Jernberg, Sweden	2:43:52.60
1932	Veli Saarinen, Finland	4:28:00.0	1968	Ole Ellefsaeter, Norway	2:28:45.80
1936	Elis Viklund, Sweden	3:30:11.0	1972	Paal Tyldum, Norway	2:43:14.75
1948	Nils Karlsson, Sweden	3:47:48.0	1976	Ivar Formo, Norway	2:37:30.05
1952	Veikko Hakulinen, Finland	3:33:33.0	1980 *	Nikolai Zimjatov, USSR	2:27:24.50
1956	Sixten Jernberg, Sweden	2:50:27.00			

SKIING: NORDIC—MEN: 40-KILOMETER RELAY

1936	Finland	2:41:33.0	1956	USSR	2:15:30.0	1968	Norway	2:08:33.50	1980 *	USSR	1:57:03.46
1948	Sweden	2:32:08.0	1960	Finland	2:18:45.6	1972	USSR	2:04:47.90			
1952	Finland	2:20:16.0	1964	Sweden	2:18:34.6	1976	Finland	2:07:59.72			

SKIING: NORDIC—MEN: COMBINED CROSS COUNTRY AND JUMPING

1924	Thorlief Haug, Norway	453.800	1960	Georg Thoma, W. Germany	457.952
1928	Johan Grottumsbraaten, Norway	427.800	1964	Tormod Knutsen, Norway	469.280
1932	Johan Grottumsbraaten, Norway	446.200	1968	Franz Keller, W. Germany	449.040
1936	Oddbjorn Hagen, Norway	430.300	1972	Ulrich Wehling, E. Germany	413.340
1948	Heikki Hasu, Finland	448.800	1976	Ulrich Wehling, E. Germany	423.390
1952	Simon Slattvik, Norway	451.621	1980	Ulrich Wehling, E. Germany	432.200
1956	Sverre Stenersen, Norway	455.000			

SKIING: NORDIC—MEN: 90-METER SKI JUMPING

1924	Jacob Thams, Norway	227.5	1960	Helmut Recknagel, W. Germany	227.2
1928	Alfred Andersen, Norway	330.5	1964	Toralf Engan, Norway	230.7
1932	Birger Ruud, Norway	228.0	1968	Vladimir Beloussov, USSR	231.3
1936	Birger Ruud, Norway	232.0	1972	Wojciech Fortuna, Poland	219.9
1948	Petter Hugsted, Norway	228.1	1976	Karl Schnabl, Austria	234.8
1952	Arnfinn Bergmann, Norway	226.0	1980	Jouko Tormanen, Finland	271.0
1956	Antti Hyvarinen, Finland	227.0			

SKIING: NORDIC—MEN: 70-METER SKI JUMPING

1964	Veikko Kankkonen, Finland	229.9	1976	Hans-Georg Aschenbach, E. Germany	252.0
1968	Jiri Raska, Czechoslovakia	216.5	1980	Anton Innauer, Austria	266.3
1972	Yukio Kasaya, Japan	244.2			

TOBOGGAN (LUGE)—MEN: SINGLES

1964	Thomas Koehler, W. Germany	3:26.77	1976	Detlef Guenther, E. Germany	3:27.688
1968 *	Manfred Schmid, Austria	2:52.48	1980	Bernhard Glass, E. Germany	2:54.796
1972	Wolfgang Scheidel, E. Germany	3:27.580			

TOBOGGAN (LUGE)—WOMEN: SINGLES

1964	Ortrun Enderlein, W. Germany	3:24.67	1976	Margit Schumann, E. Germany	2:50.621
1968 *	Erica Lechner, Italy	2:28.66	1980	Vera Zozulia, USSR	2:36.537
1972	Anna Muller, E. Germany	2:59.180			

TOBOGGAN (LUGE)—MEN: DOUBLES

1964	Austria: Josef Feistmantl, Manfred Stengl	1:41.62	1976	E. Germany: Hans Rinn, Norbert Hahn	1:25.604
1968	E. Germany: Klaus Bonsack, Thomas Koehler	1:35.85	1980 *	E. Germany: Hans Rinn, Norbert Hahn	1:19.331
1972	tie: Italy and E. Germany	1:28.35			

* Olympic record.

PAN-AMERICAN GAMES

FINAL MEDAL STANDINGS: 1983

Source: U.S. Olympic Committee

The 9th Pan-American Games were held in Caracas, Venezuela on August 14–29, 1983. The games, held every four years, became largely a contest between the U.S. and Cuban teams.

NATION	GOLD	SILVER	BRONZE	TOTAL
United States	136	92	56	284
Cuba	79	53	43	175
Canada	18	44	47	109
Venezuela	12	26	35	73
Brazil	14	20	22	56
Mexico	7	11	24	42
Argentina	2	11	22	35
Colombia	1	7	13	21
Puerto Rico	2	7	6	15
Dominican Republic	0	5	9	14
Chile	1	3	9	13
Peru	1	1	4	6
Jamaica	0	0	6	6
Uruguay	1	0	2	3
Panama	0	0	3	3
Trinidad	0	1	2	3
Ecuador	1	0	0	1
Bahamas	0	1	0	1
Nicaragua	0	1	0	1
Guatemala	0	0	1	1
Belize	0	0	1	1
Virgin Islands	0	0	1	1

PAN-AMERICAN GAMES CHAMPIONS: 1983

BASEBALL 1st Cuba **2d** Nicaragua **3d** U.S. **4th** Dominican Republic

BASKETBALL Men: 1st U.S. **2d** Brazil **3d** Mexico

BASKETBALL Women: 1st U.S. **2d** Cuba **3d** Brazil

BOXING

Super Heavyweight: Jorge Gonzales, Cuba
Heavyweight: Aurelio Toyo, Cuba
Light Heavyweight: Pablo Romero, Cuba
Middleweight: Bernardo Comas, Cuba
Light Middleweight: Orestes Solano, Cuba
Welterweight: Louis Howard, U.S.
Light Welterweight: Candelario Duvergel, Cuba
Lightweight: Pernell Whitaker, U.S.
Featherweight: Adolfo Horta, Cuba
Bantamweight: Manuel Vilchez, Venezuela
Flyweight: Pedro Reyes, Cuba
Light Flyweight: Rafael Ramos, Puerto Rico

CYCLING

Sprint: Nelson Vails, U.S. 0:10.96
Kilo Race: Rory O'Reilly, U.S. 1:05.54
4,000-Meter Pursuit: D. Grylls, U.S. 4:48.80
4,000-Meter Pursuit: U.S. 4:22.01
180-Kilometer Road Race: Luis R. Ramos, Mexico 4:44.07
100-Kilometer Team Time Trial: U.S. 2:03.20

EQUESTRIAN EVENTS

Jumping: Anne Kursinski, U.S. ....10.72 pts.
Dressage: Carole Grant, U.S. ....1,291 pts.
Team Jumping: U.S. ....16.92 pts.
Team Dressage: U.S. ....3,555 pts.

FENCING

Team Foil, Men: 1st Cuba **2d** U.S. **3d** Venezuela
Team Foil, Women: 1st Cuba **2d** U.S. **3d** Argentina
Epee: Agapito Nussa, Cuba **Sabre:** Peter Westbrook, U.S.
Foil, Women: Margarita Rodriguez, Cuba
Foil, Men: Efigenio Favier, Cuba
Team Sabre: 1st Cuba[1] **2d** Canada **3d** U.S.
Team Epee, Men: 1st Cuba[1] **2d** Canada **3d** U.S.
Team Sabre, Men: 1st Cuba **2d** U.S. **3d** Canada

FIELD HOCKEY: 1st Canada **2d** Argentina **3d** Chile

GYMNASTICS: MEN

All-Around: Casimiro Suarez, Cuba ....116.10 pts.
Team: 1st Cuba **2d** U.S. **3d** Canada
Floor Exercise: Casimiro Suarez, Cuba
Pommel Horse: Amador Lazaro, Cuba
Still Rings: Casimiro Suarez, Cuba
Vaulting: Casimiro Suarez, Cuba
Parallel Bars: Roberto Richard, Cuba
High Bar: Casimiro Suarez, Cuba

GYMNASTICS: WOMEN

All-Around: Orisel Martinez, Cuba ....76 pts.
Team: 1st U.S. **2d** Cuba **3d** Brazil
Floor Exercise: Yumi Mordre, U.S.
Balance Beam: Elsa Chivas, Cuba
Uneven Bars: Lucy Wener, U.S.
Vaulting: Orisel Martinez, Cuba

JUDO (MEN)

Open: Venacio Gomez, Cuba
+95 Kg: Mark Berger, Canada
95 Kg: Isaac Azcuy, Cuba
86 Kg: Louis Jani, Canada
78 Kg: Brett Barron, U.S.
71 Kg: Guillermo D'Nelson, Cuba
65 Kg: Gerardo Padilla, Mexico
60 Kg: Rafael Rodriguez, Cuba

ROWING

Single Sculls: 1st Argentina **2d** Canada **3d** U.S.
Double Sculls: 1st Canada **2d** U.S. **3d** Cuba
Pair without Coxswain: 1st Brazil **2d** Argentina **3d** U.S.
Quadruple Sculls: 1st Canada **2d** Cuba **3d** Argentina
Four with Coxswain: 1st U.S. **2d** Brazil **3d** Canada
Four without Coxswain: 1st Cuba **2d** U.S. **3d** Canada
Eights: 1st U.S. **2d** Chile **3d** Canada
Pair with Coxswain: 1st Cuba **2d** U.S. **3d** Peru

SHOOTING

Air Rifle, Individual: J. Meredith, U.S. ....580 pts.
Free Pistol, Individual: E. Buljung, U.S. ....558 pts.
Engl. Match, Individual: R. Fitz-Randolph, U.S. ....594 pts.
Skeet, Individual: Matt Dryke, U.S. ....199 pts.
Olympic Trap, Individual: D. Carlisle, U.S. ....200 pts.
Air Pistol, Individual: C. Hora, Peru ....579 pts.
Rapid-Fire Pistol, Individual: T. Anderson ....594 pts.
Standard Pistol: Eric Buljung, U.S. ....584 pts.
Center-Fire Pistol, Individual: E. Buljung, U.S. ....590 pts.
Air Rifle, Team: U.S. ....1,727 pts.
Free Pistol, Team: Venezuela ....1,640 pts.
English Match, Team: U.S. ....1,776 pts.
Skeet, Team: U.S. ....442 pts.
Trap, Team: U.S. ....441 pts.
Air Pistol, Team: Ecuador ....1,706 pts.
Rapid-Fire Pistol, Team: U.S. ....1,766 pts.
Standard-Pistol, Team: U.S. ....1,718 pts.
Center-Fire Pistol, Team: Venezuela ....1,752 pts.

1 Medal vacated for use of banned substances.

SOCCER

1st Uruguay **2d** Brazil **3d** Guatemala

SWIMMING AND DIVING: MEN

3-Meter Springboard: G. Louganis, U.S. ....724.02 pts.
Platform Diving: Greg Louganis, U.S. ....677.58 pts.
100-Meter Butterfly: M. Gribble, U.S. 0:54.25
100-Meter Freestyle: Rowdy Gaines, U.S. 0:50.38
100-Meter Backstroke: Rick Carey, U.S. 0:55.19*
100-Meter Breaststroke: S. Lundquist, U.S. 1:02.28*
200-Meter Freestyle: Bruce Hayes, U.S. 1:49.89
200-Meter Medley: Ricardo Prado, Brazil 2:04.51
200-Meter Backstroke: Rick Carey, U.S. 1:59.34
200-Meter Butterfly: C. Beardsley, U.S. 1:58.85
200-Meter Breaststroke: S. Lundquist, U.S. 2:19.31
400-Meter Freestyle: Bruce Hayes, U.S. 3:53.17
400-Meter Medley: Ricardo Prado, Brazil 4:21.43
400-Meter Freestyle Relay: U.S. 3:21.41
400-Meter Medley Relay: U.S. 3:40.42*
800-Meter Freestyle Relay: U.S. 7:23.63
1,500-Meter Freestyle: J. Kostoff, U.S. 15:30.67

SWIMMING AND DIVING: WOMEN

3-Meter Springboard: K. McCormick, U.S. ......500.73 pts.
10-Meter Platform Diving: W. Wyland, U.S. .....426.57 pts.
100-Meter Freestyle: C. Steinseifer, U.S. 0:56.92
100-Meter Backstroke: Sue Walsh, U.S. 1:02.48
100-Meter Breaststroke: Ann Ottenbrite, Canada ..1:10.63
100-Meter Butterfly: Laurie Lehner, U.S. 1:01.14
200-Meter Backstroke: Amy White, U.S. 2:15.66
200-Meter Breaststroke: Kathy Bald, Canada 2:25.53
200-Meter Butterfly: Mary T. Meagher, U.S. 2:10.06
200-Meter Freestyle: Sippy Woodhead, U.S. 2:01.33
200-Meter Medley: Tracy Caulkins, U.S. 2:16.22
400-Meter Freestyle: Tiffany Cohen, U.S. 4:12.27
400-Meter Medley: Tracy Caulkins, U.S. 4:51.82
400-Meter Medley Relay: U.S. 4:12.99
400-Meter Freestyle Relay: U.S. 3:46.46
800-Meter Freestyle: Tiffany Cohen, U.S. 8:35.42
Synchronized, Pairs: 1st U.S. **2d** Canada **3d** Mexico
Synchronized, Team: 1st Canada **2d** U.S. **3d** Mexico
Synchronized, Individual: Tracie Ruiz, U.S.

TENNIS

Men, Singles: 1st Greg Holmes, U.S. **2d** Fernando P. Pascal, Mexico **3d** Christian Miniussi, Argentina
Men, Doubles: 1st U.S. **2d** Mexico **3d** Venezuela
Women, Singles: 1st Gretchen Rush, U.S. **2d** Beatriz Fernandez, Puerto Rico **3d** Heliane Steden, Mexico
Women, Doubles: 1st U.S. **2d** Puerto Rico **3d** Mexico
Mixed Doubles: 1st Venezuela **2d** Mexico **3d** U.S.

TRACK AND FIELD: MEN

100-Meter Dash: Leandro Penalver, Cuba 0:10.06
200-Meter Dash: Elliott Quow, U.S. 0:20.42
400-Meter Dash: Cliff Wiley, U.S. 0:45.02
800-Meter Run: Agberto Guimares, Brazil 1:46.31
1,500-Meter Run: Agberto Guimares, Brazil 3:42.91
5,000-Meter Run: Eduardo Castro, Mexico 13:54.11
10,000-Meter Run: Jose Gomez, Mexico 29:14.75
Marathon: Jorge Gonzales, Puerto Rico 2:12.43
Triple Jump: Jorge Reyna, Cuba ....55′ 11¼″
Shot Put: Luis Delis, Cuba ....59′ 10¼″
Discus Throw: Luis Delis, Cuba ....220′ 10″
110-Meter High Hurdles: Roger Kingdom, U.S. 0:13.44
400-Meter Hurdles: Franklin Monthie, Cuba 0:50.02
3,000-Meter Steeplechase: Emilio Ulloa, Chile 8:57.62
400-Meter Relay: U.S. 0:38.49
1,600-Meter Relay: U.S. 3:00.47
20-Kilometer Walk: Ernesto Canto, Mexico 1:28.12
High Jump: Juan Centelles, Cuba ....7′ 6¼″
Pole Vault: Mike Tully, U.S. ....17′ 10½″
Long Jump: Jaime Jefferson, Cuba ....26′ 4¼″
Javelin Throw: Laslo Babits, Canada ....267′ 1″
Hammer Throw: Genovevo Morejon, Cuba ....214′ 4″
Decathlon: Dave Steen, Canada ....7,958 pts.

TRACK AND FIELD: WOMEN

100-Meter Dash: Esmeraldo Garcia, Brazil 0:11.31
200-Meter Dash: Randy Givens, U.S. 0:23.14
400-Meter Dash: Charmaine Crooks, Canada 0:51.49
800-Meter Run: Nery McKeen, Cuba 2:02.20
1,500-Meter Run: Ranza Clark, Canada 4:16.18
100-Meter Hurdles: B. Fitzgerald, U.S. 0:13.16
400-Meter Relay: U.S. 0:43.21
1,600-Meter Relay: U.S. 3:29.97
High Jump: Coleen Sommer, U.S. ....6′ 3¼″
Long Jump: Kathy McMillan, U.S. ....21′ 11¾″
Shot Put: Maria Sarria, Cuba ....63′ 5½″
Discus Throw: Maria Betancourt, Cuba ....198′ 0″
Javelin Throw: Maria Colon, Cuba ....209′ 2″
Heptathlon: Conciecao Geremias, Brazil ....6,084 pts.

VOLLEYBALL

MEN: 1st Brazil **2d** Cuba **3d** Argentina
WOMEN: 1st Cuba **2d** U.S. **3d** Peru

WATER POLO

1st U.S. **2d** Cuba **3d** Canada

WEIGHTLIFTING

Medals Won[1]: Cuba, 24; Canada, 10; U.S., 7; Venezuela, 8

WRESTLING

Heavyweight:	*Freestyle,* Candido Meza, Cuba	*Greco-Roman,* Candido Meza, Cuba
220 Pounds:	*Freestyle,* Greg Gibson, U.S.	*Greco-Roman,* Rene Vidal, Cuba
198 Pounds:	*Freestyle,* Roberto Limonta, Cuba	*Greco-Roman,* Steve Fraser, U.S.
180 Pounds:	*Freestyle,* Jose Damian, Cuba	*Greco-Roman,* Orlando Perez, Cuba
163 Pounds:	*Freestyle,* Lee Kemp, United States	*Greco-Roman,* Jeff Sturbing, Canada
149 Pounds:	*Freestyle,* Raul Cascaret, Cuba	*Greco-Roman,* Antonio Lopez, Cuba
136 Pounds:	*Freestyle,* Randy Lewis, United States	*Greco-Roman,* Rene Rodriguez, Cuba
125 Pounds:	*Freestyle,* Barry Davis, United States	*Greco-Roman,* Jesus Tejada, Cuba
114 Pounds:	*Freestyle,* Ray Takahashi, Canada	*Greco-Roman,* Edmundo Miranda, Cuba
105 Pounds:	*Freestyle,* Cristobal Gonzalez, Cuba	*Greco-Roman,* Reinaldo Jimenez, Cuba

YACHTING

Snipe: U.S. | **Laser:** Brazil | **Lightning:** Brazil | **J-24 Class:** U.S. | **470-Class:** Brazil

* World record. [1] Includes medals vacated for use of banned substances.

PETS

BEST-IN-SHOW CHAMPION DOGS AT THE WESTMINSTER KENNEL CLUB SHOW

YEAR	BREED	BEST-IN-SHOW CHAMPION	OWNER
1969	Skye Terrier	Ch. Glamoor Good News	Walter and Mrs. Adele F. Goodman
1970	Boxer	Ch. Arriba's Prima Donna	Dr. and Mrs. P.J. Pagano and Dr. T.S. Fickles
1971–72	English Springer Spaniel	Ch. Chinoe's Adamant James	Dr. Milton Prickett
1973	Standard Poodle	Ch. Acadia Command Performance	Mrs. Jo Ann Sering and Edward B. Jenner
1974	German Shorthaired Pointer	Ch. Gretchenhof Columbia River	Dr. Richard P. Smith
1975	Old English Sheepdog	Ch. Sir Lancelot of Barvan	Mr. and Mrs. Ronald Vanword
1976	Lakeland Terrier	Ch. Jo-Ni's Red Baron of Crofton	Virginia Dickson
1977	Sealyham Terrier	Ch. Dersade Bobby's Girl	Dorothy Wimer
1978	Yorkshire Terrier	Ch. Cede Higgens	Barbara and Charles Switzer
1979	Irish Water Spaniel	Ch. Oak Tree's Aristocrat	Mrs. Ann Snelling
1980	Siberian Husky	Ch. Innisfree's Sierra Cinnar	Mrs. Trish Kanzler
1981	Pug	Ch. Dandy's Favorite Woodchuck	Robert A. Hauslohner
1982	Pekingese	Ch. St. Aubrey Dragonora	Anne Snelling
1983	Afghan	Ch. Kabik's The Challenger	Chris and Marguerite Terrell

BREEDS OF DOGS

The following chart compiled by the American Kennel Club (AKC) lists the 105 largest breeds of the 1,037,149 purebred dogs registered by the AKC for the year 1982.

Poodles	88,650	Cairn Terriers	6,108	Bullmastiffs	966
Cocker Spaniels	87,218	Pugs	6,058	Australian Terriers	774
Doberman Pinschers	73,180	Keeshonden	5,977	Bearded Collies	763
Labrador Retrievers	62,465	Scottish Terriers	5,834	Papillons	696
German Shepherd Dogs	60,445	Dalmatians	5,409	Welsh Terriers	656
Golden Retrievers	51,045	Weimaraners	4,586	Standard Schnauzers	653
Miniature Schnauzers	36,502	Afghan Hounds	4,484	Giant Schnauzers	634
Beagles	35,548	Norwegian Elkhounds	4,368	Belgian Sheepdogs	605
Dachshunds	32,835	Chesapeake Bay Retrievers	4,243	Salukis	605
Shetland Sheepdogs	30,512	St. Bernards	4,296	Kerry Blue Terriers	593
Yorkshire Terriers	26,205	Akitas	3,257	Italian Greyhounds	569
Lhasa Apsos	25,945	Fox Terriers	3,815	Australian Cattle Dogs	558
Chow Chows	22,623	Bichons Frises	3,632	Manchester Terriers	519
English Springer Spaniels	22,296	Silky Terriers	2,627	Tibetan Terriers	495
Siberian Huskies	20,654	Pembroke Welsh Corgis	2,575	Belgian Tervuren	446
Shih Tzu	20,556	Newfoundlands	2,394	Bernese Mountain Dogs	424
Collies	20,084	Miniature Pinschers	2,193	Pointers	419
Pomeranians	18,456	Vizslas	1,847	Cardigan Welsh Corgis	393
Basset Hounds	17,871	Great Pyrenees	1,684	Japanese Chin	386
Pekingese	17,434	Bouviers des Flandres	1,632	Bedlington Terriers	379
Brittanys	17,349	Schipperkes	1,569	American Water Spaniels	331
Boxers	16,301	American Staffordshire Terriers	1,550	Pulik	326
Chihuahuas	15,867	Basenjis	1,517	Irish Terriers	312
Great Danes	12,092	Bloodhounds	1,503	Black and Tan Coonhounds	284
Boston Terriers	11,361	Mastiffs	1,419	Flat-Coated Retrievers	283
German Shorthaired Pointers	10,019	Whippets	1,392	Briards	277
Rottweilers	9,269	English Cocker Spaniels	1,391	Border Terriers	272
Old English Sheepdogs	8,332	Rhodesian Ridgebacks	1,368	Norwich Terriers	243
Irish Setters	8,183	Borzois	1,366	Staffordshire Bull Terriers	236
Maltese	8,050	English Setters	1,205	Kuvaszok	235
Samoyeds	7,862	Bull Terriers	1,162	Lakeland Terriers	229
West Highland White Terriers	7,397	Irish Wolfhounds	1,131	Skye Terriers	223
Alaskan Malamutes	7,209	Soft-Coated Wheaten Terriers	1,111	Welsh Springer Spaniels	200
Airedale Terriers	6,876	Gordon Setters	1,082	Brussels Griffons	199
Bulldogs	6,657	German Wirehaired Pointers	1,049	French Bulldogs	182

BREEDS OF CATS

Abyssinian: *Coat:* ruddy (brown) or red, banded or ticked with darker brown, black, or red: *Eyes:* gold, green hazel.
American Short Hair: *Body:* heavily built; *Coat:* short and lustrous, same colors as Persian.
Angora, or **Turkish Angora:** *Body and Head:* more elongated than Persian; *Coat:* long-haired, silky; *Eyes:* blue, copper, odd (one blue, one copper).
Balinese, or **Long-haired Siamese:** *Body and Coat:* like Siamese except coat is long.
Himalayan: *Body:* like Persian; *Coat:* like Balinese.
Maine Coon: *Coat:* long-haired in all colors; *Body:* long and powerful; *Head:* medium to broad.
Manx: *Body:* tailless and often hops like rabbit; *Coat:* thick, double coat in variety of colors.
Persian: *Body:* Short and cobby, wide across shoulders; *Head:* wide with small ears; *Nose:* short; *Coat:* long, flowing, glossy; *Color:* there are five color divisions—Solid, Tabby and Tortie, Smoke, Silver, and Cameo.
Rex: *Coat:* curly, like lamb fleece; *Color:* all colors.
Russian Blue: *Body:* fine-boned, slender; *Coat:* double-coated, short, thick; *Eyes:* deep green; *Color:* blue with silver tipping.
Siamese: *Body:* long, slender with long tail; *Head:* triangular; *Eyes:* deep blue, almond-shaped; *Coat:* short-haired, sandy brown with points (darker colors on face, ears, paws, tail), which from darkest to lightest are called seal, chocolate, blue, lilac, and red. Points may be tortoise or striped.

RODEOS

Source: The Rodeo Cowboys Association

ALL-AROUND RODEO COWBOY CHAMPIONS

1966	Larry Mahan	$40,358	1972	Phil Lyne	$60,852	1977	Tom Ferguson	$ 76,730
1967	Larry Mahan	$51,996	1973	Larry Mahan	$64,447	1978	Tom Ferguson	$131,233
1968	Larry Mahan	$49,129	1974	Tom Ferguson	$66,929	1979	Tom Ferguson	$117,222
1969	Larry Mahan	$57,726	1975	Leo Camarillo	$50,300	1980	Paul Tierney	$105,568
1970	Larry Mahan	$41,493		Tom Ferguson	$50,300	1981	Jimmie Cooper	$105,862
1971	Phil Lyne	$49,245	1976	Tom Ferguson	$96,913	1982	Chris Lybbert	$123,709

SHOOTING

RIFLE AND PISTOL CHAMPIONSHIPS: 1983

Source: National Rifle Association of America

EVENT AND WINNER	SCORE
U.S. International Outdoor Championships	
Smallbore Rifle—Position (Perfect Score: 2400)	
National: LTC Lones W. Wigger Jr., Ft. Benning, GA	2272
Civilian: Stephen M. Bombocz, Bethlehem, PA	2236
Service: Lones W. Wigger Jr., Ft. Benning, GA	2272
Woman: Kirsten Pasch, Hibbing, MN	2175
Senior: Donald W. Burtis, Levittown, PA	2080
Int. Senior: Robert Vangene, Minneapolis, MN	2158
Collegiate: David Passmore, Miami, FL	2187
Junior: Thomas A. Tamas, Columbus, GA	2221
Int. Junior: Matthew P. Suggs, Eugene, OR	2168
Highpower Rifle (Perfect Score: 2400)	
National: Patrick M. McCann, Staunton, IL	2364
Civilian: Patrick M. McCann, Staunton, IL	2364
Service: COL Kenneth J. Erdman, Canoga Park, CA	2345
Woman: Noma J. McCullough, Newhall, CA	2351
Senior: S. C. Burkhalter, Lake Forest, IL	2307
Collegiate: Carl L. Weston, Oak Ridge, TN	2284
Junior: Chris J. Vesy, Youngstown, OH	2348
U.S. International Championships	
English Match: E. Etzel, Morgantown, WV	1784
Smallbore Free Rifle: LTC L. Wigger, Ft. Benning, GA	3488
Air Rifle: R. Fitz-Randolph Jr., Palm Bay, FL	1744
Ladies Air Rifle: T. Smith-Ferguson, Elk Grove, CA	1158
Woman Standard Rifle Prone: D. Wigger, Ft. Benning, GA	1766
Woman Standard Rifle-3 Position: 2LT Gloria Parmentier, Ft. Benning, GA	1730
Free Pistol: E. Buljung, Ft. Benning, GA	1676
Air Pistol: D. Young, Winterburn, Canada	1740
Woman Air Pistol: Ruby E. Fox, Parker, AZ	1132
Center Fire Pistol: E. Buljung, Ft. Benning, GA	1780
Rapid Fire Pistol: J. McNally, Columbus, GA	1784
Standard Pistol: E. Buljung, Ft. Benning, GA	1729
Woman Smallbore Pistol: G. Liberty, Langley AFB, VA	1739

EVENT AND WINNER	SCORE
Smallbore Rifle—Prone (Perfect Score: 6400-640X)	
National: David P. Weaver, Oil City, PA	5599-494X
Civilian: David P. Weaver, Oil City, PA	5599-494X
Service: CPT J. Meredith, Ft. Benning, GA	5598-459X
Woman: Carolyn Millard, Tullahoma, TN	5594-452X
Senior: Richard Hanson, Punta Gorda, FL	5588-443X
Collegiate: Carolyn D. Millard, Tullahoma, TN	5594-452X
Junior: Thomas A. Tamas, Columbus, GA	5597-449X
Pistol (Perfect Score: 2700-270X)	
National: MSG Roger H. Willis, Ft. Benning, GA	2652-138X
Civilian: John J. Vespa Jr., Hibbing, MN	2640-122X
Woman: Ruby E. Fox, Parker AR	2625-108X
Police: John L. Farley, Americus, GA	2616-120X
Senior: Gil Hebard, Knoxvill, IL	2580-090X
Collegiate: Russell L. May, Sarasota, FL	2573-083X
Junior: Stanley Hayes, Ft. Worth, TX	2446-053X
National Guard: James Lenardson, Toledo, OH	2640-135X
National Police Revolver (Perfect Score: 1500-150X)	
National: K. Hile, Columbus Police Dept., OH	1491-109X
Woman: B. Critchlow, Los Angeles County, CA	1470- 73X
Federal: J. Gilleland Jr., U.S. Secret Service	1489-108X
State: R. Landreth, CA Highway Patrol, CA	1489-104X
County: M. Thompson, Madison Co. Sheriffs, IN	1488- 83X
Municipal: G. Nisbet, Detroit Police Dept., MI	1486-100X
Industrial: S. Hohansen, Embassy of Norway, Washington, D.C.	1481- 77X
Sheriff: M. Thompson, Madison County Sheriff's Department, IN	1488- 83X
Retired: T. Borgese, NY City Transit Police, NY	1484- 87X
Reserve: J. Eason, Grass Valley, CA	1485- 96X
Conservation: E. Nuse, VT Fish & Game Dept.	1476- 77X

NATIONAL SKEET SHOOTING ASSOCIATION CHAMPIONS: 1983

Source: *Skeet Shooting Review*

High Overall Championships:
Champion: Phil Murray, San Antonio, TX
Woman: Lori Desatoff, Pomona, CA
Senior: Bill Tanner, San Antonio, TX
Junior: Boah Schatz, Chicago, IL

.410-Bore Championships:
Champion: Donnie Parks, Winston Salem, NC
Woman: Lori Desatoff, Pomona, CA
Senior: R. Miller, Winter Haven, FL
Junior: Fred Yonke, Rock Is., IL

28-Gauge Championships:
Champion: Bill Rodgers, Montreal, Canada
Woman: Ila Hill, Birmingham, MI
Senior: R. Chinberg, Albuquerque, NM
Junior: Noah Schatz, Chicago, IL

20-Gauge Championships:
Champion: Tal Sprinkles, Round Rock, TX
Woman: Mary Beverly, Tallahassee, FL
Senior: Tom Hanzel, San Antonio, TX
Junior: Charles Lane, Abilene, TX

12-Gauge Championships:
Champion: Wayne Mayes, Cleveland, TN
Woman: Becky Stutzman, East Peoria, IL
Senior: Ed Scherer, Waukesha, WI
Junior: Brian Werfelman, San Pedro, CA

SHUFFLEBOARD

Source: National Shuffleboard Assn., Inc.

National Shuffleboard Association Tournament: 1983

MEN

Men's Open: Larry Faris, Cincinnati, Ohio
Men's Closed: Walter Johnson, Boynton Beach, Florida
Men's Doubles: Rosaire Biron, Quebec, Canada
Tom Brown, Lakeside, Ohio

WOMEN

Women's Open: Virginia Worden, Goldwater, Michigan
Women's Closed: Helen Grove, Columbus, Ohio
Women's Doubles: Joan Benson, Venice, Florida
Phyllis Stringer, Ontario, Canada

SKATING

WORLD SPEED SKATING RECORDS

500 METERS: MEN
Evgeny Kulikov, USSR, March 27, 1981 .... 0:36.91

1,000 METERS: MEN
Pavel Pegov, USSR, March 25, 1983 .... 1:12.58

1,500 METERS: MEN
Eric Heiden, U.S., Jan. 19, 1980 .... 1:54.79

3,000 METERS: MEN
Eric Heiden, U.S., March 2, 1978 .... 4:07.01

5,000 METERS: MEN
Kay Arne Stenshjemmet, Norway, March 19, 1977 . 6:56.90

10,000 METERS: MEN
Thomas Gustafson, Sweden, Jan. 31, 1982 ...... 14:23.59

500 METERS: WOMEN
Christa Rothenburger, E. Germany, Mar. 27, 1981 . 0:40.18

1,000 METERS: WOMEN
Natalya Petruseva, USSR, March 27, 1980 .... 1:20.21

1,500 METERS: WOMEN
Natalya Petruseva, USSR, Mar. 25, 1983 .... 2:04.04

3,000 METERS: WOMEN
Gabi Schoenbrunn, E. Germany, March 27, 1980 .. 4:21.70

5,000 METERS: WOMEN
Andrea Schone, E. Germany, Jan. 23, 1983 .... 7:40.97

WORLD SPEED SKATING CHAMPIONS: 1983

MEN
Rolf Falk-Larssen, Norway

WOMEN
Andrea Schone, East Germany

AMATEUR SKATING UNION OF THE U.S. SPEED SKATING CHAMPIONS: 1983

NATIONAL OUTDOOR (Milwaukee, Wisconsin, Feb. 5–6, 1983)

Senior Men	Michael Ralston, Streamwood, Ill.	**Senior Women**	Janet Hainstock, Alpena, Mich.
Intermediate Men	Marty Pierce, St. Francis, Wis.	**Intermediate Women**	Kim Keppler, Independence, Ohio
Junior Boys	Eric Flaim, Pembroke, Mass.	**Junior Girls**	Suzette Essman, Beaver Dam, Wis.
Juvenile Boys	Akio Tagawa, Milwaukee, Wis.	**Juvenile Girls**	Michelle Kline, Circle Pines, Minn.
Midget Boys	Michael Kangas, Midland, Mich.	**Midget Girls**	Debbie Nowell, Winchester, Mass.

NORTH AMERICAN OUTDOOR (Winnipeg, Manitoba, Canada Feb. 12–13, 1983)

Senior Men	Michael Ralston, Streamwood, Ill.	**Senior Women**	Janet Hainstock, Alpena, Mich.
Intermediate Men	Pat Seltsam, Pembroke, Mass.	**Intermediate Women**	Marg Stapley, Winnipeg, Manitoba
Junior Boys	Eric Flaim, Pembroke, Mass.	**Junior Girls**	Suzette Essman, Beaver Dam, Wis.
Juvenile Boys	Akio Tagawa, Milwaukee, Wis.	**Juvenile Girls**	Michelle Kline, Circle Pines, Minn.
Midget Boys	Michael Kangas, Midland, Mich.	**Midget Girls**	Heather Hester, White Bear Lake, Minn.

NATIONAL INDOOR (Northbrook, Illinois, March 19–20, 1983)

Senior Men (Tie)	Pat Maxwell, Saratoga Spgs., N.Y. Pat Moore, Niles, Ill.	**Senior Women**	Bonnie Blair, Champaign, Ill.
		Intermediate Women	Michelle Fang, Arlington Hts., Ill.
Intermediate Men	Marty Pierce, St. Francis, Wis.	**Junior Girls**	Tammy Rosbeck, Alpena, Mich.
Junior Boys	Michael Heldrich, Northbrook, Ill.	**Juvenile Girls**	Michelle Kline, Circle Pines, Minn.
Juvenile Boys	David Cruikshank, Northbrook, Ill.	**Midget Girls**	Debbie Nowell, Winchester, Mass.
Midget Boys	Jeff Zukowski, New Berlin, Wis.		

NORTH AMERICAN INDOOR (Wyandotte, Michigan, March 26–27, 1983)

Senior Men	Pat Moore, Niles, Ill.	**Senior Women**	Lydia Stephans, Northbrook, Ill.
Intermediate Men	David Pavlicic, Florissant, Mo.	**Intermediate Women**	Arione Loignon, Montreal, Quebec
Junior Boys	Eric Flaim, Pembroke, Mass.	**Junior Girls**	Tanny Rosbeck, Alpena, Mich.
Juvenile Boys	Bob Malleck, Dearborn, Mich.	**Juvenile Girls**	Michelle Kline, Circle Pines, Minn.
Midget Boys	Jeff Ericksen, St. Paul, Minn.	**Midget Girls**	Debbie Nowell, Winchester, Mass.

FIGURE SKATING CHAMPIONS

UNITED STATES FIGURE SKATING CHAMPIONS: MEN

1953–56	Hayes Jenkins	**1963**	Tommy Litz	**1967**	Gary Visconti	**1973–75**	Gordon McKellen Jr.
1957–60	Dave Jenkins	**1964**	Scott Allen	**1968–70**	Tim Wood	**1976**	Terry Kubicka
1961	Bradley Lord	**1965**	Gary Visconti	**1971**	John Petkvich	**1977–80**	Charles Tickner
1962	Monty Hoyt	**1966**	Scott Allen	**1972**	Ken Shelley	**1981–83**	Scott Hamilton

UNITED STATES FIGURE SKATING CHAMPIONS: WOMEN

1962	Barbara Pursley	**1964–68**	Peggy Fleming	**1974–76**	Dorothy Hamill	**1981**	Elaine Zayak
1963	Lorraine Hanlon	**1968–73**	Janet Lynn	**1977–80**	Linda Fratianne	**1982–83**	Rosalynn Sumners

WORLD FIGURE SKATING CHAMPIONS: MEN

1953–56	Hayes Jenkins, U.S.	**1965**	Alain Calmat, France	**1976**	John Curry, Britain
1957–59	Dave Jenkins, U.S.	**1966–68**	Emmerich Danzer, Austria	**1977**	Vladimir Kovalev, USSR
1960	Alain Giletti, France	**1969–70**	Tim Wood, U.S.	**1978**	Charles Tickner, U.S.
1962	Don Jackson, Canada	**1971–73**	Ondrej Nepela, Czech.	**1979**	Vladimir Kovalev, USSR
1963	Don McPherson, Canada	**1974**	Jan Hoffman, E. Germany	**1980**	Jan Hoffman, E. Germany
1964	M. Schnelldorfer, W. Germany	**1975**	Sergei Volkov, USSR	**1981–83**	Scott Hamilton, U.S.

WORLD FIGURE SKATING CHAMPIONS: WOMEN

1955	Tenley Albright, U.S.	**1971–72**	Beatrix Schuba, Austria	**1978**	Anett Poetzsch, E. Germany
1956–60	Carol Heiss, U.S.	**1973**	Karen Magnussen, Canada	**1979**	Linda Fratianne, U.S.
1962–64	Sjoukje Dijkstra, Netherlands	**1974**	Christine Errath, E. Germany	**1980**	Anett Poetzsch, E. Germany
1965	Petra Burka, Canada	**1975**	Dianne deLeeuw, Netherlands	**1981**	Denise Biellmann, Switzerland
1966–68	Peggy Fleming, U.S.	**1976**	Dorothy Hamill, U.S.	**1982**	Elaine Zayak, U.S.
1969–70	Gabriele Seyfert, E. Germany	**1977**	Linda Fratianne, U.S.	**1983**	Rosalynn Sumners, U.S.

SKIING

In March 1983, for the first time, American skiers won both the men's and women's World Cup skiing titles. Tamara McKinney, 20, of Squaw Valley, Calif., was the first American woman to win the overall title in the 17-year history of the cup. She clinched the women's championship by winning six individual races and accumulating more points than defending champion Erika Hess, who came in second over the 4-month, 24-race competition.

Phil Mahre, 25, of Yakima, Wash., won the men's World Cup title for the third consecutive year. He accumulated 248 points for the season, defeating his closest challenger, former World Cup champion Ingemar Stenmark.

At the U.S. Alpine Championships, held at Copper Mountain, Colo., in February, Tamara McKinney won the women's slalom and giant slalom, and Cindy Nelson won the combined. In men's competition, Tiger Shaw won the giant slalom, Phil Mahre the slalom, Bill Johnson the downhill, and Mike Brown, the combined.

WORLD CUP CHAMPIONS—MEN

1967–68	Jean-Claude Killy, France	**1975**	Gustavo Thoeni, Italy	**1979**	Peter Luescher, Switzerland
1969–70	Karl Schranz, Austria	**1976**	Ingemar Stenmark, Sweden	**1980**	Andreas Wenzel, Liechtenstein
1971–73	Gustavo Thoeni, Italy	**1977**	Ingemar Stenmark, Sweden	**1981–83**	Phil Mahre, U.S.A.
1974	Piero Gros, Italy	**1978**	Ingemar Stenmark, Sweden		

WORLD CUP CHAMPIONS—WOMEN

1967–68	Nancy Greene, Canada	**1976**	Rosi Mittermaier, W. Germany	**1980**	Hanni Wenzel, Liechtenstein
1969	Gertrud Gabl, Austria	**1977**	Lisa-Marie Morerod, Switzerland	**1981**	Marie Theres Nadig, Switzerland
1970	Michele Jacot, France	**1978**	Hanni Wenzel, Liechtenstein	**1982**	Erika Hess, Switzerland
1971–75	Annemarie Proell, Austria	**1979**	Annemarie Proell Moser, Austria	**1983**	Tamara McKinney, U.S.A.

NCAA SKIING CHAMPIONSHIPS

The University of Utah won the first combined NCAA Men's and Women's Skiing Championships at Bozeman, Mont., on March 9–12. Kathy Kreiner's first-place finish in the women's giant slalom was the team's only individual title, but the Utes took second place in both the men's and women's slalom and did not finish lower than 17th in any event, accumulating 696 points. Vermont was second with 650 points, followed by Wyoming with 629½.

NCAA TEAM CHAMPIONS

1954–57	Denver	**1962**	Denver	**1966**	Denver	**1972**	Colorado	**1976**	Colorado	**1981**	Utah
1958	Dartmouth	**1963**	Denver	**1967**	Denver	**1973**	Colorado		Dartmouth	**1982**	Colorado
1959-60	Colorado	**1964**	Denver	**1968**	Wyoming	**1974**	Colorado	**1977–79**	Colorado	**1983**	Utah
1961	Denver	**1965**	Denver	**1969–71**	Denver	**1975**	Colorado	**1980**	Vermont		

NCAA DOWNHILL CHAMPIONS

MEN		**1966**	Terje Overland, Denver	**1977**	Stephen Hienzsch, Colorado
1960	Dave Butts, Colorado	**1967**	Dennis McCoy, Denver	**1978**	Dale Merrill, Wyoming *
1961	Gordon Eaton, Middlebury	**1968**	Barney Peet, Fort Lewis	**1979**	Chris Mikell, Vermont *
1962	Mike Baar, Denver	**1969**	Mike Lafferty, Colorado	**1980**	John Teague, Vermont *
1963	Dave Gorusch, Western Colorado	**1970–72**	Otto Tschudi, Denver	**1981**	Tor Melander, Vermont *
	Bill Marolt, Colorado	**1973**	Bob Cochran, Vermont	**1982**	Seth Bayer, Colorado *
	Buddy Werner, Colorado	**1974**	Larry Kennison, Wyoming	**1983**	Tor Melander, Vermont *
1964	John Clough, Middlebury	**1975**	Mark Ford, Colorado	**WOMEN**	
1965	Bill Marolt, Colorado	**1976**	Dave Cleveland, Dartmouth *	**1983**	Kathy Kreiner, Utah *

* Giant Slalom

NCAA SLALOM CHAMPIONS

MEN		**1968**	Dennis McCoy, Denver	**1977**	Stephen Hienzsch, Colorado
1960	Rudy Ruana, Montana	**1969**	Paul Rachetto, Denver	**1978**	Dan Brelsford, Montana
1961	Buddy Werner, Colorado	**1970**	Mike Porcarelli, Colorado	**1979**	Per Nicholaysen, Utah
1962	Jim Gaddis, Utah	**1971**	Otto Tschudi, Denver	**1980**	Bret Williams, No. Michigan
1963	James Heuga, Colorado	**1972**	Mike Porcarelli, Colorado	**1981**	Scott Hoffman, Utah
1964	John Clough, Middlebury	**1973**	Peik Christensen, Denver	**1982**	Tiger Shaw, Dartmouth
1965	Rick Chaffee, Denver	**1974**	Bill Shaw, Boise State	**1983**	Niklas Scherrer, Colorado
1966	Bill Marolt, Colorado	**1975**	Peik Christensen, Denver	**WOMEN**	
1967	Rick Chaffee, Denver	**1976**	Mike Meleski, Wyoming	**1983**	Asa Svedmark, Wyoming

NCAA CROSS COUNTRY RELAY

MEN		**1982**	Colorado	**WOMEN**	
1981	Vermont	**1983**	Vermont	**1983**	New Mexico

NCAA CROSS COUNTRY CHAMPIONS

MEN		**1965–66**	Mike Elliot, Fort Lewis	**1978**	Sigurd Kjerpeseth, Colorado
1956	Erik Berggren, Idaho	**1967**	Ned Gillette, Dartmouth	**1979**	Svein Arne Olsen, Utah
1957	Mack Miller, W. Colorado	**1968–69**	Clark Matis, Colorado	**1980**	Pal Sjulstad, Vermont
1958–59	Clarence Servold, Denver	**1970–71**	Ole Hansen, Denver	**1981**	Berndt Lund, Utah
1960	John Denhahl, Colorado	**1972**	Stale Engen, Wyoming	**1982**	Egil Nilsen, Colorado
1961	Charles Akers, Maine	**1973–75**	Steinar Hypertsen, Wyoming	**1983**	Rune Helland, Wyoming
1962	James Page, Dartmouth	**1976**	Stan Dunklee, Vermont	**WOMEN**	
1963–64	Eddie Demers, W. Colorado	**1977**	Helge Aamodt, Colorado	**1983**	Beth Heiden, Vermont

SOCCER

The Tulsa Roughnecks won Soccer Bowl-83, the North American Soccer League championship, on Oct. 1, at the B.C. Place Stadium in Vancouver, British Columbia. Tulsa took its first league title by defeating the Toronto Blizzard, 2–0. Tulsa's two goals were scored by Njego Pesa and Ron Futcher. Pesa, voted the game's most valuable player, scored on a free kick in the 56th minute of the game. Futcher's goal came in the 62d minute.

Tulsa and Toronto were seeded third and seventh respectively among the eight teams that made the playoffs. Tulsa won the Southern Division title with a record of 17 wins and 13 losses. Toronto was third in the Eastern Division after the league-leading New York Cosmos and the Chicago Sting. Toronto ended the regular season with 16 wins and 14 losses.

New York Cosmos' Robert Cabanas led the NASL in scoring at the end of the regular season, with 25 goals and 16 assists. Karl-Heinz Granitza, of the Chicago Sting, was second in scoring, with 15 goals and 18 assists.

Vancouver's Tino Lettieri was the leading goalkeeper. He played 2,594 minutes and had 159 saves, while he allowed only 25 goals against his team. His goals-against average was .86.

In a poll conducted by *The Sporting News* at the end of the regular season, Roberto Cabanas was chosen the league's most valuable player by his fellow NASL players.

On May 20 the International Federation of Football Associations (FIFA), soccer's international governing body, announced that the 1986 World Cup tournament would be held in Mexico. Colombia had been scheduled to host the prestigious tournament, but withdrew for financial reasons. The United States and Canada joined Mexico in seeking the tournament. Mexico, which hosted the 1970 tournament, becomes the first nation to host it twice.

NORTH AMERICAN SOCCER LEAGUE

1983 FINAL STANDINGS

	Games Played	Won	Lost	Goals For	Goals Against	Bonus Points	Points
Eastern Division							
New York	30	22	8	87	49	64	194
Chicago	30	15	15	66	73	57	147
Toronto	30	16	14	51	48	45	135
Montreal	30	12	18	58	71	52	124
Southern Division							
Tulsa	30	17	13	56	49	47	145
Fort Lauderdale	30	14	16	60	63	54	136
Tampa Bay	30	7	23	48	87	41	83
Team America	30	10	20	33	54	25	79
Western Division							
Vancouver	30	24	6	63	34	51	187
Golden Bay	30	20	10	71	54	55	169
Seattle	30	12	18	62	61	51	119
San Diego	30	11	19	53	65	42	106

NASL CHAMPIONS: 1968–1983

1968	Atlanta Chiefs	1972	New York Cosmos	1976	Toronto Metros	1981	Chicago Sting
1969	Kansas City Spurs	1973	Philadelphia Atoms	1977–78	New York Cosmos	1982	New York Cosmos
1970	Rochester Lancers	1974	Los Angeles Aztecs	1979	Vancouver Whitecaps	1983	Tulsa Roughnecks
1971	Dallas Tornado	1975	Tampa Bay Rowdies	1980	New York Cosmos		

NCAA SOCCER

YEAR	CHAMPION	RUNNER-UP	SCORE	HOST
1976–77	San Francisco University	Indiana	1–0	University of Pennsylvania
1977–78	Hartwick College	San Francisco University	2–1	San Francisco University
1978–79	San Francisco University	Indiana	2–0	Tampa Stadium
1979–80	Southern Illinois, Edwardsville	Clemson	3–2	Tampa Stadium
1980–81	San Francisco University	Indiana	4–3	Tampa Stadium
1981–82	University of Connecticut	Alabama A&M	2–1	Stanford Stadium
1982–83	Indiana University	Duke	2–1	Fort Lauderdale Stadium
1983–84	Indiana University	Columbia	1–0	Ft. Lauderdale Stadium

WORLD CUP

The World Cup soccer championship is played every four years, although the cycle was broken between 1938 and 1950 because of World War II. The 1982 games were held in Spain.

YEAR	CHAMPIONSHIP FINAL	HOST	YEAR	CHAMPIONSHIP FINAL	HOST
1934	Italy 2, Czechoslovakia 1	Italy	1966	England 4, West Germany 2	England
1938	Italy 4, Hungary 2	France	1970	Brazil 4, Italy 1	Mexico
1950	Uruguay 2, Brazil 1	Brazil	1974	West Germany 2, Netherlands 1	West Germany
1954	West Germany 3, Hungary 2	Switzerland	1978	Argentina 3, Netherlands 1	Argentina
1958	Brazil 5, Sweden 2	Sweden	1982	Italy 3, West Germany 1	Spain
1962	Brazil 3, Czechoslovakia 1	Chile			

SWIMMING

U.S. SHORT COURSE SWIMMING AND DIVING NATIONAL CHAMPIONSHIPS: 1983

Held at Indianapolis, Ind., April 6–9, 1983.

MEN'S EVENTS

Freestyle:
50-Yard: Tom Jager, 0:19.64
100-Yard: Rowdy Gaines, 0:43.32
200-Yard: David Larson, 1:35.06
500-Yard: Mike O'Brien, 4:16.88
1,000-Yard: Jeff Kostoff, 8:48.57*
1,650-Yard: Jeff Kostoff, 14:46.11*
Breaststroke:
100-Yard: Steve Lundquist, 0:54.07
200-Yard: Doug Soltis, 1:58.89
Backstroke:
100-Yard: Rick Carey, 0:48.32
200-Yard: Rick Carey, 1:44.43*
Butterfly:
100-Yard: Tom Jager, 0:47.87
200-Yard: Craig Beardsley, 1:44.51
Individual Medley:
200-Yard: Steve Lundquist, 1:46.46
400-Yard: Jeff Kostoff, 3:50.56
Relay Events:
400-Yard Medley: Cincinnati Pepsi Marlins 'A' team, 3:15.89
400-Yard Freestyle: Florida Aquatics 'A' team, 2:54.76
800-Yard Freestyle: Florida Aquatic 'A' team, 6:26.41
Diving Events:[1]
One-Meter Springboard: Greg Louganis, 1,197.12 points
Three-Meter Springboard: Greg Louganis, 1,309.20 points
Platform: Bruce Kimball, 1,233.48 points
Swimming Team Champions:
Florida Aquatic Swim Team
Individual High Point Award (Kiputh Award):
Jeff Kostoff, Industry Hills

WOMEN'S EVENTS

Freestyle:
50-Yard: Tammy Thomas, 0:22.20*
100-Yard: Tammy Thomas, 0:48.89
200-Yard: Tiffany Cohen, 1:46.72
500-Yard: Tiffany Cohen, 4:37.84
1,000-Yard: Tiffany Cohen, 9:30.65
1,650-Yard: Tiffany Cohen, 15:46.54*
Breaststroke:
100-Yard: Jeanne Childs, 1:01.97
200-Yard: Jeanne Childs, 2:12.72
Backstroke:
100-Yard: Sue Walsh, 0:54.74*
200-Yard: Tracy Caulkins, 1:59.15
Butterfly:
100-Yard: Laurie Lehner, 0:53.28
200-Yard: Patty King, 1:58.26
Individual Medley:
200-Yard: Tracy Caulkins, 2:00.37
400-Yard: Tracy Caulkins, 4:14.99
Relay Events:
400-Yard Medley: Florida Aquatics, 'A' team, 3:43.82
400-Yard Freestyle: Florida Aquatics 'A' team, 3:19.15*
800-Yard Freestyle: Mission Viejo 'A' team, 7:11.98
Diving Events:[1]
One-Meter Springboard: Megan Neyer, 926.67 points
Three-Meter Springboard: Megan Neyer, 993.00 points
Platform: Wendy Wyland, 832.71 points
Swimming Team Champions:
Mission Viejo Nadadores
Individual High Point Award (Kiputh Award):
Tiffany Cohen, Mission Viejo

* New American Record. [1] Diving events held at Indianapolis, Ind., April 13–17, 1983.

WORLD SWIMMING RECORDS

Source: United States Swimming

MEN'S RECORDS

EVENTS	TIME	SWIMMER AND NATION	DATE	SITE
100-Meter Freestyle	0:49.36	Ambrose (Rowdy) Gaines, U.S.	4-3-81	Austin, Texas
200-Meter Freestyle	1:47.87	Michael Gross, West Germany	8-22-83	Rome, Italy
400-Meter Freestyle	3:48.32	Vladimir Salnikov, Soviet Union	2-19-83	Moscow, Soviet Union
800-Meter Freestyle	7:52.33	Vladimir Salnikov, Soviet Union	7-14-83	Los Angeles, California
1,500-Meter Freestyle	14:54.76	Vladimir Salnikov, Soviet Union	2-22-83	Moscow, Soviet Union
100-Meter Backstroke	0:55.19	Rick Carey, U.S.	8-21-83	Caracas, Venezuela
200-Meter Backstroke	1:58.93	Rick Carey, U.S.	8-3-83	Clovis, California
100-Meter Breaststroke	1:02.08	Steve Lundquist, U.S.	8-17-83	Caracas, Venezuela
200-Meter Breaststroke	2:14.77	Victor Davis, Canada	8-5-82	Guayaquil, Ecuador
100-Meter Butterfly	0:53.44	Matt Gribble, U.S.	8-6-83	Clovis, California
200-Meter Butterfly	1:55.05	Michael Gross, West Germany	8-26-83	Rome, Italy
200-Meter Individual Medley	2:02.25	Alex Baumann, Canada	10-4-81	Brisbane, Australia
400-Meter Individual Medley	4:19.78	Ricardo Prado, Brazil	8-1-82	Guayaquil, Ecuador
400-Meter Freestyle Relay	3:19.26	United States team	8-5-82	Guayaquil, Ecuador
800-Meter Freestyle Relay	7:20.40	West German team	8-23-83	Rome, Italy
400-Meter Medley Relay	3:40.42	United States team	8-22-83	Caracas, Venezuela

WOMEN'S RECORDS

EVENTS	TIME	SWIMMER AND NATION	DATE	SITE
100-Meter Freestyle	0:54.79	Barbara Krause, East Germany	7-21-80	Moscow, Soviet Union
200-Meter Freestyle	1:58.23	Cynthia Woodhead, U.S.	9-3-79	Tokyo, Japan
400-Meter Freestyle	4:06.28	Tracey Wickham, Australia	8-24-78	Berlin, W. Germany
800-Meter Freestyle	8:24.62	Tracey Wickham, Australia	8-5-78	Edmonton, Canada
1,500-Meter Freestyle	16:04.49	Kim Linehan, U.S.	8-19-79	Fort Lauderdale, Fla.
100-Meter Breaststroke	1:08.51	Ute Geweniger, East Germany	8-25-83	Rome, Italy
200-Meter Breaststroke	2:28.36	Lina Kachushite, Soviet Union	4-6-79	Potsdam, E. Germany
100-Meter Butterfly	0:57.93	Mary Meagher, U.S.	8-16-81	Brown Deer, Wis.
200-Meter Butterfly	2:05.96	Mary Meagher, U.S.	8-13-81	Brown Deer, Wis.
100-Meter Backstroke	1:00.86	Rica Reinisch, East Germany	7-23-80	Moscow, Soviet Union
200-Meter Backstroke	2:09.91	Cornelia Sirch, East Germany	8-7-82	Guayaquil, Ecuador
200-Meter Individual Medley	2:11.73	Ute Geweniger, East Germany	7-4-81	Berlin, East Germany
400-Meter Individual Medley	4:36.10	Petra Schneider, East Germany	8-1-82	Guayaquil, Ecuador
400-Meter Freestyle Relay	3:42.71	East German team	7-27-80	Moscow, Soviet Union
400-Meter Medley Relay	4:05.79	East German team	8-26-83	Rome, Italy
800-Meter Freestyle Relay	8:02.27	East German team	8-22-83	Rome, Italy

1983 UNITED STATES LONG COURSE SWIMMING NATIONAL CHAMPIONSHIPS

Held at Clovis, Calif., Aug. 3–6, 1983.

MEN'S EVENTS	SWIMMER AND CLUB	TIME
50-Meter Freestyle	Robin Leamy, Bruin Swim Assoc.	0:22.59
100-Meter Freestyle	Rowdy Gaines, Longhorn Aquatic Club	0:50.21
200-Meter Freestyle	Bruce Hayes, Bruin Swim Assoc.	1:49.90
400-Meter Freestyle	Matt Cetlinski, Florida Aquatic Swim Team	3:52.99
800-Meter Freestyle	Jeff Kostoff, Industry Hills	7:58.31*
1500-Meter Freestyle	Jeff Kostoff, Industry Hills	15:19.23
100-Meter Backstroke	Rick Carey, Badger Swim Club	0:55.38**
200-Meter Backstroke	Rick Carey, Badger Swim Club	1:59.27
100-Meter Breaststroke	Steve Lundquist, Mustang	1:02.34**
200-Meter Breaststroke	Steve Lundquist, Mustang	2:15.38
100-Meter Butterfly	Matt Gribble, Hurricane	0:53.64
200-Meter Butterfly	Craig Beardsley, Florida Aquatic Swim Team	1:58.76
200-Meter Individual Medley	Bill Barrett, Bruin Swim Assoc.	2:03.24*
400-Meter Individual Medley	Ricardo Prado, Mission Viejo Nadadores	4:21.26
400-Meter Medley Relay	Longhorn Aquatic Club "A"	3:45.66
400-Meter Freestyle Relay	Florida Aquatic Swim Team "A"	3:21.80
800-Meter Freestyle Relay	Florida Aquatic Swim Team "A"	7:27.49
WOMEN'S EVENTS		
50-Meter Freestyle	Dara Torres, Unattached	0:25.62**
100-Meter Freestyle	Carrie Steineifer, West Valley	0:56.52
200-Meter Freestyle	Mary Wayte, Chinook Swim Club	2:01.03
400-Meter Freestyle	Tiffany Cohen, Mission Viejo Nadadores	4:08.05
800-Meter Freestyle	Tiffany Cohen, Mission Viejo Nadadores	8:30.24
1500-Meter Freestyle	Tiffany Cohen, Mission Viejo Nadadores	16:11.97
100-Meter Backstroke	Sue Walsh, University of North Carolina	1:02.68
200-Meter Backstroke	Sue Walsh, University of North Carolina	2:13.86
100-Meter Breaststroke	Kim Rhodenbaugh, Cincinnati Pepsi Marlins	1:11.56
200-Meter Breaststroke	Kim Rhodenbaugh, Cincinnati Pepsi Marlins	2:32.96
100-Meter Butterfly	Laurie Lehner, Gold Vault	0:59.54
200-Meter Butterfly	Mary T. Meagher, Lakeside Aquatic Club	2:09.53
200-Meter Individual Medley	Tracy Caulkins, Florida Aquatic Swim Team	2:15.27
400-Meter Individual Medley	Tracy Caulkins, Florida Aquatic Swim Team	4:45.71
400-Meter Medley Relay	Longhorn Aquatic Club "A"	4:14.98
400-Meter Freestyle Relay	Florida Aquatic Swim Team "A"	3:46.71
800-Meter Freestyle Relay	Florida Aquatic Swim Team "A"	8:10.22

TEAM CHAMPIONS
MEN: Florida Aquatic Swim Team
WOMEN: Mission Viejo Nadadores

INDIVIDUAL HIGH POINT WINNERS
MEN: Steve Lundquist WOMEN: Tiffany Cohen
*New American Record **World Record

NATIONAL COLLEGIATE ATHLETIC ASSOCIATION SWIMMING CHAMPIONS

NCAA TEAM CHAMPIONS

1953	Yale	**1960**	USC	**1963–66**	USC	**1974–77**	USC	**1981**	Texas
1954–56	Ohio State	**1961**	Michigan	**1967**	Stanford	**1978**	Tenn.	**1982**	UCLA
1957–59	Michigan	**1962**	Ohio State	**1968–73**	Indiana	**1979–80**	California	**1983**	Florida

50–YARD FREESTYLE

1970 David Edgar, Tennessee 0:20.930	**1975** Joe Bottom, USC 0:20.118	**1980** Andy Coan, Tennessee 0:19.920
1971 David Edgar, Tennessee 0:20.300	**1976** Joe Bottom, USC 0:20.081	**1981** K. Kirchner, Texas 0:19.660
1972 David Edgar, Tennessee 0:20.442	**1977** Joe Bottom, USC 0:19.750	**1982** Robin Leamy, UCLA 0:19.850
1973 John Trembley, Tenn. 0:20.377	**1978** Andy Coan, Tennessee 0:20.290	**1983** P. Ang, Houston 0:19.700
1974 John Trembley, Tenn. 0:20.230	**1979** Ambrose Gaines, Auburn 0:19.990	

100–YARD FREESTYLE

1970 David Edgar, Tennessee 0:46.060	**1975** Jonty Skinner, Alabama 0:43.927	**1980** Ambrose Gaines, Auburn 0:43.360
1971 David Edgar, Tennessee 0:44.690	**1976** James Montgomery, Ind. 0:44.400	**1981** Ambrose Gaines, Auburn 0:42.380
1972 David Edgar, Tennessee 0:45.003	**1977** David Fairbank, Stanford 0:43.680	**1982** Robin Leamy, UCLA 0:43.590
1973 John Trembley, Tenn. 0:45.090	**1978** Andy Coan, Tennessee 0:44.100	**1983** Tom Jager, UCLA 0:43.060
1974 Joe Bottom, USC 0:45.067	**1979** Andy Coan, Tennessee 0:43.420	

200–YARD FREESTYLE

1970 Juan Bello, Michigan 1:42.700	**1975** G. McDonnell, UCLA 1:38.042	**1980** Ambrose Gaines, Auburn 1:34.570
1971 James McConica, USC 1:39.750	**1976** James Montgomery, Ind. 1:36.530	**1981** Ambrose Gaines, Auburn 1:33.910
1972 J. Heidenreich, So. Meth. 1:38.357	**1977** Bruce Furniss, USC 1:36.160	**1982** P. Holmhertz, Calif. 1:36.460
1973 James McConica, USC 1:39.600	**1978** Bruce Furniss, USC 1:37.020	**1983** M. Orn, Ariz. State 1:36.020
1974 James Montgomery, Ind. 1:39.188	**1979** Andy Coan, Tennessee 1:35.620	

500–YARD FREESTYLE

1970 Mike Burton, UCLA 4:37.290	**1975** John Naber, USC 4:20.450	**1980** Brian Goodell, UCLA 4:17.810
1971 John Kinsella, Indiana 4:27.390	**1976** Tim Shaw, Long Beach St. 4:19.053	**1981** Doug Towne, Arizona 4:16.540
1972 John Kinsella, Indiana 4:24.496	**1977** Tim Shaw, Long Beach St. 4:17.390	**1982** A. Astbury, Arizona St. 4:18.150
1973 John Kinsella, Indiana 4:27.593	**1978** Brian Goodell, UCLA 4:18.050	**1983** G. DiCarlo, Arizona 4:16.930
1974 John Naber, USC 4:26.855	**1979** Brian Goodell, UCLA 4:16.430	

NCAA SWIMMING AND DIVING CHAMPIONS *(continued)*

1,650-YARD FREESTYLE

1972	John Kinsella, Indiana	15:33.582	**1976**	Tim Shaw, Long Beach St.	15:06.760	**1980**	Brian Goodell, UCLA	14:54.070
1973	John Kinsella, Indiana	15:29.200	**1977**	Keith Converse, Alabama	14:57.300	**1981**	Rafael Escalas, UCLA	14:53.900
1974	Jack Tingley, USC	15:29.287	**1978**	Brian Goodell, UCLA	14:55.530	**1982**	A. Borgstrom, Alabama	15:02.240
1975	M. Bruner, Stanford	15:16.540	**1979**	Brian Goodell, UCLA	14:54.130	**1983**	T. Corbisiero, Columbia	14:46.290

100-YARD BACKSTROKE

1972	Paul Gilbert, Yale	0:51.293	**1976**	John Naber, USC	0:49.940	**1980**	Clay Britt, Texas	0:49.520
1973	Mike Stamm, Indiana	0:50.910	**1977**	John Naber, USC	0:49.360	**1981**	Clay Britt, Texas	0:49.080
1974	John Naber, USC	0:50.516	**1978**	Robert Jackson, Long Bch.	0:49.880	**1982**	Clay Britt, Texas	0:49.090
1975	John Naber, USC	0:49.947	**1979**	Carlos Berrocal, Alabama	0:49.710	**1983**	Rick Carey, Texas	0:48.250

200-YARD BACKSTROKE

1972	C. Campbell, Princeton	1:50.557	**1976**	John Naber, USC	1:46.960	**1980**	James Fowler, USC	1:47.760
1973	Mike Stamm, Indiana	1:50.560	**1977**	John Naber, USC	1:46.090	**1981**	Wade Flemons, Stanford	1:46.300
1974	John Naber, USC	1:48.950	**1978**	Pete Rocca, California	1:47.480	**1982**	Rick Carey, Texas	1:46.010
1975	John Naber, USC	1:46.827	**1979**	Pete Rocca, California	1:45.530	**1983**	Rick Carey, Texas	1:45.210

100-YARD BREASTSTROKE

1972	Thomas Bruce, UCLA	0:56.998	**1976**	John Hencken, Stanford	0:56.040	**1980**	Steve Lundquist, SMU	0:53.590
1973	John Hencken, Stanford	0:57.110	**1977**	Graham Smith, California	0:55.100	**1981**	Steve Lundquist, SMU	0:52.930
1974	David Wilkie, Miami	0:56.720	**1978**	Scott Spann, Auburn	0:56.620	**1982**	Steve Lundquist, SMU	0:53.090
1975	John Hencken, Stanford	0:55.596	**1979**	Graham Smith, California	0:54.910	**1983**	Steve Lundquist, SMU	0:52.480

200-YARD BREASTSTROKE

1972	Brian Job, Stanford	2:02.592	**1976**	David Wilkie, Miami	2:00.740	**1980**	William Barrett, UCLA	1:58.430
1973	David Wilkie, Miami	2:03.400	**1977**	Graham Smith, California	2:00.050	**1981**	Steve Lundquist, SMU	1:55.010
1974	John Hencken, Stanford	2:01.748	**1978**	Graham Smith, California	2:02.240	**1982**	Steve Lundquist, SMU	1:56.840
1975	John Hencken, Stanford	2:00.839	**1979**	Graham Smith, California	2:00.370	**1983**	Glenn Mills, Alabama	1:58.330

100-YARD BUTTERFLY

1972	Mark Spitz, Indiana	0:47.988	**1976**	Matt Vogel, Tennessee	0:48.950	**1980**	Par Arvidsson, California	0:47.360
1973	John Trembley, Tenn.	0:48.680	**1977**	Joe Bottom, USC	0:47.770	**1981**	Scott Spann, Texas	0:47.220
1974	John Trembley, Tenn.	0:48.718	**1978**	Greg Jagenburg, Long Bch.	0:48.770	**1982**	Matt Gribble, Miami (Fla.)	0:47.350
1975	Jeff Rolan, Utah	0:48.953	**1979**	Par Arvidsson, California	0:47.760	**1983**	Matt Gribble, Miami (Fla.)	0:47.260

200-YARD BUTTERFLY

1972	Mark Spitz, Indiana	1:46.898	**1976**	Steve Gregg, N.C. St.	1:47.000	**1980**	Par Arvidsson, California	1:44.430
1973	Gary Hall, Indiana	1:48.480	**1977**	Mike Bruner, Stanford	1:45.270	**1981**	Craig Beardsley, Florida	1:44.150
1974	Robin Backhaus, Wash.	1:47.040	**1978**	Greg Jagenburg, Long Bch.	1:46.010	**1982**	Craig Beardsley, Florida	1:44.100
1975	Robin Backhaus, Wash.	1:47.168	**1979**	Par Arvidsson, California	1:45.530	**1983**	Ricardo Prado, SMU	1:44.960

200-YARD INDIVIDUAL MEDLEY

1972	Gary Hall, Indiana	1:51.507	**1976**	Leroy Engstrand, Tenn.	1:50.129	**1980**	William Barrett, UCLA	1:46.250
1973	Steve Furniss, USC	1:51.385	**1977**	Scott Spann, Auburn	1:48.260	**1981**	William Barrett, UCLA	1:45.010
1974	Steve Furniss, USC	1:51.522	**1978**	Scott Spann, Auburn	1:49.300	**1982**	William Barrett, UCLA	1:45.000
1975	Fredrick Tyler, Indiana	1:50.628	**1979**	Graham Smith, California	1:48.440	**1983**	Steve Lundquist, SMU	1:45.540

400-YARD INDIVIDUAL MEDLEY

1972	Gary Hall, Indiana	3:58.717	**1976**	Rodney Strachan, USC	3:55.640	**1980**	Brian Goodell, UCLA	3:31.380
1973	Steve Furniss, USC	3:56.160	**1977**	Rodney Strachan, USC	3:54.760	**1981**	J. Vassallo, Miami (Fla.)	3:48.160
1974	Steve Furniss, USC	3:57.800	**1978**	Brian Goodell, UCLA	3:53.610	**1982**	Jeff Float, USC	3:49.000
1975	Leroy Engstrand, Tenn.	3:57.801	**1979**	Brian Goodell, UCLA	3:50.800	**1983**	Ricardo Prado, SMU	3:48.190

400-YARD FREESTYLE RELAY

1968	Yale	3:04.090	**1972**	Tennessee	3:01.118	**1976**	USC	2:57.540	**1980**	Auburn	2:55.160
1969	USC	3:02.770	**1973**	Tennessee	3:00.363	**1977**	USC	2:55.280	**1981**	Texas	2:54.840
1970	USC	3:03.910	**1974**	Indiana	3:00.359	**1978**	Tennessee	2:55.280	**1982**	UCLA	2:53.150
1971	USC	3:02.380	**1975**	Indiana	2:58.421	**1979**	Tennessee	2:54.740	**1983**	Florida	2:54.060

800-YARD FREESTYLE RELAY

1972	USC	6:38.635	**1975**	Indiana	6:36.293	**1978**	Auburn	6:31.930	**1981**	Florida	6:27.020
1973	Indiana	6:36.490	**1976**	USC	6:33.130	**1979**	Florida	6:28.010	**1982**	California	6:28.940
1974	Indiana	6:40.321	**1977**	USC	6:28.010	**1980**	Auburn	6:28.070	**1983**	Florida	6:25.290

400-YARD MEDLEY RELAY

1968	Texas Arl.	3:31.530	**1972**	USC	3:23.116	**1976**	USC	3:20.020	**1980**	Texas	3:14.590
1969	Indiana	3:25.890	**1973**	Tennessee	3:22.988	**1977**	Indiana	3:17.140	**1981**	Texas	3:12.930
1970	Stanford	3:24.990	**1974**	Tennessee	3:22.788	**1978**	California	3:18.260	**1982**	Texas	3:14.240
1971	Stanford	3:22.510	**1975**	USC	3:19.221	**1979**	California	3:15.220	**1983**	SMU	3:12.630

ONE-METER DIVING

1972	Todd Smith, Ohio St.	503.25	**1976**	James Kennedy, Tenn.	514.29	**1979**	Greg Louganis, Miami (Fla.)	513.75
1973	Tim Moore, Ohio St.	487.90	**1977**	Matthew Chelich, Mich.	503.13	**1981**	Randal Ableman, Iowa	509.30
1974	Tim Moore, Ohio St.	494.25	**1978**	Wayne Chester, Alabama	485.10	**1982**	Robert Bollinger, Indiana	554.95
1975	Tim Moore, Ohio St.	502.71	**1980**	Greg Louganis, Miami (Fla.)	557.20	**1983**	Matt Scoggin, Texas	557.25

THREE-METER DIVING

1972	Craig Lincoln, Minnesota	545.94	**1976**	Brian Bungum, Indiana	542.19	**1980**	Greg Louganis, Miami (Fla.)	608.10
1973	Tim Moore, Ohio St.	539.61	**1977**	Brian Bungum, Indiana	542.40	**1981**	Robert Bollinger, Indiana	540.70
1974	Rick McAllister, Air Force	526.41	**1978**	Christopher Snode, Florida	543.18	**1982**	Ron Merriott, Michigan	600.30
1975	Tim Moore, Ohio St.	590.61	**1979**	Matthew Chelich, Michigan	527.85	**1983**	M. Bradshaw, Ohio State	575.45

TENNIS

Wide World

Defending champion Martina Navratilova makes a backhand return to Andrea Jaeger during the Wimbledon women's singles final on July 2. Navratilova defeated Jaeger 6–0, 6–3 in 54 minutes to win her fourth Wimbledon singles crown. On Sept. 11, Navratilova won her first U.S. Open singles title, trouncing archrival Chris Evert-Lloyd 6–1, 6–3 in 73 minutes. She and Pam Shriver also won the U.S. Open women's doubles crown. Her combined earnings for the two weeks of the U.S. Open totaled $644,000, including $120,000 for the singles crown, $24,000 for her share of the doubles title, and a $500,000 bonus for winning three of four designated events that comprise the $1 Million Playtex Challenge. Those prizes pushed her 1983 prize money total over the $1 million mark for the second consecutive year, and her career prize money to more than $6 million, the highest figure for any professional tennis player.

Martina Navratilova dominated women's tennis in 1983, capturing both the Wimbledon and U.S. Open women's singles titles. She and her partner Pam Shriver won the women's doubles titles at both tournaments, as well. By the end of the U.S. Open, Navratilova had won 156 of 160 matches during the 1982-83 season.

Jimmy Connors won his fifth U.S. Open men's singles title on Sept. 11, by defeating Ivan Lendl of Czechoslovakia 6–3, 6–7, 7–5, 6–0 at the Queens, New York, tennis center. Defending champion John McEnroe was eliminated from the tournament in the fourth round when an aggressive Bill Scanlon, seeded 16th, defeated him with a surprising 7–6, 7–6, 4–6, 6–3.

Other winners at the U.S. Open included the men's doubles team of John McEnroe and Peter Fleming, of the U.S., and the mixed-doubles team of Elizabeth Sayers and John Fitzgerald of Australia.

A major surprise at the Open involved 16-year-old Aaron Krickstein, of Grosse Pointe Woods, Mich., who was entered in the men's draw because he won the Junior nationals in August. He stunned 15th-seeded Vital Gerulaitis 3–6, 3–6, 6–4, 6–3, 6–4 in the third round before losing to Yannick Noah of France in the next round. Another surprise was amateur Greg Holmes of the University of Utah, the 1983 NCAA champion, defeating sixth-seed Guillermo Vilas in the third round.

John McEnroe earned his second consecutive Wimbledon men's singles title on July 3, beating unseeded Chris Lewis 6–2, 6–2, 6–2. The young New Zealander, ranked 91st in the world, had defeated Kevin Curren, the 12th seed, in a five-set semifinal match. Earlier, Curren had served 33 aces in the fourth round to defeat Jimmy Conners 6–3, 6–7, 6–3, 7–6.

John McEnroe and Peter Fleming of the U.S. won the Wimbledon men's doubles title. John Lloyd of Britain and Wendy Turnbull of the U.S. captured the mixed doubles championship.

DAVIS CUP—MEN'S TEAM TENNIS

The most highly prized trophy of international men's team tennis, the Davis Cup, was put up in 1900 by Dwight F. Davis, an outstanding sportsman and U.S. public official.

American men's tennis teams have been awarded the trophy oftener than those of any other country, winning a total of 28 final challenge rounds. Australian or Australasian (Australian and New Zealand) teams are second, having captured the Davis Cup a total of 24 times.

DAVIS CUP CHALLENGE ROUND

YEAR	WINNER	LOSER	SCORE	YEAR	WINNER	LOSER	SCORE
1900	United States	England	5–0	1947	United States	Australia	4–1
1902	United States	England	3–2	1948	United States	Australia	5–0
1903	England	United States	4–1	1949	United States	Australia	4–1
1904	England	Belgium	5–0	1950	Australia	United States	4–1
1905	England	United States	5–0	1951	Australia	United States	3–2
1906	England	United States	5–0	1952	Australia	United States	4–1
1907	Australia	England	3–2	1953	Australia	United States	3–2
1908	Australia	United States	3–2	1954	United States	Australia	3–2
1909	Australasia	United States	5–0	1955	Australia	United States	5–0
1910	Not held	—	—	1956	Australia	United States	5–0
1911	Australasia	United States	5–0	1957	Australia	United States	3–2
1912	England	Australasia	3–2	1958	United States	Australia	3–2
1913	United States	England	3–2	1959	Australia	United States	3–2
1914	Australasia	United States	3–2	1960	Australia	Italy	4–1
1915–18	Not held	—	—	1961	Australia	Italy	5–0
1919	Australasia	England	4–1	1962	Australia	Mexico	5–0
1920	United States	Australasia	5–0	1963	United States	Australia	3–2
1921	United States	Japan	5–0	1964	Australia	United States	3–2
1922	United States	Australasia	4–1	1965	Australia	Spain	4–1
1923	United States	Australasia	4–1	1966	Australia	India	4–1
1924	United States	Australasia	5–0	1967	Australia	Spain	4–1
1925	United States	France	5–0	1968	United States	Australia	4–1
1926	United States	France	4–1	1969	United States	Romania	5–0
1927	France	United States	3–2	1970	United States	West Germany	5–0
1928	France	United States	4–1	1971	United States	Romania	3–2
1929	France	United States	3–2	1972	United States	Romania	3–2
1930	France	United States	4–1	1973	Australia	United States	5–0
1931	France	England	3–2	1974	South Africa	India[1]	—
1932	France	United States	3–2	1975	Sweden	Czechoslovakia	3–2
1933	England	France	3–2	1976	Italy	Chile	4–1
1934	England	United States	4–1	1977	Australia	Italy	4–1
1935	England	United States	5–0	1978	United States	Britain	4–1
1936	England	Australia	3–2	1979	United States	Italy	5–0
1937	United States	England	4–1	1980	Czechoslovakia	Italy	4–1
1938	United States	Australia	3–2	1981	United States	Argentina	4–1
1939	Australia	United States	3–2	1982	United States	France	4–1
1940–45	Not held	—	—				
1946	United States	Australia	5–0				

WIGHTMAN CUP—WOMEN'S TEAM TENNIS

Donated in 1923 by Mrs. Hazel Wightman, an American tennis champion and socialite, the Wightman Cup is the premier prize in women's international competition. Teams from the U.S. and Britain compete for the trophy. The site alternates between the two countries.

YEAR	WINNER	SCORE	YEAR	WINNER	SCORE	YEAR	WINNER	SCORE
1923	United States	7–0	1947	United States	7–0	1966	United States	4–3
1924	Britain	6–1	1948	United States	6–1	1967	United States	6–1
1925	Britain	4–3	1949	United States	7–0	1968	Britain	4–3
1926	United States	4–3	1950	United States	7–0	1969	United States	5–2
1927	United States	5–2	1951	United States	6–1	1970	United States	4–3
1928	Britain	4–3	1952	United States	7–0	1971	United States	4–3
1929	United States	4–3	1953	United States	7–0	1972	United States	5–2
1930	Britain	4–3	1954	United States	6–0[2]	1973	United States	5–2
1931	United States	5–2	1955	United States	6–1	1974	Britain	6–1
1932	United States	4–3	1956	United States	5–2	1975	Britain	5–2
1933	United States	4–3	1957	United States	6–1	1976	United States	5–2
1934	United States	5–2	1958	Britain	4–3	1977	United States	7–0
1935	United States	4–3	1959	United States	4–3	1978	Britain	4–3
1936	United States	4–3	1960	Britain	4–3	1979	United States	7–0
1937	United States	6–1	1961	United States	6–1	1980	United States	5–2
1938	United States	5–2	1962	United States	4–3	1981	United States	7–0
1939	United States	5–2	1963	United States	6–1	1982	United States	6–1
1940–45	Not held	—	1964	United States	5–2	1983	United States	6–1
1946	United States	7–0	1965	United States	5–2			

[1] India defaulted in protest against South Africa's racial policies. [2] One doubles match was not played because of rain.

WIMBLEDON TENNIS CHAMPIONS

WIMBLEDON MEN'S SINGLES CHAMPIONS

1922	Gerald Patterson (Australia)
1923	Bill Johnston (U.S.)
1924	Jean Borotra (France)
1925	René Lacoste (France)
1926	Jean Borotra (France)
1927	Henri Cochet (France)
1928	René Lacoste (France)
1929	Henri Cochet (France)
1930	Bill Tilden (U.S.)
1931	Sid Wood (U.S.)
1932	Ellsworth Vines (U.S.)
1933	Jack Crawford (Australia)
1934–36	Fred Perry (Britain)
1937–38	Don Budge (U.S.)
1939	Bobby Riggs (U.S.)
1940–45	No matches
1946	Yvon Petra (France)
1947	Jack Kramer (U.S.)
1948	Bob Falkenburg (U.S.)
1949	Ted Schroeder (U.S.)
1950	Budge Patty (U.S.)
1951	Dick Savitt (U.S.)
1952	Frank Sedgman (Australia)
1953	Vic Seixas (U.S.)
1954	Jaroslav Drobny (Egypt)
1955	Tony Trabert (U.S.)
1956–57	Lew Hoad (Australia)
1958	Ashley Cooper (Australia)
1959	Alex Olmedo (U.S.)
1960	Neale Fraser (Australia)
1961–62	Rod Laver (Australia)
1963	Chuck McKinley (U.S.)
1964–65	Roy Emerson (Australia)
1966	Manuel Santana (Spain)
1967	John Newcombe (Australia)
1968–69	Rod Laver (Australia)
1970–71	John Newcombe (Australia)
1972	Stan Smith (U.S.)
1973	Jan Kodes (Czech.)
1974	Jimmy Connors (U.S.)
1975	Arthur Ashe (U.S.)
1976–80	Bjorn Borg (Sweden)
1981	John McEnroe (U.S.)
1982	Jimmy Connors (U.S.)
1983	John McEnroe (U.S.)

WIMBLEDON WOMEN'S SINGLES CHAMPIONS

1924	Kitty McKane (Britain)
1925	Suzanne Lenglen (France)
1926	Kitty McK. Godfree (Britain)
1927–29	Helen Wills (U.S.)
1930	Helen Wills Moody (U.S.)
1931	Cilly Aussen (Germany)
1932–33	Helen Wills Moody (U.S.)
1934	Dorothy Round (Britain)
1935	Helen Wills Moody (U.S.)
1936	Helen Hull Jacobs (U.S.)
1937	Dorothy Round (Britain)
1938	Helen Wills Moody (U.S.)
1939	Alice Marble (U.S.)
1940–45	No matches
1946	Pauline Betz (U.S.)
1947	Margaret Osborne (U.S.)
1948–50	Louise Brough (U.S.)
1951	Doris Hart (U.S.)
1952–54	Maureen Connolly (U.S.)
1955	Louise Brough (U.S.)
1956	Shirley Fry (U.S.)
1957–58	Althea Gibson (U.S.)
1959–60	Maria Bueno (Brazil)
1961	Angela Mortimer (Britain)
1962	Karen Hantze Susman (U.S.)
1963	Margaret Smith (Australia)
1964	Maria Bueno (Brazil)
1965	Margaret Smith (Australia)
1966–68	Billie Jean King (U.S.)
1969	Ann Jones (Britain)
1970	Margaret Smith Court (Australia)
1971	Evonne Goolagong (Australia)
1972–73	Billie Jean King (U.S.)
1974	Chris Evert (U.S.)
1975	Billie Jean King (U.S.)
1976	Chris Evert (U.S.)
1977	Virginia Wade (Britain)
1978–79	Martina Navratilova (U.S.)
1980	Yvonne Goolagong (Australia)
1981	Chris Evert Lloyd (U.S.)
1982–83	Martina Navratilova (U.S.)

U.S. OPEN TENNIS CHAMPIONS

U.S. MEN'S SINGLES CHAMPIONS

1915	William M. Johnston (U.S.)
1916	R. Norris Williams II (U.S.)
1917–18	R. Lindley Murray (U.S.)
1919	William M. Johnston (U.S.)
1920–25	Bill Tilden (U.S.)
1926–27	Rene Lacoste (France)
1928	Henri Cochet (France)
1929	Bill Tilden (U.S.)
1930	John Doeg (U.S.)
1931–32	Ellsworth Vines (U.S.)
1933–34	Fred Perry (England)
1935	Wilmer Allison (U.S.)
1936	Fred Perry (England)
1937–38	Don Budge (U.S.)
1939	Bobby Riggs (U.S.)
1940	Don McNeill (U.S.)
1941	Bobby Riggs (U.S.)
1942	Ted Schroeder (U.S.)
1943	Joe Hunt (U.S.)
1944	Frank Parker (U.S.)
1945	Frank Parker (U.S.)
1946	Jack Kramer (U.S.)
1947	Jack Kramer (U.S.)
1948	Pancho Gonzales (U.S.)
1949	Pancho Gonzales (U.S.)
1950	Art Larsen (U.S.)
1951–52	Frank Sedgman (Australia)
1953	Tony Trabert (U.S.)
1954	Vic Seixas (U.S.)
1955	Tony Trabert (U.S.)
1956	Ken Rosewall (Australia)
1957	Mal Anderson (Australia)
1958	Ashley Cooper (Australia)
1959–60	Neale Fraser (Australia)
1961	Roy Emerson (Australia)
1962	Rod Laver (Australia)
1963	Rafael Osuna (Mexico)
1964	Roy Emerson (Australia)
1965	Manuel Santana (Spain)
1966	Fred Stolle (Australia)
1967	John Newcombe (Australia)
1968	Arthur Ashe (U.S.)
1969	Rod Laver (Australia)
1970	Ken Rosewall (Australia)
1971	Stan Smith (U.S.)
1972	Ilie Nastase (Romania)
1973	John Newcombe (Australia)
1974	Jimmy Connors (U.S.)
1975	Manuel Orantes (Spain)
1976	Jimmy Connors (U.S.)
1977	Guillermo Vilas (Argentina)
1978	Jimmy Connors (U.S.)
1979–81	John McEnroe (U.S.)
1982–83	Jimmy Connors (U.S.)

U.S. WOMEN'S SINGLES CHAMPIONS

1920–22	Molla Bjurstedt Mallory (U.S.)
1923–25	Helen Wills (U.S.)
1926	Molla Bjurstedt Mallory (U.S.)
1927–29	Helen Wills (U.S.)
1930	Betty Nuthall (England)
1931	Helen Wills Moody (U.S.)
1932–35	Helen Hull Jacobs (U.S.)
1936	Alice Marble (U.S.)
1937	Anita Lizana (Chile)
1938–40	Alice Marble (U.S.)
1941	Sarah Palfrey Cooke (U.S.)
1942–44	Pauline Betz (U.S.)
1945	Sarah Palfrey Cooke (U.S.)
1946	Pauline Betz (U.S.)
1947	Louise Brough (U.S.)
1948–50	Margaret O. du Pont (U.S.)
1951–53	Maureen Connolly (U.S.)
1954–55	Doris Hart (U.S.)
1956	Shirley Fry (U.S.)
1957–58	Althea Gibson (U.S.)
1959	Maria Bueno (Brazil)
1960–61	Darlene Hard (U.S.)
1962	Margaret Smith (Australia)
1963–64	Maria Bueno (Brazil)
1965	Margaret Smith (Australia)
1966	Maria Bueno (Brazil)
1967	Billie Jean King (U.S.)
1968	Virginia Wade (England)
1969	Margaret S. Court (Australia)
1970	Margaret S. Court (Australia)
1971	Billie Jean King (U.S.)
1972	Billie Jean King (U.S.)
1973	Margaret S. Court (Australia)
1974	Billie Jean King (U.S.)
1975	Chris Evert (U.S.)
1976	Chris Evert (U.S.)
1977	Chris Evert (U.S.)
1978	Chris Evert (U.S.)
1979	Tracy Austin (U.S.)
1980	Chris Evert Lloyd (U.S.)
1981	Tracy Austin (U.S.)
1982	Chris Evert Lloyd (U.S.)
1983	Martina Navratilova (U.S.)

TRACK AND FIELD

United Press Int'l.

Edwin Moses (105), of Laguna Beach, Calif., sets a new world and American record in the 400-meter hurdles on Aug. 31, his 28th birthday, at a meet in Koblenz, West Germany. In setting the new record of 0:47.02, Moses beat his old world record, set in 1980, by 11-hundredths of a second. His performance marked his 85th consecutive victory in a 400-meter-hurdles final. Andre Phillips, *right*, also of the U.S., placed second, with a time of 0:48.26.

Southern Methodist University won the NCAA Division I Men's Outdoor Track Championships at the University of Houston on May 30–June 4, defeating Tennessee. At the same time, in the women's division, UCLA successfully defended its title, edging Florida State for the championship.

A variety of outdoor track world records were set in 1983. Zhu Jianhua of China set a new high jump mark of 7′ 9¾″ at Shanghai, China, on Sept. 22. The Soviet Union's Tamara Bykova set a new women's high jump record of 6′ 8¼″ at Pisa, Italy, on Aug. 25, just four days after Ulrike Meyfarth of West Germany had set a new world record of 6′ 8″, and Bykova had tied that record.

Thierry Vigneron of France set a new world mark of 19′ 1½″ in the men's pole vault on Sept. 1 at Rome, Italy. That was just four days after France's Pierre Quinon had set a new record of 19′ 1″ on Aug. 28 at Cologne, West Germany.

Calvin Smith of the U.S. ran a new world record 100 meters in 0:9.93 at Colorado Springs, Colo., on July 2. Carl Lewis of the U.S. set a new American record of 0:19.75 for the 200 meters at Indianapolis, Ind., on June 19.

A total of 48 indoor world and American record-setting performances were turned in during 1983, according to The Athletics Congress. No formal world records are kept for indoor track-and-field events because of the wide variety of track sizes used.

Among the world-best indoor records set was Billy Olson's 19′ 0¼″ pole vault at Toronto, Canada, on Feb. 4.

In March, Britain's Sebastian Coe set world bests in the men's 800-meter and 1,000-meter runs of 1:44.91 and 2:18.58, respectively.

Mary Decker of the U.S. set a new world and American best record of 9:31.7 in the women's two-mile run at Los Angeles, Calif., on Jan. 21.

NCAA MEN'S TEAM CHAMPIONSHIPS: 1922–1983

1922 California	**1932** Indiana	**1956** UCLA	**1965** Oregon, USC	**1974** Tennessee
1923 Michigan	**1933** Louisiana State	**1957** Villanova	**1966** UCLA	**1975** Texas-El Paso
1924 No meet	**1934** Stanford	**1958** USC	**1967–68** USC	**1976** USC
1925 Stanford [1]	**1935–43** USC	**1959** Kansas	**1969** San Jose State	**1977** Arizona State
1926 USC	**1944** Illinois	**1960** Kansas	**1970** Brigham Young,	**1978** USC
1927 Illinois [1]	**1945** Navy	**1961** USC	Kansas, Oregon	**1979–82** Texas-El Paso
1928 Stanford	**1946–47** Illinois	**1962** Oregon	**1971** UCLA	**1983** SMU
1929 Ohio State	**1948** Minnesota	**1963** USC	**1972** UCLA	
1930–31 USC	**1949–55** USC	**1964** Oregon	**1973** UCLA	

TRACK AND FIELD *(continued)*

U.S.A. INDOOR TRACK AND FIELD CHAMPIONSHIPS: 1983

MEN'S EVENTS

60-Yard Dash: Carl Lewis (Santa Monica TC)	0:06.04	35-lb. Weight Throw: Robert Weir (S. Methodist/Britain)	76′ 9¾″
600-Yard Dash: Eugene Sanders (Athletic Attic)	1:08.47	Long Jump: Carl Lewis (Santa Monica TC)	27′ 4¾″
1,000-Yard Run: Mark Belger (Pacific Coast Club)	2:07.79	Triple Jump: Ajayi Agbebaku (El Paso TC/Nigeria)	55′ 2″
One-Mile Run: Eamonn Coghlan (New York AC/Ireland)	3:58.50	High Jump: Tyke Peacock (unattached)	7′ 5¾″
3-Mile Run: Doug Padilla (Athletics West)	13:08.00	Pole Vault: Billy Olson (Pacific Coast Club)	18′ 8¾″
2-Mile Walk: Ray Sharp (Team Kangaroo)	12:13.33	Sprint Medley Relay: Tiger International	2:00.25
60-Yard Hurdles: Greg Foster (Wilt's AC)	0:06.92	One-Mile Relay: Southern Methodist	3:12.92
Shot Put: Kevin Akins (Ohio TC)	67′ 8¾″	Two-Mile Relay: Santa Monica TC	7:24.43
Outstanding Athlete: Eugene Sanders (Athletic Attic)		Team Champion: (Tie) Pacific Coast Club, Athletic Attic	18 pts.

WOMEN'S EVENTS

60-Yard Dash: Evelyn Ashford (Medalist TC)	0:06.58	Shot Put: Ria Stalman (Los Angeles TC/Holland)	55′ 2¾″
220-Yard Dash: Chandra Cheeseborough (Athletics West)	0:23.52	Long Jump: Carol Lewis (Houston)	21′ 5¼″
440-Yard Dash: Diane Dixon (Ohio State)	0:53.78	High Jump: Louise Ritter (Pacific Coast Club)	6′ 3½″
880-Yard Run: Delisa Walton (Tennessee)	2:03.10	640-Yard Relay: University of Nevada–Las Vegas	1:10.55
One-Mile Run: Darlene Beckford (Liberty AC)	4:33.29	One-Mile Relay: Ms International	3:42.35
Two-Mile Run: Jan Merrill (Age Group AA)	9:40.46	One-Mile Walk: Susan Brodock (So. California Road Runners)	7:14.67
60-Yard Hurdles: Stephanie Hightower (unattached)	0:07.36	Sprint Medley Relay: California Cheetahs	1:45.38
Individual Champion: Stephanie Hightower (unattached)		Team Champion: Athletics West	16 pts.

U.S.A. OUTDOOR TRACK AND FIELD CHAMPIONSHIPS: 1983

MEN'S EVENTS

100-Meter Dash: Carl Lewis (Santa Monica TC)	0:10.27	10,000-Meter Run: Alberto Salazar (Athletics West)	28:11.64
200-Meter Dash: Carl Lewis (Santa Monica TC)	0:19.75	High Jump: Dwight Stones (Pacific Coast Club)	7′ 6″
400-Meter Dash: Sunder Nix (Indiana)	0:45.15	Pole Vault: J. Buckingham (Ath. A.), B. Olson (P.C.C.)	18′ ½″
800-Meter Run: David Patrick (Athletics West)	1:44.70	Long Jump: Carl Lewis (Santa Monica TC)	28′ 10¼″
1,500-Meter Run: Steve Scott (Sub 4 TC)	3:36.62	Triple Jump: Willie Banks (Athletics West)	56′ 7½″
5,000-Meter Run: Doug Padilla (Athletics West)	13:25.14	Shot Put: Dave Laut (Athletics West)	71′ 2¾″
110-Meter High Hurdles: Greg Foster (Wilt's AC)	0:13.15	Discus Throw: John Powell (Athletic Attic)	222′ 0″
400-Meter Hurdles: Edwin Moses (unattached)	0:47.84	Hammer Throw: Dave McKenzie (Puma & Energizer)	241′ 2″
3,000-Meter Steeplechase: Henry Marsh (Athletics West)	8:21.05	Javelin Throw: Rod Ewaliko (Athletics West)	285′ 3″
20-Kilometer Walk: Jim Heiring (Athletic Attic)	1:26:54.2	Team Champion: Athletics West	116 pts.

WOMEN'S EVENTS

100-Meter Dash: Evelyn Ashford (Medalist TC)	0:11.24	400-Meter Relay: Puma & Energizer	0:43.61
200-Meter Dash: Evelyn Ashford (Medalist TC)	0:21.88	1,600-Meter Relay: Puma & Energizer	3:34.18
400-Meter Dash: Denean Howard (Los Angeles State)	0:50.99	3,200-Meter Relay: MS International	8:38.04
800-Meter Dash: Robin Campbell (Puma & Energizer)	1:59.00	800-Meter Medley Relay: Puma & Energizer	1:37.46
1,500-Meter Run: Mary Decker (Athletics West)	4:03.50	High Jump: Louise Ritter (Pacific Coast Club)	6′ 4″
3,000-Meter Run: Mary Decker (Athletics West)	8:38.36	Long Jump: Carol Lewis (Santa Monica TC)	22′ 8″
10,000-Meter Run: Katie Ishmael (Wisconsin United)	33:24.71	Shot Put: Denise Wood (Knoxville TC)	56′ 8½″
100-Meter Hurdles: Benita Fitzgerald (Adidas)	0:12.97	Discus Throw: Leslie Deniz (unattached)	206′ 3″
400-Meter Hurdles: Sharrieffa Barksdale (Adidas)	0:56.07	Javelin Throw: Karin Smith (Athletics West)	187′ 8″
10-Kilometer Walk: Susan Liers-Westerfield (Island TC)	50:51.91	Team Champion: Puma & Energizer	108 pts.

NCAA OUTDOOR TRACK AND FIELD CHAMPIONSHIPS: 1983

MEN'S EVENTS

100-Meter Dash: Emmitt King (Alabama)	0:10.15	1,600-Meter Relay: Texas Christian	3:02.09
200-Meter Dash: Elliott Quow (Rutgers)	0:20.31	High Jump: Rickie Thompsen (Houston Baptist)	7′ 5¼″
400-Meter Dash: Bert Cameron (Texas-El Paso)	0:44.62	Polt Vault: Felix Bohni (San Jose State)	18′ 2½″
800-Meter Run: Joaquim Cruz (Oregon)	1:44.91	Hammer Throw: Robert Weir (Southern Methodist)	244′ 2″
1,500-Meter Run: Frank O'Mara (Arkansas)	3:40.51	Long Jump: Ralph Spry (Mississippi)	27′ 5½″
5,000-Meter Run: Gidamis Shahanga (Texas-El Paso)	13:54.13	Triple Jump: Keith Connor (Southern Methodist)	56′ 7½″
10,000-Meter Run: Gidamis Shahanga (Texas-El Paso)	29:10.28	Javelin Throw: Einar Vilhjalmssen (Texas)	293′ 1″
110-Meter High Hurdles: Roger Kingdom (Pittsburgh)	0:13.54	Shot Put: Michael Carter (Southern Methodist)	68′ 7″
400-Meter Hurdles: Sven Nylander (Southern Methodist)	0:48.88	Discus: Dean Crouser (Oregon)	216′ 2″
3,000-Meter Steeplechase: Brian Diemer (Michigan)	8:26.95	Decathlon: Kerry Zimmerman (Indiana)	7,810 pts.
400-Meter Relay: Tennessee	0:39.22		

WOMEN'S EVENTS

100-Meter Dash: Merlene Ottey (Nebraska)	0:11.04	400-Meter Hurdles: Judi Brown (Michigan State)	0:56.44
200-Meter Dash: Merlene Ottey (Nebraska)	0:22.39	400-Meter Relay: Florida State	0:42.94
400-Meter Dash: Florence Griffith (UCLA)	0:50.94	1,600-Meter Relay: Florida State	3:28.46
800-Meter Run: Joetta Clark (Tennessee)	2:02.28	High Jump: Disa Gisladottir (Alabama)	6′ 1½″
1,500-Meter Run: Michele Bush (UCLA)	4:14.98	Long Jump: Carol Lewis (Houston)	21′ 11¾″
3,000-Meter Run: Alison Wiley (Stanford)	9:03.51	Shot Put: Carol Cady (Stanford)	56′ 0″
5,000-Meter Run: Betty Jo Springs (N. Carolina State)	15:51.97	Discus: Leslie Deniz (Arizona State)	209′ 10″
10,000-Meter Run: Betty Jo Springs (N. Carolina State)	33:01.02	Javelin Throw: Denise Thiemard (Nebraska)	178′ 10″
100-Meter Hurdles: Benita Fitzgerald (Tennessee)	0:12.84	Heptathlon: Jackie Joyner (UCLA)	6,365 pts.

WORLD TRACK AND FIELD RECORDS: MEN

EVENT	RECORD	RECORD HOLDER	NATION	DATE	SITE
Running					
1 Mile	3:47.33	Sebastian Coe	Britain	8-28-81	Brussels, Belgium
1 Hour	20,944 meters[1]	Jos Hermens	Netherlands	5-1-76	Arnhem, Netherlands
100 Meters	*0:09.93	Calvin Smith	United States	7-3-83	Colorado Springs, Colo.
200 Meters	0:19.72	Pietro Mennea	Italy	9-12-79	Mexico City, Mexico
200 Meters (turn)	0:19.8	Donald Quarrie	Jamaica	8-3-71	Cali, Colombia
400 Meters	0:43.86	Lee Evans	United States	10-18-68	Mexico City, Mexico
600 Meters	1:14.3	Lee Evans	United States	8-31-68	Lake Tahoe, California
800 Meters	1:41.73	Sebastian Coe	Britain	8-28-81	Brussels, Belgium
1,000 Meters	2:12.18	Sebastian Coe	Britain	7-11-81	Oslo, Norway
1,500 Meters	*3:31.24	Sydney Maree	South Africa	8-28-83	Cologne, West Germany
2,000 Meters	4:51.4	John Walker	New Zealand	6-30-76	Oslo, Norway
3,000 Meters	7:32.1	Henry Rono	Kenya	6-27-78	Oslo, Norway
5,000 Meters	13:00.41	David Moorcroft	Britain	7-7-82	Oslo, Norway
10,000 Meters	27:22.4	Henry Rono	Kenya	6-11-78	Vienna, Austria
20,000 Meters	57:24.2	Jos Hermens	Netherlands	5-1-76	Arnhem, Netherlands
25,000 Meters	1:13:55.8	Toshiko Seko	Japan	3-22-81	Christchurch, New Zealand
30,000 Meters	1:29:18.8	Toshiko Seko	Japan	3-22-81	Christchurch, New Zealand
Relays					
400 Meters	*0:37.86	United States team	United States	8-10-83	Helsinki, Finland
800 Meters	1:20.26	So. California	United States	5-27-78	Tempe, Arizona
1,600 Meters	2:56.16	United States team	United States	10-20-68	Mexico City, Mexico
3,200 Meters	7:03.89	British team	Britain	8-30-82	London, England
6,000 Meters	14.38.8	West German team	West Germany	8-17-77	Cologne, West Germany
Hurdles					
110 Meters	12:93.0	Renaldo Nehemiah	United States	8-19-81	Zurich, Switzerland
400 Meters	0.47.02	Edwin Moses	United States	8-31-83	Koblenz, West Germany
3,000 Meters†	8:05.4	Henry Rono	Kenya	5-13-78	Seattle, Washington
Walking					
20 Kilometers	1:20:06.8	Daniel Bautista	Mexico	10-17-71	Montreal, Canada
30 Kilometers	2:08.00	Jose Marin	Spain	4-8-79	Barcelona, Spain
50 Kilometers	3:41.39	Raul Gonzalez	Mexico	5-25-79	Fana, Norway
2 Hours	28,165 meters[2]	Jose Marin	Spain	8-4-79	Barcelona, Spain
Jumping					
High Jump	*7′ 9¾″	Zhu Jianhua	China	9-22-83	Shanghi, China
Long Jump	29′ 2½″	Bob Beamon	United States	10-18-68	Mexico City, Mexico
Triple Jump	58′ 8½″	Joao Oliveira	Brazil	10-15-75	Mexico City, Mexico
Pole Vault	*19′ 1½″	Thierry Vigneron	France	9-1-83	Rome, Italy
Throwing					
Shot	*72′ 10¾″	Udo Beyer	East Germany	6-25-83	Los Angeles, Calif.
Discus	235′ 9″	Yuriy Dumchev	Soviet Union	5-29-83	Moscow, Soviet Union
Hammer	276′ 0″	Sergei Litvinov	Soviet Union	6-21-83	Moscow, Soviet Union
Javelin	*327′ 2″	Tom Petranoff	United States	5-15-83	Los Angeles, Calif.
Decathlon	8,779 pts.	Jurgen Hingsen	West Germany	6-4/5-83	Bernhausen, West Germany

SELECTED MEN'S OUTDOOR AMERICAN RECORDS

EVENT	RECORD	RECORD HOLDER	NATION	DATE	SITE
Running					
100 Meters	*9.93	Calvin Smith	United States	7-3-83	Colorado Springs, Colo.
200 Meters	*19.75	Carl Lewis	United States	6-19-83	Indianapolis, Indiana
400 Meters	43.86	Lee Evans	United States	10-18-68	Mexico City, Mexico
800 Meters	1:43.9	Rick Wohlhuter	United States	6-28-74	Los Angeles, California
1,000 Meters	2:13.9	Rick Wohlhuter	United States	7-30-74	Oslo, Norway
1,500 Meters	3:31.96	Steve Scott	United States	8-26-81	Koblenz, West Germany
2,000 Meters	4:54.71	Steve Scott	United States	8-31-82	Ingelheim, West Germany
3,000 Meters	*7:35.84	Doug Padilla	United States	7-9-83	Oslo, Norway
5,000 Meters	13:11.93	Alberto Salazar	United States	7-6-82	Stockholm, Sweden
10,000 Meters	27:25.61	Alberto Salazar	United States	6-26-82	Oslo, Norway
Hurdles					
110 Meters	12.93	Renaldo Nehemiah	United States	8-19-81	Zurich, Switzerland
400 Meters	*47.02	Edwin Moses	United States	8-31-83	Koblenz, West Germany
Jumping					
High Jump	*7′ 7¾″	Tyke Peacock	United States	8-17-83	Berlin, West Germany
Long Jump	29′ 2½″	Bob Beamon	United States	10-18-68	Mexico City, Mexico
Triple Jump	57′ 7½″	Willie Banks	United States	6-21-81	Sacramento, California
Pole Vault	*18′ 10¼″	Jeff Buckingham	United States	7-16-83	Lawrence, Kansas
Throwing					
Shot	72′ 3″	Brian Oldfield	United States	5-16-81	Modesto, California
Discus	237′ 4″	Ben Plucknett	United States	7-7-81	Stockholm, Sweden
Hammer	*244′ 5″	Dave McKenzie	United States	6-26-83	Los Angeles, California
Javelin	*327′ 2″	Tom Petranoff	United States	5-15-83	Los Angeles, California
Decathlon	8,617 pts.	Bruce Jenner	United States	7-29/30-76	Montreal, Canada

* Pending official recognition. † Steeplechase. [1] 13 miles, 25 yards. [2] 17 miles, 881 yards.

WORLD TRACK AND FIELD RECORDS: WOMEN

EVENT	RECORD	RECORD HOLDER	NATION	DATE	SITE
Running					
60 Meters	0:07.02	Betty Cuthbert	Australia	2-27-60	Sydney, Australia
100 Meters	*0:10.79	Evelyn Ashford	United States	7-3-83	Colorado Springs, Colorado
200 Meters	0:21.71	Marita Koch	East Germany	6-10-79	Berlin, East Germany
400 Meters	0:47.99	Jarmila Kratochvilova	Czechoslovakia	7-26-83	Munich, West Germany
800 Meters	1:53.28	Jarmila Kratochvilova	Czechoslovakia	7-31-83	Berlin, E. Germany
1,500 Meters	3:52.47	Tatiana Kazankina	Soviet Union	8-13-80	Zurich, Switzerland
1 Mile	4:17.44	Maricica Puica	Romania	9-16-82	Rieti, Italy
3,000 Meters	8:26.78	Svetlana Ulmasova	Soviet Union	7-24-82	Kiev, Soviet Union
5,000 Meters	15:08.26	Mary Decker	United States	6-5-82	Eugene, Oregon
10,000 Meters	31:27.57	Raisa Sadreidinova	Soviet Union	9-7-83	Odessa, Soviet Union
Hurdles					
100 Meters	0:12.36	Grazyna Rabsztyn	Poland	6-13-80	Warsaw, Poland
200 Meters	0:25.70	Pamela Ryan	Australia	11-25-71	Melbourne, Australia
400 Meters	0:54.02	Anna Ambrosene	Soviet Union	6-11-83	Moscow, Soviet Union
Jumping					
High Jump	*6′ 8¼″	Tamara Bykova	Soviet Union	8-25-83	Pisa, Italy
Long Jump	24′ 4½″	Anisoara Cusmir	Romania	6-4-83	Bucharest, Romania
Throwing					
Shot	73′ 8″	Ileana Slupianek	East Germany	5-11-80	Potsdam, East Germany
Discus	*240′ 4″	Galina Savinkova	Soviet Union	5-22-83	Leselidze, Soviet Union
Javelin	245′ 3″	Tiina Lillak	Finland	6-13-83	Tampere, Finland
Pentathlon	5,083 pts.	Nadyezhda Tkachenko	Soviet Union	7-24-80	Moscow, Soviet Union
Heptathlon	6,836 pts.	Ramona Neubert	East Germany	6-18/19-83	Moscow, Soviet Union
Running Relays					
400 Meters	0:41.53	East German team	East Germany	7-31-83	Berlin, East Germany
800 Meters	1:28.20	East German team	East Germany	8-9-80	Jena, East Germany
1,600 Meters	3:19.04	East German team	East Germany	9-11-82	Athens, Greece
3,200 Meters	7:52.40	Soviet team	Soviet Union	8-16-76	Podolsk, Soviet Union
Race Walking					
5,000 Meters	*22:41.40	A. Deverinskaya	Soviet Union	5-15-82	Bergen, Norway
10,000 Meters	*46:15.60	A. Underova	Soviet Union	9-1-83	Moscow, Soviet Union

SELECTED WOMEN'S OUTDOOR AMERICAN RECORDS

Running					
60 Meters	0:07.30	Barbara Ferrell	United States	8-25-68	Walnut, California
100 Meters	*0:10.79	Evelyn Ashford	United States	7-3-83	Colorado Springs, Colorado
200 Meters	0:21.83	Evelyn Ashford	United States	8-24-79	Montreal, Canada
400 Meters	0:50.62	Rosalyn Bryant	United States	7-28-76	Montreal, Canada
800 Meters	*1:57.60	Mary Decker	United States	7-31-83	Gateshead, Britain
1,500 Meters	*3:57.12	Mary Decker	United States	7-26-83	Stockholm, Sweden
1 Mile	4:18.08	Mary Decker	United States	7-9-82	Paris, France
3 Miles	15:04.10	Kathy Mills	United States	5-26-78	Knoxville, Tennessee
2,000 Meters	5:38.9	Mary Decker	United States	7-7-82	Oslo, Norway
3,000 Meters	8:29.71	Mary Decker	United States	7-7-82	Oslo, Norway
5,000 Meters	15:08.26	Mary Decker	United States	6-5-82	Eugene, Oregon
10,000 Meters	31:35.30	Mary Decker	United States	7-17-82	Eugene, Oregon
Hurdles					
100 Meters	0:12.79	Stephanie Hightower	United States	7-10-82	Karl Marx Stadt, E. Germany
200 Meters	0:26.10	Pat Hawkins	United States	7-10-71	Bakersfield, California
400 Meters	*0:55.69	Lori McCauley	United States	7-2-83	Colorado Springs, Colorado
Relays					
400 Meters	*0:41.61	United States team	United States	7-3-83	Colorado Springs, Colorado
800 Meters	1:32.60	United States team	United States	6-24-79	Bourges, France
1,600 Meters	3:22.81	United States team	United States	7-31-76	Montreal, Canada
3,200 Meters	8:17.09	Athletics West team	United States	4-24-83	Walnut, California
Race Walking					
1,500 Meters	6:46.6	Lisa Metheny	United States	6-28-75	White Plains, New York
1 Mile	7:20.1	Sue Brodock	United States	2-2-74	Los Angeles, California
5,000 Meters	23:19.1	Sue Brodock	United States	6-13-80	Walnut, California
10,000 Meters	50:32.8	Sue Brodock	United States	6-17-79	Walnut, California
Jumping					
High Jump	*6′ 7″	Louise Ritter	United States	9-1-83	Rome, Italy
Long Jump	22′ 11¾″	Jodi Anderson	United States	6-28-80	Eugene, Oregon
Throwing					
Shot	62′ 7¾″	Maren Seidler	United States	6-16-79	Walnut, California
Discus	*213′ 1″	Leslie Deniz	United States	4-2-83	Tempe, Arizona
Javelin	227′ 5″	Kate Schmidt	United States	9-10-77	Pacific Palisades, California

* Pending official recognition.

WEIGHTLIFTING

1983 U.S. WEIGHTLIFTING FEDERATION NATIONAL CHAMPIONSHIPS

52 KILOGRAMS (114½ POUNDS)
1. Dirk Yasko (Unattached), 172.5 kg. (380.3 lbs.)
2. Garrett Miyahira (IOL), 162.5 kg. (358.3 lbs.)

56 KILOGRAMS (123 POUNDS)
1. Ron Crawley (Crushers Unlimited), 200.0 kg. (440.9 lbs.)
2. Avetis Karamanian (NYC P&R), 197.5 kg. (435.4 lbs.)

60 KILOGRAMS (132¼ POUNDS)
1. Brian Miyamoto (IOL), 235.0 kg. (518.1 lbs.)
2. Wrenn Norvell (Sayre Park), 227.5 kg. (501.6 lbs.)

67.5 KILOGRAMS (148¾ POUNDS)
1. Michael Jacques (Coffee's Gym), 287.5 kg. (633.8 lbs.)
2. Don Abrahamson (Sports Palace), 280.0 kg. (617.3 lbs.)

75 KILOGRAMS (165¼ POUNDS)
1. Cal Schake (York BBC), 320.0 kg. (705.5 lbs.)
2. Gary Savage (DJ's WLC), 297.5 kg. (655.9 lbs.)

82.5 KILOGRAMS (181¾ POUNDS)
1. Curt White (York BBC), 355.0 kg. (782.6 lbs.)
2. Pete Cline (Sports Palace), (700.0 lbs.)

90 KILOGRAMS (198¼ POUNDS)
1. Michael Cohen (Howard's Gym), 352.5 kg. (777.1 lbs.)
2. Kevin Winter (Sports Palace), 352.5 kg. (777.1 lbs.)

100 KILOGRAMS (220 POUNDS)
1. Ken Clark (Sports Palace), 370.0 kg. (815.7 lbs.)
2. Rich Shanko (York BBC), 370.0 kg. (815.7 lbs.)

110 KILOGRAMS (220 POUNDS)
1. Jeff Michaels (York BBC), 407.5 kg. (898.4 lbs.)
2. Guy Carlton (York BBC), 365.0 kg. (804.7 lbs.)

SUPERHEAVYWEIGHT
1. Mario Martinez (Sports Palace), 377.5 kg. (832.2 lbs.)
2. John Bergman (Sports Palace), 350.0 kg. (771.6 lbs.)

1983 U.S. WEIGHTLIFTING FEDERATION WOMEN'S NATIONAL CHAMPIONSHIPS

44 KILOGRAMS (97 POUNDS)
1. Miriam Hoffer, 198.25 kg. (437.1 lbs.)
2. Dee Anna Hammock, 181.75 kg. (400.7 lbs.)
3. Tricia Whitcomb, 143.25 kg. (315.8 lbs.)

48 KILOGRAMS (105½ POUNDS)
1. Karen Derwin, 220.25 kg. (485.6 lbs.)
2. Mitsey Cohen, 203.75 kg. (449.2 lbs.)
3. Gayle Hall, 198.25 kg. (437.1 lbs.)

52 KILOGRAMS (114½ POUNDS)
1. Kathy Regan, 275.50 kg. (607.4 lbs.)
2. Rachel Silverman, 259.00 kg. (571.0 lbs.)
3. Sunday Zeller, 259.00 kg. (571.0 lbs.)

56 KILOGRAMS (123¼ POUNDS)
1. Mary Beth Cervenak, 336.00 kg. (740.8 lbs.)
2. Colleene Colley, 314.00 kg. (692.3 lbs.)

60 KILOGRAMS (132¼ POUNDS)
1. Jane Camp, 319.50 kg. (704.4 lbs.)
2. Cammie Lusko, 314.00 kg. (692.3 lbs.)

67.5 KILOGRAMS (148¾ POUNDS)
1. Judy Glenney, 369.25 kg. (814.1 lbs.)
2. Giselle Shepatin, 264.50 kg. (583.1 lbs.)

75 KILOGRAMS (165¼ POUNDS)
1. Lisa Long, 330.50 kg. (728.6 lbs.)
2. Jody Anderson, 314.00 kg. (692.3 lbs.)

82.5 KILOGRAMS (181¾ POUNDS)
1. Karyn Tarter, 374.75 kg. (826.2 lbs.)
2. Beneta Carswell, 314.00 kg. (692.3 lbs.)

82.5 + KILOGRAMS (+181¾ POUNDS)
1. Lorna Griffin, 413.25 kg. (911.1 lbs.)
2. Salome Hayward, 248.00 kg. (546.7 lbs.)

WRESTLING

NATIONAL COLLEGIATE ATHLETIC ASSOCIATION WRESTLING CHAMPIONSHIPS

NCAA TEAM CHAMPIONSHIPS

1928–31	Oklahoma St.	1937–46	Oklahoma St.	1954–56	Oklahoma St.	1964	Oklahoma St.	1971	Oklahoma St.
1932	Indiana	1947	Cornell Col.	1957	Oklahoma	1965	Iowa State	1972–73	Iowa State
1933(tie)	Iowa State;	1948–49	Oklahoma St.	1958–59	Oklahoma St.	1966	Oklahoma St.	1974	Oklahoma
	Oklahoma St.	1950	No. Iowa	1960	Oklahoma	1967	Michigan St.	1975–76	Iowa
1934–35	Oklahoma St.	1951–52	Oklahoma	1961–62	Oklahoma St.	1968	Oklahoma St.	1977	Iowa State
1936	Oklahoma	1953	Penn State	1963	Oklahoma	1969–70	Iowa State	1978–83	Iowa

NCAA OUTSTANDING WRESTLER AWARDS

1950	A. Gizoni, Waynesburg	1963	Mickey Martin, Oklahoma	1975	Mike Frick, Lehigh
1951	W. Romanowski, Cornell Col.	1964	Dean Lahr, Colorado	1976	Chuck Yagla, Iowa
1952	Tommy Evans, Oklahoma	1965–66	Yojiro Uetake, Okla. St.	1977	Nick Gallo, Hofstra
1953	Frank Bettucci, Cornell U.	1967	Richard Sanders, Portland St.	1978	Mark Churella, Michigan
1954	Tommy Evans, Oklahoma	1968	Dwayne Keller, Oklahoma St.	1979	Bruce Kinseth, Iowa
1955	Ed Eichelberger, Lehigh	1969	Dan Gable, Iowa St.	1980	Howard Harris, Oregon St.
1956–57	Dan Hodge, Oklahoma	1970	Larry Owings, Washington	1981	Gene Mills, Syracuse
1958	Dick Delgado, Oklahoma	1971	Darrell Keller, Oklahoma St.	1982	Mark Schultz, Oklahoma
1959	Ron Gray, Iowa St.	1972	Wade Schalles, Clarion St.	1983	Mike Sheets, Oklahoma St.
1960	Dave Auble, Cornell U.	1973	Greg Strobel, Oregon St.		
1961–62	E. Simons, Lock Haven St.	1974	Floyd Hitchcock, Bloomsburg St.		

NCAA INDIVIDUAL WRESTLING CHAMPIONS: 1983

Heavyweight	Lou Banach, Iowa	158 Pounds	Jim Zalesky, Iowa	126 Pounds	Chris Davis, Illinois
190 Pounds	Lou Banach, Iowa	150 Pounds	Nate Carr, Iowa St.	118 Pounds	Adam Cuestas, Bakersfield St.
177 Pounds	Mark Schultz, Oklahoma	142 Pounds	Darryl Burley, Lehigh		
167 Pounds	Mike Sheets, Oklahoma St.	134 Pounds	Clar Anderson, Oklahoma St.		

NATIONAL AAU FREESTYLE WRESTLING CHAMPIONSHIPS: 1983

114.5 Pounds:	David Fischer, Unattached	198 Pounds:	Dave Ruckman, Unattached
125.5 Pounds:	Robert Wimberley, Ohio University	220 Pounds:	Harold Smith, Wildcat Wrestling Club
136.5 Pounds:	Mark Mangianti, Hawkeye Wrestling Club	Heavyweight:	Matt Ghaffari, Viking Wrestling Club
149.5 Pounds:	James Martinez, Minnesota	Outstanding Wrestler:	James Martinez, Minnesota
163 Pounds:	Mike DeAnna, Hawkeye Wrestling Club	Team Championship:	Viking Wrestling Club
180.5 Pounds:	John Gregor, Ohio Wrestling Club		

YACHTING

THE AMERICA'S CUP RACES

The 25th challenge for the America's Cup was won by *Australia II,* the first foreign yacht to capture the cup since the first race in the series in 1851. The Australian entry, skippered by John Bertrand, defeated the U.S. entry *Liberty,* 4 races to 3, off Newport, R.I. in September 1983.

A feature of the London Exhibition of 1851 was a 58-mile yacht race around the Isle of Wight. Among the entries was a 100-foot schooner from the United States, named the *America* and sponsored by members of the New York Yacht Club. The *America* took the race, defeating 14 English cutters and schooners, and winning a trophy called the Hundred-Guineas Cup.

The *America* was sold and left in England, but the cup was brought back to the U.S. and presented to the New York Yacht Club. Used as a trophy for international yacht racing, it became known as the America's Cup.

The first international challenge race took place in 1870 and set a pattern that is still followed. In the first contest the America's Cup was successfully defended, as were successive challenges over the years.

Specifications for yachts in America's Cup races have undergone several changes since the first race in 1851. The race in 1881 was restricted to sloop-rigged craft. Since 1956 only 12-meter (39.4-foot) sloops have been eligible to compete.

YEAR	WINNING YACHT	SPONSOR	RESULTS	LOSING YACHT	SPONSOR
1851	America, U.S.	John C. Stevens	1 race to 0	Aurora	T. Le Marchant, England
1870	Magic, U.S.	Franklin Osgood	1 race to 0	Cambria[1]	James Ashbury, England
1871	Columbia[2], U.S.	Franklin Osgood	2 races to 0	Livonia	James Ashbury, England
	Sappho[2], U.S.	William P. Douglass	2 races to 0		
1876	Madeleine, U.S.	John S. Dickerson	2 races to 0	Countess of Dufferin	Charles Gifford Canada
1881	Mischief, U.S.	J.R. Busk	2 races to 0	Atlanta	Alexander Cuthbert, Canada
1885	Puritan, U.S.	J.M. Forbes, Charles Paine	2 races to 0	Genesta	Sir Richard Sutton, England
1886	Mayflower, U.S.	Charles Paine	2 races to 0	Galatea	William Henn, England
1887	Volunteer, U.S.	Charles Paine	2 races to 0	Thistle	James Bell, England
1893	Vigilant, U.S.	Oliver Iselin	3 races to 0	Valkyrie II	Lord Dunraven, England
1895	Defender, U.S.	Oliver Iselin, E.D. Morgan, W.K. Vanderbilt	3 races to 0	Valkyrie III	Lord Dunraven, Lord Lonsdale, Lord Wolverton, England
1899	Columbia, U.S.	Oliver Iselin, J.P. Morgan	3 races to 0	Shamrock I	Sir Thomas Lipton, Ireland
1901	Columbia, U.S.	E.D. Morgan	3 races to 0	Shamrock II	Sir Thomas Lipton, Ireland
1903	Reliance, U.S.	Cornelius Vanderbilt	3 races to 0	Shamrock III	Sir Thomas Lipton, Ireland
1920	Resolute, U.S.	Harry Walters	3 races to 2	Shamrock IV	Sir Thomas Lipton, Ireland
1930	Enterprise, U.S.	Harold S. Vanderbilt	4 races to 0	Shamrock V	Sir Thomas Lipton, Ireland
1934	Rainbow, U.S.	Harold S. Vanderbilt	4 races to 2	Endeavour	T.O.M. Sopwith, England
1937	Ranger, U.S.	Harold S. Vanderbilt	4 races to 0	Endeavour II	T.O.M. Sopwith, England
1958	Columbia, U.S.	Henry Sears	4 races to 0	Sceptre	Hugh Goodson, England
1962	Weatherly, U.S.	Henry Mercer	4 races to 1	Gretel	Sir Frank Packer, Australia
1964	Constellation, U.S.	Walter Gubelmann	4 races to 0	Sovereign	Anthony Boyden, England
1967	Intrepid, U.S.	N.Y. Yacht Club's Intrepid Syndicate	4 races to 0	Dame Pattie	Royal Sydney Yacht Squadron's Syndicate, Australia
1970	Intrepid, U.S.	N.Y. Yacht Club's Intrepid Syndicate	4 races to 1	Gretel II	Sir Frank Packer, Australia
1974	Courageous, U.S.	N.Y. Yacht Club's Courageous Syndicate	4 races to 0	Southern Cross	Royal Perth Y.C. Challenger Syndicate, Australia
1977	Courageous, U.S.	Kings Point Maritime Acad. Synd.	4 races to 0	Australia	Sun City Yacht Club, Australia
1980	Freedom, U.S.	Maritime College at Fort Schuyler Found.	4 races to 1	Australia	Sun City Yacht Club, Australia
1983	Australia II, Australia	Royal Perth Yacht Club, Australia	4 races to 3	Liberty, U.S.	Maritime College at Ft. Schuyler Found.

1 *Cambria,* the only English schooner in the race, finished tenth in a field of 24.

2 After winning the first two races, the *Columbia* was disabled. *Sappho* substituted and won the fourth and fifth races.

UNITED STATES YACHT RACING UNION CHAMPIONSHIPS

MALLORY CUP—MEN

1974	Vann Wilson, San Anselmo, California
1975	Christopher Pollak, Westport, Connecticut
1976	David J. Crockett, Los Alamitos, California
1977	Marvin Beckman, Houston, Texas
1978	Glenn Darden, Fort Worth, Texas
1979	Glenn Darden, Fort Worth, Texas
1980	Dave Ullman, Corona del Mar, California
1981	Mark Foster, Corpus Christi, Texas
1982	Mark Gollison, Long Beach, CA
1983	Peter Coleman, Larchmont, N.Y.

ADAMS CUP—WOMEN

1974	Deborah Freeman, Beachwood, New Jersey
1975	Cindy S. Batchelor, Essex, Connecticut
1976	Ellen Gerloff, Galveston, Texas
1977	Cindy Stieffel, Bay Waveland, Missouri
1978	Bonnie Shore, Newport, Rhode Island
1979	Allison Jolly, St. Petersburg, Florida
1980	Judy McKinney, Bay St. Louis, Mississippi
1981	Ann Boyd Sloger, Charleston, South Carolina
1982	Heidi Backus, Corpus Christi, Texas
1983	Martha S. Altreuter, Marblehead, MA

U.S. Postal Service

Postage stamp issued in 1984 commemorates 25th anniversary of Hawaii joining the Union as 50th state on Aug. 21, 1959. Stamp depicts a golden plover in flight, a Polynesian voyaging canoe, and volcanic eruption of Mauna Loa in background. Artist Herb Kane of Kailua-Kona, Hawaii, designed the commemorative stamp.

HIGHLIGHTS: 1983

State governors breathed easier when Congress at the last minute before adjourning for the rest of 1983 approved a three-year extension of federal revenue sharing. See page 158.

The improving economy with higher than expected consumer spending brought unexpected surpluses of revenues over expenditures for many state governments in 1983.

Federal aid to the states decreased 2.7% in fiscal 1982, according to a report from the Department of Commerce on Nov. 23. Federal aid to the states in 1982 was $66 billion of the states' total revenues of $330.9 billion. State expenditures increased 6.4% over 1981 to $310.3 billion.

While total revenues exceeded expenditures, the difference largely came from a $15.9 billion excess in employee retirement revenue over retirement expenditures.

All states continued to spend more for education than for any other function. The $103 billion spent for education was a 6.3% increase over 1981. Per capita spending for education rose from $429 to $456.

Outlays for public welfare rose to $55.3 billion, up $3.8 billion. The increase came about largely from an 11.7% rise in Medicaid payments. The federal government contributed $31.5 billion of the states' welfare expenditures.

Taxes provided $162.7 billion to the states, up 8.6% from 1981. Per capita tax revenues averaged $720. General sales and gross receipt tax revenues were $50.3 billion, individual income taxes $45.7 billion, corporation income taxes $14 billion, and motor fuel taxes $10.4 billion.

Lotteries operated by 14 states provided $3.4 billion in gross ticket sales. Pennsylvania collected the most, $523.8 million, followed by Michigan with $483.1 million and New Jersey with $480.8 million.

State debt rose $12.6 billion to $147.5 billion in 1982, an increase of 9.4%.

States with the largest expenditures were:

California $40.4 billion, New York $30.2 billion, Pennsylvania $15.3 billion, Texas $14.2 billion, Illinois $14.1 billion, Michigan $14 billion, and Ohio $13.7 billion.

HIGHLIGHTS: 1983 *(continued)*

States with the smallest expenditures were: South Dakota $829 million, Vermont $888 million, New Hampshire $1.005 billion, Delaware $1.084 billion, Wyoming $1.123 billion, Montana $1.135 billion, and North Dakota $1.191 billion.

According to new population projections by the U.S. Census Bureau, California will still be the largest state in the year 2000.

Texas, currently third, will move up to second by 2000.

Florida, now seventh, will move to third.

New York will drop from second to fourth.

The Census Bureau reported that the number of employees of state governments declined to 3,083,233 full-time and 663,734 part-time in 1982. States employ an average of 133 workers per 10,000 population.

State governments with the highest ratio of employees per 10,000 population were: Alaska 442, Hawaii 380, Delaware 277, New Mexico 241, Rhode Island 211, and Vermont 207.

Those with the lowest ratio of state employees per 10,000 population were: California 100, Illinois 102, Ohio 102, Pennsylvania 104, Florida 107, Indiana 114, New Jersey 115, and Texas 115.

25 LARGEST STATES IN AREA

RANK	STATE	SQUARE MILES
1	Alaska	591,004
2	Texas	266,807
3	California	158,706
4	Montana	147,046
5	New Mexico	121,593
6	Arizona	114,000
7	Nevada	110,561
8	Colorado	104,091
9	Wyoming	97,809
10	Oregon	97,073
11	Utah	84,899
12	Minnesota	84,402
13	Idaho	83,564
14	Kansas	82,277
15	Nebraska	77,355
16	South Dakota	77,116
17	North Dakota	70,702
18	Oklahoma	69,956
19	Missouri	69,697
20	Washington	68,139
21	Georgia	58,910
22	Florida	58,664
23	Michigan	58,527
24	Illinois	56,345
25	Iowa	56,275

25 SMALLEST STATES IN AREA

RANK	STATE	SQUARE MILES
50	Rhode Island	1,212
49	Delaware	2,044
48	Connecticut	5,018
47	Hawaii	6,471
46	New Jersey	7,787
45	Massachusetts	8,284
44	New Hampshire	9,279
43	Vermont	9,614
42	Maryland	10,460
41	West Virginia	24,231
40	South Carolina	31,113
39	Maine	33,265
38	Indiana	36,185
37	Kentucky	40,409
36	Virginia	40,767
35	Ohio	41,330
34	Tennessee	42,144
33	Pennsylvania	45,308
32	Mississippi	47,689
31	Louisiana	47,752
30	New York	49,108
29	Alabama	51,705
28	North Carolina	52,669
27	Arkansas	53,187
26	Wisconsin	56,153

25 LARGEST STATES IN POPULATION

RANK	STATE	POPULATION[1]
1	California	24,724,000
2	New York	17,659,000
3	Texas	15,280,000
4	Pennsylvania	11,865,000
5	Illinois	11,448,000
6	Ohio	10,781,000
7	Florida	10,416,000
8	Michigan	9,109,000
9	New Jersey	7,438,000
10	North Carolina	6,019,000
11	Massachusetts	5,781,000
12	Georgia	5,639,000
13	Virginia	5,491,000
14	Indiana	5,471,000
15	Missouri	4,951,000
16	Wisconsin	4,765,000
17	Tennessee	4,651,000
18	Louisiana	4,362,000
19	Maryland	4,265,000
20	Washington	4,245,000
21	Minnesota	4,133,000
22	Alabama	3,943,000
23	Kentucky	3,667,000
24	South Carolina	3,203,000
25	Oklahoma	3,177,000

25 SMALLEST STATES IN POPULATION

RANK	STATE	POPULATION[1]
50	Alaska	438,000
49	Wyoming	502,000
48	Vermont	516,000
47	Delaware	602,000
46	North Dakota	670,000
45	South Dakota	691,000
44	Montana	801,000
43	Nevada	881,000
42	New Hampshire	951,000
41	Rhode Island	958,000
40	Idaho	965,000
39	Hawaii	994,000
38	Maine	1,133,000
37	New Mexico	1,359,000
36	Utah	1,554,000
35	Nebraska	1,586,000
34	West Virginia	1,948,000
33	Arkansas	2,291,000
32	Kansas	2,408,000
31	Mississippi	2,551,000
30	Oregon	2,649,000
29	Arizona	2,860,000
28	Iowa	2,905,000
27	Colorado	3,045,000
26	Connecticut	3,153,000

[1] 1982 Census Bureau estimates.

U.S. STATES AND TERRITORIES—Important Facts: 1984

	AREA Sq. Mi.	POPULATION[1] Total	Density	GOVERNOR Name	Party	Term Years	Term Expires	LEGISLATURE Senate Majority Party	House Majority Party
Alabama	51,705	3,943,000	76.3	George C. Wallace	D	4	Jan. '87	Democratic	Democratic
Alaska	591,004	438,000	0.7	William Sheffield	D	4	Dec. '86	Tie	Democratic
Arizona	114,000	2,860,000	25.1	Bruce Babbitt	D	4	Jan. '87	Republican	Republican
Arkansas	53,187	2,291,000	43.1	Bill Clinton	D	2	Jan. '85	Democratic	Democratic
California	158,706	24,724,000	155.8	George Deukmejian	R	4	Jan. '87	Democratic	Democratic
Colorado	104,091	3,045,000	29.3	Richard D. Lamm	D	4	Jan. '87	Republican	Republican
Connecticut	5,018	3,153,000	628.3	William A. O'Neill	D	4	Jan. '87	Democratic	Democratic
Delaware	2,044	602,000	294.5	Pierre S. duPont IV	R	4	Jan. '85	Democratic	Democratic
Florida	58,664	10,416,000	177.6	Robert Graham	D	4	Jan. '87	Democratic	Democratic
Georgia	58,910	5,639,000	95.7	Joe Frank Harris	D	4	Jan. '87	Democratic	Democratic
Hawaii	6,471	994,000	153.6	George R. Ariyoshi	D	4	Dec. '86	Democratic	Democratic
Idaho	83,564	965,000	11.6	John V. Evans	D	4	Jan. '87	Republican	Republican
Illinois	56,345	11,448,000	203.2	James R. Thompson	R	4	Jan. '87	Democratic	Democratic
Indiana	36,185	5,471,000	151.2	Robert D. Orr	R	4	Jan. '85	Republican	Republican
Iowa	56,275	2,905,000	51.6	Terry Branstad	R	4	Jan. '87	Democratic	Democratic
Kansas	82,277	2,408,000	29.3	John W. Carlin	D	4	Jan. '87	Republican	Republican
Kentucky	40,409	3,667,000	90.8	Martha L. Collins	D	4	Dec. '87	Democratic	Democratic
Louisiana	47,752	4,362,000	91.4	Edwin W. Edwards	D	4	Mar. '88	Democratic	Democratic
Maine	33,265	1,133,000	34.1	Joseph E. Brennan	D	4	Jan. '87	Democratic	Democratic
Maryland	10,460	4,265,000	407.8	Harold R. Hughes	D	4	Jan. '87	Democratic	Democratic
Massachusetts	8,284	5,781,000	697.9	Michael S. Dukakis	D	4	Jan. '87	Democratic	Democratic
Michigan	58,527	9,109,000	155.6	James J. Blanchard	D	4	Jan. '87	Democratic	Democratic
Minnesota	84,402	4,133,000	49.0	Rudy Perpich	D	4	Jan. '87	Democratic	Democratic
Mississippi	47,689	2,551,000	53.5	Bill Allain	D	4	Jan. '88	Democratic	Democratic
Missouri	69,697	4,951,000	71.0	Christopher S. Bond	R	4	Jan. '85	Democratic	Democratic
Montana	147,046	801,000	5.5	Ted Schwinden	D	4	Jan. '85	Republican	Democratic
Nebraska	77,355	1,586,000	20.5	Bob Kerrey	D	4	Jan. '87	Nonpartisan	—
Nevada	110,561	881,000	8.0	Richard H. Bryan	D	4	Jan. '87	Democratic	Democratic
New Hampshire	9,279	951,000	102.5	John H. Sununu	R	2	Jan. '85	Republican	Republican
New Jersey	7,787	7,438,000	955.2	Thomas H. Kean	R	4	Jan. '86	Democratic	Democratic
New Mexico	121,593	1,359,000	11.2	Toney Anaya	D	4	Jan. '87	Democratic	Democratic
New York	49,108	17,659,000	359.6	Mario M. Cuomo	D	4	Jan. '87	Republican	Democratic
North Carolina	52,669	6,019,000	114.3	James B. Hunt Jr.	D	4	Jan. '85	Democratic	Democratic
North Dakota	70,702	670,000	9.5	Allen I. Olson	R	4	Jan. '85	Republican	Democratic
Ohio	41,330	10,791,000	261.1	Richard F. Celeste	D	4	Jan. '87	Democratic	Democratic
Oklahoma	69,956	3,177,000	45.4	George Nigh	D	4	Jan. '87	Democratic	Democratic
Oregon	97,073	2,649,000	27.3	Victor Atiyeh	R	4	Jan. '87	Democratic	Democratic
Pennsylvania	45,308	11,865,000	261.9	Richard L. Thornburgh	R	4	Jan. '87	Republican	Democratic
Rhode Island	1,212	958,000	790.4	J. Joseph Garrahy	D	2	Jan. '85	Democratic	Democratic
South Carolina	31,113	3,203,000	103.0	Richard W. Riley	D	4	Jan. '87	Democratic	Democratic
South Dakota	77,116	691,000	9.0	William J. Janklow	R	4	Jan. '87	Republican	Republican
Tennessee	42,144	4,651,000	110.4	Lamar Alexander	R	4	Jan. '87	Democratic	Democratic
Texas	266,807	15,280,000	59.5	Mark White	D	4	Jan. '87	Democratic	Democratic
Utah	84,899	1,554,000	18.3	Scott M. Matheson	D	4	Jan. '85	Republican	Republican
Vermont	9,614	516,000	53.7	Richard A. Snelling	R	2	Jan. '85	Republican	Republican
Virginia	40,767	5,491,000	134.7	Charles S. Robb	D	4	Jan. '86	Democratic	Democratic
Washington	68,139	4,245,000	62.3	John Spellman	R	4	Jan. '85	Democratic	Democratic
West Virginia	24,231	1,948,000	80.4	John D. Rockfeller IV	D	4	Jan. '85	Democratic	Democratic
Wisconsin	56,153	4,765,000	84.9	Anthony S. Earl	D	4	Jan. '87	Democratic	Democratic
Wyoming	97,809	502,000	5.1	Ed Herschler	D	4	Jan. '87	Republican	Republican
Dist. of Columbia	69	631,000	9,144.9	Marion Barry[2]	D	4	Jan. '87	Democratic	—
Am. Samoa	77	34,000	441.5	Peter T. Coleman	—	4	Jan. '85	Nonpartisan	Nonpartisan
Guam	209	111,000	526.3	Ricardo Bordallo	D	4	Jan. '87	Democratic	—
No. Marianas	184	18,000	97.8	Pedro P. Tenorio	—	4	Jan. '86	—	—
Puerto Rico	3,515	3,196,520	909.4	Carlos Romero-Barcelo[3]	—	4	Jan. '85	Pop. Dem.[4]	Pop. Dem.[4]
Virgin Islands	132	101,000	765.2	Juan Luis	I	4	Jan. '87	—	Democratic

[1] July 1, 1982, Bureau of Census estimates. [2] Mayor. [3] New Progressive Party. [4] Popular Democratic Party.

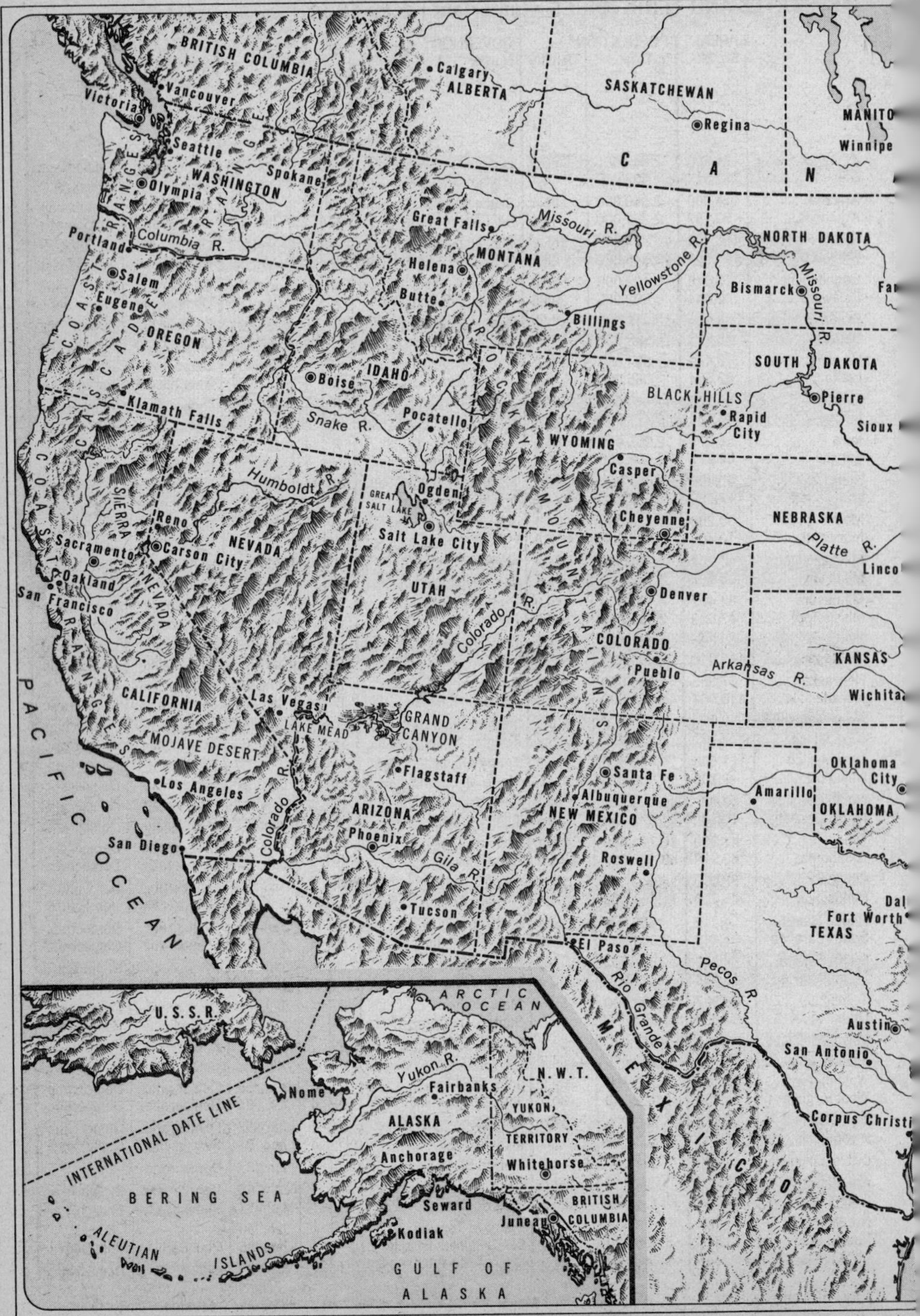
BRITISH COLUMBIA
Vancouver
Victoria
Calgary
ALBERTA
SASKATCHEWAN
Regina
MANITO
Winnipe
C A N
Seattle
WASHINGTON
Olympia
Spokane
Great Falls
Missouri R.
NORTH DAKOTA
Portland
Columbia R.
Helena
MONTANA
Yellowstone R.
Bismarck
Salem
Eugene
OREGON
Butte
Billings
SOUTH DAKOTA
Boise
IDAHO
BLACK HILLS
Pierre
Klamath Falls
Snake R.
Pocatello
Rapid City
WYOMING
Casper
Humboldt R.
GREAT SALT LAKE
Ogden
Cheyenne
NEBRASKA
Platte R.
Reno
Carson City
NEVADA
Salt Lake City
Sacramento
Oakland
San Francisco
UTAH
Denver
COLORADO
Pueblo
Arkansas R.
KANSAS
Wichita
CALIFORNIA
Las Vegas
LAKE MEAD
GRAND CANYON
MOJAVE DESERT
Flagstaff
Santa Fe
Albuquerque
NEW MEXICO
Amarillo
Oklahoma City
OKLAHOMA
Los Angeles
ARIZONA
Phoenix
Gila R.
San Diego
Roswell
Tucson
Fort Worth
TEXAS
El Paso
Pecos R.
Rio Grande
Austin
San Antonio
Corpus Christi
PACIFIC OCEAN
MEXICO
COAST RANGES
CASCADE RANGE
SIERRA NEVADA
ROCKY MOUNTAINS
Colorado R.
U.S.S.R.
ARCTIC OCEAN
Yukon R.
N.W.T.
Nome
Fairbanks
YUKON TERRITORY
ALASKA
INTERNATIONAL DATE LINE
Anchorage
Whitehorse
BERING SEA
Seward
BRITISH COLUMBIA
Juneau
Kodiak
ALEUTIAN ISLANDS
GULF OF ALASKA

UNITED STATES
JAMES BAY
St. Lawrence R.
QUEBEC
Quebec
N.B.
ONTARIO
Thunder Bay
LAKE SUPERIOR
MINNESOTA
Duluth
Montreal
MAINE
Bangor
Augusta
OTTAWA
Montpelier
Portland
VERMONT
Concord
NEW HAMPSHIRE
NEW YORK
MICHIGAN
LAKE MICHIGAN
LAKE HURON
St. Paul
Minneapolis
WISCONSIN
Mississippi R.
Toronto
L. ONTARIO
Rochester
Albany
Boston
MASSACHUSETTS
Hamilton
Buffalo
Syracuse
Providence
RHODE ISLAND
Hartford
CONNECTICUT
Hudson R.
Grand Rapids
Lansing
Flint
Madison
Detroit
Milwaukee
LAKE ERIE
Erie
New York
Rockford
Cedar Rapids
IOWA
Des Moines
Omaha
Chicago
Gary
Toledo
Cleveland
PENNSYLVANIA
Newark
Pittsburgh
Harrisburg
Trenton
Fort Wayne
OHIO
Akron
Philadelphia
NEW JERSEY
Peoria
INDIANA
Columbus
Baltimore
Annapolis
Dover
DELAWARE
ILLINOIS
Springfield
Indianapolis
Dayton
WASHINGTON D.C.
MARYLAND
Kansas City
Topeka
Jefferson City
St. Louis
Wabash R.
Ohio R.
Cincinnati
Louisville
Frankfort
Charleston
WEST VIRGINIA
Richmond
Norfolk
VIRGINIA
MISSOURI
KENTUCKY
Roanoke
APPALACHIAN MTS.
Springfield
Winston-Salem
Raleigh
NORTH CAROLINA
Nashville
Tennessee R.
Tulsa
Fort Smith
OZARK MTS.
TENNESSEE
Charlotte
Chattanooga
Greenville
Memphis
Little Rock
ARKANSAS
Columbia
SOUTH CAROLINA
Atlanta
Birmingham
Charleston
GEORGIA
Red R.
Sabine R.
MISSISSIPPI
Columbus
Savannah
Shreveport
LOUISIANA
Jackson
Meridian
Montgomery
ALABAMA
Mobile
Baton Rouge
Biloxi
Tallahassee
Jacksonville
LAKE PONTCHARTRAIN
Houston
New Orleans
Galveston
FLORIDA
GULF OF MEXICO
St. Petersburg
Tampa
LAKE OKEECHOBEE
BAHAMA ISLANDS
Miami
Key West
ATLANTIC OCEAN
NIIHAU
KAUAI
OAHU
Honolulu
MOLOKAI
LANAI
MAUI
KAHOOLAWE
HAWAII
HAWAII
MILES
0
100
200
300
400
500

PERSONAL INCOME IN STATES BY BASIC INDUSTRIES: 1982

Source: U.S. Department of Commerce, Bureau of Economic Analysis

Total personal income increased 6.9% in 1982, with average personal income rising to $11,107 per capita.

Alaska had the highest personal income per capita with $16,257. The District of Columbia, with $14,550 per capita, was higher than any state except Alaska. Mississippi's $7,778 per capita was the lowest in the country.

REGION AND STATE	PER CAPITA	TOTAL [1]	MANUFACTURING [1]	GOVERNMENT [1]	SERVICES	RETAIL TRADE [1]	CONSTRUCTION [1]	FARMING [1]	MINING [1]
United States	$11,107	$2,571,592	$446,316	$309,346	$341,671	$171,801	$96,361	$33,474	$37,301
New England	11,961	148,868	32,689	14,123	22,164	9,569	4,699	477	126
Connecticut	13,748	43,351	10,759	3,335	5,678	2,554	1,364	116	70
Maine	9,042	10,249	2,066	1,407	1,253	730	353	56	4
Massachusetts	12,088	69,882	14,431	6,806	11,899	4,550	1,966	134	26
New Hampshire	10,729	10,202	2,257	888	1,253	736	558	26	7
Rhode Island	10,723	10,278	2,151	1,175	1,440	650	275	10	5
Vermont	9,507	4,907	1,024	512	642	349	183	135	13
Mideast	12,087	513,248	87,211	63,121	78,842	29,930	15,367	1,944	1,947
Delaware	11,731	7,065	2,138	809	837	470	270[2]	116	3[2]
District of Columbia	14,550	9,186	402	7,537	4,561	627	265[2]	—	6[2]
Maryland	12,238	52,195	5,117	8,660	7,344	3,567	1,928	323	56
New Jersey	13,089	97,361	17,837	9,632	12,940	5,613	2,849	209	59
New York	12,314	217,457	33,887	24,230	35,713	11,758	5,666	543	291
Pennsylvania	10,955	129,985	27,831	12,253	17,447	7,894	4,314	753	1,533
Great Lakes	11,055	459,698	109,414	44,783	55,573	29,214	14,356	4,888	2,710
Illinois	12,100	138,519	25,730	13,409	17,977	8,498	4,633	1,434	1,025
Indiana	10,021	54,819	14,997	5,092	5,634	3,663	2,013	550	352
Michigan	10,956	99,802	27,219	10,258	12,145	6,292	2,659	749	320
Ohio	10,677	115,217	29,096	10,897	13,969	7,532	3,600	667	968
Wisconsin	10,774	51,341	12,373	5,126	5,848	3,228	1,451	1,488	46
Plains	10,789	187,104	29,538	20,688	22,354	12,677	6,759	7,021	1,563
Iowa	10,791	31,347	5,172	3,064	3,246	2,013	1,028	1,652	43
Kansas	11,765	28,325	3,985	3,217	2,959	1,733	998	1,181	578
Minnesota	11,175	46,184	8,560	4,914	5,961	3,320	1,670	1,464	334
Missouri	10,170	50,346	9,238	5,460	6,778	3,547	1,891	486	207
Nebraska	10,683	16,939	1,827	2,211	1,883	1,138	569	963	49
North Dakota	10,876	7,287	295	967	829	487	414	549	292
South Dakota	9,666	6,675	460	853	697	439	190	720	60
Southeast	9,602	520,232	81,835	70,723	61,122	36,209	21,465	7,910	9,582
Alabama	8,649	34,101	6,434	5,110	3,528	2,123	1,224	617	528
Arkansas	8,479	19,430	3,460	2,105	1,985	1,361	677	774	175
Florida	10,978	114,327	9,329	12,106	16,005	8,774	5,214	1,302	249
Georgia	9,583	54,035	9,207	7,920	6,384	4,015	2,156	777	162
Kentucky	8,934	32,762	5,532	3,959	3,324	2,120	1,178	1,065	1,817
Louisiana	10,231	44,633	5,341	5,351	5,531	3,093	2,998	376	3,094
Mississippi	7,778	19,840	3,492	2,785	1,945	1,338	890	515	343
North Carolina	9,044	54,431	13,237	7,474	5,669	3,809	1,900	1,331	94
South Carolina	8,502	27,231	6,449	4,485	2,551	1,819	1,187	282	32
Tennessee	8,906	41,420	8,862	5,148	5,186	2,961	1,477	570	232
Virginia	11,095	60,923	8,011	12,397	7,375	3,780	2,015	306	712
West Virginia	8,769	17,078	2,482	1,883	1,638	1,016	549	−5	2,144
Southwest	11,122	252,206	34,001	30,267	30,772	19,229	13,710	2,610	15,052
Arizona	10,173	29,100	3,658	3,945	3,801	2,288	1,465	345	558
New Mexico	9,190	12,492	655	2,471	1,685	929	665	189	807
Oklahoma	11,370	36,119	4,248	4,502	3,722	2,509	1,376	705	3,397
Texas	11,419	174,493	25,439	19,349	21,564	13,502	10,205	1,371	10,289
Rocky Mountain	10,754	73,837	8,292	10,441	9,370	5,460	3,884	1,264	3,799
Colorado	12,302	37,453	4,743	5,116	5,170	2,851	1,925	461	1,657
Idaho	9,029	8,716	1,017	1,117	1,037	610	410	458	109
Montana	9,580	7,673	463	1,110	868	590	366	217	290
Utah	8,875	13,788	1,850	2,222	1,740	981	661	101	605
Wyoming	12,372	6,207	220	877	557	427	520	27	1,138
Far West	12,238	397,703	62,560	50,367	58,801	28,022	14,799	7,104	2,022
California	12,567	310,704	49,601	38,596	46,906	21,715	11,163	5,390	1,732
Nevada	11,981	10,552	415	1,349	3,089	821	578	52	164
Oregon	10,335	27,373	4,478	3,415	3,293	2,084	884	526	44
Washington	11,560	49,074	8,067	7,008	5,513	3,401	2,174	1,137	83
Alaska	16,257	7,118	345	1,965	892	526	835	4	498
Hawaii	11,652	11,579	431	2,868	1,781	966	488	252	2

[1] In millions of dollars (add 000,000 to each amount shown). Figures for industries are net income. [2] 1981 data.

ALABAMA

Area: 51,705 square miles; 133,913 sq. km.
Population: 3,943,000 (1982); 3,893,978 (1980).
Capital: Montgomery.
Flower: Camellia. **Tree:** Southern (longleaf) pine.
Bird: Yellowhammer. **Nickname:** The Heart of Dixie.
Stone: Marble. **Mineral:** Hematite. **Fish:** Tarpon.
Song: *Alabama.* **Motto:** We Dare Defend Our Rights.
Flag: Diagonal red cross on white field.
Leading Industries: Manufacturing (iron, steel, aluminum, chemicals, paper), agriculture (poultry, dairy products, beef cattle, cotton, peanuts, pecans), mining (coal, iron ore, petroleum).
Climate (Montgomery): *Normal temperatures:* Jan. high 58°F., low 37°F.; July high 89°F., low 69°F. *Normal yearly precipitation:* 50" (water). *Record snowstorm:* 11" in December 1886.
Recreation Areas: National forests, 4; state parks and recreation areas, 20; Gulf Coast beaches.
Points of Interest: George C. Marshall Space Flight Center (Huntsville); Horseshoe Bend National Memorial Park; Russell Cave National Monument; White House of Confederacy in Montgomery; battleship USS *Alabama* in Mobile Bay.

KEY EVENTS IN ALABAMA

1519 **Mobile Bay believed to have been discovered** by Spanish explorer Alonso Álvarez de Piñeda.
1702 **French settlement** at Fort Louis founded; colony moves in 1711 to present site of Mobile, Ala.
1763 **Britain wins** region from France.
1783 **Spain acquires southern Alabama** from Britain, while U.S. receives northern Alabama.
1795 **U.S. obtains rest of Alabama except Mobile** from Spain in Treaty of San Lorenzo.
1813 **(April 15)** **U.S. captures Mobile** from Spain.
1814 **(March 27)** **Battle of Horseshoe Bend**: Gen. Andrew Jackson defeats Creek Indians.
1817 **(March 3)** **Territory of Alabama** organized.
1819 **(Dec. 14)** **Alabama becomes 22d U.S. state.**
1861 **First capital of Confederacy** at Montgomery.
1861 **(Jan. 11)** **Alabama** secedes from Union.
1864 **(Aug. 5–23)** **Battle of Mobile Bay:** Union Adm. David Farragut conquers Mobile's forts.
1868 **(June 25)** **Alabama readmitted** to Union.
1880 **Iron and steel industry** begins growth at Birmingham with opening of first blast furnace.
1944 **State's first oil well** produces at Gilbertown.
1949 **Space research center** established at Huntsville.
1955 **Black civil-rights crusade** by Rev. Martin Luther King Jr. begins bus boycott in Montgomery.
1961–76 **Confederate flag** flown above U.S. flag on state capitol.
1982 **State population** grows 1.3% since 1980.
1983 **George C. Wallace** becomes state's first four-term governor; served 1963–67, 1971–79.

ALASKA

Area: 591,004 square miles; 1,530,693 sq. km.
Population: 438,000 (1982); 401,851 (1980).
Capital: Juneau.
Flower: Forget-me-not. **Tree:** Sitka spruce. **Bird:** Willow ptarmigan. **Gem:** Jade. **Fish:** King salmon. **Song:** *Alaska's Flag.* **Nickname:** The Last Frontier. **Motto:** North to the Future.
Flag: Blue field with 7 gold stars on left representing Big Dipper and one on right representing Polaris.
Leading Industries: Government, mining (petroleum, gold, coal), food processing, forestry, agriculture (dairy products, poultry, cattle, hogs, sheep, potatoes, barley, oats, vegetables), tourism.
Climate (Fairbanks): *Normal temperatures:* Jan. high −2.2°F., low −22°F.; July high 72°F., low 50°F. *Normal yearly precipitation:* 11" (water). *Record snowstorm:* 20.1" in February 1966.
Recreation Areas: National parks, 8; national forests, 2; state parks and recreation areas, 64.
Points of Interest: Mt. McKinley, in Denali National Park; Mendenhall Glacier (in North Tongass National Forest); Glacier Bay and Katmai national parks; Sitka National Historical Park; Klondike Gold Rush National Historical Park; Russian-era relics in Ketchikan and Sitka; Eskimo villages.

KEY EVENTS IN ALASKA

1741 **Alaska discovered** by Danish sea captain Vitus Bering, exploring for Russia.
1784 **(Aug. 14)** **First Russian settlement** established on Kodiak Island by fur trader Grigori Shelekhov.
1867 **(Oct. 18)** **U.S. acquires Alaska** from Russia for $7.2 million.
1896–99 **Discoveries of gold** bring rush of prospectors to Klondike and Alaska.
1912 **(Aug. 24)** **Territory of Alaska** organized.
1942 **(June 12)** **Japan invades and occupies** Attu Island in Aleutians; later takes Kiska and Agattu.
1943 **(May 11–30)** **U.S. troops recapture Attu;** reoccupy Kiska on Aug. 15.
1959 **(Jan. 3)** **Alaska becomes 49th U.S. state.**
1964 **(March 27)** **Severe earthquake** in south central Alaska kills 131 persons, causes widespread damage.
1968 **Discovery of oil at Prudhoe Bay,** believed largest oil reserve in world.
1975 **(May 27)** **Alaska becomes first state to legalize use of marijuana** in ruling by state court.
1976 **Voters approve moving state capital** from Juneau to Willow, 70 miles from Anchorage.
1977 **Trans-Alaska pipeline completed** at cost of $7.7 billion; oil flows south 799 miles from Prudhoe Bay to Valdez at rate of 1.2 million barrels a day.
1978 **(Dec. 1)** **About 56 million acres of land** made into 17 national monuments by President Carter.
1980 **(April 27)** **Time zone shift** moves Juneau and nearby area to north into Yukon Time Zone.
1980 **State income tax abolished**; $185 million already collected is refunded to taxpayers; state government grows rich with 12.5% royalty on oil production.
1982 **State population** grows 8.9% since 1980.
1982 **State distributes $1,000** to each resident from oil income.
1982 **Voters reject** moving state capital to Willow.
1983 **(Oct. 30)** **Time zone shift:** Entire state, except for westernmost Aleutian Islands, moved to Yukon Time Zone, 1 hour earlier than Pacific Time Zone.

ARIZONA

Area: 114,000 square miles; 295,259 sq. km.
Population: 2,860,000 (1982); 2,718,425 (1980).
Capital: Phoenix.
Flower: Saguaro cactus blossom. **Tree:** Palo verde. **Bird:** Cactus wren. **Gemstone:** Turquoise. **Song:** *Arizona.*
Nickname: The Grand Canyon State.
Motto: *Ditat Deus* (God Enriches).
Flag: Copper-colored star centered on radiating red and yellow stripes above horizontal blue stripe.
Leading Industries: Manufacturing (machinery, smelting, metal products), mining (copper, molybdenum, gold, silver, zinc), agriculture (beef cattle, cotton, lettuce, dairy products, sheep, vegetables, fruits), tourism.
Climate (Phoenix): *Normal temperatures:* Jan. high 65°F., low 38°F.; July high 102°F., low 78°F. *Normal yearly precipitation:* 7" (water). *Record snowstorm:* 1" in January 1937.
Recreation Areas: National parks, 2; national forests, 7; national recreation area, 1; state parks and recreation areas, 11.
Points of Interest: Grand Canyon and Petrified Forest national parks; Monument Valley; Painted Desert;

ARIZONA *(continued)*
Indian reservations; Tombstone; Fort Apache: numerous national monuments (including Chiricahua, Saguaro, Organ Pipe Cactus, Pipe Spring, Canyon de Chelly, Navajo, Casa Grande Ruins, Hohokam Pima, Montezuma Castle, Tonto, Tumacacori, Tuzigoot, Walnut Canyon, Wupatki, Sunset Crater, and Marble Canyon); Oak Creek Canyon (in Coconino National Forest); Fort Bowie and Hubbell Trading Post national historical parks; Kitt Peak National Observatory.

KEY EVENTS IN ARIZONA

1539–40 Arizona explored for Spain: Marcos de Niza (1539); Francisco de Coronado (1540).
1690s Roman Catholic missions founded in Arizona by Spanish Jesuit priest Eusebio Kino.
1776 Fort Tucson established by Spaniards.
1848 U.S. acquires Arizona in Mexican War.
1853 Southern Arizona obtained from Mexico in Gadsden Purchase.
1863 Navajo Indians subdued by Kit Carson leading 400 troops against stronghold in Canyon de Chelly.
1863 (Feb. 24) Arizona Territory created.
1871–86 Apache War: Chief Geronimo captured.
1912 (Feb. 14) Arizona becomes 48th U.S. state.
1948 Indians win right to vote in Arizona.
1973 Biggest dam in world completed: New Cornelia Tailings Dam, near Ajo, containing 274,026,000 cubic yards of material, 98 feet high, 6.7 miles long.
1980 Arizona moves ahead of Oregon and Mississippi to rank 29th in population among the states.
1982 State population grows 5.2% since 1980.
1983 First new county (La Paz) created since statehood achieved in 1912.

ARKANSAS

Area: 53,187 square miles; 137,753 sq. km.
Population: 2,291,000 (1982); 2,286,419 (1980).
Capital: Little Rock.
Flower: Apple blossom. **Tree:** Pine. **Bird:** Mockingbird. **Stone:** Diamond. **Song:** *Arkansas.*
Nickname: The Land of Opportunity.
Motto: *Regnat Populus* (The People Rule).
Flag: Star-studded white diamond on red field.
Leading Industries: Food processing, manufacturing (machinery, appliances, paper), agriculture (soybeans, cotton, rice, poultry, beef cattle, dairy products), mining (petroleum, bauxite, bromine).
Climate (Little Rock): *Normal temperatures:* Jan. high 50° F., low 29° F.; July high 93° F., low 70° F. *Normal yearly precipitation:* 49″ (water). *Record snowstorm:* 13″ in January 1893.
Recreation Areas: National park, 1; national forests, 3; state parks and recreation areas, 34.
Points of Interest: Hot Springs National Park; Pea Ridge National Military Park; Arkansas Territorial Capitol Restoration (Little Rock); Fort Smith National Historic Site; Arkansas Post National Memorial; Buffalo National River; Crater of Diamonds mine near Murfreesboro; Dogpatch U.S.A., amusement park near Harrison.

KEY EVENTS IN ARKANSAS

1541 Arkansas region explored by Hernando de Soto of Spain, discoverer of Mississippi River.
1686 Arkansas Post established as fort by French explorer Henri de Tonti.
1803 U.S. acquires area in Louisiana Purchase.
1819 (March 2) Territory of Arkansas organized.
1836 (June 15) Arkansas becomes 25th U.S. state.
1861 (May 6) Arkansas secedes from Union.
1862 (March 7–8) Battle of Pea Ridge: Union troops defeat Confederate army.
1868 (June 22) Arkansas readmitted to Union.
1887 Bauxite discovered near Little Rock.
1906 Only diamond deposit in North America found near Murfreesboro.
1921 Oil production begins in El Dorado field.
1957 (Sept. 24–Nov. 27) President Eisenhower sends federal troops into Little Rock to enforce school racial desegregation barred by Gov. Orval Faubus.
1982 Population grows 0.2% since 1980.

CALIFORNIA

Area: 158,706 square miles; 411,047 sq. km.
Population: 24,724,000 (1982); 23,667,837 (1980).
Capital: Sacramento.
Flower: Golden poppy. **Tree:** California redwood. **Bird:** California valley quail. **Stone:** Serpentine. **Mineral:** Native gold. **Animal:** California grizzly bear. **Fish:** California golden trout. **Reptile:** California desert tortoise. **Insect:** California dog-face butterfly. **Marine mammal:** California gray whale. **Fossil:** Saber-toothed cat. **Song:** *I Love You, California.* **Nickname:** The Golden State.
Motto: *Eureka* (I Have Found It).
Flag: Bear and red star on white field above "California Republic " with red stripe at bottom.
Leading Industries: Manufacturing (aircraft, automobiles, electronic equipment, appliances, weapons, steel, chemicals), food processing, agriculture (beef cattle, dairying, sheep, grain, fruits, vegetables, nuts), mining (petroleum, natural gas, boron, gold), tourism.
Climate (Sacramento): *Normal temperatures:* Jan. high 53° F., low 37° F.; July high 93° F., low 58° F. *Normal yearly precipitation:* 17″ (water). *Record snowstorm:* 7.24″ in April 1880.
Recreation Areas: National parks, 5; national forests, 22; national seashore, 1; national recreation areas, 2; state parks and recreation areas, 186; many beaches.
Points of Interest: Yosemite, Kings Canyon, Sequoia, Lassen Volcanic, and Redwood national parks; Cabrillo, Channel Islands, Death Valley, Devils Postpile, Joshua Tree, Pinnacles, Lava Beds, and Muir Woods national monuments; Mt. Wilson Observatory, Disneyland, and Hollywood in Los Angeles area; Civic Center and Golden Gate Bridge and Park in San Francisco; San Simeon State Park; Point Reyes National Seashore.

KEY EVENTS IN CALIFORNIA

1542 California coast explored for Spain by Juan Rodríquez Cabrillo.
1769 First Spanish fort and mission in California established at San Diego.
1826 First American explorer reaches California by land: Jedediah Strong Smith.
1846–48 U.S. troops capture California.
1848 (Jan. 24) Gold discovered at Sutter's Mill by James W. Marshall, starting gold rush to California.
1850 (Sept. 9) California becomes 31st U.S. state.
1906 (April 18) Severe earthquake destroys most of San Francisco, killing 700 persons.
1911 First movie studio built in Hollywood.
1963 California tops New York to become largest state in population.
1968 Highest dam in U.S. built on Feather River near Oroville, 770 feet high.
1971 (Feb. 9) Earthquake in southern California kills 64 persons, causes $500 million damage.
1976 Nation's first right-to-die law approved.
1976–77 Drought causes $3 billion in farm losses.
1977 First woman appointed as state chief justice: Rose Elizabeth Bird.
1978 Voters approve Proposition 13, cutting property taxes about 60%.
1981 Fruit fly infestation threatens state's agricultural production; controlled by spraying.
1982 Population grows 4.5% since 1980.

COLORADO

Area: 104,090 square miles; 269,594 sq. km.
Population: 3,045,000 (1982); 2,889,964 (1980).
Capital: Denver.
Flower: Rocky Mountain columbine.
Tree: Colorado blue spruce.
Bird: Lark bunting. **Stone:** Aquamarine.
Animal: Rocky Mountain bighorn sheep.
Song: *Where the Columbines Grow.*
Motto: *Nil Sine Numine* (Nothing Without Providence).
Flag: Red "C" enclosing gold ball against blue, white, and blue stripes. **Nickname:** The Centennial State.
Leading Industries: Food processing, manufacturing (metal products, machinery), agriculture (beef cattle, sheep, dairy products, wheat, corn, sugar beets), tourism, mining (petroleum, molybdenum, coal, lead).
Climate (Denver): *Normal temperatures:* Jan. high 44° F., low 16° F.; July high 87° F., low 59° F. *Normal yearly precipitation:* 16" (water). *Record snowstorm:* 23" in April 1885.
Recreation Areas: National parks, 2; national forests, 12; national recreation areas, 2; state parks and recreation areas, 26.
Points of Interest: Rocky Mountain and Mesa Verde national parks; Dinosaur, Colorado, Black Canyon of Gunnison, Florissant Fossil Beds, Hovenweep, Yucca House, and Great Sand Dunes national monuments; Pikes Peak; Garden of the Gods; U.S. Air Force Academy; Durango-Silverton narrow-gauge railway; Central City; Aspen resort area; Bent's Old Fort National Historic Site.

KEY EVENTS IN COLORADO

1706 Colorado claimed for Spain by Juan de Ulibarri.
1803 U.S. acquires eastern Colorado in Louisiana Purchase.
1806 Colorado explored by Lt. Zebulon M. Pike, who discovers Pikes Peak.
1833 First permanent American settlement established at Bent's Fort, near present-day La Junta.
1845 Central Colorado acquired by U.S. with admission of Texas as state.
1848 Western Colorado obtained in Mexican War.
1858 Discovery of gold by Green Russell on Cherry Creek near present-day Denver begins gold rush.
1861 (Feb. 28) Territory of Colorado organized.
1864 Sand Creek Massacre: Settlers attack and kill hundreds of Cheyenne Indians.
1870 Railroads link Colorado with eastern states.
1875 Rich silver deposits discovered.
1876 (Aug. 1) Colorado becomes 38th U.S. state.
1891 Gold discovered at Cripple Creek.
1934–35 Drought develops "dust bowl" in eastern Colorado, causing abandonment of farms.
1974 Dwight D. Eisenhower 1.7-mile automobile tunnel completed through Rocky Mountains west of Denver, longest auto tunnel in U.S.
1976 Nation's first sunset law approved to disband agencies that do not serve public.
1977 Gem-quality diamonds discovered in northeastern Colorado.
1982 Population grows 5.3% since 1980, making Colorado 27th most populous state.

CONNECTICUT

Area: 5,018 square miles; 12,997 sq. km.
Population: 3,153,000 (1982); 3,107,576 (1980).
Capital: Hartford.
Flower: Mountain laurel. **Tree:** White oak. **Mineral:** Garnet. **Insect:** Praying mantis. **Animal:** Sperm whale. **Bird:** American robin. **Nickname:** Constitution State.
Song: *Yankee Doodle.*
Motto: *Qui Transtulit Sustinet* (He Who Transplanted Still Sustains).
Flag: State seal centered on blue field.
Leading Industries: Manufacturing (aircraft, machinery, metal products), tourism, agriculture (dairy products, poultry, tobacco).
Climate (Hartford): *Normal temperatures:* Jan. high 33° F., low 16° F.; July high 84° F., low 61° F. *Normal yearly precipitation:* 43" (water). *Record snowstorm:* 19" in February 1949.
Recreation Areas: State parks and recreation areas, 9; Long Island Sound beaches.
Points of Interest: Mystic Seaport Museum of Maritime America; Yale University (New Haven); Nathan Hale Homestead (South Coventry); Wadsworth Atheneum, Harriet Beecher Stowe House, State Capitol, and Mark Twain Memorial (Hartford); U.S. Coast Guard Academy (New London); U.S. Navy submarine base (Groton); American Shakespeare Festival Theater (Stratford).

KEY EVENTS IN CONNECTICUT

1614 Connecticut region claimed for Netherlands by Adriaen Block.
1633 Dutch build fort at site of Hartford.
1633 English colonists from Massachusetts settle Windsor.
1636–37 Pequot War: Colonists slaughter Pequot Indians near Mystic and Fairfield.
1639 (Jan. 24) Connecticut colony organized under Fundamental Orders, unifying early settlements.
1662 (May 3) Royal charter granted Connecticut: serves as constitution until 1818.
1665 Connecticut expanded, unifying with New Haven colony.
1687 Colonists save charter by hiding it in Charter Oak at Hartford to prevent being ruled by British governor of New England Sir Edmund Andros.
1776 (June 14) Independence from Britain approved in resolution by Connecticut assembly.
1788 (Jan. 9) Connecticut becomes 5th U.S. state, ratifying U.S. Constitution.
1794 Eli Whitney begins manufacture of cotton gins at New Haven; starts mass production of firearms with interchangeable parts in 1798.
1960 (Oct. 1) County governments abolished.
1974 (Nov. 5) Connecticut elects first woman governor: Ella T. Grasso; first woman governor in U.S. who was not wife or widow of preceding governor.
1977 Reorganization plan adopted by legislature reduces 256 state agencies and commissions to 23.
1982 Population increases 1.5% since 1980.

DELAWARE

Area: 2,044 square miles; 5,295 sq. km.
Population: 602,000 (1982); 594,338 (1980).
Capital: Dover.
Flower: Peach blossom.
Tree: American holly.
Bird: Blue hen chicken.
Song: *Our Delaware.*
Nickname: The First State.
Motto: Liberty and Independence.
Flag: Blue field with centered state seal in yellow diamond above date Delaware ratified U.S. Constitution (Dec. 7, 1787).
Leading Industries: Manufacturing (chemicals, plastics, leather products), food processing, agriculture (poultry, dairy products, corn, hogs, beef cattle, soybeans).
Climate (Wilmington): *Normal temperatures:* Jan. high 40° F., low 23° F.; July high 86° F., low 66° F. *Normal yearly precipitation:* 40" (water). *Record rainfall* in 24 hours: 6.5" in August 1945.

DELAWARE *(continued)*

Recreation Areas: State parks with recreation areas, 9; Rehoboth, Bethany, Dewey, and Fenwick Island beaches.
Points of Interest: Henry Francis du Pont Winterthur Museum (near Wilmington); several historic towns, including New Castle, Dover, Odessa.

KEY EVENTS IN DELAWARE

1609 Delaware Bay discovered for Dutch by Henry Hudson.
1631 First Dutch colonists settle at Zwaanendael (near Lewes).
1638 Swedish colonists found New Sweden; establish Fort Christina at Wilmington; led by Peter Minuit.
1655 New Sweden captured by Dutch led by Peter Stuyvesant.
1664 England makes Delaware part of colony of New York.
1682 Delaware region made part of Pennsylvania colony.
1704 Separate Delaware legislature granted by Pennsylvania.
1776 (Sept. 20) First state constitution adopted.
1777 (Sept. 3) Battle of Coochs Bridge: British defeat Americans in Revolutionary War battle.
1787 (Dec. 7) Delaware becomes first U.S. state, ratifying U.S. Constitution.
1802 Gunpowder manufacturing plant established by Eleuthère Irénée du Pont near Wilmington.
1861–65 In Civil War, although slave state, Delaware fights on side of Union.
1951 Delaware Memorial Bridge completed across Delaware River at Wilmington; second span opened in 1968.
1963 Delaware Turnpike opens, completing superhighway from Boston to Washington, D.C.
1982 Population grows 1.3% since 1980.

FLORIDA

Area: 58,664 square miles; 151,938 sq. km.
Population: 10,416,000 (1982); 9,746,421 (1980).
Capital: Tallahassee.
Flower: Orange blossom.
Tree: Sabal palmetto palm.
Bird: Mockingbird.
Saltwater fish: Atlantic sailfish.
Saltwater mammal: Dolphin.
Gem: Moonstone.
Shell: Horse conch.
Song: *Swanee River.* **Beverage:** Orange juice.
Nickname: The Sunshine State.
Motto: In God We Trust.
Flag: Centered state seal and diagonal red bars on white field.
Leading Industries: Tourism, manufacturing (chemicals, metal products, transportation equipment, missiles), food processing, agriculture (fruits, nuts, vegetables, tobacco, beef cattle, dairy products), mining (phosphates).
Climate (Miami): *Normal temperatures:* Jan. high 76° F., low 59° F.; July high 89° F., low 76° F. *Normal yearly precipitation:* 60″ (water). *Record snowstorm (Jacksonville):* 1.9″ in February 1899.
Recreation Areas: National park, 1; national forests, 3; national seashore, 1; state parks and recreation areas, 103; numerous beaches.
Points of Interest: Everglades National Park; Biscayne, Castillo de San Marcos, Fort Jefferson, and Fort Matanzas national monuments; Fort Caroline National Memorial near St. Augustine; Marineland; Silver Springs; Ringling museums (Sarasota); Cypress Gardens (near Winter Haven); Kennedy Space Center, Cape Canaveral; Walt Disney World; Miami Beach; Gulf Islands National Seashore.

KEY EVENTS IN FLORIDA

1513 (April 2) Florida discovered, named, and claimed for Spain by Juan Ponce de Léon.
1564 French Huguenot colonists establish Fort Caroline on St. Johns River near Jacksonville.
1565 (Sept. 8) Spaniards found St. Augustine.
1565 (Sept. 20) Spaniards under Pedro Menéndez de Avilés capture Fort Caroline, massacring French.
1763–83 Britain wins Florida in Seven Years War, but loses it back to Spain in Revolutionary War.
1810 (Oct. 27) U.S. annexes West Florida from Spain.
1814 (Nov. 7) Pensacola captured by Gen. Andrew Jackson.
1818 (April–May) East Florida captured from Spain by Gen. Jackson during First Seminole War.
1821 (Feb. 22) East Florida acquired by U.S. from Spain for $5 million in Adams-Onís Treaty (signed on Feb. 22, 1819).
1822 (March 30) Territory of Florida organized.
1835–43 Second Seminole War fought by settlers, ending with removal of Indians west of Mississippi.
1845 (March 3) Florida becomes 27th U.S. state.
1861 (Jan. 10) Florida secedes from Union.
1868 (June 25) Florida readmitted to Union.
1906 State drains Everglades near Fort Lauderdale.
1912–15 Miami Beach created as resort by Carl Fisher.
1938 Overseas Highway links Key West to mainland.
1969 First men to land on Moon launched in *Apollo 11* from Cape Canaveral.
1977 (January) Cold wave causes $385 million in agricultural losses; throws 50,000 out of work.
1982 Population grows 6.9% since 1980; fourth highest growth among the states.
1982 Overseas Highway to Key West rebuilt at cost of $238 million.

GEORGIA

Area: 58,910 square miles; 152,575 sq. km.
Population: 5,639,000 (1982); 5,463,087 (1980).
Capital: Atlanta.
Flower: Cherokee rose.
Tree: Live oak.
Bird: Brown thrasher.
Fish: Largemouth bass.
Song: *Georgia on My Mind.*
Nickname: The Empire State of the South.
Motto: Wisdom, Justice, and Moderation.
Flag: State seal on blue bar, with Confederate flag on right.
Leading Industries: Manufacturing (textiles, aircraft, automobiles), food processing, forestry, agriculture (poultry, beef cattle, hogs, peanuts, tobacco, corn, cotton), mining (kaolin, barite, bauxite).
Climate (Atlanta): *Normal temperatures:* Jan. high 51° F., low 33° F.; July high 87° F., low 69° F. *Normal yearly precipitation:* 48″ (water). *Record snowstorm:* 5.67″ in February 1961.
Recreation Areas: National forests, 2; state parks and recreation areas, 70.
Points of Interest: Okefenokee National Wildlife Refuge; Andersonville National Historic Site; Chickamauga and Chattanooga National Military Park; Little White House (Warm Springs); Sea Island; Stone Mountain; Fort Frederica, Fort Pulaski, and Ocmulgee national monuments; Kennesaw Mountain National Battlefield Park; Cumberland Island National Seashore.

KEY EVENTS IN GEORGIA

1732 (June 9) Royal charter for Georgia granted to

Gen. James Edward Oglethorpe by King George II.
1733 (Feb. 12) First permanent settlement established by Oglethorpe at site of Savannah.
1742 (July) Battle of Bloody Marsh: Oglethorpe defeats Spanish invasion at Fort Frederica on St. Simons Island.
1753 Georgia becomes royal colony.
1776 (Jan. 18) Patriots imprison last royal governor.
1777 (Feb. 5) First state constitution adopted.
1778 (Dec. 29) British capture and hold Savannah until July 11, 1782.
1788 (Jan. 2) Georgia becomes 4th U.S. state, ratifying U.S. Constitution.
1793 Eli Whitney invents cotton gin near Savannah.
1795 Yazoo Fraud: Speculators bribe legislature to sell about 50,000 square miles of western land.
1838 Cherokees forced to move to Oklahoma.
1861 (Jan. 19) Georgia secedes, joins Confederacy.
1864 (Nov. 14–Dec. 22) March to the Sea: Union Gen. William T. Sherman burns Atlanta, destroys 60-mile-wide path to coast, captures Savannah.
1870 (July 15) Georgia readmitted to Union.
1943 First state to give vote to 18-year-olds.
1961 (Aug. 30) Atlanta begins to end segregation of public schools under court order.
1972 State government reorganized by Gov. Jimmy Carter, reducing agencies from 300 to 22 departments.
1973 First black mayor of Atlanta elected: Maynard H. Jackson Jr.
1982 Population increases 3.2% since 1980. Second highest growth rate in South Atlantic states.

HAWAII

Area: 6,471 square miles; 16,759 sq. km.
Population: 994,000 (1982); 964,691 (1980).
Capital: Honolulu.
Flower: Hibiscus. **Tree:** Candlenut.
Bird: Hawaiian goose.
Song: *Hawaii Ponoi.* **Nickname:** The Aloha State.
Motto: *Ua Mau Ke Ea O Ka Aina I Ka Pono* (The Life of the Land Is Perpetuated in Righteousness).
Flag: Alternating white, red, and blue stripes, with Union Jack in upper left.
Leading Industries: Tourism, military installations, food processing, agriculture (sugarcane, pineapples, beef cattle, coffee).
Climate (Honolulu): *Normal temperatures:* Jan. high 79 ° F., low 65 ° F.; July high 87 ° F., low 73 ° F. *Normal yearly rain:* 23". *Record rainfall in 24 hours:* 17.07" in March 1958.
Recreation Areas: National parks, 2; state parks and recreation areas, 46; many fine beaches.
Points of Interest: Hawaii Volcanoes National Park (Hawaii) and Haleakala National Park (Maui); City of Refuge National Historical Park (Hawaii); Polynesian Cultural Center (Oahu, near Laie); Waimea Canyon (Kauai); USS *Arizona* Memorial (Pearl Harbor); Iolani Palace, Bishop Museum, and the Waikiki area (all in Honolulu); Nuuanu Pali (near Honolulu); Puukohola Heiau National Historic Site (Hawaii).

KEY EVENTS IN HAWAII

1778 (Jan. 18) British Capt. James Cook discovers Hawaiian Islands, naming them Sandwich Islands.
1795 Hawaii unified by King Kamehameha I.
1820 Protestant missionaries from New England led by Hiram Bingham begin converting Hawaiians.
1893 (Jan. 17) Queen Liliuokalani deposed.
1894 (July 4) Republic of Hawaii established with Sanford B. Dole as president.
1898 (Aug. 12) U.S. annexes Hawaii.
1900 (June 14) Territory of Hawaii organized.
1941 (Dec. 7) Japanese attack Pearl Harbor.
1959 (Aug. 21) Hawaii becomes 50th U.S. state.
1981 First woman mayor of Honolulu, Eileen Anderson, takes office on Jan. 2.
1982 Population grows 3.1% since 1980.

IDAHO

Area: 83,564 square miles; 216,431 sq. km.
Population: 965,000 (1982); 944,038 (1980).
Capital: Boise.
Flower: Syringa. **Tree:** White pine.
Bird: Mountain bluebird.
Horse: Appaloosa.
Gemstone: Star garnet.
Song: *Here We Have Idaho.*
Nickname: The Gem State.
Motto: *Esto Perpetua* (It Is Perpetual).
Flag: State seal and inscription "State of Idaho" centered on blue field.
Leading Industries: Agriculture (potatoes, wheat, barley, beans, hay, sugar beets, beef cattle, sheep, dairy products), food processing, forestry, mining (silver, lead, zinc, copper).
Climate (Boise): *Normal temperatures:* Jan. high 37 ° F., low 21 ° F.; July high 91 ° F., low 59 ° F. *Normal yearly precipitation:* 11.5" (water). *Record snowstorm:* 17" in December 1884.
Recreation Areas: National park, 1; national forests, 15; state parks and recreation areas, 19.
Points of Interest: Yellowstone National Park; Hells Canyon–Seven Devils scenic area; Sun Valley resort area; Shoshone Falls (near Twin Falls); Craters of the Moon National Monument; Nez Percé National Historical Park.

KEY EVENTS IN IDAHO

1805 Idaho explored by Lewis and Clark.
1846 (Aug. 5) Idaho acquired by U.S. as Oregon Treaty with Britain becomes effective.
1860 First permanent settlement established by Mormons at Franklin.
1860 (Sept. 30) Gold discovered on Orofino Creek.
1863 (March 4) Territory of Idaho established.
1877–79 Battles between U.S. troops and Nez Percé, Bannock, and Sheepeater Indians.
1880 Railroad completed to southeastern Idaho.
1890 (July 3) Idaho becomes 43d U.S. state.
1951 (Dec. 20) First electricity generated with atomic power near Idaho Falls.
1959–68 Three hydroelectric plants built on Snake River, providing over 1 million kilowatts.
1975 Snake River project opens 469-mile navigable waterway from Lewiston, Idaho, to Astoria, Oregon.
1976 (June 5) 300-foot-high Teton Dam collapses, causing 11 deaths and $1 billion in damage.
1982 Population grows 2.3% since 1980, making state 40th in population rank.

ILLINOIS

Area: 56,345 square miles; 145,933 sq. km.
Population: 11,448,000 (1982); 11,427,414 (1980).
Capital: Springfield.
Flower: Native violet. **Tree:** White oak.
Bird: Cardinal.
Mineral: Fluorite.
Insect: Monarch butterfly.
Song: *Illinois.*
Nickname: The Prairie State.
Motto: State Sovereignty–National Union.
Flag: State seal and "Illinois" centered on white field.
Leading Industries: Manufacturing (machinery, appliances, iron and steel, construction materials), food processing, agriculture (corn, hogs, oats, beef cattle, poultry, dairy products, soybeans, fruits), mining (coal, petroleum).

ILLINOIS *(continued)*

Climate (Chicago): *Normal temperatures:* Jan. high 32 ° F., low 17 ° F.; July high 84 ° F., low 65 ° F. *Normal yearly precipitation:* 34" (water). *Record snowstorm:* 19.8" in January 1967.

Recreation Areas: National forest, 1; state parks and recreation areas, 144; Lake Michigan beach and boating areas.

Points of Interest: Dickson Mounds Indian burial ground (near Lewistown); New Salem restoration; homestead and mansion of Joseph Smith (Nauvoo); Lincoln's home and burial place (Springfield). *In Chicago*: Art Institute; Field Museum; Museum of Science and Industry; Shedd Aquarium; Adler Planetarium; Merchandise Mart; Chicago Portage National Historic Site.

KEY EVENTS IN ILLINOIS

1673 Illinois explored by Louis Joliet and Jesuit priest Jacques Marquette for France.
1675 Roman Catholic mission founded at Kaskaskia, near present-day Utica, by Father Marquette.
1699 French settlers establish first permanent town at Cahokia, near present-day East St. Louis.
1763 Britain obtains region in settlement of French and Indian War.
1778 George Rogers Clark captures Kaskaskia and Cahokia during American Revoluntionary War.
1787 Region becomes part of Northwest Territory.
1809 (Feb. 3) Territory of Illinois organized.
1812 (Aug. 15–16) In War of 1812 Britain's Indian allies massacre U.S. troops and settlers at Fort Dearborn, at site of present-day Chicago.
1818 (Dec. 3) Illinois becomes 21st U.S. state.
1832 (April 6–Aug. 2) Black Hawk War fought by settlers and Indians along Mississippi River.
1844 (June 27) Carthage mob kills Joseph Smith, founder of Mormon church, and his brother Hyrum.
1848 Illinois and Michigan Canal completed, linking Great Lakes to Mississippi River.
1855 Railroad links Chicago to East Coast.
1871 (Oct. 8–9) Fire destroys most of Chicago, killing 300 persons.
1942 (Dec. 2) Atomic Age begins with first successful nuclear chain reaction achieved in Chicago.
1973 World's tallest building completed in Chicago: 1,454-foot Sears Tower.
1977 State legislature tied up 6 weeks as record 186 roll calls are taken in choosing senate president.
1982 Population grows only 0.2% since 1980.

INDIANA

Area: 36,185 square miles; 93,720 sq. km.
Population: 5,471,000 (1982); 5,490,260 (1980).
Capital: Indianapolis.
Flower: Peony.
Tree: Tulip poplar.
Bird: Cardinal.
Stone: Limestone.
Song: *On the Banks of the Wabash, Far Away.*
Nickname: The Hoosier State.
Motto: Crossroads of America.
Flag: Gold torch with 19 gold stars on blue field.
Leading Industries: Manufacturing (machinery, appliances, steel, transportation equipment), agriculture (corn, hogs, soybeans, tomatoes, wheat, sheep, poultry, dairy products), mining (coal, natural gas, petroleum).
Climate (Indianapolis): *Normal temperatures:* Jan. high 36 ° F., low 20 ° F.; July high 85 ° F., low 65 ° F. *Normal yearly precipitation:* 39" (water). *Record snowstorm:* 6.4" on Feb. 24, 1974.
Recreation Areas: National forest, 1; national lakeshore, 1; state park and recreation areas, 22.
Points of Interest: Prehistoric Indian mounds; Indiana Dunes National Lakeshore; mineral springs at French Lick; Motor Speedway (Indianapolis); Lincoln Boyhood National Memorial (near Lincoln City); George Rogers Clark National Historical Park.

KEY EVENTS IN INDIANA

1679–80 Indiana explored for France by Robert Cavelier, Sieur de La Salle.
1731–33 French settlers establish Vincennes.
1763 Britain wins region in French and Indian War.
1779 (Feb. 24) George Rogers Clark captures Vincennes from British in Revolutionary War.
1787 Becomes part of Northwest Territory.
1800 (May 7) Indiana Territory organized.
1811 (Nov. 7) Battle of Tippecanoe: Shawnees defeated near present-day Lafayette by Gen. William H. Harrison, then governor of Indiana Territory and later President of the United States.
1816 (Dec. 11) Indiana becomes 19th U.S. state.
1861–65 In Civil War Indiana supports Union with about 200,000 soldiers.
1906 Gary established as steelmaking center.
1911 First Memorial Day 500-mile auto race held at Indianapolis.
1913 (March 25–27) Floods in Indiana and Ohio kill 732 persons, cause over $180 million in damage.
1956 Indiana Turnpike opened.
1963 Studebaker Corporation ends auto production at South Bend; began as wagonmaker in 1852.
1982 Population decreases 0.4% since 1980, dropping state to 14th in rank.

IOWA

Area: 56,275 square miles; 145,752 sq. km.
Population: 2,905,000 (1982); 2,913,808 (1980).
Capital: Des Moines.
Flower: Wild rose.
Tree: Oak
Bird: Eastern goldfinch.
Stone: Geode.
Song: *The Song of Iowa.*
Nickname: The Hawkeye State.
Motto: Our Liberties We Prize and Our Rights We Will Maintain.
Flag: Blue, white, and red bars, with eagle and "Iowa" in larger white bar.
Leading Industries: Agriculture (beef cattle, hogs, corn, dairy products, poultry, soybeans, oats, hay), manufacturing (machinery, chemicals), food processing.
Climate (Des Moines): *Normal temperatures:* Jan. high 28 ° F., low 11 ° F.; July high 85 ° F.; low 65 ° F. *Normal yearly precipitation:* 31" (water). *Record snowstorm:* 19.8" in January 1942.
Recreation Areas and State Parks: 92.
Points of Interest: Herbert Hoover National Historic Site (West Branch); Amana Colonies; Fort Dodge Historical Museum, Fort, and Stockade; Effigy Mounds National Monument; Grotto of the Redemption (West Bend).

KEY EVENTS IN IOWA

1682 Iowa region claimed for France.
1762 Region ceded to Spain by France.
1788 First settler, French-Canadian Julien Dubuque, begins mining lead near present-day Dubuque.
1803 U.S. acquires region in Louisiana Purchase.
1808 Fort Madison established by U.S. Army.
1838 (June 12) Territory of Iowa organized.
1846 (Dec. 28) Iowa becomes 29th U.S. state.
1857 Des Moines becomes state capital.
1867 Railroad completed west to Council Bluffs.
1929–35 During Great Depression more than half of

Iowa's farmers lose land by mortgage foreclosures.
1960 Majority of state's people live in cities and towns for first time.
1982 Population decreases by 0.3% since 1980; one of five states that lost population since 1980.

KANSAS

Area: 82,277 square miles; 213,097 sq. km.
Population: 2,408,000 (1982); 2,364,236 (1980).
Capital: Topeka.
Flower: Native sunflower. **Tree:** Cottonwood.
Bird: Western meadowlark.
Animal: American buffalo.
Insect: Honeybee.
Song: *Home on the Range.*
Nickname: The Sunflower State.
Motto: *Ad Astra per Aspera* (To the Stars Through Difficulties).
Flag: Sunflower atop state seal on blue field.
Leading Industries: Manufacturing (aircraft, railroad equipment, chemicals, machinery), food processing, agriculture (beef cattle, wheat, hogs, sorghum grains, corn), mining (petroleum, natural gas, helium).
Climate (Topeka): *Normal temperatures:* Jan. high 38 ° F., low 18 ° F.; July high 89 ° F., low 67 ° F. *Normal yearly precipitation:* 35" (water). *Record snowstorm:* 18.7" on Feb. 27–28, 1900.
Recreation Areas: State parks and recreation areas, 29.
Points of Interest: Fort Larned and Fort Scott national historic sites; Hollenberg Pony Express Station; Fort Leavenworth; Eisenhower Library and boyhood home (Abilene); 1870s restoration of Dodge City; Kansas State Historical Society and Museum (Topeka); Museum of Art (Lawrence); John Brown Memorial State Park (Osawatomie).

KEY EVENTS IN KANSAS

1541 Region explored for Spain by Francisco de Coronado.
1682 Kansas region claimed for France.
1803 U.S. acquires Kansas in Louisiana Purchase.
1806 Kansas explored by U.S. Lt. Zebulon Pike.
1821 Santa Fe Trail route across Kansas pioneered by William Becknell.
1827 First permanent settlement: Fort Leavenworth.
1854 (May 30) Territory of Kansas created, setting off guerrilla warfare between proslavery and antislavery factions seeking to control government.
1860 (July 19) First railroad reaches Kansas.
1861 (Jan. 29) Kansas becomes 34th U.S. state.
1863 (Aug. 21) Lawrence burned and 150 settlers killed by Confederate guerrillas led by William C. Quantrill.
1865–80 Over 3,000 miles of railroad open across Kansas, making such towns as Abilene cattle-shipping centers for trail drives from Texas.
1870s Mennonite settlers introduce winter wheat, making Kansas leading wheat producer.
1892 Petroleum discovered near Neodesha.
1919 First airplane factory opens in Wichita; city becomes leading plane manufacturer in nation.
1934–35 Drought develops "dust bowl" in southwestern Kansas, driving many farmers from homes.
1982 Population grows 1.9% since 1980.

KENTUCKY

Area: 40,409 square miles; 104,660 sq. km.
Population: 3,667,000 (1982); 3,660,257 (1980).
Capital: Frankfort.
Flower: Goldenrod.
Tree: Coffee tree.
Bird: Cardinal.
Song: *My Old Kentucky Home.*
Nickname: The Bluegrass State.
Motto: United We Stand, Divided We Fall.
Flag: State seal on blue field.
Leading Industries: Manufacturing and processing (machinery, food, tobacco products, chemicals), distilling (bourbon whisky), agriculture (beef cattle, dairy products, tobacco, corn, hay, hogs, poultry, horses), mining (coal, petroleum, gas).
Climate (Louisville): *Normal temperatures:* Jan. high 42 ° F., low 25 ° F.; July high 87 ° F., low 66 ° F. *Normal yearly precipitation:* 43" (water). *Record snowstorm:* 15" in December 1917.
Recreation Areas: National park, 1; national forests, 2; state parks and recreation areas, 48.
Points of Interest: Mammoth Cave National Park; Kentucky Woodlands National Wildlife Refuge; Abraham Lincoln Birthplace National Historical Site (near Hodgenville); Cumberland Gap National Historical Park; Bluegrass region (around Lexington); Churchill Downs (Louisville); My Old Kentucky Home (Bardstown); Constitution Square restoration (Danville).

KEY EVENTS IN KENTUCKY

1750 Cumberland Gap pass in Appalachian Mountains discovered by Thomas Walker.
1774 First permanent settlement established at Harrodsburg by James Harrod.
1775 Daniel Boone blazes Wilderness Road through Cumberland Gap; established Boonesborough on Kentucky River.
1792 (June 1) Kentucky becomes 15th U.S. state.
1798 (Nov. 16) Kentucky Resolution written by Thomas Jefferson adopted by state legislature declaring federal Alien and Sedition Acts unconstitutional.
1800 (July) "Great revival" of religion begins with huge camp meeting at Gaspar River.
1815 First steamboat reaches Louisville from New Orleans.
1861–65 In Civil War Kentucky remains in Union despite opposition by state's slave owners; battles fought in Kentucky at Mill Springs on Jan. 19, 1862, at Richmond on Aug. 30, 1862, and at Perryville on Oct. 8, 1862.
1875 First Kentucky Derby horse race run at Louisville.
1982 State population grows 0.2% since 1980; lowest growth rate in East South Central states.

LOUISIANA

Area: 47,752 square miles; 123,676 sq. km.
Population: 4,362,000 (1982); 4,206,098 (1980).
Capital: Baton Rouge.
Flower: Magnolia.
Tree: Cypress.
Bird: Eastern brown pelican.
Songs: *Give Me Louisiana* and *You Are My Sunshine.*
Nickname: The Pelican State.
Motto: Union, Justice and Confidence.
Flag: Pelican atop state motto on blue field.
Leading Industries: Mining (petroleum, natural gas, salt, sulfur), manufacturing (chemicals, metal products), food processing, forestry, agriculture (beef cattle, poultry, cotton, rice, sugarcane, soybeans), services, fishing.
Climate (New Orleans): *Normal temperatures:* Jan. high 62 ° F., low 44 ° F.; July high 90 ° F., low 73 ° F. *Normal yearly precipitation:* 57" (water). *Record snowstorm:* 8.2" February 1895.
Recreation Areas: National forest, 1; state park and recreation areas, 31.
Points of Interest: New Orleans, including French Quarter, Superdome; plantation homes near Natchitoches and New Iberia; Cajun country (in Mississippi River delta region); Chalmette National Historical

LOUISIANA *(continued)*
Park; Evangeline Oak in St. Martinville; Live Oak Gardens on Jefferson Island.

KEY EVENTS IN LOUISIANA

1541 Hernando de Soto explores part of region, discovering Mississippi River for Spain.
1682 (April 9) Region claimed for France by Robert Cavelier, Sieur de La Salle.
1714 First permanent French settlement: Natchitoches.
1718 New Orleans founded by Jean Baptiste le Moyne, Sieur de Bienville.
1762 (Nov. 3) Spain acquires Louisiana.
1800 France regains Louisiana from Spain.
1803 (Dec. 20) U.S. takes formal possession of most of Louisiana after purchase from France.
1804 (March 26) Region organized by U.S. as Territory of Orleans.
1810 (Oct. 27) U.S. annexes West Feliciana District (Baton Rouge) from Spain after uprising by Americans captures area.
1812 (April 30) Louisiana becomes 18th U.S. state.
1815 (Jan. 8) Battle of New Orleans: Gen. Andrew Jackson defeats larger British army; neither side aware treaty already signed ending War of 1812.
1840 New Orleans becomes second-largest U.S. port as result of steamboat traffic on Mississippi River.
1861 (Jan. 26) Louisiana secedes from Union, joins Confederacy.
1862 (May 1) New Orleans surrenders to Union forces after Adm. David Farragut bombards its forts.
1868 (June 25) Louisiana readmitted to Union.
1877 (April 20) Reconstruction ends with withdrawal of federal troops.
1879 New Orleans becomes ocean port with dredging of Mississippi River channel by U.S. Army.
1901 Petroleum discovered near Jennings and White Castle.
1927 Mississippi River flood drives 300,000 persons from homes, causes huge property losses.
1935 (Sept. 8) Assassination in Baton Rouge of U.S. Sen. Huey P. Long, political boss of state.
1975 (Jan. 1) New constitution becomes effective, ending property taxes for homes of $30,000 or less.
1980 (March 10) First Republican governor in 103 years, David C. Treen, sworn in.
1982 Population grows 3.7% since 1980, making Louisiana 18th most populous state.
1983 (July 5) Racial designation law repealed: 1970 law had defined as black anyone with more than one thirty-second Negro blood.

MAINE

Area: 33,265 square miles; 86,156 sq. km.
Population: 1,133,000 (1982); 1,125,030 (1980).
Capital: Augusta.
Flower: White pine cone and tassel. **Tree:** Eastern white pine. **Bird:** Chickadee. **Insect:** Honeybee. **Mineral:** Tourmaline. **Fish:** Landlocked salmon.
Song: *State of Maine Song.*
Nickname: The Pine Tree State.
Motto: *Dirigo* (I Direct).
Flag: State seal centered on blue field.
Leading Industries: Manufacturing (paper, leather products, lumber), food processing, agriculture (poultry, dairy products, potatoes, oats, corn, vegetables, fruits), fishing.
Climate (Portland): *Normal temperatures:* Jan. high 31° F., low 12° F.; July high 79° F., low 57° F. *Normal yearly precipitation:* 41" (water). *Record snowstorm:* 23.3" in January 1935.
Recreation Areas: National park, 1; national forest, 1; state parks and recreation areas, 39.
Points of Interest: Bar Harbor; Acadia National Park; Allagash National Wilderness Waterway; Baxter State Park; Wadsworth-Longfellow House (Portland); Roosevelt Campobello International Park; Saint Croix Island National Monument; Old Gaol Museum (York).

KEY EVENTS IN MAINE

1498 John Cabot explores Maine coast.
1604 First French colony established at Saint Croix Island by Pierre du Guast, Sieur de Monts.
1607 First English colony founded on Kennebec River by George Popham and Raleigh Gilbert (abandoned 1608).
1622 (Aug. 10) Maine and New Hampshire granted to Sir Ferdinando Gorges and John Mason.
1623 First English settlements established.
1629 Region divided by Gorges and Mason with Gorges keeping Maine.
1677 (March 13) Massachusetts gains title to Maine by purchase for about $6,000.
1775 (June 12) First naval action of Revolutionary War: Patriots capture British sloop *Margaretta* off Machias, Me.
1775 (Oct. 18) British burn Falmouth (now Portland).
1814 In War of 1812, Eastport and eastern Maine captured and occupied by British.
1820 (March 15) Maine becomes 23d U.S. state as part of Missouri Compromise.
1838–39 Aroostook War: Militia of Maine and New Brunswick prepare to fight in boundary dispute.
1842 (Aug. 9) Webster-Ashburton Treaty signed, settling Maine's boundary with Canada.
1851 First state prohibition law enacted.
1948 First woman elected by Maine to U.S. Senate: Margaret Chase Smith.
1958 First Democrat elected to U.S. Senate by popular vote in Maine: Edmund S. Muskie.
1972 Penobscot and Passamaquoddy Indians file suit asking $300 million in damages because over 12 million acres of their land were seized illegally.
1974 First Maine governor independent of both major political parties elected: James B. Longley.
1977 Legal age raised to 20 from 18 for drinking alcoholic beverages.
1982 Population grows 0.8% since 1980.

MARYLAND

Area: 10,460 square miles; 27,092 sq. km.
Population: 4,265,000 (1982); 4,216,941 (1980).
Capital: Annapolis.
Flower: Black-eyed Susan.
Tree: White oak.
Bird: Baltimore oriole.
Animal: Chesapeake Bay retriever. **Fish:** Striped bass.
Song: *Maryland, My Maryland.*
Nickname: The Old Line State.
Motto: *Fatti Maschii, Parole Femine* (Manly Deeds, Womanly Words).
Flag: Geometric black-and-gold pattern in top left and bottom right quarters; red and white ornate crosses in other quarters.
Leading Industries: Manufacturing (steel, metal products, transportation equipment, appliances, machinery), agriculture (poultry, dairy products, corn, tobacco, soybeans), mining (stone, coal, clay), fishing.
Climate (Baltimore): *Normal temperatures:* Jan. high 42° F., low 25° F.; July high 87° F., low 67° F. *Normal yearly precipitation:* 41" (water). *Record snowstorm:* 24.5" in January 1922.
Recreation Areas: National seashore, 1; state parks and recreation areas, 49; Atlantic Ocean and Chesapeake Bay resorts.
Points of Interest: Fort McHenry National Monument; Harpers Ferry and Chesapeake and Ohio Canal national historical parks; Hampton National Historic Site; Antietam National Battlefield Site and National

Cemetery; U.S. Naval Academy (Annapolis); Assateague Island National Seashore; Catoctin Mountain and Piscataway parks; George Washington Memorial Parkway; Barbara Fritchie House in Frederick; St. Marys City restoration near Leonardtown; USS *Constellation* at Baltimore.

KEY EVENTS IN MARYLAND

1608 Chesapeake Bay explored for England by John Smith.
1631 First English settlement established by William Claiborne of Virginia on Kent Island.
1632 (June 30) Maryland colony charter granted to Cecil Calvert, 2d Lord Baltimore, by King Charles I.
1634 (March 25) English Roman Catholics land on St. Clements (now Blakistone) Island, establishing St. Marys City as capital of colony.
1649 (April 21) Religious freedom granted all Christians in Toleration Act approved by legislature.
1654–58 Revolt by Puritans led by William Claiborne takes over government, ending toleration.
1691–1715 Colonial governors appointed by British crown; Church of England established (1692), with Catholics forbidden right to vote or hold office.
1715 Calvert family regains control of colony under 4th Lord Baltimore, who renounces Catholicism.
1767 Mason and Dixon Line established as boundary between Maryland and Pennsylvania.
1774 (Oct. 19) Patriots burn British tea ship ***Peggy Stewart*** in Annapolis Harbor.
1776 (Nov. 9) First state constitution adopted.
1788 (April 28) Maryland becomes 7th U.S. state, ratifying U.S. Constitution.
1814 (Aug. 24) Battle of Bladensburg: British defeat U.S. forces in War of 1812.
1814 (Sept. 12–14) British unsuccessfully try to capture Baltimore; bombardment of Fort McHenry inspires Francis Scott Key to write *The Star-Spangled Banner.*
1828–50 Chesapeake and Ohio Canal built.
1829 Chesapeake and Delaware Canal completed.
1844 (May 24) First telegraph line opens between Baltimore and Washington, D.C.
1845 U.S. Naval Academy founded at Annapolis.
1861–65 In Civil War, although slave state, Maryland remains in Union; battles include Antietam (Sept. 17, 1862) and Monocacy (July 9, 1864).
1938 First state income tax adopted.
1952 Chesapeake Bay Bridge connects eastern and western Maryland; parallel span completed in 1973.
1977 Gov. Marvin Mandel convicted of fraud; sentenced to 4 years in jail.
1982 Population grows only 1.1% since 1980; state remains 19th in rank.

MASSACHUSETTS

Area: 8,284 square miles; 21,456 sq. km.
Population: 5,781,000 (1982); 5,737,081 (1980).
Capital: Boston.
Flower: Mayflower. **Tree:** American elm. **Bird:** Chickadee. **Fish:** Cod. **Song:** *All Hail to Massachusetts.* **Nickname:** The Bay State. **Motto:** *Ense Petit Placidam Sub Libertate Quietem* (By the Sword We Seek Peace, but Peace Only Under Liberty).
Flag: State coat of arms centered on white field.
Leading Industries: Manufacturing (machinery, appliances, printing, metal products), agriculture (dairy products, flowers, shrubs, poultry, beef cattle, hogs, hay, vegetables, tobacco).
Climate (Boston): *Normal temperatures:* Jan. high 36° F., low 23° F.; July high 81° F., low 65° F. *Normal yearly precipitation:* 43″ (water). *Record snowstorm:* 19.4″ in February 1958.
Recreation Areas: National seashore, 1; state parks and recreation areas, 68.
Points of Interest: Adams, Dorchester Heights, John F. Kennedy Birthplace, Longfellow, Salem Maritime, and Saugus Iron Works national historic sites; Minute Man National Historical Park between Lexington and Concord; Bunker Hill Memorial; Cape Cod National Seashore; Nantucket; Martha's Vineyard; Berkshire Music Festival; Salem; reconstruction of first Pilgrim village at Plymouth; Old Sturbridge Village; Basketball Hall of Fame (Springfield); *In Boston:* Old North Church, Old State House, Custom House, Quincy Market, Faneuil Hall, USS *Constitution,* and Paul Revere's House.

KEY EVENTS IN MASSACHUSETTS

c.1000 Coast believed explored by Vikings led by Leif Ericson.
1498 John Cabot explores coast for England.
1620 (Dec. 26) Pilgrims land, founding Plymouth Colony.
1628 (Sept. 6) Puritans found Salem under leadership of John Endecott, forerunner of Massachusetts Bay Colony (given royal charter March 14, 1629).
1630 (Sept. 17) Boston founded; becomes capital of Massachusetts Bay Colony in 1632.
1636 (Oct. 28) Harvard College founded.
1636–37 War fought against Pequot Indians.
1675–78 King Philip's War: Many settlers killed fighting Wampanoag Indians and their allies.
1684 (Oct. 18) Massachusetts Bay Colony charter annulled by English court.
1689 (April 18) Revolt in Boston overthrows royal governor of New England Sir Edmund Andros.
1689–1763 Massachusetts colonists take major role in French and Indian War.
1691 (Oct. 17) New royal charter for Massachusetts incorporates Plymouth and Maine in colony.
1692 Witchcraft trials result in execution of 20 persons as witches.
1775 (April 19) Revolutionary War begins with Battles of Lexington and Concord.
1775 (June 17) Battle of Bunker Hill: British defeat Massachusetts militia, but with heavy losses.
1776 (March 17) British evacuate Boston by sea after victorious 9-month siege by Continental Army.
1780 (June 15) First state constitution, written by John Adams, becomes effective; first ratified by popular referendum.
1786–87 Shays' Rebellion put down by militia.
1788 (Feb. 6) Massachusetts becomes 6th U.S. state, ratifying U.S. Constitution.
1837 (June 29) State board of education established with Horace Mann as secretary.
1853 (May 17) Labor law adopted reducing hours of work per day from 12 to 10 beginning Oct. 1, 1854.
1914 Cape Cod Canal opens.
1919 Gov. Calvin Coolidge calls out national guard to break Boston police strike.
1966 First black U.S. senator elected in U.S. since Reconstruction era: Edward W. Brooke.
1977 Islands of Martha's Vineyard and Nantucket vote to secede from state because of redistricting that would eliminate their representation in legislature.
1980 Voters approve $1.5 billion property tax cut; measure limits property tax to 2.5% of market value.
1982 Population grows only 0.8% since 1980.
1983 (March 26) Ban on Sunday store sales ends; result of 1982 legislation.

MICHIGAN

Area: 58,527 square miles; 151,844 sq. km.
Population: 9,109,000 (1982); 9,262,070 (1980).
Capital: Lansing.
Flower: Apple blossom.

MICHIGAN *(continued)*
Tree: White pine.
Bird: Robin. **Fish:** Trout.
Stone: Petoskey stone.
Gem: Chlorastrolite.
Song: *Michigan, My Michigan.*
Nickname: The Wolverine State.
Motto: *Si Quaeris Peninsulam Amoenam Circumspice* (If You Seek a Pleasant Peninsula, Look About You).
Flag: State coat of arms centered on blue field.
Leading Industries: Manufacturing (automobiles, machinery, metal products, chemicals), food processing, agriculture (dairy products, beef cattle, hogs, poultry, fruits, vegetables, corn, potatoes, soybeans, sugar beets), mining (iron ore, copper, salt, petroleum, natural gas), tourism.
Climate (Detroit): *Normal temperatures:* Jan. high 32 ° F., low 17 ° F.; July high 83 ° F., low 61 ° F. *Normal yearly precipitation:* 32″ (water). *Record snowstorm:* 19.2″ on Dec. 1–2, 1974.
Recreation Areas: National park, 1; national forests, 4; national lakeshores, 2; state parks and recreation areas, 78.
Points of Interest: Pictured Rocks and Sleeping Bear Dunes national lakeshore; Isle Royale National Park; Mackinac Island; Greenfield Village (Dearborn); Cook Nuclear Center (Bridgman); Detroit Zoological Park (Royal Oak); automobile plants in Dearborn, Detroit, Flint, Lansing, Pontiac; Soo Canals, Sault Ste. Marie.

KEY EVENTS IN MICHIGAN

c.1620 Michigan explored for France by Etienne Brulé.
1668 First permanent French settlement founded at Sault Ste. Marie by Father Jacques Marquette.
1763 Britain wins region in French and Indian War.
1783 U.S. acquires region in Revolutionary War, but British retain Detroit and other posts until 1796.
1787 Region becomes part of Northwest Territory; made part of Indiana Territory in 1800–03.
1805 (Jan. 11) Michigan Territory organized.
1812 (Aug. 16) In War of 1812 Detroit and U.S. army of 2,000 surrendered to British by territorial governor, Gen. William Hull; British troops remain on Michigan's Drummond Island until 1828.
1818 First steamboat on Lake Erie reaches Detroit.
1837 (Jan. 26) Michigan becomes 26th U.S. state.
1854 (July 6) New Republican Party given name at state convention in Jackson, Mich.
1855 First Soo Canal completed at Sault Ste. Marie, linking Lake Superior and Lake Huron.
1899 First automobile manufacturing company founded in Detroit by Ransom E. Olds.
1935–37 United Automobile Workers union uses sitdown strikes to obtain collective bargaining contracts.
1957 Straits of Mackinac bridge opens.
1967 State income tax adopted.
1980–82 Slump in auto production brings state highest unemployment rate in nation with over 15% jobless.
1981 Population decreases by 1.7% since 1980, with highest decline among states.

MINNESOTA

Area: 84,402 square miles; 218,600 sq. km.
Population: 4,133,000 (1982); 4,075,970 (1980).
Capital: St. Paul.
Flower: Pink and white lady's-slipper.
Tree: Red pine. **Grain:** Wild rice.
Bird: Common loon.
Gemstone: Lake Superior agate. **Fish:** Walleye.
Song: *Hail! Minnesota.*
Nickname: The North Star State.
Motto: *L'Etoile du Nord* (The Star of the North).
Flag: State seal and gold stars on blue field.
Leading Industries: Manufacturing (paper, automobiles, printing, lumber), food processing, agriculture (beef cattle, hogs, turkeys, poultry, sheep, dairy products, oats, corn, hay, flaxseed, potatoes, soybeans, sugar beets), mining (iron ore, taconite).
Climate (Minneapolis–St. Paul): *Normal temperatures:* Jan. high 21 ° F., low 3 ° F.; July high 82 ° F., low 61 ° F. *Normal annual precipitation:* 26″ (water). *Record snowstorm:* 16.2″ in November 1940.
Recreation Areas: National park, 1; national forests, 2; state parks and recreation areas, 98.
Points of Interest: Voyageurs National Park; North Shore Drive; Pipestone and Grand Portage national monuments; St. Croix and Lower St. Croix national scenic riverways; Lumbertown restoration in Brainerd. *In Minneapolis:* Institute of Arts; Walker Art Center; Minnehaha Park; Tyrone Guthrie Theater.

KEY EVENTS IN MINNESOTA

1679 Region explored and claimed for France by Daniel Greysolon, Sieur Duluth.
1680 Falls of St. Anthony at present-day Minneapolis named by Belgian missionary Louis Hennepin.
1762 Spain acquires western Minnesota from France.
1763 Britain obtains eastern Minnesota from France.
1783 U.S. acquires eastern Minnesota from Britain.
1800 France obtains western Minnesota from Spain.
1803 U.S. acquires western Minnesota from France in Louisiana Purchase.
1805–06 Region explored by U.S. Lt. Zebulon M. Pike.
1818 (Oct. 20) Northern Minnesota ceded to U.S. by Britain.
1820–22 Fort Snelling built by U.S. Army just south of present-day Minneapolis (first called Fort St. Anthony, renamed Fort Snelling in 1825).
1823 First Mississippi River steamboat reaches Fort Snelling from St. Louis.
1832 Lake Itasca, source of Mississippi River, discovered by Henry R. Schoolcraft.
1849 (March 3) Territory of Minnesota organized.
1858 (May 11) Minnesota becomes 32d U.S. state.
1862 Sioux Indian uprising led by Chief Little Crow kills hundreds of settlers.
1890 Rich iron-ore deposits discovered in Mesabi Range.
1894 (Sept. 1) Forest fire destroys towns of Hinkley and Sandstone, killing 418 persons.
1918 (Oct. 13–15) Forest fire in Carlton and St. Louis counties kills over 400 persons.
1955 Taconite processing plant opens at Silver Bay to extract iron from low-grade taconite ore.
1981 14,000 State employees strike for 22 days to win wage increase.
1982 Population grows 1.4% since 1980.

MISSISSIPPI

Area: 47,689 square miles; 123,515 sq. km.
Population: 2,551,000 (1982); 2,520,631 (1980).
Capital: Jackson.
Flower: Magnolia. **Tree:** Magnolia.
Bird: Mockingbird.
Song: *Go, Mississippi.*
Nickname: The Magnolia State.
Motto: *Virtute et Armis* (By Valor and Arms).
Flag: Red, white, and blue stripes, with Confederate flag in upper left.
Leading Industries: Manufacturing (clothing, lumber, chemicals, appliances), food processing, agriculture (cotton, rice, soybeans, livestock feed, beef cattle, dairy products, poultry), mining (petroleum, gas).

Climate (Jackson): *Normal temperatures:* Jan. high 58 ° F., low 36 ° F.; July high 93 ° F., low 71 ° F. *Normal annual precipitation:* 49" (water). *Record snowstorm:* 10.6" in January 1940.
Recreation Areas: National seashore, 1; national forests, 6; state parks and recreation areas, 18.
Points of Interest: Gulf Islands National Seashore; Vicksburg National Military Park; Tupelo National Battlefield; Brices Cross Roads National Battlefield Site; Jefferson Davis' homes at *Rosemont* near Woodville and *Beauvoir* at Biloxi; antebellum homes and gardens of Natchez; Old Spanish Trail; Gulf Coast beaches.

KEY EVENTS IN MISSISSIPPI

1540–41 Region explored for Spain by Hernando de Soto, who discovered Mississippi River.
1682 (April 9) Region claimed for France.
1699 (May) French found first settlement at Old Biloxi (now Ocean Springs).
1736 (May) Battle of Ackia: French defeated in attempt to destroy Chickasaw Indian fort in northeastern Mississippi, preventing French conquest of Mississippi Valley.
1763 Britain acquires region in French and Indian War.
1783 U.S. acquires northern Mississippi in Revolutionary War; Spain obtains southern Mississippi as part of West Florida.
1795 U.S. obtains part of Mississippi between 31st and 32d parallels of latitude from Spain.
1798 (April 7) Territory of Mississippi organized.
1810 (Oct. 27) U.S. annexes West Florida from Spain, including what is now southern Mississippi.
1817 (Dec. 10) Mississippi becomes 20th U.S. state.
1861 (Jan. 9) Mississippi joins Confederacy.
1861–65 In Civil War Biloxi captured by Union Navy on Dec. 31, 1861; Natchez surrenders on Sept. 10, 1862; many battles in state including Vicksburg, which surrendered on July 4, 1863, Brices Cross Roads on June 10, 1864, and Tupelo on July 14, 1864.
1870 (Feb. 17) Mississippi readmitted to Union.
1927 Mississippi River flood drives 100,000 persons from their homes, causes vast property damage.
1939 Petroleum discovered near Tinsley.
1940–60 Population declines in Mississippi.
1969 First black mayor elected since Reconstruction era, in Fayette: Charles Evers.
1982 Population grows 1.2% since 1980.

MISSOURI

Area: 69,697 square miles; 180,515 sq. km.
Population: 4,951,000 (1982); 4,916,759 (1980).
Capital: Jefferson City.
Flower: Hawthorn.
Tree: Dogwood.
Bird: Bluebird.
Stone: Mozarkite.
Song: *Missouri Waltz.*
Nickname: The Show-Me State.
Motto: *Salus Populi Suprema Lex Esto* (The Welfare of the People Shall Be the Supreme Law).
Flag: State seal centered on red, white, and blue stripes.
Leading Industries: Manufacturing (transportation equipment, chemicals, machinery), food processing, agriculture (dairy products, beef cattle, hogs, sheep, poultry, horses, soybeans, corn, cotton, wheat), mining (lead, clay, barite).
Climate (St. Louis): *Normal temperatures:* Jan. high 40 ° F., low 23 ° F.; July high 88 ° F., low 69 ° F. *Normal yearly precipitation:* 36" (water). *Record snowstorm:* 20.4" in March 1890.
Recreation Areas: Scenic riverway, 1; national forests, 2; state parks and recreation areas, 53.
Points of Interest: Mark Twain's boyhood home and Mark Twain Cave (Hannibal); Harry S. Truman Library and Museum (Independence); house where Jesse James was killed (St. Joseph); George Washington Carver National Monument near Diamond Grove; Winston Churchill Memorial and Library in Fulton; Silver Dollar City reconstruction near Branson; Wilson's Creek National Battlefield; Jefferson National Expansion Memorial National Historic Site (St. Louis); Ozark National Scenic Riverways; Lake of the Ozarks; Meramec Caverns near Stanton.

KEY EVENTS IN MISSOURI

1673 Mouth of Missouri River discovered by French explorers Louis Joliet and Jacques Marquette.
1682 (April 9) Missouri region claimed for France.
1735 First permanent settlement established at Sainte Genevieve by settlers from Kaskaskia, Ill.
1762 Spain acquires region from France.
1764 (Feb. 15) St. Louis founded by Pierre Laclede Liguest and René Auguste Chouteau.
1800 France regains region from Spain.
1803 U.S. acquires Missouri in Louisiana Purchase.
1812 (June 4) Territory of Missouri organized.
1817 (Aug. 2) Steamboat *General Pike* ascends Mississippi River to St. Louis.
1821 Kansas City established as fur trading post.
1821 (Aug. 10) Missouri becomes 24th U.S. state.
1854–65 Border warfare with Kansas as proslavery Missourians attack antislavery Kansans.
1859 First railroad crosses state.
1861–65 In Civil War Gov. Claiborne F. Jackson leads state militia in battles with Union forces; Union troops gain control of state in series of battles, but guerrilla warfare continues.
1874 (July 4) Eads Bridge opened across Mississippi River at St. Louis, longest steel-arch bridge of day.
1882 (April 3) Outlaw Jesse James slain by member of his gang in St. Joseph.
1904 World's Fair and Olympic Games held at St. Louis.
1931 Bagnell Dam completed, forming Lake of Ozarks.
1957 Truman Library opens at Independence.
1982 Population grows only 0.7% since 1980.

MONTANA

Area: 147,046 square miles; 380,846 sq. km.
Population: 801,000 (1982); 786,690 (1980).
Capital: Helena.
Flower: Bitterroot.
Tree: Ponderosa pine. **Bird:** Western meadowlark.
Stones: Sapphire and agate. **Fish:** Blackspotted cutthroat trout. **Grass:** Bluebunch wheatgrass.
Song: *Montana.*
Nicknames: The Treasure State; Big Sky Country.
Motto: *Oro y Plata* (Gold and Silver).
Flag: State seal centered on blue field.
Leading Industries: Agriculture (beef cattle, sheep, wheat) forestry, food and mineral processing, mining (petroleum, copper, gold, silver), tourism.
Climate (Helena): *Normal temperatures:* Jan. high 28 ° F., low 8 ° F.; July high 84 ° F., low 52 ° F. *Normal yearly precipitation:* 11" (water). *Record snowstorm:* 21.5" in November 1959.
Recreation Areas: National parks, 2; national forests, 11; national recreation area, 1; state parks and recreation areas, 177.
Points of Interest: Glacier National Park; Yellowstone National Park (which extends into Wyoming and Idaho); Custer Battlefield National Monument; Big Hole National Battlefield; Virginia City; Gallery '85 (Billings); Museum of the Plains Indians (Brown-

MONTANA *(continued)*
ing); Fort Union Trading Post and Grant-Kohr's Ranch national historic sites; Bighorn Canyon National Recreation Area.

KEY EVENTS IN MONTANA

1742–43 Region explored for France by François and Louis-Joseph de La Vérendrye.
1803 U.S. acquires eastern Montana in Louisiana Purchase.
1805–06 Region explored for U.S. by Meriwether Lewis and William Clark.
c.1807 First trading post established by Emanuel Lisa at junction of Bighorn and Yellowstone rivers.
1818 (Oct. 20) Northern boundary of Montana established in treaty with Britain.
1829 Fort Union trading post built for American Fur Company by Kenneth McKenzie near junction of Missouri and Yellowstone rivers.
1846 First permanent settlement established at Fort Benton on Missouri River by Alexander Culbertson.
1846 (Aug. 5) Western Montana obtained from Britain in Oregon Treaty.
1852 Gold discovered in what is now Deer Lodge County by Francis Finlay.
1860 (July 2) First steamboats reach Fort Benton.
1864 (May 26) Territory of Montana organized.
1876 (June 25) Massacre of George Custer and his troops by Sioux Indians in Battle of Little Bighorn.
1877 (Oct. 5) Chief Joseph surrenders to Col. Nelson A. Miles, ending Nez Percé War.
1882 Copper discovered at Anaconda.
1883 (Sept. 8) Railroad completed across Montana.
1889 (Nov. 8) Montana becomes 41st U.S. state.
1916 First woman elected to U.S. Congress: Jeannette Rankin.
1940 Fort Peck Dam completed on Missouri River, largest earth-fill dam in U.S.
1951 Oil wells begin production in Williston Basin.
1975 Libby Dam power project on Kootenai River begins operation.
1982 Population grows 1.8% since 1980.

NEBRASKA

Area: 77,355 square miles; 200,349 sq. km.
Population: 1,586,000 (1982); 1,569,825 (1980).
Capital: Lincoln.
Flower: Goldenrod.
Tree: Cottonwood.
Bird: Western meadowlark.
Gemstone: Blue agate. **Fossil:** Mammoth.
Grass: Little blue stem. **Insect:** Honeybee.
Rock: Chalcedony stone.
Song: *Beautiful Nebraska.*
Nickname: The Cornhusker State.
Motto: Equality Before the Law.
Flag: State seal centered on blue field.
Leading Industries: Agriculture (beef cattle, corn, hogs, wheat), meat-packing, milling, manufacturing.
Climate (Omaha): *Normal temperatures:* Jan. high 33° F., low 12° F.; July high 89° F., low 66° F. *Normal yearly precipitation:* 30" (water). *Record snowstorm:* 29.2" in March 1912.
Recreation Areas: National forests, 2; state parks and recreation areas, 93.
Points of Interest: Agate Fossil Beds, Homestead, and Scotts Bluff national monuments; Chimney Rock National Historic Site; re-created pioneer village at Minden; Boys Town near Omaha; Union stockyards in Omaha.

KEY EVENTS IN NEBRASKA

1700s French and Spanish explorers travel through parts of Nebraska.
1803 U.S. acquires Nebraska in Louisiana Purchase.
1804–06 Eastern Nebraska explored for U.S. by Meriwether Lewis and William Clark.
1812–13 Oregon Trail pioneered across Nebraska by fur trader Robert Stuart.
1819 Fort Atkinson built by U.S. Army north of present-day Omaha.
1823 First permanent settlement: Bellevue.
1848 Western Nebraska acquired in Mexican War.
1854 (May 30) Territory of Nebraska created.
1865 Construction of railroad across state begun.
1867 (March 1) Nebraska becomes 37th U.S. state.
1874–77 Plague of grasshoppers drives many farmers from state.
1934 Unicameral legislature established by amendment to state constitution; first meets in 1937.
1939 Oil discovered in southeastern Nebraska.
1966 Voters abolish state property tax; replaced with state sales and income taxes in 1967.
1982 Population increases 1.0% since 1980.

NEVADA

Area: 110,561 square miles; 286,351 sq. km.
Population: 881,000 (1982); 800,493 (1980).
Capital: Carson City.
Flower: Sagebrush.
Tree: Single-leaf piñon.
Bird: Mountain bluebird. **Animal:** Desert bighorn sheep. **Mineral:** Silver. **Grass:** Indian rice grass.
Song: *Home Means Nevada.*
Nickname: The Silver State.
Motto: All for Our Country.
Flag: Gold and green insignia in upper left on blue field.
Climate (Las Vegas): *Normal temperatures:* Jan. high 56° F., low 33° F.; July high 104° F., low 75° F. *Normal yearly precipitation:* 4" (water). *Record snowstorm:* 9" on Jan. 4–5, 1974.
Leading Industries: Gambling and tourism; mining and processing copper, mercury, gold, and silver; agriculture (beef cattle, sheep).
Recreation Areas: National forests, 4; national recreation area, 1; state parks and recreation areas, 16.
Points of Interest: Lehman Caves National Monument; Lake Tahoe area; Las Vegas; Reno; Virginia City; Liberty open-pit copper mine (near Ely); Lake Mead National Recreation Area; Hoover Dam.

KEY EVENTS IN NEVADA

1775–76 Spanish missionary Francisco Garcés crosses southern Nevada en route to California.
1825 Humboldt River discovered by fur trapper Peter Skeen Ogden of Hudson's Bay Company.
1830 Old Spanish Trail pioneered across Nevada from Santa Fe to Los Angeles by William Wolfskill.
1833 California Trail from Utah across Sierra Nevada mountains pioneered by Joseph R. Walker.
1848 U.S. acquires Nevada in Mexican War.
1849 First permanent settlement established at Mormon Station (now Genoa) by H.S. Beatie.
1850 Nevada included in new Utah Territory.
1859 (June 11) Rich Comstock silver lode discovered near Virginia City, starting rush of prospectors.
1861 (March 2) Territory of Nevada created.
1864 (Oct. 31) Nevada becomes 36th U.S. state.
1931 Nevada legalizes gambling; also reduces residence requirements for divorce to 6 weeks.
1936 Hoover Dam on Colorado River completed.
1951 Atomic weapons tests begun by U.S. government on Yucca Flats range northwest of Las Vegas.
1978 Nevada moves ahead of North Dakota to rank 45th in population.
1982 Fastest growth rate among states increases population 10.0% since 1980.

NEW HAMPSHIRE

Area: 9,279 square miles; 24,031 sq. km.
Population: 951,000 (1982); 920,610 (1980).
Capital: Concord.
Flower: Purple lilac.
Tree: White birch.
Bird: Purple finch.
Song: *Old New Hampshire.*
Nickname: The Granite State.
Motto: Live Free or Die.
Flag: State seal centered on blue field.
Leading Industries: Manufacturing (machinery, paper, leather products), tourism, food processing, agriculture (dairying, poultry, beef cattle, fruits, vegetables).
Climate (Concord): *Normal temperatures:* Jan. high 31 ° F., low 10 ° F.; July high 83 ° F., low 57 ° F. *Normal yearly precipitation:* 36" (water). *Record snowstorm:* 19" in January 1944.
Recreation Areas: National forest, 1; state parks and recreation areas, 67.
Points of Interest: Lake Winnipesaukee; White Mountains; North Conway (resort); Portsmouth (old shipbuilding town); Saint-Gaudens National Historic Site (Cornish); President Franklin Pierce's homestead (Hillsboro); Daniel Webster's birthplace (near Salisbury); Mt. Washington cog railway; Profile Mountain at Franconia Notch.

KEY EVENTS IN NEW HAMPSHIRE

1603 Mouth of Piscataqua River explored for England by Martin Pring.
1622 (Aug. 10) Region of New Hampshire and Maine granted to John Mason and Sir Ferdinando Gorges by England.
1623 First English settlements established at what are now Rye and Dover.
1629 (Nov. 7) Region divided by Mason and Gorges, with Mason keeping New Hampshire.
1641 (Oct. 9) New Hampshire settlements unite with Massachusetts.
1675–76 Many settlers killed by Indian raids in King Philip's War.
1679 (Sept. 8) New Hampshire made separate royal colony.
1689–1763 In French and Indian War New Hampshire's settlements suffer many raids.
1774 (Dec. 11–12) Patriots capture British Fort William and Mary in Portsmouth, carrying off 100 barrels of gunpowder and 15 cannon.
1776 (Jan. 5) First state constitution adopted.
1776 (June 15) New Hampshire assembly votes for independence from Britain; state's delegates receive honor of being first to vote for Declaration of Independence in Continental Congress on July 4.
1788 (June 21) New Hampshire becomes 9th U.S. state; ratification puts U.S. Constitution into effect.
1803 First cotton textile factory in state built at New Ipswich.
1838 First railroad completed in state.
1852 State abolishes property ownership qualifications for elected state officials.
1963 New Hampshire becomes first state to adopt legal lottery as support for public education.
1978–79 Only state with neither income tax nor sales tax experiences boom as industries move in.
1982 Fastest growth among New England states increases population 3.3% since 1980.

NEW JERSEY

Area: 7,787 square miles; 20,169 sq. km.
Population: 7,438,000 (1982); 7,365,011 (1980).
Capital: Trenton.
Flower: Purple violet.
Tree: Red oak.
Bird: Eastern goldfinch.
Insect: Honeybee. **Animal:** horse.
Song (unofficial): *New Jersey Loyalty Song.*
Nickname: The Garden State.
Motto: Liberty and Prosperity.
Flag: State coat of arms on yellow field.
Leading Industries: Chemicals and pharmaceuticals, machinery, food processing, electronics, industrial research, agriculture (vegetables, dairying, poultry), tourism, gambling.
Climate (Newark): *Normal temperatures:* Jan. high 39 ° F., low 24 ° F.; July high 86 ° F., low 67 ° F. *Normal yearly precipitation:* 41" (water). *Record snowstorm:* 26" in December 1947.
Recreation Areas: State parks and recreation areas, 104; numerous beach resorts.
Points of Interest: Morristown National Historical Park; Edison National Historic Site (West Orange); restored colonial village of Batsto (in Wharton Tract State Forest); Walt Whitman House (Camden); Grover Cleveland Museum (Caldwell); Princeton University; Atlantic City boardwalk; Gateway National Recreation Area; Delaware Water Gap north of Columbia, N.J.

KEY EVENTS IN NEW JERSEY

1524 New Jersey coast explored for France by Giovanni da Verrazano.
1609 Delaware Bay and Sandy Hook Bay explored by Henry Hudson for Netherlands.
1623 Dutch establish Fort Nassau near present-day Gloucester.
1660 Dutch build first permanent settlement at Bergen, now in Jersey City.
1664 Dutch surrender New Jersey to England; English found first permanent settlement at Elizabethtown.
1665 New Jersey organized as English colony under Gov. Philip Carteret.
1676 New Jersey divided into two colonies: East Jersey owned by Sir George Carteret and West Jersey owned by William Penn and other Quakers.
1682 East Jersey also acquired by William Penn and other Quakers, but colony remains divided.
1702 (April 26) Proprietors of both Jerseys surrender government control to England's Queen Anne.
1702–38 New Jersey united with own legislature, but administered by royal governor of New York.
1738–76 New Jersey separated from New York with its own royal governor.
1776 (June 17) Patriots arrest royal Gov. William Franklin, son of Benjamin Franklin.
1776 (July 2) First state constitution adopted.
1776–81 In Revolutionary War many battles fought in New Jersey, including Trenton (1776), Princeton (1777), and Monmouth (1778).
1787 (Dec. 18) New Jersey becomes 3d U.S. state, ratifying U.S. Constitution.
1800 Women first vote in Elizabethtown.
1807 Law restricts voting rights to men.
1871 System of free public schools adopted.
1952 New Jersey Turnpike opens, linking New York City and Philadelphia by superhighway.
1976 State income tax adopted to finance public schools.
1978 Legal gambling casino opens in Atlantic City.
1982 Population grows only 1.0% since 1980.

NEW MEXICO

Area: 121,593 square miles; 314,923 sq. km.
Population: 1,359,000 (1982); 1,303,046 (1980).
Capital: Santa Fe.
Flower: Yucca.

NEW MEXICO *(continued)*
Tree: Piñon.
Bird: Roadrunner.
Gem: Turquoise.
Animal: Black bear.
Fish: Cutthroat trout.
Songs: *O, Fair New Mexico* and *Asi es Nuevo Mejico.*
Nickname: The Land of Enchantment.
Motto: *Crescit Eundo* (It Grows as It Goes).
Flag: Stylized red sun centered on yellow field.
Leading Industries: Mining (petroleum, natural gas, uranium, potash, copper), agriculture (beef cattle, sheep, cotton, vegetables, wheat), food processing, atomic research, forestry.
Climate (Albuquerque): *Normal temperatures:* Jan. high 47° F., low 24° F.; July high 92° F., low 65° F. *Normal yearly precipitation:* 8" water). *Record snowstorm:* 14.2" in December 1958.
Recreation Areas: National park, 1; national forests, 7; state parks and recreation areas, 34.
Points of Interest: Carlsbad Caverns National Park; Aztec Ruins, Bandelier, Capulin Mountain, Chaco Canyon, El Morro, Fort Union, Fossil Butte, Gran Quivira, Pecos, White Sands, and Gila Cliff Dwellings national monuments; Taos and Acoma pueblos; Santa Fe; Intertribal Indian Ceremonial (Gallup); Bradbury Science Hall (Los Alamos); Gila Wilderness (near Silver City); Glorieta Battle Site (near Pecos).

KEY EVENTS IN NEW MEXICO

c.1528–39 Region explored for Spain by Alvar Núñez Cabeza de Vaca, Estéban, and Marcos de Niza.
1540–42 Spanish conquistador Francisco Vásquez de Coronado conquers Indian pueblos.
1598 First Spanish settlement established on Rio Grande River by Juan de Oñate.
1610 Santa Fe made capital of New Mexico.
1680 Revolt of Pueblo Indians led by Popé drives Spanish settlers out of New Mexico.
1692–96 Spanish rule restored by Diego de Vargas.
1821 Santa Fe Trail pioneered between New Mexico and Missouri by trader William Becknell.
1846–48 U.S. occupies and acquires New Mexico in Mexican War.
1850 (Sept. 9) Territory of New Mexico created.
1854 Southern New Mexico acquired from Mexico in Gadsden Purchase.
1861–62 Confederate troops from Texas capture New Mexico, but Union forces recapture territory; main battles at Apache Canyon and Glorieta Pass.
1862–65 Kit Carson leads New Mexican settlers in subduing Navajo and Apache Indians.
1867 (March 2) Peonage abolished by Congress.
1876–78 Lincoln County War among rival cattlemen ends after Gov. Lew Wallace declares martial law.
1878 (Nov. 30) Railroad reaches New Mexico.
1879–86 Apache Indians raid and massacre settlers until surrender of Chief Geronimo.
1881 Outlaw Billy the Kid killed by Sheriff Pat Garrett near Fort Sumner.
1912 (Jan. 6) New Mexico becomes 47th state.
1916 (March 9) Raid by Mexican bandit Pancho Villa on Columbus kills 17 persons; U.S. troops under Gen. John J. Pershing invade Mexico on March 15 in pursuit of Villa.
1945 (July 16) First atomic bomb successfully tested near Alamogordo.
1982 High growth rate increases population 4.3% since 1980.

NEW YORK

Area: 49,108 square miles; 127,189 sq. km.
Population: 17,659,000 (1982); 17,558,072 (1980).
Capital: Albany.
Flower: Rose.
Tree: Sugar maple.
Bird: Bluebird.
Animal: American beaver.
Fish: Brook trout.
Gem: Garnet.
Nickname: The Empire State.
Motto: *Excelsior* (Ever Upward).
Flag: State coat of arms centered on blue field.
Leading Industries: Manufacturing (leading state), agriculture (dairy products, fruits, vegetables), mining (iron ore, petroleum, salt).
Climate (New York City): *Normal temperatures:* Jan. high 39° F., low 26° F.; July high 85° F., low 68° F. *Normal yearly precipitation:* 40" (water). *Record snowstorm:* 26.4" in December 1947.
Recreation Areas: National seashore, 1; state parks and recreation areas, 169.
Points of Interest: Castle Clinton, Fort Stanwix, and Statue of Liberty national monuments; Niagara Falls; Saratoga National Historical Park; U.S. Military Academy (West Point); national historic sites include homes of F. D. Roosevelt at Hyde Park, of Theodore Roosevelt in Oyster Bay and New York City, Vanderbilt mansion near Hyde Park, and St. Paul's Church; national memorials include General Grant's tomb and Federal Hall in New York City; Fort Ticonderoga; Baseball Hall of Fame (Cooperstown); Finger Lakes, Adirondacks, and Catskill areas; Fire Island National Seashore; Boscobel (Garrison); Gateway National Recreation Area; skyscrapers, museums, theaters, and parks in New York City.

KEY EVENTS IN NEW YORK

1524 New York Bay explored for France by Giovanni da Verrazano.
1609 (July) Northern New York explored and claimed for France by Samuel de Champlain.
1609 (Sept. 11–Oct. 4) Hudson River explored for Dutch by Henry Hudson.
1614 First Dutch trading post, Fort Nassau, built on Castle Island at present-day Albany.
1624 First permanent Dutch settlement established in New Netherland (New York) at Fort Orange (now Albany).
1625 New Amsterdam (New York City) founded by Dutch settlers; Manhattan Island purchased from Indians for about $24 in 1626.
1664 (Sept. 8) Dutch surrender New Amsterdam to English.
1673–74 Dutch reoccupy New York but return it to England in exchange for colony of Surinam in South America.
1683 (Oct. 30) Charter of liberties adopted; freedom of religion guaranteed; taxation to be permitted only by consent of voters.
1689–1763 French and Indian War: New York is battleground for frequent battles against French and their Indian allies.
1735 (Aug. 4) Freedom of press established in trial of John Peter Zenger on basis that truth is not libel.
1775–83 In Revolutionary War British occupy New York City in 1776–83; battles in state include Ticonderoga (1775), Long Island and White Plains (1776), Saratoga (1777), Stony Point (1779).
1777 (April 20) First state constitution adopted; written largely by John Jay.
1788 (July 26) New York becomes 11th U.S. state, ratifying U.S. Constitution.
1789–90 New York City serves as first capital of the United States under Constitution.
1812–14 In War of 1812 many battles fought in state.
1825 (Oct. 26) Erie Canal opens, connecting Hudson River with Great Lakes.
1827 (July 4) Slavery abolished in state.

1831 First railroad opens: Albany to Schenectady.
1832 Cholera kills 4,000 in New York City.
1863 (July 13–16) Riots in New York City protest Civil War draft, killing about 1,000 persons.
1883 (May 24) Brooklyn Bridge opens, longest suspension bridge of its day, with span of 1,595 feet.
1904 (Oct. 27) First subway completed in New York City.
1952 UN headquarters built in New York City.
1964 Verrazano-Narrows Bridge opens across New York Harbor from Brooklyn to Staten Island; suspension span, 4,260 feet.
1974 (April 5) New York City's highest building opens: twin-tower 1,353-foot World Trade Center.
1982 Population grows only 0.6% since 1980.

NORTH CAROLINA

Area: 52,669 square miles; 136,412 sq. km.
Population: 6,019,000 (1982); 5,881,385 (1980).
Capital: Raleigh.
Flower: Dogwood.
Tree: Pine.
Bird: Cardinal.
Mammal: Gray squirrel.
Fish: Channel bass.
Song: *The Old North State.*
Nickname: The Tar Heel State.
Motto: *Esse Quam Videri* (To Be Rather Than to Seem).
Flag: Blue bar to left has letters *NC* (separated by white star) in gold; red and white stripe to right.
Leading Industries: Manufacturing (leading state in textiles and tobacco products), agriculture (tobacco, corn, peanuts, soybeans, broiler chickens), forestry.
Climate (Charlotte): *Normal temperatures:* Jan. high 52 °F., low 32 °F.; July high 88 °F., low 69 °F. *Normal yearly precipitation:* 43" (water). *Record snowstorm:* 14" in February 1902.
Recreation Areas: National park, 1; national forests, 5; national seashores, 2; state parks and recreation areas, 19.
Points of Interest: Great Smoky National Park (partly in Tennessee); the Blue Ridge Parkway; Cape Hatteras National Seashore; Guilford Courthouse and Moores Creek national military parks; Carl Sandburg home (near Hendersonville) and Fort Raleigh national historic sites; Roanoke Island; Wright Brothers National Memorial (Kitty Hawk); Tryon Palace restoration (New Bern); Alamance Battlefield (Burlington); Biltmore Estate (near Asheville); Old Salem restoration (Winston-Salem).

KEY EVENTS IN NORTH CAROLINA

1524 Coast explored for France by Giovanni da Verrazano.
1585–87 English colonists sent by Sir Walter Raleigh unsuccessfully attempt twice to settle Roanoke Island.
1653 First permanent English colonists settle on Roanoke and Chowan rivers; led from Virginia by Roger Green.
1663–65 Carolina region granted to 8 proprietors by England's King Charles II; government established for northern part of region, called Albemarle County, with appointed governor and elected assembly.
1677–78 Culpeper's Rebellion: Colonists led by John Culpeper temporarily overthrow proprietary governor.
1691 Entire Carolina region begins to be ruled by proprietary governors from Charleston (now in S.C.).
1711–13 Tuscarora War: Hundreds of settlers slain in fighting with Tuscarora Indians.
1712 North Carolina separated from South Carolina with own governor.
1718 (Nov. 21) Pirate Blackbeard (Edward Teach) killed in battle near Ocracoke Island.
1729 (July 25) North Carolina becomes royal colony as King George II buys out proprietors.
1771 (May 16) Battle of Alamance: Militia led by Gov. William Tryon defeats uprising by western Regulators who protested lack of representation in legislature.
1775 (May 20) Mecklenburg Declaration of Independence said to have been adopted by patriots in Mecklenburg County.
1776 (April 12) First colony to instruct Continental Congress delegates to vote for independence.
1776 (Dec. 18) First state constitution adopted.
1776–81 In Revolutionary War major battles in state include Moores Creek Bridge (Feb. 27, 1776) and Guilford Courthouse (March 15, 1781).
1789 (Nov. 21) North Carolina becomes 12th U.S. state, ratifying U.S. Constitution.
1801–02 Gold discovered on Meadow Creek in Cabarrus County; state leads in gold production until 1850s.
1861 (May 20) State secedes, joins Confederacy.
1861–65 In Civil War many battles fought in state until surrender of Confederate Gen. Joseph E. Johnston to Union Gen. William T. Sherman near Durham (April 26, 1865).
1868 (June 25) State readmitted to Union.
1890 American Tobacco Company founded at Durham by James Buchanan Duke; cigarette manufacturing becomes leading industry in state.
1903 (Dec. 17) First airplane flight by Orville and Wilbur Wright at Kitty Hawk.
1975 North Carolina displaces Indiana as 11th- ranking state in population.
1982 Population grows 2.3% since 1980.

NORTH DAKOTA

Area: 70,702 square miles; 183,118 sq. km.
Population: 670,000 (1982); 652,717 (1980).
Capital: Bismarck.
Flower: Wild prairie rose.
Tree: American elm.
Bird: Western meadowlark.
Stone: Teredo petrified wood.
Fish: Northern pike.
Song: *North Dakota Hymn.*
March: *Spirit of the Land.*
Nicknames: The Sioux State; The Flickertail State.
Motto: Liberty and Union, Now and Forever, One and Inseparable.
Flag: Modified Seal of U.S. on blue field.
Leading Industries: Agriculture (wheat, flaxseed, barley, rye, beef cattle, sheep, hogs), food processing, mining (petroleum, lignite).
Climate (Bismarck): *Normal temperatures:* Jan. high 19 °F., low –3 °F.; July high 84 °F., low 57 °F. *Normal yearly precipitation:* 16" (water). *Record snowstorm:* 15.5" in March 1966.
Recreation Areas: State parks and recreation areas, 20.
Points of Interest: International Peace Garden (near Dunseith); Fort Union Trading Post (partly in Montana) National Historic Site; Theodore Roosevelt National Memorial Park; State Capitol (Bismarck); Fort Lincoln State Park (south of Mandan); Fort Abercrombie; Lake Sakakawea; Slant Village restoration (near Mandan); Badlands.

KEY EVENTS IN NORTH DAKOTA

1738 Region explored for France by Pierre Gaultier de Varennes, Sieur de La Vérendrye.
1803 U.S. acquires most of North Dakota in Louisiana Purchase from France.
1804–06 Region explored for U.S. by Meriwether Lewis and William Clark; Fort Mandan built 1804.
1812 First settlement established at Pembina by Scottish and Irish families from Canada.

NORTH DAKOTA *(continued)*

1818 Northeastern part of state acquired by U.S. by treaty with Britain.
1823 (Aug. 8) U.S. takes possession of Pembina.
1832 Missouri River steamboat reaches Fort Union.
1861 (March 2) Territory of Dakota created.
1863–64 Battles fought between U.S. troops and Sioux Indians.
1872 Bismarck founded.
1872 Construction begun on railroad across state.
1889 (Nov. 2) Becomes 39th U.S. state.
1912 First presidential preference primary held.
1914 Referendum process adopted.
1920 Recall procedure adopted.
1951 Petroleum discovered near Tioga.
1960 Garrison Dam completed, forming Lake Sakakawea.
1977 Bingo and lottery gambling legalized.
1981 (July 1) Blackjack gambling legalized in bars, restaurants and motels.
1982 Population grows 2.6% since 1980.

OHIO

Area: 41,330 square miles; 107,043 sq. km.
Population: 10,791,000 (1982); 10,797,624 (1980).
Capital: Columbus.
Flower: Scarlet carnation.
Tree: Buckeye.
Bird: Cardinal.
Insect: Ladybug.
Stone: Ohio flint. **Beverage:** Tomato juice.
Song: *Beautiful Ohio.*
Nickname: The Buckeye State.
Motto: With God, All Things Are Possible.
Flag: White-bordered red circle and blue stars on blue triangle to left; red and white stripes to right.
Leading Industries: Manufacturing (transportation equipment, machinery, metals, rubber products), agriculture (hogs, beef cattle, sheep, dairy products), mining (coal, petroleum).
Climate (Cleveland): *Normal temperatures:* Jan. high 33 ° F., low 20 ° F.; July high 82 ° F., low 61 ° F. *Normal yearly precipitation:* 35" (water). *Record snowstorm:* 17.4" in November 1913.
Recreation Areas: National forest, 1; state parks and recreation areas, 62.
Points of Interest: Mound City Group National Monument (Indian burial grounds); Perry's Victory International Peace Memorial; Presidents' homes: Grant (Point Pleasant), Taft (Cincinnati), Hayes (Fremont), Harding (Marion), and Garfield (Mentor); birthplace of Thomas A. Edison (Milan); Fort Recovery; Campus Martius Museum (Marietta); Pro Football Hall of Fame (Canton); Schoenbrunn village, New Philadelphia.

KEY EVENTS IN OHIO

1669–70 Region explored for France by Robert Cavelier, Sieur de La Salle.
1763 Britain wins region in French and Indian War.
1772 Moravian settlement at Schoenbrunn near present-day New Philadelphia; abandoned in 1776.
1780 (Aug. 6–8) Shawnee Indian villages of Chillicothe and Piqua destroyed by George Rogers Clark.
1782 (March 8) Massacre of 96 Christian Indians by frontiersmen at Gnadenhutten.
1782 (June 4–6) U.S. Col. William Crawford and 480 militia defeated by British and Indians near Upper Sandusky; Crawford tortured to death on June 11.
1783 Region acquired by U.S. in Revolutionary War.
1788 (April 7) First permanent settlement established at Marietta, capital of Northwest Territory.
1790–95 Severe fighting with Indians; major battle won by Maj. Gen. Anthony Wayne at Fallen Timbers near present-day Maumee (Aug. 20, 1794).
1803 (March 1) Ohio becomes 17th U.S. state.
1812–14 In War of 1812 frontier forts withstand sieges; Commodore Oliver H. Perry defeats British in Battle of Lake Erie (Sept. 10, 1813).
1832 Ohio and Erie Canal completed.
1845 Miami and Erie Canal connects Toledo and Cincinnati.
1852 Railroad reaches Cleveland from Pittsburgh.
1863 (July 26) Raiding Confederate Gen. John H. Morgan captured near New Lisbon.
1913 (March 25–27) Floods in Ohio and Indiana kill 732 persons, cause over $180 million in damage.
1967 First black mayor elected by major U.S. city: Carl B. Stokes, in Cleveland.
1971 State income tax adopted.
1982 Population decreases 0.1% since 1980.

OKLAHOMA

Area: 69,956 square miles; 181,185 sq. km.
Population: 3,177,000 (1982); 3,025,495 (1980).
Capital: Oklahoma City.
Flower: Mistletoe.
Tree: Redbud.
Bird: Scissor-tailed flycatcher.
Fish: White bass.
Stone: Barite rose (rose rock).
Animal: American buffalo.
Reptile: Mountain boomer lizard.
Song: *Oklahoma.*
Nickname: The Sooner State.
Motto: *Labor Omnia Vincit* (Labor Conquers All Things).
Flag: Symbols above "Oklahoma" on blue field.
Leading Industries: Manufacturing and food processing, oil refining, agriculture (beef cattle, wheat), oil and natural-gas mining.
Climate (Oklahoma City): *Normal temperatures:* Jan. high 48 ° F., low 26 ° F.; July high 93 ° F., low 70 ° F. *Normal yearly precipitation:* 31" (water). *Record snowstorm:* 11.3" in March 1924.
Recreation Areas: National park, 1; national forest, 1; national recreation area, 1; state parks and recreation areas, 76.
Points of Interest: Lake Texoma recreation area; Philbrook Art Center (Tulsa); Will Rogers Memorial (Claremore); Indian City (Andarko); Fort Sill Military Reservation (Lawton); National Cowboy Hall of Fame and Oklahoma Historical Society (Oklahoma City); Chickasaw National Recreation Area (formerly Platt National Park and Arbuckle National Recreation Area).

KEY EVENTS IN OKLAHOMA

1541 Region explored for Spain by Francisco Vásquez de Coronado.
1803 U.S. acquires most of Oklahoma in Louisiana Purchase from France.
1821 Santa Fe Trail pioneered across region by American trader William Becknell.
1823–42 Eastern Indian tribes forced to move to Oklahoma region, then known as Indian Territory.
1845 Western Panhandle region of Oklahoma acquired by U.S. with annexation of Texas.
1889 (April 22) U.S. opens part of Oklahoma to settlement; some 50,000 settlers rush in on first day.
1890 (May 2) Territory of Oklahoma created.
1893 (Sept. 16) Cherokee Outlet opened to settlement; 50,000 to 100,000 settlers rush into area.
1897 First major oil well produces at Bartlesville.
1907 (Nov. 16) Oklahoma becomes 46th U.S. state.
1934–35 Drought develops "dust bowl"; farmers abandon farms; "Okies" move to California.
1970 Arkansas River made navigable, turning Tulsa and Muskogee into important river ports.
1982 Population grows 5.0% since 1980.

OREGON

Area: 97,073 square miles; 251,417 sq. km.
Population: 2,649,000 (1982); 2,633,149 (1980).
Capital: Salem.
Flower: Oregon grape.
Tree: Douglas fir.
Bird: Western meadowlark.
Stone: Thunder egg.
Animal: Beaver.
Fish: Chinook salmon.
Song: *Oregon, My Oregon.*
Nickname: The Beaver State.
Motto: The Union.
Flag: State seal with "State of Oregon" above it on blue field.
Leading Industries: Lumbering and forestry, food processing, manufacturing, agriculture (beef cattle, dairy products, wheat, vegetables, fruits, nuts, flowers).
Climate (Portland): *Normal temperatures:* Jan. high 44° F., low 33° F.; July high 79° F., low 55° F. *Normal yearly precipitation:* 38" (water). *Record snowstorm:* 16" in January 1937.
Recreation Areas: National park, 1; national forests, 15; state parks and recreation areas, 235.
Points of Interest: Crater Lake National Park; Mt. Hood; Oregon Caves National Monument; Oregon Dunes; Cape Perpetua (in Siuslaw National Forest); Columbia River gorge between The Dalles and Troutdale; Bonneville Dam; Hells Canyon; Fort Clatsop National Memorial; McLoughlin House National Historic Site; Picture Gorge and John Day Fossil Beds near Dayville; Sea Lion Caves near Florence.

KEY EVENTS IN OREGON

1500s–1600s Spanish and English sailors sight coast; Sir Francis Drake in 1579.
1770s–1780s U.S. and British ships visit coast, trading with Indians for furs.
1792 (May 7) Columbia River discovered and named by U.S. Capt. Robert Gray, establishing U.S. claim to area.
1805 Fort Clatsop built by Meriwether Lewis and William Clark near mouth of Columbia River.
1811 Astoria established as first American settlement by fur trader John Jacob Astor.
1812–13 Oregon Trail pioneered to Missouri by fur trader Robert Stuart.
1818 (Oct. 20) U.S. and Britain sign convention agreeing on joint control of Oregon region; renewed in 1827.
1819 (Feb. 2) U.S. and Spain sign Adams-Onís Treaty: Spain gives up claim to Oregon region.
1825–46 Region controlled by Hudson's Bay Company's John McLoughlin; becomes known as "Father of Oregon."
1840s American settlers arrive by hundreds along Oregon Trail.
1846 (Aug. 5) Oregon Treaty goes into effect: Britain gives up claims to Oregon region.
1848 (Aug. 14) Territory of Oregon created.
1851–58 Indian Wars in eastern Oregon.
1859 (Feb. 14) Oregon becomes 33d U.S. state.
1877–78 Fighting by settlers with Nez Percé, Paiute, and Bannock Indians.
1902 (June 2) First statewide initiative and referendum law adopted.
1908 First statewide recall law adopted.
1912 Women given right to vote.
1937 Bonneville Dam completed on Columbia River.
1964 Worst floods in state's history.
1972 First environmental "bottle law" adopted, outlawing nonreturnable beverage containers.
1978 Oregon moves ahead of Mississippi to rank 29th in population among the states.
1982 Population grows 0.6% since 1980.

PENNSYLVANIA

Area: 45,308 square miles; 117,347 sq. km.
Population: 11,865,000 (1982); 11,864,751 (1980).
Capital: Harrisburg.
Flower: Mountain laurel.
Tree: Hemlock.
Bird: Ruffed grouse.
Dog: Great Dane.
Animal: Whitetail deer.
Fish: Brook trout. **Insect:** Firefly.
Nickname: The Keystone State.
Motto: Virtue, Liberty and Independence.
Flag: Gold-bordered blue field with state coat of arms flanked by horse on either side.
Leading Industries: Manufacturing (steel, machinery, metal products), agriculture (dairy products, beef cattle, poultry, corn, mushrooms), mining (coal, petroleum, natural gas).
Climate (Philadelphia): *Normal temperatures:* Jan. high 40° F., low 24° F.; July high 87° F., low 67° F. *Normal yearly precipitation:* 40" (water). *Record snowstorm:* 21" in December 1909.
Recreation Areas: National forest, 1; state parks and recreation areas, 152.
Points of Interest: Gettysburg National Military Park; Valley Forge National Historical Park; Independence National Historical Park (in Philadelphia); Delaware Water Gap National Recreation Area; Pennsylvania Dutch region; Fort Necessity National Battlefield; national historic sites include Eisenhower farm near Gettysburg, Gloria Dei Church, Hopewell Village (near Reading); national memorials include Benjamin Franklin, Johnstown Flood, and Thaddeus Kosciusko; Cloisters restoration in Ephrata. Oliver Hazard Perry's flagship *Niagara* from War of 1812 (at Erie); Pennsylvania Farm Museum of Landis Valley (near Lancaster).

KEY EVENTS IN PENNSYLVANIA

1609 (Aug. 28) Delaware Bay explored for Netherlands by Henry Hudson.
1643 First Swedish settlements established on Tinicum Island in Schuylkill River near present-day Philadelphia, and at Upland (now Chester).
1655 Dutch from New York capture New Sweden.
1664 England acquires region with capture of New York.
1681 Philadelphia surveyed and laid out by Thomas Holme as capital of Pennsylvania.
1681 (March 14) Pennsylvania granted to William Penn by King Charles II.
1682 (Oct. 29) William Penn arrives at Upland, renaming it Chester.
1754–63 French and Indian War: Begins with skirmish at Great Meadows, Pa., between Lt. Col. George Washington and French on May 28; Washington surrenders Fort Necessity, Pa., to French (July 4, 1754).
1755 (July 9) British Maj. Gen. Edward Braddock killed and army routed by French near Fort Duquesne (Pittsburgh).
1758 (Nov. 25) British capture Fort Duquesne; rename it Fort Pitt.
1763 Indian Chief Pontiac wages war on frontier settlers.
1775–83 In Revolutionary War Congress meets in Philadelphia for most of period; major battles in state include Brandywine and Germantown (1777); Army winters at Valley Forge (1777–78).
1776 (Sept. 28) First state constitution adopted at convention presided over by Benjamin Franklin.
1787 (Dec. 12) Pennsylvania becomes 2d U.S. state, ratifying U.S. Constitution.
1790–1800 Philadelphia serves as capital of U.S.
1792 State purchases triangle of land on Lake Erie.
1794 Whisky Rebellion in western Pennsylvania as

PENNSYLVANIA *(continued)*
farmers protest federal whisky taxes; put down by militia.
1795 First paved turnpike in U.S. completed from Philadelphia to Lancaster.
1811 (Oct. 29) First Ohio River steamboat leaves Pittsburgh for New Orleans.
1829 First railroad begins operation.
1859 First successful oil well in U.S. drilled near Titusville by Edwin Drake.
1863 (July 1–3) Battle of Gettysburg: Turning point of Civil War as Union army defeats invasion of Pennsylvania by Confederate army of Gen. Robert E. Lee.
1889 (May 31) Flood caused by burst dam at Johnstown kills 2,209 persons.
1957 First full-scale atomic energy plant in U.S. to produce electricity opens at Shippingport.
1971 State income tax adopted.
1975 State drops from 3d to 4th in population rank among states.
1982 Population remains same since 1980.

RHODE ISLAND

Area: 1,212 square miles; 3,140 sq. km.
Population: 958,000 (1982); 947,154 (1980).
Capital: Providence.
Flower: Violet.
Tree: Red maple.
Bird: Rhode Island red.
Rock: Cumberlandite.
Mineral: Bowenite.
Song: *Rhode Island.*
Nickname: Little Rhody.
Motto: Hope.
Flag: White field with gold anchor with state motto underneath, surrounded by 13 gold stars.
Leading Industries: Manufacturing (jewelry, silverware, textiles, machinery), food processing, agriculture (dairy products, vegetables, poultry).
Climate (Providence): *Normal temperatures:* Jan. high 36 ° F., low 21 ° F.; July high 81 ° F., low 63 ° F. *Normal yearly precipitation:* 43" (water). *Record snowstorm:* 18.3" in February 1961.
Recreation Areas: State parks and recreation areas, 85.
Points of Interest: Roger Williams National Memorial (Providence); Samuel Slater's Mill (Pawtucket); Touro Synagogue National Historic Site (Newport); Gilbert Stuart birthplace (North Kingstown); Gen. Nathanael Greene homestead (Coventry); Vanderbilt mansions (Newport); Block Island; Narragansett Pier.

KEY EVENTS IN RHODE ISLAND

1524 Narragansett Bay explored for France by Giovanni da Verrazano.
1614 Explored for Dutch by Adriaen Block.
1636 (June) First English settlement established at Providence by Roger Williams, providing religious freedom.
1644 (March 14) England grants patent for colony of Providence Plantations; four settlements in Rhode Island unite under this patent in 1647.
1663 (July 8) Colony of Rhode Island and Providence Plantations granted new charter by King Charles II; charter remains state's constitution until 1843.
1675–76 King Philip's War: Many settlers killed in fighting with Indians; Wampanoag chief King Philip slain by settlers near present-day Bristol.
1772 (June 9) Patriots destroy British revenue schooner *Gaspée* in Narragansett Bay.
1776 (May 4) Independence from Britain declared by Rhode Island's legislature.
1776–79 British occupy Newport, defeating American-French effort to dislodge them in August 1778.
1787 State refuses to send delegates to U.S. Constitutional Convention in Philadelphia.
1790 (May 29) Rhode Island becomes 13th U.S. state, ratifying U.S. Constitution by narrow vote of 34 to 32.
1790 (Dec. 21) First textile factory in U.S. begins operation at Pawtucket, built by Samuel Slater.
1842 Dorr's Rebellion: Thomas Dorr and followers set up own state government protesting property requirements for voting.
1870 Imprisonment for debt abolished.
1888 Property qualifications for voters abolished.
1969 Newport Bridge built across Narragansett Bay with 1,600-foot suspension span.
1982 Population grows 1.2% since 1980, making state 41st in population rank.

SOUTH CAROLINA

Area: 31,113 square miles; 80,582 sq. km.
Population: 3,203,000 (1982); 3,122,814 (1980).
Capital: Columbia.
Flower: Carolina jessamine.
Tree: Palmetto.
Bird: Carolina wren.
Stone: Blue granite.
Song: *Carolina.*
Nickname: The Palmetto State.
Mottoes: *Animis Opibusque Parati* (Prepared in Mind and Resources) and *Dum Spiro Spero* (While I Breathe, I Hope).
Flag: Blue field with centered white palmetto and crescent in upper left corner.
Leading Industries: Manufacturing (textiles, chemicals, machinery), agriculture (tobacco, soybeans, cotton, beef cattle, hogs), forestry.
Climate (Columbia): *Normal temperatures:* Jan. high 57 ° F., low 34 ° F.; July high 92 ° F., low 70 ° F. *Normal yearly precipitation:* 46" (water). *Record snowstorm:* 15.7" in February 1973.
Recreation Areas: National forests, 2; state parks and recreation areas, 38; Atlantic beach resorts.
Points of Interest: Fort Sumter National Monument, Fort Moultrie, Fort Johnson, and aircraft carrier USS *Yorktown,* in Charlestown Harbor; Cowpens National Battlefield; Kings Mountain National Military Park; Middleton, Magnolia, and Cypress gardens, Charleston; Brookgreen Gardens, Georgetown; Camden and Eutaw Springs battlefields; Hilton Head resorts.

KEY EVENTS IN SOUTH CAROLINA

1521 Coast explored for Spain by Francisco de Gordillo.
1526–27 Spaniards unsuccessfully try to found colony near present-day Georgetown; led by Lucas Vásquez de Ayllón.
1562–64 French Huguenots unsuccessfully try to colonize Parris Island near Port Royal.
1566–1650 Spaniards occupy Port Royal (which they call Santa Elena).
1663–65 Carolina region granted to eight proprietors by England's King Charles II.
1670 First English settlement established at Albemarle Point on west bank of Ashley River; in 1680 settlement (renamed Charles Town) moves across river; town renamed Charlestown in 1783.
1706 French-Spanish attack on Charles Town driven off.
1711–13 Indian war between settlers and Tuscaroras.
1712 South Carolina separated from North Carolina, each with own governor.
1715 About 400 settlers killed in war with Yamassee Indians.
1719 (Nov. 28) Rebellion against proprietary government; colonists choose James Moore as governor.
1721 (May 29) New royal governor takes office.

SOUTH CAROLINA *(continued)*

1729 (July 25) South Carolina becomes royal colony as King George II buys out 7 of 8 proprietors.

1775 (Sept. 15) Last royal governor flees to British warship.

1776 (March 26) First temporary constitution adopted; new constitution adopted March 19, 1778.

1776–81 In Revolutionary War state suffers extensive fighting; British attacks on Charles Town beaten back on June 28, 1776, and May 11–12, 1779; British capture Charles Town on May 12, 1780, after two-month siege; other major battles: Stono Ferry on June 20, 1779, Camden on Aug. 16, 1780, Kings Mountain on Oct. 7, 1780, Cowpens on Jan. 17, 1781, Hobkirk's Hill on April 25, 1781, and Eutaw Springs on Sept. 8, 1781.

1788 (May 23) South Carolina becomes 8th U.S. state, ratifying U.S. Constitution.

1832 (Nov. 24) Ordinance of Nullification adopted, forbidding collection of federal tariffs in state; repealed in 1833 after President Andrew Jackson threatens force.

1860 (Dec. 20) First state to secede from Union.

1861 (April 12) Civil War begins as South Carolina troops attack federal Fort Sumter in Charleston Harbor.

1861–65 In Civil War Charleston withstands Union siege from March 1863 to February 1865; in 1865 Union Gen. William T. Sherman marches across state destroying plantations and burning capital city Columbia.

1868 (June 25) Readmitted to Union.

1877 (March) Federal troop occupation ends.

1941 Santee Dam completed, providing hydroelectric power for Charleston area.

1953 Huge $1.4 billion Savannah River plant near Aiken begins production of atomic materials.

1975–79 First elected Republican governor since Reconstruction era: James B. Edwards.

1982 Population increases 2.6% since 1980.

SOUTH DAKOTA

Area: 77,116 square miles; 199,729 sq. km.
Population: 691,000 (1982); 690,768 (1980).
Capital: Pierre.
Flower: Pasqueflower.
Tree: Black Hills spruce.
Bird: Ringnecked pheasant.
Stone: Black Hills gold.
Animal: Coyote.
Song: *Hail, South Dakota.*
Nickname: The Coyote State.
Motto: Under God the People Rule.
Flag: Blue field with centered yellow sun encircled by "South Dakota the Sunshine State."
Leading Industries: Agriculture (beef cattle, hogs, sheep, wheat, corn, soybeans), food processing, mining (gold, uranium, petroleum), tourism.
Climate (Sioux Falls): *Normal temperatures:* Jan. high 25° F., low 4° F.; July high 85° F., low 62° F. *Normal yearly precipitation:* 25" (water). *Record snowstorm:* 26" on Feb. 17–18, 1962.
Recreation Areas: National park, 1; national forests, 2; state parks and recreation areas, 1.
Points of Interest: Black Hills region (including Wind Cave National Park, Mt. Rushmore National Memorial, and Jewel Cave National Monument); Badlands National Monument near Rapid City; Deadwood; Crazy Horse memorial near Custer; Corn Palace in Mitchell.

KEY EVENTS IN SOUTH DAKOTA

1743 (March 30) Region claimed for France by Louis-Joseph and François de La Vérendrye; plant lead plate at present-day Fort Pierre (plate discovered 1913).

1803 U.S. acquires region in Louisiana Purchase.

1804–06 Region explored for U.S. by Meriwether Lewis and William Clark.

1817 Fort Pierre established as fur trading post.

1831 Missouri River steamboat reaches Fort Pierre.

1861 (March 2) Territory of Dakota created.

1873 Railroad reaches capital at Yankton.

1874–75 Gold discovered in Black Hills.

1876 Frontiersman Wild Bill Hickok shot to death in Deadwood saloon.

1889 (Nov. 2) Becomes 40th U.S. state.

1890 (Dec. 29) Wounded Knee Massacre of 300 captive Sioux Indians by federal troops; last Indian war in West.

1930–40 Drought, grasshoppers, and depression bankrupt many farmers; about 50,000 leave state.

1963 Oahe Dam completed on Missouri River at Pierre.

1972 (June 9–10) Flood at Rapid City kills 242 persons.

1973 (Feb. 27–May 8) Siege of Wounded Knee: Indians occupy village to protest federal Indian policies.

1982 Population remains same since 1980, making state 45th in population rank.

TENNESSEE

Area: 42,144 square miles; 109,151 sq. km.
Population: 4,651,000 (1982); 4,591,120 (1980).
Capital: Nashville.
Flower: Iris.
Wildflower: Passionflower.
Tree: Tulip poplar.
Bird: Mockingbird.
Animal: Raccoon.
Stone: Agate. **Rock:** Limestone.
Songs: *When It's Iris Time in Tennessee; The Tennessee Waltz; My Homeland, Tennessee;* and *My Tennessee.*
Nickname: The Volunteer State.
Motto: Agriculture and Commerce.
Flag: Three white stars in white-bordered blue circle on red field, with narrow white bar and blue bar on right.
Leading Industries: Manufacturing (chemicals, electrical equipment, clothing), food processing, agriculture (dairy products, beef cattle, hogs, soybeans, tobacco, corn, cotton), mining (coal, zinc, phosphate).
Climate (Memphis): *Normal temperatures:* Jan. high 49° F., low 32° F.; July high 92° F., low 72° F. *Normal yearly precipitation:* 49" (water). *Record snowstorm:* 18" in March 1892.
Recreation Areas: National park, 1; national forest, 1; state parks and recreation areas, 37.
Points of Interest: Great Smoky Mountains National Park; Cumberland Gap National Historical Park; Rock City Gardens (on Lookout Mountain, near Chattanooga); Chickamauga and Chattanooga, Fort Donelson, and Shiloh national military parks; The Hermitage (home of Andrew Jackson, Nashville); Andrew Johnson National Historic Site (Greeneville); American Museum of Science & Energy (Oak Ridge); Stones River National Battlefield; Parthenon reproduction (Nashville); Grand Ole Opry House and Opryland entertainment park (near Nashville).

KEY EVENTS IN TENNESSEE

1540–41 Region explored for Spain by Hernando de Soto, discovering Mississippi River.

1673 Eastern region explored for Virginia by James Needham and Gabriel Arthur; western part for France by Louis Joliet and Jacques Marquette.

1682 Region claimed for France by Robert Cavelier, Sieur de La Salle, who builds Fort Prud'homme near present-day Memphis.

1763 Britain acquires region in French and Indian War, as part of colony of North Carolina.

1784–87 State of Franklin formed by settlers, electing John Sevier as governor; disbanded when region allowed to elect representatives to North Carolina legislature.

1790 (May 26) Territory South of the River Ohio

TENNESSEE *(continued)*

created; William Blount appointed governor (Aug. 7).
1796 (June 1) Tennessee becomes 16th U.S. state.
1797 (July 7) Tennessee's U.S. Sen. William Blount becomes first person impeached (for trying to stir Indian war against Spain); expelled by U.S. Senate; impeachment dismissed in 1799.
1818 (Oct. 19) Western Tennessee purchased from Chickasaw Indians in treaty negotiated by Gen. Andrew Jackson.
1857 (March 27) Memphis and Charleston Railroad completed from Atlantic Ocean to Mississippi River.
1861 (June 24) Governor proclaims secession after people vote June 8 to join Confederacy: east Tennessee supports Union; U.S. Sen. Andrew Johnson retains seat.
1861–65 In Civil War many battles fought in state, including Fort Henry, Fort Donelson, Shiloh, Stones River, Chattanooga, Franklin, and Nashville.
1866 (July 24) Tennessee becomes first Confederate state readmitted to Union.
1878–79 Yellow-fever epidemic kills over 5,000 persons in Memphis, over fourth of population.
1933 (May 18) Tennessee Valley Authority (TVA) created by Congress, providing cheap electric power.
1942 Oak Ridge atomic-energy plant built.
1968 (April 4) Assassination of black civil-rights leader Martin Luther King Jr. at Memphis.
1979 Gov. Ray Blanton removed from office after pardoning 52 prisoners; convicted in 1981 of 11 counts of extortion, fraud, and conspiracy.
1982 Population grows 1.3% since 1980.

TEXAS

Area: 266,807 square miles; 691,026 sq. km.
Population: 15,280,000 (1982); 14,227,574 (1980).
Capital: Austin.
Flower: Bluebonnet.
Tree: Pecan.
Bird: Mockingbird.
Gem: Topaz. **Stone:** Palmwood. **Grass:** Side oats grama. **Dish:** Chili.
Song: *Texas, Our Texas.*
Nickname: The Lone Star State.
Motto: Friendship.
Flag: Lone star on blue bar on left, with red and white stripes to right.
Leading Industries: Manufacturing (chemicals, transportation equipment, petroleum refining), food processing, mining (petroleum, natural gas, sulfur, salt), agriculture (beef cattle, grain, cotton, poultry, dairy products).
Climate (Houston): *Normal temperatures:* Jan. high 63 ° F., low 42 ° F.; July high 94 ° F., low 73 ° F. *Normal yearly precipitation:* 48" (water). *Record snowstorm:* 20" on Feb. 14–15, 1895.
Recreation Areas: National parks, 2; national forests, 4; national recreation areas, 2; national seashore, 1; state parks and recreation areas, 75.
Points of Interest: Padre Island National Seashore; Big Bend and Guadalupe Mountains national parks; Gulf Coast resort area; Alamo (San Antonio); state capital (Austin); King Ranch (near Kingsville); Lyndon B. Johnson Space Center (Houston); Amistad and Lake Meredith national recreation areas; Alibates Quarries and Texas Panhandle Culture National Monument; national historic sites include Fort Davis, Lyndon B. Johnson ranch, San Jose Mission; Chamizal National Memorial; battleship USS *Texas* in Houston.

KEY EVENTS IN TEXAS

1519 Coast explored for Spain by Alonso Alvarez de Piñeda.
1682 First Spanish settlement established at Ysleta near present-day El Paso.
1685 French build Fort St. Louis at Matagorda Bay.
1821 Americans led by Stephen F. Austin settle along Brazos River in Mexican territory.
1836 (Feb. 23–March 6) Siege of Alamo: 187 Texans and frontiersmen fight to death against Mexicans.
1836 (March 2) Texas independence declared.
1836 (April 21) Battle of San Jacinto: Gen. Sam Houston defeats Mexicans; captures Mexican Gen. Antonio López de Santa Anna.
1836 (Oct. 22) Independent Republic of Texas installs Sam Houston as president.
1845 (Dec. 29) Texas becomes 28th U.S. state.
1846–48 Mexican War fought by U.S. and Mexico.
1861 (Feb. 23) Texans vote to secede; Gov. Sam Houston, who opposes secession, deposed March 20.
1861–65 In Civil War several battles fought in state; last Confederate army under Gen. Kirby Smith surrenders on May 26, 1865.
1866 Chisholm Trail for cattle drives pioneered by Jesse Chisholm from Texas to Kansas.
1870 (March 30) Texas readmitted to Union.
1900 (Sept. 8) Hurricane and tidal wave kills 6,000 persons at Galveston.
1901 Spindletop oil field opens near Beaumont.
1962 Space center built in Houston.
1963 (Nov. 22) President John F. Kennedy assassinated in Dallas.
1979 First Republican governor in 105 years takes office: William P. Clements Jr.
1982 Population grows 7.4% since 1980 with third-highest growth rate among the states.

UTAH

Area: 84,899 square miles; 219,888 sq. km.
Population: 1,554,000 (1982); 1,461,037 (1980).
Capital: Salt Lake City.
Flower: Sego lily.
Tree: Blue spruce.
Bird: Sea gull.
Gem: Topaz.
Song: *Utah, We Love Thee.*
Nickname: The Beehive State.
Motto: Industry.
Flag: State seal in gold circle on blue field.
Leading Industries: Manufacturing (primary metals, transportation equipment, machinery), food processing, mining (copper, petroleum, gold, iron, lead, coal, uranium, zinc), agriculture (beef cattle, dairy products, hay, wheat, sugar beets, fruits, vegetables).
Climate (Salt Lake City): *Normal temperatures:* Jan. high 37 ° F., low 19 ° F.; July high 93 ° F., low 61 ° F. *Normal yearly precipitation:* 15" (water). *Record snowstorm:* 18.1" in December 1972.
Recreation Areas: National parks, 5; national forests, 9; national recreation area, 1; state parks and recreation areas, 44.
Points of Interest: Bryce Canyon, Zion, Canyonlands, Arches, and Capitol Reef national parks; Cedar Breaks, Natural Bridges, Rainbow Bridge, Hovenweep, Timpanogos Cave, and Dinosaur national monuments; Mormon Tabernacle (Salt Lake City); Great Salt Lake; Glen Canyon; Monument Valley; Flaming Gorge; Golden Spike National Historic Site; Glen Canyon National Recreation Area.

KEY EVENTS IN UTAH

1776 Region explored for Spain by Franciscan friars Silvestre Vélez de Escalante and Francisco Atanasio Domínguez.
1824–25 Great Salt Lake discovered by American frontiersman James Bridger.
1847 (July 21–24) Mormons reach Great Salt Lake under leadership of Brigham Young.

1848 Grasshopper plague wiped out by sea gulls.
1848 (Feb. 2) U.S. acquires Utah in treaty ending Mexican War.
1849 State of Deseret organized by Mormons.
1850 (Sept. 9) Territory of Utah created by Congress.
1857–58 Utah War: President Buchanan removes Brigham Young as territorial governor, sends federal troops to take control of Utah from Mormons.
1862 (July 1) Polygamy practiced by Mormons made crime by act of Congress; much trouble ensues for several decades as federal authorities seek to enforce law.
1869 (May 10) First transcontinental railroad completed with driving of golden spike at Promontory Point, Utah.
1890 (Oct. 6) Mormon Church renounces polygamy.
1894 (Sept. 7) Pardon and restoration of civil rights proclaimed by President Cleveland for persons disfranchised by antipolygamy laws.
1896 (Jan. 4) Utah becomes 45th U.S. state.
1916 First non-Mormon elected governor: Democrat Simon Bamberger.
1952 Uranium discovered near Moab.
1982 Population grows 6.3% since 1980.

VERMONT

Area: 9,614 square miles; 24,900 sq. km.
Population: 516,000 (1982); 511,456 (1980).
Capital: Montpelier.
Flower: Red clover.
Tree: Sugar maple.
Animal: Morgan horse. **Insect:** Honeybee.
Bird: Hermit thrush.
Song: *Hail, Vermont!*
Nickname: The Green Mountain State.
Motto: Freedom and Unity.
Flag: State coat of arms centered on blue field.
Climate (Burlington): *Normal temperatures:* Jan. high 26° F., low 8° F.; July high 81° F., low 59° F. *Normal yearly precipitation:* 33" (water). *Record snowstorm:* 24.2" in January 1934.
Leading Industries: Manufacturing (machinery, paper), food processing, tourism, agriculture (dairy products, poultry, potatoes, apples, maple sugar), mining (granite, marble).
Recreation Areas: National forest, 1; state parks and recreation areas, 72; winter sports areas, 5.
Points of Interest: Green Mountain National Forest; Lake Champlain; Bennington Battle Monument; Calvin Coolidge Homestead (Plymouth); Shelburne Museum; Marble Exhibit (Proctor).

KEY EVENTS IN VERMONT

1609 Region explored and claimed for France by Samuel de Champlain.
1666 First French settlement established at Fort Sainte Anne on Isle La Motte in Lake Champlain.
1724 First English settlers from Massachusetts establish Fort Dummer at present-day Brattleboro.
1749–64 New Hampshire grants land to settlers.
1763 Britain wins control of region in French and Indian War.
1764 (July 20) British crown rules New York, controls Vermont region; New York begins trying to force New Hampshire settlers in Vermont to give up land.
1770–75 Green Mountain Boys organize under Ethan Allen to drive out New York settlers.
1775 (May 10) Fort Ticonderoga captured by Green Mountain Boys led by Ethan Allen.
1777 (Jan. 15) Vermont settlers declare independence as republic called New Connecticut.
1777 (July 2–8) First constitution adopted, using name Vermont; abolishes slavery; provides universal male suffrage.
1777 (Aug. 16) Battle of Bennington: British defeated just west of Bennington in New York.
1790 (Oct. 28) New York gives up claims to Vermont upon payment of $30,000 by Vermont.
1791 (March 4) Vermont becomes 14th U.S. state.
1823 Champlain Canal opens, connecting Lake Champlain to Hudson River.
1848 First railroad begins operation in state.
1864 (Oct. 19) Confederate troops rob St. Albans banks of $200,000 and escape into Canada.
1963 First Democratic governor since 1854 takes office: Philip H. Hoff.
1982 State population grows 0.9% since 1980.
1982 State's "blue law" overturned by state supreme court, permitting stores to open on Sundays.

VIRGINIA

Area: 40,767 square miles; 105,585 sq. km.
Population: 5,491,000 (1982); 5,346,797 (1980).
Capital: Richmond.
Flower: Dogwood.
Tree: Dogwood.
Animal: Foxhound.
Bird: Cardinal. **Shell:** Oyster.
Song: *Carry Me Back to Old Virginia.*
Nickname: The Old Dominion.
Motto: *Sic Semper Tyrannis* (Thus Always to Tyrants).
Flag: State seal centered on blue field.
Leading Industries: Manufacturing (chemicals, tobacco products, electrical and electronic equipment), food processing, agriculture (tobacco, beef cattle), dairy products, hogs, horses, turkeys, corn, peanuts, soybeans), mining (coal).
Climate (Norfolk): *Normal temperatures:* Jan. high 49° F., low 32° F.; July high 87° F., low 70° F. *Normal yearly precipitation:* 45" (water). *Record snowstorm:* 17.7" in December 1892.
Recreation Areas: National park, 1; national forests, 2; national seashore, 1; state parks and recreation areas, 34.
Points of Interest: Shenandoah National Park; Assateague Island National Seashore; national monuments include Booker T. Washington birthplace (near Roanoke) and George Washington birthplace (in Westmoreland County); Fredericksburg and Spotsylvania National Military Park; Petersburg National Battlefield; Manassas and Richmond National Battlefield Parks; Arlington House, Robert E. Lee National Memorial; national cemeteries at Fredericksburg, Poplar Grove, and Yorktown; Prince William Forest; Wolf Trap Farm; Skyline Drive and Blue Ridge Parkway; Monticello; Williamsburg; Mount Vernon; Appomattox Court House, Cumberland Gap, and Colonial national historical parks (last includes Jamestown and Yorktown); Alexandria; Fredericksburg; Richmond; Stratford Hall; Berkeley Plantation.

KEY EVENTS IN VIRGINIA

1607 (May 13) English colony established at Jamestown.
1619 First black slaves in English colonies in America arrive at Jamestown on Dutch ship.
1619 (July 30) First representative legislature meets in America: Virginia's House of Burgesses.
1622 Indian uprising kills over 300 colonists.
1624 Virginia made royal colony by King James I.
1644 Indian raids massacre about 500 settlers.
1676 (Sept. 19) Nathaniel Bacon burns Jamestown in rebellion against royal governor.
1693 College of William and Mary chartered.
1754–63 French and Indian War: Virginia's George

VIRGINIA *(continued)*
Washington initiates conflict with French.
1775 (March 23) Patrick Henry appeals to patriots: "Give me liberty or give me death!"
1775 (June 8) Royal governor flees to British ship.
1776 (May 15) Virginia directs delegates in Continental Congress to vote for independence.
1776 (June 12) Declaration of Rights written by George Mason adopted by Virginia Convention; state constitution adopted on June 29, also written by Mason; Patrick Henry becomes first governor.
1776–81 In Revolutionary War Virginians drive off attacks by British in 1776; British invade Virginia (1780–81) but lose Battle of Yorktown as Gen. Charles Cornwallis' army surrenders (Oct. 19, 1781).
1788 (June 25) Virginia becomes 10th U.S. state, ratifying U.S. Constitution.
1798 (Dec. 24) Virginia Resolution by James Madison adopted by legislature, declaring Alien and Sedition Acts unconstitutional.
1831 (Aug. 13–23) Slave uprising led by Nat Turner; 57 whites and about 100 blacks killed; 20 blacks including Turner executed.
1861 (April 17) Virginia secedes, joins Confederacy; western Virginians remain loyal to Union, forming separate state of West Virginia in 1863.
1861–65 In Civil War Virginia is major battleground with scores of battles; Richmond serves as Confederate capital (May 1861–April 1865); war ends in Virginia with Lee's surrender to Grant at Appomattox Court House (April 9, 1865).
1870 (Jan. 16) Virginia readmitted to Union.
1873 Railroad built from Richmond to Ohio River.
1926 Colonial Williamsburg restoration begun by John D. Rockefeller Jr.
1969 First Republican elected governor since 1869: A. Linwood Holton.
1982 State population increases 2.7% since 1980, moving state to 13th in population.

WASHINGTON

Area: 68,139 square miles; 176,478 sq. km.
Population: 4,245,000 (1982); 4,132,204 (1980).
Capital: Olympia.
Flower: Western rhododendron. **Tree:** Western hemlock.
Fish: Steelhead trout. **Bird:** Willow goldfinch.
Gem: Petrified wood.
Song: *Washington, My Home.*
Nickname: The Evergreen State.
Motto: *Alki* (By and By).
Flag: State seal centered on green field.
Leading Industries: Manufacturing (aircraft, ships, chemicals, paper, machinery), forestry, food processing, agriculture (wheat, potatoes, sugar beets, apples, beef cattle, dairy products, poultry).
Climate (Seattle): *Normal temperatures:* Jan. high 45 ° F., low 35 ° F.; July high 76 ° F., low 56 ° F. *Normal yearly precipitation:* 36 " (water). *Record snowstorm:* 21.5 " in February 1916.
Recreation Areas: National parks, 3; national forests, 9; national recreation areas, 3; state parks and recreation areas, 187.
Points of Interest: Mt. Rainier, Olympic, and North Cascades national parks; Grand Coulee Dam, Ross Lake, and Lake Chelan national recreation areas; Whitman Mission (west of Walla Walla) and Fort Vancouver national historic sites; San Juan Island National Historical Park; Pacific Science Center and Space Needle (Seattle).

KEY EVENTS IN WASHINGTON

1774 Coast explored for Spain by Juan Pérez.
1775 Region claimed for Spain by Bruno Heceta, who lands near mouth of Quinault River.
1792 (May 7) Columbia River discovered and named by American Capt. Robert Gray.
1792–94 Coast surveyed for Britain by Capt. George Vancouver.
1805–06 Lewis and Clark explore region along Columbia River and coastal area for U.S.
1810 Trading post built at present-day Spokane by Canadian explorer David Thompson.
1811 First American settlement at Okanogan by David Stuart for Pacific Fur Company.
1818 (Oct. 20) U.S. and Britain agree to joint control of region; treaty renewed in 1827.
1819 (Feb. 2) Spain gives up claim to region in Adams-Onís Treaty with U.S.
1824 Russia gives up claim to region in treaty with U.S.; ratified Jan. 12, 1825.
1825 Vancouver founded by Hudson's Bay Company's John McLoughlin, who controls region for next two decades.
1846 (Aug. 5) Britain gives up claim to region as Oregon Treaty goes into effect.
1847 (Nov. 29) Cayuse Indians massacre American missionaries Marcus and Narcissa Whitman and 11 other settlers near present-day Walla Walla, touching off Cayuse War; settlers destroy Indian villages.
1848 (Aug. 14) Territory of Oregon created, including present-day Washington.
1852 Seattle founded.
1853 (March 2) Territory of Washington created.
1855–59 Yakima Indians war with settlers in effort to protect their land.
1883 Northern Pacific Railroad completed between Washington and eastern United States.
1889 (Nov. 11) Washington becomes 42d U.S. state.
1917 Canal completed from Puget Sound to Lake Washington.
1941 Grand Coulee Dam begins operation on Columbia River, largest concrete dam and largest hydroelectric power plant in U.S.
1943 Hanford Works atomic-energy plant built.
1962 Century 21 World's Fair held at Seattle.
1974 World's first environmental exposition, Expo '74, held in Spokane.
1980 (May 18) Mount St. Helens erupts; 66 dead or missing; $1.6 billion in damage.
1982 State population increases 2.7% since 1980.

WEST VIRGINIA

Area: 24,231 square miles; 62,759 sq. km.
Population: 1,948,000 (1982); 1,950,258 (1980).
Capital: Charleston.
Flower: Big rhododendron. **Tree:** Sugar maple.
Bird: Cardinal. **Animal:** Black bear.
Fish: Brook trout.
Songs: *The West Virginia Hills; This Is My West Virginia;* and *West Virginia, My Home Sweet Home* (all official songs).
Nickname: The Mountain State.
Motto: *Montani Semper Liberi* (Mountaineers Are Always Free).
Flag: State coat of arms centered on blue-bordered white field.
Leading Industries: Manufacturing (chemicals, iron and steel, nickel, aluminum, glassware, pottery, machinery), mining (coal, natural gas, petroleum), agriculture (beef cattle, dairy products, poultry, fruits, corn).
Climate (Charleston): *Normal temperatures:* Jan. high 44 ° F., low 25 ° F.; July high 86 ° F., low 64 ° F. *Normal yearly precipitation:* 41 " (water). *Record snowstorm:* 15.1 " in November 1950.
Recreation Areas: National forests, 3; state parks and recreation areas, 34.
Points of Interest: Harpers Ferry and Chesapeake

and Ohio Canal national historical parks; White Sulphur Springs and Berkeley Springs resorts; National Radio Astronomy Observatory (Green Bank) Blennerhassett Island; scenic railroad at Cass; historic homes at Charles Town.

KEY EVENTS IN WEST VIRGINIA

1609–1863 West Virginia included in Virginia.
1726 First settler: Morgan Morgan builds cabin at Bunker Hill.
1727 German settlers from Pennsylvania found New Mecklenburg (now Shepherdstown).
1742 Coal discovered near present-day Racine.
1748 Harpers Ferry begins carrying passengers across Shenandoah River.
1754–63 French and Indian War: George Washington commands militia troops on Virginia's frontier, including what is now West Virginia.
1774 (Oct. 10) Battle of Point Pleasant: About 3,000 Virginia militia under Col. Andrew Lewis defeat 1,000 Shawnees led by Chief Cornstalk.
1775–83 In Revolutionary War Indians and British loyalists make many raids on settlers; last battle is attack on Fort Henry at present-day Wheeling (Sept. 11–13, 1782).
1859 (Oct. 16–18) John Brown seizes arsenal at Harpers Ferry; hanged at Charles Town on Dec. 2.
1860 Petroleum discovered at Burning Springs.
1861 (April 17) Opposition to secession voted by western delegates at Virginia Convention; West Virginians choose governor loyal to union (June 20).
1861–65 Many Civil War battles take place.
1863 (June 20) Becomes 35th U.S. state.
1915 U.S. Supreme Court rules West Virginia owes Virginia over $12 million as part of state debt before Civil War; debt finally paid in 1939.
1921 Miners and owners battle in Logan County.
1950–70 Poor economic conditions cause 13% decline in population from 2,005,452 in 1950.
1965 (March) Appalachian Regional Redevelopment Act brings federal aid to revitalize economy.
1972 (Feb. 26) Flood caused by collapse of coal-waste dam at Buffalo Creek kills 118 persons.
1982 Population decreases 0.1% since 1980.

WISCONSIN

Area: 56,153 square miles; 145,435 sq. km.
Population: 4,765,000 (1982); 4,705,642 (1980).
Capital: Madison.
Flower: Wood violet.
Tree: Sugar maple.
Bird: Robin.
Rock: Red granite.
Mineral: Galena.
Animal: Badger. **Wildlife Animal:** White-tailed deer.
Domestic Animal: Dairy cow.
Symbol of Peace: Mourning dove.
Fish: Muskellunge.
Song: *On, Wisconsin!*
Nickname: The Badger State.
Motto: Forward.
Flag: State coat of arms centered on blue field.
Leading Industries: Manufacturing (machinery, automobiles, electrical equipment), food processing, forestry, agriculture (dairy products, beef cattle, hogs, hay, corn, poultry, vegetables, fruits).
Climate (Milwaukee): *Normal temperatures:* Jan. high 27 °F., low 11 °F.; July high 80 °F., low 59 °F. *Normal yearly precipitation:* 29 " (water). *Record snowstorm:* 20.3 " in February 1924.
Recreation Areas: National forests, 2; national scientific reserve, 1; national lakeshore, 1; state parks and recreation areas, 65.
Points of Interest: Apostle Islands National Lakeshore; Ice Age National Scientific Reserve; Wolf, St. Croix, and Lower St. Croix national scenic riverways; Door County resort region; Wisconsin Dells; "Talie- sin," Frank Lloyd Wright's home and architectural school (Spring Green); Circus World Museum (Baraboo); Little Norway (near Mt. Horeb).

KEY EVENTS IN WISCONSIN

1634 Region explored for France by Jean Nicolet, landing at Green Bay.
1660–61 French trading post and Roman Catholic mission established near present-day Ashland.
1712–40 War between French and Fox Indians.
1763 Britain obtains region in settlement of French and Indian War.
1783 U.S. acquires region in Revolutionary War, but Britain does not turn over outposts to U.S. control until 1796.
1800–36 Region governed in turn as part of territories of Indiana, Illinois, and Michigan.
1820s American settlers begin mining lead.
1832 Black Hawk War: Settlers end power of Indians in Wisconsin.
1836 (April 20) Territory of Wisconsin created.
1837 Madison founded; becomes capital in 1838.
1848 (May 29) Wisconsin becomes 30th U.S. state.
1851 Railroad opens, Milwaukee-Waukesha.
1853 Capital punishment abolished.
1854 (Feb. 28) Formation of Republican Party first planned at meeting in Ripon.
1871 (Oct. 8–14) Forest fire kills about 800 persons, destroying village of Peshtigo.
1882 First hydroelectric power plant built on Fox River at Appleton.
1884 Ringling Brothers circus begins at Baraboo.
1911 First state income tax adopted.
1961 State sales tax adopted.
1977 (July 3–18) Illegal 15-day strike by 23,000 state workers wins higher pay.
1982 Population grows 1.3% since 1980.

WYOMING

Area: 97,809 square miles; 253,325 sq. km.
Population: 502,000 (1982); 469,557 (1980).
Capital: Cheyenne.
Flower: Indian paintbrush. **Tree:** Cottonwood.
Bird: Meadowlark. **Stone:** Jade. **Song:** *Wyoming.*
Nickname: Equality State. **Motto:** Equal Rights.
Flag: State seal and buffalo centered on red-and-white-bordered blue field.
Climate (Cheyenne): *Normal temperatures:* Jan. high 38 °F., low 15 °F.; July high 84 °F., low 55 °F. *Normal yearly precipitation:* 15 " (water). *Record snow storm:* 16.5 " in April 1955.
Leading Industries: Mining (petroleum, natural gas, coal, uranium), agriculture (beef cattle, sheep, beans, hay, sugar beets, wheat), food processing, tourism.
Recreation Areas: National parks, 2; national forests, 10; national recreation area, 1; state parks and recreation areas, 11.
Points of Interest: Grand Teton and Yellowstone national parks; Fort Laramie National Historic Site; Devils Tower and Fossil Butte national monuments; Buffalo Bill Historic Center (Cody); Flaming Gorge; Bighorn Canyon National Recreation Area.

KEY EVENTS IN WYOMING

1742–43 Believed first explored for France by Louis-Joseph and François de La Vérendrye.
1803 Region acquired in Louisiana Purchase.
1807 Yellowstone area explored by John Colter.
1833 Petroleum discovered in Wind River Basin by Capt. Benjamin de Bonneville.
1834 Fort William (later called Fort Laramie) built

WYOMING *(continued)*
by traders William Sublette and Robert Campbell.
1846–48 Western Wyoming obtained by U.S. in Oregon Treaty with Britain and in Mexican War.
1867 Cheyenne founded; first passenger train from Omaha reaches Cheyenne (Nov. 13, 1867).
1868 (July 25) Territory of Wyoming created.
1869 (Dec. 10) Women given right to vote and hold territorial offices.
1872 (March 1) Yellowstone becomes first national park in world.
1890 (July 10) Wyoming becomes 44th U.S. state; first to give women equal suffrage rights with men.
1892 Johnson County War: Cattlemen import gunmen from Texas to kill cattle rustlers.
1906 Devils Tower becomes first national monument.
1924 First woman elected governor in U.S.: Mrs. Nellie Tayloe Ross.
1951 Uranium discovered in Powder River region.
1960 First intercontinental ballistic missile (ICBM) base becomes operational near Cheyenne.
1978–80 Economic boom brings highest personal income gain in any state and lowest unemployment rate.
1981 High population growth of 6.8% since 1980; fifth-highest growth rate among states.

U.S. TERRITORIES AND DEPENDENCIES

DISTRICT OF COLUMBIA (WASHINGTON, D.C.)

Area: 69 square miles; 178 sq. km.
Population: 631,000 (1982); 638,432 (1980).
National Capital: Washington, D.C.
Flower: American beauty rose.
Bird: Wood thrush. **Tree:** Scarlet oak.
Motto: *Justitia Omnibus* (Justice for All).
Flag: Two parallel horizontal red stripes on white field; three red stars above top red stripe.
Leading Industries: Government, tourism, service industries, manufacturing (printing and publishing).
Climate: *Normal temperatures:* Jan. high 44 °F., low 28 °F.; July high 88 °F., low 69 °F. *Normal yearly precipitation:* 39 " (water). *Record snowstorm:* 25 " in January 1922.
Points of Interest: White House, U.S. Capitol, Library of Congress, Supreme Court, U.S. Botanic Garden, Folger Shakespeare Library, Museum of African Art, Smithsonian Building, National Air and Space Museum, National Museum of History and Technology, National Museum of Natural History, National Gallery of Art, Hirshhorn Museum and Sculpture Garden, Freer Gallery of Art, National Collection of Fine Arts, National Portrait Gallery, Washington Monument, Lincoln Memorial, Jefferson Memorial, Ford's Theatre, Kennedy Center for the Performing Arts, National Zoological Park, Corcoran Gallery of Art; *in Arlington, Va.:* Pentagon, Arlington National Cemetery, Marine Corps War Memorial; *in Fairfax County, Va.:* Mount Vernon (George Washington's estate).

KEY EVENTS IN DISTRICT OF COLUMBIA

1751 Georgetown laid out in 80 city lots.
1788 (Dec. 23) Maryland cedes land for capital.
1789 (Dec. 3) Virginia cedes land for capital.
1790–91 Congress establishes district as seat of national government.
1791 (March 30) President George Washington proclaims boundaries of federal district.
1791 (Sept. 9) Washington chosen as name for city by federal commissioners.
1791–92 Plan for city designed by French engineer Pierre Charles L'Enfant.
1800 (Nov. 1) President John Adams moves into White House.
1800 (Nov. 21) Congress first meets in city.
1802 (May 3) Washington incorporated by Congress.
1814 (Aug. 24–25) In War of 1812 Washington captured and burned by British.
1820 (May 15) New charter provides for mayor elected by people.
1846 (July 9) Congress retrocedes 36 square miles of district to Virginia because of lack of growth.
1871 (Feb. 21) Congress repeals charters of Washington and Georgetown; forms territorial government with officials appointed by President.
1874 (June 20) Government by three commissioners appointed by President established by Congress.
1961 (April 3) Amendment 23 to U.S. Constitution proclaimed; enables residents to vote for President and Vice President; first vote in 1964.
1967 New district government established with commissioner (mayor) appointed by President.
1970 Nonvoting delegate to represent district in U.S. House of Representatives authorized.
1974 (May 7) New home-rule charter approved, giving residents right to elect mayor and council.
1975 (Jan. 2) First elected government since 1871 sworn in.
1976 First subway begins operation in new $5 billion rapid-transit system.
1977 Racial composition of population changes to 75% black from 55% in 1960.
1978 Congress approves proposed constitutional amendment to give district voting representation in congress.
1982 (Nov. 2) Voters approve constitution to make district 51st state: "New Columbia."
1982 Population decreases 1.1% since 1980, with higher loss rate than any state except Michigan.

COMMONWEALTH OF PUERTO RICO

Area: 3,515 square miles; 9,104 sq. km.
Population: 3,259,000 (1982); 3,196,520 (1980).
Capital: San Juan, 434,849.
Other Cities: Bayamón, 196,206; Ponce, 189,046.
Nickname: Island of Enchantment.
Motto: *Joannes Est Nomen Ejus* (John Is His Name)
Animal: Lamb. **Reptile:** Coquí. **Song:** *La Borinqueña.*
Flag: Large white star on blue triangle next to staff; 3 red and 2 white horizontal stripes.
Leading Industries: Manufacturing (clothing, chemicals, electrical equipment, machinery), food processing, agriculture (sugarcane, coffee, tobacco, bananas, dairy products, poultry), tourism.
Climate (San Juan): *Normal temperatures:* Jan. high 82 °F., low 69 °F.; July high 87 °F., low 75 °F. *Normal yearly precipitation:* 60 ". *Record rainstorm:* 10.55 " in December 1910.
Points of Interest: El Morro Fortress (San Juan), Art Museum (Ponce), Caribbean National Forest with El Yunque mountain, Luquillo Beach, Phosphorescent Bay, historic buildings in Old San Juan, beaches.

KEY EVENTS IN PUERTO RICO

1493 (Nov. 19) Christopher Columbus claims Puerto Rico for Spain; names it San Juan Bautista.
1508 Spanish settlers colonize island.
1513 Black slaves first imported.
1873 Slavery abolished by Spain.
1897 Spain grants autonomous government to Puerto Ricans led by Luis Muñoz Rivera.
1898 (July 25–Aug. 13) In Spanish-American War U.S. troops invade and conquer Spanish defenders.
1898 (Dec. 10) Spain cedes Puerto Rico to U.S.

PUERTO RICO *(continued)*

1899 (Aug. 8) Hurricane kills 3,369 persons.

1917 (March 2) Territory of Puerto Rico created by Jones Act, granting U.S. citizenship to Puerto Ricans.

1946 (July 25) First island-born governor: Jesús Toribio Piñero, appointed by President Truman.

1948 Luis Muñoz Marin becomes first elected governor (son of Luis Muñoz Rivera).

1952 (July 25) Puerto Rico becomes commonwealth with own constitution (adopted March 3, 1952).

1967 (July 23) Puerto Ricans vote by 60% majority to retain commonwealth status with U.S.: 39% vote for statehood; less than 1% vote for independence.

1979 U.S. Congress passes resolution favoring a popular vote in Puerto Rico to decide on statehood.

1980 Population grows 17.9% since 1970.

1982 (Jan. 12) President Reagan pledges support for Puerto Rican statehood if islanders want it.

1982 (Sept. 24) UN General Assembly votes 70–30 to uphold Puerto Rico's status, rejecting Cuban effort to label it as a U.S. colony.

U.S. VIRGIN ISLANDS

Area: 132 square miles; 342 sq. km.
Population: 101,000 (1982); 95,591 (1980).
Capital: Charlotte Amalie, 11,756 (on St. Thomas).
Islands: St. Thomas, 32 sq. mi.; St. Croix, 82 sq. mi.; St. John, 19 sq. mi.; about 60 small islets.
Nickname: American Paradise.
Territorial Flower: Yellow elder or yellow cedar.
Bird: Yellow breast. **Song:** *Virgin Islands March.*
Flag: Golden American eagle with shield on white field; eagle between blue letters V and I.
Leading Industries: Tourism, manufacturing (rum, refined bauxite, petroleum refining, textiles), agriculture (beef cattle, dairy products, poultry, vegetables, fruits, nuts).
Normal Temperatures: Year-round, 78 ° F.
Normal Yearly Rainfall: 40–60 inches.
Points of Interest: Virgin Islands National Park on St. John; St. Thomas and Christiansted national historic sites; Buck Island Reef National Monument; ruins of castles, forts, and plantations; beaches.

KEY EVENTS IN U.S. VIRGIN ISLANDS

1493 Islands discovered by Christopher Columbus.

1500s Spaniards kill or enslave Carib Indians.

1672 (May 25) First permanent settlement established on St. Croix by Danes led by Jorgen Iverson.

1716 St. John acquired by Denmark.

1733 St. Croix bought by Denmark from France.

1848 (July 3) Slavery abolished after slave revolt.

1917 (March 31) U.S. purchases islands from Denmark for $25 million; treaty signed Aug. 4, 1916.

1927 U.S. citizenship granted to islanders.

1954 Elected legislature established by Congress.

1956 National park established on St. John.

1958 First island-born governor: John D. Merwin, appointed by President Eisenhower.

1968 Islanders given right to elect governor.

1971 (Jan. 4) First elected governor takes office: Melvin Herbert Evans.

1979 (March 6) Voters reject home rule: In 5 to 4 vote, new constitution is rejected.

1980 Population grows 53% since 1970.

1981 (Nov. 3) Voters reject home-rule constitution by 7,157 to 4,821 in referendum.

AMERICAN SAMOA

Area: 77 square miles; 199 sq. km.
Population: 34,000 (1982); 32,395 (1980).
Capital: Pago Pago, 2,451.
Islands: Tutuila and Aunu'u, 53 sq. mi.; Ta'u, 17 sq. mi.; Ofu and Olosega, 4 sq. mi.; Swain's, 1.9 sq. mi. Rose, 0.4 sq. mi.
Flower: Paogo. **Tree:** Moso'oi. **Plant:** Ava.
Motto: *Samoa—Muamua le Atua* (In Samoa, God Is First).
Song: *Amerika Samoa.*
Flag: Blue field; white triangle bordered with red with apex at midpoint of staff; American eagle at right side of triangle.
Leading Industries: Tourism, fishing, tuna canning, handicrafts, agriculture (fruits, vegetables).
Languages: Samoan and English.
Normal Temperatures: Year-round, 70 ° to 86 ° F.
Normal Yearly Rainfall: 200 inches.
Points of Interest: Villages, beaches.

KEY EVENTS IN AMERICAN SAMOA

1722 Discovered by Dutch explorer Jacob Roggeveen.

1830 British missionaries begin converting islanders.

1839–40 Survey by U.S. Navy Lt. Charles Wilkes.

1872 U.S. Navy establishes naval base at Pago Pago.

1899 (Dec. 2) U.S. and Germany agree to divide Samoan Islands between them; Britain also signs agreement, withdrawing its claims to islands.

1900–04 Chiefs of islands cede them to U.S.; formally accepted by U.S. Congress on Feb. 20, 1929.

1925 Swain's and Rose islands annexed to American Samoa.

1900–51 U.S. Navy administers islands.

1951 U.S. Department of Interior takes over administration of islands.

1966 (Nov. 19) Constitution adopted by voters gives elected legislature taxing power.

1974 Islands declared drought disaster area.

1977 (Nov. 22) Voters for first time elect Samoa-born governor: Peter T. Coleman.

1980 Population grows 19% since 1970.

GUAM

Area: 209 square miles; 541 sq. km.
Population: 111,000 (1982); 105,821 (1980).
Capital: Agana, 881.
Flower: *Puti Tai Nobio* (Bougainvillea).
Bird: *Toto* (Fruit dove). **Animal:** Iguana. **Stone:** Latte.
Tree: *Ifit* (Intsiabijuga).
Song: *Stand Ye Guamanians.*
Nickname: Pearl of the Pacific.
Flag: Territorial seal on blue field bordered in red.
Leading Industries: Military installations, manufacturing (food, beverages, printing, watches, clothing), oil refining, construction, fishing, agriculture (vegetables, fruits, poultry, hogs, beef cattle), tourism.
Languages: Chamorro and English.
Normal Temperatures: Year-round, 71 ° to 87 °F.
Normal Yearly Rainfall: 80–110 inches (mostly July through November).

KEY EVENTS IN GUAM

1521 Portuguese explorer Ferdinand Magellan believed to have visited Guam.

1668 Guam colonized by Spain.

1898 (Dec. 10) U.S. acquires Guam.

1899–1950 U.S. Navy administers Guam.

1941 (Dec. 7–13) Japan captures Guam.

1944 (July 21–Aug. 10) U.S. recaptures Guam.

1950 (Aug. 1) U.S. Territory of Guam created under U.S. Department of Interior; islanders become U.S. citizens; given right to elect own legislature.

1968 Right to elect own governor given Guam.

1976 (Sept. 4) Continued status as U.S. territory approved by voters 10,221 to 7,386.

1979 (Aug. 4) Voters reject proposed constitution by 5 to 1, demanding U.S. military give up much of the island's land to further economic development.

1980 Population grows 24.5% since 1970.

1982 (Sept. 7) Voters favor commonwealth status 3 to 1 over statehood in referendum.

COMMONWEALTH OF NORTHERN MARIANA ISLANDS

Area: *Land,* 184 square miles; 476.6 sq. km.
Population: 18,000 (1982); 16,862 (1980).
Capital: Susupe, Saipan, 7,967.
Islands: Saipan, Tinian, Rota, and 11 islets.
Legislature: 23 members.
Languages: English and Chamorro.
Leading Industries: Agriculture (coconuts); government; fishing.
Normal Temperatures: Year-round, 75 ° to 89 °F.

KEY EVENTS IN NORTHERN MARIANAS

1668 Spain colonizes Mariana Islands.
1899 Germany acquires Northern Marianas.
1947 (July 18) Northern Marianas included in U.S. Trust Territory of the Pacific Islands.
1975 (Feb. 15) U.S. signs agreement with representatives of Northern Marianas to make them U.S. commonwealth.
1976 (March 24) President Ford signs Northern Marianas Covenant establishing procedure to separate islands from Micronesia.
1976 (July 14) UN Trusteeship Council approves U.S. plan for Northern Marianas.
1978 (Jan. 9) Northern Marianas become U.S. commonwealth, pending end of trust territory; first elected governor, Carlos S. Camacho.
1982 (Jan. 9) Pedro P. Tenorio sworn in as governor for 4-year term; elected on Nov. 1, 1981.

TRUST TERRITORY OF THE PACIFIC ISLANDS

Including the many islands taken by U.S. military forces from Japan in World War II, the U.S. Trust Territory of the Pacific Islands was formally placed under American administration by the UN in 1947. The territory has been divided into four parts: (1) the Northern Marianas, a self-governing U.S. commonwealth; (2) the Federated States of Micronesia, whose capital is at Kolonia on Ponape and includes the island districts of Truk, Yap, and Kosrae of the Caroline group; (3) Belau (Palau Island) in the western Carolines, with its capital at Koror; and (4) the Marshall Islands, with its capital at Majuro.
Area: *Land,* 533 sq. mi. (1,380 sq. km.); *ocean,* 7,772 sq. mi. (20,129 sq. km.)
Population: 121,000 (1982); 116,974 (1980).
Administrative Center: Saipan in Mariana Islands.
Islands: 2,141 atolls and islands (96 inhabited).
Leading Industries: Agriculture (vegetables, fruits, poultry, copra), fishing, handicrafts.
Normal Temperatures: Year-round, 75 ° to 89 °F.
Government: High commissioner appointed by U.S.; congress of Micronesia elected by islanders.

KEY EVENTS

1885 Germany annexes Marshall Islands.
1899 Germany acquires Carolines from Spain.
1914 Japan seizes Micronesia in World War I.
1920 (Dec. 17) Japan receives League of Nations mandate over German possessions in Micronesia.
1944–45 U.S. captures Micronesia from Japan.
1946–58 U.S. test-explodes 64 nuclear weapons at Bikini and Enewetak atolls.
1947 (July 18) U.S. receives UN trusteeship over Pacific Islands.
1962 (May 7) U.S. Department of Interior given administration of entire territory.
1965 Elective congress of Micronesia established.
1975 (Nov. 8) Constitution for Federated States of Micronesia adopted.
1976 (July 14) UN Trusteeship Council approves U.S. plan for self-government for Micronesia.
1978 (Jan. 9) Northern Marianas formally separated from Micronesia.
1978 (July 12) Micronesians vote to divide into three self-governing states.
1979 (May 1) Marshall Islands becomes separate self-governing nation.
1979 (May 10) Federated States of Micronesia established as self-governing state.
1979 (Nov. 27–Dec. 3) Majuro, capital of Marshall Islands, devastated by storm with 25-foot waves.
1980 (Jan. 14) U.S. signs agreement with Marshall Islands to grant limited independence.
1980 (April 8) Enewetak restored to former residents who were removed for U.S. A-bomb tests in 1940s.
1980 (July 9) Belau (Palau) **voters ratify constitution** providing self-rule.
1981 (Jan. 1) Belau becomes self-governing.
For other developments: See separate articles on nations Belau, Marshalls, and Micronesia.

U.S. ISLAND DEPENDENCIES

The United States also occupies or claims several other islands in the Caribbean Sea and the Pacific Ocean. Altogether these islands have an area of about 15 square miles and a total population of less than 5,000 persons. They include:
BAKER ISLAND lies in the Pacific Ocean about 1,650 miles southwest of Honolulu. Barren and uninhabited, it has an area of about 380 acres. Baker was claimed by the United States in 1857.
HOWLAND ISLAND, an uninhabited Pacific island, is about 40 miles north of Baker Island. It has an area of about 1 square mile.
JARVIS ISLAND, one of the Line Islands in the central Pacific Ocean, lies about 1,500 miles south of Honolulu. Its area is 1.66 square miles.
JOHNSTON AND SAND ISLANDS have an area of less than ½ square mile. About 800 miles southwest of Honolulu, the islands were annexed by the U.S. in 1858. The U.S. Navy built an airfield on Johnston Island in World War II, and the island was used for atomic-bomb tests in 1962.
KINGMAN REEF, about 9 miles long and 5 miles wide, is in the Line Islands about 920 miles south of Honolulu.
MIDWAY ISLANDS, about 1,150 miles northwest of Honolulu, have a population of about 2,200 and an area of about 2 square miles. The two islands are Sand Island and Eastern Island. Annexed by the U.S. in 1867, the islands are controlled by the U.S. Navy. The Battle of Midway on June 4, 1942, marked the turning point of World War II in the Pacific when a Japanese fleet attempting to capture the islands was defeated by a U.S. fleet.
NAVASSA ISLAND lies midway between Jamaica and Haiti in the West Indies. It is in the Jamaica Channel about 100 miles south of Cuba. It has an area of about 2 square miles.
PALMYRA ISLAND, one of the northernmost of the Line Islands, is about 1,000 miles south of Honolulu. It has an area of 4 square miles. It was annexed by Hawaii in 1862. It became the private possession of the Fullerd-Leo family of Hawaii. In 1979 the U.S. government reported plans to purchase the island and make it a dumping ground for radioactive waste materials.
WAKE ISLAND, about 2,300 miles west of Honolulu, has an area of 3 square miles and a population of 1,647. The U.S. claimed the island in 1899 for use as a station for the transpacific telegraph cable. In World War II, Japan captured Wake Island on Dec. 23, 1941, taking more than 1,600 Americans prisoner. Japan held the island until Sept. 4, 1945.

Supreme Court

U.S. Postal Service

The U.S. Postal Service issued the 20-cent "Flag Over the Supreme Court" stamp in $4 booklets in 1983, each containing two panes of 10 stamps each. The stamp features James Earle Fraser's statue "Contemplation of Justice" in the foreground. The stamp was designed by Dean Ellis of New York City.

MAJOR SUPREME COURT DECISIONS: 1983

Perhaps the most far-reaching decision made by the Supreme Court in 1983 was its ruling striking down the use by Congress of a legislative veto on actions by the executive branch of the U.S. government (see page 21).

CITIES CAN BAN PISTOLS

In a victory for proponents of stiff gun-control laws, the Court announced on Oct. 3 that it would let stand a Court of Appeals ruling that a local ordinance can ban the possession of handguns.

The case, *Quilici* v. *Village of Morton Grove*, had sought to overturn a law adopted by the Illinois village in 1981 that forbade residents other than police and military personnel from possessing pistols. Opponents had fought the law on grounds that it violated the Bill of Rights guarantee of "the right of the people to keep and bear arms."

WOMEN'S PENSION RIGHTS

In a 5–4 ruling on July 6, the Court declared that women may not be penalized with lower monthly pension-plan payments merely because statistics indicate they live about seven years longer then men. The ruling in *Arizona Governing Committee for Tax Deferred Annuity and Deferred Compensation Plans* v. *Nathalie Norris* affects about 26 million employees in some 450,000 employer-sponsored pension plans.

The Court also ruled 5–4 that increased pension-plan payments under the ruling need not be retroactive.

Insurance companies had fought the case, fearing that it might cause sex distinctions to be banned in figuring all types of insurance benefits and payments.

In writing the majority opinion, Associate Justice Thurgood Marshall said the law "re-

MAJOR COURT DECISIONS: 1983 *(continued)*

quires employers to treat their employees as individuals not 'as simply components of a racial, religious, sexual, or national class.' "

DEATH PENALTY CASES TO BE SPEEDED

The Court in a 5–4 decision on July 6 ordered lower courts to expedite procedures in handling appeals of the 1,200 prisoners facing execution throughout the U.S. In *Barefoot* v. *Estelle* the justices upheld the procedure of the 5th Circuit Court of Appeals in rejecting a stay of execution without giving the convicted murderer a hearing for a full argument. Associate Justice Byron White in the majority opinion said:

"Federal courts are not forums in which to relitigate state trials. Even less is federal habeas a means by which a defendant is entitled to delay an execution indefinitely."

LEGISLATURES' CHAPLAINS OKAYED

The practice of state legislatures to employ chaplains to open sessions with a prayer does not violate the constitution, according to a 6–3 ruling by the Court on July 5.

In the majority opinion on *Marsh* v. *Chambers*, Chief Justice Burger wrote:

"There can be no doubt that the practice of opening legislative sessions with prayer has become part of the fabric of our society.

"To invoke Divine guidance on a public body entrusted with making the laws is not, in these circumstances, an 'establishment' of religion or a step toward establishment. It is simply a tolerable acknowledgment of beliefs widely held among the people of this country."

The finding overturned a ruling by the 8th U.S. Court of Appeals which had ordered the Nebraska legislature to end the practice of employing a Presbyterian chaplain.

TAX BENEFITS FOR TUITION EXPENSES

State tax deductions for parents paying tuition to religious and other private elementary and secondary schools were okayed by the Court on June 29 with a 5–4 decision. Although other efforts to use government funds to support parochial schools have previously been struck down by the Court, the new ruling approved a Minnesota law that allows tax deductions to parents for such expenses as tuition, textbooks, and fees.

In writing the majority opinion in *Mueller* v. *Allen*, Associate Justice William H. Rehnquist wrote:

"A state's decision to defray the cost of educational expenses incurred by parents, regardless of the type of schools their children attend, evidences a purpose that is both secular and understandable. An educated populace is essential to the political and economic health of any community, and a state's efforts to assist parents in meeting the rising cost of educational expenses plainly serves this secular purpose of insuring that the state's citizenry is well-educated. Similarly, Minnesota, like other states, could conclude that there is a strong public interest in assuring the continued financial health of private schools, both sectarian and nonsectarian. By educating a substantial number of students such schools relieve public schools of a correspondingly great burden, to the benefit of all taxpayers."

In a dissenting opinion, Associate Justice Marshall said:

"By insuring that parents will be reimbursed for tuition payments they make, the Minnesota state requires that taxpayers in general pay for the cost of parochial education and extends a financial 'incentive to parents to send their children to sectarian schools.'

"That the Minnesota statute makes some small benefit available to all parents cannot alter the fact that the most substantial benefit provided by the statute is available only to those parents who send their children to schools that charge tuition."

LIFE TERM FOR MINOR CRIME VOIDED

In a 5–4 decision on June 28 the Court invalidated a life-term sentence that had been imposed in South Dakota on a man who had passed a bad check for $100. The man had been sentenced under a habitual criminal law because he previously had been convicted of six crimes, including burglary, grand larceny, and drunk driving.

Associate Justice Lewis F. Powell, who wrote the majority opinion in *Solem* v. *Helm*, said: "We hold as a matter of principle that a criminal sentence must be proportionate to the crime."

In a bitter dissent, Chief Justice Burger wrote: "What the Court means is that a sentence is unconstitutional if it is more severe than five justices think appropriate."

STATES CAN TAX FOREIGN PROFITS

The Court in a 5–3 ruling on June 27 upheld the right of states to tax the foreign income of corporations.

Associate Justice Brennan wrote the majority opinion in *Container* v. *Franchise Tax Board.* He rejected Container Corporation's argument that the income taxed by California already had been taxed by foreign governments.

Officials estimated that California alone would have lost $500 million of annual income if the Court had struck down the tax.

AIR BAG RULE RESTORED

The Reagan administration's efforts to deregulate the automobile industry were dealt a blow on June 24 when the Court ruled unanimously that the Department of Transportation had acted improperly in revoking a federal regulation that would have forced automakers to equip new cars with air bags or automatic seat belts for greater safety.

The regulation, which had been issued in 1977 during the Carter administration, had been scheduled to go into effect in 1983. But it was rescinded by the Reagan administration in 1981.

The Court's opinion, written by Associate Justice Byron White, called the Reagan administration's action "arbitrary and capricious." The Court ordered the Department of Transportation to "examine the relevant data and articulate a satisfactory explanation for its action." No deadline was set by the Court.

The suit, *Motor Vehicle Manufacturers Association et al* v. *State Farm Mutual Automobile Insurance Co. et al*, had been pressed by the auto insurance industry which believes the use of air bags would save thousands of lives each year.

WOMEN'S ABORTION RIGHTS REAFFIRMED

In a 6–3 decision the Court on June 15 reaffirmed its 1973 ruling that government should not restrict the "fundamental right" of women to abortion.

The new ruling overturned laws in more than 20 states that had required abortion of fetuses more than three months old to be performed in hospitals. The Court's decision permits such abortions to be performed in less expensive clinics.

The Court also ruled as unconstitutional an Akron, Ohio, ordinance that had been considered a model by groups opposed to abortion. The Akron law had sought to discourage abortions by requiring a 24-hour waiting period, a complex "informed-consent" procedure between doctor and patient, parental consent for a teenager to have an abortion, and "humane" burial of the fetus.

Associate Justice Lewis F. Powell Jr. wrote the majority opinion, saying that the decision was based on an individual's "freedom of personal choice in matters of marriage and family life."

"From approximately the end of the first trimester of pregnancy," Powell wrote, "the state 'may regulate the abortion procedure to the extent that the regulation reasonably relates to the preservation and protection of maternal health.' The state's discretion to regulate on this basis does not, however, permit it to adopt abortion regulations that depart from accepted medical practice. If a state requires licensing or undertakes to regulate the performance of abortions during this period, the health standards adopted must be 'legitimately related to the objective the state seeks to accomplish.' "

Associate Justice Sandra Day O'Connor wrote the dissenting opinion, joined by Associate Justices White and William H. Rehnquist. In it she said in part:

". . . potential life is no less potential in the first weeks of pregnancy that it is at viability or afterward. At any stage in pregnancy, there is the potential for human life. The choice of viability as the point at which the state interest in potential life becomes compelling is no less arbitrary than choosing any point before viability or any point afterward. Accordingly, I believe that the state's interest in protecting potential human life exists throughout the pregnancy.

"We must always be mindful that 'the Constitution does not compel a state to fine-tune its statutes so as to encourage or facilitate abortions. To the contrary, state action encouraging childbirth except in the most urgent circumstances is rationally related to the legitimate government objective of protecting potential life.'

"The state's compelling interests in maternal physical and mental health and protection of fetal life clearly justify the waiting period. . . . The decision to abort is 'a stressful one,' and the waiting period reasonably relates to the state's interest in insuring that a woman does not make this serious decision in undue haste. The decision also has grave consequences for the fetus, whose life the state has a compelling interest to protect and preserve. The waiting period is surely a small cost to impose to insure that the woman's decision is well-considered in light of its certain and irreparable consequences on fetal life, and the possible effects on her own."

WINDFALL OIL PROFITS TAX UPHELD

The government was saved from refunding about $26 billion by a unanimous Court ruling on June 6 that upheld the constitutionality of the 1980 tax imposed by Congress on the windfall profits of oil companies that were caused by the end of oil price controls.

Because the tax exempted oil produced in Alaska, oil companies producing oil in other states had fought the measure.

Associate Justice Powell wrote the majority opinion in *U.S.* v. *Ptasynski*, saying in part:

"Congress clearly viewed exempt Alaskan oil as a unique class of oil that . . . merited favorable treatment. It had before it ample evidence of the disproportionate costs and

MAJOR COURT DECISIONS: 1983 *(continued)*

difficulties—the fragile ecology, the harsh environment, and the remote location—associated with extracting oil from this region."

SEGREGATIONISTS LOSE TAX BREAK

In an 8–1 ruling on May 24 the Court declared that private schools that practice racial discrimination are not eligible for federal tax exemption.

Chief Justice Burger wrote the majority opinion in *Bob Jones University* v. *U.S.*, saying in part:

"Over the past quarter of a century, every pronouncement of this court and myriad acts of Congress and executive orders attest a firm national policy to prohibit racial segregation and discrimination in public education . . .

"It cannot be said that educational institutions that, for whatever reasons, practice racial discrimination are institutions exercising 'beneficial and stabilizing influences in community life' . . . or should be encouraged by having all taxpayers share in their support by way of special tax status . . .

"It would be wholly incompatible with the concepts underlying tax exemption to grant the benefit of tax-exempt status to racially discriminatory educational entities. . .

"The government has a fundamental overriding interest in eradicating racial discrimination in education—discrimination that prevailed, with official approval, for the first 165 years of the nation's history. That governmental interest substantially outweighs whatever burden denial of tax benefits places on petitioners' exercise of their religious beliefs. . . ."

DRUNK DRIVERS LOSE PROTECTION

In a 7–2 decision on Feb. 22 the Court ruled that the refusal of a motorist to submit to a blood alcohol test may be used as evidence of being guilty of driving while drunk.

In *South Dakota* v. *Neville*, the South Dakota Supreme Court had ruled that the introduction of such evidence in effect forced the motorist to testify against himself.

However, the Supreme Court overturned the South Dakota ruling in an opinion written by Associate Justice O'Connor. In it she said that because the driver has the choice of whether or not to take the test, the refusal "is not protected by the privilege against self-incrimination."

AGE-BIAS LAW EXTENDED

The Court in a 5–4 ruling on March 2 upheld the rights of state and local public employes to protection from discrimination on the basis of age. The decision overturned many state and city laws and regulations that required mandatory retirement at ages younger than 70.

In *Equal Employment Opportunity Commission* v. *Wyoming*, the Court overturned a lower-court finding that the federal Age Discrimination in Employment Act impinged on states rights as protected by the 10th Amendment to the Constitution.

The case involved a game warden who had been forced by the state to retire because he had reached the age of 55.

In the majority opinion, Justice Brennan said that state and local governments should evaluate employes for retirement "in a more individualized and careful manner."

AT&T DIVESTITURE APPROVED

The Court in a 6–3 opinion on Feb. 28 upheld the reorganization agreement of the multibillion-dollar American Telephone and Telegraph Co. that had settled a federal antitrust suit in 1982.

The reorganization plan, scheduled to become effective in 1984, had been opposed by 13 states that felt it might disrupt local telephone services and cause higher rates.

The government began an antitrust suit against AT&T in 1974, charging that it was excluding competition for long-distance service and communications equipment. In the out-of-court settlement of the suit in 1982, AT&T agreed to divest itself of 22 local telephone companies and concentrate on operating long-distance phone service, selling communications equipment, and providing data processing services.

Chief Justice Burger and Associate Justices Rehnquist and White dissented from the ruling, arguing that the Court should have had a full briefing and heard arguments on the case before rendering a verdict.

OFFICIALS LIABLE FOR DAMAGES

The Court ruled 5–4 on April 20 that public officials must pay individuals for damages they have caused by indifference.

The Court upheld a jury's decision that prison guard William H. Smith should pay $25,000 compensatory damages and $5,000 in punitive damages to prisoner Daniel R. Wade for having placed in his cell other prisoners who injured Wade. The verdict said Smith "should have known" that Wade would be assaulted.

Chief Justice Burger and Associate Justices Rehnquist and Powell dissented, declaring "at least some degree of bad faith or improper motive" should be proved. In a separate dissent, Justice O'Connor said the ruling would "chill public officials in the performance of their official duties."

HISTORIC SUPREME COURT DECISIONS

1803 Judicial Review—*Marbury v. Madison:* William Marbury was appointed a justice of the peace a few weeks before President John Adams' term expired. When the next administration refused to deliver his commission, Marbury petitioned the Court for a writ of mandamus to compel Secretary of State James Madison to issue a commission. The Court dismissed the case for lack of jurisdiction. Marbury had based his case on the Judiciary Act of 1789, which authorized the Court to take original jurisdiction over such controversies. Under Article III, Section 2 of the Constitution, Supreme Court jurisdiction over such matters begins at the appellate level. Therefore, the Judiciary Act was unconstitutional and void to the extent that it gave the Court powers implicitly denied by the Constitution.

Significance: It established the principle of "judicial review," whereby the Court has jurisdiction to pass on the constitutionality of legislative acts.

1816 Federal Questions—*Martin v. Hunter's Lessee:* This case dealt with land ownership in Virginia. The Virginia Court of Appeals ruled against Martin. On appeal to the Supreme Court, that decision was reversed. In 1821 the Supreme Court asserted in *Cohens v. Virginia* that it had power to review final decisions of state courts in criminal proceedings.

Significance: The two cases established the Court's appellate power when "federal questions" (involving the Constitution, a congressional statute, or a treaty) are involved. They established that one uniform interpretation will apply for "federal questions."

1819 Constitutional Interpretation—*McCulloch v. Maryland:* Congress chartered a federal bank in 1816 to control unregulated issuances of currency by state banks. Maryland then imposed a tax on notes issued by the U.S. Bank's Baltimore branch. The branch refused to pay, and Maryland sued to collect. At the same time it challenged congressional authority to charter a bank. The Court ruled that this was within the implied powers of government, that acts of Congress not expressly authorized are valid so long as they are "necessary and proper" to carrying out express grants of power. It declared further that federal instrumentalities are not subject to state taxes.

Significance: The decision sanctioned "loose," or liberal, interpretation of the Constitution.

1824 Regulation of Commerce—*Gibbons v. Ogden:* Aaron Ogden, part owner of a steamboat operation monopoly established by New York statute, challenged the right of Thomas Gibbons to operate a rival steamboat service between New Jersey and New York under federal license. The Court declared the New York statute unconstitutional because it clearly came in conflict with congressional power to regulate commerce.

Significance: It became the basis for the sweeping exercise of federal controls over commerce. It is significant also for its statement of "pre-emption": when Congress acts within its authorized powers, it can pass legislation to invalidate contradictory laws of the states.

1852 Local Powers—*Cooley v. Wardens of the Port of Philadelphia:* The case involved the constitutionality of a Pennsylvania statute regulating navigation in the Port of Philadelphia. Much of the traffic in and out of the harbor was interstate. In its ruling the Court noted that some commerce, although technically interstate, is essentially local in character. U.S. control is not really necessary, and until it is, states and municipalities are free to act according to local needs.

Significance: The decision reasserted the authority of the Court over state regulation of commerce, and ensured a national "common market" by stating that some matters are beyond state power.

1857 Slaves as Property—*Dred Scott v. Sanford:* Dred Scott, a Missouri slave, was at one time taken into free territory, where an Act of Congress (the Missouri Compromise) prohibited slavery. Several years after his return to Missouri, Scott sued for freedom, claiming he had acquired it through residence in free territory. The decision centered on two principles: first, that Scott, being a Negro, was not a U.S. citizen and therefore could not petition federal courts; second, that the Missouri Compromise was unconstitutional. Slaves were like any other property, the Court said, and under the 5th Amendment Congress could pass no law depriving citizens of their private property.

Significance: The decision, acclaimed in the South and bitterly denounced in the North, brought the nation another step closer to civil war.

1911 Business Regulation—*Standard Oil Co. of New Jersey v. United States:* The Sherman Act (1890) outlawed "every contract, combination in the form of trust or otherwise, or conspiracy in restraint of trade." In this case the Court said that the "rule of reason" must apply, and that "every" did not mean "all" but only "unreasonable" contracts or combinations or conspiracies in restraint of trade. Later (1932) the Court ruled in *United States v. Swift & Co.* that "mere size" is not an offense against the Sherman Act.

Significance: The Court's decisions permitted the growth of huge corporate enterprises in the U.S. by watering down the stringent provisions of the congressional statute.

1925 Bill of Rights Applied to States—*Gitlow v. New York:* Gitlow was prosecuted under New York's "criminal anarchy" statute, which made it a crime to advocate or teach the propriety of overthrowing the government by force and violence. The Supreme Court upheld Gitlow's state-court conviction, over objection that it violated Gitlow's rights of freedom of speech and the press. The Court assumed that those 1st Amendment provisions were also limitations on the states because they were "incorporated" in the 14th Amendment's "due process" clause.

Significance: For the first time a part of the Bill of Rights of the Constitution was made applicable to the states.

HISTORIC SUPREME COURT DECISIONS *(continued)*

1937 Regulation of Labor—*NLRB v. Jones & Laughlin Steel Corporation:* In upholding the National Labor Relations Board's authority to regulate industrial labor relations, the Court ruled that the U.S. government has jurisdiction over any dispute that will interfere with interstate commerce. The case grew out of a labor dispute in a Pennsylvania steel plant. Manufacturing, the Court ruled, was so closely linked to interstate commerce that its control was essential to "protect that commerce from burdens and obstructions."

Significance: The decision broadened the definition of interstate commerce to include all activities that would affect its flow, either directly or indirectly, and upheld the power of Congress to regulate industrial relations.

1954 Racial Segregation—*Brown v. Board of Education of Topeka:* In this case the Court set aside a Kansas statute authorizing segregation in primary schools. The decision declared that the "separate but equal" doctrine, established in *Plessy v. Ferguson* (1896), in fact denied equal protection under the 14th Amendment and was unconstitutional. The verdict directed lower courts to use their authority to implement desegregation of public elementary schools.

Significance: This was the first time the Court declared segregation unconstitutional. From the decision evolved a body of legislation and court action aimed at eradicating discrimination in schools, housing, employment, voting, and other areas.

1962 School Prayers—*Engel v. Vitale:* A non-denominational prayer written by the N.Y. State Board of Regents for voluntary recital in the public schools was ruled unconstitutional as a violation of the 1st Amendment, which provides that Congress "shall make no laws respecting an establishment of religion or prohibiting the free exercise thereof."

A year later, in *School District of Abbington Township v. Schempp,* the Court banned legislation requiring Bible reading and recitation of the Lord's Prayer in public schools on grounds that it tended to establish a state religion.

Significance: A state may not require promotion of a specific religion in public schools.

1962 One Man, One Vote—*Baker et al. v. Carr:* The Court ruled that federal courts have the power to review legislative apportionment. As a result of large population shifts, many legislative districts were unevenly drawn and voters were denied the right to "equal protection" guaranteed by the 14th Amendment. The Baker case led to a number of decisions in 1964 calling for reapportionment on a "one man, one vote" basis. *(Reynolds v. Sims* established this rule for state legislatures, and *Wesberry v. Sanders* did the same for congressional districts.)

Significance: Political districts, which often were drawn to favor rural areas, were ordered redrawn to give increased voting strength to city and suburban residents.

1964 Libel of Officials—*New York Times v. Sullivan:* The case revolved around a full-page advertisement placed in the *Times* by Dr. Martin Luther King Jr. and other civil-rights leaders. Many statements in the ad—charging that Negroes in Montgomery, Ala., were being abused—proved false. Sullivan, a Montgomery city official, was subsequently awarded a $500,000 libel judgment. The Court reversed the judgment, ruling that criticism of official conduct cannot be termed libelous without showing actual malice.

Significance: The decision gave the news media greater freedom in reporting the news by limiting their liability for libel.

1966 Rights of Criminal Suspects—*Miranda v. Arizona:* The Court overturned the conviction of an Arizona man charged with rape and kidnapping, on grounds that his voluntary confession was obtained illegally. The decision invalidated any confessions or incriminating admissions unless the suspect is warned that he may remain silent, that anything he says may be held against him, that he has a right to have a lawyer present, and that if he cannot afford one, he is entitled to court-appointed counsel. If the suspect waives counsel and confesses, there is a "heavy burden" on the prosecution to show a waiver of rights.

Significance: The decision gives more protection to those accused of crimes.

1972 Death Penalty—*Furman v. Georgia:* The Supreme Court ruled in a 5–4 decision that the death penalty as it had been imposed by state courts was unconstitutional under the 8th and 14th Amendments.

Subsequently, in 1976, the Court ruled that the death penalty in and of itself was constitutional, upholding newly revised capital-punishment laws that provide separate consideration of sentencing after guilt had been determined.

In 1977 the Court decided that state legislatures cannot make the death penalty mandatory for the slaying of a police officer.

Significance: The decisions brought revision of capital-punishment laws to protect defendants' rights.

1972 Free Legal Counsel—*Argersinger v. Hamlin:* The Court decided that the state must provide free legal counsel for persons accused of crimes for which they may be imprisoned if they cannot afford to pay an attorney.

1973 Obscenity—*Miller v. California* and *Paris Adult Theatre I v. Slaton:* The Court redefined "obscenity," requiring a defendant prosecuted for obscenity to prove that the work as a whole shows "serious literary, artistic, political or scientific value." In addition, the Court ruled that the work must meet "contemporary community standards."

Significance: The decision gave states and local governments greater power to regulate works considered obscene.

1973 Abortion—*Roe v. Wade* and *Doe v. Bolton:* The Court overturned all state laws banning abortion during the first 6 months of pregnancy on grounds that it is a violation of the right of privacy stemming from the 14th Amendment.

Significance: The ruling broadened the rights of women in deciding whether or not to give birth to a child.

1980 New Life Forms Can Be Patented—*Diamond v. Chakrabarty:* Court recognized new science of genetic engineering, upholding patent for man-made microorganism.

UNITED STATES SUPREME COURT MEMBERS

JUSTICE (CHIEF JUSTICES IN BOLDFACE TYPE) AND STATE OF RESIDENCE	YEARS ON THE COURT	APPOINTED BY PRESIDENT:	BORN	DIED	POSITIONS BEFORE COURT APPOINTMENT
1. **John Jay** (N.Y.)	1789–95	Washington	1745	1829	President of Continental Congress; U.S. Secretary of State
2. John Rutledge (S.C.)[1]	1789–91	Washington	1739	1800	1st governor of South Carolina
3. William Cushing (Mass.)	1789–1810	Washington	1732	1810	Chief Judge, Supreme Judicial Court (Mass.)
4. James Wilson (Pa.)	1789–98	Washington	1742	1798	Private law practice
5. John Blair (Va.)	1789–96	Washington	1732	1800	State Appeals Court judge
6. James Iredell (N.C.)	1790–99	Washington	1751	1799	North Carolina Council of State
7. Thomas Johnson (Md.)	1791–93	Washington	1732	1819	Chief Judge, General Court of Maryland
8. William Paterson (N.J.)	1793–1806	Washington	1745	1806	Governor of New Jersey
9. **John Rutledge** (S.C.)[1]	1795	Washington	1739	1800	Chief Justice of South Carolina
10. Samuel Chase (Md.)	1796–1811	Washington	1741	1811	Chief Judge, General Court of Maryland
11. **Oliver Ellsworth** (Conn.)	1796–1800	Washington	1745	1807	U.S. Senator; helped write first Judiciary Act
12. Bushrod Washington (Va.)	1798–1829	John Adams	1762	1829	Private law practice
13. Alfred Moore (N.C.)	1799–1804	John Adams	1755	1810	State Superior Court judge
14. **John Marshall** (Va.)	1801–35	John Adams	1755	1835	U.S. Representative; U.S. Secretary of State
15. William Johnson (S.C.)	1804–34	Jefferson	1771	1834	Court of Common Pleas judge
16. Henry Brockholst Livingston (N.Y.)	1807–23	Jefferson	1757	1823	State Supreme Court justice
17. Thomas Todd (Ky.)	1807–26	Jefferson	1765	1826	Chief Justice, Kentucky Court of Appeals
18. Gabriel Duvall (Md.)	1812–35	Madison	1752	1844	Comptroller, U.S. Treasury
19. Joseph Story (Mass.)	1811–45	Madison	1779	1845	Massachusetts legislator
20. Smith Thompson (N.Y.)	1823–43	Monroe	1768	1843	U.S. Secretary of the Navy
21. Robert Trimble (Ky.)	1826–28	J.Q. Adams	1777	1828	U.S. District Court judge
22. John McLean (Ohio)	1829–61	Jackson	1785	1861	U.S. Postmaster General
23. Henry Baldwin (Pa.)	1830–44	Jackson	1780	1844	Private law practice
24. James Moore Wayne (Ga.)	1835–67	Jackson	1790	1867	U.S. Representative
25. **Roger Brooke Taney** (Md.)	1836–64	Jackson	1777	1864	U.S. Attorney General; private law practice
26. Philip Pendleton Barbour (Va.)	1836–41	Jackson	1783	1841	U.S. Circuit Court judge
27. John Catron (Tenn.)	1837–65	Jackson	1786	1865	Private law practice
28. John McKinley (Ala.)	1837–52	Van Buren	1780	1852	U.S. Senator-elect
29. Peter Vivian Daniel (Va.)	1841–60	Van Buren	1784	1860	U.S. District Court judge
30. Samuel Nelson (N.Y.)	1845–72	Tyler	1792	1873	Chief Justice, New York
31. Levi Woodbury (N.H.)	1845–51	Polk	1789	1851	U.S. Senator
32. Robert Cooper Grier (Pa.)	1846–70	Polk	1794	1870	State District Court judge
33. Benjamin Robbins Curtis (Mass.)	1851–57	Fillmore	1809	1874	Private law practice
34. John Archibald Campbell (Ala.)	1853–61	Pierce	1811	1889	Private law practice
35. Nathan Clifford (Maine)	1858–81	Buchanan	1803	1881	Private law practice
36. Noah Haynes Swayne (Ohio)	1862–81	Lincoln	1804	1884	Private law practice
37. Samuel Freeman Miller (Iowa)	1862–90	Lincoln	1816	1890	Private law practice
38. David Davis (Ill.)	1862–77	Lincoln	1815	1886	Judicial Circuit Court judge
39. Stephen Johnson Field (Calif.)	1863–97	Lincoln	1816	1899	State Superior Court judge
40. **Salmon Portland Chase** (Ohio)	1864–73	Lincoln	1808	1873	Governor of Ohio; U.S. Secretary of Treasury
41. William Strong (Pa.)	1870–80	Grant	1808	1895	Private law practice
42. Joseph P. Bradley (N.J.)	1870–92	Grant	1813	1892	Private law practice
43. Ward Hunt (N.Y.)	1873–82	Grant	1810	1886	N.Y. Commissioner of Appeals
44. **Morrison Remick Waite** (Ohio)	1874–88	Grant	1816	1888	President of Ohio Constitutional Convention
45. John Marshall Harlan (Ky.)	1877–1911	Hayes	1833	1911	Member, Louisiana Commission
46. William Burnham Woods (Ga.)	1881–87	Hayes	1824	1887	U.S. Circuit Court judge
47. Stanley Matthews (Ohio)	1881–89	Garfield	1824	1889	Private law practice
48. Horace Gray (Mass.)	1882–1902	Arthur	1828	1902	Chief Judge, Massachusetts
49. Samuel Blatchford (N.Y.)	1882–93	Arthur	1820	1893	U.S. Circuit Court judge
50. Lucius Quintus Cincinnatus Lamar (Miss.)	1888–93	Cleveland	1825	1893	U.S. Secretary of Interior
51. **Melville Weston Fuller** (Ill.)	1888–1910	Cleveland	1833	1910	State legislator; Chicago corporation lawyer
52. David Josiah Brewer (Kan.)	1890–1910	B. Harrison	1837	1910	U.S. Circuit Court judge

[1] Resigned as associate justice in 1791; was named Chief Justice in 1795, but Senate rejected nomination.

U.S. SUPREME COURT MEMBERS *(continued)*

JUSTICE (**CHIEF JUSTICES IN BOLDFACE TYPE**) AND STATE OF RESIDENCE	YEARS ON THE COURT	APPOINTED BY PRESIDENT:	BORN	DIED	POSITION BEFORE COURT APPOINTMENT
53. Henry Billings Brown (Mich.)	1891–1906	B. Harrison	1836	1913	U.S. District Court judge
54. George Shiras Jr. (Pa.)	1892–1903	B. Harrison	1832	1924	Private law practice
55. Howell Edmunds Jackson (Tenn.)	1893–95	B. Harrison	1832	1895	U.S. Circuit Court judge
56. **Edward Douglass White** [1] (La.)	1894–1921	Cleveland	1845	1921	U.S. Senator
57. Rufus Wheeler Peckham (N.Y.)	1896–1909	Cleveland	1838	1909	State Appeals Court judge
58. Joseph McKenna (Calif.)	1898–1925	McKinley	1843	1926	U.S. Attorney General
59. Oliver Wendell Holmes (Mass.)	1902–32	T. Roosevelt	1841	1935	Chief Justice, Massachusetts
60. William Rufus Day (Ohio)	1903–22	T. Roosevelt	1849	1923	U.S. Circuit Court judge
61. William Henry Moody (Mass.)	1906–10	T. Roosevelt	1853	1917	U.S. Attorney General
62. Horace Harmon Lurton (Tenn.)	1910–14	Taft	1844	1914	U.S. Circuit Court judge
63. Charles Evans Hughes [2] (N.Y.)	1910–16	Taft	1862	1948	Governor of New York
64. Willis Van Devanter (Wyo.)	1911–37	Taft	1859	1941	U.S. Circuit Court judge
65. Joseph Rucker Lamar (Ga.)	1911–16	Taft	1857	1916	Private law practice
66. Mahlon Pitney (N.J.)	1912–22	Taft	1858	1924	State Supreme Court judge
67. James Clark McReynolds (Tenn.)	1914–41	Wilson	1862	1946	U.S. Attorney General
68. Louis Dembitz Brandeis (Mass.)	1916–39	Wilson	1856	1941	Private law practice
69. John Hessin Clarke (Ohio)	1916–22	Wilson	1857	1945	U.S. District Court judge
70. **William Howard Taft** (Ohio)	1921–30	Harding	1857	1930	27th U.S. President
71. George Sutherland (Utah)	1922–38	Harding	1862	1942	Private law practice
72. Pierce Butler (Minn.)	1922–39	Harding	1866	1939	Private law practice
73. Edward Terry Sanford (Tenn.)	1923–30	Harding	1865	1930	U.S. District Court judge
74. **Harlan Fiske Stone** [1] (N.Y.)	1925–46	Coolidge	1872	1946	U.S. Attorney General
75. **Charles Evans Hughes** (N.Y.)	1930–41	Hoover	1862	1948	Judge, Permanent Court of International Justice
76. Owen Josephus Roberts (Pa.)	1930–45	Hoover	1875	1955	Private law practice
77. Benjamin Nathan Cardozo (N.Y.)	1932–38	Hoover	1870	1938	State Appeals Court judge
78. Hugo Lafayette Black (Ala.)	1937–71	F. Roosevelt	1886	1971	U.S. Senator
79. Stanley Forman Reed (Ky.)	1938–57	F. Roosevelt	1884	1980	U.S. Solicitor General
80. Felix Frankfurter (Mass.)	1939–62	F. Roosevelt	1882	1965	Professor of law
81. William Orville Douglas (Conn.)	1939–75	F. Roosevelt	1898	1980	Chairman of the SEC
82. Frank Murphy (Mich.)	1940–49	F. Roosevelt	1890	1949	U.S. Attorney General
83. James Francis Byrnes (S.C.)	1941–42	F. Roosevelt	1879	1972	U.S. Senator
84. Robert Houghwout Jackson (N.Y.)	1941–54	F. Roosevelt	1892	1954	U.S. Attorney General
85. Wiley Blount Rutledge (Iowa)	1943–49	F. Roosevelt	1894	1949	U.S. Circuit Court judge
86. Harold Hitz Burton (Ohio)	1945–58	Truman	1888	1964	U.S. Senator
87. **Frederick Moore Vinson** (Ky.)	1946–53	Truman	1890	1953	U.S. Secretary of Treasury
88. Tom Campbell Clark (Texas)	1949–67	Truman	1899	1977	U.S. Attorney General
89. Sherman Minton (Ind.)	1949–56	Truman	1890	1965	U.S. Circuit Court judge
90. **Earl Warren** (Calif.)	1953–69	Eisenhower	1891	1974	Governor of California
91. John Marshall Harlan (N.Y.)	1955–71	Eisenhower	1899	1971	U.S. Circuit Court judge
92.*William Joseph Brennan Jr. (N.J.)	1956–	Eisenhower	1906	—	State Supreme Court judge
93. Charles Evans Whittaker (Mo.)	1957–62	Eisenhower	1901	1973	U.S. Circuit Court judge
94. Potter Stewart (Ohio)	1958–81	Eisenhower	1915	—	U.S. Circuit Court judge
95.*Byron Raymond White (Colo.)	1962–	Kennedy	1917	—	Deputy U.S. Attorney General
96. Arthur Joseph Goldberg (Ill.)	1962–65	Kennedy	1908	—	U.S. Secretary of Labor
97. Abe Fortas [3] (D.C.)	1965–69	L. Johnson	1910	1982	Private law practice
98.*Thurgood Marshall (N.Y.)	1967–	L. Johnson	1908	—	U.S. Solicitor General
99.***Warren Earl Burger** (Minn.)	1969–	Nixon	1907	—	U.S. Circuit Court judge
100.*Harry Andrew Blackmun (Minn.)	1970–	Nixon	1908	—	U.S. Circuit Court judge
101.*Lewis Franklin Powell Jr. (Va.)	1971–	Nixon	1907	—	Private law practice
102.*William Hubbs Rehnquist (Ariz.)	1971–	Nixon	1924	—	Asst. U.S. Attorney General
103.*John Paul Stevens (Ill.)	1975–	Ford	1920	—	U.S. Court of Appeals judge
104.*Sandra Day O'Connor (Ariz.)	1981–	Reagan	1930	—	Arizona Court of Appeals judge

* Current Court members. [1] Raised from Associate to Chief Justice: White, 1910 (by President Taft); Stone, 1941 (by President F. D. Roosevelt). [2] Resigned; later named Chief Justice in 1930. [3] Senate rejected nomination as Chief Justice.

Taxes

HIGHLIGHTS: 1984

TAXES ABSORB 23% OF INCOME

The average after-tax income of U.S. households in 1980 was 23% lower than before taxes, the Census Bureau reported in August 1983.

The average 1980 after-tax household income was $16,270 compared with $21,060 before payments of federal and state income taxes, social security payroll taxes and homeowner property taxes.

Married couples with children averaged $20,520 after taxes. Households maintained by a person age 65 or older averaged $10,980, and those maintained by women with children averaged $8,890.

The report, based on a March 1981 survey of about 65,000 households, also found that three of four households paid some federal income tax and their average was $4,010. About two-thirds of the households paid state income taxes averaging $860.

Estimates show that taxes absorbed about 20% of average household income in 1974, compared with the 23% figure for 1980. Figures indicate that average household income dropped by 7% in 1974–80 after adjustment for taxes paid and changes in consumer prices.

WITHHOLDING ON DIVIDENDS REPEALED

On July 28, 1983, Congress approved a conference bill repealing a 1982 tax law that would have required financial institutions to withhold 10% of the interest and dividends paid to most clients. The withholding would have become effective Aug. 5, after having been postponed twice.

The withholding law had been part of the 1982 tax bill and was intended by 1988 to raise $13.4 to $18.2 billion in revenue that might have been lost by tax evasion. It generated intense lobbying by banks and other financial institutions. Newspaper ads and letters asked investors to write to their congressional representatives and urge repeal of the bill.

The House vote to repeal the law was 392–18, and the Senate vote was 90–7. The bill also included some provisions designed to increase compliance with interest and dividend tax collection.

One enforcement provision required "backup" withholding at a rate of 20%, effective Jan. 1, 1984, of interest and dividends for those taxpayers who had such income and failed to file a return or underreported income from interest and dividends by more than a specified amount.

President Reagan, who previously had indicated opposition to the bill, signed it into law on Aug. 5. To ensure his acceptance, Congress had added an amendment granting concessions in trade and taxes to Caribbean nations under the administration's Caribbean Basin Initiative (CBI).

PRESIDENT MAKES TAX RETURN PUBLIC

President and Mrs. Reagan filed a joint tax return for 1982, and paid federal income taxes of $292,616. Listing their occupations as "President" and "First Lady," the Reagans reported an income of $741,253, putting them in the top 0.02% of the top 1% of the nation's taxpayers, according to the Internal Revenue Service (IRS).

The Reagans, who released the documents on April 15, 1983, reported a capital gain of $256,978 from the sale of a California home, $245,061 in interest, and $4,910 in dividends from a blind trust. The President's salary was $200,000. The Reagans also reported income from pensions of $24,769.

Among their itemized deductions, the Reagans claimed $49,178 in state and local income taxes. The President and his wife gave $15,563 to charity.

ALASKA HAS HIGHEST PER CAPITA TAX BURDEN

The per capita tax burden for the U.S. was expected to be $2,482 for 1983, down 4% from 1982, according to the Tax Foundation Inc. Residents in the states with the highest income levels would pay the highest taxes on a per capita basis. The per capita tax burden for Alaska is the highest, at $3,832, with Washington, D.C., second, at $3,334. Connecticut carries the third-highest tax burden at $3,330 per capita, with New Jersey fourth at $3,115 and Illinois fifth at $2,921.

IMPORTANT TAX DATES IN 1984

February 1—Employers must provide employees with a Statement of Wages Earned and Tax Withheld (Form W-2) for 1983.

February 1—Individuals should file an income tax return for 1983 and pay the tax due, if the last installment on their 1983 estimated income tax was not paid.

April 16—Individuals must file an income tax return for the calendar year 1983. Tax due must be paid in full with the return when filed.

April 16—Those required to do so must file a declaration of estimated income tax for 1984 and pay at least 25% of such tax.

June 15—Individuals must pay second installment of 1984 estimated income tax.

September 17—Individuals must pay third installment of 1984 estimated income tax.

January 15, 1985—Individuals must pay fourth installment of 1984 estimated income tax.

FILING YOUR FEDERAL INCOME TAX IN 1984

Source: Internal Revenue Service, U.S. Department of the Treasury

BLUE, PINK, AND GREEN FORMS

Taxpayers filing 1983 federal income tax returns have a choice of the blue form 1040 (the long form), the pink form 1040A (the short form), or the green form 1040EZ.

You can only use the pink short form if all your income is from salary, wages, tips, other employee compensation, and from dividends and interest.

If you have other sources of income or if you list deductions such as medical expenses, you must use the long blue form. However, you can claim child-care credit, IRA deduction, and two-earner couple deduction on form 1040A.

However, if you are single, claim only one exemption, have an income of $50,000 or less, and received no more than $400 in interest income, you can file the short green 1040EZ form.

You can claim a limited charitable deduction on the short pink or green forms.

WHAT INCOME IS TAXABLE

The following types of income are taxable: all wages and salaries, tips and gratuities, annuities, alimony, awards, back pay, bonuses, business income, commissions, compensations for personal services, dividends, fees, estate and trust income, gambling winnings, hobby income, illegal income, interest on savings, jury duty fees, partnership income, pensions, prizes, profits from sale or exchange of real estate or other property, rents, retirement pay, rewards, royalties, severance pay, and sick pay. Also taxable, as of Jan. 1, 1984, are social security benefits of individuals whose adjusted gross income (including tax-exempt interest income), combined with half of their social security benefits, exceeds $25,000. The limit is $32,000 for a married couple filing jointly.

INCOME NORMALLY NOT TAXABLE

The following income normally is not taxable and should not be reported on the U.S. tax return: social security or welfare payments; benefits paid by the Veterans Administration; dividends paid on veterans insurance; accident, health, and casualty insurance proceeds; disability and death payments; Federal Employees Compensation Act payments; gifts; bequests; inheritances; interest on municipal bonds; insurance proceeds paid because of death; mustering-out pay; Railroad Retirement Act pensions; rental allowances of clergymen; certain scholarship and fellowship grants; workers' compensation; cost-of-living allowances paid U.S. employees abroad; and Medicare or Medicaid reimbursements. Also nontaxable are social security benefits of individuals whose adjusted gross incomes, combined with half of their social security benefits, are below $25,000. Married couples filing a joint return need not pay taxes on social security benefits if their combined adjusted gross income, including half of their social security benefits, is below $32,000.

Taxpayers should obtain IRS booklet *Taxable and Nontaxable Income* (publication 525) for more detailed information on taxable and nontaxable income.

WHO MUST FILE FEDERAL INCOME TAX RETURNS

No matter how low your income was during the year, you must file a return (1) *to get a refund* if income tax was withheld by your employer, or (2) if you qualify to receive up to $500 as an *earned income credit* (see next page).

No matter how young or how old you are, you must file a federal income tax return if you had as much income as one of the following amounts and meet the other specifications following that amount:

$400: if you received this much as net income from self-employment (such as operating your own lawn-mowing business).

$1,000: if you can be claimed as a dependent on your parent's return **and** have received this much in taxable dividends, interest, or other unearned income.

$1,000: if you are married **and** filing separately or are not living with your spouse at the end of the tax year.

$1,000: if you are entitled to exclude income from sources within U.S. possessions.

$3,300: if you are under 65 **and** you are single (or legally separated, divorced, or married living apart from your spouse for the entire year with a dependent child).

$4,300: if you are 65 or older **and** you are single (or as defined above).

$4,400: if you are under 65 **and** you are a qualifying widow or widower with a dependent child.

$5,400: if you are 65 or older **and** you are a qualifying widow or widower with a dependent child.

$5,400: if you are a married couple filing jointly **and** you both are under 65.

$6,400: if you are a married couple filing jointly **and** one of you is 65 or older.

$7,400: if you are a married couple filing jointly **and** you both are 65 or older.

IRS WILL FIGURE OUT YOUR TAX

If you do not feel capable of figuring out how much tax you owe and do not wish to pay someone to do it for you, the Internal Revenue Service (IRS) now will calculate how much tax you owe and (1) send you a refund for overpayment or (2) a bill for underpayment.

Most taxpayers qualify for this service, although some do not.

The IRS will figure out your tax for you if you meet all five of these criteria: (1) Your adjusted gross income is $50,000 or less. (2) You do not itemize such deductions as medical expenses, taxes, charitable contributions, and so on. (3) All of your income must be from wages, salaries, tips, dividends, interest, pensions, and annuities. (4) You cannot use income averaging to reduce your taxable income. (5) You cannot use an exemption for money earned abroad.

SIMPLIFIED TAX TABLES

If you do not qualify to have the IRS figure out your tax, you will find that the tax tables that come with your income tax form have been made easier to use in finding how much tax you owe.

The term "standard deduction" was removed from the Internal Revenue Code by Congress when the Tax Reduction and Simplification Act of 1977 was passed. Instead, Congress replaced the term with "zero bracket amount," which is a flat amount of income on which no tax is paid as determined by your filing status.

The zero bracket amount has been taken into account in the tax tables so that you *do not* deduct it again in determining your tax.

The tax tables show that you pay **no tax:**

(1) If you file as a single person or head of household with no dependents and have an adjusted gross income of $3,300 or less.
(2) If you are married, file jointly with two exemptions, and have an adjusted gross income of $5,400 or less.
(3) If you are married, file separately with only your own exemption, and have an adjusted gross income of $2,700 or less.

The tax tables have been extended to higher amounts of income to enable more taxpayers to determine how much tax they owe merely by finding the tax in the tables.

The maximum income included in the tax tables is $50,000.

Additional computation using tax schedules is necessary for taxpayers with higher incomes, those using income averaging, or those in other special tax situations.

EARNED INCOME CREDIT

You may be entitled to a special payment or credit of up to $500, which you could receive as a refund check or as a credit applied against taxes you owe.

You are eligible for the credit if you meet all three of these tests: (1) Your adjusted gross income was less than $10,000; (2) Your earned income was more than $1 but was less than $10,000; (3) You paid more than half the cost of keeping up a home in the United States in which you and your dependent child lived.

The credit is equal to 10% of your earned income or your adjusted gross income up to a maximum credit of $500 for an income of $5,000. If your income is larger than $5,000, the credit is scaled down so that you receive a smaller and smaller credit until it reaches zero for an income of $10,000.

If you were married, to be eligible for the earned income credit you must file a joint return (unless you did not live with your spouse at all during the year but did pay over half the cost to maintain the household where the dependent child lived).

If you are eligible for the Earned Income Credit, the IRS also will figure out this credit for you if you write "EIC" and the name of the child that qualifies you for the credit on the line specified on your tax form.

Remember, to receive the credit, you *must* file a federal income tax return, even though your income was so small that otherwise you would not have to file.

PERSONAL EXEMPTIONS AND DEPENDENTS

You can claim exemptions for yourself and your dependents whether you use the pink short form 1040A or the blue long form 1040. Each exemption reduces by $1,000 the amount of your income on which you are taxed.

Your Own Exemptions. Whether you are married or single, you receive at least one exemption for yourself. If you are 65 or older, you can claim a *second* exemption for yourself. And if you are blind, you can claim a *third* exemption for yourself.

To claim the exemption for blindness, you must submit proof with your income tax form. If you are completely blind, submit a statement saying so. If you partially blind, submit a statement from an eye physician or registered optometrist (1) that you cannot

---

TAX HOTLINE

If you need special information in preparing your income tax return, you can phone toll-free on your state's IRS hotline. To find out the phone number of your state's IRS hotline, call 800-555-1212 for toll-free directory assistance.

YOUR FEDERAL INCOME TAX *(continued)*

see over 20/200 with glasses, or (2) your field of view does not exceed 20 degrees.

Exemptions for Your Spouse. If you file a joint return with your spouse, your spouse is entitled to at least one exemption, a *second* exemption if 65 or older, and a *third* exemption if blind. Again, if a blindness exemption for your spouse is claimed, proof should be submitted with the tax form.

If you were legally divorced or separated at the end of the tax year, you cannot take an exemption for your former spouse.

If your spouse died during the year and you did not remarry, you can still claim the exemptions that you could have taken for your spouse on the date of death.

Exemptions for Dependent Children. You can claim one additional exemption for each of your dependent children who live with you, listing their first names.

Even if your child who is 19 or younger had income of $1,000 or more and has to file a tax return, you can still claim an exemption if the child lived at your home and you paid over half of his or her support.

Even if your child is 19 or older, earns $1,000 or more, and does not live at home, you can claim him or her as an exemption if the child is enrolled as a full-time student during five months of the year and receives at least half his or her support from you.

Exemptions for Children of Divorced or Separated Parents. The parent who has custody of the child during most of the year usually can claim an exemption for the child.

However, the parent who does not have custody can claim the exemption for the child (1) if that parent gave at least $600 toward the child's support during the year and the divorce or separation agreement states he or she can take the exemption, *or* (2) if that parent gave $1,200 or more for the child's support during the year and the parent having custody cannot prove he or she provided more money for the child's support.

Exemptions for Other Dependents. You also can claim exemptions for other persons who are related to you or who lived in your home for the full year if you paid more than half their support and they received less than $1,000 income.

You can take an exemption for a dependent who died during the year if he or she met the tests for a dependent while alive.

You can obtain more information about dependent exemptions from the IRS booklet *Exemptions* (publication 501).

ADJUSTMENTS TO INCOME

The blue income tax form 1040 provides space where you can deduct certain expenses to determine what is called your *adjusted gross income.*

Moving Expenses. If you had to move at least 35 miles during the year for reasons connected with your job or business, you can deduct the cost of moving your family, furniture and other household goods and personal belongings. You also can deduct such related expenses as the cost of hunting for a new home, meals and lodging while living in temporary quarters for up to 30 days, and expenses in selling or renting your old home.

For more information, obtain the IRS booklet *Moving Expenses* (publication 521).

Employee Business Expenses. You can deduct the following expenses that were not paid by your employer: (1) *Travel and transportation,* including the cost of using your car in your work. Instead of figuring your actual automobile expenses, you can take a mileage rate of 20¢ a mile for the first 15,000 miles and 11¢ for each mile over 15,000, plus parking fees and tolls. (2) *Meals and lodging* expenses while you were temporarily away overnight on business from the area of your main place of work. (3) *Selling expenses,* if you are an outside salesperson who does all selling away from your employer's place of business. For more information, obtain IRS booklet *Travel, Entertainment, and Gift Expenses* (publication 463).

Payments to a Retirement Plan. You can deduct payments to an authorized retirement plan. No additional forms are required for IRA or Keogh plans. See IRS booklets *Individual Retirement Arrangements* or *Self-Employed Retirement Plans* (publications 560 and 590).

Forfeited Interest Penalty. You can deduct a forfeited interest penalty that you have had to pay because you made a premature withdrawal from a time savings account. To do so, you must have included the interest payment you received as part of your gross income.

Alimony Paid. If you are divorced or legally separated from your spouse, you can deduct periodic payments of alimony or separate maintenance made under a court decree. You also can deduct payments made under a written separation agreement or decree for support entered into since 1954.

You *cannot deduct* lump-sum cash or property settlements, voluntary payments not made under a court order or written separation agreement, or amounts specified as child support.

The person *receiving* the alimony or separation payments must report them as taxable income.

For more information, obtain IRS booklet *Tax Information for Divorced or Separated*

Individuals (publication 504).

Disability Income Exclusion. If you are under the age of 65 and totally disabled, you may be able to exclude up to $100 a week from your income. You must enclose a physician's certification of your total disability with your return.

For information on how to figure the amount of your disability income exclusion, obtain IRS booklet *Disability Payments* (publication 522).

TAX CREDITS

You may be eligible for certain tax credits. These are amounts that are deducted directly from the taxes owed on your adjusted gross income.

Political Contributions. If you made contributions to political candidates or political organizations, you can claim a tax credit. The amount claimed cannot exceed half the amount you actually contributed and is limited to $50 on a single return or $100 on a joint return.

Credit for the Elderly. You may be able to claim this credit and reduce your tax by as much as $375 (if single) or $562.50 (if married filing jointly). To be eligible, you must be (1) 65 or older, *or* (2) under 65 but retired under a public retirement system. For more information, obtain IRS Schedules R and RP, or publication 524, *Credit for the Elderly.*

Credit for Child and Dependent Care Expenses. A taxpayer who pays for child care or care of a disabled dependent in order to be gainfully employed is eligible for a credit that can be deducted directly from taxes on blue form 1040 or 1040A. The credit amounts to up to 20% of eligible expenses for such care to a maximum of a $400 credit ($2,000 expenses) for one dependent or $800 for two or more ($4,000 expenses).

A married couple can use this credit if one spouse works full-time and the other works part-time or is a full-time student.

Under certain circumstances payments to relatives for such care can be counted in calculating the tax credit.

For more information, see IRS Form 2441, *Credit for Child Care Expenses.*

Investment Credit. You may be eligible for this credit if you have invested in certain trade or business property. For more information, obtain IRS Form 3468, *Computations of Investment Credit.*

Foreign Tax Credit. If you paid income tax to a foreign country or U.S. possession, you can claim this credit.

Work Incentive Credit. An employer can claim a credit for the salaries and wages paid to employees hired under a Work Incentive (WIN) Program or to welfare recipients.

Jobs Credit. This is a credit for business employers who hire additional employees during the year.

Energy Credits. You may be allowed a tax credit of as much as $300 for energy-conservation measures you have made to your house if it was completed before April 20, 1977. Up to a $4,000 credit may be available for improvements using renewable energy sources, such as wind, solar, or geothermal energy.

ITEMIZED DEDUCTIONS

If you had certain expenses during the year, such as contributions to a church or large medical expenses, it may be to your advantage to itemize deductions on Schedule A of blue form 1040.

Medical and Dental Expenses. Medical and dental expenses that you actually paid during the year can be deducted in part from your income for tax purposes.

You can no longer deduct separately one-half (up to $150) of the amount you paid for insurance for medical or hospital care.

The medical expenses you claim for deduction can include those for yourself, your spouse, and any dependent who received over half his or her support from you. You may *not* include amounts repaid to you, or repaid to anyone else, by hospital, health, or accident insurance. To qualify as a deduction, your medical expenses must exceed 5% of your adjusted gross income.

Taxes. You can deduct state and local income taxes, real estate taxes, sales taxes, and personal property taxes.

You *cannot* deduct federal social security tax, federal excise taxes, gasoline taxes, fees for hunting and dog licenses, fees for car inspection or drivers' licenses, taxes you paid for another person, water taxes, or taxes on liquor, beer, wine, cigarettes, and tobacco.

Interest Expenses. You can deduct interest that you have paid on a mortgage or a loan, on a bank credit-card plan, on charge accounts, and on installment-plan purchases. There are limitations on the amount of interest you can deduct on interest expense paid or accrued on debts related to investment property.

Contributions. You can deduct gifts or donations made to organizations operated for religious, charitable, educational, scientific, or literary purposes, or to prevent cruelty to animals and children.

You *cannot* deduct gifts to relatives, friends, or other persons; to social clubs, labor unions, or chambers of commerce; or to foreign organizations, organizations operated for personal profit, or organizations whose purpose is to get people to vote for new laws or for changes in old laws.

YOUR FEDERAL INCOME TAX *(continued)*

Casualty or Theft Losses. You may be able to deduct part of your loss if you had property stolen or damaged by fire, storm, automobile accident, shipwreck, and so on. The first $100 of *each* casualty or theft loss of nonbusiness property in excess of insurance reimbursement is *not* deductible.

You can only deduct a casualty or theft loss to the extent it exceeds 10% of your adjusted gross income.

Adoption Expenses. You may deduct up to $1,500 for qualified expenses incurred to adopt a child with special needs (a child eligible for adoption assistance under the Social Security Act).

Other Deductions. A variety of other expenses may be claimed as deductible as follows:

Dues paid to unions, professional organizations, and chambers of commerce.

Expenses for education that helps you keep up or improve skills you must have in your present job, trade, or business. You *cannot* deduct expenses for education to meet the minimum requirements for your job, business, or trade; or for education that is part of a course of study that will lead to your getting a new trade or business.

Gambling losses to the extent of the amount that you won and reported as income.

Cost of safety equipment, small tools, and supplies used in your job.

Expenses relating to business or office use of your home.

Certain costs of business entertainment.

Fees paid to employment agencies.

For more information, obtain IRS booklets *Business Use of Your Home* (publication 587) and *Miscellaneous Deductions and Credits* (publication 529).

TAX SAVINGS FOR HOMEOWNERS

If you own your own home, you usually can save on your income taxes by itemizing as deductions the interest on your mortgage and the local property taxes you must pay.

Any gain you realize on the sale or exchange of your home after Jan. 21, 1980, is not taxed at the time of sale if within 24 months before or after you buy and occupy another residence whose cost equals or exceeds the price of the old residence. Additional time is allowed if you construct the new residence or if you were on active duty in the U.S. armed forces. The tax is postponed; it is not forgiven.

If you are 55 or older you are entitled to a one-time exclusion of $125,000 in capital gains from the sale of your home after July 20, 1981.

For additional information, obtain IRS booklets *Tax Information for Homeowners* (publication 530) and *Tax Information on Selling or Buying Your Home* (publication 523).

INCOME AVERAGING

Certain taxpayers may benefit from a provision that provides for averaging of income. Some persons with fluctuating incomes may be eligible to pay less tax through this provision.

If the income for a given year exceeds one and one-fifth times the average annual income for the four preceding years, and the excess is more than $3,000, the taxpayer may be eligible to use this provision in figuring his tax liability.

For more information, obtain IRS booklet *Income Averaging* (publication 506).

TAX EFFECT OF CAPITAL GAINS AND LOSSES

Usually, the tax on capital gains is less than the tax on ordinary income.

If the net gains from the sale or exchange of long-term capital assets (those held longer than one year) are greater than the net losses from the sale or exchange of capital assets held for a shorter time, a maximum tax rate of 20% applies to 40% of the gain (if the sale or exchange occurred after June 9, 1981).

If the net result of all sales and exchanges of both long-term and short-term capital assets is a loss, you can deduct 50¢ from income for each $1 of loss up to a total of the loss in adjusted gross income or a $3,000 deduction for a $6,000 loss. The balance of the loss may be carried over and deducted in succeeding tax years.

INCOME FROM DIVIDENDS OR INTEREST

Similar to interest paid on savings, dividends, are distributions of cash, property, services, or accommodations by a corporation to its stockholders.

Such payments are taxable income to the stockholder. Distributions other than cash are taxed at their fair market value.

The gross amount must be reported. However, the first $100 of qualified dividends and interest may be excluded from income by a single person on Form 1040 or 1040A. To qualify for exclusion, dividends must be from taxable domestic corporations.

Husbands and wives filing a joint return are permitted up to $200 exclusions for dividends or interest.

In addition to industrial, mercantile, and other commercial corporations, the exclusion applies to dividends on the capital stock of nonexempt cooperatives, stock of the Federal National Mortgage Association, the capital stock of building and loan associations (as distinct from dividends on deposits and withdrawable accounts), and similar organizations.

Some types of corporations whose dividends do not qualify are: foreign corporations, China Trade Act corporations, exempt farmers' cooperatives, real estate investment trusts, corporations doing business in U.S. possessions (under certain conditions), and a corporation that has elected not to be taxed as a corporation.

PRESERVE ADEQUATE RECORDS

Maintain proper records to prepare federal income tax returns correctly. These records, if complete, help ensure that you will pay only the proper tax. File and store in a safe place sales slips, invoices, receipts, canceled checks, paid bills, and other documents that are used as evidence of transactions.

Copies of returns filed by the taxpayer should also be kept. These are of help in preparing future returns and if it later becomes necessary to file a claim for refund.

WHERE TO FILE AND WHEN

Individual federal income tax returns may be filed anytime on or after January 1 of the year following the year of earnings, but no later than midnight April 16, 1984, if the calendar year is the basis for these earnings.

All taxpayers—those entitled to refunds as well as those who are not—should file their returns directly with the Internal Revenue Service center that serves their state (as indicated in the tax form instructions).

If the fiscal year is used, the return is due on or before the 15th day of the fourth month after the close of the particular fiscal or tax year. Returns submitted by mail must be postmarked on or before the due date.

Payment must be made at the time the return is filed. Interest of 16% per year is charged on taxes paid after their due date, even though an extension for filing may have been authorized.

A penalty of ½% a month or part of a month to a maximum of 25% is imposed for failure to pay when due. Additional penalties are assessed for failure to file.

U.S. citizens abroad on the final filing date are allowed automatic extensions without application to June 15, 1984. Military personnel on duty outside the U.S. and Puerto Rico are allowed the same extension. Statements that the taxpayer was outside the U.S. on the due date must accompany the return.

When filing a return, you should use the preaddressed label (showing your name, address, and Social Security number) that you receive with the form 1040 or 1040A tax packages from IRS at the end of the year. Use of this label expedites processing and the issuance of any refund due.

Before filing your income tax return, make sure it is complete in every detail. It *must* include your complete name, Social Security number, amount of wages from all W-2 forms, total of personal exemptions, deductions (regardless of how computed), and signature (of both husband and wife if a joint return). Any error or omission can result in a processing delay and may slow a tax refund payment.

ESTIMATED TAX RETURN

In some instances individuals are required to file an estimated tax declaration and pay all estimated tax.

Generally a person must declare and pay an estimated tax if total tax liability is expected to exceed the amount withheld by $400 or more.

HISTORY OF THE U.S. INCOME TAX

The federal government first levied an income tax from 1862 to 1872 to help pay for the Civil War.

A new income tax law passed by Congress in 1894 was declared unconstitutional by the Supreme Court.

In 1909 the first corporate income tax law was approved by Congress.

In 1911 Wisconsin became the first state to levy an income tax on residents.

The 16th Amendment to the U.S. Constitution, adopted in 1913, made possible the present system of federal income taxes.

The first of the new income taxes began to be collected under the Underwood Tariff Act, which became law in October 1913.

Payroll taxes began in 1935, and pay-as-you-go wage deductions in 1944.

Exemptions for those who are blind or are senior citizens, as well as joint returns for married couples, took effect in 1948.

Today federal tax returns of all business and individual taxpayers in the United States are processed by computers. The system has three major features: (1) It provides a continuing updated multiple-year digest of each individual and business taxpayer's history in a master file. (2) Each taxpayer is identified in the master file by number—individuals by their social security number and businesses by their employer identification number. (3) The system centralizes processing operations in regional centers.

Individuals send their returns to one of 10 regional processing centers, where they are reviewed and remittances deposited. The center then transcribes pertinent information to the master file.

STATE INCOME TAX RATES AND EXEMPTIONS: 1983

Sources: Tax Foundation; Commerce Clearing House

Seven of the 50 states of the United States do not assess any state tax on personal incomes, including Alaska, Florida, Nevada, South Dakota, Texas, Washington, and Wyoming.

STATE	PERSONAL EXEMPTIONS			INDIVIDUAL RATES
	Single	Married	Dependent	
Alabama	$1,500	$ 3,000	$ 300	From 2% on 1st $1,000 to 5% on income over $6,000
Arizona	$1,729	$ 3,458	$1,038	From 2% on 1st $1,000 to 8% on income over $6,000
Arkansas	$17.50[1]	$ 35[1]	$ 6[1]	From 1% on 1st $2,999 to 7% on income over $25,000
California	$ 38[1]	$ 76[1]	$ 12[1]	From 1% on 1st $3,120 to 11% on income over $24,200
Colorado	$ 850	$ 1,700	$ 850	From 2.5% on 1st $1,415 to 8% on $14,153 or more; 2% surtax on intangible income over $15,000
Connecticut [2]	$ 100	$ 200	—	7% on capital gains, on dividends and interest, 6% on income between $50,000 and $59,999; 13% on income over $100,000
Delaware	$ 600	$ 1,200	$ 600	From 1.4% on 1st $1,000 to 13.5% on income over $50,000
Dist. of Col.	$ 750	$ 1,500	$ 750	From 2% on 1st $1,000 to 11% on income over $25,000
Georgia	$1,500	$ 3,000	$ 700	From 1% on 1st $1,000 to 6% on income over $10,000
Hawaii	$1,000	$ 2,000	$1,000	From 2.25% on 1st $1,000 to 11% on income over $61,000
Idaho	$ 750	$ 1,500	$ 750	From 2% on 1st $1,000 to 7.5% on income over $5,000; each person (husband and wife filing jointly are deemed one person) filing return pays additional $10
Illinois	$1,000	$ 2,000	$1,000	3% on net income
Indiana	$1,000	$ 2,000	$ 500	3% of adjusted gross income
Iowa	$ 15[1]	$ 30[1]	$ 10[1]	From 0.5% on 1st $1,023 to 13% on income over $76,725
Kansas	$1,000	$ 2,000	$1,000	From 2% on 1st $2,000 to 9% on income over $25,000
Kentucky	$ 20[1]	$ 40[1]	$ 20[1]	From 2% on 1st $3,000 to 6% on income over $8,000
Louisiana	$6,000	$12,000	$1,000	From 2% on 1st $10,000 to 6% on income over $50,000
Maine	$1,000	$ 2,000	$1,000	From 1% on 1st $2,000 to 10% on income over $25,000
Maryland	$ 800	$ 1,600	$ 800	From 2% on 1st $1,000 to 5% on income over $3,000
Massachusetts	$2,200	$ 4,400	$ 700	Interest, dividends, net capital gains, 10%; earned and business income, 5%; additional surtax, 7.5%
Michigan	$1,500	$ 3,000	$1,500	All taxable income, 6.35%
Minnesota	$ 67	$ 134	$ 67	From 1.6% on 1st $667 to 16% on income over $36,632 + 5% surtax
Mississippi	$6,000	$ 9,500	$1,500	First $5,000, 3%; over $10,000, 5%
Missouri	$1,200	$ 2,400	$ 400	From 1.5% on 1st $1,000 to 6% on income over $9,000
Montana	$ 940	$ 1,880	$ 940	From 2% on 1st $1,200 to 11% on income over $41,100
Nebraska	$ 750	$ 1,500	$ 750	20% of federal income tax liability
New Hampshire	$ 600	$ 1,200	—	5% on income from interest and dividends
New Jersey	$1,000	$ 2,000	$1,000	2.5% on 1st $20,000; 3.5% on income over $50,000
New Mexico	$ 750	$ 1,500	$ 750	0.7% on 1st $2,000 to 7.8% on income over $100,000
New York	$ 800	$ 1,600	$ 800	From 2% on 1st $1,000 to 14% on income over $23,000
North Carolina	$1,100	$ 2,200	$ 800	From 3% on 1st $2,000 to 7% on income over $10,000
North Dakota	$ 750	$ 1,500	$ 750	From 2% on 1st $3,000 to 9% on income over $50,000
Ohio	$ 650	$ 1,300	$ 650	From 0.5% on 1st $5,000 to 5% on income over $100,000; additional 83.3% surtax
Oklahoma	$1,000	$ 2,000	$1,000	From 0.5% on 1st $2,000 to 6% on income over $15,000
Oregon	$1,000	$ 2,000	$1,000	From 4.2% on 1st $500 to 10.8% on income over $5,000
Pennsylvania	—	—	—	2.45% on all taxable income
Rhode Island	$ 750	$ 1,500	$ 750	26.75% of federal income tax liability
South Carolina	$ 800	$ 1,600	$ 800	From 2% on 1st $2,000 to 7% on income over $10,000
Tennessee	—	—	—	On dividends and interest, 6%; on dividends from corporations having 75% of property taxable in state, 4%
Utah	$ 750	$ 1,500	$ 750	From 2.25% on 1st $1,500 to 7.75% on excess over $7,500
Vermont	$ 750	$ 1,500	$ 750	26% of federal income tax liability
Virginia	$ 600	$ 1,200	$ 600	From 2% on 1st $3,000 to 5¾% on income over $12,000
West Virginia	$ 700	$ 1,400	$ 700	From 2.1% on 1st $2,000 to 13% on excess over $6,000 + 12% surtax
Wisconsin	$ 20[1]	$ 40[1]	$ 20[1]	From 3.4% on 1st $3,900 to 10% on income over $51,600 + 10% surtax

[1] Credit against tax. [2] Tax applies only to adjusted gross incomes of $20,000 or more; capital gains tax applies to gains of $200 and over for joint returns and $100 or over for singles.

STATE CORPORATE INCOME TAXES: 1983[1]

Source: Tax Foundation

Only 5 of the 50 states of the United States do not levy state corporation income taxes. These states are Nevada, South Dakota, Texas, Washington, and Wyoming.

STATE	RATE	SPECIAL CONDITIONS
Alabama [2]	.... 5.0%	
Alaska	1st $ 10,000...... 1.0%	Next $ 10,000..... 5.0% Next $10,000........ 9.0%
	Next $ 10,000...... 2.0%	Next 10,000..... 6.0% $90,000 or more........ 9.4%
	Next $ 10,000...... 3.0%	Next 10,000..... 7.0%
	Next $ 10,000...... 4.0%	Next 10,000..... 8.0%
Arizona [2]	1st $ 1,000...... 2.5%	4th $ 1,000..... 6.5% 6th $ 1,000........ 9.0%
	2d $ 1,000...... 4.0%	5th $ 1,000..... 8.0% Over $ 6,000........ 10.5%
	3d $ 1,000...... 5.0%	
Arkansas	1st $ 3,000...... 1.0%	Next $ 14,000..... 5.0%
	2d $ 3,000...... 2.0%	Over $ 25,000..... 6.0%
	Next $ 5,000...... 3.0%	
California	.... 9.6%	Financial corporations except banks allowed limited offset for personal property taxes and license fees. Minimum tax: $200
Colorado	.... 5.0%	
Connecticut	.... 11.5%	Additional tax of 3.1 mills per dollar of capital stock and surplus to the extent that it exceeds net income tax
Delaware	.... 8.7%	
Dist. of Columbia	.... 9.0%	Minimum tax: $100; surtax of 10%
Florida	.... 5.0%	Exemption of $5,000 of net income allowed each corporation
Georgia	.... 6.0%	
Hawaii	$25,000 or less 5.85%	Capital gains, 3.08%
	Over $ 25,000...... 6.435%	
Idaho	.... 7.7%	
Illinois	.... 4.8%	Exemption of $1,000 of net income allowed each corporation
Indiana	.... 3.0%	Based on adjusted gross income; supplemental 4% based on net income
Iowa [2]	1st $ 25,000...... 6.0%	Financial institutions franchise tax 5% of taxable net income
	Next $ 75,000...... 8.0%	
	Next $150,000...... 10.0%	
	Over $250,000...... 12.0%	
Kansas	.... 4.5%	A 2.25% surtax imposed on taxable income over $25,000
Kentucky	$25,000 or less 3.0%	Next $ 50,000..... 5.0%
	Next $ 25,000...... 4.0%	Over $ 100,000..... 6.0%
Louisiana [2]	1st $ 25,000...... 4.0%	Next $ 100,000..... 7.0%
	2d $ 25,000...... 5.0%	Over $ 200,000..... 8.0%
	Next $ 50,000...... 6.0%	
Maine	$25,000 or less 4.95%	
	Over $ 25,000...... 6.93%	
Maryland	.... 7.0%	
Massachusetts	.... 8.33%	Net income tax supplemented by a $2.60 per $1,000 levy on tangible property not subject to local taxes, plus 8.33% of net income or $228, whichever is greater. A 14% surtax is also imposed. Interstate corporations not subject to corporate income tax pay 4% of net income plus the 14% surtax
Michigan [3]	.... 2.35%	
Minnesota	1st $25,000...... 6.0%	Over $25,000....... 12.0%
Mississippi	1st $ 5,000...... 3.0%	Next $ 5,000....... 4.0% Over $10,000.......... 5.0%
Missouri [2, 3]	.... 5.0%	
Montana	.... 6.75%	Minimum tax: $50, except $10 for small business corporations
Nebraska	1st $50,000...... 5.0%	Over $50,000..... 7.00%
New Hampshire	.... 8.0%	A 19.5% surtax is levied for fiscal year 1984.
New Jersey	.... 9.0%	Added tax on net worth
New Mexico	1st $1,000,000...... 4.8%	2d $1,000,000 .... 6% Over $2 million 7.2%
New York [3]	.... 10.0%	Alternative computing methods used if tax yield is more Minimum tax: $250. Surcharge is 20%
North Carolina	.... 6.0%	
North Dakota [2]	1st $ 3,000...... 3.0%	Next $ 10,000..... 7.5%
	Next $ 5,000...... 4.5%	Next $ 20,000..... 9.0%
	Next $ 12,000...... 6.0%	Over $ 50,000..... 10.5%
Ohio [3]	1st $ 25,000...... 5.1%	Alternative computing methods used if tax yield is more;
	Over $ 25,000...... 9.2%	5.75% surtax imposed; minimum tax $50
Oklahoma	.... 4.0%	
Oregon	.... 7.5%	
Pennsylvania	.... 10.5%	
Rhode Island	.... 8.0%	If yield is greater, tax is 40¢ on each $100 of net worth
South Carolina	.... 6.0%	
Tennessee	.... 6.0%	Additional tax on dividends and interest
Utah	.... 4.65%	Minimum tax: $50
Vermont	1st $ 10,000...... 5.0%	Minimum tax: $50
	Next $ 15,000...... 6.0%	
	Next $225,000...... 7.0%	
	Over $250,000...... 7.5%	
Virginia	.... 6.0%	
West Virginia	$50,000 or less 6.0%	15% surtax imposed
	Over $ 50,000...... 7.0%	
Wisconsin	.... 7.9%	10% surtax imposed

[1] All states levy special financial institutions tax based on net income or on value of shares of capital stock.
[2] Federal income tax is deductible in computing state tax. [3] Local taxes also imposed.

STATE TAX COLLECTIONS: WHERE THE MONEY COMES FROM [1]

Source: U.S. Department of Commerce, Bureau of the Census

STATE	TOTAL	LICENSES	INDIVIDUAL INCOME	CORPORATE INCOME	PROPERTY	DEATH AND GIFT	SEVERANCE	MISC. TAXES[2]
All states	$162,657,820	$10,099,095	$45,707,515	$14,006,175	$3,112,771	$2,350,092	$7,829,693	$2,946,368
Alabama	2,195,831	125,905	480,969	123,218	45,681	9,630	63,470	41,477
Alaska	2,539,193	54,217	1,488	703,663	142,719	335	1,571,553	5,499
Arizona	1,856,009	123,698	438,985	114,759	129,897	11,959	—	—
Arkansas	1,263,746	96,098	353,733	91,706	5,066	4,390	29,753	2,670
California	21,818,694	837,026	7,467,709	2,643,946	708,395	461,665	27,911	59,287
Colorado	1,690,034	105,900	548,944	91,400	4,967	12,979	49,184	3,632
Connecticut	2,339,524	125,348	137,726	349,283	12	79,206	—	50,375
Delaware	594,816	166,882	286,069	36,138	—	8,234	—	12,476
Florida	5,555,936	399,933	—	383,827	109,512	76,474	157,633	275,894
Georgia	3,281,065	100,220	1,182,783	267,683	12,941	12,795	—	7,085
Hawaii	1,066,225	16,929	283,000	43,202	—	5,106	—	1,453
Idaho	578,613	67,160	220,073	45,602	207	3,481	2,517	1,218
Illinois	7,429,268	469,299	2,222,143	714,196	133,356	158,245	—	43,922
Indiana	3,063,657	147,250	748,769	125,845	26,083	41,047	1,780	105
Iowa	1,996,971	193,276	720,883	147,115	—	79,842	—	2,278
Kansas	1,442,737	107,825	459,822	122,549	24,170	31,555	1,013	752
Kentucky	2,491,052	105,628	600,823	166,815	196,167	29,606	256,838	104,146
Louisiana	3,127,229	184,010	220,134	291,953	—	27,157	982,146	23,400
Maine	730,979	58,118	209,585	36,090	14,483	17,074	—	989
Maryland	3,193,087	119,532	1,354,613	148,857	112,198	23,614	—	182,276
Massachusetts	4,803,664	162,476	2,324,052	598,283	419	99,355	—	46,515
Michigan	6,307,161	316,622	2,126,630	952,280	155,167	58,002	81,603	76
Minnesota	3,799,371	231,721	1,549,121	325,295	3,853	24,568	118,609	121,771
Mississippi	1,462,293	113,501	168,471	70,987	5,166	6,587	117,012	264
Missouri	2,313,057	197,627	760,711	123,072	5,528	36,291	30	516
Montana	529,144	46,155	143,804	44,630	33,980	7,680	149,361	1,365
Nebraska	860,527	73,623	226,560	48,498	3,025	10,360	6,010	6,625
Nevada	745,460	84,173	—	—	23,695	—	—	163,554
New Hampshire	325,515	55,852	15,076	79,808	7,415	9,479	45	42,878
New Jersey	5,577,236	479,955	1,305,567	724,869	58,643	126,763	—	135,525
New Mexico	1,226,543	60,804	14,263	60,265	11,029	3,702	377,802	19,203
New York	15,438,003	533,706	8,034,066	1,342,051	—	145,976	—	221,291
North Carolina	3,790,035	286,649	1,449,370	277,460	56,871	45,336	1,217	21,883
North Dakota	532,631	48,452	35,342	37,734	2,072	3,114	186,685	7,638
Ohio	5,819,461	506,838	1,243,618	548,091	158,978	49,057	4,033	12,652
Oklahoma	2,712,960	230,882	641,428	139,022	—	41,347	742,700	82,839
Oregon	1,552,313	175,237	968,264	124,171	147	42,216	50,480	855
Pennsylvania	8,185,625	870,115	1,985,270	869,714	110,306	218,419	—	224,310
Rhode Island	674,792	23,825	215,156	52,524	7,262	9,069	—	7,023
South Carolina	1,959,205	81,413	641,838	131,546	7,783	13,348	—	29,756
South Dakota	328,785	27,395	—	1,041	—	8,135	9,299	11,097
Tennessee	2,146,242	205,169	44,469	206,835	—	29,238	2,512	35,963
Texas	9,099,849	914,070	—	—	2,496	107,849	2,378,601	637,600
Utah	950,869	38,531	331,145	40,894	242	4,514	22,295	—
Vermont	332,308	38,601	112,520	24,954	426	1,441	—	35,260
Virginia	3,235,829	164,762	1,446,187	176,965	35,345	21,756	1,280	115,184
Washington	3,528,362	198,870	—	—	615,966	56,191	46,123	65,203
West Virginia	1,468,886	80,123	305,964	34,400	1,584	14,109	—	66,522
Wisconsin	3,934,495	193,192	1,680,372	322,939	103,472	59,483	837	14,066
Wyoming	762,533	54,502	—	—	36,047	2,313	389,361	—

1 In $ thousands (add 000) for fiscal year 1982.

2 Document, stock transfer, and miscellaneous taxes.

SALES TAXES AND GROSS RECEIPTS TAXES[1]							INSURANCE TRUST FUND REVENUES [2]	STATE
General Sales Tax	Motor Fuels	Alcoholic Beverages	Tobacco Products	Insurance	Public Utilities	Pari-mutuels		
$50,342,651	$10,437,350	$2,723,456	$3,957,870	$3,457,553	$4,956,966	$730,265	$50,847,996	All states
629,453	237,698	104,364	69,947	71,696	192,323	—	544,103	Alabama
—	31,096	8,978	4,908	13,504	1,233	—	305,924	Alaska
800,921	122,343	23,341	40,766	22,000	16,463	10,877	604,807	Arizona
419,378	133,384	23,308	51,667	35,307	—	17,286	267,925	Arkansas
7,720,805	835,281	140,597	278,317	483,860	30,967	122,928	7,798,016	California
612,900	138,802	25,337	37,159	46,660	2,301	9,869	630,516	Colorado
1,004,164	149,176	25,827	74,411	72,398	214,928	56,670	438,237	Connecticut
—	34,554	5,036	12,628	13,405	18,551	843	120,611	Delaware
2,783,889	431,686	312,752	270,168	112,775	132,591	108,802	1,019,451	Florida
1,088,279	350,803	97,990	85,585	74,901	—	—	767,597	Georgia
576,927	33,196	7,701	14,011	27,713	56,987	—	303,122	Hawaii
146,206	56,805	8,164	8,240	16,915	1,753	272	187,003	Idaho
2,333,153	364,705	75,332	173,978	78,484	595,746	66,709	2,562,391	Illinois
1,510,453	286,066	34,387	85,405	56,467	—	—	558,086	Indiana
523,397	180,037	16,399	61,070	71,410	1,264	—	477,433	Iowa
470,762	116,416	34,400	33,867	38,850	756	—	322,794	Kansas
682,432	202,444	16,850	21,830	93,394	—	14,079	633,811	Kentucky
926,912	190,761	56,945	65,356	100,374	36,472	21,609	668,135	Louisiana
248,943	49,579	30,194	24,661	14,824	24,822	1,617	166,561	Maine
797,397	192,032	32,119	70,272	63,148	79,995	17,034	647,304	Maryland
917,362	269,297	85,059	145,357	122,218	—	33,271	866,920	Massachusetts
1,843,651	421,922	96,304	135,257	96,617	—	23,030	2,723,108	Michigan
875,008	258,868	55,283	88,672	75,776	70,826	—	964,824	Minnesota
767,072	101,656	35,047	35,074	41,456	—	—	396,193	Mississippi
839,003	193,579	25,022	60,979	69,868	831	—	741,797	Missouri
—	49,416	14,844	11,752	20,318	5,839	—	199,175	Montana
288,517	125,715	13,873	25,431	22,866	841	8,583	97,551	Nebraska
375,973	55,704	11,776	13,525	14,869	1,852	339	413,988	Nevada
—	59,855	5,350	26,245	15,523	671	7,318	112,105	New Hampshire
1,379,206	287,756	59,116	177,445	113,405	715,212	13,774	1,960,248	New Jersey
533,809	86,791	15,912	14,650	21,716	4,521	2,076	247,251	New Mexico
3,196,779	443,825	147,000	339,733	197,608	731,212	104,756	5,483,732	New York
779,512	372,159	115,728	18,278	93,239	272,333	—	1,004,840	North Carolina
146,935	34,711	6,021	9,724	10,215	3,988	—	143,258	North Dakota
1,819,381	527,012	73,682	198,604	156,829	494,516	26,170	4,792,502	Ohio
481,996	137,724	47,194	86,919	71,715	9,194	—	351,787	Oklahoma
—	91,303	10,836	47,078	34,261	2,163	5,302	870,619	Oregon
2,229,436	573,298	142,157	254,922	179,770	501,536	26,372	2,726,022	Pennsylvania
199,809	48,659	7,418	26,510	15,759	53,917	7,861	257,036	Rhode Island
646,544	213,882	91,574	30,199	46,628	24,694	—	558,671	South Carolina
178,687	55,609	8,800	10,973	14,874	318	2,557	79,181	South Dakota
1,117,859	280,145	57,828	79,008	68,834	18,382	—	568,755	Tennessee
3,480,790	496,415	267,682	346,038	200,115	268,193	—	1,673,672	Texas
387,624	83,615	8,161	11,139	20,226	2,483	—	394,629	Utah
48,440	25,385	14,450	9,986	6,964	12,855	1,026	64,431	Vermont
670,512	325,384	72,768	17,954	84,431	103,301	—	595,483	Virginia
1,892,066	261,403	98,666	94,254	47,182	145,657	6,781	1,588,446	Washington
781,223	95,287	6,556	37,878	32,808	—	12,432	554,767	West Virginia
961,068	285,706	47,173	114,231	47,477	104,479	—	1,236,735	Wisconsin
228,018	38,405	2,155	5,809	5,901	—	22	156,443	Wyoming

[1] Does not include miscellaneous selective sales taxes. [2] Includes contributions and earnings on investments for employee retirement, unemployment and workmen's compensation, etc.

STATE EXPENDITURES: WHERE THE TAX MONEY GOES[1]

Source: U.S. Department of Commerce, Bureau of the Census

STATE	TOTAL[2]	EDUCATION	PUBLIC WELFARE	HIGHWAYS	HOSPITALS	NATURAL RESOURCES	HEALTH	INSURANCE TRUSTS[3]
All States	$310,292,127	$102,984,441	$55,257,202	$25,131,092	$13,938,144	$5,485,297	$8,346,011	$34,663,733
Alabama	4,666,822	1,990,096	535,510	448,287	293,527	85,798	110,079	367,171
Alaska	3,280,885	812,820	174,964	259,070	16,765	205,407	81,690	139,467
Arizona	3,245,103	1,430,439	178,661	340,936	108,010	50,727	106,895	271,414
Arkansas	2,362,381	934,440	358,628	289,186	110,362	70,007	62,447	203,244
California	40,443,843	13,645,871	10,112,067	1,537,374	1,080,382	928,383	1,151,376	4,947,755
Colorado	3,635,365	1,453,517	552,968	337,405	180,433	106,382	81,371	419,559
Connecticut	3,993,741	982,480	763,521	281,164	260,111	27,322	86,560	445,202
Delaware	1,083,992	398,387	98,578	98,064	39,762	21,661	25,451	70,074
Florida	9,322,355	3,932,992	1,135,095	993,621	369,101	271,134	423,156	544,225
Georgia	6,007,075	2,370,270	914,303	840,843	271,958	131,307	226,824	483,810
Hawaii	1,994,359	644,041	290,303	94,446	82,471	46,299	68,318	168,422
Idaho	1,208,724	470,039	115,125	131,414	23,741	51,777	35,651	157,050
Illinois	14,138,237	4,412,716	3,142,803	1,168,806	473,148	132,092	301,721	2,107,286
Indiana	5,694,016	2,390,074	706,860	566,925	214,085	91,914	136,472	545,856
Iowa	3,903,183	1,525,793	586,329	471,451	242,404	85,610	35,051	358,180
Kansas	2,634,443	1,070,430	435,522	285,303	173,035	72,419	40,619	231,006
Kentucky	4,725,792	1,665,439	726,570	619,899	166,711	118,266	118,196	501,014
Louisiana	6;462,588	2,138,001	851,757	535,086	430,797	173,215	144,952	689,625
Maine	1,527,076	440,061	326,489	144,103	34,713	52,156	35,393	176,174
Maryland	6,260,305	1,735,656	911,444	756,396	348,377	84,476	174,916	655,566
Massachusetts	8,631,490	1,836,659	2,153,368	421,046	358,414	56,836	411,510	837,378
Michigan	13,996,829	3,864,049	3,254,048	894,366	690,902	140,663	552,998	2,137,295
Minnesota	6,924,688	2,784,446	1,175,282	553,520	295,925	155,837	88,150	539,443
Mississippi	3,038,846	1,147,964	440,642	354,509	142,039	87,987	68,295	219,669
Missouri	4,409,964	1,614,328	790,710	424,510	257,475	111,235	111,416	443,558
Montana	1,134,840	337,512	137,836	140,692	27,495	59,175	35,214	153,585
Nebraska	1,646,185	526,158	238,725	264,624	97,683	67,516	46,308	69,944
Nevada	1,413,147	431,320	106,798	122,700	23,781	23,589	27,228	242,142
New Hampshire	1,005,092	216,673	153,852	123,593	38,246	15,494	30,565	61,752
New Jersey	11,151,579	2,714,199	1,862,637	619,554	467,315	132,550	160,842	1,510,072
New Mexico	2,391,761	1,009,935	215,130	287,873	100,703	50,756	91,196	119,322
New York	30,159,259	7,752,257	6,736,380	1,214,221	1,910,267	131,885	752,809	2,523,083
North Carolina	6,850,703	3,030,321	790,161	555,696	353,433	150,316	189,565	670,402
North Dakota	1,190,922	448,593	104,494	147,760	53,540	43,017	20,853	72,155
Ohio	13,742,322	3,813,417	2,432,316	1,012,258	671,547	133,709	454,684	3,026,046
Oklahoma	4,162,348	1,744,930	695,616	426,541	226,678	68,052	82,348	297,809
Oregon	4,209,686	1,107,521	465,867	394,179	162,130	116,604	76,213	673,153
Pennsylvania	15,328,386	4,031,629	3,374,247	1,332,078	732,772	190,165	408,112	2,434,268
Rhode Island	1,628,042	398,184	357,077	56,645	102,814	11,227	49,344	203,131
South Carolina	4,110,192	1,541,587	470,366	247,822	201,444	77,713	120,637	356,166
South Dakota	828,962	233,587	109,090	129,822	24,562	41,509	22,387	34,487
Tennessee	4,298,381	1,541,746	662,529	510,449	215,056	68,665	126,960	485,332
Texas	14,151,809	6,749,901	1,622,657	1,963,494	812,489	227,367	256,237	962,564
Utah	1,994,176	926,614	213,426	178,629	80,293	47,564	47,381	189,583
Vermont	888,330	239,790	134,046	80,997	22,141	28,062	26,082	139,263
Virginia	6,298,334	2,240,740	888,732	677,121	470,384	73,947	186,116	402,389
Washington	7,255,537	2,966,916	863,114	626,319	170,997	167,210	155,217	1,165,244
West Virginia	2,841,679	935,591	271,400	436,707	90,380	57,265	68,260	429,642
Wisconsin	6,894,524	2,044,895	1,555,146	546,393	191,258	110,087	209,413	692,611
Wyoming	1,123,329	309,417	64,013	187,195	26,088	32,943	22,533	90,143

1 In $ thousands for fiscal year 1982. 2 Includes other expenditures not categorized. 3 Includes payments for employee retirement, unemployment compensation, workmen's compensation, and disability benefit social insurance programs.

FEDERAL MONEY GRANTED THE STATES

Source: U.S. Department of Commerce

U.S. grants to states totaled $66,026,345,000 in the fiscal year ending June 30, 1982, except for fiscal years in Alabama and Michigan (ending Sept. 30), New York (March 31), and Texas (Aug. 31).

The grants averaged $292.27 per capita.

STATE	TOTAL AID*	AID PER CAPITA	STATE	TOTAL AID*	AID PER CAPITA	STATE	TOTAL AID*	AID PER CAPITA
Alabama	$1,151,110	$295.61	Louisiana	$1,192,063	$283.42	North Dakota	$ 252,423	$386.56
Alaska	365,844	910.06	Maine	398,946	354.62	Ohio	2,414,392	223.60
Arizona	509,422	187.43	Maryland	1,266,280	300.28	Oklahoma	763,556	252.42
Arkansas	691,131	302.33	Massachusetts	1,870,100	325.97	Oregon	897,621	340.91
California	8,614,426	363.97	Michigan	2,911,081	314.30	Pennsylvania	3,263,992	275.12
Colorado	828,076	286.53	Minnesota	1,379,764	338.51	Rhode Island	387,206	408.88
Connecticut	842,799	271.17	Mississippi	862,258	342.03	South Carolina	806,603	258.36
Delaware	216,802	364.99	Missouri	1,123,395	228.47	South Dakota	243,838	352.88
Florida	1,873,540	192.24	Montana	286,719	364.32	Tennessee	1,230,529	268.03
Georgia	1,551,782	284.05	Nebraska	383,190	244.07	Texas	2,767,648	194.51
Hawaii	380,025	393.81	Nevada	225,587	281.98	Utah	552,291	378.02
Idaho	268,352	284.27	New			Vermont	253,013	495.13
Illinois	2,904,497	254.18	Hampshire	231,470	251.32	Virginia	1,305,141	244.09
Indiana	1,128,299	205.52	New Jersey	2,033,468	276.10	Washington	1,263,695	305.83
Iowa	737,540	253.10	New Mexico	454,923	349.14	West Virginia	675,404	346.36
Kansas	578,712	244.80	New York	7,316,906	416.73	Wisconsin	1,518,716	322.72
Kentucky	1,089,775	297.75	North Carolina	1,432,835	243.60	Wyoming	329,160	700.34

* In $ thousands (add 000).

STATE DEBTS

Source: U.S. Department of Commerce

The outstanding gross debt of the 50 states at the end of the 1982 fiscal year reached a new high—$147,341,980,000.

This debt averaged $650.38 per capita.

STATE	TOTAL DEBT*	DEBT PER CAPITA	STATE	TOTAL DEBT*	DEBT PER CAPITA	STATE	TOTAL DEBT*	DEBT PER CAPITA
Alabama	$1,958,569	$502.97	Louisiana	$4,146,609	$985.88	North Dakota	$ 324,836	$497.45
Alaska	3,700,774	9,205.91	Maine	860,782	765.14	Ohio	4,999,271	462.98
Arizona	240,258	88.40	Maryland	4,212,457	998.92	Oklahoma	1,171,937	387.42
Arkansas	554,540	242.58	Massachusetts	6,420,794	1,119.19	Oregon	6,220,641	2,362.57
California	10,330,999	436.50	Michigan	3,859,420	416.69	Pennsylvania	6,244,149	526.31
Colorado	741,305	256.51	Minnesota	2,659,518	652.48	Rhode Island	1,987,036	2,098.24
Connecticut	4,620,575	1,486.67	Mississippi	748,192	296.78	South Carolina	3,077,471	985.74
Delaware	1,359,539	2,288.79	Missouri	1,836,490	373.50	South Dakota	708,707	1,025.63
Florida	2,993,388	307.14	Montana	399,215	507.26	Tennessee	1,587,121	345.70
Georgia	1,645,941	301.29	Nebraska	295,479	188.20	Texas	2,458,997	172.82
Hawaii	2,109,692	2,186.21	Nevada	648,313	810.39	Utah	722,510	494.53
Idaho	427,178	452.52	New			Vermont	673,362	1,317.73
Illinois	7,470,299	653.74	Hampshire	1,270,612	1,379.60	Virginia	2,614,239	488.92
Indiana	1,024,784	186.66	New Jersey	8,795,893	1,194.28	Washington	2,492,091	603.12
Iowa	458,042	157.19	New Mexico	823,500	632.00	West Virginia	1,804,135	925.20
Kansas	397,481	168.14	New York	25,813,504	1,470.18	Wisconsin	2,647,931	562.67
Kentucky	2,659,592	726.66	North Carolina	1,591,067	270.50	Wyoming	532,745	1,133.50

* In $ thousands (add 000).

STATE RETAIL SALES TAXES: 1983[1]

Source: Tax Foundation

STATE	TAX	STATE	TAX	STATE	TAX	STATE	TAX
Alabama	4%	Indiana	5%	Nebraska	4%	South Carolina	4%
Alaska	—	Iowa	4%	Nevada	5.75%	South Dakota	4%
Arizona	5%	Kansas	3%	New Hampshire	—	Tennessee	4.5%
Arkansas	3%	Kentucky	5%	New Jersey	6%	Texas	4%
California	4.75%	Louisiana	3%	New Mexico	3.75%	Utah	4⅛%
Colorado	3.5%	Maine	5%	New York[2]	4%	Vermont	4%
Connecticut	7.5%	Maryland	5%	North Carolina	3%	Virginia	3%
Delaware	—	Massachusetts	5%	North Dakota	4%	Washington	6.5%
Florida	5%	Michigan	4%	Ohio	5%	West Virginia	5%
Georgia	3%	Minnesota	6%	Oklahoma	2%	Wisconsin	5%
Hawaii	4%	Mississippi	5%	Oregon	—	Wyoming	3%
Idaho	4.5%	Missouri	4⅛%	Pennsylvania	6%	District of	
Illinois	4%	Montana	—	Rhode Island	6%	Columbia	6%

[1] Does not include local sales taxes, which are imposed in 33 states. [2] In New York City, 8¼%.

CITY INCOME TAXES: 1983

Sources: Tax Foundation

Philadelphia has the distinction of levying the oldest and highest local income tax in effect today. Earlier efforts at such taxation, including one in Charleston, S.C., in the early 1800s, foundered on administrative difficulties.

Since the path-breaking Philadelphia enactment in 1939, however, about 4,000 localities in 10 states have followed suit. And authorizations have been granted (although no locality has acted) in Arkansas and Kansas.

In addition, a related levy has been imposed on employers: the local payroll tax, based on an employer's wage expenses. This has been enacted in Jersey City, Newark, N.J., San Francisco, and four Oregon counties.

Despite first impressions from the table that follows, the local income tax is primarily a big-city phenomenon.

Most of the taxing jurisdictions are small, but this is because many—over 3,800—small towns and school districts in Ohio and Pennsylvania use the levy. Elsewhere the tax is typically used by large jurisdictions.

Nine of the 25 largest cities in the United States, including Washington, D.C., impose their own income taxes.

Few of these local taxes are really comparable to state or U.S. taxes, since most apply only to wages and salaries—"earned" income. However, those levied by New York City, Baltimore, and cities in Michigan are closely linked, both in coverage and administration, to overlapping state taxes.

In the District of Columbia, it is similar to a state income tax.

Besides the roughly 40 million residents in localities levying income taxes, countless others who work in them but live elsewhere—commuters in Alabama, Delaware, Kentucky, Missouri, Ohio, and Pennsylvania—are subject to the levy.

Maryland's local taxes apply to residents only, as does the District of Columbia's tax.

Commuters in Michigan pay one-half the resident rates, while those in New York City pay sharply lower rates.

Where many localities in the same area tax income, special arrangements are necessary to avoid unfair treatment of those who work in one jurisdiction but live in another.

As the table below shows, local income taxes are essentially confined to the states in the Northeast and Middle Atlantic regions—with the exception of St. Louis and Kansas City, Mo., and five places in Alabama, including Birmingham and Gadsden.

The table below, compiled by the Tax Foundation from Commerce Clearing House data, lists the rates in effect as of April 1, 1983, for all U.S. localities with income taxes.

CITY AND LOCAL INCOME TAXES AND RATES [1]

STATE AND LOCALITY	RATE
Alabama	
Birmingham	1.0%
Gadsden	2.0%
3 cities under 50,000	1.0–2.0%
Delaware	
Wilmington	1.0%
Indiana	
38 counties	0.25–1.0%
Iowa	
6 school districts	1.75–4.0%
Kentucky	
Covington	2.5%
Lexington	2.0%
Louisville [2]	2.2%
Owensboro	1.0%
57 cities under 50,000	0.25–2.5%
8 counties	0.25–2.0%
Maryland	
Baltimore [3]	50.0%
24 counties [3]	20.0–50.0%
Michigan	
Detroit	3.0%
Flint	1.0%
Grand Rapids	1.0%
Michigan (continued)	
Lansing	1.0%
Pontiac	1.0%
Saginaw	1.0%
10 cities under 50,000	1.0%
Missouri	
Kansas City	1.0%
St. Louis	1.0%
New York	
New York City [4]	0.9–4.3%
Ohio	
Akron	2.0%
Canton	2.0%
Cincinnati	2.0%
Cleveland	2.0%
Cleveland Heights	2.0%
Columbus	2.0%
Dayton	1.75%
Elyria	1.0%
Euclid	2.0%
Hamilton	1.5%
Kettering	1.75%
Lakewood	1.5%
Lima	1.5%
Lorain	1.0%
Mansfield	1.0%
Parma	2.0%
Ohio (continued)	
Springfield	2.0%
Toledo	2.25%
Warren	1.5%
Youngstown	2.0%
Over 400 cities and villages under 50,000	0.25–2.0%
Pennsylvania	
Abington Township	1.0%
Allentown	1.0%
Altoona	1.0%
Bethlehem	1.0%
Chester	1.0%
Erie	1.0%
Harrisburg	1.0%
Lancaster	1.0%
Penn Hills Township	1.0%
Philadelphia	4.3125%
Pittsburgh	3.625%
Reading	1.0%
Scranton	3.5%
Wilkes-Barre	1.0%
York	1.0%
Over 3,500 other local jurisdictions	Up to 1.0%
Washington, D.C. [4]	2.0–11.0%

[1] Rates shown separately for cities of 50,000 or more. Where rates differ for resident and nonresident income, only resident rates are given. In Ohio and Pennsylvania cities, rates are the same. [2] Includes 0.75% additional tax imposed on residents of Louisville and Jefferson county for school purposes. [3] Percent of state income tax. [4] Resident income taxes are progressive.

Travel and Transportation

The Statue of Liberty holds high her torch in New York Harbor near the twin towers of the World Trade Center. However, visitors to the famous landmark may not be able to see the torch in 1984–85 because it will be removed for repairs as the statue is renovated in preparation for its 100th anniversary celebration in 1986. Chrysler Chairman Lee Iacocca led a drive in 1983 that raised $40 million in private funds to pay for the renovation.

United Press Int'l.

AUTOMOBILE HIGHLIGHTS: 1983

U.S. AUTO SALES IMPROVE

After experiencing their worst sales year in more than two decades in 1982, the three largest U.S. automakers had improved sales in 1983. In the first nine months their sales increased to a rate of 7 million automobiles, up 23% from 1982.

The three largest U.S. automobile companies each reported greatly increased profits during the first nine months of the year. Altogether their sales during the period totaled $95.4 billion with profits of $4.1 billion. In the first nine months of 1982 their sales had been $81.9 billion with net income of $662 million.

General Motors said that during the first nine months its sales totaled $53.8 billion with profits of $2.43 billion. The 1982 figures for the same period were sales of $46.2 billion and profits of $818 million.

Ford Motors reported that during the first nine months of 1983 there were $32.08 billion in sales with profits of $1.09 billion. Comparable figures for the nine months in 1982 had been sales of $27.9 billion with a loss of $422 million.

Chrysler, with 10.5% of the market, said its total revenues for the first three quarters were $9.5 billion with a profit of $582.6 million. Its comparable figures for 1982 had been sales of $7.8 billion and a profit of $266.2 million.

The fourth-largest U.S. automaker, American Motors, continued to lose money. At the end of the third quarter American Motors reported its 15th consecutive quarterly loss—$9.1 million.

U.S. automakers in 1982 had their worst sales in 21 years. They sold 5.75 million cars compared with 6.25 million in 1981. Thus, 1982 was the worst since 1961 when they sold 5.54 million automobiles. Altogether 7,978,487 cars were sold in the U.S. in 1982, with imports accounting for 2,221,829. Total sales declined 6.3% from those in 1981.

THIRD REAR STOP LAMP ORDERED

Beginning with the 1986 model year, all automobiles must have a third rear stoplight mounted at eye level under the rear window.

Secretary of Transportation Elizabeth Hanford Dole announced the new regulation on Oct. 13. It will apply to all cars manufactured after Sept. 1, 1985, although automakers may install the third stoplight on cars produced before that date if they choose.

"We expect to cut the number of rear-end collisions significantly, and eliminate 40,000 injuries as well as save an estimated $434 million in property damages annually," Secretary Dole said.

According to estimates of the department's National Highway Traffic Safety Administration (NHTSA), there were some 3.5 million rear-end collisions in 1980 that resulted in property damages and 600,000 injuries.

"We estimate that as many as 40,000 of these injuries might have been prevented if all cars had been equipped with the new eye-level stoplight," Secretary Dole said.

NHTSA estimated that about 900,000 of the 3.5 million rear-end accidents would not have occurred if the cars had had the high-mounted stoplights.

The decision to issue the regulation came after a 12-month research project involving 5,400 telephone company passenger cars. Some 2,500 of the cars were equipped with a single center high-mounted stop lamp while the remaining 2,900 had only the customary low-level stoplights. During the year-long study those cars that had the high stoplight were involved in 53% fewer rear-end accidents than the cars without the added light.

SAFE AND UNSAFE CARS

The Insurance Institute for Highway Safety released statistics on the safety records of 133 passenger cars for the model years 1980–82. The study was based on the frequency of claims for personal injury and collision damages.

The 10 cars rated as safest were:

Four-door Mercury Marquis, four-door Olds Delta 88, four-door Buick LeSabre, Olds Cutlass station wagon, Olds Custom Cruiser station wagon, four-door Ford LTD, four-door Olds Ciera, four-door Chevrolet Impala, and AMC Eagle station wagon.

The 10 with the worst injury and collision records were:

Datsun 280ZX, BMW 320i, Chevrolet Corvette, two-door Dodge Challenger, two-door Volkswagen Scirocco, two-door Datsun 200SX, Mazda RX-7, Datsun 280ZX 2+2, Toyota Celica Supra, and Chevrolet Camaro.

JAPANESE CAR QUOTAS

The Japanese government agreed on Nov. 1 to extend export restrictions for a fourth year to aid the U.S. automobile industry. However, the quota was increased to 1.85 million cars from 1.68 million.

As car sales picked up in 1983, many U.S. dealers for Japanese automobiles ran out of new cars to demonstrate. Customers often had to wait six weeks or more for delivery and even then had to agree to pay high prices because of the many optional items with which the cars were equipped. Because of the shortages, car purchasers had little leverage to bargain for lower than list price on the Japanese automobiles.

GAS SAVERS AND GAS GUZZLER

The Environmental Protection Agency (EPA) reported in September its fuel economy ratings for 1984 cars under city driving conditions. The ratings do not apply to models made for sale in California, which requires stricter emission control devices.

Two Japanese cars were rated as attaining 50 or more mpg (miles per gallon): The Honda Civic coupe with manual transmission and a four-cylinder 82-cubic-inch engine and the Datsun Nissan Sentra with manual transmission and a four-cylinder 103-cubic-inch diesel engine.

Only one car was rated as getting as low as 10 mpg. It was the Dodge B350 van with an automatic transmission and an eight-cylinder 360-cubic-inch engine.

AUTO SAFETY HOTLINE: 800-424-9393

You can phone this toll-free number day or night to report vehicle-safety problems and obtain vehicle-recall information from the National Highway Traffic Safety Administration.

HOW TO FIGURE OUT YOUR CAR'S MPG (MILES PER GALLON)

Source: General Services Administration

To check the miles-per-gallon (mpg) fuel economy of your automobile: (1) Fill your car with gasoline. (2) Write down the mileage shown on your car's odometer. (3) The next time you fill your car with gasoline, write down exactly how many gallons it takes. (4) Calculate how many miles you have gone since you last filled it. (5) Then use the following chart to discover how many miles per gallon your car gets. Locate (a) the number of gallons your car used in the row across the top of the table and (b) the number of miles it went in the left-hand column. The intersection of these two columns tells you the number of miles per gallon your car gets. For example, if it went 220 miles and used 15 gallons of gasoline, the table shows your car gets 14.7 mpg.

MILES	NUMBER OF GALLONS OF GASOLINE USED (top row)																				
	5	6	7	8	9	10	11	12	13	14	15	16	17	18	19	20	21	22	23	24	25
100	20.0	16.7	14.3	12.5	11.1	10.0	9.1	8.3	7.7	7.1	6.7	6.3	5.9	5.6	5.3	5.0	4.8	4.5	4.3	4.2	4.0
110	22.0	18.3	15.7	13.8	12.2	11.0	10.0	9.2	8.5	7.9	7.3	6.9	6.5	6.1	5.8	5.5	5.2	5.0	4.8	4.6	4.4
120	24.0	20.0	17.1	15.0	13.3	12.0	10.9	10.0	9.2	8.6	8.0	7.5	7.1	6.7	6.3	6.0	5.7	5.5	5.2	5.0	4.8
130	26.0	21.7	18.6	16.3	14.4	13.0	11.8	10.8	10.0	9.3	8.7	8.1	7.6	7.2	6.8	6.5	6.2	5.9	5.7	5.4	5.2
140	28.0	23.3	20.0	17.5	15.6	14.0	12.7	11.7	10.8	10.0	9.3	8.8	8.2	7.8	7.4	7.0	6.7	6.4	6.1	5.8	5.6
150	30.0	25.0	21.4	18.8	16.7	15.0	13.6	12.5	11.5	10.7	10.0	9.4	8.8	8.3	7.9	7.5	7.1	6.8	6.5	6.3	6.0
160	32.0	26.7	22.9	20.0	17.8	16.0	14.5	13.3	12.3	11.4	10.7	10.0	9.4	8.9	8.4	8.0	7.6	7.3	7.0	6.7	6.4
170	34.0	28.3	24.3	21.3	18.9	17.0	15.5	14.2	13.1	12.1	11.3	10.6	10.0	9.4	8.9	8.5	8.1	7.7	7.4	7.1	6.8
180	36.0	30.0	25.7	22.5	20.0	18.0	16.4	15.0	13.8	12.9	12.0	11.3	10.6	10.0	9.5	9.0	8.6	8.2	7.8	7.5	7.2
190	38.0	31.7	27.1	23.8	21.1	19.0	17.3	15.8	14.6	13.6	12.7	11.9	11.2	10.6	10.0	9.5	9.0	8.6	8.3	7.9	7.6
200	40.0	33.3	28.6	25.0	22.2	20.0	18.2	16.7	15.4	14.3	13.3	12.5	11.8	11.1	10.5	10.0	9.5	9.1	8.7	8.3	8.0
210	42.9	35.0	30.0	26.3	23.3	21.0	19.1	17.5	16.2	15.0	14.0	13.1	12.4	11.7	11.1	10.5	10.0	9.5	9.1	8.8	8.4
220	44.0	36.7	31.4	27.5	24.4	22.0	20.0	18.3	16.9	15.7	14.7	13.8	12.9	12.2	11.6	11.0	10.5	10.0	9.6	9.2	8.8
230	46.0	38.3	32.9	28.8	25.6	23.0	20.9	19.2	17.7	16.4	15.3	14.4	13.5	12.8	12.1	11.5	11.0	10.5	10.0	9.6	9.2
240	48.0	40.0	34.3	30.0	26.7	24.0	21.8	20.0	18.5	17.1	16.0	15.0	14.1	13.3	12.6	12.0	11.4	10.9	10.4	10.0	9.6
250	50.0	41.7	35.7	31.3	27.8	25.0	22.7	20.8	19.2	17.9	16.7	15.6	14.7	13.9	13.2	12.5	11.9	11.4	10.9	10.4	10.0
260	52.0	43.3	37.1	32.5	29.9	26.0	23.6	21.7	20.0	18.6	17.3	16.3	15.3	14.4	13.7	13.0	12.4	11.8	11.3	10.8	10.4
270	54.0	45.0	38.6	33.8	30.0	27.0	24.5	22.5	20.8	19.3	18.0	16.9	15.9	15.0	14.2	13.5	12.9	12.3	11.7	11.3	10.8
280	56.0	46.7	40.0	35.0	31.1	28.0	25.5	23.3	21.5	20.0	18.7	17.5	16.5	15.6	14.7	14.0	13.3	12.7	12.2	11.7	11.2
290	58.0	48.3	41.4	36.3	32.2	29.0	26.4	24.2	22.3	20.7	19.3	18.1	17.1	16.1	15.3	14.5	13.8	13.2	12.6	12.1	11.6
300	60.0	50.0	42.9	37.5	33.3	30.0	27.3	25.0	23.1	21.4	20.0	18.8	17.6	16.7	15.8	15.0	14.3	13.6	13.0	12.5	12.0
310	62.0	51.7	44.3	38.7	34.4	31.0	28.2	25.8	23.8	22.1	20.7	19.4	18.2	17.2	16.3	15.5	14.7	14.1	13.5	12.9	12.4
320	64.0	53.3	45.7	40.0	35.6	32.0	29.1	26.7	24.6	22.9	21.3	20.0	18.8	17.8	16.8	16.0	15.2	14.5	13.9	13.3	12.6
330	66.0	55.0	47.1	41.3	36.7	33.0	30.0	27.5	25.4	23.6	22.0	20.6	19.4	18.3	17.4	16.5	15.7	15.0	14.3	13.7	13.2
340	68.0	56.7	48.6	42.5	37.8	34.0	30.9	28.3	26.2	24.3	22.7	21.3	20.0	18.9	17.9	17.0	16.2	15.5	14.8	14.2	13.6
350	70.0	58.3	50.0	43.7	38.9	35.0	31.8	29.2	26.9	25.0	23.3	21.9	20.6	19.4	18.4	17.5	16.7	15.9	15.2	14.6	14.0

WHAT IS THE YEARLY COST OF FUEL FOR YOUR CAR?

Based on an average of driving 12,000 miles per year, the following table shows the annual cost of your car's fuel. For example, if you pay $1.35 per gallon, and your car gets 20 mpg (miles per gallon) for 12,000 miles, then the annual cost of fuel for your car is $810.

MPG	PRICE PER GALLON OF FUEL (top row)															
	$1.00	**$1.05**	**$1.10**	**$1.15**	**$1.20**	**$1.25**	**$1.30**	**$1.35**	**$1.40**	**$1.45**	**$1.50**	**$1.55**	**$1.60**	**$1.65**	**$1.70**	**$1.75**
50	$240	$252	$264	$276	$288	$300	$312	$324	$336	$348	$360	$372	$384	$396	$408	$420
48	250	262	275	287	300	312	325	337	350	362	375	387	400	412	425	437
46	260	273	286	300	313	326	339	352	365	378	391	404	417	430	443	456
44	272	286	300	313	327	340	354	368	381	395	409	422	436	450	463	477
42	285	300	314	328	342	357	371	385	400	414	428	442	457	471	485	500
40	300	315	330	345	360	375	390	405	420	435	450	465	480	495	510	525
38	315	331	347	363	378	394	410	426	442	457	473	489	505	521	536	552
36	333	350	366	383	400	416	433	450	466	483	500	516	533	550	566	583
34	352	370	388	405	423	441	458	476	494	511	529	547	564	582	600	617
32	375	393	412	431	450	468	487	506	525	543	562	581	600	618	637	656
30	400	420	440	460	480	500	520	540	560	580	600	620	640	660	680	700
28	428	450	471	492	514	535	557	578	600	621	642	664	685	707	728	750
26	461	484	507	530	553	576	600	623	646	669	692	715	738	761	784	807
24	500	525	550	575	600	625	650	675	700	725	750	775	800	825	850	875
22	545	572	600	627	654	681	709	736	763	790	818	845	872	900	927	954
20	600	630	660	690	720	750	780	810	840	870	900	930	960	990	1,020	1,050
18	666	700	733	766	800	833	866	900	933	966	1,000	1,033	1,066	1,100	1,133	1,166
16	750	787	825	862	900	937	975	1,012	1,050	1,087	1,125	1,162	1,200	1,237	1,275	1,312
14	857	900	942	985	1,028	1,071	1,114	1,157	1,200	1,242	1,285	1,328	1,371	1,414	1,457	1,500
12	1,000	1,050	1,100	1,150	1,200	1,250	1,300	1,350	1,400	1,450	1,500	1,550	1,600	1,650	1,700	1,750
10	1,200	1,260	1,320	1,380	1,440	1,500	1,560	1,620	1,680	1,740	1,800	1,860	1,920	1,980	2,040	2,100

WORLD'S MAJOR ENGINEERING FEATS

STRUCTURE	LOCATION	FEATURES
Longest rail tunnel	Seikan, Japan	33.5 miles long (under construction)
Longest road tunnel	St. Gotthard, Switzerland	10.01 miles long (opens in 1980)
Longest water tunnel	Delaware Aqueduct, New York	85 miles long
Tallest dam	Rojunsky, Soviet Union	1,066 feet high, 2,506 feet long
Biggest dam	New Cornelia Tailings Dam, Arizona	Filled with 274,026,000 cu. yds. of material
Longest dam	Kiev, Soviet Union	33.6 miles long, 72 feet high
Tallest building	Sears Tower, Chicago, Illinois	110 stories, 1,454 feet high
Largest building	Boeing assembly building, Everett, Wash.	205,000,000 cubic feet of space
Tallest tower, with guy wires	KTHI-TV tower, Blanchard, North Dakota	2,063 feet high
Tallest tower, no guy wires	Canadian National Railways Tower, Toronto, Ontario, Canada	1,815 feet high
Longest single bridge span	Humber Bridge, Hull, England	4,626 feet long over River Humber
Highest bridge	Royal Gorge, Colorado	1,053 feet above water
Deepest mine	Carletonville, South Africa	13,000 feet deep gold mine
Deepest oil well	Beckham County, Oklahoma	30,050 feet deep
Great Pyramid of Cheops	Egypt	481 feet high, 755 feet square
Great Wall	China	1,500 miles long, 25 feet high

WORLD'S MAJOR TUNNELS

Source: Bridge Division, Federal Highway Administration

LENGTH	NAME	LOCATION	YEAR
HIGHWAY TUNNELS			
10.01 miles	St. Gotthard	Göschenen–Airolo, Switzerland	1980
8.7 miles	Arlberg Tunnel	Austria	1978
7.2 miles	Mont Blanc	France–Italy	1965
3.6 miles	Great St. Bernard	Italy–Switzerland	1964
3.1 miles	Viella	Pobla de Segur–Viella, Spain	1948
2.8 miles	Mersey	Liverpool, England	1934
2.1 miles	Kanmon	Yamaguchi–Fukuoka, Japan	1958
2.0 miles	Elbe River	Germany	1975
1.8 miles	Reboucas	Rio de Janeiro, Brazil	1967
1.73 miles	Brooklyn–Battery	Brooklyn–Manhattan, New York	1950
1.7 miles	Dwight D. Eisenhower	60 miles west of Denver, Colorado	1973; 1979
1.6 miles	Holland	New York–New Jersey	1927
1.6 miles	Salang	Afghanistan–Soviet Union	1964
1.6 miles	Lincoln, Center	New York–New Jersey	1937
1.5 miles	Lincoln, South	New York–New Jersey	1957
1.4 miles	Baltimore Harbor	Baltimore, Maryland	1957
1.4 miles	Lincoln, North	New York–New Jersey	1945
1.4 miles	Hampton Roads	Hampton–Norfolk, Virginia	1957; 1976
1.3 miles	Copperfield	Bingham Canyon, Utah	1939
1.2 miles	Queens–Midtown	Queens–Manhattan, New York	1940
1.2 miles	Ahmed Hamdi	Under Suez Canal, Suez, Egypt	1980
RAILROAD TUNNELS[1]			
33.5 miles	Seikan	Japan	UC
13.8 miles	Dai-Shimizu	Japan	1982
12.3 miles	Simplon No. I	Switzerland–Italy	1906
12.3 miles	Simplon No. II	Switzerland–Italy	1922
11.6 miles	Kanmon	Japan	1975
11.5 miles	Apennine	Italy	1934
9.9 miles	Rokko	Japan	1972
9.3 miles	Gotthard	Switzerland	1882
9.1 miles	Lötschberg	Switzerland	1913
8.6 miles	Hokuriku	Japan	1962
8.5 miles	Mont Cenis	France–Italy	1871
8.3 miles	Shin–shimizu	Japan	1967
8.2 miles	Furka	Switzerland	1982
7.8 miles	Cascade	Washington (U.S.)	1929
7.0 miles	Flathead	Montana (U.S.)	1970
7.0 miles	Kubiki	Japan	1969
6.7 miles	Lierasen	Norway	1973
6.4 miles	Arlberg	Austria	1884
6.2 miles	Moffat	Colorado (U.S.)	1928
6.0 miles	Shimizu	Japan	1931
5.6 miles	Kvineshei	Norway	1943
5.5 miles	Rimutaka	New Zealand	1955
SHIP TUNNEL			
4.3 miles	Rove	Rhone Canal, France	1927

UC = Under construction. [1] Subway tunnels not included.

WORLD'S TALLEST BUILDINGS AND FREE-STANDING TOWERS

FEET [1]	BUILDING AND LOCATION	FLOORS	FEET [1]	BUILDING AND LOCATION	FLOORS
1,815	CNR Tower, Toronto, Canada	—	813	Chase Manhattan, New York City	60
1,454	Sears Tower [2], Chicago	110	808	Pan Am, New York City	59
1,350	World Trade Center [3], New York City	110	786	MLC Center, Sydney, Australia	68
1,250	Empire State [4], New York City	102	792	Woolworth, New York City	60
1,136	Standard Oil, Chicago	80	790	John Hancock Tower, Boston	60
1,107	John Hancock Center [5], Chicago	100	787	Sunshine 60, Tokyo, Japan	60
1,065	Centrepoint Tower, Sydney, Australia	—	787	Moscow State U. [12], Soviet Union	32
1,002	Texas Commerce Tower, Houston, Texas	75	784	Commerce Court [13], Toronto	57
985	Allied Bank, Houston, Texas	71	780	Republic Bank, Houston, Texas	54
984	Eiffel Tower [6], Paris, France	—	778	Bank of America, San Francisco	52
936	First Canadian Place, Toronto, Canada	70	774	IDS Tower, Minneapolis	57
914	Citicorp Center, New York City	59	772	One Liberty Plaza, New York City	54
899	Transco Tower, Houston, Texas	64	764	One Penn Plaza, New York City	57
866	Chrysler [7], New York City	77	757	Palace of Culture, Warsaw, Poland	40
859	Water Tower Plaza, Chicago	74	750	Exxon Building, New York City	54
858	United Calif. Bank, Los Angeles	62	750	Prudential Tower, Boston	52
853	Transamerica Pyramid, San Francisco	48	747	Detroit Plaza Hotel, Detroit	73
851	40 Wall Street [8], New York City	71	744	Interfirst Bank, Houston, Texas	55
850	RCA Building [9], New York City	70	743	U.S. Steel, New York City	50
844	First National Bank [10], Chicago	60	741	Citibank, New York City	57
841	U.S. Steel Building, Pittsburgh	64	740	Renaissance Center, Detroit	70
826	60 Wall Street Tower [11], New York City	67	740	Dominion Bank, Toronto	56

[1] Height from sidewalk to roof, floors below ground not included. [2] 1,804 ft. with TV antenna. [3] Twin towers. [4] 1,472 ft. with TV antenna. [5] 1,451 ft. with TV antenna. [6] 1,052 ft. with TV antenna. [7] 1,046 ft. with spire. [8] 927 ft. with tower. [9] 885 ft. with tower. [10] 864 ft. with tower. [11] 950 ft. with tower. [12] 994 ft. with tower. [13] 942 ft. with tower.

WORLD'S MAJOR SHIP CANALS

Source: Defense Mapping Agency Hydrographic/Topographic Center

NAME	LOCATION	YEAR OPENED	LENGTH (in nautical miles)	WIDTH OF CHANNEL OR LOCKS	MINIMUM DEPTH	LOCKS
Cape Cod	U.S.A.: Buzzards Bay to Cape Cod Bay	1914	15.1	500 ft.	32 ft.	0
Chesapeake and Delaware	U.S.A.: Chesapeake Bay to Delaware River	1829	11.3	450 ft.	35 ft.	0
Corinth	Greece: Gulf of Corinth to Aegean	1893	2.6	69 ft.	26 ft.	0
Nord-Ostee Kanal	Germany: North Sea to Baltic Sea	1895	53.0	131 ft.	36 ft.	4
Manchester Ship	England: Mersey Estuary to city of Manchester	1894	31.0	80 ft.	29 ft.	10
North Sea	Netherlands: North Sea to Amsterdam	1876	13.0	164 ft.	49 ft.	3
Panama	Panama: Atlantic to Pacific	1914	44.6	110 ft.	40 ft.	12
St. Lawrence Seaway	U.S.A.–Canada: Montreal to Lake Ontario	1959	164.0	80 ft.	27 ft.	7
Sault Ste. Marie	U.S.A.–Canada: Lake Huron to Lake Superior	1855	1.4	110 ft.	27 ft.	4
Suez	Egypt: Mediterranean Sea to Gulf of Suez	1869	104.3	525 ft.	61 ft.	0
Terneuzen Ghent	Netherlands–Belgium: Schelde River to Ghent	1827	17.3	131 ft.	44 ft.	3
Welland	Canada: Lake Ontario to Lake Erie	1932	27.0	80 ft.	27 ft.	8
White Sea—Baltic	Soviet Union: White Sea to Baltic Sea	1933	122.0	100 ft.	13 ft.	19

WORLD'S LONGEST BRIDGES

Source: Bridge Division, Federal Highway Administration

SUSPENSION BRIDGES

SPAN	BRIDGE	LOCATION	WATERWAY	OPENED
4,626 ft.	Humber	Hull, England	River Humber	1980
4,260 ft.	Verrazano-Narrows	Brooklyn to Staten Island, New York	New York Bay	1964
4,200 ft.	Golden Gate	San Francisco to Marin County, California	San Francisco Bay	1937
3,800 ft.	Mackinac	Michigan	Straits of Mackinac	1957
3,524 ft.	Bosporus	Turkey	Bosporus	1973
3,500 ft.	George Washington	New York City to Fort Lee, New Jersey	Hudson River	1931
3,323 ft.	Salazar	Lisbon, Portugal	Tagus River	1966
3,300 ft.	Forth Road	Queensferry, Scotland	Firth of Forth	1964
3,240 ft.	Severn	Bristol, England, to Chepstow, Wales	River Severn	1966
2,871 ft.	Onaruto	Kobe–Naruto, Japan	Naruto Straits	1980

SUSPENSION BRIDGES *(continued)*

SPAN	BRIDGE	LOCATION	WATERWAY	YEAR
2,800 ft.	Tacoma Narrows II	Tacoma, Washington	Puget Sound	1950
2,526 ft.	In-no-Shima Bridge	In-no-Shima, Onomichi Imbari, Japan	Seto Island Sea	1982
2,336 ft.	Kanmon Straits	Kyushu to Honshu, Japan	Kanmon Straits	1973
2,336 ft.	Angostura	Ciudad Bolívar, Venezuela	Orinoco River	1967
2,310 ft.	Transbay	San Francisco to Oakland, California	San Francisco Bay	1936
2300 ft.	Bronx-Whitestone	Bronx to Whitestone, Queens, New York	East River	1939
2,190 ft.	Pierre-LaPorte	Quebec, Canada	St. Lawrence River	1970
2,150 ft.	Delaware Memorial	Wilmington, Delaware (twin spans)	Delaware River	1951;1968
2,150 ft.	Seaway Skyway	Ogdensburg, New York, to Prescott, Ontario	St. Lawrence River	1960
2,000 ft.	Walt Whitman	South Philadelphia, Pennsylvania	Delaware River	1957
2,000 ft.	Gas Pipe Line	Louisiana	Atchafalaya River	1951
1,995 ft.	Tancarville	Tancarville, France	Seine River	1959
1,969 ft.	New Lillebaelt	Denmark	Lillebaelt Straits	1970
1,850 ft.	Ambassador	Detroit, Michigan, to Windsor, Canada	Detroit River	1929
1,800 ft.	Throgs Neck	Bronx to Queens, New York	East River	1961
1,750 ft.	Benjamin Franklin	Philadelphia, Pennsylvania, to Camden, N.J.	Delaware River	1926
1,722 ft.	Skjomen	Norway	Skjervik-Grindjord	1972
1,722 ft.	Kvalsund	Stallogargo to Kvalsund, Hammerfest, Norway	Norwegian Sea	1977
1,640 ft.	Kleve-Emmerich	Kleve to Emmerich, West Germany	Rhine River	1965
1,632 ft.	Bear Mountain	Bear Mountain to Peekskill, New York	Hudson River	1924
1,600 ft.	Newport	Rhode Island	Narragansett Bay	1969
1,600 ft.	Chesapeake Bay	Sandy Point, Maryland	Chesapeake Bay	1952
1,600 ft.	Parallel Chesapeake Bay	Sandy Point, Maryland	Chesapeake Bay	1973
1,600 ft.	Williamsburg	Manhattan to Brooklyn, New York	East River	1903
1,595 ft.	Brooklyn	Manhattan to Brooklyn, New York	East River	1883

CABLE-STAYED BRIDGES

SPAN	BRIDGE	LOCATION	WATERWAY	YEAR
1,500 ft.	Second Hooghly	Calcutta, India	Hooghly River	1980
1,325 ft.	Saint Nazaire	Saint Nazaire, France	Loire River	1975
1,312 ft.	Puente de Rande	Vigo, Spain	Vigo River	1977
1,300 ft.	Dames Point	Jacksonville, Florida	St. Johns River	—
1,222 ft.	Luling	Luling, Louisiana	Mississippi River	1983
1,205 ft.	Düsseldorf-Flehe	Düsseldorf; West Germany	Rhine River	1979
1,148 ft.	Duisburg	Duisburg, West Germany	Rhine River	1970
1,116 ft.	Mesopotamia	Mesopotamia, Argentina	Corrientas River	1972
1,102 ft.	Westgate	Melbourne to Victoria, Australia	Lower Yarra River	1977
1,083 ft.	Brazo Largo	Guazo, Argentina	Paraná River	1976
1,083 ft.	Zárate	de las Palmes, Argentina	Paraná River	1975

CANTILEVER BRIDGES

SPAN	BRIDGE	LOCATION	WATERWAY	YEAR
1,800 ft.	Quebec	Quebec, Canada	St. Lawrence River	1917
1,710 ft.	Firth of Forth	Inch-Garvie to Queensferry, Scotland	Firth of Forth	1890
1,673 ft.	Nanko	Osaka to Amagasaki, Japan	Yodo River	1974
1,644 ft.	Commodore John Barry	Chester (Pa.) to Bridgeport (N.J.)	Delaware River	1974
1,575 ft.	Greater New Orleans	New Orleans to Algiers, Louisiana	Mississippi River	1958
1,500 ft.	Howrah	Calcutta to Howrah, India	Hooghly River	1943
1,400 ft.	Transbay (East Bay)	San Francisco to Oakland, California	San Francisco Bay	1936
1,235 ft.	Baton Rouge	Baton Rouge, Louisiana	Mississippi River	1968
1,212 ft.	Tappan Zee	Tarrytown, New York	Hudson River	1955
1,200 ft.	Longview	Longview, Washington	Columbia River	1930
1,182 ft.	Queensboro	Manhattan to Queens, New York	East River	1909

CONTINUOUS-TRUSS BRIDGES

SPAN	BRIDGE	LOCATION	WATERWAY	YEAR
1,232 ft.	Astoria-Megler	Astoria, Oregon, to Megler, Washington	Columbia River	1966
1,200 ft.	Patapsco River	Outer harbor, Baltimore, Maryland	Patapsco River	1976
1,088 ft.	Commodore Point	Jacksonville, Florida	St. Johns River	1967

CONCRETE-ARCH BRIDGES

SPAN	BRIDGE	LOCATION	WATERWAY	YEAR
1,280 ft.	Krk	Krk Island to mainland Yugoslavia	Adriatic Sea	1980
1,000 ft.	Gladesville	Sydney, Australia	Parramatta River	1964

FLOATING BRIDGES*

SPAN	BRIDGE	LOCATION	WATERWAY	YEAR
7,578 ft.	Evergreen Point	Seattle to North Bellevue, Washington	Lake Washington	1963
6,561 ft.	Lacey V. Murrow	Seattle, Washington, to Mercer Island	Lake Washington	1940
6,523 ft.	Hood Canal	Puget Sound, Washington	Hood Canal	1961

STEEL-ARCH BRIDGES

SPAN	BRIDGE	LOCATION	WATERWAY	YEAR
1,700 ft.	New River Gorge	Near Fayetteville, West Virginia	New River	1976
1,652 ft.	Kill van Kull	Port Richmond, New York, to Bayonne, N.J.	Kill van Kull	1931
1,650 ft.	Sydney Harbor	Sydney, Australia	Sydney Harbor	1932
1,255 ft.	Fremont	Portland, Oregon	Willamette River	1973
1,247 ft.	Orlik Reservoir	Czechoslovakia	Orlik Reservoir	1966
1,200 ft.	Port Mann	British Columbia, Canada	Fraser River	1964
1,128 ft.	Thatcher Ferry	Balboa, Panama Canal Zone	Panama Canal	1962
1,100 ft.	Trois Rivières	Trois Rivières, Quebec, Canada	St. Lawrence River	1967

* Floating length rather than span given for floating bridges.

U.S. MOTOR VEHICLE REGISTRATIONS

Source: Federal Highway Administration, U.S. Department of Transportation

STATE	AUTO-MOBILES 1982	TRUCKS AND BUSES 1982	MOTOR-CYCLES 1982	TOTAL MOTOR VEHICLES [1] 1975	1980	1981	1982
Alabama	2,194,794	844,666	70,895	2,492,785	2,938,108	3,011,290	3,039,460
Alaska	199,956	118,594	10,462	225,575	261,527	287,595	317,750
Arizona	1,582,896	632,653	102,369	1,459,492	1,916,753	2,101,823	2,215,549
Arkansas	965,330	516,036	25,976	1,283,321	1,573,718	1,660,794	1,481,366
California	13,420,945	3,709,458	687,110	13,890,670	16,873,117	16,790,562	17,130,403
Colorado	1,843,399	658,328	118,895	1,925,198	2,342,293	2,479,317	2,501,727
Connecticut	2,099,377	158,598	75,975	1,949,239	2,147,495	2,106,516	2,257,975
Delaware	333,803	80,961	11,812	350,992	397,127	404,756	414,764
District of Columbia	212,762	18,606	5,967	255,472	267,565	272,465	231,368
Florida	6,753,616	1,580,978	226,403	5,395,372	7,613,539	7,974,098	8,334,594
Georgia	2,995,234	920,585	115,395	3,210,973	3,818,438	3,852,467	3,915,819
Hawaii	528,125	58,181	7,462	462,011	569,802	580,777	586,386
Idaho	529,194	343,442	53,495	647,446	834,068	856,663	872,636
Illinois	5,855,187	1,386,795	295,115	6,343,875	7,476,832	7,597,068	7,241,982
Indiana	2,874,145	1,009,472	161,494	3,315,371	3,825,852	3,891,297	3,883,617
Iowa	1,667,984	677,821	235,900	2,099,336	2,329,465	2,356,783	2,345,805
Kansas	1,392,762	668,412	124,694	1,805,434	2,006,868	2,023,408	2,061,174
Kentucky	1,809,711	805,630	62,551	2,245,138	2,592,714	2,593,447	2,615,341
Louisiana	2,010,151	790,276	70,994	2,187,521	2,779,457	2,822,176	2,800,427
Maine	541,222	201,635	48,166	648,131	723,612	729,251	742,857
Maryland	2,421,184	472,241	76,295	2,422,724	2,802,896	2,851,581	2,893,425
Massachusetts	3,296,631	452,937	98,711	3,107,051	3,749,243	3,758,139	3,749,568
Michigan	5,005,544	1,244,745	238,542	5,545,460	6,488,070	6,165,600	6,250,289
Minnesota	2,338,304	940,121	172,856	2,524,517	3,091,126	3,151,936	3,278,425
Mississippi	1,214,950	378,041	29,472	1,376,510	1,576,774	1,576,004	1,593,021
Missouri	2,540,190	871,315	99,523	2,866,219	3,271,286	3,333,560	3,411,505
Montana	451,097	306,827	43,675	601,957	679,532	736,152	757,924
Nebraska	804,626	410,365	47,334	1,177,845	1,254,095	1,210,957	1,214,991
Nevada	513,450	196,516	22,361	463,835	654,667	697,178	709,966
New Hampshire	660,588	112,976	56,543	485,306	704,267	761,088	773,564
New Jersey	4,389,581	527,798	104,726	4,154,542	4,761,357	4,696,536	4,917,379
New Mexico	779,944	413,217	60,367	826,568	1,067,735	1,047,936	1,193,161
New York	7,201,767	1,033,090	191,432	7,591,359	8,001,546	8,119,763	8,234,857
North Carolina	3,445,754	1,137,551	115,860	3,689,569	4,531,848	4,545,624	4,583,305
North Dakota	380,683	272,343	31,359	550,827	626,932	641,370	653,026
Ohio	6,324,670	1,311,190	279,523	7,178,933	7,771,236	7,737,264	7,635,860
Oklahoma	1,787,616	992,184	135,461	2,112,733	2,582,999	2,614,381	2,779,800
Oregon	1,467,482	607,214	83,919	1,627,592	2,080,607	2,084,546	2,074,696
Pennsylvania	5,617,934	1,106,805	228,541	7,659,305	6,925,855	7,009,902	6,724,739
Rhode Island	507,284	78,776	27,101	562,641	622,928	596,026	586,060
South Carolina	1,518,689	456,053	35,168	1,772,362	1,995,993	1,970,351	1,974,742
South Dakota	376,735	238,651	38,500	520,896	601,241	612,406	615,386
Tennessee	2,765,974	615,242	83,419	2,725,569	3,271,345	3,533,299	3,381,216
Texas	7,992,738	3,395,095	337,756	8,396,489	10,474,816	11,123,150	11,387,833
Utah	712,027	326,384	66,067	844,974	992,495	1,032,500	1,038,411
Vermont	269,966	80,915	22,237	287,109	347,323	345,214	350,881
Virginia	3,153,409	551,938	80,973	3,250,861	3,626,280	3,844,334	3,705,347
Washington	2,296,429	940,425	141,181	2,539,764	3,225,262	3,330,285	3,236,854
West Virginia	792,707	349,229	54,001	966,009	1,319,915	1,351,913	1,141,936
Wisconsin	2,560,470	601,867	206,886	2,590,709	2,940,911	3,097,621	3,162,337
Wyoming	298,847	208,754	22,274	336,824	467,289	487,342	507,601
TOTAL	123,697,863	35,811,962	5,743,463	132,950,410	155,796,219	158,456,511	159,509,825

[1] Excludes motorcycles.

U.S. MOTOR VEHICLE STATISTICS

Source: National Safety Council

YEAR	MOTOR VEHICLES	DRIVERS	VEHICLE MILES TRAVELED	HIGHWAY DEATHS	HIGHWAY DEATH RATES (Per 100 million vehicle miles)	(Per 100,000 population)
1918–22 avg.	9,200,000	14,000,000	—	12,700	—	11.9
1923–27 avg.	19,700,000	29,000,000	120,000,000,000	21,800	18.20	18.7
1928–32 avg.	25,700,000	38,000,000	199,000,000,000	31,050	15.60	25.2
1935	26,500,000	39,000,000	229,000,000,000	36,369	15.91	28.6
1940	32,500,000	48,000,000	302,000,000,000	34,501	11.42	26.1
1945	31,000,000	46,000,000	250,000,000,000	28,076	11.22	21.2
1947	37,800,000	53,000,000	371,000,000,000	32,697	8.82	22.8
1948	41,100,000	55,000,000	398,000,000,000	32,259	8.11	22.1
1949	44,700,000	59,300,000	424,000,000,000	31,701	7.47	21.3
1950	49,200,000	62,200,000	458,000,000,000	34,763	7.59	23.0
1952	53,300,000	66,800,000	514,000,000,000	37,794	7.36	24.3
1953	56,300,000	69,900,000	544,000,000,000	37,955	6.97	24.0
1954	58,600,000	72,200,000	562,000,000,000	35,586	6.33	22.1
1955	62,800,000	74,700,000	606,000,000,000	38,426	6.34	23.4
1956	65,200,000	77,900,000	631,000,000,000	39,628	6.28	23.7
1957	67,600,000	79,600,000	647,000,000,000	38,702	5.98	22.7
1958	68,800,000	81,500,000	665,000,000,000	36,981	5.56	21.3
1959	72,100,000	84,500,000	700,000,000,000	37,910	5.41	21.5
1960	74,500,000	87,400,000	719,000,000,000	38,137	5.31	21.2
1961	76,400,000	88,900,000	738,000,000,000	38,091	5.16	20.8
1962	79,700,000	92,000,000	767,000,000,000	40,804	5.32	22.0
1963	83,500,000	93,700,000	805,000,000,000	43,564	5.41	23.1
1964	87,300,000	95,600,000	847,000,000,000	47,700	5.63	25.0
1965	91,800,000	99,000,000	888,000,000,000	49,163	5.54	25.4
1966	95,900,000	101,000,000	930,000,000,000	53,041	5.70	27.1
1967	98,900,000	103,200,000	962,000,000,000	52,924	5.50	26.8
1968	103,100,000	105,400,000	1,016,000,000,000	55,862	5.40	27.5
1969	107,400,000	108,300,000	1,071,000,000,000	55,791	5.21	27.7
1970	111,200,000	111,500,000	1,120,000,000,000	54,633	4.88	26.8
1971	116,300,000	114,400,000	1,186,000,000,000	54,381	4.57	26.4
1972	122,300,000	118,400,000	1,268,000,000,000	56,278	4.43	27.0
1973	129,800,000	121,600,000	1,309,000,000,000	55,511	4.24	26.5
1974	134,900,000	125,600,000	1,290,000,000,000	46,402	3.59	22.0
1975	137,900,000	129,800,000	1,330,000,000,000	45,853	3.45	21.5
1976	143,500,000	133,800,000	1,412,000,000,000	47,038	3.33	22.0
1977	148,800,000	138,100,000	1,477,000,000,000	49,510	3.35	22.9
1978	153,600,000	140,800,000	1,548,000,000,000	52,411	3.39	24.0
1979	159,600,000	143,300,000	1,529,000,000,000	52,524	3.50	23.8
1980	161,600,000	145,000,000	1,521,000,000,000	53,300	3.50	23.5
1981	164,300,000	147,100,000	1,555,000,000,000	51,500	3.32	22.5
1982	166,500,000	149,100,000	1,571,000,000,000	46,000	2.93	19.9

INTERNATIONAL HIGHWAY AND TRAFFIC SIGNS

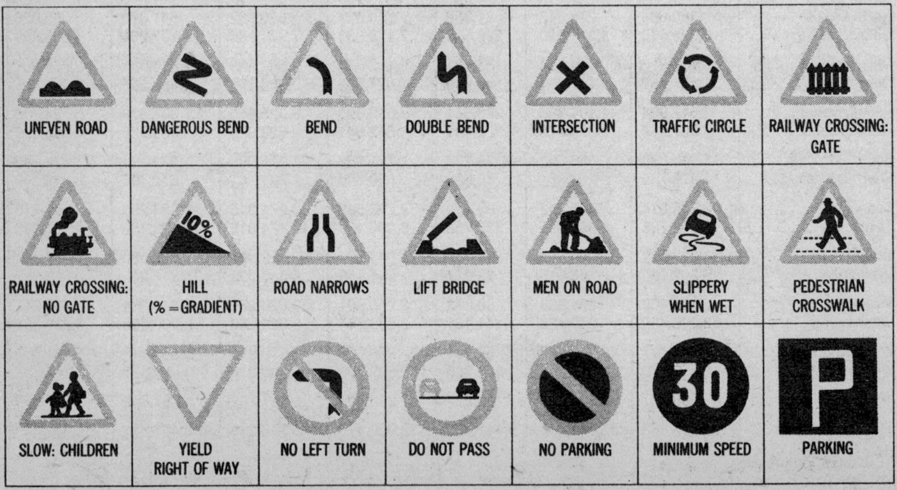

U.S. STREETS, ROADS, HIGHWAYS, AND RAILROADS

Sources: U.S. Department of Transportation; Association of American Railroads

Of the 3,866,296 miles of 1982 U.S. streets, roads, and highways, 640,556 miles (17%) are streets and highways in urban areas. Only 1%, 42,460 miles, are part of the interstate system. Of those, 9,581 miles are in urban areas.

A total of 171,178 miles of track are operated in the United States by line-haul railroads with annual gross revenues of $50 million or more. This figure excludes track used by smaller lines and by switching and terminal companies.

STATE	U.S. INTERSTATE HIGHWAY SYSTEM MILEAGE			ALL STREET, ROAD, AND HIGHWAY MILEAGE			TRACK MILEAGE OPERATED BY LARGE RAILROADS*
	Rural	Urban	Total	Rural	Urban	Total	
Alabama	642	182	824	73,755	13,728	87,483	4,299
Alaska	1,072	20	1,092	8,713	1,172	9,885	—
Arizona	1,028	115	1,143	67,400	8,890	76,290	1,801
Arkansas	425	115	540	69,296	7,353	76,649	2,708
California	1,459	804	2,263	111,374	62,514	173,888	6,476
Colorado	806	110	916	66,238	9,195	75,433	3,320
Connecticut	80	213	293	9,423	10,056	19,479	484
Delaware	7	34	41	3,910	1,359	5,269	236
District of Columbia	—	12	12	—	1,102	1,102	50
Florida	930	322	1,252	65,301	28,496	93,797	3,384
Georgia[1]	931	232	1,163	88,645	15,608	104,253	5,042
Hawaii	5	31	36	2,852	1,320	4,172	—
Idaho	551	52	603	66,150	2,245	68,395	2,381
Illinois	1,265	446	1,711	104,058	30,347	134,405	9,639
Indiana	855	259	1,114	74,032	17,622	91,654	5,608
Iowa	612	124	736	104,084	8,104	112,188	4,906
Kansas	654	154	808	123,849	8,358	132,207	7,580
Kentucky	596	141	737	61,746	6,928	68,674	3,453
Louisiana	553	134	687	46,853	10,079	56,932	3,250
Maine	282	31	313	19,713	2,240	21,953	46
Maryland	201	180	381	17,309	9,824	27,133	1,133
Massachusetts	172	380	552	13,215	20,585	33,800	1,112
Michigan	716	415	1,131	92,280	25,145	117,425	3,787
Minnesota	696	177	873	118,222	12,992	131,214	6,342
Mississippi	589	96	685	64,477	6,312	70,789	2,703
Missouri	833	286	1,119	104,745	13,865	118,610	5,677
Montana	1,085	43	1,128	69,135	2,297	71,432	3,675
Nebraska	446	35	481	87,601	4,300	91,901	4,736
Nevada	497	38	535	41,475	2,375	43,850	1,492
New Hampshire	163	38	201	12,091	2,376	14,467	461
New Jersey	108	230	338	11,457	22,235	33,692	1,506
New Mexico	916	83	999	49,325	4,427	53,752	2,075
New York	874	554	1,428	73,431	36,394	109,825	4,281
North Carolina	583	192	775	75,835	17,086	92,921	2,818
North Dakota	536	35	571	84,480	1,561	86,041	4,767
Ohio	882	655	1,537	81,935	29,215	111,150	6,999
Oklahoma	767	158	925	98,473	11,402	109,875	3,627
Oregon	583	124	707	125,318	8,416	133,734	2,941
Pennsylvania	1,174	323	1,497	88,105	27,859	115,964	6,761
Rhode Island	28	44	72	2,647	3,628	6,275	93
South Carolina	677	79	756	55,952	7,063	63,015	2,524
South Dakota	616	40	656	71,679	1,570	73,249	2,037
Tennessee	833	196	1,029	71,821	11,936	83,757	2,890
Texas	2,236	841	3,077	212,562	59,865	272,427	13,011
Utah	663	124	787	39,134	5,013	44,147	1,691
Vermont[1]	302	7	309	13,247	695	13,942	142
Virginia	805	213	1,018	52,515	12,390	64,905	3,487
Washington	471	234	705	68,517	14,807	83,324	4,281
West Virginia	359	70	429	31,634	2,934	34,568	3,604
Wisconsin	466	111	577	94,280	13,779	108,059	3,977
Wyoming	849	49	898	35,451	1,494	36,945	1,978
Total	32,879	9,581	42,460	3,225,740	640,556	3,866,296	171,178

* Class 1 railroads only. [1] 1981 data.

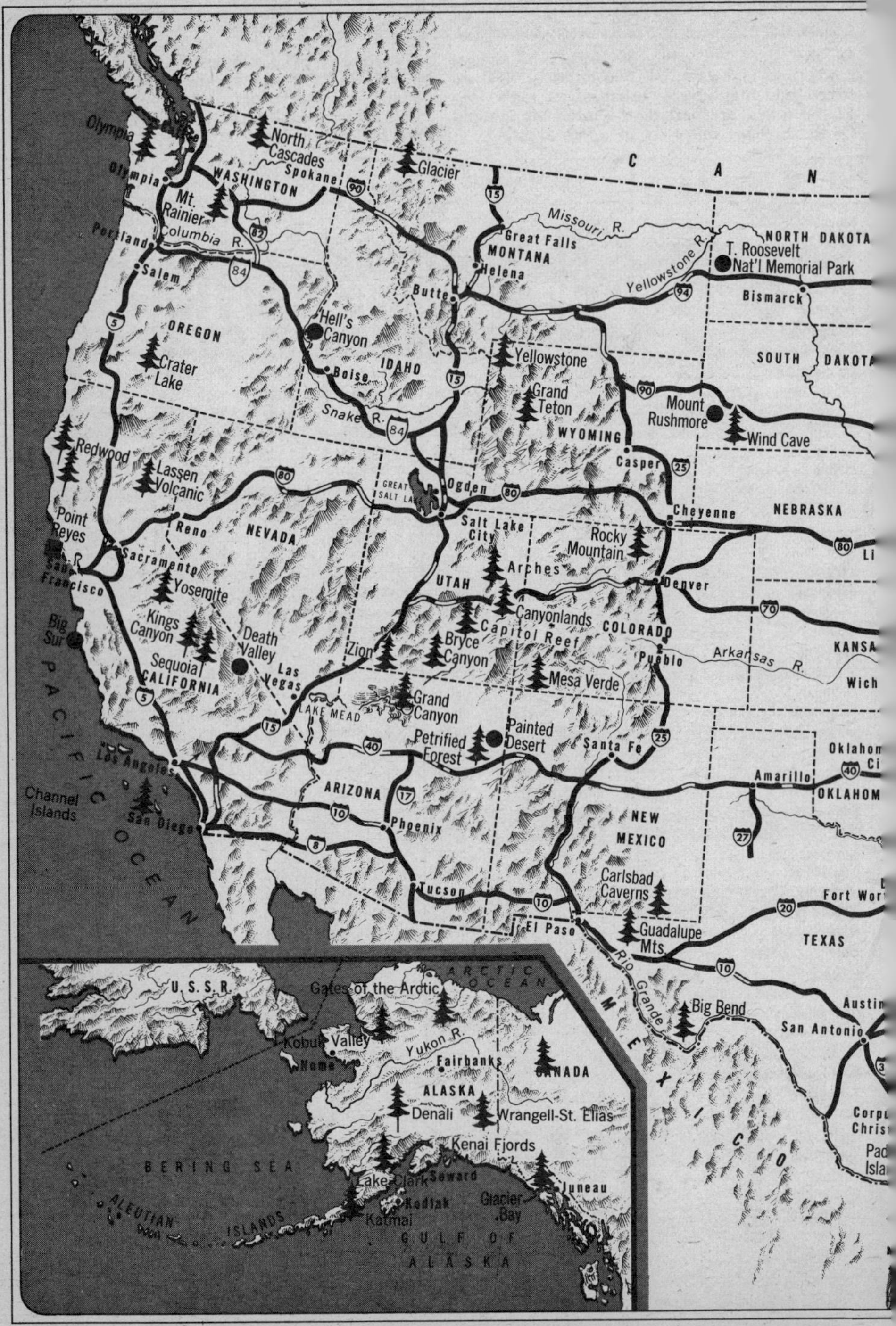
North Cascades
Olympic
Olympia
WASHINGTON
Spokane
Mt. Rainier
Glacier
C A N
Missouri R.
Great Falls
MONTANA
Helena
Butte
Portland
Columbia R.
Salem
OREGON
Crater Lake
Hell's Canyon
IDAHO
Boise
Snake R.
Yellowstone
Grand Teton
WYOMING
Yellowstone R.
NORTH DAKOTA
T. Roosevelt Nat'l Memorial Park
Bismarck
SOUTH DAKOTA
Mount Rushmore
Wind Cave
Casper
Redwood
Lassen Volcanic
Point Reyes
Reno
NEVADA
GREAT SALT LAKE
Ogden
Salt Lake City
Cheyenne
NEBRASKA
Rocky Mountain
Arches
Sacramento
San Francisco
Yosemite
UTAH
Denver
Canyonlands
Kings Canyon
Big Sur
Death Valley
Capitol Reef
COLORADO
Bryce Canyon
Zion
Pueblo
Arkansas R.
KANSAS
Sequoia
CALIFORNIA
Las Vegas
Mesa Verde
Grand Canyon
LAKE MEAD
PACIFIC OCEAN
Petrified Forest
Painted Desert
Santa Fe
Los Angeles
Channel Islands
ARIZONA
Amarillo
OKLAHOMA
San Diego
Phoenix
NEW MEXICO
Carlsbad Caverns
Tucson
El Paso
Guadalupe Mts.
Fort Worth
TEXAS
Rio Grande
MEXICO
Big Bend
San Antonio
U.S.S.R.
Gates of the Arctic
ARCTIC OCEAN
Kobuk Valley
Nome
Yukon R.
Fairbanks
CANADA
ALASKA
Denali
Wrangell-St. Elias
Kenai Fjords
BERING SEA
Lake Clark
Seward
Juneau
Kodiak
Glacier Bay
Katmai
ALEUTIAN ISLANDS
GULF OF ALASKA
5
15
82
84
90
94
25
80
70
40
17
10
8
27
20

UNITED STATES TRAVEL MAP
Interstate Highways
Completed
Under Construction or Planned
National Parks
National Seashores, Lakeshores
Other Scenic Areas
Voyageurs
Isle Royal
LAKE SUPERIOR
MINNESOTA
Pictured Rocks
Duluth
Apostle Islands
St. Paul
Minneapolis
WISCONSIN
Mississippi R.
Madison
Milwaukee
LAKE MICHIGAN
MICHIGAN
LAKE HURON
Sleeping Bear Dunes
Grand Rapids
Detroit
Indiana Dunes
Chicago
IOWA
Des Moines
Omaha
ILLINOIS
Springfield
Fort Wayne
INDIANA
Indianapolis
OHIO
Columbus
Cleveland
LAKE ERIE
Erie
Cincinnati
Ohio R.
Kansas City
St. Louis
MISSOURI
Mammoth Cave
KENTUCKY
Nashville
TENNESSEE
Great Smoky Mts
Chattanooga
Memphis
Tulsa
ARKANSAS
Little Rock
Hot Springs
Natural Bridge
Birmingham
Red R.
Shreveport
LOUISIANA
MISSISSIPPI
Jackson
ALABAMA
Montgomery
Atlanta
GEORGIA
Savannah
Charleston
SO. CAROLINA
Columbia
Charlotte
NO. CAROLINA
Cape Hatteras
Cape Lookout
Mobile
Tallahassee
Jacksonville
Cumberland Island
Canaveral
Baton Rouge
New Orleans
Houston
Galveston
Gulf Islands
GULF OF MEXICO
St. Petersburg
Tampa
FLORIDA
Miami
Everglades
Biscayne
Florida Keys
W. VIRGINIA
Pittsburgh
PENNSYLVANIA
Washington
Shenandoah
Skyline Drive
Richmond
VIRGINIA
Norfolk
MARYLAND
DELAWARE
Assateague Island
Philadelphia
NEW JERSEY
New York
Fire Island
Niagara Falls
Buffalo
L. ONTARIO
NEW YORK
Albany
Adirondacks
Montpelier
VERMONT
NEW HAMPSHIRE
White Mts.
MAINE
Augusta
Acadia
MASS.
Boston
Cape Cod
CONNECTICUT
RHODE ISLAND
ATLANTIC OCEAN
Virgin Islands Nat'l Park
San Juan
PUERTO RICO
VIRGIN ISLANDS
KAUAI
NIIHAU
OAHU
Honolulu
MOLOKAI
MAUI
LANAI
KAHOOLAWE
Haleakala Nat'l Park
HAWAII
Hawaii Volcanoes Nat'l Park
MILES
0
100
200
300
400
500

HIGHWAY DISTANCES BETWEEN U. S. AND CANADIAN CITIES

Source: American Automobile Association. Distances in statute miles.

	Albuquerque, N.M.	Atlanta, Ga.	Boston, Mass.	Chicago, Ill.	Cleveland, Ohio	Dallas, Texas	Denver, Colo.	Detroit, Mich.	Houston, Texas	Las Vegas, Nev.	Los Angeles, Calif.	Memphis, Tenn.
Albuquerque, N.M.	—	1,424	2,248	1,351	1,616	670	449	1,572	1,016	573	802	1,010
Atlanta, Ga.	1,424	—	1,115	722	734	800	1,442	735	848	1,997	2,244	394
Baltimore, Md.	1,935	711	416	729	399	1,391	1,728	570	1,524	2,535	2,755	938
Birmingham, Ala.	1,251	149	1,264	662	738	651	1,288	739	717	1,894	2,076	241
Bismarck, N.D.	1,199	1,663	1,877	865	1,220	1,275	750	1,152	1,512	1,467	1,757	1,268
Boise, Idaho	961	2,293	2,804	1,795	2,110	1,657	851	1,772	1,977	775	943	1,898
Boston, Mass.	2,248	1,115	—	1,009	654	1,795	2,016	832	1,941	2,792	3,082	1,414
Buffalo, N.Y.	1,816	928	466	546	194	1,392	1,593	259	1,649	2,369	2,659	948
Charleston, S.C.	1,753	329	974	1,051	356	1,129	1,771	970	1,177	2,326	2,573	723
Charleston, W.Va.	1,567	557	823	487	260	1,357	1,360	438	1,405	2,136	2,369	591
Charlotte, N.C.	1,651	249	843	801	574	1,049	1,569	752	1,097	2,246	2,453	621
Cheyenne, Wyo.	551	1,544	2,018	1,009	1,324	908	102	1,296	1,145	878	1,163	1,151
Chicago, Ill.	1,351	722	1,009	—	355	933	1,047	287	1,341	1,823	2,113	583
Cincinnati, Ohio	1,404	470	896	285	264	986	1,197	265	1,248	1,973	2,214	490
Cleveland, Ohio	1,616	734	654	355	—	1,198	1,362	178	1,455	2,138	2,418	754
Dallas, Texas	670	800	1,795	933	1,198	—	806	1,154	237	1,243	1,425	453
Denver, Colo.	449	1,442	2,016	1,047	1,362	806	—	1,334	1,043	776	1,066	1,047
Des Moines, Iowa	992	985	1,331	362	677	748	685	649	985	1,461	1,751	625
Detroit, Mich.	1,572	735	832	287	178	1,154	1,334	—	1,456	2,110	2,400	755
El Paso, Texas	270	1,428	2,495	1,578	1,826	628	719	1,688	746	692	797	1,081
Grand Canyon, Ariz.	409	1,833	2,657	1,760	2,025	1,079	676	1,981	1,307	336	573	1,419
Hartford, Conn.	2,210	914	101	949	594	1,694	1,940	772	2,132	2,732	2,967	1,253
Helena, Mont.	1,099	1,201	2,534	1,532	1,877	1,580	774	1,809	1,817	913	1,203	1,806
Houston, Texas	1,016	848	1,941	1,341	1,455	237	1,043	1,456	—	1,438	1,543	758
Indianapolis, Ind.	1,495	578	975	177	321	877	1,088	277	1,285	1,564	2,097	501
Jackson, Miss.	1,087	383	1,498	795	966	417	1,267	967	546	1,660	1,842	212
Kansas City, Mo.	795	848	1,447	557	815	551	594	844	788	1,370	1,597	453
Las Vegas, Nev.	573	1,997	2,792	1,823	2,138	1,243	776	2,110	1,438	—	290	1,603
Little Rock, Ark.	1,092	532	1,552	721	892	315	997	871	552	1,465	1,694	138
Los Angeles, Calif.	802	2,244	3,082	2,113	2,418	1,425	1,066	2,400	1,543	290	—	1,832
Louisville, Ky.	1,510	432	998	290	366	841	1,103	367	1,146	1,879	2,112	388
Memphis, Tenn.	1,230	394	1,414	583	754	453	1,047	755	758	1,603	1,832	—
Miami, Fla.	2,018	688	1,571	1,410	1,342	1,348	2,130	1,423	1,274	2,629	2,773	1,057
Milwaukee, Wis.	1,442	813	1,100	91	446	1,024	1,138	378	1,432	1,914	2,102	674
Minn.–St. Paul, Minn.	1,257	1,152	1,439	430	785	1,013	941	717	1,250	1,717	2,007	823
Montreal, Quebec	2,217	1,281	325	932	697	1,805	1,917	583	2,039	2,693	2,983	1,338
New Orleans, La.	1,188	485	1,578	978	1,092	518	1,324	1,093	363	1,761	1,906	395
New York, N.Y.	2,029	896	219	831	476	1,576	1,822	654	2,014	2,614	2,849	1,135
Norfolk, Va.	2,007	605	650	917	600	1,405	1,790	868	1,453	2,580	2,809	977
Oklahoma City, Okla.	756	868	1,692	795	1,060	200	661	1,016	437	1,129	1,358	474
Omaha, Nebr.	893	1,042	1,514	505	820	654	542	792	891	1,318	1,608	647
Philadelphia, Pa.	2,033	809	318	809	454	1,489	1,826	632	1,622	2,535	2,816	1,036
Phoenix, Ariz.	460	1,884	2,708	1,811	2,070	1,032	909	2,032	1,150	288	393	1,470
Pittsburgh, Pa.	1,784	778	607	496	141	1,275	1,486	319	1,626	2,262	2,503	779
Portland, Maine	2,340	1,218	103	1,115	757	1,898	2,119	865	2,336	2,895	3,185	1,517
Portland, Oreg.	1,400	2,732	3,246	2,234	2,549	2,070	1,290	2,520	2,416	983	1,063	2,337
Providence, R.I.	2,277	1,081	49	1,016	661	1,590	1,975	724	2,199	2,799	3,034	1,320
Rapid City, S.D.	841	1,581	2,012	1,044	1,358	1,198	392	1,331	1,435	1,109	1,399	1,186
Richmond, Va.	1,898	541	551	818	500	1,341	1,691	769	1,389	2,467	2,745	913
Saint John, N.B.	2,695	1,573	458	1,538	1,112	2,253	2,474	1,189	2,399	3,250	3,589	1,872
St. Louis, Mo.	1,051	564	1,197	300	565	633	844	521	1,041	1,620	1,853	238
Salt Lake City, Utah	617	1,949	2,420	1,451	1,766	1,287	507	1,738	1,633	431	721	1,554
San Antonio, Texas	830	1,038	2,068	1,206	1,471	273	961	1,427	190	1,252	1,357	726
San Francisco, Calif.	1,091	2,515	3,174	2,205	2,520	1,761	1,261	2,492	1,968	670	425	2,101
Seattle, Wash.	1,460	2,793	3,123	2,114	2,469	2,130	1,350	2,401	2,476	1,158	1,174	2,408
Toronto, Ont.	1,810	973	562	525	290	1,392	1,572	238	1,694	2,348	2,638	993
Vancouver, B.C.	1,602	2,935	3,274	2,408	2,621	2,324	1,518	2,695	2,561	1,300	1,316	2,550
Washington, D.C.	1,896	672	443	753	398	1,352	1,689	576	1,485	2,496	2,716	899
Wichita, Kans.	714	1,024	1,650	760	1,018	358	518	1,047	595	1,287	1,516	630
Yellowstone Park, Wyo.	983	2,016	2,490	1,481	1,881	1,380	574	1,768	1,617	797	1,087	1,621

Miami, Fla.	Milwaukee, Wis.	Minn.–St. Paul, Minn.	New Orleans, La.	New York, N.Y.	Philadelphia, Pa.	Phoenix, Ariz.	St. Louis, Mo.	Salt Lake City, Utah	San Francisco, Calif.	Seattle, Wash.	Washington, D.C.	
2,018	1,442	1,257	1,188	2,029	2,033	460	1,051	617	1,091	1,460	1,896	. . Albuquerque, N.M.
688	813	1,152	485	896	809	1,884	564	1,949	2,515	2,793	672	. . . . Atlanta, Ga.
1,167	820	1,159	1,161	197	98	2,420	884	2,207	2,961	2,867	39	. . . . . . Baltimore, Md.
816	753	1,064	354	1,045	923	1,683	504	1,795	2,342	2,638	786	. . . . Birmingham, Ala.
2,275	784	435	1,653	1,696	1,674	1,651	1,065	1,036	1,790	1,249	1,618	. . . . . . Bismarck, N.D.
2,981	1,784	1,579	2,149	2,586	2,564	1,063	1,695	344	649	499	2,512	. . . . Boise, Idaho
1,571	1,100	1,439	1,578	219	318	2,708	1,197	2,420	3,174	3,123	443	. . . . . . Boston, Mass.
1,536	637	979	1,286	405	419	2,264	759	1,997	2,751	2,660	420	. . . . Buffalo, N.Y.
625	1,142	1,433	814	755	668	2,213	893	2,278	2,844	3,122	531	. . . . . Charleston, S.C.
1,082	578	917	1,042	604	517	2,061	516	1,867	2,621	2,711	380	. . . Charleston, W.Va.
768	892	1,265	734	612	525	2,133	725	2,076	2,764	2,920	388	. . . . . . Charlotte, N.C.
2,232	998	941	1,426	1,800	1,778	1,011	948	442	1,196	1,285	1,791	. . . . . Cheyenne, Wyo.
1,410	91	430	978	831	809	1,811	300	1,451	2,205	2,114	753	. . . . Chicago, Ill.
1,158	376	715	955	677	602	1,858	353	1,704	2,458	2,399	523	. . . . Cincinnati, Ohio
1,342	446	785	1,092	476	454	2,070	565	1,766	2,520	2,469	398	. . . . . Cleveland, Ohio
1,348	1,024	1,013	518	1,576	1,489	1,032	633	1,287	1,761	2,130	1,352	. . . . Dallas, Texas
2,130	1,138	941	1,324	1,822	1,826	909	844	507	1,261	1,350	1,689	. . . . Denver, Colo.
1,673	351	265	1,065	1,153	1,131	1,452	387	1,089	1,843	1,894	1,069	. . . Des Moines, Iowa
1,423	378	717	1,093	654	632	2,032	521	1,738	2,492	2,401	576	. . . . Detroit, Mich.
2,009	1,567	1,482	1,109	2,204	2,115	404	1,167	887	1,222	1,730	1,980	. . . . . . El Paso, Texas
2,427	1,712	1,617	1,597	2,498	2,502	225	1,460	600	868	1,443	2,046	. Grand Canyon, Ariz.
1,470	1,040	1,379	1,464	118	217	2,601	1,096	2,360	3,114	3,063	354	. . . . . Hartford, Conn.
2,863	1,363	1,092	2,098	2,455	2,433	1,201	1,653	482	1,136	592	2,275	. . . . Helena, Mont.
1,274	1,432	1,250	363	2,014	1,622	1,150	1,041	1,633	1,968	2,476	1,485	. . . . . Houston, Texas
1,266	268	607	922	734	670	1,749	244	1,595	2,349	2,291	631	. . . . Indianapolis, Ind.
969	886	1,035	183	1,279	1,157	1,449	495	1,704	2,178	2,547	1,020	. . . . . . Jackson, Miss.
1,510	548	462	841	1,228	1,205	1,255	250	1,036	1,790	1,944	1,095	. . . . Kansas City, Mo.
2,629	1,914	1,717	1,761	2,614	2,535	288	1,620	431	670	1,158	2,496	. . . . . Las Vegas, Nev.
1,236	741	853	450	1,261	1,172	1,347	350	1,504	1,983	2,336	1,037	. . . . . Little Rock, Ark.
2,773	2,102	2,007	1,906	2,849	2,816	393	1,853	721	425	1,174	2,716	. . . Los Angeles, Calif.
1,120	381	720	726	779	704	1,764	259	1,610	2,364	2,454	637	. . . . Louisville, Ky.
1,057	674	823	395	1,123	1,036	1,470	238	1,554	2,101	2,408	899	. . . . . Memphis, Tenn.
—	1,501	1,840	900	1,352	1,167	2,413	1,286	2,637	3,147	3,481	1,128	. . . . Miami, Fla.
1,501	—	349	1,069	922	900	1,902	391	1,440	2,194	2,033	844	. . . . . Milwaukee, Wis.
1,840	349	—	1,218	1,261	1,239	1,717	540	1,251	2,005	1,684	1,183	Minn.–St. Paul, Minn.
1,698	913	1,140	1,676	385	484	2,615	1,104	2,383	3,075	2,742	609	. . . . Montreal, Quebec
900	1,069	1,218	—	1,346	1,259	1,513	678	1,805	2,279	2,648	1,122	. . . . New Orleans, La.
1,352	922	1,261	1,346	—	99	2,483	978	2,242	2,996	2,945	224	. . . . . . New York, N.Y.
1,052	1,008	1,347	1,090	432	345	2,489	946	2,297	3,051	3,141	208	. . . . Norfolk, Va.
1,572	886	813	718	1,473	1,450	1,016	495	1,168	1,647	2,011	1,391	Oklahoma City, Okla.
1,704	494	409	1,035	1,296	1,274	1,353	444	946	1,700	1,751	1,320	. . . . . . Omaha, Nebr.
1,167	900	1,239	1,259	99	—	2,493	955	2,220	2,835	3,025	137	. . . . Philadelphia, Pa.
2,413	1,902	1,717	1,513	2,552	2,493	—	1,505	719	817	1,446	2,389	. . . . Phoenix, Ariz.
1,303	587	926	1,263	388	313	2,147	642	1,907	2,661	2,610	251	. . . . . . Pittsburgh, Pa.
1,674	1,206	1,478	1,681	322	3,003	2,805	1,300	2,523	3,277	3,024	546	. . . . . Portland, Maine
3,420	2,074	1,803	2,588	2,483	3,043	1,271	2,134	774	677	175	3,010	. . . . . Portland, Oreg.
1,537	1,107	1,446	1,531	185	284	2,668	1,163	2,605	2,464	3,130	409	. . . . . Providence, R.I.
2,243	922	573	1,574	1,835	1,813	1,301	983	678	1,432	1,212	1,859	. . . . . Rapid City, S.D.
1,014	909	1,248	1,026	332	245	2,425	847	2,952	2,198	3,042	108	. . . . . . Richmond, Va.
2,029	1,662	1,746	2,036	677	776	3,150	1,655	2,927	3,681	3,349	901	. . . . . Saint John, N.B.
1,286	391	540	678	978	955	1,505	—	1,351	2,105	2,195	845	. . . . St. Louis, Mo.
2,637	1,440	1,251	1,805	2,242	2,220	719	1,351	—	754	843	2,168	. Salt Lake City, Utah
1,464	1,300	1,336	553	1,849	1,762	964	906	1,447	1,782	2,290	1,625	. . San Antonio, Texas
3,147	2,194	2,005	2,279	2,996	2,835	817	2,105	754	—	852	2,922	. San Francisco, Calif.
3,481	2,074	1,684	2,648	2,945	3,025	1,446	2,195	843	852	—	2,867	. . . . . . Seattle, Wash.
1,632	616	955	1,331	501	506	2,270	759	1,976	2,730	2,639	575	. . . . Toronto, Ont.
3,560	2,107	1,836	2,842	3,199	3,177	1,588	2,397	985	994	142	3,010	. . . . Vancouver, B.C.
1,128	844	1,183	1,122	224	137	2,389	845	2,168	2,922	2,867	—	. . . . Washington, D.C.
1,728	751	665	876	1,431	1,408	1,129	453	999	1,753	1,868	1,298	. . . . . . Wichita, Kans.
2,704	1,470	1,096	1,898	2,272	2,250	1,085	1,420	366	1,120	808	2,263	Yellowstone Park, Wyo.

NATIONAL PARK SYSTEM

The National Park Service of the U.S. Department of the Interior administers hundreds of park areas in the U.S.

Visits to national parkland areas increased by over 4 million in 1982, to set a new record of 334,448,015, a 1.4% increase over the number of such visits in 1981. National Park Service officials reported 236,940,741 visits through the first eight months of 1983, with 196,325 more visits compared with the same period in 1982.

FIRST NATIONAL PARKS AND MONUMENTS

In the early 1800s western explorers John Colter and James Bridger visited the Yellowstone region and told of its wonders.

After an official surveying party visited the Yellowstone area in 1870, a campaign was mounted to save the scenic wonders for public enjoyment.

On March 1, 1872, Congress established Yellowstone as the first national park in the world. By 1900 four more national parks had been created: Kings Canyon (at first called General Grant), Mt. Rainier, Sequoia, and Yosemite.

Under a new law to protect land of scientific value, President Theodore Roosevelt named Devils Tower, Wyo., as the first national monument in 1906.

ESTABLISHMENT OF NATIONAL PARK SERVICE

The National Park Service was created by Congress in 1916 as a bureau in the Department of the Interior.

Under direction of Stephen T. Mather from 1916 to 1929, the National Park System grew to include 25 national parks, 32 national monuments, and a national memorial.

Since 1935 the secretary of the interior has been empowered to designate historic sites, but most are established by Congress.

NATIONAL PARK SYSTEM AREAS

TYPE	AREA IN ACRES	NO.
National Battlefield Parks	8,169.08	3
National Battlefield Site	1.00	1
National Battlefields	11,047.07	10
National Capital Parks*	6,468.88	1
National Historic Sites	17,798.72	63
National Historical Parks	150,192.00	26
National Lakeshores	224,301.30	4
National Mall	146.35	1
National Memorials	8,227.61	24
National Military Parks	34,667.53	10
National Monuments	4,417,506.31	78
National Parks	47,948,623.90	48
National Parkways	163,436.55	4
National Preserves	21,106,342.48	12
National Recreation Areas	3,866,522.30	17
National Rivers	550,166.59	11
National Seashores	598,663.79	10
National Trail	101,449.56	1
Other Parks	32,026.39	10
White House	18.07	1
Total	79,365,775.48	335

* Contains 345 units.

ENTRANCE AND SERVICE FEES

Entrance fees varying from $1 to $3 are charged by the various parks and areas. The fee covers all passengers in the same car.

Anyone can purchase a "Golden Eagle Passport" for $10 that for a year provides unlimited admission to most national parklands for all passengers in one car.

Persons who are 62 or older or are permanently disabled can obtain a free "Golden Age" or "Golden Access" passport giving free admission to all national parklands and allowing a 50% discount on service fees.

Separate fees are charged within the national parklands for special services.

20 MOST VISITED NATIONAL PARKLAND AREAS: 1982

RANK	PARKLAND	LOCATION	VISITS
1	Rock Creek Park	Washington, D.C.	28,761,008
2	Golden Gate National Recreation Area	California	19,897,389
3	Blue Ridge Parkway	Virginia-North Carolina	17,849,081
4	Natchez Trace Parkway	Mississippi-Tennessee-Alabama	16,576,712
5	Great Smoky Mountains National Park	North Carolina-Tennessee	12,929,460
6	Valley Forge National Historical Park	Pennsylvania	12,470,816
7	Colonial National Historical Park	Virginia	12,161,262
8	Chickamauga & Chattanooga Natl. Military Park	Georgia-Tennessee	11,258,882
9	Gateway National Recreation Area	New York-New Jersey	10,142,226
10	George Washington Memorial Parkway	Virginia-Maryland	9,216,441
11	Kennesaw Mountain National Battlefield Park	Georgia	6,711,835
12	National Capital Parks	Washington, D.C.-Maryland	6,177,835
13	C & O Canal National Historical Park	Washington, D.C.-Maryland	6,168,698
14	Lake Mead National Recreation Area	Arizona-Nevada	5,565,467
15	Hot Springs National Park	Arkansas	5,039,737
16	Chickasaw National Recreation Area	Georgia-Tennessee	4,685,708
17	Independence National Historical Park	Pennsylvania	4,318,501
18	Cape Cod National Seashore	Massachusetts	4,047,513
19	Acadia National Park	Maine	3,755,151
20	Gulf Islands National Seashore	Florida-Mississippi	3,507,438

TIPS FOR SAFE AND ENJOYABLE CAMPING

Outdoor living has certain hazards that can be avoided by all who take basic precautions.

Know the area. Be aware of potential land and water hazards. If you are camping in one of the national recreation areas, ask the park rangers for brochures, maps, and advice.

Watch your children. Your knowledge, experience, and wisdom cannot help a child who is beyond your reach and warning voice.

Keep distant from wild animals. Do not feed bears or other wildlife. All wild animals can be dangerous. Remember too that young animals are seldom abandoned and a very protective parent is probably nearby.

Dress properly. Even in the heat of summer it is often cool in the mountains or in caves. If you are hiking on rough terrain, be sure to wear sturdy boots or shoes.

Do not hike alone. Whether on a short hike or a month-long mountain climb, a companion may save your life in an emergency.

Know your own limits. Strenuous exertion in extremes of temperature or altitude can be dangerous if you are unaccustomed to sustained exercise.

When on backcountry camping trips, at least one member of your party should be an experienced outdoorsman.

Inform the park superintendent or ranger of your route, destination, and approximate time schedule.

If you hunt, do so only in areas where it is not prohibited. Hunting is prohibited, for example, in all national parks, national monuments, and national historical areas. The use of campgrounds in these areas as base camps for hunting outside park boundaries also is prohibited. Hunting is authorized, in accordance with state laws, in designated national recreation areas.

For free camping information, write to Information Officer, Forest Service, Dept. of Agriculture, Washington, D.C. 20240; Technical Liaison Officer, Corps of Engineers, Dept. of the Army, Washington, D.C. 20315; Public Inquiry Section, National Park Service, Room 1013 Interior Building, Washington, D.C. 20240.

CAMPGROUNDS ON NATIONAL PARKLANDS

There are three classifications of camping sites:

Campground—Type A: Drinking water and sanitary facilities, including flush toilets and refuse cans, are furnished on a community basis. A typical campsite has parking space, fireplace, table and bench combination, and tent space.

There are Type A campgrounds at 32 of the 48 national parks. Parks with no Type A campgrounds are Biscayne, Canyonlands, Carlsbad Caverns, Channel Islands, Guadalupe Mountains, Isle Royale, North Cascades, Petrified Forest, Voyageurs, and all Alaska national parks except Denali.

Daily entrance fees range from $1 to $3 per car, and user fees range from $1 to $4 per night.

At most federal campgrounds, sites are assigned on a first-come, first-served basis.

Reservations may be made by mail at Cumberland Island and Point Reyes National Seashores; Acadia and Virgin Islands National Parks, Ozark National Scenic Riverways, and Dinosaur National Monument. Reservations through Ticketron are available for camping at Cape Hatteras National Seashore, Grand Canyon, Great Smoky Mountains, Rocky Mountain, Sequoia-Kings Canyon, Shenandoah, and Yosemite National Parks.

Camping Area—Type B: Relatively undeveloped sites regularly accessible by road or by trail. Facilities vary but tend to be minimal.

Group Camp—Type C: Areas used by organized groups, such as Boy Scouts and school groups. Each group space within a camp is provided with a large fireplace, several tables, and parking space for buses or a number of cars.

TYPE A CAMPGROUNDS IN ADDITION TO THOSE IN NATIONAL PARKS

Bandelier National Monument, N.M.	Glen Canyon National Recreation Area, Ariz.
Bighorn Canyon National Recreation Area, Mont.	Great Sand Dunes National Monument, Colo.
Blue Ridge Parkway, Va. and N.C.	Greenbelt Park, Md.
Buffalo National River, Ark.	Gulf Islands National Seashore, Fla.-Miss.
Canyon de Chelly National Monument, Ariz.	Hovenweep National Monument, Colo.
Cape Hatteras National Seashore, N.C.	Joshua Tree National Monument, Calif.
Catoctin Mountain Park, Md.	Lake Mead National Recreation Area, Nev.
Cedar Breaks National Monument, Utah	Lava Beds National Monument, Calif.
Chaco Culture National Historical Park, N.M.	Natchez Trace Parkway, Mo.
Chickasaw National Recreation Area, Okla.	Navajo National Monument, Ariz.
Chiricahua National Monument, Ariz.	Organ Pipe Cactus National Monument, Ariz.
Colorado National Monument, Colo.	Ozark National Scenic Riverways, Mo.
Coulee Dam National Recreation Area, Wash.	Padre Island National Seashore, Texas
Craters of the Moon National Mon., Ida.	Pinnacles National Monument, Calif.
Cumberland Gap National Historical Park, Ky.	Prince William Forest Park, Va.
Curecanti National Recreation Area, Colo.	Ross Lake National Recreation Area, Wash.
Death Valley National Monument, Calif.	Sleeping Bear Dunes National Lakeshore, Mich.
Devils Postpile National Monument, Calif.	Sunset Crater National Monument, Ariz.
Devils Tower National Monument, Wyo.	Whiskeytown National Recreation Area, Calif.
Dinosaur National Monument, Colo.	

GUIDE TO NATIONAL PARKLANDS

This guide provides brief descriptions of all 48 national parks as well as a variety of other national parklands noted as vacation attractions. Following this guide are tables listing all the parks and other areas administered by the National Park Service. Total acreages for each of the national parks and the other areas are included.

Acadia National Park. Located along the Maine coast, primarily on Mount Desert Island. The park contains campgrounds and trailer sites.

Apostle Islands National Lakeshore. A chain of islands off the coast of Wisconsin, in Lake Superior, and a stretch of mainland lakeshore along the Bayfield Peninsula. Scenic islands and a fine beach are this park's main attractions.

Arches National Park. Located in southeastern Utah, near the town of Moab. Huge, spectacular rock formations are this area's major feature. Campgrounds and trailer sites are in the park.

Assateague Island National Seashore. A 35-mile-long strip of barrier reef on the Atlantic coast of Maryland and Virginia. The park contains fine sand beaches, hiking trails, and good fishing sites. A herd of wild Chincoteague ponies inhabits the area. State campground near north end.

Badlands National Park. One of South Dakota's most popular attractions for its erosion-carved landscape, the park contains animal fossils 40 million years old. Prairie grasslands support bison, bighorn sheep, deer, and antelope.

Big Bend National Park. Located on the Texas-Mexico border some 320 miles east of El Paso, the nearest large city. This is an area of mountainous desert land and unusual geological formations along the Rio Grande. Fossils of prehistoric animals are commonly found in the area. Campsites, cabins, and motels are located in and around the park, available the year round.

Biscayne National Park. Located 20 miles southeast of Miami, Fla. Contains 25 miles of the only coral reef in North America. Access by boat only; camping permitted; no fresh water.

Bryce Canyon National Park. Located in southern Utah, about 50 miles from Cedar City. This park captures the flavor of the American West's colorful wilderness. Accommodations include tent and trailer sites, a lodge, and an inn.

Canaveral National Seashore. Lies on Florida's east coast just north of the Kennedy Space Center. Its 31 miles of waterfront are wild and undeveloped, with many bird species. Main visitor area is five-mile Playalinda Beach at the south end of the park.

Canyonlands National Park. A Utah park, this area surrounds the junction of the Colorado and Green rivers. There are water-sports facilities in the adjacent Glen Canyon National Recreation Area. Campsites open all year are located in the park.

Cape Cod National Seashore. Located on the southeastern tip of Massachusetts. A mecca for all water sports, this is an area of vast sand beaches, sand dunes, and salt marshes. The reservation adjoins towns where hotel, motel, and entertainment facilities abound.

Cape Hatteras National Seashore. Located on North Carolina's Outer Banks. Large, uncrowded beaches and fishing facilities are among this area's many assets. The park contains campsites. Hotels and motels are in several adjacent towns.

Cape Lookout National Seashore. In North Carolina, just south of Cape Hatteras, this area contains the ghost town of Portsmouth.

Capitol Reef National Park. Located in Utah, this park contains an abundance of rugged, colorful scenery. Accommodations include a motel, a guest ranch, and tent and trailer facilities.

Carlsbad Caverns National Park. Located in southeastern New Mexico, this is considered among the world's most spectacular natural caves. Guided tours are conducted through much of the 32 miles of explored caverns.

Channel Islands National Park. Includes several islands off southern California coast. Main attractions are flora and fauna. Access by boat only; camping permitted; no fresh water.

Crater Lake National Park. Located in southwest Oregon's Cascade Mountains. This park extends around a beautiful lake that fills an extinct volcano. Cottages, a hotel, and campgrounds are within the park.

Cumberland Island National Seashore. Located on the largest of Georgia's Golden Isles. Includes magnificent beaches, dunes, marshes, and lakes.

Denali National Park. A wide area of northern wilderness radiating from around Alaska's Mt. McKinley (20,320 feet), the highest peak in North America. Accommodations include campgrounds, trailer sites, and a hotel.

Everglades National Park. In southern Florida. This land of junglelike subtropical forests and swampland holds many rare species of subtropical flora and fauna. Numerous motels, cottages, and campsites are located in and around the park.

Fire Island National Seashore. A barrier island of fine Atlantic beach off Long Island's south shore. No camping facilities in the park. There are cottages and hotels in privately owned areas of Fire Island adjacent to the national seashore.

Gates of the Arctic National Park. Wilderness recreation lands near the Kobuk River in northern Alaska.

Glacier Bay National Park. Wilderness camping area in southeastern Alaska. Access by aircraft or boat only.

Glacier National Park. Located in northwestern Montana at the Canadian border. The park's chief attraction is its spectacular mountain scenery. Accommodations include campsites, cottages, and motels.

Grand Canyon National Park. The huge canyon, cutting through northwestern Arizona, was formed by the Colorado River. Camping and trailer sites as well as hotels and motels are located in and around the park.

Grand Teton National Park. Located in northwestern Wyoming, this park contains abundant camping, boating, and fishing facilities amid beautiful mountain scenery. Camping and trailer sites, hotels, and motels abound in and around the park.

Great Smoky Mountains National Park. Wooded highlands along the Tennessee–North Carolina border. This park offers extensive hiking and horse trails, with campsites along the way. A lodge and cottages are located in the park.

Guadalupe Mountains National Park. Located in far western Texas, this park is rich in geological interest and animal life, with more than 200 bird species. Carlsbad Caverns National Park in New Mexico is 34 miles away.

Gulf Islands National Seashore. Historic forts and sparkling white sand beaches near Pensacola, Fla., as well as Fort Massachusetts and primitive offshore islands in Mississippi, are included in the parkland. Facilities include campsites and boat trips from Biloxi and Gulfport to Ship Island.

Haleakala National Park. Located on Maui Island, Hawaii. Wild tropical gardens surround a volcano crater open to visitors. Volcano has not erupted for hundreds of years. Campsites and cabins are available for limited periods.

Hawaii Volcanoes National Park. Located on the island of Hawaii. This park is the site of several spectacularly smoldering active volcanoes. Campsites, cottages, and a hotel are situated within park grounds.

Hot Springs National Park. In Arkansas, adjacent to the city of Hot Springs. This attractive area is famed for its fine natural spring waters. Campgrounds and trailer sites inside the park are available the year round.

Indiana Dunes National Lakeshore. A fine stretch of sandy Lake Michigan beach between the towns of Gary and Michigan City, Ind.

Isle Royale National Park. A Michigan island in northern Lake Superior, located 15 miles from the Canadian shore. The island's woods are filled with wildlife, including wolves and moose. Accommodations include campsites, cabins, and a lodge in Rock Harbor.

Katmai National Park. Wilderness camping area in Alaska. Limited facilities include showers, stores, a lodge.

Kenai Fjords National Park. Located on Kenai Peninsula, Alaska. Limited camping available.

Kings Canyon National Park. Located in California's High Sierras. This is an area of mountain wilderness and includes a forest of giant sequoia trees. Horseback riding on trails. The park contains camping and trailer sites, as well as cabins and lodges.

Kobuk Valley National Park. Along Kobuk River in northern Alaska. Limited camping available.

Lake Clark National Park. Located in Alaska. Known for red salmon fishery watershed and habitat of caribou, Dall sheep, peregrine falcons.

Lassen Volcanic National Park. Located in northeastern California. An area of mountain wilderness, this park contains lakes, hot springs, and a volcano that was active as recently as 1921. Accommodations in and around the park, include campgrounds, cabins, and guest ranches.

Mammoth Cave National Park. A huge cavern in southwestern Kentucky, containing some 150 miles of passageways. Guided underground boat trips are a favorite attraction. Campgrounds, trailer sites, motels, and hotels are situated in and around the park.

Mesa Verde National Park. Located in southwestern Colorado. The park's main attraction is a series of prehistoric cliff dwellings used by primitive Indian tribes some 1,500 years ago. Accommodations include campgrounds, cabins, and a lodge.

Mount Rainier National Park. Located near central Washington. This park radiates from around Mt. Rainier (14,410 feet), a dormant volcano. Also within the park is a massive system of glaciers. Accommodations include campgrounds, trailer sites, and inns.

North Cascades National Park. An area at the north end of the Cascade Range in north central Washington. This region of beautiful but rugged wilderness contains numerous active glaciers. Accommodations within the park are limited to campgrounds.

Obed Wild and Scenic River. Includes 46 miles of the Obed and Emory Rivers, Clear Creek, and Daddys Creek in eastern Tennessee.

Olympic National Park. Located on Washington's Olympic Peninsula, this park is divided into two areas. The inland area is predominantly rain forest surrounding Mt. Olympus. The coastal area, a section of rugged terrain along the Pacific shoreline, is a gathering place for marine birds and other wildlife. Accommodations include camping, trailer sites, and lodges.

Ozark National Scenic Riverways. Encompassing scenic Ozark hill country in southern Missouri along the Current and Jacks Fork rivers. It has 5 campgrounds.

Padre Island National Seashore. A 113-mile stretch of narrow island beach along the Texas Gulf Coast, near Corpus Christi. This park's main attractions are its sand beaches and fine fishing areas. Campsites are available, but primitive campers must bring their own fresh water.

Petrified Forest National Park. Located in northeastern Arizona. As its name denotes, this park holds numerous ancient trees that have turned to stone. There are no campgrounds.

Pictured Rocks National Lakeshore. Located in Michigan's northern peninsula on the Lake Superior shore. This park includes good beaches, scenic forest areas, and rugged sandstone cliffs. There are campgrounds in and around the park.

Point Reyes National Seashore. A stretch of Pacific beach and rugged coastal cliffs about 45 miles north of San Francisco. The area's main attractions are its fine beaches and offshore bird and sea-lion colonies. Accommodations include a small number of campsites.

Redwood National Park. Located along the northwest California coast. Forests of coastal redwoods contain the world's tallest trees. There are campsites in the park. There are nearby trailer sites and motels.

Rocky Mountain National Park. Located about 35 miles southwest of Fort Collins, in northern Colorado. This scenic mountainous area, located on the Continental Divide, contains good fishing and skiing facilities in their respective seasons. Campgrounds are available in the park.

Sequoia National Park. This High Sierra park in California contains giant sequoia groves; part of the John Muir Trail; and Mt. Whitney, the highest peak in the lower 48 states.

Shenandoah National Park. The park's Skyline Drive along Virginia's Blue Ridge Mountains meets the scenic Blue Ridge Parkway. Nature trails and conducted field trips are major attractions. The park has campgrounds and lodges.

Theodore Roosevelt National Park. This North Dakota park features scenic badlands along the Little Missouri River and part of President Theodore Roosevelt's Elkhorn Ranch.

Virgin Islands National Park. Located on St. John, in the U.S. Virgin Islands. This park features beautiful sand beaches and tropical gardens. Camping facilities are available.

Voyageurs National Park. Located in northern Minnesota on the Canadian border. Fishing is outstanding. Other attractions include hiking trails in the thickly forested parkland.

Wind Cave National Park. Located in South Dakota's Black Hills. This park includes interesting natural caverns and ancient Indian sites. There are campgrounds and trailer sites in the park, and motels in nearby towns.

Wrangell–St. Elias National Park. Wilderness recreation lands located in Alaska mountains.

Yellowstone National Park. Located where the borders of Wyoming, Montana, and Idaho meet. This area of spectacular scenery includes about 3,000 geysers and hot springs, as well as river canyons and waterfalls that cut through beautiful forests. Accommodations include campgrounds, trailer sites, and motels.

Yosemite National Park. Located in California's Sierra Nevadas. Majestic mountain country is broken by beautiful forested valleys. The park contains campgrounds, trailer sites, cabins, hotels, and lodges.

Zion National Park. Located in the extreme southwest of Utah. A land of unusual canyons and rock formations. There are campgrounds and two lodges in the park.

NATIONAL PARK SYSTEMS AREAS

TYPE OF AREA AND STATE	ACRES
NATIONAL BATTLEFIELD PARKS (3)	
Kennesaw Mountain, Georgia	2,884.38
Manassas, Virginia	4,513.29
Richmond, Virginia	771.41
NATIONAL BATTLEFIELD SITE (1)	
Brices Cross Roads, Mississippi	1.00
NATIONAL BATTLEFIELDS (10)	
Antietam, Maryland	3,246.44
Big Hole, Montana	655.61
Cowpens, South Carolina	841.04
Fort Necessity, Pennsylvania	902.80
Monocacy, Maryland	1,659.04
Moores Creek, North Carolina	86.52
Petersburg, Virginia	1,533.68
Stones River, Tennessee	330.86
Tupelo, Mississippi	1.00
Wilson's Creek, Missouri	1,749.91
NATIONAL CAPITAL PARKS (1)	
Maryland-Virginia–D.C.	6,467.85
NATIONAL HISTORIC SITES (63)	
Adams, Massachusetts	12.17
Allegheny Portage Railroad, Pennsylvania	1,134.91
Andersonville, Georgia	475.72
Barton, Clara, Maryland	8.59
Bent's Old Fort, Colorado	800.00
Christiansted, Virgin Islands	27.15
Edison, New Jersey	21.25
Eisenhower, Pennsylvania	690.46
Ford's Theatre, Washington, D.C.	0.29
Fort Bowie, Arizona	1,000.00
Fort Davis, Texas	460.00
Fort Laramie, Wyoming	832.46
Fort Larned, Kansas	718.39
Fort Point, California	29.00
Fort Raleigh, North Carolina	157.27
Fort Scott, Kansas	16.86
Fort Smith, Arkansas	72.65
Fort Union Trading Post, N.D.-Mont.	436.45
Fort Vancouver, Washington	208.89
Friendship Hill, Point Marion, Pa.	675.00
Georgia O'Keeffe, New Mexico	4.00
Golden Spike, Utah	2,738.36
Grant-Kohrs Ranch, Montana	1,502.03
Hampton, Maryland	59.44
Hoover, Herbert, Iowa	186.80
Hopewell Village, Pennsylvania	848.06
Hubbell Trading Post, Arizona	160.09
James A. Garfield, Ohio	7.82
Jefferson National Expansion Memorial, Mo.	90.96
Johnson, Andrew, Tennessee	16.68
Kennedy, John F., Birthplace, Mass.	0.09
King Jr., Martin Luther, Atlanta, Ga.	23.16
Knife River Indian Village, North Dakota	1,293.35
Lincoln, Abraham, Birthplace, Kentucky	116.50
Lincoln, Abraham, Home, Springfield, Illinois	12.28
Longfellow, Henry W., Massachusetts	1.98
Muir, John, California	8.90
Ninety-Six, South Carolina	989.14
Olmsted, Frederick Law, Brookline, Mass.	1.75
O'Neill, Eugene, Alamo, Calif.	14.00
Palo Alto Battlefield, Texas	50.00
Poe, Edgar Allan, Philadelphia, Pa.	0.52
Puukohola Heiau, Hawaii	76.57
Roosevelt, Eleanor, New York	180.50
Roosevelt, Franklin D., Home, Hyde Park, N.Y.	264.01
Roosevelt, Theodore, Birthplace, New York	0.11
Roosevelt, Theodore, Inaugural, New York	1.03
Sagamore Hill, New York	78.00
Saint Gaudens, Augustus, New Hampshire	148.33
Salem Maritime, Massachusetts	9.10
San Juan, Puerto Rico	53.20
Sandburg, Carl, Home, North Carolina	263.52
Saugus Iron Works, Massachusetts	8.51
Sewall-Belmont House, Washington, D.C.	0.35
Springfield Armory, Massachusetts	54.93
Stone, Thomas, Maryland	328.25
Taft, William H., Ohio	3.83
Truman, Harry S, Missouri	0.86
Tuskegee Institute, Alabama	74.39
Van Buren, Martin, New York	39.58
Vanderbilt Mansion, New York	211.65
Walker, Maggie L., Virginia	1.29
Whitman Mission, Washington	98.15
NATIONAL HISTORICAL PARKS (26)	
Appomattox Court House, Virginia	1,325.08
Boston, Massachusetts	41.03
Chaco Culture, New Mexico	33,969.40
Chesapeake and Ohio Canal, Md.-W.Va.-D.C.	20,781.00
Colonial, Virginia	9,315.39

NATIONAL PARK SYSTEM AREAS *(continued)*

TYPE OF AREA AND STATE	ACRES
NATIONAL HISTORICAL PARKS *(continued)*	
Cumberland Gap, Ky.-Tenn.-Va.	20,350.90
George Rogers Clark, Indiana	24.30
Harpers Ferry, West Virginia-Maryland-Va.	2,238.64
Independence, Pennsylvania	44.85
Kalaupapa, Hawaii	10,902.10
Kaloko-Honokohau, Hawaii	1,250.24
Klondike Gold Rush, Alaska-Washington	13,270.49
Lafitte, Jean, Louisiana	20,000.00
Lowell, Massachusetts	137.08
Lyndon B. Johnson, Texas	1,477.78
Minute Man, Massachusetts	752.46
Morristown, New Jersey	1,677.65
Nez Percé, Idaho	2,108.89
Puuhonua O Homaumau, Hawaii	181.80
San Antonio Missions, Texas	477.62
San Juan Island, Washington	1,751.99
Saratoga, New York	2,604.93
Sitka, Alaska	107.71
Valley Forge, Pennsylvania	3,469.58
War in the Pacific, Guam	1,925.73
Women's Rights, New York	2.45
NATIONAL LAKESHORES (4)	
Apostle Islands, Wisconsin	67,884.84
Indiana Dunes, Indiana	12,534.82
Pictured Rocks, Michigan	72,898.86
Sleeping Bear Dunes, Michigan	70,982.78
NATIONAL MALL	
Washington, D.C.	146.35
NATIONAL MEMORIALS (23)	
Arkansas Post, Arkansas	389.18
Arlington House, Robert E. Lee Mem., Va.	27.91
Chamizal, Texas	54.90
Coronado, Arizona	4,976.77
De Soto, Florida	26.84
Federal Hall, New York	0.45
Fort Caroline, Florida	138.39
Fort Clatsop, Oregon	125.20
General Grant, New York	0.76
Hamilton Grange, New York	0.71
Jefferson, Thomas, Mem., Washington, D.C.	18.36
Johnson, Lyndon B., Memorial Grove, Washington, D.C.	17.00
John F. Kennedy Center for the Performing Arts, Washington, D.C.	17.50
Johnstown Flood, Pennsylvania	163.47
Kosciuszko, Thaddeus, Pennsylvania	0.02
Lincoln Boyhood, Indiana	197.60
Lincoln Memorial, Washington, D.C.	163.63
Mount Rushmore, South Dakota	1,278.45
Theodore Roosevelt Island, Washington, D.C.	88.50
U.S.S. Arizona Memorial, Hawaii	0.00
Vietnam Veterans National Memorial, Washington, D.C.	2.00
Washington Monument, Washington, D.C.	106.01
Williams, Roger, Rhode Island	4.56
Wright Brothers, North Carolina	431.40
NATIONAL MILITARY PARKS (10)	
Chickamauga and Chattanooga, Ga.-Tenn.	8,102.54
Fort Donelson, Tennessee	536.09
Fredericksburg and Spotsylvania, Virginia	5,908.64
Gettysburg, Pennsylvania	3,861.84
Guilford Courthouse, North Carolina	220.25
Horseshoe Bend, Alabama	2,040.00
Kings Mountain, South Carolina	3,945.29
Pea Ridge, Arkansas	4,300.35
Shiloh, Tennessee	3,837.50
Vicksburg, Mississippi	1,740.78

TYPE OF AREA AND STATE	ACRES
NATIONAL MONUMENTS (78)	
Agate Fossil Beds, Nebraska	3,055.22
Alibates Flint Quarries and Texas Panhandle Culture, Texas	1,370.97
Aniakchak, Alaska	139,500.00
Aztec Ruins, New Mexico	27.14
Bandelier, New Mexico	36,916.89
Black Canyon of the Gunnison, Colorado	13,672.13
Buck Island Reef, Virgin Islands	880.00
Cabrillo, California	143.94
Canyon de Chelly, Arizona	83,840.00
Cape Krusenstern, Alaska	660,000.00
Capulin Mountain, New Mexico	775.38
Carver, George Washington, Missouri	210.00
Casa Grande, Arizona	472.50
Castillo de San Marcos, Florida	20.48
Castle Clinton, New York	1.00
Cedar Breaks, Utah	6,154.60
Chiricahua, Arizona	11,134.80
Colorado, Colorado	20,453.95
Congaree Swamp, South Carolina	15,138.25
Craters of the Moon, Idaho	53,545.05
Custer Battlefield, Montana	765.34
Death Valley, California-Nevada	2,067,627.68
Devils Postpile, California	798.46
Devils Tower, Wyoming	1,346.91
Dinosaur, Colorado-Utah	211,272.20
Effigy Mounds, Iowa	1,474.63
El Morro, New Mexico	1,278.72
Florissant Fossil Beds, Colorado	5,998.09
Fort Frederica, Georgia	213.72
Fort Jefferson, Florida	64,700.00
Fort Matanzas, Florida	298.51
Fort McHenry, Maryland	43.26
Fort Pulaski, Georgia	5,623.10
Fort Stanwix, New York	15.52
Fort Sumter, South Carolina	66.77
Fort Union, New Mexico	720.60
Fossil Butte, New Mexico	8,198.00
Gila Cliff Dwellings, New Mexico	533.13
Grand Portage, Minnesota	709.97
Great Sand Dunes, Colorado	38,662.18
Hohokam Pima, Arizona	1,690.00
Homestead, Nebraska	194.57
Hovenweep, Utah-Colorado	785.43
Jewel Cave, South Dakota	1,273.51
John Day Fossil Beds, Oregon	14,011.90
Joshua Tree, California	559,959.50
Lava Beds, California	46,559.87
Lehman Caves, Nevada	640.00
Montezuma Castle, Arizona	857.69
Mound City Group, Ohio	217.50
Muir Woods, California	553.55
Natural Bridges, Utah	7,791.00
Navajo, Arizona	360.00
Ocmulgee, Georgia	683.48
Oregon Caves, Oregon	487.98
Organ Pipe Cactus, Arizona	330,688.86
Pecos, New Mexico	364.80
Pinnacles, California	16,221.77
Pipe Spring, Arizona	40.00
Pipestone, Minnesota	281.78
Rainbow Bridge, Utah	160.00
Russell Cave, Alabama	310.45
Saguaro, Arizona	83,573.88
Saint Croix Island, Maine	35.39
Salinas, New Mexico	1,079.94
Scotts Bluff, Nebraska	2,997.08
Statue of Liberty, New York	58.38
Sunset Crater, Arizona	3,040.00
Timpanogos Cave, Utah	250.00
Tonto, Arizona	1,120.00
Tumacacori, Arizona	16.52

NATIONAL PARK SYSTEM AREAS *(continued)*

TYPE OF AREA AND STATE	ACRES
NATIONAL MONUMENTS *(continued)*	
Tuzigoot, Arizona	809.30
Walnut Canyon, Arizona	2,249.46
Washington, Booker T., Virginia	223.92
Washington, George, Birthplace, Virginia	538.23
White Sands, New Mexico	144,458.24
Wupatki Arizona	35,253.24
Yucca House, Colorado	10.00
NATIONAL PARKS (48)	
Acadia, Maine	39,110.89
Arches, Utah	73,378.98
Badlands, South Dakota	243,302.33
Big Bend, Texas	741,118.40
Biscayne, Florida	172,845.17
Bryce Canyon, Utah	35,835.08
Canyonlands, Utah	337,570.43
Capitol Reef, Utah	241,904.26
Carlsbad Caverns, New Mexico	46,755.33
Channel Islands, California	249,353.77
Crater Lake, Oregon	160,290.33
Denali, Alaska	4,700,000.00
Everglades, Florida	1,398,800.00
Gates of the Arctic, Alaska	7,500,000.00
Glacier, Montana	1,013,594.67
Glacier Bay, Alaska	3,225,197.95
Grand Canyon, Arizona	1,218,375.24
Grand Teton, Wyoming	310,516.23
Great Smoky Mountains, Tennessee-North Carolina	520,269.44
Guadalupe Mountains, Texas	76,293.06
Haleakala, Hawaii	28,655.25
Hawaii Volcanoes, Hawaii	229,177.03
Hot Springs Arkansas	5,823.54
Isle Royale, Michigan	571,790.11
Katmai, Alaska	3,716,000.00
Kenai Fjords, Alaska	670,000.00
Kings Canyon, California	460,136.20
Kobuk Valley, Alaska	1,750,000.00
Lake Clark, Alaska	2,874,000.00
Lassen Volcanic, California	106,372.36
Mammoth Cave, Kentucky	52,369.60
Mesa Verde, Colorado	52,085.14
Mount Rainier, Washington	235,404.00
North Cascades, Washington	504,780.94
Olympic, Washington	914,578.70
Petrified Forest, Arizona	93,492.57
Redwood, California	110,130.63
Rocky Mountain, Colorado	266,944.28
Sequoia, California	402,487.83
Shenandoah, Virginia	195,057.36
Theodore Roosevelt, North Dakota	70,416.39
Virgin Islands, Virgin Islands	14,695.85
Voyageurs, Minnesota	219,128.00
Wind Cave, South Dakota	28,292.08
Wrangell-St. Elias, Alaska	8,945,000.00
Yellowstone, Wyoming-Montana-Idaho	2,219,822.70
Yosemite, California	760,917.18
Zion, Utah	146,551.10
NATIONAL PARKWAYS (4)	
Blue Ridge, North Carolina-Virginia	82,328.37
George Washington Memorial, Virginia-Maryland	7,141.63
John D. Rockefeller Jr. Memorial Parkway, Wyoming	23,777.22
Natchez Trace, Tenn.-Ala.-Miss.	50,189.33
NATIONAL PRESERVES (12)	
Aniakchak, Alaska	475,500.00
Bering Land Bridge, Alaska	2,770,000.00
Big Cypress, Florida	570,000.00

TYPE OF AREA AND STATE	ACRES
Big Thicket, Texas	85,842.48
Denali, Alaska	1,330,000.00
Gates of the Arctic, Alaska	940,000.00
Glacier Bay, Alaska	55,000.00
Katmai, Alaska	374,000.00
Lake Clark, Alaska	1,171,000.00
Noatack, Alaska	6,560,000.00
Wrangell-St. Elias, Alaska	4,255,000.00
Yukon-Charley Rivers, Alaska	2,520,000.00
NATIONAL RECREATION AREAS (17)	
Amistad, Texas	57,292.44
Bighorn Canyon, Wyoming-Montana	120,277.86
Chattahoochee River, Georgia	8,699.00
Chickasaw, Oklahoma	9,500.06
Coulee Dam, Washington	100,059.00
Curecanti, Colorado	42,114.47
Cuyahoga Valley, Ohio	32,460.19
Delaware Water Gap, Pennsylvania-N.J.	66,705.32
Gateway, New York-New Jersey	26,172.00
Glen Canyon, Arizona-Utah	1,236,880.00
Golden Gate, California	72,815.04
Lake Chelan, Washington	61,891.25
Lake Mead, Arizona-Nevada	1,496,600.52
Lake Meredith, Texas	44,977.63
Ross Lake, Washington	117,574.09
Santa Monica Mountains, California	150,000.00
Whiskeytown-Shasta-Trinity, California	42,503.43
NATIONAL RIVERS (10)	
Alagnak, Alaska	25,000.00
Big South Fork, Kentucky-Tennessee	122,960.00
Buffalo, Arkansas	94,146.00
Lower St. Croix, Minnesota-Wisconsin	9,365.05
Delaware, N.Y., Pennsylvania-New Jersey	1,973.33
New River Gorge, West Virginia	62,024.00
Obed, Tennessee	5,250.00
Ozark, Missouri	80,698.34
Rio Grande, Texas	9,600.00
St. Croix, Minnesota-Wisconsin	64,149.87
Upper Delaware, New York-Pennsylvania	75,000.00
NATIONAL SCENIC TRAIL	
Appalachian, Georgia to Maine (14 states)	101,464.40
NATIONAL SEASHORES (10)	
Assateague Island, Maryland-Virginia	39,630.93
Canaveral, Florida	57,627.07
Cape Cod, Massachusetts	44,596.43
Cape Hatteras, North Carolina	30,319.43
Cape Lookout, North Carolina	28,414.74
Cumberland Island, Georgia	36,978.28
Fire Island, New York	19,578.55
Gulf Islands, Florida-Mississippi	139,775.46
Padre Island, Texas	130,696.83
Point Reyes, California	71,046.07
OTHER PARKS (10)	
Catoctin Mountain, Maryland	5,768.90
Douglass, Frederick, Home, Wash., D.C.	8.08
Fort Benton, Montana	0.00
Fort Washington, Maryland	341.00
Greenbelt Park, Maryland	1,175.99
Perry's Victory and International Peace Memorial, Ohio	25.38
Piscataway, Maryland	4,250.84
Prince William Forest, Virginia	18,571.55
Rock Creek Park, Washington, D.C.	1,754.37
Wolf Trap Farm Park, Virginia	130.28
WHITE HOUSE	
Washington, D.C.	18.07

U.S. NATIONAL FORESTS

Source: U.S. Department of Agriculture, Forest Service; data as of Sept. 30, 1983.

STATE AND FORESTS	GROSS ACRES
UNITED STATES	
Total Forest System	223,498,256
ALABAMA	
William B. Bankhead [3]	348,917
Conecuh	171,177
Talladega	727,154
Tuskegee	15,628
ALASKA	
Chugach	6,577,301
Tongass	17,441,114
ARIZONA	
Apache [1,3,4]	1,226,686
Coconino [3]	2,010,759
Coronado [1,3]	1,782,238
Kaibab [2]	1,600,075
Prescott [3]	1,407,596
Sitgreaves	884,481
Tonto [3]	2,969,514
ARKANSAS	
Ouachita [1,2,3]	1,961,435
Ozark [2,3]	1,496,920
St. Francis	29,729
CALIFORNIA	
Angeles [3]	693,667
Calaveras Bigtree	380
Cleveland [3]	566,781
Eldorado [1,3]	884,699
Inyo [1,3]	1,843,591
Klamath [1,3,4]	1,886,758
Lassen [3]	1,374,947
Los Padres [3]	1,963,249
Mendocino [3]	1,079,483
Modoc [3]	1,979,407
Plumas [6]	1,400,305
Rogue River [1]	61,031
San Bernardino [3]	818,999
Sequoia [2,3,4]	1,180,042
Shasta [4,5]	1,634,735
Sierra [3,4]	1,412,641
Siskiyou [1]	39,668
Six Rivers	1,118,247
Stanislaus [3,4]	1,090,543
Tahoe	1,208,926
Toiyabe [1,3]	694,987
Trinity [3,4,5]	1,179,098
COLORADO	
Arapaho [3]	1,156,975
Grand Mesa	351,626
Gunnison [3]	1,767,756
Manti-LaSal [1]	27,145
Pike	1,283,790
Rio Grande [3]	1,960,466
Roosevelt [3]	1,082,537
Routt [3]	1,248,187
San Isabel	1,241,510
San Juan [3,4]	2,101,220
Uncompahgre [4]	1,044,060
White River [3]	2,089,514
FLORIDA	
Apalachicola [3]	632,000
Choctawhatchee	675
Ocala [2]	430,122
Osceola	161,814
GEORGIA	
Chattahoochee [2,3]	1,571,790
Oconee	260,855
IDAHO	
Bitterroot [1,3,4,6]	464,217
Boise [3,4,5,6]	2,959,719
Cache [1]	264,441
Caribou [1]	1,067,409
Challis [3,4,5,6]	2,487,516
Clearwater [3,6]	1,765,545
Coeur d'Alene	807,093
Kaniksu [1]	1,063,273
Kootenai [1]	46,480
Nezperce [3,4,5,6]	2,247,082
Payette [3,4,5,6]	2,425,521
St. Joe	1,074,717
Salmon [4,6]	1,794,288
Sawtooth [1,3,5]	1,805,654
Targhee [1]	1,355,419
ILLINOIS	
Shawnee	714,655
INDIANA	
Hoosier	644,139
KENTUCKY	
Daniel Boone [3]	1,360,728
Jefferson [1]	54,614
LOUISIANA	
Kisatchie [2]	1,022,703
MAINE	
White Mountain [1]	53,561
MICHIGAN	
Hiawatha	1,281,638
Huron	694,097
Manistee	1,331,673
Ottawa	1,559,892
MINNESOTA	
Chippewa	1,599,649
Superior [3]	3,260,844
MISSISSIPPI	
Bienville	382,821
De Soto	796,072
Delta	118,134
Holly Springs	519,943
Homochitto	373,497
Tombigbee	119,155
MISSOURI	
Mark Twain [3,6]	2,943,896
MONTANA	
Beaverhead [3]	2,199,446
Bitterroot [1,3]	1,188,620
Custer [1,3]	1,200,385
Deerlodge [3]	1,355,783
MONTANA *(cont.)*	
Flathead [3,6]	2,628,705
Gallatin [3,4]	2,150,710
Helena [3]	1,162,602
Kaniksu [1,3]	489,752
Kootenai [1,3]	2,097,950
Lewis & Clark [3]	1,999,022
Lolo [3]	2,614,719
NEBRASKA	
Samuel R. McKelvie	116,822
Nebraska	229,596
NEVADA	
Eldorado [1]	53
Humboldt [3]	2,680,449
Inyo [1]	62,348
Toiyabe [1]	2,681,437
NEW HAMPSHIRE	
White Mountain [1,3]	798,063
NEW MEXICO	
Apache [1,4]	650,219
Carson [3,6]	1,591,144
Cibola [3]	2,120,739
Coronado [1]	71,541
Gila [3,4]	2,797,628
Lincoln [3]	1,271,066
Santa Fe [3]	1,734,800
NORTH CAROLINA	
Cherokee [1]	327
Croatan	308,226
Nantahala [3,6]	1,349,000
Pisgah [2,3]	1,076,511
Uwharrie	219,757
OHIO	
Wayne	832,953
OKLAHOMA	
Quachita [1]	412,912
OREGON	
Deschutes [3]	1,852,274
Fremont [3]	1,710,600
Klamath [1]	26,539
Malheur [3]	1,540,754
Mt. Hood [3]	1,108,728
Ochoco	978,547
Rogue River [1]	633,780
Siskiyou [1,3,6]	1,124,256
Siuslaw [5,7]	835,261
Umatilla [1,3]	1,189,747
Umpqua	1,033,698
Wallowa [3,5,6]	1,064,634
Whitman [5]	1,311,550
Willamette [3]	1,796,866
Winema [3]	1,095,823
PENNSYVLANIA	
Allegheny	742,693
SOUTH CAROLINA	
Francis Marion [2]	414,700
Sumter [3]	965,762
SOUTH DAKOTA	
Black Hills [1,2]	1,328,013
Custer [1]	77,833
TENNESSEE	
Cherokee [1,2,3]	1,204,520
TEXAS	
Angelina	402,231
Davy Crockett	394,200
Sabine	442,705
Sam Houston	491,800
UTAH	
Ashley [1,4,5]	1,300,908
Cache [1]	954,064
Caribou [1]	8,940
Dixie	1,967,188
Fishlake	1,525,688
Manti-LaSal [1]	1,310,645
Sawtooth [1]	92,404
Uinta [3]	889,208
Wasatch [1,3,4]	1,024,321
VERMONT	
Green Mountain [3]	629,019
VIRGINIA	
George Washington [1,2]	1,638,574
Jefferson [1,3,5]	1,585,896
WASHINGTON	
Colville	1,021,028
Gifford Pinchot [3]	1,379,298
Kaniksu [1]	293,463
Mt. Baker [3]	1,312,120
Okanogan [3]	1,536,961
Olympic	715,751
Snoqualmie [3]	1,557,903
Umatilla [1,3]	319,361
Wenatchee [3]	1,902,470
WEST VIRGINIA	
George Washington [1]	157,568
Jefferson [1]	29,782
Monongahela [3,5]	1,650,951
WISCONSIN	
Chequamegon [3,6]	1,049,347
Nicolet	973,403
WYOMING	
Ashley [1]	104,701
Bighorn [4]	1,115,160
Black Hills [1]	201,136
Bridger [3]	1,744,635
Caribou [1]	9,612
Medicine Bow [2,3]	1,402,667
Shoshone [3,4]	2,466,587
Targhee [1]	333,211
Teton [3]	1,695,083
Wasatch [1]	47,704
PUERTO RICO	
Caribbean	55,665

1 Area within state boundaries; National Forest extends over two or more states. 2 Includes National Game Refuge. 3 Includes National Wilderness Area. 4 Includes Primitive Area. 5 Includes National Recreation Area. 6 Includes National Scenic River Area. 7 Includes National Scenic-Research Area.

RAILROAD HIGHLIGHTS: 1983

The 122-ton magneticaly propelled Transrapid 06 is given a hovering test at the Krauss Maffei factory in Munich, West Germany. The 184-foot-long train is designed to carry 196 passengers at speeds up to 250 mph.

RAILROAD MERGER

Santa Fe Industries Inc. announced on Sept. 2 that it would merge with Southern Pacific Co. to form the nation's third-largest railroad with 25,589 miles of track. The two that are larger are Burlington Northern with 28,937 and CSX with 26,414.

Santa Fe Chairman John J. Schmidt said his company also was considering the purchase of Conrail from the federal government. Such a combined system could become the nation's largest railroad with 40,000 miles of track, making it the first coast-to-coast railroad.

The 40,000 employees of Conrail made an offer in June to buy the 15,000-mile northeastern railroad from the federal government for $500 million. The line made a profit of $174.2 million in 1982 and $195.5 million during the first nine months of 1983. About $7 billion in federal money has been spent on Conrail since it was formed in 1976.

WYOMING LOSES PASSENGER SERVICE

For the first time in 115 years, railroad passenger service ended for the state of Wyoming on July 15, 1983, when Amtrak trains made their last runs through the state.

A federal court in May had thrown out a state lawsuit endeavoring to stop the railroad's action.

ZEPHYR'S LAST RUN

The nation's last major privately owned passenger train, the glass-domed *Rio Grande Zephyr,* made its last run through the scenic Rockies on April 24, before being replaced with regular Amtrak trains. The *Zephyr* began its Denver-Salt Lake City service in 1949.

AVIATION HIGHLIGHTS: 1983

Wide World

NASA celebrated the 200th anniversary of manned flight in 1983 by raising this giant hot-air balloon at the Kennedy Space Center in Florida. The first manned balloon flew in France on Nov. 21, 1783.

Airline labor unions began a concerted effort in 1983 to get Congress to impose new regulations on the aviation industry that could preserve the level of wages and salaries they won in the years that airlines were protected from competition. They claimed that airline safety might be jeopardized if competition continued.

Deregulation of the airlines in 1978 reduced government controls, stimulating competition by giving airlines flexibility to choose which cities to serve, what routes to fly, and how much to charge for air fares.

However, as the major airlines lost their monopolies on specific air routes, passenger fare wars developed. In the next five years airline financial statements showed losses that totaled more than $4 billion.

New smaller airlines began competing by offering passenger fares at lower prices. The new airlines could operate at lower cost by purchasing second-hand airplanes and by hiring nonunion workers at lower wages. For example, the average salary of union pilots is $69,000, but the new airlines hired pilots for half that amount or less.

In an effort to regain their profits, the major airlines began negotiating with the unions to take wage cuts and work longer hours. Some succeeded. Others did not, such as Braniff International Airways, which declared bankruptcy and went out of business in 1982.

When Continental Air Lines, the nation's eighth-largest domestic airline, lost $84 million during the first half of 1983 and was not able to

BUSIEST U.S. COMMERCIAL AIRPORTS

Source: Federal Aviation Administration

At the beginning of 1983 the United States had 12,562 airports, 2,697 heliports, and 454 seaplane bases.

A total of 258,971 civil aircraft were registered in 1982, including 4,074 air carrier planes and 254,745 general aviation aircraft.

Following is a list of leading commercial airports in the U.S. in 1982. For the 21st consecutive year Chicago's O'Hare International Airport ranked first. Leading airports for noncommercial operations include Atlanta, Ga., and Long Beach, Van Nuys, and Santa Ana, Calif.

AIRPORT	TOTAL TAKEOFFS & LANDINGS	TAKEOFFS AND LANDINGS BY TYPE OF OPERATION			
		Air Carrier	Air Taxi	General Aviation	Military
1. Chicago O'Hare Int'l, Il	604,919	438,684	119,696	42,345	4,194
2. Atlanta International, GA	571,662	484,292	44,123	34,758	8,389
3. Van Nuys, CA	507,758	0	857	503,042	3,859
4. Los Angeles International, CA	478,336	321,524	95,053	58,497	3,262
5. Long Beach, CA	476,455	3,342	10,264	461,287	1,562
6. Denver Stapleton, CO	467,279	312,481	67,544	85,986	1,268
7. Santa Ana, CA	443,929	29,655	16,428	396,029	1,817
8. Dallas/Fort Worth Regional, TX	442,770	324,766	96,712	20,592	700
9. Seattle Boeing, WA	378,640	1,482	13,270	362,074	1,814
10. Oakland, CA	378,000	42,145	35,863	298,714	1,278
11. Miami International, FL	349,841	236,108	40,641	70,599	2,493
12. Phoenix Sky Harbor Intl., AZ	348,754	136,914	35,582	167,511	8,747
13. Forth Worth Meacham, TX	339,866	0	4,805	334,098	963
14. Houston Intercontinental, TX	336,788	187,439	53,432	94,549	1,368
15. Houston Hobby, TX	336,152	84,912	21,510	228,712	1,018

AVIATION HIGHLIGHTS: 1983 *(continued)*

win wage cuts from its employees, it filed for bankruptcy on Sept. 24 and laid off 12,000 workers.

Three days later, under protection of the bankruptcy court, Continental resumed operations with a reduced schedule, hiring back about a third of its workers at wages that were 45% lower. Frank Lorenzo, head of the airline, cut his own salary from $257,000 to $43,000—the new pay for a senior pilot.

Unions representing pilots and flight attendants ordered a strike against Continental that began on Oct. 1. However, the airline kept its planes flying.

Eastern Airlines, which lost $106 million during the first half of 1983, threatened to follow Continental into bankruptcy unless its unions reduced demands for a 33% wage increase. However, to avert a strike, Eastern and its flight attendants union agreed on Oct. 12 to a new contract providing a 16.5% retroactive wage increase for 1983 and an additional 6% raise in 1984.

WORLD GROWTH OF SCHEDULED AIRLINE TRAFFIC*

Source: International Civil Aviation Organization

YEAR	MILES FLOWN	HOURS FLOWN	PASSENGERS CARRIED	PASSENGER-MILES	TON-MILES	AIRLINE TRAFFIC AVERAGES		
						Passengers per aircraft	Miles flown per passenger	Miles flown per hour
1960	1,930,000,000	8,600,000	106,000,000	67,500,000,000	8,450,000,000	35	640	224
1964	2,300,000,000	8,200,000	155,000,000	106,000,000,000	13,550,000,000	46	687	280
1965	2,550,000,000	8,700,000	177,000,000	123,000,000,000	16,060,000,000	48	699	292
1966	2,780,000,000	9,300,000	200,000,000	142,000,000,000	18,840,000,000	51	711	301
1967	3,280,000,000	10,200,000	233,000,000	169,500,000,000	22,340,000,000	52	727	323
1968	3,730,000,000	11,100,000	265,000,000	196,000,000,000	26,400,000,000	52	736	339
1969	4,160,000,000	11,800,000	293,000,000	218,000,000,000	29,690,000,000	52	742	354
1970	4,350,000,000	12,000,000	311,000,000	237,000,000,000	32,700,000,000	55	762	363
1971	4,380,000,000	12,000,000	333,000,000	252,000,000,000	34,630,000,000	58	757	365
1972	4,480,000,000	12,200,000	368,000,000	289,000,000,000	39,340,000,000	64	785	367
1973	4,670,000,000	12,700,000	404,000,000	323,000,000,000	44,230,000,000	69	800	368
1974	4,580,000,000	12,500,000	424,000,000	341,000,000,000	46,790,000,000	74	803	367
1975	4,670,000,000	12,600,000	436,000,000	357,000,000,000	48,750,000,000	76	820	371
1976	4,870,000,000	13,000,000	475,000,000	393,000,000,000	53,840,000,000	81	827	375
1977	5,030,000,000	13,300,000	517,000,000	429,000,000,000	59,040,000,000	85	830	378
1978	5,280,000,000	14,000,000	580,000,000	495,000,000,000	67,130,000,000	94	853	377
1979	5,630,000,000	14,767,000	735,000,000	651,000,000,000	86,180,000,000	99	865	381
1980	5,811,000,000	15,000,000	748,000,000	676,000,000,000	89,400,000,000	100	895	385
1981	5,647,000,000	14,601,000	749,000,000	679,000,000,000	90,410,000,000	105	924	385
1982	5,630,000,000	14,600,000	755,000,000	716,000,000,000	95,070,000,000	107	921	386

* Excludes Soviet Union; China excluded, 1960–73.

AVIATION WORLD RECORDS

Source: National Aeronautic Association, Washington, D.C., the United States representative of the Fédération Aeronautique Internationale (FAI), world governing body for aeronautical records.

JET AIRPLANE RECORDS

Jan. 10–11, 1962	**Distance in Straight Line** Maj. Clyde P. Evely, USAF; Boeing B52-H, 8 engines Kadena, Okinawa, to Madrid, Spain	U.S.A.	**12,532.28 miles** (20,168.78 km.)
June 6–7, 1962	**Distance over Closed Circuit** Capt. William Stevenson, USAF; Boeing B52-H Seymour-Johnson, North Carolina—Kindley, Bermuda—Sondrestrom, Greenland—Anchorage, Alaska—March Air Force Base, California—Key West, Florida—Seymour-Johnson, North Carolina	U.S.A.	11,336.92 miles (18,245.05 km.)
July 17, 1962	**Altitude (launched from carrier plane)** Maj. Robert M. White, USAF; North American X-15-1 (NASA Aircraft) Edwards Air Force Base, California	U.S.A.	**314,750 feet** (95,935.99 meters)
July 28, 1976	**Altitude in Horizontal Flight** Capt. Robert C. Helt, USAF; Lockheed SR-71; Beale AFB, Calif.	U.S.A.	**85,068.997 feet** (25,929.031 meters)
July 28, 1976	**Speed over Straight Course (15/25 kilometers)** Capt. Eldon W. Joersz, USAF; Lockheed SR-71; Beale AFB, Calif.	U.S.A.	**2,193.16 mph** (3,529.56 kph)
July 27, 1976	**Speed over Closed Circuit** Maj. Adolphus H. Bledsoe Jr.; USAF, Lockheed SR-71 Beale Air Force Base, California	U.S.A.	**2,092.294 mph** (3,367.221 kph)
Sept. 1, 1974	**New York to London, 3,490 miles** Maj. James V. Sullivan, USAF; SR-71, 1 hour, 54 min., 56.4 sec.	U.S.A.	**1,806.964 mph** (2,908.026 kph)
May 1–3, 1976	**Speed Around World** Capt. Walter H. Mullikin; Boeing 747 jet airliner, 4 engines Course: New York—New Delhi—Tokyo—New York Elapsed time: 1 day, 22 hours, 50 seconds	U.S.A.	**502.84 mph** (809.24 kph)

PISTON ENGINE AIRPLANE RECORDS

Sept. 29, 1946	**Distance in Straight Line** Cmdr. T.D. Davies, USN; Lockheed P2V-1 monoplane Pearce Field, Perth, Australia, to Port Columbus, Columbus, Ohio	U.S.A.	**11,235.6 miles** (18,081.99 km.)
Dec. 5–8, 1981	**Distance in Closed Circuit** Jerry D. Mullens; BD-2 airplane, 10 360-C Continental engine Oklahoma City, Okla. to Jacksonville, Florida	U.S.A.	**10,007 miles** (16,104.0 km.)
Oct. 22, 1938	**Altitude** Mario Pezzi; Caproni 161 Biplane; Montecelio, Italy	Italy	**56,046 feet** (17,083 meters)
Aug. 14, 1979	**Speed over 3-Kilometer Course** Steve Hinton, P-51D Rolls-Royce-Griffin 3800 HP engine Tonopah, Nevada	U.S.A.	**499.04 mph** (803.138 kph)
April 9, 1951	**Speed Over 15/25-Kilometer Course** Jacqueline Cochran; North American P-51 monoplane Near Indio, California	U.S.A.	**464.374 mph** (747.339 kph)
Nov. 4–9, 1977	**Speed Around World (22,868.91 miles; 36,803.95 km.)** Philander P. Claxton III and John L. Cink; Twin-engine Aero Star 601 Course: Los Angeles, Peoria, Gauder, Frankfurt, Teheran, Madras, Kota Kinabalu (Malaysia), Manila, Guam, Kwajalein Island, Wake Island, Honolulu, Los Angeles Elapsed time: 104 hours, 5 minutes, 30 seconds	U.S.A.	**219.70 mph** (353.57 kph)

HELICOPTER RECORDS

April 6–7, 1966	**Distance in Straight Line** Robert G. Ferry; Hughes YOH6A helicopter Culver City, California, to Daytona Beach, Florida	U.S.A.	**2,213,04 miles** (3,561.55 km.)
June 21, 1972	**Altitude** Jean Boulet; Alouette SA 315-001 "Lama"; Istres, France	France	**40,820 feet** (12,442 meters)
Sept. 21, 1978	**Speed over 15/25-Kilometer Course** Gourguen Karapetyan; S-A-10 helicopter, Podmoskovnoye Aerodrome	U.S.S.R.	**228.91 mph** (368.4 kph)

BALLOON RECORDS

Nov. 9–12, 1981	**Distance (transpacific)** Crew: Ben Abruzzo, Larry Newman, Ron Clark, Rocky Aoki Balloon: *Double Eagle V,* helium-filled, 400,000 cu. ft. Course: Nagashima, Japan, to Covelo, Calif. Elapsed time: 84 hours, 31 minutes	U.S.A.	**5,208.7 miles** (8,384.5 km.)
Aug. 12–17, 1978	**Distance and Duration (transatlantic)** Crew: Ben Abruzzo, Max Anderson, and Larry Newman Balloon: *Double Eagle II,* helium-filled, 5,000 cubic meters Course: Presque Isle, Maine, to Miserey, France Elapsed time: 137 hours, 5 minutes, 50 seconds	U.S.A.	**3,107.61 miles** (5,001.22 km.)
May 4, 1961	**Altitude** U.S. Navy Cmdr. Malcolm D. Ross in *Lee Lewis Memorial* over Gulf of Mexico	U.S.A.	**113,739.9 feet** (34,668 meters)

AIR DISTANCES IN THE UNITED STATES AND CANADA

Source: U. S. Civil Aeronautics Board. Distances in statute miles.

	Albuquerque, N.M.	Atlanta, Ga.	Boston, Mass.	Charleston, S.C.	Chicago, Ill.	Cincinnati, Ohio	Cleveland, Ohio	Dallas–Ft. Worth, Tx.	Denver, Colo.	Detroit, Mich.	Houston, Texas	Los Angeles, Calif.	Memphis, Tenn.
Albuquerque, N.M.	—	1,269	1,974	1,528	1,117	1,240	1,411	569	339	1,347	744	677	942
Atlanta, Ga.	1,269	—	946	259	606	373	554	721	1,208	595	689	1,946	332
Billings, Mont.	750	1,525	1,866	1,753	1,060	1,301	1,366	1,081	457	1,274	1,304	970	1,223
Birmingham, Ala.	1,138	134	1,050	392	584	396	604	597	1,091	625	562	1,815	211
Boston, Mass.	1,974	946	—	818	867	752	563	1,561	1,767	632	1,597	2,611	1,139
Buffalo, N.Y.	1,587	712	396	696	473	410	191	1,212	1,371	240	1,281	2,217	813
Charleston, S.C.	1,528	259	818	—	760	497	595	987	1,459	668	925	2,206	589
Charlotte, N.C.	1,450	227	727	168	599	335	430	936	1,348	500	913	2,125	512
Chicago, Ill.	1,117	606	867	760	—	264	316	802	901	235	925	1,745	491
Cincinnati, Ohio	1,240	373	752	497	264	—	221	811	1,081	230	871	1,900	403
Cleveland, Ohio	1,411	554	563	595	316	221	—	1,021	1,213	95	1,091	2,053	623
Columbus, Ohio	1,343	446	640	514	296	116	112	926	1,167	156	986	1,996	518
Dallas–Ft. Worth, Tx.	569	731	1,561	987	802	811	1,021	—	645	987	224	1,235	431
Dayton, Ohio	1,271	432	709	536	240	63	163	861	1,096	166	929	1,924	460
Denver, Colo.	339	1,208	1,767	1,459	901	1,081	1,213	645	—	1,135	864	849	880
Des Moines, Iowa	833	743	1,165	956	299	505	613	624	602	533	802	1,447	490
Detroit, Mich.	1,347	595	632	668	235	230	95	987	1,135	—	1,076	1,979	610
Hartford, Conn.	1,886	859	91	643	783	661	475	1,490	1,684	548	1,507	2,527	1,048
Houston, Texas	744	689	1,597	925	925	871	1,091	224	864	1,076	—	1,379	469
Indianapolis, Ind.	1,161	432	817	585	177	98	261	762	989	230	845	1,815	381
Jacksonville, Fla.	1,480	270	1,010	192	864	613	753	918	1,455	814	817	2,152	575
Kansas City, Mo.	717	693	1,257	931	403	540	695	460	543	630	643	1,363	393
Las Vegas, Nev.	487	1,747	2,381	2,005	1,514	1,678	1,825	1,056	616	1,749	1,222	236	1,416
Little Rock, Ark.	816	453	1,260	712	552	514	729	303	778	706	374	1,493	130
Los Angeles, Calif.	677	1,946	2,611	2,206	1,745	1,900	2,053	1,235	849	1,979	1,379	—	1,619
Louisville, Ky.	1,177	321	829	485	286	83	304	732	1,035	306	788	1,842	320
Memphis, Tenn.	942	332	1,139	589	491	403	623	431	880	610	469	1,619	—
Miami, Fla.	1,689	595	1,258	490	1,197	948	1,080	1,121	1,716	1,146	964	2,342	860
Milwaukee, Wis.	1,142	669	860	815	67	318	328	853	908	237	984	1,756	556
Minn.–St. Paul, Minn.	981	906	1,124	1,087	334	596	622	852	693	528	1,034	1,536	700
Montreal, Quebec	1,864	993	254	929	747	713	494	1,512	1,624	529	1,584	2,473	1,115
Nashville, Tenn.	1,123	214	943	439	409	230	448	631	1,023	457	657	1,797	200
New Orleans, La.	1,015	425	1,367	635	837	700	917	447	1,067	926	305	1,671	349
New York, N.Y.	1,825	760	187	636	740	589	425	1,391	1,638	509	1,417	2,475	964
Norfolk, Va.	1,702	516	468	351	717	485	435	1,212	1,564	529	1,201	2,371	782
Oklahoma City, Okla.	510	761	1,505	1,020	693	756	949	175	500	900	395	1,187	432
Omaha, Nebr.	725	821	1,282	1,048	416	614	730	583	485	651	781	1,330	538
Ottawa, Ontario	1,770	931	310	888	654	632	412	1,425	1,530	439	1,503	2,379	1,034
Philadelphia, Pa.	1,746	665	281	550	678	507	363	1,302	1,569	453	1,324	2,401	874
Phoenix, Ariz.	329	1,587	2,300	1,846	1,440	1,569	1,738	868	589	1,671	1,009	370	1,264
Pittsburgh, Pa.	1,486	526	496	524	412	256	105	1,066	1,302	201	1,117	2,136	652
Portland, Oreg.	1,111	2,172	2,537	2,411	1,739	1,975	2,046	1,616	985	1,953	1,825	834	1,854
Raleigh, N.C.	1,565	356	612	217	647	390	416	1,061	1,447	502	1,043	2,239	634
Rochester, N.Y.	1,643	749	343	717	528	461	244	1,265	1,425	296	1,332	2,272	863
St. Louis, Mo.	934	484	1,046	705	258	308	487	550	781	440	667	1,592	256
Salt Lake City, Utah	492	1,589	2,105	1,840	1,249	1,449	1,565	988	381	1,481	1,195	590	1,261
San Antonio, Texas	608	874	1,764	1,114	1,041	1,024	1,241	246	793	1,215	191	1,210	625
San Diego, Calif.	628	1,891	2,588	2,150	1,723	1,865	2,027	1,171	840	1,956	1,303	109	1,567
San Francisco, Calif.	896	2,139	2,704	2,395	1,846	2,036	2,161	1,465	956	2,079	1,635	337	1,807
Seattle, Wash.	1,179	2,181	2,496	2,415	1,720	1,964	2,021	1,660	1,019	1,927	1,874	954	1,870
Tampa, Fla.	1,497	406	1,185	371	1,012	773	927	928	1,513	983	787	2,158	656
Toronto, Ontario	1,554	739	446	744	437	413	193	1,199	1,328	214	1,280	2,176	812
Tulsa, Okla.	608	674	1,394	931	585	646	838	237	549	790	429	1,283	342
Vancouver, B.C.	1,290	2,248	2,514	2,475	1,764	2,014	2,057	1,754	1,110	1,962	1,971	1,080	1,943
Washington, D.C.	1,627	533	413	441	589	388	288	1,171	1,464	383	1,190	2,288	742
Wichita, Kans.	542	781	1,433	1,034	587	699	870	329	428	810	542	1,203	452
Winnipeg, Manitoba	1,130	1,299	1,354	1,467	707	971	945	1,174	793	850	1,378	1,540	1,089

Miami, Fla.	Milwaukee, Wis.	Minn.–St. Paul, Minn.	New Orleans, La.	New York, N.Y.	Oklahoma City, Okla.	Omaha, Nebr.	Philadelphia, Pa.	Portland, Oreg.	St. Louis, Mo.	Salt Lake City, Utah	San Francisco, Calif.	Seattle, Wash.	Washington, D.C.	
1,689	1,142	981	1,015	1,825	510	725	1,746	1,111	934	492	896	1,179	1,627	. . Albuquerque, N.M.
595	669	906	425	760	761	821	665	2,172	484	1,589	2,139	2,181	533	. . . . Atlanta, Ga.
2,083	1,038	748	1,472	1,776	919	706	1,727	679	1,048	387	909	664	1,648	. . . . . . Billings, Mont.
661	650	854	321	866	631	732	772	2,064	410	1,471	2,013	2,079	638	. . . Birmingham, Ala.
1,258	860	1,124	1,367	187	1,505	1,282	281	2,537	1,046	2,105	2,704	2,496	413	. . . . . . Boston, Mass.
1,185	464	734	1,097	301	1,136	887	279	2,157	674	1,710	2,309	2,122	284	. . . . Buffalo, N.Y.
490	815	1,087	635	636	1,020	1,048	550	2,411	705	1,840	2,395	2,415	441	. . . . Charleston, S.C.
651	651	930	651	541	941	914	447	2,282	575	1,727	2,296	2,279	321	. . . . . Charlotte, N.C.
1,197	67	334	837	740	693	416	678	1,739	258	1,249	1,846	1,720	589	. . . . Chicago, Ill.
948	318	596	700	589	756	614	507	1,975	308	1,449	2,036	1,964	388	. . . . Cincinnati, Ohio
1,080	328	622	917	425	949	730	363	2,046	487	1,565	2,161	2,021	288	. . . . . Cleveland, Ohio
990	331	627	806	483	866	689	405	2,034	410	1,529	2,121	2,017	299	. . . . Columbus, Ohio
1,121	853	852	447	1,391	175	583	1,302	1,616	550	988	1,465	1,660	1,171	Dallas–Ft. Worth, Tx.
998	284	574	764	554	796	621	477	1,972	339	1,460	2,051	1,957	368	. . . . Dayton, Ohio
1,716	908	693	1,067	1,638	500	485	1,569	985	781	381	956	1,019	1,464	. . . . Denver, Colo.
1,327	311	232	818	1,038	474	117	972	1,471	259	955	1,549	1,464	874	. . . Des Moines, Iowa
1,146	237	528	926	509	900	651	453	1,953	440	1,481	2,079	1,927	383	. . . . . . Detroit, Mich.
1,194	780	1,050	1,279	106	1,415	1,199	196	2,470	957	2,026	2,625	2,431	326	. . . . . Hartford, Conn.
964	984	1,034	305	1,417	395	781	1,324	1,825	667	1,195	1,635	1,874	1,190	. . . . . Houston, Texas
1,021	238	503	708	664	689	517	587	1,877	229	1,355	1,944	1,866	476	. . . Indianapolis, Ind.
335	925	1,174	513	829	983	1,088	742	2,429	753	1,834	2,366	2,443	630	. . . . Jacksonville, Fla.
1,252	436	394	690	1,113	312	152	1,039	1,481	238	919	1,498	1,489	927	. . . . Kansas City, Mo.
2,175	1,524	1,300	1,500	2,248	986	1,099	2,176	763	1,372	368	414	866	2,066	. . . . . Las Vegas, Nev.
942	613	703	346	1,088	308	495	999	1,759	296	1,155	1,689	1,782	868	. . . . Little Rock, Ark.
2,342	1,756	1,536	1,671	2,475	1,187	1,330	2,401	834	1,592	590	337	954	2,288	. . Los Angeles, Calif.
911	348	603	621	662	685	582	576	1,950	254	1,408	1,989	1,944	451	. . . . . . Louisville, Ky.
860	556	700	349	964	432	538	874	1,854	256	1,261	1,807	1,870	742	. . . . Memphis, Tenn.
—	1,259	1,501	674	1,090	1,223	1,393	1,013	2,700	1,068	2,088	2,585	2,724	921	. . . . Miami, Fla.
1,259	—	297	903	746	736	426	690	1,718	317	1,246	1,845	1,694	612	. . . . Milwaukee, Wis.
1,501	297	—	1,040	1,028	695	282	980	1,426	448	991	1,589	1,399	908	Minn.–St. Paul, Minn.
1,404	723	949	1,393	333	1,429	1,147	394	2,333	969	1,941	2,538	2,284	489	. . . Montreal, Quebec
806	475	695	471	766	615	612	675	1,972	271	1,403	1,968	1,977	542	. . . . Nashville, Tenn.
674	903	1,040	—	1,182	567	841	1,088	2,051	604	1,428	1,911	2,086	954	. . . . New Orleans, La.
1,090	746	1,028	1,182	—	1,345	1,155	94	2,454	892	1,989	2,586	2,421	228	. . . . . New York, N.Y.
802	748	1,045	939	289	1,199	1,099	211	2,454	784	1,935	2,519	2,437	157	. . . . Norfolk, Va.
1,223	736	695	567	1,345	—	418	1,261	1,484	462	865	1,383	1,519	1,136	Oklahoma City, Okla.
1,393	426	282	841	1,155	418	—	1,088	1,368	342	839	1,433	1,367	988	. . . . . . Omaha, Nebr.
1,371	629	857	1,321	337	1,339	1,053	377	2,247	880	1,848	2,446	2,200	450	. . . . Ottawa, Ontario
1,013	690	980	1,088	94	1,261	1,088	—	2,406	813	1,926	2,521	2,378	134	. . . . Philadelphia, Pa.
1,972	1,460	1,276	1,301	2,153	833	1,037	2,075	1,009	1,262	507	651	1,106	1,956	. . . . . . Phoenix, Ariz.
1,013	431	726	918	340	1,010	821	267	2,148	553	1,659	2,253	2,124	183	. . . . . Pittsburgh, Pa.
2,700	1,718	1,426	2,051	2,454	1,484	1,368	2,406	—	1,708	630	550	129	2,327	. . . . . Portland, Oreg.
700	689	981	779	426	1,058	997	336	2,363	667	1,823	2,400	2,354	224	. . . . Raleigh, N.C.
1,204	518	783	1,142	264	1,190	942	257	2,203	729	1,762	2,361	2,166	289	. . . . . Rochester, N.Y.
1,068	317	448	604	892	462	342	813	1,708	—	1,156	1,735	1,709	696	. . . . . . St. Louis, Mo.
2,088	1,246	991	1,428	1,989	865	839	1,926	630	1,156	—	599	689	1,827	. Salt Lake City, Utah
1,143	1,095	1,097	495	1,587	407	824	1,496	1,714	786	1,086	1,482	1,774	1,362	. San Antonio, Texas
2,267	1,739	1,532	1,599	2,446	1,136	1,313	2,369	933	1,557	626	447	1,050	2,253	. . . . San Diego, Calif.
2,585	1,845	1,589	1,911	2,586	1,383	1,433	2,521	550	1,735	599	—	678	2,419	San Francisco, Calif.
2,724	1,694	1,399	2,086	2,421	1,519	1,367	2,378	129	1,709	689	678	—	2,306	. . . . . . Seattle, Wash.
204	1,075	1,307	487	1,005	1,023	1,190	920	2,497	869	1,887	2,392	2,520	810	. . . . Tampa, Fla.
1,234	420	679	1,110	366	1,114	846	347	2,097	654	1,660	2,260	2,060	346	. . . . Toronto, Ontario
1,168	631	616	538	1,235	111	352	1,151	1,532	351	926	1,465	1,558	1,028	. . . . Tulsa, Okla.
2,801	1,733	1,436	2,173	2,449	1,607	1,429	2,410	250	1,770	798	800	127	2,344	. . . . Vancouver, B.C.
921	612	908	954	228	1,136	988	134	2,327	696	1,827	2,419	2,306	—	. . . Washington, D.C.
1,295	622	545	670	1,283	156	265	1,204	1,406	392	808	1,364	1,430	1,087	. . . . . . Wichita, Kans.
1,893	654	394	1,421	1,303	1,002	597	1,275	1,212	841	951	1,505	1,154	1,231	. Winnipeg, Manitoba

AIR DISTANCES BETWEEN MAJOR WORLD AIRPORTS

Source: Defense Mapping Agency Aerospace Center. Distances in nautical miles.

	Bangkok	Berlin	Cairo	Cape Town	Caracas	Chicago	Hong Kong	Honolulu	Istanbul	Lima	London	Madrid	Melbourne
Aarhus, Denmark	4,715	244	1,801	5,417	4,465	3,632	4,736	6,121	1,164	5,924	488	1,103	8,675
Accra, Ghana	5,955	2,892	2,312	2,593	3,982	5,083	6,616	8,735	2,630	4,717	2,748	2,096	8,099
Amsterdam, Netherlands	4,962	313	1,777	5,213	4,235	3,580	5,026	6,304	1,196	5,676	201	790	8,927
Anchorage, Alaska	5,220	3,946	5,339	9,111	4,647	2,473	4,408	2,413	4,688	5,547	3,902	4,502	6,713
Athens, Greece	4,283	984	603	4,306	5,054	4,742	4,623	7,261	300	6,357	1,307	1,278	8,060
Auckland, New Zealand	5,172	9,591	8,945	6,356	7,137	7,113	4,934	3,815	9,214	5,815	9,912	10,583	1,429
Baghdad, Iraq	3,274	1,766	682	4,271	6,092	5,589	3,716	7,304	871	7,368	2,221	2,313	7,032
Bangkok, Thailand	—	4,651	3,923	5,480	9,166	7,427	924	5,730	4,043	10,637	5,162	5,497	3,966
Beirut, Lebanon	3,714	1,476	305	4,162	5,666	5,305	4,138	7,419	535	6,929	1,883	1,900	7,437
Belgrade, Yugoslavia	4,413	543	1,026	4,712	4,847	4,344	4,638	6,846	440	6,225	921	1,086	8,313
Berlin, Germany	4,651	—	1,566	5,184	4,548	3,834	4,737	6,358	942	5,987	513	1,003	8,615
Bombay, India	1,628	3,402	2,348	4,438	7,847	6,999	2,327	6,972	2,605	9,031	3,899	4,066	5,289
Buenos Aires, Argentina	9,123	6,432	6,396	3,727	2,757	4,869	9,965	6,569	6,611	1,700	6,000	5,432	6,278
Cairo, Egypt	3,923	1,566	—	3,899	5,520	5,343	4,397	7,682	664	6,723	1,909	1,812	7,526
Calais, France	5,084	433	1,816	5,157	4,119	3,530	5,157	6,349	1,264	5,554	96	672	9,047
Cape Town, South Africa	5,480	5,184	3,899	—	5,542	7,398	6,404	10,025	4,517	5,289	5,209	4,617	5,577
Caracas, Venezuela	9,166	4,548	5,520	5,542	—	2,178	8,835	5,232	5,253	1,480	4,036	3,785	8,451
Chicago, Illinois	7,427	3,834	5,343	7,398	2,178	—	6,768	3,688	4,771	3,283	3,436	3,652	8,399
Copenhagen, Denmark	4,653	184	1,726	5,368	4,531	3,711	4,689	6,174	1,086	5,986	530	1,113	8,616
Denver, Colorado	7,293	4,413	5,968	8,114	2,668	784	6,496	2,913	5,353	3,463	4,071	4,366	7,621
Frankfurt, West Germany	4,850	234	1,579	5,053	4,364	3,775	4,961	6,474	1,008	5,788	354	769	8,805
Helsinki, Finland	4,257	607	1,832	5,653	4,913	3,855	4,231	5,913	1,172	6,385	1,001	1,596	8,192
Hong Kong	924	4,737	4,397	6,404	8,835	6,768	—	4,824	4,345	9,916	5,218	5,695	3,982
Honolulu, Hawaii	5,730	6,358	7,682	10,025	5,232	3,688	4,824	—	7,058	5,165	6,289	6,841	4,785
Houston, Texas	8,023	4,621	6,099	7,493	1,966	805	7,245	3,392	5,552	2,723	4,202	4,351	7,821
Istanbul, Turkey	4,043	942	664	4,517	5,253	4,771	4,345	7,058	—	6,596	1,360	1,470	7,893
Karachi, Pakistan	2,002	2,930	1,925	4,479	7,389	6,572	2,585	6,995	2,140	8,646	3,428	3,605	5,757
Keflavík, Iceland	5,469	1,303	2,864	6,181	3,705	2,558	5,257	5,288	2,243	5,182	1,027	1,564	9,158
Kinshasa, Zaire	5,191	3,410	2,257	1,778	5,013	6,178	5,994	9,720	2,811	5,506	3,441	2,880	7,033
Leningrad, U.S.S.R.	4,093	714	1,782	5,642	5,076	3,995	4,078	5,930	1,132	6,548	1,146	1,716	8,033
Lima, Peru	10,637	5,987	6,723	5,289	1,480	3,283	9,916	5,165	6,596	—	5,476	5,140	7,013
Lisbon, Portugal	5,774	1,246	2,060	4,616	3,513	3,484	5,962	6,805	1,745	4,863	845	278	9,585
London, England	5,162	513	1,909	5,209	4,036	3,436	5,218	6,289	1,360	5,476	—	673	9,127
Madrid, Spain	5,497	1,003	1,812	4,617	3,785	3,652	5,695	6,841	1,470	5,140	673	—	9,334
Melbourne, Australia	3,966	8,615	7,526	5,577	8,451	8,399	3,982	4,785	7,893	7,013	9,127	9,334	—
Mexico City, Mexico	8,499	5,253	6,690	7,405	1,933	1,466	7,641	3,300	6,174	2,285	4,816	4,904	7,334
Montreal, Canada	7,238	3,251	4,725	6,896	2,116	650	6,726	4,270	4,177	3,443	2,825	3,007	9,030
Moscow, U.S.S.R.	3,822	869	1,572	5,467	5,355	4,318	3,869	6,112	962	6,818	1,359	1,852	7,781
Nairobi, Kenya	3,905	3,437	1,904	2,205	6,240	6,971	4,738	9,333	2,567	6,797	3,684	3,336	6,210
New Delhi, India	1,578	3,130	2,383	5,003	7,675	6,504	2,042	6,445	2,466	9,061	3,642	3,926	5,494
New York, New York	7,526	3,448	4,879	6,775	1,833	644	7,013	4,331	4,359	3,153	3,000	3,119	9,016
Oslo, Norway	4,687	450	1,976	5,632	4,483	3,519	4,650	5,908	1,324	5,955	630	1,283	8,620
Panama City, Panama	12,176	5,072	6,189	6,106	740	2,020	8,766	4,575	5,857	1,268	4,567	4,408	7,873
Paris, France	5,105	477	1,734	5,023	4,113	3,610	5,213	6,481	1,214	5,533	197	557	9,056
Peking, China	1,779	3,984	4,078	6,997	7,766	5,717	1,071	4,398	3,829	8,974	4,415	4,984	4,903
Rabat, Morocco	5,776	1,406	1,948	4,310	3,577	3,732	6,043	7,107	1,736	4,864	1,081	414	9,416
Rio de Janeiro, Brazil	8,694	5,389	5,343	3,293	2,437	4,600	9,566	7,206	5,535	2,042	4,984	4,386	7,159
Rome, Italy	4,784	647	1,163	4,545	4,505	4,191	5,032	6,988	749	5,854	780	721	8,631
Saigon, Vietnam	400	5,016	4,323	5,670	9,469	7,546	813	5,475	4,434	10,584	5,524	5,882	3,608
St. Louis, Missouri	7,595	4,055	5,557	7,445	2,101	225	6,901	3,588	4,991	3,125	3,651	3,849	8,242
San Francisco, California	6,888	4,933	6,495	8,909	3,383	1,605	6,009	2,084	5,844	3,911	4,665	5,052	6,827
Santiago, Chile	9,549	6,752	6,925	4,312	2,638	4,605	10,091	5,959	7,066	1,325	6,281	5,776	6,113
Seattle, Washington	6,474	4,400	5,951	8,877	3,548	1,495	5,640	2,326	5,294	4,300	4,172	4,615	7,106
Shanghai, China	1,541	4,544	4,506	6,991	8,260	6,139	655	4,304	4,324	9,271	4,986	5,540	4,323
Shannon, Ireland	5,429	809	2,224	5,382	3,754	3,120	5,428	6,088	1,682	5,210	322	767	9,388
Singapore	775	5,363	4,460	5,220	9,910	8,132	1,389	5,836	4,678	10,163	5,876	6,147	3,256
Stockholm, Sweden	4,467	437	1,839	5,585	4,705	3,724	4,451	5,970	1,177	6,175	784	1,395	8,410
Teheran, Iran	2,952	1,899	1,058	4,551	6,357	5,648	3,348	7,013	1,106	7,688	2,389	2,575	6,798
Tokyo, Japan	2,476	4,837	5,174	7,948	7,657	5,480	1,555	3,350	4,857	8,366	5,192	5,828	4,387
Vienna, Austria	4,552	297	1,277	4,910	4,678	4,098	4,717	6,640	676	6,085	691	978	8,490
Warsaw, Poland	4,371	284	1,401	5,154	4,831	4,072	4,479	6,405	745	6,267	796	1,229	8,333
Washington, D. C.	7,645	3,631	5,064	6,866	1,774	532	7,092	4,206	4,543	3,041	3,185	3,302	8,850

Mexico City	Montreal	Moscow	New Delhi	New York	Paris	Peking	Rio de Janeiro	Rome	San Francisco	Singapore	Stockholm	Teheran	Tokyo	Vienna	Warsaw
5,065	3,063	895	3,229	3,272	546	3,929	5,464	873	4,695	5,447	298	2,058	4,728	540	441
5,800	4,478	3,511	4,578	4,443	2,587	6,389	3,047	2,269	6,661	6,244	3,329	3,359	7,470	2,687	2,981
4,979	2,981	1,162	3,443	3,166	235	4,238	5,150	701	4,756	5,676	613	2,201	5,043	521	597
3,284	2,721	3,780	4,965	2,943	4,089	3,443	7,073	4,577	1,754	5,794	3,563	4,913	3,013	4,229	4,003
6,102	4,126	1,217	2,707	4,287	1,134	4,128	5,238	580	5,914	4,891	1,308	1,332	5,156	688	865
5,917	7,761	8,754	6,748	7,672	10,027	5,617	6,631	9,953	5,663	4,546	9,191	8,114	4,759	9,643	9,377
7,019	5,017	1,393	1,714	5,212	2,083	3,422	6,019	1,599	6,500	3,857	1,884	382	4,534	1,531	1,518
8,499	7,238	3,822	1,578	7,526	5,105	1,779	8,694	4,784	6,888	775	4,467	2,952	2,476	4,552	4,371
6,698	4,706	1,332	2,151	4,882	1,726	3,782	5,627	1,200	6,357	4,290	1,684	790	4,873	1,207	1,268
5,736	3,743	933	2,845	3,921	776	4,020	5,334	397	5,475	5,075	878	1,515	4,981	251	443
5,253	3,251	869	3,130	3,448	477	3,984	5,389	647	4,933	5,363	437	1,899	4,837	297	284
8,454	6,536	2,727	613	6,778	3,789	2,576	7,250	3,349	7,306	2,113	3,368	1,514	3,641	3,220	3,123
3,984	4,872	7,280	8,531	4,590	5,963	10,414	1,077	6,014	5,606	8,577	6,783	7,444	9,914	6,384	6,657
6,690	4,725	1,572	2,383	4,879	1,734	4,078	5,343	1,163	6,495	4,460	1,839	1,058	5,174	1,277	1,401
4,911	2,920	1,292	3,557	3,096	136	4,371	5,019	695	4,749	5,793	743	2,297	5,169	597	714
7,405	6,896	5,467	5,003	6,775	5,023	6,997	3,293	4,545	8,909	5,220	5,585	4,551	7,948	4,910	5,154
1,933	2,116	5,355	7,675	1,833	4,113	7,766	2,437	4,505	3,383	9,910	4,705	6,357	7,657	4,678	4,831
1,466	650	4,318	6,504	644	3,610	5,717	4,600	4,191	1,605	8,132	3,724	5,648	5,480	4,098	4,072
5,145	3,143	836	3,159	3,351	560	3,897	5,488	828	4,769	5,381	284	1,980	4,716	474	361
1,254	1,412	4,761	6,716	1,425	4,256	5,516	5,090	4,845	831	7,881	4,230	6,104	5,057	4,695	4,622
5,166	3,172	1,096	3,312	3,351	256	4,217	5,155	517	4,953	5,549	647	2,039	5,067	337	486
5,316	3,341	474	2,824	3,578	1,045	3,415	5,973	1,208	4,723	5,004	221	1,796	4,235	791	509
7,641	6,726	3,869	2,042	7,013	5,213	1,071	9,566	5,032	6,009	1,389	4,451	3,348	1,555	4,717	4,479
3,300	4,270	6,112	6,445	4,331	6,481	4,398	7,206	6,988	2,084	5,836	5,970	7,013	3,350	6,640	6,405
663	1,377	5,123	7,277	1,233	4,369	6,252	4,360	4,938	1,421	8,631	4,526	6,451	5,803	4,876	4,865
6,174	4,177	962	2,466	4,359	1,214	3,829	5,535	749	5,844	4,678	1,177	1,106	4,857	676	745
8,035	6,086	2,272	578	6,321	3,318	2,632	7,030	2,886	7,027	2,555	2,907	1,044	3,746	2,749	2,653
4,008	2,019	1,798	4,127	2,254	1,223	4,279	5,286	1,795	3,654	6,238	1,172	3,098	4,786	1,588	1,519
6,885	5,558	3,772	4,065	5,541	3,252	6,088	3,577	2,769	7,762	5,325	3,818	3,133	7,218	3,141	3,396
5,459	3,491	324	2,663	3,731	1,174	3,279	6,101	1,271	4,817	4,841	378	1,664	4,125	852	556
2,285	3,443	6,818	9,061	3,153	5,533	8,974	2,042	5,854	3,911	10,163	6,175	7,688	8,366	6,085	6,267
4,686	2,835	2,107	4,203	2,926	777	5,227	4,153	996	4,937	6,422	1,611	2,850	6,036	1,248	1,487
4,816	2,825	1,359	3,642	3,000	197	4,415	4,984	780	4,665	5,876	784	2,389	5,192	691	796
4,904	3,007	1,852	3,926	3,119	557	4,984	4,386	721	5,052	6,147	1,395	2,575	5,828	978	1,229
7,334	9,030	7,781	5,494	9,016	9,056	4,903	7,159	8,631	6,827	3,256	8,410	6,798	4,387	8,490	8,333
—	2,003	5,782	7,926	1,817	4,974	6,726	4,135	5,529	1,635	8,972	5,178	7,105	6,120	5,499	5,505
2,003	—	3,814	6,099	290	2,993	5,655	4,411	3,566	2,206	7,998	3,189	5,112	5,628	3,501	3,503
5,782	3,814	—	2,358	4,052	1,345	3,138	6,221	1,297	5,108	4,558	657	1,344	4,057	900	623
8,006	6,322	3,430	2,927	6,391	3,490	4,988	4,828	2,906	8,349	4,037	3,741	2,357	6,086	3,141	3,301
7,926	6,099	2,358	—	6,360	3,563	2,062	7,597	3,210	6,698	2,239	3,015	1,377	3,170	3,000	2,846
1,817	290	4,052	6,360	—	3,158	5,942	4,159	3,717	2,248	8,288	3,416	5,329	5,887	3,686	3,708
4,968	2,973	883	3,241	3,196	731	3,804	5,608	1,088	4,521	5,433	226	2,139	4,563	740	580
1,302	2,197	5,818	8,175	1,912	4,671	7,733	2,856	5,119	2,884	10,149	5,161	6,945	7,339	5,240	5,354
4,974	2,993	1,345	3,563	3,158	—	4,452	4,929	590	4,860	5,801	840	2,275	5,273	570	741
6,726	5,655	3,138	2,062	5,942	4,452	—	9,353	4,410	5,139	2,417	3,632	3,043	1,131	4,035	3,760
4,878	3,084	2,237	4,198	3,154	971	5,375	3,988	1,012	5,216	6,382	1,807	2,826	6,239	1,344	1,615
4,135	4,411	6,221	7,597	4,159	4,929	9,353	—	4,943	5,739	8,509	5,762	6,399	10,024	5,322	5,602
5,529	3,566	1,297	3,210	3,717	590	4,410	4,943	—	5,444	5,427	1,075	1,854	5,353	420	716
8,446	7,436	4,173	1,972	7,726	5,475	1,830	8,947	5,172	6,812	588	4,810	3,348	2,334	4,929	4,738
1,242	843	4,543	6,718	776	3,824	5,862	4,536	4,402	1,508	8,278	3,948	5,872	5,564	4,317	4,294
1,635	2,206	5,108	6,698	2,248	4,860	5,139	5,739	5,444	—	7,343	4,674	6,406	4,486	5,227	5,099
3,549	4,718	7,619	9,140	4,429	6,276	10,271	1,586	6,413	5,132	8,866	7,054	7,982	9,299	6,751	7,002
2,027	1,985	4,529	6,137	2,105	4,368	4,699	5,975	4,943	590	7,016	4,118	5,818	4,176	4,697	4,551
6,989	6,145	3,690	2,298	6,427	5,016	581	9,848	4,942	5,360	2,040	4,203	3,451	961	4,580	4,312
4,494	2,506	1,609	3,931	2,678	491	4,573	4,862	1,078	4,387	6,157	981	2,702	5,275	1,012	1,091
8,972	7,998	4,558	2,239	8,288	5,801	2,417	8,509	5,427	7,343	—	5,210	3,573	2,860	5,237	5,080
5,178	3,189	657	3,015	3,416	840	3,632	5,762	1,075	4,674	5,210	—	1,927	4,434	678	444
7,105	5,112	1,344	1,377	5,329	2,275	3,043	6,399	1,854	6,406	3,573	1,927	—	4,158	1,707	1,627
6,120	5,628	4,057	3,170	5,887	5,273	1,131	10,024	5,353	4,486	2,860	4,434	4,158	—	4,949	4,657
5,499	3,501	900	3,000	3,686	570	4,035	5,322	420	5,227	5,237	678	1,707	4,949	—	298
5,505	3,503	623	2,846	3,708	741	3,760	5,602	716	5,099	5,080	444	1,627	4,657	298	—
1,632	423	4,224	6,521	186	3,343	6,024	4,148	3,902	2,123	8,397	3,592	5,508	5,910	3,870	3,890

OCEAN SHIPPING HIGHLIGHTS: 1983

The United States remained in 8th place among leading merchant fleets of the world in 1982, according to figures released by the U.S. Maritime Administration.

While the number of U.S.-flag ships remained the same, the fleet tonnage increased from 21,325,000 deadweight tonnage (dwt.) in 1981 to 21,886,000 by mid-1982. The total number of privately owned U.S. merchant ships decreased to 574 in 1982.

The U.S. statistics reflect a recent worldwide trend toward relatively much greater increases in tonnage than in the number of vessels, due largely to the increased size of vessels now in the merchant fleet and the construction of huge crude-oil tankers ranging to more than 500,000 dwt. This trend has established total tonnage rather than the number of ships as a more meaningful international standard for ranking merchant fleets.

The Liberian tanker *Seawise Giant,* built in Japan in 1976, is the world's largest ship, with a deadweight tonnage of 564,739. Its length of 1,504 feet 2 inches is more than five times that of a football field.

The French tanker *Pierre Guillaumat,* completed in 1977, the second-largest ship, was involved in an oil explosion in 1983.

Liberia continued to boast the world's largest merchant fleet, attracting the registry of many American and Greek-owned vessels because of its loose maritime laws.

LEADING MERCHANT FLEETS OF THE WORLD

Source: U.S. Department of Commerce, Maritime Administration

1982 RANK	COUNTRY	SHIPS	DEADWEIGHT TONNAGE	1981 RANK	COUNTRY	SHIPS	DEADWEIGHT TONNAGE
1	Liberia	2,220	146,124,000	1	Liberia	2,265	151,157,000
2	Greece	2,893	74,629,000	2	Greece	2,945	72,815,000
3	Japan	1,770	63,192,000	3	Japan	1,760	62,662,000
4	Panama	2,725	45,820,000	4	Panama	2,603	42,402,000
5	Norway	600	38,809,000	5	Britain	1,016	41,170,000
6	United Kingdom	927	37,146,000	6	Norway	609	37,967,000
7	U.S.S.R.	2,449	21,886,000	7	Soviet Union	2,541	22,067,000
8	United States *	574	21,479,000	8	United States *	578	21,325,000
9	France	317	18,516,000	9	France	339	19,229,000
10	Italy	606	16,551,000	10	Italy	621	17,091,000
11	Spain	510	12,525,000	11	Spain	505	12,336,000
12	Singapore	592	11,932,000	12	Singapore	597	11,725,000
13	China	750	10,945,000	13	Germany, West	459	11,156,000
14	Germany, West	440	10,790,000	14	China	724	10,588,000
15	India	378	9,464,000	15	India	372	9,276,000

* Privately owned ships.

SEA DISTANCES BETWEEN MAJOR WORLD PORTS

Source: Defense Mapping Agency Hydrographic/Topographic Center. Distances in nautical miles.

MAJOR WORLD PORTS	AUCKLAND (New Zealand)	BOMBAY (India)	BUENOS AIRES (Argentina)	CAPE TOWN (South Africa)	COLOMBO (Sri Lanka)	HAMBURG (W. Germany)	HONG KONG	HONOLULU	ISTANBUL (Turkey)	LE HAVRE (France)	LISBON (Portugal)
AUCKLAND	—	7,088	6,186	7,153	6,229	11,602	5,060	3,820	10,189	12,027	10,707
BOMBAY	7,088	—	8,285	4,616	896	6,613	3,895	8,328	3,853	6,153	5,278
BUENOS AIRES	6,186	8,285	—	3,719	8,161	6,625	10,587	7,764	7,101	6,159	5,339
CAPE TOWN	7,153	4,616	3,719	—	4,398	6,431	6,917	10,649	6,184	5,986	5,134
COLOMBO	6,229	896	8,161	4,398	—	7,045	3,026	7,462	4,285	6,585	5,710
HAMBURG	11,602	6,613	6,625	6,431	7,045	—	10,029	9,790	3,425	511	1,369
HONG KONG	5,060	3,895	10,587	6,917	3,026	10,029	—	4,857	7,286	12,864	8,702
HONOLULU	3,820	8,328	7,764	10,649	7,462	9,790	4,857	—	10,857	9,336	8,881
ISTANBUL	10,189	3,853	7,101	6,184	4,285	3,425	7,286	10,857	—	2,982	2,107
LE HAVRE	12,027	6,153	6,159	5,986	6,585	511	12,864	9,336	2,982	—	909
LISBON	10,707	5,278	5,339	5,134	5,710	1,369	8,702	8,881	2,107	909	—
LIVERPOOL	11,107	6,258	6,246	6,069	6,690	1,014	9,692	9,370	3,061	560	1,007
MANILA	4,653	3,771	10,445	6,742	2,911	10,033	631	4,869	7,160	9,471	8,594
MELBOURNE	1,649	5,556	6,853	5,963	4,700	11,405	4,875	4,942	8,645	10,946	10,168
NEW ORLEANS	7,945	9,515	6,237	7,290	9,961	5,111	10,628	6,129	6,358	4,659	4,345
NEW YORK	8,529	8,173	5,871	6,786	8,633	3,747	11,212	6,703	5,005	3,293	2,978
PANAMA	6,511	9,300	5,385	6,472	9,775	5,105	9,195	4,680	6,172	4,651	4,152
PORT SAID	9,383	3,049	7,202	5,402	3,480	3,564	6,480	10,970	804	3,104	2,229
RIO DE JANEIRO	7,056	7,864	1,151	3,273	7,725	5,549	10,149	8,608	6,001	5,058	4,219
SAN FRANCISCO	5,680	9,794	7,582	9,753	8,934	8,350	6,044	2,091	9,417	7,896	7,441
SINGAPORE	5,017	2,441	9,283	5,603	1,581	8,582	1,454	5,899	5,822	8,139	7,247
VALPARAISO	5,247	10,281	2,826	5,711	9,986	7,721	10,218	5,919	8,788	7,267	6,812
YOKOHAMA	4,789	5,330	10,669	8,351	4,470	11,471	1,585	3,397	8,711	11,011	10,136

WORLD'S LARGEST MERCHANT SHIPS—THE SUPERTANKERS

Source: U.S. Department of Commerce, Maritime Administration

The world's largest merchant ships are all tankers. The three largest sail under the flag of France. Each is more than eight times larger in tonnage than Britain's passenger liner *Queen Elizabeth 2*.

SHIP	FLAG	YEAR BUILT	WHERE BUILT	DWT TONNAGE	OVERALL LENGTH	EXTREME WIDTH
1. Seawise Giant	Liberia	1976	Japan	564,739	1,504 ' 2"	225 ' 9"
2. Pierre Guillaumat	France	1977	France	555,051	1,359 ' 1"	206 ' 10"
3. Prairial	France	1979	France	554,974	1,359 ' 1"	206 ' 10"
4. Batillus	France	1976	France	553,662	1,359 ' 0"	206 ' 8"
5. Bellamya	France	1976	France	553,662	1,359 ' 0"	206 ' 8"
6. Esso Atlantic	Liberia	1977	Japan	516,893	1,334 ' 0"	233 ' 2"
7. Esso Pacific	Liberia	1977	Japan	516,423	1,334 ' 0"	233 ' 2"
8. Nanny	Sweden	1978	Sweden	491,120	1,194 ' 3"	259 ' 4"
9. Nissei Maru	Japan	1975	Japan	484,337	1,243 ' 1"	203 ' 6"
10. Globtik London	Britain	1973	Japan	483,933	1,243 ' 0"	203 ' 7"

WORLD'S LARGEST PASSENGER SHIPS

Source: U.S. Department of Commerce, Maritime Administration

SHIP	FLAG	YEAR COMPLETED	PASSENGER CAPACITY	GROSS TONS	LENGTH OVERALL
1. Norway	Norway	1961	2,400	70,202	1,035 ' 2"
2. Queen Elizabeth 2	Britain	1968	1,970	67,140	963 ' 0"
3. Canberra	Britain	1961	2,400	44,807	818 ' 6"
4. Oriana	Britain	1960	2,217	41,920	804 ' 0"
5. Festivale	Panama	1961	1,146	38,175	760 ' 2"
6. Rotterdam	Netherlands	1959	1,499	37,783	748 ' 7"
7. Tropicale	Liberia	1981	1,022	36,674	671 ' 8"
8. Europa	West Germany	1981	758	34,500	655 ' 10"
9. Eugenio C	Italy	1966	1,636	30,567	713 ' 3"
10. Royal Viking Star	Norway	1972	821	28,221	674 ' 1"
11. Guglielmo Marconi	Italy	1963	1,700	28,137	700 ' 11"
12. Galileo Galilei	Italy	1963	1,700	28,084	700 ' 11"
13. Sea Princess	Britain	1966	840	27,670	660 ' 2"
14. Oceanic	Panama	1965	1,340	27,645	782 ' 3"
15. Maksim Gorkiy	Soviet Union	1969	790	24,981	638 ' 5"
16. Rhapsody	Bahamas	1957	951	24,414	642 ' 6"
17. Scandinavia	Bahamas	1982	1,606	26,747	602 ' 1"
18. Song of America	Norway	1982	1,575	37,584	703 ' 8"
19. Vistafjord	Norway	1973	670	24,292	626 ' 10"
20. Sagafjord	Norway	1965	530	24,109	619 ' 7"

LIVERPOOL (England)	MANILA (Philippines)	MELBOURNE (Australia)	NEW ORLEANS	NEW YORK	PANAMA	PORT SAID (Egypt)	RIO DE JANEIRO (Brazil)	SAN FRANCISCO	SINGAPORE	VALPARAISO (Chile)	YOKOHAMA (Japan)
11,107	4,653	1,649	7,945	8,529	6,511	9,383	7,056	5,680	5,017	5,247	4,789
6,258	3,771	5,556	9,515	8,173	9,300	3,049	7,864	9,794	2,441	10,281	5,330
6,246	10,445	6,853	6,237	5,871	5,385	7,202	1,151	7,582	9,283	2,826	10,669
6,069	6,742	5,963	7,290	6,786	6,472	5,402	3,273	9,753	5,603	5,711	8,351
6,690	2,911	4,700	9,961	8,633	9,775	3,480	7,725	8,934	1,581	9,986	4,470
1,014	10,033	11,405	5,111	3,747	5,105	3,564	5,549	8,350	8,582	7,721	11,471
9,692	631	4,875	10,628	11,212	9,195	6,480	10,149	6,044	1,454	10,218	1,585
9,370	4,869	4,942	6,129	6,703	4,680	10,970	8,608	2,091	5,899	5,919	3,397
3,061	7,160	8,645	6,358	5,005	6,172	804	6,001	9,417	5,822	8,788	8,711
560	9,471	10,946	4,659	3,293	4,651	3,104	5,058	7,896	8,139	7,267	11,011
1,007	8,594	10,168	4,345	2,978	4,152	2,229	4,219	7,441	7,247	6,812	10,136
—	9,557	11,053	4,693	3,283	4,641	3,209	5,143	7,930	8,227	7,302	11,216
9,557	—	4,515	10,809	11,388	9,370	6,348	10,001	6,299	1,330	9,710	1,758
11,053	4,515	—	9,372	9,946	7,951	7,842	8,212	6,970	3,844	6,185	4,896
4,693	10,809	9,372	—	1,721	1,564	6,491	5,136	4,678	11,526	4,049	9,115
3,283	11,388	9,946	1,721	—	2,018	5,137	4,770	5,263	10,158	4,634	9,700
4,641	9,370	7,951	1,564	2,018	—	6,294	4,284	3,245	10,529	2,616	7,680
3,209	6,348	7,842	6,491	5,137	6,294	—	6,123	9,539	5,035	8,910	7,924
5,143	10,001	8,212	5,136	4,770	4,284	6,123	—	7,573	8,846	3,670	11,523
7,930	6,299	6,970	4,678	5,263	3,245	9,539	7,573	—	7,350	5,140	4,536
8,227	1,330	3,844	11,526	10,158	10,529	5,035	8,846	7,350	—	9,902	2,880
7,302	9,710	6,185	4,049	4,634	2,616	8,910	3,670	5,140	9,902	—	9,280
11,216	1,758	4,896	9,115	9,700	7,680	7,924	11,523	4,536	2,880	9,280	—

WHAT YOU SHOULD KNOW ABOUT YOUR U.S. PASSPORT

Source: Passport Services, U.S. Department of State

A passport may be issued only to a U.S. citizen or to a person owing allegiance to the U.S. It is a travel document issued under the authority of the U.S. Secretary of State, attesting to the identity and nationality of the bearer.

Many countries require that visas issued by their consulates be stamped on a passport.

On Jan. 1, 1977, Passport Services began issuing a reduced-size passport more convenient to carry in a pocket or purse. The simplified format conforms to recommendations by the International Civil Aviation Organization (ICAO) for international standardization. The new passports no longer include height, color of hair, and color of eyes as significant identifying features.

Application. All first-time passport applications must be executed in person before one of the following: (1) a Department of State passport agent, (2) a clerk of any federal court or state court of record or a judge or clerk of any probate court accepting applications, (3) a postal employee at a post office designated to accept passport applications, or (4) a U.S. consular or diplomatic officer abroad.

A person in the U.S. who has been issued a passport within the last 8 years, in his own name and after attaining 18 years of age, may obtain a new passport by filling out, signing, and mailing "Application for Passport by Mail" (Form DSP-82), which is available at offices accepting passport applications. He or she should enclose the previous passport, two identical signed photographs taken within the last 6 months, and the $35 passport fee, and address it to the nearest passport agency or to Passport Services in Washington, D.C.

Citizenship. An applicant must prove U.S. citizenship. Acceptable documents are a previous U.S. passport or certified birth certificate. If a birth certificate is unobtainable, secondary evidence will be considered, such as a baptismal certificate or hospital birth certificate. A naturalized citizen must present a naturalization certificate.

Identification documents submitted must bear the signature and description or photograph of the applicant. Acceptable documents may include a previous U.S. passport, a driver's license, or a governmental identification card.

Photographs. Two identical photographs, taken within 6 months of the date of application and identifying the applicant, must be presented with the application.

The photo may be in color or black and white and should be 2 x 2 inches in size. The person's face should measure from 1 to 1⅜ inches from chin to top of head. Vending machine photographs are generally not acceptable.

It is no longer possible to include family members of any age in a U.S. passport. All persons are required to obtain individual passports in their own names.

Validity and Fees. An adult passport is valid for 10 years, and the passport of a minor under 18 years of age is valid for 5 years. The adult passport costs $35, the child's $20. An additional $7 fee is paid when the application is executed before an official, but is not required when the applicant applies by mail.

Offices. Passport agencies are located in Boston, Chicago, Honolulu, Houston, Los Angeles, Miami, New Orleans, New York, Philadelphia, San Francisco, Seattle, Stamford, and Washington, D.C.

Loss. Loss, theft, or destruction of a valid passport should be reported immediately to local police authorities and to Passport Services, Department of State, Washington, D.C. 20520, or, if overseas, to the nearest American embassy or consulate. A passport should be carefully guarded, as its loss could cause you unnecessary travel complications and expense.

CUSTOMS HINTS FOR RETURNING U.S. TRAVELERS

Source: U.S. Customs Service

When returning from foreign travel, a U.S. resident must declare to U.S. Customs, either orally or in writing, *all* articles acquired abroad and in his possession. Customs duty normally must be paid on most of these items.

Exemptions. You are allowed an exemption of $400 based on fair retail value of items where acquired. This duty-free exemption may include not more than 100 cigars or 200 cigarettes, and only one liter (33.8 fl. oz.) of alcoholic beverage, if you are 21 or older. Cuban tobacco products *brought directly from Cuba* may be included.

If you return directly or indirectly from the U.S. Virgin Islands, American Samoa, or Guam, your exemption is increased to $800, of which not more than $400 may be acquired elsewhere. Four liters of alcoholic beverages may be included if not more than one liter was acquired elsewhere.

If you have used the $400 resident exemption, the next $1,000 worth of items *you bring back with you* for your personal use or gifts are taxed at a flat rate of 10% (or 5% for articles from insular possessions). Articles that exceed the flat rate valuation are subject to various rates of duty as shown below.

If your purchases abroad exceed the resident exemption plus $1,000, then you must pay customs duties, such as the following:

Antiques: no duty if proof is provided that they are 100 or more years old.
Automobiles: 2.8%.
Books (foreign): free
Cameras: motion picture over $50 each, 5.3%; still cameras over $10 each, 5.3%; leather camera cases, 9.0%; lenses, 9.6%.
Candy: sweet chocolate bars, 5%; others, 7%.
Dolls and doll parts: 14.8%.
Drawings and paintings (original): free
Furniture: wood chairs, 6% to 6.9%; bentwood, 9.6%; other wood, 3.8%.
Jewelry: 9.3% to 27.5%.
Leather bags and pocketbooks: 6.9% to 10%.
Perfume: 4¢ per pound plus 6.3%.
Tape recorders: 4.7%.
Toys: 12.3%.

Rules Governing Exemptions. Except for articles acquired in the insular possessions, all articles must be with you at the time of your return. For-

CUSTOMS HINTS *(continued)*

eign purchases mailed or shipped home are subject to duty and tax. Articles purchased abroad and used during a journey must be declared. But articles acquired in the insular possessions need not accompany you. They may be sent from these islands and entered under the personal exemption or the flat rate of duty upon your return.

You must have been outside the U.S. at least 48 hours (unless entering from Mexico or the U.S. Virgin Islands) and have not claimed your customs exemption within 30 days.

Families traveling together may combine their exemptions to apply to the total value of all articles declared. Food, plants, and animals must meet U.S. Department of Agriculture or Public Health Service standards.

Duty-Free GSP Articles. Since Jan. 1, 1976, a wide range of articles have been admitted duty-free to the U.S. under the Generalized System of Preferences (GSP), designed to aid the economy of developing nations. Altogether 2,700 articles from liquor to cameras may be brought into the U.S. without paying customs duties if they were made in and purchased in any of 137 designated developing nations and dependencies.

Prohibited Articles. Certain items considered detrimental to the general welfare of the U.S. are prohibited entry by law, such as: narcotics; drugs containing narcotics in any amount; obscene articles, films, and publications; lottery tickets; wild birds or their feathers or eggs; liquor-filled candies; switchblade knives.

Restricted Articles. Firearms and ammunition are only admitted by specific authorization of the Bureau of Alcohol, Tobacco, and Firearms.

IMMUNIZATIONS REQUIRED OR RECOMMENDED FOR FOREIGN TRAVEL

Source: U.S. Public Health Service

According to international health regulations adopted by the World Health Organization (WHO), under certain conditions a country may require travelers to present international certificates of vaccination against cholera and yellow fever. For *direct* travel from the United States to most countries, no vaccinations are required. Currently, certain vaccinations are required only by some countries in Africa and Asia. Specific information on vaccinations required by these countries, vaccinations required for travel between countries, and recommendations regarding travel plans is available from health departments and private physicians. The traveler should contact the local health department at least four weeks before departure for information on countries to be visited. No vaccinations are required to return to the United States.

Cholera: Immunization is not routinely recommended for travelers to countries not requiring a cholera certificate. Cholera is acquired primarily from contaminated food and water. Persons who follow the usual tourist itinerary and use standard accommodations run virtually no risk of infection.

However, travelers to countries that require cholera vaccination should receive one injection of cholera vaccine. A cholera certificate is valid for 6 months, beginning 6 days after one injection of vaccine or on the date of revaccination if within 6 months of first injection.

Plague: Vaccination is not indicated for most travelers to countries reporting cases of plague if their travel is limited to urban areas with modern hotel accommodations.

Yellow fever: Vaccination is recommended for travel to infected areas, usually parts of Africa and South America, and for travel outside urban areas in yellow fever endemic zones.

Hepatitis prophylaxis: The risk of hepatitis-A appears small. Immune globulin is not routinely recommended for ordinary travel of less than 3 months that involves tourist routes.

However, travelers to tropical areas and developing countries off ordinary tourist routes may have a greater risk of acquiring hepatitis-A.

Immune globulin is recommended for travelers who plan to stay 3 or more months in tropical areas or developing countries where hepatitis-A is common and where they may be exposed to infected persons and contaminated food and water.

Malaria prophylaxis: There is a risk of acquiring malaria when traveling to parts of the Caribbean, Central and South America, Africa, the Middle East, the Indian subcontinent, and the Far East. All travelers to areas where malaria transmission occurs should use prophylactic drugs.

Poliomyelitis: Immunization is advised for visits to rural or remote sections of tropical areas or developing countries off the usual tourist routes where polio is epidemic or endemic.

Typhoid fever: Vaccination is recommended for travelers to areas where there is a recognized risk of exposure to the organism that causes typhoid fever. It is transmitted by contaminated food and water.

Typhoid is prevalent in many countries of Africa, Asia, and Central and South America. Therefore, immunization is recommended for travel to the smaller cities, villages, or rural areas off the usual itinerary.

Vaccination is also recommended for travel to areas with persistent typhoid epidemics.

Typhus fever: The threat of louse-borne typhus exists only in mountainous, highland, or other areas where a cold climate and other local conditions favor louse infestation. The risk for U.S. travelers is very low. Treatment with tetracycline or chloramphemicol is curative.

Production of typhus vaccine in the United States has been discontinued.

Diarrhea: The most common ailment that plagues travelers is diarrhea. Only chlorinated water sources afford significant protection against viral and bacterial waterborne diseases. In areas where chlorinated water is not available and where hygiene and sanitation are poor, only beverages made with boiled water, carbonated beverages, beer and wine may be safe to drink. Boiling is the most reliable method to make water of uncertain purity safe for drinking. Chemical disinfection with iodine is an alternative method of water treatment when boiling is not feasible. In areas of poor hygiene and sanitation, the traveler also should avoid ice cubes, unpasteurized milk and milk products, and eat only food that can be peeled or has been cooked and is still hot.

TOURIST DOCUMENTS FOR FOREIGN TRAVEL

Source: Passport Office, U.S. Department of State

When you travel to other countries, you must take with you certain documents in order to be allowed to visit them. Most countries require that you have a passport (see page 958). Some countries require that you obtain permission to visit them in advance of your arrival by getting a visa or tourist card from one of their consulates or their embassy in Washington. Some charge a fee.

To prove you are a tourist, many countries ask that you show them an air, rail, or ship ticket that will take you on to another country. Some countries also may insist that you prove you have enough funds to cover your expenses.

Some countries also require proof of immunization against some diseases. See page 959.

Americans visiting Canada, Mexico, and most Caribbean countries do not need a passport but must have proof of their citizenship with a birth certificate, voter's registration, or automobile driver's license.

Place	Documents	Fee	Limit	Place	Documents	Fee	Limit	Place	Documents	Fee	Limit
Afghanistan	PV	$14.00	3 m	Germany, East	PV	—	—	New Zealand	PO	No	30 d
Albania	S	—	—	Germany, West	P	No	3 m	Nicaragua	PV	No	—
Algeria	PV	$5.25	3 m	Ghana	PV	$8.00	14 d	Niger	PVO	$8.30	90 d
Andorra	P	No	3 m	Gibraltar	P	No	—	Nigeria	PVO	$2.55	3 m
Angola	S	—	—	Greece	P	No	3 m	Norway	P	No	3 m
Antigua	CO	—	6 m	Grenada	P	No	—	Oman	B	—	—
Argentina	PV	—	3 m	Guadeloupe	C	No	15 d	Pakistan	P	No	30 d
Australia	P	No	6 m	Guatemala	PCT	$1.00	6 m	Panama	PTO	No	4 y
Austria	P	No	3 m	Guinea	PV	—	—	Papua N. Guinea	PO	No	30 d
Azores	P	No	60 d	Guinea-Bissau	PV	—	—	Paraguay	P	No	90 d
Bahamas	CO	No	—	Guyana	PO	No	1 m	Peru	PO	—	90 d
Bahrain	PV	$14.00	—	Haiti	CT	$4.00	3 m	Philippines	PO	No	21 d
Bangladesh	PV	—	—	Honduras	PV	No	3 m	Poland	PV	$16.00	90 d
Barbados	CO	No	6 m	Hong Kong	PO	No	30 d	Portugal	P	No	60 d
Belgium	P	No	90 d	Hungary	PV	$10.00	30 d	Qatar	PV	No	6 m
Belize	CO	No	6 m	Iceland	P	No	3 m	Romania	PV	$13.00	6 m
Benin	PV	$12.00	15 d	India	P	$1.75	90 d	Rwanda	PV	$10.00	3 m
Bermuda	CO	No	—	Indonesia	P	—	2 m	St. Lucia	CO	No	6 m
Bhutan	P	—	—	Iran	PV	—	—	San Marino	P	—	3 m
Bolivia	P	No	90 d	Iraq	S	—	—	Saudi Arabia	PVO	—	72 h
Botswana	P	No	90 d	Ireland	PO	No	90 d	Senegal	PV	$5.10	3 m
Brazil	PVO	No	—	Israel	P	No	3 m	Seychelles	PO	—	—
Britain	P	No	—	Italy	P	No	3 m	Sierra Leone	PVO	$10.50	3 m
Brunei	P	No	—	Ivory Coast	PVO	No	3 m	Singapore	P	No	90 d
Bulgaria	PV	$14.00	2 m	Jamaica	CO	—	6 m	Somalia	PVO	$14.00	3 m
Burma	PVO	$4.85	1 w	Japan	PV	No	90 d	South Africa	PVO	No	1 y
Burundi	PV	$11.00	1 m	Jordan	PV	No	4 y	Soviet Union	PV	No	3 m
Cambodia	S	—	—	Kenya	PV	$6.10	6 m	Spain	P	No	6 m
Cameroon	PVO	$14.42	30d	Korea, North	PV	—	—	Sri Lanka	PO	—	1 m
Canada	C	No	—	Korea, South	PV	No	60 d	Sudan	PV	$25.63	3 m
Cape Verde	PV	$13.50	30 d	Kuwait	PV	No	1 m	Suriname	PO	No	—
Central Africa	PV	No	—	Laos	PV	—	—	Swaziland	P	No	60 d
Chad	PVO	$6.25	3 m	Lebanon	PV	$20.00	6 m	Sweden	P	No	3 m
Chile	P	No	3 m	Lesotho	PV	No	20 d	Switzerland	P	No	3 m
China	PV	$7.00	—	Liberia	PV	$2.00	3 m	Syria	PV	$8.21	6 m
Colombia	PTO	—	90 d	Libya	S	—	—	Taiwan	PV	—	6 m
Congo	PV	—	—	Liechtenstein	P	No	3 m	Tanzania	PVO	$10.50	30 d
Costa Rica	P	$5.75	6 m	Luxembourg	PO	No	3 m	Thailand	PVO	No	15 d
Cuba	PV	$6.00	—	Madagascar	PV	$47.61	1 m	Togo	P	—	90 d
Cyprus	P	—	—	Malawi	P	No	1 y	Tonga	P	—	—
Czechoslovakia	PV	$10.00	5 m	Malaysia	P	No	3 m	Trinidad-Tobago	PO	No	2 m
Denmark	P	No	3 m	Maldives	P	—	—	Tunisia	P	No	4 m
Djibouti	PV	—	—	Mali	PV	$23.25	1 w	Turkey	P	No	3 m
Dominica	CO	No	6 m	Malta	P	No	3 m	Uganda	PV	$3.15	1 y
Dominican Rep.	PT	$5.00	60 d	Martinique	C	No	15 d	United Arab Em.	PVO	$15.00	2m
Ecuador	PO	No	3 m	Mauritania	PV	$10.00	3 m	Upper Volta	PV	$2.00	3 m
Egypt	PV	$7.50	3 m	Mauritius	PV	No	—	Uruguay	P	No	3 m
El Salvador	C	—	—	Mexico	CT	No	3 m	Venezuela	PVT	No	60 d
Equat. Guinea	PV	—	—	Monaco	P	No	3 m	Vietnam	S	—	—
Ethiopia	PV	—	—	Mongolia	S	—	—	Western Samoa	PO	No	30 d
Fiji	PO	—	6 m	Morocco	P	No	3 m	Yemen, North	PV	$10.00	1 m
Finland	P	No	3 m	Mozambique	S	—	—	Yugoslavia	PV	No	1 y
France	P	No	3 m	Nauru	P	—	—	Zaire	PV	$20.00	3 m
French Guiana	P	No	3 m	Nepal	PV	$10.00	3 m	Zambia	PV	$3.50	6 m
Gabon	PV	$10.00	—	Netherlands	PO	No	90 d	Zimbabwe	PO	—	—
Gambia	PV	$8.00	—	Neth. Antilles	CO	—	14 d				

P = passport. V = visa. T = tourist card. C = proof of U.S. citizenship. O = onward ticket. S = special permission required. B = business visa only. d = days. m = months. y = years. h = hours. w = weeks.

United States

U.S. Mint

Greek discus thrower is on new U.S. silver dollar, one of three coins, 2 silver and 1 gold, issued to commemorate the Olympic Games, with proceeds to benefit the U.S. Olympic Committee and the Los Angeles Olympic Organizing Committee. The other silver dollar features a representation of the gateway to the Olympic coliseum. The $10 gold coin, the first issued by the U.S. in 50 years, shows Olympic torch bearers.

HIGHLIGHTS: 1983

OUR CHANGING POPULATION

New insights into the ways the American population is changing were revealed in a series of reports issued during the year by the Census Bureau.

The percentage of older persons in the population is increasing rapidly. At the beginning of this century, only 4% of Americans were 65 or older, but by the end of the century the percentage will have tripled with more than 13% in that age group.

The Census Bureau believes there are now more than 32,000 Americans who are 100 or older. Altogether more than 2.4 million are 85 or older, a number that has increased more than 9% since 1980.

Reflecting the nation's increasing birth rate, the number of children under 5 rose by 6.3% since 1980, climbing from 16.3 million to 17.4 million.

Despite the larger number of babies and tots, the median age of the population increased to 30.6 from 30 in 1980.

The mobility of Americans was highlighted by a finding that nearly half of the people changed their place of residence between 1975 and 1980. About 25% moved to a different home in the same county. Nearly 10% moved to another county in the same state and about the same percentage moved to a different state. Alaskans were the most mobile with nearly two-thirds of the people of that state changing residences in the 5-year period. On the other hand, Pennsylvanians were the least mobile with only about one-third moving from one home to another.

The U.S. has a young and rapidly growing Hispanic population, the Census Bureau reported. The Hispanic proportion of the U.S.

OUR GROWING POPULATION: 1790–2020

The continued growth of the United States population is shown in these figures from the Bureau of the Census. Populations from 1990 to 2020 are estimates.

YEAR	POPULATION	GROWTH	YEAR	POPULATION	GROWTH
1790	3,929,214	...	1910	92,407,000	21%
1800	5,308,483	35%	1920	106,461,000	15%
1810	7,239,881	36%	1930	123,188,000	15%
1820	9,638,453	33%	1940	132,288,000	7%
1830	12,866,020	33%	1950	151,718,000	14%
1840	17,069,453	32%	1960	180,007,000	18%
1850	23,191,876	35%	1970	204,335,000	13%
1860	31,443,321	35%	1980	226,548,861	11%
1870	39,818,449	26%	1990	249,203,000	10%
1880	50,155,783	25%	2000	267,461,600	18%
1890	62,947,714	25%	2010	283,141,000	6%
1900	76,094,000	20%	2020	296,339,000	5%

FACTS IN BRIEF ABOUT THE UNITED STATES IN 1984

Area (50 states and the District of Columbia): 3,618,770 square miles; (plus Puerto Rico, territories, and possessions): 3,623,461 sq. mi.
Population (including armed forces overseas): 233,206,000 (1983 estimate); *density:* 64.4 persons per square mile; *distribution:* 73.7% urban, 26.3% rural; *median age:* 30.0 years; *sex:* 48.6% males, 51.4% females.
Chief Cities (1980 Census): Washington, D.C., thc national capital, 638,432; New York, 7,071,639; Chicago, 3,005,072; Los Angeles, 2,968,579; Philadelphia, 1,688,210; Houston, 1,595,138; Detroit, 1,203,339; Dallas, 904,078; San Diego, 875,538; Phoenix, 789,704; Baltimore, 786,741; San Antonio, 786,023.
Main Ethnic Groups: White, 83.1%; black, 11.7%; Spanish descent, 6.4%.
Chief Religions: Protestantism, 66%; Roman Catholicism, 26%; Judaism, 3%.
Language: English (official).
Form of Government: Federal republic.
Chief of State: President Ronald Reagan, sworn in on Jan. 20, 1981.
Legislature: Senate, 100 members; House of Representatives, 435 members.
Principal Manufactures: Machinery, cement, electricity, steel, paper, automobiles, aircraft, food, chemicals, electronic equipment.
Chief Crops: Wheat, barley, corn, cotton, hay, oats, potatoes, rice, rye, sorghum, soybeans, tobacco, citrus fruits, tomatoes.
Major Minerals: Coal, iron ore, copper, gold, uranium, lead, zinc, petroleum, natural gas.
States: *Largest,* Alaska (591,004 square miles); *smallest,* Rhode Island (1,212 square miles).
Counties: *Largest,* San Bernardino, Calif. (20,064 square miles); *smallest,* New York (Manhattan Island), N.Y. (22 square miles).
Extreme Points: *Northernmost,* Point Barrow, Alaska (71° 23′ N.); *southernmost,* Ka Lae, Hawaii (18°56′ N.); *easternmost,* West Quoddy Head, Me. (66°57′ W.); *westernmost,* Attu Island, Alaska (172°27′ E.).
Highest Mountain: Mt. McKinley, Alaska (20,320 feet).
Lowest Point: Death Valley, Calif. (–282 feet).

HIGHLIGHTS: 1983 *(continued)*

population increased from 4.5% in 1970 to 6.4% in 1980. Sixty percent of the Hispanic population was of Mexican origin, 14% Puerto Rican, and 5% were Cuban. Some 39% of Hispanics were 18 or younger compared to 28% in this age group in the population as a whole.

WHITE HOUSE SECURITY

As the U.S. suffered an increasing number of attacks by terrorists abroad (see pages 15 and 27), the Secret Service became concerned that terrorists might try a truck-bomb attack in the nation's capital. On Thanksgiving Day large trucks filled with sand were parked in front of White House gates to stop anyone attempting to ram through them. Then, during the first week in December, concrete barriers were built at the gate most frequently used by foreign visitors.

GOVERNMENT CLOSES PRINTING PLANTS

The Office of Management and Budget announced in November that 130 of the government's more than 1,000 printing facilities will be closed in 1984 to save $30 million and end 1,000 jobs.

TWO STATES NEEDED FOR CONVENTION

Proponents of a Constitutional Convention to amend the U.S. Constitution were expected to step up activities in 1984 to get the needed two more states to pass resolutions for the proposal. In March the Missouri legislature made that state the 32d to call on Congress to set a date for a new Constitutional Convention—the first since 1787.

Thirty-four states must endorse the proposal to force Congress to act.

Any amendments adopted by such a convention also would have to be ratified by 34 states.

OUR AGING POPULATION*

Source: U.S. Census Bureau

YEAR	TOTAL	55 TO 64 YEARS		65 TO 74 YEARS		75 TO 84 YEARS		85 AND OVER		65 AND OVER	
		Number	Percent	Number	Percent	Number	Percent	Number	Percent	Number	Percent
1900	76,303	4,009	5.3	2,189	2.9	772	1.0	123	0.2	3,084	4.0
1910	91,972	5,054	5.5	2,793	3.0	989	1.1	167	0.2	3,950	4.3
1920	105,711	6,532	6.2	3,464	3.3	1,259	1.2	210	0.2	4,933	4.7
1930	122,775	8,397	6.8	4,721	3.8	1,641	1.3	272	0.2	6,634	5.4
1940	131,669	10,572	8.0	6,375	4.8	2,278	1.7	365	0.3	9,019	6.8
1950	150,697	13,295	8.8	8,415	5.6	3,278	2.2	577	0.4	12,270	8.1
1960	179,323	15,572	8.7	10,997	6.1	4,633	2.6	929	0.5	16,560	9.2
1970	203,302	18,608	9.2	12,447	6.1	6,124	3.0	1,409	0.7	19,980	9.8
1980	226,505	21,700	9.6	15,578	6.9	7,727	3.4	2,240	1.0	25,544	11.3
1990	249,731	21,090	8.4	18,054	7.2	10,284	4.1	3,461	1.4	31,799	12.7
2000	267,990	23,779	8.9	17,693	6.6	12,207	4.6	5,136	1.9	35,036	13.1
2010	283,141	34,828	12.3	20,279	7.2	12,172	4.3	6,818	2.4	39,269	13.9
2020	296,339	40,243	13.6	29,769	10.0	14,280	4.8	7,337	2.5	51,386	17.3
2030	304,330	33,965	11.2	34,416	11.3	21,128	6.9	8,801	2.9	64,345	21.1
2040	307,952	34,664	11.3	29,168	9.5	24,529	8.0	12,946	4.2	66,643	21.6
2050	308,856	37,276	12.1	30,022	9.7	20,976	6.8	16,063	5.2	67,061	21.7

* All population figures in thousands (add 000).

POPULATION GROWTH OF THE UNITED STATES: 1790–2000

Source: U.S. Bureau of the Census

In its first census in 1790, the United States reported a population of 3,929,214. The totals for the individual states in 1790 were: Connecticut, 237,946; Delaware, 59,096; Georgia, 82,548; Kentucky, 73,677; Maine, 96,540; Maryland, 319,728; Massachusetts, 378,787; New Hampshire, 141,885; New Jersey, 184,139; New York, 340,120; North Carolina, 393,751; Pennsylvania, 434,373; Rhode Island, 68,825; South Carolina, 249,073; Tennessee, 35,691; Vermont, 82,425; Virginia, 691,737; West Virginia, 55,873. Population growth since 1790 is shown on the chart below.

	1850	1900	1950	1970	1980[1]	1990[2]	2000[2]
UNITED STATES	**23,191,876**	**76,212,168**	**151,325,798**	**203,302,031**	**226,548,861**	**249,203,000**	**267,461,600**
Alabama	771,623	1,828,697	3,061,743	3,444,354	3,893,978	4,213,800	4,415,300
Alaska	—	63,592	128,643	302,583	401,851	522,100	630,700
Arizona	—	122,931	749,587	1,775,399	2,718,425	3,993,700	5,582,500
Arkansas	209,897	1,311,564	1,909,511	1,923,322	2,286,419	2,579,800	2,835,400
California	92,597	1,485,053	10,586,223	19,971,069	23,667,837	27,525,600	30,613,100
Colorado	—	539,700	1,325,089	2,209,596	2,889,964	3,755,100	4,656,600
Connecticut	370,792	908,420	2,007,280	3,032,217	3,107,576	3,135,600	3,062,400
Delaware	91,532	184,735	318,085	548,104	594,338	629,800	638,200
District of Columbia	51,687	278,718	802,178	756,510	638,432	501,500	376,500
Florida	87,445	528,542	2,771,305	6,791,418	9,746,421	13,316,000	17,438,000
Georgia	906,185	2,216,331	3,444,578	4,587,930	5,463,087	6,174,600	6,708,200
Hawaii	—	154,001	499,794	769,913	964,691	1,138,100	1,277,700
Idaho	—	161,772	588,637	713,015	944,038	1,213,800	1,512,200
Illinois	851,470	4,821,550	8,712,176	11,110,285	11,427,414	11,502,500	11,187,500
Indiana	988,416	2,516,462	3,934,224	5,195,392	5,490,260	5,679,300	5,679,200
Iowa	192,214	2,231,853	2,621,073	2,825,368	2,913,808	2,983,300	2,972,100
Kansas	—	1,470,495	1,905,299	2,249,071	2,364,236	2,463,400	2,494,400
Kentucky	982,405	2,147,174	3,220,711	3,220,711	3,660,257	4,073,500	4,399,900
Louisiana	517,762	1,381,625	2,683,516	3,644,637	4,206,098	4,747,000	5,159,800
Maine	583,169	694,466	913,774	993,722	1,125,030	1,229,400	1,308,000
Maryland	583,034	1,188,044	2,343,001	3,923,897	4,216,941	4,491,100	4,581,900
Massachusetts	994,514	2,805,346	4,690,514	5,689,170	5,737,081	5,703,900	5,490,400
Michigan	397,654	2,420,982	6,371,766	8,881,826	9,262,070	9,394,300	9,207,600
Minnesota	6,077	1,751,394	2,982,483	3,806,103	4,075,970	4,358,400	4,489,400
Mississippi	606,528	1,551,270	2,178,914	2,216,994	2,520,631	2,761,400	2,939,200
Missouri	682,044	3,106,665	3,954,653	4,677,623	4,916,759	5,076,800	5,080,000
Montana	—	243,329	591,024	694,409	786,690	888,400	963,000
Nebraska	—	1,066,300	1,325,510	1,485,333	1,569,825	1,639,800	1,661,900
Nevada	—	42,335	160,083	488,738	800,493	1,275,400	1,918,800
New Hampshire	317,976	411,588	553,242	737,681	920,610	1,138,800	1,363,500
New Jersey	489,555	1,883,669	4,835,329	7,171,112	7,365,011	7,513,100	7,427,600
New Mexico	61,547	195,310	681,187	1,017,055	1,303,046	1,536,000	1,727,300
New York	3,097,394	7,268,894	14,830,192	18,241,391	17,558,072	16,456,700	14,990,200
North Carolina	869,039	1,893,810	4,061,929	5,084,411	5,881,385	6,473,400	6,867,800
North Dakota	—	319,146	619,636	617,792	652,717	678,400	682,000
Ohio	1,980,329	4,157,545	7,946,627	10,657,423	10,797,624	10,763,100	10,356,800
Oklahoma	—	790,391	2,233,351	2,559,463	3,025,495	3,503,400	3,944,500
Oregon	12,093	413,536	1,521,341	2,091,533	2,633,149	3,318,600	4,025,300
Pennsylvania	2,311,786	6,302,115	10,498,012	11,800,766	11,864,751	11,720,400	11,207,600
Rhode Island	147,545	428,556	791,896	949,723	947,154	950,800	925,800
South Carolina	668,507	1,340,316	2,117,027	2,590,713	3,122,814	3,599,600	3,907,100
South Dakota	—	401,570	652,740	666,257	690,768	698,500	687,600
Tennessee	1,002,717	2,020,616	3,291,718	3,926,018	4,591,120	5,072,600	5,419,600
Texas	212,592	3,048,710	7,711,194	11,198,655	14,227,574	17,498,200	20,739,400
Utah	11,380	276,749	688,862	1,059,273	1,461,037	2,040,300	2,777,400
Vermont	314,120	343,641	377,747	444,732	511,456	574,600	625,000
Virginia	1,119,348	1,854,184	3,318,680	4,651,448	5,346,797	5,960,900	6,389,400
Washington	1,201	518,103	2,378,963	3,413,244	4,132,204	5,011,800	5,832,500
West Virginia	302,313	958,800	2,005,552	1,744,237	1,950,258	2,037,400	2,067,700
Wisconsin	305,391	2,069,042	3,434,575	4,417,821	4,705,642	5,032,700	5,215,500
Wyoming	—	92,531	290,529	332,416	469,557	701,300	1,002,200

[1] Official 1980 Census. [2] Estimates based on 1980 Census.

RACIAL POPULATION BY REGION AND STATE

Source: U.S. Census Bureau, 1980 Census

REGION AND STATE	TOTAL	WHITE	BLACK	SPANISH	ASIAN	INDIAN	ALL OTHER
New England	**12,348,907**	**11,585,633**	**474,549**	**299,145**	**81,005**	**21,597**	**185,709**
Maine	1,125,030	1,109,850	3,128	5,005	2,947	4,087	4,648
New Hampshire	920,610	910,099	3,990	5,587	2,929	1,352	2,240
Vermont	511,456	506,736	1,135	3,304	1,355	984	1,246
Massachusetts	5,737,081	5,362,836	221,279	141,043	49,501	7,743	95,678
Rhode Island	947,154	896,692	27,584	19,707	5,303	2,898	14,677
Connecticut	3,107,576	2,799,420	217,433	124,499	18,970	4,533	67,220
Middle Atlantic	**36,787,834**	**30,740,655**	**4,373,882**	**2,305,144**	**478,753**	**57,441**	**1,136,059**
New York	17,558,072	13,960,868	2,402,006	1,659,300	310,526	39,582	845,090
New Jersey	7,365,011	6,127,467	925,066	491,883	103,848	8,394	200,048
Pennsylvania	11,864,751	10,652,320	1,046,810	153,961	64,379	9,465	90,921
East North Central	**41,683,010**	**36,150,455**	**4,548,546**	**1,067,944**	**302,984**	**105,907**	**574,325**
Ohio	10,797,624	9,597,458	1,076,748	119,883	47,820	12,239	63,365
Indiana	5,490,260	5,004,394	414,785	87,047	20,557	7,836	42,652
Illinois	11,427,414	9,233,327	1,675,398	635,602	159,653	16,283	341,857
Michigan	9,262,070	7,872,241	1,199,023	162,440	56,790	40,050	93,974
Wisconsin	4,705,642	4,443,035	182,592	62,972	18,164	29,499	32,477
West North Central	**17,184,083**	**16,044,344**	**788,549**	**208,601**	**87,006**	**142,486**	**121,068**
Minnesota	4,075,970	3,935,770	53,344	32,123	26,536	35,016	25,304
Iowa	2,913,808	2,839,225	41,700	25,536	11,577	5,455	15,851
Missouri	4,916,759	4,345,521	514,276	51,653	23,096	12,321	21,472
North Dakota	652,717	625,577	2,568	3,902	1,979	20,158	2,455
South Dakota	690,768	639,669	2,144	4,023	1,738	44,968	2,249
Nebraska	1,569,825	1,490,381	48,390	28,025	7,002	9,195	14,857
Kansas	2,364,236	2,168,221	126,127	63,339	15,078	15,373	38,880
South Atlantic	**36,960,473**	**28,659,351**	**7,651,969**	**1,194,172**	**260,636**	**118,726**	**268,441**
Delaware	594,338	487,817	95,845	9,661	4,112	1,328	5,236
Maryland	4,216,941	3,158,838	958,150	64,746	64,278	8,021	27,688
District of Columbia	638,432	171,768	448,906	17,679	6,636	1,031	9,992
Virginia	5,346,797	4,229,798	1,008,668	79,868	66,209	9,454	32,689
West Virginia	1,950,258	1,874,751	65,051	12,707	5,194	1,610	3,038
North Carolina	5,881,385	4,457,507	1,318,857	56,667	21,176	64,652	19,574
South Carolina	3,122,814	2,147,224	948,623	33,426	11,834	5,757	8,382
Georgia	5,463,087	3,947,135	1,465,181	61,260	24,457	7,616	18,716
Florida	9,746,421	8,184,513	1,342,688	858,158	56,740	19,257	143,126
East South Central	**14,665,986**	**11,702,269**	**2,868,960**	**119,513**	**41,079**	**22,477**	**31,638**
Kentucky	3,660,257	3,379,006	259,477	27,406	9,970	3,610	8,714
Tennessee	4,591,120	3,835,452	725,942	34,077	13,963	5,104	10,659
Alabama	3,893,978	2,872,621	996,335	33,299	9,734	7,583	7,615
Mississippi	2,520,631	1,615,190	887,206	24,731	7,412	6,180	4,650
West South Central	**23,745,586**	**18,598,726**	**3,526,858**	**3,160,281**	**168,107**	**231,027**	**1,222,098**
Arkansas	2,286,419	1,890,322	373,768	17,904	6,740	9,428	6,177
Louisiana	4,206,098	2,912,172	1,238,241	99,134	23,779	12,065	19,643
Oklahoma	3,025,495	2,597,791	204,674	57,419	17,275	169,459	36,091
Texas	14,227,574	11,198,441	1,710,175	2,985,824	120,313	40,075	1,160,187
Mountain	**11,373,250**	**9,961,018**	**268,790**	**1,442,909**	**98,433**	**364,381**	**680,163**
Montana	786,690	740,148	1,786	9,974	2,503	37,270	4,983
Idaho	944,038	901,641	2,716	36,615	5,948	10,521	23,109
Wyoming	469,557	446,488	3,364	24,499	1,969	7,094	10,642
Colorado	2,889,964	2,571,498	101,703	339,717	29,916	18,068	168,779
New Mexico	1,303,046	977,587	24,020	477,222	6,825	106,119	188,343
Arizona	2,718,425	2,240,761	74,977	440,701	22,032	152,745	227,700
Utah	1,461,037	1,382,550	9,225	60,302	15,076	19,256	34,930
Nevada	800,493	700,345	50,999	53,879	14,164	13,308	21,677
Pacific	**31,799,732**	**24,929,171**	**1,992,922**	**4,810,964**	**1,982,436**	**356,658**	**2,538,818**
Washington	4,132,204	3,779,170	105,574	120,016	102,537	60,804	84,071
Oregon	2,633,149	2,490,610	37,060	65,847	34,775	27,314	43,346
California	23,667,837	18,030,893	1,819,281	4,544,331	1,253,818	201,369	2,362,541
Alaska	401,851	309,728	13,643	9,507	8,054	64,103	6,323
Hawaii	964,691	318,770	17,364	71,263	583,252	2,768	42,537
U.S. TOTAL	**226,548,861**	**188,371,622**	**26,495,025**	**14,608,673**	**3,500,439**	**1,420,400**	**6,758,319**

U.S. FEDERAL BUDGET FOR FISCAL 1984

President Reagan submitted to Congress in January 1983 a budget with estimated outlays of $848.5 billion for fiscal year 1984—the period Oct. 1, 1983, to Sept. 30, 1984. The estimated receipts were $659.7 billion, leaving an estimated federal budget deficit of $188.5 billion.

The Office of Management and Budget (OMB) issued revised estimates of the 1984 budget in July 1983, indicating outlays of $848.1 billion, receipts of $668.4 billion, and a deficit of $179.7 billion. For details of the revised budget of July broken down into categories of outlays, see pages 966–967.

A comparison of the estimated budget expenditures of the federal government for fiscal year 1984 with those of fiscal year 1983 shows an increase of $38.3 billion.

Over the past decade budget outlays more than tripled, increasing from $245.6 billion in 1973 to $809.8 billion in 1983.

The total federal government debt was estimated at $1,390.8 billion on Sept. 30, 1983, or about $5,924 for each person in the U.S.

WHERE THE MONEY COMES FROM

In the fiscal 1984 budget as revised in July 1983, the OMB spelled out where the money for the budget comes from in terms of each dollar of estimated receipts:

Individual income taxes	36¢
Social insurance receipts (half from employees and half from employers)	26¢
Borrowing	26¢
Corporation income taxes	4¢
Excise taxes	4¢
Other receipts	4¢

WHERE THE MONEY GOES

The OMB also indicated the major areas of spending for 1984 in terms of each dollar of estimated outlays:

Direct benefit payments to individuals	42¢
National defense	27¢
Grants to states and localities	12¢
Net interest on debt	11¢
Other federal operations	8¢

THE FEDERAL BUDGET SYSTEM

Each year's federal budget represents the President's financial plan for operating the government for 12 months. The budget states how much money the President believes the federal government should spend during the fiscal year, where the revenues are to come from, and how much money is to be spent on each government program.

The budget, therefore, is an important tool for determining what the national priorities are to be during the next year.

By increasing or decreasing the amount of taxes to be collected and the amounts of money to be spent on various programs, the government can have an important effect on the entire economy of the nation because of the huge sums involved.

The budget, however, is merely a plan. The amount of money actually spent depends on appropriations and other legislation enacted by Congress. Therefore, whether the plan of the budget really is carried out is determined through the interaction of the President, the executive agencies, and Congress.

Under traditional procedures of the past, Congress did not generally vote on budget outlays directly. Instead, it would enact a variety of bills that permitted or required the government to spend money for specific programs. However, Congress passed budget-reform measures in 1974 to improve congressional control over federal spending.

The federal fiscal year historically was from July 1 to June 30. But beginning with fiscal 1977 the budget year became October 1 to September 30. Thus fiscal 1984 runs from Oct. 1, 1983, to Sept. 30, 1984.

THE BUDGET CYCLE

The federal budget cycle is a continuous process involving four phases:

1. **Executive Submission:** The President outlines his budget proposals to Congress in January each year, climaxing months of planning and analysis throughout the executive departments and agencies.
2. **Congressional Authorizaton:** Once Congress has the President's recommended budget, it can change programs, eliminate them, or add programs not requested by the President. It can decrease or increase the amounts recommended by the President to finance existing programs and proposed new ones.

   Each September Congress is supposed to adopt a budget for the fiscal year that begins in October. Congress then cannot consider any legislation that would increase spending or decrease receipts from the adopted budget. However, Congress can adopt a new revised budget at any time.
3. **Budget Execution and Control:** Once approved, the budget becomes the basis for the operations of each department and agency during the fiscal year. Central control over most of the budget authority made available to the executive branch is maintained through a system of "apportioning" the authority.
4. **Audit.** The final step in the budget process is the audit. This involves the Office of Management and Budget in the executive branch and the General Accounting Office, which is responsible directly to Congress.

U.S. FEDERAL BUDGET OUTLAYS: FISCAL YEARS 1965–1984

Source: Office of Management and Budget; figures in $ millions (add 000,000).

	ACTUAL OUTLAYS						ESTIMATES[1]	
NATIONAL DEFENSE:	1965	1970	1975	1980	1981	1982	1983	1984
Department of Defense—Military:								
Military personnel	$13,387	$23,031	$24,968	$30,842	$36,409	$42,341	$45,308	$47,676
Retired military personnel	1,384	2,849	6,242	11,920	13,729	14,938	16,130	16,737
Operation and maintenance	12,349	21,609	26,297	44,770	51,920	59,674	64,648	69,954
Procurement	11,839	21,584	16,042	29,021	35,191	43,271	55,274	68,156
Research and development	6,236	7,166	8,866	13,127	15,278	17,729	21,430	25,734
Military construction and other	928	1,059	2,486	2,450	3,570	4,897	6,150	7,403
Atomic-energy defense activities	1,620	1,415	1,506	2,878	3,398	4,309	5,471	6,316
Defense-related activities	−137	−8	−850	142	276	263	436	301
Deductions for offsetting receipts	−150	−151	−4	−4	−4	−4	−4	−4
Total outlays	**47,456**	**78,553**	**85,552**	**135,856**	**159,765**	**187,418**	**214,843**	**242,274**
INTERNATIONAL AFFAIRS:								
Foreign economic and financial assist.	3,838	2,935	3,598	5,607	4,215	3,856	4,360	4,618
International security assistance	1,205	593	1,915	894	3,131	3,107	3,947	4,698
Conduct of foreign affairs	335	398	658	1,367	1,347	1,630	1,722	2,009
Foreign information and exchange	224	235	348	534	525	571	680	836
International financial programs	−242	357	505	2,427	2,007	911	363	1,386
Deductions for receipts and pending legislation	−114	−223	−103	−96	−95	−92	−94	−94
Total outlays	**5,245**	**4,297**	**6,922**	**10,733**	**11,130**	**9,982**	**10,978**	**13,452**
SCIENCE, SPACE, AND TECHNOLOGY:								
General science and basic research	789	947	1,038	1,381	1,483	1,607	1,662	1,873
Spaceflight	3,756	2,340	1,661	2,594	3,053	3,543	4,000	4,058
Space, science, applications, and tech.	1,017	853	958	1,346	1,384	1,457	1,533	1,656
Supporting space activities	261	370	334	405	444	473	604	757
Deductions for offsetting receipts	−2	−3	−2	−3	−5	−10	−9	−9
Total outlays	**5,821**	**4,507**	**3,989**	**5,722**	**6,359**	**7,070**	**7,791**	**8,835**
ENERGY:								
Energy supply	573	848	1,743	4,574	5,362	3,150	2,968	2,302
Energy conservation	—	—	48	568	757	518	584	585
Emergency energy preparedness	—	—	33	342	3,280	191	233	266
Energy information, policy, regulation	97	142	389	882	940	886	887	743
Deductions for offsetting receipts	—	—	−43	−53	−62	−71	−78	−81
Total outlays	**669**	**990**	**2,169**	**6,313**	**10,277**	**4,674**	**4,594**	**3,815**
NATURAL RESOURCES AND ENVIRONMENT:								
Water resources	1,607	1,539	2,634	4,294	4,215	4,032	4,187	3,681
Conservation and land management	606	717	1,300	2,328	2,576	2,746	2,672	2,211
Recreational resources	219	372	825	1,707	1,632	1,477	1,663	1,629
Pollution control and abatement	134	384	2,523	5,510	5,169	5,012	4,313	4,163
Other natural resources	293	432	762	1,412	1,485	1,526	1,574	1,443
Deductions for offsetting receipts	−337	−384	−707	−1,439	−1,553	−1,860	−1,943	−2,302
Total outlays	**2,523**	**3,061**	**7,336**	**13,812**	**13,525**	**12,934**	**12,466**	**10,825**
AGRICULTURE:								
Farm income stabilization	3,551	4,589	785	3,459	3,993	13,289	23,591	12,165
Agricultural research and services	404	577	877	1,398	1,540	1,599	1,675	1,665
Deductions for offsetting receipts	−7	−5	−2	−95	38	−14	−1	−1
Total outlays	**3,948**	**5,161**	**1,659**	**4,762**	**5,572**	**14,875**	**25,265**	**13,818**
COMMERCE AND HOUSING CREDIT:								
Mortgage credit and thrift insurance	−108	104	2,791	3,696	651	1,216	2,247	836
Postal Service	805	1,510	1,877	1,677	1,343	707	789	400
Other advancement of commerce	462	477	944	2,415	1,959	1,943	2,017	1,573
Deductions for offsetting receipts	−6	−7	−5	—	−7	−2	−1	−1
Total outlays	**1,151**	**2,108**	**5,607**	**7,788**	**3,946**	**3,865**	**5,052**	**2,808**
TRANSPORTATION:								
Ground transportation	4,105	4,678	6,501	15,079	17,100	14,326	13,910	17,804
Air transportation	944	1,422	2,408	3,762	3,850	3,564	4,097	4,960
Water transportation	730	913	1,459	2,235	2,420	2,696	3,088	3,074
Other transportation	1	26	74	104	110	90	120	118
Deductions for offsetting receipts	−34	−33	−55	−60	−99	−116	−87	−85
Total outlays	**5,746**	**7,006**	**10,388**	**21,120**	**23,381**	**20,560**	**21,128**	**25,871**
COMMUNITY AND REGIONAL DEVELOPMENT:								
Community development	413	1,449	2,297	4,878	5,111	4,583	4,721	4,993
Area and regional development	654	693	1,061	3,180	2,708	2,735	2,788	2,689
Disaster relief and insurance	53	257	398	2,043	1,604	−119	−51	132
Deductions for offsetting receipts	−8	−9	−17	−32	−30	−34	−40	−40
Total outlays	**1,114**	**2,391**	**3,738**	**10,068**	**9,394**	**7,165**	**7,419**	**7,773**

	ACTUAL OUTLAYS (in $ millions; add 000,000)						ESTIMATES [1]	
	1965	1970	1975	1980	1981	1982	1983	1984
EDUCATION, TRAINING, EMPLOYMENT, AND SOCIAL SERVICES:								
Elementary, secondary, and voc. educ.	$724	$3,107	$4,634	$6,732	$7,043	$6,780	$6,514	$6,752
Higher education	412	1,385	2,050	5,694	6,790	6,507	7,126	6,752
Research and general educ. aids	149	521	947	1,357	1,223	1,040	1,071	994
Training and employment	534	1,602	4,063	10,345	9,241	5,464	5,353	4,805
Other labor services	96	135	259	551	587	589	633	680
Social services	230	1,884	3,923	6,116	6,531	5,950	6,531	6,577
Deductions for offsetting receipts	−7	−10	−5	−28	−13	−29	−66	−99
Total outlays	**2,139**	**8,625**	**15,870**	**30,767**	**31,402**	**26,300**	**27,162**	**26,501**
HEALTH:								
Health care services [2]	881	10,206	22,335	50,075	60,351	68,350	76,436	84,739
Health research	572	1,054	1,923	3,442	3,836	3,948	4,204	4,281
Education of health-care workers	209	633	856	719	779	670	580	416
Consumer and occup. health and safety	130	226	632	1,001	1,042	1,034	1,090	1,123
Deductions for offsetting receipts	−1	−6	−5	−17	−25	−15	−28	−27
Total outlays	**1,790**	**12,115**	**25,742**	**55,220**	**65,982**	**74,017**	**82,283**	**90,532**
INCOME SECURITY:								
General retirement and disability insurance	18,124	31,303	69,348	123,684	145,024	161,805	177,361	185,608
Fed. employee retiremt. and disability	1,472	2,688	6,980	14,675	17,548	19,388	20,565	22,019
Unemployment compensation	2,787	3,364	13,459	18,023	19,664	23,756	32,326	21,783
Housing assistance	231	499	2,058	5,514	6,942	8,043	9,641	10,620
Food and nutrition assistance	299	960	6,642	14,015	16,202	15,579	18,204	16,221
Other income security	2,827	4,258	10,088	17,190	19,721	19,773	21,260	18,977
Total outlays	**25,744**	**43,073**	**108,576**	**193,100**	**225,101**	**248,343**	**279,358**	**275,229**
VETERANS' BENEFITS AND SERVICES:								
Income security for veterans	4,215	5,546	7,860	11,688	12,909	13,710	14,259	14,542
Veterans' edu., training, and rehabil.	58	1,015	4,593	2,342	2,254	1,947	1,622	1,329
Hospital and med. care for veterans	1,270	1,800	3,665	6,515	6,965	7,517	8,288	8,848
Veterans' housing	—	54	24	−23	201	102	−13	−32
Other veterans' benefits and serv.	180	263	458	665	662	682	744	769
Deductions for offsetting receipts	−2	−2	−2	−2	−3	−3	−3	−3
Total outlays	**5,721**	**8,677**	**16,597**	**21,183**	**22,988**	**23,995**	**24,897**	**25,453**
ADMINISTRATION OF JUSTICE:								
Federal law-enforcement activities	332	569	1,349	2,237	2,384	2,529	3,021	3,250
Federal litigative and judicial activities	141	236	549	1,347	1,491	1,516	1,686	1,654
Federal correctional activities	62	88	200	342	361	364	428	472
Criminal justice assistance	—	65	853	656	473	294	189	184
Deductions for offsetting receipts	−5	−6	−9	−11	−13	−32	−26	−26
Total outlays	**529**	**952**	**2,942**	**4,570**	**4,696**	**4,671**	**5,298**	**5,534**
GENERAL GOVERNMENT:								
Legislative functions	185	300	588	1,032	1,036	1,177	1,262	1,340
Executive direction and management	17	30	63	97	99	96	105	111
Central fiscal operations	638	934	1,752	2,522	2,600	2,656	3,269	3,485
General property and records manag.	602	616	418	364	169	334	548	382
Central personnel management	23	44	88	154	159	136	139	152
Other general government	39	121	423	559	745	504	727	717
Deductions for offsetting receipts	−113	−181	−199	−224	−195	−177	−286	−583
Total outlays	**1,390**	**1,857**	**3,133**	**4,505**	**4,614**	**4,726**	**5,763**	**5,604**
GENERAL PURPOSE FISCAL ASSISTANCE:								
General revenue sharing	—	—	6,130	6,835	5,140	4,575	4,573	4,574
Other general purpose fiscal assist.	238	536	1,057	1,749	1,716	1,818	1,780	2,206
Total outlays	**238**	**536**	**7,187**	**8,584**	**6,856**	**6,393**	**6,354**	**6,780**
NET INTEREST [2]:								
Interest on the public debt	11,346	19,304	32,665	74,781	95,503	117,190	128,056	148,500
Interest received by trust funds	−1,780	−3,936	−7,667	−12,045	−13,810	−16,067	−16,082	−18,969
Other interest	−987	−994	−1,754	−10,278	−12,967	−16,427	−22,996	−26,035
Total outlays [2]	**8,579**	**14,374**	**23,244**	**52,458**	**68,726**	**84,697**	**88,979**	**103,496**
ALLOWANCES:								
Civilian agency pay raises	—	—	—	—	—	—	—	—
Increased payments for employee retirement	—	—	—	—	—	—	—	949
Total outlays	—	—	—	—	—	—	—	**949**
UNDISTRIBUTED OFFSETTING RECEIPTS:								
Employer share, employee retirement	−1,329	−2,444	−3,980	−5,787	−6,371	−7,020	−8,210	−9,775
Rents and royalties on the outer continental shelf	−53	−187	−2,428	−4,101	−10,138	−6,250	−11,256	−10,200
Federal surplus property disposition	—	—	—	—	—	—	−408	−1,003
Total outlays [2]	**−1,382**	**−2,631**	**−6,408**	**−9,887**	**−16,509**	**−13,270**	**−19,873**	**−20,977**
TOTAL U.S. GOVT. OUTLAYS	**$118,430**	**$195,652**	**$324,425**	**$576,675**	**$657,204**	**$728,375**	**$809,756**	**$848,071**

[1] Based on July 1983 revisions to the 1984 Budget. [2] Revised to reflect interest received by trust funds moved from Undistributed Offsetting Receipts to the Interest function.

U.S. BUDGET AND FEDERAL DEBT: 1789–1984 [1]

Source: Office of Management and Budget; figures are in $ millions (add 000,000).

FISCAL YEAR	U.S. BUDGET RECEIPTS	U.S. BUDGET OUTLAYS	SURPLUS(+) OR DEFICIT(−)	GROSS DEBT AT END OF YEAR	FISCAL YEAR	U.S. BUDGET RECEIPTS	U.S. BUDGET OUTLAYS	SURPLUS(+) OR DEFICIT(−)	GROSS DEBT AT END OF YEAR
1789–91	$ 4	$ 4	$+ —	$ 77	1960	$ 92,492	$ 92,223	$+ 269	$ 290,862
1800	11	11	+ —	83	1961	94,389	97,795	− 3,406	292,895
1810	9	8	+ 1	48	1962	99,676	106,813	− 7,137	303,291
1820	18	18	− —	90	1963	106,560	111,311	− 4,751	310,807
1830	25	15	+ 10	39	1964	112,662	118,584	− 5,922	316,763
1840	19	24	− 5	5	1965	116,833	118,430	− 1,596	323,154
1850	44	40	+ 4	63	1966	130,856	134,652	− 3,796	329,474
1860	56	63	− 7	65	1967	148,906	157,608	− 8,702	341,348
1870	411	310	+ 101	2,436	1968	152,973	178,134	− 25,161	369,769
1880	334	268	+ 66	2,091	1969	186,882	183,645	+ 3,236	367,144
1890	403	318	+ 85	1,122	1970	192,807	195,652	− 2,845	382,603
1900	567	521	+ 46	1,263	1971	187,139	210,172	− 23,033	409,467
1905	544	567	− 23	1,132	1972	207,309	230,681	− 23,373	437,329
1910	676	694	− 18	1,147	1973	230,799	245,647	− 14,849	468,426
1915	683	746	− 63	1,191	1974	263,224	267,912	− 4,688	486,247
1920	6,649	6,358	+ 291	24,299	1975	279,090	324,245	− 45,154	544,131
1925	3,641	2,924	+ 717	20,516	1976	298,060	364,473	− 66,413	631,866
1930	4,058	3,320	+ 738	16,185	TQ [2]	81,232	94,188	− 12,956	646,379
1935	3,706	6,497	− 2,791	28,701	1977	355,559	400,506	− 44,948	709,138
1940	6,361	9,456	− 3,095	50,696	1978	399,561	448,368	− 48,807	780,425
1945	45,216	92,690	− 47,474	260,123	1979	463,302	490,997	− 27,694	833,751
1950	39,485	42,597	− 3,112	256,853	1980	517,112	576,675	− 59,563	914,317
1955	65,469	68,509	− 3,041	274,366	1981	599,272	657,204	− 57,932	1,003,941
1957	79,990	76,741	+ 3,249	272,353	1982	617,766	728,375	−110,609	1,146,987
1958	79,636	82,575	− 2,939	279,693	1983 [3]	599,926	809,756	−209,830	1,390,839
1959	79,249	92,104	− 12,855	287,767	1984 [3]	668,404	848,071	−179,667	1,611,885

[1] For 1789–1939, administrative budget. [2] TQ=Transitional Quarter, July 1 to Sept. 30, 1976. [3] July 1983 estimates.

FEDERAL BUDGET RECEIPTS BY SOURCE: 1940–1984

Source: Office of Management and Budget; figures in $ millions (add 000,000).

SOURCE	COLLECTIONS								
	1940	1950	1960	1970	1980	1981	1982	1983 [1]	1984 [1]
Individual Income Taxes	$1,110	$15,747	$40,741	$90,412	$244,069	$285,917	$297,744	$288,463	$296,050
Corporation Income Taxes	978	10,449	21,494	32,829	64,600	61,137	49,207	35,188	64,102
Social Insurance Taxes and Contributions ...	1,715	4,386	14,684	44,362	157,803	182,720	201,498	211,051	241,397
Excise Taxes	1,844	7,550	11,676	15,705	24,329	40,839	36,311	34,922	36,494
Estate and Gift Taxes	353	698	1,606	3,644	6,389	6,787	7,991	6,019	5,911
Customs Duties	331	407	1,105	2,430	7,174	8,083	8,854	8,419	9,325
Miscellaneous Receipts	30	248	1,187	3,424	12,748	13,790	16,161	15,864	15,125
Adjustment for Senate Finance Com. Bill ...						−7			
TOTAL RECEIPTS	**$6,361**	**$39,485**	**$92,492**	**$192,807**	**$517,112**	**$599,272**	**$617,766**	**$599,926**	**$668,404**

[1] July 1983 estimates.

COMPARISON OF FEDERAL RECEIPTS AND EXPENDITURES: 1975–1983 [1]

Federal Sector, National Income and Product Account (NIPA).
Source: U.S. Department of Commerce, *Survey of Current Business*; figures in $ billions (add 000,000,000).

	1975	1978	1979	1980	1981	1982	1983 Q1 [2]	1983 Q2 [2]
Federal government receipts	**$286.2**	**$431.6**	**$493.6**	**$540.7**	**$628.2**	**$627.8**	**$623.3**	**$652.0**
Personal tax and nontax receipts ...	125.4	194.9	230.6	257.5	298.1	310.4	297.7	304.3
Corporate profits tax accruals	42.8	71.3	74.2	70.3	67.3	51.3	48.6	59.0
Indirect business tax and nontax accruals.	23.9	28.1	29.4	38.9	58.5	50.3	56.2	54.7
Contributions for social insurance ..	94.2	137.2	159.5	174.1	204.3	215.7	228.5	232.6
Federal government expenditures ...	**$356.8**	**$461.0**	**$509.7**	**$602.1**	**$688.2**	**$740.0**	**$806.6**	**$815.7**
Purchases of goods and services ...	123.1	153.6	168.3	197.2	228.9	251.0	273.5	272.7
Transfer payments	149.1	185.6	209.2	251.4	286.6	310.2	340.3	345.7
Grants-in-aid to state and local govts.	54.6	77.3	80.5	88.7	87.7	83.4	85.8	86.8
Net interest paid	23.2	35.2	42.4	53.1	71.9	82.2	88.4	91.6
Subsidies less current surplus of government enterprises	6.8	9.5	9.2	11.7	13.1	13.2	18.6	17.6
Deficit (−)	**$-70.6**	**$-29.5**	**$-16.1**	**$-61.4**	**$-60.0**	**$-112.2**	**$-183.3**	**$-163.7**

[1] Calendar years. [2] First and second quarters 1983 at annual rates.

U.S. GOVERNMENT CIVILIAN EMPLOYEES

Source: Office of Personnel Management

The total number of civilian employees of the U.S. government increased by over 50,000 in the 12 months from Oct. 1, 1982, to Sept. 30, 1983. More than one-third of the employees work for the Department of Defense, which added about 37,000 civilian workers during the 12-month period.

	TOTAL[1]
TOTAL, ALL BRANCHES	**2,874,869***
LEGISLATIVE BRANCH	**39,167***
Congress	19,806*
Architect of the Capitol	2,246
General Accounting Office	5,320*
Government Printing Office	5,763
Library of Congress	5,308
U.S. Tax Court	256
Congressional Budget Office	215*
Office of Technology Assessment	176
Botanic Garden	58
Copyright Royalty Tribunal	7
JUDICIAL BRANCH	**16,626**
United States Courts	16,293
Supreme Court	333
EXECUTIVE BRANCH	**2,819,076**
Executive Office of the President:	**1,621**
White House Office	384
White House Executive Residence	87
Office of the Vice President	22
Office of Management and Budget	611
Office of Administration	209
Domestic Policy Staff	41
National Security Council	60
Office of the U.S. Trade Representative	140
Council of Economic Advisers	33
Office of Science and Technology Policy	23
Council on Environmental Quality	11
Executive Departments:	**1,737,735**
State	23,961
Treasury	124,602
Defense	1,026,461
Army	369,229
Navy	333,756
Air Force	240,977
Defense Logistics Agency	46,695
Other defense activities	35,804
Justice	58,869
Interior	79,582
Agriculture	123,987
Commerce	35,576
Labor	19,083
Health and Human Services	147,162
Housing and Urban Development	12,996
Transportation	62,959
Energy	17,229
Education	5,268
Independent Agencies:	**1,079,720**
ACTION	524
Advisory Commission on Intergovernmental Relations	34
Advisory Council on Historic Preservation	40

	TOTAL[1]
Independent Agencies (continued)	
Alaska Natural Gas Transportation System	32
American Battle Monuments Commission	392
Arms Control and Disarmament Agency	174
Board of Governors, Federal Reserve System	1,551
Civil Aeronautics Board	441
Commission on Civil Rights	259
Commodity Futures Trading Comm.	477
Consumer Product Safety Commission	633
Environmental Protection Agency	11,931
Equal Employment Opportunity Comm.	3,183
Export-Import Bank of the U.S.	335
Farm Credit Administration	308
Federal Communications Comm.	1,897
Federal Deposit Insurance Corp.	3,660
Federal Election Commission	219
Federal Emergency Management Agency	2,509
Federal Home Loan Bank Board	1,534
Federal Labor Relations Authority	290
Federal Maritime Commission	245
Federal Mediation and Conciliation Service	359
Federal Mine Safety and Health Review Commission	60
Federal Trade Commission	1,323
General Services Administration	29,586
Inter-American Foundation	65
International Trade Commission	420
Interstate Commerce Commission	1,245
Merit Systems Protection Board	524
National Aeronautics and Space Administration	22,784
National Capital Planning Commission	49
National Credit Union Administration	615
National Endowment for the Arts	277
National Endowment for the Humanities	259
National Labor Relations Board	2,726
National Mediation Board	57
National Science Foundation	1,257
National Transportation Safety Board	337
Navajo and Hopi Indian Relocation Commission	51
Nuclear Regulatory Commission	3,534
Occupational Safety and Health Review Commission	103
Office of Personnel Management	6,369
Panama Canal Commission	8,356
Peace Corps	1,026
Pennsylvania Ave. Development Corp.	46
Pension Benefit Guaranty Corporation	466
Postal Rate Commission	65
Railroad Retirement Commission	1,565
Securities and Exchange Commission	1,897
Selective Service System	284
Small Business Administration	5,100
Smithsonian Institution	4,696
Soldiers' and Airmen's Home	990
Tennessee Valley Authority	37,181
U.S. Information Agency	7,983
U.S. International Development Cooperation Agency	5,418
U.S. Metric Board	—
U.S. Postal Service	663,027
Veterans Administration	238,739
Water Resources Council	—
Other boards and agencies (27)	213

* Preliminary data. [1] As of Sept. 30, 1983. Excludes Central Intelligence Agency and National Security Agency.

U.S. GOVERNMENT AGENCIES AND DEPARTMENTS

The President is the administrative head of the executive branch of the government, which includes cabinet-level executive departments and independent agencies.

The cabinet functions at the pleasure of the President to advise him on matters of importance. The Vice President participates in all cabinet meetings. Others who regularly attend cabinet meetings include the heads of the executive departments, the counsel to the President, the special representative for trade negotiations, the director of the Office of Management and Budget, the U.S. ambassador to the UN, and presidential staff aides.

The President's salary is $200,000 a year plus $50,000 official allowance and $100,000 travel allowance.

EXECUTIVE OFFICE OF PRESIDENT REAGAN

This office consists of the individuals, agencies, and special commissions charged with aiding the President in carrying out the many activities incident to his office.

THE WHITE HOUSE OFFICE

1600 Pennsylvania Avenue, N.W., and Old Executive Office Building,
Washington, D.C. 20500
Phone: (202) 456-1414

Assistants to the President: Edwin Meese III, Counselor to the President; James A. Baker III, Chief of Staff; Michael K. Deaver, Deputy Chief of Staff; James S. Brady, Press Secretary; Richard G. Darman, Deputy to the Chief of Staff; John F.W. Rogers, Management and Administration; Larry M. Speakes, Deputy Press Secretary; M.B. Oglesby, Legislative Affairs; Fred F. Fielding, Counsel to the President; Craig L. Fuller, Cabinet Affairs; David R. Gergen, Communications; John A. Svahn, Policy Development; Edward V. Hickey Jr., Director of Special Support Services; James E. Jenkins, Deputy Counselor; Lee Verstandig, Intergovernmental Affairs; Faith Ryan Whittlesey, Public Liaison

Deputy Assistants to the President: Bentley T. Elliott, Director of Speechwriting; Michael Baroody, Director of Public Affairs; Jack L. Courtemanche, Public Liaison; T. Kenneth Cribb Jr., Assistant Counselor; Richard A. Hauser, Deputy Counsel; John M. Poindexter, National Security Affairs; Michael A. McManus, Deputy to the Deputy Chief of Staff; Roger B. Porter, Director of the Office of Policy Development; Becky N. Dunlop, Presidential Personnel; Pamela J. Turner, Legislative Affairs (Senate); Charles P. Tyson, National Security Affairs; Bruce Chapman, Director of Office of Planning and Evaluation; Rick J. Neal, Intergovernmental Affairs; W. Dennis Thomas, Legislative Affairs (House); James S. Rosebush; Karna Small, Director of Media Relations and Planning

Special Assistants to the President: Robert B. Sims, Deputy Press Secretary; Richard S. Beal, Director of Planning and Evaluation; Morton C. Blackwell, Public Liaison; Ralph C. Bledsoe, Executive Secretary of the Cabinet Council on Management and Administration; Catalina Villalpando, Public Liaison; Melvin L. Bradley, Policy Development; Robert B. Carleson, Policy Development; James W. Cicconi, Special Assistant to the Chief of Staff; Sherrie M. Cooksey, Associate Counsel; Anthony Dolan, Chief Speechwriter; Michael A. W. Evans, Personal Photographer to the President; David C. Fisher; Wendell W. Gunn, Policy Development; William Henkel, Director of Presidential Advance; Anne Higgins, Director of Correspondence; Kevin R. Hopkins, Policy Development; Robert J. Kabel, Legislative Affairs; Mary Jo T. Livingston, Director of the Office of Presidential Messages; Andrew H. Card, Jr., Intergovernmental Affairs; Nancy J. Risque, Legislative Affairs; John G. Roberts Jr., Associate Counsel; Peter H. Roussel, Deputy Press Secretary; Peter J. Rusthoven, Associate Counsel; John F. Scruggs, Legislative Affairs; William F. Sittmann, Assistant to the Deputy Chief of Staff; David L. Swanson, Legislative Affairs; Margaret D. Tutwiler, Executive Assistant to the Chief of Staff; Michael M. Uhlmann, Policy Development; David B. Waller, Senior Associate Counsel; D. Edward Wilson Jr., Associate Counsel; David L. Wright, Legislative Affairs; Robert M. Kimmitt, National Security Affairs; Carlton E. Turner, Drug Abuse Policy; Pamela G. Bailey, Deputy Director of Public Affairs; Judith A. Buckalew, Public Liaison; James K. Coyne, Private Sector Initiatives; Randall E. Davis, Legislative Affairs; Thomas R. Donnelly Jr., Legislative Affairs; Max Marlin Fitzwater, Deputy Press Secretary for Domestic Affairs; Donbald R. Fortier, National Security Affairs; H. Lawrence Garret III, Associate Counsel; Robert R. Gleason, Intergovernmental Affairs; Edmund S. Hawley, Intergovernmental Affairs; C.A. Howlett, Intergovernmental Affairs; Mary Jo Jacobi, Public Liaison; Geoffrey T.H. Kemp, National Security Affairs; Nancy M. Kennedy, Legislative Affairs; Christopher M. Lehman, National Security Affairs; Jack F. Matlock Jr., National Security Affairs; Walter Raymond Jr., National Security Affairs; Douglas A. Riggs, Public Liaison; Frederick J. Ryan Jr., Director of Scheduling; Gaston J. Sigur Jr., National Security Affairs; Robert H. Tuttle

Chief of Protocol: Selwa Roosevelt
Personal Secretary to the President: Kathleen Osborne
Physician to the President: Dr. Daniel Rugee
Chief Usher: Rex W. Scouten

EXECUTIVE OFFICE OF THE PRESIDENT *(cont.)*

CENTRAL INTELLIGENCE AGENCY (CIA)

Washington, D.C. 20505
Director: William J. Casey
Duties: To keep National Security Council informed on national-security matters; to coordinate intelligence from government agencies and from its agents in other countries. The CIA has no police or law-enforcement powers and no internal-security functions.

COUNCIL OF ECONOMIC ADVISERS (CEA)

Executive Office Building,
Washington, D.C. 20506
Established: 1946
Chairman: Martin S. Feldstein
Members: William A. Niskanen Jr., William Pode VII
Duties: To analyze trends in the national economy; to appraise economic programs and policies of the federal government; to assist in the preparation of the President's economic reports to Congress.

COUNCIL ON ENVIRONMENTAL QUALITY

722 Jackson Place, N.W.,
Washington, D.C. 20006
Established: 1969
Chairman: A. Alan Hill
Duties: To develop and recommend national policies to promote environmental quality and to administer guidelines for the environmental impact statement process.

DOMESTIC POLICY STAFF

The White House,
Washington, D.C. 20500
Established: 1977
Director: John A. Svahn
Purpose: To administer the Presidential Domestic Policy Review System to coordinate the work of the departments and agencies in developing the administration's position on selected key domestic-policy issues.

INTELLIGENCE OVERSIGHT BOARD

Executive Office Building,
Washington, D.C. 20500
Established: 1975
Chairman: W. Glenn Campbell
Membership: W. Glenn Campbell, Charles Jarvis Meyers, Charles Tyroler II
Duties: To review and assess foreign-intelligence activities and bring to the President's attention any abuses that might occur.

NATIONAL SECURITY COUNCIL

Executive Office Building,
Washington, D.C. 20506
Established: 1947
Director: Assistant to the President for National Security Affairs Robert C. McFarlane
Membership: The President, Vice President, Secretary of State, Secretary of Defense
Advisers: Chairman of the Joint Chiefs of Staff and director of the Central Intelligence Agency
Duties: To advise the President on national- security problems, formulating plans to promote the best interests of the United States in international relations.

OFFICE OF ADMINISTRATION

The White House,
Washington, D.C. 20500
Established: 1977
Director: John F. W. Rogers
Purpose: To provide administrative services to the components of the Executive Office, including accounting and payroll, mail and messengers, library facilities, and computer facilities; to coordinate the zero-base budgeting system.

OFFICE OF MANAGEMENT AND BUDGET (OMB)

Executive Office Building,
Washington, D.C. 20503
Established: 1970
Director: David A. Stockman
Duties: To aid the President in the preparation and administration of the budget and make recommendations for the more efficient organization of the federal government.

OFFICE OF SCIENCE AND TECHNOLOGY POLICY

Executive Office Building,
Washington, D.C. 20503
Established: May 11, 1976
Director: George A. Keyworth II
Duties: To advise the President on science, engineering, and technology; to evaluate the overall federal-government efforts in science and technology.

OFFICE OF THE SPECIAL REPRESENTATIVE FOR TRADE NEGOTIATIONS

1800 G Street, N.W.,
Washington, D.C. 20506
Established: 1963
Special Representative for Trade Negotiations: William E. Brock III
Duties: To facilitate implementation of the trade-agreements program; to assist and advise the President in coordinating international trade policy; and to administer the negotiation and implementation of international trade agreements.

OFFICE OF THE VICE PRESIDENT

Executive Office Building,
Washington, D.C. 20501
Chief of Staff: Daniel J. Murphy
Executive Functions: Participation in all cabinet meetings and meetings of the National Security Council; member of Board of Regents of the Smithsonian Institution; chairs executive committee that develops the President's long-term agenda.

PRESIDENT'S FOREIGN INTELLIGENCE ADVISORY BOARD

Executive Office Building
Washington, D.C. 20500
Established: 1981
Chairman: Anne L. Armstrong
Vice Chairman: Leo Cherne
Membership: 19 members
Duties: To assess the quality, quantity, and adequacy of intelligence collection and other intelligence activities.

CABINET-LEVEL EXECUTIVE DEPARTMENTS

AGRICULTURE, DEPARTMENT OF

14th Street and Independence Avenue, N.W., Washington, D.C. 20250
Established: 1889 as an executive department
Secretary of Agriculture: John R. Block
Administrator, Farmers Home Administration: Charles W. Shuman
Purpose: To carry out agricultural research, education, conservation, marketing, regulatory work, agricultural adjustment, and rural development. It also collects and distributes agricultural information.

COMMERCE, DEPARTMENT OF

14th Street and Constitution Avenue, N.W., Washington, D.C. 20230
Established: 1913
Secretary: Malcolm Baldrige
Director of the Census: C.L. Kincannon
Director, National Oceanic and Atmospheric Administration: John V. Byrne
Purpose: To promote full development of the economic resources of the U.S. It conducts censuses; disseminates commercial statistics; compiles nautical and aeronautical charts; establishes weights, measures, and standards; issues patents and registers trademarks; provides weather forecasting.

DEFENSE, DEPARTMENT OF

The Pentagon, Washington, D.C. 20301
Established: 1949
Secretary: Caspar W. Weinberger
Deputy Secretary: Frank G. Carlucci
Functions: To defend the U.S. against all enemies; to ensure the security of the U.S. and areas vital to its interest.
Secretary of the Army: John O. Marsh Jr.
Secretary of the Navy: John F. Lehman
Secretary of the Air Force: Verne Orr

EDUCATION, DEPARTMENT OF

400 Maryland Ave., S.W., Washington, D.C. 20202
Established: 1979
Secretary: Terrel H. Bell
Under Secretary: Gary L. Jones
Purpose: To administer and coordinate federal education programs.
Commissioner, Rehabilitation Services Administration: George A. Conn

ENERGY, DEPARTMENT OF

1000 Independence Avenue, S.W., Washington, D.C. 20585
Established: 1977
Secretary: Donald P. Hodel
Purpose: To carry out the national energy policy, including conservation, resource development and production, research, data management, and environmental protection and regulation related to energy.
Chairman, Federal Energy Regulatory Commission: Charles M. Butler III

HEALTH AND HUMAN SERVICES, DEPARTMENT OF

200 Independence Avenue, S.W., Washington, D.C. 20201
Established: 1953 as Department of Health, Education, and Welfare; name changed 1979.
Secretary: Margaret M. Heckler
Under Secretary: Vacant
Purpose: To administer and coordinate federal activities in health and welfare.
Commissioner Food and Drug Administration: Mark Novitch
Commissioner on Aging: Lennie-Marie Tolliver
Surgeon General, Public Health Service: Dr. C. Everett Koop
Director, National Institutes of Health: James B. Wyngaarden
Director, National Cancer Institute: Dr. Vincent T. DeVita Jr.
Commissioner of Social Security: Martha A. McSteen

HOUSING AND URBAN DEVELOPMENT, DEPARTMENT OF

451 7th Street, N.W., Washington, D.C. 20410
Established: 1965
Secretary: Samuel R. Pierce
Under Secretary: Philip Abrams
Purpose: To administer housing and urban-development programs and offer technical aid to states, cities, and counties.

INTERIOR, DEPARTMENT OF THE

18th and C Streets, N.W., Washington, D.C. 20240
Established: 1849
Secretary: William P. Clark
Under Secretary: Vacant
Purpose: To formulate and administer programs for the conservation and development of natural resources. It supervises the Bureau of Mines, Geological Survey, Bureau of Indian Affairs, Bureau of Land Management, National Park Service, Fish and Wildlife Service, and Water and Power Resources Service.

JUSTICE, DEPARTMENT OF

Constitution Avenue and 10th Street, N.W., Washington, D.C. 20530
Established: 1870
Attorney General: William French Smith
Deputy Attorney General: Edward C. Schmults
Director, Federal Bureau of Investigation: William Webster
Solicitor General: Rex E. Lee
Purpose: To provide means for enforcing federal laws, to furnish legal counsel in federal cases, and to construe the laws under which other departments act.

LABOR, DEPARTMENT OF

200 Constitution Avenue, N.W.,
Washington, D.C. 20210
Established: 1913
Secretary: Raymond J. Donovan
Under Secretary: Malcolm R. Lovell Jr.
Purpose: To administer and enforce laws designed to advance the public interest by promoting the welfare of U.S. wage earners, improving their working conditions, and advancing their opportunities for profitable employment.

STATE, DEPARTMENT OF

2201 C Street, N.W.,
Washington, D.C. 20520
Established: 1789
Secretary: George P. Shultz
Deputy Secretary: Kenneth W. Dam
Administrator, Agency for International Development (AID): M. Peter McPherson
Purpose: The President, who has overall responsibility for U.S. foreign policy, looks to the Department of State for primary advice in formulating and executing that policy. The department's primary objective is to promote U.S. interest in international relations.

TRANSPORTATION, DEPARTMENT OF

400 7th Street, S.W.,
Washington, D.C. 20590
Established: 1966
Secretary: Elizabeth Dole
Deputy Secretary: James Burnley IV
Administrator, Federal Aviation Administration: J. Lynn Helms
Administrator, Federal Highway Administration: Ray Barnhart
Administrator, Federal Railroad Administration: John H. Riley
Administrator, National Highway Safety Administration: Diane K. Steed
Purpose: To develop national policies to provide fast, safe, efficient, convenient, and economical transportation. It also directs the Federal Aviation Administration, St. Lawrence Seaway Development Corporation, and, in peacetime, the U.S. Coast Guard.

TREASURY, DEPARTMENT OF THE

15th Street and Pennsylvania Avenue, N.W.,
Washington, D.C. 20220
Established: 1789
Secretary: Donald T. Regan
Deputy Secretary: R.T. McNamar
Treasurer of the U.S.: Katherine D. Ortega
Comptroller of the Currency: C. T. Conover
Commissioner, Internal Revenue Service: Roscoe L. Egger Jr.
Purpose: To manage national finances; provide coined and printed currency; maintain U.S. credit; represent the U.S. in international banking and monetary organizations; collect U.S. taxes through the Internal Revenue Service; and supervise the Secret Service.

INDEPENDENT AGENCIES OF THE U.S. GOVERNMENT

ACTION

806 Connecticut Avenue, N.W.,
Washington, D.C. 20525
Established: 1971
Director: Thomas W. Pauken
Deputy Director: Betty H. Breaker
Activities: Coordinates citizen volunteer action programs, including the Peace Corps, VISTA, foster grandparents, and retired volunteers.

ARMS CONTROL AND DISARMAMENT AGENCY

Department of State Building,
Washington, D.C. 20451
Established: 1961
Director: Kenneth L. Adelman
Deputy Director: Robert T. Grey Jr.
Activities: Participates in nuclear-test-ban and general disarmament negotiations at Geneva and in the United Nations; conducts research on arms control and disarmament.

BOARD FOR INTERNATIONAL BROADCASTING

Department of State Building,
Washington, D.C. 20451
Established: 1973
Chairman: Frank Shakespeare
Activities: To provide assistance to Radio Free Europe and Radio Liberty and to encourage a flow of information to people of the communist nations of Europe.

CIVIL AERONAUTICS BOARD (CAB)

1825 Connecticut Avenue, N.W.,
Washington, D.C. 20428
Established: 1938
Membership: Five members
Chairman: Clinton Dan McKinnon
Activities: Regulates economic aspects of U.S. air-carrier operations, and of foreign common-carrier operations to and from the U.S.

COMMISSION OF FINE ARTS

708 Jackson Place, N.W.,
Washington, D.C. 20006
Established: 1910
Membership: Seven expert fine-arts judges
Chairman: J. Carter Brown
Activities: Advises, assists on matters relating to art, monuments, and public works.

COMMISSION ON CIVIL RIGHTS

1121 Vermont Avenue, N.W.,
Washington, D.C. 20425
Established: 1957
Chairman: Clarence M. Pendleton Jr.
Activities: Investigates complaints of persons being deprived of their civil rights because of race, color, religion, sex, or national origin.

COMMODITY FUTURES TRADING COMMISSION

2033 K Street N.W.,
Washington, D.C. 20581
Established: 1974
Chairman: Susan Meredith Phillips
Activities: Seeks to strengthen the regulation of futures trading and to bring under regulation all agricultural and other commodities that are traded on commodity exchanges, and to protect market users against abuses.

INDEPENDENT AGENCIES *(continued)*

CONSUMER PRODUCT SAFETY COMMISSION

1111 18th Street, N.W.,
Washington, D.C. 20207
Established: Oct. 27, 1972
Chairman: Nancy H. Steorts
Membership: Five members
Activities: Studies consumer-product safety; orders unsafe products taken off the market; establishes product-safety standards to reduce risks to consumers.

ENVIRONMENTAL PROTECTION AGENCY (EPA)

401 M Street, S.W.,
Washington, D.C. 20460
Established: 1970
Administrator: William D. Ruckelshaus
Deputy Administrator: Alvin L. Alm
Activities: To assure the protection of the environment by monitoring, regulating, abating, and controlling pollution of the environment on a systematic basis.

EQUAL EMPLOYMENT OPPORTUNITY COMMISSION (EEOC)

2401 E Street, N.W.,
Washington, D.C. 20506
Established: 1965
Membership: Five members, appointed to 5-year terms by the President
Chairman: Clarence Thomas
Activities: Coordinates federal efforts to end discrimination in employment.

EXPORT-IMPORT BANK OF THE U.S.

811 Vermont Avenue, N.W.,
Washington, D.C. 20571
Established: 1934
President: William H. Draper III
Activities: Aids in financing and facilitating trade between the U.S. and foreign countries.

FARM CREDIT ADMINISTRATION (FCA)

490 L'Enfant Plaza West, S.W.,
Washington, D.C. 20578
Established: 1916
Governor: Donald E. Wilkinson
Activities: Supervises and coordinates a cooperative credit system for agriculture, providing long-term and short-term credits to farmers and their cooperative organizations.

FEDERAL COMMUNICATIONS COMMISSION (FCC)

1919 M Street, N.W.,
Washington, D.C. 20554
Established: 1934
Membership: Five members, appointed to 7-year terms by the President.
Chairman: Mark S. Fowler
Activities: Regulates interstate and foreign commerce in communication by radio and wire to make available a rapid, efficient radio communication service at reasonable cost.

FEDERAL DEPOSIT INSURANCE CORPORATION (FDIC)

550 17th Street, N.W.,
Washington, D.C. 20429
Established: 1933
Membership: The Board of Directors comprises three members. Two are appointed to 6-year terms by the President. The chairman is one of the presidential appointees. The Comptroller of the Currency serves ex-officio as the third member of the corporation.
Chairman: William M. Isaac
Activities: Insures the deposits of all banks entitled to benefits of insurance under the law, paying depositors of insured banks that close without adequate funds to meet claims against them; acts as a receiver for national banks placed in receivership and, under certain conditions, for state banks placed in receivership.

FEDERAL ELECTION COMMISSION

1325 K Street, N.W.,
Washington, D.C. 20005
Established: 1975
Chairman: Danny Lee McDonald
Activities: Enforces federal laws on election campaign financing.

FEDERAL EMERGENCY MANAGEMENT AGENCY

1725 Eye St., N.W.
Washington, D.C. 20472
Established: 1979
Director: Louis O. Giuffrida
Purpose: To oversee federal programs that assist areas and individuals affected by civil emergencies.

FEDERAL HOME LOAN BANK BOARD

1700 G Street, N.W.,
Washington, D.C. 20552
Established: 1955
Chairman: Richard T. Pratt
Activities: Provides credit reserve for savings and home-financing institutions; supervises the Federal Home Loan Bank System, the Federal Savings and Loan System, and the Federal Savings and Loan Insurance Corporation.

FEDERAL MARITIME COMMISSION

1100 L Street, N.W.,
Washington, D.C. 20573
Established: 1961
Membership: Five members, appointed to 4 year terms by the President.
Chairman: Alan Green Jr.
Activities: Regulates rates, fares, charges, classifications, tariffs, regulations, and practices of common carriers engaged in maritime commerce within U.S. jurisdiction.

FEDERAL MEDIATION AND CONCILIATION SERVICE

2100 K Street, N.W.,
Washington, D.C. 20427
Established: 1947
Director: Kay McMurray
Activities: Assists in the solution of labor disputes affecting interstate commerce by offering conciliation and mediation services.

FEDERAL RESERVE SYSTEM

Board of Governors of the Federal Reserve System
20th Street and Constitution Avenue, N.W.,
Washington, D.C. 20551
Established: 1913
Membership: The Board of Governors of the Federal Reserve System has seven members appointed by the President.
Chairman: Paul A. Volcker
Activities: Provides for establishment of Federal

Reserve Banks to furnish an elastic currency, to afford means of rediscounting commercial paper, and to establish effective supervision of banking in the United States.

FEDERAL SAVINGS AND LOAN INSURANCE CORPORATION (FSLIC)

1700 G Street, N.W.,
Washington, D.C. 20552
Established: 1934
Director: H. Brent Beesley
Activities: Insures each depositor's account in approved savings and loan associations; to prevent default of an insured institution, the corporation can make loans or purchase assets of the institution; income is from premiums paid by the insured institutions.

FEDERAL TRADE COMMISSION (FTC)

Pennsylvania Avenue at 6th Street, N.W.,
Washington, D.C. 20580
Established: 1915
Membership: Five members, appointed to 7-year terms by the President. Not more than three commissioners may be members of the same political party.
Chairman: James C. Miller III
Activities: Promotes fair and free competition in interstate commerce by prevention of price fixing, boycotts, combinations in restraint of trade, and other practices; safeguards consumers from unfair advertising and sales techniques.

GENERAL SERVICES ADMINISTRATION (GSA)

18th and F Streets, N.W.,
Washington, D.C. 20405
Established: 1949
Administrator: Gerald P. Carmen
Activities: Manages government property and records, including the construction and operation of buildings, procurement and distribution of supplies, disposal of surplus property, management of traffic and communications, stockpiling of strategic and critical materials, and care of records.

INTER-AMERICAN FOUNDATION

1515 Wilson Blvd.,
Rosslyn, Va. 22209
Established: Dec. 30, 1969
Chairman: Vacant
Purpose: Supports small-scale local social-development projects in Latin America.

INTERNATIONAL DEVELOPMENT COOPERATION AGENCY, U.S.

2201 C Street, N.W.,
Washington, D.C. 20520
Established: 1979
Director: M. Peter McPherson
Purpose: To consolidate policy direction of developing agencies and control budgets of various international development agencies.

INTERNATIONAL TRADE COMMISSION, U.S.

E and 8th Streets, N.W.,
Washington, D.C. 20436
Established: 1916
Chairman: Alfred E. Eckes Jr.
Activities: Serves Congress and the President as an advisory, fact-finding agency on tariff, commercial policy, and foreign-trade matters.

INTERSTATE COMMERCE COMMISSION (ICC)

12th Street and Constitution Avenue, N.W.,
Washington, D.C. 20423
Established: 1887
Membership: Seven members
Chairman: Reese H. Taylor Jr.
Activities: Regulates interstate commerce, and foreign import and export commerce to the extent that it takes place in the United States.

NATIONAL AERONAUTICS AND SPACE ADMINISTRATION (NASA)

400 Maryland Avenue, S.W.,
Washington, D.C. 20546
Established: 1958
Administrator: James M. Beggs
Activities: Conducts research on flight within and outside the Earth's atmosphere; develops, constructs, tests, and operates aeronautical and space vehicles.

NATIONAL CREDIT UNION ADMINISTRATION

2025 M Street, N.W.,
Washington, D.C. 20456
Established: March 10, 1970
Chairman: Edgar F. Callahan
Activities: Regulates credit unions.

NATIONAL FOUNDATION ON THE ARTS AND HUMANITIES

806 15th Street, N.W.,
Washington, D.C. 20506
Established: 1965
Chairman, National Endowment for the Arts: Francis S. M. Hodsoll
Chairman, National Endowment for the Humanities: William J. Bennett
Purpose: To encourage and support national programs in the humanities and the arts. The Arts Endowment awards grants to groups (and some individuals) engaged in or concerned with the arts, awards grants-in-aid to assist state art agencies, and conducts special studies.

NATIONAL LABOR RELATIONS BOARD (NLRB)

1717 Pennsylvania Avenue, N.W.,
Washington, D.C. 20570
Established: 1935
Membership: Five members, appointed to 4-year terms by the President
Chairman: Donald L. Dotson
Activities: Prevents, through a variety of powers, unfair labor practices.

NATIONAL MEDIATION BOARD

1425 K Street, N.W.,
Washington, D.C. 20572
Established: 1934
Chairman: Robert O. Harris
Activities: Mediates differences between the railroads and airlines on one hand and their employees on the other.

INDEPENDENT AGENCIES *(continued)*

NATIONAL SCIENCE FOUNDATION (NSF)
1800 G Street, N.W.,
Washington, D.C. 20550
Established: 1950
Director: Edward A. Knapp
Purpose: Strengthens basic research and education in the sciences in the U.S.

NATIONAL TRANSPORTATION SAFETY BOARD
800 Independence Avenue, S.W.,
Washington, D.C. 20594
Established: 1966
Chairman: James Eugene Burnett Jr.
Activities: Investigates major accidents in civil aviation, railroads, highways, pipelines, and ships; reports the facts and circumstances of accidents; and makes recommendations for legislation to prevent accidents.

NUCLEAR REGULATORY COMMISSION (NRC)
1717 H Street, N.W.,
Washington, D.C. 20555
Established: Oct. 11, 1974
Chairman: Nunzio J. Palladino
Membership: Five members
Responsibilities: Took over duties of former Atomic Energy Commission (AEC) to regulate, license, and supervise the security and safety of peaceful uses of nuclear power.

OFFICE OF PERSONNEL MANAGEMENT
1900 E Street, N.W.,
Washington, D.C. 20415
Established: 1979
Director: Donald J. Devine
Purpose: Administration of a merit system for federal-government employees.

OVERSEAS PRIVATE INVESTMENT CORPORATION
1129 20th Street, N.W.,
Washington, D.C. 20527
Established: 1971
President: Craig A. Nalen
Purpose: To provide incentives (including insurance against loss by expropriation) for U.S. private investors in 90 developing nations.

POSTAL RATE COMMISSION
2000 L Street, N.W.,
Washington, D.C. 20268
Established: Aug. 12, 1970
Chairman: Janet D. Steiger
Activities: Holds hearings and submits recommendations to the Postal Service on postage rates, fees, and mail classifications.

POSTAL SERVICE, UNITED STATES
475 L'Enfant Plaza, S.W.,
Washington, D.C. 20260
Established: 1970 (The U.S. Postal Service, which began operations July 1, 1971, replaced the cabinet-level Post Office Department established by Congress in 1872. The first Postal Service was created in 1775.)
Postmaster General: William F. Bolger
Activities: To provide postal services.

RAILROAD RETIREMENT BOARD
884 Rush Street
Chicago, Ill. 60611
Established: 1935
Chairman: William P. Adams
Purpose: Administers payment of retirement and disability annuities to railroad employees and their families.

SECURITIES AND EXCHANGE COMMISSION (SEC)
500 N. Capitol Street, N.W.,
Washington, D.C. 20549
Established: 1934
Membership: Five members, appointed by the President to 5-year terms. Only three may be members of the same political party.
Chairman: John S. R. Shad
Activities: Protects the interests of the public and investors against malpractices in securities and financial markets.

SMALL BUSINESS ADMINISTRATION (SBA)
1441 L Street, N.W.,
Washington, D.C. 20416
Established: 1953
Administrator: James C. Sanders
Activities: Aids, counsels, and protects the interests of small business; ensures that small business concerns receive a fair proportion of government purchases and contracts, and of the sales of government property; makes loans to small business concerns, state and local development companies, and the victims of floods and disasters.

SMITHSONIAN INSTITUTION
1000 Jefferson Drive, S.W.,
Washington, D.C. 20560
Established: 1846
Secretary of the Institution: S. Dillon Ripley
Activities: Performs fundamental research; maintains library, theater, and museum facilities; engages in programs of national and international cooperative research.

TENNESSEE VALLEY AUTHORITY (TVA)
New Sprankle Building,
Knoxville, Tenn. 37902
Woodward Building, 15th and H Streets, N.W.,
Washington, D.C. 20444
Established: 1933
Membership: Three-member Board of Directors appointed by the President.
Chairman: Charles H. Dean Jr.
Activities: Develops the Tennessee River system through construction of a series of dams; conducts forestry programs; assists in flood control; and is an important supplier of electricity to the surrounding region.

UNITED STATES INFORMATION AGENCY (USIA)
1750 Pennsylvania Avenue, N.W.,
Washington, D.C. 20547
Established: 1977
Director: Charles Z. Wick
Deputy Director: Gilbert A. Robinson
Activities: Voice of America broadcasts to other countries and international educational and cultural-exchange activities

VETERANS ADMINISTRATION (VA)
Vermont Avenue and H Street, N.W.,
Washington, D.C. 20420
Established: 1930
Administrator of Veterans Affairs: Harry N. Walters
Activities: Administers benefits for former members of the armed forces, their eligible dependents and beneficiaries.

Women's Rights

United Press Int'l.

Miss America 1984, Vanessa Williams, 20, of Millwood, N.Y., leaps for joy in Atlantic City, N.J., on Sept. 18, the morning after she became the first black to win the coveted title. She had entered the contest as Miss New York.

HIGHLIGHTS: 1983

ERA REVIVAL DEFEATED IN CONGRESS

The House of Representatives on Nov. 15, 1983, narrowly defeated a move to revive the proposed Equal Rights Amendment (ERA) to the Constitution. The 278–147 vote was six short of the majority needed to approve an amendment to the Constitution.

House Speaker Thomas P. (Tip) O'Neill Jr. (D-Mass.) brought the measure to the floor under special rules permitting no amendments and allowing each side only 20 minutes for debate. Normally, such rules are used only for noncontroversial legislation. O'Neill's action infuriated the Republican minority in the House, and the vote appeared to be a reflection of anger rather than principle. Many of the bill's sponsors voted against it because of unhappiness over the procedures.

O'Neill explained later that some Republicans had planned to offer amendments, and that if those amendments had been added during normal procedures, hard-core ERA backers would have then voted against the measure. Thus, it appeared the ERA would not have been approved in its original form in any case.

The amendment, stating "Equality of rights under the law shall not be denied or abridged by the United States or any state on account of sex," was approved by Congress in 1972 and sent to the states for ratification. Despite an extension of the ratification period, only 35 of the required 38 states ratified the measure by the deadline, June 30, 1982.

NEWSCASTER'S SEX-BIAS SUIT OVERTURNED

A federal judge in Kansas City, Mo., on Oct. 31, overturned a jury's award of $500,000 to a TV news achorwoman who had charged she was a victim of sex discrimination.

In the suit, Christine Craft, 37, had contended that her employer, Metromedia Inc., owner of KMBC-TV, in Kansas City, Mo., demoted her on a television news program because she was "too old, too unattractive, and not deferential enough to men." She also contended that the company had been fraudulent in saying it

HIGHLIGHTS: 1983 *(continued)*

was hiring her for her journalistic abilities, not her appearance. On Aug. 8, the jury awarded Craft $375,000 in actual damages and $125,000 in punitive damages on the fraud charge. It did not agree that Metromedia had violated federal equal-pay laws but recommended to Judge Joseph E. Stevens Jr. that he find Metromedia guilty of practicing sex discrimination.

The judge found that Craft was not a victim of sex discrimination and threw out the $500,000 award as "excessive" and influenced by "the pervasive publicity" in the case. He ordered a new trial, on the fraud charges, to begin Jan. 4, 1984.

After leaving the Kansas City station in 1981, rather than accept a demotion to reporter after being a co-anchor on the nightly news, she took a job with a TV station in Santa Barbara, Calif., until the end of August, when she began a lecture tour about her court case.

WOMEN STILL EARN LESS THAN MEN

Despite two decades of struggle for equality, women working at full-time jobs earn only 62% of what men do, according to data released by the Census Bureau in October. Women working full time in 1982 had median annual earnings of $13,014, while men had median incomes of $21,077.

More women are working today, however, than ever before. According to the Bureau of Labor Statistics, an estimated 48.1 million women were working outside their homes in March 1983, comprising 52.6% of all adult women. In 1960, 23 million women worked outside the home, representing only 38% of adult women over 16.

The earnings gap seemed to affect older women more significantly than younger women. The Labor Department reported that in 1982, women 16 to 24 years of age earned 82% as much of men the same age.

The Census Bureau reported, however, that of all the women who worked in 1982, only 10% earned more than $20,000.

Sally K. Ride became the first U.S. woman astronaut when she rode the space shuttle *Challenger* on its second flight, June 18–24. Ride, a physicist, accompanied four male astronauts on the "nearly perfect" mission.

United Press Int'l.

CHANGES SINCE 1950

A profile of American women in the years 1950–1980 was issued by the Census Bureau in October. It traced changes that have taken place over the three decades in the lives of women.

The profile found that fertility decreased sharply, dipping from 24.1 births per 1,000 population in 1950 to 16.1 in 1980. The total fertility rate was 3.3 children per woman in 1950 but only 1.8 per woman in 1980.

In 1950 a woman's average age at her first marriage was 20.3, but by 1980 it had risen to 22.1 years of age. The proportion of women aged 20–24 who had never married rose from approximately 25% in 1950 to 45% in 1980.

The proportion of divorced women rose in the three decades, also, with divorcées representing 2.4% of adult women in 1950, and 6.6% in 1980.

The report also found that just over one-fourth of adult women headed a household in 1980, up from 15% in 1950. Unfortunately, these households account for an increasing proportion of those in poverty.

Although college enrollment was about the same for women and men, women earn fewer professional and graduate degrees.

MATERNITY LEAVE AWARDED ADOPTIVE MOM

A working mother won the right to an unpaid maternity leave to take care of her adopted baby daughter, after a nine-month fight.

Carol Fezar, 39, a tax clerk in Ambridge, Ohio, filed a grievance with her union, a local chapter of the Federation of State, County and Municipal Employees, after she was denied maternity leave when she and her husband, Michael, 45, a chemistry professor, adopted their daughter, Kristin Marie, in May 1983.

The Ambridge Borough Council had denied the leave because it felt that maternity benefits were meant for a female worker who "conceived and got pregnant." The union, however, argued that "maternity leave is a contractual right that cannot be denied."

Federal arbitrator Carl Stoltenberg of Pittsburgh, Pa., handed down his decision on Oct. 31, saying that the concept of maternity "encompasses the duties and responsibilities of motherhood" and that since maternity leaves can cover up to a year, a major portion of the time must be considered for child-rearing.

The borough was directed to grant Mrs. Fezar maternity leave retroactive to May 18, 1982, her last day of work. She had been offered a six-month "reasonable purpose" leave, then a 90-day leave of absence, but she felt that she was entitled to the six-month maternity leave guaranteed in her contract, with an option for an additional six months.

NEWSWORTHY WOMEN

Actress **Patricia Neal** was honored in May as Mother of the Year by the Hebrew Home for the Aged in New York City. . . . **Geraldine Lawhorn,** 67, of Chicago, Ill., became the sixth deaf and blind person in the U.S. to receive a college degree when she graduated from Northeastern University in June.

One thousand sorority women at the University of California voted in May to choose the ten most influential women of the year. Included were First Lady **Nancy Reagan,** columnist **Erma Bombeck,** singers **Lena Horne** and **Juice Newton,** newscaster **Connie Chung,** puppeteer **Shari Lewis,** TV commentator **Sonya Friedman,** UN Ambassador **Jeane Kirkpatrick,** and golfer **Jan Stephenson.** . . . UN **Ambassador Kirkpatrick** received the Henrietta Szold Award, the highest honor bestowed by Hadassah, in August.

Roman Catholic nun **Agnes Mansour** left her religious order in Detroit after the Vatican ordered her to resign her post as director of the Michigan Department of Social Services or else denounce the agency's policy of funding abortions for the poor. Mansour had been on leave from the Religious Sisters of Mercy, but chose to leave the order when faced with the choice. She stressed she felt abortion is wrong, but as long as it is legal, it should be funded.

Daphne Reese and **Angela Dennis,** both 22, became the first black women to graduate from the U.S. Coast Guard Academy in May. . . . In February the U.S. Postal Service named **Jackie Strange** postmaster general for the Southern Postal Region, the highest post ever held by a woman in the agency.

Eight centuries of men-only tradition were broken in September when **Mary Donaldson,** 62, was elected Lord Mayor of London. The wife of England's leading appeals-court judge, **Sir John Donaldson,** took office as London's first lady Lord Mayor in November. . . . **Jihan al-Sadat,** widow of late Egyptian President **Anwar al-Sadat,** delivered the convocation address at the University of Vermont graduation ceremonies in May. She predicted peace for the Middle East and reminded graduates not to take their education for granted.

United Press Int'l.

Police officer Susan McKenna, 25, models a new uniform for pregnant policewomen at New York City police headquarters in January. Judy Loeb, *right,* designed the new uniform.

In September **Betty Anne Williams** was sworn in as the first black president of the Washington (D.C.) Press Club. . . . Also in September, **Cathleen Black,** publisher of *New York* magazine, was named president of Gannett Co. Inc.'s daily newspaper *USA TODAY.*

In October, Radcliffe College honored nine of its women graduates for outstanding lifetime achievement. The honorees were **Dr. Mary Calderone,** 79, founder of the Sex Information and Education Council of the U.S.; consumer activist **Esther Peterson,** 76; NAACP executive **Jean E. Fairfax,** 63; lawyer **Lucy Somerville Howorth,** 88; physicist **Prof. Chien-Shiung Wu,** 71; writer **Eudora Welty,** 74; pediatric cardiologist **Dr. Helen B. Taussig,** 85; historian **Barbara Tuchman,** 71; and artist **Georgia O'Keeffe,** 95.

IMPORTANT DATES IN THE HISTORY OF AMERICAN WOMEN

1773 First play by American woman playwright: *The Adulateur,* a satire by Mercy Otis Warren (1728–1814).

1774–83 First American woman secret agent abroad: Patience Lovell Wright (1725–26), who sent back secret reports while doing wax sculptures of George III and others in London.

1779 First woman to fight as a uniformed U.S. soldier (disguised as a man): Deborah Sampson (1760–1827), who was wounded twice.

1790 Publication of first popular novel by an American woman: *Charlotte Temple* by Susanna Haswell Rowson (c.1762–1824).

1800 Women first vote in local election in Elizabethtown, N.J.

1821 First college-level school for women: the Troy (N.Y.) Female Seminary, founded by Emma Willard (1787–1870).

1824 First strike by women workers at Pawtucket, R.I., weaving mill.

1830 First major women's magazine: *Lady's Book* (later *Godey's Lady's Book*).

1835 Oberlin College in Ohio admits women, becoming first coeducational college; awards first degrees to women in 1841.

1836 First American stage actress to become a star: Charlotte Cushman (1816–76) debuts in New York City as Lady Macbeth.

1836–37 First permanent women's colleges founded: Georgia Female College at Macon, Ga. (later Wesleyan College) and Mt. Holyoke Female Seminary at South Hadley, Mass. (later Mt. Holyoke College).

1847 First American woman astronomer discovers a comet: Maria Mitchell (1818–89).

1848 Married women given right to own real estate in own name by New York legislature.

1848 (July 19–20) First women's rights convention held in Seneca Falls, N.Y.; planned by Elizabeth Cady Stanton (1815–1902) and Lucretia C. Mott (1793–1880).

1849 First woman doctor granted M.D. degree by medical school at Geneva N.Y.: Elizabeth Blackwell (1821–1910).

1850 Founding of first school of medicine for women: Women's College of Pennsylvania.

1852 Publication of first bestselling reform novel by a woman: *Uncle Tom's Cabin* by Harriet Beecher Stowe (1811–96).

1861 First superintendent of women nurses appointed for Union forces in Civil War: Dorothea Lynde Dix (1802–87).

1862 An 8-hour-day law for women and children workers enacted by Wisconsin legislature.

1869 First law giving women right to vote and hold office by Wyoming territorial legislature.

1869 National American Woman Suffrage Association founded; Susan B. Anthony (1820–1906) served as president from 1892 to 1900.

1870 (Aug. 1) Women vote in territorial election for first time in Utah.

1874 National Woman's Christian Temperance Union (WCTU) founded in Cleveland, Ohio.

1881 American Red Cross organized by Clara Barton (1821–1912).

1883 First international organization for women, World's Woman's Christian Temperance Union, founded by Frances E. Willard (1839–98).

1887 First woman mayor elected: Susanna Madora Salter (1860–1961) in Argonia, Kan.

1889 Woman reporter sets record for trip around the world in 72 days, 6 hours, and 11 minutes: Nellie Bly (1867?–1922).

1890 Wyoming provides equal voting rights for women in its constitution.

1895 First American woman interpretive dancer debuts in New York City: Isadora Duncan (1878–1927).

1910 Congress passes Mann Act: forbids interstate transport of women for immoral purposes.

1912 First minimum-wage act for women and children enacted in Massachusetts.

1913 First woman movie star: Pearl White (1889–1938) in the serial *Perils of Pauline.*

1916 First woman elected to Congress: Jeannette Rankin (1880–1973), U.S. representative from Montana; the only member of Congress to vote against U.S. declarations of war both in World War I and World War II.

1918 Woman-in-Industry Service established in U.S. Department of Labor as first agency for women; became Women's Bureau in 1920.

1920 (Aug. 26) Women win right to vote in national elections for first time with proclamation of Amendment 19 to the United States Constitution.

1922 First woman appointed U.S. senator: Rebecca Latimer Felton (1835–1930; D-Ga.) attended sessions on only two days.

1924 First woman elected state governor in Wyoming: Nellie Tayloe Ross (1876–1977).

1931 First American woman to win the Nobel Peace Prize: Jane Addams (1860–1935).

1932 First woman pilot to solo across the Atlantic Ocean from Newfoundland to Ireland: Amelia Earhart (1897–1937).

1932 (Jan. 12) First woman elected to U.S. Senate: Hattie Wyatt Caraway (1878–1950) was reelected to full 6-year terms in 1932 and 1938.

1933 First woman appointed as member of presidential cabinet: Frances Perkins (1882–1965), secretary of labor under President Franklin D. Roosevelt in 1933–45.

1938 First American woman to win the Nobel Prize for Literature: Pearl S. Buck (1892–1973).

1955 First American black woman opera star debuts at New York City's Metropolitan Opera: Marian Anderson (born 1902).

1964 Job discrimination against women forbidden by U.S. Civil Rights Act.

1966 National Organization for Women (NOW) founded by Betty Friedan as leading organization in women's liberation movement.

1972 Equal rights for women amendment to U.S. Constitution approved by Congress.

1973 (Jan. 22) Supreme Court orders repeal of abortion laws in 46 states; rules that women must be allowed to receive abortions on demand during first 6 months of pregnancy.

1974 (June 3) Supreme Court rules women must receive equal wages for same work as men.

1978 (Nov. 1) First women report for sea duty aboard U.S. Navy noncombat ships.

1980 (May) U.S. military service academies graduate women officers for first time.

1981 (Sept. 25) First woman justice of U.S. Supreme Court, Sandra Day O'Connor, sworn in.

1982 (June 30) Equal Rights Amendment defeated; ratified by only 35 states.

1983 (Sept. 17) First black Miss America named: Vanessa Williams, of Millwood, N.Y., honored.

Deaths: 1983

Persons who died from Jan. 1 through Dec. 31, 1983, are listed below and on the following pages. Some gained such fame that their names are instantly recognizable. Others are included because of noteworthy activities or achievements in their lifetimes, even though their names are less well known.

Ibrahim Abboud, 82, chief of state of Sudan in 1958–64: in Khartoum, Sudan, on Sept. 8.
George Abell, 57, astronomer, cosmologist; discovered Abell Galaxy: in Los Angeles, Calif., on Oct. 7.
Edwin Ross Adair, 75, U.S. representative (R-Ind.) in 1950–71: in Fort Wayne, Ind., on May 7.
Claus Adam, 65, composer and cellist: in New York City on July 4.
Frank Aiken, 85, deputy prime minister and foreign minister of Ireland in 1951–69; cofounder of Fianna Fail party: in Dublin, Ireland, on May 18.
Ivan Le Lorraine Albright, 86, American-born painter of "magic realism" style: in Woodstock, Vt., on Nov. 18.
Robert Aldrich, 65, film director known for *The Dirty Dozen*: in Los Angeles, Calif., on Dec. 5.
Miguel Alemán, 79, president of Mexico in 1946–52: in Mexico City, Mexico, on May 14.
Jim Ameche, 68, 1930s radio star: in Tucson, Ariz., on Feb. 4.
Maxie Anderson, 48, American balloonist; made trans-Atlantic balloon flight in 1978: during balloon race near Würzburg, West Germany, on June 27.
Tex Antoine, 59, New York City TV weather forecaster: in New York City on Jan. 12.
Benigno S. Aquino Jr., 50, major Philippines opposition leader; assassinated on arrival in Manila, Philippines, at end of 3-year exile in U.S., on Aug. 21.
Peter Arne, 62, British character actor: found murdered in London, England, apartment on Aug. 1.
Wayne N. Aspinall, 87, U.S. representative (D-Colo.) in 1948–72: in Palisade, Colo., on Oct. 9.
Georges Auric, 84, composer for French films: in Paris, France, on July 23.
Earl Averill, 81, major league baseball outfielder in 1929–41; had lifetime .318 batting average: in Everett, Wash., on Aug. 16.

Bert Bacharach, 85, former fashion editor, syndicated columnist; father of composer Burt Bacharach: in New York City on Sept. 15.
George Balanchine, 79, Russian-born ballet dancer and choreographer; cofounder of New York City Ballet and its director in 1948–83; director of ballet at Metropolitan Opera in 1934–37: in New York City on April 30.
Billy Baldwin, 80, considered dean of American interior decorators: in Nantucket, Mass., on Nov. 25.
Lesley Ballantine, 84, American-born author of children's books; daughter of poet Robert Frost: in Fairfield, Conn., on July 9.
Frank B. Bane, 89, first administrator of Social Security system in 1931–38: in Alexandria, Va., on Jan. 23.
Paul J. Barnes, 64, radio announcer, actor; known as "man of a thousand voices:" in Elgin, Ill., on May 16.
Emma Barrett, 85, jazz pianist: in New Orleans, La., on Jan. 27.
Henry Barton, 85, first director, in 1931–57, of American Institute of Physics: in Greensboro, Vt., on Oct. 11.
Clair Bee, 87, Long Island University basketball coach in 1931–52: in Cleveland, Ohio, on May 20.
Kiko Bejines, 20, Mexican boxer: of head injuries suffered in match Sept. 1, in Los Angeles, Calif., on Sept. 4.
Madison (Matty) Bell, 84, Southern Methodist University football coach in 1935–41, 1945–49: in Dallas, Tex., on June 30.
Ben Benn, 91, Russian-born painter of still lifes and landscapes: early advocate of Cubism: in Connecticut on Jan. 7.
Cathy Berberian, 54, American mezzo-soprano known for unusual performances of contemporary music: in Rome, Italy, on March 6.
Ted Berrigan, 48, American poet: in New York City on July 4.
Georges Bidault, 83, prime minister and foreign minister of France in 1940s and 1950s: in Cambo-les-Bains, France, on Jan. 27.
William Black, 80, founder and chairman of Chock Full o'Nuts Corporation: in New York City on March 7.
Eubie Blake, 100, jazz pianist, composer of *I'm Just Wild About Harry* and others; in New York City on Feb. 12.
Felix Bloch, 77, physicist; shared 1952 Nobel Prize in Physics for development of new methods for nuclear-magnetic precision measurements and related discoveries: in Zurich, Switzerland, on Sept. 10.
Charles G. Bluhdorn, 56, founder, chairman of Gulf and Western Industries: in airplane en route to New York City from Dominican Republic, on Feb. 19.
Anthony Blunt, 75, former art adviser to Queen Elizabeth II of Britain; exposed as Soviet spy in 1979: in London, England, on March 25.
Willie Bobo, 49, musician; blended jazz, Latin, and blues rhythms: in Los Angeles, Calif., on Sept. 15.
Geoffrey Bocca, 59, British author, historian: in London, England, on July 7.
Bart J. Bok, 77, astronomer; authority on Milky Way: in Tucson, Ariz., on Aug. 5.
George Bond, 67, Navy medical officer who pioneered Sealab project in 1960s that proved man could live on ocean floor: in Charlotte, N.C., on Jan. 3.
Henry Botkin, 86, abstract painter known for collage paintings: in New York City on March 4.
Adrian Boult, 93, conductor of BBC Symphony Orchestra in 1930–49 and London Philharmonic in 1950s and 60s: in Kent, England, on Feb. 23.
Sydney Box, 76, film producer known for *The Seventh Veil*; author of one-act plays: in Perth, Australia, on May 25.
Robert F. Bradford, 80, Republican governor of Massachusetts in 1947–48: in Boston, Mass., on March 18.
Caroline Bradley, 37, foremost British equestrian: in Ipswich, England, on June 1.
Peter Brandon, 57, stage and television actor: in Rochester, N.Y., on Nov. 27.
James Breasted Jr., 74, art historian; director of Los Angeles County Museum in 1946–51: in Laconia, N.H., on May 4.
Paul (Bear) Bryant, 69, University of Alabama football coach in 1958–82; compiled record of 323 wins, 85 losses, 17 ties in entire career: in Tuscaloosa, Ala., on Jan. 26.
Luis Bunuel, 83, Spanish-born film director: in Mexico City, Mexico, on July 29.
James A. Burke, 73, U.S. representative (D-Mass.) in 1959–79: in Boston, Mass., on Oct. 13.
Phillip Burton, 56, U.S. representative (D-Calif.) since 1964: in San Francisco, Calif., on April 10.

DEATHS: 1983 *(continued)*

Arthur Cady, 63, painter known for cityscapes and landscapes: in Brewster, N.Y., on April 5.

Rod Cameron, 73, actor: in Gainesville, Ga., on Dec. 21.

Marcolino G. Candau, 71, director-general of World Health Organization (WHO) in 1953–73: in Geneva, Switzerland, on Jan. 24.

Judy Canova, 66, comedienne, singer, actress: in Hollywood, Calif., on Aug. 5.

Raymond Carlson, 76, editor of *Arizona Highways* magazine in 1938–71: in Scottsdale, Ariz., on Feb. 28.

Karen Carpenter, 32, popular singer, member of singing duo The Carpenters, with brother Richard: in Downey, Calif., on Feb. 4.

John A. Carroll, 82, U.S. senator (D-Colo.) in 1957–63, U.S. representative in 1947–49: in Denver, Colo., on Aug. 31.

Robert Carson, 73, screenwriter; won 1937 Academy Award for *A Star Is Born:* in Los Angeles on Jan. 19.

Lillian Carter, 85, mother of former President Jimmy Carter, nurse, Peace Corps volunteer, champion of civil rights: in Americus, Ga., on Oct. 30.

William Cary, 72, chairman of Securities and Exchange Commission (SEC) in 1961–64: in New York City on Feb. 7.

Mario Cardinal Casariego, 74, archbishop of Guatemala since 1963: in Guatemala, on June 15.

Turner Catledge, 82, managing editor of *New York Times* in 1951–64, executive editor in 1964–68: in New Orleans, La., on April 27.

Alfonso J. Cervantes, 62, mayor of St. Louis, Mo., in 1965–73: in St. Louis, Mo., on June 23.

Henry Chapin, 89, American poet, author: in Peterborough, N.H., on Sept. 4.

Prince Charles of Belgium, 79, served as Belgian regent in 1944–50 when brother, King Leopold II, was in exile: in Brussels, Belgium, on June 1.

Robert Christian, 42, actor; won 1976 Obie award for *Blood Knot*: in New York City on Jan. 27.

Barney Clark, 62, dentist; first human to have artificial heart implanted on Dec. 2, 1982: of massive circulatory collapse in Salt Lake City, Utah, on March 23.

Kenneth Clark, 79, art historian; author and narrator of *Civilisation* TV series: in Hythe, England, on May 21.

Albert Claude, 84, winner of 1974 Nobel Prize in Medicine for pioneering in use of electron microscope to study living cells, and discovering such cell parts as ribosomes and lysosomes: in Belgium on May 22.

Jan Clayton, 66, actress known for role of mother in *Lassie* TV show: in Los Angeles, Calif., on Aug. 28.

Edith Coates, 74, British opera mezzo-soprano since 1924: in London, England, on Jan. 7.

Peter T. Coffield, 38, TV and theater actor: in New York City on Nov. 19.

Blanton Collier, 76, coach of University of Kentucky football team in 1954–61; coach of Cleveland Browns in 1963–70: in Houston, Tex., on March 22.

Michael Conrad, 58, actor; won Emmy award for role in *Hill Street Blues*: in Los Angeles, Calif., on Nov. 22.

Terence Cardinal Cooke, 62, leader of Roman Catholic Archdiocese of New York since 1968, cardinal since 1969: in New York City on Oct. 6.

Erastus Corning 2d, 73, Democratic mayor of Albany, N.Y., since 1942: in Boston, Mass., on May 28.

Don Costa, 57, record conductor, arranger, producer for popular singers: in New York City on Jan. 19.

John Cowles Sr., 84, Minneapolis newspaper publisher in 1940s to 1960s: in Minneapolis, Minn., on Feb. 25.

Buster Crabbe, 75, Olympic swimming champion in 1928 and 1932; later was movie actor: in Scottsdale, Ariz., on April 23.

Burrill B. Crohn, 99, physician, medical researcher; in 1932 defined and identified ileitis disease: in New Milford, Conn., on July 29.

George Cukor, 83, film director for 53 years; won 1964 Academy Award for *My Fair Lady* and 1975 Emmy Award for *Love Among the Ruins*: in Los Angeles, Calif., on Jan. 24.

Leora Dana, 60, stage actress: in New York City on Dec. 13.

Jean D'Arcy, 69, French television pioneer; founder of Eurovision in 1954: in Paris, France, on Jan. 19.

Toni Darney, 61, stage, screen, TV actress: in New York City on Jan. 5.

Maurice E. (Jake) Day, 90, animator for Disney studios; drew deer for *Bambi:* in Darariscotta, Maine, on May 15.

Louis de Funes, French comedian: in Nantes, France, on Jan. 27.

Roy Andries de Groot, 73, wine and food critic: suicide in New York City on Sept. 16.

Ernesto de La Guardia, 79, president of Panama in 1956–60: in Panama City, Panama, on May 2.

Peter Dejongh, 86, engineer, designer, developed Quonset hut during World War II: in Arlington, N.J., on July 3.

Dolores Del Rio, 77, Mexican-born film actress: in Newport Beach, Calif., on April 11.

Joe Delaney, 24, Kansas City Chiefs running back since 1981: drowned while trying to rescue two boys in amusement park pond in Monroe, La., on June 29.

William Demarest, 91, film actor: in Hollywood, Calif., on Dec. 28.

Jimmy Demaret, 73, golfer: in Houston, Texas, on Dec. 28.

Jack Dempsey, 87, heavyweight boxing champion in 1919–26: in New York City on May 31.

Edwin Denby, 80, poet and dance critic: suicide in Searsport, Me., on July 12.

Reginald Denham, 89, actor, playwright, theatrical director: in Englewood, N.J., on Feb. 4.

Robert C. Dennis, 67, TV scriptwriter for *Charlie's Angels, Hawaii Five-O, Dragnet*, others: in Hollywood, Calif., on Sept. 14.

Howard Dietz, 86, lyricist for songs for musicals, including *Dancing in the Dark, You and the Night and the Music:* in New York City on July 30.

Farrell Dobbs, 76, Socialist Workers Party presidential candidate in 1948, 1952, 1956, 1960: in Pinole, Calif., on Oct. 31.

Robert Docking, 57, Democratic governor of Kansas in 1966–74: in Arkansas City, Kan., Oct. 8.

Owen Dodson, 68, poet, novelist, influence on African-American drama: in New York City on June 21.

Anton Dolin, 79, British ballet dancer, choreographer; performed with Diaghilev's Ballet Russe in 1920-25, 1928-29, and Ballet Theater in New York; formed several ballet companies: in Paris, France, on Nov. 25.

Florence Dolowitz, 94, founder in 1927 of Women's American ORT in U.S.: in Brooklyn, N.Y., on July 23.

Fifi D'Orsay, 79, Canadian-born film actress in 1930s: in Los Angeles, Calif., on Dec. 2.

Osvaldo Dorticós, 64, president of Cuba in 1959–76: a suicide in Havana, Cuba, on June 23.

Roscoe Drummond, 81, political columnist for more than 50 years: in Princeton, N.J., on Sept. 30.

Werner Egk, 82, German-born composer known for *Peer Gynt* (1938): in Inning, West Germany, on July 10.

Simcha Ehrlich, 67, deputy prime minister of Israel, leader of Liberal Party: in Jerusalem, Israel, on June 19.

C. Bruce Elbrick, 75, former U.S. ambassador to Portugal, Yugoslavia, and Brazil: in Washington, D.C., on April 13.

Faye Emerson, 65, actress, TV personality: in Majorca, Spain, on March 9.

Dick Emery, 63, British comedian: in London, England, on Jan. 2.

Rip Engle, 76, Penn State University football coach in 1950–65: in Bellefonte, Pa., on March 7.
Benjamin Epstein, 70, national director of Anti-Defamation League of B'nai B'rith in 1947–78: in New York City on May 2.

Princess Faika, 55, sister of late King Farouk of Egypt: in Cairo, Egypt, on Jan. 7.
Paul Feigay, 64, producer of Broadway shows, including *On the Town*: in Brewster, N.Y. on Feb. 26.
Temple Fielding, 69, author of travel books used by millions: in Palma, Majorca, on May 18.
Adrian S. Fisher, 69, first deputy director of United States Arms Control and Disarmament Agency in 1961–69; dean of Georgetown University Law Center in 1969–77: in Washington, D.C., on March 18.
Yakov L. Fishman, 70, chief rabbi of Moscow's Choral Synagogue: in Moscow, Soviet Union, on June 3.
Paul Fix, 82, character actor: in Santa Monica, Calif., on Oct. 14.
Lynn Fontanne, 95, actress; formed husband-and-wife team with Alfred Lunt: in Genesee Depot, Wis., on July 30.
Aaron Ford, 80, U.S. representative (D-Miss.) in 1935–43: in auto accident near Jackson, Miss., on July 8.
Eddie Foy Jr., 78, vaudevillian; member of Eddie Foy and the Seven Little Foys act: in Woodland Hills, Calif., on July 15.
Philip Fradkin, 61, musical director of *42d Street, Gypsy,* and *Timbuktu!*: in New York City on May 20.
Alfred Friendly, 71, managing editor of the *Washington Post* in 1955–65; won 1968 Pulitzer Prize for investigative reporting from abroad for coverage of 1967 Arab-Israeli War: in Washington, D.C., on Nov. 7.
R. Buckminster Fuller, 87, American inventor; designed Dymaxion prefabricated metal home in 1927; invented geodesic dome of triangular elements in 1960s: in Los Angeles, Calif., on July 1.
Bill Fury, 42, British pop singer: in London, England, on Jan. 28.

Kay Gable, 65, widow of film star Clark Gable: in Houston, Tex., on May 25.
Barry Galbraith, 63, guitarist in 1950s and 1960s: in Bennington, Vt., on Jan. 13.
Thomas S. Gates Jr., 76, secretary of Navy and Defense departments in Eisenhower administration: in Philadelphia, Pa., on March 25.
Christopher George, 54, TV actor: in Los Angeles, Calif., on Nov. 28.
James M. Geraghty, 78, art editor of *The New Yorker* in 1939–73: in Venice, Fla., on Jan. 16.
Ira Gershwin, 86, lyricist; with brother George wrote scores for such Broadway musicals as *Porgy and Bess* and many songs: in Beverly Hills, Calif., on Aug. 17.
Julian H. Gibbs, 58, president of Amherst College since 1979: in Springfield, Mass., on Feb. 20.
Carl Joyce Gilbert, 77, special representative for trade negotiations in 1969–71: in Boston, Mass., on Nov. 13.
Alberto Ginastera, 67, Argentine composer: in Geneva, Switzerland, on June 25.
Arthur Godfrey, 79, radio and TV personality: in New York City on March 16.
Leopold Godowsky II, 82, developed Kodachrome color photography process with Leopold Mannes in 1920s: in New York City on Feb. 18.
Larry Gordon, 29, linebacker with Miami Dolphins since 1976: in Phoenix, Ariz., on June 25.
Rex Gosden, 45, writer of country-music songs: in Riverdale, Ga., on May 23.
Donald Gramm, 56, American bass-baritone; appeared with Metropolitan Opera and New York City Opera: in New York City on June 2.
Ernest Graves, 64, classical actor: in New York City on June 1.
Charlie Grimm, 85, major league baseball player in 1915–34; manager of Chicago Cubs in 1932–38, 1944–49, and 1959–60: in Scottsdale, Ariz., on Nov. 15.
Alfred M. Gruenther, 84, supreme commander of NATO forces in 1953–56: in Washington, D.C., on May 30.

Joan Hackett, 49, stage and screen actress: in Encino, Calif., on Oct. 9.
George Halas, 88, founder and coach of Chicago Bears football team in 1920–68; a founder of professional football: in Chicago, Ill., on Oct. 31.
Roswell Ham, 92, president of Mount Holyoke College in 1936–57: in Santa Barbara, Calif., on July 20.
Nancy Hanks, 55, head of National Endowment for the Arts and National Council on the Arts in 1969–77: in New York City on Jan. 7.
H. Keffer Hartline, 79, biophysicist; co-winner of 1967 Nobel Prize in medicine for discoveries concerning primary chemical and physiological visual processes in the eye: in Fallston, Md., on March 17.
Johnny Hartman, 60, jazz singer: in New York City on Sept. 15.
James Hayden, 29, actor portraying drug addict in Broadway play *American Buffalo*: in New York City of apparent drug overdose, on Nov. 8.
Leonard Heaton, 80, surgeon general of the Army in 1959–69: in Washington, D.C., on Sept. 10.
Joel Hildebrand, 101, chemist; on staff of University of California in 1913–52: in Kensington, Calif., on April 30.
Earl (Fatha) Hines, 77, father of modern jazz piano: in Oakland, Calif., on April 22.
Carmelita Chase Hinton, 92, educator; founded Putney School in Putney, Vt., in 1935: in Concord, Mass., on Jan. 16.
Eric Hoffer, 80, itinerant farm worker, then longshoreman, who became author and philosopher; known for *In Our Time*, others: in San Francisco, Calif., on May 21.
Anna Rosenberg Hoffman, 81, assistant secretary of defense in 1950–53: in New York City on May 9.
Julius J. Hoffman, 87, judge who presided over 1969–70 Chicago Seven conspiracy trial: in Chicago, Ill., on July 1.
Keith Holyoake, 79, governor general of New Zealand in 1977–80, prime minister in 1957, 1960–72: in Wellington, New Zealand, on Dec. 8.
Clemens Holzmeister, 97, Austrian architect; designed Turkish Parliament Building in Ankara: in Hallein, Austria, on June 12.
William Hornbeck, 82, film editor; won 1951 Academy Award for *A Place in the Sun*: in Ventura, Calif., on Oct. 11.
Frederick Lawson Hovde, 75, president of Purdue University in 1946–71: in Lafayette, Ind., on March 1.
Maurice Hutcheson, 85, president of United Brotherhood of Carpenters and Joiners of America in 1952–72: in Lakeland, Fla., on Jan. 9.

Don Ida, 49, American balloonist: during balloon race near Würzburg, West Germany, on June 27.
Idris I, 93, king of Libya in 1951-69: in Cairo, Egypt, on May 25.
Arturo Illia, 83, president of Argentina in 1963–66: in Córdoba, Argentina, on Jan. 18.
Stuart H. Ingersoll, 84, retired Navy vice admiral; commanded Sixth and Seventh fleets; was superintendent of U.S. Naval Academy and headed Naval War College in 1957–60: in Newport, R.I., on Jan. 29.
Graham Washington Jackson, 79, Navy musician whose face became famous in 1945 photo in which he played *'Going Home'* on accordion at death of Franklin D. Roosevelt: in Atlanta, Ga., on Jan. 15.
Henry M. (Scoop) Jackson, 71, U.S. senator (D-

DEATHS: 1983 *(continued)*

Wash.) since 1941: in Everett, Wash., on Sept. 1.

Paul Jacobs, 53, pianist and harpsicordist of New York Philharmonic: in New York City on Sept. 25.

Harry James, 67, trumpeter, bandleader: in Las Vegas, Nev., on July 5.

Harold Johnson, 71, Army chief of staff in 1964–68: in Washington, D.C., on Sept. 24.

Rachel Harris Johnson, 95, founded Girls Clubs of America Inc., in 1945: in Worcester, Mass., on Aug. 9.

Carolyn Jones, 54, film and TV actress: in Hollywood, Calif., on Aug. 3.

Len B. Jordan, 84, U.S. senator (R-Ida.) in 1962–73, governor of Idaho in 1951–55: in Boise, Idaho, on June 30.

Lewis Jordan, 70, news editor of *New York Times* in 1960–76; author of writing and editing manual used by staff of *Times*: in Sharon, Conn., on Nov. 17.

Herman Kahn, 61, founder of Hudson Institute: in Chappaqua, N.Y., on July 7.

Aline Kaplan, 60, executive director of Hadassah, Women's Zionist Organization of America: in New York City on Sept. 29.

Mordecai Kaplan, 102, rabbi, founder of Jewish Reconstructionist movement in 1922: in New York City on Nov. 8.

Barbara Karinska, 97, designer of costumes for New York City Ballet and its precursor since 1946; won 1948 Academy Award for costume design for *Joan of Arc*: in New York City on Oct. 18.

Ezra J. Keats, 67, writer, illustrator of children's books: in New York City on May 6.

Mike Kellin, 61, stage, screen, TV actor; won 1976 Obie award for *American Buffalo*: in Nyack, N.Y., on Aug. 26.

Reamer Kline, 72, president of Bard College (N.Y.) in 1960–74: in Annandale-on-Hudson, N.Y., on March 9.

Revone W. Kluckman, 54, chairman and chief executive officer of Zenith Radio Corp. since 1982: in Elk Grove Village, Ill., on July 18.

Arthur Koestler, 77, British-Hungarian novelist known for *Darkness at Noon* (1941): in suicide pact with wife, Cynthia, in London, England, on March 3.

Pola Kostrukoff, 83, fashion designer of 1940s and 50s: in Island Park, N.Y., on Feb. 25.

Doug Kotar, 32, New York Giants running back in 1974-81: in Pittsburgh, Pa., on Dec. 16.

Charles Kullman, 80, operatic tenor; sang at Metropolitan Opera in 1935–60: in New Haven, Conn., on Feb. 8.

Suzanne La Follette, 89, author, editor, founder of *National Review* magazine: in Palo Alto, Calif., on April 23.

Meyer Lansky, 81, reputed financial genius of organized crime: in Miami Beach, Fla., on Jan. 15.

Doris Emrick Lee, 78, painter and book illustrator: in Clearwater, Fla., on June 16.

Carolyn Leigh, 57, lyricist, known for *Hey Look Me Over*, songs from *Peter Pan*: in New York City on Nov. 19.

Hans Leip, 89, lyricist; wrote words to *Lili Marlene*: in Fruthwilen, Switzerland, on June 6.

Emil (Dutch) Leonard, 74, major league baseball pitcher in 1933–53: in Springfield, Ill., on April 17.

King Leopold III, 81, king of Belgium in 1934–51; forced to abdicate in favor of son Baudouin as a result of surrendering to invading Nazis during World War II: in Brussels, Belgium, on Sept. 25.

Robert A. Lewis, 65, copilot of *Enola Gay*, B-29 that dropped atomic bomb on Hiroshima in 1945: in Newport News, Va., on June 18.

George Liberace, 71, orchestra leader, violinist: in Las Vegas, Nev., on Oct. 16.

George Lichty, 78, cartoonist; created *Grin and Bear It* series in 1932: in Santa Rosa, Calif., on July 18.

Mary Livingstone, 77, radio star, sidekick for husband Jack Benny: in Holmby Hills, Calif., on June 30.

Richard Llewellyn, 76, Welsh playwright, author; known for *How Green Was My Valley*: in Dublin, Ireland, on Nov. 30.

Nora Lofts, 79, author of historical novels: in Bury St. Edmunds, England, on Sept. 10.

Richard Loo, 80, Chinese-American actor: in Los Angeles, Calif., on Nov. 20.

Ross Macdonald (Kenneth Millar), 67, American-born author of Lew Archer mystery novels: in Santa Barbara, Calif., on July 11.

John A. Mackay, 94, president of Princeton Theological Seminary in 1936–59: in Heightstown, N.J., on June 9.

Donald Maclean, 69, British diplomat who defected to Soviet Union in 1951 after betraying United States atomic secrets: in Moscow, Soviet Union, on March 6.

Gertrude Macy, 79, Broadway producer: in New York City on Oct. 18.

Donald Madden, 49, actor known for classical roles on Broadway: in Central Islip, N.Y., on Jan. 22.

Paul Mann, 72, pianist, composer known for *Put Your Dreams Away*: in New York City on May 27.

Igor Markevitch, 70, conductor of orchestras in Cuba, Europe, and Canada: in Antibes, France, on March 7.

Catherine Marshall, 68, author of inspirational books: in Boynton Beach, Fla., on March 18.

Freddy Martin, 76, big-band leader for more than 50 years: in Newport Beach, Calif., on Sept. 30.

William E. Martz, 37, American chess player; co-champion of 1982 U.S. Open: in Milwaukee, Wis., on Jan. 17.

Raymond Massey, 86, stage, film, TV actor; known for film portrayal of Abraham Lincoln: in Los Angeles, Calif., on July 29.

John Masters, 68, author; known for *Bhowani Junction:* in Albuquerque, N.M., on May 6.

Lloyd McBride, 67, president of United Steelworkers of America since 1977: in Whitehall, Pa., on Nov. 6.

Tom McCall, 69, Republican governor of Oregon in 1967–75: in Portland, Ore., on Jan. 8.

John McCulloch, 74, president of English-Speaking Union of the United States since 1972: in Southampton, N.Y., on Aug. 15.

Lawrence P. McDonald, 48, U.S. representative (D-Ga.) since 1975; chairman of John Birch Society: in plane shot down by Soviet fighter in Sea of Japan on Aug. 31.

Henry McLaughlin, 90, vaudevillian who played Clarabelle the Clown on *Howdy Doody* TV show in 1954–56: in Long Beach, Calif., on July 24.

George McLean, 78, owner and publisher of the *Northeast Mississippi Daily Journal* since 1934: in Tupelo, Miss., on March 1.

Humberto Cardinal Medeiros, 67, archbishop of Boston: in Boston, Mass., on Sept. 17.

John Gaw Meem, 88, American architect known for "Santa Fe" style: in Santa Fe, N.M., on Aug. 4.

Peter Mennin, 60, American composer; president of Juilliard School of Music since 1963: in New York City on June 17.

Robert Merriman, 66, stage actor, producer, director: in Bennington, Vt., on Feb. 2.

John Ayers Merritt, 57, Tennessee State football coach since 1963; ranked sixth in number of victories among all college football coaches, with 233: in Nashville, Tenn., on Dec. 15.

Otto Messmer, 91, film animator who created Felix the Cat in 1919: in Teaneck, N.J., on Oct. 28.

Michel Micombero, 43, president of Burundi in 1966–76: in Mogadishu, Somalia, on July 16.

Michael Miller, 51, actor: in Harpers Ferry, W.Va., on May 4.

William E. Miller, 69, U.S. representative (R-N.Y.) in 1951–65; Republican vice-presidential candidate in 1964 election: in Buffalo, N.Y., on June 24.
Joan Miró, 90, Spanish surrealist painter and sculptor: in Palma on Spanish island Majorca on Dec. 25.
Marion Monroe, 85, child psychologist; coauthor of *Dick, Jane and Sally* reading textbooks, used in 1940s to 1970s: in Long Beach, Calif., on June 25.
Jerome Moross, 69, composer for theater and films: in Miami, Fla., on July 25.

John Needham, 65, national commander of Salvation Army since 1982: in Montclair, N.J., on April 13.
Jess Neely, 85, college football coach at Rice University in 1940–66: in Weslaco, Tex., on April 9.
David Niven, 73, British-born actor; won 1958 Academy Award for *Separate Tables*: in Chateau-d'Oex, Switzerland, on July 29.
Marian Nixon, 78, actress; first leading lady for Spencer Tracy in *Face the Sky* (1933): in Los Angeles, Calif., on Feb. 13.
Harry Nkumbula, 67, Zambian politician; president of African National Congress in 1951–58: in Lusaka, Zambia, on Oct. 8.
John Notte, 73, Democratic governor of Rhode Island in 1961–63: in Providence, R.I., on March 6.

Simon Oakland, 61, character actor: in Cathedral City, Calif., on Aug. 29.
Pat O'Brien, 83, American actor known for roles as priests and policemen: in Santa Monica, Calif., on Oct. 15.
Richard O'Brien, 65, character actor: in Los Angeles, Calif., on March 29.
David Oyite Ojok, 49, chief of staff of Ugandan army: in helicopter crash in Uganda, on Dec. 2.
Walter O'Keefe, 82, humorist, lyricist, radio quiz show host: in Torrance, Calf., on June 25.
F. J. O'Neill, 83, majority owner of Cleveland Indians baseball team since 1978: in Cleveland, Ohio, on Aug. 29.

Harriet Parsons, 76, film producer of *I Remember Mama, Clash by Night, Susan Slept Here,* and others: in Hollywood, Calif., on Jan. 2.
Norbert Pearlroth, 89, researcher for *Ripley's Believe It or Not* in 1923–75: in New York City on April 14.
Arvid Y. Pelshe, 84, oldest member of Soviet Politburo: in Moscow, Soviet Union, on May 29.
Alfred E. Perlman, 80, president of N.Y. Central Railroad in 1954–68: in San Francisco, Calif., on April 30.
Lorraine Collett Petersen, 90, model for the young woman on Sun-Maid raisin box in 1915: in Fresno, Calif., on March 30.
Frederick V. Peterson, 80, Republican governor of Nebraska in 1947–53: in Freemont, Neb., on Oct. 16.
Slim Pickens, 64, cowboy actor: in Modesto, Calif., on Dec. 8.
José Batista Pinheiro de Azevedo, 66, prime minister of Portugal in 1975–76: in Lisbon, Portugal, on Aug. 10.
Nikolai V. Podgorny, 79, president of Soviet Union in 1965–77: in the Soviet Union on Jan. 10.
Zelda F. Popkin, 84, novelist, former newspaper reporter: in Silver Spring, Md., on May 25.
Peter Potter, 78, radio and TV show host: in Rancho Mirage, Calif., on April 17.

Qiao Guanhua, 70, Chinese foreign minister in 1974–76; ousted because of connections with radical Gang of Four: in Peking, China, on Sept. 22.

Sam Raphaelson, 87, playwright; known for *The Jazz Singer*: in New York City on July 16.
Danny Rapp, 41, leader of 1950s rock group Danny and the Juniors: suicide in Quartzsite, Ariz., on April 4.
Francis Reichelderfer, 87, chief of U.S. Weather Bureau in 1938–63: in Washington, D.C., on Jan. 25.
Walter Reisch, 79, Austrain-born writer of films, including *Ninotchka, The Great Waltz,* and *Titanic*: in Los Angeles, Calif., on March 28.
Georges Remi, 75, creator of comic book hero Tintin: in Brussels, Belgium, on March 3.
Mary Renault, 78, British-born author of novels about ancient Greece: in Cape Town, South Africa, on Dec. 13.
Frank Reynolds, 59, ABC News anchorman since 1978: in Washington, D.C., on July 20.
Sir Ralph Richardson, 80, British stage and screen actor: in London, England, on Oct. 10.
Waldeck Rochet, 77, leader of French Communist Party in 1964–72: in Paris, France, on Feb. 15.
Will Rogers, 84, U.S. respresentative (D-Okla.) in 1933–43: in Falls Church, Va., on Aug. 3.
Maurice Ronet, 55, French actor: in Paris, France, on March 14.
Benjamin Rosenthal, 59, U.S. representative (D-N.Y.) since 1963; a day after being sworn in for his 11th term: in Washington, D.C., on Jan. 4.
Tino Rossi, 76, French singer: in Neuilly, France, on Sept. 27.
David Rounds, 53, state and TV actor: in Lamontville, N.Y., on Dec. 9.
Selena Royle, 78, stage and film actress: in Guadalajara, Mexico, on April 23.

Bill Sackter, 70, mildly retarded man who spent 44 years in school for retarded and was portrayed by Mickey Rooney in television film *Bill*: in Iowa City, Ia., on June 16.
Katharine Price Collier St. George, 86, English-born U.S. representative (R-N.Y.) in 1946–64: in Tuxedo Park, N.Y., on May 2.
Antonio Cardinal Samore, 77, Vatican mediator, specialist in Latin American affairs: in Rome, Italy, on Feb. 3.
Issam Sartawi, 48, European coordinator of Palestine Liberation Organization (PLO): assassinated in Albufeira, Portugal, on April 10.
Jessica Savitch, 35, NBC television reporter since 1977: in auto accident near New Hope, Pa., on Oct. 23.
Murray Seasongood, 104, mayor of Cincinnati in 1920s: in Cincinnati, Ohio, on Feb. 22.
Anna Seghers, 82, author of *The Seventh Cross*: in Berlin, East Germany, on June 1.
Jason Seley, 64, sculptor, dean of Cornell University College of Architecture, Art and Planning since 1980: in Ithaca, N.Y., on June 23.
Josep L. Sert, 80, Spanish-born architect; dean of Graduate School of Design at Harvard University in 1953–69: in Barcelona, Spain, on March 15.
Whitney North Seymour Sr., 82, president of American Bar Association in 1960, trial lawyer; member of administration of Herbert Hoover: in New York City on May 21.
Norma Shearer, 79, film star of 1920s and 30s; won Oscar in 1929–30 for *The Divorcee*: in Woodland Hills, Calif., on June 12.
Aleksandr Shirov, 24, Soviet Alpine skier: in auto accident in Soviet Union on May 20.
David M. Shoup, 78, commandant of Marine Corps in 1959–63: in Alexandria, Va., on Jan. 13.
Elizabeth Siefert, 84, author of more than 80 novels about doctors: in Moberly, Mo., on June 17.
Sidney Skolsky, 78, Hollywood reporter for more than 50 years: in Los Angeles, Calif., on May 3.
Martha Sleeper, 72, film and stage actress: in Beaufort, S.C., on March 25.
Walter Slezak, 80, film and stage actor: suicide in Flower Hill, N.Y., on April 22.
Avraham Soltes, 66, rabbi, served as Jewish chaplain at

DEATHS: 1983 *(continued)*

U.S. Military Academy at West Point, N.Y., since 1963: in New York City on May 23.

Jack Somack, 64, stage, film, TV actor: in Hollywood, Calif., on Aug. 29.

Arthur Space, 74, stage, screen, TV actor: in Hollywood, Calif., on Jan. 13.

Richard Stankiewicz, 60, American sculptor who used scrap-iron construction to create "scrap art": in Worthington, Mass., on March 27.

Ruth Carter Stapleton, 54, evangelist, sister of former President Jimmy Carter: in Fayetteville, N.C., on Sept. 26.

Christina Stead, 80, Australian-born novelist known for *The Man Who Loved Children* (1940): in Sydney, Australia, on March 31.

Tom Steed, 79, U.S. representative (D-Okla.) in 1947–79: in Shawnee, Okla., on June 8.

Robert T. Stevens, 83, secretary of the Army in 1953–55: in Edison, N.J., on Jan. 31.

Shepperd Strudwick, 75, stage, screen, TV character actor: in New York City on Jan. 15.

Gloria Swanson, 84, 1920s film idol: in New York City on April 4.

Neil H. Swanson, 86, historical novelist; former executive editor of Baltimore Sunpapers: in Baltimore, Md., on Feb. 5.

Charles P. Taft, 85, mayor of Cincinnati, Ohio, in 1955–57; son of President William Howard Taft: in Cincinnati, Ohio, on June 24.

Germaine Tailleferre, 91, French composer: in Paris, France, on Nov. 7.

Thurairajah Tambimuttu, 67, Indian poet and editor: in London, England, on June 22.

James Tate, 73, Democratic mayor of Philadelphia, Pa., in 1962–72: in Somers Point, N.J., on May 27.

Corrie Ten Boom, 91, Dutch author of *The Hiding Place,* later a film: in Placentia, Calif., on April 15.

Shuji Terayama, 47, Japanese playwright: in Tokyo, Japan, on May 4.

Frederick Thompson, 75, orthopedic surgeon: led development in 1950 of artificial hip replacement procedure: in New York City on April 13.

Frank Tonestein, 80, demographer; founded Office of Population Research at Princeton University in 1936; president of The Population Council in 1959–68; first director of UN population division in 1946–48: in Langhorne, Pa., on Feb. 19.

Ivan Tors, 66, film and TV producer known for *Flipper*: in Brazil on June 4.

Shepard Traube, 76, theatrical director, producer known for *Angel Street* and others: in New York City on July 23.

Merle Travis, 65, country music singer: in Tahlequah, Okla., on Oct. 20.

Roger J. Traynor, 83, chief justice of California Supreme Court 1964–70: in Berkeley, Calif., on May 14.

Jean Troisgros, 56, renowned French chef: in Vittel, France, on Aug. 8.

William M. Tuck, 86, Democratic governor of Virginia in 1946–50; U.S. representative (D-Va.) in 1953–68: in South Boston, Va., on June 9.

Earl S. Tupper, 76, created Tupperware line of plastic containers in 1942: in Costa Rica on Oct. 3.

Umberto II, 78, king of Italy for one month in 1946; lived in exile in Portugal since Italy voted to become republic: in Geneva, Switzerland, on March 18.

Norm Van Brocklin, 57, football quarterback for Los Angeles Rams and Philadelphia Eagles in 1949–60: in Atlanta, Ga., on May 2.

James Van Der Zee, 96, photographer noted for pictures of Harlem: in Washington, D.C., on May 15.

Raymond Vitte, 33, actor on *The Quest* TV show: in Los Angeles, Calif., on Feb. 20.

Ulf von Euler, 78, Swedish biochemist; won 1970 Nobel Prize in Medicine for research in chemistry of nerve transmission: in Stockholm, Sweden, on March 10.

John Vorster, 67, prime minister of South Africa in 1966–78: in Cape Town, South Africa, on Sept. 10.

Alfred Wallenstein, 84, cellist, conductor, music director of Los Angeles Philharmonic in 1943–56: in New York City on Feb. 8.

William Walton, 80, British composer; works included oratorio *Belshazzar's Feast* (1931) and opera *Troilus and Cressida* (1954): in Ischia, Italy, on March 8.

Theodore Ward, 80, playwright known for *Big White Fog* and *Our Land*: in Chicago, Ill., on May 8.

Bob Waterfield, 62, college and professional football quarterback in 1940s and 1950s: in Burbank, Calif., on March 25.

Muddy Waters, 68, blues musician: in Chicago, Ill., on April 30.

Barbara M. Watson, 64, first black and first woman to serve as assistant secretary of state in 1968–74; administrator of Bureau of Security and Consular Affairs in 1977–80: in Washington, D.C., on Feb. 17.

Doodles Weaver, 71, comedian: suicide in Burbank, Calif., on Jan. 15.

James A. Wechsler, 67, columnist and former editor of *New York Post:* in New York City on Sept. 11.

Louise Weiss, 90, French feminist, oldest member of European Parliament: in Paris, France, on May 26.

Hennes Weisweiler, 63, coach, New York Cosmos soccer team in 1980–82: in Aesch, Switzerland, on July 5.

J. Bernard West, 70, chief usher of White House in 1937–69: in Arlington, Va., on July 18.

Rebecca West, 90, British journalist and novelist known for *The Return of the Soldier* (1918): in London, England, on March 15.

Michael Whitney, 52, actor, husband of actress Twiggy: in New York City on Nov. 30.

Leonard Wibberley, 68, journalist, author, known for *The Mouse That Roared:* in Santa Monica, Calif., on Nov. 22.

Charmion von Wiegand, 85, abstract artist: in New York City on June 9.

John Williams, 80, British-born actor: in La Jolla, Calif., on May 7.

John Bell Williams, 64, Democratic governor of Mississippi in 1968–72: in Brandon, Miss., on March 26.

Tennessee Williams, 71, American playwright known for *The Glass Menagerie* (1944), *The Rose Tattoo* (1950); *A Streetcar Named Desire* (1947) and *Cat on a Hot Tin Roof* (1955) won Pulitzer Prizes: in New York City on Feb. 25.

Frances E. Willis, 84, first career officer in State Department Foreign Service to serve as U.S. ambassador; had posts in Switzerland, Norway, and Ceylon in 1953–64: in Redlands, Calif., on July 20.

Carroll L. Wilson, 72, first general manager of Atomic Energy Commission in 1946–50: in Providence, R.I., on Jan. 12.

Dennis Wilson, 39, Beach Boys' drummer: in Los Angeles on Dec. 28.

Kai Winding, 60, Danish-born jazz trombonist: in Yonkers, N.Y., on May 6.

Arthur M. Wirtz, 82, owner of Chicago Black Hawks hockey team: in Chicago, Ill., on July 21.

Mel Wright, 55, former pitcher; bullpen coach for Montreal Expos: in Houston, Tex., on May 16.

Milton R. Young, 85, U.S. senator (R-N.D.) in 1945–81: in Sun City, Ariz., on May 31.

Clement J. Zablocki, 71, U.S. representative (D-Wis.) since 1949: chairman of House Foreign Affairs Committee since 1977: in Washington, D.C., on Dec. 3.

Index